The Broadview Anthology of

AMERICAN LITERATURE

Concise Edition

Volume 1
Beginnings to Reconstruction

The Broadview Anthology of
AMERICAN LITERATURE

Concise Edition

Volume 1
Beginnings to Reconstruction

GENERAL EDITORS:

Derrick R. Spires, Cornell University
Rachel Greenwald Smith, Saint Louis University
Christina Roberts, Seattle University
Joseph Rezek, Boston University
Justine S. Murison, University of Illinois, Urbana-Champaign
Laura L. Mielke, University of Kansas
Christopher Looby, University of California, Los Angeles
Rodrigo Lazo, University of California, Irvine
Alisha Knight, Washington College
Hsuan L. Hsu, University of California, Davis
Michael Everton, Simon Fraser University
Christine Bold, University of Guelph

broadview press

BROADVIEW PRESS – www.broadviewpress.com
Peterborough, Ontario, Canada

Founded in 1985, Broadview Press remains a wholly independent publishing house. Broadview's focus is on academic publishing: our titles are accessible to university and college students as well as scholars and general readers. With over 800 titles in print, Broadview has become a leading international publisher in the humanities, with world-wide distribution. Broadview is committed to environmentally responsible publishing and fair business practices.

Library and Archives Canada Cataloguing in Publication

Title: The Broadview Anthology of American literature / general editors: Derrick R. Spires (Cornell University), Rachel Greenwald Smith (Saint Louis University), Christina Roberts (Seattle University), Joseph Rezek (Boston University), Justine S. Murison (University of Illinois, Urbana-Champaign), Laura L. Mielke (University of Kansas), Christopher Looby (University of California, Los Angeles), Rodrigo Lazo (University of California, Irvine), Alisha Knight (Washington College), Hsuan L. Hsu (University of California, Davis), Michael Everton (Simon Fraser University), Christine Bold (University of Guelph).
Names: Spires, Derrick Ramon, editor.
Description: Concise edition. | Includes bibliographical references and index. | Contents: Volume I. Beginnings to reconstruction
Identifiers: Canadiana (print) 20220472734 | Canadiana (ebook) 20220472769 | ISBN 9781554816194 (v. 1 ; softcover) | ISBN 9781770488885 (v. 1 ; PDF) | ISBN 9781460408209 (v. 1 ; EPUB)
Subjects: LCSH: American literature. | LCGFT: Literature.
Classification: LCC PS507 .B76 2023 | DDC 810.8—dc23

Broadview Press handles its own distribution in North America:
PO Box 1243, Peterborough, Ontario K9J 7H5, Canada
555 Riverwalk Parkway, Tonawanda, NY 14150, USA
Tel: (705) 743-8990; Fax: (705) 743-8353
email: customerservice@broadviewpress.com

For all territories outside of North America, distribution is handled by Eurospan Group.

Broadview Press acknowledges the financial support of the Government of Canada for our publishing activities.

Canada

Cover design by Lisa Brawn
Typesetting by Alexandria Stuart

PRINTED IN CANADA

CONTRIBUTING EDITORS AND WRITERS

MANAGING EDITORS:	Laura Buzzard, Don LePan
DEVELOPMENTAL EDITORS AND STAFF WRITERS:	Jennifer McCue, Brett McLenithan, Nora Ruddock, Helena Snopek, Maxwell Uphaus
GENERAL ACADEMIC AND TEXTUAL EDITORS:	Joe Davies, Michel Pharand
DESIGN COORDINATOR:	Alexandria Stuart

ASSOCIATE GENERAL EDITORS:

Gina Caison	John Marsh	Benjamin Railton
Drew Lopenzina	Koritha Mitchell	Julia Stern
Jason Haslam	Susan Scott Parrish	Kelly Wisecup

CONTRIBUTING EDITORS:

David Anthony	Christopher Hager	Jason Shaffer
Kristin Boudreau	Clayton McCarl	Christopher B. Teuton
Tim Cassedy	Laura K. Muñoz	Willow White
Scott Cave	Tiffany Potter	Caroline Wigginton
Matthew Cohen	Birgit Brander Rasmussen	Kelly Wisecup
Alejandra Dubcovsky	David Read	Brian Yothers
Jenny Marie Forsythe	Ashley Reed	
John R. Funchion	Siân Silyn Roberts	

CONTRIBUTING WRITERS:

Michael Everton	John Marsh	Joseph Rezek
Emily Farrell	Zoe McKenna	Alexandria Stuart
Jenny Marie Forsythe	Laura Mielke	Kelly Wisecup
Genevieve Kirk	Bethany Qualls	Braedan Zimmer
Rodrigo Lazo	Andrew Reszitnyk	

LAYOUT AND TYPESETTING:
Alexandria Stuart

PRODUCTION COORDINATORS:
Tara Lowes   Tara Trueman

PERMISSIONS COORDINATOR:
Jacqueline Kwan

PROOFREADERS:

Joe Davies	Judith Earnshaw	Michel Pharand
Bethany Qualls		

TEXT PREPARATION:

Caileigh Broach	Genevieve Kirk	Jennifer McCue
Alexandria Stuart	Braedan Zimmer	

Ana Schwartz, University of Texas at Austin

Seminole Nation Historic Preservation Office

E. Thomson Shields, Jr., East Carolina University

Reiner Smolinski, Georgia State University

Carole Lynn Stewart, Brock University

Matthew Teutsch, Piedmont University

Margaret Thickstun, Hamilton College

Zachary Turpin, University of Idaho

Abram Van Engen, Washington University in St. Louis

Lindsay Van Tine, Gilder Lehrman Institute of American History

Megan Walsh, St. Bonaventure University

James Warren, Washington and Lee University

Ed White, Tulane University

Edward Whitley, Lehigh University

Maria Windell, University of Colorado Boulder

Chad Wriglesworth, University of Waterloo

Jonathan Yeager, University of Tennessee at Chattanooga

Michael Ziser, University of California, Davis

Contents

This anthology's online component is available at sites.broadviewpress.com/baalonline/

[Note to Instructors: *The Interesting Narrative* is among over 400 available editions from Broadview, any one of which may be packaged together with this anthology volume.]

[Note to Instructors: *Secret History* is among over 400 available editions from Broadview, any one of which may be packaged together with this anthology volume.]

1820 TO RECONSTRUCTION

[Note to Instructors: The Last of the Mohicans is among over 400 available editions from Broadview, any one of which may be packaged together with this anthology volume.]

[Note to Instructors: *The Scarlet Letter* is among over 400 available editions from Broadview, any one of which may be packaged together with this anthology volume.]

[Note to Instructors: *Uncle Tom's Cabin* is among over 400 available editions from Broadview, any one of which may be packaged together with this anthology volume.]

[Note to Instructors: *Billy Budd, Sailor (An Inside Narrative)* is among over 400 available editions from Broadview, any one of which may be packaged together with this anthology volume.]

[Note to Instructors: *Little Women* is among over 400 available editions from Broadview, any one of which may be packaged together with this anthology volume.]

APPENDICES

[Note to Instructors and Students: See the anthology's companion website for further supplemental resources, including a selection of historical maps and an interactive timeline.]

PREFACE

A Concise Edition

Publication in 2022 of the first two volumes of the full *Broadview Anthology of American Literature* was met with near-universal acclaim—but was met as well with numerous requests that we publish a concise edition as soon as possible. For some instructors, the breadth and depth of a two-volume package is extraordinarily attractive for a survey course. Even if these instructors are able to assign only a small percentage of the material included, they are confident that many of their students will value the whole—and will find it highly useful as they continue to explore American literature in courses beyond the introductory survey. Other instructors, though, are of the view that the majority of their students will not want to hold on to their anthology volumes once the survey course has been completed; they thus feel that they cannot justify assigning such a substantial package for their students—regardless of quality, regardless of price. Many of this latter group have let us know that they would love to adopt the Broadview as a course text for their survey course, but that they would not feel justified in doing so unless or until we published a single volume covering the Beginnings to Reconstruction period. The present volume has been published in response to such requests.

A Fresh Approach

The broadening of the canon of American literature in recent generations has made the task of assembling and editing an anthology that fully and vibrantly reflects the ways in which American literary traditions are studied and taught an extraordinarily daunting one. The sheer amount of work involved in creating an anthology is enormous, but so too is the amount of expertise that must be called on. With that background very much in mind, we decided when we embarked on this project to involve a large number of contributors in the process (as the pages following the title page to

this volume attest), and to encourage a high degree of collaboration at every level. First and foremost have been the distinguished academics who serve as General Editors for the anthology, but in all there have been hundreds of people involved at various stages in advising, researching, drafting headnotes or annotations, reviewing material, editing material, and carrying out the work of designing and typesetting the texts and other materials. That approach has allowed us to prepare a large anthology of high quality with unusual speed—but we have throughout remained acutely aware of the importance of maintaining a high degree of consistency. Material has been reviewed and revised in-house at Broadview, by outside editors, and by a variety of academics with an extraordinarily diverse range of backgrounds and academic specialities, as well as by members of the group of General Editors for the project as a whole. The aim has been not only to ensure accuracy but also to make sure that the same standards are applied throughout the anthology to matters such as extent and coverage in author introductions, level of annotation, tone of writing, and student accessibility.

The General Editors have throughout taken the lead in the process of making selections for the anthology. Along the way we have been guided by several core principles. We have endeavored to provide a selection that is broadly representative, while also being mindful of the importance of choosing texts that have the capacity to engage readers' interest today. We have included a select number of longer works (among them Mary Rowlandson's *Narrative*, Frederick Douglass's *Narrative*, Herman Melville's *Benito Cereno*, and Rebecca Harding Davis's *Life in the Iron-Mills*) in their entirety in the anthology's bound book component, and many more (among them Benjamin Franklin's *Autobiography*, Elizabeth Ashbridge's *Account*, Susanna Rowson's *Slaves in Algiers*, Hannah Webster Foster's *The Coquette*, and Henry David Thoreau's *Walden*) in the anthology's online component. On the other hand, where inexpensive high-quality editions of particular works are available in our series of Broadview Editions, we have often decided to omit these works here, on the grounds that those wishing to teach one or more such works may easily order them in a special-price combination package with the anthology; on these grounds we have decided against including Nathaniel Hawthorne's *The Scarlet Letter*, for example. With a number of works (among them Olaudah Equiano's *Interesting Narrative*, Thomas Paine's *Common Sense*, Harriet Beecher Stowe's *Uncle Tom's Cabin*, Harriet Jacobs's *Incidents in the Life of a Slave Girl*, and Herman Melville's *Moby-Dick*), we have provided a substantial selection of excerpts.

Overall, our aim has always been to present American literature in the round—literature from the South and West as well as the Northeast, literature by a wide range of black and Indigenous as well as white writers, literature by Hispanic writers, literature reflective of different sexual orientations, and popular literature as well as literature established by scholarly and pedagogical convention as "literary." We have aimed to represent all genres—including oral literature and oratory as well as prose non-fiction, fiction, poetry, and drama. Throughout, we have aimed to include a wide range of selections by lesser-known writers as well as a full selection of works long accepted as part of the canon. From Elizabeth Ashbridge to Lucy Terry to Briton Hammon, and from William Apess to José María Heredia to Margaret Jane Mussey Sweat, you will find many writers here who are not represented in most general anthologies of American literature. Nor is the anthology's expanded range a matter only of including writers who have never been part of the established canon of American literature. We have also taken a fresh look at the history of the canon in other ways; we acknowledge, for example, the central place that Henry Wadsworth Longfellow held in the literary imagination of nineteenth- and early twentieth-century America by according him more space than has any general anthology of American literature for at least a half century.

When publishers issue "concise" or "shorter" editions of literary anthologies, they typically take a "major authors" approach, focusing on the most canonical authors and works. Selections from Benjamin Franklin's writings tend to remain largely untouched, while the likes of Sor Juana Inés de la Cruz and William Wells Brown and Jane Johnston Schoolcraft disappear entirely. Breadth and diversity, in short, tend to be sacrificed. In this case, the General Editors and the publisher have been determined to resist that tendency—to ensure that the diversity of American literature is reflected as fully as possible within the confines of a concise anthology. Readers will find a generous selection of works by canonical authors; Bradstreet, Franklin, Equiano, Irving, Emerson, Thoreau, Douglass, Jacobs, Hawthorne, Poe, Dickinson, and Whitman are all well represented. But readers will also find Sor Juana and Brown and Schoolcraft—and Canassatego, and Judith Sargent Murray, and William Apess, and Lydia Huntley Sigourney, and José María Heredia, and Sarah Moore Grimké, and Elias Boudinot, and David Walker, and Frances Ellen Watkins Harper—and many more. To be sure, some of the selections by authors such as Sor Juana and Horton and Schoolcraft that appear in the full anthology's bound book volumes appear in the Concise Edition's website component—as is also the case with authors such as Emerson and Hawthorne. And there are of course a few authors who are included in the full anthology but who do not appear at all in the concise edition, in either the bound book or the website components. But these are few and far between. Overall, the levels of representation in the Concise Edition of women authors, African American authors, Indigenous authors, and Hispanic authors are very much as they are in the full anthology.

As with the full anthology, the inclusion of such a great range of material is made possible simply by the format we have adopted; a two-column, large trim-size format allows us to include, in a similar number of pages, a greater amount of material than do the formats adopted by other anthologies. It's also facilitated by the hybrid nature of this anthology. The key point here is that the Broadview is *not* simply a bound-book anthology; a very large amount of material is included as part of its online component. These website selections are not "add-ons" prepared to a lower editorial standard and meant to be accorded a subsidiary status; as their inclusion in the anthology's main table of contents suggests, they are an integral part of the anthology itself, presented in the same format, and edited and annotated according to the same principles as the material included in the bound book volume. Our research has suggested that most of the authors and works which we have included as part of the anthology's website component are likely to be taught somewhat less frequently than are the authors and works included in the bound book volume. But we fully expect that a majority of instructors will wish to teach at least *some* of the selections that are to be found in the anthology's online component rather than in the bound book. (In some cases, too, we have gone against what our research has suggested about current pedagogical practice, and have included in the bound-book volume works by lesser-known writers who we believe deserve to be more widely taught—just as, in the other direction, we have included in the anthology's website component a number of works that have long been part of the established canon.) In the end, of course, instructors will make their own choices, with the needs of their own students in mind; our aim with this Concise Edition—as with the full anthology—is simply to provide instructors with the widest possible range of materials to choose from, prepared to a high editorial standard, and accompanied by the widest possible range of contextual materials.

How does this hybrid approach work in practice? A few examples may help to make plain the various ways in which it can work. Excerpts from Cotton Mather's *The Wonders of the Invisible World* are included in the bound book, while a package of contextual materials relating to the Salem Witch Trials is included in the anthology's online component; Parts 1 and 2 of Franklin's *Autobiography* are included in the bound book (together with "Remarks Concerning the Savages of North America" and "On the Slave Trade"), while the full *Autobiography* is made available in the anthology's website component. Substantial excerpts from two of Crèvecoeur's *Letters from an American Farmer* are included in the bound book, while substantial excerpts from two others (together with a selection of contextual materials) are included in the anthology's website component. Lydia Maria Child's letter on "Woman's Rights" appears in these pages; a more substantial selection from her writings appears in the online component. Twelve pages of excerpts from the *Life of Mà-Ka-Tai-Me-She-Kià-Kiàk, or Black Hawk* appear in these pages, while the full text is included in the online component. Substantial excerpts from Thoreau's *Walden* (together with "Resistance to Civil Government") are included in the bound book, while the complete text of *Walden* is made available in the anthology's website component, together with contextual materials and other Thoreau selections. In a small number of cases, audio and video selections are included in the online component alongside written texts, in recognition of the value of oral traditions.

The online component of the anthology is also important when it comes to the overview introductions to each volume. At the request of the large number of instructors we consulted on this matter, these overviews cover significant developments in American history as well as developments in American literary history. Indeed (and somewhat to our surprise), a substantial majority of those we surveyed felt that it was more important to include overviews of key aspects of the historical background in the bound book volume than it was to include overviews of the literary genres. The genre introductions for each period are thus included (together with certain of the historical overview sections, and with an overview of the development of language during the period) in the anthology's website component.

The way in which we have treated the poets George Moses Horton and Sarah Morgan Bryan Piatt is a good example of the degree to which a hybrid approach makes possible unprecedented opportunities for an anthology to be truly inclusive. Neither of these two writers has at this point a clearly established place in the canon; there is no handful of poems by either poet that have become familiar to all Americanists and that are included again and again in anthologies. Horton, author of the first book by a black Southerner and one of the most interesting poetic voices of the mid-nineteenth century, is rarely included in anthologies of any sort; even *The Norton Anthology of African American Literature* accords him only four pages. Piatt is more widely recognized, and is now represented by at least one or two poems in most anthologies of American literature—but, with the partial exception of "The Palace-Burner," there is no consensus on which of her poems most deserve to be read and studied. For each of these poets we present well over a dozen selections. Our hope is that this approach may facilitate wider reading by both instructors and students, perhaps leading to some lively class discussions as to which poems by each poet are most engaging, most interesting—and most deserving of finding a place in the American literary canon.

One further point about a "hybrid" anthology such as this one deserves to be made; when an anthology comprises both bound book and website components, there is no need to remove any author or any work from the anthology—ever. Almost every academic who has been teaching for a few years has experienced the frustration that occurs when a new edition of a favorite anthology appears—and some of the selections that have *made* it a favorite anthology have been removed. With this anthology (as with Broadview's acclaimed anthology of British literature), any selections that, upon publication of a new edition, no longer appear in the bound book anthology, will readily be found in the anthology's website component.

In a number of cases the distinctive format of the anthology facilitates the presentation of content in an engaging and practical fashion. Notably, the adoption of a two-column format allows for different versions of texts to be presented in parallel column format. That provides an opportunity for ready comparison, for example, of the Bay Psalm Book version of Psalm 21 with the King James version, and of various different versions of several of Emily Dickinson's poems. It provides an opportunity as well to show translated material alongside the original. We present several of Sor Juana's poems both in the Spanish originals and in a facing-column translation; we present one of Jane Johnston Schoolcraft's Ojibwe-language poems with her own English translation; and we present the original Spanish text of Heredia's "To Washington" alongside an English translation specially prepared for this anthology. The translated material in the section "Popular Literature and Print Culture, 1820–Reconstruction"—Wilhelm Weitling's "The Little Communist" and an excerpt from Ignace Nau's poem of Haiti, "Dessalines"—is presented in the same way. Readers are thus provided with an accessible translation while at the same time being able to experience something of the flavor of the original, in a format that provides for maximum convenience in comparing the two.

The large trim-size, two-column format also allows for greater flexibility in the presentation of visual materials. Throughout we have aimed to make this an anthology that is fully alive to the visual aspects of print culture, and, more broadly, to the connections between literary and visual culture. Readers will thus find an abundance of illustrations from the original texts, of facsimiles of title pages, of newspaper clippings of relevant articles, and of other relevant images. Wherever possible we include with each author headnote an image of the author—and, with authors such as Sojourner Truth, Douglass, Whitman, and Longfellow, we include a portfolio of other author images. In all there are hundreds of black-and-white illustrations in this volume—and we include as well twenty-four pages of color images.

Visual materials are also a key component of the background contextual materials that form an important part of the anthology. These materials are presented in two ways. Several "Contexts" sections on particular topics or themes appear for each period, presented independent of any particular text or author. These include broadly based groupings of material on such topics as "Slavery and Resistance," "Gender and Sexuality," and "Expansion, Native American Expulsion, and 'Manifest Destiny.'" Groups of "In Context" materials, on the other hand, each relate to a particular text or author. They range from "Indigenous Experiences of Metacom's War" (presented as "In Context" material accompanying Rowlandson's *Narrative*); to "Images of Rip Van Winkle"; to a fugitive slave advertisement for Harriet Jacobs; to a selection of materials on the California Gold Rush (presented as "In Context" material accompanying excerpts from the memoirs of Vicente Pérez Rosales); to a selection of "Nineteenth-Century Images of Whales and Whaling" and "The Story of the Essex" (both presented as "In Context" material accompanying the anthology's selection of *Moby-Dick* excerpts).

We also take a rather different approach to popular literature than do competing anthologies. For decades now, the leading college-level anthologies of American literature have been making some space for texts that were popular in the eighteenth or nineteenth centuries but dropped from view in the early twentieth; works such as *The Coquette* and *Clotel* have found their way into anthologies—as, of course, has *Uncle Tom's Cabin*. This renewed interest in popular and influential works of other eras, though, has often not extended to works that remained highly popular well into the twentieth century. This is particularly true of poems; works such as Longfellow's *Hiawatha* and "Paul Revere's Ride" and Whitman's "O Captain, My Captain," which were etched into the memories of generations of Americans, have been considered somehow inappropriate for inclusion in twenty-first-century anthologies. That is not the approach we take here; *The Coquette, Clotel*, and *Uncle Tom's Cabin* are certainly to be found in this anthology, but so too are *Hiawatha*, "Paul Revere's Ride," and "O Captain, My Captain." And so too are dozens of other works of popular literature—some within author entries, others in the two substantial "Popular Literature and Print Culture" sections that are included in the anthology's online component. Our aim is to provide a broad-ranging representation of American literature that includes as full a sense as possible of American literary history and print culture.

Nor does the anthology neglect oral literature and oral culture. We provide a remarkably wide-ranging selection of Indigenous and African American oral literatures, and we incorporate a diverse array of speeches in this volume. In anthologizing oral literatures in written form, we have aimed to be as transparent as possible in identifying when—and by whom—the oral works were recorded, and where possible we have included versions produced by writers from the communities to whom the stories belong. In the case of Indigenous traditions, we have also included a variety of visual pieces (such as wampum, story poles, and painted boxes). Indigenous oral and visual literatures are concentrated at the beginning of the anthology in recognition of Indigenous cultural precedence, but we have also endeavored to recognize the continued presence of Indigenous peoples and the continuing vitality of these forms—both by including some stories in contemporary versions and by including further examples of Indigenous oral and visual literature throughout this Concise Edition.

Overall, then, we have striven to make the Concise Edition more wide-ranging and comprehensive than any other "concise" or "shorter" anthology of American literature. But it must inevitably be a good deal less comprehensive than is the full anthology; by its very nature, any "concise" or "shorter" edition must leave a fair amount out. If instructors find themselves wanting to go beyond the material that is included in the Concise Edition of the Broadview in its bound book and online components, they may in some cases find that the material they are looking for is available as part of the online component of the main anthology (which is accessible through the same website as the online component of the Concise Edition). In many cases, though, they may not be able to find what they were looking for; a good many selections that appear in the bound book volumes of the full anthology are simply not available to those using the Concise Edition. If instructors who would like to choose the Concise Edition for their students find themselves hesitating to do so because one or two pieces that they would very much like to teach have been omitted from the Concise Edition, we hope they will contact their Broadview representative or our editorial team; in some cases it may be possible for us to accommodate special requests and add material to the online component of the Concise Edition website—or to arrange for a small coursepack (whether digital or hard copy) to be prepared as a supplement.

"AMERICAN": "American" is of course a slippery term. As used in expressions such as "American history" and "American literature," "American" is typically understood to mean "relating to the United States of America," rather than to all of the Americas, from Cape Horn to the North Pole. But we adopt a broad definition of "American" in this anthology, offering coverage that begins with the literatures of the people who inhabited what is now the United States, and contiguous areas; we include the literatures of Indigenous peoples first of all, and then those of settler colonists from Spain, France, and elsewhere as well as from Britain.

The fact that the United States of America as an independent nation existed first on the eastern seaboard has traditionally led to a strong emphasis in the teaching of early American literature on the literature of the east coast—and especially of the Northeast. Americanists in recent decades have pushed to broaden that scholarly and pedagogical focus, and those efforts have been reflected in recent editions of the main anthologies. This anthology partakes of that broadening, and carries it further. In our coverage of Indigenous literatures, for example, we provide a range of materials from groups in the South, the Southwest, and the Northwest as well as from the East and Northeast. Similarly, the "Civilizations in Contact" section includes extensive coverage of civilizations in contact throughout North America. Hispanic authors—among them Sor Juana Inés de la Cruz, José María Heredia, and Vicente Pérez Rosales—are here given considerably more space than they are conventionally accorded. More space too is provided for Indigenous voices. And, whereas many anthologies of the past have treated the writings of Indigenous authors primarily as contextual material, we have chosen to accord author entries to a significant number of Indigenous authors, including Canassatego, Sagoyewatha, Tecumseh, Jane Johnston Schoolcraft / Bamewawagezhikaquay, Black Hawk / Mà-ka-tai-me-she-kià-kiàk, Elias Boudinot / Gallegina, and John Rollin Ridge / Yellow Bird.

CHRONOLOGY, PERIODIZATION, AND REPRESENTATION: Like the other major anthologies of American literature, this anthology uses chronology as its primary organizing principle. But we nevertheless aim to challenge established conventions of periodization in important ways. Significantly, we end this first concise volume not at 1865 but rather with Reconstruction; we include in the latter half of the volume a wide selection of material covering the 1865–77 period. The most common point at which to break the two halves of an American Literature survey course has long been the end of the Civil War in 1865, and all other American literature anthologies use 1865 as a break point. Why take a different approach? One reason is simply that the amount of literary material any full survey course must at least touch on keeps expanding. Some of that expansion occurs as a result of the ongoing process of recovering lesser-known authors and texts, but the majority occurs simply as a result of the march of time. Moving the break from 1865 to 1877 runs the risk of giving short shrift to some important antebellum writers and texts. On balance, however, more and more Americanists are coming round to the view that the higher priority is to give somewhat more weight to

more recent material; it is in part for that reason that an increasing number of institutions now break the survey at 1877 rather than 1865.

But achieving an appropriate balance between the more recent past and earlier eras is not the only reason for choosing 1877 rather than 1865 as a break point. The two dates send different messages as to the arc of American history—and of American literary history. Choosing 1865 as a break point suggests a new beginning, a fresh start, with America having finally put the wrenching issue of slavery behind it. Choosing the end of Reconstruction as a break point suggests, arguably, something closer to reality: that, much as slavery itself may have ended, the legacy of slavery carried on as an enormously powerful shaping force in American history and literature. In making this choice, we recognize that historians no longer see 1877 as representing a clean break point, a precise moment at which Reconstruction's hopes of achieving equality were dashed and Reconstruction's ideals finally betrayed. They and we see it rather as one important moment in a continuum. But choosing such a moment emphasizes the importance of that continuum to the history and the literature of America. That is not to suggest that other topics that have received more emphasis in other anthologies—industrialization and urbanization, for example, or realism and regionalism[1]—are unimportant; far from it. We are confident that the coverage we provide of these and other related topics compares favorably to that of any other available anthology. But throughout the anthology we accord a place of utmost

---

[1] Through to the end of the twentieth century, the degree to which anthologies of American literature placed very little emphasis on racial inequality after the end of the Civil War is striking. Through to at least its 1994 fourth edition, for example, *The Norton Anthology of American Literature* included in its introduction to the history and literature of 1865–1914 America just one short paragraph on "the problem of racial inequality, more specifically what came to be known as the 'Negro problem.'" The 11-line paragraph—included almost at the end of the introduction—includes a brief discussion of Booker T. Washington and W.E.B. Du Bois; in the rest of the introduction, the only mention of a black author is the appearance of Charles Chesnutt in a list of "southern local colorists." The introduction's emphasis is entirely on the economic "transformation of a nation" ushered in by the Civil War—on industrialization and urbanization, in short—and, in literature, on realism and naturalism and regionalism. The authors never use the word "slavery"—or, indeed, the word "Reconstruction."

significance to slavery, the legacy of slavery, and, more generally, the ongoing struggle for equality.

In taking this approach, we recognize that a majority of institutions still break the survey course at 1865; for that reason, we will also include material covering the period 1865–77 in volume 2 of the Concise Edition (which will cover the second half of the survey). Much as the editors of this anthology may feel that the end of Reconstruction is a more appropriate break point than 1865, we have no desire to inconvenience those working within the traditional framework of the American Literature survey.

At several points in the anthology, we challenge the traditional periodization of—and the traditional emphases on—the scholarship and the pedagogy of American literature through departures from strict chronology. The first three authors we included in the "1820 to Reconstruction" period, for example, are William Apess, Catharine Sedgwick, and James Fenimore Cooper—in that order. Had we followed strict chronology according to each author's birthdate (the guideline through most of the anthology), that order would be reversed, with Cooper appearing first (just as he appears before Sedgwick and Apess in the Norton and in other leading anthologies). Cooper was born a few months earlier than Sedgwick in 1789, and Apess was born almost a decade later—in 1798. To open the "1820 to Reconstruction" period with Apess, then, signals a difference in approach. Presentation involves issues of representation, and this anthology aims to represent Indigenous perspectives—like those of African Americans and other previously under-represented groups—more fully and more prominently than has traditionally been done in presenting the chronology of American literature. Foregrounding Apess rather than Cooper is one important signal. Including Sedgwick before Cooper is another—a sign that we feel it to be at *least* as important to represent the traditions in nineteenth-century American literature that Sedgwick was so influential in forging as it is to represent the influence of Cooper and his famous "Leatherstocking" series.

One other point is worth making about the presentation of William Apess in this anthology. We have chosen to foreground in the bound book portion of the anthology his "An Indian's Looking-Glass for the White Man"; excerpts from his more frequently anthologized autobiographical work, *Son of the Forest*, are included as part of the anthology's website component (along with excerpts from his *Eulogy on King Philip*). This anthology's emphasis, then, runs counter to what has long been a powerful tendency in anthologizing authors from under-represented groups. Far too often, in our view, such authors (and such groups) are represented exclusively by memoirs and other autobiographical writings, while their analytical or argumentative works are ignored. Here as in other respects we aim to present American literature more fully and fairly than it often has been presented—and to represent Indigenous writers, black writers, and so on more fully and fairly than they have been represented. Readers will find an abundance of autobiographical writings in this anthology, by writers traditionally underrepresented as well as by canonical writers such as Jacobs and Douglass. But they will also find fiction, poetry, and analytic and argumentative writings by such authors as Lemuel Haynes, Elias Boudinot, Harriet Wilson, George Moses Horton, Maria Stewart, David Walker, Martin R. Delany, and John Rollin Ridge.

AMERICAN LITERATURE AND AMERICAN HISTORY IN THE TWENTY-FIRST CENTURY: This anthology is being published at a time when, in many parts of the U.S., broad-minded approaches to the teaching of American history, culture, and literature are under severe pressure. Most notably, it is argued in numerous states that the teaching of "divisive concepts" (as the phrasing of Oklahoma's legislation puts it) is to be discouraged in public institutions—at the post-secondary level as well as in schools. Students, it is argued, should not be exposed to "overly negative" portrayals of America—by which is often implied portrayals of the nation's checkered history with respect to gender equality, its dispossession and mistreatment of Indigenous peoples, and its long history of racial oppression. Even a cursory glance through the contents of this anthology will be enough to make clear we do not share that view. In these as in other respects, we have made every effort to present American literature in the context of a full and honest presentation of American culture and American history—which, in our view, has to include a full acknowledgment of the central role that settler colonialism, slavery, and racial oppression have played in that history, from the arrival of enslaved people in St. Augustine in 1565 and in Jamestown in 1619 through to our own time. But we do not present only the negative: far from it. Throughout the anthology we present a wide range of the texts that have reflected—and have shaped—the development of American ideals. Yes, we present Crèvecoeur's farmer's reflections on slavery and his jaundiced comments on the American Revolution—but we present too the glowing reflections on the American character that he puts forward in his "What Is an American?" letter. Yes, we provide the background on how the matter of slavery came to be omitted from the Declaration of Independence—but, in presenting Jefferson's original draft as well as the final text, we encourage a full and open discussion of the document that has been foundational in shaping American ideals. Literature that is straightforwardly expressive of the highest of those ideals—from John Winthrop and Roger Williams, to Phillis Wheatley and Canassatego and Benjamin Franklin, and on to Abraham Lincoln, Julia Ward Howe, Walt Whitman, and many others—features prominently in the anthology. But we believe too that many of the high points in American history and literature have been moments of resistance. From Thomas Paine and Absalom Jones to Lemuel Haynes and Judith Sargent Murray, from Tecumseh and William Apess to Lydia Maria Child and Margaret Fuller, from Henry David Thoreau to William Lloyd Garrison, Sarah Moore Grimké, and Sojourner Truth, and on to David Walker, Frederick Douglass, Rebecca Harding Davis, Frances Harper—the list is a long one—some of America's finest literature has come from writers who struggled for justice and, in doing so, placed themselves in eloquent opposition to the tendencies of their time.[1] Authors such as these are featured prominently throughout the anthology;

in this as in other respects, we have striven to take a broad view, and to present American literature—and America—in the round.

COURSE TEXT OPTIONS: Our primary aim has been to provide an anthology of extraordinary quality and extraordinary range for use in American Literature survey courses of the sort that are found in the vast majority of North American colleges and universities. For courses surveying Transatlantic Literature rather than American Literature only—and for many courses organized thematically—an attractive option may be to create a custom text (either electronically or through Broadview's bound custom coursepack option), bringing together an instructor's preferred readings from this anthology and from *The Broadview Anthology of British Literature*—the format of which is almost identical to that of *The Broadview Anthology of American Literature*. Together, these anthologies offer several thousand pages of material to choose from in assembling your own custom course text. (We offer an easy and intuitive Custom Text Builder, and our Custom Text Administrator welcomes inquiries.)

Even for many teaching a standard American Literature survey course, the Broadview custom text option may be an appealing one. If, for example, you typically build your survey course around a small number of complete works, together with a relatively modest number of poems, short stories, essays, etc., you might bring together the shorter materials in a custom text of 200 pages or so, and then choose a special-price package of Broadview editions. (Broadview's list of American literature editions list now includes more than 80 titles, from *The Female American*, Equiano's *Interesting Narrative*, and Paine's *Common Sense* to Wharton's *The Age of Innocence* and Fitzgerald's *The Great Gatsby*.) Editions may be packaged together for special savings—or, if you decide to choose just one or two editions for use with the anthology, the edition(s) may be packaged together with the anthology for a nominal additional charge.

---

[1] We give considerably less prominence to the authors who reflect sides of the American character that virtually everyone today finds deeply repugnant—but even these we do not entirely hide from view. In certain Contexts sections and as part of the anthology's website component readers can find, for example, excerpts from racist "anti-Indian" writings, excerpts from "anti-Tom" novels written in defense of slavery, and so on. Here too, our aim is to further in every way possible students' understanding of the literatures of America, both in the context of today and in their historical context.

Editorial Procedures, Conventions, and Apparatus

The in-house set of editorial guidelines for *The Broadview Anthology of American Literature* now runs to over 40 pages, covering everything from conventions for the spacing of marginal notes, to the use of small caps for the abbreviations CE and BCE, to the approach we have adopted to references in author headnotes to name changes. Perhaps the most important core principle in the introductions to the various volumes, in the headnotes for each author, in the introductions in "Contexts" sections, and in annotations throughout the anthology, is to endeavor to provide a sufficient amount of information to enable students to read and interpret these texts, but without making evaluative judgments or imposing particular interpretations. In practice that is all a good deal more challenging than it sounds; it is often extremely difficult to describe why a particular author is considered to be important without using language that verges on the interpretive or the evaluative. But it is a fine line that we have all agreed is worth trying to walk; we hope that readers will find that the anthology achieves an appropriate balance.

INTRODUCTIONS AND AUTHOR HEADNOTES: Introductory headnotes are provided for each author included in the anthology; each "Contexts" section includes its own substantial introduction; and coverage of each period begins with an introduction that endeavors to provide a sense not only of the broad picture of literary developments in the period, but also of the historical, social, and political background, and of the cultural climate. Readers should be cautioned that, while there is inevitably some overlap between information presented here and information presented in the author headnotes, an effort has been made to avoid such repetition as much as possible; the introduction to each period should thus be read in conjunction with the author headnotes and the introductions to the Contexts sections.

We aim throughout to be factual in the information we provide in author headnotes, and not to direct students' response with a particular evaluative or interpretive emphasis. But at the same time, we aim to engage student interest by making clear the degree to which and the ways in which a particular author's works have provoked a deep response or excited controversy, whether in their own day or in more recent times. Of necessity we provide something by way of conventional biographies of the authors—an overview of each author's life and works. But we strive as well in each case to provide what might be called a biography of the texts themselves: a summary of the reception history for key works, and an indication of why—in their own day, in our era, and in the intervening decades—the works have been considered worthy of attention and engagement (or, in some cases, have been unjustly neglected).

ANNOTATION: It is also often difficult to make judgments as to where it is appropriate to provide an explanatory annotation for a word or phrase. Our policy has been to annotate where we believe that most second-year undergraduates are likely to have difficulty understanding the denotative meaning. (We have made it a practice not to provide notes discussing connotative meanings.) But in practice the vocabularies of undergraduates at any given level may vary enormously, both from institution to institution and within any given college or university class. Where a word might not be known to many students but is not extraordinarily unusual or obscure, we will leave it to students unfamiliar with the word to look up its meaning. In the other direction, we make it a practice to annotate seemingly familiar words where they are being used in a text in ways that many undergraduates may not be familiar with; if a child is described as having grown up in "mean circumstances," we will gloss *mean* as *humble, impoverished*. On the whole, we provide somewhat more annotation than most competitors, and somewhat less interpretation. Again, we hope that readers will find that the anthology has struck an appropriate balance.

SPELLING AND PUNCTUATION: The level of capitalization in many seventeenth-, eighteenth-, and early nineteenth-century texts can be a distraction for students coming for the first time to the literature of these periods—as can the ways in which such texts are often punctuated. Our general policy has been to use modern conventions of capitalization, and to lightly modernize spelling and punctuation, while also providing samples of important texts in the original (and indicating in the margin where the original spelling and punctuation have been retained). Where capitalization and italicization are concerned, we have made an exception in the case of certain authors and texts—Benjamin Franklin's *Autobiography* is a notable example[1]—where spelling and punctuation choices are known (or believed on reliable authority) to represent conscious choice on the part of the author rather than simply reflecting the common practice of the time.

Much as spelling and punctuation in the great majority of texts included in the anthology are lightly modernized, we aim to provide for readers a real sense of the historical development of the language and of print culture. To that end we have included in this volume many examples of texts in their original form—in some cases through the use of pages shown in facsimile, in others by providing short passages in original spelling and punctuation as described above. We have also included a section of the history of the language as part of the introduction to each period. And throughout the anthology we include materials—visual as well as textual—relating to the history of print culture. While the anthology is intended for English-language courses, we have also made an effort through facsimile pages and facing-column translations to gesture toward the diversity of languages that are encompassed in American literature, including Spanish, French, and Indigenous languages such as Ojibwe and Massachusett.

We of course use modern conventions of American spelling and punctuation in all material newly prepared for the anthology (period introductions, author headnotes, annotations, etc.). We have not, however, "Americanized" all spellings in the texts themselves; texts from earlier periods of course use spellings that we would now categorize as British rather than American, which have been retained. (Instructors who wish to discuss with their students the development of American spelling can thus find in the anthology a wealth of material that is relevant.)

THE ETHICS AND POLITICS OF ANNOTATION, CAPITALIZATION, ETC.: Anthologies of American literature have traditionally allowed many offensive words or phrases (racist, sexist, anti-Semitic, anti-Muslim, anti-gay, etc.) either to pass entirely without comment, or to be glossed with apologist comments that leave the impression that such terms were excusable in the past, and may even be unobjectionable in the present. Most obviously, many anthologies print "the n-word" where it appears in various texts without remarking on its presence; our view is that, where such terms appear, they should be annotated, with a footnote making clear the degree to which such terms are highly offensive—and saying something as well about the history of their use. Derogatory comments about Jews and money and about the supposed cultural inferiority of Indigenous peoples are other examples. *The Broadview Anthology* endeavors in such cases, first of all, not to allow such words and phrases to pass without comment; and second, to gloss without glossing over. A few unacceptable slurs—such as the word "savage"—are unfortunately so omnipresent that we have elected not to gloss them at every usage.

Issues of ethics and politics often arise as well over debated points of present-day usage. Some of these—such as the decision whether or not to use "slave"—involve word choice. Our policy has been to avoid the use of this noun wherever possible; "enslaved people" may be somewhat more wordy than "slaves," but it has the advantage of emphasizing the essential humanity of those being referred to.

Other issues involve capitalization. As is the case with many other issues in the often-fraught history of racial and ethnic terminology, there may here be reasonable arguments that point in somewhat different directions. After much discussion, we have decided to capitalize the word "Indigenous" wherever it has been judged an appropriate term to use, but to refer wherever possible to specific groups (Ojibwe, Diné, etc.). We have chosen not to capitalize "black," however (except, of course, where it is capitalized in the literary texts themselves); though many respected media outlets have in recent years made it a policy to capitalize "black," our view is that the capitalization of "black" may be taken to implicitly encourage the

---

[1]   For those who may prefer to teach the *Autobiography* with modernized spelling and punctuation, we provide a lightly modernized text in the anthology's website component.

highly questionable assumption that a single, mono-lithic "black" ethnicity or culture exists.

TEXTS: Each author entry concludes with a note on the text(s), addressing issues regarding different versions and source texts. In some cases, we have also used footnotes to clarify one or more textual issues or to indicate what translation has been used. Copyright information for texts and translations that are not in the public domain is provided on the website and within the bound books, in a section listing Permissions Acknowledgments.

We make it a practice to include the date when the work was first made public, whether through publication in print or, in the case of dramatic works, made public through the first performance of the play (or in the case of oratory, when the speech was first delivered). Where that date is known to differ substantially from the date of composition, a note to this effect is included in parentheses.

TIMELINES: The "Texts and Contexts" timelines provide in each volume a convenient parallel reference guide to the dates of literary texts and historical developments.

GLOSSARY: Here we have adopted an integrated approach, including political and religious terms along with literary ones in a convenient general glossary. While we recognize that googling for information of this sort is often the student's first resort (and we recognize too the value of searching the web for the wealth of background reference information available there), we also recognize that information culled from the Internet is often far from reliable; it is our intent, through this glossary, through our introductions and headnotes, and through the wealth of accessible annotation in the anthology, to provide as part of the anthology a reliable core of information in the most convenient and accessible form possible.

MAPS: Also appearing within the bound book is a selection of maps specially prepared for this anthology.

ONLINE COMPANION MATERIALS: In addition to the website component of the anthology itself, the main anthology website includes a range of companion materials. "Reading Poetry" provides a concise but comprehensive introduction to the study of poetry; it includes discussions of diction, imagery, poetic figures, and of various poetic forms, as well as offering an introduction to prosody. We provide as well a comprehensive glossary of poetic terms. Also appearing online is a selection of historical maps; these may supplement the maps in the bound book volume in a variety of interesting ways. Additional companion materials on the anthology website include an interactive timeline and lists of the anthology's contents grouped by theme and author background.

ACKNOWLEDGMENTS

In addition to those whose assistance is acknowledged formally on the contributors' pages following the title page of this anthology, and those who were kind enough to grant permission to reprint copyrighted material (listed in the Permissions Acknowledgments at the back of each volume) the General Editors and all of us in-house at Broadview owe an enormous debt of gratitude to the hundreds of academics who have offered advice and assistance at various stages of this project. In particular, we would like to express our appreciation and our thanks to the following:

Mary Grace Albanese, Binghamton University, State University of New York

Christopher Apap, Oakland University

Stephen Arch, Michigan State University

Marybeth Baggett, Liberty University

Lindsey Banco, University of Saskatchewan

Brad Bannon, University of Tennessee, Knoxville

Margarita Barcelo, Metropolitan State University of Denver

Wesley Beal, Lyon College

Phillip Beard, Auburn University

William Bedford Clark, Texas A&M University

Ann Beebe, University of Texas at Tyler

Martin Bickman, University of Colorado, Boulder

John Blair, Texas State University

Anne Boyd Rioux, University of New Orleans

Nicholas Bradley, University of Victoria

Ashlee Brand, Cuyahoga Community College

Vince Brewton, University of North Alabama

Neil Brooks, Huron University College

Miriam Brown Spiers, Kennesaw State University

Michelle Burnham, Santa Clara University

Sandra Burr, Northern Michigan University

Cari Carpenter, West Virginia University

Vincent Casaregola, St. Louis University

John Casey, University of Illinois, Chicago

Abigail Chandler, University of Massachusetts Lowell

Mary Chapman, University of British Columbia

Schuyler Chapman, Glenville State College

Ben Child, Colgate University

Amanda Claybaugh, Harvard

Jim Coby, Indiana University

Michael Cohen, University of California, Los Angeles

Jeffrey Lamar Coleman, St. Mary's College of Maryland

Melissa Daniels-Rauterkus, University of Southern California

Clark Davis, University of Denver

David Davis, Mercer University

Richard De Prospo, Washington College

Christopher Diller, Berry College

Joseph A. Dimuro, University of California, Los Angeles

Don Dingledine, University of Wisconsin, Oshkosh

Kathleen Donegan, University of California, Berkeley

Virginia Dow, Liberty University

Paul Downes, University of Toronto

J. Michael Duvall, College of Charleston

Amy Earhart, Texas A&M University

S. Max Edelson, University of Virginia

Gregory Eiselein, Kansas State University

Berton Emerson, Whitworth University

Anna Esquivel, Jackson State Community College

Mike Everton, Simon Fraser University

Vera Foley, Gustavus Adolphus College

Laura Furlan, University of Massachusetts, Amherst

Brian Gazaille, University of Oregon

Melissa Gniadek, University of Toronto

Lisa Gordis, Barnard College

Robin Grey, University of Illinois, Chicago

John Griffith, University of Washington

Christopher Hager, Trinity College

Kenneth Haley, Paris Junior College

Faye Halpern, University of Calgary

William Hammersmith, Liberty University

Lawrence Hanley, San Francisco State University

Lucas Hardy, Youngstown State University

Tamara Harvey, George Mason University

Jason Haslam, Dalhousie University

Heather Hathaway, Marquette University

John Hay, University of Las Vegas, Nevada
Desiree Henderson, University of Texas at Arlington
Elizabeth Hewitt, The Ohio State University
Melvin Hill, University of Tennessee at Martin
Andrew Hoberek, University of Missouri
Michael Hoberman, Fitchburg State University
Larry Howe, Roosevelt University
Zach Hutchins, Colorado State University
Coleman Hutchison, University of Texas at Austin
Gordon Hutner, University of Illinois
Mark Kamrath, University of Central Florida
Amelia Katanski, Kalamazoo College
Pam Kingsbury, University of North Alabama
Dana Kinnison, University of Missouri
Nadine M. Knight, College of the Holy Cross
Andrew Kopec, Purdue University, Fort Wayne
Cynthia Kuhn, Metropolitan State University, Denver
Laura Laffrado, Western Washington University
Kimberli Lawson, Brigham Young University
William Lawton, James Madison University
Hellen Lee, California State University, Sacramento
Lisa Logan, University of Central Florida
Laura Lorhan, University of California, Los Angeles
Christopher Love, University of Alabama
Alyssa MacLean, Western University
David Magill, Longwood University
Joshua Masters, University of West Georgia
Kristin Matthews, Brigham Young University
Barbara McCaskill, University of Georgia
Gabrielle McIntire, Queen's University
Marilou McKenna, York University
Diego Millan, Washington and Lee University
Keith Mitchell, University of Massachusetts, Lowell
Koritha Mitchell, Ohio State University
Lisa Moody, Southeastern Louisiana University
Heather Moulton, Central Arizona College
Erich Nunn, Auburn University
Nadia Nurhussein, Johns Hopkins University
Jeffrey Ostler, University of Oregon
Keri Overall, Weatherford College
Robert Dale Parker, University of Illinois
    Urbana-Champaign
Jason Payton, University of Georgia
KJ Peters, Loyola Marymount University
Jason Potts, St. Francis Xavier University
Ben Railton, Fitchburg State University

Arthur Redding, York University
Peter Reed, University of Mississippi
Karen Renner, Northern Arizona University
James Riemer, Marshall University
Sian Roberts, Queens College
Elizabeth Robinson, Tennessee Technological University
Karen Roggenkamp, Texas A&M University-Commerce
Eric Russell, Central Michigan University
Elissa Minor Rust, Portland Community College
Debra Ryals, Pensacola State College
James Salazar, Temple University
Rebecca Saulsbury Bravard, Florida Southern College
Jennifer Schell, University of Alaska, Fairbanks
Sarah Schuetze, University of Wisconsin, Green Bay
Susan Schulten, University of Denver
Ormond Seavey, George Washington University
Jason Shaffer, United States Naval Academy
Cherene Sherrard-Johnson, University of
    Wisconsin-Madison
Mark Silverberg, Cape Breton University
Scott Simkins, Auburn University
Avery Slater, University of Toronto
Scott Slawinski, Western Michigan University
Angela Sorby, Marquette University
Sunny Stalter-Pace, Auburn University
Nicole Stamant, Agnes Scott College
Jordan Stein, Fordham University
Carole Lynn Stewart, Brock University
Nancy Sweet, California State University, Sacramento
Brynnar Swenson, Butler University
Matthew Teutsch, Auburn University
Brianna Thompson, Kenyon College
David Thoreen, Assumption University
Michael Thurston, Smith College
Kathryn Walkiewicz, University of California, San Diego
Sarah Wasserman, University of Delaware
Ed White, Tulane University
Natasha Whitton, Southeastern Louisiana University
Caroline Wigginton, University of Mississippi
Maria Windell, University of Colorado, Boulder
Nathan Wolff, Tufts University
Chad Wriglesworth, University of Waterloo
Joan Wylie Hall, University of Mississippi
Hilary Wyss, Trinity College
Elissa Zellinger, Texas Tech University
Michael Ziser, University of California, Davis

AMERICA AND AMERICAN LITERATURE, BEGINNINGS TO 1820

INDIGENOUS NORTH AMERICAN CULTURES AND LITERATURES

"**M**y elders say this was how our world was created," writes Cherokee scholar Christopher B. Teuton:

> Before there was this solid earth on which we live, the place we call Elohi, there was only Galunlati, the Sky World, which exists high above the arch of the Sky-Vault. A long time ago, before humans, the ancient animals grew crowded in there; they needed more space to live and grow. … In the ancient time they were still changing; this was before their forms were finally shaped by their thoughts and actions.

The animals held a council and agreed to search the "vast world of water" below them to find a place where they could live. One by one, the animals failed in their search until Dayunisi, the small and unassuming water beetle, dove into the water and brought up a handful of mud from the depths:

> She places that dark mud on the surface of the dark blue water, and with the help of others it begins to spread out in all directions, growing and drying. And it becomes the world on which we now stand[.] …

All of the hundreds of Indigenous cultures in North America have their own narratives of creation. Each is unique, but there are sometimes commonalities; many, for example, feature an "earth diver" who, like the water beetle, obtains materials for the first land

from deep under water. Some include the emergence of humankind from an underground realm, or a series of emergences into a series of higher worlds. According to Lakota tradition, while the earth was being prepared for human habitation, people lived underground in a spirit lodge; those who emerged too early were punished by transformation into buffalo, who would sustain the humans who came up to the land at the appropriate time. In Tlingit oral literature, the world was created by Raven, but it was in darkness until Raven cleverly stole the stars, moon, and sun to light it.

For many Indigenous peoples of North America, chronological precision is unimportant to traditional knowledge, and it is simply not a part of the narratives of origin—and, often, migration—that tell how each people came to be in its homeland. (Ethnological and archaeological consensus, too, are not specific as to when human society first emerged on the continent, though the earliest estimates are that it did so more than thirty thousand years ago.) But Indigenous traditional literatures evoke a deep, complex past and a history of environmental and cultural change. Some stories suggest that the people they belong to have been rooted in the same place from their very beginning; others suggest evolution through a series of metaphorical or geographical movements, and sometimes through merging or cultural interchange with other groups encountered along the way. Chickasaw knowledge-keepers, for example, say that their people traveled from the west under guidance from the Creator until they had crossed a great river, when there was disagreement as to where they should stop; those who stopped first became the Choctaw Nation, and those who continued eastward became Chickasaw.

Some migration stories are far less literal. The Diné (Navajo) creation story, for instance, involves the emergence of people from a dark first world into a succession of supernatural realms until they reach the Fifth World, where humans now live; in the Fourth World, they first encounter the Pueblo people. Some scholars see parallels between this Indigenous account and settler ethnographic accounts, which hold that the people of the Navajo Nation are descended from Athapaskans who journeyed from subarctic North America before settling in the Dinétah (an area including parts of what are now also called New Mexico, Colorado, Utah, and Arizona). There, they developed diplomatic relations with the Pueblo people whose civilization had long been established in the region; the Diné came to flourish not far from places abandoned early in the second millennium CE by Ancestral Puebloans, whose civilization had served as a continental center of trade and who had left behind massive buildings—many with hundreds of rooms—and hundreds of miles of roads.

Cultural exchange and historical change like this occurred in every part of North America. In the first half of the second millennium CE, there were many hundreds of different languages spoken on the continent by thousands of distinct cultures. Every type of landscape, from woodland to tundra to desert, supported a diversity of cultures—a diversity reflected in the fact that agricultural societies had cultivated as many as seven hundred species of corn alone (a staple crop across much of the continent). Agriculture, sometimes facilitated by vast irrigation systems, fed the Aztec Empire and other city-states in what would later be called Mexico and the southern U.S., while many peoples of the plains, the coast, and the northern woodlands regions developed specialized hunting and gathering skills, often practicing these skills alongside agriculture. Some peoples constructed imposing cities, while others moved freely through large territories, and some traveled seasonally between temporary settlements and permanent villages. Political systems were

This photograph, taken as part of the Historic American Buildings Survey in the mid-twentieth century, shows the ruins of Pueblo Bonito, the largest of the "great houses" built by Ancestral Puebloans. The complex, built between 850 and 1150, was four storeys tall and had more than 350 rooms on the ground floor alone.

equally varied, including small bands loosely linked by intermarriage; the aristocratic, expansionist Aztec Empire; and the democratic Haudenosaunee (Iroquois Confederacy), whose Great Law of Peace provides for each of its five (later, six) component nations to send delegates to a Grand Council where decisions affecting the whole Confederacy are made by consensus.

Such structures were not impervious to change; far from it. The fact that we do not in many cases have detailed written records of the histories of Indigenous societies should not be taken to suggest that those societies were static—that their histories began to unfold only with the arrival of Europeans. Take, for example, the case of the Great Law of Peace of the Haudenosaunee. When Europeans first encountered these peoples, their Great League was a long-established understanding—effectively, a pact of mutual non-aggression. But that had not always been the case; indeed, the formation of the pact had been preceded by a long period of wars and recriminations among the five—a period described in the Dekanawida legend (as set down in English in the early twentieth century by Mohawk Seth Newhouse and revised by Onondaga-Tuscarora Albert Cusick):

> The Ongweoweh [the original people] had fought long and bravely. So long had they fought that they became lustful for war, and many times Endeka-Gakwa, the Sun, came out of the East to find them fighting. It was thus because the Ongweoweh were so successful that they said the Sun loved war and gave them power. All the Ongweoweh fought other nations, sometimes together and sometimes singly, and oftimes they fought among themselves. … Everywhere there was peril and everywhere mourning. Men were ragged with sacrifice and the women scarred with the flints, and everywhere there was misery. Feuds with outer nations, feuds with brother nations, feuds of sister towns and feuds of families and of clans made every warrior a stealthy man who liked to kill. Then in those days there was no great law.

It was after a long period of such conflict that the prophet Dekanawida and his disciple Hayonhwatha (variously spelled Deganawida and Hiawatha, respectively) arranged a series of meetings of the feuding nations, and managed to negotiate a lasting peace accord—the Great Law of Peace.

Historians have not reached a consensus as to precisely when these momentous developments occurred; some say that the peak period of feuding among the Five Nations occurred in the fifteenth century, and the peace efforts of Deganawida and Hiawatha in the early sixteenth century, while others argue that the same succession of events transpired as much as several centuries earlier. But all agree that the events chronicled in the legend of Deganawida were crucial to the formation of what became the most powerful and influential Indigenous group in the northeast of the continent.

Diplomatic and economic links between Indigenous groups throughout the continent spanned vast distances; trade networks allowed for the movement of resources including seashells, ceramics, buffalo hides from the Great Plains, and fish oil from the Pacific Northwest. Turquoise, a valuable gemstone mined by Puebloans, was used as a trade currency as far north as the Great Lakes and as far south as the Aztec Empire. Trade was facilitated by roads spanning much of the continent, such that from Muscogee lands in present-day Georgia it was possible to trace travel routes all the way to the Pacific coast, where a road connected what is now northern Mexico to present-day Alaska.

North American Indigenous traditional literatures are as diverse and complex as the cultures they belong to, but generally speaking, oral literature historically played and continues to play—a prominent role in Indigenous cultural expression. In the centuries before colonization, as now, Indigenous oral literatures spanned many genres, including songs; political speeches; chants, rituals, and other ceremonial works; and stories. It can serve a vast range of aesthetic, cultural, and spiritual aims, as Anishinaabe (Ojibwe) academic Niigaanwewidam James Sinclair describes:

> Now, as before, stories reflect the experiences, thoughts, and knowledge important to Anishinaabeg, and collectively map the creative and critical relationships, and philosophies and histories of kin. Among other reasons, stories create, define, and maintain our relations with each other and the world around us, and when shared, cause us to reflect, to learn, to grow, as families, communities, and a People. Stories also

indicate where we are in the universe, how we got here/there, and often indicate where we need to go.

Many peoples' most important works of oral literature have a long history of performance by skilled practitioners in a ceremonial context. Some such ceremonies, and the narratives they incorporate, can extend over multiple days; a recitation of the Haudenosaunee Great Law of Peace might take a week to ten days, while some Diné ceremonies last nine. Scholar Drew Lopenzina argues that ceremonial narratives play an important and distinctive role in the perpetuation of culture and of human and natural relationships:

> ... [W]hen the storyteller relates the creation of the world in a ceremonial setting, it is perceived not as mere invocation of ancient occurrences, but rather as an indispensable component of the world's continuance. It is the ceremony that keeps the world in motion, informing all its beings of right action and a proper ordering of events. The story itself is generative and it may change with each telling, just as the world itself is changing and reshaping the narrative order of our existence, but it is framed within a certain form and tradition that must be properly understood and enacted for the ceremony itself to be successful.

The ability of a story to change with each iteration, within the framework of tradition, is part of the particular power of oral literature. Each expert performance of a traditional Indigenous oral story—whether it occurs today or six hundred years ago—partakes of a long cultural lineage that shapes the content of the story and the method of its performance. But each performance is also shaped by the choices of the storyteller, whose gestures, vocal inflections, phrasing, and selection of what story elements to emphasize can all reflect the historical and cultural moment, the needs of the audience, and other aspects of the specific context in which the story is told.

Scholars have often attempted to impose universal categories on Indigenous stories. Culture hero stories, for example, are so called because they feature figures whose actions shape the world, such as Gluskap, who, according to the traditions of the Wabanaki Confederacy, played a role in the world's creation, taught humans the

skills they needed to live, and has saved humans from various monsters—often by transforming them into animals after defeating them. In Indigenous literature, culture heroes often overlap with trickster figures—multifaceted beings who are clever and powerful, but tend to be led astray by their appetites in ways that can be variously funny, ribald, sinister, philosophically profound, and morally or practically instructive. Tricksters may also be creators, like Raven of Tlingit stories, and they may have a shaping effect on the world after its creation, like Coyote, who brings death and sickness into the world in the stories of Maidu people, Caddo people, and many others. But while there are commonalities in the figures and motifs that appear in the traditional literatures of different Indigenous cultures, each must be understood as its own independent body of literature founded in the landscape, history, and moral and aesthetic standards of its people.

Nowhere are Indigenous literatures more diverse than in the vast array of visual modes of communication that peoples have developed across the continent. Ideas, stories, histories, diplomatic agreements, and messages of all kinds have long been recorded and communicated in literary forms specific to particular regions or nations. These forms include symbolic carvings and engravings, painted baskets, tattoos, scrolls, wampum belts and strings, maps, books, arrangements of stones or sticks—all carrying meanings legible to those with the knowledge necessary to read them. For example, many peoples of Dawnland (an Algonquian name for what are now New England, the Canadian Maritime provinces, and parts of Quebec) possess pictographic traditions with many uses, including map-making and long-distance communication. Pictographs inscribed into a tree might indicate where the author had experienced a successful hunt, or inform friends and family of the length and destination of the author's journey. Further north, Innu tshissinuatshitakana (message sticks), pieces of spruce placed according to symbolic conventions, were similarly developed to communicate with fellow travelers.

Many traditional literacies occupy a space between what European tradition would consider writing and visual art, sometimes combining visual with oral forms as well. Mayan writing, developed in Mesoamerica as early as the first millennium BCE, is so complex that interpreting books aloud was an art form of its own: glyphs represented both syllabic sounds and entire words or concepts, and books incorporated pictures as well as glyphs that together conveyed the text's complete meaning. Among Haudenosaunee and other Northern woodlands peoples, an important form of communication and record-keeping is wampum—purple and white shell beads that can be patterned so as to convey ideas. For many hundreds of years, belts of wampum woven in symbolic patterns have been made to document diplomatic agreements and other significant events. The full meaning of the pattern is preserved in oral tradition, as wampum keepers in each generation learn to read the belts, using them as a guide to memory that enables them to speak at length on the knowledge held in the wampum. In the case of diplomatic agreements, wampum readings can function as diplomatic events in themselves, in which the involved parties gather to hear, discuss, and reinvigorate the agreement made concrete in the belt.

Many traditions recognize visual literacy as possessing a sacred power. In Anishinaabe tradition, for example, images inscribed on birchbark scrolls record important spiritual and historical knowledge; the scrolls, kept by the Midéwiwin or Great Medicine Society, serve as a complement to an oral tradition in which one must be educated in order to interpret them. Diné ceremonies generally employ both sacred chants and sandpaintings, detailed and symbolically rich images made by dropping sand, pollen, and other colored powders in precise ways. These sacred visual texts are intended to be destroyed in the course of the ceremony, and are sufficiently powerful that it is considered dangerous to oneself and one's community to capture them in permanent form.

The colonization of the Americas brought about a great deal of loss in Indigenous literatures, as the actions of settler-colonists— sometimes intentionally—destroyed whole cultures and interfered in numerous ways with the knowledge-keeping practices of the cultures that survived. Colonization also brought change to Indigenous literatures, as Indigenous people adapted European languages, genres, and forms of writing to their purposes, and as each people's oral and visual traditions have continued to evolve through centuries of political and cultural upheaval.

CONTACT, AND THE LITERATURES OF CONTACT

As Lenape elder Nora Thompson Dean recounted in the late twentieth century,

> Long ago there was a Lenape man who had remarkable powers. He would often go and meditate. He was able to foresee the future. One day he told his people, "Soon we will have visitors. They will be real white, fair skinned people, and they will come from the east in a huge vessel. They are a people who will change our way of life."
>
> Not many people believed him, but finally one day the Lenape people saw a ship coming in. And when these men got out of their boat, the Lenape people were much amazed as they had light skin, blue eyes, and light hair. They were very stunned and dumbfounded, but most of the Lenape were so glad that these visitors had come that they put down furs for them to walk on.

The arrival of Europeans elicited various reactions on different parts of the continent—surprise, aggression, and gracious welcome among them. But one common thread is undeniable: contact brought tremendous change to Indigenous ways of life, as well as to the ways of life of the Europeans who came to the Americas. Christopher Columbus and his crew were not the first white people to reach the Atlantic coast of the Americas; Norse people, having established themselves on Greenland slightly before 1000 CE, had briefly settled in small numbers on the northeastern North American coast, while seafarers from various regions of the western European seaboard, including England and the Basque country, may have fished the Grand Banks off the coast of Newfoundland in the late Middle Ages. The extraordinary and destructive cultural, environmental, and political transformation initiated by Columbus's arrival in the Caribbean in 1492, however, was different from anything that had come before.

Columbus's actions during his early voyages presaged much of what was to follow as Europeans explored and colonized what they would call the New World: on his first voyage, he took Taíno prisoners and established a military base on Hispaniola, where Haiti and the Dominican Republic are now located; he subsequently enslaved hundreds of Taíno people for sale in

Mayans invented paper around 500 CE, and Mayan cities possessed libraries housing thousands of books. During the colonial era, almost all of these were deliberately destroyed by Spanish clergy. This image shows two pages from one of the few books known to have survived, known as the Paris Codex (for the city where it is now kept). Among other things, the codex contains precise astronomical information and a calendar denoting the appropriate rituals for a 360-year period.

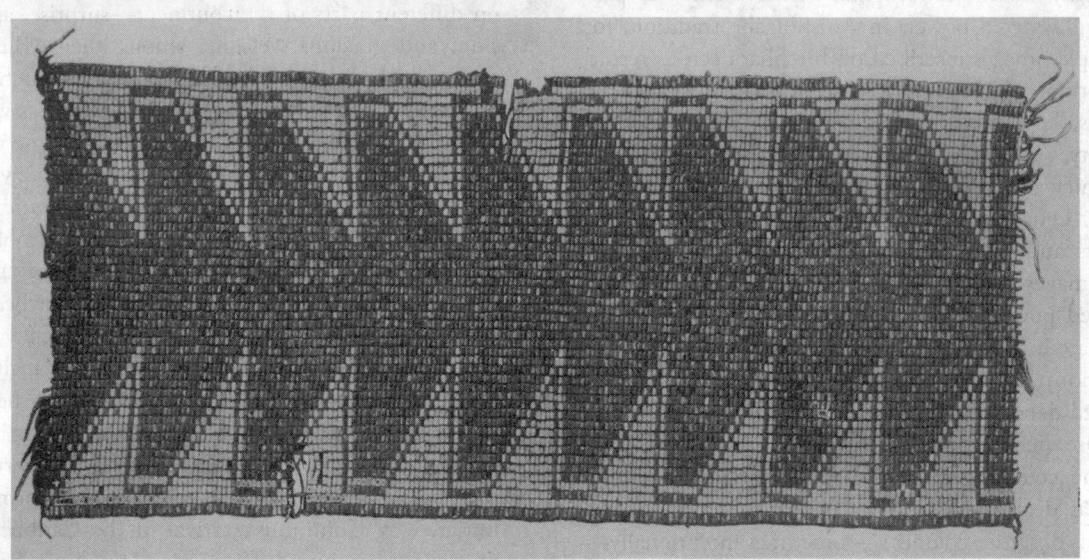

This wampum belt, known as the Dust Fan Belt, is kept by the Onondaga Nation. According to its keepers, it was made at the foundation of the Haudenosaunee Confederacy, and its imagery evokes the confederacy's principles. The Onondaga interpret the belt as evoking two powerful symbols, first of the Tree of Peace, a giant white pine that was uprooted at the foundation of the Haudenosaunee Confederacy of Five Nations. Into the cavity of the uprooted pine, the nations threw their weapons of war, which were then buried when the tree was replanted; an eagle was placed at the top to guard the Confederacy against potential dangers. The white pine is also symbolic of the Confederacy itself, as the tree's needles grow in bundles of five, the number of nations originally in the Confederacy. The pattern of the belt also suggests the shape of a dust fan, a reminder of the need for clear vision. There is no beginning or ending to the belt—the pattern continues beyond its borders—suggesting the long continuity of the Confederacy and its values.

Spain. Believing there to be vast gold deposits in one area of Hispaniola, he demanded each of its inhabitants produce as tribute an impossible quota of gold—and cut off the hands of those who inevitably failed. Before 1500, more than half of the island's Indigenous population was dead, mostly due to execution, forced overwork, or suicide, and the Spanish began to bring in enslaved Africans to replace them as a source of labor. "Who in future generations will believe this?" wrote the friar and historian Bartolomé de las Casas, reflecting on the scale of the destruction. "I myself writing as a knowledgeable eyewitness can hardly believe it."

Columbus's ventures marked the beginning of an age of exploration and colonization by European powers. These efforts were dominated by Spain in the sixteenth century, and increasingly by England from the seventeenth century onward, though many other nations competed to secure for themselves the labor, resources, and land of the Americas. Often, Indigenous people were affected by colonization even before their own territories were occupied, as invasive species, disruptions to trade patterns, and, above all, foreign diseases caused immense suffering, dramatically reduced Indigenous populations, and created political and economic instability. The shrewdest colonizers—who were, in the early phases of colonization, vastly outnumbered by Indigenous people—did not hesitate to take advantage of these weaknesses, or to exploit pre-existing diplomatic tensions between Indigenous groups.

The Spanish conquistador Hernán Cortés, for example, would have had very little chance at defeating the powerful Aztecs with only the small force at his command—and did, in fact, fail disastrously in his early attempts. But the capital city of Tenochtitlan was soon ravaged by smallpox and famine, and Cortés formed an alliance with the nearby Tlaxcalans, who saw an opportunity to free themselves from Aztec dominance. With ten thousand Tlaxcalan warriors and mere hundreds of Spanish soldiers, Cortés massacred

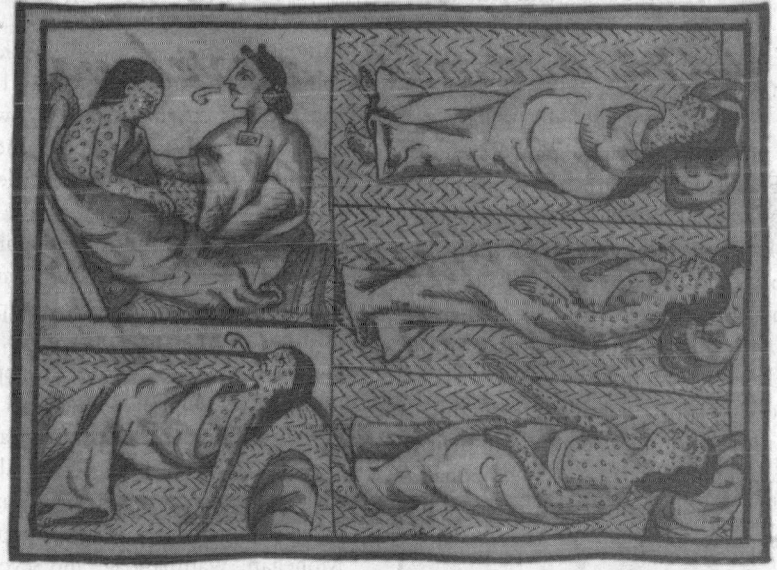

Illustration from *The General History of the Things of New Spain*, sixteenth century. Known as the Florentine Codex for the city in which it is now held, *The General History of the Things of New Spain* is a massive compendium of Aztec history, culture, and knowledge written in Spanish and Nahuatl (the language spoken by Aztecs). The book is the result of a decades-long collaboration between the Spanish friar Bernardino de Sahagún and dozens of Nahua scholars and artist-scribes. The illustration reproduced here depicts an epidemic of smallpox that occurred shortly after Europeans introduced the disease to the Americas. Most of the book is lavishly colored, but the last portion, from which this image was taken, is not; another epidemic struck, forcing the book's creators to sequester themselves, and they ran out of pigment before completing the project.

the people of Tenochtitlan in 1521. Less than a decade later, an anonymous poet wrote of the siege in Nahuatl (the language spoken by Aztecs):

> Broken spears lie in the roads;
> we have torn our hair in our grief.
> The houses are roofless now, and their walls
> are red with blood.
>
> Worms are swarming in the streets and plazas,
> and the walls are splattered with gore.
> The water has turned red, as if it were dyed,
> and when we drink it,
> it has the taste of brine. ...

The European settler-colonizing presence spread quickly: after failed attempts earlier in the century, Spanish colonizers founded presidios (fortified settlements) at St. Augustine, Florida, in 1565 and Santa Fe, New Mexico, in 1610. Exploration of the Pacific, led by Spanish and Portuguese explorers, was not as thorough as Atlantic exploration, but by the late sixteenth century Spain's trade routes crossed both Pacific and Atlantic Oceans, with some ships stopping to replenish their fresh water on the California coast as they completed the treacherous route between the Philippines and South America. The English, too, explored the Pacific coast, primarily as privateers seeking Spanish trade goods—though Sir Francis Drake alarmed the Spanish government in 1579 by making diplomatic contact with Indigenous inhabitants of northern California and declaring it "Nova Albion" (New England). (As it turned out, California would indeed be settled by the Spanish, beginning in the mid-eighteenth century with the presidio of San Diego.)

As they staked their claims, colonists frequently overwrote North American place names with their own; California, for example, was named for a fictional island described in the early sixteenth-century Spanish romance *Las Sergas de Esplandián*:

> Know, then, that, on the right hand of the Indies, there is an island called California, very close to the side of the Terrestrial Paradise, and it was peopled by black women, without any man among them, for they lived in the fashion of Amazons. ... Their arms were all of gold, and so was the harness

of the wild beasts which they tamed and rode. For, in the whole island, there was no metal but gold.

Many colonizers, especially in the early period, were motivated by genuine belief in myths such as that of the fantastically wealthy city of El Dorado, which was sought by Antonio de Berrio, Walter Ralegh, and numerous other explorers.

English settler-colonization did not begin in earnest until the seventeenth century, when English colonizers established settlements concentrated in the Caribbean; in what are now Virginia and the Carolinas; and in New England, the location of Plymouth Colony (1620), the Massachusetts Bay Colony (1630), and several others. When John Smith named this last region "New England" in 1616, English settlement in North America was far from fully established. On the contrary, the small population of early colonists in New England and Virginia frequently struggled merely to survive. With little knowledge of the landscape or the local economies, they relied on the knowledge of Indigenous people—some they had kidnapped and some they communicated with peacefully—and on Indigenous food stores, both stolen and traded for. As John Smith wrote in 1617, "had the savages not fed us" the Virginia colonists "directly [would have] starved." On the New England coast, Indigenous homes still significantly outnumbered settler-colonist dwellings a decade after the arrival of the *Mayflower*. Cultural interchange was multidirectional: Indigenous people adopted aspects of European homes and fortifications; Europeans adopted canoes; wampum came to be used as a currency across the region; and pidgins (simple languages used for trade) developed out of different, mutually intelligible Indigenous languages, influencing both Indigenous and European speech.

Even as English settlement became more developed, power relations in New England were far from straightforward. The Narragansett, Abenaki, Pequot, Mohegan, Wampanoag, and several other Indigenous peoples who lived there each had their own internal and external conflicts, diplomatic connections, and agendas, and some found opportunities for advancement in forming alliances with colonist communities. Colonists turned diplomatic instabilities to their advantage, most infamously during the genocidal Pequot War (1636–38). An alliance of English colonies

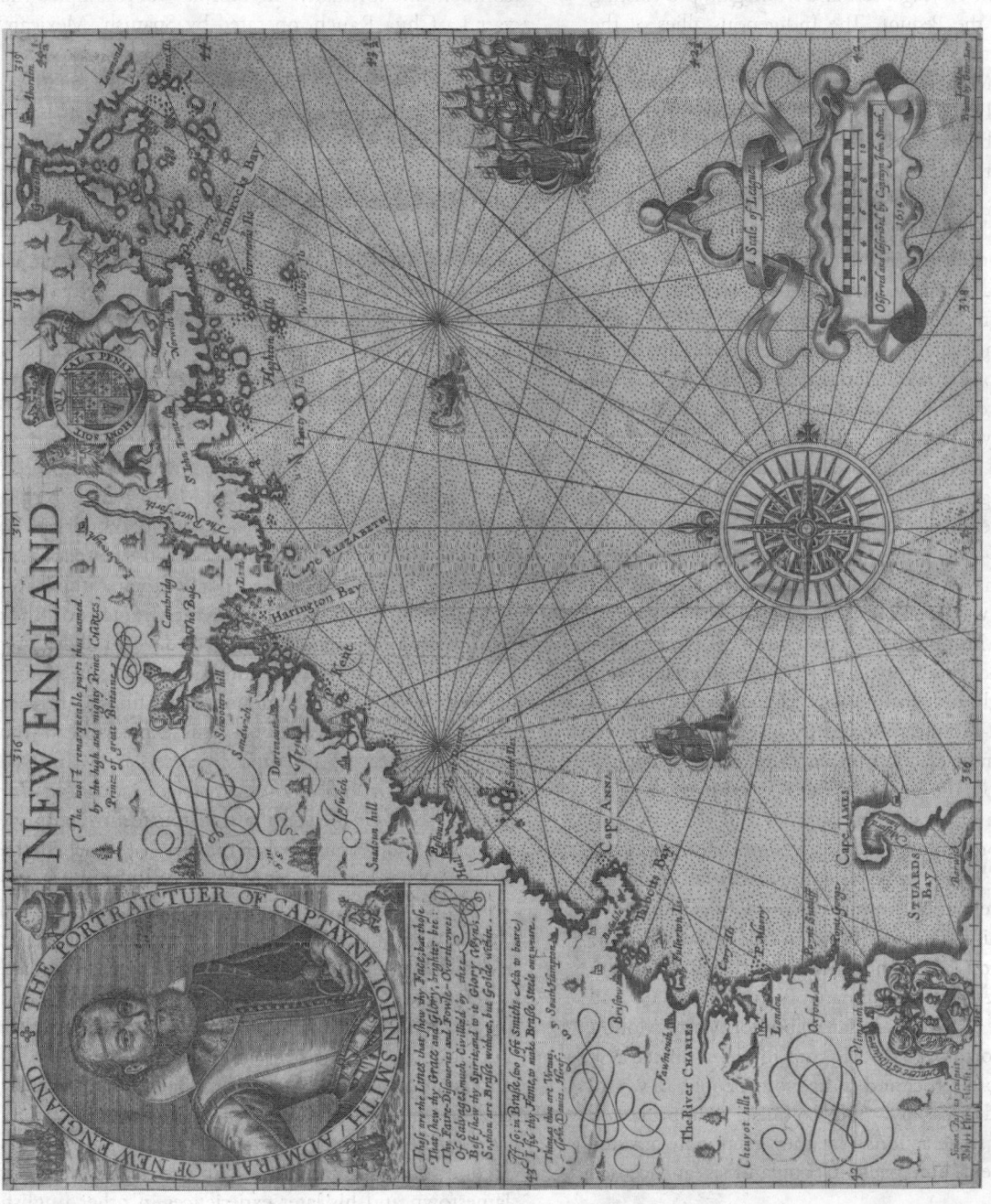

This map, which appeared in John Smith's *A Description of New England* (1616), is the first to apply the name "New England" to the region formerly known to colonists as "North Virginia." The map features place names selected by the teenaged Prince Charles (1600–49), later King Charles I, and Smith included a table showing "the correspondence of the old names to the new." Most of the place names assigned on the map were not retained in the long term, but a few were: Accomack, for example, was renamed Plymouth, and the Massachusetts River was to be known as the Charles.

including Massachusetts and Plymouth singled out the powerful Pequot for elimination and formed an alliance with the Narragansett and Mohegan, pre-existing enemies of the Pequot. The Indigenous allies of the English were appalled when the war culminated in the Mystic Massacre, during which English soldiers set fire to the Pequot fortress and killed everyone inside, including children and civilians as well as warriors. The Narragansett disclaimed the massacre, declaring that the English were "too furious, and slay[ed] too many men," but the damage was done: the English enslaved the survivors, forbade them from calling themselves Pequot, and demanded that all Indigenous people of the area bring them the heads of any Pequot they discovered. The war brought about a fundamental shift in the region's power relations by revealing what the English were capable of, and even the Narragansett and Mohegan, who had entered the war thinking themselves equal allies, ended in a position of subservience. To the Indigenous groups who had been neutral in the conflict, the English had replaced the Pequot as the dominant group in the area; the Montaukett sachem Wyandanch, for example, agreed to give the colonists "tribute, as we did the Pequots."

On the European side, too, conflicts were multifaceted. The Dutch settlers of New Netherland were threateningly near to the New England colonies, and in the mid-seventeenth century, New Netherlanders found themselves confronting, according to council minutes, "on the one side the war with the savages and on the other side the approach of the English." According to colony records, the English similarly feared that "at the same time they shall fall upon the English: the Dutch from their ships, the Indians by land." Enmity even arose between colonies of the same parent nations, as demonstrated in the bitter rivalry between the Puritan-dominated Plymouth Colony and the nearby, relatively secular colony of Ma-re Mount. Thomas Morton, Ma-re Mount's founder, hosted revelries for both settler and Indigenous people, to whom he also sold guns; Plymouth colonists disapproved so strongly of these actions that they eventually arrested him and sent him back to England as an accused criminal.

In other contact regions of North America, as in New England, settler-colonists—often from more than one European nation—shared with diverse Indigenous groups a complex web of trade, cultural interchange, conflict, and brutality. In Florida, for example, the vast La Chua Ranch, operated by Spanish, Mexican, Native American, and enslaved African people, was at the center of a trade not only in beef but also in Cuban rum and Indigenous-grown corn. In the Great Lakes region, French missionaries converted large numbers of Wendat (Huron) people and allied with them against their Haudenosaunee rivals. There, too, the French were vastly outnumbered by Indigenous people and relied on them for the success of their colonial enterprise; as Mary McKey, a Wendat elder, phrased it in an oral history, "When the white man was first seen here, in the old time, he began to barter with our ancestors. Nowhere could he step without coming across some red man."

In European literature of contact, writers attempted to understand but also to lay claim to an unfamiliar land, and occasionally to condemn but more often to advocate colonization. The accuracy of narratives of discovery varies tremendously, but all are shaped at least to some degree by the agendas of their authors and by the European cultural and literary frameworks they used to interpret what they witnessed. Columbus's first letter of discovery (1493), for example, is an explicit request to the Spanish monarchy to finance further expeditions. Its description of his exploits bears the influence of earlier travel narratives set largely in Asia, such as *The Travels of Marco Polo* (c. 1300) and *The Travels of Sir John Mandeville* (mid-fourteenth century), reflecting Columbus's belief that he had reached the Asian coast. Cortés, in his "Letters of Relation" (1519–26)—another blatant attempt to secure royal support through the medium of print—describes the Aztec ruler Moctezuma's palace as having "a large patio, laid with pretty tiles in the manner of a chessboard." This feature is unlike anything in Indigenous Mesoamerica but quite common in the architecture of the Moors, an enemy whom the Spanish monarchy had recently defeated in Granada. *The General History of Virginia, New England, and the Summer Isles* (1624), John Smith's account of his prominent role in the establishment of Jamestown and his later experiences in other English settlements, includes some self-aggrandizing passages that similarly call into question the accuracy of his

Samuel de Champlain, "Defeat of the Iroquois at Lake Champlain," 1613. Samuel de Champlain, an explorer who played a key role in the early colonization of New France, was also an artist and writer who illustrated his own accounts of his experiences. The above image depicts Champlain at the center of a battle in which Haudenosaunee warriors were defeated by a group consisting of a few French people and a number of Wendat, Innu, and Algonquin people. Champlain described the incident as follows:

When I saw [the Haudenosaunee] make a move to draw their bows upon us, I took aim with my arquebus and shot straight at one of the three chiefs, and with this shot two fell to the ground and one of their companions was wounded who died thereof a little later. I had put four bullets into my arquebus. As soon as our people saw this shot so favourable for them, they began to shout so loudly that one could not have heard it thunder, and meanwhile the arrows flew thick on both sides. The Iroquois were much astonished that two men should have been killed so quickly, although they were provided with shields made of cotton thread woven together and wood, which were proof against their arrows. This frightened them greatly. As I was reloading my arquebus, one of my companions fired a shot from within the woods, which astonished them again so much that, seeing their chiefs dead, they lost courage and took to flight, abandoning the field and their fort, and fleeing into the depth of the forest, whither I pursued them and laid low still more of them. Our Indians also killed several and took ten or twelve prisoners.

work. Most famous among these is an encounter with Wahunsonacock, chief of the Powhatan Confederacy, who, according to Smith, was about to execute him when the chief's daughter, Pocahontas, supposedly risked her own life to prevent the execution.

Alongside personal and national ambition, religious conviction was a key motive for colonization—and one that was often invoked in discovery and settlement accounts. To some Spanish colonizers, bringing Catholicism to Indigenous people was the predominant goal; according to the memoirs of Bernal Díaz del Castillo, a participant in the conquest of Tenochtitlan, the conquistadors came "to serve God and his Majesty, to give light to those who were in the darkness"—if also, Castillo adds, "to grow rich as all men desire to do." Though Spanish missions and civil governments were often in conflict, the twin purposes of wealth and proselytization were in many respects complementary, as Spanish missionaries tended to make the closest contact with Indigenous villages, cultivating diplomatic relationships with Indigenous groups as potential sources of labor. In the Great Lakes region at the center of New France, religious proselytization motivated missionaries to learn Indigenous languages and ways of living; this facilitated the development of the diplomatic and economic relationships underlying the fur trade. Many of the settlers of New England were Puritans, Protestants who believed the Anglican Church to be corrupted by Catholic influence. They saw settlement in the New World as a way to establish a spiritually upright society in which they could live according to their principles. For these settlers, their experiences paralleled those of the Israelites, God's chosen people, recounted in the Bible: hardships were tests of faith, and successes were signs that their colonization of the land was willed by divine providence.

"Many good religious devout men have made it a great question," John Smith acknowledged in his *Advertisements for the Unexperienced Planters of New England, or Any Where* (1631), "as a matter of conscience, by what warrant they might go to possess those countries, which are none of theirs, but the poor salvages [savages']." Indeed, writings about colonization often struggled to justify the exploitation, dispossession, and killing of Indigenous people, especially as these facts conflicted with settler-colonists' belief in

Seal of the Massachusetts Bay Colony, 1629. The original seal of the Massachusetts Bay Colony, developed when the colony received its charter in 1629, depicts an Indigenous man saying "come over and help us." He holds an arrow pointing down, a symbol of peace.

their religious purpose or their political right to the territory. The justifications colonists used were sometimes mutually contradictory. Robert Cushman, a Plymouth supporter, argued that there was a spiritual imperative to "conver[t] … the heathens" but also described the land as "empty." At the same time, many colonists went so far as to interpret the devastating epidemics that swept Indigenous communities as a divine blessing that reflected God's support for the settlers. Even the relatively Indigenous-friendly colonist Thomas Morton praised "the wondrous wisdom and love of God, … shown by sending to the place his Minister [i.e., disease], to sweep away by heaps the Salvages." Belief that God had granted them the right to settle North America was used to excuse even extreme violence; John Underhill, a soldier who commanded the massacre of the Pequot, wrote that "We had sufficient light from the word of God for our proceedings."

Often, narratives of discovery were inconsistent in the degree to which they acknowledged that North America was even occupied. John Smith wrote, for example, that settlers should come because "the country of the Massachusetts" was a "Paradise ... for here are many isles all planted with corn; groves, mulberries, salvage gardens, and good harbors." On the other hand, William Bradford, a leader of the Plymouth colonists, wrote of "those vast and unpeopled countries of America, which are fruitful and fit for habitation, being devoid of all civil inhabitants, where there are only salvage and brutish men, which range up and down, little otherwise than the wild beasts of the same." Even as, in actuality, the English relied on Indigenous knowledge and resources to establish their settlements, they argued that the Indigenous inhabitants had limited rights to the land because they had failed to cultivate it. Cushman claimed that "[t]hey are not industrious, neither have art, science, skill or faculty to use either the land or the commodities of it, but all spoils, rots, and is marred for want of manuring, gathering, ordering, etc."

Even the size of European territorial claims could represent a distortion of the facts. Seventeenth-century New France, for example, consisted of only a few settlements, but the French claimed to have "discovered" and to possess a vast area of the North American interior. For much of the colonial period, the reach of colonists beyond the east coast and the southern portion of the continent was limited, and much of North America remained mostly or wholly Indigenous in population. As late as 1782, J. Hector St. John de Crèvecoeur marveled that

> Many ages will not see ... the unknown bounds of North America entirely peopled. Who can tell how far it extends? ... for no European foot has as yet travelled half the extent of this mighty continent!

The continent was, of course, already "peopled." For the societies of the north and west, disruptions were relatively small in the first centuries, but for those in contact regions change was harsh and abrupt. Some Indigenous people migrated out of contact regions, others tried military resistance, and others attempted to make economic and diplomatic opportunities for themselves out of the changes. For many, this latter approach involved selectively adopting European cultural practices, including writing in European languages. In Mexico, scribes who were already trained in their own complex writing system quickly acquired the alphabet used by the Spanish. Through their early adoption, they preserved pre-contact works as well as accounts of colonization that might otherwise not have survived in written form, as Spanish clergy systematically destroyed Aztec and Mayan books.

In New England, many seventeenth-century sachems enlisted settlers to write diplomatic letters on their behalf, and some Indigenous students soon began to seek a European education that would help them advocate for their communities. A number of these students attended Harvard. The college had a mandate to educate them for the purposes of proselytization, but they learned Latin, Hebrew, and Greek and studied classical literature and philosophy as well as Christian theology. North America's first printing

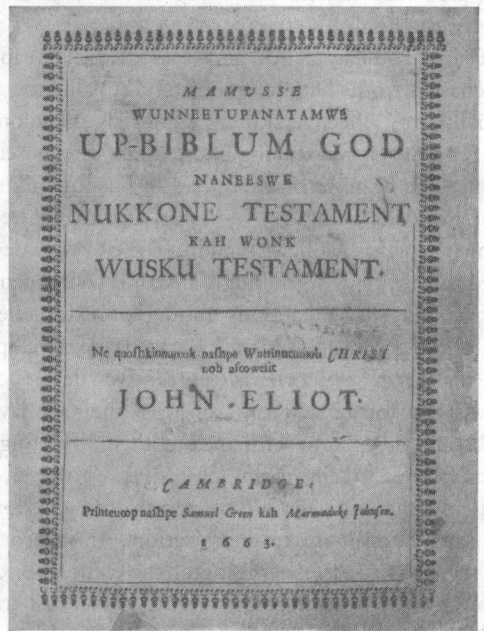

Title page of *Mamusse Wunneetupanatamwe Up-Biblum God*, also known as the Eliot Indian Bible or Algonquian Bible, 1663.

press, the Cambridge Press, was operated by Wowaus, a Nipmuc man also known as James Printer. Among its publications was the first Bible to be printed in North America, an Algonquian translation known as the Eliot Indian Bible (1663) for its overseer, the Puritan settler John Eliot, but written largely by Indigenous scholars.

Some Indigenous groups responded to settler-colonial encroachment with immediate violence. The Calusa of what the Spanish called La Florida, for example, responded aggressively to almost every Spanish attempt at diplomatic or missionary engagement, a strategy that kept them independent until the early eighteenth century. More often, Indigenous groups were friendly at first, but came to consider diplomatic efforts futile as settler-colonists claimed dominance over ever-expanding territory and demonstrated their willingness to exploit and brutalize Indigenous people. One famous early attempt at a military solution to the threat posed by colonization was King Philip's War (1675–76), named for the Wampanoag sachem Metacom (also known as King Philip). Metacom's leadership helped to unite a large number of New England Indigenous peoples—Nipmuc, Narragansett, and Wabanaki among them—against their common enemy, the English settlers.

Using guerilla tactics and armed with weapons purchased from Dutch colonists, the alliance was initially very effective, killing hundreds of colonists and completely destroying more than fifteen settlements. The English, however, had Indigenous allies of their own, including the Mohegan and the powerful Kanien'kehá:ka (Mohawk), and in the end they devastated their opponents, killing thousands of Indigenous people and enslaving many more, some for sale to Caribbean colonists. A lucrative slave trade developed, but it proved to be brief as the captives developed a reputation for tenaciously resisting their enslavers, and planters began to refuse to buy them. The English accomplished their main objectives, however, in reducing the Indigenous population and discouraging armed resistance to colonization. At the end of the seventeenth and beginning of the eighteenth centuries, people from more than thirty east coast tribes fled to the less fully colonized Great Plains, where they formed hybrid cultures with the tribes already living there. Through this migration, they achieved almost another hundred years relatively free from the direct interference of settler-colonists.

While in reality Indigenous people faced captivity in much larger numbers than colonists, the colonial genre of the "Indian captivity narrative," typically written by and for white readers, focuses on the sufferings of colonists held captive by Indigenous groups. The genre began to develop not long after North American colonization itself, with the earliest first-person captivity accounts published in the mid-sixteenth century. *The Relation of Álvar Núñez Cabeza de Vaca* (1542) was a particularly early and influential firsthand narrative. In it, Cabeza de Vaca recounts the growth of his Catholic faith and of his respect for Indigenous peoples during the eight years he spent lost between what the Spanish called La Florida and Mexico, including a period of enslavement in what is now Texas. The secondhand narrative of Juan Ortiz, retold by numerous authors but most famously in Inca Garcilaso de la Vega's *La Florida del Inca* (1605), was also influential. Ortiz's account of his capture by the people of Uzita, where the daughter of the cacique (chief) saves him from execution, may have inspired John Smith's account of his salvation by Pocahontas.

In English, the most influential early captivity narrative by far was Mary Rowlandson's *The Sovereignty and Goodness of God* (1682), an account of her abduction and captivity during King Philip's War. Rowlandson's story established a pattern that many (though not all) English-language captivity narratives would follow: a white protagonist, especially a white woman, whose suffering is the primary subject of the account; a focus on the testing and development of the protagonist's Christian faith; and detailed but also frequently inaccurate and racist depictions of Indigenous people and cultures. In this respect, captivity narratives are like much of the early American literary canon, in which Indigenous experiences of contact are usually obscured or distorted. These experiences are, however, more directly communicated in colonial-era Indigenous people's own writings and nonalphabetic works; in their dictated letters, transcribed speeches, and legal documents; and in oral histories that Native American peoples continue to preserve.

RELIGION IN EARLY AMERICA

When the subject of religion among the settlers of what would become the United States arises, the Puritans of New England come to many minds first. Primary school students dress up as Pilgrims and learn how these early English settlers journeyed from Europe to the New World in search of religious liberty. But long before the Plymouth settlers arrived aboard the Mayflower in 1620, or even before their fellow English colonists in Virginia founded Jamestown in 1607, Spanish-speaking Catholics had traversed North America, seeking to convert—and to conquer—the Indigenous peoples of Florida and much of what are now the states of Texas, New Mexico, Arizona, and California. Indeed, throughout the sixteenth and seventeenth centuries, many of the areas that would eventually become the United States were explored and settled by French- and Spanish-speaking Catholics. Maryland, founded in 1632 as a Catholic colony, is estimated to have had a Catholic population of 3,000 in 1700; the combined Catholic population of what are now the southwestern states, Louisiana, and Florida, though difficult to estimate, was certainly far, far larger. Indeed, the oldest known Christian church in what is now the continental United States stands, not in Plymouth or Jamestown, but in Santa Fe: San Miguel Mission, built between 1610 and 1626.

Though the Puritans may not deserve quite so central a place in early American history as they have often been accorded, there is no question of their importance. The Puritans were not originally a denomination unto themselves, but rather a large group within the established Church of England; they took their name from their desire to purify the church by ridding it of its more "popish" or Roman Catholic elements. They embraced the doctrines laid out by John Calvin, a French theologian who argued from biblical proofs that only a small number of individuals (the "elect") had been predestined for salvation from the time they were born. Because the Puritans felt that the Church of England's clerical hierarchy discouraged individual congregations from making their own decisions, they organized their churches as congregational polities, in which each male member of the church participated in decision-making. (This organization was less egalitarian

Timothy H. O'Sullivan, *The Church of San Miguel, Santa Fe*, 1873.

than it sounds, since only those who had proven they were among the elect could be members of the church.) And because they objected to the sumptuous display in Anglican church decoration and clerical dress, the Puritans held their services in unadorned meeting-houses and would not even allow musical instruments during worship. Though they had been persecuted for their religious beliefs in England, this did not make the Puritans more inclined toward religious tolerance when they reached America. The Massachusetts Bay colonists, for instance, drove Quakers and members of other denominations out of the colony, and banished dissenters such as Roger Williams and Anne Hutchinson. In creating such laws and following such practices, British colonies in North America were following the same sorts of discriminatory patterns that had long been followed in Britain itself.

Whether Catholic or Protestant, European migrants to North America offered the conversion of natives as a primary goal of exploration and settlement. They regarded Indigenous peoples as heathens or pagans who needed both the light of Christian revelation and the refinement of European civilization. Because they regarded Indigenous religions as devilish, European

Tituba and the Children.

Tituba, a central figure in the Salem Witch Trials, as she was imagined in a nineteenth-century engraving.

Few episodes in American history have sparked greater or longer lasting interest than the Salem witch trials of 1692–93, in which thirty people were found guilty of witchcraft following the accusations of several young women. Nineteen of the convicted were executed and one more was pressed to death for refusing to confess. Horrific as this episode was, it pales by comparison with various seventeenth-century outbreaks of hysteria over alleged witchcraft in Europe (in the Bamberg witch trials alone, some 1,000 people are believed to have been executed).

The causes of such outbreaks are still widely discussed and disputed; anxiety over emergent capitalism and the rise of scientific rationalism have been suggested, as have (in the case of the Salem episode) issues of race and trauma. Certain of the accusers had evidently been captured for some time by an Abenaki group and during that period had been traumatized by witnessing various atrocities. Tituba, one of the first three women accused of witchcraft and a key figure in the saga, is now believed to have been of Arawak (northeastern South American Indigenous) background, and to have come to Salem after some time enslaved in Barbados.

Important literary works with a connection to this historical episode include Nathaniel Hawthorne's 1835 story "Young Goodman Brown" and Arthur Miller's 1953 play *The Crucible*. For more on this subject, see the section "In Context: The Salem Witch Trials" in the online component of this anthology.

colonists could not see the commonalities shared by their cultures. Indigenous North Americans possessed complex cosmologies that nearly always included faith in a Supreme Being responsible for Creation, belief in other, lesser supernatural entities, and visions of an afterlife. In outline, then, Indigenous belief systems had a good deal in common with those of Christians, whether Catholic or Protestant, who also believed in a Supreme Being, in angels and other lesser supernatural beings, and in an afterlife of either punishment or reward. Rather than appreciating these shared spiritual traits, however, European settlers sought either to graft a Christian cosmology onto native beliefs and practices or to eradicate them altogether. English settlers in New England frequently combined their conversion efforts with "civilizing" requirements: natives who converted were expected to adopt English standards of dress and kinship and to come out of their tribal homes to

The Serra Chapel at the Mission San Juan Capistrano, built of adobe blocks, which dates from 1777–83. The Spanish decided in 1768 to colonize "Alta California" ("Upper California"); they had already established missions in Baja California. The Spanish approach to colonization was highly structured, and (in theory at least) powerfully oriented toward conversion of the Indigenous peoples to Christianity. Forts ("Presidios") were established at San

Diego, Santa Barbara, Monterrey, and San Francisco, with each of the four presidios responsible for the defense of several substantial Catholic missions, each to be run by the Franciscan order. The Padre of each mission assumed overall authority for the surrounding area; the declared plan was, after a ten-year transition period, to hand over control of lands claimed by each mission to the Indigenous population—though in practice, no plan to cede control was ever enacted.

Church authorities at these missions made much of the large numbers baptized, but scholars now believe that a relatively small percentage of the local population were true converts to Catholicism; most are thought to have adhered to their traditional religion, which—like Catholicism—posited an all-powerful Creator, and vested substantial secular authority in the local religious leaders.

The Spanish influx into Alta California was led by Franciscan missionary Junípero Serra (1713–84), who established the first nine Spanish missions in the area. Serra (after whom the chapel shown above is named) has become a highly controversial figure. He has been widely condemned by anti-colonialists as an oppressor of Indigenous peoples in Alta California—and for his earlier work for the Inquisition in Mexico. But he has long been lauded by Catholic authorities for the number of people who converted to Catholicism on his watch and for his enthusiasm for the work of conversion; when he first came into contact with unbaptized Indigenous peoples (in San Diego, in 1769), he wrote that he "kissed the ground and thanked God for giving me what I have longed for for so many years." He was declared a saint by Pope Francis in 2015.

form villages of "praying Indians" at the outskirts of English settlements. While Catholic missionaries were less insistent on erasing native cultural forms, their conversion efforts also often proceeded through violent means: historians now estimate that, by the late eighteenth century, genizaros—Indigenous people in what are now the southwestern states who had been "de-tribalized," usually by being enslaved—accounted for one-third of the population of New Mexico.

As English colonists on the Eastern seaboard drove Indigenous people off their land and became more politically and territorially entrenched, they created

strong ties between church and state by establishing one religion as official. It was the Puritan church—officially named the Congregational Church—that became the established church in Massachusetts, Connecticut, and New Hampshire. In most of the other colonies (which had been founded largely from economic motives), including South Carolina, North Carolina,[1] Georgia, Virginia, and, somewhat later, Maryland, the Anglican Church (the Church of England) became the

---

1   From 1669 to 1712 these were a single colony—Carolina—that was divided into two provinces.

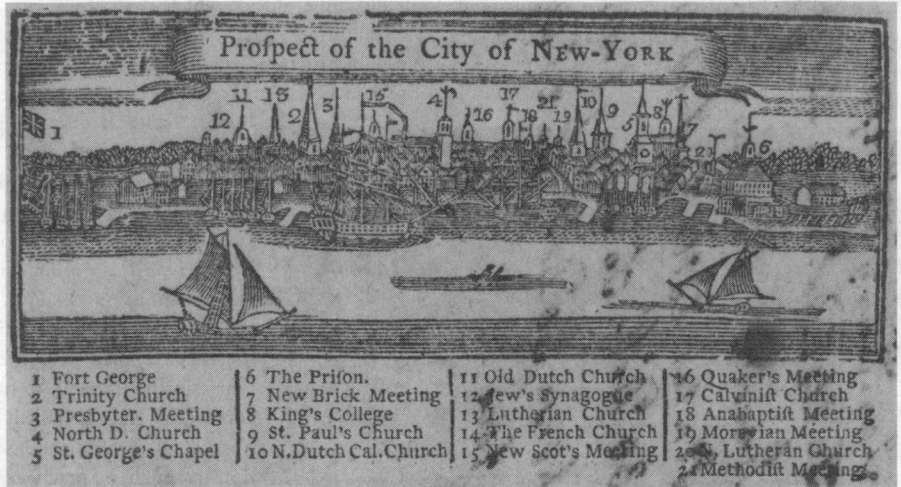

Prospect of the City of New-York

1 Fort George	6 The Prison.	11 Old Dutch Church	16 Quaker's Meeting
2 Trinity Church	7 New Brick Meeting	12 Jew's Synagogue	17 Calvinist Church
3 Presbyter. Meeting	8 King's College	13 Lutheran Church	18 Anabaptist Meeting
4 North D. Church	9 St. Paul's Church	14 The French Church	19 Moravian Meeting
5 St. George's Chapel	10 N.Dutch Cal.Church	15 New Scot's Meeting	20 N. Lutheran Church
			21 Methodist Meeting.

New York City (woodblock), 1771. Broadly speaking, England's mainland colonies may be divided into three groups: New England colonies, in which Puritans dominated and in which the Congregational Church was accorded established status; southern colonies, in which mainstream Anglicans dominated and the Church of England became the established church; and the middle colonies, in which no denomination was accorded the status of an established religion. New York does not quite fit the pattern; although the Church of England became the established religion in several counties of New York, it was never adopted by the colony as a whole. In the Hudson Valley and some other areas, the Dutch Reformed Church remained strong, while in various northern and western areas Lutherans predominated. As this 1771 image illustrates, New York City offered (by eighteenth-century standards) a spiritual smorgasbord.

established religion.[1] That did not simply mean that one church had slightly favored status over others. It typically meant that all citizens were required to support the established church through the payment of tithes or other taxes; it also often meant that those who did not belong to the established church were precluded from holding public office. In some colonies, restrictions went a good deal further. In Virginia, all white Virginians were required not only to pay taxes to support the established church, but also to be members of it and to attend services. Prejudice against those suspected of belonging to other denominations sometimes ran high; in the 1760s and 1770s, for example, those alleged to be Baptist were frequently subject to physical violence.

In most colonies, then, freedom of religion was an entirely alien concept; the formation of churches in non-approved denominations was in many cases prohibited, as in some cases was private worship. Even in colonies that had embraced the concept of "liberty of conscience" and not established any Christian denomination as the state religion, "liberty of conscience" was a long way removed from twenty-first-century notions of religious freedom. Colonies such as New Jersey and Georgia proclaimed that "liberty of conscience" applied to all except "papists" (as Catholics were derogatively termed), and the practice of non-Christian religions such as Judaism and Islam was often outlawed entirely.

There were two notable exceptions to this rule. In 1636 The Colony of Rhode Island and Providence Plantations (as it was officially known), founded by Roger Williams, became the first English colony to

---

[1] The Anglican Church was also the established faith in Maine (which became part of Massachusetts in 1691 and did not separate from it until 1820). Vermont—an unorganized area on the edge of the New England and New York colonies until 1777, when it briefly declared itself an independent republic—was largely Puritan / Congregationalist, but it required only that office holders "profess the Protestant religion." In Delaware there was no officially established religion, but Anglicans came eventually to predominate. In New Jersey too there was no established religion, and in this case a variety of Christian denominations flourished, with Presbyterians the largest group and Quakers the second largest. In Pennsylvania, William Penn (1644–1718) founded a Quaker colony, but its laws mandated religious tolerance.

declare freedom of religion for all Christian denominations—including Catholicism. But religious freedom in Rhode Island went further still; there was no prohibition placed on non-Christian religions. In his writings, Williams expressed the view that "none of the papists, Protestants, Jews, or Turks" should be forced to come to "prayers or worship, nor be compelled from their own particular prayers or worship." In other words, the world of religion would be kept entirely separate from the world of politics and law. This principle of the separation of church and state—a "wall of separation between the garden of the church and the wilderness of the world," in Williams's words—would later be enshrined in the First Amendment to the U.S. Constitution.

The second major exception was Pennsylvania, the charter for which was granted in 1681 to William Penn, who sought a safe haven far from England for himself and other members of the Society of Friends (also known as the Quakers). The charter provided a substantial measure of religious freedom, and its provisions created a lasting difference between Pennsylvania and all other colonies except Rhode Island—a difference that did not please everyone. The dissatisfied immigrant Gottlieb Mittelberger, for instance, writing in the early 1750s, complained that the "preachers throughout Pennsylvania ha[d] no power to punish anyone, or to compel anyone to go to church," with the result that "many sects lead people astray, and ma[de] them heterodox."[1] And yet, as Mittelberger begrudgingly admitted, religious tolerance seemed to result in greater general kindliness: "To speak truth, one seldom hears a quarrel among [the Pennsylvanians]. ... Americans live more quietly and peacefully together than the Europeans—and all this is the result of the

The first Jewish cemetery in America was established in Rhode Island in 1677, and the first synagogue—the Touro Synagogue, the interior of which is pictured here—in the same colony in 1763.

liberty which they enjoy and which makes them all equal."

If church and state were so closely entwined in the majority of the colonies, and freedom of religion such an alien concept in all but a few, how did it come to pass that the United States, after it was founded, could so swiftly embrace the principle of religious freedom?[2] One reason was simply that, even among those who would have preferred that America establish a single religion, there was no agreement as to *which* religious denomination it should be. Theological differences even between Protestant denominations could be rancorous and protracted, making the choice of a single established sect all but impossible. Another reason was

[1]   To illustrate his point, Mittelberger described "a German neighbor, who had been a Lutheran but had re-baptized himself in running water; some time afterwards he circumcised himself and believed only in the Old Testament; finally, however, shortly before his death, he baptized himself again by sprinkling water upon his head." The different modes of baptism suggest that Mittelberger's neighbor had cycled through a number of different Protestant denominations that conducted their baptismal ceremonies differently. The references to circumcision and to belief "only in the Old Testament" suggest that the neighbor flirted with Judaism, which requires that male believers be circumcised; the Hebrew Bible is roughly co-extensive with the Christian Old Testament.

[2]   Article 1 of the 1791 Bill of Rights (the First Amendment to the Constitution) declares that "Congress shall make no law respecting an establishment of religion, or prohibiting the free exercise thereof."

that rates of religiosity in early America were highly inconsistent from one decade to the next. The religious observances of seventeenth-century Christians—whether of Puritans in New England, Quakers in Pennsylvania, or Anglicans in the southern colonies—were generally restrained in character. But in the 1730s and 1740s a series of revivals swept both the North American colonies and Western Europe. This period, known as the Great Awakening, saw a marked increase in religious practice in the colonies.

Beginning in the Massachusetts church led by Jonathan Edwards, a Congregationalist minister and theologian, the revival soon attracted preachers from both North America and England who sought to fan the flames of religious fervor. Like Edwards, the English evangelists John Wesley and George Whitefield (both Anglicans) sought to engage the emotions as well as the souls and minds of their listeners. But unlike Edwards, who quickly became concerned about what he considered the excesses of the revival he himself had sparked, Wesley and Whitefield sought to take preaching and religious instruction beyond the walls of the church (traveling widely and often preaching outdoors) and to inspire a spirit of intense personal commitment in believers. Whitefield, like Edwards, embraced a Calvinist theology: though he preached passionately to anyone who would listen, only the elect, both men believed, would be enabled to heed Christ's call. Wesley, by contrast, preached an Arminian theology that emphasized that salvation was open to all—not just to a predestined elect. A new denomination—the Methodists—developed out of Wesley's teaching, and within other denominations the evangelical revival movement became so powerful that it divided both the Congregationalists and the Presbyterians in two, with evangelical factions within both denominations breaking away from the traditional mainstream.

In the second half of the century, however, the revival quickly lost strength; far fewer Americans were attending outdoor revival meetings in the 1770s than had done so in the 1740s. And for the most part, they did not return to the churches of traditional Christian denominations. The result was that by the late eighteenth century, it is estimated, no more than ten per cent of Americans were churchgoers. The Revolutionary decades were arguably the most

John Wollaston, *George Whitefield*, c. 1742. Whitefield was one of the most powerful figures of the Great Awakening—on both sides of the Atlantic. A close associate of John Wesley, he chose to go his own way, preaching to large crowds outdoors rather than affiliating with any church. He was universally agreed to possess extraordinary power as a speaker, as the actor David Garrick's fervently expressed wish attests: "I would give a hundred guineas, if I could say 'Oh!' like Mr. Whitefield." Whitefield has sometimes been called America's first celebrity. Accounts of his preaching filled newspapers from Maine to Georgia; Benjamin Franklin wrote in his autobiography of hearing Whitefield preach; and Phillis Wheatley first gained fame in Boston for her poem "Elegy on the Death of the Rev. Mr. George Whitefield."

secular era in American history. During these decades, many influential Americans adopted deism—the view that humans should base their faith on reason, and that reason justifies belief in a Supreme Being who is responsible for Creation, but that much of what is recounted in the Bible cannot be confirmed by human means. Some deists, such as Thomas Paine, rejected Christianity and all other organized religion and came to believe that God, having created the world, played no part in human affairs thereafter; others, such as Thomas Jefferson, continued to believe in the historical reality of Jesus Christ and the moral efficacy of his teachings but nevertheless held beliefs far removed from those of any traditional Christian denomination. James Madison and Benjamin Franklin were also deists; indeed, historian Jill Lepore has concluded that "most of the Founding Fathers were deists," though she concedes that "not all of them were as skeptical as Jefferson" about the value of traditional Christianity.

Regardless of their varying, occasionally skeptical attitudes towards traditional religious belief, the founders nevertheless recognized religion as a central aspect of social life, and the new Constitution, while prohibiting a federal establishment of religion, did nothing to interfere with state church establishments, some of which persisted into the early decades of the nineteenth century. But men like Jefferson, Madison, and many of their contemporaries also possessed a then-unprecedented openness toward non-Christian religions. Royall Tyler's popular 1797 novel *The Algerine Captive*, for instance, stages a debate between a Christian adherent and a Muslim mullah; while the Christian feels he should be able to best the mullah easily, he finds himself confounded by the logic of the other man's arguments. John Adams, negotiating real-life protection for Americans traveling off the coast of North Africa, included the following wording in the 1797 Treaty of Tripoli:

> As the government of the United States of America is not in any sense founded on the Christian Religion, as it has in itself no character of enmity against the laws, religion or tranquility of Musselmen [Muslims], and as the said States never have entered into any war or act of hostility against any Mehomitan [Muslim] nation, it is declared by the parties that no pretext arising from religious opinions shall ever produce an interruption of the harmony existing between the two countries.

And in 1784, Massachusetts author Hannah Adams published *A View of Religions*, an early work of comparative religious studies that, instead of dismissing or denigrating non-Christian religions, sought to understand them on their own terms.

This respect rarely extended to the religious traditions of the enslaved people who were brought from Africa to labor in the American colonies. As many as twenty per cent of them may have been followers of Islam, but the majority almost certainly did not hold monotheistic beliefs. The religious traditions in many areas of West Africa (the center of the trade in enslaved people on the east side of the Atlantic) were animistic: adherents of religions that allow for the possibility of objects and places as well as living creatures possessing spiritual qualities—of things and places being in a real sense alive.[1] It is unclear for how long or to what extent animism and other elements of African religions persisted in the religious practices of African Americans; with families subject to dispersal at the whim of enslavers, with high death rates, and with precious little time available to carry on traditions, much was inevitably lost. In certain cases, however—particularly in areas in which Catholic missionaries allowed or even encouraged the blending of Christian with non-Christian religious elements—hybrid sets of religious beliefs set down deep roots. Such was the case with Voodoo (originally "Vaudou") in Haiti, and also with Santeria in Cuba.

It is also possible to see elements of animism persisting in the spirituals through which enslaved African Americans began in the eighteenth century to express

---

[1]   It may also be worth noting that some variants of Christianity have certain affinities with animism. Such is arguably the case with the sort of Nature-worship that we often associate with English Romantic poetry, or with certain moods of the spirituality of transcendentalists such as Emerson. Here, for example, is how Emerson expresses (in "Woodnotes II") the view that a "Universal Spirit" is not a Supreme Being sitting above the natural world, but is rather embedded in every aspect of nature:

> He is the axis of the star;
> He is the sparkle of the spar;
> He is the heart of every creature;
> He is the meaning of each feature;
> And his mind is the sky.

John Rose, *The Old Plantation* (Beaufort County, South Carolina), c. 1785.

a distinctive brand of Christianity. Spirituals such as "Roll, Jordan, Roll" have often been read with reference to the institution of slavery, as in the Bible, crossing the Jordan River marked the entrance of the formerly enslaved Israelites into the "Promised Land" where they would be free. But in the river and in the tree of life with which the spiritual begins, it does not seem too much of a stretch to hear traces of West African animism. In one spiritual, African American voices proclaimed: "If you want to find Jesus, go in the wilderness," subverting a Methodist hymn about coming *out of* the wilderness. Through small acts of meaning-making like this, many enslaved people combined West African spiritual traditions with Christian doctrine and practice, building religions that were uniquely their own.

SLAVERY AND AMERICA: BEGINNINGS TO 1820

[See also the "Contexts: Slavery and Resistance" section in the website component of this volume.]

Until relatively recently, American slavery has been associated mainly with the period leading up to the Civil War—the period of Frederick Douglass's *Narrative*, of Harriet Beecher Stowe's *Uncle Tom's Cabin*, and of Solomon Northup's *Twelve Years a Slave*. Many Americans have tended to think of slavery as a "peculiar institution"[1] that, horrible as it undoubtedly

---

[1] This term is thought to have been first used by the Southern politician John C. Calhoun, an outspoken defender of slavery; while he was Vice President during the years 1825–32, Calhoun began to refer both to the "peculiar labor" of enslaved people and to the "peculiar domestic institution" of slavery in the Southern states. The intent was to suggest that, however pernicious slavery might be in other contexts or in other parts of the world, the form it had taken in the American South was entirely benign—and, in any case, was "peculiar" to that region and could not be judged by outsiders.

A 1671 engraving of St. Augustine.

was, existed for only a limited time in America, and left few lingering after-effects. But the more thoroughly American history is explored, the more clear it becomes that this long-held view of slavery flies in the face of the facts. Slavery played a central role in American life from long before the United States existed, and the legacy of slavery has carried on through to our own day.

In the Thirteen Colonies, the system known as chattel slavery began not in the late eighteenth century but "about the latter end of August" in 1619, when a ship called the *White Lion*, carrying "twenty and odd" enslaved Africans, arrived in the colony of Virginia. (In Portuguese- and Spanish-controlled territories, African chattel slavery was by that time long established. The Portuguese had first enslaved West African people in 1441; enslaved African people had first arrived in St. Augustine in Spanish Florida in 1565.) Early on, systems of chattel slavery were not codified to the extent they later would be, and such slavery was not fully racialized in the way that it later became; English colonists in

America, for example, purchased people not only from Africa but also from various Native American peoples.[1]

In the late 1600s the Thirteen Colonies began to codify the status of enslaved people—and of all black people, whether enslaved or not. Between 1662 and 1723 Virginia passed a series of laws that declared enslaved people to be property; determined that any child born to an enslaved mother would be enslaved from birth; and restricted the rights of black people who were not enslaved. By 1723, a "free" black person would be required to pay at least as much tax as a white person, but would not be free to own property, vote, occupy any position of civil or ecclesiastical authority, or marry a white person. Other colonies enacted similar laws, firmly embedding racism into American

---

[1]   Certain forms of slavery had been common among Native American peoples before the arrival of Europeans; those captured in war, for example, were often then enslaved. But Native American practices did not classify enslaved people as property (or "chattel")— and did not regard "slave" as a status that would be passed on from generation to generation.

society long before the Revolution. That was the case not only in the South, but also in much of the North. In New York City, for example (where the Dutch had introduced slavery, with the English later codifying it), enslaved people made up twenty per cent of the city's population by the middle of the eighteenth century.

When the Northern colonies finally did move to abolish slavery, in most cases they adopted a policy of gradualism. In some states emancipation legislation affected only those born after it was enacted, so that those who were already enslaved when the legislation was passed would remain enslaved for life; thus it was, for example, that in Pennsylvania (which in 1780 became the first of the Thirteen Colonies to pass legislation abolishing slavery) there were still enslaved people in the late 1840s. In other states, legislation to "free" enslaved people altered their status not to "free person"—let alone to "citizen"[1]—but rather to indentured servant, and mandated that the children of enslaved people were also required to spend extended periods as indentured servants. In New Jersey, the last of the Northern states to pass such legislation, formerly enslaved people became "apprenticed for life"; considerable numbers were still effectively enslaved when the Civil War broke out.

While the role of slavery in Northern states has been underemphasized, it remains true that the role played by enslaved people was far more prominent in the Southern states. In New Jersey, the Northern state with the highest concentration of enslaved people, these constituted six per cent of the population in 1800; in South Carolina, the Southern state with the highest concentration, forty-two per cent of the population was enslaved. Overwhelmingly, Southern enslaved people worked on farms or—especially from the late eighteenth and early nineteenth centuries—on large plantations. It would be difficult to exaggerate the value of the labor provided by enslaved people. Florida slaveholder and plantation owner Zephaniah Kingsley—author in the 1820s of one of the most

popular proslavery tracts—was among those who were quite straightforward on that score:

> In short, the greatest value of agricultural product for export, and nearly all the springs of national and individual prosperity, flow from slave labor[.] … The labor of the negro, under the wholesome restraint of intelligent direction, is like a constant stream[.] …

Engraved portrait of Alice, an enslaved Pennsylvanian woman, 1804. Born around 1686 to enslaved parents who had been brought to Philadelphia from Barbados, Alice—who lacked a surname but was known as Alice of Dunk's Ferry, after the ferry crossing where she collected tolls for her enslaver—died, still enslaved, in 1802 (more than twenty years after Pennsylvania adopted a law to gradually abolish slavery in 1780). In her later years, she became a well-known recounter of stories about colonial Pennsylvania's early days—"being," as the writer Isaiah Thomas (in one of whose works this portrait was published) put it, "a sensible intelligent woman, and having a good memory."

---

1   This word was left undefined in the American constitution, but beginning in the late 1780s the practice developed in most states of classifying "Negroes" (along with women, children, and Indigenous people) as "inhabitants" who were not to be allowed the privilege of voting or otherwise participating in government. Not until the Fourteenth Amendment was passed in 1868 did that situation begin to change.

1. Negre qui ejambe le tabac.
2. Negre qui torque le tabac.
3. Negre qui le met en rolle.
4. Tabac a la pente.

Anonymous eighteenth-century engraving showing enslaved black people processing harvested tobacco. While American slavery is today often associated with cotton cultivation, the cotton industry only took off—and began making large demands on the labor of enslaved African Americans—at the very end of the eighteenth century. For most of the seventeenth and eighteenth centuries, tobacco was the primary cash crop produced by enslaved labor throughout much of the American South—including in areas, such as Virginia, where cotton production never became widespread.

If slavers such as Kingsley were frank about how much economic benefit enslaved people provided them with, they were utterly disingenuous when they asserted that slavery amounted to "wholesome restraint." Every American schoolchild nowadays has some sense of the physical brutality to which enslaved people were subjected. But the full extent of the systemic cruelty is still often not appreciated; many today, for example, remain unaware of the degree to which family life was often made utterly impossible for enslaved people, as parents and children were sold off separately.

As slavery became more widespread in the eighteenth century, restrictions on the lives of enslaved people became tighter and tighter. In South Carolina, for example, a substantial 1739 uprising of enslaved people—the Stono Rebellion—prompted the government to pass an updated version of the law known as the "Negro Act"—more formally, An Act for the Better Ordering and Governing of Negroes and Other Slaves in this Province. The 1740 version expanded considerably on the previous iterations of the act in several respects; notably, it prohibited enslaved people from assembling in groups, and made it illegal to teach any slave how to write:

> … [T]he having of slaves taught to write, or suffering them to be employed in writing, may be attended with great inconveniences; Be it therefore enacted by the authority aforesaid, That all and every person and persons whatsoever, who shall hereinafter teach or cause any slave or slaves to be taught to write, or shall use or employ any slave as a scribe in any manner of writing whatsoever, hereafter taught to write, every such person and persons, shall, for every such offense, forfeit the sum of one hundred pounds current money.

The South Carolina legislation was subsequently used as a model for similar legislation in Georgia and other states.

By 1776, then, the institution of slavery had become very firmly entrenched in America. The ironies, paradoxes, and contradictions inherent in the manner in which America's founders dealt with the issue of slavery—or, perhaps more accurately, refused to deal with it—have been the subject of much discussion. At its center is the figure of Thomas Jefferson, a believer in the superiority of whites over blacks, and an enslaver who fathered numerous children with Sally Hemings, whom he had enslaved, but also the drafter of the Declaration of Independence, with its ringing assertion that "all men are created equal." In the original draft of that document Jefferson also included a clause denouncing the British king for allowing slavery, an "execrable commerce" and an "assemblage of horrors." That clause was, as Jefferson recounted later, "struck out in compliance to South Carolina and Georgia," though he admitted that representatives of the Northern states had not fought to retain it. Between 1777 and 1804 those Northern states all enacted legislation that would bring about emancipation within their borders (albeit extremely gradually). And many whites during this era—in the South as well as the North—expected as well as hoped that slavery would somehow fade away in every state. But no state was willing to press for an end to slavery throughout the nation sooner rather than later—and, once the three-fifths clause was embedded in the Constitution (see below), it is doubtful if any could have succeeded in doing so had they tried.

In 1808, following Britain, the United States abolished the transatlantic slave trade; people could no longer be brought legally from Africa to America to be sold into slavery.[1] But that move did not bring with it any improvement in conditions for enslaved people in America; for many, indeed, conditions became even worse. The cotton and sugar industries were both growing rapidly in the early nineteenth century, and both were characterized by extraordinarily harsh conditions; in short order, enslaved people were literally worked

A remnant of the signage for one of the New Orleans slave markets still exists at the corner of St. Louis and Chartres in the French Quarter: the faint outline ("… change") of what was once the sign for the Slave Exchange at the St. Louis Hotel.

to death. That the slaveholders continued after 1808 to be able to obtain replacements was due to the growth of America's internal slave trade—which, unlike the transatlantic trade, remained entirely legal. In certain of the Atlantic states—most notably, Virginia, where the soil had become depleted after generations of tobacco growing, and where there grew to be three times as many enslaved women as enslaved men—supplying the internal slave trade became a highly profitable business. From early adolescence onward, women were expected to be pregnant continually; sexual partners were chosen for them—or, in many cases, they were raped by their enslavers. Their children were then shipped to the Gulf Coast to be sold at the New Orleans slave market—the most important source of labor for the sugar and cotton industries.

Before 1820 the literature of slavery is far less voluminous than it is in the 1820–60 period, but it includes a number of foundational texts. Chief among them is Olaudah Equiano's *Interesting Narrative*, published in 1789 in London and three years later in New York, but the writings of others who were enslaved also deserve attention, among them the narratives of Ukawsaw Gronniosaw (*A Narrative of the Most Remarkable Particulars in the Life of James Albert Ukawsaw Gronniosaw, an African Prince, as Related by Himself,*

---

[1]   Considerable numbers of enslaved people from abroad continued to be brought into the United States illegally—some smuggled through Atlantic ports, some brought from (Spanish-controlled) Florida and Texas.

For Sale,

THE under mentioned Property, situate in the parish of Plaquemine, to wit:

A fine Sugar Plantation and Saw Mill, having 50 arpents front on the river with the usual depth for 30, and a double concession for 20 arpents, situate at 8 leagues from New Orleans and on the same side; together with

51 head of Slaves
12 yoke of Draught Oxen
32 Horses or mules
6 Carts and all the Plantation Tools necessary.

Notice of sale, *Louisiana State Gazette* (New Orleans), 1 November 1819. The sale of enslaved people through auction at slave markets grew steadily through the late eighteenth and early nineteenth centuries, but many enslaved people were also sold— as in this case—along with the plantation where they were enslaved.

1772); of Venture Smith (*A Narrative of the Life and Adventures of Venture, a Native of Africa: But Resident above Sixty Years in the United States of America, Related by Himself*, 1798); and of Jeffrey Brace (*The Blind African Slave, Or Memoirs of Boyrereau Brinch, Nicknamed Jeffrey Brace, as Told to Benjamin F. Prentiss, Esq.*). These early slave narratives are a varied group; in the late eighteenth and early nineteenth centuries the slave narrative genre had not yet become firmly established—and the narratives of enslaved people were not inextricably associated with the abolitionist cause in the ways that they later came to be. The theme of Christian spiritual development figures prominently in a number of these early narratives. Gronniosaw's narrative, for example, was published not in order to promote antislavery causes, but to demonstrate (as Calvinist preacher Walter Shirley puts it in his preface to the volume) that God may choose to save "those whom he hath foreknown" even in "those benighted parts of the world where the gospel of Jesus Christ hath never reached"; as Shirley would have it, God undertook to bring Gronniosaw "by a way he knew not, out of darkness into His marvelous light." Equiano's narrative did spur antislavery feeling to some degree when it was published—but it appears to have done so only in Britain. The American edition, published

in 1792, excited little interest, and to the extent that it did, it seems to have been valued as a travel narrative as much as for what Equiano has to say about slavery (see the author headnote on Equiano for a discussion of the reception history of the book). The narratives of Venture Smith and of Jeffrey Brace are more tightly focused on the subject of slavery than are those of Gronniosaw or Equiano, but they appear to have attracted little attention on publication. Interestingly, Smith's story is framed in the preface as of importance less for drawing attention to the horrors of slavery in the way that later slave narratives do (with their extended descriptions of whippings and other horrific abuses), than it is for demonstrating the lost potential that slavery represented for a "great mind" such as Smith's:

> The subject of the following pages, had he received only a common education, might have been a man of high respectability and usefulness; and had his education been suited to his genius, he might have been an ornament and an honor to human nature. ... It may perhaps, not be unpleasing to see the efforts of a great mind wholly uncultivated, enfeebled and depressed by slavery, and struggling under every disadvantage—the reader may here see a Franklin and a Washington, in a state of nature, or rather in a state of slavery.

Several early narratives of slavery are represented in the contents of this anthology—as are Phillis Wheatley's poems on the subject of slavery. Included as well are a number of commentaries on slavery by black writers such as clergymen Absalom Jones (*The Petition of People of Color*) and Lemuel Haynes (*Liberty Further Extended: Or Free Thoughts on the Illegality of Slave-keeping*). It was black writers such as Jones and Haynes who pointed out most directly the contradictions inherent in the approach to freedom taken by America's founders: "Liberty" in Haynes's words, "is equally as precious to a black man as it is to a white one, and bondage equally as intolerable to the one as it is to the other." Haynes's text, though, remained unpublished.

The writings of eighteenth and early nineteenth-century white authors on the subject of slavery— J. Hector St. John de Crèvecoeur and Thomas Jefferson notable among them—are also represented

THE
FEMALE COMBATANTS

I'll force you to Obedience you Rebellious Slut

Liberty Liberty for ever Mother while I exist

OR WHO SHALL
Publish'd According to Act Jan.ʳ 26. 1776.   Price 6.ᵈ

The Female Combatants, 1776. This illustration, probably printed in London, was published in the early days of the American Revolution; it depicts the incipient conflict as a face-off between an elegantly dressed older woman, representing Britain, and a younger, bare-breasted and tattooed woman in Indigenous garb, representing the American colonies. The British figure declares, "I'll force you to Obedience you Rebellious Slut," while the American figure responds, "Liberty, Liberty forever Mother while I exist." Notably, while the illustration appropriates Native American imagery to represent the American colonies, it leaves out of the picture the actual Indigenous peoples who were caught between—and variously manipulated, exploited, or attacked by—the rebellious colonies and their "mother country."

substantially in these pages. It is striking, however, that the highest profile late eighteenth-century works of fiction and drama on the subject of slavery, Susanna Rowson's 1794 *Slaves in Algiers* and Royall Tyler's 1797 *The Algerine Captive*, concern the enslavement of white people in North Africa rather than the enslavement of black people in America.

"BEGIN THE WORLD OVER AGAIN":
AN AGE OF REBELLION AND REVOLUTION

[See also this volume's "Contexts: Rebellions and Revolutions" section.]

To the white European colonizers of North America in the seventeenth and early eighteenth centuries, rebellions and revolts were occurrences to be feared. The pattern was largely the same: members of an oppressed group rebelled against oppressors of European background. Examples include the 1680 Pueblo Revolt against Spanish rule; the 1729 Natchez revolt against French rule; the 1663 rebellion of enslaved Africans (together with indentured servants) in Virginia; the 1712 rebellion of enslaved Africans (together with Native Americans) in New York; the 1739 rebellion of enslaved Africans in South Carolina; and Metacom's Rebellion of 1675–78 (also known as King Philip's War—see above under "Contact, and the Literatures of Contact"). Colonizers reacted to such events by waging War against Indigenous nations, passing strict slave codes, and terrorizing the black population. Although these rebellions were largely defeated, their legacy helped set the stage for the complicated era historians often call the "age of revolutions," beginning with the American Revolution (1775–83) and ending with the European revolutions of the mid-nineteenth century.

It is one irony of American history, though not a surprising one, that when colonists in mainland North America[1] rebelled against British rule, they largely sidelined, ignored, and continued to terrorize members of the oppressed groups who had fought,

---

[1] It is sometimes forgotten that Britain had in the 1770s not thirteen but twenty-six American colonies, ranging from icy Newfoundland in the north to Grenada, just off the coast of South America. Britain considered her Caribbean possessions—especially sugar-producing Barbados—to be the most valuable.

and continued to fight, for a better life. Indeed, the American Revolution was first understood as a rebellion. The idea that colonists might revolt against the "mother country," as white people across the economic spectrum did in the 1770s, and as the Spanish colonists of Mexico did in 1810, was inconceivable almost right up until those events actually happened. Even when the conflict now known as the American Revolution began, it was not until the British were finally defeated that it came to be understood as a Revolutionary War or a War of Independence.

The most radical event of the age of revolutions occurred not in British North America but in Haiti, the former French colony of Saint-Domingue, where between 1791 and 1804 enslaved Africans overthrew French rule, eradicated the institution of slavery, defeated Napoleon's attempts at re-enslavement, and established the first independent black nation in the Americas (and the second independent nation in the Americas overall, after the U.S.). While the Haitian Revolution aimed to overthrow white supremacy, the American Revolution was initially not a matter of high principles. When Britain began to directly tax the colonies[1]—particularly the Thirteen Colonies that it had paid for an army to defend against the French in the war of 1756–63—the resistance was at first merely economic. Soon came an appeal to a broader principle about self-sovereignty—not just "No taxation!" but instead "No taxation without representation." With the Declaration of Independence of 1776 would come the most powerful principle: "all men are created equal" and possess the "inalienable rights" to "life, liberty, and the pursuit of happiness." The success of a war that white men fought nominally for that grand principle influenced revolutionary movements in Europe, the Americas, and around the world, while Haitian independence was largely dismissed and denigrated—except by black people in the African diaspora who continued to look to it for inspiration.

During the long years of the American Revolution itself, the conflict also played out as a "civil war," as J. Hector St. John de Crèvecoeur's American farmer called it in 1782. Particularly in states such as New York and Pennsylvania, a great many people, much as they might dislike the measures imposed by Britain, did not favor a complete break with the Crown. The Quaker poet Hannah Griffitts, for example, who had stood in resolute opposition to measures such as the Sugar Act and the Townsend Duties, was in 1776 just as resolute in her opposition to Thomas Paine's arguments for independence; in her poem "Upon Reading a Book Entitled Common Sense" she argues that there is "subtlety" (in the now-archaic sense of treachery or cunning) in "ev'ry page of this fallacious tale." Overall, historians have estimated that some twenty per cent of American free citizens remained loyal to Britain, with up to forty-five per cent becoming active supporters of independence.[2]

About twenty per cent of the non-Indigenous population of 1770s North America[3] was enslaved rather than free, and enslaved people seem to have supported independence in much smaller numbers. Once the British announced, in November 1775, that anyone who escaped slavery and joined the British army would thereby attain their freedom, the black American population was overwhelmingly (if very quietly) pro-British. Many enslaved people did escape and try to join the British forces; although many were re-captured, several thousand remained free and did indeed join the British. (Two of the most important black American writers of the time, Phillis Wheatley and Lemuel Haynes, are in this respect both interesting exceptions—supporters of the Patriot rather than Loyalist cause.) At the end of the war, the 75,000 Loyalists to the crown who left the United States at war's end included between 15,000 and 20,000 formerly enslaved people.

While the Declaration of Independence expressed with great eloquence the classic Enlightenment principles of equality, the clarity of its rhetoric also effectively

---

[1] The now-infamous series of taxes included those imposed under the Sugar Act (1764); the Stamp Act (1765); the Townshend Acts of 1767 and 1768; and the series of 1774 measures known as the "Coercive Acts" in Britain and as the "Intolerable Acts" in the American colonies.

[2] Estimates of the percentage of the population that remained loyal to the Crown are generally based on enlistment figures or other indicators of the behavior of the male citizenry. Did women support or oppose independence in the same proportion as men? The anecdotal evidence is unclear, and we have no statistical indicators.

[3] The Indigenous population living within American borders may still have been as large as 500,000 in the late eighteenth century, though estimates of the Indigenous population at any time before Native Americans were fully included in the census (in 1900) vary widely.

John Singleton Copley, *The Death of Major Peirson, 6 January 1781*, 1783. Copley (1738–1815), an American-born artist, made his name as a portrait painter in New England but moved to Britain in 1774, never to return. This painting depicts the defense of the British island of Jersey against invading French forces (allied to the rebellious Thirteen Colonies) during the Revolutionary War. The inclusion of a black man in the British ranks, while of debatable historical accuracy in terms of this specific battle, reflects the real participation of black Americans on the British side of the war.

Portrait of an unidentified American Revolutionary War sailor, c. 1780. Many black people—including the writers Olaudah Equiano and Briton Hammon—served in the British navy or on merchant ships during the eighteenth century. Because of their frequently extensive maritime experience, black Americans, both free and enslaved, were recruited to the navy of the Thirteen Colonies from the very start of the Revolutionary War; while some performed menial jobs, others became ships' pilots—a skilled and prestigious position. The American Revolutionary naval officer James Barron, in his memoirs, identified several black men whom he served with as "courageous patriots who ... in justice to their merits should not be forgotten," including "Captain" Mark Starlins, an enslaved man who became a pilot. Other African Americans, however, served in the British Royal Navy, in the belief that—in the reported words of one black fisher and pilot who was executed in Charleston in 1775 for allegedly plotting a pro-British insurrection—"the War was come to help the poor Negroes."

obscured not only the hypocrisy inherent in that document (as an argument for equality that pertained only to white men) but also a complicated history of rebellion and revolution that preceded and followed the year 1776. Some of the most talented writers of the age engaged with that history as it immediately unfolded and also for decades to come.

What is the difference between a revolt or rebellion and a revolution? The best short answer is perhaps that a revolution succeeds; a rebellion doesn't. But the word "revolution" has come to suggest something more: it has typically been applied to changes in society that are about much more than mere power. As we have grown used to thinking of it, a revolution is founded in some way on a set of ideas.

There were many reasons why the balance of opinion in the thirteen North American colonies finally swung decisively in 1776 toward open rebellion, but the most important was arguably the influence of a short pamphlet whose author claimed to offer "nothing more than simple facts, plain arguments, and common sense." Thomas Paine's *Common Sense*, published in January of 1776, went through twenty-five editions in under a year; it was by far the best-selling pamphlet in an era when the norm was to share books, pamphlets, and newspapers rather than for individuals to purchase their own copy. (Historians debate how many copies were sold—Paine himself guessed that the number was 120,000, but the current thinking is now in the range of 40,000–70,000.) Paine argued more persuasively than anyone else that Britain could never be expected to act in the interest of American colonies; that the principle of hereditary succession on which the British monarchy was founded was foolish and wicked; that in the colonies "the *law* ought to be king"; and that "a government of our own" was the "natural right" of the people. More perhaps than any other writer, he ensured that a rebellion became an ideas-based revolution. *Common Sense* provided the world with a rhetoric of Revolution that survives to this day. To his fellow colonists, he wrote:

> We have it in our power to begin the world over again. A situation, similar to the present, hath not happened since the days of Noah until now. The birth day of a new world is at hand.

John Singleton Copley, *Paul Revere*, c. 1770. Revere (1735–1818) was a prosperous and well-respected silversmith both before and after the famous role he played in the American Revolution. See the In Context materials accompanying Henry Wadsworth Longfellow's poem "The Midnight Ride of Paul Revere" (in the online component of this anthology) for Revere's own account.

In the American Revolution, the primary principle of "freedom" that the rebels were fighting for was self-governance—independence from their colonial rulers.[1] In another pamphlet, *American Liberty; A Poem* (1775),

---

[1] Particularly given that it was the British forces who offered freedom to enslaved Americans willing to fight for their side in the war, the vocabulary of the era's literature is often deeply paradoxical; Freneau is among the many patriots who write of America fighting to escape the "slavery" of control by Britain but have nothing to say on the subject of offering freedom to Americans who are literally enslaved. The ironies are particularly tangled in Freneau's case; horrified by the cruelties of slavery in the West Indies that he witnessed when he traveled there in 1776 (and that he wrote about in his "Sir Toby" poems), Freneau nevertheless did not at the time call for the abolition of slavery—and indeed he later became an enslaver himself when he lived in New Jersey. He did free his enslaved people, however, before New Jersey in 1804 passed a law mandating gradual emancipation.

John Singleton Copley, *John Adams*, 1783. In this painting, Adams—the American commissioner to the negotiations that produced the Treaty of Paris that ended the Revolutionary War—is shown gesturing toward a map of his newly independent country. The statue in the background contains imagery of peace, including an olive branch and a lowered torch. Adams was later appointed the first American ambassador to Britain; when a counterpart assumed that he had family in England, he replied:

> Neither my father nor mother, grandfather or grandmother, great grandfather or great grandmother, nor any other relation that I know of, nor care a farthing for, has been in England these one hundred and fifty years; so that you see I have not one drop of blood in my veins, but what is American.

Philip Freneau set out a vision of the future that many held—a vision of a nation that gives "all for freedom," that frees itself from the chains of control by Britain, and that thereby emboldens itself to expand in all directions, including out west by colonizing lands ruled by sovereign Native American nations. Freneau's rhetoric embodies the central paradox of the revolution, which was that the vision of freedom it attempted to universalize in fact was white supremacist and inherently, if silently, limited to white men:

> Thrice happy we who long attacks have stood
> And swam to Liberty thro' seas of blood;
> The time shall come when strangers rule no more,
> Nor cruel mandates vex from Britain's shore;
> When Commerce shall extend her short'ned wing,
> And her free freights from every climate bring;

> When mighty towns shall flourish free and great,
> Vast their dominion, opulent their state;
> When one vast cultivated region teems,
> From ocean's edge to Mississippi's streams[.] ...

In the same year that Freneau issued his *American Liberty* pamphlet, John Adams urged "the people of every colony" to "set up governments of their own, under their own authority; for the people [are] the source of all authority." But who exactly were "the people"? Enslaved people were not considered part of "the people"—and neither were women. Nor, indeed, were all adult white males accorded full rights. Though some states—notably Pennsylvania—went further than others in declaring rights for all, even in Pennsylvania the right to vote was restricted to those who were resident in the state and paid taxes. States such as Massachusetts required that men own property in order to vote, or to hold office. The United States was making unprecedented strides in the direction of what we now call democracy—but many elite Americans maintained a powerful fear of it. Following Aristotle[1] and a long tradition of European thought, they saw in unrestrained democracy the danger of "mob rule." It was a fear that was reinforced in the 1790s by the course that the French Revolution ended up taking.

The freedoms that were fought for in France beginning in 1789 were considerably more wide-ranging than those which had motivated the American Revolution, even though the National Assembly in France drew heavily on the Declaration of Independence in its own Declaration of the Rights of Man and the Citizen (a document that Thomas Jefferson helped his friend the Marquis de Lafayette draft when Jefferson was the American Minister to France). Not just monarchical rule but economic and social hierarchies of any sort were under attack. "Men are born and remain free and equal in rights," Article 1 of the Declaration states; "social distinctions," it added, "may be founded only upon the general good." For a time, many radicals in the United States voiced a degree of pride at the obvious debt the French owed to American revolutionary rhetoric. That enthusiasm was dampened considerably beginning in 1793, however, as the horrific violence known as "the terror" began.

Even as France descended into violence, a new group of revolutionaries were fighting in Saint-Domingue to transform the brutal slave regime that had long terrorized the majority of the colony's inhabitants. Saint-Domingue was the center of Caribbean sugar production—and the center too of the region's most horrific levels of oppression. Its population was composed of approximately 30,000 white people, approximately 30,000 free people of color, and some 500,000 enslaved black people. While some of the white colonists of Saint-Domingue petitioned the central government in France for the same kinds of rights white colonists in America had achieved, Toussaint Louverture, a former slave, held the great radical ambition to abolish slavery and extend equal rights to all. While the long tradition of slave revolt and rebellion in the Americas lay behind the ambitions and actions of Louverture, he also credited events in France as an inspiration. Louverture's initial aim was to rule an autonomous Haiti as a colonial governor still within the French Empire. Several articles in the Haitian Constitution of 1801 (known as "Toussaint's Constitution") make his radicalism quite clear:

> There cannot exist slaves on this territory, servitude is therein forever abolished. All men[2] are born, live and die free and French.

> There shall exist no distinction other than those based on virtue and talent, and other superiority afforded by law in the exercise of a public function.

> The law is the same for all whether in punishment or in protection.

These demands, backed up by military might, terrified white people all over the Atlantic world, and especially in those portions of the United States with large enslaved black populations. The Haitian Revolution unfolded over many years, and at different stages involved interventions by the British and the Spanish as well as by numerous factions within Haiti itself; the Haitian army defeated Napoleon's final attempt at invasion in 1803. Jean Jacques Dessalines, a former slave, declared total independence from France on 1 January 1804. (Louverture had earlier been captured and imprisoned in France, where he died in 1803.)

The events in Saint-Domingue inspired considerable fear in the American south, and the United States government remained hostile to Haitian autonomy throughout the nineteenth century (during the Revolution, the U.S. provided both arms and financial aid to the losing cause). Haiti also inspired a number

---

[1] Aristotle posited three broad types of government: a monarchy—the corrupt version of which is a tyranny; an aristocracy—the corrupt version of which is an oligarchy; and a polity—the corrupt version of which is a democracy.

[2] Like the revolutionary declarations of America and France, those of Haiti made no mention of women. The European and English trail blazers in that regard were the 1791 *Declaration of the Rights of Woman and the Female Citizen* (French: *Déclaration des droits de la femme et de la citoyenne*) by Olympe de Gouges and Mary Wollstonecraft's *A Vindication of the Rights of Woman* (1792). Of note is the fact that Judith Sargent Murray's *On the Equality of the Sexes* (1790) predates both of these works—though there is no evidence that either de Gouges or Wollstonecraft was aware of Murray's work.

of revolts in the United States on the part of enslaved black people—and horrific reprisals on the part of enslavers. But it did not entirely sour white American opinion generally on "the spirit of revolution." In the second decade of the nineteenth century freedom continued (as Thomas Paine had predicted it would) to be "hunted round the globe." The period 1810–25 saw successful revolutions and the establishment of numerous republics in former Spanish and Portuguese colonies throughout much of Central and South America. Americans for the most part celebrated the creation of these new free republics, saw the situation of the South Americans as parallel to their own struggles against a colonial oppressor, and swelled with pride at the part they saw themselves as having played in inspiring the revolutionary activity. "If national policy forbids our lending active and open service to their cause," the *Alexandria Gazette* opined in 1817, "it may surely be permitted us to wish them success, and … afford them our prayers and wishes."

Below the surface of this pan-American revolutionary camaraderie, however, lay a number of unresolved tensions. Some of these were rooted in ethnicity and religion. Most of the newly independent republics were Spanish speaking, and in all of them the Catholic Church was prominent—whereas English-speaking Americans were overwhelmingly Protestant, and often virulently anti-Catholic when it came to matters closer

Toussaint Louverture, c. 1800. This engraving was made as part of a series of portraits of generals of the French Revolution.

Engraved portrait of Simón Bolívar, 1819. Known as *El Libertador* (The Liberator), Bolívar (1783–1830) successfully led the struggles of what are now Venezuela, Bolivia, Colombia, Ecuador, Peru, and Panama for independence from Spain. While he drew inspiration from the American Revolution and admired George Washington (to whom he has often been compared), Bolívar was disturbed by American slavery, which he encountered when he visited the U.S. in 1807; while fighting for Venezuelan independence in 1816, he proclaimed "absolute freedom for the slaves who have groaned under the Spanish yoke during the three previous centuries"—on the condition that all emancipated enslaved men of military age join the independence struggle.

to home. The Monroe Doctrine, established in 1823, rejected European rule in the Americas but paternalistically cast the United States as protector of the hemisphere. A further source of tension was slavery; though circumstances in the new Central American and South American republics were in every case very different from those in Haiti, the new republics in almost every case resolved to abolish slavery—typically, through the same sort of gradualist approach that the Northern U.S. states were following. That put them very much at odds with attitudes increasingly being adopted by whites in the Southern states, where slavery (which had often in the eighteenth century been defended on circumstantial grounds, as an institution that for the moment represented the least of all possible evils) was increasingly defended as a positive good. These tensions in American public opinion would be brought to the surface in the 1820s, when the newly formed Democratic Party began to vigorously stir up feeling against the Central and South American republics on the bases of religion and of race.

By then the American Revolution itself had become a subject of historical romance and playful literary satire. In Washington Irving's "Rip Van Winkle," the eponymous hero famously sleeps through the Revolution and wakes up only to find all the great social changes it established both bothersome and bewildering. But especially among enslaved people in the Americas, who continued to rebel, and also throughout Europe—whose autocratic regimes contended with numerous revolutions from below—a great hope lived on, that ordinary people can somehow begin the world over again.

THE SHAPE OF A PEOPLE

American literature from the colonial and early national periods serves as an illuminating record of how residents understood themselves as people and as *a* people. Oral narratives, folk songs, political records, life writing, fictional narratives, sermons, poetry, scientific prose, and so many other writings from this era take up fundamental questions: What is the basis for community and how does it perpetuate itself? Which individuals are recognized by and included in a community, why, and how? What are the obligations of individuals to their communities and vice versa?

The shape of the people in colonial North America was never static. The original inhabitants of the lands claimed by Europeans—from the Taínos of the Caribbean to the Salish of the Pacific Northwest to the Mi'kmaq in present-day Maine and the Canadian Atlantic Provinces—had their own understandings of personhood and community. One finds in oral literatures such as the Diné (Navajo) creation story and the Wampanoag "Origin of the Island of Nantucket" accounts of how a people is formed and sustained through the natural environment. A wide range of Indigenous metaphysics informed diplomatic and martial responses of various tribes to the arrival of Europeans—and to the disease, war, and displacement they brought to Indigenous peoples. As waves of European settlers and enslaved Africans arrived in North America over three centuries, the Native American population decreased by as much as ninety per cent. Native Americans pursued their own migrations and alliances, forming new communities and political structures in the interest of survival.

According to one scholarly estimate, from the seventeenth century through to the Revolutionary War the net[1] migration of Europeans to British North America (including the Caribbean) was in the range of 700,000 Europeans immigrated. Immigrants to what would become the Thirteen Colonies came primarily from England in the first half of the seventeenth century; in the eighteenth century they came increasingly from Scotland, Ireland, and the Rhineland (now part of Germany) as well. After 1650, the majority of these European immigrants were indentured servants, contractually obligated to labor for a term in exchange for the cost of their relocation. The vast majority of immigrating servants were men, with a ratio of roughly 4:1 in the seventeenth century. Indeed, men outnumbered women among Euro-American immigrants in every North American colony, including New England, to which more family units migrated. This demographic

---

[1]   It is important to use net figures in considering totals; considerable numbers of immigrants returned to Europe after spending a few years in America. (Gottlieb Mittelberger, for example, whose observations are quoted in the next paragraph, emigrated from the Duchy of Württemberg in what is now Germany in 1750, but returned to Württemberg in 1754.)

Benjamin West, *Penn's Treaty with the Indians*, 1771–72. The legendary "Great Treaty" negotiated between the Lenni Lenape (Delaware) leader Tamanend and William Penn, the founder of Pennsylvania, is frequently celebrated in art and literature, perhaps most famously in this painting by Benjamin West. In the mid-seventeenth century, the Lenape occupied territory from New York to Maryland, including what became eastern Pennsylvania. Unlike the overwhelming majority of colonists, who wholly disregarded the prior land claims of Indigenous populations, Penn paid the Lenape for their territory in Pennsylvania; nonetheless, conflict between the colonists and the Lenape continued during Penn's lifetime and afterward—and usually the Lenape were forced to give way to the colonists' desires. No text of a "Great Treaty" survives, but a wampum belt given to Penn by the Lenape as part of peace negotiations in 1682 is depicted below.

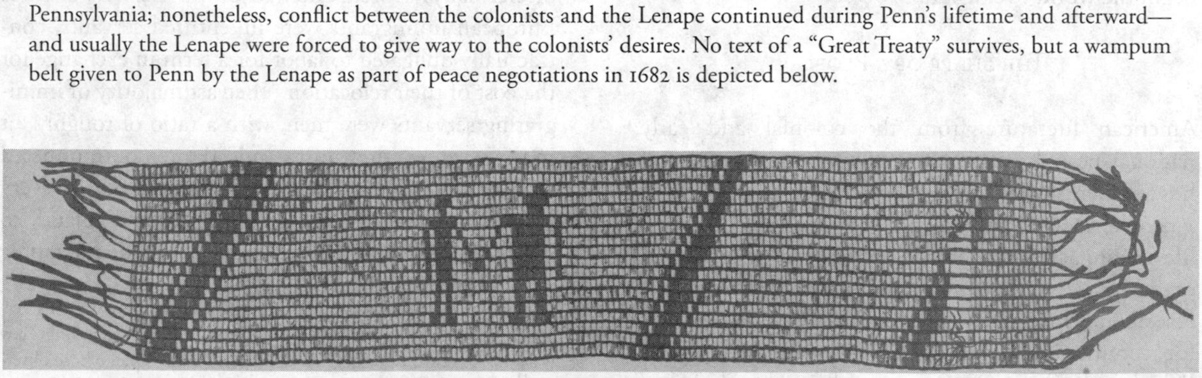

Shackamoxon Treaty Belt [Penn Wampum Belt], 1682.

imbalance gradually leveled out over the eighteenth century.

The transport of indentured servants and the sale of their contracts was a significant business, and the merchants engaged in this business did not shy away from treating their indentured passengers as commodities. Often, prospective immigrants were imprisoned as soon as they signed their contracts and confined until their ship's departure in case they thought better of their decision. On the ship itself, profit was maximized at the cost of extremely cramped conditions and subpar food and water in insufficient quantities. The German immigrant Gottlieb Mittelberger offers a vivid picture of the deplorable circumstances:

> [D]uring the voyage there is on board these ships terrible misery, stench, fumes, horror, vomiting, many kinds of sea-sickness, fever, dysentery, headache, heat, constipation, boils, scurvy, cancer [i.e., cankers], mouth-rot, and the like, all of which come from old and sharply salted food and meat, also from very bad and foul water, so that many die miserably.

Conditions could be better than those Mittelberger describes, but they could also be worse. In one particularly egregious example, the *Sea-Flower* departed from Ireland in 1741 with more than one hundred indentured passengers; the trip to Boston took four months, several weeks longer than expected, and by the time the *Sea-Flower* arrived more than half the passengers had starved to death. A few had eaten their shipmates.

Why did migrants lease their own freedom to undertake such voyages? Some were taken in by the rhetoric of those who profited from the indenture system; Mittelberger speaks disparagingly of "those who suffer themselves to be persuaded and enticed away by the man-thieves" who convince them that "roasted pigeons will fly into their mouths in America or Pennsylvania without their working for them." But for many migrants, the prospects were genuinely worse at home. For the least wealthy Europeans, standards of living were very poor in the sixteenth and seventeenth centuries as land that had once been held in common was privatized and rural peasants were forced into the cities. In England, where circumstances were especially bad, more than half of the nation's peasant class was

without land by the beginning of the seventeenth century, and the number rose as the century progressed. Overpopulation in urban centers fostered rampant disease, while frequent food shortages and price increases left many people unable to afford to feed themselves. Even so, some regretted the decision to try their luck in America; Richard Frethorne, a twelve-year-old indentured servant writing home to his parents, told them that "people cry out day and night—Oh! That they were in England without their limbs—and would not care to lose any limb to be in England again, yea, though they beg from door to door." Frethorne—like many other indentured servants in the colonies—did not survive his term of servitude.

Indentured servants found their rights and freedoms severely curtailed in America. Servants' masters commonly whipped, beat, raped, and otherwise abused them, and they could not marry without permission. Nonetheless, for some indentured servants, America did provide a greater degree of opportunity than they would have had in Europe. In early seventeenth-century Maryland, for example, many servants acquired land and political standing in the community after completing their contracts. But such opportunities diminished through the century as class divisions solidified; by the mid-seventeenth century, Maryland immigrants who had completed indentures were much less likely to end up acquiring their own land than to become tenant farmers, continuing to work for the landowning classes that had exploited them as indentured labor. Similar patterns can be found throughout the colonies. In Boston, for example, in the 1680s, the top one per cent of the population possessed about twenty-five per cent of the wealth in the city; by 1770, that number had risen to forty-four per cent of the city's wealth.

Transportation to America was also common as a punishment for a wide range of crimes committed in Britain, and by some estimates a full quarter of the British immigrants to America in the eighteenth century were convicts. Like indenture, transportation was a profitable system of unfree labor; merchants were paid by the government to transport prisoners and, upon arrival in America, could then sell the convicts for the duration of their sentences (usually seven years). Many convicts attempted to escape, even though the penalty for returning to Britain before one's sentence expired was death.

Between 1600 and 1776, more than three million enslaved Africans were forcibly brought to British colonies, with about 660,000 arriving in mainland North America. From the beginning, the lot of enslaved Africans was worse than that of indentured Europeans, but, especially in the first half of the seventeenth century, enslaved black people and indentured white people often found a great deal of common ground in their experiences. Initially, enslaved and indentured people frequently socialized together, formed romantic relationships, ran away together, and occasionally rebelled together. This community between indentured and enslaved people made colonial elites uneasy, and they encouraged division between white and black people with a variety of laws. Interracial sex was punishable by whipping as early as 1630 in Virginia, while laws prohibiting marriage between black and white people began to be passed throughout the colonies in the 1660s. Indentured servants also, increasingly, received privileges that were denied to enslaved people; white servants, for example, were sometimes permitted to join militias while enslaved people were not, and white defendants generally received lesser sentences than black defendants for the same crimes. In the early eighteenth century, colonies passed laws requiring indentured servants' masters to furnish them with goods upon completion of the indenture—while for black people enslavement had become lifelong and hereditary.

While the majority of those who came to early America were taken by force or driven by economic motives, scholars of American literature long privileged the writings and history of the Puritans and related Protestant groups who came to New England for a different reason: to live according to their religious beliefs without interference. These British immigrants who led the colonization of the Algonquian homelands understood themselves to have entered into a covenant with God as a chosen people, to be obligated to obey God's Law and to live in close community with one another. In 1630, John Winthrop offered the Puritans founding Massachusetts Bay Colony a scriptural type

Robert W. Weir, *Embarkation of the Pilgrims*, 1843, U.S. Capitol Rotunda.

for their social formation: a body of distinct parts "knit together by [Christ's] bond of love." That love took the form of placing the welfare of the community above all else. Residents who were not church members were literally known as Strangers, and early on the Puritan leadership expelled Quakers, Catholics, Antinomians, and others who disagreed with ministers. The concept of covenanted community contributed to the remarkable success of Anglo-Protestant colonization in New England, despite high mortality, harsh weather, theological disagreements, military conflict, and conflict with British investors and the crown. Accounts of faith-based resilience abound in the literature of New England, from the poetry of Anne Bradstreet to the captivity narrative of Mary Rowlandson.

The focus on New England writing in the study of early American literature has contributed to a long-lasting narrative of American exceptionalism (the belief that America is in important ways exceptional—not merely different but extraordinarily different, and in ways that mark it as superior). This belief in America's fundamental difference is commonly traced back to Winthrop's now-famous assertion that the Massachusetts Bay Colony "shall be as a city upon a hill. The eyes of all people are upon us." According to this narrative, the covenanted communities of Winthrop and others—freedom-seeking dissenters chosen by God and committed to one another—gave rise over time to freedom-loving revolutionaries who envisioned a nation conceived in liberty. Certainly, many participants in the American Revolution claimed for America a unique and important place in history, arguing that its deliberate foundation on a set of developed political principles set it apart from other nations that had evolved organically. Alexander Hamilton put it this way:

> It seems to have been reserved to the people of this country, by their conduct and example, to decide the important question, whether societies of men are really capable or not of establishing good government from reflection and choice, or whether they are forever destined to depend for their political constitutions on accident and force.

The idea of the U.S. as a political experiment and an example to the world has been ubiquitous in American

Engraving from Pere Joseph François Lafitau, *Customs of the American Indians Compared with the Customs of Primitive Times* (*Moeurs des Sauvages Amériquains, Comparées aux Moeurs des Premiers Temps*), 1724. This engraving from the work of an eighteenth-century French ethnologist shows a European imagining of the peace negotiations that led to the foundation of the Haudenosaunee Confederacy. It shows leaders from five Iroquois nations (Cayuga, Mohawk, Oneida, Onondaga, and Seneca) assembled around Dekanawida, a leader of the negotiations.

politics since the Revolution, but the phrase "city upon a hill" did not become a commonplace shorthand for this idea until the mid-twentieth century, when it was revived by John F. Kennedy. Since then, American politicians from Ronald Reagan to Barack Obama have used it in key speeches.

Alongside the narrative of exceptional American community, the narrative of the exceptional individual has been a part of American literature since the colonial era. This idea is particularly prominent in works from the Chesapeake and Mid-Atlantic regions such as John Smith's self-promotional *General History of Virginia, New England, and the Summer Isles* (1624), in which Smith presents himself as a rugged hero who pursues his vision of righteous, thrilling conquest in the face of immense opposition. Benjamin Franklin (who was born in Boston but made his name in Philadelphia) produced an *Autobiography* (1791) that some have read as evidence that the nation was made great through citizens' dogged pursuit of self-interest and self-improvement.

In recent decades, scholars of American literary history have looked more broadly at the different literatures of American communities before 1820. They have taken a more expansive approach to reading the Puritan works that have long been part of the canon—reading, for example, with an eye to the Indigenous voices that are overwritten in William Bradford's account of the Pequot War or Rowlandson's account of King Philip's War. And they have broadened the canon considerably.

Even among the white settlers of New England, not everyone was a Puritan; Thomas Morton's *New English Canaan* (1637), for instance, offers an alternative vision of a society in which there is no place for Puritan religious authority, for the practice of indentureship, or for the violent expulsion of Indigenous neighbors. Examples abound beyond seventeenth-century New England. In the eighteenth-century life writing of Quakers Elizabeth Ashbridge and John Woolman, for instance, we learn about the alternative social structures created through Quaker faith and receive firsthand testimony as to the cruelties of indentureship, as to violence against women (both domestic and public), and as to the practice of slavery. Indigenous oral literatures preserve the knowledge of various forms of political community practiced across the continent—including that of the Iroquois Confederacy (Haudenosaunee), a democratic governmental system established centuries before the Continental Congress. Indigenous political ideologies are also reflected in the transcribed speeches of powerful rhetoricians such as Sagoyewatha / Red Jacket (Seneca), Canassatego (Onondaga), and Tecumseh (Shawnee).

Early African American expression has in the past been approached primarily through the neoclassical poetry of Phillis Wheatley and through Olaudah Equiano's *Interesting Narrative* (1789), with an emphasis placed on individual resistance to oppression. In recent decades, the range of African American voices and genres included under the umbrella of "American Literature" has expanded, as has the understanding of African American writing in civic contexts. In addition to Wheatley's and Equiano's groundbreaking publications, readers take up such contributions of African Americans as Belinda Sutton's 1783 petition to the Massachusetts General Court—of interest both as an autobiography and as, some argue, the first successful petition for slavery reparations—and the life writings of preachers such as John Marrant and David George.

Some black writers argued openly against African American oppression, but by its very publication even the most conservative African American writing testified against the commonly held view that, as Benjamin Banneker phrased it in a widely circulated letter to Thomas Jefferson, black people were "scarcely capable of mental endowments." (Banneker, a freeborn African American, presented his achievements in surveying and astronomy as evidence against this view.) Oral forms of literature also retained an important place in African American literature of the period, from rhetorically powerful sermons and abolitionist speeches (which often appeared in print as well) to works such as Lucy Terry's "Bars Fight" (composed c. 1746), a ballad that was preserved in oral tradition for more than a century before its print publication.

Title page of Samson Occom's *A Sermon Preached at the Execution of Moses Paul, an Indian*, 1772. Samson Occom, a Mohegan minister and community leader, is now best known for his autobiographical narrative, unpublished until the twentieth century. He was, however, famous in his lifetime as a preacher, and the text of his *Sermon Preached at the Execution of Moses Paul* (1772) is generally acknowledged to be the first bestseller by a Native American. The text appeared in a remarkable nineteen editions; the title page pictured here is from the fourth.

Title page of Benjamin Banneker's 1795 *Almanac*. Banneker, a self-taught mathematician, published a series of almanacs (annual publications including, among other things, astronomical and weather information for the coming year). His 1795 volume features a woodcut portrait of the author.

Engraving by Hébert after Auguste Raffet, *Attack and Capture of the Crête-à Pierrot*, 1839.

If American exceptionalism has understood the Revolutionary era and the first decades of the republic as establishing unprecedented freedom for early Americans, then an expanded body of American literature makes plain the founding exclusions as well as inclusions. Thomas Paine imagined a people formed out of shared emotion and rational discernment—that is, out of a *common sense* that would sustain them in revolution and in the work of nation building. But Abigail Adams suspected that when men alone were entrusted with that work, they would omit their female compatriots. In 1776, she wrote to her husband, who was away at the Continental Congress, that in addition to declaring independence from Britain they should also "Remember the Ladies, and be more generous and favorable to them than your ancestors." Sure enough, patriarchal tyranny did not end in the revolutionary era. A little over a decade later, as the founding fathers framed the U.S. Constitution in the late 1780s, they assumed the political agency of "We the people" for men alone and established that an enslaved American would constitute 3/5 of a person for the purposes of representation. Subsequently, the U.S. refused to recognize in 1804 the newly established and first black-led republic in the Americas, Haiti, despite a supposedly shared commitment to liberty and equality.

One evocative account of the shape of the people at the end of the eighteenth century is J. Hector St. John de Crèvecoeur's *Letters from an American Farmer* (1782), in which the fictional Farmer James poses the question "What then is the American, this new man?" and concludes that he is a European immigrant transformed by the freedom and prosperity the land affords. His love of country, James insists, is inspired by the fact that "his labour is founded on the basis of nature, SELF-INTEREST." Yet in travels to South Carolina, James witnesses slavery's brutal negation of black personhood. When, at the end of *Letters*, Revolutionary War approaches his farmstead, James and his family flee to a nearby Native American community, determining they had best ride out the brutal war among a people less impacted—at least in Crèvecoeur's romantic telling—by the disagreement between the British crown and colonists who wished to form their own nation.

By the first decades of the nineteenth century, two interrelated questions from the Revolution remained: Who was considered equal to whom? And who would enjoy true liberty? There was not a single shape to American society, though there were many narratives or theories of who belonged and how they understood their communal identity. If anything was certain, it was the perpetual possibility of reshaping "a people"—of reimagining community by way of individual rights and public values.

"A STATE OF INDEPENDENCY": THE REPUBLIC'S FIRST DECADES

What was created in 1776 when the Continental Congress issued the Declaration of Independence? While Thomas Jefferson's ringing words have served as an inspiration for democratic ideals ever since, they did not at the time herald an intent to form a democratic nation in anything like the modern sense. In practice, the claim that "all men" possessed "certain inalienable rights" was understood to apply only to adult white males. Nor did the founders intend in 1776 to create a nation state in anything like the modern sense; the Declaration was consistently plural in its language, referring to the former colonies as "free and independent states," with no suggestion of any overarching body that would speak for them all collectively. Similarly, the Articles of Confederation that the Continental Congress adopted in 1777 (and that were ratified by the individual states over the next four years) asserted the "sovereignty, freedom, and independence" of each of the individual states, not of the collective entity. The colonies had entered collectively into what was often termed a "state of independency," but the national government existed almost exclusively as an entity to conduct the war and other matters of foreign affairs; it had no power over any of the individual states in any sphere, and no power to levy taxes or to undertake any other financial or economic measures.

Before long it became clear that more power would need to be granted to the federal government if the Confederation were to last—that a national government would need to have the power to regulate commerce and to raise money without relying solely on contributions from the individual states, and that a judiciary and other permanent national institutions would need to be created. But what should be the extent, and the limits, of federal power?

When a Constitutional Convention was finally held in May 1787 and a Constitution for the United States proposed, the debate about this question was fierce. Under the constitution's provisions, the individual states would be barred from charging import or export taxes, interfering with property rights, or in any way obstructing interstate commerce. Moreover, in the statement of purpose drafted by Gouverneur Morris (a native New Yorker who represented Pennsylvania at the convention), the national government was tasked with overarching duties such as establishing justice, promoting the general welfare of the people, and securing the blessings of liberty; the preamble, which in its original draft had referred to "We, the people of the states of New-Hampshire, Massachusetts, Rhode Island and Providence Plantations, Connecticut, New York," etc., was given a more collectivist emphasis: "We, the people of the United States ..."

Supporters of the proposed constitution, known as the Federalists, put their case persuasively—most notably in the 85 essays by Alexander Hamilton, James Madison, and John Jay that were collectively known as *The Federalist Papers*. But to many, the proposed constitution's provisions granted too much power to the national government, and did too little to protect the rights of individual citizens—rights that had been given robust expression in the constitutions of many of the individual states. It was in that context that Madison, in order to win support for ratification, proposed that the first Congress put into place a Bill of Rights, "to make the Constitution better in the opinion of those who are opposed to it." The ten amendments that together constitute the Bill of Rights were put forward in 1789; among other things, they protect "freedom of speech, or of the press," protect "the right of the people peaceably to assemble," prohibit "unreasonable searches and seizures," protect the right to not "be deprived of life, liberty, or property, without due process of law," and assure anyone accused of a crime of the right to "a speedy and public trial." In the 1780s the Bill of Rights was a constitutional add-on, but it has come in the twentieth and twenty-first centuries to be regarded as of central importance to the Constitution.

By 21 June 1788 the Constitution in its original form had been ratified by the required number of states; by 15 December 1791 the Bill of Rights had also been ratified by the required number of states.

The numbers in the different States, according to the most accurate accounts which could be obtained by the late Federal Convention, were as follow :	
In New-Hampshire,	102,000
In Massachusetts,	360,000
In Rhode-Island,	58,000
In Connecticut,	202,000
In New-York,	238,000
In New-Jersey,	130,000
In Pennsylvania,	360,000
In Delaware,	37,000
In Maryland, (including three-fifths of 80,000 negroes)	218,000
In Virginia, (including three-fifths of 280,000 negroes)	420,000
In North-Carolina, (including three-fifths of 60,000 negroes)	200,000
In South-Carolina, (including three-fifths of 80,000 negroes)	150,000
In Georgia, (including three-fifths of 20,000 negroes)	90,000

From the *Hartford Courant*, 25 February 1788; similar notices appeared in newspapers throughout the states.

The Constitution's "We, the people" preamble was understood to exclude the Indigenous peoples of North America (excepting those few who had accepted assimilation and were paying taxes), and also to exclude enslaved people. The words "person," "persons," and "people" in the Bill of Rights were understood similarly. Enslaved people do appear in the Constitution obliquely when they are referred to in the notorious "three-fifths" clause, according to the terms of which additional political power was granted to slaveholding states. Enslaved people themselves were of course granted no political power and no rights. But whenever population was taken into account (in apportioning each state's number of representatives in the House of Representatives, and each state's number of votes for the presidential electoral college), slave states would be granted representation based on the total number of their white population plus "three fifths of all other persons." The three-fifths clause played a key role in maintaining slavery—and in giving Southern states an outsized say in national politics up to the Civil War.

In the debates over the Constitution, the "Federalists" and the "Anti-Federalists" were loose groupings of individuals, not organized political parties. In these early days of the republic most Americans had strong feelings against "faction"—what we would call division along party lines. There were thus no parties in the nation's earliest days; those who had been elected gave speeches and voted as independent individuals, not as the members of any formal group. But in the years following the ratification of the Constitution and the Bill of Rights, large, informal groupings took shape—most notably, on one side, supporters of the ideas that George Washington, Alexander Hamilton, and John Adams (who succeeded Washington as President) gave voice to, and on the opposing side, supporters of the ideas that Thomas Jefferson and James Madison gave voice to. Washington, Hamilton, and Adams advocated a relatively strong central government, a standing army, a national bank, and other measures to bring order to the monetary and financial system, and support for manufacturing and other industries. Pointing to the excesses of the French Revolution, they opposed measures that would broaden the franchise so as to allow men who did not own property to vote, and they tended to think of inequality not as an issue to be addressed but as an inevitable, even desirable feature of any properly functioning society. Federalist preacher (and textbook author) Jedediah Morse made this principle quite explicit in *A Discourse, Delivered at the African Meeting House in Boston, July 14 1808*:

> Distinctions of rank and condition in life are requisite to the perfection of the social state. There must be rulers and ruled, masters and servants, rich and poor. ... There is nevertheless a kind of equality among the members: all are free; all are useful and necessary; all are to be regarded and honored according to their station and use.[1]

Jefferson and Madison, on the other hand, were more sympathetic to democratic and egalitarian ideals, more supportive of farmers (both slaveholding Southern plantation owners and small "yeomen" owning family farms), and suspicious of institutions such as a permanent national army or a national bank, which they regarded as signs of a dangerous centralization of power in the hands of the federal government.

In the 1790s these loose groupings coalesced into two political parties: the Federalists, supporting Washington and Hamilton, and the Republicans,[2] supporting Jefferson and Madison. Disagreements between the two became more and more heated as the decade wore on, and partisans on both sides accused their opponents of holding treasonous views. The fiercely contested 1800 election turned largely on the Federalists' imposition of several pieces of legislation that aimed to reduce dissent. The Alien and Sedition Acts of 1798 made it more difficult to obtain American citizenship and gave the federal government broad powers to imprison or deport non-citizens and to prosecute those expressing views critical of the government. The resolution of the election was extraordinarily complicated and prolonged, but in the end Thomas Jefferson was elected president, on the slogan "Jefferson and Liberty."

The election of Jefferson is commonly thought of as a watershed moment in American history—not least of all because it demonstrated that a peaceful transition of power could be accomplished in the young republic. (Jefferson's endeavor to bring unity to the fractious country was demonstrated by his famous declaration, "We are all republicans, we are all federalists.") But it has also often been seen as a triumph of democratic ideals and of the values of "the common man" over what had become the overly controlling habits of Adams and the Federalists. Jefferson did pardon those who had been convicted under the Sedition Act (which Congress allowed to expire in 1801), and he restored the period required before one could obtain citizenship to five years from fourteen. But his administration proved to be no more willing than those of Washington or Adams had been to respect the rights of Indigenous peoples or of free African Americans.

---

[1]   Morse made these statements in the course of arguing that freeing enslaved people should not be imagined to entail a general leveling of society. (While asserting repeatedly that, for all people, "the greatest slavery is sin," Morse celebrated the abolition of the international slave trade and expressed hope that the "gradual and ultimate extinction of African slavery" would come to pass.)

[2]   The Republican party of this era (also known as the Democratic-Republican Party) broke up in the 1820s; the Republican Party that was founded in 1854 and that still exists today is an entirely different entity.

Ancestral Pueblo storage jar, c. 1050–1100. This Ancestral Pueblo storage jar, likely used to preserve food in preparation for drought, is painted in a style known as "Socorro black-on-white" for the region of the Upper Rio Grande Valley where it originated. The abstract pattern on the jar probably references the movement of water, with the black portions evoking clouds while the lines represent rain; the hand-shaped symbol may be the painter's personal mark.

Shingwaukonse, Mishipeshu with canoe and serpents, c. early nineteenth century. This rock painting, part of an important Ojibwe pictograph site at Agawa Rock on the east coast of Lake Superior, depicts the powerful spirit Mishipeshu, sometimes called the Great Lynx, who governs the dangerous waters of Lake Superior and possesses the region's copper. The prominent shaman and chief Shingwaukonse (1773–1854) told the anthropologist Henry Rowe Schoolcraft that, while many of Agawa Rock's paintings are substantially older, he himself had drawn Mishipeshu as part of a ritual to gather power before leading a resistance effort against copper miners. Indigenous knowledge-keepers and settler anthropologists have also found a variety of other meanings in the image.

Alejo Fernández, *The Virgin of the Navigators*, 1531–36. This painting forms the central panel of an altarpiece painted by the prominent Seville-based artist Alejo Fernández under a commission from the House of Trade, the government entity that oversaw the commercial aspects of the Spanish Empire. Scholars continue to discuss the identities of the figures sheltered under the Virgin Mary's cloak, but some of the most likely candidates include Hernán Cortés, leader of the conquest of Mexico, on a bent knee in a red cape; Charles I of Spain (also Holy Roman Emperor as Charles V) behind Cortés with a red beard; explorer Amerigo Vespucci, holding a cane; and, in a gold robe, Christopher Columbus. Behind these figures are Indigenous people of the Americas. One possible explanation for their simple cloth attire, unlike anything Indigenous Americans would have worn in daily life, is that they are dressed for baptism.

John White, *The Manner of Their Fishing*, c. 1585. English artist John White accompanied the first attempt to colonize Roanoke Island, off the coast of what is now North Carolina, where he made watercolors such as this one depicting the plants, animals, and Indigenous people of the region. Etchings based on his paintings were made for a 1590 edition of Thomas Hariot's *A Brief and True Report of the New Found Land of Virginia* (first published in 1588), an account of the same expedition; these etchings circulated widely and strongly influenced European understandings of the Americas and the people who lived there. In Hariot's caption for the etching based on this painting, he notes a number of the fishing methods depicted, including the building of fishing weirs, rows of stakes placed in the water so as to trap fish. He writes of them that "[t]here was never seen among us so cunning a way to take fish," commenting that "it is a pleasant sight to see the people, sometimes wading, and going sometimes sailing in those rivers, which are shallow and not deep, free from all care of heaping up riches for their posterity, content with their state, and living friendly together of those things which god of his bounty has given to them, yet without giving him any thanks according to his desert."

For further examples of John White's work and selections from Hariot's *Brief and True Report*, see "Civilizations in Contact" elsewhere in this anthology.

Anonymous, *Elizabeth Clarke Freake and Baby Mary*, 1671–74.

Anonymous, *John Freake*, 1671–74.

The anonymous painter of these works, sometimes known as the "Freake Painter" in reference to them, painted around ten portraits in the Boston area in the early 1670s; the painter appears to have received English training in the Elizabethan style of portraiture, which was no longer popular in England by this time. The subjects of the portraits, John Freake and Elizabeth Clarke Freake, were Boston Puritans whose wealth is reflected in the expensive and fashionable clothing they wear. Elizabeth was born near Boston to a wealthy merchant family, and John, who had immigrated to Boston from England, was also a very successful merchant. Elizabeth originally held a fan in her portrait, but it was altered a few years later to include her youngest daughter.

Detail, anonymous casta painting, eighteenth century. Popular among eighteenth-century Spanish elites in the Americas, casta paintings represent complex racial classifications or "castes" through a series of images showing the offspring of various mixed-race couples. Each set begins with white, black, and Indigenous parents, applying separate terms to their children and grandchildren in various racial combinations. Like many sets of casta paintings do, the image reproduced here includes sixteen classifications:

1. Spaniard with Indigenous person: Mestizo.
2. Mestizo with Spaniard: Castizo.
3. Castizo with Spaniard: Spaniard.
4. Spaniard with African: Mulatto.
5. Mulatto with Spaniard: Morisca ("Moorish").
6. Morisca with Spaniard: Chino (literally "Chinese").
7. Chino with Indigenous person: Salta atrás ("throwback").
8. Salta atrás with Mulatto: Lobo ("wolf").
9. Lobo with Chino: Gíbaro.
10. Gíbaro with Mulatto: Albarazado ("white-spotted").
11. Albarazado with African: Cambujo.
12. Cambujo with Indigenous person: Sanbaigo.
13. Sanbaigo with Loba: Calpamulato.
14. Calpamulto with Cambujo: Tente en el aire ("hold yourself in the air").
15. Tente en el aire with Mulatto: No te entiendo (literally "I don't understand you").
16. No te entiendo with Indigenous person: Torna atrás ("return backwards").

Beyond terms such as "mestizo" and "mulatto," this precise (and, generally speaking, offensive) terminology was little used in practice, but its complexity can be taken as an indication of eighteenth-century Euro-American fascination both with race and with taxonomy. The categories also reflect differences in Spanish racism toward Indigenous and black people: most casta paintings assert that a person with one Indigenous grandparent could be considered Spanish, while a person with one African grandparent could not.

Agostino Brunias, *Free Women of Colour with Their Children and Servants in a Landscape*, c. 1770–96. The Italian-born painter Agostino Brunias spent much of his career on Dominica and other Caribbean islands colonized by Britain. His paintings, which often focus on the islands' mixed-race elites, had admirers on both sides of the abolition debate. His proslavery audience in Europe and the colonies enjoyed his idyllic and exotic depictions of plantation life—and the absence of any representation of the brutality of slavery. At the same time, his work was welcomed by black and mixed-race Caribbeans who appreciated his celebration of the Creole culture emerging in the region; the Haitian revolutionary Touissant Louverture, for example, wore a jacket with buttons featuring miniature scenes painted by Brunias.

Robert Dighton, *Keep Within Compass and You Shall Be Sure, to Avoid Many Troubles which Others Endure*, 1784 and 1785. Designed by the painter and printmaker Robert Dighton and printed by the London publisher Carington Bowles, these images circulated widely in the colonies as well as in Britain, appearing not only as prints but also on everyday objects such as fans and teapots. The man in the print on the left points to sacks of coins; on the edge of the illustration are smaller scenes of a man ruined by gambling, a man being robbed by a prostitute, a ship crashed on rocks, and prisoners in jail. The woman in the print on the right holds a book that reads "The Pleasures of Imagination Realized"; the chest at her feet is labeled "The Reward of Virtue." The scenes surrounding her feature women ruined by gambling, dropping a baby in a bout of drunkenness, being arrested by watchmen, and performing manual labor in prison.

Joshua Johnson, *Adelina Morton*, c. 1810. Generally considered the first known professional African American painter, Joshua Johnson was born into slavery in Maryland, and after his enslaver (who was also his father) granted him his freedom he earned his living making portraits of Baltimore elites. In one newspaper advertisement offering his services, he writes that, "As a self-taught genius, deriving from nature and industry his knowledge of the Art; and having experienced many insuperable obstacles in the pursuit of his studies, it is highly gratifying to him to make assurances of his ability to execute all commands with an effect, and in a style, which must give satisfaction."

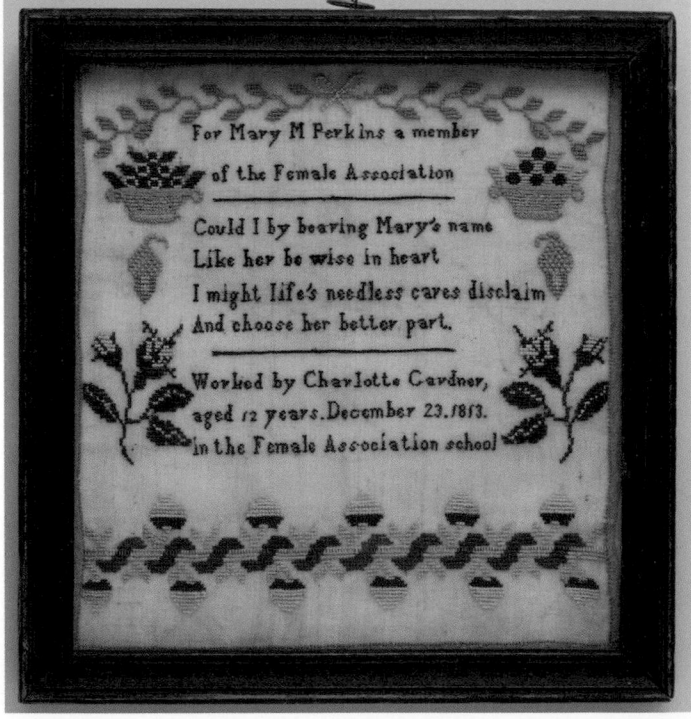

Charlotte Cardner, Quaker School Sampler, 1813. At the beginning of the nineteenth century, the New York Female Association, a Quaker organization, founded New York's first public school for girls—a project motivated by the Quaker belief that education should be accessible to all. Students learned reading, writing, arithmetic, and embroidery; the latter skill is evident in this sampler made for one of the school's patrons.

The First, Second, and Last Scene of Mortality. Prudence Punderson.

Prudence Punderson, *The First, Second, and Last Scene of Mortality*, c. 1776–83. Needlework artist Prudence Punderson's family supported the British side during the American Revolution, and as a result they were forced to flee their home in Connecticut. While living in exile and relative poverty in Long Island, Punderson created her best-known works, including this self-portrait. On the right, Punderson appears as a baby, cared for by a servant (probably an enslaved woman named Jenny, whom the family owned); in the center, she appears as an adult drawing at a table; on the left is depicted a covered mirror above a coffin bearing the initials "P.P." The interior depicted is likely based on the home the Pundersons left behind in Connecticut, as their Long Island lodgings would not have been so comfortable. As soon as the war ended, Punderson returned to Connecticut and married; she died less than a year later, at the age of 26.

Anonymous, *Benjamin Hawkins and the Creek Indians*, c. 1805. In 1796, Benjamin Hawkins, a former senator, was appointed "Principal Temporary Agent for Indian Affairs South of the Ohio River" and charged with implementing the so-called "plan of civilization," according to which the Indigenous peoples of the region would replace hunting and Indigenous farming practices with a Euro-American style of farming cash crops and keeping livestock. On the surface, this plan was intended to help Indigenous groups flourish economically—ignoring the fact that they were quite capable of supporting themselves already—but the covert goal was to undermine Indigenous claims to hunting lands to make more room for settler-colonists. Hawkins saw himself as an ally to the Indigenous groups and believed the "plan of civilization" was the best way forward, since the other likely possibility was the violent expulsion of the Indigenous peoples from the region. He moved to a Muscogee-Creek community, where he found that many people were already selectively adopting Euro-American farming practices and appreciated his support. Disagreement among the Muscogee about how to respond to the "plan of civilization" culminated in a civil war (1813–14); the U.S. government intervened brutally and forced the Muscogee to sign a treaty that ceded two-thirds of their land. Hawkins resigned in protest.

Anonymous Chinese artist after John James Barralet, *Apotheosis of Washington*, early nineteenth century (original c. 1802). After George Washington's death in 1799, the commemoration of his life and passing became a tremendously fashionable subject for artists. The print this work is based on, by the Irish-born illustrator John James Barralet, was so popular that it was issued several times. One copy was taken to China to be copied onto porcelain—or, in examples such as the one reproduced here, glass—for sale in the United States. The work depicts Washington lifted from his tomb by allegorical figures of Immortality and Father Time; in the background are figures of Faith, Hope, and Charity. In front of the tomb are an Indigenous figure and Lady Liberty, who holds a liberty cap on a pole, a symbol of the revolution. Liberty and the Indigenous man are placed in poses reminiscent of the sleeping soldiers often depicted in scenes of Christ's resurrection, while the image of Washington ascending on a cloud, aided by winged figures, reflects typical images of the Virgin Mary being taken up into heaven.

John Quidor, *The Return of Rip Van Winkle*, 1849. New York painter John Quidor devoted much of his career to depicting scenes from literature, especially from the work of Washington Irving—most famously "The Legend of Sleepy Hollow" (1820) and "Rip Van Winkle" (1819), the latter of which was a popular subject for nineteenth-century artists generally. In this interpretation of Rip's dramatic homecoming following his twenty-year nap, Quidor frames the character's extreme body language with the chaos and change occasioned by the American Revolution. See Washington Irving's author section, elsewhere in this anthology, for another Quidor painting based on "Rip Van Winkle."

John Lewis Krimmel, *Independence Day Celebration in Centre Square*, 1819. Born in Germany, John Lewis Krimmel emigrated to Philadelphia in 1809, where he became best-known for his scenes of everyday life. This painting of the city's 1819 Fourth of July celebrations shows a crowd engaging in the festivities while, on the right, a woman attempts to distribute temperance literature. On the left, a black child runs away from the scene—an allusion to the risk of racist violence that generally kept African American Philadelphians from participating in city revelries such as this. In the central foreground, officers of the army and navy point to a Pennsylvania flag, a portrait of George Washington, and banners referencing American victories in the War of 1812 (1812–15).

Early nineteenth-century criteria as to who counted as a citizen and who could vote were extremely narrow by modern standards—and they narrowed even further during the years Jefferson was in power (1801–09). In most states only citizens who owned a considerable amount of property (fifty acres or more was a common requirement) were allowed to vote. In the early years of the republic many states did not specify that "citizen"

The Providential Detection, c. 1797–1800. This anti-Jeffersonian political cartoon depicts Thomas Jefferson being prevented by an American eagle (and by God, symbolized by an eye peering out of a cloud in the top right corner) from burning the U.S. Constitution on an "Altar to Gallic Despotism"—referring to the radical and, to Federalists, extremist policies of the French Revolution, which influenced Jeffersonian Republicanism. The document Jefferson is dropping from his right hand, labeled "To Mazzei," refers to a private letter Jefferson wrote to his friend Philip Mazzei in 1796, in which he condemned the "Anglo-Monarchico-Aristocratic party"—i.e., the Federalists—currently controlling the U.S. government; the letter's publication in 1797 made Jefferson the target of intense Federalist criticism.

was intended to mean "white male"; in several states (theoretically at least) both women and free black people could vote.[1] By 1807, however, almost every state had passed legislation specifically restricting the franchise to white men, excluding women and black people of either sex from voting. Overall, then, it is difficult to argue that democratic vistas widened in America in the early nineteenth century.

Nowhere are the paradoxes inherent in Jeffersonian "democratic ideals" more evident than in the history of American expansion during this period. Federalists in this era were wary of expansion, fearing the unpredictable consequences of taking on new responsibilities and of trying to assimilate the inhabitants of new territories. Jefferson, on the other hand, was keen to acquire more land for the white farmers and would-be western settlers who were a key constituency for the Republicans, envisaging "an empire of liberty" that would eventually stretch to the Pacific. For white would-be settlers on western lands, he made this prospect more appealing by requiring settlers to purchase no more than 160 acres of public land (compared to the former requirement of 640 acres) with a down payment of only $16 and at a price of $2 an acre—or sometimes less. (By contrast, when land was purchased under the terms of treaties imposed on Indigenous peoples, the price was typically no more than 2 cents per acre; Jefferson wrote in 1803 that he felt it "important to press on the Indians, as steadily and strenuously as they can bear, the extension of our purchases.")

The primary U.S. territorial acquisition for which Jefferson was responsible, the Louisiana Purchase of 1803, has often been seen primarily through the lens of the negotiations between Jefferson's government and that of Napoleon; it should also be seen in an international context that includes the Caribbean as well as Europe and continental North America—and it should be seen as part of a process rather than in isolation. In the 1780s and 1790s the Spanish authorities in

---

1   The original constitutions of Massachusetts, New Hampshire, Vermont, and Maine had all granted the vote to free black people, but by the early nineteenth century they all passed legislation denying black people the right to vote. In New Jersey, both free black males and property-owning women were able to vote until 1807; thereafter, the franchise was restricted to white men—as it was in New York, Pennsylvania, Connecticut, Maryland, Tennessee, and North Carolina.

James Peale, *The Artist and His Family*, 1795. This painting of Peale, his wife Mary, and five of their eventual six children helped promote the ideology of "Republican Motherhood": the idea that women had a key role to play in fostering the fledgling U.S.'s republican values by instilling these values in their children. "Republican Motherhood" vested women's traditional domestic roles with great political importance while reinforcing the belief that the private home, rather than the public sphere, was women's proper place—a belief conveyed in this painting by the way in which only Peale himself looks outward at the painting's viewer, while his wife confines her focus to her children.

Florida and Louisiana,[1] anxious that the white populations there not be heavily outnumbered by Indigenous people and enslaved people, were eager to attract white American settlers. At the urging of Jefferson (then Secretary of State), President George Washington

made a show of complaining of "this seduction of our inhabitants" while secretly encouraging white Americans to settle in those Spanish territories. "I wish a hundred thousand of our inhabitants would accept the invitation," Jefferson wrote; "it will be the means of delivering to us peaceably, what may otherwise cost us a war." When in 1801 France acquired the Louisiana territory from Spain the fundamentals did not change.[2] Indeed, the transfer of colonial control ended up hastening the process by which the U.S. acquired the vast territory. The unexpectedly stiff resistance that Napoleon's French forces had met when they tried to retake Haiti from the enslaved people who had rebelled there[3] persuaded Napoleon that he could not afford to defend the huge territory of Louisiana at the same time as he was fighting a war in Europe. Thanks very largely to the strength of a black-led revolution that the American government deplored, the United States was able to buy all of Louisiana for a mere $15 million. For the most part, of course, the French were selling land that was not theirs to sell; the colonial powers had laid claim to the vast Louisiana territory without having negotiated treaties with its Indigenous inhabitants that could give them any legitimate claim to ownership. But such niceties did not trouble Jefferson or the American Congress any more than they had the European colonial powers.

The acquisition of the Louisiana Territory represented the most substantial expansion of the United States during the first decades of the new republic, but Americans looked to expand in a number of other directions as well during these years—to the south and to the north as well as westward. The War of 1812 has traditionally not been framed as a war of American expansionism; at the time, indeed, works of popular literature such as Samuel Woodworth's "The Patriotic Diggers" framed it as a defensive war in the face of British aggression. But were it not for American expansionism the war would surely not have occurred; its roots lie in the spread of white settlement westward in the late eighteenth and early nineteenth centuries.

---

[1]   "Louisiana" initially referred to a vast area of the North American interior, stretching from the Great Lakes to the Gulf of Mexico and from the Appalachian to the Rocky Mountains, explored and colonized by France in the late seventeenth and eighteenth centuries (the name "Louisiana" came from King Louis XIV of France). The Louisiana Territory purchased by the U.S. in 1803 comprised only part of this, but still consisted of a huge stretch of land between the Mississippi and the Rockies, of which the present-day U.S. state of Louisiana is only the southernmost portion.

---

[2]   France had previously ceded the Louisiana Territory to Spain in 1762.

[3]   For more on the Haitian Revolution and its impact on American history and literature, see the "Contexts: Revolutions and Rebellions" section of this volume.

J.L. Bouqueto de Woiseri, *Under My Wings Everything Prospers*, 1803. The Louisiana Purchase was widely and often extravagantly praised. At a 10 August 1803 gathering of the citizens of Lexington, Kentucky, to celebrate the purchase, for example, the following toast was made: "To Thomas Jefferson, President of the United States. Can he, by whose wise measures we have acquired a new world, continue still to have enemies?"

The above painting of New Orleans by a local artist dates from just after the Louisiana Purchase. The bird holding the banner is a somewhat puzzling feature. The bald eagle had been selected as the national symbol of the United States in 1782; the bird pictured here is clearly not a mature bald eagle, though it is possible that it is a juvenile. (Not until they are three to five years old do bald eagles acquire their distinctive white head feathers.)

Without any formal authorization, close to 400,000 American settler colonists had by 1800 taken land west of the Appalachians. It was in response to these encroachments that a number of allied Indigenous peoples challenged the Americans in a succession of wars, culminating in what became known as Tecumseh's War (see the Tecumseh author entry). And it was in large part in response to British support (some real, some imagined) for this Indigenous resistance[1] that the U.S. in 1812 declared war on Britain. Kentuckian Henry Clay, the leader of the congressional group known as the War Hawks, argued bluntly to his fellow congressmen that the "conquest of Canada" could readily be accomplished even "by the militia of Kentucky acting alone," and that Congress should act to "extinguish the torch that lights up savage warfare,"

and to "acquire the entire fur trade connected with that country [i.e., the entire fur trade in Canada]." The Federalists and not a few Republicans thought Clay and the War Hawks to be misguided extremists, but in the end the War Hawks prevailed; the bill authorizing the declaration of war passed in the Senate by 19 to 13.

The war itself was inconclusive; when it ended in 1815 the boundary between the United States and the British colonies to the north was unchanged. But the end of the war did not bring an end to American expansionism. As had happened in what became Ohio, and as would happen later in what would become the state of Texas, American settlers had also begun without formal authorization in the late eighteenth century to spill over the country's southern border; many thousands had settled in the Spanish colonies of East Florida and West Florida (whose combined area extended from St. Augustine on the Atlantic coast to what is now southeastern Louisiana). Though the territories

---

[1] This account is necessarily oversimplified; other irritants included a variety of disputes over trade and shipping issues.

Julia Plantou (artist) and Alexis Chataigner (engraver), *Peace of Ghent 1814 and Triumph of America*, c. 1815. This elaborate allegorical image projects a celebratory, patriotic view of the Peace of Ghent, the treaty between Britain and the United States that ended the War of 1812. At the right, Columbia, the allegorical representation of the U.S., is being crowned with the laurels of victory; at the left, Britannia, the allegorical representation of Britain, is being compelled to accept peace terms by Minerva and Hercules—Roman gods personifying, respectively, wisdom and strength.

were nominally under Spanish control, fewer than 15,000 Spanish settlers lived there (most of them in the centers of St. Augustine, Pensacola, and Mobile); those of Spanish descent were substantially outnumbered by Seminole, Muscogee (Creek), and other Indigenous peoples, together with "maroons" who had escaped from slavery. (In the eighteenth century, Spain had held out the prospect of freedom to enslaved Africans in British colonies, on the condition that they convert to Catholicism.) Americans who settled in the Floridas coveted what they saw as underutilized land, and feared that the maroons would foment unrest among those still enslaved. But by 1810 many thousands of white Americans who had settled in Spanish territory

in the Floridas were chafing at Spanish laws—not least of all the web of laws designed to protect enslaved workers from mistreatment. When in that year a group of Americans in West Florida rebelled against Spanish rule and declared themselves to be "a free and independent state," the administration of President James Madison invaded, and Congress annexed what had been a large part of West Florida to the United States. A similar process unfolded over the course of the next decade in the remainder of West Florida and in East Florida; through pressure, subterfuge, and outright war (against the Muscogee and the Seminole as well as the Spanish), the United States had by 1821 acquired the entirety of the two Floridas.

Texts and Contexts:
A Chronological Chart

In the chart below, dates generally refer to the year when a work was first made public, whether published in print or, in the case of speeches and plays, made public through the first performance. Where that date is known to differ substantially from the date of composition, the difference is generally noted; for manuscript works whose exact date of composition is unknown, we have provided an estimated date range.

For events from 1820 to Reconstruction, see the chart in the second half of this volume.

TEXTS		CONTEXTS	
before 10,500 BCE	The oral traditions of North American Indigenous people can in some cases be traced back to the last Ice Age	before 10,500 BCE	Migration of small groups from Asia to the Americas over several thousand years
		c. 3000 BCE –500 BCE	Red Paint Culture flourishes in the Northeast
		c. 200–900	Peak of Maya civilization; city of Teotihuacàn flourishes
		c. 700–1600	Mississippian Culture flourishes in Midwest and Southeast
		c. 750 CE	Ancestral Puebloans of the Southwest begin living in pueblo complexes
		982–1015	Norse people establish settlements in North America and encounter Inuit, Beothuk, Mi'kmaq
c. 1021–1154	Maya Codex of Mexico	c. 1142–1500	Formation of Haudenosaunee (Iroquois) Confederacy (exact date is controversial)
c. 1200–50	Dresden Codex	c. 1200–1400	Ndee (Apache) and Diné (Navajo) migrate into Southwest
			Beginning of the migration of the Ojibwe people from the Atlantic to the Great Lakes

1542	Álvar Núñez Cabeza de Vaca, *The Relation of Álvar Núñez Cabeza de Vaca*		1542	Juan Rodríguez Cabrillo's voyage to California begins
1552	Bartolomé de las Casas, *A Short Account of the Destruction of the Indies*		1558–1603	Reign of Elizabeth I
			1565	Permanent Spanish settlement founded at St. Augustine, Florida; approximately 800 Spanish colonists bring with them approximately 50 enslaved Africans
			1585	English colonizers land on Roanoke Island near modern-day North Carolina but abandon the settlement a year later
			1587	Second expedition to Roanoke, led by John White (later called the Lost Colony due to the disappearance of the colonists)
1588	Thomas Hariot, *A Brief and True Report of the New Found Land of Virginia*		1603–10	Samuel de Champlain explores the St. Lawrence River and Acadia, establishing a settlement in the Bay of Fundy (1604) and founding Quebec (1608)
1605	Inca Garcilaso de la Vega, *La Florida del Inca*		1607	The Virginia Company establishes a settlement at Jamestown
				Under the leadership of Wahunsonacock, Powhatan people provide food and supplies to starving Jamestown colonists
			1609	Henry Hudson explores Staten Island, Manhattan Island, and river valley of what is known today as the Hudson River
1610	Gaspar de Villagrá, *Historia de la Nueva Mexico*		1610–14	First Anglo-Powhatan War
1611	King James Bible (a new translation prompted in part by English Puritans)		1612	First commercial tobacco crop grown in Jamestown
1613	Samuel de Champlain, *The Voyages of the Sieur de Champlain*		1613	Two Row Wampum establishes the Convenant Chain between settlers and member nations of the Haudenosaunee
			1619	"20. and odd" enslaved persons from the African Kingdom of Ndongo, or "Angola," arrive in Virginia aboard a privateer ship flying the Dutch flag

		1620	Approximately 100 Separatists arrive aboard the *Mayflower*, found Plymouth Colony
		1621	Settlers and local Wampanoag together celebrate successful harvest
		1622–26	Second Anglo-Powhatan War
1624	John Smith, *The General History of Virginia, New England, and the Summer Isles*	1624	First permanent Dutch settlement in New Netherland (later called New York)
1630	John Winthrop, "A Model of Christian Charity" (pub. 1838)	1630–43	English Puritans establish Massachusetts Bay Colony.
1630–50	William Bradford's journal, *Of Plymouth Plantation* (pub. 1856)	1634	First English settlers arrive in Maryland
		1636	Harvard College founded
		1636–38	Pequot War between the Pequot tribe and English colonists from the Massachusetts Bay, Plymouth, and Connecticut colonies (with Narragansett and Mohegan allies)
			Mystic Massacre of 1637; colonists set fire to a Pequot fort, killing most of the occupants (between 500 and 700 Pequot)
1637	Thomas Morton, *New English Canaan*	1637	*Desire*, first slave ship built in the American colonies, sets sail for the British West Indies
		1638	First printing press arrives in the colonies
			Anne Hutchinson tried, convicted, and banished for challenging Puritan religious beliefs
1640	*Bay Psalm Book*	1641	Massachusetts legalizes slavery; it is the first British colony to do so
			Sugar exports from the Caribbean begin
		1642–51	English Civil War
1643	Roger Williams, *A Key into the Language of America*	1644–46	Third Anglo-Powhatan War
		1649	Execution of Charles I of England
1650	Anne Bradsteet, *The Tenth Muse*	1651	Thomas Hobbes's *Leviathan* is published in London
		1660	Restoration of British monarchy; end of Puritan rule in England

1662	Michael Wigglesworth, *The Day of Doom*	1662	Hereditary slavery established in Virginia
1663	Algonquian-language Bible (first Bible printed in North America)	1663	Rebellion by enslaved blacks and white indentured servants in Virginia
1673–1729	Samuel Sewall's *Diary* (pub. 1878–82)	1675–76	Metacom's War (King Philip's War)
		1676	Bacon's Rebellion
		1680	Pueblo Revolt
		1681	William Penn founds Pennsylvania
1682	Mary Rowlandson, *A Narrative of the Captivity and Restoration of Mrs. Rowlandson*		
1682–1725	Edward Taylor, *Preparatory Meditations* (pub. 1939, 1960)	1688	Quakers pass first formal antislavery resolution
		1689	John Locke's *Second Treatise of Government* is published in London
		1689–97	King William's War
1692	Sor Juana Inés de la Cruz, *First Dream*	1692–93	Salem witchcraft trials
1693	Cotton Mather, *The Wonders of the Invisible World*		
		1694	Rice cultivation introduced in the Carolinas
		1695	Gold discovered in Brazil
1702	Cotton Mather, *Magnalia Christi Americana*	1702–13	Queen Anne's War
		1708	South Carolina becomes first English colony with a black majority
		1718	French found New Orleans
		1720–80	Peak years of the slave trade to British North America
		1722	Tuscarora join the Haudenosaunee
		1726–56	The Great Awakening
1741	Jonathan Edwards, "Sinners in the Hands of an Angry God"		
		1744–48	King George's War
c. 1746	Lucy Terry, "Bars Fight" (pub. 1854)		
		1752	Benjamin Franklin invents the lightning rod

1760	Briton Hammon, *A Narrative of the Uncommon Sufferings, and Surprizing Deliverance of Briton Hammon, A Negro Man*
1761	Jupiter Hammon, "An Evening Thought: Salvation by Christ, with Penitential Cries"
1762–1801	John and Abigail Adams's correspondence (pub. 1840, 1875)
1772	James Gronniosaw, *A Narrative of the Most Remarkable Particulars in the Life of James Albert Ukawsaw Gronniosaw, an African Prince, as Related by Himself* Samson Occom, *Sermon Preached at the Execution of Moses Paul*
1773	Phillis Wheatley, *Poems on Various Subjects*
1776	Thomas Paine, *Common Sense* Declaration of Independence
1780s	Annis Boudinot Stockton publishes poems in various newspapers

1754–63	French and Indian War Seven Years' War
1760–1820	Reign of King George III
1763	Pontiac's rebellion Royal Proclamation of 1763
1765	Stamp Act
1767	Survey of Mason-Dixon line completed
1769	Father Junípero Serra founds Mission San Diego (first Spanish mission in "Alta California")
1770	Boston Massacre
1773	Boston Tea Party
1774	First Continental Congress
1775	American Revolutionary War begins Anthony Benezet founds America's first abolitionist society (Benjamin Franklin becomes its president in 1787)
1777	The Stars and Stripes is adopted as the national flag by the Continental Congress Vermont Republic abolishes slavery

1782	J. Hector St. John de Crèvecoeur, *Letters from an American Farmer*		
		1783	Treaty of Paris ends the Revolutionary War; Britain cedes the Northwest Territory to the United States, doubling the land area of the new country
1785	John Marrant, *A Narrative of the Lord's Wonderful Dealings with John Marrant, a Black*		
1786	Philip Freneau, *Poems*		
	Jupiter Hammon, "Address to the Negroes of New York State"		
1787	Thomas Jefferson, *Notes on the State of Virginia*	1787	U.S. Constitution signed at constitutional convention in Philadelphia; ratified a year later by 9 of 13 states
	Royall Tyler, *The Contrast*		
1787–88	Alexander Hamilton, James Madison, and John Jay, *The Federalist* papers		Free African Society founded by Absalom Jones and Richard Allen
1789	Olaudah Equiano, *The Interesting Narrative of the Life of Olaudah Equiano* (American edition pub. 1792)	1789	French Revolution begins
			George Washington elected first president
			Bill of Rights (ratified 1791)
1790	Judith Sargent Murray, "On the Equality of the Sexes"	1790	U.S. Supreme Court meets for first time
			First U.S. census; population of 3.9 million (including 694,280 enslaved people; Indigenous people are not counted)
1791	Benjamin Franklin, *Autobiography* (Part 1 is first published in France in translation; Parts 1, 2, and 3 are published in English in 1817)	1791	Washington, D.C., established as U.S. capital
			Haitian Revolution begins
	Susanna Haswell Rowson, *Charlotte Temple*		
		1792	United States Dollar approved as currency
			New York Stock Exchange founded
		1793	U.S. Congress passes first Fugitive Slave Act
		1794	Patent issued for Eli Whitney's cotton gin
		1795	First Naturalization Act, restricting citizenship to free white persons
1797	Hannah Webster Foster, *The Coquette*		
1798	Venture Smith, *A Narrative of the Life and Adventures of Venture, A Native of Africa*	1798	Alien and Sedition Acts
	Charles Brockden Brown, *Wieland*		

1799	Code of Handsome Lake (Gaihwi:io), orally transmitted with the aid of wampum	1799	Napoleon Bonaparte seizes power in France
		1800	Thomas Jefferson elected President
		1803	Louisiana Purchase
		1804	Haitian Declaration of Independence
		1804–06	Lewis and Clark expedition, aided by Shoshone guide Sacagawea
1805	Sagoyewatha, "Reply to the Missionary Jacob Cram"	1807	United States Congress passes Act Prohibiting Importation of Slaves (went into effect 1808)
			Britain passes Act for the Abolition of the Slave Trade (went into effect 1808)
1808	Leonora Sansay, *Secret History; or, the Horrors of St. Domingo*	1808	Under the leadership of Tecumseh and proclaiming the teachings of Tenskwatawa, Tecumseh's confederacy evolves to promote tribal unity and the rejection of English-American culture
		1810	Mexican War of Independence begins
		1812–14	War of 1812
		1813–14	Creek War
1814	Francis Scott Key, "The Star-Spangled Banner"	1814	Burning of Capitol Building in Washington
			Francis Cabot Lowell introduces new systems to the textile industry at the Boston Manufacturing Company
		1815	Nathan Hale founds the *North American Review*, the nation's first literary magazine
			Battle of Waterloo
		1816–18	First Seminole War
1817	William Cullen Bryant, "Thanatopsis" First Cherokee Women's Petition (a second and third followed in 1818 and 1831)		
		1819	First steamship to cross the Atlantic
			Spain cedes East Florida to the United States and renounces claim to West Florida
			Attorney General of Upper Canada confirms that formerly enslaved people who have fled the United States and entered Upper Canada are "protected by the laws of England" and cannot be forced to return

INDIGENOUS ORAL AND VISUAL LITERATURES

Indigenous traditional literatures are the oldest literatures produced on the North American continent, and they are still heard, read, interpreted, translated, and published in Indigenous nations today, as part of continuous literary and intellectual histories, political deliberations, and ceremonies. These literatures appear in a vast array of media, each with their own complex aesthetics, from oral literatures—told in hundreds of languages across the continent—to visual texts, some of which use alphabetic writing and some of which use nonalphabetic forms. Nonalphabetic Indigenous traditional literatures include, for example, carved house posts, painted baskets, pictographic texts, and wampum belts; they can express narratives and ideas, record laws, and document events, among other purposes. The stories told in traditional literatures—both oral and written—are enormously varied, ranging from stories of the creation of the world and of humans and other animals to stories of how communities and cultures were formed, stories of alliances and conflicts among Indigenous communities and other historical events, and stories engaging with questions of how people should live.

Indigenous traditional literatures challenge conceptions of "America" and of "American literature" oriented around European colonization and settlement and around alphabetic writing. In many recent American literature anthologies, including this one, a cluster of "traditional literatures" from several tribal traditions is located in the opening pages as a signal of their firstness. Yet before the late twentieth century, it was far more common for anthologies to ignore Native American literatures and position works by the Virginia settler John Smith or the Massachusetts Bay colony settler John Winthrop as the first American literatures. When these older anthologies did acknowledge Indigenous literary traditions, they rarely depicted Indigenous people as authors and presented traditional literatures without context. To take just a few examples, the 1968 anthology *O Brave New World: American Literature 1600–1840* begins with a section titled "The Mythological Inheritance," which consists of captivity narratives by colonists, including John Smith's 1624 *Generall History of Virginia*. In 1976, the anthology *Colonial American Literature from Wilderness to Independence* opened with a section titled "Before the Settlers" that placed two "Indian Myths" alongside European travel narratives and an excerpt from William Shakespeare's *The Tempest*. These selections gave the impression that Indigenous traditional literatures were scarce and that settlers' narratives were better suited to exemplify early literatures from the Americas. In 1989, the *Heath Anthology* was the first to begin with a section—titled "Native American Traditions"—featuring Indigenous literatures from across the continent and acknowledging Indigenous peoples' place as the first peoples of the land.

Foregrounding traditional literatures can complicate the linear timelines through which American literary histories are often told, in which European settlement is soon followed by nation formation and in which "American" (i.e., settler) literatures replace Indigenous ones. Contrary to those linear timelines, Indigenous traditional literatures existed long before settler literatures, and their complex histories of retelling, translation, and publication reach into the present. As active, living texts, they invoke a tense that Timothy Powell, in his collaborations with Eastern Band Cherokee storyteller Freeman Owle, calls "ancient present tense." By this, Powell and Owle mean that Indigenous stories have roots that go back for thousands of years, and when those stories are told, they bring "this deep past into the immediacy of the present," as if the events are occurring now.[1] Traditional literatures require an understanding of literary history that transcends linear time to account for stories' active tellings and retellings in Indigenous communities and for the ways that Indigenous stories bring multiple timescales together. At the same

---

[1] See Timothy Powell, William Weems, and Freeman Owle, "Native/American Digital Storytelling: Situating the Cherokee Oral Tradition within American Literary History," *Literary Compass* 4.1 (2007).

time, interpreting traditional literatures in the context of the specific tribal communities and histories to which they belong can call into question the category of "American literature" itself: traditional literatures not only originate from a period before the existence of an "America" but also are cultivated and kept within Indigenous tribal nations that have histories, governance systems, languages, and cultural practices distinct from those of settler nation states such as the United States and Canada.

European settlers have often evaluated Indigenous literatures in terms of a binary between oral literature—which settlers saw as untrustworthy and ephemeral—and written literature, which they saw as superior and more durable. In fact, traditional literatures cannot be understood according to this binary: traditional stories and knowledge are carefully preserved over centuries in oral form, and traditional literatures have always existed in a wide array of non-alphabetic visual forms as well, as shown in many of the following selections including pictographs, petroglyphs, wampum, and wood carvings. In this sense, traditional literatures exemplify what Cherokee scholar Christopher B. Teuton calls the "textual continuum," a spectrum of oral, graphic (pictographic, hieroglyphic, and other non-alphabetic texts), and alphabetic texts.[1] This multi-media continuum also corresponds to practices of preserving knowledge, making new knowledge, and questioning knowledge. Teuton explains that "The oral and graphic build on the premise that oral discourses are living forms of cultural knowledge, kept alive in the memory of members of a group; graphic discourses record tradition for posterity, to live beyond the lives of those who record them." Meanwhile, what Teuton calls the "critical impulse" questions and disrupts, making the process of keeping knowledge one of continual construction, rather than of static reproduction.

Many of the works gathered here were recorded in English alphabetic script between the eighteenth and twenty-first centuries. Each of these versions reflects a centuries-long process of translation and circulation by Indigenous people and, sometimes, European settlers. The traditional literatures selected here were first told in an Indigenous language, and they continue to be told in Indigenous languages such as Anishinaabemowin, Wôpanâak, Mohegan, K'iche', Onöndowa'ga:' Gawë:nö' (Seneca), and Kanien'kéha (Mohawk). They were also, at various points in their histories, translated and transcribed in English, Spanish, or French, often by Indigenous intellectuals or knowledge keepers who made strategic decisions about when and how to translate stories and circulate them in manuscript or in print networks. Some of these decisions occurred in the context of pressure from settler historians and anthropologists to record and "preserve" Indigenous literatures. At other times, settlers themselves transcribed Indigenous stories or made copies of pictographic texts, usually to serve their own research interests. Such stories recorded by settlers should be read with an especially critical eye; as scholar Craig Womack suggests, because they reflect the recorder's own separation from the stories' culture of origin, they are often stripped of important cultural context and rendered as "artifacts" rather than living works.[2]

In the eighteenth and nineteenth centuries, settlers often acted under the assumption that Indigenous people could not maintain their own literary histories. Yet despite the destruction of Indigenous codices by Spanish priests, boarding schools throughout the U.S. and Canada that were deliberately designed to separate Indigenous children from their own communities and traditions, and many other settler efforts to eliminate Indigenous people and cultures, Indigenous peoples and stories survived. And Indigenous writers, artists, and historians continue to engage with traditional literatures today, renewing the stories again.

⌘⌘⌘

---

[1]   See Christopher B. Teuton, *Deep Waters: The Textual Continuum in American Indian Literature* (University of Nebraska Press, 2010).

[2]   For an example of this issue discussed in detail, see Womack's *Red on Red: Native American Literary Separatism* (University of Minnesota Press, 1999).

Mi'kmaq

The examples below of Mi'kmaq petroglyphs, or pictographs carved on rocks, attest to the material and spatial qualities of Indigenous writing systems. Pictographic writing systems are not alphabetic, meaning that they are not oriented by letters representing sounds that combine to form words; instead, they include images that represent ideas. Indigenous people in the northeast, including Mi'kmaq people, traced pictographs on rocks as well as on birchbark. Petroglyphs such as the ones below could serve several purposes: as maps that oriented travelers in place and in stories; as signals that someone had already traveled along the route; and as territorial markers. For the Mi'kmaq—whose homelands extend throughout the oceans and northeastern coast of what are now eastern Canada and the United States, and whose knowledge of river and ocean travel took them along the east coast as far as what is now Florida—petroglyphs are part of what Abenaki scholar Lisa Brooks calls a "spatialized writing system" that "represented the relationships between people, between places, between humans and nonhumans, between the waterways that joined them."[1]

Europeans observed Mi'kmaq writing systems carefully with the goal of using them to represent European concepts. Seventeenth-century French priest Chrestien LeClercq developed an ideographic script, inspired by his observation of older Mi'kmaq writing practices, that spread quickly in Mi'kmaq communities. LeClercq's goal in developing the script was to translate prayer books that could be used to convert Mi'kmaq people to Catholicism; his books attest to the influence of Indigenous writing systems on European practices of translation. Mi'kmaq people used the writing system for their own ends, which included but were not limited to religious practices.

Mi'kmaq people made contact with Europeans as early as the sixteenth century, and they conducted diplomacy with both French and British officials as European nations vied for access to Indigenous lands and trading networks. Alliances with the French provided some protection against British settlers and soldiers who sought to claim Mi'kmaq lands. Mi'kmaq leaders continued diplomacy even when the British founded Halifax, Nova Scotia, in 1749 and Governor Edward Cornwallis attempted a genocidal campaign to eliminate Mi'kmaq people by offering a bounty to British settlers for killing them. Treaties made with British, French, and U.S. governments in the eighteenth and nineteenth centuries protected hunting and fishing rights throughout Mi'kmaq territories and provided a foundation for more recent court decisions affirming Mi'kmaq sovereignty. These protections came after an extended period in which Canada and the U.S. refused to honor those treaties and instituted policies to remove Mi'kmaq people from their lands and require Mi'kmaq children to attend boarding schools intended to force their assimilation to settler culture. Mi'kmaq territories currently extend to Newfoundland, St Pierre et Miquelon, Nova Scotia, New Brunswick, the Magdalen archipelago, and the Gaspé Peninsula of Quebec, with traditional homelands reaching to the state of Maine in the United States. Alongside this insistence on political sovereignty, Mi'kmaq artists such as Louis Esme Cruz continue to use pictographs in their visual art, attesting to the ways Mi'kmaq people are keeping their writing systems alive.

---

[1]   See Lisa Brooks, *The Common Pot: The Recovery of Native Space in the Northeast* (University of Minnesota Press, 2008).

PETROGLYPH OF HUMAN FIGURE AND SUN
Bedford, Nova Scotia (undated)

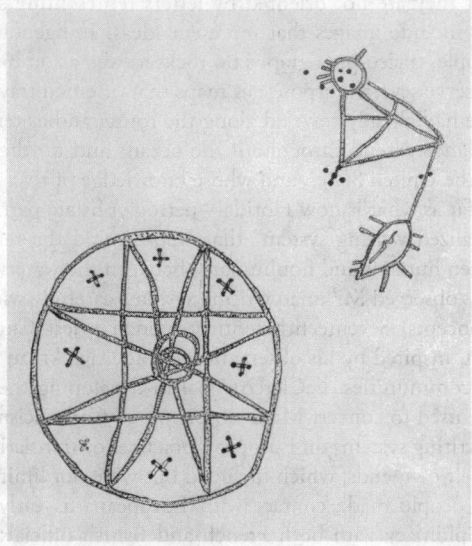

PETROGLYPH TRACING
traced by George Creed (1888)

The undated petroglyph represented in this tracing evokes a fish and four sticks that were inscribed on a rock pointing to the west; with two sticks lying across them. This may communicate the message "I am going fishing to the west for two days."

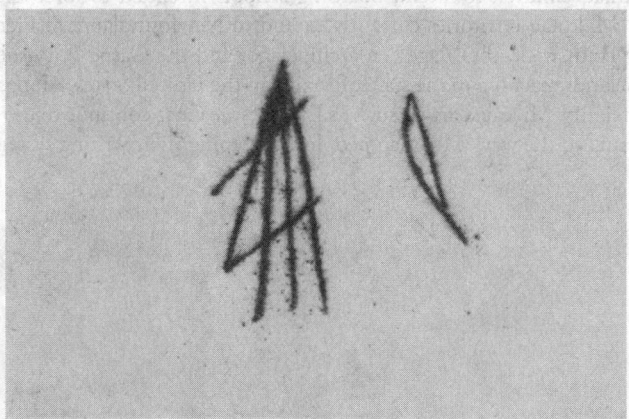

PAGE OF A MI'KMAQ PRAYER BOOK
(c. 1790)

Mohegan

The basket pictured here is woven from wood splints and painted with pink, green, and white images of medallions, trails, and plants. Its design, decoration, and construction process reflect Mohegan textual traditions that extend far beyond alphabetic literature: as the Cree scholar Stephanie Fitzgerald points out, the Mohegan word for painting, wuskuswang, is also the word for writing. Alphabetic literature—such as the work of the Mohegan minister Samson Occom, included elsewhere in this anthology—can be understood as a newcomer to a longstanding textual tradition that includes painted images on baskets, pictographs inscribed on rocks and birchbark, and wampum belts.

The process of making a basket requires one to select a log, soak it, strip the bark, and weave the strips together before painting the basket. This work is collaborative, often performed by women (though in the nineteenth century more men also made baskets to support their communities). Basket making is a time for sharing stories and knowledge, some of which are inscribed in images on the baskets themselves. As Mohegan women Gladys Tantaquidgeon and Jayne Fawcett note, basket makers adorn their baskets by drawing on a "Mohegan symbolic 'vocabulary,'" which includes designs that tell certain stories.[1] For example, the domed medallions on this basket represent the four directions; the leaves and pink dots represent strawberries and other plants that sustain Mohegan people; and the trails represent the trail of life as well as specific Mohegan journeys.

PAINTED WOOD-SPLINT STORAGE BASKET
(c. 1817)

---

[1]   See Gladys Tantaquidgeon and Jayne G. Fawcett, "Symbolic Motifs on Painted Baskets of the Mohegan-Pequot," *A Key into the Language of Woodsplint Baskets,* eds. Ann McMullen and Russell G. Handsman (American Indian Archaeological Institute, 1987).

Haudenosaunee (Iroquois)

The works below come from the Haudenosaunee or Iroquois Confederacy ("Iroquois" is derived from the word French colonists called Haudenosaunee people; "Haudenosaunee" is the peoples' own name for themselves). The Confederacy originally consisted of five nations, the Seneca, Mohawk, Onondaga, Oneida, and Cayuga, who formed a league by uniting around the Great Law of Peace. The Five Nations later accepted the Tuscarora nation into the Confederacy. The Tuscarora had historical and linguistic ties to Haudenosaunee people, and when, in the early eighteenth century, British settlers began to invade Tuscarora lands in the Carolinas, the Confederacy agreed to provide protection, and the Tuscarora moved north in 1722 to become one of the Six Nations. The Confederacy still exists today, having survived the 1779–80 Sullivan Campaign, a series of scorched earth campaigns by American forces on Haudenosaunee lands and fields during the U.S. Revolutionary War, which destroyed nearly all the villages of the Onondaga, Cayuga, and Seneca. Haudenosaunee people also lived through a series of illegal land cessions and removals in the nineteenth century, the forced education of Haudenosaunee children in boarding schools, and sweeping anti-Indian laws in Canada and the United States that denied legal rights to Indigenous people. Despite these events, as the selection of Haudenosaunee literatures here attests, Haudenosaunee people are keeping stories of their creation and of the Confederacy's formation alive.

The Haudenosaunee story of the world's creation is, as Susan M. Hill (Mohawk) comments, not only an account of how the world began; it also "holds many of our beliefs regarding the relationship intended to exist between humans and the rest of the natural world."[1] The stories regarding the formation of the Haudenosaunee Confederacy continue this account of the relationship among humans and with the natural world. These stories tell how the Peacemaker and his helper Hiawatha united Haudenosaunee people during a time when they were ruled by greed and violence. The Peacemaker brought the Great Law of Peace, which provided the Haudenosaunee with means for resolving conflict through peace rather than war and established practices of good governance and leadership. The more recently recorded versions of "The Creation"[2] and "Thanksgiving Address" attest to the ways that Haudenosaunee people continue to tell and live by these stories and to recite and share the precedents established in the Great Law. The Thanksgiving Address is spoken in greeting and gratitude to all of creation, to recognize the reliance of humans on the natural world and to bring those assembled into agreement. The Address is also invoked before ceremonies and government meetings.

Haudenosaunee people have maintained these stories and laws for generations, in the form of oral texts, speeches, and wampum belts as well as, in more recent centuries, written texts. The works gathered here represent an attempt to reflect, as far as possible, the range of forms Haudenosaunee stories take. The first two works were written by Seneca and Tuscarora men who translated stories into English and, at least in part, into terms white settler readers could comprehend. They are less authors—in the sense of a writer who owns their work—than linguistic and cultural translators who continued longstanding practices of sharing, remembering, and transcribing stories and laws. Some Haudenosaunee people, such as the Seneca scholar Arthur C. Parker and his great-uncle Ely S. Parker, collaborated with white anthropologists whose work was deeply distorted by colonialist ideology and often positioned Haudenosaunee people as racially and culturally inferior. The Parkers used these collaborations to circulate versions of Haudenosaunee stories of the world's creation and of the formation of the Haudenosaunee Confederacy, even as anthropologists' assumptions and queries sometimes framed those stories' final forms. By contrast, some printed versions of Haudenosaunee stories were strictly Haudenosaunee productions: the first edition of Cusick's *Sketches of the Ancient History of the Six Nations*, for example, was translated, printed, and distributed

---

[1] See Susan M. Hill, *The Clay We Are Made Of: Haudenosaunee Land Tenure on the Grand River* (University of Manitoba Press, 2017).

[2] This selection appears in the anthology's website component.

by Tuscarora people in New York. Cusick described his process of writing and translating *Sketches* as one undertaken to provide a history of the Six Nations from a Haudenosaunee perspective. He wrote in his preface that he "had long been waiting" for some of "my people" to write a history, and when he found that no such history existed, Cusick himself "determined to commence the work." Cusick's preface emphasizes the importance of tribal histories told by tribal members, an act that laid the groundwork for more recent editions of Haudenosaunee histories and stories.

from [CREATION STORY]

as recorded and translated by David Cusick, *Sketches of the Ancient History of the Six Nations* (1827)

PART I

A TALE OF THE FOUNDATION OF THE GREAT ISLAND, NOW NORTH AMERICA—THE TWO INFANTS BORN, AND THE CREATION OF THE UNIVERSE

Among the ancients there were two worlds in existence. The lower world was in great darkness—the possession of the great monster—but the upper world was inhabited by humankind; and there was a woman conceived[1] and would have the twin born. When her travail[2] drew near, and her situation seemed to produce a great distress on her mind, and she was induced by some of her relations to lay herself on a mattress which was prepared, so as to gain refreshments to her wearied body; but while she was asleep the very place sunk down towards the dark world.

The monsters of the great water were alarmed at her appearance of descending to the lower world; in consequence all the species of the creatures were immediately collected into where it was expected she would fall. When the monsters were assembled, and they made consultation, one of them was appointed in haste to search the great deep, in order to procure some earth, if it could be obtained; accordingly the monster descends, which succeeds, and returns to the place. Another requisition was presented, who would be capable to secure the woman from the terrors of the great water, but none was able to comply except a large turtle came forward and made proposal to them to endure her lasting weight, which was accepted.

The woman was yet descending from a great distance. The turtle executes[3] upon the spot, and a small quantity of earth was varnished on the back part of the turtle. The woman alights on the seat prepared, and she receives a satisfaction.[4] While holding her, the turtle increased every moment and became a considerable island of earth, and apparently covered with small bushes. The woman remained in a state of unlimited darkness, and she was overtaken by her travail to which she was subject.

While she was in the limits of distress one of the infants in her womb was moved by an evil opinion and he was determined to pass out under the side of the parent's arm, and the other infant in vain endeavored to prevent his design. The woman was in a painful condition during the time of their disputes, and the infants entered the dark world by compulsion, and their parent expired in a few moments. They had the power of sustenance without a nurse,[5] and remained in the dark regions.

After a time the turtle increased to a great Island and the infants were grown up, and one of them possessed with a gentle disposition, and named Enigorio, i.e. the good mind. The other youth possessed an insolence of character, and was named Enigonhahetgea, i.e. the bad mind. The good mind was not contented to remain in a dark situation, and he was anxious to create a great light in the dark world; but the bad mind was desirous that the world should remain in a natural state.

The good mind determines to prosecute his designs, and therefore commences the world of creation. At first he took the parent's head, (the deceased) of which he created an orb, and established it in the centre of the

---

[1]   *conceived*   I.e., pregnant (with twins).

[2]   *travail*   Labor of childbirth.

[3]   *executes*   Carries out the plan.

[4]   *satisfaction*   I.e., solution to her problem.

[5]   *a nurse*   Someone to provide them with milk.

firmament,[1] and it became of a very superior nature to bestow light to the new world (now the sun), and again he took the remnant of the body and formed another orb, which was inferior to the light (now moon). In the orb a cloud of legs appeared to prove it was the body of the good mind (parent). The former was to give light to the day and the latter to the night; and he also created numerous spots of light (now stars): these were to regulate the days, nights, seasons, years, etc.

Whenever the light extended to the dark world the monsters were displeased and immediately concealed themselves in the deep places, lest they should be discovered by some human beings. The good mind continued the works of creation, and he formed numerous creeks and rivers on the Great Island, and then created numerous species of animals of the smallest and the greatest, to inhabit the forests, and fishes of all kinds to inhabit the waters. When he had made the universe he was in doubt respecting some beings to possess the Great Island; and he formed two images of the dust of the ground in his own likeness, male and female, and by his breathing into their nostrils he gave them the living souls, and named them Ea-gwe-howe, i.e. a real people; and he gave the Great Island all the animals of game for their maintenance; and he appointed thunder to water the earth by frequent rains, agreeable of the nature of the system; after this the Island became fruitful and vegetation afforded the animals subsistence.

The bad mind, while his brother was making the universe, went throughout the Island and made numerous high mountains and falls of water, and great steeps, and also creates various reptiles which would be injurious to mankind; but the good mind restored the Island to its former condition. The bad mind proceeded further in his motives and he made two images of clay in the form of humankind; but while he was giving them existence they became apes; and when he had not the power to create mankind he was envious against his brother; and again he made two of clay. The good mind discovered his brother's contrivances, and aided in giving them living souls[2] (it is said these had the most knowledge of good and evil).

The good mind now accomplishes the works of creation, notwithstanding the imaginations of the bad mind were continually evil; and he attempted to enclose all the animals of game in the earth, so as to deprive them from mankind; but the good mind released them from confinement (the animals were dispersed, and traces of them were made on the rocks near the cave where it was closed).

The good mind experiences that his brother was at variance with the works of creation, and feels not disposed to favor any of his proceedings, but gives admonitions of his future state. Afterwards the good mind requested his brother to accompany him, as he was proposed to inspect the game, etc., but when a short distance from their nominal residence, the bad mind became so unmanly that he could not conduct his brother anymore.

The bad mind offered a challenge to his brother and resolved that who gains the victory should govern the universe; and appointed a day to meet the contest. The good mind was willing to submit to the offer, and he enters the reconciliation with his brother; which he falsely mentions that by whipping with flags would destroy his temporal life;[3] and he earnestly solicits his brother also to notice the instrument of death, which he manifestly relates by the use of deer horns, beating his body he would expire. On the day appointed the engagement commenced, which lasted for two days: after pulling up the trees and mountains as the track of a terrible whirlwind, at last the good mind gained the victory by using the horns, as mentioned the instrument of death, which he succeeded in deceiving his brother and he crushed him in the earth; and the last words uttered from the bad mind were, that he would have equal power over the souls of humankind after death; and he sinks down to eternal doom, and became the Evil Spirit. After this tumult the good mind repaired to the battle ground, and then visited the people and retires from the earth.

---

[1] *firmament* Sky or heavens.

[2] [Cusick's note] It appears by the fictitious accounts, that the said beings became civilized people and made their residence in the southern parts of the Island; but afterwards they were destroyed by the barbarous nations, and their fortifications were ruined unto this day.

[3] *he falsely ... life* He says that a whipping with rushes (grasslike plants) would kill him, which is a lie.

ORIGIN OF FOLK STORIES
as recorded by Arthur C. Parker, *Seneca Myths and Folk Tales* (1923)

There was once a boy who had no home. His parents were dead and his uncles would not care for him. In order to live this boy, whose name was Gaqka, or Crow, made a bower of branches for an abiding place and hunted birds and squirrels for food.

He had almost no clothing but was very ragged and dirty. When the people from the village saw him they called him Filth-Covered-One, and laughed as they passed by, holding their noses. No one thought he would ever amount to anything, which made him feel heavy-hearted. He resolved to go away from his tormentors and become a great hunter.

One night Gaqka found a canoe. He had never seen this canoe before, so he took it. Stepping in he grasped the paddle, when the canoe immediately shot into the air, and he paddled above the clouds and under the moon. For a long time he went always southward. Finally the canoe dropped into a river and then Gaqka paddled for shore.

On the other side of the river was a great cliff that had a face that looked like a man. It was at the forks of the river where this cliff stood. The boy resolved to make his home on the top of the cliff and so climbed it and built a bark cabin.

The first night he sat on the edge of the cliff he heard a voice saying, "Give me some tobacco." Looking around the boy, seeing no one, replied, "Why should I give tobacco?"

There was no answer and the boy began to fix his arrows for the next day's hunt. After a while the voice spoke again, "Give me some tobacco."

Gaqka now took out some tobacco and threw it over the cliff. The voice spoke again: "Now I will tell you a story."

Feeling greatly awed the boy listened to a story that seemed to come directly out of the rock upon which he was sitting. Finally the voice paused, for the story had ended. Then it spoke again saying, "It shall be the custom hereafter to present me with a small gift for my stories." So the boy gave the rock a few bone beads. Then the rock said, "Hereafter when I speak, announcing that I shall tell a story you must say, 'Nio,' and as I speak you must say 'Hĕⁿ'',' that I may know that you

are listening. You must never fall asleep but continue to listen until I say 'Dā´neho nigagā´is.' (So thus finished is the length of my story.) Then you shall give me presents and I shall be satisfied."

The next day the boy hunted and killed a great many birds. These he made into soup and roasts. He skinned the birds and saved the skins, keeping them in a bag.

That evening the boy sat on the rock again and looked westward at the sinking sun. He wondered if his friend would speak again. While waiting he chipped some new arrow-points, and made them very small so that he could use them in a blow gun. Suddenly, as he worked, he heard the voice again. "Give me some tobacco to smoke," it said. Gaqka threw a pinch of tobacco over the cliff and the voice said, "Hau'nio," and commenced a story. Long into the night one wonderful tale after another flowed from the rock, until it called out, "So thus finished is the length of my story." Gaqka was sorry to have the stories ended but he gave the rock an awl made from a bird's leg and a pinch of tobacco.

The next day the boy hunted far to the east and there found a village. Nobody knew who he was but he soon found many friends. There were some hunters who offered to teach him how to kill big game, and these went with him to his own camp on the high rock. At night he allowed them to listen to the stories that came forth from the rock, but it would speak only when Gaqka was present. He therefore had many friends with whom to hunt.

Now after a time Gaqka made a new suit of clothing from deer skin and desired to obtain a decorated pouch. He, therefore, went to the village and found one house where there were two daughters living with an old mother. He asked that a pouch be made and the youngest daughter spoke up and said, "It is now finished. I have been waiting for you to come for it." So she gave him a handsome pouch.

Then the old mother spoke, saying, "I now perceive that my future son-in-law has passed through the door and is here." Soon thereafter, the younger woman brought Gaqka a basket of bread and said, "My mother greatly desires that you should marry me." Gaqka looked at the girl and was satisfied, and ate the bread.

The older daughter was greatly displeased and frowned in an evil manner.

That night the bride said to her husband, "We must now go away. My older sister will kill you for she is jealous." So Gaqka arose and took his bride to his own lodge. Soon the rock spoke and began to relate wonder stories of things that happened in the old days. The bride was not surprised, but said, "This standing rock, indeed, is my grandfather. I will now present you with a pouch into which you must put a trophy for every tale related."

All winter long the young couple stayed in the lodge on the great rock and heard all the wonder tales of the old days. Gaqka's bag was full of stories and he knew all the lore of former times.

As springtime came the bride said, "We must now go north to your own people and you shall become a great man." But Gaqka was sad and said, "Alas, in my own country I am an outcast and called by an unpleasant name." The bride only laughed, saying, "Nevertheless we shall go north."

Taking their pelts and birdskins, the young couple descended the cliff and seated themselves in the canoe. "This is my canoe," said the bride. "I sent it through the air to you."

The bride seated herself in the bow of the canoe and Gaqka in the stern. Grasping a paddle he swept it through the water, but soon the canoe arose and went through the air. Meanwhile the bride was singing all kinds of songs, which Gaqka learned as he paddled.

When they reached the north, the bride said, "Now I shall remove your clothing and take all the scars from your face and body. She then caused him to pass through a hollow log, and when Gaqka emerged from the other end he was dressed in the finest clothing and was a handsome man.

Together the two walked to the village where the people came out to see them. After a while Gaqka said, "I am the boy whom you once were accustomed to call 'Cia′′dōdă'.' I have now returned." That night the people of the village gathered around and listened to the tales he told, and he instructed them to give him small presents and tobacco. He would plunge his hand in his pouch and take out a trophy, saying, "Ho ho'! So here is another one!" and then looking at his trophy would relate an ancient tale.

Everybody now thought Gaqka a great man and listened to his stories. He was the first man to find out all about the adventures of the old-time people. That is why there are so many legends now.

THANKSGIVING ADDRESS
as crafted by Rokwaho (Dan Thompson) and translated by John Stokes and Kanawahienton (David Benedict) (1993)

(Ohén:ton Karihwatéhkwen—Words Before All Else)

THE PEOPLE

Today we have gathered and we see that the cycles of life continue. We have been given the duty to live in balance and harmony with each other and all living things. So now, we bring our minds together as one as we give greetings and thanks to each other as People. *Now our minds are one.*

THE EARTH MOTHER

We are all thankful to our Mother, the Earth, for she gives us all that we need for life. She supports our feet as we walk about upon her. It gives us joy that she continues to care for us as she has from the beginning of time. To our Mother, we send greetings and thanks. *Now our minds are one.*

THE WATERS

We give thanks to all the Waters of the world for quenching our thirst and providing us with strength. Water is life. We know its power in many forms— waterfalls and rain, mists and streams, rivers and oceans. With one mind, we send greetings and thanks to the spirit of Water. *Now our minds are one.*

THE FISH

We turn our minds to all the Fish life in the water. They were instructed to cleanse and purify the water. They also give themselves to us as food. We are grateful that we can still find pure water. So, we turn now to the

Fish and send our greetings and thanks.
Now our minds are one.

THE PLANTS

Now we turn toward the vast fields of Plant life. As far as the eye can see, the Plants grow, working many wonders. They sustain many life forms. With our minds gathered together, we give thanks and look forward to seeing Plant life for many generations to come.
Now our minds are one.

THE FOOD PLANTS

With one mind, we turn to honor and thank all the Food Plants we harvest from the garden. Since the beginning of time, the grains, vegetables, beans and berries have helped the people survive. Many other living things draw strength from them too. We gather all the Plant Foods together as one and send them a greeting and thanks.
Now our minds are one.

THE MEDICINE HERBS

Now we turn to all the Medicine Herbs of the world. From the beginning, they were instructed to take away sickness. They are always waiting and ready to heal us. We are happy there are still among us those special few who remember how to use these plants for healing. With one mind, we send greetings and thanks to the Medicines and to the keepers of the Medicines.
Now our minds are one.

THE ANIMALS

We gather our minds together to send greetings and thanks to all the Animal life in the world. They have many things to teach us as people. We see them near our homes and in the deep forests. We are glad they are still here and we hope that it will always be so.
Now our minds are one.

THE TREES

We now turn our thoughts to the Trees. The Earth has many families of Trees who have their own instructions and uses. Some provide us with shelter and shade, others with fruit, beauty and other useful things. Many people of the world use a Tree as a symbol of peace and strength. With one mind, we greet and thank the Tree life.
Now our minds are one.

THE BIRDS

We put our minds together as one and thank all the Birds who move and fly about over our heads. The Creator gave them beautiful songs. Each day they remind us to enjoy and appreciate life. The Eagle was chosen to be their leader. To all the Birds—from the smallest to the largest—we send our joyful greetings and thanks.
Now our minds are one.

THE FOUR WINDS

We are all thankful to the powers that we know as the Four Winds. We hear their voices in the moving air as they refresh us and purify the air we breathe. They help to bring the change of seasons. From the four directions they come, bringing us messages and giving us strength. With one mind, we send our greetings and thanks to the Four Winds.
Now our minds are one.

THE THUNDERERS

Now we turn to the west where our Grandfathers, the Thunder Beings, live. With lightning and thundering voices, they bring with them the water that renews life. We bring our minds together as one to send greetings and thanks to our Grandfathers, the Thunderers.
Now our minds are one.

THE SUN

We now send greetings and thanks to our eldest Brother, the Sun. Each day without fail he travels the

sky from east to west, bringing the light of a new day. He is the source of all the fires of life. With one mind, we send greetings and thanks to our Brother, the Sun.
Now our minds are one.

GRANDMOTHER MOON

We put our minds together and give thanks to our oldest Grandmother, the Moon, who lights the night-time sky. She is the leader of women all over the world, and she governs the movement of the ocean tides. By her changing face we measure time, and it is the Moon who watches over the arrival of children here on Earth. With one mind, we send greetings and thanks to our Grandmother, the Moon.
Now our minds are one.

THE STARS

We give thanks to the Stars who are spread across the sky like jewelry. We see them in the night, helping the Moon to light the darkness and bringing dew to the gardens and growing things. When we travel at night, they guide us home. With our minds gathered together as one, we send greetings and thanks to all the Stars.
Now our minds are one.

THE ENLIGHTENED TEACHERS

We gather our minds to greet and thank the Enlightened Teachers who have come to help throughout the ages. When we forget how to live in harmony, they remind us of the way we were instructed to live as people. With one mind, we send greetings and thanks to these caring Teachers.
Now our minds are one.

THE CREATOR

Now we turn our thoughts to the Creator, or Great Spirit, and send greetings and thanks for all the gifts of Creation. Everything we need to live a good life is here on this Mother Earth. For all the love that is still around us, we gather our minds together as one and send our choicest words of greetings and thanks to the Creator.
Now our minds are one.

CLOSING WORDS

We have now arrived at the place where we end our words. Of all the things we have named, it was not our intention to leave anything out. If something was forgotten, we leave it to each individual to send such greetings and thanks in their own way.
Now our minds are one.

IROQUOIS OR CONFEDERACY OF THE FIVE NATIONS
as recorded by Ely S. Parker (manuscript c. 1848)

By the tradition of the Five Nations it appears that in their early history, they were frequently engaged in petty wars one with another, as well also with tribes living north of the lakes. The Five Nations, on account of their small numbers, suffered more by these wars than their neighbors, until there sprang up among the Onondagas a man more formidable in war than a whole tribe or nation. He consequently became the terror of all the surrounding nations, especially of the Cayugas and Senecas. This man, so formidable and whose cabin was as impregnable as a tower, is said to have had a head of hair, the ends of each terminating in a living snake; the ends of his fingers, and toes, his ears, nose and lips, eyebrows and eyelashes all terminated in living snakes. He required in war, no bow and arrow, no battle axe or war club, for he had but to look upon his enemies, and they fell dead—so great was the power of the snakes that enshrouded him. He was a warrior by birth, and by his great power he had become the military despot of all the surrounding nations. And when he marched against his enemies they fled before his fatal sight.

Among the Onondagas there lived a man renowned for his wisdom, and his great love of peace. For a long time he had watched with great anxiety the increasing power of this military despot who on account of his snakey habiliments,[1] was known by the applicable name Tadodahoh, or Atotahoh, signifying tangled because the snakes seemed to have tangled themselves into his hair; he saw bands of noble warriors fall before his fatal look. He revolved in his mind by what means he could take from the Tadodahoh his power, and also

---

[1]   *habiliments* Attire.

to divest him of his snakey appendages. He well knew that he could not wrest his power from him, unless he could put into his hands some means by which he could still exercise power and influence. He therefore concluded to call a general council, of the Five Nations, and to invite to this council the Tadodahoh, at which council he proposed to lay before the wise men a plan of Union that would secure not only amity and peace among themselves, and a perpetual existence as a confederacy, but they would render themselves formidable and superior in power to any nation on the Continent. He accordingly called a council to be held upon the east bank of the Onondaga Lake, and to this council the Tadodahoh was invited, who it is said lived near the shores of Lake Ontario a short distance from Irondequoit Bay. He accepted the invitation and proceeded to the place. He occupied the council grounds alone, for no one would approach near to him, although great numbers had come to attend. The projector of the alliance alone proceeded to the grounds and into the presence of the Tadodahoh. He proceeded to divulge his plan when he was informed that his daughter had died whom he had left at home sick. He drew his robe about him, covering himself completely, and mourned for her. (His style of mourning was afterwards adopted by the Confederacy as the custom to mourn for sachems just before another was to be installed in his place.) He mourned night and day, and in his mourning which he did in a kind of song, he repeated the whole plan of Union. And when he had finished, no one of the wise men seemed to understand or comprehend his meaning and objects. Daganowedah, the projector of the play of alliance, being provoked at their dullness of comprehension, which resulted more from their ignorance of civil matters than dullness of comprehension, arose in the night and travelled towards the east. He had not travelled far when he struck a small lake, and anyone could go around it sooner than to cross it in a canoe. Yet he chose to make a canoe of bark and go across it. It seems that he did not wish to deviate from a straight line. While he was crossing the lake, his canoe ran upon what he supposed to be a sand bar; he put his paddle down into the water to ascertain the cause of the stopping of the boat; in taking out his paddle he found a quantity of small shells, he took pains to put

a sufficient quantity into his canoe, and after going ashore, he made a pouch of a young deer skin, and put these shells into it, after having first made a number of belts, and put the rest into strings of equal lengths. To this he gave the name of wampum, and the belts and strings he had made of the shells, he converted into the records of his wise sayings and the entire plan of his project of alliance.

He then proceeded on his journey, and he had not travelled far when he came to an Indian castle.[1] Without calling a council he began to rehearse his plan of alliance, by means of his belts and strings of wampum. But the people of this castle were unable to comprehend the benefits of his project, and talked of him as crazy. When he heard what they were saying concerning him, he proceeded on his journey, sorrowing that he could not find a people who would listen to the words of wisdom. He at length came to another settlement, which was one of the Mohawk castles. Here again he rehearsed his plan of Union. Still his sayings were incomprehensible to that people. They however listened carefully for the purpose of ascertaining what it was that he could talk so long upon. All that they could understand of it, was the manner in which councils were to be called. A council was accordingly called and he invited to attend. They invited him for the purpose of giving him an opportunity to say in council and before a large number what he had been so long saying in the open fields. But after he had taken his seat in council and nothing was said or done, no exchange of wampum belts (for he had lent them a belt with which to call a council), he arose and again went into the fields and there repeated his speeches. He concluded by saying that they too were ignorant, and knew nothing about transacting civil matters. This was reported to the Grand Chief of the Mohawks and again he called another council and invited Daganowedah. When the council was opened and the wise man had taken his seat, the Mohawk Chief presented to him a belt of wampum, with a request that whatever he should have to say, should be said in open council. If he was a messenger from another tribe, they would hear in open council what were their wishes. He merely replied that he was the messenger of no one; that he had conceived a noble plan of alliance, but had not

---

[1]   *castle*   Most important village of a given Indigenous group.

found a nation wise enough to comprehend its benefits and thus he had travelled and should continue so to travel until he found support. He then rehearsed in open council his plan of Union which though they could not comprehend it, was pronounced by all to be a noble project. Daganowedah the Onondaga wise man was immediately adopted into the Mohawk Nation, nor could the Onondagas afterwards claim him, since they first rejected his project of Alliance. He was also made a chief of the Mohawk Nation, and was to exercise equal power with the original Mohawk chief. They were to live in the same lodge, and to be in every respect, equals.

But he had lived with the original chief but a short time, when he was ordered about as though he had been a mere servant. To this a free spirit will ever revolt, he therefore left him, and again went into the fields. He was asked why he left the house of his friend. He replied that he had not been treated as a friend or visitor, but as a slave. The original chief begged his pardon, and solicited him to return. He did, and was thenceforth treated with great regard. Daganowedah at length suggested the propriety of sending runners to the west, from whence he had come, to ascertain what may be doing from whence he had come. He wanted runners to go and seek the smoke of the council fire. The chief of the Mohawks at once called upon some runners to go towards the west in search of the smoke of a council fire. The guardian bird of the runners was the heron; they accordingly took upon themselves the form of herons. They went towards the west, but flying too high they did not see the smoke of the council fire of Onondaga. They proceeded as far west as Sandusky in Ohio, where they were unable to transform or change themselves again into men. Another set of runners were then sent out who took upon them the form or shape of crows. They found the smoke of the council fire at Onondaga and so reported.

Daganowedah then proposed to send a few runners to the council to inform them that they had found a wise man of the Onondaga nation, who had conceived a plan of Union, and to request that he might be heard before the Great Tadodahoh. This was done; and as soon as the council at Onondaga heard where their wise man had gone, they sent a deputation to recall him. Daganowedah had in the mean time made arrangement with the Mohawk Chief to act as his spokesman when they should be in council. He was also to take the lead in the file, and to perform all the duties necessary to the completion of the Alliance, but he was to act as Daganowedah should direct. His reason for choosing a spokesman, was that he had not been heard when the council first opened, and that probably they might listen to a wise man of the Mohawks. To this arrangement the Mohawk agreed. He agreed also to divest Tadodahoh of his snakes, and to make him as other men, except that he should clothe him in civil power as the Head of the Confederacy that should be formed. They then proceeded with a delegation of the Mohawks to the council grounds at Onondaga. When they had arrived they addressed Tadodahoh the great military despot. The Mohawk divested him of his snakes, and for this reason he was styled Hayowenthah, or one who takes away or divests.

The plan of alliance was at first simple. It provided for the establishment of a confederacy, enjoying a democratic form of government. The civil and legislative power was to be vested in a certain number of wise men who should be styled civil sachems, and the military and executive power in another set of men who should be styled military sachems. The Union was to be established as a family organization, the Mohawks, Onondagas and Senecas to compose the Fathers and the Cayugas and Oneidas the children. This plan was adopted.

WAMPUM BELTS

These images of wampum belts (white, purple, and black beads made from quahog shells and whelk and woven together) represent important texts of diplomacy, law, and memory. Wampum belts encode Haudenosaunee history, political agreements, and cultural knowledge. According to Haudenosaunee histories, Hiawatha received wampum when he was grieving the loss of his three daughters and wife. The Peacemaker taught him how to string wampum beads together and how to conduct ceremonies to clear the mind and heart and assuage grief. Hiawatha brought wampum to Haudenosaunee people, using the Condolence Ceremony to clear peoples' minds, eyes, ears, and throats of grief and negativity.

Wampum belts also record alliances and other political agreements. For example, the Two Row Belt pictured here records the first treaty, made in 1613, between the Haudenosaunee Confederacy and a settler nation, in this case Dutch settlers. As Seneca-descended scholar Penelope Kelsey has explained, the two dark lines represent the Haudenosaunee and Dutch, respectively. These lines do not share common origins, and they do not intersect, but they are fashioned from the same materials. The belt records an agreement between two different peoples who will continue to pursue different paths while existing together; it is a map for how the two peoples will interact. The Two Row wampum recognizes settler practices but insists on maintaining specifically Haudenosaunee practices and knowledge for Haudenosaunee people.

While some settler translators learned and participated in wampum protocols in order to respect their powerful diplomatic purposes, settlers, including anthropologists and ethnographers working closely within these communities, also stole belts, removing some to museums and keeping others in private collections. Haudenosaunee people continue to work to secure the return of stolen belts to the Confederacy; some have been recovered, while others remain in settler institutions. The belts depicted here are held by the Onondaga Nation.

Ha:yëwënta' (Hiawatha) Belt

Two Row Wampum

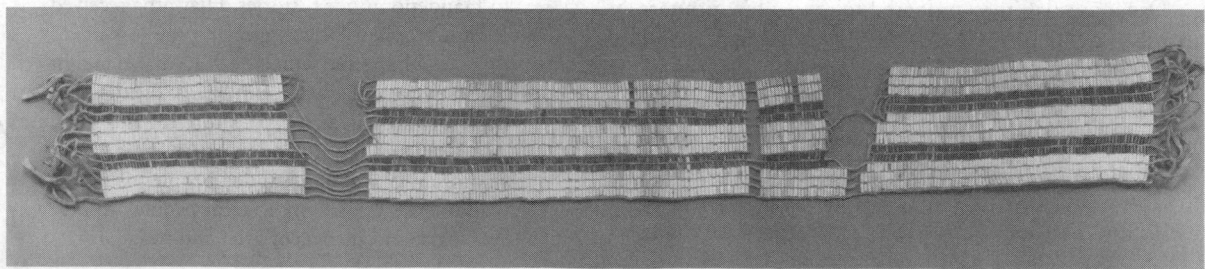

Ojibwe

Ojibwe tribal nations are part of the Anishinaabeg peoples, the linguistically and historically related peoples who include the Ojibwe, Odawa, and Potawatomi tribal nations. There are now multiple Ojibwe tribal nations on homelands stretching from the Great Lakes to the Plains and extending across more recent boundary lines between the United States and Canada. Ojibwe stories place the peoples' origin in the northeast. After the receding of the glaciers at the end of the last ice age, Ojibwe people traveled west, keeping pictographic records that show a migration route following rivers from the Atlantic to the upper Great Lakes. By the time some of the stories included here were recorded in print in the nineteenth century, Ojibwe tribes had hundreds of years of experience pursuing diplomacy and conflict with other Indigenous nations, including but not limited to the Haudenosaunee and Dakota, and with the French, British, and United States traders and settlers who desired access to Indigenous trading routes and homelands.

Anishinaabemowin, the language Ojibwe people speak, differentiates among several kinds of stories: aadizookaanag are traditional stories that carry values and philosophies, while dibaajimowinan are historical in nature, including family and tribal stories.[1] The stories below are aadizookaanag, traditional stories of creation and of the Ojibwe hero or trickster Nanaboozhoo (also spelled Nanabush and Nenabozho). These stories articulate the values people need to live well together and demonstrate the behaviors that build or destroy communities. And these stories continue in the work of Ojibwe writers and artists today: as the poet Heid E. Erdrich writes, "We write into and out of a great telling that brings us stories and songs, that teaches us to look and listen. This is not some mystic tradition; it is simply how it is to be aware of where you are, who you are, and who your people are when they create with words."[2]

The stories selected here center around Nanaboozhoo, a shape-shifting figure who can take human and animal forms. These selections also highlight the range of Nanaboozhoo stories, from his role in creation stories to some of the humorous adventures he undertakes. Many of Nanaboozhoo's stories are funny, ribald accounts in which he plays the role of a prankster. Nanaboozhoo can be self-interested, pursuing his own appetites and desires, but he can also be selfless. His actions often escape usual human expectations for behavior, and their surprising qualities can encourage listeners to understand a problem or phenomenon from a new perspective or to realize that their current expectations may be limited.[3]

William Jones and George Copway, the Indigenous scholars who recorded for print some of the stories and pictographs included here, did so as part of work that also included translating and defending Ojibwe linguistic and historical knowledge. Jones is a Meskwakie (or Fox) man who studied with the anthropologist Franz Boas at Columbia University before becoming the first Indigenous anthropologist to work at Chicago's Field Museum. Jones made Anishinaabemowin dictionaries that Ojibwe people use today for language study; he also kept linguistic and botanical records on the Field Museum's collections of seeds from Meskwakie people, which are being used today in the Field Museum's rematriation (or return) of seeds to the Meskwakie.

George Copway, a Mississauga Ojibwe missionary and writer, also recorded Ojibwe pictographs and histories that Ojibwe people continue to study and use today. His transcription of pictographs appears in his history of Ojibwe people, *The Traditional History and Characteristic Sketches of the Ojibway Nation.* Far from the decontextualized ethnographic reporting that characterized many settler histories of Ojibwe people, Copway's *Traditional History* defended pictographic writing systems against settlers' disparaging of them. Copway represented Ojibwe people as drawing on multiple

---

[1]   See Jill Doerfler, Niigaanwewidam James Sinclair, and Heidi Kiiwetinepinesiik Stark, "Bagijige: Making an Offering," in their 2013 collection *Centering Anishinaabeg Studies: Understanding the World Through Stories.*

[2]   See Heid E. Erdrich, "'Name': Literary Ancestry as Presence," *Centering Anishinaabeg Studies.*

[3]   For further discussion of Nanaboozhoo, see John Borrows, "The Trickster: Integral to a Distinctive Culture," *Forum Constitutionnel* 8.2 (1997).

forms of inscription and communication, from pictographs to wampum to alphabetic writing. Ojibwe leaders used pictographs representing their clans, or patrilineal kinship identities, to sign treaties with European and North American settler nations, while pictographs carved on stone marked territory, sent messages, and recorded songs. Copway's own work exemplifies the diverse languages and media in which Ojibwe literatures appear: he participated in a Great Lakes network of Ojibwe Methodists who translated English-language hymns into Anishinaabemowin and who wrote some of the first English-language Ojibwe histories and personal autobiographies. Copway's history, as well as his autobiography and political writings in defense of Ojibwe peoples, are part of an extensive and ongoing Ojibwe literary tradition, in both English and Anishinaabemowin.

from "The Birth of Nenabozho"

as told by Waasaagoneshkang, recorded by William Jones, and translated by Rand Valentine, from *Voices from Four Directions: Contemporary Translations of the Native Literatures of North America* (2004)

The following story was told near Pelican Lake, Minnesota, in the early twentieth century by Waasaagoneshkang (Ojibwe: He Who Leaves the Imprint of His Foot Shining in the Snow), an Ojibwe man who spent his formative years near the border between Minnesota and Ontario. Waasaagoneshkang dictated this and many other traditional stories to the anthropologist William Jones; the version excerpted here is a 2004 translation by the linguist Rand Valentine based on Jones's transcription.

I

Once some people were living in a wigwam,
  an old woman and her daughter.
And at some point she said to her daughter,
  "Listen, my daughter, be on your guard.
  Take careful heed of what I'm about to tell you.
  I'm terribly afraid, I fear for your well-being.
  Never ever sit facing the west when you go outside
    to relieve yourself.[1]
  Something bad will happen to you if you sit facing
    in that direction.
  That's the basis of my fear for you.
  Take heed of what I'm telling you,
    because you could bring great harm on yourself.
  That's what I want to tell you now."

Well, it seems that that young woman was exceedingly careful.

No man ever came within sight of her.
But then once she forgot,
    and at that instant she heard the wind rushing
      toward her.
And she felt the rush of a cool breeze there at her
  going out.
And she leapt to her feet.
  "Mother, look at me, this state I'm in.
  Perhaps it's happened to me as you said it might."

Well, the old woman said to her daughter:
  "Oh, most assuredly you've brought great harm on
    yourself!"

And the old woman began to weep.
  "That's how it is, you've brought harm on your
    body.
  Listen to what's going to happen to you.
  Beings have entered your body, and that's what has
    left you so pitiable.
  They're not humans, those who entered your body.
  And it won't be long until they're born.
  Alas, it's the very ones I feared."

Well, after a while the old woman heard the sound of
  them arguing with each other.
And then she knew for sure that her daughter
  wouldn't survive.
She heard them arguing;
  there within her daughter's belly they rumbled.
And this they were heard to say:
  "It's I who shall be firstborn!"
"No" was heard another,
  "You will not be firstborn—*I* shall be!"

And always the old woman wept when she heard
  them contending in this way.
She knew what a large number they were.

---

[1] [Valentine's note]   Nenabozho's brothers and father were traditionally associated with the cardinal points of the compass.

Well, as they spoke they pushed each other back,
  seeking in vain to exit.
Some of them said: "Don't! We're going to harm our
  mother.
    Let us exit in an orderly fashion," some said, in
      vain.

But those who wanted to be firstborn weren't happy
  with this.
And so they declared that they would exit through
  various routes.
One of them saw a light.
    "Well, as for me, I'm going straight in that
      direction."
And so as they contended as to who would be
  firstborn,
    they tore their mother apart.

And some time later as the old woman was looking
  about,
    she found a bit of blood.
And so she peeled some birch bark.
And into the birch bark she placed the blood, repeatedly folding the bark,
    and then she laid it away.

Well, from time to time she took a look at it.
And once, when she unwrapped it,
    she beheld a child.
And she was spoken to by the child,
    this is what she was told:
        "Grandmother!"
she was told when she was spoken to.

And then it spoke to her again:
"Do you know who I am?
Why, I am Nenabozho."

2

So the old woman began to raise him.
And at some point he said to his grandmother:
    "Might you not know of people living anywhere
      here on the earth?"

"Yes," he was told by his grandmother,
    "across Gichigami there are people."[1]

"And by any chance might they not be in possession
  of fire?"

"Yes," he was told by his grandmother,
    "most certainly they possess fire."

And this he said to his grandmother:
    "Well, guess what, I'm going to go get that fire!"
he said to his grandmother.

And this his grandmother said to him:
    "You won't be able to do it.
    They keep very close guard over their home.
    There's an old man living there.
    Every day he works at making a net.
    He never goes out but always remains inside.
    But he has two daughters; they're the only ones
        who ever venture out."

And this he said to his grandmother:
    "Nevertheless, I'm going,"
he said to his grandmother.

"Very well," he was told by his grandmother.

Well, at some point then he said:
    "Let Gichigami freeze over,
    let Gichigami freeze as thick as a sheet of birch
        bark covering the lodge."

And truly, it happened just as he said.

"And this is what I'll look like," he said.
    "I'll look like a bunny."

And then truly, that's how he looked.

And so he set off across the ice,
    and most assuredly he didn't break through.

---

[1]   [Valentine's note]   I use the Ojibwe designation for Lake
Superior, Gichigami, throughout, assuming that it is known from
Longfellow's *The Song of Hiawatha*, though the correct pronunciation is GitCh—ih—guh—mih or gih—Chi—guh—mih, with all
the *i*s short as in English *pin*.

And eventually he came in sight of where the people
 were living.
And when he arrived at the place from which they
 drew their water,
  he arranged this at the place where they would
   come to draw their water:
  he was thrown up on the shore by Gichigami;
  he was rolled up there, precisely where the woman
   drew her water.

And this he said: "Let her find me irresistibly cute."

And so he lay in wait for her to come to fetch water.

And what do you know, but indeed he saw her walking toward him.
And when she arrived where he was,
 she drew up some water.
And he was noticed by her,
 and he was picked up by her,
And so, he was wrung out by her,
 and he was carried away home,
  tucked inside the bosom of her dress, he was.

And when he had been taken inside the lodge,
 indeed he beheld an old man sitting there.
And, truly, the old man was making a net.
And the woman said this to her elder sister:
 "Look at this!"
 She said secretly to her elder sister.

  "Look at what I found, a little bunny rabbit!"

And this she was told by her elder sister:
 "Our father's going to take us to task,"
 she was told by her elder sister;
 that is, secretly she was told this by her elder sister.

And then she searched inside the bosom of her dress,
and she extracted him and set him down beside the
 fire to dry off his fur.

And the women were laughing it up,
 they found the bunny so irresistibly cute.
And as a result, they were discovered by their father.
 "Pipe down!" he told them.

"Take a look at this bunny!"

"What!" they were told by their father.
 "Haven't you heard that manitous[1] were recently
  born?
 And might not this indeed be one of them?
 Go and put it outside,"
 they were told by their father.

But this the woman said:
 "How could it be that a bunny rabbit be a
  manitou?"
 she said to her father.

And this he said:
 "Truly you're not in the habit of listening.
 Have you never noticed how advanced in years I
  am?"

But this is what the woman did:
 she exposed the bunny to the heat of the fire,
 and to make its fur dry,
 she kept turning it over and over by the fire.

And this then thought Nenabozho:
"I must be dry by now."

Well, the women kept amusing themselves with him.

And this he thought: "Let a spark fall on me!"

And truly a spark alit on him.
And after he was on fire,
 he leaped out of the lodge.

And the women said this:
 "Look, it's racing out with the fire!"
 they said to their father.

"Oh, no!" said the old man.
 "Truly you don't know how to listen,
  even though people try to tell you.
 Undoubtedly it's a manitou,
 come to rob us of our fire!"

---

[1] *manitous* Spirits.

And the old man leaped up
   and ran to his canoe,
   intending to toss it into the water.
But it was of no use,
   because the water had been frozen into ice.

And so they were left to watch helplessly
   as far out in the midst of the great expanse of
      Gichigami,
   it began to flicker with a blue flame,
   until it faded from their sight.
They were utterly helpless to do anything.

And he came in sight of where they were staying.
And this he had said to his grandmother before setting off:
      "Be prepared because I may indeed return with
         fire,"
   he had said to his grandmother.

And so he spoke to her as he came in sight of their
   home;
   this he said to his grandmother upon entering:
   "Extinguish me, grandma, I'm on fire!"
And that is how they came to have fire.

And this said Nenabozho:
   "And thus shall the rabbit appear mottled in the
      summer."

                    3

And thus they came to be in possession of fire.

And Nenabozho remained there with his
   grandmother,
   and all this time the waters of Gichigami were
      heaving.
Seated-Rabbit is the name of that portion of
   Gichigami.
And always he went there to sit.

And this he said to his grandmother:
   "So be it, Grandma, that this be the duration of
      my being a rabbit."

And at that place there was evidently a promontory,
   and there on the height of the rock he would sit.
Indeed, that is the appearance that the rock has there.
And then he said,
   "Seated-Rabbit is what the people shall call it."

And afterward he took on human form.
But no longer did he have the appearance of a child.
And this he said to his grandmother:
   "Do you know who I am?"

"No," he was told.

"I am Nenabozho."

And this he said to his grandmother:
   "Can it really be that I am an only child?"
   he said to his grandmother.

"Yes," he was told.
   "Truly you're an only child," he was told.

And this he answered:
   "Can you tell me this, then?"
he said to his grandmother,
   "Might not I have had a father?"

"Yes," he was told,
   "but whoever it might have been was not visible,"
   he was told.

And this too he was told,
   "She who was your mother is dead.
   That's all I can tell you.
   I would not hide anything from you."

And this Nenabozho said to her:
   "How could it be that I be an only child?
   You must be hiding something from me,"
   he said to his grandmother.

And then he said:
   "Why do you do this,
   hiding from me what transpired with us?
   But be that as it may, I haven't forgotten what
      happened."

I know that I have brothers.
So tell me the truth of what happened to us."

Well, these words frightened the old woman.
And this she said to her grandchild:
    "Very well, I will tell you,
    it's true that you weren't alone when you were
        born.

"As truly as I speak,
    this is what happened to you:
You and your brothers killed your mother when you
    were born.
But steadfastly I held to what I had purposed,
and that is why I have raised you."

And this he said to his grandmother:
    "Oh, so that's what happened to me at my birth!
    It was not I who killed my mother."

And then he thought:
    "I'm going to go looking for those brothers of
        mine,"
    he thought.

Well, then he said to his grandmother,
    "I'm going to go look for the one who made me
        an orphan."

"Don't!" his grandmother said in vain to him.
    "What is to be gained in your doing this,
    going into battle against your brother?"

"Nevertheless," he said, "I'm going to do it."

And then he set to work making his arrows.
And when he had prepared,
    he set off;
    directly to the south he went,
    because he knew that that was where his brother
        was.

And when he was near the home of his brother,
    he made four caches of arrows.

And then he came to the place where his brother was.

And Nenabozho said, "So, are you ready to do battle
    with me?"

"Indeed," his brother said to him.

"Well, then, let the battle begin."

And so they began fighting,
    and they were firing at each other.
And as he was being forced back,
    Nenabozho came to the place where his arrows
        were,
    where he had cached them.

And from there in turn he drove the other back,
    almost to the place where he lived,
    Nenabozho drove him back.

And from there once more Nenabozho was driven
    back,
    once again he was driven back to a place where
    he had cached his arrows.
And once more, futilely, he drove the other back,
    near to where he lived.

And then once more Nenabozho was driven back,
    until yet again he reached a cache of arrows.

And at that point he thought:
    "It seems likely now that I'll be vanquished."
He had only a very few arrows left,
    and they were very small.

And so he began to weep.

And this he thought:
    "It's likely now that I'll be killed,"
    he thought.

And then he was addressed by the weasel.
    "What's the matter with you,
        you look as if you've been weeping, Nenabozho,"
    he was told by the weasel.
    "Nothing's going to happen to you.
    Listen, I'll tell you what you must do,"
        said the weasel to him.

"Listen, shoot him there …"
"Shoot him at the base of his hair knot."

So then Nenabozho gave a war cry.
And no sooner had he begun driving his brother back,
   than he shot him at the base of the hair knot.
And his brother fell forward.
Nenabozho raced up to him,
   and this he said: "Die!"

And this he was told by his brother:
   "You're doing vast harm to those who are yet to
      live."
And his brother wept;
   he wept for the people.
In vain he sought to avoid being killed.

But Nenabozho was thoroughly determined to kill
   him.

And at last he succeeded in killing his younger sibling.
And for a short time his brother was out of his wits.

And Nenabozho said,
   "In return, you will be leader over there
   where those who cease to live will come.
   It's there you shall be,
   and there you shall be leader."

And then after his brother had consented,
   he said to him,
   "You've done vast harm to the people who are
      soon to live."

"Well, the earth would fill up with people.
   And where might those people live who are soon
      to be born?
   That is why it shall come to pass that people die,
      because otherwise the earth would soon be
      filled,
   and although we could arrange it such that
      only the aged might die among those who are
      to come,
   nowhere would they have room were this to
      come to pass.

You see, that's why they will also die while yet
   children.
Yes, that is what I foresee,
that it will happen thus to those who are soon to die,
that it will happen as it now does with you.
Because it is only a change of place from one earth
   to another.
Where you are those who have ceased to live shall
   meet you." …

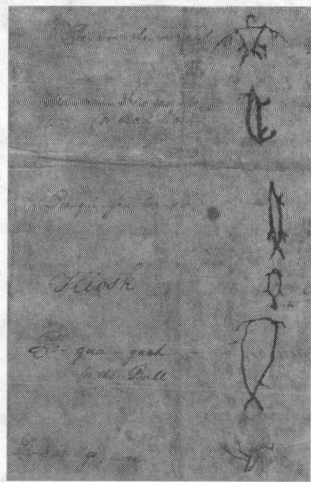

Alphabetic and pictographic signatures on a treaty between the U.S. Government and the Odawa, Ojibwe, Wendat, and Potawatomi peoples, 1807.

Anishinaabe (probably Ojibwe) shoulder bag with pictographic imagery, c. 1800.

OJIBWE PICTOGRAPHS
recorded and translated by George Copway, from *The Traditional History and Characteristic Sketches of the Ojibway Nation* (1851)

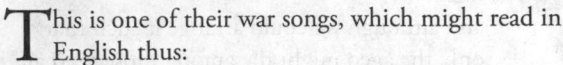

This is one of their war songs, which might read in English thus:

1.

I will haste to the land of the foe,
With warriors clad with the bow.

2.

I will drink the blood of their very heart;
I will change their joy into sorrow's smart
Their braves, their sires will I defy,
And a Nation's vengeance satisfy.

3.

They are in their homes, now happy and free;
No frowning cloud o'er their camp they see;

Yet the youngest of mine shall see the tall
Braves, scattered, wandering, and fall.

The warrior is represented by the figure of a man with a bow about him, and arrows in his hand; with the plume of the eagle waving over his head, indicative of his acquaintance with war life. The next figure represents a watching warrior, equally brave, but the heart is represented as dead. The curve of his mouth shows that he is shouting. The next figure represents a person with long hair, an indication that the best of the enemy's warriors were to fall, and their wail must be heard like the wail of a woman. The wigwam with its smoke curling upwards, indicates a council fire and the defiance of an attack. The other wigwams are seen without fire; and the black one signifies silence and death.

When I was young I was taught this, and while singing I could, in imagination, see the enemy, though none were within a hundred miles. ...

... These are some of the figures used by us in writing. With these, and from others of a similar class, the Ojibways can write their war and hunting songs.

An Indian well versed in these can send a communication to another Indian, and by them make himself as well understood as a pale face can by letter.

There are over two hundred figures in general use for all the purposes of correspondence. Material things are represented by pictures of them.

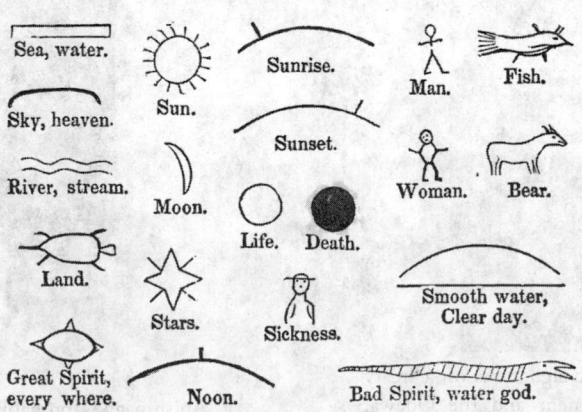

Invitations to Indians to come and worship in the spring are made in the following form:

The whole story would thus read:

"Hark to the words of the Sa-ge-mah."

"The Great Medicine Lodge will be ready in eight days."

"Ye who live in the woods and near the Lakes and by streams of water, come with your canoes or by land to the worship of the Great Spirit."

In the above, the wigwam and the medicine pale or worship, represent the depositories of medicine, record and work. The Lodge is represented with men in it; the dots above indicate the number of days.

These picture representations were used by the Ojibways until the introduction of European manners among them. …

Cherokee

By the time Cherokee people first made contact with colonists in 1540, Cherokees had been living in what is now called southern Appalachia for thousands of years and had established numerous permanent communities supported by a combination of hunting, fishing, and agriculture, structured around a two-season rhythm of summer and winter. Cherokee oral stories convey values and wisdom that have been shaped by relationship to the landscape over this long duration, and that continue to evolve as Cherokee history unfolds. According to Cherokee scholar Sandra Muse Isaacs, two key principles that recur in her people's oral traditions are Gadugi, a community-oriented commitment to generosity and support of other beings, and Duyvkta, the "right path" of harmony, balance, self-respect, and care for oneself as well as others.

Cherokee people also have a long tradition of writing. An indispensable contributor to this tradition is the blacksmith, silversmith, warrior, inventor, and political figure Sequoyah (c. 1770–1843), best known as the creator of the Cherokee Syllabary, a method of writing in the Cherokee language that he developed and popularized in the early nineteenth century. According to ethnographic accounts, Sequoyah created the syllabary independently, inspired by European writing systems, but Cherokee oral history holds that he was also inspired by an earlier form of writing that had been used by some Cherokee knowledge-keepers. Each symbol in Sequoyah's system represents an entire syllable, which makes it far more efficient to learn than the English alphabet; it spread quickly and was adopted by a majority of Cherokee speakers by the mid-1820s. It contributed to the development of a written constitution for the nation, completed in 1827, and to the creation of the bilingual Cherokee-English newspaper the *Cherokee Phoenix*, founded in 1828. The syllabary remains in common use today.

By the time the stories presented here were recorded in English in the late nineteenth and twentieth centuries, a series of atrocities perpetrated by the American government had wreaked havoc on Cherokee culture for generations. The most infamous of these, known as Expulsion or Removal, occurred in the late 1830s, as the majority of Cherokee people were forced to leave their homes and travel west of the Mississippi River; thousands of people died of disease and starvation during the journey or shortly afterward. As a result of these events, there are now Western Cherokee-speaking communities in Oklahoma, where the people were forcibly relocated, and Eastern Cherokee-speaking communities in the original homeland of Appalachia, as some resisters had managed to escape expulsion.

Myths of the Cherokee, the collection from which the first of the stories below was taken, was compiled by the white ethnographer James Mooney, who spent several years with the Eastern Band of Cherokees in the mountains of North Carolina toward the end of the nineteenth century. During this time, Mooney worked with a number of knowledgeable storytellers, most notably the shaman A'yûñ'inĭ (Swimmer). It appears that Mooney pressured the storytellers he worked with to share restricted knowledge, but also that they were motivated by a desire to preserve a record of their literature, which was then under threat from the pressures of colonization; present-day Cherokee scholars disagree regarding the extent to which Mooney exploited his collaborators. Mooney believed himself to be preserving the literature of a dying culture, but in fact Cherokee oral traditions continue to flourish.

WHY THE POSSUM'S TAIL IS BARE
as recorded by James Mooney, *Myths of the Cherokee* (1902)

James Mooney writes of the following text that "This story was heard from several informants, east and west. In one variant the hair clipping was done by the Moth, and in another by the spells of the Snail, who is represented as a magician. The version here given is the most common."

The Possum used to have a long, bushy tail, and was so proud of it that he combed it out every morning and sang about it at the dance, until the Rabbit, who had had no tail since the Bear pulled it out, became very jealous and made up his mind to play the Possum a trick.

There was to be a great council and a dance at which all the animals were to be present. It was the Rabbit's business to send out the news, so as he was passing the Possum's place he stopped to ask him if he intended to be there. The Possum said he would come if he could have a special seat, "because I have such a handsome tail that I ought to sit where everybody can see me." The Rabbit promised to attend to it and to send someone besides to comb and dress the Possum's tail for the dance, so the Possum was very much pleased and agreed to come.

Then the Rabbit went over to the Cricket, who is such an expert hair cutter that the Indians call him the barber, and told him to go next morning and dress the Possum's tail for the dance that night. He told the Cricket just what to do and then went on about some other mischief.

In the morning the Cricket went to the Possum's house and said he had come to get him ready for the dance. So the Possum stretched himself out and shut his eyes while the Cricket combed out his tail and wrapped a red string around it to keep it smooth until night. But all this time, as he wound the string around, he was clipping off the hair close to the roots, and the Possum never knew it.

When it was night the Possum went to the townhouse where the dance was to be and found the best seat ready for him, just as the Rabbit had promised. When his turn came in the dance he loosened the string from his tail and stepped into the middle of the floor.

The drummers began to drum and the Possum began to sing, "See my beautiful tail." Everybody shouted and he danced around the circle and sang again, "See what a fine color it has." They shouted again and he danced around another time, singing, "See how it sweeps the ground." The animals shouted more loudly than ever, and the Possum was delighted. He danced around again and sang, "See how fine the fur is." Then everybody laughed so long that the Possum wondered what they meant. He looked around the circle of animals and they were all laughing at him. Then he looked down at his beautiful tail and saw that there was not a hair left upon it, but that it was as bare as the tail of a lizard. He was so much astonished and ashamed that he could not say a word, but rolled over helpless on the ground and grinned, as the Possum does to this day when taken by surprise.

SEQUOYAH, CHEROKEE SYLLABARY (NINETEENTH CENTURY)

This syllabary was hand written by Sequoyah himself.

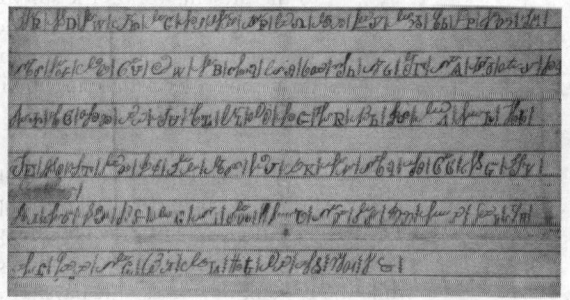

Navajo (Diné)

Much of the Navajo (Diné) creation story takes place between the four sacred mountains that define the limits of Dinétah, the Navajo traditional homeland, which spans parts of what are now also called Arizona, Colorado, New Mexico, and Utah. Traditional Navajo ways of life involve seasonal movement through this land. Initially, hunting and gathering were the only sources of food, but Navajo people also adopted agriculture from their Pueblo neighbors, and later, adopted the keeping of livestock herds from the Spanish, whom they first encountered in the late sixteenth century. Having resisted colonization by violent Spanish forces for more than a century, Navajo people began to face hostility from U.S. forces in the mid-1800s, and in 1863 were compelled to surrender to the U.S. The military forced them to march to central New Mexico, where they were held in an internment camp for four years; many people died both on the march, known as the Long Walk, and as a result of conditions in the camp, where sanitation, provisions, and shelter were inadequate. After four years, the Navajo were permitted to return to a reservation in a portion of Dinétah; since then, they have expanded their territory to include more of their traditional homeland.

An extended telling of the creation story plays a central role in the Blessingway rite, an important ceremony known in the Diné language as hózhóojí, meaning "way of hózhó." The complex philosophical concept of hózhó, meaning something like "beauty," "harmony," or "goodness," is taught and made manifest through the telling of the creation story and the other actions of the rite. Navajo anthropologist Rain Parrish describes the "interrelationships of stories, chants and rituals" as part of this process:

> At the beginning of the ceremony the practitioners introduce the surroundings of the dwellings, and the practitioner and patient's relationship to the natural and supernatural worlds. The origin of the Navajo is traced and we then return to the present world. The story of the myths is related with all its appropriate rituals. The key to the restoration of harmony and well being is in carefully acquiring the knowledge or ritual actions and their powers. By participating in this process, by actualizing the myths, we are composing a profound sense of unity with spirit and substance.

The Blessingway is one of many traditional ceremonies incorporating song, poetry, movement, and drypainting (visual art made by dropping sand and other colored powders). All the elements of a given ceremony are informed by the specific narratives included in it, which are often episodes drawn from the creation story. Ceremonies differ dramatically in duration—some last one night, while the Blessingway takes nine days. They also differ in many other respects; the drypaintings of the Blessingway are a few inches across, for example, while some drypaintings used in other ceremonies are so large that they must be painted in buildings made for the purpose. Specific ceremonies have particular functions, including to establish harmony, to cure sickness, or to oppose evil.

The portion of the creation story transcribed below is from *Navajo Creation Myth: The Story of the Emergence*, an early-twentieth-century collaboration between the white anthropologist Mary Cabot Wheelwright and the Navajo knowledge-keeper Hasteen Klah. Klah escaped attending the boarding schools intended to force assimilation to settler culture that were inflicted on many of his peers, and instead received training in traditional practices; as a nádleehí, a person whose gender does not fully conform to the roles of either men or women, he developed an unusual breadth of expertise that encompassed weaving (traditionally a women's art) as well as ceremony (traditionally conducted by men). Fearing that his knowledge, threatened by boarding schools and other oppressive government tactics, would be otherwise lost, Klah disregarded prohibitions against the sharing of ceremonial knowledge in order to record, with Wheelwright, not only the creation story itself but also an extensive body of drypaintings and other ceremonial practices.

from the Creation Story
as recorded by Hasteen Klah with Mary C. Wheelwright,
Navajo Creation Myth: The Story of the Emergence (1942)

The creation story begins with the creation of the First World, followed by the emergence of beings from that place into a series of higher worlds, until they reach the Fourth World (or, in some versions, the Fifth), where people currently live. The episode transcribed below begins after the birth of twins to Estsan-ah-tlehay, Changing Woman, an important figure in the narrative. At this point in the story the world is plagued by numerous monsters, which the twins will eventually slay.

from Birth of Nayenezgani and Tohbachischin

... When they were sixteen years old, they were quite grown up, and they looked so much alike no one could tell them apart. They wanted very much to find out who their father was. They asked this four times before the Sun had risen, but their mother was ashamed to tell them. But when the Sun had come up about half way, she pointed to it and said: "That is your father."

Etsay-Hasteen[1] made the twins bows and arrows, and they went about hunting and enjoying themselves. Once in their wanderings they came close to the edge of the mountain and they saw a Yehtso, a Gray Monster, coming up, and they shot at him with their bows and arrows and he was so frightened that he ran away.

One day when they were out hunting, Begochiddy[2] met them and sitting down between them said: "The Sun is your father and you must go and visit him." To help them, and to tell them what would happen in the future, and to show them the way, he gave them wind spirits, Niltche-beyazh. And he gave Nayenezgani the elder, the rainbow, Natseelit, to carry him wherever he wanted to go. And he gave Tohbachischin a ray of light, Shah-bekloth. He told the boys that when they came to their father's house they would be shown all sorts of clothing and other things, but that they must choose only the flint armor, Bezh; the lightning arrows,

Iknee-kah; and the stone knife, also the big cyclones and the big hail, and the kehtahn or magic cigarette named Kehtahn-de-konth; and he repeated: "You must be sure to ask for that." (Their mother, Estsan-ah-tlehay, did not know that they were starting on this journey.) …

[The twins journey to the house of the Spirit of the Sun.]

from Test of the Twins by the Sun

Inside on the east side of the house there was a black cloud rolled up, on the south side a blue cloud, on the west a yellow cloud, and on the north a white cloud. The twins met the Moon spirit there, though the moon itself was not present as it was wandering about. And the Spirit asked them: "What are you doing here, my boys? Your father is a fierce man and I will try to protect you." So the Spirit wrapped the two boys in the white cloud to hide them.

After they were hidden in the white cloud, the Sun Spirit came in and asked the Moon Spirit: "Who was speaking?" and the Moon Spirit answered: "No one except myself." The Sun Spirit did not believe this and went to the black cloud and unrolled it but found nothing there, and he unrolled the south cloud and the west cloud, and finally in the north cloud he found the boys. He seized them by the hair of their heads and threw them against some great spikes of obsidian which were turned edge-wise like knives set in the floor at the east side of the hogahn.[3] He said: "I hope these boys are my sons" (for if they were really his sons they would not be hurt by anything). They were not harmed by the knives; and then the Sun Spirit threw them onto the knives on the south, west and north, and they were still unharmed.

The Sun Spirit called the Moon spirit and said: "Uncle, heat the sweat-house." So the Moon Spirit heated the sweat-house, and on one side he dug a hole large enough to contain the two boys and covered it with a little Moon. He brought the boys over to the sweat-house and showed them the hole where they could hide, and they hid themselves in it. Then the Sun

---

[1] *Etsay-Hasteen* The first man.

[2] *Begochiddy* Introduced earlier in the narrative as the "great god."

[3] *hogahn* Dwelling constructed from wood and mud.

Spirit came to the house bringing a jug of water and poured it on a bar of obsidian which had been heated red hot; and it filled the house with much steam, and he asked the boys: "Are you too warm in there?" and the boys answered: "No." He asked this of the boys four times and they answered each time: "No, we are all right," so the Sun Spirit went back to his hogahn and the boys came out of the sweat-house.

Each night while they were at the Sun's house they slept on the roof, and they had a robe of white clouds to cover them and the Sun Spirit gave them another robe also, but they were very cold there and would have frozen except that the Otter Woman came and gave them her fur robe to spread over them. It hailed and stormed all night, and the Sun thought that they would be frozen, but thanks to the fur robe which the Otter Woman gave them, they were warm.

When the Sun went into his home again, he filled a turquoise pipe, a white shell pipe, an abalone pipe, and a jet pipe with poison smoke. On their way back to the Sun's house from the sweat-house, the twins met a caterpillar who gave them some medicine weeds to eat so that they could not be killed if they smoke the poison pipes of the Sun. Back in the Sun's house again the boys were given a blue pipe to smoke, and the Sun lighted it with a little Sun. They smoked all of the pipes easily.

Finding that he could not kill them with the poison smoke, the Sun Spirit caught the boys by the hair and threw them into a big black jar on the east side of the room. He then hung a huge stone by a stream of water to the roof over the jar and let the stone fall to crush the twins; but when he looked into the jar, he saw the boys in it unharmed. He tried this four times, and even made the great stone drop more heavily but he could not hurt the twins. Then he took the boys into his arms, holding one on either side of him, for he knew now that they were really his sons, because they had not been harmed by his tests.

The Sun Spirit had four children by a spirit woman named Yoodi-yenai, who had been in the Fourth World. Her eldest daughter was called Turquoise Girl, Doklizhe-etahdeh, and the younger was called White Shell Girl, Yolthkai-etahdeh. The older boy was called Abalone Boy, Dichithli-eshki, and the younger boy was called Jet Boy, Baszhini-eshki. The Sun Spirit said to his daughters: "Bring some water to your brothers," and the Turquoise Girl brought a blue basket and a jug of water, and the White Shell Girl brought a white basket and a jug of water, and also they brought soap-root, and the twins washed their hair and their sisters bathed them and dried them first with fine white corn meal and then with corn pollen. Then the Sun and his spirit wife went to the eastern room and brought the sweet-smelling flowers with which they rubbed the twins. And they were made beautiful and looked just like the other children of the Sun. And they sat down on a turquoise bench. The Sun Spirit told his daughters to feed the twins and they gave them Yolthkai-tahn (corn meal mush, ceremonially called White-Shell-Food).

The Sun Spirit then asked the twins: "Why did you come to me?" And they answered: "There are monsters killing all of our people and we want to be able to kill them." The Sun Spirit did not answer but took the boys to the east room which was reached by steps. He opened the door, and there they saw many rainbows, and the Sun Spirit asked the twins if that was what they wanted, but the boys said: "No, we do not want that sort of thing." Then the Sun took them to a door at the south and opened it, and there were many plants, corn, beans, and so forth. And the Sun Spirit said: "Is that what you wanted?" The boys said: "No." So the west door was opened, and there they saw clothing and jewelry, and the Sun asked them: "Did you come for this sort of thing?" And they said: "No"; but the boys had forgotten what they wanted and the Sun then showed them many more things.

Then Niltche-beyazh, the Spirit Wind, spoke in their ears and said: "Begochiddy told you to ask for flint armor and the other weapons." So they said to the Sun: "We want the flint armor and the stone knife, lightning arrows, cyclones, hail, and the magic kehtahn." The Sun said to them: "What do you want them for? They are dangerous." And they answered: "We want to dress in that armor and use the weapons to kill the giants and the monsters." When the twins answered thus, the Sun Spirit sat down with his head in his hands and said sadly: "You must not kill your brother," for he claimed the giants as his children. But finally he decided to grant their request and said: "Very well, I will give you what you have asked for." And he taught them how to wear the armor, and how to shoot the lightning arrows, and how to use the stone knife, the big hail, the cyclones, and also how to use the magic kehtahn. And they then told him how they were going to kill the monsters, the bears, and other creatures who were harming the people.

Then the Sun Spirit gave them the gifts that they had asked for and they started to go back to Tsoll-tsilth on the clouds, the Sun accompanying them. And when they reached there, they rested above the mountain sitting on the clouds, and the Sun Spirit asked them many questions to test their cleverness. He pointed to Siss-nah-jini and asked them its name and the boys answered correctly. The Sun asked the names of all the mountains and they named them correctly. He also pointed to Huerfano Peak[1] below and the boys recognized their home, so the Sun was satisfied that they were intelligent and asked them no more questions.

Tse' Hone / Newspaper Rock

Known in Diné (Navajo) as Tse' Hone (rock that tells a story), this rock contains a large collection of petroglyphs that were carved over a period of more than a thousand years, and by a variety of peoples, including Ancestral Puebloans, Fremont people, Diné (Navajo) people, Pueblo people, and Europeans, among other groups. Tse' Hone is in present day Utah, to the north of the Diné homeland

---

[1] *Huerfano Peak* Sacred mountain at the center of the Navajo homeland.

CIVILIZATIONS IN CONTACT

The Caribbean

Christopher Columbus never recanted his claim that the Caribbean islands he reached in his world-changing 1492 expedition were on the east coast of Asia. Like the early explorers and colonists who came after him, he interpreted the unfamiliar places and people he encountered in terms familiar to him. He had set out from Portugal believing Japan was less than 3,000 miles away (a quarter of the actual distance) and with expectations of what he would find there that had been shaped by his reading. From the writings of Marco Polo, who had visited Asia in the late thirteenth century, he expected to find the prosperous kingdom of a Great Khan, abundant with spices and gold. In *The Travels of Sir John Mandeville* (mid-fourteenth century), a widely read travel narrative that merged fact with fantastical fiction, he read of Southeast Asian islands populated by "folk of diverse shape and marvelously disfigured"—one-eyed giants, headless people with eyes in their shoulders, and people with enormous lips or ears. But the *Travels* also described places of great wealth and magnificence, including a Christian empire in India and an "isle, great and good and plenteous" where the people are unfamiliar with Christianity but are "full of all virtue, and they eschew all … sins."

Echoes of the monsters and riches Columbus had read about appear in his accounts of his own travels, including in his personal journal and in his public letter describing his first voyage, both of which are represented in translation below. The letter was published in numerous editions in the 1490s, and its purpose was largely to maintain public support for Columbus's operations, which were financed with the help of the Spanish queen, Isabella I of Castile. Thus, it reflects the religious and economic goals that Columbus and the monarchy shared. Columbus was invested in the possibility of bringing Catholicism to new peoples, a missionary project he appears to have personally believed in and that provided what was seen as an honorable purpose for his voyages and settlement attempts. Profit was another key motive for his exploration and colonization—a motive that would sometimes complement and sometimes contradict the goal of religious conversion. Belief in the importance of conversion provided justification for Spanish control of the Indigenous people whose labor colonization relied upon, but it also made the exploitation of the Taíno controversial, since many Spanish people, including Isabella I, thought it immoral to enslave those they had converted to Catholicism.

With some exceptions, the Taíno and other Indigenous groups the European crew encountered on the first voyage received them peacefully, though Columbus frequently took Indigenous prisoners. When he departed the island now known as Haiti and the Dominican Republic, he left a fortified encampment occupied by a small number of crew members who were all killed before his return. When Columbus undertook his second voyage in 1494, he returned to the island with a much larger number of settlers, many of whom were prisoners released on the condition of their participation in the colonizing project. He established the colony of Hispaniola with the intention of extracting vast quantities of gold, but the island did not turn out to be the wellspring of gold and other expensive goods that he had expected. He attempted to increase the colony's profits by exploiting the Taíno people who lived there; clinging to his belief that the island concealed extraordinary gold deposits, he required every Taíno person over 14 to produce a nearly unachievable quota of gold and imposed gruesome punishment on those who refused or failed to comply. Colonists also enslaved Taíno and other Indigenous people to sell in Spain, and many settlers raped or undertook at best dubiously consensual relationships with Indigenous women. In a letter excerpted below, the Italian aristocrat Michele de Cuneo, a friend of Columbus who participated in the second voyage, offers a chillingly matter-of-fact account of sexual violence and enslavement perpetrated by the colonists.

Conditions for the Taíno worsened in 1499, when Columbus returned to Hispaniola on a third voyage to find the settlers in rebellion against him, forcing him to implement a system whereby control over the land and people was parcelled out to individual settlers. This was soon codified into the encomienda system, according to which the Indigenous laborers were nominally free and said to receive the benefits of civilization and Christianity as recompense for their work. But in reality, the system was tantamount to slavery. Columbus himself—never as skilled a leader as he was a sailor—was soon ousted from power altogether and sent back to Spain to face criminal charges. He regained enough status to make one more voyage across the Atlantic, but he was forbidden to return to Hispaniola and instead focused his exploration on the Central American mainland. This expedition was plagued by shipwreck and mutiny, and Columbus spent more than a year stranded on Jamaica before he was finally rescued. His health compromised by the experience, he returned to Spain, where he died two years later. He had explored a remarkable amount of territory, encompassing much of the Caribbean and portions of the South and Central American coast, and he had amassed a great deal of personal wealth, but he continued to resent his loss of authority in Hispaniola.

Another participant in the early settlement of Hispaniola was Bartolomé de las Casas, a Spanish merchant's son who first came to the colony in 1502 and crossed the Atlantic many times in the following decades. Initially a participant in the conquest of the Caribbean and a plantation operator under the encomienda system, and also educated as a priest, Las Casas came to believe that the violent and exploitative way the Spanish treated Indigenous people in the colonies was profoundly sinful. He gave up his own encomienda and took up a campaign against the oppression he had witnessed and participated in. Las Casas remained focused on this cause for the rest of his life, and in numerous writings and speeches he attempted to convince both colonists and Spanish authorities of the injustice of their behavior toward Indigenous populations. His views intensified as his career progressed: once a proponent of the enslavement of Africans (who were more resistant to European diseases) as a replacement for Indigenous enslavement, he came to oppose slavery altogether, and to advocate not just freedom from slavery but also limited self-governance for colonized Indigenous societies.

Las Casas had some impact on the policies of the Church and of the Spanish state. He joined the Dominican order and took up a leadership role in missionary efforts in the colonies, serving for a time as bishop in the Mexican colony of Chiapas. The pressure he placed on the government contributed to some attempts at political change, the most significant of which was the passage of the New Laws of the Indies (1542). These laws were intended to free most Indigenous people from enslavement and would have substantially reformed settler-Indigenous relations in other important ways, but the reaction to them in the colonies was so forceful that the laws were soon partially repealed. Seeking a wider audience for his appeals, Las Casas published the arguments and testimony he had given in support of the New Laws as *A Short Account of the Destruction of the Indies* in 1552. Presented as an account of Las Casas's personal experience, the book is also a persuasive document intended not only to evoke the extent of the atrocities committed by colonists but also to convince readers of the humanity of the Indigenous victims. For Spanish authorities, it was at this time an open question whether Indigenous people should be considered worthy of the rights accorded to other peoples. In 1550 Las Casas had, at the request of the monarchy, formally debated the theologian Juan Ginés de Sepúlveda, who argued that Indigenous people were naturally suited to enslavement, describing them as "*homunculi* in whom hardly a vestige of humanity remains."

As Las Casas hoped, *Destruction of the Indies* was widely read both in Spain and, in translation, in other European countries. It was both influential and controversial. Some considered Las Casas a heretic or a traitor—and, indeed, his forceful condemnation of Spanish actions in the colonies would long be used by Spain's Protestant enemies as fodder for the "Black legend," a distorted narrative that exaggerated the evils committed by the Spanish Empire while downplaying those of Protestant colonizing nations. But Las Casas also found an audience sympathetic to his aims, and his work is considered an important contribution to the development of the philosophy of universal human rights.

The following section begins with excerpts from Columbus's diary of his first voyage to North America, a document that bears the mark both of Columbus and of Las Casas. While the full, original text of the diary has not survived, a substantial portion of the record is preserved in an abridged copy made by Las Casas, probably several decades after Columbus's death. Las Casas intersperses passages quoted directly from the diary with his own summaries of omitted portions, and scholars continue to debate the extent to which his objectivity as an editor might have been compromised by his own strong views. In the passages included below, direct quotations from Columbus appear in quotation marks.

⌘ ⌘ ⌘

from Christopher Columbus with Bartolomé de las Casas, *Journal of the First Voyage to America*[1]

Friday, 12th of October

The vessels were hove to,[2] waiting for daylight; and on Friday they arrived at a small island of the Lucayos,[3] called, in the language of the Indians, Guanahani.[4] Presently they saw naked people. The Admiral[5] went on shore in the armed boat, and Matin Alonso Pinzon, and Vicente Yañez, his brother, who was captain of the *Niña*. The Admiral took the royal standard,[6] and the captain went with two banners of the green cross, which the Admiral took in all the ships as a sign, with an F and a Y[7] and a crown over each letter, one on one side of the cross and the other on the other. Having landed, they saw trees very green, and much water, and fruits of diverse kinds. The Admiral called to the two captains, and to the others who leaped on shore, and to Rodrigo Escovedo, secretary of the whole fleet, and to Rodrigo Sanchez of Segovia, and said that they should bear faithful testimony that he, in presence of all, had taken, as he now took, possession of the said island for the King and for the Queen his Lords, making the declarations that are required, as is now largely set forth in the testimonies which were then made in writing.

Presently many inhabitants of the island assembled. What follows is in the actual words of the Admiral in his book of the first navigation and discovery of the Indies. "I," he says, "that we might form great friendship, for I knew that they were a people who could be more easily freed and converted to our holy faith by love than by force, gave to some of them red caps, and glass beads to put round their necks, and many other things of little value, which gave them great pleasure, and made them so much our friends that it was a marvel to see. They afterwards came to the ship's boats where we were, swimming and bringing us parrots, cotton threads in skeins, darts, and many other things; and we exchanged them for other things that we gave them, such as glass beads and small bells. In fine,[8] they took all, and gave what they had with good will. It appeared to me to be a race of people very poor in everything. They go as naked as when their mothers bore them, and so do the women, although I did not see more than one young girl. All I saw were youths, none more

---

[1]   Translated by Clements R. Markham, 1893.

[2]   *hove to*   I.e., stopped.

[3]   *Lucayos*   Spanish name for the Taíno people who inhabited the islands.

[4]   *Guanahani*   The island renamed San Salvador by Columbus.

[5]   *Admiral*   Columbus, given the title of Admiral of the Ocean Sea in recognition of his 1492 exploration.

[6]   *standard*   Flag.

[7]   *an F and a Y*   Signifying King Ferdinand II of Aragon and Queen Isabella I of Castile, the Catholic monarchs of Spain. The flag described here, featuring a green cross and the monarchs' initials, represented Columbus's fleet.

[8]   *In fine*   In short.

than thirty years of age. They are very well made, with very handsome bodies, and very good countenances.[1] Their hair is short and coarse, almost like the hairs of a horse's tail. They wear the hairs brought down to the eyebrows, except a few locks behind, which they wear long and never cut. They paint themselves black, and they are the color of the Canarians,[2] neither black nor white. Some paint themselves white, others red, and others of what color they find. Some paint their faces, others the whole body, some only round the eyes, others only on the nose. They neither carry nor know anything of arms, for I showed them swords, and they took them by the blade and cut themselves through ignorance. They have no iron, their darts being wands without iron, some of them having a fish's tooth at the end, and others being pointed in various ways. They are all of fair stature and size, with good faces, and well made. I saw some with marks of wounds on their bodies, and I made signs to ask what it was, and they gave me to understand that people from other adjacent islands came with the intention of seizing them, and that they defended themselves. I believed, and still believe, that they come here from the mainland to take them prisoners. They should be good servants and intelligent, for I observed that they quickly took in what was said to them, and I believe that they would easily be made Christians, as it appeared to me that they had no religion. I, our Lord being pleased, will take hence, at the time of my departure, six natives for your Highness, that they may learn to speak. I saw no beast of any kind except parrots, on this island." The above is in the words of the Admiral.

Saturday, 13th of October

"… They brought skeins of cotton thread, parrots, darts, and other small things which it would be tedious to recount, and they give all in exchange for anything that may be given to them. I was attentive, and took trouble to ascertain if there was gold. I saw that some of them had a small piece fastened in a hole they have in the nose, and by signs I was able to make out that to the south, or going from the island to the south, there

was a king who had great cups full, and who possessed a great quantity. I tried to get them to go there, but afterwards I saw that they had no inclination. I resolved to wait until tomorrow in the afternoon and then to depart, shaping a course to the S.W., for, according to what many of them told me, there was land to the S., to the S.W., and N.W., and that the natives from the N.W. often came to attack them, and went on to the S.W. in search of gold and precious stones. …"

Sunday, 14th of October

"At dawn I ordered the ship's boat and the boats of the caravels[3] to be got ready, and I went along the coast of the island and to the N.N.E., to see the other side, which was on the other side to the east, and also to see the villages. Presently I saw two or three, and the people all came to the shore, calling out and giving thanks to God. Some of them brought us water, others came with food, and when they saw that I did not want to land, they got into the sea, and came swimming to us. We understood that they asked us if we had come from heaven. One old man came into the boat, and others cried out, in loud voices, to all the men and women, to come and see the men who had come from heaven, and to bring them to eat and drink. Many came, including women, each bringing something, giving thanks to God, throwing themselves on the ground and shouting to us to come on shore. But I was afraid to land, seeing an extensive reef of rocks which surrounded the island, with deep water between it and the shore forming a port large enough for as many ships as there are in Christendom,[4] but with a very narrow entrance. It is true that within this reef there are some sunken rocks, but the sea has no more motion than the water in a well. In order to see all this I went this morning, that I might be able to give a full account to your Highnesses, and also where a fortress might be established. I saw a piece of land which appeared like an island, although it is not one, and on it there were six houses. It might be converted into an island in two days, though I do not see that it would be necessary, for these people are very simple as regards the use of arms, as your Highnesses will see from the

---

[1]   *countenances* Facial appearances.

[2]   *Canarians* Canary Islanders. In 1492, Castile was in the last few years of a decades-long campaign to conquer the Canary Islands, which the monarchy achieved complete control over in 1496.

[3]   *caravels* Portuguese sailing ships designed for exploration. The *Pinta* and *Niña* were this type of ship.

[4]   *Christendom* The entire Christian world.

seven that I caused to be taken, to bring home and learn our language and return; unless your Highnesses should order them all to be brought to Castile,[1] or to be kept as captives on the same island; for with fifty men they can all be subjugated and made to do what is required of them. Close to the above peninsula there are gardens of the most beautiful trees I ever saw, and with leaves as green as those of Castile in the month of April and May, and much water. I examined all that port, and afterwards I returned to the ship and made sail. I saw so many islands that I hardly knew how to determine to which I should go first. Those natives I had with me said, by signs, that there were so many that they could not be numbered, and they gave the names of more than a hundred. At last I looked out for the largest, and resolve to shape a course for it, and so I did. It will be distant five leagues[2] from this of *San Salvador*, and the others some more, some less. All are very flat, and all are inhabited. The natives make war on each other, although these are very simple-minded and handsomely-formed people."

Tuesday, 27th of November
… The Admiral also says: "How great the benefit that is to be derived from this country would be, I cannot say. It is certain that where there are such lands there must be an infinite number of things that would be profitable. But I did not remain long in one port, because I wished to see as much of the country as possible, in order to make a report upon it to your Highnesses; and besides, I do not know the language, and these people neither understand me nor any other in my company; while the Indians I have on board often misunderstand. Moreover, I have not been able to see much of the natives, because they often take to flight. But now, if our Lord pleases, I will see as much as possible, and will proceed by little and little, learning and comprehending; and I will make some of my followers learn the language. For I have perceived that there is only one language up to this point. After they understand the advantages, I shall labor to make all these people Christians. They will become so readily, because they have no religion nor idolatry, and your

Highnesses will send orders to build a city and fortress, and to convert the people. I assure your Highnesses that it does not appear to me that there can be a more fertile country nor a better climate under the sun, with abundant supplies of water. This is not like the rivers of Guinea, which are all pestilential. I thank our Lord that, up to this time, there has not been a person of my company who has had so much as a headache, or been in bed from illness, except an old man who has suffered from the stone[3] all his life, and he was well again in two days. I speak of all three vessels. If it will please God that your Highnesses should send learned men out here, they will see the truth of all I have said. I have related already how good a place Rio de Mares[4] would be for a town and fortress, and this is perfectly true; but it bears no comparison with this place, nor with the Mar de Nuestra Señora.[5] For here there must be a large population, and very valuable productions, which I hope to discover before I return to Castile. I say that if Christendom will find profit among these people, how much more will Spain, to whom the whole country should be subject. Your Highnesses ought not to consent that any stranger should trade here, or put his foot in the country, except Catholic Christians, for this was the beginning and end of the undertaking; namely, the increase and glory of the Christian religion, and that no one should come to these parts who was not a good Christian." …

Sunday, 16th of December
At midnight the Admiral made sail with the land-breeze to get clear of that gulf.[6] Passing along the coast of Española on a bowline,[7] for the wind had veered to the east, he met a canoe in the middle of the gulf, with a single Indian in it. The Admiral was surprised how he could have kept afloat with such a gale blowing. Both

---

[1] *Castile* Kingdom in Spain at the time of writing.

[2] *leagues* One league is approximately three miles, and three nautical miles at sea.

[3] *the stone* Kidney stones.

[4] *Rio de Mares* Name Columbus gave to the area surrounding a bay he encountered while exploring Cuba.

[5] *Mar de Nuestra Señora* Name Columbus gave to a region of numerous mountainous islands.

[6] *made sail … that gulf* Due to unfavorable winds, Columbus had struggled to depart from his anchorage near what is now Port-de-Paix, Haiti.

[7] *on a bowline* With the sails tied so as to move the boat close to the opposite direction of the wind.

the Indian and his canoe were taken on board, and he was given glass beads, bells, and brass trinkets, and taken in the ship, until she was off a village 17 miles from the former anchorage, where the Admiral came to again. The village appeared to have been lately built, for all the houses were new. The Indian then went on shore in his canoe, bringing the news that the Admiral and his companions were good people; although the intelligence had already been conveyed to the village[.] … Presently more than five hundred natives with their king came to the shore opposite the ships, which were anchored very close to the land. Presently one by one, then many by many, came to the ship without bringing anything with them, except that some had a few grains of very fine gold in their ears and noses, which they readily gave away. The Admiral ordered them all to be well treated; and he says: "for they are the best people in the world, and the gentlest; and above all I entertain the hope in our Lord that your Highnesses will make them all Christians, and that they will be all your subjects, for as yours I hold them." He also saw that they all treated the king with respect, who was on the seashore. The Admiral sent him a present, which he received in great state. He was a youth of about 21 years of age, and he had with him an aged tutor, and other councillors who advised and answered him, but he uttered very few words. One of the Indians who had come in the Admiral's ship spoke to him, telling him how the Christians had come from Heaven, and how they came in search of gold, and wished to find the island of Baneque.[1] He said that it was well, and that there was much gold in the said island. He explained to the alguazil[2] of the Admiral that the way they were going was the right way, and that in two days they would be there; adding, that if they wanted anything from the shore he would give it them with great pleasure. This king, and all the others, go naked as their mothers bore them, as do the women without any covering, and these were the most beautiful men and women that had yet been met with. They are fairly white, and if they were clothed and protected from the sun and air, they would be almost as fair as people in Spain. This land is cool, and the best that words

can describe. It is very high, yet the top of the highest mountain could be ploughed with bullocks;[3] and all is diversified with plains and valleys. In all Castile there is no land that can be compared with this for beauty and fertility. All this island, as well as the island of Tortuga, is cultivated like the plain of Cordova. They raise on these lands crops of yams, which are small branches, at the foot of which grow roots like carrots, which serve as bread. They powder and knead them, and make them into bread; then they plant the same branch in another part, which again sends out four or five of the same roots, which are very nutritious, with the taste of chestnuts. Here they have the largest the Admiral had seen in any part of the world, for he says that they have the same plant in Guinea. At this place they were as thick as a man's leg. All the people were stout and lusty, not thin, like the natives that had been seen before, and of a very pleasant manner, without religious belief. The trees were so luxuriant that the leaves left off being green, and were dark coloured with verdure. It was a wonderful thing to see those valleys, and rivers of sweet water, and the cultivated fields, and land fit for cattle, though they have none, for orchards, and for anything in the world that a man could seek for.

In the afternoon the king came on board the ship, where the Admiral received him in due form, and caused him to be told that the ships belonged to the Sovereigns of Castile, who were the greatest princes in the world. But neither the Indians who were on board, who acted as interpreters, nor the king, believed a word of it. They maintained that the Spaniards came from Heaven, and that the Sovereigns of Castile must be in Heaven, and not in this world. They placed Spanish food before the king to eat, and he ate a mouthful, and gave the rest to his councillors and tutor, and to the rest who came with him.

"Your Highnesses may believe that these lands are so good and fertile, especially these of the island of Española,[4] that there is no one who would know how to describe them, and no one who could believe if he had not seen them. And your Highnesses may believe that this island, and all the others, are as much yours as Castile. Here there is only wanting a settlement and

---

[1] *Baneque* Indigenous people had told the explorers that a great deal of gold could be found on this island.

[2] *alguazil* Member of a ship's crew responsible for policing.

[3] *bullocks* Castrated bulls.

[4] *Española* Hispaniola, now the location of Haiti and the Dominican Republic.

the order to the people to do what is required. For I, with the force I have under me, which is not large, could march over all these islands without opposition. I have seen only three sailors land, without wishing to do harm, and a multitude of Indians fled before them. They have no arms, and are without warlike instincts; they all go naked, and are so timid that a thousand would not stand before three of our men. So that they are good to be ordered about, to work and sow, and do all that may be necessary, and to build towns, and they should be taught to go about clothed and to adopt our customs."

—WRITTEN 1492–93

Christopher Columbus, *Letter of Columbus to Various Persons Describing the Results of His First Voyage and Written on the Return Journey*[1]

Since I know that you will be pleased at the great success with which the Lord has crowned my voyage, I write to inform you how in thirty-three days I crossed from the Canary Islands to the Indies, with the fleet which our most illustrious sovereigns gave me. I found very many islands with large populations and took possession of them all for their Highnesses; this I did by proclamation and unfurled the royal standard.[2] No opposition was offered.

I named the first island that I found "San Salvador," in honour of our Lord and Saviour who has granted me this miracle. The Indians call it "Guanahani." The second island I named "Santa Maria de Conception," the third "Fernandina," the fourth "Isabela" and the fifth "Juana"; thus I renamed them all.[3]

When I reached Cuba, I followed its north coast westwards, and found it so extensive that I thought this must be the mainland, the province of Cathay.[4] Since there were no towns or villages on the coast, but only small groups of houses whose inhabitants fled as soon as we approached, I continued on my course, thinking that I should undoubtedly come to some great towns or cities. We continued for many leagues[5] but found no change, except that the coast was bearing me northwards. This I wished to avoid, since winter was approaching and my plan was to journey south. As the wind was carrying me on I decided not to wait for a change of weather but to turn back to a remarkable harbor which I had observed. From here I sent two men inland to discover whether there was a king or any great cities. They travelled for three days, finding only a large number of small villages and great numbers of people, but nothing more substantial. Therefore they returned.

I understood from some Indians whom I had captured elsewhere that this was an island, and so I followed its coast for 107 leagues to its eastward point. From there I saw another eighteen leagues eastwards which I then named "Hispaniola." I crossed to this island and followed its northern coast eastwards for 188 leagues continuously, as I had followed the coast of Cuba. All these islands are extremely fertile and this one is particularly so. It has many large harbors finer than any I know in Christian lands, and many large rivers. All this is marvelous. The land is high and has many ranges of hills, and mountains incomparably finer than Tenerife.[6] All are most beautiful and various in shape, and all are accessible. They are covered with tall trees of different kinds which seem to reach the sky. I have heard that they never lose their leaves, which I can well believe, for I saw them as green and lovely as they are in Spain in May; some were flowering, some bore fruit and others were at different stages according to their nature. It was November but everywhere I went the nightingale and many other birds were singing. There are palms of six or eight different kinds—a marvelous sight because of their great variety—and the other trees, fruit and plants are equally marvelous. There are splendid pine woods and broad fertile plains, and there is honey. There are many kinds of birds and

---

[1]   Translated by J.M. Cohen, 1969.

[2]   *standard*   Flag.

[3]   *The second … them all*   These names reference Catholic saints, with the exception of islands named for King Ferdinand II of Aragon and Queen Isabella I of Castile, the Catholic monarchs of Spain, who supported Columbus's venture.

[4]   *Cathay*   China.

[5]   *leagues*   One league is approximately three miles, and three nautical miles at sea.

[6]   *Tenerife*   One of the Canary Islands, and the last to be conquered by Castile; its people surrendered to the Castilian monarchy in 1496.

varieties of fruit. In the interior are mines and a very large population.

Hispaniola is a wonder. The mountains and hills, the plains and meadow lands are both fertile and beautiful. They are most suitable for planting crops and for raising cattle of all kinds, and there are good sites for building towns and villages. The harbors are incredibly fine and there are many great rivers with broad channels and the majority contain gold. The trees, fruits and plants are very different from those of Cuba. In Hispaniola there are many spices and large mines of gold and other metals. …

The inhabitants of this island, and all the rest that I discovered or heard of, go naked, as their mothers bore them, men and women alike. A few of the women, however, cover a single place with a leaf of a plant or piece of cotton which they weave for the purpose. They have no iron or steel or arms and are not capable of using them, not because they are not strong and well built but because they are amazingly timid. All the weapons they have are canes cut at seeding time, at the end of which they fix a sharpened stick, but they have not the courage to make use of these, for very often when I have sent two or three men to a village to have conversation with them a great number of them have come out. But as soon as they saw my men all fled immediately, a father not even waiting for his son. And this is not because we have harmed any of them; on the contrary, wherever I have gone and been able to have conversation with them, I have given them some of the various things I had, a cloth and other articles, and received nothing in exchange. But they have still remained incurably timid. True, when they have been reassured and lost their fear, they are so ingenuous and so liberal with all their possessions that no one who has not seen them would believe it. If one asks for anything they have they never say no. On the contrary, they offer a share to anyone with demonstrations of heartfelt affection, and they are immediately content with any small thing, valuable or valueless, that is given them. I forbade the men to give them bits of broken crockery, fragments of glass or tags of laces, though if they could get them they fancied them the finest jewels in the world. One sailor was known to have received gold to the weight of two and a half castellanos[1] for the tag of a breeches lace, and other received much more for things of even less value. For newly minted blancas[2] they would give everything they possessed, even two or three castellanos of gold or an arroba[3] or two of spun cotton. They even took bits of broken hoops from the wine barrels and, as simple as animals, gave what they had. This seemed to me to be wrong and I forbade it.

I gave them a thousand pretty things that I had brought, in order to gain their love and incline them to become Christians. I hoped to win them to the love and service of their Highnesses and of the whole Spanish nation and to persuade them to collect and give us of the things which they possessed in abundance and which we needed. They have no religion and are not idolaters; but all believe that power and goodness dwell in the sky and they are firmly convinced that I have come from the sky with these ships and people. In this belief they gave me a good reception everywhere, once they had overcome their fear; and this is not because they are stupid—far from it, they are men of great intelligence, for they navigate all those seas, and give a marvelously good account of everything—but because they have never before seen men clothed or ships like these.

As soon as I came to the Indies, at the first island I discovered I seized some natives, intending them to inquire and inform me about things in these parts. These men soon understood us, and we them, either by speech or signs, and they were very useful to us. I still have them with me, and despite all the conversation they have had with me they are still of the opinion that I come from the sky and have been the first to proclaim this wherever I have gone. The others have gone running from house to house and to the neighboring villages shouting: "Come, come and see the people from the sky," so, once they were reassured about us, all have come, men and women alike, and not one, old or young, has remained behind. All have brought us something to eat and drink which they have given with a great show of love. In all the islands they have very many canoes like oared fustas.[4]

---

[1] *castellanos* Castilian gold coins.

[2] *blancas* Castilian copper coins.

[3] *arroba* Unit measuring weight; the precise weight of an arroba varied by region, but was in the range of two to three dozen pounds.

[4] *fustas* Long, narrow ships with mast and sails, used by the Portuguese for expedition and cargo.

They are of various sizes, some as large as a fusta of eighteen benches. But they are not as broad, since they are hollowed out of a single tree. A fusta would not be able to keep up with them, however, for they are rowed at an incredible speed. In these they travel and transport their goods between the islands, which are innumerable. I have seen some of these canoes with eighty men in them, all rowing.

In all these islands I saw no great difference in the looks of the people, their customs or their language. On the other hand, all understand one another, which will be of singular assistance in the work of their conversion to our holy faith, on which I hope your Highnesses will decide, since they are very well disposed towards it.

I have already told of my voyage of 107 leagues in a straight line from west to east along the coast of Cuba, according to which I reckon that the island is larger than England and Scotland put together.

One of these provinces is called Avan and there the people are born with tails, and these provinces cannot have a length of less than fifty or sixty leagues, according to the information I received from those Indians whom I have with me and who know all the islands.

The other island, Hispaniola, is greater in circumference than the whole of Spain from Collioure to Fuenterabia[1] in the Basque province, since I travelled along one side for 188 great leagues in a straight line from west to east.

These islands are richer than I yet know or can say and I have taken possession of them in their Majesties' name and hold them all on their behalf and as completely at their disposition as the Kingdom of Castile. In the island of Hispaniola I have taken possession of a large town which is most conveniently situated for the goldfields and for communications with the mainland both here, and there in the territories of the Grand Khan,[2] with which there will be very profitable trade. I have named this town Villa de Navidad and have built a fort there. Its fortifications will by now be

finished and I have left sufficient men to complete them. They have arms, artillery and provisions for more than a year, and a fusta; also a skilled shipwright who can build more.

I have established warm friendship with the king of that land, so much so, indeed, that he was proud to call me and treat me as a brother. But even should he change his attitude and attack the men of La Navidad, he and his people know nothing about arms and go naked, as I have already said; they are the most timorous people in the world. In fact, the men that I have left there would be enough to destroy the whole land, and the island holds no dangers for them so long as they maintain discipline.

In all these islands the men are seemingly content with one woman, but their chief or king is allowed more than twenty. The women appear to work more than the men and I have not been able to find out if they have private property. As far as I could see whatever a man had was shared among all the rest and this particularly applies to food.

I have not found the human monsters which many people expected. On the contrary, the whole population is very well made. They are not Negroes as in Guinea, and their hair is straight, for where they live the sun's rays do not strike too harshly, but they are strong nevertheless, despite the fact that Hispaniola is 20 to 21 degrees from the Equator.[3]

There are high mountains in these islands and it was very cold this winter but the natives are used to this and withstand the weather, thanks to their food, which they eat heavily seasoned with very hot spices. Not only have I found no monster but I have had no reports of any except the island called "Quaris," which is the second as you approach the Indies from the east, and which is inhabited by a people who are regarded in these islands as extremely fierce and who eat human flesh. They have many canoes in which they travel throughout the islands of the Indies, robbing and taking all they can. They are no more ill-shaped than any other natives of the Indies, though they are in the habit of wearing their hair long like women. They have

---

[1]   *Collioure … Fuenterabia* Collioure and Fuenterabia (now Hondarríbia) are today at opposite ends of the border between France and Spain; Collioure is on the east coast, and Fuenterabia is on the west coast.

[2]   *Grand Khan* I.e., the Mongolian emperor. At the time of writing, Columbus persisted in his belief that he had reached Asia.

[3]   *despite … Equator* Reference to longstanding European beliefs that the equatorial region was too hot to allow for human flourishing. Some who held these beliefs thought the region was entirely uninhabitable; others thought it was populated by monstrous or weak and unhealthy races.

bows and arrows with the same canes as the others, tipped with splinters of wood, for the lack of iron which they do not possess. They behave most savagely to the other peoples but I take no more account of them than the rest. It is these men who have relations with the women of Matinino, where there are no men and which is the first island you come to on the way from Spain to the Indies. These women do not follow feminine occupations but use cane bows and arrows like those of the men and arm and protect themselves with plates of copper, of which they have much.

In another island, which I am told is larger than Hispaniola, the people have no hair. Here there is a vast quantity of gold, and from here and the other islands I bring Indians as evidence.

In conclusion, to speak only of the results of this very hasty voyage, their Highnesses can see that I will give them as much gold as they require, if they will render me some very slight assistance; also I will give them all the spices and cotton they want, and as for mastic,[1] which has so far been found only in Greece and the island of Chios and which the Genoese authorities have sold at their own price, I will bring back as large a cargo as their Highnesses may command. I will also bring them as much aloes as they ask and as many slaves, who will be taken from the idolaters. I believe also that I have found rhubarb and cinnamon and there will be countless other things in addition, which the people I have left there will discover. For I did not stay anywhere unless delayed by lack of wind except at the town of La Navidad, which I had to leave secure and well established. In fact I should have done much more if the ships had been reasonably serviceable, but this is enough.

Thus the eternal God, Our lord, grants to all those who walk in his way victory over apparent impossibilities, and this voyage was pre-eminently a victory of this kind. For although there was much talk and writing of these lands, all was conjectural, without ocular evidence. In fact, those who accepted the stories judged rather by hearsay than on any tangible information. So all Christendom will be delighted that our Redeemer has given victory to our most illustrious King and Queen and their renowned kingdoms, in this great matter. They should hold great celebrations and render solemn thanks to the Holy Trinity with many solemn prayers, for the great triumph which they will have, by the conversion of so many peoples to our holy faith and for the temporal benefits which will follow, for not only Spain, but all Christendom will receive encouragement and profit.

This is a brief account of the facts.

Written in the caravel[2] off the Canary Islands.

15 February 1493

At your orders

The Admiral

After this was written, when I was already in Spanish waters, I was struck by such a strong south-south-west wind that I was compelled to lighten ship,[3] but today by a great miracle I made the port of Lisbon, from which I decided to write letters to their Highnesses. Throughout the Indies, I have always found weather like that of May; I went there in thirty-three days and returned in twenty-eight. I met with no storms except these which held me up for fourteen days, beating about in these seas. The sailors here say that there has never been so bad a winter nor so many ships lost.

Written on 4 March —1493

from Michele de Cuneo, letter [Concerning Columbus's Second Voyage][4] (1495)

From [the] island of Guadalupe, which belongs … to the Caribs,[5] we set sail on 10 November and on the 13th of the same month we came to another island of Caribs very beautiful and fertile, and we arrived at a very beautiful harbor. As soon as the Caribs saw us they ran away to the mountains like those of the other island and they emptied their houses, into which we went and took whatever pleased us. In these few days we found many islands where we did not go

---

1 *mastic* Tree resin used to make varnish, as well as for other purposes.

2 *caravel* Ship.

3 *lighten ship* I.e., throw cargo and other heavy items into the water; a lighter ship can withstand stormy weather more easily.

4 Translated by Samuel Eliot Morison, 1963.

5 *Caribs* Kalinago people, neighbors and historical enemies of the Taíno people.

ashore. A few times we anchored, that is, for the night; and when we did not anchor we kept the ship hove-to,[1] and this in order not to make any headway and for fear of running afoul of the said islands, to which, because they were close one to the other the Lord Admiral gave the name of Eleven Thousand Virgins; and to the one previously mentioned, Santa Cruz.

One of those days while we were lying at anchor we saw coming from a cape a canoe, that is to say a boat, which is how they call it in their language, going along with oars so that it looked like a well-manned bergantino,[2] on which there were three or four Carib men with two Carib women and two Indian slaves, of whom (that is the way the Caribs treat their other neighbors in those other islands), they had recently cut the genital organ to the belly, so that they were still sore; and we having the flagship's boat ashore, when we saw that canoe coming, quickly jumped into the boat and gave chase to that canoe. While we were approaching her the Caribs began shooting at us with their bows in such manner that, had it not been for the shields, half of us would have been wounded. But I must tell you that to one of the seamen who had a shield in his hand came an arrow, which went through the shield and penetrated his chest three inches, so that he died in a few days. We captured that canoe with all the men, and one Carib was wounded by a spear in such a way that we thought he was dead, and cast him for dead into the sea, but instantly saw him swim. In so doing we caught him and with the grapple hauled him over the bulwarks of the ship where we cut his head with an axe. The other Caribs, together with those slaves, we later sent to Spain. While I was in the boat I captured a very beautiful Carib woman, whom the said Lord Admiral gave to me, and with whom, having taken her into my cabin, she being naked according to their custom, I conceived desire to take pleasure. I wanted to put my desire into execution but she did not want it and treated me with her finger nails in such a manner that I wished I had never begun. But seeing that, to tell you the end of it all, I took a rope and thrashed her well, for which she raised such unheard of screams that you would not have believed your ears. Finally we came to an agreement in such manner that

I can tell you that she seemed to have been brought up in a school of harlots. To that cape of that island the Admiral gave the name Cape of the Arrow because of the one who had died of the arrow. …

… Sailing to Hispaniola I was the first to sight land. Therefore the Lord Admiral in that very place ordered us ashore at a cape where there was an excellent harbor and he called it el cavo de San Michele Saonese,[3] out of respect for me, and this he wrote down in his book. Sailing always along the coast we found mountainous shores and good harbors and several times we landed, and everywhere we found innumerable people of the usual sort. And thus ranging the coast toward our settlement we found not too far from a cape a very beautiful island which also I was the first to sight, the which was some 25 leagues in circumference, and again out of love for me, the Lord Admiral called it *La Bella Saonese*. He gave it to me as a present; and I took possession of it according to the appropriate modes and forms, as the Lord Admiral was doing of the other islands in the name of His Majesty the King, that is by virtue of a document signed by a notary public. On the above mentioned island I uprooted grass and cut trees and planted the cross and also the gallows, and in the name of God I baptized it with the name *La Bella Saonese*. And well it is called beautiful for in it there are 37 villages with at least 30,000 souls; and all this too the Lord Admiral noted down in his book. …

When our caravels[4] in which I wished to go home had to leave for Spain, we gathered together in our settlement 1600 people male and female of those Indians, of whom, among the best males and females, we embarked on our caravels on 17 February 1495, 550 souls. Of the rest who were left the announcement went around that whoever wanted them could take as many as he pleased; and this was done. And when everybody had been supplied there were some 400 of them left to whom permission was granted to go wherever they wanted. Among them there were many women who had infants at the breast. They, in order to better escape us, since they were afraid we would turn

---

[1] *hove-to* With sails positioned to inhibit movement.

[2] *bergantino* Sailing ship.

[3] *el cavo … Saonese* The cape of St. Michael of Savona. Cuneo was from Savona, in northern Italy.

[4] *caravels* Ships.

to catch them again, left their infants anywhere on the ground and started to flee like desperate people; and some fled so far that they were removed from our settlement of Isabela 7 or 8 days beyond mountains and across huge rivers; wherefore from now on scarcely any will be had. Among these people who were taken was one of their kings with two chiefs, who it was decided should be killed with arrows on the following day, so they were tied up; but in the night they knew so well how to gnaw one another's ropes with their teeth, that they were freed from their bonds and escaped. …

Meanwhile I departed for Spain with those caravels. Sailing with terrible and contrary winds we had to turn back thrice so that we spent a month among those islands. Wherefore, seeing the few provisions that we had, we turned north and proceeded in that direction for about 600 Roman miles;[1] and when it pleased God the winds turned favorable to our sails and we passed from the island of Boriquen to the island of Madeira in 23 days. But when we reached the waters around Spain about 200 of those Indians died, I believe because of the unaccustomed air, colder than theirs. We cast them into the sea. The first land we saw was Cape Spartel and very soon after we reached Cadiz, in which place we disembarked all the slaves, half of whom were sick. For your information they are not working people and they very much fear cold, nor have they long life. …

—1495

from Bartolomé de las Casas, *A Short Account of the Destruction of the Indies*[2]

[PREFACE]

The Americas were discovered in 1492, and the first Christian settlements established by the Spanish the following year. It is accordingly forty-nine years now since Spaniards began arriving in numbers in this part of the world. They first settled the large and fertile island of Hispaniola, which boasts six hundred leagues[3] of coastline and is surrounded by a great many other large islands, all of them, as I saw for myself, with as high a native population as anywhere on earth. Of the coast of the mainland, which, at its nearest point, is a little over two hundred and fifty leagues from Hispaniola, more than ten thousand leagues had been explored by 1541, and more are being discovered every day. This coastline, too, was swarming with people and it would seem, if we are to judge by those areas so far explored, that the Almighty selected this part of the world as home to the greater part of the human race.

God made all the peoples of this area, many and varied as they are, as open and as innocent as can be imagined. The simplest people in the world—unassuming, long-suffering, unassertive, and submissive—they are without malice or guile, and are utterly faithful and obedient both to their own native lords and to the Spaniards in whose service they now find themselves. Never quarrelsome or belligerent or boisterous, they harbour no grudges and do not seek to settle old scores; indeed, the notions of revenge, rancor, and hatred are quite foreign to them. At the same time, they are among the least robust of human beings: their delicate constitutions make them unable to withstand hard work or suffering and render them liable to succumb to almost any illness, no matter how mild. Even the common people are no tougher than princes or than other Europeans born with a silver spoon in their mouths and who spend their lives shielded from the rigors of the outside world. They are also among the poorest people on the face of the earth; they own next to nothing and have no urge to acquire material possessions. As a result they are neither ambitious nor greedy, and are totally uninterested in worldly power. Their diet is every bit as poor and as monotonous, in quantity and in kind, as that enjoyed by the Desert Fathers.[4] Most of them go naked, save for a loincloth to cover their modesty; at best they may wrap themselves in a piece of cotton material a yard or two square. Most sleep on matting, although a few possess a kind of hanging net, known in the language of Hispaniola as a hammock. They are innocent and pure in mind and have a lively intelligence, all of which makes them particularly receptive to learning and understanding the truths of our Catholic faith and to being instructed in virtue; indeed, God has invested them with fewer

---

[1] *Roman miles* Unit of distance slightly shorter than a modern mile.

[2] Translated by Nigel Griffin, 1992.

[3] *leagues* One league is approximately three miles.

[4] *Desert Fathers* Early Christian hermits who lived very austerely.

impediments in this regard than any other people on earth. Once they begin to learn of the Christian faith they become so keen to know more, to receive the Sacraments, and to worship God, that the missionaries who instruct them do truly have to be men of exceptional patience and forbearance; and over the years I have time and again met Spanish laymen who have been so struck by the natural goodness that shines through these people that they frequently can be heard to exclaim: "These would be the most blessed people on earth if only they were given the chance to convert to Christianity."

It was upon these gentle lambs, imbued by the Creator with all the qualities we have mentioned, that from the very day they clapped eyes on them the Spanish fell like ravening wolves upon the fold, or like tigers and savage lions who have not eaten meat for days. The pattern established at the outset has remained unchanged to this day, and the Spaniards still do nothing save tear the natives to shreds, murder them and inflict upon them untold misery, suffering and distress, tormenting, harrying and persecuting them mercilessly. We shall in due course describe some of the many ingenious methods of torture they have invented and refined for this purpose, but one can get some idea of the effectiveness of their methods from the figures alone. When the Spanish first journeyed there, the indigenous population of the island of Hispaniola stood at some three million; today only two hundred survive. The island of Cuba, which extends for a distance almost as great as that separating Valladolid from Rome,[1] is now to all intents and purposes uninhabited; and two other large, beautiful and fertile islands, Puerto Rico and Jamaica, have been similarly devastated. Not a living soul remains today on any of the islands of the Bahamas, which lie to the north of Hispaniola and Cuba, even though every single one of the sixty or so islands in the group, as well as those known as the Isles of Giants and others in the area, both large and small, is more fertile and more beautiful than the Royal Gardens in Seville and the climate is as healthy as anywhere on earth. The native population, which once numbered some five hundred thousand, was wiped out by forcible expatriation to the island of Hispaniola, a policy

adopted by the Spaniards in an endeavor to make up losses among the indigenous population of that island. One God-fearing individual was moved to mount an expedition to seek out those who had escaped the Spanish trawl and were still living in the Bahamas and to save their souls by converting them to Christianity, but, by the end of a search lasting three whole years, they had found only the eleven survivors I saw with my own eyes. A further thirty or so islands in the region of Puerto Rico are also now uninhabited and left to go to rack and ruin as a direct result of the same practices. All these islands, which together must run to over two thousand leagues, are now abandoned and desolate.

On the mainland, we know for sure that our fellow-countrymen have, through their cruelty and wickedness, depopulated and laid waste an area which once boasted more than ten kingdoms, each of them larger in area than the whole of the Iberian Peninsula. The whole region, once teeming with human beings, is now deserted over a distance of more than two thousand leagues: a distance, that is, greater than the journey from Seville to Jerusalem and back again.

At a conservative estimate, the despotic and diabolical behaviour of the Christians has, over the last forty years, led to the unjust and totally unwarranted deaths of more than twelve million souls, women and children among them, and there are grounds for believing my own estimate of more than fifteen million to be nearer the mark.

There are two main ways in which those who have traveled to this part of the world pretending to be Christians have uprooted these pitiful peoples and wiped them from the face of the earth. First, they have waged war on them: unjust, cruel, bloody and tyrannical war. Second, they have murdered anyone and everyone who has shown the slightest sign of resistance, or even of wishing to escape the torment to which they have subjected him. This latter policy has been instrumental in suppressing the native leaders, and, indeed, given that the Spaniards normally spare only women and children, it has led to the annihilation of all adult males, whom they habitually subject to the harshest and most iniquitous and brutal slavery that man has ever devised for his fellow-men, treating them, in fact, worse than animals. All the many and infinitely varied ways that have been devised for oppressing these

---

[1] *Valladolid from Rome* Valladolid, in western Spain, is about a thousand miles from Rome; Cuba is close to 800 miles long.

peoples can be seen to flow from one or other of these two diabolical and tyrannical policies.

The reason the Christians have murdered on such a vast scale and killed anyone and everyone in their way is purely and simply greed. They have set out to line their pockets with gold and to amass private fortunes as quickly as possible so that they can then assume a status quite at odds with that into which they were born. Their insatiable greed and overweening[1] ambition know no bounds; the land is fertile and rich, the inhabitants simple, forbearing and submissive. The Spaniards have shown not the slightest consideration for these people, treating them (and I speak from first-hand experience, having been there from the outset) not as brute animals—indeed, I would to God they had done and had shown them the consideration they afford their animals—so much as piles of dung in the middle of the road. They have had as little concern for their souls as for their bodies, all the millions that have perished having gone to their deaths with no knowledge of God and without the benefit of the Sacraments. One fact in all this is widely known and beyond dispute, for even the tyrannical murderers themselves acknowledge the truth of it: the indigenous peoples never did the Europeans any harm whatever; on the contrary, they believed them to have descended from the heavens, at least until they or their fellow-citizens had tasted, at the hands of these oppressors, a diet of robbery, murder, violence, and all other manner of trials and tribulations.

HISPANIOLA

As we have said, the island of Hispaniola was the first to witness the arrival of the Europeans and the first to suffer the wholesale slaughter of its people and the devastation and depopulation of the land. It all began with the Europeans taking native women and children both as servants and to satisfy their own base appetites; then, not content with what the local people offered them of their own free will (and all offered as much as they could spare), they started taking for themselves the food the natives contrived to produce by the sweat of their brows, which was in all honesty little enough. Since what a European will consume in a single day normally

supports three native households of ten persons each for a whole month, and since the newcomers began to subject the locals to other vexations, assaults, and iniquities, the people began to realize that these men could not, in truth, have descended from the heavens. Some of them started to conceal what food they had, others decided to send their women and children into hiding, and yet others took to the hills to get away from the brutal and ruthless cruelty that was being inflicted on them. The Christians punched them, boxed their ears and flogged them in order to track down the local leaders, and the whole shameful process came to a head when one of the European commanders raped the wife of the paramount chief of the entire island. It was then that the locals began to think up ways of driving the Europeans out of their lands and to take up arms against them. Their weapons, however, were flimsy and ineffective both in attack and in defence (and, indeed, war in the Americas is no more deadly than our jousting, or than many European children's games) and, with their horses and swords and lances, the Spaniards easily fended them off, killing them and committing all kinds of atrocities against them.

They forced their way into native settlements, slaughtering everyone they found there, including small children, old men, pregnant women, and even women who had just given birth. They hacked them to pieces, slicing open their bellies with their swords as though they were so many sheep herded into a pen. They even laid wagers on whether they could manage to slice a man in two at a stroke, or cut an individual's head from his body, or disembowel him with a single blow of their axes. They grabbed suckling infants by the feet and, ripping them from their mothers' breasts, dashed them headlong against the rocks. Others, laughing and joking all the while, threw them over their shoulders into a river, shouting: "Wriggle, you little perisher." They slaughtered anyone and everyone in their path, on occasion running through a mother and her baby with a single thrust of their swords. They spared no one, erecting especially wide gibbets[2] on which they could string up their victims with their feet just off the ground and then burn them alive thirteen at a time, in honour of our Saviour and the twelve Apostles, or tie dry straw to their bodies and set fire to

---

[1] *overweening* Overly proud.

[2] *gibbets* I.e., wooden frames upon which bodies could be hung.

it. Some they chose to keep alive and simply cut their wrists, leaving their hands dangling, saying to them: "Take this letter"—meaning that their sorry condition would act as a warning to those hiding in the hills. The way they normally dealt with the native leaders and nobles was to tie them to a kind of griddle consisting of sticks resting on pitchforks driven into the ground and then grill them over a slow fire, with the result that they howled in agony and despair as they died a lingering death.

It once happened that I myself witnessed their grilling of four or five local leaders in this fashion (and I believe they had set up two or three other pairs of grills alongside so that they might process other victims at the same time) when the poor creatures' howls came between the Spanish commander and his sleep. He gave orders that the prisoners were to be throttled, but the man in charge of the execution detail, who was more bloodthirsty than the average common hangman (I know his identity and even met some relatives of his in Seville), was loath to cut short his private entertainment by throttling them and so he personally went round ramming wooden bungs[1] into their mouths to stop them making such a racket and deliberately stoked the fire so that they would take just as long to die as he himself chose. I saw all these things for myself and many others besides. And, since all those who could do so took to the hills and mountains in order to escape the clutches of these merciless and inhuman butchers, these mortal enemies of humankind trained hunting dogs to track them down—wild dogs who would savage a native to death as soon as look at him, tearing him to shreds and devouring his flesh as though he were a pig. These dogs wrought havoc among the natives and were responsible for much carnage. And when, as happened on the odd occasion, the locals did kill a European, as, given the enormity of the crimes committed against them, they were in all justice fully entitled to, the Spanish came to an unofficial agreement among themselves that for every European killed one hundred natives would be executed.

… Indeed, they invented so many new methods of murder that it would be quite impossible to set them all down on paper and, however hard one tried to chronicle them, one could probably never list a thousandth part of what actually took place. All I can say is that I know it to be an incontrovertible fact and do here so swear before Almighty God, that the local peoples never gave the Spanish any cause whatever for the injury and injustice that was done to them in these campaigns. On the contrary, they behaved as honorably as might the inmates of a well-run monastery, and for this they were robbed and massacred, and even those who escaped death on this occasion found themselves condemned to a lifetime of captivity and slavery. I would go further. It is my firm belief that not a single native of the island committed a capital offence, as defined in law, against the Spanish while all this time the natives themselves were being savaged and murdered. Despite the enormous provocation, very few of the natives, I hazard, were guilty of even those sins which do not lie within the ambit[2] of human law but are properly the province of God, such as hatred and anger, or the thirst for revenge against those who committed such enormities upon them. It is my own experience of these peoples, gained over many years, that they are no more given to impetuous actions or to harboring thoughts of retribution than are boys of ten or twelve years of age. I know beyond any shadow of a doubt that they had, from the very beginning, every right to wage war on the Europeans, while the Europeans never had just cause for waging war on the local peoples. The actions of the Europeans, throughout the New World, were without exception wicked and unjust: worse, in fact, than the blackest kind of tyranny.

After the fighting was over and all the men had been killed, the surviving natives—usually, that is, the young boys, the women, and the children—were shared out between the victors. One got thirty, another forty, a third as many as a hundred or even twice that number; everything depended on how far one was in the good books of the despot who went by the title of governor. The pretext under which the victims were parceled out in this way was that their new masters would then be

---

[1]   *bungs* Plugs.

[2]   *ambit* Scope.

in a position to teach them the truths of the Christian faith; and thus it came about that host of cruel, grasping and wicked men, almost all of them pig-ignorant, were put in charge of these poor souls. And they discharged this duty by sending the men down the mines, where working conditions were appalling, to dig for gold, and putting the women to labor in the fields and on their master's estates, to till the soil and raise the crops, properly a task only for the toughest and strongest of men. Both women and men were given only wild grasses to eat and other unnutritious foodstuffs. The mothers of young children promptly saw their milk dry up and their babies die; and, with the women and the men separated and never seeing each other, no new children were born. The men died down the mines from overwork and starvation, and the same was true of the women who perished out on the estates. The islanders, previously so numerous, began to die out as would any nation subjected to such appalling treatment. For example, they were made to carry burdens of three and four arrobas[1] for distances of up to a hundred or even two hundred leagues, and were forced to carry their Christian masters in hammocks, which are like nets slung from the shoulders of the bearers. In short, they were treated as beasts of burden and developed huge sores on their shoulders and backs as happens with animals made to carry excessive loads. And this is not to mention the floggings, beatings, thrashings, punches, curses and countless other vexations and cruelties to which they were routinely subjected and to which no chronicle could ever do justice nor any reader respond save with horror and disbelief.

It is of note that all these island territories began to go to the dogs once news arrived of the death of our most gracious Queen Isabella, who departed this life in 1504. Up to then, only a small number of provinces had been destroyed through unjust military action, not the whole area, and news of even this partial destruction had by and large been kept from the Queen, because, she—may her soul rest in peace—took a close personal interest in the physical and spiritual welfare of the native peoples, as those of us who lived through those years and saw examples of it with our own eyes can attest. There is one other general rule in all this, and it is that, wherever the Spaniards set foot, right throughout the Americas, they subjected the native inhabitants to the cruelties of which we have spoken, killing these poor and innocent people, tyrannizing them, and oppressing them in the most abominable fashion. The longer they spent in the region the more ingenious were the torments, each crueller than the last, that they inflicted on their victims, as God finally abandoned them and left them to plummet headlong into a life of full-time crime and wickedness.

—1552

---

[1]   *three and four arrobas*   Around 44 to 60 kilograms.

New Mexico: The Pueblo Revolt

From its beginning in the sixteenth century, the Spanish colonization of "New Mexico" was characterized by exploitation and often brutality toward the diverse peoples to whom the land belonged, whom the Spanish collectively called Pueblos. As the colony became more established, many Pueblo individuals and communities converted to Catholicism, some out of genuine belief, and some out of a hope that missionaries might provide some protection from the abuses they endured from commercial colonists under the encomienda system, which entitled individual settlers to receive tribute from Indigenous communities. These Pueblos found, however, that conversion came with its own array of abuses. Missionaries imposed oppressive discipline on converts, requiring forced labor, destroying sacred objects of importance to the community, and using corporal punishment to enforce their authority.

In the 1660s and 70s, the struggles of Pueblo people intensified as an extensive drought brought food shortages, along with Navajo and Apache raiders seeking to feed their own communities—hardships that exacerbated the burdens of colonization as the Spanish continued to demand labor and resources from the Pueblos. Many Pueblos returned with renewed vigor to their longstanding spiritual practices, including, importantly, ritual dances in which the dancers embody specific katsinas (spirits) in order to bring rain. Missionaries' brutal attempts to stamp out these rituals and persecute their leaders served only to galvanize Pueblo rejection of Catholicism. This combination of circumstances provoked an unprecedented mass resistance known as the Pueblo Revolt of 1680.

The organization of the revolt was an extraordinary feat involving dozens of independent villages and a number of distinct cultures, including several mutually unintelligible languages. Before 1680, these barriers had prevented Indigenous people—who vastly outnumbered settlers in New Mexico—from coordinating their efforts against the Spanish. At the center of this organizational effort was Po'pay, a Tewa man from Ohkay Owingeh (San Juan Pueblo) who, in 1675, was one of almost fifty religious leaders whipped for witchcraft and sentenced to enslavement. Before the leaders could be sold, a group of Pueblo warriors successfully demanded their release from prison, and Po'pay went into hiding in Taos, a pueblo far north of Santa Fe, the locus of Spanish power in the region. Here, according to accounts some Pueblo people gave to the Spanish, he communed with spirits including Po'se yemu, a teacher of traditions and bringer of rain who is revered in most Pueblo cultures. Po'pay coordinated the attack with the help of a circle of war captains recruited from many different pueblos.

The Spanish learned that an attack was coming but did not anticipate its scale, and they were both unprepared and wholly outnumbered. Within weeks, the rebellion had ended in a decisive victory for the Pueblos, who killed hundreds of colonists and two-thirds of the missionaries but allowed the majority of the 2,500 settlers and their remaining Pueblo allies to flee hundreds of miles south to El Paso, on the southern border of New Mexico. The success of the rebellion was in many respects unprecedented, and the sudden loss of an entire established province dismayed Spanish settlers and authorities. In a letter reprinted in translation below, the province's governor, Antonio de Otermín, describes this loss from a Spanish perspective and attempts to justify his failure to prevent what was, in Spanish eyes, an unthinkable catastrophe.

The extent of the provocations the Pueblos endured and the violence with which they responded are reflected in the account of one community's participation in the rebellion given below by Hopi scholar Edmund Nequatewa, from his oral literature collection *Truth of a Hopi* (1936). As Nequatewa's story suggests, a key motive for the rebels was religion—a desire both to expel oppressive missionaries and to revitalize traditional spirituality. In many communities, the victors burned churches, destroyed Christian relics, rebuilt their kivas (underground ritual buildings), and relearned the important ceremonial dances that missionaries had only partially succeeded in erasing from community knowledge. Many people ceremonially washed themselves in the river to cleanse themselves of their Catholic baptism. In 1681, Fray Francisco de Ayeta, who traveled to New Mexico as part of a failed reconquest attempt, reported that "not a sign has been visible of [the Pueblos] ever having been Christians." Spanish influence was not, however, entirely erased. The Pueblos—almost all of whom had been born under Spanish rule and many of whom had Spanish as well as Indigenous heritage—did choose to maintain some technologies, crops, and livestock of Spanish origin.

The Pueblos succeeded in maintaining their independence for thirteen years. A reconquest campaign beginning in 1692 secured most of New Mexico for Spain—with the exception of Hopi, which remained independent for another century. Even though the rebels did not achieve permanent independence for New Mexico, they did substantially improve conditions under colonialism; afraid to provoke another rebellion, the colonial government did not reinstate the exploitative encomienda system, and missionaries were less violent in their efforts to suppress Pueblo spiritual practices.

NOTE ON THE TEXTS: The text of the letter of Antonio de Otermín appears as translated in C.W. Hackett's *Historical Documents Relating to New Mexico, Nueva Vizcaya, and Approaches Thereto, to 1773*; the story by Nequatewa is based on the version appearing in his collection *Truth of a Hopi*. Spelling and punctuation have been modernized in accordance with the practices of this anthology.

⌘ ⌘ ⌘

Antonio de Otermín, letter on the Pueblo Revolt of 1680, 8 September 1680

My very reverend father, Sir, and friend, most beloved Fray Francisco de Ayeta:[1]

The time has come when, with tears in my eyes and deep sorrow in my heart, I commence to give an account of the lamentable tragedy, such as has never before happened in the world, which has occurred in this miserable kingdom and holy *custodia*,[2] His Divine Majesty[3] having thus permitted it because of my grievous sins. Before beginning my narration I desire, as one obligated and grateful, to give your reverence the thanks due for the demonstrations of affection and kindness which you have given in your solicitude in ascertaining and inquiring for definite notices about both my life

and those of the rest in this miserable kingdom, in the midst of persistent reports which had been circulated of the deaths of myself and the others, and for sparing neither any kind of effort nor large expenditures. For this, only Heaven can reward your reverence, though I do not doubt that his Majesty (may God keep him) will do so.

After I sent my last letter to your reverence by the *maese de campo*,[4] Pedro de Leyba, while the necessary things were being made ready alike for the escort and in the way of provisions, for the most expeditious dispatch of the returning carts and their guards, as your reverence had enjoined me, I received information that a plot for a general uprising of the Christian Indians was being formed and was spreading rapidly. This was wholly contrary to the existing peace and tranquility in this miserable kingdom, not only among the Spaniards and natives, but even on the part of the heathen enemy, for it had been a long time since they had done us any considerable damage. It was my misfortune that I learned of it on the eve of the day set for the beginning

---

[1] *Fray Francisco de Ayeta* Custos (guardian) of the New Mexico missions from 1676 to 1683.

[2] *custodia* Administrative area that had its own government but was also subject to the authority of a province. New Mexico was under the authority of the province of Santo Evangelio, in Mexico.

[3] *His Divine Majesty* I.e., God.

[4] *maese de campo* Spanish: field master, a high-ranking military official.

of the said uprising, and though I immediately, at that instant, notified the lieutenant general on the lower river and all the other *alcaldes mayores*[1]—so that they could take every care and precaution against whatever might occur, and so that they could make every effort to guard and protect the religious ministers and the temples—the cunning and cleverness of the rebels were such, and so great, that my efforts were of little avail. To this was added a certain degree of negligence by reason of the [report of the] uprising not having been given entire credence, as is apparent from the ease with which they captured and killed both those who were escorting some of the religious,[2] as well as some citizens in their houses, and, particularly, in the efforts that they made to prevent my orders to the lieutenant general passing through. This was the place where most of the forces of the kingdom were, and from which I could expect some help, but of three orders which I sent to the said lieutenant general, not one reached his hands. The first messenger was killed and the others did not pass beyond Santo Domingo,[3] because of their having encountered on the road the certain notice of the deaths of the religious who were in that convent, and of the *alcalde mayor*, some other guards, and six more Spaniards whom they captured on that road. Added to this is the situation of this kingdom which, as your reverence is aware, makes it so easy for the said [Indian] alcaldes[4] to carry out their evil designs, for it is entirely composed of *estancias*,[5] quite distant from one another.

On the eve [of the day] of the glorious San Lorenzo,[6] having received notice of the said rebellion from the governors of Pecos and Tanos, who said that two Indians had left the Theguas, and particularly the

pueblos of Thesuque,[7] to which they belonged, to notify them to come and join the revolt, and that they [the governors] came to tell me of it and of how they were unwilling to participate in such wickedness and treason, saying that they now regarded the Spaniards as their brothers, I thanked them for their kindness in giving the notice and told them to go to their pueblos and remain quiet. I busied myself immediately in giving the said orders which I mentioned to your reverence, and on the following morning as I was about to go to mass there arrived Pedro Hidalgo,[8] who had gone to the pueblo of Thesuque, accompanying Father Fray Pio, who went there to say mass. He told me that the Indians of the said pueblo had killed the said Father Fray Pio and that he himself had escaped miraculously. [He told me also] that the said Indians had retreated to the sierra with all the cattle and horses belonging to the convent, and with their own.

The receipt of this news left us all in the state that may be imagined. I immediately and instantly sent the *maese de campo*, Francisco Gómez, with a squadron of soldiers sufficient to investigate this case and also to attempt to extinguish the flame of the ruin already begun. He returned here on the same day, telling me that [the report] of the death of the said Fray Juan Pio was true. He said also that there had been killed that same morning Father Fray Tomás de Torres, *guardián*[9] of Nambé, and his brother, with the latter's wife and a child, and another resident of Taos, and also Father Fray Luis de Morales, *guardián* of San Ildefonso, and the family of Francisco de Anaya;[10] and in Poxuaque Don Joseph de Goitia, Francisco de Ximénez,[11] his wife and family, and Doña Petronila de Salas[12] with ten sons and daughters; and that they had robbed and profaned the convents and [had robbed] all the haciendas[13] of

---

[1]   *alcaldes mayores*   I.e., government officials with authority over one of the regions into which New Mexico was divided (with the exception of Santa Fe, which had its own municipal government).

[2]   *religious*   I.e., religious officials.

[3]   *Santo Domingo*   Spanish name for Kewa Pueblo, about 35 miles southwest of Santa Fe.

[4]   *the said ... alcaldes*   I.e., Indigenous officials involved in the revolt.

[5]   *estancias*   Ranches.

[6]   *On the eve ... Lorenzo*   St. Lawrence's feast day is 10 August.

[7]   *Pecos and Tanos ... Thesuque*   Unless otherwise indicated, all the places mentioned in this passage are Indigenous communities.

[8]   *Pedro Hidalgo*   Spanish soldier.

[9]   *guardián*   Official in charge of a mission.

[10]   *Franciso de Anaya*   Spanish military captain.

[11]   *Francisco de Ximénez*   Spanish military captain.

[12]   *Doña Petronila de Salas*   Spanish woman born in New Mexico.

[13]   *haciendas*   Estates.

those murdered and also all the horses and cattle of that jurisdiction and La Cañada.[1]

Upon receiving this news I immediately notified the *alcalde mayor* of that district to assemble all the people in his house in a body, and told him to advise at once the *alcalde mayor* of Los Taos to do the same. On this same day I received notice that two members of a convoy had been killed in the pueblo of Santa Clara, six others having escaped by flight. Also at the same time the *sargento mayor*,[2] Bernabe Marquez, sent to ask me for assistance, saying that he was surrounded and hard pressed by the Indians of the Queres and Tanos nations.[3] Having sent the aid for which he asked me, and an order for those families of Los Cerrillos[4] to come to the villa, I instantly arranged for all the people in it and its environs to retire to the *casas reales*.[5] Believing that the uprising of the Tanos and Pecos might endanger the person of the reverend father custodian, I wrote him to set out at once for the villa, not feeling reassured even with the escort which the lieutenant took, at my orders, but when they arrived with the letter they found that the Indians had already killed the said father custodian; Father Fray Domingo de Vera; Father Fray Manuel Tinoco, the minister *guardián* of San Marcos, who was there; and Father Fray Fernando de Velasco, *guardián* of Los Pecos, near the pueblo of Galisteo, he having escaped that far from the fury of the Pecos. The latter killed in that pueblo Fray Juan de la Pedrosa, two Spanish women, and three children. There died also at the hands of the said enemies in Galisteo Joseph Nieto, two sons of *Maestre de Campo* Leiva, Francisco de Anaya, the younger, who was with the escort, and the wives of *Maestre de Campo* Leiva and Joseph Nieto, with all their daughters and families. I also learned definitely on this day that there had died in the pueblo of Santo Domingo Fathers Fray Juan de Talabán, Fray Francisco Antonio Lorenzana, and Fray Joseph de Montesdoca, and the *alcalde mayor*, Andrés

de Peralta, together with the rest of the men who went as escort.

Seeing myself with notices of so many and such untimely deaths, and that not having received any word from the lieutenant-general was probably due to the fact that he was in the same exigency and confusion, or that the Indians had killed most of those on the lower river, and considering also that in the pueblo of Los Taos the fathers *guardianes* of that place and of the pueblo of Pecuries might be in danger, as well as the *alcalde mayor* and the residents of that valley, and that at all events it was the only place from which I could obtain any horses and cattle—for all these reasons I endeavored to send a relief of soldiers. Marching out for that purpose, they learned that in La Cañada, as in Los Taos and Pecuries, the Indians had risen in rebellion, joining the Apaches of the Achos nation. In Pecuries they had killed Francisco Blanco de la Vega; a *mulata* belonging to[6] the *maese de campo*, Francisco Xavier; and a son of the said *mulata*. Shortly thereafter I learned that they also killed in the pueblo of Taos the father *guardián*, Fray Francisco de Mora, and Father Fray Mathías Rendón, the *guardián* of Pecuries; and Fray Antonio de Pro; and the *alcalde mayor*, as well as another fourteen or fifteen soldiers, along with all the families of the inhabitants of that valley, all of whom were together in the convent. Thereupon I sent an order to the *alcalde mayor*, Luis de Quintana, to come at once to the villa with all the people whom he had assembled in his house, so that, joined with those of us who were in the *casas reales*, we might endeavor to defend ourselves against the enemy's invasions. It was necessarily supposed that they would join all their forces to take our lives, as was seen later by experience.

On Tuesday, the thirteenth of the said month, at about nine o'clock in the morning, there came in sight of us in the suburb of Analco,[7] in the cultivated field of the hermitage[8] of San Miguel, and on the other side of the river from the villa, all the Indians of the Tanos and Pecos nations and the Querez of San Marcos, armed and giving war-whoops. As I learned that one of

---

[1]   *La Cañada*   Spanish name given to the settlements in the Santa Cruz River valley, north of Santa Fe.

[2]   *sargento mayor*   Sergeant major.

[3]   *Queres and Tanos nations*   Keres territory includes a number of pueblos to the southwest of Santa Fe; Southern Tewa (also known as Tano) territory is to the south of Santa Fe.

[4]   *Los Cerrillos*   Spanish name given to a district south of Santa Fe.

[5]   *casas reales*   Spanish: royal houses; i.e., the governor's palace.

[6]   *mulata*   Person of mixed black and white heritage;   *belonging to* I.e., employed or enslaved by.

[7]   *Analco*   Settlement near Santa Fe inhabited by Tlaxcalans (Indigenous Mexicans) who had accompanied the Spanish colonists.

[8]   *hermitage*   I.e., church.

the Indians who was leading them was from the villa and had gone to join them shortly before, I sent some soldiers to summon him and tell him on my behalf that he could come to see me in entire safety, so that I might ascertain from him the purpose for which they were coming. Upon receiving this message he came to where I was, and, since he was known, as I say, I asked him how it was that he had gone crazy too—being an Indian who spoke our language, was so intelligent, and had lived all his life in the villa among the Spaniards, where I had placed such confidence in him—and was now coming as a leader of the Indian rebels. He replied to me that they had elected him as their captain, and that they were carrying two banners, one white and the other red, and that the white one signified peace and the red one war. Thus if we wished to choose the white it must be [upon our agreeing] to leave the country, and if we chose the red, we must perish, because the rebels were numerous and we were very few; there was no alternative, inasmuch as they had killed so many religious and Spaniards.

On hearing this reply, I spoke to him very persuasively, to the effect that he and the rest of his followers were Catholic Christians, [asking] how they expected to live without the religious; and said that even though they had committed so many atrocities, still there was a remedy, for if they would return to obedience to his Majesty they would be pardoned; and that thus he should go back to this people and tell them in my name all that had been said to him, and persuade them to [agree to] it and to withdraw from where they were; and that he was to advise me of what they might reply. He came back from there after a short time, saying that his people asked that all classes of Indians who were in our power be given up to them, both those in the service of the Spaniards and those of the Mexican nation of that suburb of Analco. He demanded also that his wife and children be given up to him, and likewise that all the Apache men and women whom the Spaniards had captured in war [be turned over to them], inasmuch as some Apaches who were among them were asking for them. If these things were not done they would declare war immediately, and they were unwilling to leave the place where they were because they were awaiting the Taos, Percuries, and Theguas nations, with whose aid they would destroy us.

Seeing his determination, and what they demanded of us, and especially the fact that it was untrue that there were any Apaches among them, because they were at war with all of them, and that these parleys were intended solely to obtain his wife and children and to gain time for the arrival of the other rebellious nations to join them and besiege us, and that during this time they were robbing and sacking what was in the said hermitage and the houses of the Mexicans, I told him (having given him all the preceding admonitions as a Christian and a Catholic) to return to his people and say to them that unless they immediately desisted from sacking the houses and dispersed, I would send to drive them away from there. Whereupon he went back, and his people received him with peals of bells and trumpets, giving loud shouts in sign of war.

With this, seeing after a short time that they not only did not cease the pillage but were advancing toward the villa with shamelessness and mockery, I ordered all the soldiers to go out and attack them until they succeeded in dislodging them from that place. Advancing for this purpose, they joined battle, killing some at the first encounter. Finding themselves repulsed, they took shelter and fortified themselves in the said hermitage and the houses of the Mexicans, from which they defended themselves a part of the day with the firearms that they had and with arrows. Having set fire to some of the houses in which they were, thus having them surrounded and at the point of perishing, there appeared on the road from Thesuque a band of the people whom they were awaiting, who were all the Teguas. Thus it was necessary to go to prevent these latter from passing on to the villa, because the *casas reales* were poorly defended; whereupon the said Tanos and Pecos fled to the mountains and the two parties joined together, sleeping that night in the sierra of the villa. Many of the rebels remained dead and wounded, and our men retired to the *casas reales* with one soldier killed and the *maese de campo*, Francisco Gómez, and some fourteen or fifteen soldiers wounded, to attend them and entrench and fortify ourselves as best we could.

On the morning of the following day, Wednesday, I saw the enemy come down all together from the sierra where they had slept, toward the villa. Mounting my horse, I went out with the few forces that I had to meet them, above the convent. The enemy saw me and halted, making ready to resist the attack. They took up a better position, gaining the eminence[1] of some ravines and thick timber,[2] and began to give war-whoops, as if daring me to attack them.

I paused thus for a short time, in battle formation, and the enemy turned aside from the eminence and went nearer the sierras, to gain the one which comes down behind the house of the *maese de campo*, Francisco Gómez. There they took up their position, and this day passed without our having any further engagements or skirmishes than had already occurred, we taking care that they should not throw themselves upon us and burn the church and the houses of the villa.

The next day, Thursday, the enemy obliged us to take the same step as on the day before of mounting on horseback in fighting formation. There were only some light skirmishes to prevent their burning and sacking some of the houses which were at a distance from the main part of the villa. I knew well enough that these dilatory tactics were to give time for the people of the other nations who were missing to join them in order to besiege and attempt to destroy us, but the height of the places in which they were, so favorable to them and on the contrary so unfavorable to us, made it impossible for us to go and drive them out before they should all be joined together.

On the next day, Friday, the nations of the Taos, Pecuries, Hemes,[3] and Querez having assembled during the past night, when dawn came more than 2,500 Indians fell upon us in the villa, fortifying and entrenching themselves in all its houses and at the entrances of all the streets, and cutting off our water, which comes through the *arroyo*[4] and the irrigation canal in front of the *casas reales*. They burned the holy temple and many houses in the villa. We had several skirmishes over possession of the water, but, seeing that it was impossible to hold even this against them, and almost all the soldiers of the post being already wounded, I endeavored to fortify myself in the *casas*

reales and to make a defense without leaving their walls. [The Indians were] so dexterous[5] and so bold that they came to set fire to the doors of the fortified tower of Nuestra Señora de las Casas Reales,[6] and, seeing such audacity, and the manifest risk that we ran of having the *casas reales* set on fire, I resolved to make a sally[7] into the plaza of the said *casas reales* with all my available force of soldiers, without any protection, to attempt to prevent the fire which the enemy was trying to set. With this endeavor we fought the whole afternoon, and, since the enemy, as I said above, had fortified themselves and made embrasures[8] in all the houses, and had plenty of arquebuses,[9] powder, and balls, they did us much damage. Night overtook us and God was pleased that they should desist somewhat from shooting us with arquebuses and arrows. We passed this night, like the rest, with much care and watchfulness, and suffered greatly from thirst because of the scarcity of water.

On the next day, Saturday, they began at dawn to press us harder and more closely with gunshots, arrows, and stones, saying to us that now we should not escape them, and that besides their own numbers, they were expecting help from the Apaches whom they had already summoned. They fatigued us greatly on this day, because all was fighting, and above all we suffered from thirst, as we were already oppressed by it. At nightfall, because of the evident peril in which we found ourselves by their gaining the two stations where cannon were mounted, which we had at the doors of the *casas reales*, aimed at the entrances of the streets, in order to bring them inside it was necessary to assemble all the forces that I had with me, because we realized that this was their [the Indians'] intention. Instantly all the said Indian rebels began a chant of victory and raised war-whoops, burning all the houses of the villa, and they kept us in this position the entire night, which I assure your reverence was the most horrible that could be thought of or imagined, because the

---

[1] *eminence* Height.

[2] *timber* I.e., trees.

[3] *Hemes* Towa-speaking people whose territory is located to the east of Santa Fe.

[4] *arroyo* Desert creek or river.

[5] *dexterous* I.e., cunning.

[6] *Nuestra … Reales* Spanish: Our Lady of the Royal Palace; i.e., the church.

[7] *sally* Sudden attack made by a force that is under siege.

[8] *embrasures* Openings made in a fortification so that fighters can shoot out.

[9] *arquebuses* Long guns similar to muskets.

whole villa was a torch and everywhere were war chants and shouts. What grieved us most were the dreadful flames from the church and the scoffing and ridicule which the wretched and miserable Indian rebels made of the sacred things, intoning the *alabado*[1] and the other prayers of the church with jeers.

Finding myself in this state, with the church and the villa burned, and with the few horses, sheep, goats, and cattle which we had without feed or water for so long that many had already died, and the rest were about to do so, and with such a multitude of people, most of them children and women, so that our numbers in all came to about a thousand persons, perishing with thirst—for we had nothing to drink during these two days except what had been kept in some jars and pitchers that were in the *casas reales*—surrounded by such a wailing of women and children, with confusion everywhere, I determined to take the resolution of going out in the morning to fight with the enemy until dying or conquering. Considering that the best strength and armor were prayers to appease the Divine wrath, though on the preceding days the poor women had made them with such fervor, that night I charged them to do so increasingly, and told the father *guardián* and the other two religious to say mass for us at dawn, and exhort all alike to repentance for their sins and to conformance with the Divine will, and to absolve us from guilt and punishment. These things being done, all of us who could mounted our horses, and the rest [went] on foot with their arquebuses, and some Indians who were in our service with their bows and arrows, and in the best order possible we directed our course toward the house of the *maese de campo*, Francisco Xavier, which was the place where (apparently) there were the most people and where they had been most active and boldest. On coming out of the entrance to the street it was seen that there was a great number of Indians. They were attacked in force, and though they resisted the first charge bravely, finally they were put to flight, many of them being overtaken and killed. Then turning at once upon those who were in the streets leading to the convent, they also were put to flight with little resistance. The houses in the direction of the house of the said *maese de campo*, Francisco Xavier, being still full of Indians who had taken refuge in them, and

seeing that the enemy with the punishment and deaths that we had inflicted upon them in the first and second assaults were withdrawing toward the hills, giving us a little room, we laid siege to those who remained fortified in the said houses. Though they endeavored to defend themselves, and did so, seeing that they were being set afire and that they would be burned to death, those who remained alive surrendered and much was made of them. The deaths of both parties in this and the other encounters exceeded three hundred Indians.

Finding myself a little relieved by this miraculous event, although I had lost much blood from two arrow wounds which I had received in the face and from a remarkable gunshot wound in the chest on the day before, I immediately had water given to the cattle, the horses, and the people. Because we now found ourselves with very few provisions for so many people, and without hope of human aid, considering that our not having heard in so many days from the people on the lower river would be because of their all having been killed, like the others in the kingdom, or at least of their being or having been in dire straits, with the view of aiding them and joining with them into one body, so as to make the decisions most conducive to his Majesty's service, on the morning of the next day, Monday, I set out for La Isleta,[2] where I judged the said comrades on the lower river would be. I trusted in Divine Providence, for I left without a crust of bread or a grain of wheat or maize,[3] and with no other provision for the convoy of so many people except four hundred animals and two carts belonging to private persons, and, for food, a few sheep, goats, and cows.

In this manner, and with this fine provision, besides a few small ears of maize that we found in the fields, we went as far as the pueblo of La Alameda,[4] where we learned from an old Indian whom we found in a maize-field that the lieutenant-general with all the residents of his jurisdictions had left some fourteen or fifteen days before to return to El Paso[5] to meet the

---

[1]   *alabado*   Praise hymn.

[2]   *La Isleta*   Spanish name given to a Tiwa Pueblo more than 70 miles southwest of Santa Fe.

[3]   *maize*   Corn.

[4]   *La Alameda*   Spanish name given to a Tiwa Pueblo about 60 miles southwest of Santa Fe.

[5]   *El Paso*   Settlement at the southern border of New Mexico, about 300 miles south of Santa Fe.

carts. This news made me very uneasy, alike because I could not be persuaded that he would have left without having news of me as well as of all the others in the kingdom, and because I feared that from his absence there would necessarily follow the abandonment of this kingdom. On hearing this news I acted at once, sending four soldiers to overtake the said lieutenant-general and the others who were following him, with orders that they were to halt wherever they should come up with them. Going in pursuit of them, they overtook them at the place of Fray Cristóbal.[1] The lieutenant-general, Alonso Garcia, overtook me at the place of Las Nutrias,[2] and a few days' march thereafter I encountered the *maese de campo*, Pedro de Leiva, with all the people under his command, who were escorting these carts and who came to ascertain whether or not we were dead, as your reverence had charged him to do, and to find me, ahead of the supply train. I was so short of provisions and of everything else that at best I should have had a little maize for six days or so.

Thus, after God, the only succor and relief that we have rests with your reverence and in your diligence. Wherefore, and in order that your reverence may come immediately, because of the great importance to God and the king of your reverence's presence here, I am sending the said *maese de campo*, Pedro de Leyba, with the rest of the men whom he brought so that he may come as escort for your reverence and the carts or mule-train in which we hope you will bring us some assistance of provisions. Because of the haste which the case demands I do not write at more length, and for the same reason I cannot make a report at present concerning the above to the señor viceroy,[3] because the *autos*[4] are not verified and there has been no opportunity to conclude them. I shall leave it until your reverence's arrival here. For the rest I refer to the account which will be given to your reverence by the father secretary, Fray Buene Ventura de Berganza. I am slowly overtaking the other party, which is sixteen leagues from here, with the view of joining them and discussing whether

or not this miserable kingdom can be recovered. For this purpose I shall not spare any means in the service of God and of his Majesty, losing a thousand lives if I had them, as I have lost my estate and part of my health, and shedding my blood for God. May He protect me and permit me to see your reverence in this place at the head of the relief. September 8, 1680. Your servant, countryman, and friend kisses your reverence's hand.

Don Antonio de Otermín
—1680

HOW THE SPANIARDS CAME TO SHUNG-OPOVI,[5] HOW THEY BUILT A MISSION, AND HOW THE HOPI DESTROYED THE MISSION
as recorded by Edmund Nequatewa in *Truth of a Hopi* (1936)

It may have taken quite a long time for these villages to be established. Anyway, every place was pretty well settled down when the Spanish came. The Spanish were first heard of at Zuni[6] and then at Awatovi.[7] They came on to Shung-opovi, passing Walpi.[8] At First Mesa, Si-kyatki was the largest village then, and they were called Si-kyatki, not Walpi. The Walpi people were living below the present village on the west side. When the Spaniards came, the Hopi thought that they were the ones they were looking for—their white brother, the Bahana,[9] their savior.

The Spaniards visited Shung-opovi several times before the missions were established. The people of Mishongovi[10] welcomed them so the priest who was with the white men built the first Hopi mission at

---

[1] *Fray Cristóbal* Stopping place about halfway between Santa Fe and El Paso.

[2] *Las Nutrias* Stopping place about 50 miles south of La Alameda.

[3] *viceroy* I.e., senior government official in charge of New Spain.

[4] *autos* Legal documents.

---

[5] *SHUNG-OPOVI* One of the villages of Second Mesa, one of the three mesas (flat-topped elevated areas) where Hopi villages are located.

[6] *Zuni* Pueblo of the Zuni people, southeast of the Hopi mesas.

[7] *Awatovi* A large, important village before Spanish conquest, Awatovi was destroyed near the end of the eighteenth century and was never rebuilt.

[8] *Walpi* Hopi village on the First Mesa.

[9] *Bahana* According to Nequatewa, the Bahana (the "white man") came into the world at the same time as the Hopi people and left to find great knowledge; the true Bahana would one day return bearing this knowledge and would "make peace and do away with all evil."

[10] *Mishongovi* Another village of the Second Mesa.

Mishongovi. The people of Shung-opovi were at first afraid of the priests but later they decided he was really the Bahana, the savior, and let him build a mission at Shung-opovi.

Well, about this time the Strap Clan were ruling at Shung-opovi and they were the ones that gave permission to establish the mission. The Spaniards, whom they called Castilla, told the people that they had much more power than all their chiefs and a whole lot more power than the witches. The people were very much afraid of them, particularly if they had much more power than the witches. They were so scared that they could do nothing but allow themselves to be made slaves. Whatever they wanted done must be done. Any man in power that was in this position the Hopi called *Tota-achi*, which means a grouchy person that will not do anything himself, like a child. They couldn't refuse, or they would be slashed to death or punished in some way. There were two *Tota-achi*.

The missionary did not like the ceremonies. He did not like the Kachinas[1] and he destroyed the altars and the customs. He called it idol worship and burned up all the ceremonial things in the plaza.

When the Priests started to build the mission, the men were sent away over near the San Francisco peaks to get the pine or spruce beams. These beams were cut and put into shape roughly and were then left till the next year when they had dried out. Beams of that size were hard to carry and the first few times they tried to carry these beams on their backs, twenty to thirty men walking side by side under the beam. But this was rather hard in rough places and one end had to swing around. So finally they figured out a way of carrying the beam in between them. They lined up two by two with the beam between the lines. In doing this, some of the Hopis were given authority by the missionary to look after these men and to see if they all did their duty. If any man gave out on the way he was simply left to die. There was great suffering. Some died for lack of food and water, while others developed scabs and sores on their bodies.

It took a good many years for them to get enough beams to Shung-opovi to build the mission. When this mission was finally built, all the people in the village had to come there to worship, and those that did not come were punished severely. In that way their own religion was altogether wiped out, because they were not allowed to worship in their own way. All this trouble was a heavy burden on them and they thought it was on account of this that they were having a heavy drought at this time. They thought their gods had given them up because they weren't worshiping the way they should.

Now during this time the men would go out pretending they were going on a hunting trip and they would go to some hiding place, to make their prayer offerings. So today, a good many of these places are still to be found where they left their little stone bowls in which they ground their copper ore to paint the prayer sticks. These places are called *Puwa-kiki*, cave places. If these men were caught they were severely punished.

Now this man, Tota-achi (the Priest), was going from bad to worse. He was not doing the people any good and he was always figuring what he could do to harm them. So he thought out how the water from different springs or rivers would taste and he was always sending some man to these springs to get water for him to drink, but it was noticed that he always chose the men who had pretty wives. He tried to send them far away so that they would be gone two or three days, so it was not very long until they began to see what he was doing. The men were even sent to the Little Colorado River[2] to get water for him, or to Moencopi.[3] Finally, when a man was sent out he'd go out into the rocks and hide, and when the night came he would come home. Then, the priest, thinking the man was away, would come to visit his wife, but instead the man would be there when he came. Many men were punished for this.

All this time the priest, who had great power, wanted all the young girls to be brought to him when they were about thirteen or fourteen years old. They had to live with the priest. He told the people they would become better women if they lived with him for

---

[1]   *Kachinas* Katsinas, spirits who play a central role in Hopi belief. Katsina dances (in which masked dancers embody katsinas) were particular targets of suppression by missionaries.

[2]   *Little Colorado River* River almost 50 miles away from Shung-opovi at its closest points.

[3]   *Moencopi* Moenkopi Wash is a tributary of the Little Colorado River; it is now the site of a Hopi village about 50 miles west of Shung-opovi.

about three years. Now one of these girls told what the Tota-achi were doing and a brother of the girl heard of this and he asked his sister about it, and he was very angry. This brother went to the mission and wanted to kill the priest that very day, but the priest scared him and he did nothing. So the Shung-opovi people sent this boy, who was a good runner, to Awatovi to see if they were doing the same thing over there, which they were. So that was how they got all the evidence against the priest.

Then the chief at Awatovi sent word by this boy that all the priests would be killed on the fourth day after the full moon. They had no calendar and that was the best way they had of setting the date. In order to make sure that everyone would rise up and do this thing on the fourth day the boy was given a cotton string with knots in it and each day he was to untie one of these knots until they were all out and that would be the day for the attack.

Things were getting worse and worse so the chief of Shung-opovi went over to Mishongnovi and the two chiefs discussed their troubles. "He is not the savior and it is your duty to kill him," said the chief of Shung-opovi. The chief of Mishongnovi replied, "If I end his life, my own life is ended."

Now the priest would not let the people manufacture prayer offerings, so they had to make them among the rocks in the cliffs out of sight, so again one day the chief of Shung-opovi went to Mishongnovi with tobacco and materials to make prayer offerings. He was joined by the chief of Mishongnovi and the two went a mile north to a cave. For four days they lived there

heartbroken in the cave, making pahos.[1] Then the chief of Mishongnovi took the prayer offerings and climbed to the top of the Corn Rock and deposited them in the shrine, for according to the ancient agreement with the Mishongnovi people it was their duty to do away with the enemy.

He then, with some of his best men, went to Shung-opovi, but he carried no weapons. He placed his men at every door of the priest's house. Then he knocked on the door and walked in. He asked the priest to come out but the priest was suspicious and would not come out. The chief asked the priest four times and each time the priest refused. Finally, the priest said, "I think you are up to something."

The chief said, "I have come to kill you." "You can't kill me," cried the priest, "you have no power to kill me. If you do, I will come to life and wipe out your whole tribe."

The chief returned, "If you have this power, then blow me out into the air; my gods have more power than you have. My gods have put a heart into me to enter your home. I have no weapons. You have your weapons handy, hanging on the wall. My gods have prevented you from getting your weapons."

The old priest made a rush and grabbed his sword from the wall. The chief of Mishongnovi yelled and the doors were broken open. The priest cut down the chief and fought right and left but was soon overpowered, and his sword taken from him.

They tied his hands behind his back. Out of the big beams outside they made a tripod. They hung him on the beams, kindled a fire and burned him.

---

1   *pahos*   Prayer feathers, which are ritually prepared and then used for ceremonial purposes.

Northeastern Woodlands

In the northeastern part of North America, the first Indigenous people to come into contact with early modern Europeans were probably Beothuk, whose home settlers would come to call Newfoundland. Beothuk people may have made contact with English sailors or Basque whalers even before Columbus landed in the Caribbean, but they certainly had solidified trade relationships with Europeans early in the sixteenth century—as did Mi'kmaq people, whose territory extended from Newfoundland to what is now Maine. Many Indigenous peoples further inland and further south along the coast made first contact with European explorers and settlers as the sixteenth century unfolded, and some experienced first contact in the seventeenth century. The transcriptions below of Lenni Lenape (Delaware) oral accounts of "the arrival of the whites" likely reflect encounters with English explorer Henry Hudson's Dutch-financed expedition in 1609. The Lenape accounts appear below in three versions, told and transcribed in the nineteenth, twentieth, and twenty-first centuries. In some versions of the account, the settlers steal land from the Lenape using a trick from classical legend: they asked for as much land as could be encompassed by an animal hide, then, having obtained agreement, cut up the hide into small strips to enclose a larger territory. Scholars disagree as to whether Europeans really attempted to employ this ruse or whether this part of the story is a later addition, borrowed from Western tradition as a metaphor for settlers' actual behavior.

North of La Florida, European attempts to establish settler-colonies were largely not successful until the seventeenth century. But while they did not result in permanent settlements, sixteenth-century explorations and colonization attempts in northeastern North America did inform literary depictions of the continent and its people that would shape the way Europeans thought and wrote about the "New World" in following centuries. Mathematician, scientist, and navigator Thomas Hariot's *A Brief and True Report of the New Found Land of Virginia* (1588), for example, written after his participation in the first failed Roanoke colony in what is now North Carolina, was the first published account of a visit to the Americas to be written in English. As such, it helped to establish a pattern for English-language documents that, as its title page indicates, were addressed to "the adventurers, favourers, and wellwillers of the action, for the inhabiting and planting" of North American settlements. Like many of the later pro-colonization pamphlets it influenced, Hariot's report focuses on the economic advantages colonization could offer to settlers and traders, and most of the document addresses the land's natural resources and suitability for farming. In the portion of the pamphlet excerpted here, Hariot discusses the region's Algonquian-speaking peoples with an eye to their potential as allies or enemies of English colonies. He was better prepared than most of the English to forge connections with the colony's Indigenous neighbors, having learned Algonquian from the Croatoan chief Manteo and the Roanoke Wanchese, when the two Indigenous men had made a diplomatic visit to London in 1584. Hariot's account, together with the watercolors made by the painter John White based on his experiences of the same Roanoke expedition, constitute the most detailed surviving observations of Indigenous lives by very early English colonists. White's paintings in particular, which were published as engravings in later printings of Hariot's book, had a shaping influence on the way the English imagined Indigenous people during the era.

In seventeenth-century Dawnland—known to English settlers as New England—English settlers were somewhat less focused on religious conversion than their French counterparts to the north,[1] and Puritan attempts at proselytization were largely not as effective as those of Catholic missionaries in other regions. One early attempt at indoctrination of the local Indigenous people was undertaken at Harvard, which in the 1660s began to offer an education in Christian religion and ancient Western languages to Indigenous students, most of whom were members of prominent families seeking insight into the culture of the encroaching settler-colonists. Of the first class of such students, many died, some at least in part because of the unfamiliar way of living; the only one to

---

[1]   See the online component of this anthology for materials related to French colonization centered on the St. Lawrence and Great Lakes regions.

graduate, a Wampanoag sachem's son named Caleb Cheeshateaumauk, died of tuberculosis the following year. During his time at Harvard, Cheeshateaumauk is believed to have authored the oldest surviving document written by an Indigenous person in the English colonies: a letter to the Society for the Propagation of the Gospel in New England, an English organization that funded conversion efforts such as those undertaken at Harvard. Cheeshateaumauk's letter, written in Latin, reflects its author's education in Western classics as well as his family background in diplomacy.

The Society for the Propagation of the Gospel in New England also funded a translation of the Bible into Massachusett, an undertaking accomplished by the missionary John Eliot and a team of Indigenous translators, many of whom were Harvard students. Eliot's missionary efforts led some Massachusett-speaking Indigenous groups not only to adopt Christianity but also to adopt alphabetic writing in the Massachusett language. One such piece of writing is the legal document reprinted below, according to which the sachem Mittark and his community made a formal agreement never to sell their territory in Aquinnah (Gay Head). In 1703, when two community members attempted to sell their portions of the land, other residents of Gay Head brought forward this document to argue against the legality of the sale. The commission deciding the case heard testimony that the document was in fact a forgery written after Mittark's death; the document was then declared invalid and the sales were allowed to proceed. While it remains unclear whether the document is the 1681 agreement it purports to be or a forgery made two decades later, it is in either case an illustrative example of an Indigenous community harnessing the power of the written document to advocate for itself in an English colonial system that did not recognize the legitimacy of Indigenous forms of record-keeping. While many Indigenous people in other tribes near the English colonies also wrote or dictated letters and other documents for diplomatic purposes, Massachusett-speakers were unusual in the extent of their early adoption of alphabetic literacy. The body of legal and religious documents written in Massachusett from the mid-seventeenth to mid-eighteenth centuries is expansive enough that, in the twenty-first century, it is now being used to facilitate the language's revival after a period of extinction.

Even as Indigenous communities and individuals were quick to make strategic use of the written word, oral tradition never ceased to play a key role in Indigenous literary cultures. The continued importance of orality—and the fact that oral literature continued to develop in response to historical change even as traditional elements were preserved—is illustrated by the career of the Seneca prophet Handsome Lake in the late eighteenth and early nineteenth centuries. Handsome Lake's teachings, known as the Gai'wiio' (Good Message), merge traditional Haudenosaunee practice with Christian (and especially Quaker) influences. Also known as the Code of Handsome Lake, the teachings were carried orally by Handsome Lake and then by his followers; they were eventually written down in the mid-nineteenth century but are still recited formally by adherents. The final selection below is a story that was first transcribed for publication with the Code in 1913, having been passed from Handsome Lake to his relative Chief Edward Cornplanter, who told it to the Seneca scholar Arthur C. Parker. First told hundreds of years after European and Indigenous people encountered each other on the continent's northeastern coast, the story reflects on early colonization and its consequences.

Lenni Lenape (Delaware) Accounts of the Arrival of the Whites

Each of the following accounts of first contact between Lenni Lenape and European people is mediated in a number of ways. The first was told by Willie Longbone (1868–1946), a fluent Lenape-speaker of Oklahoma, who made extensive recordings of his people's language and literature with the assistance of the settler anthropologist Carl Vogelin; the translation was made by Jim Rementer, a settler scholar who has worked for decades on the preservation and revitalization of the Lenape language. The second version, also transcribed by Rementer, is based on the storytelling of Nora Thompson Dean (1907–84), a prominent Lenape knowledge-keeper. These two accounts from the twentieth- and twenty-first centuries are followed by a much earlier version, by the English-born John Heckewelder (1743–1823), a missionary for the Moravian Church who included it in his book on the Lenape and neighboring peoples; he did not give the name of the storyteller who told him the account. This last version communicates at least as much about Heckewelder's own views of the Lenape as it does about Lenape perspectives on Europeans.

THE COMING OF THE WHITES
as told in 1939 by Willie Longbone, recorded by Carl Vogelin, and translated by Jim Rementer, from *Algonquian Spirit: Contemporary Translations of the Algonquian Literatures of North America* (2005)

A long time ago when the whites came across the water the Lenape did not know that they were coming. One man said in his vision song, "Someone wants to come to see us. He will come across the water." A warrior said, "I'll kill him when I see him."

The next year they saw a ship coming in this direction, and the chief [who had the vision] said, "Now that's the one. The one coming is our elder brother," but the warrior said, "Not mine!" When the whites had arrived, the warrior began to say, "I want to overpower him," but the man [chief] said, "This one is our older brother, that's what I said! [Na nën ndëluwèn.]" The white man said, "Oh, [repeating the Lenape word

ndëluwèn], you must be a Delaware!" That is the reason they began to call the Lenape "Delaware." [At this point the sound on the record becomes very distorted, but then it resumes as] "What do you want?" He [the white man] said, "I want a little piece of land, only as much as a cowhide will cover. Will you give it to me?"

[The Lenape answered], "Oh yes, we can give you that much." Ah, but they did not use just the cowhide. They began to cut it into little thin strips so that when stretched out it encircled a large piece of land. [End of recording.]

PREDICTION OF THE ARRIVAL OF THE WHITE PEOPLE
as transcribed by Jim Rementer from multiple tellings by Nora Thompson Dean, from *Algonquian Spirit: Contemporary Translations of the Algonquian Literatures of North America* (2005)

Long ago there was a Lenape man who had remarkable powers. He would often go and meditate. He was able to foresee the future. One day he told his people, "Soon we will have visitors. They will be real white, fair-skinned people, and they will come from the east in a huge vessel. They are a people who will change our way of life."

Not many people believed him, but finally one day the Lenape people saw a ship coming in. And when these men got out of their boat, the Lenape people were much amazed as they had light skin, blue eyes, and light hair. They were very stunned and dumbfounded, but most of the Lenape were so glad that these visitors had come that they put down furs for them to walk on.

But some Lenape wanted to kill the white people and said, "We don't want these people here. We'll just kill them." But the powerful man said, "No, they came to me in a vision. We will not kill them. They might be our brothers. They might bring us good things. They are going to bring us good things, eventually. We want to treat them good."

And so they did. They put furs down for the white people to sit and walk on. They gave the white people seeds, food, and other things they needed. That's the way the prediction was told a long time ago about the arrival of the white people.

INDIAN ACCOUNT OF THE FIRST ARRIVAL OF THE DUTCH AT NEW YORK ISLAND

as recorded by John Heckewelder, *History, Manners, and Customs of the Indian Nations Who Once Inhabited Pennsylvania and the Neighboring States* (1818)

The Lenni Lenape claim the honour of having received and welcomed the Europeans on their first arrival in the country, situated between New England and Virginia. It is probable, however, that the Mahicanni or Mohicans, who then inhabited the banks of the Hudson, concurred in the hospitable act. The relation I am going to make was taken down many years since from the mouth of an intelligent Delaware Indian, and may be considered as a correct account of the tradition existing among them of this momentous event. I give it as much as possible in their own language.[1]

A great many years ago, when men with a white skin had never yet been seen in this land, some Indians who were out a fishing, at a place where the sea widens, espied at a great distance something remarkably large floating on the water, and such as they had never seen before. These Indians immediately returning to the shore, apprised their countrymen of what they had observed, and pressed them to go out with them and discover what it might be. They hurried out together, and saw with astonishment the phenomenon which now appeared to their sight, but could not agree upon what it was; some believed it to be an uncommonly large fish or animal, while others were of opinion it must be a very big house floating on the sea. At length the spectators concluded that this wonderful object was moving towards the land, and that it must be an animal or something else that had life in it; it would therefore be proper to inform all the Indians on the inhabited islands of what they had seen, and put them on their guard. Accordingly they sent off a number of runners and watermen to carry the news to their scattered chiefs, that they might send off in every direction for the warriors, with a message that they should come immediately. These arriving in numbers, and having themselves viewed the strange appearance, and observing that it was actually moving towards the entrance of the river or bay; concluded it to be a remarkably large house in which the Mannitto (the Great or Supreme Being) himself was present, and that he probably was coming to visit them.[2] By this time the chiefs were assembled at York island, and deliberating in what manner in which they should receive their Mannitto on his arrival. Every measure was taken to be well provided with plenty of meat for a sacrifice. The women were desired to prepare the best victuals.[3] All the idols or images were examined and put in order, and a grand dance was supposed not only to be an agreeable entertainment for the Great Being, but it was believed that it might, with the addition of a sacrifice, contribute to appease him if he was angry with them. The conjurers were also set to work, to determine what this phenomenon portended, and what the possible result of it might be. To these and to the chiefs and wise men of the nations, men, women, and children were looking up for advice and protection. Distracted between hope and fear, they were at a loss what to do; a dance, however, commenced in great confusion. While in this situation, fresh runners arrive declaring it to be a large house of various colours, and crowded with living creatures. It appears now to be certain, that it is the great Mannitto, bringing them some kind of game,[4] such as he had not given them before, but other runners soon after arriving declare that it is positively a house full of human beings, of quite a different colour from that of the Indians, and dressed differently from them; that in particular one of them was dressed entirely in red, who must be the Mannitto himself. They are hailed from the vessel in a language they do not understand, yet they shout or yell in return by way of answer, according to the custom of their country; many are for running off to the woods, but are pressed by others to stay, in order not to give offence to their visitor, who might find them out and destroy them. The house, some say, large canoe, at last stops, and a canoe of a

---

[1] *in their own language* I.e., following their manner of telling.

[2] [Heckewelder's note] Henry Hudson, a British navigator and discoverer in the employ of the Dutch East India Company, sailed from Amsterdam in command of the *Half Moon*, in April of 1609, in search of a north-eastern passage. Foiled by the ice in the higher latitudes, he turned southwards, and in September anchored in New York bay.

[3] *victuals* Foods.

[4] *game* I.e., animals for hunting.

smaller size comes on shore with the red man, and some others in it; some stay with his canoe to guard it. The chiefs and wise men, assembled in council, form themselves into a large circle, towards which the man in red clothes approaches with two others. He salutes them with a friendly countenance,[1] and they return the salute after their manner. They are lost in admiration; the dress, the manners, the whole appearance of the unknown strangers is to them a subject of wonder; but they are particularly struck with him who wore the red coat all glittering with gold lace, which they could in no manner account for. He, surely, must be the great Mannitto, but why should he have a white skin? Meanwhile, a large *Hackhack*[2] is brought by one of his servants, from which an unknown substance is poured out into a small cup or glass, and handed to the supposed Mannitto. He drinks—has the glass filled again, and hands it to the chief standing next to him. The chief receives it, but only smells the contents and passes it on to the next chief, who does the same. The glass or cup thus passes through the circle, without the liquor being tasted by anyone, and is upon the point of being returned to the red clothed Mannitto, when one of the Indians, a brave man and a great warrior, suddenly jumps up and harangues the assembly on the impropriety of returning the cup with its contents. It was handed to them, says he, by the Mannitto, that they should drink out of it, as he himself had done. To follow his example would be pleasing to him; but to return what he had given them might provoke his wrath, and bring destruction on them. And since the orator believed it for the good of the nation that the contents offered them should be drunk, and as no one else would do it, he would drink it himself, let the consequence be what it might; it was better for one man to die, than that a whole nation should be destroyed. He then took the glass, and bidding the assembly a solemn farewell, at once drank up its whole contents. Every eye was fixed on the resolute chief, to see what effect the unknown liquor would produce. He soon began to stagger, and at last fell prostrate on the ground. His companions now bemoan his fate, he falls into a sound

sleep, and they think he has expired. He wakes again, jumps up and declares, that he has enjoyed the most delicious sensations, and that he never before felt himself so happy as after he had drunk the cup. He asks for more, his wish is granted; the whole assembly then imitate him, and all become intoxicated.

After this general intoxication had ceased, for they say that while it lasted the whites had confined themselves to their vessel, the man with the red clothes returned again, and distributed presents among them, consisting of beads, axes, hoes, and stockings such as the white people wear. They soon became familiar with each other, and began to converse by signs. The Dutch made them understand that they would not stay here, that they would return home again, but would pay them another visit the next year, when they would bring them more presents, and stay with them awhile; but as they could not live without eating, they should want a little land of them to sow seeds, in order to raise herbs and vegetables to put into their broth. They went away as they had said, and returned in the following season, when both parties were much rejoiced to see each other; but the whites laughed at the Indians, seeing that they knew not the use of the axes and hoes they had given them the year before; for they had these hanging to their breasts as ornaments, and the stockings were made use of as tobacco pouches. The whites now put handles to the former for them, and cut trees down before their eyes, hoed up the ground, and put the stockings on their legs. Here, they say, a general laughter ensued among the Indians, that they had remained ignorant of the use of such valuable implements, and had borne the weight of such heavy metal hanging to their necks, for such a length of time. They took every white man they saw for an inferior Mannitto attendant upon the supreme Deity who shone superior in the red and laced clothes.

As the whites became daily more familiar with the Indians, they at last proposed to stay with them, and asked only for so much ground for a garden spot as, they said, the hide of a bullock would cover or encompass, which hide was spread before them. The Indians readily granted this apparently reasonable request; but the whites then took a knife, and beginning at one end of the hide, cut it up to a long rope, not thicker than a child's finger, so that by the time the whole was cut

---

[1]   *countenance* Facial expression.

[2]   [Heckewelder's note]   Hackhack is properly a gourd; but since they have not seen glass bottles and decanters, they call them by the same name.

up, it made a great heap; they then took the rope at one end, and drew it gently along, carefully avoiding its breaking. It was drawn out into a circular form, and being closed at its ends, encompassed a large piece of ground. The Indians were surprised at the superior wit of the whites,[1] but did not wish to contend with them about a little land, as they had still enough themselves. The white and red men lived contentedly together for a long time, though the former from time to time asked for more land, which was readily obtained, and thus they gradually proceeded higher up the Mahicannittuck,[2] until the Indians began to believe that they would soon want all their country, which in the end proved true.

from Thomas Hariot, *A Brief and True Report of the New Found Land of Virginia*[3]

OF THE NATURE AND MANNERS OF THE PEOPLE

It resteth I speak[4] a word or two of the natural inhabitants, their natures and manners, leaving large discourse thereof until time more convenient hereafter: now only so far forth, as that you may know, how that they in respect of troubling our inhabiting and planting, are not to be feared; but that they shall have cause both to fear and love us, that shall inhabit with them.

They are a people clothed with loose mantles[5] made of deer skins, and aprons of the same round about their middles; all else naked; of such a difference of statures only as we in England; having no edge tools or weapons of iron or steel to offend us withal, neither know they how to make any: those weapons that they have, are only bows made of Witch-hazel, and arrows of reeds; flat edged truncheons also of wood about a yard long, neither have they anything to defend themselves

but targets[6] made of barks; and some armors made of sticks wickered[7] together with thread.

Their towns are but small, and near the sea coast but few, some containing but 10 or 12 houses, some 20; the greatest that we have seen have been but of 30 houses; if they be walled it is only done with barks of trees made fast to stakes, or else with poles only fixed upright and close one by another.

Their houses are made of small poles made fast[8] at the tops in round form after the manner as is used in many arbories[9] in our gardens in England, in most towns covered with barks, and in some with artificial[10] mats made of long rushes; from the tops of the houses down to the ground. The length of them is commonly double to the breadth, in some places they are but 12 and 16 yards long, and in other some we have seen of four and twenty.

In some places of the country one only town belongeth to the government of a *Wiróans* or chief Lord; in other some two or three, in some six, eight, and more; the greatest *Wiróans* that yet we had dealing with had but eighteen towns in his government, and able to make not above seven or eight hundred fighting men at the most: The language of every government is different from any other, and the farther they are distant the greater is the difference.

Their manner of wars amongst themselves is either by sudden surprising one another most commonly about the dawning of the day, or moonlight; or else by ambushes, or some subtle devices:[11] Set battles are very rare, except it fall out where there are many trees, where either part may have some hope of defence, after the delivery of every arrow, in leaping behind some or other.

If there fall out any wars between us and them, what their fight is likely to be, we having advantages against so many manner of ways, as by our discipline, our strange weapons and devices else; especially by ordnance great and small, it may be easily imagined; by

---

[1] [Heckewelder's note] These Dutchmen were probably acquainted with what is related of Queen Dido in ancient history, and thus turned their classical knowledge to a good account. [According to classical legend, Dido founded Carthage by obtaining land using a similar trick.]

[2] *Mahicannittuck* Known to settlers as the Hudson River.

[3] The present text is based on the first edition (1588).

[4] *It resteth I speak* It remains for me to speak.

[5] *mantles* Cloaks or other loose garments.

[6] *targets* Light shields.

[7] *wickered* I.e., woven.

[8] *fast* Secure.

[9] *arbories* Orchards.

[10] *artificial* Human-made.

[11] *devices* Stratagems.

the experience we have had in some places, the turning up of their heels against us in running away was their best defence.

In respect of us they are a people poor, and for want[1] of skill and judgement in the knowledge and use of our things, do esteem our trifles before things of greater value: Notwithstanding in their proper manner considering the want of such means as we have, they seem very ingenious; for although they have no such tools, nor any such crafts, sciences and arts as we; yet in those things they do, they show excellency of wit. And by how much they upon due consideration shall find our manner of knowledges and crafts to exceed theirs in perfection, and speed for doing or execution, by so much the more is it probable that they should desire our friendships and love, and have the greater respect for pleasing and obeying us. Whereby may be hoped if means of good government be used, that they may in short time be brought to civility, and the embracing of true religion.

Some religion they have already, which although it be far from the truth, yet being as it is, there is hope it may be the easier and sooner reformed.

They believe that there are many Gods which they call *Montóac*, but of different sorts and degrees; one only chief and great God, which hath been from all eternity. Who as they affirm when he purposed to make the world, made first other gods of a principal order to be as means and instruments to be used in the creation and government to follow; and after the Sun, Moon, and Stars, as petty gods and the instruments of the other order more principal. First they say were made waters, out of which by the gods was made all diversity of creatures that are visible or invisible.

For mankind they say a woman was made first, which by the working of one of the gods, conceived and brought forth children: And in such sort they say they had their beginning.

But how many years or ages have passed since, they say they can make no relation, having no letters nor other such means as we to keep records of the particularities of times past, but only tradition from father to son.

They think that all the gods are of human shape, and therefore they represent them by images in the forms of men, which they call *Kewasówok* (one alone is called *Kewás*); them they place in houses appropriate or temples which they call *Machicómuck*; where they worship, pray, sing, and make many times offerings unto them. In some *Machicómuck* we have seen but one *Kewás*, in some two, and in other some three; the common sort think them to be also gods.

They believe also the immortality of the soul, that after this life as soon as the soul is departed from the body according to the works it hath done, it is either carried to heaven the habitacle[2] of gods, there to enjoy perpetual bliss and happiness, or else to a great pit or hole, which they think to be in the furthest parts of their part of the world toward the sunset, there to burn continually: the place they call *Popogusso*.

For the confirmation of this opinion, they told me two stories of two men that had been lately dead and revived again, the one happened but few years before our coming into the country of a wicked man which having been dead and buried, the next day the earth of the grave being seen to move, was taken up again; who made the declaration where his soul had been, that is to say very near entering into *Popogusso*, had not one of the gods saved him and gave him leave to return again, and teach his friends what they should do to avoid that terrible place of torment.

The other happened in the same year we were there, but in a town that was threescore miles from us, and it was told me for strange news that one being dead, buried and taken up again as the first, showed that although his body had lain dead in the grave, yet his soul was alive, and had traveled far in a long broad way, on both sides whereof grew most delicate and pleasant trees, bearing more rare and excellent fruits than ever he had seen before or was able to express, and at length came to most brave and fair houses near which he met his father, that had been dead before, who gave him great charge to go back again and show his friends what good they were to do to enjoy the pleasures of that place, which when he had done he should after come again.

What subtlety soever be in the *Wiroances* and Priests, this opinion worketh so much in many of the common and simple sort of people that it maketh them have great respect to their Governors, and also

---

[1]   *want* Lack.

[2]   *habitacle* Home.

great care what they do, to avoid torment after death, and to enjoy bliss; although notwithstanding there is punishment ordained for malefactors, as stealers, whoremongers, and other sorts of wicked doers; some punished with death, some with forfeitures, some with beating, according to the greatness of the facts.

And this is the sum of their religion, which I learned by having special familiarity with some of their priests. Wherein they were not so sure grounded, nor gave such credit to their traditions and stories but through conversing with us they were brought into great doubts of their own, and no small admiration of ours, with earnest desire in many, to learn more than we had means for want of perfect utterance in their language to express.

Most things they saw with us, as mathematical instruments, sea compasses, the virtue of the lodestone in drawing iron,[1] a perspective glass[2] whereby was showed many strange sights, burning glasses,[3] wildfire works,[4] guns, books, writing and reading, spring clocks that seem to go of themselves, and many other things that we had, were so strange unto them, and so far exceeded their capacities to comprehend the reason and means how they should be made and done, that they thought they were rather the works of gods than of men, or at the leastwise they had been given and taught us of the gods. Which made many of them to have such opinion of us, as that if they knew not the truth of god and religion already, it was rather to be had from us, whom God so specially loved than from a people that were so simple, as they found themselves to be in comparison of us. Whereupon greater credit was given unto that we spake of concerning such matters.

Many times and in every town where I came, according as I was able, I made declaration of the contents of the Bible; that therein was set forth the true and only GOD, and his mighty works, that therein was contained the true doctrine of salvation through Christ, with many particularities of Miracles and chief points of religion, as I was able to then utter, and

thought fit for the time. And although I told them the book materially and of itself was not of any such virtue, as I thought they did conceive, but only the doctrine therein contained; yet would many be glad to touch it, to embrace it, to kiss it, to hold it to their breasts and heads, and stroke over all their body with it; to show their hungry desire of that knowledge which was spoken of.

The *Wiroans* with whom we dwelt called Wingina, and many of his people would be glad many times to be with us at our prayers, and many times call upon us both in his own town, as also in others whither he sometimes accompanied us, to pray and sing Psalms; hoping thereby to be partaker of the same effects which we by that means also expected.

Twice this *Wiroans* was so grievously sick that he was like to die, and as he lay languishing, doubting of any help by his own priests, and thinking he was in such danger for offending us and thereby our god, sent for some of us to pray and be a means to our God that it would please him either that he might live or after death dwell with him in bliss, so likewise were the requests of many others in the like case.

On a time also when their corn began to wither by reason of a drought which happened extraordinarily, fearing that it had come to pass by reason that in some thing they had displeased us, many would come to us and desire us to pray to our God of England, that he would preserve their corn, promising that when it was ripe we also should be partakers of the fruit.

There could at no time happen any strange sicknesses, losses, hurts, or any other cross[5] unto them, but that they would impute to us the cause or means thereof for offending or not pleasing us.

One other rare and strange accident, leaving others, will I mention before I end, which moved the whole country that either knew or heard of us, to have us in wonderful admiration.

There was no town where we had any subtle device practised against us, we leaving it unpunished or not revenged (because we sought by all means possible to win them by gentleness) but that within a few days after our departure from every such town, the people began to die very fast, and many in short space; in some towns about twenty, in some forty, in some sixty,

---

[1] *virtue ... iron* Power of magnets to attract iron.

[2] *perspective glass* Viewing device used to see distant objects more clearly, or a viewing device used to produce an interesting distortion or other visual effect.

[3] *burning glasses* Lenses or mirrors that can be used to start fires.

[4] *wildfire works* Flammable substances used as weapons of war.

[5] *cross* Adversity.

and in one six score, which in truth was very many in respect of their numbers. This happened in no place that we could learn but where we had been, where they used some practice against us, and after such time; the disease also so strange, that they neither knew what it was, nor how to cure it; the like by report of the oldest men in the country never happened before, time out of mind. A thing specially observed by us as also by the natural inhabitants themselves.

Insomuch that when some of the inhabitants which were our friends and especially the *Wiroans* Wingina had observed such effects in four or five towns to follow their wicked practises, they were persuaded that it was the work of our God through our means, and that we by him might kill and slay whom we would without weapons and not come near them.

And thereupon when it had happened that they had understanding that any of their enemies had abused us in our journeys, hearing that we had wrought no revenge with our weapons, and fearing upon some cause the matter should so rest: did come and entreat us that we would be a means to our God that they as others that had dealt ill with us might in like sort die; alleging how much it would be for our credit and profit, as also theirs; and hoping furthermore that we would do so much at their requests in respect of the friendship we profess them.

Whose entreaties although we showed that they were ungodly, affirming that our God would not subject himself to any such prayers and requests of men: that indeed all things have been and were to be done according to his good pleasure as he had ordained: and that we to show ourselves his true servants ought rather to make petition for the contrary, that they with them might live together with us, be made partakers of his truth and serve him in righteousness; but notwithstanding in such sort, that we refer that as all other things, to be done according to his divine will and pleasure, and as by his wisdom he had ordained to be best.

Yet because the effect fell out so suddenly and shortly after according to their desires, they thought nevertheless it came to pass by our means, and that we in using such speeches unto them did but dissemble the matter, and therefore came unto us to give us thanks in their manner that although we satisfied them

not in promise, yet in deeds and effect we had fulfilled their desires.

This marvelous accident in all the country wrought so strange opinions of us, that some people could not tell whether to think us gods or men, and the rather because that all the space of their sickness, there was no man of ours known to die, or that was especially sick: they noted also that we had no women amongst us, neither that we did care for any of theirs.[1]

Some therefore were of opinion that we were not born of women, and therefore not mortal, but that we were men of an old generation many years past then risen again to immortality.

Some would likewise seem to prophesy that there were more of our generation yet to come, to kill theirs and take their places, as some thought the purpose was by that which was already done.

Those that were immediately come after us they imagined to be in the air, yet invisible and without bodies, and that they by our entreaty and for the love of us did make the people die in that sort as they did by shooting invisible bullets into them.

To confirm this opinion their physicians to excuse their ignorance in curing the disease, would not be ashamed to say, but earnestly make the simple people believe, that the strings of blood that they sucked out of the sick bodies, were the strings wherewithal the invisible bullets were tied and cast.

Some also thought that we shot them ourselves out of our pieces[2] from the place where we dwelt, and killed the people in any such town that had offended us as we listed,[3] how far distant from us soever it were.

And other some said that it was the special work of God for our sakes, as we ourselves have cause in some sort to think no less, whatsoever some do or may imagine to the contrary, especially some astrologers knowing of the eclipse of the sun which we saw the same year before in our voyage thitherward, which unto them appeared very terrible. And also of a comet which began to appear but a few days before the beginning of the said sickness. But to conclude them from being the

---

[1]   *neither that … of theirs*   I.e., they also noted that we did not show sexual interest in the women of their communities.

[2]   *pieces*   Firearms.

[3]   *listed*   Wished.

special causes of so special an accident[1] there are farther reasons than I think fit at this present to be alleged.

These their opinions I have set down the more at large that it may appear unto you that there is good hope they may be brought through discreet dealing and government to the embracing of the truth, and consequently to honour, obey, fear and love us.

And although some of our company towards the end of the year, showed themselves too fierce, in slaying some of the people, in some towns, upon causes that on our part, might easily enough have been borne withal: yet notwithstanding because it was on their part justly deserved, the alteration of their opinions generally and for the most part concerning us is the less to be doubted.[2] And whatsoever else they may be, by carefulness of ourselves need nothing at all to be feared.[3]

The best nevertheless in this as in all actions besides is to be endeavoured and hoped, and of the worst that may happen notice to be taken with consideration, and as much as may be eschewed.

—1588

John White, Selected Watercolors

The English artist and colonist John White participated in the first two attempts to found an English colony in the Americas, on Roanoke Island, off the coast of present-day North Carolina. White himself would lead the second attempt, which famously ended in disaster with the disappearance of the entire colony's population while he was in England obtaining more supplies. The following illustrations were based on observations made during his first voyage, in 1585, when he was commissioned to document the people, plants, and animals the settlers encountered. White appears to have aimed for accuracy in his depictions, but his drawings tend to focus on elements of particular relevance to the colonizing project—potential sources of food, prospective trade goods and markets, and Indigenous technologies. The Roanoke Colony was established on territory belonging to Roanoke people, but there were many Indigenous groups in the area, and White also visited nearby towns such as Secotan and Pomeiooc. White's watercolors provided the basis for a series of etchings included in a 1590 edition of Hariot's *Brief and True Report*; these etchings circulated widely and had a significant impact on the way Europeans thought about and portrayed Indigenous people in the following centuries.

This illustration of a prominent woman and her daughter in Pomeiooc shows the woman holding a gourd; Hariot identifies it as "a gourd full of some kind of pleasant liquor" but such vessels typically held water. The woman's daughter holds an English doll of high quality—likely a gift recognizing her high status. Hariot's caption notes that the young girls of the community "are greatly delighted with puppets and babes [dolls] which were brought out of England."

---

[1] *accident* Event, especially one that occurs by chance.

[2] *doubted* Feared.

[3] *by carefulness … feared* I.e., they are so attentive in caring for us that we need not fear them.

This illustration shows the Algonquian-speaking community of Secoton. White's descriptions identify, from top to bottom, "Their ripe corn," "Their green corn," and "Corn newly sprung"; "Their sitting at meat"; "Their place of solemn prayer"; "The house wherein the tomb of their herounds [chiefs] standeth"; and "A ceremony in their prayers with strange gestures and songs, dancing about posts carved on the tops like men's faces."

This image, titled "Their Sitting at Meat," does not specify a particular community, but shows people enjoying foods commonly eaten along the coast near Roanoke Island. Hariot writes that "Their meat [food] is maize sodden ... of very good taste, deer's flesh, or of some other beast, and fish. They are very sober in their eating, and drinking, and consequently very long lived because they do not oppress nature."

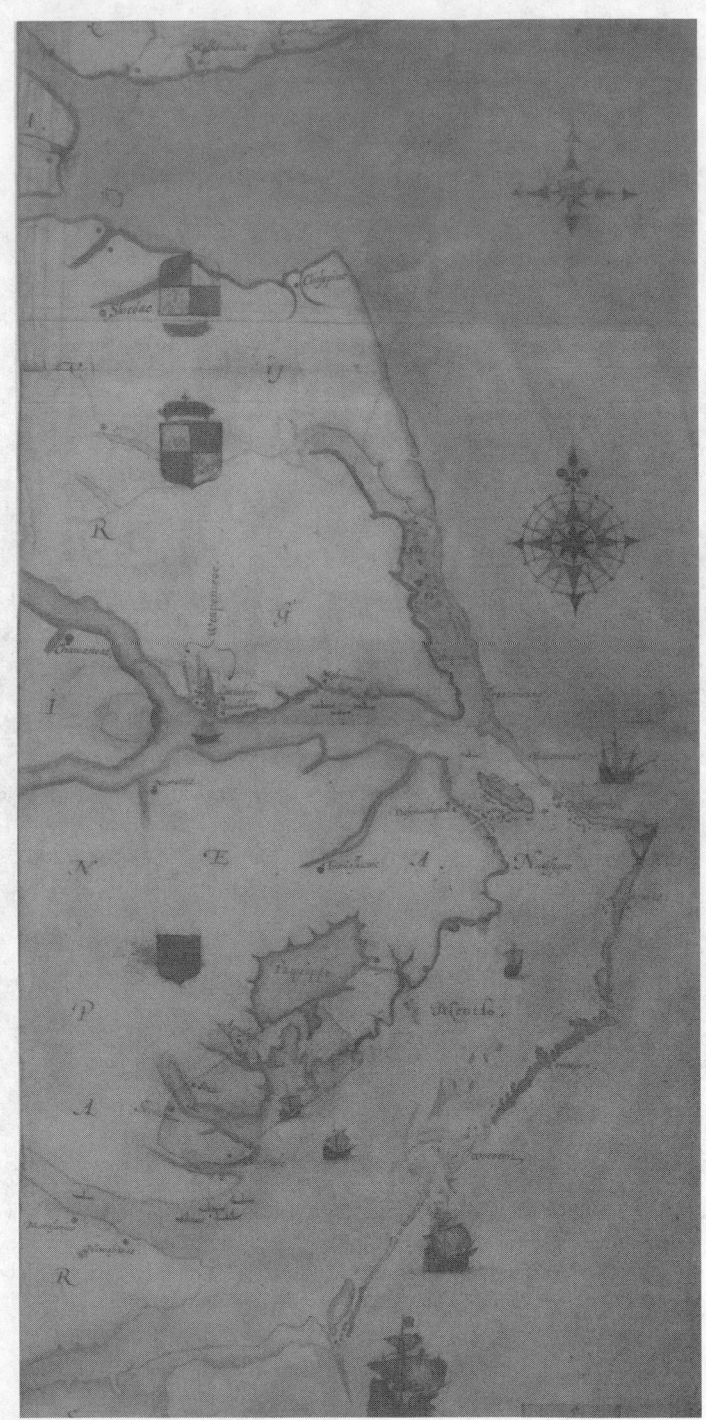

White drew this map of the region surrounding Roanoke based on measurements taken by Hariot and probably other surveyors.

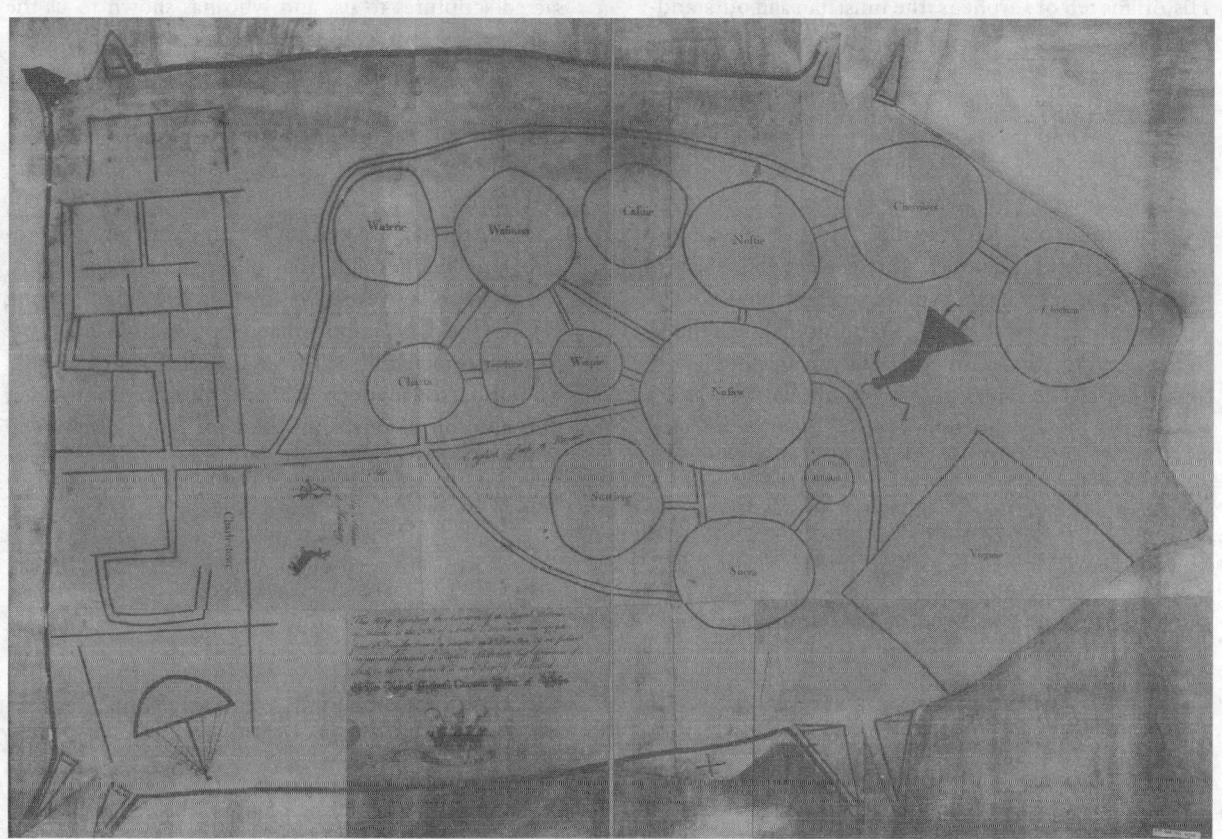

[Catawba Deerskin Map], based on a 1721 original. This map is a paper copy of a lost deerskin original presented by Catawba people to Francis Nicholson, governor of the colony of South Carolina, in 1721. The map shows Indigenous nations between Charles Town in South Carolina (represented to the south at the left side of the map) and Virginia (represented to the northwest in the bottom right corner of the map).

Caleb Cheeshateaumauk, letter to the Society for the Propagation of the Gospel in New England,[1] 1663

Most honored benefactors,

Historians tell of Orpheus, the musician and outstanding poet, that he received a lyre from Apollo, and that he was so excellent with it that he moved the forests and rocks by his song. He made huge trees follow behind him, and indeed rendered tamer the most ferocious beasts. After he took up the lyre he descended into the nether world, lulled Pluto and Proserpina with his song, and led Eurydice, his wife, out of the underworld into the upper.[2] The ancient philosophers say that this serves as a symbol to show how powerful are the force and virtue of education and refined literature in the transformation of the nature of barbarians. They are like trees, rocks, and brute beasts, and a substantive change (metamorphosis) must be effected in them. They have to be secured like tigers and must be induced to follow.[3]

God delegated you to be our patrons, and He endowed you with all wisdom and intimate compassion, so that you might perform the work of bringing blessings to us pagans, who derive our life and origin from our forebears. We used to be naked in soul and body, alien from all humanity, led around in the desert by all sorts of errors.

Oh threefold and fourfold most illustrious and most loving men, what kind of thanks, if not the greatest and most immense, should we give you, for you have supported us with an abundance of all things for our education and for the sustenance of our bodies. You have poured forth immense—the greatest—resources.

And we will especially give great thanks to God the most excellent and highest, who has revealed the sacred scriptures to us, and who has shown to us the Lord Jesus Christ, who is the way of truth and of life.[4] Besides all this, another hope is left us through the depths of divine mercy: that we may become instruments to spread and propagate the gospel among our kin and neighbors, so that they also may know God, and Christ.

Even though we cannot commensurately reciprocate your kindness and that of our other benefactors, we do hope, however. We are not left alone praying before God with importunate supplications for those pious and merciful men who are still in old England, who disbursed so much gold and silver for us to obtain the salvation of our souls, and for you as well, who were instruments like aqueducts in bestowing all these benefits on us.

Most devoted to your dignity:

Caleb Cheeshateaumauk

—1663

Mittark, Agreement of Mittark and His People Not to Sell Land to the English[5]

I am Muttaak, sachem of Gay Head and Nashaquitsa[6] as far as Wanemessit. Know this all people. I Muttaak and my chief men[7] and my children and my people, these are our lands. Forever we own them, and our posterity forever shall own them. I Muttaak and we the chief men, and with our children and all our

---

[1] Translation by Wolfgang Hochbruck and Beatrix Dudensing-Reichel, 1992, 1996.

[2] *Historians tell … the upper* The story of Orpheus and Eurydice appears in numerous classical sources, including Ovid's *Metamorphoses.* Orpheus is permitted to retrieve his dead wife from the underworld on the condition that he not look back at her as she follows him to the surface; he looks back slightly before she reaches the world of the living, and she vanishes. Some early and medieval Christian interpretations of the story, which position Orpheus as a Christ-like or priest-like figure saving souls from hell, do not include this ending; *Apollo* Ancient Greek god associated with the sun and poetry; *Pluto and Proserpina* Latin names for the king and queen of the underworld in classical mythology.

[3] *They are like … to follow* See Horace's *The Art of Poetry* (19 BCE), in which Orpheus is described as "the priest and Interpreter of the gods" who "deterred the savage race of men from slaughters and inhuman diet" and was "once said to tame tigers and furious lions."

[4] *who is the … life* See John 14.6: "Jesus saith unto him, I am the way, the truth, and the life: no man cometh unto the Father, but by me."

[5] Translated by Ives Goddard and Kathleen Joan Bragdon, 1988.

[6] *Gay Head and Nashaquitsa* Territory on the southwestern portion of Noepe, now also called Martha's Vineyard, off the coast of Massachusetts.

[7] *chief men* Members of a sachem's council.

[common] people[1] [present], have agreed that no one [shall] sell land. But if anyone larcenously sells land, you shall take [back] your land, because it is forever your possession. But if anyone does not keep this agreement, he shall fall [and] have nothing more of this land at Gay Head and Nashaquitsa at all forever. I Muttaak and we the chief men, and our posterity, [say]: And it shall be so forever. I Ummuttaak say this, and my chief men: if any of these sons of mine protects my sachemship, he shall forever be a sachem. But if [any of] my sons does not protect my sachemship and sells it, he shall fall forever. And we chief men say this, and our sachem: if any of these sons of ours protects our chieftainship, he shall forever be a chief man. But if any of our sons does not protect our chieftainship and sells it, he shall fall forever. I Umuttaag, sachem, say this and my chief men; [this is] our agreement. We say it before God. It shall be so forever. I Ummuttaak, this is my hand [X], on the date September 11, 1681.

We chief men say this [and] our sachem; this is our agreement. [We say it] before God. It shall be so forever. These are our hands [X — X — X].

I John Keeps am a witness and this is my hand concerning the agreement of Ummuttaak and his chief men of Gay Head and Nashaquitsa, all [and] both. I Puttukquannan am a witness. I witnessed this agreement of Ummuttaak and his chief men of Gay Head and Nashaquitsa, both. No one forever [shall] sell it; they [shall] keep it. I Puttakquannan, this is my hand [X].

I Sasauwapinnoo am a witness. I witnessed the agreement of Ummuttaak and his chief men of Gay Head and Nashaquitsa, all [and] both. I Sasauwapinnoo, my hand.
—1681

Mittark, Agreement of Mittark and His People Not to Sell Land to the English, 1681. An English translation of this Massachusett-language legal document appears above.

HANDSOME LAKE, "HOW THE WHITE RACE CAME TO AMERICA AND WHY THE GAI'WIIO[2] BECAME A NECESSITY"

originally told by Handsome Lake in the early nineteenth century; appearing here as told by Chief Edward Cornplanter (So-son-do-wa) to Arthur C. Parker for *The Code of Handsome Lake, the Seneca Prophet* (1913)

Now this happened a long time ago across the great salt sea, odji′ke′dāgi ga, that stretches east. There is, so it seems, a world there and soil like ours. There in the great queen's country where swarmed many people—so many that they crowded upon one another and had no place for hunting—there lived a great queen. Among her servants was a young preacher of the queen's religion, so it is said.

---

[1] *[common] people* People subject to the sachem. The consent of the common people was essential to decisions regarding the dispensation of land; *[common]* Words believed to be erroneously omitted by the clerk who copied the document have been inserted in square brackets.

[2] *GAI'WIIO* Literally "Good Message," the religious movement founded by Handsome Lake.

Now this happened. The great queen requested the preacher to clean some old volumes which she had concealed in a hidden chest. So he obeyed and when he had cleaned the last book, which was at the bottom of the chest, he opened it and looked about and listened, for truly he had no right to read the book and wanted no one to detect him. He read. It was a great book and told him many things which he never knew before. Therefore he was greatly worried. He read of a great man who had been a prophet and the son of the Great Ruler. He had been born on the earth and the white men to whom he preached killed him. Now moreover the prophet had promised to return and become the King. In three days he was to come and then in forty to start his kingdom. This did not happen as his followers had expected and so they despaired. Then said one chief follower, "Surely he will come again sometime, we must watch for him."

Then the young preacher became worried for he had discovered that his god was not on earth to see. He was angry moreover because his teachers had deceived him. So then he went to the chief of preachers and asked him how it was that he had deceived him. Then the chief preacher said, "Seek him out and you will find him for indeed we think he does live on earth." Even so, his heart was angry but he resolved to seek.

On the morning of the next day he looked out from the opening of his room and saw out in the river a beautiful island and he marveled that he had never seen it before. He continued to gaze and as he did he saw among the trees a castle of gold and he marveled that he had not seen the castle of gold before. Then he said, "So beautiful a castle on so beautiful an isle must indeed be the abode of him whom I seek." Immediately he put on his clothes and went to the men who had taught him and they wondered and said, "Indeed it must be as you say." So then together they went to the river and when they came to the shore they saw that it was spanned by a bridge of shining gold. Then one of the great preachers fell down and read from his book a long prayer and arising he turned his back upon the island and fled for he was afraid to meet the lord. Then with the young man the other crossed the bridge and he knelt on the grass and he cried loud and groaned his prayer but when he arose to his feet he too fled and would not look again at the house—the castle of gold.

Then was the young man disgusted and boldly he strode toward the house to attend to the business which he had in mind. He did not cry or pray and neither did he fall to his knees for he was not afraid. He knocked at the door and a handsome smiling man welcomed him in and said, "Do not be afraid of me." Then the smiling man in the castle of gold said, "I have wanted a young man such as you for some time. You are wise and afraid of nobody. Those older men were fools and would not have listened to me (direct) though they might listen to some one whom I had instructed. Listen to me and most truly you shall be rich. Across the ocean that lies toward the sunset is another world and a great country and a people whom you have never seen. Those people are virtuous, they have no unnatural evil habits and they are honest. A great reward is yours if you will help me. Here are five things that men and women enjoy: take them to these people and make them as white men are. Then shall you be rich and powerful and you may become the chief of all great preachers here."

So then the young man took the bundle containing the *five things* and made the bargain. He left the island and looking back saw that the bridge had disappeared and before he had turned his head the castle had gone and then as he looked the island itself vanished.

Now then the young man wondered if indeed he had seen his lord for his mind had been so full of business that he had forgotten to ask. So he opened his bundle of five things and found a flask of rum, a pack of playing cards, a handful of coins, a violin and a decayed leg bone. Then he thought the things very strange and he wondered if indeed his lord would send such gifts to the people across the water of the salt lake; but he remembered his promise.

The young man looked about for a suitable man in whom to confide his secret and after some searching he found a man named Columbus and to him he confided the story. Then did Columbus secure some big canoes and raise up wings and he sailed away. He sailed many days and his warriors became angry and cried that the chief who led them was a deceiver. They planned to behead him but he heard of the plan and promised that on the next day he would discover the new country. The next morning came and then did Columbus discover America. Then the boats turned back and reported their find to the whole world. Then did great ships come, a good many. Then did they bring many bundles of the five things and spread the gifts to all the men of the great earth island.

Then did the invisible man of the river island laugh and then did he say, "These cards will make them gamble away their wealth and idle their time: this money will make them dishonest and covetous and they will forget their old laws: this fiddle will make them dance with their arms about their wives and bring about a time of tattling and idle gossip: this rum will turn their minds to foolishness and they will barter their country for baubles; then will this secret poison eat the life from their blood and crumble their bones." So said the invisible man he was Hanĭsse´ono, the evil one.

Now all this was done and when afterward he saw the havoc and the misery his work had done he said, "I think I have made an enormous mistake for I did not dream that these people would suffer so." Then did even the devil himself lament that his evil had been so great.

So after the swarms of white men came and misery was thrust upon the Ongwe-oweh[1] the Creator was sorry for his own people whom he had molded from the soil of the earth of this Great Island, and he spoke to his four messengers and many times they tried to tell right men the revelations of the Creator but none would listen. Then they found our head man sick. Then they heard him speak to the sun and to the moon and they saw his sickness. Then they knew that he suffered because of the cunning evils that Hanĭsse´ono had given the Ongwe-oweh. So then they knew that he was the one. He was the one who should hear and tell Gai´wiio‘. But when Ganio‘dai´io‘[2] spoke the evil being ceased his lament and sought to obstruct Gai´wiio‘, for he claimed to be master.

The Gai´wiioi‘ came from Hodiänok´doo[n] Hĕd´iohe‘, the Great Ruler, to the Hadiöyä´geono[n], the four messengers.[3] From them it was transmitted to Ganio‘dai´io‘, Handsome Lake who taught it to Skandyo[n]´gwadĭ (Owen Blacksnake) and to his own grandson, Sos´heowă (James Johnson). Blacksnake taught it to Henry Stevens (Ganishando), who taught it to Soson´dowa, Edward Cornplanter. "So I know that I have the true words and I preach them," adds Cornplanter.

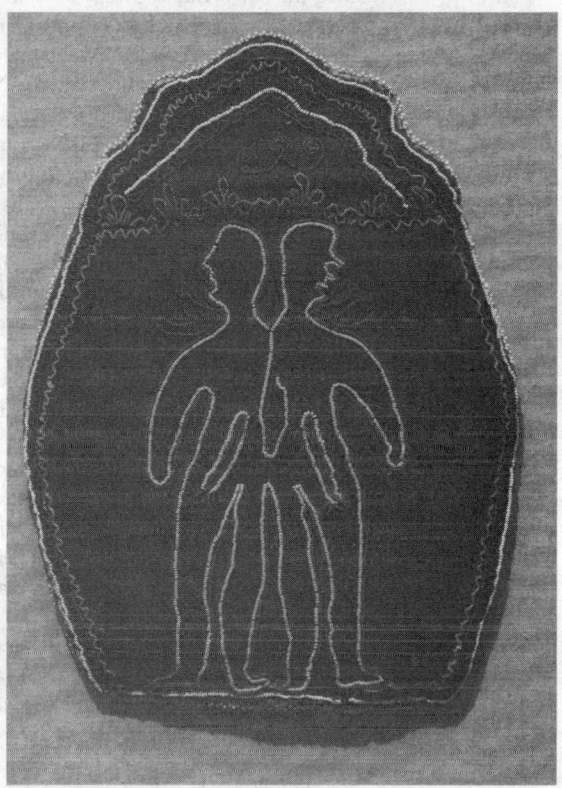

Seneca pouch, early nineteenth century. This pouch, embroidered with an image of the twin brothers central to the Haudenosaunee creation story, references internal divisions among the Haudenosaunee during the American Revolutionary War (1775–84), when members disagreed as to whether to support the American or British sides.

---

[1] *Ongwe-oweh* Literally, "original people," i.e., the Haudenosaunee.

[2] *Ganio‘dai´io‘* Handsome Lake.

[3] *four messengers* Beings who delivered the Creator or Great Ruler's message to Handsome Lake.

In Context

The Myth of Thanksgiving[1]

The American celebration of Thanksgiving has changed over the course of the four centuries since the "first Thanksgiving" of 1621. The holiday has come to represent for many people a celebration of food, family, and friends—all centered on the story and iconography of a myth concerning the Pilgrims of Plymouth and their "friendly relations" with the Wampanoag people of what came to be known as New England. Parades, pageants, costumes, and other revelries have often attended the holiday, perpetuating a myth of harmonious relationships between the Wampanoag and the Puritans and a subsequent gradual, benevolent expansion of the European colony across the territory that became the United States, in the course of which Indigenous peoples gave up their lands and gradually disappeared. Yet very little of this story is based in truth. The first Thanksgiving feast took place during a brief time when a treaty of mutual defense existed between the Pilgrims and the Wampanoag, in what was otherwise a long history of slaughter, domination, and duplicity on the part of the colonists.

The earliest roots of what developed into the American holiday of Thanksgiving can be traced to two accounts of the Plymouth colony's plentiful harvest of 1621, excerpts of which are both printed below: a letter by Edward Winslow printed in *Mourt's Relation* (1622), and a journal entry by Governor William Bradford in *Of Plymouth Plantation* (1651). The successful harvest of 1621, the year following the colonists' first arrival in Plymouth, was crucial to the survival of the fledgling community. For Puritans, a day of Thanksgiving was a solemn occasion declared by the community at any time of year when it saw evidence of God's favor in worldly events. The day would be dedicated to fasting and prayer; similarly, the community would declare days of humiliation or penitence, in which the people would pray for forgiveness when outward events revealed signs that God was displeased. Neither Winslow nor Bradford identified the event they described as a day of Thanksgiving; as there was feasting involved, it was evidently not a formal Thanksgiving but more a day of social celebration. Winslow relates how the sachem of the Wampanoag, Massasoit, came to see the colonists with ninety men. The Wampanoag had made a mutual defense pact with the Pilgrims the year before, and, when the Wampanoag heard gunfire at the colony, brought an army to aid in the colonists' defense. Finding the gunfire was not hostile, the Wampanoag brought additional food to the feast and stayed for three days.

This peaceful meeting was not repeated on a yearly basis, and there was little future occasion to celebrate harmony with the Indigenous peoples of the area. The Puritans continued to hold Thanksgivings and Humiliations, but in response to events in the moment—for example, when grateful for their victories in battle against the friends they had feasted with in 1621. The Thanksgiving held in 1676 was one such occasion, when the Pilgrims stuck the head of Metacom, the son of Massasoit, on a spike, where it was to stay for twenty-five years. The settlers also worked ceaselessly to acquire Indigenous lands using dubious methods, including threats, violence, debt, and false promises.

The modern holiday of Thanksgiving was shaped by more than simply the "origin story" of the 1621 Wampanoag-Pilgrim feast. In 1841, a Unitarian minister named Alexander Young wrote notes in his copy of *Mourt's Relation*, to the effect that the celebration described by Winslow was the "first thanksgiving ... of New England." Then, two decades later, a magazine editor named Sarah Josepha Hale repurposed this language and wrote a letter urging

---

[1]   The editors are indebted to Philip Deloria's excellent article "The Invention of Thanksgiving: Massacres, Myths, and the Making of the Great November Holiday" (*The New Yorker*, 18 November 2019).

Abraham Lincoln to declare a national Thanksgiving holiday to celebrate the union. In 1863, Lincoln agreed. He declared that there would be a national holiday on the last Thursday of November—"Thanksgiving"—a day of national unity in the midst of civil war. Families and friends gathered to share foodways, customs, and leisure activities, and also to pray and mourn the losses from the ongoing civil conflict. From that point on, Thanksgiving began to resemble the holiday we are familiar with today, a celebration of American identity, family, food, and sport. By the early twentieth century, the story of the 1621 feast was woven within this unionist fabric, and the holiday gradually became increasingly celebratory and consumerist, having mainly lost the undertones of war remembrance that Lincoln had urged.

For the Wampanoag and other Indigenous nations of New England, Thanksgiving is observed as a National Day of Mourning. Since 1970, the United American Indians of New England have held protests and vigils on Thanksgiving; Linda Coombs, a member of the Wampanoag nation, has powerfully described what the holiday has come to represent for her people: "When the colonists came over in the 17th century, they had to get rid of us in one form or fashion or another, whether it was converting us, moving us, annihilating us, or shipping us out of the country into slavery, and I just wish people knew that, because this history is not yet well known, but that's what it took for America to be what it is today and for people to sit down to have their Thanksgiving dinner."[1]

from Edward Winslow, "A Letter Sent from New England to a Friend in These Parts," 12 December 1621, published in *Mourt's Relation* (1622)

L oving, and old friend,

Although I received no letter from you by this ship, yet forasmuch as I know you expect the performance of my promise, which was, to write unto you truly and faithfully of all things, I have therefore at this time sent unto you accordingly. …

You shall understand, that in this little time, that a few of us have been here, we have built seven dwelling-houses, and four for the use of the plantation, and have made preparation for diverse[2] others. We set the last spring some twenty acres of Indian corn, and sowed some six acres of barley and peas, and according to the manner of the Indians, we manured our ground with herrings or rather shads, which we have in great abundance, and take with great ease at our doors. Our corn did prove[3] well, and God be praised, we had a good increase of Indian corn, and our barley indifferent good, but our peas not worth the gathering, for we feared they were too late sown, they came up very well, and blossomed, but the sun parched them in the blossom.

Our harvest being gotten in, our governor[4] sent four men on fowling, that so we might after a special manner rejoice together after we had gathered the fruit of our labors; they four in one day killed as much fowl, as with a little help beside, served the company almost a week, at which time amongst other recreations, we exercised our arms, many of the Indians coming amongst us, and among the rest their greatest King Massasoit,[5] with some ninety men, whom for three days we entertained and feasted, and they went out and killed five deer, which they brought to the plantation and bestowed on our governor,

---

[1]   Quoted in Olivia B. Waxman, "400 Years after the 'First Thanksgiving,' the Tribe that Fed the Pilgrims Continues to Fight for Its Land amid Another Epidemic," 23 November 2020, *Time Magazine*.

[2]   *diverse*   Several.

[3]   *prove*   Thrive.

[4]   *governor*   William Bradford (1590–1657).

[5]   *King Massasoit*   Sachem of the Wampanoag confederacy, also known as Ousamequin (c. 1581–1661).

and upon the captain, and others. And although it be not always so plentiful as it was at this time with us, yet by the goodness of God, we are so far from want that we often wish you partakers of our plenty. …

Your loving friend,

E.W.

from William Bradford, *Of Plymouth Plantation*, Chapter 12 Anno Domini 1621 (1856; written 1630–51)

They began now to gather in the small harvest they had, and to fit up their houses and dwellings against winter, being all well recovered in health and strength and had all things in good plenty. For as some were thus employed in affairs abroad, others were exercised in fishing, about cod and bass and other fish, of which they took good store, of which every family had their portion. All the summer there was no want; and now began to come in store of fowl, as winter approached, of which this place did abound when they came first (but afterward decreased by degrees). And besides waterfowl there was great store of wild turkeys, of which they took many, besides venison, etc. Besides they had about a peck[1] a meal a week to a person, or now since harvest, Indian corn to that proportion. Which made many afterwards write so largely of their plenty here to their friends in England, which were not feigned but true reports.

Abraham Lincoln, A Proclamation, 3 October 1863

The year that is drawing towards its close, has been filled with the blessings of fruitful fields and healthful skies. To these bounties, which are so constantly enjoyed that we are prone to forget the source from which they come, others have been added, which are of so extraordinary a nature, that they cannot fail to penetrate and soften even the heart which is habitually insensible to the ever watchful providence of Almighty God. In the midst of a civil war of unequalled magnitude and severity, which has sometimes seemed to foreign States to invite and to provoke their aggression,[2] peace has been preserved with all nations, order has been maintained, the laws have been respected and obeyed, and harmony has prevailed everywhere except in the theatre of military conflict; while that theatre has been greatly contracted by the advancing armies and navies of the Union. Needful diversions of wealth and of strength from the fields of peaceful industry to the national defence, have not arrested the plough, the shuttle[3] or the ship; the axe has enlarged the borders of our settlements, and the mines, as well of iron and coal as of the precious metals, have yielded even more abundantly than heretofore. Population has steadily increased, notwithstanding the waste that has been made in the camp, the siege and the battlefield; and the country, rejoicing in the consciousness of augmented strength and vigor, is permitted to expect continuance of years with large increase of freedom. No human counsel hath devised nor hath any mortal hand worked out these great things. They are the gracious gifts of the Most High God, who, while dealing with us in anger for our sins, hath nevertheless remembered mercy. It has seemed to me fit and proper that they should be solemnly, reverently and gratefully acknowledged as with one heart and one voice by the whole American People. I do therefore invite my fellow citizens in every part of the United States, and also those who are at sea and those who are sojourning in foreign lands, to set apart and observe the last Thursday of November next, as a day of Thanksgiving and Praise to our beneficent Father who dwelleth

---

[1] *peck*   Unit of measurement equivalent to about eight quarts.

[2] *foreign States … aggression*   Confederate forces had hoped for military support from Britain and France, a threat that never materialized.

[3] *shuttle*   I.e., the shuttle used on a loom for weaving.

in the Heavens. And I recommend to them that while offering up the ascriptions[1] justly due to Him for such singular deliverances and blessings, they do also, with humble penitence for our national perverseness and disobedience, commend to His tender care all those who have become widows, orphans, mourners or sufferers in the lamentable civil strife in which we are unavoidably engaged, and fervently implore the interposition of the Almighty Hand to heal the wounds of the nation and to restore it as soon as may be consistent with the Divine purposes to the full enjoyment of peace, harmony, tranquility and Union.

In testimony whereof, I have hereunto set my hand and caused the Seal of the United States to be affixed.

Thomas Nast, *Thanksgiving-Day*, 26 November 1863. This print was inserted as a centerfold in *Harper's Weekly* in 1863, after Lincoln's Thanksgiving Proclamation of the same year. Lady Liberty at prayer is the central figure, with other groups of citizens also praying in the surrounding vignettes, including, at the bottom, a group of enslaved people praying for freedom and giving thanks for emancipation (the Emancipation Proclamation had been issued by Lincoln on 1 January 1863).

---

[1]   *ascriptions*   I.e., prayers (an ascription is the term for the closure of a sermon, when the speaker offers thanks and praise to God).

J.L.G. Ferris, *The First Thanksgiving, 1621*, c. 1912–15. This painting presents an idealized, romantic depiction of the Wampanoag and Plymouth settlers sharing a meal ("the first Thanksgiving") at Plymouth—though the presence of various weapons in the image hints at the precariousness of peace. Ferris produced this painting as part of a series, *Pageant of a Nation*, that presented key moments in U.S. history. Many aspects of this painting have been proven historically inaccurate—for example, there is no evidence that women took part in the feast, and the Wampanoag did not wear feathered headdresses. Their clothes in the painting, too, are more typical of tribes from the Plains.

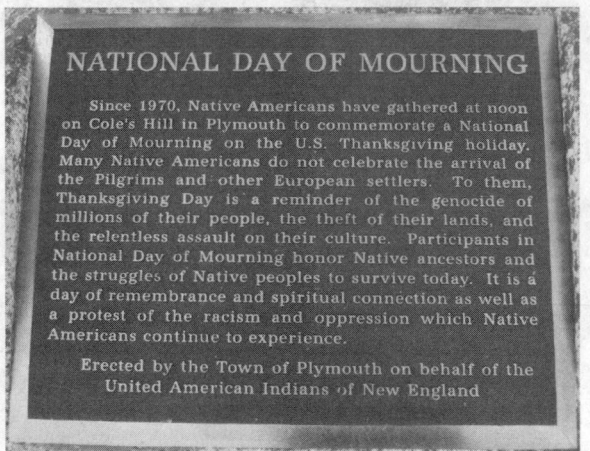

National Day of Mourning plaque, 1998. This plaque was erected by the town of Plymouth as part of a settlement with the United American Indians of New England, after peaceful protesters had been arrested on Thanksgiving Day in Plymouth on 27 November 1997. The settlement not only led to all charges being dropped against the protesters and to the erection of this plaque, but also, according to the statement by the United American Indians of New England, to other reparations: "Plymouth has acknowledged our right to walk on our own land without a permit on National Day of Mourning. Plymouth has agreed to make the truth part of its celebration of the pilgrim myth of thanksgiving. Under the terms of this agreement, we will have a number of important opportunities to address the lies and inaccuracies about 'thanksgiving' and the history of Indigenous peoples that have been disseminated not only in Plymouth but throughout the country. We are confident that this agreement represents a tremendous victory for the struggle of Native people to have our voices heard and respected."

Álvar Núñez Cabeza de Vaca

c. 1490 – c. 1560

In 1542, a work was published in Spain to widespread acclaim, *La relación y comentarios* ["The Account and Commentaries"], a text which told of the travels of a small group of failed conquistadors through the peopled wilderness of North America. To the surprise of many in Europe, the would-be colonizers were, on numerous occasions, assisted by the Indigenous peoples of the region, who seemed to possess substantial riches. One of the few survivors of a disastrous Spanish expedition to colonize Florida (a name that during this period referred to a vast swath of unexplored territory north of New Spain, stretching from the Florida Peninsula to the Pacific coast), Álvar Núñez Cabeza de Vaca was the Spanish explorer and political leader who composed this account. Widely read by Spanish politicians, explorers, and missionaries for its detailed information on the geography, material resources, and Indigenous cultures of North America, the *relación* won its author great fame and political rewards, and inspired many to become conquistadors.

Born in Jerez de la Frontera, Castile (now Spain), Cabeza de Vaca was a member of a minor aristocratic family. In 1527—six years after the Spanish conquest of the Aztec Empire—he was appointed treasurer and chief constable for the expedition of Pánfilo de Narváez, who had been directed by the Spanish king to "discover and conquer and settle" the coast of the Gulf of Mexico. In April 1528, the expedition landed near modern-day Tampa Bay, Florida, then marched inland in search of plunder. Their provisions ran low, and the colonizers suffered serious losses from disease, starvation, environmental hazards, and conflicts with Indigenous groups. By November 1528, only eighty of the approximately six hundred original expeditioners were left alive.

Weakened by illness and hunger, Cabeza de Vaca and a few other survivors had by then made it to an island off the coast of present-day Texas, where they threw themselves upon the mercy of the local Indigenous people. At times, he and his companions were permitted to engage in trade or made to perform faith healing, which they accomplished by reciting Christian prayers over the bodies of the sick. On other occasions, he and his cohort were enslaved, beaten, and forced to perform difficult labor; he was also separated from his companions on several occasions. In September 1534, Cabeza de Vaca and the three others who remained alive—two Spaniards named Andrés Dorantes de Carranza and Alonso del Castillo Maldonado, and an enslaved Moroccan named Estevanico—escaped their captors and set out to connect with the Spanish settlements in what is now western Mexico.

Over the course of their journey, the travelers appear to have earned a reputation among the Indigenous population as faith healers and amassed hundreds of followers, for whom there may have been a religious or ritual element to the relationship. The journey came to an end in the spring of 1536, when Cabeza de Vaca and his party stumbled upon a group of Spanish enslavers near the Gulf of California. Having arrived in Spanish colonial territory, Cabeza de Vaca was disgusted by the mistreatment of local Indigenous peoples, a fact that he claims caused conflict between him and certain New Spanish authorities. Nevertheless, he joined with resident Franciscan missionaries to begin the work of Christianizing the population, commanding them to "build churches and put crosses in them." While here, Cabeza de Vaca and the two other Spanish survivors of the Narváez expedition produced a joint report of the mission, presenting it to the New Spanish viceroy.

In the summer of 1537, Cabeza de Vaca returned home to Spain, where he presented the king a new report on his experiences—one he hoped would win him political favor. A detailed version of this report was released to the public in 1542 as *La relación y comentarios*. A further modified edition of that text was published in 1555 under the title *Naufragios* ["Shipwrecks"]. In an effort to ensure that his report would be "of no trivial value for those who go in [the king's] name to subdue those countries," Cabeza de Vaca made mention of everything that might prove profitable to Spain. He described the various Indigenous nations' languages, physical attributes, forms of social organization, and approaches to war, while taking careful stock of their wealth, agriculture, and material resources.

In 1540, Cabeza de Vaca was appointed governor of Rio de la Plata—today, Paraguay—a region in which Spanish authorities feared warfare with Indigenous peoples was likely to break out. His subjects chafed under his administration, and he was arrested in April 1544 and sent to Spain in chains. In 1551, he was found guilty of political misconduct by the Royal Council of the Indies and stripped of his titles. In 1555, he released an account of his governorship, *Comentarios* ["Commentaries"], which presented him as an honest and peaceful administrator, who was resented by his subordinates for the kindness and mercy he showed in his dealings with Indigenous peoples.

Cabeza de Vaca's self-portrayal as a champion of Indigenous people has proven controversial. Throughout the *relación*, he frequently alludes to their virtuousness, and emphasizes that it is possible to "bring them to a knowledge of the true faith and true Lord." Some scholars maintain that Cabeza de Vaca genuinely appreciated the Indigenous peoples' humanity, suggesting that he advocated for cooperation with—rather than domination of—the Indigenous communities. According to this point of view, the *relación* should be seen as an apology for a peaceful form of colonization, which ought to be considered in conjunction with works such as Bartholomé de las Casas's 1542 text *Brevísima relación de la destrucción de las Indias* ["A Short Account of the Destruction of the Indies"]. Other scholars view Cabeza de Vaca's sympathetic remarks toward Indigenous peoples more cynically, arguing that his remarks were part of a rhetorical strategy to curry favor with the imperial administration. In the eyes of these scholars, rather than view the *relación* as a humane reflection upon the customs of Indigenous nations, we should see it as the reflections of a failed conqueror, whose sole aim was to get away from a population he viewed as irredeemably alien.

Whatever Cabeza de Vaca's true views on Indigenous peoples, the information that he provided about the people and land of North America proved invaluable in Spanish colonization efforts. His report to the king provided intelligence that was used during Hernando de Soto's 1539 expedition to Florida, Fray Marcos de Niza's 1539 search for the legendary Seven Cities of Gold (which was aided by Cabeza de Vaca's former companion Estevanico), and Francisco Vásquez de Coronado's expedition into modern-day Arizona and New Mexico. The ultimate effect of *La relación* was to accelerate the conquest, forced conversion, and displacement of the very people Cabeza de Vaca claimed to admire.

NOTE ON THE TEXT: The excerpts presented below are reprinted with permission from Volume 1 of *Alvar Núñez Cabeza de Vaca: His Account, His Life, and the Expedition of Pánfilo de Narváez* (1999), translated into English by Rolena Adorno and Patrick Charles Pautz. Their translation is based on the 1542 Zamora edition of Cabeza de Vaca's *Relación*.

⌘ ⌘ ⌘

from *The Relación of Álvar Núñez Cabeza de Vaca*

The account that Álvar Núñez Cabeza de Vaca gave of what occurred in the Indies on the expedition of which Pánfilo de Narváez served as governor, from the year [15]27 to [15]36, when he returned to Seville with three members of his company.

Holy, Imperial, Catholic Majesty:[1]

Among as many princes as we know there have been in the world, I think none could be found whom men have tried to serve with truer will or greater diligence and desire than we see men honoring Your Majesty today. It is quite evident that this is not without great cause and reason; nor are men so ignorant that all of them blindly and arbitrarily pursue this course, since we see not only countrymen, whom faith and duty oblige to do this, but even foreigners strive to exceed their efforts. But even when the desire and will of all makes them equal in this matter, beyond the particular advantage that anyone can secure for himself, there is a very great disparity not caused by the shortcoming of any one of them, but only by fortune, or more certainly through no fault of one's own, but only by the will and judgment of God, where it happens that one may come away with more notable services than he expected, while to another everything occurs so to the contrary that he cannot demonstrate any greater witness to his intention than his diligence, and even this is sometimes so obscured that it cannot make itself evident. For myself I can say that on the expedition that by command of Your Majesty I made to the mainland, well I thought that my deeds and services would be as illustrious and self-evident as those of my ancestors, and that I would not have any need to speak in order to be counted among those who with complete fidelity and great solicitude administer and carry out the mandates of Your Majesty, and whom you favor. But since neither my counsel nor diligence prevailed in order that the endeavor upon which we were embarked be completed as service to Your Majesty, and since no expedition of as many as have gone to those lands ever saw itself in such grave dangers or had such a wretched and disastrous end as that which God permitted us to suffer on account of our sins, I had no opportunity to perform greater service than this, which is to bring to Your Majesty an account of all that I was able to observe and learn in the nine years that I walked lost and naked through many and very strange lands, as much regarding the locations of the lands and provinces and the distances among them, as with respect to the foodstuffs and animals that are produced in them, and the diverse customs of many and very barbarous peoples with whom I conversed and lived, plus all the other particulars that I could come to know and understand, so that in some manner Your Majesty may be served. Because although the hope that I had of coming out from among them was always very little, my care and effort to remember everything in details was always very great. This I did so that if at some time our Lord God should wish to bring me to the place where I am now,[2] I would be able to bear witness to my will and serve Your Majesty, inasmuch as the account of it all is, in my opinion, information not trivial for those who in your name might go to conquer those lands and at the same time bring them to knowledge of the true faith and the true Lord and service to Your Majesty. I wrote all this with such sure knowledge that although some very novel things may be read in it, very difficult for some to believe, they can absolutely give them credence and be assured that I am in everything brief rather than lengthy, and it will suffice for this purpose to have offered it to Your Majesty as such, for which I ask that it be received in the name of service, because this alone is what a man who came away naked could carry out with him.

CHAPTER 4
HOW WE ENTERED INLAND

And the next day[3] the governor[4] decided to go inland to explore the land and see what it contained. The commissary, the inspector of mines, and I went with

---

[1]   *Holy, Imperial, Catholic Majesty*   Charles V, who served as Holy Roman emperor from 1519 to 1556 and as king of Spain from 1515 to 1556.

[2]   *the place where I am now*   I.e., his home in Castile.

[3]   *the next day*   The expeditioners landed near modern-day Tampa Bay, Florida, on 12 April 1528. Their intended destination after leaving Cuba had been the Río de las Palmas (believed to be the present-day Río Soto la Marina in northeastern Mexico), where they intended to establish a settlement, but poor weather had landed the ships on the opposite end of the Gulf of Mexico.

[4]   *the governor*   Pánfilo de Narváez, leader of the expedition.

him, with forty men, and among them six horsemen, whose horses were of little use to us. We followed to the north until, at the hour of vespers,[1] we arrived at a very large bay[2] that seemed to us to go far inland. We remained there that night, and the next day we returned to where the ships and crew were stationed. The governor ordered that the brigantine[3] go along the coast toward Florida and look for the port that Miruelo, the pilot, had said he knew. But he had already miscalculated, and he did not know where we were nor where the port was. And the brigantine was ordered, in case it did not find the port, to travel to Havana and pick up Álvaro de la Cerda's ship,[4] and after taking on some provisions, to come to search for us. When the brigantine had departed, the same group of us as before, along with some others, again went inland, and we followed along the coast of the bay we had found and, having gone four leagues,[5] we took four Indians. And we showed them maize to see if they recognized it, because up to that point we had not seen any sign of it. They told us that they would take us to where it can be found. And thus they took us to their village, which is at the back of the bay near there and in which they showed us a little maize that was not yet ready to harvest. There we found many crates belonging to Castilian[6] merchants, and in each one of them was the body of a dead man, and the bodies were covered with painted deer hides. This seemed to the commissary to be a type of idolatry, and he burned the crates with the bodies in them. We also found pieces of linen cloth and plumes that seemed to be from New Spain. In addition, we found samples of gold. By means of signs we asked the Indians where those things had come from. They indicated to us by gestures that very far away from there there was a province called Apalachen,[7] in which there was much gold, and they made signs to

indicate that there were very great quantities of everything we held in esteem. They said that in Palachen[8] there was great bounty. And taking those Indians as guides we departed from there. And going some ten or twelves leagues we found another village of fifteen houses where there was a good-sized plot of sown maize that was ready to be harvested, and we also found some that was dry. And after being there two days, we returned to where the comptroller and the crew and the ships were located, and we told the comptroller and the pilots about what we had seen and the news that the Indians had given us. And the next day, which was the first of May, the governor called aside the commissary, the comptroller, and the inspector, and myself, as well as a sailor named Bartolomé Fernández, and a notary named Jerónimo de Alaniz. And thus all together, he told us that it was his will to enter inland, and that the ships should go along the coast until they arrived at the port,[9] and that the pilots said and believed that going in the direction of the Río de Palmas they were very close to there. And on this matter he requested that we give him our opinion. I responded that it seemed to me that by no means should he leave the ships without first assuring that they remained in a secure and inhabited port, and that he should take notice that the pilots were not convinced, nor were they all affirming the same thing, nor did they know where they were, and that beyond all this, the horses were in such condition that we could not make use of them in any need that might present itself, and that above all we were traveling mute, that is, without interpreters, through an area where we could hardly make ourselves understood by the Indians or learn about the land what we desired to know, and that we were entering into a land about which we had no information, nor did we know what it was like, nor what was stored in it, nor by what people it was populated, nor in which part of it we were located, and that beyond all this, we did not have adequate provisions to enter a place of which we were ignorant, because having seen the stores of the ships, no more than a pound of hardtack and another of salt pork could be given to each man as a ration to take in exploring the land, and that in my opinion we should set sail and go

---

1   *vespers*   In Catholic worship, the evening prayer.

2   *a very large bay*   I.e., Tampa Bay.

3   *brigantine*   Type of small sailing ship that can also be rowed.

4   *Álvaro de la Cerda's ship*   Ship that had been left behind in Havana, Cuba.

5   *leagues*   One league is equivalent to approximately three miles.

6   *Castilian*   From Castile, a region of Spain (the Kingdom of Spain had been formed from the union of the Kingdoms of Aragon and Castile in 1516).

7   *Apalachen*   Region in what is now called the Florida Panhandle.

8   *Palachen*   I.e., Apalachen.

9   *the port*   I.e., on the Río de las Palmas.

to seek a port and a land better for settling, since what we had seen was in itself as unpopulated and as poor as any place that had been discovered in those parts. To the commissary it seemed quite the opposite, he saying that it was not necessary to embark, but rather that, always going along the coast, they should go in search of the port (because the pilots said that going in the direction of Pánuco[1] it would not be but ten or fifteen leagues from there, and that it was not possible, always going along the coast, for us to miss it, because they said that it entered twelve leagues inland), and that the first ones to find it should wait there for the others, and that to embark was to tempt God, because since we departed from Castile we had suffered so many hardships and had experienced so many storms, so many losses of ships and men until arriving there, and that for these reasons he should go along the coast until reaching the port and that the ships with the other men should go along the same route until arriving at the same port. To all the others who were there assembled it seemed appropriate to do this in this manner, except for the notary, who said that, rather than abandoning the ships, they should be left in a known and secure port and in an area that was inhabited; that once this was done, he [the governor] could enter inland and do whatever seemed best to him. The governor followed his opinion as well as what the others counseled him. I, having seen his resolution, requested on behalf of Your Majesty that he not leave the ships without their being in port and secure, and thus I asked that my request be certified by the notary we had there with us. He [the governor] responded that since he agreed with the assessment of the majority of the other officials and the commissary, I had no right to make these demands of him. And he asked the notary to certify that on account of there not being adequate foodstuffs in that land to establish a settlement or a port for the ships, he was moving the settlement that he had established there and was going with it in search of the port and of land that would be better. And then he commanded that the people who were going to go with him be advised to supply themselves with whatever was necessary for the journey. And when this was done, in the presence of those who were there he said to me that since I objected so much and feared the inland expedition, I should stay and take charge of the ships and the people who remained on them and settle the land if I arrived before him. I refused to do this. And after having gone from there that same afternoon, saying that it did not seem to him that he could entrust it to anyone else, he sent me a messenger to say that he was beseeching me to take charge of it. And he, seeing that in spite of entreating me so much I still declined to accept it, asked me why I avoided doing so, to which I responded that I refused to take that responsibility because I was certain and knew that he would not see the ships again nor the ships him, and that I understood this on seeing how unprepared they were to go inland, and that I was more willing than he and the others to expose myself to danger and endure whatever he and the others were to endure than to take charge of the ships and give occasion that it be said, as I had opposed the overland expedition, that I remained out of fear, for which my honor would be under attack, and that I preferred risking my life to placing my honor in jeopardy. He, seeing that he could not prevail upon me, beseeched many others to speak with me about it and beg me to do it, to whom I responded the same as I had to him. And thus, through his lieutenant, he dispatched an order by which an *alcalde*[2] he brought with him, named Caravallo, was to remain with the ships.

from CHAPTER 5
HOW THE GOVERNOR LEFT THE SHIPS

Saturday, the first of May, the same day that this happened, he [the governor] commanded that each one of those who was to go with him be given two pounds of hardtack and half a pound of salt pork. And thus we set out to enter inland. We took with us a total of three hundred men. Among them went the commissary, Fray Juan Suárez, and another friar, who was called Fray Juan de Palos, and three clerics, and the [royal] officials. We the horsemen who went with them numbered forty. And thus we traveled with those provisions, which we carried for fifteen days without finding anything to eat other than hearts of palm of

---

[1] *Pánuco* The crew also hoped eventually to reach the Spanish settlement of Santisteban de Puerto on the Río Pánuco—also on the opposite side of the Gulf of Mexico, south of the Río de las Palmas.

[2] *alcalde* Town government official with administrative and judicial powers.

the type found in Andalusia.[1] During this entire time we did not find a single Indian, nor did we see a single house or village. And at the end [of the fifteen days] we came to a river[2] that we crossed by swimming on rafts with very great difficulty. It took us an entire day to cross it because it had a very strong current. Having crossed to the other side, nearly two hundred Indians, more or less, confronted us. The governor went out to them, and after having spoken to them by means of signs, they gestured to us in such a way that we had to turn on them. And we captured five or six of them, and these Indians took us to their houses, which were a half league from there, where we found great quantities of maize ready to be harvested. And we gave infinite thanks to our Lord for having aided us in so great a need, because since we were most certainly new to these hardships, beyond the fatigue we suffered, we came very worn out from hunger. … [W]e departed from there, always going in pursuit of that province of Apalachen that the Indians had told us about, taking as guides the ones from among them whom we had captured. And thus we walked until the seventeenth of June, during which time we found no Indians who dared to face us. And there, a native lord, carried on the shoulders of an Indian and covered with a painted deer hide, came forth to meet us. He brought with him many people, and before him they came playing reed flutes. And thus he arrived to where the governor was and he spent an hour with him. And by gestures we gave him to understand that we were going to Palachen, and by those which he made, it seemed to us that he was an enemy of the people of Apalachen, and that he would go to help us against them. We gave him beads and bells and other items in exchange, and he gave the governor the deerskin garment he was wearing, and thus he returned. And we went following him in the direction that he took. That night we reached a river that was very deep and very wide and had a very strong current. And because we did not dare to cross it with rafts, we made a canoe for the purpose, and it took us a day to cross it. And if the Indians had wanted to attack us, they could easily have obstructed our passage, and even with their help we had great difficulty. One of the horsemen, who was named Juan Velázquez, a native of Cuéllar,[3] because he did not want to wait, went into the river on his horse, and the current, since it was strong, swept him off his horse, and he held tight to the reins, and thus he drowned and drowned the horse as well. And those Indians of that lord, who was called Dulchanchellin, found the horse and told us where we could find him [Velázquez] downstream, and thus they went to retrieve him. And his death gave us much grief, because up to that point none of us had perished. The horse fed many that night. Once departed from there, we arrived the next day at the village of that lord, and there he sent us maize. That night, where they went to get water, they shot at one of our Christians, and God willed that they not wound him. The next day we left from there without even one of the Indians of that area appearing, because all of them had fled. But following our course, there appeared Indians who came prepared for war. And although we called to them, they refused to return or even hold their ground, but, rather, they retreated, following us along the same road we were traveling. The governor left some of the horsemen behind as an ambush on the road, so that as the Indians passed, they assaulted them and took three or four Indians. And we took these Indians as guides from that point onward; they took us through land very difficult to maneuver and glorious to see, because in it there are very great forests, and the trees wonderfully tall, and there are so many that are fallen upon the ground that they hindered our progress, so that we could not pass without making many detours and having very great difficulty. Of those trees that were not downed, many were split from top to bottom by lightning bolts that strike in that land where there are always great storms and tempests. With these difficulties we walked until the day after the Day of Saint John,[4] when we arrived within sight of Apalachen without being perceived by the Indians of the area. We gave many thanks to God upon seeing ourselves so near it (believing that what they had told us about that land was true, that there the great hardships that we had suffered would end), as much because of the long and difficult road we had walked as because of the great hunger we had suffered. Because although sometimes we found maize, most

---

1   *Andalusia*   Province of southern Spain.

2   *a river*   The Withlacoochee River in what is now central Florida.

3   *Cuéllar*   Prominent town in north-central Spain.

4   *the Day of Saint John*   Catholic feast day in honor of Saint John the Baptist, observed on 24 June.

of the time we walked seven or eight leagues without finding any. And there were many among us who, apart from the great fatigue and hunger they suffered and, since there was no other recourse, had wounds on their backs from carrying their weapons on their shoulders. But on finding ourselves where we desired to be, and where they told us there were so many foodstuffs and so much gold, it seemed to us that a great portion of our hardship and weariness had been lifted from us. …

[The expeditioners remain briefly in Apalachen, raiding a village for supplies and warring with the Indigenous inhabitants. They then continue their journey in search of the Río de las Palmas, with many members of the expedition dying of hunger and thirst along the way. At the end of an arduous sea voyage, during which many more men die, the expeditioners finally land on an island off the coast of what is now Texas. The Indigenous inhabitants of the region prove willing to lend their aid to the weakened crew; it now being winter, they determine to remain on the island until conditions improve.]

from CHAPTER 14
HOW FOUR CHRISTIANS DEPARTED

… [T]he weather turned so cold and there were such great storms that the Indians could not pull up the roots.[1] And from the waterways where they fished there was no yield whatsoever. And as the houses were so unprotected, the people began to die. And five men who were in Xamho on the coast came to such dire need that they ate one another until only one remained, who because he was alone, had no one to eat him. The names of these men were: Sierra, Diego López, Corral, Palacios, Gonzalo Ruiz. The Indians became very upset because of this and it produced such a great scandal among them that without a doubt, if at the start they had seen it, they would have killed them, and all of us would have been in grave danger. Finally, in a very short time, of us eighty men who arrived there from both ends [of the island], only fifteen remained alive. And after these men had died, a stomach ailment befell the Indians of the land, from which half of them died. And they thought that we

were the ones who had killed them. And taking this to be very true, they planned among themselves to kill those of us who remained. When they came to put it into effect, an Indian in whose possession I had been placed told them that they should not believe that we were the ones who killed them, because if we had such power, we would not have allowed so many of our own to die, as they saw, without our being able to prevent it, and that since no more than a few of us now remained, and since none of us did any harm or ill, the best thing to do would be to leave us alone. And our Lord God granted that the others followed this advice and opinion, and thus they were diverted from their intention. To this island we gave the name Malhado.[2] The people we found there are large and well proportioned. They have no weapons other than bows and arrows, which they employ with great skill. The men have one pierced nipple and some have both pierced. And through the hole they make, they wear a reed up to two and a half spans long and as thick as two fingers. They also have their lower lip pierced and a piece of reed as thin as half a finger placed in it. The women are given to hard work. They inhabit this island from October to the end of February. They sustain themselves on the roots that I have mentioned, which they dig out from under water in November and December. They have waterways and they do not have fish apart from this period; from then on they eat the roots. At the end of February they go to other places to look for food because at that time the roots begin to sprout and become inedible. These people love their children more and treat them better than any people in the world. And when it happens that one of their children dies, the parents and the relatives and all the rest of the people weep. And the weeping lasts a whole year, that is, each day in the morning before sunrise, first the parents begin to weep, and after this the entire community also weeps. And they do this at noon, and at daybreak. And after a year of mourning has passed, they perform the honors of the dead and wash and cleanse themselves of the ashes they wear. They mourn all the dead in this manner, except for the elderly, to whom they pay no attention, because they

---

[1] *pull up the roots*   I.e., harvest root vegetables.

[2] *Malhado*   Spanish: Misfortune. Many historians have posited that Malhado, or the Isle of Misfortune, is present-day Galveston Island, off the Texas coast near present-day Houston; others have suggested different possibilities.

say they have lived past their time, and from them no gain is to be had, rather, they occupy land and deprive the children of their share of the food. Their custom is to bury their dead, except those among them who are physicians,[1] whose remains they burn. And while the fire burns, they all dance and make a great celebration. And afterward they pulverize the bones. And a year later, upon paying homage to them, they all lacerate themselves, and to the relatives they give the powdered bones so that they may drink them in water. Each of them has one wife. Among them, the physicians are the most unconstrained; they can have two or three wives, among whom there is great friendship and harmony. When one gives his daughter in marriage, from the day that the one who takes her as his wife marries her, everything that he kills hunting or fishing is taken by his wife to the house of her father without daring to take or eat anything of it. And from the house of the father-in-law, food is brought to the husband, and in all this time [neither] the father-in-law nor the mother-in-law enters his house, nor is he to enter the house of any of his in-laws. And if it should happen that they meet anywhere, they veer a crossbow's shot from their course, and as they go distancing themselves from one another, they carry their heads lowered and their eyes to the ground, because they consider it a bad thing to see or speak with one another. The women are at liberty to communicate and converse with their parents-in-law and relatives. And this custom is common from the island [of Malhado] to more than fifty leagues inland. They have another custom, which is that when a child or sibling dies, in the household in which the death occurs they cease to seek food for three months, but rather they allow themselves to starve. And their relatives and neighbors supply them with the food they are to eat. And because in the time we were there so many of them died, in most of the houses there was very great hunger in the effort to also keep their custom and ceremony. And those who sought food, in spite of their great labors, could find but very little, because the weather was so severe. And for this reason, the Indians who held me left the island, and in some canoes crossed to the mainland to certain bays that had many oysters. And for three months of the year they eat nothing else and drink very bad water. There is a great scarcity of firewood, and there are mosquitoes in great abundance. Their houses are built of woven reeds on top of beds of oyster shells. And they sleep on them on animal skins, if they happen to have them. And thus we were there until the end of April when we went to the seacoast where we ate blackberries the entire month, during which time they do not cease to perform their *areitos*[2] and celebrations.

CHAPTER 15
OF WHAT HAPPENED TO US IN THE VILLA OF MALHADO[3]

On that island about which I have spoken, they tried to make us physicians without examining us or asking us for our titles, because they cure illnesses by blowing on the sick person, and with that breath of air and their hands they expel the disease from him. And they demanded that we do the same and make ourselves useful. We laughed about this, saying that it was a mockery and that we did not know how to cure. And because of this, they took away our food until we did as they told us. And seeing our resistance, an Indian told me that I didn't know what I was saying when I said that what he knew how to do would do no good, because the stones and other things that the fields produce have powers, and that he, by placing a hot stone on the abdomen, restored health and removed pain, and that it was certain that we,[4] because we were

---

[1] *physicians* The original Spanish word here, "fisico," would have had a somewhat broader meaning for Cabeza de Vaca than "physician" does today. Adorno and Pautz note that "fisico" indicated a person who (according to the thirteenth-century Castilian statutory code *Siete Partidas*) understood "the nature of things and their interactions; knowing such things, one can do much good and remove evil, particularly preserving the life and health of men and preventing them from falling ill."

[2] *areitos* Religious songs and dances. The word is derived from the Taíno language, spoken by various Indigenous peoples in the Caribbean, but was adopted by Spanish colonists in reference to many different Indigenous cultures.

[3] THE VILLA OF MALHADO The use of the term "villa" (town) here is misleading and may be the result of an editor's error; the Spanish did not establish any sort of municipality on the island they named Malhado.

[4] *we* I.e., human beings (including both the Spanish travelers and the Indigenous people).

men, had greater virtue and capacity.[1] In short, we found ourselves in such need that we had to do it, without fearing that anyone would bring us to grief for it. The manner in which they perform cures is as follows: on becoming sick, they call a physician and after being cured they not only give him everything they possess, but they also seek things to give him from among their relatives. What the physician does is to make some incisions where the sick person has pain, and then sucks all around them. They perform cauterizations with fire, which is a thing among them considered to be very effective, and I have tried it and it turned out well for me. And after this, they blow upon the area that hurts, and with this they believe that they have removed the malady. The manner in which we performed cures was by making the sign of the cross over them and blowing on them, and praying a Pater Noster and an Ave Maria,[2] and as best we could, beseeching our Lord God that he grant them health and move them to treat us well. Our Lord God in his mercy willed that all those on whose behalf we made supplication, after we had made the sign of the cross over them, said to the others that they were restored and healthy, and on account of this they treated us well, and refrained from eating in order to give their food to us, and they gave us skins and other things. The hunger that we suffered there was so extreme that many times I went three days without eating anything, and they also suffered the same, and it seemed impossible to me to remain alive, although many times afterward, I found myself in even greater hunger and necessity, as I will recount later.

The Indians who held Alonso del Castillo and Andrés Dorantes and the others who had remained alive, since they spoke another language and were of a different lineage,[3] crossed to a different part of the mainland to eat oysters, and they remained there until the first day of the month of April, and afterward they returned to the island, which is probably about two leagues from there at the point where the water is the widest, and the island is a half league wide and five long. All the people of this land go about naked. Only the women cover part of their bodies with a type of fiber that grows on trees.[4] The young women cover themselves with deerskins. They are people who freely share what they have with one another. There is no lord among them. All who are of a single lineage band together. On the island live people of two different languages: some are called of Capoques, and the others, of Han. They have as a custom that, when they know one another and meet from time to time, before they speak they weep for half an hour and when this is done, the one who receives the visit rises first and gives to the other everything he possesses, and the other receives it. And a little while later he goes away with it, and it even happens sometimes that after receiving the goods, they part without speaking a single word. They have other strange customs, but I have told the most important and most notable ones so that I may go and tell what else happened to us. ...

—1542

---

1   *greater virtue and capacity*   I.e., than the stones and other natural healing objects.

2   *a Pater Noster and an Ave Maria*   Latin names for the Lord's Prayer (literally, the Our Father) and the Hail Mary.

3   *The Indians ... a different lineage*   Upon their first arrival on the island they later name Malhado, Cabeza de Vaca and his crew encounter these two other expeditioners who had become separated from the initial expedition. Cabeza de Vaca identifies the Indigenous peoples by whom del Castillo and Dorantes are held as the Yguase and the Mariame.

4   *fiber that grows on trees*   Probably Spanish moss.

John Smith
1580 – 1631

In 1624, fifteen years after his departure in disgrace from the Jamestown colony, John Smith published *The General History of Virginia, New England, and the Summer Isles* in England, commenting on his experiences of the emerging colonization endeavor, on his ambivalent relationship with the region's Native American leaders, and on what he saw as the shameful failures of the people in charge of the colony. "Had we been in Paradise itself, with those governors," he scoffed, "it would not have been much better." The *General History* was Smith's third publication based on his colonial experiences, and he would go on to write several more over the next seven years, earning a reputation both as a writer who had played a significant role in the colonial endeavor and as one who could not be trusted to report the truth. Smith's complex legacy has become only more fraught in the centuries since his death, and he has been simultaneously derided as a self-aggrandizing braggart and hailed as a founding figure of American history and literature.

Smith was baptized in Willoughby, Lincolnshire on 9 January 1580, the first son of well-to-do tenant farmers George and Alice Rickard Smith. Though educated at a respectable grammar school and encouraged by his parents to pursue a merchant career, Smith would later describe himself as having a mind "set upon brave adventures." Shortly after his father's death in 1596, Smith left England and joined a company of soldiers fighting the Spanish in the war for Dutch independence; in 1600 he joined the Habsburg armies in the war against the Ottoman Empire. In his later autobiographical works Smith would colorfully describe his many exploits across northern and eastern Europe, which included the "good success" of decapitating three Turkish soldiers in single combat as well as a subsequent period of enslavement which took him as far as what is now southern Russia before he managed to kill his captor and escape. For his feats of daring in the Long Turkish War, Smith was awarded a coat of arms for which he devised his own motto: "Vincere est vivere"—"To conquer is to live."

Smith's American ventures began in 1606, after King James I of England had signed the "First Charter of Virginia," granting settlement rights in North America to the newly formed Virginia Company. Impressed by Smith's experience, the company's partners named him to the governing committee of the new settlement, making him something of an exception in a group made up primarily of wealthy gentlemen. In December of that year Smith joined the company's first colonial expedition. Tensions between Smith and the upper-class governors began early in the voyage—he was accused of planning a mutiny during the voyage and briefly sentenced to death—and they persisted throughout the next several years, even after Smith was elected to the Company's presidency in September 1608.

The colonists struggled immensely to establish themselves; some historians (and Smith himself) have attributed this to their poor work ethic and lack of competent leadership, though others have pointed out that the Company arrived in Virginia during a period of severe drought. Regardless, Smith's presidency was certainly more austere than that of his predecessors, who had relied primarily on supply missions from England for their survival. By contrast, Smith emphasized agricultural labor and famously declared that "he that will not work shall not eat." Smith also developed a wide knowledge of the region's geography, and cultivated important if frequently ambivalent trade relationships with the local Algonquian nations, including with various leaders of the Powhatan Confederacy; as he writes in a letter to Queen Anne published in the *General History*, "had the savages not fed us, we directly [would have] starved."

By 1609, however, Smith had—like many of the colony's previous leaders—been discredited in the eyes of the council; he was wounded in a gunpowder explosion that autumn, and returned to England in October. He would never visit Virginia again, though he traveled to New England in 1614 on another colonizing venture (and planned other voyages there).

The events of 1606–08 were first recorded in Smith's *A True Relation of Such Occurrences and Accidents of Note as Happened in Virginia* (1608). He revisited this subject several times, most famously in his *General History*, which was published many years after his removal from the colony. It expands significantly on the earlier work, and includes the famous, previously unmentioned account of his near-execution by Powhatan chief Wahunsonacock (sometimes spelled Wahunsenacawh); according to his 1624 account, Smith was on the point of being clubbed to death when the chief's favored young daughter (a historical figure known by several names—Pocahontas, most famously, but also Amonute, Matoaka, and Lady Rebecca Rolfe), put "his head in her arms, and laid her own upon his to save him from death."

Smith's aims as a writer were manifold; in part, he sought to elevate himself as an exemplary colonist, while also—especially in his later writings—publicizing the various failures of his rivals in Jamestown. Texts such as the *General History* were produced within an established tradition of writings about the emerging colonial effort. To that point the genre had mostly comprised works by writers who had themselves never made the Atlantic crossing: as Smith proudly declared, "I am no compiler by hearsay, but have been a real actor."

Smith's later years as a would-be adventurer, however, were marked more by frustration than by triumph. He failed to persuade the Pilgrims to choose him as their guide in 1620, and he failed in a 1621 petition to the London Company to recompense him for his services in Virginia; repeated attempts to regain employment with that Company also proved fruitless. After his last trip to North America, which formed the basis of his *A Description of New England* (1616), he remained in England as a writer. He published the successful *An Accidence, or the Pathway to Experience Necessary for All Young Seamen* (1626), a manual of sailors' terms, and followed up with *A Sea Grammar* (1627), the first sailor's handbook in English. He remained a tireless self-promoter; his autobiography, *The True Travels, Adventures, and Observations of Captain John Smith, in Europe, Asia, Africa, and America, from* Anno Domini *1593 to 1629*, appeared in 1630. Smith's last work, *Advertisements for the Inexperienced Planters of New England, or Anywhere* (1631), again saw him setting himself up as a model for the planters of the "New World."

Smith never married or had children, and died in London on 21 June 1631. His reputation by that point was mixed; his publications had certainly helped spur English interest in the colonization of New England, but his unreliability as a writer was already widely suspected. David Lloyd's ballad *The Legend of Captain Jones*—widely believed to be a satire of Smith—was published the same year that he died.

It was in the nineteenth century that American writers and historians began to perceive and extol Smith as a national hero; Southern author William Gilmore Simms, for instance, declared Smith the "Founder of Virginia" in his 1846 *The Life of Captain John Smith*. Smith's adventures in Jamestown and among the Indigenous peoples of Virginia were the subject for numerous stage plays and works of poetry in the 1800s. In particular, many white writers began to romanticize the story of his relationship with Pocahontas (who had in fact married another English colonist, John Rolfe, in 1614).

In the 1860s and 70s, however, some historians began again to cast doubt upon Smith's reliability as a writer, beginning a scholarly feud that continued well into the early twentieth century. The feud was to a large extent fueled by cultural conflicts between the anti-Smith North and the pro-Smith South. In 1930, prolific Massachusetts-based historian Samuel Eliot Morison concluded that Smith was "a liar, if you will, but a thoroughly cheerful and generally harmless liar." Today, scholars are more likely to concede that Smith provides what he believes to be a factually accurate account of his travels, though his work is inevitably tainted by colonialist as well as other biases—as well as by ambition. Despite the heated debates that still circulate about Smith, about his writings, and about the colonial mission itself, he continues to occupy a prominent position in the mythology of America.

NOTE ON THE TEXT: The excerpts from *The General History of Virginia, New England, and the Summer Isles* are based on the 1624 edition; various transcriptions, including that of the University of North Carolina's Documenting the South project and that prepared by Philip Barbour for his three-volume *Complete Works of John Smith* (1986) have been consulted, as have some older editions (notably Edward Arber and A.G. Bradley's 1910 *Travels and Works of Captain John Smith*). Spelling and punctuation have largely been modernized in accordance with the practices of this anthology, although we have left Smith's rambling sentence structures intact in many cases where modern punctuation practice would call for more periods (and fewer colons, semi-colons, and commas). In the text of Chapter 2 we include a passage in which Smith's original spelling and punctuation have been preserved.

The editors gave serious consideration to the question of whether the speeches by Wahunsonacock (also known as Powhatan) that are embedded within the Smith text should be presented independent of that text; given that the speeches are not reported in other sources and have come down to us in no other form than that mediated by Smith, however, we decided that it would be preferable to present them only in that context. A fuller discussion of the role Wahunsonacock played in the history of the area now known as Virginia is provided in the anthology's online component along with excerpts from Smith's *A True Relation of Such Occurrences and Accidents of Note as Hath Happened in Virginia*.

⌘ ⌘ ⌘

from *The General History of Virginia, New England, and the Summer Isles*

from THE THIRD BOOK

from CHAPTER 1

It might well be thought, a country so fair (as Virginia is) and a people so tractable[1] would long ere this have been quietly possessed, to the satisfaction of the adventurers,[2] and the eternizing of the memory of those that effected it. But because all the world does see a defailment,[3] this following treatise shall give satisfaction to all indifferent[4] readers, how the business hath been carried [out]: where no doubt they will easily understand and answer to their question, how it came to pass there was no better speed and success in those proceedings.

Captain Bartholomew Gosnold, one of the first movers[5] of this plantation, having many years solicited many of his friends, but found small assistance, at last prevailed with some gentlemen, as Captain John Smith,[6] Mr. Edward-Maria Wingfield, Mr. Robert Hunt,[7] and diverse others, who depended[8] a year upon his projects; but nothing could be effected, till by their great charge and industry, it came to be apprehended by certain of the nobility, gentry, and merchants, so that his Majesty, by his letters patents, gave commission for establishing councils, to direct here [in London]; and to govern, and to execute there [in

Virginia].[9] To effect this, was spent another year, and by that [time] three ships were provided, one of 100 tons, another of 40, and a pinnace[10] of 20. The transportation of the company was committed to Captain Christopher Newport, a mariner well practiced for the western parts of America. But their orders for government[11] were put in a box, not to be opened, nor the governors known, until they arrived in Virginia.

On the 19 of December, 1606 we set sail from Blackwall,[12] but by unprosperous winds were kept six weeks in the sight of England; all which time Mr. Hunt, our preacher, was so weak and sick that few expected his recovery. Yet although he were but twenty miles from his habitation ([at] the time we were in the Downs[13]) and notwithstanding the stormy weather, nor the scandalous imputations (of some few, little better than atheists, of the greatest rank[14] amongst us) suggested against him,[15] all this could never force from him so much as a seeming desire to leave the business, but [he] preferred the service of God, in so good a voyage, before any affection[16] to contest with his godless foes, whose disastrous designs[17] (could they have prevailed) had even then overthrown the business, so many discontents did then arise, had he not with the water of patience, and his godly exhortations (but chiefly by his true devoted examples) quenched those flames of

---

[1] *tractable* Tame, easily governable.

[2] *quietly possessed* Peacefully colonized; *adventurers* Investors in the colony.

[3] *all the world ... defailment* I.e., all the world has perceived this venture to have been a failure.

[4] *indifferent* Impartial, open-minded.

[5] *first movers* Initiators.

[6] *Captain John Smith* Smith frequently refers to himself in the third person throughout this text, possibly in part because the *General History* incorporated writing from several other authors.

[7] *Mr. Edward-Maria Wingfield* Soldier and Member of Parliament in England (1550–1631); *Mr. Robert Hunt* Minister who joined the Virginia expedition (1568–1608).

[8] *diverse* Various; *depended* Anticipated.

[9] *his Majesty* King James I of England (1566–1625); *by his letters ... Virginia* In 1606 James I signed the First Charter of Virginia, granting the colonists of the Virginia Company land rights in America. The charter also established corresponding ruling councils in London and Virginia, whose members, while needing to meet the King's approval, could govern relatively freely.

[10] *pinnace* Small sailing vessel, generally with two masts, usually meant to accompany a larger ship. The pinnace was named the *Discovery*; the two other, larger ships were the *Susan Constant*, on board which Smith sailed, and the *Godspeed*.

[11] *orders for government* I.e., decisions regarding who would be appointed to the colony's governing council.

[12] *Blackwall* I.e., Blackwall Yarn, a shipyard on the River Thames.

[13] *the Downs* Anchorage off the coast of Kent in the English Channel, in which ships might seek shelter from storms before venturing into the open ocean.

[14] *greatest rank* Highest status.

[15] *nor ... against him* It was rumored that Hunt had committed adultery with his servant in England, among other accusations.

[16] *affection* Inclination.

[17] *designs* Schemes.

envy and dissention. We watered at the Canaries;[1] we traded with the savages at Dominica;[2] three weeks we spent in refreshing ourselves amongst these West-India Isles. In Guadeloupe we found a bath so hot, as in it we boiled pork as well as over the fire. And at a little isle called Monito, we took from the bushes with our hands near two hogsheads[3] full of birds in three or four hours. In Nevis, Mona, and the Virgin Isles we spent some time, where, with a loathsome beast like a crocodile (called an iguana), tortoises, pelicans, parrots, and fishes, we daily feasted. Gone from thence in search of Virginia, the company was not a little discomforted, seeing the mariners had 3 days passed their reckoning[4] and found no land, so that Captain Ratcliffe (captain of the pinnace) rather desired to bear up the helm to return for England, than [to] make further search. But God the guider of all good actions, forcing them by an extreme storm to hull[5] all night, did drive them by his providence to their desired port, beyond all their expectations, for never any of them had seen that coast.

The first land they made they called Cape Henry,[6] where thirty of them, recreating[7] themselves on shore, were assaulted by five savages, who hurt two of the English very dangerously. That night was the box opened,[8] and the orders read, in which Bartholomew Gosnold, John Smith, Edward Wingfield, Christopher Newport, John Ratcliffe, John Martin, and George Kendall were named to be the Council, and [instructed] to choose a President amongst them for a year, who with the Council should govern. Matters of moment[9] were to be examined by a jury, but determined by the major part of the Council, in which the President had two voices.[10] Until the 13 of May they sought a place to plant[11] in. Then the Council was sworn; Mr. Wingfield was chosen President, and an oration made, [explaining] why Captain Smith was not admitted of the Council as the rest.[12]

Now falleth every man to work: the Council contrive[13] the fort, the rest cut down trees to make place to pitch their tents; some provide clapboard to relade[14] the ships, some make gardens, some nets, etc. The savages often visited us kindly. The President's overweening jealousy[15] would admit no exercise at arms, or fortification, but the boughs of trees cast together in the form of a half moon by the extraordinary pains and diligence of Captain Kendall. Newport, Smith, and twenty others were sent to discover the head of the river: by diverse small habitations they passed, [and] in six days they arrived at a town called Powhatan, consisting of some twelve houses, pleasantly seated on a hill; before it three fertile isles, about it many of their cornfields; the place is very pleasant, and strong by nature; of this place the Prince is called Powhatan,[16] and his people

---

1   *watered* Supplied the ship with fresh water; *Canaries* The Canary Islands, an archipelago off the southern coast of present-day Morocco.

2   *savages at Dominica* The Carib people were at the time the inhabitants of this Caribbean island; Smith uses the pejorative word "savage" indiscriminately to name the Indigenous inhabitants of any location.

3   *near two hogsheads* Almost two barrels.

4   *3 days ... reckoning* I.e., it had been three days since their calculated date of arrival.

5   *hull* Ride by force of the wind alone with furled sails.

6   *Cape Henry* Named for King James's son, Henry Frederick (1594–1612), this cape on the coast of Virginia, along with Cape Charles, forms the entrance to Chesapeake Bay.

7   *recreating* Refreshing or restoring their physical health.

8   *the box opened* An unusual aspect of the venture was that Smith and the others had sailed with a box that contained a list of those the Virginia Company had appointed to govern the colony, and had been given strict instructions not to open the box and read the list until they had arrived.

9   *moment* Immediate importance.

10   *voices* Votes.

11   *plant* Settle.

12   *why Captain Smith ... as the rest* During the voyage Smith had been charged with sedition, treason, and a plot to "make himself king," and had consequently been sentenced to death. When orders arrived from London assigning Smith a leadership position in the colony, he was reprieved from his sentence, though not immediately permitted to take his seat on council.

13   *contrive* Designed. (In this passage Smith alternates between present and past verb tenses.)

14   *clapboard* Thin, overlapping wooden planks used in building as protection from the elements; *relade* Reload.

15   *overweening jealousy* Excessive prudence; the council had been warned by the English investors to avoid inciting any conflict with the local Indigenous peoples.

16   *Prince ... Powhatan* The chief's personal name was Wahunsonacock; that the English referred to him simply as "Powhatan" was likely the result of a misunderstanding based on him having been introduced to them as the Chief of Powhatan.

Powhatans; to this place the river is navigable, but higher[1] within a mile, by reason of the rocks and isles, there is not passage for a small boat; this they call the Falls. The people in all parts kindly intreated[2] them, till being returned within twenty miles of Jamestown, they [the Powhatans] gave just cause of jealousy,[3] but had God not blessed the discoverers otherwise than those at the fort, there had then been an end of that plantation; for at the fort, where they arrived the next day, they found 17 men hurt, and a boy slain by the savages, and had it not chanced [that] a cross-bar shot[4] from the ships struck down a bough from a tree amongst them [the Powhatans], that caused them to retire, our men had all been slain, being securely all at work, and their arms in dry vats.[5]

Hereupon the President was contented the fort should be palisaded,[6] the ordnance mounted,[7] his men armed and exercised, for many were the assaults and ambuscades[8] of the savages, and our men by their disorderly straggling were often hurt, when the savages by the nimbleness of their heels well escaped. What toil we had, with so small a power to guard our workmen a-day, watch all night, resist our enemies, and effect our business, to relade the ships, cut down trees, and prepare the ground to plant our corn,[9] etc., I refer to the reader's consideration. Six weeks being spent in this manner, Captain Newport (who was hired only for our transportation) was to return [to England] with the ships. Now Captain Smith, who all this time from their departure from the Canaries was restrained as a prisoner upon the scandalous suggestions of some of the chief [colonists] (envying his

repute), who feigned[10] [that] he intended to usurp the government, murder the Council, and make himself king; that his confederates[11] were dispersed in all the three ships; and that diverse of his confederates that revealed it, would affirm it. For this he was committed as a prisoner; thirteen weeks he remained thus suspected, and by that time the ships should return they [the Council members] pretended out of their commiserations[12] to refer him to the Council in England to receive a check,[13] rather than by particulating[14] his designs make him so odious to the world, as to touch his life, or utterly overthrow his reputation. But he so much scorned their charity, and publicly defied the uttermost of their cruelty, [that] he wisely prevented their policies, though he could not suppress their envies, yet so well he demeaned[15] himself in this business, as all the company did see his innocence, and his adversaries' malice, and those suborned to accuse him accused his accusers of subornation; many untruths were alleged against him; but being so apparently disproved, begat a general hatred in the hearts of the company against such unjust commanders that the President was adjudged to give him £200 so that all he [President Wingfield] had was seized upon, in part of satisfaction, which Smith presently returned to the store for the general use of the colony. Many were the mischiefs that daily sprung from their ignorant (yet ambitious) spirits; but the good doctrine and exhortation of our preacher Mr. Hunt reconciled them, and caused Captain Smith to be admitted of the Council; the next day all received the Communion,[16] the day following the savages voluntarily desired peace, and Captain Newport returned for England with news; leaving in Virginia 100 [colonists] the 15 of June 1607.

By this observe:
Good men did ne'r their country's ruin bring.

---

[1] *higher* Upstream.

[2] *intreated* Treated.

[3] *jealousy* Anger and mistrust.

[4] *cross-bar shot* Cannonball with a spike protruding from either side.

[5] *arms* Weapons; *dry vats* Storage containers.

[6] *palisaded* Enclosed by a wooden fence.

[7] *ordnance mounted* Cannon or other large artillery positioned for use.

[8] *ambuscades* Ambushes.

[9] *corn* Grain (such as the seeds of wheat and barley); it is only through trade with the Native Americans that the colonists begin to consume maize.

[10] *feigned* Falsely alleged.

[11] *confederates* Alleged co-conspirators.

[12] *commiserations* Compassion.

[13] *check* Reprimand.

[14] *particulating* Making known in detail.

[15] *demeaned* Conducted.

[16] *received the Communion* Took part in the Eucharist, the Christian sacrament in which blessed bread and wine are ingested.

But when evil men shall injuries begin;
Not caring to corrupt and violate
The judgements'-seat for their own lucre's[1] sake:
Then look that country cannot long have peace,
Though for the present it have rest and ease.[2] …

from CHAPTER 2
WHAT HAPPENED TILL THE FIRST SUPPLY

Being thus left to our fortunes, it fortuned that within ten days[3] scarce ten amongst us could either go,[4] or well stand, such extreme weakness and sickness oppressed us. And thereat none need marvel, if they consider the cause and reason, which was this: whilst the ships stayed, our allowance was somewhat bettered by a daily proportion of biscuit, which the sailors would pilfer to sell, give, or exchange with us, for money, sassafras, furs, or love.[5] But when they departed, there remained neither tavern, beer-house, nor place of relief, but the common kettle.[6] Had we been as free from all sins as [we were from] gluttony and drunkenness, we might have been canonized for Saints; but our President would never have been admitted,[7] for engrossing to his private[8] oatmeal, sack, oil, *aqua vitæ*,[9] beef, eggs, or what not, but the kettle;[10] that indeed he allowed equally to be distributed, and that was half a pint of wheat, and as much barley boiled with water for a man a day, and this, having fried some 26 weeks in the ship's hold, contained as many worms as grains; so that we might truly call it rather so much bran than corn.[11] Our drink was water,[12] our lodgings castles in the air. With this lodging and diet, our extreme toil in bearing and planting palisades, so strained and bruised us, and our continual labour in the extremity of the heat had so weakened us, as were cause sufficient to have made us as miserable in our native country, or any other place in the world. From May to September, those that escaped lived upon sturgeon, and sea-crabs; fifty [men] in this time we buried. The rest, seeing the President's projects[13] to escape these miseries in our pinnace by flight[14] (who all this time had neither felt want nor sickness) so moved our dead spirits, as we deposed him, and established Ratcliffe in his place (Gosnold being dead Kendall deposed).[15] Smith newly recovered, Martin and Ratcliffe were by his care preserved and relieved, and the most of the soldiers recovered, with the skillful diligence of Mr. Thomas Wotton our surgeon[16] general. But now was all our provision spent, the sturgeon gone, all helps abandoned, each hour expecting the fury of the savages; when God, the patron of all good endeavours, in that desperate extremity so changed the hearts of the savages that they brought such plenty of their fruits, and provision, as no man wanted.[17]

And now where some affirmed it was ill done of the Council to send forth men so badly provided, this incontradictable reason will show them plainly they are too ill advised to nourish such ill conceits. First, the

---

1 *lucre's* Profit's.

2 *Then look … ease* Smith quotes a translation of Greek poet Theognis of Megara (c. 6th century BCE) found in Martin Fotherby's *Atheomastix: Clearing Four Truths against Atheists and Infidels* (1622), a work that seems to be the source of most of the poetic quotations Smith includes in the *General History*.

3 *within ten days* I.e., by 25 June 1607 (within ten days of Captain Newport's 15 June departure for England to give news of the colony and to bring back fresh supplies).

4 *go* Walk.

5 *pilfer* Plunder or steal; *sassafras* Tree native to eastern North America and Asia, whose leaves, roots, and bark were used for medicinal purposes; *love* Presumably, sexual favors provided by the settlers for the sailors.

6 *common kettle* I.e., collective supplies.

7 *would never … admitted* I.e., would not have been admitted to sainthood.

8 *engrossing to his private* Keeping for his personal use.

9 *sack* White wine from Spain; *aqua vitæ* Latin: water of life; term for a variety of alcoholic distillates, such as brandy or whisky.

10 *but the kettle* Except the communal supplies.

11 *so that … than corn* I.e., the grains had been so damaged by worms and rot that there was not much left other than the bran, or husks.

12 *Our drink … water* I.e., as opposed to beer or wine, the preferred beverages of the colonists and indeed what the noun "drink" would ordinarily refer to.

13 *the President's projects* I.e., Wingfield's plans.

14 *flight* I.e., retreat; running away.

15 *Gosnold being … Kendall deposed* Gosnold had died in August of 1607, while Kendall had been removed from the council and arrested under a charge of mutiny; as later described by Smith, he was soon executed.

16 *surgeon* Medical doctor (without the specific connotation of specializing in surgery).

17 *as no man wanted* Such that no man was in need.

fault of our going was our own, what could be thought fitting or necessary we had, but what we should find, or want, or where we should be, we were all ignorant [of], and supposing to[1] make our passage in two months, with victual to live,[2] and the advantage of the spring to work; we were at sea five months, where we both spent our victual and lost the opportunity of the time and season to plant, by the unskillful presumption of our ignorant transporters, that understood not at all what they undertook.

Such actions have ever since the world's beginning been subject to such accidents, and everything of worth is found full of difficulties, but nothing so difficult as to establish a Commonwealth so far remote from men and means, and where men's minds are so untoward[3] as neither do well [to] themselves, nor suffer others.

But to proceed. The new President[4] and Martin, being little beloved, of weak judgment in dangers, and less industry[5] in peace, committed the managing of all things abroad[6] to Captain Smith; who by his own example, good words, and fair promises, set some to mow, others to bind thatch, some to build houses, others to thatch them, himself always bearing the greatest task for his own share, so that in short time he provided most of them lodgings, neglecting any for himself.

This done, seeing [that] the savages' superfluity[7] begin to decrease, [Smith] (with some of his workmen) shipped himself in the shallop[8] to search the country for trade. The want of the language,[9] knowledge to manage his boat without sails, the want of a sufficient power (knowing the multitude of the savages), apparel for his men, and other necessaries, were infinite impediments, yet no discouragement. Being but six or seven

in company he went down the river to Kecoughtan,[10] where at first they scorned him as a famished man, and would in derision offer him a handful of corn, a piece of bread, for their [the colonists'] swords and muskets, and such like proportions also for their apparel. But seeing by trade and courtesy there was nothing to be had, he made bold to try such conclusions as necessity enforced, though contrary to his commission:[11] [Smith] let fly[12] his muskets, [and] ran his boat on shore, whereat they all fled into the woods. So marching towards their houses, they might see great heaps of corn;[13] much ado[14] he had to restrain his hungry soldiers from present taking of it, expecting as it happened that the savages would assault them, as not long after they did with a most hideous noise. Sixty or seventy of them, some [painted] black, some red, some white, some parti-coloured,[15] came in a square order, singing and dancing out of the woods, with their *Okee* (which was an idol made of skins, stuffed with moss, all painted and hung with chains and copper) borne before them; and in this manner being well-armed, with clubs, targets,[16] bows and arrows, they charged the English, that so kindly received them,[17] with their muskets loaded with pistol shot, that down fell their God, and diverse[18] lay sprawling on the ground; the rest fled again to the woods, and ere long sent one of their *Quiyoughkasoucks*[19] to offer peace, and redeem their *Okee*. Smith told them, [that] if only six of them would come unarmed and load his boat, he would not

---

[1] *supposing to* Having assumed we would.

[2] *victual to live* Provisions necessary to survive.

[3] *untoward* Unruly or inept.

[4] *new President* I.e., Ratcliffe.

[5] *industry* Industriousness; willingness to work.

[6] *abroad* I.e., beyond the palisade.

[7] *superfluity* Generosity.

[8] *shallop* Smaller, shallow-water boat used for communications to and from a larger ship.

[9] *want of the language* Not knowing the local language.

[10] *Kecoughtan* Village on the mouth of the James River, home to the Kecoughtan people, who were part of the Powhatan Confederacy and whose leader or weroance was Pochins, son of Wahunsonacock,

[11] *commission* Instructions.

[12] *let fly* Fired.

[13] *towards their … heaps of corn* Towards the Powhatan houses, they [Smith's soldiers] could see great heaps of grain.

[14] *ado* Difficulty.

[15] *parti-coloured* Multicolored (i.e., wearing body paint).

[16] *targets* Shields.

[17] *that so kindly received them* Who responded to their attack in the same manner (i.e., as strongly).

[18] *diverse* Several of them.

[19] *Quiyoughkasoucks* Smith uses this term in various contexts throughout his writings, sometimes to refer to Algonquian deities, and sometimes, as here, to refer to their priests. "Quiyoughcohannock" is also the name of a member tribe of the Powhatan Confederacy.

only be their friend, but restore [to] them their *Okee*, and give them beads, copper, and hatchets besides; which on both sides was to their contents performed, and then they brought him venison, turkeys, wild fowl, bread, and what they had, singing and dancing in sign of friendship till they departed. In his return he discovered the town and country of Warraskoyack.[1]

> Thus God unboundless by his power,
> Made them thus kind, would us devour.

Smith, perceiving [that]—notwithstanding their late[2] misery—not any [of the colonists] regarded but from hand to mouth[3] (the company being well recovered), caused the pinnace to be provided with things fitting to get provision for the year following; but in the interim he made 3 or 4 journeys and discovered the people of Chickahominy.[4] Yet what he carefully provided the rest carelessly spent. Wingfield and Kendall living in disgrace, seeing all things at random[5] in the absence of Smith … strengthened themselves with[6] the sailors and other confederates to regain their former credit and authority, or at least such means aboard the pinnace (being fitted to sail as Smith had appointed for trade) to alter her course and to go for England. Smith, unexpectedly returning, had the plot discovered[7] to him, [and] much trouble he had to prevent it, till with store of saker[8] and musket shot he forced them [to] stay or sink in the river, which action cost the life of Captain Kendall. These brawls are so disgustful, as some will say they were better forgotten, yet all men of good judgement will conclude [that] it were better their baseness should be manifest to the world, than the business bear

the scorn and shame of their excused disorders.[9] The President and Captain Archer[10] not long after intended also to have abandoned the country, which project also was curbed and suppressed by Smith. The Spaniard never more greedily desired gold than he [Smith] victual, nor his soldiers more to abandon the country, than he to keep it.[11] But, finding plenty of corn in the river of Chickahominy where hundreds of savages in diverse places stood with baskets expecting his coming, and now the winter approaching, the rivers became so covered with swans, geese, ducks, and cranes, that we daily feasted with good bread, Virginia peas, pumpkins, and putchamins,[12] fish, fowl, and diverse sorts of wild beasts as fat as we could eat them: so that none of our Tuftaffety humorists[13] desired to go for England.

But our comedies never endured long without a tragedy; some idle exceptions[14] being muttered against Captain Smith, for not discovering the head of Chickahominy River, and taxed[15] by the Council to be too slow in so worthy an attempt.[16] The next voyage he proceeded so far that with much labour by cutting of trees asunder he made his passage, but when his barge could pass no farther, he left her in a broad bay out of danger of shot, commanding none should go ashore till his return: himself with two English and two savages went up higher in a canoe, but he was not long absent

---

1   *Warraskoyack*   Village on the mouth of the Pagan River, a tributary of the James River.

2   *late*   Recent.

3   *regarded but … to mouth*   I.e., considered anything beyond their immediate needs.

4   *Chickahominy*   Region along the Chickahominy River, which flows south into the James River and was named after the nation who inhabited it.

5   *at random*   In disorder.

6   *strengthened themselves with*   Made themselves popular among.

7   *discovered*   Revealed.

8   *saker*   Shot for cannon.

9   *it were better … disorders*   I.e., it would be better to let the guilt of the responsible persons be known, rather than have the entire company be seen as at fault.

10   *Captain Archer*   Gabriel Archer (1575–1609/10) had traveled to New England with Bartholomew Gosnold in 1602, and was among the first colonists at Chesapeake Bay in 1607; well-known as a rival to Smith, he left for England with Captain Christopher Newport on a so-called Supply Mission. Archer returned the next year and the rivalry continued until he died in the brutal following winter.

11   *The Spaniard … keep it*   Smith desired to provide food for the colony as eagerly as Spaniards desire gold, and Smith just as strongly to preserve the colony as his soldiers to abandon it. (Contemporary stereotypes among the English often depicted Spanish people as cruel and greedy, especially during the early period of American colonization when the British and Spanish empires were in conflict.)

12   *putchamins*   Persimmons.

13   *Tuftaffety humorists*   Frivolous, luxury-loving people; *Tuftaffety* Variety of taffeta, a high-end silk fabric.

14   *exceptions*   Complaints.

15   *taxed*   Accused.

16   *so … attempt*   Such an important duty.

but[1] his men went ashore, whose want of government[2] gave both occasion and opportunity to the savages to surprise one George Cassen,[3] whom they slew, and much failed not to have cut off the boat and all the rest. Smith little dreaming of that accident, being got to the marshes at the river's head, twenty miles in the desert,[4] had his[5] two men slain (as is supposed) sleeping by the canoe, whilst himself by fowling sought them victual, who finding he was beset with 200 savages, two of them he slew, still defending himself with the aid of a savage his guide, whom he bound to his arm with his garters, and used him as a buckler,[6] yet he was shot in his thigh a little, and had many arrows that stuck in his clothes but no great hurt, till at last they took him prisoner. When this news came to Jamestown, much was their sorrow for his loss, few expecting what ensued. Six or seven weeks those barbarians kept him prisoner; many strange triumphs and conjurations they made of him, yet he so demeaned himself amongst them, as he not only diverted them from surprising the fort, but procured his own liberty, and got himself and his company such estimation amongst them, that those savages admired him more than their own *Quiyoughkasoucks*. The manner how they used and delivered him, is as followeth.

The savages having drawn from George Cassen whither Captain Smith was gone, prosecuting that opportunity they followed him with 300 bowmen, conducted by the King of Pamunkey,[7] who in divisions searching the turnings of the river, found Robinson and Emry by the fireside; those they shot full of arrows and slew. Then finding the Captain, as is said, that used the savage that was his guide as his shield (three of them being slain and diverse others so galled[8]), all the rest would not come near him. Thinking thus to have returned to his boat, regarding them, as he marched, more than his way, [he] slipped up to the middle in an oozy creek, and his savage with him, yet durst[9] they not come to him till, being near dead with cold, he threw away his arms. Then according to their composition they drew him forth and led him to the fire, where his men were slain. Diligently they chafed his benumbed limbs. He demanding for their Captain, they showed him Opechancanough, King of Pamunkey, to whom he gave a round ivory double compass dial. Much they marveled at the playing of the fly[10] and needle, which they could see so plainly, and yet [could] not touch it, because of the glass that covered them. But when he demonstrated by that globe-like jewel the roundness of the earth, and skies, the sphere of the sun, moon, and stars, and how the sun did chase the night round about the world continually; the greatness of the land and sea, the diversity of nations, variety of complexions, and how we were to them antipodes,[11] and many other such like matters, they all stood as amazed with admiration. Notwithstanding, within an hour after they tied him to a tree, and as many as could stand about him prepared to shoot him; but the King holding up the compass in his hand, they all laid down their bows and arrows, and in a triumphant manner led him to Orapaks,[12] where he was after their manner kindly feasted, and well used.[13]

Their order in conducting him was thus; Drawing themselves all in fyle, the King in the middest had all their Peeces[14] and Swords borne before him. Captaine *Smith* was led after him by three great Salvages, holding him fast by each arme: and on each side six went in fyle with their Arrowes nocked.[15] But arriving at the Towne (which was but onely thirtie or fortie hunting houses made of Mats, which they remove as they please, as we our tents) all the women and children

[1] *but* Until.

[2] *want of government* Lack of discipline.

[3] *George Cassen* Listed as a "labourer" in the records of the Jamestown colonists.

[4] *desert* Wilderness.

[5] [Smith's note] Jehu Robinson and Thomas Emry, slain. [*had his* Found his.]

[6] *buckler* Shield.

[7] *King of Pamunkey* Opechancanough, younger brother of Chief Wahunsonacock and chief of the Pamunkey, an Algonquian-speaking tribe, part of the Powhatan Confederacy.

[8] *galled* Injured.

[9] *durst* Dared.

[10] *fly* Card showing the points on a compass.

[11] *antipodes* Living on the opposite side of the earth.

[12] *Orapaks* Village further west, near the head of the Chickahominy River.

[13] *used* Treated.

[14] *Peeces* Firearms.

[15] *Arrowes nocked* Arrows notched (onto their bowstrings).

original spelling

staring to behold him, the souldiers first all in fyle performed the forme of a *Bissom*[1] so well as could be; and on each flanke, officers as Serieants[2] to see them keepe their order. A good time they continued this exercise, and then cast themselves in a ring, dauncing in such severall[3] Postures, and singing and yelling out such hellish notes and screeches; being strangely painted, every one [had] his quiver of Arrowes, and at his backe a club; on his arme a Fox or an Otters skinne, or some such matter for his vambrace;[4] their heads and shoulders painted red, with Oyle and *Pocones*[5] mingled together, which Scarlet-like colour made an exceeding handsome shew; his Bow in his hand, and the skinne of a Bird with her wings abroad[6] dryed, tyed on his head, a peece of copper, a white shell, a long feather, with a small rattle growing at the tayles of their snakes tyed to it, or some such like toy. All this while *Smith* and the King stood in the middest guarded, as before is said, and after three dances they all departed. *Smith* they conducted to a long house, where thirtie or fortie tall fellowes did guard him, and ere long more bread and venison was brought him then would have served twentie men, I thinke his stomacke at that time was not very good; what he left they put in baskets and tyed over his head. About midnight they set the meate againe before him, all this time not one of them would eate a bit with him, till the next morning they brought him as much more, and then did they eate all the old, & reserved the new as they had done the other, which made him thinke they would fat him to eate him. Yet in this desperate estate to defend him from the cold, one [whose name was] Maocassater brought him his gowne, in requitall of[7] some beads and toyes *Smith* had given him at his first arrivall in *Virginia*.

Two days after a man would have slain him (but that the guard prevented it) for the death of his son, to whom they conducted him [Smith] to recover the poor man then breathing his last. Smith told them that at Jamestown he had a water would do it,[8] if they would let him fetch it, but they would not permit that; but made all the preparations they could to assault Jamestown, craving his advice, and for recompense he should have life, liberty, land, and women. In part of a table book[9] he wrote his mind to them at the fort,[10] what was intended, how they should follow that direction to affright the messengers, and without fail send him such things as he wrote for. And an inventory with them. The difficulty and danger, he told the savages, of the mines, great guns, and other engines exceedingly affrighted them, yet according to his request they went to Jamestown, in as bitter weather as could be of frost and snow, and within three days returned with an answer.

But when they came to Jamestown, seeing men sally[11] out as he had told them they would, they fled; yet in the night they came again to the same place where he had told them they should receive an answer, and such things as he had promised them, which they found accordingly, and with which they returned with no small expedition,[12] to the wonder of them all that heard it, that he could either divine,[13] or the paper could speak. Then they led him to the Youghtanunds, the Mattapanients, the Piankatanks, the Nantaughtacunds, and Onawmanients upon the rivers of Rappahannock, and Potomac, over all those rivers, and back again by diverse other several nations, to the King's habitation at Pamunkey, where they entertained him with most strange and fearful conjurations:

As if near led to hell,
Amongst the devils to dwell.[14]

---

1 *Bissom* Military formation in which soldiers march in a twisting line.

2 *Serieants* Sergeants.

3 *severall* Various.

4 *vambrace* Forearm armor.

5 *Pocones* Dyes made from the roots of any of several eastern North American plants.

6 *abroad* Spread out.

7 *in requitall of* In return for.

---

8 *water … it* I.e., medicine.

9 *table book* Notebook.

10 *In part … the fort* He took a page from his notebook and wrote a warning to the colonists at the fort.

11 *sally* Rush.

12 *expedition* Promptness.

13 *divine* Communicate through magic.

14 *As if … dwell* Smith paraphrases a translation of the Roman poet Seneca (c. 4 BCE–65 CE) found in Martin Fotherby's *Atheomastix*.

Not long after, early in a morning a great fire was made in a long house, and a mat spread on the one side, as on the other; on the one they caused him to sit, and all the guard went out of the house, and presently came skipping in a great grim fellow, all painted over with coal, mingled with oil; and many snakes' and weasels' skins stuffed with moss, and all their tails tied together, so as they met on the crown of his head in a tassel; and round about the tassel was as a coronet of feathers, the skins hanging round about his head, back, and shoulders, and in a manner covered his face, with a hellish voice and a rattle in his hand. With most strange gestures and passions he began his invocation, and environed the fire with a circle of meal;[1] which done, three more such like devils came rushing in with the like antic tricks, painted half black, half red; but all their eyes were painted white, and some red strokes like mutchatos[2] along their cheeks. Round about him those fiends danced a pretty while, and then came in three more as ugly as the rest, with red eyes, and white strokes over their black faces, at last they all sat down right against him; three of them on the one hand of the chief priest, and three on the other. Then all with their rattles began a song, which ended, the chief priest laid down five wheat corns.[3] Then, straining his arms and hands with such violence that he sweat, and his veins swelled, he began a short oration.[4] At the conclusion they all gave a short groan; and then laid down three grains more. After that, began their song again, and then another oration, ever laying down so many corns as before, till they had twice encircled the fire; that done, they took a bunch of little sticks prepared for that purpose, continuing still their devotion, and at the end of every song and oration, they laid down a stick betwixt the divisions of corn. Till night, neither he nor they did either eat or drink, and then they feasted merrily, with the best provisions they could make. Three days they used this ceremony; the meaning whereof, they told him, was to know if he intended them well or no. The circle of meal signified their country, the circles of corn the bounds of the sea, and the sticks his country.

They imagined the world to be flat and round, like a trencher,[5] and they in the midst. After this they brought him a bag of gunpowder, which they carefully preserved till the next spring, to plant as they did their corn, because they would be acquainted with the nature of that seed. Opitchapam the King's brother invited him to his house, where, with as many platters of bread, fowl, and wild beasts as did environ him,[6] he bid him welcome; but not any of them would eat a bit with him, but put up all the remainder in baskets. At his return to Opechancanough's, all the King's women, and their children flocked about him for their parts,[7] as a due by custom to be merry with such fragments.

But his waking mind in hideous dreams did
oft see wondrous shapes,
    Of bodies strange, and huge in growth, and
of stupendous makes.[8]

At last they brought him to Werowocomoco,[9] where was Powhatan, their emperor. Here more than two hundred of those grim courtiers stood wondering at him, as [if] he had been a monster; till Powhatan and his train had put themselves in their greatest braveries.[10] Before a fire upon a seat like a bedstead, he sat covered with a great robe, made of rarowcun[11] skins, and all the tails hanging by. On either hand did sit a young wench of 16 to 18 years, and along on each side [of] the house two rows of men, and behind them as many women, with all their heads and shoulders painted red; many of their heads bedecked with the white down of birds; but everyone with something, and a great chain of white beads about their necks. At his entrance before the King, all the people gave a great

---

[1] *meal* Ground maize.

[2] *mutchatos* Mustaches.

[3] *corns* Kernels.

[4] *oration* Prayer.

[5] *trencher* Plate.

[6] *as did environ him* As it took to encircle him.

[7] *parts* Gifts or offerings.

[8] *But his … makes* Smith quotes Fotherby's translation of Roman poet Lucretius (c. 99–c. 55 BCE).

[9] *Werowocomoco* Village on the York River, Powhatan's political center.

[10] *braveries* Fine formal costumes.

[11] *rarowcun* Raccoon. This English word is derived from an Algonquian word which Smith attempts to represent with various spellings throughout his writings.

shout. The Queen of Appamatuck[1] was appointed to bring him water to wash his hands, and another brought him a bunch of feathers, instead of a towel to dry them. Having feasted him after their best barbarous manner they could, a long consultation was held, but the conclusion was [that] two great stones were brought before Powhatan. Then as many as could laid hands on him [Smith] dragged him to them, and thereon laid his head, and being ready with their clubs to beat out his brains, Pocahontas, the King's dearest daughter, when no entreaty could prevail, got his head in her arms, and laid her own upon his to save him from death; whereat the emperor was contented he should live to make him hatchets, and her bells, beads, and copper; for they thought him as well of[2] all [these] occupations as themselves. For the King himself will make his own robes, shoes, bows, arrows, pots; plant, hunt, or do anything so well as the rest.

> They say he bore a pleasant show,
> But sure his heart was sad.
> For who can pleasant be, and rest,
> That lives in fear and dread:
> And having life suspected, doth
> It still suspected lead.[3]

Two days after, Powhatan having disguised himself in the most fearfulest manner he could, [he] caused Captain Smith to be brought forth to a great house in the woods, and there upon a mat by the fire to be left alone. Not long after, from behind a mat that divided the house was made the most dolefulest[4] noise he ever heard; then Powhatan, more like a devil than a man, with some two hundred more as black as himself, came unto him and told him now they were friends, and presently he should go to Jamestown to send him two great guns, and a grindstone, for which he would give

him the country of Capahowosick,[5] and forever esteem him as[6] his son Nantaquoud. So to Jamestown with 12 guides Powhatan sent him. That night they quartered[7] in the woods, he still expecting (as he had done all this long time of his imprisonment) every hour to be put to one death or other, for all their feasting. But almighty God (by his divine providence) had mollified the hearts of those stern barbarians with compassion. The next morning betimes they came to the fort, where Smith, having used the savages with what kindness he could, he showed Rawhunt, Powhatan's trusty servant, two demi-culverins[8] and a millstone to carry [to] Powhatan. They found them somewhat too heavy; but when they did see him discharge them, being loaded with stones, among the boughs of a great tree loaded with icicles, the ice and branches came so tumbling down that the poor savages ran away half dead with fear. But at last we regained some conference with them, and gave them such toys; and sent to Powhatan [and] his women and children such presents as gave them in general full content.

Now in Jamestown they were all in combustion,[9] the strongest preparing once more to run away with the pinnace; which with the hazard of his life, with saker falcon and musket shot, Smith [was] forced now the third time to stay or sink. Some, no better than they should be, had plotted with the President the next day to have put him to death by the Levitical law,[10] for the lives of Robinson and Emry, pretending the fault was his that had led them to their ends: but he quickly took such order with such lawyers[11] that he laid them by the heels,[12] till he sent some of them prisoners for England. Now every once in four or five days, Pocahontas with her attendants brought him so much provision that

---

[1]   *Queen of Appamatuck* Opossunoquonuske, leader of this Algonquian-speaking tribe which resided along the Appomattox River.

[2]   *as well of* I.e., as skilled at.

[3]   *They say ... lead* Smith paraphrases Fotherby's translation of Greek playwright Euripides (c. 480–406 BCE).

[4]   *dolefulest* Doleful; sorrowful.

[5]   *Capahowosick* Village located just southwest of Werowocomoco on Smith's map of Virginia.

[6]   *as* I.e., as well as.

[7]   *quartered* I.e., took up quarters; lodged.

[8]   *demi-culverins* Large, long cannons.

[9]   *combustion* Disorder.

[10]   *Levitical law* See Leviticus 24.17: "And he that killeth any man shall surely be put to death."

[11]   *lawyers* Those who execute Mosaic law (the laws set down in the first five books of the Torah or Old Testament, including the Book of Leviticus).

[12]   *laid them ... heels* Arrested them.

saved many of their lives, that else for all this had[1] starved with hunger.

> Thus from numb death our good God sent relief,
> The sweet assuager of all other grief.[2]

His relation[3] of the plenty he had seen, especially at Werawocomoco, and of the state and bounty of Powhatan (which till that time was unknown), so revived their dead spirits (especially [the story of] the love of Pocahontas)[4] [that] all men's fear was abandoned. Thus you may see what difficulties still crossed any good endeavour: and the good success of the business being thus oft brought to the very period of destruction; yet you see by what strange means God hath still delivered it. As for the insufficiency of them admitted in Commission, that error could not be prevented by the Electors,[5] there being no other choice, and all strangers to each other's education, qualities, or disposition. And if any deem it a shame to our nation to have any mention made of those enormities, let them peruse the histories of the Spaniards' discoveries and plantations, where they may see how many mutinies, disorders, and dissentions have accompanied them, and crossed their attempts. …

from Chapter 8
Captain Smith's Journey to Pamunkey

… The 12 of January we arrived at Werowocomoco, where the river was frozen near half a mile from the shore; but to neglect[6] no time, the President[7] with his barge so far had approached by breaking the ice, as the ebb left him amongst those oozy shoals. Yet rather than to lie there frozen to death, by his own example he taught them to march near middle deep, a flight shot through this muddy frozen ooze. When the barge floated, he appointed two or three to return her aboard the pinnace. Where, for want of water in melting the ice, they made fresh water, for the river there was salt. But in this march Mr. Russell (whom none could persuade to stay behind), being somewhat ill, and exceeding heavy, so overtoiled himself as the rest had much ado (ere he got ashore) to regain[8] life into his dead benumbed spirits. Quartering in the next houses we found, we sent to Powhatan for provision, who sent us plenty of bread, turkeys, and venison; the next day having feasted us after his ordinary manner, he began to ask us when we would be gone, saying he [had] sent not for us, neither had he any corn; and his people much less.[9] Yet for forty swords he would procure us forty baskets. The President, showing him the men there present that brought him the message and conditions, asked Powhatan how it chanced he became so forgetful; thereat the King concluded the matter with a merry laughter, asking for our commodities, but none he liked without guns and swords, valuing a basket of corn more precious than a basket of copper; saying he could eat his corn, but not the copper.

Captain Smith, seeing the intent of this subtle[10] savage, began to deal with him after this manner:

> Powhatan, though I had many courses to have made my provision, yet believing your promises to supply my wants, I neglected all to satisfy your desire: and to testify my love, I sent you my men for your building, neglecting mine own. What your people had you have increased, forbidding them our trade: and now you think by consuming the time, we shall consume for want, not having to fulfill your strange demands. As for swords and guns, I told you long ago I had none to spare; and you must know those I have can keep me from want: yet steal or wrong you

---

[1] *else for all this had*   Otherwise would have.

[2] *Thus from … grief*   The first line appears to be Smith's own, while the second is quoted from Fotherby's translation of Euripides.

[3] *relation*   Telling the story.

[4] *especially … Pocahontas*   I.e., especially Smith's relation of Pocahontas's apparent love for him.

[5] *them admitted in Commission*   Those appointed to govern the colony in the Virginia Company's original instructions; *Electors*   Those elected by the Virginia Company's stockholders to direct the company's business.

[6] *neglect*   Waste.

[7] *the President*   Smith, who had been elected President the previous September.

[8] *regain*   Restore.

[9] *saying … less*   Pretending that he had not sent for us, that he did not have any grain, and that his people had much less food [than they needed].

[10] *subtle*   Cunning.

I will not, nor dissolve that friendship we have mutually promised, except you constrain us by our bad usage.

The King, having attentively listened to this discourse, promised that both he and his country would spare him what he could, the which within two days they should receive. "Yet Captain Smith," sayeth the King,

> some doubt I have of your coming hither that makes me not so kindly seek to relieve you as I would. For many do inform me [that] your coming hither is not for trade but to invade my people, and possess my country, who dare not come to bring you corn, seeing you thus armed with your men. To free us of this fear, leave aboard your weapons, for here they are needless, we being all friends, and forever Powhatans.[1]

With many such discourses they spent the day, quartering that night in the King's houses. The next day he renewed his building, which he little intended should proceed. For, the Dutchmen[2] finding his plenty, and knowing our want, and perceiving his preparations to surprise us, little thinking we could escape both him and famine; to obtain his favour, revealed to him so much as they knew of our estates and projects, and how to prevent them. One of them being of so great a spirit, judgement, and resolution, and a hireling that was certain of his wages for his labour, and ever well used both he and his countrymen; that the President knew not whom better to trust; and not knowing any fitter for that employment, had sent him as a spy to discover Powhatan's intent, then little doubting his honesty, nor could ever be certain of his villainy till near half a year after.

Whilst we expected the coming in of the country, we wrangled out of the King ten quarters[3] of corn for a copper kettle, the which the President perceiving him much to affect,[4] valued it at a much greater rate. But in regard of his scarcity he would accept it [the corn], provided we should have as much more the next year, or else the country of Monacan.[5] Wherewith each seemed well contented, and Powhatan began to expostulate the difference of peace and war after this manner:

> Captain Smith, you may understand that I, having seen the death of all my people thrice, and not any one living of these three generations but myself; I know the difference of peace and war better than any in my country. But now I am old and ere long must die; my brethren, namely Opitchapam, Opechancanough, and Kecoughtan, my two sisters, and their two daughters, are distinctly each other's successors. I wish their experience [to be] no less than mine, and your love to them no less than mine to you. But this bruit from Nansemond,[6] that you are come to destroy my country, so much affrighteth all my people as they dare not visit you. What will it avail[7] you to take that by force [which] you may quickly have by love, or to destroy them that provide you food? What can you get by war, when we can hide our provisions and fly to the woods, whereby you must famish, by wronging us your friends? And why are you thus jealous[8] of our loves, seeing us unarmed, and [that we] both do, and are willing still to feed you, with that [which] you cannot get but by our labours? Think you I am so simple not to know it is better to eat good meat, lie well, and sleep quietly with

---

1   *being all … Powhatans* Chief Wahunsonacock had previously adopted Smith as a son and granted him chiefdom over Capahowosick, a nearby village on the York River. Some historians believe that what Smith had understood to be his near execution by Chief Wahunsonacock earlier was in fact an adoption ritual.

2   *the Dutchmen* With the second supply ship Jamestown had imported several "Dutchmen" (elsewhere Smith indicates that they were from Germany), as well as several Polish people, to work as builders and artisans. Smith later came to believe that the Dutchmen had betrayed him to Powhatan.

3   *quarters* Units of measure used for grains and other dry commodities.

4   *affect* Admire.

5   *Monacan* Siouan-speaking tribe who were at this time in conflict with the Powhatan Confederacy.

6   *bruit* Rumor; *Nansemond* Tribe under the Powhatan Confederacy who lived along the Nansemond River, a tributary of the James; in 1608 the English had raided their town in search of corn, burning and destroying their houses and canoes.

7   *avail* Benefit.

8   *jealous* Mistrustful.

my women and children, laugh and be merry with you, have copper, hatchets, or what I want being your friend, than be forced to fly from all, to lie cold in the woods, feed upon acorns, roots, and such trash, and be so hunted by you, that I can neither rest, eat, nor sleep; but my tired men must watch, and if a twig but break, everyone cryeth, "there commeth Captain Smith"? Then must I fly I know not whither: and thus with miserable fear end my miserable life, leaving my pleasures to such youths as you, which through your rash unadvisedness may quickly as miserably end, for want of that [which] you never know where to find. Let this therefore assure you of our loves, and every year our friendly trade shall furnish you with corn; and now also, if you would come in friendly manner to see us, and not thus with your guns and swords as to invade your foes.

To this subtle discourse, the President thus replied:

Seeing [that] you will not rightly conceive of our words, we strive to make you know our thoughts by our deeds; the vow I made you of my love, both myself and my men have kept. As for your promise, I find it every day violated by some of your subjects. Yet we, finding your love and kindness, our custom is so far from being ungrateful, that, for your sake only, we have curbed our thirsting desire of revenge; else had they[1] known as well the cruelty we use to our enemies, as our true love and courtesy to our friends. And I think your judgment sufficient to conceive, as well by the adventures we have undertaken, as by the advantage we have (by our arms) of yours: that had we intended you any hurt, long ere this we could have effected it. Your people coming to Jamestown are entertained[2] with their bows and arrows without any exceptions; we esteeming it with you as it is with us, to wear our arms as our apparel. As for the danger of our enemies, in such wars consist our chiefest pleasure. For your riches we have no use; as for

the hiding your provision, or by your flying to the woods, we shall not so unadvisedly starve as you conclude; your friendly care in that behalf is needless, for we have a rule to find beyond your knowledge.[3]

Many other discourses they had, till at last they began to trade. But the King, seeing his will would not be admitted as a law, [neither] our guard dispersed, nor our men disarmed, he (sighing) breathed his mind once more in this manner:

Captain Smith, I never use any Weroance[4] so kindly as yourself, yet from you I receive the least kindness of any. Captain Newport gave me swords, copper, clothes, a bed, towels, or what I desired; ever taking what I offered him, and would send away his guns when I entreated him. None doth deny to lie at my feet, or refuse to do what I desire, but only you, of whom I can have nothing but what you regard not,[5] and yet you will have whatsoever you demand. Captain Newport you call father, and so you call me; but I see for all us both you will do what you list,[6] and we must both seek to content you. But if you intend [to be] so friendly as you say, send hence your arms, that I may believe you; for you see the love I bear you doth cause me thus nakedly[7] to forget myself.

Smith, seeing this savage but trifle the time to cut his throat,[8] procured the savages to break the ice, that his boat might come to fetch his corn and him, and gave order for more men to come on shore, to surprise the King, with whom also he but trifled the time till his men were landed, and to keep him from suspicion, entertained the time with this reply:

---

1 *they* I.e., Wahunsonacock's people.

2 *entertained* Armed.

3 *we have … knowledge* I.e., we have ways beyond your knowledge to acquire provisions.

4 *Weroance* Algonquin word for "chief" or "leader."

5 *what you regard not* What you don't want; worthless things.

6 *list* Want.

7 *nakedly* Defenselessly.

8 *but trifle … throat* Only putting in time before cutting his throat.

Powhatan you must know, as I have but one God, I honour but one King; and I live not here as your subject, but as your friend to pleasure you with what I can. By the gifts you bestow on me, you gain more than by trade: yet would you visit me as I do you, you should know it is not our custom, to sell our courtesies as a vendible commodity. Bring all your country with you for your guard; I will not dislike it as being over jealous. But to content you, tomorrow I will leave my arms, and trust to your promise. I call you father indeed, and as a father you shall see I will love you: but the small care you have of such a child caused my men persuade me to look to myself.

By this time Powhatan, having knowledge his men were ready, whilst the ice was a breaking, with his luggage, women and children, fled. Yet to avoid suspicion, [he] left two or three of the women talking with the Captain, whilst he secretly ran away, and his men that secretly beset the house. Which being presently discovered to Captain Smith, with his pistol, sword, and target he made such a passage among these naked devils, that at his first shot, they next him tumbled one over another, and the rest quickly fled, some one way, some another: so that without any hurt, only accompanied with John Russell, he obtained the *corps de guard*.[1] When they [the Powhatans] perceived him so well escaped, and with his eighteen men (for he had no more with him ashore) to the uttermost of their skill they sought excuses to dissemble the matter: and Powhatan to excuse his flight and the sudden coming of this multitude, sent our Captain a great bracelet and a chain of pearl, by an ancient orator that bespoke us to this purpose, perceiving even then from our pinnace, a barge and men departing and coming unto us.

Captain Smith, our Weroance is fled, fearing your guns, and knowing when the ice was broken there would come more men, sent these numbers but to guard his corn from stealing, that might happen without your knowledge:

now, though some be hurt by your misprision,[2] yet Powhatan is your friend and so will forever continue. Now, since the ice is open, he would have you send away your corn, and if you would have his company, send away also your guns, which so affrighteth his people, that they dare not come to you as he promised they should.

Then having provided baskets for our men to carry our corn to the boats, they kindly offered their service to guard our arms, that none should steal them. A great many they were of goodly well proportioned fellows, as grim as devils; yet the very sight of cocking our matches,[3] and being to let fly, a few words caused them to leave their bows and arrows to our guard, and bear down our corn on their backs; we needed not importune them to make dispatch.[4] But our barges being left on the ooze by the ebb,[5] caused us [to] stay till the next high-water, so that we returned again to our old quarter. Powhatan and his Dutchmen, [who were] bursting with desire to have the head of Captain Smith, for if they could but kill him, they thought all was theirs, neglected not any opportunity to effect his purpose. The Indians with all the merry sports they could devise, spent the time till night; then they all returned to Powhatan, who all this time was making ready his forces to surprise the house and him at supper. Notwithstanding, the eternal all-seeing God did prevent him, and by a strange means. For Pocahontas, his dearest jewel and daughter, in that dark night came through the irksome woods, and told our Captain great cheer should be sent us by and by, but Powhatan and all the power he could make would after come kill us all, if they that brought it could not kill us with our own weapons when we were at supper. Therefore, if we would live, she wished us presently to be gone. Such things as she delighted in, he [Smith] would have given her, but with the tears running down her cheeks she said she durst not be seen to have any; for if Powhatan should know it, she were but dead, and so she ran away by herself as she came.

---

[2] *misprision* Misconduct.

[3] *cocking our matches* Readying our firearms for use.

[4] *needed ... dispatch* I.e., it was not necessary to insist that they do as the colonists wish and bear the corn.

[5] *ebb* Tide.

---

[1] *corps de guard* French: guardhouse; military construction which defends the entrance to a fort.

Within less than an hour came eight or ten lusty[1] fellows, with great platters of venison and other victual, very importune to have us put out our matches (whose smoke made them sick) and sit down to our victual. But the Captain made them taste every dish, which [having been] done he [then] sent some of them back to Powhatan, to bid him make haste, for he was prepared for his coming. As for them, he knew they came to betray him at his supper: but he would prevent them and all their other intended villainies, so that they might be gone. Not long after came more messengers, to see what news; not long after them [came] others. Thus we spent the night as vigilantly as they, till it was high-water, yet [we] seemed to the savages as friendly as they to us[.] …

—1624

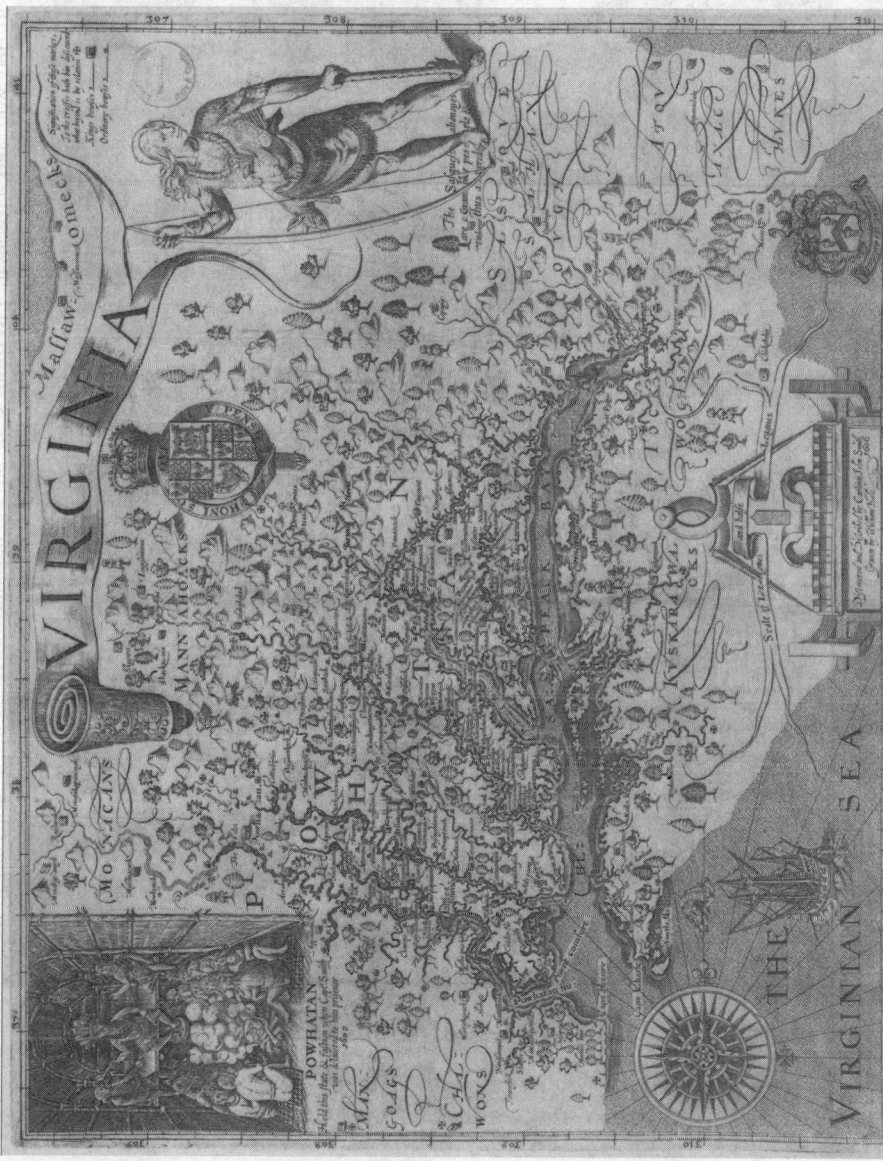

John Smith's map of Virginia was first published in 1612, and also included a "description of the country, the commodities, people, government and religion." In the upper left-hand corner of the map is a depiction of Wahunsonacock as he is said to have appeared when Smith was his prisoner. The image was later reproduced in Smith's *General History*.

---

1 *lusty* Strong, vigorous.

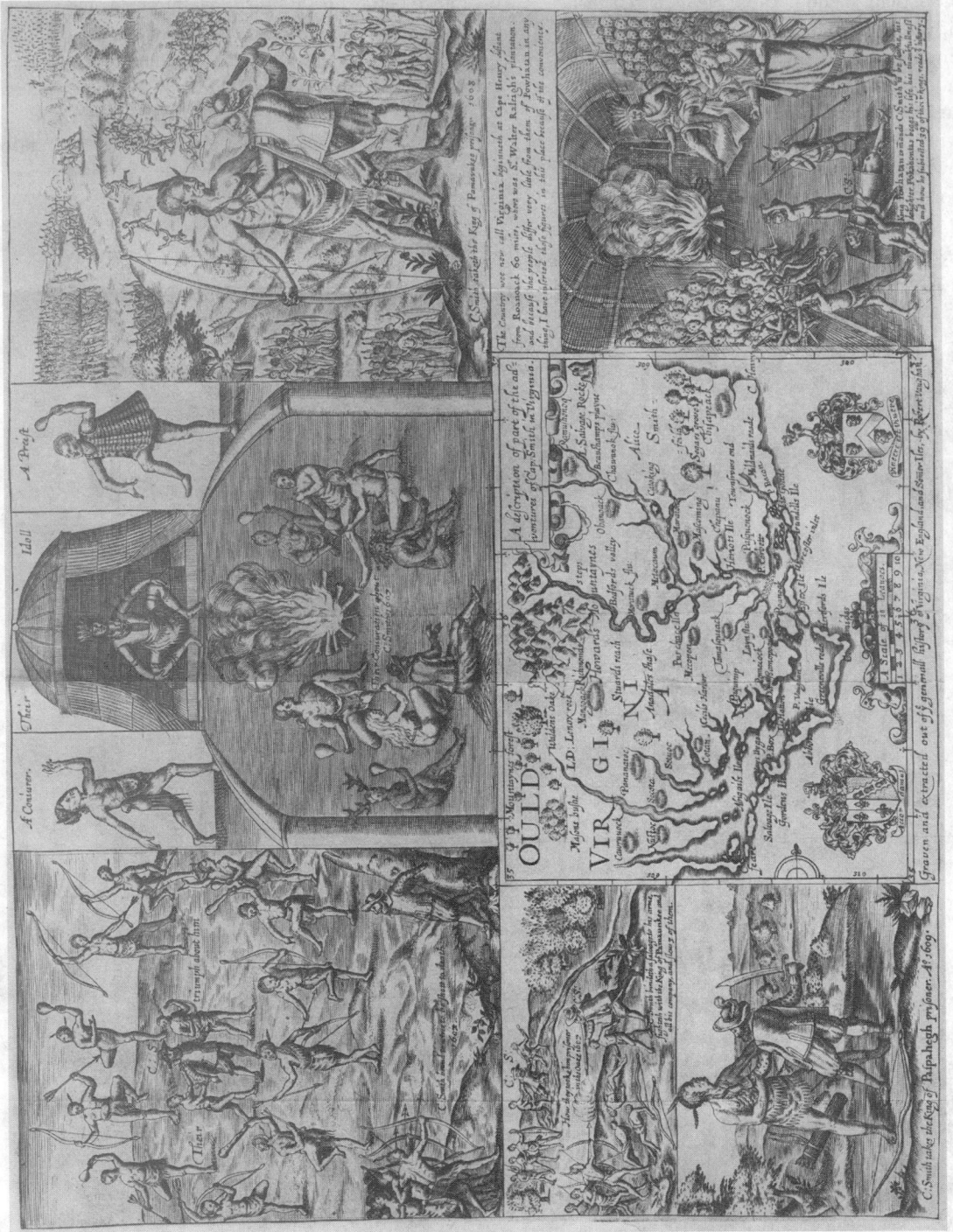

Known as the "Map of the Ould Virginia," this map depicts the areas south of Chesapeake Bay, now part of North Carolina, that had been settled under Sir Walter Ralegh's patent in the 1580s. The whole image, which was designed by Robert Vaughan for Smith's *General History*, also includes numerous depictions of Smith's encounters with the Powhatan and other Indigenous peoples around Virginia.

—1624

William Bradford

1590 – 1657

One of the famous group of settlers who came to Cape Cod on the *Mayflower,* William Bradford was a Puritan Separatist, writer, and politician who served for decades as the governor of Plymouth, one of the earliest European settlements in New England. His historical account of the journey and the first thirty years of settlement—*Of Plymouth Plantation* (1630–51)—helped shape the mythology of early American history. Bradford himself soon became mythologized as the "father of American history"; Cotton Mather described him in 1702 as an Adam figure, "the father of them all," and also as a Moses, "the leader of a people in a wilderness." While the Puritans' colonialist belief in their divine right to settle America has been soundly criticized, Bradford's journal is still widely considered foundational to the American story, and an early example of the Puritan consciousness that shaped New England history for generations.

Bradford was born in 1590 in Austerfield, Yorkshire, to a family with considerable farmland. Orphaned as a child, he was brought up by two of his uncles. He loved to read and began to study the Geneva Bible at an early age; at seventeen, he joined a Separatist Puritan congregation. Unlike most Puritans, who sought to reform the Anglican Church from within, the Separatists took their beliefs far enough to break with the established church—a move that was considered treasonous, putting them at odds not only with the powerful clergy but also with the government.

Persecution of Separatists under King James I led Bradford's community (known as the Scrooby congregation) to move to Holland, a country that allowed them religious freedom. They went first to Amsterdam in 1607, and then to Leiden, where Bradford became a weaver. He struggled financially until he inherited his family's estate in 1611, and two years later he married Dorothy May, an Englishwoman living in Amsterdam. Most members of the Scrooby congregation, however, continued to find it difficult to earn a living in Leiden, and they worried that their children might be assimilated into Dutch culture and lose their English Separatist identity. Bradford was among a group of community members who decided to leave Leiden and establish a new colony in what is now New York State, in part of a region the English then referred to as Virginia. These "Pilgrims" departed in 1620, having obtained a grant of land from the English government and secured financing through a profit-sharing agreement with the Merchant Adventurers, a London trading company.

Instead of Virginia, however, the *Mayflower* touched down at Cape Cod. Prevented by the weather from sailing further south, the leaders of the community decided to settle in a place they called Plymouth, known to the local Indigenous people as Patuxet. Many historians think that the settlement might have encountered more resistance from Indigenous people had not an epidemic killed ninety per cent of the Patuxet (the local Wampanoag band) between 1617 and 1619, leaving the area sparsely populated when the Pilgrims arrived. Instead, relationships with Indigenous people would prove crucial for the colony's survival, as Indigenous supporters taught the colonists how to fish, how to cultivate the land, and other essential skills. This help was sorely needed: in the first year after arrival, more than half of the hundred settlers died of scurvy and other illnesses. Bradford survived a serious illness, but his wife drowned in November 1620 when she fell off the deck of the *Mayflower*, which was moored in Plymouth harbor.

Following the death of John Carver, the first governor of Plymouth, Bradford was elected to take up the role; he would serve as governor for thirty of the first thirty-five years of the colony's existence. The governor, along with his elected assistants, made crucial decisions on the colony's behalf, including political and economic decisions, but also practical everyday ones about land allocation and farming practices; the governor also presided as a judge over criminal and civil disagreements. Bradford proved to be an effective leader, making careful decisions to ensure the colony's survival; he was also, however, capable of ruthlessness—of sentencing a community member to death for bestiality, for example. His dealings with the neighboring Indigenous peoples, while he intended them to be fair and measured, were nonetheless affected by his racial and religious prejudices. The Plymouth community grew over the course of Bradford's lifetime from the 101 *Mayflower* passengers in 1620 to 1,360 members in 1657. By the end of his life, however, he was distressed by the number of new settlements unconnected to the Separatist church; Baptists and Quakers, for example, had begun to form their own congregations. This splintering of the original intimate church community was, for him, a source of sorrow and regret.

In 1630, Bradford began writing *Of Plymouth Plantation*, which tells the story of the settlers' journey from Holland and of the first thirty years of colonization. The narrative resolutely keeps its focus on the colony's economic prosperity and moral status, revealing little about Bradford's own personal life. He speaks of himself in the third person, barely mentioning his wife's death, and there is no mention at all of his remarriage to Alice Southworth or of the births of his three children (he and his first wife had left their first son in Holland, but he eventually followed Bradford to America). *Of Plymouth Plantation* records, in Bradford's "plain style" of writing, detailed and vivid accounts of the voyage, contact with Indigenous peoples, the work of settlement, and various iconic incidents, some of which made their way into American mythology.

Of Plymouth Plantation is composed of two books, the first detailing the Pilgrims' journey and early days of settlement, and the second providing a year-by-year account of the principal concerns of the colony. Book One is written confidently in the genre of providential histories not uncommon among Puritans at the time, in which the hand of God is at times clearly, and at other times mysteriously, guiding events. The histories recorded in the Bible are the most important precursors of this kind of writing; the story in Exodus, for example, of the people of Israel escaping captivity in Egypt, was for Bradford and other American Puritans a prefiguration of their own journey across the sea to find religious freedom. In taking up the genre, Bradford was influenced by earlier providential histories such as John Foxe's *Acts and Monuments* (1563), a popular work that told the stories of Protestant martyrs in sixteenth-century England. Book Two of *Plymouth Plantation*, however, shifts away from a providential tone and style, coming to resemble an economic history, as Bradford finds himself detailing the complex financial and political negotiations of Plymouth with its various trade partners: Indigenous communities, nearby settlements, and the Merchant Adventurers in England. Book Two also becomes more elegiac in tone, as Bradford struggles to square the gradual dissolution of the community with his faith in Plymouth's God-given destiny.

The manuscript of *Of Plymouth Plantation* was passed down in Bradford's family for several generations. The family made it available to seventeenth- and eighteenth-century historians such as Nathaniel Morton, Cotton Mather, and Thomas Prince, and it remained a central source for information about the early years of New England history (along with Edward Winslow's 1622 publication *A Relation or Journal of the Beginning and Proceedings of the English Plantation Settled at Plymouth in New England*, to which Bradford also contributed). The manuscript made its way to a Boston library, from which it is thought to have been stolen by a British soldier during the Boston occupation of 1775–76. New England scholars had a copy of the first portion of the text but considered the rest lost until 1855, when they noticed that British scholars were citing it. Thus began a 42-year-long legal battle to return the text to America. This conflict was finally decided in favor of the United States in 1897, when the manuscript was returned and placed in the Massachusetts State House, where it remains.

Because the manuscript was outside America for so many decades, *Of Plymouth Plantation* was not printed in its entirety until 1856. Once published, it was received with enthusiasm both as a literary work and as a valuable history of early New England. Its readership increased further with the publication of an accessible scholarly edition of Bradford's history by Worthington C. Ford in 1912, and by the 1960s the book was on most course syllabi dealing with American studies. In the twentieth century, Bradford came to be more appreciated as a literary writer, with greater attention being paid to his style and influences. Scholars have also argued that Bradford's narrative has influenced writers of immigration such as Willa Cather, as well as writers of "frontier" fiction such as Catherine Maria Sedgwick and James Fenimore Cooper. As a document of colonialism, the bias inherent in Bradford's work has come into focus, and *Of Plymouth Plantation* has been compared to other colonial narratives outside of New England, such as Álvar Núñez Cabeza de Vaca's *La relación y comentarios* (1542). Indigenous responses to the text have also enriched the critical dialogue; Cherokee writer Betty Booth Donahue argues in *Bradford's Indian Book* (2011), for example, that the structure of the text is profoundly influenced by Indigenous forms of storytelling.

In 1647, Bradford stopped adding entries to *Of Plymouth Plantation*, but he continued to write, composing dialogues and poems on theological topics. While not generally considered exceptional in literary terms, these works are often read for further insight into the colonial period and into Bradford's roles—as historiographer, politician, and writer—in shaping our perceptions of early American history. Bradford died in Plymouth in 1657, where a stone monument on Burial Hill commemorates his contributions to the community. In his last poem, "Epitaphium Meum" ("My Epitaph"), he describes himself as "a man of sorrows," waiting for his "happy change." Despite the disappointment he felt at the dispersal of the Plymouth community, he passed down his history in the hope that the Pilgrims' story would be an example to future generations: "As one small candle may light a thousand, so the light here kindled hath shone unto many, yea in some sort to our whole nation." Bradford's text remains a rich resource for readers seeking to understand the complex cultural, economic, political, and religious histories of early America.

NOTE ON THE TEXT: Several editions of Bradford's *Of Plymouth Plantation* have been consulted in the preparation of the text reprinted here, including Worthington Chauncey Ford's 1912 edition and Samuel Eliot Morison's 1952 edition. Spelling and punctuation have been lightly modernized in accordance with the practices of this anthology.

⌘ ⌘ ⌘

from *Of Plymouth Plantation*

And first of the occasion and inducements there unto; the which that I may truly unfold, I must begin at the very root and rise of the same. The which I shall endeavour to manifest in a plain style, with singular regard unto the simple truth in all things; at least as near as my slender judgment can attain the same.

from THE FIRST BOOK

from CHAPTER I
[THE SEPARATIST INTERPRETATION OF THE REFORMATION IN ENGLAND, 1550–1607]

It is well known unto the godly and judicious, how since the first breaking out of the light of the gospel[1] in our honourable nation of England (which was the first of nations whom the Lord adorned therewith, after the gross darkness of popery which had covered and overspread the Christian world), what wars, and oppositions ever since, Satan hath raised, maintained, and continued against the Saints,[2] from time to time, in one sort or other. Sometimes by bloody death and cruel torments; other whiles imprisonments, banishments, and other hard usages; as being loath his kingdom should go down, the truth prevail and the churches of God revert to their ancient purity and recover their primitive order, liberty, and beauty. ...

Mr. Foxe[3] recordeth how that besides those worthy martyrs and confessors which were burned in Queen Mary's days[4] and otherwise tormented, "Many (both students and others) fled out of the land to the number of 800, and became several congregations, at Wesel, Frankfurt, Basel, Emden, Markpurge, Strasburg and Geneva, etc." Amongst whom (but especially those

---

1   *first breaking out ... gospel* Dawn of Protestantism. The Church of England, a Protestant church, was founded in the 1530s, though Protestant ideology had taken hold in some quarters in England in the preceding decades.

2   *Saints* Term used by some Puritan sects to describe their members; Bradford is using it here more generally to refer to Protestants. The implication is that members are themselves saints and do not need priests to act as intermediaries between them and God.

3   [Bradford's note] Acts and Mon[uments]: pag. 1587 edition 2. [This book is commonly known as *The Book of Martyrs* (first published in 1563), an account of Christian martyrs in Western history; it was written by John Foxe, an English historian and member of the clergy.]

4   *burned in Queen Mary's days* Mary I (1516–58) was a Roman Catholic, and in her attempt to reverse the Reformation set in motion by her father, Henry VIII, she burned almost 300 Protestant dissenters at the stake. Upon Queen Mary's death, her half-sister Elizabeth became Queen, and England became Protestant again.

at Frankfurt) began that bitter war of contention and persecution about the ceremonies and service book,[1] and other popish and antichristian stuff, the plague of England to this day, which are like the high places in Israel which the prophets cried out against, and were their ruin.[2] ...

And this contention died not with Queen Mary, nor was left beyond the seas. But at her death these people[3] returning into England under gracious Queen Elizabeth, many of them being preferred to bishoprics and other promotions according to their aims and desires, that inveterate hatred against the holy discipline of Christ in His church[4] hath continued to this day. Insomuch that for fear it should prevail, all plots and devices have been used to keep it out, incensing the Queen and State against it as dangerous for the commonwealth; and that it was most needful that the fundamental points of religion should be preached in those ignorant and superstitious times. And to win the weak and ignorant they might retain diverse harmless ceremonies; and though it were to be wished that diverse things were reformed, yet this was not a season for it. And many the like, to stop the mouths of the more godly, to bring them on to yield to one ceremony after another, and one corruption after another; by these wiles beguiling some and corrupting others till at length they began to persecute all the zealous professors[5] in the land (though they knew little what this discipline meant) both by word and deed, if they would not submit to their ceremonies and become slaves to them and their popish trash, which have no ground

in the Word of God, but are relics of that man of sin.[6] And the more the light of the gospel grew, the more they urged their subscriptions to[7] these corruptions. So as (notwithstanding all their former pretenses and fair colors) they whose eyes God had not justly blinded might easily see whereto these things tended. And to cast contempt the more upon the sincere servants of God, they opprobriously[8] and most injuriously gave unto and imposed upon them that name of Puritans, which is said the Novatians[9] out of pride did assume and take unto themselves. And lamentable it is to see the effects which have followed. Religion hath been disgraced, the godly grieved, afflicted, persecuted and many exiled; sundry[10] have lost their lives in prisons and other ways. On the other hand, sin hath been countenanced; ignorance, profaneness, and atheism[11] increased, and the papists encouraged to hope again for a day. ...

So many, therefore, of these professors as saw the evil of these things in these parts, and whose hearts the Lord had touched with heavenly zeal for His truth, they shook off this yoke of antichristian bondage, and as the Lord's free people joined themselves (by a covenant of the Lord) into a church estate, in the fellowship of the gospel, to walk in all His ways made known, or to be made known unto them, according to their best endeavours, whatsoever it should cost them, the Lord assisting them. And that it cost them something this ensuing history will declare. ...

Yet seeing themselves thus molested, and that there was no hope of their continuance there, by a joint consent they resolved to go into the Low Countries, where they heard was freedom of religion for all men; as also

---

[1] *contention ... service book*   Puritans such as Bradford objected to many practices of the Church of England, including its rituals, Book of Common Prayer, and hierarchical clergy; they considered such things to be distractions reminiscent of Catholicism.

[2] *high places in Israel ... ruin*   See 1 Kings 13.1–3. These passages describe the coming of a "man of God" who speaks against the altars in "high places" in Bethel, where idolatrous worship and sacrifice took place; the man of God predicts the coming of a prophet, Josiah, who will destroy these idols and their worshippers.

[3] *these people*   Anglican Protestants who had fled England to avoid persecution under Queen Mary.

[4] *holy discipline ... His church*   I.e., the discipline and practices of Puritan congregations.

[5] *professors*   Those who openly claim to believe in Christianity.

[6] *Word of God*   I.e., the Gospels; *that man of sin*   Following Martin Luther's lead, Puritans viewed the Pope, and the church he leads, as the "man of sin," the antichrist—a figure opposed to Christ that seeks to supplant him at the Second Coming. See 2 Thessalonians 2.3–4.

[7] *subscriptions to*   Approvals of.

[8] *opprobriously*   Scornfully.

[9] *Novatians*   Followers of Novatian (200–258), a Greek theologian whose sect did not allow lapsed Christians to be accepted back into the rites of communion.

[10] *sundry*   Many.

[11] *atheism*   In the seventeenth century, the term was used to refer not only to a disbelief in God, but more broadly to godlessness, wickedness, or corruption.

how sundry from London and other parts of the land had been exiled and persecuted for the same cause, and were gone thither, and lived at Amsterdam and in other places of the land. So after they had continued together about a year, and kept their meetings every Sabbath in one place or other, exercising the worship of God amongst themselves, notwithstanding all the diligence and malice of their adversaries, they seeing they could no longer continue in that condition, they resolved to get over into Holland as they could. Which was in the year 1607 and 1608; of which more at large in the next chapter.

from CHAPTER 4
SHOWING THE REASONS AND
CAUSES OF THEIR REMOVAL

After they had lived in this city[1] about some eleven or twelve years (which is the more observable being the whole time of that famous truce between that state and the Spaniards)[2] and sundry of them were taken away by death and many others began to be well stricken in years (the grave mistress of Experience having taught them many things), those prudent governors with sundry of the sagest members began both deeply to apprehend their present dangers and wisely to foresee the future and think of timely remedy. In the agitation of their thoughts, and much discourse of things hereabout, at length they began to incline to this conclusion: of removal to some other place. Not out of any newfangledness or other such like giddy humor by which men are oftentimes transported to their great hurt and danger, but for sundry weighty and solid reasons, some of the chief of which I will here briefly touch.

And first, they saw and found by experience the hardness of the place and country to be such as few in comparison would come to them, and fewer that would bide it out and continue with them. For many that came to them, and many more that desired to be with them, could not endure that great labour and hard fare, with other inconveniences which they underwent and were contented with. ... For many, though they desired to enjoy the ordinances of God in their purity and the liberty of the gospel with them, yet (alas) they admitted of bondage with danger of conscience, rather than to endure these hardships. Yea, some preferred and chose the prisons in England rather than this liberty in Holland with these afflictions. But it was thought that if a better and easier place of living could be had, it would draw many and take away these discouragements. Yea, their pastor would often say that many of those who both wrote and preached now against them, if they were in a place where they might have liberty and live comfortably, they would then practice as they did.

Secondly. They saw that though the people generally bore all these difficulties very cheerfully and with a resolute courage, being in the best and strength of their years; yet old age began to steal on many of them; and their great and continual labours, with other crosses and sorrows, hastened it before the time. So as it was not only probably thought, but apparently seen, that within a few years more they would be in danger to scatter, by necessities pressing them, or sink under their burdens, or both. And therefore according to the divine proverb, that a wise man seeth the plague when it cometh, and hideth himself, Proverbs 22.3, so they like skillful and beaten soldiers were fearful either to be entrapped or surrounded by their enemies so as they should neither be able to fight nor fly. And therefore thought it better to dislodge betimes[3] to some place of better advantage and less danger, if any such could be found.

Thirdly. As necessity was a taskmaster over them so they were forced to be such, not only to their servants but in a sort to their dearest children, the which as it did not a little wound the tender hearts of many a loving father and mother, so it produced likewise sundry sad and sorrowful effects. For many of their children that were of best dispositions and gracious inclinations, having learned to bear the yoke in their youth[4] and willing to bear part of their parents' burden, were oftentimes so oppressed with their heavy labours that though their minds were free and willing, yet their bodies bowed under the weight of the same,

---

[1] *this city* Leiden, Holland.

[2] *truce between ... Spaniards* The Twelve Years' Truce (1609–21), a break in the hostilities of the Eighty Years' War between Spain and the Southern Netherlands.

[3] *betimes* Quickly, before it was too late.

[4] *bear the yoke in their youth* See Lamentations 3.27.

and became decrepit in their early youth, the vigour of nature being consumed in the very bud as it were. But that which was more lamentable, and of all sorrows most heavy to be borne, was that many of their children, by these occasions and the great licentiousness of youth in that country,[1] and the manifold temptations of the place, were drawn away by evil examples into extravagant and dangerous courses, getting the reins off their necks and departing from their parents. Some became soldiers, others took upon them far voyages by sea, and others some worse courses tending to dissoluteness and the danger of their souls, to the great grief of their parents and dishonour of God. So that they saw their posterity would be in danger to degenerate and be corrupted.

Lastly (and which was not least), a great hope and inward zeal they had of laying some good foundation, or at least to make some way thereunto, for the propagating and advancing the gospel of the kingdom of Christ in those remote parts of the world; yea, though they should be but even as stepping-stones unto others for the performing of so great a work.

These and some other like reasons moved them to undertake this resolution of their removal; the which they afterward prosecuted with so great difficulties, as by the sequel will appear. …

CHAPTER 9
OF THEIR VOYAGE, AND HOW THEY PASSED THE SEA; AND OF THEIR SAFE ARRIVAL AT CAPE COD

September 6.   These troubles[2] being blown over, and now all being compact together in one ship,

they put to sea again with a prosperous wind, which continued diverse days together, which was some encouragement unto them; yet, according to the usual manner, many were afflicted with seasickness. And I may not omit here a special work of God's providence. There was a proud and very profane young man, one of the seamen, of a lusty,[3] able body, which made him the more haughty; he would always be contemning the poor people in their sickness and cursing them daily with grievous execrations; and did not let to tell them that he hoped to help to cast half of them overboard before they came to their journey's end, and to make merry with what they had; and if he were by any gently reproved, he would curse and swear most bitterly. But it pleased God before they came half seas over, to smite this young man with a grievous disease, of which he died in a desperate manner, and so was himself the first that was thrown overboard. Thus his curses light on his own head, and it was an astonishment to all his fellows for they noted it to be the just hand of God upon him. …

But to omit other things (that I may be brief) after long beating at sea they fell with that land which is called Cape Cod; the which being made and certainly known to be it, they were not a little joyful. After some deliberation had amongst themselves and with the master of the ship, they tacked about and resolved to stand for the southward (the wind and weather being fair) to find some place about Hudson's River[4] for their habitation. But after they had sailed that course about half the day, they fell amongst dangerous shoals and roaring breakers, and they were so far entangled therewith as they conceived themselves in great danger; and the wind shrinking upon them withal, they resolved to bear up again for the Cape and thought themselves happy to get out of those dangers before night overtook them, as by God's providence they did. And the next day they got into the Cape Harbor[5] where they rid in safety.

---

[1]   *great licentiousness … country*   The English Puritans objected to many aspects of Dutch life, particularly their habit of socializing after church on Sundays, which the Puritans felt ought to be kept holy and spent in contemplation. There was also concern among the Puritan leaders that if they remained in the Netherlands their children would eventually become Dutch and not English, which they wanted to prevent.

[2]   *These troubles*   In Book 1, Chapters 7–8 (omitted here) the Pilgrims set sail in two ships. The smaller one, the *Speedwell*, leaks, and they return to Dartmouth, England, to have it repaired. A second sailing produces the same result, and the ships return to Plymouth, England, where the *Speedwell* is deemed unseaworthy. Some of its passengers decide not to take the journey after all, but some board the larger ship (the *Mayflower*), which then becomes rather crowded with passengers, crew, and supplies.

[3]   *lusty*   Strong and healthy.

[4]   *Hudson's River*   Prominent waterway in New York state and the *Mayflower*'s original destination.

[5]   *Cape Harbor*   Today called Provincetown Harbor.

A word or two by the way of this cape. It was thus first named by Captain Gosnold and his company,[1] Anno[2] 1602, and after by Captain Smith[3] was called Cape James; but it retains the former name amongst seamen. Also, that point which first showed those dangerous shoals unto them they called Point Care, and Tucker's Terror; but the French and Dutch to this day call it Malabar[4] by reason of those perilous shoals and the losses they have suffered there.

Being thus arrived in a good harbor, and brought safe to land, they fell upon their knees and blessed the God of Heaven[5] who had brought them over the vast and furious ocean, and delivered them from all the perils and miseries thereof, again to set their feet on the firm and stable earth, their proper element. And no marvel if they were thus joyful, seeing wise Seneca[6] was so affected with sailing a few miles on the coast of his own Italy, as he affirmed, that he had rather remain twenty years on his way by land than pass by sea to any place in a short time, so tedious and dreadful was the same unto him.[7]

But here I cannot but stay and make a pause, and stand half amazed at this poor people's present condition; and so I think will the reader, too, when he well considers the same. Being thus passed the vast ocean, and a sea of troubles before in their preparation (as may be remembered by that which went before), they had now no friends to welcome them nor inns to entertain or refresh their weatherbeaten bodies no houses or much less towns to repair to, to seek for succor. It is recorded in Scripture[8] as a mercy to the Apostle[9] and his shipwrecked company, that the barbarians showed them no small kindness in refreshing them, but these savage barbarians, when they met with them (as after will appear) were readier to fill their sides full of arrows than otherwise. And for the season it was winter, and they that know the winters of that country know them to be sharp and violent, and subject to cruel and fierce storms, dangerous to travel to known places, much more to search an unknown coast. Besides, what could they see but a hideous and desolate wilderness, full of wild beasts and wild men—and what multitudes there might be of them they knew not. Neither could they, as it were, go up to the top of Pisgah[10] to view from this wilderness a more goodly country to feed their hopes; for which way soever they turned their eyes (save upward to the heavens) they could have little solace or content in respect of any outward objects. For summer being done, all things stand upon them with a weatherbeaten face, and the whole country, full of woods and thickets, represented a wild and savage hue. If they looked behind them, there was the mighty ocean which they had passed and was now as a main bar and gulf to separate them from all the civil parts of the world. If it be said they had a ship to succor them, it is true; but what heard they daily from the master and company? But that with speed they should look out a place (with their shallop[11]) where they would be, at some near distance; for the season was such as he would not stir from thence till a safe harbor was discovered by them, where they would be, and he might go without danger; and that victuals[12] consumed apace but he must and would keep sufficient for themselves and their return. Yea, it was muttered by some that if they got not a place in time, they would turn them and their goods ashore and leave them. Let it also be considered what weak hopes of supply and succor they left behind them, that might

---

[1]   [Bradford's note]   Because they took much of that fish there. [I.e., they caught a great deal of codfish there.]

[2]   *Anno*   Latin: Year.

[3]   *Captain Gosnold*   Bartholomew Gosnold (1571–1607), English explorer and lawyer, led the first recorded European expedition to Cape Cod;   *Captain Smith*   John Smith (c. 1580–1631), English explorer, author, and cartographer.

[4]   *Point Care … Malabar*   These names probably refer to Nauset Harbor, Cape Cod.

[5]   *blessed the God of Heaven*   See Daniel 2.19.

[6]   *Seneca*   Seneca the Younger (c. 4 BCE–65 CE), a Roman stoic philosopher.

[7]   [Bradford's note]   Epistle 53. [Bradford is paraphrasing from Seneca's "Epistle 53" from *The Moral Epistles to Lucius* (c. 65 CE).]

[8]   [Bradford's note]   Acts 28[.2].

[9]   *the Apostle*   Paul the Apostle (c. 5–c. 64 or 67), also known as Saint Paul, an early Christian missionary who is traditionally considered the author of thirteen books of the New Testament.

[10]   *Pisgah*   Mount Pisgah. On its peak, God shows Moses the Promised Land. See Deuteronomy 34.1–4.

[11]   *shallop*   Open row-boat used in shallow waters to move between a larger boat and land.

[12]   *victuals*   Food or provisions.

bear up their minds in this sad condition and trial they were under; and they could not but be very small. It is true, indeed, the affections and love of their brethren at Leiden was cordial and entire towards them, but they had little power to help them or themselves; and how the case stood between them and the merchants at their coming away hath already been declared.[1]

What could now sustain them but the Spirit of God and His grace? May not and ought not the children of these fathers rightly say: "Our fathers were Englishmen which came over this great ocean, and were ready to perish in this wilderness; but they cried unto the Lord, and He heard their voice and looked on their adversity,"[2] etc. "Let them therefore praise the Lord, because He is good: and His mercies endure forever."[3] "Yea, let them which have been redeemed of the Lord, show how He hath delivered them from the hand of the oppressor. When they wandered in the desert wilderness out of the way, and found no city to dwell in, both hungry and thirsty, their soul was overwhelmed in them. Let them confess before the Lord His loving kindness and His wonderful works before the sons of men."[4]

from CHAPTER 10
SHOWING HOW THEY SOUGHT OUT A PLACE OF HABITATION; AND WHAT BEFELL THEM THEREABOUT

Being thus arrived at Cape Cod the 11th of November, and necessity calling them to look out a place for habitation (as well as the master's and mariners' importunity); they having brought a large shallop with them out of England, stowed in quarters in the ship, they now got her out and set their carpenters to work to trim her up; but being much bruised and shattered in the ship with foul weather, they saw she would be long in mending. Whereupon a few of them tendered themselves to go by land and discover those nearest places, whilst the shallop was in mending; and the rather because as they went into that harbor there seemed to be an opening some two or three leagues off, which the master judged to be a river.[5] It was conceived there might be some danger in the attempt, yet seeing them resolute, they were permitted to go, being sixteen of them well armed under the conduct of Captain Standish,[6] having such instructions given them as was thought meet.[7]

They[8] set forth the 15th of November; and when they had marched about the space of a mile by the sea side, they espied five or six persons with a dog coming towards them, who were savages; but they fled from them and ran up into the woods, and the English followed them, partly to see if they could speak with them, and partly to discover if there might not be more of them lying in ambush. But the Indians seeing themselves thus followed, they again forsook the woods and ran away on the sands as hard as they could, so as they could not come near them but followed them by the tracks of their feet sundry miles and saw that they had come the same way. So, night coming on, they made their rendezvous and set out their sentinels, and rested in quiet that night; and the next morning followed their tracks till they had headed a great creek[9] and so left the sands, and turned another way into the woods. But they still followed them by guess, hoping to find their dwellings; but they soon lost both them and themselves, falling into such thickets as were ready to tear their clothes and armor in pieces; but were most distressed for want of drink. But at length they found

---

1   *how the case stood ... been declared* The relationship between the Pilgrims and the Merchant Adventurers—the group of capitalists led by Thomas Weston (c. 1584–c. 1647) who helped fund Plymouth Plantation—had fallen out over several conditions of their agreement. Most contentiously, the Adventurers changed the original agreement that would grant the Pilgrims ownership of their houses and lands (and the profits made from them) after seven years; an amendment to that original agreement stated that such property would be *divided* between the Pilgrims and the Adventurers after seven years. The disagreement between the parties delayed the *Mayflower*'s departure and did not end amicably, with Weston refusing any further financial aid.

2   [Bradford's note]   Deuteronomy 26.5,7.

3   *Let them therefore praise ... endure forever* See Psalm 106.1.

4   [Bradford's note]   Psalm 107.1–5, 8.

5   *river* From where the Pilgrims were, the land near Plymouth looks like an island in certain conditions, hence the assumption a river divides the land from the sea.

6   *Captain Standish* Myles Standish (c. 1584–1656), English ex-soldier hired by the Merchant Adventurers as a military advisor to the Pilgrims. He became a good friend and supporter to the Pilgrims.

7   *meet* Suitable.

8   *They* Bradford was included in this group.

9   *headed a great creek* Went around the source of the creek, in this case East-Harbor Creek.

water and refreshed themselves, being the first New England water they drunk of, and was now in great thirst as pleasant unto them as wine or beer had been in foretimes.

Afterwards they directed their course to come to the other shore, for they knew it was a neck of land they were to cross over, and so at length got to the seaside and marched to this supposed river, and by the way found a pond of clear, fresh water, and shortly after a good quantity of clear ground where the Indians had formerly set corn, and some of their graves. And proceeding further they saw new stubble where corn had been set the same year, also they found where lately a house had been, where some planks and a great kettle was remaining, and heaps of sand newly paddled[1] with their hands. Which, they digging up, found in them diverse fair Indian baskets filled with corn, and some in ears, fair and good, of diverse colors, which seemed to them a very goodly sight (having never seen any such before). This was near the place of that supposed river they came to seek, unto which they went and found it to open itself into two arms with a high cliff of sand in the entrance but more like to be creeks of salt water than any fresh, for aught they saw; and that there was good harborage for their shallop, leaving it further to be discovered by their shallop, when she was ready. So, their time limited them being expired, they returned to the ship lest they should be in fear of their safety; and took with them part of the corn and buried up the rest. And so, like the men from Eshcol, carried with them of the fruits of the land and showed their brethren;[2] of which, and their return, they were marvelously glad and their hearts encouraged.

After this, the shallop being got ready, they set out again for the better discovery of this place,[3] and the master of the ship desired to go himself. So there went some thirty men but found it to be no harbor for ships but only for boats. There was also found two of their houses covered with mats, and sundry of their implements in them, but the people were run away and could not be seen.[4] Also there was found more of their corn and of their beans of various colors; the corn and beans they brought away, purposing to give them full satisfaction[5] when they should meet with any of them as, about some six months afterward they did, to their good content.

And here is to be noted a special providence of God, and a great mercy to this poor people, that here they got seed to plant them corn the next year, or else they might have starved, for they had none nor any likelihood to get any till the season had been past, as the sequel did manifest. Neither is it likely they had had this, if the first voyage had not been made, for the ground was now all covered with snow and hard frozen; but the Lord is never wanting unto His in their greatest needs; let His holy name have all the praise.

The month of November being spent in these affairs, and much foul weather falling in, the 6th of December they sent out their shallop again with ten of their principal men[6] and some seamen, upon further discovery, intending to circulate that deep bay of Cape Cod. The weather was very cold and it froze so hard as the spray of the sea lighting on their coats, they were as if they had been glazed. Yet that night betimes they got down into the bottom of the bay, and as they drew near the shore they saw some ten or twelve Indians very busy about something. They landed about a league or two from them, and had much ado to put ashore anywhere—it lay so full of flats. Being landed, it grew late and they

---

[1]   *paddled* Flattened down. In Champlain's *Voyages* (1632), the author notes that Indigenous peoples of this area would dig large sand trenches, put their corn in grass sacks, and cover it with several feet of sand, thereby preserving it very effectively.

[2]   *Eshcol ... brethren* In Numbers 13, God tells Moses to send men to explore the land of Canaan, which God gives to the Israelites. The leaders of the various tribes set out and explore the wilderness, bringing back grapes, pomegranates, and figs to prove to their people the fertility of the land they found. See Numbers 13.23–26.

[3]   *this place* This second expedition explored the areas around the Pamet and Little Pamet Rivers, returning to Cape Cod Harbor on 30 November.

[4]   *their houses ... could not be seen* This area was inhabited by Nauset people, who spoke the Massachusett language; their round wigwams were constructed with bent boughs stuck into the ground on each side, interwoven with smaller boughs and covered with mats of woven bark. The implements mentioned were likely for farming and fishing.

[5]   *satisfaction* Payment.

[6]   *ten of their principal men* According to *Mourt's Relation* (1622), a first-hand account of the colony's beginnings, these were Standish, Carver, Bradford, Edward Winslow, John Tilley, Edward Tilley, John Howland, Richard Warren, Steven Hopkins, Edward Doten, John Alderton, Thomas English, Clarke, Copin, and four more unnamed sailors.

made themselves a barricado with logs and boughs as well as they could in the time, and set out their sentinel and betook them to rest, and saw the smoke of the fire the savages made that night. When morning was come they divided their company, some to coast along the shore in the boat, and the rest marched through the woods to see the land, if any fit place might be for their dwelling. They came also to the place where they saw the Indians the night before, and found they had been cutting up a great fish like a grampus,[1] being some two inches thick of fat like a hog, some pieces where of they had left by the way. And the shallop found two more of these fishes dead on the sands, a thing usual after storms in that place, by reason of the great flats of sand that lie off.

So they ranged up and down all that day, but found no people, nor any place they liked. When the sun grew low, they hasted out of the woods to meet with their shallop, to whom they made signs to come to them into a creek hard by,[2] the which they did at high water; of which they were very glad, for they had not seen each other all that day since the morning. So they made them a barricado as usually they did every night, with logs, stakes and thick pine boughs, the height of a man, leaving it open to leeward, partly to shelter them from the cold and wind (making their fire in the middle and lying round about it) and partly to defend them from any sudden assaults of the savages, if they should surround them; so being very weary, they betook them to rest. But about midnight, they heard a hideous and great cry, and their sentinel called "Arm! arm!" So they bestirred them and stood to their arms and shot off a couple of muskets, and then the noise ceased. They concluded it was a company of wolves or such like wild beasts, for one of the seamen told them he had often heard such a noise in Newfoundland.

So they rested till about five of the clock in the morning; for the tide, and their purpose to go from thence, made them be stirring betimes. So after prayer they prepared for breakfast, and it being day dawning it was thought best to be carrying things down to the boat. But some said it was not best to carry the arms down, others said they would be the readier, for they had lapped them up in their coats from the dew; but some three or four would not carry theirs till they went themselves. Yet as it fell out, the water being not high enough, they laid them down on the bank side and came up to breakfast.

But presently, all on the sudden, they heard a great and strange cry, which they knew to be the same voices they heard in the night, though they varied their notes; and one of their company being abroad came running in and cried, "Men, Indians! Indians!" And withal, their arrows came flying amongst them. Their men ran with all speed to recover their arms, as by the good providence of God they did. In the meantime, of those that were there ready, two muskets were discharged at them, and two more stood ready in the entrance of their rendezvous but were commanded not to shoot till they could take full aim at them. And the other two charged again with all speed, for there were only four had arms there, and defended the barricado, which was first assaulted. The cry of the Indians was dreadful, especially when they saw their men run out of the rendezvous towards the shallop to recover their arms, the Indians wheeling about upon them. But some running out with coats of mail on, and cutlasses in their hands, they soon got their arms and let fly amongst them and quickly stopped their violence. Yet there was a lusty man, and no less valiant, stood behind a tree within half a musket shot, and let his arrows fly at them; he was seen [to] shoot three arrows, which were all avoided. He stood three shots of a musket, till one taking full aim at him and made the bark or splinters of the tree fly about his ears, after which he gave an extraordinary shriek and away they went, all of them. They[3] left some to keep the shallop and followed them about a quarter of a mile and shouted once or twice, and shot of two or three pieces, and so returned. This they did that they might conceive that they were not afraid of them or any way discouraged.

Thus it pleased God to vanquish their enemies and give them deliverance; and by His special providence so to dispose that not any one of them were either hurt or hit, though their arrows came close by them and on every side [of] them; and sundry of their coats, which hung up in the barricado, were shot through and through. Afterwards they gave God solemn thanks and

---

1   *grampus*   Name applied to several species of whale and dolphin.

2   *creek*   Herring River, also called Great Meadow Creek; *hard by*   Nearby.

3   *They*   The English.

praise for their deliverance, and gathered up a bundle of their arrows and sent them into England afterward by the master of the ship, and called that place the First Encounter. ...

from THE SECOND BOOK

The rest of this History (if God give me life and opportunity) I shall, for brevity's sake, handle by way of annals,[1] noting only the heads of principal things, and passages as they fell in order of time, and may seem to be profitable to know or to make use of. And this may be as the Second Book.

from CHAPTER 11
THE REMAINDER OF ANNO 1620
[THE MAYFLOWER COMPACT][2]

I shall a little return back, and begin with a combination made by them before they came ashore; being the first foundation of their government in this place. Occasioned partly by the discontented and mutinous speeches that some of the strangers[3] amongst them had let fall from them in the ship: That when they came ashore they would use their own liberty, for none had power to command them, the patent they had being for Virginia and not for New England, which belonged to another Government, with which the Virginia Company had nothing to do.[4] And partly that such an act by them done, this their condition considered,[5] might be as firm as any patent, and in some respects more sure.

The form was as followeth:

IN THE NAME OF GOD, AMEN.

original spelling

We whose names are underwritten, the loyall subjects of our dread[6] soveraigne Lord, King James, by the grace of God of Great Britain, France and Ireland king, defender of the faith, etc.

Haveing undertaken, for the glorie of God and advancement of the Christian faith and honour of our king and countrie, a voyage to plant the first colonie in the Northerne parts of Virginia, doe by these presents[7] solemnly and mutualy in the presence of God, and one of another, covenant and combine our selves together into a civill body politick, for our better ordering and preservation and furrherance of the ends aforesaid; and by vertue hereof to enacte, constitute, and frame such just and equall lawes, ordinances, acts, constitutions and offices, from time to time, as shall be thought most meete and convenient for the generall good of the Colonie, unto which we promise all due submission and obedience. In witness whereof we have hereunder subscribed our names at Cape-Codd, the 11 of November, in the year of the raigne of our soveraigne lord, King James, of England, France and Ireland, the eighteenth, and of Scotland the fifty-fourth. Anno Dom. 1620.

After this they chose, or rather confirmed, Mr. John Carver (a man godly and well approved amongst them) their Governor for that year. And after they had provided a place for their goods, or common store (which were long in unlading for want of boats, foulness of winter weather and sickness of diverse) and begun some small cottages for their habitation; as time would admit, they met and consulted of laws and orders, both for their civil and military government as the necessity of their condition did require, still adding thereunto as urgent occasion in several times, and as cases did require.

In these hard and difficult beginnings they found some discontents and murmurings arise amongst some, and mutinous speeches and carriages[8] in other; but they were soon quelled and overcome by the

---

[1] *annals* A narrative of events organized according to year.

[2] *MAYFLOWER COMPACT* Written agreement created by the male passengers of *The Mayflower*, declaring that, once disembarked, they intended to live together within a common political body governed by laws and a constitution.

[3] *strangers* Those who traveled on *The Mayflower* but were not members of the Separatist congregation.

[4] *patent ... nothing to do* The Pilgrims had brought a patent— a land grant from the King—for "the Northern parts of Virginia," but weather forced a landing further north, outside the jurisdiction specified in the patent. In this state of legal uncertainty, some of the ship's passengers threatened to abandon the group once they reached land. The Mayflower Compact averted this threat of mutiny.

[5] *this ... considered* Considering their circumstances.

[6] *dread* Revered.

[7] *by these presents* In these statements.

[8] *carriages* Ways of behaving.

wisdom, patience and just and equal[1] carriage of things by the Governor and better part, which clave[2] faithfully together in the main.

[THE STARVING TIME]

But that which was most sad and lamentable was, that in two or three months' time half of their company died, especially in January and February, being the depth of winter, and wanting houses and other comforts; being infected with the scurvy and other diseases which this long voyage and their inaccomodate condition had brought upon them. So as there died sometimes two or three of a day in the foresaid time, that of 100 and odd persons, scarce fifty remained. And of these, in the time of most distress, there was but six or seven sound persons who to their great commendations be it spoken, spared no pains night nor day, but with abundance of toil and hazard of their own health, fetched them wood, made them fires, dressed them meat, made their beds, washed their loathsome clothes, clothed and unclothed them. In a word, did all the homely and necessary offices for them which dainty and queasy stomachs cannot endure to hear named; and all this willingly and cheerfully, without any grudging in the least, showing herein their true love unto their friends and brethren; a rare example and worthy to be remembered. Two of these seven were Mr. William Brewster, their reverend Elder, and Myles Standish, their Captain and military commander, unto whom myself and many others were much beholden in our low and sick condition. And yet the Lord so upheld these persons as in this general calamity they were not at all infected either with sickness or lameness. And what I have said of these I may say of many others who died in this general visitation, and others yet living; that whilst they had health, yea, or any strength continuing, they were not wanting to any that had need of them. And I doubt not but their recompense is with the Lord. ...

[INDIAN RELATIONS]

All this while the Indians came ·skulking about them, and would sometimes show themselves aloof off, but when any approached near them, they would run away; and once they stole away their tools where they had been at work and were gone to dinner. But about the 16th of March, a certain Indian came boldly amongst them and spoke to them in broken English, which they could well understand but marveled at it. At length they understood by discourse with him, that he was not of these parts, but belonged to the eastern parts where some English ships came to fish, with whom he was acquainted and could name sundry of them by their names, amongst whom he had got his language. He became profitable to them in acquainting them with many things concerning the state of the country in the east parts where he lived, which was afterwards profitable unto them; as also of the people here, of their names, number and strength, of their situation and distance from this place, and who was chief amongst them. His name was Samoset.[3] He told them also of another Indian whose name was Squanto,[4] a native of this place, who had been in England and could speak better English than himself.

Being, after some time of entertainment and gifts dismissed, a while after he came again, and five more with him, and they brought again all the tools that were stolen away before, and made way for the coming of their great Sachem, called Massasoit.[5] Who, about four or five days after, came with the chief of his friends and other attendance, with the aforesaid Squanto. With whom, after friendly entertainment and some gifts given him, they made a peace with him (which hath now continued this 24 years) in these terms:

---

1   *equal* Impartial.

2   *clave* Cleaved, stuck.

3   *Samoset* Sagamore—a type of chief—of the Pemaquid Abenaki people (c. 1590–1653). Samoset's people lived in what is now Maine.

4   *Squanto* Tisquantum (1585–1622), a member of the Patuxet tribe that lived in the area around Plymouth. Squanto was kidnapped by English sailors in 1617 and returned to New England in 1619 to find his village empty as the result of an epidemic.

5   *Sachem* High chief; *Massasoit* Sachem of the Wampanoag (c. 1581–1661).

1. That neither he nor any of his should injure or do hurt to any of their people.

2. That if any of his did any hurt to any of theirs, he should send the offender, that they might punish him.

3. That if anything were taken away from any of theirs, he should cause it to be restored; and they should do the like to his.

4. If any did unjustly war against him, they would aid him; if any did war against them, he should aid them.

5. He should send to his neighbors confederates to certify them of this, that they might not wrong them, but might be likewise comprised in the conditions of peace.

6. That when their men came to them, they should leave their bows and arrows behind them.

After these things he returned to his place called Sowams,[1] some 40 miles from this place, but Squanto continued with them and was their interpreter and was a special instrument sent of God for their good beyond their expectation. He directed them how to set their corn, where to take fish, and to procure other commodities, and was also their pilot to bring them to unknown places for their profit, and never left them till he died. …

from CHAPTER 12
ANNO DOMINI 1621
[*MAYFLOWER* DEPARTS AND CORN PLANTED]

They now began to dispatch the ship away which brought them over, which lay till about this time, or the beginning of April.[2] The reason on their parts why she stayed so long, was the necessity and danger that lay upon them; for it was well towards the end of December before she could land anything here, or they able to receive anything ashore. Afterwards, the 14th of January, the house which they had made for a general rendezvous by casualty fell afire, and some were fain to retire aboard for shelter; then the sickness began to fall sore amongst them, and the weather so bad as they could not make much sooner any dispatch. Again, the Governor and chief of them, seeing so many die and fall down sick daily, thought it no wisdom to send away the ship, their condition considered and the danger they stood in from the Indians, till they could procure some shelter; and therefore thought it better to draw some more charge[3] upon themselves and friends than hazard all. The master and seamen likewise, though before they hasted[4] the passengers ashore to be gone, now many of their men being dead, and of the ablest of them (as is before noted), and of the rest many lay sick and weak; the master durst not put to sea till he saw his men begin to recover, and the heart of winter over.

Afterwards they (as many as were able) began to plant their corn, in which service Squanto stood them in great stead, showing them both the manner how to set it, and after how to dress and tend it. Also he told them, except they got fish and set with it in these old grounds it would come to nothing.[5] And he showed them that in the middle of April they should have store enough come up the brook by which they began to build, and taught them how to take it,[6] and where to get other provisions necessary for them. All which they found true by trial and experience. Some English seed they sowed, as wheat and peas, but it came not to good, either by the badness of the seed or lateness of the season or both, or some other defect. …

[INDIAN DIPLOMACY]

Having in some sort ordered their business at home, it was thought meet to send some abroad to see their new friend Massasoit, and to bestow upon him some gratuity[7] to bind him the faster unto them; as also that hereby they might view the country and see in what

---

1   *Sowams*   This village is now named Warren, Rhode Island.

2   *the ship … April*   The *Mayflower* sailed from New Plymouth on 5 April and reached England on 6 May.

3   *charge*   Expense.

4   *hasted*   Hurried.

5   *fish … come to nothing*   Squanto taught them to use fish as fertilizer for the crops. In Captain John Smith's *Advertisements for the Unexperienced*, he wrote that in New England they "stick at every plant of corn, a herring or two; which cometh in that season in such abundance, they may take more than they know what to do with." It was a very effective method to gain high yields of corn.

6   *he showed them … how to take it*   Squanto taught the settlers how to set up a fishing weir across the brook to catch large quantities of migrating herring in the spring.

7   *gratuity*   Gift.

manner he lived, what strength he had about him, and how the ways were to his place, if at any time they should have occasion. So the second of July they sent Mr. Edward Winslow and Mr. Hopkins,[1] with the foresaid Squanto for their guide; who gave him a suit of clothes and a horseman's coat, with some other small things, which were kindly accepted; but they found but short commons[2] and came both weary and hungry home. For the Indians used then to have nothing so much corn as they have since the English have stored[3] them with their hoes, and seen their industry in breaking up new grounds therewith.[4]

They found his place to be forty miles from hence, the soil good and the people not many, being dead and abundantly wasted in the late great mortality, which fell in all these parts about three years before the coming of the English, wherein thousands of them died. They not being able to bury one another, their skulls and bones were found in many places lying still above ground where their houses and dwellings had been, a very sad spectacle to behold. But they brought word that the Narragansetts[5] lived but on the other side of that great bay, and were a strong people, and many in number, living compact together, and had not been at all touched with this wasting plague.

About the later end of this month, one John Billington lost himself in the woods, and wandered up and down some five days, living on berries and what he could find. At length he light on an Indian plantation twenty miles south of this place, called Manomet; they conveyed him further off, to Nauset among those people that had before set upon the English when they were coasting whilst the ship lay at the Cape, as is before noted. But the Governor caused him to be inquired for among the Indians, and at length Massasoit sent word

where he was, and the Governor sent a shallop for him and had him delivered. Those people[6] also came and made their peace; and they gave full satisfaction to those whose corn they had found and taken when they were at Cape Cod.

Thus their peace and acquaintance was pretty well established with the natives about them. ...

[First Thanksgiving[7]]

They began now to gather in the small harvest they had, and to fit up their houses and dwellings against winter, being all well recovered in health and strength and had all things in good plenty. For as some were thus employed in affairs abroad, others were exercised in fishing, about cod and bass and other fish, of which they took good store, of which every family had their portion. All the summer there was no want; and now began to come in store of fowl, as winter approached, of which this place did abound when they came first (but afterward decreased by degrees). And besides waterfowl there was great store of wild turkeys, of which they took many, besides venison, etc. Besides they had about a peck[8] a meal a week to a person, or now since harvest, Indian corn to that proportion. Which made many afterwards write so largely of their plenty here to their friends in England, which were not feigned but true reports.

---

[1] *Mr. Hopkins* Stephen Hopkins (1581–1644), an English tanner and merchant recruited to join the Pilgrims by the Company of Merchant Adventurers.

[2] *short commons* Scarce rations, little food.

[3] *stored* Supplied.

[4] *industry ... therewith* The Indigenous peoples in this area used clamshells to till the earth for their corn; the English supplied them with hoes, which dig up more earth more quickly. There are records, however, suggesting that cultivation by clamshell was superior than that which resulted from European tools.

[5] *Narragansetts* Algonquian tribe living in what is now Rhode Island.

[6] *Those people* I.e., the Nauset.

[7] *First Thanksgiving* The feast described here is not explicitly identified as a "thanksgiving" in Bradford's account, but it was a practice of Puritan congregations to declare days of thanksgiving—special days set aside for prayer, to thank God for favorable events such as a good harvest. The modern holiday is based on this tradition. See also "The Myth of Thanksgiving," included in the "Civilizations in Contact" section of this volume.

[8] *peck* Unit of measurement for dry goods, equivalent to about eight dry quarts.

from CHAPTER 14
ANNO DOMINI 1623
[END OF THE "COMMON COURSE AND CONDITION"[1]]

All this while no supply was heard of, neither knew they when they might expect any. So they began to think how they might raise as much corn as they could, and obtain a better crop than they had done, that they might not still thus languish in misery. At length, after much debate of things, the Governor (with the advice of the chiefest amongst them) gave way that they should set corn every man for his own particular,[2] and in that regard trust to themselves; in all other things to go on in the general way as before. And so assigned to every family a parcel of land, according to the proportion of their number, for that end, only for present use (but made no division for inheritance) and ranged all boys and youth under some family. This had very good success, for it made all hands very industrious, so as much more corn was planted than otherwise would have been by any means the Governor or any other could use, and saved him a great deal of trouble, and gave far better content. The women now went willingly into the field, and took their little ones with them to set corn; which before would allege weakness and inability; whom to have compelled would have been thought great tyranny and oppression.

The experience that was had in this common course and condition, tried sundry years and that amongst godly and sober men, may well evince the vanity of that conceit of Plato's and other ancients, applauded by some of later times; that the taking away of property and bringing in community into a commonwealth would make them happy and flourishing; as if they were wiser than God.[3] For this community (so

far as it was) was found to breed much confusion and discontent and retard much employment that would have been to their benefit and comfort. For the young men, that were most able and fit for labor and service, did repine that they should spend their time and strength to work for other men's wives and children without any recompense. The strong, or man of parts, had no more in division of victuals and clothes than he that was weak and not able to do a quarter the other could; this was thought injustice. The aged and graver men to be ranked and equalized in labors and victuals, clothes, etc., with the meaner and younger sort, thought it some indignity and disrespect unto them. And for men's wives to be commanded to do service for other men, as dressing their meat, washing their clothes, etc., they deemed it a kind of slavery, neither could many husbands well brook[4] it. Upon the point all being to have alike, and all to do alike, they thought themselves in the like condition, and one as good as another; and so, if it did not cut off those relations that God hath set amongst men, yet it did at least much diminish and take of the mutual respects that should be preserved amongst them. And would have been worse if they had been men of another condition. Let none object this is men's corruption, and nothing to the course itself. I answer, seeing all men have this corruption in them, God in His wisdom saw another course fitter for them. …

from CHAPTER 28
ANNO DOMINI 1637
[THE PEQUOT WAR]

In the fore part of this year, the Pequots[5] fell openly upon the English at Connecticut, in the lower parts of the river, and slew sundry of them as they were at work in the fields, both men and women, to the great terror of the rest; and went away in great pride and triumph, with many high threats. They also assaulted

---

[1] *COMMON COURSE AND CONDITION* The economic system at Plymouth was from the beginning one in which all members labored for the common stock—each person worked and contributed, and everyone was fed and clothed and housed. This began to cause some tension in the colony among those who felt that not all members were contributing equally (and that harder work was not rewarded with more gain).

[2] *every man for his own particular* Each man for himself, i.e., all members would harvest—and keep—their own crops.

[3] *conceit of Plato's … wiser than God* In Jean Bodin's *Les Six livres de la République* (1576), a translated copy of which Bradford owned, Bodin writes: "But he [Plato] understood not that by making all

things thus common, a Commonweal must needs perish: for nothing can be public, where nothing is private." In *Republic*, Plato argues that the ruling classes should give up private property to ensure their transcendence of personal interest, and that their needs would be taken care of by the state.

[4] *brook* Tolerate.

[5] *Pequots* Indigenous people living in what is now southeastern Connecticut.

a fort at the river's mouth, though strong and well defended; and though they did not there prevail, yet it struck them with much fear and astonishment to see their bold attempts in the face of danger. Which made them in all places to stand upon their guard and to prepare for resistance, and earnestly to solicit their friends and confederates in the Bay of Massachusetts to send them speedy aid, for they looked for more forcible assaults. Mr. Vane, being then Governor, writ from their General Court to them here to join with them in this war. To which they were cordially willing, but took opportunity to write to them about some former things, as well as present, considerable hereabout. …

In the meantime, the Pequots, especially in the winter before, sought to make peace with the Narragansetts, and used very pernicious arguments to move them thereunto: as that the English were strangers and began to overspeed their country, and would deprive them thereof in time, if they were suffered to grow and increase. And if the Narragansetts did assist the English to subdue them, they did but make way for their own overthrow, for if they were rooted out, the English would soon take occasion to subjugate them. And if they would hearken to them they should not need to fear the strength of the English, for they would not come to open battle with them but fire their houses, kill their cattle and lie in ambush for them as they went abroad upon their occasions; and all this they might easily do without any or little danger to themselves. The which course being held, they well saw the English could not long subsist but they would either be starved with hunger or be forced to forsake the country. With many the like things; insomuch that the Narragansetts were once wavering and were half minded to have made peace with them, and joined against the English. But again, when they considered how much wrong they had received from the Pequots, and what an opportunity they now had by the help of the English to right themselves; revenge was so sweet unto them as it prevailed above all the rest, so as they resolved to join with the English against them, and did.

The Court here agreed forthwith to send fifty men at their own charge; and with as much speed as possibly they could, got them armed and had made them ready under sufficient leaders, and provided a bark to carry them provisions and tend upon them for all occasions.

But when they were ready to march, with a supply from the Bay, they had word to stay; for the enemy was as good as vanquished and there would be no need.

I shall not take upon me exactly to describe their proceedings in these things, because I expect it will be fully done by themselves who best know the carriage and circumstances of things. I shall therefore but touch them in general. From Connecticut, who were most sensible of the hurt sustained and the present danger, they set out a party of men, and another party met them from the Bay, at the Narragansetts', who were to join with them. The Narragansetts were earnest to be gone before the English were well rested and refreshed, especially some of them which came last. It should seem their desire was to come upon the enemy suddenly and undiscovered. There was a bark of this place, newly put in there, which was come from Connecticut, who did encourage them to lay hold of the Indians' forwardness, and to show as great forwardness as they, for it would encourage them, and expedition might prove to their great advantage. So they went on, and so ordered their march as the Indians brought them to a fort[1] of the enemy's (in which most of their chief men were) before day. They approached the same with great silence and surrounded it both with English and Indians, that they might not break out; and so assaulted them with great courage, shooting amongst them, and entered the fort with all speed. And those that first entered found sharp resistance from the enemy, who both shot at and grappled with them; others ran into their houses and brought out fire and set them on fire, which soon took in their mat; and standing close together, with the wind all was quickly on a flame, and thereby more were burnt to death than was otherwise slain. It burnt their bowstrings and made them unserviceable; those that escaped the fire were slain with the sword; some hewed to pieces, others run through with their rapiers, so as they were quickly dispatched and very few escaped. It was conceived they thus destroyed about 400 at this time. It was a fearful sight to see them thus frying in the fire and the streams of blood quenching the same, and horrible was the stink and scent thereof; but the victory seemed a sweet sacrifice,[2] and they gave the praise thereof to God, who had wrought so

---

[1] *fort* This was Fort Mystic, on the bank of the Mystic River.

[2] *sweet sacrifice* See Leviticus 2.2.

wonderfully for them, thus to enclose their enemies in their hands and give them so speedy a victory over so proud and insulting an enemy. …

That I may make an end of this matter, this Sassacus (the Pequots' chief sachem) being fled to the Mohawks, they cut off his head, with some other of the chief of them, whether to satisfy the English or rather the Narragansetts (who, as I have since heard, hired them to do it) or for their own advantage, I well know not; but thus this war took end. The rest of the Pequots were wholly driven from their place, and some of them submitted themselves to the Narragansetts and lived under them. Others of them betook themselves to the Mohegans under Uncas, their sachem, with the approbation of the English of Connecticut, under whose protection Uncas lived; and he and his men had been faithful to them in this war and done them very good service. But this did so vex the Narragansetts, that they had not the whole sway over them, as they have never ceased plotting and contriving how to bring them under; and because they cannot attain their ends, because of the English who have protected them, they have sought to raise a general conspiracy against the English, as will appear in another place. …

from Chapter 32
Anno Domini 1642
[Wickedness Breaks Forth]

Marvelous it may be to see and consider how some kind of wickedness did grow and break forth here, in a land where the same was so much witnessed against and so narrowly looked unto, and severely punished when it was known, as in no place more, or so much, that I have known or heard of; insomuch as they have been somewhat censured even by moderate and good men for their severity in punishments. And yet all this could not suppress the breaking out of sundry notorious sins (as this year, besides other, gives us too many sad precedents and instances), especially drunkenness and uncleanness.[1] Not only incontinency[2] between persons unmarried, for which many both men and women have been punished sharply enough, but some married persons also. But that which is worse, even

sodomy and buggery[3] (things fearful to name) have broke forth in this land oftener than once.

I say it may justly be marveled at and cause us to fear and tremble at the consideration of our corrupt natures, which are so hardly bridled, subdued and mortified; nay, cannot by any other means but the powerful work and grace of God's Spirit. But (besides this) one reason may be that the Devil may carry a greater spite against the churches of Christ and the gospel here, by how much the more they endeavour to preserve holiness and purity amongst them and strictly punisheth the contrary when it ariseth either in church or commonwealth; that he might cast a blemish and stain upon them in the eyes of [the] world, who use to be rash in judgment. I would rather think thus, than that Satan hath more power in these heathen lands, as some have thought, than in more Christian nations, especially over God's servants in them.

2. Another reason may be, that it may be in this case as it is with waters when their streams are stopped or dammed up. When they get passage they flow with more violence and make more noise and disturbance than when they are suffered to run quietly in their own channels; so wickedness being here more stopped by strict laws, and the same more nearly looked unto so as it cannot run in a common road of liberty as it would and is inclined, it searches everywhere and at last breaks out where it gets vent.

3. A third reason may be, here (as I am verily persuaded) is not more evils in this kind, nor nothing near so many by proportion as in other places; but they are here more discovered and seen and made public by due search, inquisition and due punishment; for the churches look narrowly to their members, and the magistrates over all, more strictly than in other places. Besides, here the people are but few in comparison of other places which are full and populous and lie hid, as it were, in a wood or thicket and many horrible evils by that means are never seen nor known; whereas here, they are, as it were, brought into the light and set in the plain field, or rather on a hill, made conspicuous to the view of all. …

—1856 (written 1630–51)

---

[1] *uncleanness* Sexual impurity.

[2] *incontinency* Lack of self-restraint.

[3] *buggery* Anal intercourse, as well as any intercourse with an animal.

IN CONTEXT

Mapping Colonial Conflict

The following are historical mappings of conflicts between settlers and Indigenous peoples in seventeenth-century New England. The first map depicts the genocide of the Pequot known as the Mystic Massacre (1637); the second documents Indigenous oral records of the boundaries of Pequot territory before the Pequot War (1636–38); and the third is a settler map marking sites of conflict across New England.

John Underhill, "The Figure of the Indians' Fort or Palizado in New England and the Manner of Destroying It by Captain Underhill and Captain Mason," *News from America* **(1638)**

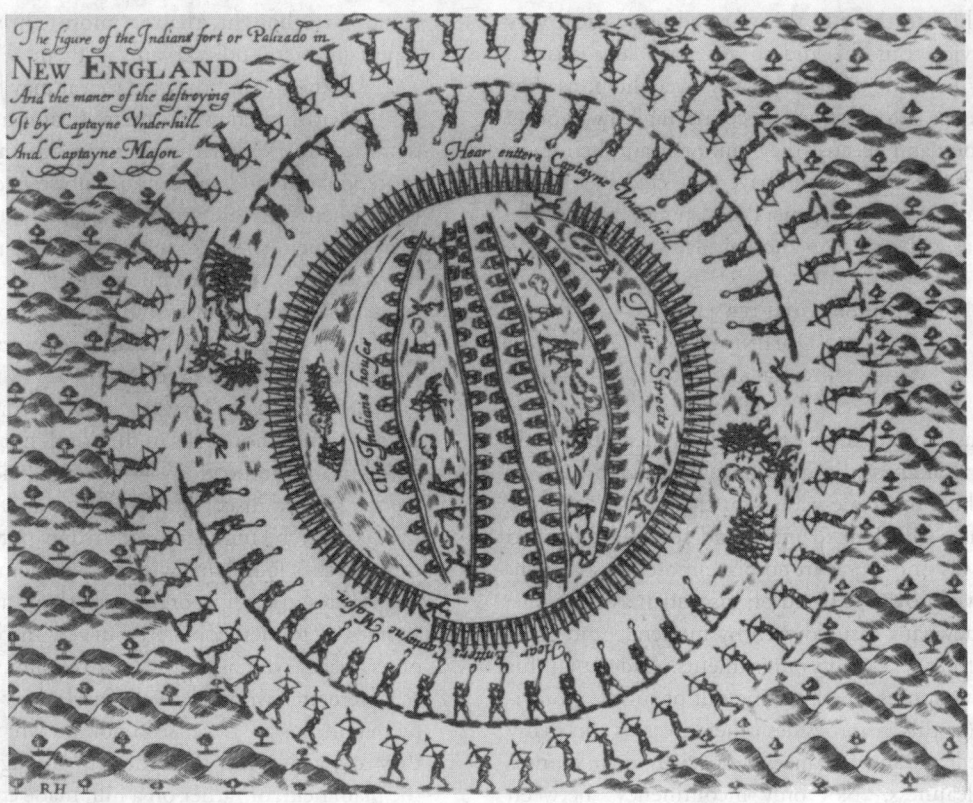

John Underhill and John Mason, colonists from Connecticut, led a genocide of the Pequots at their fortress on the Mystic River on 26 May 1637, killing everyone inside—including children and the elderly. The death toll of 400 people constituted a large percentage of the Pequot population, and the attack marked a devastating turning point in the Pequot War; after the massacre, almost all surviving Pequots were hunted down and killed or enslaved by settlers and their Indigenous allies, and were for a time not permitted to call themselves Pequot. It was not until 1983 that the Mashantucket Pequot Tribal Nation was recognized by the federal government; another tribal nation, the Eastern Pequot, is still pursuing federal recognition.

This map depicting the massacre appeared in Underhill's *News from America*, an account of his experiences as a militia captain during the Pequot War. Underhill describes the Mystic Massacre as follows:

Captain Mason entering into a wigwam, brought out a firebrand, after he had wounded many in the house, then he set fire on the west side where he entered, myself set fire on the south end with a train of powder. The fires of both meeting in the center of the fort blazed most terribly, and burnt all in the space of half an hour; many courageous fellows were unwilling to come out, and fought most desperately through the pallisadoes, so as they were scorched and burnt with the very flame, and were deprived of their arms, in regard the fire burnt their very bowstrings, and so perished valiantly: mercy they did deserve for their valour, could we have had opportunity to have bestowed it; many were burnt in the Fort, both men, women, and children, others forced out, and came in troops to the Indians [the colonists' Narragansett and Mohegan allies], twenty, and thirty at a time, which our soldiers received and entertained with the point of the sword; down fell men, women, and children. Those that scaped us, fell into the hands of the Indians, that were in the rear of us; it is reported by themselves, that there were about four hundred souls in this Fort, and not above five of them escaped out of our hands. Great and doleful was the bloody sight to the view of young soldiers that never had been in war, to see so many souls lie gasping on the ground so thick in some places, that you could hardly pass along. It may be demanded, Why should you be so furious (as some have said) should not Christians have more mercy and compassion? But I would refer you to David's war, when a people is grown to such a height of blood, and sin against God and man … there he hath no respect to persons, but harrows them, and saws them, and puts them to the sword, and the most terriblest death that may be: sometimes the Scripture declares women and children must perish with their parents; sometime[s] the case alters: but we will not dispute it now. We had sufficient light from the word of God for our proceedings.

John Tinker, Uncas, Wesawegun, Cassacinamon, Harry Wright, and Ninigret, "Plan of the Pequot Country and Testimony of Uncas, Cassacinamon, and Wesawegun" (1662)

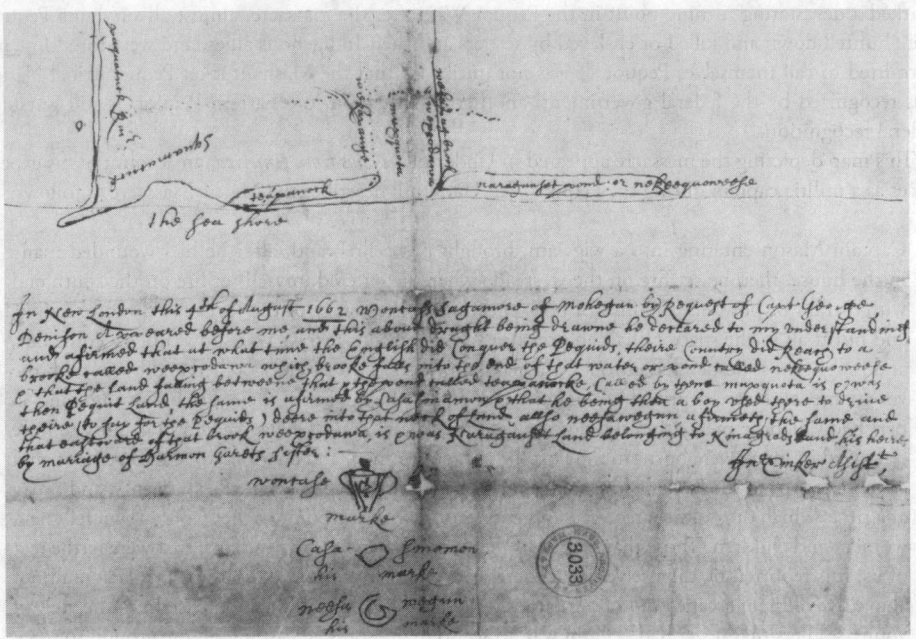

This image shows the extent of Pequot territory before the Pequot War, with testimony of Uncas, Cassacinamon, and Wesawegun regarding the borders of the land. The map is made by the war's victors: the colonists and the Mohegan and the Narragansett, the Indigenous tribes that fought alongside the colonists. The 1638 Treaty of Hartford had declared Pequot territory to be the property of the English colonists. In 1662, however, there was conflict among the colonists after Charles II issued the Connecticut charter, which transferred the Pequot lands from Massachusetts to Connecticut. There were disagreements among the colonists as to the extent of the land, and disagreements between the Mohegan and the Narragansett as well, who each claimed some portion of the land as spoils of war. To help sort out the various claims, Indigenous leaders were gathered together at the General Court in New London to document their knowledge of the territory's boundaries. John Tinker and Harry Wright, two colonial representatives, were joined by Uncas; other signatories to the map were Pequot survivors Wesawegun and Cassacinamon. The following is a lightly modernized transcription of the writing on the map:

In New London this 4th of August 1662 Woncass [Uncas] Sagamore of Mohegan by request of Captain George Denison appeared before me, and this above draft being drawn he declared to my understanding and affirmed that at what time the English did conquer the Pequids [Pequots], their country did reach to a brook called Weex-co-da-wa, which brook falls into the end of that water or pond called Nekeequoweese, and that the land falling between that and the pond called Teapanocke, called by them Muxquota, is and was then Pequot land, the same is affirmed by Cassacinamon, and that he being then a boy used there to drive their (to say for the Pequots) deer into that neck of land, also Wesawegun affirmeth the same, and that eastward of that brook Weexcodawa, is and was Narragansett land belonging to Ninagrads [Ninigret] and his heirs by marriage of Hermon Garret's sister:

John Tinker, Assist.

—Woncase [Uncas] his mark
—Cassasinomon his mark
—Wesawegun his mark

William Hubbard, "A Map of New-England" (1677)

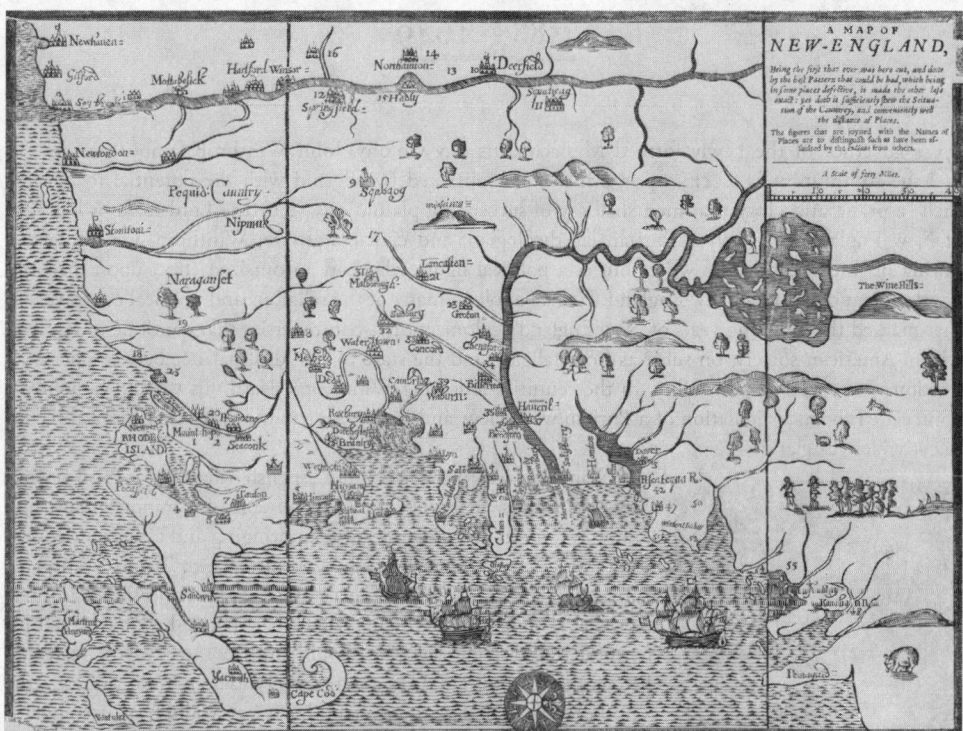

This is the first map printed in America, issued by Boston printer John Foster. It was an illustration in English-born writer and clergy member William Hubbard's book *The Present State of New England: Being a Narrative of the Troubles with the Indians* (1677). The description in the upper right corner identifies the map as "the first that ever was here [in America] cut, and done by the best pattern that could be had, which being in some places defective, it made the other less exact: yet doth it sufficiently show the situation of the country, and conveniently well the distance of places." The crowns on the map mark European settlements; the numbers mark places where there had been conflicts with Indigenous peoples.

John Winthrop

1588 – 1649

As governor of the newly formed Massachusetts Bay Colony, John Winthrop famously envisaged the community as a "city upon a hill" to be observed by all, and with the potential to become such "a praise and glory that men shall say of succeeding plantations, 'may the Lord make it like that of New England.'" A lawyer, Puritan lay theologian, and civil magistrate, Winthrop was recognized during his lifetime not as a writer but as a political figure who had an outsized effect upon the early development of colonial New England. He had a role in many of the religious and political controversies that marked the fledgling years of New England's colonization—controversies that continue to resonate within American society, on subjects from religion and the state to the ideal balance between personal freedom and social responsibility. In the centuries following Winthrop's death, his writing came to be appreciated for its articulation of a Puritan worldview, and for its contributions to the historical record of early New England.

Winthrop was born in a rural English village in 1588 to devout Calvinist parents, his father the younger son of a minor landowning family. Winthrop had a comfortable upbringing and a rigorous education, and at age fourteen he gained admittance to Trinity College in Cambridge, intending to become a minister. This education was interrupted at seventeen, when he married Mary Forth; he later turned his attention to studying law. He would outlive three wives, marrying Thomasine Clopton in 1615, Margaret Tyndal in 1618, and Martha Rainsborough in 1648; among them, his wives would bear sixteen children, only half of whom lived to adulthood.

In 1613, Winthrop came into ownership of his family's estate in Groton, Suffolk—lands which had been expropriated from the Catholic Church and sold to Winthrop's grandfather—where he served as Lord of the Manor. Winthrop felt a calling to participate in public life, reflecting that "surer peace and joy in Christianity must not aim at a condition retired from the world." In 1615 he was appointed to the Suffolk Commission of the Peace, and in 1627 he was named attorney for the Court of Wards.

During this time, Winthrop grew increasingly concerned with the kingdom's spiritual welfare. Like other Puritans, he was alarmed by the policies of James I and his successor Charles I, both of whom had shifted the Church of England away from Calvinist orthodoxy. Winthrop became convinced that it would be necessary to emigrate from England in order to live a godly life. By 1629, he was meeting with the Massachusetts Bay Company, a group of Puritans who had already begun to establish their own commonwealth in America. Winthrop quickly rose to prominence within the company and in October 1629 was elected governor. The following year, on a ship with about 700 fellow emigrants, he set sail for America to assume command of the colony itself.

Tradition holds that while en route to the colony, Winthrop delivered the inspirational lay sermon *A Model of Christian Charity*, which includes his description of the American colony as "a city upon a hill." The ideas in *A Model of Christian Charity* were not particularly groundbreaking to Winthrop's audience, and the sermon was not remarked upon by his contemporaries—or even by Winthrop himself in his journals. This makes it difficult if not impossible to confirm the date of the sermon's composition and delivery—if indeed he ever delivered it—and some scholars have questioned whether Winthrop was even the sermon's author, positing such figures as the minister George Phillips, his fellow passenger, as more likely candidates. Though the text circulated among some readers during Winthrop's lifetime, no seventeenth-century response hints at the impact the sermon would have in later centuries.

Winthrop ultimately served as Governor of Massachusetts for twelve non-consecutive annual terms during the colony's first two decades. His leadership was instrumental in bringing the first large waves of English settlers into the Massachusetts Bay Colony. In his role as a colonial leader, Winthrop participated in numerous political and theological clashes, many of them involving dissenters such as Thomas Morton, Roger Williams, and Anne Hutchinson. Winthrop was neither the most nor the least tolerant colonial leader in New England at the time: while he despised what he called their "dangerous errors" in matters of religion, he nevertheless professed respect for the "bold spirit" and "godl[iness]" of radical figures such as Williams and Hutchinson. Winthrop's chief concern was to preserve the cohesion of the Puritan commonwealth, and believed that it was necessary "to entertain all means that may conduce to [its] welfare … and to keep off whatever appears to tend to [its] damage."

In addition to the colony's internal social and religious crises, Winthrop was involved in conflicts between the colonists and the Indigenous nations of the region: the colony occupied territory that belonged to Massachusett, Nipmuc, and other Algonquian-speaking peoples. Relations between the settlers and Indigenous people were relatively friendly in the first few years, during which Winthrop entertained a few Algonquian leaders at his home but had little sustained communication with them. The Pequot War of 1636–38, however, demanded a greater degree of diplomacy; Winthrop appealed to Roger Williams, who convinced the Narragansett people to join the fight against their traditional rivals, the Pequot, in an alliance that also included the Mohegan and all the other New England colonies. At the conclusion of the Pequot War, Winthrop oversaw the enslavement of Pequot captives, some of whom were kept by the victors (including Winthrop himself), while others were exchanged in Barbados for enslaved people from Africa.

Throughout the decades he spent in the government of the Massachusetts Bay Colony, Winthrop kept a journal. He began the project as he crossed the Atlantic, intending to record his experience of the journey so he could tell later waves of settlers what to expect. He then decided to continue the journal as a record of the colony's foundation; gradually the journal developed from an up-to-the-minute diary into a work more closely resembling a historical account. By the second volume, Winthrop's notes indicate that he had come to consider his project to be a sacred history documenting the suffering and eventual triumph of God's "subjects and soldiers." The work was thus part of a tradition of earlier Christian historians such as the English Protestant John Foxe, whose *Acts and Monuments* (1563), commonly known as the *Book of Martyrs* for its focus on the persecution of righteous Christians, was beloved by Puritan readers.

Winthrop's journal includes a wealth of information not found in the colony's official records, including the details of political controversies too sensitive for official documentation. Given the spiritual purpose of his task, Winthrop strove to be candid, and this often makes the journal both engaging and informative—though it is by no means unbiased, as he often takes great pains to justify his political decisions and show his opponents to have been in the wrong. Winthrop, who died in March 1649 after a lengthy illness, worked on the journal right up until the last weeks of his life, when he became too ill to write.

None of the writing for which Winthrop would come to be remembered was in circulation at the time of his death. Though later portions of his journal seem to have been intended for wider readership, the work did not appear in print until 1790, when the first two of his three journal notebooks were published. In 1825/26, after the third was rediscovered, all three volumes were released under the title *Winthrop's Journal, The History of New England from 1630–1649*. Winthrop's account began to shape conceptions of American history even before its first printing—the manuscript was frequently lent out to scholars of New England history—and since its publication it has been more widely considered invaluable as a historical record. *A Model of Christian Charity* remained unpublished even longer, finally appearing in print in 1838, while Winthrop's other writings were published as the *Winthrop Papers* in 1929–47.

In the early eighteenth century, Winthrop was lionized as a historical and spiritual figure; in 1702, fellow Puritan Cotton Mather praised him for "a certain *greatness of soul*, which rendered him grave, generous, courageous, resolved, well-applied, and every way a *gentleman* in his demeanour." More recently, his popular image has been more complex; he is envisioned by some as a repressive authoritarian, and by others as a pragmatic moderate within the context of the seventeenth-century Puritan political spectrum.

A major contributor to his enduring reputation is the rise in popularity of *A Model of Christian Charity*, which since the mid-twentieth century has been required reading for many students of American history and literature. Now often invoked as an early example of American exceptionalism, Winthrop's characterization of his colony as a "city upon a hill" continues to strike a deep patriotic chord, and twentieth-century American leaders such as John F. Kennedy and Ronald Reagan quoted the phrase in their own speeches.

NOTE ON THE TEXT: This text of *A Model of Christian Charity* is based upon the 1838 version published by the Massachusetts Historical Society. Biblical references are taken from the 1599 Geneva Bible, the translation of the Christian scriptures that Winthrop would have used.

⌘ ⌘ ⌘

A Model of Christian Charity

God Almighty, in his most holy and wise providence,[1] hath so disposed of the condition of mankind, as in all times some must be rich, some poor, some high and eminent in power and dignity; others mean and in submission.

THE REASON HEREOF

1 *Reas.*[2] First, to hold conformity with the rest of his world, being delighted to show forth the glory of his wisdom in the variety and difference of the creatures,[3] and the glory of his power in ordering all these differences for the preservation and good of the whole, and the glory of his greatness, that as it is the glory of princes to have many officers, so this great king will have many stewards, counting himself more honored in dispensing his gifts to man by man, than if he did it by his own immediate hands.

2 *Reas.* Secondly, that he might have the more occasion to manifest the work of his Spirit: first upon the wicked in moderating and restraining them, so that the rich and mighty should not eat up the poor, nor the poor and despised rise up against and shake off their yoke. Secondly, in the regenerate,[4] in exercising his graces in them, as in the great ones, their love, mercy, gentleness, temperance etc., in the poor and inferior sort, their faith, patience, obedience, etc.

3 *Reas.* Thirdly, that every man might have need of others, and from hence they might be all knit more nearly together in the bonds of brotherly affection. From hence it appears plainly that no man is made more honorable than another or more wealthy etc., out of any particular and singular respect to himself, but for the glory of his creator and the common good of the creature, man. Therefore God still reserves the property of these gifts to himself as [in] Ezekiel 16.17.[5] He there calls wealth, "his gold and his silver," and Proverbs 3.9,[6] he claims their service as his due, "Honor the Lord with thy riches," etc.—all men being thus (by divine providence) ranked into two sorts, rich and poor; under the first are comprehended all such as are able to live comfortably by their own means duly improved; and all others are poor according to the former distribution.

There are two rules whereby we are to walk one towards another: justice and mercy. These are always distinguished in their act and in their object, yet may they both concur in the same subject in each respect; as sometimes there may be an occasion of showing mercy to a rich man in some sudden danger or distress, and

---

[1] *providence*   Divine control and foreknowledge.

[2] *Reas.*   Reason.

[3] *creatures*   Created beings.

[4] *the regenerate*   Those saved, or reborn, through the sacrifice of Jesus Christ.

[5] *Ezekiel 16.17*   "Thou hast also taken thy fair jewels of my gold and of my silver, which I had given thee, and madest to thyself images of men, and didst commit whoredom with them."

[6] *Proverbs 3.9*   "Honour the Lord with thy riches, and with the first fruits of all thine increase."

also doing of mere justice to a poor man in regard of some particular contract, etc.

There is likewise a double law by which we are regulated in our conversation[1] towards another: in both the former respects, the law of nature and the law of grace, or the moral law or the law of the gospel, to omit the rule of justice as not properly belonging to this purpose otherwise than it may fall into consideration in some particular cases. By the first of these laws, man as he was enabled so withal is commanded to love his neighbor as himself.[2] Upon this ground stands all the precepts of the moral law, which concerns our dealings with men. To apply this to the works of mercy, this law requires two things. First, that every man afford his help to another in every want or distress; secondly, that he perform this out of the same affection which makes him careful of his own goods, according to the words of our Savior (Matthew 7.12): "whatsoever ye would that men should do to you."[3] This was practiced by Abraham and Lot in entertaining the angels and the old man of Gibeah.[4]

The law of grace or of the gospel hath some difference from the former (the law of nature), as in these respects: First, the law of nature was given to man in the estate of innocence—this of the gospel in the estate of regeneracy.[5] Secondly, the former propounds one man to another, as the same flesh and image of God. This as a brother in Christ also, and in the communion of the same Spirit, and so teacheth to put a difference between Christians and others. "Do good to all, especially to the household of faith."[6] Upon this ground the Israelites were to put a difference between the brethren of such as were strangers, though not of the Canaanites.[7]

Thirdly, the law of nature would give no rules for dealing with enemies, for all are to be considered as friends in the state of innocence, but the gospel commands love to an enemy. Proof: "If thine enemy hunger, feed him; Love your enemies, do good to them that hate you." Matthew 5.44.[8]

This law of the gospel propounds likewise a difference of seasons and occasions. There is a time when a Christian must sell all and give to the poor, as they did in the Apostles' times.[9] There is a time also when Christians (though they give not all yet) must give beyond their ability, as they of Macedonia, 2 Corinthians 8.[10] Likewise, community of perils calls for extraordinary liberality, and so doth community in some special service for the church. Lastly, when there is no other means whereby our Christian brother may be relieved in his distress, we must help him beyond our ability rather than tempt God in putting him upon[11] help by miraculous or extraordinary means.

This duty of mercy is exercised in the kinds:[12] giving, lending and forgiving.[13]

Question: What rule shall a man observe in giving in respect of the measure?

---

[1] *conversation* Way of behaving in society.

[2] *love his neighbor as himself* See Matthew 19.19: "Honour thy father, and mother: and, Thou shalt love thy neighbour as thyself"; and Matthew 5.43: "Ye have heard that it hath been said, Thou shalt love thy neighbour, and hate thine enemy."

[3] *whatsoever ye … to you* See Matthew 7.12: "Therefore whatsoever ye would that men should do to you: even so do ye to them: for this is the Law and the Prophets."

[4] *Abraham … of Gibeah* In Genesis 18, Abraham is a gracious host to three angels who visit him in human form. In Genesis 19, Abraham's nephew Lot hosts two angels, whom he defends from an angry mob, offering his own daughters to the mob in place of his guests. Judges 19 includes the story of an old man in Gibeah who similarly shelters travelers and defends them from a horde of "wicked" people, offering his own daughter to placate them.

[5] *estate of innocence* I.e., state before original sin; *estate of regeneracy* I.e., state of salvation through Christ.

[6] *Do good … of faith* See Galatians 6.10.

[7] *Canaanites* People of Canaan, the Promised Land of the Israelites, who were expelled upon the Israelites' arrival. God instructed the Israelites to have "no compassion" for the Canaanites, and to "utterly destroy them." See Deuteronomy 7.1–4.

[8] *Matthew 5.44* The full text reads, "But I say unto you, Love your enemies, bless them that curse you, do good to them that hate you, and pray for them which hurt you, and persecute you."

[9] *There is a time … Apostles' times* See Luke 18.22, where Jesus tells a rich man seeking eternal life to "Sell all that ever thou hast, and distribute unto the poor, and thou shalt have treasure in heaven, and come follow me."

[10] *2 Corinthians 8* Winthrop refers to verses 1–3: "We do you also to wit, brethren, of the grace of God bestowed upon the Churches of Macedonia. Because in great trial of affliction their joy abounded, and their most extreme poverty abounded unto their rich liberality. For to their power (I bear record) yea, and beyond their power they were willing."

[11] *putting him upon* I.e., forcing our brother to rely upon.

[12] *kinds* Categories.

[13] *forgiving* I.e., of a debt.

Answer: If the time and occasion be ordinary he is to give out of his abundance. "Let him lay aside as God hath blessed him."[1] If the time and occasion be extraordinary, he must be ruled by them; taking this withal, that then a man cannot likely do too much, especially if he may leave himself and his family under probable means of comfortable subsistence.

Objection: A man must lay up for posterity, the fathers lay up for posterity and children, and he is worse than an infidel that providⁿeth not for his own.[2]

Answer: For the first, it is plain that it being spoken by way of comparison, it must be meant of the ordinary and usual course of fathers, and cannot extend to times and occasions extraordinary. For the other place the Apostle[3] speaks against such as walked[4] inordinately, and it is without question, that he is worse than an infidel who through his own sloth and voluptuousness shall neglect to provide for his family.

Objection: "The wise man's eyes are in his head," saith Solomon,[5] "and foreseeth the plague"; therefore he must forecast and lay up against evil times when he or his may stand in need of all he can gather.

Answer: This very argument Solomon useth to persuade to liberality (Ecclesiastes 11[6]), "Cast thy bread upon the waters ... for thou knowest not what evil may come upon the land." Luke [16.9], "Make you friends of the riches of iniquity ..."[7] You will ask how this shall

be? Very well. For first he that gives to the poor, lends to the Lord[8] and he will repay him even in this life an hundredfold to him or his. "The righteous is ever merciful and lendeth, and his seed enjoyeth the blessing,"[9] and besides we know what advantage it will be to us in the day of account when many such witnesses shall stand forth for us to witness the improvement of our talent.[10] And I would know of those who plead so much for laying up for time to come, whether they hold that to be gospel Matthew [6.19],[11] "Lay not up for yourselves treasures upon earth," etc. If they acknowledge it, what extent will they allow it? If only to those primitive[12] times, let them consider the reason whereupon our Savior grounds it. The first is that they are subject to the moth, the rust, the thief. Secondly, they will steal away the heart: "where the treasure is there will your heart be also."

The reasons are of like force at all times. Therefore the exhortation must be general and perpetual, withallways in respect of the love and affection to riches and in regard of the things themselves when any special service for the church or particular distress of our brother do call for the use of them; otherwise it is not only lawful but necessary to lay up as Joseph did[13] to have ready upon such occasions, as the Lord (whose stewards we are of them) shall call for them from us. Christ gives us an instance of the first, when he sent his disciples for the donkey, and bids them answer the

---

1   *Let him ... blessed him*   See 1 Corinthians 16.2.

2   *he is worse ... his own*   See 1 Timothy 5.8;   *infidel*   Unbeliever.

3   *Apostle*   St. Paul, traditionally considered the author of many books of the New Testament, including 1 Timothy.

4   *walked*   Lived one's life. See Ephesians 5.15: "Take heed therefore that ye walk circumspectly, not as fools, but as wise."

5   *Solomon*   King of Israel who is traditionally considered the author of Ecclesiastes and a contributor to Proverbs. See Ecclesiastes 2.14 and Proverbs 22.3 for the passages quoted.

6   *Ecclesiastes 11*   See Ecclesiastes 11.1–2: "Cast thy bread upon the waters: for after many days thou shalt find it. Give a portion to seven, and also to eight: for thou knowest not what evil shall be upon the earth."

7   *Make you ... iniquity*   See Luke 16.9: "Make you friends with the riches of iniquity, that when ye shall want, they may receive you into everlasting habitations." This statement follows the parable of a steward who is about to lose his position keeping his master's accounts; the steward alters the records to reduce the debts owed to his master, thus ensuring that he will be taken in by his master's debtors.

8   *he that gives ... Lord*   See Proverbs 19.17: "He that hath mercy upon the poor, lendeth unto the Lord: and the Lord will recompense him that which he hath given."

9   *The righteous ... the blessing*   See Psalms 37.26.

10   *improvement of our talent*   Increase of our riches and wealth. See Matthew 25.14–30, a parable in which a master gives each of his servants coins; he rewards the servants who increase their wealth by lending it and punishes the one who hoards it instead.

11   *Matthew [6.19]*   See Matthew 6.19–21: "Lay not up treasures for yourselves upon the earth, where the moth and canker corrupt, and where thieves break through and steal: But lay up for yourselves treasures in heaven, where neither moth nor rust doth corrupt, and where thieves do not break through nor steal. For where your treasure is, there will your heart be also."

12   *primitive*   I.e., early. The early Christian period was often called the era of the "primitive church," with no connotation of inferiority.

13   *lay up as Joseph did*   Joseph, son of Jacob and Rachel, rose from slavery to high office in the Pharaoh's court. He averted a crisis by storing grain in anticipation of a famine. See Genesis 41.

owner thus, "the Lord hath need of him."[1] So when the Tabernacle[2] was to be built, he sends to his people to call for their silver and gold, etc., and yields no other reason but that it was for his work. When Elisha comes to the widow of Sareptah[3] and finds her preparing to make ready her pittance for herself and family, he bids her first provide for him, he challenges first God's part which she must first give before she must serve her own family. All these teach us that the Lord looks that when he is pleased to call for his right in any thing we have, our own interest we have must stand aside till his turn be served. For the other, we need look no further than to that of 1 John 3.17, "He who hath this world's goods and seeth his brother to need and shuts up his compassion from him, how dwelleth the love of God in him?" Which comes punctually to this conclusion: If thy brother be in want and thou canst help him, thou needst not make doubt of what thou shouldst do; if thou lovest God thou must help him.

Question: What rule must we observe in lending?

Answer: Thou must observe whether thy brother hath present or probable or possible means of repaying thee, if there be none of those, thou must give him according to his necessity, rather than lend [to] him as he requires.[4] If he hath present means of repaying thee, thou art to look at him not as an act of mercy, but by way of commerce, wherein thou art to walk by the rule of justice; but if his means of repaying thee be only probable or possible, then he is an object of thy mercy, thou must lend him, though there be danger of losing it. Deuteronomy 15.7–8: "If any of thy brethren be poor ... thou shalt lend him sufficient." That men might not shift off this duty by the apparent hazard, he tells them that though the year of Jubilee[5] were at hand (when he must remit it, if he were not able to repay it before), yet he must lend him, and that cheerfully.[6] It may not grieve thee to give him, saith he. And because

some might object, why so I should soon impoverish myself and my family, he adds, with all thy work, etc., for our Savior said (Matthew 5.42),[7] "From him that would borrow of thee turn not away."

Question: What rule must we observe in forgiving?[8]

Answer: Whether thou didst lend by way of commerce or in mercy, if he hath nothing to pay thee, thou must forgive (except in cause where thou hast a surety or a lawful pledge). Deuteronomy 15.1–2—Every seventh year the creditor was to quit that which he lent to his brother if he were poor, as appears in verse 4: "Save when there shall be no poor with thee." In all these and like cases, Christ gives a general rule (Matthew 7.12), "Whatsoever ye would that men should do to you, do ye the same to them."

Question: What rule must we observe and walk by in cause of community of peril?[9]

Answer: The same as before, but with more enlargement towards others and less respect towards ourselves and our own right. Hence it was that in the primitive church they sold all, had all things in common, neither did any man say that which he possessed was his own. Likewise in their return out of the captivity, because the work was great for the restoring of the church and the danger of enemies was common to all, Nehemiah[10] directs the Jews to liberality and readiness in remitting their debts to their brethren, and disposing liberally to such as wanted, and stand not upon their own dues which they might have demanded of them. Thus did some of our forefathers in times of persecution in England, and so did many of the faithful of other churches, whereof we keep an honorable remembrance of them; and it is to be observed that both in Scriptures and latter stories of the churches that such as have been most bountiful to the poor saints, especially in those extraordinary times and occasions, God hath left them highly commended to posterity, as Zaccheus, Cornelius, Dorcas, Bishop Hooper, the

---

1   *the Lord hath need of him*   See Luke 19.31.

2   *Tabernacle*   Tent containing the Ark of the Covenant, the vessel that held the Ten Commandments. See Exodus 25.

3   *the widow of Sareptah*   See 1 Kings 17.

4   *requires*   I.e., requests.

5   *Jubilee*   Biblically mandated observance supposed to occur every 50 years where debts and enslaved people are released and fields left uncultivated. See Leviticus 25.

6   *though the year ... cheerfully*   See Deuteronomy 15.7–10.

7   *Matthew 5.42*   The full passage reads: "Give to him that asketh, and from him that would borrow of thee, turn not away."

8   *forgiving*   I.e., forgiving debt.

9   *in cause ... of peril*   I.e., in situations when the community is in danger.

10   *Nehemiah*   An Old Testament prophet, Nehemiah oversaw repairs on the walls of Jerusalem and persuaded moneylenders to think of the common good and charge no interest.

Cutler of Brussels and diverse others.[1] Observe again that the Scripture gives no caution to restrain any from being over liberal this way; but all men to the liberal and cheerful practice hereof by the sweeter promises; as to instance one for many (Isaiah 58.6–9) "Is not this the fast I have chosen to loose the bonds of wickedness, to take off the heavy burdens, to let the oppressed go free and to break every yoke ... to deal thy bread to the hungry and to bring the poor that wander into thy house, when thou seest the naked to cover them ... and then shall thy light brake forth as the morning and thy health shall grow speedily, thy righteousness shall go before God, and the glory of the Lord shalt embrace thee; then thou shall call and the Lord shall answer thee," etc. [Isaiah 58.]10: "If thou pour out thy soul to the hungry, then shall thy light spring out in darkness, and the Lord shall guide thee continually, and satisfy thy soul in draught, and make fat thy bones, thou shalt be like a watered garden, and they shalt be of thee that shall build the old waste places," etc. On the contrary most heavy curses are laid upon such as are straitened[2] towards the Lord and his people (Judges 5.23), "Curse ye Meroshe ... because they came not to help the Lord." "He who shutteth his ears from hearing the cry of the poor, he shall cry and shall not be heard."[3] Matthew 25: "Go ye cursed into everlasting fire," etc. "I was hungry and ye fed me not."[4] 2 Corinthians 9.6: "He that soweth sparingly shall reap sparingly."

Having already set forth the practice of mercy according to the rule of God's law, it will be useful to lay open the grounds of it also, being the other part of the Commandment and that is the affection from which this exercise of mercy must arise, the Apostle tells us that this love is the fulfilling of the law,[5] not that it is enough to love our brother and so no further; but in regard of the excellency of his parts giving any motion to the other as the soul to the body and the power it hath to set all the faculties at work in the outward exercise of this duty; as when we bid one make

the clock strike, he doth not lay hand on the hammer, which is the immediate instrument of the sound, but sets on work the first mover or main wheel; knowing that will certainly produce the sound which he intends. So the way to draw men to the works of mercy, is not by force of argument from the goodness or necessity of the work; for though this cause may enforce a rational mind to some present act of mercy, as is frequent in experience, yet it cannot work such a habit in a soul, as shall make it prompt upon all occasions to produce the same effect, but by framing these affections of love in the heart which will as naturally bring forth the other, as any cause doth produce the effect.

The definition which the Scripture gives us of love is this: Love is the bond of perfection.[6] First it is a bond or ligament.[7] Secondly, it makes the work perfect. There is no body but consists of parts and that which knits these parts together, gives the body its perfection, because it makes each part so contiguous to others as thereby they do mutually participate with each other, both in strength and infirmity, in pleasure and pain. To instance in the most perfect of all bodies: Christ and his church make one body. The several parts of this body considered a part before they were united, were as disproportionate and as much disordering as so many contrary qualities or elements, but when Christ comes, and by his spirit and love knits all these parts to himself and each to other, it is become the most perfect and best proportioned body in the world (Ephesians 4.15–16).[8] Christ, by whom all the body being knit together by every joint for the furniture thereof, according to the effectual power which is in the measure of every perfection of parts, a glorious body without spot or wrinkle; the ligaments hereof being Christ, or his love, for Christ is love (1 John 4.8).[9] So this definition is right. Love is the bond of perfection.

---

[1] *Zaccheus ... and diverse others*   Christian martyrs.

[2] *straitened*   I.e., unsympathetic.

[3] *He who ... be heard*   See Proverbs 21.13.

[4] *Go ye cursed ... me not*   See Matthew 25.41–45, where Jesus equates refusal to help the poor and in need with refusal to help Jesus himself.

[5] *love is ... the law*   See Romans 13.10.

[6] *Love is ... perfection*   See Colossians 3.14.

[7] *ligament*   Connection.

[8] *Ephesians 4.15–16*   "But let us follow the truth in love, and in all things, grow up into him, which is the head, that is, Christ. By whom all the body being coupled and knit together by every joint, for the furniture thereof ... receiveth increase of the body, unto the edifying of itself in love."

[9] *1 John 4.8*   "He that loveth not, knoweth not God, for God is love."

From hence we may frame these conclusions. 1. First of all, true Christians are of one body in Christ (1 Corinthians 12[.12]). Ye are the body of Christ and members of their part. All the parts of this body being thus united are made so contiguous in a special relation as they must needs partake of each other's strength and infirmity; joy and sorrow, weal and woe. If one member suffers, all suffer with it, if one be in honor, all rejoice with it. Secondly, the ligaments of this body which knit together are love. Thirdly, no body can be perfect which wants its proper ligament. Fourthly, all the parts of this body being thus united are made so contiguous in a special relation as they must needs partake of each other's strength and infirmity, joy and sorrow, weal and woe. 1 Corinthians 12.26: If one member suffers, all suffer with it; if one be in honor, all rejoice with it. Fifthly, this sensitivity and sympathy of each other's conditions will necessarily infuse into each part a native desire and endeavor, to strengthen, defend, preserve and comfort the other.

To insist a little on this conclusion being the product of all the former, the truth hereof will appear both by precept and pattern. 1 John 3.16, "We ought to lay down our lives for the brethren." Galatians 6.2, "Bear ye one another's burdens and so fulfill the law of Christ." For patterns we have that first of our Savior who, out of his good will in obedience to his father, becoming a part of this body and being knit with it in the bond of love, found such a native sensitivity of our infirmities and sorrows as he willingly yielded himself to death to ease the infirmities of the rest of his body, and so healed their sorrows. From the like sympathy of parts did the Apostles and many thousands of the Saints lay down their lives for Christ. Again the like we may see in the members of this body among themselves. Romans 9—Paul could have been contented to have been separated from Christ, that the Jews might not be cut off from the body. It is very observable what he professeth of his affectionate partaking with every member; "Who is weak" (saith he) "and I am not weak? Who is offended and I burn not?"[1] And again (2 Corinthians 7.13), "Therefore we are comforted because ye were comforted." Of Epaphroditus[2]

he speaketh (Philippians 2.25–30) that he regarded not his own life to do him service. So Phebe[3] and others are called the servants of the church. Now it is apparent that they served not for wages, or by constraint, but out of love. The like we shall find in the histories of the church, in all ages; the sweet sympathy of affections which was in the members of this body one towards another; their cheerfulness in serving and suffering together; how liberal they were without repining, harbourers without grudging, and helpful without reproaching; and all from hence, because they had fervent love amongst them; which only makes the practice of mercy constant and easy.

The next consideration is how this love comes to be wrought. Adam in his first estate[4] was a perfect model of mankind in all their generations, and in him this love was perfected in regard of the habit. But Adam, himself rent[5] from his Creator, rent all his posterity also one from another; whence it comes that every man is born with this principle in him to love and seek himself only, and thus a man continueth till Christ comes and takes possession of the soul and infuseth another principle, love to God and our brother, and this latter having continual supply from Christ, as the head and root by which he is united, gets predominant in the soul, so by little and little expels the former. 1 John 4.7 "Love cometh of God and every one that loveth is born of God," so that this love is the fruit of the new birth, and none can have it but the new creature. Now when this quality is thus formed in the souls of men, it works like the Spirit upon the dry bones. Ezekiel 37.7—"Bone came to bone."[6] It gathers together the scattered bones, or perfect old man Adam,[7] and knits them into one body again in Christ, whereby a man is become again a living soul.

---

1   *Who … I burn not?*   See 2 Corinthians 11.29.

2   *Epaphroditus*   In his letter to the Philippians, Paul writes of Epaphroditus that "for the work of Christ he was near unto death,

and regarded not his life, to fulfill that service which was lacking on your part toward me" (Philippians 2.30).

3   *Phebe*   Paul praises the service of Phebe, a deacon in the early Church. See Romans 16.1–2.

4   *first estate*   State of innocence, before the first sin.

5   *rent*   Torn away.

6   *Bone came to bone*   See Ezekiel 37.1–10, in which Ezekiel revives a field of dry bones to form a living army.

7   *old man Adam*   Adam, the first human, guilty of original sin (as opposed to Jesus Christ, sometimes called "new Adam" in reference to his role as redeemer of original sin).

The third consideration is concerning the exercise of this love, which is twofold, inward or outward. The outward hath been handled in the former preface of this discourse. From unfolding the other we must take in our way that maxim of philosophy, "*simile simili gaudet*,"[1] or like will to like; for as of things which are turned with disaffection to each other, the ground of it is from a dissimilitude or arising from the contrary or different nature of the things themselves; for the ground of love is an apprehension of some resemblance in the things loved to that which affects it. This is the cause why the Lord loves the creature, so far as it hath any of his Image in it; he loves his elect[2] because they are like himself, he beholds them in his beloved son. So a mother loves her child, because she thoroughly conceives a resemblance of herself in it. Thus it is between the members of Christ; each discerns, by the work of the Spirit, his own Image and resemblance in another, and therefore cannot but love him as he loves himself. Now when the soul, which is of a sociable nature, finds anything like to itself, it is like Adam when Eve was brought to him. She must be one with himself. "This is flesh of my flesh"[3] (saith he) "and bone of my bone." So the soul conceives a great delight in it; therefore she desires nearness and familiarity with it. She hath a great propensity to do it good and receives such content[4] in it, as fearing the miscarriage of her beloved, she bestows it in the inmost closet of her heart. She will not endure that it shall want any good which she can give it. If by occasion she be withdrawn from the company of it, she is still looking towards the place where she left her beloved. If she heard it groan, she is with it presently. If she find it sad and disconsolate, she sighs and moans with it. She hath no such joy as to see her beloved merry and thriving. If she see it wronged, she cannot hear it without passion. She sets no bounds to her affections, nor hath any thought of reward. She finds recompense enough in the exercise of her love towards it. We may see this acted to life in Jonathan and David.[5] Jonathan a valiant man endued[6] with the spirit of love, so soon as he discovered the same spirit in David had presently his heart knit to him by this ligament of love; so that it is said he loved him as his own soul, he takes so great pleasure in him, that he strips himself to adorn his beloved. His father's kingdom was not so precious to him as his beloved David, David shall have it with all his heart. Himself desires no more but that he may be near to him to rejoice in his good. He chooseth to converse with him in the wilderness even to the hazard of his own life, rather than with the great Courtiers in his father's palace. When he sees danger towards him, he spares neither rare pains nor peril to direct it. When injury was offered his beloved David, he would not bear it, though from his own father. And when they must part for a season only, they thought their hearts would have broke for sorrow, had not their affections found vent by abundance of tears. Other instances might be brought to show the nature of this affection; as of Ruth and Naomi,[7] and many others; but this truth is cleared enough.

If any shall object that it is not possible that love shall be bred or upheld without hope of requital, it is granted; but that is not our cause; for this love is always under reward. It never gives, but it always receives with advantage. First, in regard that among the members of the same body, love and affection are reciprocal in a most equal and sweet kind of commerce. Secondly, in regard of the pleasure and content that the exercise of love carries with it, as we may see in the natural body. The mouth is at all the pains[8] to receive and mince the food which serves for the nourishment of all the other parts of the body; yet it hath no cause to complain; for first the other parts send back, by several passages, a due proportion of the same nourishment, in a better form for the strengthening and comforting the mouth. Secondly, the labor of the mouth is accompanied with such pleasure and content as far exceeds the pains it takes. So is it in all the labor of love among Christians.

---

[1]   *simile simili gaudet*   Medieval Latin proverb roughly meaning "like rejoices in like."

[2]   *elect*   People chosen to receive salvation.

[3]   *This is flesh of my flesh*   In Christian doctrine, God created Eve from Adam's rib. See Genesis 2.22–23.

[4]   *content*   Satisfaction, contentment.

[5]   *Jonathan and David*   Jonathan defies his father to maintain his friendship with David in 1 Samuel 19.

[6]   *endued*   Endowed.

[7]   *Ruth and Naomi*   After the death of her son, Naomi urges his widow, Ruth, to return to her parents. She chooses instead to remain with Naomi. See Ruth 1.16.

[8]   *at all the pains*   Solely responsible for the labor.

The party loving, reaps love again, as was showed before, which the soul covets more than all the wealth in the world. Thirdly, nothing yields more pleasure and content to the soul than when it finds that which it may love fervently; for to love and live beloved is the soul's paradise both here and in heaven. In the state of wedlock there be many comforts to learn out of the troubles of that condition; but let such as have tried the most, say if there be any sweetness in that condition comparable to the exercise of mutual love.

From the former considerations arise these conclusions: First, this love among Christians is a real thing, not imaginary. Secondly, this love is as absolutely necessary to the being of the body of Christ, as the sinews and other ligaments of a natural body are to the being of that body. Thirdly, this love is a divine, spiritual, nature; free, active, strong, courageous, permanent; undervaluing[1] all things beneath its proper object; and of all the graces, this makes us nearer to resemble the virtues of our heavenly father. Fourthly, it rests in the love and welfare of its beloved. For the full certain knowledge of those truths concerning the nature, use, and excellency of this grace, that which the holy ghost hath left recorded, 1 Corinthians 13,[2] may give full satisfaction, which is needful for every true member of this lovely body of the Lord Jesus, to work upon their hearts by prayer, meditation, continual exercise at least of the special [influence] of this grace, till Christ be formed in them and they in him, all in each other, knit together by this bond of love.

It rests now to make some application of this discourse, by the present design, which gave the occasion of writing of it. Herein are four things to be propounded; first the persons, secondly the work, thirdly the end,[3] fourthly the means.

First, for the persons. We are a company professing ourselves fellow members of Christ, in which respect only, though we were absent from each other many miles, and had our employments as far distant, yet we ought to account ourselves knit together by this bond of love and live in the exercise of it, if we would have comfort of our being in Christ. This was notorious in the practice of the Christians in former times; as is testified of the Waldenses,[4] from the mouth of one of the adversaries Aeneas Sylvius "*mutuo ament pene antequam norunt*,"[5] they used to love any of their own religion even before they were acquainted with them.

Secondly, for the work we have in hand. It is by a mutual consent, through a special overvaluing providence[6] and a more than an ordinary approbation of the churches of Christ, to seek out a place of cohabitation and consortship[7] under a due form of government both civil and ecclesiastical. In such cases as this, the care of the public must oversway all private respects, by which, not only conscience, but mere civil policy, doth bind us. For it is a true rule that particular estates cannot subsist in the ruin of the public.

Thirdly, the end is to improve our lives to do more service to the Lord; the comfort and increase of the body of Christ, whereof we are members, that ourselves and posterity may be the better preserved from the common corruptions of this evil world, to serve the Lord and work out our salvation under the power and purity of his holy ordinances.

Fourthly, for the means whereby this must be effected. They are twofold, a conformity with the work and end we aim at. These we see are extraordinary, therefore we must not content ourselves with usual ordinary means. Whatsoever we did, or ought to have done, when we lived in England, the same must we do, and more also, where we go. That which the most in their churches maintain as truth in profession only, we must bring into familiar and constant practice; as in this duty of love, we must love brotherly without dissimulation, we must love one another with a pure heart fervently. We must bear one another's burdens. We must not look only on our own things, but also

---

[1]   *undervaluing* I.e., considering to be inferior.

[2]   *1 Corinthians 13* This chapter extols the virtue of love, concluding, "And now abideth faith, hope, and love, even these three: but the greatest of these is love" (1 Corinthians 13.13).

[3]   *end* Purpose.

[4]   *Waldenses* Christian sect founded in the late twelfth century. Its members were persecuted by the Catholic Church, and the movement later adopted the theology of the Protestant Reformation.

[5]   *Aeneas Sylvius* Historian and scholar Pope Pius II (Aeneas Sylvius Piccolomini, 1405–64); *mutuo ament pene antequam norunt* Latin phrase more accurately rendered as "mutuo solent amare pene antequam norunt." Winthrop follows the phrase with its translation.

[6]   *overvaluing providence* I.e., providence that exceeds everything else in value.

[7]   *consortship* Fellowship.

on the things of our brethren. Neither must we think that the Lord will bear with such failings at our hands as he doth from those among whom we have lived; and that for these three reasons: First, in regard of the more near bond of marriage between him and us, wherein he hath taken us to be his, after a most strict and peculiar manner, which will make him the more jealous of our love and obedience. So he tells the people of Israel, you only have I known of all the families of the earth, therefore will I punish you for your transgressions.[1] Secondly, because the Lord will be sanctified in them that come near Him. We know that there were many that corrupted the service of the Lord; some setting up altars before his own; others offering both strange fire and strange sacrifices also; yet there came no fire from heaven, or other sudden judgment upon them, as did upon Nadab and Abihu,[2] whom yet we may think did not sin presumptuously. Thirdly, when God gives a special commission he looks to have it strictly observed in every article; When he gave Saul a commission to destroy Amaleck,[3] He indented[4] with him upon certain articles, and because he failed in one of the least, and that upon a fair pretense, it lost him the kingdom, which should have been his reward, if he had observed his commission.

Thus stands the cause between God and us. We are entered into covenant with him for this work. We have taken out a commission. The Lord hath given us leave to draw our own articles. We have professed to enterprise these and those accounts, upon these and those ends. We have hereupon besought him of favor and blessing. Now if the Lord shall please to hear us, and bring us in peace to the place we desire, then hath he ratified this covenant and sealed our commission, and will expect a strict performance of the articles contained in it; but if we shall neglect the observation of these articles which are the ends we have propounded, and, dissembling with our God, shall fall to embrace this present world and prosecute our carnal intentions, seeking great things for ourselves and our posterity, the Lord will surely break out in wrath against us, and be revenged of such a people, and make us know the price of the breach of such a covenant.

Now the only way to avoid this shipwreck, and to provide for our posterity, is to follow the counsel of Micah,[5] to do justly, to love mercy, to walk humbly with our God. For this end, we must be knit together, in this work, as one man. We must entertain each other in brotherly affection. We must be willing to abridge ourselves of our superfluities, for the supply of others' necessities. We must uphold a familiar commerce together in all meekness, gentleness, patience and liberality. We must delight in each other; make others' conditions our own; rejoice together, mourn together, labor and suffer together, always having before our eyes our commission and community in the work, as members of the same body. So shall we keep the unity of the spirit in the bond of peace. The Lord will be our God, and delight to dwell among us, as his own people, and will command a blessing upon us in all our ways, so that we shall see much more of his wisdom, power, goodness and truth, than formerly we have been acquainted with. We shall find that the God of Israel is among us, when ten of us shall be able to resist a thousand of our enemies; when he shall make us a praise and glory that men shall say of succeeding plantations, "may the Lord make it like that of New England." For we must consider that we shall be as a city upon a hill.[6] The eyes of all people are upon us. So that if we shall deal falsely with our God in this work we have undertaken, and so cause him to withdraw his present help from us, we shall be made a story and a by-word through the world. We shall open the mouths of enemies to speak evil of

---

[1]   *you only … your transgressions*   See Amos 3.2.

[2]   *Nadab and Abihu*   In Leviticus 9–10, the high priest Aaron is instructed to make offerings, which God sends a fire to consume; Aaron's sons, Nadab and Abihu disregard God's instructions by lighting their own fire at the altar. See Leviticus 10.1–2: "But Nadab and Abihu, the sons of Aaron … offered strange fire before the Lord, which he had not commanded them. Therefore a fire went out from the Lord, and devoured them."

[3]   *commission to destroy Amaleck*   In 1 Samuel 15, God (speaking through the prophet Samuel) instructs Saul, King of Israel, to destroy all the people of Amalek and their livestock. Saul has most of the Amalekites killed but spares the king of Amalek and the best of the livestock; as a punishment, God declares that Saul will cease to be king of Israel.

[4]   *indented*   Made a binding agreement.

[5]   *counsel of Micah*   See Micah 6.8: "He hath showed thee, O man, what is good, and what the Lord requireth of thee: surely to do justly, and to love mercy, and to humble thyself, to walk with thy God."

[6]   *city upon a hill*   See Matthew 5.14: "Ye are the light of the world. A city that is set on an hill, cannot be hid."

the ways of God, and all professors for God's sake. We shall shame the faces of many of God's worthy servants, and cause their prayers to be turned into curses upon us till we be consumed out of the good land whither we are going.

I shall shut up this discourse with that exhortation of Moses,[1] that faithful servant of the Lord, in his last farewell to Israel, Deuteronomy 30. "Beloved, there is now set before us life and death, good and evil," in that we are commanded this day to love the Lord our God, and to love one another, to walk in his ways and to keep his Commandments and his ordinance and his laws, and the articles of our covenant with Him, that we may live and be multiplied, and that the Lord our God may bless us in the land whither we go to possess it. But if our hearts shall turn away, so that we will not obey, but shall be seduced, and worship other Gods, our pleasure and profits, and serve them; it is propounded unto us this day, we shall surely perish out of the good land whither we pass over this vast sea to possess it.

Therefore let us choose life,
that we, and our seed
may live, by obeying his
voice and cleaving to him,
for he is our life and our prosperity.[2]

—1838 (Written 1630)

---

[1] *Moses* One of the most important Hebrew prophets, best known for delivering the Israelites from captivity in Egypt to the promised land, and for transmitting God's laws to the people.

[2] *Beloved, there is now … our prosperity* This passage paraphrases Deuteronomy 30.15–20.

ANNE HUTCHINSON

1591 – 1643

To the leaders of the Massachusetts Bay Colony, Anne Hutchinson was an unspeakably vile woman, an "American Jezebel" and an "instrument of Satan." The figurehead of a theological controversy that divided Massachusetts Bay Puritans, Hutchinson was long remembered as a symbol of the supposedly monstrous consequences of outspoken religious criticism and of what writer Nathaniel Hawthorne later called her "feminine ambition." Today, she is considered one of the first significant American public women—one who voiced her spiritual convictions in opposition to a powerful and patriarchal church and government.

Hutchinson was born in Lincolnshire, England, the daughter of Anglican deacon Francis Marbury and his second wife Bridget; both her parents were from prominent families. A religious conformist in his old age, Marbury had been far more rebellious in his youth, when he defied the Bishop of London and was imprisoned for heresy. It appears that he gave Anne an uncommonly rigorous education for a woman of the time, including reading, writing, and biblical interpretation. In her early twenties, she married cloth merchant William Hutchinson.

In 1612, Hutchinson began attending Saint Botolph's Church in Boston, Lincolnshire, where the young, dynamic minister John Cotton proclaimed a radical Puritan spiritual message. Upon hearing Cotton's sermons, which pronounced the freely given grace of God to be the sole pathway to salvation, Hutchinson began to see the Anglican clergy as an alliance of "antichrists"—a view common among the most fervid Puritans. She also found a mentor in her similarly radical brother-in-law, the preacher John Wheelwright.

In 1633, Cotton fled to North America to escape religious persecution. The following year, Hutchinson joined him, along with her husband and ten children—as did Wheelwright and his family. They settled in Boston, the capital of the Massachusetts Bay Colony and a refuge for Puritans. Hutchinson quickly became a leading member of the Church of Boston, serving the community as a widely sought spiritual counselor, healer, and midwife. She hosted discussion groups in which she and other parishioners debated ecclesiastical matters, beginning with discussion of Cotton's sermons but quickly extending beyond them; it wasn't long before Hutchinson and her group began to criticize many of the colony's church leaders for their spiritual failings. Hutchinson hosted both mixed-gender and women-only groups, and she ran the latter meetings herself—a practice that was not outside the bounds of Puritan propriety but that in Hutchinson's case proved threatening to church officials. Even her political enemy John Winthrop conceded that Hutchinson was "a woman of a ready wit and a bold spirit" but maintained that she was disseminating "dangerous errors," which spread like "Plague" from women to men.

Hutchinson's disagreement with the colony's religious authorities stemmed from deep-seated theological concerns: she differed from the colony's ministers—with the exception of outliers such as Cotton and Wheelwright—on the question of how one could know that one had been saved by God. The established view was that one might never be certain during one's lifetime, but could find evidence of salvation by examining one's thoughts and actions for evidence of "sanctification"—godly behavior that demonstrated the presence of God's grace. This, Hutchinson claimed, was incorrect: in her view, people who had been saved would know it immediately, never doubt their salvation, and therefore have no need to scrutinize their actions for evidence. In this way, Hutchinson took an extreme position on the question of whether "works" (an individual's good acts) or "grace" (given unconditionally by God) were necessary for a person to be saved. Generally, Puritans considered souls to be saved by grace alone, not works, but Hutchinson went further: to her, the established ministers, by suggesting that individual behavior could be interpreted as evidence of the presence of grace, were essentially endorsing works as a part of salvation.

Hutchinson's position was endorsed by Henry Vane the Younger, a youthful aristocrat who served for a single year as colonial governor. With his support, she attracted a large following, and underlying tensions blossomed into a heated, public controversy—one long known as the Antinomian Controversy,[1] now more often called the Free Grace Controversy. The conflict escalated in early 1637, when Wheelwright delivered a lay sermon that denounced all the colony's ministers, with the exception of Cotton.

Massachusetts's rulers took action. In May of 1637, Vane was succeeded as governor by John Winthrop, who sought to quash dissent in the colony. In August, the ministers in power held a council enumerating and denouncing the "erroneous opinions" of the Free Grace proponents. Cotton was forced to tone down his sermons, and, that autumn, Wheelwright was banished. Many of his and Hutchinson's allies were brought to trial as well, though most received lesser punishments. Hutchinson, too, was tried by civil authorities.

At her two-day trial, held in November, Hutchinson expertly cited scripture to defend herself. On the first day, several ministers testified to the erroneous views they had heard her express. At the beginning of the second day, she shrewdly demanded that the ministers testify again—this time under oath—and tension heightened in the court as many of the witnesses were reluctant to do so. With the question of the repeated testimonies still unresolved, a few people were allowed to speak on Hutchinson's behalf; one of these was John Cotton, whose longwinded and awkward testimony was by no means unambiguous in support of her. Hutchinson interrupted him with an extraordinary testimony of her own, during which she avowed that she had received direct revelations from God and prophesied that ruin would come to the colony should the ministers continue to persecute her. After this apparently heretical and treasonous statement, the trial concluded fairly quickly; two of the previous day's witnesses agreed to repeat their testimonies under oath, and soon afterward Hutchinson was declared "deluded by the devil" and sentenced to banishment.

Hutchinson spent four months under house arrest and was then excommunicated at a second trial conducted by church officials. She and some of her supporters left for Aquidneck Island, where fellow Free Grace proponents were already at work on a new colony. They had been invited to settle there by Roger Williams, who had been banished from Massachusetts for his religious views two years earlier and had since founded his own colony on another part of Aquidneck. Together, these settlements would develop into Rhode Island.

According to Winthrop, in Aquidneck Hutchinson delivered lay sermons on Sundays to a mixed-gender audience—now openly defying Puritan gender norms—and continued to condemn the Massachusetts Bay churches. During these years, she also experienced a series of misfortunes, including a stillbirth, which Massachusetts authorities triumphantly interpreted as signs of God's disapproval. In 1641, her husband died. In 1642, as Massachusetts threatened to take over Rhode Island, Hutchinson left the new settlement and traveled with many of her children to New Netherland. She settled near what is now Westchester, New York, on territory whose ownership was contested by the local Siwanoy people. The following year, in retaliation for a Dutch massacre of a Lenape village, a Siwanoy raiding party attacked Hutchinson's homestead. All except her nine-year-old daughter Susanna were killed.

No writing by Hutchinson is known to have survived, but several of her contemporaries recorded their experiences of the Free Grace Controversy. The best-known of these accounts are given by John Winthrop in his *Journal* and in *A Short Story of the Rise, Reign, and Ruin of the Antinomians, Familists and Libertines* (1644), his extended argument against the positions held by Hutchinson and her allies. For political expediency, the accounts of Winthrop and others tended to heap blame upon Hutchinson while downplaying the importance of players such as Cotton (who remained an influential Boston minister) and Vane (who had returned to England and become politically powerful there). As a result, she was long demonized by conformists, while her memory inspired radicals such as Quaker activist Mary Dyer.

Hutchinson's reputation in the nineteenth century is suggested in a sketch by Hawthorne, who ambivalently describes her as "a woman of extraordinary talent and strong imagination" and as "a burden too grievous for our fathers." Twentieth-century accounts were similarly clouded by sexism: some scholars

---

[1]   Antinomianism is the belief that those who have been saved by grace are not obligated to follow moral codes.

represented her as a mere accessory to Cotton, while in 1962 Emery Battis, in what was for decades the standard account of the Free Grace Controversy, argued that Hutchinson's increased extremism was a symptom of menopause. Some recent scholars champion Hutchinson as a proto-feminist combating a patriarchal church, while others present her as a liberal fighting a repressive theocracy. Others have seen her not as a progressive but as a committed Puritan whose radicalism and conviction exceeded even that of other Puritans.

NOTE ON THE TEXT: The transcript of Hutchinson's civil trial survives in two forms, neither entirely reliable. One is a condensed account by John Winthrop included as part of *A Short Story of the Rise, Reign, and Ruin of the Antinomians, Familists and Libertines.* The other, more extensive account appears as an appendix to *History of the Colony and Province of Massachusetts Bay* (1767), by the prominent historian Thomas Hutchinson, Hutchinson's own great-grandson. Thomas Hutchinson, who collected documents of historical import, claimed that his transcript was based upon "an ancient manuscript of the trial at large, having been preserved," but unfortunately this manuscript no longer survives and its authorship remains a mystery. Selections from the appendix to Thomas Hutchinson's book appear below; the editors have consulted the text as it appears in Hutchinson's *History* and in David D. Hall's *The Antinomian Controversy, 1636–1638: A Documentary History* (1990). Portions of Winthrop's account are included in the online portion of this anthology as contextual material.

⌘ ⌘ ⌘

The Examination of Mrs. Anne Hutchinson at the Court at Newtown

MR. WINTHROP, GOVERNOR. Mrs. Hutchinson, you are called here as one of those that have troubled the peace of the commonwealth and the churches here; you are known to be a woman that hath had a great share in the promoting and divulging of those opinions that are causes of this trouble, and to be nearly joined not only in affinity and affection with some of those the court had taken notice of and passed censure upon, but you have spoken diverse things, as we have been informed, very prejudicial to the honour of the churches and ministers thereof, and you have maintained a meeting and an assembly in your house that hath been condemned by the general assembly as a thing not tolerable nor comely in the sight of God nor fitting for your sex, and notwithstanding that was cried down you have continued the same. Therefore we have thought good to send for you to understand how things are, that if you be in an erroneous way we may reduce[1] you that so you may become a profitable member here among us. Otherwise if you be obstinate in your course that then the court may take such course that you may trouble us no further. Therefore I would intreat you to express whether you do not hold and assent in practice to those opinions and factions that have been handled in court already, that is to say, whether you do not justify Mr. Wheelwright's sermon and the petition.[2]

MRS. HUTCHINSON. I am called here to answer before you but I hear no things laid to my charge.

GOV. I have told you some already and more I can tell you.

[MRS. H.] Name one, Sir.

GOV. Have I not named some already?

MRS. H. What have I said or done?

GOV. Why for your doings, this you did harbour and countenance those that are parties in this faction that you have heard of.

---

[1]   *reduce*   Restore to correct spiritual conduct.

[2]   *Mr. Wheelwright's ... petition*   Earlier in 1637, Hutchinson's brother-in-law John Wheelwright was tried in court after delivering a rebellious sermon critical of most Massachusetts church authorities. His supporters submitted a petition arguing, among other things, that Wheelwright's actions were a matter of "conscience"—that is, of personal spiritual belief—and that it was therefore inappropriate to try him in civil court before he was tried by the church. The court dismissed the petition, and Wheelwright was convicted and banished for "contempt and sedition."

[MRS. H.] That's matter of conscience, Sir.

GOV. Your conscience you must keep or it must be kept for you. ...

GOV. Why do you keep such a meeting at your house as you do every week upon a set day?

MRS. H. It is lawful for me to do so, as it is all your practices, and can you find a warrant for yourself[1] and condemn me for the same thing? ...

GOV. For this, that you appeal to our practice you need no confutation. ... [B]ut I will say that there was no meeting of women alone, but your meeting is of another sort for there is sometimes men among you.

MRS. H. There was never any man with us.

GOV. Well, admit there was no man at your meeting and that you was sorry for it, there is no warrant for your doings, and by what warrant do you continue such a course?

MRS. H. I conceive there lies a clear rule in Titus, that the elder women should instruct the younger,[2] and then I must have a time wherein I must do it.

GOV. All this I grant you, I grant you a time for it, but what is this to the purpose that you Mrs. Hutchinson must call a company together from their callings to come to be taught of you?

MRS. H. Will it please you to answer me this and to give me a rule, for then I will willingly submit to any truth. If any come to my house to be instructed in the ways of God what rule have I to put them away?

GOV. But suppose that a hundred men come unto you to be instructed; will you forbear to instruct them?

MRS. H. As far as I conceive I cross a rule in it.

GOV. Very well, and do you not so here?

MRS. H. No Sir, for my ground is they are men.

GOV. Men and women all is one for that, but suppose that a man should come and say, "Mrs. Hutchinson, I hear that you are a woman that God hath given his grace unto and you have knowledge in the word of God, I pray instruct me a little," ought you not to instruct this man?

MRS. H. I think I may. Do you think it not lawful for me to teach women and[3] why do you call me to teach the court?

GOV. We do not call you to teach the court but to lay open yourself.

MRS. H. I desire you that you would then set me down a rule by which I may put them away that come unto me and so have peace in so doing.

GOV. You must show your rule to receive them.

MRS. H. I have done it.

GOV. I deny it because I have brought more arguments than you have. ...

MRS. H. ... [I]f you look upon the rule in Titus it is a rule to me. If you convince me that it is no rule I shall yield.

GOV. You know that there is no rule that crosses another, but this rule crosses that in the Corinthians.[4] But you must take it in this sense: that elder women must instruct the younger about their business, and to love their husbands and not to make them to clash.

MRS. H. I do not conceive but that it is meant for some public times.

GOV. Well, have you no more to say but this?

MRS. H. I have said sufficient for my practice.

GOV. Your course is not to be suffered for, besides that we find such a course as this to be greatly prejudicial[5] to the state, besides the occasion that it is to seduce many honest persons that are called to those meetings and your opinions, being known to be different from the word of God, may seduce many simple souls that resort unto you. Besides that the occasion which hath come of late hath come from none but such as have frequented your meetings, so that now they are flown off from magistrates and ministers, and this since they have come to you. And besides

---

1   *a warrant for yourself* Justification for your own actions.

2   *clear rule ... younger* See Titus 2.1–5, where it is presented as "wholesome doctrine" that "the elder women" be "teachers of honest things. That they may instruct the young women to be sober minded, that they love their husbands, that they love their children, that they be temperate, chaste, keeping at home, good and subject unto their husbands, and the word of God be not evil spoken of." Unless otherwise indicated, biblical quotations included in footnotes to this selection are from the 1560 Geneva Bible, which appears to be the translation Hutchinson references most frequently in this transcript.

3   *and* But then.

4   *that in the Corinthians* See 1 Corinthians 14.34–35: "Let your women keep silence in the Churches: for it is not permitted unto them to speak: but they ought to be subject, as also the Law saith. And if they will learn anything, let them ask their husbands at home: for it is a shame for women to speak in the Church."

5   *prejudicial* Harmful.

that it will not well stand with the commonwealth that families should be neglected for so many neighbours and dames and so much time spent. We see no rule of God for this. We see not that any should have authority to set up any other exercises besides what authority hath already set up, and so what hurt comes of this you will be guilty of and we for suffering you.

MRS. H. Sir, I do not believe that to be so.

GOV. Well, we see how it is. We must therefore put it away from you,[1] or restrain you from maintaining this course.

MRS. H. If you have a rule for it from God's word you may.

GOV. We are your judges, and not you ours and we must compel you to it. …

[The trial continues into a second day, and several witnesses are questioned, including John Cotton, whose examination Hutchinson interrupts with the following speech.]

MRS. H. If you please to give me leave I shall give you the ground of what I know to be true. Being much troubled to see the falseness of the constitution of the church of England, I had like to have turned separatist.[2] Whereupon I kept a day of solemn humiliation and pondering of the thing; this scripture was brought unto me—he that denies Jesus Christ to be come in the flesh is antichrist.[3] This I considered of and in considering found that the papists[4] did not deny him to be come in the flesh, nor we did not deny him—who then was antichrist? Was the Turk[5] antichrist only? The Lord knows that I could not open[6] scripture; he must by his prophetical office open it unto me. So after that being unsatisfied in the thing, the Lord was pleased to bring this scripture out of the Hebrews: He that denies the testament denies the testator,[7] and in this did open unto me and give me to see that those which did not teach the new covenant[8] had the spirit of antichrist, and upon this he did discover[9] the ministry unto me; and ever since, I bless the Lord, he hath let me see which was the clear ministry and which the wrong. Since that time I confess I have been more choice[10] and he hath let me to distinguish between the voice of my beloved and the voice of Moses, the voice of John Baptist[11] and the voice of antichrist, for all those voices are spoken of in scripture. Now if you do condemn me for speaking what in my conscience I know to be truth I must commit myself unto the Lord.

MR. NOWELL.[12] How do you know that was the spirit?

---

1   *put it away from you*   I.e., remove it from you, put it out of your mind.

2   *turned separatist*   Become part of a movement to separate from the state-sponsored Church of England.

3   *he that … antichrist*   See 1 John 4.3. In his first epistle, John argues against those who claim that Jesus was not both fully human and fully God, but instead a spirit who only had the appearance of humanity. In the Geneva Bible, footnotes to 1 John 4 interpret this passage as applying to ministers (described as "[t]hey which boast that they have the spirit to preach or prophesy"), who possess "the spirit of God" only if they preach that Christ is both human and divine;   *antichrist*   One who falsely pretends to be Christ, but who in fact denies and subverts Jesus' message.

4   *papists*   Disparaging term for Catholics.

5   *the Turk*   Hutchinson uses the word as a stand-in for "Muslim."

6   *open*   I.e., explicate in the manner of a minister. Puritan sermons generally involved the close examination of a passage from the Bible.

7   *He that … testator*   I.e., those who deny the existence of a testament declared by God for humanity deny the existence and death of the one who established the testament, Jesus. See Hebrews 9.16–18.

8   *new covenant*   The covenant of grace established between God and humankind, according to which God freely dispenses his grace and saves the elect. According to Puritan theology, the covenant of grace was established by Christ, who atoned for humanity's sins by sacrificing himself, thereby making it possible for the righteous to attain salvation. The covenant of grace replaced the covenant of works, the first covenant between God and humanity, according to which God granted eternal life in exchange for obedience. This earlier covenant was broken after Adam, the first human, defied God.

9   *discover*   Reveal.

10   *choice*   Discerning.

11   *my beloved*   I.e., Jesus. See Song of Songs 2.8. and 5.2 in the King James Bible for references to "the voice of my beloved";   *Moses*   Hebrew prophet who first delivered God's law and the ten commandments to the ancient Israelites;   *John Baptist*   Prophet who first announced the coming of Christ.

12   *MR. NOWELL*   Increase Nowell, one of the magistrates judging Hutchinson's trial; he also served as court secretary.

MRS. H. How did Abraham know that it was God that bid him offer his son, being a breach of the sixth commandment?[1]

DEP. GOV. THOMAS DUDLEY.[2] By an immediate voice.

MRS. H. So to me by an immediate revelation.

DEP. GOV. THOMAS DUDLEY. How! an immediate revelation.

MRS. H. By the voice of his own spirit to my soul. I will give you another scripture, Jeremiah 46.27–28[3]—out of which the Lord showed me what he would do for me and the rest of his servants. But after he was pleased to reveal himself to me I did presently, like Abraham, run to Hagar.[4] And after that he did let me see the atheism[5] of my own heart, for which I begged of the Lord that it might not remain in my heart, and being thus, he did show me this (a twelvemonth after) which I told you of before. Ever since that time I have been confident of what he hath revealed unto me.

   … another place out of Daniel 7 and he … and for us all,[6] wherein he showed me the sitting of the judgment and the standing of all high and low before the Lord and how thrones and kingdoms were cast down before him. When our teacher[7] came to New-England it was a great trouble unto me, my brother Wheelwright being put by also. I was then much troubled concerning the ministry under which I lived, and then that place in the 30th of Isaiah was brought to my mind. Though the Lord give thee bread of adversity and water of affliction yet shall not thy teachers be removed into corners any more, but thine eyes shall see thy teachers.[8] The Lord giving me this promise and they being gone there was none then left that I was able to hear, and I could not be at rest but I must come hither.[9] Yet that place of Isaiah did much follow me, though the Lord give thee the bread of adversity and water of affliction. This place lying I say upon me, then this place in Daniel was brought unto me and did show me that though I should meet with affliction yet I am the same God that delivered Daniel out of the lion's den,[10] I will also deliver thee.

   Therefore I desire you to look to it, for you see this scripture fulfilled this day, and therefore I desire you that as you tender the Lord and the church and commonwealth to consider and look what you do. You have power over my body but the Lord Jesus hath power over my body and soul; and assure yourselves thus much, you do as much as in you lies to put the Lord Jesus Christ from you, and if you go on in this course you begin, you will bring a curse upon you and your posterity, and the mouth of the Lord hath spoken it.

DEP. GOV. THOMAS DUDLEY. What is the scripture she brings?

MR. STOUGHTON.[11] Behold I turn away from you.

---

[1] *Abraham … commandment* In Genesis 22.1–2, God speaks directly to Abraham, ordering him to offer his own son as a sacrifice. This would break the commandment "Thou shalt not kill."

[2] *THOMAS DUDLEY* One of the magistrates judging Hutchinson's trial.

[3] *Jeremiah 46.27–28* "But fear not thou, O my servant Jacob, and be not thou afraid, O Israel: for behold, I will deliver thee from a far country, and thy seed from the land of their captivity, and Jacob shall return and be in rest, and prosperity, and none shall make him afraid. Fear thou not, O Jacob my servant, saith the Lord, for I am with thee, and I will utterly destroy all the nations, whither I have driven thee: but I will not utterly destroy thee, but correct thee by judgment, and not utterly cut thee off."

[4] *run to Hagar* I.e., choose the covenant of works instead of the covenant of grace. The biblical patriarch Abraham had one son with his servant, Hagar, and one son with his wife, Sarai. The annotations accompanying Galatians 4.21–24 in the Geneva Bible link the covenant of works to Hagar and the covenant of grace to Sarai.

[5] *atheism* In the seventeenth century, the term was used to refer not only to a disbelief in God, but more broadly to godlessness, wickedness, or corruption.

[6] *… another … us all* The manuscript was unclear here, and may have been deliberately defaced; *Daniel 7* This portion of Daniel describes a vision of four kingdoms, depicted as beasts, that will hold great power on earth but be conquered by divine judgment. The "little horn" (Daniel 7.8) of the fourth, most terrible beast is often interpreted as an image of the antichrist.

[7] *our teacher* John Cotton, who left England in 1633.

[8] *Though the … teachers* See Isaiah 30.20 (King James Bible).

[9] *must come hither* Hutchinson and her family left England for Massachusetts in 1634.

[10] *Daniel … lion's den* See Daniel 6. Daniel's political rivals contrive to have him imprisoned overnight in a den of lions as a means of execution; God protects him because of his faith, and he emerges unharmed.

[11] *MR. STOUGHTON* Israel Stoughton, one of the magistrates at the trial.

MRS. H. But now having seen him which is invisible I fear not what man can do unto me.[1]

Gov. Daniel was delivered by miracle; do you think to be delivered so too?

MRS. H. I do here speak it before the court. ...

Gov. The case is altered and will not stand with us now, but I see a marvellous providence of God to bring things to this pass that they are. We have been hearkening about the trial of this thing and now the mercy of God by a providence hath answered our desires and made her to lay open herself and the ground of all these disturbances to be by revelations[.] ... [T]he ground work of her revelations is the immediate revelation of the spirit and not by the ministry of the word,[2] and that is the means by which she hath very much abused the country[.] ...

Gov. The court hath already declared themselves satisfied concerning the things you hear, and concerning the troublesomeness of her spirit and the danger of her course amongst us, which is not to be suffered.

Therefore if it be the mind of the court that Mrs. Hutchinson for these things that appear before us is unfit for our society, and if it be the mind of the court that she shall be banished out of our liberties[3] and imprisoned till she be sent away, let them hold up their hands.

[Thirty-seven of the forty magistrates and deputies in attendance vote to banish Hutchinson, with two votes against and one abstention.]

Gov. Mrs. Hutchinson, the sentence of the court you hear is that you are banished from out of our jurisdiction as being a woman not fit for our society, and are to be imprisoned till the court shall send you away.

MRS. H. I desire to know wherefore I am banished?

Gov. Say no more. The court knows wherefore and is satisfied.

—1767 (TRANSCRIPT OF 1637 TRIAL)

---

[1] *But now ... unto me* See Hebrews 11.27, which says of Moses, "By faith he forsook Egypt, and feared not the fierceness of the king: for he endured, as he that saw him which is invisible."

[2] *[T]he ground ... of the word* I.e., the teachings she is spreading are not grounded in the instruction of a minister.

[3] *our liberties* The area subject to our jurisdiction; i.e., the Massachusetts Bay Colony.

ROGER WILLIAMS

c. 1603 – 1683

Long before the separation of church and state was proclaimed by American founders, Roger Williams attested the need for "a wall of separation between the Garden of the church and the wilderness of the world." Like other Massachusetts Puritans such as John Winthrop and John Cotton, Williams was deeply committed to the truth of his Puritan beliefs. But whereas Winthrop had envisaged a government that would foster correct worship, Williams held up a different ideal: the removal of everything, including state interference, that might stand in the way of each individual's relationship to God. Though his ideas were too radical even for most other Puritans, he managed to found a colony that put them into practice—and, a century after his death, his work would influence the shape of American government.

Born around 1603 to a respected middle-class family, Williams was raised in one of London's centers of Separatist activity, the Smithfield district. He entered Cambridge University's Pembroke College with the assistance of prominent jurist Sir Edward Coke, and went on to earn scholarships for his skill in Latin, Hebrew, and Greek. He graduated with a BA in 1627, but he soon abandoned his MA and began to focus on Puritan theology and practice; he took holy orders and began serving as a chaplain two years later. His beliefs grew increasingly radical: Williams came to oppose any formal connection between the Church of England and the state, and he advocated freedom of worship—dangerous opinions to hold in the political landscape of the time.

Williams married Mary Barnard, a reverend's daughter, in 1629, and shortly thereafter the two set sail for Massachusetts Bay Colony, seeking the freedom to worship safely. Williams was a charming and charismatic speaker, and many in Massachusetts welcomed the intelligent, scholarly, and pious preacher. He was offered the prestigious post of minister at Boston's First Church, but turned the post down, saying that he "durst not officiate to an unseparated people." His belief that Puritans must separate from the Church of England was deeply controversial, as such a move would destabilize the colony's relationship with its parent country. He also expressed other controversial views: he thought, for instance, that the English king had no power to grant colonists ownership of Native Americans' lands, a position that called the colony's legitimacy into question. He asserted, too, that the authority of civil magistrates should be limited to civil matters, not extending to religious belief or practice. Not surprisingly, these ideas were threatening to those who followed Governor John Winthrop's vision for a highly structured society administered by Puritan believers with the guidance of the clergy. Williams's attempt to find a congregation with whom he could speak openly took him to Salem, then to Plymouth, and back to Salem again.

Williams's conflict with Winthrop and with the General Court of the Massachusetts Bay Colony escalated, and in 1635 he was indicted for "heresy and divisiveness." (He and Winthrop nonetheless remained lifelong friends—and even political allies—who frequently exchanged letters.) Williams avoided deportation by fleeing south, and he was welcomed by the people of Narragansett Bay. He purchased land from the Narragansett chiefs Canonicus and Mianotonomo in what is now Rhode Island, and named his new home Providence; here he and Mary raised six children. The settlers of Providence were largely on good terms with the Narragansett, and during the Pequot War (1636–38) Williams's diplomacy secured them as allies with the English colonists against the Pequot. (After the war, he would also be instrumental in persuading the Narragansett to help recapture Pequots who had escaped from slavery.)

Williams remained committed to the separation of religion and government, advocating freedom from persecution even for those whose views he despised (among them Quakers, whom he called "the cursed sect"). Providence became a sanctuary for Quakers, Baptists, Jews, and other religious minorities who found the Massachusetts colony too oppressive. Increasing suppression in Massachusetts brought an influx of Puritan dissenters such as Anne Hutchinson, some of whom founded the new settlements of Pocasset (later Portsmouth) and Newport nearby. Williams himself abandoned the idea of membership in any specific church, though he remained deeply devout in his own beliefs.

In 1643, encroachment by the Massachusetts Bay Colony forced Williams to return to England to seek a charter for the colony of Rhode Island (which included Providence and the other tolerant settlements). During this voyage he gathered what he knew of Narragansett language and customs into *A Key into the Language of America* (1643), which has become one of his best-known works. Ostensibly a phrasebook, the *Key* also examines Narragansett culture, language, beliefs, and other elements of life. It is a remarkable example of what we would now call anthropology and provides considerable insight into early relations between Indigenous Americans and Europeans. In the twentieth century, it would be a useful source of information for a revival of Narragansett language and culture.

While in London, Williams wrote another major work: the 400-page *Bloody Tenet of Persecution, for Cause of Conscience, in a Conference between Truth and Peace* (1644). This thorough articulation of his views on freedom of religion was part of an ongoing debate on the subject with Massachusetts Puritan minister John Cotton that would extend into the next decade. While Williams succeeded in obtaining a charter for Rhode Island, there remained significant resistance in England to the idea of religious toleration: *The Bloody Tenet* was greeted with public outrage, and Parliament ordered all copies burned. Williams's argument nonetheless had an impact on the debate in England, and it is likely that his ideas influenced those of prominent English intellectuals such as John Milton (1608–74) and, later, John Locke (1632–1704).

Williams returned to Providence in 1644. For several decades, his friendly relations with the Narragansett helped to cultivate a generally peaceful relationship between the Indigenous peoples and the English settlers of the region. During King Philip's War (1675–76), his diplomatic efforts finally failed; the New England settlers massacred a Narragansett village, and in response the Narragansett joined other tribes in attacking and burning Providence. Williams lived to see his home rebuilt, though he never recovered financially. The Narragansett numbers, however, were severely depleted. Many died during the conflict, and Williams oversaw the sale of many of the captives into indentured servitude in Rhode Island—or outright slavery on English plantations in the Caribbean. The few remaining Narragansett were forced to flee their land.

Williams spent his last years living in poverty in Providence, where he died around 1683. He was a prolific writer throughout his life, but much of his work became scattered after his death. Shortly after the Civil War, a group in Rhode Island collected his works and compiled them in a six-volume set released as *The Complete Writings of Roger Williams* (1867). Later editions were expanded into seven volumes. Since the publication of his collected works, many scholars have praised Williams as a liberal ahead of his time for his views on colonization and religious freedom, while others have stressed the need to interpret his ideas in the context of his extremely devout seventeenth-century theology.

A few colonies founded after Rhode Island adopted similar statements of religious toleration, and at the time of the American Revolution the nation's founders embraced Williams's ideal as it had been adapted by Locke and other liberal theorists. More than a century after Williams's death, the First Amendment to the United States Constitution would declare that "Congress shall make no law respecting an establishment of religion, or prohibiting the free exercise thereof."

NOTE ON THE TEXT: The text of *A Key into the Language of America* is based upon the 1643 edition. Spelling and punctuation have been modernized in accordance with the practices of this anthology.

⌘ ⌘ ⌘

from *A Key into the Language of America*[1]

To my Dear and Well-beloved Friends and Countrymen, in Old and New England.

I present you with a key; I have not heard of the like,[2]
yet framed, since it pleased God to bring that mighty
continent of America to light. Others of my countrymen have often, and excellently, and lately written of
the country (and none that I know beyond the goodness and worth of it).

This key respects the native language of it, and happily[3] may unlock some rarities concerning the natives
themselves, not yet discovered.

I drew the materials in a rude lump at sea, as a private help to my own memory, that I might not by my
present absence lightly lose what I had so dearly bought
in some few years' hardship, and charges among the
barbarians; yet being reminded by some, what pity it
were to bury those materials in my grave at land or
sea; and withal, remembering how often I have been
importuned by worthy friends, of all sorts, to afford
them some help this way. I resolved (by the assistance
of the most high) to cast those materials into this key,
pleasant and profitable for all, but especially for my
friends residing in those parts.

A little key may open a box, where lies a bunch of
keys. With this I have entered into the secrets of those
countries, wherever English dwell about two hundred
miles, between the French and Dutch plantations; for
want of this, I know what gross mistakes myself and
others have run into.

There is a mixture of this language north and south,
from the place of my abode, about six hundred miles;
yet within the two hundred miles (aforementioned)
their dialects do exceedingly differ; yet not so, but
(within that compass) a man may, by this help, converse with thousands of natives all over the country; and

by such converse it may please the Father of Mercies[4]
to spread civility and (in his own most holy season)
Christianity; for one candle will light ten thousand,
and it may please God to bless a little leaven[5] to season
the mighty lump of those peoples and territories.

It is expected, that having had so much converse
with these natives, I should write some little of them.

Concerning them (a little to gratify expectation), I
shall touch upon four heads:

First, by what names they are distinguished.

Secondly, their original[6] and descent.

Thirdly, their religion, manners, customs, etc.

Fourthly, that great point of their conversion.

To the first, their names are of two sorts:

First, those of the English giving: as natives, savages,
Indians, wildmen (so the Dutch call them *wilden*),
Abergeny[7] men, pagans, barbarians, heathen.

Secondly, their names which they give themselves.

I cannot observe that they ever had (before the
coming of the English, French or Dutch amongst
them) any names to difference themselves from strangers, for they knew none; but two sorts of names they
had, and have amongst themselves:

First, general, belonging to all natives, as *Nínnuock,
Ninnimissinnûwock, Eniskeetompaûwog*, which signifies
Men, Folk, or People.

Secondly, particular names, peculiar to several nations,
of them amongst themselves, as Nanhigganûck,
Massachusêuck, Cawasumsêuck, Cowwesûck, Quin-
tikóok, Qunnipiûck, Pequttóog, etc.

They have often asked me, why we call them Indians,
natives, etc. And understanding the reason, they will
call themselves Indians, in opposition to English, etc.

For the second head proposed, their original and
descent:

From Adam and Noah[8] that they spring, it is granted
on all hands.

---

1   Subtitled *An Help to the Language of the Natives in That Part of
America, Called New England.*

2   *I have … the like*   Williams's *Key* was the first substantial
English-language text to study Indigenous languages in detail,
although William Wood's 1634 *New England's Prospect* did dedicate
five pages to the subject.

3   *respects*   Is concerned with; *happily*   Perhaps.

4   *Father of Mercies*   I.e., God.

5   *leaven*   Literally, a raising agent, such as yeast. Cf. Matthew
13.33: "The kingdom of heaven is like unto leaven, which a woman
took, and hid in three measures of meal, till the whole was leavened."

6   *original*   Origin.

7   *Abergeny*   Aboriginal.

8   *Adam*   According to Christian tradition, the first human created by God; *Noah*   Biblical figure who, under God's direction,
spared himself and a small number of humans and other animals
from a flood that destroyed all other living beings. Cf. Genesis 7.23.

But for their later descent, and whence they came into those parts, it seems as hard to find, as to find the wellhead of some fresh stream, which running many miles out of the country to the salt ocean, hath met with many mixing streams by the way. They say, themselves, that they have sprung and grown up in that very place, like the very trees of the wilderness.

They say that their great god Kautántowwì created those parts, as I observed in the chapter of their religion. They have no clothes, books, nor letters, and conceive their fathers never had; and therefore they are easily persuaded that the God that made Englishmen is a greater God, because He hath so richly endowed the English above themselves. But when they hear that about sixteen hundred years ago, England and the inhabitants thereof were like unto themselves, and since have received from God, clothes, books, etc. they are greatly affected with a secret hope concerning themselves.

Wise and judicious men, with whom I have discoursed, maintain their original to be northward from Tartaria:[1] and at my now taking ship, at the Dutch plantation, it pleased the Dutch Governor (in some discourse with me about the natives) to draw their line from Iceland, because the name Sackmakan (the name for an Indian prince, about the Dutch) is the name for a prince in Iceland.

Other opinions I could number up: under favour I shall present (not mine opinion, but) my observations to the judgment of the wise.

First, others (and myself) have conceived some of their words to hold affinity with the Hebrew.[2]

Secondly, they constantly anoint their heads as the Jews did.

Thirdly, they give dowries for their wives, as the Jews did.

Fourthly (and which I have not so observed amongst other nations as amongst the Jews, and these): they constantly separate their women (during the time of their monthly sickness) in a little house alone by themselves four or five days, and hold it an irreligious thing for either father or husband or any male to come near them.

They have often asked me if it be so with women of other nations, and whether they are so separated, and for their practice they plead nature and tradition. Yet again I have found a greater affinity of their language with the Greek tongue.

2. As the Greeks and other nations, and ourselves call the seven stars (or Charles' Wain, the Bear)[3] so do they *Mosk* or *Paukunnawaw*, the Bear.

3. They have many strange relations of one Wétucks,[4] a man that wrought great miracles amongst them, and walking upon the waters, etc., with some kind of broken resemblance to the Son of God.

Lastly, it is famous that the Sowwest (*Sowaniu*) is the great subject of their discourse, from thence their traditions. There they say (at the southwest) is the court of their great god Kautántowwì. At the southwest are their forefathers' souls; to the southwest they go themselves when they die; from the southwest came their corn, and beans out of their great god Kautántowwì's field; and indeed the further northward and westward from us their corn will not grow, but to the southward better and better. I dare not conjecture in these uncertainties. I believe they are lost, and yet hope (in the Lord's holy season) some of the wildest of them shall be found to share in the blood of the Son of God. To the third head, concerning their religion, customs, manners etc. I shall here say nothing, because in those 32 chapters of the whole book,[5] I have briefly touched those of all sorts, from their birth to their burials, and have endeavored (as the nature of the work would give way) to bring some short observations and applications home to Europe from America.

Therefore fourthly, to that great point of their conversion, so much to be longed for, and by all New English so much pretended,[6] and I hope in truth.

---

1   *Tartaria*   Region of Central Asia.

2   *affinity with the Hebrew*   Many Europeans hypothesized a connection between Native Americans and the ancient Israelites.

3   *Charles' ... Bear*   Charlemagne's wagon, the constellation Ursa Major, also known as The Great Bear.

4   *Wétucks*   Legendary giant of Narragansett oral literature, called Moshup by neighboring tribes; he has transformative powers and his actions are said to have shaped the geographical features of the region.

5   *whole book*   The *Key*.

6   *by all ... much pretended*   Reference to exaggerated claims about the conversion of Indigenous people made by the Puritans, most notably in the 1643 text *New England's First Fruits*.

For myself I have uprightly labored to suit my endeavors to my pretenses, and of later times (out of desire to attain their language) I have run through varieties of intercourses with them day and night, summer and winter, by land and sea. Particular passages tending to this, I have related diverse,[1] in the chapter of their religion.

Many solemn discourses I have had with all sorts of nations of them, from one end of the country to another (so far as opportunity, and the little language I have could reach).

I know there is no small preparation in the hearts of multitudes of them. I know their many solemn confessions to myself, and one to another of their lost wandering conditions. I know strong convictions upon the consciences of many of them, and their desires uttered that way.

I know not with how little knowledge and grace of Christ the Lord may save, and therefore, neither will despair, nor report much.

But since it hath pleased some of my worthy countrymen to mention (of late in print) Wequash,[2] the Péquot captain, I shall be bold so far to second their relations, as to relate mine own hopes of him (though I dare not be so confident as others).

Two days before his death, as I passed up to Qunníhticut River, it pleased my worthy friend Mr. Fenwick[3] (whom I visited at his house in Saybrook Fort at the mouth of that river) to tell me that my old friend Wequash lay very sick. I desired to see him, and himself was pleased to be my guide two miles where Wequash lay.

Amongst other discourse concerning his sickness and death (in which he freely bequeathed his son to Mr. Fenwick) I closed with him concerning his soul: he told me that some two or three years before he had lodged at my house, where I acquainted him with the condition of all mankind, and his own in particular; how God created man and all things; how man fell from God, and of his present enmity against God, and the wrath of God against him until repentance. Said he, "Your words were never out of my heart to this present," and said he, "Me much pray to Jesus Christ." I told him so did many English, French, and Dutch, who had never turned to God, nor loved Him. He replied in broken English: "Me so big naughty heart, me heart all one stone!"; savory expressions using to breathe from compunct[4] and broken hearts, and a sense of inward hardness and unbrokenness. I had many discourses with him in his life, but this was the sum of our last parting until our General Meeting.[5]

Now, because this is the great inquiry of all men: What Indians have been converted? What have the English done in those parts? What hopes of the Indians receiving the knowledge of Christ?

And because to this question, some put an edge from the boast of the Jesuits in Canada and Maryland, and especially from the wonderful conversions made by the Spaniards and Portugals in the West Indies; besides what I have here written, as also, beside what I have observed in the chapter of their religion, I shall further present you with a brief additional discourse concerning this great point, being comfortably persuaded that the Father of Spirits, who was graciously pleased to persuade Japhet (the Gentiles) to dwell in the tents of Shem[6] (the Jews), will, in His holy season (I hope approaching), persuade these gentiles of America to partake of the mercies of Europe, and then shall be fulfilled what is written by the prophet Malachi,[7] from the rising of the sun (in Europe) to the going down of the same (in America), My name shall be great among the Gentiles. So I desire to hope and pray.

Your unworthy countryman,

Roger Williams

---

[1]   *I have ... diverse* I have recounted a variety.

[2]   *Wequash* Member of the Pequot tribe who famously converted to Christianity. Wequash's conversion was given special attention by the authors of *New England's First Fruits*.

[3]   *Qunníhticut* Connecticut; *Mr. Fenwick* George Fenwick (c. 1603–57), an English politician and early colonizer of Connecticut.

[4]   *compunct* Pricked by knowledge of wrongdoing.

[5]   *General Meeting* Reunion at Judgment Day.

[6]   *Japhet* Noah's third son, traditionally seen as the progenitor of European, and some Asian, peoples; *Shem* Noah's eldest son, considered the progenitor of Semitic peoples. Cf. Genesis 9.27.

[7]   *written by ... Malachi* Cf. Malachi 1.11: "For from the rising of the sun even unto the going down of the same my name shall be great among the Gentiles; and in every place incense shall be offered unto my name, and a pure offering: for my name shall be great among the heathen, saith the Lord of hosts."

DIRECTIONS FOR THE USE OF THE LANGUAGE

1. A dictionary or grammar way I had consideration of, but purposely avoided, as not so accommodate to the benefit of all, as I hope this form is.

2. A dialogue also I had thoughts of, but avoided for brevity's sake, and yet (with no small pains) I have so framed every chapter and the matter of it, as I may call it an implicit dialogue.

3. It is framed chiefly after the Narrogánset dialect, because most spoken in the country, and yet (with attending to the variation of peoples and dialects) it will be of great use in all parts of the country.

4. Whatever your occasion be either of travel, discourse, trading, etc., turn to the table which will direct you to the proper chapter.

5. Because the life of all languages is in the pronunciation, I have been at the pains and charges[1] to cause the accents, tones, or sounds to be affixed (which some understand, according to the Greek language, acutes, graves, circumflexes), for example in the second leaf,[2] in the word *Ewò* (He): the sound or tone must not be put on *E* but *wò* where the grave accent is.

In the same leaf, in the word *Ascowequássin*, the sound must not be on any of the syllables, but on *quáss*, where the acute or sharp sound is.

In the same leaf in the word *Anspaumpmaùntam*, the sound must not be on any other syllable but *maûn*, where the circumflex or long sounding accent is.

6. The English for every Indian word or phrase stands in a straight line directly against the Indian: yet sometimes there are two words for the same thing (for their language is exceeding copious, and they have five or six words sometimes for one thing) and then the English stands against them both: for example in the second leaf,

Cowáunckamish and *Cuckquénamish.*	I pray your favour.

1   *I have ... charges*   I have worked painstakingly under a heavy load.

2   *leaf*   Page.

from CHAPTER 1
OF SALUTATION

Observation

The Natives are of two sorts (as the English are). Some more rude and clownish,[3] who are not so apt to salute, but upon salutation resalute[4] lovingly. Others, and the general, are sober and grave, and yet cheerful in a mean,[5] and as ready to begin a salutation as to resalute, which yet the English generally begin, out of desire to civilize them.

What cheer *Nétop*? is the general salutation of all English toward them. *Nétop* is friend.

Netompaüog	Friends.

They are exceedingly delighted with salutations in their own language.

Neèn, Keèn, Ewò	I, you, he.
Keén ka neen	You and I.
Asco wequássin	
Asco wequassunnúm-mis	Good morrow.
Askuttaaquompsin?	How do you?
Asnpaumpmaùntam	I am very well.
Taubot paump maúntaman	I am glad you are well.
Cowaúnckamish	My service to you. ...

From these courteous salutations observe in general: There is a savour[6] of civility and courtesy even amongst these wild Americans, both amongst themselves and towards strangers.

More Particular

1. The courteous pagan shall condemn
Uncourteous Englishmen,
Who live like foxes, bears and wolves,
Or lion in his den.

2. Let none sing blessings to their souls,
For that they courteous are:
The wild barbarians with no more
Than nature, go so far:

3   *rude and clownish*   Rustic and unrefined.

4   *salute*   Offer a greeting;   *resalute*   Return a greeting.

5   *in a mean*   On average, typically.

6   *savour*   Understanding.

3. If nature's sons both wild and tame,
    Humane and courteous be:
    How ill becomes it sons of God
    To want[1] humanity?

from Chapter 21

Of Religion, the Soul, Etc.

| *Manìt-manittó-wock* | God, Gods |

Obs.[2] He that questions whether God made the World, the Indians will teach him. I must acknowledge I have received in my converse with them many confirmations of those two great points, Hebrews 11.6.[3] viz.:[4]

1. That God is.

2. That he is a rewarder of all them that diligently seek him.

They will generally confess that God made all: but then in special, although they deny not that Englishman's God made English Men, and the Heavens and Earth there; yet their Gods made them and the Heaven, and Earth where they dwell.

| *Nummusquauna- múckqun manit* | God is angry with me? |

Obs. I have heard a poor Indian lamenting the loss of a child at break of day, call up his wife and children and all about him to lamentation, and with abundance of tears cry out! O God thou hast taken away my child! thou art angry with me: O turn thine anger from me, and spare the rest of my children.

If they receive any good in hunting, fishing, harvest etc. they acknowledge God in it.

Yea, if it be but an ordinary accident, a fall, etc. they will say God was angry and did it. *Musquantum manit.* God is angry. But herein is their Misery.

First they branch their Godhead[5] into many Gods.

Secondly, attribute it to creatures.

First, many Gods: they have given me the names of thirty seven ... which in their solemn worships they invocate as:

Kautántowwit The great South-West God, to whose house all souls go, and from whom came their corn, beans, as they say.

Wompanand	The Eastern God.
Chekesuwànd	The Western God.
Wunnauaméanit	The Northern God.
Sowwanànd	The Southern God.
Wetuómanit	The House God.

Even as the Papists have their he and she saint protectors as St. George, St. Patrick, St. Denis, Virgin Mary,[6] etc.

| *Squáuanit* | The Woman's God. |
| *Muckquachuck- quànd* | The Children's God. |

Obs. I was once with a Native dying of wound, given him by some murderous English (who robbed him and run him through with a rapier, from whom in the heat of his wound, he at present escaped from them, but dying of his wound, they suffered death at new Plymouth, in New England) this native dying called much upon Muckquachuckquànd, which of other natives I understood (as they believed) had appeared to the dying young man, many years before, and bid him whenever he was in distress call upon him.

Secondly, as they have many of these feigned deities: so worship they the creatures in whom they conceive doth rest some deity:

Keesuckquànd	The Sun God.
Nanepaushat	The Moon God.
Paumpágussit	The Sea.
Yotáanit	The Fire God.

Supposing that Deities be in these, etc.

When I have argued with them about their Fire-God: can it, say they, be, but this fire must be a God, or divine power, that out of a stone will arise in a spark, and when a poor naked Indian is ready to starve with cold in the house and especially in the woods, often saves his life, doth dress all our food for us, and if it be angry will burn the house about us, yea if a spark fall into the dry wood, burns up the country, (though this burning of the wood to them they count a benefit both

---

[1] *want* Lack.

[2] *Obs.* Observation.

[3] *Hebrews 11.6* "But without faith it is impossible to please him: for he that cometh to God must believe that he is, and that he is a rewarder of them that diligently seek him."

[4] *viz.* Abbreviation of the Latin videlicet, meaning "namely," or "that is to say."

[5] *Godhead* God's essence; in Christianity the term is often used in reference to the trinity, God understood as a unified whole made up of three "persons": father, son, and holy spirit.

[6] *St. George ... Virgin Mary* Saints of the Catholic Church.

for destroying of vermin, and keeping down the weeds and thickets)? …

Besides there is a general custom amongst them, at the apprehension of any excellency in men, women, birds, beasts, fish, etc. to cry out *Manittóo*, that is, it is a God, as thus if they see one man excel others in wisdom, valour, strength, activity etc. they cry out *Manittóo*, a God: and therefore when they talk amongst themselves of the English ships, and great buildings, of the plowing of their fields, and especially of books and letters, they will end thus: *Manittôwock*, they are Gods; *Cummanitôo*, you are a God, etc. A strong conviction natural in the soul of man, that God is filling all things, and places, and that all excellencies dwell in God, and proceed from him, and that they only are blessed who have that Jehovah their portion.

from CHAPTER 29
OF THEIR WAR, ETC.

Obs. Their wars are far less bloody and devouring than the cruel wars of Europe; and seldom twenty slain in a pitched field:[1] partly because when they fight in a wood every tree is a buckler.[2]

When they fight in a plain, they fight with leaping and dancing, that seldom an arrow hits, and when a man is wounded, unless he that shot follows upon the wounded, they soon retire and save the wounded: and yet having no Swords, nor guns, all that are slain are commonly slain with great valour and courage: for the conqueror ventures into the thickest, and brings away the head of his enemy.

Niss-nissoke	Kill kill.
Kunnish	I will kill you.
Kunnishickqun ewò	He will kill you.
Kunnishickquock	They will kill you.
Siuckissûog	They are stout men.
Nickummissūog	They are weak.
Nnickummaunámaûog	I shall easily vanquish them.
Neene núppamen	I am dying?
Cowaúnckamish	Quarter, quarter.

Kunnanaumpasúmmish	Mercy, mercy.
Kekuttokaúntá	Let us parley.
Aquétuck	Let us cease arms.
Wunnishaúnta	Let us agree.
Cowammáunsh	I love you.
Wunnêtu ntá	My heart is true.
Tuppaûntash	Consider what I say.
Tuppaûntamoke	Do you all consider.
Cummequaunum cummittamussussuck ka cummuckiaûg	Remember your wives and children.
Eatch kèen anawâyean	Let all be as you say.
Cowawwunnaûwem	You speak truly.
Cowauôntam	You are a wise man.
Wetompátitea	Let us make friends.

General Observations of Their Wars

How dreadful and yet how righteous is it with the most righteous judge of the whole world, that all the generations of men being turned enemies against, and fighting against him who gives them breath and being, and all things (whom yet they cannot reach, should stab, kill, burn, murder and devour each other)?

More Particular

The Indians count of men as dogs,
It is no wonder then:
They tear out one another's throats!
But now that English men,
(That boast themselves God's children, and
Members of Christ to be)
That they should thus break out in flames.
Sure 'tis a mystery!
The second sealed mystery or red horse,[3]
Whose rider hath power and will,
To take away peace from earthly men,
They must each other kill.
—1643

---

[1]   *pitched field*   I.e., planned battle.
[2]   *buckler*   Shield.

[3]   *second sealed … red horse*   In Revelation, John envisions God opening seven seals, each of which precipitates a cataclysmic event. The second seal releases a rider on a red horse who signifies War. Cf. Revelation 6.3–4.

ANNE BRADSTREET

c. 1612 – 1672

A Puritan colonist born in England, Anne Bradstreet is distinguished as one of the first poets to write in English in North America. As such, she has always been closely associated with the historical archive of early colonial America. But why do we read Anne Bradstreet in the modern world? For many decades now, a lively debate has centered on that question. Is it merely for historical and sociological reasons—"because she was the first American poet, and a woman at that" (as Louisa Hall puts it)? Or is her poetry of real value to us today *as poetry*?

Though Bradstreet was praised by some in her own time as an accomplished versifier, her work attracted little attention in the seventeenth and eighteenth centuries, and for much of the nineteenth and early twentieth centuries discussions of her poetry tended to be politely patronizing. The 1858 *American Cyclopedia* praised her "singular quaintness"; William P. Trent's 1904 *Brief History of American Literature* concluded that she "was a good, true woman, well read in the poets of her day, and possessed of genuine though very slight literary powers." Then, in the 1950s and 60s the poet John Berryman reimagined Bradstreet's life through the 57 stanzas of his 1956 "Homage to Mistress Bradstreet"—and brought a new bluntness to discussions of what he described at one point as Bradstreet's "spiritless poems." He went on in a 1965 essay to characterize Bradstreet as a "boring, high minded Puritan woman who may have been our first American poet but was not a good one." (It was "as a woman," rather than "as a poetess" that Bradstreet interested Berryman.) A number of poets and literary scholars piled on, describing Bradstreet's verse as "dull," "awkward," "insipid"—at best, "endearingly competent." But in the 1960s and 70s those critics met with a strong riposte; in 1966, for example, Ann Stanford argued that Bradstreet's work was characterized by powerful tensions—a "clash of feeling and dogma that keeps her poetry alive." In 1967 the distinguished poet Adrienne Rich made a strong case that Bradstreet's more personal work in particular displayed both honesty and emotional intensity. Late twentieth-century feminist critics fleshed out the picture of a poet of considerable range, and in this century Eavan Boland persuasively argued in a 2006 essay for the merits of "the neighbourly, definite voice" with which Bradstreet tells her story. (Boland's 2012 poem "Becoming Anne Bradstreet" makes the case in a different fashion for the earlier poet's "home truths.")

Bradstreet was born Anne Dudley in Northampton, England, to Dorothy Yorke and Thomas Dudley. In 1619 her father became steward to the Earl of Lincoln, and Anne lived in comfort on the Earl's estate in her youth. Though not educated formally, she was an ardent reader and made use of her access to an extensive library, encouraged by her parents to pursue learning in many subjects. She married her father's assistant, Cambridge graduate Simon Bradstreet, in 1628; two years later, the couple joined her parents and hundreds of other Puritan colonists on a journey to join the new Massachusetts Bay Colony in America.

Their ship, the *Arbella*, arrived in Salem after three difficult months. The eighteen-year-old Bradstreet, as she later wrote, "found a new world and new manners at which my heart rose [in revolt]. But after I was convinced it was the way of God, I submitted to it and joined the church at Boston." Bradstreet's body of work gives expression, from a variety of angles, both to her Puritan beliefs and to her experience of everyday life in seventeenth-century America.

We do not know if Bradstreet wrote any poems before she came to America; the first of her extant poems, "Upon a Fit of Sickness," was composed in 1632, when she was twenty. After their first years in Salem, the family lived in several increasingly remote communities, including Charlestown, Newtown, and Ipswich; they eventually settled in Andover (now called North Andover). Bradstreet and her husband also began to establish their own family, with their first child Samuel born in 1633 and seven more following over the next nineteen years (all of whom, remarkably, survived into adulthood). Bradstreet's husband and father both worked as administrators in the colony, spending a great deal of time away from home and often leaving her as the sole manager of the household; she nonetheless found time to compose poems, which she shared with her social circle but made no effort to publish. (Print technology was not yet well established in America, and even in Europe authors often still preferred to circulate manuscripts by hand rather than have them printed).

In 1650, a collection of Bradstreet's poems was published in London under the title *The Tenth Muse Lately Sprung Up in America*. The publication seems to have been orchestrated by several friends, chief among them her brother-in-law John Woodbridge, who had brought copies of a number of her poems with him when he returned to England. In his epistle to the reader, Woodbridge expresses his rationale:

> ... I fear the displeasure of no person in the publishing of these poems but the author, without whose knowledge, and contrary to her expectation, I have presumed to bring to public view, what she resolved should (in such a manner) never see the sun; but I found [that various people] had gotten some scattered papers ... [and] were likely to have sent forth broken pieces, to the author's prejudice, which I thought to prevent, as well as to pleasure those that earnestly desired the view of the whole.

Though some have suggested that Bradstreet herself may have approved of Woodbridge's actions, most scholars have taken the evidence at face value and concluded that Bradstreet very likely did indeed (as she later put it in her poem "The Author to Her Book") find herself "blushing" at the unexpected and unplanned publication.

Whatever the circumstances of its publication, the writing in the collection demonstrates not only the author's facility with poetic forms but also her very considerable knowledge of philosophy, history, science, and literature. Her "quaternions" (four-part poems) discuss the four elements, seasons, humors of human beings, and stages of life; her elegies praise such figures as Elizabeth I and Sir Philip Sidney; and her "Dialogue Between Old England and New" depicts the political relationship between her old and new homes as personified by a mother and daughter. Though *The Tenth Muse* was a commercial success for the printer, it would be the only collection of Bradstreet's work published during her lifetime.

The poems in *The Tenth Muse* are largely public poems, but Bradstreet's writing could also be highly personal, drawing on her life experiences as a wife, mother, and Puritan, and including elegies for her parents, poems responding to the deaths of several grandchildren, and love letters to her husband. (The publication history has led many to assume that the formal, public poems were essentially apprentice work, and that it was only later in her life that Bradstreet's writing took a personal turn, but recent scholarship has shown that there can be no precise correlation of her public poems and her personal poems with different stages of her life.) With her children as her imagined audience, she wrote *Meditations Divine and Moral*, a work containing observations and wisdom which she hoped could serve as a guide for her descendants after her death. Also among her unpublished writings were poems documenting personal trials (such as the fire that destroyed her home), as well as happy occasions such as her son's safe return from a trip to England. In addition to providing a glimpse into Bradstreet's lived experiences, her personal poems are notable for the tensions between their speaker's attachment to earthly life and a Puritan insistence that heavenly concerns take priority over all temporal ones.

Rich, Boland, and numerous others have been of the view that Bradstreet's public poetry is less successful aesthetically than her more personal poems—but on that subject too there has been lively disagreement, with Louisa Hall and others suggesting that what earlier commentators had read as instances of poetic incompetence (in, for example, Bradstreet's early elegies) are in fact "purposeful strategies"— intentional breaches of formal literary convention. A spirit of lively engagement with the poetry itself, then, has increasingly come to prevail in discussions of Bradstreet, with the pious and patronizing voices that were for so long dominant now increasingly relegated to the sidelines.

At sixty, Bradstreet succumbed to consumption. Six years later, her writing was published in North America for the first time as *Several Poems Compiled with Great Variety of Wit and Learning* (1678), a volume that brought together the poems from *The Tenth Muse* both with poems not previously published—some of which (such as the love poems to her husband) the editors acknowledged that she "never meant should come to public view"—and with various later poems about Bradstreet's life. Other personal poems, however, remained in the possession of her son Simon; these would not appear in print until 1867, when John Harvard Ellis published a complete collection of her writing.

Not many material artifacts from Bradstreet's life remain—her place of burial is unmarked and no portraits of her as an adult have survived.

———

NOTE ON THE TEXTS: Unless otherwise noted, the texts here are based on those found in the 1678 edition of *Several Poems Compiled with Great Variety of Wit and Learning, Full of Delight Wherein Especially Is Contained a Compleat Discourse, and Description of the Four Elements, Constitutions, Ages of Man, Seasons of the Year, Together with an Exact Epitome of the Three by a Gentlewoman in New-England*—or, in the case of poems not included in the seventeenth-century publications, the 1867 John Harvard Ellis edition of *The Works of Mrs. Bradstreet in Prose and Verse* (the first collection to include her later, personal poems). The ordering of the texts follows that found in these volumes—though, as scholars such as Margaret Olofson Thickstun have pointed out, we do not have any evidence that Bradstreet had any input herself into this ordering—or, indeed, whether she was responsible for the titles assigned to many of the poems.

Transcriptions of the 1678 volume may be found both on the University of Michigan Early English Books site and the University of Pennsylvania Celebration of Women Writers site. Other editions consulted include the 1897 Frank E. Hopkins edition (with introduction by Charles Eliot Norton) of *Poems of Mrs. Bradstreet, Together with Her Prose Remains*, and the 1967 Jeannine Hensley edition (with introduction by Adrienne Rich) of *The Works of Anne Bradstreet*. Thickstun was among those who raised concerns over some of the editorial practices followed in the Hensley volume; she has now published a new edition of Bradstreet's work—*Anne Bradstreet, Poems and Meditations* (2019)—which addresses those concerns, presenting the works in ways that helpfully clarify their publication history for the reader. (The editors of this anthology gratefully acknowledge Thickstun's assistance.)

Spelling and punctuation have been modernized in accordance with the practices of this anthology.

⌘ ⌘ ⌘

Prologue[1]

1

To sing of wars, of captains, and of kings,
  Of cities founded, commonwealths begun,
For my mean° pen are too superior things,   *humble*
And how they all, or each, their dates have run:
5 Let poets and historians set these forth,
My obscure verse shall not so dim their worth.

2

But when my wond'ring eyes and envious heart
Great Bartas'[2] sugared lines do but read o'er,

Fool, I do grudge, the muses did not part
10 'Twixt him and me that over-fluent store;[3]
A Bartas can do what a Bartas will,
But simple I, according to my skill.

3

From school-boy's tongue, no rhetoric we expect,
Nor yet a sweet consort° from broken strings,   *harmony*
15 Nor perfect beauty where's a main defect,
My foolish, broken, blemished Muse so sings;
And this to mend, alas, no art is able,
'Cause nature made it so irreparable.

---

[1] This poem serves as the prologue for *The Tenth Muse* (1650).

[2] *Bartas* Guillaume de Salluste, seigneur du Bartas (1544–90), French writer of epic poetry.

[3] *muses* Nine classical sister goddesses responsible for the arts; *did not ... store* Did not divide between the two of us the overabundance of talent they gave him.

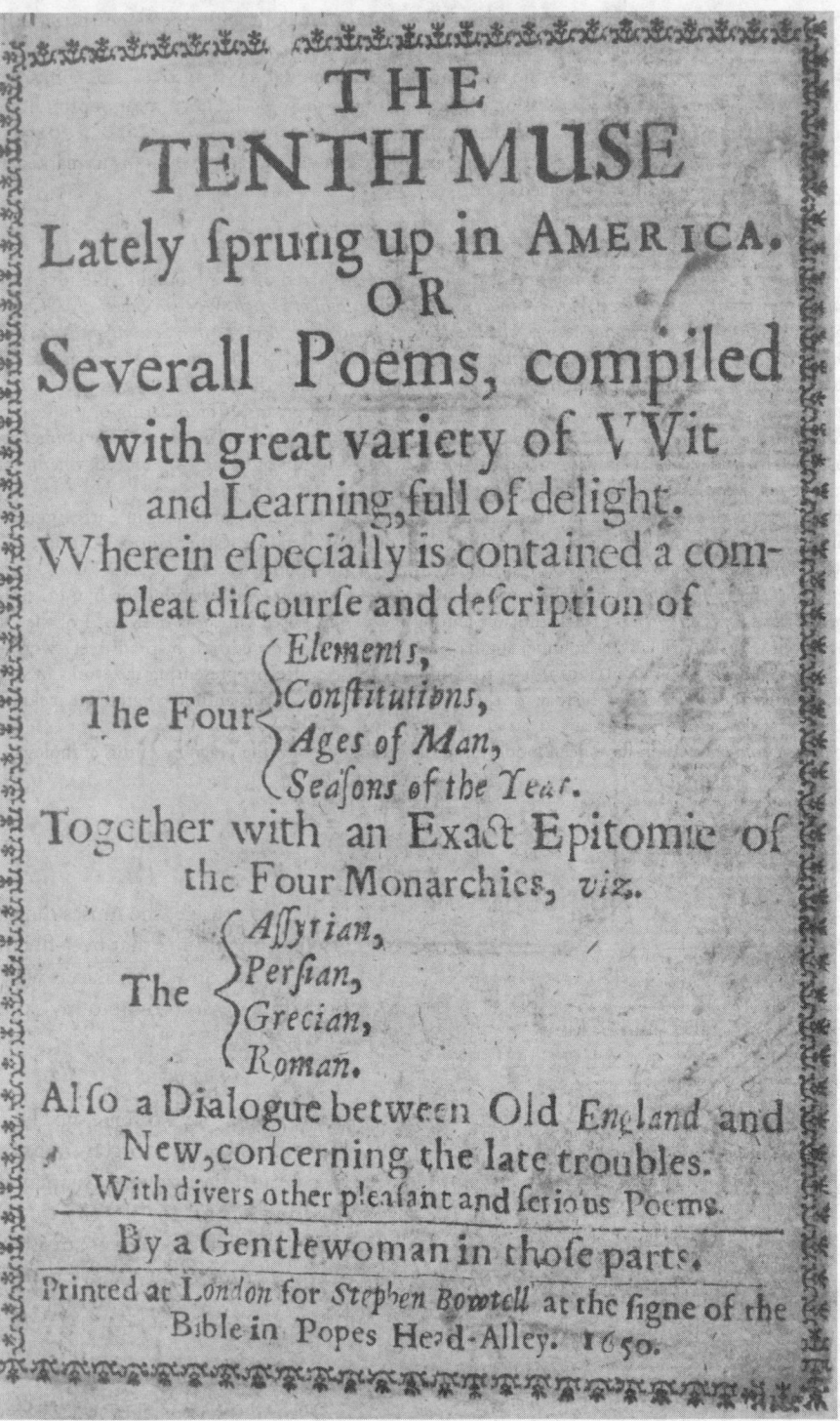

THE
TENTH MUSE

Lately sprung up in AMERICA.
OR

Severall Poems, compiled
with great variety of VVit
and Learning, full of delight.
Wherein especially is contained a compleat discourse and description of

The Four
{
Elements,
Constitutions,
Ages of Man,
Seasons of the Year.
}

Together with an Exact Epitomie of
the Four Monarchies, *viz.*

The
{
Assyrian,
Persian,
Grecian,
Roman.
}

Also a Dialogue between Old *England* and
New, concerning the late troubles.
With divers other pleasant and serious Poems.

By a Gentlewoman in those parts.

Printed at London for *Stephen Bowtell* at the signe of the
Bible in Popes Head-Alley. 1650.

Title page of the 1650 edition of *The Tenth Muse*.

4

Nor can I, like that fluent sweet-tongued Greek[1]
20 Who lisped at first, speak afterwards more plain;
By art, he gladly found what he did seek,
A full requital of his striving pain:
Art can do much, but this maxim's most sure,
A weak or wounded brain admits no cure.

5

25 I am obnoxious° to each carping tongue   *vulnerable*
Who says my hand a needle better fits.
A poet's pen, all scorn, I should thus wrong;
For such despite° they cast on female wits: *spite*
If what I do prove well, it won't advance,
30 They'll say it's stol'n, or else, it was by chance.

6

But sure the antique Greeks were far more mild,
Else of our sex, why feigned° they those nine,[2]   *invented*
And poesy made, Calliope's[3] own child,
So 'mongst the rest, they placed the arts divine:
35 But this weak knot they will full soon untie,
The Greeks did nought, but play the fool and lie.[4]

7

Let Greeks be Greeks, and women what they are,
Men have precedency, and still excel,
It is but vain unjustly to wage war;
40 Men can do best, and women know it well.
Preeminence in each, and all is yours,
Yet grant some small acknowledgement of ours.

8

And oh, ye high flown quills that soar the skies,
And ever with your prey, still catch your praise,
45 If e'er you deign these lowly lines your eyes,

Give wholesome parsley wreath, I ask no bays:[5]
This mean and unrefined stuff of mine,
Will make your glistering gold but more to shine.
—1650, 1678

Contemplations

1

Sometime now past in the autumnal tide,
When Phoebus wanted but one hour to bed,[6]
The trees all richly clad, yet void of pride,
Were gilded o'er by his rich golden head.
5 Their leaves and fruits seemed painted, but was true,
Of green, of red, of yellow, mixèd hue;
Rapt° were my senses at this delectable view.   *overwhelmed*

2

I wist° not what to wish, yet sure thought I,   *knew*
If so much excellence abide below,
10 How excellent is he that dwells on high,
Whose power and beauty by his works we know?
Sure he is goodness, wisdom, glory, light,
That hath this under world so richly dight:°   *decorated*
More Heaven than Earth was here, no winter and no
    night.

3

15 Then on a stately oak I cast mine eye,
Whose ruffling top the clouds seemed to aspire;[7]
How long since thou wast in thine infancy?
Thy strength, and stature, more thy years admire;[8]
Hath hundred winters passed since thou wast born?
20 Or thousand since thou breakest thy shell of horn?
If so, all these as nought, eternity doth scorn.

---

[1] *fluent … Greek*   Demosthenes of Athens (384–322 BCE), famous orator, who suffered from a speech defect and trained himself to speak clearly.

[2] *those nine*   I.e., the Muses.

[3] *Calliope*   Muse of epic poetry.

[4] *But this … lie*   I.e., my critics will pull apart my argument by dismissing the ancient Greeks as liars and fools.

[5] *bays*   In classical times, wreaths of bay laurel were awarded for poetic and other achievements.

[6] *Phoebus wanted but one hour to bed*   I.e., the sun was only an hour away from setting; Phoebus is a name given to the classical god Apollo, referring to his role as sun god.

[7] *the clouds seemed to aspire*   Seemed to try to reach to the clouds.

[8] *Thy strength … admire*   Your strength and stature, and even more so your years, give rise to admiration. (The use of the verb *admire* in this way, meaning cause someone to feel admiration or wonder, is now obsolete.)

4

Then higher on the glistering sun I gazed,
Whose beams was shaded by the leafy tree.
The more I looked, the more I grew amazed,
25 And softly said, what glory's like to thee?
Soul of this world, this universe's eye,
No wonder some made thee a deity:
Had I not better known, (alas), the same had I.[1]

5

Thou as a bridegroom from thy chamber rushes,
30 And as a strong man joys to run a race,[2]
The morn doth usher thee, with smiles and blushes;
The Earth reflects her glances in thy face.
Birds, insects, animals with vegative,[3]
Thy heat from death and dullness doth revive:
35 And in the darksome womb of fruitful nature dive.

6

Thy swift annual and diurnal course,
Thy daily straight, and yearly oblique path,
Thy pleasing fervor, and thy scorching force,
All mortals here the feeling knowledge hath.[4]
40 Thy presence makes it day, thy absence night,
Quaternal seasons causèd by thy might:
Hail creature, full of sweetness, beauty and delight.

7

Art thou so full of glory that no eye
Hath strength thy shining rays once to behold?
45 And is thy splendid throne erect so high
As to approach it, can no earthly mold?°   *form, thing*
How full of glory then must thy creator be,
Who gave this bright light luster unto thee?
Admired, adored for ever, be that majesty.

---

[1]   *Had I not better … had I*   If I had not known better (i.e., been told of the existence of a Christian God), I'm sorry to say that I too would have treated the great tree as a god.

[2]   *Thou as … a race*   See Psalm 19.1–5: "The heavens declare the glory of God; and the firmament sheweth his handiwork. … In them he set a tabernacle for the sun, / Which is as a bridegroom coming out of his chamber, and rejoiceth as a strong man to run a race."

[3]   *animals with vegative*   The animal as well as the plant world.

[4]   *All mortals … hath*   I.e., all mortal beings on earth feel this knowledge.

8

50 Silent alone, where none or° saw, or heard,   *either*
In pathless paths I led my wand'ring feet,
My humble eyes to lofty skies I reared
To sing some song, my mazèd° muse   *bewildered*
    thought meet.°   *appropriate*
My great Creator I would magnify,
55 That nature had thus decked liberally:
But ah, and ah, again, my imbecility!

9

I heard the merry grasshopper then sing,
The black-clad cricket, bear a second part;
They kept one tune, and played on the same string,
60 Seeming to glory in their little art.
Shall creatures abject thus their voices raise
And in their kind resound their maker's praise:
Whilst I, as mute, can warble forth no
    higher lays?°   *songs, poems*

10

When present times look back to ages past,
65 And men in being fancy those are dead,[5]
It makes things gone perpetually to last,
And calls back months and years that long since fled.
It makes a man more agèd in conceit,°   *imagination*
Than was Methuselah, or's grand-sire great,[6]
70 While of their persons and their acts his mind doth
    treat.

11

Sometimes in Eden fair, he seems to be,
Sees glorious Adam there made Lord of all,
Fancies the Apple, dangle on the Tree,
That turn'd his Sovereign to a naked thral.°   *slave*
75 Who like a miscreant's driven from that place,

---

[5]   *men in … dead*   Living people think of (or imagine) those who are dead.

[6]   *Methuselah*   Old Testament figure said to have lived to be 969 years old (Genesis 5.27);   *or's grand-sire great*   Or his great grandfather. Methuselah's great grandfather, Mahalaleel, lived 895 years (Genesis 5.17), though the speaker may be alluding to Adam, from whom Methuselah is of course also descended.

To get his bread with pain, and sweat of face:[1]
A penalty impos'd on his backsliding Race.

12

Here sits our Grandame in retired place,[2]
And in her lap, her bloody Cain[3] new born,
The weeping Imp oft looks her in the face,
Bewails his unknown hap,° and fate forlorn;   *fortune*
His Mother sighs, to think of Paradise,
And how she lost her bliss, to be more wise,
Believing him that was, and is, Father of lyes.[4]

13

85 Here Cain and Abel come to sacrifice,
Fruits of the earth and fatlings[5] each do bring,
On Abel's gift the fire descends from skies,
But no such sign on false Cain's offering;
With sullen hateful looks he goes his ways,
90 Hath thousand thoughts to end his brother's days,
Upon whose blood his future good he hopes to raise.

14

There Abel keeps his sheep, no ill he thinks,
His brother comes, then acts his fratricide,
The virgin Earth, of blood her first draught drinks
95 But since that time she often hath been cloyed;[6]
The wretch with ghastly face and dreadful mind
Thinks each he sees will serve him in his kind,
Though none on Earth but kindred near then could
    he find.

15

Who fancies not his looks now at the bar,[7]
100 His face like death, his heart with horror fraught,
Nor malefactor° ever felt like war,   *evildoer*
When deep despair with wish of life hath fought,
Branded with guilt, and crushed with
    treble° woes,   *triple*
A vagabond to land of Nod he goes,
105 A city builds,[8] that walls might him secure from foes.

16

Who thinks not oft upon the fathers' ages,
Their long descent, how nephews' sons they saw,
The starry observations of those sages,
And how their precepts to their sons were law,
110 How Adam sighed to see his progeny,
Clothed all in his black sinful livery,[9]
Who neither guilt nor yet the punishment
    could fly.°   *escape*

17

Our life compare we with their length of days
Who to the tenth of theirs doth now arrive?[10]
115 And though thus short, we shorten many ways,
Living so little while we are alive;
In eating, drinking, sleeping, vain delight—
So, unawares, comes on perpetual night,
And puts all pleasures vain unto eternal flight.

18

120 When I behold the heavens as in their prime,
And then the earth (though old) still clad in green,
The stones and trees, insensible of time,
Nor age nor wrinkle on their front are seen;
If winter come, and greenness then do fade,
125 A spring returns, and they more youthful made;

---

1 *To get ... face* Part of the condemnation spoken by God after driving Adam and Eve out of the Garden of Eden for eating the forbidden fruit: "In the sweat of thy face shalt thou eat bread" (Genesis 3.19).

2 *our Grandame ... place* Our grandmother (i.e., Eve), in the location she inhabited after she was exiled.

3 *Cain* One of Adam and Eve's sons. In Genesis 4.1–16, when his brother Abel's sacrifice of a lamb pleased God more than Cain's offering of crops, Cain became enraged and killed Abel. After becoming the first murderer, Cain was forced to wander the earth as an exile.

4 *Father of lyes* Title bestowed on the devil in John 8.44. In Genesis 3.15, a serpent convinced Eve to eat the forbidden fruit that would give her knowledge of good and evil; in conventional interpretations of the Bible, this serpent is equated with the devil.

5 *fatlings* Young animals raised for meat.

6 *cloyed* Sickened, especially by over-feeding.

7 *at the bar* Before the judge.

8 *land of ... builds* Cain finally settled in a location east of Eden known as Nod, where he built a city and named it after his son Enoch (Genesis 4.16–17).

9 *Clothed ... livery* I.e., Adam's children wear his sinfulness as if wearing his house uniform; they have inherited his sinfulness.

10 *Our life ... arrive* The early patriarchs of the Old Testament were said to have enjoyed lifespans of hundreds of years.

But man grows old, lies down, remains where once
   he's laid.

19

By birth more noble than those creatures all,
Yet seems by nature and by custom cursed,
No sooner born, but grief and care makes fall
130 That state obliterate he had at first;
Nor youth, nor strength, nor wisdom spring again,
Nor habitations long their names retain,
But in oblivion to the final day[1] remain.

20

Shall I then praise the heavens, the trees, the earth
135 Because their beauty and their strength last longer?
Shall I wish there, or never to had birth,
Because they're bigger, and their bodies stronger?
Nay, they shall darken, perish, fade and die,
And when unmade, so ever shall they lie,
140 But man was made for endless immortality.

21

Under the cooling shadow of a stately elm
Close sat I by a goodly river's side,
Where gliding streams the rocks did overwhelm;
A lonely place, with pleasures dignified.
145 I once that loved the shady woods so well,
Now thought the rivers did the trees excel,
And if the sun would ever° shine, there   *always*
   would I dwell.

22

While on the stealing stream I fixed mine eye,
Which to the longed-for ocean held its course,
150 I marked nor crooks nor rubs[2] that there did lie
Could hinder aught,° but still augment its force. *anything*
"O happy flood," quoth I, "that holds thy race
Till thou arrive at thy belovèd place,
Nor is it rocks or shoals that can obstruct thy pace,

23

155 "Nor is't enough, that thou alone mayst slide,
But hundred brooks in thy clear waves do meet,
So hand in hand along with thee they glide
To Thetis'[3] house, where all embrace and greet.
Thou emblem true of what I count the best,
160 O could I lead my rivulets[4] to rest,
So may we press to that vast mansion, ever blest."

24

Ye fish which in this liquid region 'bide,
That for each season have your habitation,
Now salt, now fresh where you think best to glide
165 To unknown coasts, to give a visitation,
In lakes and ponds, you leave your numerous
   fry;°   *hatchlings*
So nature taught, and yet you know not why,
You wat'ry folk that know not your felicity.

25

Look how the wantons frisk to taste the air,[5]
170 Then to the colder bottom straight they dive;
Eftsoon° to Neptune's[6] glassy hall repair *soon after*
To see what trade the great ones there do drive,
Who forage o'er the spacious sea-green field,
And take the trembling prey before it yield,
175 Whose armour is their scales, their spreading fins their
   shield.

26

While musing thus with contemplation fed,
And thousand fancies buzzing in my brain,
The sweet-tongued Philomel[7] perched o'er my head,
And chanted forth a most melodious strain
180 Which rapt me so with wonder and delight,
I judged my hearing better than my sight,
And wished me wings with her a while to take my
   flight.

---

1   *final day* I.e., Judgment Day, for which bodies will be resurrected and reunited with souls.

2   *marked nor crooks ... rubs* Observed that neither bends nor obstructions.

3   *Thetis* Classical sea nymph.

4   *rivulets* Small branches of a river or stream.

5   *wantons ... air* The lively ones leap up above the surface.

6   *Neptune* Classical sea god.

7   *Philomel* Nightingale, so named for the Greek mythological figure Philomela, who was transformed into a nightingale.

27

"O merry bird," (said I) "that fears no snares,
That neither toils nor hoards up in thy barn,[1]
185 Feels no sad thoughts nor
   cruciating° cares   *tormenting, painful*
To gain more good or shun what might thee harm.
Thy clothes ne'er wear, thy
   meat° is everywhere,   *food (of any sort)*
Thy bed a bough, thy drink the water clear,
Reminds not what is past, nor what's to come dost
   fear.

28

190 "The dawning morn with songs thou dost
   prevent,°   *anticipate*
Sets hundred notes unto thy feathered crew,
So each one tunes his pretty instrument,
And warbling out the old, begins anew,
And thus they pass their youth in summer season,
195 Then follow thee into a better region,
Where winter's never felt by that sweet airy legion."

29

Man at the best a creature frail and vain,
In knowledge ignorant, in strength but weak,
Subject to sorrows, losses, sickness, pain,
200 Each storm his state, his mind, his body break,
From some of these he never finds cessation,
But day or night, within, without, vexation,
Troubles from foes, from friends, from dearest, near'st
   relation.

30

And yet this sinful creature, frail and vain,
205 This lump of wretchedness, of sin and sorrow,
This weather-beaten vessel wracked with pain,
Joys not in hope of an eternal morrow;
Nor all his losses, crosses, and vexation,
In weight, in frequency and long duration
210 Can make him deeply groan for that divine
   translation.°   *transformation*

---

1 *That neither toils ... thy barn* See Matthew 6.28.

31

The mariner that on smooth waves doth glide,
Sings merrily, and steers his barque° with ease,   *ship*
As if he had command of wind and tide,
And now becomes great master of the seas;
215 But suddenly a storm spoils all the sport,
And makes him long for a more quiet port,
Which 'gainst all adverse winds may serve for fort.

32

So he that saileth in this world of pleasure,
Feeding on sweets, that never bit of th' sour,
220 That's full of friends, of honour and of treasure,
Fond° fool, he takes this earth ev'n   *silly*
   for heav'n's bower,[2]
But sad affliction comes and makes him see
Here's neither honour, wealth, nor safety;
Only above is found all with security.

33

225 O Time the fatal wrack° of mortal things,   *ruination*
That draws oblivion's curtains over kings;
Their sumptuous monuments, men know them not,
Their names without a record are forgot,
Their parts, their ports, their pomp's all laid in th'
   dust
230 Nor wit, nor gold, nor buildings 'scape time's rust;
But he whose name is graved in the white stone[3]
Shall last and shine when all of these are gone.
—1678

The Flesh and the Spirit

In secret place where once I stood
Close by the banks of lacrim flood°   *flood of tears*
I heard two sisters reason on
Things that are past, and things to come;
5 One Flesh was called, who had her eye
On worldly wealth and vanity;
The other Spirit, who did rear
Her thoughts unto a higher sphere:

---

2 *bower* Shaded, comfortable sanctuary.

3 *white stone* See Revelation 2.17: "To him that overcometh will I give ... a white stone, and in the stone a new name written."

Sister, quoth Flesh, what liv'st thou on,
10 Nothing but meditation?
Doth contemplation feed thee so
Regardlessly to let earth go?[1]
Can speculation satisfy
Notion without reality?
15 Dost dream[2] of things beyond the moon
And dost thou hope to dwell there soon?
Hast treasures there laid up in store
That all in the world thou count'st but poor?
Art fancy-sick[3] or turned a sot°   fool
20 To catch at shadows which are not?
Come, come, I'll show unto thy sense,
Industry hath its recompense.°   compensation
What canst desire, but thou may'st see
True substance in variety?
25 Dost honour like? Acquire the same,
As some to their immortal fame:
And trophies to thy name erect
Which wearing time shall ne'er deject.
For riches dost thou long full sore?
30 Behold enough of precious store.
Earth hath more silver, pearls, and gold
Than eyes can see, or hands can hold.
Affect's thou pleasure?[4] Take thy fill,
Earth hath enough of what you will.
35 Then let not go what thou may'st find,
For things unknown, only in mind.

Spirit: Be still thou unregenerate[5] part,
Disturb no more my settled heart,
For I have vowed, (and so will do)
40 Thee as a foe, still to pursue.
And combat with thee will and must,
Until I see thee laid in the dust.
Sisters we are, yea twins we be
Yet deadly feud twixt thee and me;
45 For from one father are we not,

Thou by old Adam wast begot,[6]
But my arise is from above
Whence my dear father I do love.
Thou speak'st me fair but hat'st me sore;
50 Thy flatt'ring shows I'll trust no more.
How oft thy slave, hast thou me made,
When I believed what thou hast said,
And never had more cause of woe
Than when I did what thou bad'st do.[7]
55 I'll stop mine ears at these thy charms
And count them for my deadly harms.
Thy sinful pleasures I do hate,
Thy riches are to me no bait,
Thine honours do nor will I love;[8]
60 For my ambition lies above.
My greatest honour it shall be
When I am victor over thee,
And triumph shall, with laurel head,[9]
When thou my captive shalt be led,
65 How I do live, thou need'st not scoff,
For I have meat° thou know'st not of;   food
The hidden manna[10] I do eat;
The word of life it is my meat.
My thoughts do yield° me more   give
    content°   contentment
70 Than can thy hours in pleasure spent.
Nor are they shadows which I catch,
Nor fancies vain at which I snatch.
But reach at things that are so high,
Beyond thy dull capacity;
75 Eternal substance I do see,
With which enrichèd I would be:

---

[1] *Doth contemplation ... earth go* I.e., are you fed so full by contemplation that you can thoughtlessly ignore earthly things?

[2] *Dost dream* Do you dream.

[3] *Art fancy-sick* Are you imagining things?

[4] *Affect's thou pleasure?* Do you seek pleasure?

[5] *unregenerate* Not recognized as a member of God's elect.

---

[6] *Adam wast begot* Spirit suggests here that Flesh is a descendant of Adam, the first human, and is thus contaminated by Adam's original sin of disobedience to God.

[7] *bad'st do* Bids or commands me to do.

[8] *Thine honours do ... love* I.e., I will not honor you, nor will I love you. Both the 1650 and 1678 editions read "Thine honours do ..." but this may be a misprint for "Thine honors due," which would offer other interpretations.

[9] *laurel head* In Ancient Greece and Rome, laurels were traditionally granted those victorious in athletic competitions or in battle.

[10] *manna* In the Book of Exodus, manna was the food God provided for the sustenance of the Israelites during their forty years wandering the desert. Cf. Exodus 16.1 and Psalm 78.24–25.

Mine eye doth pierce the heavens, and see
What is invisible to thee.
My garments are not silk nor gold,
80 Nor such like trash which earth doth hold,
But royal robes I shall have on,
More glorious than the glistering° sun;   *gleaming*
My crown not diamonds, pearls, and gold,
But such as angels' heads enfold.
85 The city where I hope to dwell,
There's none on earth can parallel;
The stately walls both high and strong,
Are made of precious jasper stone,
The gates of pearl, both rich and clear,
90 And angels are for° porters there;   *act as*
The streets thereof transparent gold,
Such as no eye did e're behold,
A crystal river there doth run,
Which doth proceed from the Lamb's[1] throne:
95 Of life, there are the waters sure,
Which shall remain forever pure;
Nor° sun, nor moon, they have no need,   *of*
For glory doth from God proceed:
No candle there, nor yet torch light,
100 For there shall be no darksome night.

From sickness and infirmity,
For evermore they shall be free,
Nor withering age shall e're come there,
But beauty shall be bright and clear.
105 This city pure is not for thee,
For things unclean there shall not be:
If I of heaven may have my fill,
Take thou the world, and all that will.
—1678

The Author to Her Book[2]

Thou ill-formed offspring of my feeble brain,
Who after birth did'st by my side remain,

Till snatched from thence by friends, less wise than true
Who, thee abroad, exposed to public view,[3]
5 Made thee in rags, halting to th' press to trudge,
Where errors were not lessened (all may judge).
At thy return my blushing was not small,
My rambling brat (in print) should mother call,
I cast thee by as one unfit for light,
10 Thy visage was so irksome in my sight;
Yet being mine own, at length affection would
Thy blemishes amend, if so I could:
I washed thy face, but more defects I saw,
And rubbing off a spot, still made a flaw.
15 I stretched thy joints to make thee even feet,[4]
Yet still thou run'st more hobbling than is meet;°   *suitable*
In better dress to trim thee was my mind,
But nought save home-spun cloth, i' th' house I find.
In this array, 'mongst vulgars[5] mayst thou roam.
20 In critics' hands, beware thou dost not come;
And take thy way where yet thou art not known,
If for thy father asked, say, thou hadst none:
And for thy mother, she alas is poor,
Which caused her thus to send thee out of door.
—1678

Before the Birth of One of Her Children

All things within this fading world hath end,
Adversity doth still our joys attend;
No ties so strong, no friends so clear and sweet,
But with death's parting blow is sure to meet.
5 The sentence passed is most irrevocable,
A common thing, yet oh, inevitable;
How soon, my dear, death may my steps attend,[6]
How soon't may be thy lot to lose thy friend,

---

[1] *Lamb's* Jesus is often referred to as the "Lamb of God," as he offered himself as a sacrifice for the atonement of humankind's sin. Cf. John 1.29 and Revelation 22.3.

[2] This poem first appeared in the posthumous *Several Poems* (1678), a collection that included both new writing and revised versions of previously published poems.

[3] *Till … view* Bradstreet's first book, *The Tenth Muse* (1650), was published in London, apparently without her knowledge or permission. Her brother-in-law John Woodbridge had brought her writings to England and arranged for the publication.

[4] *make thee … feet* Make your poetic rhythm regular. (Poetic feet are units made up of stressed and unstressed syllables in regular patterns; they are the building blocks of accentual syllabic meter.)

[5] *vulgars* Common people.

[6] *How soon … attend* Reference to the dangers associated with childbirth; it is estimated that the odds of a seventeenth-century woman dying while giving birth were greater than [continued …]

We both are ignorant, yet love bids me
10 These farewell lines to recommend to thee,
That when that knot's untied that made us one,
I may seem thine, who in effect am none.
And if I see not half my days that's due,
What nature would, God grant to yours and you;
15 The many faults that well you know I have,
Let be interred in my oblivious grave;
If any worth or virtue were in me,
Let that live freshly in thy memory,
And when thou feel'st no grief, as I no harms,
20 Yet love thy dead, who long lay in thine arms,
And when thy loss shall be repaid with gains,
Look to my little babes, my dear remains.
And if thou love thyself, or loved'st me,
These oh protect from step dame's[1] injury.
25 And if chance to thine eyes shall bring this verse,
With some sad sighs honour my absent hearse;[2]
And kiss this paper for thy love's dear sake,
Who with salt tears this last farewell did take.
—1678

To My Dear and Loving Husband

If ever two were one, then surely we.
If ever man were loved by wife, then thee;
If ever wife was happy in a man,
Compare with me, ye women, if you can.
5 I prize thy love more than whole mines of gold,
Or all the riches that the East doth hold.
My love is such that rivers cannot quench,
Nor ought° but love from thee give recompense.   *anything*
Thy love is such I can no way repay,
10 The heavens reward thee manifold, I pray.
Then while we live, in love let's so persever,
That when we live no more, we may live ever.
—1678

----

one per cent per birth. (Given that most women gave birth several times, the lifetime risk for a woman was much higher.)

1 *step dame* Stepmother.

2 *hearse* Frame upon which a body was placed during a funeral; in Puritan funerary practices, prose and poems in praise of the deceased were sometimes pinned to the hearse. "Hearse" can also refer to the dead body itself.

A Letter to Her Husband, Absent upon Public Employment[3]

My head, my heart, mine eyes, my life, nay more,
My joy, my magazine of earthly store,[4]
If two be one, as surely thou and I,
How stayest thou there, whilst I at Ipswich[5] lie?
5 So many steps, head from the heart to sever,
If but a neck, soon should we be together:
I, like the earth this season, mourn in black,
My sun is gone so far in's° zodiac,[6]   *in its*
Whom whilst I joyed, nor storms, nor frosts I felt,
10 His warmth such frigid colds did cause to melt.
My chilled limbs now numbèd lie forlorn;
Return, return sweet Sol from Capricorn;[7]
In this dead time, alas, what can I more
Than view those fruits which through thy heat I bore?[8]
15 Which sweet contentment yield me for a space,
True living pictures of their father's face.
O strange effect! now thou art southward gone,
I weary grow, the tedious day so long;
But when thou northward to me shalt return,
20 I wish my sun may never set, but burn
Within the Cancer[9] of my glowing breast,
The welcome house of him my dearest guest.
Where ever, ever stay, and go not thence,
Till nature's sad decree shall call thee hence;
25 Flesh of thy flesh, bone of thy bone,[10]
I here, thou there, yet both but° one.   *only*
—1678

----

3 *Public Employment* Civil service. Bradstreet's husband Simon worked as an administrator for the Massachusetts Bay Colony, and often traveled to the outlying communities.

4 *magazine … store* Storehouse of earthly values.

5 *Ipswich* Isolated community in Massachusetts.

6 *zodiac* Ring of constellations extending across the sky; the sun appears to travel through each in the course of a year.

7 *Sol* Sun; also the name of the Roman sun god; *Capricorn* Goat-shaped constellation marking the portion of the sky in which the sun appears from late December through most of January.

8 *those fruits … bore* I.e., the speaker's children.

9 *Cancer* Crab-shaped constellation marking the portion of the sky in which the sun appears from late June through much of July.

10 *Flesh … thy bone* See Genesis 2.23: "And Adam said, This is now bone of my bones, and flesh of my flesh: she shall be called Woman."

In Memory of My Dear Grand-Child Elizabeth Bradstreet, Who Deceased August, 1665 Being a Year and Half Old

1

Farewell dear babe, my heart's too much content,[1]
Farewell sweet babe, the pleasure of mine eye,
Farewell fair flower that for a space was lent,
Then ta'en away unto Eternity.
5 Blest babe, why should I once bewail thy fate,
Or sigh thy days so soon were terminate,
Sith° thou art settled in an everlasting state?   *since*

2

By nature trees do rot when they are grown,
And plums and apples throughly° ripe do fall,   *thoroughly*
10 And corn and grass are in their season mown,
And time brings down what is both strong and tall.
But plants new set to be eradicate,
And buds new blown° to have so short a date,   *blossomed*
Is by his hand alone that guides nature and fate.
—1678

In Memory of My Dear Grand-Child Anne Bradstreet, Who Deceased June 20, 1669, Being Three Years and Seven Months Old

With troubled heart and trembling hand I write,
The heavens have changed to sorrow my delight.
How oft with disappointment have I met,
When I on fading things my hopes have set?
5 Experience might 'fore this have made me wise,
To value things according to their price:
Was ever stable joy yet found below,°   *i.e., on Earth*
Or perfect bliss without mixture of woe?
I knew she was but as a withering flower,
10 That's here today, perhaps gone in an hour;
Like as a bubble, or the brittle glass,
Or like a shadow turning as it was.
More fool then I to look on that was lent
As if mine own, when thus impermanent.

---

[1] *my heart's too much content* I.e., who gave my heart too much happiness.

Farewell dear child, thou ne'er shall come to me;
But yet a while, and I shall go to thee.
Meantime my throbbing heart's cheered up with this:
Thou with thy Saviour art in endless bliss.
—1678

On My Dear Grand-Child Simon Bradstreet, Who Died on 16 November, 1669, Being but a Month and One Day Old

No sooner come, but gone, and fall'n asleep,
Acquaintance short, yet parting caused us weep,
Three flowers, two scarcely blown,[2] the last i'th' bud,
Cropped by th' Almighty's hand; yet is he good.
5 With dreadful awe before him let's be mute,
Such was his will, but why, let's not dispute,
With humble hearts and mouths put in the dust,
Let's say he's merciful, as well as just.
He will return, and make up all our losses,
10 And smile again, after our bitter crosses.
Go pretty babe, go rest with sisters twain;°   *two*
Among the blest in endless joys remain.
—1678

For Deliverance from a Fever

When sorrows had begirt° me round,   *beseiged*
And pains within and out,
When in my flesh no part was found,[3]
Then didst Thou rid me out.[4]
5 My burning flesh in sweat did boil,
My aching head did break,
From side to side for ease I toil,
So faint I could not speak.
Beclouded was my soul with fear

---

[2] *two scarcely blown* Two of Bradstreet's other grandchildren died in early childhood; her poems in response to their deaths are included above; *blown* Blossomed.

[3] *no part was found* No attribute was found. The meaning of *part* in this context is not entirely clear, and there are several archaic meanings of the word; to read it as meaning *quality* or *attribute* (as the word is used in the phrase *a person of many parts*) seems plausible.

[4] *didst Thou rid me out* Then did you [God] clean me out.

10 Of Thy displeasure sore,
    Nor could I read my evidence
    Which oft I read before.
    "Hide not Thy face from me!" I cried,
    "From burnings keep my soul.
15 Thou know'st my heart, and hast me tried;°   tested
    I on Thy mercies roll."
    "O heal my soul," Thou know'st I said,
    "Though flesh consume to nought,
    What though in dust it shall be laid,
20 To glory 't shall be brought."
    Thou heard'st, Thy rod Thou didst remove
    And spared my body frail
    Thou show'st to me Thy tender love,
    My heart no more might quail.
25 O, praises to my mighty God,
    Praise to my Lord, I say,
    Who hath redeemed my soul from pit,°   damnation
    Praises to Him for aye.°   forever
    —1867

Some Verses upon the Burning of
Our House, July 10th, 1666[1]

In silent night when rest I took
For sorrow near I did not look,
I wakened was with thund'ring noise
And piteous shrieks of dreadful voice.
5   That fearful sound of "fire" and "fire,"
    Let no man know is my desire.
    I, starting up, the light did spy,
    And to my God my heart did cry
    To strengthen me in my distress
10 And not to leave me succourless.°   without aid
    Then, coming out, beheld a space[2]

The flame consume my dwelling place,
And when I could no longer look,
I blest his name that gave and took,
15 That laid my goods now in the dust.
    Yea, so it was, and so 'twas just.
    It was His own, it was not mine,
    Far be it that I should repine;
    He might of all justly bereft,
20 But yet sufficient for us left.
    When by the ruins oft I past
    My sorrowing eyes aside did cast
    And here and there the places spy
    Where oft I sat and long did lie:
25 Here stood that trunk, and there that chest,
    There lay that store I counted best.
    My pleasant things in ashes lie,
    And them behold no more shall I.
    Under thy roof no guest shall sit,
30 Nor at thy table eat a bit.
    No pleasant tale shall e'er be told,
    Nor things recounted done of old.
    No candle e'er shall shine in thee,
    Nor bridegroom's voice e'er heard shall be.
35 In silence ever shalt thou lie,
    Adieu, adieu, all's vanity.
    Then straight I 'gin my heart to chide,
    And did thy wealth on earth abide,
    Didst fix thy hope on mould'ring dust,
40 The arm of flesh didst make thy trust?
    Raise up thy thoughts above the sky
    That dunghill mists away may fly.
    Thou hast a house on high erect,
    Framed by that mighty architect,
45 With glory richly furnished
    Stands permanent, though this be fled.
    It's purchasèd and paid for too
    By Him who hath enough to do.
    A price so vast as is unknown
50 Yet by his gift is made thine own.
    There's wealth enough, I need no more;
    Farewell my pelf,° farewell my store.   worldly riches
    The world no longer let me love;[3]
    My hope and treasure lies above.
    —1867

---

1   The following poem appears in a handwritten collection of Bradstreet's personal writings known as the Andover Manuscript, which contains some texts in Bradstreet's own hand, and others— including this poem—transcribed by her son Simon from papers that are now lost. The full text of the heading given the poem by Simon Bradstreet reads as follows: "Here follow some verses upon the burning of our house, July 10th, 1666. Copied out of a loose paper." This and the other poems from the Andover Manuscript were first published in 1867.

2   *beheld a space*   Saw that within a brief time.

3   *The world ... me love*   Let me love the world no longer.

To My Dear Children[1]

This book by any yet unread,
I leave for you when I am dead,
That, being gone, here you may find
What was your living mother's mind.
Make use of what I leave in love
And God shall bless you from above.

A.B.

My dear children:
Knowing by experience that the exhortations of parents take most effect when the speakers leave to speak,[2] and those especially sink deepest which are spoke latest—and being ignorant whether on my death-bed I shall have opportunity to speak to any of you, much less to all—thought it the best, whilst I was able, to compose some short matters (for what else to call them I know not) and bequeath [them] to you, that[3] when I am no more with you, yet I may be daily in your remembrance (although that is the least in my aim in what I now do), but that[4] you may gain some spiritual advantage by my experience. I have not studied in this you read to show my skill, but to declare the truth—not to set forth myself, but the glory of God. If I had minded the former, it had been perhaps better pleasing to you,—but seeing the last is the best, let it be best pleasing to you. The method I will observe shall be this—I will begin with God's dealing with me from my childhood to this day. In my young years, about 6 or 7 as I take it, I began to make conscience of my ways, and what I knew was sinful, as[5] lying, disobedience to parents, etc., I avoided it. If at any time I was overtaken with the like evils, it was a great trouble. I could not be at rest till by prayer I had confessed it unto God.

I was also troubled at the neglect of private duties,[6] though too often tardy that way.[7] I also found much comfort in reading the scriptures, especially those places I thought most concerned my condition, and as I grew to have more understanding, so the more solace I took in them.

In a long fit of sickness which I had on my bed I often communed with my heart, and made my supplication to the most high,[8] who set me free from that affliction.

But as I grew up to be about 14 or 15 I found my heart more carnal, and sitting loose from God, vanity, and the follies of youth take hold of me. About 16, the Lord laid his hand sore[9] upon me, and smote me with the smallpox. When I was in my affliction, I besought the Lord, and confessed my pride and vanity and he was entreated of me, and again restored me. But I rendered not to him according to the benefit received.

After a short time I changed my condition and was married, and came into this country, where I found a new world and new manners, at which my heart rose. But after I was convinced it was the way of God, I submitted to it and joined to the church at Boston.

After some time I fell into a lingering sickness like a consumption, together with a lameness, which correction I saw the Lord sent to humble and try me and do me good; and it was not altogether ineffectual.

It pleased God to keep me a long time without a child, which was a great grief to me, and cost me many prayers and tears before I obtained one, and after him gave me many more, of whom I now take the care, that as I have brought you into the world, and with great pains, weakness, cares, and fears, brought you to this, I now travail[10] in birth again of you till Christ be formed in you.

Among all my experiences of God's gracious dealings with me I have constantly observed this, that he

---

[1] This short poem and prose message appears to have been transcribed by Bradstreet's son Simon from an earlier manuscript in Bradstreet's own hand; "To My Dear Children" was first published along with the other Andover Manuscript material in the 1867 collection *The Works of Anne Bradstreet in Prose and Verse*.

[2] *leave to speak* Cease to speak.

[3] *that* So that.

[4] *but that* Only so that.

[5] *as* Such as.

[6] *private duties* Prayers, devotions.

[7] *though too often tardy that way* I.e., though I was often slower than I should have been (to feel guilty for neglecting my duties).

[8] *most high* I.e., God.

[9] *sore* Heavily.

[10] *travail* Labor. The apostle Paul uses this metaphor in Galatians 4.19 ("My little children, of whom I travail in birth again until Christ be formed in you").

hath never suffered[1] me long to sit loose from him, but by one affliction or other hath made me look home, and search what was amiss, so usually thus it hath been with me that I have no sooner felt my heart out of order, but I have expected correction for it, which most commonly hath been upon my own person, in sickness, weakness, pains, sometimes on my soul, in doubts and fears of God's displeasure, and my sincerity towards him. Sometimes he hath smote a child with sickness, sometimes chastened by losses in estate,[2]—and these times (through his great mercy) have been the times of my greatest getting and advantage, yea I have found them the times when the Lord hath manifested the most love to me. Then have I gone to searching, and have said with David, Lord search me and try me,[3] see what ways of wickedness are in me, and lead me in the way everlasting; and seldom or never but I have found either some sin I lay under which God would have reformed, or some duty neglected which he would have performed. And by his help I have laid vows and bonds upon my soul to perform his righteous commands.

If at any time you are chastened of God, take it as thankfully and joyfully as in greatest mercies, for if ye be His, ye shall reap the greatest benefit by it. It hath been no small support to me in times of darkness when the Almighty hath hid His face from me, that yet I have had abundance of sweetness and refreshment after affliction, and more circumspection in my walking after I have been afflicted. I have been with God like an untoward[4] child, that no longer than the rod has been on my back (or at least in sight) but I have been apt to forget him and myself too. Before I was afflicted I went astray, but now I keep thy statutes.[5]

I have had great experience of God's hearing my prayers, and returning comfortable answers to me, either in granting the thing I prayed for, or else in satisfying my mind without it; and I have been confident it hath been from him, because I have found my heart through his goodness enlarged in thankfulness to him.

I have often been perplexed that I have not found that constant joy in my pilgrimage and refreshing which I supposed most of the servants of God have; although he hath not left me altogether without the witness of his holy spirit, who hath oft given me his word and set to his seal that it shall be well with me. I have sometimes tasted of that hidden manna[6] that the world knows not, and have set up my Ebenezer,[7] and have resolved with myself that against such a promise, such tastes of sweetness, the gates of Hell shall never prevail. Yet have I many times sinkings and droopings, and not enjoyed that felicity that sometimes I have done. But when I have been in darkness and seen no light, yet have I desired to stay myself upon the Lord. And, when I have been in sickness and pain, I have thought if the Lord would but lift up the light of his countenance upon me, although he ground me to powder, it would be but light to me; yea, oft have I thought [that] if I were in hell itself, and could there find the love of God toward me, it would be a heaven. And, could I have been[8] in heaven without the love of God it would have been a hell to me; for in truth, it is the absence and presence of God that makes heaven or hell.

Many times hath Satan troubled me concerning the verity of the scriptures, many times by atheism: how could I know whether there was a God? I never saw any miracles to confirm me, and those which I read of— how did I know but they were feigned? That there is a God my reason would soon tell me by the wondrous works that I see, the vast frame of the heaven and the earth, the order of all things, night and day, summer and winter, spring and autumn, the daily providing for this great household upon the earth, the preserving and directing of all to its proper end. The consideration of

---

[1]   *suffered*   Allowed.

[2]   *sometimes chastened by losses in estate*   Sometimes rebuked (me) by making me suffer financial losses.

[3]   *David … try me*   King David was a biblical king of Israel. Several biblical psalms are attributed to him, including the one to which Bradstreet refers here, Psalm 26.

[4]   *untoward*   Unruly, disobedient.

[5]   *I keep thy statutes*   Bradstreet alludes to Psalm 119.8, a prayer offered to God by one who obeys God and "keep[s] [his] statutes."

[6]   *manna*   In the Book of Exodus, manna was the food God provided for the sustenance of the Israelites during their forty years wandering the desert. See Exodus 16.31 and Psalm 78.24–25.

[7]   *Ebenezer*   Hebrew for "stone of help," a commemoration of the assistance of God. See 1 Samuel 7.12.

[8]   *could I have been*   If I could have been.

these things would with amazement certainly resolve me that there is an Eternal Being.

But how should I know He is such a God as I worship in Trinity, and such a savior as I rely upon? Though this hath thousands of times been suggested to me, yet God hath helped me ever. I have argued this with myself. That there is a God, I see. If ever this God hath revealed himself, it must be in his word, and this must be it, or none. Have I not found that operation by it that no human invention can work upon the soul? Hath not judgments befallen diverse[1] who have scorned and condemned it? Hath it not been preserved through all ages maugre[2] all the heathen tyrants and all of the enemies who have opposed it? Is there any story but that which shows the beginnings of times, and how the world came to be as we see? Do we not know the prophecies in it fulfilled, which could not have been so long foretold by any but God himself?

When I have got over this block, then have I another put in my way. that, admit[3] this be the true God whom we worship, and that be His word, yet why may not the Popish religion[4] be the right? They have the same God, the same Christ, the same word; they only interpret it one way, we another. This hath sometimes stuck with me, and more it would, but the vain fooleries that are in their religion, together with their lying miracles and cruel persecutions of the saints, which admit were they as they term them, yet not so to be dealt withal. The consideration of these things and many the like would soon turn me to my own religion again. But some new troubles I have had since the world has been filled with blasphemy, and sectaries,[5] and some who have been accounted sincere Christians have been carried away with them, that[6] sometimes I have said, "Is there faith upon the earth?" and I have not known what to think. But then I have remembered the words of Christ that so it must be, and that, if it were possible, the very elect[7] should be deceived. "Behold, saith our Savior, I have told you before." That hath stayed my heart, and I can now say, "Return, O my soul, to thy rest; upon this rock Christ Jesus will I build my faith,[8] and if I perish, I perish." But I know all the powers of Hell shall never prevail against it. I know whom I have trusted, and whom I have believed, and that He is able to keep that I have committed to his charge. Now to the king, immortal, eternal, and invisible, the only wise God, be honor and glory forever and ever![9] Amen.

This was written in much sickness and weakness, and is very weakly and imperfectly done, but, if you can pick any benefit out of it, it is the mark which I aimed at.[10]

—1867

---

[1] *diverse* Different kinds of people.

[2] *maugre* In spite of.

[3] *admit* Even if it is admitted that.

[4] *the Popish religion* Roman Catholicism.

[5] *sectaries* Dissenters; those of different religious sects.

[6] *have been carried away with them, that* Have been so persuaded by them (i.e., by these dissenting versions of Christianity) that.

[7] *elect* Those who have been predestined by God for salvation.

[8] *upon this ... my faith* Bradstreet alludes to Matthew 16.18, in which Jesus says to his disciple Peter, "And I say also unto thee, That thou art Peter, and upon this rock I will build my church; and the gates of hell shall not prevail against it."

[9] *Now to ... forever and ever* Bradstreet echoes Paul's address to God in the epistle Philippians 4.20.

[10] *it is the mark which I aimed at* (Then I have achieved) the goal I aimed at.

Mary Rowlandson

1637 – 1711

The Sovereignty and Goodness of God, Puritan settler Mary Rowlandson's narrative of her time held hostage by an Indigenous community, was the first prose work by a woman to be published in English in British North America. An immediate success on both sides of the Atlantic, it would become one of the most popular works of early American literature. Rowlandson's dramatic story has been read as spiritual allegory, anti-Indigenous propaganda, ethnographic document, and historical record. It is today widely acknowledged to be, as a narrative, among the most vivid accounts of early New England settler experience—and, as a cultural artifact, among the seventeenth century's most deeply fraught examples of the rhetoric of colonization.

Born in England in 1637, Rowlandson sailed for the Massachusetts Bay Colony as a young child with her parents John and Joan White in 1639. The Whites were part of a massive wave of Puritan migration to a region the Indigenous peoples already living there called Dawnland. The early Europeans who came to Dawnland encountered thriving Indigenous communities and trade networks; they brought with them diseases that soon devastated the coastal communities, a catastrophe the Puritans interpreted as evidence of divine support for their invasion of the region. The Whites, who settled in Salem, acquired a significant amount of land over the next thirteen years, but they wanted more. In 1653, they left their son in charge and moved to the new town of Lancaster, situated fifty miles inland on Nipmuc territory.

In 1660, the English monarchy was restored to power, ending the Puritan regime in England. As a result, Puritan migration to Dawnland increased—as did tensions with the region's Indigenous occupants, the Nipmuc, Narragansett, and Wampanoag. A longstanding alliance between the Wampanoag and the English deteriorated after the death of sachem Ousamequin (known to settlers by his title Massasoit) in 1662. Ousamequin was succeeded by his eldest son Wamsutta, who soon died mysteriously, with many suspecting he had been poisoned. His younger brother Metacom (called "King Philip" by the English) and other Indigenous leaders—such as Pocasset saunkskaw (female sachem) Weetamoo, who also appears in Rowlandson's narrative—built an alliance to defend their territories, resources, and ways of life.

A wave of Indigenous resistance formed and began to crest in the summer of 1675. The ensuing conflict, now known as King Philip's War, lasted a year and devastated the region, leaving about five per cent of the colonists and as many as forty per cent of the Indigenous inhabitants dead. Many of the Indigenous survivors were either distributed among colonists as indentured servants, or shipped to Bermuda or the West Indies to be sold into slavery.

Settler histories tended to treat King Philip's War as an isolated event ending in a decisive victory for colonists, but the arc of resistance—and of tragedy—is a long one. Indigenous peoples had been resisting colonization in multiple ways long before 1675 and would continue to do so afterward. But the odds against them only grew; over the course of the seventeenth century the Indigenous population of what the colonizers now called "New England" fell from almost 150,000 to fewer than 10,000 (their numbers reduced by disease and starvation even more than by armed conflict), while the number of colonists rose from nothing to well over 50,000.

Rowlandson's narrative opens dramatically at the beginning of the attack that led to her capture. Eliding the context of Puritan expansion, it presents the attack as senseless violence perpetrated by "merciless Heathens" whom she describes in dehumanizing terms as "hell-hounds" and "ravenous beasts." The Preface, not written by Rowlandson, holds to the same racist ideas, even as it acknowledges the context of colonial violence that preceded and precipitated the attack: "the Narrhagansets were now driven quite from their own Country, and all their provisions there hoarded up, to which they durst not at present return, and being so numerous as they were, soon devoured those to whom they went [i.e., the Nipmuc], whereby both the one and their other were now reduced to extreme straits."

At the time of the attack on Lancaster, Rowlandson was in charge of her large household because her husband, Joseph Rowlandson, had traveled to Boston with several other men from the settlement to ask for military reinforcements. The property was already partially garrisoned, but it could not withstand the attack that came on 10 February 1676. An alliance of Nipmuc, Narragansett, and Wampanoag fighters killed several inhabitants and took hostage twenty-four others, among them Mary Rowlandson and three of her children. Following her capture, Rowlandson was separated from her two older children, while six-year-old Sarah, who had been badly injured in the attack, died in her arms nine days later. Rowlandson was held jointly in captivity by Weetamoo and her husband, the Narragansett sachem Quinnapin. Over the next eleven weeks she traveled widely with her captors; all frequently went hungry, and they undertook a level of physical exertion far beyond what the average Puritan woman would have been used to.

In early May, Rowlandson was ransomed for a sum of twenty pounds, a price she set herself at the request of her captors. The Rowlandson family never returned to Lancaster; they lived in Boston for ten months before moving to Connecticut. Joseph Rowlandson died not long thereafter. As was common among settlers, Rowlandson soon remarried. In 1679, she became Mrs. Samuel Talcott, marrying a former officer who had served in the colonial militia during the war. She outlived her second husband and died in 1711.

Rowlandson likely began writing the memoir of her capture not long after her release. At first, Rowlandson's account circulated in manuscript form, but public demand for her narrative grew, and it was published in 1682 under the title *The Sovereignty and Goodness of God, together, with the Faithfulness of His Promises Displayed; Being a Narrative of the Captivity and Restoration of Mrs. Mary Rowlandson*. Puritans generally thought it inappropriate for writings by women to appear in print unless under the auspices of male authority; in its published form Rowlandson's narrative was preceded by a male-authored preface and followed by the text of her husband's final sermon. The anonymous preface—thought by most modern scholars to be the work of influential preacher, historian, and colonial administrator Increase Mather—emphasized Rowlandson's appropriately modest reluctance to publish, and described the book as a work of pious public service that offered important lessons on faith and providence. Mather also saw into print several other settler captivity narratives that, like Rowlandson's, vilify Indigenous people and argue for a return to Puritan orthodoxy.

Structured as a series of twenty "Removes"—each one recounting the travels of Rowlandson and her captors from one camp to another—Rowlandson's narrative dramatically depicts her emotional trauma and details her spiritual as well as her physical journey. Puritans tended to see mourning as a sinful and even idolatrous attachment to worldly relationships, and to be of the view that believers ought instead to celebrate God's will. It is in this context that Rowlandson portrays her efforts to come to terms with her own suffering; she makes liberal use of biblical references and quotations to reaffirm her faith.

The Sovereignty and Goodness of God was an immediate success. The first Boston edition sold out quickly, leading to the publication of two more editions in Cambridge, Massachusetts, that same year, and one more in England. In the first of many renamings and re-envisionings of Rowlandson's account, the English edition was retitled as *A True History of the Captivity and Restoration of Mrs. Mary Rowlandson, A Minister's Wife in New-England. Wherein Is Set forth, The Cruel and Inhumane Usage She Underwent amongst the Heathens, for Eleven Weeks Time: And Her Deliverance from Them*. The new title repositioned the narrative to appeal to a more religiously diverse audience, and foregrounded its exotic appeal as an eyewitness account. In the eighteenth century, as nationalist sentiment intensified, Rowlandson's narrative was seen as a dramatic depiction of the struggle of Anglo-American civilization against Indigenous "savagery." Once again, a shift in interpretive emphasis was reflected in the titles given the work; *A Narrative of the Captivity, Sufferings, and Removes of Mrs. Mary Rowlandson, Who Was Taken Prisoner by the Indians with Several Others, and Treated in the Most Barbarous and Cruel Manner by These Vile Savages* is one late eighteenth-century example.

In the early twentieth century, critics began increasingly to value Rowlandson's text for its historical and ethnographic significance. A 1903 edition, for example, suggested in its introduction that the work was "an authentic and graphic delineation of the manners and customs of the primitive children of the soil from whom our ancestors relentlessly wrested their beautiful and beloved heritage in order to enrich us and our posterity." From the late twentieth century onwards, Rowlandson's account has been increasingly studied by literary scholars and historians not only for its portrayal of the trauma of war, but also for the ways in which it is shaped by cultural prejudices and by the ideology of colonization.

Today, Rowlandson's narrative is acknowledged to have played a central role in setting the pattern for an entire literary genre—the "Indian captivity narrative." Conventions of the genre include a focus on the perspective and suffering of white captives; a tendency towards dehumanizing and racist representations of Native Americans—portrayals often presented in order to justify colonial violence; and detailed, but also biased descriptions of Indigenous customs and ways of life. Arguably, use of the term "Indian captivity narrative" has had the effect of obscuring the much higher incidence of captivity experienced by Indigenous people and other people of color in colonial America. Indigenous people's accounts of their abduction, enslavement, forced indenture, imprisonment, and occasional deliverance are to be found embedded in legal documents, verse, sermons, letters, and Native American oral histories, but during Rowlandson's era these narratives were not generally published for white readers. The fact that settler readers frequently devoured the stories of captives such as Rowlandson but rarely encountered the stories of Indigenous captives is one of the many ironies surrounding Rowlandson's narrative. Increasingly, it is because of such ironies (rather than in spite of them) that the text is recognized as foundational to early American culture.

NOTE ON THE TEXT: The text of the work presented below is based on the second "corrected and amended" edition of Rowlandson's *The Sovereignty and Goodness of God, together, with the Faithfulness of His Promises Displayed; Being a Narrative of the Captivity and Restoration of Mrs. Mary Rowlandson*, published in Cambridge, Massachusetts in 1682; this is the earliest surviving edition. Spelling and punctuation have been modernized in accordance with the practices of this anthology. Biblical citation formats have been made consistent for the sake of clarity. Rowlandson's inconsistent capitalization of the second-person pronoun when referring to God has been retained. Italics have been removed except when signifying foreign-language words or when clearly intended for emphasis.

⌘ ⌘ ⌘

The Sovereignty and Goodness of God, together, with the Faithfulness of His Promises Displayed; Being a Narrative of the Captivity and Restoration of Mrs. Mary Rowlandson

THE PREFACE TO THE READER[1]

It was on Tuesday Feb. 1, 1675,[2] in the afternoon, when the Narragansetts' quarters (in or toward the

Nipmuc country, whither they are now retired for fear of the English army lying in their own country) were the second time beaten up by the forces of the United Colonies,[3] who thereupon soon betook themselves to flight, and were all the next day pursued by the English, some overtaken and destroyed. But on Thursday Feb. 3rd, the English having now been six days on their march from their headquarters at Wickford, in the Narragansett country, toward and

---

[1]   This preface is generally thought to have been written by Increase Mather (1639–1723), the influential Puritan minister who was partially responsible for the publication of Rowlandson's narrative.

[2]   *Tuesday Feb. 1, 1675* By the modern Gregorian calendar, 11 February 1676. England continued to observe the Julian calendar until 1752, long after the Gregorian calendar had been adopted by

most other European countries and colonies. (The discrepancy in the year is accounted for by the fact that, according to the Julian calendar, the new year began on 25 March.)

[3]   *United Colonies* Also known as the New England Confederation, the United Colonies of New England was founded in 1643 and allied the Puritan colonies of Massachusetts Bay, Plymouth, Connecticut, and New Haven for military, political, and religious reasons. (The Puritan-dominant but religiously tolerant colony of Rhode Island was excluded from the alliance.)

after the enemy, and provision grown exceeding short, insomuch that they were fain to kill some horses for the supply, especially of their Indian friends, they were necessitated to consider what was best to be done. And about noon (having hitherto followed the chase as hard as they might) a council was called, and though some few were of another mind, yet it was concluded by far the greater part of the council of war, that the army should desist the pursuit and retire, the forces of Plymouth and the Bay[1] to the next town of the Bay, and Connecticut forces to their own next towns; which determination was immediately put in execution. The consequent whereof, as it was not difficult to be foreseen by those that knew the causeless enmity of these barbarians against the English, and the malicious and revengeful spirit of these heathen: so it soon proved dismal.

The Narragansetts were now driven quite from their own country, and all their provisions there hoarded up, to which they durst not at present return, and being so numerous as they were, soon devoured those to whom they went,[2] whereby both the one and other were now reduced to extreme straits, and so necessitated to take the first and best opportunity for supply, and very glad, no doubt, of such an opportunity as this, to provide for themselves, and make spoil of the English at once; and seeing themselves thus discharged of their pursuers, and a little refreshed after their flight, the very next week on Thursday Feb. 10, they fell with mighty force and fury upon Lancaster: which small town, remote from aid of others, and not being garrisoned as it might, the army being now come in, and as the time indeed required (the design[3] of the Indians against that place being known to the English some time before) was not able to make effectual resistance: but notwithstanding utmost endeavour of the inhabitants, most of the buildings were turned into ashes; many people (men, women and children) slain, and others captivated.[4] The most solemn and remarkable part of this tragedy, may that justly be reputed, which

fell upon the family of that reverend servant of God, Mr. Joseph Rowlandson, the faithful Pastor of Christ in that place, who being gone down to the council of the Massachusetts to seek aid for the defence of the place, at his return found the town in flames, or smoke, his own house being set on fire by the enemy, through the disadvantage of a defective fortification, and all in it consumed: his previous yoke-fellow,[5] and dear children, wounded and captivated (as the issue evidenced, and following narrative declares) by these cruel and barbarous savages. A sad catastrophe! Thus all things come alike to all: none knows either love or hatred by all that is before him. It is no new thing for God's precious ones to drink as deep as others, of the cup of common calamity. Take just Lot[6] (yet captivated) for instance beside others. But it is not my business to dilate[7] on these things, but only in few words introductively to preface to the following script, which is a narrative of the wonderfully awful, wise, holy, powerful, and gracious providence of God, towards that worthy and precious gentlewoman, the dear consort of the said Reverend Mr. Rowlandson, and her children with her, as in casting of her into such a waterless pit, so in preserving, supporting, and carrying through so many such extreme hazards, unspeakable difficulties and disconsolateness, and at last delivering her out of them all, and her surviving children also. It was a strange and amazing dispensation, that the Lord should so afflict his precious servant and handmaid; it was as strange, if not more, that he should so bear up the spirits of his servant under such bereavements and of his handmaid under such captivity, travels and hardships (much too hard for flesh and blood) as he did, and at length deliver and restore. But he was their Saviour, who hath said, *When thou passest through the Waters, I will be with thee, and through the Rivers, they shall not overflow thee: When thou walkest through the fire thou shalt not be burnt, nor shall the flame kindle upon thee,* Isaiah 43.2.; and again, *He woundeth and his hands make whole. He shall deliver thee in six troubles, yea in seven there shall no evil touch thee: In Famine*

---

[1] *the Bay* I.e., the Massachusetts Bay Colony.

[2] *devoured those ... they went* I.e., depleted the food supply of the allied tribes, including the Nipmuc.

[3] *design* Plan; objective.

[4] *captivated* I.e., taken captive.

[5] *yoke-fellow* Wife (i.e., Mary Rowlandson).

[6] *just Lot* Virtuous biblical figure who is held captive during the conflict sometimes known as the War of Nine Kings; see Genesis 14.12–16.

[7] *dilate* Expound upon; discuss at length.

he shall redeem thee from Death, and in War from the power of the sword. Job 5.18–20. Methinks this dispensation doth bear some resemblance to those of Joseph, David, and Daniel, yea, and of the three children[1] too, the stories whereof do represent us with the excellent textures of divine providence, curious pieces of divine work: and truly so doth this, and therefore not to be forgotten, but worthy to be exhibited to, and viewed, and pondered by all, that disdain not to consider the operation of his hands.

The works of the Lord (not only of creation, but of providence also, especially those that do more peculiarly concern his dear ones, that are as the apple of his eye, as the signet[2] upon His hand, the delight of his eyes, and the object of his tenderest care) are great, sought out of all those that have pleasure therein. And of these verily this is none of the least.

This narrative was penned by the gentlewoman herself, to be to her a memorandum of God's dealing with her, that she might never forget, but remember the same, and the several[3] circumstances thereof, all the days of her life. A pious scope which deserves both commendation and imitation: some friends having obtained a sight of it, could not but be so much affected with the many passages of working providence discovered therein, as to judge it worthy of public view, and altogether unmeet[4] that such works of God should be hid from present and future generations. And therefore, though this gentlewoman's modesty would not thrust it into the press, yet her gratitude unto God made her not hardly persuadable to let it pass, that God might have his due glory, and others benefit by it as well as herself. I hope by this time none will cast any reflection[5] upon this gentlewoman, on the score of this publication of her affliction and deliverance.

If any should, doubtless they may be reckoned with the nine lepers, of whom it is said, *Were there not ten cleansed, where are the nine? but one returning to give God thanks.*[6] Let such further know that this was a dispensation of public note, and of universal concernment, and so much the more, by how much the nearer this gentlewoman stood related to that faithful Servant of God, whose capacity and employment was public in the house of God, and his name on that account of a very sweet savour in the Churches of Christ, who is there of a true Christian spirit, that did not look upon himself much concerned in this bereavement, this captivity in the time thereof, and in his deliverance when it came, yea more than in many others; and how many are there, to whom so concerned, it will doubtless be a very acceptable thing to see the way of God with this gentlewoman in the aforesaid dispensation, thus laid out and portrayed before their eyes.

To conclude whatever any coy phantasies may deem, yet it highly concerns those that have so deeply tasted, how good the Lord is, to enquire with David, *What shall I render to the Lord for all his benefits to me?* Psalm 116.12. He thinks nothing too great; yea, being sensible of his own disproportion to the due praises of God he calls in help. *Oh, magnify the Lord with me, let us exalt his Name together*, Psalm 34.3. And it is but reason, that our praises should hold proportion with our prayers: and that as many hath helped together by prayer for the obtaining of his mercy, so praises should be returned by many on this behalf; and forasmuch as not the general but particular knowledge of things makes deepest impression upon the affections, this narrative particularizing the several passages of this providence will not a little conduce thereunto. And therefore holy David in order to the attainment of that end, accounts himself concerned to declare what God had done for his soul, Psalm 66.16. *Come and hear, all ye that fear God, and I will declare what God hath done for my soul*, i.e. *for his life*, see verses 9–10. *He holdeth our soul in life, and suffers not our feet to be moved, for thou our God hast proved us, thou hast tried us, as silver is tried.*[7] Life-mercies are

---

[1]   *Joseph, David, and Daniel*   Heroic biblical figures who are saved by divine intervention in Genesis 39, 1 Samuel 17, and Daniel 6, respectively;   *the three children*   Shadrach, Meshach, and Abednego are three youths who are cast into a burning furnace as punishment for their worship of God, but their lives are saved by divine intervention; see Daniel 3.

[2]   *signet*   Ring into which a mold is fixed for the stamping of wax seals.

[3]   *several*   Different; individual.

[4]   *unmeet*   Inappropriate.

[5]   *reflection*   Criticism; censure.

---

[6]   *Were there … give God thanks*   See Luke 17.11–19: Jesus heals ten lepers, but only one of them—a Samaritan—comes back to praise and thank God for his healing.

[7]   *as silver is tried*   To "try" in this context means to extract a metal by means of heat.

heart-affecting mercies, of great impression and force, to enlarge pious hearts in the praises of God, so that such know not how but to talk of God's acts, and to speak of and publish[1] his wonderful works. Deep troubles, when the waters come into thy soul, are wont to produce vows: vows must be paid. *It is better not vow, than vow and not to pay.*[2] I may say, that as none knows what it is to fight and pursue such an enemy as this, but they that have fought and pursued them: so none can imagine what it is to be captivated, and enslaved to such atheistical, proud, wild, cruel, barbarous, brutish—in one word—diabolical creatures are these, the worst of the heathen; nor what difficulties, hardships, hazards, sorrows, anxieties and perplexities do unavoidably wait upon such a condition, but those that have tried it. No serious spirit then (especially knowing anything of this gentlewoman's piety) can imagine but that the vows of God are upon her. Excuse her then if she come thus into public, to pay those vows. Come and hear what she hath to say.

I am confident that no friend of divine Providence will ever repent his time and pains spent in reading over these sheets, but will judge them worth pursuing again and again.

Here, Reader, you may see an instance of the Sovereignty of God, who doth what he will with his own as well as others; and who may say to him, *What dost thou?*[3] Here you may see an instance of the faith and patience of the Saints, under the most heart-sinking trials; here you may see, the promises are breasts full of consolation, when all the world besides is empty, and gives nothing but sorrow. That God is indeed the supreme Lord of the world, ruling the most unruly, weakening the most cruel and savage, granting his people mercy in the sight of the unmerciful, curbing the lusts of the most filthy, holding the hands of the violent, delivering the prey from the mighty, and gathering together the outcasts of Israel. Once and again you have heard, but here you may see, *that power belongeth unto God*; that our God is the God of Salvation, and to him belong the issues from Death. That our God is in the Heavens, and doth whatever pleases him.

Here you have Sampson riddle exemplified, and that great promise, Romans 8.28. verified, *Out of the Eater comes forth meat, and sweetness out of the strong.*[4] The worst of evils working together for the best good. How evident is it that the Lord hath made this gentlewoman a gainer by all this affliction, that she can say, 'tis good for her, yea better that she hath been, than that she should not have been, thus afflicted.

Oh how doth God shine forth in such things as these!

Reader, if thou gettest no good by such a declaration as this, the fault must needs be thine own. Read therefore; peruse, ponder, and from hence lay up something from the experience of another, against thine own turn comes, that so thou also through patience and consolation of the Scripture mayest have hope.

TER AMICAM[5]

A Narrative of the Captivity and Restoration of Mrs. Mary Rowlandson

On the tenth of February 1675 came the Indians with great numbers upon Lancaster. Their first coming was about sunrising; hearing the noise of some guns, we looked out; several houses were burning, and the smoke ascending to Heaven. There were five persons taken in one house; the father, and the mother and a sucking child, they knocked on the head; the other two they took and carried away alive. There were two others, who being out of their garrison upon some occasion were set upon; one was knocked on the head, the other escaped. Another there was who running along was shot and wounded, and fell down; he begged of them his life, promising them money (as they told me), but they would not hearken to him but knocked him in head, and stripped him naked, and split open his bowels. Another seeing many of the Indians about his barn, ventured and went out, but was quickly shot down. There were three others belonging to the same

---

[1] *publish* I.e., proclaim, announce.

[2] *It is … to pay* See Ecclesiastes 5.5.

[3] *What dost thou?* See Job 9.12.

[4] *Sampson riddle … the strong* Reference to the riddle Samson poses to the Philistines in Judges 14.14, which itself refers back to an incident in which Samson killed a lion and later found a swarm of bees that had nested in its carcass and made honey. His reference to Romans 8.28 is to the moment in which the apostle Paul promises that "And we know that all things work together for good to them that love God, to them who are the called according to his purpose."

[5] *TER AMICAM* Apparently a misprint for "Per Amicam," meaning "For my friend."

garrison who were killed; the Indians getting up upon the roof of the barn, had advantage to shoot down upon them over their fortification. Thus these murderous wretches went on, burning and destroying before them.

At length they came and beset our own house, and quickly it was the dolefullest day that ever mine eyes saw. The house stood upon the edge of a hill; some of the Indians got behind the hill, others into the barn, and others behind anything that could shelter them; from all which places they shot against the house, so that the bullets seemed to fly like hail; and quickly they wounded one man among us, then another, and then a third. About two hours (according to my observation, in that amazing time) they had been about the house before they prevailed to fire it (which they did with flax and hemp, which they brought out of the barn, and there being no defence about the house, only two flankers[1] at two opposite corners, and one of them not finished). They fired it once, and one ventured out and quenched it, but they quickly fired it again, and that took. Now is that dreadful hour come, that I have often heard of (in time of war, as it was the case of others), but now mine eyes see it. Some in our house were fighting for their lives, others wallowing in their blood, the house on fire over our heads, and the bloody heathen ready to knock us on the head, if we stirred out. Now might we hear mothers and children crying out for themselves, and one another, *Lord, what shall we do?* Then I took my children (and one of my sisters, hers) to go forth and leave the house: but as soon as we came to the door and appeared, the Indians shot so thick that the bullets rattled against the house, as if one had taken an handful of stones and threw them, so that we were fain to give back.[2] We had six stout dogs belonging to our garrison, but none of them would stir, though another time, if any Indian had come to the door, they were ready to fly upon him and tear him down. The Lord hereby would make us the more acknowledge his hand, and to see that our help is always in him. But out we must go, the fire increasing, and coming along behind us, roaring, and the Indians gaping before us with their guns, spears and hatchets to devour us. No sooner were we out of the house, but

my brother in law (being before wounded, in defending the house, in or near the throat) fell down dead, whereat the Indians scornfully shouted, and hallowed,[3] and were presently upon him, stripping off his clothes, the bullets flying thick, one went through my side, and the same (as would seem) through the bowels and hand of my dear child[4] in my arms. One of my elder sister's children, named William, had then his leg broken, which the Indians perceiving, they knocked him on head. Thus were we butchered by those merciless heathen, standing amazed, with the blood running down to our heels. My eldest sister being yet in the house, and seeing those woeful sights, the infidels hauling mothers one way, and children another, and some wallowing in their blood: and her elder son telling her that her son William was dead, and my self was wounded, she said, *And Lord let me die with them*; which was no sooner said, but she was struck with a bullet, and fell down dead over the threshold. I hope she is reaping the fruit of her good labours, being faithful to the service of God in her place. In her younger years she lay under much trouble upon spiritual accounts, till it pleased God to make that precious Scripture take hold of her heart, 2 Corinthians 12.9, *And he said unto me my Grace is sufficient for thee*. More then twenty years after I have heard her tell how sweet and comfortable that place was to her. But to return: the Indians laid hold of us, pulling me one way, and the children another, and said, *Come go along with us*; I told them they would kill me; they answered, if I were willing to go along with them, they would not hurt me.

Oh the doleful sight that now was to behold at this house! *Come, behold the works of the Lord, what desolations he has made in the Earth.*[5] Of thirty-seven persons who were in this one house, none escaped either present death, or a bitter captivity, save only one, who might say as he, Job 1.15. *And I only am escaped alone to tell the News.* There were twelve killed, some shot, some stabbed with their spears, some knocked down with their hatchets. When we are in prosperity, oh the little that we think of such dreadful sights, and to see our dear friends and relations lie bleeding out their

---

[1]   *flankers*   Projecting defense structures.

[2]   *fain to give back*   Obliged to retreat.

[3]   *hallowed*   Hallooed; shouted.

[4]   *my dear child*   Sarah Rowlandson, about six-and-a-half years old.

[5]   *Come ... in the Earth*   See Psalm 46.8.

heart-blood upon the ground. There was one who was chopped into the head with a hatchet, and stripped naked, and yet was crawling up and down. It is a solemn sight to see so many Christians lying in their blood, some here, and some there, like a company of sheep torn by wolves. All of them stripped naked by a company of hell-hounds, roaring, singing, ranting and insulting, as if they would have torn our very hearts out; yet the Lord by his Almighty power preserved a number of us from death, for there were twenty-four of us taken alive and carried captive.

I had often before this said, that if the Indians should come, I should choose rather to be killed by them than taken alive, but when it came to the trial my mind changed; their glittering weapons so daunted my spirit, that I chose rather to go along with those (as I may say) ravenous beasts, than that moment to end my days; and that I may the better declare what happened to me during that grievous captivity, I shall particularly speak of the several removes[1] we had up and down the wilderness.

THE FIRST REMOVE

Now away we must go with those barbarous creatures, with our bodies wounded and bleeding, and our hearts no less than our bodies. About a mile we went that night, up upon a hill within sight of the town, where they intended to lodge. There was hard by a vacant house (deserted by the English before, for fear of the Indians). I asked them whether I might not lodge in the house that night? to which they answered, *What, will you love English men still?* This was the dolefullest night that ever my eyes saw. Oh, the roaring, and singing and dancing, and yelling of those black creatures in the night, which made the place a lively resemblance of hell. And as miserable was the waste that was there made, of horses, cattle, sheep, swine, calves, lambs, roasting pigs, and fowls (which they had plundered in the town), some roasting, some lying and burning, and some boiling to feed our merciless enemies, who were joyful enough though we were disconsolate. To add to the dolefulness of the former day, and the dismalness of the present night, my thoughts ran upon my losses and sad bereaved condition. All was gone: my husband

gone (at least separated from me, he being in the Bay; and to add to my grief, the Indians told me they would kill him as he came homeward), my children gone, my relations and friends gone, our house and home and all our comforts within door, and without, all was gone except my life, and I knew not but the next moment that might go too. There remained nothing to me but one poor wounded babe, and it seemed at present worse than death that it was in such a pitiful condition, bespeaking compassion, and I had no refreshing for it, nor suitable things to revive it. Little do many think what is the savageness and brutishness of this barbarous enemy! even those that seem to profess more than others among them, when the English have fallen into their hands.

Those seven that were killed at Lancaster the summer before upon a Sabbath day, and the one that was afterward killed upon a weekday, were slain and mangled in a barbarous manner, by one-eyed John, and Marlborough's Praying Indians, which Capt. Mosely brought to Boston, as the Indians told me.[2]

THE SECOND REMOVE

But now, the next morning, I must turn my back upon the town, and travel with them into the vast and desolate wilderness, I knew not whither. It is not my tongue or pen can express the sorrows of my heart, and bitterness of my spirit, that I had at this departure: but God was with me in a wonderful manner, carrying me along and bearing up my spirit, that it did not quite fail. One of the Indians carried my poor wounded babe upon a horse; it went moaning all along, *I shall die, I shall die.* I went on foot after it, with sorrow that cannot be expressed. At length I took it off the horse, and carried it in my arms till my strength failed, and I fell down with it. Then they set me upon a horse with my wounded child in my lap, and there being no furniture[3]

---

[1]   *removes*   Changes of place.

[2]   *Those seven ... Indians told me*   On 22 August 1675, a group of Nipmuc and Wampanoag warriors carried out the first significant attack on the town of Lancaster, killing seven colonists. The Indigenous fighters were led by Nipmuc sachem Monoco, known to the English as "One-Eyed John"; many of the English also suspected, probably falsely, the involvement of Nipmuc "Praying Indians"—Indigenous converts to Christianity—from the town of Marlborough.

[3]   *furniture*   I.e., saddle, stirrups, etc.

upon the horse's back, as we were going down a steep hill, we both fell over the horse's head, at which they like inhumane creatures laughed, and rejoiced to see it, though I thought we should there have ended our days, as overcome with so many difficulties. But the Lord renewed my strength still, and carried me along, that I might see more of his power; yea, so much that I could never have thought of, had I not experienced it.

After this it quickly began to snow, and when night came on, they stopped: and now down I must sit in the snow, by a little fire, and a few boughs behind me, with my sick child in my lap; and calling much for water, being now (through the wound) fallen into a violent fever. My own wound also growing so stiff, that I could scarce sit down or rise up; yet so it must be, that I must sit all this cold winter night upon the cold snowy ground, with my sick child in my arms, looking that every hour would be the last of its life; and having no Christian friend near me, either to comfort or help me. Oh, I may see the wonderful power of God, that my Spirit did not utterly sink under my affliction: still the Lord upheld me with his gracious and merciful Spirit, and we were both alive to see the light of the next morning.

THE THIRD REMOVE

The morning being come, they prepared to go on their way: One of the Indians got up upon a horse, and they set me up behind him, with my poor sick babe in my lap. A very wearisome and tedious day I had of it, what with my own wound, and my child's being so exceeding sick, and in a lamentable condition with her wound. It may be easily judged what a poor feeble condition we were in, there being not the least crumb of refreshing that came within either of our mouths, from Wednesday night to Saturday night, except only a little cold water. This day in the afternoon, about an hour by sun, we came to the place where they intended, *viz.*[1] an Indian town called Wenimesset, northward of Quahaug. When we were come, oh the number of pagans (now merciless enemies) that there came about me, that I may say as David, Psalm 27.13, *I had fainted, unless I had believed,* etc. The next day was the

Sabbath: I then remembered how careless I had been of God's holy time: how many Sabbaths I had lost and misspent, and how evilly I had walked in God's sight; which lay so close unto my spirit, that it was easy for me to see how righteous it was with God to cut off the thread of my life, and cast me out of his presence forever. Yet the Lord still showed mercy to me, and upheld me; and as he wounded me with one hand, so he healed me with the other. This day there came to me one Robert Pepper (a man belonging to Roxbury) who was taken in Captain Beers his fight,[2] and had been now a considerable time with the Indians; and up with them almost as far as Albany, to see King Philip, as he told me, and was now very lately come into these parts. Hearing, I say, that I was in this Indian town, he obtained leave to come and see me. He told me, he himself was wounded in the leg at Captain Beers his fight; and was not able some time to go, but as they carried him, and as he took oaken leaves and laid to his wound, and through the blessing of God he was able to travel again. Then I took oaken leaves and laid to my side, and with the blessing of God it cured me also; yet before the cure was wrought, I may say, as it is in Psalm 38.5–6, *My wounds stink and are corrupt, I am troubled, I am bowed down greatly, I go mourning all the day long.* I sat much alone with a poor wounded child in my lap, which moaned night and day, having nothing to revive the body, or cheer the spirits of her, but instead of that, sometimes one Indian would come and tell me one hour, that *Your master will knock your child in the head,* and then a second, and then a third, *Your master will quickly knock your child in the head.*

This was the comfort I had from them, miserable comforters are ye all, as he said.[3] Thus nine days I sat upon my knees, with my babe in my lap, till my flesh was raw again; my child being even ready to depart this sorrowful world, they bade me carry it out to another wigwam (I suppose because they would not be troubled with such spectacles), whither I went with a very heavy heart, and down I sat with the picture of death in my lap. About two hours in the night, my sweet babe, like a lamb, departed this life, on Feb. 18,

---

[1]   *viz.*   Abbreviation for the Latin videlicet, meaning "namely" or "that is to say."

[2]   *Robert Pepper … his fight*   I.e., Robert Pepper, a man from the town of Roxbury, Massachusetts, who was taken captive during a battle with Captain Richard Beers's troops.

[3]   *This was … as he said*   See Job 16.1–2.

1675, it being about six years and five months old. It was nine days from the first wounding, in this miserable condition, without any refreshing of one nature or other, except a little cold water. I cannot but take notice, how at another time I could not bear to be in the room where any dead person was, but now the case is changed; I must and could lie down by my dead babe, side by side all the night after. I have thought since of the wonderful goodness of God to me, in preserving me in the use of my reason and senses, in that distressed time, that I did not use wicked and violent means to end my own miserable life. In the morning, when they understood that my child was dead, they sent for me home to my master's wigwam (by my master in this writing must be understood Quanopin, who was a Sagamore,[1] and married King Philip's wife's sister;[2] not that he first took me, but I was sold to him by another Narraganset Indian, who took me when first I came out of the garrison). I went to take up my dead child in my arms to carry it with me, but they bid me let it alone: there was no resisting, but go I must and leave it. When I had been at my master's wigwam, I took the first opportunity I could get, to go look after my dead child: when I came I asked them what they had done with it? then they told me it was upon the hill: then they went and showed me where it was, where I saw the ground was newly digged, and there they told me they had buried it. There I left that child in the wilderness, and must commit it, and myself also in this wilderness-condition, to him who is above all. God having taken away this dear child, I went to see my daughter Mary, who was at this same Indian town, at a wigwam not very far off, though we had little liberty or opportunity to see one another; she was about ten years old, and taken from the door at first by a Praying Indian and afterward sold for a gun. When I came in sight, she would fall a-weeping; at which they were provoked, and would not let me come near her, but bade me be gone; which was a heart-cutting word to me. I had one child dead, another in the wilderness, I knew not where, the

third they would not let me come near to: *Me* (as he said) *have ye bereaved of my children, Joseph is not, and Simeon is not, and ye will take Benjamin also, all these things are against me.*[3] I could not sit still in this condition, but kept walking from one place to another. And as I was going along, my heart was even overwhelmed with the thoughts of my condition, and that I should have children, and a nation which I knew not ruled over them. Whereupon I earnestly entreated the Lord, that he would consider my low estate, and show me a token for good, and if it were his blessed will, some sign and hope of some relief. And indeed quickly the Lord answered, in some measure, my poor prayers; for as I was going up and down mourning and lamenting my condition, my son came to me, and asked me how I did; I had not seen him before, since the destruction of the town, and I knew not where he was, till I was informed by himself, that he was amongst a smaller parcel of Indians, whose place was about six miles off. With tears in his eyes, he asked me whether his sister Sarah was dead; and told me he had seen his sister Mary; and prayed me, that I would not be troubled in reference to himself. The occasion of his coming to see me at this time, was this: There was, as I said, about six miles from us, a small plantation[4] of Indians, where it seems he had been during his captivity; and at this time, there were some forces of the Indians gathered out of our company, and some also from them (among whom was my son's master) to go to assault and burn Medfield. In this time of the absence of his master, his dame brought him to see me. I took this to be some gracious answer to my earnest and unfeigned desire. The next day, *viz.* to this, the Indians returned from Medfield, all the company, for those that belonged to the other small company, came through the town that now we were at. But before they came to us, oh! the outrageous roaring and hooping[5] that there was. They began their din about a mile before they came to us. By their noise and hooping they signified how many they had destroyed (which was at that time twenty-three). Those that were with us at home, were gathered together as soon as they heard the hooping, and every time that the other went over their number, these at

---

[1] *Sagamore* Algonquian political leader; the term is sometimes used interchangeably with Sachem.

[2] *King Philip's wife's sister* The Wampanoag *saunkskaw*, or female sachem, Weetamoo (c. 1635–76); the Narraganset Quinnapin was her fourth and final husband.

[3] *Me … against me* See Genesis 42.36.

[4] *plantation* I.e., settlement.

[5] *hooping* Whooping.

home gave a shout, that the very earth rung again; and thus they continued till those that had been upon the expedition were come up to the Sagamore's wigwam; and then, oh, the hideous insulting and triumphing that there was over some English men's scalps that they had taken (as their manner is) and brought with them. I cannot but take notice of the wonderful mercy of God to me in those afflictions, in sending me a Bible. One of the Indians that came from Medfield fight, had brought some plunder, came to me, and asked me, if I would have a Bible, he had got one in his basket. I was glad of it, and asked him, whether he thought the Indians would let me read? He answered, yes; so I took the Bible, and in that melancholy time, it came into my mind to read first the 28th chapter of Deuteronomy,[1] which I did; and when I had read it, my dark heart wrought on this manner: That there was no mercy for me, that the blessings were gone, and the curses come in their room,[2] and that I had lost my opportunity. But the Lord helped me still to go on reading till I came to Chapter 30, the seven first verses, where I found, *There was mercy promised again, if we would return to him by repentance; and though we were scattered from one end of the Earth to the other, yet the Lord would gather us together, and turn all those curses upon our Enemies.* I do not desire to live to forget this Scripture, and what comfort it was to me.

Now the Indians began to talk of removing from this place, some one way, and some another. There were now, besides myself, nine English captives in this place (all of them children, except one woman). I got an opportunity to go and take my leave of them; they being to go one way, and I another, I asked them whether they were earnest with God for deliverance, they told me, they did as they were able, and it was some comfort to me, that the Lord stirred up children to look to him. The woman, *viz.* Goodwife[3] Joslin, told me she should never see me again, and that she could find in her heart to run away; I wished her not to run away by any means, for we were near thirty miles from any English town, and she very big with child, and had but one week to reckon,[4] and another child in her arms, two years old, and bad rivers there were to go over, and we were feeble with our poor and coarse entertainment.[5] I had my Bible with me, I pulled it out, and asked her whether she would read; we opened the Bible and lighted on Psalm 27, in which Psalm we especially took notice of that, *ver. ult., Wait on the Lord, Be of good courage, and he shall strengthen thine Heart, wait I say on the Lord.*[6]

The Fourth Remove

And now I must part with that little company I had. Here I parted from my daughter Mary (whom I never saw again till I saw her in Dorchester, returned from captivity), and from four little cousins and neighbours, some of which I never saw afterward: the Lord only knows the end of them. Amongst them also was that poor woman before mentioned, who came to a sad end, as some of the company told me in my travel: she having much grief upon her spirit, about her miserable condition, being so near her time,[7] she would be often asking the Indians to let her go home; they not being willing to that, and yet vexed with her importunity, gathered a great company together about her, and stripped her naked, and set her in the midst of them; and when they had sung and danced about her (in their hellish manner) as long as they pleased, they knocked her on head, and the child in her arms with her; when they had done that, they made a fire and put them both into it, and told the other children that were with them, that if they attempted to go home, they would serve them in like manner. The children said she did not shed one tear, but prayed all the while. But to return to my own journey, we travelled about half a day or little more, and came to a desolate place in the wilderness, where there were no wigwams or inhabitants

---

1   *28th chapter of Deuteronomy* The first 30 chapters of this book consist of sermons delivered by Moses to the Israelites; the first verse of chapter 28 is, "And it shall come to pass, if thou shalt hearken diligently unto the voice of the Lord thy God, to observe and to do all his commandments which I command thee this day, that the Lord thy God will set thee on high above all nations of the earth."

2   *in their room* I.e., in their place.

3   *Goodwife* Polite form of address for a married woman of ordinary social status.

4   *but one week to reckon* I.e., one week remaining in her pregnancy.

5   *entertainment* Food and other provisions.

6   *ver. ult.* Latin: final verse; *Wait on … the Lord* See Psalm 27.14.

7   *being so near her time* I.e., having so recently given birth.

before; we came about the middle of the afternoon to this place; cold and wet, and snowy, and hungry, and weary, and no refreshing, for man, but the cold ground to sit on, and our poor Indian cheer.

Heart-aching thoughts here I had about my poor children, who were scattered up and down among the wild beasts of the forest. My head was light and dizzy (either through hunger or hard lodging, or trouble or all together), my knees feeble, my body raw by sitting double night and day, that I cannot express to man the affliction that lay upon my spirit, but the Lord helped me at that time to express it to himself. I opened my Bible to read, and the Lord brought that precious Scripture to me, Jeremiah 31.16: *Thus saith the Lord, refrain thy voice from weeping, and thine eyes from tears, for thy work shall be rewarded, and they shall come again from the Land of the Enemy.* This was a sweet cordial to me, when I was ready to faint, many and many a time have I sat down, and wept sweetly over this Scripture. At this place we continued about four days.

THE FIFTH REMOVE

The occasion (as I thought) of their moving at this time, was, the English army it being near and following them; for they went, as if they had gone for their lives, for some considerable way, and then they made a stop, and chose some of their stoutest men, and sent them back to hold the English army in play whilst the rest escaped. And then, like Jehu, they marched on furiously,[1] with their old, and with their young: some carried their old decrepit mothers, some carried one, and some another. Four of them carried a great Indian upon a bier; but going through a thick wood with him, they were hindered, and could make no haste; whereupon they took him upon their backs, and carried him, one at a time, till they came to Banquaug River. Upon a Friday, a little after noon, we came to this river. When all the company was come up, and were gathered together, I thought to count the number of them, but they were so many, and being somewhat in motion, it was beyond my skill. In this travel,

because of my wound, I was somewhat favoured in my load; I carried only my knitting work and two quarts of parched meal: Being very faint I asked my mistress to give me one spoonful of the meal, but she would not give me a taste. They quickly fell to cutting dry trees, to make rafts to carry them over the river, and soon my turn came to go over. By the advantage of some brush which they had laid upon the raft to sit upon, I did not wet my foot (which many of themselves at the other end were mid-leg deep), which cannot but be acknowledged as a favour of God to my weakened body, it being a very cold time. I was not before acquainted with such kind of doings or dangers. *When thou passeth through the waters I will be with thee, and through the Rivers they shall not overflow thee*, Isaiah 43.2. A certain number of us got over the river that night, but it was the night after the Sabbath before all the company was got over. On the Saturday they boiled an old horse's leg which they had got, and so we drank of the broth, as soon as they thought it was ready, and when it was almost all gone, they filled it up again.

The first week of my being among them, I hardly ate anything; the second week, I found my stomach grow very faint for want of something; and yet it was very hard to get down their filthy trash; but the third week, though I could think how formerly my stomach would turn against this or that, and I could starve and die before I could eat such things, yet they were sweet and savoury to my taste. I was at this time knitting a pair of white cotton stockings for my mistress, and had not yet wrought[2] upon a Sabbath day. When the Sabbath came they bade me go to work; I told them it was the Sabbath day, and desired them to let me rest, and told them I would do as much more tomorrow; to which they answered me, they would break my face. And here I cannot but take notice of the strange providence of God in preserving the heathen; they were many hundreds, old and young, some sick, and some lame; many had papooses[3] at their backs. The greatest number at

---

[1]   *they marched on furiously*   See 2 Kings 9.20: "He came even unto them, and cometh not again: and the driving is like the driving of Jehu the son of Nimshi; for he driveth furiously." Jehu was King of Israel from c. 842–c. 815 BCE.

[2]   *wrought*   I.e., done work.

[3]   *papooses*   The word *papoòs* was recorded in Roger Williams's *A Key into the Language of America* in 1643, where it was listed as the Narragansett word for "child." The term became popular with colonists as a general referent for any Native American child, but eventually took on a distinctly negative connotation—though it would have been considered a more-or-less neutral term by Rowlandson and her contemporaries.

this time with us were squaws,[1] and they travelled with all they had, bag and baggage, and yet they got over this river aforesaid; and on Monday they set their wigwams on fire, and away they went. On that very day came the English army after them to this river, and saw the smoke of their wigwams, and yet this river put a stop to them. God did not give them courage or activity to go over after us. We were not ready for so great a mercy as victory and deliverance; if we had been, God would have found out a way for the English to have passed this river, as well as for the Indians with their squaws and children, and all their luggage. *Oh that my People had hearkened to me, and Israel had walked in my ways, I should soon have subdued their Enemies, and turned my hand against their Adversaries.* Psalm 81.13–14.

The Sixth Remove

On Monday (as I said) they set their wigwams on fire, and went away. It was a cold morning, and before us there was a great brook with ice on it; some waded through it, up to the knees and higher, but others went till they came to a beaver dam, and I amongst them, where through the good providence of God, I did not wet my foot. I went along that day mourning and lamenting, leaving farther my own country, and travelling into the vast and howling wilderness, and I understood something of Lot's wife's temptation, when she looked back.[2] We came that day to a great swamp, by the side of which we took up our lodging that night. When I came to the brow of the hill that looked toward the swamp, I thought we had been come to a great Indian town (though there were none but our own company). The Indians were as thick as the trees; it seemed as if there had been a thousand hatchets going at once. If one looked before one, there was nothing but Indians, and behind one, nothing but Indians, and so on either hand, I myself in the midst, and no Christian soul near me, and yet how hath the Lord preserved me in safety? *Oh the experience that I have had of the goodness of God, to me and mine!*

The Seventh Remove

After a restless and hungry night there, we had a wearisome time of it the next day. The swamp by which we lay was, as it were, a deep dungeon, and an exceeding high and steep hill before it. Before I got to the top of the hill, I thought my heart and legs and all would have broken, and failed me. What through faintness and soreness of body, it was a grievous day of travel to me. As we went along, I saw a place where English cattle had been: that was comfort to me, such as it was. Quickly after that we came to an English path, which so took with me, that I thought I could have freely lain down and died. That day, a little after noon, we came to Squaukheag, where the Indians quickly spread themselves over the deserted English fields, gleaning what they could find; some picked up ears of wheat that were crickled[3] down, some found ears of Indian corn; some found groundnuts,[4] and others sheaves of wheat that were frozen together in the shock, and went to threshing of them out. My self got two ears of Indian corn, and whilst I did but turn my back, one of them was stolen from me, which much troubled me. There came an Indian to them at that time, with a basket of horse liver. I asked him to give me a piece. *What*, says he, *can you eat horse liver?* I told him I would try, if he would give a piece, which he did, and I laid it on the coals to roast; but before it was half ready, they got half of it away from me, so that I was fain to take the rest and eat it as it was, with the blood about my mouth, and yet a savoury bit it was to me. *For to the hungry Soul every bitter thing is sweet.*[5] A solemn sight methought it was, to see fields of wheat and Indian

---

1   *squaws* The earliest recorded use of the word "squaw" in English was in *Mourt's Relation* (1622), where it is used as an adjective roughly analogous to "Native American female." The term's etymology has been widely contested, though it is generally agreed that it was borrowed by colonists from the Massachusett *squa*, and from similar words in other Algonquian languages. While the term's use by English speakers in Rowlandson's era was, like *papoose*, intended to be generally neutral, over time the word developed a severely derogatory connotation and an association with various negative stereotypes of Indigenous women.

2   *Lot's wife's … looked back* See Genesis 19.24; Lot's wife looks back as the family flees the city of Sodom—which is being destroyed by God for its inhabitants' wickedness—and is turned into a pillar of salt.

3   *crickled* Crackled; broken.

4   *groundnuts* Tuberous vegetables that bear some resemblance to potatoes, native to North America and part of the staple diets of many Indigenous people at the time.

5   *For to … is sweet* See Proverbs 27.7.

corn forsaken and spoiled, and the remainders of them to be food for our merciless enemies. That night we had a mess of wheat for our supper.

THE EIGHTH REMOVE

On the morrow morning we must go over the river, i.e. Connecticut, to meet with King Philip. Two canoes full they had carried over; the next turn I myself was to go, but as my foot was upon the canoe to step in, there was a sudden outcry among them, and I must step back; and instead of going over the river, I must go four or five miles up the river farther Northward. Some of the Indians ran one way, and some another. The cause of this route was, as I thought, their espying some English scouts who were thereabout. In this travel up the river, about noon, the company made a stop, and sat down; some to eat, and others to rest them. As I sat amongst them, musing of things past, my son Joseph unexpectedly came to me. We asked of each other's welfare, bemoaning our doleful condition, and the change that had come upon us. We had husbands and father, and children, and sisters, and friends, and relations, and house, and home, and many comforts of this life; but now we may say, as Job, *Naked came I out of my Mother's womb, and naked shall I return: The Lord gave, the Lord hath taken away, Blessed be the Name of the Lord.*[1] I asked him whether he would read; he told me, he earnestly desired it, I gave him my Bible, and he lighted upon that comfortable Scripture, Psalm 118.17–18. *I shall not die but live, and declare the works of the Lord: the Lord hath chastened me sore, yet he hath not given me over to death.* Look here, Mother (says he), did you read this? And here I may take occasion to mention one principal ground of my setting forth these lines: even as the Psalmist says, *To declare the Works of the Lord*, and his wonderful power in carrying us along, preserving us in the wilderness, while under the enemy's hand, and returning of us in safety again. And His goodness in bringing to my hand so many comfortable and suitable Scriptures in my distress. But to return. We travelled on till night; and in the morning, we must go over the river to Philip's crew.

When I was in the canoe, I could not but be amazed at the numerous crew of pagans that were on the bank on the other side. When I came ashore, they gathered all about me, I sitting alone in the midst. I observed they asked one another questions, and laughed, and rejoiced over their gains and victories. Then my heart began to fail: and I fell a-weeping, which was the first time, to my remembrance, that I wept before them. Although I had met with so much affliction, and my heart was many times ready to break, yet could I not shed one tear in their sight, but rather had been all this while in a maze,[2] and like one astonished. But now I may say as, Psalm 137.1: *By the Rivers of Babylon, there we sate down: yea, we wept when we remembered Zion.* There one of them asked me why I wept; I could hardly tell what to say. Yet I answered, they would kill me. No, said he, none will hurt you. Then came one of them and gave me two spoonfuls of meal to comfort me, and another gave me half a pint of peas, which was more worth than many bushels at another time. Then I went to see King Philip. He bade me come in and sit down, and asked me whether I would smoke it (a usual compliment nowadays amongst saints and sinners), but this no way suited me. For though I had formerly used tobacco, yet I had left it ever since I was first taken. It seems to be a bait the Devil lays to make men lose their precious time. I remember with shame how formerly, when I had taken two or three pipes, I was presently ready for another, such a bewitching thing it is; but I thank God, he has now given me power over it. Surely there are many who may be better employed than to lie sucking a stinking tobacco-pipe.

Now the Indians gather their forces to go against Northampton. Overnight one went about yelling and hooting to give notice of the design.[3] Whereupon they fell to boiling of groundnuts and parching of corn (as many as had it) for their provision; and in the morning away they went. During my abode in this place, Philip spoke to me to make a shirt for his boy, which I did, for which he gave me a shilling. I offered the money to my master, but he bade me keep it, and with it I bought a piece of horse flesh. Afterwards he asked me to make a cap for his boy, for which he invited me

---

[1]　*Naked came ... the Lord*　God allowed Satan to inflict numerous hardships upon the devout Job, as a test of his faithfulness; the line referenced comes from Job 1.21.

[2]　*in a maze*　I.e., in amazement; in shock.

[3]　*design*　Plan.

to dinner. I went, and he gave me a pancake, about as big as two fingers; it was made of parched wheat, beaten and fried in bear's grease, but I thought I never tasted pleasanter meat[1] in my life. There was a squaw who spoke to me to make a shirt for her *sannup*,[2] for which she gave me a piece of bear. Another asked me to knit a pair of stockings, for which she gave me a quart of peas. I boiled my peas and bear together, and invited my master and mistress to dinner; but the proud gossip, because I served them both in one dish, would eat nothing, except one bit that he gave her upon the point of his knife. Hearing that my son was come to this place, I went to see him, and found him lying flat upon the ground. I asked him, how he could sleep so? He answered me, that he was not asleep, but at prayer, and lay so that they might not observe what he was doing. I pray God he may remember these things now he is returned in safety. At this place (the sun now getting higher), what with the beams and heat of the sun, and the smoke of the wigwams, I thought I should have been blind, I could scarce discern one wigwam from another. There was here one Mary Thurston of Medfield, who seeing how it was with me, lent me a hat to wear; but as soon as I was gone, the squaw who owned that Mary Thurston came running after me, and got it away again. Here was the squaw that gave me one spoonful of meal. I put it in my pocket to keep it safe. Yet notwithstanding somebody stole it, but put five Indian corns in the room of it, which corns were the greatest provisions I had in my travel for one day.

The Indians returning from Northampton, brought with them some horses, and sheep, and other things which they had taken. I desired them, that they would carry me to Albany, upon one of those horses, and sell me for powder; for so they had sometimes discoursed. I was utterly hopeless of getting home on foot, the way that I came. I could hardly bear to think of the many weary steps I had taken, to come to this place.

---

[1]   *meat*   In the seventeenth century, a word that could be used to refer to any meal, regardless of whether or not it included animal meat.

[2]   *sannup*   Massachusett: husband (or, more generally, any married man).

THE NINTH REMOVE

But instead of going either to Albany or homeward, we must go five miles up the river, and then go over it. Here we abode a while. Here lived a sorry Indian, who spoke to me to make him a shirt; when I had done it, he would pay me nothing. But he living by the riverside, where I often went to fetch water, I would often be putting of him in mind, and calling for my pay; at last he told me, if I would make another shirt, for a papoose not yet born, he would give me a knife, which he did when I had done it. I carried the knife in, and my master asked me to give it him, and I was not a little glad that I had any thing that they would accept of, and be pleased with. When we were at this place, my master's maid came home; she had been gone three weeks into the Narraganset country, to fetch corn, where they had stored up some in the ground. She brought home about a peck and half of corn. This was about the time that their great captain, Naananto, was killed in the Narraganset country. My son being now about a mile from me, I asked liberty to go and see him. They bade me go, and away I went; but quickly lost myself, travelling over hills and through swamps, and could not find the way to him. And I cannot but admire at the wonderful power and goodness of God to me, in that, though I was gone from home, and met with all sorts of Indians, and those I had no knowledge of, and there being no Christian soul near me; yet not one of them offered the least imaginable miscarriage to me. I turned homeward again, and met with my master; he showed me the way to my son. When I came to him I found him not well; and withal he had a boil on his side, which much troubled him. We bemoaned one another a while, as the Lord helped us, and then I returned again. When I was returned, I found myself as unsatisfied as I was before. I went up and down mourning and lamenting: and my spirit was ready to sink, with the thoughts of my poor children; my son was ill, and I could not but think of his mournful looks, and no Christian friend was near him, to do any office of love for him, either for soul or body. And my poor girl, I knew not where she was, nor whether she was sick, or well, or alive, or dead. I repaired under these thoughts to my Bible (my great comfort in that time) and that Scripture came to my hand, *Cast thy burden upon the Lord, and He shall sustain thee*, Psalm 55.22.

But I was fain to go and look after something to satisfy my hunger, and going among the wigwams, I went into one, and there found a squaw who showed herself very kind to me, and gave me a piece of bear. I put it into my pocket, and came home, but could not find an opportunity to broil it, for fear they would get it from me, and there it lay all that day and night in my stinking pocket. In the morning I went to the same squaw, who had a kettle of groundnuts boiling; I asked her to let me boil my piece of bear in her kettle, which she did, and gave me some groundnuts to eat with it; and I cannot but think how pleasant it was to me. I have sometime seen bear baked very handsomely among the English, and some liked it, but the thoughts that it was bear, made me tremble; but now that was savoury to me that one would think was enough to turn the stomach of a brute creature.

One bitter cold day, I could find no room to sit down before the fire. I went out, and could not tell what to do, but I went in to another wigwam, where they were also sitting round the fire, but the squaw laid a skin for me, and bid me sit down, and gave me some groundnuts, and bade me come again, and told me they would buy me, if they were able, and yet these were strangers to me that I never saw before.

THE TENTH REMOVE

That day a small part of the company removed about three quarters of a mile, intending further the next day. When they came to the place where they intended to lodge, and had pitched their wigwams, being hungry I went again back to the place we were before at, to get something to eat, being encouraged by the squaw's kindness, who bade me come again; when I was there, there came an Indian to look after me, who when he had found me, kicked me all along. I went home and found venison roasting that night, but they would not give me one bit of it. Sometimes I met with favour, and sometimes with nothing but frowns.

THE ELEVENTH REMOVE

The next day in the morning they took their travel, intending a day's journey up the river. I took my load at my back, and quickly we came to wade over the river, and passed over tiresome and wearisome hills. One hill was so steep that I was fain to creep up upon my knees, and to hold by the twigs and bushes to keep myself from falling backward. My head also was so light, that I usually reeled as I went; but I hope all these wearisome steps that I have taken, are but a forewarning to me of the heavenly rest. *I know, O Lord, that thy judgments are right, and that thou in faithfulness hast afflicted me*, Psalm 119.71.[1]

THE TWELFTH REMOVE

It was upon a Sabbath-day morning that they prepared for their travel. This morning I asked my master whether he would sell me to my husband; he answered me *Nux*,[2] which did much rejoice my spirit. My mistress, before we went, was gone to the burial of a papoose, and returning, she found me sitting and reading in my Bible; she snatched it hastily out of my hand, and threw it out of doors. I ran out and catched it up, and put it into my pocket, and never let her see it afterward. Then they packed up their things to be gone, and gave me my load; I complained it was too heavy, whereupon she gave me a slap in the face, and bade me go. I lifted up my heart to God, hoping the Redemption was not far off, and the rather because their insolency grew worse and worse.

But the thoughts of my going homeward (for so we bent our course) much cheered my spirit, and made my burden seem light, and almost nothing at all. But (to my amazement and great perplexity) the scale was soon turned; for when we had gone a little way, on a sudden my mistress gives out, she would go no further, but turn back again, and said I must go back again with her; and she called her *sannup*, and would have had him gone back also, but he would not, but said he would go on, and come to us again in three days. My spirit was, upon this, I confess, very impatient, and

---

[1]   *119.71*   The actual citation is Psalm 119.75.

[2]   *Nux*   Yes.

almost outrageous.[1] I thought I could as well have died as went back; I cannot declare the trouble that I was in about it, but yet back again I must go. As soon as I had an opportunity, I took my Bible to read, and that quieting Scripture came to my hand, Psalm 46.10—*Be still, and know that I am God*—which stilled my spirit for the present. But a sore time of trial, I concluded, I had to go through. My master being gone, who seemed to me the best friend that I had of an Indian, both in cold and hunger, and quickly so it proved. Down I sat, with my heart as full as it could hold, and yet so hungry that I could not sit neither. But going out to see what I could find, and walking among the trees, I found six acorns, and two chestnuts, which were some refreshment to me. Towards night I gathered me some sticks for my own comfort, that I might not lie a-cold; but when we came to lie down they bade me to go out, and lie somewhere else, for they had company (they said) come in more than their own. I told them, I could not tell where to go. They bade me go look; I told them, if I went to another wigwam they would be angry, and send me home again. Then one of the company drew his sword, and told me he would run me through if I did not go presently. Then was I fain to stoop to this rude fellow, and to go out in the night, I knew not whither. Mine eyes have seen that fellow afterwards walking up and down Boston, under the appearance of a Friend-Indian, and several others of the like cut. I went to one wigwam, and they told me they had no room. Then I went to another, and they said the same. At last an old Indian bade me to come to him, and his squaw gave me some groundnuts; she gave me also something to lay under my head, and a good fire we had: and through the good providence of God, I had a comfortable lodging that night. In the morning, another Indian bade me come at night, and he would give me six groundnuts, which I did. We were at this place and time about two miles from Connecticut River. We went in the morning to gather groundnuts, to the river, and went back again that night. I went with a good load at my back (for they when they went, though but a little way, would carry all their trumpery[2] with them). I told them the skin was off my back, but I had no other comforting answer from them than this, that it would be no matter if my head were off too.

The Thirteenth Remove

Instead of going toward the Bay, which was that I desired, I must go with them five or six miles down the river into a mighty thicket of brush, where we abode almost a fortnight. Here one asked me to make a shirt for her papoose, for which she gave me a mess of broth, which was thickened with meal made of the bark of a tree, and to make it the better, she had put into it about a handful of peas, and a few roasted groundnuts. I had not seen my son a pretty while, and here was an Indian of whom I made inquiry after him, and asked him when he saw him. He answered me, that such a time his master roasted him, and that himself did eat a piece of him, as big as his two fingers, and that he was very good meat. But the Lord upheld my spirit under this discouragement, and I considered their horrible addictedness to lying, and that there is not one of them that makes the least conscience of speaking of truth. In this place, on a cold night, as I lay by the fire, I removed a stick that kept the heat from me; a squaw moved it down again, at which I looked up, and she threw a handful of ashes in mine eyes. I thought I should have been quite blinded, and have never seen more, but lying down, the water run out of my eyes, and carried the dirt with it, that by the morning, I recovered my sight again. Yet upon this, and the like occasions, I hope it is not too much to say with Job, *Have pity upon me, have pity upon me, O ye my Friends, for the Hand of the Lord has touched me.*[3] And here I cannot but remember how many times sitting in their wigwams, and musing on things past, I should suddenly leap up and run out, as if I had been at home, forgetting where I was, and what my condition was. But when I was without, and saw nothing but wilderness, and woods, and a company of barbarous heathens, my mind quickly returned to me, which made me think of that spoken concerning Sampson, who said, *I will go out and shake myself as at other times, but he wist not that the Lord was departed from him.*[4] About this time I began to think that all my hopes of restoration

---

[1]   *outrageous* Outraged.

[2]   *trumpery* Trifling objects; trash.

[3]   *Have pity ... touched me* See Job 19.21.

[4]   *I will ... from him* See Judges 16.20; *wist* Knew.

would come to nothing. I thought of the English army, and hoped for their coming, and being taken by them, but that failed. I hoped to be carried to Albany, as the Indians had discoursed before, but that failed also. I thought of being sold to my husband, as my master spake, but instead of that, my master himself was gone, and I left behind, so that my spirit was now quite ready to sink. I asked them to let me go out and pick up some sticks, that I might get alone, and pour out my heart unto the Lord. Then also I took my Bible to read, but I found no comfort here neither, which many times I was wont to find. So easy a thing it is with God to dry up the streams of Scripture-comfort from us. Yet I can say, that in all my sorrows and afflictions, God did not leave me to have my impatience work towards himself, as if his ways were unrighteous. But I knew that he laid upon me less than I deserved. Afterward, before this doleful time ended with me, I was turning the leaves of my Bible, and the Lord brought to me some Scriptures, which did a little revive me, as that Isaiah 55.8, *For my thoughts are not your thoughts, neither are your ways my ways, saith the Lord.* And also that, Psalm 37.5, *Commit thy way unto the Lord, trust also in him, and he shall bring it to pass.* About this time they came yelping from Hadley, where they had killed three Englishmen, and brought one captive with them, *viz.* Thomas Read. They all gathered about the poor man, asking him many questions. I desired also to go and see him; and when I came, he was crying bitterly, supposing they would quickly kill him. Whereupon I asked one of them, whether they intended to kill him; he answered me, they would not. He being a little cheered with that, I asked him about the welfare of my husband; he told me he saw him such a time in the Bay, and he was well, but very melancholy. By which I certainly understood (though I suspected it before) that whatsoever the Indians told me respecting him was vanity and lies. Some of them told me he was dead, and they had killed him; some said he was married again, and that the governor wished him to marry, and told him he should have his choice, and that all persuaded I was dead. So like were these barbarous creatures to him who was a liar from the beginning.[1]

As I was sitting once in the wigwam here, Philip's maid came in with the child in her arms, and asked me to give her a piece of my apron, to make a flap for it. I told her I would not. Then my mistress bade me give it, but still I said no; the maid told me if I would not give her a piece, she would tear a piece off it. I told her I would tear her coat then. With that my mistress rises up, and takes up a stick big enough to have killed me, and struck at me with it, but I stept out, and she struck the stick into the mat of the wigwam. But while she was pulling of it out, I ran to the maid and gave her all my apron, and so that storm went over.

Hearing that my son was come to this place, I went to see him, and told him his father was well, but very melancholy. He told me he was as much grieved for his father as for himself; I wondered at his speech, for I thought I had enough upon my spirit in reference to myself, to make me mindless of my husband and everyone else, they being safe among their friends. He told me also, that a while before, his master (together with other Indians) were going to the French for powder;[2] but by the way the Mohawks met with them, and killed four of their company, which made the rest turn back again, for which I desire that myself and he may bless the Lord; for it might have been worse with him, had he been sold to the French, than it proved to be in his remaining with the Indians.[3]

I went to see an English youth in this place, one John Gilberd of Springfield. I found him lying without doors,[4] upon the ground. I asked him how he did? He told me he was very sick of a flux,[5] with eating so much blood. They had turned him out of the wigwam, and with him an Indian papoose, almost dead (whose parents had been killed), in a bitter cold day, without fire or clothes: the young man himself had nothing on but his shirt and waistcoat. This sight was enough to melt a heart of flint. There they lay quivering in the cold, the youth round like a dog, the papoose stretched out, with his eyes and nose and mouth full of dirt, and yet alive,

[1]   *him who was ... the beginning*   I.e., Satan.

[2]   *powder*   I.e., gunpowder.

[3]   *going to the French ... the Indians*   Rowlandson expresses common Puritan anti-Catholic prejudice by suggesting that living under the rule of the Mohawk, who had allied themselves with the New England Confederation, would be preferable to capture by the Catholic French.

[4]   *without doors*   Outdoors.

[5]   *flux*   Early name for dysentery, a disease characterized by severe diarrhea and bleeding.

and groaning. I advised John to go and get to some fire; he told me he could not stand, but I persuaded him still, lest he should lie there and die, and with much ado I got him to a fire, and went myself home. As soon as I was got home, his master's daughter came after me, to know what I had done with the English man. I told her I had got him to a fire in such a place. Now had I need to pray Paul's Prayer, 2 Thessalonians 3.2, *That we may be delivered from unreasonable and wicked men.* For her satisfaction I went along with her, and brought her to him; but before I got home again, it was noised about, that I was running away and getting the English youth along with me; that as soon as I came in, they began to rant and domineer, asking me where I had been, and what I had been doing? and saying they would knock him on the head. I told them I had been seeing the English youth, and that I would not run away. They told me I lied, and taking up a hatchet, they came to me, and said they would knock me down if I stirred out again, and so confined me to the wigwam. Now may I say with David, 2 Samuel 24.14, *I am in a great strait.* If I keep in, I must die with hunger, and if I go out, I must be knocked in head. This distressed condition held that day, and half the next; and then the Lord remembered me, whose mercies are great. Then came an Indian to me with a pair of stockings that were too big for him, and he would have me ravel them out, and knit them fit for him. I showed myself willing, and bid him ask my mistress if I might go along with him a little way; she said yes, I might, but I was not a little refreshed with that news, that I had my liberty again. Then I went along with him, and he gave me some roasted groundnuts, which did again revive my feeble stomach.

Being got out of her sight, I had time and liberty again to look into my Bible, which was my guide by day, and my pillow by night. Now that comfortable Scripture presented itself to me, Isaiah 54.7: *For a small moment have I forsaken thee, but with great mercies will I gather thee.* Thus the Lord carried me along from one time to another, and made good to me this precious promise, and many others. Then my son came to see me, and I asked his master to let him stay a while with me, that I might comb his head, and look over him, for he was almost overcome with lice. He told me, when I had done, that he was very hungry, but I had nothing

to relieve him; but bid him go into the wigwams as he went along, and see if he could get anything among them. Which he did, and it seems tarried a little too long, for his master was angry with him, and beat him, and then sold him. Then he came running to tell me he had a new master, and that he had given him some groundnuts already. Then I went along with him to his new master, who told me he loved him, and he should not want. So his master carried him away, and I never saw him afterward, till I saw him at Pascataqua in Portsmouth.

That night they bade me go out of the wigwams again; my mistress's papoose was sick, and it died that night, and there was one benefit in it, that there was more room. I went to a wigwam, and they bade me come in, and gave me a skin to lie upon, and a mess of venison and groundnuts, which was a choice dish among them. On the morrow they buried the papoose, and afterward, both morning and evening, there came a company to mourn and howl with her: though I confess, I could not much condole with them. Many sorrowful days I had in this place, often getting alone. *Like a Crane or a Swallow, so did I chatter: I did mourn as a Dove, mine eyes fail with looking upward. Oh, Lord I am oppressed, undertake for me,* Isaiah 38.14. I could tell the Lord as Hezekiah, verse 3. *Remember now O Lord, I beseech thee, how I have walked before thee in truth.* Now had I time to examine all my ways: my conscience did not accuse me of unrighteousness toward one or other, yet I saw how in my walk with God, I had been a careless creature. As David said, *Against thee, thee only have I sinned;*[1] and I might say with the poor publican, *God be merciful unto me a sinner.*[2] On the Sabbath days, I could look upon the sun and think how people were going to the house of God, to have their souls refreshed; and then home, and their bodies also: but I was destitute of both; and might say as the poor prodigal, *He would fain have filled his belly with the husks that the Swine did eat, and no man gave unto him,* Luke 15.16. For I must say with him, *Father I have sinned against Heaven, and in thy sight,* verse 21. I remembered how on the night before and after the Sabbath, when my family was about me, and relations and neighbours with us, we could pray and sing, and then refresh our

---

[1]   *As David … sinned*   See Psalm 51.4.

[2]   *poor publican … a sinner*   See Luke 18.13.

bodies with the good creatures of God; and then have a comfortable bed to lie down on; but instead of all this, I had only a little swill for the body, and then like a swine, must lie down on the ground. I cannot express to man the sorrow that lay upon my spirit, the Lord knows it. Yet that comfortable Scripture would often come to my mind, *For a small moment have I forsaken thee, but with great mercies will I gather thee.*[1]

THE FOURTEENTH REMOVE

Now must we pack up and be gone from this Thicket, bending our course toward the Bay-towns I haveing nothing to eat by the way this day, but a few crumbs of Cake, that an Indian gave my girls the same day we were taken. She gave it me, and I put it in my pocket: there it lay, till it was so mouldy (for want of good baking) that one could not tell what it was made of; it fell all to crumbs, & grew so dry and hard, that it was like little flints; & this refreshed me many times, when I was ready to faint. It was in my thoughts when I put it into my mouth, that if ever I returned, I would tell the World what a blessing the Lord gave to such mean food. As we went along, they killed a Deer, with a young one in her. they gave me a piece of the Fawn, and it was so young and tender, that one might eat the bones as well as the flesh, and yet I thought it very good. When night came on we sate down; it rained, but they quickly got up a Bark Wigwam, where I lay dry that night. I looked out in the morning, and many of them had line[2] in the rain all night, I saw by their Reaking. Thus the Lord dealt mercifully with me many times, and I fared better than many of them. In the morning they took the blood of the Deer and put it into the Paunch, and so boyled it; I could eat nothing of that, though they ate it sweetly. And yet they were so nice[3] in other things, that when I had fetcht water, and had put the Dish I dipt the water with, into the Kettle of water which I brought, they would say, they would knock me down; for they said, it was a sluttish trick.[4]

original spelling

We went on our travel. I having got one handful of groundnuts for my support that day they gave me my load, and I went on cheerfully (with the thoughts of going homeward), having my burden more on my back than my spirit. We came to Baquang River again that day, near which we abode a few days. Sometimes one of them would give me a pipe, another a little tobacco, another a little salt, which I would change for a little victuals.[5] I cannot but think what a wolfish appetite persons have in a starving condition: for many times when they gave me that which was hot, I was so greedy, that I should burn my mouth, that it would trouble me hours after, and yet I should quickly do the same again. And after I was thoroughly hungry, I was never again satisfied. For though sometimes it fell out,[6] that I got enough, and did eat till I could eat no more, yet I was as unsatisfied as I was when I began. And now could I see that Scripture verified (there being many Scriptures which we do not take notice of, or understand till we are afflicted) Micah 6.14. *Thou shalt eat and not be satisfied.* Now might I see more than ever before, the miseries that sin hath brought upon us. Many times I should be ready to run out against the heathen, but the Scripture would quiet me again, Amos 3.6. *Shall there be evils in the City, and the Lord hath not done it?* The Lord help me to make a right improvement of His Word, and that I might learn that great lesson, Micah 6.8–9, *He hath shewed thee (Oh Man) what is good, and what doth the Lord require of thee, but to do justly, and love mercy, and walk humbly with thy God? Hear ye the rod, and who hath appointed it.*

THE SIXTEENTH REMOVE

We began this remove with wading over Baquag River; the water was up to the knees, and the stream very swift, and so cold that I thought it would have cut me in sunder. I was so weak and feeble that I reeled as I went along, and thought there I must end my days at last, after my bearing and getting through so many difficulties. The Indians stood laughing to see me staggering along, but in my distress the Lord gave me experience

---

[1] *For a ... gather thee* See Isaiah 54.7.

[2] *line* Lain.

[3] *nice* Scrupulous; having refined tastes or habits.

[4] *sluttish* Unclean or disgusting; *trick* Thoughtless or stupid action.

---

[5] *victuals* Food.

[6] *it fell out* It so happened.

of the truth, and goodness of that promise, Isaiah 43.2, *When thou passest thorough the Waters, I will be with thee, and through the Rivers, they shall not overflow thee.* Then I sat down to put on my stockings and shoes, with the tears running down mine eyes, and many sorrowful thoughts in my heart, but I got up to go along with them. Quickly there came up to us an Indian, who informed them that I must go to Wachusett to my master, for there was a letter come from the council to the Sagamores about redeeming the captives, and that there would be another in fourteen days, and that I must be there ready. My heart was so heavy before that I could scarce speak or go in the path; and yet now so light that I could run. My strength seemed to come again, and recruit my feeble knees, and aching heart; yet it pleased them to go but one mile that night, and there we stayed two days. In that time came a company of Indians to us, near thirty, all on horseback. My heart skipped within me, thinking they had been Englishmen at the first sight of them, for they were dressed in English apparel, with hats, white neckcloths, and sashes about their waists, and ribbons upon their shoulders; but when they came near, there was a vast difference between the lovely faces of Christians, and the foul looks of those heathens, which much damped my spirit again.

The Seventeenth Remove

A comfortable remove it was to me, because of my hopes. They gave me a pack, and along we went cheerfully, but quickly my will proved more than my strength; having little or no refreshing, my strength failed me, and my spirit were almost quite gone. Now may I say with David, Psalm 119.22–24, *I am poor and needy, and my heart is wounded within me. I am gone like the shadow when it declineth: I am tossed up and down like the locusts; my knees are weak through fasting, and my flesh faileth of fatness.*[1] At night we came to an Indian town, and the Indians sat down by a wigwam discoursing, but I was almost spent, and could scarce speak. I laid down my load, and went into the wigwam, and there sat an Indian boiling of horses' feet (they being wont to eat the flesh first, and when the feet were old and dried, and they had nothing else, they would

cut off the feet and use them). I asked him to give me a little of his broth, or water they were boiling in; he took a dish, and gave me one spoonful of samp,[2] and bid me take as much of the broth as I would. Then I put some of the hot water to the samp, and drank it up, and my spirit came again. He gave me also a piece of the ruff or ridding[3] of the small guts, and I broiled it on the coals; and now may I say with Jonathan, *See, I pray you, how mine eyes have been enlightened, because I tasted a little of this honey,* 1 Samuel 14.29. Now is my Spirit revived again, though means be never so inconsiderable, yet if the Lord bestow his blessing upon them, they shall refresh both soul and body.

The Eighteenth Remove

We took up our packs and along we went, but a wearisome day I had of it. As we went along I saw an Englishman stripped naked, and lying dead upon the ground, but knew not who it was. Then we came to another Indian town, where we stayed all night. In this town there were four English children, captives; and one of them my own sister's. I went to see how she did, and she was well, considering her captive condition. I would have tarried that night with her, but they that owned her would not suffer it. Then I went into another wigwam, where they were boiling corn and beans, which was a lovely sight to see, but I could not get a taste thereof. Then I went to another wigwam, where there were two of the English children; the squaw was boiling horses' feet, then she cut me off a little piece, and gave one of the English children a piece also. Being very hungry I had quickly eat[4] up mine, but the child could not bite it, it was so tough and sinewy, but lay sucking, gnawing, chewing and slabbering of it in the mouth and hand; then I took it of the child, and eat it myself, and savoury it was to my taste. Then I may say as Job, chapter 6.7, *The things that my soul refused to touch, are as my sorrowful meat.* Thus the Lord made that pleasant refreshing, which another time would have been an abomination. Then I went home to my mistress's wigwam, and they told me I disgraced my master with begging, and if I did so any more, they

---

[1] *I am ... of fatness* This is actually from Psalm 109.

[2] *samp* Cornmeal porridge.

[3] *ruff or ridding* Parts that were being cast aside.

[4] *eat* Ate.

would knock me in head. I told them, they had as good knock me in head as starve me to death.

The Nineteenth Remove

They said, when we went out, that we must travel to Wachusett this day. But a bitter weary day I had of it, travelling now three days together, without resting any day between. At last, after many weary steps, I saw Wachusett hills, but many miles off. Then we came to a great swamp, through which we travelled up to the knees, in mud and water, which was heavy going to one tired before. Being almost spent, I thought I should have sunk down at last, and never got out; but I may say, as in Psalm 94.18, *When my foot slipped, thy mercy, O Lord held me up*. Going along, having indeed my life, but little spirit, Philip, who was in the company, came up and took me by the hand, and said, *Two weeks more and you shall be Mistress again*. I asked him, if he spoke true? he answered, *Yes, and quickly you shall come to your master again*; who had been gone from us three weeks. After many weary steps we came to Wachusett, where he was, and glad I was to see him. He asked me, when I washed me? I told him not this month, then he fetched me some water himself, and bid me wash, and gave me the glass[1] to see how I looked, and bid his squaw give me something to eat; so she gave me a mess of beans and meat, and a little groundnut cake. I was wonderfully revived with this favour showed me, Psalm 106.46, *He made them also to be pitied, of all those that carried them Captives*.

My master had three squaws, living sometimes with one, and sometimes with another one, this old squaw, at whose wigwam I was, and with whom my master had been those three weeks. Another was Wettimore,[2] with whom I had lived and served all this while. A severe and proud dame she was, bestowing every day in dressing herself neat as much time as any of the gentry of the land: powdering her hair, and painting her face, going with necklaces, with jewels in her ears, and bracelets upon her hands. When she had dressed herself, her work was to make girdles of wampum and beads. The third squaw was a younger one, by whom he had two papooses. By that time I was refreshed by the old squaw, with whom my master was, Wettimore's maid came to call me home, at which I fell a-weeping. Then the old squaw told me, to encourage me, that if I wanted victuals, I should come to her, and that I should lie there in her wigwam. Then I went with the maid, and quickly came again and lodged there. The squaw laid a mat under me, and a good rug over me; the first time I had any such kindness showed me. I understood that Wettimore thought that if she should let me go and serve with the old squaw, she would be in danger to lose not only my service, but the redemption-pay[3] also. And I was not a little glad to hear this, being by it raised in my hopes, that in God's due time there would be an end of this sorrowful hour. Then came an Indian, and asked me to knit him three pair of stockings, for which I had a hat, and a silk handkerchief. Then another asked me to make her a shift, for which she gave me an apron.

Then came Tom and Peter, with the second letter from the council, about the captives. Though they were Indians, I got them by the hand, and burst out into tears. My heart was so full that I could not speak to them; but recovering myself, I asked them how my husband did, and all my friends and acquaintance? They said, *They are all very well, but melancholy*. They brought me two biscuits, and a pound of tobacco. The tobacco I quickly gave away; when it was all gone, one asked me to give him a pipe of tobacco, I told him it was all gone; then began he to rant and threaten. I told him when my husband came I would give him some. *Hang him rogue* (says he), *I will knock out his brains, if he comes here*. And then again, in the same breath they would say, that if there should come an hundred without guns, they would do them no hurt. So unstable and like madmen they were. So that fearing the worst, I durst not send to my husband, though there were some thoughts of his coming to redeem and fetch me, not knowing what might follow; for there was little more trust to them then to the master they served. When the letter was come, the Saggamores met to consult about the captives, and called me to them to enquire how much my husband would give to redeem me, when I came I sat down among them, as I was wont to do, as their manner is. Then they bade me stand up, and said, they were the General Court.

---

[1] *glass* Mirror.

[2] *Wettimore* I.e., Weetamoo.

[3] *redemption-pay* I.e., the ransom price.

They bid me speak what I thought he would give. Now knowing that all we had was destroyed by the Indians, I was in a great strait: I thought if I should speak of but a little, it would be slighted, and hinder the matter; if of a great sum, I knew not where it would be procured. Yet at a venture, I said twenty pounds, yet desired them to take less; but they would not hear of that, but send that message to Boston, that for twenty pounds I should be redeemed. It was a Praying Indian that wrote their letter for them. There was another Praying Indian, who told me, that he had a brother, that would not eat horse, his conscience was so tender and scrupulous (though as large as hell, for the destruction of poor Christians). Then he said, he read that Scripture to him, 2 Kings, 6.25: *There was a famine in Samaria, and behold they besieged it, until an Ass's head was sold for fourscore pieces of silver, and the fourth part of a Kab[1] of Doves' dung, for five pieces of silver.* He expounded this place to his brother, and showed him that it was lawful to eat that in a famine which is not at another time. And now, says he, he will eat horse with any Indian of them all. There was another Praying Indian who, when he had done all the mischief that he could, betrayed his own father into the English hands, thereby to purchase his own life. Another Praying Indian was at Sudbury fight,[2] though, as he deserved, he was afterward hanged for it. There was another Praying Indian so wicked and cruel as to wear a string about his neck, strung with Christians' fingers. Another Praying Indian, when they went to Sudbury fight, went with them, and his squaw also with him, with her papoose at her back. Before they went to that fight, they got a company together to Powwow; the manner was as followeth. There was one that kneeled upon a deer skin, with the company round him in a ring who kneeled, and striking upon the ground with their hands, and with sticks, and muttering or humming with their mouths. Besides him who kneeled in the ring, there also stood one with a gun in his hand. Then he on the deerskin made a speech, and all manifested assent to it: and so they did many times together. Then they bade him with the gun go out of the ring, which he did, but when he was out, they called him in again; but he seemed to make

a stand, then they called the more earnestly, till he returned again. Then they all sang. Then they gave him two guns, in either hand one. And so he on the deerskin began again; and at the end of every sentence in his speaking, they all assented, humming or muttering with their mouths, and striking upon the ground with their hands. Then they bade him with the two guns go out of the ring again; which he did, a little way. Then they called him in again, but he made a stand; so they called him with greater earnestness, but he stood reeling and wavering as if he knew not whether he should stand or fall, or which way to go. Then they called him with exceeding great vehemency, all of them, one and another: after a little while he turned in, staggering as he went, with his arms stretched out, in either hand a gun. As soon as he came in, they all sang and rejoiced exceedingly a while. And then he upon the deer skin made another speech, unto which they all assented in a rejoicing manner: and so they ended their business, and forthwith went to Sudbury fight. To my thinking they went without any scruple, but that they should prosper, and gain the victory. And they went out not so rejoicing, but they came home with as great a victory. For they said they had killed two captains and almost an hundred men. One Englishman they brought along with them: and he said, it was too true, for they had made sad work at Sudbury, as indeed it proved. Yet they came home without that rejoicing and triumphing over their victory, which they were wont to show at other times, but rather like dogs (as they say) which have lost their ears. Yet I could not perceive that it was for their own loss of men. They said they had not lost above five or six, and I missed none, except in one wigwam. When they went, they acted as if the Devil had told them that they should gain the victory: and now they acted as if the Devil had told them they should have a fall. Whether it were so or no, I cannot tell, but so it proved, for quickly they began to fall, and so held on that summer, till they came to utter ruin. They came home on a Sabbath day, and the Powwow[3] that kneeled upon the deer skin came home (I may say, without abuse) as black as the Devil. When my master came home, he came to me and bid me make a shirt for his papoose, of a Holland-laced pillowbeer.[4] About

---

[1] *Kab* Measurement of volume.

[2] *Sudbury fight* Battle that took place in the town of Sudbury, Massachusetts on 21 April 1676.

[3] *Powwow* Shaman.

[4] *Holland-laced pillowbeer* Pillowcase made from Dutch linen.

that time there came an Indian to me and bid me come to his wigwam at night, and he would give me some pork and groundnuts. Which I did, and as I was eating, another Indian said to me, he seems to be your good friend, but he killed two Englishmen at Sudbury, and there lie their clothes behind you. I looked behind me, and there I saw bloody clothes, with bullet-holes in them; yet the Lord suffered not this wretch to do me any hurt. Yea, instead of that, he many times refreshed me: five or six times did he and his squaw refresh my feeble carcass. If I went to their wigwam at any time, they would always give me something, and yet they were strangers that I never saw before. Another squaw gave me a piece of fresh pork, and a little salt with it, and lent me her pan to fry it in; and I cannot but remember what a sweet, pleasant and delightful relish that bit had to me, to this day. So little do we prize common mercies when we have them to the full.

THE TWENTIETH REMOVE

It was their usual manner to remove, when they had done any mischief, lest they should be found out: and so they did at this time. We went about three or four miles, and there they built a great wigwam, big enough to hold an hundred Indians, which they did in preparation to a great day of dancing. They would say now amongst themselves, that the Governor would be so angry for his loss as Sudbury, that he would send no more about the captives, which made me grieve and tremble. My sister being not far from the place where we now were, and hearing that I was here, desired her master to let her come and see me; and he was willing to it, and would go with her. But she being ready before him, told him she would go before, and was come within a mile or two of the place; then he overtook her, and began to rant as if he had been mad, and made her go back again in the rain, so that I never saw her till I saw her in Charlestown. But the Lord requited many of their ill doings, for this Indian, her master, was hanged afterward at Boston. The Indians now began to come from all quarters, against their merry dancing day. Among some of them came one Goodwife Kettle. I told her my heart was so heavy that it was ready to break. So is mine too, said she, but yet said, I hope we shall hear some good news shortly. I

could hear how earnestly my sister desired to see me, and I as earnestly desired to see her: and yet neither of us could get an opportunity. My daughter was also now about a mile off, and I had not seen her in nine or ten weeks, as I had not seen my sister since our first taking. I earnestly desired them to let me go and see them: yea, I intreated, begged, and persuaded them, but to let me see my daughter; and yet so hard hearted were they, that they would not suffer it. They made use of their tyrannical power whilst they had it: but through the Lord's wonderful mercy, their time was now but short.

On a Sabbath day, the sun being about an hour high in the afternoon, came Mr. John Hoar[1] (the Council permitting him, and his own forward spirit inclining him) together with the two fore-mentioned Indians, Tom and Peter, with their third letter from the Council. When they came near, I was abroad. Though I saw them not, they presently called me in, and bade me sit down and not stir. Then they catched up their guns, and away they ran, as if an enemy had been at hand, and the guns went off apace. I manifested some great trouble,[2] and they asked me what was the matter? I told them, I thought they had killed the Englishman (for they had in the meantime informed me that an Englishman was come). They said, *No*; they shot over his horse and under, and before[3] his horse; and they pushed him this way and that way, at their pleasure, showing what they could do. Then they let them come to their wigwams. I begged of them to let me see the Englishman, but they would not. But there was I fain to sit their pleasure. When they had talked their fill with him, they suffered me to go to him. We asked each other of our welfare, and how my husband did, and all my friends? He told me they were all well, and would be glad to see me. Amongst other things which my husband sent me, there came a pound of tobacco, which I sold for nine shillings in money: for many of the Indians, for want of tobacco, smoked hemlock and ground ivy. It was a great mistake in any who thought I sent for tobacco: for through the favour of God, that

---

[1] *Mr. John Hoar* Prominent Massachusetts militia leader and lawyer.

[2] *manifested some great trouble* I.e., had the appearance of being in great distress.

[3] *before* In front of.

desire was overcome. I now asked them, whether I should go home with Mr. Hoar? They answered *No*, one and another of them: and it being night, we lay down with that answer; in the morning, Mr. Hoar invited the Sagamores to dinner; but when we went to get it ready, we found that they had stolen the greatest part of the provision Mr. Hoar had brought, out of his bags, in the night: And we may see the wonderful power of God, in that one passage,[1] in that when there was such a great number of the Indians together, and so greedy of a little good food, and no English there, but Mr. Hoar and myself, that there they did not knock us in the head, and take what we had, there being not only some provision, but also trading-cloth,[2] a part of the twenty pounds agreed upon. But instead of doing us any mischief, they seemed to be ashamed of the fact, and said, it were some *matchit*[3] Indian that did it. Oh, that we could believe that there is no thing too hard for God! God showed his power over the heathen in this, as he did over the hungry lions when Daniel was cast into the den.[4] Mr. Hoar called them betime to dinner, but they ate very little, they being so busy in dressing themselves, and getting ready for their dance, which was carried on by eight of them, four men and four squaws. My master and mistress being two. He was dressed in his Holland shirt, with great laces sewed at the tail of it, and he had his silver buttons, his white stockings, his garters were hung round with shillings, and he had girdles of wampum upon his head and shoulders. She had a kersey[5] coat, and [was] covered with girdles of wampum from the loins upward; her arms from her elbows to her hands were covered with bracelets, there were handfuls of necklaces about her neck, and several sorts of jewels in her ears. She had fine red stockings, and white shoes, her hair powdered and face painted red, that was always before black. And all the dancers were after the same manner. There were two other singing and knocking

on a kettle for their music. They kept hopping up and down one after another, with a kettle of water in the midst, standing warm upon some embers, to drink of when they were dry. They held on till it was almost night, throwing out wampum to the standers by. At night I asked them again, if I should go home? They all as one said No, except[6] my husband would come for me. When we were lain down, my master went out of the wigwam, and by and by sent in an Indian called James the Printer,[7] who told Mr. Hoar that my master would let me go home tomorrow, if he would let him have one pint of liquors. Then Mr. Hoar called his own Indians, Tom and Peter, and bid them go and see whether he would promise it before them three: and if he would, he should have it; which he did, and he had it. Then Philip smelling the business called me to him, and asked me what I would give him, to tell me some good news, and speak a good word for me. I told him, I could not tell what to give him, I would anything I had, and asked him what he would have? He said, two coats and twenty shillings in money, and half a bushel of feed corn, and some tobacco. I thanked him for his love: but I knew the good news as well as the crafty fox. My master, after he had had his drink, quickly came ranting into the wigwam again, and called for Mr. Hoar, drinking to him, and saying, *He was a good man*; and then again he would say, *Hang him rogue*. Being almost drunk, he would drink to him, and yet presently say he should be hanged. Then he called for me; I trembled to hear him, yet I was fain to go to him, and he drank to me, showing no incivility. He was the first Indian I saw drunk all the while that I was amongst them. At last his squaw ran out, and he after her, round the wigwam, with his money jingling at his knees, but she escaped him. But having an old squaw, he ran to her; and so through the Lord's mercy, we were no more troubled that night. Yet I had not a comfortable night's rest, for I think I can say, I did not sleep

---

[1]   *passage*   Event.

[2]   *trading-cloth*   Pieces of cloth used as a form of currency.

[3]   *matchit*   From *machétu* (recorded in Williams's *Key*, probably Narragansett): poor.

[4]   *as he … the den*   See Daniel 6, where God sends an angel to restrain the lions in whose den the prophet Daniel has been imprisoned.

[5]   *kersey*   Rough woven fabric made from wool.

[6]   *except*   Unless.

[7]   *James the Printer*   James Printer (1640–1709), born Wowaus, was a literate Nipmuc Christian who had become well known among Massachusetts colonials for his printing of the first translation of the Bible into the Massachusett language in 1663. He appears to have come to sympathize with Metacom's cause over the course of the war, and he subsequently worked as an interpreter and scribe for Metacom, for which many of the English colonists branded him as a traitor.

for three nights together. The night before the letter came from the council, I could not rest. I was so full of fears and troubles, God many times leaving us most in the dark, when deliverance is nearest: yea, at this time I could not rest night nor day. The next night I was overjoyed, Mr. Hoar being come, and that with such good tidings. The third night I was even swallowed up with the thoughts of things, *viz.* that ever I should go home again; and that I must go, leaving my children behind me in the wilderness; so that sleep was now almost departed from mine eyes.

On Tuesday morning they called their General Court (as they call it) to consult and determine whether I should go home or no. And they all as one man did seemingly consent to it, that I should go home, except Philip, who would not come among them.

But before I go any further, I would take leave to mention a few remarkable passages of providence, which I took special notice of in my afflicted time.

1. Of the fair opportunity, lost in the long march, a little after the fort fight, when our English army was so numerous, and in pursuit of the enemy, and so near as to take several and destroy them, and the enemy in such distress for food, that our men might track them by their rooting in the earth for groundnuts whilst they were flying for their lives. I say, that then our army should want provision, and be forced to leave their pursuit and return homeward; and the very next week, the enemy came upon our town, like bears bereft of their whelps, or so many ravenous wolves, rending us and our lambs to death. But what shall I say? God seemed to leave his people to themselves, and order all things for his own holy ends. *Shall there be evil in the City and the Lord hath not done it?*[1] *They are not grieved for the affliction of Joseph, therefore shall they go Captive, with the first that go Captive.*[2] It is the Lord's doing, and it should be marvelous in our eyes.

2. I cannot but remember how the Indians derided the slowness and dullness of the English army, in its setting out. For after the desolations at Lancaster and Medfield, as I went along with them, they asked me when I thought the English army would come after them? I told them I could not tell. It may be they will come in May, said they. Thus did they scoff at us, as if the English would be a quarter of a year getting ready.

3. Which also I have hinted before, when the English army with new supplies were sent forth to pursue after the enemy, and they understanding it, fled before them till they came to Baquaug River, where they forthwith went over safely; that that river should be impassable to the English. I can but admire to see the wonderful providence of God in preserving the heathen for farther affliction to our poor country. They could go in great numbers over, but the English must stop: God had an over-ruling hand in all those things.

4. It was thought if their corn were cut down, they would starve and die with hunger; and all their corn that could be found was destroyed, and they driven from that little they had in store, into the woods in the midst of winter; and yet how to admiration did the Lord preserve them for his holy ends, and the destruction of many still amongst the English! Strangely did the Lord provide for them, that I did not see (all the time I was among them) one man, woman, or child die with hunger.

Though many times they would eat that, that a hog or a dog would hardly touch, yet by that God strengthened them to be a scourge to his people.

The chief and commonest food was groundnuts. They eat also nuts and acorns, harty choaks,[3] lily roots, ground-beans, and several other weeds and roots, that I know not.

They would pick up old bones and cut them to pieces at the joints, and if they were full of worms and maggots, they would scald them over the fire to make the vermin come out, and then boil them, and drink up the liquor, and then beat the great ends of them in a mortar, and so eat them. They would eat horses' guts and ears, and all sorts of wild birds which they could catch; also bear, venison, beaver, tortoise, frogs, squirrels, dogs, skunks, rattlesnakes—yea, the very bark of trees—besides all sorts of creatures, and provision which they plundered from the English. I can but stand in admiration to see the wonderful power of God, in providing for such a vast number of our enemies in the wilderness, where there was nothing to

---

1   *Shall ... done it*   See Amos 3.6.

2   *They are ... Captive*   See Amos 6.6–7.

3   *harty choaks* Artichokes; presumably referring to what is also known today as the Jerusalem artichoke or sunchoke, a wild-growing tuber.

be seen, but from hand to mouth. Many times in a morning, the generality of them would eat up all they had, and yet have some further supply against they wanted. It is said, Psalm 81.13–14. *Oh, that my People had hearkened to me, and Israel had walked in my ways, I should soon have subdued their Enemies, and turned my hand against their Adversaries.* But now our perverse and evil carriages in the sight of the Lord, have so offended him, that instead of turning his hand against them, the Lord feeds and nourishes them up to be a scourge to the whole land.

5. Another thing that I would observe is the strange providence of God in turning things about when the Indians was at the highest, and the English at the lowest. I was with the enemy eleven weeks and five days, and not one week passed without the fury of the enemy, and some desolation by fire and sword upon one place or other. They mourned (with their black faces) for their own losses, yet triumphed and rejoyced in their inhumane, and many times devilish cruelty to the English. They would boast much of their victories, saying that in two hours time they had destroyed such a captain and his company at such a place; and such a captain and his company in such a place; and such a captain and his company in such a place; and boast how many towns they had destroyed, and then scoff and say, *They had done them a good turn, to send them to Heaven so soon.* Again, they would say, *This summer that they would knock all the rogues in the head, or drive them into the sea, or make them fly the country;* thinking surely, Agag-like, *The bitterness of Death is past.*[1] Now the heathen begins to think all is their own, and the poor Christians' hopes to fail (as to man) and now their eyes are more to God, and their hearts sigh heaven-ward, and to say in good earnest, *Help, Lord, or we perish.* When the Lord had brought his people to this, that they saw no help in anything but himself, then he takes the quarrel into his own hand; and though they had made a pit, in their own imaginations, as deep as hell for the Christians that summer, yet the Lord hurled themselves into it. And the Lord had not so many ways before to preserve them, but now he hath as many to destroy them.

But to return again to my going home, where we may see a remarkable change of providence. At first they were all against it, except my husband would come for me; but afterwards they assented to it, and seemed much to rejoice in it. Some asked me to send them some bread, others some tobacco, others shaking me by the hand, offering me a hood and scarf to ride in; not one moving hand or tongue against it. Thus hath the Lord answered my poor desire, and the many earnest requests of others put up unto God for me. In my travels an Indian came to me, and told me, if I were willing, he and his squaw would run away, and go home along with me. I told him no, I was not willing to run away, but desired to wait God's time, that I might go home quietly, and without fear. And now God hath granted me my desire. O the wonderful power of God that I have seen, and the experience that I have had. I have been in the midst of those roaring lions and savage bears that feared neither God, nor man, nor the Devil; by night and day, alone and in company; sleeping all sorts together; and yet not one of them ever offered me the least abuse of unchastity to me, in word or action. Though some are ready to say I speak it for my own credit; but I speak it in the presence of God, and to his glory. God's power is as great now, and as sufficient to save, as when he preserved Daniel in the lions' den; or the three children in the fiery furnace. I may well say as his Psalm 107.12, *Oh give thanks unto the Lord for he is good, for his mercy endureth for ever.* Let the redeemed of the Lord say so, whom he hath redeemed from the hand of the enemy, especially that I should come away in the midst of so many hundreds of enemies quietly and peacably, and not a dog moving his tongue. So I took my leave of them, and in coming along my heart melted into tears, more than all the while I was with them, and I was almost swallowed up with the thoughts that ever I should go home again. About the sun going down, Mr. Hoar and myself, and the two Indians, came to Lancaster, and a solemn sight it was to me. There had I lived many comfortable years amongst my relations and neighbours, and now not one Christian to be seen, nor one house left standing. We went on to a farm house that was yet standing, where we lay all night: and a comfortable lodging we had, though nothing but straw to lie on. The Lord preserved us in safety that night, and raised

---

1   *The bitterness of Death is past*   See 1 Samuel 15.32. Agag, king of Amalek, thought his life had been spared after his defeat by Saul, but he was then killed by Samuel.

us up again in the morning, and carried us along, that before noon, we came to Concord. Now was I full of joy, and yet not without sorrow; joy to see such a lovely sight, so many Christians together, and some of them my neighbours. There I met with my brother, and my brother in law, who asked me if I knew where his wife was? Poor heart! he had helped to bury her, and knew it not; she being shot down by the house was partly burnt, so that those who were at Boston at the desolation of the town, and came back afterward and buried the dead, did not know her. Yet I was not without sorrow, to think how many were looking and longing, and my own children amongst the rest, to enjoy that deliverance that I had now received; and I did not know whether ever I should see them again. Being recruited[1] with food and raiment, we went to Boston that day, where I met with my dear husband; but the thoughts of our dear children, one being dead, and the other we could not tell where, abated our comfort each to other. I was not before so much hemmed in with the merciless and cruel heathen, but now as much with pitiful, tender-hearted, and compassionate Christians. In that poor, and distressed, and beggarly condition I was received in, I was kindly entertained in several houses; so much love I received from several (some of whom I knew, and others I knew not) that I am not capable to declare it. But the Lord knows them all by name: The Lord reward them sevenfold into their bosoms of his spirituals, for their temporals.[2] The twenty pounds, the price of my redemption, was raised by some Boston gentlemen, and Ms. Usher, whose bounty and religious charity I would not forget to make mention of. Then Mr. Thomas Shepard of Charlestown received us into his house, where we continued eleven weeks; and a father and mother they were to us. And many more tender-hearted friends we met with in that place. We were now in the midst of love, yet not without much and frequent heaviness of heart for our poor children, and other relations, who were still in affliction. The week following, after my coming in, the governor and Council sent forth to the Indians again, and that not without success; for they brought in my sister, and Goodwife Kettle. Their not knowing where our children were was a sore trial to us still, and

yet we were not without secret hopes that we should see them again. That which was dead[3] lay heavier upon my spirit, than those which were alive and amongst the heathen; thinking how it suffered with its wounds, and I was no way able to relieve it, and how it was buried by the heathen in the wilderness from[4] among all Christians. We were hurried up and down in our thoughts. Sometime we should hear a report that they were gone this way, and sometimes that, and that they were come in, in this place or that. We kept enquiring and listning to hear concerning them, but no certain news as yet. About this time the Council had ordered a day of public thanksgiving: though I thought I had still cause of mourning, and being unsettled in our minds, we thought we would ride toward the Eastward, to see if we could hear anything concerning our children. And as we were riding along (God is the wise disposer[5] of all things) between Ipswich and Rowly we met with Mr. William Hubbard,[6] who told us that our son Joseph was come in to Major Waldren's,[7] and another with him, which was my sister's son. I asked him how he knew it? He said, the Major himself told him so. So along we went till we came to Newbury; and their minister being absent, they desired my husband to preach the thanksgiving for them; but he was not willing to stay there that night, but would go over to Salisbury, to hear further, and come again in the morning, which he did, and preached there that day. At night, when he had done, one came and told him that his daughter was come in at Providence.[8] Here was mercy on both hands. Now hath God fulfilled that precious Scripture which was such a comfort to me in my distressed condition, when my heart was ready to sink into the earth (my children being gone I could not tell whither), and my knees trembling under me. *And I was walking through the valley of the shadow of Death.*[9] Then the Lord brought, and now has fulfilled that

---

1 *recruited* Refreshed.

2 *for their temporals* I.e., in return for their worldly generosity.

3 *That which was dead* I.e., Rowlandson's daughter Sarah.

4 *from* Away from.

5 *disposer* Ruler; one who puts things in order.

6 *Mr. William Hubbard* Minister—and later a historian of King Philip's War—based in Ipswich, Massachusetts (1621–1704).

7 *Major Waldren* Colonial soldier Richard Waldron (1615–89).

8 *Providence* I.e., the settlement in Rhode Island.

9 *And I ... of Death* See Psalm 23.4.

reviving word unto me: Thus saith the Lord, *Refrain thy voice from weeping, and thine eyes from tears, for thy Work shall be rewarded*, saith the Lord, *and they shall come again from the Land of the Enemy*.[1] Now we were between them, the one on the East, and the other on the West; our son being nearest, we went to him first, to Portsmouth, where we met with him, and with the Major also, who told us he had done what he could, but could not redeem him under seven pounds, which the good people thereabouts were pleased to pay. The Lord reward the Major, and all the rest, though unknown to me, for their labour of love. My sister's son was redeemed for four pounds, which the Council gave order for the payment of. Having now received one of our children, we hastened toward the other. Going back through Newbury, my husband preached there on the Sabbath day, for which they rewarded him many fold.

On Monday we came to Charlestown, where we heard that the governor of Rhode Island had sent over for our daughter, to take care of her, being now within his jurisdiction, which should not pass without our acknowledgments. But she being nearer Rehoboth than Rhode Island, Mr. Newman went over, and took care of her, and brought her to his own house. And the goodness of God was admirable to us in our low estate, in that he raised up passionate friends on every side to us, when we had nothing to recompense any for their love. The Indians were now gone that way, that it was apprehended dangerous to go to her. But the carts which carried provision to the English army, being guarded, brought her with them to Dorchester, where we received her safe: blessed be the Lord for it, for great is his power, and He can do whatsoever seemeth him good. Her coming in was after this manner: She was travelling one day with the Indians, with her basket at her back; the company of Indians were got before her, and gone out of sight, all except one squaw; she followed the squaw till night, and then both of them lay down, having nothing over them but the heavens, and under them but the earth. Thus she travelled three days together, not knowing whither she was going, having nothing to eat or drink but water, and green hirtle-berries.[2] At last they came into Providence, where she was kindly entertained by several of that town. The Indians often said that I should never have her under twenty pounds; but now the Lord hath brought her in upon free cost, and given her to me the second time. The Lord make us a blessing indeed, each to others.[3] Now have I seen that Scripture also fulfilled, Deuteronomy 30.4–7. *If any of thine be driven out to the outmost parts of heaven, from thence will the Lord thy God gather thee, and from thence will he fetch thee. And the Lord thy God will put all these curses upon thine enemies, and on them which hate thee, which persecuted thee*. Thus hath the Lord brought me and mine out of that horrible pit, and hath set us in the midst of tender-hearted and compassionate Christians. It is the desire of my soul, that we may walk worthy of the mercies received, and which we are receiving.

Our family being now gathered together (those of us that were living), the South Church in Boston hired an house for us. Then we removed from Mr. Shepard's, those cordial friends, and went to Boston, where we continued about three quarters of a year. Still the Lord went along with us, and provided graciously for us. I thought it somewhat strange to set up housekeeping with bare walls; but as Solomon says, *Money answers all things*;[4] and that we had through the benevolence of Christian friends, some in this town, and some in that, and others; and some from England; that in a little time we might look, and see the house furnished with love. The Lord hath been exceeding good to us in our low estate, in that when we had neither house nor home, nor other necessaries, the Lord so moved the hearts of these and those towards us, that we wanted neither food, nor raiment for our selves or ours, Proverbs 18.24. *There is a Friend which sticketh closer than a Brother*. And how many such friends have we found, and now living amongst? And truly such a friend have we found him to be unto us, in whose house we lived, *viz.* Mr. James Whitcomb, a friend unto us near hand, and afar off.

---

[1]   *Thus saith … the Enemy*   See Jeremiah 31.16.

[2]   *hirtle-berries*   Whortleberries; any of a number of species in the genus Vaccinium, which includes huckleberries and blueberries.

[3]   *each to others*   I.e., to each other.

[4]   *Money answers all things*   See Ecclesiastes 10.19.

I can remember the time, when I used to sleep quietly without workings in my thoughts, whole nights together, but now it is other ways with me. When all are fast[1] about me, and no eye open, but his who ever waketh, my thoughts are upon things past, upon the awful dispensation of the Lord towards us; upon his wonderful power and might, in carrying of us through so many difficulties, in returning us in safety, and suffering none to hurt us. I remember in the night season, how the other day I was in the midst of thousands of enemies, and nothing but death before me; it is then hard work to persuade myself, that ever I should be satisfied with bread again. But now we are fed with the finest of the wheat, and, as I may say, *With honey out of the rock.*[2] Instead of the husk, we have the fatted calf. The thoughts of these things in the particulars of them, and of the love and goodness of God towards us, make it true of me, what David said of himself, Psalm 6.6. *I watered my Couch with my tears.* Oh! the wonderful power of God that mine eyes have seen, affording matter enough for my thoughts to run in, that when others are sleeping mine eyes are weeping.

I have seen the extreme vanity of this world.[3] One hour I have been in health, and wealth, wanting nothing; but the next hour in sickness and wounds, and death, having nothing but sorrow and affliction.

Before I knew what affliction meant, I was ready sometimes to wish for it. When I lived in prosperity, having the comforts of the world about me, my relations by me, my heart cheerful, and taking little care for anything; and yet seeing many, whom I preferred before myself, under many trials and afflictions, in sickness, weakness, poverty, losses, crosses, and cares of the world, I should be sometimes jealous least I should have my portion in this life, and that Scripture would come to my mind, Hebrews 12.6. *For whom the Lord loveth he chasteneth, and scourgeth every Son whom he receiveth.* But now I see the Lord had his time to scourge and chasten me. The portion of some is to have their afflictions by drops, now one drop and then another, but the dregs of the cup, the wine of astonishment: like a sweeping rain that leaveth no food, did the Lord prepare to be my portion. Affliction I wanted, and affliction I had full measure (I thought), pressed down and running over: yet I see, when God calls a person to anything, and through never so many difficulties, yet he is fully able to carry them through and make them see, and say they have been gainers thereby. And I hope I can say in some measure, as David did, *It is good for me that I have been afflicted.*[4] The Lord hath showed me the vanity of these outward things. That they are the vanity of vanities, and vexation of spirit; that they are but a shadow, a blast, a bubble, and things of no continuance. That we must rely on God himself, and our whole dependence must be upon him. If trouble from smaller matters begin to arise in me, I have something at hand to check myself with, and say, why am I troubled? It was but the other day that if I had had the world, I would have given it for my freedom, or to have been a servant to a Christian. I have learned to look beyond present and smaller troubles, and to be quieted under them, as Moses said, Exodus 14.13. *Stand still and see the salvation of the Lord.*

FINIS

1682

---

[1] *fast*   I.e., fast asleep.

[2] *fed with … the rock*   See Psalm 81.16.

[3] *vanity of this world*   Seventeenth-century meanings of *vanity* are only distantly related to the sense in which the word is most commonly used nowadays (i.e., to denote excessive regard for one's physical appearance). In the way that it is frequently used in sixteenth- and seventeenth-century translations of Ecclesiastes and other books of the Bible, *vanity* derives from a Hebrew word meaning *mist* or *vapor*—by extension, anything that does not last long, and that is insubstantial. According to Christian doctrine, all earthly things fall into that category.

---

[4] *It is … afflicted*   See Psalm 119.71.

IN CONTEXT

Editions of Rowlandson's Narrative

Only eight pages of the first edition of *The Sovereignty and Goodness of God*, published in Boston in 1682, have survived to today. Three more editions were, however, published that same year, two in Cambridge, Massachusetts, and one in London.

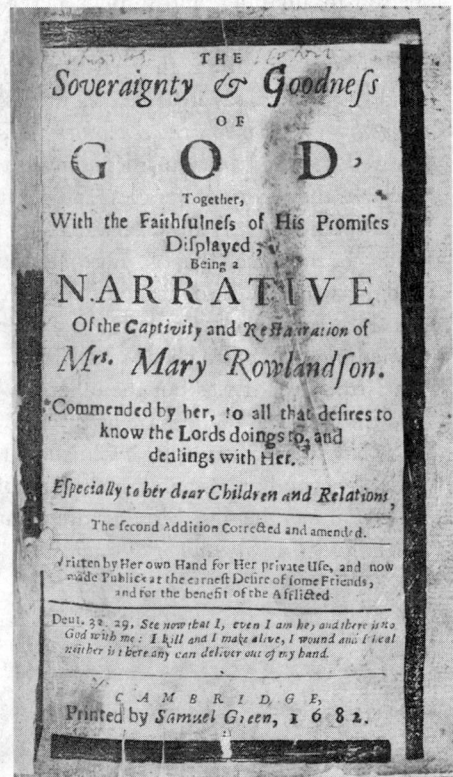

Title page to the first of two editions—called, respectively, the "second Addition" and the "second edition"—printed by Cambridge printer Samuel Green in 1682. Together, these two printings sold over one thousand copies.

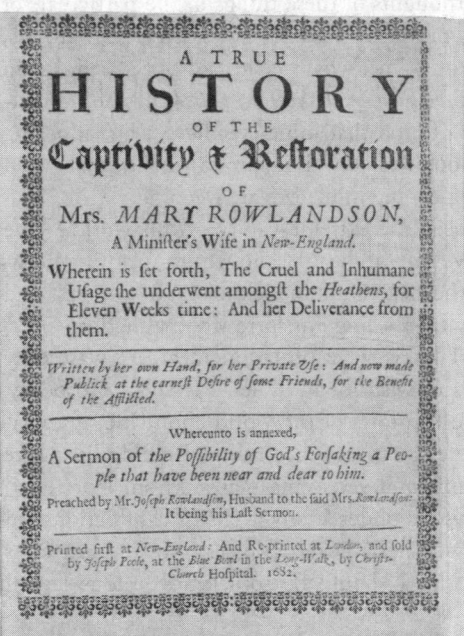

Title page to the London edition of Rowlandson's narrative, also printed in 1682.

IN CONTEXT

Picturing Mary Rowlandson

Editions of Rowlandson's narrative continued to be reissued well into the eighteenth century. Two such editions were notably accompanied by illustrations that seem intended to portray Rowlandson, though both these portrayals took significant liberties with the text's account of events.

This edition of Rowlandson's narrative, retitled to suit the tastes of the revolutionary era, was first released in 1773 (though the title page reproduced below is from a 1791 reprinting). Here, Rowlandson—who did not engage in combat at any point during the Lancaster raid—is depicted single-handedly fighting off a group of attackers armed with tomahawks and rifles.

This image was initially created for the frontispiece of a 1762 book called *The Life and Adventures of a Female Soldier*, which told the story of Hannah Snell, an English woman who had famously donned men's clothing and joined the British Navy earlier in the century. In 1770 the engraving was reused by the same printer in a new edition of Rowlandson's narrative; note the musket and gunpowder horn, the British flag over the fort in the distance, and the figure's distinctly eighteenth-century clothing, including a cocked hat.

IN CONTEXT

Indigenous Experiences of Metacom's War

Far more Indigenous people than settlers were held captive during and after King Philip's War. Some were taken as captives by other Indigenous people, sometimes including their own relations, but most were held captive by English settlers in a variety of ways: they were held in appalling conditions in internment camps; they were imprisoned for acts of war on the basis of little to no evidence; and, especially after the war, they were enslaved in large numbers.

Many of the documents included below relate to the forms of captivity experienced by "praying Indians," Indigenous allies of the English who had converted to Christianity and partially adopted European ways of living. These Indigenous Christians occupied a uniquely uncomfortable position in the conflict. As they struggled to maintain the diplomatic relationships they had entered into with the English, they often found themselves siding against their own relatives from outside the "praying towns"; some were even taken and held as captives by Metacom's forces. But the English—far more likely than Indigenous people to view the world in racial terms—tended to lump their Indigenous enemies and allies together and did not trust the Indigenous Christians regardless of their efforts to prove their loyalty. During the war, the English interned hundreds of their Indigenous allies, most infamously transporting many hundreds to Deer Island on the Massachusetts coast where, inadequately provisioned and deprived of their usual livelihoods, about half died over the winter.

By the summer of 1676, English forces were roaming the countryside capturing or killing Indigenous combatants, non-combatants, and allies almost indiscriminately. The petitions at the end of this selection represent the efforts of Indigenous leaders with longstanding relationships to the English—many of whom had gone to extraordinary lengths to aid the English side during the war—to negotiate the safe surrender of their families and communities. These efforts did succeed in obtaining some individuals' lives and freedoms, but overall the English were ruthless in punishing as criminals almost any Indigenous people who could not concretely prove their constant loyalty to the English, including those who had surrendered in response to offers of amnesty. Many were publicly executed, indentured for long periods (a fate especially common for children), or enslaved for life and either kept locally or forcibly transported for sale in Barbados, Bermuda, and other colonies.

NOTE ON THE TEXTS: Unless otherwise indicated, the editors have consulted several sources, including the manuscript versions, in preparing the following texts for the anthology; we are especially indebted to the work of Lisa Brooks, who discusses many of them in her landmark work *Our Beloved Kin: A New History of King Philip's War* (2018) and includes many of them on a website associated with the book. Several of the selections below are based on their transcriptions in *An Historical Account of the Doings and Sufferings of the Christian Indians in New England in the Years 1675, 1676, 1677* (1677) by Daniel Gookin, who was "Superintendent of the Praying Indians" and whose account of King Philip's War is more sympathetic and reliable than most other settler accounts from the period.

from John Easton, letter to Josiah Winslow, 26 May 1675

John Easton, Deputy Governor of Rhode Island, wrote the following letter to Plymouth Governor Josiah Winslow on behalf of Weetamoo, the saunkskaw (woman sachem) of the Pocasset, a Wampanoag tribe. Written a month before King Philip's War began, the letter articulates the concerns that would lead Weetamoo to join the war against the English: namely that English settlements were, increasingly, interfering with Pocasset territory and disrupting Pocasset livelihoods. Weetamoo had substantial troops at her disposal and played a major role in King Philip's War until her death during the conflict; she also appears (as Wettimore) in Rowlandson's *Narrative*.

Friend Josiah Winslow, Governor of Plymouth Colony,

Weetamoo the queen of Pocasset and her husband showed me a letter—Constant Southworth[1] and other names to it, dated April 30, 75—by which they have great fear of oppression from the English, [so] that they could not tell how to trust me, but [feared] that I would to please the English join to do them wrong. ... [W]hat they would now have [as] their bounds north and south is to maintain a river at each end by which they have great dependence for fish, but are free to accommodate thee or whom they shall admit with thee of four mile square of land at least[.] ... But by having their other bounds confirmed in their records they shall agree to what more they will give them. They prefer so fair and as it appeareth to me desire only of you what is their reasonable due that I have large hope you will not deny it, and to have the difference decided as to them it may appear not to be by such as determine in their own case.[2] I am persuaded both may be so satisfied. I am largely engaged in myself to manifest to them that I am not false, but to endeavor they may have right according to English law, and hope it will not be in any opposition to your desires or to your rule in your colony. I know about 60 have confirmed to the queen's right to be to a far greater tract of land beside what now she and they would be contented with. ...

John Easton

James Quannapaquait with unnamed magistrates, *The Examination and Relation of James Quannapaquait, alias James Rumny-Marsh*[3] (January 1676)

James Quannapaquait and Job Kattenanit, two Indigenous Christians being held at Deer Island, were enlisted as spies and sent to learn about the plans of Metacom's followers; after their service, they were sent back to Deer Island. Quannapaquait's extensive account of their experiences, excerpted here, was recorded by the magistrates who heard his testimony, and offers insight into the experiences and motivations of Indigenous people on both sides of King Philip's War.

The examination and relation of James Quannapaquait, alias James Rumny-Marsh, being one of the Christian Indians belonging to Natick;[4] taken the 24th day of January 1675/6,[5] on which day he returned from his journey (for this man and another called Job of Magunkaquog,[6] a Christian man also)

---

[1] *Constant Southworth* Treasurer of the Plymouth Colony. Southworth was one of many people in the colony hoping to expand their own land holdings into Pocasset territory.

[2] *to have ... own case* I.e., I hope you will agree to have the dispute resolved by judges who will not appear to decide the matter according to their own interests.

[3] The present text is based upon the version reprinted in Josiah Howard Temple's *History of North Brookfield, Massachusetts* (1887).

[4] *Natick* Indigenous praying community.

[5] *1675/6* The writers here employ the practice of dual dating, which accounts for the fact that the date of the beginning of the new year varied among countries still using the Julian calendar, such as Britain and its colonies, where the new year was marked on 25 March.

[6] *Magunkaquog* Indigenous praying community.

were sent forth by order of the council of Massachusetts upon the last of December (as spies) to discover the enemies' quarters and motions and his state and condition, and to gain what intelligence they could; for which end they had particular instruction. Though when first they were moved to go [on] this journey, they saw it would be a hazardous undertaking, and that they should run the hazard of their lives in it, yet they were willing to venture upon these and like considerations. First, that they might declare their readiness to serve the English. Secondly, one of them, namely Job, had three children (even all he had) that were carried away with the Hassanamesit Indians and, as he conceived were with the enemy, and he was willing to know their state as well as the condition of the praying Indians of Hassanamesit and Magunkaquog that were he thought in the power of the enemy. Third, they hoped to suggest something in order to the enemy's submission to the English and making peace if they found the enemy in a temper fit for it. And if that could be effected then they hoped the poor Christian Indians at the Deer Island and in other places possibly might be restored to their places again, and be freed from much suffering they are now in by this war, and thereby the jealousies[1] that the English have now of them might be removed. These and other reasons induced them to run this adventure for which also if they returned in safety they had a promise of a reward.

They doubted[2] the Indian enemy would mistrust them for spies, and that they would move the fight for them against the English, unto which doubts they were advised to tell the Indian enemy a lamentable story (and yet agreeable to truth) of their deep sufferings by the English; that Job was imprisoned several days (as he was) where he suffered much, though he had served the English faithfully as an interpreter and in actual arms being with the Mohegans at the fight near Secunke with Philip, the beginning of August last, but imprisonment and suspicions the English had of him was part of his reward for that service to the English. …

… [Y]et after all these services both they and their wives and children and all their country men that lived at Natick were mistrusted by the English and thereupon (at a few hours warning) brought away from their place and fort and houses at Natick and carried down in boats to Deer Island, leaving and losing much of their substance, cattle, swine, horse and corn, and at the island were exposed to great sufferings having little wood for fuel, a bleak place and poor wigwams such as they could make a shift to make themselves with a few mats. And here at the island had very little provision, many of them, and diverse other sorrows and troubles they were exposed to, and were about 350 souls men, women, and children; and that now having an opportunity to get off the island they came to see how things were with the Indians in the woods; and if they preferred them to fight with and for them they were advised to manifest all readiness and forwardness and not show any averseness. Things being thus prepared these two spies were sent away without arms excepting hatchets and with a little parched meal[3] for provision. …

… At this place among these Indians they found all the Christian Indians belonging to Hassanamesit and Magunkaquog, which are about 40 men and about 80 women and children; these praying Indians were carried away by the enemy. Some went willingly, others of them unwillingly, as they told him, for before they went away they were in a great strait, for if they came to the English they knew they should be sent to Deer Island, as others were, and their corn being at such a distance about 40 miles from Boston, it could not be caried to sustain their lives and so they should be in danger to famish and others feared they should be sent away to Barbados, or other places. And to stay at Hassanamesit these Indians or enemies would not permit them, but said they must have the corn, but promised them if they would go with them they should not die but be preserved. These being in this condition most of them thought it best to go with them though they feared death every way. …

Further he saith that he understood by the chief men and old men yet they were inclinable to have peace again with the English, but the young men (who are their principal soldiers) say "We will have no peace. We are all or most of us alive yet and the English have killed very few of us last summer. Why shall

---

[1]   *jealousies* Suspicions.

[2]   *doubted* Feared.

[3]   *parched meal* Dried ground grain.

we have peace to be made slaves, and either be killed or sent away to sea to Barbadoes, etc.? Let us live as long as we can and die like men, and not live to be enslaved." …

Massachusetts Council, order regarding Indigenous allies[1] (30 August 1675)

Even before the Massachusetts Council began to confine its Indigenous allies to sites such as Deer Island, it imposed substantial restrictions on their freedom of movement. The following Massachusetts Council order was imposed near the beginning of the war.

At a Council held in Boston, August 30th, 1675

The Council judging it of absolute necessity for security of the English and Indians in amity with us, that they be restrained their usual commerce with the English and hunting in the woods, during the time of hostility with those that are our enemies; do order, that all those Indians that are desirous to approve themselves faithful to the English be confined to the several places underwritten, until the Council shall take further order, and that they so order the setting of their wigwams that they may stand compact in one place of their plantations respectively, where it may be best for their own provision and defence, and that none of them do presume to travel above one mile from the centre of such of their dwellings unless in company of some English, or in their service, excepting for gathering in their corn with one Englishman in company, on peril of being taken as our enemies, or their abettors. And in case any of them be taken without the limits aforesaid except as above said, and do lose their lives, or be otherwise damnified[2] by English or Indians; the Council do hereby declare that they shall account themselves wholly innocent, and their blood, or other damage by them sustained, will be upon their own heads. Also, it shall not be lawful for any Indians that are now in amity with us to entertain any strange Indians, or to receive any of our enemies' plunder, but shall from time to time make discovery thereof to some English[3] that shall be appointed for that end to sojourn with them, on penalty of being accounted our enemies, and to be proceeded against as such.

Also, whereas it is the manner of the heathen that are now in hostility with us, contrary to the practice of civil nations, to execute their bloody insolences by stealth, and skulking in small parties, declining all open decision of the controversy, either by treaty or by the sword; the Council do therefore order, that after the publication of the provision aforesaid, it shall be lawful for any person, whether English or Indian, that shall find any Indian travelling in any of our towns or woods, contrary to the limits above-named, to command them under their guard and examination, or to kill and destroy them as they best may or can. The Council hereby declaring, that it will be most acceptable to them that none be killed or wounded that are willing to surrender themselves into custody.

The places of the Indians' residence are Natick, Punkapoag, Nashobah, Wamesit, and Hassanamesit. And if there be any that belong to other places, they are to repair to some one of these.

By the Council.

Edward Rawson, *Secretary*.

Numphow and John Line, letter to Thomas Henchman, November 1675

In November 1675, a group of vigilantes from Chelmsford attacked the people of Wamesit, a nearby praying town. The vigilantes falsely believed people from Wamesit to be responsible for

---

[1] The present text is based on the version included in Gookin's *Historical Account*.

[2] *damnified* Injured.

[3] *but shall … English* Unless they declare it to an English person.

the burning of a barn full of hay and grain, and in retaliation they shot six noncombatants, including a child who died of his wounds. This was not the first retaliatory attack Chelmsford had made on Wamesit, its ostensible ally, but for many in Wamesit it was the last straw. The following letter was written by Wamesit leaders Numphow and John Line as they led a group north in an attempt to escape conflict with the English. The letter is addressed to Thomas Henchman, a Chelmsford resident with authority over Wamesit, who at the request of the Massachusetts Council had sent a messenger, Wepocositt, to try to persuade them to come back.

First, Numphow, and John a Line, we send a messenger to you again (Wepocositt) with this answer, we cannot come home again, we go towards the French, we go where Wannalancet[1] is; the reason is we went away from our home, we had help from the Council, but that did not do us good, but we had wrong by the English. Secondly, the reason is we went away from the English, for when there was any harm done in Chelmsford, they laid it to us, and said we did it, but we know ourselves we never did any harm to the English, but we go away peaceably and quietly. Thirdly, as for the Island,[2] we say there is no safety for us, because many English be not good, and may be they come to us and kill us, as in the other case. We are not sorry for what we leave behind, but we are sorry the English have driven us from our praying to God and from our teacher. We did begin to understand a little of praying to God. We thank humbly the Council. We remember our love to Mr. Henchman and James Richardson.[3]

James Printer

James Printer, also known to his Nipmuc community as Wowaus, began an apprenticeship at Cambridge Press at a young age. During his career there he worked on, among many other texts, the first Bible published in North America. Though he attempted to maintain neutrality during King Philip's War, Printer was held captive by both sides. First, he was one of eleven Indigenous Christians who were falsely accused of a 1675 raid on Lancaster, the settlement where Rowlandson would herself be abducted in another attack later in the war. As Daniel Gookin's account below details, these falsely accused men, Printer included, were incarcerated for weeks and almost killed by an angry mob during the trial that ultimately found all but one of them innocent. After Printer returned to his hometown of Hassanamesit, which had become a praying community allied with the English, he and other residents were captured by Metacom's fighters. During his captivity Printer appears to have come to sympathize with the resisters' aims and to have worked as a scribe on Metacom's behalf; the note reprinted below is widely attributed to him.

Printer never gave up his ties to the English. After the war, he helped to negotiate amnesty for some of the Indigenous survivors and returned to his trade of typesetting. One of the works he would eventually typeset was Rowlandson's *The Sovereignty and Goodness of God*.

---

[1] *Wannalancet* Penacook sachem (c. 1619–97) who had led his community north to what is now New Hampshire, hoping to escape the English. Generally speaking, the areas immediately to the north of the English colonies on the Atlantic coast were occupied by the French or disputed between the French and English.

[2] *the Island* Deer Island, where the English forced many of their Indigenous allies to live during the war.

[3] *James Richardson* Chelmsford resident who, along with Henchman, had been given some authority over the Wamesit community. The burned barn belonged to him, but he had maintained his belief in the innocence of the people of Wamesit and attempted to act as their ally.

from DANIEL GOOKIN, *AN HISTORICAL ACCOUNT OF THE DOINGS AND SUFFERINGS OF THE CHRISTIAN INDIANS IN NEW ENGLAND IN THE YEARS 1675, 1676, 1677* (1677)

... [T]he pretence for seizing these fifteen Marlborough Indians and sending them down as prisoners was this, that eleven of them had committed a notorious murder upon seven English persons at Lancaster upon a Lord's day, August 22nd. The next and immediate accuser of these Indians was one David, an Indian, one of the fifteen, who being suspected for shooting at a lad belonging to the English of Marlborough that was sent out by his master to look up some sheep, this David being apprehended by the aforesaid captain upon the former suspicion, and fastened to a tree to be shot to death, and fearing to drink of the same cup as his brother Andrew had done a fortnight before, being shot to death by some soldiers at the same place. ... But David, as aforesaid, being fastened to a tree, and guns bent at him, feared death, and being offered a reprieve if he would confess truth, he promised something, and so was unbound, and then accused eleven of the Indians then at the fort, and now prisoners, to be murderers of the English at Lancaster before mentioned; "but," said he, "I did not see it done, neither was I there, but I heard some speak so."

David was hereupon released from present death, but yet was sent down prisoner with the rest, and being examined before the Council, he at first owned[1] that he had said so to the Captain, at Marlborough; but afterward, upon the trial before the court and jury, he said he had accused those Indians falsely. Indeed some of the accused Indians, particularly one named James Akompanet, a very understanding fellow, pleaded in behalf of himself and the rest, that what David said against them, was, first, to save his own life when he was bound to the tree, secondly, to revenge himself of them because they had seized upon his brother Andrew, and his son, and delivered them to the English, one whereof was put to death, and the other sent out of the country, a slave.

... [All the people on] trial were acquitted, except one man, who was found guilty of being accessory to the murder; but this man, named Joseph Spoonant, was tried by another jury, not the same that tried the others. Upon what ground the jury went, I know not; but the man was sold for a slave and sent out of the country. Also, the first adviser of them all, called David, was condemned to be sold, his crime alleged for suspicion of shooting an Irish boy at Marlborough, and for accusing the others falsely; but all the rest were discharged. ...

But before this business was fully examined and issued, the clamors of the people were very great upon this occasion, and all things against those praying Indians accused (as one of the most intelligent of the magistrates said) were represented as very great, as things appear in mist or fog. Some men were so violent that they would have had these Indians put to death by martial law, and not tried by a jury, though they were subjects under the English protection, and not in hostility with us; others had received such impressions in their minds, that they could hardly extend charity to the jurors and magistrates that acquitted them. ... Although I mention the story of this matter in this place, yet it was towards the latter end of September, before these Indians were tried and acquitted, all which time they remained in prison, under great sufferings. ...

ATTRIBUTED TO JAMES PRINTER, NOTE TACKED TO A TREE, C. 1676

Though English man hath provoked us to anger and wrath and we care not though we have war with you this 21 years—for there are many of us, 300 of which have fought with you at this town. We have nothing but our lives to lose, but thou hast many fair houses, cattle, and much good things.

---

[1] *owned* Admitted.

from Andrew Pittimee, Quanahpohkit, John Mague, and James Speen, petition to the Governor and Council of the Massachusetts Colony,[1] June 1676

In the following petition, a group of Indigenous officers who had served on the English side attempt to secure the freedom of a number of individuals being imprisoned by the English. The subjects of the petition include "Captain Tom" Wuttasacomponom, a Hassanamesit leader who had been held captive twice during the war. First, he was captured by Metacom's forces when they invaded Hassanamesit; he and his family eventually escaped or were freed but, they would later say, were too afraid to return to the English. In the spring of 1676, Indigenous scouts working for the English found him and his family and brought them in.

The success of the petition was limited but significant. The English publicly hanged Wuttasacomponom but did free the women and children the officers had requested. English authorities also responded to the suggestion "that others that are out, and love the English, may be encouraged to come in" by implementing a two-week period during which Indigenous individuals could request amnesty from the settlers. This negotiation undoubtedly saved some lives—though, as they would discover, those seeking amnesty could not be assured of a friendly reception.

To the Honourable the Governor and Council of the Massachusetts Colony, Assembled at Boston this —— of June 1676

The humble petition of Andrew Pittimee, Quanahpohkit, *alias* James Rumney Marsh, John Magus, and James Speen, officers unto the Indian soldiers, now in your service, with the consent of the rest of the Indian soldiers being about eighty men;

Humbly imploreth your favour and mercies to be extended to some of the prisoners taken by us, (most of them) near Lancaster, Marlborough, etc., in whose behalf we are bold to supplicate your Honours. And we have three reasons for this humble supplication. First, because the persons we beg pardon for, as we are informed, are innocent, and have not done any wrong or injury unto the English, all this war time, only were against their wills taken and kept among the enemy. Secondly, because it pleased your Honours to say to some of us, to encourage us to fidelity and activity in your service, that you would be ready to do anything for us that was fit for us to ask and you to grant. Thirdly, that others that are out, and love the English, may be encouraged to come in. More that we humbly intercede for, is the lives and liberties of those few of our poor friends and kindred, that, in this time of temptation and affliction, have been in the enemy's quarters; we hope it will be no grief of heart to you to show mercy, and especially to such who have (as we conceive) done no wrong to the English. If we did think, or had any ground to conceive that they were naught, and were enemies to the English, we would not intercede for them, but rather bear our testimony against them, as we have done. We have (especially some of us) been sundry times in your service to the hazard of our lives, both as spies, messengers, scouts, and soldiers, and have through God's favour acquitted ourselves faithfully, and shall do as long as we live endeavour with all fidelity to fight in the English cause, which we judge is our cause, and also God's cause, to oppose the wicked Indians, enemies to God and all goodness. In granting this our humble request, you will much oblige us who desire to remain,

Your Honour's Humble and Faithful Servants

Andrew Pittimee,
James Quanapohkhit,
Job,
John Magus,
James Speen

---

[1]   The present text is based on the version included in Gookin's *Historical Account*.

Sor Juana Inés de la Cruz
1648 – 1695

During the latter decades of the seventeenth century, Sor Juana Inés de la Cruz, a Hieronymite nun based in Mexico City, was among the best-known writers in the Spanish-speaking world. Her poetry and plays, on themes ranging from the religious to the secular, were read and performed at the courts in both New Spain and Madrid. Though her status as a woman writer certainly invoked criticism from conservative religious leaders, for much of her career her work was overwhelmingly well-received, and Sor Juana herself was praised as the "Tenth Muse of America."

Juana Inés Ramírez was born in the village of San Miguel Nepantla in 1648, the daughter of unmarried parents; baptized as a "daughter of the Church," she went by her mother's surname and was brought up by her mother and various wealthier maternal relatives. Extremely precocious as a child, Juana claimed in her autobiographical writings to have learned to read and write at the age of three. Different historical sources conflict as to the order of events, but it is clear that as a child she read voraciously from her grandfather's substantial library, that she mastered Latin at a young age, and that around the age of eight or ten she was sent to the viceregal court in Mexico City, where she astonished the high society with her wit, intellectual avidity, and vivacious personality, and where she wrote her first poems. It was during this period that she was introduced to the New Spanish vicereine, Leonor Carreto, and later to her successor, María Luisa Manrique de Lara Y Gonzaga—both of whom would become important patrons of Juana's writing. Sor Juana, who wrote love poetry with both male and female subjects, dedicated several passionate lyrics to María Luisa.

Given her apparently rich life at court—and lack of any particularly strong religious inclination—Juana's choice to enter the monastic life may seem puzzling. It is worth noting, however, that the Catholic convents of New Spain were a common refuge for young women who were either unwilling or unable to marry. In 1667 Juana entered the Discalced Carmelite order as a novice, but found the lifestyle there far too austere, and left after only three months. Two years later, however, she joined the Convent of Santa Paula (later San Jéronimo), which was known for its comparative leniency in the enforcement of rules. Here she lived for the remaining twenty-six years of her life, taking on the name Sor (Sister) Juana Inés de la Cruz (of the Cross).

Though officially cloistered from the outside, secular world, in reality the convent allowed its members a large degree of connectedness to the Mexican metropolis, as well as a greater amount of independence than would have been available to them as either married or unmarried laywomen. The nuns were accorded private cells, often consisting of several rooms, were allowed to acquire personal possessions such as jewelry and books, and were often given paid work; Sor Juana, for instance, was employed as the convent's accounts keeper. Though they were expected to adhere to a regular schedule of prayer and to participate in some communal meals and needlework sessions, they were also permitted to spend much of their time alone, and to receive visitors in the convent's outer parlor. Many of the sisters had personal servants, and Sor Juana herself owned at least one enslaved maidservant during her time at the convent. During her apparently ample personal time, Sor Juana studied the sciences, mathematics, philosophy, architecture, music theory, theology, and literature, over the years amassing one of the largest private libraries in the colonial Americas. Perhaps most significantly, she kept up a vibrant correspondence with the outside world, including with several New Spanish viceroyals, who corresponded with her both from New Spain and from the court at Madrid.

Throughout the 1680s, Sor Juana took advantage of her close personal connection to New Spain's colonial nobility, and her literary writings became highly sought after at the Mexican court. Her writings included plays, various forms of secular and religious song to be performed at courtly ceremonies and religious services, odes in honor of important personages or public occasions, and lyric poems—many of them dealing with romantic themes. Her work reflects mastery of a Baroque Mexican literary aesthetic, which includes highly ornate, often exaggerative language, intricate metaphors, and copious references to classical literature and philosophy; some of her villancicos (poetic compositions sung during religious services) also incorporate the Indigenous Nahuatl language. Though her works show the influence of eminent Spanish Baroque poets such as Luis de Góngora, poems such as her epic *First Dream* (first published 1692) have also been likened by recent scholars to the works of much-later symbolist poets such as Stéphane Mallarmé and modernist poets such as T.S. Eliot; *First Dream*, a mythologically inspired, gender-fluid depiction of a soul's pursuit of intellectual knowledge, has also been extensively analyzed for its resonances with later feminist thought.

Little evidence has survived to indicate a first date of composition for many of Sor Juana's works. A first volume of her poetry was published in Spain in 1689 as *The Overflowing of the Castalian Spring, by the Tenth Muse of America* (the "Castalian Spring" refers to a fountain in Greek mythology said to inspire poetic genius). Two more volumes would follow, with the *Second Volume of Her Works* published in Seville in 1692 and *Fame and Posthumous Works of the Mexican Phoenix* in Madrid in 1700. Sor Juana's name became mired in controversy near the end of 1690, when her tract criticizing a sermon by venerated Portuguese Jesuit António Vieira was published without her consent. The document raised the ire of a number of religious authority figures, who began to pressure her to desist from her literary and intellectual interests. It is unclear whether Sor Juana continued to write after 1691; she fell into relative obscurity until her death during an epidemic in 1695.

Over the following two centuries, Sor Juana was largely ignored by scholars and readers; no volumes of her poetry were re-issued between 1725 and 1940. Interest in her oeuvre was reignited in the mid-twentieth century, especially after the publication of Mexican poet Octavio Paz's influential biography *Sor Juana, or The Traps of Faith* in 1982. Since then, her poetry has been extensively studied by both Mexican and international scholars, and Sor Juana has become regarded once again as one of the most important figures of seventeenth-century colonial literature.

NOTE ON THE TEXTS: The English-language texts presented below are based upon those appearing in Alan S. Trueblood's edition, *A Sor Juana Anthology* (1988), whose translations are in turn based on the Spanish versions appearing in *Obras selectas* (Georgina Sabat de Rivers and Elias L. Rivers, 1976) and *Obras completas* (Alfonso Méndez Plancarte, 1952 and 1955). Trueblood's in-line translations of Latin material quoted by Sor Juana have been moved to the footnotes. The Spanish-language text of poem 82 presented here is based on the version first published in *Inundacion Castalida de la Unica Poetisa, Musa Dezima, Soror Juana Inés de la Cruz* (1689). The spelling and punctuation of the Spanish have not been modernized.

⌘ ⌘ ⌘

82

Expressa su respecto amoroso, y dize el sentido en que llama suya, à la Señora Virreyna.

Divina Lysi mía:
perdona, si me atrevo,
à llamarte assi, quando
aun, de ser tuya, el nombre no merezco.

5   A èsto, no osadia
es llamarte assi; puesto,
que à ti te sobran rayos,
si en mi pudiera aver atrevimientos.
Error es de la lengua;

10   que lo que dize Imperio
del dueño, en el dominio,
parezcan possessiones, en el siervo.
Mi Rey, dize el Vassallo,
mi Carcel, dize el preso,

15   y el mas humilde Esclavo,
sin agraviarlo, llama suyo, al dueño.
Assi, quando yo mia,
te llamo, no pretendo,
que juzguen, que eres mia,

20   sino solo, que yo ser tuya, quiero.
Yo te vi; pero basta,
que à publicar incendios,
basta apuntar la causa;
sin añadir la culpa del efecto.

25   Que mirarte tan alta,
no impide à mi denuedo;
que no ay Deidad segura
al altivo volar del pensamiento.
Y aunque otras más merezcan;

30   en distancia del Cielo,
lo mismo dista el valle
mas humilde, que el monte más sobervio.
En fin yo de adorarte
el delito confiesso;

35   si quieres castigarme,
esse mismo castigo serà premio.
—1689

82

She expresses her loving respect, explaining what she means when she says Her Ladyship the Vicereine, Marquise de la Laguna, belongs to her[1]

My divine Lysis:
do forgive my darling,
if so I address you,
unworthy though I am to be known as yours.

5   I cannot think it bold
to call you so, well knowing
you've ample thunderbolts
to shatter any overweening[2] of mine.
It's the tongue that misspeaks

10   when what is called dominion—
I mean, the master's rule—
is made to seem possession by the slave.
The vassal says: my king;
my prison, the convict says;

15   and any humble slave
will call the master his without offense.
Thus, when I call you mine,
it's not that I expect
you'll be considered such—

20   only that I hope I may be yours.
I saw you—need more be said?
To broadcast a fire,
telling the cause suffices—
no need to apportion blame for the effect.

25   Seeing you so exalted
does not prevent my daring;
no god is ever secure
against the lofty flight of human thought.
There are women more deserving,

30   yet in distance from heaven
the humblest of valleys
seems no farther than the highest peak.
In sum, I must admit
to the crime of adoring you;

35   should you wish to punish me,
the very punishment will be reward.
—1988

---

[1]   *She expresses … to her*   These headings were included in the first editions of Sor Juana's collected works; scholars are unsure as to who wrote them.

[2]   *overweening*   Presumptuousness.

92

She demonstrates the inconsistency of men's wishes in blaming
women for what they themselves have caused

Silly, you men—so very adept
at wrongly faulting womankind,
not seeing you're alone to blame
for faults you plant in woman's mind.

5   After you've won by urgent plea
the right to tarnish her good name,
you will expect her to behave—
you, that coaxed her into shame.

You batter her resistance down
10 and then, all righteousness, proclaim
that feminine frivolity,
not your persistence, is to blame.

When it comes to bravely posturing,
your witlessness must take the prize:
15 you're the child that makes a bogeyman,
and then recoils in fear and cries.

Presumptuous beyond belief,
you'd have the woman you pursue
be Thais[1] when you're courting her,
20 Lucretia[2] once she falls to you.

For plain default of common sense,
could any action be so queer
as oneself to cloud the mirror,
then complain that it's not clear?

25 Whether you're favored or disdained,
nothing can leave you satisfied.
You whimper if you're turned away,
you sneer if you've been gratified.

With you, no woman can hope to score;
30 whichever way, she's bound to lose;
spurning you, she's ungrateful;
succumbing, you call her lewd.

Your folly is always the same:
you apply a single rule
35 to the one you accuse of looseness
and the one you brand as cruel.

What happy mean could there be
for the woman who catches your eye,
if, unresponsive, she offends
40 yet whose complaisance you decry?

Still, whether it's torment or anger—
and both ways you've yourselves to blame—
God bless the woman who won't have you,
no matter how loud you complain.

45 It's your persistent entreaties
that change her from timid to bold.
Having made her thereby naughty,
you would have her good as gold.

So where does the greater guilt lie
50 for a passion that should not be:
with the man who pleads out of baseness
or the woman debased by his plea?

Or which is more to be blamed—
though both will have cause for chagrin:
55 the woman who sins for money
or the man who pays money to sin?

So why are you men all so stunned
at the thought you're all guilty alike?
Either like them for what you've made them
60 or make of them what you can like.

If you'd give up pursuing them,
you'd discover, without a doubt,
you've a stronger case to make
against those who seek you out.

65 I well know what powerful arms
you wield in pressing for evil:
your arrogance is allied
with the world, the flesh, and the devil!
—1689 (TRANSLATION 1988)

---

[1] *Thais* Ancient Greek courtesan (c. 4th century BCE) who followed the troops of Alexander the Great during his conquests. She was known as a lover of one of Alexander's generals and possibly of Alexander himself.

[2] *Lucretia* Ancient Roman noblewoman (c. 6th century BCE) who is said to have been raped by Sextus Tarquinus, the son of the last king of Rome, and to have subsequently died by suicide.

COTTON MATHER

<u>1663 – 1728</u>

Puritan minister and intellectual Cotton Mather is often vilified as a repressive fanatic responsible for the deadly moral panic known as the Salem witch trials. But the real Mather was far more complex: while he was the key spokesperson for the trials' legitimacy, his earlier work advocated the sympathetic treatment of witches; in addition to his religious studies he was a popularizer of scientific advances and, for his accomplishments in the sciences, was made a fellow of the Royal Society; he argued strenuously in support of gender hierarchy, class divisions, and slavery, but he also asserted the potential equality of all souls. Some American historians have viewed Mather's work as expressing the last gasp of Puritan dominance in New England, while others have seen him as a participant in a cultural shift, transforming older religious ideas into a form that could be carried forward into the eighteenth century.

Born in Boston, the capital of the Massachusetts Bay Colony, Cotton Mather was the son of the spiritual leader Increase Mather, and the grandson of Richard Mather and John Cotton, Puritan clerics who were instrumental in the colony's foundation. A gifted child, Mather enrolled in Harvard (where his father was president) at age eleven, the youngest person to be admitted to the college. Mather firmly believed that his parentage obliged him to accomplish great things; he also, like many Puritans, believed in the Calvinist doctrine that he—like all humans—was a depraved creature who deserved any suffering he experienced. Mather's classmates found his piety insufferable, and he was frequently subjected to physical violence from his peers. For much of his youth, Mather worked to overcome a stutter that threatened to prevent him from becoming a minister.

Mather applied himself to his studies, and he graduated from Harvard in 1678 with an education in Latin, Greek, and Hebrew, having read deeply across the sciences and humanities. He continued to expand his knowledge throughout his life; in addition to accessing his father's library and the Harvard library, he would come to own more than three thousand books, forming one of the largest personal libraries in America. Writing in an ornate, allusive writing style more common to writers of the sixteenth century, he published almost four hundred books and pamphlets over his lifetime—by some estimates, more than the output of all other New England ministers combined. Of these, his most celebrated work during his lifetime was the *Magnalia Christi Americana* (1702), a religious history of seventeenth-century New England. At the same time, he spent decades of his life working on his *Biblia Americana*, a sprawling work of biblical commentary that totaled forty-five hundred manuscript pages at the time of his death; largely because of its size and complexity, this work remained unpublished until the twenty-first century.

In 1685, Mather was ordained as pastor of North Boston Church, the same post once held by his father. Massachusetts was in the midst of major cultural and political changes: in the 1680s, the English government revoked the Massachusetts Bay Colony's charter, a move that destabilized the power of the Puritan ruling class Mather belonged to. At the same time, the dogmatically religious society that the Puritans had established was giving way to a more secular and rationalistic culture. Mather's preaching called upon individuals to deepen their relationships with God and come to see, as Mather and other Puritans did, the divine and the demonic as fully entangled with everyday life. In one typical sermon, he encouraged Christians to feel the warmth of God's love, saying, "There is nothing that will bring you so near Heaven, or help you lead a Heavenly life, as to keep alive a comfortable persuasion ... that God your savior has loved you." Mather also undertook many community projects, including extensive efforts to convert the enslaved people of Boston to Christianity. He put forward his ideas regarding the importance of good works in the widely read book *Bonifacius, or Essays to Do Good* (1710)—a work Benjamin Franklin would later satirize through his writing persona "Silence Dogood," but which he would also come to credit with inspiring his own desire to be "a useful citizen."

Mather's life took a dramatic turn in 1688, when a family was afflicted by what Boston's spiritual and medical authorities considered a case of demonic possession. After an Irish Catholic washerwoman was held responsible and executed for witchcraft, Mather took it upon himself to care for one of the affected children. He undertook a study of her symptoms and published his findings in *Memorable Providences, Relating to Witchcrafts and Possessions* (1689). Widely read in England and America, the text established Mather as an expert on witchcraft and popularized the notion that the devil was at work in Massachusetts.

In 1692, reports of witchcraft emerged from Salem Village, and a special court was established to investigate the situation. In an ambiguous letter to the judges, Mather voiced support for the trial, but also urged caution. "[I]t is necessary that all proceedings thereabout be managed with an exceeding tenderness towards those that may be complained of," his letter declared, but he appeared to contradict this warning with the closing statement that "[n]evertheless, we cannot but humbly recommend unto the government, the speedy and vigorous prosecution" of witches. Mather's letter was either disregarded or taken as an endorsement of the proceedings: nineteen people were convicted and executed on spurious evidence, and one man was crushed to death when he refused to enter a plea. Mather was not present for the trials, but he may have attended at least one execution.

After the executions were carried out, Mather composed an account of events, *Wonders of the Invisible World* (1692), with the endorsement of the lieutenant governor, William Stoughton, one of the trials' fiercest judges. Though the book expresses occasional reservations regarding the trials, its overall thrust is to justify the proceedings and vindicate the judges' decisions. *Wonders of the Invisible World* would be followed by an outpouring of oppositional tracts, the most famous of which was Robert Calef's *More Wonders of the Invisible World* (1700). Calef, who appears to have hated Mather, accused him of "carrying both fire to increase, and water to quench, the conflagration." The portrait of Mather put forward in *More Wonders* helped to shape his popular image in later centuries as a figure of oppression and superstition.

Mather studied natural phenomena with the same experimental eye he used to study witchcraft. He was one of the strongest advocates for science and modern medicine in Massachusetts. In 1721, when Boston was struck by a smallpox epidemic, Mather publicly endorsed inoculation, a practice he had learned of from the Proceedings of the Royal Society (a prestigious scientific organization of which he was a fellow) as well as from Onesimus, an enslaved man he held for many years. Smallpox inoculation had long been practiced in parts of Africa, and was already spreading among black people in America, but Mather's endorsement persuaded hundreds of white Bostonians to undergo inoculation. (Many more, however, were not persuaded, and one opponent of inoculation attempted to bomb Mather's house.)

Mather died in 1728, survived by his third wife and only two of his fifteen children. His obituaries tended to praise him effusively, glossing over his involvement in the witch trials and other controversies; according to one publication, he was "perhaps the principal ornament of this country, and the greatest scholar that was ever bred in it." But by the nineteenth and twentieth centuries, Mather's reputation was overshadowed by his association with the executions at Salem. In popular culture, he was interpreted as a villain: in a series of Marvel comics, an evil "witch-slayer" bore his name. Today, academics are more likely to recognize Mather as a complex figure attempting to respond to large-scale changes in American religious and political life. Some contemporary scholars suggest that his personal, passionate approach to faith laid the groundwork for a new religious movement that would come to exercise a profound influence upon American culture and politics: evangelicalism.

NOTE ON THE TEXT: The text presented here is based on the original 1693 edition. Spelling and punctuation have been modernized in accordance with the practices of this anthology.

⌘ ⌘ ⌘

from *The Wonders of the Invisible World*

from ENCHANTMENTS ENCOUNTERED

The New-Englanders are a people of God settled in those which were once the Devil's territories; and it may easily be supposed that the Devil was exceedingly disturbed when he perceived such a people here accomplishing the promise of old made unto our blessed Jesus that He should have the utmost[1] parts of the earth for His possession. There was not a greater uproar among the Ephesians[2] when the gospel was first brought among them than there was among the powers of the air[3] (after whom those Ephesians walked) when first the silver trumpets of the gospel here made the joyful sound. The Devil, thus irritated, immediately tried all sorts of methods to overturn this poor plantation: and so much of the church as was fled into this wilderness immediately found the Serpent cast out of his mouth a flood[4] for the carrying of it away. I believe, that never were more satanical devices used for the unsettling of any people under the sun,[5] than what have been employed for the extirpation[6] of the vine which God has here planted, casting out the heathen, and preparing a room before it, and causing it to take deep root, and fill the land; so that it sent its boughs unto the Atlantic Sea eastward, and its branches unto the Connecticut River westward, and the hills were covered with the shadows thereof.[7] But

all those attempts of hell have hitherto been abortive, many an Ebenezer[8] has been erected unto the praise of God, by His poor people here; and, having obtained help from God, we continue to this Day.

Wherefore[9] the Devil is now making one attempt more upon us; an attempt more difficult, more surprising, more snarled with unintelligible circumstances than any that we have hitherto encountered; an attempt, so critical, that if we get well through, we shall soon enjoy halcyon days[10] with all the vultures of hell trodden under our feet. He has wanted his incarnate legions to persecute us, as the people of God have in the other hemisphere been persecuted: he has therefore drawn forth his more spiritual[11] ones to make an attack upon us. We have been advised, by some credible Christians yet alive, that a malefactor accused of witchcraft as well as murder, and executed in this place more than forty years ago, did then give notice of an horrible plot against the country by witchcraft, and a foundation of witchcraft then laid, which if it were not seasonably[12] discovered would probably blow up and pull down all the churches in the country.

And we have now with horror seen the discovery of such a witchcraft! An army of devils is horribly broke in upon the place which is the center and, after a sort, the first-born of our English settlements:[13] and the houses of the good people there are filled with the doleful shrieks of their children and servants, tormented by

---

[1] *utmost* Most remote.

[2] *Ephesians* Residents of the Ancient Greek city of Ephesus. A riot broke out during the apostle Paul's ministry in Ephesus when he denounced the goddess Diana, whom the majority of Ephesians worshipped. See Acts 19.23–41.

[3] *powers of the air* Diabolical forces. See Ephesians 2.2: "in time past ye walked according to the course of this world, according to the prince of the power of the air, the spirit that now worketh in the children of disobedience."

[4] *the Serpent* I.e., Satan; *the Serpent … a flood* I.e., Satan unleashed a host of maladies to destroy the Christian settlements. See Revelation 12.15.

[5] *under the sun* Phrase used frequently in Ecclesiastes to refer to the worldly realm.

[6] *extirpation* Uprooting.

[7] *vine which … thereof* See Psalm 80.8–11: "Thou hast brought a vine out of Egypt: thou hast cast out the heathen, and planted it.

Thou preparedst room before it, and didst cause it to take deep root, and It filled the land. The hills were covered with the shadow of it, and the boughs thereof were like the goodly cedars. She sent out her boughs unto the sea, and her branches unto the river."

[8] *Ebenezer* Hebrew: Stone of help. In 1 Samuel 7.12, the Israelite prophet Samuel erects a stone by this name to commemorate God's assistance in defeating the Philistines, enemies of the Israelites.

[9] *Wherefore* For this reason.

[10] *we shall … days* At the time of this writing, Mather believed that the Second Coming of Christ was likely to happen in 1697; *halcyon* Prosperous and happy.

[11] *spiritual* Supernatural.

[12] *seasonably* In a timely manner.

[13] *first-born of our English settlements* Mather's claim is not literally true: Jamestown, founded in 1607, was the first permanent English settlement in North America. The Salem region was, however, home to one of the first English settlements that would become a part of the Massachusetts Bay Colony.

invisible hands, with tortures altogether preternatural.[1] After the mischiefs there endeavoured,[2] and since in part conquered, the terrible plague of evil angels hath made its progress into some other places, where other persons have been in like manner diabolically handled. These our poor afflicted neighbours, quickly after they became infected and infested with these demons, arrive to a capacity of discerning those which they conceive the shapes of their troublers;[3] and notwithstanding the great and just suspicion that the demons might impose the shapes of innocent persons in their spectral exhibitions[4] upon the sufferers (which may perhaps prove no small part of the witch plot in the issue[5]), yet many of the persons thus represented,[6] being examined, several of them have been convicted of a very damnable witchcraft: yea, more than one twenty have confessed that they have signed unto a book, which the Devil showed them, and engaged in his hellish design of bewitching and ruining our land.

We know not, at least I know not, how far the delusions of Satan may be interwoven into some circumstances of the confessions; but one would think all the rules of understanding humane affairs are at an end if after so many most voluntary harmonious confessions, made by intelligent persons of all ages, in sundry towns, at several times, we must not believe the main strokes wherein those confessions all agree: especially when we have a thousand preternatural things every day before our eyes, wherein the confessors do acknowledge their concernment,[7] and give demonstration of their being so concerned. If the devils now can strike the minds of men, with any poisons of so fine a composition and operation, that scores of innocent people shall unite in confessions of a crime, which we see actually committed, it is a thing prodigious, beyond the wonders of the former ages, and it threatens no less than a sort of a dissolution upon the world.

Now, by these confessions 'tis agreed that the Devil has made a dreadful knot[8] of witches in the country, and by the help of witches has dreadfully increased that knot; that these witches have driven a trade of commissioning their confederate spirits to do all sorts of mischiefs to the neighbours, whereupon there have ensued such mischievous consequences upon the bodies and estates of the neighbourhood, as could not otherwise be accounted for; yea, that at prodigious witch-meetings, the wretches have proceeded so far as to concert and consult the methods of rooting out the Christian religion from this country, and setting up instead of it, perhaps a more gross diabolism[9] than ever the world saw before. And yet it will be a thing little short of miracle, if in so spread a business as this, the Devil should not get in some of his juggles,[10] to confound the discovery of all the rest. …

Doubtless, the thoughts of many will receive a great scandal against New England from the number of persons that have been accused or suspected for witchcrafts in this country: But it were easy to offer many things that may answer and abate the scandal. If the Holy God should anywhere permit the devils to hook two or three wicked scholars into witchcraft, and then by their assistance to range with their poisonous insinuations among ignorant, envious, discontented people till they have cunningly decoyed them into some sudden act, whereby the toils of hell shall be perhaps inextricably cast over them: what country in the world would not afford witches, numerous to a prodigy?[11] Accordingly, the kingdoms of Sweden, Denmark, Scotland, yea, and England itself, as well as the Province of New England, have had their storms of witchcrafts breaking upon them, which have made most lamentable devastations: which also I wish may be the last. And it is not uneasy to be imagined that God has not brought out all the witchcrafts in many other lands with such a speedy, dreadful, destroying jealousy as burns forth upon such high treasons committed here in a land of uprightness. Transgressors may more quickly here than elsewhere

---

[1] *preternatural* Out of the ordinary, unnatural.

[2] *endeavoured* Attacked.

[3] *arrive to … their troublers* I.e., become able to identify the witches.

[4] *spectral exhibitions* Ghostly phenomena, experienced through visions.

[5] *in the issue* In the end.

[6] *represented* Portrayed by the demons seen in the accusers visions.

[7] *concernment* Involvement.

[8] *knot* Association of people.

[9] *diabolism* Devil worship.

[10] *juggles* Occult deceptions.

[11] *numerous to a prodigy* I.e., amazingly numerous.

become a prey to the vengeance of Him who has eyes like a flame of fire, and who walks in the midst of the golden candlesticks. Moreover, there are many parts of the world, who if they do upon this occasion insult over this people of God, need only to be told the story of what happened at Loim, in the Duchy of Gulic,[1] where, a popish curate, having ineffectually tried many charms to eject the Devil out of a damsel there possessed, he passionately bid the Devil to come out of her, into himself; but the Devil answered him, *Quid mihi Opus est eum tentare, quem Novissimo Die, Jure Optimo sum Possessurus?* that is, What need I meddle with one, whom I am sure to have and hold at the Last Day, as my own forever![2]

But besides all this, give me leave to add: it is to be hoped, that among the persons represented by the spectres which now afflict our neighbours, there will be found some that never explicitly contracted[3] with any of the evil angels. The witches have not only intimated, but some of them acknowledge, that they have plotted the representations of innocent persons, to cover and shelter themselves in their witchcrafts; now, although our good God has hitherto generally preserved us from the abuse therein designed by the Devils for us, yet who of us can exactly state how far our God may for our chastisement permit the Devil to proceed in such an abuse? …

from THE TRIAL OF MARTHA CARRIER[4]

1. Martha Carrier was indicted for the bewitching of certain persons, according to the form usual in such cases. Pleading Not Guilty to her indictment, there were first brought in a considerable number of the bewitched persons, who not only made the court sensible[5] of an horrid witchcraft committed upon them, but also deposed that it was Martha Carrier, or her shape,[6] that grievously tormented them by biting, pricking, pinching, and choking of them. It was further deposed, that while this Carrier was on her examination before the magistrates, the poor people were so tortured that everyone expected their death upon the very spot; but that upon the binding of Carrier, they were eased. Moreover the look of Carrier then laid[7] the afflicted people for dead; and her touch, if her eye at the same time were off them, raised them again. Which things were also now seen upon her trial. And it was testified, that upon the mention of some having their necks twisted almost round by the shape of this Carrier, she replied, It's no matter, though their necks had been twisted quite off.

2. Before the trial of this prisoner, several of her own children had frankly and fully confessed not only that they were witches themselves, but that this their mother had made them so. This confession they made with great shows of repentance, and with much demonstration of truth. They related place, time, occasion; they gave an account of journeys, meetings, and mischiefs by them performed; and were very credible in what they said. Nevertheless, this evidence was not produced against the prisoner at the bar,[8] inasmuch as there was other evidence enough to proceed upon.

3. Benjamin Abbot gave in his testimony that last March was a twelve month,[9] this Carrier was very angry with him upon laying out some land near her husband's. Her expressions in this anger were that she would stick as close to Abbot as the bark stuck to the tree, and that he should repent of it afore seven years came to an end, so as Doctor Prescot should[10] never cure him. These words were heard by others, besides Abbot himself; who also heard her say, She would hold his nose as close to the grindstone as ever it was held[11] since his name was Abbot. Presently after this, he was taken with a swelling in his foot, and then with a pain in his side, and exceedingly tormented. It

---

1   *Duchy of Gulic*   State in what is now Germany.

2   *What need … own forever*   I.e., the Devil has no need to possess the cleric because, as a Catholic, the cleric is already destined for damnation.

3   *contracted*   Entered into an agreement.

4   *MARTHA CARRIER*   Woman born between 1643 and 1650 and hanged for witchcraft in 1692. She had been a resident of Billerica, Massachusetts, but lived in Andover, Massachusetts, by the time of her trial.

5   *sensible*   Cognizant.

6   *her shape*   I.e., a spectral vision of Martha Carrier.

7   *laid*   Cast to the ground.

8   *at the bar*   I.e., in court.

9   *a twelve month*   One year prior.

10   *so as … should*   In such a way that Doctor Prescot could.

11   *hold his nose … was held*   Treat him cruelly and dominate him as much as anyone ever had.

bred unto a sore, which was lanced by Doctor Prescot, and several gallons of corruption[1] ran out of it. For six weeks it continued very bad; and then another sore bred in his groin, which was also lanced by Doctor Prescot. Another sore then bred in his groin, which was likewise cut, and put him to very great misery. He was brought unto death's door, and so remained until Carrier was taken, and carried away by the constable; from which very day, he began to mend, and so grew better every day, and is well ever since. Sarah Abbot, also his wife, testified that her Husband was not only all this while afflicted in his body, but also that strange, extraordinary and unaccountable calamities befell his cattle; their death being such as they could guess at no natural reason for.

4. Allin Toothaker[2] testified that Richard, the son of Martha Carrier, having some difference with him, pulled him down by the hair of the head. When he rose again, he was going to strike at Richard Carrier; but fell down flat on his back to the ground, and had not power to stir hand or foot, until he told Carrier he yielded; and then he saw the shape of Martha Carrier go off his breast. This Toothaker had received a wound in the wars; and he now testified that Martha Carrier told him he should never be cured. Just afore the apprehending of Carrier, he could thrust a knitting needle into his wound, four inches deep; but presently after her being seized, he was thoroughly healed. He further testified that when Carrier and he sometimes were at variance,[3] she would clap her hands at him, and say, he should get nothing by it.[4] Whereupon he several times lost his cattle by strange deaths whereof no natural causes could be given.

5. John Rogger[5] also testified that upon the threatening words of this malicious Carrier, his cattle would be strangely bewitched; as was more particularly then described.

6. Samuel Preston[6] testified, that about two years ago, having some difference with Martha Carrier, he lost a cow in a strange preternatural unusual manner; and about a month after this, the said Carrier, having again some difference with him, she told him he had lately lost a cow, and it should not be long before he lost another! Which accordingly came to pass; for he had a thriving and well-kept Cow, which without any known cause quickly fell down and Died.

7. Phebe Chandler[7] testified, that about a fortnight before the apprehension of Martha Carrier, on a Lord's Day,[8] while the psalm was singing in the Church, this Carrier then took her by the shoulder and shaking her, asked her where she lived. She made her no answer, although as Carrier, who lived next door to her father's house, could not in reason but know[9] who she was. Quickly after this, as she was at several times crossing the fields, she heard a voice that she took to be Martha Carrier's and it seemed as if it was over her head. The voice told her she should within two or three days be poisoned. Accordingly, within such a little time, one half of her right hand became greatly swollen, and very painful; as also part of her face; whereof she can give no account how it came. It continued very bad for some days; and several times since, she has had a great pain in her breast; and been so seized on her legs, that she has hardly been able to go. She added that lately, going well to the House of God,[10] Richard, the son of Martha Carrier, looked very earnestly upon her, and immediately her hand, which had formerly been poisoned, as is above said, began to pain her greatly, and she had a strange burning at her stomach; but was then struck deaf, so that she could not hear any of the prayer or singing till the two or three last words of the psalm.

8. One Foster,[11] who confessed her own share in the witchcraft for which the prisoner stood indicted, affirmed that she had seen the prisoner at some of their witch meetings, and that it was this Carrier, who persuaded her to be a witch. She confessed that the Devil

---

[1] *corruption* Fetid material.

[2] *Allin Toothaker* Resident (c. 1670–?) of Billerica and nephew of Martha Carrier.

[3] *at variance* In conflict.

[4] *should get nothing by it* Gain no advantage (from their quarrel).

[5] *John Rogger* John Rogers (1641–95), who had lived near Martha Carrier in Billerica.

[6] *Samuel Preston* Farmer and innkeeper (1649–1738) in Salem.

[7] *Phebe Chandler* Resident (1680–1720) of Andover.

[8] *Lord's Day* Sunday.

[9] *could not … know* I.e., must know.

[10] *House of God* Church.

[11] *Foster* Ann Foster (c. 1617–92), an Andover resident who died in prison after being accused of witchcraft.

carried them on a pole to a witch meeting, but the pole broke, and she hanging about Carrier's neck they both fell down, and she then received an hurt by the fall, whereof she was not at this very time recovered.

9. One Lacy,[1] who likewise confessed her share in this witchcraft, now testified that she and the prisoner were once bodily present at a witch meeting in Salem Village; and that she knew the prisoner to be a witch, and to have been at a diabolical sacrament,[2] and that the prisoner was the undoing of her and her children by enticing them into the snare of the Devil.

10. Another Lacy,[3] who also confessed her share in this witchcraft, now testified that the prisoner was at the witch meeting in Salem Village where they had bread and wine administered unto them.[4]

11. In the time of this prisoner's trial, one Susanna Shelden[5] in open court had her hands unaccountably tied together with a wheel-band, so fast[6] that without cutting, it could not be loosed. It was done by a spectre; and the sufferer affirmed it[7] was the prisoner's.

Memorandum. This rampant hag, Martha Carrier, was the person of whom the confessions of the witches and of her own children among the rest agreed that the Devil had promised her she should be Queen of Hell.

—1693

---

1 *Lacy* Mary Lacy (1652–1707), resident of Andover and daughter of Ann Foster.

2 *diabolical sacrament* Ritual parodying the sacrament of the Lord's Supper performed by Christians.

3 *Another Lacy* Mary Lacy Kempe (1674–1744), daughter of Mary Lacy.

4 *had bread ... unto them* I.e., held a diabolical sacrament; bread and wine are consumed during the Lord's Supper.

5 *Susanna Shelden* One of the principal accusers (c. 1674–?) during the Salem Witch Trials.

6 *fast* Tight.

7 *it* I.e., the specter.

CANASSATEGO

c. 1684 – 1750

In June 1750, two Moravian Christian missionaries paid an unannounced visit to the Onondaga diplomat and orator Canassatego. The missionaries wrote that Canassatego "knew at once who we were, called us by name, and seemed very much pleased to see us. He began to laugh for joy, in his peculiar manner, and one felt and saw that we were welcome guests." The skill with which, on this occasion, Canassatego put his Euro-American visitors at ease encapsulates his adroit management, for nearly a decade, of the complex, sensitive relationship between the Haudenosaunee Confederacy, which he represented as an emissary, and the British North American colonies. Canassatego's recorded speeches provide an evocative example of how eighteenth-century Native Americans drew on and reworked their oral literary traditions as they navigated the increasing pressures of white colonial expansion. His diplomatic and rhetorical abilities also gained Canassatego a noteworthy afterlife in Euro-American culture; in particular, the famous closing words of a speech he gave to colonial delegates in Lancaster, Pennsylvania, in 1744—"We are a powerful confederacy; and by your observing the same methods our wise forefathers have taken, you will acquire fresh strength and power"—arguably influenced the movement for colonial unity that underlies the very idea of the United States itself.

Little is known about Canassatego's early life; he was "about 60 years of age" in 1744, according to one white observer. By the time he first appears in the historical record in 1742, Canassatego had become one of the "chief men" of the Onondaga nation, a founding member of the Haudenosaunee Confederacy. He seems not to have had any connections to the Onondaga's hereditary sachems, however, and apparently gained his position purely by dint of his political and rhetorical skill, charisma, and ambition.

By the 1730s, the Haudenosaunee—caught between the contending colonial empires of Britain and France, embroiled in conflict with various Indigenous rivals, and ravaged by epidemics, famine, and alcohol abuse—were in danger of losing the powerful position they had long held in the politics of northeastern North America. In an attempt to strengthen its hand, the confederacy began forging closer ties with the British colony of Pennsylvania. In 1736, in a council that Canassatego likely attended, Pennsylvania agreed to recognize Haudenosaunee supremacy over all Indigenous peoples in its region and to deal only with the Haudenosaunee when negotiating any further land acquisitions; in exchange, the Haudenosaunee would help protect Pennsylvania's borderlands and take responsibility for managing disputes between Pennsylvania and other Indigenous nations.

This 1736 agreement set the stage for Canassatego's emergence as a leading Haudenosaunee representative in their subsequent dealings with Pennsylvania and its neighboring colonies. In 1742, Canassatego served in this capacity in negotiations meant to finalize territorial acquisitions Pennsylvania had made in the previous few years from the Haudenosaunee and Lenape (Delaware). After collecting the asking price for land the Haudenosaunee had sold, Canassatego shrewdly maneuvered the Pennsylvanian delegates into making an additional payment with a speech that sharply refuted Euro-American stereotypes of Indigenous simplicity or ignorance: "We know our lands are now become more valuable; the white people think we don't know their value, but we are sensible that the land is everlasting, and the few goods we receive for it are soon worn out and gone." Canassatego also held up the Haudenosaunee side of their pact with Pennsylvania while simultaneously asserting Haudenosaunee supremacy over other Indigenous peoples with a withering address to the Lenape, who were attempting to dispute an underhanded treaty (the so-called "Walking Purchase" of 1737) that had ceded more of their territory to Pennsylvania. Canassatego told the Lenape delegates, "We conquered you, we made women of you, you know you are women, and can no more sell land than women," and demanded that they relinquish the disputed land to Pennsylvania: "Take the advice of a wise man and remove immediately."

In addition to his rhetorical dexterity, Canassatego's stature as a diplomat stemmed from his mastery of the protocols of Haudenosaunee diplomacy and his fluency with the elaborate metaphorical language that the Haudenosaunee used to describe their relations with other peoples. (Some of these metaphors, such as "burying the tomahawk," have made their way into modern American vernacular.) This fluency is particularly on display in the speeches that Canassatego gave at Lancaster in 1744, during a conference to resolve territorial disputes between the Haudenosaunee and several colonies. The Haudenosaunee were demanding compensation for land they claimed to have conquered from the Susquehannock nation, while the colonial representatives asserted that they had previously purchased the land in question from the Susquehannock and thus owed the Haudenosaunee nothing. Canassatego defended the primacy of the Haudenosaunee's territorial claims over those of the Euro-American newcomers in a series of powerful speeches, forcing the colonial delegates to acknowledge the Haudenosaunee's claims in practice, if not in theory, by paying the compensation the Haudenosaunee had demanded. (Canassatego's speeches at Lancaster, like those he gave in the other major councils in which he took part, were probably translated by Conrad Weiser, a German-born Pennsylvanian interpreter; Canassatego developed a close partnership with Weiser that further contributed to Canassatego's diplomatic successes.)

After Lancaster, Canassatego took part in at least two more Haudenosaunee–colonial conferences, at Albany, New York, in 1745 and Philadelphia in 1749, in which he continued to use all his skills to keep the Haudenosaunee both friendly with and independent of the British colonies and to derive the greatest possible material benefit to the Haudenosaunee from the sale of Indigenous land. He died in 1750. The most common explanation of his death, both at the time and today, is that he was assassinated, but whether his assassins were French agents, pro-French Haudenosaunee, or compatriots angered by a deal he had allegedly made to sell communal Haudenosaunee land (the three main prevailing theories) remains unknown.

Canassatego's diplomatic speeches were printed by Benjamin Franklin, the official publisher of the records of Pennsylvania's Indigenous treaty negotiations. These published records were widely read in both the colonies and Britain; as a result, Canassatego became, after his death, something of a transatlantic celebrity. The English author John Shebbeare, for example, made Canassatego a character in his satirical novel *Lydia, or Filial Piety* (1755), using him to critique various aspects of British society from a conventional "noble savage" perspective. Scholars have also argued that Canassatego directly influenced Franklin's political thought, and hence fundamental U.S. political ideas, by his recommendations that the disparate and sometimes fractious British colonies forge a united confederacy after the model of the Haudenosaunee—a recommendation he made most famously in his closing speech at the 1744 Lancaster conference. Canassatego's presentation of the Haudenosaunee as a model for colonial unity, it has been suggested, shaped the plan for a unified colonial government that Franklin proposed at the 1754 Albany Congress and ultimately the U.S. Constitution—another example of the way in which Canassatego's oratory, by drawing powerfully on his people's rhetorical and literary traditions, gave those traditions a compelling new form.

NOTE ON THE TEXT: The text presented here of Canassatego's 26 June 1744 speech at Lancaster is based on the version of the speech printed by Benjamin Franklin in Philadelphia in 1744. Spelling and punctuation have been modernized according to the practices of this anthology.

⌘ ⌘ ⌘

from *Speech at Lancaster, 26 June 1744*

… Brother, the Governor of Maryland,

When you mentioned the affair of the land yesterday,[1] you went back to old times, and told us, you had been in possession of the province of Maryland above one hundred years; but what is one hundred years in comparison of the length of time since our claim began—since we came out of this ground? For we must tell you, that long before one hundred years our ancestors came out of this very ground, and their children have remained here ever since. You came out of the ground in a country that lies beyond the seas; there you may have a just claim, but here you must allow us to be your elder brethren, and the lands to belong to us long before you knew anything of them. It is true, that above one hundred years ago the Dutch came here in a ship, and brought with them several goods, such as awls, knives, hatchets, guns, and many other particulars, which they gave us. And when they had taught us how to use their things, and we saw what sort of people they were, we were so well pleased with them, that we tied their ship to the bushes on the shore; and afterwards, liking them still better the longer they stayed with us, and thinking the bushes too tender, we removed the rope, and tied it to the trees; and as the trees were liable to be blown down by high winds, or to decay of themselves, we, from the affection we bore them, again removed the rope, and tied it to a strong and big rock [here the interpreter said, "They mean the Oneida[2] country"] and not content with this, for its further security we removed the rope to the big mountain [here the interpreter said, "They mean the Onondaga[3] country"] and there we

tied it very fast, and rolled wampum[4] about it; and, to make it still more secure, we stood upon the wampum, and sat down upon it, to defend it, and to prevent any hurt coming to it, and did our best endeavours that it might remain uninjured forever. During all this time the newcomers, the Dutch, acknowledged our right to the lands, and solicited us, from time to time, to grant them parts of our country, and to enter into league and covenant with us, and to become one people with us.[5]

After this the English came into the country, and, as we were told, became one people with the Dutch.[6] About two years after the arrival of the English, an English governor[7] came to Albany, and finding what great friendship subsisted between us and the Dutch, he approved it mightily, and desired to make as strong a league, and to be upon as good terms with us as the Dutch were, with whom he was united, and to become one people with us. And by his further care in looking into what had passed between us, he found that the rope which tied the ship to the great mountain was only fastened with wampum, which was liable to break and rot, and to perish in a course of years; he therefore told us, he would give us a silver chain, which would be much stronger, and would last forever. This we accepted, and fastened the ship with it, and it

---

[1] *When you … yesterday* Haudenosaunee diplomatic protocol dictated that responses to any major proposals or statements be delivered the day after the proposal or statement in question was made; this was a way of showing that the recipients of the proposal or statement had taken it seriously and given it respectful consideration before delivering their response.

[2] *Oneida* One of the five founding nations of the Haudenosaunee Confederacy; the name means "people of the standing stone."

[3] *Onondaga* Another of the five founding Haudenosaunee nations; the name means "hill place people." Canassatego was an Onondaga.

[4] *wampum* Belts and strings of wampum, a type of bead made from shells, are used among the Indigenous nations of eastern North America for numerous purposes, including the recording of treaties, stories, and historical events as well as ceremonial exchange, trade, and decorative art.

[5] *above one hundred … with us* In Haudenosaunee oral tradition, the treaty the Haudenosaunee made with the Dutch (in 1613, according to the tradition) is known as the Two Row Wampum Treaty; the Haudenosaunee consider it to be the basis for all their subsequent treaties with European and Euro-American governments and to still be in effect.

[6] *After this … the Dutch* The Dutch settlement of New Amsterdam—the nucleus of what is now New York City—was surrendered to the British in 1664; Britain took over the rest of New Netherland, the Dutch colony on the northeastern Atlantic seaboard, in 1674.

[7] *an English governor* Edmund Andros, governor of New York colony from 1674 to 1683. In 1675, Andros asked for Haudenosaunee assistance in the conflicts then engulfing many of the British North American colonies, including King Philip's War in New England and Bacon's Rebellion in Virginia. Andros's agreement with the Haudenosaunee formed the basis for the series of treaties and alliances between the Haudenosaunee and the British colonies that came to be called the Covenant Chain.

has lasted ever since. Indeed we have had some small differences with the English, and, during these misunderstandings, some of their young men would, by way of reproach, be every now and then telling us, that we should have perished if they had not come into the country and furnished us with strouds[1] and hatchets, and guns, and other things necessary for the support of life; but we always gave them to understand that they were mistaken—that we lived before they came amongst us, and as well, or better, if we may believe what our forefathers have told us. We had then room enough, and plenty of deer, which was easily caught; and though we had not knives, hatchets, or guns, such as we have now, yet we had knives of stone, and hatchets of stone, and bows and arrows, and those served our uses as well then as the English ones do now. We are now straitened,[2] and sometimes in want of deer, and liable to many other inconveniencies since the English came among us, and particularly from that pen-and-ink work that is going on at the table (pointing to the secretary), and we will give you an instance of this. Our Brother Onas,[3] a great while ago, came to Albany to buy the Susquehanna lands[4] of us, but our Brother, the Governor of New York, who, as we suppose, had not a good understanding with our Brother Onas, advised us not to sell him any land, for he would make an ill use of it. And pretending to be our good friend, he advised us, in order to prevent Onas's, or any other person's imposing upon us, and that we might always have our land when we should want it, to put it into his hands, and told us, he would keep it for our life, and never open his hands, but keep them close shut, and not part with any of it, but at our request. Accordingly we trusted him, and put our land into his hands, and charged him to keep it safe for our use; but, some time after, he went to England, and carried our land with him, and there sold it to our Brother Onas for a large sum of money. And when, at the instance of our Brother Onas, we were minded to sell him some lands, he told us, we had sold the Susquehanna lands already to the Governor of New York, and that he had bought them from him in England, though when he came to understand how the Governor of New York had deceived us, he very generously paid us for our lands over again.

Though we mention this instance of an imposition put upon us by the Governor of New York, yet we must do the English the justice to say, we have had their hearty assistances in our wars with the French, who were no sooner arrived amongst us than they began to render us uneasy, and to provoke us to war, and we have had several wars with them, during all which we constantly received assistance from the English, and, by their means, we have always been able to keep up our heads against their attacks.

We now come nearer home. We have had your deeds interpreted to us, and we acknowledge them to be good and valid, and that the Conestoga or Susquehannock Indians had a right to sell those lands to you, for they were then theirs; but since that time we have conquered them, and their country now belongs to us, and the lands we demanded satisfaction for are no part of the lands comprised in those Deeds. They are the Cohongorontas[5] lands; those, we are sure, you have not possessed one hundred years—no, nor above ten years, and we made our demands so soon as we knew your people were settled in those parts. These have never been sold, but remain still to be disposed of; and we are well pleased to hear you are provided with goods, and do assure you of our willingness to treat with you for those unpurchased lands; in confirmation whereof, we present you with this belt of wampum.

Which was received with the usual ceremonies.
—1744

---

[1] *strouds*   Blankets made of stroud (a coarse woolen fabric) that were sold or traded to Indigenous people.

[2] *straitened*   Reduced in means; impoverished.

[3] *Onas*   Treaty name, meaning "quill pen," that the Haudenosaunee used for the governors of Pennsylvania Colony.

[4] *Susquehanna lands*   I.e., lands in the valley of the Susquehanna River, which flows through parts of New York and Pennsylvania.

---

[5] [Franklin's note] I.e., Potomac. ["Cohongorontas" was the Haudenosaunee name for the Potomac River west of the Blue Ridge Mountains.]

JONATHAN EDWARDS

1703 – 1758

On 8 July 1741, Jonathan Edwards visited the congregation of Enfield, Connecticut—one of the few communities in New England to remain unmoved by the explosion of religious enthusiasm known as the First Great Awakening. To this initially aloof crowd, Edwards delivered "Sinners in the Hands of an Angry God," an oration that would become one of the best-known sermons in American history. "O sinner! Consider the fearful danger that you are in," Edwards warned, soon eliciting outbursts of emotion from his transformed audience. "The God that holds you over the pit of hell, much as one holds a spider … abhors you." A prominent theologian and philosopher, Edwards is best known for inspiring—and then theorizing—religious revivals, first in his own congregation in the mid-1730s and then as a participant in the larger Great Awakening that swept New England in the early 1740s. His religious writings had a lasting effect upon Protestant theology in New England, and his philosophical works helped to shape American views on free will, aesthetics, and history for generations. Edwards remains an influential thinker for American Calvinists, and his work continues to be studied for its innovative fusion of Protestant Christianity and Enlightenment philosophy.

Born in East Windsor, Connecticut, in 1703, Jonathan Edwards was the fifth child of Esther Stoddard and minister Timothy Edwards. At thirteen, he enrolled at Yale, where he was shocked to discover what he described as his classmates' "monstrous impieties." A dutiful student who immersed himself in the literature of Enlightenment thinkers such as Isaac Newton and John Locke, in college Edwards struggled with his religious beliefs until he underwent a conversion experience that filled him, he would later write, with "constant delight and pleasure." In 1727, he was ordained in Northampton, Massachusetts, as an assistant pastor to his grandfather, Solomon Stoddard.

Two years later, Edwards succeeded Stoddard as the sole pastor of the Congregational Church in Northampton. In this role, he developed his characteristic style of preaching. Following in the footsteps of such Puritan ministers as William Perkins and William Ames, Edwards adopted a "plain style" of speech, which focused on making clear connections between divine wisdom and everyday life. His sermons typically derive a theme from scripture, outline theological assertions related to the theme, and then discuss some practical applications of those theological points. Edwards believed that New England was at risk of falling into depravity: taverns were becoming widespread, premarital sex was common, and young people were spending less time in prayer. "Arminianism"—a catch-all term used by strict Calvinists to refer to a range of views in which humans can play a role in their own salvation—was also growing in popularity. In response to these developments, Edwards delivered a public lecture in Boston in 1731, "God Glorified in Man's Dependence," which stirringly defended the Calvinist tenet that humankind relies completely on God.

Beginning in 1733, Edwards sought to rejuvenate his congregation's passion for Calvinist spirituality. He encouraged the town elders to persuade the younger generation to take religion more seriously. By 1735, partly due to Edwards's moving sermons, religious fervor had taken hold of the town. Hundreds of people made open professions of faith. "All the conversation in all companies and upon all occasions was upon [spiritual and eternal things] only," Edwards recalled in *A Faithful Narrative of the Surprising Work of God* (1737). "Other discourse than of the things of religion would scarcely be tolerated." The spiritual awakening came to a conclusion in early June 1735, when Edwards's uncle, overwhelmed by fear for his spiritual state, died by suicide.

The larger-scale revival of Calvinist spirituality that became known as the First Great Awakening gathered momentum in 1740. All across New England, expressions of religious ecstasy grew commonplace. Believing this to be a sign of Christianity's imminent triumph over evil, Edwards wrote and preached in support of the revival. In the process, he established himself as a leading representative of a growing community of New England ministers, known as the New Lights, who believed that the revivals represented the work of God.

During the First Great Awakening, Edwards was recognized by his fellow ministers as an exceptionally skilled author of sermons, and he was sometimes called upon to inspire spiritual awakening in disinterested congregations—most famously in the congregation of Enfield, to which he preached "Sinners in the Hands of an Angry God." Although Edwards was not a particularly passionate speaker, his words inspired many parishioners to weep and cry out so excessively that, as a member of the congregation recorded in his diary, Edwards was unable to finish the sermon. He is now best known for this undeniably provocative sermon, but it is actually an outlier; only two of his sermons focus on hell and its torments. He spoke far more frequently about God's benevolence and the beauty of God's creation.

The spiritual renewal that Edwards helped to inspire was not universally celebrated. For a faction of New England's religious establishment known as the Old Lights, the revival spirit precipitated by Edwards and other so-called "New Light" preachers was, as the Boston pastor Charles Chauncy put it, "a disease, a sort of madness" masquerading as real piety. As the Great Awakening spread through New England, Edwards frequently wrote and spoke in response to the concern that many of the converts were driven by emotional frenzy, rather than true apprehensions of divine grace. In *A Treatise Concerning Religious Affections* (1746), his most thorough work on the matter, he drew upon the philosophy of John Locke to differentiate authentic religious experiences from mere enthusiasm.

Once the fervor of the Great Awakening died out in the mid-1740s, Edwards began to lose favor with his own congregation, and in 1750 he was dismissed as pastor. He then became a missionary to the Mahican of Stockbridge, a town founded for the purpose of colonizing and converting Indigenous people through integration with settler families. Edwards believed that unconverted Mahican were in a state of sin and ignorance, and that it was the responsibility of the English to spread the gospel and give them sufficient education to read and understand the Bible: "we do no more than our duty in it," he said to his Indigenous congregation, "for it was once with our forefathers as 'tis with you. They formerly were in great darkness." While in Stockbridge, Edwards composed *Freedom of Will* (1754), a dense work of philosophy in which he considered the compatibility of divine power with human free will.

In 1758, just weeks after being appointed president of the College of New Jersey—now called Princeton—Edwards died following complications from an inoculation against smallpox. (Unlike modern vaccination, eighteenth-century inoculation carried some risk of infection with the disease.) After his death, Edwards's disciples would go on to found a theological movement known as New Divinity, in which a significant number of New England ministers would be schooled. Throughout the eighteenth and nineteenth centuries, many American authors and religious figures felt compelled either to embrace or debunk the worldview Edwards had argued for. Harriet Beecher Stowe shared Edwards's belief that the second coming of Christ would take place after the Church had overthrown the antichristian forces of evil, saved a vast number of souls, and instituted a paradisiacal global society. Edwards, however, had owned enslaved people, and, in Stowe's view, his chief failing was that he had not explicitly recognized slavery as an antichristian force. Ralph Waldo Emerson, by contrast, considered Edwards's theology to be a "disease" that prevented people from recognizing their own inherent dignity. For the United States to progress as a society, Emerson believed, it would need to leave the spirituality of Puritan-inspired thinkers such as Edwards behind.

Throughout the nineteenth century, Edwards was viewed as the culmination of the Puritan tradition that preceded him and the spiritual forefather of the evangelical movements that followed. He proved to be a significant influence upon the writers and preachers of the Second Great Awakening of the 1790s to 1830s, and his ideas shaped the theology that dominated nineteenth-century New England seminaries. By the turn of the twentieth century, however, Edwards was treated as a "Great Anachronism" for his attachment to old-fashioned religiosity. His reputation was resurrected in the mid-twentieth century, when he was hailed by critics such as Perry Miller and Sacvan Bercovitch as one of the first figures in colonial America to be recognized as an important intellectual on both sides of the Atlantic. In the twenty-first century, Edwards's direct influence has been largely limited to Calvinist institutions, although his work continues to be widely anthologized. "It is safe to say," early Americanist Edward Gallagher suggests, "that there will never be an American literature without 'Sinners in the Hands of an Angry God.' It is simply too compelling."

NOTE ON THE TEXT: The text of "Sinners in the Hands of an Angry God" is based on the 1741 edition published in Boston by S. Kneeland and T. Green. Spelling and punctuation have been modernized in accordance with the practices of this anthology.

⌘ ⌘ ⌘

Sinners in the Hands of an Angry God

Deuteronomy 32.35[1]
—Their Foot shall slide in due Time—

In this verse is threatened the vengeance of God on the wicked unbelieving Israelites, that were God's visible people, and lived under means of grace;[2] and that, notwithstanding all God's wonderful works that he had wrought towards that people, yet remained, as is expressed (Deuteronomy 32.28) void of counsel, having no understanding in them;[3] and that, under all the cultivations of heaven, brought forth bitter and poisonous fruit; as in the two verses next preceding the text.[4]

The expression I have chosen for my text, *Their foot shall slide in due time*, seems to imply the following things relating to the punishment and destruction that these wicked Israelites were exposed to.

1. That they were *always* exposed to destruction; as one that stands or walks in slippery places is always exposed to fall. This is implied in the manner of their destruction's coming upon them, being represented by their foot sliding. The same is expressed, Psalm 73.18: *Surely thou didst set them in slippery places; thou castedst them down into destruction.*

2. It implies that they were always exposed to *sudden* unexpected destruction. As he that walks in slippery places is every moment liable to fall; he can't foresee one moment whether he shall stand or fall the next; and when he does fall, he falls at once without warning. Which is also expressed in Psalm 73.18–19: *Surely thou didst set them in slippery places; thou castedst them down into destruction: How are they brought into desolation as in a moment?*

3. Another thing implied is, that they are liable to fall *of themselves*, without being thrown down by the hand of another. As he that stands or walks on slippery ground, needs nothing but his own weight to throw him down.

4. That the reason why they are not fallen already, and do not fall now, is only that God's appointed time

---

[1] *Deuteronomy 32.35*   "To me belongeth vengeance and recompence; their foot shall slide in due time: for the day of their calamity is at hand, and the things that shall come upon them make haste."

[2] *lived under means of grace*   Lived under the terms of the covenant of grace, according to which humans cannot be saved through their own actions, but only by the grace of God.

[3] *void of ... them*   See Deuteronomy 32.28–29: "For they are a nation void of counsel, neither is there any understanding in them. O that they were wise, that they understood this, that they would consider their latter end!"

[4] *two verses ... text*   See Deuteronomy 32.32–33: "For their vine is of the vine of Sodom, and of the fields of Gomorrah: their grapes are grapes of gall, their clusters are bitter: their wine is the poison of dragons, and the cruel venom of asps." In this passage, Sodom and Gomorrah refer to two biblical cities populated by wicked people,

which God consumed with fire and brimstone in a demonstration of divine judgment.

is not come. For it is said, that when that due time, or appointed time comes, *their foot shall slide*. Then they shall be left to fall as they are inclined by their own weight. God won't hold them up in these slippery places any longer, but will let them go; and then, at that very instant, they shall fall into destruction; as he that stands in such slippery declining ground, on the edge of a pit that he can't stand alone, when he is let go he immediately falls and is lost.

The observation from the words that I would now insist upon is this: *There is nothing that keeps wicked men at any one moment out of hell, but the mere pleasure of God.* By the mere pleasure of God, I mean his sovereign pleasure, his arbitrary will, restrained by no obligation, hindered by no manner of difficulty, any more than if nothing else but God's mere will had in the least degree, or in any respect whatsoever, any hand in the preservation of wicked men one moment. The truth of this observation may appear by the following considerations.

1. There is no want[1] of *power* in God to cast wicked men into hell at any moment. Men's hands can't be strong when God rises up. The strongest have no power to resist him, nor can any deliver out of his hands. He is not only able to cast wicked men into hell, but he can most *easily* do it. Sometimes an earthly prince meets with a great deal of difficulty to subdue a rebel, that he has found means to fortify himself, and has made himself strong by the numbers of his followers. But it is not so with God. There is no fortress that is any defense from the power of God. Though hand join in hand, and vast multitudes of God's enemies combine and associate themselves, they are easily broken in pieces. They are as great heaps of light chaff before the whirlwind; or large quantities of dry stubble before devouring flames.[2] We find it easy to tread on and crush a worm that we see crawling on the earth; so 'tis easy for us to cut or singe a slender thread that anything hangs by: thus easy is it for God when he pleases to cast his enemies down to hell. What are we,

that we should think to stand before him, at whose rebuke the earth trembles, and before whom the rocks are thrown down?[3]

2. They *deserve* to be cast into hell; so that divine justice never stands in the way, it makes no objection against God's using his power at any moment to destroy them. Yea, on the contrary, justice calls aloud for an infinite punishment of their sins. Divine justice says of the tree that brings forth such grapes of Sodom, *Cut it down, why cumbereth it the ground?*, Luke 13.7. The sword of divine justice is every moment brandished over their heads, and 'tis nothing but the hand of arbitrary mercy, and God's mere will, that holds it back.

3. They are *already* under a sentence of condemnation to hell. They do not only justly deserve to be cast down thither, but the sentence of the law of God, that eternal and immutable rule of righteousness that God has fixed between him and mankind, is gone out against them, and stands against them; so that they are bound over[4] already to hell. John 3.18: *He that believeth not is condemned already.* So that every unconverted man[5] properly belongs to hell; that is his place; from thence he is. John 8.23: *Ye are from beneath.* And thither he is bound; 'tis the place that justice, and God's word, and the sentence of his unchangeable law assign to him.

4. They are now the objects of that very *same* anger and wrath of God that is expressed in the torments of hell. And the reason why they don't go down to hell at each moment, is not because God, in whose power they are, is not then very angry with them; as angry as he is with many of those miserable creatures now tormented in hell, who there feel and bear the fierceness of his wrath. Yea, God is a great deal more angry with great numbers that are now on earth. Yea, doubtless with many that are now in this congregation, that it

---

[1] *want* Lack.

[2] *They are ... whirlwind* See Psalm 1.4: "The ungodly are not so: but are like the chaff which the wind driveth away"; *large quantities ... devouring flames* See Isaiah 5.24: "Therefore as the fire devoureth the stubble, and the flame consumeth the chaff, so their root shall be as rottenness, and their blossom shall go up as dust: because they have cast away the law of the Lord of hosts, and despised the word of the Holy One of Israel."

[3] *earth trembles* See Jeremiah 10.10: "But the Lord is the true God, he is the living God, and an everlasting king: at his wrath the earth shall tremble, and the nations shall not be able to abide his indignation"; *before whom ... down* See Nahum 1.6: "Who can stand before his indignation? And who can abide in the fierceness of his anger? His fury is poured out like fire and the rocks are thrown down by him."

[4] *bound over* Condemned.

[5] *unconverted man* The unconverted include not only those who have not converted to Christianity, but also those who have not publicly proclaimed a conversion experience of being personally saved by God.

may be are at ease and quiet, than he is with many of those who are now in the flames of hell.[1]

So that it is not because God is unmindful of their wickedness, and does not resent it, that he does not let loose his hand and cut them off. God is not altogether such a one as themselves, though they may imagine him to be so. The wrath of God burns against them, their damnation does not slumber; the pit is prepared, the fire is made ready, the furnace is now hot, ready to receive them, the flames do now rage and glow. The glittering sword is whet, and held over them, and the pit hath opened her mouth under them.[2]

5. The *Devil* stands ready to fall upon them, and seize them as his own, at what moment God shall permit him. They belong to him; he has their souls in his possession, and under his dominion. The scripture represents them as his goods, Luke 11.21.[3] The devils watch them; they are ever by them at their right hand; they stand waiting for them, like greedy hungry lions that see their prey,[4] and expect to have it, but are for the present kept back. If God should withdraw his hand, by which they are restrained, they would in one moment fly upon their poor souls. The old serpent[5] is gaping for them; hell opens its mouth wide to receive them; and if God should permit it, they would be hastily swallowed up and lost.

6. There are in the souls of wicked men those hellish *principles* reigning, that would presently kindle and flame out into hell fire, if it were not for God's restraints. There is laid in the very nature of carnal men, a foundation for the torments of hell. There are those corrupt principles, in reigning power in them, and in full possession of them, that are seeds of hell fire. These principles are active and powerful, exceeding violent in their nature, and if it were not for the restraining hand of God upon them, they would soon break out, they would flame out after the same manner as the same corruptions, the same enmity does in the hearts of damned souls, and would beget the same torments as they do in them.[6] The souls of the wicked are in scripture compared to the troubled sea, Isaiah 57.20.[7] For the present, God restrains their wickedness by his mighty power, as he does the raging waves of the troubled sea, saying, *Hitherto shalt thou come, but no further*;[8] but if God should withdraw that restraining power, it would soon carry all before it. Sin is the ruin and misery of the soul; it is destructive in its nature; and if God should leave it without restraint, there would need nothing else to make the soul perfectly miserable. The corruption of the heart of man is immoderate and boundless in its fury; and while wicked men live here, it is like fire pent up by God's restraints, whereas if it were let loose, it would set on fire the course of nature; and as the heart is now a sink of sin, so if sin was not restrained, it would immediately turn the soul into a fiery oven, or a furnace of fire and brimstone.

7. It is no security to wicked men for one moment, that there are no *visible means* of *death* at hand.[9] 'Tis no security to a natural man,[10] that he is now in health, and that he does not see which way he should now

---

[1]   *Yea, God … hell* Edwards alludes to the Reformed Protestant concept of "the invisible church"—the idea that there is a community of Christians, the elect, who have already received or are destined to receive salvation, and whose identities are known by God alone. Not all members of the "visible church"—the institutional communities of worship—are members of the invisible church: some apparent Christians are destined for hell.

[2]   *The glittering sword* See Deuteronomy 32.41: "If I whet my glittering sword, and mine hand take hold on judgment; I will render vengeance to mine enemies, and will reward them that hate me"; *pit hath … under them* See Numbers 16.30: "But if the Lord make a new thing, and the earth open her mouth, and swallow them up, with all that appertain unto them, and they go down quick into the pit; then ye shall understand that these men have provoked the Lord."

[3]   *Luke 11.21* In Luke 11.20–22, Jesus metaphorically describes demons as "strong men" who treat human beings as property, and describes God as an even stronger man who can take away the demons' possessions with ease.

[4]   *greedy hungry … their prey* See Psalm 104.21: "The young lions roar after their prey, and seek their meat from God."

[5]   *old serpent* Satan. See Revelation 12.9.

[6]   *These principles … in them* I.e., wicked people are governed by powerful forces of sin, and if God did not hold these forces in check the wicked would be just as tormented on earth as they are in hell.

[7]   *Isaiah 57.20* "But the wicked are like the troubled sea, when it cannot rest, whose waters cast up mire and dirt."

[8]   *Hitherto shalt thou … no further* See Job 38.11.

[9]   *It is … at hand* I.e., wicked people should not take any comfort in the fact that there may not appear to be any immediate risk of dying.

[10]   *natural man* Person who remains in a state of original sin. See 1 Corinthians 2.14: "But the natural man receiveth not the things of the Spirit of God: for they are foolishness unto him: neither can he know them, because they are spiritually discerned."

immediately go out of the world by any accident, and that there is no visible danger in any respect in his circumstances. The manifold[1] and continual experience of the world in all ages, shows this is no evidence that a man is not on the very brink of eternity, and that the next step will not be into another world. The unseen, unthought-of ways and means of persons going suddenly out of the world are innumerable and inconceivable. Unconverted men walk over the pit of hell on a rotten covering, and there are innumerable places in this covering so weak that they will not bear their weight, and these places are not seen. The arrows of death fly unseen at noonday;[2] the sharpest sight cannot discern them. God has so many different unsearchable ways of taking wicked men out of the world and sending them to hell, that there is nothing to make it appear that God had need to be at the expense of a miracle, or go out of the ordinary course of his providence,[3] to destroy any wicked man, at any moment. All the means that there are of sinners going out of the world, are so in God's hands, and so universally and absolutely subject to his power and determination, that it does not depend at all the less on the mere will of God whether sinners shall at any moment go to hell, than if means were never made use of or at all concerned in the case.[4]

8. Natural men's *prudence* and *care* to preserve their own *lives*, or the care of others to preserve them, do not secure them a moment.[5] To this, divine providence and universal experience do also bear testimony. There is this clear evidence that men's own wisdom is no security to them from death; that if it were otherwise we should see some difference between the wise and politic men of the world, and others, with regard to their liableness to early and unexpected death: but how is it in fact? Ecclesiastes 2.16: *How dieth the wise man? even as the fool.*

9. All wicked men's *pains* and *contrivance*[6] which they use to escape hell, while they continue to reject Christ, and so remain wicked men, do not secure them from hell one moment. Almost every natural man that hears of hell, flatters himself that he shall escape it; he depends upon himself for his own security; he flatters himself in what he has done, in what he is now doing, or what he intends to do. Every one lays out matters in his own mind how he shall avoid damnation, and flatters himself that he contrives well for himself, and that his schemes will not fail. They hear indeed that there are but few saved, and that the greater part of men that have died heretofore are gone to hell; but each one imagines that he lays out matters better for his own escape than others have done. He does not intend to come to that place of torment; he says within himself, that he intends to take effectual care, and to order matters so for himself as not to fail.

But the foolish children of men miserably delude themselves in their own schemes, and in confidence in their own strength and wisdom; they trust to nothing but a shadow. The greater part of those who heretofore have lived under the same means of grace, and are now dead, are undoubtedly gone to hell; and it was not because they were not as wise as those who are now alive: it was not because they did not lay out matters as well for themselves to secure their own escape. If we could speak with them and inquire of them, one by one, whether they expected, when alive and when they used to hear about hell, ever to be the subjects of misery: we doubtless, should hear one and another reply, "No, I never intended to come here: I had laid out matters otherwise in my mind; I thought I should contrive well for myself; I thought my scheme good. I intended to take effectual care; but it came upon me unexpected; I did not look for it at that time, and in that manner; it came as a thief;[7] Death outwitted me: God's wrath was too quick for me. Oh, my cursed foolishness! I was flattering myself, and pleasing myself with vain dreams of what I would do hereafter;

---

[1]   *manifold* Diverse.

[2]   *The arrows ... noonday* See Psalm 91.5: "Thou shalt not be afraid for the terror by night; nor for the arrow that flieth by day."

[3]   *providence* Divine foresight, power, and governance.

[4]   *All the ... the case* I.e., all factors that can make a person die are ultimately controlled by God. Consequently, people's lives are just as much in God's hands as they would be if God directly caused people to die without the mediation of seemingly external factors (such as disease and war).

[5]   *Natural men's ... a moment* I.e., it does not matter how much one takes care of one's health or avoids risky behaviors: anyone can die at an unexpected time.

[6]   *contrivance* Scheming, clever planning.

[7]   *came as a thief* See 1 Thessalonians 5.2: "the day of the Lord so cometh as a thief in the night."

and when I was saying peace and safety, then sudden destruction came upon me."[1]

10. God has laid himself under *no obligation*, by any promise to keep any natural man out of hell one moment. God certainly has made no promises either of eternal life, or of any deliverance or preservation from eternal death, but what are contained in the covenant of grace,[2] the promises that are given in Christ, in whom all the promises are yea and amen. But surely they have no interest in the promises of the covenant of grace who are not the children of the covenant, who do not believe in any of the promises, and have no interest in the Mediator[3] of the covenant.

So that, whatever some have imagined and pretended about promises made to natural men's earnest seeking and knocking,[4] 'tis plain and manifest, that whatever pains a natural man takes in religion, whatever prayers he makes, till he believes in Christ, God is under no manner of obligation to keep him a moment from eternal destruction.

So that thus it is that natural men are held in the hand of God over the pit of hell; they have deserved the fiery pit, and are already sentenced to it; and God is dreadfully provoked, his anger is as great towards them as to those that are actually suffering the executions of the fierceness of his wrath in hell, and they have done nothing in the least to appease or abate that anger, neither is God in the least bound by any promise to hold them up one moment; the devil is waiting for them, hell is gaping for them, the flames gather and flash about them, and would fain lay hold on them, and swallow them up; the fire pent up in their own hearts is struggling to break out: and they have no interest in any Mediator, there are no means within reach that can be any security to them. In short, they have no refuge, nothing to take hold of; all that preserves them every moment is the mere arbitrary will, and uncovenanted, unobliged forbearance of an incensed God.

APPLICATION

The use may be of *awakening* unconverted persons[5] in this congregation. This that you have heard is the case of every one of you that are out of Christ.[6] That world of misery, that lake of burning brimstone, is extended abroad under you. *There* is the dreadful pit of the glowing flames of the wrath of God; there is hell's wide gaping mouth open; and you have nothing to stand upon, not anything to take hold of; there is nothing between you and hell but the air; 'tis only the power and mere pleasure of God that holds you up.

You probably are not sensible of this; you find you are kept out of hell, but do not see the hand of God in it; but look at other things, as the good state of your bodily constitution, your care of your own life, and the means you use for your own preservation. But indeed these things are nothing; if God should withdraw his hand, they would avail no more to keep you from falling, than the thin air to hold up a person that is suspended in it.

Your wickedness makes you as it were heavy as lead[7] and to tend downwards with great weight and pressure towards hell; and if God should let you go, you would immediately sink and swiftly descend and plunge into the bottomless gulf, and your healthy constitution, and your own care and prudence, and best contrivance, and all your righteousness, would have no more influence to uphold you and keep you out of hell than a spider's web would have to stop a falling rock. Were it not for the sovereign pleasure of God, the earth would not bear you one moment; for you are a burden to it; the creation groans with you; the creature[8] is made subject to the bondage of your corruption, not willingly; the sun does not willingly shine upon you to give you light to serve sin and Satan; the earth does not willingly yield her increase to satisfy your lusts; nor is it willingly

---

1   *peace and safety ... upon me*   See 1 Thessalonians 5.3.

2   *God certainly ... of grace*   Edwards alludes to the Calvinist tenet of "limited atonement," which holds that salvation is granted only to those members of God's elect.

3   *the Mediator*   I.e., Christ.

4   *seeking and knocking*   See Matthew 7.7: "Ask, and it shall be given you; seek, and ye shall find; knock, and it shall be opened."

5   *unconverted persons*   Parishioners who had not yet publicly proclaimed their experience of salvation, and thus had not obtained full church membership.

6   *out of Christ*   Not saved, not a member of the elect.

7   *heavy as lead*   See Exodus 15.10, where God is praised for drowning the Egyptians, enemies of the Israelites, in the sea: "Thou didst blow with thy wind, the sea covered them: they sank as lead in the mighty waters."

8   *creature*   Thing or being created by God.

a stage for your wickedness to be acted upon; the air does not willingly serve you for breath to maintain the flame of life in your vitals, while you spend your life in the service of God's enemies. God's creatures are good, and were made for men to serve God with, and do not willingly subserve to[1] any other purpose, and groan when they are abused to purposes so directly contrary to their nature and end. And the world would spew you out, were it not for the sovereign hand of him who hath subjected it in hope.[2] There are the black clouds of God's wrath now hanging directly over your heads, full of the dreadful storm, and big with thunder; and were it not for the restraining hand of God, it would immediately burst forth upon you. The sovereign pleasure of God, for the present, stays his rough wind; otherwise it would come with fury, and your destruction would come like a whirlwind,[3] and you would be like the chaff on the summer threshing floor.

The wrath of God is like great waters that are dammed for the present; they increase more and more, and rise higher and higher, till an outlet is given; and the longer the stream is stopped, the more rapid and mighty is its course, when once it is let loose. 'Tis true, that judgment against your evil works has not been executed hitherto; the floods of God's vengeance have been withheld; but your guilt in the meantime is constantly increasing, and you are every day treasuring up more wrath; the waters are constantly rising, and waxing more and more mighty; and there is nothing but the mere pleasure of God that holds the waters back that are unwilling to be stopped and press hard to go forward. If God should only withdraw his hand from the flood-gate, it would immediately fly open, and the fiery floods of the fierceness and wrath of God, would rush forth with inconceivable fury and would come upon you with omnipotent power; and if your strength were ten thousand times greater than it is, yea, ten thousand times greater than the strength of the stoutest, sturdiest devil in hell, it would be nothing to withstand or endure it.

The bow of God's wrath is bent,[4] and the arrow made ready on the string, and justice bends the arrow at your heart, and strains the bow, and it is nothing but the mere pleasure of God, and that of an angry God, without any promise or obligation at all, that keeps the arrow one moment from being made drunk with your blood.

Thus all you that never passed under a great change of heart, by the mighty power of the Spirit of God upon your souls; all you that were never born again,[5] and made new creatures, and raised from being dead in sin, to a state of new, and before altogether unexperienced light and life, are in the hands of an angry God. However you may have reformed your life in many things, and may have had religious affections, and may keep up a form of religion in your families and closets,[6] and in the house of God, 'tis nothing but his mere pleasure that keeps you from being this moment swallowed up in everlasting destruction. However unconvinced you may now be of the truth of what you hear, by and by you will be fully convinced of it. Those that are gone from being in the like circumstances with you, see that it was so with them; for destruction came suddenly upon most of them; when they expected nothing of it, and while they were saying, Peace and safety: now they see, that those things on which they depended for peace and safety, were nothing but thin air and empty shadows.

The God that holds you over the pit of hell, much as one holds a spider, or some loathsome insect over the fire, abhors you, and is dreadfully provoked: his wrath towards you burns like fire; he looks upon you as worthy of nothing else, but to be cast into the fire; he is of purer eyes than to bear to have you in his sight; you are ten thousand times more abominable in his eyes, than the most hateful venomous serpent is in ours. You have offended him infinitely more than ever a stubborn rebel did his prince; and yet 'tis nothing but his

---

[1] *subserve to* Serve, facilitate.

[2] *him who … in hope* See Romans 8.20: "the creature was made subject to vanity, not willingly, but by reason of him who hath subjected the same in hope."

[3] *your destruction … whirlwind* See Proverbs 1.26–27, where wisdom addresses "fools," saying "I also will laugh at your calamity; I will mock when your fear cometh; when your fear cometh as desolation, and your destruction cometh as a whirlwind."

[4] *The bow … bent* See Psalm 7.11–12: "God judgeth the righteous, and God is angry with the wicked every day. If he turn not, he will whet his sword; he hath bent his bow, and made it ready."

[5] *born again* I.e., saved; spiritually reborn through faith in Christ.

[6] *closets* I.e., private rooms.

hand that holds you from falling into the fire every moment. 'Tis to be ascribed to nothing else, that you did not go to hell the last night; that you was suffered to awake again in this world, after you closed your eyes to sleep. And there is no other reason to be given, why you have not dropped into hell since you arose in the morning, but that God's hand has held you up. There is no other reason to be given why you have not gone to hell, since you have sat here in the house of God, provoking his pure eyes by your sinful wicked manner of attending his solemn worship. Yea, there is nothing else that is to be given as a reason why you do not this very moment drop down into hell.

O sinner! Consider the fearful danger you are in: 'Tis a great furnace of wrath, a wide and bottomless pit, full of the fire of wrath, that you are held over in the hand of that God, whose wrath is provoked and incensed as much against you, as against many of the damned in hell. You hang by a slender thread, with the flames of divine wrath flashing about it, and ready every moment to singe it, and burn it asunder; and you have no interest in any Mediator, and nothing to lay hold of to save yourself, nothing to keep off the flames of wrath, nothing of your own, nothing that you ever have done, nothing that you can do, to induce God to spare you one moment.

And consider here more particularly several things concerning that wrath that you are in such danger of.

1. *Whose* wrath it is: it is the wrath of the infinite God. If it were only the wrath of man, though it were of the most potent prince, it would be comparatively little to be regarded. The wrath of kings is very much dreaded, especially of absolute monarchs, who have the possessions and lives of their subjects wholly in their power, to be disposed of at their mere will. Proverbs 20.2: *The fear of a king is as the roaring of a lion: Whoso provoketh him to anger, sinneth against his own soul.* The subject that very much enrages an arbitrary prince, is liable to suffer the most extreme torments that human art can invent, or human power can inflict. But the greatest earthly potentates in their greatest majesty and strength, and when clothed in their greatest terrors, are but feeble, despicable worms of the dust in comparison of the great and almighty Creator and King of heaven and earth. It is but little that they can do, when most enraged and when they have exerted the utmost of their fury. All the kings of the earth, before God, are as grasshoppers;[1] they are nothing and less than nothing: both their love and their hatred is to be despised. The wrath of the great king of kings[2] is as much more terrible than theirs, as his majesty is greater. Luke 12.4–5: *And I say unto you, my friends, Be not afraid of them that kill the body, and after that, have no more that they can do. But I will forewarn you whom you shall fear: fear him, which after he hath killed, hath power to cast into hell: yea, I say unto you, fear him.*

2. 'Tis the *fierceness* of his wrath that you are exposed to. We often read of the fury of God; as in Isaiah 59.18: *According to their deeds, accordingly he will repay fury to his adversaries.* So Isaiah 66.15: *For behold, the Lord will come with fire, and with his chariots like a whirlwind, to render his anger with fury, and his rebuke with flames of fire.* And in many other places. So, Rev. 19.15, we read of *The wine press of the fierceness and wrath of Almighty God.* The words are exceeding terrible. If it had only been said, *the wrath of God,* the words would have implied that which is infinitely dreadful: but 'tis not only said so, but *the fierceness and wrath of God.* The fury of God! The fierceness of Jehovah! Oh, how dreadful that must be! Who can utter or conceive what such expressions carry in them! But it is not only said so, but *the fierceness and wrath of almighty God.* As though there would be a very great manifestation of his almighty power in what the fierceness of his wrath should inflict, as though omnipotence should be as it were enraged and excited, as men are wont to exert their strength in the fierceness of their wrath. Oh! Then, what will be the consequence! What will become of the poor worms that shall suffer it! Whose hands can be strong? And whose heart endure? To what a dreadful, inexpressible, inconceivable depth of misery must the poor creature be sunk who shall be the subject of this!

Consider this, you that are here present, that yet remain in an unregenerate state. That God will execute the fierceness of his anger implies that he will inflict wrath without any pity. When God beholds the ineffable extremity of your case, and sees your torment to be so vastly disproportioned to your strength, and sees how your poor soul is crushed, and sinks down, as it

---

[1]   *grasshoppers*   See Isaiah 40.22: "It is he that sitteth upon the circle of the earth, and the inhabitants thereof are as grasshoppers."

[2]   *king of kings*   God.

were, into an infinite gloom; he will have no compassion upon you, he will not forbear the executions of his wrath, or in the least lighten his hand; there shall be no moderation or mercy, nor will God then at all stay his rough wind; he will have no regard to your welfare, nor be at all careful lest you should suffer too much in any other sense, than only that you shall not suffer beyond what strict justice requires. Nothing shall be withheld, because it's so hard for you to bear. Ezekiel 8.18: *Therefore will I also deal in fury: mine eye shall not spare, neither will I have pity; and though they cry in mine ears with a loud voice, yet I will not hear them.* Now God stands ready to pity you; this is a day of mercy; you may cry now with some encouragement of obtaining mercy. But when once the day of mercy is past, your most lamentable and dolorous[1] cries and shrieks will be in vain; you will be wholly lost and thrown away of God, as to any regard to your welfare. God will have no other use to put you to but to suffer misery; you shall be continued in being to no other end, for you will be a vessel of wrath fitted to destruction; and there will be no other use of this vessel, but to be filled full of wrath. God will be so far from pitying you when you cry to him, that 'tis said he will only *laugh and mock,* Proverbs 1.25–26, etc.

How awful[2] are those words, Isaiah 63.3, which are the words of the great God. *I will tread them in mine anger, and will trample them in my fury, and their blood shall be sprinkled upon my garments, and I will stain all my raiment.*[3] 'Tis perhaps impossible to conceive of words that carry in them greater manifestations of these three things, *viz.*[4] contempt, and hatred, and fierceness of indignation. If you cry to God to pity you, he will be so far from pitying you in your doleful case, or showing you the least regard or favour, that instead of that, he will only tread you under foot. And though he will know that you cannot bear the weight of omnipotence treading upon you, yet he will not regard that, but he will crush you under his feet without mercy; he will crush out your blood, and make it fly, and it shall be sprinkled on his garments, so as to stain all his raiment.

He will not only hate you, but he will have you in the utmost contempt: no place shall be thought fit for you, but under his feet to be trodden down as the mire of the streets.

3. The misery you are exposed to is that which God will inflict to that end, that he might *show* what that *wrath* of Jehovah is. God hath had it on his heart to show to angels and men, both how excellent his love is and also how terrible his wrath is. Sometimes earthly kings have a mind to show how terrible their wrath is by the extreme punishments they would execute on those that would provoke them. Nebuchadnezzar, that mighty and haughty monarch of the Chaldean empire, was willing to show his wrath when enraged with Shadrach, Meshach, and Abednego;[5] and accordingly gave orders that the burning fiery furnace should be heated seven times hotter than it was before; doubtless, it was raised to the utmost degree of fierceness that human art could raise it. But the great God is also willing to show his wrath, and magnify his awful majesty and mighty power in the extreme sufferings of his enemies. Romans 9.22: *What if God, willing to show his wrath, and to make his power known, endured with much long-suffering the vessels of wrath fitted to destruction?* And seeing this is his design, and what he has determined, even to show how terrible the unrestrained wrath, the fury and fierceness of Jehovah is, he will do it to effect. There will be something accomplished and brought to pass that will be dreadful with a witness. When the great and angry God hath risen up and executed his awful vengeance on the poor sinner, and the wretch is actually suffering the infinite weight and power of his indignation, then will God call upon the whole universe to behold that awful majesty and mighty power that is to be seen in it. Isaiah 33.12–14: *And the people shall be as the burnings of lime, as thorns cut up shall they be burnt in the fire. Hear ye that are far off, what I have done; and ye that are near, acknowledge my might. The sinners in Zion are afraid; fearfulness hath surprised the hypocrites,* etc.

Thus it will be with you that are in an unconverted state, if you continue in it; the infinite might, and

---

[1] *dolorous* Sorrowful, marked by suffering.

[2] *awful* Awe-inspiring.

[3] *raiment* Clothing.

[4] *viz.* Abbreviation of the Latin videlicet, meaning "namely," or "that is to say."

[5] *Shadrach, Meshach, and Abednego* Three Jewish youths in the book of Daniel who refused to bow before an image of Nebuchadnezzar, the king of Babylon, and were punished by being cast into a furnace. God prevented the flames from harming them. See Daniel 3.

majesty, and terribleness of the Omnipotent GOD shall be magnified upon you, in the ineffable strength of your torments. You shall be tormented in the presence of the holy angels, and in the presence of the Lamb;[1] and when you shall be in this state of suffering, the glorious inhabitants of heaven shall go forth and look on the awful spectacle, that they may see what the wrath and fierceness of the Almighty is; and when they have seen it, they will fall down and adore that great power and majesty. Isaiah 66.23–24: *And it shall come to pass, that from one new moon to another, and from one sabbath to another, shall all flesh come to worship before me, saith the Lord. And they shall go forth and look upon the carcasses of the men that have transgressed against me; for their worm shall not die, neither shall their fire be quenched, and they shall be an abhorring unto all flesh.*

4. 'Tis *everlasting* wrath. It would be dreadful to suffer this fierceness and wrath of Almighty God one moment; but you must suffer it to all eternity. There will be no end to this exquisite horrible misery. When you look forward, you shall see a long forever, a boundless duration before you, which will swallow up your thoughts, and amaze your soul; and you will absolutely despair of ever having any deliverance, any end, any mitigation, any rest at all. You will know certainly that you must wear out long ages, millions of millions of ages, in wrestling and conflicting with this almighty merciless vengeance; and then when you have so done, when so many ages have actually been spent by you in this manner, you will know that all is but a point to what remains. So that your punishment will indeed be infinite. Oh, who can express what the state of a soul in such circumstances is! All that we can possibly say about it, gives but a very feeble, faint representation of it; 'tis inexpressible and inconceivable: For *who knows the power of God's anger?*[2]

How dreadful is the state of those that are daily and hourly in the danger of this great wrath and infinite misery! But this is the dismal case of every soul in this congregation that has not been born again, however moral and strict, sober and religious, they may otherwise be. Oh that you would consider it, whether you be young or old! There is reason to think that there are many in this congregation now hearing this discourse, that will actually be the subjects of this very misery to all eternity. We know not who they are, or in what seats they sit, or what thoughts they now have. It may be they are now at ease, and hear all these things without much disturbance, and are now flattering themselves that they are not the persons, promising themselves that they shall escape. If we knew that there was one person, and but one, in the whole congregation, that was to be the subject of this misery, what an awful thing would it be to think of! If we knew who it was, what an awful sight would it be to see such a person! How might all the rest of the congregation lift up a lamentable and bitter cry over him! But, alas! instead of one, how many is it likely will remember this discourse in hell? And it would be a wonder, if some that are now present should not be in hell in a very short time, even before this year is out. And it would be no wonder if some persons, that now sit here, in some seats of this meeting-house,[3] in health, quiet and secure, should be there before tomorrow morning. Those of you that finally continue in a natural condition, that shall keep out of hell longest will be there in a little time! Your damnation does not slumber; it will come swiftly, and, in all probability, very suddenly upon many of you. You have reason to wonder that you are not already in hell. 'Tis doubtless the case of some whom you have seen and known that never deserved hell more than you, and that heretofore appeared as likely to have been now alive as you. Their case is past all hope; they are crying in extreme misery and perfect despair; but here you are in the land of the living and in the house of God, and have an opportunity to obtain salvation. What would not those poor damned hopeless souls give for one day's opportunity such as you now enjoy!

And now you have an extraordinary opportunity, a day wherein Christ has thrown the door of mercy wide open, and stands in calling and crying with a loud voice to poor sinners; a day wherein many are flocking to him, and pressing into the kingdom of God.[4] Many are daily coming from the east, west, north and south; many that were very lately in the same miserable condition that you are in, are now in a happy state, with

---

[1]   *the Lamb*   Christ.

[2]   *who knows … God's anger*   See Psalm 90.11: "Who knoweth the power of thine anger? Even according to thy fear, so is thy wrath."

[3]   *meeting-house*   Place of worship.

[4]   *And now … of God*   At the time Edwards delivered this sermon, the First Great Awakening, a surge of religious enthusiasm, was spreading across New England.

their hearts filled with love to him who has loved them, and washed them from their sins in his own blood, and rejoicing in hope of the glory of God. How awful is it to be left behind at such a day! To see so many others feasting, while you are pining and perishing! To see so many rejoicing and singing for joy of heart, while you have cause to mourn for sorrow of heart, and howl for vexation of spirit! How can you rest one moment in such a condition? Are not your souls as precious as the souls of the people at Suffield,[1] where they are flocking from day to day to Christ?

Are there not many here who have lived *long* in the world, and are not to this day born again? And so are aliens from the commonwealth of Israel,[2] and have done nothing ever since they have lived, but treasure up wrath against the day of wrath? Oh, sirs, your case, in an especial manner, is extremely dangerous. Your guilt and hardness of heart is extremely great. Do you not see how generally persons of your years are passed over and left in the present remarkable and wonderful dispensation of God's mercy? You had need to consider yourselves and awake thoroughly out of sleep. You cannot bear the fierceness and wrath of the infinite God.

And you that are *young men* and *young women*, will you neglect this precious season which you now enjoy, when so many others of your age are renouncing all youthful vanities, and flocking to Christ? You especially have now an extraordinary opportunity; but if you neglect it, it will soon be with you as with those persons who spent all the precious days of youth in sin, and are now come to such a dreadful pass in blindness and hardness.

And you, *children* that are unconverted, do not you know that you are going down to hell, to bear the dreadful wrath of that God, who is now angry with you every day and every night? Will you be content to be the children of the devil, when so many other children in the land are converted, and are become the holy and happy children of the king of kings?

And let everyone that is yet out of Christ, and hanging over the pit of hell, whether they be old men and women, or middle aged, or young people, or little children, now hearken to the loud calls of God's word and providence. This acceptable year of the Lord, a day of such great favour to some, will doubtless be a day of as remarkable vengeance to others. Men's hearts harden, and their guilt increases apace at such a day as this, if they neglect their souls; and never was there so great danger of such persons being given up to hardness of heart and blindness of mind. God seems now to be hastily gathering in his elect in all parts of the land; and probably the greater part of adult persons that ever shall be saved will be brought in now in a little time, and that it will be as it was on the great outpouring of the Spirit upon the Jews in the apostles' days; the election will obtain, and the rest will be blinded.[3] If this should be the case with you, you will eternally curse this day, and will curse the day that ever you was born, to see such a season of the pouring out of God's Spirit, and will wish that you had died and gone to hell before you had seen it. Now undoubtedly it is, as it was in the days of John the Baptist, the axe is in an extraordinary manner laid at the root of the trees, that every tree which brings not forth good fruit, may be hewn down and cast into the fire.[4]

Therefore, let every one that is out of Christ, now awake and fly from the wrath to come. The wrath of Almighty God is now undoubtedly hanging over a great part of this congregation. Let every one fly out of Sodom: *Haste and escape for your lives, look not behind you, escape to the mountain, lest you be consumed.*[5]

—1741

---

[1] *Suffield*   A neighboring town in Massachusetts where, two days earlier, Edwards had delivered a sermon that was enthusiastically received by an audience of more than two hundred people.

[2] *aliens from ... of Israel*   People who are estranged from the church, i.e., are not members of the elect.

[3] *the election ... be blinded*   See Romans 11.7: "Israel hath not obtained that which he seeketh for; but the election hath obtained it, and the rest were blinded."

[4] *the axe ... the fire*   See Luke 3.9: "And now also the axe is laid unto the root of the trees: every tree therefore which bringeth not forth good fruit is hewn down, and cast into the fire."

[5] *Haste and ... consumed*   See Genesis 19.17, where an angel warns Lot to flee the city of Sodom before it is destroyed by God: "Escape for thy life; look not behind thee, neither stay thou in all the plain; escape to the mountain, lest thou be consumed."

LUCY TERRY
c. 1724/30 – 1821

Lucy Terry is celebrated as the author of the first known work of literature by an African American. That work, the short occasional poem "Bars Fight," was transmitted orally by her community members for decades after its composition circa 1746, before being published in the mid-nineteenth century.

Terry (whose birth name is unknown), is thought by several scholars to have been born around 1730 (though some others have argued that she was born as early as 1724), probably in West Africa. She was brought enslaved to Rhode Island in early childhood; her name was likely given her by the slaveholder who first purchased her, Samuel Terry. She grew up in Deerfield, Massachusetts—then a frontier settlement that was home to a significant number of enslaved individuals—as the legal property of Ebenezer and Abigail Wells. She was baptized in 1735 and admitted into full church communion in 1744. In Deerfield, Terry developed a reputation as a compelling storyteller, reportedly attracting enthusiastic audiences at the local tavern. Josiah Holland's *History of Western Massachussetts* describes her as follows:

> One of the most noteworthy characters in the early history of Deerfield was a colored woman, known as "Luce Bijah."[1] She was … known for her wit and shrewdness. Her house was the constant resort of the boys, to hear her talk. She removed with her husband and children to Vermont, and purchased a tract of land, the title to which proved imperfect. A suit was brought to dispossess her, and she argued her case against Stephen R. Bradley and Royal Tyler (afterwards, Chief Justice of Vermont). Judge Chase, who held the court, said that Luce made a better argument than he had heard at the bar of Vermont. Luce was a poetess, and commemorated in verse the end of the "Bars Fight."

The "Bars fight" itself occurred on 25 August 1746. A group of approximately fifty Abenaki warriors, under the command of the French army, launched an attack, targeting a field known locally as "the Bars" where a group of (largely or entirely white) villagers had gathered to begin their haymaking. The villagers were unaware of the recent capture of Fort Massachusetts by the French army and their Indigenous allies, a small part of the mounting hostilities that would lead to the French and Indian War in the following decade. The attack led to the deaths of five villagers, with one young girl, Eunice Allen, surviving a severe head injury, and her younger brother, Samuel Allen, taken captive. Much of what is known today of this incident is owed to Terry's poem, which was presumably composed not long after the attack, and which nineteenth-century historian George Sheldon would later describe as "the fullest contemporary account of that bloody tragedy which has been preserved."

Stylistically the poem is a striking mix, with some elements suggestive of the ballad form (often the means of memorializing local history), some suggestive of other verse forms—and with interesting differences between the stylistic features of the first eighteen lines and those of the last ten. Clearly the poem (which may well have been intended to be sung) struck a chord; through one means or another it was preserved orally for decades. Its first appearance in print was on the front page of the *Springfield Republican* on 20 November 1854, shortly prior to its inclusion in Holland's two-volume work.

In May 1756, Terry married Abijah Prince, a free African American. Not long thereafter, she was freed from slavery, possibly through purchase by her husband; the couple's six children—two of whom likely fought for the American army during the Revolutionary War—would all be born into freedom. The family eventually settled in Vermont in the 1770s, where they came to own a substantial amount of property and to hold positions of considerable respect in the community. That said, the Princes remained

---

[1]   Though she is most often referred to as "Lucy Terry," various records refer to her as "Bijah's Luce," "Lucy Abijah," and "Luce Bijah" (after the name of her husband, Abijah Prince).

subject to racial prejudice; the continual violence and harassment of one neighbor who sought to drive them off their land led to the court case Holland refers to, in which Terry successfully petitioned for legal protection. (Numerous other accounts exist of Terry defending herself and her family in court, though most of these have not been substantiated by surviving court documents.)

Terry died in 1821, likely in her nineties. Her funeral was attended by the well-known African American minister and writer Lemuel Haynes, who composed an antislavery poem to be read at the occasion. A long obituary in the *Vermont Gazette* foregrounded her respectability and religiosity as well as her intelligence and narrative talents, claiming that "the fluency of her speech captivated all around her, and was not destitute of instruction and edification."

"Bars Fight" remains Terry's only known composition. Though dismissed by some scholars in the twentieth century as "doggerel," the poem is highly valued today—as a historical document recounting one part of the struggle between white settlers and the Indigenous peoples of early America; as a work revealing the talents and the sympathies of a young African American woman in the mid-eighteenth century; and as an important text in the ongoing exploration of the liminal space between the cultures of orality and those of the written word.

NOTE ON THE TEXT: The text presented below is based on that printed as part of the history of Deerfield, in Volume Two of Josiah Holland's *History of Western Massachusetts* (1855). Spelling and punctuation have been modernized in accordance with the practices of this anthology.

⌘ ⌘ ⌘

Bars[1] Fight

August 'twas the twenty-fifth,
Seventeen hundred forty-six;
The Indians did in ambush lay,
Some very valiant men to slay,
5 The names of whom I'll not leave out.
Samuel Allen like a hero fought.
And though he was so brave and bold,
His face no more shall we behold.
Eleazer Hawks was killed outright,
10 Before he had time to fight—
Before he did the Indians see,
Was shot and killed immediately.
Oliver Amsden he was slain,
Which caused his friends much grief and pain.
15 Simeon Amsden they found dead,
Not many rods[2] distant from his head.
Adonijah Gillett we do hear

Did lose his life which was so dear.
John Sadler fled across the water,
20 And thus escaped the dreadful slaughter.
Eunice Allen see the Indians coming,
And hopes to save herself by running,
And had not her petticoats stopped her,
The awful creatures had not catched her,
25 Nor tommy hawked her on the head,
And left her on the ground for dead.[3]
Young Samuel Allen, Oh lack-a-day!
Was taken and carried to Canada.[4]
—1855 (COMPOSED C. 1746)

---

3 *Eunice Allen … for dead* Eunice Allen, who was thirteen at the time of the attack, survived her injuries, reportedly living to over eighty years of age.

4 *Young Samuel … to Canada* The eight-year-old son of the Samuel Allen whose death is noted earlier in the poem, young Samuel Allen was taken captive by the attackers and held for ransom for a year and nine months, during which period he was said to have assimilated into Abenaki society; contemporary reports suggest that he was reluctant to return to his previous Massachusetts life. It is with reference to these concluding lines and the story of Samuel Allen that some scholars have drawn connections between Terry's poem and the captivity narrative tradition within American literature.

---

1 *Bars* Local name for a meadow outside Deerfield, Massachusetts.

2 *rods* Units of measurement, equalling approximately five and a half yards.

SAGOYEWATHA

c. 1758 – 1830

Popularly known as Red Jacket, Sagoyewatha was a Seneca chief and orator. Renowned for his powers of persuasion in Indigenous councils—and for his ability to adapt Haudenosaunee rhetoric to the persuasion of settler audiences—he often spoke on behalf of the Seneca at treaty councils from the 1780s to the 1820s, articulating the positions that Seneca leaders had collectively agreed upon. He sought peace whenever possible, as the diplomatic tradition of the Haudenosaunee dictated, while also defending Seneca land and culture, often with an ironic wit. He is best known for his rhetorically powerful speeches in defense of Indigenous land rights and religious practices, and for his diplomatic efforts on behalf of the Haudenosaunee—efforts that Haudenosaunee negotiators continue to build on in the present day.

Sagoyewatha was most likely born in Canoga, New York (the exact location of his birthplace is unclear); his father was Cayuga, and his mother was a member of an influential Senecan family that included other important figures such as the war chief Cornplanter and the religious leader Handsome Lake. The Seneca are a matrilineal society, and Sagoyewatha was born into his mother's clan, the Wolf clan. In childhood he received the name Otetiani ("Always Ready"). Legend has it that early in his life he attended an important council of Indigenous leaders on the Shenandoah river, where he heard Logan the Orator—a war leader of the Haudenosaunee—speak. This experience sparked an ambition, and it is said that the young Sagoyewatha would spend a great deal of time alone in the forest "playing Logan": practicing his skills of persuasion. He also served as a runner, a messenger tasked with accurately recounting council proceedings to other communities.

The role of diplomat and peacemaker is vitally important in Haudenosaunee culture, the orator acting as a steward for the Great Law of Peace of the People of the Longhouse.[1] Sagoyewatha's ambition was to join the long history of respected Indigenous orators, including Garangula, Hendrick, Skenandoah, Adario, and Logan. In the 1770s, the young Otetiani was given a new name, Sagoyewatha, often translated as "the keeper awake" and considered a tribute to his rhetorical power to captivate his audience. (Recently, it has been suggested that the name may simply mean "he wakes them up early," with no particular reference to Sagoyewatha's oratorical gifts.)

During the American Revolutionary War the Seneca generally supported a neutral position, but most eventually sided with the British. While Sagoyewatha was not a successful soldier—in fact, accusations of cowardice from his political rivals would follow him for the rest of his life—he was more successful in his diplomatic role as a runner, and British officers gave him a British military jacket in recognition of his services. He wore such a jacket from then on, embracing the name of "Red Jacket." The British government did not, however, prove to be a reliable ally to the Seneca: as part of the treaty that ended the war, Britain gave America large portions of land that earlier agreements had recognized as belonging to Indigenous peoples. Many Seneca migrated to Canada as a result, but Sagoyewatha stayed in the Genesee River Valley in New York and became a key negotiator representing the Seneca who remained to the American government.

President Washington requested a meeting with Sagoyewatha in 1792, in an effort to convince the Seneca chiefs to support efforts to contain wars with Indigenous peoples in the West. Sagoyewatha's speech on the historical context of the wars impressed Washington so greatly that he gave the chief a

---

[1]   An oral constitution of the Haudenosaunee, or Six Nations (originally Five Nations), the Great Law of Peace enshrines individual rights and creates a consensus-based federation among the nations.

silver "peace medal." Sagoyewatha was also influential in the negotiation of the Treaty of Canandaigua in 1794—the "peace and friendship" treaty between the Six Nations of the Iroquois and the new government of the United States. The treaty, to which Sagoyewatha was a signatory, did not secure as much land as he had wanted for the Seneca, but it did acknowledge the right of Indigenous nations to negotiate directly with the American government. While the federal government did not consistently adhere to the terms of the treaty, it remains in force in the twenty-first century and is still the legal basis for the sovereignty of Haudenosaunee nations.

In 1805, Sagoyewatha gave the speech for which he is most famous, his "Reply to Jacob Cram," sometimes titled "Religion for the White Man and the Red," or "We Never Quarrel about Religion." In this speech, Sagoyewatha explains Haudenosaunee leadership's refusal to allow missionaries to establish churches on Seneca reservations. By 1807, however, he faced opposition from those within his own community who had converted to Christianity, and this schism among the people deepened, becoming a crisis in 1826 when Christian Seneca sold land to the Ogden company—a private land developer— against the wishes of those chiefs who followed the traditional religion. When Sagoyewatha and thirty or forty other leaders from the "Pagan party" protested this sale, which had been obtained through bribery and threats, the agreement was not ratified. The Ogden company ignored this, however, and succeeded in buying, under extortionate terms, almost all of the Seneca reservation in Western New York. Sagoyewatha was for a time deposed from his leadership role, probably as a result of this controversy and certainly on account of his continued resistance to Christianity. He did, however, regain his position before his death. His later years were shadowed by alcoholism, by the deaths of his children, and by a period of separation from his wife following her conversion to Christianity. He died of cholera in 1830.

As an orator whose speeches were delivered in Seneca but recorded in English translation, Sagoyewatha left behind a written record that at best only partially captures his achievements. His work, however, is far better documented than is typical for a Native American orator of this period; many of his most important speeches took place on occasions that were facilitated by first-rate interpreters and thoroughly recorded, and much (though by no means all) of the writing attributed to him has a consistency of tone and style that suggests a certain degree of accuracy. Beginning in the mid-1810s, Seneca leadership began consciously to harness the reach of print media, and it appears that many of Sagoyewatha's speeches from this point onward were intended not only for performance but also for transcription in newspapers and pamphlets.

By the time of his death, Sagoyewatha's reputation was such that, a decade later, his biographer could write that "[t]he name of Red-Jacket, the great orator of the Six Nations, is among those most familiar to the American ear." Several biographies were written about Sagoyewatha in the nineteenth and twentieth centuries, and his speeches were frequently distributed in pamphlets and schoolbooks. Competing narratives of his life, however, have long circulated. One such image, promulgated by his political opponents, emphasized his military failures and his alcoholism, portraying him as a self-serving coward. Another, at least as false, romanticized his wisdom and eloquence and eulogized him as the "last of the Senecas"—invoking the common stereotype of the vanishing "noble savage" who is worthy of respect but whose era has sadly passed. In recent decades, scholarship has focused on Sagoyewatha as a major contributor to an ongoing tradition of Haudenosaunee diplomacy. Scholars have analyzed his speeches with reference to Haudenosaunee rhetoric and ideology, and have emphasized the foundation he helped to lay for later generations of Indigenous resistance.

NOTE ON THE TEXT: This text is based on the first printing of the speech in the *Monthly Anthology and Boston Review*, April 1809; additions made by the *Monthly Anthology* appear in square brackets below. The history of the transmission of this speech is somewhat unclear; it was published almost three years after it was delivered, and scholars believe that the council probably took place in November rather than, as the *Monthly Anthology* suggests, in the summer. Sagoyewatha kept track of what was published about him, however, and there is no evidence that he disputed the text's accuracy.

⌘ ⌘ ⌘

[*Reply to the Missionary Jacob Cram*][1]

[In the summer of 1805, a number of the principal Chiefs and Warriors of the Six Nations of Indians,[2] principally Senecas, assembled at Buffalo Creek, in the State of New York, at the particular request of a gentleman Missionary from the State of Massachusetts.[3] The Missionary being furnished with an Interpreter, and accompanied by the Agent of the United States for Indian affairs,[4] met the Indians in Council, when the following talk took place.]

FIRST, BY THE AGENT.

Brothers of the Six Nations; I rejoice to meet you at this time, and thank the Great Spirit, that he has preserved you in health, and given me another opportunity of taking you by the hand.

Brothers; The person who sits by me is a friend who has come a great distance to hold a talk with you. He will inform you what his business is, and it is my request that you would listen with attention to his words.

MISSIONARY. *My Friends*; I am thankful for the opportunity afforded us of uniting together at this time. I had a great desire to see you, and inquire into your state and welfare; for this purpose I have travelled a great distance, being sent by your old friends, the Boston Missionary Society. You will recollect they formerly sent missionaries among you, to instruct you in religion, and labour for your good. Although they have not heard from you for a long time, yet they have not forgotten their brothers the Six Nations, and are still anxious to do you good.

Brothers; I have not come to get your lands or your money, but to enlighten your minds, and to instruct you how to worship the Great Spirit agreeably to his mind and will, and to preach to you the gospel of his son Jesus Christ. There is but one religion, and but one way to serve God, and if you do not embrace the right way, you cannot be happy hereafter. You have never worshipped the Great Spirit in a manner acceptable to him; but have, all your lives, been in great errors and darkness. To endeavour to remove these errors, and open your eyes, so that you might see clearly, is my business with you.

Brothers; I wish to talk with you as one friend talks with another; and, if you have any objections to receive the religion which I preach, I wish you to state them; and I will endeavour to satisfy your minds, and remove the objections.

Brothers; I want you to speak your minds freely; for I wish to reason with you on the subject, and, if possible, remove all doubts, if there be any on your minds. The subject is an important one, and it is of consequence that you give it an early attention while the offer is made you. Your friends, the Boston Missionary Society, will continue to send you good and faithful ministers, to instruct and strengthen you in religion, if, on your part, you are willing to receive them.

Brothers; Since I have been in this part of the country, I have visited some of your small villages, and talked with your people. They appear willing to receive instruction, but, as they look up to you as their older brothers in council, they want first to know your opinion on the subject.

You have now heard what I have to propose at present. I hope you will take it into consideration, and give me an answer before we part.

---

[1]   Originally published under the title Indian Speech;   *Jacob Cram* New England missionary and author of *Journal of a Missionary Tour* (1808).

[2]   *Six Nations of Indians* Also known as the Haudenosaunee Confederacy or Iroquois Confederacy, this alliance of Iroquoian-speaking nations—including the Mohawk, Onondaga, Oneida, Cayuga, Seneca, and later the Tuscarora—constituted a powerful political and trading community in Northeastern North America from the seventeenth to nineteenth centuries. The Haudenosaunee Confederacy, though now much reduced in population, continues to advocate for its sovereign communities in both the United States and Canada.

[3]   [Note from the *Monthly Anthology*]   Rev. Mr. Cram.

[4]   *Agent of the United States for Indian affairs* Person authorized by the U.S. government to act on its behalf during negotiations with Indigenous peoples. Agents oversaw trade, distributed annual payments to the sachems, attempted to manage conflicts, and enacted the forced removal of Indigenous peoples from their land and onto reservations. This role was largely unsupervised and involved the handling of a great deal of money and trade goods; while some agents were honest, many were corrupt and self-serving, inflicting untold damage on the Indigenous communities.

[After about two hours consultation amongst themselves, the Chief commonly called, by the white people, Red Jacket,[1] rose and spoke as follows:]

Friend and Brother; It was the will of the Great Spirit that we should meet together this day. He orders all things, and has given us a fine day for our Council. He has taken his garment from before the sun, and caused it to shine with brightness upon us. Our eyes are opened, that we see clearly; our ears are unstopped, that we have been able to hear distinctly the words you have spoken. For all these favours we thank the Great Spirit; and Him *only*.

Brother; This council fire was kindled by you. It was at your request that we came together at this time. We have listened with attention to what you have said. You requested us to speak our minds freely. This gives us great joy; for we now consider that we stand upright before you, and can speak what we think. All have heard your voice, and all speak to you now as one man. Our minds are agreed.

Brother; You say you want an answer to your talk before you leave this place. It is right you should have one, as you are a great distance from home, and we do not wish to detain you. But we will first look back a little, and tell you what our fathers have told us, and what we have heard from the white people.

Brother; Listen to what we say.

There was a time when our forefathers owned this great island. Their seats[2] extended from the rising to the setting sun. The Great Spirit had made it for the use of Indians. He had created the buffalo, the deer, and other animals for food. He had made the bear and the beaver. Their skins served us for clothing. He had scattered them over the country, and taught us how to take them. He had caused the earth to produce corn for bread. All this He had done for his red children, because He loved them. If we had some disputes about our hunting ground, they were generally settled without the shedding of much blood. But an evil day came upon us. Your forefathers crossed the great water, and landed on this island. Their numbers were small. They found friends and not enemies. They told us they had fled from their own country for fear of wicked men, and had come here to enjoy their religion. They asked for a small seat. We took pity on them, granted their request; and they sat down amongst us. We gave them corn and meat, they gave us poison [alluding, it is supposed, to ardent spirits[3]] in return.

The white people had now found our country. Tidings were carried back, and more came amongst us. Yet we did not fear them. We took them to be friends. They called us brothers. We believed them, and gave them a larger seat. At length their numbers had greatly increased. They wanted more land; they wanted our country. Our eyes were opened, and our minds became uneasy. Wars took place. Indians were hired to fight against Indians, and many of our people were destroyed. They also brought strong liquor amongst us. It was strong and powerful, and has slain thousands.

Brother; Our seats were once large and yours were small. You have now become a great people, and we have scarcely a place left to spread our blankets. You have got our country, but are not satisfied; you want to force your religion upon us.

Brother; Continue to listen.

You say that you are sent to instruct us how to worship the Great Spirit agreeably to his mind, and, if we do not take hold of the religion which you white people teach, we shall be unhappy hereafter. You say that you are right and we are lost. How do we know this to be true? We understand that your religion is written in a book. If it was intended for us as well as you, why has not the Great Spirit given to us, and not only to us, but why did he not give to our forefathers the knowledge of that book, with the means of understanding it rightly? We only know what you tell us about it. How shall we know when to believe, being so often deceived by the white people?

Brother; You say there is but one way to worship and serve the Great Spirit. If there is but one religion; why do you white people differ so much about it? Why not all agreed, as you can all read the book?

Brother; We do not understand these things.

We are told that your religion was given to your forefathers, and has been handed down from father to son. We also have a religion, which was given to our

---

1   [Note from the *Monthly Anthology*]   His Indian name is, Sagu-yu-whàt-hah; which interpreted is, *Keeper-awake*.

2   *seats* Lands.

3   *ardent spirits* I.e., alcohol. It is also possible that Sagoyewatha uses "poison" here to refer to disease rather than to alcohol.

forefathers, and has been handed down to us their children. We worship in that way. It teaches us to be thankful for all the favours we receive; to love each other, and to be united. We never quarrel about religion.

Brother; The Great Spirit has made us all, but he has made a great difference between his white and red children. He has given us different complexions and different customs. To you He has given the arts. To these He has not opened our eyes. We know these things to be true. Since He has made so great a difference between us in other things; why may we not conclude that He has given us a different religion according to our understanding? The Great Spirit does right. He knows what is best for his children; we are satisfied.

Brother; We do not wish to destroy your religion, or take it from you. We only want to enjoy our own.

Brother; We are told that you have been preaching to the white people in this place. These people are our neighbours. We are acquainted with them. We will wait a little while, and see what effect your preaching has upon them. If we find it does them good, makes them honest, and less disposed to cheat Indians; we will then consider again of what you have said.

Brother; You have now heard our answer to your talk, and this is all we have to say at present.

As we are going to part, we will come and take you by the hand, and hope the Great Spirit will protect you on your journey, and return you safe to your friends.

As the Indians began to approach the missionary, he rose hastily from his seat and replied, that he could not take them by the hand; that there was no fellowship between the religion of God and the works of the devil.

This being interpreted to the Indians, they smiled, and retired in a peaceable manner.

It being afterwards suggested to the missionary that his reply to the Indians was rather indiscreet;[1] he observed, that he supposed the ceremony of shaking hands would be received by them as a token that he assented to what they had said. Being otherwise informed, he said he was sorry for the expressions.

—1805 (PUBLISHED 1809)

---

1   *indiscreet*   Inconsiderate, rude.

BENJAMIN FRANKLIN
1706 – 1790

Benjamin Franklin, though best known as one of the founders of the United States, played staggeringly diverse roles in the course of his transatlantic career: diplomat, political theorist, inventor, scientist, entrepreneur, humorist, and autobiographer. He is often put forward—and in many ways put himself forward—as an exemplar of the mythical "self-made man," the ambitious yet unpretentious person whose success relies on nothing but his own hard work and perhaps a touch of shrewd talent.

Though he spent decades of his life in England, and his politics, values, and prose style were in many ways shaped by European influences, Franklin repurposed these influences for an American context; his contributions to the ideological and intellectual traditions of the United States have ensured his enduring reputation as an exemplary figure of American culture.

Franklin was born in Boston in 1706, the youngest son of seventeen children raised in the household of Josiah Franklin—who had left England as a Calvinist dissident in the previous century—and his second wife Abiah Folger. Josiah initially intended Benjamin for the ministry, but removed him from the necessary grammar school after only two years, likely for financial reasons. After a short period working in his father's soap and candle making business, Benjamin was apprenticed to his brother James, who was soon to found the innovative, satirical, and frequently controversial newspaper *The New-England Courant*.

Although he would later describe James as a "harsh and tyrannical" master, the printing trade suited Franklin well, not least because the work exposed him to reading material beyond that of his father's religious library. In particular, Franklin became a dedicated student of pre-Enlightenment philosophers such as John Locke and Francis Bacon; essayists Daniel Defoe, Joseph Addison, and Richard Steele; and classical Greek and Roman philosophers.

In 1722, Franklin secretly submitted the first in a series of fourteen satirical letters to the *Courant* under the pseudonym "Silence Dogood," the purported widow of a country minister. Like much of Franklin's later writing, the Dogood letters blend lighthearted humor with genuine social commentary; they poke fun at contemporary fashions and also address subjects from religious hypocrisy to the poor education of women. The revelation that James's sixteen-year-old brother was the true author of these remarkably popular—and frequently provocative—letters caused a significant rift in an already strained relationship, as did James's subsequent imprisonment for publishing articles that were critical of the religious and political authorities. In 1723, Franklin moved to Pennsylvania—a Quaker-led state, and hence more progressive than Puritan Boston—to begin establishing an independent career. This decision to strike out on his own became an integral part of Franklin's legend of self-made success.

In Philadelphia, Franklin found brief employment at a printing house; he then traveled to London, England, where he worked as a typesetter and frequented coffeehouses, participating in London's intellectual scene. While in England, he published *A Dissertation on Liberty and Necessity, Pleasure and Pain* (1725), a pamphlet in which he concluded that traditional religion was useless and illogical. (In later years, Franklin regretted this argument and burned all extant copies of the pamphlet he could find.) In 1729, having returned to Philadelphia, he partnered with fellow-printer Hugh Meredith to purchase the *Pennsylvania Gazette*, which soon became the most successful newspaper in the colonies and a leader in the burgeoning field of American news publishing. On occasion, Franklin wrote for the paper himself.

In the meantime, he also engaged with his "Junto," an intellectual club formed of likeminded friends who gathered regularly to share essays and discuss ideas. In 1730 he entered a common-law marriage with Deborah Read, a love interest from his youth who had been abandoned by her first husband; Read would later manage Franklin's businesses while he was living in England. The couple had two children, and also raised the future Loyalist leader William Franklin, Franklin's illegitimate son whose mother's identity he never revealed.

The year 1732 saw the launch of *Poor Richard's Almanack*, Franklin's most ambitious project yet and for many years his best-known achievement. Annual almanacs were staples of nearly all colonial homes, providing weather forecasts, astronomical and astrological predictions, and bits of entertainment and advice suitable for general readers—the latter of which Franklin's almanac took to remarkable heights. In the persona of poor country man Richard Saunders, Franklin filled the almanac with countless catchy proverbs and aphorisms, many of which, as Franklin openly acknowledged, were adaptations of well-known European proverbs. As Saunders, Franklin espoused what many have come to think of as quintessential values of modern capitalism: thrift, industriousness, productivity, and painstaking self-improvement. The *Almanack* was extraordinarily successful, selling upwards of 10,000 copies in one year. Many of the *Poor Richard* maxims—particularly those that Franklin compiled in "The Way to Wealth," an essay he wrote as part of the preface to the final issue of the almanac published under his supervision in 1758—have become almost inescapably ingrained in the American vernacular.

Franklin continued to publish essays over the course of the following decades, though from the late 1740s onwards his time was increasingly devoted to research into natural phenomena such as electricity, as well as to civic and political pursuits. (Franklin is credited with several inventions, including the lightning rod; his findings regarding electricity were initially ridiculed but eventually earned him the prestigious Copley Medal.) Franklin was elected to the Pennsylvania Assembly in 1751, and from 1757 to 1775 worked as a colonial representative in London. During this time, he became agent to the Crown for several of the Thirteen Colonies and published writing in support of colonial interests. Once a steadfast loyalist, by the outbreak of the American Revolution Franklin was a reluctant revolutionary, and in 1776 he was invited to join the committee responsible for drafting the Declaration of Independence; some of the document's most famous lines, including the line beginning "We hold these truths to be self-evident," were refined by him. In addition to signing the Declaration, he was among the signatories to the Treaty of Paris (1783) that ended the Revolutionary War and to the U.S. Constitution (1787).

Franklin first began composing what came to be known as his *Autobiography* (1791) in 1771, at the age of sixty-five. While incomplete, the memoir remains his most renowned literary creation. Franklin himself never used the term "autobiography," but the text is considered a foundational work of the genre, blending the common "confessional" mode often associated with religious writers with a more secular mode focused at least as much on his public as his private affairs. The *Autobiography* is often considered Franklin's fullest exploration of what it means to live virtuously; it recounts, as he writes in Part Two, his "bold and arduous project of arriving at moral perfection." The carefully selected, self-consciously crafted chronicle of Franklin's life was quickly interpreted as a prototypical American narrative; as his friend Benjamin Vaughan asserted in a letter of 1783, "All that has happened to you is also connected with the detail of the manners and situation of a rising people."

After the Revolutionary War, Franklin continued to work on his political writings. His 1784 pamphlet "Information to Those Who Would Remove to America," directed at prospective immigrants, influentially characterized the United States as a "land of labor," a country of opportunity for those ambitious enough to pursue it. In "Remarks Concerning the Savages" (1784), Franklin commented directly on the country's racial politics, criticizing American mistreatment of Indigenous cultures. In a later pamphlet, "On the Slave Trade" (1790), he continued his critique of racial injustice, this time focusing on the hypocrisy of slave ownership. Like many well-off white Americans throughout the eighteenth century, Franklin owned enslaved people for much of his adulthood; later in life, he became increasingly skeptical of the ethics of the slave trade, and was elected president of the country's first abolitionist society in 1787.

Franklin's funeral in 1790 was attended by about 20,000 people. By the time of his death, he had witnessed and taken an active part in the most dramatic social and political transformations America had experienced since the earliest years of colonialism. His personal myth has since become so strongly entwined with mainstream ideas of American national character that he has often been embraced or rejected on this basis, even as his writings have remained widely read and broadly influential. The Transcendentalists of the early nineteenth century tended to feel that, as Emerson phrased it, "Franklin's man is a frugal, inoffensive, thrifty citizen, but savors of nothing heroic"—a position that anticipates the censure of later critics such as D.H. Lawrence. Franklin's fierce independence, entrepreneurial innovation, and sense of social responsibility, however, have been cited as inspiration by industrialists from Andrew Carnegie to Elon Musk, even as scholars—perhaps most influentially, Max Weber in his 1905 work *The Protestant Ethic and the Spirit of Capitalism*—have criticized Franklin as an advocate of damaging capitalistic values. Yet Franklin's body of work and achievements are more varied and complex than any of these assessments suggests, and as his biographer Walter Isaacson notes, his multifaceted image is continually reinterpreted "to reflect, or refract, the attitudes of each succeeding era."

NOTE ON THE TEXTS: The texts of "Remarks Concerning the Savages of North America" and "On the Slave Trade" presented below are based on the versions that appear in Albert Henry Smyth's *The Writings of Benjamin Franklin* (ten volumes, 1905–07). The spelling and punctuation of these texts have been modernized in accordance with the practices of this anthology. The text of Franklin's *Autobiography* (Parts One and Two of which are presented below, with the full text appearing in the website component) is based on that published in J.A. Leo Lemay's *Benjamin Franklin: Writings* (1987). This edition provides a clean edition of the "genetic text" first prepared by Lemay and Paul M. Zall for the University of Tennessee Press in 1981, which is in turn based on Franklin's original, unpublished manuscript. The spelling and punctuation of the *Autobiography* have not been modernized here, with the exception of Franklin's superscript abbreviations (for example, *corrg* for *correcting*, or *4to* for *quarto*), which have been modernized throughout. A fully modernized version of the text is included in the website component of this anthology.

⌘ ⌘ ⌘

Remarks Concerning the Savages of North America

Savages we call them, because their manners differ from ours, which we think the perfection of civility; they think the same of theirs.

Perhaps, if we could examine the manners of different nations with impartiality, we should find no people so rude,[1] as to be without any rules of politeness; nor any so polite, as not to have some remains of rudeness.

The Indian men, when young, are hunters and warriors; when old, counsellors; for all their government is by counsel of the sages; there is no force, there are no prisons, no officers to compel obedience, or inflict punishment. Hence they generally study oratory, the best speaker having the most influence. The Indian

women till the ground, dress the food, nurse and bring up the children, and preserve and hand down to posterity the memory of public transactions. These employments of men and women are accounted as natural and honourable. Having few artificial wants, they have abundance of leisure for improvement by conversation. Our laborious manner of life, compared with theirs, they esteem slavish and base; and the learning, on which we value ourselves, they regard as frivolous and useless. An instance of this occurred at the Treaty of Lancaster,[2] in Pennsylvania, *anno* 1744, between the Government of Virginia and the Six Nations. After the principal business was settled, the commissioners from Virginia acquainted the Indians, by a speech, that there was at Williamsburg a college, with a fund for

---

[1] *rude* Uncivilized.

[2] *Treaty of Lancaster* Treaty in which the Six Nations Confederacy (also known as the Iroquois or Haudenosaunee) ceded their lands in the Shenandoah Valley to the British.

educating Indian youth;[1] and that, if the Six Nations would send down half a dozen of their young lads to that college, the government would take care that they should be well provided for, and instructed in all the learning of the white people. It is one of the Indian rules of politeness not to answer a public proposition the same day that it is made; they think it would be treating it as a light matter, and that they show it respect by taking time to consider it, as of a matter important. They therefore deferred their answer till the day following; when their speaker began, by expressing their deep sense of the kindness of the Virginia government, in making them that offer; "for we know," says he, "that you highly esteem the kind of learning taught in those colleges, and that the maintenance of our young men, while with you, would be very expensive to you. We are convinced, therefore, that you mean to do us good by your proposal; and we thank you heartily. But you, who are wise, must know that different nations have different conceptions of things; and you will therefore not take it amiss, if our ideas of this kind of education happen not to be the same with yours. We have had some experience of it; several of our young people were formerly brought up at the colleges of the northern provinces; they were instructed in all your sciences; but, when they came back to us, they were bad runners, ignorant of every means of living in the woods, unable to bear either cold or hunger, knew neither how to build a cabin, take a deer, or kill an enemy, spoke our language imperfectly, were therefore neither fit for hunters, warriors, nor counsellors; they were totally good for nothing. We are however not the less obliged by your kind offer, though we decline accepting it; and, to show our grateful sense of it, if the gentlemen of Virginia will send us a dozen of their sons, we will take great care of their education, instruct them in all we know, and make *men* of them."

Having frequent occasions to hold public councils, they have acquired great order and decency in conducting them. The old men sit in the foremost ranks, the warriors in the next, and the women and children in the hindmost. The business of the women is to take exact notice of what passes, imprint it in their memories (for they have no writing), and communicate it to their children. They are the records of the council, and they preserve traditions of the stipulations in treaties 100 years back; which, when we compare with our writings, we always find exact. He that would speak, rises. The rest observe a profound silence. When he has finished and sits down, they leave him 5 or 6 minutes to recollect, that, if he has omitted anything he intended to say, or has anything to add, he may rise again and deliver it. To interrupt another, even in common conversation, is reckoned highly indecent. How different this is from the conduct of a polite British House of Commons, where scarce a day passes without some confusion, that makes the Speaker hoarse in calling *to order*; and how different from the mode of conversation in many polite companies of Europe, where, if you do not deliver your sentence with great rapidity, you are cut off in the middle of it by the impatient loquacity of those you converse with, and never suffered to finish it!

The politeness of these savages in conversation is indeed carried to excess, since it does not permit them to contradict or deny the truth of what is asserted in their presence. By this means they indeed avoid disputes; but then it becomes difficult to know their minds, or what impression you make upon them. The missionaries who have attempted to convert them to Christianity, all complain of this as one of the great difficulties of their mission. The Indians hear with patience the truths of the Gospel explained to them, and give their usual tokens of assent and approbation; you would think they were convinced. No such matter. It is mere civility.

A Swedish minister, having assembled the chiefs of the Susquehanah Indians, made a sermon to them, acquainting them with the principal historical facts on which our religion is founded; such as the fall of our first parents by eating an apple, the coming of Christ to repair the mischief, his miracles and suffering, etc. When he had finished, an Indian orator stood up to thank him. "What you have told us," says he, "is all very good. It is indeed bad to eat apples. It is better to make them all into cider. We are much obliged by your kindness in coming so far, to tell us these things which you have heard from your mothers. In return, I will tell you some of those we have heard from ours. In the

---

[1]   *at Williamsburg … Indian youth*   In its early years, the College of William and Mary, established in 1693, was conceived of in part as a place of higher education for Indigenous men.

beginning, our fathers had only the flesh of animals to subsist on; and if their hunting was unsuccessful, they were starving. Two of our young hunters, having killed a deer, made a fire in the woods to broil some part of it. When they were about to satisfy their hunger, they beheld a beautiful young woman descend from the clouds, and seat herself on that hill, which you see yonder among the blue mountains. They said to each other, it is a spirit that has smelled our broiling venison, and wishes to eat of it; let us offer some to her. They presented her with the tongue; she was pleased with the taste of it, and said, 'Your kindness shall be rewarded; come to this place after thirteen moons, and you shall find something that will be of great benefit in nourishing you and your children to the latest generations.' They did so, and, to their surprise, found plants they had never seen before; but which, from that ancient time, have been constantly cultivated among us, to our great advantage. Where her right hand had touched the ground, they found maize; where her left hand had touched it, they found kidney beans; and where her backside had sat on it, they found tobacco." The good missionary, disgusted with this idle tale, said, "What I delivered to you were sacred truths; but what you tell me is mere fable, fiction, and falsehood." The Indian, offended, replied, "My brother, it seems your friends have not done you justice in your education; they have not well instructed you in the rules of common civility. You saw that we, who understand and practise those rules, believed all your stories; why do you refuse to believe ours?"

When any of them come into our towns, our people are apt to crowd round them, gaze upon them, and incommode them, where they desire to be private; this they esteem great rudeness, and the effect of the want[1] of instruction in the rules of civility and good manners. "We have," say they, "as much curiosity as you, and when you come into our towns, we wish for opportunities of looking at you; but for this purpose we hide ourselves behind bushes, where you are to pass, and never intrude ourselves into your company."

Their manner of entering one another's village has likewise its rules. It is reckoned uncivil in travelling strangers to enter a village abruptly, without giving notice of their approach. Therefore, as soon as they arrive within hearing, they stop and hollow,[2] remaining there till invited to enter. Two old men usually come out to them, and lead them in. There is in every village a vacant dwelling, called *the Strangers' House*. Here they are placed, while the old men go round from hut to hut, acquainting the inhabitants, that strangers are arrived, who are probably hungry and weary; and everyone sends them what he can spare of victuals,[3] and skins to repose on. When the strangers are refreshed, pipes and tobacco are brought; and then, but not before, conversation begins, with enquiries who they are, whither bound, what news, etc.; and it usually ends with offers of service, if the strangers have occasion[4] of guides, or any necessaries for continuing their journey; and nothing is exacted for the entertainment.

The same hospitality, esteemed among them as a principal virtue, is practised by private persons; of which Conrad Weiser,[5] our interpreter, gave me the following instance. He had been naturalized among the Six Nations, and spoke well the Mohock[6] language. In going through the Indian country, to carry a message from our Governor to the council at Onondaga, he called at the habitation of Canassatego,[7] an old acquaintance, who embraced him, spread furs for him to sit on, placed before him some boiled beans and venison, and mixed some rum and water for his drink. When he was well refreshed, and had lit his pipe, Canassatego began to converse with him; asked how he had fared the many years since they had seen each other; whence he then came; what occasioned the journey, etc. Conrad answered all his questions; and when the discourse began to flag, the Indian, to continue it, said, "Conrad, you have lived long among the white people, and know something of their customs; I have been sometimes

---

[1]   *want*   Lack.

[2]   *hollow*   I.e., holler; shout.

[3]   *victuals*   Food.

[4]   *occasion*   Need.

[5]   *Conrad Weiser*   Pennsylvanian diplomat (1696–1760) who worked as an interpreter between the Pennsylvania Colony and various local Indigenous groups.

[6]   *Mohock*   I.e., Mohawk, the Iroquoian language spoken by the Mohawk people (who are members of the Six Nations Confederacy).

[7]   *Canassatego*   Onondaga political leader and diplomat for the Six Nations (c. 1684–1750), renowned for his oratorical abilities; Franklin oversaw the printing of several of Canassatego's speeches, including two excerpted elsewhere in this volume (see both the bound book and online components).

at Albany, and have observed, that once in seven days they shut up their shops, and assemble all in the great house; tell me what it is for? What do they do there?" "They meet there," says Conrad, "to hear and learn *good things.*" "I do not doubt," says the Indian, "that they tell you so; they have told me the same; but I doubt the truth of what they say, and I will tell you my reasons. I went lately to Albany to sell my skins and buy blankets, knives, powder, rum, etc. You know I used generally to deal with Hans Hanson; but I was a little inclined this time to try some other merchant. However, I called first upon Hans, and asked him what he would give for beaver. He said he could not give any more than four shillings a pound; 'but,' says he, 'I cannot talk on business now; this is the day when we meet together to learn *good things,* and I am going to the meeting.' So I thought to myself, 'Since we cannot do any business today, I may as well go to the meeting too,' and I went with him. There stood up a man in black, and began to talk to the people very angrily. I did not understand what he said; but, perceiving that he looked much at me and at Hanson, I imagined he was angry at seeing me there; so I went out, sat down near the house, struck fire, and lit my pipe, waiting till the meeting should break up. I thought too, that the man had mentioned something of beaver, and I suspected it might be the subject of their meeting. So, when they came out, I accosted my merchant. 'Well, Hans,' says I, 'I hope you have agreed to give more than four shillings a pound.' 'No,' says he, 'I cannot give so much; I cannot give more than three shillings and sixpence.' I then spoke to several other dealers, but they all sung the same song—three and sixpence—three and sixpence. This made it clear to me, that my suspicion was right; and, that whatever they pretended of meeting to learn *good things,* the real purpose was to consult how to cheat Indians in the price of beaver. Consider but a little, Conrad, and you must be of my opinion. If they met so often to learn *good things,* they would certainly have learnt some before this time. But they are still ignorant. You know our practice. If a white man, in travelling through our country, enters one of our cabins, we all treat him as I treat you; we dry him if he is wet, we warm him if he is cold, we give him meat and drink, that he may allay his thirst and hunger; and we spread soft furs for him to rest and sleep on; we demand nothing in return. But, if I go into a white

man's house at Albany, and ask for victuals and drink, they say, 'Where is your money?' and if I have none, they say, 'Get out, you Indian dog.' You see they have not yet learned those little *good things,* that we need no meetings to be instructed in, because our mothers taught them to us when we were children; and therefore it is impossible their meetings should be, as they say, for any such purpose, or have any such effect; they are only to contrive *the cheating of Indians in the price of beaver.*"[1]
—c. 1783–84

On the Slave Trade

This letter is Franklin's last known work, published in *The Federal Gazette* on 25 March 1790, less than a month before his death. An example of Franklin's many literary hoaxes, the piece claims to present a speech by Algerian political leader Sidi Mehemet Ibrahim, in defense of the trade in Christian slaves; in reality, both Ibrahim and his speech are inventions of Franklin's.

To the Editor of the *Federal Gazette*

March 23d, 1790

Sir,

Reading last night in your excellent paper the speech of Mr. Jackson[2] in Congress against their meddling with the affair of slavery, or attempting to mend

[1]   [Franklin's note]   It is remarkable that in all ages and countries hospitality has been allowed as the virtue of those whom the civilized were pleased to call barbarians. The Greeks celebrated the Scythians for it. The Saracens possessed it eminently, and it is to this day the reigning virtue of the wild Arabs. St. Paul, too, in the relation of his voyage and shipwreck on the island of Melita says the barbarous people showed us no little kindness; for they kindled a fire, and received us every one, because of the present rain, and because of the cold.—F. [*Scythians* Nomadic people who flourished in parts of Eastern Europe and Central Asia in the first millennium BCE; *Saracens* Medieval term used to denote Muslim Arabs; *St. Paul … Melita* See Acts 27–28; "Melita" here refers to the island of Malta.]

[2]   *Mr. Jackson* Georgia politician James Jackson (1757–1806), who opposed the abolition of slavery.

the condition of the slaves, it put me in mind of a similar one made about 100 years since by Sidi Mehemet Ibrahim, a member of the Divan of Algiers,[1] which may be seen in Martin's Account of his Consulship, anno 1687.[2] It was against granting the petition of the sect called *Erika*, or Purists, who prayed for the abolition of piracy and slavery as being unjust. Mr. Jackson does not quote it; perhaps he has not seen it. If, therefore, some of its reasonings are to be found in his eloquent speech, it may only show that men's interests and intellects operate and are operated on with surprising similarity in all countries and climates, when under similar circumstances. The African's speech, as translated, is as follows.

"*Allah Bismillah, etc. God is great, and Mahomet is his Prophet.*"

Have these *Erika* considered the consequences of granting their petition? If we cease our cruises against the Christians, how shall we be furnished with the commodities their countries produce, and which are so necessary for us? If we forbear to make slaves of their people, who in this hot climate are to cultivate our lands? Who are to perform the common labours of our city, and in our families? Must we not then be our own slaves? And is there not more compassion and more favour due to us as Mussulmen,[3] than to these Christian dogs? We have now above 50,000 slaves in and near Algiers. This number, if not kept up by fresh supplies, will soon diminish, and be gradually annihilated. If we then cease taking and plundering the infidel ships, and making slaves of the seamen and passengers, our lands will become of no value for want of cultivation; the rents of houses in the city will sink one half; and the revenues of government arising from its share of prizes be totally destroyed! And for what? To gratify the whims of a whimsical sect, who would have us, not only forbear making more slaves, but even to manumit those we have.

But who is to indemnify[4] their masters for the loss? Will the state do it? Is our treasury sufficient? Will the

Erika do it? Can they do it? Or would they, to do what they think justice to the slaves, do a greater injustice to the owners? And if we set our slaves free, what is to be done with them? Few of them will return to their countries; they know too well the greater hardships they must there be subject to; they will not embrace our holy religion; they will not adopt our manners; our people will not pollute themselves by intermarrying with them. Must we maintain them as beggars in our streets, or suffer our properties to be the prey of their pillage? For Men long accustomed to slavery will not work for a livelihood when not compelled. And what is there so pitiable in their present condition? Were they not slaves in their own countries?

Are not Spain, Portugal, France, and the Italian states governed by despots, who hold all their subjects in slavery, without exception? Even England treats its sailors as slaves; for they are, whenever the government pleases, seized, and confined in ships of war, condemned not only to work, but to fight, for small wages, or a mere subsistence, not better than our slaves are allowed by us. Is their condition then made worse by their falling into our hands? No; they have only exchanged one slavery for another, and I may say a better; for here they are brought into a land where the sun of Islamism gives forth its light, and shines in full splendor, and they have an opportunity of making themselves acquainted with the true doctrine, and thereby saving their immortal souls. Those who remain at home have not that happiness. Sending the slaves home then would be sending them out of light into darkness.

I repeat the question, What is to be done with them? I have heard it suggested that they may be planted in the wilderness, where there is plenty of land for them to subsist on, and where they may flourish as a free state; but they are, I doubt, too little disposed to labour without compulsion, as well as too ignorant to establish a good government, and the wild Arabs would soon molest and destroy or again enslave them. While serving us, we take care to provide them with everything, and they are treated with humanity. The labourers in their own country are, as I am well informed, worse fed, lodged, and clothed. The condition of most of them is therefore already mended, and requires no further improvement. Here their lives are in safety. They are not liable to be impressed for soldiers,[5] and forced to cut one another's Christian

---

[1] *Divan of Algiers* Council of senior officials of the Regency of Algiers, the term for Algeria when it was under the rule of the Ottoman Empire.

[2] *Martin's Account … 1687* A fictional account.

[3] *Mussulmen* I.e., Muslims.

[4] *indemnify* Compensate.

---

[5] *impressed for soldiers* Forced into military service, often by means of a "press gang" who would seize men without notice.

throats, as in the wars of their own countries. If some of the religious mad bigots, who now tease[1] us with their silly petitions, have in a fit of blind zeal freed their slaves, it was not generosity, it was not humanity, that moved them to the action; it was from the conscious burden of a load of sins, and hope, from the supposed merits of so good a work, to be excused damnation.

How grossly are they mistaken in imagining slavery to be disallowed by the Alcoran![2] Are not the two precepts, to quote no more, "*Masters, treat your slaves with kindness; slaves, serve your masters with cheerfulness and fidelity,*" clear proofs to the contrary? Nor can the plundering of infidels be in that sacred book forbidden, since it is well known from it, that God has given the world, and all that it contains, to his faithful Mussulmen, who are to enjoy it of right as fast as they conquer it. Let us then hear no more of this detestable proposition, the manumission of Christian slaves, the adoption of which would, by depreciating our lands and houses, and thereby depriving so many good citizens of their properties, create universal discontent, and provoke insurrections, to the endangering of government and producing general confusion. I have therefore no doubt, but this wise council will prefer the comfort and happiness of a whole nation of true believers to the whim of a few *Erika*, and dismiss their petition.

The result was, as Martin tells us, that the Divan came to this resolution; "The doctrine, that plundering and enslaving the Christians is unjust, is at best *problematical*; but that it is the interest of this state to continue the practice is clear; therefore let the petition be rejected."

And it was rejected accordingly.

And since like motives are apt to produce in the minds of men like opinions and resolutions, may we not, Mr. Brown,[3] venture to predict, from this account, that the petitions to the Parliament of England for abolishing the slave trade, to say nothing of other legislatures, and the debates upon them,

will have a similar conclusion? I am, Sir, your constant reader and humble servant,

HISTORICUS

—1790

---

from *The Autobiography*

The work known today as the *Autobiography* of Benjamin Franklin has complicated origins, both in its composition and its publication history. Franklin worked on the manuscript over the course of four distinct periods of his life, beginning it in 1771 as a letter to his son William Franklin, and leaving it unfinished upon his death in April 1790, nearly twenty years later. Despite its incomplete state—the narrative ends with Franklin's arrival in London in 1757—the work quickly achieved international renown, and was by the mid-1800s considered a seminal work of American literature.

Several copies of Franklin's original manuscript came to be circulated in North America and Europe shortly after his death. This led to the first publication of the *Autobiography* in France in 1791, titled *Mémoirs de la vie privée de Benjamin Franklin* (*Memoirs of the Private Life of Benjamin Franklin*). This translated text, based on a flawed copy that included only Part 1, nevertheless became the basis for subsequent publications of the work, including English versions re-translated from the French. Franklin's grandson William Temple Franklin published a more accurate edition that included Parts 1, 2, and 3 in 1817, but this version was nevertheless heavily edited. In the 1860s, Franklin's original manuscript made its way into the hands of American diplomat John Bigelow, who proceeded to edit and publish the first version of the work to include all four parts in 1868.

In 1981, Franklin scholars J.A. Leo Lemay and Paul M. Zall published *The Autobiography of Benjamin Franklin: A Genetic Text*, the first version to reproduce all of Franklin's copious revisions and amendments to the manuscript. The text presented below is based on the version published in Lemay's *Benjamin Franklin: Writings* (1987), which is a revised "clear text" based on the genetic text. Spelling and punctuation have not been modernized.

---

1   *tease* Irritate.

2   *the Alcoran* The Qur'an; the notable 1647 translation of the Qur'an into French, in turn translated into English in 1649, was titled *L'Alcoran de Mahomet*.

3   *Mr. Brown* Andrew Brown (c. 1744–97), editor of the *Federal Gazette*.

PART 1

Twyford, at the Bishop of St Asaph's[1]
1771.

Dear Son,

I have ever had a Pleasure in obtaining any little Anecdotes of my Ancestors. You may remember the Enquiries I made among the Remains of my Relations when you were with me in England;[2] and the Journey I took for that purpose. Now imagining it may be equally agreeable to you to know the Circumstances of *my* Life, many of which you are yet unacquainted with; and expecting a Weeks uninterrupted Leisure in my present Country Retirement, I sit down to write them for you. To which I have besides some other Inducements. Having emerg'd from the Poverty & Obscurity in which I was born & bred, to a State of Affluence & some Degree of Reputation in the World, and having gone so far thro' Life with a considerable Share of Felicity, the conducing Means I made use of, which, with the Blessing of God, so well succeeded, my Posterity may like to know, as they may find some of them suitable to their own Situations, & therefore fit to be imitated.—That Felicity, when I reflected on it, has induc'd me sometimes to say, that were it offer'd to my Choice, I should have no Objection to a Repetition of the same Life from its Beginning, only asking the Advantage Authors have in a second Edition to correct some Faults of the first. So would I if I might, besides correcting the Faults, change some sinister Accidents & Events of it for others more favourable, but tho' this were deny'd, I should still accept the Offer. However, since such a Repetition is not to be expected, the Thing most like living one's Life over again, seems to be a *Recollection* of that Life; and to make that Recollection as durable as possible, the putting it down in Writing.—Hereby, too, I shall indulge the Inclination so natural in old Men, to be talking of themselves and their own past Actions, and I shall indulge it, without being tiresome to others who thro' respect to Age might think themselves oblig'd to give me a Hearing, since this may be read or not as any one pleases. And lastly, (I may as well confess it, since my Denial of it will be believ'd by no body) perhaps I shall a good deal gratify my own *Vanity*. Indeed, I scarce ever heard or saw the introductory Words, *Without Vanity I may say*, &c. but some vain thing immediately follow'd. Most People dislike Vanity in others whatever Share they have of it themselves, but I give it fair Quarter wherever I meet with it, being persuaded that it is often productive of Good to the Possessor & to others that are within his Sphere of Action: And therefore in many Cases it would not be quite absurd if a Man were to thank God for his Vanity among the other Comforts of Life.—

And now I speak of thanking God, I desire with all Humility to acknowledge, that I owe the mention'd Happiness of my past Life to his kind Providence, which lead me to the Means I us'd & gave them Success.—My Belief of This, induces me to *hope*, tho' I must not *presume*, that the same Goodness will still be exercis'd towards me in continuing that Happiness, or in enabling me to bear a fatal Reverso,[3] which I may experience as others have done, the Complexion of my future Fortune being known to him only: and in whose Power it is to bless to us even our Afflictions.

The Notes one of my Uncles (who had the same kind of Curiosity in collecting Family Anecdotes) once put into my Hands, furnish'd me with several Particulars, relating to our Ancestors. From those Notes I learnt that the Family had liv'd in the same Village, Ecton in Northamptonshire, for 300 Years, & how much longer he knew not, (perhaps from the Time when the Name *Franklin* that before was the Name of an Order of People, was assum'd by them for a Surname, when others took Surnames all over

---

[1] *Twyford … St Asaph's* At the time he began writing his memoirs, Franklin was living with his friend Jonathan Shipley, the Bishop of St. Asaph (1714–88), at his home in Twyford, near London. In the years leading up to the American Revolution, Shipley became a vocal opponent of George III's management of the American colonies.

[2] *You may remember … England* In 1757, Franklin traveled with his son William to London on a political appointment. While there, in July 1758, the two of them visited their ancestral homes in Ecton and Banbury. The diplomatic proceedings of this trip to England are described in Part Four of Franklin's *Autobiography*, included in the website component of this anthology.

[3] *Reverso* Latin: Return; i.e., reversal of fortunes. Franklin may also have in mind the dueling technique of "riverso," a backhanded cut.

the Kingdom.—[1]) on a Freehold of about 30 Acres, aided by the Smith's Business which had continued in the Family till his Time, the eldest Son being always bred to that Business. A Custom which he & my Father both followed as to their eldest Sons.—When I search'd the Register at Ecton, I found an Account of their Births, Marriages and Burials, from the Year 1555 only, there being no Register kept in that Parish at any time preceding.—By that Register I perceiv'd that I was the youngest Son of the youngest Son for 5 Generations back. My Grandfather Thomas, who was born in 1598, lived at Ecton till he grew too old to follow Business longer, when he went to live with his Son John, a Dyer at Banbury in Oxfordshire, with whom my Father serv'd an Apprenticeship. There my Grandfather died and lies buried. We saw his Gravestone in 1758. His eldest Son Thomas liv'd in the House at Ecton, and left it with the Land to his only Child, a Daughter, who with her Husband, one Fisher of Wellingborough sold it to Mr Isted, now Lord of the Manor there. My Grandfather had 4 Sons that grew up, viz. Thomas, John, Benjamin and Josiah. I will give you what Account I can of them at this distance from my Papers, and if those are not lost in my Absence, you will among them find many more Particulars. Thomas was bred a Smith under his Father, but being ingenious, and encourag'd in Learning (as all his Brothers like wise werre,) by an Esquire Palmer then the principal Gentleman in that Parish, he qualify'd himself for the Business of Scrivener,[2] became a considerable Man in the County Affairs, was a chief Mover[3] of all publick Spirited Undertakings, for the County or Town of Northampton & his own Village, of which many Instances were told us at Ecton, and he was much taken Notice of and patroniz'd by the then Lord Halifax. He died in 1702 Jan. 6. old Stile,[4] just 4 Years to a Day before I was born. The Account we receiv'd of his Life & Character from some old People at Ecton, I remember struck you as something extraordinary from its Similarity to what you knew of mine. Had he died on the same Day, you said one might have suppos'd a Transmigration.[5]—John was bred a Dyer, I believe of Woollens. Benjamin, was bred a Silk Dyer, serving an Apprenticeship at London. He was an ingenious Man, I remember him well, for when I was a Boy he came over to my Father in Boston, and lived in the House with us some Years. He lived to a great Age. His Grandson Samuel Franklin[6] now lives in Boston. He left behind him two Quarto Volumes, M.S. of his own Poetry, consisting of little occasional Pieces[7] address'd to his Friends and Relations, of which the following sent to me, is a Specimen.

---

[1] [Franklin's note] As a proof that Franklin was anciently the common name of an order or rank in England, see Judge Fortescue, *De laudibus Legum Angliae*, written about the year 1412, in which is the following passage, to show that good juries might easily be formed in any part of England.

"Regio etiam illa, ita respersa refertaque est *possessoribus terrarum* et agrorum, quod in ea, villula tam parva reperiri non poterit, in qua non est *miles*, *armiger*, vel pater-familias, quails ibidem *Franklin* vulgariter nuncupatur, magnis ditatus possessionibus, nec non libere tenentes et alii *valecti* plurimi, suis patrimoniis sufficientes ad faciendum juratum, in forma praenotata."

"Moreover, the same country is so filled and replenished with landed menne, that therein so small a Thorpe cannot be found werein dweleth not a knight, an esquire, or such a householder, as is there commonly called a *Franklin*, enriched with great possessions; and also other freeholders and many yeomen able for their livelihoods to make a jury in form aforementioned."—(*Old Translation*.)

Chaucer too calls his Country Gentleman, a *Franklin*, and after describing his good housekeeping thus characterises him:

"This worthy Franklin bore a purse of silk,
Fix'd to his girdle, white as morning milk.
Knight of the Shire, first Justice at th' Assize,
To help all the poor, the doubtful to advise.
In all employments, generous, just, he proved;
Renown'd for courtesy, by all beloved."

[*Chaucer* English poet Geoffrey Chaucer (c. 1340–1400); Franklin provides a loose paraphrase of several lines in Chaucer's *Canterbury Tales*.]

---

2   *Scrivener* One who writes or copies documents, especially legal documents, professionally; scribe.

3   *Mover* I.e., one who brings actions or ideas into motion.

4   *old Stile* I.e., according to the Julian calendar, which was in use in Britain and its colonies until 1752. By the Gregorian calendar, Benjamin Franklin was born 17 January 1706.

5   *Transmigration* I.e., transferral of a deceased person's soul into another's body.

6   *Samuel Franklin* Benjamin Franklin's cousin, a cutler by trade.

7   *Quarto* Book format which employs large sheets of paper folded to produce four pages each; *M.S.* Manuscript; *occasional Pieces* I.e., poems written in honor of specific occasions.

Sent to My Name upon a Report
of his Inclination to Martial affaires
7 July 1710

Beleeve me Ben. It is a Dangerous Trade
The Sword has Many Marr'd as well as Made
By it doe many fall Not Many Rise
Makes Many poor few Rich and fewer Wise
Fills Towns with Ruin, fields with blood beside
Tis Sloths Maintainer, And the Shield of pride
Fair Cities Rich to Day, in plenty flow
War fills with want, Tomorrow, & with woe
Ruin'd Estates, The Nurse of Vice, broke limbs
  & scars
     Are the Effects of Desolating Warrs

    Sent to B. F. in N. E.[1] 15 July 1710

B e to thy parents an Obedient Son
E ach Day let Duty constantly be Done
N ever give Way to sloth or lust or pride
I f free you'd be from Thousand Ills beside
A bove all Ills be sure Avoide the shelfe[2]
M ans Danger lyes in Satan sin and selfe
I n vertue Learning Wisdome progress Make
N ere shrink at Suffering for thy saviours sake
F raud and all Falsehood in thy Dealings Flee
R eligious Always in thy station be
A dore the Maker of thy Inward part
N ow's the Accepted time, Give him thy Heart
K eep a Good Conscience 'tis a constant Frind
L ike Judge and Witness This Thy Acts Attend
I n Heart with bended knee Alone Adore
N one but the Three in One forevermore.

He had form'd a Shorthand of his own, which he taught me, but never practising it I have now forgot it. I was nam'd after this Uncle, there being a particular Affection between him and my Father. He was very pious, a great Attender of Sermons of the best Preachers, which he took down in his Shorthand and had with him many Volumes of them.—He was also much of a Politician, too much perhaps for his Station. There fell lately into my Hands in London a Collection he had made of all the principal Pamphlets relating to Publick

Affairs from 1641 to 1717. Many of the Volumes are wanting,[3] as appears by the Numbering, but there still remains 8 Vols. Folio, and 24 in quarto & octavo.[4]—A Dealer in old Books met with them, and knowing me by my sometimes buying of him, he brought them to me. It seems my Uncle must have left them here when he went to America, which was about 50 Years since. There are many of his Notes in the Margins.—

This obscure Family of ours was early in the Reformation, and continu'd Protestants thro' the Reign of Queen Mary, when they were sometimes in Danger of Trouble on Account of their Zeal against Popery.[5] They had got an English Bible,[6] & to conceal & secure it, it was fastned open with Tapes under & within the Frame of a Joint Stool. When my Great Great Grandfather read in it to his Family, he turn'd up the Joint Stool upon his Knees, turning over the Leaves then under the Tapes. One of the Children stood at the Door to give Notice if he saw the Apparitor coming, who was an Officer of the Spiritual Court. In that Case the Stool was turn'd down again upon its feet, when the Bible remain'd conceal'd under it as before. This Anecdote I had from my Uncle Benjamin.—The Family continu'd all of the Church of England till about the End of Charles the Second's Reign,[7] when some of the Ministers that had been outed for Nonconformity, holding Conventicles[8] in Northamptonshire,

---

[1] *N. E.* New England.

[2] *the shelfe* Uselessness (referring to the phrase "on the shelf," designating something that is out of the way or inactive).

[3] *wanting* Missing.

[4] *Folio* Book format involving single large sheets of paper folded once; *octavo* Book format produced by folding a standard-sized printing sheet three times to form eight leaves.

[5] *early in the Reformation* I.e., early supporters of the Protestant Reformation, a sixteenth-century religious movement that sought to reform the Catholic Church and ultimately established the Protestant form of Christianity. The Protestant Church of England was established under Henry VIII's reign in 1534; *continu'd Protestants ... Queen Mary* The Catholic Church was re-established in England under the reign of Mary I (1553–58), initiating a brief period of severe persecution of dissenters; *Popery* Derogatory term for Catholicism.

[6] *English Bible* The translation of the Bible into vernacular languages was a central element of the Protestant Reformation; the reference here is likely to the Geneva Bible, the favored translation of the Puritans, so named because of its creation by English dissenters who fled to Switzerland during Mary I's reign.

[7] *the End ... Reign* 1685.

[8] *Conventicles* Meetings held by nonconformists to the Church of England; such dissention was outlawed by the Conventicle Act of 1664.

Benjamin & Josiah adher'd to them, and so continu'd all their Lives. The rest of the Family remain'd with the Episcopal Church.[1]

Josiah, my Father, married young, and carried his Wife[2] with three Children unto New England, about 1682. The Conventicles having been forbidden by Law, & frequently disturbed, induced some considerable Men of his Acquaintance to remove to that Country, and he was prevail'd with to accompany them thither, where they expected to enjoy their Mode of Religion with Freedom.—By the same Wife he had 4 Children more born there, and by a second Wife ten more, in all 17, of which I remember 13 sitting at one time at his Table, who all grew up to be Men & Women, and married;—I was the youngest Son and the youngest Child but two, & was born in Boston, N. England.

My Mother the second Wife was Abiah Folger, a Daughter of Peter Folger, one of the first Settlers of New England, of whom honourable mention is made by Cotton Mather,[3] in his Church History of that Country, (entitled Magnalia Christi Americana) as a *godly learned Englishman*, if I remember the Words rightly.—I have heard that he wrote sundry small occasional Pieces, but only one of them was printed which I saw now many Years since. It was written in 1675, in the homespun Verse of that Time & People, and address'd to those then concern'd in the Government there. It was in favour of Liberty of Conscience, & in behalf of the Baptists, Quakers, & other Sectaries, that had been under Persecution; ascribing the Indian Wars[4] & other Distresses, that had befallen the Country to that Persecution, as so many Judgments of God, to punish so heinous an Offence; and exhorting a Repeal of those uncharitable Laws. The whole appear'd to me as written with a good deal of Decent Plainness & manly Freedom. The six concluding Lines I remember, tho'

I have forgotten the two first of the Stanza, but the Purport of them was that his Censures proceeded from *Goodwill*, & therefore he would be known as the Author,

> because to be a Libeller, (says he)
>   I hate it with my Heart.
> From Sherburne Town[5] where now I dwell,
>   My Name I do put here,
> Without Offence, your real Friend,
>   It is Peter Folgier.

My elder Brothers were all put Apprentices to different Trades. I was put to the Grammar School at Eight Years of Age, my Father intending to devote me as the Tithe of his Sons[6] to the Service of the Church. My early Readiness in learning to read (which must have been very early, as I do not remember when I could not read) and the Opinion of all his Friends that I should certainly make a good Scholar, encourag'd him in this Purpose of his. My Uncle Benjamin too approv'd of it, and propos'd to give me all his Shorthand Volumes of Sermons I suppose as a Stock to set up with, if I would learn his Character.[7] I continu'd however at the Grammar School not quite one Year, tho' in that time I had risen gradually from the Middle of the Class of that Year to be the Head of it, and farther was remov'd into the next Class above it, in order to go with that into the third at the End of the Year. But my Father in the mean time, from a View of the Expence of a College Education which, having so large a Family, he could not well afford, and the mean Living many so educated were afterwards able to obtain, Reasons that he gave to his Friends in my Hearing, altered his first Intention, took me from the Grammar School, and sent me to a School for Writing & Arithmetic kept by a then famous Man, Mr Geo. Brownell, very successful in his Profession generally, and that by mild encouraging Methods. Under him I acquired fair Writing pretty soon, but I fail'd in the Arithmetic, & made no Progress in it.—At Ten Years old, I was taken home to assist

---

[1] *Episcopal Church*   American branch of the Anglican Church.

[2] *his Wife*   Josiah Franklin's first wife was Anne Child, who died in 1689 of complications from childbirth.

[3] *Cotton Mather*   Colonial religious leader and historian; his *Magnalia Christi Americana* was published in 1702 and tells of various significant events in the history of New England.

[4] *the Indian Wars*   The most serious seventeenth-century conflict between the New England colonies and Indigenous peoples (in this case the Wampanoag and several allied nations), known in English as King Philip's War, broke out in 1675, the same year that Folger's poem was written.

[5] [Franklin's note]   In the Island of Nantucket.

[6] *the Tithe of his Sons*   Traditionally, a tithe is one-tenth of one's earnings, given annually to the Church; the implication here is that Franklin's father intended his youngest son to enter into the ministry, in place of the traditional tithe.

[7] *his Character*   I.e., his method of shorthand.

my Father in his Business, which was that of a Tallow Chandler and Sope-Boiler.[1] A Business he was not bred to, but had assumed on his Arrival in New England & on finding his Dying Trade[2] would not maintain his Family, being in little Request. Accordingly I was employed in cutting Wick for the Candles, filling the Dipping Mold, & the Molds for cast Candles, attending the Shop, going of Errands, &c.—I dislik'd the Trade and had a strong Inclination for the Sea; but my Father declar'd against it; however, living near the Water, I was much in and about it, learnt early to swim well, & to manage Boats, and when in a Boat or Canoe with other Boys I was commonly allow'd to govern,[3] especially in any case of Difficulty; and upon other Occasions I was generally a Leader among the Boys, and sometimes led them into Scrapes, of which I will mention one Instance, as it shows an early projecting public Spirit, tho' not then justly conducted. There was a Salt Marsh that bounded part of the Mill Pond, on the Edge of which at Highwater, we us'd to stand to fish for Minews.[4] By much Trampling, we had made it a mere Quagmire. My Proposal was to build a Wharf there fit for us to stand upon, and I show'd my Comrades a large Heap of Stones which were intended for a new House near the Marsh, and which would very well suit our Purpose. Accordingly in the Evening when the Workmen were gone, I assembled a Number of my Playfellows, and working with them diligently like so many Emmets,[5] sometimes two or three to a Stone, we brought them all away and built our little Wharff.—The next Morning the Workmen were surpriz'd at Missing the Stones; which were found in our Wharff; Enquiry was made after the Removers; we were discovered & complain'd of; several of us were corrected by our Fathers; and tho' I pleaded the Usefulness of the Work, mine convinc'd me that nothing was useful which was not honest.—

I think you may like to know something of his Person[6] & Character. He had an excellent Constitution of Body, was of middle Stature, but well set and very strong. He was ingenious, could draw prettily, was skill'd a little in Music and had a clear pleasing Voice, so that when he play'd Psalm Tunes on his Violin & sung withal as he some times did in an Evening after the Business of the Day was over, it was extreamly agreeable to hear. He had a mechanical Genius too, and on occasion was very handy in the Use of other Tradesmen's Tools. But his great Excellence lay in a sound Understanding, and solid Judgment in prudential Matters, both in private & publick Affairs. In the latter indeed he was never employed, the numerous Family he had to educate & the Straitness of his Circumstances, keeping him close to his Trade, but I remember well his being frequently visited by leading People, who consulted him for his Opinion on Affairs of the Town or of the Church he belong'd to & show'd a good deal of Respect for his Judgment and Advice. He was also much consulted by private Persons about their Affairs when any Difficulty occur'd, & frequently chosen an Arbitrator between contending Parties.—At his Table he lik'd to have as often as he could, some sensible Friend or Neighbour, to converse with, and always took care to start some ingenious or useful Topic for Discourse, which might tend to improve the Minds of his Children. By this means he turn'd our Attention to what was good, just, & prudent in the Conduct of Life; and little or no Notice was ever taken of what related to the Victuals on the Table, whether it was well or ill drest, in or out of season, of good or bad flavour, preferable or inferior to this or that other thing of the kind; so that I was bro't up in such a perfect Inattention to those Matters as to be quite Indifferent what kind of Food was set before me; and so unobservant of it, that to this Day, if I am ask'd I can scarce tell, a few Hours after dinner, what I din'd upon.—This has been a Convenience to me in travelling, where my Companions have been sometimes very unhappy for want of a suitable Gratification of their more delicate because better instructed Tastes and Appetites.—

My Mother had likewise an excellent Constitution. She suckled all her 10 Children. I never knew either my Father or Mother to have any Sickness but that of

---

[1] *Tallow Chandler and Sope-Boiler* Manufacturer of candles (made of tallow, a cheap preparation of animal fats) and soap.

[2] *Dying Trade* I.e., his work as a dyer. (During this period, the vast majority of textiles used in the English colonies were imported from England, which may help explain the lack of business opportunities for a dyer in New England.)

[3] *govern* I.e., steer the boat.

[4] *Minews* Minnows.

[5] *Emmets* Ants.

[6] *Person* I.e., physical appearance.

which they dy'd, he at 89 & she at 85 Years of age. They lie buried together at Boston, where I some Years since plac'd a Marble over their Grave with this Inscription

> Josiah Franklin
> And Abiah his Wife
> Lie here interred.
> They lived lovingly together in Wedlock
> Fifty-five Years.—
> Without an Estate or any gainful Employment,
> By constant Labour and Industry,
> With God's Blessing,
> They maintained a large Family
> Comfortably;
> And brought up thirteen Children,
> And seven Grandchildren
> Reputably.
> From this Instance, Reader,
> Be encouraged to Diligence in thy Calling,
> And distrust not Providence.
> He was a pious & prudent Man,
> She a discreet and virtuous Woman.
> Their youngest Son,
> In filial Regard to their Memory,
> Places this Stone.
> J. F. born 1655—Died 1744. Ætat[1] 89
> A. F. born 1667—died 1752 —— 85.

By my rambling Digressions I perceive my self to be grown old. I us'd to write more methodically.—But one does not dress for private Company as for a publick Ball. 'Tis perhaps only Negligence.—

To return. I continu'd thus employ'd in my Father's Business for two Years, that is till I was 12 Years old; and my Brother John, who was bred to that Business having left my Father, married and set up for himself at Rhodeisland, there was all Appearance that I was destin'd to supply his Place and be a Tallow Chandler. But my Dislike to the Trade continuing, my Father was under Apprehensions that if he did not find one for me more agreable, I should break away and get to Sea, as his Son Josiah had done to his great Vexation. He therefore sometimes took me to walk with him, and see Joiners, Bricklayers, Turners, Braziers,[2] &c. at their Work, that he might observe my Inclination, & endeavour to fix it on some Trade or other on Land.— It has ever since been a Pleasure to me to see good Workmen handle their Tools; and it has been useful to me, having learnt so much by it, as to be able to do little Jobs my self in my House, when a Workman could not readily be got; & to construct little Machines for my Experiments while the Intention of making the Experiment was fresh & warm in my Mind. My Father at last fix'd upon the Cutler's[3] Trade, and my Uncle Benjamin's Son Samuel who was bred to that Business in London being about that time establish'd in Boston, I was sent to be with him some time on liking. But his Expectations of a Fee with me displeasing my Father, I was taken home again.

From a Child I was fond of Reading, and all the little Money that came into my Hands was ever laid out in Books. Pleas'd with the Pilgrim's Progress,[4] my first Collection was of John Bunyan's Works, in separate little Volumes. I afterwards sold them to enable me to buy R. Burton's[5] Historical Collections; they were small Chapmen's Books[6] and cheap, 40 or 50 in all.— My Father's little Library consisted chiefly of Books in polemic Divinity,[7] most of which I read, and have since often regretted, that at a time when I had such a Thirst for Knowledge, more proper Books had not fallen in my Way, since it was now resolv'd I should not be a Clergyman. Plutarch's Lives[8] there was, in which I read abundantly, and I still think that time spent to great Advantage. There was also a Book of Defoe's

---

[1]   *Ætat*   Abbreviation for the Latin *aetatis*, meaning "aged."

[2]   *Joiners*   Woodworkers, especially of ornamental or small pieces; *Turners*   Those who manufacture objects on a lathe; *Braziers*   Makers of brass objects.

[3]   *Cutler*   Maker of cutlery.

[4]   *the Pilgrim's Progress*   Christian allegorical novel (1678) by English Puritan John Bunyan; in the eighteenth century it was among the most widely read works of fiction in the English language.

[5]   *R. Burton*   Robert or Richard Burton, pseudonym of English writer and bookseller Nathaniel Crouch (born 1632); his popular historical works consisted primarily of material rewritten on the basis of other historians' work.

[6]   *Chapmen's Books*   Chapbooks; small, cheaply bound booklets.

[7]   *polemic Divinity*   I.e., argumentative works on theological questions.

[8]   *Plutarch's Lives*   Collection of biographical writings on important historical figures by ancient Greek writer Plutarch (46 CE–c. 120 CE).

called an Essay on Projects and another of Dr Mather's call'd Essays to do Good,[1] which perhaps gave me a Turn of Thinking that had an Influence on some of the principal future Events of my Life.

This Bookish Inclination at length determin'd my Father to make me a Printer, tho' he had already one Son, (James) of that Profession. In 1717 my Brother James return'd from England with a Press & Letters[2] to set up his Business in Boston. I lik'd it much better than that of my Father, but still had a Hankering for the Sea.—To prevent the apprehended Effect of such an Inclination, my Father was impatient to have me bound[3] to my Brother. I stood out some time, but at last was persuaded and signed the Indentures,[4] when I was yet but 12 Years old.—I was to serve as an Apprentice till I was 21 Years of Age, only I was to be allow'd Journeyman's Wages during the last Year. In a little time I made great Proficiency in the Business, and became a useful Hand to my Brother. I now had Access to better Books. An Acquaintance with the Apprentices of Booksellers, enabled me sometimes to borrow a small one, which I was careful to return soon & clean. Often I sat up in my Room reading the greatest Part of the Night, when the Book was borrow'd in the Evening & to be return'd early in the Morning lest it should be miss'd or wanted.—And after some time an ingenious Tradesman[5] who had a pretty[6] Collection of Books, & who frequented our Printing House, took Notice of me, invited me to his Library, & very kindly lent me such Books as I chose to read. I now took a Fancy to Poetry, and made some little Pieces. My Brother, thinking it might turn to account encourag'd me, & put me on composing two occasional Ballads. One was called the *Light House Tragedy*, & contain'd an Account of the drowning of Capt. Worthilake with

his Two Daughters; the other was a Sailor Song on the Taking of *Teach* or Blackbeard the Pirate.[7] They were wretched Stuff, in the Grubstreet Ballad Stile,[8] and when they were printed he sent me about the Town to sell them. The first sold wonderfully, the Event being recent, having made a great Noise. This flatter'd my Vanity. But my Father discourag'd me, by ridiculing my Performances, and telling me Verse-makers were generally Beggars; so I escap'd being a Poet, most probably a very bad one. But as Prose Writing has been of great Use to me in the Course of my Life, and was a principal Means of my Advancement, I shall tell you how in such a Situation I acquir'd what little Ability I have in that Way.

There was another Bookish Lad in the Town, John Collins by Name, with whom I was intimately acquainted. We sometimes disputed, and very fond we were of Argument, & very desirous of confuting one another. Which disputatious Turn, by the way, is apt to become a very bad Habit, making People often extreamly disagreable in Company, by the Contradiction that is necessary to bring it into Practice, & thence, besides souring & spoiling the Conversation, is productive of Disgusts & perhaps Enmities where you may have occasion for Friendship. I had caught it by reading my Father's Books of Dispute about Religion. Persons of good Sense, I have since observ'd, seldom fall into it, except Lawyers, University Men, and Men of all Sorts that have been bred at Edinborough.[9] A Question was once some how or other started between Collins & me, of the Propriety of educating the Female Sex in Learning, & their Abilities for Study. He was of Opinion that it was improper; & that they were naturally unequal to it. I took the contrary Side, perhaps

---

1   *Essay on Projects* 1697 prose work by English writer Daniel Defoe, discussing subjects such as banking, economic development, and women's education; *Essays to do Good* Mather's 1710 collection of essays on morality and religious piety.

2   *Letters* I.e., type for printing.

3   *bound* Apprenticed.

4   *Indentures* Contract of indentured apprenticeship, by which one was obliged to work, generally without any pay, for a set period of years.

5   [Franklin's note] Mr Matthew Adams.

6   *pretty* Commendable, admirable.

7   *the drowning ... Two Daughters* The Boston lighthouse keeper George Worthylake was drowned on 3 November 1718 along with his wife, daughters, a friend, a servant, and an enslaved man; *Taking of ... the Pirate* The famous English pirate Edward Teach—better known as Blackbeard—was killed in a battle with the Royal Navy on 22 November 1718.

8   *Grubstreet Ballad Stile* Grub Street was an impoverished area of London known for its proliferation of hack writers who sold cheap, hastily written pamphlets and ballads on current subjects of interest.

9   *Men of ... at Edinborough* Franklin alludes generally to contemporary stereotypes about Scottish people, including the idea that they are prone to argumentation; in a 1766 letter to Benjamin Rush and Jonathan Potts, Franklin describes the people of Edinburgh as being "very shrewd and observing."

a little for Dispute sake. He was naturally more eloquent, had a ready Plenty of Words, and sometimes
as I thought bore me down more by his Fluency than
by the Strength of his Reasons. As we parted without settling the Point, & were not to see one another
again for some time, I sat down to put my Arguments
in Writing, which I copied fair & sent to him. He
answer'd & I reply'd. Three or four Letters of a Side had
pass'd, when my Father happen'd to find my Papers,
and read them. Without entring into the Discussion,
he took occasion to talk to me about the Manner of
my Writing, observ'd that tho' I had the Advantage of
my Antagonist in correct Spelling & pointing[1] (which
I ow'd to the Printing House) I fell far short in elegance
of Expression, in Method and in Perspicuity, of which
he convinc'd me by several Instances. I saw the Justice
of his Remarks, & thence grew more attentive to the
Manner in Writing, and determin'd to endeavour at
Improvement.—

About this time I met with an odd Volume of the
Spectator.[2] I had never before seen any of them. I
bought it, read it over and over, and was much delighted
with it. I thought the Writing excellent, & wish'd if
possible to imitate it. With that View, I took some of
the Papers, & making short Hints of the Sentiment
in each Sentence, laid them by a few Days, and then
without looking at the Book, try'd to compleat the
Papers again, by expressing each hinted Sentiment at
length & as fully as it had been express'd before, in any
suitable Words that should come to hand.

Then I compar'd my Spectator with the Original,
discover'd some of my Faults & corrected them. But
I found I wanted[3] a Stock of Words or a Readiness in
recollecting & using them, which I thought I should
have acquir'd before that time, if I had gone on making
Verses, since the continual Occasion for Words of
the same Import but of different Length, to suit the
Measure, or of different Sound for the Rhyme, would
have laid me under a constant Necessity of searching

for Variety, and also have tended to fix that Variety in
my Mind, & make me Master of it. Therefore I took
some of the Tales & turn'd them into Verse: And after
a time, when I had pretty well forgotten the Prose,
turn'd them back again. I also sometimes jumbled my
Collections of Hints into Confusion, and after some
Weeks endeavour'd to reduce them into the best Order,
before I began to form the full Sentences & compleat the Paper. This was to teach me Method in the
Arrangement of Thoughts. By comparing my Work
afterwards with the original, I discover'd many faults
and amended them; but I sometimes had the Pleasure
of Fancying that in certain Particulars of small Import,
I had been lucky enough to improve the Method or
the Language and this encourag'd me to think I might
possibly in time come to be a tolerable English Writer,
of which I was extreamly ambitious.

My Time for these Exercises & for Reading, was
at Night after Work, or before Work began in the
Morning; or on Sundays, when I contrived to be in
the Printing House alone, evading as much as I could
the common Attendance on publick Worship, which
my Father used to exact of me when I was under his
Care:—And which indeed I still thought a Duty; tho'
I could not, as it seemed to me, afford the Time to
practise it.

When about 16 Years of Age I happen'd to meet
with a Book written by one Tryon,[4] recommending a
Vegetable Diet. I determined to go into it. My Brother
being yet unmarried, did not keep House, but boarded
himself & his Apprentices in another Family. My refusing to eat Flesh occasioned an Inconveniency, and I
was frequently chid for my singularity.[5] I made my self
acquainted with Tryon's Manner of preparing some of
his Dishes, such as Boiling Potatoes, or Rice, making
Hasty Pudding,[6] & a few others, and then propos'd
to my Brother, that if he would give me Weekly half
the Money he paid for my Board, I would board my
self. He instantly agreed to it, and I presently found
that I could save half what he paid me. This was an
additional Fund for buying Books: But I had another

---

[1] *pointing* Punctuation.

[2] *the Spectator* Short-lived but highly influential London periodical published daily by Joseph Addison and Richard Steele from
1711 to 1712, and by Addison alone for several months in 1714; its
essays discussed morality, manners, and literature, all with a distinctively witty prose style.

[3] *wanted* Lacked; needed.

[4] *Tryon* English writer Thomas Tryon, whose 1691 *A Way to
Health* recommended vegetarianism as a healthful diet and advocated for better treatment of animals.

[5] *singularity* Unusualness.

[6] *Hasty Pudding* Quick porridge made of grains or cornmeal.

Advantage in it. My Brother and the rest going from the Printing House to their Meals, I remain'd there alone, and dispatching presently my light Repast, (which often was no more than a Bisket or a Slice of Bread, a Handful of Raisins or a Tart from the Pastry Cook's, and a Glass of Water) had the rest of the Time till their Return, for Study, in which I made the greater Progress from that greater Clearness of Head & quicker Apprehension which usually attend Temperance in Eating & Drinking. And now it was that being on some Occasion made asham'd of my Ignorance in Figures, which I had twice fail'd in learning when at School, I took Cocker's[1] Book of Arithmetick, & went thro' the whole by my self with great Ease.—I also read Seller's & Sturmy's[2] Books of Navigation, & became acquainted with the little Geometry they contain, but never proceeded far in that Science.—And I read about this Time Locke On Human Understanding and the Art of Thinking by Messrs du Port Royal.[3]

While I was intent on improving my Language, I met with an English Grammar (I think it was Greenwood's[4]) at the End of which there were two little Sketches of the Arts of Rhetoric and Logic, the latter finishing with a Specimen of a Dispute in the Socratic Method.[5] And soon after I procur'd Xenophon's[6] Memorable Things of Socrates, wherein there are many Instances of the same Method. I was charm'd with it, adopted it, dropt my abrupt Contradiction, and positive Argumentation, and put on the humble Enquirer & Doubter. And being then, from reading Shaftsbury & Collins,[7] become a real Doubter in many Points of our Religious Doctrine, I found this Method safest for my self & very embarrassing to those against whom I used it, therefore I took a Delight in it, practis'd it continually & grew very artful & expert in drawing People even of superior Knowledge into Concessions the Consequences of which they did not foresee, entangling them in Difficulties out of which they could not extricate themselves, and so obtaining Victories that neither my self nor my Cause always deserved.—I continu'd this Method some few Years, but gradually left it, retaining only the Habit of expressing my self in Terms of modest Diffidence, never using when I advance any thing that may possibly be disputed, the Words, *Certainly, undoubtedly*, or any others that give the Air of Positiveness to an Opinion; but rather say, *I conceive*, or *I apprehend* a Thing to be so or so, *It appears to me*, or *I should think it so or so for such & such Reasons*, or *I imagine* it to be so, or *it is so if I am not mistaken*.—This Habit I believe has been of great Advantage to me, when I have had occasion to inculcate my Opinions & persuade Men into Measures that I have been from time to time engag'd in promoting.—And as the chief Ends of Conversation are to *inform*, or to be *informed*, to *please* or to *persuade*, I wish well meaning sensible Men would not lessen their Power of doing Good by a Positive assuming Manner that seldom fails to disgust, tends to create Opposition, and to defeat every one of those Purposes for which Speech was given us, to wit, giving or receiving Information, or Pleasure: For If you would *inform*, a positive dogmatical Manner in advancing your Sentiments, may provoke Contradiction & prevent a candid Attention. If you wish Information & Improvement from the Knowledge of others and yet at the same time express your self as firmly fix'd in your present Opinions, modest sensible Men, who do not love Disputation, will probably leave you undisturb'd in the Possession of your Error; and by such a Manner you can seldom

---

[1] *Cocker* English engraver Edward Cocker, credited as the author of the popular 1677 textbook *Cocker's Arithmetick*.

[2] *Seller's & Sturmy's* John Seller (1632–97) and Samuel Sturmy (1633–69), popular English writers on marine navigation.

[3] *Locke On Human Understanding* John Locke's influential philosophical work *An Essay on Human Understanding* (1689); *Art of … Port Royal* 1662 treatise on logic by French philosophers Antoine Arnauld and Pierre Nicole.

[4] *Greenwood* English grammarian James Greenwood, author of *An Essay Towards a Practical English Grammar* (1711).

[5] *Socratic Method* Common term for the method of philosophical discourse exemplified by the Greek philosopher Socrates (c. 470–399 BCE), characterized by the continual asking of probing questions rather than making definitive statements.

[6] *Xenophon* Greek historian and philosopher (c. 430–354 BCE), a friend and disciple of Socrates who defended the controversial elder philosopher in numerous works.

[7] *Shaftsbury & Collins* Anthony Ashley Cooper, 1st Earl of Shaftesbury (1621–83), politician who supported religious freedom (within the bounds of Protestantism), and Anthony Collins (1676–1729), freethinker and religious skeptic.

hope to recommend your self in *pleasing* your Hearers, or to persuade those whose Concurrence you desire.—Pope[1] says, judiciously,

> *Men should be taught as if you taught them not,*
> *And things unknown propos'd as things forgot,—*

farther recommending it to us,

> *To speak tho' sure, with seeming Diffidence.*

And he might have couple'd with this Line that which he has coupled with another, I think less properly,

> *For want of Modesty is want of Sense.*[2]

If you ask why *less properly*, I must repeat the Lines;

> "Immodest Words admit of *no* Defence;
> "*For* Want of Modesty is Want of Sense."

Now is not *Want of Sense*, (where a Man is so unfortunate as to want it) some Apology for his *Want of Modesty*? and would not the Lines stand more justly thus?

> Immodest Words admit *but this* Defence,
> That Want of Modesty is Want of Sense.

This however I should submit to better Judgments.—

My Brother had in 1720 or 21, begun to print a Newspaper. It was the second that appear'd in America,[3] & was called *The New England Courant*. The only one before it, was *the Boston News Letter*. I remember his being dissuaded by some of his Friends from the Undertaking, as not likely to succeed, one Newspaper being in their Judgment enough for America.—At this time 1771 there are not less than five & twenty.—He went on however with the Undertaking, and after having work'd in composing the Types & printing off the Sheets I was employ'd to carry the Papers thro' the Streets to the

Customers.—He had some ingenious Men among his Friends who amus'd themselves by writing little Pieces for this Paper, which gain'd it Credit, & made it more in Demand; and these Gentlemen often visited us.—Hearing their Conversations, and their Accounts of the Approbation their Papers were receiv'd with, I was excited to try my Hand among them. But being still a Boy, & suspecting that my Brother would object to printing any Thing of mine in his Paper if he knew it to be mine, I contriv'd to disguise my Hand, & writing an anonymous Paper[4] I put it in at Night under the Door of the Printing House. It was found in the Morning & communicated to his Writing Friends when they call'd in as Usual. They read it, commented on it in my Hearing, and I had the exquisite Pleasure, of finding it met with their Approbation, and that, in their different Guesses at the Author none were named but Men of some Character among us for Learning & Ingenuity.—I suppose now that I was rather lucky in my Judges: And that perhaps they were not really so very good ones as I then esteem'd them. Encourag'd however by this, I wrote and convey'd in the same Way to the Press several more Papers, which were equally approv'd, and I kept my Secret till my small Fund of Sense for such Performances was pretty well exhausted, & then I discovered[5] it; when I began to be considered a little more by my Brother's Acquaintance, and in a manner that did not quite please him, as he thought, probably with reason, that it tended to make me too vain. And perhaps this might be one Occasion of the Differences that we began to have about this Time. Tho' a Brother, he considered himself as my Master, & me as his Apprentice; and accordingly expected the same Services from me as he would from another; while I thought he demean'd me too much in some he requir'd of me, who from a Brother expected more Indulgence. Our Disputes were often brought before our Father, and I fancy I was either generally in the right, or else a better Pleader, because the Judgment was generally in my favour. But my Brother was passionate & had often

---

[1] *Pope* English poet Alexander Pope (1688–1744); Franklin quotes (loosely) below from his *An Essay on Criticism*, lines 576–77 and 569.

[2] *For want ... of Sense* This line is in fact a misquotation from Wentworth Dillon's *Essay on Translated Verse* (1684).

[3] *It was ... in America* James Franklin's newspaper was in fact the fifth newspaper to be printed in America.

[4] *an anonymous Paper* Franklin refers here to his "Silence Dogood" papers, a series of letters purported to be written by the widow Silence Dogood, published between 12 April and 8 October 1722. Letters 1, 2, and 5 are included in the online component of this anthology.

[5] *discovered* Revealed.

beaten me, which I took extreamly amiss;[1] and thinking my Apprenticeship very tedious, I was continually wishing for some Opportunity of shortening it, which at length offered in a manner unexpected.

One of the Pieces in our News-Paper, on some political Point which I have now forgotten, gave Offence to the Assembly.[2] He was taken up, censur'd and imprison'd for a Month by the Speaker's Warrant, I suppose because he would not discover his Author.[3] I too was taken up & examin'd before the Council; but tho' I did not give them any Satisfaction, they contented themselves with admonishing me, and dismiss'd me; considering me perhaps as an Apprentice who was bound to keep his Master's Secrets. During my Brother's Confinement, which I resented a good deal, notwithstanding our private Differences, I had the Management of the Paper; and I made bold to give our Rulers some Rubs[4] in it, which my Brother took very kindly, while others began to consider me in an unfavourable Light, as a young Genius that had a Turn for Libelling & Satyr.[5] My Brother's Discharge was accompany'd with an Order of the House, (a very odd one) *that James Franklin should no longer print the Paper called the New England Courant.* There was a Consultation held in our Printing House among his Friends what he should do in this Case. Some propos'd to evade the Order by changing the Name of the Paper; but my Brother seeing Inconveniences in that, it was finally concluded on as a better Way, to let it be printed for the future under the Name of *Benjamin Franklin*. And to avoid the Censure of the Assembly that might fall on him, as still printing it by his Apprentice, the Contrivance was, that my old Indenture should be return'd to me with a full Discharge on the Back of it, to be shown on Occasion;[6] but to secure to him the

Benefit of my Service I was to sign new Indentures for the Remainder of the Term, which were to be kept private. A very flimsy Scheme it was, but however it was immediately executed, and the Paper went on accordingly under my Name for several Months. At length a fresh Difference[7] arising between my Brother and me, I took upon me to assert my Freedom, presuming that he would not venture to produce the new Indentures. It was not fair in me to take this Advantage, and this I therefore reckon one of the first Errata[8] of my Life: But the Unfairness of it weigh'd little with me, when under the Impressions of Resentment, for the Blows[9] his Passion too often urg'd him to bestow upon me. Tho' He was otherwise not an ill-natur'd Man: Perhaps I was too saucy & provoking.—

When he found I would leave him, he took care to prevent my getting Employment in any other Printing-House of the Town, by going round & speaking to every Master, who accordingly refus'd to give me Work. I then thought of going to New York as the nearest Place where there was a Printer: and I was the rather inclin'd to leave Boston, when I reflected that I had already made my self a little obnoxious, to the governing Party; & from the arbitrary Proceedings of the Assembly in my Brother's Case it was likely I might if I stay'd soon bring my self into Scrapes; and farther that my indiscrete Disputations about Religion began to make me pointed at with Horror by good People, as an Infidel or Atheist; I determin'd on the Point: but my Father now siding with my Brother, I was sensible that if I attempted to go openly, Means would be used to prevent me. My Friend Collins therefore undertook to manage a little for me. He agreed with the Captain of a New York Sloop[10] for my Passage, under the Notion of my being a young Acquaintance of his that had got a naughty Girl with Child, whose Friends would compel me to marry her, and therefore I could not appear or come away publickly. So I sold some of my Books to raise a little Money, Was taken on board privately, and as we had a fair Wind, in three Days I found my self in New York near 300 Miles from home, a Boy of but 17,

---

1   [Franklin's note]   I fancy his harsh & tyrannical Treatment of me, might be a means of impressing me with that Aversion to arbitrary Power that has stuck to me thro' my whole Life.

2   *One of ... the Assembly*   The article in question suggested that certain public figures in Boston had connections to local piracy.

3   *discover his Author*   I.e., reveal who had written the controversial article.

4   *Rubs*   Criticisms.

5   *Satyr*   I.e., satire.

6   *my old Indenture ... Occasion*   I.e., Franklin was to be freed of his prior indenture, and given papers of discharge to display to the authorities if need be.

7   *Difference*   Conflict.

8   *Errata*   Errors in a printed book, marked out for correction in the second edition.

9   *Blows*   Beatings.

10   *Sloop*   Small, single-masted sailing vessel.

without the least Recommendation to or Knowledge of any Person in the Place, and with very little Money in my Pocket.—

My Inclinations for the Sea, were by this time worne out, or I might now have gratify'd them.—But having a Trade, & supposing my self a pretty good Workman, I offer'd my Service to the Printer of the Place, old Mr William Bradford.[1]—He could give me no Employment, having little to do, and Help enough already: But, says he, my Son at Philadelphia has lately lost his principal Hand, Aquila Rose, by Death. If you go thither I believe he may employ you.—Philadelphia was 100 Miles farther. I set out, however, in a Boat for Amboy;[2] leaving my Chest and Things to follow me round by Sea. In crossing the Bay we met with a Squall that tore our rotten Sails to pieces, prevented our getting into the Kill,[3] and drove us upon Long Island. In our Way a drunken Dutchman, who was a Passenger too, fell over board; when he was sinking I reach'd thro' the Water to his shock Pate[4] & drew him up so that we got him in again.—His Ducking sober'd him a little, & he went to sleep, taking first out of his Pocket a Book which he desir'd I would dry for him. It prov'd to be my old favourite Author Bunyan's Pilgrim's Progress in Dutch, finely printed on good Paper with copper Cuts,[5] a Dress better than I had ever seen it wear in its own Language. I have since found that it has been translated into most of the Languages of Europe, and suppose it has been more generally read than any other Book except perhaps the Bible.—Honest John[6] was the first that I know of who mix'd Narration & Dialogue, a Method of Writing very engaging to the Reader, who in the most interesting Parts finds himself as it were brought into the Company, & present at the Discourse. De foe in his Cruso, his Moll Flanders, Religious Courtship, Family Instructor,[7] & other Pieces, has imitated it with Success. And Richardson has done the same in his Pamela,[8] &.—

When we drew near the Island[9] we found it was at a Place where there could be no Landing, there being a great Surff on the stony Beach. So we dropt Anchor & swung round towards the Shore. Some People came down to the Water Edge & hallow'd to us, as we did to them. But the Wind was so high & the Surff so loud, that we could not hear so as to understand each other. There were Canoes on the Shore, & we made Signs & hallow'd that they should fetch us, but they either did not understand us, or thought it impracticable. So they went away, and Night coming on, we had no Remedy but to wait till the Wind should abate, and in the mean time the Boatman & I concluded to sleep if we could, and so crouded into the Scuttle[10] with the Dutchman who was still wet, and the Spray beating over the Head of our Boat, leak'd thro' to us, so that we were soon almost as wet as he. In this Manner we lay all Night with very little Rest. But the Wind abating the next Day, we made a Shift to reach Amboy before Night, having been 30 Hours on the Water without Victuals, or any Drink but a Bottle of filthy Rum:—The Water we sail'd on being salt.—

In the Evening I found my self very feverish, & went ill to Bed. But having read somewhere that cold Water drank plentifully was good for a Fever, I follow'd the Prescription, sweat plentifully most of the Night, my Fever left me, and in the Morning crossing the Ferry, proceeded on my Journey, on foot, having 50 Miles to Burlington,[11] where I was told I should find Boats that would carry me the rest of the Way to Philadelphia.

---

[1]   *William Bradford*   William Bradford (1660–1752), English-born printer who pioneered the American printing trade.

[2]   *Amboy*   Perth Amboy, New Jersey, located just across from the southern point of Staten Island.

[3]   *the Kill*   Narrow body of water separating northern Staten Island from New Jersey, known as Kill van Kull; the Kill branches west off the Upper New York Bay, which divides Long Island from New Jersey.

[4]   *shock Pate*   Head covered with rough, shaggy hair.

[5]   *copper Cuts*   Copper-plate engravings.

[6]   *John*   I.e., John Bunyan. (*The Pilgrim's Progress* is often considered one of the first novels in the English language.)

[7]   *Cruso … Family Instructor*   List of works by Daniel Defoe; today, *Robinson Crusoe* (1719) and *Moll Flanders* (1722) are considered novels, while *Religious Courtship* (1722) and *The Family Instructor* (1715) are considered nonfiction conduct manuals.

[8]   *Pamela*   1740 epistolary novel by Samuel Richardson.

[9]   *the Island*   I.e., Staten Island.

[10]   *Scuttle*   Covered square hole that is a means of moving between decks.

[11]   *Burlington*   City in New Jersey, on the bank of the Delaware River, which forms the border between New Jersey and Pennsylvania.

It rain'd very hard all the Day, I was thoroughly soak'd, and by Noon a good deal tir'd, so I stopt at a poor Inn, where I staid all Night, beginning now to wish that I had never left home. I cut so miserable a Figure too, that I found by the Questions ask'd me I was suspected to be some runaway Servant, and in danger of being taken up on that Suspicion.——However, I proceeded the next Day, and got in the Evening to an Inn within 8 or 10 Miles of Burlington, kept by one Dr Brown.——

He entred into Conversation with me while I took some Refreshment, and finding I had read a little, became very sociable and friendly. Our Acquaintance continu'd as long as he liv'd. He had been, I imagine, an itinerant Doctor, for there was no Town in England, or Country in Europe, of which he could not give a very particular Account. He had some Letters,[1] & was ingenious, but much of an Unbeliever, & wickedly undertook some Years after to travesty the Bible in doggrel Verse as Cotton had done Virgil.[2]——By this means he set many of the Facts in a very ridiculous Light, & might have hurt weak minds if his Work had been publish'd:——but it never was.——At his House I lay that Night, and the next Morning reach'd Burlington.——But had the Mortification to find that the regular Boats were gone, a little before my coming, and no other expected to go till Tuesday, this being Saturday. Wherefore I return'd to an old Woman in the Town of whom I had bought Gingerbread to eat on the Water, & ask'd her Advice; she invited me to lodge at her House till a Passage by Water should offer; & being tired with my foot Travelling, I accepted the Invitation. She understanding I was a Printer, would have had me stay at that Town & follow my Business, being ignorant of the Stock necessary to begin with. She was very hospitable, gave me a Dinner of Ox Cheek with great Goodwill, accepting only of a Pot of Ale in return. And I tho't my self fix'd till Tuesday should come. However walking in the Evening by the Side of the River a Boat came by, which I found was going towards Philadelphia, with several People in her. They took me in, and as there was no Wind, we row'd all the Way; and about Midnight, not having yet seen the City, some of the Company were confident we must have pass'd it, and would row no farther, the others knew not where we were, so we put towards the Shore, got into a Creek, landed near an old Fence with the Rails of which we made a Fire, the Night being cold, in October, and there we remain'd till Daylight. Then one of the Company knew the Place to be Cooper's Creek a little above Philadelphia, which we saw as soon as we got out of the Creek, and arriv'd there about 8 or 9 a Clock, on the Sunday morning, and landed at the Market street Wharff.——

I have been the more particular in this Description of my Journey, & shall be so of my first Entry into that City, that you may in your Mind compare such unlikely Beginning with the Figure I have since made there. I was in my working Dress, my best Cloaths being to come round by Sea. I was dirty from my Journey; my Pockets were stuff'd out with Shirts & Stockings; I knew no Soul, nor where to look for Lodging. I was fatigu'd with Travelling, Rowing & Want of Rest. I was very hungry; and my whole Stock of Cash consisted of a Dutch Dollar[3] and about a Shilling in Copper. The latter I gave the People of the Boat for my Passage, who at first refus'd it on Account of my Rowing; but I insisted on their taking it, a Man being sometimes more generous when he has but a little Money than when he has plenty, perhaps thro' Fear of being thought to have but little. Then I walk'd up the Street, gazing about, till near the Market House I met a Boy with Bread. I had made many a Meal on Bread, & inquiring where he got it, I went immediately to the Baker's he directed me to in second Street; and ask'd for Bisket, intending such as we had in Boston, but they it seems, were not made in Philadelphia, then I ask'd for a threepenny Loaf, and was told they had none such: so not considering or knowing the Difference of Money & the greater Cheapness nor the Names of his Bread, I bad him give me three pennyworth of any sort. He gave me accordingly three great Puffy Rolls. I was surpriz'd at the Quantity, but took it, and having no Room in my Pockets, walk'd off, with a Roll under each Arm, & eating the other. Thus I went up Market Street as far as fourth Street, passing by the Door of Mr Read, my future Wife's Father, when she standing at the Door

---

[1]   *Letters*   I.e., academic or literary education.

[2]   *as Cotton … Virgil*   Reference to *Scarronides: or, Virgil travestie* (1664–70), English writer Charles Cotton's notoriously vulgar parody of the *Aeneid* (29–19 BCE) by the Roman poet Virgil.

[3]   *Dutch Dollar*   Also known as the guilder, a Dutch coin that was circulated in colonial America.

saw me, & thought I made as I certainly did a most awkward ridiculous Appearance. Then I turn'd and went down Chestnut Street and part of Walnut Street, eating my Roll all the Way, and coming round found my self again at Market street Wharff, near the Boat I came in, to which I went for a Draught of the River Water, and being fill'd with one of my Rolls, gave the other two to a Woman & her Child that came down the River in the Boat with us and were waiting to go farther. Thus refresh'd I walk'd again up the Street, which by this time had many clean dress'd People in it who were all walking the same Way; I join'd them, and thereby was led into the great Meeting House of the Quakers[1] near the Market. I sat down among them, and after looking round a while & hearing nothing said, being very drowzy thro' Labour & want of Rest the preceding Night, I fell fast asleep, and continu'd so till the Meeting broke up, when one was kind enough to rouse me. This was therefore the first House I was in or slept in, in Philadelphia.—

Walking down again towards the River, & looking in the Faces of People, I met a young Quaker Man whose Countenance I lik'd, and accosting him requested he would tell me where a Stranger could get Lodging. We were then near the Sign of the Three Mariners. Here, says he, is one Place that entertains Strangers, but it is not a reputable House; if thee[2] wilt walk with me, I'll show thee a better. He brought me to the Crooked Billet in Water-Street. Here I got a Dinner. And while I was eating it, several sly Questions were ask'd me, as it seem'd to be suspected from my youth & Appearance, that I might be some Runaway. After Dinner my Sleepiness return'd: and being shown to a Bed, I lay down without undressing, and slept till Six in the Evening; was call'd to Supper; went to Bed again very early and slept soundly till the next Morning. Then I made my self as tidy as I could, and went to Andrew Bradford the Printer's.—I found in the Shop the old Man his Father, whom I had seen at New York, and who travelling on horse back had got to Philadelphia

before me.—He introduc'd me to his Son, who receiv'd me civilly, gave me a Breakfast, but told me he did not at present want a Hand, being lately supply'd with one. But there was another Printer in town lately set up, one Keimer,[3] who perhaps might employ me; if not, I should be welcome to lodge at his House, & he would give me a little Work to do now & then till fuller Business should offer.

The old Gentleman said, he would go with me to the new Printer: And when we found him, Neighbour, says Bradford, I have brought to see you a young Man of your Business, perhaps you may want such a One. He ask'd me a few Questions, put a Composing Stick[4] in my Hand to see how I work'd, and then said he would employ me soon, tho' he had just then nothing for me to do. And taking old Bradford whom he had never seen before, to be one of the Towns People that had a Good Will for him, enter'd into a Conversation on his present Undertaking & Prospects; while Bradford not discovering[5] that he was the other Printer's Father; on Keimer's Saying he expected soon to get the greatest Part of the Business into his own Hands, drew him on by artful Questions and starting little Doubts, to explain all his Views, what Interest he rely'd on, & in what manner he intended to proceed.—I who stood by & heard all, saw immediately that one of them was a crafty old Sophister,[6] and the other a mere Novice. Bradford left me with Keimer, who was greatly surpriz'd when I told him who the old Man was.

Keimer's Printing House I found, consisted of an old shatter'd Press, and one small worn-out Fount[7] of English, which he was then using himself, composing in it an Elegy on Aquila Rose before-mentioned, an ingenious young Man of excellent Character much respected in the Town, Clerk of the Assembly, & a pretty[8] Poet. Keimer made Verses, too, but very indif-

---

[1] *Quakers* Members of the religious denomination formally known as the Society of Friends; the group had a significant presence in Pennsylvania, which had been founded by the Quaker William Penn in 1681.

[2] *thee* Quakers were known for their use of the pronouns "thee" and "thou" and related turns of phrase that were otherwise considered outdated in everyday speech by the eighteenth-century.

[3] *Keimer* English-born printer Samuel Keimer, who had emigrated to Pennsylvania after a stint in debtors' prison shortly before Franklin's arrival.

[4] *Composing Stick* Printing tool on which one arranges pieces of movable type into lines, and which is then set into a printing galley.

[5] *discovering* Revealing.

[6] *Sophister* Clever and conniving person.

[7] *Fount* Assemblage of type in a given size and style.

[8] *pretty* I.e., skillful, talented.

ferently.[1]—He could not be said to write them, for his Manner was to compose them in the Types directly out of his Head; so there being no Copy, but one Pair of Cases, and the Elegy likely to require all the Letter, no one could help him.—I endeavour'd to put his Press (which he had not yet us'd, & of which he understood nothing) into Order fit to be work'd with; & promising to come & print off his Elegy as soon as he should have got it ready, I return'd to Bradford's, who gave me a little Job to do for the present, & there I lodged & dieted. A few Days after Keimer sent for me to print off the Elegy. And now he had got another Pair of Cases, and a Pamphlet to reprint, on which he set me to work.—

These two Printers I found poorly qualified for their Business. Bradford had not been bred to it, & was very illiterate; and Keimer tho' something of a Scholar, was a mere Compositor, knowing nothing of Presswork.[2] He had been one of the French Prophets[3] and could act their enthusiastic Agitations. At this time he did not profess any particular Religion, but something of all on occasion; was very ignorant of the World, & had, as I afterwards found, a good deal of the Knave in his Composition. He did not like my Lodging at Bradford's while I work'd with him. He had a House indeed, but without Furniture, so he could not lodge me; But he got me a Lodging at Mr Read's beforementioned, who was the Owner of his House. And my Chest & Clothes being come by this time, I made rather a more respectable Appearance in the Eyes of Miss Read, than I had done when she first happen'd to see me eating my Roll in the Street.—

I began now to have some Acquaintance among the young People of the Town, that were Lovers of Reading with whom I spent my Evenings very pleasantly and gaining Money by my Industry & Frugality, I lived very agreably, forgetting Boston as much as I could, and not desiring that any there should know where I resided except my Friend Collins who was in my Secret, & kept it when I wrote to him.—At length an Incident happened that sent me back again much sooner than I had intended.—

I had a Brother-in-law, Robert Holmes, Master of a Sloop, that traded between Boston and Delaware. He being at New Castle,[4] 40 Miles below Philadelphia, heard there of me, and wrote me a Letter, mentioning the Concern of my Friends in Boston at my abrupt Departure, assuring me of their Goodwill to me, and that every thing would be accommodated to my Mind if I would return, to which he exhorted me very earnestly.—I wrote an Answer to his Letter, thank'd him for his Advice, but stated my Reasons for quitting Boston fully, & in such a Light as to convince him I was not so wrong as he had apprehended.—Sir William Keith[5] Governor of the Province, was then at New Castle, and Capt. Holmes happening to be in Company with him when my Letter came to hand, spoke to him of me, and show'd him the Letter. The Governor read it, and seem'd surpriz'd when he was told my Age. He said I appear'd a young Man of promising Parts, and therefore should be encouraged: The Printers at Philadelphia were wretched ones, and if I would set up there, he made no doubt I should succeed; for his Part, he would procure me the publick Business, & do me every other Service in his Power. This my Brother-in-Law afterwards told me in Boston. But I knew as yet nothing of it; when one Day Keimer and I being at Work together near the Window, we saw the Governor and another Gentleman (which prov'd to be Col. French, of New Castle) finely dress'd, come directly across the Street to our House, & heard them at the Door. Keimer ran down immediately, thinking it a Visit to him. But the Governor enquir'd for me, came up, & with a Condescension[6] & Politeness I had been quite unus'd to, made me many Compliments, desired to be acquainted with me, blam'd me kindly for not having made my self known to him when I first came to the Place, and would have me away with him to the Tavern where he was going with Col. French to taste

---

1   *indifferently*   In inferior quality.

2   *a mere Compositor ... Presswork*   I.e., familiar with the work of setting type (composing) but not with operating the printing press.

3   *French Prophets*   Millenarian group originating in the Protestant Camisard sect of early-eighteenth-century France; following a period of violent persecution under the Catholic Louis XIV between 1702 and 1715, a small group of Camisards emigrated to London, where they and their followers became known as the French Prophets. The Prophets became infamous for undergoing wild, violent fits during meetings.

4   *New Castle*   Town in Delaware.

5   *William Keith*   The Scottish-born Sir William Keith served as Governor of Pennsylvania and Delaware from 1717 to 1726.

6   *Condescension*   Gracious behavior shown to a social inferior.

as he said some excellent Madeira.[1] I was not a little surpriz'd, and Keimer star'd like a Pig poison'd. I went however with the Governor & Col. French, to a Tavern the Corner of Third Street, and over the Madeira he propos'd my Setting up my Business, laid beforre me the Probabilities of Success, & both he & Col French, assur'd me I should have their Interest & Influence in procuring the Publick Business of both Governments. On my doubting whether my Father would assist me in it, Sir William said he would give me a Letter to him, in which he would state the Advantages,—and he did not doubt of prevailing with him. So it was concluded I should return to Boston in the first Vessel with the Governor's Letter recommending me to my Father. In the mean time the Intention was to be kept secret, and I went on working with Keimer as usual, the Governor sending for me now & then to dine with him, a very great Honour I thought it, and conversing with me in the most affable, familiar, & friendly manner imaginable. About the End of April 1724. a little Vessel offer'd for Boston. I took Leave of Keimer as going to see my Friends. The Governor gave me an ample Letter, saying many flattering things of me to my Father, and strongly recommending the Project of my setting up at Philadelphia, as a Thing that must make my Fortune.—We struck on a Shoal in going down the Bay & sprung a Leak, we had a blustring time at Sea, and were oblig'd to pump almost continually, at which I took my Turn.—We arriv'd safe however at Boston in about a Fortnight.—I had been absent Seven Months and my Friends had heard nothing of me, for my Br. Holmes was not yet return'd; and had not written about me. My unexpected Appearance surpriz'd the Family; all were however very glad to see me and made me Welcome, except my Brother. I went to see him at his Printing-House: I was better dress'd than ever while in his Service, having a genteel new Suit from Head to foot, a Watch, and my Pockets lin'd with near Five Pounds Sterling in Silver. He receiv'd me not very frankly,[2] look'd me all over, and turn'd to his Work again. The Journey-Men were inquisitive where I had been, what sort of a Country it was, and how I lik'd it? I prais'd it much, & the happy Life I led in it; expressing strongly my Intention of returning to it; and one

of them asking what kind of Money we had there, I produc'd a handful of Silver, and spread it before them, which was a kind of Raree-Show[3] they had not been us'd to, Paper being the Money of Boston.[4] Then I took an Opportunity of letting them see my Watch: and lastly, (my Brother still grum & sullen) I gave them a Piece of Eight[5] to drink & took my Leave.—This Visit of mine offended him extreamly. For when my Mother some time after spoke to him of a Reconciliation, & of her Wishes to see us on good Terms together, & that we might live for the future as Brothers, he said, I had insulted him in such a Manner before his People that he could never forget or forgive it.—In this however he was mistaken.—

My Father receiv'd the Governor's Letter with some apparent Surprize; but said little of it to me for some Days; when Capt. Holmes returning, he show'd it to him, ask'd if he knew Keith, and what kind of a Man he was: Adding his Opinion that he must be of small Discretion,[6] to think of setting a Boy up in Business who wanted yet 3 Years of being at Man's Estate.[7] Ho[l]mes said what he could in favor of the Project; but my Father was clear in the Impropriety of it; and at last gave a flat Denial to it. Then he wrote a civil Letter to Sir William thanking him for the Patronage he had so kindly offered me, but declining to assist me as yet in Setting up, I being in his Opinion too young to be trusted with the Management of a Business so important; & for which the Preparation must be so expensive.—

My friend & Companion Collins, who was a Clerk at the Post-Office, pleas'd with the Account I gave him of my new Country, determin'd to go thither also:—And while I waited for my Fathers Determination, he set out before me by Land to Rhodeisland, leaving his Books which were a pretty Collection of Mathematicks

---

1   *Madeira*   Portuguese fortified wine.

2   *frankly*   I.e., openly or warmly.

3   *Raree-Show*   Peep show.

4   *Paper being the Money of Boston*   Paper money had only been introduced in Pennsylvania in the previous year.

5   *Piece of Eight*   Spanish dollar (a common form of currency in the colonies).

6   *small Discretion*   Poor judgment.

7   *wanted yet … Man's Estate*   I.e., was still three years short of being considered a grown man. (Franklin was at this time eighteen years old.)

& Natural Philosophy,[1] to come with mine & me to New York where he propos'd to wait for me. My Father, tho' he did not approve Sir William's Proposition was yet pleas'd that I had been able to obtain so advantageous a Character from a Person of such Note where I had resided, and that I had been so industrious & careful as to equip my self so handsomely in so short a time: therefore seeing no Prospect of an Accommodation between my Brother & me, he gave his Consent to my Returning again to Philadelphia, advis'd me to behave respectfully to the People there, endeavour to obtain the general Esteem, & avoid lampooning & libelling to which he thought I had too much Inclination;—telling me, that by steady Industry and a prudent Parsimony,[2] I might save enough by the time I was One and Twenty to set me up, & that if I came near the Matter, he would help me out with the Rest.—This was all I could obtain, except some small Gifts as Tokens of his & my Mother's Love, when I embark'd again for New-York, now with their Approbation & their Blessing.—

The Sloop putting in at Newport, Rhodeisland, I visited my Brother John, who had been married & settled there some Years. He received me very affectionately, for he always lov'd me.—A Friend of his, one Vernon, having some Money due to him in Pensilvania, about 35 Pounds Currency, desired I would receive it for him, and keep it till I had his Directions what to remit it in. Accordingly he gave me an Order.—This afterwards occasion'd me a good deal of Uneasiness.—At Newport we took in a Number of Passengers for New York: Among which were two young Women, Companions, and a grave, sensible Matron-like Quaker-Woman with her Attendants.—I had shown an obliging Readiness to do her some little Services which impress'd her I suppose with a degree of Good-will towards me.— Therefore when she saw a daily growing Familiarity between me & the two Young Women, which they appear'd to encourage, she took me aside & said, Young Man, I am concern'd for thee, as thou hast no Friend with thee, and seems not to know much of the World, or of the Snares Youth is expos'd to; depend upon it those are very bad Women, I can see it in all their Actions, and if thee art not upon thy Guard, they will draw thee into some Danger: they are Strangers to thee,—and I advise thee in a friendly Concern for thy Welfare, to have no Acquaintance with them.—As I seem'd at first not to think so ill of them as she did, she mention'd some Things she had observ'd & heard that had escap'd my Notice; but now convinc'd me she was right. I thank'd her for her kind Advice, and promis'd to follow it.—When we arriv'd at New York, they told me where they liv'd, & invited me to come and see them: but I avoided it. And it was well I did: For the next Day, the Captain miss'd a Silver Spoon & some other Things that had been taken out of his Cabbin, and knowing that these were a Couple of Strumpets,[3] he got a Warrant to search their Lodgings, found the stolen Goods, and had the Thieves punish'd.—So tho' we had escap'd a sunken Rock which we scrap'd upon in the Passage, I thought this Escape of rather more Importance to me. At New York I found my Friend Collins, who had arriv'd there some Time before me. We had been intimate from Children, and had read the same Books together. But he had the Advantage of more time for Reading, & Studying and a wonderful Genius for Mathematical Learning in which he far outstript me. While I liv'd in Boston most of my Hours of Leisure for Conversation were spent with him, & he continu'd a sober as well as an industrious Lad; was much respected for his Learning by several of the Clergy & other Gentlemen, & seem'd to promise making a good Figure in Life: but during my Absence he had acquir'd a Habit of Sotting with Brandy; and I found by his own Account & what I heard from others, that he had been drunk every day since his Arrival at New York, & behav'd very oddly. He had gam'd too and lost his Money, so that I was oblig'd to discharge his Lodgings,[4] & defray his Expences to and at Philadelphia:—Which prov'd extreamly inconvenient to me.—The then Governor of N York, Burnet,[5] Son of Bishop Burnet hearing from the Captain that a young Man, one of his Passengers, had a great many Books, desired he would bring me to see him. I waited

---

[1] *Determination* Decision; *Natural Philosophy* Branch of study which would today broadly be termed "science."

[2] *Parsimony* Thriftiness.

[3] *Strumpets* Derogatory term for prostitutes.

[4] *discharge his Lodgings* I.e., pay the remainder of his rent.

[5] *Burnet* William Burnet, English-born governor of New York and New Jersey from 1720 to 1728, and of Massachusetts and New Hampshire from 1728 to 1729. His father was the Scottish philosopher Gilbert Burnet, Bishop of Salisbury.

upon him accordingly, and should have taken Collins with me but that he was not sober. The Governor treated me with great Civility, show'd me his Library, which was a very large one, & we had a good deal of Conversation about Books & Authors. This was the second Governor who had done me the Honour to take Notice of me, which to a poor Boy like me was very pleasing.—We proceeded to Philadelphia. I received on the Way Vernon's Money, without which we could hardly have finish'd our Journey.—Collins wish'd to be employ'd in some Counting House; but whether they discover'd his Dramming[1] by his Breath, or by his Behaviour, tho' he had some Recommendations, he met with no Success in any Application, and continu'd Lodging & Boarding at the same House with me & at my Expence. Knowing I had that Money of Vernon's he was continually borrowing of me, still promising Repayment as soon as he should be in Business. At length he had got so much of it, that I was distress'd to think what I should do, in case of being call'd on to remit it.—His Drinking continu'd, about which we sometimes quarrel'd, for when a little intoxicated he was very fractious. Once in a Boat on the Delaware with some other young Men, he refused to row in his Turn: I will be row'd home, says he. We will not row you, says I. You must says he, or stay all Night on the Water, just as you please. The others said, Let us row; What signifies it? But my Mind being soured with his other Conduct, I continu'd to refuse. So he swore he would make me row, or throw me overboard; and coming along stepping on the Thwarts[2] towards me, when he came up & struck at me, I clapt my Hand under his Crutch, and rising pitch'd him head-fore-most into the River. I knew he was a good Swimmer, and so was under little Concern about him; but before he could get round to lay hold of the Boat, we had with a few Strokes pull'd her out of his Reach.—And ever when he drew near the Boat, we ask'd if he would row, striking a few Strokes to slide her away from him.—He was ready to die with Vexation, & obstinately would not promise to row; however seeing him at last beginning to tire, we lifted him in; and brought him home dripping wet in the Evening. We hardly exchang'd a civil Word afterwards; and a West India Captain who

had a Commission to procure a Tutor for the Sons of a Gentleman at Barbadoes, happening to meet with him, agreed to carry him thither. He left me then, promising to remit me the first Money he should receive in order to discharge the Debt. But I never heard of him after.—The Breaking into this Money of Vernon's was one of the first great Errata of my Life. And this Affair show'd that my Father was not much out in his Judgment when he suppos'd me too Young to manage Business of Importance. But Sir William, on reading his Letter, said he was too prudent. There was great Difference in Persons, and Discretion did not always accompany Years, nor was Youth always without it. And since he will not set you up, says he, I will do it my self. Give me an Inventory of the Things necessary to be had from England, and I will send for them. You shall repay me when you are able; I am resolv'd to have a good Printer here, and I am sure you must succeed. This was spoken with such an Appearance of Cordiality, that I had not the least doubt of his meaning what he said.—I had hitherto kept the Proposition of my Setting up a Secret in Philadelphia, & I still kept it. Had it been known that I depended on the Governor, probably some Friend that knew him better would have advis'd me not to rely on him, as I afterwards heard it as his known Character to be liberal of Promises which he never meant to keep.—Yet unsolicited as he was by me, how could I think his generous Offers insincere? I believ'd him one of the best Men in the World.—

I presented him an Inventory of a little Printing House, amounting by my Computation to about 100£ Sterling. He lik'd it, but ask'd me if my being on the Spot in England to chuse the Types & see that every thing was good of the kind, might not be of some Advantage. Then, says he, when there, you may make Acquaintances & establish Correspondencies in the Bookselling, & Stationery Way. I agreed that this might be advantageous. Then says he, get yourself ready to go with Annis;[3] which was the annual Ship, and the only one at that Time usually passing between London and Philadelphia. But it would be some Months before Annis sail'd, so I continu'd working with Keimer, fretting about the Money Collins had got from me, and in

---

[1]   *Dramming*   Drinking.

[2]   *Thwarts*   Rower's seat on a boat.

[3]   *Annis*   I.e., Thomas Annis, captain of the packet *London Hope*.

daily Apprehensions of being call'd upon by Vernon, which however did not happen for some Years after.—

I believe I have omitted mentioning that in my first Voyage from Boston, being becalm'd off Block Island,[1] our People set about catching Cod & hawl'd up a great many. Hitherto I had stuck to my Resolution of not eating animal Food; and on this Occasion, I consider'd with my Master Tryon the taking every Fish as a kind of unprovok'd Murder, since none of them had or ever could do us any Injury that might justify the Slaughter. —All this seem'd very reasonable.—But I had formerly been a great Lover of Fish, & when this came hot out of the Frying Pan, it smelt admirably well. I balanc'd some time between Principle & Inclination: till I recollected, that when the Fish were opened, I saw smaller Fish taken out of their Stomachs:—Then, thought I, if you eat one another, I don't see why we mayn't eat you. So I din'd upon Cod very heartily and continu'd to eat with other People, returning only now & then occasionally to a vegetable Diet. So convenient a thing is it to be a *reasonable Creature*, since it enables one to find or make a Reason for every thing one has a mind to do.—

Keimer & and I liv'd on a pretty good familiar Footing & agreed tolerably well: for he suspected nothing of my Setting up. He retain'd a great deal of his old Enthusiasms, and lov'd an Argumentation. We therefore had many Disputations. I us'd to work him so with my Socratic Method, and had trapann'd[2] him so often by Questions apparently so distant from any Point we had in hand, and yet by degrees led to the Point, and brought him into Difficulties & Contradictions, that at last he grew ridiculously cautious, and would hardly answer me the most common Question, without asking first, *What do you intend to infer from that?* However it gave him so high an Opinion of my Abilities in the Confuting Way, that he seriously propos'd my being his Colleague in a Project he had of setting up a new Sect. He was to preach the Doctrines, and I was to confound all Opponents. When he came to explain with me upon the Doctrines, I found several Conundrums which I objected to, unless I might have my Way a little too, and introduce some of mine. Keimer wore his

Beard at full Length, because somewhere in the Mosaic Law it is said, *thou shalt not mar the Corners of thy Beard.*[3] He likewise kept the seventh day Sabbath;[4] and these two Points were Essentials with him.—I dislik'd both, but agreed to admit them upon Condition of his adopting the Doctrine of using no animal Food. I doubt,[5] says he, my Constitution will not bear that. I assur'd him it would, & that he would be the better for it. He was usually a great Glutton, and I promis'd my self some Diversion in half-starving him. He agreed to try the Practice if I would keep him Company. I did so and we held it for three Months. We had our Victuals dress'd and brought to us regularly by a Woman in the Neighbourhood, who had from me a List of 40 Dishes to be prepar'd for us at different times, in all which there was neither Fish Flesh nor Fowl, and the Whim suited me the better at this time from the Cheapness of it, not costing us above 18^{d}[6] Sterling each, per Week.— I have since kept several Lents[7] most strictly, Leaving the common Diet for that, and that for the common, abruptly, without the least Inconvenience: So that I think there is little in the Advice of making those Changes by easy Gradations.—I went on pleasantly, but Poor Keimer suffer'd grievously, tir'd of the Project, long'd for the Flesh Pots of Egypt,[8] and order'd a roast Pig; He invited me & two Women Friends to dine with him, but it being brought too soon upon table, he could not resist the Temptation, and ate it all up before we came.—

---

[1]   *Block Island*   About thirty miles northeast of the tip of Long Island, part of Rhode Island.

[2]   *trapann'd*   Ensnared.

[3]   *Mosaic Law*   Series of strictures laid down in the Torah, or the first five books of the Hebrew Bible (the Old Testament);   *thou shalt … thy Beard*   See Leviticus 19.27. Wearing a long beard was considered unusual by western eighteenth-century standards of grooming.

[4]   *seventh day Sabbath*   I.e., observance of the Sabbath, or day of rest, on Saturday rather than Sunday. The practice is upheld by numerous Christian denominations as well as within Judaism.

[5]   *doubt*   Fear; suspect.

[6]   *18^{d}*   Eighteen pence.

[7]   *Lents*   The Christian observance of Lent, the forty-day period preceding Easter, traditionally involves various forms of fasting, often including abstaining from meat.

[8]   *long'd for … Egypt*   Common expression referring to a longing for indulgent bodily pleasures; see Exodus 16.3: "And the children of Israel said unto them, Would to God we had died by the hand of the Lord in the land of Egypt, when we sat by the flesh pots, and when we did eat bread to the full; for ye have brought us forth into this wilderness, to kill this whole assembly with hunger."

I had made some Courtship during this time to Miss Read, I had a great Respect & Affection for her, and had some Reason to believe she had the same for me: but as I was about to take a long Voyage, and we were both very young, only a little above 18. it was thought most prudent by her Mother to prevent our going too far at present, as a Marriage if it was to take place would be more convenient after my Return, when I should be as I expected set up in my Business. Perhaps too she thought my Expectations not so well founded as I imagined them to be.—

My chief Acquaintances at this time were, Charles Osborne, Joseph Watson, & James Ralph; All Lovers of Reading. The two first were Clerks to an eminent Scrivener or Conveyancer[1] in the Town, Charles Brogden; the other was Clerk to a Merchant. Watson was a pious sensible young Man, of great Integrity.— The others rather more lax in their Principles of Religion, particularly Ralph, who as well as Collins had been unsettled by me, for which they both made me suffer.—Osborne was sensible, candid, frank, sincere, and affectionate to his Friends; but in litterary Matters too fond of Criticising. Ralph, was ingenious, genteel in his Manners, & extreamly eloquent; I think I never knew a prettier Talker.—Both of them were great Admirers of Poetry, and began to try their Hands in little Pieces. Many pleasant Walks we four had together, on Sundays into the Woods near Skuylkill,[2] where we read to one another & conferr'd on what we read. Ralph was inclin'd to pursue the Study of Poetry, not doubting but he might become eminent in it and make his Fortune by it, alleging that the best Poets must when they first began to write, make as many Faults as he did.—Osborne dissuaded him, assur'd him he had no Genius for Poetry, & advis'd him to think of nothing beyond the Business he was bred to; that in the mercantile way tho' he had no Stock, he might by his Diligence & Punctuality recommend himself to Employment as a Factor,[3] and in time acquire wherewith to trade on his own Account. I approv'd the amusing one's Self with Poetry now & then, so far as to improve one's Language, but no farther. On this it was propos'd that we should each of us at our next Meeting produce a Piece of our own Composing, in order to improve by our mutual Observations, Criticisms & Corrections. As Language & Expression were what we had in View, we excluded all Considerations of Invention, by agreeing that the Task should be a Version of the 18th Psalm,[4] which describes the Descent of a Deity. When the Time of our Meeting drew nigh, Ralph call'd on me first, & let me know his Piece was ready. I told him I had been busy, & having little Inclination had done nothing.—He then show'd me his Piece for my Opinion; and I much approv'd it, as it appear'd to me to have great Merit. Now, says he, Osborne never will allow the least Merit in any thing of mine, but makes 1000 Criticisms out of mere Envy. He is not so jealous of you. I wish therefore you would take this Piece, & produce it as yours. I will pretend not to have had time, & so produce nothing: We shall then see what he will say to it.—It was agreed, and I immediately transcrib'd it that it might appear in my own hand. We met. Watson's Performance was read: there were some Beauties in it: but many Defects. Osborne's was read: It was much better. Ralph did it Justice, remark'd some Faults, but applauded the Beauties. He himself had nothing to produce. I was backward,[5] seem'd desirous of being excus'd, had not had sufficient Time to correct, &c. but no Excuse could be admitted, produce I must. It was read and repeated; Watson and Osborne gave up the Contest; and join'd in applauding it immoderately. Ralph only made some Criticisms & propos'd some Amendments, but I defended my Text. Osborne was against Ralph, & told him he was no better a Critic than Poet; so he dropt the Argument. As they two went home together, Osborne express'd himself still more strongly in favour of what he thought my Production, having restrain'd himself before as he said, lest I should think

---

[1]   *Conveyancer*   Lawyer who specializes in drafting property deeds.

[2]   *Skuylkill*   Main river running through Philadelphia.

[3]   *Factor*   Agent.

[4]   *18th Psalm*   See Psalm 18.6–10: "In my distress I called upon the Lord, and cried unto my God: he heard my voice out of his temple, and my cry came before him, even into his ears. Then the earth shook and trembled; the foundations also of the hills moved and were shaken, because he was wroth. There went up a smoke out of his nostrils, and fire out of his mouth devoured: coals were kindled by it. He bowed the heavens also, and came down: and darkness was under his feet. And he rode upon a cherub, and did fly: yea, he did fly upon the wings of the wind."

[5]   *backward*   I.e., reluctant.

it Flattery. But who would have imagin'd, says he, that Franklin had been capable of such a Performance; such Painting, such Force! such Fire! he has even improv'd the Original! In his common Conversation, he seems to have no Choice of Words; he hesitates and blunders; and yet, good God, how he writes!—When we next met, Ralph discover'd the Trick we had plaid him, and Osborne was a little laught at. This Transaction fix'd Ralph in his Resolution of becoming a Poet. I did all I could to dissuade him from it, but He continued scribbling Verses, till *Pope*[1] cur'd him.—He became however a pretty good Prose Writer. More of him hereafter. But as I may not have occasion again to mention the other two, I shall just remark here, that Watson died in my Arms a few Years after, much lamented, being the best of our Set. Osborne went to the West Indies, where he became an eminent Lawyer & made Money, but died young. He and I had made a serious Agreement, that the one who happen'd first to die, should if possible make a friendly Visit to the other, and acquaint him how he found things in that separate State. But he never fulfill'd his Promise.

The Governor, seeming to like my Company, had me frequently to his House; & his Setting me up was always mention'd as a fix'd thing. I was to take with me Letters recommendatory to a Number of his Friends, besides the Letter of Credit, to furnish me with the necessary Money for purchasing the Press & Types, Paper, &c. For these Letters I was appointed to call at different times, when they were to be ready, but a future time was still named.—Thus he went on till the Ship whose Departure too had been several times postponed was on the Point of sailing. Then when I call'd to take my Leave & receive the Letters, his Secretary, Dr Bard, came out to me and said the Governor was extreamly busy, in writing, but would be down at Newcastle before the Ship, & there the Letters would be deliverd to me.

Ralph, tho' married & having one Child, had determined to accompany me in this Voyage. It was thought he intended to establish a Correspondence, & obtain Goods to sell on Commission. But I found

afterwards, that thro' some Discontent with his Wifes Relations, he purposed to leave her on their Hands, & never return again.—Having taken leave of my Friends, & interchang'd some Promises with Miss Read, I left Philadelphia in the Ship, which anchor'd at Newcastle. The Governor was there. But when I went to his Lodging, the Secretary came to me from him with the civillest Message in the World, that he could not then see me being engag'd in Business of the utmost Importance, but should send the Letters to me on board, wish'd me heartily a good Voyage and a speedy Return, &c. I return'd on board, a little puzzled, but still not doubting.—

Mr Andrew Hamilton, a famous Lawyer of Philadelphia, had taken Passage in the same Ship for himself and Son: and with Mr Denham a Quaker Merchant, & Messrs Onion & Russel Masters of an Iron Work in Maryland, had engag'd the Great Cabin; so that Ralph and I were forc'd to take up with a Birth in the Steerage:[2]—And none on board knowing us, were considered as ordinary Persons.— But Mr Hamilton & his Son (it was James, since Governor)[3] return'd from New Castle to Philadelphia, the Father being recall'd by a great Fee to plead for a seized Ship.—And just before we sail'd Col. French coming on board, & showing me great Respect, I was more taken Notice of, and, with my Friend Ralph invited by the other Gentlemen to come into the Cabin, there being now Room. Accordingly we remov'd thither.

Understanding that Col. French had brought on board the Governor's Dispatches,[4] I ask'd the Captain for those Letters that were to be under my Care. He said all were put into the Bag together; and he could not then come at them; but before we landed in England, I should have an Opportunity of picking them out. So I was satisfy'd for the present, and we proceeded on our Voyage. We had a sociable Company in the Cabin, and lived uncommonly well, having the Addition of all Mr Hamilton's Stores, who had laid in plentifully. In this Passage Mr Denham contracted a

---

[1] *Pope* Alexander Pope (1688–1744), who was during the eighteenth century widely considered an exemplary poet. Ralph's work would later be parodied in Pope's *Dunciad* (1728–43), which satirizes the hack writers of contemporary England.

[2] *Birth* I.e., berth; lodging on board a ship; *Steerage* Lower cargo deck, often the cheapest and most unpleasant place of accommodation.

[3] *James, since Governor* James Hamilton, who served as governor of Pennsylvania from 1748 to 1754 and from 1759 to 1763.

[4] *Dispatches* Letters and other communications.

Friendship for me that continued during his Life. The Voyage was otherwise not a pleasant one, as we had a great deal of bad Weather.——

When we came into the Channel,[1] the Captain kept his Word with me, & gave me an Opportunity of examining the Bag for the Governor's Letters. I found none upon which my Name was put, as under my Care; I pick'd out 6 or 7 that by the Handwriting I thought might be the promis'd Letters, especially as one of them was directed to Basket the King's Printer, and another to some Stationer.[2] We arriv'd in London the 24th of December, 1724.——I waited upon the Stationer who came first in my Way, delivering the Letter as from Governor Keith. I don't know such a Person, says he: but opening the Letter, O, this is from Riddlesden; I have lately found him to be a compleat Rascal, and I will have nothing to do with him, nor receive any Letters from him. So, putting the Letter into my Hand, he turn'd on his Heel & left me to serve some Customer.——I was surprized to find these were not the Governor's Letters. And after recollecting and comparing Circumstances, I began to doubt his Sincerity. I found my Friend Denham, and opened the whole Affair to him. He let me into Keith's Character; told me there was not the least Probability that he had written any Letters for me, that no one who knew him had the smallest Dependence on him, and he laught at the Notion of the Governor's giving me a Letter of Credit, having as he said no Credit to give.——On my expressing some Concern about what I should do: He advis'd me to endeavour getting some Employment in the Way of my Business. Among the Printers here, says he, you will improve yourself; and when you return to America, you will set up to greater Advantage.

We both of us happen'd to know, as well as the Stationer, that Riddlesden the Attorney, was a very Knave. He had half ruin'd Miss Read's Father by persuading him to be bound for him.[3] By his Letter it appear'd, there was a secret Scheme on foot to the Prejudice of Hamilton, (Suppos'd to be then coming over with us,) and that Keith was concern'd in it with

Riddlesden. Denham, who was a Friend of Hamilton's, thought he ought to be acquainted with it. So when he arriv'd in England, which was soon after, partly from Resentment & Ill-Will to Keith & Riddlesden, & partly from Good Will to him: I waited on him, and gave him the Letter. He thank'd me cordially, the Information being of Importance to him. And from that time he became my Friend, greatly to my Advantage afterwards on many Occasions.

But what shall we think of a Governor's playing such pitiful Tricks, & imposing so grossly on a poor ignorant Boy! It was a Habit he had acquired. He wish'd to please every body; and having little to give, he gave Expectations.——He was otherwise an ingenious sensible Man, a pretty good Writer, & a good Governor for the People, tho' not for his Constituents the Proprietaries,[4] whose Instructions he sometimes disregarded.——Several of our best Laws were of his Planning, and pass'd during his Administration.——

Ralph and I were inseparable Companions. We took Lodgings together in Little Britain[5] at 3/6[6] per Week, as much as we could then afford.——He found some Relations, but they were poor & unable to assist him. He now let me know his Intentions of remaining in London, and that he never meant to return to Philadelphia——He had brought no Money with him, the whole he could muster having been expended in paying his Passage.——I had 15 Pistoles:[7] So he borrowed occasionally of me, to subsist while he was looking out for Business.——He first endeavoured to get into the Playhouse, believing himself qualify'd for an Actor; but Wilkes,[8] to whom he apply'd, advis'd him candidly not to think of that Employment, as it was impossible he should succeed in it. Then he propos'd to Roberts,

---

[1]   *the Channel* I.e., the English Channel, body of water separating England from the European continent.

[2]   *Basket* John Baskett (c. 1665–1742); *Stationer* Seller of books and stationery.

[3]   *bound for him* Legally responsible for paying his debts.

[4]   *his Constituents the Proprietaries* As a proprietary colony, the land of Pennsylvania was legally owned by its proprietaries (William Penn and his descendants), who continued to reside in England. In the coming decades conflicts of interest would frequently arise between Pennsylvania's proprietaries and the political leaders who resided in the colony.

[5]   *Little Britain* Small district of London, known for its many booksellers.

[6]   *3/6* Three shillings and sixpence.

[7]   *Pistoles* Gold coins used as currency internationally.

[8]   *Wilkes* Irish-born actor and prominent theater manager Robert Wilks (c. 1665–1732).

a Publisher in Paternoster Row,[1] to write for him a Weekly Paper like the Spectator, on certain Conditions, which Roberts did not approve. Then he endeavour'd to get Employment as a Hackney Writer to copy for the Stationers & Lawyers about the Temple:[2] but could find no Vacancy.—

I immediately got into Work at Palmer's then a famous Printing House in Bartholomew Close;[3] and here I continu'd near a Year. I was pretty diligent; but spent with Ralph a good deal of my Earnings in going to Plays & other Places of Amusement. We had together consum'd all my Pistoles, and now just rubb'd on from hand to mouth. He seem'd quite to forget his Wife & Child, and I by degrees my Engagements with Miss Read, to whom I never wrote more than one Letter, & that was to let her know I was not likely soon to return. This was another of the great Errata of my Life, which I should wish to correct if I were to live it over again.—In fact, by our Expences, I was constantly kept unable to pay my Passage.

At Palmer's I was employ'd in Composing for the second Edition of Woollaston's Religion of Nature.[4] Some of his Reasonings not appearing to me well-founded, I wrote a little metaphysical Piece, in which I made Remarks on them. It was entitled, *A Dissertation on Liberty & Necessity, Pleasure and Pain*.[5]—I inscrib'd it to my Friend Ralph.—I printed a small Number. It occasion'd my being more consider'd by Mr Palmer, as a young Man of some Ingenuity, tho' he seriously expostulated with me upon the Principles of my Pamphlet which to him appear'd abominable. My printing this Pamphlet was another Erratum.

While I lodg'd in Little Britain I made an Acquaintance with one Wilcox a Bookseller, whose Shop was at the next Door. He had an immense Collection of second-hand Books. Circulating Libraries were not then in Use; but we agreed that on certain reasonable Terms which I have now forgotten, I might take, read & return any of his Books. This I esteem'd a great Advantage, & I made as much Use of it as I could.—

My Pamphlet by some means falling into the Hands of one Lyons, a Surgeon, Author of a Book intituled *The Infallibility of Human Judgment*, it occasioned an Acquaintance between us; he took great Notice of me, call'd on me often, to converse on those Subjects, carried me to the Horns a pale Ale-House in [blank] Lane, Cheapside, and introduc'd me to Dr Mandevile, Author of the Fable of the Bees[6] who had a Club there, of which he was the Soul, being a most facetious[7] entertaining Companion. Lyons too introduc'd me to Dr Pemberton, at Batson's Coffee House, who promis'd to give me an Opportunity some time or other of seeing Sir Isaac Newton,[8] of which I was extreamly desirous; but this never happened.

I had brought over a few Curiosities among which the principal was a Purse made of the Asbestos, which purifies by Fire.[9] Sir Hans Sloane[10] heard of it, came to see me, and invited me to his House in Bloomsbury Square; where he show'd me all his Curiosities, and

---

[1] *Paternoster Row*   Street near Little Britain, known as a center of the book and printing trade.

[2] *about the Temple*   Around the notable central London legal district known as the Temple.

[3] *Bartholomew Close*   Near Little Britain.

[4] *Woollaston's Religion of Nature*   1722 philosophical work by Anglican priest William Woolaston, which proposed a system of morality that could be discerned directly from "nature" rather than from religious doctrine; the work had a substantial influence on the development of Deism later in the eighteenth century.

[5] *A Dissertation ... and Pain*   Franklin's pamphlet argues against commonplace conceptions of free will and morality, to the point of claiming that virtue and vice are nonexistent. He later destroyed all copies of the work that he could find, though a few have survived to the twenty-first century.

[6] *the Fable of the Bees*   1714 work by Dutch-born philosopher Bernard Mandeville, which proposes, through an allegory depicting a hive of bees, that social cohesion and economic prosperity are ultimately the result of the individual pursuit of personal gain, rather than of virtuous action or generosity.

[7] *facetious*   Elegantly amusing and agreeable.

[8] *Dr Pemberton*   English physician and mathematician Henry Pemberton (1694–1771); *Sir Isaac Newton*   English physicist and mathematician (1642–1727) who formulated a number of revolutionary theories about the physical world, including the law of gravity; he was a friend of Pemberton's.

[9] *a Purse ... by Fire*   The mineral asbestos—widely known as an effective fire retardant—is formed of thin fibrous crystals, which can be spun and woven into a coarse sort of cloth—though this product never came into widespread use.

[10] *Sir Hans Sloane*   Anglo-Irish naturalist and collector (1660–1753), whose collections would form the basis of the British Museum and the Natural History Museum; Franklin's asbestos purse remains part of the Natural History Museum's collection.

persuaded me to let him add that to the Number, for which he paid me handsomely.—

In our House there lodg'd a young Woman; a Millener,[1] who I think had a Shop in the Cloisters. She had been genteelly bred; was sensible & lively, and of most pleasing Conversation.—Ralph read Plays to her in the Evenings, they grew intimate, she took another Lodging, and he follow'd her. They liv'd together some time, but he being still out of Business, & her Income not sufficient to maintain them with her Child, he took a Resolution of going from London, to try for a Country School, which he thought himself well qualify'd to undertake, as he wrote an excellent Hand, & was a Master of Arithmetic & Accounts.—This however he deem'd a Business below him, & confident of future better Fortune when he should be unwilling to have it known that he once was so meanly employ'd, he chang'd his Name, & did me the Honour to assume mine.—For I soon after had a Letter from him, acquainting me, that he was settled in a small Village in Berkshire, I think it was, where he taught reading & writing to 10 or a dozen Boys at 6 pence each per Week, recommending Mrs T. to my Care, and desiring me to write to him directing for Mr Franklin Schoolmaster at such a Place. He continu'd to write frequently, sending me large Specimens of an Epic Poem, which he was then composing, and desiring my Remarks & Corrections.—These I gave him from time to time, but endeavour'd rather to discourage his Proceeding. One of Young's[2] Satires was then just publish'd. I copy'd & sent him a great Part of it, which set in a strong Light the Folly of pursuing the Muses[3] with any Hope of Advancement by them. All was in vain. Sheets of the Poem continu'd to come by every Post. In the mean time Mrs T. having on his Account lost her Friends & Business, was often in Distresses, & us'd to send for me, and borrow what I could spare to help her out of them. I grew fond of her Company, and being at that time under no Religious Restraint, & presuming on my Importance to her, I attempted Familiarities, (another Erratum) which she repuls'd with a proper

Resentment, and acquainted him with my Behaviour. This made a Breach between us, & when he return'd again to London, he let me know he thought I had cancel'd all the Obligations he had been under to me.—So I found I was never to expect his Repaying me what I lent to him or advanc'd for him. This was however not then of much Consequence, as he was totally unable.—And in the Loss of his Friendship I found my self reliev'd from a Burthen. I now began to think of getting a little Money beforehand; and expecting better Work, I left Palmer's to work at Watts's near Lincoln's Inn Fields, a still greater Printing House. Here I continu'd all the rest of my Stay in London.

At my first Admission into this Printing House, I took to working at Press, imagining I felt a Want of the Bodily Exercise I had been us'd to in America, where Presswork is mix'd with Composing.[4] I drank only Water; the other Workmen, near 50 in Number, were great Guzzlers of Beer. On occasion I carried up & down Stairs a large Form of Types in each hand, when others carried but one in both Hands. They wonder'd to see from this & several Instances that the Water-American as they call'd me was *stronger* than themselves who drunk *strong* Beer. We had an Alehouse Boy who attended always in the House to supply the Workmen. My Companion at the Press, drank every day a Pint before Breakfast, a Pint at Breakfast with his Bread and Cheese; a Pint between Breakfast and Dinner; a Pint at Dinner; a Pint in the Afternoon about Six o'clock, and another when he had done his Day's-Work. I thought it a detestable Custom.—But it was necessary, he suppos'd, to drink *strong* Beer that he might be *strong* to labour. I endeavour'd to convince him that the Bodily Strength afforded by Beer could only be in proportion to the Grain or Flour of the Barley dissolved in the Water of which it was made; that there was more Flour in a Pennyworth of Bread, and therefore if he would eat that with a Pint of Water, it would give him more Strength than a Quart of Beer.—He drank on however, & had 4 or 5 Shillings to pay out of his Wages every Saturday Night for that muddling Liquor; an Expence

---

[1] *Millener* Milliner; purveyor of hats and other accessories.

[2] *Young* English poet Edward Young, who published a series of satirical works between 1725 and 1728.

[3] *the Muses* I.e., an artistic or literary career; the Muses are Greek mythological figures representing the arts.

[4] *where Presswork … with Composing* I.e., where the task of setting type is done by the same workers as the more physically active task of working the printing press.

I was free from.—And thus these poor Devils keep themselves always under.[1]

Watts after some Weeks desiring to have me in the Composing-Room, I left the Pressmen. A new *Bienvenu* or Sum for Drink, being 5/, was demanded of me by the Compostors. I thought it an Imposition, as I had paid below.[2] The Master thought so too, and forbad my Paying it. I stood out two or three Weeks, was accordingly considered as an Excommunicate, and had so many little Pieces of private Mischief done me, by mixing my Sorts, transposing my Pages, breaking my Matter,[3] &c. &c. if I were ever so little out of the Room, & all ascrib'd to the Chapel Ghost, which they said ever haunted those not regularly admitted, that notwithstanding the Master's Protection, I found myself oblig'd to comply and pay the Money; convinc'd of the Folly of being on ill Terms with those one is to live with continually. I was now on a fair Footing with them, and soon acquir'd considerable Influence. I propos'd some reasonable Alterations in their[4] Chapel Laws, and carried them against all Opposition. From my Example a great Part of them, left their muddling Breakfast of Beer & Bread & Cheese, finding they could with me be supply'd from a neighbouring House with a large Porringer[5] of hot Water-gruel, sprinkled with Pepper, crumb'd with Bread, & a Bit of Butter in it, for the Price of a Pint of Beer, viz, three half-pence. This was a more comfortable as well as cheaper Breakfast, & kept their Heads clearer.—Those who continu'd sotting with Beer all day, were often, by not paying, out of Credit at the Alehouse, and us'd to make Interest with me to get Beer, *their Light*, as they phras'd it, *being out*. I watch'd the Pay table on Saturday Night, & collected what I stood engag'd for them, having to pay some times near Thirty Shillings a Week

on their Accounts.—This, and my being esteem'd a pretty good Riggite, that is a jocular verbal Satyrist, supported my Consequence in the Society.—My constant Attendance, (I never making a St. Monday[6]), recommended me to the Master; and my uncommon Quickness at Composing, occasion'd my being put upon all Work of Dispatch[7] which was generally better paid. So I went on now very agreably.—

My Lodging in Little Britain being too remote, I found another in Duke-street opposite to the Romish[8] Chapel. It was two pair of Stairs backwards at an Italian Warehouse. A Widow Lady kept the House; she had a Daughter & a Maid Servant, and a Journey-man who attended the Warehouse, but lodg'd abroad.— After sending to enquire my Character at the House where I last lodg'd, she agreed to take me in at the same Rate 3/6 per Week, cheaper as she said from the Protection she expected in having a Man lodge in the House. She was a Widow, an elderly Woman, had been bred a Protestant, being a Clergyman's Daughter, but was converted to the Catholic Religion by her Husband, whose Memory she much revered, had lived much among People of Distinction, and knew a 1000 Anecdotes of them as far back as the Times of Charles the second.[9] She was lame in her Knees with the Gout, and therefore seldom stirr'd out of her Room, so sometimes wanted Company; and hers was so highly amusing to me; that I was sure to spend an Evening with her whenever she desired it. Our Supper was only half an Anchovy each, on a very little Strip of Bread & Butter, and half a Pint of Ale between us.—But the Entertainment was in her Conversation. My always keeping good Hours, and giving little Trouble in the Family, made her unwilling to part with me; so that, when I talk'd of a Lodging I had heard of, nearer my Business, for 2/[10] a Week, which, intent as I now was

---

[1]   *under* I.e., poor.

[2]   *A new Bienvenu ... below* I.e., because Franklin was employed in a new position, the "compostors" or typesetters demanded of him the fee ordinarily exacted of new employees, despite the fact that he had already paid that same fee when he began his previous job as a pressman; *5/* Five shillings.

[3]   *Sorts* Individual pieces of type; *Matter* Types arranged and ready for printing.

[4]   [Franklin's note] A Printing House is always called a Chappel by the Workmen.—

[5]   *Porringer* Small, handled bowl for soups and porridges.

[6]   *making a St. Monday* Treating Monday as a holiday (presumably implying missing or being late for work due to the previous night's merriment).

[7]   *Work of Dispatch* I.e., work that needs to be completed promptly.

[8]   *Romish* Roman Catholic.

[9]   *Charles the second* King of England, Scotland, and Ireland from 1660 to 1685.

[10]   *2/* Two shillings.

on saving Money, made some Difference; she bid me not think of it, for she would abate me two Shillings a Week for the future, so I remain'd with her at 1/6[1] as long as I staid in London.—

In a Garret of her House there lived a Maiden Lady of 70 in the most retired[2] Manner, of whom my Landlady gave me this Account, that she was a Roman-Catholic, had been sent abroad when young & lodg'd in a Nunnery with an Intent of becoming a Nun: but the Country not agreeing with her, she return'd to England, where there being no Nunnery, she had vow'd to lead the Life of a Nun as near as might be done in those Circumstances: Accordingly She had given all her Estate to charitable Uses, reserving only Twelve Pounds a Year to live on, and out of this Sum she still gave a great deal in Charity, living her self on Watergruel only, & using no Fire but to boil it.—She had lived many Years in that Garret, being permitted to remain there gratis by successive catholic Tenants of the House below, as they deem'd it a Blessing to have her there. A Priest visited her, to confess her every Day. I have ask'd her, says my Landlady, how she, as she liv'd, could possibly find so much Employment for a Confessor? O, says she, it is impossible to avoid *vain Thoughts*. I was permitted once to visit her: She was chearful & polite, & convers'd pleasantly. The Room was clean, but had no other Furniture than a Matras, a Table with a Crucifix & Book, a Stool, which she gave me to sit on, and a Picture over the Chimney of St. *Veronica*, displaying her Handkerchief with the miraculous Figure of Christ's bleeding Face on it,[3] which she explain'd to me with great Seriousness. She look'd pale, but was never sick, and I give it as another Instance on how small an Income Life & Health may be supported.—

At Watts's Printinghouse I contracted an Acquaintance with an ingenious young Man, one Wygate, who having wealthy Relations, had been better educated than most Printers, was a tolerable Latinist, spoke French, & lov'd Reading. I taught him, & a Friend of his, to swim, at twice going into the River, & they soon became good Swimmers. They introduc'd me to some Gentlemen from the Country who went to Chelsea by Water to see the College and Don Saltero's Curiosities.[4] In our Return, at the Request of the Company, whose Curiosity Wygate had excited, I stript & leapt into the River, & swam from near Chelsea to Blackfryars,[5] performing on the Way many Feats of Activity both upon & under Water, that surpriz'd & pleas'd those to whom they were Novelties.—I had from a Child been ever delighted with this Exercise, had studied & practis'd all Thevenot's[6] Motions & Positions, added some of my own, aiming at the graceful & easy, as well as the Useful.—All these I took this Occasion of exhibiting to the Company, & was much flatter'd by their Admiration.—And Wygate, who was desirous of becoming a Master, grew more & more attach'd to me on that account, as well as from the Similarity of our Studies. He at length propos'd to me travelling all over Europe together, supporting ourselves every where by working at our Business. I was once inclin'd to it. But mentioning it to my good Friend Mr Denham, with whom I often spent an Hour, when I had Leisure. He dissuaded me from it; advising me to think only of returning to Pensilvania, which he was now about to do.—

I must record one Trait of this good Man's Character. He had formerly been in Business at Bristol, but fail'd in Debt to a Number of People, compounded[7] and went to America. There, by a close Application to Business as a Merchant, he acquir'd a plentiful Fortune in a few Years. Returning to England in the Ship with

---

[1] *1/6* One shilling and sixpence.

[2] *retired* Reclusive.

[3] *St. Veronica … on it* Saint Veronica is said to have witnessed Christ on his journey to his execution at Calvary, and to have been moved by his suffering to offer him her veil to wipe his bleeding head. According to Christian legend, an image of Christ's face was then imprinted upon the veil, which became known as the Veil of Veronica, a sacred relic in Catholic worship and a common subject of Catholic artwork.

[4] *Chelsea … Don Saltero's Curiosities* Don Saltero's was a well-known coffeehouse in the riverside district of Chelsea, founded in 1695 by a former servant of Hans Sloane and remarkable for its housing of many artifacts and curiosities. The College Franklin refers to is in fact the Chelsea Hospital, founded in 1682 on the former site of the Chelsea theological college.

[5] *Blackfryars* District of central London, approximately four miles downriver from Chelsea.

[6] *Thevenot* Melchisédech Thévenot, French scientist, cartographer, and diplomat whose *The Art of Swimming* (1696) was among the first published works to discuss swimming and give instruction on swimming techniques.

[7] *compounded* Made an agreement for paying only part of his debts.

me, He invited his old Creditors to an Entertainment, at which he thank'd them for the easy Composition[1] they had favour'd him with, & when they expected nothing but the Treat, every Man at the first Remove,[2] found under his Plate an Order on a Banker for the full Amount of the unpaid Remainder with Interest.

He now told me he was about to return to Philadelphia, and should carry over a great Quantity of Goods in order to open a Store there: He propos'd to take me over as his Clerk, to keep his Books (in which he would instruct me) copy his Letters, and attend the Store. He added, that as soon as I should be acquainted with mercantile Business he would promote me by sending me with a Cargo of Flour & Bread &c to the West Indies, and procure me Commissions from others; which would be profitable, & if I manag'd well, would establish me handsomely. The Thing pleas'd me, for I was grown tired of London, remember'd with Pleasure the happy Months I had spent in Pennsylvania, and wish'd again to see it. Therefore I immediately agreed, on the Terms of Fifty Pounds a Year Pensylvania Money; less indeed than my present Gettings as a Compostor, but affording a better Prospect.—

I now took Leave of Printing, as I thought for ever, and was daily employ'd in my new Business; going about with Mr Denham among the Tradesmen, to purchase various Articles, & see them pack'd up, doing Errands, calling upon Workmen to dispatch, &c. and when all was on board, I had a few Days Leisure. On one of these Days I was to my Surprize sent for by a great Man I knew only by Name, a Sir William Wyndham[3] and I waited upon him. He had heard by some means or other of my Swimming from Chelsey to Blackfryars, and of my teaching Wygate and another young Man to swim in a few Hours. He had two Sons about to set out on their Travels;[4] he wish'd to have them first taught Swimming; and propos'd to gratify me handsomely if I would teach them.—They were not yet come to Town and my Stay was uncertain, so I could not undertake it. But from this Incident I thought it likely, that if I were to remain in England and open a Swimming School, I might get a good deal of Money.—And it struck me so strongly, that had the Overture been sooner made me, probably I should not so soon have returned to America.—After Many Years, you & I had something of more Importance to do with one of these Sons of Sir William Wyndham, become Earl of Egremont, which I shall mention in its Place.[5]—

Thus I spent about 18 Months in London. Most Part of the Time, I work'd hard at my Business, & spent but little upon my self except in seeing Plays, & in Books.—My Friend Ralph had kept me poor. He owed me about 27 Pounds; which I was now never likely to receive; a great Sum out of my small Earnings. I lov'd him notwithstanding, for he had many amiable Qualities.—tho' I had by no means improv'd my Fortune.—But I had pick'd up some very ingenious Acquaintance whose Conversation was of great Advantage to me, and I had read considerably.

We sail'd from Gravesend on the 23d of July 1726.— For The Incidents of the Voyage, I refer you to my Journal, where you will find them all minutely related. Perhaps the most important Part of that Journal is the *Plan*[6] to be found in it which I formed at Sea, for regulating my future Conduct in Life. It is the more remarkable, as being form'd when I was so young, and yet being pretty faithfully adhered to quite thro' to old Age.—We landed in Philadelphia the 11th of October, where I found sundry Alterations. Keith was no longer Governor, being superseded by Major Gordon;[7] I met him walking the Streets as a common Citizen. He seem'd a little asham'd at seeing me, but pass'd without saying any thing. I should have been as much asham'd

---

[1]   *Composition* I.e., the settlement of his debts.

[2]   *Remove* I.e., of plates.

[3]   *Sir William Wyndham* English politician (c. 1688–1740) who during this period was serving as leader of the Tory opposition in the House of Commons.

[4]   *their Travels* Throughout the eighteenth century (and well into the nineteenth) it was common for young British men of means to travel the European continent upon the completion of their formal education.

[5]   *something of … its Place* The son referred to is Charles Wyndham, 2nd Earl of Egremont, who as Secretary of State for the Southern Department (1761–63) in the British Cabinet had oversight of the American colonies. Franklin does not in fact return to this subject in the *Autobiography*.

[6]   *my Journal … the Plan* This plan seems to have been lost, not appearing in the version of the journal that survives; a small segment Franklin referred to as "the preamble and heads of it" has survived through a 1785 copy by his friend William Rawle.

[7]   *Major Gordon* Patrick Gordon, a military veteran who served as Pennsylvania's governor from 1726 to 1736.

at seeing Miss Read, had not her Friends despairing with Reason of my Return, after the Receipt of my Letter, persuaded her to marry another, one Rogers, a Potter, which was done in my Absence. With him however she was never happy, and soon parted from him, refusing to cohabit with him, or bear his Name It being now said that he had another Wife. He was a worthless Fellow tho' an excellent Workman which was the Temptation to her Friends. He got into Debt, ran away in 1727 or 28, went to the West Indies, and died there. Keimer had got a better House, a Shop well supply'd with Stationary, plenty of new Types, a number of Hands tho' none good, and seem'd to have a great deal of Business.

Mr Denham took a Store in Water Street, where we open'd our Goods. I attended the Business diligently, studied Accounts, and grew in a little Time expert at selling.—We lodg'd and boarded together, he counsell'd me as a Father, having a sincere Regard for me: I respected & lov'd him: and we might have gone on together very happily: But in the Beginning of February 1726/7[1] when I had just pass'd my 21st Year, we both were taken ill. My Distemper was a Pleurisy,[2] which very nearly carried me off:—I suffered a good deal, gave up the Point in my own mind, & was rather disappointed when I found my self recovering; regretting in some degree that I must now sometime or other have all that disagreeable Work to do over again.—I forget what his Distemper was. It held him a long time, and at length carried him off. He left me a small Legacy in a nuncupative[3] Will, as a Token of his Kindness for me, and he left me once more to the wide World. For the Store was taken into the Care of his Executors, and my Employment under him ended:—My Brother-in-law Homes, being now at Philadelphia, advis'd my Return to my Business. And Keimer tempted me with an Offer of large Wages by the Year to come & take the Management of his Printing-House that he might better attend his

Stationer's Shop.—I had heard a bad Character of him in London, from his Wife & her Friends, & was not fond of having any more to do with him. I try'd for farther Employment as a Merchant's Clerk; but not readily meeting with any, I clos'd again with Keimer.—

I found in *his* House these Hands; Hugh Meredith a Welsh-Pensilvanian, 30 Years of Age, bred to Country Work: honest, sensible, had a great deal of solid Observation, was something of a Reader, but given to drink:—Stephen Potts, a young Country Man of full Age, bred to the Same:—of uncommon natural Parts, & great Wit & Humour, but a little idle.— These he had agreed with at extream low Wages, per Week, to be rais'd a Shilling every 3 Months, as they would deserve by improving in their Business, & the Expectation of these high Wages to come on hereafter was what he had drawn them in with.—Meredith was to work at Press, Potts at Bookbinding, which he by Agreement, was to teach them, tho' he knew neither one nor t'other. John —— a wild Irishman brought up to no Business, whose Service for 4 Years Keimer had purchas'd from the Captain of a Ship. He too was to be made a Pressman. George Webb, an Oxford Scholar, whose Time for 4 Years he had likewise bought, intending him for a Compositor: of whom more presently. And David Harry, a Country Boy, whom he had taken Apprentice. I soon perceiv'd that the Intention of engaging me at Wages so much higher than he had been us'd to give, was to have these raw cheap Hands form'd thro' me, and as soon as I had instructed them, then, they being all articled to him, he should be able to do without me.—I went on however, very cheerfully; put his Printing House in Order, which had been in great Confusion, and brought his Hands by degrees to mind their Business and to do it better.

It was an odd Thing to find an Oxford Scholar in the Situation of a bought Servant. He was not more than 18 Years of Age, & gave me this Account of himself; that he was born in Gloucester, educated at a Grammar School there, had been distinguish'd among the Scholars for some apparent Superiority in performing his Part when they exhibited Plays; belong'd to the Witty Club there, and had written some Pieces in Prose & Verse which were printed in the Gloucester Newspapers.—Thence he was sent to Oxford; where

---

[1] *February 1726/7* According to the Gregorian calendar, the year of Franklin's and Denham's illnesses was 1727. Franklin here employs the practice of dual dating, which accounts for the fact that the date of the beginning of the new year varied among countries still using the Julian calendar, such as Britain and its colonies, where the new year was marked on 25 March.

[2] *Pleurisy* Painful inflammation of the lungs.

[3] *nuncupative* Given orally rather than written down.

he continu'd about a Year, but not well-satisfy'd, wishing of all things to see London & become a Player.[1] At length receiving his Quarterly Allowance of 15 Guineas, instead of discharging his Debts, he walk'd out of Town, hid his Gown in a Furz[2] Bush, and footed it to London, where having no Friend to advise him, he fell into bad Company, soon spent his Guineas, found no means of being introduc'd among the Players, grew necessitous, pawn'd his Cloaths & wanted Bread. Walking the Street very hungry, & not knowing what to do with himself, a Crimp's Bill[3] was put into his Hand, offering immediate Entertainment & Encouragement to such as would bind themselves to serve in America. He went directly, sign'd the Indentures, was put into the Ship & came over; never writing a Line to acquaint his Friends what was become of him. He was lively, witty, good-natur'd and a pleasant Companion; but idle, thoughtless & imprudent to the last Degree.

John the Irishman soon ran away. With the rest I began to live very agreeably, for they all respected me, the more as they found Keimer incapable of instructing them, and that from me they learnt something daily. We never work'd on Saturday, that being Keimer's Sabbath. So I had two Days for Reading. My Acquaintance with ingenious People in the Town, increased. Keimer himself treated me with great Civility & apparent Regard; and nothing now made me uneasy but my Debt to Vernon, which I was yet unable to pay being hitherto but a poor Oeconomist.[4] He however kindly made no Demand of it.

Our Printing House often wanted Sorts, and there was no Letter Founder[5] in America. I had seen Types cast at James's in London, but without much Attention to the Manner: However I now contriv'd a Mould, made use of the Letters we had, as Puncheons, struck the Matrices[6] in Lead, and thus supply'd in a pretty tolerable way all Deficiencies. I also engrav'd several Things on occasion. I made the Ink, I was Warehouseman & every thing, in short quite a Factotum.[7]—

But however serviceable I might be, I found that my Services became every Day of less Importance, as the other Hands improv'd in the Business. And when Keimer paid my second Quarter's Wages, he let me know that he felt them too heavy, and thought I should make an Abatement. He grew by degrees less civil, put on more of the Master, frequently found Fault, was captious[8] and seem'd ready for an Out-breaking. I went on nevertheless with a good deal of Patience, thinking that his incumber'd Circumstances were partly the Cause. At length a Trifle snapt our Connexion. For a great Noise happening near the Courthouse, I put my Head out of the Window to see what was the Matter. Keimer being in the Street look'd up & saw me, call'd out to me in a loud Voice and angry Tone to mind my Business, adding some reproachful Words, that nettled me the more for their Publicity, all the Neighbours who were looking out on the same Occasion being Witnesses how I was treated. He came up immediately into the Printing-House, continu'd the Quarrel, high Words pass'd on both Sides, he gave me the Quarter's Warning[9] we had stipulated, expressing a Wish that he had not been oblig'd to so long a Warning: I told him his Wish was unnecessary for I would leave him that Instant; and so taking my Hat walk'd out of Doors; desiring Meredith whom I saw below to take care of some Things I left, & bring them to my Lodging.—

Meredith came accordingly in the Evening, when we talk'd my Affair over. He had conceiv'd a great Regard for me, & was very unwilling that I should leave the House while he remain'd in it. He dissuaded me from returning to my native Country which I began to think of. He reminded me that Keimer was in debt for all he possess'd, that his Creditors began to be uneasy, that he kept his Shop miserably, sold often without Profit for ready Money, and often trusted without keeping Accounts. That he must therefore fail; which

---

[1] *Player* Actor.

[2] *Gown* Scholar's robes; *Furz* Furze, thorny shrub common throughout England, also known as gorse.

[3] *Crimp's Bill* A "crimp" is an agent for a shipping company, especially one who procures or impresses workers. Here, the "crimp's bill" is presumably an advertisement for a position of indentured servitude in the colonies.

[4] *Oeconomist* Economist; manager of one's finances.

[5] *Letter Founder* One who casts metal into types.

[6] *Puncheons* Stamps; *Matrices* Molds.

[7] *Factotum* Person who does all manner of work.

[8] *captious* Inclined to criticize or find fault.

[9] *Quarter's Warning* I.e., notice of dismissal, to be given a quarter-year in advance.

would make a Vacancy I might profit of.—I objected my Want of Money. He then let me know, that his Father had a high Opinion of me, and from some Discourse that had pass'd between them, he was sure would advance Money to set us up, if I would enter into Partnership with him.—My Time, says he, will be out with Keimer in the Spring. By that time we may have our Press & Types in from London:—I am sensible I am no Workman. If you like it, Your Skill in the Business shall be set against the Stock I furnish; and we will share the Profits equally.—The Proposal was agreable, and I consented. His Father was in Town, and approv'd of it, the more as he saw I had great Influence with his Son, had prevail'd on him to abstain long from Dramdrinking, and he hop'd might break him of that wretched Habit entirely, when we came to be so closely connected. I gave an Inventory to the Father, who carry'd it to a Merchant; the Things were sent for; the Secret was to be kept till they should arrive, and in the mean time I was to get Work if I could at the other Printing House.—But I found no Vacancy there, and so remain'd idle a few Days, when Keimer, on a Prospect of being employ'd to print some Paper-money, in New Jersey, which would require Cuts & various Types that I only could supply, and apprehending Bradford might engage me & get the Jobb from him, sent me a very civil Message, that old Friends should not part for a few Words the Effect of sudden Passion, and wishing me to return. Meredith persuaded me to comply, as it would give more Opportunity for his Improvement under my daily Instructions.—So I return'd, and we went on more smoothly than for some time before.— The New Jersey Jobb was obtain'd. I contriv'd a Copper-Plate Press for it, the first that had been seen in the Country.—I cut several Ornaments and Checks for the Bills.[1] We went together to Burlington, where I executed the Whole to Satisfaction, & he received so large a Sum for the Work, as to be enabled thereby to keep his Head much longer above Water.—

At Burlington I made an Acquaintance with many principal People of the Province. Several of them had been appointed by the Assembly a Committee to attend the Press, and take Care that no more Bills were printed than the Law directed. They were therefore by Turns constantly with us, and generally he who attended brought with him a Friend or two for Company. My Mind having been much more improv'd by Reading than Keimer's, I suppose it was for that Reason my Conversation seem'd to be more valu'd. They had me to their Houses, introduc'd me to their Friends and show'd me much Civility, while he, tho' the Master, was a little neglected. In truth he was an odd Fish, ignorant of common Life, fond of rudely opposing receiv'd Opinions, slovenly to extream dirtiness, enthusiastic in some Points of Religion, and a little Knavish withal. We continu'd there near 3 Months, and by that time I could reckon among my acquired Friends, Judge Allen, Samuel Bustill, the Secretary of the Province, Isaac Pearson, Joseph Cooper & several of the Smiths, Members of Assembly, and Isaac Decow the Surveyor General. The latter was a shrewd sagacious old Man, who told me that he began for himself when young by wheeling Clay for the Brickmakers, learnt to write after he was of Age, cary'd the Chain[2] for Surveyors, who taught him Surveying, and he had now by his Industry acquir'd a good Estate; and says he, I foresee, that you will soon work this Man out of his Business & make a Fortune in it at Philadelphia. He had not then the least Intimation of my Intention to set up there or any where.—These Friends were afterwards of great Use to me, as I occasionally was to some of them.—They all continued their Regard for me as long as they lived.—

Before I enter upon my public Appearance in Business, it may be well to let you know the then State of my Mind, with regard to my Principles and Morals, that you may see how far those influenc'd the future Events of my Life. My Parent's had early given me religious Impressions, and brought me through my Childhood piously in the Dissenting Way.[3] But I was scarce 15 when, after doubting by turns of several Points as I found them disputed in the different Books I read, I began to doubt of Revelation[4] it self. Some Books

---

[1]   *cut several ... the Bills* I.e., made engravings for the ornamental designs and checked patterns for the paper money.

[2]   *Chain* Surveying tool used for measuring distance; the length of one chain is sixty-six feet.

[3]   *in the Dissenting Way* I.e., as a Congregationalist rather than an Episcopalian (Anglican).

[4]   *Revelation* I.e., the idea that the Bible is the word of God revealed to humanity.

against Deism[1] fell into my Hands; they were said to be the Substance of Sermons preached at Boyle's[2] Lectures. It happened that they wrought an Effect on me quite contrary to what was intended by them: For the Arguments of the Deists which were quoted to be refuted, appeared to me much Stronger than the Refutations. In short I soon became a thorough Deist. My Arguments perverted some others, particularly Collins & Ralph: but each of them having afterwards wrong'd me greatly without the least Compunction, and recollecting Keith's Conduct towards me, (who was another Freethinker) and my own towards Vernon & Miss Read which at Times gave me great Trouble, I began to suspect that this Doctrine tho' it might be true, was not very useful.—My London Pamphlet, which had for its Motto those Lines of Dryden

> ———Whatever is, is right
> Tho' purblind Man / Sees but a Part of
> The Chain, the nearest Link,
> His Eyes not carrying to the equal Beam,
> That poizes all above.[3]

And from the Attributes of God, his infinite Wisdom, Goodness & Power concluded that nothing could possibly be wrong in the World, & that Vice & Virtue were empty Distinctions, no such Things existing: appear'd now not so clever a Performance as I once thought it; and I doubted whether some Error had not insinuated itself unperceiv'd, into my Argument, so as to infect all that follow'd, as is common in metaphysical Reasonings.—I grew convinc'd that *Truth, Sincerity & Integrity* in Dealings between Man & Man, were

of the utmost Importance to the Felicity of Life, and I form'd written Resolutions, (which still remain in my Journal Book) to practise them ever while I lived. Revelation had indeed no weight with me as such; but I entertain'd an Opinion, that tho' certain Actions might not be bad *because* they were forbidden by it, or good *because* it commanded them; yet probably those Actions might be forbidden *because* they were bad for us, or commanded *because* they were beneficial to us, in their own Natures, all the Circumstances of things considered. And this Persuasion, with the kind hand of Providence, or some guardian Angel, or accidental favourable Circumstances & Situations, or all together, preserved me (thro' this dangerous Time of Youth & the hazardous Situations I was sometimes in among Strangers, remote from the Eye & Advice of my Father,) without any *wilful* gross Immorality or Injustice that might have been expected from my Want of Religion.—I say *wilful*, because the Instances I have mentioned, had something of *Necessity* in them, from my Youth, Inexperience, & the Knavery of others.—I had therefore a tolerable Character to begin the World with, I valued it properly, & determin'd to preserve it.—

We had not been long return'd to Philadelphia, before the New Types arriv'd from London.—We settled with Keimer, & left him by his Consent before he heard of it.—We found a House to hire near the Market, and took it. To lessen the Rent, (which was then but 24£ a Year tho' I have since known it to let for 70) We took in Thomas Godfrey a Glazier, & his Family, who were to pay a considerable Part of it to us, and we to board with them. We had scarce opened our Letters & put our Press in Order, before George House, an Acquaintance of mine, brought a Countryman to us; whom he had met in the Street enquiring for a Printer. All our Cash was now expended in the Variety of Particulars we had been obliged to procure, & this Countryman's Five Shillings, being our First Fruits & coming so seasonably, gave me more Pleasure than any Crown[4] I have since earn'd; and the Gratitude I felt towards House, has made me often more ready than perhaps I should otherwise have been to assist young Beginners.—

---

1   *Deism* School of religious and philosophical thought that grew to prominence during the Enlightenment, proposing that God exists only as the creator of the universe, and has had little or no influence on the world since creation; more generally, Deists deny the literal truth or importance of the Bible and other teachings of formal religion.

2   *Boyle* English chemist and Anglican priest Robert Boyle (1627–91), who lectured against Deism and other forms of religious skepticism.

3   *Whatever is … all above* Franklin's quotation and attribution is slightly mistaken. The first line is in fact from Alexander Pope's *An Essay on Man* (1733–34), the final line of Epistle 1—though it bears a resemblance to a line from John Dryden's 1679 play *Oedipus*: "What ever is, is in its causes just" (3.1.243). The remainder of the quotation is from Dryden's *Oedipus*, 3.1.245–48.

4   *Crown* Five-shilling coin.

There are Croakers[1] in every Country always boding its Ruin. Such a one then lived in Philadelphia, a Person of Note, an elderly Man, with a wise Look and very grave Manner of Speaking. His Name was Samuel Mickle. This Gentleman, a Stranger to me, stopt one Day at my Door, and ask'd me if I was the young Man who had lately opened a new Printing-house: Being answer'd in the Affirmative; He said he was sorry for me; because it was an expensive Undertaking, & the Expence would be lost, for Philadelphia was a sinking Place, the People already half Bankrupts or near being so; all Appearances to the contrary such as new Buildings & the Rise of Rents, being to his certain Knowledge fallacious; for they were in fact among the Things that would soon ruin us. And he gave me such a Detail of Misfortunes now existing or that were soon to exist, that he left me half-melancholy. Had I known him before I engag'd in this Business, probably I never should have done it.—This Man continu'd to live in this decaying Place, & to declaim[2] in the same Strain, refusing for many Years to buy a House there, because all was going to Destruction, and at last I had the Pleasure of seeing him give five times as much for one as he might have bought it for when he first began his Croaking.—

I should have mention'd before, that in the Autumn of the preceding Year, I had form'd most of my ingenious Acquaintance into a Club, for mutual Improvement, which we call'd the Junto.[3] We met on Friday Evenings. The Rules I drew up, requir'd that every Member in his Turn should produce one or more Queries on any Point of Morals, Politics or Natural Philosophy, to be discuss'd by the Company, and once in three Months produce and read an Essay of his own Writing on any Subject he pleased. Our Debates were to be under the Direction of a President, and to be conducted in the sincere Spirit of Enquiry after Truth, without fondness for Dispute, or Desire of Victory; and to prevent Warmth,[4] all Expressions of Positiveness in Opinions, or of direct Contradiction, were after some time made

contraband & prohibited under small pecuniary Penalties. The first Members were, Joseph Brientnal, a Copyer of Deeds for the Scriveners; a good-natur'd friendly middle-ag'd Man, a great Lover of Poetry, reading all he could meet with, & writing some that was tolerable; very ingenious in many little Nicknackeries, & of sensible Conversation. Thomas Godfrey, a self-taught Mathematician, great in his Way, & afterwards Inventor of what is now call'd Hadley's Quadrant.[5] But he knew little out of his way, and was not a pleasing Companion, as like most Great Mathematicians I have met with, he expected unusual Precision in every thing said, or was forever denying or distinguishing upon Trifles,[6] to the Disturbance of all Conversation.—He soon left us.—Nicholas Scull, a Surveyor, afterwards Surveyor-General, Who lov'd Books, & sometimes made a few Verses. William Parsons, bred a Shoemaker, but loving Reading, had acquir'd a considerable Share of Mathematics, which he first studied with a View to Astrology that he afterwards laught at. He also became Surveyor General.—William Maugridge, a Joiner, & a most exquisite Mechanic, & a solid sensible Man. Hugh Meredith, Stephen Potts, & George Webb, I have Characteris'd before. Robert Grace, a young Gentleman of some Fortune, generous, lively & witty, a Lover of Punning and of his Friends. And William Coleman, then a Merchant's Clerk, about my Age, who had the coolest clearest Head, the best Heart, and the exactest Morals, of almost any Man I ever met with. He became afterwards a Merchant of great Note, and one of our Provincial Judges: Our Friendship continued without Interruption to his Death, upwards of 40 Years. And the Club continu'd almost as long and was the best School of Philosophy, Morals & Politics that then existed in the Province; for our Queries which were read the Week preceding their Discussion, put us on reading with Attention upon the several Subjects, that we might speak more to the purpose: and here too we acquired better Habits of Conversation, every thing being studied in our Rules which might

---

[1] *Croakers* Those who speak prophesies of doom.

[2] *declaim* Recite passionately.

[3] *Junto* In its origins, the term refers to a small committee who gather together for the advancement of mutual political goals or of the public interest.

[4] *Warmth* Passionate debate; anger.

---

[5] *Hadley's Quadrant* Navigational tool better known today as the octant; similar devices were invented around the same time, independently, by both Thomas Godfrey and the English mathematician John Hadley (1682–1744).

[6] *distinguishing upon Trifles* I.e., drawing attention to minute or petty distinctions between things.

prevent our disgusting each other. From hence the long Continuance of the Club, which I shall have frequent Occasion to speak farther of hereafter; But my giving this Account of it here, is to show something of the Interest I had, every one of these exerting themselves in recommending Business to us.—Brientnal particularly procur'd us from the Quakers, the Printing 40 Sheets of their History, the rest being to be done by Keimer: and upon this we work'd exceeding hard, for the Price was low. It was a Folio, Pro Patria Size, in Pica with Long Primer Notes.[1] I compos'd of it a Sheet a Day, and Meredith work'd it off at Press. It was often 11 at Night and sometimes later, before I had finish'd my Distribution for the next days Work: For the little Jobbs sent in by our other Friends now & then put us back. But so determin'd I was to continue doing a Sheet a Day of the Folio, that one Night when having impos'd my Forms, I thought my Days Work over, one of them by accident was broken and two Pages reduc'd to Pie,[2] I immediately distributed & compos'd it over again before I went to bed. And this Industry visible to our Neighbours began to give us Character and Credit; particularly I was told, that mention being made of the new Printing Office at the Merchants Every-night-Club, the general Opinion was that it must fail, there being already two Printers in the Place, Keimer & Bradford; but Doctor Baird (whom you and I saw many Years after at his native Place, St. Andrews in Scotland) gave a contrary Opinion; for the Industry of that Franklin, says he, is superior to any thing I ever saw of the kind: I see him still at work when I go home from Club; and he is at Work again before his Neighbours are out of bed. This struck the rest, and we soon after had Offers from one of them to supply us with Stationary. But as yet we did not chuse to engage in Shop Business.

I mention this Industry the more particularly and the more freely, tho' it seems to be talking in my own Praise, that those of my Posterity who shall read it, may know the Use of that Virtue, when they see its Effects in my Favour throughout this Relation.—

George Webb, who had found a Friend that lent him wherewith to purchase his Time of Keimer,[3] now came to offer himself as a Journeyman to us. We could not then imploy him, but I foolishly let him know, as a Secret, that I soon intended to begin a Newspaper, & might then have Work for him.—My Hopes of Success as I told him were founded on this, that the then only Newspaper,[4] printed by Bradford, was a paltry thing, wretchedly manag'd, no way entertaining; and yet was profitable to him.—I therefore thought a good Paper could scarcely fail of good Encouragement I requested Webb not to mention it, but he told it to Keimer, who immediately, to be beforehand with[5] me, published Proposals for Printing one himself,—on which Webb was to be employ'd.—I resented this, and to counteract them, as I could not yet begin our Paper, I wrote several Pieces of Entertainment for Bradford's Paper, under the Title of the Busy Body which Brientnal continu'd some Months.[6] By this means the Attention of the Publick was fix'd on that Paper, & Keimers Proposals which we burlesqu'd and ridicul'd, were disregarded. He began his Paper however, and after carrying it on three Quarters of a Year, with at most only 90 Subscribers, he offer'd it to me for a Trifle, & I having been ready some time to go on with it, took it in hand directly and it prov'd in a few Years extreamly profitable to me.[7]—

I perceive that I am apt to speak in the singular Number, though our Partnership still continu'd. The Reason may be, that in fact the whole Management of the Business lay upon me. Meredith was no Compositor, a poor Pressman, & seldom sober. My Friends lamented my Connection with him, but I was to make the best of it.

---

[1] *Pro Patria Size* According to Frank Woodworth Pine's 1916 edition of the *Autobiography*, this term refers to "A sheet 8-½ by 13-½ inches, having the words *pro patria* [Latin: for the fatherland] in translucent letters in the body of the paper"; *in Pica with Long Primer Notes* I.e., the main text is in pica (the font size today standardized as size 12), with footnotes in size 10.

[2] *Pie* Printer's term for a confused jumble of types.

[3] *wherewith to … of Keimer* Money to pay Keimer for his remaining years of servitude and thereby be released from his contract of indenture.

[4] *then only Newspaper* Andrew Bradford's *The American Weekly Mercury* was published from 1719 to 1749.

[5] *be beforehand with* I.e., get ahead of.

[6] *several Pieces … some Months* Thirty-two of these letters were published in the *Mercury* over the course of 1729.

[7] *his Paper … to me* This was the paper that later became known as the *Pennsylvania Gazette*, which under Franklin's ownership (1729–48) became one of the most prominent newspapers in the North American colonies.

Our first Papers made a quite different Appearance from any before in the Province, a better Type & better printed: but some spirited Remarks[1] of my Writing on the Dispute then going on between Governor Burnet and the Massachusetts Assembly, struck the principal People, occasion'd the Paper & the Manager of it to be much talk'd of, & in a few Weeks brought them all to be our Subscribers. Their Example was follow'd by many, and our Number went on growing continually.—This was one of the first good Effects of my having learnt a little to scribble.—Another was, that the leading Men, seeing a News Paper now in the hands of one who could also handle a Pen, thought it convenient to oblige & encourage me.—Bradford still printed the Votes & Laws & other Publick Business. He had printed an Address of the House[2] to the Governor in a coarse blundering manner; We reprinted it elegantly & correctly, and sent one to every Member. They were sensible of the Difference, it strengthen'd the Hands of our Friends in the House, and they voted us their Printers for the Year ensuing.

Among my Friends in the House I must not forget Mr Hamilton before mentioned, who was then returned from England & had a Seat in it. He interested himself for me strongly in that Instance, as he did in many others afterwards, continuing his Patronage till his Death.[3] Mr Vernon about this time put me in mind of the Debt I ow'd him:—but did not press me.—I wrote him an ingenuous Letter of Acknowledgments, crav'd his Forbearance a little longer which he allow'd me, & as soon as I was able I paid the Principal with Interest & many Thanks.—So that *Erratum* was in some degree corrected.—

But now another Difficulty came upon me, which I had never the least Reason to expect. Mr. Meredith's Father, who was to have paid for our Printing House according to the Expectations given me, was able to advance only one Hundred Pounds, Currency, which had been paid, & a Hundred more was due to the Merchant; who grew impatient & su'd us all. We gave Bail, but saw that if the Money could not be rais'd in time, the Suit must come to a Judgment & Execution, & our hopeful Prospects must with us be ruined, as the Press & Letters must be sold for Payment, perhaps at half-Price.—In this Distress two true Friends whose Kindness I have never forgotten nor ever shall forget while I can remember any thing, came to me separately unknown to each other, and without any Application from me, offering each of them to advance me all the Money that should be necessary to enable me to take the whole Business upon my self, if that should be practicable, but they did not like my continuing the Partnership with Meredith, who as they said was often seen drunk in the Streets, & playing at low Games in Alehouses, much to our Discredit. These two Friends were *William Coleman* & *Robert Grace*. I told them I could not propose a Separation while any Prospect remain'd of the Merediths fulfilling their Part of our Agreement. Because I thought my self under great Obligations to them for what they had done & would do if they could. But if they finally fail'd in their Performance, & our Partnership must be dissolv'd, I should then think myself at Liberty to accept the Assistance of my Friends. Thus the matter rested for some time. When I said to my Partner, perhaps your Father is dissatisfied at the Part you have undertaken in this Affair of ours, and is unwilling to advance for you & me what he would for you alone: If that is the Case, tell me, and I will resign the whole to you & go about my Business. No—says he, my Father has really been disappointed[4] and is really unable; and I am unwilling to distress him farther. I see this is a Business I am not fit for. I was bred a Farmer, and it was a Folly in me to come to Town & put my self at 30 Years of Age an Apprentice to learn a new Trade. Many of our Welsh People are going to settle in North

---

[1]   A long footnote in Franklin's original manuscript reprints the text of these "Remarks," which was published in the *Gazette* on 9 October 1729; that footnote has been omitted here in the interest of clarity and brevity. The dispute referred to centered on Governor Burnet's demands, supported by the Board of Trade in England, to receive a fixed salary from the Massachusetts Assembly, when it had previously been the practice of the Assembly to simply reward the governor with periodic grants "according to their sense of his merit and services." Burnet remained rigidly attached to his demand until his death, as did his successors, until the matter was put to rest in favor of the Assembly during the governorship of Jonathan Belcher (1730–41).

[2]   *the House*   I.e., the Assembly.

[3]   [Franklin's note]   I got his Son once 500£.

[4]   *disappointed*   I.e., in financial matters.

Carolina[1] where Land is cheap: I am inclin'd to go with them, & follow my old Employment. You may find Friends to assist you. If you will take the Debts of the Company upon you, return to my Father the hundred Pound he has advanc'd, pay my little personal Debts, and give me Thirty Pounds & a new Saddle, I will relinquish the Partnership & leave the whole in your Hands. I agreed to this Proposal. It was drawn up in Writing, sign'd & seal'd immediately. I gave him what he demanded & he went soon after to Carolina; from whence he sent me next Year two long Letters, containing the best Account that had been given of that Country, the Climate, Soil, Husbandry, &c. for in those Matters he was very judicious. I printed them in the Papers, and they gave grate Satisfaction to the Publick.

As soon as he was gone, I recurr'd to my two Friends; and because I would not give an unkind Preference to either, I took half what each had offered & I wanted, of one, & half of the other; paid off the Company Debts, and went on with the Business in my own Name, advertising that the Partnership was dissolved. I think this was in or about the Year 1729.[2]—

About this Time there was a Cry among the People for more Paper-Money, only 15,000£ being extant in the Province & that soon to be sunk. The wealthy Inhabitants oppos'd any Addition, being against all Paper Currency, from an Apprehension that it would depreciate as it had done in New England to the Prejudice of all Creditors.[3]—We had discuss'd this Point in our Junto, where I was on the Side of an Addition, being persuaded that the first small Sum struck in 1723 had done much good, by increasing the Trade Employment, & Number of Inhabitants in the Province, since I now saw all the old Houses inhabited, & many new ones building, where as I remember'd well, that when I first walk'd about the Streets of Philadelphia, eating my Roll, I saw most of the Houses in Walnut street between Second & Front streets with Bills on their Doors, to be let; and many likewise in Chestnut Street, & other Streets; which made me then think the Inhabitants of the City were one after another deserting it.—Our Debates possess'd me so fully of the Subject, that I wrote and printed an anonymous Pamphlet on it, entituled, *The Nature & Necessity of a Paper Currency*. It was well receiv'd by the common People in general; but the Rich Men dislik'd it; for it increas'd and strengthen'd the Clamour for more Money; and they happening to have no Writers among them that were able to answer it, their Opposition slacken'd, & the Point was carried by a Majority in the House. My Friends there, who conceiv'd I had been of some Service, thought fit to reward me, by employing me in printing the Money, a very profitable Jobb, and a great Help to me.—This was another Advantage gain'd by my being able to write. The Utility of this Currency became by Time and Experience so evident, as never afterwards to be much disputed, so that it grew soon to 55,000£ and in 1739 to 80,000£ since which it arose during War to upwards of 350,000£. Trade, Building & Inhabitants all the while increasing. Tho' I now think there are Limits beyond which the Quantity may be hurtful.—

I soon after obtain'd, thro' my Friend Hamilton, the Printing of the NewCastle[4] Paper Money, another profitable Jobb, as I then thought it; small Things appearing great to those in small Circumstances. And these to me were really great Advantages, as they were great Encouragements.—He procured me also the Printing of the Laws and Votes of that Government which continu'd in my Hands as long as I follow'd the Business.—

I now open'd a little Stationer's Shop. I had in it Blanks[5] of all Sorts the correctest that ever appear'd

---

[1] *Welsh People ... North Carolina* The royal colony of North Carolina was founded in 1729; many of its earliest European settlers were Welsh Presbyterians, who settled in Cape Fear in an area eventually known as the Welsh Tract.

[2] *I think ... 1729* In fact, Franklin's partnership with Meredith was dissolved in July 1730, and officially announced in 1732, once he had paid off all the company debts.

[3] *About this ... all Creditors* Pennsylvania's first paper currency had been issued in a fixed installment in 1723. Paper money was at this period still a relatively new and ill-defined concept in the colonies, with paper bills having no intrinsic value but acting instead as "bills of credit," backed by real estate collateral and intended to be eventually redeemed and retired (or "sunk") by the colonial government. Poor management of the issuing of paper currency had led to extreme inflation in New England and South Carolina, which had most negatively affected wealthy creditors in the colony.

[4] *NewCastle* Political center of Delaware, which was owned by the same proprietaries as Pennsylvania.

[5] *Blanks* I.e., documents with blank spaces, designed for various purposes.

among us, being assisted in that by my Friend Brientnal; I had also Paper, Parchment, Chapmen's Books, &c. One Whitemash a Compositor I had known in London, an excellent Workman now came to me & work'd with me constantly & diligently, and I took an Apprentice the Son of Aquila Rose. I began now gradually to pay off the Debt I was under for the Printing-House.—In order to secure my Credit and Character as a Tradesmen, I took care not only to be in *Reality* Industrious & frugal, but to avoid all *Appearances* of the Contrary. I drest plainly; I was seen at no Places of idle Diversion; I never went out a-fishing or shooting; a Book, indeed, sometimes debauch'd me from my Work; but that was seldom, snug,[1] & gave no Scandal: and to show that I was not above my Business, I sometimes brought home the Paper I purchas'd at the Stores, thro' the Streets on a Wheelbarrow. Thus being esteem'd an industrious thriving young Man, and paying duly for what I bought, the Merchants who imported Stationary solicited my Custom, others propos'd supplying me with Books, & I went on swimmingly.—In the mean time, Keimer's Credit & Business declining daily, he was at last forc'd to sell his Printing-house to satisfy his Creditors. He went to Barbadoes, & there lived some Years, in very poor Circumstances.

His Apprentice David Harry, whom I had instructed while I work'd with him, set up in his Place at Philadelphia having bought his Materials. I was at first apprehensive of a powerful Rival in Harry, as his Friends were very able, & had a good deal of Interest. I therefore propos'd a Partnership to him; which he, fortunately for me, rejected with Scorn. He was very proud, dress'd like a Gentleman, liv'd expensively, took much Diversion & Pleasure abroad, ran in debt, & neglected his Business, upon which all Business left him; and finding nothing to do, he follow'd Keimer to Barbadoes; taking the Printinghouse with him. There this Apprentice employ'd his former Master as a Journeyman. They quarrel'd often. Harry went continually behind-hand, and at length was forc'd to sell his Types, and return to his Country Work in Pensilvania. The Person that bought them, employ'd Keimer to use them, but in a few years he died. There remain'd now no Competitor with me at Philadelphia, but the old one, Bradford, who was rich & easy, did a

little Printing now & then by straggling Hands, but was not very anxious about the Business. However, as he kept the Post Office, it was imagined he had better Opportunities of obtaining News, his Paper was thought a better Distributer of Advertisements than mine, & therefore had many more, which was a profitable thing to him & a Disadvantage to me. For tho' I did indeed receive & send Papers by the Post, yet the publick Opinion was otherwise; for what I did send was by Bribing the Riders[2] who took them privately: Bradford being unkind enough to forbid it: which occasion'd some Resentment on my Part; and I thought so meanly of him for it, that when I afterwards came into his Situation, I took care never to imitate it.

I had hitherto continu'd to board with Godfrey who lived in Part of my House with his Wife & Children, & had one Side of the Shop for his Glazier's Business, tho' he work'd little, being always absorb'd in his Mathematics.—Mrs Godfrey projected a Match for me with a Relation's Daughter, took Opportunities of bringing us often together, till a serious Courtship on my part ensu'd the Girl being in herself very deserving. The old Folks encourag'd me by continual Invitations to Supper, & by leaving us together, till at length it was time to explain. Mrs Godfrey manag'd our little Treaty. I let her know that I expected as much Money with their Daughter as would pay off my Remaining Debt for the Printing-house, which I believe was not then above a Hundred Pounds.[3] She brought me Word they had no such Sum to spare. I said they might mortgage their House in the Loan Office.—The Answer to this after some Days was, that they did not approve the Match; that on Enquiry of Bradford they had been inform'd the Printing Business was not a profitable one, the Types would soon be worn out & more wanted, that S. Keimer & D. Harry had fail'd one after the other, and I should probably soon follow them; and therefore I was forbidden the House, & the Daughter shut up.—Whether this was a real Change of Sentiment, or only Artifice, on a Supposition of our being too far engag'd in Affection to retract, & therefore that we

1   *snug*   Unseen; private.

2   *Riders*   Postal delivery workers.

3   *I let her know … Pounds*   Such financial settlements were commonly involved in drawing up marriage contracts in the eighteenth century.

should steal a Marriage,[1] which would leave them at Liberty to give or withhold what they pleas'd, I know not: But I suspected the latter, resented it, and went no more. Mrs Godfrey brought me afterwards some more favourable Accounts of their Disposition, & would have drawn me on again: But I declared absolutely my Resolution to have nothing more to do with that Family. This was resented by the Godfreys, we differ'd, and they removed, leaving me the whole House, and I resolved to take no more Inmates. But this Affair having turn'd my Thoughts to Marriage, I look'd round me, and made Overtures of Acquaintance in other Places; but soon found that the Business of a Printer being generally thought a poor one, I was not to expect Money with a Wife unless with such a one, as I should not otherwise think agreable.—In the mean time that hard-to-be-govern'd Passion of Youth, had hurried me frequently into Intrigues with low Women that fell in my Way, which were attended with some Expence & great Inconvenience, besides a continual Risque to my Health by a Distemper which of all Things I dreaded,[2] tho' by great good Luck I escaped it.—

A friendly Correspondence as Neighbours & old Acquaintances, had continued between me & Mrs Read's Family who all had a Regard for me from the time of my first Lodging in their House. I was often invited there and consulted in their Affairs, wherein I sometimes was of Service.—I pity'd poor Miss Read's unfortunate Situation, who was generally dejected, seldom chearful, and avoided Company. I consider'd my Giddiness & Inconstancy when in London as in a great degree the Cause of her Unhappiness; tho' the Mother was good enough to think the Fault more her own than mine, as she had prevented our Marrying before I went thither, and persuaded the other Match in my Absence. Our mutual Affection was revived, but there were now great Objections to our Union. That Match was indeed look'd upon as invalid, a preceding Wife being said to be living in England; but this could not easily be prov'd, because of the Distance &c. And tho' there was a Report of his Death, it was not certain. Then, tho' it should be true, he had left many Debts which his Successor might be call'd upon to pay. We ventured however, over all these Difficulties, and I took

her to Wife[3] Sept. 1. 1730. None of the Inconveniencies happened that we had apprehended, she prov'd a good & faithful Helpmate, assisted me much by attending the Shop, we throve together, and have ever mutually endeavour'd to make each other happy.—Thus I corrected that great *Erratum* as well as I could.

About this Time our Club meeting, not at a Tavern, but in a little Room of Mr Grace's set apart for that Purpose; a Proposition was made by me, that since our Books were often referr'd to in our Disquisitions upon the Queries, it might be convenient to us to have them all together where we met, that upon Occasion they might be consulted; and By thus clubbing our Books to a common Library, we should, while we lik'd to keep them together, have each of us the Advantage of using the Books of all the other Members, which would be nearly as beneficial as if each owned the whole. It was lik'd and agreed to, & we fill'd one End of the Room with such Books as we could best spare. The Number was not so great as we expected; and tho' they had been of great Use, yet some Inconveniencies occurring for want of due Care of them, the Collection after about a Year was separated, & each took his Books home again.

And now I set on foot my first Project of a public Nature, that for a Subscription Library. I drew up the Proposals, got them put into Form by our great Scrivener Brockden, and by the help of my Friends in the Junto, procur'd Fifty Subscribers of 40/[4] each to begin with & 10/ a Year for 50 Years, the Term our Company was to continue. We afterwards obtain'd a Charter, the Company being increas'd to 100. This was the Mother of all the N American Subscription Libraries now so numerous. It is become a great thing itself, & continually increasing.—These Libraries have improv'd the general Conversation of the Americans, made the common Tradesmen & Farmers as intelligent as most Gentlemen from other Countries, and perhaps have contributed in some degree to the Stand so generally made throughout the Colonies in Defence of their Privileges.—

---

1   *steal a Marriage*   I.e., elope.

2   *a Distemper ... I dreaded*   I.e., syphilis.

3   *took her to Wife*   Due to the uncertainty regarding Read's first husband, her marriage to Franklin was never considered legal; their union was nevertheless considered legitimate and acceptable by most within the community, and they referred to one another as husband and wife.

4   *40/*   Forty shillings.

Memorandum

Thus far was written with the Intention express'd in the Beginning and therefore contains several little family Anecdotes of no Importance to others. What follows was written many Years after in compliance with the Advice contain'd in these Letters, and accordingly intended for the Publick. The Affairs of the Revolution occasion'd the Interruption.[1]

PART 2

Letter from Mr. Abel James,[2] with Notes on my Life, (received in Paris.)

My dear & honored Friend.

I have often been desirous of writing to thee, but could not be reconciled to the Thought that the Letter might fall into the Hands of the British, lest some Printer or busy Body should publish some Part of the Contents & give our Friends Pain & myself Censure.

Some Time since there fell into my Hands to my great Joy about 23 Sheets in thy own hand-writing containing an Account of the Parentage & Life of thyself, directed to thy Son ending in the Year 1730 with which there were Notes likewise in thy writing, a Copy of which I inclose in Hopes it may be a means if thou continuedst it up to a later period, that the first & latter part may be put together; & if it is not yet continued, I hope thou wilt not delay it, Life is uncertain as the Preacher tells us,[3] and what will the World say if kind, humane & benevolent Ben Franklin should leave his Friends & the World deprived of so pleasing & profitable a Work, a Work which would be useful & entertaining not only to a few, but to millions.

The Influence Writings under that Class have on the Minds of Youth is very great, and has no where appeared so plain as in our public Friends' Journals. It almost insensibly leads the Youth into the Resolution of endeavouring to become as good and as eminent as the Journalist. Should thine for Instance when published, and I think it could not fail of it, lead the Youth to equal the Industry & Temperance of thy early Youth, what a Blessing with that Class would such a Work be. I know of no Character living nor many of them put together, who has so much in his Power as Thyself to promote a greater Spirit of Industry & early Attention to Business, Frugality and Temperance with the American Youth. Not that I think the Work would have no other Merit & Use in the World, far from it, but the first is of such vast Importance, that I know nothing that can equal it.

———

The foregoing letter and the minutes accompanying it being shewn to a friend, I received from him the following:

LETTER FROM MR. BENJAMIN VAUGHAN.[4]

Paris, January 31, 1783.

MY DEAREST SIR,

When I had read over your sheets of minutes of the principal incidents of your life, recovered for you by your Quaker acquaintance; I told you I would send you a letter expressing my reasons why I thought it would be useful to complete and publish it as he desired. Various concerns have for some time past prevented this letter being written, and I do not know whether it was worth any expectation: happening to be at leisure however at present, I shall by writing at least interest and instruct myself; but as the terms I am inclined to use may tend to offend a person of your manners, I shall only tell you how I would address any other person, who was as good and as great as yourself, but less diffident. I would say to him, Sir, I *solicit* the history of your life from the following motives.

Your history is so remarkable, that if you do not give it, somebody else will certainly give it; and perhaps so as nearly to do as much harm, as your own management of the thing might do good.

It will moreover present a table of the internal circumstances of your country, which will very much

---

[1]   *Thus far … the Interruption*   Part One of the *Autobiography* was written in 1771; Franklin began Part Two while working as the U.S. Minister to France in 1784.

[2]   *Abel James*   A Quaker merchant friend from Philadelphia. This letter was written in 1782.

[3]   *Life is … tells us*   The uncertainty of life and death is a major theme of the Book of Ecclesiastes, whose wisdom-dispensing narrator, Kohelet, is often referred to as simply "the Preacher."

[4]   *BENJAMIN VAUGHAN*   British politician (1751–1835) who supported the American Revolution. He later became a member of the American Philosophical Society founded by Franklin and his associates.

tend to invite to it settlers of virtuous and manly minds. And considering the eagerness with which such information is sought by them, and the extent of your reputation, I do not know of a more efficacious advertisement than your Biography would give.

All that has happened to you is also connected with the detail of the manners and situation of *a rising people*; and in this respect I do not think that the writings of Caesar and Tacitus[1] can be more interesting to a true judge of human nature and society.

But these, Sir, are small reasons in my opinion, compared with the chance which your life will give for the forming of future great men; and in conjunction with your *Art of Virtue*,[2] (which you design to publish) of improving the features of private character, and consequently of aiding all happiness both public and domestic.

The two works I allude to, Sir, will in particular give a noble rule and example of *self-education*. School and other education constantly proceed upon false principles, and shew a clumsy apparatus pointed at a false mark; but your apparatus is simple, and the mark a true one; and while parents and young persons are left destitute of other just means of estimating and becoming prepared for a reasonable course in life, your discovery that the thing is in many a man's private power, will be invaluable!

Influence upon the private character late in life, is not only an influence late in life, but a weak influence. It is in *youth* that we plant our chief habits and prejudices; it is in youth that we take our party as to profession, pursuits, and matrimony. In youth therefore the turn is given; in youth the education even of the next generation is given; in youth the private and public character is determined; and the term of life extending but from youth to age, life ought to begin well from youth; and more especially *before* we take our party as to our principal objects.

---

[1] *Caesar and Tacitus* Roman military leader and dictator Gaius Julius Caesar (100–44 BCE), who wrote two memoirs of his experience of the Gallic Wars, and Roman historian Publius Cornelius Tacitus (c. 56–c. 120 CE).

[2] *Art of Virtue* Franklin appears to have first proposed this work in a 1760 letter to the Scottish philosopher Henry Home, Lord Kames (1696–1782). This distinct work was never begun, though Part Two of the *Autobiography* is generally considered to have been written with some of its ambitions in mind.

But your Biography will not merely teach self-education, but the education of *a wise man*; and the wisest man will receive lights and improve his progress, by seeing detailed the conduct of another wise man. And why are weaker men to be deprived of such helps, when we see our race has been blundering on in the dark, almost without a guide in this particular, from the farthest trace of time. Shew then, Sir, how much is to be done, *both to sons and fathers*; and invite all wise men to become like yourself; and other men to become wise.

When we see how cruel statesmen and warriors can be to the humble race, and how absurd distinguished men can be to their acquaintance, it will be instructive to observe the instances multiply of pacific acquiescing manners; and to find how compatible it is to be great and *domestic*; enviable and yet *good-humoured*.

The little private incidents which you will also have to relate, will have considerable use, as we want above all things, *rules of prudence in ordinary affairs*; and it will be curious to see how you have acted in these. It will be so far a sort of key to life, and explain many things that all men ought to have once explained to them, to give them a chance of becoming wise by foresight.

The nearest thing to having experience of one's own, is to have other people's affairs brought before us in a shape that is interesting; this is sure to happen from your pen. Your affairs and management will have an air of simplicity or importance that will not fail to strike; and I am convinced you have conducted them with as much originality as if you had been conducting discussions in politics or philosophy; and what more worthy of experiments and system, (its importance and its errors considered) than human life!

Some men have been virtuous blindly, others have speculated fantastically, and others have been shrewd to bad purposes; but you, Sir, I am sure, will give under your hand, nothing but what is at the same moment, wise, practical, and good.

Your account of yourself (for I suppose the parallel I am drawing for Dr. Franklin, will hold not only in point of character but of private history), will shew that you are ashamed of no origin; a thing the more important, as you prove how little necessary all origin is to happiness, virtue, or greatness.

As no end likewise happens without a means, so we shall find, Sir, that even you yourself framed a plan by which you became considerable; but at the same time we may see that though the event is flattering, the means are as simple as wisdom could make them; that is depending upon nature, virtue, thought, and habit.

Another thing demonstrated will be the propriety of every man's waiting for his time for appearing upon the stage of the world. Our sensations being very much fixed to the moment, we are apt to forget that more moments are to follow the first, and consequently that man should arrange his conduct so as to suit the *whole* of a life. Your attribution appears to have been applied to your *life*, and the passing moments of it have been enlivened with content and enjoyment, instead of being tormented with foolish impatience or regrets. Such a conduct is easy for those who make virtue and themselves their standard, and who try to keep themselves in countenance by examples of other truly great men, of whom patience is so often the characteristic.

Your Quaker correspondent, Sir, (for here again I will suppose the subject of my letter resembling Dr. Franklin,) praised your frugality, diligence, and temperance, which he considered as a pattern for all youth; but it is singular that he should have forgotten your modesty, and your disinterestedness,[1] without which you never could have waited for your advancement, or found your situation in the mean time comfortable; which is a strong lesson to shew the poverty of glory, and the importance of regulating our minds.

If this correspondent had known the nature of your reputation as well as I do, he would have said; your former writings and measures would secure attention to your Biography, and Art of Virtue; and your Biography and Art of Virtue, in return, would secure attention to them. This is an advantage attendant upon a various character,[2] and which brings all that belongs to it into greater play; and it is the more useful, as perhaps more persons are at a loss for the *means* of improving their minds and characters, than they are for the time or the inclination to do it.

But there is one concluding reflection, Sir, that will shew the use of your life as a mere piece of biography. This style of writing seems a little gone out of vogue, and yet it is a very useful one; and your specimen of it may be particularly serviceable, as it will make a subject of comparison with the lives of various public cut-throats and intriguers, and with absurd monastic self-tormentors, or vain literary triflers. If it encourages more writings of the same kind with your own, and induces more men to spend lives fit to be written; it will be worth all Plutarch's Lives put together.

But being tired of figuring to myself a character of which every feature suits only one man in the world, without giving him the praise of it; I shall end my letter, my dear Dr. Franklin, with a personal application to your proper self.

I am earnestly desirous then, my dear Sir, that you should let the world into the traits of your genuine character, as civil broils[3] may otherwise tend to disguise or traduce it. Considering your great age, the caution of your character, and your peculiar style of thinking, it is not likely that any one besides yourself can be sufficiently master of the facts of your life, or the intentions of your mind.

Besides all this, the immense revolution of the present period, will necessarily turn our attention towards the author of it; and when virtuous principles have been pretended in it, it will be highly important to shew that such have really influenced; and, as your own character will be the principal one to receive a scrutiny, it is proper (even for its effects upon your vast and rising country, as well as upon England and upon Europe), that it should stand respectable and eternal. For the furtherance of human happiness, I have always maintained that it is necessary to prove that man is not even at present a vicious and detestable animal; and still more to prove that good management may greatly amend him; and it is for much the same reason, that I am anxious to see the opinion established, that there are fair characters existing among the individuals of the race; for the moment that all men, without exception, shall be conceived abandoned,[4] good people will cease efforts deemed to be hopeless, and perhaps think of

---

[1]   *singular* Strange; *disinterestedness* I.e., impartiality, lack of prejudice.

[2]   *a various character* I.e., a person of varied abilities, interests, and achievements.

[3]   *broils* Conflicts.

[4]   *abandoned* Unrestrained; immoral.

taking their share in the scramble of life, or at least of making it comfortable principally for themselves.

Take then, my dear Sir, this work most speedily into hand: shew yourself good as you are good, temperate as you are temperate; and above all things, prove yourself as one who from your infancy have loved justice, liberty, and concord, in a way that has made it natural and consistent for you to have acted, as we have seen you act in the last seventeen years of your life. Let Englishmen be made not only to respect, but even to love you. When they think well of individuals in your native country, they will go nearer to thinking well of your country; and when your countrymen see themselves well thought of by Englishmen, they will go nearer to thinking well of England. Extend your views even further; do not stop at those who speak the English tongue, but after having settled so many points in nature and politics, think of bettering the whole race of men.

As I have not read any part of the life in question, but know only the character that lived it, I write some what at hazard.[1] I am sure however, that the life, and the treatise I allude to (on the *Art of Virtue*), will necessarily fulfil the chief of my expectations; and still more so if you take up the measure of suiting these performances to the several views above stated. Should they even prove unsuccessful in all that a sanguine admirer of yours hopes from them, you will at least have framed pieces to interest the human mind; and whoever gives a feeling of pleasure that is innocent to man, has added so much to the fair side of a life otherwise too much darkened by anxiety, and too much injured by pain.

In the hope therefore that you will listen to the prayer addressed to you in this letter, I beg to subscribe myself, my dearest Sir, &c. &c.
Signed   BENJ. VAUGHAN.

Continuation of the Account of my Life.
Begun at Passy[2] 1784

It is some time since I receiv'd the above Letters, but I have been too busy till now to think of complying with the Request they contain. It might too be much better done if I were at home among my Papers, which would aid my Memory, & help to ascertain Dates. But my Return being uncertain, and having just now a little Leisure, I will endeavour to recollect & write what I can; If I live to get home, it may there be corrected and improv'd.

Not having any Copy here of what is already written, I know not whether an Account is given of the means I used to establish the Philadelphia publick Library, which, from a small Beginning is now become so considerable, though I remember to have come down to near the Time of that Transaction, 1730. I will therefore begin here, with an Account of it, which may be struck out if found to have been already given.—

At the time I establish'd my self in Pensylvania, there was not a good Bookseller's Shop in any of the Colonies to the Southward of Boston. In New-York & Philadelphia the Printers were indeed Stationers, they sold only Paper, &c. Almanacks,[3] Ballads, and a few common School Books. Those who lov'd Reading were oblig'd to send for their Books from England.—The Members of the Junto had each a few. We had left the Alehouse where we first met, and hired a Room to hold our Club in. I propos'd that we should all of us bring our Books to that Room, where they would not only be ready to consult in our Conferences, but become a common Benefit, each of us being at Liberty to borrow such as he wish'd to read at home. This was accordingly done, and for some time contented us. Finding the Advantage of this little Collection, I propos'd to render the Benefit from Books more common by commencing a Public Subscription Library. I drew a Sketch of the Plan and Rules that would be necessary, and got a skilful Conveyancer Mr Charles Brockden to put the whole in Form of Articles of Agreement to be subscribed, by which each Subscriber engag'd to pay a certain Sum down for the first Purchase of Books and an annual Contribution for encreasing them.—So few were the Readers at that time in Philadelphia, and the Majority of us so poor, that I was not able with great Industry to find more than Fifty Persons, mostly young Tradesmen, willing to pay down for this purpose Forty shillings each, & Ten Shillings per Annum. On this

---

[1] *at hazard* I.e., running the risk of being mistaken in his assumptions about the *Autobiography*.

[2] *Passy* Wealthy suburb of Paris in which Franklin and his grandson resided while he was working as U.S. Minister to France.

[3] *Almanacks* Annual publications including calendars and predictions for the agricultural year.

little Fund we began. The Books were imported. The Library was opened one Day in the Week for lending to the Subscribers, on their Promisory Notes to pay Double the Value if not duly returned. The Institution soon manifested its Utility, was imitated by other Towns and in other Provinces, the Librarys were augmented by Donations, Reading became fashionable, and our People having no publick Amusements to divert their Attention from Study became better acquainted with Books, and in a few Years were observ'd by Strangers to be better instructed & more intelligent than People of the same Rank generally are in other Countries.—

When we were about to sign the above-mentioned Articles, which were to be binding on us, our Heirs, &c for fifty Years, Mr Brockden, the Scrivener, said to us, "You are young Men, but it is scarce probable that any of you will live to see the Expiration of the Term fix'd in this Instrument." A Number of us, however, are yet living: But the Instrument was after a few Years rendred null by a Charter that incorporated & gave Perpetuity to the Company.—

The Objections, & Reluctances I met with in Soliciting the Subscriptions, made me soon feel the Impropriety of presenting one's self as the Proposer of any useful Project that might be suppos'd to raise one's Reputation in the smallest degree above that of one's Neighbours, when one has need of their Assistance to accomplish that Project. I therefore put my self as much as I could out of sight, and stated it as a Scheme of *a Number of Friends*, who had requested me to go about and propose it to such as they thought Lovers of Reading. In this way my Affair went on more smoothly, and I ever after practis'd it on such Occasions; and, from my frequent Successes, can heartily recommend it. The present little Sacrifice of your Vanity will afterwards be amply repaid. If it remains a while uncertain to whom the Merit belongs, some one more vain than yourself will be encourag'd to claim it, and then even Envy will be dispos'd to do you Justice, by plucking those assum'd Feathers, & restoring them to their right Owner.

This Library afforded me the Means of Improvement by constant Study, for which I set apart an Hour or two each Day; and thus repair'd in some Degree the Loss of the Learned Education my Father once intended for me. Reading was the only Amusement I allow'd my self. I spent no time in Taverns, Games, or Frolicks of any kind. And my Industry in my Business continu'd as indefatigable as it was necessary. I was in debt for my Printing-house, I had a young Family[1] coming on to be educated, and I had to contend with for Business two Printers who were establish'd in the Place before me. My Circumstances however grew daily easier: my original Habits of Frugality continuing. And My Father having among his Instructions to me when a Boy, frequently repeated a Proverb of Solomon, "*Seest thou a Man diligent in his Calling, he shall stand before Kings, he shall not stand before mean Men.*"[2] I from thence consider'd Industry as a Means of obtaining Wealth and Distinction, which encourag'd me; tho' I did not think that I should ever literally stand before Kings, which however has since happened.—for I have stood before five,[3] & even had the honour of sitting down with one, the King of Denmark, to Dinner.

We have an English Proverb that says,

He that would thrive
Must ask his Wife;

it was lucky for me that I had one as much dispos'd to Industry & Frugality as my self. She assisted me chearfully in my Business, folding & stitching Pamphlets, tending Shop, purchasing old Linen Rags for the Paper-makers, &c &c. We kept no idle Servants, our Table was plain & simple, our Furniture of the cheapest. For instance my Breakfast was a long time Bread & Milk, (no Tea,) and I ate it out of a twopenny earthen Porringer with a Pewter Spoon. But mark how Luxury will enter Families, and make a Progress, in Spite of Principle. Being Call'd one Morning to Breakfast, I found it in a China Bowl with a Spoon of Silver. They had been bought for me without my Knowledge by my Wife, and had cost her the enormous Sum of three and

---

1   *a young Family* Franklin's first son, William Franklin, was born in 1730 to an unknown mother, and raised by Franklin and Read together. The couple had two more children: Francis Folger (1732–36), and Sarah (1743–1808).

2   *Seest thou … mean Men* See Proverbs 22.29.

3   *I have stood before five* Franklin met kings Louis XV (r. 1715–74) and Louis XVI (r. 1774–92) of France, George II (r. 1727–60) and George III (r. 1760–1820) of the United Kingdom, and Christian VII of Denmark and Norway (r. 1766–1808), who invited Franklin for dinner when both men were in London in 1768.

twenty Shillings, for which she had no other Excuse or Apology to make, but that she thought *her* Husband deserv'd a Silver Spoon & China Bowl as well as any of his Neighbours. This was the first Appearance of Plate[1] & China in our House, which afterwards in a Course of Years as our Wealth encreas'd, augmented gradually to several Hundred Pounds in Value.—

I had been religiously educated as a Presbyterian; and tho' some of the Dogmas of that Persuasion, such as the Eternal Decrees of God, Election, Reprobation,[2] &c. appear'd to me unintelligible, others doubtful, & I early absented myself from the Public Assemblies of the Sect, Sunday being my Studying-Day, I never was without some religious Principles; I never doubted, for instance, the Existence of the Deity, that he made the World, & govern'd it by his Providence; that the most acceptable Service of God was the doing Good to Man; that our Souls are immortal; and that all Crime will be punished & Virtue rewarded either here or hereafter; these I esteem'd the Essentials of every Religion, and being to be found in all the Religions we had in our Country I respected them all, tho' with different degrees of Respect as I found them more or less mix'd with other Articles which without any Tendency to inspire, promote or confirm Morality, serv'd principally to divide us & make us unfriendly to one another.— This Respect to all, with an Opinion that the worst had some good Effects, induc'd me to avoid all Discourse that might tend to lessen the good Opinion another might have of his own Religion; and as our Province increas'd in People and new Places of worship were continually wanted, & generally erected by voluntary Contribution, my Mite[3] for such purpose, whatever might be the Sect, was never refused.—

Tho' I seldom attended any Public Worship, I had still an Opinion of its Propriety, and of its Utility when rightly conducted, and I regularly paid my annual Subscription for the Support of the only Presbyterian Minister or Meeting we had in Philadelphia. He us'd

to visit me sometimes as a Friend, and admonish me to attend his Administrations, and I was now and then prevail'd on to do so, once for five Sundays successively. Had he been, *in my Opinion*, a good Preacher perhaps I might have continued, notwithstanding the occasion I had for the Sunday's Leisure in my Course of Study: But his Discourses were chiefly either polemic Arguments, or Explications of the peculiar Doctrines of our Sect, and were all to me very dry, uninteresting and unedifying, since not a single moral Principle was inculcated or enforc'd, their Aim seeming to be rather to make us Presbyterians than good Citizens. At length he took for his Text that Verse of the 4th Chapter of Philippians, *Finally, Brethren, Whatsoever Things are true, honest, just, pure, lovely, or of good report, if there be any virtue, or any praise, think on these Things*; & I imagin'd in a Sermon on such a Text, we could not miss of having some Morality: But he confin'd himself to five Points only as meant by the Apostle,[4] viz. 1. Keeping holy the Sabbath Day. 2. Being diligent in Reading the Holy Scriptures. 3. Attending duly the Publick Worship. 4. Partaking of the Sacrament.[5] 5. Paying a due Respect to God's Ministers.—These might be all good Things, but as they were not the kind of good Things that I expected from that Text, I despaired of ever meeting with them from any other, was disgusted, and attended his Preaching no more.— I had some Years before compos'd a little Liturgy or Form of Prayer for my own private Use, viz, in 1728. entitled, *Articles of Belief & Acts of Religion.*[6] I return'd to the Use of this, and went no more to the public Assemblies. My Conduct might be blameable, but I leave it without attempting farther to excuse it, my present purpose being to relate Facts, and not to make Apologies for them.—

It was about this time I conceiv'd the bold and arduous Project of arriving at moral Perfection. I wish'd to live without committing any Fault at any time; I would conquer all that either Natural Inclination,

---

[1] *Plate* I.e., silverware.

[2] *Eternal Decrees of God* God's eternal plan for and sovereign control over the universe; *Election* The Calvinist doctrine that God has predetermined the members of the "elect" (those whose souls will be saved upon death), without any reference to their earthly actions; *Reprobation* Eternal damnation.

[3] *Mite* Small donation.

[4] *the Apostle* The Apostle Paul, said to be the author of the Epistle to the Philippians.

[5] *Partaking of the Sacrament* I.e., participating in the ceremony of the Eucharist, the consuming of the bread and wine that are believed to be spiritual representations of the body and blood of Christ.

[6] *Articles of … Religion* Much of this private liturgy has survived in manuscript form.

Custom, or Company might lead me into. As I knew, or thought I knew, what was right and wrong, I did not see why I might not *always* do the one and avoid the other. But I soon found I had undertaken a Task of more Difficulty than I had imagined: While my Care was employ'd in guarding against one Fault, I was often surpriz'd by another. Habit took the Advantage of Inattention. Inclination was sometimes too strong for Reason. I concluded at length, that the mere speculative Conviction that it was our Interest to be compleatly virtuous, was not sufficient to prevent our Slipping, and that the contrary Habits must be broken and good Ones acquired and established, before we can have any Dependance on a steady uniform Rectitude of Conduct. For this purpose I therefore contriv'd the following Method.—

In the various Enumerations of the moral Virtues I had met with in my Reading, I found the Catalogue more or less numerous, as different Writers included more or fewer Ideas under the same Name. Temperance, for Example, was by some confin'd to Eating & Drinking, while by others it was extended to mean the moderating every other Pleasure, Appetite, Inclination or Passion, bodily or mental, even to our Avarice & Ambition. I propos'd to myself, for the sake of Clearness, to use rather more Names with fewer Ideas annex'd to each, than a few Names with more Ideas; and I included under Thirteen Names of Virtues all that at that time occurr'd to me as necessary or desirable, and annex'd to each a short Precept, which fully express'd the Extent I gave to its Meaning.—

These Names of Virtues with their Precepts were

1. TEMPERANCE.
Eat not to Dulness.
Drink not to Elevation.
2. SILENCE.
Speak not but what may benefit others or your self. Avoid trifling Conversation.
3. ORDER.
Let all your Things have their Places. Let each Part of your Business have its Time.
4. RESOLUTION.
Resolve to perform what you ought. Perform without fail what you resolve.

5. FRUGALITY.
Make no Expence but to do good to others or yourself: i.e. Waste nothing.
6. INDUSTRY.
Lose no Time.—Be always employ'd in something useful.—Cut off all unnecessary Actions.—
7. SINCERITY.
Use no hurtful Deceit.
Think innocently and justly; and, if you speak; speak accordingly.
8. JUSTICE.
Wrong none, by doing Injuries or omitting the Benefits that are your Duty.
9. MODERATION.
Avoid Extreams. Forbear resenting Injuries so much as you think they deserve.
10. CLEANLINESS.
Tolerate no Uncleanness in Body, Cloaths or Habitation.—
11. TRANQUILITY.
Be not disturbed at Trifles, or at Accidents common or unavoidable.
12. CHASTITY.
Rarely use Venery[1] but for Health or Offspring; Never to Dulness, Weakness, or the Injury of your own or another's Peace or Reputation.—
13. HUMILITY.
Imitate Jesus and Socrates.—

My intention being to acquire the *Habitude* of all these Virtues, I judg'd it would be well not to distract my Attention by attempting the whole at once, but to fix it on one of them at a time, and when I should be Master of that, then to proceed to another, and so on till I should have gone thro' the thirteen. And as the previous Acquisition of some might facilitate the Acquisition of certain others, I arrang'd them with that View as they stand above. *Temperance* first, as it tends to procure that Coolness & Clearness of Head, which is so necessary where constant Vigilance was to be kept up, and Guard maintained, against the unremitting Attraction of ancient Habits, and the Force of perpetual Temptations. This being acquir'd & establish'd, *Silence* would be more easy, and my Desire being to gain Knowledge at the same

---

[1] *use Venery* Have sex.

time that I improv'd in Virtue, and considering that in Conversation it was obtain'd rather by the Use of the Ears than of the Tongue, & therefore wishing to break a Habit I was getting into of Prattling, Punning, & Joking, which only made me acceptable to trifling Company, I gave *Silence* the second Place. This and the next, *Order*, I expected would allow me more Time for attending to my Project and my Studies; RESOLUTION once become habitual, would keep me firm in my Endeavours to obtain all the subsequent Virtues; *Frugality* & *Industry*, by freeing me from my remaining Debt, & producing Affluence & Independance would make more easy the Practice of *Sincerity* and *Justice*, &c. &c. Conceiving then that agreeable to the Advice of Pythagoras in his Golden Verses,[1] daily Examination would be necessary, I contriv'd the following Method for conducting that Examination.

I made a little Book in which I allotted a Page for each of the Virtues. I rul'd each Page with red Ink so as to have seven Columns, one for each Day of the Week, marking each Column with a Letter for the Day. I cross'd these Columns with thirteen red Lines, marking the Beginning of each Line with the first Letter of one of the Virtues, on which Line & in its proper Column I might mark by a little black Spot every Fault I found upon Examination, to have been committed respecting that Virtue upon that Day.

---

[1] [Franklin's note] *Let not the stealing God of Sleep surprize,*
Nor creep in Slumbers on thy weary Eyes,
Ere ev'ry Action of the former Day,
Strictly *thou dost, and* righteously *survey.*
With Rev'rence at thy own Tribunal stand,
And answer justly to thy own Demand.
Where have I been? In what have I transgrest?
What Good or Ill has this Day's Life exprest?
Where have I fail'd in what I ought to do?
In what to GOD, to Man, or to myself I owe?
Inquire severe whate'er from first to last,
From Morning's Dawn till Ev'nings Gloom has past.
If Evil were thy Deeds, repenting mourn,
And let thy Soul with strong Remorse be torn:
If Good, the Good with Peace of Mind repay,
And to thy secret Self with Pleasure say,
Rejoice, my Heart, for all went well to Day.
[The "Golden Verses" to which Franklin refers are a work of uncertain origin most famously published in Latin in 1494 by the Greek scholar Constantine Lascaris, and attributed to the ancient Greek philosopher Pythagoras (c. 570–c. 495 BCE); the lines included here are Franklin's own translation.]

Form of the pages.

		S.	M.	T.	W.	T.	F.	S.
	TEMPERANCE. EAT NOT TO DULLNESS; DRINK NOT TO ELEVATION.							
T.								
S.		*	*		*		*	
O.		* *	*	*		*	*	*
R.				*			*	
F.			*			*		
I.				*				
S.								
J.								
M.								
C.								
T.								
C.								
H.								

I determined to give a Week's strict Attention to each of the Virtues successively. Thus in the first Week my great Guard was to avoid every the least Offence against Temperance, leaving the other Virtues to their ordinary Chance, only marking every Evening the Faults of the Day. Thus if in the first Week I could keep my first Line marked T clear of Spots, I suppos'd the Habit of that Virtue so much strengthen'd and its opposite weaken'd, that I might venture extending my Attention to include the next, and for the following Week keep both Lines clear of Spots. Proceeding thus to the last, I could go thro' a Course compleat in Thirteen Weeks, and four Courses in a Year.—And like him who having a Garden to weed, does not attempt to eradicate all the bad Herbs at once, which would exceed his Reach and his Strength, but works on one of the Beds at a time, & having accomplish'd the first proceeds to a second; so I should have, (I hoped) the encouraging Pleasure of seeing on my Pages the Progress I made in Virtue, by clearing successively my Lines of their Spots, till in the End by a Number of Courses, I should be happy in viewing a clean Book after a thirteen Weeks daily Examination.

This my little Book had for its Motto these Lines from *Addison's Cato*;

Here will I hold: If there is a Pow'r above us,
(And that there is, all Nature cries aloud
Thro' all her Works) he must delight in Virtue,
And that which he delights in must be happy.[1]

Another from *Cicero*.

O Vitæ Philosophia Dux! O Virtutum indagatrix, expul-
trixque vitiorum! Unus dies bene, & ex preceptis tuis
actus, peccanti immortalitati est anteponendus.[2]

Another from the Proverbs of Solomon speaking of
Wisdom or Virtue;

Length of Days is in her right hand, and in her Left
Hand Riches and Honours; Her Ways are Ways of
Pleasantness, and all her Paths are Peace.[3] III, 16, 17.

And conceiving God to be the Fountain of Wisdom,
I thought it right and necessary to solicit his Assistance
for obtaining it; to this End I form'd the following little
Prayer, which was prefix'd to my Tables of Examination;
for daily Use.

O powerful Goodness! bountiful Father! merciful Guide!
Increase in me that Wisdom which discovers my truest
Interests; Strengthen my Resolutions to perform what
that Wisdom dictates. Accept my kind Offices to thy other
Children, as the only Return in my Power for thy con-
tinual Favours to me.

I us'd also sometimes a little Prayer which I took
from *Thomson's* Poems. viz

Father of Light and Life, thou Good supreme,
O teach me what is good, teach me thy self!
Save me from Folly, Vanity and Vice,
From every low Pursuit, and fill my Soul

With Knowledge, conscious Peace, & Virtue pure,
Sacred, substantial, neverfading Bliss![4]

The Precept of *Order* requiring that *every Part of
my Business should have its allotted Time,* one Page
in my little Book contain'd the following Scheme of
Employment for the Twenty-four Hours of a natural
Day,

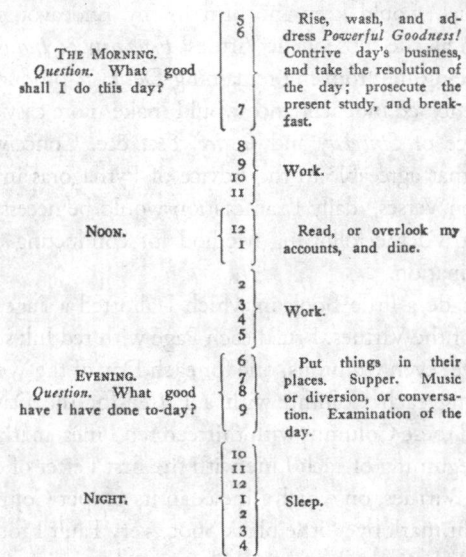

THE MORNING. *Question.* What good shall I do this day?	5 6 7	Rise, wash, and address *Powerful Goodness!* Contrive day's business, and take the resolution of the day; prosecute the present study, and breakfast.
	8 9 10 11	Work.
NOON.	12 1	Read, or overlook my accounts, and dine.
	2 3 4 5	Work.
EVENING. *Question.* What good have I have done to-day?	6 7 8 9	Put things in their places. Supper. Music or diversion, or conversation. Examination of the day.
NIGHT.	10 11 12 1 2 3 4	Sleep.

I enter'd upon the Execution of this Plan for Self
Examination, and continu'd it with occasional
Intermissions for some time. I was surpriz'd to find
myself so much fuller of Faults than I had imagined,
but I had the Satisfaction of seeing them diminish. To
avoid the Trouble of renewing now & then my little
Book, which by scraping out the Marks on the Paper
of old Faults to make room for new Ones in a new
Course, became full of Holes: I transferr'd my Tables
& Precepts to the Ivory Leaves of a Memorandum
Book, on which the Lines were drawn with red Ink
that made a durable Stain, and on those Lines I mark'd
my Faults with a black Lead Pencil, which Marks I
could easily wipe out with a wet Sponge. After a while
I went thro' one Course only in a Year, and afterwards
only one in several Years; till at length I omitted them
entirely, being employ'd in Voyages & Business abroad
with a Multiplicity of Affairs, that interfered. But I

---

[1]   *Here will ... be happy*   See Joseph Addison's 1713 play *Cato, A Tragedy*, 5.1.15–18.

[2]   *O Vitæ ... est anteponendus*   Latin: O philosophy, guide of life! O searcher out of virtue and exterminator of vice! One day spent well and in accordance with thy precepts is worth an immortality of sin; partial quotation from Roman philosopher Marcus Tullius Cicero's *Tusculan Disputations* (c. 45 BCE), translated here by Frank Woodworth Pine (1916).

[3]   *Length of ... are Peace*   See Proverbs 3.16–17; the Book of Proverbs is traditionally attributed to King Solomon.

[4]   *Father of ... neverfading Bliss!*   See James Thomson's 1726 poem *The Seasons*, "Winter," lines 218–23.

always carried my little Book with me. My Scheme of ORDER, gave me the most Trouble, and I found, that tho' it might be practicable where a Man's Business was such as to leave him the Disposition of his Time, that of a Journey-man Printer for instance, it was not possible to be exactly observ'd by a Master, who must mix with the World, and often receive People of Business at their own Hours.—Order too, with regard to Places for Things, Papers, &c. I found extreamly difficult to acquire. I had not been early accustomed to it, & having an exceeding good Memory, I was not so sensible of the Inconvenience attending Want of Method. This Article therefore cost me so much painful Attention & my Faults in it vex'd me so much, and I made so little Progress in Amendment, & had such frequent Relapses, that I was almost ready to give up the Attempt, and content my self with a faulty Character in that respect. Like the Man who in buying an Ax of a Smith my Neighbour, desired to have the whole of its Surface as bright as the Edge; the Smith consented to grind it bright for him if he would turn the Wheel. He turn'd while the Smith press'd the broad Face of the Ax hard & heavily on the Stone, which made the Turning of it very fatiguing. The Man came every now & then from the Wheel to see how the Work went on; and at length would take his Ax as it was without farther Grinding. No, said the Smith, Turn on, turn on; we shall have it bright by and by; as yet 'tis only speckled. Yes, says the Man; but—*I think I like a speckled Ax best.*—And I believe this may have been the Case with many who having for want of some such Means as I employ'd found the Difficulty of obtaining good, & breaking bad Habits, in other Points of Vice & Virtue, have given up the Struggle, & concluded that *a speckled Ax was best.* For something, that pretended to be Reason was every now and then suggesting to me, that such extream Nicety as I exacted of my self might be a kind of Foppery[1] in Morals, which, if it were known would make me ridiculous; that a perfect Character might be attended with the Inconvenience of being envied and hated; and that a benevolent Man should allow a few Faults in himself, to keep his Friends in Countenance. In Truth I found myself incorrigible with respect to *Order*; and now I am grown old, and

my Memory bad, I feel very sensibly[2] the want of it. But on the whole, tho' I never arrived at the Perfection I had been so ambitious of obtaining, but fell far short of it, yet I was by the Endeavour made a better and a happier Man than I otherwise should have been, if I had not attempted it; As those who aim at perfect Writing by imitating the engraved Copies, tho' they never reach the wish'd for Excellence of those Copies, their Hand[3] is mended by the Endeavour, and is tolerable while it continues fair & legible.—

And it may be well my Posterity should be informed, that to this little Artifice, with the Blessing of God, their Ancestor ow'd the constant Felicity of his Life down to his 79th Year in which this is written. What Reverses may attend the Remainder is in the Hand of Providence: But if they arrive the Reflection on past Happiness enjoy'd ought to help his Bearing them with more Resignation. To *Temperance* he ascribes his long-continu'd Health, & what is still left to him of a good Constitution; to *Industry* and *Frugality* the early Easiness of his Circumstances, & Acquisition of his Fortune, with all that Knowledge that enabled him to be a useful Citizen, and obtain'd for him some Degree of Reputation among the Learned. To *Sincerity* & *Justice* the Confidence of his Country, and the honourable Employs it conferr'd upon him. And to the joint Influence of the whole Mass of the Virtues, even in the imperfect State he was able to acquire them, all that Evenness of Temper, & that Chearfulness in Conversation which makes his Company still sought for, & agreable even to his younger Acquaintance. I hope therefore that some of my Descendants may follow the Example & reap the Benefit.—

It will be remark'd that, tho' my Scheme was not wholly without Religion there was in it no Mark of any of the distinguishing Tenets of any particular Sect.—I had purposely avoided them; for being fully persuaded of the Utility and Excellency of my Method, and that it might be serviceable to People in all Religions, and intending some time or other to publish it, I would not have any thing in it that should prejudice any one of any Sect against it.—I purposed writing a little Comment on each Virtue, in which I would have shown the Advantages of possessing it, & the Mischiefs attending

---

[1] *Nicety* Fastidiousness; *Foppery* Excessive vanity or affectation.

[2] *sensibly* Strongly.

[3] *Hand* I.e., handwriting.

its opposite Vice; and I should have called my Book the ART *of Virtue*, because it would have shown the *Means & Manner* of obtaining Virtue; which would have distinguish'd it from the mere Exhortation to be good, that does not instruct & indicate the Means; but is like the Apostle's Man of verbal Charity, who only, without showing to the Naked & the Hungry *how* or where they might get Cloaths or Victuals, exhorted them to be fed & clothed.[1] *James* II, 15, 16.——

But it so happened that my Intention of writing & publishing this Comment was never fulfilled. I did indeed, from time to time put down short Hints of the Sentiments, Reasonings, &c. to be made use of in it; some of which I have still by me: But the necessary close Attention to private Business in the earlier part of my Life, and public Business since, have occasioned my postponing it. For it being connected in my Mind with a *great and extensive Project* that required the whole Man to execute, and which an unforeseen Succession of Employs prevented my attending to, it has hitherto remain'd unfinish'd.——

In this Piece it was my Design to explain and enforce this Doctrine, that vicious Actions are not hurtful because they are forbidden, but forbidden because they are hurtful, the Nature of Man alone consider'd: That it was therefore every ones Interest to be virtuous, who wish'd to be happy even in this World. And I should from this Circumstance, there being always in the World a Number of rich Merchants, Nobility, States and Princes, who have need of honest Instruments for the Management of their Affairs, and such being so rare, have endeavoured to convince young Persons, that no Qualities were so likely to make a poor Man's Fortune as those of Probity & Integrity.

My List of Virtues contain'd at first but twelve: But a Quaker Friend having kindly inform'd me that I was generally thought proud; that my Pride show'd itself frequently in Conversation; that I was not content with being in the right when discussing any Point, but was overbearing & rather insolent; of which he convinc'd me by mentioning several Instances;——I determined endeavouring to cure myself if I could

of this Vice or Folly among the rest, and I added *Humility* to my List, giving an extensive Meaning to the Word.——I cannot boast of much Success in acquiring the *Reality* of this Virtue; but I had a good deal with regard to the *Appearance* of it.——I made it a Rule to forbear all direct Contradiction to the Sentiments of others, and all positive Assertion of my own. I even forbid myself agreable to the old Laws of our Junto, the Use of every Word or Expression in the Language that imported a fix'd Opinion; such as *certainly, undoubtedly,* &c. and I adopted instead of them, *I conceive, I apprehend,* or *I imagine* a thing to be so or so, or it so appears to me at present.——When another asserted something that I thought an Error, I deny'd my self the Pleasure of contradicting him abruptly, and of showing immediately some Absurdity in his Proposition; and in answering I began by observing that in certain Cases or Circumstances his Opinion would be right, but that in the present case there *appear'd* or *seem'd* to me some Difference, &c. I soon found the Advantage of this Change in my Manners. The Conversations I engag'd in went on more pleasantly. The modest way in which I propos'd my Opinions, procur'd them a readier Reception and less Contradiction; I had less Mortification when I was found to be in the wrong, and I more easily prevail'd with others to give up their Mistakes & join with me when I happen'd to be in the right. And this Mode, which I at first put on, with some violence to natural Inclination, became at length so easy & so habitual to me, that perhaps for these Fifty Years past no one has ever heard a dogmatical Expression escape me. And to this Habit (after my Character of Integrity) I think it principally owing, that I had early so much Weight with my Fellow Citizens, when I proposed new Institutions, or Alterations in the old; and so much Influence in public Councils when I became a Member. For I was but a bad Speaker, never eloquent, subject to much Hesitation in my choice of Words, hardly correct in Language, and yet I generally carried my Points.[2]——

In reality there is perhaps no one of our natural Passions so hard to subdue as *Pride*. Disguise it, struggle with it, beat it down, stifle it, mortify it as much as one pleases, it is still alive, and will every now and then peep out and show itself. You will see it perhaps often

---

1   *the Apostle's ... clothed*   See James 2.15–16: "If a brother or sister be naked, and destitute of daily food, And one of you say unto them, Depart in peace, be ye warmed and filled; notwithstanding ye give them not those things which are needful to the body; what doth it profit?"

2   *carried my Points*   Was successful in my arguments.

in this History. For even if I could conceive that I had compleatly overcome it, I should probably be proud of my Humility.—

      Thus far written at Passy 1784

—1987 (WRITTEN 1771–90)

[The full text of Benjamin Franklin's *Autobiography* is included in the website component of this anthology.]

In Context

Portraits of Benjamin Franklin

David Martin, portrait of Benjamin Franklin, 1767. Scottish artist David Martin painted this portrait of Franklin while he was in London protesting British taxation of the colonies. Franklin is overlooked by a bust of Isaac Newton (1643–1727), the famed English mathematician and physicist.

Line engraving by Augustin de Saint-Aubin, after Charles Nicolas Cochin, 1777. The caption under his name reads, "Born in Boston, in New England, on 17 January 1706."

Joseph Siffred Duplessis, portrait of Benjamin Franklin, c. 1785. Likely the most famous portrait of Franklin, this was painted by the well-known French portrait artist Duplessis while Franklin was living in Passy, shortly before his replacement as minister plenipotentiary to France by Thomas Jefferson.

Louis Joseph Masquelier, *Mirabeau Arrive Aux Champs Élisées* ("Mirabeau Arrives at the Elysian Fields"), 1792. This remarkable engraving depicts the recently deceased French revolutionary politician the Comte de Mirabeau, who had eulogized Franklin in June 1790, arriving at the Elysian Fields, the location of the afterlife for virtuous and heroic individuals in Greek mythology. Benjamin Franklin offers Mirabeau a crown of laurels; they are surrounded by other eminent men of the eighteenth century, including French philosophers Jean-Jacques Rousseau and Voltaire.

Benjamin West, *Benjamin Franklin Drawing Electricity from the Sky*, c. 1816. This posthumous portrait commemorates Franklin's famous 1753 kite experiment, in which he proved that lightning is derived from electricity. Franklin is surrounded by *putti*: symbolic figures, commonly found in European art from the Renaissance to the nineteenth century, that can represent various passions, states of being, or mental faculties. West (who had been a friend of Franklin's) is also known for his historical paintings depicting events such as the 1759 Battle of Quebec, and political paintings such as that commemorating the signing of the Treaty of Paris in 1783.

Samson Occom

1723 – 1792

Today, the Mohegan minister Samson Occom is best known for his autobiographical narrative, a rhetorically powerful account of his life as an Indigenous leader skilled in the language, and following the religion, of the English settlers. In his own lifetime, he was a famous and admired preacher whose books were popular and influential across racial and cultural lines. He was also an accomplished community leader, forming diplomatic connections between tribes and using his knowledge of settler legal and political systems to preserve the independence and land rights of Native Americans.

Samson Occom was born in 1723 in Ben's Town, Connecticut, to Joshua Occom, a prominent Mohegan, and Sarah Samson, a descendant of Pequot leaders. Occom was educated in the skills of hunting and fishing, as well as in the arts, particularly oratory and the interpretation of wampum.[1] He also taught himself to read and write in English. Occom was raised with traditional Mohegan spiritual beliefs, but the evangelical movement known as the Great Awakening brought changes to his family's religious life. His mother converted to Christianity in 1739, and Occom had his own conversion experience at eighteen, when he heard the preaching of Great Awakening radical John Davenport.

In 1742, Occom joined the Mohegan Tribal Council, and, in an effort to become a more effective advocate for his people, he sought further education. He approached the white minister Eleazar Wheelock, who taught Occom higher skills in English, as well as Greek, Latin, and Hebrew. Occom's success inspired Wheelock to found Moor's Indian Charity School, whose curriculum included Bible study and writing skills in classical languages as well as English. Occom helped to recruit Indigenous students for the new school, but difficulties with his eyesight prevented him from attending Yale as planned.

In 1749, Occom established himself as a schoolteacher in Montauk, Long Island, where he also served the Montaukett people in various ways: as a minister; as a healer practicing local Indigenous medicine; and as a judge and counselor resolving community disputes. At first he received no compensation for this work, and later he was given a salary far below what would have been offered to a white minister in the same position. While Great Awakening theology presented black and Indigenous people as the spiritual equals of white people, this view was largely not upheld in practice by the movement's white leadership, many of whom felt that, as Wheelock claimed, "an Indian Missionary may be supported with less than half the expense, that will be necessary to support an Englishman." To supplement his paltry missionary income, Occom labored as a woodworker, bookbinder, farmer, hunter, and fisher.

The financial pressures on Occom increased after he married Mary Fowler, a woman from a powerful Montaukett family, in 1751; the couple would eventually have twelve children. Through his marriage, Occom joined the Montaukett community, and he described some of their cultural practices in "An Account of the Montauk Indians, on Long-Island" (1761, published 1809). Although he lived among the Montaukett, Occom maintained his leadership role as a Mohegan. In particular, he was for decades an important player in the Mason Case, a drawn-out and controversial legal battle against the Connecticut Colony regarding the sale of Mohegan territory to settlers. Occom, like many other Mohegan, objected to settler encroachment on communal lands, arguing that pre-existing treaties and deeds made the sales

---

[1] Wampum, shell beads, are used for many purposes including trade and record keeping. The white and purple beads are arranged in belts or strands to form patterns that can be interpreted by an expert reader.

illegal. The dispute lasted for much of the eighteenth century, and was, in the end, decided in favor of the colony.

At Wheelock's urging, in 1765 Occom undertook a two-year trip to Britain to raise funds for the Indian Charity School. The decision to send him was controversial, with white religious leaders either questioning Occom's authenticity as an example of a converted "heathen" or claiming he did not really have the skills of a minister: as Occom phrased it in a letter to Wheelock, "some say I can't talk Indian, others say I can't read." In response to these accusations, Occom produced "The True Account of My Education," the first draft of his famous autobiographical narrative. His career remained a subject of controversy, however, and two years later he felt compelled to write a significantly expanded version of the autobiography.

During his preaching tour of Britain, Occom was treated, he later wrote, as a "gazing stock" for curious audiences—but his oratorical skill made his trip an unqualified success. He met prominent religious and political figures including the king, rejected an invitation from the archbishop of Canterbury to join the Anglican Church, and befriended the influential Great Awakening evangelist George Whitefield. He returned to America having raised a remarkable twelve thousand pounds for the Charity School—only to discover that Wheelock instead planned to spend the money on the foundation of Dartmouth College, which would, almost exclusively, serve white students. Meanwhile, Wheelock had not followed through on his promise to look after Occom's family, who were destitute and starving. Disillusioned, Occom left the missionary society and cut his ties to Wheelock.

As an independent traveling preacher, Occom continued to develop his oratorical style. While his sermons of the 1750s and 60s tend to offer straightforward explication of Bible verses, his later sermons expand their interpretive scope, moving beyond individual moral applications to touch on wider cultural and political issues. This more sophisticated approach is exemplified in Occom's *A Sermon, Preached at the Execution of Moses Paul, an Indian* (1772). The occasion for the sermon was the execution of a Mohegan man, Moses Paul, for murder; Paul, who claimed that he had been sentenced by a racist court for a killing made in self-defense, had invited Occom to speak. Occom, preaching on the idea that "the wages of sin is death" (Romans 6.23), asked all the attending audience to consider their own imminent demise and punishment, urged Paul to accept salvation before his execution, and concluded by exhorting the Indigenous audience members in particular to forsake alcohol, which had been involved in the incident.

A Sermon, Preached at the Execution of Moses Paul was a significant event in both its oral and written forms. An impressive crowd of black, Indigenous, and white listeners gathered, according to the Hartford *Courant*, "as much excited to hear Mr. Occum preach, as to see the execution." The sermon was revised and published in book form—the only one of Occom's sermons to appear in print during his lifetime—and was among the most popular works of the decade, issued in nineteen editions. The work made Occom famous in New England; by 1773 he found he had "continual calls to preach both by the English and the Indians."

Occom followed his sermon with another, perhaps equally influential publication: *A Choice Collection of Hymns and Spiritual Songs* (1774). The collection of over 100 hymns featured work by prominent English writers such as Isaac Watts and John and Charles Wesley, selected from a substantial personal hymnal library Occom had gathered while in Britain. Alongside these appeared previously unpublished American hymns collected by Occom during his years of itinerant preaching; the book also includes hymns written by Occom himself. According to its subtitle, the hymnal was "Intended for the Edification of Sincere Christians, of All Denominations," and it helped establish a pattern for the nascent genre of interdenominational hymnals in America. The collection remained popular across the colonies into the nineteenth century, and "Throughout the Saviour's Life We Trace," one of Occom's own contributions, remains a standard in many hymnals.

Also in the early 1770s, Occom began to work with his brother-in-law David Fowler to establish a new settlement, where Indigenous Christians from across New England could practice their religion and culture with minimal interference from Anglo-Americans. They negotiated a land grant from the Oneida in the colony of New York, and in the 1780s Occom and his family were among the hundreds of Indigenous Christians who emigrated to the new community, called Brotherton or Eeyamequittoowauconnuck. As a resident, he continued to advocate on behalf of the settlement, at one point successfully petitioning the government to restore two thousand acres that had been illegally leased to white occupants. In the nineteenth century, Brotherton was relocated to Wisconsin, where it remains a distinct Indigenous community.

Occom moved to New Stockbridge, near Brotherton, less than a year before his death in 1792. He maintained his status as a community leader up to the end of his life, preaching to both white and Indigenous audiences multiple times a week, and hundreds of people attended his funeral. The extent of his literary importance, however, was not widely recognized until the late twentieth century. In the 1980s, Bernd Peyer rediscovered Occom's autobiographical narrative and published it for the first time, presenting him as "the 'father' of modern Native American literature"; later in the century, LaVonne Brown Ruoff identified *A Sermon, Preached at the Execution of Moses Paul* as the first bestseller by an Indigenous American. Since then, scholarship has often focused on Occom's status as a cross-cultural figure; while some critics interpret his adoption of Christianity and English literary arts as a loss of his own Indigenous culture, others admire what they see as his savvy deployment of Anglo-American ideas and rhetorical strategies in defense of Indigenous communities and ways of life.

NOTE ON THE TEXTS: The text of the autobiographical narrative, unpublished in Occom's lifetime, is based upon the original manuscript, scans of which are available online at The Occom Circle, while the text of "The Sufferings of Christ" is based upon that appearing in the first edition of *A Choice Collection of Hymns and Spiritual Songs* (1774). Spelling and punctuation have been modernized according to the practices of this anthology.

⌘⌘⌘

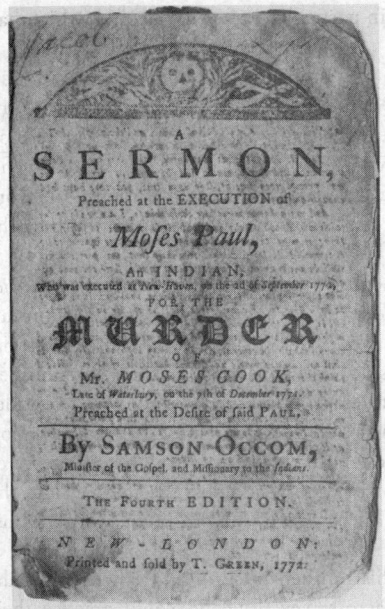 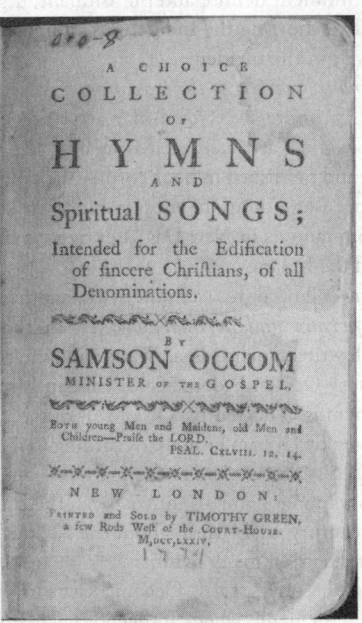

Title pages of *A Sermon Preached at the Execution of Moses Paul* (fourth edition, 1772) and *A Choice Collection of Hymns and Spiritual Songs* (third edition, 1774).

[Autobiographical Narrative]

Having seen and heard several representations, in England and Scotland, made by some gentlemen in America, concerning me, and finding many gross mistakes in their account—I thought it my duty to give a short plain and honest account of myself, that those who may hereafter see it, may know the truth concerning me.

FROM MY BIRTH TILL I RECEIVED THE CHRISTIAN RELIGION

I was born a heathen and brought up in heathenism, till I was between 16 and 17 years of age, at a place called Mohegan, in New London, Connecticut, in New England. My parents lived a wandering life, as did all the Indians at Mohegan; they chiefly depended upon hunting, fishing, and fowling for their living and had no connection with the English, excepting to [traffic] with them in their small trifles—and they strictly maintained and followed their heathenish ways, customs and religion—though there was some preaching among them. Once a fortnight, in the summer season, a minister from N[ew] London used to come up, and the Indians to attend; not that they regarded[1] the Christian religion, but they had blankets given to them every fall of the year, and for these things they would attend. And there was a sort of school kept, when I was quite young, but I believe there never was one that ever learned to read anything.[2] And when I was about 10 years of age there was a man who went about among the Indian wigwams, and where ever he could find the Indian children, would make them read; but the children used to take care to keep out of his way; and he used to catch me sometimes and make me say over my letters; and I believe I learnt some of them. But this was soon over too—and all this time there was not one amongst us, that made a profession of Christianity. Neither did we cultivate our land, nor kept any sort of creatures except dogs, which we used in hunting; and we dwelt in wigwams. These are a sort of tents, covered with mats made of flags.[3] And to this time we were unacquainted with the English tongue in general, though there were a few, who understood a little of it.

FROM THE TIME OF OUR REFORMATION TILL I LEFT MR. WHEELOCK[4]

When I was 16 years of age, we heard a strange rumor among the English, that there were extraordinary ministers preaching from place to place and a strange concern among the white people. This was in the spring of the year. But we saw nothing of these things, till some time in the summer, when some ministers began to visit us and preach the word of god; and the common people also came frequently and exhorted us to the things of god. Which it pleased the lord, as I humbly hope, to bless and accompany with divine influence to the conviction and saving conversion of a number of us; amongst whom I was one that was impressed with the things we had heard. These preachers did not only come to us, but we frequently went to their meetings and churches. Constantly, after I was awakened and converted, I went to all the meetings I could come at; and continued under trouble of mind about 6 months; at which time I began to learn the English letters; got me a primer and used to go to my English neighbours frequently for assistance in reading, but went to no school. And when I was 17 years of age, I had, as I trust, a discovery of the way of salvation through Jesus, and was enabled to put my trust in him alone for life and salvation. From this time the distress and burden of my mind was removed, and I found serenity and pleasure of soul, in serving god. By this time I just began to read in the New Testament without spelling[5]—and I had a stronger desire still to learn to read the word of god, and at the same time had an uncommon pity and compassion to my poor brethren according to the flesh. I used to wish I was capable of instructing my poor kindred. I used to think, if I could once learn to read I would instruct the poor children in reading—and used frequently to talk with our Indians concerning

---

[1] *regarded* Respected or cared about.

[2] *there never … anything* I.e., no one who attended the school learned to read.

[3] *flags* Rushes, or grasslike plants.

[4] MR. WHEELOCK Eleazar Wheelock (1711–79), Connecticut minister and educator.

[5] *without spelling* I.e., easily; without having to pronounce the individual letters.

religion. Thus I continued till I was in my 19th year: by this time I could read a little in the Bible. At this time my poor mother was going to Lebanon, and having had some knowledge of Mr. Wheelock and hearing he had a number of English youth under his tuition, I had a great inclination to go to him and be with him a week or a fortnight,[1] and desired my mother to ask Mr. Wheelock whether he would take me a little while to instruct me in reading. Mother did so, and when she came back, she said Mr. Wheelock wanted to see me as soon as possible. So I went up, thinking I should be back again in a few days; when I got up there, he received me with kindness and compassion and in stead of staying a fortnight or 3 weeks, I spent 4 years with him.

After I had been with him some time, he began to acquaint his friends of my being with him, and of his intentions of educating me, and my circumstances. And the good people began to give some assistance to Mr. Wheelock, and gave me some old and some new clothes. Then he represented the case to the honorable commissioners at Boston, who were commissioned by the Honorable Society in London for Propagating the Gospel among the Indians in New England and parts adjacent, and they allowed him 60£ in old tenor,[2] which was about 6£ sterling, and they continued it 2 or 3 years, I can't tell exactly. While I was at Mr. Wheelock's, I was very weakly and my health much impaired, and at the end of 4 years, I over strained my eyes to [such a] degree, I could not pursue my studies any longer; and out of these 4 years I lost just about one year—and was obliged to quit my studies.

FROM THE TIME I LEFT MR. WHEELOCK TILL I WENT TO EUROPE

As soon as I left Mr. Wheelock, I endeavoured to find some employ among the Indians; went to Nahantuck,[3] thinking they may want a school master, but they had one; then went to Narraganset,[4] and they were indifferent about school, and went back to Mohegan, and heard a number of our Indians were going to Montauk, on Long Island, and I went with them. And the Indians there were very desirous to have me keep a school amongst them, and I consented, and went back a while to Mohegan; and some[time] in November I went on the island, I think it is 17 years ago last November. I agreed to keep school with them half a year, and left it with them to give me what they pleased; and they took turns to provide food for me. I had near 30 scholars this winter; I had evening school too for those that could not attend the day school— and began to carry on their meetings, though they had a minister, one Mr. Horton, the Scotch Society's[5] missionary; but he spent, I think, two thirds of his time at Shenecock, 30 miles from Montauk. We met together 3 times for divine worship every sabbath and once on every Wednesday evening. I read the scriptures to them and used to expound upon some particular passages in my own tongue;[6] visited the sick and attended their burials. When the half year expired, they desired me to continue with them, which I complied with, for another half year. When I had fulfilled that, they were urgent to have me stay longer, so I continued till I was married, which was about 2 years after I went there.

And continued to instruct them in the same manner as I did before. After I was married a while, I found there was need of a support more than I needed while I was single—and I made my case known to Mr. Buell and to Mr. Wheelock, and also the needy circumstances and the desires of these Indians of my continuing amongst them, and the commissioners were so good as to grant £15 per an. sterling—and I kept on in my service as usual, yea I had additional service. I kept school as I did before and carried on the religious meetings as often as ever, and attended the sick and their funerals, and did what writings they wanted, and often sat as a judge to reconcile and decide their matters between them, and had visitors of Indians from

---

[1]   *a fortnight*   Two weeks.

[2]   *old tenor*   I.e., Connecticut currency, which was worth much less than the British pound sterling; both types of money circulated in the colony.

[3]   *Nahantuck*   Also called Niantic, territory of the Niantic people on the Connecticut coast.

[4]   *Narraganset*   Territory of the Narragansett people on the coast of Rhode Island.

[5]   *Scotch Society*   The Scottish Society for the Propagation of Christian Knowledge, a missionary society.

[6]   *my own tongue*   Mohegan-Pequot, a language closely related to Montauk.

all quarters; and, as our custom is, we freely entertain all visitors. And was fetched often from my tribe and from others to see into their affairs both religious [and] temporal—besides my domestic concerns—and it pleased the Lord to increase my family fast. And soon after I was married, Mr. Horton left these Indians and the Shenecock Indians, and after this I was licenced to p[reach] and then I had the whole care of these Indians at Montauk, and visited the Shenecock Indians often. Used to set out Saturdays towards night and come back again Mondays. I have been obliged to set out from home after sun set, and ride 30 miles in the night, to preach to these Indians. And some Indians at Shenecock sent their children to my school at Montauk, I kept one of them some time, and had a young man a half year from Mohegan, a lad from Nahantuck, who was with me almost a year; and had little or nothing for keeping them.

My method in the school was, as soon as the children got together, and took their proper seats, I prayed with them, then began to hear them.[1] I generally began (after some of them could spell and read) with those that were yet in their alphabets, so around, as they were properly seated, till I got through, and I obliged them to study their books, and to help one another. When they could not make out a hard word they brought [it] to me—and I usually heard them, in the summer season 8 times a day, 4 in the morning, and in the afternoon. In the winter season 6 times a day, as soon as they could spell, they were obliged to spell when ever they wanted to go out. I concluded with prayer; I generally heard my evening scholars 3 times round, and as they go out the school, everyone that can spell is obliged to spell a word, and to go out leisurely one after another. I catechised[2] 3 or 4 times a week according to the assembly's shorter catechism, and many times proposed questions of my own, and in my own tongue. I found difficulty with some children, who were somewhat dull; most of these can soon learn to say over their letters, they distinguish the sounds by the ear, but their eyes can't distinguish the letters, and the way I took to cure them was by making an alphabet on small bits of paper, and glued them on small chips of cedar after this manner: A, B, etc. I put these on letters in order on a bench then point to one letter and bid a child to take notice of it, and then I order the child to fetch me the letter from the bench; if it brings the letter, it is well, if not it must go again and again till it brings the right letter. When they can bring any letters this way, then I just jumble them together, and bid them to set them in alphabetical order, and it is a pleasure to them; and they soon learn their letters this way.

I frequently discussed or exhorted my scholars, in religious matters. My method in our religious meetings was this: sabbath morning we assemble together about 10 o'c[lock] and begin with singing; we generally sung Dr. Watts's[3] psalms or hymns. I distinctly read the psalm or hymn first, and then gave the meaning of it to them, after that sing, then pray, and sing again after prayer. Then proceed to read some suitable portion of scripture, and so just give the plain sense of it in familiar discourse and apply it to them, so conclude with prayer and singing. In the after noon and evening we proceed in the same manner, and so in Wednesday evening. Some time after Mr. Horton left these Indians, there was a remarkable revival of religion among these Indians and many were hopefully converted to the saving knowledge of god in Jesus. It is to be observed before Mr. Horton left these Indians they had some prejudices infused in their minds, by some enthusiastical exhorters from New England, against Mr. Horton, and many of them had left him; by this means he was discouraged, and sued a dismission[4] and was dismissed from these Indians. And being acquainted with the enthusiasts in New England and the make and the disposition of the Indians, [I] took a mild way to reclaim them. I opposed them not openly but let them go on in their way, and whenever I had an opportunity, I would read such passages of the scriptures, and I thought would confound their notions, and I would come to them with all authority, saying, "thus saith the Lord"; and by this means, the Lord was pleased to bless my poor endeavours, and they were reclaimed, and brought to hear almost any of the ministers.

---

1   *hear them* I.e., hear them read or recite their lessons.

2   *catechised* Taught the fundamentals of religious belief, especially by questioning students with reference to a catechism, a book summarizing a religion's official theology.

3   *Dr. Watts* Isaac Watts (1674–1748), English minister best known as the author of numerous hymns.

4   *sued a dismission* Asked to be released from his post.

I am now to give an account of my circumstances and manner of living. I dwelt in a wigwam, a small hut with small poles and covered with mats made of flags, and I was obliged to move twice a year, about 2 miles distance, by reason of the scarcity of wood, for in one neck of land they planted their corn, and in another, they had their wood, and I was obliged to have my corn carted and my hay also—and I got my ground plowed every year, which cost me about 12 s[hillings] an acre; and I kept a cow and a horse, for which I paid 21 shillings every year York currency,[1] and went 18 miles to mill for every dust of meal we used in my family. I hired or joined with my neighbours to go to mill, with a horse or ox cart, or on horseback, and sometimes went myself. My family increasing fast, and my visitors also, I was obliged to contrive every way to support my family; I took all opportunities, to get something to feed my family daily. I planted my own corn, potatoes, and beans; I used to be out hoeing my corn sometimes before sun rise and after my school is dismissed, and by this means I was able to raise my own pork, for I was allowed to keep 5 swine. Some mornings and evenings I would be out with my hook and line to catch fish, and in the fall of year and in the spring, I used my gun, for we lived very handy for fowl, and I was very expert with [a] gun, and fed my family with fowl. I could more than pay for my powder and shot with feathers. At other times I bound old books for Easthampton people, made wooden spoons and ladles, stocked guns, and worked on cedar to make pails, piggins,[2] and churns etc. Besides all these difficulties I met with adverse providence: I bought a mare, had it but little while, and she fell into the quick sands and died. After a while bought another, I kept her about half year, and she was gone, and I never heard nor seen her from that day to this; it was supposed some rogue stole her. I got another and [it] died with a distemper, and last of all I bought a young mare, and kept her till she had one colt, and she broke her leg and died, and presently after the colt died also. In the whole I lost 5 horse kind; all these losses helped to pull me down; and by this time I got greatly in debt, and acquainted my circumstances to some of my friends, and they represented my case to the commissioners of Boston, and interceded with them for me, and they were pleased to vote [£]15 for my help, and soon after sent a letter to my good friend at N[ew] London, acquainting him that they had superseded[3] their vote; and my friends were so good as to represent my needy circumstances still to them, and they were so good at last, as to vote £15 and sent it, for which I am very thankful. And the Reverend Mr. Buell was so kind as to write in my behalf to the gentlemen of Boston; and he told me they were much displeased with him, and heard also once and again that they blamed me for being extravagant. I can't conceive how these gentlemen would have me live. I am ready to impute [it] to their ignorance, and I would wish they had changed circumstances with me but one month, that they may know by experience what my case really was; but I am now fully convinced, that it was not ignorance, for I believe it can be proved to the world that these same gentlemen gave a young missionary, a single man, *one hundred pounds* for one year, and fifty pounds for an interpreter, and thirty pounds for an introducer; so it cost them one hundred and eighty pounds in one single year, and they sent too where there was no need of a missionary.

Now you see what difference they made between me and other missionaries; they gave me 180 pounds for 12 years service, which they gave for one year's service in another mission. In my service (I speak like a fool,[4] but I am constrained) I was my own interpreter. I was both a school master and minister to the Indians, yea I was their ear, eye and hand, as well as mouth. I leave it with the world, as wicked as it is, to judge whether I ought not to have had half as much, they gave a young man just mentioned, which would have been but £50 a year; and if they ought to have given me that, I am not under obligations to them, I owe them nothing at all. What can be the reason that they used me after this manner? I can't think of anything, but this as a poor Indian boy said, who was bound out to an English family, and he used to drive plow for a young man, and he whipped and beat him almost every day, and the young man found fault with him, and complained of him to his master and the poor boy was called to

---

[1]   *York currency*   Money printed by the colony of New York.

[2]   *piggins*   Small buckets or deep ladles.

[3]   *superseded*   Suspended or retracted.

[4]   *I speak like a fool*   See 2 Corinthians 11.23: "Are they ministers of Christ? (I speak as a fool) I am more; in labours more abundant, in stripes above measure, in prisons more frequent, in deaths oft."

answer for himself before his master, and he was asked, what it was he did, that he was so complained of and beat almost every day. He said, he did not know, but he supposed it was because he could not drive any better; but says he, I drive as well as I know how; and at other times he beats me, because he is of a mind to beat me; but says he, I believe he beats [me] for the most of the time because I am an Indian.

So I am ready to say, they have used [me] thus, because I can't instruct the Indians so well as other missionaries; but I can assure *them* I have endeavoured to teach them as well as I [know] how—but I must say, I believe it is because I am a poor Indian. I can't help that god has made me so; I did not make my self so.—
—1982 (WRITTEN 1765, 1768)

The Sufferings of Christ

1

Throughout the Saviour's life we trace,
   Nothing but shame and deep disgrace,
No period else is seen;
Till he a spotless victim fell,
5 Tasting in soul a painful Hell,
Caused by the creature's sin.[1]

2

On the cold ground methinks I see
My Jesus kneel, and pray for me;
For this I him adore;
10 Seized with a chilly sweat throughout,
Blood-drops did force their passage out
Through ev'ry opened pore.

3

A pricking thorn his temples bore;
His back with lashes all was tore,
15 Till one the bones might see;
Mocking, they pushed him here and there,
Marking his way with blood and tear,
Pressed by the heavy tree.°   *cross*

4

Thus up the hill he painful came,
20 Round him they mock, and make their game,
At length his cross they rear;
And can you see the mighty God,
Cry out beneath sin's heavy load,
Without one thankful tear?

5

25 Thus veiled in humanity,
He dies in anguish on the tree;
What tongue his grief can tell?
The shudd'ring rocks their heads recline,
The mourning sun refuse to shine,
30 When the creator fell.

6

Shout, brethren, shout in songs divine,
He drank the gall, to give us wine,[2]
To quench our parching thirst;
Seraphs° advance your voices higher;   *angels*
35 Bride of the Lamb,[3] unite the choir,
And laud thy precious Christ.
—1774

---

1 *the creature's sin* The sin of created beings. According to most Christian theology, Jesus' crucifixion was a sacrifice made necessary by the sin committed by the first humans, Adam and Eve.

2 *drank the gall* See Matthew 27.34, in which the soldiers supervising Jesus' crucifixion give him "vinegar to drink mixed with gall"; *give us wine* In John 2.1–11, Jesus miraculously transforms water into wine.

3 *the Lamb* Jesus. The phrase "the bride, the Lamb's wife" appears in Revelation 21.9 and has been interpreted to refer to the city of heaven, to the soul, or to the Christian church as a whole.

Elm Bark Box

Samson Occom sent this decorated box, made from elm bark, to his sister Lucy in Mohegan; it is possible that he carved the box himself. The box documents his journey to Brotherton, a pantribal separatist community he was instrumental in helping to establish on former Oneida territory in the colony of New York. The pattern on the side of the box is called the "Trail of Life" or "Path of the Sun," reflecting both the cycle of life from birth to death and the course of the sun, from sunrise in the east to sunset in the west. The journey from Mohegan to Brotherton was also, literally, a movement westward, from Connecticut to New York. Markings on the top of the box represent each of the tribes from which the migrants to Brotherton originated.

—C. 1780S–1790S

J. Hector St. John de Crèvecoeur

1735 – 1813

At once intimately familiar with and yet in ways an outsider to American culture, French-born J. Hector St. John de Crèvecoeur earned renown in his life as an authority on Americanness, during the very years when the nation's political character was being challenged and defined. His *Letters from an American Farmer* (1782) vividly brought both the successes and the failures of American society to life for European audiences, and earned him a smaller but still substantial reputation in the country they depicted. Long interpreted as the literal thoughts of their creator, the *Letters*, written in the persona of Pennsylvania-born "Farmer James," have a complex reception history that has been shaped by changing tastes and political currents, and complicated by the fact that different and sometimes conflicting versions of the text were published during Crèvecoeur's lifetime. For over two centuries readers have struggled to reconcile the different sides of "Farmer James," who writes that America is "the most perfect society now existing in the world," but who concludes, upon witnessing the horrors of American slavery, that Americans "certainly are not that class of beings which we vainly think ourselves to be."

Born to members of the petty nobility in Normandy in 1735, Michel-Guillaume Jean de Crèvecoeur received an austere classical education under the tutorship of Catholic Jesuits in Caen, before moving to England in 1754 to live with distant relatives. He moved to French Canada the following year, after the untimely death of his English fiancée, and was employed by the French militia as a surveyor and map-maker during the French and Indian War. He became widely commended for his skills as a cartographer, but a battle wound and his subsequent disgrace after an undisclosed controversy led Crèvecoeur to again seek a different life. By late 1759 Crèvecoeur was making his way southwards to the British colonies, intent on making a living as an American farmer.

Though he did not settle immediately—spending approximately a decade working on an itinerant basis as a tradesperson and surveyor throughout New York, New England, and the Great Lakes region—by 1769 Crèvecoeur had become a British subject, had changed his name to James Hector St. John, and had purchased a large tract of land in Orange County, New York. It was shortly after his marriage to the Protestant Mehitable Tippett that Crèvecoeur began his work on a series of pieces reflecting upon the burgeoning American culture he now found himself a part of. When the American Revolution broke out in 1776, Crèvecoeur was conflicted; his wife's family were staunch Loyalists, but many of his other acquaintances supported the colonial rebels. Crèvecoeur himself decided to evade the conflict by heading back to France with his son in 1780, ostensibly with the aim of securing his children's inheritance—though he was hindered in his efforts by a few months' stint as British prisoner of war, on suspicion of being a Patriot spy.

Having eventually reached England, Crèvecoeur sought a publisher for his now-complete series of literary pieces in the popular eighteenth-century genre of epistolary writing. The collection aroused the interest of publisher Thomas Davies (a friend of Samuel Johnson), and *Letters from an American Farmer; Describing Certain Provincial Situations, Manners, and Customs Not Generally Known; and Conveying Some Idea of the Late and Present Interior Circumstances of the British Colonies in North America* was printed in London in 1782. The letters are narrated by the self-described "humble American Planter" Farmer James—a farmer in Pennsylvania rather than New York—and addressed to a "Mr. F.B.," a refined Englishman who is described as having visited Farmer James and his wife on their homestead, and who is said to be still curious about the state of affairs in the colonies. They describe a good deal of the culture, industry, geography, and politics of early America—and convey too a good deal of emotional content, as Mr. F.B. is said in Letter 2 to have requested: "… you used, in your refined style, to denominate me the farmer of feelings. How rude must those feelings be in him who daily holds the ax or the plough! … Those feelings, however, I will delineate as well as I can, agreeably to your earnest request."

With peace negotiations now well under way between Britain and the United States, Davies advertised the work as the unvarnished truth, asserting that the letters contained "much authentic information, little known on this side the Atlantic. They cannot, therefore, fail of being highly interesting, to the people of England, at a time when everybody's attention is directed toward the affairs of America." The collection was an immediate success in England. The *Letters*'s blend of sentimentality, romanticism, and Enlightenment political values rendered them highly interesting to a wide variety of audiences; a second edition was soon printed in London, and translations into Dutch and German ensued. Crèvecoeur's narrator both praises America as a farmer's paradise (and cultural melting pot) and condemns it as a place of horrendous enslavement and violent warfare, but many readers appeared to pay attention primarily to the more optimistic opening letters; indeed, the collection received some criticism on both sides of the Atlantic for what George Washington, otherwise an admirer of the work, described as a "too flattering" portrait of the nation.

Crèvecoeur soon returned to France, where he found himself a celebrity and began associating with members of the Parisian intellectual elite, while also working on a substantially altered French version of the *Lettres d'un Cultivateur Américain* (1784; 1787). Though he had appeared to harbor a degree of Loyalist sympathy while living in the rebelling colonies, here Crèvecoeur was embraced by the French as a specimen of an American Patriot, an image underscored by the intensely anti-British stance taken by many of the letters in the French-language edition. Largely abandoning the framing conceit of Farmer James, the French text provides a more explicitly philosophical exploration of Crèvecoeur's themes; the influence of French *philosophes* such as Rousseau and Voltaire is evident.

The growing tension between Crèvecoeur's French and American identities only increased when he was sent to the United States as a consul by the French government in 1783. Crèvecoeur's return to New York late that year was marked by tragedy: he found that his wife had been killed, his homestead destroyed in a raid, and that his two other children had barely escaped death themselves, and been taken in by strangers in Boston. After several politically successful but emotionally exhausting years working in the United States, Crèvecoeur eventually resigned from his French governmental position. He returned to France permanently in 1790.

The timing of his return was unfortunate. Once again, the pacifist Crèvecoeur was surrounded by political turmoil as the French Revolution took hold; many of his acquaintances were executed or sent into exile during the Reign of Terror in 1793–94. Crèvecoeur himself fled Paris for Germany. Later in the decade he supported himself by writing agricultural pamphlets in Normandy. His last major work, *Voyage dans la Haute-Pennsylvanie et dans l'état de New-York* (1801), was virtually ignored upon publication; some found the work's philosophical ambitiousness to be at odds with their vision of the quaint, artless sentimentality of Farmer James. Crèvecoeur died of heart complications in 1813.

In the decades following his death, *Letters from an American Farmer* fell into obscurity, remaining out of print for many decades. Some nineteenth-century critics admired it as a quaint historical curiosity; the 1856 *Cyclopaedia of American Literature* describes the text as "pleasing and agreeable" but "all sentiment and susceptibility … looking at homely American life in the Claude Lorraine glass of fanciful enthusiasm." New editions published in 1904 and 1912 signaled a revival of scholarly interest; still, the *Letters* were read primarily as interesting sociological documents rather than as literary works—although D.H. Lawrence in his 1923 *Studies in Classic American Literature* acknowledged Crèvecoeur as the emotional "prototype of the American." That year also saw the publication of *Sketches of Eighteenth Century America*, a collection of letters that had not made it into Crèvecoeur's original collection, though some of them had provided the basis for portions of the French *Lettres*.

It was only in the latter half of the twentieth century that literary scholars began to read the *Letters* with a view to their almost novelistic quality, acknowledging Crèvecoeur's Farmer James as a literary creation rather than as simply a version of his author, and taking into fuller consideration the thematic progression of the twelve letters considered as a whole. Interest among historians increased as well, as scholars came to see Crèvecoeur's influence on contemporary works such as Thomas Jefferson's *Notes on the State of Virginia* (1787), as well as on early sociological writings such as Alexis de Tocqueville's monumental *Democracy in America* (1835–40). In the twenty-first century scholarly interest has grown further, particularly in the wake of Dennis D. Moore's edition (2013), which brings together the twelve *Letters* with more than a dozen other essays by Crèvecoeur.

NOTE ON THE TEXT: The text presented below is based on the two earliest London editions of *Letters from an American Farmer; Describing Certain Provincial Situations, Manners, and Customs, Not Generally Known; and Conveying Some Idea of the Late and Present Interior Circumstances of the British Colonies in North America* (1782 and 1783); the 1783 edition includes numerous corrections made by the author. Various modern editions—notably Dennis D. Moore's *Letters from an American Farmer and Other Essays* (2013)—have also been consulted. Spelling and punctuation have been modernized in accordance with the practices of this anthology.

⌘ ⌘ ⌘

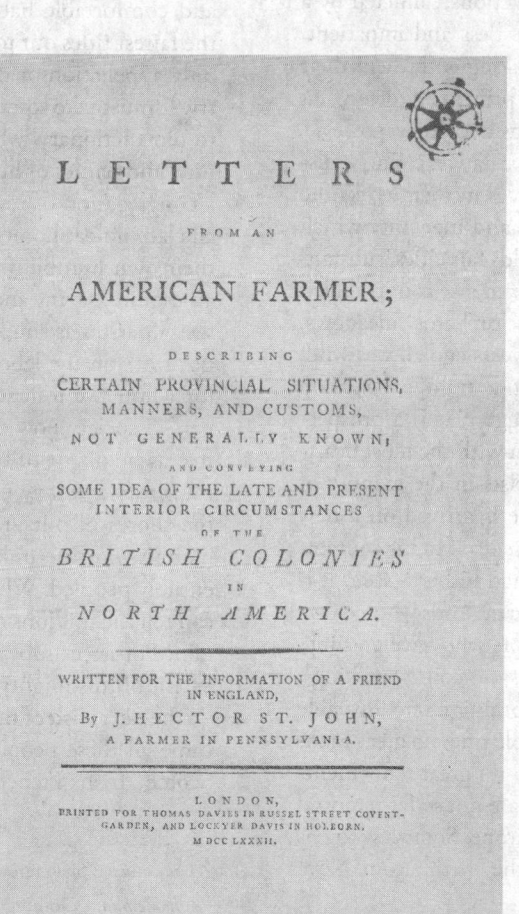

LETTERS

FROM AN

AMERICAN FARMER;

DESCRIBING

CERTAIN PROVINCIAL SITUATIONS,
MANNERS, AND CUSTOMS,

NOT GENERALLY KNOWN;

AND CONVEYING

SOME IDEA OF THE LATE AND PRESENT
INTERIOR CIRCUMSTANCES

OF THE

BRITISH COLONIES

IN

NORTH AMERICA.

WRITTEN FOR THE INFORMATION OF A FRIEND
IN ENGLAND,

By J. HECTOR ST. JOHN,
A FARMER IN PENNSYLVANIA.

LONDON,
PRINTED FOR THOMAS DAVIES IN RUSSEL STREET COVENT-
GARDEN, AND LOCKYER DAVIS IN HOLBORN.
M DCC LXXXII.

from *Letters from an American Farmer*

from Letter 3
What Is an American?

I wish I could be acquainted with the feelings and thoughts which must agitate the heart and present themselves to the mind of an enlightened Englishman when he first lands on this continent. He must greatly rejoice that he lived at a time to see this fair country discovered and settled; he must necessarily feel a share of national pride, when he views the chain of settlements which embellishes these extended shores. When he says to himself, "This is the work of my countrymen, who, when convulsed by factions,[1] afflicted by a variety of miseries and wants, restless and impatient, took refuge here. They brought along with them their national genius,[2] to which they principally owe what liberty they enjoy, and what substance they possess." Here he sees the industry of his native country displayed in a new manner, and traces in their works the embryos of all the arts, sciences, and ingenuity which flourish in Europe. Here he beholds fair cities, substantial villages, extensive fields, an immense country filled with decent houses, good roads, orchards, meadows, and bridges, where an hundred years ago all was wild, woody and uncultivated! What a train of pleasing ideas this fair spectacle must suggest; it is a prospect which must inspire a good citizen with the most heartfelt pleasure. The difficulty consists in the manner of viewing so extensive a scene. He is arrived on a new continent; a modern society offers itself to his contemplation, different from what he had hitherto seen. It is not composed, as in Europe, of great lords who possess everything, and of a herd of people who have nothing. Here are no aristocratical families, no courts, no kings, no bishops, no ecclesiastical dominion, no invisible power giving to a few a very visible one; no great manufacturers employing thousands, no great refinements of luxury. The rich and the poor are not so far removed from each other as they are in Europe. Some few towns excepted, we are all tillers of the earth, from Nova Scotia to West Florida. We are a people of cultivators, scattered over an immense territory, communicating with each other by means of good roads and navigable rivers, united by the silken bands of mild government, all respecting the laws, without dreading their power, because they are equitable. We are all animated with the spirit of an industry which is unfettered and unrestrained, because each person works for himself. If he travels through our rural districts he views not the hostile castle, and the haughty mansion, contrasted with the clay-built hut and miserable cabin, where cattle and men help to keep each other warm, and dwell in meanness, smoke, and indigence.[3] A pleasing uniformity of decent competence appears throughout our habitations. The meanest of our log-houses is a dry and comfortable habitation. Lawyer or merchant are the fairest titles our towns afford; that of a farmer is the only appellation of the rural inhabitants of our country. It must take some time ere he can reconcile himself to our dictionary, which is but short in words of dignity, and names of honour. There, on a Sunday, he sees a congregation of respectable farmers and their wives, all clad in neat homespun,[4] well mounted, or riding in their own humble wagons. There is not among them an esquire, saving the unlettered[5] magistrate. There he sees a parson as simple as his flock, a farmer who does not riot[6] on the labour of others. We have no princes for whom we toil, starve, and bleed; we are the most perfect society now existing in the world. Here man is free as he ought to be; nor is this pleasing equality so transitory as many others are. Many ages will not see the shores of our great lakes replenished with inland nations, nor the unknown bounds of North America entirely peopled. Who can tell how far it extends? Who can tell the millions of men whom it will feed and contain? For no European foot has as yet travelled half the extent of this mighty continent!

The next wish of this traveller will be to know whence came all these people. They are a mixture of English, Scotch, Irish, French, Dutch, Germans, and Swedes.

---

[1] *convulsed by factions*   I.e., distressed or agitated by disputes.

[2] *national genius*   I.e., the distinctive spirit and qualities of their respective nations.

[3] *meanness*   Shabbiness or squalor; *indigence*   Poverty.

[4] *homespun*   Clothing made from yarn or thread spun at home.

[5] *saving*   Except for; *unlettered*   Unsophisticated; having a limited education.

[6] *riot*   Make merry; live indulgently.

From this promiscuous[1] breed, that race now called Americans have arisen. The eastern provinces[2] must indeed be excepted, as being the unmixed descendants of Englishmen. I have heard many wish that they had been more intermixed also: for my part, I am no wisher, and think it much better as it has happened. They exhibit a most conspicuous figure in this great and variegated picture; they too enter for a great share in the pleasing perspective displayed in these thirteen provinces. I know it is fashionable to reflect on[3] them, but I respect them for what they have done; for the accuracy and wisdom with which they have settled their territory; for the decency of their manners; for their early love of letters;[4] their ancient college,[5] the first in this hemisphere; for their industry,[6] which to me who am but a farmer, is the criterion of everything. There never was a people, situated as they are, who with so ungrateful a soil have done more in so short a time. Do you think that the monarchical ingredients, which are more prevalent in other governments, have purged them from all foul stains? Their histories assert the contrary.

In this great American asylum,[7] the poor of Europe have by some means met together, and in consequence of various causes; to what purpose should they ask one another what countrymen they are? Alas, two thirds of them had no country. Can a wretch who wanders about, who works and starves, whose life is a continual scene of sore affliction or pinching penury;[8] can that man call England or any other kingdom his country? A country that had no bread for him, whose fields procured him no harvest, who met with nothing but the frowns of the rich, the severity of the laws, with jails and punishments; who owned not a single foot of the extensive surface of this planet? No! urged by a variety of motives, here they came. Everything has tended to regenerate them: new laws, a new mode of living, a new social system. Here they are become men; in Europe they were as so many useless plants, wanting vegetative mould,[9] and refreshing showers. They withered, and were mowed down by want, hunger, and war; but now by the power of transplantation, like all other plants they have taken root and flourished! Formerly they were not numbered in any civil lists[10] of their country, except in those of the poor; here they rank as citizens. By what invisible power has this surprising metamorphosis been performed? By that of the laws and that of their industry. The laws, the indulgent[11] laws, protect them as they arrive, stamping on them the symbol of adoption; they receive ample rewards for their labours; these accumulated rewards procure them lands; those lands confer on them the title of freemen, and to that title every benefit is affixed which men can possibly require. This is the great operation daily performed by our laws. From whence proceed these laws? From our government. Whence the government? It is derived from the original genius and strong desire of the people ratified and confirmed by the crown. This is the great chain which links us all, this is the picture which every province exhibits, Nova Scotia excepted.[12] There the crown has done all; either there were no people who had genius, or it was not much attended to: the consequence is, that the province is very thinly inhabited indeed; the power of the crown in conjunction with the musketos[13] has prevented men from settling there. Yet some parts of it flourished once, and it contained a mild, harmless set of people. But for the fault of a few leaders, the whole were banished. The greatest political error the crown ever committed in America, was to cut off men from a country which wanted nothing but men!

What attachment can a poor European emigrant have for a country where he had nothing? The knowledge of

---

[1] *promiscuous*   Varied; mixed.

[2] *eastern provinces*   I.e., New England.

[3] *reflect on*   Criticize or portray negatively.

[4] *letters*   Learning.

[5] *ancient college*   Harvard College in Massachusetts, established in 1636.

[6] *industry*   Industriousness.

[7] *asylum*   Place of shelter or sanctuary.

[8] *pinching penury*   Biting poverty.

[9] *wanting vegetative mould*   I.e., lacking fertilizer.

[10] *civil lists*   Government records of significant members of a society.

[11] *indulgent*   Tolerant.

[12] *Nova Scotia excepted*   Reference to the 1755 Expulsion of the Acadians, which occurred in the wake of the French and Indian War, when longtime French Acadian settlers were forcibly removed from Nova Scotia by the British government for refusing to sign an oath of allegiance.

[13] *musketos*   Mosquitos.

the language, the love of a few kindred as poor as himself, were the only cords that tied him: his country is now that which gives him land, bread, protection, and consequence; *Ubi panis ibi patria*,[1] is the motto of all emigrants. What then is the American, this new man? He is either an European, or the descendant of an European, hence that strange mixture of blood, which you will find in no other country. I could point out to you a family whose grandfather was an Englishman, whose wife was Dutch, whose son married a French woman, and whose present four sons have now four wives of different nations. *He* is an American, who leaving behind him all his ancient prejudices and manners, receives new ones from the new mode of life he has embraced, the new government he obeys, and the new rank he holds. He becomes an American by being received in the broad lap of our great *Alma Mater*.[2] Here individuals of all nations are melted into a new race of men, whose labours and posterity will one day cause great changes in the world. Americans are the western pilgrims, who are carrying along with them that great mass of arts, sciences, vigour, and industry which began long since in the east; they will finish the great circle. The Americans were once scattered all over Europe; here they are incorporated into one of the finest systems of population which has ever appeared, and which will hereafter become distinct by the power of the different climates they inhabit. The American ought therefore to love this country much better than that wherein either he or his forefathers were born. Here the rewards of his industry follow with equal steps the progress of his labour; his labour is founded on the basis of nature, *self-interest*; can it want a stronger allurement? Wives and children, who before in vain demanded of him a morsel of bread, now, fat and frolicksome, gladly help their father to clear those fields whence exuberant crops are to arise to feed and to clothe them all; without any part being claimed, either by a despotic prince, a rich abbot, or a mighty lord. Here religion demands but little of him; a small voluntary salary to the minister,[3] and gratitude to God; can

he refuse these? The American is a new man, who acts upon new principles; he must therefore entertain new ideas, and form new opinions. From involuntary idleness, servile dependence, penury, and useless labour, he has passed to toils of a very different nature, rewarded by ample subsistence. This is an American.

British America is divided into many provinces, forming a large association, scattered along a coast 1,500 miles extent and about 200 wide. This society I would fain examine, at least such as it appears in the middle provinces; if it does not afford that variety of tinges and gradations which may be observed in Europe, we have colours peculiar to ourselves. For instance, it is natural to conceive that those who live near the sea must be very different from those who live in the woods; the intermediate space will afford a separate and distinct class.

Men are like plants; the goodness and flavour of the fruit proceeds from the peculiar soil and exposition in which they grow. We are nothing but what we derive from the air we breathe, the climate we inhabit, the government we obey, the system of religion we profess, and the nature of our employment. Here you will find but few crimes; these have acquired as yet no root among us. I wish I were able to trace all my ideas; if my ignorance prevents me from describing them properly, I hope I shall be able to delineate a few of the outlines, which are all I propose.

Those who live near the sea, feed more on fish than on flesh, and often encounter that boisterous element. This renders them more bold and enterprising; this leads them to neglect the confined occupations of the land. They see and converse with a variety of people; their intercourse[4] with mankind becomes extensive. The sea inspires them with a love of traffic,[5] a desire of transporting produce from one place to another; and leads them to a variety of resources which supply the place of labour. Those who inhabit the middle settlements, by far the most numerous, must be very different; the simple cultivation of the earth purifies them, but the indulgences of the government, the soft remonstrances of religion, the rank of independent freeholders,[6] must

---

[1]   *Ubi panis ibi patria*   Latin: Where there is bread, there is my homeland.

[2]   *Alma Mater*   Latin: Bountiful Mother.

[3]   *voluntary ... minister*   In parts of Europe, payment of tithes to the established church—which funded the salaries of the clergy—was

compulsory, even for those who did not belong to the established church.

[4]   *intercourse*   Interactions.

[5]   *traffic*   Trade.

[6]   *freeholders*   Landowners.

necessarily inspire them with sentiments very little known in Europe among people of the same class. What do I say? Europe has no such class of men; the early knowledge they acquire, the early bargains they make, give them a great degree of sagacity. As freemen they will be litigious; pride and obstinacy are often the cause of lawsuits; the nature of our laws and governments may be another. As citizens it is easy to imagine that they will carefully read the newspapers, enter into every political disquisition, freely blame or censure governors and others. As farmers they will be careful and anxious to get as much as they can, because what they get is their own. As northern men they will love the cheerful cup. As Christians, religion curbs them not in their opinions; the general indulgence leaves everyone to think for themselves in spiritual matters; the laws inspect our actions, our thoughts are left to God. Industry, good living, selfishness, litigiousness, country politics, the pride of freemen, religious indifference, are their characteristics. If you recede still farther from the sea, you will come into more modern settlements; they exhibit the same strong lineaments, in a ruder[1] appearance. Religion seems to have still less influence, and their manners are less improved.

Now we arrive near the great woods, near the last inhabited districts;[2] there men seem to be placed still farther beyond the reach of government, which in some measure leaves them to themselves. How can it pervade every corner? As they were driven there by misfortunes, necessity of beginnings, desire of acquiring large tracks of land, idleness, frequent want of economy,[3] ancient debts; the reunion of such people does not afford a very pleasing spectacle. When discord, want of unity and friendship; when either drunkenness or idleness prevail in such remote districts, contention, inactivity, and wretchedness must ensue. There are not the same remedies to these evils as in a long-established community. The few magistrates they have are in general little better than the rest; they are often in a perfect state of war; that of man against man, sometimes decided by blows, sometimes by means of the law; that of man against every wild inhabitant of these venerable woods,

of which they are come to dispossess them. There men appear to be no better than carnivorous animals of a superior rank, living on the flesh of wild animals when they can catch them, and when they are not able, they subsist on grain. He who would wish to see America in its proper light, and have a true idea of its feeble beginnings and barbarous rudiments, must visit our extended line of frontiers where the last settlers dwell, and where he may see the first labours of settlement, the mode of clearing the earth, in their different appearances; where men are wholly left dependent on their native tempers, and on the spur of uncertain industry, which often fails when not sanctified by the efficacy of a few moral rules. There, remote from the power of example, and check of shame,[4] many families exhibit the most hideous parts of our society. They are a kind of forlorn hope, preceding by ten or twelve years the most respectable army of veterans[5] which come after them. In that space, prosperity will polish some, vice and the law will drive off the rest, who uniting again with others like themselves will recede still farther; making room for more industrious people, who will finish their improvements, convert the log house into a convenient habitation, and rejoicing that the first heavy labours are finished, will change in a few years that hitherto barbarous country into a fine, fertile, well-regulated district. Such is our progress, such is the march of the Europeans toward the interior parts of this continent. In all societies there are off-casts; this impure part serves as our precursors or pioneers; my father himself was one of that class,[6] but he came upon honest principles, and was therefore one of the few who held fast; by good conduct and temperance he transmitted to me his fair inheritance, when not above one in fourteen of his contemporaries had the same good fortune.

Forty years ago this smiling country was thus inhabited; it is now purged, a general decency of manners prevails throughout, and such has been the fate of our best countries.

Exclusive of those general characteristics, each province has its own, founded on the government,

---

[1]   *ruder*   Less refined.

[2]   *last inhabited districts*   I.e., the "frontier" regions beyond the borders of the Thirteen Colonies.

[3]   *want of economy*   Poor management of personal finances.

[4]   *check of shame*   I.e., the power of shame to change or restrain one's behavior.

[5]   *veterans*   Experienced settlers.

[6]   *my father … that class*   Crèvecoeur's own father was a country gentleman in France who never visited America.

climate, mode of husbandry,[1] customs, and peculiarity of circumstances. Europeans submit insensibly to these great powers, and become, in the course of a few generations, not only Americans in general, but either Pennsylvanians, Virginians, or provincials under some other name. Whoever traverses the continent must easily observe those strong differences, which will grow more evident in time. The inhabitants of Canada, Massachusetts, the middle provinces, the southern ones will be as different as their climates; their only points of unity will be those of religion and language.

As I have endeavoured to show you how Europeans become Americans, it may not be disagreeable to show you likewise how the various Christian sects introduced wear out, and how religious indifference becomes prevalent. When any considerable number of a particular sect happen to dwell contiguous to each other, they immediately erect a temple, and there worship the Divinity agreeably to their own peculiar ideas. Nobody disturbs them. If any new sect springs up in Europe, it may happen that many of its professors[2] will come and settle in America. As they bring their zeal with them, they are at liberty to make proselytes if they can, and to build a meeting and to follow the dictates of their consciences; for neither the government nor any other power interferes. If they are peaceable subjects, and are industrious, what is it to their neighbours how and in what manner they think fit to address their prayers to the Supreme Being? But if the sectaries are not settled close together, if they are mixed with other denominations, their zeal will cool for want of fuel, and will be extinguished in a little time. Then the Americans become as to religion, what they are as to country, allied to all. In them the name of Englishman, Frenchman, and European is lost, and in like manner, the strict modes of Christianity as practised in Europe are lost also. This effect will extend itself still farther hereafter, and though this may appear to you as a strange idea, yet it is a very true one. I shall be able perhaps hereafter to explain myself better; in the meanwhile, let the following example serve as my first justification.

Let us suppose you and I to be travelling. We observe that in this house, to the right, lives a Catholic, who prays to God as he has been taught, and believes in transubstantiation;[3] he works and raises wheat, he has a large family of children, all hale and robust; his belief, his prayers offend nobody. About one mile farther on the same road, his next neighbour may be a good honest plodding German Lutheran, who addresses himself to the same God, the God of all, agreeably to the modes he has been educated in, and believes in consubstantiation;[4] by so doing he scandalizes nobody; he also works in his fields, embellishes the earth, clears swamps, etc. What has the world to do with his Lutheran principles? He persecutes nobody, and nobody persecutes him; he visits his neighbours, and his neighbours visit him. Next to him lives a seceder,[5] the most enthusiastic of all sectaries; his zeal is hot and fiery, but separated as he is from others of the same complexion, he has no congregation of his own to resort to, where he might cabal[6] and mingle religious pride with worldly obstinacy. He likewise raises good crops, his house is handsomely painted, his orchard is one of the fairest in the neighbourhood. How does it concern the welfare of the country, or of the province at large, what this man's religious sentiments are, or really whether he has any at all? He is a good farmer, he is a sober, peaceable, good citizen. … This is the visible character; the invisible one is only guessed at, and is nobody's business. … Each of these people instruct their children as well as they can, but these instructions are feeble compared to those which are given to the youth of the poorest class in Europe. Their children will therefore grow up less zealous and more indifferent in matters of religion than their parents. The foolish vanity, or rather the fury of making proselytes, is unknown here; they have no time, the seasons call for all their attention, and thus in a few years, this mixed neighbourhood will exhibit a strange religious medley, that will be neither pure Catholicism

---

[1]   *husbandry* Farming.

[2]   *professors* Followers.

[3]   *transubstantiation* Central belief of Catholicism that the bread and wine consumed during the ritual of the Eucharist literally transform into the body and blood of Christ.

[4]   *consubstantiation* As opposed to transubstantiation, this doctrine holds that the bread and wine taken at communion represent the spiritual presence of Christ, but are not actually transformed into his body and blood.

[5]   *seceder* One who has withdrawn participation from any formal religious organization.

[6]   *cabal* Conspire with others; mingle dangerously.

nor pure Calvinism.[1] A very perceptible indifference, even in the first generation, will become apparent; and it may happen that the daughter of the Catholic will marry the son of the seceder, and settle by themselves at a distance from their parents. What religious education will they give their children? A very imperfect one. If there happens to be in the neighbourhood any place of worship—we will suppose a Quaker's meeting—rather than not show their fine clothes,[2] they will go to it, and some of them may perhaps attach themselves to that society. Others will remain in a perfect state of indifference; the children of these zealous parents will not be able to tell what their religious principles are, and their grandchildren still less. ... Thus all sects are mixed as well as all nations; thus religious indifference is imperceptibly disseminated from one end of the continent to the other; which is at present one of the strongest characteristics of the Americans. Where this will reach no one can tell; perhaps it may leave a vacuum fit to receive other systems. Persecution, religious pride, the love of contradiction, are the food of what the world commonly calls religion. These motives have ceased here. Zeal in Europe is confined; here it evaporates in the great distance it has to travel. There it is a grain of powder enclosed;[3] here it burns away in the open air, and consumes without effect.

But to return to our back settlers. I must tell you that there is something in the proximity of the woods which is very singular. It is with men as it is with the plants and animals that grow and live in the forests; they are entirely different from those that live in the plains. I will candidly tell you all my thoughts, but you are not to expect that I shall advance any reasons. By living in or near the woods, their actions are regulated by the wildness of the neighbourhood. The deer often come to eat their grain, the wolves to destroy their sheep, the bears to kill their hogs, the foxes to catch their poultry. This surrounding hostility immediately puts the gun into their hands; they watch these animals, they kill some; and thus by defending their property, they soon become professed hunters; this is the progress; once hunters, farewell to the plough. The chase renders them ferocious, gloomy, and unsociable; a hunter wants no neighbour, he rather hates them, because he dreads the competition. In a little time their success in the woods makes them neglect their tillage. They trust to the natural fecundity of the earth, and therefore do little; carelessness in fencing often exposes what little they sow to destruction; they are not at home to watch; in order therefore to make up the deficiency, they go oftener to the woods. That new mode of life brings along with it a new set of manners, which I cannot easily describe. These new manners, being grafted on the old stock, produce a strange sort of lawless profligacy, the impressions of which are indelible. The manners of the Indian natives are respectable, compared with this European medley. Their wives and children live in sloth and inactivity; and having no proper pursuits, you may judge what education the latter receive. Their tender minds have nothing else to contemplate but the example of their parents; like them they grow up a mongrel breed, half civilized, half savage, except nature stamps on them some constitutional propensities. That rich, that voluptuous sentiment is gone which struck them so forcibly; the possession of their freeholds no longer conveys to their minds the same pleasure and pride. To all these reasons you must add, their lonely[4] situation, and you cannot imagine what an effect on manners the great distances they live from each other has! Consider one of the last settlements in its first view: of what is it composed? Europeans who have not that sufficient share of knowledge they ought to have, in order to prosper; people who have suddenly passed from oppression, dread of government, and fear of laws, into the unlimited freedom of the woods. This sudden change must have a very great effect on most men, and on that class particularly. Eating of wild meat, whatever you may think, tends to alter their temper; though all the proof I can adduce is that I have seen it: and having no place of worship to resort to, what little society this might afford is denied them. ... Thus our bad people are those who are half cultivators and half hunters; and the worst of them are those who have degenerated altogether into the hunting state. As old ploughmen and new men of the woods, as Europeans

---

1   *Calvinism*   Branch of Protestant belief based on the teachings of French dissenter John Calvin (1509–64), presented here as diametrically opposed to Catholicism.

2   *Quaker's meeting ... fine clothes*   Quakers were known for their adherence to principles of plain dress.

3   *powder enclosed*   I.e., as gunpowder is enclosed in a gun.

4   *lonely*   I.e., remote and unpopulated.

and new-made Indians, they contract the vices of both; they adopt the moroseness and ferocity of a native, without his mildness, or even his industry at home. If manners are not refined, at least they are rendered simple and inoffensive by tilling the earth; all our wants are supplied by it, our time is divided between labour and rest, and leaves none for the commission of great misdeeds. As hunters it is divided between the toil of the chase, the idleness of repose, or the indulgence of inebriation. Hunting is but a licentious idle life, and if it does not always pervert good dispositions; yet, when it is united with bad luck, it leads to want: want stimulates that propensity to rapacity and injustice, too natural to needy men, which is the fatal gradation. After this explanation of the effects which follow by living in the woods, shall we yet vainly flatter ourselves with the hope of converting the Indians? We should rather begin with converting our back-settlers; and now if I dare mention the name of religion, its sweet accents would be lost in the immensity of these woods. Men thus placed, are not fit either to receive or remember its mild instructions; they want temples and ministers, but as soon as men cease to remain at home, and begin to lead an erratic life, let them be either tawny or white, they cease to be its disciples. …

Europe contains hardly any other distinctions but lords and tenants; this fair country alone is settled by freeholders, the possessors of the soil they cultivate, members of the government they obey, and the framers of their own laws, by means of their representatives. This is a thought which you have taught me to cherish; our distance from Europe, far from diminishing, rather adds to our usefulness and consequence as men and subjects. Had our forefathers remained there, they would only have crouded it, and perhaps prolonged those convulsions which had shook it so long. Every industrious European who transports himself here, may be compared to a sprout growing at the foot of a great tree; it enjoys and draws but a little portion of sap; wrench it from the parent roots, transplant it, and it will become a tree bearing fruit also. Colonists are therefore intitled to the consideration due to the most useful subjects; a hundred families barely existing in some parts of Scotland, will here in six years, case an annual exportation of 10,000 bushels of wheat: 100 bushels being but a common quantity for an industrious family to sell, if they cultivate good land. It is here then that the idle may be employed, the useless become useful, and the poor become rich; but by riches I do not mean gold and silver, we have but little of those metals; I mean a better sort of wealth, cleared lands, cattle, good houses, good cloaths, and an increase of people to enjoy them.

There is no wonder that this country has so many charms, and presents to Europeans so many temptations to remain in it. A traveller in Europe becomes a stranger as soon as he quits his own kingdom; but it is otherwise here. We know, properly speaking, no strangers; this is every person's country; the variety of our soils, situations, climates, governments, and produce, hath something which must please every body. No sooner does an European arrive, no matter of what condition, than his eyes are opened upon the fair prospect; he hears his language spoke, he retraces many of his own country manners, he perpetually hears the names of families and towns with which he is acquainted; he sees happiness and prosperity in all places disseminated; he meets with hospitality, kindness, and plenty every where; he beholds hardly any poor, he seldom hears of punishments and executions; and he wonders at the elegance of our towns, those miracles of industry and freedom. He cannot admire enough our rural districts, our convenient roads, good taverns, and our many accommodations; he involuntarily loves a country where every thing is so lovely. When in England, he was a mere Englishman; here he stands on a larger portion of the globe, not less than its fourth part, and may see the productions of the north, in iron and naval stores; the provisions of Ireland, the grain of Egypt, the indigo, the rice of China. He does not find, as in Europe, a crouded society, where every place is over-stocked; he does not feel that perpetual collision of parties, that difficulty of beginning, that contention which oversets so many. There is room for every body in America; has he any particular talent, or industry? he exerts it in order to procure a livelihood, and it succeeds. Is he a merchant? the avenues of trade are infinite; is he eminent in any respect? he will be employed and respected. Does he love a country life? pleasant farms present themselves; he may purchase what he wants, and thereby become an American farmer. Is he a labourer, sober and industrious? he

original spelling

original spelling

need not go many miles, nor receive many informations before he will be hired, well fed at the table of his employer, and paid four or five times more than he can get in Europe. Does he want uncultivated lands? thousands of acres present themselves, which he may purchase cheap. Whatever be his talents or inclinations, if they are moderate, he may satisfy them. I do not mean that every one who comes will grow rich in a little time; no, but he may procure an easy, decent maintenance, by his industry. Instead of starving he will be fed, instead of being idle he will have employment; and these are riches enough for such men as come over here. The rich stay in Europe, it is only the middling and poor that emigrate. Would you wish to travel in independent idleness, from north to south, you will find easy access, and the most chearful reception at every house; society without ostentation, good cheer without pride, and every decent diversion which the country affords, with little expense. It is no wonder that the European who has lived here a few years, is desirous to remain; Europe with all its pomp, is not to be compared to this continent, for men of middle stations, or labourers.

An European, when he first arrives, seems limited in his intentions, as well as in his views; but he very suddenly alters his scale; two hundred miles formerly appeared a very great distance, it is now but a trifle; he no sooner breathes our air than he forms schemes, and embarks in designs he never would have thought of in his own country. There the plenitude of society confines many useful ideas, and often extinguishes the most laudable schemes which here ripen into maturity. Thus Europeans become Americans. …

… It is of very little importance how, and in what manner an indigent man arrives; for if he is but sober, honest, and industrious, he has nothing more to ask of heaven. Let him go to work, he will have opportunities enough to earn a comfortable support, and even the means of procuring some land; which ought to be the utmost wish of every person who has health and hands to work. I knew a man who came to this country, in the literal sense of the expression, stark naked; I think he was a Frenchman, and a sailor on board an English man-of-war.[1] Being discontented, he had stripped himself and swam ashore; where finding clothes and friends, he settled afterwards at Maraneck, in the county of Chester, in the province of New-York: he married and left a good farm to each of his sons. I knew another person who was but twelve years old when he was taken on the frontiers of Canada by the Indians; at his arrival at Albany he was purchased by a gentleman, who generously bound him apprentice to a tailor. He lived to the age of ninety, and left behind him a fine estate and a numerous family, all well settled; many of them I am acquainted with. Where is then the industrious European who ought to despair?

After a foreigner from any part of Europe is arrived, and become a citizen, let him devoutly listen to the voice of our great parent, which says to him, "Welcome to my shores, distressed European; bless the hour in which thou didst see my verdant fields, my fair navigable rivers, and my green mountains! If thou wilt work, I have bread for thee;[2] if thou wilt be honest, sober, and industrious, I have greater rewards to confer on thee—ease and independence. I will give thee fields to feed and clothe thee; a comfortable fireside to sit by, and tell thy children by what means thou hast prospered; and a decent bed to repose on. I shall endow thee beside with the immunities of a freeman.[3] If thou wilt carefully educate thy children, teach them gratitude to God, and reverence to that government, that philanthropic government, which has collected here so many men and made them happy. I will also provide for thy progeny; and to every good man this ought to be the most holy, the most powerful, the most earnest wish he can possibly form, as well as the most consolatory prospect when he dies. Go thou and work and till; thou shalt prosper, provided thou be just, grateful and industrious." … In the year 1770, I purchased some lands in the county of ——, which I intended for one of my sons; and was obliged to go there in order to see them properly surveyed and marked out: the soil is good, but the country has a very wild aspect. However, I observed with pleasure that land sells very fast; and I am in hopes when the lad gets a wife, it

---

1   *man-of-war* Large warship.

2   *thee* In late eighteenth-century America, the use of *thee* and *thou* as second person singular pronouns was often a sign of membership of the Society of Friends (the Quakers), who had been the first European settlers in Pennsylvania. Farmer James and (especially) his wife use these pronouns with some frequency in certain of the *Letters*.

3   *immunities of a freeman* Rights of a free person.

will be a well-settled decent country. Agreeable to our customs, which indeed are those of nature, it is our duty to provide for our eldest children while we live, in order that our homesteads may be left to the youngest, who are the most helpless. Some people are apt to regard the portions given to daughters as so much lost to the family; but this is selfish, and is not agreeable to my way of thinking; they cannot work as men do; they marry young: I have given an honest European a farm to till for himself, rent free, provided he clears an acre of swamp every year, and that he quits it whenever my daughter shall marry. It will procure her a substantial husband, a good farmer—and that is all my ambition.

Whilst I was in the woods I met with a party of Indians; I shook hands with them, and I perceived they had killed a cub; I had a little peach brandy, they perceived it also, we therefore joined company, kindled a large fire, and ate an hearty supper. I made their hearts glad, and we all reposed on good beds of leaves. Soon after dark, I was surprised to hear a prodigious hooting through the woods; the Indians laughed heartily. One of them, more skillful than the rest, mimicked the owls so exactly, that a very large one perched on a high tree over our fire. We soon brought him down; he measured five feet seven inches from one extremity of the wings to the other. By Captain —— I have sent you the talons, on which I have had the heads of small candlesticks fixed. Pray keep them on the table of your study for my sake. …

from LETTER 9
DESCRIPTION OF CHARLES-TOWN;[1] THOUGHTS ON SLAVERY; ON PHYSICAL EVIL; A MELANCHOLY SCENE

Charles-Town is, in the north, what Lima is in the south; both are capitals of the richest provinces of their respective hemispheres: you may therefore conjecture that both cities must exhibit the appearances necessarily resulting from riches. Peru abounding in gold, Lima is filled with inhabitants who enjoy all those gradations of pleasure, refinement, and luxury, which proceed from wealth. Carolina produces commodities more valuable perhaps than gold, because they are gained by greater

industry; it exhibits also on our northern stage a display of riches and luxury, inferior indeed to the former, but far superior to what are to be seen in our northern towns. Its situation is admirable, being built at the confluence of two large rivers, which receive in their course a great number of inferior streams; all navigable in the spring, for flat boats. Here the produce of this extensive territory concentres; here therefore is the seat of the most valuable exportation; their wharfs, their docks, their magazines,[2] are extremely convenient to facilitate this great commercial business. The inhabitants are the gayest in America; it is called the centre of our beau monde, and is always filled with the richest planters of the province, who resort hither in quest of health and pleasure. Here are always to be seen a great number of valetudinarians from the West Indies, seeking for the renovation of health, exhausted by the debilitating nature of their sun, air, and modes of living. Many of these West Indians have I seen, at thirty, loaded with the infirmities of old age; for nothing is more common in those countries of wealth, than for persons to lose the abilities of enjoying the comforts of life, at a time when we northern men just begin to taste the fruits of our labour and prudence. The round of pleasure, and the expenses of those citizens' tables, are much superior to what you would imagine: indeed the growth of this town and province have been astonishingly rapid. It is pity that the narrowness of the neck on which it stands prevents it from increasing; and which is the reason why houses are so dear. The heat of the climate, which is sometimes very great in the interior parts of the country, is always temperate in Charles-Town; though sometimes when they have no sea breezes the sun is too powerful. The climate renders excesses of all kinds very dangerous, particularly those of the table; and yet, insensible or fearless of danger, they live on, and enjoy a short and a merry life: the rays of their sun seem to urge them irresistibly to dissipation and pleasure: on the contrary, the women, from being abstemious,[3] reach to a longer period of life, and seldom die without having had several husbands. An European at his first arrival must be greatly surprised when he sees the elegance of their houses, their sumptuous furniture, as well as the

---

[1] *DESCRIPTION OF CHARLES-TOWN*   It is likely that Crèvecoeur himself never traveled to South Carolina, and that what knowledge he had of the region was second-hand.

[2] *magazines* Storehouses.

[3] *abstemious* Moderate in their habits.

magnificence of their tables; can he imagine himself in a country, the establishment of which is so recent?

The three principal classes of inhabitants are lawyers, planters, and merchants; this is the province which has afforded to the first the richest spoils, for nothing can exceed their wealth, their power, and their influence. They have reached the *ne plus ultra*[1] of worldly felicity; no plantation is secured, no title is good, no will is valid, but what they dictate, regulate, and approve. The whole mass of provincial property is become tributary to this society—which, far above priests and bishops, disdain to be satisfied with the poor Mosaical portion of the tenth.[2] I appeal to the many inhabitants, who, while contending perhaps for their right to a few hundred acres, have lost by the mazes of the law their whole patrimony. These men are more properly law givers than interpreters of the law; and have united here, as well as in most other provinces, the skill and dexterity of the scribe with the power and ambition of the prince: who can tell where this may lead in a future day? The nature of our laws, and the spirit of freedom, which often tends to make us litigious,[3] must necessarily throw the greatest part of the property of the colonies into the hands of these gentlemen. In another century, the law will possess in the north, what now the church possesses in Peru and Mexico.

While all is joy, festivity, and happiness in Charles-Town, would you imagine that scenes of misery overspread in the country? Their ears by habit are become deaf, their hearts are hardened; they neither see, hear, nor feel for the woes of their poor slaves, from whose painful labours all their wealth proceeds. Here the horrors of slavery, the hardship of incessant toils, are unseen; and no one thinks with compassion of those showers of sweat and of tears which from the bodies of Africans daily drop, and moisten the ground they till. The cracks of the whip urging these miserable beings to excessive labour, are far too distant from the gay Capital to be heard. The chosen race eat, drink, and live happy, while the unfortunate one grubs up the ground,

raises indigo, or husks the rice; exposed to a sun full as scorching as their native one; without the support of good food, without the cordials of any cheering liquor. This great contrast has often afforded me subjects of the most afflicting meditation. On the one side, behold a people enjoying all that life affords most bewitching and pleasurable, without labour, without fatigue, hardly subjected to the trouble of wishing. With gold, dug from Peruvian mountains, they order vessels to the coasts of Guinea; by virtue of that gold, wars, murders, and devastations are committed in some harmless, peaceable African neighbourhood, where dwelt innocent people, who even knew not but that all men were black.[4] The daughter torn from her weeping mother, the child from the wretched parents, the wife from the loving husband; whole families swept away and brought through storms and tempests to this rich metropolis! There, arranged like horses at a fair, they are branded like cattle, and then driven to toil, to starve, and to languish for a few years on the different plantations of these citizens. And for whom must they work? For persons they know not, and who have no other power over them than that of violence; no other right than what this accursed metal has given them! Strange order of things! Oh, Nature, where art thou? Are not these blacks thy children as well as we? On the other side, nothing is to be seen but the most diffusive misery and wretchedness, unrelieved even in thought or wish! Day after day they drudge on without any prospect of ever reaping for themselves; they are obliged to devote their lives, their limbs, their will, and every vital exertion to swell the wealth of masters; who look not upon them with half the kindness and affection with which they consider their dogs and horses. Kindness and affection are not the portion of those who till the earth, who carry burdens, who convert the logs into useful boards. This reward, simple and natural as one would conceive it, would border on humanity; and planters must have none of it!

If negroes are permitted to become fathers, this fatal indulgence only tends to increase their misery: the poor companions of their scanty pleasures are likewise the companions of their labours; and when at some critical seasons they could wish to see them relieved, with

---

[1]   *ne plus ultra*   Highest point; pinnacle.

[2]   *the poor ... tenth*   I.e., tithes, taxes paid to the church equivalent to one-tenth of one's annual earnings. Tithe laws are set out in the Old Testament or the Torah as part of what is called Mosaic Law.

[3]   *litigious*   Inclined towards having disputes, particularly legal disputes.

[4]   *who even ... black*   I.e., who did not even know that not all men are black.

tears in their eyes they behold them perhaps doubly oppressed, obliged to bear the burden of nature—a fatal present—as well as that of unabated tasks. How many have I seen cursing the irresistible propensity, and regretting that, by having tasted of those harmless joys, they had become the authors of double misery to their wives. Like their masters, they are not permitted to partake of those ineffable sensations with which nature inspires the hearts of fathers and mothers; they must repel them all, and become callous and passive. This unnatural state often occasions the most acute, the most pungent of their afflictions; they have no time, like us, tenderly to rear their helpless offspring, to nurse them on their knees, to enjoy the delight of being parents. Their paternal fondness is embittered by considering that, if their children live, they must live to be slaves like themselves; no time is allowed them to exercise their pious office.[1] The mothers must fasten them on their backs, and, with this double load, follow their husbands in the fields, where they too often hear no other sound than that of the voice or whip of the task-master, and the cries of their infants, broiling in the sun. These unfortunate creatures cry and weep like their parents, without a possibility of relief; the very instinct of the brute, so laudable, so irresistible, runs counter here to their master's interest; and to that god all the laws of nature must give way. Thus planters get rich; so raw, so unexperienced am I in this mode of life, that were I to be possessed of a plantation, and my slaves treated as in general they are here, never could I rest in peace; my sleep would be perpetually disturbed by a retrospect of the frauds committed in Africa, in order to entrap them; frauds surpassing in enormity everything which a common mind can possibly conceive. I should be thinking of the barbarous treatment they meet with on shipboard; of their anguish, of the despair necessarily inspired by their situation, when torn from their friends and relations; when delivered into the hands of a people differently coloured, whom they cannot understand; carried in a strange machine over an ever agitated element, which they had never seen before; and finally delivered over to the severities of the whippers, and the excessive labours of the field. Can it be possible that the force of custom should ever make me deaf to all these reflections, and as insensible

to the injustice of that trade, and to their miseries, as the rich inhabitants of this town seem to be? What then is man; this being who boasts so much of the excellence and dignity of his nature, among that variety of inscrutable mysteries, of unsolvable problems with which he is surrounded? The reason why man has been thus created is not the least astonishing! It is said, I know, that they are much happier here than in the West-Indies; because land being cheaper upon this continent than in those islands, the fields allowed them to raise their subsistence from are in general more extensive. The only possible chance of any alleviation depends on the humour of the planters, who, bred in the midst of slaves, learn from the example of their parents to despise them; and seldom conceive either from religion or philosophy any ideas that tend to make their fate less calamitous; except[2] some strong native tenderness of heart, some rays of philanthropy, overcome the obduracy[3] contracted by habit.

I have not resided here long enough to become insensible of pain for the objects which I every day behold. In the choice of my friends and acquaintance, I always endeavour to find out those whose dispositions are somewhat congenial with my own. We have slaves likewise in our northern provinces;[4] I hope the time draws near when they will be all emancipated: but how different their lot, how different their situation, in every possible respect! They enjoy as much liberty as their masters, they are as well clad, and as well fed; in health and sickness they are tenderly taken care of; they live under the same roof, and are, truly speaking, a part of our families. Many of them are taught to read and write, and are well instructed in the principles of religion; they are the companions of our labours, and treated as such; they enjoy many perquisites,[5] many established holidays, and are not obliged to work more than white people. They marry where inclination leads

---

[1]   *office*   Role; duty.

[2]   *except*   Unless.

[3]   *obduracy*   Inability to be moved by pity; hard-heartedness.

[4]   *We have … northern provinces*   Pennsylvania (the home state of Farmer James) began a process of gradual abolition in 1780; New York State (Crèvecoeur's residence while he was writing the bulk of the *Letters*) did likewise in 1799. The last enslaved people in New York State were not freed until 1827.

[5]   *enjoy many perquisites*   I.e., receive many rewards or forms of compensation for their labor.

them; visit their wives every week; are as decently clad as the common people; they are indulged in educating, cherishing, and chastising their children, who are taught subordination to them as to their lawful parents. In short, they participate in many of the benefits of our society, without being obliged to bear any of its burdens. They are fat, healthy, and hearty, and far from repining at their fate; they think themselves happier than many of the lower class whites: they share with their masters the wheat and meat provision they help to raise; many of those whom the good Quakers have emancipated have received that great benefit with tears of regret, and have never quitted, though free, their former masters and benefactors.

But is it really true, as I have heard it asserted here, that those blacks are incapable of feeling the spurs of emulation,[1] and the cheerful sound of encouragement? By no means; there are a thousand proofs existing of their gratitude and fidelity: those hearts in which such noble dispositions can grow, are then like ours, they are susceptible of every generous sentiment, of every useful motive of action; they are capable of receiving lights, of imbibing ideas that would greatly alleviate the weight of their miseries. But what methods have in general been made use of to obtain so desirable an end? None; the day in which they arrive and are sold, is the first of their labours; labours, which from that hour admit of no respite; for though indulged by law with relaxation on Sundays, they are obliged to employ that time which is intended for rest, to till their little plantations.[2] What can be expected from wretches in such circumstances? Forced from their native country, cruelly treated when on board, and not less so on the plantations to which they are driven; is there anything in this treatment but what must kindle all the passions, sow the seeds of inveterate resentment, and nourish a wish of perpetual revenge? They are left to the irresistible effects of those strong and natural propensities; the blows they receive, are they conducive to extinguish them, or to win their

affections? They are neither soothed by the hopes that their slavery will ever terminate but with their lives; [n]or yet encouraged by the goodness of their food, or the mildness of their treatment. The very hopes held out to mankind by religion, that consolatory system so useful to the miserable, are never presented to them; neither moral nor physical means are made use of to soften their chains; they are left in their original and untutored state, that very state wherein the natural propensities of revenge and warm passions are so soon kindled. Cheered by no one single motive that can impel the will, or excite their efforts, nothing but terrors and punishments are presented to them; death is denounced[3] if they run away; horrid dilaceration[4] if they speak with their native freedom; perpetually awed by the terrible cracks of whips, or by the fear of capital punishments, while even those punishments often fail of their purpose.

A clergyman settled a few years ago at George-Town, and feeling as I do now, warmly recommended to the planters, from the pulpit, a relaxation of severity; he introduced the benignity of Christianity, and pathetically made use of the admirable precepts of that system to melt the hearts of his congregation into a greater degree of compassion toward their slaves than had been hitherto customary; "Sir (said one of his hearers) we pay you a genteel salary to read to us the prayers of the liturgy, and to explain to us such parts of the Gospel as the rule of the church directs; but we do not want you to teach us what we are to do with our blacks." The clergyman found it prudent to withhold any farther admonition. Whence this astonishing right, or rather this barbarous custom, for most certainly we have no kind of right beyond that of force? We are told, it is true, that slavery cannot be so repugnant to human nature as we at first imagine, because it has been practised in all ages, and in all nations: the Lacedemonians themselves, those great assertors of liberty, conquered the Helotes with the design of making them their slaves;[5] the Romans, whom we consider as

---

1 *emulation* Ambition.

2 *indulged by law ... plantations* In many areas, enslaved people were legally required to be given "leisure time" from their ordinary labor on Sundays, a fact held up by many enslavers as proof that American slavery was not as cruel as their opponents claimed; however, as the narrator here points out, enslaved individuals generally had to use this time for the tending of their own small vegetable allotments and for other tasks required for their sustenance.

3 *denounced* Threatened.

4 *dilaceration* Tearing of the body; i.e., severe physical abuse.

5 *Lacedemonians ... their slaves* The Helots were a class of people subjugated by the Lacedemonians (or the Spartans) in the ancient world. Historians have long debated whether the Helots were truly members of an enslaved class or whether their status was something between that of enslaved and free.

our masters in civil and military policy, lived in the exercise of the most horrid oppression; they conquered to plunder and to enslave. What a hideous aspect the face of the earth must then have exhibited! Provinces, towns, districts, often depopulated; their inhabitants driven to Rome, the greatest market in the world, and there sold by thousands! The Roman dominions were tilled by the hands of unfortunate people, who had once been, like their victors free, rich, and possessed of every benefit society can confer; until they became subject to the cruel right of war, and to lawless force. Is there then no superintending power who conducts the moral operations of the world, as well as the physical? The same sublime hand which guides the planets round the sun with so much exactness, which preserves the arrangement of the whole with such exalted wisdom and paternal care, and prevents the vast system from falling into confusion; doth it abandon mankind to all the errors, the follies, and the miseries, which their most frantic rage, and their most dangerous vices and passions can produce?

The history of the earth! doth it present anything but crimes of the most heinous nature, committed from one end of the world to the other? We observe avarice, rapine,[1] and murder, equally prevailing in all parts. History perpetually tells us of millions of people abandoned to the caprice of the maddest princes, and of whole nations devoted to the blind fury of tyrants. Countries destroyed; nations alternately buried in ruins by other nations; some parts of the world beautifully cultivated, returned again to the pristine state; the fruits of ages of industry, the toil of thousands in a short time destroyed by few! If one corner breathes in peace for a few years, it is, in turn subjected, torn, and levelled; one would almost believe the principles of action in man, considered as the first agent of this planet, to be poisoned in their most essential parts. We certainly are not that class of beings which we vainly think ourselves to be; man an animal of prey, seems to have rapine and the love of bloodshed implanted in his heart; nay, to hold it the most honourable occupation in society: we never speak of a hero of mathematics, a hero of knowledge or humanity; no, this illustrious appellation is reserved for the most successful butchers of the world. If Nature has given us a fruitful soil to inhabit, she has refused us such inclinations and propensities as would afford us the full enjoyment of it. Extensive as the surface of this planet is, not one half of it is yet cultivated, not half replenished; she created man, and placed him either in the woods or plains, and provided him with passions which must forever oppose his happiness: everything is submitted to the power of the strongest; men, like the elements, are always at war; the weakest yield to the most potent; force, subtilty, and malice, always triumph over unguarded honesty, and simplicity. Benignity, moderation, and justice, are virtues adapted only to the humble paths of life: we love to talk of virtue and to admire its beauty, while in the shade of solitude, and retirement; but when we step forth into active life, if it happen to be in competition with any passion or desire, do we observe it to prevail? Hence so many religious impostors have triumphed over the credulity of mankind, and have rendered their frauds the creeds of succeeding generations, during the course of many ages; until worn away by time, they have been replaced by new ones. Hence the most unjust war, if supported by the greatest force, always succeeds; hence the most just ones, when supported only by their justice, as often fail. Such is the ascendancy of power; the supreme arbiter of all the revolutions which we observe in this planet: so irresistible is power, that it often thwarts the tendency of the most forcible causes, and prevents their subsequent salutary effects, though ordained for the good of man by the Governor of the universe. Such is the perverseness of human nature; who can describe it in all its latitude?

In the moments of our philanthropy we often talk of an indulgent nature, a kind parent, who for the benefit of mankind has taken singular pains to vary the genera of plants, fruits, grain, and the different productions of the earth, and has spread peculiar blessings in each climate. This is undoubtedly an object of contemplation which calls forth our warmest gratitude; for so singularly benevolent have those parental intentions been, that where barrenness of soil or severity of climate prevail, there she has implanted in the heart of man sentiments which overbalance every misery, and supply the place of every want. She has given to the inhabitants of these regions an attachment to their savage rocks and wild shores, unknown to those who inhabit the fertile fields of the temperate zone. Yet if

---

[1]   *rapine* Plunder.

we attentively view this globe, will it not appear rather a place of punishment than of delight? And what misfortune! that those punishments should fall on the innocent, and its few delights be enjoyed by the most unworthy. Famine, diseases, elementary convulsions, human feuds, dissensions, etc., are the produce of every climate; each climate produces, besides, vices and miseries peculiar to its latitude. View the frigid sterility of the north, whose famished inhabitants, hardly acquainted with the sun, live and fare worse than the bears they hunt—and to which they are superior only in the faculty of speaking. View the arctic and antarctic regions, those huge voids where nothing lives; regions of eternal snow; where winter in all his horrors has established his throne, and arrested every creative power of nature. Will you call the miserable stragglers in these countries by the name of men? Now contrast this frigid power of the north and south with that of the sun; examine the parched lands of the torrid zone, replete with sulphureous exhalations; view those countries of Asia subject to pestilential infections which lay nature waste; view this globe often convulsed both from within and without; pouring forth from several mouths, rivers of boiling matter, which are imperceptibly leaving immense subterranean graves, wherein millions will one day perish! Look at the poisonous soil of the equator, at those putrid slimy tracks, teeming with horrid monsters, the enemies of the human race; look next at the sandy continent, scorched perhaps by the fatal approach of some ancient comet, now the abode of desolation. Examine the rains, the convulsive storms of those climates, where masses of sulphur, bitumen, and electrical fire, combining their dreadful powers, are incessantly hovering and bursting over a globe threatened with dissolution. On this little shell, how very few are the spots where man can live and flourish! Even under those mild climates which seem to breathe peace and happiness, the poison of slavery, the fury of despotism, and the rage of superstition, are all combined against man! There only the few live and rule, whilst the many starve and utter ineffectual complaints: there, human nature appears more debased perhaps than in the less favoured climates. The fertile plains of Asia, the rich low lands of Egypt and of Diarbeck,[1] the fruitful fields bordering on the Tigris and the Euphrates,[2] the extensive country of the East Indies in all its separate districts; all these must to the geographical eye seem as if intended for terrestrial paradises: but though surrounded with the spontaneous riches of nature, though her kindest favours seem to be shed on those beautiful regions with the most profuse hand, yet there in general we find the most wretched people in the world. Almost everywhere, liberty, so natural to mankind, is refused, or rather enjoyed but by their tyrants; the word slave is the appellation of every rank, who adore as a divinity a being worse than themselves; subject to every caprice, and to every lawless rage which unrestrained power can give. Tears are shed, perpetual groans are heard, where only the accents of peace, alacrity, and gratitude should resound. There the very delirium of tyranny tramples on the best gifts of nature, and sports with the fate, the happiness, the lives of millions: there the extreme fertility of the ground always indicates the extreme misery of the inhabitants!

Everywhere one part of the human species are taught the art of shedding the blood of the other; of setting fire to their dwellings; of levelling the works of their industry: half of the existence of nations regularly employed in destroying other nations. What little political felicity is to be met with here and there has cost oceans of blood to purchase; as if good was never to be the portion of unhappy man. Republics, kingdoms, monarchies, founded either on fraud or successful violence, increase by pursuing the steps of the same policy, until they are destroyed in their turn, either by the influence of their own crimes, or by more successful but equally criminal enemies.

If from this general review of human nature, we descend to the examination of what is called civilized society; there the combination of every natural and artificial want, makes us pay very dear for what little share of political felicity we enjoy. It is a strange heterogeneous assemblage of vices and virtues, and of a variety of other principles, forever at war, forever jarring, forever producing some dangerous, some distressing extreme. Where do you conceive then that nature intended we should be happy? Would you prefer the state of men in the woods, to that of men in a more

---

[1] *Diarbeck* Diyarbakir, significant city in Turkey.

[2] *Tigris and the Euphrates* River system in western Asia; part of a historically significant region known as the Fertile Crescent.

improved situation? Evil preponderates in both; in the first they often eat each other for want of food, and in the other they often starve each other for want of room. For my part, I think the vices and miseries to be found in the latter, exceed those of the former; in which real evil is more scarce, more supportable, and less enormous. Yet we wish to see the earth peopled; to accomplish the happiness of kingdoms, which is said to consist in numbers. Gracious God! to what end is the introduction of so many beings into a mode of existence in which they must grope amidst as many errors, commit as many crimes, and meet with as many diseases, wants, and sufferings!

The following scene will I hope account for these melancholy reflections, and apologize for the gloomy thoughts with which I have filled this letter: my mind is, and always has been, oppressed since I became a witness to it. I was not long since invited to dine with a planter who lived three miles from ——, where he then resided. In order to avoid the heat of the sun, I resolved to go on foot, sheltered in a small path, leading through a pleasant wood. I was leisurely travelling along, attentively examining some peculiar plants which I had collected, when all at once I felt the air strongly agitated; though the day was perfectly calm and sultry. I immediately cast my eyes toward the cleared ground, from which I was but at a small distance, in order to see whether it was not occasioned by a sudden shower; when at that instant a sound resembling a deep rough voice, uttered, as I thought, a few inarticulate monosyllables. Alarmed and surprized, I precipitately looked all round, when I perceived at about six rods distance[1] something resembling a cage, suspended to the limbs of a tree; all the branches of which appeared covered with large birds of prey, fluttering about, and anxiously endeavouring to perch on the cage. Actuated by an involuntary motion of my hands more than by any design of my mind, I fired at them; they all flew to a short distance, with a most hideous noise: when, horrid to think and painful to repeat, I perceived a negro, suspended in the cage, and left there to expire! I shudder when I recollect that the birds had already picked out his eyes; his cheek bones were bare; his arms had been attacked in several places, and his body seemed covered with a multitude of wounds. From the edges of the hollow sockets and from the lacerations with which he was disfigured, the blood slowly dropped, and tinged the ground beneath. No sooner were the birds flown, than swarms of insects covered the whole body of this unfortunate wretch, eager to feed on his mangled flesh and to drink his blood. I found myself suddenly arrested by the power of affright and terror; my nerves were convulsed; I trembled, I stood motionless, involuntarily contemplating the fate of this negro, in all its dismal latitude. The living spectre, though deprived of his eyes, could still distinctly hear, and in his uncouth dialect begged me to give him some water to allay his thirst. Humanity herself would have recoiled back with horror; she would have balanced whether to lessen such reliefless distress, or mercifully with one blow to end this dreadful scene of agonizing torture! Had I had a ball in my gun, I certainly should have dispatched[2] him; but finding myself unable to perform so kind an office, I sought, though trembling, to relieve him as well as I could. A shell ready fixed to a pole, which had been used by some negroes, presented itself to me; filled it with water, and with trembling hands I guided it to the quivering lips of the wretched sufferer. Urged by the irresistible power of thirst, he endeavoured to meet it, as he instinctively guessed its approach by the noise it made in passing through the bars of the cage. "Tankè, you whitè man, tankè you, puté somè poyson and givè me." How long have you been hanging there? I asked him. "Two days, and me no die; the birds, the birds; aaah me!" Oppressed with the reflections which this shocking spectacle afforded me, I mustered strength enough to walk away, and soon reached the house at which I intended to dine. There I heard that the reason for this slave being thus punished, was on account of his having killed the overseer of the plantation. They told me that the laws of self-preservation rendered such executions necessary; and supported the doctrine of slavery with the arguments generally made use of to justify the practice; with the repetition of which I shall not trouble you at present.

Adieu

—1782, 1783.

---

[1]   *at about … rods distance*   About thirty yards away.

[2]   *dispatched*   Killed.

In Context

Nantucket and Charles-Town

Nantucket and its environs and Charles-Town and its environs present contrasting faces of America to Crèvecoeur's Farmer James. Images of both are provided here. (For Crèvecoeur's account of Nantucket, see the excerpt from Letter 4 included in the anthology's website component.)

The Town of Sherbourne on the Island of Nantucket.

"The inhabitants are the gayest in America; [Charles-Town] is called the centre of our beau monde," wrote Crèvecoeur in the late eighteenth century. Many of the buildings from that era are still standing—including the building now known as "the Pink House," which dates from 1712 and which served as a tavern for much of the eighteenth century. Photograph by Brian Stansberry, 2010. (Licensed under CC BY 3.0.)

Indigo Processing, St Stephen's Parish [approximately 30 miles north of Charlestown], 1762.

Thomas Paine

1737 – 1809

Born in obscurity and buried in ignominy 72 years later, Thomas Paine nevertheless played a significant role in the histories of three nations. After failing in numerous early careers, Paine became an overnight success with the publication of his first pamphlet in the American colonies, *Common Sense* (1776), and his talent for political rhetoric and persuasion made him an important influence in the Revolutionary War effort in America, in the drafting of Jefferson's Declaration of Independence, and in the formation of the French National Assembly.

Paine was born in the town of Thetford in Norfolk, England, the only son of a Quaker couple, Joseph Pain (a shopkeeper of modest means who made and sold "stays" or corsets) and his wife Frances (Cocke) Pain.[1] Thomas spent several years at the local grammar school before beginning an apprenticeship with his father. At sixteen he ran away from home and briefly signed on with a privateer before returning to Thetford. Three years later he is reported to have worked for a time in London for "a very noted stay-maker," but the next year he again signed on with a privateer—this time for six months. On his return he moved to Dover, where he took up the stay-maker's trade once more. In 1759 he borrowed ten pounds to finance his own stay-making shop in the nearby town of Sandwich; here he met and married Mary Lambert, a maid in a local shopkeeper's household, whose father worked for the Customs and Excise Service. But Paine was unable to make a living for himself in the stay-making business; his shop failed, and at about the same time—in 1760—Mary died in childbirth, together with the infant.

Between 1756 and 1774 Paine lived several times for brief periods in London, where in his spare time he attended lectures and met several leading intellectual figures of the day—among them the astronomer John Bevis, the mathematician (and Commissioner of the Board of Excise) George Lewis Scott, and the renowned scientist and intellectual Benjamin Franklin.

Paine continued to live a peripatetic life through his twenties and thirties, working for varying lengths of time as a tobacco-shop proprietor, a grocer, a teacher, and an exciseman (a traveling tax collector)—a profession that he may have become interested in through the influence of Mary's father. Though twice dismissed from excise positions, he had something of an impact on that profession, agitating for better pay and working conditions for excisemen, and publishing in 1772 a pamphlet arguing these points, *The Case of the Officers of Excise*. During the years 1768 to 1774 Paine lived in Lewes, Sussex (a town that had suffered from economic hardship and that had something of a tradition of radical political activity); here he joined the White Hart Inn's debating club, and became politically active. In 1771 he married Elizabeth Ollive, the daughter of a prominent Lewes shopkeeper. In 1774, however, his life fell apart again; he was dismissed for the second time as an excise officer, the shop he had inherited from Elizabeth's father failed, and he was threatened with debtor's prison. He and Elizabeth formally separated, and Paine moved to London.

In London he was befriended by Franklin; when Paine decided to emigrate, Franklin provided him with letters of introduction. Paine arrived in Philadelphia in November 1774 in very poor health, but by the following spring he had been hired by printer Robert Aiken to edit a new publication, the *Pennsylvania Magazine*. Paine had finally found his calling; under his editorship the magazine's circulation rose to over 1,500 (said by some to have been higher than any other American magazine of its day).

---

1   At some point before 1769 Paine added an "e" to his surname.

Paine began to contribute pieces to the magazine himself, beginning in March 1775 with an essay on "African Slavery in America" in which he argued that those who had been enslaved had "a natural, perfect right" to freedom. The essay led to the formation the following month of the Society for the Relief of Free Negroes, Unlawfully Held in Bondage (America's earliest known antislavery society); Paine would later play a significant role in the drafting of the 1780 legislation that initiated the gradual abolition of slavery in Pennsylvania.

As hostilities between Britain and its American colonies were escalating in December 1775, Paine was able to put his writing skills to further use when he was commissed by Franklin and other prominent figures to write a pamphlet; on 9 January 1776 he issued *Common Sense*, one of the first publications to argue that America should immediately declare full independence from Britain. The pamphlet was an extraordinary success; even scholars such as Trish Loughran who have helpfully called into question a number of unverifiable claims concerning the number of copies circulated have affirmed that it was "immensely popular." In plain and forceful language, Paine called on ordinary people to give their energy to a higher purpose—the creation of America. His accessible prose, compelling logic, and gift for dismissing opposing arguments made him for a time the American Revolution's most adept promoter.

Dubbing Britain a "tyrannical oppressor," *Common Sense* argues that government, at best "a necessary evil," should serve to protect its citizens and preserve their freedom. A subsequent series of letters, entitled *The American Crisis* (1776–83), continued to muster support for the revolution in the face of military setbacks and public fear and despondency. One such letter's rousing and powerful rhetoric— "These are times that try men's souls…"—was read to George Washington's troops on Christmas Eve in an effort to boost their morale.

After the Revolutionary War ended, Paine spent considerable time in Britain and France. The publication of Edmund Burke's conservative pamphlet attacking the French Revolution, *Reflections on the Revolution in France* (1790), spurred him to publish a rebuttal, based largely on the account of the Revolution he had been working on at the time. Part 1 of Paine's *Rights of Man* (1791) came in the midst of a pamphlet storm of replies to Burke (among them Mary Wollstonecraft's *A Vindication of the Rights of Men*). Demonstrating once again his powers of persuasion, and leaning on the weight of his experience in the American Revolution (the work was dedicated to George Washington), Paine challenged Burke's view of the French Revolution. *Rights of Man* insists that each generation, rather than being ruled by preceding generations, "must be as free to act for itself, in all cases, as the ages and generations which preceded it." Paine argues that men have certain natural rights, existent from birth and given by their creator, which society is formed to protect and to enforce through the provision of civil rights. Part 2 of *Rights of Man* (1792) went further, arguing that American independence had set in motion the changes that would bring down the tyranny of hereditary government in Europe. This attack on the monarchy and aristocracy saw Paine charged with treason in England; he took refuge in France, where he had been made an honorary citizen.

Paine was in 1792 elected to the French National Assembly, and the following year he was appointed to a committee that had been tasked with the job of drafting a new French constitution. With the coming to power of the Jacobin government of Maximilien Robespierre, however, Paine fell from favor; he was imprisoned during the Reign of Terror (1793–94), and narrowly avoided the guillotine. Paine (who blamed George Washington for not having secured his release from prison earlier) was finally freed following Robespierre's execution in 1794. Paine—whose opinionated nature, disdain for social convention, and carefree habits of spending and of borrowing had cost him many friends and supporters—once more found himself at the center of controversy, this time for his last major work, *The Age of Reason* (1794–95). This deist denunciation of the Bible and of organized Christianity (along with religious institutions of all denominations) met with widespread hostility; Paine, who returned to America in 1802, was labeled an infidel and an atheist. Ostracised, he spent the final years of his life in poverty. When he died Paine was buried on his farm in New Rochelle, under a tombstone stating simply—at his request—"The author of Common Sense"; his request to be buried in a Quaker graveyard had been refused. A decade later the famed radical writer and politician William Cobbett arranged for his remains to be exhumed, with the intent of according Paine a more honored burial place in Britain. Cobbett's plans were frustrated, however, and the whereabouts of Paine's remains has been unknown ever since.

If Paine's reputation had its ups and downs during his lifetime, so too has his posthumous reputation. The disgrace he had suffered following the publication of *The Age of Reason* lingered in many minds long after his death, and disapproval of Paine's character continued to color many discussions of his writings. Thus, for example, an 1851 article in the Philadelphia magazine *Arthur's Home Gazette* by Arthur J. Stanbury attacked Paine as "an infidel, a debauchee, a drunkard, a liar, a blasphemer, and a profane swearer." An answering opinion piece in William Lloyd Garrison's newspaper *The Liberator* offered a defense that ridiculed Stanbury's *ad hominem* reasoning, as well as its hypocrisy: "Paine was a drunkard, and therefore his opinions were detestable. [Famous American statesman Daniel] Webster was a drunkard, but his opinions are worthy of all deference. Paine was licentious, and therefore unfit to receive distinguished consideration; Webster is licentious, but is worthy of the highest national honor." (The *Liberator* piece ended on a note of optimism: "the good shall yet triumph," it predicted, in the ways that Paine had striven for.)

Paine was celebrated by many (Walt Whitman among them) in the late nineteenth and early twentieth centuries, but he continued to be disparaged as well (particularly by those of a conservative bent); one 1924 history of American literature dismisses him in a couple of lines as "an obscure Englishman of whiggish temper [who became] the fiercest advocate of American independence." And some twentieth-century anthologists and literary historians ignore him altogether; Barrett Wendell's 1925 literary history of America makes no more mention of Paine than does Samuel Knapp's 1829 overview. But for the most part Paine's positive contribution to American literature was, by the early twentieth century, at least grudgingly recognized—as, for example, William P. Trent's 1903 literary history acknowledges it: "Time has not made more palatable [the] vulgarity [of Paine's writings], but it has made us see that even if the man never ceased to be a philistine, he was of greater service to his race than most children of 'sweetness and light' are wont to be."

By mid-century writers were no longer judged so harshly on grounds such as "vulgarity" and "philistinism," and the acknowledgments of Paine's importance ceased to be grudging. Throughout the later decades of the twentieth century and the early decades of this century Paine's centrality both to the history of America and to its literature has been universally recognized. Included in every major anthology of American literature, his writing has been lauded not only for its rhetorical power and persuasiveness but also for helping to shape a plain style of American prose writing.

NOTE ON THE TEXTS: The early publishing history of *Common Sense* is a tangled one. When printer Robert Bell's first printing of 1,000 copies of the 47-page pamphlet quickly sold out, Bell ordered a second printing—but without having paid Paine, as had earlier been agreed, half the profits from the first printing. Paine then contracted a new edition with another printer (Thomas and William Bradford), while Bell himself also issued further editions (adding the phrase "by an Englishman" to the title page). Paine and the Bradfords arranged to price their edition of the pamphlet significantly lower than Bell had priced his, and the Bradford edition substantially outsold Bell's. The Bradford version included a new introduction and (as it declared on the title page) "several additions in the body of the work," as well as "an appendix; together with an address to the people called Quakers." The additions to "the body of the work" were primarily charts and tables; most of the text was unrevised. Nevertheless, it was the text of this second edition (and that of the near-identical third edition) which reached the greatest number of Americans in 1776; for that reason, it is the second rather than the first edition that we have used as a base text here.

Paine issued three editions of "The American Crisis" in late 1776; the text excerpted here is that issued third (dated 23 December).

Except where otherwise noted, spelling and punctuation have been modernized according to the practices of this anthology.

⌘ ⌘ ⌘

COMMON SENSE;

ADDRESSED TO THE

INHABITANTS

OF

AMERICA,

On the following interesting

SUBJECTS.

I. Of the Origin and Design of Government in general,
with concise Remarks on the English Constitution.

II. Of Monarchy and Hereditary Succession.

III. Thoughts on the present State of American Affairs.

IV. Of the present Ability of America, with some miscellaneous Reflections.

Man knows no Master save creating HEAVEN,
Or those whom choice and common good ordain.
                                        THOMSON.

PHILADELPHIA;

Printed, and Sold, by R. BELL, in Third-Street.

MDCCLXXVI.

Title page of the first edition of Paine's pamphlet, showing its full, 52-word title: *Common Sense: addressed to the inhabitants of America, on the following interesting subjects. I. Of the origin and design of government in general, with concise remarks on the English Constitution. II. Of monarchy and hereditary succession. III. Thoughts on the present state of American affairs. IV. Of the present ability of America, with some miscellaneous reflections.* The quotation ("Man knows no master save creating Heaven, / Or those whom choice and common good ordain") is from Part 4: Britain of James Thomson's long poem *Liberty* (1736). The context is a passage discussing the history of the early Britons—"sons of nature," as Thomson presents them— who were "unsubdued" by either "tyrant force" or "tyrant custom." It is from their experience that the general moral is drawn that humankind is not to be ruled except by "creating Heaven" or, alternatively, by such principles as our own choices and the interests of the common good command us to follow.

from *Common Sense*

INTRODUCTION

Perhaps the sentiments contained in the following pages, are not yet sufficiently fashionable to procure them general favor; a long habit of not thinking a thing *wrong*, gives it a superficial appearance of being right, and raises at first a formidable outcry in defense of custom. But the tumult soon subsides. Time makes more converts than reason.

As a long and violent abuse of power, is generally the Means of calling the right of it in question (and in Matters too which might never have been thought of, had not the Sufferers been aggravated into the inquiry) and as the King of England hath undertaken in his own Right, to support the Parliament in what he calls Theirs, and as the good people of this country are grievously oppressed by the combination, they have an undoubted privilege to inquire into the pretensions of both, and equally to reject the usurpation of either.

In the following sheets, the author hath studiously avoided every thing which is personal among ourselves. Compliments as well as censure to individuals make no part thereof. The wise, and the worthy, need not the triumph of a pamphlet; and those whose sentiments are injudicious, or unfriendly, will cease of themselves unless too much pains are bestowed upon their conversion.

The cause of America is in a great measure the cause of all mankind. Many circumstances hath, and will arise, which are not local, but universal, and through which the principles of all Lovers of Mankind are affected, and in the Event of which, their Affections are interested. The laying a Country desolate with Fire and Sword, declaring War against the natural rights of all Mankind, and extirpating the Defenders thereof from the Face of the Earth, is the Concern of every Man to whom Nature hath given the Power of feeling; of which Class, regardless of Party Censure, is the

AUTHOR.

P.S. The Publication of this new Edition hath been delayed, with a View of taking notice (had it been necessary) of any Attempt to refute the Doctrine of Independance: As no Answer hath yet appeared, it is now presumed that none will, the Time needful for getting such a Performance ready for the Public being considerably past.

Who the Author of this Production is, is wholly unnecessary to the Public, as the Object for Attention is the *Doctrine* itself, not the Man. Yet it may not be unnecessary to say, That he is unconnected with any Party, and under no sort of Influence public or private, but the influence of reason and principle.

Philadelphia, February 14, 1776

THOUGHTS ON THE PRESENT STATE OF AMERICAN AFFAIRS

In the following pages I offer nothing more than simple facts, plain arguments, and common sense; and have no other preliminaries to settle with the reader, than that he will divest himself of prejudice and prepossession, and suffer his reason and his feelings to determine for themselves; that he will put *on*, or rather that he will not put *off*, the true character of a man, and generously enlarge his views beyond the present day.

Volumes have been written on the subject of the struggle between England and America. Men of all ranks have embarked in the controversy, from different motives, and with various designs; but all have been ineffectual, and the period of debate is closed. Arms, as the last resource, decide the contest; the appeal was the choice of the king, and the continent hath accepted the challenge.

It hath been reported of the late Mr. Pelham[1] (who, though an able minister, was not without his faults) that on his being attacked in the House of Commons, on the score that his measures were only of a temporary kind, replied "they will last my time." Should a thought so fatal and unmanly possess the colonies in the present contest, the name of ancestors will be remembered by future generations with detestation.

The sun never shined on a cause of greater worth. 'Tis not the affair of a city, a country, a province, or a kingdom, but of a continent—of at least one eighth part of the habitable globe. 'Tis not the concern of a

---

1   *Mr. Pelham*   Henry Pelham (1694–1754), English prime minister from 1743 until his death.

day, a year, or an age; posterity are virtually involved in the contest, and will be more or less affected, even to the end of time, by the proceedings now. Now is the seed time of continental union, faith and honor. The least fracture now will be like a name engraved with the point of a pin on the tender rind of a young oak; the wound will enlarge with the tree, and posterity read it in full grown characters.

By referring the matter from argument to arms, a new era for politics is struck; a new method of thinking hath arisen. All plans, proposals, etc. prior to the nineteenth of April, i.e., to the commencement of hostilities,[1] are like the almanacs of the last year; which, though proper then, are superseded and useless now. Whatever was advanced by the advocates on either side of the question then, terminated in one and the same point, viz. a union with Great Britain; the only difference between the parties was the method of effecting it; the one proposing force, the other friendship; but it hath so far happened that the first hath failed, and the second hath withdrawn her influence.

As much hath been said of the advantages of reconciliation, which, like an agreeable dream, hath passed away and left us as we were, it is but right, that we should examine the contrary side of the argument, and inquire into some of the many material injuries which these colonies sustain, and always will sustain, by being connected with, and dependant on Great Britain. To examine that connection and dependence, on the principles of nature and common sense, to see what we have to trust to, if separated, and what we are to expect, if dependant.

I have heard it asserted by some, that as America hath flourished under her former connection with Great Britain, that the same connection is necessary towards her future happiness, and will always have the same effect. Nothing can be more fallacious than this kind of argument. We may as well assert that because a child has thrived upon milk, that it is never to have meat, or that the first twenty years of our lives is to become a precedent for the next twenty. But even this is admitting more than is true, for I answer roundly,

that America would have flourished as much, and probably much more, had no European power had anything to do with her. The commerce by which she hath enriched herself are the necessaries of life, and will always have a market while eating is the custom of Europe.

But she has protected us, say some. That she has engrossed[2] us is true, and defended the continent at our expense as well as her own is admitted—and she would have defended Turkey from the same motive, viz. the sake of trade and dominion.

Alas, we have been long led away by ancient prejudices, and made large sacrifices to superstition. We have boasted the protection of Great Britain, without considering, that her motive was interest, not attachment; that she did not protect us from our enemies on our account, but from her enemies on her own account, from those who had no quarrel with us on any other account, and who will always be our enemies on the same account. Let Britain wave her pretensions to the continent, or the continent throw off the dependence, and we should be at peace with France and Spain were they at war with Britain. The miseries of Hanover's last war ought to warn us against connections.[3]

It has lately been asserted in parliament that the colonies have no relation to each other but through the parent country—i.e., that Pennsylvania and the Jerseys,[4] and so on for the rest, are sister colonies by the way of England; this is certainly a very roundabout way of proving relationship, but it is the nearest and only true way of proving enemyship, if I may so call it. France and Spain never were, nor perhaps ever will be our enemies as Americans, but as our being the *subjects of Great-Britain*.

But Britain is the parent country, say some. Then the more shame upon her conduct. Even brutes do not

---

[1]   *commencement of hostilities* On 19 April 1775, fifteen months before the Declaration of Independence, British and American forces clashed at Lexington, Massachusetts, in what is often thought of as the first battle of the American Revolution.

[2]   *engrossed* Dominated.

[3]   *The miseries … connections* Paine here refers to the Seven Years' War (1756–63), a major military conflict that involved a number of European powers, including Britain and France. Though Britain was eventually largely successful militarily, success did not come easily; heavy losses were suffered (not least of all in the American colonies), and Britain doubled its national debt in order to finance the war. The British monarchs during this period—George II and then George III—were both of the House of Hanover.

[4]   *Jerseys* Between 1674 and 1702 New Jersey was divided into East and West Jersey.

devour their young, nor savages make war upon their families; wherefore the assertion, if true, turns to her reproach. But it happens not to be true, or only partly so, and the phrase *parent* or *mother country* hath been jesuitically[1] adopted by the king and his parasites, with a low papistical[2] design of gaining an unfair bias on the credulous weakness of our minds. Europe, and not England, is the parent country of America. This new world hath been the asylum for the persecuted lovers of civil and religious liberty from *every part* of Europe. Hither have they fled, not from the tender embraces of the mother, but from the cruelty of the monster; and it is so far true of England, that the same tyranny which drove the first emigrants from home, pursues their descendants still.

In this extensive quarter of the globe, we forget the narrow limits of three hundred and sixty miles (the extent of England) and carry our friendship on a larger scale; we claim brotherhood with every European Christian, and triumph in the generosity of the sentiment.

It is pleasant to observe by what regular gradations we surmount the force of local prejudice, as we enlarge our acquaintance with the world. A man born in any town in England divided into parishes, will naturally associate most with his fellow parishioners (because their interests in many cases will be common) and distinguish him by the name of neighbour; if he meet him but a few miles from home, he drops the narrow idea of a street, and salutes him by the name of townsman; if he travel out of the county, and meet him in any other, he forgets the minor divisions of street and town, and calls him countryman, i.e. county-man; but if in their foreign excursions they should associate in France or any other part of Europe, their local remembrance would be enlarged into that of Englishmen. And by a just parity of reasoning, all Europeans meeting in

America, or any other quarter of the globe, are countrymen; for England, Holland, Germany, or Sweden, when compared with the whole, stand in the same places on the larger scale which the divisions of street, town, and county do on the smaller ones; distinctions too limited for continental minds. Not one third of the inhabitants, even of this province,[3] are of English descent. Wherefore I reprobate the phrase of parent or mother country applied to England only, as being false, selfish, narrow, and ungenerous.

But admitting that we were all of English descent— what does it amount to? Nothing. Britain, being now an open enemy, extinguishes every other name and title: And to say that reconciliation is our duty, is truly farcical. The first king of England, of the present line (William the Conqueror) was a Frenchman, and half the peers of England[4] are descendants from the same country; wherefore, by the same method of reasoning, England ought to be governed by France.

Much hath been said of the united strength of Britain and the colonies, that in conjunction they might bid defiance to the world. But this is mere presumption; the fate of war is uncertain, neither do the expressions mean anything; for this continent would never suffer itself to be drained of inhabitants to support the British arms in either Asia, Africa, or Europe.

Besides, what have we to do with setting the world at defiance? Our plan is commerce, and that, well attended to, will secure us the peace and friendship of all Europe; because, it is the interest of all Europe to have America a free port. Her trade will always be a protection, and her barrenness of gold and silver secure her from invaders.

I challenge the warmest advocate for reconciliation to show a single advantage that this continent can reap by being connected with Great Britain. I repeat the challenge; not a single advantage is derived. Our corn[5] will fetch its price in any market in Europe, and our imported goods must be paid for, buy them where we will.

---

[1] *jesuitically* Paine is here partaking in a long tradition of anti-Catholic prejudice. The Jesuits—a Catholic religious order—were known for the rigorous training in logic and argumentation that they provided in their schools. Non-Catholics often disparaged Jesuitical practices of argumentation as conniving and deceitful.

[2] *papistical* Of a sort that one would expect from the pope and his followers. It was a common slur among the English (and among many Protestants elsewhere) to suggest that the Pope and, more generally, the Catholic church exercised undue influence over its credulous followers.

[3] *this province* Pennsylvania.

[4] *peers of England* Members of the upper house of the British parliament, the House of Lords, who were at the time all members of the English nobility.

[5] *corn* Grain.

But the injuries and disadvantages which we sustain by that connection are without number; and our duty to mankind at large, as well as to ourselves, instruct us to renounce the alliance, because any submission to, or dependence on Great Britain tends directly to involve this continent in European wars and quarrels; and sets us at variance with nations who would otherwise seek our friendship, and against whom we have neither anger nor complaint. As Europe is our market for trade, we ought to form no partial connection with any part of it. It is the true interest of America to steer clear of European contentions, which she never can do while, by her dependence on Britain, she is made the make-weight in the scale of British politics.

Europe is too thickly planted with kingdoms to be long at peace, and whenever a war breaks out between England and any foreign power, the trade of America goes to ruin because of her connection with Britain. The next war may not turn out like the last,[1] and should it not, the advocates for reconciliation now will be wishing for separation then, because neutrality, in that case, would be a safer convoy than a man-of-war.[2] Every thing that is right or natural pleads for separation. The blood of the slain, the weeping voice of Nature cries, "'Tis time to part." Even the distance at which the Almighty hath placed England and America is a strong and natural proof that the authority of the one, over the other, was never the design of Heaven. The time likewise at which the continent was discovered adds weight to the argument, and the manner in which it was peopled increases the force of it. The Reformation[3] was preceded by the discovery of America, as if the Almighty graciously meant to open a sanctuary to the persecuted in future years, when home should afford neither friendship nor safety.

The authority of Great Britain over this continent is a form of government which sooner or later must have an end. And a serious mind can draw no true pleasure by looking forward, under the painful and positive conviction that what he calls "the present constitution" is merely temporary. As parents, we can have no joy, knowing that this government is not sufficiently lasting to ensure anything which we may bequeath to posterity. And by a plain method of argument, as we are running the next generation into debt, we ought to do the work of it; otherwise we use them meanly[4] and pitifully. In order to discover the line of our duty rightly, we should take our children in our hand, and fix our station a few years farther into life; that eminence will present a prospect which a few present fears and prejudices conceal from our sight.

Though I would carefully avoid giving unnecessary offence, yet I am inclined to believe that all those who espouse the doctrine of reconciliation may be included within the following descriptions: interested men,[5] who are not to be trusted; weak men, who cannot see; prejudiced men, who *will not* see; and a certain set of moderate men, who think better of the European world than it deserves; and this last class, by an ill-judged deliberation, will be the cause of more calamities to this continent, than all the other three.

It is the good fortune of many to live distant from the scene of sorrow; the evil is not sufficiently brought to their doors to make them feel the precariousness with which all American property is possessed. But let our imaginations transport us for a few moments to Boston; that seat of wretchedness[6] will teach us wisdom, and instruct us for ever to renounce a power in whom we can have no trust. The inhabitants of that unfortunate city, who but a few months ago were in ease and affluence, have now, no other alternative than to stay and starve, or turn out to beg. Endangered by the fire of their friends if they continue within the city, and plundered by the soldiery if they leave it, in their present condition they are prisoners without the hope of redemption, and in a general attack for their relief, they would be exposed to the fury of both armies.

Men of passive tempers look somewhat lightly over the offences of Britain, and, still hoping for the best, are apt to call out, "Come, come, we shall be friends

---

1   *may not ... like the last*   I.e., may not end with Britain as the victor (as did the Seven Years' War).

2   *man-of-war*   Large, heavily armed naval warship.

3   *The Reformation*   I.e., the emergence of Protestantism in Europe, which in its early years (and in areas where Catholicism remained the dominant religion) led to the persecution of many dissenters by the Catholic Church.

4   *meanly*   Stingily.

5   *interested men*   I.e., people who have a financial interest or some other personal involvement in a particular matter.

6   *Boston ... wretchedness*   At the time Paine was writing, Boston was blockaded and occupied by the British military.

again, for all this." But examine the passions and feelings of mankind, bring the doctrine of reconciliation to the touchstone of nature, and then tell me whether you can hereafter love, honour, and faithfully serve the power that hath carried fire and sword into your land? If you cannot do all these, then are you only deceiving yourselves, and by your delay bringing ruin upon posterity. Your future connection with Britain, whom you can neither love nor honour, will be forced and unnatural, and, being formed only on the plan of present convenience, will in a little time fall into a relapse more wretched than the first. But if, you say, you can still pass the violations over, then I ask, Hath your house been burnt? Hath your property been destroyed before your face? Are your wife and children destitute of a bed to lie on, or bread to live on? Have you lost a parent or a child by their hands, and yourself the ruined and wretched survivor? If you have not, then are you not a judge[1] of those who have. But if you have, and still can shake hands with the murderers, then are you unworthy[2] of the name of husband, father, friend, or lover, and whatever may be your rank or title in life; you have the heart of a coward, and the spirit of a sycophant.

This is not inflaming or exaggerating matters, but trying them by those feelings and affections which nature justifies, and without which we should be incapable of discharging the social duties of life, or enjoying the felicities of it. I mean not to exhibit horror for the purpose of provoking revenge, but to awaken us from fatal and unmanly slumbers, that we may pursue determinately some fixed object. It is not in the power of Britain or of Europe to conquer America, if she do not conquer herself by delay and timidity. The present winter is worth an age if rightly employed, but if lost or neglected, the whole continent will partake of the misfortune; and there is no punishment which that man will not deserve, be he who, or what, or where he will, that may be the means of sacrificing a season so precious and useful.

It is repugnant to reason, to the universal order of things, to all examples from former ages, to suppose that this continent can longer remain subject to any external power. The most sanguine in Britain does not think so. The utmost stretch of human wisdom cannot, at this time, compass a plan short of separation which can promise the continent even a year's security. Reconciliation is now a fallacious dream. Nature hath deserted the connection, and Art cannot supply her place. For, as Milton wisely expresses, "never can true reconcilement grow where wounds of deadly hate have pierced so deep."[3] ...

As to government matters, it is not in the power of Britain to do this continent justice; the business of it will soon be too weighty and intricate to be managed with any tolerable degree of convenience by a power so distant from us, and so very ignorant of us—for if they cannot conquer us, they cannot govern us. To be always running three or four thousand miles with a tale or a petition, waiting four or five months for an answer (which, when obtained, requires five or six more to explain it in), will in a few years be looked upon as folly and childishness. There was a time when it was proper, and there is a proper time for it to cease.

Small islands not capable of protecting themselves are the proper objects for kingdoms to take under their care; but there is something very absurd in supposing a continent to be perpetually governed by an island. In no instance hath nature made the satellite larger than its primary planet, and as England and America, with respect to each other, reverses the common order of nature, it is evident they belong to different systems: England to Europe, America to itself.

I am not induced by motives of pride, party, or resentment to espouse the doctrine of separation and independence; I am clearly, positively, and conscientiously persuaded that it is the true interest of this continent to be so; that everything short of that is mere patchwork, that it can afford no lasting felicity—that it is leaving the sword to our children, and shrinking back at a time when a little more, a little farther, would have rendered this continent the glory of the earth. ...

But where, says some, is the King of America? I'll tell you, Friend; he reigns above, and doth not make havoc of mankind like the Royal Brute of Britain. Yet, that we may not appear to be defective even in earthly honors, let a day be solemnly set apart for proclaiming the charter; let it be brought forth placed on the divine law, the word of God; let a crown be placed thereon, by

---

1   *then are you not a judge*   I.e., then it is not your place to judge.

2   *are you unworthy*   You are unworthy.

3   *never can ... so deep*   See John Milton's 1667 poem *Paradise Lost*, 4.98–99. (Ironically, the words are spoken by Lucifer.)

which the world may know, that, so far as we approve of monarchy, that in America the law is king. For, as in absolute governments the King is law, so in free countries the law ought to be King; and there ought to be no other. But, lest any ill use should afterwards arise, let the crown at the conclusion of the ceremony be demolished, and scattered among the people whose right it is.

A government of our own is our natural right. And when a man seriously reflects on the precariousness of human affairs, he will become convinced that it is infinitely wiser and safer to form a constitution of our own in a cool deliberate manner, while we have it in our power, than to *trust* such an interesting event to time and chance. If we omit it now,[1] some Massanello[2] may hereafter arise who, laying hold of popular disquietudes, may collect together the desperate and the discontented, and by assuming to themselves the powers of government, may sweep away the liberties of the continent like a deluge. Should the government of America return again into the hands of Britain, the tottering situation of things will be a temptation for some desperate adventurer to try his fortune; and in such a case, what relief can Britain give? Ere she could hear the news, the fatal business might be done; and ourselves suffering like the wretched Britons under the oppression of the Conqueror. Ye that oppose independence now, ye know not what ye do; ye are opening a door to eternal tyranny by keeping vacant the seat of government. There are thousands, and tens of thousands, who would think it glorious to expel from the continent that barbarous and hellish power which hath stirred up the Indians and Negroes to destroy us. The cruelty hath a double guilt; it is dealing brutally by us, and treacherously by them.

To talk of friendship with those in whom our reason forbids us to have faith, and our affections wounded through a thousand pores instruct us to detest, is madness and folly. Every day wears out the little remains of kindred between us and them, and can there be any reason to hope that, as the relationship expires, the affection will increase; or that we shall agree better, when we have ten times more and greater concerns to quarrel over than ever?

Ye that tell us of harmony and reconciliation, can ye restore to us the time that is past? Can ye give to prostitution its former innocence? Neither can ye reconcile Britain and America. The last cord now is broken; the people of England are presenting addresses against us.[3] There are injuries which Nature cannot forgive; she would cease to be Nature if she did. As well can the lover forgive the ravisher of his mistress, as the continent forgive the murders of Britain. The Almighty hath implanted in us these unextinguishable feelings for good and wise purposes. They are the guardians of His image in our hearts. They distinguish us from the herd of common animals. The social compact would dissolve, and justice be extirpated the earth (or have only a casual existence) were we callous to the touches of affection. The robber and the murderer would often escape unpunished, did not the injuries which our tempers sustain provoke us into justice.

O ye that love mankind! Ye that dare oppose, not only the tyranny, but the tyrant, stand forth! Every spot of the old world is overrun with oppression. Freedom hath been hunted round the globe. Asia and Africa have long expelled her. Europe regards her like a stranger, and England hath given her warning to depart. O! receive the fugitive, and prepare in time an asylum for mankind. ...

—1776

---

1   *omit it now*   Neglect to do it now.

2   [Paine's note]   Thomas Anello, otherwise Massanello, a fisherman of Naples who, after spiriting up his countrymen in the public marketplace, against the oppression of the Spaniards, to whom the place was then subject, prompted them to revolt, and in the space of a day became king. [The rebel leader is more commonly referred to as Tommaso Aniello (1620–47).]

3   *presenting addresses against us*   Initiating conflict with us.

In Context

A Response to *Common Sense*

from Charles Inglis, *The Deceiver Unmasked; or, Loyalty and Interest United in Answer to a Pamphlet Entitled* Common Sense (1776)

Charles Inglis (1734–1816) emigrated to the American colonies in 1755; he worked for some years as a priest in Delaware before being appointed to Trinity Church in New York. Vehemently opposed to Paine's suggestion that the colonies declare independence from Britain, Inglis was one of several loyalists who issued pamphlets in response to Paine's *Common Sense*. When Inglis first issued his pamphlet under the provocative title *The Deceiver Unmasked* (in an edition printed by Samuel Loudon), it met with a violent reaction from the Sons of Liberty group—as Hugh Hughes described in a 31 March letter to John Adams:

> There has been a Pamphlet written and published here against our natural rights and "Common Sense." It has met with its demerit. Some of our sturdy Sons seized between 1,500 and 2,000 of them at Sam Loudon's, and consigned them to the flames. This has given great umbrage to several of our pretended friends, but they are forced to pocket the affront.

Following this act of vandalism, Inglis re-issued the pamphlet with a different printer under a less incendiary title: *The True Interest of America Impartially Stated, in Certain Strictures on a Pamphlet Entitled* Common Sense (1776).

In the face of the success of the Revolution, Inglis returned to England (in 1783), but in 1787 he emigrated again to the British colonies—this time to Nova Scotia, where he became the Anglican Church's first bishop to be based in North America.

Preface

The following pages contain an answer to one of the most artful, insidious, and pernicious pamphlets I have ever met with. It is addressed to the passions of the populace, at a time when their passions are much inflamed. At such juncture, cool reason and judgement are too apt to sleep: the mind is easily imposed on. …

The author of *Common Sense* has availed himself of all these circumstances. Under the mask of friendship to America, in the present calamitous situation of affairs, he gives vent to his own private resentment and ambition, and recommends a scheme which must infallibly prove ruinous. He proposes that we should renounce our allegiance to the sovereign, break off all connection with Great Britain, and set up an independent empire of the republican kind. Sensible that such a proposal must, even at this time, be shocking to the ears of Americans, he insinuates that the novelty of his sentiments is the only obstacle to their success. …

I find no common sense in this pamphlet, but much uncommon frenzy. It is an outrageous insult on the common sense of Americans—an insidious attempt to poison their minds and seduce them from their loyalty and truest interest. The principles of government laid down in it are not only false, but too absurd to have ever entered the head of a crazy politician before. …

The author calls himself an Englishman, but whether he is a native of Old England or new England is a thing I neither know nor care about. I am only to know him by the features he hath here exhibited of himself, which are those of an avowed republican, utterly averse and unfriendly to the English constitution. …

From our former connection with Great Britain we have already derived numberless advantages and benefits; from a closer union with her, on proper principles, we may derive still greater benefits in future. Duty, gratitude, interest, nay, providence, by its all-wise dispensations, loudly call on both countries to unite, and would join them together; and may infamy be the portion of that wretch who would put them asunder.

February 16, 1776

---

from *The American Crisis*[1]

These are the times that try men's souls. The summer soldier and the sunshine patriot will, in this crisis, shrink from the service of their country; but he that stands it now[2] deserves the love and thanks of man and woman. Tyranny, like hell, is not easily conquered; yet we have this consolation with us, that the harder the conflict, the more glorious the triumph. What we obtain too cheap, we esteem too lightly: it is dearness[3] only that gives every thing its value. Heaven knows how to put a proper price upon its goods; and it would be strange indeed if so celestial an article as freedom should not be highly rated. Britain, with an army to enforce her tyranny, has declared that she has a right (not only to tax) but "to bind us in all cases whatsoever,"[4] and if being bound in that manner is not slavery, then is there not such a thing as slavery upon earth. Even the expression is impious; for so unlimited a power can belong only to God.

Whether the independence of the continent was declared too soon, or delayed too long, I will not now enter into as an argument; my own simple opinion is, that had it been eight months earlier, it would have been much better. We did not make a proper use of last winter; neither could we, while we were in a dependent state. However, the fault, if it were one, was all our own;[5] we have none to blame but ourselves. But no great deal is lost yet. All that Howe[6] has been doing for this month past, is rather a ravage than a conquest, which the spirit of the Jerseys,[7] a year ago, would have quickly repulsed, and which time and a little resolution will soon recover.

I have as little superstition in me as any man living, but my secret opinion has ever been, and still is, that God Almighty will not give up a people to military destruction, or leave them unsupportedly to perish, who have so earnestly and so repeatedly sought to avoid the calamities of war, by every decent method which wisdom could invent. Neither have I so much of the infidel in me as to suppose that He has relinquished the government of the world, and given us up to the care of devils; and as I do not, I cannot see on what grounds the king of Britain can look up to heaven for help against us; a common murderer, a highwayman, or a house-breaker, has as good a pretence as he. ...

—1776

---

1   This was the first in a series of "Crisis" pamphlets that Paine issued between December 1776 and December 1783.

2   *stands it now*   Endures the crisis now.

3   *dearness*   Great expense.

4   *to bind ... whatsoever*   Reference to a statement made in the Declaratory Act (1766): "[the British government] had, hath, and of right ought to have, full power and authority to make laws and statutes of sufficient force and validity to bind the colonies and people of America, subjects of the crown of great Britain, in all cases whatsoever."

5   [Paine's note]   The present winter is worth an age, if rightly employed; but, if lost or neglected, the whole continent will partake of the evil; and there is no punishment that man does not deserve, be he who, or what, or where he will, that may be the means of sacrificing a season so precious and useful. [Paine is here quoting from *Common Sense*.]

6   *Howe*   Sir William Howe (1729–1814), commander of the British forces during the Revolutionary War.

7   *the Jerseys*   East New Jersey and West New Jersey; Paine is referring to Washington's successful surprise attack on Christmas Day of the previous year.

THOMAS JEFFERSON
1743 – 1826

From his own time through to the twenty-first century, Thomas Jefferson has remained one of the most admired figures in American history. Yet his legacy is extraordinarily complex and, in many ways, controversial; it has been interpreted and re-interpreted in myriad ways since his death. As the primary author of the Declaration of Independence, Jefferson penned some of the most cherished and quintessentially American phrases in the nation's history, setting out the ideals of democracy, equality, and religious freedom that remain close to its political heart. Yet many historians have seen Jefferson's position as an advocate of freedom and equality as deeply conflicted, given his status as a lifelong slaveholder and his troubling comments on natural racial difference. Jefferson embodies the profound contradictions at the heart of America's political and cultural history.

Jefferson was born into relative privilege in Shadwell, Virginia, the son of well-to-do plantation owner Peter Jefferson and his wife Jane Randolph Jefferson. He inherited the plantation—and its numerous enslaved people—upon the death of his father in 1757. Jefferson was educated privately for several years; at the age of sixteen he entered William and Mary College in Williamsburg, where he became immersed in the study of ethics, law, history, and natural philosophy. After leaving the college in 1762, Jefferson pursued further study of the law, and continued to work in the legal profession until the end of the decade, when he was elected to the colonial legislature of Virginia. In 1772 Jefferson married Martha Wayles, who brought well over one hundred enslaved people into the marriage upon her father's death; the couple would go on to have six children, though only two would live into adulthood.

Among the notable efforts of Jefferson's early political career was a failed attempt to repeal the 1691 legislation that effectively made manumission illegal in Virginia. In later years, he would reflect bitterly on the rejection of his proposed bill, writing that, "indeed, during the regal government, nothing liberal could expect success. Our minds were circumscribed within narrow limits, by an habitual belief that it was our duty to be subordinate to the mother country in all matters of government." As tensions between America and the "mother country" increased, so did Jefferson's prominence as a political figure and writer of political documents. In 1774, in response to the political unrest following the Boston Tea Party, Jefferson was called upon to draft the *Summary View of the Rights of British America*, arguably the strongest written expression of antipathy against British rule published in the American colonies up to that point. While it did not expressly support separation from the Crown, the article contained many ideas that anticipated those expressed two years later in the Declaration of Independence; the *Summary View* argued that the British monarch had no legitimate right to impose laws on the colonists without their consent, and that to do so was an infringement upon their God-given rights. The document was controversial, and was not officially adopted by the First Virginia Convention of 1774; nevertheless, it was widely circulated as a pamphlet among patriotically inclined readers, and its ideas soon became central to the philosophy of what was increasingly appearing to be an inevitable war.

In 1776, Jefferson became the unofficial leader of a committee of five chosen by the Second Continental Congress to draft a Declaration of Independence. The influence of John Locke's *Two Treatises* (in which the British philosopher argues that the authority of monarchs is founded on the consent of the people) on the Declaration has long been recognized, but Jefferson's approach may have owed at least as much to the influence of other thinkers, especially to Scottish Enlightenment philosophers such as Francis Hutcheson (1694–1746), who contributed significantly to developing the idea of natural, "unalienable" rights. The now-famous phrasings of the Declaration were refined through numerous revisions, some of which were highly significant. In his *Autobiography*, Jefferson emphasises his role as the document's primary author while drawing attention to the differences between the draft he presented before the Congress and the edited version that would become the official document of the Revolution; the passages removed by the Congress include some of Jefferson's strongest indictments of the British King, as well as a vehement and controversial passage censuring Britain for its role in the "execrable commerce" of the slave trade. The final work was approved on the fourth of July, though it was not in fact signed until August.

Jefferson returned to Virginia after the Declaration was signed; he was elected to the House of Delegates in September 1776 and to the position of Governor in 1779. His time in state politics was marked by the introduction of a number of rejected bills, including a bill for providing free public education for both boys and girls, and "A Bill for Establishing Religious Freedom," which became the basis for the Virginia Statute for Religious Freedom in 1786; Jefferson later considered this last to be among his greatest achievements.

Shortly after the end of his second term as Virginia's governor, Jefferson began working on *Notes on the State of Virginia* (1787), the only book he published during his lifetime. It was prompted by a questionnaire sent him and other state representatives in 1780 by French diplomat François Marbois, as part of an endeavor by France to learn more about its new allies (France, too, was then at war with the British). In answering Marbois's twenty-two queries about Virginia's laws, geographical features, economy, Indigenous population, and other matters, Jefferson, who had long been a keen historian and collector of historical documents, took the endeavor far more seriously than any of the other delegates, only a handful of whom had responded with even brief replies. Over the following two years, Jefferson expanded his initial response—to which Marbois had responded with delight in December 1781—into a multifaceted examination of the political, social, and economic constitution of the emerging United States, as seen through the lens of the state of Virginia. The text's meticulous collation of information, as well as its blending of areas of study that might today be seen as disparate, reflects Enlightenment-era ideas about the interconnectedness of rational knowledge. Many parts of the text are direct responses to the ideas and writings of contemporary European thinkers, most notably those of French naturalist the Comte de Buffon, whose theories about the physical inferiority of American species Jefferson takes pains to refute. Interspersed through Jefferson's recitals of facts are many passages expressing his views on matters such as emigration, religion, slavery, and race. His reflections on the latter two subjects are of particular interest to modern readers. At the time of the text's publication, Jefferson expressed fears that his condemnation of slavery would prove controversial; today, it is the apparently incongruous racism expressed throughout the text (especially in Query 14, where he offers some deeply disturbing opinions about the intellectual inferiority of African Americans, as well as in his less pejorative but still troubling comments about Indigenous Americans) that prompts in many readers disconcerted questions about Jefferson's intellectual legacy.

Jefferson did not initially intend his *Notes* for broad circulation, and it was not until 1787 that he succumbed to increasing public demand and arranged for the general publication of the text in London. Though his contemporary readers were generally enthusiastic, Jefferson himself often dismissed the work as a mere collection of notes. Many nineteenth-century readers likewise criticized the text's heterogeneity; today, however, *Notes on the State of Virginia* is widely acknowledged to be among the most important American books of the eighteenth century.

When *Notes* was published, Jefferson was himself living in Paris, where he had been appointed in 1785 to take over Benjamin Franklin's position as U.S. Minister to France. (Here he struck up an acquaintance with the Comte de Buffon, to whom he presented both a cougar skin and a stuffed moose as proof of the great size of American species.) Jefferson returned to America in 1790, after which he served in a string of increasingly powerful political roles: Secretary of State, Vice President to John Adams, and eventually—though it was not a role he much desired—President. His Presidency was marked by, among many things, an emphasis on states' rights and on Western expansion. Through the 1803 purchase of the Louisiana Territory from France, Jefferson's government almost doubled the geographical size of the young republic, acquiring undisputed control of the strategically and commercially important New Orleans and the Mississippi River—and also acquiring nominal control over vast areas occupied by Native Americans. The purchase seems an extraordinary bargain in hindsight; the Americans had been willing to pay $10 million for New Orleans and its environs alone, and were astonished to find the French, who were preoccupied both with war in Europe and with the unexpected strength of rebel forces in their Caribbean colony of Saint-Domingue, willing to part with the entire territory for $15 million (well under $1 billion in today's money). Yet the transaction was highly controversial at the time, with many Americans opposing the purchase on the grounds that it could unnecessarily involve the republic in European quarrels—and could worsen divisions between North and South over slavery. Notably, Jefferson made no move to limit the expansion of slavery into the new territory. He was, however, responsible for enacting the 1808 Act Prohibiting the Importation of Slaves, a small step toward abolition that was celebrated by many abolitionists at the time.

Jefferson retired from public life in 1809, after two terms as President, and spent his last years embracing life as an agriculturalist at his now-famous plantation, Monticello. He began writing his memoirs in 1821 after many requests from friends and admirers; though today known generally as *The Autobiography of Thomas Jefferson*, this short text was first published only as part of the collected *Papers of Thomas Jefferson*, released posthumously in 1829. In a coincidence that has now reached the status of myth, Jefferson died on the fourth of July on the fiftieth anniversary of the Declaration of Independence, just hours before the death of his friend, adversary, and fellow Declaration drafter John Adams. After his death, the vast majority of Jefferson's enslaved people were sent to the auction block.

In recent years, one of the most controversial aspects of Jefferson's life has been his long-term sexual relationship with Sally Hemings, an enslaved mixed-race woman approximately thirty years his junior. The relationship likely began soon after Martha Jefferson's 1782 death. Rumors of the relationship were first made public in 1802 by newspaper scandalmonger James T. Callender, and they surfaced repeatedly in the following decades (perhaps most famously in William Wells Brown's 1853 novel *Clotel; or, The President's Daughter*). Until the late twentieth century, however, the vast majority of historians and scholars dismissed the allegation that Jefferson had fathered several children with Hemings; it was only in the 1990s that an increasing willingness to accept the oral testimonies that had been given by Hemings's descendants since the 1800s—together with DNA testing—finally persuaded mainstream historians to accept the reality of the relationship. This aspect of Jefferson's life—along with the fact that, of the approximately six hundred enslaved people he owned throughout his life, Jefferson freed only nine—continues to complicate the reputation of a figure who prided himself on his lifelong opposition to slavery as an industry, and who wrote with such memorable eloquence about the fundamental rights and equality of all people.

NOTE ON THE TEXTS: The excerpt from Thomas Jefferson's *Autobiography*, which includes the Declaration of Independence, has been taken from the A.A. Lipscomb and A.E. Bergh's 1903 edition of *The Writings of Thomas Jefferson*. As is now standard practice in anthologies of this sort, the differences between Jefferson's original version of the Declaration and that finally adopted by the Second Continental Congress are indicated, here with the omitted text underlined, and text added by the Congress placed in square brackets. The text of *Notes on the State of Virginia* is taken from the London edition of 1787. Except in the Declaration, spelling and punctuation have been modernized in accordance with the practices of this anthology.

⌘ ⌘ ⌘

from *The Autobiography of Thomas Jefferson*

Congress proceeded the same day[1] to consider the Declaration of Independence, which had been reported and lain on the table the Friday preceding, and on Monday referred to a committee of the whole. The pusillanimous idea that we had friends in England worth keeping terms with still haunted the minds of many. For this reason, those passages which conveyed censures on the people of England were struck out, lest they should give them offence. The clause, too, reprobating the enslaving the inhabitants of Africa, was struck out in complaisance to South Carolina and Georgia, who had never attempted to restrain the importation of slaves, and who, on the contrary, still wished to continue it. Our northern brethren also, I believe, felt a little tender under those censures; for though their people had very few slaves themselves, yet they had been pretty considerably carriers of them to others. The debates, having taken up the greater parts of the 2nd, 3rd, and 4th days of July, were, on the evening of the last, closed; the Declaration was reported by the committee, agreed to by the House, and signed by every member present, except Mr. Dickinson.[2] As the sentiments of men are known not only by what they receive, but what they reject also, I will state the form of the Declaration as originally reported. The parts struck out by Congress shall be distinguished by a black line drawn under them; and those inserted by them shall be placed in the margin, or in a concurrent column.[3]

A DECLARATION BY THE REPRESENTATIVES OF THE UNITED STATES OF AMERICA, IN GENERAL CONGRESS ASSEMBLED

When, in the course of human events, it becomes necessary for one people to dissolve the political bands which have connected them with another, and to assume among the powers of the earth the separate and equal station to which the laws of nature and of nature's God entitle them, a decent respect to the opinions of mankind requires that they should declare the causes which impel them to the separation.

We hold these truths to be self evident:[4] that all men are created equal; that they are endowed by their Creator with [certain] <u>inherent and</u> inalienable rights;[5] that among these are life, liberty, and the pursuit of happiness;[6] that to secure these rights, governments are instituted among men, deriving their just powers from the consent of the governed; that whenever any form of government becomes destructive of these ends, it is the right of the people to alter or to abolish it, and to institute new government, laying its foundation on such principles, and organizing its powers in such form, as to them shall seem most likely to effect their safety and happiness. Prudence, indeed, will dictate that governments long established should not be changed for light and transient causes; and accordingly all experience hath shown that mankind are more disposed to suffer while evils are sufferable, than to right themselves by abolishing the forms to which they are accustomed. But when a long train of abuses and usurpations, <u>begun at a distinguished[7] period and</u> pursuing invariably the same object, evinces a design to reduce them under absolute despotism, it is their right, it is their duty to throw off such government, and to provide new guards for their future security. Such has been the patient sufferance of these colonies; and such is not the necessity

---

[1]   *the same day*   1 July 1776.

[2]   *Mr. Dickinson*   John Dickinson (1732–1808), the representative from Pennsylvania. He was generally resistant to the idea of violent revolution, and believed that declaring independence was inadvisable until the colonies had finished drafting the Articles of Confederation and established foreign allies.

[3]   *those inserted ... column*   In this reproduction of the Declaration, text added by the committee has been indicated with square brackets.

[4]   *self evident*   An earlier draft of the text had the words "sacred and undeniable" here.

[5]   *inalienable rights*   The idea of "unalienable rights" has been traced by some to Scottish philosopher Francis Hutcheson's *Inquiry into the Original of Our Ideas of Beauty and Virtue* (1726), which was widely influential in eighteenth-century America.

[6]   *life ... happiness*   Compare with John Locke's *Two Treatises of Government* (1689), where it is argued that "man" has a natural right to preserve his "life, liberty, and estate [property]."

[7]   *distinguished*   Distinct; particular.

which constrains them to <u>expunge</u> [alter] their former systems of government. The history of the present king of Great Britain[1] is a history of <u>unremitting</u> injuries and usurpations, <u>among which appears no solitary fact to contradict the uniform tenor of the rest, but all have</u> [all having] in direct object the establishment of an absolute tyranny over these states. To prove this, let facts be submitted to a candid world <u>for the truth of which we pledge a faith yet unsullied by falsehood</u>.

He has refused his assent to laws the most wholesome and necessary for the public good.

He has forbidden his governors to pass laws of immediate and pressing importance, unless suspended in their operation till his assent should be obtained; and, when so suspended, he has utterly neglected to attend to them.

He has refused to pass other laws for the accommodation of large districts of people, unless those people would relinquish the right of representation in the legislature, a right inestimable to them, and formidable to tyrants only.

He has called together legislative bodies at places unusual, uncomfortable, and distant from the depository of their public records, for the sole purpose of fatiguing them into compliance with his measures.

He has dissolved representative houses repeatedly <u>and continually</u> for opposing with manly firmness his invasions on the rights of the people.

He has refused for a long time after such dissolutions to cause others to be elected, whereby the legislative powers, incapable of annihilation, have returned to the people at large for their exercise, the state remaining, in the meantime, exposed to all the dangers of invasion from without and convulsions within.

He has endeavored to prevent the population of these states; for that purpose obstructing the laws for naturalization of foreigners, refusing to pass others to encourage their migrations hither, and raising the conditions of new appropriations of lands.

He has <u>suffered</u> [obstructed] the administration of justice <u>totally to cease in some of these states</u> [by] refusing his assent to laws for establishing judiciary powers.

He has made <u>our</u> judges dependent on his will alone for the tenure of their offices, and the amount and payment of their salaries.

He has erected a multitude of new offices, <u>by a self-assumed power</u> and sent hither swarms of new officers to harass our people and eat out their substance.[2]

He has kept among us in times of peace standing armies <u>and ships of war</u> without the consent of our legislatures.

He has affected to render the military independent of, and superior to, the civil power.

He has combined with others to subject us to a jurisdiction foreign to our constitutions and unacknowledged by our laws, giving his assent to their acts of pretended legislation for quartering large bodies of armed troops among us; for protecting them by a mock trial from punishment for any murders which they should commit on the inhabitants of these states; for cutting off our trade with all parts of the world; for imposing taxes on us without our consent; for depriving us [in many cases] of the benefits of trial by jury; for transporting us beyond seas to be tried for pretended offences; for abolishing the free system of English laws in a neighboring province, establishing therein an arbitrary government, and enlarging its boundaries,[3] so as to render it at once an example and fit instrument for introducing the same absolute rule into these <u>states</u> [colonies]; for taking away our charters, abolishing our most valuable laws, and altering fundamentally the forms of our governments; for suspending our own legislatures, and declaring themselves invested with power to legislate for us in all cases whatsoever.

He has abdicated government here <u>withdrawing his governors, and declaring us out of his allegiance and protection</u> [by declaring us out of his protection, and waging war against us].

He has plundered our seas, ravaged our coasts, burnt our towns, and destroyed the lives of our people.

---

[1] *present king of Great Britain* George III (r. 1760–1820).

[2] *eat out their substance* Consume their food and produce.

[3] *for abolishing ... boundaries* The reference is to the Quebec Act of 1774, a controversial act of British Parliament granting numerous special rights to the French inhabitants of the Province of Quebec, which territory Britain had recently acquired from France following the Seven Years' War. The Act extended the province's borders significantly and gave its French inhabitants the right to practice Catholicism, among other things. This was seen by many in the Thirteen Colonies as a threat to Protestantism, as an unjust concession to the French designed to placate them, and moreover as a show of Britain's arbitrary power; it was often referred to as one of the "Intolerable Acts" instigating the American Revolution.

He is at this time transporting large armies of foreign mercenaries[1] to complete the works of death, desolation and tyranny already begun with circumstances of cruelty and perfidy [scarcely paralleled in the most barbarous ages, and totally] unworthy the head of a civilized nation.

He has constrained our fellow citizens taken captive on the high seas, to bear arms against their country, to become the executioners of their friends and brethren, or to fall themselves by their hands.

He has [excited domestic insurrection among us, and has] endeavored to bring on the inhabitants of our frontiers, the merciless Indian savages, whose known rule of warfare is an undistinguished destruction of all ages, sexes and conditions of existence.

He has incited treasonable insurrections of our fellow citizens, with the allurements of forfeiture and confiscation of our property.

He has waged cruel war against human nature itself, violating its most sacred rights of life and liberty in the persons of a distant people who never offended him, captivating and carrying them into slavery in another hemisphere, or to incur miserable death in their transportation thither. This piratical warfare, the opprobrium of INFIDEL powers, is the warfare of the CHRISTIAN king of Great Britain. Determined to keep open a market where MEN should be bought and sold, he has prostituted his negative[2] for suppressing every legislative attempt to prohibit or to restrain this execrable commerce. And that this assemblage of horrors might want no fact of distinguished die,[3] he is now exciting those very people to rise in arms among us, and to purchase that liberty of which he has deprived them,[4] by murdering the people on whom he also obtruded them: thus paying off former crimes committed against the LIBERTIES of one people, with crimes which he urges them to commit against the LIVES of another.

In every stage of these oppressions we have petitioned for redress in the most humble terms: our repeated petitions have been answered only by repeated injuries.

A prince whose character is thus marked by every act which may define a tyrant is unfit to be the ruler of a [free] people who mean to be free. Future ages will scarcely believe that the hardiness of one man adventured, within the short compass of twelve years only, to lay a foundation so broad and so undisguised for tyranny over a people fostered and fixed in principles of freedom.

Nor have we been wanting in attentions to our British brethren. We have warned them from time to time of attempts by their legislature to extend a [an unwarrantable] jurisdiction over these our states [us]. We have reminded them of the circumstances of our emigration and settlement here, no one of which could warrant so strange a pretension: that these were effected at the expense of our own blood and treasure, unassisted by the wealth or the strength of Great Britain: that in constituting indeed our several forms of government, we had adopted one common king, thereby laying a foundation for perpetual league and amity with them: but that submission to their parliament was no part of our constitution, nor ever in idea, if history may be credited: and, we [have] appealed to their native justice and magnanimity as well as to [and we have conjured them by] the ties of our common kindred to disavow these usurpations which were likely to [would inevitably] interrupt our connection and correspondence. They too have been deaf to the voice of justice and of consanguinity, and when occasions have been given them, by the regular course of their laws, of removing from their councils the disturbers of our harmony, they have, by their free election, re-established them in power. At this very time too, they are permitting their chief magistrate to send over not only soldiers of our common blood, but Scotch and foreign mercenaries to

---

[1] *foreign mercenaries* As the revolutionary conflict mounted, Britain entered into treaties with a number of small German states, primarily Hesse-Kassel and Hesse-Hanau, and hired their troops for support in the coming war. These German soldiers—who were not, technically, mercenaries—were referred to as Hessians and came to be known for their brutality and penchant for plundering.

[2] *negative* Right of veto.

[3] *that this ... die* The meaning here is unclear, though a variety of possible interpretations have been put forward. One possible reading might be: "And that this list of horrors might lack no distinctive fact," with "die" possibly being a variant spelling of "dye." Others have put forward that "fact" is a misprint for "facet," with the meaning thus being: "in order that this horrific combination [of evils] might lack nothing in completeness [like a six-sided die with distinct markings on all six sides]."

[4] *exciting those ... deprived them* Lord Dunmore's 1775 Proclamation promised freedom to any enslaved persons who would join the Loyalist army.

invade and destroy us. These facts have given the last stab to agonizing affection, and manly spirit bids us to renounce forever these unfeeling brethren. We must endeavor to forget our former love for them, and hold them as we hold the rest of mankind, enemies in war, in peace friends. We might have been a free and a great people together; but a communication of grandeur and of freedom, it seems, is below their dignity. Be it so, since they will have it. The road to happiness and to glory is open to us, too. We will tread it apart from them, and [We must therefore] acquiesce in the necessity which denounces our eternal separation [and hold them as we hold the rest of mankind, enemies in war, in peace friends]!

[Draft version][1]

We therefore the representatives of the United States of America in General Congress assembled, do in the name, and by the authority of these states reject and renounce all allegiance and subjection to the kings of Great Britain and all others who may hereafter claim by, through or under them; we utterly dissolve all political connection which may heretofore have subsisted between us and the people or parliament of Great Britain: and finally we do assert and declare these colonies to be free and independent states, and that as free and independent states, they have full power to levy war, conclude peace, contract alliances, establish commerce, and to do all other acts and things which independent states may of right do.

And for the support of this declaration, we mutually pledge to each other our lives, our fortunes, and our sacred honor.

[End of facing-column]

The Declaration thus signed on the 4th, on paper was engrossed[2] on parchment, & signed again on the 2d. of August.
—1829 (WRITTEN 1821; DECLARATION WRITTEN 1776)

[Final Version]

We, therefore, the representatives of the United States of America in General Congress assembled, appealing to the supreme judge of the world for the rectitude of our intentions, do in the name, and by the authority of the good people of these colonies, solemnly publish and declare, that these united colonies are, and of right ought to be free and independent states; that they are absolved from all allegiance to the British crown, and that all political connection between them and the state of Great Britain is, and ought to be, totally dissolved; and that as free and independent states, they have full power to levy war, conclude peace, contract alliances, establish commerce, and to do all other acts and things which independent states may of right do.

And for the support of this declaration, with a firm reliance on the protection of divine providence, we mutually pledge to each other our lives, our fortunes, and our sacred honor.

---

[1]   To show the substantial revisions made to these closing paragraphs, the editors here follow the standard practice of presenting them in facing-column format, with Jefferson's original (deletions underlined) in the left-hand column and the final text in the right-hand column.

[2]   *engrossed*   Written out in clear, formal handwriting.

from *Notes on the State of Virginia*

from QUERY 14
THE ADMINISTRATION OF JUSTICE AND
DESCRIPTION OF THE LAWS?

... The following variations from the British model[1] are perhaps worthy of being specified. Debtors unable to pay their debts, and making faithful delivery of their whole effects,[2] are released from confinement, and their persons forever discharged from restraint for such previous debts; but any property they may afterwards acquire will be subject to their creditors.

The poor, unable to support themselves, are maintained by an assessment on the titheable persons in their parish. This assessment is levied and administered by twelve persons in each parish, called vestrymen, originally chosen by the housekeepers of the parish, but afterwards filling vacancies in their own body by their own choice. These are usually the most discreet[3] farmers, so distributed through their parish that every part of it may be under the immediate eye of some one of them. They are well acquainted with the details and economy[4] of private life, and they find sufficient inducements to execute their charge[5] well, in their philanthropy, in the approbation of their neighbours, and the distinction which that gives them. The poor who have neither property, friends, nor strength to labour, are boarded in the houses of good farmers, to whom a stipulated sum is annually paid. To those who are able to help themselves a little, or have friends from whom they derive some succours, inadequate however to their full maintenance, supplementary aids are given, which enable them to live comfortably in their own houses, or in the houses of their friends. Vagabonds, without visible property or vocation, are placed in workhouses, where they are well clothed, fed, lodged, and made to labour. Nearly the same method of providing for the poor prevails through all our states; and from Savannah to Portsmouth you will seldom meet a beggar. In the larger towns indeed they sometimes present themselves. These are usually foreigners, who have never obtained a settlement in any parish. I never yet saw a native American[6] begging in the streets or highways. A subsistence is easily gained here; and if, by misfortunes, they are thrown on the charities of the world, those provided by their own country are so comfortable and so certain, that they never think of relinquishing them to become strolling beggars. Their situation too, when sick, in the family of a good farmer, where every member is emulous[7] to do them kind offices, where they are visited by all the neighbours, who bring them the little rarities which their sickly appetites may crave, and who take by rotation the nightly watch over them, when their condition requires it, is without comparison better than in a general hospital, where the sick, the dying, and the dead are crammed together, in the same rooms, and often in the same beds. The disadvantages inseparable from general hospitals are such as can never be counterpoised by all the regularities of medicine and regimen. Nature and kind nursing save a much greater proportion in our plain way, at a smaller expense, and with less abuse. One branch only of hospital institution is wanting with us; that is, a general establishment for those labouring under difficult cases of chirurgery.[8] The aids of this art are not equivocal. But an able chirurgeon cannot be had in every parish. Such a receptacle should therefore be provided for those patients; but no others should be admitted.

Marriages must be solemnized either on special licence, granted by the first magistrate of the county, on proof of the consent of the parent or guardian of either party under age, or after solemn publication, on three several[9] Sundays, at some place of religious worship in the parishes where the parties reside. The act of solemnization may be by the minister of any society of Christians, who shall have been previously licensed for this purpose by the court of the county. Quakers and

---

1   *British model*   I.e., British parliamentary law, which Jefferson discusses in the preceding paragraphs; here he contrasts this system with certain laws adopted in the United States.

2   *effects*   Property.

3   *discreet*   Prudent; trustworthy.

4   *economy*   Management (especially of household affairs).

5   *charge*   Duty.

6   *native American*   I.e., a person of European descent born and raised in America.

7   *emulous*   Desirous (especially in a competitive manner).

8   *chirurgery*   Surgery.

9   *several*   Successive.

Menonists[1] however are exempted from all these conditions, and marriage among them is to be solemnized by the society itself.

A foreigner of any nation not in open war with us becomes naturalized by removing to the state to reside, and taking an oath of fidelity, and thereupon acquires every right of a native citizen; and citizens may divest themselves of that character by declaring, by solemn deed or in open court, that they mean to expatriate themselves, and no longer to be citizens of this state.

Conveyances of land must be registered in the court of the county wherein they lie, or in the general court, or they are void, as to creditors, and subsequent purchasers.

Slaves pass by descent and dower[2] as lands do. Where the descent is from a parent, the heir is bound to pay an equal share of their value in money to each of his brothers and sisters.

Slaves, as well as lands, were entailable[3] during the monarchy; but, by an act of the first republican assembly, all donees in tail,[4] present and future, were vested with the absolute dominion of the entailed subject.

Bills of exchange, being protested, carry 10 per cent interest from their date.

No person is allowed, in any other case, to take more than five per cent per annum simple interest for the loan of monies.

Gaming debts are made void, and monies actually paid to discharge such debts (if they exceeded 40 shillings) may be recovered by the payer within three months, or by any other person afterwards.

Tobacco, flour, beef, pork, tar, pitch, and turpentine, must be inspected by persons publicly appointed, before they can be exported. ...

Many of the laws which were in force during the monarchy being relative merely to that form of government, or inculcating principles inconsistent with republicanism, the first assembly which met after the establishment of the commonwealth appointed a committee to revise the whole code, to reduce it into proper form and volume, and report it to the assembly. This work has been executed by three gentlemen,[5] and reported, but probably will not be taken up till a restoration of peace shall leave to the legislature leisure to go through such a work.

The plan of the revisal was this. The common law of England—by which is meant, that part of the English law which was anterior to the date of the oldest statutes extant—is made the basis of the work. It was thought dangerous to attempt to reduce it to a text; it was therefore left to be collected from the usual monuments of it. Necessary alterations in that, and so much of the whole body of the British statutes, and of acts of assembly, as were thought proper to be retained, were digested into 126 new acts, in which simplicity of style was aimed at, as far as was safe. The following are the most remarkable alterations proposed:

To change the rules of descent, so as that the lands of any person dying intestate[6] shall be divisible equally among all his children, or other representatives, in equal degree.

To make slaves distributable among the next of kin, as other moveables.

To have all public expenses, whether of the general treasury, or of a parish or county (as for the maintenance of the poor, building bridges, courthouses, etc.), supplied by assessments on the citizens, in proportion to their property.

To hire undertakers for keeping the public roads in repair, and indemnify individuals through whose lands new roads shall be opened.

To define with precision the rules whereby aliens should become citizens, and citizens make themselves aliens.

To establish religious freedom on the broadest bottom.

To emancipate all slaves born after passing the act. The bill reported by the revisors does not itself contain this proposition; but an amendment containing

---

1   *Menonists* Mennonites.

2   *dower* I.e., the property inherited by a widow upon the death of her husband.

3   *entailable* An entail was a rule of settlement limiting who could inherit one's property in successive generations, legally preventing future owners from bequeathing any of the inherited estate to any person at will.

4   *donees in tail* Those in possession of a previously entailed property.

5   *three gentlemen* The three revisors Jefferson refers to are himself, George Wythe (1726–1806), and Edmund Pendleton (1721–1803).

6   *intestate* Not having left a will.

it was prepared, to be offered to the legislature whenever the bill should be taken up, and further directing that they should continue with their parents to a certain age, then be brought up, at the public expense, to tillage, arts or sciences, according to their geniuses,[1] till the females should be eighteen, and the males twenty-one years of age, when they should be colonized to such place as the circumstances of the time should render most proper, sending them out with arms,[2] implements of household and of the handicraft arts, seeds, pairs of the useful domestic animals, etc.; to declare them a free and independent people, and extend to them our alliance and protection, till they have acquired strength; and to send vessels at the same time to other parts of the world for an equal number of white inhabitants, to induce whom to migrate hither, proper encouragements were to be proposed. It will probably be asked, Why not retain and incorporate the blacks into the state, and thus save the expense of supplying, by importation of white settlers, the vacancies they will leave? Deep rooted prejudices entertained by the whites; ten thousand recollections, by the blacks, of the injuries they have sustained; new provocations; the real distinctions which nature has made; and many other circumstances, will divide us into parties, and produce convulsions which will probably never end but in the extermination of the one or the other race. To these objections, which are political, may be added others, which are physical and moral. The first difference which strikes us is that of colour. Whether the black of the negro resides in the reticular membrane between the skin and scarf-skin,[3] or in the scarf-skin itself; whether it proceeds from the colour of the blood, the colour of the bile, or from that of some other secretion—the difference is fixed in nature, and is as real as if its seat and cause were better known to us. And is this difference of no importance? Is it not the foundation of a greater or less share of beauty in the two races? Are not the fine mixtures of red and white, the expressions of every passion by greater or less suffusions of colour in the one, preferable to that eternal monotony, which reigns in the countenances,

that immoveable veil of black which covers all the emotions of the other race? Add to these, flowing hair, a more elegant symmetry of form, their own judgment in favour of the whites, declared by their preference of them, as uniformly as is the preference of the Oranootan[4] for the black women over those of his own species. The circumstance of superior beauty is thought worthy attention in the propagation of our horses, dogs, and other domestic animals; why not in that of man? Besides those of colour, figure, and hair, there are other physical distinctions proving a difference of race. They have less hair on the face and body. They secrete less by the kidneys, and more by the glands of the skin, which gives them a very strong and disagreeable odour. This greater degree of transpiration renders them more tolerant of heat, and less so of cold, than the whites. Perhaps too a difference of structure in the pulmonary apparatus, which a late ingenious[5] experimentalist has discovered to be the principal regulator of animal heat, may have disabled them from extricating, in the act of inspiration, so much of that fluid from the outer air, or obliged them in expiration, to part with more of it. They seem to require less sleep. A black, after hard labour through the day, will be induced by the slightest amusements to sit up till midnight or later, though knowing he must be out with the first dawn of the morning. They are at least as brave, and more adventuresome. But this may perhaps proceed from a want of forethought, which prevents their seeing a danger till it be present. When present, they do not go through it with more coolness or steadiness than the whites. They are more ardent after their female, but love seems with them to be more an eager desire, than a tender delicate mixture of sentiment and sensation. Their griefs are transient. Those numberless afflictions, which render it doubtful whether heaven has given life to us in mercy or in wrath, are less felt, and sooner forgotten with them. In general, their existence appears to participate more of sensation than reflection. To this must be ascribed their disposition to sleep when abstracted from their diversions, and unemployed in labour. An

---

[1] *geniuses* Particular skills or inclinations.

[2] *arms* Weapons.

[3] *scarf-skin* Epidermis, or outermost layer of skin.

[4] *Oranootan* Orangutan.

[5] [Jefferson's note] Crawford. [Adair Crawford (1748–95), English physicist and chemist who studied the relationship between heat and respiration.]

animal whose body is at rest, and who does not reflect, must be disposed to sleep of course. Comparing them by their faculties of memory, reason, and imagination, it appears to me, that in memory they are equal to the whites; in reason much inferior, as I think one could scarcely be found capable of tracing and comprehending the investigations of Euclid;[1] and that in imagination they are dull, tasteless, and anomalous. It would be unfair to follow them to Africa for this investigation. We will consider them here, on the same stage with the whites, and where the facts are not apocryphal on which a judgment is to be formed. It will be right to make great allowances for the difference of condition, of education, of conversation, of the sphere in which they move. Many millions of them have been brought to, and born in, America. Most of them indeed have been confined to tillage, to their own homes, and their own society; yet many have been so situated, that they might have availed themselves of the conversation of their masters; many have been brought up to the handicraft arts, from that circumstance have always been associated with the whites. Some have been liberally educated, and all have lived in countries where the arts and sciences are cultivated to a considerable degree, and have had before their eyes samples of the best works from abroad. The Indians, with no advantages of this kind, will often carve figures on their pipes not destitute of design and merit. They will crayon[2] out an animal, a plant, or a country, so as to prove the existence of a germ[3] in their minds which only wants cultivation. They astonish you with strokes of the most sublime oratory, such as prove their reason and sentiment strong, their imagination glowing and elevated. But never yet could I find that a black had uttered a thought above the level of plain narration; never see even an elementary trait of painting or sculpture. In music they are more generally gifted than the whites with accurate ears for tune and time, and they have

been found capable of imagining a small catch.[4] Whether they will be equal to the composition of a more extensive run of melody, or of complicated harmony, is yet to be proved. Misery is often the parent of the most affecting touches in poetry. Among the blacks is misery enough, God knows, but no poetry. Love is the peculiar *æstrum*[5] of the poet. Their love is ardent, but it kindles the senses only, not the imagination. Religion indeed has produced a Phyllis Whately;[6] but it could not produce a poet. The compositions published under her name are below the dignity of criticism. The heroes of the *Dunciad* are to her, as Hercules to the author of that poem.[7] Ignatius Sancho[8] has approached nearer to merit in composition; yet his letters do more honour to the heart than the head. They breathe the purest effusions of friendship and general philanthropy, and show how great a degree of the latter may be compounded with strong religious zeal. He is often happy in the turn of his compliments, and his style is easy and familiar, except

---

1 *Euclid* Ancient Greek mathematician (c. 300 BCE), whose *Elements* was frequently used for the teaching of mathematics during this period.

2 *crayon* Sketch.

3 *germ* Seed.

4 [Jefferson's note] The instrument proper to them is the Banjar, which they brought hither from Africa, and which is the original of the guitar, its chords being precisely the four lower chords of the guitar. [The banjo originated in enslaved communities in the Caribbean and American colonies, and can possibly trace its roots to a number of West African musical instruments. The origin of the guitar, however, is unrelated to either the banjo or its West African ancestors. *catch* Short, simple tune.]

5 *æstrum* Something, especially a kind of passion, which incites a given activity.

6 *Phyllis Whatley* Phillis Wheatley, an enslaved, West African-born woman whose *Poems on Various Subjects, Religious and Moral* (1773) was the first book of poetry to be published by an African American woman. It brought her a great deal of fame on both sides of the Atlantic; Wheatley was emancipated shortly after the volume's publication. A great many of her poems centered on religious (especially Methodist) themes.

7 *The heroes … that poem* The *Dunciad* (1728–43) is a mock-heroic epic poem written by English satirical poet Alexander Pope. Jefferson's comparison of Pope to Hercules is meant to allude to Pope's short and disfigured stature, caused by a number of childhood illnesses.

8 *Ignatius Sancho* British African author, composer, and actor born into slavery in 1729. His *Letters of the Late Ignatius Sancho, an African* were published posthumously in 1782, and included extensive commentary on political, domestic, and artistic life in eighteenth-century England, as well as on his early period of enslavement.

when he affects a Shandean[1] fabrication of words. But his imagination is wild and extravagant, escapes incessantly from every restraint of reason and taste, and, in the course of its vagaries, leaves a tract of thought as incoherent and eccentric, as is the course of a meteor through the sky. His subjects should often have led him to a process of sober reasoning, yet we find him always substituting sentiment for demonstration. Upon the whole, though we admit him to the first place among those of his own colour who have presented themselves to the public judgment, yet when we compare him with the writers of the race among whom he lived, and particularly with the epistolary class, in which he has taken his own stand, we are compelled to enroll him at the bottom of the column. This criticism supposes the letters published under his name to be genuine, and to have received amendment from no other hand—points which would not be of easy investigation.

The improvement of the blacks in body and mind, in the first instance of their mixture with the whites, has been observed by everyone, and proves that their inferiority is not the effect merely of their condition of life. We know that among the Romans, about the Augustan age[2] especially, the condition of their slaves was much more deplorable than that of the blacks on the continent of America. The two sexes were confined in separate apartments, because to raise a child cost the master more than to buy one. Cato,[3] for a very restricted indulgence to his slaves in this particular, took from them a certain price. But in this country the slaves multiply as fast as the free inhabitants. Their situation and manners place the commerce between the two sexes almost without restraint. The same Cato, on a principle of economy, always sold his sick and superannuated slaves. He gives it as a standing precept to a master visiting his farm, to sell his old oxen, old waggons, old tools, old and diseased servants, and

everything else become useless. ... The American slaves cannot enumerate this among the injuries and insults they receive. It was the common practice to expose in the island of Aesculapius, in the Tyber,[4] diseased slaves, whose cure was like to become tedious. The Emperor Claudius,[5] by an edict, gave freedom to such of them as should recover, and first declared, that if any person chose to kill rather than to expose them, it should be deemed homicide. The exposing them is a crime of which no instance has existed with us; and were it to be followed by death, it would be punished capitally. We are told of a certain Vedius Pollio, who, in the presence of Augustus, would have given a slave as food to his fish, for having broken a glass.[6] With the Romans, the regular method of taking the evidence of their slaves was under torture. Here it has been thought better never to resort to their evidence. When a master was murdered, all his slaves, in the same house, or within hearing, were condemned to death. Here punishment falls on the guilty only, and as precise proof is required against him as against a freeman. Yet notwithstanding these and other discouraging circumstances among the Romans, their slaves were often their rarest artists. They excelled too in science, insomuch as to be usually employed as tutors to their master's children. Epictetus, Terence, and Phaedrus[7] were slaves. But they were of the race of whites. It is not their condition then, but nature, which has produced the distinction. Whether further observation will or will not verify the conjecture that nature has been less bountiful to them in the endowments of the head, I believe that in those of the heart she will be found to have done them justice. That disposition to theft with which they have been branded, must be ascribed to their situation, and not to any depravity of the moral sense. The man in whose favour no laws of property exist, probably feels

---

[1]   *Shandean* Allusion to Laurence Sterne's 1759–67 novel *The Life and Opinions of Tristram Shandy*, known for its imaginative use of language. Ignatius Sancho famously wrote to Sterne in 1766 to ask that he more strongly publicize his antislavery opinions.

[2]   *Augustan age* Period of the reign of Augustus, first emperor of the Roman Empire (r. 27 BCE–14 CE).

[3]   *Cato* Cato the Elder (234–149 BCE), Roman politician and historian. Below, Jefferson cites Cato's writings on slavery from *De Re Rusticâ* or *De Agri Cultura* (*On Agriculture*).

[4]   *expose* Leave to die; *Aesculapius, in the Tyber* Tiber Island, named after the river which flows through Rome, was then the site of a temple to Aesculapius, the god of medicine and healing.

[5]   *Emperor Claudius* Emperor of Rome from 41 to 54 CE.

[6]   *Vedius Pollio ... a glass* Pollio was notorious even during his lifetime for his luxurious tastes and excessive cruelty. It is indeed said that he regularly punished those he enslaved by feeding them to his eels.

[7]   *Epictetus* Greek-Roman Stoic philosopher (c. 55–135 CE); *Terence* Roman playwright (c. 190–c. 159 BCE); *Phaedrus* Roman fabulist from the first century CE.

himself less bound to respect those made in favour of others. When arguing for ourselves, we lay it down as a fundamental that laws, to be just, must give a reciprocation of right—that, without this, they are mere arbitrary rules of conduct, founded in force, and not in conscience; and it is a problem which I give to the master to solve, whether the religious precepts against the violation of property were not framed for him as well as his slave? And whether the slave may not as justifiably take a little from one who has taken all from him, as he may slay one who would slay him? That a change in the relations in which a man is placed should change his ideas of moral right and wrong, is neither new, nor peculiar to the colour of the blacks. Homer tells us it was so 2600 years ago.

Ημισυ, γαζ τ᾽ ἀρετῆς ἀποαίνυιαι ευρύθπα Ζευς
Ανερς, ευτ᾽ ἀν μιν κατά δθλιον ἡμαζ ἑλησιν.
                                        Od. 17. 323.

... Jove fix'd it certain, that whatever day
Makes man a slave, takes half his worth away.[1]

But the slaves of which Homer speaks were whites. Notwithstanding these considerations which must weaken their respect for the laws of property, we find among them numerous instances of the most rigid integrity, and as many as among their better instructed masters, of benevolence, gratitude, and unshaken fidelity. The opinion that they are inferior in the faculties of reason and imagination, must be hazarded with great diffidence. To justify a general conclusion requires many observations, even where the subject may be submitted to the anatomical knife, to optical glasses,[2] to analysis by fire, or by solvents. How much more then where it is a faculty, not a substance, we are examining; where it eludes the research of all the senses; where the conditions of its existence are various and variously combined; where the effects of those which are present or absent bid defiance to calculation; let me add too, as a circumstance of great tenderness, where our conclusion would degrade a whole race of men from the rank in the scale of beings which their Creator may perhaps have given them. To our reproach it must be said, that though for a century and a half we have had under our eyes the races of black and of red men, they have never yet been viewed by us as subjects of natural history. I advance it therefore as a suspicion only, that the blacks, whether originally a distinct race, or made distinct by time and circumstances, are inferior to the whites in the endowments both of body and mind. It is not against experience to suppose that different species of the same genus, or varieties of the same species, may posses different qualifications. Will not a lover of natural history then, one who views the gradations in all the races of animals with the eye of philosophy, excuse an effort to keep those in the department of man as distinct as nature has formed them? This unfortunate difference of colour, and perhaps of faculty, is a powerful obstacle to the emancipation of these people. Many of their advocates, while they wish to vindicate the liberty of human nature, are anxious also to preserve its dignity and beauty. Some of these, embarrassed by the question "What further is to be done with them?" join themselves in opposition with those who are actuated by sordid avarice only. Among the Romans emancipation required but one effort. The slave, when made free, might mix with, without staining, the blood of his master. But with us a second is necessary, unknown to history. When freed, he is to be removed beyond the reach of mixture. ...

—1787

---

[1] *Jove ... worth away* Jefferson quotes from Book 17 of Alexander Pope's translation of *The Odyssey of Homer* (1715–20); *Jove* Roman name for the Greek god Zeus.

[2] *optical glasses* I.e., microscopes or magnifying glasses.

The Federalist

During and immediately after the American Revolution (1776–83), the thirteen former colonies which had become the first thirteen states of the United States had been governed by the Articles of Confederation, which was presented to Congress in 1776 and ratified in 1781. In the wake of the Revolutionary War, however, the political context shifted, and the Articles were not proving sufficient to meet new challenges. Political factions and protest movements began to cause civil unrest, and in 1787 twelve states sent delegates to Philadelphia to revise the Articles. The delegates decided that the revisions needed were so extensive that it would be better to draft a new Constitution. Once the Constitution was written, each state was to hold a convention and either ratify or reject it, setting up one of the stormiest political debates in American history. On one side were the Federalists—who urged ratification—and on the other were the Anti-Federalists, who worried that the Constitution would impinge on individual freedom. It was out of this debate that the eighty-five essays that comprise *The Federalist* were born.

The Federalist essays were published in the pages of several New York newspapers from 27 October 1787 to 28 May 1788, in an effort to sway the delegates of New York state to support ratification. They were originally published under the pen name "Publius" in honor of Roman consul Publius Valerius Publicola (d. 503 BCE), whose surname means "friend of the people." They were actually written by three men: Alexander Hamilton (1757–1804), James Madison (1751–1836), and John Jay (1745–1829). Each of these authors was a prominent lawmaker, and each made significant contributions to the United States in its infancy: Hamilton was the first Secretary of the Treasury, Madison the fourth President of the United States, and Jay the first Chief Justice of the Supreme Court.

In 1787 prominent Anti-Federalists, using the pen names "Cato," "Centinel," and "Brutus," began publishing letters and essays in newspapers, arguing against the proposed Constitution. In October 1787, Cato wrote that the Constitution's "principles, and the exercise of them will be dangerous to your liberty and happiness"; earlier in the same month, Centinel claimed that the Constitution was "the most daring attempt to establish a despotic aristocracy among freemen, that the world has ever witnessed." Hamilton, Madison, and Jay responded by writing in support of the Constitution, detailing how checks and balances were built in to divide power and protect the rights of the states and the citizens. In "The Federalist No. 1," Hamilton wrote that the series of essays would "endeavour to give a satisfactory answer to all the objections which shall have made their appearance, that may seem to have any claim to your attention." And *The Federalist* does cover a great deal of ground, including the military, international relations, economic issues, taxation, and executive power. Its central argument, however, is that a strong federal union would be far more beneficial for the growing nation, economically and politically, than a looser collection of independent states. The authors warn against the oppressive powers of sectarianism and advocate a strong constitutional union to protect individuals.

Although the authorship of a few essays is still debated, it is generally accepted that, of the 85 essays, Hamilton wrote 51, Madison 29, and Jay 5. Madison later explained that "though carried on in concert, the writers are not mutually answerable for all the ideas of each other, there being seldom time for even a perusal of the pieces by any but the writer before they were wanted at the press." The pace of writing was indeed swift—all 85 of the papers were written within six months, and sometimes three or four articles would appear within a single week. New York ratified the Constitution on 26 July 1788, and the main object of *The Federalist* was achieved. Government under the new constitution was scheduled to begin on 4 March 1789.

The Anti-Federalists, however, also achieved some of their aims, most notably the addition of a Bill of Rights, designed to secure individual freedoms and to prevent a strong central government from devolving into tyranny. James Madison wrote twelve amendments for the Constitution that would address the Anti-Federalist concerns and limit the power of government. Madison argued that these should be incorporated into the Constitution, but instead they were adopted as codicils. Ten of the amendments were ratified in 1790, forming the American Bill of Rights.

As works of persuasive writing, *The Federalist* papers have been the subject of much analysis in regard to their rhetorical style, and in regard to the perceived similarities and differences between the styles of their three authors. Madison's contributions have been seen by many as the most carefully intellectual of the three. Although the *Papers* were intended as persuasive commentary on a pertinent contemporary matter, they were immediately recognized for their wider significance as outstanding contributions to Western political thought. George Washington wrote to Hamilton that he believed the essays would "merit the notice of posterity" even after the "transient circumstances" of their conception were over; and in a letter to Madison, Thomas Jefferson wrote that *The Federalist* comprised "the best commentary on the principles of government which ever was written." Today *The Federalist* is acknowledged as vitally important for interpreting the provisions of the American Constitution; the essays continue to be cited as touchstones by the Supreme Court of the United States in rendering decisions, and by leading politicians and political writers in discussing current political issues.

NOTE ON THE TEXTS: The texts presented here are based on the original newspaper printings: for *The Federalist* No. 1, this was the version printed in *The Independent Journal* on 27 October 1787; for *The Federalist* No. 10, this was the version printed in *The Daily Advertiser* on 22 November 1787. Jacob Cooke's 1961 edition, *The Federalist,* was also consulted.

⌘⌘⌘

from *The Federalist*

NO. 1 [ALEXANDER HAMILTON]

October 27, 1787

To the People of the State of New York.

AFTER an unequivocal experience of the inefficiency of the subsisting[1] Federal Government, you are called upon to deliberate on a new Constitution for the United States of America. The subject speaks its own importance; comprehending in its consequences, nothing less than the existence of the UNION, the safety and welfare of the parts of which it is composed, the fate of an empire, in many respects, the most interesting in the world. It has been frequently remarked, that it seems to have been reserved to the people of this country, by their conduct and example, to decide the important question, whether societies of men are really capable or not of establishing good government from reflection and choice, or whether they are forever destined to depend, for their political constitutions, on accident and force. If there be any truth in the remark, the crisis at which we are arrived may with propriety be regarded as the era in which that decision is to be made; and a wrong election[2] of the part we shall act, may, in this view, deserve to be considered as the general misfortune of mankind.

This idea will add the inducements of philanthropy to those of patriotism to heighten the solicitude which all considerate and good men must feel for the event. Happy will it be if our choice should be directed by a judicious estimate of our true interests, unperplexed and unbiased by considerations not connected with the public good. But this is a thing more ardently to be wished, than seriously to be expected. The plan offered to our deliberations affects too many particular interests, innovates upon too many local institutions, not to involve in its discussion a variety of objects foreign to its merits, and of views, passions and prejudices little favourable to the discovery of truth.

1 *subsisting* Existing, current.

2 *election* Choice.

Among the most formidable of the obstacles which the new Constitution will have to encounter may readily be distinguished the obvious interest of a certain class of men in every State to resist all changes which may hazard a diminution of the power, emolument[1] and consequence of the offices they hold under the State-establishments—and the perverted[2] ambition of another class of men, who will either hope to aggrandize themselves by the confusions of their country, or will flatter themselves with fairer prospects of elevation from the subdivision of the empire into several partial confederacies, than from its union under one government.

It is not, however, my design to dwell upon observations of this nature. I am well aware that it would be disingenuous to resolve indiscriminately the opposition of any set of men (merely because their situations might subject them to suspicion) into interested or ambitious views. Candour will oblige us to admit that even such men may be actuated by upright intentions; and it cannot be doubted that much of the opposition which has made its appearance, or may hereafter make its appearance, will spring from sources, blameless at least, if not respectable, the honest errors of minds led astray by preconceived jealousies and fears. So numerous indeed and so powerful are the causes, which serve to give a false bias to the judgment, that we, upon many occasions, see wise and good men on the wrong as well as on the right side of questions, of the first magnitude to society. This circumstance, if duly attended to, would furnish a lesson of moderation to those, who are ever so much persuaded of their being in the right, in any controversy. And a further reason for caution, in this respect, might be drawn from the reflection, that we are not always sure, that those who advocate the truth are influenced by purer principles than their antagonists. Ambition, avarice, personal animosity, party opposition, and many other motives not more laudable than these, are apt to operate as well upon those who support as upon those who oppose the right side of a question. Were there not even these inducements to moderation, nothing could be more ill-judged than that intolerant spirit which has, at all times, characterised political parties. For, in politics as

in religion, it is equally absurd to aim at making proselytes by fire and sword. Heresies in either can rarely be cured by persecution.

And yet however just these sentiments will be allowed to be, we have already sufficient indications, that it will happen in this as in all former cases of great national discussion. A torrent of angry and malignant passions will be let loose. To judge from the conduct of the opposite parties, we shall be led to conclude, that they will mutually hope to evince the justness of their opinions, and to increase the number of their converts by the loudness of their declamations, and by the bitterness of their invectives. An enlightened zeal for the energy and efficiency of government will be stigmatized, as the offspring of a temper fond of despotic power and hostile to the principles of liberty. An overscrupulous jealousy[3] of danger to the rights of the people, which is more commonly the fault of the head than of the heart, will be represented as mere pretence and artifice; the bait for popularity at the expense of public good. It will be forgotten, on the one hand, that jealousy is the usual concomitant of violent love, and that the noble enthusiasm of liberty is too apt to be infected with a spirit of narrow and illiberal distrust. On the other hand, it will be equally forgotten, that the vigour of government is essential to the security of liberty; that, in the contemplation of a sound and well-informed judgment, their interest can never be separated; and that a dangerous ambition more often lurks behind the specious mask of zeal for the rights of the people, than under the forbidding appearance of zeal for the firmness and efficiency of government. History will teach us, that the former has been found a much more certain road to the introduction of despotism, than the latter, and that of those men who have overturned the liberties of republics the greatest number have begun their career, by paying an obsequious court to the people,[4] commencing Demagogues and ending Tyrants.

In the course of the preceding observations I have had an eye, my Fellow Citizens, to putting you upon your guard against all attempts, from whatever quarter, to influence your decision in a matter of the utmost

---

1   *emolument* Profit.

2   *perverted* Misguided.

3   *jealousy* Fear or suspicion.

4   *paying an obsequious … people* I.e., being overly eager to gratify popular demands.

moment to your welfare by any impressions other than those which may result from the evidence of truth. You will, no doubt, at the same time, have collected from the general scope of them that they proceed from a source not unfriendly to the new Constitution. Yes, my Countrymen, I own to you, that, after having given it an attentive consideration, I am clearly of opinion, it is your interest to adopt it. I am convinced, that this is the safest course for your liberty, your dignity, and your happiness. I effect not reserves,[1] which I do not feel. I will not amuse you with an appearance of deliberation, when I have decided. I frankly acknowledge to you my convictions, and I will freely lay before you the reasons on which they are founded. The consciousness of good intentions disdains ambiguity. I shall not however multiply professions on this head. My motives must remain in the depository of my own breast: my arguments will be open to all, and may be judged of by all. They shall at least be offered in a spirit, which will not disgrace the cause of truth.

I propose in a series of papers to discuss the following interesting particulars—*The utility of the* UNION *to your political prosperity—The insufficiency of the present Confederation to preserve that Union—The necessity of a government at least equally energetic with the one proposed to the attainment of this object—The conformity of the proposed constitution to the true principles of republican government—Its analogy to your own state constitution—* and lastly, *The additional security, which its adoption will afford to the preservation of that species of government, to liberty and to property.*

In the progress of this discussion I shall endeavour to give a satisfactory answer to all the objections which shall have made their appearance that may seem to have any claim to your attention.

It may perhaps be thought superfluous to offer arguments to prove the utility of the UNION, a point, no doubt, deeply engraved on the hearts of the great body of the people in every state, and one, which it may be imagined has no adversaries. But the fact is, that we already hear it whispered in the private circles of those who oppose the new constitution, that the Thirteen States are of too great extent for any general system, and that we must of necessity resort to separate confederacies of distinct portions of the whole.[2] This doctrine will, in all probability, be gradually propagated, till it has votaries enough to countenance an open avowal of it. For nothing can be more evident, to those who are able to take an enlarged view of the subject, than the alternative of an adoption of the new Constitution, or a dismemberment of the Union. It will therefore be of use to begin by examining the advantages of that Union, the certain evils and the probable dangers, to which every State will be exposed from its dissolution. This shall accordingly constitute the subject of my next address.

PUBLIUS.

NO. 10 [JAMES MADISON]

November 22, 1787

To the People of the State of New York.

AMONG the numerous advantages promised by a well-constructed Union, none deserves to be more accurately developed[3] than its tendency to break and control the violence of faction.[4] The friend of popular[5] governments, never finds himself so much alarmed for their character and fate, as when he contemplates their propensity to this dangerous vice. He will not fail therefore to set a due value on any plan which, without violating the principles to which he is attached, provides a proper cure for it. The instability, injustice and confusion introduced into the public councils, have in truth been the mortal diseases under which popular governments have everywhere perished; as they continue to be the favorite and fruitful topics from which the adversaries to liberty derive their most specious declamations.[6] The valuable improvements made by the American constitutions on the popular models, both ancient and modern, cannot certainly

---

[1] *effect not reserves* Will not pretend to have reservations.

[2] [Hamilton's note] The same idea, tracing the arguments to their consequences, is held out in several of the late publications against the New Constitution. (Publius)

[3] *developed* Discussed, explained.

[4] *faction* Conflicting interest groups or political parties.

[5] *popular* I.e., democratic.

[6] *specious* Attractive, but false; *declamations* Public rhetoric.

be too much admired; but it would be an unwarrantable partiality, to contend that they have as effectually obviated[1] the danger on this side as was wished and expected. Complaints are everywhere heard from our most considerate and virtuous citizens, equally the friends of public and private faith, and of public and personal liberty; that our governments are too unstable; that the public good is disregarded in the conflicts of rival parties; and that measures are too often decided, not according to the rules of justice, and the rights of the minor party; but by the superior force of an interested[2] and overbearing majority. However anxiously we may wish that these complaints had no foundation, the evidence of known facts will not permit us to deny that they are in some degree true. It will be found indeed, on a candid review of our situation, that some of the distresses under which we labor, have been erroneously charged on the operation of our governments; but it will be found, at the same time, that other causes will not alone account for many of our heaviest misfortunes; and particularly, for that prevailing and increasing distrust of public engagements, and alarm for private rights, which are echoed from one end of the continent to the other. These must be chiefly, if not wholly, effects of the unsteadiness and injustice, with which a factious spirit has tainted our public administrations.

By a faction I understand a number of citizens, whether amounting to a majority or minority of the whole, who are united and actuated by some common impulse of passion, or of interest, adverse to the rights of other citizens, or to the permanent and aggregate interests of the community.

There are two methods of curing the mischiefs of faction: the one, by removing its causes; the other, by controlling its effects.

There are again two methods of removing the causes of faction: the one by destroying the liberty which is essential to its existence; the other, by giving to every citizen the same opinions, the same passions, and the same interests.

It could never be more truly said than of the first remedy, that it is worse than the disease. Liberty is to faction, what air is to fire, an aliment[3] without which it instantly expires. But it could not be a less folly to abolish liberty, which is essential to political life, because it nourishes faction, than it would be to wish the annihilation of air, which is essential to animal life, because it imparts to fire its destructive agency. The second expedient is as impracticable, as the first would be unwise. As long as the reason of man continues fallible, and he is at liberty to exercise it, different opinions will be formed. As long as the connection subsists between his reason and his self-love, his opinions and his passions will have a reciprocal influence on each other; and the former will be objects to which the latter will attach themselves. The diversity in the faculties of men from which the rights of property originate, is not less an insuperable obstacle to a uniformity of interests. The protection of these faculties is the first object of government. From the protection of different and unequal faculties of acquiring property, the possession of different degrees and kinds of property immediately results: and from the influence of these on the sentiments and views of the respective proprietors, ensues a division of the society into different interests and parties.

The latent causes of faction are thus sown in the nature of man; and we see them everywhere brought into different degrees of activity, according to the different circumstances of civil society. A zeal for different opinions concerning religion, concerning government and many other points, as well of speculation as of practice; an attachment to different leaders ambitiously contending for pre-eminence and power; or to persons of other descriptions whose fortunes have been interesting to the human passions, have in turn divided mankind into parties, inflamed them with mutual animosity, and rendered them much more disposed to vex and oppress each other, than to cooperate for their common good. So strong is this propensity of mankind to fall into mutual animosities, that where no substantial occasion presents itself, the most frivolous and fanciful distinctions have been sufficient to kindle their unfriendly passions, and excite their most violent conflicts. But the most common and durable source of factions, has been the various and unequal distribution of property. Those who hold, and those who are without property, have ever formed distinct interests

---

[1]   *obviated* Avoided.

[2]   *interested* Concerned with private advantage.

[3]   *aliment* Nourishment.

in society. Those who are creditors, and those who are debtors, fall under a like discrimination. A landed[1] interest, a manufacturing interest, a mercantile interest, a monied interest, with many lesser interests, grow up of necessity in civilized nations, and divide them into different classes, actuated by different sentiments and views. The regulation of these various and interfering interests forms the principal task of modern legislation, and involves the spirit of party and faction in the necessary and ordinary operations of government.

No man is allowed to be a judge in his own cause; because his interest would certainly bias his judgment, and, not improbably, corrupt his integrity. With equal, nay with greater reason, a body of men, are unfit to be both judges and parties, at the same time; yet, what are many of the most important acts of legislation, but so many judicial determinations, not indeed concerning the rights of single persons, but concerning the rights of large bodies of citizens; and what are the different classes of legislators, but advocates and parties to the causes which they determine? Is a law proposed concerning private debts? It is a question to which the creditors are parties on one side, and the debtors on the other. Justice ought to hold the balance between them. Yet the parties are and must be themselves the judges; and the most numerous party, or, in other words, the most powerful faction must be expected to prevail. Shall domestic manufactures be encouraged, and in what degree, by restrictions on foreign manufactures? are questions which would be differently decided by the landed and the manufacturing classes; and probably by neither, with a sole regard to justice and the public good. The apportionment of taxes on the various descriptions of property, is an act which seems to require the most exact impartiality; yet, there is perhaps no legislative act in which greater opportunity and temptation are given to a predominant party, to trample on the rules of justice. Every shilling[2] with which they overburden the inferior number, is a shilling saved to their own pockets.

It is in vain to say, that enlightened statesmen will be able to adjust these clashing interests, and render them all subservient to the public good. Enlightened statesmen will not always be at the helm: nor, in many cases, can such an adjustment be made at all, without taking into view indirect and remote considerations, which will rarely prevail over the immediate interest which one party may find in disregarding the rights of another, or the good of the whole.

The inference to which we are brought, is, that the *causes* of faction cannot be removed; and that relief is only to be sought in the means of controlling its *effects*.

If a faction consists of less than a majority, relief is supplied by the republican principle, which enables the majority to defeat its sinister views by regular vote. It may clog the administration, it may convulse the society; but it will be unable to execute and mask its violence under the forms of the Constitution. When a majority is included in a faction, the form of popular government on the other hand enables it to sacrifice to its ruling passion or interest, both the public good and the rights of other citizens. To secure the public good, and private rights, against the danger of such a faction, and at the same time to preserve the spirit and the form of popular government, is then the great object to which our enquiries are directed. Let me add that it is the great desideratum,[3] by which alone this form of government can be rescued from the opprobrium[4] under which it has so long labored, and be recommended to the esteem and adoption of mankind.

By what means is this object attainable? Evidently by one of two only. Either the existence of the same passion or interest in a majority at the same time, must be prevented; or the majority, having such co-existent passion or interest, must be rendered, by their number and local situation, unable to concert and carry into effect schemes of oppression. If the impulse and the opportunity be suffered[5] to coincide, we well know that neither moral nor religious motives can be relied on as an adequate control. They are not found to be such on the injustice and violence of individuals, and lose their efficacy in proportion to the number combined together; that is, in proportion as their efficacy becomes needful.

From this view of the subject, it may be concluded, that a pure democracy,[6] by which I mean, a society,

---

1   *landed*   Relating to the class of people who own land.

2   *shilling*   Coin worth twelve pennies.

3   *desideratum*   Latin: thing which is desired.

4   *opprobrium*   Reproach.

5   *suffered*   Permitted.

6   *pure democracy*   Also known as direct democracy.

consisting of a small number of citizens, who assemble and administer the government in person, can admit of no cure for the mischiefs of faction. A common passion or interest will, in almost every case, be felt by a majority of the whole; a communication and concert[1] results from the form of government itself; and there is nothing to check the inducements to sacrifice the weaker party, or an obnoxious[2] individual. Hence it is, that such democracies have ever been spectacles of turbulence and contention; have ever been found incompatible with personal security, or the rights of property; and have in general been as short in their lives, as they have been violent in their deaths. Theoretic politicians, who have patronized[3] this species of government, have erroneously supposed, that by reducing mankind to a perfect equality in their political rights, they would, at the same time, be perfectly equalized and assimilated in their possessions, their opinions, and their passions.

A republic, by which I mean a government in which the scheme of representation takes place, opens a different prospect, and promises the cure for which we are seeking. Let us examine the points in which it varies from pure democracy, and we shall comprehend both the nature of the cure, and the efficacy which it must derive from the Union.

The two great points of difference between a democracy and a republic are, first, the delegation of the government, in the latter, to a small number of citizens elected by the rest: secondly, the greater number of citizens, and greater sphere of country, over which the latter may be extended.

The effect of the first difference is, on the one hand to refine and enlarge the public views, by passing them through the medium of a chosen body of citizens, whose wisdom may best discern the true interest of their country, and whose patriotism and love of justice, will be least likely to sacrifice it to temporary or partial considerations. Under such a regulation, it may well happen that the public voice pronounced by the representatives of the people, will be more consonant to the public good, than if pronounced by the people themselves convened for the purpose. On the other hand, the effect may be inverted. Men of factious tempers, of local prejudices, or of sinister designs, may by intrigue, by corruption or by other means, first obtain the suffrages,[4] and then betray the interests of the people. The question resulting is, whether small or extensive republics are most favorable to the election of proper guardians of the public weal:[5] and it is clearly decided in favor of the latter by two obvious considerations.

In the first place it is to be remarked that however small the republic may be, the representatives must be raised to a certain number, in order to guard against the cabals[6] of a few; and that however large it may be, they must be limited to a certain number, in order to guard against the confusion of a multitude. Hence the number of representatives in the two cases, not being in proportion to that of the constituents, and being proportionally greatest in the small republic, it follows, that if the proportion of fit characters, be not less, in the large than in the small republic, the former will present a greater option, and consequently a greater probability of a fit choice.

In the next place, as each representative will be chosen by a greater number of citizens in the large than in the small republic, it will be more difficult for unworthy candidates to practice with success the vicious arts, by which elections are too often carried; and the suffrages of the people being more free, will be more likely to center on men who possess the most attractive merit, and the most diffusive[7] and established characters.

It must be confessed, that in this, as in most other cases, there is a mean, on both sides of which inconveniencies will be found to lie. By enlarging too much the number of electors, you render the representative too little acquainted with all their local circumstances and lesser interests; as by reducing it too much, you render him unduly attached to these, and too little fit to comprehend and pursue great and national objects. The federal Constitution forms a happy combination in this respect; the great and aggregate interests being referred to the national, the local and particular, to the state legislatures.

The other point of difference is, the greater number of citizens and extent of territory which may be brought

---

1   *concert* Agreement.

2   *obnoxious* Vulnerable.

3   *patronized* Supported.

4   *suffrages* Votes.

5   *weal* Wellbeing.

6   *cabals* Intrigues.

7   *diffusive* Generous and broad-minded.

within the compass of Republican, than of Democratic Government; and it is this circumstance principally which renders factious combinations less to be dreaded in the former, than in the latter. The smaller the society, the fewer probably will be the distinct parties and interests composing it; the fewer the distinct parties and interests, the more frequently will a majority be found of the same party; and the smaller the number of individuals composing a majority, and the smaller the compass within which they are placed, the more easily will they concert and execute their plans of oppression. Extend the sphere, and you take in a greater variety of parties and interests; you make it less probable that a majority of the whole will have a common motive to invade the rights of other citizens; or if such a common motive exists, it will be more difficult for all who feel it to discover their own strength, and to act in unison with each other. Besides other impediments, it may be remarked, that where there is a consciousness of unjust or dishonorable purposes, communication is always checked by distrust, in proportion to the number whose concurrence is necessary.

Hence it clearly appears, that the same advantage, which a republic has over a democracy, in controlling the effects of faction, is enjoyed by a large over a small republic—is enjoyed by the Union over the states composing it. Does this advantage consist in the substitution of representatives, whose enlightened views and virtuous sentiments render them superior to local prejudices, and to schemes of injustice? It will not be denied, that the representation of the Union will be most likely to possess these requisite endowments. Does it consist in the greater security afforded by a greater variety of parties, against the event of any one party being able to outnumber and oppress the rest? In an equal degree does the increased variety of parties, comprised within the Union, increase this security? Does it, in fine,[1] consist in the greater obstacles opposed to the concert and accomplishment of the secret wishes of an unjust and interested majority? Here, again, the extent of the Union gives it the most palpable advantage.

The influence of factious leaders may kindle a flame within their particular states, but will be unable to spread a general conflagration through the other states: a religious sect, may degenerate into a political faction in a part of the confederacy; but the variety of sects dispersed over the entire face of it, must secure the national councils against any danger from that source: a rage for paper money,[2] for an abolition of debts, for an equal division of property, or for any other improper or wicked project, will be less apt to pervade the whole body of the Union, than a particular member of it; in the same proportion as such a malady is more likely to taint a particular county or district, than an entire state.

In the extent and proper structure of the Union, therefore, we behold a republican remedy for the diseases most incident to republican government. And according to the degree of pleasure and pride, we feel in being republicans, ought to be our zeal in cherishing the spirit, and supporting the character of Federalists.

PUBLIUS.

—1787

---

1 *in fine* In conclusion.

2 *rage for paper money* Coin money was often in short supply in colonial America, leading to various experiments with paper money (still a novel and ill-defined concept at this time) starting in the late 1600s; waves of inflation and depreciation of currency persisted well into the 1700s, resulting in parliamentary acts that limited the issuing of paper currency.

OLAUDAH EQUIANO OR GUSTAVUS VASSA

c. 1745 – 1797

Olaudah Equiano's *The Interesting Narrative of the Life of Olaudah Equiano* was one of the first slave narratives written in English, and is now universally acknowledged to be among the most significant and influential of all eighteenth-century texts. His narrative was a document of central importance for the abolitionist movement, showing readers the horrors of slavery while also demonstrating the eloquence of a native-born African who had been educated in the Western tradition, and displaying to the devout that black people were as capable of spiritual enlightenment as were whites.

Until the beginning of this century Equiano's account of his early years was generally taken entirely at face value: it was accepted that he had been born in what is now southern Nigeria, into the Igbo nation; that he had been kidnaped at the age of eleven and enslaved for some time in Africa; and that he was eventually brought across the Atlantic in slavery. In a 1999 article and then in his 2005 biography of Equiano, historian Vincent Carretta challenged his account, citing two documents suggesting that Equiano had been born not in Africa, but in Carolina. The issue remains disputed and may never be entirely resolved. It is significant, however, that neither Carretta nor other scholars have challenged the authenticity of the information Equiano provides about life in Africa, the passage across the Atlantic, and so on; if Equiano himself was indeed born into American slavery, he would have obtained such information directly from enslaved Africans he knew. At issue, then, is not the fundamental reality of the account Equiano provides, but only whether the early part of his narrative represents a first-hand account or an act of creative imagination based on first-hand research.

Equiano's account of his life following his purchase in Virginia by the British naval captain Michael Henry Pascal is not in dispute. While enslaved by Pascal (who renamed him "Gustavus Vassa") Equiano began his career as a mariner. For the next ten or eleven years, Equiano traveled widely around the Mediterranean, Europe, and the Americas with a series of enslavers; he was engaged in several battles during the Seven Years' War (1756–63), including the 1758 siege of Louisbourg in what is now Nova Scotia. He was sold in May of 1763 for £40 to Robert King, a Philadelphia Quaker who owned property on the Caribbean island of Monserrat and had various shipping interests. After working for King for approximately three years, Equiano was by 1766 able to purchase his freedom.

After securing his freedom, Equiano settled in England. (While slavery was still permitted in England's overseas colonies, it had no legal standing in England itself, where there was a relatively large population of free blacks.) From time to time he earned his living there—working for some time as a hairdresser, for example—but for many years he kept returning to the sea to earn a living, working on vessels traveling not only to American ports such as Savannah and Charleston but also to Turkey, to the Caribbean, and to South America. In 1773 he served on a scientific expedition to the Arctic, and in 1775–76 he was hired to assist in the setting up of a plantation colony in Central America, where his duties included acting as an overseer of enslaved workers.

He had been taught to read and write while still enslaved and in the 1780s Equiano began to use these skills to draw attention to the plight of enslaved people and to petition for the abolition of slavery. He played a key role in helping to bring to the attention of the public the 1781 case of the slave ship *Zong*, from which 132 enslaved people had been thrown overboard; he was a founder (together with Ottobah Cugoano and others) of the Sons of Africa, which became an influential abolitionist group; he worked closely over many years with prominent white abolitionists (including Granville Sharpe, Thomas Clarkson, and William Wilberforce); his narrative made a deep impression on John Wesley, the Methodist leader (Equiano himself became a Methodist, as he recounts in his narrative); and it made an impression too on the hundreds of influential Britons whose support Equiano enlisted when he published his *Interesting Narrative* in 1789. By that time Equiano was himself a leader of the campaign against the slave trade, and he was as tireless—and as effective—in promoting the book after it had been published as he had been in soliciting support beforehand.

When in 1792 he married Susannah Cullen, a woman he had met while promoting his book in Cambridge, the occasion was considered worthy of notice in the provincial press as well as in London. The *Derby Mercury* was among the newspapers reporting on the event:

> On the 9th instant was married at Soham, in Cambridgeshire, Gustavus Vassa, the African, well known in England as the champion and advocate for procuring a suppression of the slave trade, to Miss Cullen, daughter of Mr. Cullen, of Ely. A vast number of people were assembled on the occasion.

The change in Equiano's circumstances occasioned only a brief pause in Equiano's efforts on behalf of the abolitionist cause: "when I have given her eight or ten days comfort," he wrote a friend, "I mean directly to go to Scotland and sell my fifth editions."

The *Interesting Narrative* went through several more English editions in Equiano's lifetime, and he appears to have become quite well-to-do in his later years, both from the proceeds of book sales and from other ventures (including as a money-lender to some of his influential London contacts). He and Susannah had two children—both daughters. He died in London of unknown causes, on the 31st of March 1797.

The reception history of the *Interesting Narrative* in America differs strikingly from that in Britain. When the book was first published in London in 1789, it was prefaced by a letter addressed jointly to the British Houses of Parliament and accompanied by a list of 311 subscribers, including not only prominent names associated with the British abolitionist movement but also many names from the highest ranks of British society (among them the Prince of Wales, the Duke of York, and the Bishop of London). The book was widely reviewed in Britain, and widely read; several other editions followed, typically including the names of additional influential subscribers, together with fresh testimonials. Reviewers' discussions of the book typically focused on those aspects of the *Interesting Narrative* to which Equiano had drawn attention in his letter to Parliament, and treated the book as a whole as "an instrument" that aimed to bring change to Equiano's "suffering countrymen" who had been enslaved: "may the God of heaven inspire benevolence on that important day when the question of Abolition is to be discussed," Equiano implored the members of the House of Lords and House of Commons.

The circumstances were quite different when the book was published in the United States in 1791. The book was published by a New York printer largely known for publishing religious books. It included a list of just 113 subscribers, none of them particularly prominent in society and none of them especially notable as abolitionists. Indeed (as the research of Akiyo Ito has revealed), the American subscribers were very largely of the artisan class—"bakers, grocers, cartmen, cabinetmakers, carpenters, tailors, watchmakers, blacksmiths" and so on, many of whom owned enslaved people. Ito persuasively suggests that these early American readers may have valued Equiano's narrative less as an antislavery tract than as a travel and adventure narrative. Interestingly, even when Equiano's *Interesting Narrative* was re-issued in America (some thirty years after its initial edition had received so little attention), this aspect of the book seems to have been emphasized; a bookseller's 1837 description that was published more than once in William Lloyd Garrison's antislavery newspaper *The Liberator* mentions that Equiano had "lived as a slave," but places more emphasis on the book's "great variety of wonderful scenes, which give his narrative an interest scarcely surpassed by Robinson Crusoe."

It is perhaps unsurprising that, as an abolitionist text, the *Interesting Narrative* exerted far less influence in America than in Britain. For one thing, Equiano himself declared a strong connection to "old England," and little if any to America; for another, relatively little of the time that Equiano had spent enslaved had been in any part of what later became the United States. The text nevertheless has a good deal to say about slavery in the continental American colonies; the various encounters that Equiano reports (in Chapters 6, 7, and 8) having experienced in Savannah alone provide a searing indictment of the institution as it existed in the Thirteen Colonies.

Interest in Equiano's narrative—along with interest in slave narratives generally—dropped off in the late nineteenth and early twentieth centuries, and it was not until the latter part of the twentieth century that the *Interesting Narrative* began to be again widely read and widely studied. By the early twenty-first century, however, it had become one of the most widely taught texts in the canons of British and American literature—and in the newly formed canon of transatlantic literature. For the most part it has been studied fruitfully as an abolitionist text; an awareness of the book's early American reception history is a reminder that the *Interesting Narrative* can also be appreciated from numerous other angles as well. It is among other things a lively adventure narrative, a Christian conversion narrative, a remarkable tour of the transatlantic economic world—and a richly layered portrait of a man of extraordinary and sometimes contradictory character. Curious about all manner of things, blessed with seemingly boundless entrepreneurial energy, and blessed as well with keen descriptive and storytelling powers, Equiano reveals himself to be a highly talented self-fashioner. He is by turns boastful and self-deprecating; deeply religious and highly worldly. An impassioned and effective opponent of slavery, he was also an apologist for the slave trade within Africa, and a man who allowed himself to be employed for a time as an overseer of enslaved people. "My life and fortune have been extremely chequered, and my adventures various," Equiano declares near the end of the *Interesting Life*. His narrative has often been read, in the words of Joanna Brooks, as "a collective autobiography for millions who survived the slave trade," and unquestionably the text has much to tell us of that collective experience. But—as its earliest American readers appear to have recognized—it has much to tell us too of one of the most extraordinary individuals of his time.

NOTE ON THE TEXT: The texts of the various editions of the *Interesting Narrative* do not vary greatly; the changes Equiano made for the later British editions very largely involved the addition of testimonials and quotations from favorable reviews of the book. The American edition carried a different title page and subscriber list, but the text itself closely followed that of the first two London editions. The first edition, published in 1789, has here been used as a base text. Some paragraph breaks have been added, and spelling and punctuation have been modernized in accordance with the practices of this anthology.

⌘ ⌘ ⌘

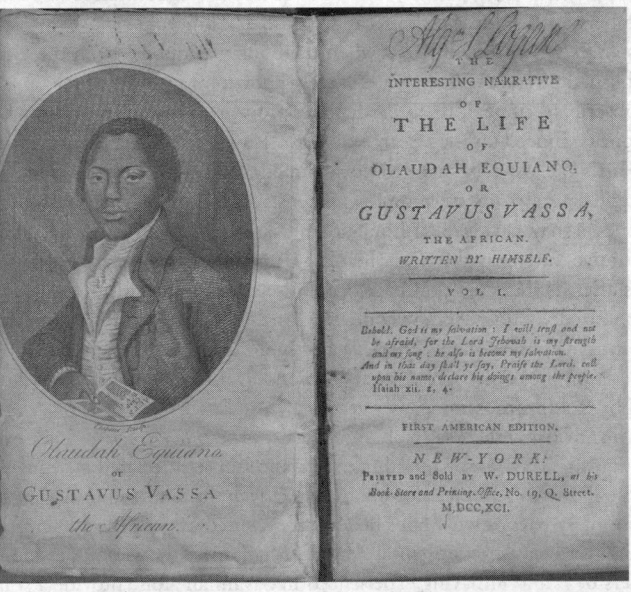

Frontispiece and title page of the first American edition of Equiano's *Interesting Narrative*, 1791.

from *The Interesting Narrative of the Life
of Olaudah Equiano
or Gustavus Vassa, the African.
Written by Himself*

from CHAPTER I[1]

The author's account of his country, and their manners and customs—Administration of justice—Embrenche—Marriage ceremony, and public entertainments—Mode of living—Dress—Manufactures—Buildings—Commerce—Agriculture—War and religion—Superstition of the natives—Funeral ceremonies of the priests or magicians—Curious mode of discovering poison—Some hints concerning the origin of the author's countrymen, with the opinions of different writers on that subject.

I believe it is difficult for those who publish their own memoirs to escape the imputation of vanity; nor is this the only disadvantage under which they labour: it is also their misfortune that what is uncommon is rarely, if ever, believed, and what is obvious we are apt to turn from with disgust, and to charge the writer with impertinence. People generally think those memoirs only worthy to be read or remembered which abound in great or striking events, those, in short, which in a high degree excite either admiration or pity: all others they consign to contempt and oblivion. It is therefore, I confess, not a little hazardous in a private and obscure individual, and a stranger too, thus to solicit the indulgent attention of the public; especially when I own[2] I offer here the history of neither a saint, a hero, nor a tyrant. I believe there are few events in my life which have not happened to many: it is true the incidents of it are numerous; and, did I consider myself an European, I might say my sufferings were great: but when I compare my lot with that of most of my countrymen, I regard myself as a particular favourite of Heaven, and acknowledge the mercies of Providence in every occurrence of my life. If then the following narrative does not appear sufficiently interesting to engage general attention, let my motive be some excuse for its publication. I am not so foolishly vain as to expect from it either immortality or literary reputation. If it affords any satisfaction to my numerous friends, at whose request it has been written, or in the smallest degree promotes the interests of humanity, the ends for which it was undertaken will be fully attained, and every wish of my heart gratified. Let it therefore be remembered that, in wishing to avoid censure, I do not aspire to praise.

That part of Africa, known by the name of Guinea, to which the trade for slaves is carried on, extends along the coast above 3400 miles, from the Senegal to Angola, and includes a variety of kingdoms. Of these the most considerable is the kingdom of Benin,[3] both as to extent and wealth, the richness and cultivation of the soil, the power of its king, and the number and warlike disposition of the inhabitants. It is situated nearly under the line,[4] and extends along the coast about 170 miles, but runs back into the interior part of Africa to a distance hitherto I believe unexplored by any traveller; and seems only terminated at length by the empire of Abyssinia, near 1500 miles from its beginning. This kingdom is divided into many provinces or districts: in one of the most remote and fertile of which, called Eboe, I was born, in the year 1745, in a charming fruitful vale named Essaka. The distance of this province from the capital of Benin and the sea coast must be very considerable; for I had never heard of white men or Europeans, nor of the sea. And our subjection to the king of Benin was little more than nominal, for every transaction of the government, as far as my slender observation extended, was conducted by the chiefs or elders of the place. The manners and government of a people who have little commerce with other countries are generally very simple, and the history of what passes in one family or village may serve as a specimen of a nation. My father was one of those elders or chiefs I have spoken of, and was styled Embrenche; a term, as I remember, importing the highest distinction, and signifying in our language a *mark* of grandeur. This mark is conferred on the person

---

[1] The entire first chapter is included in the website component of this anthology.

[2] *own* Admit.

[3] *kingdom of Benin* This kingdom extended over part of present-day Nigeria as well as present-day Benin.

[4] *under the line* South of the equator.

entitled to it by cutting the skin across at the top of the forehead, and drawing it down to the eyebrows; and while it is in this situation applying a warm hand, and rubbing it until it shrinks up into a thick weal[1] across the lower part of the forehead. Most of the judges and senators were thus marked; my father had long borne it. I had seen it conferred on one of my brothers, and I was also *destined* to receive it by my parents. Those Embrenche, or chief men, decided disputes and punished crimes, for which purpose they always assembled together. The proceedings were generally short, and in most cases the law of retaliation prevailed. I remember a man was brought before my father and the other judges for kidnapping a boy; and, although he was the son of a chief or senator, he was condemned to make recompense by a man or woman slave. Adultery, however, was sometimes punished with slavery or death, a punishment which I believe is inflicted on it throughout most of the nations of Africa, so sacred among them is the honour of the marriage bed, and so jealous are they of the fidelity of their wives. Of this I recollect an instance: a woman was convicted before the judges of adultery, and delivered over, as the custom was, to her husband to be punished. Accordingly he determined to put her to death; but it being found, just before her execution, that she had an infant at her breast; and no woman being prevailed on to perform the part of a nurse, she was spared on account of the child. The men, however, do not preserve the same constancy to their wives which they expect from them; for they indulge in a plurality, though seldom in more than two. Their mode of marriage is thus: both parties are usually betrothed when young by their parents (though I have known the males to betroth themselves). On this occasion a feast is prepared, and the bride and bridegroom stand up in the midst of all their friends, who are assembled for the purpose, while he declares she is thenceforth to be looked upon as his wife, and that no other person is to pay any addresses to her. This is also immediately proclaimed in the vicinity, on which the bride retires from the assembly. Some time after she is brought home to her husband, and then another feast is made, to which the relations of both parties are invited. Her parents then deliver her to the bridegroom, accompanied with a number of

blessings, and at the same time they tie round her waist a cotton string of the thickness of a goose-quill, which none but married women are permitted to wear: she is now considered as completely his wife; and at this time the dowry is given to the new married pair, which generally consists of portions of land, slaves, and cattle, household goods, and implements of husbandry. These are offered by the friends of both parties; besides which the parents of the bridegroom present gifts to those of the bride, whose property she is looked upon before marriage; but after it she is esteemed the sole property of her husband. The ceremony being now ended, the festival begins, which is celebrated with bonfires, and loud acclamations of joy, accompanied with music and dancing.

We are almost a nation of dancers, musicians, and poets. Thus every great event, such as a triumphant return from battle or other cause of public rejoicing, is celebrated in public dances, which are accompanied with songs and music suited to the occasion. The assembly is separated into four divisions which dance either apart or in succession, and each with a character peculiar to itself. The first division contains the married men, who in their dances frequently exhibit feats of arms, and the representation of a battle. To these succeed the married women, who dance in the second division. The young men occupy the third; and the maidens the fourth. Each represents some interesting scene of real life, such as a great achievement, domestic employment, a pathetic[2] story, or some rural sport; and as the subject is generally founded on some recent event, it is therefore ever new. This gives our dances a spirit and variety which I have scarcely seen elsewhere.[3] We have many musical instruments, particularly drums of different kinds, a piece of music which resembles a guitar, and another much like a stickado.[4] These last are chiefly used by betrothed virgins, who play on them on all grand festivals.

As our manners are simple, our luxuries are few. The dress of both sexes is nearly the same. It generally consists of a long piece of calico, or muslin, wrapped loosely round the body, somewhat in the form of a highland

---

[1]   *weal*   Mark; welt.

[2]   *pathetic*   Conveying a sense of pathos; emotionally affecting.

[3]   [Equiano's note]   When I was in Smyrna I have frequently seen the Greeks dance after this manner.

[4]   *stickado*   Musical instrument similar to a xylophone.

plaid. This is usually dyed blue, which is our favourite colour. It is extracted from a berry, and is brighter and richer than any I have seen in Europe. Besides this, our women of distinction wear golden ornaments; which they dispose with some profusion on their arms and legs. When our women are not employed with the men in tillage, their usual occupation is spinning and weaving cotton, which they afterwards dye and make it into garments. They also manufacture earthen vessels, of which we have many kinds. Among the rest tobacco pipes, made after the same fashion, and used in the same manner, as those in Turkey.[1]

Our manner of living is entirely plain; for as yet the natives are unacquainted with those refinements in cookery which debauch the taste: bullocks, goats, and poultry supply the greatest part of their food. These constitute likewise the principal wealth of the country, and the chief articles of its commerce. …

As we live in a country where nature is prodigal of her favours, our wants are few and easily supplied; of course, we have few manufactures. They consist for the most part of calicoes, earthen ware, ornaments, and instruments of war and husbandry. But these make no part of our commerce, the principal articles of which, as I have observed, are provisions. In such a state money is of little use; however, we have some small pieces of coin, if I may call them such. They are made something like an anchor, but I do not remember either their value or denomination. We have also markets, at which I have been frequently with my mother. These are sometimes visited by stout mahogany-coloured men from the south west of us: we call them Oye-Eboe, which term signifies "red men living at a distance." They generally bring us firearms, gunpowder, hats, beads, and dried fish. The last we esteemed a great rarity, as our waters were only brooks and springs. These articles they barter with us for odoriferous woods and earth, and our salt of wood ashes. They always carry slaves through our land; but the strictest account is exacted of their manner of procuring them before they are suffered to pass. Sometimes indeed we sold slaves to them, but they were only prisoners of war, or such among us

as had been convicted of kidnapping, or adultery, and some other crimes which we esteemed heinous. …

As to religion, the natives believe that there is one Creator of all things, and that he lives in the sun and is girded round with a belt; that he may never eat or drink; but, according to some, he smokes a pipe, which is our own favourite luxury. They believe he governs events, especially our deaths or captivity; but, as for the doctrine of eternity, I do not remember to have ever heard of it: some however believe in the transmigration of souls in a certain degree. Those spirits which are not transmigrated, such as our dear friends or relations, they believe always attend them and guard them from the bad spirits or their foes. For this reason they always before eating, as I have observed, put some small portion of the meat, and pour some of their drink, on the ground for them; and they often make oblations of the blood of beasts or fowls at their graves. I was very fond of my mother, and almost constantly with her. When she went to make these oblations at her mother's tomb, which was a kind of small solitary thatched house, I sometimes attended her. There she made her libations and spent most of the night in cries and lamentations. I have been often extremely terrified on these occasions. The loneliness of the place, the darkness of the night, and the ceremony of libation, naturally awful and gloomy, were heightened by my mother's lamentations; and these, concurring with the cries of doleful birds by which these places were frequented, gave an inexpressible terror to the scene.

We compute the year from the day on which the sun crosses the line, and on its setting that evening there is a general shout throughout the land—at least, I can speak from my own knowledge, throughout our vicinity. The people at the same time make a great noise with rattles, not unlike the basket rattles used by children here, though much larger, and hold up their hands to heaven for a blessing. It is then the greatest offerings are made, and those children whom our wise men foretell will be fortunate are then presented to different people. I remember many used to come to see me, and I was carried about to others for that purpose. …

---

[1] [Equiano's note] The bowl is earthen, curiously figured, to which a long reed is fixed as a tube. This tube is sometimes so long as to be borne by one, and frequently out of grandeur by two boys.

CHAPTER 2

The author's birth and parentage—His being kid-napped with his sister—Their separation—Surprise at meeting again—Are finally separated—Account of the different places and incidents the author met with till his arrival on the coast—The effect the sight of a slave ship had on him—He sails for the West Indies—Horrors of a slave ship—Arrives at Barbadoes, where the cargo is sold and dispersed.

I hope the reader will not think I have trespassed on his patience in introducing myself to him with some account of the manners and customs of my country.[1] They had been implanted in me with great care, and made an impression on my mind which time could not erase, and which all the adversity and variety of fortune I have since experienced served only to rivet and record; for, whether the love of one's country be real or imaginary, or a lesson of reason, or an instinct of nature, I still look back with pleasure on the first scenes of my life, though that pleasure has been for the most part mingled with sorrow.

I have already acquainted the reader with the time and place of my birth. My father, besides many slaves, had a numerous family, of which seven lived to grow up, including myself and a sister, who was the only daughter. As I was the youngest of the sons, I became, of course, the greatest favourite with my mother, and was always with her; and she used to take particular pains to form my mind. I was trained up from my ear-liest years in the art of war; my daily exercise was shoot-ing and throwing javelins, and my mother adorned me with emblems after the manner of our greatest war-riors. In this way I grew up till I was turned the age of eleven, when an end was put to my happiness in the following manner. Generally, when the grown people in the neighbourhood were gone far in the fields to labour, the children assembled together in some of the neighbours' premises to play; and commonly some of us used to get up a tree to look out for any assailant or kidnapper that might come upon us; for they some-times took those opportunities of our parents' absence to attack and carry off as many as they could seize. One day, as I was watching at the top of a tree in our yard, I saw one of those people come into the yard of our next neighbour but one, to kidnap, there being many stout[2] young people in it. Immediately on this I gave the alarm of the rogue, and he was surrounded by the stoutest of them, who entangled him with cords, so that he could not escape till some of the grown people came and secured him. But alas! ere long it was my fate to be thus attacked, and to be carried off, when none of the grown people were nigh. One day, when all our people were gone out to their works as usual, and only I and my dear sister were left to mind the house, two men and a woman got over our walls and in a moment seized us both, and, without giving us time to cry out or make resistance, they stopped our mouths and ran off with us into the nearest wood. Here they tied our hands and continued to carry us as far as they could, till night came on, when we reached a small house where the robbers halted for refreshment and spent the night. We were then unbound, but were unable to take any food; and, being quite overpowered by fatigue and grief, our only relief was some sleep, which allayed our misfortune for a short time.

The next morning we left the house and continued travelling all the day. For a long time we had kept the woods, but at last we came into a road, which I believed I knew. I had now some hopes of being deliv-ered, for we had advanced but a little way before I dis-covered some people at a distance, on which I began to cry out for their assistance. But my cries had no other effect than to make them tie me faster and stop my mouth, and then they put me into a large sack. They also stopped my sister's mouth and tied her hands, and in this manner we proceeded till we were out of the sight of these people. When we went to rest the follow-ing night they offered us some victuals, but we refused it, and the only comfort we had was in being in one another's arms all that night, and bathing each other with our tears. But alas! we were soon deprived of even the small comfort of weeping together. The next day proved a day of greater sorrow than I had yet experi-enced, for my sister and I were then separated while we lay clasped in each other's arms. It was in vain that we besought them not to part us; she was torn from me and immediately carried away, while I was left in a state

---

[1]   *my country* Equiano says he was born in Essaka, a country located in the interior of present-day Nigeria.

[2]   *stout* Sturdily built; strong.

of distraction not to be described. I cried and grieved continually, and for several days I did not eat anything but what they forced into my mouth.

At length, after many days travelling, during which I had often changed masters, I got into the hands of a chieftain in a very pleasant country. This man had two wives and some children, and they all used[1] me extremely well, and did all they could to comfort me—particularly the first wife, who was something like my mother. Although I was a great many days' journey from my father's house, yet these people spoke exactly the same language with us. This first master of mine, as I may call him, was a smith,[2] and my principal employment was working his bellows, which were the same kind as I had seen in my vicinity. They were in some respects not unlike the stoves here in gentlemen's kitchens, and were covered over with leather; and in the middle of that leather a stick was fixed, and a person stood up and worked it in the same manner as is done to pump water out of a cask with a hand pump. I believe it was gold he worked, for it was of a lovely bright yellow colour, and was worn by the women on their wrists and ankles.

I was there I suppose about a month, and they at last used to trust me some little distance from the house. This liberty I used in embracing every opportunity to inquire the way to my own home; and I also sometimes, for the same purpose, went with the maidens in the cool of the evenings to bring pitchers of water from the springs for the use of the house. I had also remarked where the sun rose in the morning and set in the evening as I had travelled along, and I had observed that my father's house was towards the rising of the sun. I therefore determined to seize the first opportunity of making my escape, and to shape my course for that quarter; for I was quite oppressed and weighed down by grief after my mother and friends; and my love of liberty, ever great, was strengthened by the mortifying circumstance of not daring to eat with the free-born children, although I was mostly their companion.

While I was projecting my escape, one day an unlucky event happened which quite disconcerted my plan and put an end to my hopes. I used to be sometimes employed in assisting an elderly woman slave to cook and take care of the poultry, and one morning while I was feeding some chickens, I happened to toss a small pebble at one of them, which hit it on the middle and directly killed it. The old slave, having soon after missed the chicken, inquired after it; and on my relating the accident (for I told her the truth, because my mother would never suffer me to tell a lie), she flew into a violent passion, threatened that I should suffer for it, and, my master being out, she immediately went and told her mistress what I had done. This alarmed me very much, and I expected an instant flogging, which to me was uncommonly dreadful, for I had seldom been beaten at home. I therefore resolved to fly, and accordingly I ran into a thicket that was hard by and hid myself in the bushes. Soon afterwards my mistress and the slave returned, and, not seeing me, they searched all the house; but, not finding me, and I not making answer when they called to me, they thought I had run away, and the whole neighbourhood was raised in the pursuit of me. In that part of the country (as in ours) the houses and villages were skirted with woods, or shrubberies, and the bushes were so thick that a man could readily conceal himself in them so as to elude the strictest search. The neighbours continued the whole day looking for me, and several times many of them came within a few yards of the place where I lay hid. I then gave myself up for lost entirely and expected every moment, when I heard a rustling among the trees, to be found out and punished by my master. But they never discovered me, though they were often so near that I even heard their conjectures as they were looking about for me; and I now learned from them that any attempt to return home would be hopeless. Most of them supposed I had fled towards home, but the distance was so great, and the way so intricate, that they thought I could never reach it, and that I should be lost in the woods. When I heard this I was seized with a violent panic and abandoned myself to despair. Night too began to approach, and aggravated all my fears. I had before entertained hopes of getting home, and I had determined when it should be dark to make the attempt; but I was now convinced it was fruitless, and I began to consider that, if possibly I could escape all other animals, I could not those of the human kind, and that, not knowing the way, I must perish in the woods. Thus was I like the hunted deer:

---

[1]   *used*   Treated.

[2]   *smith*   One who works with metals.

Ev'ry leaf and ev'ry whisp'ring breath
Conveyed a foe, and ev'ry foe a death.[1]

I heard frequent rustlings among the leaves, and, being pretty sure they were snakes, I expected every instant to be stung by them. This increased my anguish, and the horror of my situation became now quite insupportable. I at length quitted the thicket, very faint and hungry, for I had not eaten or drank anything all the day, and crept to my master's kitchen, from whence I set out at first, and which was an open shed, and laid myself down in the ashes with an anxious wish for death to relieve me from all my pains. I was scarcely awake in the morning when the old woman slave, who was the first up, came to light the fire and saw me in the fireplace. She was very much surprised to see me, and could scarcely believe her own eyes. She now promised to intercede for me, and went for her master, who soon after came and, having slightly reprimanded me, ordered me to be taken care of and not to be ill-treated.

Soon after this my master's only daughter, and child by his first wife, sickened and died, which affected him so much that for some time he was almost frantic, and really would have killed himself, had he not been watched and prevented. However, in a small time afterwards he recovered, and I was again sold. I was now carried to the left of the sun's rising, through many different countries and a number of large woods. The people I was sold to used to carry me very often, when I was tired, either on their shoulders or on their backs. I saw many convenient, well built sheds along the roads, at proper distances to accommodate the merchants and travellers, who lay in those buildings along with their wives, who often accompany them; and they always go well armed.

From the time I left my own nation, I always found somebody that understood me, till I came to the sea coast. The languages of different nations did not totally differ,[2] nor were they so copious as those of the Europeans, particularly the English. They were therefore easily learned, and while I was journeying thus through Africa I acquired two or three different tongues. In this manner I had been travelling for a considerable time when one evening, to my great surprise, whom should I see brought to the house where I was but my dear sister! As soon as she saw me she gave a loud shriek and ran into my arms. I was quite overpowered: neither of us could speak, but for a considerable time clung to each other in mutual embraces, unable to do any thing but weep. Our meeting affected all who saw us; and indeed I must acknowledge, in honour of those sable[3] destroyers of human rights, that I never met with any ill treatment, or saw any offered to their slaves, except tying them when necessary, to keep them from running away. When these people knew we were brother and sister they indulged us together, and the man to whom I supposed we belonged lay with us, he in the middle, while she and I held one another by the hands across his breast all night; and thus for a while we forgot our misfortunes in the joy of being together. But even this small comfort was soon to have an end, for scarcely had the fatal morning appeared when she was again torn from me forever! I was now more miserable, if possible, than before. The small relief which her presence gave me from pain was gone, and the wretchedness of my situation was redoubled by my anxiety after her fate and my apprehensions lest her sufferings should be greater than mine, when I could not be with her to alleviate them. Yes, thou dear partner of all my childish sports! thou sharer of my joys and sorrows! happy should I have ever esteemed myself to encounter every misery for you, and to procure your freedom by the sacrifice of my own. Though you were early forced from my arms, your image has been always riveted in my heart, from which neither time nor fortune have been able to remove it; so that, while the thoughts of your sufferings have damped my prosperity, they have mingled with adversity and increased its bitterness. To that Heaven which protects the weak from the strong, I commit the care of your innocence and virtues, if they have not already received their full reward, and if your youth and delicacy have not long since fallen victims to the violence of the African trader, the pestilential stench of a Guinea ship,[4] the seasoning in the

---

1   *Ev'ry ... death* See lines 287–88 of John Denham's "Cooper's Hill": "Now every leaf, and every moving breath / Presents a foe, and every foe a death."

2   *languages ... differ* The Igbo languages and other languages in the Niger-Congo language family share many features not only with each other but also with many Bantu languages.

3   *sable* Dark skinned.

4   *Guinea ship* Slave ship from Guinea.

European colonies, or the lash and lust of a brutal and unrelenting overseer.

I did not long remain after my sister. I was again sold and carried through a number of places, till, after travelling a considerable time, I came to a town called Tinmah, in the most beautiful country I had yet seen in Africa. It was extremely rich, and there were many rivulets which flowed through it and supplied a large pond in the centre of the town, where the people washed. Here I first saw and tasted cocoa-nuts, which I thought superior to any nuts I had ever tasted before; and the trees, which were loaded, were also interspersed amongst the houses, which had commodious shades adjoining and were in the same manner as ours, the insides being neatly plastered and whitewashed. Here I also saw and tasted for the first time sugar cane. Their money consisted of little white shells the size of the fingernail. I was sold here for one hundred and seventy-two of them by a merchant who lived, and brought me, there. I had been about two or three days at his house when a wealthy widow, a neighbour of his, came there one evening and brought with her an only son, a young gentleman about my own age and size. Here they saw me; and, having taken a fancy to me, I was bought of the merchant and went home with them. Her house and premises were situated close to one of those rivulets I have mentioned, and were the finest I ever saw in Africa: they were very extensive, and she had a number of slaves to attend her. The next day I was washed and perfumed, and when mealtime came I was led into the presence of my mistress, and ate and drank before her with her son. This filled me with astonishment, and I could scarce help expressing my surprise that the young gentleman should suffer[1] me, who was bound, to eat with him, who was free; and not only so, but that he would not at any time either eat or drink till I had taken first, because I was the eldest (which was agreeable to our custom). Indeed, everything here, and all their treatment of me, made me forget that I was a slave. The language of these people resembled ours so nearly that we understood each other perfectly. They had also the very same customs as we. There were likewise slaves daily to attend us, while my young master and I with other boys sported with our darts and bows and arrows, as I had been used to do at home. In this resemblance to my former happy state I passed about two months; and I now began to think I was to be adopted into the family, and was beginning to be reconciled to my situation and to forget by degrees my misfortunes, when all at once the delusion vanished; for, without the least previous knowledge, one morning early, while my dear master and companion was still asleep, I was wakened out of my reverie to fresh sorrow, and hurried away even amongst the uncircumcised.[2]

Thus at the very moment I dreamed of the greatest happiness I found myself most miserable, and it seemed as if fortune wished to give me this taste of joy only to render the reverse more poignant. The change I now experienced was as painful as it was sudden and unexpected. It was a change indeed from a state of bliss to a scene which is inexpressible by me, as it discovered[3] to me an element I had never before beheld, and till then had no idea of, and wherein such instances of hardship and cruelty continually occurred, as I can never reflect on but with horror.

All the nations and people I had hitherto passed through resembled our own in their manners, customs, and language, but I came at length to a country, the inhabitants of which differed from us in all those particulars. I was very much struck with this difference, especially when I came among a people who did not circumcise, and ate without washing their hands. They cooked also in iron pots, and had European cutlasses and cross bows, which were unknown to us, and fought with their fists amongst themselves. Their women were not so modest as ours, for they ate and drank and slept with their men. But, above all, I was amazed to see no sacrifices or offerings among them. In some of those places the people ornamented themselves with scars, and likewise filed their teeth very sharp. They wanted sometimes to ornament me in the same manner, but I would not suffer them, hoping that I might sometime be among a people who did not thus disfigure themselves, as I thought they did. At last I came to the banks of a large river which was covered with canoes, in which the people appeared to live with their household utensils and provisions of all kinds. I was beyond measure astonished at this, as I had never before seen

---

[1] *suffer* Permit.

[2] *uncircumcised* I.e., heathens, foreigners.

[3] *discovered* Revealed.

any water larger than a pond or a rivulet, and my surprise was mingled with no small fear when I was put into one of these canoes and we began to paddle and move along the river. We continued going on thus till night; and when we came to land and made fires on the banks, each family by themselves, some dragged their canoes on shore, others stayed and cooked in theirs and laid in them all night. Those on the land had mats, of which they made tents, some in the shape of little houses. In these we slept, and after the morning meal we embarked again and proceeded as before. I was often very much astonished to see some of the women, as well as the men, jump into the water, dive to the bottom, come up again, and swim about.

Thus I continued to travel, sometimes by land, sometimes by water, through different countries and various nations, till, at the end of six or seven months after I had been kidnapped, I arrived at the seacoast. It would be tedious and uninteresting to relate all the incidents which befell me during this journey, and which I have not yet forgotten; of the various hands I passed through, and the manners and customs of all the different people among whom I lived. I shall therefore only observe that in all the places where I was the soil was exceedingly rich; the pumpkins, eadas,[1] plantains, yams, etc., etc., were in great abundance, and of incredible size. There were also vast quantities of different gums, though not used for any purpose, and everywhere a great deal of tobacco. The cotton even grew quite wild, and there was plenty of redwood. I saw no mechanics[2] whatever in all the way, except such as I have mentioned. The chief employment in all these countries was agriculture, and both the males and females, as with us, were brought up to it, and trained in the arts of war.

The first object which saluted my eyes when I arrived on the coast was the sea, and a slave ship, which was then riding at anchor and waiting for its cargo. These filled me with astonishment, which was soon converted into terror when I was carried on board. I was immediately handled and tossed up, to see if I were sound, by some of the crew; and I was now persuaded that I had gotten into a world of bad spirits, and that they were going to kill me. Their complexions, too, differing so

much from ours, their long hair, and the language they spoke (which was very different from any I had ever heard) united to confirm me in this belief. Indeed, such were the horrors of my views and fears at the moment that, if ten thousand worlds had been my own, I would have freely parted with them all to have exchanged my condition with that of the meanest[3] slave in my own country. When I looked round the ship, too, and saw a large furnace of copper boiling, and a multitude of black people of every description chained together, every one of their countenances expressing dejection and sorrow, I no longer doubted of my fate; and, quite overpowered with horror and anguish, I fell motionless on the deck and fainted. When I recovered a little I found some black people about me who I believed were some of those who brought me on board and had been receiving their pay; they talked to me in order to cheer me, but all in vain. I asked them if we were not to be eaten by those white men with horrible looks, red faces, and loose hair. They told me I was not, and one of the crew brought me a small portion of spirituous liquor in a wine glass; but, being afraid of him, I would not take it out of his hand. One of the blacks therefore took it from him and gave it to me, and I took a little down my palate, which, instead of reviving me as they thought it would, threw me into the greatest consternation at the strange feeling it produced, having never tasted any such liquor before.

Soon after this the blacks who brought me on board went off, and left me abandoned to despair. I now saw myself deprived of all chance of returning to my native country, or even the least glimpse of hope of gaining the shore, which I now considered as friendly; and I even wished for my former slavery in preference to my present situation, which was filled with horrors of every kind, still heightened by my ignorance of what I was to undergo. I was not long suffered to indulge my grief; I was soon put down under the decks, and there I received such a salutation in my nostrils as I had never experienced in my life; so that, with the loathsomeness of the stench and crying together, I became so sick and low that I was not able to eat, nor had I the least desire to taste anything. I now wished for the last friend, death, to relieve me; but soon, to my grief, two of the white men offered me eatables; and, on my refusing to

---

1   *eadas* Eddoes (a variety of tropical vegetable).

2   *mechanics* Artisans.

3   *meanest* Most lowly; worst treated.

eat, one of them held me fast by the hands and laid me across, I think, the windlass,[1] and tied my feet while the other flogged me severely. I had never experienced anything of this kind before; and although, not being used to the water, I naturally feared that element the first time I saw it, yet nevertheless, could I have got over the nettings, I would have jumped over the side. But I could not, and besides, the crew used to watch us very closely who were not chained down to the decks, lest we should leap into the water, and I have seen some of these poor African prisoners most severely cut for attempting to do so, and hourly whipped for not eating. This indeed was often the case with myself.

In a little time after, amongst the poor chained men I found some of my own nation, which in a small degree gave ease to my mind. I inquired of these what was to be done with us; they gave me to understand we were to be carried to these white people's country to work for them. I then was a little revived and thought, if it were no worse than working, my situation was not so desperate. But still I feared I should be put to death; the white people looked and acted, as I thought, in so savage a manner—for I had never seen among any people such instances of brutal cruelty, and this not only shown towards us blacks, but also to some of the whites themselves. One white man in particular I saw, when we were permitted to be on deck, flogged so unmercifully with a large rope near the forecast that he died in consequence of it, and they tossed him over the side as they would have done a brute.[2] This made me fear these people the more, and I expected nothing less than to be treated in the same manner. I could not help expressing my fears and apprehensions to some of my countrymen. I asked them if these people had no country, but lived in this hollow place (the ship). They told me they did not, but came from a distant one. "Then," said I, "how comes it in all our country we never heard of them?" They told me because they lived so very far off. I then asked, where were their women? had they any like themselves? I was told they had. "And why," said I, "do we not see them?" They answered, because they were left behind. I asked how the vessel could go. They told me they could not tell, but that

there were cloths put upon the masts by the help of the ropes I saw, and then the vessel went on; and the white men had some spell or magic they put in the water when they liked in order to stop the vessel. I was exceedingly amazed at this account, and really thought they were spirits. I therefore wished much to be from amongst them,[3] for I expected they would sacrifice me. But my wishes were vain, for we were so quartered that it was impossible for any of us to make our escape.

While we stayed on the coast I was mostly on deck, and one day, to my great astonishment, I saw one of these vessels coming in with the sails up. As soon as the whites saw it, they gave a great shout, at which we were amazed; and the more so as the vessel appeared larger by approaching nearer. At last she came to an anchor in my sight, and when the anchor was let go I and my countrymen who saw it were lost in astonishment to observe the vessel stop, and were now convinced it was done by magic. Soon after this the other ship got her boats out, and they came on board of us, and the people of both ships seemed very glad to see each other. Several of the strangers also shook hands with us black people and made motions with their hands, signifying, I suppose, we were to go to their country; but we did not understand them.

At last, when the ship we were in had got in all her cargo, they made ready with many fearful noises, and we were all put under deck, so that we could not see how they managed the vessel. But this disappointment was the least of my sorrow. The stench of the hold while we were on the coast was so intolerably loathsome that it was dangerous to remain there for any time, and some of us had been permitted to stay on the deck for the fresh air, but now that the whole ship's cargo were confined together, it became absolutely pestilential. The closeness of the place and the heat of the climate, added to the number in the ship, which was so crowded that each had scarcely room to turn himself, almost suffocated us. This produced copious perspirations, so that the air soon became unfit for respiration from a variety of loathsome smells, and brought on a sickness among the slaves, of which many died, thus falling victims to the improvident avarice, as I may call it, of their purchasers. This wretched situation was again aggravated

---

1 *windlass* On board ship, a mechanical contrivance used for winding ropes or chains.

2 *brute* Non-human animal.

3 *from amongst them* Away from them.

by the galling[1] of the chains, now become insupportable, and the filth of the necessary tubs,[2] into which
the children often fell, and were almost suffocated.
The shrieks of the women and the groans of the dying
rendered the whole a scene of horror almost inconceivable. Happily perhaps for myself, I was soon reduced
so low here that it was thought necessary to keep me
almost always on deck; and from my extreme youth
I was not put in fetters. In this situation I expected
every hour to share the fate of my companions, some
of whom were almost daily brought upon deck at the
point of death, which I began to hope would soon put
an end to my miseries. Often did I think many of the
inhabitants of the deep much more happy than myself.
I envied them the freedom they enjoyed, and as often
wished I could change my condition for theirs. Every
circumstance I met with served only to render my state
more painful and heighten my apprehensions and my
opinion of the cruelty of the whites.

One day they had taken a number of fishes; and
when they had killed and satisfied themselves with as
many as they thought fit, to our astonishment who
were on the deck, rather than give any of them to us
to eat as we expected, they tossed the remaining fish
into the sea again, although we begged and prayed for
some as well as we could, but in vain; and some of my
countrymen, being pressed by hunger, took an opportunity, when they thought no one saw them, of trying
to get a little privately; but they were discovered, and
the attempt procured them some very severe floggings.

One day, when we had a smooth sea and moderate wind, two of my wearied countrymen who were
chained together (I was near them at the time),
preferring death to such a life of misery, somehow
made through the nettings and jumped into the sea.
Immediately another quite dejected fellow, who, on
account of his illness, was suffered to be out of irons,
also followed their example; and I believe many more
would very soon have done the same if they had not
been prevented by the ship's crew, who were instantly
alarmed. Those of us that were the most active were
in a moment put down under the deck, and there was
such a noise and confusion amongst the people of the
ship as I never heard before, to stop her and get the
boat out to go after the slaves. However, two of the
wretches were drowned; but they got the other, and
afterwards flogged him unmercifully for thus attempting to prefer death to slavery.

In this manner we continued to undergo more
hardships than I can now relate, hardships which are
inseparable from this accursed trade. Many a time we
were near suffocation from the want of fresh air, which
we were often without for whole days together. This,
and the stench of the necessary tubs, carried off many.

During our passage I first saw flying fishes, which
surprised me very much: they used frequently to fly
across the ship, and many of them fell on the deck. I
also now first saw the use of the quadrant;[3] I had often
with astonishment seen the mariners make observations with it, and I could not think what it meant.
They at last took notice of my surprise, and one of
them, willing to increase it, as well as to gratify my
curiosity, made me one day look through it. The clouds
appeared to me to be land, which disappeared as they
passed along. This heightened my wonder, and I was
now more persuaded than ever that I was in another
world, and that everything about me was magic.

At last we came in sight of the island of Barbados, at
which the whites on board gave a great shout and made
many signs of joy to us. We did not know what to think
of this, but as the vessel drew nearer we plainly saw the
harbour and other ships of different kinds and sizes,
and we soon anchored amongst them off Bridgetown.
Many merchants and planters now came on board,
though it was in the evening. They put us in separate
parcels[4] and examined us attentively. They also made
us jump, and pointed to the land, signifying we were
to go there. We thought by this we should be eaten
by these ugly men, as they appeared to us; and, when
soon after we were all put down under the deck again,
there was much dread and trembling among us, and
nothing but bitter cries to be heard all the night from
these apprehensions, insomuch that at last the white
people got some old slaves from the land to pacify us.
They told us we were not to be eaten, but to work, and
were soon to go on land, where we should see many of
our country people. This report eased us much; and

---

1   *galling* Chafing.

2   *necessary tubs* Containers for human excrement.

3   *quadrant* Instrument used for taking altitudes.

4   *parcels* Groups.

sure enough, soon after we were landed, there came to us Africans of all languages.

We were conducted immediately to the merchant's yard, where we were all pent up together like so many sheep in a fold, without regard to sex or age. As every object was new to me, everything I saw filled me with surprise. What struck me first was that the houses were built with stories, and in every other respect different from those in Africa. But I was still more astonished on seeing people on horseback. I did not know what this could mean, and indeed I thought these people were full of nothing but magical arts. While I was in this astonishment, one of my fellow prisoners spoke to a countryman of his about the horses, who said they were the same kind they had in their country. I understood them, though they were from a distant part of Africa, and I thought it odd I had not seen any horses there; but afterwards, when I came to converse with different Africans, I found they had many horses amongst them, and much larger than those I then saw.

We were not many days in the merchant's custody before we were sold after their usual manner, which is this: on a signal given (as the beat of a drum), the buyers rush at once into the yard where the slaves are confined, and make choice of that parcel they like best. The noise and clamour with which this is attended, and the eagerness visible in the countenances of the buyers, serve not a little to increase the apprehensions of the terrified Africans, who may well be supposed to consider them as the ministers of that destruction to which they think themselves devoted. In this manner, without scruple, are relations and friends separated, most of them never to see each other again. I remember in the vessel in which I was brought over, in the men's apartment there were several brothers who, in the sale, were sold in different lots; and it was very moving on this occasion to see and hear their cries at parting. O ye nominal Christians![1] Might not an African ask you, "Learned you this from your God, who says unto you, 'Do unto all men as you would men should do unto you'? Is it not enough that we are torn from our country and friends to toil for your luxury and lust of gain?[2] Must every tender feeling be likewise sacrificed to your avarice? Are the dearest friends and relations, now rendered more dear by their separation from their kindred, still to be parted from each other, and thus prevented from cheering the gloom of slavery with the small comfort of being together and mingling their sufferings and sorrows? Why are parents to lose their children, brothers their sisters, or husbands their wives?" Surely this is a new refinement in cruelty, which, while it has no advantage to atone for it, thus aggravates distress and adds fresh horrors even to the wretchedness of slavery.

from Chapter 3[3]

> The author is carried to Virginia—His distress— Surprise at seeing a picture and a watch—Is bought by Captain Pascal, and sets out for England—His terror during the voyage—Arrives in England—His wonder at a fall of snow—Is sent to Guernsey, and in some time goes on board a ship of war with his master—Some account of the expedition against Louisbourg under the command of Admiral Boscawen, in 1758.

I now totally lost the small remains of comfort I had enjoyed in conversing with my countrymen; the women too, who used to wash and take care of me, were all gone different ways, and I never saw one of them afterwards.

I stayed in this island for a few days; I believe it could not be above a fortnight; when I and some few more slaves, that were not saleable amongst the rest, from very much fretting, were shipped off in a sloop for North America. On the passage we were better treated than when we were coming from Africa, and we had plenty of rice and fat pork. We were landed up a river a good way from the sea, about Virginia county, where we saw few or none of our native Africans, and not one soul who could talk to me. I was a few weeks weeding grass, and gathering stones in a plantation; and at last all my companions were distributed different ways, and only myself was left. I was now exceedingly miserable, and thought myself worse off than any of the rest of my companions; for they could talk to each other, but I had no person to speak to that I could understand.

---

[1] *nominal Christians* So-called Christians.

[2] *lust of gain* Desire for riches.

[3] A longer selection of excerpts from this chapter is included as part of the website component of this anthology.

In this state I was constantly grieving and pining,[1] and wishing for death rather than anything else.

While I was in this plantation the gentleman, to whom I suppose the estate belonged, being unwell, I was one day sent for to his dwelling house to fan him; when I came into the room where he was I was very much affrighted at some things I saw, and the more so as I had seen a black woman slave as I came through the house, who was cooking the dinner, and the poor creature was cruelly loaded with various kinds of iron machines; she had one particularly on her head, which locked her mouth so fast that she could scarcely speak; and could not eat nor drink. I was much astonished and shocked at this contrivance, which I afterward learned was called the iron muzzle. Soon after I had a fan put into my hand, to fan the gentleman while he slept; and so I did indeed with great fear. While he was fast asleep, I indulged myself a great deal in looking about the room, which to me appeared very fine and curious. The first object that engaged my attention was a watch which hung on the chimney, and was going. I was quite surprised at the noise it made and was afraid it would tell the gentleman anything I might do amiss: and when I immediately after observed a picture hanging in the room, which appeared constantly to look at me, I was still more affrighted, having never seen such things as these before. At one time I thought it was something relative to magic; and not seeing it move I thought it might be some way the whites had to keep their great men when they died, and offer them libation as we used to do to our friendly spirits. In this state of anxiety I remained till my master awoke, when I was dismissed out of the room, to my no small satisfaction and relief; for I thought that these people were all made up of wonders. In this place I was called Jacob; but on board the *African Snow* I was called Michael.

I had been some time in this miserable, forlorn, and much dejected state, without having anyone to talk to, which made my life a burden, when the kind and unknown hand of the Creator (who in very deed leads the blind in a way they know not) now began to appear, to my comfort; for one day the captain of a merchant ship, called the *Industrious Bee*, came on some business to my master's house. This gentleman, whose name was Michael Henry Pascal, was a lieutenant in the royal navy, but now commanded this trading ship, which was somewhere in the confines of the county many miles off. While he was at my master's house it happened that he saw me, and liked me so well that he made a purchase of me. I think I have often heard him say he gave thirty or forty pounds sterling for me; but I do not now remember which. However, he meant me for a present to some of his friends in England: and I was sent accordingly from the house of my then master, one Mr. Campbell, to the place where the ship lay; I was conducted on horseback by an elderly black man (a mode of travelling which appeared very odd to me). When I arrived I was carried on board a fine large ship, loaded with tobacco, etc. and just ready to sail for England. I now thought my condition much mended; I had sails to lie on, and plenty of good vitals[2] to eat; and everybody on board used me very kindly, quite contrary to what I had seen of any white people before; I therefore began to think that they were not all of the same disposition. A few days after I was on board we sailed for England.

I was still at a loss to conjecture my destiny. By this time, however, I could smatter a little imp'rfect English; and I wanted to know as well as I could where we were going. Some of the people of the ship used to tell me they were going to carry me back to my own country, and this made me very happy. I was quite rejoiced at the sound of going back; and thought if I should get home what wonders I should have to tell. But I was reserved for another fate, and was soon undeceived when we came within sight of the English coast. While I was on board this ship, my captain and master named me Gustavus Vassa.[3] I at that time began to understand him a little, and refused to be called so, and told him as well as I could that I would be called Jacob; but he said I should not, and still called me Gustavus; and when I refused to answer to my new name, which at first I did, it gained me many a cuff; so at length I submitted, and was obliged to bear the present name, by which I have been known ever since.

---

1   *pining* Becoming exhausted with mental suffering.

2   *vitals* Nutritious foods.

3   *Gustavus Vassa* The sixteenth-century Swedish monarch Gustav Vasa was widely regarded as a hero to his people; a 1739 play by Henry Brooke, *Gustavus Vasa, the Deliverer of His Country*, helped to make Vasa well-known in the English-speaking world.

The ship had a very long passage; and on that account we had very short allowance of provisions. Towards the last we had only one pound and a half of bread per week, and about the same quantity of meat, and one quart of water a day. We spoke with only one vessel the whole time we were at sea, and but once we caught a few fishes. In our extremities the captain and people told me in jest they would kill and eat me; but I thought them in earnest, and was depressed beyond measure, expecting every moment to be my last. While I was in this situation one evening they caught with a good deal of trouble, a large shark, and got it on board. This gladdened my poor heart exceedingly, as I thought it would serve the people to eat instead of their eating me; but very soon, to my astonishment, they cut off a small part of the tail, and tossed the rest over the side. This renewed my consternation; and I did not know what to think of these white people, though I very much feared they would kill and eat me.

There was on board the ship a young lad who had never been at sea before, about four or five years older than myself: his name was Richard Baker. He was a native of America, had received an excellent education, and was of a most amiable temper. Soon after I went on board he shewed me a great deal of partiality and attention, and in return I grew extremely fond of him. We at length became inseparable; and, for the space of two years, he was of very great use to me, and was my constant companion and instructor. Although this dear youth had many slaves of his own, yet he and I have gone through many sufferings together on shipboard; and we have many nights lain in each other's bosoms when we were in great distress. Thus such a friendship was cemented between us as we cherished till his death, which, to my very great sorrow, happened in the year 1759, when he was up the Archipelago, on board his majesty's ship the *Preston*: an event which I have never ceased to regret, as I lost at once a kind interpreter, an agreeable companion, and a faithful friend; who, at the age of fifteen, discovered a mind superior to prejudice; and who was not ashamed to notice, to associate with, and to be the friend and instructor of one who was ignorant, a stranger, of a different complexion, and a slave! My master had lodged in his mother's house in America: he respected him very much, and made him always eat with him in the cabin. He used often to tell

him jocularly that he would kill me to eat. Sometimes he would say to me the black people were not good to eat, and would ask me if we did not eat people in my country. I said, No: then he said he would kill Dick (as he always called him) first, and afterwards me. Though this hearing relieved my mind a little as to myself, I was alarmed for Dick and whenever he was called I used to be very much afraid he was to be killed; and I would peep and watch to see if they were going to kill him: nor was I free from this consternation till we made the land.

One night we lost a man overboard; and the cries and noise were so great and confused in stopping the ship, that I, who did not know what was the matter, began, as usual, to be very much afraid, and to think they were going to make an offering with me, and perform some magic; which I still believed they dealt in. As the waves were very high, I thought the ruler of the seas was angry, and I expected to be offered up to appease him. This filled my mind with agony, and I could not any more that night close my eyes again to rest. However, when daylight appeared I was a little eased in my mind; but still every time I was called, I used to think it was to be killed.

Sometime after this we saw some very large fish, which I afterwards found were called grampusses.[1] They looked to me extremely terrible, and made their appearance just at dusk and were so near as to blow the water on the ship's deck. I believed them to be the rulers of the sea; and, as the white people did not make any offerings at anytime, I thought they were angry with them: and, at last, what confirmed my belief was, the wind just then died away, and a calm ensued, and in consequence of it the ship stopped going. I supposed that the fish had performed this, and I hid myself in the fore part of the ship, through fear of being offered up to appease them, every minute peeping and quaking: but my good friend Dick came shortly towards me, and I took an opportunity to ask him, as well as I could, what these fish were. Not being able to talk much English, I could but just make him understand my question; and not at all, when I asked him if any offerings were to be made to them: however, he told me these fish would swallow anybody; which

---

[1] *grampusses* The name "grampus" is applied to several species of whale and dolphin.

sufficiently alarmed me. Here he was called away by the captain, who was leaning over the quarter-deck railing and looking at the fish; and most of the people were busied in getting a barrel of pitch to light, for them to play with. The captain now called me to him, having learned some of my apprehensions from Dick; and having diverted himself and others for some time with my fears, which appeared ludicrous enough in my crying and trembling, he dismissed me. The barrel of pitch was now lighted and put over the side into the water: by this time it was just dark, and the fish went after it; and, to my great joy, I saw them no more.

However, all my alarms began to subside when we got sight of land; and at last the ship arrived at Falmouth, after a passage of thirteen weeks. Every heart on board seemed gladdened on our reaching the shore, and none more than mine. The captain immediately went on shore, and sent on board some fresh provisions, which we wanted very much: we made good use of them, and our famine was soon turned into feasting, almost without ending. It was about the beginning of the spring 1757 when I arrived in England; and I was nearly twelve years of age at that time. I was very much struck with the buildings and the pavement of the streets in Falmouth; and, indeed, any object I saw filled me with new surprise. One morning when I got upon deck, I saw it covered all over with the snow that fell overnight: as I had never seen anything of the kind before, I thought it was salt; so I immediately ran down to the mate and desired him, as well as I could, to come and see how somebody in the night had thrown salt all over the deck. He, knowing what it was, desired me to bring some of it down to him: accordingly I took up a handful of it, which I found very cold indeed; and when I brought it to him he desired me to taste it. I did so, and I was surprised beyond measure. I then asked him what it was; he told me it was snow: but I could not in anywise understand him. He asked me if we had no such thing in my country; and I told him, No. I then asked him the use of it, and who made it; he told me a great man in the heavens, called God: but here again I was to all intents and purposes at a loss to understand him; and the more so when a little after I saw the air filled with it, in a heavy shower, which fell down on the same day. After this I went to church; and having never been at such a place before, I was again amazed at seeing and hearing the service. I asked all I could about it; and they gave me to understand it was worshipping God, who made us and all things. I was still at a great loss, and soon got into an endless field of inquiries, as well as I was able to speak and ask about things. However, my little friend Dick used to be my best interpreter; for I could make free with him, and he always instructed me with pleasure: and from what I could understand by him of this God, and in seeing these white people did not sell one another, as we did, I was much pleased; and in this I thought they were much happier than we Africans. I was astonished at the wisdom of the white people in all things I saw; but was amazed at their not sacrificing, or making any offerings, and eating with unwashed hands, and touching the dead. I likewise could not help remarking the particular slenderness of their women, which I did not at first like; and I thought they were not so modest and shamefaced as the African women.

I had often seen my master and Dick employed in reading; and I had a great curiosity to talk to the books, as I thought they did; and so to learn how all things had a beginning: for that purpose I have often taken up a book, and have talked to it, and then put my ears to it, when alone, in hopes it would answer me; and I have been very much concerned when I found it remained silent.[1] …

---

[1]   *I had often ... remained silent* A similar episode is recounted in James Albert Ukawsaw Gronniosaw's 1772 *A Narrative of the Most Remarkable Particulars in the Life of James Albert Ukawsaw Gronniosaw, an African Prince, as Related by Himself.* Before he learned to read, Gronniosaw reports that he believed that books could talk:

> I was never so surprised in my whole life as when I saw the book talk to my master, for I thought it did, as I observed him to look upon it and move his lips. I wished it would do so to me. As soon as my master had done reading, I followed him to the place where he put the book, being mightily delighted with it, and when nobody saw me, I opened it and put my ear down close upon it in great hope that it would say something to me, but was very sorry and greatly disappointed when I found it would not speak.

As Henry Louis Gates has noted, the "trope of the talking book" appears in at least five slave narratives between 1770 and 1815 (those of Gronniosaw, Equiano, John Marant [1785], Ottobah Cuguano [1787], and John Jea [1811]).

from Chapter 4

The author is baptized—Narrowly escapes drowning—Goes on an expedition to the Mediterranean—Incidents he met with there—Is witness to an engagement between some English and French ships—A particular account of the celebrated engagement between Admiral Boscawen and Mons. Le Clue, off Cape Logas, in August 1759—Dreadful explosion of a French ship—The author sails for England—His master appointed to the command of a fire ship—Meets a negro boy, from whom he experiences much benevolence—Prepares for an expedition against Belle-Isle—A remarkable story of a disaster which befell his ship—Arrives at Belle-Isle—Operations of the landing

It was now between two and three years since I first came to England, a great part of which I had spent at sea; so that I became inured to that service,[1] and began to consider myself as happily situated; for my master treated me always extremely well; and my attachment and gratitude to him were very great. From the various scenes I had beheld on ship-board, I soon grew a stranger to terror of every kind, and was, in that respect at least, almost an Englishman. I have often reflected with surprise that I never felt half the alarm at any of the numerous dangers I have been in, that I was filled with at the first sight of the Europeans, and at every act of theirs, even the most trifling, when I first came among them, and for some time afterwards. That fear, however, which was the effect of my ignorance, wore away as I began to know them. I could now speak English tolerably well, and I perfectly understood everything that was said. I now not only felt myself quite easy with these new countrymen, but relished their society and manners. I no longer looked upon them as spirits, but as men superior to us; and therefore I had the stronger desire to resemble them; to imbibe their spirit, and imitate their manners; I therefore embraced every occasion of improvement; and every new thing that I observed I treasured up in my memory. I had long wished to be able to read and write; and for this purpose I took every opportunity to gain instruction, but had made as yet very little progress.

However, when I went to London with my master, I had soon an opportunity of improving myself, which I gladly embraced. Shortly after my arrival, he sent me to wait upon the Miss Guerins,[2] who had treated me with much kindness when I was there before; and they sent me to school.

While I was attending these ladies their servants told me I could not go to Heaven unless I was baptized. This made me very uneasy; for I had now some faint idea of a future state: accordingly I communicated my anxiety to the eldest Miss Guerin, with whom I was become a favourite, and pressed her to have me baptized; when to my great joy she told me I should. She had formerly asked my master to let me be baptized, but he had refused; however she now insisted on it; and he being under some obligation to her brother complied with her request; so I was baptized in St. Margaret's Church, Westminster, in February 1759, by my present name. The clergyman, at the same time, gave me a book, called *A Guide to the Indians*,[3] written by the Bishop of Sodor and Man. On this occasion Miss Guerin did me the honour to stand as godmother, and afterwards gave me a treat. I used to attend these ladies about the town, in which service I was extremely happy; as I had thus many opportunities of seeing London, which I desired of all things. I was sometimes, however, with my master at his rendezvous house, which was at the foot of Westminster Bridge. Here I used to enjoy myself in playing about the bridge stairs, and often in the watermen's wherries,[4] with other boys. On one of these occasions there was another boy with me in a wherry, and we went out into the current of the river: while we were there two more stout boys came to us in another wherry, and, abusing us for taking the boat, desired me to get into the other wherry-boat. Accordingly I went to get out of the wherry I was in; but just as I had got one of my feet into the other boat the boys shoved it off, so that I fell into the Thames; and, not being able to swim, I should unavoidably have been

---

[1] *became inured to that service* Grew accustomed to life at sea.

[2] *the Miss Guerins* Elizabeth Martha Guerin and Mary Guerin, cousins of Michael Henry Pascal.

[3] *A Guide to the Indians* Bishop Thomas Wilson's *An Essay Towards an Instruction for the Indians* was published in London in 1740; this is likely the book Equiano is thinking of.

[4] *watermen's wherries* Small boats belonging to those offering ferry services on the river.

drowned, but for the assistance of some watermen who providentially came to my relief.

The *Namur* being again got ready for sea, my master, with his gang,[1] was ordered on board; and, to my no small grief I was obliged to leave my school-master, whom I liked very much, and always attended[2] while I stayed in London, to repair on board with my master. Nor did I leave my kind patronesses, the Miss Guerins, without uneasiness and regret. They often used to teach me to read, and took great pains to instruct me in the principles of religion and the knowledge of God. I therefore parted from those amiable ladies with reluctance; after receiving from them many friendly cautions how to conduct myself, and some valuable presents.

When I came to Spithead, I found we were destined for the Mediterranean, with a large fleet, which was now ready to put to sea. We only waited for the arrival of the admiral, who soon came on board; and about the beginning of the spring, 1759, having weighed anchor and got under way, sailed for the Mediterranean; and in eleven days from the Land's End, we got to Gibraltar. While we were here I used to be often on shore, and got various fruits in great plenty, and very cheap.

I had frequently told several people, in my excursions on shore, the story of my being kidnapped with my sister, and of our being separated, as I have related before; and I had as often expressed my anxiety for her fate, and my sorrow at having never met her again. One day, when I was on shore, and mentioning these circumstances to some persons, one of them told me he knew where my sister was, and, if I would accompany him, he would bring me to her. Improbable as this story was I believed it immediately, and agreed to go with him, while my heart leaped for joy: and, indeed, he conducted me to a black young woman, who was so like my sister that at first sight I really thought it was her: but I was quickly undeceived; and, on talking to her, I found her to be of another nation.

While we lay here the *Preston* came in from the Levant. As soon as she arrived, my master told me I should now see my old companion, Dick, who had gone in her when she sailed for Turkey. I was much rejoiced at this news, and expected every minute to embrace him; and when the captain came on board of our ship, which he did immediately after, I ran to inquire after my friend; but, with inexpressible sorrow, I learned from the boat's crew that the dear youth was dead! and that they had brought his chest, and all his other things, to my master. These he afterwards gave to me, and I regarded them as a memorial of my friend, whom I loved, and grieved for as a brother.

While we were at Gibraltar, I saw a soldier hanging by his heels, at one of the moles:[3] I thought this a strange sight, as I had seen a man hanged in London by his neck. At another time I saw the master of a frigate towed to shore on a grating, by several of the men-of-war boats, and discharged the fleet, which I understood was a mark of disgrace for cowardice. On board the same ship there was also a sailor hung up at the yard-arm. …

After the taking of this island [Belle-Isle] our ships, with some others commanded by Commodore Stanhope in the *Swiftsure*, went to Basse-road, where we blocked up a French fleet. Our ships were there from June till February following; and in that time I saw a great many scenes of war, and stratagems on both sides to destroy each other's fleet. Sometimes we would attack the French with some ships of the line; at other times with boats; and frequently we made prizes.[4] Once or twice the French attacked us by throwing shells with their bomb-vessels: and one day as a French vessel was throwing shells at our ships she broke from her springs, behind the isle of I de Re: the tide being complicated, she came within a gun shot of the *Nassau* but the *Nassau* could not bring a gun to bear upon her, and thereby the Frenchman got off. We were twice attacked by their fire-floats, which they chained together, and then let them float down with the tide; but each time we sent boats with graplings, and towed them safe out of the fleet.

We had different commanders while we were at this place, Commodores Stanhope, Dennis, Lord Howe, etc. From hence, before the Spanish war began, our ship and the *Wasp* sloop were sent to St. Sebastian in Spain, by Commodore Stanhope; and Commodore Dennis afterwards sent our ship as a cartel to Bayonne in France, after which we went in February in 1762 to

---

1   *gang* Crew.

2   *attended* Called on; was friendly towards.

3   *moles* Stone structures forming breakwaters or piers.

4   *made prizes* Captured enemy ships with valuable cargo aboard.

Belle-Isle, and there stayed till the summer, when we left it, and returned to Portsmouth.

After our ship was fitted out again for service, in September she went to Guernsey, where I was very glad to see my old hostess, who was now a widow, and my former little charming companion, her daughter. I spent some time here very happily with them, till October, when we had orders to repair to Portsmouth. We parted from each other with a great deal of affection; and I promised to return soon, and see them again, not knowing what all-powerful fate had determined for me. Our ship having arrived at Portsmouth, we went into the harbour, and remained there till the latter end of November, when we heard great talk about a peace;[1] and, to our very great joy, in the beginning of December we had orders to go up to London with our ship to be paid off. We received this news with loud huzzas, and every other demonstration of gladness; and nothing but mirth was to be seen throughout every part of the ship. I too was not without my share of the general joy on this occasion. I thought now of nothing but being freed, and working for myself and thereby getting money to enable me to get a good education; for I always had a great desire to be able at least to read and write; and while I was on ship-board I had endeavoured to improve myself in both. While I was in the *Aetna* particularly, the captain's clerk taught me to write, and gave me a smattering of arithmetic as far as the rule of three.[2] There was also one Daniel Queen, about forty years of age, a man very well educated, who messed with me on board this ship, and he likewise dressed and attended the captain.

Fortunately, this man soon became very much attached to me, and took very great pains to instruct me in many things. He taught me to shave and dress hair a little, and also to read in the Bible, explaining many passages to me, which I did not comprehend. I was wonderfully surprised to see the laws and rules of my country written almost exactly here; a circumstance which I believe tended to impress our manners and customs more deeply on my memory. I used to tell him of this resemblance; and many a time we have

sat up the whole night together at this employment. In short, he was like a father to me; and some even used to call me after his name; they also styled me the black Christian. Indeed, I almost loved him with the affection of a son. Many things I have denied myself that he might have them; and when I used to play at marbles or any other game, and won a few halfpence, or got any little money, which I sometimes did, for shaving any one, I used to buy him a little sugar or tobacco, as far as my stock of money would go. He used to say, that he and I never should part; and that when our ship was paid off, as I was as free as himself or any other man on board, he would instruct me in his business, by which I might gain a good livelihood. This gave me new life and spirits and my heart burned within me, while I thought the time long till I obtained my freedom. For though my master had not promised it to me, yet, besides the assurances I had received that he had no right to detain me, he always treated me with the greatest kindness, and reposed in me an unbounded confidence; he even paid attention to my morals; and would never suffer me to deceive him, or tell lies, of which he used to tell me the consequences; and that if I did so God would not love me; so that, from all this tenderness, I had never once supposed, in all my dreams of freedom, that he would think of detaining me any longer than I wished.

In pursuance of our orders, we sailed from Portsmouth for the Thames, and arrived at Deptford the 10th of December, where we cast anchor just as it was high water. The ship was up about half an hour, when my master ordered the barge to be manned; and all in an instant, without having before given me the least reason to suspect anything of the matter, he forced me into the barge; saying, I was going to leave him, but he would take care I should not. I was so struck with the unexpectedness of this proceeding, that for some time I did not make a reply, only I made an offer to go for my books and chest of clothes, but he swore I should not move out of his sight; and if I did, he would cut my throat, at the same time taking his hanger.[3] I began, however, to collect myself and, plucking up courage, I told him I was free, and he could not by law serve[4] me so. But this only enraged him the

---

[1] *a peace* The Seven Years' War ended in February of 1763 with the signing of the Treaty of Paris.

[2] *the rule of three* Method for discovering a fourth number in a series involving proportions, once the first three are known.

[3] *hanger* Short, curved sword.

[4] *serve* Treat.

more; and he continued to swear, and said he would soon let me know whether he would or not, and at that instant sprung himself into the barge from the ship, to the astonishment and sorrow of all on board. The tide, rather unluckily for me, had just turned downward, so that we quickly fell down the river along with it, till we came among some outward-bound West Indiamen; for he was resolved to put me on board the first vessel he could get to receive me. The boat's crew, who pulled against their will, became quite faint different times, and would have gone ashore; but he would not let them. Some of them strove them to cheer me, and told me he could not sell me, and that they would stand by me, which revived me a little; and I still entertained hopes; for as they pulled along he asked some vessels to receive me, but they could not. But, just as we had got a little below Gravesend, we came alongside of a ship which was going away the next tide for the West Indies; her name was the *Charming Sally*, Captain James Doran; and my master went on board and agreed with him for me; and in a little time I was sent for into the cabin.

When I came there, Captain Doran asked me if I knew him; I answered that I did not; "Then," said he, "you are now my slave." I told him my master could not sell me to him, nor to anyone else. "Why," said he, "did not your master buy you?" I confessed he did. "But I have served him," said I, "many years, and he has taken all my wages and prize-money,[1] for I only got one sixpence during the war; besides this I have been baptized; and by the laws of the land no man has a right to sell me." And I added, that I had heard a lawyer and others at different times tell my master so. They both then said that those people who told me so were not my friends; but I replied, it was very extraordinary that other people did not know the law as well as they. Upon this Captain Doran said I talked too much English; and if I did not behave myself well, and be quiet, he had a method on board to make me. I was too well convinced of his power over me to doubt what he said; and, my former sufferings in the slave ship presenting themselves to my mind, the recollection of them made me shudder. However, before I retired I told them that as I could not get any right

among men here I hoped I should hereafter in Heaven; and I immediately left the cabin, filled with resentment and sorrow. The only coat I had with me my master took away with him, and said if my prize-money had been £10,000 he had a right to it all, and would have taken it. I had about nine guineas, which, during my long sea-faring life, I had scraped together from trifling perquisites and little ventures; and I hid it that instant, lest my master should take that from me likewise, still hoping that by some means or other I should make my escape to the shore; and indeed some of my old shipmates told me not to despair, for they would get me back again; and that, as soon as they could get their pay, they would immediately come to Portsmouth to me, where this ship was going. But, alas! all my hopes were baffled, and the hour of my deliverance was yet far off. My master, having soon concluded his bargain with the captain, came out of the cabin, and he and his people got into the boat and put off; I followed them with aching eyes as long as I could, and when they were out of sight I threw myself on the deck, while my heart was ready to burst with sorrow and anguish.

from CHAPTER 5[2]

The author's reflections on his situation—Is deceived by a promise of being delivered—His despair at sailing for the West Indies—Arrives at Montserrat, where he is sold to Mr. King—Various interesting instances of oppression, cruelty, and extortion, which the author saw practiced upon the slaves in the West Indies during his captivity from the year 1763 to 1766—Address on it to the planters.

Thus, at the moment I expected all my toils to end, was I plunged, as I supposed, in a new slavery;[3] in

---

[1]   *prize-money*   Share of the valuables seized when capturing other vessels.

[2]   The entire fifth chapter is included in the website component of this anthology.

[3]   *Thus ... slavery*   Equiano was sold to Captain James Doran in December 1762. The sale came as a shock, as Equiano had expected to become a free man at the conclusion of the Seven Years' War, in which he had served as a sailor. Given the somewhat ambiguous legal status of slavery in England at the time—enslaved people were typically but unofficially held to be freemen upon arrival in England—Michael Pascal, the British Royal Navy Lieutenant who had bought Equiano on his arrival in Virginia, had a difficult time finding a new enslaver for Equiano. Eventually, he contacted Doran,

comparison to which all my service hitherto had been "perfect freedom"; and whose horrors, always present to my mind, now rushed on it with tenfold aggravation. I wept very bitterly for some time: and began to think that I must have done something to displease the Lord, that he thus punished me so severely. This filled me with painful reflections on my past conduct; I recollected that on the morning of our arrival at Deptford[1] I had rashly sworn that as soon as we reached London I would spend the day in rambling and sport. My conscience smote me for this unguarded expression: I felt that the Lord was able to disappoint me in all things, and immediately considered my present situation as a judgment of Heaven on account of my presumption in swearing: I therefore, with contrition of heart, acknowledged my transgression to God, and poured out my soul before him with unfeigned repentance, and with earnest supplications I besought him not to abandon me in my distress, nor cast me from his mercy for ever. In a little time my grief, spent with its own violence, began to subside; and after the first confusion of my thoughts was over I reflected with more calmness on my present condition: I considered that trials and disappointments are sometimes for our good, and I thought God might perhaps have permitted this in order to teach me wisdom and resignation; for he had hitherto shadowed me with the wings of his mercy, and by his invisible but powerful hand brought me the way I knew not. These reflections gave me a little comfort, and I rose at last from the deck with dejection and sorrow in my countenance, yet mixed with some faint hope that the *Lord would appear* for my deliverance. ...

... On the 13th of February 1763, from the masthead, we descried our destined island Montserrat; and soon after I beheld those

> Regions of sorrow, doleful shades, where peace
> And rest can rarely dwell. Hope never comes

That comes to all, but torture without end
Still urges.[2]

At the sight of this land of bondage,[3] a fresh horror ran through all my frame, and chilled me to the heart. My former slavery now rose in dreadful review to my mind, and displayed nothing but misery, stripes, and chains; and, in the first paroxysm of my grief, I called upon God's thunder, and his avenging power, to direct the stroke of death to me, rather than permit me to become a slave, and be sold from lord to lord.

In this state of my mind our ship came to an anchor, and soon after discharged her cargo. I now knew what it was to work hard; I was made to help to unload and load the ship. And, to comfort me in my distress in that time, two of the sailors robbed me of all my money, and ran away from the ship. I had been so long used to an European climate that at first I felt the scorching West India sun very painful, while the dashing surf would toss the boat and the people in it frequently above high water mark. Sometimes our limbs were broken with this, or even attended with instant death, and I was day by day mangled and torn.

About the middle of May, when the ship was got ready to sail for England, I all the time believing that Fate's blackest clouds were gathering over my head, and expecting their bursting would mix me with the dead, Captain Doran sent for me ashore one morning, and I was told by the messenger that my fate was then determined. With trembling steps and fluttering heart I came to the captain, and found with him one Mr. Robert King, a Quaker,[4] and the first merchant in the place. The captain then told me my former master had sent me there to be sold; but that he had desired him to get me the best master he could, as he told him I was a very deserving boy, which Captain Doran said

2   *Regions of sorrow ... Still urges* Cf. John Milton, *Paradise Lost* (1.65–68). This verse offers the poem's first view of hell, but Equiano somewhat mitigates the bleaker meaning of Milton's lines, changing "rest can never dwell" to "rest can rarely dwell."

3   *land of bondage* Phrase often used in reference to Egypt as the site of the Israelites' captivity and slavery in the Old Testament.

4   *Quaker* The Quakers (formally known as the Society of Friends) are a Protestant sect that was and is committed to pacifism, equality of the sexes, and social reform. They typically sought to avoid worldly vanities, adhering to customs of plain dress, and using an old-fashioned diction (employing the pronouns thee and thou for example).

captain of the merchant ship *Charming Sally*, who agreed to act as agent, transporting Equiano to be sold in Montserrat, in the West Indies.

1   *Deptford* Southeast London area on the River Thames's south bank. Equiano arrived at Deptford on 10 December 1762.

he found to be true; and if he were to stay in the West Indies he would be glad to keep me himself; but he could not venture to take me to London, for he was very sure that when I came there I would leave him. I at that instant burst out a crying, and begged much of him to take me to England with him, but all to no purpose. He told me he had got me the very best master in the whole island, with whom I should be as happy as if I were in England, and for that reason he chose to let him have me, though he could sell me to his own brother-in-law for a great deal more money than what he got from this gentleman. Mr. King, my new master, then made a reply, and said the reason he had bought me was on account of my good character; and, as he had not the least doubt of my good behaviour, I should be very well off with him. He also told me he did not live in the West Indies, but at Philadelphia, where he was going soon; and, as I understood something of the rules of arithmetic, when we got there he would put me to school, and fit me for a clerk. This conversation relieved my mind a little, and I left those gentlemen considerably more at ease in myself than when I came to them; and I was very grateful to Captain Doran, and even to my old master, for the character they had given me; a character which I afterward found of infinite service to me. I went on board again, and took leave of all my shipmates; and the next day the ship sailed. When she weighed anchor I went to the waterside and looked at her with a very wishful and aching heart, and followed her with my eyes and tears until she was totally out of sight. I was so bowed down with grief that I could not hold up my head for many months; and if my new master had not been kind to me I believe I should have died under it at last. And indeed I soon found that he fully deserved the good character which Captain Doran had given me of him; for he possessed a most amiable disposition and temper, and was very charitable and humane. If any of his slaves behaved amiss he did not beat or use them ill, but parted with them. This made them afraid of disobliging him; and as he treated his slaves better than any other man on the island, so he was better and more faithfully served by them in return. By this kind treatment I did at last endeavour to compose myself; and with fortitude, though moneyless, determined to face whatever fate had decreed for me. Mr. King soon asked me what I could do; and at the same time said he did not mean to treat me as a common slave. I told him I knew something of seamanship, and could shave and dress hair pretty well; and I could refine wines, which I had learned on shipboard, where I had often done it; and that I could write, and understood arithmetic tolerably well as far as the Rule of Three. He then asked me if I knew anything of gauging;[1] and, on my answering that I did not, he said one of his clerks should teach me to gauge.

Mr. King dealt in all manner of merchandise, and kept from one to six clerks. He loaded many vessels in a year; particularly to Philadelphia, where he was born, and was connected with a great mercantile house in that city. He had besides many vessels and droggers,[2] of different sizes, which used to go about the island; and others to collect rum, sugar, and other goods. I understood pulling and managing those boats very well; and this hard work, which was the first that he set me to, in the sugar seasons used to be my constant employment. I have rowed the boat, and slaved at the oars, from one hour to sixteen in the twenty-four; during which I had fifteen pence sterling per day to live on, though sometimes only ten pence. However this was considerably more than was allowed to other slaves that used to work with me, and belonged to other gentlemen on the island: those poor souls had never more than nine pence per day, and seldom more than six pence, from their masters or owners, though they earned them three or four pisterines:[3] for it is a common practice in the West Indies for men to purchase slaves though they have not plantations themselves, in order to let them out to planters and merchants at so much a piece by the day, and they give what allowance they choose out of this produce of their daily work to their slaves for subsistence; this allowance is often very scanty. My master often gave the owners of these slaves two and a half of these pieces per day, and found the poor fellows in victuals[4] himself, because he thought the owners did not feed them well enough according to the work

---

[1] *gauging*   Calculating the holding capacity or contents of a ship or other container.

[2] *drogger*   Slow, awkward coasting vessel used in the West Indies.

[3] [Equiano's note]   These pisterines are of the value of a shilling [twelve pence].

[4] *found … victuals*   I.e., gave them food.

they did. The slaves used to like this very well; and, as they knew my master to be a man of feeling, they were always glad to work for him in preference to any other gentleman: some of whom, after they had been paid for these poor people's labours, would not give them their allowance out of it. Many times have I even seen these unfortunate wretches beaten for asking for their pay; and often severely flogged by their owners if they did not bring them their daily or weekly money exactly to the time; though the poor creatures were obliged to wait on the gentlemen they had worked for sometimes for more than half the day before they could get their pay; and this generally on Sundays, when they wanted the time for themselves. In particular, I knew a countryman of mine who once did not bring the weekly money directly that it was earned; and though he brought it the same day to his master, yet he was staked to the ground for this pretended negligence, and was just going to receive a hundred lashes, but for a gentleman who begged him off fifty. ...

Once, for a few days, I was let out to fit a vessel, and I had no victuals allowed me by either party; at last I told my master of this treatment, and he took me away from it. In many of the estates, on the different islands where I used to be sent for rum or sugar, they would not deliver it to me, or any other negro; he was therefore obliged to send a white man along with me to those places; and then he used to pay him six to ten pisterines a day. From being thus employed, during the time I served Mr. King, in going about the different estates on the island, I had all the opportunity I could wish for to see the dreadful usage of the poor men; usage that reconciled me to my situation, and made me bless God for the hands into which I had fallen.

I had the good fortune to please my master in every department in which he employed me; and there was scarcely any part of his business, or household affairs, in which I was not occasionally engaged. I often supplied the place of a clerk,[1] in receiving and delivering cargoes to the ships, in tending stores, and delivering goods: and, besides this, I used to shave and dress my master when convenient, and take care of his horse; and when it was necessary, which was very often, I worked likewise on board of different vessels of his. By these means I became very useful to my master; and

saved him, as he used to acknowledge, above a hundred pounds a year. Nor did he scruple to say I was of more advantage to him than any of his clerks; though their usual wages in the West Indies are from sixty to a hundred pounds current[2] a year.

I have sometimes heard it asserted that a negro cannot earn his master the first cost;[3] but nothing can be further from the truth. I suppose nine tenths of the mechanics throughout the West Indies are negro slaves; and I well know the coopers[4] among them earn two dollars a day; the carpenters the same, and oftentimes more; as also the masons, smiths, and fishermen, etc. and I have known many slaves whose masters would not take a thousand pounds current for them. But surely this assertion refutes itself; for, if it be true, why do the planters and merchants pay such a price for slaves? And, above all, why do those who make this assertion exclaim the most loudly against the abolition of the slave trade? So much are men blinded, and to such inconsistent arguments are they driven by mistaken interest! I grant, indeed, that slaves are sometimes, by half-feeding, half-clothing, over-working and stripes,[5] reduced so low, that they are turned out as unfit for service, and left to perish in the woods, or expire on a dunghill.

My master was several times offered by different gentlemen one hundred guineas for me; but he always told them he would not sell me, to my great joy: and I used to double my diligence and care for fear of getting into the hands of those men who did not allow a valuable slave the common support of life. Many of them even used to find fault with my master for feeding his slaves so well as he did; although I often went hungry, and an Englishman might think my fare very indifferent; but he used to tell them he always would do it, because the slaves thereby looked better and did more work.

While I was thus employed by my master I was often witness to cruelties of every kind, which were exercised on my unhappy fellow slaves. I used frequently to have different cargoes of new negroes in my care for sale; and it was almost a constant practice with our clerks, and

---

[1] *supplied the place of a clerk* Filled the position of clerk.

[2] *current* Currency.

[3] *first cost* Price paid for an enslaved person.

[4] *coopers* Makers of wooden casks, barrels, and other vessels for storing goods.

[5] *stripes* Whip lashes.

other whites, to commit violent depredations on the chastity of the female slaves; and these I was, though with reluctance, obliged to submit to at all times, being unable to help them. When we have had some of these slaves on board my master's vessels to carry them to other islands, or to America, I have known our mates to commit these acts most shamefully, to the disgrace, not of Christians only, but of men. I have even known them gratify their brutal passion with females not ten years old; and these abominations some of them practised to such scandalous excess, that one of our captains discharged the mate and others on that account. And yet in Montserrat I have seen a negro-man staked to the ground, and cut most shockingly,[1] and then his ears cut off bit by bit, because he had been connected with a white woman who was a common prostitute: as if it were no crime in the whites to rob an innocent African girl of her virtue; but most heinous in a black man only to gratify a passion of nature, where the temptation was offered by one of a different colour, though the most abandoned woman of her species.[2]

Another negro man was half-hanged, and then burnt, for attempting to poison a cruel overseer. Thus by repeated cruelties are the wretched first urged to despair, and then murdered, because they still retain so much of human nature about them as to wish to put an end to their misery, and retaliate on their tyrants! These overseers are indeed for the most part persons of the worst character of any denomination of men in the West Indies. Unfortunately, many humane gentlemen, by not residing on their estates, are obliged to leave the management of them in the hands of these human butchers, who cut and mangle the slaves in a shocking manner on the most trifling occasions, and altogether treat them in every respect like brutes. They

pay no regard to the situation of pregnant women, nor the least attention to the lodging of the field negroes. Their huts, which ought to be well covered, and the place dry where they take their little repose, are often open sheds, built in damp places; so that, when the poor creatures return tired from the toil of the field, they contract many disorders, from being exposed to the damp air in this uncomfortable state, while they are heated, and their pores are open. This neglect certainly conspires with many others to cause a decrease in the births as well as in the lives of the grown negroes. I can quote many instances of gentlemen who reside on their estates in the West Indies, and then the scene is quite changed; the negroes are treated with lenity and proper care, by which their lives are prolonged, and their masters are profited. To the honour of humanity, I knew several gentlemen who managed their estates in this manner; and they found that benevolence was their true interest. And, among many I could mention in several of the islands, I knew one in Montserrat[3] whose slaves looked remarkably well, and never needed any fresh supplies of negroes; and there are many other estates, especially in Barbadoes, which, from such judicious treatment, need no fresh stock of negroes at any time. I have the honour of knowing a most worthy and humane gentleman, who is a native of Barbadoes, and has estates there.[4] This gentleman has written a treatise on the usage of his own slaves. He allows them two hours for refreshment at mid-day; and many other indulgencies and comforts, particularly in their lying; and, besides this, he raises more provisions on his estate than they can destroy; so that by these attentions he saves the lives of his negroes, and keeps them healthy, and as happy as the condition of slavery can admit. I myself, as shall appear in the sequel,[5] managed an estate, where, by those attentions, the negroes were uncommonly cheerful and healthy, and did more work by half than by the common mode of treatment they usually do. For want,[6] therefore, of such care and

---

1   *cut most shockingly* The likely punishment implied here is castration.

2   The following paragraph was added here by Equiano in some later editions: "One Mr. D[rummond] told me that he had sold 41,000 negroes, and that he once cut off a negro-man's leg for running away.—I asked him if the man had died in the operation, how he, as a Christian, could answer for the horrid act before God? and he told me, answering was a thing of another world, but what he thought and did were policy. I told him that the Christian doctrine taught us to do unto others as we would that others should do unto us. He then said that his scheme had the desired effect—it cured that man and some others of running away."

3   [Equiano's note] Mr. Dubury, and many others, Montserrat.

4   [Equiano's note] Sir Philip Bibbes, Baronet, Barbadoes.

5   *in the sequel* Hereafter. The first three editions of *The Interesting Narrative* were published in two volumes, with Chapters 1–6 included in the first volume and Chapters 7–12 in the second. See Chapter 11 for Equiano's account of his time spent as an overseer.

6   *want* Lack.

attention to the poor negroes, and otherwise oppressed as they are, it is no wonder that the decrease should require 20,000 new negroes annually to fill up the vacant places of the dead.

Even in Barbadoes, notwithstanding those humane exceptions which I have mentioned, and others I am acquainted with, which justly make it quoted as a place where slaves meet with the best treatment, and need fewest recruits of any in the West Indies, yet this island requires 1000 negroes annually to keep up the original stock, which is only 80,000. So that the whole term of a negro's life may be said to be there but sixteen years![1] And yet the climate here is in every respect the same as that from which they are taken, except in being more wholesome. Do the British colonies decrease in this manner? And yet what a prodigious difference is there between an English and West India climate?

While I was in Montserrat I knew a negro man, named Emanuel Sankey, who endeavoured to escape from his miserable bondage, by concealing himself on board of a London ship: but fate did not favour the poor oppressed man; for, being discovered when the vessel was under sail, he was delivered up again to his master. This *Christian master* immediately pinned the wretch down to the ground at each wrist and ankle, and then took some sticks of sealing wax, and lighted them, and dropped it all over his back. There was another master who was noted for cruelty; and I believe he had not a slave but what had been cut, and had pieces fairly taken out of the flesh: and, after they had been punished thus, he used to make them get into a long wooden box or case he had for that purpose, in which he shut them up during pleasure.[2] It was just about the height and breadth of a man; and the poor wretches had no room, when in the case, to move.

It was very common in several of the islands, particularly in St. Kitt's, for the slaves to be branded with the initial letters of their master's name; and a load of heavy iron hooks hung about their necks. Indeed on the most trifling occasions they were loaded with chains; and often instruments of torture were added. The iron muzzle, thumb-screws, etc. are so well known, as not to need a description, and were sometimes applied for the slightest faults. I have seen a negro beaten till some

of his bones were broken, for even letting a pot boil over.[3] ...

from Chapter 6[4]

Some account of Brimstone-Hill in Montserrat—Favourable change in the author's situation—He commences merchant with three pence—His various success in dealing in the different islands, and America, and the impositions he meets with in his transactions with Europeans—A curious imposition on human nature—Danger of the surfs in the West Indies—Remarkable instance of kidnapping a free mulatto—The author is nearly murdered by Doctor Perkins in Savannah.

In the preceding chapter I have set before the reader a few of those many instances of oppression, extortion, and cruelty, which I have been a witness to in the West Indies: but, were I to enumerate them all, the catalogue would be tedious and disgusting. The punishments of the slaves on every trifling occasion are so frequent, and so well known, together with the different instruments with which they are tortured, that it cannot any longer afford novelty to recite them; and they are too shocking to yield delight either to the writer or the reader. I shall therefore hereafter only mention such as incidentally befell myself in the course of my adventures. ...

Some time in the year 1763 kind Providence seemed to appear rather more favourable to me. One of my master's vessels, a Bermudas sloop, about sixty tons, was commanded by one Captain Thomas Farmer, an Englishman, a very alert and active man, who gained my master a great deal of money by his good

---

1   [Equiano's note] Benezet's "Account of Guinea," p. 16.

2   *during pleasure* At discretion.

3   The following lines appear in some later editions: "It is not uncommon after a flogging, to make slaves go on their knees, and thank their owners, and pray, or rather say, God bless them. I have often asked many of the men slaves (who used to go several miles to their wives, and late in the night, after having been wearied with a hard day's labour) why they went so far for wives, and why they did not take them of their own master's negro women, and particularly those who lived together as household slaves? Their answers have ever been—'Because when the master or mistress choose to punish the women, they make the husbands flog their own wives, and that they could not bear to do.'"

4   A longer selection of excerpts is included in the website component of this anthology.

management in carrying passengers from one island to another; but very often his sailors used to get drunk and run away from the vessel, which hindered him in his business very much. This man had taken a liking to me; and many different times begged of my master to let me go a trip with him as a sailor; but he would tell him he could not spare me, though the vessel sometimes could not go for want of hands, for sailors were generally very scarce in the island. However, at last, from necessity or force, my master was prevailed on, though very reluctantly, to let me go with this captain; but he gave great charge to him to take care that I did not run away, for if I did he would make him pay for me. This being the case, the captain had for some time a sharp eye upon me whenever the vessel anchored; and as soon as she returned I was sent for on shore again. Thus was I slaving as it were for life, sometimes at one thing, and sometimes at another; so that the captain and I were nearly the most useful men in my master's employment. I also became so useful to the captain on shipboard, that many times, when he used to ask for me to go with him, though it should be but for twenty-four hours, to some of the islands near us, my master would answer he could not spare me, at which the captain would swear, and would not go the trip; and tell my master I was better to him on board than any three white men he had; for they used to behave ill in many respects, particularly in getting drunk; and then they frequently got the boat stove,[1] so as to hinder the vessel from coming back as soon as she might have done. This my master knew very well; and at last, by the captain's constant entreaties, after I had been several times with him, one day, to my great joy, my master told me the captain would not let him rest, and asked me whether I would go aboard as a sailor, or stay on shore and mind the stores, for he could not bear any longer to be plagued in this manner. I was very happy at this proposal, for I immediately thought I might in time stand some chance by being on board to get a little money, or possibly make my escape if I should be used ill: I also expected to get better food, and in greater abundance; for I had felt much hunger oftentimes, though my master treated his slaves, as I have observed, uncommonly well. I therefore, without hesitation, answered him, that I would go and be

a sailor if he pleased. Accordingly, I was ordered on board directly. Nevertheless, between the vessel and the shore, when she was in port, I had little or no rest, as my master always wished to have me along with him. Indeed, he was a very pleasant gentleman, and but for my expectations on shipboard I should not have thought of leaving him. But the captain liked me also very much, and I was entirely his right-hand man. I did all I could to deserve his favour, and in return I received better treatment from him than any other I believe ever met with in the West Indies in my situation.

After I had been sailing for some time with this captain, at length I endeavoured to try my luck and commence merchant. I had but a very small capital to begin with; for one single half bit, which is equal to three pence in England,[2] made up my whole stock. However I trusted to the Lord to be with me; and at one of our trips to St. Eustatia, a Dutch island, I bought a glass tumbler with my half bit, and when I came to Montserrat I sold it for a bit, or sixpence. Luckily we made several successive trips to St. Eustatia (which was a general mart for the West Indies, about twenty leagues from Montserrat); and in our next, finding my tumbler so profitable, with this one bit I bought two tumblers more; and when I came back I sold them for two bits, equal to a shilling sterling. When we went again, I bought with these two bits four more of these glasses, which I sold for four bits on our return to Montserrat; and in our next voyage to St. Eustatia I bought two glasses with one bit, and with the other three I bought a jug of Geneva,[3] nearly about three pints in measure. When we came to Montserrat I sold the gin for eight bits, and the tumblers for two, so that my capital now amounted in all to a dollar, well husbanded[4] and acquired in the space of a month or six weeks, when I blessed the Lord that I was so rich. As we sailed to different islands, I laid this money out in various things occasionally, and it used to turn out to very good account, especially when we went

---

[1] *got the boat stove* Stove the boat in; made a hole in the boat.

[2] *single half bit … England* A half bit was a unit of Spanish currency; three English pence would be the equivalent of perhaps a couple of American dollars today in purchasing power.

[3] *Geneva* Geneva gin (in the late eighteenth century a very inexpensive and widely available type of liquor).

[4] *well husbanded* Carefully managed.

to Guadaloupe, Grenada, and the rest of the French islands.

Thus was I going all about the islands upwards of four years, and ever trading as I went, during which I experienced many instances of ill usage, and have seen many injuries done to other negroes in our dealings with Europeans: and, amidst our recreations, when we have been dancing and merry-making, they, without cause, have molested and insulted us. Indeed, I was more than once obliged to look up to God on high, as I had advised the poor fisherman some time before. And I had not been long trading for myself in the manner I have related above, when I experienced the like trial in company with him as follows: This man being used to the water, was upon an emergency put on board of us by his master to work as another hand, on a voyage to Santa Cruz; and at our sailing he had brought his little all for a venture, which consisted of six bits' worth of limes and oranges in a bag; I had also my whole stock, which was about twelve bits' worth of the same kind of goods, separate in two bags; for we had heard these fruits sold well in that island. When we came there, in some little convenient time he and I went ashore with our fruits to sell them; but we had scarcely landed when we were met by two white men, who presently took our three bags from us. We could not at first guess what they meant to do; and for some time we thought they were jesting with us; but they too soon let us know otherwise, for they took our ventures immediately to a house hard by, and adjoining the fort, while we followed all the way begging of them to give us our fruits, but in vain. They not only refused to return them, but swore at us, and threatened if we did not immediately depart they would flog us well. We told them these three bags were all we were worth in the world, and that we brought them with us to sell when we came from Montserrat, and shewed them the vessel. But this was rather against us, as they now saw we were strangers as well as slaves. They still therefore swore, and desired us to be gone, and even took sticks to beat us; while we, seeing they meant what they said, went off in the greatest confusion and despair. Thus, in the very minute of gaining more by three times than I ever did by any venture in my life before, was I deprived of every farthing I was worth. An insupportable misfortune! But how to help ourselves we knew not.

In our consternation we went to the commanding officer of the fort and told him how we had been served[1] by some of his people; but we obtained not the least redress: he answered our complaints only by a volley of imprecations against us, and immediately took a horse-whip, in order to chastise us, so that we were obliged to turn out much faster than we came in. I now, in the agony of distress and indignation, wished that the ire of God in his forked lightning might transfix these cruel oppressors among the dead.

Still however we persevered; went back again to the house, and begged and besought them again and again for our fruits, till at last some other people that were in the house asked if we would be contented if they kept one bag and gave us the other two. We, seeing no remedy whatever, consented to this; and they, observing one bag to have both kinds of fruit in it, which belonged to my companion, kept that; and the other two, which were mine, they gave us back. As soon as I got them, I ran as fast as I could, and got the first negro man I could to help me off; my companion, however, stayed a little longer to plead; he told them the bag they had was his, and likewise all that he was worth in the world; but this was of no avail, and he was obliged to return without it. The poor old man, wringing his hands, cried bitterly for his loss; and, indeed, he then did look up to God on high, which so moved me with pity for him, that I gave him nearly one third of my fruits. We then proceeded to the markets to sell them; and Providence was more favourable to us than we could have expected, for we sold our fruits uncommonly well; I got for mine about thirty-seven bits. Such a surprising reverse of fortune in so short a space of time seemed like a dream to me, and proved no small encouragement for me to trust the Lord in any situation. My captain afterwards frequently used to take my part, and get me my right, when I have been plundered or used ill by these tender Christian depredators; among whom I have shuddered to observe the unceasing blasphemous execrations which are wantonly thrown out by persons of all ages and conditions, not only without occasion, but even as if they were indulgences and pleasure.

At one of our trips to St. Kitt's I had eleven bits of my own; and my friendly captain lent me five bits

---

[1] *served* Treated.

more, with which I bought a Bible. I was very glad to get this book, which I scarcely could meet with anywhere. I think there was none sold in Montserrat; and, much to my grief, from being forced out of the *Aetna* in the manner I have related, my Bible, and the Guide to the Indians, the two books I loved above all others, were left behind.

While I was in this place, St. Kitt's, a very curious imposition on human nature took place. A white man wanted to marry in the church a free black woman that had land and slaves in Montserrat: but the clergyman told him it was against the law of the place to marry a white and a black in the church. The man then asked to be married on the water, to which the parson consented, and the two lovers went in one boat, and the parson and clerk in another, and thus the ceremony was performed. After this the loving pair came on board our vessel, and my captain treated them extremely well, and brought them safe to Montserrat.

The reader cannot but judge of the irksomeness of this situation to a mind like mine, in being daily exposed to new hardships and impositions, after having seen many better days, and having been as it were in a state of freedom and plenty; added to which, every part of the world I had hitherto been in seemed to me a paradise in comparison of the West Indies. My mind was therefore hourly replete with inventions and thoughts of being freed, and, if possible, by honest and honourable means; for I always remembered the old adage; and I trust it has ever been my ruling principle, that honesty is the best policy; and likewise that other golden precept—to do unto all men as I would they should do unto me. However, as I was from early years a predestinarian,[1] I thought whatever fate had determined must ever come to pass; and therefore, if ever it were my lot to be freed nothing could prevent me, although I should at present see no means or hope to obtain my freedom; on the other hand, if it were my fate not to be freed, I never should be so, and all my endeavours for that purpose would be fruitless.

In the midst of these thoughts, I therefore looked up with prayers anxiously to God for my liberty; and at the same time I used every honest means, and endeavoured all that was possible on my part to obtain it. In process of time I became master of a few pounds, and in a fair way of[2] making more, which my friendly captain knew very well; this occasioned him sometimes to take liberties with me: but whenever he treated me waspishly I used plainly to tell him my mind, and that I would die before I would be imposed on as other negroes were, and that to me life had lost its relish when liberty was gone. This I said although I foresaw my then well-being or future hopes of freedom (humanly speaking) depended on this man. However, as he could not bear the thoughts of my not sailing with him, he always became mild on my threats. I therefore continued with him; and, from my great attention to his orders and his business, I gained him credit, and through his kindness to me I at last procured my liberty. While I thus went on, filled with the thoughts of freedom, and resisting oppression as well as I was able, my life hung daily in suspense, particularly in the surfs I have formerly mentioned, as I could not swim. These are extremely violent throughout the West Indies, and I was ever exposed to their howling rage and devouring fury in all the islands. I have seen them strike and toss a boat right up an end, and maim several on board. Once in the Grenada islands, when I and about eight others were pulling a large boat with two puncheons[3] of water in it, a surf struck us, and drove the boat and all in it about half a stone's throw, among some trees, and above the high-water mark. We were obliged to get all the assistance we could from the nearest estate to mend the boat, and launch it into the water again. At Montserrat one night, in pressing hard to get off the shore on board, the punt[4] was overset with us four times; the first time I was very near being drowned; however the jacket I had on kept me up above water a little space of time, while I called on a man near me who was a good swimmer, and told him I could not swim; he then made haste to me, and, just as I was sinking, he caught hold of me, and brought me to sounding,[5] and then he went and brought the punt also. As soon as we had turned the water out of her, lest we should

---

[1] *predestinarian* One who believes that all that occurs is predestined by God. (The question of to what degree human events are predestined was the subject of heated dispute at the time within the Methodist church, which Equiano joined in 1774.)

[2] *in a fair way of* On the way to.

[3] *puncheons* Barrels.

[4] *punt* Small boat.

[5] *to sounding* To where one could find sound footing underwater.

be used ill for being absent, we attempted again three times more, and as often the horrid surfs served us as at first; but at last, the fifth time we attempted, we gained our point, at the imminent hazard of our lives.

One day also, at Old Road in Montserrat, our captain, and three men besides myself, were going in a large canoe in quest of rum and sugar, when a single surf tossed the canoe an amazing distance from the water, and some of us even a stone's throw from each other: most of us were very much bruised; so that I and many more often said, and really thought, that there was not such another place under the heavens as this. I longed therefore much to leave it, and daily wished to see my master's promise performed of going to Philadelphia. While we lay in this place a very cruel thing happened on board of our sloop which filled me with horror; though I found afterwards such practices were frequent. There was a very clever and decent free young mulatto-man who sailed a long time with us: he had a free woman for his wife, by whom he had a child; and she was then living on shore, and all very happy. Our captain and mate, and other people on board, and several elsewhere, even the natives of Bermudas, all knew this young man from a child that he was always free, and no one had ever claimed him as their property: however, as might too often overcomes right in these parts, it happened that a Bermudas captain, whose vessel lay there for a few days in the road, came on board of us, and seeing the mulatto-man, whose name was Joseph Clipson, he told him he was not free, and that he had orders from his master to bring him to Bermudas. The poor man could not believe the captain to be in earnest; but he was very soon undeceived, his men laying violent hands on him: and although he shewed a certificate of his being born free in St. Kitt's, and most people on board knew that he served his time to boat building,[1] and always passed for a free man, yet he was taken forcibly out of our vessel. He then asked to be carried ashore before the secretary or magistrates, and these infernal invaders of human rights promised him he should; but, instead of that, they carried him on board of the other vessel: and the next day, without giving the poor man any hearing on shore, or suffering him even to see his wife or child, he was carried away,

and probably doomed never more in this world to see them again.

Nor was this the only instance of this kind of barbarity I was a witness to. I have since often seen in Jamaica and other islands free men, whom I have known in America, thus villainously trepanned[2] and held in bondage. I have heard of two similar practices even in Philadelphia—and, were it not for the benevolence of the Quakers in that city, many of the sable[3] race, who now breathe the air of liberty, would, I believe, be groaning indeed under some planter's chains. These things opened my mind to a new scene of horror to which I had been before a stranger. Hitherto I had thought only slavery dreadful; but the state of a free negro appeared to me now equally so at least, and in some respects even worse, for they live in constant alarm for their liberty; and even this is but nominal, for they are universally insulted and plundered without the possibility of redress; for such is the equity of the West Indian laws, that no free negro's evidence will be admitted in their courts of justice. In this situation, is it surprising that slaves, when mildly treated, should prefer even the misery of slavery to such a mockery of freedom? I was now completely disgusted with the West Indies, and thought I never should be entirely free until I had left them. ...

About the latter end of the year 1764 my master bought a larger sloop, called the *Providence*, about seventy or eighty tons, of which my captain had the command. I went with him into this vessel, and we took a load of new slaves for Georgia and Charlestown.[4] My master now left me entirely to the captain, though he still wished for me to be with him; but I, who always much wished to lose sight of the West Indies, was not a little rejoiced at the thoughts of seeing any other country. Therefore, relying on the goodness of my captain, I got ready all the little venture I could; and, when the vessel was ready, we sailed, to my great joy. When we got to our destined places, Georgia and Charlestown, I expected I should have an opportunity of selling my little property to advantage: but here, particularly in Charlestown, I met with buyers, white men, who imposed on me as in other places. Notwithstanding, I

---

[1] *served his time to boat building* Was apprenticed as a boat builder.

[2] *trepanned* Taken by force.

[3] *sable* Dark skinned.

[4] *Charlestown* Charleston, South Carolina.

was resolved to have fortitude; thinking no lot or trial is too hard when kind Heaven is the rewarder.

We soon got loaded again, and returned to Montserrat; and there, amongst the rest of the islands, I sold my goods well; and in this manner I continued trading during the year 1764; meeting with various scenes of imposition, as usual.

After this, my master fitted out his vessel for Philadelphia, in the year 1765; and during the time we were loading her, and getting ready for the voyage, I worked with redoubled alacrity, from the hope of getting money enough by these voyages to buy my freedom in time, if it should please God; and also to see the town of Philadelphia, which I had heard a great deal about for some years past; besides which, I had always longed to prove my master's promise the first day I came to him. In the midst of these elevated ideas, and while I was about getting my little merchandize in readiness, one Sunday my master sent for me to his house. When I came there, I found him and the captain together; and, on my going in, I was struck with astonishment at his telling me he heard that I meant to run away from him when I got to Philadelphia: "And therefore," said he, "I must sell you again: you cost me a great deal of money, no less than forty pounds sterling; and it will not do to lose so much. You are a valuable fellow," continued he; "and I can get any day for you one hundred guineas, from many gentlemen in this island." And then he told me of Captain Doran's brother-in-law, a severe master, who ever wanted to buy me to make me his overseer. My captain also said he could get much more than a hundred guineas for me in Carolina. This I knew to be a fact; for the gentleman that wanted to buy me came off several times on board of us, and spoke to me to live with him, and said he would use me well.

When I asked what work he would put me to he said, as I was a sailor, he would make me a captain of one of his rice vessels. But I refused: and fearing, at the same time, by a sudden turn I saw in the captain's temper, he might mean to sell me, I told the gentleman I would not live with him on any condition, and that I certainly would run away with his vessel: but he said he did not fear that, as he would catch me again; and then he told me how cruelly he would serve me if I should do so. My captain, however, gave him to understand that I knew something of navigation, so he thought better of it; and, to my great joy, he went away. I now told my master I did not say I would run away in Philadelphia; neither did I mean it, as he did not use me ill, nor yet the captain: for if they did I certainly would have made some attempts before now; but as I thought that if it were God's will I ever should be freed it would be so, and, on the contrary, if it was not his will it would not happen; so I hoped, if ever I were freed, whilst I was used well, it should be by honest means; but, as I could not help myself, he must do as he pleased; I could only hope and trust to the God of Heaven; and at that instant my mind was big with inventions and full of schemes to escape. I then appealed to the captain whether he ever saw any sign of my making the least attempt to run away; and asked him if I did not always come on board according to the time for which he gave me liberty; and, more particularly, when all our men left us at Gaurdeloupe and went on board of the French fleet, and advised me to go with them, whether I might not, and that he could not have got me again. To my no small surprise, and very great joy, the captain confirmed every syllable that I had said: and even more; for he said he had tried different times to see if I would make any attempt of this kind, both at St. Eustatia and in America, and he never found that I made the smallest; but, on the contrary, I always came on board according to his orders; and he did really believe, if I ever meant to run away, that, as I could never have had a better opportunity, I would have done it the night the mate and all the people left our vessel at Gaurdeloupe.

The captain then informed my master, who had been thus imposed on by our mate, though I did not know who was my enemy, the reason the mate had for imposing this lie upon him; which was, because I had acquainted the captain of the provisions the mate had given away or taken out of the vessel. This speech of the captain was like life to the dead to me, and instantly my soul glorified God; and still more so on hearing my master immediately say that I was a sensible fellow, and he never did intend to use me as a common slave; and that but for the entreaties of the captain, and his character of me, he would not have let me go from the stores about as I had done; that also, in so doing, he thought by carrying one little thing or other to different places to sell I might make money. That he also intended to encourage me in this by crediting me with half a puncheon of rum and half a hogshead of sugar at a time; so that, from being careful, I might have money enough, in some time, to purchase my freedom; and, when that was the case, I might depend upon it he would let me have it for forty pounds sterling money, which was only the same price he gave for me. This sound gladdened my poor heart beyond measure; though indeed it was no more than the very idea I had formed in my mind of my master long before, and I immediately made him this reply: "Sir, I always had that very thought of you, indeed I had, and that made me so diligent in serving you." He then gave me a large piece of silver coin, such as I never had seen or had before, and told me to get ready for the voyage, and he would credit me with a tierce[1] of sugar, and another of rum; he also said that he had two amiable sisters in Philadelphia, from whom I might get some necessary things. Upon this my noble captain desired me to go aboard; and, knowing the African metal,[2] he charged me not to say anything of this matter to anybody; and he promised that the lying mate should not go with him any more. This was a change indeed; in the same hour to feel the most exquisite pain, and in the turn of a moment the fullest joy. It caused in me such sensations as I was only able to express in my looks; my heart was so overpowered with gratitude that I could have kissed both of their feet. When I left the room I immediately went, or rather flew, to the vessel, which being loaded, my master, as good as his word, trusted me with a tierce of rum, and another of sugar, when we sailed, and arrived safe at the elegant town of Philadelphia. I soon sold my goods here pretty well; and in this charming place I found everything plentiful and cheap.

While I was in this place a very extraordinary occurrence befell me. I had been told one evening of a wise woman, a Mrs. Davis, who revealed secrets, foretold events, etc. I put little faith in this story at first, as I could not conceive that any mortal could foresee the future disposals[3] of Providence, nor did I believe in any other revelation than that of the Holy Scriptures;

however, I was greatly astonished at seeing this woman in a dream that night, though a person I never before beheld in my life; this made such an impression on me that I could not get the idea the next day out of my mind, and I then became as anxious to see her as I was before indifferent; accordingly in the evening, after we left off working, I inquired where she lived, and being directed to her, to my inexpressible surprise, beheld the very woman in the very same dress she appeared to me to wear in the vision. She immediately told me I had dreamed of her the preceding night; related to me many things that had happened with a correctness that astonished me; and finally told me I should not be long a slave: this was the more agreeable news, as I believed it the more readily from her having so faithfully related the past incidents of my life. She said I should be twice in very great danger of my life within eighteen months, which, if I escaped, I should afterwards go on well; so, giving me her blessing, we parted. After staying here some time till our vessel was loaded, and I had bought in my little traffic, we sailed from this agreeable spot for Montserrat, once more to encounter the raging surfs.

We arrived safe at Montserrat, where we discharged our cargo; and soon after that we took slaves on board for St. Eustatia, and from thence to Georgia. I had always exerted myself and did double work, in order to make our voyages as short as possible; and from thus overworking myself while we were at Georgia I caught a fever and ague. I was very ill for eleven days and near dying; eternity was now exceedingly impressed on my mind, and I feared very much that awful event. I prayed the Lord therefore to spare me; and I made a promise in my mind to God, that I would be good if ever I should recover. At length, from having an eminent doctor to attend me, I was restored again to health; and soon after we got the vessel loaded, and set off for Montserrat. During the passage, as I was perfectly restored, and had much business of the vessel to mind, all my endeavours to keep up my integrity, and perform my promise to God, began to fail; and, in spite of all I could do, as we drew nearer and nearer to the islands, my resolutions more and more declined, as if the very air of that country or climate seemed fatal to piety. When we were safe arrived at Montserrat, and I had got ashore, I forgot my former resolutions. Alas! How prone is the heart to leave that God it wishes

---

[1]   *a tierce*   One third of a barrel.

[2]   *metal*   Character.

[3]   *disposals*   Arrangements.

to love! and how strongly do the things of this world strike the senses and captivate the soul!

After our vessel was discharged, we soon got her ready, and took in, as usual, some of the poor oppressed natives of Africa, and other negroes; we then set off again for Georgia and Charlestown. We arrived at Georgia, and, having landed part of our cargo, proceeded to Charlestown with the remainder. While we were there, I saw the town illuminated; the guns were fired, and bonfires and other demonstrations of joy shown, on account of the repeal of the Stamp Act.[1]

Here I disposed of some goods on my own account; the white men buying them with smooth promises and fair words, giving me however but very indifferent payment. ...

We soon came to Georgia, where we were to complete our lading; and here worse fate than ever attended me: for one Sunday night, as I was with some negroes in their master's yard in the town of Savannah, it happened that their master, one Doctor Perkins, who was a very severe and cruel man, came in drunk; and, not liking to see any strange negroes in his yard, he and a ruffian of a white man he had in his service beset me in an instant, and both of them struck me with the first weapons they could get hold of. I cried out as long as I could for help and mercy; but, though I gave a good account of myself, and he knew my captain, who lodged hard by him, it was to no purpose. They beat and mangled me in a shameful manner, leaving me near dead. I lost so much blood from the wounds I received that I lay quite motionless, and was so benumbed that I could not feel anything for many hours. Early in the morning they took me away to the jail. As I did not return to the ship all night, my captain, not knowing where I was, and being uneasy that I did not then make my appearance, he made inquiry after me; and, having found where I was, immediately came to me. As soon as the good man saw me so cut and mangled, he could not forbear weeping; he soon got me out of jail to his lodgings, and immediately sent for the best doctors in the place, who at first declared it as their opinion that I could not recover. My captain

on this went to all the lawyers in the town for their advice, but they told him they could do nothing for me as I was a negro. He then went to Doctor Perkins, the hero who had vanquished me, and menaced him, swearing he would be revenged of him, and challenged him to fight. But cowardice is ever the companion of cruelty—and the Doctor refused.

However, by the skilfulness of one Doctor Brady of that place, I began at last to mend; but, although I was so sore and bad with the wounds I had all over me that I could not rest in any posture, yet I was in more pain on account of the captain's uneasiness about me than I otherwise should have been. The worthy man nursed and watched me all the hours of the night; and I was, through his attention and that of the doctor, able to get out of bed in about sixteen or eighteen days. All this time I was very much wanted on board, as I used frequently to go up and down the river for rafts, and other parts of our cargo, and stow them when the mate was sick or absent.

In about four weeks I was able to go on duty; and in a fortnight after, having got in all our lading, our vessel set sail for Montserrat; and in less than three weeks we arrived there safe towards the end of the year. This ended my adventures in 1764 [1765]; for I did not leave Montserrat again till the beginning of the following year.

END OF THE FIRST VOLUME

from CHAPTER 7[2]

The author's disgust at the West Indies—Forms schemes to obtain his freedom—Ludicrous disappointment he and his Captain meet with in Georgia—At last, by several successful voyages, he acquires a sum of money sufficient to purchase it—Applies to his master, who accepts it, and grants his manumission, to his great joy—He afterwards enters as a freeman on board one of Mr. King's ships, and sails for Georgia—Impositions on free negroes as usual—His venture of turkeys—Sails for Montserrat, and on his passage his friend, the Captain, falls ill and dies.

---

1   *Stamp Act* The 1765 Stamp Act (requiring that various printed papers be produced on stamped paper of English manufacture) was a form of tax imposed on the American colonies by the British colonial government. The Stamp Act inspired outrage in the colonies, and was repealed the following year.

2   This chapter is included in its entirety in the website component of this anthology.

Every day now brought me nearer my freedom, and I was impatient till we proceeded again to sea, that I might have an opportunity of getting a sum large enough to purchase it. I was not long ungratified; for, in the beginning of the year 1766, my master bought another sloop, named the *Nancy*, the largest I had ever seen. She was partly laden, and was to proceed to Philadelphia; our Captain had his choice of three, and I was well pleased he chose this, which was the largest; for, from his having a large vessel, I had more room, and could carry a larger quantity of goods with me. Accordingly, when we had delivered our old vessel, the *Prudence*, and completed the lading of the *Nancy*, having made near three hundred per cent, by four barrels of pork I brought from Charlestown, I laid in as large a cargo as I could, trusting to God's providence to prosper my undertaking.

With these views I sailed for Philadelphia. On our passage, when we drew near the land, I was for the first time surprised at the sight of some whales, having never seen any such large sea monsters before; and as we sailed by the land one morning I saw a puppy whale close by the vessel; it was about the length of a wherry boat, and it followed us all the day till we got within the Capes.[1] We arrived safe and in good time at Philadelphia, and I sold my goods there chiefly to the Quakers. They always appeared to be a very honest discreet sort of people, and never attempted to impose on me;[2] I therefore liked them, and ever after chose to deal with them in preference to any others.

One Sunday morning while I was here, as I was going to church, I chanced to pass a meeting-house.[3] The doors being open, and the house full of people, it excited my curiosity to go in. When I entered the house, to my great surprise, I saw a very tall woman standing in the midst of them, speaking in an audible voice something which I could not understand. Having never seen anything of this kind before, I stood and stared about me for some time, wondering at this odd scene. As soon as it was over I took an opportunity to make inquiry about the place and people, when I was informed they were called Quakers. I particularly asked what that woman I saw in the midst of them had said, but none of them were pleased to satisfy me; so I quitted them, and soon after, as I was returning, I came to a church crowded with people; the church-yard was full likewise, and a number of people were even mounted on ladders, looking in at the windows. I thought this a strange sight, as I had never seen churches, either in England or the West Indies, crowded in this manner before. I therefore made bold to ask some people the meaning of all this, and they told me the Rev. Mr. George Whitfield[4] was preaching. I had often heard of this gentleman, and had wished to see and hear him; but I had never before had an opportunity. I now therefore resolved to gratify myself with the sight, and I pressed in amidst the multitude. When I got into the church, I saw this pious man exhorting the people with the greatest fervour and earnestness, and sweating as much as I ever did while in slavery on Montserrat beach. I was very much struck and impressed with this; I thought it strange I had never seen divines exert themselves in this manner before, and I was no longer at a loss to account for the thin congregations they preached to.

When we had discharged our cargo here, and were loaded again, we left this fruitful land once more, and set sail for Montserrat. My traffic had hitherto succeeded so well with me, that I thought, by selling my goods when we arrived at Montserrat, I should have enough to purchase my freedom. But, as soon as our vessel arrived there, my master came on board, and gave orders for us to go to St. Eustatia, and discharge our cargo there, and from thence proceed for Georgia. I was much disappointed at this; but thinking, as usual, it was of no use to encounter with the decrees of fate, I submitted without repining, and we went to St. Eustatia. After we had discharged our cargo there we took in a live cargo, as we call a cargo of slaves. Here I sold my goods tolerably well; but, not being able to lay out all my money in this small island to as much advantage as in many other places, I laid out

---

[1] *got within the Capes* Delaware Bay (which leads to the Delaware river and the city of Philadelphia) is entered as one passes between Cape May to the north and Cape Henlopen to the south.

[2] *impose on me* Treat me unfairly or dishonestly.

[3] *meeting-house* In early America churches were often referred to as meeting houses.

[4] *Rev. Mr. George Whitfield* Whitfield (also spelled Whitefield) (1714–70) was originally an Anglican minister; renowned for his charismatic preaching, he became one of the founders of Methodism and one of the leaders of the Great Awakening of the 1730s and 1740s.

only part, and the remainder I brought away with me net.[1] We sailed from hence for Georgia, and I was glad when we got there, though I had not much reason to like the place from my last adventure in Savannah; but I longed to get back to Montserrat and procure my freedom, which I expected to be able to purchase when I returned. …

We set sail once more for Montserrat, and arrived there safe; but much out of humour with our friend the silversmith. When we had unladen the vessel, and I had sold my venture, finding myself master of about forty-seven pounds, I consulted my true friend, the Captain, how I should proceed in offering my master the money for my freedom. He told me to come on a certain morning, when he and my master would be at breakfast together. Accordingly, on that morning I went, and met the Captain there, as he had appointed. When I went in, I made my obeisance to my master, and with my money in my hand, and many fears in my heart, I prayed him to be as good as his offer to me, when he was pleased to promise me my freedom as soon as I could purchase it. This speech seemed to confound him; he began to recoil: and my heart that instant sunk within me. "What," said he, "give you your freedom? Why, where did you get the money? Have you got forty pounds sterling?" "Yes, sir," I answered. "How did you get it?" replied he. I told him, very honestly. The Captain then said he knew I got the money very honestly and with much industry, and that I was particularly careful. On which my master replied, I got money much faster than he did; and said he would not have made me the promise he did if he had thought I should have got money so soon. "Come, come," said my worthy Captain, clapping my master on the back, "Come, Robert, (which was his name) I think you must let him have his freedom; you have laid your money out very well; you have received good interest for it all this time, and here is now the principal at last. I know Gustavus has earned you more than an hundred a-year, and he will still save you money, as he will not leave you—Come, Robert, take the money." My master then said he would not be worse than his promise; and, taking the money, told me to go to the Secretary at the Register Office, and get my manumission[2] drawn up.

These words of my master were like a voice from heaven to me: in an instant all my trepidation was turned into unutterable bliss; and I most reverently bowed myself with gratitude, unable to express my feelings, but by the overflowing of my eyes, while my true and worthy friend, the Captain, congratulated us both with a peculiar degree of heartfelt pleasure.

As soon as the first transports of my joy were over, and that I had expressed my thanks to these my worthy friends in the best manner I was able, I rose with a heart full of affection and reverence, and left the room, in order to obey my master's joyful mandate of going to the Register Office. As I was leaving the house I called to mind the words of the Psalmist, in the 126th Psalm, and like him, "I glorified God in my heart, in whom I trusted."[3] These words had been impressed on my mind from the very day I was forced from Deptford to the present hour, and I now saw them, as I thought, fulfilled and verified. My imagination was all rapture as I flew to the Register Office, and, in this respect, like the apostle Peter,[4] (whose deliverance from prison was so sudden and extraordinary, that he thought he was in a vision) I could scarcely believe I was awake. Heavens! who could do justice to my feelings at this moment! Not conquering heroes themselves, in the midst of a triumph—Not the tender mother who has just regained her long-lost infant, and presses it to her heart—Not the weary hungry mariner, at the sight of the desired friendly port—Not the lover, when he once more embraces his beloved mistress, after she had been ravished from his arms!—All within my breast was tumult, wildness, and delirium! My feet scarcely touched the ground, for they were winged with joy, and, like Elijah, as he rose to heaven,[5] they "were with lightning sped as I went on." Every one I met I told of my happiness, and blazed about the virtue of my amiable master and captain.

---

[1] *net* Without having made any additional payments.

[2] *manumission* Release from enslavement.

[3] *the Psalmist … trusted* The words quoted by Equiano do not appear in this psalm; it is not entirely clear what passage he may have had in mind—possibly Psalm 28.

[4] [Equiano's note] Acts, Ch. 12, verse 9.

[5] *rose to heaven* See 2 Kings 2.1–18.

When I got to the office and acquainted the Register with my errand he congratulated me on the occasion, and told me he would draw up my manumission for half price, which was a guinea. I thanked him for his kindness; and, having received it and paid him, I hastened to my master to get him to sign it, that I might be fully released. Accordingly, he signed the manumission that day, so that, before night, I who had been a slave in the morning, trembling at the will of another, was become my own master, and completely free. I thought this was the happiest day I had ever experienced; and my joy was still heightened by the blessings and prayers of the sable race, particularly the aged, to whom my heart had ever been attached with reverence.

As the form of my manumission has something peculiar in it, and expresses the absolute power and dominion one man claims over his fellow, I shall beg leave to present it before my readers at full length:

Montserrat—To all men unto whom these presents shall come:[1] I Robert King, of the parish of St. Anthony in the said island, merchant, send greeting: Know ye, that I, the aforesaid Robert King, for and in consideration of the sum of seventy pounds current money of the said island, to me in hand paid, and to the intent that a negro man-slave, named Gustavus Vassa, shall and may become free, have manumitted, emancipated, enfranchised, and set free, and by these presents do manumit, emancipate, enfranchise, and set free, the aforesaid negro man-slave, named Gustavus Vassa, for ever, hereby giving, granting, and releasing unto him, the said Gustavus Vassa, all right, title, dominion, sovereignty, and property, which, as lord and master over the aforesaid Gustavus Vassa, I had, or now I have, or by any means whatsoever I may or can hereafter possibly have over him the aforesaid negro, for ever. In witness whereof I the abovesaid Robert King have unto these presents set my hand and seal, this tenth day of July, in the year of our Lord one thousand seven hundred and sixty-six.
Robert King

Signed, sealed, and delivered in the presence of Terrylegay, Montserrat.

Registered the within manumission at full length, this eleventh day of July, 1766, in liber[2]
D. Terrylegay, Register.

In short, the fair as well as black people immediately styled me by a new appellation, to me the most desirable in the world, which was Freeman, and at the dances I gave,[3] my Georgia superfine blue clothes made no indifferent appearance, as I thought. Some of the sable females, who formerly stood aloof, now began to relax and appear less coy; but my heart was still fixed on London, where I hoped to be ere long. So that my worthy captain and his owner, my late master, finding that the bent of my mind was towards London, said to me, "We hope you won't leave us, but that you will still be with the vessels." Here gratitude bowed me down; and none but the generous mind can judge of my feelings, struggling between inclination and duty. However, notwithstanding my wish to be in London, I obediently answered my benefactors that I would go in the vessel, and not leave them; and from that day I was entered on board as an able-bodied sailor, at thirty-six shillings per month, besides what perquisites I could make. My intention was to make a voyage or two, entirely to please these my honoured patrons; but I determined that the year following, if it pleased God, I would see Old England once more, and surprise my old master, Capt. Pascal, who was hourly in my mind; for I still loved him, notwithstanding his usage of me, and I pleased myself with thinking of what he would say when he saw what the Lord had done for me in so short a time, instead of being, as he might perhaps suppose, under the cruel yoke of some planter.

With these kind of reveries, I used often to entertain myself, and shorten the time till my return; and now, being as in my original free African state, I embarked on board the Nancy, after having got all things ready for our voyage. In this state of serenity, we sailed for St. Eustatia; and, having smooth seas and calm weather, we soon arrived there: after taking our cargo on board, we proceeded to Savannah in Georgia, in August, 1766. ...

---

1   these presents shall come   The present words shall be shown.

2   liber   Latin: book.

3   gave   Attended.

from Chapter 8

The author, to oblige Mr. King, once more embarks for Georgia in one of his vessels—A new captain is appointed—They sail, and steer a new course—Three remarkable dreams—The vessel is shipwrecked on the Bahama bank, but the crew are preserved, principally by means of the author—He sets out from the island with the captain, in a small boat, in quest of a ship—Their distress—Meet with a wrecker—Sail for Providence—Are overtaken again by a terrible storm, and are all near perishing—Arrive at New Providence—The author, after some time, sails from thence to Georgia—Meets with another storm, and is obliged to put back and refit—Arrives at Georgia—Meets new impositions—Two white men attempt to kidnap him—Officiates as a parson at a funeral ceremony—Bids adieu to Georgia, and sails for Martinico.

… We stayed in New Providence[1] about seventeen or eighteen days; during which time I met with many friends, who gave me encouragement to stay there with them: but I declined it; though, had not my heart been fixed on England, I should have stayed, as I liked the place extremely, and there were some free black people here who were very happy, and we passed our time pleasantly together, with the melodious sound of the catguts,[2] under the lime and lemon trees. At length Captain Phillips hired a sloop to carry him and some of the slaves that he could not sell to Georgia; and I agreed to go with him in this vessel, meaning now to take my farewell of that place. When the vessel was ready, we all embarked; and I took my leave of New Providence, not without regret. We sailed about four o'clock in the morning, with a fair wind, for Georgia; and about eleven o'clock the same morning a short and sudden gale sprung up and blew away most of our sails; and, as we were still amongst the keys, in a very few minutes it dashed the sloop against the rocks. Luckily for us the water was deep; and the sea was not so angry but that, after having for some time laboured hard, and being many in number, we were saved through God's

mercy; and, by using our greatest exertions, we got the vessel off. The next day we returned to Providence, where we soon got her again refitted. Some of the people swore that we had spells set upon us by somebody in Montserrat; and others that we had witches and wizards amongst the poor helpless slaves; and that we never should arrive safe at Georgia. But these things did not deter me; I said, "Let us again face the winds and seas, and swear not, but trust to God, and he will deliver us." We therefore once more set sail; and, with hard labour, in seven days' time arrived safe at Georgia.

After our arrival we went up to the town of Savannah; and the same evening I went to a friend's house to lodge, whose name was Mosa, a black man. We were very happy at meeting each other; and after supper we had a light till it was between nine and ten o'clock at night. About that time the watch or patrol came by; and, discerning a light in the house, they knocked at the door: we opened it; and they came in and sat down, and drank some punch with us: they also begged some limes of me, as they understood I had some, which I readily gave them. A little after this they told me I must go to the watch-house with them: this surprised me a good deal, after our kindness to them; and I asked them, why so? They said that all negroes who had light in their houses after nine o'clock were to be taken into custody, and either pay some dollars or be flogged. Some of those people knew that I was a free man; but, as the man of the house was not free, and had his master to protect him, they did not take the same liberty with him they did with me. I told them that I was a free man, and just arrived from Providence; that we were not making any noise, and that I was not a stranger in that place, but was very well known there: "Besides," said I, "what will you do with me?"—"That you shall see," replied they, "but you must go to the watch-house with us." Now whether they meant to get money from me or not I was at a loss to know; but I thought immediately of the oranges and limes at Santa Cruz: and seeing that nothing would pacify them I went with them to the watch-house, where I remained during the night. Early the next morning these imposing ruffians flogged a negro man and woman that they had in the watch-house, and then they told me that I must be flogged too. I asked why? and if there was no law for free men? And told them if there was I would

---

1   *New Providence* The largest of the Bahama Islands.

2   *the melodious sound of the catguts* Catgut was commonly used to make strings for stringed instruments (such as fiddles).

have it put in force against them. But this only exasperated them the more; and instantly they swore they would serve[1] me as Doctor Perkins had done; and they were going to lay violent hands on me; when one of them, more humane than the rest, said that as I was a free man they could not justify stripping me by law. I then immediately sent for Doctor Brady, who was known to be an honest and worthy man; and on his coming to my assistance they let me go.

This was not the only disagreeable incident I met with while I was in this place; for, one day, while I was a little way out of the town of Savannah, I was beset by two white men, who meant to play their usual tricks with me in the way of kidnapping. As soon as these men accosted me, one of them said to the other, "This is the very fellow we are looking for that you lost": and the other swore immediately that I was the identical person. On this they made up to me, and were about to handle me; but I told them to be still and keep off; for I had seen those kind of tricks played upon other free blacks, and they must not think to serve me so. At this they paused a little, and one said to the other—it will not do; and the other answered that I talked too good English. I replied, I believed I did; and I had also with me a revengeful stick equal to the occasion; and my mind was likewise good. Happily however it was not used; and, after we had talked together a little in this manner, the rogues left me. I stayed in Savannah some time, anxiously trying to get to Montserrat once more to see Mr. King, my old master, and then to take a final farewell of the American quarter of the globe. At last I met with a sloop called the *Speedwell*, Captain John Bunton, which belonged to Grenada, and was bound to Martinico, a French island, with a cargo of rice, and I shipped myself on board of her. Before I left Georgia a black woman, who had a child lying dead, being very tenacious of the church burial service,[2] and not able to get any white person to perform it, applied to me for that purpose. I told her I was no parson; and besides, that the service over the dead did not affect the soul. This, however, did not satisfy her; she still urged me very hard: I therefore complied with her earnest entreaties, and at last consented to act the parson for

the first time in my life. As she was much respected, there was a great company both of white and black people at the grave. I then accordingly assumed my new vocation, and performed the funeral ceremony to the satisfaction of all present; after which I bade adieu to Georgia, and sailed for Martinico.

from Chapter 9[3]

The author arrives at Martinico—Meets with new difficulties—Gets to Montserrat, where he takes leave of his old master, and sails for England—Meets Capt. Pascal—Learns the French horn—Hires himself with Doctor Irving, where he learns to freshen sea water—Leaves the doctor, and goes a voyage to Turkey and Portugal; and afterwards goes a voyage to Grenada, and another to Jamaica—Returns to the Doctor, and they embark together on a voyage to the North Pole, with the Hon. Capt. Phipps—Some account of that voyage, and the dangers the author was in—He returns to England.

I thus took a final leave of Georgia; for the treatment I had received in it disgusted me very much against the place; and when I left it and sailed for Martinico I determined never more to revisit it. My new captain conducted his vessel safer than my former one; and, after an agreeable voyage, we got safe to our intended port. While I was on this island I went about a good deal, and found it very pleasant: in particular I admired the town of St. Pierre, which is the principal one in the island, and built more like an European town than any I had seen in the West Indies. In general also, slaves were better treated, had more holidays, and looked better than those in the English islands. After we had done our business here, I wanted my discharge, which was necessary; for it was then the month of May, and I wished much to be at Montserrat to bid farewell to Mr. King, and all my other friends there, in time to sail for Old England in the July fleet. ...

We had a most prosperous voyage, and, at the end of seven weeks, arrived at Cherry-Garden stairs.[4] Thus

---

[1] *serve* Treat.

[2] *very tenacious of the church burial service* Determined to have a church burial service for her child.

[3] A longer selection of excerpts from this chapter is included as part of the website component of this anthology.

[4] *Cherry-Garden stairs* Landing area on the Thames, in London's east end.

were my longing eyes once more gratified with a sight of London, after having been absent from it above four years. I immediately received my wages, and I never had earned seven guineas so quick in my life before; I had thirty-seven guineas in all, when I got cleared of the ship. I now entered upon a scene, quite new to me, but full of hope.

In this situation my first thoughts were to look out for some of my former friends, and amongst the first of those were the Miss Guerins. As soon, therefore, as I had regaled myself I went in quest of those kind ladies, whom I was very impatient to see; and with some difficulty and perseverance, I found them at May's-hill, Greenwich. They were most agreeably surprised to see me, and I quite overjoyed at meeting with them. I told them my history, at which they expressed great wonder, and freely acknowledged it did their cousin, Capt. Pascal, no honour. He then visited there frequently; and I met him four or five days after in Greenwich Park. When he saw me he appeared a good deal surprised, and asked me how I came back? I answered, "In a ship." To which he replied dryly, "I suppose you did not walk back to London on the water." As I saw, by his manner, that he did not seem to be sorry for his behaviour to me, and that I had not much reason to expect any favour from him, I told him that he had used me very ill, after I had been such a faithful servant to him for so many years; on which, without saying any more, he turned about and went away. A few days after this I met Capt. Pascal at Miss Guerin's house, and asked him for my prize-money.[1] He said there was none due to me; for, if my prize-money had been £.10,000, he had a right to it all. I told him I was informed otherwise; on which he bade me defiance; and, in a bantering tone, desired me to commence a lawsuit against him for it: "There are lawyers enough," said he, "that will take the cause in hand, and you had better try it." I told him then that I would try it, which enraged him very much; however, out of regard to the ladies, I remained still, and never made any farther demand of my right.

Some time afterwards these friendly ladies asked me what I meant to do with myself, and how they could assist me. I thanked them, and said, if they pleased, I would be their servant; but if not, as I had thirty-seven guineas, which would support me for some time, I would be much obliged to them to recommend me to some person who would teach me a business whereby I might earn my living. They answered me very politely, that they were sorry it did not suit them to take me as their servant, and asked me what business I should like to learn? I said, hair-dressing. They then promised to assist me in this; and soon after they recommended me to a gentleman whom I had known before, one Capt. O'Hara, who treated me with much kindness, and procured me a master, a hair-dresser, in Coventry-court, Haymarket, with whom he placed me. I was with this man from September till the February following.

In that time we had a neighbour in the same court who taught the French horn. He used to blow it so well that I was charmed with it, and agreed with him to teach me to blow it. Accordingly he took me in hand, and began to instruct me, and I soon learned all the three parts. I took great delight in blowing on this instrument, the evenings being long; and besides that, I was fond of it. I did not like to be idle, and it filled up my vacant hours innocently.

At this time also I agreed with the Rev. Mr. Gregory, who lived in the same court, where he kept an academy and an evening-school, to improve me in arithmetic. This he did as far as barter and alligation; so that all the time I was there I was entirely employed. In February 1768 I hired myself to Dr. Charles Irving, in Pall Mall, so celebrated for his successful experiments in making sea water fresh; and here I had plenty of hair-dressing to improve my hand. This gentleman was an excellent master; he was exceedingly kind and good tempered; and allowed me in the evenings to attend my schools, which I esteemed a great blessing; therefore I thanked God and him for it, and used all my diligence to improve the opportunity.

This diligence and attention recommended me to the notice and care of my three preceptors, who on their parts bestowed a great deal of pains in my instruction, and besides were all very kind to me. My wages, however, which were by two thirds less than I ever had in my life (for I had only £.12 per annum) I soon found would not be sufficient to defray this extraordinary expense of masters, and my own necessary expenses; my old thirty-seven guineas had by this time worn all

---

[1]   *prize-money*   Share of the valuables seized when capturing other vessels.

away to one. I thought it best, therefore, to try the sea again in quest of more money, as I had been bred to it, and had hitherto found the profession of it successful. I had also a very great desire to see Turkey, and I now determined to gratify it. Accordingly, in the month of May, 1768, I told the doctor my wish to go to sea again, to which he made no opposition; and we parted on friendly terms.

The same day I went into the city in quest of a master. I was extremely fortunate in my inquiry; for I soon heard of a gentleman who had a ship going to Italy and Turkey, and he wanted a man who could dress hair well. I was overjoyed at this, and went immediately on board of his ship, as I had been directed, which I found to be fitted up with great taste, and I already foreboded no small pleasure in sailing in her. Not finding the gentleman on board, I was directed to his lodgings, where I met with him the next day, and gave him a specimen of my dressing. He liked it so well that he hired me immediately, so that I was perfectly happy; for the ship, master, and voyage, were entirely to my mind. The ship was called the *Delaware*, and my master's name was John Jolly, a neat smart good-humoured man, just such a one as I wished to serve. We sailed from England in July following, and our voyage was extremely pleasant. We went to Villa Franca, Nice, and Leghorn;[1] and in all these places I was charmed with the richness and beauty of the countries, and struck with the elegant buildings with which they abound. We had always in them plenty of extraordinary good wines and rich fruits, which I was very fond of; and I had frequent occasions of gratifying both my taste and curiosity; for my captain always lodged on shore in those places, which afforded me opportunities to see the country around. I also learned navigation of the mate, which I was very fond of. When we left Italy we had delightful sailing among the Archipelago islands, and from thence to Smyrna in Turkey. This is a very ancient city; the houses are built of stone, and most of them have graves adjoining to them; so that they sometimes present the appearance of church-yards. Provisions are very plentiful in this city, and good wine less than a penny a pint. The grapes, pomegranates, and many other fruits, were also the richest and largest I ever tasted. The natives are well looking and strong made, and treated me always with great civility. In general, I believe they are fond of black people; and several of them gave me pressing invitations to stay amongst them, although they keep the franks, or Christians,[2] separate, and do not suffer them to dwell immediately amongst them. I was astonished in not seeing women in any of their shops, and very rarely any in the streets; and whenever I did they were covered with a veil from head to foot, so that I could not see their faces, except when any of them out of curiosity uncovered them to look at me, which they sometimes did. I was surprised to see how the Greeks are, in some measure, kept under by the Turks,[3] as the negroes are in the West Indies by the white people. The less refined Greeks, as I have already hinted, dance here in the same manner as we do in my nation. On the whole, during our stay here, which was about five months, I liked the place and the Turks extremely well. I could not help observing one very remarkable circumstance there: the tails of the sheep are flat, and so very large, that I have known the tail even of a lamb to weigh from eleven to thirteen pounds. The fat of them is very white and rich, and is excellent in puddings, for which it is much used. Our ship being at length richly loaded with silk, and other articles, we sailed for England.

In May 1769, soon after our return from Turkey, our ship made a delightful voyage to Oporto in Portugal, where we arrived at the time of the carnival.[4] On our arrival, there were sent on board to us thirty-six articles to observe, with very heavy penalties if we should break any of them; and none of us even dared to go on board any other vessel or on shore till the Inquisition had sent on board and searched for every thing illegal, especially bibles.[5] Such as were produced, and

---

[1]   *Leghorn*   Livorno (a seaport in northwest Italy).

[2]   *franks, or Christians*   "Frank," originally a term for members of the ancient tribes that inhabited what is now France, came in medieval times to be widely used in the Middle East as a term for Western European Christians; this usage persisted into the eighteenth century and beyond.

[3]   *the Greeks … the Turks*   Greece was under the control of the Turkish Ottoman Empire from late medieval times until Greek independence was declared in 1832.

[4]   *the carnival*   Probably the festival of São João (St. John), a major celebration held in Porto in June.

[5]   *Inquisition … bibles*   From the thirteenth until the early nineteenth centuries the Roman Catholic church operated a set of institutions known collectively as the "Holy Inquisition," the purpose of which was to combat heresy. Roman Catholic [continued …]

certain other things, were sent on shore till the ships were going away; and any person in whose custody a bible was found concealed was to be imprisoned and flogged, and sent into slavery for ten years. I saw here many very magnificent sights, particularly the garden of Eden, where many of the clergy and laity went in procession in their several orders with the Host,[1] and sung Te Deum.[2] I had a great curiosity to go into some of their churches, but could not gain admittance without using the necessary sprinkling of holy water at my entrance. From curiosity, and a wish to be holy, I therefore complied with this ceremony, but its virtues were lost on me, for I found myself nothing the better for it. This place abounds with plenty of all kinds of provisions. The town is well built and pretty, and commands a fine prospect. Our ship having taken in a load of wine, and other commodities, we sailed for London, and arrived in July following. Our next voyage was to the Mediterranean. The ship was again got ready, and we sailed in September for Genoa. This is one of the finest cities I ever saw; some of the edifices were of beautiful marble, and made a most noble appearance; and many had very curious fountains before them. The churches were rich and magnificent, and curiously adorned both in the inside and out. But all this grandeur was in my eyes disgraced by the galley slaves,[3] whose condition both there and in other parts of Italy is truly piteous and wretched. After we had stayed there some weeks, during which we bought many different things which we wanted, and got them very cheap, we sailed to Naples, a charming city, and remarkably clean. The bay is the most beautiful I ever saw; the moles[4] for shipping are excellent. I thought it extraordinary to see grand operas acted here on Sunday nights, and even attended by their majesties. I too, like these great ones, went to those sights, and vainly served God in the day while I thus served mammon effectually at night. While we remained here there happened an eruption of Mount Vesuvius, of which I had a perfect view. It was extremely awful; and we were so near that the ashes from it used to be thick on our deck.

After we had transacted our business at Naples we sailed with a fair wind once more for Smyrna, where we arrived in December. A seraskier[5] or officer took a liking to me here, and wanted me to stay, and offered me two wives; however I refused the temptation. The merchants here travel in caravans or large companies. I have seen many caravans from India, with some hundreds of camels, laden with different goods. The people of these caravans are quite brown. Among other articles, they brought with them a great quantity of locusts,[6] which are a kind of pulse, sweet and pleasant to the palate, and in shape resembling French beans, but longer. Each kind of goods is sold in a street by itself, and I always found the Turks very honest in their dealings. They let no Christians into their mosques or churches, for which I was very sorry; as I was always fond of going to see the different modes of worship of the people wherever I went. The plague broke out while we were in Smyrna, and we stopped taking goods into the ship till it was over. She was then richly laden, and we sailed in about March 1770 for England. One day in our passage we met with an accident which was near burning the ship. A black cook, in melting some fat, overset the pan into the fire under the deck, which immediately began to blaze, and the flame went up very high under the foretop. With the fright the poor cook became almost white, and altogether speechless. Happily however we got the fire out without doing much mischief. After various delays in this passage, which was tedious, we arrived in Standgate Creek[7] in July; and, at the latter end of the year, some new event occurred, so that my noble captain, the ship, and I all separated.

In April 1771 I shipped myself as a steward with Capt. Wm. Robertson of the ship *Grenada Planter*,

---

practice did not encourage private study of the Bible by individuals; preferred practice was for the clergy to interpret the Bible to the laity. (Protestant denominations, in contrast, encouraged individuals to read and study the Bible on their own.)

[1]   *the Host* Communion wafers.

[2]   *Te Deum* Latin: To God. The *Te Deum* prayer is recited or sung during Catholic services.

[3]   *galley slaves* Galleys were ships propelled either by sail or by oars—with the rowing done by enslaved people (generally, war captives).

[4]   *moles* Stone structures forming breakwaters or piers.

[5]   *seraskier* High-ranking military official.

[6]   *locusts* Locust beans (also known as iru beans), legumes from a tree common in much of West Africa.

[7]   *Standgate Creek* Harbor located near the mouth of the Thames in southeast England.

once more to try my fortune in the West Indies; and we sailed from London for Madeira, Barbadoes, and the Grenades. ...

[At the end of the voyage] we arrived in England, and I got clear of this ship. But, being still of a roving disposition, and desirous of seeing as many different parts of the world as I could, I shipped myself soon after, in the same year, as steward on board of a fine large ship, called the *Jamaica*, Captain David Watt; and we sailed from England in December 1771 for Nevis and Jamaica. I found Jamaica to be a very fine large island, well peopled, and the most considerable of the West India islands. There was a vast number of negroes here, whom I found as usual exceedingly imposed upon by the white people, and the slaves punished as in the other islands. There are negroes whose business it is to flog slaves; they go about to different people for employment, and the usual pay is from one to four bits. I saw many cruel punishments inflicted on the slaves in the short time I stayed here. In particular I was present when a poor fellow was tied up and kept hanging by the wrists at some distance from the ground, and then some half hundred weights were fixed to his ancles, in which posture he was flogged most unmercifully. There were also, as I heard, two different masters noted for cruelty on the island, who had staked up two negroes naked, and in two hours the vermin stung them to death. I heard a gentleman I well knew tell my captain that he passed sentence on a negro man to be burnt alive for attempting to poison an overseer. I pass over numerous other instances, in order to relieve the reader by a milder scene of roguery.

Before I had been long on the island, one Mr. Smith at Port Morant bought goods of me to the amount of twenty-five pounds sterling; but when I demanded payment from him, he was going each time to beat me, and threatened that he would put me in jail. One time he would say I was going to set his house on fire, at another he would swear I was going to run away with his slaves. I was astonished at this usage from a person who was in the situation of a gentleman, but I had no alternative; I was therefore obliged to submit. When I came to Kingston, I was surprised to see the number of Africans who were assembled together on Sundays; particularly at a large commodious place, called Spring Path. Here each different nation of Africa meet and dance after the manner of their own country. They still retain most of their native customs: they bury their dead, and put victuals, pipes and tobacco, and other things, in the grave with the corpse, in the same manner as in Africa. Our ship having got her loading we sailed for London, where we arrived in the August following. On my return to London, I waited on my old and good master, Dr. Irving, who made me an offer of his service again. Being now tired of the sea I gladly accepted it. I was very happy in living with this gentleman once more; during which time we were daily employed in reducing old Neptune's dominions by purifying the briny element and making it fresh. Thus I went on till May 1773, when I was roused by the sound of fame, to seek new adventures, and to find, towards the North Pole, what our Creator never intended we should, a passage to India. ...

—1789

IN CONTEXT

Equiano's Narrative as a Philadelphia Abolitionist Pamphlet

The first illustrated edition of any part of Equiano's *Interesting Narrative* seems to have been a 36-page pamphlet largely made up of excerpts from Equiano's work. The pamphlet was issued in 1829 in Philadelphia by Samuel Wood, a Quaker printer who had been publishing abolitionist broadsides and pamphlets since the early years of the century. As illustrations, Wood included several woodcuts (several of which had appeared in his earlier publications and were now re-purposed); he also appended to the Equiano material "the following *Remarks upon the Slave Trade*," which Wood had originally published in 1807 as a reprint of "a pamphlet lately published by a society at Plymouth, in Great Britain, from which the Philadelphia Society for Promoting the Abolition of Slavery have taken the following extracts, and have added a copy of the plate, which accompanied it." The plate (shown right) bears a close resemblance to Thomas Clarkson's 1787 diagram of the hold of the slave ship *Brooks*, which had been widely reprinted and was credited with helping significantly to spur abolitionist sentiment.

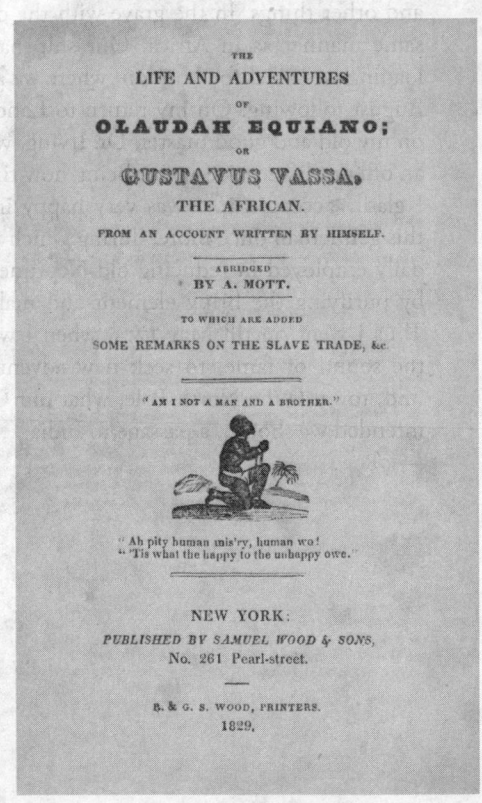 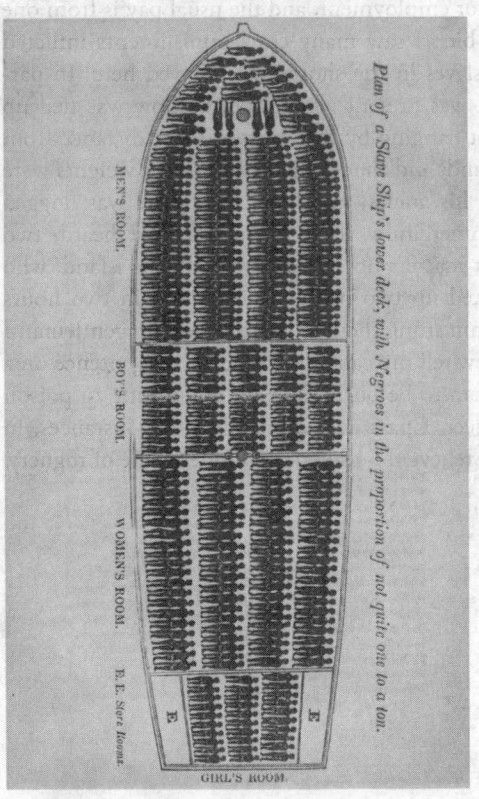

Title page and illustration, *The Life and Adventures of Olaudah Equiano* (1829).

IN CONTEXT

Reactions to Olaudah Equiano's Work

from *The Analytic Review* (May 1789)[1]

The life of an African, written by himself, is certainly a curiosity, as it has been a favourite philosophic whim to degrade the numerous nations, on whom the sun-beams more directly dart, below the common level of humanity, and hastily to conclude that nature, by making them inferior to the rest of the human race, designed to stamp them with a mark of slavery. ... If these volumes do not exhibit extraordinary intellectual powers, sufficient to wipe off the stigma, yet the activity and ingenuity, which conspicuously appear in the character of Gustavus, place him on a par with the general mass of men, who fill the subordinate stations in a more civilized society than that which he was thrown into at his birth.

from *The Monthly Review* (June 1789)

We entertain no doubt of the general authenticity of this very intelligent African's story; though it is not improbable that some English writer has assisted him in the compilement, or, at least, the correction of his book; for it is sufficiently well-written. The Narrative wears an honest face; and we have conceived a good opinion of the man, from the artless manner in which he has detailed the variety of adventures and vicissitudes which have fallen to his lot. His publication appears very seasonable, at a time when negro-slavery is the subject of public investigation; and it seems calculated to increase the odium that has been excited against the West-India planters, on account of the cruelties that some are said to have exercised on their slaves, many instances of which are here detailed.

from "Descriptive Catalogue of Anti-Slavery Works for Sale by Isaac Knaap, at the Depository, No. 25, Cornhill," published in *The Liberator*, 27 October 1837, and again 17 November 1837.

In all, Knapp's list includes 68 works; among the more notable listed ahead of Equiano's *Interesting Narrative* are "Mrs. Child's Appeal" (Lydia Child's *An Appeal in Favor of That Class of Americans Called Africans*), listed at number 2; Archy Moore's *The Slave*, listed at number 4; Charles Ball's *A Narrative of the Life and Adventures of Charles Ball*, listed at number 5; Phillis Wheatley's *Memoir and Poems*, listed at number 18; Whittier's *Poems*, listed at number 20; and a collection of Lemuel Haynes's writings, listed at number 30.

36.   GUSTAVUS VASSA.   294 pp. 12 mo. Cloth 62 1-2-
The life of Olaudah Equiano, or Gustavus Vassa, the African, written by himself. With two lithographic Prints.
This is the life of a native African, of powerful intellect, who was "stolen out of his own land," lived as a slave in Pennsylvania, went several voyages to the West Indies, and to several ports in Europe, narrowly escaped death several times, and passed through a great variety of wonderful scenes, which give his narrative an interest scarcely surpassed by Robinson Crusoe.

---

[1]   Though published anonymously, this review is now known to have been written by Mary Wollstonecraft.

Rebellions and Revolutions
Contexts

The late eighteenth and early nineteenth centuries were a time of great change and turmoil, both in the Americas and in Britain and Europe. Enlightenment philosophers such as Voltaire, John Locke, Jean-Jacques Rousseau, and Thomas Paine had set forth powerful ideas about the natural rights of individuals. These rights, they argued, existed regardless of social class; the old hierarchal institutions that had long structured European society—the monarchy, the aristocracy, and the church—came to be seen by many as upholding a system that benefitted the few while depriving the many of their rights and livelihoods. The Enlightenment voices that called for throwing off the yokes of absolute monarchy and state religion resonated strongly in Europe, and also in the European colonies, including in North America. White settler colonists grew increasingly enraged at being controlled by an overseas power even as they largely saw freedom in terms that excluded people of other races. Meanwhile, for some enslaved and Indigenous people in the European colonies, the new rhetoric of freedom and equality provided useful terms to make their own struggles for emancipation—which long pre-dated these Enlightenment-era revolutions—legible on the world stage.

The different revolutions, then, saw issues of rights and of freedoms from different perspectives. In America the right to hold private property ranked high—and, much as the "founding fathers" did not wish to replicate the hierarchies of England, nor did they wish to embrace unfettered democracy, which they associated with mob rule. The revolutionaries in France in 1789–90, on the other hand, placed far more emphasis on equality—and far less on private property rights. The same was true, at least initially, in Haiti (though the early ideals of both the Haitian and French Revolutions were widely betrayed later during periods of horrific violence). In the United States, opinion was divided with regard to the French Revolution. Most white Americans were dismayed by the Haitian Revolution (even half a century later, the prospect of "a negro nation, a sort of Hayti on the continent" being formed in the United States—or in Texas—was deployed to inspire racist and reactionary fears among America's white population), but the Haitian Revolution offered a vision of hope to black Americans, both enslaved and free. The Haitian Revolution affected mainland North America in other ways too; not least of all, in imposing such military and financial costs on Napoleon's France that he sold the territory of Louisiana, the vast majority of it still inhabited and controlled by Native Americans, to the United States for a bargain price. The conflicts that resulted from these passionate strivings for different freedoms were manifold, complex, and interwoven.

The following selections may be read alongside the many other materials in this anthology that relate to the themes of freedom and revolution. The period introduction to this volume offers an overview of the revolutionary period, from its beginnings in Indigenous uprisings such as Pontiac's War (1763) to the American, Haitian, and French Revolutions that followed. The online section entitled "Contexts: Slavery and Resistance" offers further readings on enslaved people's struggle for freedom in the Americas and Caribbean. And many relevant texts also appear under various author entries, both within this volume and in the website component—including those of Benjamin Franklin, John and Abigail Adams, Thomas Jefferson, Thomas Paine, Philip Freneau, Phillis Wheatley, Susanna Rowson, Royall Tyler, and Lemuel Haynes.

⌘ ⌘ ⌘

"Pontiac's War"

from anonymous [believed to be Robert Navarre], *Journal of the Pontiac Conspiracy* (1763)[1]

At the conclusion of the Seven Years' War in 1763, the French ceded their territory in North America to the British (with the exception of Louisiana, which was ceded to Spain). To the Indigenous tribes of the Ohio Valley and Great Lakes, the departure of the French and arrival of the British was viewed with alarm. Many of the peoples from this area, known as the upper country or *pays-d'en-haut*, had built trusted trade relationships with the French and believed that the British were comparatively treacherous and disrespectful. And, more broadly, the defeat of the French in North America left a power vacuum; in a variety of earlier conflicts, Indigenous peoples had often been able to use the power struggle between the English and the French to their advantage, shifting allegiances according to which power offered them better protection.

Throughout the British colonies, the encroachment of white settlers on land occupied by Indigenous peoples (and in many cases supposedly protected by treaty rights) was an ongoing issue. Pontiac, an Odawa war chief, drew on the visions of the Lenape prophet Neolin to gather an armed force to resist this encroachment. Pontiac drew on several of Neolin's ideas, including his vision of a shared identity among the various tribes of Indigenous peoples, and his conviction that there should be a return to pre-contact ways of life. Neolin's religious prophecies also include a clear divine instruction to drive the British off Indigenous lands. Pontiac successfully amplified Neolin's message in his speeches to Indigenous councils, and, in 1763, an attack was launched on Fort Detroit, marking the beginning of the war that the British termed "Pontiac's Rebellion" (though it involved a large coalition of Indigenous groups, and Pontiac was only one leader among many).

The war lasted until 1766; over the course of it, the Indigenous coalition captured several British forts and killed hundreds of white settlers, prompting a violent British response.

The rebellion's consequences were far-reaching. An increased sense among Indigenous peoples of a "pan-Indian" identity was one important consequence. Another was the British decision during the war to issue the Proclamation of 1763, under the terms of which lands west of the Appalachian Mountains were declared to be reserved for Indigenous peoples, and sales of Indigenous land to private individuals were to be prohibited. The British authorities proved unable (or in some cases unwilling) to enforce these new regulations, however. Settlers, infuriated by these restrictions, largely ignored them. One further consequence, then, was a fraying of relations between American colonists and British authorities. All in all, the rebellion of 1763 helped set the stage for the complicated era historians often call the "age of revolutions," beginning with the American Revolution (1775–83) and ending with the European Revolutions of the mid-nineteenth century.

The excerpts that follow are drawn from *Journal of the Pontiac Conspiracy* (1763), which is usually attributed to Robert Navarre. Navarre was in charge of mediating land and property disputes for the French authorities in Detroit, and he continued to work as a translator and interpreter after the British took over (he could speak several Indigenous languages). As an eyewitness of the events leading up to Pontiac's Rebellion, Navarre provides valuable, detailed accounts of Neolin's visions and of Pontiac's speeches; it is important to be aware, however, that Navarre's relation of these events is mediated by his own Eurocentric perspective.

The council of the three nations, Ottawas, ... Pottawattamies, and the bad Huron band,[2]

---

[1]   The text presented here is based on the 1912 Burton edition, translated from the French by R.C. Ford.

[2]   *Ottawas, Pottawattamies ... Huron band* These tribes all became involved in Pontiac's War. Of those mentioned here, the Odawa and Pottawatomi were members of the alliance of the Council of Three Fires (along with the Ojibwe). Most of the Wendat (Huron) groups living in the area had built longstanding alliances with the French.

took place and was presided over by Pontiac in his capacity of head chief of all the northern nations. He made a speech, and as a reason for his action exhibited war-belts which he claimed he had received from his Great Father, the King of France, to induce him to attack the English. ...

They listened to him as chief, and in order to flatter his vanity and excite his pride they promised to do whatever he wished. Delighted to find so much loyalty among the three nations which numbered four hundred and sixty men, he craftily made use of their weakness to get complete control over them. To accomplish this he related in the council the story of a Wolf (Delaware) Indian,[1] who had journeyed to Heaven and talked with the Master of Life.[2] He spoke with so much eloquence that his narrative had just the effect upon them that he desired.

This story deserves a place here since it contains in blackest aspect the reason of the attack upon the English, and upon the French too, perhaps, if God in His mercy had not disposed differently. It is as follows:

An Indian of the Wolf nation, eager to make the acquaintance of the Master of Life—this is the name for God among all the Indians—resolved to undertake the journey to Paradise, where he knew He resided, without the knowledge of any of his tribe or village. But the question was how to succeed in his purpose and find the way thither. Not knowing anyone who had been there and was thus able to teach him the road, he had recourse to incantation in the hope of deriving some good augury from his trance. As a rule all the Indians, even those who are enlightened, are subject to superstition, and put a good deal of credence in their dreams and those things which one has a good deal of trouble to wean them from. This episode will be proof of what I say.

This Wolf Indian in his dream imagined that he had only to set out and by dint of travelling would arrive at the celestial dwelling. This he did the next day. Early in the morning he arose and equipped himself for a hunting journey, not forgetting to take provisions and

ammunition, and a big kettle. Behold him then setting out like that on his journey to Heaven to see the Master of Life.

The first seven days of his journey were quite favorable to his plans; he walked on without growing discouraged, always with a firm belief that he would arrive at his destination, and eight days went by without his encountering anything which could hinder him in his desire. On the evening of the eighth day he halted at sunset as usual, at the opening to a little prairie upon the bank of a stream which seemed to him a suitable camping place. As he was preparing his shelter for the night he beheld at the other end of this prairie where he camped, three roads, wide and plainly marked. ... [After false starts down two of the roads, he took] the third road which he followed for a day without discovering anything. Suddenly he saw before him what appeared to be a mountain of marvelous whiteness and he stopped, overcome with astonishment. Nevertheless, he again advanced, firmly determined to see what this mountain could be, but when he arrived at the foot of it he no longer saw any road and was sad. At this juncture, not knowing what to do to continue his way, he looked around in all directions and finally saw a woman of this mountain, of radiant beauty, whose garments dimmed the whiteness of the snow. And she was seated.

This woman addressed him in his own tongue: "Thou appearest to me surprised not to find any road to lead thee where thou wishest to go. I know that for a long while thou hast been desirous of seeing the Master of Life and of speaking with him; that is why thou hast undertaken this journey to see him. The road which leads to his abode is over the mountain, and to ascend it thou must forsake all that thou hast with thee, and disrobe completely, and leave all thy trappings and clothing at the foot of the mountain. No one shall harm thee; go and bathe thyself in a river which I shall show thee, and then thou shalt ascend."

The Wolf was careful to obey the words of the woman, but one difficulty yet confronted him, namely, to know how to reach the top of the mountain which was perpendicular, pathless, and smooth as ice. He questioned this woman how one should go about climbing up, and she replied that if he was really anxious to see the Master of Life he would have to ascend,

---

[1]   *Wolf (Delaware) Indian*   Neolin, who is being referred to here, was a member of the Wolf clan of the Lenape people, an Indigenous tribe of the Northeastern Woodlands.

[2]   *Master of Life*   Another name for the Indigenous concept of the Great Spirit or primary life force.

helping himself only with his hand and his left foot. This appeared to him impossible, but encouraged by the woman he set about it and succeeded by dint of effort. ...

Here he saw the Master of Life who took him by the hand and gave him a hat all bordered with gold to sit down upon. The Wolf hesitated to do this for fear of spoiling the hat, but he was ordered to do so, and obeyed without reply.

After the Indian was seated the Lord said to him: "I am the Master of Life, and since I know what thou desirest to know, and to whom thou wishest to speak, listen well to what I am going to say to thee and to all the Indians:

"I am He who hath created the heavens and the earth, the trees, lakes, rivers, all men, and all that thou seest and hast seen upon the earth. Because I love you, ye must do what I say and love, and not do what I hate. I do not love that ye should drink to the point of madness, as ye do; and I do not like that ye should fight one another. Ye take two wives, or run after the wives of others; ye do not well, and I hate that. Ye ought to have but one wife, and keep her till death. When ye wish to go to war, ye conjure and resort to the medicine dance, believing that ye speak to me; ye are mistaken—it is to Manitou that ye speak, an evil spirit who prompts you to nothing but wrong, and who listens to you out of ignorance of me.

"This land where ye dwell I have made for you and not for others. Whence comes it that ye permit the Whites upon your lands? Can ye not live without them? I know that those whom ye call the children of your Great Father[1] supply your needs, but if ye were not evil, as ye are, ye could surely do without them. Ye could live as ye did live before knowing them—before those whom ye call your brothers had come upon your lands. Did ye not live by the bow and arrow? Ye had no need of gun or powder, ... I do not forbid you to permit among you the children of your Father;[2] I love them. They know me and pray to me, and I supply their wants and all they give you. But as to those who come to trouble your lands[3]—drive them out, make war upon them. I do not love them at all; they know me not, and are my enemies, and the enemies of your brothers. Send them back to the lands which I have created for them and let them stay there. Here is a prayer which I give thee in writing to learn by heart and to teach to the Indians and their children."

The Wolf replied that he did not know how to read. He was told that when he should have returned to earth he would have only to give the prayer to the chief of his village who would read it and teach him and all the Indians to know it by heart; and he must say it night and morning without fail, and do what he has just been told to do. ...

The Wolf promised to do faithfully what the Master of Life told him, and that he would recommend it well to the Indians, and that the Master of Life would be pleased with them. ...

This adventure was soon noised about among the people of the whole village who came to hear the message of the Master of Life, and then went to carry it to the neighboring villages. The members of these villages came to see the pretended traveller, and the news was spread from village to village and finally reached Pontiac. He believed all this, as we believe an article of faith, and instilled it into the minds of all those in his council. They listened to him as to an oracle, and told him that he had only to speak and they were all ready to do what he demanded of them.

Pontiac, delighted at the success of his harangue, told the Hurons and Pottawattamies to return to their villages, and that in four days he would go to the Fort[4] with his young men for the peace-pipe dance,[5] and that while the dancers were engaged some other young men would roam around in the Fort to spy out all that was being done, the number of men the English had in the garrison, the number of traders, and the houses they occupied. All of this happened as he had said. ...

---

[1]   *children of your Great Father*   Colonial authorities often referred to their monarchs as the "Great Father" or "Great Mother" in their treaties with Indigenous peoples; in this context, the king of France, Louis XV, is being referenced.

[2]   *children of your Father*   The French.

[3]   *those ... lands*   The English.

[4]   *Fort*   Fort Detroit, a French stronghold that had been taken over by the British in 1760.

[5]   *peace-pipe dance*   Ceremonial dance involving smoking sacred pipes. Europeans often referred to ceremonial pipe-smoking as "peace-pipes," because such smoking took place at treaty agreements; pipes were smoked, however, for many other sacred and political decision-making ceremonies, including that of going to war.

Pontiac, wholly occupied with his project and nourishing in his heart a poison which was to be fateful for the English, and perhaps for the French, sent runners the following day, Monday, the 2nd of May, to each of the Huron and Pottawattamy villages to discover the real feeling of each of these two nations, for he feared to be crossed in his plans. These emissaries had orders to notify these nations for him that Thursday, the 5th of May, at mid-day, a grand council would be held in the Pottawattamy village which was situated between two and three miles below the Fort toward the southwest, and that the three nations should meet there and that no woman should be allowed to attend for fear of betraying their plans.

When the appointed day had come all the Ottawas with Pontiac at their head, and the bad band of the Hurons in [the] charge of Takay,[1] repaired to the Pottawattamy village where the expected council was to be held. Care had been taken to send the women out of the village so that they might not hear anything of what should be decided. Pontiac ordered sentinels to be placed around the village in order not to be disturbed in their council. When all these precautions had been taken each Indian seated himself in the circle according to rank, and Pontiac at the head, as great chief of all, began to speak. He said:

"It is important for us, my brothers, that we exterminate from our lands this nation which seeks only to destroy us. You see as well as I that we can no longer supply our needs, as we have done, from our brothers, the French. The English sell us goods twice as dear as the French do, and their goods do not last. Scarcely have we bought a blanket or something else to cover ourselves with before we must think of getting another; and when we wish to set out for our winter camps they do not want to give us any credit as our brothers, the French, do.

"When I go to see the English commander and say to him that some of our comrades are dead, instead of bewailing their death, as our French brothers do, he laughs at me and at you. If I ask anything for our sick, he refuses with the reply that he has no use for us. From all this you can well see that they are seeking our ruin. Therefore, my brothers, we must all swear their

destruction and wait no longer. Nothing prevents us; they are few in numbers, and we can accomplish it. All the nations who are our brothers attack them—why should we not attack? Are we not men like them? Have I not shown you the wampum belts[2] which I received from our Great Father, the Frenchman? He tells us to strike them—why do we not listen to his words? What do we fear? It is time. Do we fear that our brothers, the French, who are here among us will prevent us? They do not know our plans, and they could not hinder anyway, if they would. You all know as well as I that when the English came upon our lands to drive out our Father, Belestre,[3] they took away all the Frenchmen's guns and that they now have no arms to protect themselves with. Therefore, it is time for us to strike. If there are any French who side with them, let us strike them as well as the English. Remember what the Master of Life told our brother, the Wolf, to do. That concerns us all as well as others. I have sent wampum belts and messengers to our brothers, the Chippewas of Saginaw, and to our brothers, the Ottawas of Michillimackinac, and to those of the Thames River to join us. They will not be slow in coming, but while we wait let us strike anyway. There is no more time to lose. When the English are defeated we shall then see what there is left to do, and we shall stop up the ways hither so that they may never come again upon our lands."

The speech, which Pontiac delivered in such an energetic tone, produced its desired effect upon the members of the council, and they all swore with one accord the complete destruction of the English. ...

from George III, The Royal Proclamation of 1763

Responding to the outbreak of Pontiac's War (see above), King George III issued the following Proclamation, which sets out rules for future land settlement in British North America. Pontiac's War had shown Britain

---

[1]   *Takay*   Chief of the people the French called the Huron, but who call themselves the Wendat or Wyandot people.

[2]   *wampum belts*   Belts of shell beads used by Indigenous peoples for numerous purposes, including sending messages, record-keeping, and trade.

[3]   *Belestre*   François Marie Picote, Sieur de Bellestre was the commander of Fort Detroit until he surrendered in the autumn of 1760.

that the Indigenous peoples would not accept the theft of their lands passively, and the Proclamation attempted to quell rebellion by asserting Indigenous rights and the legitimacy of Indigenous land titles, as well as by creating a land barrier between settler and Indigenous populations. All territory west of the Appalachians was deemed an Indigenous reserve, and any land purchased by settlers to the east had to be first bought by the Crown from the Indigenous people. Any European-settled land held in contradiction to these rules was required to be vacated immediately. These restrictions, as outlined in the Proclamation below, became a source of significant tension between settlers and the British authorities in the years leading up to the American Revolutionary War. As the British did not uphold the promises made to Indigenous peoples in this Proclamation, the document did little in the long run to secure their goodwill.

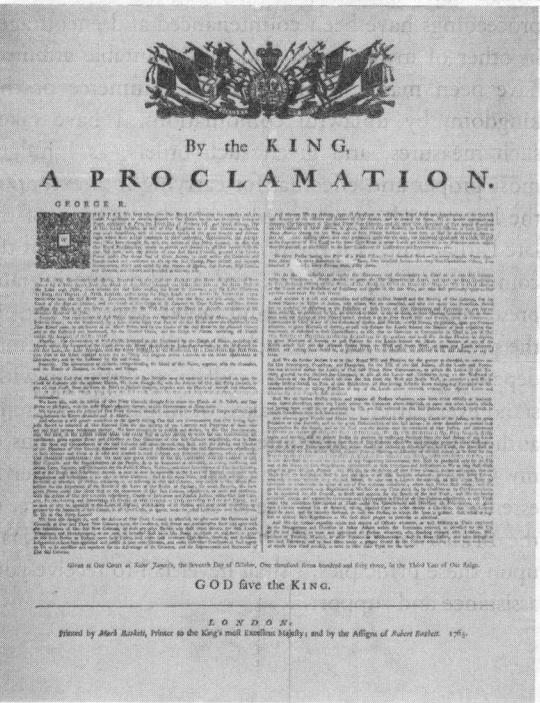

The Royal Proclamation of 1763.

And whereas it is just and reasonable, and … essential to our interest, and the security of our colonies, that the several nations or tribes of Indians with whom we are connected, and who live under our protection, should not be molested or disturbed in the possession of such parts of our dominions and territories as, not having been ceded to or purchased by us, are reserved to them, or any of them, as their hunting grounds—We do therefore, with the advice of our Privy Council, declare it to be our royal will and pleasure, that no Governor or Commander in Chief in any of our colonies of Quebec, East Florida, or West Florida, do presume, upon any pretence whatever, to grant warrants of survey, or pass any patents for lands beyond the bounds of their respective governments, as described in their commissions: as also that no Governor or Commander in Chief in any of our other colonies or plantations in America do presume for the present, and until our further pleasure be known, to grant warrants of survey, or pass patents for any lands beyond the heads or sources of any of the rivers which fall into the Atlantic ocean from the West and North West, or upon any lands whatever, which, not having been ceded to or purchased by us as aforesaid, are reserved to the said Indians, or any of them.

And we do further declare it to be our royal will and pleasure, for the present as aforesaid, to reserve under our sovereignty, protection, and dominion, for the use of the said Indians, all the lands and territories not included within the limits of our said three new governments, or within the limits of the territory granted to the Hudson's Bay Company, as also all the lands and territories lying to the westward of the sources of the rivers which fall into the sea from the West and North West as aforesaid.

And we do hereby strictly forbid, on pain of our displeasure, all our loving subjects from making any purchases or settlements whatever, or taking possession of any of the lands above reserved, without our especial leave and licence for that purpose first obtained.

And we do further strictly enjoin and require all persons whatever who have either wilfully or inadvertently seated themselves upon any lands within the countries above described, or upon any other lands which, not having been ceded to or purchased by us, are still reserved to the said Indians as aforesaid, forthwith to remove themselves from such settlements.

And whereas great frauds and abuses have been committed in purchasing lands of the Indians, to the great prejudice of our interests, and to the great dissatisfaction of the said Indians: In order, therefore, to prevent such irregularities for the future, and to the end that the Indians may be convinced of our justice and determined resolution to remove all reasonable cause of discontent, we do, with the advice of our Privy Council strictly enjoin and require, that no private person do presume to make any purchase from the said Indians of any lands reserved to the said Indians, within those parts of our colonies where we have thought proper to allow settlement: but that, if at any time any of the said Indians should be inclined to dispose of the said lands, the same shall be purchased only for us, in our name, at some public meeting or assembly of the said Indians, to be held for that purpose by the Governor or Commander in Chief of our colony respectively within which they shall lie: and in case they shall lie within the limits of any proprietary government, they shall be purchased only for the use and in the name of such proprietaries, conformable to such directions and instructions as we or they shall think proper to give for that purpose:

Given at our Court at St. James's the 7th Day of October 1763, in the third year of our reign.

GOD SAVE THE KING

The Revolutionary War

from George III, Speech to Parliament, 30 November 1774

At the end of the year 1774, tensions between Britain and the American colonists were at a high pitch. Britain, with the intention of quelling rebellion in America in the wake of the Boston Tea Party, had passed the Coercive Acts (more widely known as the Intolerable Acts), which effectively placed Boston harbor under martial law. In response, the Continental Congress met in Philadelphia that September, and they drafted a list of grievances for the king; they also passed

a resolution that, if the Intolerable Acts were not repealed by 1 December 1774, the colonies would begin to boycott British imports. The Acts were not repealed. George III delivered the following speech in the British Parliament the day before the colonial resolution was to take effect; the excerpts below include a response from the British House of Commons, underscoring Parliament's support for the king.

As with all news in this period, word of this speech took some time to cross the Atlantic. The text of the full speech, together with relevant speeches made in Parliament, was printed as a broadside in Boston, 31 January 1775.

My Lords and Gentlemen,

It gives me much concern, that I am obliged, at the opening of this Parliament, to inform you, that a most daring spirit of resistance and disobedience to the law still unhappily prevails in the province of the Massachusetts Bay, and has in diverse[1] parts of it broke forth in fresh violences of a very criminal nature. These proceedings have been countenanced and encouraged in other of my colonies and unwarrantable attempts have been made to obstruct the commerce of this kingdom, by unlawful combinations. I have taken such measures, and given such orders, as I judged most proper and effectual for carrying into execution the laws which were passed in the last session of the late Parliament,[2] for the protection and security of the commerce of my subjects, and for the restoring and preserving peace, order, and good government, in the province of the Massachusetts Bay; and you may depend upon my firm and steadfast resolution to withstand every attempt to weaken or impair the supreme authority of this legislature over all the dominions of my Crown; the maintenance of which I consider as essential to the dignity, the safety, and the welfare, of the British empire; assuring myself, that, while I act upon these principles, I shall never fail to receive your assistance and support. ...

---

[1] *diverse* Several.

[2] *laws ... Parliament* I.e., the Intolerable Acts. See headnote, above.

from Response of the House of Commons,
8 December 1774

The House of Commons Address of Thanks to his Majesty, for his most gracious Speech from the Throne, is as follows:

Most gracious Sovereign,

We, your Majesty's most dutiful and loyal subjects, the Commons of Great Britain in Parliament assembled, return your Majesty our humble thanks for your most gracious speech from the throne.

Permit us to assure your Majesty, that we receive with the highest sense of your Majesty's goodness the early information which you have been pleased to give us, of the state of the province of the Massachusetts Bay.

We feel the most sincere concern, that a spirit of disobedience and resistance to the law should still unhappily prevail in that province, and that it has broke forth in fresh violences of a most criminal nature; and we cannot but lament that such proceedings should have been countenanced and encouraged in any other of your Majesty's colonies; and that any of your subjects should have been so far deluded and misled, as to make rash and unwarrantable attempts to obstruct the commerce of your Majesty's kingdoms by unlawful combinations.[1]

We beg leave to present our most dutiful thanks to your Majesty, for having taken such measures as your Majesty judged most proper and effectual, for carrying into execution the laws which were passed in the last session of the late Parliament, for the protection and security of the commerce of your Majesty's subjects, and for restoring and preserving peace, order, and good government, in the province of the Massachusetts Bay.

The Able Doctor, or America Swallowing the Bitter Draught, 1774. This political cartoon originally appeared in Britain in *London Magazine*. In it, Lord North, Britain's prime minister, is forcing the Intolerable Acts—pictured as tea—down the throat of a woman who, the caption tells us, is "America." The Intolerable Acts (officially known as the Coercive Acts) imposed taxes on the American colonies for tea and other goods, and placed Boston harbor under martial law.

---

1   *combinations* Conspiracies.

Your faithful Commons, animated by your Majesty's gracious assurances, will use every means in their power to assist your Majesty in maintaining entire and inviolate the supreme authority of this legislature over all the dominions of your Crown; being truly sensible that we should betray the trust reposed in us, and be wanting in every duty which we owe to your Majesty and to our fellow subjects, if we failed to give our most zealous support to those great constitutional principles which govern your Majesty's conduct in this important business, and which is so essential to the dignity, safety, and welfare of the British empire. ...

We assure your Majesty, that we will, with the utmost cheerfulness, grant to your Majesty every necessary supply; and that we consider ourselves bound by gratitude, as well as duty, to give every proof of our most affectionate attachment to a prince,[1] who, during the whole course of his reign, has made the happiness of his people the object of all his views, and the rule of all his actions.

from William Wirt, *Sketches of the Life and Character of Patrick Henry* (1817)

Virginia lawyer Patrick Henry (later to become governor) first attracted notice for his impassioned resistance to the Stamp Act. He gained attention again as a delegate to the First Continental Congress in 1774, when he called for voting by the colonies to be tied to population, with each colony's delegates casting a number of votes proportionate to that colony's white population. No colony's votes should be weighted more heavily than others, argued Henry: "the distinction between Virginians, Pennsylvanians, New Yorkers, and New Englanders is no more. I am not a Virginian but an American."

Early 1775 brought word to the American colonies of the resolve of George III and the British government to take a firm stand against the "daring spirit of resistance and disobedience to the laws, which so strongly prevails in the province of the Massachusetts Bay" (see above). The Continental Congress had sent the king a petition setting out its grievances; Britain had been increasing its military presence in the American colonies. In various states, conventions were held to discuss the next course of action; the Second Virginia Convention brought together 120 delegates (among them George Washington, Thomas Jefferson, and Patrick Henry).

Henry's famous "Give Me Liberty or Give Me Death" speech was delivered to the convention on March 23. No written text of the speech has survived; the only versions we have are based on the one reconstructed by biographer William Wirt over thirty years later, relying on the memories of those who had heard the speech. (Had any of them taken notes? Even that is unclear.) Notwithstanding the doubts over the accuracy of the version that has come down to us, Henry's speech has become a foundational text of American history and oratory; it remains interesting as an example not only of impassioned speech-making but also of martial argumentation—and the entire episode remains interesting for the light it sheds on differences of opinion in the Revolutionary era (differences of opinion not only between Virginia and Britain and among the Virginians themselves, but also between colonial Virginians and colonial Jamaicans).

Frontispiece, William Wirt, *Sketches of the Life and Character of Patrick Henry*, 1817.

---

1   *prince* I.e., leader.

from Section 4

On Monday, the 20th of March, 1775, the convention of delegates from the several counties and corporations of Virginia, met for the second time. This assembly was held in the old church in the town of Richmond. Mr. Henry was a member of that body also. The reader will bear in mind the tone of the instructions given by the convention of the preceding year to their deputies in congress. He will remember, that while they recite with great feeling, the series of grievances under which the colonies had laboured, and insist with firmness on their constitutional rights, they give nevertheless, the most explicit and solemn pledge of their faith and true allegiance to his majesty King George the III and avow their determination to support him with their lives and fortunes, in the legal exercise of all his just rights and prerogatives. He will remember, that these instructions contain, also, an expression of their sincere approbation of a connection with Great Britain, and of their ardent wishes for a return of that friendly intercourse, from which this country had derived so much prosperity and happiness. These sentiments still influenced many of the leading members of the convention of 1775. They could not part with the fond hope, that those peaceful days would again return, which had shed so much light and warmth over the land; and the report of the king's gracious reception of the petition from Congress, tended to cherish and foster that hope, and to render them averse to any measure of violence. But Mr. Henry saw things with a steadier eye and a deeper insight. His judgment was too solid to be duped by appearances; and his heart too firm and manly to be amused by false and flattering hopes. He had long since read the true character of the British Court; and saw that no alternative remained for his country but abject submission or heroic resistance. It was not for a soul like Henry's to hesitate between these courses. He had offered upon the altar of liberty no divided heart. The gulf of war which yawned before him, was indeed fiery and fearful; but he saw that the awful plunge was inevitable. The body of the convention however, hesitated. They cast around "a longing lingering look"[1] on those flowery fields, on which peace, and ease, and joy, were still sporting; and it required all the energies of a mentor like Henry, to push them from the precipice, and conduct them over the stormy sea of the revolution, to liberty and glory.

The convention being formed and organized for business, proceeded, in the first place, to express their unqualified approbation of the measures of Congress, and to declare, that they considered "this whole continent as under the highest obligations to that respectable body, for the wisdom of their counsels, and their unremitted endeavours to maintain and preserve inviolate the just rights and liberties of his majesty's dutiful and loyal subjects in America."

They next resolve, that "the warmest thanks of the convention, and of all the inhabitants of this colony, were due, and that this just tribute of applause be presented to the worthy delegates, deputed by a former convention, to represent this colony in general congress, for their cheerful undertaking and faithful discharge of the very important trust reposed in them."

The morning of the 23d March was opened, by reading a petition and memorial from the assembly of Jamaica[2] to the king's most excellent majesty: whereupon it was "resolved, that the unfeigned thanks and most grateful acknowledgments of the convention be presented to that very respectable assembly, for the exceeding generous and affectionate part they have so nobly taken, in the unhappy contest between Great Britain and her colonies; and for their truly patriotic endeavours to fix the just claims of the colonists upon the most permanent constitutional principles: that the assembly be assured, that it is the most ardent wish of this colony (and they were persuaded of the whole continent of North America) to see a speedy return of those halcyon days, when we lived a free and happy people."

These proceedings were not adapted to the taste of Mr. Henry; on the contrary, they were "gall and wormwood"[3] to him. The house required to be wrought

---

[1] *a longing lingering look* See Thomas Gray's "An Elegy Written in a Country Churchyard" (1751), line 81.

[2] *petition ... of Jamaica* Reference to *The Humble Petition and Memorial of the Assembly of Jamaica*, 28 December 1774. The Jamaican colonists petitioned the king to respect the constitutional rights of settlers throughout the empire, while simultaneously assuring the king of their own unwavering loyalty.

[3] *gall and wormwood* See Lamentations 3.19: "Remembering mine affliction and my misery, the wormwood and the gall"; *gall* Bile; *wormwood* Bitter herb.

up to a bolder tone. He rose, therefore, and moved the following manly resolutions:

"Resolved, That a well-regulated militia, composed of gentlemen and yeomen,[1] is the natural strength and only security of a free government; that such a militia in this colony, would forever render it unnecessary for the mother country to keep among us for the purpose of our defence, any standing army of mercenary soldiers, always subversive of the quiet, and dangerous to the liberties of the people, and would obviate the pretext of taxing us for their support.

"That the establishment of such a militia is, *at this time*, peculiarly necessary, by the state of our laws, for the protection and defence of the country, some of which are already expired, and others will shortly be so; and that the known remissness of government in calling us together in legislative capacity, renders it too insecure, in this time of danger and distress, to rely that opportunity will be given of renewing them, in general assembly, *or making any provision to secure our inestimable rights and liberties, from those further violations with which they are threatened.*

"Resolved, therefore, That this colony be immediately put into a state of defence, and that [there] be a committee to prepare a plan for embodying, arming, and disciplining such a number of men, as may be sufficient for that purpose."

The alarm which such a proposition must have given to those who had contemplated no resistance of a character more serious than petition, non-importation,[2] and passive fortitude, and who still hung with suppliant tenderness on the skirts of Britain, will be readily conceived by the reflecting reader. The shock was painful. It was almost general. The resolutions were opposed as not only rash in policy, but as harsh and well-nigh impious in point of feeling. Some of the warmest patriots of the convention opposed them. Richard Bland, Benjamin Harrison, and Edmund Pendleton, who had so lately drunk of the fountain of patriotism in the continental congress, and Robert C. Nicholas, one of the best as well as ablest men and patriots in the state, resisted them with all their influence and abilities.

They urged the late gracious reception of the Congressional petition[3] by the throne. They insisted that national comity, and much more filial respect, demanded the exercise of a more dignified patience. That the sympathies of the parent country were now on our side. That the friends of American liberty in parliament, were still with us, and had, as yet, had no cause to blush for our indiscretion. That the manufacturing interests of Great Britain, already smarting under the effects of our non-importation, co-operated powerfully towards our relief. That the sovereign himself had relented, and showed that he looked upon our sufferings with an eye of pity. "Was this a moment," they asked, "to disgust our friends, to extinguish all the conspiring sympathies which were working in our favour; to turn their friendship into hatred, their pity into revenge? And what was there, they asked, in the situation of the colony, to tempt us to this? Were we a great military people? Were we ready for war? Where were our stores—where were our arms—where our soldiers—where our generals—where our money, the sinews of war? They were nowhere to be found. In truth, we were poor—we were naked—we were defenceless. …

These arguments and topics of persuasion, were so well justified by the appearance of things, and were moreover so entirely in unison with that love of ease and quiet which is natural to man, and that disposition to hope for happier times, even under the most forbidding circumstances, that an ordinary man, in Mr. Henry's situation, would have been glad to compound with the displeasure of the house, by being permitted to withdraw his resolutions in silence.

Not so, Mr. Henry. His was a spirit fitted to raise the whirlwind, as well as to ride in it. His was that comprehensive view, that unerring prescience, that perfect command over the actions of men, which qualified him not merely to guide, but almost to create the destinies of nations.

---

[1]   *yeomen* Respectable small landowners that nonetheless rank under gentlemen.

[2]   *non-importation* I.e., a boycott of British goods.

[3]   *Congressional petition* On 24 October 1774, the First Continental Congress sent a petition, written by John Dickinson, to George III protesting the Intolerable Acts. The petition asserted that the colonists would remain loyal if the Acts were repealed and other grievances were addressed.

He rose at this time with a majesty unusual to him in an exordium,[1] and with all that self-possession by which he was so invariably distinguished. "No man," he said, "thought more highly than he did, of the patriotism, as well as abilities, of the very worthy gentlemen who had just addressed the house. But different men often saw the same subject in different lights; and therefore, he hoped it would not be thought disrespectful to those gentlemen, if, entertaining as he did, opinions of a character very opposite to theirs, should speak forth his sentiments freely, and without reserve. This," he said, "was no time for ceremony. The question before the house was one of awful moment to this country. For his own part, he considered it as nothing less than a question of freedom or slavery. And in proportion to the magnitude of the subject, ought to be the freedom of the debate. It was only in this way that they could hope to arrive at truth, and fulfil the great responsibility which they held to God and their country. Should he keep back his opinions, at such a time, through fear of giving offence, he should consider himself as guilty of treason towards his country, and of an act of disloyalty toward the majesty of Heaven, which he revered above all earthly kings."

"Mr. President,"[2] said he, "it is natural to man to indulge in the illusions of hope. We are apt to shut our eyes against a painful truth—and listen to the song of that siren, till she transforms us into beasts.[3] Is it," he asked, "the part of wise men, engaged in a great and arduous struggle for liberty? Were we disposed to be of the number of those, who having eyes, see not, and having ears, hear not, the things which so nearly concern their temporal salvation? For his part, whatever anguish of spirit it might cost, he was willing to know the whole truth to know the worst, and to provide for it."

"He had," he said, "but one lamp by which his feet were guided: and that was the lamp of experience. He knew of no way of judging of the future, but by the past. And judging by the past, he wished to know what there had been in the conduct of the British ministry for the last ten years, to justify those hopes with which gentlemen had been pleased to solace themselves and the house? Is it that insidious smile with which our petition has been lately received? Trust it not, sir; it will prove a snare to your feet.[4] Suffer not yourselves to be betrayed with a kiss.[5] Ask yourselves how this gracious reception of our petition, comports with those warlike preparations which cover our waters and darken our land? Are fleets and armies necessary to a work of love and reconciliation? Have we shown ourselves so unwilling to be reconciled, that force must be called in to win back our love? Let us not deceive ourselves, sir. These are the implements of war and subjugation—the last arguments to which kings resort. I ask gentlemen, sir, what means this martial array, if its purpose be not to force us to submission? Can gentlemen assign any other possible motive for it? Has Great Britain any enemy in this quarter of the world, to call for all this accumulation of navies and armies? No, sir: she has none. They are meant for us: they can be meant for no other. They are sent over to bind and rivet upon us those chains, which the British ministry have been so long forging. And what have we to oppose to them? Shall we try argument? Sir, we have been trying that for the last ten years. Have we anything new to offer upon the subject? Nothing. We have held the subject up in every light of which it is capable; but it has been all in vain. Shall we resort to entreaty and humble supplication? What terms shall we find, which have not been already exhausted? Let us not, I beseech you, sir, deceive ourselves longer. Sir, we have done everything that could be done, to avert the storm which is now coming on. We have petitioned—we have remonstrated—we have supplicated—we have prostrated ourselves before the throne, and have implored its interposition to arrest the tyrannical hands of the ministry and parliament. Our petitions have been slighted; our remonstrances have produced additional violence and insult; our supplications have been disregarded; and we have been spurned, with contempt, from the foot of the throne.

---

1   *exordium*   The beginning of a speech.

2   *Mr. President*   The presiding officer of the First Congressional Congress, Peyton Randolph (1721–75).

3   *siren ... beasts*   This is a conflation of two of the many dangers that Odysseus uses his wits to escape in Homer's *Odyssey*: the Sirens are creatures whose song can enchant sailors to their deaths by shipwreck, and Circe is a sorceress who turns men into beasts.

4   *snare ... feet*   See Job 18.8: "For he is cast into a net by his own feet, and he walketh upon a snare."

5   *betrayed with a kiss*   Judas marks his betrayal of Christ with a kiss. See Matthew 26.47–49.

In vain, after these things, may we indulge the fond hope of peace and reconciliation. There is no longer any room for hope. If we wish to be free—if we mean to preserve inviolate those inestimable privileges for which we have been so long contending—if we mean not basely to abandon the noble struggle in which we have been so long engaged, and which we have pledged ourselves never to abandon, until the glorious object of our contest shall be obtained—we must fight!—I repeat it, sir; we must fight!! An appeal to arms and to the God of Hosts, is all that is left us!"[1]

"They tell us, sir," continued Mr. Henry, "that we are weak—unable to cope with so formidable an adversary. But when shall we be stronger? Will it be the next week, or the next year? Will it be when we are totally disarmed; and when a British guard shall be stationed in every house? Shall we gather strength by irresolution and inaction? Shall we acquire the means of effectual resistance, by lying supinely on our back, and hugging the delusive phantom of hope, until our enemies shall have bound us, hand and foot? Sir, we are not weak, if we make a proper use of those means which the God of nature hath placed in our power. Three millions of people, armed in the holy cause of liberty, and in such a country as that which we possess, are invincible by any force which our enemy can send against us. Besides, sir, we shall not fight our battles alone. There is a just God who presides over the destinies of nations; and who will raise up friends to fight our battles for us. The battle, sir, is not to the strong alone; it is to the vigilant, the active, the brave. Besides, sir, we have no election.[2] If we were base enough to desire it, it is now too late to retire from the contest. There is no retreat, but in submission and slavery! Our chains are forged. Their clanking may be heard on the plains of Boston! The war is inevitable—and let it come!! I repeat it, sir; let it come!!!

"It is in vain, sir, to extenuate the matter. Gentlemen may cry, peace, peace—but there is no peace. The war is actually begun! The next gale that sweeps from the north, will bring to our ears the clash of resounding arms! Our brethren are already in the field! Why stand we here idle? What is it that gentlemen wish? What would they have? Is life so dear; or peace so sweet, as to be purchased at the price of chains, and slavery? Forbid it, Almighty God!—I know not what course others may take; but as for me," cried he, with both his arms extended aloft, his brows knit, every feature marked with the resolute purpose of his soul, and his voice swelled to its boldest note of exclamation—"give me liberty, or give me death!"

He took his seat. No murmur of applause was heard. The effect was too deep. After the trance of a moment, several members started from their seats. The cry, "to arms," seemed to quiver on every lip, and gleam from every eye! Richard H. Lee[3] arose and supported Mr. Henry, with his usual spirit and elegance. But his melody was lost amidst the agitations of that ocean, which the master spirit of the storm had lifted up on high. That supernatural voice still sounded in their ears, and shivered along their arteries. They heard, in every pause, the cry of liberty or death. They became impatient of speech—their souls were on fire for action. . . .

---

[1] [Wirt's note] "Imagine to yourself," says my correspondent, (judge Tucker), "this sentence delivered with all the calm dignity of Cato, of Utica; imagine to yourself the Roman senate, assembled in the capitol, when it was entered by the profane Gauls, who, at first, were awed by their presence, as if they had entered an assembly of the gods! Imagine that you heard that Cato addressing such a senate— imagine that you saw the hand-writing on the wall of Belshazzar's palace—imagine you heard a voice as from heaven uttering the words, 'We must fight,' as the doom of fate, and you may have some idea of the speaker, the assembly to whom he addressed himself, and the auditory, of which I was one." [*Cato* Cato the Younger (95–46 BCE) was a Roman senator famous for his integrity; he died by suicide rather than accept Julius Caesar's dictatorship; *handwriting . . . Belshazzar* In Daniel 5, a disembodied hand writes King Belshazzar's fate on the wall; no astrologer or fortuneteller in the land could decipher it, but the prophet Daniel is called, and he tells Belshazzar that his ungodly ways have been weighed in the balance and found wanting, and that his kingdom will fall.]

[2] *election* Choice.

[3] *Richard H. Lee* Politician from Virginia, best known for the Lee Resolution of 1776, which called for American independence from Great Britain.

Benjamin Franklin, "What Would Satisfy the Americans?" (1775); "Join, or Die" (1754)

Benjamin Franklin played an important role over several decades in the events that led to the formation of the American republic. One early contribution was his publication of the "Join, or Die" image in the 9 May 1754 issue of his *Pennsylvania Gazette*. It is the earliest extant image depicting the concept of the unification of the British colonies of eastern North America, but it was not conceived of with a view to the unification of the colonies as an independent nation. The intent was rather to encourage the formation of a united front against the French and the Indigenous peoples who were allied to them. The French, in Franklin's view (as he put it in the editorial accompanying the drawing), intended to "establish themselves, settle their Indians, ... kill, seize, and imprison our traders ... , murder and scalp our farmers, with their wives and children, and take an easy posses sion of such parts of British territory as they find most convenient for them." The image was later repurposed by others in a variety of ways. During the 1765 Stamp Act controversy it was used as part of an effort to unify the colonies against the imposition by Britain of what were seen to be unfair taxes, and it was repurposed again during the American Revolution, when Paul Revere and others used the image as a way of visualizing the imperative for uniting in the effort to win independence.

Franklin continued to participate in American affairs of the utmost gravity until a few years before his death (see his author entry elsewhere in this volume), but he was always capable of a light-hearted take on even the most serious of circumstances—as the anecdote below from 1775 illustrates. (At the time Franklin was nearing the end of the almost two decades he spent in London.)

"WHAT WOULD SATISFY THE AMERICANS?"

Doctor Franklin, being in England in the Year 1775 was asked by a Nobleman, what would satisfy the Americans? Answered, That it might easily be comprised in a few Re's

Which he immediately wrote on a piece of Paper Thus,

Re {
call your Forces,
store Castle William,
pair the Damage done to Boston,
peal your unconstitutional Acts,
nounce your pretentions to Tax us,
fund the duties you have extorted; after this quire, and
ceive payment for the destroyed Tea,[1] with the voluntary grants of the Colonies, And then joice in a happy
conciliation.
}

"JOIN, OR DIE"

JOIN, or DIE.

---

[1] *destroyed Tea* During the Boston Tea Party uprising against the British imposition of the Tea Tax, the American colonists threw 92,000 pounds of tea belonging to the East India Company into Boston harbor.

In 1782, twenty-one-year-old Deborah Sampson joined the 4th Massachusetts Regiment under the name Robert Shurtliff. Sampson fought under this disguise in a number of skirmishes over the course of seventeen months, and was promoted to the status of an orderly before an injury led to the discovery of her biological sex and she was honorably discharged. Though Sampson is far from the only "female soldier" known to have fought for the Continental Army, her story reached a wider audience than most, and eventually became the basis for Herman Mann's (heavily embellished) 1797 biography *The Female Review*, which he wrote based on interviews he had conducted with Sampson. While some readers balked at Sampson's rejection of traditional gender roles, most found reason to praise the patriotic sentiment that had prompted this course of action. The portrait reproduced here was painted from life in 1797 by Joseph Stone, and likely commissioned by Mann; a version of the portrait was used as the frontispiece to *The Female Review*. Substantial excerpts from that work are included in the author entry for Mann/Sampson in the website component of this anthology.

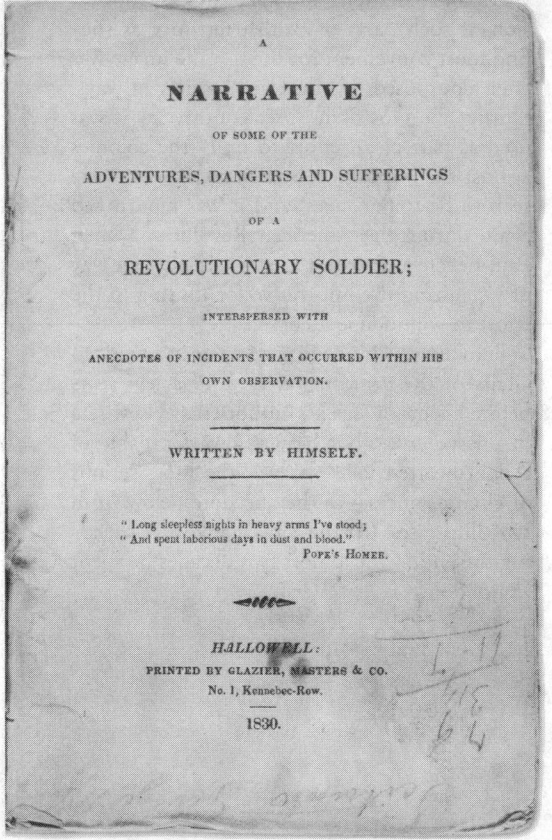

Title page, Joseph Plumb Martin, *A Narrative of Some of the Adventures, Dangers, and Sufferings of a Revolutionary Soldier; Interspersed with Anecdotes of Incidents that Occurred within His Own Observation*, 1830. Though not published until several decades after the war, the narrative by Joseph Plumb Martin (1760–1850) of his years as a soldier is arguably the best record we have of the experience of ordinary soldiers during the Revolutionary War. With a wealth of anecdotes, Martin (who was an enlisted soldier from 1776 to 1783) provides a vivid sense of the hardships endured by enlisted men, and of the poor treatment they received not only during the course of the war but also after it was over.

Poems and Songs

During the Revolutionary War and the decades preceding it, patriotic songs and poems flourished in American oral and print culture. These popular tunes were important propaganda tools for stirring the emotions—both on the revolutionaries' side and among those who supported the British. As one Revolutionary army chaplain put it at the beginning of the war, "One good song is worth a dozen addresses or proclamations."

anonymous ("A Young Woman of Virginia"), "Virginia Banishing Tea" (1774)

In protest against various British tax measures, and against the Tea Act (which granted a monopoly on tea sales in the colonies to the British East India Company, thereby making illegal the sale of the less expensive teas imported from other sources, which the colonists had grown accustomed to drinking), colonists were encouraged to boycott tea and to consume locally made herbal teas instead. In Virginia, more active measures were also taken, including the Yorktown Tea Party on 1 November 1774, in which two half-chests of tea were thrown overboard. Although far less tea was destroyed than in the Boston Tea Party, the Yorktown protest convinced many merchants in Virginia to sign on to the Continental Association, which had been formed for the express purpose of boycotting British goods. The following poem was written by an anonymous young woman, about whom nothing is known except that she was "a native of Virginia, endowed with all the graces of a cultivated mind, pleasant external qualities, and a model of patriotism worthy the emulation of many more conspicuous."

Begone, pernicious baneful tea,
With all Pandora's ills,[1] possessed;

Hyson,[2] no more beguiled by thee,
My noble sons shall be oppressed.

5   To Britain fly; where gold enslaves
And venal men their birth-right sell:
Tell North[3] and his bribed clan of knaves
Their bloody acts were made in hell.

In Henry's reign those acts began,[4]
10   Which sacred rules of justice broke;
North now pursues the hellish plan,
To fix on us his slavish yoke.

But we oppose, and will be free,
This great good cause we will defend;
15   Nor bribe, nor Gage,[5] nor North's decree,
Shall make us "at his feet to bend."[6]

From Anglia's[7] ancient sons we came,
Those heroes who for freedom fought;
In Freedom's cause we'll match their fame,
20   By their example greatly taught.

Our king we love, but North we hate,[8]
Nor will to him submission own;
If death's our doom, we'll brave our fate,
But pay allegiance to the throne.

---

[1]   *Pandora's ills*   In Greek mythology, Pandora is given a box containing all the sorrows of mortality and is told not to open it, but her curiosity gets the better of her; she opens the box, and the sorrows are unleashed on the world.

[2]   *Hyson*   Brand of green tea.

[3]   *North*   Frederick North, 2nd Earl of Guilford, better known as Lord North, who served as Britain's prime minister from 1770 to 1782.

[4]   *Henry's reign ... began*   King Henry VIII (r. 1509–47) made increased use of the Star Chamber, a court that came to be considered an oppressive tool used to override Parliament and enforce the king's proclamations.

[5]   *Gage*   General Thomas Gage served as commander-in-chief of the British forces in North America from 1763 to 1775.

[6]   *at his feet to bend*   Phrase from "To His Excellency Governor Belcher, on the Death of His Lady," a poem by the American poet Mather Byles (1706–88); Byles was a firm Royalist.

[7]   *Anglia*   I.e., England.

[8]   *king ... hate*   Power to impose taxation in Britain lay with Parliament—of which Lord North was the leader—not with the king.

25 Then rouse, my sons; from slavery; free
    Your suffering homes from God's high wrath!
    Gird on your steel:[1] give liberty
    To all who follow in our path!

Attributed to Philip Dawe, *The Bostonians Paying the Excise-man, or Tarring and Feathering*, 1774. This image shows five Patriots tarring, feathering, and forcing tea down the throat of John Malcolm, a Loyalist and the Commissioner of Customs, who was in charge of collecting the taxes imposed by the British. In the background, the Boston Tea Party is taking place, an event which in fact occurred a month earlier than the tarring and feathering of John Malcolm on 5 January 1774.

from Lemuel Haynes, "The Battle of Lexington" (1775)

Lemuel Haynes (1753–1833) was a black writer, clergyman, and poet. Abandoned shortly after birth, he grew up as an indentured servant in the Rose family in Connecticut, where he was encouraged to pursue an independent course of reading and religious study. He became a minuteman in 1774 and fought in the early battles of the American Revolution. After the war, he studied theology and Classics with Congregationalist clergymen in Connecticut, becoming a minister himself in 1785. He wrote significant works on abolition, including "Liberty Further Extended" (1776) and *The Nature and Importance of True Republicanism* (1801). The following patriotic ballad commemorates the first battles of the Revolutionary War in Lexington and Concord, which took place on 19 April 1775. (See also the Lemuel Haynes author entry included in the website component of this volume.)

A poem on the inhuman tragedy perpetrated on the 19th of April 1775 by a number of the British troops under the command of Thomas Gage,[2] which parricides and ravages are shocking displays of ministerial & tyrannic vengeance composed by Lemuel a young mulatto[3] who obtained what little knowledge he possesses, by his own application to letters.

…

The nineteenth day of April last
    We ever shall retain
As monumental of the past
Most bloody shocking scene

5 Then tyrants filled with horrid rage
    A fatal journey went
    And unmolested to engage
    And slay the innocent …

---

1   *Gird ... steel* Buckle on your swords.

2   *Thomas Gage* General Thomas Gage served as commander-in-chief of the British forces in North America from 1763 to 1775.

3   *mulatto* Term, now considered offensive, for a person of both black and white ancestry.

At Lexington they did appear
10 Arrayed in hostile form
And though our friends were peaceful there
Yet on them fell the storm

Eight most unhappy victims fell
Into the arms of death
15 Unpitied by those tribes of hell
Who cursed them with their breath

The savage band still march along
For Concord they were bound
While oaths and curses from their tongue
20 Accent with hellish sound

To prosecute their fell° desire   *villainous*
At Concord they unite
Two sons of freedom there expire
By their tyrannic spite

25 Thus did our friends endure their rage
Without a murm'ring word
Till die they must or else engage
And join with one accord

Such pity did their breath inspire
30 That long they bore the rod¹
And with reluctance they conspire
To shed the human blood

But pity could no longer sway
Tho' 'tis a pow'rful band
35 For liberty now bleeding lay
And called them to withstand

The awful conflict now begun
To rage with furious pride
And blood in great effusion run
40 From many a wounded side

For liberty, each freedman strives
As it's a gift of God
And for it willing yield their lives
And seal it with their blood

45 Thrice happy they who thus resign
Into the peaceful grave
Much better there, in death confined
Than a surviving slave …

Although our numbers were but few
50 And they a num'rous throng
Yet we their armies do pursue
And drive their hosts along

One son of freedom could annoy
A thousand tyrant fiends
55 And their despotic tribe destroy
And chase them to their dens

Thus did the sons of Britain's king
Receive a sore disgrace
Whilst sons of freedom join to sing
60 The vict'ry they embrace

Oh! Britain how art thou become
Infamous in our eye
Nearly allied to ancient Rome
That seat of popery²

65 Our fathers, though a feeble band
Did leave their native place
Exiled to a desert land
This howling wilderness

A num'rous train of savage brood
70 Did then attack them round
But still they trusted in their God
Who did their foes confound

Our fathers' blood did freely flow
To buy our freedom here
75 Nor will we let our freedom go
The price was much too dear …

---

¹ *bore the rod* Endured the burden of tyranny.

² *popery* A pejorative term for Roman Catholicism.

Ruth Bryant, "The American Maid's Choice: An Extempore" (1776)

The following poem is drawn from Ruth Bryant's manuscript booklet from the Revolutionary era, which was brought to light in 2010 by historian Rachel Hope Cleves. Bryant (1760–83), who was just fifteen when she composed the earliest of the poems, was the daughter of middle-class parents in North Bridgewater, Massachusetts (her parents kept a small farm, and her father was also a doctor). She had seven siblings, four of whom are known to have also written poetry; William Cullen Bryant, the well-known nineteenth-century poet and abolitionist, was the son of Ruth's brother Peter. As Cleves has written, the poems are interesting both in themselves and in demonstrating that "being banned from fighting" did not prevent young women such as Bryant from "vicarious involvement in the war."

The manuscript booklet was transcribed by Cleves for her article "'Heedless Youth': The Revolutionary War Poetry of Ruth Bryant" (2010).

B etter is he that ruleth his spirit than
He that taketh a city—Solomon[1]—

I choose the gallant warrior brave
Who ne'er will yield to be a slave;
5   Good government he will maintain
But nobly spurns the galling chain.

His steady spirit's always free
From each fell passion's tyranny;
He wields his sword with martial skill
10   And lays internal rebels still.

Then fortifies on every side,
Nor fears the force of wind and tide;
He keeps his guards and sentries out
And puts insulting foes to rout.

15   He to his country turns his views;
The meanest place he'll not refuse
If so he can advance the cause,
And keep the God of Nature's laws.

True courage doth his mind inspire,
20   Tempered with virtue's heavenly fire;
He burns within with ardent zeal—
Not vainly blazes—for our weal.°   *well-being*

Convinced that justice prompts our wars,
He boldly seeks the field of Mars;[2]
25   Calm and serene he meets the foe,
Resolved to give, or take the blow.

He is determined to be free,
He'll risk his life for liberty,
Of moral worth and mind serene,
30   Polite, and of engaging mien.°   *manner*

This noble patriot I admire
Who glows with such heroic fire;
This is the man that I approve
If he and I agree in love.

Hannah Griffitts, "Upon Reading a Book Entitled *Common Sense*" (1776)

Writing poems under the name "Fidelia," meaning "Faithful," Quaker poet Hannah Griffitts (1727–1817) composed over sixty poems that she circulated among her friends and family (many of whom were supportive of the American colonists' struggle against the British). As a Quaker pacifist, however, Griffitts could not support the war. She viewed the writer Thomas Paine, who supported revolution in his pamphlet *Common Sense* (1775–76), as incendiary, and wished that more moderate voices would prevail and find a peaceful solution to the conflict.

---

[1] *Better is he ... Solomon*   See Proverbs 16.32 (traditionally considered to be written by the prophet King Solomon): "He that is slow to anger is better than the mighty; and he that ruleth his spirit than he that taketh a city."

---

[2] *Mars*   In Roman mythology, the god of war.

The vizard° dropped, see subtlety prevail,   *mask*
Thro' ev'ry page of this fallacious tale,
Sylvania° let it not unanswered pass,   *Pennsylvania*
But heed the well guess'd snake beneath the grass,[1]
5   A deeper wound at freedom ne'er was made,
Then by this Oliverian[2] is displayed.
Orders confounded—Dignities thrown down,
Charters degraded equal with the Crown,
The impartial press, most partially maintained
10 Freedom infringed & conscience is restrained,
The moderate man is held to public view,
"The friend of tyranny & foe to you,"
Denied the common right to represent
Forbid to give his reasons for dissent,
15 Whilst base informers (owned° a   *acknowledged*
     public pest)
Are round the land encouraged & caressed
Our representatives the people's choice
Are held contemptuous by this daring voice.
Persons are seized & posts monopolized
20 And all our form of government despised
Then from this "specimen of rule" beware,
Behold the serpent & avoid his snare.
'Tis not in names, our present danger lies
Sixty as well as one can tyrannize,
25 Ah! then awake Sylvania & beware,
The fatal danger of this subtle snare,
Hold fast your own, your charter'd rights maintain
Nor let them weave the snare into the chain,
And whilst firm union stands° the British   *withstands*
     foes,
30 Let not the native hand your date of freedom close.

---

[1]   *snake … grass* Common saying that can be traced back to the
Roman poet Virgil's (70–19 BCE) *Eclogues*; the idea is that beneath a
fair exterior something dangerous lurks.

[2]   *Oliverian* Similar to Oliver Cromwell, the British politician
who led the parliamentary revolt against King Charles I and ruled
England as Lord Protector from 1653 to 1658. Cromwell persecuted
Catholics and any Protestant sect that he didn't approve of, including
Quakers (which is why Griffitts, in particular, would view him as a
tyrant).

Francis Hopkinson, "A Camp Ballad"[3] (1778)

American politician, judge, composer, designer,
and writer Francis Hopkinson (1737–91) was
widely known for his poems, songs, and satires,
which were considered vital contributions to
the patriotic literature of the day. Hopkinson
was born into Pennsylvania's cultured political
class, and after studying law took up various
posts, moving eventually to New Jersey, where
he became a representative in the Continental
Congress of 1776. A firm supporter of the
Revolution and signee of the Declaration of
Independence, Hopkinson continued serving as a judge and, by the 1880s, had secured
a reputation as one of the early republic's most
prominent literary figures.

Make room, oh! ye kingdoms in hist'ry renowned
    Whose arms have in battle with glory been
    crowned,
Make room for America, another great nation,
Arises to claim in your council a station.

5   Her sons fought for freedom, and by their own brav'ry
Have rescued themselves from the shackles of slav'ry.
America's free, and though Britain abhorred it,
Yet fame a new volume prepares to record it.

Fair freedom in Briton her throne had erected,
10 But her sons growing venal,° and she   *corrupt*
    disrespected;
The goddess offended forsook the base nation,
And fixed on our mountains a more honoured
    station.

With glory immortal she here sits enthroned,
Nor fears the vain vengeance of Britain disowned,
15 Whilst Washington guards her with heroes surrounded,
Her foes shall with shameful defeat be confounded.

---

[3]   *A Camp Ballad* During the winter of 1777–78, George Washington set up camp with the Continental Army at Valley Forge,
Pennsylvania. While at this camp and despite its harsh conditions,
the army recovered from a series of defeats and engaged in military
training that resulted in the Continental Army becoming a far more
powerful force capable of defeating the British.

To arms then, to arms, 'tis fair freedom invites us;
The trumpet shrill sounding to battle excites us;
The banners of virtue unfurled,[1] shall wave o'er us,
20 Our hero lead on, and the foe fly before us.

On Heav'n and Washington placing reliance,
We'll meet the bold Briton, and bid him defiance:
Our cause we'll support, for 'tis just and 'tis glorious
When men fight for freedom they must be victorious.

Jonathan Odell, "The Old Year and the New: A Prophecy" (1779)

Loyalist poet and minister Jonathan Odell (1737–1818) became well-known for his poetry in support of the British monarchy and in opposition to the Revolution. He came before the New Jersey Provincial Congress on account of his Loyalist writing, where he was forced to swear loyalty to America; he soon left for New York to continue his Loyalist work. After the war, Odell left the United States for New Brunswick, then part of the British colony of Nova Scotia.

So convinced was Odell in 1779 that the British would finally subdue the American rebellion that he wrote the following optimistic song to ring in the New Year of 1780. Moses Colt Tyler first ascribed authorship of this poem to Odell in 1897, and it has since generally been accepted to be his work.

What though last year be past and gone,
  Why should we grieve or mourn about it?
As good a year is now begun,
  And better too—let no one doubt it.

5   'Tis New Year's morn; why should we part?
  Why not enjoy what heaven has sent us?
  Let wine expand the social heart,
  Let friends, and mirth, and wine content us.

10 War's rude alarms disturbed last year;
  Our country bled and wept around us;
  But this each honest heart shall cheer,
  And peace and plenty shall surround us.

Last year "King Congo,"[2] through the land,
  Displayed his thirteen stripes[3] to fright us;
15 But George's[4] power, in Clinton's[5] hand,
  In this New Year shall surely right us.

Last year saw many honest men
  Torn from each dear and sweet connection;
  But this° shall see them home again,   *this year*
20 And happy in their king's protection.

Last year vain Frenchmen braved our coasts,
  And baffled Howe,[6] and 'scaped from Byron;[7]
  But this shall bring their vanquished hosts
  To crouch beneath the British lion.

25 Last year rebellion proudly stood,
  Elate, in her meridian glory;
  But this shall quench her pride in blood—
  George shall avenge each martyred Tory.[8]

Then bring us wine, full bumpers° bring: *glasses*
30 Hail this New Year in joyful chorus;

---

[1] *banners ... unfurled* Hopkinson was a member of the committee in charge of creating a design for the flag of the United States in 1776; in 1777, the committee adopted the Stars and Stripes. Hopkinson is credited as the designer of this flag, as well as of the flag for the U.S. Navy.

[2] *King Congo* Dismissive term for the American Continental Congress. In late eighteenth-century America (as in Britain), the word "Congo" was generally understood to refer not to the region of central Africa that now bears its name but rather to the black Chinese tea known as Congou or, more commonly, Congo, which was among the most popular varieties of tea at the time; the epithet is thus in all probability a reference to the Americans' determination to retain control of their tea supply.

[3] *thirteen stripes* American flag; the thirteen stripes represent the thirteen colonies.

[4] *George* King George III of Great Britain and Ireland (r. 1760–1820).

[5] *Clinton* General Sir Henry Clinton served from 1778 to 1782 as the British army's commander-in-chief in North America.

[6] *Howe* William Howe served as commander-in-chief of the British land forces in North America from 1775 to 1778.

[7] *Byron* John Byron, also known as "Foul-Weather Jack," served as a vice-admiral in the British Navy. He unsuccessfully attacked a French fleet in July 1779.

[8] *Tory* American loyal to Britain.

God bless great George our gracious king,
And crush rebellion down before us!

'Tis New Year's morn; why should we part?
Why not enjoy what heaven has sent us?
35   Let wine expand the social heart,
Let friends, and mirth, and wine content us.

---

from Dunmore's Proclamation, 1775

In the spring of 1775, the governor of the colony of Virginia, John Murray, the 4th Earl of Dunmore, became increasingly alarmed at reports of an impending attack by American Patriots on the state capitol of Williamsburg. Tensions continued to build, and in November of the same year Dunmore issued a proclamation that offered freedom to the enslaved and indentured male population in the state, on the condition that those freed join the British army to help stifle the rebellion. While the Proclamation secured Dunmore's immediate goal—within a month, 800 new soldiers had joined the British—in the longer term, the threat the Proclamation presented to the slave system alienated the Southern colonies even further from Britain. Patriot and Loyalist slaveholders alike were alarmed by the Proclamation, as it stirred long-held fears of a slave revolt and threatened slaveholders' economic interests. While Dunmore's Proclamation did not secure British victory in the Revolutionary War, it was never revoked by Britain: over the course of the war thousands of enslaved people joined the British army. The British public's sympathy with the plight of the enslaved grew over the course of the conflict, and many historians view Dunmore's Proclamation as a key step on the way to the eventual abolition of slavery in the British Empire (1833–34).

A PROCLAMATION

As I have ever entertained hopes that an accommodation might have taken place between Great Britain and this colony, without being compelled by my duty to this most disagreeable but now absolutely necessary step, rendered so by a body of armed men unlawfully assembled, ... and the formation of an army, and that army now on their march to attack His Majesty's troops and destroy the well-disposed[1] subjects of this colony. To defeat such unreasonable purposes, and [so] that all such traitors and their abettors may be brought to justice, and that the peace and good order of this colony may be again restored, which the ordinary course of the civil law is unable to effect; I have thought fit to issue this, my proclamation, hereby declaring that until the aforesaid good purposes can be obtained, I do in virtue of the power and authority to me given, by His Majesty, determine to execute martial law, and cause the same to be executed throughout this colony. ... And I do hereby further declare all indentured servants, negroes, or others, (appertaining to rebels,) free that are able and willing to bear arms, they joining His Majesty's troops as soon as may be, for the more speedily reducing this colony to a proper sense of their duty[,] ... till such time as peace may again be restored to this at present most unhappy country. ...

Given under my Hand on board the ship *William*, off Norfolk, the 7th day of November, in the sixteenth year of His Majesty's reign.

Dunmore

(God save the king.)

from Edward Rutledge, letter to Ralph Izard, 8 December 1775

The following excerpt from American politician Edward Rutledge's letter reveals that Dunmore's Proclamation (see above) was received by slaveholding Americans as yet another British abuse: "our slaves emancipated for the express purpose of massacring their masters." Rutledge represented South Carolina in the Continental Congress (1774–76) and signed the Declaration of Independence; he also owned over 50 enslaved people. The recipient of this letter, Ralph Izard,

---

[1] *well-disposed*   I.e., loyal to Britain.

was a large landowner from South Carolina who was living in England at the time; he was thus in a position to report on British sentiment regarding the conflict. Izard was an American politician and loyal to the Revolutionary cause, and he acted as a diplomat and raised funds for the Revolution while living abroad. Izard owned at least 602 enslaved people on his 2,353-acre plantation in South Carolina; after the Revolutionary War he became one of the first South Carolina senators elected to Congress.

You will receive by this conveyance a proclamation issued by Lord Dunmore—tending, in my judgement, more effectively to work an eternal separation between Great Britain and the Colonies than any other expedience which could possibly have been thought of.

Tell me then, I beseech you (before it is too late) what are the sentiments of the English nation—are the people of that country determined to force us into independence? Or do they really imagine that we are so insensitive to the calls of reason to every injury? Do they expect that after our towns have been destroyed, our liberties repeatedly invaded, our women and children driven from their habitations, our nearest relatives sacrificed, our slaves emancipated for the express purpose of massacring their masters—can they, I say, after all their injuries, expect that we shall return to our former connection with a forgiving and a cordial disposition? …

Declaration by the Representatives of the People of the Colony and Dominion of Virginia, Assembled in General Convention, 14 December 1775

Shaken by the prospect of a widespread slave revolt that would swell the army of the British, the Virginia Congress responded to Dunmore's Proclamation (see above) with a threatening reminder that enslaved people who took up arms to free themselves were subject to the death penalty in Virginia; the Declaration simultaneously suggested that those who returned to enslavement might be pardoned.

By the Representatives of the People of the Colony and Dominion of VIRGINIA, assembled in GENERAL CONVENTION

A DECLARATION

Whereas lord Dunmore, by his proclamation, dated on board the ship *William*, off Norfolk, the 7th day of November 1775, hath offered freedom to such able-bodied slaves as are willing to join him, and take up arms, against the good people of this colony, giving thereby encouragement to a general insurrection, which may induce a necessity of inflicting the severest punishments upon those unhappy people, already deluded by his base and insidious arts; and whereas, by an act of the General Assembly now in force in this colony, it is enacted, that all negro or other slaves, conspiring to rebel or make insurrection, shall suffer death, and be excluded all benefit of clergy:[1] We think it proper to declare, that all slaves who have been, or shall be, seduced, by his lordship's proclamation, or other arts, to desert their masters' service, and take up arms against the inhabitants of this colony, shall be liable to such punishment as shall hereafter be directed by the General Convention. And to that end all such, who have taken this unlawful and wicked step, may return in safety to their duty, and escape the punishment due to their crimes, we hereby promise pardon to them, they surrendering themselves to Col. William Woodford, or any other commander of our troops, and not appearing in arms after the publication hereof. And we do farther earnestly recommend it to all humane and benevolent persons in this colony to explain and make known this our offer of mercy to those unfortunate people.

EDMUND PENDLETON, president.

---

[1] *benefit of clergy*   In British and American law, the benefit of the clergy was a means of avoiding the death penalty by petitioning for a lesser punishment. In this context, the crime of inciting or participating in insurrection was punishable by death with no possibility of avoiding the sentence.

The French Revolution, and the Revolutionary Call for Women's Rights

The Enlightenment ideal of liberty that had fueled the American Revolution resonated powerfully in France, and the Americans' success in defeating the British and in creating a republic based on the rights and liberties of the citizenry (at least of the white male citizenry) inspired the French. Beginning in 1789, the French began the process of overthrowing and replacing their monarchy and much of their hierarchical social structure; many hoped to create a republic based on equal rights for all citizens. Many Americans responded at first with enthusiasm to the French Revolution; the French had been their allies against the British, and the American people were largely sympathetic to an ideology that seemed so similar to their own. But as the French Revolution grew more violent—and as the depth of the French Revolution's commitment to equality became fully apparent (in 1794 France proclaimed the freedom of all enslaved people in its colonies[1])—Americans became more divided in their response. Thomas Jefferson and the Republican party remained supportive (albeit with reservations), while Alexander Hamilton and the Federalists became increasingly hostile to the Revolution. Officially, the Americans maintained neutrality as Britain and Spain opposed the new French regime in a series of wars that lasted until 1802.

The Declaration of the Rights of Man and of the Citizen was produced by France's National Constituent Assembly in 1789; it was written by the Marquis de Lafayette, working closely with Thomas Jefferson. The Declaration is the central document outlining the core values of the French Revolution, and it had a significant impact on framing the conversation around democracy and human rights worldwide. As with the American Declaration of Independence, however, it had limitations—rights were only accorded to male citizens, despite some voices petitioning at the time to include women and people of color. (Nicolas de Condorcet, for example, put the matter quite simply: "he who votes against the right of another, whatever the religion, color, or sex of that other, has henceforth abjured his own.")

The French Revolution was also a watershed moment in the history of women's rights; writers such as Olympe de Gouges and Mary Wollstonecraft broke new ground in arguing for women's equality.

Declaration of the Rights of Man and of the Citizen (1789)[2]

Approved by the National Assembly of France, August 26, 1789

The representatives of the French people, organized as a National Assembly, believing that the ignorance, neglect, or contempt of the rights of man are the sole cause of public calamities and of the corruption of governments, have determined to set forth in a solemn declaration the natural, unalienable, and sacred rights of man, in order that this declaration, being constantly before all the members of the social body, shall remind them continually of their rights and duties; in order that the acts of the legislative power, as well as those of the executive power, may be compared at any moment with the objects and purposes of all political institutions and may thus be more respected, and, lastly, in order that the grievances of the citizens, based hereafter upon simple and incontestable principles, shall tend to the maintenance of the constitution and redound to the happiness of all. Therefore the National Assembly recognizes and proclaims, in the presence and under the auspices of the Supreme Being, the following rights of man and of the citizen:

Articles:

1. Men are born and remain free and equal in rights. Social distinctions may be founded only upon the general good.

2. The aim of all political association is the preservation of the natural and imprescriptible rights of man. These

---

[1] Emancipation in France's colonies was short-lived; Napoleon Bonaparte reinstated slavery in 1802.

[2] Translation from "The French Revolution, 1789–1791," ed. James Harvey Robinson, in *Translations and Reprints from the Original Sources of European History*, 1894.

rights are liberty, property, security, and resistance to oppression.

3. The principle of all sovereignty resides essentially in the nation. No body nor individual may exercise any authority which does not proceed directly from the nation.

4. Liberty consists in the freedom to do everything which injures no one else; hence the exercise of the natural rights of each man has no limits except those which assure to the other members of the society the enjoyment of the same rights. These limits can only be determined by law.

5. Law can only prohibit such actions as are hurtful to society. Nothing may be prevented which is not forbidden by law, and no one may be forced to do anything not provided for by law.

6. Law is the expression of the general will. Every citizen has a right to participate personally, or through his representative, in its foundation. It must be the same for all, whether it protects or punishes. All citizens, being equal in the eyes of the law, are equally eligible to all dignities and to all public positions and occupations, according to their abilities, and without distinction except that of their virtues and talents.

7. No person shall be accused, arrested, or imprisoned except in the cases and according to the forms prescribed by law. Anyone soliciting, transmitting, executing, or causing to be executed, any arbitrary order, shall be punished. But any citizen summoned or arrested in virtue of the law shall submit without delay, as resistance constitutes an offense.

8. The law shall provide for such punishments only as are strictly and obviously necessary, and no one shall suffer punishment except it be legally inflicted in virtue of a law passed and promulgated before the commission of the offense.

9. As all persons are held innocent until they shall have been declared guilty, if arrest shall be deemed indispensable, all harshness not essential to the securing of the prisoner's person shall be severely repressed by law.

10. No one shall be disquieted on account of his opinions, including his religious views, provided their manifestation does not disturb the public order established by law.

11. The free communication of ideas and opinions is one of the most precious of the rights of man. Every citizen may, accordingly, speak, write, and print with freedom, but shall be responsible for such abuses of this freedom as shall be defined by law.

12. The security of the rights of man and of the citizen requires public military forces. These forces are, therefore, established for the good of all and not for the personal advantage of those to whom they shall be intrusted.

13. A common contribution is essential for the maintenance of the public forces and for the cost of administration. This should be equitably distributed among all the citizens in proportion to their means.

14. All the citizens have a right to decide, either personally or by their representatives, as to the necessity of the public contribution; to grant this freely; to know to what uses it is put; and to fix the proportion, the mode of assessment and of collection and the duration of the taxes.

15. Society has the right to require of every public agent an account of his administration.

16. A society in which the observance of the law is not assured, nor the separation of powers defined, has no constitution at all.

17. Since property is an inviolable and sacred right, no one shall be deprived thereof except where public necessity, legally determined, shall clearly demand it, and then only on condition that the owner shall have been previously and equitably indemnified.

"The Rights of Woman" in America

Though it was in London that the "bluestockings" became famous in the 1790s, the early response to the ideas put forward in Olympe de Gouges's 1791 "Declaration of the Rights of Woman" and Mary Wollstonecraft's 1792 *A Vindication of the Rights of Woman* may well have been (as political historian Eileen Hunt Botting has suggested) more positive in the United States than it was in Britain. The first American edition of Wollstonecraft's book was published in 1792, and by 1794 three more editions had appeared, the *Lady's Magazine* in Philadelphia had published substantial excerpts from the book, and Wollstonecraft's ideas had been widely discussed in newspapers. The impact of these ideas in 1790s America is shown here in excerpts from a 1792 letter by Annis Boudinot Stockton (an accomplished poet and a strong supporter of the American Revolution) and from an anonymous 1795 poem "by a lady" published in a Philadelphia weekly newspaper.

By century's end, however, American opinion had become less receptive to the ideas of writers such as de Gouges and Wollstonecraft. Wollstonecraft died in 1797 and her reputation suffered because her husband, William Godwin, published a scandalous biography about her private life. The reaction against Jacobin excesses in France following The Terror made revolutionary ideas in general suspect in many quarters, while revolutionary ideas about gender were to a large extent being damped down by a growing cult of sentiment. It would not be until much later in the nineteenth century that Wollstonecraft's ideas would inspire significant numbers of American women, including literary giant Margaret Fuller, to begin to press for revolutionary change.

from ANNIS BOUDINOT STOCKTON, LETTER TO HER DAUGHTER [JULIA STOCKTON RUSH], 22 MARCH 1793

My dear Julia,
I have been engaged these two days with reading the rights of women, which I never could procure before, though it has been much longer in the neighborhood. I have been musing upon the subject over my solitary fire till I took up the resolution to give you my sentiments upon it though I suppose it is an old thing with you—I wonder you never sent me your critique—I am much pleased with her strength of reasoning, and her sentiment in general—but think that she like many other great geniuses—establish an hypothesis and lay such weight upon it as to cause the superstructure to destroy the foundation. ... I have always contended that the education of women was not made a matter of that importance, which it ought to be—but we see that error daily correcting—and in this country, the empire of reason is not monopolized by men; there is great pains taken to improve our sex, and store their minds with that knowledge best adapted to make them useful in the situation that their creator has placed them—and we do not often see those efforts opposed by the other sex, but rather disposed to assist them by every means in their power, and men of sense generally prefer such women, as Companions through life—The state of society may be different in Europe from what it is here in America—but from the observation I have been able to make in my own country, I do not think any of that slavish obedience exists, that she talks so much of—I think the women have their equal right of everything, Latin and Greek excepted. And I believe women of the most exalted minds, and the most improved understanding, will be most likely to practice that conciliating mode of conduct, which she seems to condemn, as blind obedience, and slavish submission, to the caprice of an arbitrary tyrant, which character she seems to apply to men as a sex ... you know that it is a favourite tenet with me, that there is no sex in soul—I believe it as firmly as I do my existence—but at the same time I do not think that the sexes were made to be independent of each other—I believe that our creator intended us for different walks in life—and that it takes equal powers of mind, and understanding, properly to fulfil the duties that he has marked out for us—as it does for the other sex, to gain knowledge of the arts and sciences, and if our education was the same, our improvement would be the same—but there is no occasion for exactly the same education. I think we may draw the conclusion that there is no sex in soul, from the following illustrations—that there are many men, that have been taught, and have *not* obtained any great degree of knowledge in the

circle of the sciences—and that there *have* been women who have excelled in every branch, when they have had an opportunity of instruction, and I have no doubt if those advantages were oftener to occur, we should see more instances. …

[S]ome of her expressions are by far, too strong for my ideas—but *she* writes like a philosopher, and *I* think as a novice—yet to sum up my poor judgement upon this wonderful book, I do really think a great deal of instruction may be gathered from it—and I am sure that no one can read it, but they may find something or other, that will correct their conduct and enlarge their ideas. …

Adieu my love, may heaven bless you and yours and protect you this night, prays your ever affectionate

    mother A Stockton—

from ANONYMOUS ("A LADY"), *THE PHILADELPHIA MINERVA* (17 OCTOBER 1795)

Man boasts the noble cause
  Nor yields supine to laws
Tyrants ordain;
Let woman have a sphere
5 Nor yield to slavish fear,
  Her equal rights declare,
  And well maintain.
  …

Let snarling critics frown,
  Their maxims I disown,
10 Their ways detest;
By man, your tyrant lord,
  Females, no more be awed.
Let freedom's sacred word
  Inspire your breast.

The Haitian Revolution

The latter half of the eighteenth century saw numerous slave insurrections in colonial holdings throughout the West Indies and South America, notably in Panama, Jamaica, Surinam, and Guyana. But the only successful revolution took place in Saint-Domingue, the French colony that would later become Haiti. Beginning in 1791 and ending in 1804, the Haitian Revolution spanned thirteen years and led to the foundation of a black state free from slavery. In America, the Haitian Revolution divided opinion sharply. For a majority of white Americans the revolution was a source of considerable concern. Southern enslavers and their supporters feared that similar events would occur on their plantations—and many whites who had no fondness for slavery shared to some degree a fear of the instability that inevitably accompanied revolutionary change. As former plantation owners fled Haiti for the United States, they fanned the flames of fear. During the early stages of the revolution, American governments provided hundreds of thousands of dollars in assistance to the Haitian plantation owners as they tried to quell the rebellion, and to white Haitians who fled the island to take refuge in the United States. The American government also sought to undermine the new nation of Haiti after the revolution had finally succeeded; with the support of Congress, the Jefferson administration refused to grant diplomatic recognition to the Haitian government, and in 1806 they placed a trade embargo on Haiti.

Black Americans, on the other hand, together with many white abolitionists, were supportive and saw the conflict as further proof that societies built on slavery were inherently unstable. Haiti became a source of hope to enslaved people across the world, and to black resistance in America particularly. It continued to be a source of inspiration throughout the nineteenth century. As Frederick Douglass said in 1893, "Until [Haiti] spoke no Christian nation had abolished Negro slavery. Until she spoke no Christian nation had given to the world an organized effort to abolish slavery. Until she spoke the slave ship, followed by hungry sharks, greedy to devour the dead and dying slaves flung overboard to feed them, ploughed in peace the South Atlantic, painting the sea with the Negro's blood."

Toussaint Louverture, Proclamation, 29 August 1793

Beginning in the autumn of 1791, a leader of the rebel army named Toussaint Bréda started living in the mountains on the west coast of Saint-Domingue among a group of formerly enslaved soldiers leagued with the Spanish and waging a guerilla war against the French colonial authorities and slaveholders. On 29 August 1793 at a fortification named Camp Turel, Bréda announced himself to the world under a different name, Toussaint Louverture, declaring at the same time his determination to free the enslaved people of Saint-Domingue. Scholars believe that Louverture had had advance knowledge of the intention of the French representative Léger Félicité Sonthonax to announce the abolition of slavery in Saint-Domingue on that very same day. Most historians believe that Louverture intended this brief statement to deflect support away from Sonthonax—a white newcomer from France—and instead to Louverture himself, a black leader who shared their interests.

Brothers and friends, I am Toussaint Louverture; perhaps my name has made itself known to you. I have undertaken vengeance. I want Liberty and Equality to reign in St Domingue. I am working to make that happen. Unite yourselves to us, brothers, and fight with us for the same cause.

Your very humble and obedient servant, Toussaint Louverture,

General of the armies of the king,[1] for the public good

Toussaint Louverture displaying a copy of the Haitian Constitution, 1801 (with the apparent blessing of the Catholic Church). The document was in many ways paradoxical; Louverture proclaimed a Constitution framed as if Haiti were an independent state, even though it was officially still a colony of France; the Constitution abolished slavery, but required that farmhands not leave their domicile in search of employment elsewhere; it purportedly guaranteed freedom and security for all, but its provisions left almost all power ultimately in the hands of the governor—"Citizen Toussaint Louverture."

from Jean-Jacques Dessalines, "Liberty or Death. Proclamation. Jean-Jacques Dessalines, Governor General, to the People of Hayti"[2] (1804)

When Haiti became an independent country, Jean-Jacques Dessalines (1758–1806) declared himself the state's governor general-for-life; he then ruled as emperor of Haiti until his assassination in 1806. One of the earliest state documents printed by the new country was his

---

[1] *king* Likely a reference to the Spanish king Charles IV (r. 1788–1808); the rebel fighters were allied with the Spanish at this point in the Revolution.

[2] This anonymous translation from the French appeared in 1804 in several American papers; it appears here as it did in the *Connecticut Herald*. See Writ's account of Patrick Henry's "Liberty or Death" speech, above.

"Liberty or Death" speech, excerpted below. In part, the speech is offered as a justification for a series of massacres of the remaining white population of Haiti that Dessalines had ordered in the early months of 1804.

Crimes, the most atrocious, such as were until then unheard of, and would cause nature to shudder, have been perpetrated. The measure was overheaped. At length the hour of vengeance has arrived, and the implacable enemies of the rights of man have suffered the punishment due to their crimes.

My arm, raised over their heads, has too long delayed to strike. At that signal, which the justice of God has urged, your hands, righteously armed, have brought the axe upon the ancient tree of slavery and prejudices. In vain had time, and more especially the infernal politics of Europeans, surrounded it with triple brass; you have stripped it of its armour; you have placed it upon your hearts, that you may become (like your natural enemies) cruel and merciless. Like an overflowing mighty torrent that tears down all opposition, your vengeful fury has carried away everything in its impetuous course. Thus perish all tyrants over innocence, all oppressors of mankind!

What then? bent for many ages under an iron yoke; the sport of the passions of men, of their injustice, and of the caprice of fortune; mutilated victims of the cupidity of white Frenchmen? after having fattened with our toils these insatiate blood-suckers, with a patience and resignation unexampled, we should again have seen that sacrilegious horde make an attempt upon our destruction, without any distinction of sex or age; and we, men without energy, of no virtue, or no delicate sensibility, should not we have plunged in their breast the dagger of desperation? Where is that vile Haytian, so unworthy of his regeneration, who thinks he has not accomplished the decrees of the Eternal, by exterminating these bloody thirsty tigers! If there is one, let him fly; indignant nature discards him from our bosom; let him hide his shame far from hence; the air we breathe is not suited to his gross organs; it is the pure air of Liberty, august and triumphant.

Yes, we have rendered to these true cannibals war for war, crime for crime, outrage for outrage.

Yes, I have saved my country—I have avenged America.[1] The avowal I make of it in the face of earth and heaven, constitutes my pride and my glory. Of what consequence to me is the opinion which contemporary and future generations will pronounce upon my conduct? I have performed my duty; I enjoy my own approbation; for me that is sufficient. But what do I say? The preservation of my unfortunate brothers, the testimony of my own conscience are not my only recompence: I have seen two classes of men, born to cherish, assist and succour one another—mixed, in a word, and blended together—crying for vengeance, and disputing the honour of the first blow. ...

[S]ooner or later Divine Justice will unchain on earth some mighty winds, above the weakness of the vulgar, for the destruction and terror of the wicked; tremble, tyrants, usurpers, scourges of the new world! our daggers are sharpened; your punishment is ready! sixty thousand men, equipped, inured to war, obedient to my orders, burn to offer a new sacrifice to the manes of their assassinated brothers. Let that nation come who may be mad and daring enough to attack me. Already at its approach, the irritated genius[2] of Hayti, rising out of the bosom of the ocean, appears; his menacing aspect throws the waves into commotion, excites tempests, and with his mighty hand disperses ships, or dashes them in pieces; to his formidable voice the laws of nature pay obedience; diseases, plague, famine, conflagration, poison, are his constant attendants. But why calculate on the assistance of the climate and of the elements? Have I forgot that I command a people of no common cast, brought up in adversity, whose audacious daring frowns at the obstacles and increases by dangers? Let them come, then, these homicidal Cohorts! I wait for them with firmness and with a steady eye. I abandon to them freely the sea-shore, and the places where cities have existed; but woe to those who may approach too near the mountains! It were better for them that the sea received them into its profound abyss, than to be devoured by the anger of the children of Hayti.

---

1   *America* Dessalines is referring to all the colonies in the Americas (North, South, and Central).

2   *genius* Guardian spirit.

"War and Death to Tyrants!" this is my motto;
"Liberty! Independence!" this is our rallying cry

Generals, officers, soldiers, a little unlike him who has preceded me, the ex-general Toussaint Louverture, I have been faithful to the promise which I made to you when I took up arms against tyranny, and whilst the last spark of life remains in me I shall keep my oath. Never again shall a colonist or an European set his foot upon this territory with the title of master or proprietor. This resolution shall henceforward form the fundamental basis of our constitution.

Should other chiefs, after me, by pursuing a conduct diametrically opposite to mine, dig their own graves and those of their species, you will have to accuse only the law of destiny which shall have taken me away from the happiness and welfare of my fellow-citizens. May my successors follow the path I shall have traced out for them! It is the system best adapted for consolidating their power; it is the highest homage they can render to my memory.

As it is derogatory to my character and my dignity to punish the innocent for the crimes of the guilty, a handful of whites, commendable by the religion they have always professed, and who have besides taken the oath to live with us in the woods, have experienced my clemency. I order that the sword respect them, and that they be unmolested.

I recommend anew and order to all the generals of department, etc. to grant succours, encouragement, and protection, to all neutral and friendly nations who may wish to establish commercial relations in this island.

The Governor-General
(Signed) Dessalines
A true Copy. The Sec'y-General
Juste Chanlatte

Gabriel's Rebellion and Other Rebellions by Enslaved Americans

If the American and French Revolutions helped inspire the Haitian Revolution, so too did the Haitian Revolution help inspire rebellions and revolutions elsewhere—including revolutions in Mexico (1810–21) and other Spanish-controlled territories, and several rebellions by enslaved blacks in the United States—perhaps most notably Gabriel's Rebellion in Virginia in 1800. Gabriel and his fellow rebels—including his brother Solomon, who like Gabriel was an enslaved blacksmith—worked with others enslaved in and around the state capital, Richmond, to formulate a plan of rebellion; their hope was that if they could capture the state's governor, James Monroe, they would be able to demand the abolition of slavery in return for their hostage. The plan was discovered before they could put it into effect; Gabriel and 25 others were hanged.

Newspaper Reports

The newspaper reports below give a sense of the ways in which Gabriel's Rebellion and other rebellions of enslaved blacks in the newly formed United States were seen as linked to Toussaint Louverture and the Haitian Revolution, as well as to the French Revolution (and, by extension, Frenchmen).

from the *Virginia Argus*
(Richmond, Virginia, 3 October 1800)

Was not the slave *Gabriel* of Virginia, as fit an object for negociation, and as fit for command as *Toussaint*—unhappily it is only the difference of situation which entitles Toussaint to a present of *three carriages* from a British agent in Philadelphia, and marks the slave of Prosser, an object for the gibbet.

from THE *FEDERAL GALAXY*
(BRATTLEBORO, VERMONT, 11 OCTOBER 1800)

Fredericksburg, Sept. 23
Extract of a letter to the Editor

"I left Richmond yesterday morning, all was confusion and alarm. The minutiae of the conspiracy which has been detected have not been detailed to the public, and perhaps, through a mistaken notion of prudence and policy, will not be detailed in the Richmond papers. Indeed, fear seems to have put an imprimateur[1] on the press.

"But as I conceive it a matter of great moment that the origin of this evil should be known, I now communicate to you such circumstances as I was enabled, by much industry, to collect from the most authentic sources.

"On the Saturday night when the deluge of rain fell, the plot was to have been carried into execution. One thousand negroes were to have entered the town in three directions with fire and sword. The penitentiary house, which the executive had made a magazine[2] of a few days before, and of which the conspirators were apprized, was to have been seized on in the first place, then the treasury, then the mills, and then the bridge across James river. The first would have supplied them arms and ammunition for many thousand men, the second with money, the third with bread, and the fourth would have enabled them to let in their friends and keep out their enemies from the south side of James river.

"The metropolis being in their possession, which in a few hours would have been the case, a proclamation was to have been issued, by which the negroes from the country and the southern states would have been invited to rally round their standard. In less than one week they might have calculated on 50,000 men in arms. For in addition to friends of their colour, they expected that every Frenchman would join them, every negro and mulatto,[3] and many of the most redoubtable democrats in the state. It came out in evidence on the trial of the six who were condemned on Thursday, that in the general massacre of the white males which was determined on, not a Frenchman was to be touched. It also appeared on the trial, that two Frenchmen had planned the plot, and that the General Gabriel, who is not yet caught had procured it from them. The names of those Frenchmen were not known, when I left town, but it is probable that the criminals will make some further discoveries[4] under the gallows, and that such information may be at length obtained as will enable us to drag forth those diabolical monsters from their lurking places, and bring them to condign[5] punishment. ..."

October 1
Letters are received in town from Richmond which mention new discoveries relative to the intended revolt of the negroes. A plan was systemically laid for a general insurrection throughout the state, and the most brutal acts were to have been perpetrated. Several respectable characters, obnoxious to these wretches, were to be singled out for their barbarity in the massacre. Two of the most distinguished beauties of Richmond were to be devoted to the filthy embraces of the commander in chief, Gabriel, and the white women generally were to be preserved for rewards to his followers. ...

from Robert Sutcliff, *Travels in Some Parts of North America in the Years 1804, 1805, and 1806* (1815)

This report of a statement given c. 1804 to a lawyer (who in turn reported it to an English traveler) by one of those accused of plotting a rebellion has often been quoted without attribution in connection with Gabriel's Rebellion of 1800. That it in fact dates from a few years later does not make it any less notable as a statement of principle.

---

[1]   *imprimateur*   Usually refers to an official license to print; here, it suggests "seal."

[2]   *magazine*   Storehouse where ammunition and weaponry are kept.

[3]   *mulatto*   Term, now considered offensive, for people of both black and white ancestry.

[4]   *make ... discoveries*   Give up some more information.

[5]   *condign*   Deserved, appropriate.

I pursued my way to Richmond [Virginia] in the mail stage,[1] through a beautiful country, but clouded and debased by negro slavery. At the house where I breakfasted, which is called the Bowling Green, I was told that the owner had in his possession 200 slaves. In one field near the house, planted with tobacco, I counted nearly 20 women and children, picking grubs from the plants. In the afternoon I passed by a field in which several poor slaves had lately been executed, on the charge of having an intention to rise against their masters. A lawyer who was present at their trials at Richmond informed me that, on one of them being asked what he had to say to the court in his defence, he replied in a manly tone of voice, "I have nothing more than what General Washington would have had to offer, had he been taken by the British and put to trial by them. I have adventured my life in endeavoring to obtain the liberty of my countrymen, and I beg, as a favour, that I may be immediately led to execution. I know that you have pre-determined to shed my blood; why then all this mockery of a trial?"

---

[1] *mail stage*   Stage coach carrying mail as well as passengers.

Judith Sargent Murray

1751 – 1820

"I think," writes Judith Sargent Murray in her first published essay on female education, "to teach young minds to aspire, ought to be the ground work of education[.] … Ambition is a noble principle, which properly directed, may be productive of the most valuable consequences." At a time when such aspirations, especially among women, were more likely to be seen as vices than as positive attributes, Murray boldly pronounced them to be laudable, encouraging girls and women to embrace ambitions beyond those of marriage and feminine domesticity, and to have pride in themselves and their mental capabilities. Aside from her essays, which comprise her most enduring work, Murray was also a poet, playwright, and religious writer. Her 1790 essay "On the Equality of the Sexes" (which preceded both Olympe de Gouges's *Declaration of the Rights of Woman and the Female Citizen* and Mary Wollstonecraft's *A Vindication of the Rights of Woman*) broke new ground by extending the Enlightenment hope for a rational society, and the American hope for an equal one, into the sphere of gender.

Born in Gloucester, Massachusetts, in 1751, Judith Sargent was the eldest child of Winthrop Sargent and Judith Saunders Sargent. The family belonged to the merchant class; their wealth stemmed from the marine trade. Judith showed exceptional intellectual promise from a young age, and while it was not possible at the time for girls to receive a formal education equivalent to that of boys, her parents ensured that she and her brother (who was preparing for Harvard) received the same level of home tutorship in subjects such as Latin and Greek. Beyond this she studied voraciously on her own, and became exceptionally well-read; nevertheless, she always regretted her lack of a formal education. As she later lamented in a letter, "It was the mode to confine the female intellect within the narrowest bounds."

At the age of eighteen, Judith married John Stevens, a prosperous sea merchant. The marriage was not founded on love; in her future writings, Murray would press for the broadening of respectable women's options beyond marriage and the raising of a family.

Murray began composing poems with some degree of seriousness in her early twenties, submitting them for publication in Boston's *The Gentleman's and Lady's Town and Country Magazine* in the 1780s. In 1782 she also wrote a catechism for Universalism, the religion to which she and her parents had (somewhat controversially) converted in the previous decade, and to which she became highly devoted. With the heightening of the American Revolutionary War, Murray became invested in the dominant spirit of liberation, and highly interested in issues related to independence and human rights. Her first secular prose publication was an essay on female education entitled "Desultory Thoughts upon the Utility of Encouraging a Degree of Self-Complacency, Especially in Female Bosoms" (1784), which was published under the pen name "Constantia." (The use of pen names was very common at the time, especially among women, who, if they published, rarely did so under their own names.) Here Murray laid the groundwork on which her future career would be built, embracing the principle of intellectual equality of the sexes, and drawing attention to the need for women to be educated and taught to value their selves.

In 1786, John Stevens died in disgrace in the West Indies (having gone there to escape debtor's prison); Judith resolved to remain unmarried and to commit the rest of her life to the Universalist church. Two years later, she married John Murray, the minister who had established the first Universalist congregation in Gloucester. Unlike her first marriage, her union with Murray was based firmly on love and mutual intellectual admiration.

In 1789, Murray submitted a poem, "Lines Occasioned by the Death of an Infant," to *The Massachusetts Magazine*, a work occasioned by her grief over the miscarriage of her son and the painful illness she suffered thereafter. The following year saw the publication of "On the Equality of the Sexes" (which she had first drafted over a decade previously) in the same magazine. The piece is in many ways a natural development of Enlightenment ideas concerning the seat of reason in the soul, the division of body and soul, and the pre-eminence of the latter over the former. Murray argued against the then-common view that women were by nature intellectually inferior to men, and therefore best-suited only to helpful domesticity and frivolous amusements. She was highly gratified when Wollstonecraft's *Vindication*, which expressed similar ideas, was released two years later. In 1792 Murray took on a new pen name, "The Gleaner," under which she published many more essays on politics and literary criticism, two plays, and the serialized novel *The Story of Margaretta*, which appeared in 1798. In that same year she acknowledged the work of "The Gleaner" to be that of "Constantia."

The Murrays had one daughter, Julia Maria, to whom they endeavored to give the best education possible. Murray published little after 1798, focusing most of her efforts on caring for her husband and editing his writings, which she helped complete and publish after his death in 1815. Julia married a Southern landowner, Adam Bingaman, and in 1818 Murray joined them on Bingaman's Natchez, Mississippi plantation, where she died two years later. For many generations after her death Murray was almost entirely forgotten. The multi-volume *American Cyclopedia* of 1866 devotes a half-page to her husband ("the father of Universalism in America") but makes no mention of her—and the same is true of histories and anthologies of American literature of the early and mid-twentieth century. Only in the 1970s, with the rise of feminist scholarship, did her ground-breaking contributions begin to be again acknowledged. As Murray's personal correspondence makes clear, she equivocated over the issue of whether or not the principle of human equality should apply to races other than her own, or even to white women of the laboring class; her limited vision in matters such as these inevitably colors the way we read her work today. But Murray remains a figure of vital importance to the spreading of the idea that women are equal to men, and deserving of the same education and the same opportunities.

NOTE ON THE TEXT: The text of "On the Equality of the Sexes" is based on the first version printed in *The Massachusetts Magazine, or, Monthly Museum of Knowledge and Rational Entertainment* for March–April 1790. Spelling and punctuation have been modernized in accordance with the practices of this anthology.

⌘ ⌘ ⌘

On the Equality of the Sexes

PART I

That minds are not alike, full well I know,
This truth each day's experience will show;
To heights surprising some great spirits soar,
With inborn strength mysterious depths explore;
5   Their eager gaze surveys the path of light,
Confessed it stood to Newton's[1] piercing sight.

Deep science, like a bashful maid retires,
And but° the *ardent* breast her worth inspires;   °only
By perseverance the coy fair is won,
10 And Genius, led by Study, wears the crown.
But some there are who wish not to improve,
Who never can the path of knowledge love,
Whose souls almost with the dull body one,
With anxious care each mental pleasure shun;
15 Weak is the leveled, enervated mind,
And but while here to vegetate designed.
The torpid spirit mingling with its clod,
Can scarcely boast its origin from God;

---

[1]   *Newton*   Sir Isaac Newton (1642–1727), English mathematician and physicist who experimented with the refraction of light.

Stupidly dull—they move progressing on—
20   They eat, and drink, and all their work is done.
While others, emulous of sweet applause,
Industrious seek for each event a cause,
Tracing the hidden springs whence knowledge flows,
Which nature all in beauteous order shows.
25   Yet cannot I their sentiments imbibe,[1]
Who this distinction to the sex ascribe,
As if a woman's form must needs enroll°   *incorporate*
A weak, a servile, an inferior soul;
And that the guise of man must still proclaim,
30   Greatness of mind, and him, to be the same.
Yet as the hours revolve fair proofs arise,
Which the bright wreath of growing fame supplies;
And in past times some men have *sunk so low*,
That female records nothing *less* can show.
35   But imbecility is still confined,
And by the lordly sex to us consigned;
They rob us of the power t'improve,
And then declare we only trifles love;
Yet haste the era, when the world shall know
40   That such distinctions only dwell below;
The soul unfettered, to no sex confined,
Was for the abodes of cloudless day designed.
     Meantime we emulate their manly fires,
Though erudition all their thoughts inspires,
45   Yet nature with *equality* imparts,
And *noble passions*, swell e'en *female hearts*.

Is it upon mature consideration we adopt the idea
that nature is thus partial[2] in her distributions? Is it
indeed a fact that she hath yielded to one half of the
human species so unquestionable a mental superiority? I know that to both sexes elevated understandings,
and the reverse, are common. But, suffer[3] me to ask,
in what the minds of females are so notoriously deficient, or unequal. May not the intellectual powers be
ranged under these four heads—imagination, reason,
memory and judgment? The province of imagination
hath long since been surrendered up to us, and we have
been crowned undoubted sovereigns of the regions of
fancy.[4] Invention is perhaps the most arduous effort of
the mind; this branch of imagination hath been particularly ceded to us, and we have been time out of
mind invested with that creative faculty. Observe the
variety of fashions (here I bar the contemptuous smile)
which distinguish and adorn the female world; how
continually are they changing, insomuch that they
almost render the wise man's assertion problematical,
and we are ready to say, *there is something new under
the sun*.[5] Now what a playfulness, what an exuberance
of fancy, what strength of inventive imagination, doth
this continual variation discover? Again, it hath been
observed, that if the turpitude[6] of the conduct of our
sex hath been ever so enormous, so extremely ready
are we, that the very first thought presents us with an
apology so plausible as to produce our actions even
in an amiable light. Another instance of our creative
powers is our talent for slander; how ingenious are we
at inventive scandal? What a formidable story can we
in a moment fabricate merely from the force of a prolific imagination? How many reputations, in the fertile
brain of a female, have been utterly despoiled? How
industrious are we at improving[7] a hint? Suspicion how
easily do we convert into conviction, and conviction,
embellished by the power of eloquence, stalks abroad
to the surprise and confusion of unsuspecting innocence. Perhaps it will be asked if I furnish these facts
as instances of excellency in our sex. Certainly not; but
as proofs of a creative faculty, of a lively imagination.
Assuredly great activity of mind is thereby discovered,
and was this activity properly directed, what beneficial
effects would follow.

Is the needle and kitchen sufficient to employ the
operations of a soul thus organized? I should conceive
not. Nay, it is a truth that those very departments leave
the intelligent principle vacant, and at liberty for speculation. Are we deficient in reason? We can only reason
from what we know, and if an opportunity of acquiring
knowledge hath been denied us, the inferiority of our
sex cannot fairly be deduced from thence. Memory, I
believe, will be allowed us in common, since everyone's
experience must testify that a loquacious old woman is
as frequently met with as a communicative old man;

---

[1]   *imbibe* Swallow; accept.

[2]   *partial* Biased.

[3]   *suffer* Allow.

[4]   *fancy* Imagination; fancifulness.

[5]   *there is … the sun* See Ecclesiastes 1.9: "and there is no new
thing under the sun."

[6]   *turpitude* Baseness.

[7]   *improving* Intensifying or exaggerating.

their subjects are alike drawn from the fund of other times, and the transactions of their youth, or of maturer life, entertain, or perhaps fatigue you, in the evening of their lives. "But our judgment is not so strong—we do not distinguish so well." Yet it may be questioned, from what doth this superiority, in this determining faculty of the soul, proceed? May we not trace its source in the difference of education, and continued advantages? Will it be said that the judgment of a male of two years old is more sage[1] than that of a female's of the same age? I believe the reverse is generally observed to be true. But from that period what partiality! How is the one exalted, and the other depressed, by the contrary modes of education which are adopted! The one is taught to aspire, and the other is early confined and limited. As their years increase, the sister must be wholly domesticated, while the brother is led by the hand through all the flowery paths of science. Grant that their minds are by nature equal, yet who shall wonder at the *apparent* superiority, if indeed custom becomes *second nature*; nay if it taketh place of nature, and that it doth the experience of each day will evince.

At length arrived at womanhood, the uncultivated fair one feels a void which the employments allotted her are by no means capable of filling. What can she do? To books she may not apply; or if she doth, *to those only of the novel kind,*[2] lest she merit the appellation of a *learned lady*; and what ideas have been affixed to this term, the observation of many can testify. Fashion, scandal, and sometimes what is still more reprehensible, are then called in to her relief; and who can say to what lengths the liberties she takes may proceed? Meantime she herself is most unhappy; she feels the want[3] of a cultivated mind. Is she single, she in vain seeks to fill up time from sexual[4] employments or amusements. Is she united to a person whose soul nature made equal to her own? Education hath set him so far above her that in those entertainments which are productive of such rational felicity, she is not qualified to accompany him. She experiences a mortifying consciousness of inferiority which embitters every enjoyment. Doth the person to whom her adverse fate hath consigned her possess a mind incapable of improvement, she is equally wretched in being so closely connected with an individual whom she cannot but despise.

Now, was she[5] permitted the same instructors as her brother (with an eye however to their particular departments), for the employment of a rational mind an ample field would be opened. In astronomy she might catch a glimpse of the immensity of the Deity, and thence she would form amazing conceptions of the august and supreme Intelligence. In geography she would admire Jehovah in the midst of his benevolence; thus adapting this globe to the various wants and amusements of its inhabitants. In natural philosophy[6] she would adore the infinite majesty of heaven, clothed in condescension;[7] and as she traversed the reptile world, she would hail the goodness of a creating God. A mind, thus filled, would have little room for the trifles with which our sex are, with too much justice, accused of amusing themselves, and they would thus be rendered fit companions for those who should one day wear them as their crown.[8] Fashions, in their variety, would then give place to conjectures, which might perhaps conduce to the improvement of the literary world; and there would be no leisure for slander or detraction. Reputation would not then be blasted, but serious speculations would occupy the lively imaginations of the sex. Unnecessary visits would be precluded, and that custom would only be indulged by way of relaxation, or to answer the demands of consanguinity and friendship. Females would become discreet,[9] their judgments would be invigorated, and their partners for life being circumspectly chosen, an unhappy Hymen[10] would then be as rare as is now the reverse.

---

[1] *sage* Wise.

[2] *those … novel kind* Throughout much of the eighteenth and early nineteenth centuries, novels were considered by many to be light and unserious in nature, appropriate only for women readers; moreover, many criticized novels as indulgent and morally unsound escapism.

[3] *want* Lack.

[4] *sexual* I.e., appropriate to her sex; feminine.

[5] *was she* If she were.

[6] *natural philosophy* I.e., the sciences.

[7] *condescension* Indifference toward one's own superiority.

[8] *those who … their crown* See Proverbs 12.4: "A virtuous woman is a crown to her husband." The phrase was used in a contemporary illustration which advised women on their duties, and to "keep within compass"; see the color plates in this anthology.

[9] *discreet* Prudent.

[10] *Hymen* In Greek mythology, the god of marriage; thus, marriage itself.

Will it be urged that those acquirements would supersede our domestic duties? I answer that every requisite in female economy[1] is easily attained; and with truth I can add that, when once attained, they require no further *mental attention*. Nay, while we are pursuing the needle, or the superintendency of the family, I repeat, that our minds are at full liberty for reflection; that imagination may exert itself in full vigor; and that if a just foundation is early laid, our ideas will then be worthy of rational beings. If we were industrious we might easily find time to arrange them upon paper, or should avocations[2] press too hard for such an indulgence, the hours allotted for conversation would at least become more refined and rational. Should it still be vociferated, "Your domestic employments are sufficient"—I would calmly ask, is it reasonable that a candidate for immortality, for the joys of heaven, an intelligent being who is to spend an eternity in contemplating the works of Deity, should at present be so degraded as to be allowed no other ideas than those which are suggested by the mechanism of a pudding, or the sewing the seams of a garment? Pity that all such censurers of female improvement do not go one step further and deny their future existence; to be consistent they surely ought.

Yes, ye lordly, ye haughty sex, our souls are by nature *equal* to yours; the same breath of God animates, enlivens, and invigorates us; and that we are not fallen lower than yourselves, let those witness who have greatly towered above the various discouragements by which they have been so heavily oppressed; and though I am unacquainted with the list of celebrated characters on either side, yet from the observations I have made in the contracted circle in which I have moved, I dare confidently believe that, from the commencement of time to the present day, there hath been as many females as males who, by the *mere force of natural powers*, have merited the crown of applause; who, *thus unassisted*, have seized the wreath of fame. I know there are [those] who assert that, as the animal[3] powers of the one sex are superior, of course their mental faculties also must be stronger (thus attributing strength of mind to the transient organization of this earth-born

tenement[4]). But if this reasoning is just, man must be content to yield the palm[5] [to] many of the brute creation,[6] since by not a few of his brethren of the field he is far surpassed in bodily strength. Moreover, was this argument admitted, it would prove too much, for ocular demonstration evinceth that there are many robust masculine ladies and effeminate gentlemen. Yet I fancy that Mr. Pope,[7] though clogged with an enervated body, and distinguished by a diminutive stature, could nevertheless lay claim to greatness of soul; and perhaps there are many other instances which might be adduced to combat so unphilosophical an opinion. Do we not often see that when the clay-built tabernacle[8] is well nigh dissolved, when it is just ready to mingle with the parent soil, the immortal inhabitant aspires to and even attaineth heights the most sublime, and which were before wholly unexplored? Besides, were we to grant that animal strength proved anything, taking into consideration the accustomed impartiality of Nature, we should be induced to imagine that she had invested the female mind with superior strength as an equivalent for the bodily powers of man. But waiving this however palpable advantage, for *equality only* we wish to contend.

PART 2

I am aware that there are many passages in the sacred oracles which seem to give the advantage to the other sex, but I consider all these as wholly metaphorical. Thus David was a man after God's own heart,[9] yet see him enervated by his licentious passions! Behold him

---

1   *economy* Household management.

2   *avocations* Employments.

3   *animal* I.e., physical.

4   *this earth-born tenement* I.e., the body.

5   *palm* Honor.

6   *the brute creation* I.e., the realm of non-human animals.

7   *Mr. Pope* Alexander Pope (1688–1744), English poet, highly regarded throughout the eighteenth century; Pope had a spinal deformity that was likely caused by a form of spinal tuberculosis, and also suffered numerous chronic illnesses as an adult.

8   *tabernacle* House or dwelling-place; in other words, the body, as the dwelling-place of the soul.

9   *Thus David ... own heart* See 1 Samuel 13.14: "The Lord hath sought him a man after his own heart." David was the second king of Israel, portrayed in the Old Testament.

following Uriah to the death,[1] and show me wherein could consist the immaculate Being's complacency. Listen to the curses which Job bestoweth upon the day of his nativity,[2] and tell me where is his perfection, where his patience—*literally* it existed not. David and Job were types[3] of him who was to come; and the superiority of man, as exhibited in scripture, being also emblematical, all arguments deduced from thence of course fall to the ground. The exquisite delicacy of the female mind proclaimeth the exactness of its texture, while its nice[4] sense of honor announceth its innate, its native grandeur. And indeed, in one respect, the preeminence seems to be tacitly allowed us, for after an education which limits and confines, and employments and recreations which naturally tend to enervate the body and debilitate the mind; after we have from early youth been adorned with ribbons and other gewgaws,[5] dressed out like the ancient victims previous to a sacrifice, being taught by the care of our parents in collecting the most showy materials that the ornamenting our exterior ought to be the principal object of our attention; after, I say, fifteen years thus spent, we are introduced into the world,[6] amid the united adulation of every beholder. Praise is sweet to the soul; we are immediately intoxicated by large draughts of flattery which, being plentifully administered, is to the pride of our hearts the most acceptable incense. It is expected that with the other sex we should commence immediate war, and that we should triumph over the machinations of the most artful. We must be constantly upon our guard; prudence and discretion must be our characteristics; and we must rise superior to, and obtain a complete victory over those who have been long adding to the native strength of their minds by an unremitted study of men and books, and who have, moreover, conceived from the loose characters which they have seen portrayed in the extensive variety of their reading a most contemptible opinion of the sex.

Thus unequal, we are, notwithstanding, forced to the combat, and the infamy which is consequent upon the smallest deviation in our conduct proclaims the high idea which was formed of our native strength; and thus, indirectly at least, is the preference acknowledged to be our due. And if we are allowed an equality of acquirement, let serious studies equally employ our minds, and we will bid our souls arise to equal strength. We will meet upon even ground, the despot man; we will rush with alacrity to the combat, and, crowned by success, we shall then answer the exalted expectations which are formed. Though sensibility,[7] soft compassion, and gentle commiseration are inmates in the female bosom, yet against every deep laid art, altogether fearless of the event, we will set them in array; for assuredly the wreath of victory will encircle the spotless brow. If we meet an equal, a sensible friend, we will reward him with the hand of amity, and through life we will be assiduous to promote his happiness; but from every deep laid scheme for our ruin, retiring into ourselves, amid the flowery paths of science, we will indulge in all the refined and sentimental pleasures of contemplation. And should it still be urged that the studies thus insisted upon would interfere with our more peculiar department,[8] I must further reply that *early hours*, and close application, will do wonders; and to her who is from the first dawn of reason taught to fill up time rationally, both the requisites will be easy.

I grant that niggard[9] fortune is too generally unfriendly to the mind; and that much of that valuable treasure, time, is necessarily expended upon the wants of the body; but it should be remembered that in embarrassed[10] circumstances our companions[11] have as little leisure for literary improvement as is afforded to us; for most certainly their provident care is at least

---

[1]   *Behold him … the death*   David arranged the death of Uriah the Hittite, so that he could marry Uriah's wife Bathsheba. See 2 Samuel 11.2–27.

[2]   *the curses … his nativity*   Job endured many earthly punishments at the hands of God, as a trial of his faith; though he remained faithful at the end, Job in his suffering cursed the day he was born. See Job 3; *nativity*   Birth.

[3]   *types*   Prefigurations, i.e., of Christ in the New Testament.

[4]   *nice*   Virtuous.

[5]   *gewgaws*   Ornaments.

[6]   *introduced into the world*   In polite society of the time, for a girl to be "brought out," usually in her late teens, meant she was considered to be marriageable and allowed to engage in social affairs, such as balls.

[7]   *sensibility*   Heightened emotional or aesthetic awareness.

[8]   *our more peculiar department*   I.e., the duties particular to female life.

[9]   *niggard*   Stingy.

[10]   *embarrassed*   Difficult.

[11]   *our companions*   I.e., men.

as requisite as our exertions. Nay, we have even more leisure for sedentary pleasures, as our avocations are more retired, much less laborious, and, as hath been observed, by no means require that avidity of attention which is proper to the employments of the other sex. In high life, or, in other words, where the parties are in possession of affluence, the objection respecting time is wholly obviated,[1] and of course falls to the ground; and it may also be repeated that many of those hours which are at present swallowed up in fashion and scandal might be redeemed, were we habituated to useful reflections. But in one respect, O ye arbiters of our fate! we confess that the superiority is indubitably yours; you are by nature formed for our protectors; we pretend not to vie with you in bodily strength; upon this point we will never contend for victory. Shield us then, we beseech you, from external evils, and in return *we* will transact *your* domestic affairs. Yes, *your*, for are you not equally interested in those matters with ourselves? Is not the elegancy of neatness as agreeable to your sight as to ours? Is not the well-flavored viand[2] equally delightful to your taste? And doth not your sense of hearing suffer as much from the discordant sounds prevalent in an ill-regulated family, produced by the voices of children and many *et ceteras*?

CONSTANTIA

By way of supplement to the foregoing pages, I subjoin the following extract from a letter, wrote to a friend in the December of 1780.

And now assist me, O thou genius of my sex, while I undertake the arduous task of endeavouring to combat that vulgar, that almost universal errour, which hath, it seems, enlisted even Mr. P—— under its banners. The superiority of your sex hath, I grant, been time out of mind esteemed a truth incontrovertible; in consequence of which persuasion, every plan of education hath been calculated to establish this favourite tenet. Not long since;[3] weak and presuming as I was, I amused myself with selecting some arguments from nature, reason, and experience, against this so generally received idea. I confess that to sacred testimonies I had

original spelling

not recourse. I held them to be merely metaphorical, and thus regarding them, I could not persuade myself that there was any propriety in bringing them to decide in this *very important debate*. However, as you, sir, confine yourself entirely to the sacred oracles, I mean to bend the whole of my artillery against those supposed proofs which you have from thence provided, and from which you have formed an intrenchment *apparently* so invulnerable. And first, to begin with our great progenitors;[4] but here, suffer me to premise, that it is for mental strength I mean to contend, for with respect to animal powers, I yield them undisputed to that sex which enjoys them in common with the lion, the tyger, and many other beasts of prey; therefore your observations respecting the *rib under the arm*,[5] *at a distance from the head*, &c. &c. in no sort militate against my view. Well, but the woman was first in the transgression.[6] Strange how blind *self love* renders you men; were you not wholly absorbed in a partial[7] admiration of your own abilities, you would long since have acknowledged the force of what I am now going to urge. It is true some ignoramuses have absurdly enough informed us that the beauteous fair of paradise,[8] was seduced from her obedience, by a malignant demon, *in the guise of a baleful serpent*; but we, who are better informed, know that the fallen spirit presented himself to her view, *a shining angel still*; for thus, saith the criticks in the Hebrew tongue, ought the word to be rendered.[9] Let us examine her motive— Hark! the seraph[10] declares that she shall attain a perfection of knowledge; for is there aught which is not comprehended under one or other of the terms *good*

original spelling

---

[1]   *obviated*   Made irrelevant.

[2]   *viand*   Meal.

[3]   *since*   Ago.

[4]   *our great progenitors*   Adam and Eve.

[5]   *the rib … the arm*   See Genesis 2.22: "And the rib, which the Lord God had taken from man, made he a woman, and brought her unto the man."

[6]   *the transgression*   I.e., eating the fruit of the tree of knowledge of good and evil, which was forbidden.

[7]   *partial*   Biased.

[8]   *the beauteous fair of paradise*   I.e., Eve.

[9]   *the fallen spirit … rendered*   The appropriate translation of *nachash*, the word used to describe what is generally referred to as the serpent in Genesis, has been much debated by biblical scholars; one possible translation is "shining one." The serpent is often understood to be Satan or Lucifer, who was once an angel; the name Lucifer, in Latin, means "light bringer."

[10]   *seraph*   Angel.

and *evil*. It doth not appear that she was governed by any one sensual appetite, but merely by a desire of adorning her mind; a laudable ambition fired her soul, and a thirst for knowledge impelled the predilection so fatal in its consequences. Adam could not plead the same deception; assuredly he was not deceived; nor ought we to admire his superior strength, or wonder at his sagacity, when we so often confess that example is much more influential than precept. His gentle partner stood before him, a melancholy instance of the direful effects of disobedience; he saw her not possessed of that wisdom which she had fondly hoped to obtain, but he beheld the once blooming female, disrobed of that innocence which had heretofore rendered her so lovely. To him, then, deception became impossible, as he had proof positive of the fallacy of the argument which the deceiver had suggested. What then could be his inducement to burst the barriers, and to fly directly in the face of that command, which *immediately* from the mouth of deity *he* had received, since, I say, he could not plead that fascinating stimulus, the accumulation of knowledge, as indisputable conviction was so visibly portrayed before him. What mighty cause impelled him to sacrifice myriads of beings yet unborn, and by one impious act, which *he saw* would be productive of such fatal effects, entail undistinguished ruin upon a race of beings which he was yet to produce? Blush, ye vaunters of fortitude, ye boasters of resolution, ye haughty lords of the creation; blush when ye remember that he was influenced by no other motive than a bare pusillanimous attachment to a woman! By sentiments so exquisitely soft that all his sons have, from that period, when they have designed to degrade them, described as highly feminine. Thus it should seem that all the arts of the grand deceiver (since means adequate to the purpose are, I conceive, invariably pursued) were requisite to mislead our general mother, while the father of mankind forfeited his own, and relinquished the happiness of posterity, merely in compliance with the blandishments of a female. The subsequent subjection the apostle Paul explains as a figure; after enlarging upon the subject, he adds, "*This is a great mystery; but I speak concerning Christ and the church.*"[1] Now we know with what consummate wisdom the unerring father of eternity hath formed his plans; all the types which he

hath displayed, he hath permitted *materially* to fail, in the very virtue for which *they* were famed. The reason for this is obvious; we might otherwise mistake his economy,[2] and render that honor to the creature which is due only to the creator. I know that Adam was a figure of him who was to come.[3] The grace contained in this figure is the reason of my rejoicing, and while I am very far from prostrating before the shadow, I yield joyfully in all things the preeminence to the second federal head.[4] Confiding faith is prefigured by Abraham, yet he exhibits a contrast to affiance when he says of his fair companion, she is my sister.[5] Gentleness was the characteristic of Moses, yet he hesitated not to reply to Jehovah himself. With unsaintlike tongue he murmured at the waters of strife,[6] and with rash hands he break the tables which were inscribed by the finger of divinity.[7] David, dignified with the title of the man after God's own heart, and yet how stained was his life. Solomon[8] was celebrated for wisdom, but folly is wrote in legible characters upon his almost every action. Lastly, let us turn our eyes to man in the aggregate. He is manifested as the figure of strength, but that we may not regard him as anything more than a figure, his soul is formed in no sort superior, but every way equal to the mind of her who is the emblem of weakness, and whom he hails the gentle companion of his better days.

—1790

---

[2] *economy* Management (of his created world).

[3] *him who … to come* Jesus.

[4] *second federal head* Jesus. Both Adam and Jesus are considered "federal heads" in Christian theology, meaning they represent humanity in a covenant with God; Jesus is the second, because Adam broke his covenant with God.

[5] *Confiding faith … my sister* Upon entering Egypt, Abraham fears that the Egyptians will kill him in order to abduct his wife Sarah, so he asks that Sarah say she is his sister. See Genesis 12.11–13; *affiance* Faith, trust; also, marriage.

[6] *With unsaintlike … of strife* See Exodus 17: the Israelites become angry with Moses for bringing them into a land where there is no water; in fear of their discontent, Moses confronts God, who commands Moses to strike his rod upon a rock out of which water then flows. Moses calls this water Meribah, or "strife."

[7] *Gentleness was … of divinity* Moses, leader of the Israelites who received the Ten Commandments from God, is described as very meek. In a moment of anger, he breaks one of the "tables" or stone tablets upon which the Ten Commandments are written.

[8] *Solomon* Successor to David, King Solomon was considered to be very wise, but committed sins such as idolatry.

---

[1] *This is … the church* See Ephesians 5.32.

BRITON HAMMON
fl. c. 1760

On Christmas Day 1747, Massachusetts "servant" Briton Hammon embarked, with the permission of his "Master" John Winslow, on a sea voyage to Jamaica, little knowing that what should have been a half-year engagement would turn into thirteen years of captivity and displacement on both sides of the Atlantic before he could return to his home in the British colonies. Within a month of Hammon's homecoming, a pamphlet titled *A Narrative of the Uncommon Sufferings and Surprising Deliverance of Briton Hammon, A Negro Man* (1760) appeared in Boston. It purported to be a dramatic account of faith, divine Providence, and the "barbarous" savagery of Hammon's Indigenous captors. Yet to modern readers, this text is far more than a conventional—and conventionally xenophobic—captivity narrative. As the first black-authored text published in North America, and thus the first published written work in the canon of African American literature, Briton Hammon's *Narrative* is a work of unquestionable historical importance. It is also a work of very considerable interest as literature. Hammon's ambiguous social status, and his confession that the text omits "a great many things," complicate matters considerably—as do the ways in which race was constructed in the early Atlantic world. These factors call into question any simple or literal interpretations of Hammon's account of captivity, or of his "deliverance."

In June 1748, following a successful harvest in the Caribbean, the ship on which Hammon was employed was cast away off the coast of Florida, where the entire crew—aside from Hammon himself—were subsequently killed by a group of Indigenous Floridians. (Though Hammon's *Narrative* does not attempt to specify this group, some modern historians have speculated that they were of the Calusa people, whose population had, by the 1700s, been severely depleted through slaving raids encouraged by the English.) The *Narrative* goes on to describe Hammon's series of sufferings as a captive first of the Floridians and next of the Spanish in colonial Cuba; it recounts as well his later years aboard a number of English trading vessels and Royal Navy warships during the Seven Years' War, before his eventual reunion with John Winslow in London.

The account of these events in the *Narrative* is the only record we have of Hammon's life, though various conjectures have been made in recent decades on the basis of a handful of documents and census records in which his name appears. The *Narrative* itself tells us remarkably little about Hammon's life or status before and after his Atlantic adventures. Most notably, it is left unclear whether Hammon—whose race is only mentioned in the title of the work—was an enslaved person, an indentured servant, or a free employee to John Winslow. (The loose usage of the terms "master" and "servant" during the eighteenth century does not rule out any of these possibilities.) While there is increasing historical consensus that Hammon was probably enslaved (with some historians pointing out that the unambiguous term "slave" was often evaded in the slaveholding North), there continues to be disagreement as to the circumstances that led Winslow to allow Hammon to temporarily leave his service in the first place.

Likewise, the circumstances surrounding the creation and publication of Hammon's *Narrative* are almost completely obscure. Readers have generally assumed that the text, like the texts of many African American captivity narratives later in the century, would have been written by a white amanuensis based on Hammon's retelling, though again, this is conjecture. What we do know is that Hammon's *Narrative* was printed by eminent Boston publishers John Green and Joseph Russell in 1760, and that earlier that year another text had been printed by Green & Russell's frequent associates Fowle & Draper, bearing a remarkably similar title: *A Plain Narrative of the Uncommon Sufferings, and Remarkable Deliverance of Thomas Brown, of Charlestown, in New England.*

These and other circumstances surrounding Hammon's text bring to the fore questions about literary genre in the eighteenth-century literary world, as well as questions about interpretation and about black literary history as a whole. It seems at times clear that the *Narrative* falls into the genre of the captivity narrative, an extraordinarily popular and also highly homogeneous genre in both Britain and the colonial Americas; captivity narratives were often deeply spiritual in tone and almost always centered on the literal and psychological resistance of the (usually white) captives to the culture of their Indigenous captors. Throughout his own tale, the Protestant Hammon emphasizes God's role in saving him from both the pagan Native Americans and the Catholic Spanish, and the text ends with impassioned praise of God's Providence in finally reuniting him with his "good Master" Winslow. Yet the degree to which the *Narrative*'s language reflects Hammon's private experience, rather than simply reflecting the literary and social conventions of the era, remains in doubt. Can Hammon's *Narrative* be considered a captivity narrative in the traditional sense, if he was never free to begin with? To what degree might the captivity narrative genre have provided Hammon with a language for thinking through enslavement? If Hammon's exact status is unclear, to what degree does that fact complicate the relationship of this text to earlier and later texts in the literature of slavery? Readers have been wrestling with such questions since Hammon's text was rediscovered by African American bibliographer Dorothy Porter in the mid-twentieth century; there is scant evidence for a wide readership of the text before this point.

It is accepted that in 1762 Hammon married Hannah, an African American woman and member of Plymouth's First Church, with whom he had one child. For many years this was all that was known of Hammon's life after his return to New England. More recent research, however, has revealed that Hammon probably changed his name to Nichols some time in the late 1770s, after the family with whom he and his master were living when Winslow died in 1774. Briton Nichols is listed as having fought for the Continental Army in the American Revolutionary War, as did many members of the white Nichols family (Winslow's surviving descendants remained staunch Loyalists). In later census records, Briton Nichols is described as a free husband and father. This information may further complicate interpretations of an intriguing text that provides a unique perspective on the lives of enslaved and free people of African descent in eighteenth-century America.

NOTE ON THE TEXT: The text of the work presented below is based on the 1760 edition of *A Narrative of the Uncommon Sufferings and Surprizing Deliverance of Briton Hammon, A Negro Man,—Servant to General Winslow, of Marshfield, in New-England; Who returned to* Boston, *after having been absent almost Thirteen Years.* Spelling and punctuation have been modernized in accordance with the practices of this anthology.

⌘⌘⌘

A Narrative of the Uncommon Sufferings and Surprising Deliverance of Briton Hammon, A Negro Man

To the reader,

As my capacities and condition of life are very low, it cannot be expected that I should make those remarks on the sufferings I have met with, or the kind Providence of a good God for my preservation, as one in a higher station; but shall leave that to the reader as he goes along, and so I shall only relate matters of fact as they occur to my mind.

On Monday, 25th day of December, 1747, with the leave of my Master, I went from Marshfield,[1] with an intention to go a voyage to sea, and the next day, the 26th, got to Plymouth, where I immediately shipped myself on board of a sloop,[2] Capt. John Howland, Master,[3] bound to Jamaica and the Bay.[4] We sailed from Plymouth in a short time, and after a pleasant passage of about thirty days arrived at Jamaica. We was

---

[1] *Marshfield* Town in Plymouth County, Massachusetts.

[2] *sloop* Small sailing ship.

[3] *Capt. John Howland, Master* Throughout the text Hammon frequently follows the mention of a ship with the name of its captain, common practice in writing of this era.

[4] *the Bay* The Bay of Capeche, in the Gulf of Mexico.

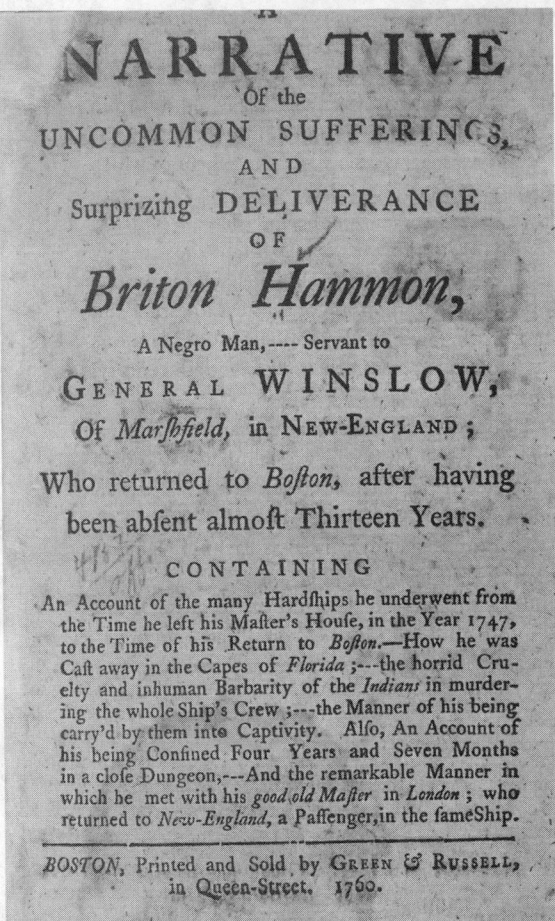

NARRATIVE
Of the
UNCOMMON SUFFERINGS,
AND
Surprizing DELIVERANCE
OF
Briton Hammon,
A Negro Man,---- Servant to
GENERAL WINSLOW,
Of *Marshfield,* in NEW-ENGLAND;
Who returned to *Boston,* after having
been absent almost Thirteen Years.

CONTAINING
An Account of the many Hardships he underwent from
the Time he left his Master's House, in the Year 1747,
to the Time of his Return to *Boston.*—How he was
Cast away in the Capes of *Florida;*---the horrid Cruelty and inhuman Barbarity of the *Indians* in murdering the whole Ship's Crew;---the Manner of his being
carry'd by them into Captivity. Also, An Account of
his being Confined Four Years and Seven Months
in a close Dungeon,---And the remarkable Manner in
which he met with his *good old Master* in *London;* who
returned to *New-England,* a Passenger, in the same Ship.

BOSTON, Printed and Sold by GREEN & RUSSELL,
in Queen-Street. 1760.

detained at Jamaica only five days, from whence we sailed for the Bay, where we arrived safe in ten days. We loaded our vessel with logwood,[1] and sailed from the Bay the 25th day of May following, and the 15th day of June, we were cast away[2] on Cape Florida, about five leagues from the shore. Being now destitute of every help, we knew not what to do or what course to take in this our sad condition. The Captain was advised, intreated, and begged on, by every person on board, to heave over[board] but only twenty ton of the wood, and we should get clear—which if he had done, might have saved his vessel and cargo, and not only so, but

his own life, as well as the lives of the mate and nine hands,[3] as I shall presently relate.

After being upon this reef two days, the Captain ordered the boat[4] to be hoisted out, and then asked who were willing to tarry[5] on board? The whole crew was for going on shore at this time, but as the boat would not carry twelve persons at once, and to prevent any uneasiness, the Captain, a passenger, and one hand tarried on board, while the mate, with seven hands besides myself, were ordered to go on shore in the boat, which as soon as we had reached, one half were to be landed, and the other four to return to the sloop, to fetch the Captain and the others on shore. The Captain ordered us to take with us our arms,[6] ammunition, provisions and necessaries for cooking, as also a sail to make a tent of, to shelter us from the weather. After having left the sloop, we stood towards the shore, and being within two leagues of the same, we espied a number of canoes, which we at first took to be rocks, but soon found our mistake, for we perceived they moved towards us. We presently saw an English colour[7] hoisted in one of the canoes, at the sight of which we were not a little rejoiced, but on our advancing yet nearer, we found them, to our very great surprise, to be Indians, of which there were sixty. Being now so near them [that] we could not possibly make our escape, they soon came up with and boarded us, took away all our arms, ammunition, and provision. The whole number of canoes (being about twenty) then made for the sloop, except two which they left to guard us, who ordered us to follow on with them; the eighteen which made for the sloop went so much faster than we that they got on board above three hours before we came alongside, and had killed Captain Howland, the passenger and the other hand. We came to the larboard[8] side of the sloop, and they ordered us round to the starboard, and as we were passing round

---

1   *logwood* Tree native to Mexico and Central America, extensively harvested during this period for its use as a dye.

2   *cast away* Ran aground.

3   *hands* Members of the ship's crew.

4   *boat* I.e., the lifeboat.

5   *tarry* Wait.

6   *arms* Weapons.

7   *colour* Flag.

8   *larboard* Port or left side of a ship; the right side is known as the starboard.

the bow,[1] we saw the whole number of Indians advancing forward and loading their guns, upon which the mate said, "*my lads, we are all dead men*," and before we had got round, they discharged their small arms upon us, and killed three of our hands, viz.[2] Reuben Young of Cape Cod, Mate; Joseph Little; and Lemuel Doty of Plymouth, upon which I immediately jumped overboard, choosing rather to be drowned than to be killed by those barbarous and inhuman savages. In three or four minutes after, I heard another volley, which dispatched[3] the other five, viz. John Nowland, and Nathaniel Rich, both belonging to Plymouth; and Elkanah Collymore, and James Webb, strangers;[4] and Moses Newmock, Mulatto.[5] As soon as they had killed the whole of the people, one of the canoes paddled after me, and soon came up with me, hauled me into the canoe, and beat me most terribly with a cutlass. After that they tied me down; then this canoe stood for[6] the sloop again and as soon as she came alongside, the Indians on board the sloop betook themselves to their canoes, then set the vessel on fire, making a prodigious shouting and hallowing[7] like so many devils. As soon as the vessel was burnt down to the water's edge, the Indians stood for the shore, together with our boat, on board of which they put five hands. After we came to the shore, they led me to their huts, where I expected nothing but immediate death, and as they spoke broken English, were often telling me, while coming from the sloop to the shore, that they intended to roast me alive. But the Providence of God ordered it otherwise, for He appeared for my help in this mount of difficulty, and they were better to me than my fears, and soon unbound me, but set a guard over me every night. They kept me with them about five weeks, during which time they used me pretty well, and gave me boiled corn, which was what they often eat themselves.

The Way I made my Escape from these Villains was this; A Spanish Schooner arriving there from St. Augustine,[8] the Master of which, whose Name was Romond, asked the Indians to let me go on board his Vessel, which they granted, and the Captain[9] knowing me very well, weigh'd Anchor and carry'd me off to the Havanna,[10] and after being there four Days the Indians came after me, and insisted on having me again, as I was their Prisoner;—They made Application to the Governor,[11] and demanded me again from him; in answer to which the Governor told them, that as they had put the whole Crew to Death, they should not have me again, and so paid them Ten Dollars for me, adding, that he would not have them kill any Person hereafter, but take as many of them as they could, of those that should be cast away, and bring them to him, for which he would pay them Ten Dollars a-head. At the Havanna I lived with the Governor in the Castle about a Twelve-month, Where I was walking thro' the Street, I met with a Press Gang[12] who immediately prest me, and put me into Goal,[13] and with a Number of others I was confin'd till next Morning, when we were all brought out, and ask'd who would go on board the King's Ships, four of which having been lately built, were bound to Old-Spain, and on my refusing to serve on board, they put me in a close[14] Dungeon, where I was confin'd *Four Years and seven months*; during which

---

[1] *bow* Front end of a ship.

[2] *viz.* Abbreviation of the Latin videlicet, meaning "namely," or "that is to say."

[3] *dispatched* Killed.

[4] *strangers* Foreigners.

[5] *Mulatto* Term, now considered offensive, that was commonly used in the eighteenth century in Britain and North America to classify individuals of mixed racial background; while "mulatto" generally meant a person with one white and one black parent, the term was often used rather loosely and might refer more to a person's physical appearance than to his or her actual known ancestry.

[6] *stood for* Steered towards.

[7] *hallowing* Hallooing; shouting.

[8] *St. Augustine* Then the capital of Spanish Florida.

[9] [Hammon's note] The way I came to know this gentleman was, by his being taken last war by an English privateer, and brought into Jamaica, while I was there. [*last war* The War of Jenkins' Ear (1739–48), a conflict between Britain and Spain fought primarily in the Caribbean. Hammon's master, John Winslow, had led an attack on Cartagena in 1740.]

[10] *the Havanna* Capital of Spanish Cuba.

[11] *the Governor* I.e., the Governor of Cuba, Francisco Cajigal de la Vega (1691–1777).

[12] *Press-Gang* Group authorized to seize men (generally, though not always, those appearing to be of "seafaring habits") off the streets and force them into military or naval service; *Press* Impress; compel into service.

[13] *Goal* Gaol; jail.

[14] *close* Narrow; enclosed.

original spelling

time I often made application to the Governor, by Persons who came to see the Prisoners, but they never acquainted him with it, nor did he know all this Time what became of me, which was the means of[1] my being confin'd there so long. But kind Providence so order'd it, that after I had been in this Place so long as the Time mention'd above the Captain of a Merchantman,[2] belonging to Boston, having sprung a Leak was obliged to put into the Havanna to refit, and while he was at Dinner at Mrs. Betty Howard's, she told the Captain of my deplorable Condition, and said she would be glad, if he could by some means or other relieve me; The Captain told Mrs. Howard he would use his best Endeavours for my Relief and Enlargement.[3]

Accordingly, after dinner, [the Captain] came to the prison and asked the keeper if he might see me; upon his request I was brought out of the dungeon, and after the Captain had interrogated me, [he] told me he would intercede with the Governor for my relief out of that miserable place, which he did, and the next day the Governor sent an order to release me. I lived with the Governor about a year after I was delivered from the dungeon, in which time I endeavoured three times to make my escape, the last of which proved effectual. The first time I got on board of Captain Marsh, an English twenty-gun ship, with a number of others, and lay on board concealed that night; and the next day the ship being under sail, I thought myself safe, and so made my appearance upon deck, but as soon as we were discovered the Captain ordered the boat out, and sent us all on shore. I entreated the Captain to let me, in particular,[4] tarry on board, begging and crying to him to commiserate my unhappy condition, and added that I had been confined almost five years in a close dungeon, but the Captain would not hearken to any entreaties, for fear of having the Governor's displeasure, and so I was obliged to go on shore.

After being on shore another twelvemonth, I endeavoured to make my escape the second time by trying to get on board of a sloop bound to Jamaica, and as I was going from the city to the sloop, was unhappily taken by the guard, and ordered back to the castle, and there

confined. However, in a short time I was set at liberty, and ordered with a number of others to carry the[5] Bishop from the castle through the country to confirm the old people,[6] baptize children, etc., for which he receives large sums of money. I was employed in this service about seven months, during which time I lived very well, and then returned to the castle again, where I had my liberty to walk about the city, and do work for myself. The *Beaver*, an English Man of War,[7] then lay in the harbour, and having been informed by some of the ship's crew that she was to sail in a few days, I had nothing now to do but to seek an opportunity how I should make my escape.

Accordingly, one Sunday night the Lieutenant of the ship with a number of the barge crew were in a tavern, and Mrs. Howard, who had before been a friend to me, interceded with the Lieutenant to carry me on board. The Lieutenant said he would with all his heart, and immediately I went on board in the barge. The next day the Spaniards came alongside the *Beaver* and demanded me again, with a number of others who had made their escape from them and got on board the ship, but just before I did; but the Captain, who was a true Englishman, refused them, and said he could not answer it, to deliver up any Englishmen under English colours. In a few days we set sail for Jamaica, where we arrived safe, after a short and pleasant passage.

After being at Jamaica a short time we sailed for London, as convoy to a fleet of merchantmen, who all arrived safe in the Downs.[8] I was turned over to another ship, the *Arcenceil*, and there remained about a month. From this ship I went on board the *Sandwich* of 90 guns; on board the *Sandwich* I tarried six weeks, and then was ordered on board the *Hercules*, Capt. John Porter, a 74-gun ship. We sailed on a cruise, and met with a French 84-gun ship, and had a very smart

---

1   *means of* Reason for.

2   *Merchantman* Merchant vessel.

3   *Enlargement* Release.

4   *in particular* I.e., as an exception from the others.

5   [Hammon's note] He is carried (by way of respect) in a large two-arm chair; the chair is lined with crimson velvet, and supported by eight persons.

6   *confirm the old people* I.e., administer the Catholic sacrament of confirmation. (It is usually administered around the age of thirteen; it is unclear whether "old" here refers to young people who have come of age, or older Catholics who never received the rite during their youth.)

7   *Man of War* Warship.

8   *the Downs* Anchorage off the coast of Kent in the English Channel.

engagement[1] in which about seventy of our hands were killed and wounded. The Captain lost his leg in the engagement, and I was wounded in the head by a small shot. We should have[2] taken this ship, if they had not cut away the most of our rigging; however, in about three hours after, a 64-gun ship came up with and took her. I was discharged from the *Hercules* the 12th day of May 1759 (having been on board of that ship three months), on account of my being disabled in the arm and rendered incapable of service, after being honourably paid the wages due to me. I was put into the Greenwich Hospital, where I stayed and soon recovered. I then shipped myself a cook[3] on board *Captain Martyn*, an armed ship in the King's service. I was on board this ship almost two months, and after being paid my wages was discharged in the month of October. After my discharge from *Captain Martyn*, I was taken sick in London of a fever, and was confined about six weeks, where I expended all my money and [was] left in very poor circumstances; and unhappy for me I knew nothing of my good Master's[4] being in London at this my very difficult time. After I got well of my sickness, I shipped myself on board of a large ship bound to Guinea,[5] and being in a public house[6] one evening, I overheard a number of persons talking about rigging a vessel bound to New England. I asked them to what part of New England this vessel was bound? [and] they told me, to Boston; and having asked them who was Commander? they told me, Captain Watt. In a few minutes after this the mate of the ship came in, and I asked him if Captain Watt did not want a cook, who told me he did, and that the Captain would be in in a few minutes; and in about half an hour the Captain came in, and then I shipped myself at once, after begging off from the ship bound to Guinea. I worked on board Captain Watt's ship

almost three months before she sailed, and one day, being at work in the hold,[7] I overheard some persons on board mention the name of Winslow, at the name of which I was very inquisitive, and having asked what Winslow they were talking about, they told me it was General Winslow, and that he was one of the passengers. I asked them what General Winslow? for I never knew my good Master by that title before; but after enquiring more particularly I found it must be Master, and in a few days' time the truth was joyfully verified by a happy sight of his person, which so overcome me that I could not speak to him for some time. My good Master was exceeding glad to see me, telling me that I was like one arose from the dead, for he thought I had been dead a great many years, having heard nothing of me for almost thirteen years.

I think I have not deviated from truth, in any particular of this my narrative, and though I have omitted a great many things, yet what is wrote may suffice to convince the reader, that I have been most grievously afflicted, and yet through the Divine Goodness, as miraculously preserved, and delivered out of many dangers; of which I desire to retain a grateful remembrance, as long as I live in the world.

And now, that in the Providence of that God who delivered his servant David out of the paw of the lion and out of the paw of the bear,[8] I am freed from a long and dreadful captivity, among worse savages than they; and am returned to my own native land, to show how great things the Lord hath done for me. I would call upon all men, and say, O Magnify the Lord with me, and let us exalt his name together! O that men would praise the Lord for His goodness, and for his wonderful works to the children of men![9]

—1760

---

[1] [Hammon's note] A particular account of this engagement has been published in the Boston newspapers. [*smart engagement* Fierce battle.]

[2] *should have* Would have.

[3] *shipped myself a cook* I.e., was hired as a ship's cook.

[4] *my good Master* I.e., John Winslow.

[5] *Guinea* At this period the name Guinea was often used to refer to West Africa as a whole; in this instance, the ship was probably headed there to buy enslaved people for trade.

[6] *public house* Pub.

[7] *hold* Inner chamber of a ship in which cargo is held.

[8] *who delivered ... bear* See 1 Samuel 17.37: "David said moreover, The Lord that delivered me out of the paw of the lion, and out of the paw of the bear, he will deliver me out of the hand of this Philistine."

[9] *children of men* See Psalm 90.3: "Thou turnest man to destruction; and sayest, Return, ye children of men."

PHILLIS WHEATLEY
1753? – 1784

Phillis Wheatley was the first author of African descent to publish a book of poetry in English, *Poems on Various Subjects, Religious and Moral* (London, 1773). During her life she gained an international readership on both sides of the Atlantic. Born in Africa and kidnapped by slave traders when she was six or seven years old, Wheatley was purchased by an evangelical family in Boston who taught her to read. She immersed herself in biblical and classical traditions and soon taught herself to write, publishing her first poem in a Rhode Island newspaper when she was a young teenager. A deeply religious poet who drew on John Milton and Alexander Pope, Wheatley was praised in her time by Voltaire, Benjamin Franklin, and George Washington. She is best known for writing about her experience of slavery and the slave trade, including the controversial poem "On Being Brought from Africa to America." More recently, scholars have come to recognize and appreciate the wide diversity of Wheatley's work, including elegies, lyrics, hymns, and narrative poems inspired by the Old Testament and Ovid's *Metamorphoses*. Long recognized as the founding author of the African American literary tradition, she is now also considered one of the most important poets of colonial North America.

Wheatley was probably born in 1753 near the West coast of sub-Saharan Africa, although the precise place and date of her birth are unknown. She was brought to Boston in 1761 on the slave ship *Phillis*, after which her new enslavers, John and Susanna Wheatley, saw fit to name her. She first became famous in 1770 after the transatlantic reprinting of her elegy for George Whitefield, a founder of Methodism who preached frequently in North America and believed in the spiritual equality of Africans. Wheatley soon advertised in Boston for subscriptions to a book of twenty-eight poems but was unable to gather enough support for publication; Great Britain, however, proved friendlier ground. While visiting London with her enslavers' son, Nathaniel, in the summer of 1773, Wheatley helped arrange for her book's publication under the patronage of Selina Hastings, the Countess of Huntingdon, a Methodist leader to whom Whitefield had been personal chaplain. Wheatley was celebrated in London by many prominent historical figures, including Benjamin Franklin, Granville Sharp (the famous abolitionist), the Earl of Dartmouth (for whom Dartmouth College had been named), and Sir Brook Watson, eventual Lord Mayor of London. She wrote effusively of how she had been welcomed: "I was received in England with such kindness, complaisance, and so many marks of esteem and real friendship as astonishes me on the reflection." Wheatley soon returned to Boston, however, to care for the ailing Susanna.

As a poet, Wheatley was particularly adept at the heroic couplet, the dominant poetic form of the eighteenth century. Her devotion to Protestant Christianity is revealed in elegies that exhort surviving relatives to seek comfort in the glory of salvation. As with Milton before her, Wheatley mingled biblical references with frequent allusions to Greek and Roman myth, often invoking the Muses to her aid. A few meditative poems explore the workings of the mind ("On Recollection," "On Imagination"), while more explicitly political poems such as "To the Right Honourable William, Earl of Dartmouth" display her commitment to freedom and equality. Wheatley's letters to prominent individuals and personal friends —including Obour Tanner, an enslaved black woman living in Newport, Rhode Island—address her religious faith, her transatlantic travels, the sale of her book of poems, and her strident antislavery beliefs.

Wheatley's poetry challenged Western culture's racist belief—evidenced in the writings of David Hume, Immanuel Kant, and Thomas Jefferson—that people of African descent were inferior to whites—even that Africans were less than fully human. Her patrons and publishers rightly assumed that many readers would be incredulous that an enslaved woman and native of Africa could have written a volume of poetry. *Poems on Various Subjects* thus includes a preface by Wheatley's enslaver verifying her authorship, and an attestation of her poetic abilities signed by eighteen prominent Bostonians, including Thomas Hutchison, Governor of Massachusetts, and John Hancock, future signer of the Declaration of Independence. Her poetic achievement remained an important touchstone in debates about race and slavery well into the nineteenth century.

Immediately after *Poems on Various Subjects* was published, many readers expressed outrage that such an accomplished poet was still enslaved. Responding to this pressure, John Wheatley manumitted Phillis in 1773. Throughout the period of the American Revolution she continued to write and publish poems—among them a panegyric to George Washington. The war disrupted the transatlantic network of Methodist patrons that had supported her early career, however, and she never garnered enough support to publish a second book. She married John Peters, a free black man, in 1778. Wheatley took her husband's last name as her own, thereafter publishing poetry and signing letters as Phillis Peters. The Peters were ambitious and resourceful, but the couple faced serious misfortune; it is likely they had at least one child who died in infancy, and John Peters was in prison for debt when Wheatley Peters herself died in 1784. The unpublished work she left behind does not survive, but *Poems on Various Subjects* received renewed attention beginning in the mid-nineteenth century, when Wheatley was adopted as an icon of the American antislavery movement.

NOTE ON THE TEXTS: Unless otherwise noted, the texts of the poems presented here are from the 1773 first London edition of *Poems on Various Subjects, Religious and Moral*. Some of Wheatley's poems from that volume also exist in other versions; as an example, we have presented "On the Death of the Rev. Mr. George Whitefield" in facing column format, with a broadside version first published in Boston in 1770 alongside the 1773 version. We also include a poem that dates from later than 1773 and a number of Wheatley's letters; information on those texts is provided in footnotes. Spelling and punctuation have been modernized in accordance with the practices of this anthology.

⌘⌘⌘

To Maecenas[1]

Maecenas, you, beneath the myrtle shade,
Read o'er what poets sung, and shepherds played.
What felt those poets but you feel the same?
Does not your soul possess the sacred flame?
5 Their noble strains° your equal genius shares   *verses*
In softer language, and diviner airs.

    While Homer[2] paints lo! circumfused°   *dispersed*
        in air,
Celestial Gods in mortal forms appear;
Swift as they move hear each recess rebound,
10 Heav'n quakes, earth trembles, and the shores resound.

Great Sire of verse, before my mortal eyes,
The lightnings blaze across the vaulted skies,
And, as the thunder shakes the heav'nly plains,
A deep-felt horror thrills through all my veins.
15 Where gentler strains demand thy graceful song,
The length'ning line moves languishing along.
When great Patroclus[3] courts Achilles' aid,
The grateful tribute of my tears is paid;
Prone on the shore he feels the pangs of love,
20 And stern Pelides[4] tend'rest passions move.

    Great Maro's[5] strain in heav'nly numbers flows,
The Nine[6] inspire, and all the bosom glows.

[1] *Maecenas* Wealthy Roman patron (d. 8 BCE) and the dedicatee of poems by Horace (56–8 BCE) and Virgil (70–19 BCE), including *The Georgics* (36–29 BCE).

[2] *Homer* Ancient Greek poet, traditionally believed to be the author of the *Iliad* and *Odyssey*. Wheatley read Homer in a popular English translation by Alexander Pope (1688–1744).

[3] *Patroclus* In the *Iliad*, the character who pleads with Achilles, the great Greek warrior, to return to battle.

[4] *Pelides* Another name in the *Iliad* for Achilles, the son of Peleus.

[5] *Maro* Common name for Virgil.

[6] *Nine* The Muses, nine goddesses who preside over the arts.

O could I rival thine and Virgil's page,
Or claim the Muses with the Mantuan Sage;[1]
25 Soon the same beauties should my mind adorn,
And the same ardors in my soul should burn:
Then should my song in bolder notes arise,
And all my numbers pleasingly surprize;
But here I sit, and mourn a grov'ling mind,
30 That fain would mount, and ride upon the wind.

    Not you, my friend, these plaintive strains become,
Not you, whose bosom is the Muses home;
When they from tow'ring Helicon[2] retire,
They fan in you the bright immortal fire,
35 But I less happy, cannot raise the song,
The fault'ring music dies upon my tongue.

    The happier Terence[3] all the choir inspir'd,
His soul replenished, and his bosom fir'd;
But say, ye Muses, why this partial grace,
40 To one alone of Afric's sable race;
From age to age transmitting thus his name
With the first glory in the rolls of fame?

    Thy virtues, great Maecenas! shall be sung
In praise of Him, from those virtues sprung:
45 While blooming wreaths around thy temples spread,
I'll snatch a laurel from thine honoured head,
While you indulgent smile upon the deed.

    As long as Thames[4] in streams majestic flows,
Or Naiads[5] in their oozy beds repose,
50 While Phoebus[6] reigns above the starry train,
While bright Aurora[7] purples o'er the main,
So long, great Sir, the muse thy praise shall sing,
So long thy praise shall make Parnassus[8] ring:

Then grant, Maecenas, thy paternal rays,
55 Hear me propitious,° and defend my lays.   *with favor*
—1773

To the University of Cambridge,[9] in New-England

While an intrinsic ardor prompts to write,
    The muses promise to assist my pen;
'Twas not long since I left my native shore
The land of errors, and Egyptian[10] gloom:
5 Father of mercy, 'twas thy gracious hand
Brought me in safety from those dark abodes.

    Students, to you 'tis giv'n to scan the heights
Above, to traverse the ethereal space,
And mark the systems of revolving worlds.
10 Still more, ye sons of science ye receive
The blissful news by messengers from heav'n,
How Jesus' blood for your redemption flows.
See him with hands out-stretched upon the cross;
Immense compassion in his bosom glows;
15 He hears revilers, nor resents their scorn:
What matchless mercy in the Son of God!
When the whole human race by sin had fall'n,
He deigned to die that they might rise again,
And share with him in the sublimest skies,
20 Life without death, and glory without end.

    Improve your privileges while they stay,
Ye pupils, and each hour redeem, that bears
Or good or bad report of you to heav'n.
Let sin, that baneful evil to the soul,
25 By you be shunned, nor once remit your guard;
Suppress the deadly serpent in its egg.
Ye blooming plants of human race divine,
An Ethiop[11] tells you 'tis your greatest foe;
Its transient sweetness turns to endless pain,
30 And in immense perdition sinks the soul.
—1773 (WRITTEN 1767)

---

1   *Mantuan Sage*   Another name for Virgil, born in Mantua.

2   *Helicon*   Mountain sacred to the Muses.

3   [Wheatley's note]   He was an African by birth. [Terence was a dramatist (d. c. 159 BCE) born in Carthage, in North Africa, who lived for a time as an enslaved person in Rome.]

4   *Thames*   The great river that flows through London.

5   *Naiads*   Nymphs dwelling in springs and rivers.

6   *Phoebus*   Apollo, god of the sun.

7   *Aurora*   Goddess of the dawn.

8   *Parnassus*   Sacred mountain in Greece associated with Apollo and the Muses.

---

9   *University of Cambridge*   Harvard University, in Cambridge, Massachusetts.

10   *Egyptian*   Egypt was often substituted as a name for the entire continent of Africa.

11   *Ethiop*   Ethiopian; i.e., African. Like Egypt, Ethiopia was often substituted as a name for Africa.

To the King's Most Excellent Majesty[1]

Your subjects hope, dread Sire—
The crown upon your brows may flourish long,
And that your arm may in your God be strong!
O may your sceptre num'rous nations sway,
5 And all with love and readiness obey!

But how shall we the British king reward!
Rule thou in peace, our father, and our lord!
Midst the remembrance of thy favours past,
The meanest peasants most admire the last.[2]
10 May George, belov'd by all the nations round,
Live with heav'ns choicest constant blessings crown'd!

Great God, direct, and guard him from on high,
And from his head let ev'ry evil fly!
And may each clime with equal gladness see
15 A monarch's smile can set his subjects free!
—1773 (WRITTEN 1768)

On Being Brought from Africa to America

'Twas mercy brought me from my Pagan land,
Taught my benighted soul to understand
That there's a God, that there's a Saviour too:
Once I redemption neither sought nor knew.
5 Some view our sable race with scornful eye,
"Their colour is a diabolic die."
Remember, *Christians*, *Negros*, black as Cain,[3]
May be refined and join th' angelic train.
—1773

---

[1] As Wheatley's note to line 9 indicates, this poem, addressed to King George III (1738–1820), celebrates the repeal of the Stamp Act, a controversial measure that taxed printed material (such as newspapers and legal documents) throughout the American colonies. It was repealed in 1766.

[2] [Wheatley's note] The Repeal of the Stamp Act.

[3] *Cain* The oldest son of Adam and Eve, who kills his younger brother, Abel, in Genesis 4. As punishment, God exiles Cain from Eden and sets a mark of sin upon him. Some in Wheatley's time believed this mark took the form of dark skin, and attempted to justify slavery on the grounds that Africans were descended from Cain.

On Imagination

Thy various works, imperial queen, we see,
How bright their forms! how decked with pomp
by thee!
Thy wond'rous acts in beauteous order stand,
And all attest how potent is thine hand.

5 From Helicon's[4] refulgent° heights attend;   *radiant*
Ye sacred choir, and my attempts befriend:
To tell her glories with a faithful tongue,
Ye blooming graces, triumph in my song.

Now here, now there, the roving Fancy flies,
10 Till some loved object strikes her wand'ring eyes,
Whose silken fetters all the senses bind,
And soft captivity involves the mind.

Imagination! who can sing thy force?
Or who describe the swiftness of thy course?
15 Soaring through air to find the bright abode,
Th' empyreal° palace of the thund'ring God,   *heavenly*
We on thy pinions° can surpass the wind,   *wings*
And leave the rolling universe behind:
From star to star the mental optics rove,
20 Measure the skies, and range the realms above.
There in one view we grasp the mighty whole,
Or with new worlds amaze th' unbounded soul.

Though Winter frowns to Fancy's raptured eyes
The fields may flourish, and gay scenes arise;
25 The frozen deeps° may break their iron bands,   *seas*
And bid their waters murmur o'er the sands.
Fair Flora[5] may resume her fragrant reign,
And with her flow'ry riches deck the plain;
Sylvanus[6] may diffuse his honours round,
30 And all the forest may with leaves be crowned;
Show'rs may descend, and dews their gems disclose,
And nectar sparkle on the blooming rose.

Such is thy pow'r, nor are thine orders vain,
O thou the leader of the mental train:

---

[4] *Helicon* Mountain sacred to the Muses.

[5] *Flora* Roman goddess of spring.

[6] *Sylvanus* Roman god of the forest.

35 In full perfection all thy works are wrought,
    And thine the sceptre o'er the realms of thought.
    Before thy throne the subject-passions bow,
    Of subject-passions sov'reign ruler thou;
    At thy command joy rushes on the heart,
40 And through the glowing veins the spirits dart.

        Fancy might now her silken pinions° try   *wings*
    To rise from earth, and sweep th' expanse on high;
    From Tithon's[1] bed now might Aurora rise,
    Her cheeks all glowing with celestial dies,°   *colors*
45 While a pure stream of light o'erflows the skies.
    The monarch of the day I might behold,
    And all the mountains tipt with radiant gold,
    But I reluctant leave the pleasing views,
    Which Fancy dresses to delight the Muse;
50 Winter austere forbids me to aspire,
    And northern tempests damp the rising fire;
    They chill the tides of Fancy's flowing sea,
    Cease then, my song, cease the unequal lay.
    —1773

To the Right Honourable William, Earl of Dartmouth, His Majesty's Principal Secretary of State for North-America[2]

Hail, happy day, when, smiling like the morn,
Fair Freedom rose, New-England to adorn:
The northern clime beneath her genial ray,
Dartmouth, congratulates thy blissful sway:
5 Elate with hope her race no longer mourns,
Each soul expands, each grateful bosom burns,

While in thine hand with pleasure we behold
The silken reins, and Freedom's charms unfold.
Long lost to realms beneath the northern skies
10 She shines supreme, while hated faction dies:
Soon as appeared the Goddess° long desired,   *freedom*
Sick at the view, she° languished and expired;   *faction*
Thus from the splendors of the morning light
The owl in sadness seeks the caves of night.

15   No more, America, in mournful strain
Of wrongs, and grievance unredressed complain,
No longer shall thou dread the iron chain,
Which wanton Tyranny with lawless hand
Had made, and with it meant t' enslave the land.

20   Should you, my lord, while you peruse my song,
Wonder from whence my love of freedom sprung,
Whence flow these wishes for the common good,
By feeling hearts alone best understood,
I, young in life, by seeming cruel fate
25 Was snatch'd from Afric's fancy'd happy seat:
What pangs excruciating must molest,°   *disturb*
What sorrows labour in my parent's breast?
Steeled° was that soul and by no misery moved   *hardened*
That from a father seized his babe belov'd:
30 Such, such my case.[3] And can I then but pray
Others may never feel tyrannic sway?

        For favours past, great Sir, our thanks are due,
And thee we ask thy favours to renew,
Since in thy pow'r, as in thy will before,
35 To soothe the griefs, which thou did'st once deplore.
May heav'nly grace the sacred sanction° give   *blessing*
To all thy works, and thou forever live
Not only on the wings of fleeting fame,
Though praise immortal crowns the patriot's name,
40 But to conduct to heav'ns refulgent°   *radiant*
    fane,°   *temple*
May fiery coursers° sweep th' ethereal plain,   *horses*
And bear thee upwards to that blest abode,
Where, like the prophet, thou shalt find thy God.
—1773

---

1 *Tithon* Trojan prince, mortal lover of Aurora, goddess of the dawn.

2 *William ... North-America* William Legge (1731–1801), Second Earl of Dartmouth, in 1772 appointed Secretary of State for the Colonies by Lord North (1732–92). Dartmouth's support for the repeal of the Stamp Act in 1766 had earned him a favorable reputation among colonists angered by British taxation policies; expectations upon his appointment were therefore high. Wheatley initially wrote this poem at the instigation of Thomas Wooldridge, who suggested Dartmouth's appointment as a subject when he visited the Wheatleys in Boston in October 1772. Wheatley revised the poem for its inclusion in *Poems on Various Subjects*; that is the version printed here.

---

3 *Steeled ... my case* Wheatley references being stolen from her father's arms by a slave trader unmoved by his abominable task.

To S.M.,[1] a Young African Painter, on Seeing His Works

To show the lab'ring bosom's deep intent,
And thought in living characters to paint,
When first thy pencil did those beauties give,
And breathing figures learnt from thee to live,
How did those prospects give my soul delight,   5
A new creation rushing on my sight?
Still, wond'rous youth! each noble path pursue,
On deathless glories fix thine ardent view:
Still may the painter's and the poet's fire
To aid thy pencil, and thy verse conspire!   10
And may the charms of each seraphic[2] theme
Conduct thy footsteps to immortal fame!
High to the blissful wonders of the skies
Elate thy soul, and raise thy wishful eyes.
Thrice happy, when exalted to survey   15
That splendid city, crowned with endless day,
Whose twice fix gates on radiant hinges ring:
Celestial Salem blooms in endless spring.[3]

Calm and serene thy moments glide along,
And may the muse inspire each future song!   20
Still, with the sweets of contemplation bless'd,
May peace with balmy wings your soul invest!
But when these shades of time are chased away,
And darkness ends in everlasting day,
On what seraphi pinions°   25   wings
    shall we move,
And view the landscapes in the realms above?
There shall thy tongue in heav'nly murmurs flow,

And there my muse with heav'nly transport glow:
No more to tell of Damon's[4] tender sighs,
Or rising radiance of Aurora's[5] eyes,   30
For nobler themes demand a nobler strain,
And purer language on th'ethereal plain.
Cease, gentle muse! the solemn gloom of night
Now seals the fair creation from my sight.
—1773

To His Excellency General Washington[6]

The following letter and verses were written by the famous Phillis Wheatley, the African Poetess, and presented to his Excellency Gen. Washington.[7]

Sir,

I have taken the freedom to address your Excellency in the enclosed poem, and entreat your acceptance, though I am not insensible of its inaccuracies. Your being appointed by the Grand Continental Congress to be Generalissimo of the armies of North America, together with the fame of your virtues, excite sensations not easy to suppress. Your generosity, therefore, I presume, will pardon the attempt. Wishing your Excellency all possible success in the great cause you are so generously engaged in. I am,

Your Excellency's most obedient humble servant,

Phillis Wheatley.

---

1   *S.M.*   The painter Scipio Moorhead (fl. 1773), a person enslaved by John Moorhead of Boston. The engraving of Wheatley's reproduced in this anthology is copied from a portrait that some scholars attribute to this artist.

2   *seraphic* Angelic, heavenly; the angels surrounding God's throne are referred to as seraphim.

3   *That splendid ... endless spring* Reference to "new Jerusalem," an earthly paradise that, according to Revelation 21, will descend from heaven after the end times. This city experiences no night and is surrounded by twelve gates, each named for one of the twelve tribes of Israel; *Salem* Another name for Jerusalem.

4   *Damon*   Generic name in pastoral poetry for a farmer, dating back to Virgil.

5   *Aurora* Goddess of the dawn.

6   Wheatley sent this poem to George Washington on 26 October 1775. At the time she was in Providence, Rhode Island, having fled there with the Wheatleys during the British Occupation of Boston, and Washington was in Cambridge, Massachusetts, commanding the troops of the colonial army. Washington replied on 28 February 1776, writing, "I thank you most sincerely for your polite notice of me, in the elegant lines you enclosed; and however underserving I may be of such encomium and panegyrick, the style and manner exhibit a striking proof of your poetical talents." The poem was first published in the *Virginia Gazette* on 20 March 1776.

7   *The following ... Gen. Washington* The poem appears here as it was published in the *Pennsylvania Magazine*, edited by Thomas Paine (1763–1809)—together with this headnote and Wheatley's letter.

Celestial choir! enthroned in realms of light,
Columbia's[1] scenes of glorious toils I write.
While freedom's cause her anxious breast alarms,
She flashes dreadful in refulgent° arms.   *radiant*
5   See mother earth her offspring's fate bemoan,
And nations gaze at scenes before unknown!
See the bright beams of heaven's revolving light
Involved in sorrows and the veil of night!
       The goddess comes, she moves divinely fair,
10 Olive and laurel binds her golden hair:
Wherever shines this native of the skies,
Unnumbered charms and recent graces rise.
       Muse! Bow propitious° while my pen relates   *favorably*
How pour her armies through a thousand gates,
15 As when Eolus[2] heaven's fair face deforms,
Enwrapped in tempest and a night of storms;
Astonished ocean feels the wild uproar,
The refluent° surges beat the sounding shore;   *flowing*
Or thick as leaves in Autumn's golden reign,
20 Such, and so many, moves the warrior's train.
In bright array they seek the work of war,

Where high unfurled the ensign° waves in air.   *flag*
Shall I to Washington their praise recite?
Enough thou know'st them in the fields of fight.
25 Thee, first in peace and honors—we demand
The grace and glory of thy martial band.
Famed for thy valour, for thy virtues more,
Hear every tongue thy guardian aid implore!
       One century scarce performed its destined round,
30 When Gallic° powers Columbia's fury found;[3]   *French*
And so may you, whoever dares disgrace
The land of freedom's heaven-defended race!
Fix'd are the eyes of nations on the scales,
For in their hopes Columbia's arm prevails.
35 Anon Britannia° droops the pensive head,   *Great Britain*
While round increase the rising hills of dead.
Ah! cruel blindness to Columbia's state!
Lament thy thirst of boundless power too late.
       Proceed, great chief, with virtue on thy side,
40 Thy ev'ry action let the goddess guide.
A crown, a mansion, and a throne that shine,
With gold unfading, Washington! Be thine.
—1775

On the Death of the Rev. Mr. George Whitefield

Phillis Wheatley revised her poems throughout her career and especially for her 1773 book *Poems on Various Subjects, Religious and Moral*. Many important poems exist in earlier versions, including "To the Right Honourable William, Earl of Dartmouth" and "Farewell to America." Wheatley significantly revised the poem that first brought her transatlantic fame, her elegy for George Whitefield, the Methodist minister. Whitefield toured the American colonies multiple times, delivering sermons outdoors to thousands of people during the Great Awakening of the 1730s and 1740s. He was well known as a philanthropist and advocate for the spiritual equality of black people, although, notably, he was not an abolitionist. Wheatley's elegy circulated as a broadside and was reprinted widely in Britain and North America. Included here are two versions: the first published within weeks of Whitefield's death in 1770, and the later version published in *Poems on Various Subjects*. In the book version, Wheatley's poem is divorced from its initial context to fit with the other poems in the collection: the long headnote from the broadside, included here, was replaced in the book with a brief title and the date of its original publication. Wheatley also shortened the poem by over a dozen lines; made many subtle changes to her language ("Inflame the soul" in line 8, for example, becomes "Inflame the heart"); and cut a passage about the Boston Massacre.

---

1   *Columbia* The personification of America, a term derived from Christopher Columbus. Columbia is the "Goddess" referenced throughout the poem (see line 9).

2   *Eolus* Aeolus, god of the wind.

3   *Gallic ... found* Wheatley references the French and Indian War (1754–63), which pitted Anglo-Americans against France and their Native American allies. It was during this war that Washington initially made his reputation as a military commander.

On the Death of the Rev. Mr. George Whitefield

[Broadside version (1770)]

An elegiac poem, on the death of that celebrated divine, and eminent servant of Jesus Christ, the late Reverend, and pious George Whitefield, Chaplain to the Right Honorable the Countess of Huntingdon,[1] &c. &c., who made his exit from this transitory state, to dwell in the celestial realms of bliss, on Lord's Day, 30th of September, 1770, when he was seized with a fit of the asthma, at Newbury-Port, near Boston, in New England. In which is a condolatory address to his truly noble benefactress, the worthy and pious Lady Huntingdon—and the Orphan-Children in Georgia;[2] who, with many thousands, are left, by the death of this great man, to lament the loss of a father, friend, and benefactor.

By Phillis, a servant girl[3] of 17 years of age, belonging to Mr. J. Wheatley, of Boston:—and has been but 9 years in this country from Africa.

Hail happy saint on thy immortal throne!
To thee complaints of grievance are unknown;
We hear no more the music of thy tongue,
Thy wonted° auditories° cease to throng.   *usual / audiences*
5 Thy lessons in uncqualled° accents flowed!   *unparalleled*
While emulation in each bosom glowed;
Thou didst, in strains of eloquence refined,
Inflame the soul, and captivate the mind.
Unhappy we, the setting sun deplore!
10 Which once was splendid, but it shines no more.
He leaves this earth for Heaven's unmeasured height:
And worlds unknown, receive him from our fight;
There Whitefield wings, with rapid course his way,
And sails to Zion,[4] through vast seas of day.

---

1 *Countess of Huntingdon* Selina Hastings (1707–91), an evangelical who founded the "Huntingdon Connexion," a group of radical Methodists who broke from the Church of England in 1782. Whitefield was her personal Chaplain at the time of his death.

2 *Orphan-Children in Georgia* Whitefield founded an orphanage in Bethesda, Georgia, in 1738, and throughout his career solicited funds for its upkeep.

3 *servant girl* In Boston at this time "servant" was a common euphemism for "slave."

4 *Zion* Heaven, or the promised land.

On the Death of the Rev. Mr. George Whitefield

[Poems on Various Subjects *version (1773)*]

Hail, happy saint, on thine immortal throne,
Possessed of glory, life, and bliss unknown;
We hear no more the music of thy tongue,
Thy wonted° auditories° cease to throng.   *usual / audiences*
5 Thy sermons in uncqualled° accents flowed,   *unparalleled*
And ev'ry bosom with devotion glowed;
Thou didst in strains of eloquence refined
Inflame the heart, and captivate the mind.
Unhappy we the setting sun deplore,
10 So glorious once, but ah! it shines no more.

Behold the prophet in his tow'ring flight!
He leaves the earth for heav'n's unmeasured height,
And worlds unknown receive him from our fight.
There Whitefield wings with rapid course his way,
15 And sails to Zion through vast seas of day.

15   When his Americans were burdened sore,[1]
When streets were crimsoned with their guiltless gore![2]
Unrivaled friendship in his breast now strove:
The fruit thereof was charity and love
Towards America—couldst thou do more
20   Than leave thy native home, the British shore,
To cross the great Atlantic's wat'ry road,
To see America's distressed abode?
Thy prayers, great saint, and thy incessant cries,
Have pierced the bosom of thy native skies!
25   Thou moon hast seen, and ye bright stars of light
Have witness been of his requests by night!
He prayed that grace in every heart might dwell:
He longed to see America excel;
He charged its youth to let the grace divine
30   Arise, and in their future actions shine;
He offered that he did himself receive,
A greater gift not God himself can give:
He urged the need of Him to every one;
It was no less than God's co-equal Son!
35   Take Him ye wretched for your only good,
Take Him ye starving souls to be your food.
Ye thirsty, come to this life giving stream:
Ye preachers, take him for your joyful theme:
Take Him, "my dear Americans," he said,
40   Be your complaints in his kind bosom laid:
Take Him ye Africans, he longs for you;
Impartial Saviour, is his title due;
If you will choose to walk in grace's road,
You shall be sons, and kings, and priests to God.

45   Great Countess! We Americans revere
Thy name, and thus condole[3] thy grief sincere:
We mourn with thee, that tomb obscurely placed,
In which thy Chaplain undisturbed doth rest.

Thy prayers, great saint, and thine incessant cries
Have peirced the bosom of thy native skies.
Thou moon hast seen, and all the stars of light,
How he has wrestled with his God by night.
20   He prayed that grace in ev'ry heart might dwell,
He longed to see America excel;
He charged its youth that ev'ry grace divine
Should with full lustre in their conduct shine;
That Saviour, which his soul did first receive,
25   The greatest gift that ev'n a God can give,
He freely offered to the num'rous throng,
That on his lips with list'ning pleasure hung.

"Take him, ye wretched, for your only good,
Take him ye starving sinners, for your food;
30   Ye thirsty, come to this life-giving stream,
Ye preachers, take him for your joyful theme;
Take him my dear Americans, he said,
Be your complaints on his kind bosom laid:
Take him, ye Africans, he longs for you,
35   Impartial Saviour is his title due:
Washed in the fountain of redeeming blood,
You shall be sons, and kings, and priests to God."

Great Countess,[4] we Americans revere
Thy name, and mingle in thy grief sincere;
40   New England deeply feels, the Orphans mourn,
Their more than father will no more return.

---

1   *burdened sore*   Burdened with much suffering.

2   *streets ... gore*   Reference to the Boston Massacre on 5 March 1770, which Whitefield condemned. British troops fired without orders into a group of civilians, killing three and setting off a firestorm of anti-British sentiment in the colonies.

3   *condole*   Sympathize with.

---

4   [Wheatley's note]   The Countess of Huntingdon, to whom Mr. Whitefield was Chaplain.

[Broadside version (1770) cont'd]

New England sure, doth feel the orphan's smart;[1]
50 Reveals the true sensations of his heart:
Since this fair Sun, withdraws his golden rays,
No more to brighten these distressful days!
His lonely Tabernacle, sees no more
A Whitefield landing on the British shore:
55 Then let us view him in yon azure skies:
Let every mind with this loved object rise.
No more can he exert his lab'ring breath,
Seized by the cruel messenger of death.
What can his dear America return?
60 But drop a tear upon his happy urn,
Thou tomb, shalt safe retain thy sacred trust,
Till life divine re-animate his dust.
—1770

[Poems on Various Subjects version (1773) cont'd]

But, though arrested by the hand of death,
Whitefield no more exerts his lab'ring breath,
Yet let us view him in th' eternal skies,
45 Let ev'ry heart to this bright vision rise;
While the tomb safe retains its sacred trust,
Till life divine re-animates his dust.
—1773

In Context

Preface to Phillis Wheatley's *Poems on Various Subjects, Religious and Moral* (1773)

Phillis Wheatley's publishers included extensive introductory material to convince readers that she was in fact the author of the poems that followed. Such material included a letter from John Wheatley, her enslaver, and an attestation signed by more than a dozen prominent citizens of Boston. Prefaces like this were not unusual for texts written by unlikely authors; when *Poems, on Several Occasions* (1785) appeared, by Wheatley's contemporary Anne Yearsley, a poor "milk-woman," the volume featured a preface by Hannah More. Nevertheless, the stakes were different for black authors who faced a predominantly racist society who thought them unequal to the task of expressing imaginative thoughts in writing. More than half a century later, this practice still continued; Frederick Douglass's *Narrative* (1845) featured two prefaces by white patrons and sponsors, the abolitionists William Lloyd Garrison and Wendell Phillips.

The following is a Copy of a Letter sent by the Author's Master to the Publisher.

Phillis was brought from Africa to America, in the Year 1761, between seven and eight years of age. Without any assistance from school education, and by only what she was taught in the family, she, in sixteen months' time from her arrival, attained the English language, to which she was an utter stranger before, to such a degree, as to read any, the most difficult parts of the sacred writings, to the great astonishment of all who heard her.

---

1 *smart* Suffering. A reference to the orphanage Whitefield supported in Georgia.

As to her writing, her own curiosity led her to it; and this she learnt in so short a time, that in the year 1765, she wrote a letter to the Rev. Mr. Occom,[1] the Indian minister, while in England.

She has a great inclination to learn the Latin tongue, and has made some progress in it. This relation is given by her master who bought her and with whom she now lives.

John Wheatley

Boston, 14 November, 1772

To the Public

As it has been repeatedly suggested to the publisher, by persons, who have seen the manuscript, that numbers would be ready to suspect they were not really the writings of Phillis, he has procured the following attestation, from the most respectable characters in Boston, that none might have the least ground for disputing their original.

We whose names are under-written, do assure the world, that the poems specified in the following Page,[2] were (as we verily believe) written by Phillis, a young Negro girl, who was but a few years since, brought an uncultivated barbarian[3] from Africa, as has ever since been, and now is, under the disadvantage of serving as a slave in a family in this town. She has been examined by some of the best judges,[4] and is thought qualified to write them.

His Excellency THOMAS HUTCHINSON, Governor,
The Hon. ANDREW OLIVER, Lieutenant-Governor.

The Hon. Thomas Hubbard,	The Rev. Charles Cheuney, D.D.[5]
The Hon. John Erving,	The Rev. Mather Byles, D.D.
The Hon. James Pitts,	The Rev. Ed. Pemberton, D.D.
The Hon. Harrison Gray,	The Rev. Andrew Elliot, D.D.
The Hon. James Bowdoin,	The Rev. Samuel Cooper, D.D.
John Hancock, Esq;	The Rev. Samuel Mather, D.D.
Joseph Green, Esq;	The Rev. Mr. John Moorhead,
Richard Carey, Esq;	Mr. John Wheatley, her Master.

N.B. The original attestation, signed by the above gentlemen, may be seen by applying to Archibald Bell, Bookseller, No. 8, Aldgate-Street.

---

[1] *Mr. Occom* Samson Occom (1723–92), Mohegan minister, who toured England as a minister in the 1760s. This early letter does not survive.

[2] [original note] The words "following page" allude to the contents of the manuscript copy, which are wrote at the back of the above attestation.

[3] *uncultivated barbarian* Uncivilized and uncultured, without the connotation of rudeness or violence (as in modern usage).

[4] *examined ... judges* Most notable among the signatories are: Thomas Hutchinson (1711–80), current Governor of Massachusetts; Andrew Oliver (1706–74), Lieutenant Governor; Thomas Hubbard (1702–73), at the time treasurer of Harvard College; James Bowdoin (1726–90), future Governor of Massachusetts for whom Bowdoin college would be named; John Hancock (1737–93), famous signatory of the Declaration of Independence; Samuel Cooper (1725–83), minister of the Brattle Street Congregational Church; Samuel Mather (1706–85), son of Cotton Mather (1663–1728), prominent Puritan minister; and John Moorhead (1703–73), enslaver of Scipio Moorhead, the African painter to whom Wheatley addressed a poem in 1772 (see above).

[5] *D.D.* Doctor of Divinity.

POPULAR LITERATURE AND PRINT CULTURE
IN EARLY AMERICA: A VISUAL SAMPLER

The following images offer only a glimpse of the variety of forms printed material took in American literature in the seventeenth and eighteenth centuries. For a more thorough sampling of popular literature and print culture, see the "Popular Literature and Print Culture" omnibus sections in this anthology's online component.

⌘⌘⌘

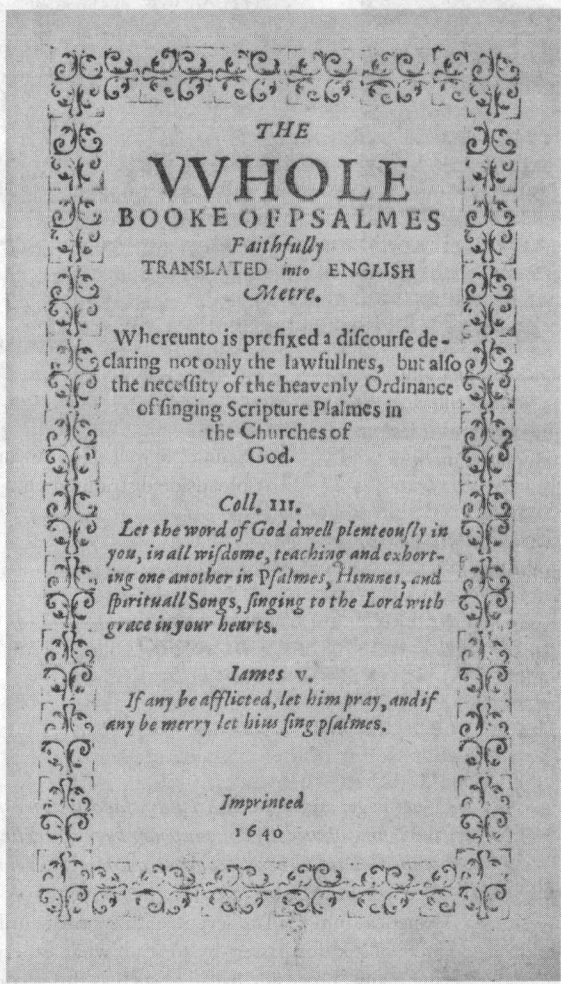

Title page from the *Bay Psalm Book* (1640), the first book to be printed in the English Colonies.

G As runs the *Glaſs*
   Mans life doth paſs.

H *My Book* and *Heart*
   Shall never part.

J *Job* feels the Rod
   Yet bleſſes GOD.

K Our *KING* the
   good
   No man of blood.

L The *Lion* bold
   The *Lamb* doth hold.

M The *Moon* gives light
   In time of night.

Page from *The New England Primer*, 1727. First published by Benjamin Harris in the late seventeenth century and frequently reissued under various titles, this book remained in common use in American schools for more than 150 years.

WEDNESDAY, *January* 1. 1701.
A little before Break-a-Day, at *Boſton* of the *Maſſachuſets.*

ONCE more! Our GOD, vouchſafe to Shine:
Tame Thou the Rigour of our Clime.
Make haſte with thy Impartial Light,
And terminate this long dark Night.

Let the tranſplanted **Engliſh** Vine
Spread further ſtill : ſtill Call it Thine.
Prune it with Skill : for yield it can
More Fruit to Thee the Huſbandman.

Give the poor **Indians** Eyes to ſee
The Light of Life : and ſet them free ;
That they Religion may profeſs,
Denying all Ungodlineſs.

From hard'ned **Jews** the Vail remove,
Let them their Martyr'd JESUS love ;
And Homage unto Him afford,
Becauſe He is their Rightfull LORD.

So falſe Religions ſhall decay,
And Darkneſs fly before bright Day :
So Men ſhall GOD in CHRIST adore ;
And worſhip Idols vain, no more.

So **Aſia**, and **Africa**,
Europa, with **America** ;
All Four, in Conſort join'd, ſhall Sing
The Songs of Praiſe to CHRIST our KING.

Samuel Sewall, ["Verses upon a New Century"], a broadside distributed on 1 January 1701.

Next Page: anonymous, *New England Bravery, Being a Full and True Account of the Taking of the City of Louisbourg by the New England Forces under the Command of the Gallant General Pepperell, on the 17th of June, 1745.* Broadsides, large sheets of paper printed on one side, were a common format for popular literature in America from the late seventeenth century until well into the nineteenth. Some were posted for passers-by to read, while others were printed for sale—including many "broadside ballads," such as this account of the capture of the French fortress of Louisburg by colonial forces during King George's War.

New-England Bravery:

Being a full and true Account of the taking of the City of *Louisbourg*, by the *New-England* Forces under the Command of the gallant General *Pepperell*, on the 17th of *June*, 1745.

Tune of, *Chivey-Chace*.

COme all *New-England*'s gallant Lads,
　and lend to me an Ear,
And of your Brethren's mighty Acts
　I will in short declare.
Brave PEP'RELL with three Thousand Men,
　(perhaps some hundreds more)
Did land the very first of *May*,
　upon *Cape-Breton* Shore:
And tho' opposed by *Morepang*
　with full two hundred Men,
A handful of our gallant Lads
　did drive them back again.
Some few were taken Prisoners,
　and many kill'd out-right,
Which taught the *French* at *Louisbourg*
　New-England Men can fight.
The *Monsieurs* all astonished
　to see our Armament,
Were griev'd to see that they must be
　within Stone Walls all pent.
In haste they call in to their Aid
　the Men upon the Isle,
Forgetting their own Poverty,
　(such Things would make one smile)
But what is vastly more absurd
　Than any thing like this,
They quitted the *Grand Battery*,
　the Glory of the Place.
Of which our *English* Lads did take
　Possession quick,
And with the Guns did ever since
　the Enemy annoy.
They also did with mighty Toil
　their Batteries erect,
Against the Town and Citidel,
　which play'd with good Effect.
They sent such Showers of Bombs and Balls
　as made the *Frenchmen* quake,
And sputter out such Words as these,
　Those Dogs the Place will take.
Our Men did also batter down
　the West Gate and the Wall,
And made therein so large a Breach
　that to the *French* they'd call ;
Come out, Jack Frenchman, *come to us,*
　and drink a Bowl of Punch,

The Frenchmen cry, *you English Dogs,*
　come, here's a pretty Wench.
But by and by they change their Tones,
　and offer Terms of Peace,
Which if consented to they would
　surrender up the Place.
(For they were so severely maul'd
　by Cannon Shot and Shells,
That they no Place of Safety found
　on Platforms or in Cells.)
Their Island Battery likewise,
　on which they much depended,
Was so annoyed by our Men
　it could not be defended.
For they did wisely plant some Guns
　upon the Light-House Point,
And also one good Mortar Piece,
　which put them out of Joint.
Our Lads they fir'd so furiously
　into that Island Fort,
The Soldiers jump'd into the Sea,
　which made our Men good Sport.
Our Gen'ral upon this Success
　did send *Monsieurs* Word,
If they would not give up the Place,
　He'd put them to the Sword.
And now not daring to withstand
　the Force of all our Bands,
They gave up all their Fortresses
　into our *English* Hands.
With Beat of Drums and Colours spread,
　the Seventeenth of *June*,
Our gallant Army marched in,
　'bout Twelve o'Clock at Noon.
The Gentlemen and Ladies too
　they did caress our Men,
For having them delivered
　from worse than Lion's Den.
They all are to be sent to *France*,
　with all the Islanders,
Which needs must ease our Countrymen
　of many Cares and Fears.
And all the Men are strictly bound
　(that is as we do hear)
Not to bear Arms against King GEORGE,
　at least for one whole Year.

Sold at the Heart and Crown in Cornhill, Boston.

Jonathan Livermore His Verses

TECUMSEH

c. 1768 – 1813

One of the most energetic and eloquent exponents of Native American unity and resistance to U.S. expansion, the Shawnee leader Tecumseh was also, ironically, one of the first Native Americans to become a full-blown U.S. folk hero. His foremost adversary, the military officer and politician William Henry Harrison, summarized Tecumseh's insurgent stature while also anticipating his appropriation by the very white American society he fought so hard against: "The implicit obedience and respect which the followers of Tecumseh pay him bespeaks him one of those uncommon geniuses, which spring up occasionally to produce revolutions and overturn the established order of things." Together with his brother Tenskwatawa, also known as "The Prophet," Tecumseh envisioned and worked indefatigably to create a confederation of the Indigenous nations of the Great Lakes region (and beyond) that would be able to halt the relentless march of white colonization and form an independent Indigenous state. Much of his reputation and many of his achievements stemmed from the universally acknowledged power of his oratory, which drew on and reshaped longstanding Indigenous rhetorical traditions, and his legacy looms large in both white American and Native American history and culture.

Tecumseh's nation, the Shawnee, had been scattered by Haudenosaunee expansion into the Ohio River valley during the century before his birth; at the time Tecumseh was born, they were attempting to return to their traditional territories in what is now Ohio. Tecumseh was born around 1768 in those traditional territories (most likely in the vicinity of present-day Chillicothe, Ohio), although his parents had met and married in what is now Alabama and his mother may have been Muscogee (Creek). No sooner had the Shawnee begun reestablishing themselves in their Ohio Valley homelands than they found themselves facing a new foreign influx, this time that of Euro-American colonists. Tecumseh spent much of the 1780s and 1790s alternately taking part in the fight against American expansion into the Ohio Country—in the course of which both his father and his older brother died in battle—and traveling further afield in an (unsuccessful) attempt to outpace that expansion. In 1794, an American victory at the Battle of Fallen Timbers (at which Tecumseh was present) ended the so-called Northwest Indian War and caused the collapse of the Indigenous confederation that had formed to resist the Americans. Many Indigenous leaders signed the subsequent Treaty of Greenville (1795), ceding most of present-day Ohio to the U.S., but Tecumseh did not.

In 1805, Tecumseh's younger brother Lalawéthika reportedly experienced a series of visions that earned him the new name "Tenskwatawa," meaning "Open Door." Tenskwatawa began preaching a new religion, which held that white Americans were "the children of the Evil Spirit" who "poisoned the land," and enjoined Native Americans to forswear alcohol and other Euro-American products and customs, to revive their traditional ways of life, and to surrender no more land to the whites. Tecumseh joined Tenskwatawa in proclaiming that Indigenous land was the common possession of all Indigenous nations, which could not be ceded without the consent of all, and in calling for the fractured Indigenous confederacy to reunite around this imperative. White writers have long tended to apportion Tenskwatawa and Tecumseh to separate "religious" and "political" spheres and to build up Tecumseh at Tenskwatawa's expense. It is clear from the historical record, however, that the two brothers shared the same beliefs and ideas—and that, at least in the early days of their movement, Tenskwatawa overshadowed Tecumseh. The originality of the brothers' message has also been exaggerated, when in fact they were building on prior movements for political unity, and related spiritual revivalist movements, among the Indigenous peoples of the Great Lakes region, including the earlier confederacies organized by the Odawa leader Pontiac (in conjunction with the religious revival led by the Lenape prophet Neolin) and the Mohawk Joseph Brant (who anticipated the later course of Tecumseh's career by allying with the British against the Americans during the Revolutionary War).

Tenskwatawa and Tecumseh's new movement spread quickly, and in 1808 they founded (in what is now Indiana) a base for it, known in English as "Prophetstown," which soon grew into a large multinational Indigenous community. The brewing conflict between the brothers' movement and U.S. authorities came to a head after the signing of the Treaty of Fort Wayne in 1809, whereby accommodationist Indigenous leaders ceded millions more acres of present-day Indiana and Illinois in negotiations at which other Indigenous groups with a stake in the land in question were not represented. Tecumseh, outraged, met in August 1810 with William Henry Harrison, the governor of the Indiana Territory, in an attempt to get the treaty rescinded. The encounter was tense and left both sides convinced that war was impending.

Tecumseh's speech at his meeting with Harrison, in which he laid out his objections to the Fort Wayne treaty in the context of a broader history of Indigenous relations with white colonizers, is one of the first extant examples of his oratory. Like the other speeches attributed to him, the speech has roots in Shawnee political and rhetorical culture, with its emphasis on using public speaking to foster consensus; it also shows how Tecumseh, like other Indigenous leaders at the time, adapted his rhetoric for white audiences and in response to the exigencies of Indigenous–white contact. Tecumseh's recorded speeches also attest—however imperfectly, given their translation and likely embellishment by white writers—to his oratory's incisive power. In the words of one white American recollection of Tecumseh from shortly after his death, "His eloquence was nervous [i.e., forceful], concise, impressive, figurative and sarcastic."

During the two years following his meeting with Harrison, Tecumseh devoted himself to building a common front among Indigenous peoples both near and far, visiting nations as distant as the Choctaw, Chickasaw, and Muscogee (Creek) of what is now Mississippi and Alabama and the Osage of what is now Missouri and Arkansas. Tecumseh's travels, and the speeches and anecdotes that stem from them, bear ample witness to his political and diplomatic abilities; however, few of the more distant Indigenous nations he visited ended up joining his confederacy. In November 1811, William Henry Harrison took advantage of Tecumseh's absence to launch a preventive strike on Prophetstown, defeating Tenskwatawa at the Battle of Tippecanoe and burning the town—although this battle was not the crippling blow to the Indigenous confederacy that American propaganda later made it out to be.

When war broke out between the U.S. and Britain in 1812, Tecumseh's war with the U.S. bled into this broader conflict. Tecumseh quickly made common cause with the British and fought successfully with them in the first year of the war, helping to fend off an American invasion of Canada and later to capture Detroit. The esteem in which Tecumseh was held by his British allies gave rise to the mistaken belief that he was made a general in the British army. By the fall of 1813, however, the British had been forced to retreat into Canada, reluctantly accompanied by Tecumseh. When the British and Indigenous force confronted their American pursuers at the Battle of the Thames, in what is now the Canadian province of Ontario, the British contingent fled the field, and Tecumseh, left to fight alone, was killed. After his death, his confederacy crumbled, leaving the way clear for U.S. domination of the entire region between the Ohio River, the Great Lakes, and the Mississippi.

Tecumseh's death in battle sealed his swift transformation, in white American culture, into the paradigmatic "noble Indian": a worthy foe whose courageous but doomed struggle (as American commentators characterized it) underscored the supposed inevitability of U.S. conquest. As a contributor to the *Indiana Sentinel* put it in 1820, "Every schoolboy in the Union now knows that Tecumseh was a great man. He was truly great—and his greatness was his own, unassisted by science or the aid of education." His legend inspired and was embroidered by works such as the 1841 biography *Life of Tecumseh*, the 1844 play *Tecumseh; or, The Prophet of the West*, and a slew of similar novels, poems, plays, and films that continued into the twentieth century. At the same time, Tecumseh's words and actions—together with those of his brother—helped inspire an ongoing lineage of Indigenous resistance and assertion of autonomy. The Sauk leader Black Hawk, who led his own war against U.S. expansion twenty years after Tecumseh's death, was reported to have "often boasted of his being at the right hand of Tecumseh," and his 1833 autobiography—a landmark in Native American literature—refers specifically and prophetically to Tenskwatawa (who also inspired Black Hawk's spiritual counterpart, Wabokieshiek). In the late nineteenth century, the kind of apocalyptic Indigenous spiritual ideas, transcending tribal boundaries and blending aspects of various religions, that were developed by Tenskwatawa and articulated in Tecumseh's speeches reemerged in the Ghost Dance movement, while in the twentieth century, Tecumseh's example was frequently cited by the organizers of the American Indian Movement. Scholars today continue to work to counteract Tecumseh's mythologization by the people who defeated him, demonstrating the extent of his collaboration with Tenskwatawa and the way in which his speeches and ideas built on existing Indigenous political, religious, and rhetorical traditions.

NOTE ON THE TEXT: The text of Tecumseh's 1810 speech to William Henry Harrison is based on the manuscript text of the English translation of the speech included in the collection of Harrison's papers held by the Indiana Historical Society, a facsimile of which appears on the society's website. Spelling and punctuation have been modernized according to the practices of this anthology.

⌘ ⌘ ⌘

Speech to William Henry Harrison

Brother, I wish you to listen to me well. I wish to reply to you more explicitly, as I think you do not clearly understand what I before said to you. I shall explain it again.

When we were first discovered it was by the French,[1] who told us that they would adopt us as their children and gave us presents, without asking anything in return but our considering them as our fathers. Since we have changed our fathers, we find it different.

Brother, this is the manner that the treaty was made by us with the French. They gave us many presents and treated us well. They asked us for a small piece of country to live on, which they were not to leave, and continued to treat us as their children. After some time, the British and French came to quarrel.[2] The British

were victorious, yet the French promised to think of us as their child and if they ever could serve us, to do it: "Now, my red children, I know I was obliged to abandon you in disagreeable circumstances, but we have never ceased to look upon you, and if we now could be of service to you, we would still be your friends."

The next father we found was the British, who told us that they would now be our fathers and treat us in the same manner as our former fathers the French. They would occupy the same land they did and not trouble us on ours, but would look on us as their children.

Brother, we were very glad to hear the British promise to treat us [as] our fathers the French had done. They began to treat us in the same way, but at last they changed their good treatment by raising the tomahawk against the Americans and put it into our hands, by which we have suffered the loss of a great many of our young men.

Brother, now we began to discover the treachery of the British. They never troubled us for our lands, but they have done worse by inducing us to go to war. The Hurons have particularly suffered during the war and have at length become certain of it—they have told us we must bury the British tomahawk entirely—that if we do not, they (the British) would ere long ask us to take it up.

---

[1] *When we ... the French* Explorers from the French colonies in Canada and the Illinois Country first encountered Shawnee along the Ohio River in the seventeenth century.

[2] *the British ... quarrel* Conflicts between the French and British colonies in North America over control of the Great Lakes region and the Ohio River valley, in which both sides were supported by their respective mother countries and by Native American allies, took place regularly throughout the late seventeenth and early eighteenth centuries. These conflicts culminated in the French and Indian War (1754–63), in which Britain forced France to give up nearly all of its North American possessions. The Shawnee supported the French in

the early stages of the war but made peace with the British colonies in 1758.

You ought to know that after we agreed to bury the tomahawk at Greenville[1] we then found new fathers in the Americans, who told us they would treat us well, not like the British who gave us but a small piece of pork every day.

I want now to remind you of the promises of the white people. You recollect that the time the Delawares lived near the white people (Americans) and [were] satisfied with the promises of friendship and remained in security, yet one of their towns was surprised and the men, women and children murdered.[2]

The same promises were given to the Shawnees. Flags were given to them and [they] were told by the Americans that they were now children of the Americans: "These flags will be as security for you; if the white people intend to do you harm hold up your flags and no harm will be done you." This was at length practised, and the consequence was that the person bearing the flag was murdered with others in their village.[3] How, my Brother, after this conduct can you blame me for placing little confidence in the promises of our fathers the Americans?

Brother, since the peace was made you have killed some of the Shawnees, Winebagoes, Delawares and Miamies, and you have taken our lands from us, and I do not see how we can remain at peace with you if you continue to do so. You have given goods to the Kickapoos for the sale of their land, which has been the cause of many deaths among them. You have promised us assistance, but I do not see that you have given us any.

You try to force the red people to do some injury. It is you that is pushing them on to do mischief. You endeavour to make distinctions. You wish to prevent the Indians to do as we wish them: to unite and let them consider their land common property of the whole. You take tribes aside and advise them not to come into this measure, and until our design is accomplished, we do not wish to accept of your invitation to go and visit the President.

The reason I tell you this is—you want by your distinctions of Indian tribes, in allotting to each a particular track of land, to make them to war with each other. You never see an Indian come and endeavour to make the white people do so. You are continually driving the red people; when at last you will drive them into the great Lake where they can't either stand or walk.

Brother, you ought to know what you are doing with the Indians. Perhaps it is by direction of the President to make those distinctions. It is a very bad thing and we do not like it. Since my residence at Tippecanoe,[4] we have endeavoured to level all the distinctions, to destroy village chiefs, by whom all mischief is done. It is they who sell our land to the Americans. Our object is to let all our affairs be transacted by warriors.

Brother, this land that was sold and the goods that [were] given for it was only done by a few. The treaty was afterwards brought here and the Weas[5] were induced to give their consent because of their small numbers. The treaty at Fort Wayne[6] was made through

---

[1] *we agreed ... Greenville* Reference to the 1795 Treaty of Greenville, which ended the Northwest Indian War (1785–95). Under the terms of the treaty, the defeated Northwestern Confederacy of Native American nations, including the Shawnee, ceded most of the present-day state of Ohio in exchange for yearly grants of money and supplies.

[2] *one ... murdered* In the Gnadenhutten Massacre of 1782, ninety-six men, women, and children from the Lenape (Delaware) and other Indigenous nations, who had converted to the pacifist Moravian Christian denomination and were living in a Moravian missionary settlement in Gnadenhutten, Ohio, were killed by American militia who suspected them of spying for the British.

[3] *the consequence ... their village* Reference to the murder of the Shawnee chief Moluntha during Logan's raid, an American military expedition led by General Benjamin Logan against largely undefended Shawnee villages in October 1786, during the Northwest Indian War. Moluntha had signed the Treaty of Fort Finney between the United States and the Shawnee the year before, in token of which he was flying an American flag over his lodge, and he met Logan's troops holding a copy of the treaty, but he was killed (against Logan's orders) by one of Logan's officers.

[4] *Tippecanoe* Known in English as Prophetstown, the community of Indigenous people from various nations founded by Tecumseh and his brother Tenskwatawa ("The Prophet") at the confluence of the Tippecanoe and Wabash Rivers in what is now Indiana.

[5] *Weas* Indigenous nation whose traditional territory is located in what is now western Indiana.

[6] *The treaty at Fort Wayne* In 1809, William Henry Harrison, governor of the Indiana Territory, began negotiations at Fort Wayne with representatives of the Potawatomi, Lenape (Delaware), Eel Rivers, and Miami nations—although not with the Shawnee—to open a large swath of Indigenous land in the territory to white American settlement. The Treaty of Fort Wayne, signed in the fall of 1809 and finalized in 1810, sold over three million acres of Indigenous land to the United States. Opposition to the treaty by other Native Americans led to attacks on white settlements in 1810; Tecumseh was particularly incensed by the treaty, and his hostility to it motivated the negotiations with Harrison during which he gave this speech.

the threats of Winamac,[1] but in the future we are prepared to punish those chiefs who may come forward to propose to sell their land. If you continue to purchase of them, it will produce war among the different tribes, and at last I do not know what will be the consequence to the white people.

Brother, I was glad to hear your speech. You said if we could show that the land was sold by persons that had no right to sell, you would restore it. Those that did sell did not own it. It was *me*—these tribes set up a claim but the tribes with me will not agree to their claim. If the land is not restored to us, you will soon see, when we return to our homes, how it will be settled. We shall have a great council at which all the tribes shall be present, when we will show to those who sold that they had no right to sell the claim they set up, and we shall see what will be done with those chiefs that did sell the land to you. I am not alone in this determination. It is the determination of all the warriors and red people that listen to me.

I now wish you to listen to me. If you do not, it will appear as if you wished me to kill all the chiefs that sold you the land. I tell you so because I am authorized by all the tribes to do so. I am at the head of them all. I am a warrior, and all the warriors will meet together in two or three moons from this. Then I will call for those chiefs that sold you the land and shall know what to do with them. If you do not restore the land, you will have a hand in killing them.

Brother, do not believe that I came here to get presents from you. If you offer us anything we will not take it. By taking goods from you, you will hereafter say that with them you purchased another piece of land from us. If we want anything we are able to buy it from your traders. Since the land was sold to you, no traders come among us. I now wish you would clear all the roads and let the traders come among us. Then perhaps some of our young men will occasionally call on you to get their guns repaired. This is all the assistance we ask of you.

Brother, I should now be very glad to know immediately: what is your determination about the land, also of the traders I have mentioned?

Brother, it has been the object of both myself and my brother[2] from the beginning to prevent the lands being sold. Should you not return the land, it will occasion us to call a great council that will meet at the Huron Village,[3] where the council fire has already been lighted, at which those who sold the land shall be called and shall suffer for their conduct.

Brother, I wish you would take pity on all the red people and do what I have requested. If you will not give up the land and do cross the boundary of your present settlement, it will be very hard and produce great troubles among us. How can we have confidence in the white people? When Jesus Christ came upon the earth, you killed and nailed him on a cross. You thought he was dead, but you were mistaken. You have Shakers[4] among you, and you laugh and make light of their worship.

Everything I have said to you is the truth. The Great Spirit has inspired me, and I speak nothing but the truth to you. In two moons we shall assemble at the Huron Village (addressing himself to the Weas and Pottawatomies), where the great belts of all the tribes[5] are kept, and there settle our differences.

---

[2] *my brother* I.e., Tenskwatawa, also known as "The Prophet" (1775–1836), Tecumseh's younger brother. An influential religious figure, Tenskwatawa led a separatist Indigenous spiritual movement that provided much of the basis for unified Indigenous opposition to further U.S. expansion in the Great Lakes region in the first decades of the nineteenth century.

[3] *the Huron Village* Today the site of Brownstown, Michigan, near Detroit; the Wendat (Huron) community located there in the early nineteenth century was the symbolic headquarters of the alliance of Indigenous nations around the Great Lakes that formed to resist U.S. expansion in 1783 and of which Tecumseh's confederacy was the continuation.

[4] *Shakers* Christian sect, founded in England in the mid-eighteenth century, that settled in America in the 1770s and 1780s; their ecstatic worship services (which earned them the name "Shakers"), celibate and communal lifestyle, pacifism, and egalitarian beliefs, which particularly emphasized equality of the sexes, prompted bemusement or hostility among many other Americans. A group of Shaker missionaries visited Tecumseh and Tenskwatawa's community in 1807, under the belief that it represented a religious revival similar to that which had given rise to the Shakers themselves, and were cordially received there.

[5] *the great … tribes* Belts and strings of wampum, a type of bead made from shells, are used among the Indigenous nations of eastern North America for numerous purposes, including the recording of treaties, stories, and historical events as well as ceremonial exchange, trade, and decorative art.

---

[1] *Winamac* Potawatomi chief, whose name is also spelled Winnemac; he led the Potawatomi delegation in the negotiations that led to the Treaty of Fort Wayne and played a key part in persuading other, more reluctant Indigenous representatives to sign the treaty.

Now, Brother, I hope you will confess that you ought not to have listened to those bad birds who bring you bad news. I have declared myself freely to you, and if you want any explanation from our town, send a man who can speak to us.

If you think [it] proper to give us any presents, and we can be convinced that they are given through friendship alone, we will accept them. As we intend to hold our council at the Huron Village that is near the British, we may probably make them a visit. Should they offer us any presents of goods, we will not take them, but should they offer us powder[1] and the tomahawk, we will take the powder and refuse the tomahawk.

I wish you, Brother, to consider [that] everything I have said is true and that it is the sentiments of all the red people who listen to me.

By your giving goods to the Kickapoos, you killed many. They were seized with the smallpox, by which many died.

—1810

Illustration by John Reuben Chapin, engraved by William Ridgway, of the 1810 confrontation between Tecumseh and William Henry Harrison (c. 1818). This illustration has been characterized as "extremely inaccurate," especially for its depiction of the clothing of Tecumseh and his party, but it exemplifies white American culture's rapid appropriation of Tecumseh.

---

1   *powder*   I.e., gunpowder.

WASHINGTON IRVING
1783 – 1859

Washington Irving was the United States' first literary celebrity, and among the first American writers to be widely read and respected—including in Britain, where critics had long scoffed at literature in America. Over the course of his highly varied career, Irving earned fame for his urbane satire and ambitious, pseudohistorical parody; for his small-scale literary portraits of rural New York; and for works of nonfiction that capitalized on the emerging cultural importance of the American "frontier." As an important advocate for writers' financial rights, and one of the first Americans to attain financial success through his writings alone, Irving played a vital role in giving shape to an American literary market—and stature to a national literature that was struggling for recognition.

Born to English and Scottish parents in Manhattan in 1783, Irving was raised primarily in the growing metropolis, but also experienced the landscapes and cultural heritage of rural Dutch New York, whose influence would be seen in some of his earliest writings. Though he was initially pushed toward a career in the law, Irving had by his early twenties established a local reputation as a satirist and occasional theater critic; he wrote a popular series of letters under the pen name of Jonathan Oldstyle for New York's *Morning Chronicle* in 1802, and from 1807 to 1808 collaborated with his brother William and friend James Kirke Paulding on the periodical *Salmagundi*, which was among the first publications to refer to New York City by the nickname "Gotham."

By 1809, Irving was piecing together his first major book, a unified work that quickly evolved from an extension of the satirical *Salmagundi* project into a work of much broader literary and cultural scope. Published late that year, *A History of New York, from the Beginning of the World to the End of the Dutch Dynasty* was a lively parody of American historical publications. Written in the persona of the elderly and rather unreliable Dutch historian Diedrich Knickerbocker, the book's account of New York's colonial history was composed of both farce and fact; though parodic in tone, the text was nevertheless based on serious archival research on Irving's part, and worked to feed the growing post-revolutionary hunger of Euro-Americans for an account of their national heritage. In this sense, Irving's *History* responded to the appeals of writers like Charles Brockden Brown, who had in the *American Review* of 1802 called for an American historian who could "vie with those who have so recently shone in Great-Britain." The *History* became the most lucrative single literary work yet published in the United States. Abroad, its humor won the admiration (and won Irving the friendship) of Scottish Romantic poet Sir Walter Scott, who claimed the volume had given him an "uncommon degree of entertainment," and who favorably compared Irving's writing to that of the famous satirists Jonathan Swift and Laurence Sterne. The immensely popular Scott would prove an important influence on Irving's later fiction.

Irving's next publication, written while he was living abroad in England, constituted a considerable change in his literary vision. The stories and sketches that made up *The Sketch Book of Geoffrey Crayon, Gent.* (1819–20) were written under yet another pseudonym. Lightly comic in tone, they also exhibited Irving's increasingly romantic sensibility and interest in European myth. Much of the text was inspired by Irving's recent readings of German folktales, to which he had been introduced by Scott; "Rip Van Winkle," for example, is an Americanized adaptation of the German tale "Peter Klaus."

The *Sketch Book* was published in the United States between 1819 and 1820 to extraordinary and lasting acclaim; years later, American poet Henry Wadsworth Longfellow would call the collection his "first book," "the one book among all others" that first captivated him as a chid. The *Sketch Book* was soon re-published in Britain by the prestigious publisher John Murray. In an age of rampant and unchecked book piracy—especially when it came to international publication—Irving established a copyright in England and subsequently became one of the first American authors to make a profit from books printed abroad. The English volumes of the *Sketch Book* contained a number of both major and minor revisions, some likely designed to capitalize on the new literary market; particularly noteworthy were two added sketches depicting and commenting on Native American culture and life. In England, the *Sketch Book* was admired by writers such as Lord Byron and Charles Dickens; Irving's numerous tales of English Christmas traditions contributed to a tradition that would later influence Dickens's famous Christmas tales. Overall, indeed, the *Sketch Book*'s focus was almost overwhelmingly English—yet its most popularly enduring stories, "Rip Van Winkle" and "The Legend of Sleepy Hollow," have acquired near-mythic status as quintessentially American fables.

Irving's next two books, *Bracebridge Hall* (1822) and *Tales of a Traveller* (1824), were also written under the Geoffrey Crayon pseudonym and inspired by Irving's European travels. He then wrote *The Life and Voyages of Christopher Columbus* (1828) while on a political assignment in Madrid. Though a rather fanciful account of the explorer's life, the work long remained a standard educational text in American schools; as such, it contributed to an enduring historical misconception: the notion that Europeans had believed the earth to be flat until Columbus's voyage had proved them wrong.

After seventeen years abroad Irving finally returned to the United States and was recognized there as a celebrity. He embarked on a tour of the western regions of the country, which provided the raw material for three lucrative volumes of travel writing. These books—*A Tour on the Prairies* (1833), *Astoria: Or, Enterprise Beyond the Rocky Mountains* (1836), and *The Adventures of Captain Bonneville* (1837)—represent another significant shift in Irving's literary vision and cultural focus. Irving encourages his readers to take excursions into the west such as he had done. He wrote, in *A Tour*: "We send our youth abroad to grow luxurious and effeminate in Europe; it appears to me that a previous tour on the prairies would be more likely to produce that manliness, simplicity, and self-dependence most in unison with our political institutions." These books both contributed to and were shaped by the growing culture of western expansion—exemplified in fiction by the works of James Fenimore Cooper—with *A Tour* influentially describing the frontier as a place "between civilized and savage life." Though Irving shows some sympathy for the struggles of Indigenous Americans, he nevertheless portrays western expansion—reliant on the genocidal Indian Removal Act—in broadly romantic terms.

The travel volumes proved lucrative, and allowed Irving to purchase property in the region that has since 1996 been named Sleepy Hollow in his honor. He spent the last two decades of his life writing several biographical works, including a life of Irish writer Oliver Goldsmith (whose *Citizen of the World* [1760–61] Irving had admired as a child), and the substantial *Life of George Washington* (1855–59). Irving died a few months after the release of the latter work's final volume, and was buried in the cemetery at Sleepy Hollow. Upon Irving's death, the English novelist William Makepeace Thackeray described him as "the first ambassador whom the New World of Letters sent to the Old." In that so-called New World, Irving's work had bolstered and brought life to American literature as a whole, and the American short story in particular. Though American authors would continue throughout much of the nineteenth century to struggle against a literary market that privileged British writing, Irving helped open the door to the idea that American writers could be worth reading. His depictions of the American landscape, from the Hudson River and the Catskill Mountains to Oregon, helped define a whole set of romantic associations with those regions in America's popular imagination.

NOTE ON THE TEXT: The text of "Rip Van Winkle" presented here is based on that which appears in the first edition of *The Sketch Book of Geoffrey Canyon, Gent.* (1819–20). Spelling and punctuation have been modernized in accordance with the practices of this anthology.

⌘ ⌘ ⌘

Rip Van Winkle

[The following Tale was found among the papers of the late Diedrich Knickerbocker, an old gentleman of New York, who was very curious in the Dutch history of the province,[1] and the manners of the descendants from its primitive settlers. His historical researches, however, did not lay so much among books, as among men; for the former are lamentably scanty on his favourite topics; whereas he found the old burghers,[2] and still more, their wives, rich in that legendary lore, so invaluable to true history. Whenever, therefore, he happened upon a genuine Dutch family, snugly shut up in its low-roofed farm house, under a spreading sycamore, he looked upon it as a little clasped volume of black-letter,[3] and studied it with the zeal of a bookworm.

The result of all these researches was a history of the province, during the reign of the Dutch governors, which he published some years since. There have been various opinions as to the literary character of his work, and, to tell the truth, it is not a whit better than it should be. Its chief merit is its scrupulous accuracy, which, indeed, was a little questioned, on its first appearance, but has since been completely established; and it is now admitted into all historical collections, as a book of unquestionable authority.

The old gentleman died shortly after the publication of his work, and now, that he is dead and gone, it cannot do much harm to his memory, to say, that his time might have been much better employed in weightier labours. He, however, was apt to ride his hobby his own way; and though it did now and then kick up the dust a little in the eyes of his neighbours, and grieve the spirit of some friends, for whom he felt the truest deference and affection; yet his errors and follies are remembered "more in sorrow than in anger,"[4] and it begins to be suspected, that he never intended to injure or offend. But however his memory may be appreciated by critics, it is still held dear among many folk, whose good opinion is well worth having; particularly certain biscuit bakers, who have gone so far as to imprint his likeness on their new year cakes, and have thus given him a chance for immortality, almost equal to being stamped on a Waterloo medal, or a Queen Anne's farthing.[5]]

Rip Van Winkle
A Posthumous Writing of Diedrich Knickerbocker

By Woden, God of Saxons,
From whence comes Wensday, that is Wodensday,
Truth is a thing that ever I will keep
Unto thylke day in which I creep into
My sepulchre—

CARTWRIGHT[6]

Whoever has made a voyage up the Hudson[7] must remember the Kaatskill mountains. They are a dismembered branch of the great Appalachian family, and are seen away to the west of the river, swelling up to a noble height, and lording it over the surrounding country. Every change of season, every change of weather, indeed, every hour of the day, produces some change in the magical hues and shapes of these

---

[1]   *Diedrich Knickerbocker*   Allusion to the fictional author of Irving's parody *History of New York* (1809);   *curious*   interested;   *Dutch history … province*   In the early to mid-seventeenth century, the Dutch Republic colonized land on the east coast of North America, calling this territory New Netherland. The territory was ceded to Britain in 1664 and renamed the Province of New York, with the town of New Amsterdam also being named New York.

[2]   *burghers*   Citizens.

[3]   *black-letter*   Gothic-style typeface used in early printed material; black-letter books were regarded as valuable and important, and therefore often fitted with clasps and locks.

[4]   [Irving's note]   Vide the excellent discourse of G.C. Verplanck, Esq. before the New-York Historical Society. [Gulian C. Verplanck was a politician, writer, and founder of the New York Historical Society, who had disparaged Irving's parodic *History of New York*; also see Horatio's description of the King's ghost in Shakespeare's *Hamlet* 1.2.232: "A countenance more in sorrow than in anger."]

[5]   *Waterloo medal … Anne's farthing*   Waterloo medals were widely distributed to those who fought in the battles leading up to the defeat of Napoleon in 1815; Queen Anne's farthings, small coins worth a quarter of a penny, were only accidentally circulated after the Queen's death in 1714, and then incorrectly believed to be highly valuable.

[6]   *By Woden … CARTWRIGHT*   Excerpt from William Cartwright's 1635 play *The Ordinary* (3.1.1050–54), lines spoken by a pedantic antiquarian named Moth;   *Woden*   Foremost god in Norse mythology.

[7]   *Hudson*   Hudson River, which runs through what is now New York State; the river was named after English explorer Henry Hudson, who sailed for the Dutch East India Company in the early seventeenth century.

mountains, and they are regarded by all the good wives, far and near, as perfect barometers. When the weather is fair and settled, they are clothed in blue and purple, and print their bold outlines on the clear evening sky; but sometimes, when the rest of the landscape is cloudless, they will gather a hood of gray vapours about their summits, which, in the last rays of the setting sun, will glow and light up like a crown of glory.

At the foot of these fairy mountains, the voyager may have descried[1] the light smoke curling up from a village, whose shingle roofs gleam among the trees, just where the blue tints of the upland melt away into the fresh green of the nearer landscape. It is a little village of great antiquity, having been founded by some of the Dutch colonists, in the early times of the province, just about the beginning of the government of the good Peter Stuyvesant[2] (may he rest in peace!), and there were some of the houses of the original settlers standing within a few years, with lattice windows, gable fronts surmounted with weathercocks, and built of small yellow bricks brought from Holland.

In that same village, and in one of these very houses (which, to tell the precise truth, was sadly time-worn and weather-beaten), there lived many years since, while the country was yet a province of Great Britain, a simple, good-natured fellow, of the name of Rip Van Winkle. He was a descendant of the Van Winkles who figured so gallantly in the chivalrous days of Peter Stuyvesant, and accompanied him to the siege of Fort Christina.[3] He inherited, however, but little of the martial character of his ancestors. I have observed that he was a simple, good-natured man; he was moreover a kind neighbour, and an obedient, henpecked husband. Indeed, to the latter circumstance might be owing that meekness of spirit which gained him such universal popularity; for those men are most apt to be obsequious and conciliating abroad, who are under the discipline of shrews[4] at home. Their tempers, doubtless, are

rendered pliant and malleable in the fiery furnace of domestic tribulation, and a curtain lecture[5] is worth all the sermons in the world for teaching the virtues of patience and long suffering. A termagant[6] wife may, therefore, in some respects, be considered a tolerable blessing; and if so, Rip Van Winkle was thrice blessed.

Certain it is, that he was a great favourite among all the good wives of the village, who, as usual with the amiable sex, took his part in all family squabbles, and never failed, whenever they talked those matters over in their evening gossippings, to lay all the blame on Dame Van Winkle. The children of the village, too, would shout with joy whenever he approached. He assisted at their sports, made their playthings, taught them to fly kites and shoot marbles, and told them long stories of ghosts, witches, and Indians. Whenever he went dodging about the village, he was surrounded by a troop of them, hanging on his skirts, clambering on his back, and playing a thousand tricks on him with impunity; and not a dog would bark at him throughout the neighbourhood.

The great error in Rip's composition was an insuperable aversion to all kinds of profitable labour.[7] It could not be for the want of assiduity or perseverance; for he would sit on a wet rock, with a rod as long and heavy as a Tartar's lance, and fish all day without a murmur, even though he should not be encouraged by a single nibble. He would carry a fowling piece[8] on his shoulder for hours together, trudging through woods and swamps, and up hill and down dale, to shoot a few squirrels or wild pigeons. He would never even refuse to assist a neighbour in the roughest toil, and was a foremost man at all country frolics for husking Indian corn, or building stone fences; the women of the village, too, used to employ him to run their errands, and to do such little odd jobs as their less obliging husbands would not do for them—in a word, Rip was ready to attend to anybody's business but his own; but

---

1   *descried*   Discerned; caught sight of.

2   *Peter Stuyvesant*   Last director-general of the colony of New Netherland, from 1647 until 1664, when he ceded the territory to the English.

3   *Fort Christina*   Swedish colony in what is now the state of Delaware, where Swedish troops were defeated by Stuyvesant in 1655, effectively ending Swedish colonialism in North America.

4   *shrews*   Derogatory term for controlling or nagging women.

5   *curtain lecture*   Archaic term describing the scolding by a wife of her husband, with the further implication that she denies his sexual advances, while behind the curtains of their bed.

6   *termagant*   Bad-tempered; shrewish.

7   *The great error ... profitable labour*   I.e., Rip's greatest character flaw was his constant distaste for doing useful work.

8   *fowling piece*   Small gun for hunting wild birds.

as to doing family duty, and keeping his farm in order, it was impossible.

In fact, he declared it was no use to work on his farm; it was the most pestilent little piece of ground in the whole country; everything about it went wrong, and would go wrong, in spite of him. His fences were continually falling to pieces; his cow would either go astray, or get among the cabbages; weeds were sure to grow quicker in his fields than anywhere else; the rain always made a point of setting in just as he had some outdoor work to do. So that though his patrimonial estate had dwindled away under his management, acre by acre, until there was little more left than a mere patch of Indian corn and potatoes, yet it was the worst conditioned farm in the neighbourhood.

His children, too, were as ragged and wild as if they belonged to nobody. His son Rip, an urchin begotten in his own likeness, promised to inherit the habits, with the old clothes of his father. He was generally seen trooping like a colt at his mother's heels, equipped in a pair of his father's cast-off galligaskins,[1] which he had much ado to hold up with one hand, as a fine lady does her train in bad weather.

Rip Van Winkle, however, was one of those happy mortals, of foolish, well-oiled dispositions, who take the world easy, eat white bread or brown, whichever can be got with least thought or trouble, and would rather starve on a penny than work for a pound. If left to himself, he would have whistled life away in perfect contentment; but his wife kept continually dinning in his ears about his idleness, his carelessness, and the ruin he was bringing on his family. Morning, noon, and night, her tongue was incessantly going, and everything he said or did was sure to produce a torrent of household eloquence. Rip had but one way of reply-ing to all lectures of the kind, and that, by frequent use, had grown into a habit. He shrugged his shoulders, shook his head, cast up his eyes, but said nothing. This, however, always provoked a fresh volley from his wife, so that he was fain to draw off his forces,[2] and take to the outside of the house—the only side which, in truth, belongs to a henpecked husband.

Rip's sole domestic adherent was his dog Wolf, who was as much henpecked as his master; for Dame Van Winkle regarded them as companions in idleness, and even looked upon Wolf with an evil eye, as the cause of his master's so often going astray. True it is, in all points of spirit befitting an honourable dog, he was as courageous an animal as ever scoured the woods—but what courage can withstand the ever-during and all-besetting terrors of a woman's tongue? The moment Wolf entered the house, his crest fell, his tail drooped to the ground, or curled between his legs, he sneaked about with a gallows air,[3] casting many a sidelong glance at Dame Van Winkle, and at the least flourish of a broomstick or ladle, would fly to the door with yelping precipitation.

Times grew worse and worse with Rip Van Winkle as years of matrimony rolled on; a tart temper never mel-lows with age, and a sharp tongue is the only edge tool that grows keener[4] by constant use. For a long while he used to console himself, when driven from home, by frequenting a kind of perpetual club of the sages, philosophers, and other idle personages of the village, that held its sessions on a bench before a small inn, des-ignated by a rubicund portrait of his majesty George the Third.[5] Here they used to sit in the shade, of a long lazy summer's day, talk listlessly over village gossip, or tell endless sleepy stories about nothing. But it would have been worth any statesman's money to have heard the profound discussions that sometimes took place, when by chance an old newspaper fell into their hands, from some passing traveller. How solemnly they would listen to the contents, as drawled out by Derrick Van Bummel, the schoolmaster, a dapper, learned little man, who was not to be daunted by the most gigan-tic word in the dictionary; and how sagely they would deliberate upon public events some months after they had taken place.

The opinions of this junto[6] were completely con-trolled by Nicholas Vedder, a patriarch of the village,

---

1   *galligaskins*   Loose-fitting style of breeches or trousers.

2   *fain to … his forces*   I.e., inclined to withdraw from the interaction.

3   *gallows air*   Appearance of one ready for the gallows, to be hanged.

4   *keener*   Sharper.

5   *George the Third*   King of Great Britain from 1760 to 1820, and the last British monarch to rule over the Thirteen Colonies preceding the American Revolutionary War.

6   *junto*   Self-organized political committee or club.

and landlord of the inn, at the door of which he took his seat from morning till night, just moving sufficiently to avoid the sun, and keep in the shade of a large tree; so that the neighbours could tell the hour by his movements as accurately as by a sun dial. It is true, he was rarely heard to speak, but smoked his pipe incessantly. His adherents, however (for every great man has his adherents), perfectly understood him, and knew how to gather his opinions. When anything that was read or related displeased him, he was observed to smoke his pipe vehemently, and send forth short, frequent, and angry puffs; but when pleased, he would inhale the smoke slowly and tranquilly, and emit it in light and placid clouds, and sometimes taking the pipe from his mouth, and letting the fragrant vapour curl about his nose, would gravely nod his head in token of perfect approbation.

From even this stronghold the unlucky Rip was at length routed by his termagant wife, who would suddenly break in upon the tranquility of the assemblage, [and][1] call the members all to nought; nor was that august personage, Nicholas Vedder himself, sacred from the daring tongue of this terrible virago,[2] who charged him outright with encouraging her husband in habits of idleness.

Poor Rip was at last reduced almost to despair; and his only alternative to escape from the labour of the farm and the clamour of his wife, was to take gun in hand, and stroll away into the woods. Here he would sometimes seat himself at the foot of a tree, and share the contents of his wallet[3] with Wolf, with whom he sympathised as a fellow sufferer in persecution. "Poor Wolf," he would say, "thy mistress leads thee a dog's life of it; but never mind, my lad, while I live thou shalt never want a friend to stand by thee!" Wolf would wag his tail, look wistfully in his master's face, and if dogs can feel pity, I verily believe he reciprocated the sentiment with all his heart.

In a long ramble of the kind on a fine autumnal day, Rip had unconsciously scrambled to one of the highest parts of the Kaatskill mountains. He was after his favourite sport of squirrel shooting, and the still solitudes had echoed and re-echoed with the reports of his gun. Panting and fatigued, he threw himself, late in the afternoon, on a green knoll, covered with mountain herbage, that crowned the brow of a precipice. From an opening between the trees, he could overlook all the lower country for many a mile of rich woodland. He saw at a distance the lordly Hudson, far, far below him, moving on its silent but majestic course, the reflection of a purple cloud, or the sail of a lagging bark,[4] here and there sleeping on its glassy bosom, and at last losing itself in the blue highlands.

On the other side he looked down into a deep mountain glen, wild, lonely, and shagged, the bottom filled with fragments from the impending cliffs, and scarcely lighted by the reflected rays of the setting sun. For some time Rip lay musing on this scene, evening was gradually advancing, the mountains began to throw their long blue shadows over the valleys, he saw that it would be dark long before he could reach the village, and he heaved a heavy sigh when he thought of encountering the terrors of Dame Van Winkle.

As he was about to descend, he heard a voice from a distance, hallooing, "Rip Van Winkle! Rip Van Winkle!" He looked around, but could see nothing but a crow winging its solitary flight across the mountain. He thought his fancy must have deceived him, and turned again to descend, when he heard the same cry ring through the still evening air; "Rip Van Winkle! Rip Van Winkle!"—at the same time Wolf bristled up his back, and giving a low growl, skulked to his master's side, looking fearfully down into the glen. Rip now felt a vague apprehension stealing over him; he looked anxiously in the same direction, and perceived a strange figure slowly toiling up the rocks, and bending under the weight of something he carried on his back. He was surprised to see any human being in this lonely and unfrequented place, but supposing it to be someone of the neighbourhood in need of his assistance, he hastened down to yield it.

On nearer approach, he was still more surprised at the singularity of the stranger's appearance. He was a short, square-built old fellow, with thick bushy hair, and a grizzled beard. His dress was of the antique Dutch fashion—a cloth jerkin[5] strapped round the

---

1   [and]   Irving added this word in later editions.

2   *virago*   Fierce woman.

3   *wallet*   Knapsack.

4   *bark*   Small type of sailing boat.

5   *jerkin*   Style of jacket fashionable during the seventeenth century, but no longer worn by the time of this story.

waist—several pairs of breeches, the outer one of ample volume, decorated with rows of buttons down the sides, and bunches at the knees. He bore on his shoulder a stout keg, that seemed full of liquor, and made signs for Rip to approach and assist him with the load. Though rather shy and distrustful of this new acquaintance, Rip complied with his usual alacrity, and mutually relieving each other, they clambered up a narrow gully, apparently the dry bed of a mountain torrent. As they ascended, Rip every now and then heard long rolling peals, like distant thunder, that seemed to issue out of a deep ravine, or rather cleft between lofty rocks, toward which their rugged path conducted. He paused for an instant, but supposing it to be the muttering of one of those transient thunder showers which often take place in mountain heights, he proceeded. Passing through the ravine, they came to a hollow, like a small amphitheatre, surrounded by perpendicular precipices, over the brinks of which impending trees shot their branches, so that you only caught glimpses of the azure sky, and the bright evening cloud. During the whole time, Rip and his companion had laboured on in silence; for though the former marvelled greatly what could be the object[1] of carrying a keg of liquor up this wild mountain, yet there was something strange and incomprehensible about the unknown, that inspired awe, and checked familiarity.[2]

On entering the amphitheatre, new objects of wonder presented themselves. On a level spot in the centre was a company of odd-looking personages playing at nine-pins.[3] They were dressed in a quaint, outlandish fashion: some wore short doublets,[4] others jerkins, with long knives in their belts, and most had enormous breeches, of similar style with that of the guide's. Their visages, too, were peculiar: one had a large head, broad face, and small piggish eyes; the face of another seemed to consist entirely of nose, and was surmounted by a white sugarloaf hat,[5] set off with a little red cockstail. They all had beards, of various shapes and colours. There was one who seemed to be the commander. He was a stout old gentleman, with a weather-beaten countenance; he wore a laced doublet, broad belt and hanger,[6] high crowned hat and feather, red stockings, and high-heeled shoes, with roses in them. The whole group reminded Rip of the figures in an old Flemish painting, in the parlour of Dominie[7] Van Schaick, the village parson, and which had been brought over from Holland at the time of the settlement.

What seemed particularly odd to Rip was that, though these folks were evidently amusing themselves, yet they maintained the gravest faces, the most mysterious silence, and were, withal, the most melancholy party of pleasure he had ever witnessed. Nothing interrupted the stillness of the scene, but the noise of the balls, which, whenever they were rolled, echoed along the mountains like rumbling peals of thunder.

As Rip and his companion approached them, they suddenly desisted from their play, and stared at him with such fixed statue-like gaze, and such strange, uncouth, lacklustre countenances, that his heart turned within him, and his knees smote together. His companion now emptied the contents of the keg into large flagons, and made signs to him to wait upon the company. He obeyed with fear and trembling;[8] they quaffed the liquor in profound silence, and then returned to their game.

By degrees, Rip's awe and apprehension subsided. He even ventured, when no eye was fixed upon him, to taste the beverage, which he found had much of the flavour of excellent Hollands.[9] He was naturally a thirsty soul, and was soon tempted to repeat the draught. One taste provoked another, and he reiterated his visits to the flagon so often, that at length his senses were overpowered, his eyes swam in his head, his head gradually declined, and he fell into a deep sleep.

---

[1]   *object* Purpose.

[2]   *checked familiarity* I.e., discouraged overt friendliness.

[3]   *nine-pins* Lawn game similar to modern-day bowling.

[4]   *doublets* Another form of male upper-body garment.

[5]   *sugarloaf hat* Tall, conical sort of hat, often associated with English Puritans and Pilgrims who settled the eastern Americas in the early 1600s.

[6]   *hanger* Short sword worn at the belt.

[7]   *old Flemish painting* Flemish art, hailing from Belgium and the Netherlands, developed its distinctive style during the late Renaissance; *Dominie* Title for a minister or parson, commonly used in the former Dutch colonies.

[8]   *fear and trembling* Cf. Philippians 2.12: "Wherefore, my beloved, as ye have always obeyed, not as in my presence only, but now much more in my absence, work out your own salvation with fear and trembling."

[9]   *Hollands* Dutch gin.

On awakening, he found himself on the green knoll from whence he had first seen the old man of the glen. He rubbed his eyes—it was a bright sunny morning. The birds were hopping and twittering among the bushes, and the eagle was wheeling aloft, and breasting the pure mountain breeze. "Surely," thought Rip, "I have not slept here all night." He recalled the occurrences before he fell asleep. The strange man with the keg of liquor—the mountain ravine—the wild retreat among the rocks—the woebegone party at nine-pins—the flagon—"Oh! that flagon! that wicked flagon!" thought Rip—"what excuse shall I make to Dame Van Winkle?"

He looked round for his gun, but in place of the clean, well-oiled fowling piece, he found an old firelock lying by him, the barrel encrusted with rust, the lock falling off, and the stock worm-eaten. He now suspected that the grave roysters[1] of the mountain had put a trick upon him, and having dosed him with liquor, had robbed him of his gun. Wolf, too, had disappeared, but he might have strayed away after a squirrel or partridge. He whistled after him, shouted his name, but all in vain; the echoes repeated his whistle and shout, but no dog was to be seen.

He determined to revisit the scene of the last evening's gambol,[2] and if he met with any of the party, to demand his dog and gun. As he arose to walk he found himself stiff in the joints, and wanting in his usual activity.[3] "These mountain beds do not agree with me," thought Rip, "and if this frolic should lay me up with a fit of the rheumatism, I shall have a blessed time with Dame Van Winkle." With some difficulty he got down into the glen: he found the gully up which he and his companion had ascended the preceding evening, but to his astonishment a mountain stream was now foaming down it, leaping from rock to rock, and filling the glen with babbling murmurs. He, however, made shift to scramble up its sides, working his toilsome way through thickets of birch, sassafras, and witch hazel, and sometimes tripped up or entangled by the wild grape vines that twisted their coils and tendrils from tree to tree, and spread a kind of network in his path.

At length he reached to where the ravine had opened through the cliffs, to the amphitheatre; but no traces of such opening remained. The rocks presented a high impenetrable wall, over which the torrent came tumbling in a sheet of feathery foam, and fell into a broad deep basin, black from the shadows of the surrounding forest. Here, then, poor Rip was brought to a stand. He again called and whistled after his dog; he was only answered by the cawing of a flock of idle crows, sporting high in air about a dry tree that overhung a sunny precipice; and who, secure in their elevation, seemed to look down and scoff at the poor man's perplexities. What was to be done? the morning was passing away, and Rip felt famished for his breakfast. He grieved to give up his dog and gun; he dreaded to meet his wife; but it would not do to starve among the mountains. He shook his head, shouldered the rusty firelock, and, with a heart full of trouble and anxiety, turned his steps homeward.

As he approached the village, he met a number of people, but none that he knew, which somewhat surprised him, for he had thought himself acquainted with everyone in the country round. Their dress, too, was of a different fashion from that to which he was accustomed. They all stared at him with equal marks of surprise, and whenever they cast eyes upon him, invariably stroked their chins. The constant recurrence of this gesture induced Rip, involuntarily, to do the same, when, to his astonishment, he found his beard had grown a foot long!

He had now entered the skirts of the village. A troop of strange children ran at his heels, hooting after him, and pointing at his gray beard. The dogs, too, not one of which he recognized for his old acquaintances, barked at him as he passed. The very village seemed altered: it was larger and more populous. There were rows of houses which he had never seen before, and those which had been his familiar haunts had disappeared. Strange names were over the doors—strange faces at the windows—everything was strange. His mind now began to misgive him, that both he and the world around him were bewitched. Surely this was his native village, which he had left but the day before. There stood the Kaatskill mountains—there ran the silver Hudson at a distance—there was every hill and dale precisely as it had always been—Rip was sorely

---

[1]   *roysters*   Revelers.

[2]   *gambol*   Festivity; frolic.

[3]   *wanting in his usual activity*   I.e., lacking his usual energy.

perplexed. "That flagon last night," thought he, "has addled my poor head sadly!"

It was with some difficulty he found the way to his own house, which he approached with silent awe, expecting every moment to hear the shrill voice of Dame Van Winkle. He found the house gone to decay—the roof fallen in, the windows shattered, and the doors off the hinges. A half-starved dog, that looked like Wolf, was skulking about it. Rip called him by name, but the cur snarled, showed his teeth, and passed on. This was an unkind cut indeed. "My very dog," sighed poor Rip, "has forgotten me!"

He entered the house, which, to tell the truth, Dame Van Winkle had always kept in neat order. It was empty, forlorn, and apparently abandoned. This desolateness overcame all his connubial fears—he called loudly for his wife and children—the lonely chambers rung for a moment with his voice, and then all again was silence.

He now hurried forth, and hastened to his old resort, the little village inn—but it too was gone. A large rickety wooden building stood in its place, with great gaping windows, some of them broken, and mended with old hats and petticoats, and over the door was painted, "The Union Hotel, by Jonathan Doolitle." Instead of the great tree that used to shelter the quiet little Dutch inn of yore, there now was reared a tall naked pole, with something on top that looked like a red night cap,[1] and from it was fluttering a flag, on which was a singular assemblage of stars and stripes—all this was strange and incomprehensible. He recognized on the sign, however, the ruby face of King George, under which he had smoked so many a peaceful pipe, but even this was singularly metamorphosed. The red coat was changed for one of blue and buff,[2] a sword was stuck in the hand instead of a sceptre, the head was decorated with a cocked hat,[3] and underneath was painted in large characters, GENERAL WASHINGTON.

There was, as usual, a crowd of folk about the door, but none that Rip recollected. The very character of the people seemed changed. There was a busy, bustling, disputatious tone about it, instead of the accustomed phlegm and drowsy tranquillity. He looked in vain for the sage Nicholas Vedder, with his broad face, double chin, and fair long pipe, uttering clouds of tobacco smoke instead of idle speeches; or Van Bummel, the schoolmaster, doling forth the contents of an ancient newspaper. In place of these, a lean, bilious-looking fellow, with his pockets full of handbills, was haranguing vehemently about rights of citizens—election—members of congress—liberty—Bunker's hill—heroes of seventy-six[4]—and other words, that were a perfect Babylonish jargon[5] to the bewildered Van Winkle.

The appearance of Rip, with his long, grizzled beard, his rusty fowling piece, his uncouth dress, and the army of women and children that had gathered at his heels, soon attracted the attention of the tavern politicians. They crowded around him, eyeing him from head to foot, with great curiosity. The orator bustled up to him, and drawing him partly aside, inquired "which side he voted?" Rip stared in vacant stupidity. Another short but busy little fellow pulled him by the arm, and raising on tiptoe, inquired in his ear, "whether he was Federal or Democrat."[6] Rip was equally at a loss to comprehend the question, when a knowing, self-important old gentleman, in a sharp cocked hat, made his way through the crowd, putting them to the right and left with his elbows as he passed, and planting

---

[4] *Bunker's hill* First major battle of the Revolutionary war; *heroes of seventy-six* The Declaration of Independence was drafted in 1776.

[5] *Babylonish jargon* Incomprehensible gibberish, referring to the biblical story of the Tower of Babel (Genesis 11.1–9), which relates how it came to be that humans speak different languages and cannot understand one another; technically, the more correct term would be "Babelish."

[6] *Federal or Democrat* Opposing political parties that arose in the 1790s, led respectively by Alexander Hamilton (1755–1804) and Thomas Jefferson (1743–1826); the policies of the Federalists emphasized a strong central government and favored stronger ties to Britain in foreign affairs, while Jefferson's Democratic-Republicans placed more emphasis on states' rights, defended the values of an agrarian society in opposition to the perceived elitism of the Federalists, and believed in the capability of common people to participate fully in democracy.

---

[1] *tall naked pole … red night cap* The pole and the red cap were both widespread symbols of liberty, especially after their use in the French Revolution; similar loose-fitting caps had been worn in ancient Rome by people emancipated from slavery.

[2] *blue and buff* Colors worn by American Revolutionary soldiers.

[3] *cocked hat* Style of hat worn in the late eighteenth century (especially as part of military uniforms), worn with one side of the brim folded up or "cocked."

himself before Van Winkle, with one arm akimbo, the other resting on his cane, his keen eyes and sharp hat penetrating, as it were, into his very soul, demanded, in an austere tone, "what brought him to the election with a gun on his shoulder, and a mob at his heels, and whether he meant to breed a riot in the village?" "Alas! gentlemen," cried Rip, somewhat dismayed, "I am a poor quiet man, a native of the place, and a loyal subject of the King, God bless him!"

Here a general shout burst from the bystanders—"A tory![1] a tory! a spy! a refugee! hustle him! away with him!" It was with great difficulty that the self-important man in the cocked hat restored order; and having assumed a tenfold austerity of brow, demanded again of the unknown culprit, what he came there for, and whom he was seeking. The poor man humbly assured them that he meant no harm, but merely came there in search of some of his neighbours, who used to keep about the tavern.

"Well—who are they?—name them."

Rip bethought himself a moment, and inquired, "where's Nicholas Vedder?"

There was a silence for a little while, when an old man replied, in a thin piping voice, "Nicholas Vedder? why he is dead and gone these eighteen years! There was a wooden tombstone in the churchyard that used to tell all about him, but that's rotted and gone too."

"Where's Brom Dutcher?"

"Oh he went off to the army in the beginning of the war; some say he was killed at the battle of Stoney Point—others say he was drowned in a squall, at the foot of Antony's Nose.[2] I don't know—he never came back again."

"Where's Van Bummel, the schoolmaster?"

"He went off to the wars too, was a great militia general, and is now in Congress."

Rip's heart died away, at hearing of these sad changes in his home and friends, and finding himself thus alone in the world. Every answer puzzled him, too, by treating of such enormous lapses of time, and of matters which he could not understand:

war—congress—Stoney Point—he had no courage to ask after any more friends, but cried out in despair, "does nobody here know Rip Van Winkle?"

"Oh, Rip Van Winkle!" exclaimed two or three, "Oh, to be sure! that's Rip Van Winkle yonder, leaning against the tree."

Rip looked, and beheld a precise counterpart of himself as he went up the mountain: apparently as lazy, and certainly as ragged. The poor fellow was now completely confounded. He doubted his own identity, and whether he was himself or another man. In the midst of his bewilderment, the man in the cocked hat demanded who he was, and what was his name?

"God knows," exclaimed he, at his wit's end; "I'm not myself—I'm somebody else—that's me yonder—no—that's somebody else, got into my shoes—I was myself last night, but I fell asleep on the mountain, and they've changed my gun, and everything's changed, and I'm changed, and I can't tell what's my name, or who I am!"

The bystanders began now to look at each other, nod, wink significantly, and tap their fingers against their foreheads. There was a whisper, also, about securing the gun, and keeping the old fellow from doing mischief; at the very suggestion of which, the self-important man in the cocked hat retired with some precipitation. At this critical moment a fresh likely[3] woman pressed through the throng to get a peep at the graybearded man. She had a chubby child in her arms, which, frightened at his looks, began to cry. "Hush, Rip," cried she, "hush, you little fool, the old man won't hurt you." The name of the child, the air of the mother, the tone of her voice, all awakened a train of recollections in his mind.

"What is your name, my good woman?" asked he.

"Judith Gardenier."

"And your father's name?"

"Ah, poor man, his name was Rip Van Winkle; it's twenty years since he went away from home with his gun, and never has been heard of since—his dog came home without him; but whether he shot himself, or was carried away by the Indians, nobody can tell. I was then but a little girl."

Rip had but one question more to ask; but he put it with a faltering voice:

---

1   *tory* Royalist.

2   *Stoney Point* British fortress which was captured by the Continental Army in 1779; *Antony's Nose* Small mountain along the Hudson River, which is also mentioned in Irving's *History of New York*.

3   *likely* Pretty (later revised editions have "comely" here).

"Where's your mother?"

Oh, she too had died but a short time since; she broke a blood vessel in a fit of passion at a New England pedlar.

There was a drop of comfort, at least, in this intelligence. The honest man could contain himself no longer. He caught his daughter and her child in his arms. "I am your father!" cried he—"Young Rip Van Winkle once—old Rip Van Winkle now! Does nobody know poor Rip Van Winkle?"

All stood amazed, until an old woman, tottering out from among the crowd, put her hand to her brow, and peering under it in his face for a moment, exclaimed, "Sure enough! it is Rip Van Winkle—it is himself. Welcome home again, old neighbour—why, where have you been these twenty long years?"

Rip's story was soon told, for the whole twenty years had been to him but as one night. The neighbours stared when they heard it; some were seen to wink at each other, and put their tongues in their cheeks; and the self-important man in the cocked hat, who, when the alarm was over, had returned to the field, screwed down the corners of his mouth, and shook his head—upon which there was a general shaking of the head throughout the assemblage.

It was determined, however, to take the opinion of old Peter Vanderdonk, who was seen slowly advancing up the road. He was a descendant of the historian of that name,[1] who wrote one of the earliest accounts of the province. Peter was the most ancient inhabitant of the village, and well versed in all the wonderful events and traditions of the neighbourhood. He recollected Rip at once, and corroborated his story in the most satisfactory manner. He assured the company that it was a fact, handed down from his ancestor the historian, that the Kaatskill mountains had always been haunted by strange beings. That it was affirmed that the great Hendrick Hudson, the first discoverer of the river and country, kept a kind of vigil there every twenty years, with his crew of the Half-moon,[2]

being permitted in this way to revisit the scenes of his enterprise, and keep a guardian eye upon the river, and the great city called by his name. That his father had once seen them in their old Dutch dresses playing at nine pins in a hollow of the mountain; and that he himself had heard, one summer afternoon, the sound of their balls, like long peals of thunder.

To make a long story short, the company broke up, and returned to the more important concerns of the election. Rip's daughter took him home to live with her; she had a snug, well-furnished house, and a stout cheery farmer for a husband, whom Rip recollected for one of the urchins that used to climb upon his back. As to Rip's son and heir, who was the ditto of himself, seen leaning against the tree, he was employed to work on the farm; but evinced an hereditary disposition to attend to anything else but his business.

Rip now resumed his old walks and habits; he soon found many of his former cronies, though all rather the worse for the wear and tear of time; and preferred making friends among the rising generation, with whom he soon grew into great favour.

Having nothing to do at home, and being arrived at that happy age when a man can do nothing with impunity, he took his place once more on the bench, at the inn door, and was reverenced as one of the patriarchs of the village, and a chronicle of the old times "before the war." It was some time before he could get into the regular track of gossip, or could be made to comprehend the strange events that had taken place during his torpor. How that there had been a revolutionary war—that the country had thrown off the yoke of old England—and that, instead of being a subject of his Majesty George the Third, he was now a free citizen of the United States. Rip, in fact, was no politician; the change of states and empires made but little impression on him. But there was one species of despotism under which he had long groaned, and that was—petticoat government. Happily, that was at an end; he had got his neck out of the yoke of matrimony, and could go in and out whenever he pleased, without dreading the tyranny of Dame Van Winkle. Whenever her name was mentioned, however, he shook his head, shrugged his shoulders, and cast up his eyes; which might pass either for an expression of resignation to his fate, or joy at his deliverance.

---

[1]   *historian of that name*   Adriaen van der Donk, who wrote *Description of New Netherland* (1655).

[2]   *crew of the Half-moon*   Referring to Hudson's ship, the *Halve Maen*; following a mutiny in 1611, Hudson and seven other crew members disappeared into the Hudson Bay, their fates remaining unknown.

He used to tell his story to every stranger that arrived at Mr. Doolittle's hotel. He was observed, at first, to vary on some points every time he told it, which was doubtless owing to his having so recently awakened. It at last settled down precisely to the tale I have related, and not a man, woman, or child in the neighbourhood, but knew it by heart. Some always pretended to doubt the reality of it, and insisted that Rip had been out of his head, and that this was one point on which he always remained flighty. The old Dutch inhabitants, however, almost universally gave it full credit. Even to this day they never hear a thunderstorm of a summer afternoon about the Kaatskill, but they say Hendrick Hudson and his crew are at their game of nine pins; and it is a common wish of all henpecked husbands in the neighbourhood, when life hangs heavy on their hands, that they might have a quieting draught out of Rip Van Winkle's flagon.

NOTE

The foregoing tale, one would suspect, had been suggested to Mr. Knickerbocker by a little German superstition about Charles V.[1] and the Kypphauser mountain; the subjoined note, however, which he had appended to the tale, shows that it is an absolute fact, narrated with his usual fidelity:

"The story of Rip Van Winkle may seem incredible to many, but nevertheless I give it my full belief, for I know the vicinity of our old Dutch settlements to have been very subject to marvellous events and appearances. Indeed, I have heard many stranger stories than this, in the villages along the Hudson; all of which were too well authenticated to admit of a doubt. I have even talked with Rip Van Winkle myself, who, when last I saw him, was a very venerable old man, and so perfectly rational and consistent on every other point, that I think no conscientious person could refuse to take this into the bargain; nay, I have seen a certificate on the subject taken before a country justice, and signed with a cross, in the justice's own hand writing. The story, therefore, is beyond the possibility of doubt.
D.K."

—1819

---

[1] *Charles V.* Holy Roman Emperor from 1519 to 1556. In later editions, Irving changed this to "the Emperor Frederick der Rothbart," another Holy Roman Emperor who reigned from 1152 to 1190. According to legend, der Rothbart, also known as Frederick Barbarossa ("redbeard"), did not die but rather fell asleep in the Kyffhäuser mountains in Germany, and will one day reawaken and return Germany to its past greatness. In reality, Irving's source for "Rip Van Winkle" is likely the German folktale "Peter Klaus," which was written down by Johann Karl Christoph Nachtigal in 1800.

IN CONTEXT

Images of Rip Van Winkle

John Quidor, *Rip Van Winkle and His Companions at the Inn Door of Nicholas Vedder*, 1839.

John Quidor, *The Return of Rip Van Winkle*, 1849 (see also the color insert).

The first illustrated edition of Irving's *Sketch Book* appeared in 1848, with 17 illustrations by Felix O.C. Darley. (Irving contributed a new preface for the edition, but made no comment in it on the addition of illustrations to the texts.) Darley's one illustration for "Rip Van Winkle," which appeared without a caption, is reproduced here.

F.O.C. Darley, *Rip Van Winkle Awaking*, 1848.

Joseph Jefferson (1829–1905) became famous in the latter half of the nineteenth century very largely for his portrayals of Rip Van Winkle in the dramatic adaptation by Irish playwright Dion Boucicault (*Rip Van Winkle, or The Sleep of Twenty Years* [1865]); the play was a hit for many years in London as well as throughout America. The 30 September 1865 issue of *The Illustrated London News* featured the following short piece on the new play. The same issue included an illustration of Jefferson starring in the production. Both that image and a photograph of Jefferson starring in the same role almost thirty years later are reproduced on the following pages.

> The new play of "Rip Van Winkle," a dramatised version, by Mr. Dion Boucicault, of Washington Irving's most genial and humorous story—in which the hero, one of the early Dutch settlers in New York, falls in with the goblins who haunt the Katskill mountains, and drinks their magic liquor, causing him a sleep of twenty years—is likely to have a long run at the Adelphi Theatre. The new American actor, Mr. Jefferson, who appears as Rip Van Winkle, seems as though he had created the character himself, so perfectly does he enter into the author's conception of the loose-lived, lazy, lounging fellow, who lets his wife turn him out of doors and then becomes the victim of the mischievous imps, with the ghost of the old pirate, Hendrik Hudson, at their head. Our Illustration shows the scene in which poor Rip Van Winkle is compelled to quaff the fatal potion.

Scene from "Rip Van Winkle," at the Adelphi Theatre, 1865.

Benjamin Joseph Falk, *Joseph Jefferson as Rip Van Winkle*, c. 1894.

AMERICA AND AMERICAN LITERATURE, 1820 TO RECONSTRUCTION

[Overview introductory sections on the following topics appear in the website component of the anthology:

Money and Machines, Capital and Labor
Individualism and Self-Reliance
Religion and Culture, 1820 to Reconstruction
The Civil War and Its Literature
Reconstruction and the Literature of Reconstruction
Language in America, 1820 to Reconstruction

Literary Genres, 1820 to Reconstruction
Poetry
Prose Fiction
Prose Non-fiction
Drama]

CHANGING VIEWS OF AMERICAN LITERATURE

In October 1840, the first issue appeared of what was termed by a British newspaper "an American periodical without a parallel in the history of the world." This was the *Lowell Offering*, "a repository of original articles on various subjects written by factory operatives," specifically, "females employed in the mills."[1] Though this publication survived for only a few years, it seems to have gained a surprisingly wide readership—and certainly it gained extraordinary respect, lauded in dozens of newspapers and magazines on both sides of the Atlantic, including in a review by Charles Dickens. With its mix of stories and poems (including pieces on such highly charged subjects as British oppression of Ireland as well as many on more familiar "poetical" subjects), together with essays on subjects ranging from nature, the arts, aesthetics, and astronomy, to "Time," "Contentment," "Indolence and Industry," and "The Nature of Man," the publication succeeded magnificently in challenging readers' assumptions as to what young working-class women might be capable of.

That challenge to conventional assumptions was made explicit by "A Factory Girl," the pseudonym of an unknown Lowell worker who set out, in the lead article of the *Lowell Offering*'s second issue, to rebut a characterization of female factory employees like herself that had been made by Orestes Brownson, an important figure in New England's intellectual establishment. Brownson had asserted that the phrase "She has worked in a factory, *is sufficient to damn to infamy the most worthy and virtuous girl.*" "A Factory Girl" scathingly refuted Brownson's assertion, thereby demonstrating, in her own words, that "a *factory girl* is not afraid to oppose herself to the *Editor of the Boston Quarterly Review.*" She was not afraid of opposing the influential arbiter of taste Sara Josepha Hale either. In the following issue of the *Lowell Offering* appeared "Gold Watches," in which "A Factory Girl"[2] took issue with Hale's lament that, with even some Lowell working girls having taken to wearing gold watches, all markers of class distinction were in danger of disappearing. In challenging Hale, "A Factory Girl" replied with an essay of strikingly incisive class commentary:

> Those who do not labor for their living have more time for the improvement of their minds, for the cultivation of conversational powers, and graceful manners; if, with all these advantages, they still need richer dress to distinguish them from us, the fault must be their own. ... [The factory girls] see things more as they really are, and not through the false medium which misleads the aristocracy.

The *Lowell Offering* was itself subject to challenging criticisms; some accused it of being, in its eagerness to "show what factory girls had power to do," too upbeat about working-class circumstances, too

---

[1] The city of Lowell, Massachusetts, founded in the 1820s as a planned manufacturing center for textiles, was the first large-scale factory town in the United States and a center of the industrial revolution in America.

[2] Most *Lowell Offering* contributions were anonymous; the most common practice was for authors to be identified by their first names or their initials. It is possible that the pieces by an author identified as "A Factory Girl" were in fact by different authors, but given the similarities in theme, tone, and style, it seems likely that they were written by the same author.

Cover of the May 1845 issue of the *Lowell Offering*.

keen to present "only one side of the question," too reluctant to "expose all the evils, and miseries, and mortifications attendant upon a factory life." But the fact that the *Lowell Offering* was widely read, praised, and reviewed is a testament to the diversity and openness that American literature was capable of in the 1820–Reconstruction period. Even the most partial of lists gives some sense of that range and openness: from Frederick Douglass's *North Star* in Rochester, New York to the *North Star* in Danville, Vermont that reprinted the *Lowell Offering* story "Abby's Year in Lowell"; from the popular prose of Fanny Fern, Bret Harte, and Mark Twain and the popular poetry of Lydia Sigourney and Henry Longfellow to the political writings of David Walker, Angelina Grimké, and Lydia Maria Child; from the sermons of Theodore Parker to the speeches of Abraham Lincoln; from the groundbreaking works of George Copway and John Rollin Ridge to the impassioned poetry of George Moses Horton and Frances Harper; from William Alcott's *Vegetable Diet* to Louisa May Alcott's *Little Women*; from the reformist prose of William Lloyd Garrison

and the reformist poetry of John Greenleaf Whittier to the reactionary prose of William Gilmore Simms; from the poems of the Seminole Wars to the 1867 anthology *Slave Songs of the United States*; from New Englander Richard Henry Dana Jr.'s enormously popular 1840 account of sailing to California and back to Chilean Vicente Pérez Rosales's equally engaging account of the California Gold Rush. Even in the face of the sort of censorship and repression that made *Uncle Tom's Cabin* unavailable in the South and led William Wells Brown to publish *Clotel* in England rather than America, American literature may fairly be said to have undergone an astonishing expansion and diversification in the 1820–Reconstruction period. Driven by an array of technological, economic, demographic, infrastructural, and educational changes, the number and variety of publications, and the speed and volume with which they could be circulated around the country, increased massively. And that in turn enabled many more Americans from all communities and walks of life, including people like the Lowell "Factory Girl," to join the national literary conversation.

In a passage from his 1849 novel *Redburn*, one of the writers who has come to be seen as central to nineteenth-century American literature, Herman Melville, powerfully conveys the expansiveness and diversity of that literature, and of nineteenth-century America as a whole. The passage reflects on America's identity as a nation of immigrants:

> Settled by the people of all nations, all nations may claim [America] for their own. You cannot spill a drop of American blood without spilling the blood of the whole world. Be he Englishman, Frenchman, German, Dane, or Scot; the European who scoffs at an American, calls his own brother *Raca*, and stands in danger of the judgment.[1] We are not a narrow tribe of men[.] … No: our blood is as the flood of the Amazon, made up of a

---

1   Melville here alludes to Matthew 5.22, part of Jesus' Sermon on the Mount, in which Jesus quotes the Ten Commandments' injunction "Thou shalt not kill" and then continues: "But I say unto you, That whosoever is angry with his brother without a cause shall be in danger of the judgment; and whosoever shall say to his brother, Raca, shall be in danger of the council." "Raca" is the Greek rendering of a word in Aramaic, the language spoken by Jesus, that means "empty-headed" or "foolish."

thousand noble currents all pouring into one. We are not a nation, so much as a world.

Like America as a whole, as Melville describes it here, nineteenth-century American literature, as it took shape through the contributions of writers as different as Melville and "A Factory Girl," could be said to consist of "a thousand noble currents all pouring into one," and in that sense to be "not a nation, so much as a world."

A century later, though, literary scholars had considerably narrowed down their view of nineteenth-century American literature from the breadth and variety of Melville's vision in *Redburn*. By the mid-twentieth century, scholars came to see American literature of the time of *Redburn* and the *Lowell Offering* in exactly the way that *Redburn* rejects in describing America as a whole: as consisting of, or at least exemplified by, "a narrow tribe of men." Within this "narrow tribe" of canonized nineteenth-century authors—most of them white, upper-class men—Melville himself, ironically, was given an integral place, while the likes of the Lowell factory girl, and the many other nineteenth-century writers who made the literature of that period so multifaceted and capacious, were minimized or forgotten altogether. One of the main stories of nineteenth-century American literature is thus the story of how it grew to become a "world" in its own time; how twentieth-century scholars shrank it down to a "narrow tribe"; and how, since the mid-twentieth century, it has expanded again.

The United States in the early and mid-nineteenth century was, to an extent possibly unparalleled by any previous society in history, a nation of readers and writers. Developments in printing technology in the early decades of the century, especially the invention of cast-iron printing presses and steam-powered printing, lowered the production costs of books, newspapers, and periodicals and increased the speed and volume with which they could be published, while new transportation technologies such as the railroad and steamship greatly heightened how far and how fast such publications could be distributed. The nation's lax copyright laws afforded authors, especially international ones, little control over their works after publication, thereby encouraging a "culture of reprinting" that further fed the proliferation of printed material.

Albert Sands Southworth and/or Josiah Johnson Hawes, *Classroom in the Emerson School for Girls*, c. 1850. This school—established in 1823 by George Barrell Emerson, second cousin of Ralph Waldo Emerson—was the most prominent girls' school in Boston.

At the same time, the U.S. was becoming one of the most literate countries in the world. Public schools were rapidly established in the northern states after the Revolution; universal, free, compulsory primary education was introduced in the mid-nineteenth century, and every state had tax-subsidized elementary schools by 1870. These educational measures further raised a literacy rate that in some regions—and among white Americans—already exceeded ninety per cent at the start of the century.[1]

The result of this congruence of developments was a large and growing popular demand for printed material and a burgeoning publishing industry to feed that popular demand. This interconnected expansion of print culture and readership is perhaps best exemplified

---

[1]   Literacy rates in the North far outstripped those among white Southerners in the decades leading up to the Civil War. During these same decades, the Southern states, in turn, steadily restricted the already limited ability of enslaved African Americans to learn to read and write.

by the growth, beginning in the 1830s, of the "penny press": a new variety of mass-produced newspaper, priced at one cent rather than the six cents that traditional newspapers cost. Such papers made news media affordable for the first time to the urban working classes and brought about a concomitant change in journalistic practices, as well as in ideas about what "the news" was.[1] However, the country's expanding print culture did not just create more readers; it also created more writers. As Catharine Maria Sedgwick's 1830 short story "Cacoethes Scribendi" satirically illustrates, the proliferation of books, periodicals, newspapers, and other kinds of publication both reflected and fostered the growth of an "irresistible urge to write" (the English translation of the story's Latin title) among numerous Americans, including many people—such as the homebound women of Sedgwick's story—who had previously been discouraged or excluded from authorship.

Alexander Gardner, *Virginia. Newspaper Vendor and Cart in Camp,* 1863. This depiction of a seller of "Philadelphia, N.Y. and Baltimore papers" to soldiers of the U.S. Army during the Civil War illustrates the extent of newspaper distribution and consumption by the 1860s.

Sedgwick was part of a significant surge in literary production in the 1820s. This surge yielded the first cohort of major post-Revolutionary American writers, including Sedgwick, James Fenimore Cooper, William Cullen Bryant, Lydia Maria Child, and their older contemporary Washington Irving (who appears elsewhere in this volume). All these writers met with great popular success between 1819 and 1829 and quickly became among the most highly regarded and highest-selling authors of their day, a status they retained for much of the nineteenth century. Notably, they achieved this status in Europe, especially Britain, as well as in America. The writers of the 1820s thereby counteracted European prejudices against American literature as crude and derivative and won recognition for it, at least in some quarters, as a body of writing that could stand on par with that of any other country. In 1820, the English critic Sydney Smith had famously mocked American literature with his rhetorical question, "In the four quarters of the globe, who reads an American book?" By 1847, however, an article in the British periodical *Bentley's Miscellany*, which serialized work by both Cooper and Sedgwick, could assert with only some degree of exaggeration that American books—specifically, Cooper's—were read all over the world: "He has been the chosen companion of the prince and the peasant on the borders of the Volga, the Danube, and the Guadalquivir, by the Indus and the Ganges, the Paraguay and the Amazon." While plenty of Europeans would continue to look down on American literature for decades to come (if not longer), the literary generation of the 1820s firmly established the idea, both domestically and internationally, that a distinctive, reputable American literature existed and deserved further cultivation. It could fairly be said of this generation collectively what *Bentley's* said in 1847 of Cooper's *The Spy* (1821): "it gave an extraordinary impulse to literature in the United States, more than anything that had before occurred; it roused the people from their feelings of intellectual dependence."

One of the primary venues whereby this "impulse to literature" was cultivated was the literary society; these sprang up all over the country during this period, especially among the working classes. Typically, members of these societies paid a regular fee, which was used to subscribe jointly to newspapers and journals or to stock

---

[1]   Important penny papers included the *Transcript* in Boston (founded in 1830), the *Picayune* in New Orleans (1837), and the *Sun* (1833), *Herald* (1835), *Tribune* (1841), and *Daily Times* (1851) in New York—this last the progenitor of today's *New York Times*.

a library. Literary societies provided opportunities for their members to teach and learn from one another; to read and discuss a range of literary works; and frequently to compose, share, and even publish their own writing. The *Lowell Offering*, for example, was an outgrowth of the seven "Mutual Self-Improvement Clubs" that the Lowell factory workers had founded by the early 1840s, in which they met to read original compositions to one another. The Lowell literary societies, and the periodical they gave rise to, helped launch the career of at least one significant literary figure: the poet Lucy Larcom, who began working at a Lowell mill at age eleven, first printed her work in the *Offering*, and went on to become one of only three nineteenth-century American female poets to have a volume of her collected poems published in her lifetime.

Literary societies were also an important part of the lives of free African Americans in the North, for whom they played an equally significant intellectual, social, and political role. Black men in Philadelphia formed the Reading Room Society for Men of Colour in 1828, and many other such societies quickly followed in the ensuing years, including societies for black women. Speaking in 1837, James Forten Jr., a leading figure in Philadelphia's black community, summed up the significance literary societies held for African Americans:

> As soon as we engage in any enterprise having for its foundation the mighty principles of mental illumination, we are at once noticed and respected. Thus we see that, whatever tends to disseminate the principles of education, tends to raise us above the tide of popular prejudice; and whatever tends to raise us above the chilling influence of prejudice, must of reason tend to elevate our condition. ... Such, I conceive, our Literary Institutions to have the power of doing.

African American literary societies were often venues not just for "reading, ... examining, ... [and] exercising the great faculty of thinking," in Forten's words, but also for writing. In an 1832 article, the white abolitionist William Lloyd Garrison described the Female Literary Association of Philadelphia, the members of which "assemble[d] every Tuesday evening for the purpose of mutual improvement in moral and literary pursuits": "Nearly all of them write, almost weekly,

original pieces, which are put anonymously into a box, and afterward criticized by a committee." With the members' permission, Garrison printed some of their compositions in his newspaper, the *Liberator*, but other participants in black literary societies published their work on their own initiative. For example, Sarah Forten, a member of the Female Literary Association and the sister of James Forten Jr., regularly published her essays and poetry in the *Liberator* and other such periodicals—albeit under the pen names "Ada" and "Magawisca" (the latter a name she had gleaned from the writing of Catharine Sedgwick).

Even members of groups as comprehensively marginalized or subordinated as Indigenous Americans and enslaved people asserted their ability and right to participate in the country's enormous literary expansion, and furthered that expansion in significant ways. The same vast growth in the pace, volume, and variety of publication that produced the penny papers and the *Lowell Offering* also enabled the founding, in 1828, of the *Cherokee Phoenix*, the first Native American-run newspaper (printed in both English and Cherokee), as well as the printing of the first published Native American autobiography, the Pequot minister and writer William

Alfred R. Waud, *"Zion" School for Colored Children, Charleston, South Carolina*, 1866. The Zion School was one of several schools founded by Northern missionaries for recently emancipated people in Charleston in the wake of the Civil War. The caption that accompanied this illustration when it was published in *Harper's Weekly* in December 1866 noted, "It is a peculiarity of this school that it is entirely under the superintendence of colored teachers."

Apess's *A Son of the Forest* (1829). Enslaved people in the South were legally barred not just from printing their own newspapers or publishing their life stories but from learning to read and write at all, but they still seized whatever opportunities they could to educate themselves and enter the literary sphere. One of the most striking examples of this was the career of George Moses Horton, a self-taught enslaved poet in North Carolina who had three volumes of his work published between 1829 and 1865. Similar aspirations are evident in the "sabbath school" that Frederick Douglass organized before his escape from slavery in 1838, in which he surreptitiously taught "my loved fellow-slaves how to read," and in the intense desire for education that emancipated African Americans demonstrated after the Civil War: what Booker T. Washington described as "a whole race trying to go to school." And outside the circles of formal education and print culture, enslaved people created a rich and powerful oral literature of their own—one that, once it began to see its way into print, swiftly became a major influence on the further development of America's written literature.

Popular understandings of literature throughout the early and mid-nineteenth century were broader and more fluid than the definition of the literary that, in the twentieth century, would shape the formation of the nineteenth-century canon. The folktales, work songs, and spirituals circulated orally by enslaved African Americans highlight the limitations, even the arbitrariness, of a conception of literature tied exclusively to print culture and literacy. Even within the sphere of literate print culture, though, nineteenth-century notions of what counted as literature were malleable and expansive. The supposedly firm boundary between "high culture" and "popular culture" that would become so important to twentieth-century conceptions of the literary was much more porous in the nineteenth century: poetry and popular song shaded into each other, and the self-consciously artistic fiction of such writers as Melville, Nathaniel Hawthorne, and Edgar Allan Poe was shaped by, and even arose out of, mass-market "sensation literature," with its fixation on adventure, sexuality, and violence. Similarly, most nineteenth-century Americans would have recognized no hard-and-fast distinction between, for example, a historical study or devotional tract, on the one hand,

and a novel or poem on the other. Novels and poems could equally be vehicles of moral or historical instruction, and history books and religious tracts could equally be manifestations of linguistic artistry and sources of diversion and pleasure.

In this extensive, diverse, and expanding literary field, with its broad ideas about what constituted "the literary," the authors who would be canonized in the twentieth century were for the most part seen as quite marginal.[1] Poe barely eked out a living from his pen and was known more for his criticism than his creative writing; Melville perplexed and frustrated readers and critics by turning away from the popular travel narratives with which he began his career and sank into obscurity; and Henry David Thoreau and Walt Whitman won notoriety but only a limited readership. Even Hawthorne—whose *The Scarlet Letter* (1850) was an instant success that sold out its initial 2,500-volume print run in just ten days—felt unappreciated in comparison to more popular female writers such as Harriet Beecher Stowe and Maria Susanna Cummins, infamously complaining in 1855 that "America is now given over to a damned mob of scribbling women, and I should have no chance of success while the public taste is occupied with their trash—and should be ashamed of myself if I did succeed." The institutionalization by twentieth-century scholars of Hawthorne's sense of the superior merit of his work, and that of fellow figures like his admirer Melville, has long obscured the extent to which female writers such as Stowe and Cummins actually became among the most celebrated authors of the time, or the fact that African Americans such as Frederick Douglass and William Wells Brown achieved a popularity overseas, especially in Britain, that outstripped that of many white American writers.

The elevation of the likes of Hawthorne and Melville above the likes of Stowe, Douglass, and Brown, and the reconceptualization of nineteenth-century American

---

[1] The writers of the generation of the 1820s discussed above *were* immediately recognized as major literary figures, and most of them have continued to be recognized as such ever since—although Catharine Sedgwick, for one, was sidelined in the twentieth century and has only been restored to prominence relatively recently.

Among the now canonical mid-century writers, Emily Dickinson is of course a special case, given that she published fewer than a dozen of her poems during her lifetime, all anonymously, and was otherwise read until the 1890s by only a small circle of family and acquaintances.

literature in terms of this narrow, elevated canon, took some time. Anthologies of American literature published in the early twentieth century tended to include a relatively capacious selection of nineteenth-century writers (as long as those writers were white) in a way that approximated the full breadth and variety of the early and mid-nineteenth century literary scene, as well as the breadth of what "the literary" encompassed during that period. During the early twentieth century, however, few American universities required students to take courses in American literature, and its study was widely looked down upon: in 1936, one scholar of American literature called his subject "the orphan child of the curriculum." Making American literature respectable in the eyes of the academic establishment required demonstrating that American literature could be both aesthetically and politically edifying, and in order to do that, scholars narrowed their focus to those works and authors who best matched their own conceptions of what "great literature" was, and of what America was.

The most important contribution to this narrower reconceptualization of nineteenth-century American literature in the mid-twentieth century was the Harvard scholar F.O. Matthiessen's 1941 book *American Renaissance*, which remains one of the single most influential books on American literature ever written. Matthiessen argued that mid-nineteenth-century American literature was best understood in terms of a "renaissance" exemplified by the works of just five writers, all of them white men from New England or New York: Ralph Waldo Emerson, Thoreau, Hawthorne, Whitman, and Melville.[1] According to Matthiessen, these five writers best exemplified "devotion to the possibilities of democracy" and thus "provide[d] a culture commensurate with America's political opportunity" in a way that warranted putting them at the core of the nineteenth-century American canon.[2] This project

of narrowing nineteenth-century American literature down to those figures deemed to have best enshrined, in literary form, a vision of America amenable to the nation's mid-twentieth-century cultural and political establishment also reflected the agenda of the United States government, which strongly promoted the study and teaching of American literature, at home and abroad, as a way of defending and elevating the nation's status during World War II and the Cold War. As a result of these scholarly and governmental efforts, American literature exploded as an academic subject in the 1940s and 50s, but the body of literature studied and taught became much more constricted than it had been earlier in the century. After World War II, for example, it became common practice for survey courses to include only eight writers from the 1820–Reconstruction period: Matthiessen's five plus Poe, Dickinson, and Mark Twain. A strong tendency to concentrate on this authorial canon—expanded slightly with the eventual inclusion of figures such as Douglass—persisted for much of the rest of the twentieth century and lingers into the twenty-first.

Ironically, though, this twentieth-century narrowing-down of nineteenth-century literature was driven, in part, by one of the same forces that also drove the original development of nineteenth-century literature, in all its true expansive diversity: American cultural nationalism. In and through their studies of nineteenth-century literature, mid-twentieth-century scholars such as Matthiessen sought to define a distinctive American national identity and culture. Many nineteenth-century American writers had similar motives. The first half of the nineteenth century was a period in which Americans sought earnestly to assert the distinctiveness and value of their national culture—to create, or demonstrate the existence of, an American literature that would not stand in Europe's shadow and would represent the originality, uniqueness, importance, and greatness that they saw in themselves. As the influential writer, editor, critic, and literary promoter John Neal—whose 1824 essay series on "American Writers" can claim to be the first history of American literature—put it in 1828, numerous Americans felt the need

---

[1]   Matthiessen's conception of the "American Renaissance" was even narrower than this list itself suggests: his exploration of these five writers focused on the works they published in a span of just six years, from 1850 to 1855.

[2]   While *American Renaissance* played a crucial part in this narrowing of the American literary canon, it should also be noted that Matthiessen himself—as a gay man whose fear of persecution for his left-wing political views during the McCarthy era contributed to his death by suicide in 1950—resisted the exclusionary forces at work in

---

American politics and culture during his time and represented some of the people and views those forces sought to exclude.

to announce "another Declaration of Independence, in the great *Republic of Letters*."

Such literary declarations of independence resound across the breadth of early and mid-nineteenth-century American literature—including in most of the examples given so far in this introduction. One of the Lowell "Factory Girl's" most withering critiques of Orestes Brownson was that his disrespect for industrial labor blurred the difference between European and American factory workers and perpetuated aristocratic European attitudes: "we often hear the condition of the factory population of England, and the station which the operatives hold in society there, referred to as descriptive of *our* condition. As well might it be said, as say the *nobility* of England, that *labor itself* is disgraceful, and that all

Portrait of John Neal by Sarah Miriam Peale, 1823. A leading American literary nationalist, Neal called for "faithful representations of native character" in American literature, urging American writers to cultivate the "abundant and hidden sources of fertility … in the northern, as well as the southern Americas." His literary criticism helped launch the careers of John Greenleaf Whittier, Edgar Allan Poe, Henry Wadsworth Longfellow, and Nathaniel Hawthorne.

who work should be consigned to contempt, if not to infamy." Melville's description of immigration and American national character in *Redburn* trumpets America's diverse expansiveness as the basis of the country's difference from the "narrow tribes" of Europe and cautions Europeans against "scoff[ing] at" Americans. Much of the work of the generation of the 1820s was devoted to Americanizing European literary genres, such as the historical novel, and to exploring stories and themes that could be considered distinctively American, such as the history of contact and conflict between Indigenous peoples and European settlers. And black and white writers alike singled out African American literature—in particular, the slave narrative—as the best basis for an American claim to literary independence, in both negative and positive terms: Frederick Douglass wrote of one slave narrative that "America has the melancholy honor of being the sole producer of books such as this," while the white abolitionist Theodore Parker posited that, because slave narratives best represented the urge for freedom at the core of American identity, "all the original romance of Americans is in them, not in the white man's novel." These writers, like most of their fellow Americans, would have rejected the idea that American literature could or should be completely *separate* from the European literary tradition: Douglass, for one, made a point, in the newspapers he edited, of printing works by both black and white American writers alongside the work of British authors. But an urge to establish American equality and distinctiveness within that ongoing conversation with European literature lay at the core of much nineteenth-century American literary creation, forming one of the unifying threads amid that literature's multifarious diversity.

This diversity began to be recovered in the latter decades of the twentieth century. Indeed, "recovery" could serve as the characteristic keyword for the prevailing scholarly approach to nineteenth-century literature in the late twentieth century and into the twenty-first, in the same way that "narrowing" can serve as a keyword for the prevailing mid-twentieth-century approach. Increasingly, as dominant assumptions about American history, culture, and identity came to be challenged, scholars began as well to challenge the established canon of nineteenth-century literature and to recover the writers and works that the process of canon-formation had marginalized, neglected, or forgotten. This recovery effort started with the works of white women, propelled by the rise of feminist theory in the 1970s and 80s; as post-colonial theory and queer theory developed in the ensuing decades, African American, Indigenous, and queer writing (including queer elements in canonical works) began to be recovered as well. At the same time, scholars went "beneath the American Renaissance"—to quote the title of one important 1988 study—to uncover the ways in which the canonical authors of the early and mid-nineteenth century were influenced by the vast array of other writing that existed around them. Scholarship on print culture and book history highlighted the diversity of that vast array of nineteenth-century writing and the speed with which it was changing during the period; more recently, digitization and related methods have made that huge nineteenth-century archive more accessible, thereby further facilitating recovery; and "hemispheric" approaches have recovered the suppressed political, cultural, and literary ties between the United States and the rest of the Americas, thereby prompting fundamental redefinition of what "American" literature is. All these developments, and more, continue to yield new views of nineteenth-century American literature, expanding and sharpening our picture of that literature's expansive "world."

RACE, SLAVERY, AND AMERICA, 1820–1860[1]

By 1820, settler colonists had been enslaving Africans and their descendants in what is now the United States for well over two hundred years.[2] Over that time chattel slavery and modern racism had developed together and become mutually reinforcing: white people enslaved black people because most white people viewed black people as inferior, and most white people viewed black people as inferior in part because most black people were enslaved. This connection between slavery and racism strengthened during the first half of the nineteenth century. In 1787, Thomas Jefferson, in his *Notes on the State of Virginia*, hedged his assertion that "the blacks … are inferior to the whites in the endowments both of body and mind," advancing this thought as "a suspicion only"; like many of America's founders, he also anticipated that slavery would come to a gradual end. By the 1850s, racist ideas had become more dogmatic and proslavery voices less apologetic—not just in the South but in the North as well. In 1852, for example, New York *Herald* publisher James Gordon Bennett proclaimed that "the negro is and always will be, to the end of time, inferior to the white race, and, therefore, doomed to subjection,"[3] while in 1854 the leading antislavery activist William Lloyd Garrison reported that, in "justification of slaveholding," a dozen reasons "are popularly urged in all parts of the country," the most common being simply that "the victims are black" and that they thereby "belong to an inferior race."

As these interconnected ideas about race and slavery became more deep-seated and pervasive in the proslavery camp, so too did opposition to them grow. "No compromise with Slavery!" was the ringing call of Garrison and other abolitionists; "Liberty for each, for all, forever!" The battle-lines, then, were clear. Yet within each camp, and between the two, a wide variety of complex and sometimes contradictory views about race and slavery continued to proliferate.

When Jefferson drafted the Declaration of Independence, the northern as well as the southern colonies all still enslaved black people. The self-proclaimed Vermont Republic abolished slavery outright in 1777, and the rest of the Northern states had by 1804 adopted measures to end slavery, though most states implemented abolition gradually (in some cases, *very* gradually). Slavery was also forbidden in the Northwest Territory—the recently-settled area between the Appalachian Mountains, the Great Lakes, and the Ohio

---

[1]   Please note that a "Contexts" section on the topic of "Slavery and Abolition" appears in the body of this volume.

[2]   The first recorded Africans to be enslaved in the Thirteen Colonies arrived at Jamestown, Virginia, in 1619. The enslavement of Africans in the Spanish colonies founded in present-day South Carolina and Florida had begun much earlier; Spanish settler colonists brought enslaved people to the short-lived colony of San Miguel de Gualdape (at Winyah Bay, South Carolina) in 1526, where these enslaved Africans staged the first known slave rebellion in what would become the continental United States.

[3]   The context is interesting: Bennett was drawing a parallel between what he saw as the permanently inferior status of women (on account purely of their biological sex) and what he saw as the permanently inferior status of black people to "the white race." The woman is happier in a state of subjection "than she would be in any other condition," he concluded, "because it is the law of her nature."

and Mississippi Rivers—and in the new states created from it. In the South, by contrast, economic and technological developments reinforced slavery's hold. The success in the Carolinas of wetlands systems of cultivating rice (the know-how for which had been brought from Africa by enslaved workers) was making Carolina plantation owners wealthier and wealthier. The invention of the cotton engine (or "cotton gin") in 1793 facilitated the production of cotton fiber for textiles on an industrial scale—but the cotton mills required an ever-larger supply of cotton, picked by hand by an ever-growing population of enslaved people in an ever-expanding area across the "Deep South." And (in territory that would before long become part of the United States) the introduction into Louisiana in 1795 of the technology for sugar granulation led to tremendous growth of sugar plantations, whose owners likewise relied on a large enslaved workforce. (Especially large numbers of enslaved workers were required to support the Louisiana sugar industry, because the horrendous conditions the workers were forced to endure led to extraordinarily high death rates.) The growth of the cotton and sugar industries spread slavery westward from its original base on the Atlantic seaboard in Virginia, Georgia, and the Carolinas, into Alabama, Mississippi, and Louisiana in particular.[1]

At first, the crucial divergence between Northern "free states" and Southern "slave states" (as the states in which slavery was outlawed and those in which it was permitted were respectively termed) was accompanied by relatively little national conversation about slavery itself. In the words of historian John Jay Chapman, the issue of slavery in the late eighteenth and early nineteenth centuries was for the white majority "a sleeping serpent"—an issue that "was always in everyone's *mind*" but "not always on his tongue." The ban on slavery in the Northwest Territory had been passed in 1787 without much controversy, and twenty years later Congress outlawed the international slave trade as soon

as it was constitutionally permitted to do so,[2] also with little controversy.[3] The addition of new states to the union similarly took place in an uncontentious, carefully evenhanded way, in free state–slave state pairs, so as to preserve the overall balance of power between North and South.

The "sleeping serpent" was loudly roused during the 1818–1820 debate over the proposed entry of Missouri into the union as a slave state. Missouri had been created out of federal territory, as opposed to land previously claimed by existing states; however, unlike the Northwest Territory, Congress had not made any ruling on slavery's legality in the territory acquired in the 1803 Louisiana Purchase, including Missouri.[4] Missouri's admission to the union thus became an important and divisive test case of the federal government's ability to regulate slavery's expansion into new states. Northerners generally wished to limit the expansion of slavery westwards and thus favored a broad interpretation of the government's authority to do so, whereas white Southerners generally supported a narrow interpretation. The debate was resolved by the 1820 Missouri Compromise, which balanced Missouri's admission as a slave state with that of Maine as a free state and

---

[1] In 1860 the United States cotton crop was valued at $217,000,000, the sugar cane crop at $39,000,000; the value of the rice crop ($3,200,000), however, had grown by only a million dollars since 1800. By comparison, the leading crops in the North were wheat (valued in 1860 at $151,000,000) and corn (valued in 1860 at $69,000,000).

[2] The question of whether and how the U.S. Constitution would deal with the slave trade and—more centrally—with slavery itself was the most contentious issue at the 1787 constitutional convention. The compromises that resulted from these debates included the lack of any specific constitutional mention of slavery as such; the inclusion of a provision permitting Congress to ban the importation of enslaved people into the country after an interval of twenty years; the adoption of a so-called "fugitive slave clause" mandating the return of people "held to service or labor" who escaped into another state; and the infamous "Three Fifths Compromise" that based congressional representation on "the whole Number of free Persons" in each state plus "three fifths of all other Persons"—i.e., of enslaved people. This "representation" of enslaved people did not allow them any political voice, but it gave slave states, and thus enslavers, far more seats and influence in the federal government than they would otherwise have had.

[3] In Congress, the ban was promoted by Thomas Jefferson and had substantial support from other white Southerners—especially in Virginia, where the economy was transitioning from a tobacco economy to one based on the cultivation of wheat and other crops that required less labor to grow, as well as on profits from the internal slave trade (the sale of "surplus" enslaved people to markets in the Deep South).

[4] The future state of Louisiana itself, in which slavery was well-established by 1803, was an exception.

established the 36°30' line of latitude—Missouri's southern boundary—as a dividing line for the westward expansion of slavery going forward: slavery would be banned in all Louisiana Purchase territory lying north of the line, but would be permitted in all Louisiana Purchase territory lying south of it. The compromise codified and entrenched the division between free and slave states in a manner that deeply troubled many observers. The elderly Thomas Jefferson, for example, deemed the Missouri Compromise "the [death] knell of the Union": "A geographical line, coinciding with a marked principle, moral and political, once conceived and held up to the angry passions of men, will never be obliterated; and every new irritation will mark it deeper and deeper."

In the years following the Missouri Compromise, the controversy over race and slavery broadened and deepened,[1] due in part to a significant expansion of African American literary and political activity in the North. *Freedom's Journal*, the first newspaper in the United States to be published by African Americans, was founded in New York City in 1827—the same year that the last enslaved person in New York state was freed. Black Northerners did not need convincing as to the evils of slavery or the merits of abolition, but they did want to vindicate and uplift themselves in the face of the racism that shadowed their lives almost as pervasively, if generally less violently, as it did the lives of enslaved black Southerners. Racial vindication and uplift were the explicit aims of *Freedom's Journal*—whose editors intended, as they put it, "to plead our own cause" and to dispel the "misrepresentations" of black people that had "deceived" white Americans. African American literary societies such as the Female Literary Association of Philadelphia (founded in 1831) asserted "equality with those of our fellow beings who differ from us in complexion, but who are, with ourselves, children of one Eternal Parent." Sarah Mapps Douglass, a black Philadelphian who helped found the Female Literary Association, urged her fellow free black Northerners to dare "to assert that the black man

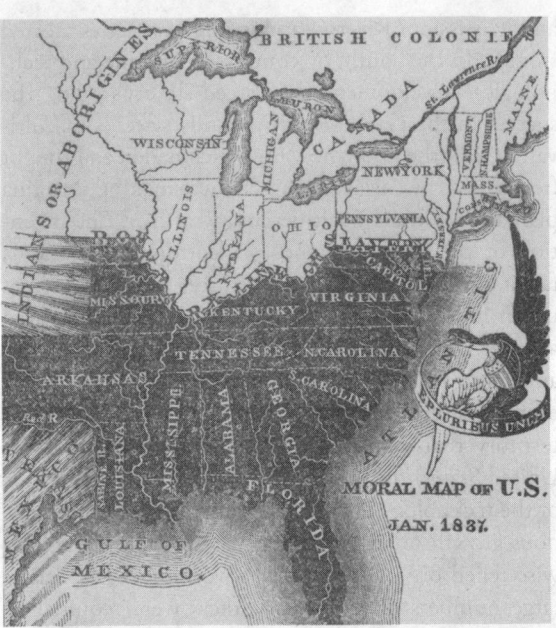

Julius Rubens Ames, "Moral Map of the U.S.," 1837. At the time Ames, an artist and abolitionist, published this map visualizing the divide between free states (in white) and slave states (in black), Texas had not yet been annexed by the U.S., but white American settlers had established slavery there. The map also shows slavery spreading west from Missouri, in defiance of the 1820 Missouri Compromise banning slavery in areas north of Missouri's southern boundary.

is equal by nature to the white, and that slavery and not his color has debased him." She also reminded them of the need for solidarity with their enslaved compatriots, and of the essential identity of the antiracist and antislavery causes: "we [i.e., free and enslaved African Americans] rise or fall together and ... we can never be elevated to our proper standing while they are in bondage."[2]

In the 1830s, this upsurge of Northern black writing and activism helped inspire the rise of the abolitionist movement, which led to wider and wider discussion

---

1   A policy of silence about slavery was, however, perpetuated in the U.S. Congress: from 1836 to 1844, a series of "gag rules" imposed by the proslavery majority in the House of Representatives banned any mention of slavery on the House floor, while similar measures to prevent the consideration of antislavery petitions were adopted in the Senate.

---

2   This essay by Douglass was published in *The Liberator*, William Lloyd Garrison's abolitionist newspaper, on 13 October 1832—one of the many examples of African American writing, particularly including works by African American women, that Garrison printed.

of the issue of slavery.[1] Abolitionism's emergence onto the national stage is conventionally dated to 1831, when William Lloyd Garrison began publishing *The Liberator*, his influential antislavery newspaper (printed weekly, without interruption, until 1865), with its call for the immediate and uncompensated abolition of slavery throughout the United States. In his introductory editorial to *The Liberator*'s first issue, Garrison famously declared "I will be heard," and he was: his efforts, and those of the array of other antislavery activists that gathered around him (and, in some cases, broke away from him), made slavery itself—its morality and continued existence, not just the question of its expansion—an active, enduring political issue.

Abolitionists did not confine their agitation to slavery per se. Leading activists such as Garrison, Theodore S. Wright, and Lucretia Mott linked the abolition of slavery in the South to a broader struggle. The 1833 constitution of the Philadelphia Female Anti-Slavery Society (one of the many abolitionist organizations that sprang up throughout the North beginning in the early 1830s) made clear that an important part of their mission was combatting racial prejudice and inequality throughout the country:

> The object of this Society shall be to collect and disseminate correct information of the character of slavery, and of the actual conditions of the slaves and free people of color for the purpose of inducing the community to adopt such measures as may be in their power to dispel the prejudice against the people of color, to improve their condition and to bring about the speedy abolition of slavery.[2]

Theodore Sedgwick Wright, 1845. A Presbyterian minister and influential abolitionist, Wright was a leader among those who linked the struggle to abolish slavery with the broader struggle against racial prejudice. Even those nominally "free" people "colored with skin like my own," he declared in 1837, "are still slaves—everywhere we feel the chain galling us," as a result of "this prejudice," which "excludes us from all stations of profit, usefulness and honor; takes away from us all motive for pressing forward," and "destroys souls."

Not every abolitionist was of the same mind on this point; for some time both in New York and in Boston, for example, antislavery societies formed by white women admitted no black members (unlike the Philadelphia society, which was multiracial). The Boston female Anti-Slavery Society was persuaded by Garrison to change its policies, while in New York an almost entirely black Manhattan Abolition Society was formed in 1840 in response to the all-white Ladies' New York City Anti-Slavery Society.

---

[1]   In addition to the work of earlier American antislavery activists, both white and black, the concerted abolitionist movement that took off in the 1830s had roots in the evangelical Protestant religious fervor of the Second Great Awakening and in the late eighteenth- and early nineteenth-century transatlantic campaign to abolish the international slave trade.

[2]   In its commitment to neither *immediate* nor *gradual* but rather to "the *speedy* abolition of slavery," the Philadelphia Female Anti-Slavery Society adopted an intermediate position on what would become one of the main points of disagreement among opponents of slavery. Garrisonian abolitionists demanded slavery's immediate end, while more moderate antislavery reformers were prepared to accept gradualism. The abolitionist movement also split—in some cases quite bitterly—over whether abolition could be achieved under the auspices of the Constitution as it existed (Garrison and his allies thought it could not, while other abolitionists such as Frederick

---

Douglass thought it could) and over the morality and efficacy of armed resistance to slavery (which was rejected by Garrison and Douglass alike but was embraced, for example, by John Brown).

The ongoing efforts by enslaved people themselves to resist their bondage also became more prominent in the post-1820 political environment. News of the debate about Missouri's admission—which seemed to indicate to many people in the South, black as well as white, that slavery itself was under threat—may have helped inspire the planned revolt of enslaved people in Charleston, South Carolina, supposedly organized by the freed black man Denmark Vesey, that was pre-emptively quashed by white authorities in 1822.[1] In 1831 Nat Turner, an enslaved preacher in Southampton County, Virginia, led a revolt by around seventy enslaved people. He believed that the right time to rise up had now come: as he (reportedly) put it, "the great day of judgment" was at hand and the time was "fast approaching when the first should be last and the last should be first."

Turner's rebellion was bloodily suppressed, with ter-rified and vengeful white mobs arbitrarily murdering large numbers of black people in Virginia and through-out the South, and in its wake the slave states inten-sified efforts to regulate enslaved people and stamp out potential resistance—for example, by forbidding enslaved people from learning to read and write. News of Turner's rebellion circulated widely, however, and later uprisings by enslaved people on the slave ships *Amistad* in 1839 and *Creole* in 1841 were more success-ful. Both of these later uprisings resulted in high-profile court cases. In the *Amistad* case, Northern abolitionists argued before the U.S. Supreme Court on behalf of the enslaved people who had rebelled and taken over the ship—and won their case.

The "Underground Railroad" that developed in the 1840s and grew considerably in the 1850s was a much broader effort to help enslaved people win their freedom. This was an informal but extensive network of secret routes, safe houses, and personal connections within and between local groups (made up both of free blacks and of white abolitionists) that in one way or another helped thousands of enslaved

people—according to one estimate, as many as 100,000—to escape to the free states, to Canada, or, in some cases, to Mexico.

As antislavery agitation in the North intensified, so too did Southern enslavers' insistence on slavery's necessity and value. Slavery became ever more cru-cial to the Southern economy; by the time the Civil War began, it has been estimated that over twenty per cent of private wealth in the U.S. was in the form of enslaved people. In the first decades of the nineteenth century, most enslavers had still tended to characterize slavery in the way that Jefferson had done in 1787: as a necessary evil which they were reluctantly obliged to maintain, at least for the time being. But by the 1830s enslavers were increasingly praising slavery as altruis-tic, civilizing, and altogether beneficial. This so-called "positive good" depiction of slavery began to circulate around the time of the Missouri Compromise. It was expanded upon in the 1830s by Southern politicians such as John C. Calhoun, who became the most influ-ential proponent of the view that (as he expressed it in an 1837 speech)

> in the present state of civilization, where two races of different origin, and distinguished by colour, and other physical differences, as well as intel-lectual, are brought together, the relation now existing in the slaveholding states between the two [races] is, instead of an evil, a good—a positive good.

Enslavers such as Calhoun continued to propound such views of slavery, in ever-more-hyperbolic terms, down to the Civil War, thereby further widening the gulf between them and their Northern antislavery opponents.

The vehemence of the rhetoric of "free states" versus "slave states," which proliferated at the time and has remained common ever since, should not be allowed to obscure the differences that existed within these regions—or the fact that the divide between them was in some respects a good deal blurrier than the rheto-ric suggests. The stereotype of the antebellum white Southern family is that of a rich plantation owner with dozens or even hundreds of enslaved workers. Such families did exist, and the men who headed them wielded enormous power over the entire South

---

[1]   Recently, some historians have proposed that the Missouri Compromise and its aftermath inspired the Vesey "conspiracy" in a different way: namely, that the anxiety about the survival of slavery that the compromise prompted in white enslavers drove them to concoct evidence of an intended revolt by enslaved people that did not actually exist, so as to give them an excuse for clamping down on enslaved African Americans and thus reasserting their hegemony.

and indeed the entire nation. Only a small minority of Southern white families fit that description, however. Even in 1860, when the population of enslaved people had reached a high of four million (one-third of the overall Southern population of twelve million), only about a quarter of free families in the slave states owned enslaved people, and most of those who did own enslaved people owned fewer than five.[1] The social division between the enslaving class, especially the large enslavers, and the so-called "poor whites" was and would remain a significant factor in Southern politics, intensifying but also complicating the fundamental racial divide between free whites and enslaved blacks.

An equally important distinction existed between more northerly slave states such as Kentucky, Virginia, and Maryland—the so-called "Upper South"—and the "Deep South," consisting of South Carolina, Georgia, Alabama, Mississippi, Louisiana, Florida, and Texas. Cotton cultivation, and that of other large-scale plantation crops such as sugar, indigo, and rice, flourished in the Deep South but, by the 1820s, scarcely existed in the Upper South, where environmental conditions for it were unsuitable (and where, in many cases, the soil had been exhausted by up to two centuries of intensive plantation agriculture). As a result, the economy of the Upper South came to rely increasingly on the sale of enslaved people born there to the large, labor-intensive plantations of the Deep South. Because the condition and treatment of enslaved people on such Deep Southern plantations tended to be even worse, and because sellers and traders of enslaved people frequently broke up the families of the people they dealt in, being "sold south"—or "sold down the river," in reference to the Mississippi—became a fate that enslaved people in the Upper South greatly feared for themselves and their loved ones. Nearly one million African Americans, however, were forced to endure it. Meanwhile, the economic distinction between Upper South and Deep South took on increasing political significance. It is telling that, while all seven states of the Deep South seceded in the winter of 1860–61, four of the Upper South states (Virginia, North Carolina, Tennessee, and Arkansas) did not join them until several months later, and the other four (Missouri, Kentucky, Maryland, and Delaware) never did secede.[2]

The North, for its part, had its own important regional differentiations. The Puritan and Quaker traditions of New England and Pennsylvania lent strength to abolitionism in those states, and abolitionist sentiment was strong as well in parts of the former Northwest Territory that had been settled largely by New Englanders. Other areas of Ohio, Indiana, and

Timothy H. O'Sullivan, *Five Generations on Smith's Plantation, Beaufort, South Carolina*, 1862. O'Sullivan took this photograph of an African American family whose members had been enslaved on the plantation of J.J. Smith, on one of the Sea Islands off the coast of South Carolina, shortly after the U.S. Army occupied the area early in the Civil War, liberating its enslaved population.

---

[1]   These statistics should be qualified in two ways. First, many white farm families who could not afford ownership rented enslaved people at certain times of the year. Second, many white men who neither owned nor rented enslaved people seem nevertheless to have had no objection to the institution of slavery—with many aspiring to become enslavers themselves.

[2]   Substantial popular opinion against secession also persisted even in parts of the Upper South states that did secede—for example, in eastern Tennessee and northwestern Virginia (which, when Virginia seceded, promptly seceded from Virginia, becoming the new state of West Virginia). These areas tended to have particularly low numbers of enslaved people and enslavers.

Illinois, however, had been settled by Southerners, and popular sentiment in those areas, as well as local laws, remained friendly to slavery. Much of the North, including New England, also retained a strong economic interest in slavery: enslaved labor provided cotton for northern textile mills such as those of Lowell, Massachusetts, while the banking, shipping, and manufacturing sectors of New York City—far and away the North's, and the nation's, biggest city—were all closely linked to slavery. An anonymous black member of the Female Literary Association of Philadelphia, writing in the 25 August 1832 issue of *The Liberator* under the pen name "Bera," emphasized these connections when she reminded "residents in the non-slaveholding states" who "consume[d] the produce of slave labor" that they too were implicated in slavery's crimes: "every citizen of the United States who withholds any exertion [against slavery that is] in his power to make," she insisted, "is in reality a kidnapper, a slave-trader, and a slaveholder."

It should be pointed out as well that various forms of involuntary servitude, including outright slavery, persisted even in the "free states." Indenture lingered as a labor arrangement well into the nineteenth century, and—as works by black Northerners such as Austin Reed's *Life and Adventures of a Haunted Convict* (c. 1858) and Harriet Wilson's *Our Nig* (1859) attest—it was frequently racialized and was in some cases virtually indistinguishable from slavery. Penal servitude (also documented in Austin Reed's remarkable memoir), which expanded significantly in the nineteenth century, could also in practice be very similar to slavery. And it should not be forgotten that the gradualism of the abolition laws passed by most Northern states meant that some African Americans remained enslaved there for decades after the legislation had been passed. New Jersey, the final Northern state to adopt an abolition measure, began a process of gradual emancipation in 1804, but the last enslaved people in the state were not freed until 1865, when the Thirteenth Amendment abolished slavery nationwide.

Above all, racism seems to have been just as pervasive among white Northerners as it was among white Southerners; indeed, some observers found white Northerners to be even more virulent in their racism, or at least more outspoken. The French traveler Alexis de Tocqueville, for instance, wrote in the wake of his 1831–32 visit to the United States, "The prejudice of race appears to be stronger in the states that have abolished slavery than those where it still exists." Racial prejudice shaped and was reflected by such popular cultural institutions in the North as blackface minstrelsy, as well as by laws such as Pennsylvania's disenfranchisement in 1838 of its black male population (the wealthier among whom, at least, had previously been able to vote). The decades between 1820 and 1860 also saw specific white Northern communities, including working-class men (both native-born and immigrants) and middle-class women, become more strongly invested in their whiteness. For members of these segments of the population—both of which were relatively disempowered or marginalized, albeit in different ways—emphasizing their whiteness provided a way of claiming empowerment and privilege by differentiating themselves from even more disempowered or marginalized non-white people. Whiteness offered a particularly important path to acceptance and empowerment for Irish immigrants—targets of both religious and racialized prejudice during this period. The views expressed in an 1852 article in the *Buffalo Morning Express* on the subject of immigration were widely shared among native-born white Americans:

> The Germans show their Teutonic blood by becoming land holders as soon as they settle among us. This is a remarkably good feature, as it leads to permanent location, stability of industry, and a thrifty method of living. The Irish lack this disposition, much to their detriment.

Over the course of the nineteenth century the Irish slowly but steadily became more accepted by the white establishment, in part by espousing antiblack racism and supporting slavery.[1]

---

1   Habits of racial classification in the nineteenth century were (and are) often confusing. Though many used the word "race" when referring to perceived national or ethnic characteristics (e.g., "Anglo-Saxon race," "Teutonic race," "Irish race"), all these groups were usually understood to be part of the wider "white race"—and certainly they were classed as such in the census. The Irish were by far the largest group of immigrants in the first half of the nineteenth century. The 1850 census, for instance, reported the following totals for "citizens of foreign birth": Ireland 961,719; Germany 573,225; England 278,675; British America 147,700; Scotland 70,550.

Given the obstacles, it is remarkable how many African Americans achieved great success during the 1820–Reconstruction period. Pictured on the right is Frances Ellen Watkins Harper; employed as a seamstress and domestic worker when in her teens, she published her first book at around the age of 20, and in 1854 became the first black woman to be hired by an antislavery society as a lecturer, eventually becoming a distinguished writer and campaigner for gender equality and racial equality (see her author entry in the body of this volume). Pictured on the left is Mifflin Wistar Gibbs, a Philadelphian who worked first as a carpenter, became a leading figure in the antislavery movement, moved to San Francisco during the 1849 Gold Rush, moved to Canada in 1858 in the face of discriminatory laws and became the first black person elected to public office in British Columbia before moving back to the U.S., where he settled in Arkansas, became an attorney and, in 1873, the first black judge elected in the U.S. His final public post was as American Consul in Madagascar.

Racial prejudice among white Northerners not infrequently prompted violent opposition to the abolitionist movement. William Lloyd Garrison was nearly lynched by a Boston mob in 1835, and two years later another high-profile antislavery activist, Elijah P. Lovejoy, was murdered by proslavery citizens of Alton, Illinois. Conversely, even some abolitionists or abolitionist sympathizers remained hostile to the notion that black people—or Indigenous Americans—could be accorded equal status. The British phrenologist[1] George Combe, for example, who visited the U.S. in 1838–39, described Native Americans and African Americans in the following terms in 1842: "The one is like the wolf or the fox, the other like the dog. In both the brain is inferior in size, particularly in the moral and intellectual regions, to that of the Anglo-Saxon race, and hence the foundation of the natural superiority of the latter over both." Yet Combe was repulsed by slavery; he wrote of the enslaved people from the *Amistad* that he found it "impossible to look without horror and indignation on these young and unoffending men and children deprived of their liberty, reduced to slavery, and converted into mere 'property,' by *Christians*."

A combination of dislike for slavery and racial prejudice was also widespread in the colonization movement, which sought to emancipate enslaved black people and then resettle them out of the country, primarily to Liberia in West Africa. Represented in particular by the American Colonization Society, an organization founded in 1816 by an uneasy alliance of Northern abolitionists and Southern enslavers, colonization was overwhelmingly opposed by

---

[1] Phrenology was a pseudoscience, widely popular throughout the nineteenth century, that claimed to be able to identify inherent differences in the character and capacities both of different individuals and different races from the shape of human skulls; it contributed greatly to the growth of "scientific" racism during this period.

African Americans but long remained popular with white Americans; Abraham Lincoln backed it as late as 1862 (and even in the preliminary version of his Emancipation Proclamation). Near the end of her 1859 autobiographical novel *Our Nig*, the black New Englander Harriet Wilson offered a withering commentary on such "professed abolitionists, who didn't want slaves at the South, nor [black people] in their own houses, North."

As hostile as many white Northerners thus were to African American equality and even to the existence of free African Americans in the United States, and as comfortable as many of them were with enslaving black people, opposition to Southern slavery continued to rise in the North, if often for reasons that had little to do with the sufferings or aspirations of enslaved people themselves. To many in the North, the slaveholding South constituted a threatening "Slave Power": the quasi-aristocratic social order in the slave states made the South fundamentally undemocratic, and the economic importance of "King Cotton," together with the extra sway in the federal government the South held as a result of the Constitution's "Three Fifths Clause" (allotting disproportionate representation to slave states), made Northerners fear that Southern slavery would ultimately destroy democracy in the nation as a whole. These fears particularly motivated Northern opposition to slavery's expansion—an issue that came to the fore again in the 1840s in response to the massive territorial acquisitions the U.S. made in that decade, especially from Mexico. By the 1840s, the question of slavery—and particularly that of its expansion—was causing the country's existing two-party political system to break down; in the North, antislavery members of both major political parties, the Whigs and Democrats, formed in 1848 the Free Soil Party, dedicated to keeping slavery out of the new western territories. Bitter debate ensued between Free Soil Northerners and Southern enslavers committed to the institution's expansion, in the course of which some Southern extremists began seriously to advocate secession.[1]

This renewed debate resulted in a new compromise, the Compromise of 1850, which admitted California as a free state (but required it to send one proslavery and one antislavery senator to Congress so as to preserve the free state–slave state balance of power in the Senate); empowered the inhabitants of other western territories to decide for themselves whether or not slavery would be permitted there; banned the slave trade in the District of Columbia; and—most controversially—implemented a new, much more draconian Fugitive Slave Act. By effectively requiring all citizens to assist in the capture and return of escapees from slavery, the 1850 Fugitive Slave Act inflamed popular opinion in the North and insured that, the compromise notwithstanding, the national divide regarding slavery would only deepen further in the ensuing decade.

The key signposts of this deepening divide can be briefly enumerated. In 1852, Harriet Beecher Stowe's antislavery novel *Uncle Tom's Cabin* became an enormous bestseller, strengthening opposition to slavery in the North and prompting proslavery writers to pen numerous would-be rebuttals. In 1854, the Kansas–Nebraska Act gave the settlers of those territories the

Eastman Johnson, *A Ride for Liberty—The Fugitive Slaves*, 1862. Johnson (1824–1906), an artist who had acquired a national reputation by the late 1850s, created three versions of this painting, which he based on a scene he claimed to have witnessed firsthand near Manassas, Virginia, during the Civil War.

---

[1]   Seceding from the union was not, however, a course of action contemplated only in the slave states: some abolitionists supported Northern secession from the United States under the slogan "No Union with Slaveholders," which William Lloyd Garrison added to the masthead of *The Liberator*.

authority to vote for or against the existence of slavery there, resulting in years of bloodshed between pro- and antislavery factions in Kansas—a mini-civil war that has come to be called "Bleeding Kansas." In 1857, the Supreme Court's decision in *Dred Scott v. Sandford* declared that African Americans were not U.S. citizens under the Constitution, that the Missouri Compromise was unconstitutional, and that the federal government had no ability to restrict the expansion of slavery at all. In 1859, John Brown, an abolitionist who had fought in Kansas, mounted an armed raid on Harpers Ferry, Virginia, in an attempt to galvanize a mass resistance movement by enslaved people throughout the South; the failed raid, and Brown's subsequent trial and execution by the state of Virginia, polarized the country even more. And in 1860, the presidential election was won by Abraham Lincoln, the candidate of the new Republican Party (into which the Free Soil Party had evolved), who ran on a platform opposed to slavery's further expansion and who did not even appear on the ballot in slave states. Lincoln's election convinced the states of the Deep South that slavery's continued existence was at stake; even before Lincoln had taken office, they began to secede. Lincoln mobilized federal troops to suppress their rebellion, and four other slave states joined them, thus bringing on the Civil War.

By the time the war began, the great national debate about race and slavery that precipitated it had taken some participants to startling extremes. The Virginian social theorist George Fitzhugh, for example, argued that slavery was simply the best way of organizing labor for all people, white as well as black: he contended that Northern industrial workers would be better off enslaved outright than in their current condition of supposed "wage slavery" and called it "a libel on white men to say they are unfit for slavery." Other white commentators in both halves of the country had taken to racializing the country's division itself, by questioning whether the white inhabitants of the country's other half were, in fact, truly "white." A January 1860 article entitled "The Basis of Northern Hostility to the South" published in *De Bow's Review*, a New Orleans periodical, asserted that, in comparison to white Northerners, their Southern counterparts were a superior "race of the pure Anglo-Saxon blood"; another 1860 article in the *Southern Literary Messenger* similarly claimed that white Northerners belonged to a "branch of the human family" that had "acquired differences so marked as almost to constitute them a 'permanent variety' in the classification of Race." Conversely, the English artist Barbara Bodichon, who visited the South in 1857–58, declared that Southern enslavement of African Americans had deracinated Southern whites: "There is a recklessness and carelessness about these Southerners which I did not think the Anglo-Saxon race could attain under any circumstances." Such opinions should not be taken as broadly representative of popular feeling in either the North or the South, but they are a telling measure of how profoundly divisive slavery had become.

As the Civil War progressed, many long-held views began to be altered—not least of all those of Lincoln. Over the course of the war, the battle on the Union side was not only against the secessionist states but also—in part at least—against prejudice in the North. And it was fought within the hearts and minds of individuals as well as in society as a whole. When in 1863 Frederick Douglass petitioned the President to provide equal wages and equal treatment for black troops fighting in the federal army, Lincoln equivocated (according to Douglass's account),

> saying that the employment of colored troops at all was a great gain to the colored people; that the measure could not have been successfully adopted at the beginning of the war; that the wisdom of making colored men soldiers was still doubted; that their enlistment was a serious offense to popular prejudice.

By war's end Lincoln (and many others) had come round on this point, as he had come round on the question of "recolonization" and on other issues; black troops were finally receiving equal wages and equal rations, and with the Thirteenth Amendment of 1865, slavery was finally brought to an end. But "popular prejudice" against people of color would continue to plague America—and to distance it from the realization of its ideals.

EXPANSION, EXPULSION, AND "MANIFEST DESTINY"[1]

From the very start of their colonization of the Americas, Europeans conceived of that colonization as a providential process and used such conceptions to legitimize their dispossession of the Americas' Indigenous inhabitants. Such ideas took root in the thirteen colonies and became integral to the identity of the new nation formed from those colonies, which in the eyes of many of its citizens seemed "destined by Divine Providence"—as future president John Quincy Adams put it in an 1811 letter to his father, former president John Adams—to encompass "the whole continent of North America." Adams's claim reflected the way in which his young country had in fact been expanding energetically since its inception: in the first four decades of its existence, the United States began colonizing the vast territories between the Appalachian Mountains and the Mississippi River, crushing Indigenous resistance there in the Northwest Indian War (1785–95), Tecumseh's War (1810–13), and the Creek War (1813–14); purchased from France the even vaster Louisiana Territory west of the Mississippi in 1803; negotiated joint occupation, with the British-chartered Hudson's Bay Company, of the Oregon Country on the Pacific coast in 1818;[2] and obtained Florida by treaty with Spain in 1819.

Beginning in the 1820s, the westward push of the U.S.'s territory and population became more formalized, more concerted, and more intense than ever before—as did the expulsion, subordination, or outright destruction of the communities that resisted U.S. expansion or simply stood in its way, be they Native Americans or descendants of other European colonial empires. This accelerated expansionism was driven by the same fundamental dynamics that had propelled settler colonialism in North America from its beginning: the ready availability of abundant and therefore cheap land, which white colonists—disregarding the Indigenous peoples already occupying it—believed to be theirs for the taking, and the perception that settling such land could provide a fresh start, especially to those who lacked economic opportunities in their place of origin.[3] Contrary to the claims of its propagandists at the time, however, American expansion, and the horrendous cruelties it entailed for those who stood in its way, were neither destined nor inevitable. Mid-century expansionism emerged in tandem with "Jacksonian democracy"—the populist political movement spearheaded by Andrew Jackson, who rose from relatively humble origins to serve two terms as President, from 1829 to 1837. Jackson championed the "common man" against what he characterized as a political and economic establishment dominated by aristocratic elites. His administration encouraged intensified migration westward, promising rapid access to cheap land for all migrants (in contrast to the more measured pace of settlement—in which public land would be sold at a price high enough to cover the federal government's costs—that was favored by Jackson's opponents).

Jackson's pro-expansionary policy gained additional strength after the financial crisis known as the Panic of 1837. During the economic depression that followed, members of Jackson's Democratic Party advocated westward migration, and the territorial annexation that would facilitate it, as a "safety-valve" for the labor unrest and class conflict they feared were brewing among the afflicted working classes in the industrializing Northeast. This supposed interest of the industrial North in westward expansion paralleled the longstanding desire of slaveholders in the South to extend slavery to new territories—something that Southern enslavers deemed necessary for the survival of their plantation economy (which quickly exhausted the soil and thus required the regular acquisition of fertile new land). Mississippi senator Albert G. Brown epitomized such

---

[1]   Please note that a "Contexts" section on this topic appears in the body of this volume.

[2]   This was a territory much larger than present-day Oregon; it included all of what are now the states of Washington, Oregon, and Idaho, together with parts of present-day Montana and Wyoming, and substantial portions of what is now the Canadian province of British Columbia. The British referred to the territory (which remained jointly occupied until 1846) as the Columbia District.

[3]   The myth of western settlement as offering endless opportunity for poor, landless people to become self-sufficient proprietors did not always match its reality. Of the 38 million acres of recently colonized public lands that were sold between 1835 and 1837, for example, 29 million ended up in the hands of real estate speculators rather than independent farmers. And according to one 1846 observer in the recently settled state of Indiana, one-third of that state's voters were "tenants or day laborers or young men who have acquired no property." Newly colonized territory in the South, meanwhile, came under the grip of the most inequitable and disempowering economic system of all: plantation slavery.

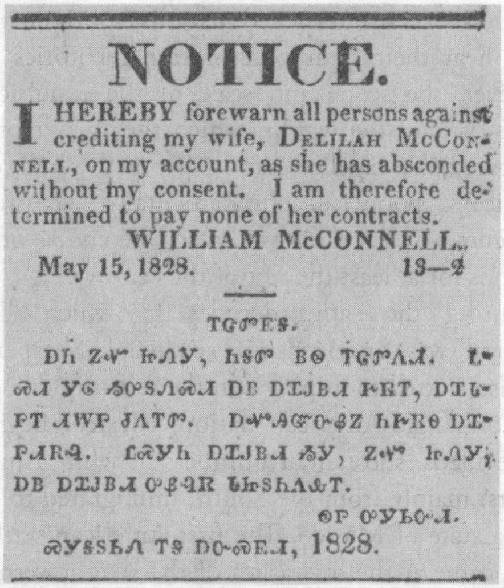

NOTICE.

I HEREBY forewarn all persons against crediting my wife, DELILAH McCONNELL, on my account, as she has absconded without my consent. I am therefore determined to pay none of her contracts.
WILLIAM McCONNELL.
May 15, 1828.   13—2

TGᏃᎬᏏ.

DᏂ ᏃᏌ ᏏᎯᎩ, ᏂᏍᏉ ᏃᎬ TGᏃᎯᎯᏗ. ᎿᏉ ᏗᏗ �YᏫ ᏓᎣᏌᎯᏗᏗ ᎠᏣ ᎠᎢᏣᎯ ᏏᎬᏘ, ᎠᎢᎤ ᏆᏘ ᎯᏪᏈ ᎫᎯᏔ. ᎠᏫᎠᏰᎣ-ᎦᏃ ᎯᎢᏲ ᎠᏘ ᏆᏗᏅ. ᎶᏚᏴᏂ ᎠᎢᏣᎯ ᎠᏳ, ᏃᏫ ᏏᎯᎩ, ᎠᎬ ᎠᎢᏣᎯ ᎣᏘᏁ ᏔᏏᎯᏌ.

                                ᎣᏘ ᎤᏴᏓᎤᎥ.
ᏫᎩᏍᏍᏞᎯ ᎢᎦ ᎠᎣ-ᎦᎬᎥ, 1828.

This bilingual notice announcing a husband's refusal to pay the debts of his "absconded" wife was published in 1828 in the *Cherokee Phoenix*, the Cherokee national newspaper, in both English and Cherokee script.

proslavery expansionism in an 1858 speech urging the wholesale annexation of Mexican and other Latin American territory, a decade after the U.S. had already wrested vast areas from Mexico: "I want Cuba[.] ... I want Tamaulipas, Potosi, and one or two other Mexican States; and I want them all ... for the planting or spreading of slavery. ... I would spread the blessings of slavery, like the religion of our Divine Master, to the uttermost ends of the earth."

The first major target of Jacksonian America's drive to expand was the remaining territory of the Indigenous nations east of the Mississippi. By the 1820s, despite several wars and numerous territorial cessions, nearly 100,000 Native Americans still lived on millions of acres between the Great Lakes and the Gulf of Mexico.[1] Many of them had formed close economic and familial ties with their white neighbors and—in line with federal policies that officially encouraged their assimilation—had adopted such Euro-American institutions and practices as they thought would benefit them. They learned to speak and write English (and, in the case of the Cherokee, devised a writing system for their

own language); they formed centralized governments with written constitutions; they participated in the market economy; and they often adopted Christianity. The so-called "Five Civilized Tribes" in the South (the Choctaw, Chickasaw, Cherokee, Muscogee [Creek], and Seminole) led the way in this acceptance of white American norms, which in their case extended to the enslavement, by their wealthiest citizens, of African Americans.[2] Even as members of these nations developed a form of plantation slavery themselves, however, the slaveholding white elites around them coveted their lands and feared that the continued existence of such well-organized, autonomous non-white communities in the South would weaken white supremacy there. Other white Americans with no vested interest in slavery wanted to open up Indigenous land to white settlement, and many expressed the view—some out of pure self-interest, others out of misguided but sincerely held philanthropic beliefs—that Indigenous people could not survive in close contact with whites and needed to be "removed" for their own good.

This mixture of motivations gave rise to a course of action that the Choctaw leader George Colbert called an "act of usurpation ... unparalleled in history": the systematic, state-administered deportation beyond the bounds of the United States of the entire Indigenous population east of the Mississippi. In 1830, Congress passed the Indian Removal Act, which mandated that the Indigenous nations east of the Mississippi either cede their remaining lands and relocate to an allotted "Indian Territory" farther west or accept the jurisdiction of the states in which they lived—a measure that entailed their dissolution as autonomous nations. Many Indigenous people strenuously protested this measure, aided by considerable numbers of white American allies. Such protests notwithstanding, between 1831 and 1838, most members of the five Indigenous nations in the south, and numerous smaller nations in the north, were forced to move (for the Indigenous nations practicing slavery, the deportees included enslaved African

---

[1]   25,000 Native Americans lived north of the Ohio River and 66,000 south of it.

[2]   By 1830, enslaved African Americans made up over five per cent of the combined population of these five nations. The Cherokee nation contained the largest number of enslaved people; seven to eight per cent of Cherokee families were slaveowners. As was the general case throughout the South, only a further small fraction of this enslaving minority owned more than a few enslaved people. The large majority of Cherokee enslavers claimed some white ancestry.

Wabokieshiek (c. 1794–c. 1841), a spiritual leader of the Sauk and Ho-Chunk nations of the upper Mississippi Valley. Wabokieshiek (also known as White Cloud) called for the preservation of traditional Indigenous ways of life and played a major part in Black Hawk's War (1832), the campaign waged by members of the Sauk and allied nations to retain their lands east of the Mississippi. George Catlin, a white American artist known for his depictions of Native Americans, painted this portrait in 1832.

Americans). During their various long journeys to the new territories designated for them, the deportees suffered from disease, harsh weather, meager rations, and administrative incompetence; thousands died. These deadly treks westward have come to be known, in American memory, by the name originally coined for the last and most famous deportation, that of the Cherokee: the Trail of Tears. Some Indigenous people from several nations, in both the north and the south, took up arms—unsuccessfully—against their expulsion; others managed to avoid being expelled, and

members of some expelled nations continue to live in or near their traditional eastern territories today. However, the scope and scale of the expulsions of the 1830s, and the way in which they geographically segregated the expelled nations from the bulk of the American populace, fundamentally transformed Indigenous–U.S. relations and set the course of those relations for at least the rest of the century.[1]

During the same decades in which "Indian Removal" was conceived and executed, U.S. expansionism also started to impinge on the territory of a different non-Anglo-American nation: Mexico. Beginning in the 1820s, substantial numbers of white American settlers, mainly from the South, immigrated to Texas, then a state of Mexico. The first American settlers in Texas came at the invitation of the state government, but many others arrived without official sanction. By the 1820s, many *Tejanos* (descendants of the original Hispanic colonists of Texas) were already agitating for greater political autonomy within Mexico. The American settlers also wanted to distance themselves from the authority of the Mexican government—and to form strong ties to the United States. They engaged in widespread defiance of Mexican authority and law—including, in particular, Mexico's abolition of slavery in 1829. These pressures, together with the Mexican government's corresponding fear of losing control of Texas, led in 1835 to the conflict known as the Texas Revolution; the American settlers, together with the Tejanos, took arms against the Mexican government. The bloodshed included the annihilation of the Texan garrison of the Alamo (a former Spanish mission in San Antonio), the massacre of several hundred Texan prisoners at Goliad, and the Texan slaughter of Mexican soldiers at the climactic Battle of San Jacinto. By the end of April 1836, Mexico had been defeated and Texas had declared its independence—which, however, the Mexican government refused to recognize. In part because of the persistence of tense relations between Texas and Mexico that resulted, Tejanos in the new Republic of Texas, including those who had fought for independence, were often ill treated; one of them, Juan Seguín—who had carried the Alamo defenders' final

---

[1]   For a fuller discussion of Native American expulsion and resistance during the 1830s, see the following section of this introduction.

Carl Nebel, *General Scott's Entrance into Mexico*, 1851. This painting depicts American troops led by General Winfield Scott occupying Mexico City in 1847 during the Mexican–American War.

message requesting reinforcements—described himself as "a foreigner in my native land."

The vast majority of independent Texas's Anglo-American inhabitants favored annexation by the United States, as did American President John Tyler, but the fact that Texas was a slaveholding region whose entry into the union would upset the delicate balance of slave and free states made this a highly contentious issue in America. The debate over whether to annex Texas featured prominently in the 1844 presidential election, which was won by James K. Polk, a Jacksonian Democrat, slaveholding Southerner, and strong proponent of national expansion. Texas was accordingly admitted into the union in 1845—the first step in the enormous expansion of U.S. territory that the Polk administration oversaw. In the 1844 election some elements in Polk's party had demanded that the United States annex large tracts of territory in the Pacific Northwest as well, including what is now the Canadian province of British Columbia to the border

of Russian America (today's Alaska) at latitude 54°40'; "fifty-four forty or fight" became an annexationist rallying cry. In the other direction, the British claimed all territory south to the mouth of the Columbia River. In 1846, with war looming against Mexico over the annexation of Texas (which Mexico still claimed), Polk did not want to risk conflict on two different fronts; instead, he negotiated a treaty that divided the Oregon Country, leaving in American hands what are today the states of Oregon, Washington, and Idaho, as well as parts of Montana and Wyoming. The compromise was widely considered to be a negotiating victory for the United States, but it left those in Polk's own Democratic Party who had demanded the acquisition of "all of Oregon" less than fully satisfied.

That same year, Polk used a dispute over the Texas–Mexico boundary to provoke the long-anticipated war with Mexico. The Mexican–American War lasted for two years and remains, in terms of the percentage of military fatalities, the second-deadliest war in U.S.

Daniel A. Jenks, *Camp 100—Humbolt River*, 1859. This drawing of an emigrant encampment on the Humboldt River, in what is now western Nevada, comes from the sketchbook that Jenks kept of his journey overland to California.

history (exceeded only by the Civil War). Over 13,000 American soldiers—nearly seventeen per cent of those who served—died in the war, while as many as 25,000 Mexicans perished, including an estimated 4,000 civilians.[1] The war, which Polk's opponents in the Whig Party justifiably characterized as a war of aggression, was deeply unpopular with much of the civilian population and even with many soldiers, thousands of whom deserted—including a significant number who switched sides to fight for Mexico.[2] The United States, however, was the clear victor, and when U.S. forces occupied the Mexican heartland and captured Mexico City, some of the same Americans who had demanded "all of Oregon" called for the annexation of "all of Mexico." Polk did not go quite that far, but when the war ended in 1848, Mexico was forced not only to surrender its claim to Texas but also to cede to the United States a vast amount of additional land, including all or most of the present-day states of California, Nevada, Utah, Arizona, New Mexico, and Colorado.[3]

As had been the case with Texas, Americans began colonizing the huge territories the U.S. took over during the Polk administration well before those territories formally became U.S. possessions. American missionaries, followed by small groups of emigrants, began journeying to the Oregon Country along the 2,170-mile route that would come to be called the Oregon Trail in the mid-1830s; the first large body of settlers traversed the route in 1843, and by 1869, about 400,000 westward migrants had used it. A further 300,000 people from the U.S. and around the world surged into California after gold was discovered there in January 1848, shortly before California was officially ceded to the U.S. The first group of the approximately

---

[1]   As was typically the case during this period, most military deaths were due to disease.

[2]   Most of the U.S. soldiers who did so were immigrants; Irish Catholic troops, who shared a religious affiliation with their Catholic Mexican opponents and who faced considerable anti-immigrant and anti-Catholic prejudice in the U.S., were especially likely to change sides. (Most U.S. soldiers in the Mexican–American War had been born outside the U.S.; about a quarter were Irish.)

[3]   The 1848 Mexican Cession, which amounted to one-third of Mexico's original territory, also included portions of what is now Texas, Oklahoma, Kansas, and Wyoming. In return, the U.S. paid $15 million (the equivalent of over $400 million today) and assumed $3.25 million worth of Mexican state debt owed to U.S. citizens. The continental U.S. reached its present-day form a few years later with the Gadsden Purchase (1853), in which Mexico sold a further small portion of what is now Arizona and New Mexico.

Anonymous, *The Plantation*, 1825.

Deborah Goldsmith, *Family Portrait*, c. 1832. Deborah Goldsmith (1808–36) earned her living as a traveling portrait painter in New York State—a very unusual career for a woman at the time. While she worked predominantly in watercolor, the family portrait reproduced here was painted with oils. The woman depicted holding a baby in the upper left corner would have been a servant rather than enslaved, as slavery had been abolished in New York in the 1820s.

Sarah Mapps Douglass, *A Token of Love from Me to Thee*, 1833. Especially popular among younger women of the mid-nineteenth century, friendship albums are collections of poems and drawings—sometimes original, sometimes copied—contributed by the owner's friends. The painting included here, an original work by educator, writer, and activist Sarah Mapps Douglass, appears in the album of her friend and fellow activist Amy Cassey; Cassey and Douglass were both members of the Philadelphia Female Anti-Slavery Society, a mixed-race abolitionist organization, and of the Female Literary Association, a society of women intellectuals from Philadelphia's flourishing free black community. Mapps Douglass and the other middle-class black women in her circle laid claim to arts, such as writing and floral painting, that were in most of America considered the province of white women.

Thomas Cole, *The Course of Empire: The Consummation of Empire*, 1836. In 1833, Cole, an English-born painter, began work on a series of five allegorical paintings that would, in his words, show the changes "effected by man in his progress from Barbarism to Civilization, to Luxury, the Vicious state or state of destruction and to the state of Ruin & Desolation." The series' title was taken from a line from an eighteenth-century poem, "Verses on the Prospect of Planting Arts and Learning in America," that was frequently cited by nineteenth-century exponents of American national expansion: "Westward the Course of Empire takes its way." Each painting in the series depicts the same riverbank location, first as a village of nomadic hunters, then as a small agricultural settlement; in this painting, the third, the setting has developed into a magnificent—but also militaristic and decadent—imperial capital.

Thomas Cole, *The Course of Empire: Destruction*, 1836. This, the fourth painting in Cole's series, depicts the great city shown in the previous painting being sacked by a hostile army. *Destruction*, like the rest of *The Course of Empire*, was greeted with acclaim when the full series was exhibited in New York in 1836; the *New-York Mirror* wrote that it portrayed "the merited downfall of all the empires which the earth has heretofore known." Like some of his literary and artistic peers, Cole harbored fears of the U.S. experiencing a similar fate. In an 1835 journal entry, he wrote of his fears that the republic of America could face its downfall as a result of internal division and conflict: "I have of late felt a presentiment that the Institutions of the U[nited] States will ere long undergo a change— that there will be a separation of the States."

George Catlin, *Wi-jún-jon, Pigeon's Egg Head (The Light) Going to and Returning from Washington*, 1837–39. Catlin made it his artistic mission to create a visual record of traditional Native American ways of life—which, like many nineteenth-century white Americans, he believed to be headed for inevitable extinction. In the course of several journeys through the American West in the 1830s, Catlin created hundreds of portraits and other depictions of Native Americans, assembling them in what he called his "Indian Gallery." This painting is a double portrait of Ah-jon-jon, a leader of the Assiniboine nation of the northern Great Plains whose name, meaning "The Light," Catlin mistranslated as "Pigeon's Egg Head." The Light visited Washington, D.C. in 1831–32; while there, in Catlin's words, he "exchanged his beautifully garnished and classic costume" for a U.S.-style military uniform. "In this fashion," Catlin continued, "was poor Wi-jun-jon metamorphosed."

Edmonia Lewis, *Hiawatha*, 1868. A sculptor of black and Ojibwe parentage, Edmonia Lewis spent much of her career in a community of women artists in Rome, where she said she was "practically driven" because "the land of liberty had no room for a colored sculptor." Lewis sometimes took up subject matter that capitalized on her American audience's fascination with her racial background. The bust represented here depicts the Haudenosaunee (Iroquois) leader Hiawatha; Lewis paired it with a bust of Minnehaha, his fictional beloved in Longfellow's famous poem *The Song of Hiawatha* (1855).

Robert S. Duncanson, *Uncle Tom and Little Eva*, 1853. Born to a free black family in New York State, Robert S. Duncanson achieved international acclaim as, in the words of one American critic, "the best landscape painter in the West." The painting reproduced here, of characters from *Uncle Tom's Cabin*, is unusual in that Duncanson did not generally comment directly on racial issues in his work, although he did paint other scenes drawn from literature. *Uncle Tom's Cabin* was a common source of inspiration for mid-nineteenth-century artists, who were especially drawn to this scene in which Tom and Eva discuss religion; see Stowe's author section for further examples of art inspired by her novel.

Winslow Homer, *The Veteran in a New Field*, 1865, New England artist Winslow Homer spent part of the Civil War on the front lines as an illustrator depicting events for *Harper's Weekly*; following this experience, he produced a number of paintings reflecting on the war and its meaning. In this painting, completed a few months after the war ended, the figure is identified as a Union veteran by his jacket and canteen in the bottom right corner, almost obscured by the stalks of grain he is harvesting.

Samuel Colman Jr., *Storm King on the Hudson*, 1866. Colman belonged to the so-called "second generation" of the Hudson River School, an artistic movement founded in the 1820s and 30s that sought to capture what its practitioners considered to be the unique power of the American natural landscape—and the drama of its (white) human settlement. By the 1860s, many Hudson River School artists had taken to depicting scenes from (or inspired by) the trans-Mississippi West, but this painting maintains the school's traditional focus on the northeastern Hudson Valley landscapes. By the time Colman painted this depiction of the Hudson River near Storm King Mountain (a peak famous for dramatic weather), steam technology was transforming the river's extensive commercial traffic—as the painting illustrates.

Emily Dickinson, Seq. 32, *Herbarium*, c. 1839–46. When she was about nine years old, Emily Dickinson began to keep a detailed herbarium of flowers labeled with their Latin names and carefully pressed into a clothbound book. By the time she completed the book, around the age of sixteen, she had accumulated more than sixty pages of preserved flowers. The flowers on the page depicted here include *Solanum tuberosum* (the potato flower; upper left), *Veronica serpyllifolia* (thyme-leaved speedwell; middle row, second from left), and *Digitalis purpurea* (common foxglove; upper right).

After John Gast, *American Progress*, c. 1873 (painting produced 1872). *American Progress*, the best-known painting by Brooklyn-based artist John Gast, was commissioned by the publisher George Crofutt, who distributed it widely as the color print reproduced here and used it as a frontispiece in one of his popular tourist guides to the American West. In an advertisement offering the print to his subscribers, Crofutt describes it as a

> beautiful picture, which … represents the United States' portion of the American Continent in its beauty and variety, from the Atlantic to the Pacific Ocean, illustrating at a glance the grand drama of Progress in the civilization, settlement and history of this country.
>
> In the foreground, the central and principal figure, a beautiful and charming female, is floating westward through the air, bearing on her forehead the "Star of Empire." … In her right hand she carries a book—common schools—the emblem of education and the testimonial of our national enlightenment, while with the left hand she unfolds and stretches the slender wires of the telegraph, that are to flash intelligence throughout the land. On the right of the picture, is a city, steamships, manufactures, schools and churches, over which beams of light are streaming and filling the air—indicative of civilization. The general tone of the picture on the left, declares darkness, waste and confusion. … Fleeing from "Progress," and towards the blue waters of the Pacific, … are the Indians, buffaloes, wild horses, bears, and other game, moving westward—ever westward—the Indians … turn their despairing faces towards, as they flee from, the presence of the wondrous vision. The "Star" is *too much for them*. …

Howling Wolf, *At the Sand Creek Massacre*, 1874–75. Southern Cheyenne warrior and artist Howling Wolf was one of his era's most important practitioners of ledger art, a form that adapted Plains Indigenous painting styles and methods to Euro-American materials, including the ledger paper that was commonly used by traders and government officials. Howling Wolf here depicts the Sand Creek Massacre (1864), where a U.S. government force of 675 soldiers attacked a Cheyenne and Arapaho camp on a reservation, ignoring the inhabitants' clear attempts to surrender. While most of the estimated 150 to 230 people the soldiers killed were children and unarmed civilians, Howling Wolf was one of a small number of Cheyenne and Arapaho warriors who attempted to defend their community—but with little success, as they possessed only bows and rifles while the U.S. forces were well-armed with heavy artillery at their disposal. The soldiers scalped and mutilated the bodies of those they had killed, and the extraordinary brutality of the event evoked national disgust; their colonel, John Chivington, was condemned by a congressional committee for leading "a foul and dastardly massacre." Survivors of the massacre preserved its history in oral literature, and in hide paintings and other visual works such as the one reproduced here.

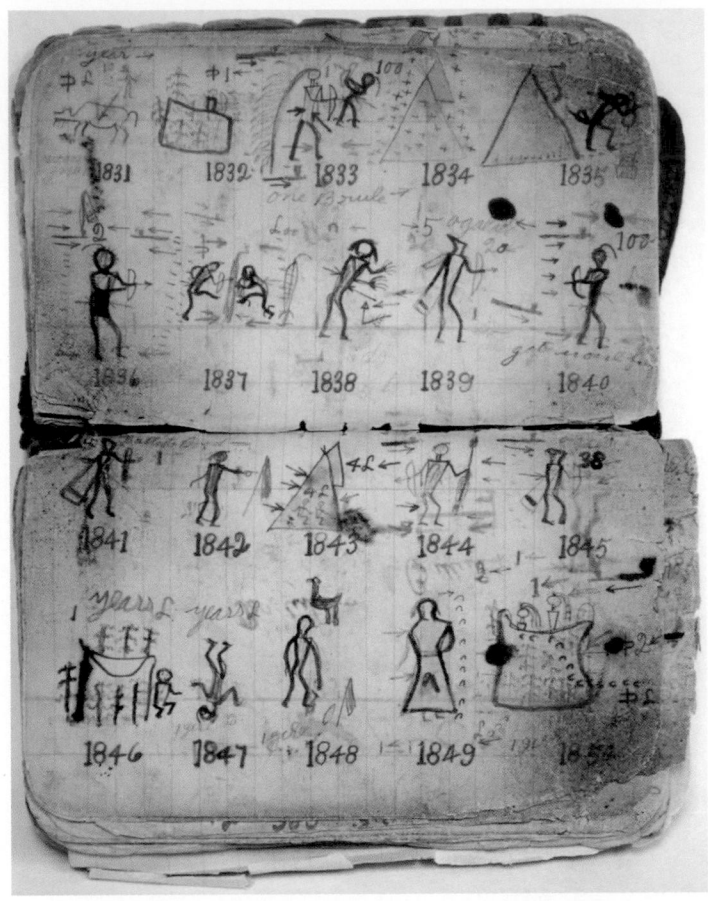

Battiste Good / Wapostangi, page of a winter count documenting 1831–52 (copy produced 1880). Winter counts, kept by Lakota, Kiowa, and other Plains peoples, are community records. In a Lakota winter count, each year is marked at the end of winter by a symbol indicating what the community has determined to be the most memorable event of that year; this symbol, drawn by the winter count's keeper, serves as a record of the year's name and a memory aid for the telling of the community's history. Winter counts were initially kept on buffalo hides and, increasingly as buffalo became scarce, cloth or paper. Battiste Good (Wapostangi), a winter count keeper of the Sicangu Lakota, kept his community's count on cloth, but the page reproduced here is drawn from a ledger-paper copy he made for a white collector. Many year names reference deaths, injuries, and battles; a selection of the year names for this page as given by Good may be translated as follows:

1830–31: "Shot-many-white-buffalo-cows winter"

1832–33: "Stiff-Leg-with-War-Bonnet-on-died winter," during which Stiff Leg died in a battle with Pawnee warriors

1833–34: "Storm-of-stars winter," the year of an exceptional meteor shower

1834–35: "Killed-the-Cheyenne-who-came-to-camp winter"

1839–40: "Came-home-from-the-starve-to-death-war-path winter," during which many Lakota peoples united against the Pawnee, succeeding in battle but nearly starving in the process

1845–46: "Broke-out-on-faces-had-sore-throats-and-camped-under-the-bluff winter"

1847–48: "The-Teal-broke-his-leg winter," the symbol for which shows The Teal's arm pointing toward the fractured leg, with a teal (a species of bird) near his head to suggest his identity

70,000 Mormons who escaped persecution in the eastern U.S. by moving to Utah arrived there in 1847, at a time when it too was still nominally Mexican territory. These numbers attest to the tremendous appeal of the new western territories and the opportunities they afforded to many Americans. Many others, though, suffered from the risks, sacrifices, disruptions, and costs inevitably involved in such transcontinental migrations. One such person, a woman named Elizabeth Cress, who moved with her husband from North Carolina to Illinois but then refused to accompany him further westward, wrote a letter to her parents in 1851 that provides another perspective on, and another part of the story of, mid-nineteenth-century American expansion: "my old man has left me & has gone to California and took my wagon and left me and my Children in a bad situation."

The roughly 80,000 Hispanic inhabitants of the territories taken from Mexico experienced even more profound disruptions. Contempt for this Hispanic population featured prominently in U.S. expansionary thinking, according to which the Hispanic Mexicans were—as Richard Henry Dana put it in *Two Years Before the Mast* (1840), his account of his voyage to California by sea in the 1830s—"an idle, thriftless

Edward Vischer, *A Californian Magnate in His Home*, 1865. By the time this painting of Los Angeles landowner General Don Andres Pico was made, many such large Californio estates had been taken over, broken up, or whittled away by white American settlers.

people" who could "make nothing for themselves."[1] Many in the U.S. felt it to be only just that the land of these Hispanic settlers be taken over by supposedly more industrious and politically enlightened white Americans. The 1848 treaty that ended the Mexican–American War theoretically extended full U.S. citizenship to former Mexican citizens, and it also would have guaranteed property rights for holders of Mexican land grants; however, Congress removed this last provision from the treaty, stipulating instead that property rights would be guaranteed only to those who could prove ownership—a stipulation that was often difficult and financially ruinous to meet. Racialized prejudice and lack of adequate legal protections combined to relegate most Mexican Americans to the status of second-class citizens, and the influx of white American settlers to California and Texas soon also made them a minority. Mariano Guadalupe Vallejo, a prominent Californio who initially supported California's entrance into the U.S., voiced the resulting bitterness of many Hispanic Americans in his 1875 memoirs, in which he castigated "the swollen torrent of shysters, who came from Missouri and other states of the Union" in the Gold Rush: "[T]hese legal thieves, clothed in the robes of the law, took from us our lands and our houses and without the least scruple enthroned themselves in our homes like so many powerful kings." Similar injustices drove the Tejano Juan Cortina to armed resistance; in September 1859, he briefly occupied the border town of Brownsville, Texas, with a force of seventy men, issuing a proclamation that asserted the right of Mexican Americans to defend themselves against those who "persecute and rob us without reason and for no other motive or crime than that of being of Mexican origin" and avowed, "Our personal enemies will not possess our land, except by paying for it with their own blood."

Racialized discrimination was by no means confined to Hispanic Mexicans. Californian legislation such as the 1850 foreign miners' tax and the 1855 anti-vagrancy laws imposed restrictions on those of Mexican, Asian, Indigenous, and African backgrounds. Oregon's

---

[1]   Dana's comparisons of the lives of the Hispanic colonizers with those of the Indigenous peoples of California are of considerable interest: "Among the Mexicans," he observed, "there is no working class; (the Indians being slaves and doing all the hard work); and every rich man looks like a grandee, and every poor scamp like a broken-down gentleman."

original Negro Exclusion Law and additional exclusion laws of 1862 (levying special taxes on Hawaiians, Asians, and those of mixed race as well as on blacks) made it clear that, while Oregon might not be a slave state, it was emphatically not a state in which all were welcome or would be treated equally.

Arguably the greatest injustices were directed toward the Indigenous nations of the U.S.'s new western acquisitions; much of what had occurred to Native Americans east of the Mississippi up until the 1830s was repeated after 1848 in the West—in some cases, on an even larger and more terrible scale. When the Dakota of Minnesota rose up in 1862 in response to neglect and abuse by federal authorities, the rebellion was viciously suppressed; the American response included the largest mass execution in American history—the hanging of 38 Dakota men.[1] In 1864, the Navajo of the southwest followed in the footsteps of the Cherokee and so many other eastern nations when, in the "Long Walk of the Navajo," they too were deported *en masse* from their traditional territories (although unlike their eastern counterparts, they were eventually able to return). The Cherokee expulsion had been precipitated, in part, by the discovery of gold on their lands in Georgia in 1829; two decades later, the much larger gold rush in California had even grimmer consequences for California's Indigenous peoples. By 1900, the massacres and enslavement perpetrated by white American settlers, and the disease and starvation they spread, had reduced an Indigenous Californian population that numbered as high as 150,000 in 1848 to just 16,000.

One phrase introduced during the Polk administration has come to define American expansionism, a phrase that was used again and again both to celebrate the progress of expansion and to gloss over or rationalize the many wrongs committed in pursuing it: "manifest destiny." The phrase first appeared, more or less in passing, in an 1845 article advocating the annexation of Texas that was published in *The United States Magazine and Democratic Review*, a Jacksonian Democratic periodical edited by the Irish American journalist John L. O'Sullivan. The article proclaimed that Texas's incorporation into the U.S. was key to "the

Wife and two children of Little Crow, one of the leaders of the 1862 Dakota uprising in Minnesota, during their internment after the uprising's suppression; photograph by Benjamin Upton, 1864. Little Crow himself was killed by white settlers in 1863.

fulfillment of our manifest destiny to overspread the continent allotted by Providence for the free development of our yearly multiplying millions." This first use of the term "manifest destiny" did not have much immediate impact, but when the phrase appeared again in another *Democratic Review* article a few months later that asserted the U.S.'s right, in its dispute with Britain over the Oregon Country, to claim "the whole of Oregon," it began to catch on.[2] The idea of an American "manifest destiny" was cited by both

---

[1]   A further 265 Dakota prisoners had their death sentences commuted by President Lincoln.

[2]   As the phrase "manifest destiny" became more and more widespread, its origins were forgotten, and the *Democratic Review*'s role in coining it was not recognized until 1927. The two articles in which the phrase first appeared were both published anonymously; they have traditionally been credited to O'Sullivan, but several scholars have posited that the first, at least, was actually written by Jane Cazneau, a journalist for the *Democratic Review* and other periodicals and an avid expansionist.

sides in the congressional debate over the Oregon issue in early 1846, and in the late 1840s and 1850s the term became ubiquitous. By 1858, the writer and Army wife Teresa Griffin Vielé could use it as a commonplace to describe how, in her eyes, Anglo-American settlement in Texas displayed "the marks of inevitable progress … otherwise called 'manifest destiny.'" Other writers repurposed the phrase to refer not to the supposed inevitability of (white) American expansion but to the supposed inevitability of Native American disappearance in the face of that expansion—a fate that Mary Eastman, in her 1849 book *Dahcotah; or, Life and Legends of the Sioux around Fort Snelling*, termed the "manifest destiny of the aborigines."

In context, however, Eastman's use of "manifest destiny" demonstrates trepidation about, rather than confidence in, "the giant strides of civilization" before which Indigenous people supposedly were "receding rapidly, and with feeble resistance": "We should be better reconciled to this manifest destiny of the aborigines, if the inroads of civilization were worthy of it." Such misgivings were widespread: if many Americans enthusiastically endorsed and sought to realize their self-proclaimed "manifest destiny" to possess the continent and dispossess those who preceded them there, many others were troubled by this idea or opposed it outright. In the 1820s and 1830s, "Indian Removal" met with fervent opposition. In 1829, for example, a group of women (including the poet Lydia Sigourney and the educator Catharine Beecher, sister of Harriet Beecher Stowe) organized a grassroots campaign against Native American expulsion that resulted in almost 1,500 women submitting anti-removal petitions to Congress, in what has been identified as a landmark moment in the history of women's activism in the U.S. Even figures as reactionary as the Southern writer William Gilmore Simms, a strong supporter of slavery, condemned what, in 1845, he called "the reckless and unsparing hand with which we have smitten [Indigenous people] in their habitations, and expelled them from their country." Other commentators specifically warned against justifying the country's "unsparing" policies toward Native Americans by abstract invocations of destiny. As the pioneering anthropologist Lewis Henry Morgan put it in 1851: "It cannot be forgotten, that in after years our Republic must render

an account, to the civilized world, for the disposal which it makes of the Indian. It is not sufficient, before this tribunal, to plead inevitable destiny."

Aggression toward Mexico, the other major means whereby the U.S. pursued its "manifest destiny," was opposed just as strongly, sometimes in surprising ways or by surprising voices. John Quincy Adams, for example, whose 1811 characterization of American expansion as "destined by Divine Providence" was quoted earlier, had by 1836 become one of the staunchest opponents of American expansionism, as he demonstrated in an impassioned speech to his fellow members of the House of Representatives:

> What will be your *cause* in such a war [with Mexico]? Aggression, conquest, and the re-establishment of slavery where it has been abolished. In that war, Sir, the banners of *freedom* will be the banners of Mexico; and your banners—I blush to speak the word—will be the banners of *slavery*.

When the U.S. eventually went to war with Mexico a decade later, many New Englanders opposed the war because, like Adams, they considered it an attempt to expand slavery. Many white Southerners opposed it as well—on the grounds either that it would be too difficult to reimpose slavery in Mexico or that incorporating a large non-white (and non-Protestant) population into the United States would undermine white supremacy.[1] The common thread linking opposition to Indigenous expulsion and to war with Mexico, as parallel attempts to seize the rightful patrimony of others, was highlighted by the use, in both causes, of the biblical story of Naboth's vineyard, in which the Israelite King Ahab is condemned by God for arranging the death of his neighbor Naboth in order to obtain his vineyard, which Naboth had refused to sell.[2] In 1825, the New

---

[1]   The Mexican–American War, and the accompanying debates about whether to annex Mexican territory (and if so, how much), highlighted inherent, unresolved tensions in the concept of "manifest destiny" itself. Was America's destiny associated primarily with its supposed political superiority, as a constitutional democracy, or its supposed racial superiority, as an ostensibly "Anglo-Saxon" nation? Was America called to spread the benefits of its democratic political institutions (an argument made by proponents of annexing all of Mexico) or to consolidate and extend white supremacy (one of the arguments used to oppose that course of action)?

[2]   See 1 Kings 21.

York newspaper editor William Leete Stone likened the Georgia state government's attempts to dispossess the Muscogee (Creek) to Ahab "wickedly wresting from Naboth *the inheritance of his fathers*," while in 1848, the abolitionist minister Theodore Parker compared Ahab's designs on Naboth's vineyard to President Polk's designs on Mexico in his "Sermon of the Mexican War"—a piece of oratory that, scholars have suggested, helped inspire Herman Melville's *Moby-Dick* (1851).

African Americans had an especially complicated relationship with the idea of "manifest destiny." Many black people identified slavery as the root of U.S. expansionism and condemned it accordingly, as did Mary Ann Shadd in *A Plea for Emigration* (1852), her treatise advocating black emigration to Canada: "The pro-slavery party of the United States is the aggressive party on this continent. It is the serpent that aims to swallow all others." But "manifest destiny" thinking appealed to other African Americans. In 1848, for example, the clergyman Henry Highland Garnet celebrated the U.S. victory over Mexico as an event that would augment America's diversity and thereby make it more peaceful and democratic: "This republic, and this continent, are to be the theatre in which the grand drama of our triumphant Destiny is to be enacted." Still other black thinkers appropriated the language of "manifest destiny" to voice black separatist aspirations: the poet James Monroe Whitfield, arguing like Shadd in favor of African American emigration, asserted in 1853, "I … consider it a part of [black people's] 'manifest destiny' to possess all the tropical regions of this continent," and the abolitionist minister Richard Harvey Cain entitled his 1862 lecture advocating the creation of an African American colony in Africa "Manifest Destiny of the African Race." As African Americans elaborated these various responses to the concept of manifest destiny, the question of whether slavery was to be permitted in the new western territories became more and more polarizing, bringing the country closer and closer to civil war.

The debates over national expansion and Native American expulsion that consumed the country as a whole between the 1820s and the Civil War also took place in and through American literature. These issues took center stage, in particular, in the wave of novels about Indigenous–settler relations that swept the national literary scene in the 1820s and 30s, including (among many others) Lydia Maria Child's *Hobomok* (1824), Catharine Maria Sedgwick's *Hope Leslie* (1827), William Gilmore Simms's *The Yemassee* (1835), and James Fenimore Cooper's Leatherstocking Tales (1823–41). While most of these works were set during colonial times a century or more previously, their subject-matter unavoidably resonated with the crisis in U.S.–Native American relations that was unfolding when they were published, and their popularity thrust the questions at stake in that crisis upon readers who otherwise might not have had to confront them. Cooper's *The Last of the Mohicans* (1827), for example, evokes the burgeoning issue of "Indian Removal" in passages such as the following, in which an Indigenous character denounces white expansionism: "[The white man's] gluttony makes him sick. God gave him enough, and yet he wants all. Such are the pale-faces!" It should be noted, though, that this speech is delivered by Magua, the novel's Huron (Wendat) villain; such novels' perspectives on the matters they address are far from consistent or univocal. If some writers, such as Child, outspokenly condemned Indigenous expulsion, others, such as Cooper, could voice reservations about the march of white civilization, and sympathetically portray Indigenous resistance to it, while also doing as much as anyone to foster the myths—of intrepid backwoodsmen, regenerative violence, and Native Americans who were either noble or savage but, in either case, inevitably doomed—that helped motivate and sustain American expansionism.

Similar ambivalence on the question of national expansion pervades the mid-nineteenth-century American literary canon. Many of the writers at the core of this canon endorsed and perpetuated ideas of American exceptionalism, of America's special destiny, and even of America's providential right to claim the continent. William Cullen Bryant and Walt Whitman, in their capacity as editors of Jacksonian Democratic newspapers, supported Indigenous expulsion and the Mexican–American War, respectively. Herman Melville was largely supportive of the idea of American exceptionalism, which the protagonist of his 1850 novel *White-Jacket; or, The World in a Man-of-War* endorses in ringing terms: "Americans are the peculiar, the chosen people—the Israel of our time; we bear the ark of the liberties of the world. God has pre-destined, mankind expects, great things from our race; and great things we feel in our souls."[1] Ralph Waldo Emerson declared that "Nature says to the American … 'I give you the land and sea, the forest and the mine, the elemental forces'"; and Henry David Thoreau celebrated "the westward tendency" that he saw as "the prevailing tendency of my countrymen." Yet Whitman also came to consider Mexico "the only one to whom we have ever really done wrong"; Thoreau went to jail rather than pay a tax to fund the Mexican–American War; Emerson called invocations of "*Manifest Destiny, Democracy, Freedom*" "fine names for an ugly thing"; and Melville's writing also includes numerous condemnations of imperialism, including U.S. imperialism, and the prejudice that propelled it, from the negative portrayals of white incursions on Indigenous Pacific Islander life in *Typee* (1846) to the searing portrait of an obsessive, genocidal "Indian-hater" in *The Confidence-Man* (1857).

But to read the works of these canonical writers—most of whom had little firsthand acquaintance with what was occurring in the course of their country's enlargement—is barely to scratch the surface of nineteenth-century American literature's engagement with national expansion. Westward migration and settlement also generated a large body of writing, to which women, in particular, contributed significantly. Many depictions of newly colonized areas were promotional, meant to encourage western settlement and guide settlers in their new life; notable examples include *Texas: Observations, Historical, Geographical and Descriptive* (1833) by Mary Austin Holley—cousin of Stephen F. Austin, the founder of the first major Anglo-American colony in Texas—and *Life in Prairie Land* (1846) by Eliza Farnham. Margaret Fuller's *Summer on the Lakes* (1844), an account of a tour of newly colonized areas in the Great Lakes region in 1843, is promotional as well, but Fuller—a notable Transcendentalist and women's rights advocate—also documented settler colonialism's impact on Native Americans (albeit from the widely held white perspective that saw Indigenous people as

inevitably bound for "speedy extinction"). Fuller also registers environmental concern for the land itself, recording her fears that the settlers' "mode of cultivation will, in the course of twenty, perhaps ten years, obliterate the natural expression of the country." Other writers pushed back against promotional literature in their efforts to realistically depict the struggle and privation of settler life. Caroline Kirkland's *A New Home—Who'll Follow?* (1839), a lightly fictionalized portrayal of colonizer life in a new settlement in Michigan, became an acclaimed bestseller as it generated intense controversy for its unromanticized truth-telling; Alice Cary's *Clovernook; Or Recollections of Our Neighborhood in the West* (1852), also a bestseller, followed suit some years later.

The West became a common setting in the sentimental and domestic fiction that rose to popularity in the 1850s. Works such as Maria Susanna Cummins's *Mabel Vaughan* (1857) and Caroline Soule's *The Pet of the Settlement* (1860) celebrated the West as a place where, in the words of the latter novel, "struggling, debt-ridden, homeless and hungry men and women from the crowded cities of the older States" could find regeneration in cohesive rural communities. Similarly, in Mary Hayden Pike's *Ida May* (1854) and E.D.E.N. Southworth's *India: The Pearl of Pearl River* (1856), the free soil of the West redeems Southerners from the taint of slavery. Sensation fiction—the frequently lurid and violent, stereotypically "masculine" counterpart to stereotypically "feminine" sentimental fiction—also gravitated westward and dealt with national expansion in ways that are often more nuanced than readers might expect. The hero of *The Volunteer: or, the Maid of Monterey* (1847), by the prolific and influential popular writer Ned Buntline (the pen name of E.Z.C. Judson), calls the Mexican–American War a "war of invasion," and a character in Southworth's *The Hidden Hand* (1859) reflects similarly on his participation in the war: "what had I to do with invading another's country?" Such works prefigured the rise, in the 1860s, of the dime novel, a new form of cheap popular literature priced, as its name suggests, at ten cents; the titles of some of the first dime novels—*Malaeska, the Indian Wife of the White Hunter* and *Seth Jones; or, The Captives of the Frontier* (both 1860)—attest to the way in which western expansion was integral to this genre

---

[1]   This oft-quoted passage is prompted by a commentary on the practice of flogging on board ship; White-Jacket, the protagonist and narrator, is directly addressing the reader as he argues that America need not and should not follow the example of other nations: "in things of this kind England should be nothing to us, except an example to be shunned."

Cover of *Esther: A Story of the Oregon Trail* (1862), by the prolific dime novelist Ann S. Stephens.

from its start. And as the following passage from Ann S. Stephens's *Esther: A Story of the Oregon Trail* (1862) demonstrates, dime novels could reflect on "manifest destiny" and Indigenous expulsion in ways that were multifaceted and ambivalent, quite as much as could more canonical literary works:

> The star that leads civilization westward shines sadly upon the graves of a people almost extinct— a people that have been hunted ruthlessly from their greenwood haunts till every year has seen their graves multiplying thicker and thicker in the wilderness. Then the Anglo-Saxon comes to plow it up and plant corn above the dead warriors, stopping now and then to pick up a stone arrowhead from his furrow, and examine it curiously, as if he did not know what soil his sacrilegious plow was upturning. ... Yon star that leads westward has no halting place for him till it sets on the calm Pacific, writing on its blue waters the history of a people that have perished.

These popular works, like their "highbrow" canonical counterparts, were largely written and published in the East, which remained the location of the country's literary establishment, but a vibrant literary and publishing scene quickly arose in the West as well. Western migrants brought nineteenth-century America's robust, deep-rooted print culture with them to their new homes, founding newspapers and printing shops and publishing a tremendous variety of journalism, essays, fiction, and poetry. By 1867, California had developed a literary culture big enough and busy enough to yield an anthology—*Poetry of the Pacific*, published in San Francisco—that was more than 400 pages long and featured the work of over sixty poets (half of them women). One of the leading Californian writers was Bret Harte, who moved there in 1853. Harte gained a reputation in the 1860s for his colorful, frequently satirical depictions of Gold Rush life—as well as for his condemnations of violence against Indigenous Californians, which earned him death threats from some of his white compatriots. The young Missourian Samuel Clemens, who spent the Civil War years in Nevada Territory and then California (where he met Harte), similarly made a name for himself in the West with his writing, in his case literally: his publications in Nevada newspapers in the 1860s included his first use of the pen name "Mark Twain." A different kind of Western writing is exemplified by the work of Eliza R. Snow, the so-called "Mormon poetess"—and plural wife (first of Joseph Smith, the Mormon founder, and then of Brigham Young, the leader of the Mormon exodus to Utah)—whose poetic depictions of Mormon westward migration and life in their new settlements filled two volumes, the first published in Britain in 1856 and the second in Salt Lake City in 1877.

The experience of U.S. expansion also gave rise to a rich and varied body of literature among America's Indigenous peoples and among the Hispanic inhabitants of the territories taken from Mexico. The petitions, essays, letters, poems, and narratives written during the expulsion crisis by members of those Indigenous nations that had adopted literacy and written languages are an eloquent record of Native Americans' various attempts to resist, survive, or come to terms with their dispossession. These texts run the gamut from the polished political prose of John Ross, the

Eliza R. Snow, c. 1852.

Cherokee Principal Chief, to the blunt, world-weary verse penned by an anonymous Choctaw during his nation's deportation: "On my way to the Arkansas / God damn the white mans laws / O come and go along with me / O come and go along with me." A particular standout among this corpus is the autobiography of Black Hawk, the Sauk chieftain who led an attempt to reclaim his nation's lands in Illinois and Wisconsin in the 1832 war named after him. Black Hawk dictated his autobiography to a U.S. government interpreter during his imprisonment after the war; published in 1833, it became a frequently reprinted bestseller. Alongside this written literature, Native Americans enshrined and interpreted their experiences in oral stories, many of which continue to be related today.

Mid-nineteenth-century Hispanic American liter-ary culture is also characterized by both a vibrant writ-ten literature and a popular, largely oral counterpart. This culture includes, at one end of the spectrum, the memoirs of elite figures such as Mariano Guadalupe Vallejo and Juan Seguín, and the fiction of María Ruiz de Burton, a Californio woman from a similarly elite background who was the first female Mexican American author to write in English; her first novel,

Who Would Have Thought It? (1872), critiques white American racial hypocrisy and "manifest destiny" doctrine. At the other end of the spectrum, Hispanic American literature comprises popular dramas, such as the play *Los Tejanos* (probably written between 1841 and 1846), and anonymous corridos (ballads), such as the many composed about Joaquín Murrieta, a legend-ary Californio outlaw who is supposed to have fought back against Anglo-American injustice during the Gold Rush. These works also attest to Hispanic American grievances and resistance: *Los Tejanos*, which depicts a failed Texan expedition into New Mexico (then still part of Mexico) in 1841, ends with a Hispanic charac-ter telling a captured Anglo-American Texan general, "Die, you dog! Now you are going to pay for all the evil you had planned," while one of the Murrieta corridos pushes back against white American avowals of their "manifest destiny" in its declaration that "California is Mexico's / Because God wanted it that way."

Such ballads provided inspiration for a writer who brings together Native American, Hispanic American, and white American literary cultures in one complex combination: the Cherokee author John Rollin Ridge (Chees-quat-a-law-ny). The son and grandson of prom-inent Cherokee who were killed by fellow members of their nation for their support for, and role in bringing about, Cherokee "removal," Ridge was born on the Cherokee's traditional lands in Georgia but ended up in California, where he embarked on a career in journal-ism and literature. While he wrote poetry and essays, his most significant work was *The Life and Adventures of Joaquín Murieta: The Celebrated California Bandit* (1854), the first published Native American novel and the first novel written in California, which codi-fied the Murrieta corridos in what would prove to be a popular and influential form. The novel condemns white American racism toward Mexican Americans, but is virtually silent about the treatment of California's Indigenous population. While Ridge occasionally spoke out against their mistreatment, his writing also traffics in the degrading characterization of Indigenous Californians as primitive "Diggers,"[1] a stereotype that

---

[1]   This derogatory term reflected the contempt that white American settlers felt for the hunter-gatherer way of life—including digging up roots to eat—practiced by many of California's Indigenous peoples; the term is today rightly considered highly offensive.

helped drive their near-total extermination. Ridge, as a Native American writer who adapted Hispanic American material and who suffered from, criticized, and participated in settler colonialism, arguably exemplifies more fully than any other single writer of the period the complex history of U.S. expansion.

NATIVE AMERICAN WRITING—AND WRITING ABOUT NATIVE AMERICANS

The complex case of John Rollin Ridge exemplifies a larger truth about American literature of the 1820– Reconstruction period: namely, that this literature cannot be understood apart from the violence visited upon Indigenous communities and the vital, persistent expression of Native Americans whose writings contradicted settler narratives about the supposed disappearance of Indigenous people and cultures. The United States pursued its grand narrative of settler rule, or self-proclaimed "manifest destiny," through a strategy of Indigenous expulsion that was then referred to as *Indian removal*—a polite term for the pilfering of Indigenous lands through questionable and broken treaties, and the forced relocation of approximately 100,000 Indigenous people from their homelands east of the Mississippi River to insufficient territories to the west. The strategy of expulsion went back to the beginnings of colonialism in North America, but its pursuit as official federal policy was a nineteenth-century phenomenon—articulated by Thomas Jefferson, passed narrowly by the House and Senate in 1830, signed into law by President Andrew Jackson, and implemented over subsequent decades.

Expulsion was always controversial; Native American leaders and non-Indigenous allies questioned it on both political and moral grounds. President Jackson—whose reputation stemmed, in part, from the brutal military campaigns he had conducted against the Muscogee (Creek) in 1813–14 and the Seminole in 1818—expressed his frustration over such protest, asking in his 1830 address to Congress, "What good man would prefer a country covered with forests and ranged by a few thousand savages to our extensive Republic, studded with cities, towns, and prosperous farms embellished with all the improvements which art can devise or industry execute, occupied by more than

12,000,000 happy people, and filled with all the blessings of liberty, civilization and religion?" Opponents of expulsion posed their own questions. In a petition to the U.S. Congress in December 1829, the Cherokee Nation queried, "what better right can a people have to a country, than the right of *inheritance* and *immemorial peaceable possession?*" No less an authority than the U.S. Supreme Court upheld the sovereignty of the Cherokee Nation in its 1832 *Worcester v. Georgia* decision, but ultimately to little effect: as Andrew Jackson is said—probably apocryphally—to have commented after the ruling was issued, "John Marshall [the Chief Justice] has made his decision; now let him enforce it!"

The most famous, or infamous, expulsion is the Cherokee Trail of Tears, in which, over the course of six months in 1838–39, approximately 16,000 members of the Cherokee Nation were forcibly removed from the southeast to lands in what had been designated as "Indian Territory" (a large and vaguely-defined area west of the Mississippi, centering on what is now Oklahoma). At least 4,000 died as a direct result. The basis for Cherokee expulsion was the controversial Treaty of New Echota (1835), signed by a faction of Cherokee leaders who, in contradiction of Principal Chief John Ross, had concluded that the nation's options for political resistance had run out. The federal government also expelled members of the Muscogee (Creek), Chickasaw, Choctaw, Sauk (Sac), Meskwaki (Fox), Seminole, Kickapoo, Shawnee, Ho-Chunk (Winnebago), and Potawatomi nations, among others, in deportations that were often as deadly as that of the Cherokee.

Native Americans resisted these efforts in a variety of ways. In the south, members of the Muscogee nation took up arms in the Second Creek War (1836), while the Seminole of Florida—including associated groups of African American escapees from slavery, the so-called Black Seminole—resisted until 1842. The Second Seminole War, the longest and most expensive (in both human and monetary terms) of all U.S.-Native American conflicts, cost the lives of 1,466 U.S. soldiers and an unknown number of militia members, as well as between thirty and forty million dollars, an unheard-of amount of money at the time; as many as a thousand Seminole—a number that would amount to twenty per cent of their total population—were killed,

Henry Lewis, *The Battle of Bad Axe*, 1857. In his 2020 book *Surviving Genocide*, Jeffrey Ostler describes this image as "an especially striking example of colonial evasion; the caption refers to the event as a battle," but what is being portrayed in the image "is clearly a massacre."

and 3,824 were eventually deported. In the north, the Sauk leader Black Hawk and his band of warriors from several Indigenous nations defended their land holdings with force in 1832. But they were badly outnumbered, and the brief war ended with a massacre near the mouth of the Bad Axe River in what is now Wisconsin. When they surrendered, the Sauk and their allies were forced to sign a document ceding "to the United States forever all the lands to which the said tribes have title or claims"; the American government termed the document a "Treaty of Peace, Friendship, and Cession." In an autobiographical account dictated after his capture and detention by federal forces, Black Hawk commented on this sort of deceptive language: "How smooth must be the language of the whites, when they can make right look like wrong, and wrong like right." The hypocrisy of U.S. actions was a theme reiterated by all who spoke, wrote, and took up arms in defense of Indigenous sovereignty.

One of the most powerful critics of settler ideology in this era was the Pequot activist, orator, and minister William Apess, who insisted on a biblical basis for racial equality. In essays, and speeches, and his autobiography, Apess declared that the U.S., in dispossessing Indigenous people and enslaving Africans, was in violation of God's law. His brilliant "An Indian's Looking-Glass for the White Man" (1833) challenged white Americans to engage in self-reckoning regarding the "blackness" of their sins. In *Eulogy on King Philip* (1836), Apess linked seventeenth-century colonial violence with that of antebellum America, and confronted his audience directly: "Who, my dear sirs, were wanting of the name of savages—whites, or Indians? Let justice answer." Apess's inversion of the white framework of savagery and civilization echoes through political writings by settler activists, from Jeremiah Evarts's "William Penn" essays (1829) to Ralph Waldo Emerson's April 1838 letter to President Martin Van Buren, in which he angrily asked, "Sir, does this government think that the people of the United States are become savage and mad?"

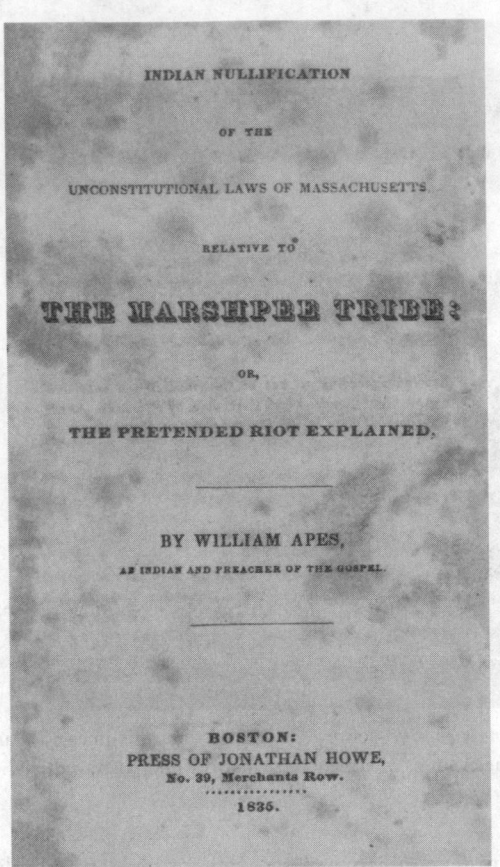

INDIAN NULLIFICATION

OF THE

UNCONSTITUTIONAL LAWS OF MASSACHUSETTS

RELATIVE TO

THE MARSHPEE TRIBE:

OR,

THE PRETENDED RIOT EXPLAINED,

BY WILLIAM APES,

AN INDIAN AND PREACHER OF THE GOSPEL.

BOSTON:
PRESS OF JONATHAN HOWE,
No. 39, Merchants Row.

1835.

Title page of William Apess's *Indian Nullification of the Unconstitutional Laws of Massachusetts Relative to the Marshpee Tribe* (1835).

William Apess was just one of a growing number of Indigenous authors who, in the years prior to the Civil War, produced periodicals, histories, collections of tales and songs, life writing, poetry, and fiction, in Indigenous languages as well as English. After Sequoyah (George Gist) completed a syllabary for the Cherokee language in 1821, the Cherokee Nation adopted it as an official writing system. That syllabary led to the publication of the bilingual *Cherokee Phoenix*, edited by Elias Boudinot (Buck Watie) from 1828 to 1834. The first newspaper in an Indigenous language, the *Phoenix* was read not only by most Cherokee households but also by subscribers across the U.S. and in Europe. Other newspapers followed— among them the Shawnee-language *Siwinowe Kesibwi*

(*The Shawnee Sun*) in 1835, *The Choctaw Telegraph* in 1848, and the bilingual Sioux and English *Iapi Oaye, the Word Carrier* in 1871. Indigenous people also began to write novels, beginning with John Rollin Ridge's *The Life and Adventures of Joaquín Murieta* (1854).

During this period, Indigenous historians also made efforts to document Indigenous history and traditional literatures from the perspective of their own peoples. Tuscarora writer and artist David Cusick was among the first to do so in print with *Sketches of Ancient History of the Six Nations* (1828), offering an Indigenous history of the people of the Haudenosaunee (Iroquois Confederacy) that combines Haudenosaunee and English literary traditions. George Copway (Ojibwe) achieved literary celebrity with his volumes of Ojibwe history and memoir, including *Life, History, and Travels of Kah-ge-ga-gah-bowh* (1847) and *The Traditional History and Characteristic Sketches of the Ojibway Nation* (1850).

Ojibwe author Jane Johnston Schoolcraft (Bamewa-wagezhikaquay) composed poetry in both English and Ojibwe, and translated a number of traditional oral stories into written English. Though she circulated much of her work in manuscript form rather than print, Schoolcraft's impact on nineteenth-century literary culture was profound. Her linguistic and cultural knowledge informed publications by her white husband, Henry Rowe Schoolcraft, beginning with an 1839 collection of Ojibwe oral traditions titled *Algic Researches*, to which her contributions were so extensive that her colleague Elizabeth Oakes Smith described her as "unquestionably, nearly, if not quite" its author. Henry's work, which failed to give adequate credit to his wife, inspired Henry Wadsworth Longfellow's 1855 epic *The Song of Hiawatha*.

This abundance of Native American literary production served as a demonstration of Indigenous humanity in the face of dehumanizing U.S. policy, and affirmed cultural and political sovereignty in a prolonged period of upheaval. Such work existed in conjunction with the variety of nonalphabetic Indigenous literacies including basketry, pictographs, wampum, tattoos, beadwork, scrolls, oral traditions, and orations. Most of these literacies had existed long before contact with Europeans, but some developed later. For example, the ledger art of the Cheyenne, Lakota, Kiowa, and other

THE FLYING HEAD PUT TO FLIGHT BY A WOMAN PARCHING ACORNS

David Cusick, "The Flying Head Put to Flight by a Woman Parching Acorns," *Sketches of Ancient History of the Six Nations*, 1828. This drawing by Cusick illustrates a story in which the people were plagued by monstrous flying heads until, one night, one of the monsters saw a woman parching acorns and mistakenly believed she was eating coals directly from the fire. The flying heads were so frightened by the sight that they left the community alone thereafter.

Plains Indigenous people adapted the traditions of narrative painting to a nineteenth-century context. Before the pressures of colonization dramatically reduced buffalo populations, buffalo hides had been the most common material for narrative painting on the Plains; in the latter half of the nineteenth century, many artists replaced hides with paper from ledger books obtained from government agents and other settlers, integrating Euro-American drawing and painting implements into their artistic practice.

The interest of non-Indigenous people in Indigenous culture was fostered by U.S. cultural nationalism—somewhat ironically, given the close relationship between ideas of American exceptionalism and "manifest destiny." White Americans appropriated the images, histories, material objects, and languages of Native Americans as fodder for the creation of uniquely "American" art, from painting to music to literature.

This was an era in which an ever-growing number of white authors—among them James Fenimore Cooper, Catharine Maria Sedgwick, Washington Irving, William Gilmore Simms, Henry David Thoreau, Lydia Huntley Sigourney, William Cullen Bryant, Margaret Fuller, Lydia Maria Child, and Henry Wadsworth Longfellow—recounted their travels into "Indian country" or spun fictional narratives of often noble Native Americans offering courageous but futile resistance in the face of European conquest. Stereotypes of the "noble savage," of the doomed "Indian warrior," and of the beautiful "Indian princess" pervade these texts. The presentation of Indigenous people in these ways often signaled authorial sympathy for the nations targeted for displacement, yet collectively these works reinforced a myth of the inevitability of Indigenous disappearance and white settlement and conquest, from the Atlantic to the Pacific.

Sitting Bull Counting Coup on an Indian Enemy, c. 1870. This copy of an illustration by the Lakota leader Sitting Bull (c. 1831–90) was drawn on the back of a roster sheet for the U.S. Army's Thirty-First Infantry Regiment. The illustration depicts Sitting Bull's first "coup"—an exploit in which a warrior touched an enemy in battle and escaped unharmed, thereby winning great prestige—at the age of fourteen.

Among the most famous and influential examples of what is sometimes called the "vanishing Indian" myth is Cooper's novel *The Last of the Mohicans: A Narrative of 1757* (1826). As the title suggests, the novel imagines the inevitable demise of the people Cooper calls Mohicans; the culture he imagines combines traits of the Mohican and Mohegan peoples, both of whom in fact continue to survive in the twenty-first century. The novel is admiring in its portrayal of most of its Indigenous characters and poignantly laments the loss of their cultures, but it also presents that loss as a foregone conclusion: at the novel's tragic end, the Lenni Lenape sage Tamenund declares that "The pale-faces are masters of the earth, and the time of the red-men has not yet come again. My day has been too long." *The Last of the Mohicans* retained its popularity and

influence into the twentieth century and has been adapted for film and television numerous times. The myth of the "vanishing Indian" that it helped to popularize persists in twenty-first-century popular culture, from Hollywood films to professional sports—and is present throughout the U.S. Capitol building.

A notable counterpoint to Cooper's work is Herman Melville's 1857 satirical novel *The Confidence-Man*, which focused not on the romanticized Native American but the inverse: Melville exposed the nation's reliance on narratives of the "Indian Hater," a "captain in the vanguard of conquering civilization" whose metaphysics entail "that a brother is to be loved, and an Indian to be hated." Melville knew that works such as Robert Montgomery Bird's *Nick of the Woods* (1837) and Simms's *The Yemassee* (1844) gave expression to the nation's genocidal impulse through the reduction of human beings to caricatures of evil incarnate. In *Nick of the Woods*, for example, the white Quaker Nathan Slaughter roams the Kentucky forest disguised as a monster, murdering Indigenous people to avenge the death of his family. Yet it is Slaughter's Shawnee enemy, the chief Wenonga, whom Bird villainizes. The racism inherent in the portrayal of Wenonga is crude and virulent; at one point Wenonga is portrayed as saying this to Slaughter: "'Me kill all white-man! Me Wenonga: me drink white-man blood; me no heart!'"

Ultimately, the appetite for the Indian Hater narrative and the perpetual representation of Native Americans in non-Indigenous literature, oratory, drama, visual art, music, and even place names, points to a deep disease—and a deep unease—at the heart of white America. The abundance of Indigenous writing and performance in a period of supposed Native American disappearance confirms the foundational role of Indigenous peoples at the moment of American literature's invention.

William H. Powell, *Discovery of the Mississippi by De Soto,* 1855, one of eight historical paintings commissioned by Congress and displayed in the U.S. Capitol rotunda. The painting depicts Hernando De Soto (1500–42) arriving at the shore of the Mississippi near Natchez, 8 May 1541.

First page of the serialization of Elizabeth Oakes Smith, *The Western Captive; or, The Times of Tecumseh*, 1842. Smith, a popular novelist and poet and an acquaintance of Jane Johnston Schoolcraft and Henry Rowe Schoolcraft, was influenced by the Schoolcrafts' work in her depictions of Indigenous lives and cultures. Her novel *The Western Captive* is unusual in its portrayal of Indigenous people not as inevitable casualties of history but as vital participants in an ongoing American struggle. She presents the Shawnee Chief Tecumseh as a "patriot," writing that

> slowly but surely is the race advancing to a goal where the chain shall of itself fall from the free limb; and the eye, wandering backward through the long vista of despotism and revolution, shall behold how strong men were stricken in the race, that they might become heralds and guide-marks for others. Such was the fate of Tecumseh[.]

While Oakes Smith's writings do not partake in the sort of hostile stereotyping of Indigenous peoples that permeates the writing of so many white writers of this period, they are sometimes informed by Rousseauian "noble savage" stereotypes, however; later in the same passage, for example, she comments that "the untutored savage being nearer the threshold of truth, may be better able to expound her doctrines."

Women's Rights and Women's Roles[1]

Insofar as gender is defined by the law, it is not unreasonable to suggest that women barely existed in early nineteenth-century America. For the first half of the century, marriage was in most of the country governed by the law of coverture, by which all of a woman's property was subsumed under that of her husband upon marriage. The injustice of this law was captured in the 1848 "Declaration of Sentiments," a pioneering women's-rights manifesto: "[man] has made [woman], if married, in the eye of the law, civilly dead." The practice of coverture, a hold-over from English common law, essentially rendered married women, with few exceptions, legally dependent upon their husbands, with no ability to own property in their own names. A married woman could, in a limited number of situations, sue for divorce, but if successful she could not claim custody of the couple's children, except under extreme circumstances.

Though there was little by way of an organized movement for women's rights before the 1840s, some legal changes began to take place in the 1830s; beginning in 1839, several states began passing laws marginally increasing married women's rights to own property under limited circumstances. A significant stride came in April 1848, when the state of New York enacted the Married Women's Property Act, enabling married women to own property and financial assets under their own names. This legislation (which was a direct result of the petitioning of activists such as Elizabeth Cady Stanton and Ernestine Rose) became a model for similar acts passed throughout the United States in subsequent months and years.[2]

By this time increasing numbers of women were beginning to call for far more wide-reaching change. In 1843, Margaret Fuller published her monumental essay "The Great Lawsuit," calling for acknowledgment of women's intellectual equality and challenging her era's conventional conceptions of gender. Most famously, a formalized women's rights movement began to take shape at the Seneca Falls Convention in July 1848. The document that resulted from the convention, the Declaration of Sentiments, took the Declaration of Independence as its model, claiming that "all men and women are created equal" and structuring itself as a demand for government with the consent of the governed. Its signatories included sixty-eight women, including such leading activists as Elizabeth Cady Stanton and Lucretia Mott, and thirty-two men, including Frederick Douglass.

Elizabeth Cady Stanton with her sons Daniel and Henry, 1848.

Even among the group of activists attending the convention, the question of women's *suffrage* remained at this time highly controversial. The Declaration of Sentiments included a demand for women's suffrage rights, but only after robust debate; Frederick Douglass was among the delegates of the Seneca Falls Convention who argued most vigorously and persuasively for the inclusion of this demand in the document.

The only African American at Seneca Falls was Douglass; not a single black woman was invited to attend the convention. Often excluded from activist

---

[1] Please note that "Contexts: Gender and Sexuality," included in the website component of this volume, addresses women's rights in further detail.

[2] Not all women saw such laws as a complete victory, however. New York poet Frances Sargent Locke Osgood lamented in 1848 that the bill offered only financial protection to women, and therefore only improved the lives of those who had access to wealth in the first place—doing little to protect women who were poor, or "whose all of wealth / Is in their souls and faces."

organizations on account of their race, gender, or both, black women nonetheless found means to make their voices heard in favor of progressive causes. The extent of the barriers they faced is suggested by the fact that the Colored National Convention did not allow the participation of women delegates until 1848—and that the woman allowed to speak at the convention that year to persuade them to do so, Rebecca Sanford, was white. Despite such barriers, one of the best-remembered women's rights campaigners of the era was Sojourner Truth, who addressed the question of universal suffrage again and again in the 1850s, 60s, and 70s: "There is a great stir about colored men getting their rights, but not a word about the colored women; and if colored men get their rights, and not colored women theirs, you see the colored men will be masters over the women, and it will be just as bad as it was before."

The struggle against the oppression of women and the struggle to end slavery were indeed closely linked during this period; as Fuller remarked in 1843, "the warmest appeal in behalf of women" came from abolitionists, "partly in consequence of a natural following out of principles, partly because many women have been prominent in that cause." Yet women were often excluded from participation in formal abolitionist meetings and conventions, most famously from the 1840 World Anti-Slavery Convention. This exclusion not only triggered a split in the abolitionist movement but also, in many ways, triggered the development of the formalized women's rights movement.

That said, much as there tended to be strong lines of connection between the various progressive causes—most notably, abolitionism and women's rights—we should not assume that there was any *necessary* connection. In fact, several of the most prominent white women's rights leaders were lukewarm in their support of rights for African Americans—or outright opposed the idea that black men might obtain the vote before white women. Elizabeth Cady Stanton, for example, lamented in 1868, "To what a depth of degradation must the women of this nation have fallen to be willing to stand aside, silent and indifferent spectators in the reconstruction of the nation, while all the lower stratas of manhood are to legislate in their interests." On the other hand, the popular poet Lydia Sigourney—who was strongly supportive of abolition, opposed the Mexican–American war, and spoke out against child labor—was reluctant to support the cause of women's rights; in "Women's patriotism," which appeared in the same year that the Seneca Falls convention took place, Sigourney wrote against the "loud clamor" for "women's rights" (a term she put in quotation marks), and recommended instead that the truly patriotic American woman stay "In her own place, the hearth beside."

There is a powerful irony in the path that the struggle for equitable gender roles took over the course of this period: progressive notions were given greater currency in public conversation at mid-century, but for the most part they were brought no closer to realization in society at large. Speakers and writers received considerable attention when they argued, for example, that women should be free to vote or should receive equal pay for equal work, or when they asserted (as Lucy Stone did) that women should not be required to give up their names upon marriage. But while such notions of equality were being circulated more widely, in its actual practices with regard to gender roles in the mid-to-late nineteenth century, mainstream American society was arguably becoming more restrictive rather than less so.

The middle decades of the nineteenth century saw the crystallization of the ideology of separate spheres: the concept that men and women could best contribute to their communities and attain self-fulfilment by committing themselves to the "spheres" on their respective sides of the gender binary—the public sphere for men, and the private or domestic sphere for women. While women's participation in the public sphere—including politics and the marketplace—had been frequently discouraged by the dominant social norms of much of western history, during the nineteenth century this ideology became increasingly mythologized. "The cult of true womanhood," as it was defined by historian Barbara Welter in the 1960s, was a set of cultural values that defined women as essentially domestic, family-oriented, emotional, physically weak, and selfless beings; women who did not conform to these ideals were often considered to be either morally deficient or simply unfortunate anomalies.

As Sarah Moore Grimké pointed out in the 1830s, marriage was "often held up to the view of girls as the *sine qua non* of human happiness and human existence." As early as 1819, Washington Irving's "The Wife" gave succinct expression to the nineteenth-century feminine ideal as it was beginning to take shape. The story, which tells of a newly married couple who unexpectedly fall into poverty, presents the view that "woman, who is the mere dependant and ornament of man in his happier hours, should be his stay and solace when smitten with sudden calamity ..., tenderly supporting the drooping head, and binding up the broken heart." Two decades later, the doctrine of separate spheres was summarized—and applauded—by French social theorist Alexis de Tocqueville, in his monumental *Democracy in America* (1835–40):

> In no country has such constant care been taken as in America to trace two clearly distinct lines of action for the two sexes, and to make them keep pace one with the other, but in two pathways which are always different. American women never manage the outward concerns of the family, or conduct a business, or take a part in political life; nor are they, on the other hand, ever compelled to perform the rough labor of the fields, or to make any of those laborious exertions which demand the exertion of physical strength. No families are so poor as to form an exception to this rule. If on

"Little Lessons for Little Ladies," *Harper's New Monthly Magazine*, August 1851. "Fan-ny Fal-lal, al-though she was not rich, nor a per-son of rank, was a ve-ry fine La-dy. She would pass all her time reading novels and work-ing cro-chet, but would neg-lect her house-hold du-ties; so her hus-band, who was a ve-ry nice man, and fond of a nice din-ner, be-came a mem-ber of a Club, and used to stop out ve-ry late at night, which led to ma-ny quar-rels. How fool-ish it was of Fan-ny to neg-lect her house-hold du-ties, and not to make her Al-bert hap-py at home."

the one hand an American woman cannot escape from the quiet circle of domestic employments, on the other hand she is never forced to go beyond it. Hence it is that the women of America, who often exhibit a masculine strength of understanding and a manly energy, generally preserve great delicacy of personal appearance and always retain the manners of women, although they sometimes show that they have the hearts and minds of men.

The shift toward hard-and-fast gender roles is closely connected to the shift toward a more urban society gathering steam during this period. Whereas between 1790 and 1820 the percentage of city-dwelling Americans increased only slightly (from 5.1% to 7.2%), by 1870 25.7% of Americans lived in cities. That is of course a long way from twenty-first-century America (in which roughly 80% are urban dwellers),

Albert Sands Southworth and/or Josiah Johnson Hawes, *Girl with Portrait of George Washington*, c. 1850. Women activists began in the 1840s and 1850s to rethink the ideas of the founders on the matter of gender equality; as Elizabeth Cady Stanton put it in her *Declaration of Sentiments*, "we hold these truths to be self-evident, that all men and women are created equal."

but it nonetheless represented a substantial movement away from American conventions of farm life circa 1800, which often involved husband and wife toiling together in the fields.

By the 1830s the ideology of separate spheres was strengthening even in rural areas. But for many families, the gendered ideal remained by necessity primarily aspirational in nature. In his assertion that no family was "so poor as to form an exception to this rule," de Toqueville was clearly mistaken. In the 1830s many women did indeed contribute to the "rough labor of the fields," and many were compelled to leave home to find paid employment. Moreover, since many employers were reluctant to hire women, paid work was often undertaken from the home. Sarah Moore Grimké described this difficult situation in one of her *Letters on the Equality of the Sexes*: "I have known a widow, left with four or five children to provide for, unable to leave home because her helpless babes demand her attention, compelled to earn a scanty subsistence, by making coarse shirts at 12 ½ cents a piece, or by taking in washing, for which she was paid by some wealthy persons 12 ½ cents per dozen."

The transition from rural to urban family life is often imagined to have resulted in the husband finding paid work and the wife taking care of the home and the children. Though such arrangements were not uncommon, it was common as well for the young women of the family to be the first to take up paid employment in the city. Indeed, one of the first templates for factory employment in the United States, the scheme developed by Francis Cabot Lowell, was intended specifically for young women. Lowell intended his scheme to be a more humane and forward-looking alternative to the English system, in which factory girls were often overworked, underpaid, and generally exploited. Factories that made use of this scheme—most famously the textile mills in Lowell, Massachusetts—initially promised their employees (relatively) good wages, clean and comfortable housing (the vast majority of female employees lived communally in on-site boarding houses), and a companionable environment in which the "mill girls" were given broader educational and cultural opportunities than would normally have been available to them. The scheme offered an allure of independence for young women that seemed almost

Winslow Homer, *New England Factory Life—"Bell Time,"* in *Harper's Weekly*, 25 July 1868.

revolutionary at the time. But by the mid-1830s, facing increased competition, many such mills began lowering the young women's wages, and conditions began deteriorating in other ways. In 1845 the mill employees formed the Female Labor Reform Organization, but to little avail. Factory work was not without stigma, either (as noted in the opening paragraphs of this introduction). By 1850, most of the factory owners, seeking ever-cheaper labor, had begun hiring immigrants instead of native-born women.

As the world of work became more and more organized into separate spheres, certain occupations became female-gendered to such an extent that men were regarded with amusement, suspicion, or distrust if they were so employed. Many retail sales jobs, for example, came to be considered the province of "shop girls"; though men often worked in such jobs, the pay was not enough to support a family, and the handling of fabric and other domestic items was a far cry from the rough physical labor that was considered the province of working-class men. The 1860 poem "Opening Day" makes the stereotype clear in its lament for the

dry goods salesmen said to grow "thinner, weaker, feebler" through their employment:

> Ah, would they try
> To live—or die—
> By manly toil, despairing never!
> But no, each soul
> Plays woman's role,
> And tape and yardstick rule forever![1]

In many areas of nineteenth century America, women were more likely to work in domestic service than any other occupation. A life "in service" in the nineteenth century is stereotypically associated with Victorian Britain, but statistics suggest that the percentage of the population employed as domestic servants in the U.S. in 1870—7.7%—may well have been as high as in Britain at the time. Employment as a governess, however (a situation common throughout

---

[1] For more on dry-goods salesmen and on ideas of masculinity during this period, see "Contexts: Gender and Sexuality" in this volume's website component.

Britain during this period), was far less common in the United States.

The ideology of separate spheres, and related ideas of women's physical capabilities, did not apply to enslaved women, who often performed excruciatingly hard work. Many activists picked up on this double standard—particularly activists who had experience of slavery, such as Sojourner Truth. In her famous 1851 speech, Truth pointed out, "I have as much muscle as any man, and can do as much work as any man. I have plowed and reaped and husked and chopped and mowed, and can any man do more than that?" Yet, while enslaved women's gender was not considered when they were exploited in the fields, their gender *was* considered when their enslavers exploited them for their sexual and reproductive abilities. Formerly enslaved abolitionist Harriet Jacobs wrote that "Slavery is terrible for men; but it is far more terrible for women. Superadded to the burden common to all, they have wrongs, and sufferings, and mortifications peculiarly their own."

In the other direction, white attitudes toward slavery were gendered to a significant degree. Indeed, if Harriet Martineau is to be believed, it is entirely possible that a majority of the overall population of the South was in fact opposed to slavery. On the basis of her extensive travels in the United States in 1834, the famed British writer reported that she had "never met a lady of Southern origin who did not speak of slavery as a sin and a curse—the burden which oppressed their lives." If it were indeed the case that a majority of white Southern women were in fact quietly opposed to slavery, they, together with the roughly one-third of the population who were black,[1] would have constituted well over fifty per cent of the population of the South.

What Martineau does not make clear is that many of the white Southern women who detested slavery did so not because of fellow-feeling with enslaved African Americans, but in disgust at the damage to their own families caused by slaveholding men who routinely raped the women and girls they had enslaved. "God forgive us, but ours is a monstrous system," Mary Chesnut lamented: "our men live all in one house with their wives and their concubines, and the mulattoes one sees in every family exactly resemble the white children—and every lady tells you who is the father of all mulatto children in everybody's household, but those in her own she seems to think drop from the clouds, or pretends so to think."

Another subject of debate commonly linked to nineteenth-century women activists is the temperance movement, which played a vitally important role in the shaping of American social and political life from the 1820s onwards. In the twenty-first century, the puritanical temperance crusader demanding that people abstain from alcohol has become a quaint stereotype—but such a position seems far from absurd when one looks at the numbers. In 1790 the average American adult consumed 2.5 gallons of ethanol annually—very close to today's level of 2.4 gallons. But by 1810 Americans' per capita consumption had risen to 4.5 gallons, and by 1830 to a level far higher than that of any nation in the twenty-first century—7.1 gallons; those Americans who drank alcohol were on average consuming the equivalent of almost two bottles of whisky every week. The toll on family life was unprecedented.

It should not surprise us, then, that the fight for women's rights and the belief that women should work as society's moral leaders were tied closely to the movement for temperance. Among the most prominent temperance activists were Elizabeth Cady Stanton, Susan B. Anthony, and the poet Frances Harper. Harper, known today largely for her abolitionist and anti-racist writings, also wrote myriad poems on the subject of temperance (among them "The Drunkard's Child" and "The Revel") and spoke on the subject extensively in the years following the Civil War.

At the beginning of the 1820–Reconstruction period, Washington Irving was proving that it was possible for a man to earn a living by his pen in America. By the end of it, a very considerable number of women had proven that the same was possible for them. In the middle decades of the century, indeed, the leading women writers were at least as successful as the men. Though works such as Hawthorne's

---

[1]   The ratio of black people to white people in the South remained quite consistent throughout the period, even as the overall population increased. In 1820 enslaved African Americans constituted thirty-three per cent of the total population (4,507,845) of the Southern states, with free people of color comprising an additional three per cent; in 1860 enslaved African Americans constituted thirty-two per cent of the overall population of 12,240,293, with free people of color comprising an additional two per cent.

Scarlet Letter, Melville's *Moby-Dick*, and Whitman's *Leaves of Grass* have become central to the canon of American literature, they did not sell overly well at the time. Far more successful were Harriet Beecher Stowe's *Uncle Tom's Cabin* (1851–52) and Susan Warner's *The Wide, Wide World* (1850), a novel of a young woman who struggles to find her way after the death of her mother; the book was issued in fourteen editions in its first two years. Fiction writers Susanna Cummins, E.D.E.N. Southworth, Elizabeth Oakes Smith, and Ann Sophia Stephens were hugely successful as well, as was the poet Lydia Sigourney; by the 1850s there could be no question that women were just as capable as men of earning a living out of literature. Yet women who wrote for publication were still frowned upon by some more conservative members of society (leading many women, especially at the beginnings of their careers, to publish anonymously or pseudonymously). And—as Louisa May Alcott makes clear in *Little Women*—there were still significant barriers for women to overcome if they wished to make writing their career. Writers such as Sigourney—who wrote both on conventional poetic themes and on issues such as slavery and the oppression of Indigenous peoples, and whose writing often provided the main source of income in a household in which the husband suffered various financial reverses—had to work hard to maintain a veneer of middle-class feminine respectability. When Sigourney published a volume of verse without her husband's knowledge, his response told much of the era's conception of women: "Who wants, or would value, a wife who is to be the public property of the whole community?"

Nathaniel Currier, *The Drunkard's Progress. From the First Glass to the Grave*, 1846. "Step 1. A glass with a Friend." "Step 2. A glass to keep the cold out." "Step 3. A glass too much." "Step 4. Drunk and riotous." "Step 5. The summit attained. Jolly companions. A confirmed drunkard." "Step 6. Poverty and Disease." "Step 7. Forsaken by Friends." "Step 8. Desperation and crime." "Step 9. Death by suicide."

Much is often made in discussions of gender in mid-nineteenth-century America of women's clothing of the era and of dress reform movements such as the development of bloomers in the 1850s. Named after their first prominent proponent, Amelia Bloomer, bloomers (loose-fitting trousers inspired by Turkish fashions, designed to be worn under knee-length skirts) did represent—for the middle and upper classes, at least—a strikingly different new option. But the backlash against women who challenged conventional gender norms through their dress was so extreme that the vast majority of bloomer-wearers abandoned the garment after a few years; as with votes for women and other matters of women's rights, it would not be until well into the twentieth century that more practical clothing for women in certain social or occupational classes became socially acceptable.

Bloomers represented one approach to the matter of how to design practical clothing for women. Others tried to adopt a more straightforward approach—wearing clothing designed for men. Yet in many jurisdictions, and increasingly as the century progressed, wearing garments conventionally associated with the opposite sex was punishable by law. The famous journalist Fanny Fern spoke out against such absurd laws, and herself experimented with wearing her husband's clothing for rainy walks. Fern's is far from the only case of a woman dressing in men's clothing during this period. But for the most part these were driven by concerns very far from a wish to enjoy greater comfort in everyday life; the largest number of women dressing as men during the period was probably during the Civil War, when numerous cases were reported of women assuming men's garb in order to enlist.[1] The majority of women, to be sure, dressed in ways that adhered strictly to the period's norms. But as these examples suggest, various women in this period cross-dressed in a number of different ways and for a variety of different reasons: some passed as men in daily life, some wore men's clothes without attempting to pass as men; some were women in romantic or sexual relationships with other women; some who consistently passed as men did so to travel more safely or to pursue careers

Nathaniel Currier, *The Bloomer Costume*, 1851.

not open to women, while others did so because they considered themselves men.[2]

MARRIAGE AND SEXUALITY[3]

At the beginning of the nineteenth century the idea that most people have an innate, fixed sexual orientation had not yet surfaced in public discourse. By the end of the century, that idea was taking root strongly in America (as in Britain and elsewhere)—but there is disagreement both as to when exactly it began to do so, and about how quickly the change occurred. Undoubtedly, a key point in the development of the idea of discrete homosexual and heterosexual identities is the coining of the words "homosexual" and "heterosexual" themselves; they are first recorded as having been used by the Austrian writer Karl-Maria Kertbeny

---

[1]   Similar behavior was at least as common during the Revolutionary War in the late eighteenth century, but it seems to have entirely died out by the time of the First and Second World Wars in the twentieth.

[2]   Because the word "transgender" was coined in the twentieth century, it can be difficult to determine what language should apply to people of earlier centuries whose experience of gender does not appear to have matched the gender they were assigned at birth. For real and fictional examples of such lives, see "Contexts: Gender and Sexuality" in the website component of this volume.

[3]   Please note that a "Contexts" section on the topic of "Gender and Sexuality" appears in the website component of this volume.

in the late 1860s, but they took decades to become established in the English language. (The first modern usage of "bisexual" followed in the 1880s.) Before this, other terms existed to describe people who engaged in same-sex sexual activity; terms such as "lesbian" and "sapphic" are recorded as early as the mid-eighteenth century, and for men "sodomite" was long the term most commonly used. "Sodomite" and "homosexual" are, however, far from precise equivalents. Whereas the term "homosexual" references an inherent desire for sexual activity with members of one's own sex, the term "sodomy" references a particular act—an act that, as an early nineteenth-century Maryland law put it, "involved the penetration of a penis inside the rectum of an animal, woman or girl, or another man or a boy." To be sure, "sodomy" and "sodomite" seem often to have been used with particular reference to acts involving two men, but it was often assumed that those who engaged in such acts would have preferred an encounter with a woman—or alternatively, as in the arguments put forward in one newspaper in 1859 concerning the alleged proclivity of Chinese immigrants in San Francisco for sodomy, that it was a vice which one could be induced to abandon, so long as one had the good example of others to follow.

One result of these views is that same-sex sexuality was in many respects heavily regulated—both socially and, for men, legally, in that sodomy was a crime carrying long prison sentences and, under some circumstances, the threat of execution. Some environments (such as the navy) were more permissive than others, but there was always a threat of both legal and extra-legal punishment; in 1854, for example, a Presbyterian minister convicted of sodomy in Mobile, Alabama, was forced to "flee from the city or risk the chances of life in the hands of an infuriated mob." Yet despite such repressive norms, the absence of clearly defined sexual orientations also meant that individuals' experiences and expressions of desire were in some respects more fluid than they would be in the following century. Individuals might engage in same-sex intimacy—forbidden or otherwise—in ways that do not quite map on to later models of homo-, bi-, or heterosexuality. And not all forms of same-sex passion were forbidden: especially for young women, passionate connections of great intensity were permitted and even welcome.

Women in such friendships might openly kiss, cuddle, and share a bed, though it was expected that their physical intimacy would stop there—and in individual cases it is often difficult to determine whether it did or not.

The eroticism of passionate friendship—and its limits—are articulated by the writer Margaret Sweat in

Frances Shimer and Cindarella Gregory, 1869. Shimer and Gregory co-founded Mount Carroll Seminary—a pioneering higher-education institution in northwestern Illinois—in 1853 and ran it together until 1870; they had an extremely close relationship that one modern scholar has characterized as a "passionate friendship." Shimer married in 1857; she and her husband lived in separate quarters throughout their marriage.

her only novel, *Ethel's Love Life* (1859), whose description of a woman's connections with other women extends further into erotic territory than is typical of discussions of romantic friendship. When in that novel Ethel writes to her fiancé Ernest that "women often love each other with as much fervor and excitement as they do men," she also specifies that such love is "[f]reed from all the grosser elements of passion, as it exists between the sexes," while "it retains its energy, its abandonment, its flush, its eagerness, its palpitation, and its rapture." While a twenty-first-century reader might be tempted to speculate as to where Sweat would draw the line between "the grosser elements of passion" and the "rapture" that remained, it would be difficult to argue that there is nothing sexual in the novel's vision of same-sex love:

I have had my passionate attachments among women, which swept like whirlwinds over me, sometimes scorching me with a furnace blast[.] … I have loved so intensely that the daily and nightly communion I have held with my beloved ones has not sufficed to slake my thirst for them, nor the lavishness of their love for me been able to satisfy the demands of my exacting nature.

A high percentage of the most canonical of mid- and late nineteenth-century American authors—including Dickinson, Emerson, and Melville as well as Whitman and James—have been thought by many of their biographers to have felt or, in some cases, acted on same-sex desires. Of these, it was Whitman who became most famous for foregrounding what he referred to in 1856 in a letter to Emerson as "manly friendship." At

Daguerreotype of two women, c. 1859. The woman on the right has been identified as Catherine Mary ("Kate") Scott Turner, an old friend of Sue Gilbert Dickinson, who (along with Austin Dickinson, her husband and Emily's brother) lived next door to Emily Dickinson. Some have argued that the figure on the left is Emily Dickinson. Kate Scott Turner and Emily Dickinson developed a warm friendship beginning in January 1859, but had a falling out in 1860. Turner's husband had died in 1857; in 1866 she married John Hone Anthon (and is thus also often referred to as Kate Anthon).

that time, he complained, there was little or nothing to be heard on the subject: "As to manly friendship, everywhere observed in the States, there is not the first breath of it to be observed in print." That would change in subsequent decades, as same-sex romantic friendship would become a commonplace element in literary fiction by the end of the century. Whitman's own view of such friendships was perhaps more sexual and certainly more ideological than that of most of his contemporaries. In *Democratic Vistas* (1871) he praised the "fervid comradeship" of same-sex love, and described it as a "counterbalance and offset of our materialistic and vulgar American democracy, and for the spiritualization thereof."

Whitman's poetry aroused substantial controversy among Americans in the nineteenth century—but not for the reasons we might assume today. Indeed, Whitman's most controversial poems appear not to have been those we are likely to interpret as homoerotic but rather those that celebrated too openly things such as heterosexual intercourse and prostitution, such as the

Portrait of Bayard Taylor by Thomas Hicks, 1855. A well-known author and lecturer in the mid-nineteenth century, Taylor gained fame as a poet and travel writer; his accounts of his journeys to the Middle East and to other locations prompted Hicks to paint him in Arab attire in this portrait. While traveling in Egypt, Taylor lived on a boat on the Nile with a middle-aged German business-man, later describing their time together as "happy and care-free as two Adams in a Paradise without Eves." Taylor is perhaps best-known today for his 1870 novel *Joseph and His Friend*, which has been described as "America's first gay novel"; Taylor addressed it to those "who believe in the truth and tenderness of man's love for man."

Herman Melville, c. 1860; Elizabeth Shaw Melville, c. 1860. He was an occasionally disloyal and some-times abusive husband; she copied and edited his manuscripts and is said to have remained devoted to him.

The Longfellows with friends, Newport, Rhode Island, 1852. Henry Wadsworth Longfellow is to the right, Frances ("Fanny") Longfellow in the center. The photo is a reminder of how tightly knit much of nineteenth-century literary society was; the Longfellows and the Melvilles were well acquainted with each other; Frances Appleton (as she had been before she married Longfellow) and Elizabeth Shaw had grown up in the same neighborhood of Boston. Another friend was poet Julia Ward Howe, the woman in the photograph with her hand on Fanny Longfellow's shoulder.

sexually explicit "A Woman Waits for Me." That said, Whitman has long been celebrated by many as a gay poet, especially since the late twentieth century, with his "Calamus" series in particular now well-known for its lyrical depiction of same-sex love.

When it came to sexuality between men and women, social norms largely restricted its expression to the confines of marriage. Women risked much more than men by contravening these norms—not only the possibility of pregnancy but also, especially for middle- and upper-class women, social ostracism. This is not to say, however, that sexual purity mores were not applied to men at all. Social reformer Sylvester Graham was among those who zealously advocated that men refrain from indulging their sexual impulses outside marriage, and his *Lecture to Young Men, on Chastity* (1837) also vigorously condemns what he calls "the worst form of venereal indulgence," masturbation. The disgust with which masturbation was considered by those who were willing to publicly mention it speaks to the profound suspicion with which all sexual activity outside the bounds of what was considered "natural"—i.e., inter-course between a married man and woman, engaged in primarily to produce children—was widely viewed at the time.

As to marriage, a wide variety of conduct books offered advice. Matthew Hale Smith's *Counsels Addressed to Young Ladies and Young Men* (1846), for example, advised those contemplating marriage not to "expect, nor insist upon, perfection," and not to be "misled by beauty, rank, or wealth; they are not to be despised, but they cannot alone make you happy." A young person was advised not to marry unless there is ... a sincere attachment. Sordid, conventional marriages, or marriages for convenience, are frightful things. ... [But] if your hearts are bound together by love; if both are yielding and true; if both cultivate the spirit of meekness, forbearance, and kindness, you will be blessed in your home and in the journey of life.

10   DIRECTORY.

Mrs. Stewart,

Now residing in Orange street, near Chatham, but formerly of 37 Reade street. Keeps a very respectable house, with but few girls.

Lucretia Perry,

Lives at Mrs. Stewart's above named house, and is about 18 years of age, rather tall, but not handsome. She has been kept for the last few months, and is now, by a fellow of a dubious kind of occupation.

Mother Gallagher,

122 West Broadway, next door to Riley's Hotel. A house of the highest order. Generally 8 or 9 girls of uncommon beauty.

Mrs. Williams,

Keeps at 21 Sullivan-street, a very pretty Magdalen, with but 3 or 4 of the sisterhood under her charge; very quiet and a genteel resort.

Mrs. Ellis,

Keeps an excellent house No. 102 Church-st. She was despoiled at 23 Crosby-st.

Maria Wood,

Lives at 102 Church-st. and is sister-in-law to an ex-alderman—rather ordinary—on the town 6 years, and consequently well worn. Seduced by Capt. B. late of the Custom house.

DEDICATION.

TO THE

"LADIES' REFORM ASSOCIATION,"

FOR THE SUPPRESSION OF ONANISM,

This little Volume is respectfully Dedicated, with the thanks of the author, that their praiseworthy endeavors have contributed so largely to suppress the evil.

Gift of Leo Hershkowitz
14 February 2003

Pages from *Prostitution Exposed* (1839), the earliest known American brothel guide. These publications, marketed to middle- or upper-class men, provided directories of houses of prostitution in major cities (in the case of *Prostitution Exposed*, New York City), together with brief descriptions of the establishments. The dedication page of *Prostitution Exposed* parodies the rhetoric of contemporary moral reformers—specifically, those who sought to prevent the practice of masturbation—by dedicating the book "to the 'Ladies' Reform Association,' for the suppression of onanism," i.e., masturbation; the implication is that the "ladies" in question are sex workers, who prevent "onanism" by offering sexual services to men.

Daguerreotype of Edgar Allan Poe, 1848; daguerreotype of Sara Helen Whitman, c. 1856. The two were engaged to be married in 1848, but broke off the engagement. Whitman, a widow, was herself an accomplished poet; after Poe's death she became active in the struggle for women's rights, and did not again marry.

Such was the ideal—and yet both the conduct books and the marriage vows also made clear to young women that, in Hale Smith's words, that they must "be obedient. So God expressly commands. ... The head of the woman is the man; he must control and direct." In most American jurisdictions the law permitted corporal punishment by the husband of the wife, and it also accepted the view of the famous seventeenth-century British jurist Matthew Hale, who had ruled during the colonial period that a "husband cannot be guilty of rape committed by himself upon his lawful property throughout the marriage."

Among the most interesting opponents of such views was Lucy Stone; when she married abolitionist Henry Blackwell in 1855 the couple refused to make any reference to obedience in their marriage vows, and they prepared a special statement to be read at the ceremony. (Thomas Wentworth Higginson, who read the statement and performed the marriage, later encouraged others to follow the same principles.) Stone and Blackwell also negotiated a private agreement regarding

sexual and reproductive rights; following principles that had been set out in Henry C. Wright's highly unconventional manual *Marriage and Parentage; or The Reproductive Element in Man, as a Means to His Elevation and Happiness* (1854), the two agreed that the woman should be in control of "the reproductive element."

Divorce also became more common during the nineteenth century, as the power to grant divorce shifted from the legislature to the judiciary and the conditions for being granted a divorce expanded in most states. At mid-century, the United States had the highest divorce rate in the western world.[1] In this regard as well, men and women were held to different standards, especially when it came to adultery and the custody of children, and laws varied widely across the

---

1   The rate was 0.3 divorces per 1,000 Americans in the 1860s; by the end of the century it had climbed to 0.7 per 1,000. (The rate peaked in the late 1970s at 5.1 per 1,000; by 2017 it had fallen to just under 3.0 per 1,000.)

country. States in New England and especially in the West had, on the whole, the most liberal divorce laws.

Black Americans, especially those who were enslaved, had far less choice when it came to marriage. Under both federal and state law, indeed, there could be no such thing as a marriage between two enslaved people; their status as property precluded any acknowledgment under law of familial ties. There was thus no legal obstacle to the breaking up of families. It has been estimated that at least one third of enslaved children in the Upper South experienced the breakup of family life through their own sale or the sale of one or more parents or siblings, and the figure may well have been higher in the Deep South, where conditions for enslaved people were, in many ways, even worse. When we read a poem such as Frances Harper's "The Fugitive's Wife," we are movingly reminded of the reality of life for those who could never be legally married, and whose children could never legally belong to them.

Daguerreotype, Unidentified couple, c. 1864. Even after emancipation (as historian Tera Hunter has detailed), numerous barriers to marriage for black people continued to be erected in many states.

Alfred R. Waud, *Marriage of a Colored Soldier at Vicksburg by Chaplain Warren of the Freedmen's Bureau*, 1866.

Herbert Gleason, *Walden Pond in Winter*. Gleason spent many years following Thoreau's footsteps and photographing scenes described in *Walden* and other writings; over 100 of his photographs were included in the 1906 edition of *The Writings of Henry David Thoreau*. The above image shows Walden Pond in winter; in the background is a passing train—or, as Thoreau described it, an "iron horse" that can "make the hills echo with his snort like thunder, shaking the earth with his feet, and breathing fire and smoke from his nostrils." (Additional Gleason images are included as "In Context" material in the Thoreau author section.)

NATURE AND THE ENVIRONMENT[1]

To think of nature and the environment in the context of mid-nineteenth-century America is to think first and foremost of Emerson and Thoreau—and, in the visual arts, of Thomas Cole, Frederick Church, and Albert Bierstadt—figures who invested an idealized Nature with near-spiritual qualities, who saw Nature as standing apart from humanity, but also as possessing restorative powers for the human soul. "In the woods," as Emerson famously put it, "we return to reason and faith. There I feel that nothing can befall me ... which nature cannot repair."

Emerson and Thoreau were far from alone; nature writing became during this period a mainstay of American literature. The prose (as well as the art) of John James Audubon broke new ground scientifically as well as aesthetically. And—very much in the same spirit as Emerson and Thoreau—increasing numbers of poets sang nature's praises in much of their work. William Cullen Bryant wrote of the prairies that "man hath no part in all this glorious work" and called forest groves "God's first temples"; in similar fashion later in the century, Longfellow (in "My Cathedral") likened the "stately pines" to "cathedral towers," and John Greenleaf Whittier regarded "the wood giant" with a blending of "Pagan awe" and "Christian reverence."

But as Thoreau was retreating from the world to commune with nature at Walden Pond, General

---

[1]   Please note that a "Contexts" section on this topic appears in the website component of this volume.

Stephen Watts Kearny was leading the Army of the West into California, charged not only with defeating any Mexicans in his path but also with clearing a road through the mountains and forests across which settlers could travel. As put into words in a poem by Thomas D'Arcy McGee that celebrates the mission and extends it into a metaphor for western expansion in general, the goal of "the Army of the West"—both the literal army and its metaphorical counterpart in the "army" of westward-moving American settlers—was not only to "lay low the foes of liberty" (the Mexicans) and "annex their lands"; it was also to "pluck the primal forests up, and sow their sites with corn," to clear the way for "the plough that frees the soil." To McGee the forest was a "tangled waste"—and nowhere does he acknowledge it to be already inhabited by Indigenous peoples. It would be hard to imagine a literary work more antithetical to the sorts of values that we now call environmentalism.

The set of attitudes with which McGee approached the "tangled waste" of the California forest in verse—and with which Kearny approached California itself—is not often reflected in the literature that is most frequently taught today, but it was the dominant mode of thinking in America throughout this period. Trees were to be felled, and the earth was to be exploited without restriction for its mineral wealth. In 1840 the number of tons of coal mined in America exceeded 1 million for the first time; by 1860 the total had reached 20 million tons, and by 1880, 80 million tons. Non-human animals too were to be exploited for the benefit of humans; Bronson Alcott was almost alone in not only finding the consumption by humans of other animals morally repugnant but also environmentally unsound. ("It is calculated," he and his collaborator Charles Lane wrote in 1843, "that if no animal food were consumed, one-fourth of the land now used would suffice for human sustenance.") The building of mills and ironworks and factories was to be encouraged—as was the growth of cities—without regard to the effect they might have on the land, the air, and the water. Canals, steamships, and railways made the exploitation of the land and the waterways ever easier. In 1850 there were 9,000 miles of railway track in America; by 1880 that number had risen to 93,200.

Settler colonists steadily moved westward, and as they did so, imposed a new order on the land,

using the grid system that had been first proposed by Thomas Jefferson as a model. They expressed little concern as to the ways in which they might damage the environment, but many—following the naturalist and western explorer Josiah Gregg—expressed unbounded optimism as to the ways in which their activity would improve not only the land but also the climate. Gregg argued in his 1844 *Commerce of the Prairies, or, The Journal of a Santa Fe Trader* that "the extensive cultivation of the earth" on the high plains might "operate a change … upon the seasons" and "might contribute to the multiplication of showers." Later in the century some prominent agriculturalists lent spurious academic support to these ideas, hypothesizing that the soil would be better able to absorb the rain once it had been broken by the plough, that the absorbed moisture would then slowly evaporate, and that the result would be increased rainfall. The science turned out to be wrong, but generations of settlers bought the idea that "rain follows the plough."

A few commentators offered spirited resistance to the easy acceptance of environmental degradation in the face of "progress." Lydia Sigourney, for example, described in her 1854 poem "Fallen Forests" the terrible toll of "Man's warfare on the trees," and passionately lamented the loss of old-growth forests: "every echo of the axe doth hew / The iron heart of centuries away." The painter and poet Thomas Cole lamented such loss too—and was explicit in blaming human greed for the destruction: "each hill and dale," he wrote, had "become / An altar unto Mammon." But—particularly before 1850—the voices raised in support of conservation tended to be drowned out by those raised in support of the unbridled pursuit of material wealth.

Not everyone, of course, was allowed to share in that pursuit equally; the pursuit of wealth (and wealth itself—especially in the form of land) was in effect reserved for white men. The government soon reneged on the "40 acres and a mule" promise it made in 1865 to emancipated African Americans, and the Homestead Acts that resulted in the granting of almost 250 million acres of western land to homesteaders at virtually no cost effectively applied only to white people. Native Americans, for their part, were pushed by government fiat ever further westward into "Indian Country"—land supposedly reserved for them by the government,

Thomas Cole, *The Falls of the Kaaterskill*, 1826. On the rocky ledge beside the falls, Cole depicts an Indigenous man, face upraised, calling. By the time Cole painted the picture, the Indigenous peoples of the area had been almost entirely displaced; the painting dates from the same year in which James Fenimore Cooper's *The Last of the Mohicans* was published. Three years earlier, Cooper had included in *The Pioneers* a passage in which Natty Bumppo, a white scout who has lived among Native Americans, describes the view from the falls:

"There's a place in them hills that I used to climb to, when I wanted to see the carryings on of the world. ... The place I mean is next to the river, where one of the ridges juts out a little from the rest, and where the rocks fall for the best part of a thousand feet. ..."

"What see you when you get there?" asked Edwards.

"Creation!" said Natty, dropping the end of his rod into the water, and sweeping one hand around him in a circle—"all creation, lad. ..."

but under terms that kept shifting and that proved to be entirely unreliable. These "removals" were in many cases driven at least as much by issues of land use as they were by simple growth of the non-Indigenous population. In much of the South, for example, land was in capitalist terms undervalued; white plantation owners had invested little in the land they occupied, but often paid large amounts to create an enslaved labor force. When the cotton fields had exhausted the fertility of the soil (as cotton monocultures, with the limited fertilizers available at the time, tended to do fairly quickly), plantation owners looked to relocate to fresh land. What stood in their way initially were the agreements the government had made with peoples such as the Chickasaw, Choctaw, Muscogee (Creek), and Cherokee, giving them the right to occupy much of the land between the Appalachians and the Mississippi. The plantation owners lobbied the government to have Indigenous peoples forced west of the Mississippi—and successive American administrations (most notably that of Andrew Jackson) were happy to oblige.

The amount of land that constituted "Indian Country" was still fairly large at the beginning of this period; "Indian Country" in 1834 included most of the land between the Mississippi and the Rockies, and from the 49th parallel to the Mexican border. But by 1854 "Indian Country" constituted little more than the present state of Oklahoma. The remnants of more than a dozen peoples had been forced to relocate there—and the original Indigenous peoples of the region had been forced to share their space with the influx of newcomers. (In 1889, that territory too would be taken from Native Americans.) Indigenous peoples were prevented from controlling even the smaller and smaller parcels of land that they had been allotted. In a landmark 1823 decision, the Supreme Court ruled that Native Americans could deal only with the federal government regarding the purchase or sale of any land; no private transactions would be allowed.

Not all whites acquiesced in these moves. A significant minority of white Americans deplored the continuing annexation of Native American land—and many more acknowledged it to be a tragedy. But for most it was a tragedy with an air of inevitability to it; Indigenous people would simply have to make way for progress as settlers took over more and more of the land. Even early on in the century, displaced Indigenous people were often portrayed as adding color to the landscape, picturesque additions to grand images of the wilderness. So it is that a lone Native American stands by the waterfall in Thomas Cole's 1826 *Falls of the Kaaterskill*. William Cullen Bryant assumed a Native American voice as he imagined the end point of continuous westward pressure on the Indigenous population: "… they shall fill the land, and we /Are driven to the western sea." White Antelope is said to have provided a blunter summary just before his death at Wounded Knee: "Nothing lives long. Only the earth and the mountains."

A few voices during this period also began to insist that the wilderness itself must be preserved. Increasingly, "the wilderness" came to be associated with the West. Thoreau's 1862 maxim on "wildness" is often quoted; less often noted is the degree to which he associated that wildness with the American West: "The West of which I speak is but another name for the Wild; and what I have been preparing to say is, that in Wildness is the preservation of the world."

John Muir's 1869 visit to the Sierra Nevada mountains was in this connection a key moment in American environmental history. A direct line can be drawn between the feelings the wilderness engendered in the young Muir during that summer and the landmark conservation efforts of the late nineteenth and early twentieth centuries that involved Muir, Theodore Roosevelt, and many others.[1] More important during the 1820–Reconstruction period, however, were the calls to action of George Perkins Marsh. Marsh shared the sense of loss expressed by Cole, Sigourney, and others at the loss of the old growth forests, but, as a congressman (and former farmer, lawyer, and businessman) he brought to bear on the matter a

---

[1] In such contexts the word "wilderness" should arguably always appear in quotation marks, for in almost all cases it was used to denote land that was in fact inhabited to a greater extent than white explorers and adventurers were keen to acknowledge. John Muir, for example, described the flora of the Bloody Cañon of the Sierra Nevada as being "as yet untrodden" when he first beheld it in 1869—yet later in the same passage he describes an encounter with several local "Mono Indians," whom he describes as "mostly ugly, and some of them altogether hideous. … Somehow they seemed to have no right place in the landscape."

practical ecological perspective that has led some to call him America's first environmentalist. In an 1847 lecture Marsh offered practical reasons (including the value of trees to "succeeding generations") why "trees are no longer what they were in our fathers' time, an incumbrance." And in the same lecture he warned that "climate itself has in many instances" been "gradually changed and ameliorated or deteriorated by human action." Marsh's ideas—summed up in his influential 1864 book *Man and Nature: or, Physical Geography as Modified by Human Action*—had much to do with the marked increase in environmental awareness beginning around mid-century; it was not entirely by coincidence that in the same year *Man and Nature* was published, Abraham Lincoln set aside the Yosemite region for "public use, resort and recreation," or that, early in the following decade, Ulysses S. Grant made Yellowstone the first national park. There may have been more degradation than preservation of the American environment between the 1820s and the 1870s, but the hardy seeds of American environmentalism had also been sown.

They had been sown in the cities as well as in the wild. Here the key figure of the period is Frederick Law Olmstead, famous as one of the most important individuals shaping the American urban environment in the nineteenth century—the moving force behind the designs of Central Park in New York, Franklin Park in Boston, and Jackson Park in Chicago. Less well known is that Olmstead was also a leading voice for the preservation of non-human American environments. His 1865 report on Yosemite laid out the principle of setting aside scenery that "shall never be private property but that ... shall be held solely for public purposes." In the same document, Olmstead took issue with the destructive aspects of capitalism's driving force, recognizing that the duty of government was "to provide means of protection for all its citizens in the pursuit of happiness against the obstacles, otherwise insurmountable, which the selfishness of individuals or combinations of individuals is liable to interpose to that pursuit." Environmental issues, Olmstead realized, were inextricably intertwined with America's economic and political structures—and with its psyche.

TEXTS AND CONTEXTS:
A CHRONOLOGICAL CHART

In the chart below, dates generally refer to the year when a work was first made public, whether published in print or, in the case of speeches and plays, made public through the first performance. Where that date is known to differ substantially from the date of composition, the difference is generally noted; for manuscript works whose exact date of composition is unknown, we have provided an estimated date range.

⌘ ⌘ ⌘

TEXTS		CONTEXTS	
1820	Washington Irving, *The Sketch Book*	1820	Missouri Compromise admits Missouri to the union as a slave state, Maine as a free state, and prohibits slavery in all new states in the Louisiana Purchase lands north of latitude 36° 30′
1821	William Cullen Bryant, *Poems*	1821	Mexico becomes independent
			Sequoyah creates syllabary for the Cherokee language
		1823	President James Monroe proclaims that the United States will consider any attempt by European powers to expand the area under their control in the Western hemisphere as a threat to the "health and safety" of the United States
1824	Mary Jemison and James E. Seaver, *A Narrative of the Life of Mrs. Mary Jemison*		
	Lydia Maria Child, *Hobomok*		
1825	José María Heredia, "Niagara"	1825	Erie Canal opens

1826	Elias Boudinot, "An Address to the Whites"	1826	American Temperance Society founded
	James Fenimore Cooper, *The Last of the Mohicans*		Landscapes by Thomas Cole exhibited at the American Academy of the Fine Arts
	Jane Johnston Schoolcraft begins to publish poems in *The Literary Voyager*		
1827	James John Audubon begins to publish *The Birds of America*	1827	Last enslaved people in New York state freed
			Freedom's Journal founded
	David Cusick, *Sketches of Ancient History of the Six Nations*		
	Lydia Sigourney, *Poems*		
	Catharine Sedgwick, *Hope Leslie*		
		1827–28	The newspaper *The Cherokee Phoenix* founded (Elias Boudinot, editor)
		1828	First performances of "Jump Jim Crow" by Thomas Dartmouth Rice
1829	William Apess, *A Son of the Forest*	1829	First steam locomotive to operate on a U.S. railroad, "The Stourbridge Lion"
	David Walker, *An Appeal to the Coloured Citizens of the World*		Slavery abolished in Mexico
	Cherokee Council, "Memorial of the Cherokees"		
	George Moses Horton, *The Hope of Liberty*		
		1830	Indian Removal Act
			Opening of Baltimore and Ohio Railroad (first U.S. railway chartered for commercial transportation)
			Louis A. Godey begins publishing *The Lady's Book* (subsequently known as *Godey's Lady's Book* and as *Godey's Magazine and Lady's Book*)
1831	Edgar Allan Poe, *Poems*	1831	William Lloyd Garrison begins publishing *The Liberator*
			Nat Turner leads a slave rebellion in Virginia; 55 white people are killed, and roughly 200 black people are either executed or killed by white mobs in retaliation
			Tim Rice escapes from slavery in Kentucky into Ohio. Over the next 34 years many thousands of enslaved people are aided in their escape north, often to Canada

		1832	New York and Harlem Railroad begins service (a harbinger of rapid mass transit)
			Samuel Morse applies for a patent for an electric telegraph
1833	Black Hawk, *Life of Ma-Ka-Tai-Me-She-Kia-Kiak, or Black Hawk*	1833	American Anti-Slavery Society founded
	Lydia Maria Child, *An Appeal in Favor of That Class of Americans Called Africans*		Britain: Slavery Abolition Act passed (begins to take effect in 1834)
			Benjamin Day founds the *New York Sun*, ushering in the era of the penny press
1835	First volume of *Democracy in America*, by Alexis de Tocqueville	1835	Texas Revolution begins
	First *Davy Crockett Almanac* published		Second Seminole War begins
	William Gilmore Simms, *The Yemassee: A Romance of Carolina*		
1836	Angelina Grimké, *Appeal to the Christian Women of the South*	1836	Samuel Colt obtains a patent for a revolver
	Ralph Waldo Emerson, *Nature*		Migrant wagon train organized in Missouri; travel begins on what becomes known as the Oregon Trail
			Republic of Texas established, formally requests annexation by the United States
1837	Nathaniel Hawthorne, *Twice-Told Tales*	1837	Panic of 1837 initiates an economic depression that lasts until the mid-1840s
	Victor Séjour, "Le Mulatre" ("The Mulatto")	1838–39	Trail of Tears: Approximately 60,000 Cherokee, Muscogee, Seminole, Chickasaw, Choctaw, and other Indigenous people are forcibly removed by federal troops and relocated to Indian Territory in modern-day Oklahoma
		1839	*Amistad* Rebellion
1840	Richard Henry Dana Jr., *Two Years before the Mast*		
1841	Ralph Waldo Emerson, "Self Reliance"	1841	Experiment in communal living at Brook Farm begins
		1842	Term "underground railroad" appears in *The Liberator*
			Harriet Jacobs escapes to the Northern States

1851	Herman Melville, *Moby-Dick, or The Whale*	1851	Indian Appropriations Act creates the Indian reservation system; Native Americans require permission to leave their reservations
	Sojourner Truth delivers speech later titled "Ain't I a Woman?" (pub. 1851, 1863)		Isaac Merritt Singer patents his sewing machine
1852	Harriet Beecher Stowe, *Uncle Tom's Cabin*	1852	Wells Fargo founded
	Frederick Douglass, "What to the Slave Is the Fourth of July?"		
	Mary Ann Shadd, *A Plea for Emigration*		
1853	William Wells Brown, *Clotel*	1853	Otis Elevator Company founded
	Solomon Northup, *Twelve Years a Slave*		
1854	Henry David Thoreau, *Walden*	1854	Republican Party formed in opposition to slavery
	Frances Ellen Watkins Harper, *Poems on Miscellaneous Subjects*		Kansas-Nebraska Act repeals the Missouri Compromise, allowing new states to determine by popular vote whether or not to allow slavery
	John Rollin Ridge, *The Life and Adventures of Joaquín Murieta*		
	Fanny Fern, *Ruth Hall*		
1855	Herman Melville, *Benito Cereno*	1855–58	Third Seminole War
	Walt Whitman, *Leaves of Grass*		
	Henry Wadsworth Longfellow, *The Song of Hiawatha*		
1857	Frank J. Webb, *The Garies and Their Friends*	1857	*Dred Scott v. Sandford*: Supreme Court rules that black people "are not included, and were not intended to be included, under the word 'citizens' in the Constitution"
			Frederic Edwin Church's *Niagara* exhibited in New York to extraordinary acclaim
			The Atlantic Monthly founded
1858	Abraham Lincoln, "A House Divided"		
1859	E.D.E.N. Southworth, *The Hidden Hand*	1859	John Brown leads raid on Harpers Ferry
	Frances Ellen Watkins Harper, "The Two Offers"		Charles Darwin's *On the Origin of Species* is published in London
	Harriet Wilson, *Our Nig, or Sketches from the Life of a Free Black*		
	Dion Boucicault, *The Octoroon*		

1860	Ann S. Stephens, *Malaeska* (1839 serial) republished as the first dime novel
	Edward S. Ellis, *Seth Jones; Or, the Captives of the Frontier*
1861	Harriet Jacobs, *Incidents in the Life of a Slave Girl*
	Rebecca Harding Davis, *Life in the Iron-Mills*
	Frederick Law Olmstead, *The Cotton Kingdom*
	Elizabeth Stoddard, *The Morgesons*
	Emily Dickinson, "I taste a liquor never brewed –" published in the *Springfield Republican* under the title "The May-Wine." (Of the many hundreds of poems Dickinson wrote, only ten were published in her lifetime.)
1862	Louisa May Alcott, "The Brothers" (later republished as "My Contraband")
1865	Mark Twain, "The Celebrated Jumping Frog of Calaveras County"
	Henry James, "The Story of a Year"
1866	John Greenleaf Whittier, *Snow-Bound: A Winter Idyl*
1867	Horatio Alger, *Ragged Dick; or Street Life in New York with the Boot Blacks* serialized (book publication in 1868)
	Slave Songs of the United States (earliest published collection of African-American spirituals)

1860	South Carolina secedes from the Union
1861	Abraham Lincoln becomes 16th president
	Southern states variously secede from the Union and form the Confederate States of America; Civil War begins
1862	Land-Grant Colleges Act (leading ultimately to the establishment of 102 state colleges and universities)
1863	Emancipation Proclamation
	Battle of Gettysburg
1864	Yosemite Grant (first instance of land being set aside by the Federal government for preservation and public use)
	Sand Creek Massacre
1865	Lincoln is assassinated
	The Ku Klux Klan is formed
	Major General Gordon Granger advises the people of Texas that "all slaves are free"
	Thirteenth Amendment abolishes slavery
1866	Civil Rights Act (first federal law to define citizenship)

1868	Louisa May Alcott, *Little Women* (Volume 1)	1868	Fourteenth Amendment redefines citizenship to include those born with "slave" status
		1869	Completion of the Pacific Railroad (the first transcontinental railroad in the United States)
1870	Thomas Bailey Aldrich, *The Story of a Bad Boy*	1870	Fifteenth Amendment grants black men the right to vote
	Bayard Taylor, *Joseph and His Friend*		John D. Rockefeller incorporates Standard Oil
		1871	Great Chicago Fire
		1872	Yellowstone becomes first national park
1873	William Dean Howells, *A Chance Acquaintance*	1874	Gold discovered in South Dakota; U.S. troops invade the Black Hills territory despite treaty
1876	Mark Twain, *The Adventures of Tom Sawyer*	1876	Battle of the Little Bighorn (Greasy Grass)
			Alexander Graham Bell patents his telephone
1877	Henry James, *The American*	1877	Thomas Edison patents his phonograph
			Anna Sewell's *Black Beauty* is published in London; by 1880 more than one million copies are circulating in the U.S.
			Great Sioux War ends; Sitting Bull escapes to Canada; Crazy Horse killed
			Compromise of 1877 leads to the end of Reconstruction

WILLIAM APESS
1798 – 1839

Near the end of his renowned 1836 speech on King Philip's War, Pequot writer and activist William Apess declared:

> We want trumpets that sound like thunder, and men to act as though they were going at war with those corrupt and degrading principles that rob one of all rights, merely because he is ignorant and of a little different color. Let us have principles that will give everyone his due; and then shall wars cease, and the weary find rest.

In that speech, the apex of a remarkable career, he laid claim to Indigenous history, finding in King Philip (also known by his Massachusett name of Metacom) an exemplary forefather—and a focus for his ongoing critique of the injustice and brutality of colonization. As a preacher, Apess harnessed Christian principles to call for racial equality and to condemn colonial hypocrisy. As a historian, memoirist, and political activist, he was among the early nineteenth century's most eloquent defenders of the principle of Indigenous self-determination, powerfully challenging the white settler myth that the Euro-American colonial project was the destined will of God.

Almost all that we know of Apess's early life comes from his own account in his first published work, the autobiographical *A Son of the Forest* (1829). He was born in Colrain, Massachusetts, in 1798, and was of mixed white, Pequot, and possibly African American ancestry. Following his parents' early separation, he was sent to live with his maternal grandparents in Colchester, Connecticut, where he and his siblings endured dire poverty and frequent abuse until Apess was removed from the home by neighbors. He lived for a time as a "ward" of the town in the care of the white Furman family, and after a year was sold to them as an indentured servant—an extremely common circumstance for Indigenous children in the region.

Apess's account of his time with the Furmans (whom he describes as "poor" but who were also sufficiently financially comfortable to have several servants, and possibly enslaved people, in their household) is deeply ambivalent. Mr. and Mrs. Furman are described at different points as akin both to surrogate parents and to masters, and Mr. Furman clearly subjected Apess to regular (and often racially motivated) abuse, including teaching Apess to fear Indigenous people, thereby inflicting profound psychological trauma. Under their care, Apess received "six successive winters" of formal education, roughly the minimum that the Furmans would have been legally required to provide. Mrs. Furman also introduced him to the principles of Christianity, which soon took an intense hold on him, especially after he began attending Methodist camp meetings—a habit to which the Baptist Mr. Furman eventually put an end. When Apess was eleven years old, the Furmans sold his indenture to a new master, who promptly ended his formal schooling. After a few years, Apess ran away to New York, where he was conscripted into the army by a press gang (who gave his age as seventeen rather than fifteen). The War of 1812 was already well underway when he was enlisted, and he served until its conclusion in 1815.

Apess returned to Colrain in 1818 and was officially baptized into the Methodist Church, embarking then on an informal career as a preacher and missionary. In 1829 he released his autobiography, *A Son of the Forest*, a work heavily influenced by the popular genre of the conversion narrative as well as by the slave narrative. It also represented Apess's first published foray into historical writing; the appendix, which constitutes half the book, is an exploration of the history of Indigenous peoples and of European colonization. While Apess may also have included Indigenous oral history in his research, this appendix largely repurposes the scholarship of white colonists such as Elias Boudinot, whose 1816 book *A Star in the West* argues that North American Indigenous peoples are the descendants of the biblical lost tribes of Israel. Despite making use of such narratives, Apess is painfully aware of their inadequacy:

> The Indian character, I have observed before, has been greatly misrepresented. Justice has not and, I may add, justice cannot be fully done to them by the historian. My people have had no press to record their sufferings or to make known their grievances; on this account many a tale of blood and woe has never been known to the public.

Apess was ordained as a minister in 1831; he spent the following years traveling around the northeastern states, where he frequently spoke in Indigenous and mixed-race communities, forming connections with intellectuals in Indigenous and antislavery resistance movements and developing his ideas regarding religion, justice, and racial equality. For Apess, these issues were connected; as he had written in his autobiography, he was "convinced that Christ died for all mankind—that age, sect, colour, country, or situation, made no difference." Apess also collaborated with four other Pequot Christians in 1833 to produce a collection of short conversion narratives entitled *The Experiences of Five Christian Indians of the Pequod Tribe*. The text concludes with "An Indian's Looking-Glass for the White Man," a damning essay criticizing white Christians for their hypocritical treatment of Native Americans. In its arguments and rhetorical strategies, this essay displays the influence of abolitionist writers and speakers such as David Walker, as well as of Indigenous figures such as Cherokee editor and anti-Removal activist Elias Boudinot/Gallegina (named for the white politician mentioned above).

Later that year, Apess arrived in Mashpee, Massachusetts, where he became involved in agitating for the rights of the Mashpee tribe. Apess acquired regional notoriety for his role in helping draft what is sometimes known as the Mashpee Indian Declaration of Independence—a document that called for Mashpee self-government and jurisdiction over resources. He was briefly imprisoned and given a hefty fine of $100 following a non-violent confrontation over logging rights, but the Mashpee struggle was ultimately successful, and the tribe obtained some degree of self-government and resource control. Apess, who was adopted as a member of the tribe, described the Mashpee's accomplishments in *The Indian Nullification of the Unconstitutional Laws of Massachusetts, Relative to the Marshpee Tribe; or, the Pretended Riot Explained* (1835), where he recounts the tribe's resolution: "That we, as a tribe, will rule ourselves, and have the right to do so; for all men are born free and equal, says the Constitution of the country."

In 1836, Apess delivered a lecture at the Odeon in Boston on King Philip's War (1675–78), the conflict that had broken out between the Wampanoag and English Puritans after a longstanding peace treaty was repeatedly violated by the English settlers. Notorious for its high death toll, the war's violence disproportionately affected the Indigenous population, nearly eliminating the Wampanoag and their allies. King Philip's War already loomed large in American historical narratives—narratives in which the Wampanoag leader Metacom, or "King Philip," seemed to have only two possible roles. To some he personified the villainous "savage," described by Puritan historian Thomas Church as a "great, naked, dirty beast" in *The Entertaining History of King Philip's War* (1716); to others he was the embodiment of the "vanishing Indian," tragically representing a noble but inevitably declining race. (The latter approach is exemplified in John Augustus Stone's play *Metamora: or, The Last of the Wampanoags* [1829], whose title character is based on Metacom.) Apess's lecture powerfully re-envisioned this history, representing Metacom as a military hero. The speech's condemnation of the unchristian conduct of the Puritan settlers—and its linking of the same conduct to the ongoing oppression of people of color in America—made such an impression that Apess was asked to speak again two weeks later. The speech was published as *Eulogy on King Philip* (1836) and released in a second edition the following year; Apess also took the *Eulogy* on tour to several other cities.

Apess spent most of the last years of his life in New York City, during which time he made public appearances there and in Washington to speak about politics, religion, and Indigenous history. Upon his death in 1839, Apess was mentioned in a small handful of obituaries, which acknowledged him as a preacher and the author of a work on Metacom, but which did not mention his political activism in New England, or give any sense of the range and importance of his intellectual output. For many decades Apess's work was largely left out of the narrative of American history and literature. Since the 1990s, he has been increasingly acknowledged as a leading figure in the nineteenth century's culture of reform and activism and celebrated for his penetrating exposition of American racism and hypocrisy. Today he is widely seen as a visionary thinker, writer, and speaker, who broke new ground with his autobiographical self-fashioning and his radical reworking of the narratives of Indigenous history.

NOTE ON THE TEXT: The text included below is based upon the first Boston printing of *The Experiences of Five Christian Indians of the Pequod Tribe* (1833). Spelling and punctuation have been modernized in accordance with the practices of this anthology.

⌘ ⌘ ⌘

An Indian's Looking-Glass for the White Man[1]

Having a desire to place a few things before my fellow creatures who are traveling with me to the grave, and to that God who is the maker and preserver both of the white man and the Indian, whose abilities are the same, and who are to be judged by one God, who will show no favor to outward appearances, but will judge righteousness. Now I ask if degradation has not been heaped long enough upon the Indians? And if so, can there not be a compromise; is it right to hold and promote prejudices? If not, why not put them all away? I mean here amongst those who are civilized. It may well be that many are ignorant of the situation of many of my brethren within the limits of New England. Let me for a few moments turn your attention to the reservations in the different states of New England, and, with but few exceptions, we shall find them as follows: The most mean, abject,

miserable race of beings in the world—a complete place of prodigality[2] and prostitution.

Let a gentleman and lady of integrity and respectability visit these places, and they would be surprised; as they wandered from one hut to the other they would view with the females who are left alone, children half starved, and some almost as naked as they came into the world. And it is a fact that I have seen them as much so—while the females are left without protection, and are seduced by white men, and are finally left to be common prostitutes for them, and to be destroyed by that burning, fiery curse, that has swept millions, both of red and white men, into the grave with sorrow and disgrace—Rum. One reason why they are left so is, because their most sensible and active men are absent at sea.[3] Another reason is, because they are made to believe they are minors[4] and have not the abilities given them from God, to take care of themselves, without it is to see to a few little articles, such

---

2   *prodigality* Wastefulness.

3   *most sensible ... absent at sea* Whaling was at the time a lucrative, though highly dangerous, industry that attracted many highly skilled Indigenous men. Few of these men, however, were ever granted positions of significant authority, and few were as well-remunerated as white whalers, especially since they were often obligated to give a percentage of their earnings to white overseers.

4   *minors* American law designated Indigenous people as legal minors.

---

1   This text is Apess's epilogue to a longer collaborative work, *The Experiences of Five Christian Indians of the Pequod Tribe* (1833), which contains brief conversion narratives from Apess and his wife Mary, as well as three others.

as baskets and brooms. Their land is in common stock, and they have nothing to make them enterprising.

Another reason is because those men who are Agents,[1] many of them are unfaithful, and care not whether the Indians live or die; they are much imposed upon by their neighbors who have no principle. They would think it no crime to go upon Indian lands and cut and carry off their most valuable timber, or anything else they chose; and I doubt not but they think it clear gain.[2] Another reason is because they have no education to take care of themselves; if they had, I would risk them[3] to take care of their own property.

Now I will ask, if the Indians are not called the most ingenious people amongst us? And are they not said to be men of talents? And I would ask, could there be a more efficient way to distress and murder them by inches than the way they have taken? And there is no people in the world but who may be destroyed in the same way. Now if these people are what they are held up in our view to be, I would take the liberty to ask why they are not brought forward and pains taken to educate them? to give them all a common education, and those of the brightest and first-rate talents put forward and held up to office? Perhaps some unholy, unprincipled men would cry out, the skin was not good enough; but stop friends—I am not talking about the skin, but about principles. I would ask if there cannot be as good feelings and principles under a red skin as there can be under a white? And let me ask, is it not on the account of a bad principle, that we who are red children have had to suffer so much as we have? And let me ask, did not this bad principle proceed from the whites or their forefathers? And I would ask, is it worth while to nourish it any longer? If not, then let us have a change; although some men no doubt will spout their corrupt principles against it, that are in the halls of legislation and elsewhere. But I presume this kind of talk will seem surprising and horrible. I do not see why it

should so long as they (the whites) say that they think as much of us as they do of themselves.

This I have heard repeatedly, from the most respectable gentlemen and ladies—and having heard so much precept, I should now wish to see the example. And I would ask who has a better right to look for these things than the naturalist[4] himself—the candid man would say none.

I know that many say that they are willing, perhaps the majority of the people, that we should enjoy our rights and privileges as they do. If so, I would ask why are not we protected in our persons and property throughout the Union? Is it not because there reigns in the breast of many who are leaders, a most unrighteous, unbecoming and impure black principle, and as corrupt and unholy as it can be—while these very same unfeeling, self-esteemed characters pretend to take the skin as a pretext to keep us from our unalienable and lawful rights? I would ask you if you would like to be disfranchised from all your rights, merely because your skin is white, and for no other crime? I'll venture to say, these very characters who hold the skin to be such a barrier in the way, would be the first to cry out, injustice! awful injustice!

But, reader, I acknowledge that this is a confused world, and I am not seeking for office; but merely placing before you the black inconsistency that you place before me—which is ten times blacker than any skin that you will find in the Universe. And now let me exhort you to do away that principle, as it appears ten times worse in the sight of God and candid men, than skins of color—more disgraceful than all the skins that Jehovah ever made. If black or red skins, or any other skin of color is disgraceful to God, it appears that he has disgraced himself a great deal—for he has made fifteen colored people to one white, and placed them here upon this earth.

Now let me ask you, white man, if it is a disgrace for to eat, drink and sleep with the image of God,[5] or sit, or walk and talk with them? Or have you the folly to think that the white man, being one in fifteen or sixteen, are the only beloved images of God? Assemble all nations together in your imagination, and then let

---

1   *Agents*   White overseers appointed by the federal government to enforce federal policy in Indigenous communities and to represent Indigenous individuals in legal matters. Agents were ostensibly supposed to care for Indigenous people, whom white authorities deemed incapable of self-government, but many agents exploited their extreme power for personal gain.

2   *clear gain*   I.e., gain without accompanying debt, loss, or legal burden.

3   *risk them*   I.e., trust them.

4   *naturalist*   I.e., Indigenous person.

5   *image of God*   See Genesis 1.26: "And God said, Let us make man in our image, after our likeness."

the whites be seated amongst them, and then let us look for the whites, and I doubt not it would be hard finding them; for to the rest of the nations, they are still but a handful. Now suppose these skins were put together, and each skin had its national crimes written upon it—which skin do you think would have the greatest? I will ask one question more. Can you charge the Indians with robbing a nation almost of their whole Continent, and murdering their women and children, and then depriving the remainder of their lawful rights, that nature and God require them to have? And to cap the climax, rob another nation[1] to till their grounds, and welter out their days under the lash with hunger and fatigue under the scorching rays of a burning sun? I should look at all the skins, and I know that when I cast my eye upon that white skin, and if I saw those crimes written upon it, I should enter my protest against it immediately, and cleave to that which is more honorable. And I can tell you that I am satisfied with the manner of my creation, fully—whether others are or not.

But we will strive to penetrate more fully into the conduct of those who profess to have pure principles, and who tell us to follow Jesus Christ and imitate him and have his Spirit. Let us see if they come anywhere near him and his ancient disciples. The first thing we are to look at, are his precepts, of which we will mention a few. "Thou shalt love the Lord thy God with all thy heart, with all thy soul, with all thy mind, and with all thy strength. The second is like unto it. Thou shalt love thy neighbor as thyself. On these two precepts hang all the law and the prophets."—Matt. xxii. 37, 38, 39, 40. "By this shall all men know that they are my disciples, if ye have love one to another."—John xiii. 35. Our Lord left this special command with his followers, that they should love one another.

Again, John in his Epistles says, "He who loveth God, loveth his brother also."—iv. 21. "Let us not love in word but in deed."—iii. 18. "Let your love be without dissimulation. See that ye love one another with a pure heart fervently."—1. Peter viii. 22. "If any man say, I love God, and hateth his brother, he is a liar."—John iv. 20. "Whosoever hateth his brother is a murderer, and no murderer hath eternal life abiding in him." The first thing that takes our attention, is the saying of

Jesus, "Thou shalt love," &c. The first question I would ask my brethren in the ministry, as well as that of the membership, What is love, or its effects? Now if they who teach are not essentially affected with pure love, the love of God, how can they teach as they ought? Again, the holy teachers of old said, "Now if any man have not the spirit of Christ, he is none of his."—Rom. viii. 9. Now my brethren in the ministry, let me ask you a few sincere questions. Did you ever hear or read of Christ teaching his disciples that they ought to despise one because his skin was different from theirs? Jesus Christ being a Jew, and those of his Apostles certainly were not whites—and did not he who completed the plan of salvation complete it for the whites as well as for the Jews, and others? And were not the whites the most degraded people on the earth at that time, and none were more so; for they sacrificed their children to dumb idols! And did not St. Paul labor more abundantly for building up a Christian nation amongst you than any of the Apostles. And you know as well as I that you are not indebted to a principle beneath a white skin for your religious services, but to a colored one.

What then is the matter now; is not religion the same now under a colored skin as it ever was? If so I would ask why is not a man of color respected; you may say as many say, we have white men enough. But was this the spirit of Christ and his Apostles? If it had been, there would not have been one white preacher in the world—for Jesus Christ never would have imparted his grace or word to them, for he could forever have withheld it from them. But we find that Jesus Christ and his Apostles never looked at the outward appearances. Jesus in particular looked at the hearts, and his Apostles through him being discerners of the spirit, looked at their fruit without any regard to the skin, color or nation; as St. Paul himself speaks, "Where there is neither Greek nor Jew, circumcision nor uncircumcision, Barbarian nor Scythian, bond nor free—but Christ is all and in all."[2] If you can find a spirit like Jesus Christ and his Apostles prevailing now in any of the white congregations, I should like to know it. I ask, is it not the case that everybody that is not white

---

[1]   *another nation* I.e., the African continent.

[2]   *Where there is … in all* See Colossians 3.11; *Greek* Gentile; non-Jewish person; *Scythian* Eurasian nomadic ethnic group, often used in ancient rhetoric as an example of "barbaric" peoples.

is treated with contempt and counted as barbarians? And I ask if the word of God justifies the white man in so doing? When the prophets prophesied, of whom did they speak? When they spoke of heathens, was it not the whites and others who were counted Gentiles? And I ask if all nations with the exception of the Jews were not counted heathens? and according to the writings of some, it could not mean the Indians, for they are counted Jews.[1] And now I would ask, why is all this distinction made among these Christian societies? I would ask what is all this ado about Missionary Societies, if it be not to Christianize those who are not Christians? And what is it for? To degrade them worse, to bring them into society where they must welter out their days in disgrace, merely because their skin is of a different complexion. What folly it is to try to make the state of human society worse than it is. How astonished some may be at this—but let me ask, is it not so? Let me refer you to the churches only. And my brethren, is there any agreement? Do brethren and sisters love one another? Do they not rather hate one another? Outward forms and ceremonies, the lusts of the flesh, the lusts of the eye and pride of life is of more value to many professors,[2] than the love of God shed abroad in their hearts, or an attachment to his altar, to his ordinances or to his children. But you may ask who are the children of God? perhaps you may say none but white. If so, the word of the Lord is not true.

I will refer you to St. Peter's precepts—Acts 10. "God is no respecter of persons"—&c. Now if this is the case, my white brother, what better are you than God? And if no better, why do you who profess his gospel and to have his spirit, act so contrary to it? Let me ask why the men of a different skin are so despised, why are not they educated and placed in your pulpits? I ask if his services well performed are not as good as if a white man performed them? I ask if a marriage or a funeral ceremony, or the ordinance of the Lord's house would not be as acceptable in the sight of God as though he was white? And if so, why is it not to you? I ask again, why is it not acceptable to have men to exercise their office in one place as well as in another? Perhaps you will say that if we admit you to all of these privileges you will want more. I expect that I can guess what that is—Why, say you, there would be intermarriages. How that would be I am not able to say—and if it should be, it would be nothing strange or new to me; for I can assure you that I know a great many that have intermarried, both of the whites and the Indians—and many are their sons and daughters—and people too of the first respectability. And I could point to some in the famous city of Boston and elsewhere. You may now look at the disgraceful act in the statute law passed by the Legislature of Massachusetts,[3] and behold the fifty pound fine levied upon any Clergyman or Justice of the Peace that dare to encourage the laws of God and nature by a legitimate union in holy wedlock between the Indians and whites. I would ask how this looks to your law makers. I would ask if this corresponds with your sayings—that you think as much of the Indians as you do of the whites. I do not wonder that you blush many of you while you read; for many have broken the ill-fated laws made by man to hedge up the laws of God and nature. I would ask if they who have made the law have not broken it—but there is no other state in New England that has this law but Massachusetts; and I think as many of you do not, that you have done yourselves no credit.

But as I am not looking for a wife, having one of the finest cast,[4] as you no doubt would understand while you read her experience and travail of soul in the way to heaven, you will see that it is not my object. And if I had none, I should not want anyone to take my right from me and choose a wife for me; for I think that I or any of my brethren have a right to choose a wife for themselves as well as the whites—and as the whites have taken the liberty to choose my brethren, the Indians, hundreds and thousands of them as partners in life, I believe the Indians have as much right to choose their partners amongst the whites if they wish. I would ask you if you can see anything inconsistent in your conduct and talk about the Indians? And if

---

[1] *the Indians ... counted Jews* Some early racial theories posited that North American Indigenous peoples were descended from one of the Ten Lost Tribes of Israel.

[2] *professors* I.e., people who profess to follow Christianity.

[3] *disgraceful act ... Legislature of Massachusetts* Massachusetts had banned intermarriage between whites and those defined as "negro or mulatto" in 1705, and in 1786 it expanded this law to apply to Indigenous people as well. Interracial marriage was not legalized in Massachusetts until 1843.

[4] *cast* Character; also complexion or physical form.

you do, I hope you will try to become more consistent. Now if the Lord Jesus Christ, who is counted by all to be a Jew, and it is well known that the Jews are a colored people, especially those living in the East, where Christ was born—and if he should appear amongst us, would he not be shut out of doors by many, very quickly? and by those too, who profess religion?

By what you read, you may learn how deep your principles are. I should say they were skin deep. I should not wonder if some of the most selfish and ignorant would spout a charge of their principles now and then at me. But I would ask, how are you to love your neighbors as yourself? Is it to cheat them? Is it to wrong them in anything? Now to cheat them out of any of their rights is robbery. And I ask, can you deny that you are not robbing the Indians daily, and many others? But at last you may think I am what is called a hard and uncharitable man. But not so. I believe there are many who would not hesitate to advocate our cause; and those too who are men of fame and respectability—as well as ladies of honor and virtue. There is a Webster, an Everett, and a Wirt,[1] and many others who are distinguished characters—besides an host of my fellow citizens, who advocate our cause daily. And how I congratulate such noble spirits—how they are to be prized and valued; for they are well calculated to promote the happiness of mankind. They well know that man was made for society, and not for hissing stocks[2] and outcasts. And when such a principle as this lies within the hearts of men, how much it is like its God—and how it honors its Maker—and how it imitates the feelings of the good Samaritan, that had his wounds bound up, who had been among thieves and robbers.[3]

Do not get tired, ye noble-hearted—only think how many poor Indians want their wounds done up daily; the Lord will reward you, and pray you stop not till this tree of distinction shall be levelled to the earth, and the mantle of prejudice torn from every American heart—then shall peace pervade the Union.

WILLIAM APES.[4]

—1833

---

1   *Webster* Daniel Webster (1782–1852), orator, lawyer, and Massachusetts senator, who spoke for the defense of Muscogee lands against Georgia State's expansionist ambitions; *Everett* Edward Everett (1794–1865), Massachusetts governor and Harvard professor, who opposed the Indian Removal Act; *Wirt* William Wirt (1772–1834), the longest-serving Attorney General in United States history, who represented (unsuccessfully) the Cherokee nation in the case *Cherokee Nation v. Georgia* (1831).

2   *for hissing stocks* To be objects of scorn or mockery (i.e., "laughing stocks").

3   *the good Samaritan ... and robbers* See Luke 10.30–37.

4   *WILLIAM APES* Apess began adding the second "s" to his surname around the summer of 1836; this has since become the standard spelling.

James Fenimore Cooper
1789 – 1851

James Fenimore Cooper was one of the most popular U.S. novelists of the nineteenth century. The author of more than thirty novels, he was the first to adapt Walter Scott's genre of the historical novel to an American context, with *The Spy* (1821), and he founded the popular genre of the sea tale with *The Pilot* (1824). Cooper is most famous and celebrated for his Leatherstocking Tales (1823–41), a series of historical novels that depict the life and times of Natty Bumppo, a soldier and hunter who makes his way on the edge of Anglo-American settlements during the colonial era and early national period. As a simple-spoken, illiterate, brave, self-reliant, and sharp-shooting white adventurer who rejects civilization, Natty Bumppo became the prototype for the masculine heroes of the American Western. Cooper earned fame and fortune around the world for his celebration of U.S. national identity and his

representations of Native Americans, who appear in many of his novels. One of the first U.S. writers to succeed as a professional author, Cooper fashioned himself as an international man of letters, writing about politics, culture, history, and the law; he was in his day, as he is now, a polarizing figure in American culture.

Born in Burlington, New Jersey, Cooper spent his early life in Otsego, New York—later called "Cooperstown" in honor of his father, the village's first settler and founder. As a young man, Cooper studied briefly at Yale University and then spent time as a sailor on merchant ships and in the U.S. Navy. A sizable inheritance from his father, received in 1809, allowed him to retire from the Navy, and in 1811, he married Susan DeLancey, the daughter of a well-established New York family. Over the next eight years, Cooper experienced a series of family deaths and business failures; the ensuing financial troubles may have led him to seek his fortune with novel writing. In 1820, Cooper published his first novel, *Precaution*, an imitation of the English domestic novel. It was a moderate success, but nothing compared to his best-selling next novel, *The Spy*, a tale of a double agent operating between British and Continental armies during the American Revolution. Inspired by Scott—who fictionalized great historical events through the perspective of ordinary characters—Cooper turned to American history.

Cooper's third novel, *The Pioneers* (1823), inaugurated the Leatherstocking Tales and was the first to feature Natty Bumppo. Set in the 1790s in a New York village modeled loosely on Cooperstown, this novel reckoned with historical changes in the settlements from the perspective of Judge Temple, a figure for Cooper's father, and from the perspective of Bumppo and his Indigenous friend, Chingachgook, who resist the encroaching laws, culture, and institutions of the modern nation-state. Later Leatherstocking tales included *The Last of the Mohicans* (1826), *The Prairie* (1827), *The Pathfinder* (1840), and *The Deerslayer* (1841). These works were some of the first American novels to express concern about the destruction of the natural world at the hands of human beings.

For his depictions of Native Americans, Cooper drew on the writings of other Anglo-Americans, especially John Heckewelder, a Moravian missionary to the Lenape. At times Cooper's work communicates a sympathy for Indigenous peoples, but overall his novels reinforce damaging stereotypes and inaccurate myths, including the notion that Native Americans were incapable of integrating into or coexisting with white society. Such ideas were challenged by a few of Cooper's Anglo-American contemporaries, especially Lydia Maria Child and Catharine Maria Sedgwick, who offer alternative portraits of Indigenous peoples in their respective historical romances *Hobomok* (1824) and *Hope Leslie* (1827). On the whole, however, Cooper's work helped to popularize the belief that Native American cultures were inevitably in decline—a position that was used by nineteenth-century politicians to justify the forced migration and extermination of Indigenous populations.

Cooper's fourth novel, *The Pilot* (1824), is widely considered the first major work of nautical fiction. It has had many successors, including novels by Herman Melville and Joseph Conrad. Although Cooper was initially celebrated in the United States—New York chief justice James Kent called him "the genius which has rendered our native soil classic ground"—some American critics soon soured on his work. A staunch backer of Andrew Jackson and the Democratic party, Cooper was made the target of a smear campaign by reviewers affiliated with the anti-Jacksonian Whig party. To these reviewers, Cooper was motivated solely by greed; he was a class traitor for lending his support to Jackson's efforts to reign in the power of moneyed elites and increase popular sovereignty. "[A]ll that I see and hear gives me reason to believe that there is a great falling off in popular favor at home," Cooper wrote in an 1832 letter from Europe, where he and his family—his wife and their five children—had by that time been living for six years. "I rarely see my name mentioned even with respect in any American publication."

Cooper returned to America in 1833, and was soon living again at Cooperstown, but he had been sufficiently stung by the criticisms of his work that, in his 1834 *Letter to His Countrymen*, he declared his intention to renounce his career as a writer. The resolution proved hard to keep; he was soon publishing more works of non-fiction, including a history of the U.S. Navy, and by the end of the decade he had begun writing the last two of his Leatherstocking tales, *The Pathfinder* and *The Deerslayer*. In another series, the "Littlepage" novels—including *Satanstoe* (1845), *The Chainbearer* (1845), and *The Redskins* (1846)—Cooper defended landowners against tenants, now earning the ire of Democrats who accused him of the worst kind of aristocratic values. Despite such controversies, Cooper's novels continued to sell astonishingly well in the U.S., in Britain, and on the European Continent. After his death in 1851, he was lionized by fellow literary giants Washington Irving, Herman Melville, and Ralph Waldo Emerson. His major works were then republished in New York in a lavish edition illustrated by F.O.C. Darley in 1859–61, which solidified Cooper's stature in the canon of American literature.

Mark Twain famously ridiculed Cooper in his 1895 satire "Fenimore Cooper's Literary Offenses." But Twain, who also hated Walter Scott, in fact owed many debts to both novelists, and his opinion went against the grain of the common consensus. In the twentieth century, Marxist literary theorist Georg Lukács ranked Cooper along with historical novelists Balzac and Tolstoy, calling him the only "worthy successor" to Scott in the English language, while D.H. Lawrence, in *Studies in Classic American Literature* (1923), compared the Leatherstocking Tales to the *Odyssey* and praised Cooper's romantic depictions of nature: "No man could sufficiently praise the beauty and glamorous magnificence of Cooper's presentation of the aboriginal American landscape, the New World." Cooper's reputation declined significantly with the rise of Modernism. But it was his vision of the magnificence of nature, and his placement of the white settler and outcast seemingly alone at its center, that lasted far into the twentieth century and that marks Cooper's major contribution to the myth of American innocence.

NOTE ON THE TEXT: The text presented below is based on that of the first 1826 edition of *The Last of the Mohicans; a Narrative of 1757*. Spelling and punctuation have been modernized in accordance with the practices of this anthology.

⌘ ⌘ ⌘

from *The Last of the Mohicans;*
a Narrative of 1757

Set in the Province of New York during the 1754–63 conflict known by Anglo-Americans as the French and Indian War, *The Last of the Mohicans* (1826) was the second published installment of Cooper's Leatherstocking Tales (though chronologically its storyline precedes that of *The Pioneers* by several decades). Like the other Leatherstocking Tales, the novel is defined by the presence of character Nathaniel "Natty" Bumppo, who also bears the nicknames Hawk-eye, La Longue Carabine, and Leatherstocking. A white hunter and adventurer who was raised in a Lenape community, he now works as a British Army scout with his Mohican companions Chingachgook and his son Uncas. The novel takes place in the days leading up to and following the Siege of Fort William Henry (1757), part of the French and Indian War (1754–63), a territorial dispute in which French colonists and a diverse group of Indigenous allies fought British colonists and their Indigenous allies, including Mohican fighters.

The novel begins at Ford Edward, where half-sisters Alice and Cora Munro are preparing for a journey to meet their father, Colonel George Munro, at Fort William Henry. Along with their escort, Major Duncan Heyward, the party soon meet a Huron named Magua, who offers to guide them through the woods; they are also joined by an eccentric and out-of-place psalmodist named David Gamut. After they encounter Hawk-eye and his companions in the forest, it is revealed that Magua—who holds a personal grudge against Colonel Munro—has been intentionally leading the group astray. In the brawl that follows, Magua kidnaps the sisters, intending to force Cora to marry him. The rest of the novel follows the adventures of Hawk-eye, Uncas, and Heyward as they seek to rescue the captives from Magua and his fellow Huron, who are depicted as treacherous and villainous. Uncas, the eponymous "last of the Mohicans," emerges as a powerful leader of the favorably depicted Lenape, heroically motivated by his love for Cora. The portrayals of Uncas and Cora (who is eventually revealed to be of partially African ancestry) would become the prototypes for many depictions of Indigenous and mixed-race characters in later American literature.

Volume 2

from Chapter 12

[At this point in the narrative, Hawk-eye, Heyward, Alice, and Cora are in hiding from Magua and the Hurons at a Lenape camp; Magua arrives, and seeks to convince the Lenape to give up those he considers to be his lawful prisoners.]

"The Spirit that made men, colored them differently," commenced the subtle Huron.[1] "Some are blacker than the sluggish bear. These he said should be slaves; and he ordered them to work forever, like the beaver. You may hear them groan, when the south wind blows, louder than the lowing buffaloes, along the shores of the great salt water, where the big canoes come and go with them in droves. Some he made with faces paler than the ermine[2] of the forests, and these he ordered to be traders; dogs to their women, and wolves to their slaves. He gave this people the nature of the pigeon: wings that never tire; young, more plentiful than the leaves on the trees, and appetites to devour the earth. He gave them tongues like the false call of the wildcat; hearts like rabbits; the cunning of the hog (but none of the fox); and arms longer than the legs of the moose. With his tongue he stops the ears of the Indians; his heart teaches him to pay warriors to fight his battles; his cunning tells him how to get together the goods of the earth; and his arms enclose the land from the shores of the salt water, to the islands of the great lake. His gluttony makes him sick. God gave him enough, and yet he wants all. Such are the pale faces.

"Some the Great Spirit made with skins brighter and redder than yonder sun," continued Magua, pointing impressively upward to the lurid luminary, which was struggling through the misty atmosphere of the horizon; "and these did he fashion to his own mind. He gave them this island as he had made it, covered with trees, and filled with game. The wind made their clearings; the sun and rain ripened their fruits; and the snows came to tell them to be thankful. What need had they of roads to journey by! They saw through the

---

[1]   *subtle Huron*   Magua, who is also known by the French nickname "le Renard subtil," or "the cunning fox."

[2]   *ermine*   Species of weasel known for its white winter coat.

hills! When the beavers worked, they lay in the shade, and looked on. The winds cooled them in summer; in winter, skins kept them warm. If they fought among themselves, it was to prove that they were men. They were brave; they were just; they were happy."

Here the speaker paused, and again looked around him, to discover if his legend had touched the sympathies of his listeners. He met everywhere with eyes riveted on his own, heads erect, and nostrils expanded, as if each individual present felt himself able and willing, singly, to redress the wrongs of his race.

"If the Great Spirit gave different tongues to his red children," he continued, in a low, still, melancholy voice, "it was that all animals might understand them. Some he placed among the snows, with their cousin, the bear. Some he placed near the setting sun, on the road to the happy hunting grounds. Some on the lands around the great fresh waters; but to his greatest, and most beloved, he gave the sands of the salt lake. Do my brothers know the name of this favored people?"

"It was the Lenape!" exclaimed twenty eager voices in a breath.

"It was the Lenni Lenape," returned Magua, affecting to bend his head in reverence to their former greatness. "It was the tribes of the Lenape! The sun rose from the water that was salt, and set in water that was sweet, and never hid himself from their eyes. But why should I, a Huron of the woods, tell a wise people their own traditions? Why remind them of their injuries; their ancient greatness; their deeds; their glory; their happiness—their losses; their defeats; their misery? Is there not one among them who has seen it all, and who knows it to be true? I have done. My tongue is still, but my ears are open."

[Though the elderly Lenape sage Tamenund considers Magua's arguments, in Chapter 13 he declares Uncas to be a rightful leader of the Lenape. Uncas is free to take back Hawk-eye, Heyward, and Alice, but Cora—with whom Uncas has now fallen in love—remains in Magua's grasp.]

from CHAPTER 15

"'Tis the maiden!"[1] shouted the scout. "Courage, lady; we come—we come."

The chase was renewed with a diligence rendered tenfold encouraging, by this glimpse of the captive. But the way was now rugged, broken, and, in spots, nearly impassable. Uncas abandoned his rifle, and leaped forward with headlong precipitation. Heyward rashly imitated his example, though both were, a moment afterwards, admonished of its madness, by hearing the bellowing of a piece,[2] that the Hurons found time to discharge down the passage in the rocks, the bullet from which even gave the young Mohican a slight wound.

"We must close!" said the scout, passing his friends by a desperate leap; "the knaves will pick us all off at this distance; and see, they hold the maiden so as to shield themselves!"

Though his words were unheeded, or rather unheard, his example was followed by his companions, who, by incredible exertions, got near enough to the fugitives to perceive that Cora was borne along between the two warriors, while Magua prescribed the direction and manner of their flight. At this moment, the forms of all four were strongly drawn against an opening in the sky, and then they disappeared. Nearly frantic with disappointment, Uncas and Heyward increased efforts that already seemed superhuman, and they issued from the cavern on the side of the mountain, in time to note the route of the pursued. The course lay up the ascent, and still continued hazardous and laborious.

Encumbered by his rifle, and, perhaps, not sustained by so deep an interest in the captive as his companions, the scout suffered the latter to precede him a little, Uncas, in his turn, taking the lead of Heyward. In this manner, rocks, precipices, and difficulties, were surmounted, in an incredibly short space, that at another time, and under other circumstances, would have been deemed almost insuperable. But the impetuous young men were rewarded, by finding, that, encumbered with Cora, the Hurons were rapidly losing ground in the race.

---

1   *the maiden* Cora.

2   *a piece* I.e., a rifle.

"Stay, dog of the Wyandots!" exclaimed Uncas, shaking his bright tomahawk at Magua; "a Delaware girl calls stay!"

"I will go no farther," cried Cora, stopping unexpectedly on a ledge of rocks, that overhung a deep precipice, at no great distance from the summit of the mountain. "Kill me if thou wilt, detestable Huron, I will go no farther!"

The supporters of the maiden raised their ready tomahawks with the impious joy that fiends are thought to take in mischief, but Magua suddenly stayed their uplifted arms. The Huron chief, after casting the weapons he had wrested from his companions over the rock, drew his knife, and turned to his captive, with a look in which conflicting passions fiercely contended.

"Woman," he said, "choose; the wigwam or the knife of le Subtil!"

Cora regarded him not; but dropping on her knees, with a rich glow suffusing itself over her features, she raised her eyes and stretched her arms towards Heaven, saying, in a meek and yet confiding voice—

"I am thine! do with me as thou seest best!"

"Woman," repeated Magua, hoarsely, and endeavouring in vain to catch a glance from her serene and beaming eye, "choose."

But Cora neither heard nor heeded his demand. The form of the Huron trembled in every fibre, and he raised his arm on high, but dropped it again, with a wild and bewildered air, like one who doubted. Once more he struggled with himself, and lifted the keen weapon again—but just then a piercing cry was heard above them, and Uncas appeared, leaping frantically, from a fearful height, upon the ledge. Magua recoiled a step, and one of his assistants, profiting by the chance, sheathed his own knife in the bosom of the maiden.

The Huron sprang like a tiger on his offending and already retreating countryman, but the falling form of Uncas separated the unnatural combatants. Diverted from his object by this interruption, and maddened by the murder he had just witnessed, Magua buried his weapon in the back of the prostrate Delaware, uttering an unearthly shout, as he committed the dastardly deed. But Uncas arose from the blow, as the wounded panther turns upon his foe, and struck the murderer of Cora to his feet, by an effort, in which the last of his failing strength was expended. Then, with a stern and

steady look, he turned to le Subtil, and indicated, by the expression of his eye, all that he would do, had not the power deserted him. The latter seized the nerveless arm of the unresisting Delaware, and passed his knife into his bosom three several times, before his victim, still keeping his gaze riveted on his enemy with a look of inextinguishable scorn, fell dead at his feet.

"Mercy! mercy! Huron," cried Heyward, from above, in tones nearly choked by horror; "give mercy, and thou shalt receive it!"

Whirling the bloody knife up at the imploring youth, the victorious Magua uttered a cry, so fierce, so wild, and yet so joyous, that it conveyed the sounds of savage triumph to the ears of those who fought in the valley, a thousand feet below. He was answered by an appalling burst from the lips of the scout, whose tall person was just then seen moving swiftly towards him, along those dangerous crags, with steps as bold and reckless, as if he possessed the power to move in middle air. But when the hunter reached the scene of the ruthless massacre, the ledge was tenanted only by the dead.

His keen eye took a single look at the victims, and then shot its glances over the difficulties of the ascent in his front. A form stood at the brow of the mountain, on the very edge of the giddy height, with uplifted arms, in an awful attitude of menace. Without stopping to consider his person, the rifle of Hawk-eye was raised, but a rock, which fell on the head of one of the fugitives below, exposed the indignant and glowing countenance of the honest Gamut. Then Magua issued from a crevice, and, stepping with calm indifference over the body of the last of his associates, he leaped a wide fissure, and ascended the rocks at a point where the arm of David could not reach him. A single bound would carry him to the brow of the precipice, and assure his safety. Before taking the leap, however, the Huron paused, and shaking his hand at the scout, he shouted—

"The pale-faces are dogs! the Delawares women! Magua leaves them on the rocks, for the crows!"

Laughing hoarsely, he made a desperate leap, and fell short of his mark; though his hands grasped a shrub on the verge of the height. The form of Hawk-eye had crouched like a beast about to take its spring, and his frame trembled so violently with eagerness, that the muzzle of the half raised rifle played like a leaf fluttering in the wind. Without exhausting himself with fruitless efforts, the cunning Magua suffered[1] his body to drop to the length of his arms, and found a fragment for his feet to rest upon. Then, summoning all his powers, he renewed the attempt, and so far succeeded, as to draw his knees on the edge of the mountain. It was now, when the body of his enemy was most collected together, that the agitated weapon of the scout was drawn to his shoulder. The surrounding rocks, themselves, were not steadier than the piece became for the single instant that it poured out its contents.

The arms of the Huron relaxed, and his body fell back a little, while his knees still kept their position. Turning a relentless look on his enemy, he shook a hand in grim defiance. But his hold loosened, and his dark person was seen cutting the air with its head downward, for a fleeting instant, until it glided past the fringe of shrubbery which clung to the mountain, in its rapid flight to destruction.

—1826

[NOTE: Additional selections from *The Last of the Mohicans* are included in the online component of this anthology.]

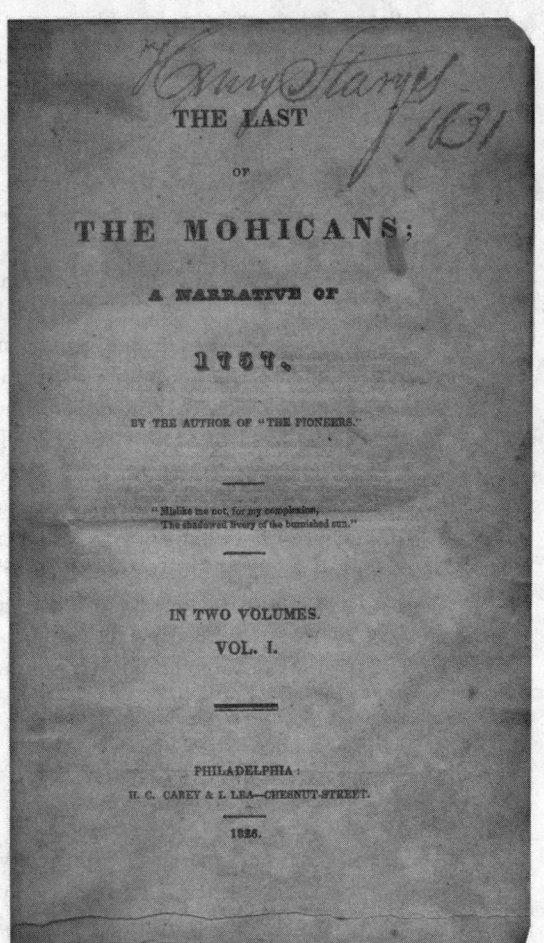

Title page of volume 1 of the 1826 first edition of *The Last of the Mohicans*. The quotation—"Mislike me not, for my complexion, / The shadowed livery of the burnished sun"—is from a speech in Shakespeare's *The Merchant of Venice* by the dark-skinned Prince of Morocco, who is attempting to woo the light-skinned Portia.

---

[1]   *suffered* Allowed.

LYDIA HUNTLEY SIGOURNEY

1791 – 1865

One of the first American literary superstars, Lydia Sigourney had a tremendous impact on nineteenth-century popular culture. An adept professional, she established herself as an icon of middle-class American womanhood and repurposed European Romantic forms for an American audience. Her prolific body of work includes fifteen volumes of poetry, as well as works of history, children's books, conduct manuals, a novel, and over two thousand articles in nearly three hundred different periodicals. Deftly exploiting the popular appeal of the sentimental mode, she wrote on a wide range of politically and socially important subjects, including the environment, the role of women, and government policies that she felt threatened the integrity of the union, such as slavery and the genocide of Indigenous peoples.

Sigourney was born in Norwich, Connecticut, the only child of Ezekiel and Zerviah Huntley. The Huntleys lived in the mansion of the wealthy Lathrop family, for whom Ezekiel Huntley was a gardener. Mrs. Lathrop took a keen interest in the development of Lydia's intelligence, and Lydia received one of the best educations available to girls at this time. She studied both at home and at various local schools, where she learned the usual domestic skills taught to girls, as well as mathematics, grammar, literature, and classical languages. At the age of twenty, she opened her own school.

Sigourney thrived as a teacher, and, in 1814 moved to Hartford, where she ran a school for the daughters of wealthy families. The following year, she published her first book: *Moral Pieces, in Prose and Verse,* a collection of poems, advice, and homilies addressed to young women. This volume's emphasis on nature, subjectivity, originality, and deep feeling reflects Sigourney's extensive reading in British sentimental and Romantic literature, particularly the works of evangelical poets such as Hannah More and William Cowper. In *Moral Pieces,* however, as in many of her later works, Sigourney adapts Romantic aesthetics and poetic forms to American cultural, political, and religious life, particularly the lives of American women and children, and to the American landscape.

In 1819 Sigourney accepted the proposal of Charles Sigourney, an upper-class businessperson. Social mores required her to abandon teaching for a married upper-class woman's domestic duties. Charles also disapproved of her literary ambitions and persuaded her to publish anonymously; this would remain a source of conflict for much of their marriage. In the first three years of their marriage, the couple conceived three children, all of whom died at birth or shortly afterwards. In 1824, she published—anonymously—the long poem *Traits of the Aborigines of America.* In this and her other poems about Indigenous peoples, Sigourney takes part in her culture's propensity to romanticize and elegize Indigenous people, thereby participating in their erasure, but she also turns a fierce critical eye on the cruelty and greed of white settlers, acting, as she did on many subjects, as a kind of national conscience for the American middle and upper classes.

In 1827, Sigourney published *Poems,* by "the Author of 'Moral Pieces in Prose and Verse,'" without informing her husband. His response was furious: "Who wants or would value, a wife who is to be the public property of the whole community?" Sigourney tried and failed to convince Charles to agree to a formal separation, and in the end she agreed to his demands that she slow down her literary activity and bear children; by 1830, she had borne a daughter and a son. In her writing during this period, she came increasingly to represent herself as an exemplar of feminine virtue, shifting her focus to women's domestic duties in works such as *Letters to Young Ladies* (1833). To build on the popular success of *Letters to Young Ladies,* she began to publish under her own name, achieving widespread international fame with *Poems* (1834).

Sigourney's philanthropic activity also gained momentum in these years. In 1828 she helped found the Hartford campaign to aid in the Greek War of Independence; in 1829 she formed the Hartford Female African Society and the Hartford County Temperance Society, as well as a protest movement, the "Ladies' Circular" to petition against the Indian Removal Act (which was passed in 1830). While Sigourney opposed slavery and viewed it as a stain on the republic, she argued that enslaved people should be freed and then helped to emigrate to Africa, rather than being accorded citizenship in America.

In 1836 her husband's business interests began to suffer, and Sigourney's income as a writer took on more importance to the family's finances. She produced a great deal of material, much of which appeared in magazines and was then repurposed for inclusion in books. She also continued to write for the lucrative "advice" or "conduct" book market, publishing volumes such as *Letters to Mothers* (1838), a discussion of women's place in the republic. In works such as these, Sigourney located women's influence in the home and in philanthropic endeavors; she did not advocate for suffrage or for other political power for women. Meanwhile, rumors circulated that Charles denied food and writing paper to Sigourney, that he had threatened her with a sword, and that his daughters (from his previous marriage) attempted to poison her and her baby. In 1840 Sigourney signed a note Charles had written stating that these rumors were untrue. She then departed to Europe for a long reading tour that expanded her transatlantic audience.

After returning home, Sigourney published a travel memoir, *Pleasant Memories of Pleasant Lands* (1842). She also began to write collections of verse that her readers could copy out in their own scrapbooks or letters: poems in *The Voice of Flowers* (1846), for example, could be inscribed in valentines, while *The Weeping Willow* (1847) contained elegies for use in funeral readings or sympathy cards. She also collected her poems on certain social topics; *Water-Drops* (1843) contains her verses on temperance, and *Poetry for Seamen* (1845) collects poems aimed at reforming the morality of sailors. Her middle- and upper-class readership thereby connected to her poems in an intimate way, sharing them among themselves on the defining occasions of their lives, and looking to Sigourney for moral leadership.

Sigourney's later publications include *The Faded Hope* (1850), a memoir of her son who had died of tuberculosis, as well as several collections of her writing for periodicals and an advice book about aging, *Past Meridian* (1854). She died in Hartford in 1865, and her autobiography *Letters of Life* (1866) was published posthumously. Her fame, while greatest in America, was transatlantic, and by the time she died, countless societies and organizations had been named after her, as had a town in Iowa.

During Sigourney's lifetime, most critics praised her for the devout morality underlying her poetry, and for her feminine, sentimental style: as one critic phrased it, "Her womanly delicacy gilds every page traced by her pen, and sheds a beautiful halo around her genius. … [H]er name has become a household word in all lands where Christian virtues are cherished." As tastes changed toward the end of the nineteenth century, however, her reputation declined rapidly. With the rise of literary modernism, the critical establishment largely dismissed Sigourney, viewing her achievement as saccharine, feminine, and didactic. It was not until the 1970s that interest in Sigourney's work was revived, as attention turned to the important role that nineteenth-century sentimentalism played in spurring social reform, and to the role that Sigourney in particular played in shaping American cultural identity. Interest in Sigourney's work has since flourished, uncovering her importance as a professional writer, political activist, and advocate for domestic and sentimental values.

NOTE ON THE TEXTS: The texts of all poems included here are based upon their earliest printings in book form. The texts of "Indian Names" and "Slavery" are based on those published in *Poems* (1834); the text of "To a Shred of Linen" is based on that published in *Select Poems* (1838). Spelling and punctuation have been modernized in accordance with the practices of this anthology.

⌘ ⌘ ⌘

Indian Names[1]

"How can the red men be forgotten, while so many of our
states and territories, bays, lakes and rivers, are indelibly
stamped by names of their giving?"

Ye say they all have passed away,
    That noble race and brave,
That their light canoes have vanished
    From off the crested wave;
5 That, 'mid the forests where they roamed,
    There rings no hunter shout,
But their name is on your waters,
    Ye may not wash it out.

'Tis where Ontario's billow°   *wave*
10   Like Ocean's surge is curled,
Where strong Niagara's thunders wake
    The echo of the world.
Where red Missouri bringeth
    Rich tribute from the west,
15 And Rappahannock[2] sweetly sleeps
    On green Virginia's[3] breast.

Ye say their cone-like cabins,[4]
    That clustered o'er the vale,
Have fled away like withered leaves
20   Before the autumn gale,
But their memory liveth on your hills,
    Their baptism on your shore,
Your everlasting rivers speak
    Their dialect of yore.

25 Old Massachusetts wears it,
    Within her lordly crown,
And broad Ohio bears it,
    Amid his young renown;
Connecticut hath wreathed it

30   Where her quiet foliage waves,
And bold Kentucky breathes it hoarse
    Through all her ancient caves.

Wachuset[5] hides its lingering voice
    Within his rocky heart,
35 And Alleghany[6] graves° its tone   *engraves*
    Throughout his lofty chart;[7]
Monadnock,[8] on his forehead hoar°   *gray*
    Doth seal the sacred trust,
Your mountains build their monument,
40   Though ye destroy their dust.

Ye call these red-brown brethren
    The insects of an hour,
Crushed like the noteless° worm amid   *unnoticed*
    The regions of their power;
45 Ye drive them from their father's lands,
    Ye break of faith the seal,
But can ye from the court of Heaven
    Exclude their last appeal?

Ye see their unresisting tribes
50   With toilsome step and slow,
On through the trackless desert pass,
    A caravan of woe;[9]
Think ye the Eternal's ear is deaf?
    His sleepless vision dim?
55 Think ye the *soul's blood* may not cry
    From that far land to him?
—1834

---

1 This poem was republished in *Selections from the American Poets* (1840), with the last two stanzas omitted.

2 *Rappahannock* River in eastern Virginia.

3 *Virginia* Unlike the other place names mentioned in this poem, Virginia does not derive from Indigenous languages, but is derived from the Latin "virgo," which means "virgin" or "maiden."

4 *cone-like cabins* I.e., tepees, traditional dwellings of many Indigenous tribes from the Great Plains.

5 *Wachuset* Mountain in Massachusetts.

6 *Alleghany* Mountain range in the eastern United States and Canada.

7 *chart* Outline, especially as recorded on a map.

8 *Monadnock* Mountain in New Hampshire.

9 *unresisting tribes … caravan of woe* The 1830 Indian Removal Act, signed into law by President Andrew Jackson, forced southeastern Indigenous tribes—the Chickasaw, Cherokee, Muscogee (Creek), Seminole, and Choctaw—to leave their ancestral lands and move west of the Mississippi river. This forced removal of 60,000 people, known as the Trail of Tears, has been described as cultural genocide, and thousands of people died of disease and starvation during the journey or shortly afterward. Sigourney's description of the removals as "unresisting," however, is not true; the Cherokee, in particular, put forward strong resistance, but were ultimately unsuccessful.

Slavery

"Slavery is a dark shade on the map of
the United States."
—La Fayette[1]

<small>Written for the Celebration of the
Fourth of July</small>

We have a goodly clime,
   Broad vales and streams we boast,
Our mountain frontiers frown sublime,
   Old Ocean guards our coast;
5 Suns bless our harvest fair,
   With fervid° smile serene,   *glowing*
But a dark shade is gathering there—
   What can its blackness mean?

We have a birthright proud,
10   For our young sons to claim,
An eagle soaring o'er the cloud,
   In freedom and in fame;
We have a scutcheon[2] bright,
   By our dead fathers bought,
15 A fearful blot distains° its white—   *stains*
   Who hath such evil wrought?

Our banner o'er the sea
   Looks forth with starry eye,
Emblazoned, glorious, bold and free,
20   A letter on the sky,
What hand with shameful stain
   Hath marred its heavenly blue?
The yoke, the fasces,[3] and the chain,
   Say, are these emblems true?

25 This day[4] doth music rare
   Swell through our nation's bound,
But Afric's wailing mingles there,
   And Heaven doth hear the sound:
O God of power! we turn
30   In penitence to thee,
Bid our loved land the lesson learn—
   To bid the slave *be free.*
—1834

To a Shred of Linen

Would they swept cleaner!
               Here's a littering shred
Of linen left behind—a vile reproach
To all good housewifery. Right glad am I,
That no neat lady, trained in ancient times
5 Of pudding-making, and of sampler-work,[5]
And speckless sanctity of household care,
Hath happened here, to spy thee. She, no doubt,
Keen looking through her spectacles, would say,
"*This comes of reading books*": or some spruce[6] beau
10 Essenced and lily-handed, had he chanced
To scan thy slight superfices,°   *outward appearance*
   'twould be
"*This comes of writing poetry.*" Well—well—
Come forth—offender!—hast thou aught to say?
Canst thou by merry thought, or quaint conceit,[7]
15 Repay this risk, that I have run for thee?
—Begin at alpha,[8] and resolve thyself
Into thine elements. I see the stalk
And bright, blue flower of flax,[9] which
   erst° o'erspread   *formerly*
That fertile land, where mighty Moses stretched

---

[1] *La Fayette* The Marquis de Lafayette (1757–1834) fought in the American Revolution commanding American troops; he also supported the French Revolution and was a prominent abolitionist throughout his life. The quoted statement was widely attributed to him.

[2] *scutcheon* Coat of arms represented on a shield.

[3] *fasces* Group of rods, often birch rods, with an axe in the middle. The symbol is prominent in American iconography, including, for example, the seal of the Senate and the frieze of the Supreme Court. It represents the power of unity and order of law, but has also long been associated with corporal punishment.

[4] *This day* I.e., the fourth of July.

[5] *sampler-work* Type of needlework done to display one's expertise in embroidery.

[6] *spruce* Tidy and good-looking.

[7] *quaint conceit* Ingenious metaphor.

[8] *alpha* The first letter of the Greek alphabet; i.e., the beginning.

[9] *flax* Linen is woven from flax fibers.

His rod miraculous.[1] I see thy bloom
Tinging, too scantly, these New England vales.
But, lo! the sturdy farmer lifts his flail,[2]
To crush thy bones unpitying, and his wife
With 'kerchiefed head, and eyes brimful of dust,
Thy fibrous nerves, with hatchel-tooth[3] divides.
—I hear a voice of music—and behold!
The ruddy damsel singeth at her wheel,[4]
While by her side the rustic lover sits.
Perchance, his shrewd eye secretly doth count
The mass of skeins, which, hanging on the wall,
Increaseth day by day. Perchance his thought
(*For men have deeper minds than women—sure!*)
Is calculating what a thrifty wife
The maid will make; and how his dairy shelves
Shall groan beneath the weight of golden cheese,
Made by her dexterous hand, while many a keg
And pot of butter, to the market borne,
May, transmigrated, on his back appear,
In new thanksgiving coats.
            Fain would I ask,
Mine own New England, for thy once loved wheel,

By sofa and piano quite displaced.
Why dost thou banish from thy parlor-hearth
That old Hygeian harp,[5] whose magic ruled
Dyspepsia,° as the minstrel-shepherd's skill   *indigestion*
Exorcised Saul's ennui?[6] There was no need,
In those good times, of trim callisthenics,

And there was less of gadding,° and far more   *gallivanting*
Of home-born, heart-felt comfort, rooted strong
In industry, and bearing such rare fruit,
As wealth might never purchase.
            But come back,
Thou shred of linen. I did let thee drop,
In my harangue, as wiser ones have lost
The thread of their discourse. What was thy lot
When the rough battery of the loom had stretched
And knit thy sinews, and the chemist sun
Thy brown complexion bleached?
            Methinks I scan
Some idiosyncrasy, that marks thee out
A defunct pillow-case. Did the trim guest,
To the best chamber ushered, e'er admire
The snowy whiteness of thy freshened youth
Feeding thy vanity? or some sweet babe
Pour its pure dream of innocence on thee?
Say, hast thou listened to the sick one's moan,
When there was none to comfort? or shrunk back
From the dire tossings of the proud man's brow?
Or gathered from young beauty's restless sigh
A tale of untold love?
            Still, close and mute!
Wilt tell no secrets, ha? Well then, go down,
With all thy churl-kept[7] hoard of curious lore,
In majesty and mystery, go down
Into the paper-mill,[8] and from its jaws,
Stainless and smooth, emerge. Happy shall be
The renovation, if on thy fair page
Wisdom and truth, their hallowed lineaments
Trace for posterity. So shall thine end
Be better than thy birth, and worthier bard
Thine apotheosis[9] immortalize.
—1838

---

[1] *fertile land ... rod miraculous* See Exodus 9.23: "And Moses stretched forth his rod toward heaven: and the Lord sent thunder and hail, and the fire ran along upon the ground, and the Lord rained hail upon the land of Egypt." Exodus 9.31 describes the hail damage: "And the flax and the barley was smitten: for the barley was in the ear, and the flax was bolled [ripe]."

[2] *flail* Instrument used for threshing.

[3] *hatchel-tooth* Instrument with sharp teeth used to comb out flax.

[4] *wheel* Spinning-wheel, used to create thread out of the combed flax.

[5] *Hygeian harp* I.e., spinning-wheel. In Greek mythology, Hygeia is a goddess of health and cleanliness; the implication is that the activity of spinning could prevent illnesses associated with luxury or idleness.

[6] *minstrel-shepherd's ... Saul's ennui* See 1 Samuel 16.23: "And it came to pass, when the evil spirit from God was upon Saul, that David took an harp, and played with his hand: so Saul was refreshed, and was well, and the evil spirit departed from him."

[7] *churl-kept* Stingily kept. "Churl" could also refer to a rural or unrefined person.

[8] *paper-mill* Scraps of cloth would be shredded and reused to make paper.

[9] *apotheosis* Transformation into a god; deification.

Nature and the Environment:
A Visual Sampler

The following paintings, drawings, and photographs evoke some of the myriad ways in which nineteenth-century Americans viewed the natural world. For a fuller survey of nature in American literature and culture of this period, see "Contexts: Nature and the Environment" in this anthology's online component.

⌘⌘⌘

Nature and the Environment: Changing Views

John James Audubon, Bird Paintings
(1827–38)

In the 1820s, John James Audubon (1785–1851), a Franco-American ornithologist, naturalist, and painter, undertook a massive project: a book that would compile paintings of every species of bird in North America, based on fourteen years of field observations and drawings. The completed book, *The Birds of America*, comprises 435 images (printed in installments from 1827 to 1838) of 497 bird species; it was hailed internationally as a great scientific and artistic accomplishment. While aspects of Audubon's methods and accuracy have been called into question, as has his character as an enslaver, his work wielded enormous influence on how subsequent nineteenth-century scientists and artists alike viewed and represented the natural world.

John James Audubon, *Great Horned Owl,* 1827.

John James Audubon, *Golden Eagle*, 1833–34.

Hugh Lee Pattinson, *Horseshoe Falls,* 1840. Pattinson (1796–1858), an English chemist and entrepreneur, took this photograph while visiting Canada in 1840; the image is the first known photograph of Niagara Falls as well as the first photograph known to have been taken in Canada.

Edward Hicks, *The Peaceable Kingdom,* c. 1848. Hicks (1780–1849) was a Quaker minister as well as a painter. Between about 1820 and his death, he painted 62 versions of *The Peaceable Kingdom,* drawing inspiration and imagery from the famous description of the kingdom of God in Isaiah 11.6–7: "The wolf also shall dwell with the lamb, and the leopard shall lie down with the kid; and the calf and the young lion and the fatling together; and a little child shall lead them. … [A]nd the lion shall eat straw like the ox."

Marian Hooper Adams, *Umbrella Tree at Smith's Point*, 1883. Adams (1843–85), who was married to the renowned historian Henry Adams and known to friends and family as "Clover" Adams, was admired for both her portraits and her landscape photographs.

The Hudson River School

The mode of representing natural scenes developed by the artists of the Hudson River School—realistic but also idealized and symbolically rich, and attuned to both the beneficent and the threatening sides of nature (or, as Romantic aesthetic theory termed them, the beautiful and the sublime)—is especially well-exemplified by Thomas Cole's *View from Mount Holyoke, Northampton, Massachusetts, after a Thunderstorm—The Oxbow*. This painting by Cole (1801–48), an English-born artist typically considered the founder of the Hudson River School, depicts the Oxbow, a well-known landscape created by a bend of the Connecticut River in western Massachusetts, as seen from a nearby mountaintop. With its combination of sweeping natural vista and wealth of symbolic detail, it has become one of the most famous and representative Hudson River School paintings.

After Cole's untimely death in 1848, his older contemporary Asher Durand (1796–1886) inherited his widely acknowledged status as the leader of what was becoming an emerging school of New York-based landscape artists. Durand paid tribute to Cole shortly after the latter's death in his *Kindred Spirits*, which was commissioned by the New York businessman and art patron Jonathan Sturges as a gift for the poet William Cullen Bryant, a friend of Cole's. As Sturges explained to Bryant, he had "requested Mr. Durand to paint a picture in which he should associate our departed friend and yourself as kindred spirits." The painting portrays Cole and Bryant surveying a landscape based on Kaaterskill Clove, a valley in the Catskill Mountains of New York state that was frequently painted by Hudson River School artists and that Bryant also described in his poetry. After receiving the painting, Bryant noted to Durand that "everybody admires it greatly," and it was praised by critics when it was exhibited publicly in 1849.

Nearly a decade after Durand used it as the basis for *Kindred Spirits*, Harriet Cany Peale (1799–1869) also depicted Kaaterskill Clove in her own painting of that name. Cany had studied with Rembrandt Peale, a member of a famous artistic family whom she later married, and her association with him and his family long overshadowed her own accomplishments. After her death, she was largely remembered only as a copyist, but she has recently begun to gain increased recognition as more of her original work is rediscovered.

The achievements of Cole, Durand, and Cany Peale's generation were built on by the second generation of Hudson River School artists. Emerging in the 1850s, this second generation perpetuated the Hudson River School into the post-Civil War period; many of them extended the school's aesthetic approach to the western landscapes being intensively opened up during that period. Robert S. Duncanson (1821–72), a Cincinnati, Ohio-based African American painter with no formal art education, was one of these; in 1861, the *Daily Cincinnati Gazette* dubbed him "the best landscape painter in the west," and another Cincinnati newspaper called his *Landscape with Rainbow* "one of the most beautiful pictures painted on this side of the [Allegheny] mountains." *Landscape with Rainbow*, together with Duncanson's other landscape paintings of the 1850s and 60s, helped him become the first black American artist to achieve an international reputation, winning acclaim in Canada and Britain as well as the United States.

Thomas Cole, *View from Mount Holyoke, Northampton, Massachusetts, after a Thunderstorm—The Oxbow*, 1836.

Asher Durand, *Kindred Spirits*, 1849. The right-hand figure pointing to the landscape is the painter Thomas Cole; the poet William Cullen Bryant is on the left.

Harriet Cany Peale, *Kaaterskill Clove*, 1858.

Robert S. Duncanson, *Landscape with Rainbow*, 1859.

Plains Ledger Art

The Indigenous peoples of the Great Plains have a rich artistic tradition that, in the mid-nineteenth century, included a variety of different kinds of painting on bison and other animal hides. By convention, types of hide painting were apportioned by gender: women traditionally painted abstract, geometrical designs, while men painted representational art, including scenes of combat and hunting, depictions of important events such as treaty signings, renderings of supernatural visions, and pictorial calendars (known as winter counts) in which individual years were represented by pictograms.

Starting in the 1860s, as the United States began settling the Great Plains in earnest and clamping down on the autonomous existence of the region's Indigenous inhabitants, these artistic practices began to change dramatically. As the great bison herds of the Plains were systematically destroyed by industrial hunting, Indigenous artists largely had to shift from hides to paper, often taken from accounting ledger books—because of which this transitional art form has come to be called "ledger art." The content of this art changed as well. In addition to the conventional representation of hunting and warfare, Indigenous artists depicted the Euro-American people and technologies that were radically altering their way of life and environment, and they also began increasingly to portray rituals and other aspects of their daily life from before intensive Euro-American encroachment began, as a way of both documenting these threatened aspects of their traditional way of life and asserting continuity with a past from which official U.S. policy was striving to sever them. Similar aims also guided the Indigenous artists who revived ledger art in the 1960s and 70s and who continue to practice it into the twenty-first century.

As an art form that both depicts and was shaped by profound cultural and environmental change—including the near-eradication of bison that necessitated the use of ledger paper in the first place—Plains ledger art provides a rich record of how the Indigenous people of this region related to and used their environment before Euro-American intrusion into it, as well as of how they adapted to this environment's dramatic transformation.

Shave Head (O-uk-ste-uh), *Hunting Buffalo*, 1875–78. Shave Head, also known as John Wicks, was a Cheyenne man in his twenties who was one of seventy-two men and one woman from various Indigenous nations of the Great Plains (mainly Cheyenne, Kiowa, and Comanche) incarcerated at Fort Marion, Florida, from 1875 to 1878. During their imprisonment, the fort commander provided them with art supplies; twenty-six of the prisoners took up drawing, including Shave Head. In the image reproduced here, four Cheyenne warriors are depicted hunting a herd of bison (four of which have been wounded), while a fifth warrior above them is wounding a lone elk. All five warriors wear full headdresses, and four of them carry elaborate, symbolically powerful mountain lion bows and quivers, indicating the hunt's ceremonial importance.

Black Hawk, Images from the Black Hawk Ledger (1880–81)

Black Hawk (Čhetáŋ Sápa' or Cetan Sapa, c. 1832–90)[1] was a medicine man and spiritual leader of the Sans Arc (Itázipčho) Lakota. During the very severe winter of 1880–81, William Edward Caton, a trader at the Cheyenne River reservation in what is now South Dakota, commissioned Black Hawk—who, according to Caton's son, "was in great straits," having "absolutely nothing, no food, and would not beg"—to create a series of drawings based on "a wonderful dream" Black Hawk was said to have had. Caton paid Black Hawk 50 cents per drawing (at the time, a generous compensation) and had the 76 completed drawings bound into a book; the collection was later lost and was not rediscovered until 1993. Black Hawk himself is believed to have been killed in the Wounded Knee Massacre in 1890.

The Black Hawk Ledger, as it is now called, contains depictions of warfare, rituals, and supernatural visions, and is regarded as a valuable visual record of Lakota religion and culture. The ledger also contains seventeen scenes of animal life, including the first image reproduced below. The view of non-human animals underlying such scenes is well described by the twentieth-century Lakota medicine man Archie Fire Lame Deer (Tȟáȟča Hušté): "all wild animals have power because Wakan Tanka [the Great Spirit] dwells in all of them, even in a tiny ant. The white man has built a wall between himself and that power. To understand what the animals are telling us needs time and patience, and the white man never has time."

The second image presented here, one of the ledger's many ceremonial depictions, portrays what has been described as a "buffalo transformation ceremony": a ritual in which members of a society of holy men called "Buffalo Dreamers" don bison masks, initiating a process whereby they are believed to acquire the animal's identity and power.

Black Hawk, *Great Horned Owls, Sandhill Crane, Crow.*

---

[1] *Black Hawk ... 90* Not to be confused with Black Hawk (Mà-ka-tai-me-she-kià-kiàk [1767–1838]), the famous Sauk leader.

Black Hawk, *Buffalo Dreamers*.

George Moses Horton

c. 1797 – after 1867

George Moses Horton aptly summarized his own importance in American literary history in a letter he wrote in 1852: "I am the only public or recognized poet of color in my native state or perhaps in the union, born in slavery but yet craving that scope and expression whereby my literary labor of the night may be circulated throughout the whole world." Horton was not only one of the first published African American poets, but also the only one to have multiple volumes of poetry published while enslaved, arguably the first one to advocate openly for release from enslavement in his work, and the first black person to publish a book of any kind in the American South. In a literary career that spanned five decades, Horton explored a wide variety of subjects in an equally wide variety of verse forms and poetic styles, leaving behind a body of work that would be significant by any standard but is all the more so considering the circumstances in which it was produced. His poetry balances the conventional and the colloquial, the influence of the white-dominated literary canon and the poet's own experiences of racialization and enslavement, in a way that makes it a major contribution to the development of a distinctively American poetry in the mid-nineteenth century—a development that Horton advocated and in which he saw himself as an integral participant.

Horton was enslaved from his birth, in 1797 or 98, on the North Carolina estate of William Horton, a small tobacco farmer who, as was common, imposed his surname on the people he enslaved; the names of Horton's parents are unknown. As a child, Horton was put to work herding cattle, but he quickly exhibited an inclination toward books. He taught himself to read by acquiring "old parts of spelling books" and laboriously working through them in his free time on Sundays and by night. In his autobiographical introduction to his second poetry collection, which is one of the few sources of information about his life, Horton vividly describes this labor: "by close application to my book at night, my visage became considerably emaciated by extreme perspiration[.] … I had to sit sweating and smoking over my incompetent bark or brush light, almost exhausted by the heat of the fire, and almost suffocated with smoke." From spelling books, he moved on to the New Testament, Methodist hymns, and especially poetry. Soon, being able to read but not yet able to write, he was composing his own poetry in his head.

In the 1820s, Horton found a market for this skill at the University of North Carolina in Chapel Hill, where he would walk on Sundays from his enslaver's farm to sell produce. Horton quickly became acquainted with students at the university, who would frequently force him, as a prank, to deliver off-the-cuff speeches for them but also began paying him to compose poems to order. Horton came to specialize in acrostic poems on the names of his clients' love interests; he charged between 25 and 75 cents a poem and eventually was making three to four dollars a week—a considerable amount of money at the time. This income enabled him to buy his own time from his enslaver and spend more time in Chapel Hill. Some of the university students he knew gave him books, including works by Homer, Virgil, Shakespeare, Milton, and Byron, which influenced his emerging style. Horton's burgeoning literary career was further assisted by his friendship with Caroline Lee Hentz, the wife of a university faculty member, who helped him get his first poems into print in 1828. (Ironically, Hentz would later have her own literary career as a proslavery novelist.)

The wider attention these first publications won for Horton provided the impetus for his first collection, *The Hope of Liberty* (1829)—a booklet that appears to have been produced without Horton's participation, or possibly even his knowledge. The publisher of *The Hope of Liberty* was a member of the American Colonization Society (ACS), an organization that sought to resettle free black Americans in the African colony of Liberia; he seems to have had Horton's work distributed for free, in the hope of obtaining sufficient charitable contributions to buy Horton's freedom and send him to the colony. (It is unclear whether or not Horton himself, at this time, had any interest in emigrating to Liberia.) As the volume's title suggests, Horton's resistance to his enslavement and desire for release from it provide the collection's main theme, evident in poems such as "The Slave's Complaint" and "On Hearing of the Intention of a Gentleman to Purchase the Poet's Freedom." The collection also incorporates poems on numerous other topics, including love lyrics, reflections on nature, and religious meditations. Besides exhibiting Horton's range, this thematic variety helped make the collection publishable in North Carolina, as did the way in which, in his poems addressing enslavement, Horton concentrates on his personal situation and aspirations rather than condemning slavery more broadly. A more sustained and open poetic attack on slavery as an institution, especially coming from an author who was himself enslaved, would likely have been suppressed—and the volume's publisher appears to have edited Horton's more aggrieved or forceful descriptions of his condition accordingly. Even so, *The Hope of Liberty* did not garner enough contributions to the ACS to pay for Horton's freedom.

Instead, Horton's ambiguous life as an enslaved professional poet continued for another three-and-a-half decades. Although marriages between enslaved people were illegal, he married sometime in the 1830s and had two children. He also finally learned to write in the early 1830s and continued to hire his time from his enslaver, despite the fact that, during these years, North Carolina made it illegal to teach enslaved people to read and write—and illegal to allow them to buy their own time. The growing restrictions Horton faced in the 1830s and 40s, as slavery in North Carolina became ever more stringent, are indirectly reflected in his second collection, *The Poetical Works of George M. Horton* (1845). This volume was not an ACS venture, and Horton was actively involved in its publication, even penning an autobiographical introduction for it, but it shared the same goal as *The Hope of Liberty*: raising sufficient money to buy Horton out of enslavement. Unlike *The Hope of Liberty*, however, *The Poetical Works* contains hardly any direct references to slavery and nowhere openly expresses a desire for freedom. Such desire, though, can be glimpsed in Horton's treatment of other subjects, such as his celebration of the intellectual freedom enjoyed by the white students at UNC in "On the Pleasures of College Life." *The Poetical Works* also includes poems in a more colloquial style on such everyday topics as drinking, indebtedness, and itching skin, which Horton treats with humane detail and wry, often self-deprecating humor. This second collection once again demonstrates Horton's range and versatility, but it fell short of its financial goal.

Horton remained enslaved up until the arrival of Union troops in North Carolina in the spring of 1865, at the end of the Civil War. After his emancipation, Horton, then nearly seventy, became friends with a Union officer, William H.S. Banks, who sponsored the publication of Horton's third and final collection, *Naked Genius* (1865). Horton's newfound freedom enabled him to return, in these poems, to direct reflections on slavery and liberation, but the volume also expresses a sense of age and decline, as in "George Moses Horton, Myself," and a feeling of displacement, as in "The Southern Refugee." Subsequently, Horton went north to Philadelphia, where he published at least two more poems in local newspapers. He disappears from the historical record in 1866, and his ultimate fate is unknown. According to one testimony, he was still living in Philadelphia in 1883 and died later that year, but recent scholarship suggests that he ended up emigrating to Liberia after all, arriving in 1867 and likely dying there.

Horton was a strong defender of American literature and proponent of its further growth. As he wrote in an 1849 letter to a North Carolina newspaper, "I am for developing *our own* resources, and cherishing native genius. ... Why *go abroad* for poetry when we have an infinitely superior article of domestic manufacture?" He went on to say that "I am too modest to speak of my own [poetry]" as a case in point, but he clearly did think of himself as an American poet who was playing a part in cultivating a "native" poetic canon. It took well over a century, however, for literary scholarship to see Horton in the way that he saw himself. In what is probably the last evaluation of Horton written during his lifetime, the Philadelphia *Evening Telegraph* described him in 1866 as "a profound and prolific writer" with "an intelligence, a bright intellectual fire, that would have made an imperishable name for him had he enjoyed the benefits of an ordinary education," but such positive, if patronizing, assessments of him did not long endure. Up through the 1960s, the few formal studies of Horton that were undertaken, all by white scholars, tended to be openly condescending and even racist in their treatment of him, acknowledging the significance of the fact that he wrote but largely dismissing the value of his work itself. Horton's rehabilitation began in the 1970s and is ongoing: new writing by him continues to be discovered in archival collections, and his critical reputation, together with appreciation of his importance to American literature, continues to grow. Horton is now increasingly recognized as one of the figures who helped bring mid-nineteenth-century American poetry into its own.

NOTE ON THE TEXTS: The texts of Horton's poems presented here are mainly based on the first editions of the three collections of Horton's poetry published in his lifetime. "The Lover's Farewell," "On Liberty and Slavery," "The Slave's Complaint," and "On Hearing of the Intention of a Gentleman to Purchase the Poet's Freedom" are based on the versions of these poems printed in *The Hope of Liberty* (1829); "The Fearful Traveler in the Haunted Castle" is based on the version printed in *The Poetical Works of George M. Horton* (1845); and "Death of an Old Carriage Horse" is based on the version printed in *Naked Genius* (1865). Spelling and punctuation have been modernized according to the practices of this anthology.

⌘⌘⌘

The Lover's Farewell

And wilt thou, love, my soul display,
And all my secret thoughts betray?
I strove but could not hold thee fast,
My heart flies off with thee at last.

5 The favorite daughter of the dawn,
On love's mild breeze will soon be gone;
I strove, but could not cease to love,
Nor from my heart the weight remove.

And wilt thou, love, my soul beguile,
10 And gull° thy favorite with a smile?   *trick, deceive*
Nay, soft affection answers, nay,
And beauty wings my heart away.

I steal on tiptoe from these bowers,°   *wooded enclosures*
All spangled° with a thousand flowers;   *adorned*
15 I sigh, yet leave them all behind,
To gain the object of my mind.

And wilt thou, love, command my soul,
And waft° me with a light control?—   *carry, propel*
Adieu to all the blooms of May,
20 Farewell—I fly with love away!

I leave my parents here behind,
And all my friends—to love resigned—
'Tis grief to go, but death to stay:
Farewell—I'm gone with love away!
—1829

On Liberty and Slavery

Alas! and am I born for this,
To wear this slavish chain?
Deprived of all created bliss,
Through hardship, toil and pain!

5 How long have I in bondage lain,
And languished to be free!
Alas! and must I still complain—
Deprived of liberty.

Oh, Heaven! and is there no relief
10 This side the silent grave—
To soothe the pain—to quell the grief
And anguish of a slave?

Come Liberty, thou cheerful sound,
Roll through my ravished[1] ears!

---

[1] *ravished* Overwhelmed with delight or ecstasy; or, forcibly stolen.

15   Come, let my grief in joys be drowned,
And drive away my fears.

Say unto foul oppression, Cease:
Ye tyrants rage no more,
And let the joyful trump° of peace,   *trumpet*
20   Now bid the vassal soar.

Soar on the pinions° of that dove   *wings*
Which long has cooed for thee,
And breathed her notes from Afric's° grove,   *Africa's*
The sound of Liberty.

25   Oh, Liberty! thou golden prize,
So often sought by blood—
We crave thy sacred sun to rise,
The gift of nature's God:[1]

Bid Slavery hide her haggard face,
30   And barbarism fly:
I scorn to see the sad disgrace
In which enslaved I lie.

Dear Liberty! upon thy breast,
I languish to respire;°   *rest*
35   And like the swan unto her nest,
I'd to thy smiles retire.

Oh, blest asylum—heavenly balm!
Unto thy boughs I flee—
And in thy shades the storm shall calm,
40   With songs of Liberty!
—1829

The Slave's Complaint

Am I sadly cast aside,
On misfortune's rugged° tide?   *stormy*
Will the world my pains deride
    Forever?

5   Must I dwell in Slavery's night,
And all pleasure take its flight,

Far beyond my feeble sight,
    Forever?

Worst of all, must Hope grow dim,
10   And withhold her cheering beam?
Rather let me sleep and dream
    Forever!

Something still my heart surveys,°   *perceives*
Groping through this dreary maze;
15   Is it Hope?—then burn and blaze
    Forever!

Leave me not a wretch confined,
Altogether lame and blind—
Unto gross[2] despair consigned,
20   Forever!

Heaven! in whom can I confide?
Canst thou not for all provide?
Condescend° to be my guide   *graciously consent*
    Forever:

25   And when this transient life shall end,
Oh, may some kind eternal friend
Bid me from servitude ascend,
    Forever!
—1829

On Hearing of the Intention of a Gentleman to Purchase the Poet's Freedom

When on life's ocean first I spread my sail,
I then implored° a mild auspicious gale;   *prayed to*
And from the slippery strand° I took my flight,   *shore*
And sought the peaceful haven° of delight.   *harbor*

5   Tyrannic storms arose upon my soul,
And dreadful did their mad'ning[3] thunders roll;
The pensive° muse[4] was shaken from her sphere,   *anxious*
And hope, it vanished in the clouds of fear.

---

[1] *nature's God* The introduction to the Declaration of Independence asserts that the American colonies are entitled to independence by "the Laws of Nature and of Nature's God."

[2] *gross* Enormous; thick; deep.

[3] *mad'ning* So overwhelming as to cause madness.

[4] *muse* Figure of inspiration for poetry or art, so called after the nine Muses, classical goddesses who presided over the arts and learning.

At length a golden sun broke through the gloom,
10   And from his smiles arose a sweet perfume—
A calm ensued, and birds began to sing,
And lo! the sacred muse resumed her wing.

With frantic° joy she chanted as she flew,   *delirious*
And kissed the clement° hand that bore her   *merciful*
   through
15   Her envious foes did from her sight retreat,
Or prostrate fall beneath her burning feet.

'Twas like a proselyte,° allied to Heaven—   *converted person*
Or rising spirits' boast of sins forgiven,
Whose shout dissolves the adamant[1] away
20   Whose melting[2] voice the stubborn rocks obey.

'Twas like the salutation of the dove,
Borne on the zephyr[3] through some lonesome grove,
When Spring returns, and Winter's chill is past,
And vegetation smiles above the blast.

25   'Twas like the evening of a nuptial pair,[4]
When love pervades the hour of sad despair—
'Twas like fair Helen's sweet return to Troy,
When every Grecian bosom swelled with joy.[5]

The silent harp which on the osiers° hung,   *willow trees*
30   Was then attuned,° and manumission[6] sung: *tuned*
Away by hope the clouds of fear were driven,
And music breathed my gratitude to Heaven.

Hard was the race to reach the distant goal,
The needle oft was shaken from the pole;[7]
35   In such distress, who could forbear to weep?[8]
Tossed by the headlong billows° of the deep!   *waves*

The tantalizing beams which shone so plain,
Which turned my former pleasures into pain—
Which falsely promised all the joys of fame,
40   Gave way, and to a more substantial flame.

Some philanthropic souls as from afar,
With pity strove to break the slavish bar;
To whom my floods of gratitude shall roll,
And yield with pleasure to their soft control.

45   And sure of Providence this work begun—
He shod my feet this rugged° race to run;   *strenuous*
And in despite° of all the swelling tide,   *defiance*
Along the dismal path will prove my guide.

Thus on the dusky° verge of deep despair,   *dark*
50   Eternal Providence was with me there;
When pleasure seemed to fade on life's gay dawn,
And the last beam of hope was almost gone.
—1829

The Fearful Traveller in the Haunted Castle

Oft do I hear those windows ope°   *open*
    And shut with dread surprise,
And spirits murmur as they grope,
    But break not on the eyes.

5   Still fancy° spies the winding sheet,[9]   *imagination*
    The phantom and the shroud,
And bids the pulse of horror beat
    Throughout my ears aloud.

---

[1]   *adamant*   Stone or mineral of extraordinary hardness.

[2]   *melting*   I.e., causing to melt.

[3]   *zephyr*   West wind, synonymous with a gentle and pleasant breeze. In Greek mythology, Zephyrus, the god of the west wind, was considered to be the messenger of spring.

[4]   *nuptial pair*   Newly married couple.

[5]   *'Twas like … joy*   Horton's reference to the story of Helen and the Trojan War here seems muddled: according to the story, Helen was seduced away from her husband, the Greek king Menelaus, by the Trojan prince Paris, and the Greeks attacked Troy in order to win her back.

[6]   *manumission*   Release from enslavement.

[7]   *The needle … pole*   I.e., the compass needle was frequently driven to point in other directions than north (towards "the pole"). Many enslaved people in America escaped to northern free states, or further north to Canada.

[8]   *forbear to weep*   Refrain from weeping.

[9]   *winding sheet*   Burial shroud.

Some unknown finger thumps the door,
    From one of faltering voice,
Till someone seems to walk the floor
    With an alarming noise.

The drum of horror holds her sound,
    Which will not let me sleep,
When ghastly breezes float around,
    And hidden goblins creep.

Methinks I hear some constant groan,
    The din of all the dead,
While trembling thus I lie alone,
    Upon this restless bed.

At length the blaze of morning broke
    On my impatient view,
And truth or fancy told the joke,
    And bade the night adieu.

'Twas but the noise of prowling rats,
    Which ran with all their speed,
Pursued in haste by hungry cats,
    Which on the vermin feed.

The cat growled as she held her prey,
    Which shrieked with all its might,
And drove the balm of sleep away
    Throughout the live-long night.

Those creatures crumbling off the cheese
    Which on the table lay;
Some cats, too quick the rogues to seize,
    With rumbling lost their prey.

Thus man is often his own elf,[1]
    Who makes the night his ghost,
And shrinks with horror from himself,
    Which is to fear the most.
—1845

___

[1] *elf* Supernatural creature; demon.

Death of an Old Carriage Horse

I was a harness horse,
    Constrained to travel weak or strong,
With orders from oppressing force,
    Push along, push along.

I had no space of rest,
    And took at forks the roughest prong,
Still by the cruel driver pressed,
    Push along, push along.

Vain strove the idle bird
    To charm me with her artless° song,   *simple, sincere*
But pleasure lingered from the word,
    Push along, push along.

The order of the day
    Was push, the peal of every tongue,
The only word was all the way,
    Push along, push along.

Thus to my journey's end,
    Had I to travel right or wrong,
'Till death, my sweet and favored friend,
    Bade me from life to push along.
—1865

JOHN BROWN

1800 – 1859

According to Frederick Douglass, John Brown was "the man of this nineteenth century." By taking up arms against slavery, first in Kansas Territory and then in a failed raid on Harpers Ferry, Virginia, Brown helped bring to a boiling point the long-simmering tensions between abolitionist and proslavery factions in America. Indeed, historians view his armed resistance as a key trigger of the Civil War,

nineteenth-century America's defining conflict. Cutting to the heart of the question sundering his country, Brown instantly became, and has always remained, an intensely polarizing figure. The passionately religious and deeply personal fervor of his abolitionism, and his conviction that armed struggle against slavery was necessary for its eradication, have led Brown's critics throughout history to characterize him as a violent, fanatical madman, but his advocates have viewed those same attributes as evidence of a perceptive, even visionary outlook, for it did take a terrible war to end slavery in America. Brown was an eloquent spokesperson for his cause—Ralph Waldo Emerson ranked his so-called "Last Speech" with the Gettysburg Address as "the two best specimens of eloquence we have had in this country"—but his vision was played out more fully in his actions, through which he sought to bring into being a rejuvenated America, free of slavery. As two modern scholars of Brown have put it, he had "a rich imagination—a sense of alternate reality more common to writers and artists than to militant political leaders." Not surprisingly, Brown captured the imaginations of many of the foremost literary figures of his era—Douglass, Emerson, Henry David Thoreau, Herman Melville, Walt Whitman, Lydia Maria Child, and John Greenleaf Whittier, to name a few—who responded powerfully to him in their own work.

Abolitionism was part of Brown's upbringing from his birth in Connecticut in 1800. His father, Owen Brown, was a stern New England Calvinist and a vocal opponent of slavery; after moving his family to Ohio in 1805, he operated a safe house on the Underground Railroad, as his son was also later to do. John Brown was educated at an abolitionist-run academy and briefly studied for the ministry before setting up as a tanner (his father's trade). In 1837, the widely-publicized murder of the antislavery clergy member and newspaper editor Elijah Lovejoy caused Brown to declare that "from this time, I consecrate my life to the destruction of slavery." As Brown became more involved in the national antislavery movement, however, he came to disagree with the white abolitionist establishment, whose commitment to emancipation through nonviolent persuasion he deemed "hopeless": he once voiced a desire that the leading abolitionist orators would have their tongues cut out, so that, being no longer able to say anything, they would be forced to "do something." Instead, Brown preferred to align himself with black abolitionists and formerly enslaved people, whose stake in the struggle against slavery was more personal and urgent. He drew inspiration particularly from the ideas and tactics of black revolutionaries such as Nat Turner, Joseph Cinqué, and Toussaint Louverture.

Brown first acted on these ideas amid the civil strife between pro- and antislavery settlers in the Kansas Territory in the 1850s, a period that became known as "Bleeding Kansas." Brown moved to Kansas in 1855, after learning about the apparent helplessness of the antislavery settlers (known as Free-Staters) in the face of proslavery violence. This aggression came to a head on 21 May 1856, when proslavery raiders sacked the Free-State town of Lawrence. To avenge the raid and pre-empt further such attacks, Brown and his followers, including four of his sons, murdered five proslavery settlers at Pottawatomie Creek on the night of 23–24 May. The brutality of these killings, and Brown's role in and motivation for them, remain a source of controversy. Brown went on to stage a brave but unsuccessful defense of the Free-State town of Osawatomie against a much larger proslavery force, and by late 1856 his actions in Kansas had gained him nationwide prominence.

After returning east in the autumn of 1856, Brown began enlisting support for a more ambitious plan. He proposed establishing a guerilla force in the Appalachian Mountains of western Virginia, modeled on the "Maroon" communities of fugitive blacks in the Caribbean, which would stage raids into the surrounding lowlands to free enslaved people. Brown maintained that as more and more enslaved people joined this group, and as other groups sprang up to emulate it, the whole slave system would eventually break down. As part of the preparation for this plan, and while staying in the home of Frederick Douglass, Brown wrote a "Provisional Constitution" that would govern his guerilla organization and provide the basis for a new government for the United States in the wake of slavery's collapse. The constitution condemned slavery as a betrayal of the country's founding ideals and as an institutionalization of a state of war between one group of citizens and another. It also set forth a vision of a new society organized on egalitarian and explicitly religious principles, in which "filthy conversation" would be forbidden, the Sabbath universally observed, all property held in common, and all people—male and female alike—encouraged to bear arms and to "labor in some way for the general good." (Brown practiced what he preached in his own household, requiring his sons as well as his daughters—he had a total of twenty children by two marriages—to share in domestic chores.) The constitution helped Brown raise funding from white abolitionist backers, but his plans were viewed with skepticism by Douglass, who believed the scheme was doomed by Brown's lack of firsthand acquaintance with the region and the enslaved people living there.

Douglass's fears came to pass when Brown and his followers launched their plan on 16 October 1859 with a raid on Harpers Ferry, Virginia, which housed a federal armory from which Brown intended to equip the enslaved people he believed would join him. Brown's party seized the armory and took hostages (whom he treated well, including ordering them breakfast from the town's hotel) but was cut off and surrounded by local militia and then by U.S. Marines, who crushed the raiders and captured Brown on 18 October. The raid resulted in seventeen deaths, including Brown's sons Watson and Oliver and eight others from Brown's party, and electrified the nation, as did Brown's subsequent trial by the state of Virginia for murder, treason, and incitement of slave insurrection. Brown refused his defense team's attempt to present his provisional constitution as evidence of his insanity, and in his "Last Speech," after being found guilty on all counts, he denied any criminal intent, defended his actions as motivated by the Golden Rule, and declared himself ready to die a martyr for his cause. He held to this intention up to his execution on 2 December 1859, rejecting a friend's attempt to spring him from jail. On his way to be hanged, he handed one of his jailers a note: "I, John Brown, am now quite certain that the crimes of this guilty land will never be purged away but with blood."

Brown and his actions immediately inspired contradictory interpretations and have remained divisive ever since. Opponents of abolition viewed Brown as, in Nathaniel Hawthorne's words, a "bloodstained fanatic," and the Harpers Ferry raid caused panic about potential slave revolts throughout the South, convincing many Southerners that Northern abolitionism threatened not just their livelihoods but their lives. Conversely, Northern abolitionists—including many committed to pacifism—came to hail Brown as a Christ-like martyr: Emerson said that Brown's hanging would "make the gallows glorious like the cross," while Thoreau called him "meteor-like, flashing through the darkness in which we live." (Later, Whitman and Melville both wrote poems about Brown's execution in which they echoed Thoreau's meteor image.) As the nation careened toward civil war, these competing interpretations of Brown made him an ongoing force; in the words of the "John Brown Song," popular in the Union during the war and later rewritten by poet Julia Ward Howe as "The Battle Hymn of the Republic," Brown's "soul" kept "marching on."

In the late nineteenth and early twentieth centuries, many white Americans embraced a view of the Civil War as a tragic, unnecessary fratricide, and the depiction of Brown as an unhinged perpetrator of needless violence accordingly became dominant. Later in the twentieth century, Brown was variously praised and condemned all across the political spectrum: he has been claimed as a model for revolutionary armed resistance by the right-wing terrorist Timothy McVeigh and the left-wing Weather Underground group, and castigated as a progenitor of American domestic terrorism by mainstream and extremist voices alike. Many African American activists, from Harriet Tubman to W.E.B. Du Bois to Malcolm X, have seen Brown as a clear-eyed opponent of the systemic, state-supported terrorism that was slavery. Present-day scholarship continues to debate Brown and his legacy, paying particular attention to his provisional constitution as an important landmark in a long history of grassroots American attempts to change what the country was and re-envision what it could be.

NOTE ON THE TEXT: The text included here of "John Brown's Last Speech" is based on the transcript printed in the *New York Herald* on 3 November 1859; the text of the speech included in *John Brown's Trial*, by Brian McGinty (2009), was also consulted. Spelling and punctuation have been modernized in accordance with the practices of this anthology.

⌘ ⌘ ⌘

John Brown's Last Speech[1]

I have, may it please the Court, a few words to say.

In the first place, I deny everything but what I have all along admitted, of a design on my part to free slaves. I intended certainly to have made a clean thing of that matter, as I did last winter, when I went into Missouri, and there took slaves without the snapping of a gun on either side, moving them through the country, and finally leaving them in Canada.[2] I designed to have done the same thing again on a larger scale. That was all I intended. I never did intend murder or treason, or the destruction of property, or to excite or incite slaves to rebellion, or to make insurrection.[3]

I have another objection, and that is that it is unjust that I should suffer such a penalty. Had I interfered in the manner in which I admit, and which I admit has been fairly proved—for I admire the truthfulness and candor of the greater portion of the witnesses who have testified in this case—had I so interfered in behalf of the rich, the powerful, the intelligent, the so-called great, or in behalf of any of their friends, either father, mother, brother, sister, wife or children, or any of that class, and suffered and sacrificed what I have in this interference, it would have been all right; every man in this court would have deemed it an act worthy of reward rather than punishment.

This court acknowledges, too, as I suppose, the validity of the law of God. I see a book kissed, which I suppose to be the Bible, or at least the New Testament, which teaches me that all things whatsoever I would that men should do to me, I should do even so to them.[4] It teaches me, further, to remember them that are in bonds, as bound with them.[5] I endeavored to act up to that instruction. I say I am yet too young to understand that God is any respecter of persons. I believe that to have interfered as I have done, as I

---

1   Brown gave this speech in court before being sentenced to death on 2 November 1859 on charges of murder, treason, and inciting a slave insurrection resulting from his raid on Harpers Ferry, Virginia. He had just been invited by the clerk of the court to "say why sentence should not be pronounced upon him." The extent to which Brown had prepared the speech in advance is not clear; in a subsequent letter, he claimed that "I was taken wholly by surprise" by the clerk's invitation. According to some eyewitnesses, Brown spoke "timidly—hesitatingly, indeed," but others found him "composed" and judged that he spoke "with perfect calmness of voice and mildness of manner." Newspaper reporters transcribed his words as he spoke, and in the ensuing days they were widely printed around the country.

2   *as I did ... Canada*   Brown refers here to a raid he led into the slave state of Missouri in December 1858, during which his party liberated eleven enslaved people and led them to Canada. Contrary to Brown's assertion, this raid was not entirely free of violence, as one enslaver was killed during it.

3   *I never ... insurrection*   This claim led hostile observers to accuse Brown of lying, since aiding enslaved people to revolt was his avowed

purpose in undertaking the Harpers Ferry raid. When Brown's prosecuting attorney pointed out this contradiction to him during the month between Brown's trial and execution, Brown replied in a letter that, in the "hurry of the moment" when he was called on to speak, he "did not consider the full bearing of what I then said." He went on to admit that his aim at Harpers Ferry had in fact been to arm enslaved people in the South rather than to "run them out of the slave States."

4   *all things ... them*   See Matthew 7.12.

5   *remember ... them*   See Hebrews 13.3.

have always freely admitted I have done, in behalf of His despised poor, is no wrong, but right. Now, if it is deemed necessary that I should forfeit my life for the furtherance of the ends of justice, and mingle my blood further with the blood of my children[1] and with the blood of millions in this slave country, whose rights are disregarded by wicked, cruel, and unjust enactments, I say let it be done.

Let me say one word further. I feel entirely satisfied with the treatment I have received on my trial. Considering all the circumstances, it has been more generous than I expected; but I feel no consciousness of guilt. I have stated from the first what was my intention and what was not. I never had any design against the liberty of any person, nor any disposition to commit treason or excite slaves to rebel or make any general insurrection. I never encouraged any man to do so, but always discouraged any idea of that kind.

Let me say also, in regard to the statements made by some of those who were connected with me. I fear it has been stated by some of them that I have induced them to join me, but the contrary is true. I do not say this to injure them, but as regretting their weakness. Not one joined me but of his own accord, and the greater part of them at their own expense. A number of them I never saw and never had a word of conversation with till the day they came to me, and that was for the purpose I have stated.

Now, I have done.

—1859

---

[1] *the blood of my children* Two of Brown's sons had been killed when federal troops put down his Harpers Ferry raid; another son had been killed by proslavery militia in Kansas three years earlier.

Jane Johnston Schoolcraft / Bamewawagezhikaquay

1800 – 1842

Bamewawagezhikaquay, also known as Jane Johnston Schoolcraft, translated her Ojibwe name into English as "Woman of the Sound the Stars Make Rushing through the Sky." A Métis writer well-educated in both Ojibwe and British traditions, she created a sophisticated body of writing that is at once Métis, Ojibwe, and Euro-American in its content and style. She wrote formal English poetry, translations of traditional Ojibwe stories and love songs, and original poetry in Ojibwe—the first poetry known to have been composed in writing by an Indigenous author in an Indigenous language. Although little of her work was formally published in her lifetime, and her career was overshadowed by that of her husband, the ethnographer Henry Rowe Schoolcraft, her significance is coming to be appreciated in the twenty-first century.

Schoolcraft was born Jane Johnston in Sault Ste. Marie, in what is now the state of Michigan's upper peninsula, in 1800. Her mother, Ozhaguscodaywayquay, also known as Susan Johnston, was part of a prominent Ojibwe family; her father, John Johnston, was a Scotch-Irish trader. Schoolcraft was thus born into a Métis culture—a midwestern culture blending Indigenous, French, and Anglo ancestries and traditions—that was already well established in the area. Each of her parents preserved their own traditions and languages, and Schoolcraft and her seven siblings all received thorough Ojibwe- and English-language educations at home, where their father amassed an unusually extensive library of literature, theology, and history (despite their rural location, the family owned about a thousand books). Schoolcraft traveled to Ireland in 1809 and may have received a few months of formal schooling there, but a change in the family's finances prompted an early return to the Sault in 1810.

Schoolcraft probably began to write literature in her teens, and continued to write for most of her life; her oldest surviving dated poem was completed when she was fifteen years old. Many poems appear only in Ojibwe or, more often, English, while in some cases she composed the same content in English and Ojibwe versions. Most of her English poetry employs the formal conventions and style of Euro-American Romanticism; her Ojibwe poetry, on the other hand, tends to use formal techniques drawn from Ojibwe oral traditions. While her translations of Ojibwe traditional songs are sometimes literal, without a new poetic form imposed, others adapt the content to the Euro-American verse forms that Schoolcraft's English-language readers would have recognized as poetry. Similarly, Schoolcraft appears to have varied her approach to the translation of traditional Ojibwe stories. Some appear to preserve the original narrative structure, giving the impression of a direct translation, while others are creative adaptations employing the tone and structure of Euro-American folk stories, suggesting the influence of the Brothers Grimm and other Romantic-era collectors of folk and fairytales.

Schoolcraft's work was deeply entwined with her husband's. She met Henry Rowe Schoolcraft in 1822 when he came to the Sault as a United States Indian agent; they were married in 1823. They had four children, though the eldest, William, died before age three. As writers, she and Henry had a complex and mutually influential relationship: her expertise shaped much of the ethnographic work on Indigenous peoples that made him famous, and he encouraged and preserved her writing—some of which he published, often without clear attribution, as part of his own books. Henry, whose attitude toward Native Americans was generally condescending, appears to have enjoyed his wife's combination of Indigeneity and Euro-American refinement; in his *Personal Memoirs* (1851), he describes their reception during a 1824–25 trip to New York as "something like a sensation in every circle," observing that many wanted "to see the northern Pocahontas" who was educated, had traveled abroad, and wrote with "grammatical skill and taste." Henry's commentary offers a glimpse of the patronizing, exoticizing attitudes Schoolcraft often faced at home and abroad.

During her lifetime, Jane Schoolcraft's work appeared only once in a "publication" under her own name. This was in a handwritten magazine edited by Henry during the winter of 1826–27, which he titled *The Muzzeniegun, or Literary Voyager*. The *Muzzeniegun* (Ojibwe: "book") circulated among their friends, and it included at least nine poems and five Ojibwe stories by Jane (some appearing under pseudonyms), including the poem "By an Ojibwa Female Pen," the story "Mishösha, or the Magician and His Daughters," and poems about her eldest son's death. One recipient, the Schoolcrafts' friend Charles Christopher Trowbridge, praised "the pathos of style and the singular felicity of expression" of Schoolcraft's poem "To My Ever Beloved & Lamented Son William Henry" and asked for permission to have it published, but his request appears to have been declined.

In 1833, the Schoolcrafts moved to Michigan's Mackinac Island, separating Jane Schoolcraft from her mother and siblings. Henry, who became Superintendent of Indian Affairs for Michigan in 1836, began to travel more extensively to support his political career (which included the negotiation of a treaty that deprived the Ojibwe of a vast portion of their land). In a letter to her husband, Schoolcraft describes herself as "chained at home ... like a domestic bear, who ever & anon, growls out his dissatisfaction at his circumscribed limits." During this period, she was also frequently ill and became addicted to the opium mixture doctors prescribed to treat her pain.

In 1839, Henry published some of Jane's English versions of traditional Ojibwe oral stories in the collection *Algic Researches*. He did not identify her translations specifically—though he did acknowledge "Mrs. Henry R. Schoolcraft" as one of the volume's contributors—and she may have been involved in the preparation of the rest of the book as well. After Henry was dismissed from his role as superintendent, the Schoolcrafts moved to New York City to start afresh in 1841. The following year, Jane Schoolcraft died unexpectedly while visiting her sister in Dundas, a town in what is now Ontario, Canada. The writer Margaret Fuller, a friend of the Schoolcrafts, lamented that "by the premature death of Mrs. Schoolcraft was lost a mine of poesy, to which few had access."

After Schoolcraft's death, her husband continued to publish her work—generally in his own books and periodicals, though with some direct acknowledgment of her authorship. He also gathered a collection of her poetry that appears to have been intended for publication but was never printed. He did, however, save much of her work in manuscript form, and it would probably not have survived if not for its inclusion in archive collections dedicated to his writings. Though some of these materials are in her handwriting, many more were copied out by Henry and probably revised by him. Because he is known to have freely intervened in the revision and translation of her work—and whether he did so with or without her approval is unclear—it is often difficult to determine how closely the surviving documents reflect their original author's intentions.

For a century, Schoolcraft's importance was barely acknowledged in print, though her work in *Algic Researches* would exert a significant influence on Henry Wadsworth Longfellow's famous poem *The Song of Hiawatha* (1855). She began to receive some recognition in 1962, when Philip P. Mason edited a print edition of *Literary Voyager*, which included footnotes clarifying the extent of her contributions. No collection dedicated to her writing was released until 2007, when the scholar Robert Dale Parker collected her work in *The Sound the Stars Make Rushing through the Sky: The Writings of Jane Johnston Schoolcraft*. Parker's recovery efforts brought Schoolcraft to broader attention and quickly established her as a writer of significance, important not only for her erudition in multiple languages and traditions but also for her skill and versatility as a poet and storyteller.

NOTE ON THE TEXTS: The following texts are based upon those appearing in Robert Dale Parker's collection of Schoolcraft's writings, *The Sound the Stars Make Rushing through the Sky* (2007); the original sources employed by Parker are noted in footnotes at the beginning of each text. In Schoolcraft's time, Ojibwe did not yet have a standardized orthography, and her work in Ojibwe thus employs spelling and word divisions that differ significantly from those of the present day. Her original spellings have been preserved in the Ojibwe texts, while the English texts have been modernized in accordance with the practices of this anthology.

⌘⌘⌘

To the Pine Tree

*on first seeing it
on returning from Europe*[1]

Shing wauk! Shing wauk! nin ge ik id,
Waish kee wau bum ug, shing wauk
Tuh quish in aun nau aub, ain dak nuk i yaun.
Shing wauk, shing wauk No sa
5 Shi e gwuh ke do dis au naun
Kau gega way zhau wus co zid.

Mes ah nah, shi egwuh tah gwish en aung
Sin da mik ke aum baun
Kag ait suh, ne meen wain dum
10 Me nah wau, wau bun dah maun
Gi yut wi au, wau bun dah maun een
Shing wauk, shing wauk nosa
Shi e gwuh ke do dis au naun.

Ka ween ga go, kau wau bun duh e yun
15 Tib isht co, izz henau gooz ze no an
Shing wauk wah zhau wush co zid
Ween Ait ah kwanaudj e we we
Kau ge gay wa zhau soush ko zid
—2007 (WRITTEN 1822–40)

Translation[2]

The pine! the pine! I eager cried,
The pine, my father! see it stand,
As first that cherished tree I spięd,
Returning to my native land.
5 The pine! the pine! oh lovely scene!
The pine, that is forever green.

Ah beauteous tree! ah happy sight!
That greets me on my native strand°   *shore*
And hails me, with a friend's delight,
10 To my own dear bright mother land
Oh 'tis to me a heart-sweet scene,
The pine—the pine! that's ever green.

Not all the trees of England bright,
Not Erin's° lawns of green and light   *Ireland's*
15 Are half so sweet to memory's eye,
As this dear type of northern sky
Oh 'tis to me a heart-sweet scene,
The pine—the pine! that ever green.
—2007 (WRITTEN 1822–40)

---

1 *returning from Europe* Schoolcraft visited Ireland and England with her father in 1809, returning to her native North America in 1810.

---

2 The translation reprinted here is Schoolcraft's own.

By an Ojibwa Female Pen[1]

Invitation to sisters to a walk in the Garden, after a shower

Come, sisters come! the shower's past,
The garden walks are drying fast,
The Sun's bright beams are seen again,
And nought within, can now detain.
5   The rain drops tremble on the leaves,
Or drip expiring, from the eaves;
But soon the cool and balmy air,
Shall dry the gems that sparkle there,
With whisp'ring breath shake ev'ry spray,
10 And scatter every cloud away.

Thus sisters! shall the breeze of hope,
Through sorrow's clouds a vista ope;°   open
Thus, shall affliction's surly blast,
By faith's bright calm be stilled at last;
15 Thus, pain and care—the tear and sigh,
Be chased from every dewy eye;
And life's mixed scene itself, but cease,
To show us realms of light and peace.
—1962 (WRITTEN BEFORE 1826)

To My Ever Beloved and Lamented Son William Henry[2]

Who was it, nestled on my breast,
"And on my cheek sweet kisses prest"[3]
And in whose smile I felt so blest?
                              Sweet Willy.

5   Who hailed my form as home I stept,
And in my arms so eager leapt,
And to my bosom joyous crept?
                              My Willy.

Who was it, wiped my tearful eye,
10 And kissed away the coming sigh,
And smiling bid me say "good boy"?
                              Sweet Willy.

Who was it, looked divinely fair,
Whilst lisping sweet the evening prayer,
15 Guileless and free from earthly care?
                              My Willy.

Whither has fled the rose's hue?
The lily's whiteness blending grew,
Upon thy cheek—so fair to view.
20   My Willy.

Oft have I gazed with rapt delight,
Upon those eyes that sparkled bright,
Emitting beams of joy and light!
                              Sweet Willy.

25 Oft have I kissed that forehead high,
Like polished marble to the eye,
And blessing, breathed an anxious sigh.
                              For Willy.

My son! Thy coral lips are pale,
30 Can I believe the heart-sick tale,
That I, thy loss must ever wail?
                              My Willy.

The clouds in darkness seemed to low'r,
The storm has passed with awful pow'r,
35 And nipped my tender, beauteous flow'r!
                              Sweet Willy.

But soon my spirit will be free,
And I, my lovely son shall see,
For God, I know, did this decree!
40   My Willy.

—1827

---

1   This poem appeared in the first issue of *The Muzzeniegun, or Literary Voyager*, a handwritten manuscript magazine edited by Henry Rowe Schoolcraft in 1826 and 1827, under the pseudonym "Rosa." This magazine seems to have circulated among the Schoolcrafts' friends in the region, and the poem was not formally published until 1962.

2   *William Henry*   Schoolcraft's son, who was less than three years old when he died of croup in 1827.

3   *And on … prest*   From English poet Ann Taylor's "My Mother" (1804), a popular poem in which a child praises its mother. Schoolcraft here employs the same form as Taylor's poem but replaces the original refrain, "My mother," with "My Willy" or "Sweet Willy."

On Leaving My Children John and Jane at School, in the Atlantic States, and Preparing to Return to the Interior

In 1839, the eldest living Schoolcraft children were sent to elite, predominately white boarding schools in Philadelphia and Princeton when Jane (called Janee) was eleven and Johnston (called John) nine years old. Though the forced enrollment of Native American children in boarding schools would become a tool of cultural assimilation in the later nineteenth century, this was not yet a commonplace practice; the Schoolcraft children went to boarding school following the wishes of their father.

The following poem appeared in Henry Rowe Schoolcraft's *Personal Memoirs of a Residence of Thirty Years with the Indian Tribes on the American Frontiers* (1851), where he introduced them with the statement that "Mrs. Schoolcraft, having left her children at school, at Philadelphia and Princeton, remained pensive, and wrote the following lines in the Indian tongue, on parting from them, which I thought so just that I made a translation of them." Henry subtitles his version a "Free Translation," and it diverges in many respects from Jane's Ojibwe original. A twenty-first-century translation more faithful to the original text, prepared by Dennis Jones, Heidi Stark, and James Vukelich for *The Sound the Stars Make Rushing through the Sky*, appears in facing column with the Ojibwe; it is followed by Henry's English version.

Nyau nin de nain dum
May kow e yaun in
Ain dah nuk ki yaun
Waus sa wa kom eg
5 Ain dah nuk ki yaun

Ne dau nis ainse e
Ne gwis is ainse e
Ishe nau gun ug wau
Waus sa wa kom eg

10 She gwau go sha ween
Ba sho waud e we
Nin zhe ka we yea
Ishe ez hau jau yaun
Ain dah nuk ke yaun

15 Ain dah nuk ke yaun
Nin zhe ke we yea
Ishe ke way aun e
Nyau ne gush kain dum
—1851 (WRITTEN 1839)

As I am thinking
When I find you
My land
Far in the west
5 My land

My little daughter
My little son
I leave them behind
Far away land

10 [emphatically] But soon
It is close however
To my home I shall return
That is the way that I am, my being
My land

15 My land
To my home I shall return
I begin to make my way home
Ahh but I am sad
—2007

Free Translation

Ah! when thought reverts to my country so dear,
My heart fills with pleasure, and throbs with a fear:
My country, my country, my own native land,
So lovely in aspect, in features so grand,
5 Far, far in the West. What are cities to me,
Oh! land of my mother, compared unto thee?

Fair land of the lakes! thou are blest to my sight,
With thy beaming bright waters, and landscapes of
    light;
The breeze and the murmur, the dash and the roar,
10 That summer and autumn cast over the shore,
They spring to my thoughts, like the lullaby tongue,
That soothed me to slumber when youthful and
    young.

One feeling more strongly still binds me to thee,
There roved my forefathers, in liberty free—
15 There shook they the war lance, and sported the
    plume,
Ere Europe had cast o'er this country a gloom;

Nor thought they that kingdoms more happy could be,
White lords of a land so resplendent and free.

Yet it is not alone that my country is fair,
20 And my home and my friends are inviting me there;
While they beckon me onward, my heart is still here,
With my sweet lovely daughter, and bonny boy dear;
And oh! what's the joy that a home can impart,
Removed from the dear ones who cling to my heart.

25 It is learning that calls them; but tell me, can schools
Repay for my love, or give nature new rules?
They may teach them the lore of the wit and the sage,
To be grave in their youth, and be gay in their age;
But ah! my poor heart, what are schools to thy view,
30 While severed from children thou lovest so true!

I return to my country, I haste on my way,
For duty commands me, and duty must sway;
Yet I leave the bright land where my little ones dwell,
With a sober regret, and a bitter farewell;
35 For there I must leave the dear jewels I love,
The dearest of gifts from my Master above.
    —1851

JOSÉ MARÍA HEREDIA

1803 – 1839

In 1888, José Martí, a Cuban poet and political exile, declared José María Heredia "the first poet of America." A leader of the Romantic movement in Spanish-language literature, and now the national poet of Cuba, Heredia was a pioneering figure in hemispheric American literary history whose innova-

tive poetry responded to locations and histories specific to the Americas. Heredia was also an important "poet of America" in a narrower sense, in that he spent a short but formative part of his life in the United States, where he published the first edition of his only poetry collection to appear in his lifetime, *Poesías* (*Poems*, 1825). Heredia's time in the U.S. strengthened his commitment to independence for all the Americas, especially Cuba, and his encounters with the U.S. literary scene and with North American landscapes shaped some of his most characteristic and famous poems, such as "Niágara" ("Niagara," 1825). Heredia's poetry, in turn, was celebrated and translated by U.S. writers. Accordingly, his work claims a place in U.S. literary history, highlighting the connections between U.S.-American literature and the multi-lingual and multi-national literatures of the rest of the Americas.

Born in the Cuban city of Santiago de Cuba on the last day of 1803, Heredia belonged to the elite ruling class of Spain's American colonies. His family came from the Spanish colony of Santo Domingo, where they had owned coffee plantations worked by enslaved laborers. When the Haitian Revolution broke out in the neighboring French portion of the island, the family fled to Cuba. Heredia's father, a Spanish colonial magistrate, went on to hold a succession of posts in Florida, Venezuela, and Mexico as well as Cuba, so Heredia spent his early years moving frequently throughout Spanish America. During this itinerant upbringing, Heredia received a classical education and soon proved himself something of a child prodigy: capable, when he was only eight, of translating from Latin the work of the Roman poet Horace. Heredia's burgeoning poetic imagination was also fed, in a different way, by the wars of independence being waged throughout Spanish America during his youth. The ongoing freedom struggles he witnessed in Venezuela and Mexico aligned with his own spontaneous, creative temperament to give rise to what would become his central commitment to *libertad* (liberty) in all forms, personal and literary as well as public and political. This emerging commitment shaped the poetry Heredia began writing in his teens, as well as the political activity he undertook as a law student in Cuba in the early 1820s, which included advocating for Cuban independence and the abolition of slavery. In 1823, charged with participation in an anti-colonial conspiracy, he had to flee Cuba and went into exile in the United States.

Heredia's time in the U.S. is amply documented in his letters, which describe the genesis of much of his poetry together with his personal sufferings and aspirations as an exile, his dislike of the English language and northern winters, and his admiration for U.S. political institutions and for the places he saw in the course of his travels. After arriving in Boston in the dead of winter, he stated his intention, in one of his first letters, "to deal head on with the English language, or to work a bit more on my poetry" before noting that "I don't know whether you will understand these last paragraphs because the ink is well nigh frozen." He quickly resettled in New York City and began dealing "head on" with English by translating into Spanish an array of English-language works, including the poetry of Lord Byron and the republican political rhetoric of the U.S. orator Daniel Webster. Heredia's translating spurred his own poetry-writing, as did his travels throughout the U.S.: a visit to sites from the country's revolutionary history, including Philadelphia and Mount Vernon, inspired his "Ode to Washington," while a trip to Niagara Falls prompted "Niágara."

Heredia's poetry was further encouraged by—and capitalized on—a surge of U.S.-American interest in Spanish language and literature; as one New York newspaper put it at the time, "The great business of the day is learning Spanish and Italian." The publishing houses of New York and Philadelphia also did extensive business printing Spanish-language books for distribution in Latin America. When Heredia's *Poesías* appeared in New York in the summer of 1825, it was targeted at domestic as well as international markets: a foreword in both Spanish and English explained that Heredia had endeavored "to make these poems useful to Americans learning the Spanish language," but the publisher also set aside copies for sale in Cuba and Mexico.

Poesías showcases Heredia's classical roots, as well as the qualities that made him a trailblazing American Romantic. He worked largely in established poetic forms, especially the *silva*, a form popular with Heredia's poetic generation that consists of hendecasyllabic (eleven-syllable) lines, together with occasional heptasyllabic (seven-syllable) lines; Spanish poets of the period—Heredia very much included—built intricate variations of rhyme and stanza length into this form. (Both of the poems by Heredia included below are *silvas*.) Heredia's poetry, however, balances formal polish with a deliberately unrefined diction and style. He used *cultismos* (learned words) and classical allusions sparingly, aiming instead for a freer, more direct poetic style that hews closer to living, spoken language. This goal aligns with Heredia's poetic emphasis on spontaneity, emotional sincerity, and depth of feeling. In these respects, Heredia's poetry reflects the Romanticism that, by the time he started writing, was well-established in British and German literature but was only beginning to make itself felt in both Spanish-language literature and the literatures of the Americas. A further quintessentially Romantic aspect of Heredia's poetry is his receptiveness to nature and the sublime—a quality abundantly on display in poems such as "Niágara."

Yet Heredia's poetry differentiates itself from its European Romantic antecedents by its focus on distinctively American locations and features: not just Niagara Falls, but also the hurricanes of his native Caribbean, as in "En una tempestad" ("In a Storm," 1822), or the pyramids and volcanos of Mexico, as in "En el teocalli de Cholula" ("In the Pyramid of Cholula," 1820). As Martí contended when hailing Heredia as "the first poet of America," "Only he has put in his verses the sublimity, pomp, and fire of [America's] nature. He is volcanic like its core, and serene like its heights." In addition, Heredia's poetry reinvents, in a specifically American form, another hallmark of much European literary Romanticism: its revolutionary politics. Heredia transmutes this aspect of his literary inheritance into a consistent call for anticolonial liberation, in Cuba and throughout the Americas. In the words of an 1849 U.S.-American review of Heredia's work, "Thoughts of sorrow or of hope for Cuba underlie almost all his poems."

Poesías met with acclaim in the United States and throughout the Americas, as well as in Western Europe. As Heredia himself put it in a letter to his mother, "These poems have been rather well received here; and the periodicals have praised them to exaggeration." The *New-York American* described the poems as possessing "traits of the truest genius" and went on to print a lengthy Spanish review asserting that Heredia "may be as sure of the esteem of his compatriots as he is the hatred of tyrants." Heredia's work was also applauded by fellow Latin American exiles and by Spanish intellectuals. This international acclaim brought to a close Heredia's U.S. period: at the personal invitation of the Mexican president, he left the U.S. in August 1825 for Mexico, where he spent most of the rest of his life. In Mexico, Heredia served in various governmental and educational positions, wrote and staged plays, edited literary reviews and newspapers, translated English-language works such as Sir Walter Scott's *Waverley*, and revised and expanded *Poesías*, a second edition of which was published in 1832. His continued involvement in plots to liberate Cuba from Spain earned him a death sentence *in absentia* in 1831, but near the end of his life he was able to make an arrangement with the colonial authorities that allowed him to visit Cuba to see his mother. He died of tuberculosis in Mexico in 1839.

If Heredia's time in the U.S. played a pivotal role in his literary career, his poetry also had an impact on U.S. literary culture. Through at least the mid-nineteenth century, U.S. critics continued to praise Heredia as, in the words of one 1849 reviewer, one of "the noblest and loftiest poets of Spanish America" and "first among the poets of his country." In particular, William Cullen Bryant, a leading U.S. poet, was influenced by Heredia's work, which he greatly admired. Bryant used a free translation of "En una tempestad" as the basis for his poem "The Hurricane," and he was also involved in writing a popular, anonymously published translation of "Niágara" that helped disseminate Heredia's poetry in North America. In Latin America, and especially in Cuba, Heredia's reputation went from strength to strength: new editions of his poetry appeared consistently throughout the nineteenth century and into the twentieth, and today, "El Cantor del Niagara," as he is known, is securely canonized within Latin American literary history. Scholarly interest in Heredia's U.S. period and the poetry resulting from it began to increase in the mid-twentieth century, and contemporary scholarship continues to explore his work's implications for evolving definitions of "American" literature and for efforts to trace the enduring links among the literatures of the Americas.

———————

NOTE ON THE TEXTS: Two different versions of "Niágara" were published in Heredia's lifetime, in the 1825 and 1832 editions of *Poesías*. The English-language version of the poem presented below is based on the translation of the 1825 version, by Thatcher Taylor Payne and William Cullen Bryant, that was printed anonymously in *The United States Review and Literary Gazette* in 1827. The text of this translation has been modernized in accordance with the practices of this anthology. The full Spanish-language text of the 1832 version of "Niágara" appears in the anthology's website portion, along with the scholar Frederick Luciani's 2020 translation of this version.

The text of the original Spanish excerpt of Heredia's "A Washington" ("To Washington") included below is based on that of the 1832 edition of *Poesías*, in which this poem was first printed; we present this Spanish-language excerpt together with a new English translation, completed especially for this anthology by Rodrigo Lazo.

⌘ ⌘ ⌘

Niagara

From the Spanish of José Maria Heredia

My lyre![1] give me my lyre! my bosom feels
The glow of inspiration. Oh how long
Have I been left in darkness since this light
Last visited my brow. Niagara!
5   Thou with thy rushing waters dost restore
The heavenly gift that sorrow took away.

    Tremendous torrent! for an instant hush
The terrors of thy voice and cast aside
Those wide involving° shadows, that my eyes   *enveloping*
10 May see the fearful beauty of thy face!
I am not all unworthy of thy sight,
For from my very boyhood have I loved,
Shunning the meaner° track of common minds,   *cruder*
To look on nature in her loftier moods.
15 At the fierce rushing of the hurricane,
At the near bursting of the thunderbolt
I have been touched with joy; and when the sea,

Lashed by the wind, hath rocked my bark°   *ship*
and showed
Its yawning caves beneath me, I have loved
20 Its dangers and the wrath of elements.
But never yet the madness of the sea
Hath moved me as thy grandeur moves me now.

    Thou flowest on in quiet, till thy waves
Grow broken 'midst the rocks; thy current then
25 Shoots onward like the irresistible course
Of destiny. Ah, terribly they rage—
The hoarse and rapid whirlpools there! My brain
Grows wild, my senses wander, as I gaze
Upon the hurrying waters, and my sight
30 Vainly would follow, as toward the verge
Sweeps the wide torrent—waves innumerable
Meet there and madden—waves innumerable
Urge on and overtake the waves before,
And disappear in thunder and in foam.

35   They reach—they leap the barrier—the abyss
Swallows insatiable the sinking waves.
A thousand rainbows arch them, and woods
Are deafened with the roar. The violent shock
Shatters to vapor the descending sheets—

———————

[1]   *lyre*   Stringed instrument resembling a harp, traditionally used (for example, in ancient Greece) to accompany song or the performance of poetry.

40 A cloudy whirlwind fills the gulf, and heaves
The mighty pyramid of circling mist
To heaven. The solitary hunter near
Pauses with terror in the forest shades.

What seeks my restless eye? Why are not here,
45 About the jaws of this abyss, the palms—
Ah—the delicious° palms, that on the plains   *delightful*
Of my own native Cuba, spring and spread
Their thickly foliaged summits to the sun,
And, in the breathings of the ocean air,
50 Wave soft beneath the heaven's unspotted blue?

But no, Niagara—thy forest pines
Are fitter coronal° for thee. The palm,   *garland, crown*
The effeminate myrtle, and frail rose may grow
In gardens, and give out their fragrance there,
55 Unmanning him who breathes it. Thine it is
To do a nobler office. Generous minds
Behold thee, and are moved, and learn to rise
Above earth's frivolous pleasures; they partake
Thy grandeur at the utterance of thy name.

60 God of all truth! in other lands I've seen
Lying philosophers,[1] blaspheming men,
Questioners of thy mysteries, that draw
Their fellows deep into impiety,
And therefore doth my spirit seek thy face
65 In earth's majestic solitudes. Even here
My heart doth open all itself to thee.
In this immensity of loneliness
I feel thy hand upon me. To my ear
The eternal thunder of the cataract brings
70 Thy voice, and I am humbled as I hear.

Dread torrent! that with wonder and with fear
Dost overwhelm the soul of him that looks

Upon thee, and dost bear it from itself,
Whence hast thou thy beginning? Who supplies,
75 Age after age, thy unexhausted springs?
What power hath ordered, that, when all thy weight
Descends into the deep, the swollen waves
Rise not, and roll to overwhelm the earth?

The Lord hath opened his omnipotent hand,
80 Covered thy face with clouds, and given his voice
To thy down-rushing waters; he hath girt
Thy terrible forehead with his radiant bow.[2]
I see thy never-resting waters run,
And I bethink me how the tide of time
85 Sweeps to eternity. So pass of man—
Pass, like a noon-day dream—the blossoming days,
And he awakes to sorrow. I, alas!
Feel that my youth is withered, and my brow
Ploughed early with the lines of grief and care.

90 Never have I so deeply felt as now
The hopeless solitude, the abandonment,
The anguish of a loveless life. Alas!
How can the impassioned, the unfrozen heart
Be happy without love? I would that one
95 Beautiful—worthy to be loved and joined
In love with me—now shared my lonely walk
On this tremendous brink. 'T were sweet to see
Her dear face touched with paleness, and become
More beautiful from fear, and overspread
100 With a faint smile while clinging to my side!
Dreams—dreams. I am an exile, and for me
There is no country and there is no love.

Hear, dread Niagara, my latest voice!
Yet a few years and the cold earth shall close
105 Over the bones of him who sings thee now
Thus feelingly. Would that this, my humble verse,
Might be like thee, immortal. I, meanwhile,
Cheerfully passing to the appointed rest,
Might raise my radiant forehead in the clouds
110 To listen to the echoes of my fame.
—1825 (TRANSLATION PUBLISHED 1827)

1 *God … Lying philosophers* In the revised version of "Niágara" that Heredia published in the 1832 edition of *Poesías*, an additional eight lines appear between these two. These further lines, which Heredia either composed later and added to the 1832 version of the poem or deliberately excluded from the poem's 1825 publication, are translated as follows in Frederick Luciani's 2020 translation of the 1832 version (which appears in full in the website portion of this anthology): "I have seen execrable men / Your holy name blaspheme, / Impious fanaticism sow, / Fields engulf in blood and tears, / Lay waste in war the very earth, / And turn brother into foe. / I saw these, and my heart would swell / In righteous wrath."

2 *What power … bow* See Genesis 9.9–17, in which, after the Flood, God makes the rainbow the sign of his promise to never again send another flood to destroy all life.

from *To Washington*

A Washington

(Escrita en Monte Vernon)

Primero en paz y en guerra.
primero en el afecto de tu patria
Y en la veneración del universo.
Viva imagen de Dios sobre la tierra,
5   libertador, legislador y justo,
Washington inmortal, oye benigno
el débil canto de tu gloria indigno,
con que voy a ensalzar tu nombre augusto.

¿Te pintaré indignado
10   a la voz de la patria dolorida
volar al arduo campo de la gloria,
y como Jove en el Olimpo, armado,
a la suerte mandar y a la victoria?
Magnánimo apareces;
15   ríndese Boston, y respira libre.
Vanamente el tirano
cuarenta mil esclavos lanza fiero
para extirpar el nombre americano.

To Washington[1]

(Composed at Mount Vernon[2])

"First in war, first in peace,
first in the hearts of your countrymen,"[3]
and the veneration of the globe.
A liberator, a legislator, a just leader,
5   living image of God on earth,
immortal Washington, kindly hear
my humble and unworthy song
which will exalt your respected name.

Should I portray you alarmed
10   at your country's suffering cry,
flying to the glory of the battlefield,
armed, like Jove on Olympus,[4]
to command fortune and victory?
Benevolent you appear;
15   Boston surrenders and breathes freely.[5]
Vainly does the proud tyrant
send forty-thousand slave-troops[6]
to erase the name "American."

---

[1]   Translated by Rodrigo Lazo for Broadview Press, 2021.

[2]   *Mount Vernon*   Washington's plantation estate on the banks of the Potomac River in Virginia, which he owned from 1761 until his death in 1799. At the time of Heredia's stay in the United States, the estate was still owned by the Washington family but was falling into disrepair.

[3]   *First ... countrymen*   Heredia's opening lines play on a well-known passage from Washington's funeral oration, delivered in 1799 by Henry Lee: "First in war, first in peace, and first in the hearts of his countrymen."

[4]   *Jove on Olympus*   "Jove" is a Roman name for Zeus, king of the Greek gods, said to dwell on Mount Olympus.

[5]   *Boston ... freely*   After the outbreak of the Revolutionary War in April 1775, American militia laid siege to the British troops occupying Boston; Washington took command of the besieging forces in July 1775, and the British were eventually forced out of the city in March 1776.

[6]   *slave-troops*   In the nineteenth century, the word "slavery" was commonly used in general terms, including by Heredia and his circle, to describe subjugation to tyrannical authority. Heredia is here characterizing the troops sent to America by King George III as servile subjects of such authority.

[A Washington *cont'd*]

Tú, sin baldón, al número cediste,
20 y acallando el espíritu guerrero,
a tu gloria, la patria, preferiste.
Así del pueblo eterno los caudillos
al vencedor Aníbal contemplaron
con inmutable frente,
25 y la invasión rugiente
a la púnica rechazaron.

Mas luego, una noche de feliz memoria,
del Delaware el vacilante hielo
ofreció a tu valor y patrio celo,
30 el camino del triunfo y de la gloria.
La sobervia británica humillada
es por ultimo en York, y su caudillo
tinde a tus pies la ponderosa espada.
El universo atónito saluda
35 a la triunfante América, y te adora,

[To Washington *cont'd*]

With honor, you retreat before the number[1]
20 and, tempering the martial spirit,
Protect your true glory, your country.
Just so, the leaders of the Eternal City
looked down on triumphant Hannibal,
keeping a calm front,[2]
25 and on the Punic coast turned away
the bellowing invasion.[3]

And later, on a memorable brilliant night,
the unsteady ice on the Delaware
honored your bravery and love of country,
30 opening a route to triumph and glory.[4]
Proud Britain is finally trampled
at York,[5] and her kingpin[6]
yields the sword at your feet.
The astonished world salutes
35 triumphant America, and adores you,

---

[1] *you ... number* In the summer and fall of 1776, Washington gradually withdrew his Continental Army from New York City and its vicinity in the face of a much larger British force.

[2] [Translator's note] My use of "front" here draws from the Spanish "frente," which can also mean forehead.

[3] *Just so ... invasion* In the Second Punic War (218–201 BCE), the second of three wars between Rome ("the Eternal City") and the North African city-state of Carthage, Carthaginian (also known as Punic) forces led by the general Hannibal invaded Roman territory in Italy. Hannibal won several significant victories, but the Romans were eventually able to wear his army down by avoiding major battles and waging a prolonged war of attrition; in the meantime, another Roman army attacked Carthaginian territory ("the Punic coast"), compelling Hannibal to leave Italy and pursue them there, where he was conclusively defeated. Heredia is here comparing Washington's strategic withdrawals in the face of overwhelming British strength to the delaying tactics that ultimately enabled Rome to defeat Hannibal.

[4] *And later ... glory* Reference to Washington's famous crossing of the icy Delaware River on the night of 25–26 December 1776, a daring move that enabled him to launch a successful surprise attack on the garrison of Hessians (German mercenaries fighting for the British) in Trenton, New Jersey, the following day.

[5] *Proud Britain ... York* Reference to Washington's victory at the Battle of Yorktown (1781), the final British defeat of the Revolutionary War, which compelled the British to recognize American independence.

[6] *kingpin* The Spanish word Heredia uses here, "caudillo," connotes an authoritarian ruler who wields power arbitrarily and coercively.

[A Washington *cont'd*]

mientras que la metrópoli sañuda
tu gloria bella y su baldón devora.
Mas cuando por la paz inutil viste
de libertad la espada en tu alta mano,
40   el poder soberano
como insufrible carga depusiste.

Alzado a la primer magistratura,
de tu patria la suerte coronaste,
y en cimientos eternos afirmaste
45   la paz, la libertad sublime y pura. ...

En la tumba modesta,
que guarda tus cenizas por Tesoro,
ni luce el mármol, ni centella el oro,
ni entallado laurel ni palmas veo.
50   ¿Para qué, si es un mundo
a tu gloria inmortal digno trofeo?
Con estupor profundo
por tu genio creador lo miro alzado
hasta la cumbre de moral grandeza.
55   Potente y con virtud; libre y tranquilo;
esclavo de las leyes;[1]
del universe asilo;
Asombro de naciones y de reyes.
    —1832 (WRITTEN 1824)

[To Washington *cont'd*]

while the empire chokes on its disgrace,
rages at your beautiful glory.
But when peace covers with liberty
The sword in your august hand,
40   Sovereign power over the land
You decline as insufferable misery.

Elected to the highest office,
you crowned your country with prosperity
and set an eternal foundation of peace
45   based on pure and sublime liberty. ...

At your humble tomb[2]
that guards your ashes as a treasure,
I see neither laurel nor palm[3]
Neither gold nor marble adornments.
50   Why bother, if your trophy
is a world of immortal glory?
With profound modesty, I watch
Your ingenious creation rise
to the summit of moral greatness.
55   Peace, liberty and virtue disburse
Laws that bring cooperation;
Refuge for the universe;
Astonishment for monarchs and nations.
    —2021

---

[1]   [Translator's note]   Heredia invokes slavery to emphasize subservience to laws in the new republic. An alternate interpretation and potential translation would take the word "esclavo" as an enslaved person under the new constitution, and thus that image would clash with the veneration of the new country in the surrounding lines. [Washington enslaved African Americans throughout his life, but—unlike most other slaveholding founders—he emancipated all enslaved people he owned in his will. By the time of Heredia's stay in the United States, both pro- and antislavery factions were claiming Washington's legacy to support their own positions. Heredia voiced antislavery sentiments elsewhere in his work, but his writing from his U.S. period is silent on the subject of American slavery.]

[2]   *your humble tomb*   Washington was initially buried in a modest family vault at Mount Vernon. He had left instructions for the construction of a new funeral vault in his will, but this was not carried out until 1831.

[3]   *neither laurel nor palm*   In ancient Greece and Rome, laurel wreaths were given in recognition of high achievement, including victory in battle; palm leaves are also traditional symbols of victory and honor.

Lydia Maria Child

1802 – 1880

Lydia Maria Child's work was so diverse, so prolific, and so widely read that, as her first biographer wrote, "she seemed to supply a sufficient literature for any family through her own unaided pen" as the author of novels, domestic handbooks, stories for children, and more. But Child rapidly fell from the height of her popularity when she began to publish abolitionist writing far too radical for the mainstream taste she had served. For portions of her career, her uncompromising articulation of her views on slavery—and on other matters such as interracial marriage, Indigenous-settler relations, gender roles, and the equality of religions—garnered her boycotts and mainstream derision. It also produced an incisive and rich body of fiction and nonfiction addressing the concerns most pertinent to nineteenth-century American society.

Child was born in Massachusetts in 1802, the youngest daughter of Convers and Susannah Rand Francis. Her devoutly Calvinist parents generally disapproved of academic pursuits—especially for girls—so her formal education was limited to that offered by local public schools. Her literary interests were encouraged, however, by her elder brother Convers. In 1815, following the deaths of her mother and several other family members, Child was sent to live with a married elder sister in rural Maine, where Child worked briefly as a schoolteacher but was expected primarily to cultivate her domestic skills. In 1821, however, she had the opportunity to live again with her brother Convers near Boston; here she became increasingly immersed in the study of literature, history, religion, and philosophy, and met other future literary luminaries such as Ralph Waldo Emerson.

As early as the publication of her first novel, *Hobomok: A Tale of Early Times* (1824), Child began to court both the controversy and the popularity that together would define her career. The novel, which she wrote in a matter of weeks, was set in early colonial Massachusetts and largely inspired by Child's encounter with J.W. Eastburn and R.C. Sands's epic poem *Yamoyden: A Tale of the Wars of King Philip* (1820). *Hobomok* itself dramatized the settler-Indigenous relations of early colonial Massachusetts and Plymouth, and depicted a short-lived marriage between its Puritan heroine and the Native American Hobomok. It was this element that was perceived as scandalous by many white readers, who balked at the depiction of an interracial marriage as well as at Child's generally sympathetic—if stereotypical—portrayal of Massachusett Indigenous culture. One article in the *North American Review* called the subject matter "revolting," and initial sales of the book's one-thousand-copy print run were slow. Nevertheless, *Hobomok* was received favorably by an influential minority. Child actively sought out the support of respected literary scholar George Ticknor; he took her on as a protégée, and she soon became a minor celebrity in Boston circles.

Buoyed by the support of the Boston literary establishment and motivated to achieve financial independence, Child continued to mine the increasingly popular field of colonial history for her subsequent publications. Her novel *The Rebels, or Boston before the Revolution* (1825) centered on the American Revolution; *The First Settlers of New England* (1828) was a nonfiction book aimed at children. Child furthered her reputation by founding *The Juvenile Miscellany*, a very successful magazine in the burgeoning genre of children's literature, and she cemented her celebrity in 1829 with *The Frugal Housewife*, a wildly popular handbook whose topics encompassed cookery, domestic economy, and parenting. In 1828 she married David Lee Child, a struggling lawyer and journalist; together they edited *The Massachusetts Journal*, while Child's more lucrative publications continued to provide their primary income. By the time Child released *The Mother's Book*, a parenting handbook, in 1831, she was one of the most popular writers in the country; as a critic for the *North American Review* asserted in July 1833, Child was, as an author and public figure, "just the woman we want for the mothers and daughters of the present generation."

A month after that review was published, Child released *An Appeal in Favor of that Class of Americans Called Africans*—a work unlike anything she had published before. Partially instigated by Child's recent friendship with radical abolitionist William Lloyd Garrison, the *Appeal* was the result of three years' study, informed by abolitionist editorials, Southern newspaper reports and registers of enslaved people, and histories of Africa and of the slave trade. While Child's writings had previously hinted at moderately antislavery sentiments, the majority of her audience were unprepared for the exhaustively researched and fervently articulated abolitionism of her *Appeal*. The work condemned Southern slavery in the strongest terms, denounced racism in the North, and went so far as to express sympathy for enslaved people who engaged in violent resistance, comparing it to the "blood [shed] for the sake of liberty" during the American Revolution. The influence on her argument of African American writers such as David Walker—whose *Appeal to the Colored Citizens of the World* had caused a storm of controversy in 1829— was clear. Readers were scandalized, and many canceled their subscriptions to the *Juvenile Miscellany* in response, causing Child to relinquish her editorial position; she also lost the patronage of Ticknor. At the same time, the abolitionist press welcomed the text; numerous anecdotes were shared of enslavers who had "converted" to the abolitionist cause upon reading her work. Child's *Appeal* would prove to be among the most influential antislavery texts of the era. One review in *The Unionist* called it "altogether one of the most valuable publications which have for a long time fallen under our eye."

Child continued to be a household name, but her sphere of influence changed and her work was for several decades dominated by antislavery activism, as well as by a wide range of other influential nonfiction works such as *History of the Condition of Women, In Various Ages and Nations* (1835). She also continued to write short stories, many of them centered on the subjects of slavery and racism, for various publications. In 1841, she began writing for New York City's *National Anti-Slavery Standard*, to which she contributed a popular column that came to be known as "Letters from New York"; her 1843 collection of these letters sold out within months. The epistles covered a wide variety of social, moral, and philosophical topics that were generally deemed inappropriate for women writers, including prison reform, prostitution, and gender equality. Child also vehemently criticized Indian Removal and other federal policies concerning Native Americans, though her proposed alternatives were often paternalistic and assimilationist, grounded in the view that Indigenous people were inherently equal to but "less advanced" than Europeans.

As the Civil War broke out, Child often expressed frustration with the Lincoln administration for its emphasis on preserving the Union over abolishing slavery; during Reconstruction, she criticized the regressive racial policies that characterized much of the post-slavery nation. Her 1865 reader *The Freedmen's Book* was a diverse collection of inspirational biographies, poems, and other writings by both white and African American authors, dedicated by Child "to the freedmen" with the hope that readers would "derive fresh strength and courage from this true record of what colored men have accomplished, under great disadvantages." Child published her final novel, *A Romance of the Republic*, in 1867; it returned to the subject of interracial marriage, this time envisioning a positive future relationship between African Americans and white Americans.

Child died in 1880, two years after the death of her husband. A funeral address was given by abolitionist and orator Wendell Phillips, who celebrated both her literary achievements and her lifelong pursuit of social justice. In the late nineteenth century, a decline in interest in abolitionist figures led to reduced attention to Child's work, but the breadth of her intellectual contributions helped to ensure that she was regularly discussed—as an essayist, as a novelist, as a writer for children—throughout much of the twentieth century and into the twenty-first. Recent criticism has focused increasingly on her fiction, addressing the ways in which her depictions of colonialism and Indigenous societies both challenge and conform to nineteenth-century prejudices. Yet Child's nonfiction remains central to her importance—and her *Appeal* in particular remains a seminal work of historical scholarship, as well as a salient condemnation of racism and a prescient analysis of the social, political, and economic effects of slavery on the United States.

NOTE ON THE TEXT: The text presented here is based on that appearing in the 1843 edition of Child's *Letters from New-York*. Spelling and punctuation have been modernized in accordance with the practices of this anthology.

⌘ ⌘ ⌘

from *Letters from New-York*

LETTER 34
WOMAN'S RIGHTS

January, 1843

You ask what are my opinions about "Woman's Rights." I confess a strong distaste for the subject, as it has been generally treated. On no other theme, probably, has there been uttered so much of false, mawkish sentiment, shallow philosophy, and sputtering, farthing-candle wit. If the style of its advocates has often been offensive to taste, and unacceptable to reason, assuredly that of its opponents have been still more so. College boys have amused themselves with writing dreams in which they saw women in hotels, with their feet hoisted, and chairs tilted back, or growling and bickering at each other in legislative halls, or fighting at the polls, with eyes blackened by fisticuffs. But it never seems to have occurred to these facetious writers that the proceedings which appear so ludicrous and improper in women are also ridiculous and disgraceful in men. It were well that men should learn not to hoist their feet above their heads, and tilt their chairs backward, not to growl and snap in the halls of legislation, or give each other black eyes at the polls.

Maria Edgeworth[1] says, "We are disgusted when we see a woman's mind overwhelmed with a torrent of learning; that the tide of literature has passed over it should be betrayed only by its fertility." This is beautiful and true; but is it not likewise applicable to man? The truly great never seek to display themselves. If they carry their heads high above the crowd, it is only made manifest to others by accidental revelations of their extended vision. "Human duties and proprieties do not lie so very far apart," said Harriet Martineau;[2] "if they did, there would be two gospels, and two teachers, one for man, and another for woman."

It would seem, indeed, as if men were willing to give women the exclusive benefit of gospel-teaching. "Women should be gentle," say the advocates of subordination; but when Christ said, "Blessed are the meek," did he preach to women only? "Girls should be modest," is the language of common teaching, continually uttered in words and customs. Would it not be an improvement for men, also, to be scrupulously pure in manners, conversation and life? Books addressed to young married people abound with advice to the wife, to control her temper, and never to utter wearisome complaints, or vexatious words, when the husband comes home fretful or unreasonable, from his out-of-door conflicts with the world. Would not the advice be as excellent and appropriate, if the husband were advised to conquer his fretfulness, and forbear his complaints, in consideration of his wife's ill-health, fatiguing cares, and the thousand disheartening influences of domestic routine? In short, whatsoever can be named as loveliest, best, and most graceful in woman, would likewise be good and graceful in man. You will perhaps remind me of courage? If you use the word in its highest

---

[1] *Maria Edgeworth* Anglo-Irish writer who wrote widely on subjects such as education and the intellectual equality of women; Child may be alluding to a passage from Edgeworth's *Letters for Literary Ladies* (1795): "When you say that men of superior understanding dislike the appearance of extraordinary strength of mind in the fair sex, you probably mean that the display of that strength is disgusting."

[2] *Harriet Martineau* English writer and social theorist who had written in support of Child's abolitionist writing in 1838. Child is likely paraphrasing from Martineau's *Society in America* (1837), which was written after her extended tour of the United States.

signification, I answer that woman, above others, hath abundant need of it, in her pilgrimage; and the true woman wears it with a quiet grace. If you mean mere animal courage, that is not mentioned in the sermon on the Mount, among those qualities which enable us to inherit the earth, or become the children of God. That the feminine ideal approaches much nearer to the gospel standard than the prevalent idea of manhood is shown by the universal tendency to represent the Saviour and his most beloved disciple with mild, meek expression, and feminine beauty. None speak of the bravery, the might, or the intellect of Jesus; but the devil is always imagined as a being of acute intellect, political cunning, and the fiercest courage. These universal and instinctive tendencies of the human mind reveal much.

That the present position of women in society is the result of physical force is obvious enough; whosoever doubts it, let her reflect why she is afraid to go out in the evening without the protection of a man. What constitutes the danger of aggression? Superior physical strength, uncontrolled by the moral sentiments. If physical strength were in complete subjection to moral influence, there would be no need of outward protection. That animal instinct and brute force now govern the world is painfully apparent in the condition of women everywhere; from the Morduan Tartars,[1] whose ceremony of marriage consists in placing the bride on a mat, and consigning her to the bridegroom, with the words, "Here, wolf, take thy lamb"—to the German remark, that "stiff ale, stinging tobacco, and a girl in her smart dress, are the best things." The same thing, softened by the refinements of civilization, peeps out in Stephen's remark, that "woman never looks so interesting, as when leaning on the arm of a soldier";[2] and in Hazlitt's complaint that "it is not easy to keep up a conversation with women in company. It is thought a piece of rudeness to differ from them; it is not quite fair to ask them a reason for what they say."[3]

This sort of politeness to women is what men call gallantry; an odious word to every sensible woman,

because she sees that it is merely the flimsy veil which foppery[4] throws over sensuality, to conceal its grossness.[5] So far is it from indicating sincere esteem and affection for women, that the profligacy of a nation may, in general, be fairly measured by its gallantry. This taking away rights, and condescending to grant privileges, is an old trick of the physical force principle; and with the immense majority, who only look on the surface of things, this mask effectually disguises an ugliness, which would otherwise be abhorred. The most inveterate slave-holders are probably those who take most pride in dressing their household servants handsomely, and who would be most ashamed to have the name of being unnecessarily cruel. And profligates, who form the lowest and most sensual estimate of women, are the very ones to treat them with an excess of outward deference.

There are few books which I can read through without feeling insulted as a woman; but this insult is almost universally conveyed through that which was intended for praise. Just imagine, for a moment, what impression it would make on men if women authors should write about their "rosy lips," and "melting eyes," and "voluptuous forms," as they write about us! That women in general do not feel this kind of flattery to be an insult, I readily admit; for, in the first place, they do not perceive the gross chattel-principle,[6] of which it is the utterance; moreover, they have, from long habit, become accustomed to consider themselves as household conveniences, or gilded toys. Hence, they consider it feminine and pretty to abjure all such use of their faculties as would make them co-workers with man in the advancement of those great principles, on which the progress of society depends. "There is perhaps no animal," says Hannah More,[7] "so much indebted to subordination, for its good behaviour, as

---

[1]   *Morduan Tartars*   Turkic ethnic group residing in central Asia.

[2]   *Stephen's remark … soldier*   Paraphrased from American explorer and diplomat John Lloyd Stephen's *Incidents of Travel in the Russian and Turkish Empires* (1839).

[3]   *Hazlitt's … they say*   From English writer William Hazlitt's essay "On the Conversation of Authors" (1820).

[4]   *foppery*   Affected elegance.

[5]   *grossness*   Unrefined nature.

[6]   *chattel-principle*   I.e., the principle that women are the property of men.

[7]   *Hannah More*   English poet, playwright, and religious writer (1745–1833) who advocated education for women but also criticized many of the proto-feminist writings of her era. More and her sister Martha ran a number of so-called "Charity Schools" for the poor. The quotation is from a 1793 letter More wrote to the Earl of Orford.

woman." Alas, for the animal age, in which such utterance could be tolerated by public sentiment!

Martha More, sister of Hannah, describing a very impressive scene at the funeral of one of her Charity School teachers, says, "The spirit within seemed struggling to speak, and I was in a sort of agony; but I recollected that I had heard, somewhere, a woman must not speak in the church. Oh, had she been buried in the church-yard, a messenger from Mr. Pitt[1] himself should not have restrained me; for I seemed to have received a message from a higher Master within."

This application of theological teaching carries its own commentary.

I have said enough to show that I consider prevalent opinions and customs highly unfavourable to the moral and intellectual development of women: and I need not say that, in proportion to their true culture,[2] women will be more useful and happy, and domestic life more perfected. True culture in them, as in men, consists in the full and free development of individual character, regulated by their own perceptions of what is true, and their own love of what is good.

This individual responsibility is rarely acknowledged, even by the most refined, as necessary to the spiritual progress of women. I once heard a very beautiful lecture from R.W. Emerson, on Being and Seeming.[3] In the course of many remarks, as true as they were graceful, he urged women to be, rather than seem. He told them that all their laboured education of forms, strict observance of genteel etiquette, tasteful arrangement of the toilette,[4] etc., all this seeming would not gain hearts like being truly what God made them; that earnest simplicity, the sincerity of nature, would kindle the eye, light up the countenance, and give an inexpressible charm to the plainest features.

The advice was excellent, but the motive by which it was urged brought a flush of indignation over my face. Men were exhorted to be, rather than to seem, that they

might fulfil the sacred mission for which their souls were embodied; that they might, in God's freedom, grow up into the full stature of spiritual manhood; but women were urged to simplicity and truthfulness, that they might become more pleasing.

Are we not all immortal beings? Is not each one responsible for himself and herself? There is no measuring the mischief done by the prevailing tendency to teach women to be virtuous as a duty to man, rather than to God—for the sake of pleasing the creature,[5] rather than the Creator. "God is thy law, thou mine,"[6] said Eve to Adam. May Milton be forgiven for sending that thought "out into everlasting time" in such a jewelled setting. What weakness, vanity, frivolity, infirmity of moral purpose, sinful flexibility of principle—in a word, what soul-stifling, has been the result of thus putting man in the place of God!

But while I see plainly that society is on a false foundation, and that prevailing views concerning women indicate the want of wisdom and purity, which they serve to perpetuate—still, I must acknowledge that much of the talk about women's rights offends both my reason and my taste. I am not of those who maintain there is no sex in souls; nor do I like the results deducible from that doctrine. Kinmont,[7] in his admirable book, called *The Natural History of Men*, speaking of the warlike courage of the ancient German women, and of their being respectfully consulted on important public affairs, says, "You ask me if I consider all this right, and deserving of approbation; or that women were here engaged in their appropriate tasks? I answer, yes; it is just as right that they should take this interest in the honour of their country, as the other sex. Of course, I do not think that women were made for war and battle; neither do I believe that men were. But since the fashion of the times had made it so, and settled it that war was a necessary element of greatness, and that no safety was to be procured without it, I argue that it shows a healthful state of feeling in other respects, that the

---

[1] *Mr. Pitt* William Pitt the Younger, English politician who served as Prime Minister of Great Britain from 1783 to 1801 and of the United Kingdom from 1801 to 1806.

[2] *culture* I.e., cultivation.

[3] *R.W. Emerson ... Seeming* Child alludes to a lecture given in Boston by Transcendentalist thinker Ralph Waldo Emerson on 10 January 1838.

[4] *toilette* Dressing and personal grooming.

[5] *creature* Created being.

[6] *God is ... mine* See Book 4 of *Paradise Lost* (1667, 1674), John Milton's epic poem about the fall of Adam and Eve from the Garden of Eden: "God is thy law, thou mine: To know no more / Is woman's happiest knowledge, and her praise."

[7] *Kinmont* Alexander Kinmont, Scottish-American ethnologist. Child refers to his collection *Twelve Lectures on the Natural History of Man* (1839).

feelings of both sexes were equally enlisted in the cause; that there was no division in the house, or the State; and that the serious pursuits and objects of the one were also the serious pursuits and objects of the other."

The nearer society approaches to divine order, the less separation will there be in the characters, duties, and pursuits of men and women. Women will not become less gentle and graceful, but men will become more so. Women will not neglect the care and education of their children, but men will find themselves ennobled and refined by sharing those duties with them; and will receive, in return, co-operation and sympathy in the discharge of various other duties, not deemed inappropriate to women. The more women become rational companions, partners in business and in thought, as well as in affection and amusement, the more highly will men appreciate home—that blessed word, which opens to the human heart the most perfect glimpse of Heaven, and helps to carry it thither, as on an angel's wings.

> Domestic bliss,
> That can, the world eluding, be itself
> A world enjoyed; that wants no witnesses
> But its own sharers, and approving heaven;
> That, like a flower deep hid in rocky cleft,
> Smiles, though 'tis looking only at the sky.[1]

Alas, for these days of Astor houses, and Tremonts, and Albions![2] where families exchange comforts for costliness, fireside retirement for flirtation and flaunting, and the simply, healthful, cozy meal, for gravies and gout, dainties and dyspepsia. There is no characteristic of my countrymen which I regret so deeply, as their slight degree of adhesiveness to home. Closely intertwined with this instinct is the religion of a nation. The home and the church bear a near relation to each other. The French have no such word as home in their language, and I believe they are the least reverential and religious of all the Christian nations. A Frenchman had been in the habit of visiting a lady constantly for several years, and being alarmed at a report that she was sought in marriage, he was asked why he did not marry her himself. "Marry her!" exclaimed he; "good heavens! where should I spend my evenings?" The idea of domestic happiness was altogether a foreign idea to his soul, like a word that conveyed no meaning. Religious sentiment in the French leads the same roving life as the domestic affections; breakfasting at one restaurateur's, and supping at another's. When some wag in Boston reported that Louis-Philippe[3] had sent over for Dr. Channing[4] to manufacture a religion for the French people, the witty significance of the joke was generally appreciated.

There is a deep spiritual reason why all that relates to the domestic affections should ever be found in close proximity with religious faith. The age of chivalry was likewise one of unquestioning veneration, which led to the crusade for the holy sepulchre.[5]

The French Revolution, which tore down churches, and voted that there was no God, likewise annulled marriage; and the doctrine that there is no sex in souls has usually been urged by those of infidel tendencies. Carlyle[6] says, "But what feeling it was in the ancient, devout, deep soul, which of marriage made a sacrament; this, of all things in the world, is what Diderot will think of for aeons without discovering; unless, perhaps, it were to increase the vestry fees."[7]

The conviction that woman's present position in society is a false one, and therefore re-acts disastrously on the happiness and improvement of man, is pressing, by slow degrees, on the common consciousness, through all the obstacles of bigotry, sensuality, and selfishness. As man approaches to the truest life, he will perceive more and more that there is no separation or discord in their mutual duties. They will be one; but it will be as affection and thought are one; the treble and bass of the same harmonious tune.

—1843

---

1   *Domestic bliss ... the sky*   From Scottish-born poet Rann Kennedy's "A Poem on the Death of Her Royal Highness, the Princess Charlotte of Wales" (1817).

2   *Astor houses ... Albions!*   Names of well-known, elegant hotels.

3   *Louis-Philippe*   King of France from 1830 to 1848.

4   *Dr. Channing*   William Ellery Channing (1780–1842), an influential Unitarian preacher known for his liberal and tolerant religious views.

5   *holy sepulchre*   Site of Jesus' burial, in Jerusalem.

6   *Carlyle*   Thomas Carlyle, English essayist. The following paraphrase is from his 1833 essay on Denis Diderot (1713–84), in which he strongly criticizes the French Enlightenment philosopher.

7   *vestry fees*   Fees paid for the use of chapels or other special seats in a church.

Expansion, Native American Expulsion, and "Manifest Destiny"

CONTEXTS

By the start of the nineteenth century, Euro-American settlers had been steadily dispossessing Native Americans of what had become the eastern United States for nearly two hundred years. With the adoption of the Indian Removal Act of 1830, which mandated the wholesale expulsion of the eastern U.S.'s Indigenous communities, this steady dispossession reached a dreadful climax. Indigenous people throughout the U.S. were facing the immediate threats of the country's westward expansion well before the Removal Act was signed into law, however. By 1820, the Indigenous nations of the Old Northwest (the region bounded by the Appalachian Mountains, the Great Lakes, and the Ohio and Mississippi Rivers) had been fragmented and marginalized by the tide of white settlement. The larger Indigenous nations in the South—the Choctaw, Chickasaw, Cherokee, Muscogee (Creek), and Seminole—more successfully maintained their cohesion while adopting many Euro-American institutions and practices, because of which white Americans dubbed them the "Five Civilized Tribes," but that did not prevent them from facing intense pressure, like their fellow Indigenous peoples to the north, to surrender their territories and relocate west of the Mississippi. This pressure not infrequently took the form of outright aggression, as in the 1818 attack by white militia on a friendly Muscogee community described in the newspaper article "Destruction of Chehaw Village." Some Native Americans gave in to the pressures directed toward them—including the parents of Catharine Brown, a young Cherokee convert to Christianity, as she describes in the letter included below. As the petitions addressed by Cherokee women to their leaders in 1817 and 1818 make clear, though, many other Indigenous people were firmly opposed to "part[ing] with any more of our land."

Calls to open up the remaining Indigenous territory east of the Mississippi to white settlement, and to move its inhabitants out of the way of that settlement, continued to increase during the 1820s. A wide variety of groups and individuals at different levels of government and civil society joined in advocating for Indigenous expulsion: state and territorial governors, U.S. congressional committees, citizen groups, religious organizations, Indian agents, the heads of the federal Office of Indian Affairs (later the Bureau of Indian Affairs), and even some Indigenous leaders. This widespread, decentered movement for expulsion came to a head, and received powerful centralized endorsement, when Andrew Jackson became president in 1829. Jackson had made his name, in part, as the leader of brutal military campaigns against Native Americans, and his administration made "Indian removal"—as the plan for Indigenous expulsion was euphemistically termed—a policy priority. Debate about this policy quickly came to the forefront of the national conversation. Some of the policy's strongest supporters were Southern enslavers (such as Jackson himself), who wanted to spread plantation slavery onto Indigenous land, but "removal" was also championed in the North by members of Jackson's Democratic Party, as the poet and newspaper editor William Cullen Bryant's editorials on the topic demonstrate. This nationwide support enabled the passage of the Removal Act, according to which all Indigenous people east of the Mississippi had to either cede their remaining lands and relocate to designated "Indian Territory" west of the river or accept the jurisdiction of the U.S. states in which they lived. In December 1830, Jackson himself—whose name has remained indelibly associated with Indigenous expulsion ever since—applauded this act, and defended the policy underlying it, in his "Message to Congress on Indian Removal."

The Indian Removal Act only passed Congress by a very narrow margin, however, and many white Americans, especially in the North, opposed the government's plans to deport Native Americans (a fact that Bryant's editorials acknowledge). One of the leaders of this opposition was the well-known poet Lydia Sigourney, who helped organize the so-called "Ladies' Circular" campaign that petitioned Congress to reject the Removal Act—a milestone in the history of American female political advocacy. After the act passed, Sigourney then lamented its consequences, as she imagined them, in "The Cherokee Mother," a poem she published in 1831 in *The Cherokee Phoenix*, the Cherokee national newspaper.

Despite such opposition, the federal government, empowered by the Removal Act, quickly began negotiating removal treaties—many of dubious legitimacy—with Indigenous nations and then deporting them piecemeal. The first nation to be expelled was the Choctaw people of Mississippi and Alabama; part of their deportation, which occurred between 1831 and 1833 and caused thousands of Choctaw deaths, was witnessed by the visiting French writer Alexis de Tocqueville, who recorded its "air of ruin and destruction." The Muscogee (Creek) and Chickasaw in the South, and numerous nations in the North, followed suit in the next few years. The Cherokee strenuously protested their own planned expulsion, even after a minority of Cherokee leaders formally ceded their nation's land—despite lacking the legal authority to do so—in the Treaty of New Echota in 1835. John Ross, the Cherokee Principal Chief, led the Cherokee opposition to "removal," making its case in documents such as the 1836 petition to Congress written by Ross and signed by thousands of other Cherokee. Joining the Cherokee in these efforts were white allies such as Ralph Waldo Emerson, whose open letter to Jackson's successor as president, Martin Van Buren, was written early in 1838. Such protests notwithstanding, the Cherokee were deported in 1838, the last major "removal" to take place. Two accounts of the ensuing "Trail of Tears" appear below: the testimony of Eliza Whitmire, an enslaved African American whose family made the deadly trek to Indian Territory along with their Cherokee enslavers, and a narrative by the modern-day Cherokee storyteller Freeman Owle.

Because the Cherokee and their fellow Southeastern nations were the largest, wealthiest, and most politically prominent Indigenous nations, and because their expulsion involved a massive movement of people over a vast distance, their case commanded public attention at the time and has often been taken to be representative of "Indian removal" ever since. Many other Indigenous nations besides the five major Southeastern ones, though, were deported during the 1820s and 30s: the Shawnee, for instance, were expelled from their homelands in the Old Northwest just as thoroughly as the Cherokee and were moved just as far, but their expulsion inspired nothing like as intense of a public debate. Indigenous expulsion in other parts of the country also often took a quite different form than it did in the South. The expulsion of the Ojibwe, for example, involved many local, small-scale relocations or confinements and took them a much shorter distance from their traditional territories than the Cherokee, Shawnee, or other nations were forced to move.

Expulsion undoubtedly was an enormous, traumatic rupture for the Indigenous people who underwent it, and it decisively moved most of the Indigenous population of the eastern U.S. beyond the sphere of daily lived experience for the bulk of the country's white population. By no means, however, should expulsion be seen as the end of the story. The deported nations survived and in some cases even thrived, and an important part of the history of Indigenous expulsion is the history of what Indigenous people did after it: re-establish livelihoods, including farms and plantations, and institutions, including schools and academies, printing offices, and governments, in their new territories, and envision and negotiate new political relationships, both between deported nations that found themselves living next to one another and between deportees and the local Indigenous communities whose lands, in some cases, the deportees were now occupying.

The expulsions of the 1830s also sparked several wars, as various groups of Native Americans throughout the country fought back against the effort to expel them. U.S. forces were tasked with quelling armed resistance by members of the Sauk and allied nations, led by Black Hawk, in Illinois and Wisconsin and by members of the Muscogee nation in Alabama. The longest and costliest conflict was the war fought against the Seminole of Florida, who took up arms in 1835 and held out until 1842, when the remaining few hundred Seminole who had not been killed or deported were permitted to remain on an unofficial reservation. (Further white encroachment onto this residual territory led to another U.S.–Seminole war, the third, from 1855 to 1858.) The war's great expense in both money and lives, together with its flimsy moral justification, made it unpopular both with many civilians and many soldiers—as is attested by some of the documents presented in this section, including the diary of U.S. Army officer

Ethan Allen Hitchcock (in the section's website component) and the political cartoon criticizing the tactics used against the Seminole by General Zachary Taylor.

At the same time as the Seminole War was breaking out, another conflict erupted on one of the other fronts of American expansion: Texas. By the 1830s, large numbers of white Americans had settled in that territory, then part of Mexico, and their resistance to Mexican authority—together with the desire for greater political autonomy of many Hispanic Tejanos—led to war in 1835. After initial defeats at the Alamo, where a small Texan garrison fought to the death, and Goliad, where Mexican troops executed several hundred Texan prisoners, Texan forces ultimately prevailed in the spring of 1836, gaining the Republic of Texas *de facto* independence. Among the texts included in this section's website component, R.M. Potter's "Hymn of the Alamo" extols the defense of the Alamo as a self-sacrificial stand that helped win "Freedom," while U.S. Senator Daniel S. Dickinson's 1845 speech likens the Texas Revolution to America's Revolutionary War in the course of an argument in favor of annexing the Republic of Texas to the United States.

The heated debate over Texas annexation that occasioned Dickinson's speech also gave rise to the term that has come to epitomize American expansion: "manifest destiny." This term first appeared in an article, entitled "Annexation," published in 1845 in *The United States Magazine and Democratic Review,* a Jacksonian Democratic periodical that had already made clear its commitment to American exceptionalism and its exalted view of American national destiny in its 1839 article "The Great Nation of Futurity." The term quickly caught on among advocates of national expansion, but the idea that America had an expansionary destiny that legitimized its seizure of others' territory was just as quickly condemned—for example, by Democratic Congressman Charles Goodyear, who gave a speech in early 1846 in which he scathingly characterized "manifest destiny" as "the robber's title."

The stakes of this debate became even higher when war broke out with Mexico later in 1846—largely at U.S. provocation—over the annexation of Texas, which Mexico still claimed. Some Americans, including a young Walt Whitman in his editorials for the *Brooklyn Daily Eagle,* welcomed the war as an opportunity for the country to realize its "manifest destiny" at Mexico's expense, while others opposed the war as an unjustified imperialistic land-grab. U.S. forces swiftly surpassed the goals set for them by the likes of Whitman, conquering New Mexico and California before invading the Mexican heartland; the account of Rosalía Vallejo (in this section's online component), describing her experiences at the hands of the white American settlers in California who rebelled against Mexican rule at the beginning of the war, provides a Hispanic perspective on these conquests. After Mexico was defeated and gave up these and other vast stretches of its territory in 1848, the Irish American politician and poet Thomas D'Arcy McGee elaborated the campaign waged during the war by the U.S. "Army of the West," in his poem of that title, into a metaphor for American westward expansion and colonization writ large.

During the 1850s, in the wake of the enormous territorial acquisitions that had occurred between 1845 and 1848, the idea of "manifest destiny" further proliferated and diversified. The African American poet James Monroe Whitfield's 1853 open letter to Frederick Douglass advocating black emigration out of the United States illustrates how widely the term had spread and the different uses to which it was being put. The conventional white American understanding of the country's "manifest destiny" also continued to run strong in the 1850s. However, as the Whig presidential administrations of Zachary Taylor and Millard Fillmore moved away from overtly expansionist policies, and as the debate over the extension of slavery into the western territories intensified, attempts to continue the country's expansion during that decade generally took the unofficial form of "filibustering": the practice by U.S. citizens of inciting insurrections in Latin American countries, frequently with the aim of enabling U.S. annexation of the country in question in the insurrection's wake. This practice is skewered in the popular 1854 poem "Filibustering Ethics," which also serves as a withering critique of "manifest destiny" thinking more generally. A different kind of critique of such thinking, from the point of view of one of the communities recently taken over by American expansion, can be seen in Francisco Ramírez's 1855 editorial from *El Clamor Público,* his pioneering Spanish-language Californian newspaper.

The two chronologically latest pieces in this section, by John Rollin Ridge (in the bound book) and Henry David Thoreau (in the website component), exemplify the variety and complexity of the ways in which Americans of all stripes responded to American national expansion, its justifications, and its consequences. Ridge's "Poem (Delivered at Commencement of Oakland College, California, June 6th 1861)" demonstrates how Ridge—the son and grandson of Cherokee leaders killed in the internal Cherokee dispute over their nation's "removal"—could imbue certain of his works with "manifest destiny" ideas, even as others criticize the effects of U.S. expansion on some of the people it subordinated. Thoreau's essay "Walking" demonstrates the powerful appeal that the idea of America's "westward tendency" had even for such a writer as Thoreau, whose uncompromising opposition to the Mexican–American War had landed him in jail. By the time Ridge's poem was written and Thoreau's essay published, the debate over how to incorporate the new western territories—specifically, whether or not slavery would be allowed there—had helped precipitate the Civil War: a further consequence of the great national "westering" that both works, in their different ways, celebrate.

⌘ ⌘ ⌘

Catharine Brown (Kä tý), letter to Loring S. Williams and Matilda Loomis Williams, 5 July 1819

By late 1818, the family of Catharine Brown (c. 1800–23), having suffered repeated acts of theft and violence on their land from encroaching settlers, had determined to move westwards in the hopes of escaping further white aggression. For Catharine, however—a Cherokee student at the American Board of Commissioners for Foreign Missions school in Brainerd, Tennessee, and a recent convert to Christianity—moving west would mean leaving behind the Christian community to which she now felt profoundly connected. Brown was herself a minor celebrity, known throughout the United States both for her renowned piety and for her letters to missionary friends, which were widely published in newspapers and religious periodicals. Though her parents temporarily removed her from the Brainerd school in November 1818, their move westwards ultimately did not take place until after Brown's death. Nevertheless, her letters from the period vividly recount the agony of having to choose between what she had come to think of as her two families.

To MR. AND MRS. WILLIAMS
Brainerd, July 5, 1819

My dear Brother and Sister,[1]

Although I have long omitted answering your affectionate letters, my heart has been often with you. Yes, dear brother and sister, I do not forget you, and all the pleasant meetings we had together, when you were here. But pain is mixed with pleasure when I think they are gone, no more to return! When I remember the kind instruction I received from you, before you left this place, my heart swells with gratitude. I feel much indebted to you, but more particularly to that God, who sent you here to instruct the poor ignorant Indians in the way that leads to everlasting life. Oh, my dear friends, may the Lord ever bless you, and make you the instrument of doing great good where he has called you.

You may pass through many trials; but remember, beloved brother and sister, all our trials here will only make us richer there when we arrive at our home. A few more days, and then, I hope, our weary souls will be at rest in our Saviour's kingdom, where we shall enjoy His blessed presence forever.

---

[1] *Brother and Sister* Like many devout Christians at the time, Brown refers to all of her fellow believers as brothers and sisters, not just her siblings by blood.

When I wrote you before, I expected to go to the Arkansas,[1] and never to see this place again. But the Lord has in mercy ordered it otherwise. He has permitted me to live with the dear missionaries here again, though my parents could not bear to think of leaving me behind. My mother said, if I remained here, she did not expect to see me again in this world. Indeed, she wished she had never sent me to this school, and that I had never received religious instruction. I told her, if she was a Christian, she would not feel so: she would be willing to give me, and all she had, up to Christ. I told her I did not wish to stay on account of my own pleasure, but that I wished to get more instruction, so that it might be for her good, as well as for mine.

I felt very sorry for my poor parents. I thought it was my duty to go in obedience to their commands, and commit myself to the will of God. I knew the Lord could change the hearts of my parents.

They are now perfectly willing that I should stay here two years longer. I left them in March. They expected to set out in that month for the Arkansas. They had already prepared for the journey. But the Lord has so ordered, that they have concluded not to go until next fall. I don't know whether they will go then. I hope you will pray for them, and also for me, that I may be useful to their immortal souls. O that I might be made the means of turning many souls from darkness unto marvellous light.[2] My dear brother and sister, I love you much, and feel that the time is short when we shall sit down with our Saviour, and experience that love which no words can describe.

From your affectionate sister in Christ,

Catharine Brown

---

[1]   *the Arkansas*   I.e., Arkansas Territory, which became the state of Arkansas in 1836. Groups of Cherokee had begun relocating there as early as the Revolutionary era, and a substantial number, who became known as the "Old Settlers," moved to the territory after the federal government established a Cherokee reservation there in 1815.

[2]   *turning ... unto marvellous light*   See Acts 26.18: "To open their eyes, and to turn them from darkness to light, and from the power of Satan unto God, that they may receive forgiveness of sins, and inheritance among them which are sanctified by faith that is in me."

Cherokee Women's Petitions (1817, 1818, 1831)

The Cherokee traditionally accorded an important place to women, not just symbolically but also socially and economically. The Cherokee kinship system was matrilineal, meaning descent was traced through women; in addition, Cherokee women were responsible for agriculture, which gave them significant economic status. As the Cherokee adopted Euro-American culture and institutions in the early nineteenth century, Cherokee society became more overtly male-dominated. However, Cherokee women still wielded substantial influence (even if this was often overlooked) and frequently acted as preservers of traditional values. These roles are particularly on display in the three petitions that, between 1817 and 1831, Cherokee women presented to the male leaders of the Cherokee Nation in response to white American pressure for Cherokee "removal." All three petitions oppose removal or the relinquishment of further Cherokee land, but they frame this opposition in different ways that reflect the development of Cherokee society, and women's place in it, throughout the early nineteenth century.

The text of the petitions is based on their original manuscript (1817) or published (1818 and 1831) versions.

PETITION (2 MAY 1817)

The Cherokee ladies now being present at the meeting of their chiefs and warriors in council have thought it their duty as mothers to address their beloved chiefs and warriors now assembled.

Our beloved children and head men of the Cherokee Nation, we address you as warriors in council. We have raised all of you on the land which we now have, which God gave us to inhabit and raise provisions. We know that our country has once been extensive, but by repeated sales has become circumscribed to a small track, and [we] never have thought it our duty to interfere in the disposition[3] of it till now. If a father or mother was to sell all their lands which they had to depend on, which their children had to raise their living on, which would be indeed bad and to be

---

[3]   *disposition*   Administration, disposal.

removed to another country. We do not wish to go [to] an unknown country [to] which we have understood some of our children wish to go over the Mississippi, but this act of our children would be like destroying your mothers.

Your mothers, your sisters ask and beg of you not to part with any more of our land. We say ours. You are our descendants; take pity on our request. But keep it for our growing children, for it was the good will of our creator to place us here, and you know our father, the great president,[1] will not allow his white children to take our country away. Only keep your hands off of paper talks for it's our own country. For [if] it was not, they would not ask you to put your hands to paper, for it would be impossible to remove us all. For as soon as one child is raised, we have others in our arms, for such is our situation and will consider our circumstance.

Therefore, children, don't part with any more of our lands but continue on it and enlarge your farms and cultivate and raise corn and cotton and we, your mothers and sisters, will make clothing for you which our father the president has recommended to us all. We don't charge anybody for selling any lands, but we have heard such intentions of our children. But your talks become true at last; it was our desire to forewarn you all not to part with our lands.

Nancy Ward[2] to her children: Warriors to take pity and listen to the talks of your sisters. Although I am very old yet cannot but pity the situation in which you will hear of their minds. I have great many grandchildren which [I] wish them to do well on our land.

---

[1]   *the great president*   At the time of this petition, the President of the United States was James Monroe.

[2]   *Nancy Ward*   English name of Nanyehi (c. 1738–1822 or 1824), a Cherokee political leader. In recognition for battlefield heroism during her youth, she was named a "Beloved Woman," a Cherokee title conferring great honor and responsibility: Beloved Women headed the Council of Women, could vote in the Council of Chiefs, decided the fate of prisoners taken in war, and could serve as ambassadors on behalf of the Cherokee Nation. As a Beloved Woman, Nanyehi was known for her support for the American colonists during the Revolutionary War (at a time when most Cherokee supported the British) and for her advocacy of peaceful coexistence with white Americans.

PETITION (30 JUNE 1818)

Beloved Children,

We have called a meeting among ourselves to consult on the different points now before the council, relating to our national affairs. We have heard with painful feelings that the bounds of the land we now possess are to be drawn into very narrow limits. The land was given to us by the Great Spirit above as our common right, to raise our children upon, and to make support for our rising generations. We therefore humbly petition our beloved children, the head men and warriors, to hold out to the last in support of our common rights, as the Cherokee nation have been the first settlers of this land; we therefore claim the right of the soil.

We well remember that our country was formerly very extensive, but by repeated sales it has become circumscribed to the very narrow limits we have at present. Our Father the President advised us to become farmers, to manufacture our own clothes, and to have our children instructed. To this advice we have attended in everything as far as we were able. Now the thought of being compelled to remove to the other side of the Mississippi is dreadful to us, because it appears to us that we, by this removal, shall be brought to a savage state[3] again, for we have, by the endeavor of our Father the President, become too much enlightened to throw aside the privileges of a civilized life.

We therefore unanimously join in our meeting to hold our country in common as hitherto.

Some of our children have become Christians. We have missionary schools among us. We have heard the gospel in our nation. We have become civilized and enlightened, and are in hopes that in a few years our nation will be prepared for instruction in other branches of sciences and arts, which are both useful and necessary in civilized society.

There are some white men among us, who have been raised in our country from their youth, are connected with us by marriage, and have considerable families, who are very active in encouraging the emigration of

---

[3]   *savage state*   The authors of this petition have here assimilated the use of the derogatory term "savage," common among white Americans in the nineteenth century, to characterize Indigenous society and culture.

our nation. These ought to be our truest friends but prove our worst enemies. They seem to be only concerned how to increase their riches, but do not care what becomes of our Nation, nor even of their own wives and children.

PETITION (17 OCTOBER 1831[1])

To the Committee and Council,

We the females, residing in Salequoree and Pine Log,[2] believing that the present difficulties and embarrassments under which this nation is placed demands a full expression of the mind of every individual, on the subject of emigrating to Arkansas,[3] would take upon ourselves to address you. Although it is not common for our sex to take part in public measures, we nevertheless feel justified in expressing our sentiments on any subject where our interest is as much at stake as any other part of the community.

We believe the present plan of the General Government to effect our removal West of the Mississippi, and thus obtain our lands for the use of the State of Georgia, to be highly oppressive, cruel and unjust. And we sincerely hope there is no consideration which can induce our citizens to forsake the land of our fathers of which they have been in possession from time immemorial, and thus compel us, against our will, to undergo the toils and difficulties of removing with our helpless families hundreds of miles to unhealthy and unproductive country. We hope therefore the Committee and Council will take into deep consideration our deplorable situation, and do everything in their power to avert such a state of things. And we trust by a prudent course their transactions with the General Government will enlist in our behalf the sympathies of the good people of the United States.

---

[1] *1831* This petition, dated "1821" in its original text, was published as a letter in the *Cherokee Phoenix* on 12 November 1831; the 1821 dating is almost certainly a typographical error.

[2] *Salequoree and Pine Log* Cherokee communities in northern Georgia.

[3] *Arkansas* I.e., Arkansas Territory, which became the state of Arkansas in 1836. Groups of Cherokee had begun relocating there as early as the Revolutionary era, and a substantial number, who became known as the "Old Settlers," moved to the territory after the federal government established a Cherokee reservation there in 1815.

Andrew Jackson, message to Congress on Indian Removal (1830)

One of the most famous of Andrew Jackson's numerous defenses of the policy of Native American expulsion is the portion excerpted below of his annual message to Congress on 6 December 1830, after the passage of the Indian Removal Act earlier that year. The text of the excerpt is based on that contained in the U.S. National Archives (in the Records of the United States Senate, 1789–1990) and published on the National Archives website.

It gives me pleasure to announce to Congress that the benevolent policy of the Government, steadily pursued for nearly thirty years, in relation to the removal of the Indians beyond the white settlements is approaching to a happy consummation. Two important tribes have accepted the provision made for their removal at the last session of Congress,[4] and it is believed that their example will induce the remaining tribes also to seek the same obvious advantages.

The consequences of a speedy removal will be important to the United States, to individual States, and to the Indians themselves. The pecuniary advantages which it promises to the Government are the least of its recommendations. It puts an end to all possible danger of collision between the authorities of the General and State Governments on account of the Indians. It will place a dense and civilized population in large tracts of country now occupied by a few savage hunters. By opening the whole territory between Tennessee on the north and Louisiana on the south to the settlement of the whites it will incalculably strengthen the southwestern frontier and render the adjacent States strong enough to repel future invasions without remote aid. It will relieve the whole State of Mississippi and the western part of Alabama of Indian occupancy, and enable those States to advance rapidly in population, wealth, and power. It will separate the Indians from immediate contact with settlements of whites; free them from the

---

[4] *Two important ... Congress* At the time Jackson spoke, elements of the leadership of the Chickasaw and Choctaw nations had signed removal treaties in August and September 1830, respectively. (The Chickasaw later deemed the land allotted to them west of the Mississippi unacceptable and renegotiated a new treaty in 1832.)

power of the States; enable them to pursue happiness in their own way and under their own rude[1] institutions; will retard the progress of decay, which is lessening their numbers, and perhaps cause them gradually, under the protection of the Government and through the influence of good counsels, to cast off their savage habits and become an interesting,[2] civilized, and Christian community.

What good man would prefer a country covered with forests and ranged by a few thousand savages to our extensive Republic, studded with cities, towns, and prosperous farms embellished with all the improvements which art can devise or industry execute, occupied by more than 12,000,000 happy people, and filled with all the blessings of liberty, civilization and religion?

The present policy of the Government is but a continuation of the same progressive change by a milder process. The tribes which occupied the countries now constituting the Eastern States were annihilated or have melted away to make room for the whites. The waves of population and civilization are rolling to the westward, and we now propose to acquire the countries occupied by the red men of the South and West by a fair exchange, and, at the expense of the United States, to send them to land where their existence may be prolonged and perhaps made perpetual. Doubtless it will be painful to leave the graves of their fathers; but what do they more than our ancestors did or than our children are now doing? To better their condition in an unknown land our forefathers left all that was dear in earthly objects. Our children by thousands yearly leave the land of their birth to seek new homes in distant regions. Does Humanity weep at these painful separations from everything, animate and inanimate, with which the young heart has become entwined? Far from it. It is rather a source of joy that our country affords scope where our young population may range unconstrained in body or in mind, developing the power and facilities of man in their highest perfection. These remove[3] hundreds and almost thousands of miles at their own expense, purchase the lands they occupy, and support themselves at their new homes from the moment of their arrival. Can it be cruel in

this Government when, by events which it cannot control, the Indian is made discontented in his ancient home to purchase his lands, to give him a new and extensive territory, to pay the expense of his removal, and support him a year in his new abode? How many thousands of our own people would gladly embrace the opportunity of removing to the West on such conditions! If the offers made to the Indians were extended to them, they would be hailed with gratitude and joy.

Andrew Jackson as the Great Father, c. 1835. "Great Father" was a title frequently used in the context of Indigenous–settler relations, by both Euro-American authorities and Indigenous people, to refer to the leaders of settler-colonial nations, including the Kings of France and Britain and later the U.S. President. The title was meant to evoke the President or other Euro-American leader's supposedly beneficent care for his Indigenous "children"—an idea literalized by this cartoon's unknown illustrator. The framed painting in the top right-hand corner of the illustration depicts Columbia—the allegorical female personification of the United States—standing with her foot on the head of a subjugated foe.

---

[1]   *rude*   Uncivilized.

[2]   *interesting*   Important, worthy of consideration.

[3]   *remove*   Relocate.

And is it supposed that the wandering savage has a stronger attachment to his home than the settled, civilized Christian? Is it more afflicting to him to leave the graves of his fathers than it is to our brothers and children? Rightly considered, the policy of the General Government toward the red man is not only liberal, but generous. He is unwilling to submit to the laws of the States and mingle with their population. To save him from this alternative, or perhaps utter annihilation, the General Government kindly offers him a new home, and proposes to pay the whole expense of his removal and settlement.

Lydia Sigourney, "The Cherokee Mother" (1831)

By the time of the Indian Removal Act, the celebrated white American poet Lydia Huntley Sigourney had already demonstrated, in poems such as *Traits of the Aborigines of America* (1822), a sympathetic—if also romanticizing and condescending—interest in Indigenous people and history. This poem, written in response to the Removal Act and published in 1831 in *The Cherokee Phoenix*, the Cherokee national newspaper, further exemplifies that interest. The poem was never republished in any of Sigourney's collections.

Ye bid us hence.[1] These vales are dear,
 To infant hope, to patriot pride,
These streamlets tuneful to our ear,
Where our light shallops[2] peaceful glide.

5 Beneath yon consecrated mounds
Our fathers' treasured ashes rest,
Our hands have tilled these corn-clad grounds,
Our children's birth these homes have blest.

Here, on our souls a Saviour's love
10 First beamed with renovating° ray,   *regenerating, redeeming*
Why should we from these haunts° remove?   *habitations*
But still you warn us hence away.

Child, ask not where! I cannot tell,
Save where wide wastes uncultured° spread,   *uncultivated*

15 Where unknown waters fiercely roll,
And savage monsters howling tread;

Where no blest Church with hallowed train,[3]
Nor hymns of praise, nor voice of prayer,
Like angels soothe the wanderer's pain;
20 Ask me no more. I know not where.

Go seek thy Sire. The anguish charm[4]
That shades his brow like frowning wrath,
Divide the burden from his arm,[5]
And gird him for his pilgrim-path.

25 Come, moaning babe! Thy mother's arms
Shall bear thee on our weary course,
Shall be thy shield from midnight harms,
And baleful dews, and tempests hoarse.°   *rough*

John Ross, letter to the Senate and House of Representatives, 28 September 1836

As the momentum for expulsion intensified in the wake of the Indian Removal Act and Andrew Jackson's landslide re-election in 1832, the leadership of the Cherokee Nation became divided over how to respond. A majority, headed by Principal Chief John Ross (1790–1866), remained strongly opposed to giving up their traditional lands. However, a minority of Cherokee, including some influential leaders, decided that it was in the nation's best interest to come to terms with the federal government; this faction became known as the "Treaty Party." In late 1835, without any sanction from Ross or the Cherokee National Council, members of the Treaty Party separately negotiated the Treaty of New Echota with federal representatives, whereby they consented to removal. The outraged response of the Cherokee majority, and their continued opposition to removal even after the Treaty of New Echota was ratified by the Senate in May 1836, is illustrated by the following petition, addressed to the U.S. Congress in September 1836 by Ross and thousands of other Cherokee.

---

1   *Ye bid us hence*   I.e., you command us to leave.

2   *shallops*   Shallow-water boats.

3   *train*   Assembly of people.

4   *The anguish charm*   I.e., charm away the anguish.

5   *Divide ... arm*   I.e., take a share of the "burden" he is carrying.

Red Clay Council Ground,[1] Cherokee Nation
September 28, 1836

Most respectfully, and most humbly showeth: That your memorialists,[2] the Chiefs, National Committee and Council, and people of the Cherokee Nation in General Council assembled, solicit permission to approach your honorable bodies, under circumstances peculiar in the history of nations; circumstances of distress and anxiety beyond our power to express. We earnestly bespeak your patience, therefore, while we lay before you a brief epitome[3] of our griefs.

It is well known that for a number of years past we have been harassed by a series of vexations, which it is deemed unnecessary to recite in detail, but the evidence of which our delegation will be prepared to furnish. With a view to bringing our troubles to a close, a delegation was appointed on the 23rd of October, 1835, by the General Council of the nation, clothed with full powers to enter into arrangements with the Government of the United States, for the final adjustment of all our existing difficulties. The delegation, failing to effect an arrangement with the United States commissioner then in the nation, proceeded, agreeably to[4] their instructions in that case, to Washington City, for the purpose of negotiating a treaty with the authorities of the United States.

After the departure of the Delegation, a contract was made by the Rev. John F. Schermerhorn,[5] and certain individual Cherokees, purporting to be a "treaty, concluded at New Echota, in the State of Georgia, on the 29th day of December, 1835, by General William Carroll and John F. Schermerhorn, commissioners on the part of the United States, and the chiefs, headmen, and people of the Cherokee tribes of Indians." A spurious Delegation, in violation of a special injunction of the general council of the nation, proceeded to Washington city with this pretended treaty, and by false and fraudulent representations supplanted in the favor of the Government the legal and accredited Delegation of the Cherokee people, and obtained for this instrument, after making important alterations in its provisions, the recognition of the United States Government. And now it is presented to us as a treaty, ratified by the Senate, and approved by the President Andrew Jackson, and our acquiescence in its requirements demanded, under the sanction of the displeasure of the United States, and the threat of summary compulsion, in case of refusal. It comes to us, not through our legitimate authorities, the known and usual medium of communication between the Government of the United States and our nation, but through the agency of a complication[6] of powers, civil and military.

By the stipulations of this instrument, we are despoiled of our private possessions, the indefeasible property of individuals. We are stripped of every attribute of freedom and eligibility for legal self-defence. Our property may be plundered before our eyes; violence may be committed on our persons; even our lives may be taken away, and there is none to regard our complaints. We are denationalized; we are disfranchised. We are deprived of membership in the human family! We have neither land nor home, nor resting place that can be called our own. And this is effected by the provisions of a compact which assumes the venerated, the sacred appellation of treaty.

We are overwhelmed! Our hearts are sickened, our utterance is paralyzed, when we reflect on the condition in which we are placed, by the audacious practices of unprincipled men, who have managed their stratagems with so much dexterity as to impose on[7] the Government of the United States, in the face of our earnest, solemn, and reiterated protestations.

The instrument in question is not the act of our Nation; we are not parties to its covenants; it has not received the sanction of our people. The makers of

---

1   *Red Clay Council Ground*   Capital of the Cherokee Nation, located in extreme southeastern Tennessee, just north of the state border with Georgia. Because of laws passed by the state of Georgia restricting the right of the Cherokee to hold public meetings, the Cherokee had officially moved their seat of government from New Echota, Georgia, to Red Clay Council Ground in 1832.

2   *memorialists*   Petitioners.

3   *epitome*   Summary.

4   *agreeably to*   In accordance with.

5   *Rev. John F. Schermerhorn*   Minister and personal friend of Andrew Jackson, whom Jackson appointed as an Indian Commissioner in 1832 with a mandate to accomplish the removal of the Cherokee and Chickasaw nations.

6   *complication*   Complex combination.

7   *impose on*   Deceive.

it sustain no office nor appointment in our Nation, under the designation of Chiefs, Head men, or any other title, by which they hold, or could acquire, authority to assume the reins of Government, and to make bargain and sale of our rights, our possessions, and our common country. And we are constrained solemnly to declare, that we cannot but contemplate the enforcement of the stipulations of this instrument on us, against our consent, as an act of injustice and oppression, which, we are well persuaded, can never knowingly be countenanced by the Government and people of the United States; nor can we believe it to be the design of these honorable and highminded individuals, who stand at the head of the Government, to bind a whole Nation, by the acts of a few unauthorized individuals. And, therefore, we, the parties to be affected by the result, appeal with confidence to the justice, the magnanimity, the compassion, of your honorable bodies, against the enforcement, on us, of the provisions of a compact, in the formation of which we have had no agency.

In truth, our cause is your own; it is the cause of liberty and of justice; it is based upon your own principles, which we have learned from yourselves; for we have gloried to count your George Washington and your Thomas Jefferson our great teachers; we have read their communications to us with veneration; we have practised their precepts with success. And the result is manifest. The wildness of the forest has given place to comfortable dwellings and cultivated fields, stocked with the various domestic animals. Mental culture, industrious habits, and domestic enjoyments, have succeeded the rudeness of the savage[1] state.

We have learned your religion also. We have read your Sacred books. Hundreds of our people have embraced their doctrines, practised the virtues they teach, cherished the hopes they awaken, and rejoiced in the consolations which they afford. To the spirit of your institutions, and your religion, which has been imbibed by our community, is mainly to be ascribed that patient endurance which has characterized the conduct of our people, under the laceration of their keenest woes. For assuredly, we are not ignorant of our condition; we are not insensible to our sufferings. We feel them! we groan under their pressure! And anticipation[2] crowds our breasts with sorrows yet to come. We are, indeed, an afflicted people! Our spirits are subdued! Despair has well nigh seized upon our energies! But we speak to the representatives of a Christian country; the friends of justice; the patrons of the oppressed. And our hopes revive, and our prospects brighten, as we indulge the thought. On your sentence, our fate is suspended; prosperity or desolation depends on your word. To you, therefore, we look! Before your august assembly we present ourselves, in the attitude of deprecation,[3] and of entreaty. On your kindness, on your humanity, on your compassion, on your benevolence, we rest our hopes. To you we address our reiterated prayers. Spare our people! Spare the wreck of our prosperity! Let not our deserted homes become the monuments of our desolation! But we forbear! We suppress the agonies which wring our hearts, when we look at our wives, our children, and our venerable sires! We restrain the forebodings of anguish and distress, of misery and devastation and death, which must be the attendants on the execution of this ruinous compact.

In conclusion, we commend to your confidence and favor, our well-beloved and trustworthy brethren and fellow-citizens, John Ross, Principal Chief, Richard Taylor, Samuel Gunter, John Benge, George Sanders, Walter S. Adair, Stephen Foreman, and Kalsateehee of Aquohee, who are clothed with full powers to adjust all our existing difficulties by treaty arrangements with the United States, by which our destruction may be averted, impediments to the advancement of our people removed, and our existence perpetuated as a living monument, to testify to posterity the honor, the magnanimity, the generosity of the United States. And your memorialists, as in duty bound, will ever pray. Signed by Ross, George Lowrey, Edward Gunter, Lewis Ross, thirty-one members of the National Committee and National Council, and 2,174 others.

---

[1] *rudeness* Ignorance; lack of refinement; primitiveness; *savage* Ross here adopts the common nineteenth-century use of the disparaging term "savage" by white Americans to describe the society and culture of Indigenous peoples.

[2] *anticipation* Fear.

[3] *august* Exalted; *deprecation* Sincere plea.

Ralph Waldo Emerson, letter to Martin Van Buren, 23 April 1838

After the ratification of the Treaty of New Echota, the U.S. government set a deadline of 23 May 1838 for the Cherokee to voluntarily remove in accordance with the treaty, after which they would be forcibly expelled. As the deadline approached, opponents of the treaty continued to petition the government not to enforce removal. One of the most prominent such petitioners was Ralph Waldo Emerson, who addressed this open letter on the subject directly to President Martin Van Buren. Judging by his journals, Emerson composed this letter with a great deal of difficulty, and he himself doubted its efficacy: he called it "merely a scream," before adding that "sometimes a scream is better than a thesis." A similar ambivalence about the letter was exhibited by its first publishers, the editors of the Washington, D.C., *Daily National Intelligencer*, who printed it "with some reluctance" on 14 May 1838. The present text is based on that reprinted in the *New-Bedford Mercury* on 25 May 1838.

Letter to Martin Van Buren, President of the United States

A Protest Against the Removal of the Cherokee Indians from the State of Georgia

SAY, what is Honour? 'Tis the finest sense
Of justice which the human mind can frame,
Intent each lurking frailty to disclaim,
And guard the way of life from all offence,
Suffered or done.[1]

Concord, Mass.
April 23, 1838

SIR:

The seat you fill places you in a relation of credit and nearness to every citizen. By right and natural position, every citizen is your friend. Before any acts contrary to his own judgment or interest have repelled the affections of any man, each may look with trust and living anticipation to your government. Each has the highest right to call your attention to such subjects as are of a public nature, and properly belong to the chief magistrate;[2] and the good magistrate will feel a joy in meeting such confidence. In this belief and at the instance[3] of a few of my friends and neighbors, I crave of your patience a short hearing for their sentiments and my own: and the circumstance that my name will be utterly unknown to you will only give the fairer chance to your equitable construction[4] of what I have to say.

Sir, my communication respects the sinister rumors that fill this part of the country concerning the Cherokee people. The interest always felt in the aboriginal population—an interest naturally growing as that decays[5]—has been heightened in regard to this tribe. Even in our distant State some good rumor of their worth and civility has arrived. We have learned with joy their improvement in the social arts. We have read their newspapers. We have seen some of them in our schools and colleges. In common with the great body of the American people, we have witnessed with sympathy the painful labors of these red men to redeem their own race from the doom of eternal inferiority, and to borrow and domesticate in the tribe the arts and customs of the Caucasian race. And notwithstanding the unaccountable apathy with which of late years the Indians have been sometimes abandoned to their enemies, it is not to be doubted that it is the good pleasure and the understanding of all humane persons in the Republic, of the men and the matrons sitting in the thriving independent families all over the land, that they shall be duly cared for; that they shall taste justice

---

[1]   *SAY ... done*   From one of the "Sonnets Dedicated to Liberty" (1802–03) by the English poet William Wordsworth.

[2]   *chief magistrate*   I.e., president. This term was used frequently to refer to the President of the United States in the early decades of the nation's existence but is rare today.

[3]   *instance*   Urging.

[4]   *equitable construction*   Fair interpretation.

[5]   *as that decays*   I.e., as "the aboriginal population" declines. A belief that Native Americans were in terminal decline and inevitably bound for extinction—an idea known as the "vanishing Indian" trope—was widespread among white Americans in the nineteenth century, even those such as Emerson who sympathized with Indigenous people and sought to prevent their further dispossession.

and love from all to whom we have delegated the office of dealing with them.

The newspapers now inform us that, in December, 1835, a treaty contracting for the exchange of all the Cherokee territory was pretended to be made by an agent on the part of the United States with some persons appearing on the part of the Cherokees; that the fact afterwards transpired that these deputies did by no means represent the will of the nation; and that, out of eighteen thousand souls composing the nation, fifteen thousand six hundred and sixty-eight have protested against the so-called treaty. It now appears that the government of the United States choose to hold the Cherokees to this sham treaty, and are proceeding to execute the same. Almost the entire Cherokee Nation stand up and say, "This is not our act. Behold us. Here are we. Do not mistake that handful of deserters for us"; and the American President and the Cabinet, the Senate and the House of Representatives, neither hear these men nor see them, and are contracting to put this active nation into carts and boats, and to drag them over mountains and rivers to a wilderness at a vast distance beyond the Mississippi. And a paper purporting to be an army order fixes a month from this day as the hour for this doleful removal.

In the name of God, sir, we ask you if this be so. Do the newspapers rightly inform us? Men and women with pale and perplexed faces meet one another in the streets and churches here, and ask if this be so. We have inquired if this be a gross misrepresentation from the party opposed to the government[1] and anxious to blacken it with the people. We have looked in the newspapers of different parties[2] and find a horrid confirmation of the tale. We are slow to believe it. We hoped the Indians were misinformed, and that their remonstrance was premature, and will turn out to be a needless act of terror.

The piety, the principle that is left in the United States, if only in its coarsest form, a regard to the speech of men—forbid us to entertain it as a fact. Such a dereliction of all faith and virtue, such a denial of justice, and such deafness to screams for mercy were never heard of in times of peace and in the dealing of a nation with its own allies and wards,[3] since the earth was made. Sir, does this government think that the people of the United States are become savage and mad? From their mind are the sentiments of love and a good nature wiped clean out? The soul of man, the justice, the mercy that is the heart's heart in all men, from Maine to Georgia, does abhor this business.

In speaking thus the sentiments of my neighbors and my own, perhaps I overstep the bounds of decorum. But would it not be a higher indecorum coldly to argue a matter like this? We only state the fact that a crime is projected that confounds our understandings by its magnitude—a crime that really deprives us as well as the Cherokees of a country, for how could we call the conspiracy that should crush these poor Indians our government, or the land that was cursed by their parting and dying imprecations our country, any more? You, sir, will bring down that renowned chair in which you sit into infamy if your seal is set to this instrument of perfidy; and the name of this nation, hitherto the sweet omen of religion and liberty, will stink to the world.

You will not do us the injustice of connecting this remonstrance with any sectional and party feeling. It is in our hearts the simplest commandment of brotherly love. We will not have this great and solemn claim upon national and human justice huddled aside under

---

[1] *the party opposed to the government* I.e., the Whig Party, the main opposition party in the United States at the time; Van Buren and his predecessor, Andrew Jackson, were both Democrats. The Whigs took shape in the 1830s in opposition to Jackson's presidency; they tended to oppose both an overly powerful executive branch and territorial expansion and drew their support mainly from the urban middle classes, in contrast to the poor farmers and working-class men who formed the Democrats' base.

[2] *the newspapers of different parties* Most U.S. newspapers in the 1830s had explicit partisan affiliations.

[3] *wards* Dependants—people (such as minor children) under the protection or custody of someone else. Emerson's characterization here of the relationship between the U.S. government and Indigenous nations reflects the idea—widespread among white Americans at the time—that this relationship was one of guardianship or tutelage of weaker, supposedly more "childlike" people by a stronger, supposedly more "mature" state. This view can be seen, for example, in the common portrayal—as in the political cartoon of Andrew Jackson included elsewhere in this Contexts section—of Indigenous people as "children" of the "Great Father" (i.e., the U.S. president); it was also enshrined in federal law, for instance in Supreme Court Chief Justice John Marshall's ruling in *Cherokee Nation v. Georgia* (1831), which asserted that the relationship of Indigenous nations to the U.S. resembled "that of a ward to their guardian."

the flimsy plea of its being a party act. Sir, to us the questions upon which the government and the people have been agitated during the past year, touching the prostration of the currency and of trade,[1] seem but motes[2] in comparison. These hard times, it is true, have brought the discussion home to every farmhouse and poor man's house in this town; but it is the chirping of grasshoppers beside the immortal question whether justice shall be done by the race of civilized to the race of savage man—whether all the attributes of reason, of civility, of justice, and even of mercy, shall be put off by the American people, and so vast an outrage upon the Cherokee Nation and upon human nature shall be consummated.

One circumstance lessens the reluctance with which I intrude at this time on your attention, my conviction that the government ought to be admonished of a new historical fact, which the discussion of this question has disclosed, namely, that there exists in a great part of the Northern people a gloomy diffidence[3] in the *moral* character of the government.

On the broaching of this question, a general expression of despondency, of disbelief that any good will accrue from a remonstrance on an act of fraud and robbery, appeared in those men to whom we naturally turn for aid and counsel. Will the American government steal? Will it lie? Will it kill?—We ask triumphantly. Our counsellors and old statesmen here say that ten years ago they would have staked their lives on the affirmation that the proposed Indian measures could not be executed; that the unanimous country would put them down. And now the steps of this crime follow each other so fast, at such fatally quick time, that the millions of virtuous citizens, whose agents the government are, have no place to interpose, and must shut their eyes until the last howl and wailing of these tormented villages and tribes shall afflict the ear of the world.

I will not hide from you, as an indication of this alarming distrust, that a letter addressed as mine is, and suggesting to the mind of the Executive the plain obligations of man, has a burlesque character in the apprehensions[4] of some of my friends. I, sir, will not beforehand treat you with the contumely[5] of this distrust. I will at least state to you this fact, and show you how plain and humane people, whose love would be honor, regard the policy of the government, and what injurious inferences they draw as to the minds of the governors. A man with your experience in affairs must have seen cause to appreciate the futility of opposition to the moral sentiment. However feeble the sufferer and however great the oppressor, it is in the nature of things that the blow should recoil upon the aggressor. For God is in the sentiment, and it cannot be withstood. The potentate and the people perish before it; but with it, and as its executor, they are omnipotent.

I write thus, sir, to inform you of the state of mind these Indian tidings have awakened here, and to pray with one voice more that you, whose hands are strong with the delegated power of fifteen millions of men, will avert with that might the terrific[6] injury which threatens the Cherokee tribe.

With great respect, sir, I am your fellow citizen, Ralph Waldo Emerson.

from Eliza Whitmire, interview (1936)

One of the white American institutions assimilated by the so-called "Five Civilized Tribes," especially the Cherokee, as they adapted to the settler-colonial culture encroaching upon them in the early nineteenth century was African American chattel slavery. When the remaining Cherokee were expelled in 1838, the small minority who owned enslaved people brought their "property" with them. Among the enslaved African Americans caught up in the Cherokee expulsion was the family of Eliza Whitmire, who was about five years old at the time. Nearly

---

1   *the prostration ... trade* In 1837, various economic developments (including a sharp drop in the price of cotton and a collapsing land bubble) sparked a severe financial crisis, known as the Panic of 1837. The panic caused an economic depression that lasted into the mid-1840s.

2   *motes* Trifles.

3   *diffidence* Distrust.

4   *burlesque* Grotesquely comic; *apprehensions* Understandings.

5   *beforehand* I.e., in anticipation (of the president not being worthy of his trust); *contumely* Insolent contempt.

6   *terrific* I.e., terrible.

a century later, she was interviewed as part of an oral history project conducted by the federal Works Progress Administration under the New Deal, during which she gave the account of the Cherokee expulsion presented below.

M y name is Eliza Whitmire. I live on a farm near Estella[1] where I settled shortly after the Civil War and where I have lived ever since. I was born in slavery in the state of Georgia, my parents having belonged to a Cherokee Indian of the name of George Sanders who owned a large plantation in the old Cherokee Nation in Georgia. He also owned a large number of slaves but I was too young to remember how many he owned.

I do not know the exact date of my birth, although my mother told me I was about five years old when President Andrew Jackson[2] ordered General Scott[3] to proceed to the Cherokee country in Georgia, with two thousand troops and remove the Cherokees by force to the Indian Territory. This bunch of Indians were called the Eastern Emigrants. The Old Settler Cherokees had moved themselves in 1835 when the order was first given to the Cherokees to move out.

The weeks that followed General Scott's order to remove the Cherokees were filled with horror and suffering for the unfortunate Cherokees and their slaves. The women and children were driven from their homes, sometimes with blows, and close on the heels of the retreating Indians came greedy whites to pillage the Indians' homes, drive off their cattle, horses and hogs, and they even rifled the graves for any jewelry or other ornaments that might have been buried with the dead.

The Cherokees, after being driven from their homes, were divided into detachments of nearly equal size and late in October, 1838, the first detachment started, the others following one by one. The aged, sick and the young children rode in the wagons, which carried the provisions and bedding, while others went on foot. The trip was made in the dead of winter and many died from exposure from sleet and snow, and all who lived to make this trip, or had parents who made it, will long remember it as a bitter memory.

Freeman Owle, "The Trail of Tears" (1996)

Born in 1947, Freeman Owle is a member of the Eastern Band of Cherokee Indians, who are descended from Cherokee living in the mountains of southwestern North Carolina who managed to escape expulsion. He grew up hearing and learning his family's traditional stories and eventually became a storyteller himself. He related the story below, which combines a family history of the Trail of Tears with an account of the origin of the Cherokee Eastern Band, in October 1996; the story was collected in *Living Stories of the Cherokee*, edited by Barbara R. Duncan (1998), on which the present text is based.

I found that out[4] as I was growing up,
and my parents began to tell me this story of the
    Trail of Tears.
And you look at me and you say,
    "Well, he's probably as much Scots-Irish[5] as I am."
Yes, I am.
But I am Oogoku tsiskayi Tsalagi ashkaya.[6]

---

1   *Estella*   Town in the Cherokee Nation, in the northeastern portion of what is now the state of Oklahoma.

2   *President Andrew Jackson*   Although Jackson was the most prominent advocate of "Indian removal" and is the president most closely associated with the policy, the expulsion of the Cherokee was in fact carried out under the authority of Jackson's successor, Martin Van Buren, who became president in 1837.

3   *General Scott*   Winfield Scott (1786–1866), Army general who oversaw the Cherokee expulsion. The combined force of militiamen, Army regulars, and volunteers with which Scott enforced the expulsion totaled 7,000, far more than the 2,000 Whitmire goes on to estimate.

4   *I found that out*   A segue from the previous story Owle told in the session at which this story was collected, which ends with the affirmation that "Never again will there be a person like you in this world[.] … [W]e're all very, very special."

5   *Scots-Irish*   Descendants of Protestants from Scotland and England who settled in Ulster, the northern province of Ireland, during the seventeenth century, many of whom then re-emigrated to the American colonies. In America, most Scots-Irish settled in the Appalachian Mountains from Pennsylvania southward, where they lived in close proximity to Native Americans, including the Cherokee, and frequently intermarried with them.

6   *Oogoku … ashkaya*   Cherokee: Owl Birdtown Cherokee man. (The editors wish to thank Professor Christopher Teuton of the Cherokee Nation for his translation of this line.)

My name is Owle, I live in Birdtown,[1]
   and I happened to grow up on the reservation.
Sort of like a little story that Marsha was reading to
   our daughter last night
      about the zebra.
Says, "Are you white with black stripes or black with
   white stripes?"
Are you Scots-Irish with Indian, or Indian with
   Scots-Irish?
I don't know, I really don't.
All I know is I'm different from anyone who's ever
   lived,
      and different than anyone who ever will.
And my fingerprints are different, so I must be special.
They told me that
   my family was, in 1838, in a log cabin near
      Murphy, North Carolina.
And all of a sudden,
   someone was banging on the door
   early that morning.
And they opened up the door and they looked out,
   and fifty Georgia soldiers were standing in the yard.
They said,
   "Come out of the cabin."
And when my great-grandfather—
   I'll just call him grandfather—
   did,
      they burned the cabin to the ground.
He and his wife and small baby were taken to
   Murphy, North Carolina,
      put into a stockade,
      stayed there for six weeks.
There was no roof, only a line of poles
   encircling the stockade.
They say that
   the mud was deep,
   there wasn't much food,
   no one had anything to cover themselves with,
   but the baby survived because the mother was
      feeding it.
Early one morning,
   on that October morning
   when the frost was heavy

and the ground was frozen hard enough for
   wagons to travel,
General Winfield Scott[2] began to march the
   people out of this fort.
So he marched them across the frozen ground
   and across the Santeetlah Mountains
   into Tennessee.
There was a woman by the name of Martha Ross,
   Scots-Irish and Cherokee.
She had a beautiful coat,
   and she began to look, late that night,
   and the rain was coming down, and it was cold,
   and she heard a baby crying.
She went to the sound of the baby and found the child
   very cold
   and wet—
   it had pneumonia.
She covered the child with her coat,
   and two days later she died of pneumonia herself.
It is people like this
   who have made contributions to the Cherokee
      society.
It is people like the people of North Carolina
   who allowed those people living in North Carolina
      to remain there.
The history is written,
   the history says
   that North Carolina did not remove its
      Cherokees.[3]
They were called the Oconaluftee Cherokees.
And you go see *Unto These Hills*,[4] it doesn't mention
   this.

---

[1]   *Birdtown* Town in the Qualla Boundary, the area in south-western North Carolina that is the territory of the Eastern Band of Cherokee Indians, held in trust for them by the federal government.

[2]   *Winfield Scott* Army general (1786–1866) who oversaw the Cherokee expulsion.

[3]   *It is people like the people … its Cherokees* Several hundred Cherokee living in the remote mountains of southwestern North Carolina were able to evade the troops sent to round them up for deportation; others managed to negotiate exemptions from being expelled, in some cases under the condition that they give up Cherokee citizenship and assimilate as U.S. and North Carolina citizens. The name "Oconaluftee Cherokees," which Owle gives in the following line, comes from the Oconaluftee River, along which most of the North Carolina Cherokee who escaped expulsion lived and which the Cherokee consider to be sacred.

[4]   *Unto These Hills* Historical drama about Cherokee history up to the Trail of Tears. The drama has been staged consistently at an outdoor theater in Cherokee, North Carolina, the headquarters of the Eastern Band, since 1950.

But they didn't make them leave.
The other fifteen thousand began to march on toward
  Oklahoma.
When they got to the Mississippi, they asked my
  grandfather
    if he would count the Cherokees who crossed the
      river.
And he said,
    "Yes, 1 will."
But he told his wife in Cherokee,
    "Go hide in the cane brake and take the baby with
      you.
    And I will tell them you're here.
    And we'll go back home."
So he counted the Cherokees as they crossed the
  flatboat across the Mississippi,
    and he told the soldiers,
    "All the Cherokees are accounted for."
And they said,
    "Are you sure?
    Go back to the river and check again."
And this was what he wanted,
    and he goes back to the river,
    and he looks into the bushes and the brush,
    and all of a sudden he leaps into the water.
They come running behind, and they shoot many
  times into the water.
They look into the black, swirling waters of the
  Mississippi,
    and this Cherokee doesn't surface.
So—for a long time.
And they give him up as being dead.
He's breathing through a reed all this time.
And after he gives the soldiers time enough to go away,
    he comes up and he swims back
    across the Mississippi.
He looks for his wife on the other side,
    and—she heard the gunshots.
She ran
    with the baby in her arms,
    she would run all night long,
    and then find a briar patch to sleep in in the
      daytime,
    or a farmer's haystack.
Took her several weeks to get back home,

but she came on back to the old burned-out cabin
  site
    because that's all she knew as home.
She waited there week after week,
    and her husband didn't return.
She went down to the village,
    to the Scots-Irish settlers,
    and they gladly gave her food.
And they were feeding those Cherokees
    that were hiding in the mountains.
If the North Carolina people had been caught by the
  Georgia guard
    handing out food to the Cherokees,
    they too would have lost their land and been put
      in prison
    as Cherokee sympathizers.
But the Scots-Irish people were feeding her
    one morning, a year later,
    when she heard a noise up on the hill,
    and she looked and there was someone coming.
And so she ran and hid with the baby.
And after a while it was her husband
    coming out of the woods.
They were reunited,
    and we still live
    in a little place where they came and rebought
      with their own money
    called Birdtown.
And the reason they were able to rebuy it was:
    there was a wagon train coming through here,
    and it had a little baby on it—
    a little white child
    who was very sick.
And the parents were smart enough to say,
    "If we go on with this child, it's going to die."
And they said—
    have you ever heard the term, "Give it to the
      Indians"?[1]
    They gave the child to the Indians.

---

[1] *Give it … Indians* Variation of "Give it back to the Indians," a
phrase that was widespread in white American usage in the mid- and
late twentieth century. The phrase was used of a place or thing that
had become so spoiled or run-down as to be undesirable, with the
implication either that it was now fit only for Indigenous people or
that it would be better off in the hands of Indigenous people, who
would take better care of it than white Americans had. The phrase was
popularized by a 1939 Broadway show tune, "Give [continued …]

Chief Yonaguska[1] made the child better.
His name was William Holland Thomas.[2]
Will Thomas was already a citizen of the United
    States,
        and the Cherokees could go and buy up land
        and put it in this child's name
        by the thousands of acres,
        and we are still here.
But in the early 1920s
    my grandfather, Solomon Owle,
    was living in this little place called Birdtown
    and paying his taxes to Swain County,[3]
    and I think was a good citizen.
The federal government looked down and said,
    "This can't be.
    This bunch of savages are not supposed to be able
        to take care of themselves."
And they came down and took the deeds away from
    those people
    and set up what they called the Qualla Indian
        Boundary.
They couldn't call it a reservation,
    because a reservation is land that is given to the
        Indians,
    and the Indians are forced upon it.
This land was bought back
    under Will Thomas's name—
    see, it's not a reservation
    it's a little different.
You know, I came here tonight to tell you
    that the Cherokee people don't really hold any
        hatred

or animosity in their heart
    for those things that happened in the past.
We can take our hats off to the past,
    but as one great gentleman said,
    "We should take our shirts off to the future."
The reason the Cherokee people survived
    is because they loved their neighbors
    and were good neighbors.
The Cherokees of today
    still welcome even all the visitors in the '41 Chevys
    and the '40 Ford coupes
    and the bears and everything—
    they were glad to see the tourists come.
And we're glad to see the tourists come, even today.

from John O'Sullivan or Jane Cazneau, "Annexation," *The United States Magazine and Democratic Review* (1845)

The first recorded appearance of the term "manifest destiny" was in the article below, published in the July–August 1845 issue of *The United States Magazine and Democratic Review*, a Jacksonian Democratic periodical founded by the Irish American editor John L. O'Sullivan (1813–95). The article, which makes the case for the U.S. annexation of what was then the independent Republic of Texas (a hotly debated issue at the time), was originally published anonymously; it has traditionally been credited to O'Sullivan, but several historians have posited that it was actually written by Jane Cazneau (1807–78), a journalist for the *Democratic Review* and other periodicals who was an avid expansionist.

It is now time for the opposition to the Annexation of Texas to cease, all further agitation of the waters of bitterness and strife, at least in connection with this question—even though it may perhaps be required of us as a necessary condition of the freedom of our institutions, that we must live on forever in a state of unpausing struggle and excitement upon some subject of party division or other. But, in regard to Texas, enough has now been given to party. It is time for the common duty of Patriotism to the Country to succeed—or if this claim will not be recognized, it is at

---

It Back to the Indians," which jocularly proposes returning New York City to the Indigenous people from whom it was first purchased.

[1] *Yonaguska* Cherokee chief (1759–1839) whose name translates to "Drowning Bear"; he led the North Carolina Cherokee who managed to avoid expulsion and remain on their homelands, where they eventually reorganized as the Eastern Band of Cherokee Indians.

[2] *William Holland Thomas* White adopted son of Yonaguska (1805–93) who negotiated on behalf of the North Carolina Cherokee with the federal government, purchased land in North Carolina to be used by the Cherokee, and eventually succeeded Yonaguska as chief of the Eastern Band, despite the fact that he had no Cherokee ancestry himself. The written historical record of the circumstances of Thomas's adoption by Yonaguska does not match the version related in this story.

[3] *Swain County* County in the southwestern corner of North Carolina on the border with Tennessee.

James S. Baillie, *Hunting Indians in Florida with Blood Hounds*, 1848. This lithograph by Baillie, a prolific mid-nineteenth-century lithograph artist, was printed by opponents of Zachary Taylor's successful 1848 presidential campaign. The lithograph criticizes Taylor's conduct during his period (1838–40) as commander of U.S. military forces in the Second Seminole War—specifically, his use of bloodhounds against the Seminole. In fact, blood-hounds were used only to track Seminole through the Florida wetlands (often unsuccessfully), not—as depicted here—to physi-

cally attack them, but the misconception reflects the revulsion many white Americans felt toward the war and the country's treatment of Native Americans in general. Taylor's speech bubble reads: "Hurra! Captain, we've got them at last, the dogs are at them—now forward with the Rifle and Bayonet and 'give them Hell Brave Boys,' let not a red nigger escape—, show no mercy—, exterminate them,—this day we'll close the Florida War, and write its history in the blood of the Seminole—but remember Captn., as I have written to our Government to say that the dogs are intended to ferret out the Indians, (not to worry [i.e., bite] them) for the sake of consistency and the appearance of Humanity, you will appear not to notice the devastation they commit."

Charles Bird King, *Tuko-See-Mathla, a Seminole Chief*, 1844. Also known as John Hicks, Tuko-See-Mathla was a member of a Seminole delegation to Washington, D.C. in 1826, where King painted his portrait. This lithograph, based on King's portrait, was later printed as part of *History of the Indian Tribes of North America*, a three-volume collection of biographies of Indigenous leaders, with accompanying portraits, published by Thomas McKenney and James Hall; the collection remains an important source for biographical and visual information about early nineteenth-century Native American life.

least time for common sense to acquiesce with decent grace in the inevitable and the irrevocable.

Texas is now ours. Already, before these words are written, her Convention has undoubtedly ratified the acceptance, by her Congress, of our proffered invitation into the Union; and made the requisite changes in her already republican form of constitution to adapt it to its future federal relations. Her star and her stripe may already be said to have taken their place in the glorious blazon of our common nationality; and the sweep of our eagle's wing already includes within its circuit the wide extent of her fair and fertile land. She is no longer to us a mere geographical space—a certain combination of coast, plain, mountain, valley, forest and stream. She is no longer to us a mere country on the map. She comes within the dear and sacred designation of Our Country; no longer a "*pays*," she is a part of "*la patrie*";[1] and that which is at once a sentiment and a virtue, Patriotism, already begins to thrill for her too within the national heart. ... The next session of Congress will see the representatives of the new young State in their places in both our halls of national legislation, side by side with those of the old Thirteen. Let their reception into "the family" be frank, kindly, and cheerful, as befits such an occasion, as comports not less with our own self-respect than patriotic duty towards them. Ill betide those foul birds that delight to file[2] their own nest, and disgust the ear with perpetual discord of ill-omened croak.

Why, were other reasoning wanting, in favor of now elevating this question of the reception of Texas into the Union, out of the lower region of our past party dissensions, up to its proper level of a high and broad nationality, it surely is to be found, found abundantly, in the manner in which other nations have undertaken to intrude themselves into it, between us and the proper parties to the case, in a spirit of hostile interference against us, for the avowed object of thwarting our policy and hampering our power, limiting our greatness and checking the fulfillment of our manifest destiny to overspread the continent allotted by Providence for the free development of our yearly multiplying millions. This we

have seen done by England, our old rival and enemy; and by France, strangely coupled with her against us[.][3] ... The zealous activity with which this effort to defeat us was pushed by the representatives of those governments, together with the character of intrigue accompanying it, fully constituted that case of foreign interference, which Mr. Clay[4] himself declared should and would unite us all in maintaining the common cause of our country against foreigner and the foe. ...

It is wholly untrue, and unjust to ourselves, the pretence that the Annexation has been a measure of spoliation, unrightful and unrighteous—of military conquest under forms of peace and law—of territorial aggrandizement at the expense of justice, and justice due by a double sanctity to the weak. This view of the question is wholly unfounded[.] ... The independence of Texas was complete and absolute. It was an independence, not only in fact, but of right. No obligation of duty towards Mexico tended in the least degree to restrain our right to effect the desired recovery of the fair province once our own—whatever motives of policy might have prompted a more deferential consideration of her feelings and her pride, as involved in the question. If Texas became peopled with an American population, it was by no contrivance of our government, but on the express invitation of that of Mexico herself[.] ... [Texas] was released, rightfully and absolutely released, from all Mexican allegiance, or duty of cohesion to the Mexican political body, by the acts and fault of Mexico herself, and Mexico alone.[5] There never was a clearer case. ... What then can be more preposterous than all this clamor by Mexico and the Mexican interest, against Annexation, as a violation of any rights of hers, any duties of ours? ...

---

1   *pays ... la patrie*   In French, "pays" means "land," while "patrie" means "fatherland," i.e., nation.

2   *file*   Defile, pollute. The phrase "It's a foul bird that files its own nest" was proverbial.

---

3   *England ... us*   When the administration of U.S. President John Tyler began to push for the annexation of Texas in 1844, Britain and France attempted to forestall it by proposing a treaty between Texas and Mexico whereby Mexico would recognize Texan independence and Texas would agree not to seek incorporation into the United States.

4   *Mr. Clay*   Henry Clay (1777–1852), politician from Kentucky. As a leading figure in the generally anti-expansionist Whig Party who was the party's candidate in the 1844 presidential election, Clay strongly opposed Texas annexation.

5   *If Texas ... Mexico alone*   See the section on "Expansion, Expulsion, and 'Manifest Destiny'" in the introduction to this anthology volume for an overview of the history of American settlement in Texas and of Texas's revolt against Mexican rule referred to here.

Nor is there any just foundation for the charge that Annexation is a great pro-slavery measure—calculated to increase and perpetuate that institution. Slavery had nothing to do with it. Opinions were and are greatly divided, both at the North and South, as to the influence to be exerted by it on Slavery and the Slave States. ...

... The country which was the subject of Annexation in this case, from its geographical position and relations, happens to be—or rather the portion of it now actually settled, happens to be—a slave country. But a similar process might have taken place in proximity to a different section of our Union; and indeed there is a great deal of Annexation yet to take place, within the life of the present generation, along the whole line of our northern border. Texas has been absorbed into the Union in the inevitable fulfilment of the general law which is rolling our population westward; the connection of which with that ratio of growth in population which is destined to swell our numbers to the enormous population of *two hundred and fifty millions* (if not more), is too evident to leave us in doubt of the manifest design of Providence in regard to the occupation of this continent. It was disintegrated from Mexico in the natural course of events, by a process perfectly legitimate on its own part, blameless on ours; and in which all the censures due to wrong, perfidy and folly, rest on Mexico alone. And possessed as it was by a population which was in truth but a colonial detachment from our own, and which was still bound by myriad ties of the very heart-strings to its old relations, domestic and political, their incorporation into the Union was not only inevitable, but the most natural, right and proper thing in the world—and it is only astonishing that there should be any among ourselves to say it nay. ...

... With no friendship for slavery, though unprepared to excommunicate to eternal damnation, with bell, book, and candle, those who are, we see nothing in the bearing of the Annexation of Texas on that institution to awaken a doubt of the wisdom of that measure, or a compunction for the humble part contributed by us towards its consummation.

California will, probably, next fall away from the loose adhesion which, in such a country as Mexico, holds a remote province in a slight equivocal kind of dependence on the metropolis. Imbecile[1] and distracted, Mexico never can exert any real governmental authority over such a country. The impotence of the one and the distance of the other, must make the relation one of virtual independence; unless, by stunting the province of all natural growth, and forbidding that immigration which can alone develop its capabilities and fulfil the purposes of its creation, tyranny may retain a military dominion, which is no government in the legitimate sense of the term. In the case of California this is now impossible. The Anglo-Saxon[2] foot is already on its borders. Already the advance guard of the irresistible army of Anglo-Saxon emigration has begun to pour down upon it, armed with the plough and the rifle, and marking its trail with schools and colleges, courts and representative halls, mills and meeting-houses.[3] A population will soon be in actual occupation of California, over which it will be idle for Mexico to dream of dominion. They will necessarily become independent. All this without agency of our government, without responsibility of our people—in the natural flow of events, the spontaneous working of principles, and the adaptation of the tendencies and wants of the human race to the elemental circumstances in the midst of which they find themselves placed. And they will have a right to independence—to self-government—to the possession of the homes conquered from the wilderness by their own labors and dangers, sufferings and sacrifices—a better and a truer right than the artificial title of sovereignty in Mexico, a thousand miles distant, inheriting from Spain a title good only against those who have none better. Their right to independence will be the natural right of self-government belonging to any community strong enough to maintain it—distinct in position, origin and character, and free from any mutual obligations of membership of a common political body,

---

[1] *Imbecile* Weak (though also with derogatory connotations of intellectual deficiency).

[2] *Anglo-Saxon* This term, which originally referred to the Germanic cultural group that settled in and ruled England in the early Middle Ages, was widely used in both Britain and the United States in the nineteenth century to refer to white people inhabiting or stemming from England (or the British Isles more generally). In such contexts, the term often carried—and still carries—racist connotations of inherent racial superiority.

[3] *meeting-houses* I.e., churches, specifically those of Protestant denominations.

binding it to others by the duty of loyalty and compact of public faith. This will be their title to independence; and by this title, there can be no doubt that the population now fast streaming down upon California will both assert and maintain that independence. Whether they will then attach themselves to our Union or not, is not to be predicted with any certainty. Unless the projected railroad across the continent to the Pacific be carried into effect, perhaps they may not; though even in that case, the day is not distant when the Empires of the Atlantic and Pacific would again flow together into one, as soon as their inland border should approach each other. But that great work, colossal as appears the plan on its first suggestion, cannot remain long unbuilt. Its necessity for this very purpose of binding and holding together in its iron clasp our fast-settling Pacific region with that of the Mississippi valley—the natural facility[1] of the route—the ease with which any amount of labor for the construction can be drawn in from the overcrowded populations of Europe, to be paid in the lands made valuable by the progress of the work itself—and its immense utility to the commerce of the world with the whole eastern coast of Asia, alone almost sufficient for the support of such a road—these considerations give assurance that the day cannot be distant which shall witness the conveyance of the representatives from Oregon and California to Washington within less time than a few years ago was devoted to a similar journey by those from Ohio; while the magnetic telegraph will enable the editors of the "San Francisco Union," the "Astoria Evening Post," or the "Nootka Morning News,"[2] to set up in type the first half of the President's Inaugural before the echoes of the latter half shall have died away beneath the lofty porch of the Capitol, as spoken from his lips.

---

[1]   *facility*   Ease, expediency.

[2]   *Astoria ... News*   Astoria and Nootka are both places in the Pacific Northwest. While Astoria is in what would become the U.S. state of Oregon, Nootka Island is adjacent to Vancouver Island, which today belongs to the Canadian province of British Columbia. A year after this article was published, the so-called Oregon Country was divided between Britain and the U.S. along the 49th parallel, with all territory to the south of the parallel entering the U.S. and all territory to the north of it remaining in British hands (and eventually becoming part of Canada). As the article makes clear, however, expansionist Americans in the early 1840s desired and expected to annex the entire Pacific Northwest.

Away, then, with all idle French talk of *balances of power* on the American Continent. There is no growth in Spanish America! Whatever progress of population there may be in the British Canadas, is only for their own early severance of their present colonial relation to the little island three thousand miles across the Atlantic; soon to be followed by Annexation, and destined to swell the still accumulating momentum of our progress. And whosoever may hold the balance, though they should cast into the opposite scale all the bayonets and cannon, not only of France and England, but of Europe entire, how would it kick the beam against the simple, solid weight of the two hundred and fifty, or three hundred millions—and American millions—destined to gather beneath the flutter of the stripes and stars, in the fast hastening year of the Lord 1945!

from Walt Whitman, *Brooklyn Daily Eagle* editorials

In 1846, Walt Whitman, then twenty-seven years old, took over the editorship of *The Brooklyn Daily Eagle and Kings County Democrat*, a newspaper with strong Democratic Party affiliations. As editor, Whitman authored a series of columns that year that enthusiastically endorsed "manifest destiny" thinking: the editorials supported the Mexican–American War and advocated the annexation of Mexican territory, especially California. However, Whitman soon grew more uneasy about the war, and particularly about the possibility that slavery would be extended to the areas seized from Mexico; he supported the Wilmot Proviso—Democratic Congressman David Wilmot's unsuccessful attempt to ban slavery in conquered Mexican territory—and was eventually fired from the *Daily Eagle* for his embrace of such "free soil" policies. The text of the excerpts from Whitman's editorials given below is based on their original newspaper publications.

SHALL WE FIGHT IT OUT? (11 MAY 1846)

Yes: Mexico must be thoroughly chastised! We have reached a point, in our intercourse[3] with that

---

[3]   *intercourse*   Interactions.

Frances Flora Bond Palmer, *Across the Continent: "Westward the Course of Empire Takes Its Way,"* 1868. The title of this lithograph, produced for the popular Currier and Ives printmaking firm that sold inexpensive colored engravings to a mass audience, alludes to both a line from a 1726 poem, "Verses on the Prospect of Planting Arts and Learning in America," by the British philosopher George Berkeley, and a well-known mural, painted in 1861 for the U.S. Capitol Building by the artist Emmanuel Leutze, that took Berkeley's line for its title. (Another example of the widespread quotation and misquotation of the line in nineteenth-century American culture occurs in Henry David Thoreau's essay 'Walking' [1862], excerpted in the website portion of this Contexts section.) Born and raised in Britain, Frances Palmer (1812–76) moved to the U.S. in the 1840s, where she became a successful illustrator; another of her lithographs appears in the "Nature and the Environment" Contexts section in the website component of this volume.

country, when prompt and effectual demonstrations of force are enjoined upon us by every dictate of right and policy. The news of yesterday[1] has added the last argument wanted to prove the necessity of an immediate Declaration of War by our government toward its southern neighbor.

We are justified in the face of the world, in having treated Mexico with more forbearance than we have ever yet treated an enemy—for Mexico, though contemptible in many respects, is an enemy deserving a vigorous "lesson." We have coaxed, excused, listened with deaf ears to the insolent gasconade[2] of her government, submitted thus far to a most offensive rejection of an Ambassador personifying the American nation, and waited for years without payment of the claims of our injured merchants. We have sought peace through

---

[1]   *news of yesterday*   In late April 1846, Mexican forces attacked a U.S. patrol in the territory between the Nueces and Rio Grande rivers—territory that was disputed between Mexico, which claimed the Nueces as Texas's boundary (and refused to recognize Texan independence from Mexico in any case), and the U.S., which claimed the Rio Grande as the boundary. U.S. President James K. Polk had ordered U.S. troops to move into the disputed area, fully aware that this would likely provoke conflict. News of the clash reached the U.S. east coast in early May (by which time Mexican and U.S. troops in the disputed region had fought several other battles), and Congress declared war on Mexico on 13 May.

[2]   *gasconade*   Extravagant boasting.

every avenue, and shut our eyes to many things, which, had they come from England or France, the President would not have dared to pass over without stern and speedy resentment. We have dammed up our memory, of what has passed in the South years ago—of the devilish massacres of some of our bravest and noblest sons, the children not of the South alone, but of the North and the West—massacres, not only in defiance of ordinary humanity, but in violation of all the rules of war.[1] Who has read the sickening story of those brutal wholesale massacres, so useless for any purpose except gratifying the cowardly appetite of a nation of bravos,[2] willing to shoot down men by the hundred in cold blood—without panting for the day when the prayer of that blood should be listened to[3]—when the vengeance of a retributive God should be meted out to those who so ruthlessly and needlessly slaughtered His image?

That day has arrived. We think there can be no doubt of the truth of yesterday's news; and we are sure the people here, ten to one, are for prompt and *effectual* hostilities. ... Let our arms now be carried with a spirit which shall teach the world that, while we are not forward with a quarrel, America knows how to crush, as well as how to expand!

from OUR TERRITORY ON THE PACIFIC (7 JULY 1846)

However soon the passage-at-arms between this republic and Mexico be closed, we hope—since things have resolved themselves into the state they now hold—that the United States will (in some way) fix their mark of ownership on the American coast of the Pacific[.] ...

We love to indulge in thoughts of the future extent and power of this republic—because all its increase is the increase of human happiness and liberty. Therefore hope we that the U.S. will keep a fast grip on California. What has miserable, inefficient Mexico—with her superstition, her burlesque[4] of freedom, her actual tyranny by the few over the many—what has she to do with the great mission of peopling the new world with a noble race? Be it ours, to achieve that mission! Be it ours to roll down all of the upstart leaven[5] of old despotism, that comes in our way!

Alfred Jones, *Mexican News*, 1851. Jones (1819–1900), an Anglo-American engraver, made this copy of an 1848 painting, *War News from Mexico*, by the artist Richard Caton Woodville, Sr. (1825–55); the copy was distributed to members of the American Art-Union, a subscription-based organization founded to promote awareness of (and the sale of) work by American artists. Both the original painting and this copy effectively convey the intensity with which Americans followed, and debated, the Mexican–American War, and the works' metaphorically rich composition and detail have made them enduringly famous.

---

1   *We have dammed up ... war*   Reference to the battles of the Alamo and Goliad, fought between the Mexican Army and rebel Texans during the Texan Revolution in 1836. At the Alamo, the entire Texan garrison of between 182 and 257 men was killed, several of them after they had surrendered; at Goliad, hundreds of Texan prisoners (the exact number is unknown) were executed. Whitman later included a description of the Goliad Massacre in his poem "Song of Myself," first published in 1855.

2   *bravos*   Men who fight and kill for hire.

3   *when ... listened to*   See Genesis 4.10, in which God tells Cain, who has just murdered his brother Abel, "the voice of thy brother's blood crieth unto me from the ground."

4   *burlesque*   Ridiculous parody.

5   *leaven*   Undesirable holdover. See 1 Corinthians 5.7: "Purge out therefore the old leaven, that ye may be a new lump, as ye are unleavened."

Thomas D'Arcy McGee, "The Army of the West" (c. 1849)

During the Mexican–American War, an American military unit called the Army of the West, commanded by General Stephen Watts Kearny, marched west from Fort Leavenworth, Kansas, to invade New Mexico and California. The army was charged not only with defeating any Mexicans in its path but also with clearing a road through the mountains and forests across which settlers could travel. The poem presented below, by the Irish-born politician and writer Thomas D'Arcy McGee (1825–68), takes the Army of the West's successful campaign as its backdrop but broadens and deepens the actual army's metaphorical significance. McGee, whose advocacy for Irish revolution against British rule forced him to move to the U.S. in 1848, supported Irish American settlement in the west as a way of preserving Irish Catholic identity from dilution in the big eastern cities—as well as protecting Irish Catholics themselves from the anti-immigrant and anti-Catholic prejudice they frequently encountered there. McGee's own experiences in the U.S. eventually soured him on American-style democracy and republicanism, and in the 1850s he abandoned revolutionary politics in favor of Irish Catholic conservatism. He left the U.S. in 1857 and moved to Montreal, where he became a strong advocate of Canadian confederation and an outspoken critic of American expansionism. His opposition to the Fenians—Irish American radicals who sought to strike a blow against the British Empire by seizing Canada from Britain—probably led to his assassination in 1868, one year after he had helped bring about a confederated Canada.

"The Army of the West" was first published in 1849 in the New York *Nation*, an Irish American newspaper McGee edited. The text presented below is based on that published in *The Poems of Thomas D'Arcy McGee* (1870).

We fight upon a new-found plan, our Army of the West—
Our brave brigades, along the line, will leave the foe no rest—
Our battle-axes, bright and keen, with every day's swift sands,
Lay low the foes of Liberty, and then annex their lands;
5 On, onward through the Western woods our standard saileth ever
And shadows many a nameless peak and unbaptizèd river—
The Army of the Future we, the champions of the Unborn—
We pluck the primal forests up, and sow their sites with corn.

That ruggèd standard beareth the royal arms of toil—
10 The axe, and pike, and ponderous sledge, and plough that frees the soil—
The field is made of stripes, and the stars the crest supplies,
And the living eagles hover round the flagstaffs where it flies.
And thus beneath our standard, right merrily we go,
The Future for our heritage, the tangled Waste our foe:
15 The Army of the Future we, the champions of the Unborn—
We pluck the primal forests up, and sow their sites with corn.

Down in yon glade the anvil rings beneath the arching oaks,
Behind yon hills our neighbors drive young oxen in the yokes,
Yon laughing boys now boating down the rapid river's tide,
20 Go to the learnèd man who keeps the log-house on its side
Like suckers° of the pine they grow,   *offshoots*
elastic, rugged, tall,
They will hit a swallow on the wing with a single rifle ball—
The cadets of our army they, from "the West-Point"[1] of the unborn,
They too will pluck the forests up, and sow their sites with corn.

---

[1] *West-Point* Since 1802, West Point, New York, has been the site of the United States Military Academy, where cadets are trained to become officers in the U.S. Army.

²⁵ Oh ye who dwell in cities, in the self-conceited East,
    Do you ever think how by our toils your comforts are
        increased?
    When you walk upon your carpets, and sit on your
        easy chairs,
    And read self-applauding stories, and give yourselves
        such airs—
    Do you ever think upon us, Backwoodsmen of the
        West,
³⁰ Who, from the Lakes[1] to Texas, have given the foe no
        rest?
    On the Army of the Future, and the champions of the
        Unborn,
    Who pluck the primal forests up, and sow their sites
        with corn?

from J.M. Whitfield in reply to F. Douglass [Letter on Emigration], 25 September 1853

> The African American poet James Monroe
> Whitfield (1822–71) wrote the letter excerpted
> below in response to Frederick Douglass's
> criticism of a call by Martin Delany—like
> Douglass, a friend and patron of Whitfield's—
> for a convention to discuss potential African
> American emigration out of the United States.
> The letter initiated an extended public debate
> between Whitfield, on one side, and Douglass
> and his allies, on the other, over the necessity
> and efficacy of African American emigration.
> The text of the excerpt from Whitfield's letter
> presented here is based on that published by
> Whitfield in *Arguments, Pro and Con, on the
> Call for a National Emigration Convention*
> (1854).

... [C]olored men can never be fully and
fairly respected as the equals of the
whites, in this country, or any other, until they are
able to show in some part of the world, men of their
own race occupying a primary and independent position, instead of a secondary and inferior one, as is
now the case everywhere. In short, that they must
show a powerful nation in which the black is the
ruling element, capable of maintaining a respectable

position among the *great* nations of the earth; and I
believe that the reflex influence of such a power with
the increased activity that its reaction will excite in
the colored people of this country will be the only
thing sufficiently powerful to remove the prejudices
which ages of unequal oppression have engendered,
unless the bleaching theory of Henry Clay should
prevail,[2] and be carried into practice, by which the
negro race in this country is to be absorbed, and its
identity lost in that of the Caucasian—a consummation in my opinion not to be wished for.[3] I believe
it to be the destiny of the negro to develop a higher
order of civilization and Christianity than the world
has yet seen. I also consider it a part of his "manifest
destiny" to possess all the tropical regions of this continent, with the adjacent islands. That the negro is to
be the predominant race in all that region in regard to
numbers, is beyond doubt. The only question is, shall
they exercise the power and influence their numbers
entitle them to, and become the ruling political element of the land in which they live? Or shall they, as
too many of our brethren in this country seem to be
willing to do, tamely submit to the usurpation of a
white aristocracy, naturally inferior to themselves in
physical, moral, and mental power, and devote their
lives to building up a power whose every energy will
be wielded to crush them?

anonymous, "Filibustering Ethics" (1854)

> First published in a San Francisco newspaper
> (exactly which one is a matter of dispute), this
> comic parody of "filibustering"—the practice by
> Americans of attempting to foment instability
> in, and then seize, Latin American countries—
> quickly went the mid-nineteenth-century

---

¹   *the Lakes*   I.e., the Great Lakes.

²   *the bleaching … prevail*   Henry Clay was a prominent politician
who, as senator for Kentucky, had recently helped put together the
Compromise of 1850, an arrangement between slave states and free
states that was regarded by abolitionists as a sellout. Clay enslaved
African Americans throughout his life but supported the gradual
abolition of slavery; however, he believed a multiracial society was
impossible and that free African Americans would therefore either
have to merge with white Americans or leave the country.

³   *a consummation … wished for*   See Shakespeare's *Hamlet* 3.1.71–
72, in which Hamlet calls death "a consummation / Devoutly to be
wished."

equivalent of viral: during the first five months of 1854, it was reprinted (under various titles) from Wisconsin to Louisiana and as far afield as Honolulu, in newspapers that ran the political gamut from abolitionism to the defense of "Southern Rights." The text given below is based on that printed in the *Milwaukee Daily Sentinel*, 20 May 1854.

Says Captain Robb to Farmer Cobb,
    "Your farm is very fine, sir;
Please give me up your title-deeds,
    I claim it all as mine, sir."
5 "Pray, how can it be thine?" says Cobb;
    "I'm sure I never sold it:
'Twas left me by my father, sir;
    I only ought to hold it."

"Nay, Cobb, the 'march of destiny'—
10   'Tis strange you don't perceive it—
Is sure to make it mine someday,
    I solemnly believe it."
"But have you not already got
    More land than you can till, sir?
15 More rocks than you can ever blast?
    More weeds than you can kill, sir?"

"Aye, Cobb; but something whispers me—
    A sort of inspiration—
That I've a *right* to every farm
20   Not under cultivation.
I'm of the 'Anglo-Saxon race,'[1]
    A people known to fame, sir;
But you—what right have you to land?
    Who ever heard your name, sir?

25 "I deem you, Cobb, a lazy lout,
    Poor, trodden down, and blind, sir;
And if I take your useless land,
    You ought to think it kind, sir!
And with my scientific skill,

30   I set it down as true, sir,
That I can gather from the farm
    Full twice as much as you, sir.

"To be explicit: 'Tis an age
    Of freedom and progression;
35 No longer, dog in manger-like,[2]
    Can you retain possession.
The farm you long since forfeited
    Because you failed to till it;
To me it clearly now belongs,
40   Simply because—*I will it.*

"My logic if you disapprove,
    Or fail of comprehending,
Or do not feel convinced that I
    Your welfare am attending,
45 I've plenty more of arguments
    To which I can resort, sir!
Six-shooters, rifles, bowie-knives,[3]
    Will indicate the sort, sir.

"So prithee, Cobb, take my advice;
50   Make over your domains, sir;
Or, sure as I am Captain Robb,
    Will I blow out your brains, sir!"
Poor Cobb can only grind his teeth
    And grumble protestations
55 That *might* should be the rule of *right*
    Among *enlightened nations.*

---

1 *Anglo-Saxon race* The term "Anglo-Saxon," which originally referred to the Germanic cultural group that settled in and ruled England in the early Middle Ages, was widely used in both Britain and the United States in the nineteenth century as a name for white people inhabiting or stemming from England (or the British Isles more generally). In such contexts, the term often carried—and still carries—racist connotations of inherent racial superiority.

2 *dog in manger-like* Reference to a traditional fable about a dog lying in a manger, who does not eat the grain contained in the manger but, by lying there, also prevents a horse from eating it. The fable is typically used to criticize someone who has no use for an object or resource in their possession but who prevents others, for whom it would be useful, from accessing it.

3 *bowie-knives* Type of fighting-knife associated with the American South. It was created for and named after Jim Bowie (c. 1796–1836), a soldier and slave trader who gained a reputation in the South for his violent exploits; he later moved to Texas, where he became a leader in the Texas Revolution and was killed at the Alamo.

This 1848 political cartoon caricatures Lewis Cass (1782–1866), the Democratic candidate in that year's presidential election. Cass had had a long political career up to that point, serving, among many other capacities, as Andrew Jackson's Secretary of War; he was one of the primary architects and leading exponents of Native American expulsion and had become known as a strong advocate of American expansion. The cartoon depicts Cass holding a bloodstained sword labeled "Manifest Destiny"; his leg, along with many other parts of his body, is a cannon firing "Gas" (a reference to Cass's nickname, "General Gas"); and his speech bubble lays out his annexationist agenda: "New Mexico, California, Chihuahua, Zacatecas, MEXICO, Peru, Yucatan, Cuba."

Francisco P. Ramírez, editorial from *El Clamor Público*, 24 July 1855

Born in Los Angeles, California, Francisco Ramírez (1837–1908) was just seventeen when, in 1855, he founded *El Clamor Público* ("The Public Outcry"), southern California's first Spanish-language newspaper. The paper was created, as Ramírez put it in 1856, "to serve as an organ for the general perspective of the Spanish race as a means of manifesting the atrocious injuries of which they have been victims in this country where they were born and in which they now live in a state inferior to the poorest of their persecutors." In his writing for the newspaper, Ramírez consistently celebrated the values enshrined in the U.S. Constitution, especially freedom of expression and freedom of the press,

while tirelessly condemning the hypocrisy with which the white Americans who had come to dominate his native land applied these values. His stewardship of the paper, which shut down in 1859, made *El Clamor Público* a landmark in the development of a Hispanic American ethnic and political consciousness in the United States. Ramírez later came to support the Republican Party because of its opposition to the expansion of slavery; he was active in Republican state politics until 1880, when he fled to Mexico to avoid a charge of bank fraud, never returning to California.

The editorial presented below exemplifies Ramírez's critique of white American racism and "manifest destiny" doctrine. The editorial was written, in part, in response to the passage of California's Anti-Vagrancy Act, which authorized the incarceration of all "vagrants," defined as people who did not have or accept employment, as well as sex workers and alcoholics. Section Two of the act specifically singled out "All persons who are commonly known as 'Greasers' or the issue of Spanish and Indian blood" as especially worthy of suspicion and prosecution; this racist provision led to the law being dubbed "the Greaser Act." The present text is based on a translation of the editorial first published by Arte Público Press and reprinted in *Herencia: The Anthology of Hispanic Literature of the United States* (2001).

The United States' conception of freedom is truly curious. This much-lauded freedom is imaginary. We think that a man is not truly free when he is obligated to pay a tax for so many doors and windows, even for the air he breathes. In our opinion, freedom is what all rational creation has a right to make use of as it sees fit, conforming to reason and justice. There are three species of freedom: natural, civil, and political, or rather, freedom of man, freedom of the citizen, and freedom of the nation. Natural freedom is the right man enjoys by nature to make use of it according to his free will, in keeping with the purpose for which he was raised. Civil freedom is the right that links all citizens to society so that they can do as they please when it is not to the contrary of the established laws. And lastly, political or national freedom is the right that all nations have to work for themselves independently of another nation, to be subject or servile to no tyrant. But here in this fabulous[1] country, he who robs and assassinates the most is he who enjoys freedom. Certain people have no kind of freedom—this freedom, we say, is that which the courts deny to all individuals of color. To buy a man for money, to hang or burn him alive arbitrarily, is another great liberty which any individual has here, according to his likes. This happens in the United States, where slavery is tolerated, where the most vile despotism reigns unchecked—in the middle of a nation that they call the "Model Republic." It is enough that these institutions are unique in a country that tries to consume everything due to its "Manifest Destiny." Ultimately, we here in California have been favored by our "Model Legislature," with two laws so original that they have no equal in the annals of any civilized nation. These are the Sunday law[2] and the famous vagrant law. The former prohibits dances and other innocent diversions on Sunday, on pain of incarceration and fine for all those who infringe on the decree, as if to force people to stay at home to fast and pray to the Almighty for our welfare. (Wouldn't it be better to pray so that he would free us from such legislatures?) The supposition that people are made more moral by taking away their pastimes and diversions is truly ridiculous. The latter is that which affects our Californian and Mexican population directly. They particularly distinguish us by the title of Greasers. This law has served to widen the gap that has existed for some time between the foreigners and the natives.

from John Rollin Ridge, "Poem (Delivered at Commencement of Oakland College, California, June 6th 1861)" (1861)

John Rollin Ridge (1827–67) was the son and grandson of prominent Cherokee signatories to the Treaty of New Echota, the 1836 treaty—unsanctioned by the Cherokee leadership—that ceded the Cherokee's traditional lands and agreed that the Cherokee people would relocate west of the Mississippi. Because of this, both were killed in 1839 by supporters of John Ross, the Cherokee Principal Chief and an opponent of removal; Ridge, then twelve years old, witnessed his father's murder. Ridge's writing after his move to California in the 1850s includes poetry and journalism as well as the first novel by an Indigenous author, *The Life and Adventures of Joaquín Murieta* (1854). His work contains condemnations of white American racism and advocacy for California's Indigenous population, but he was also capable of espousing the expansionism and condescension toward Indigenous Californians that typified the white settler-colonial society he had joined—as the poem presented here (the text of which is based on that printed in 1868 in *The Poems of John Rollin Ridge*) demonstrates.

Excerpts from Ridge's *The Life and Adventures of Joaquín Murieta* can be found in the author section for him in this anthology's website component.

The waves that murmur at our feet,
  Through many an age had rolled
Ere fortune found her favorite seat
Within this land of gold.

5 The Digger,[3] searching for his roots,
  Here roamed the region wide—
Or, wearied with the day's pursuits,
Slept by this restless tide.

The dream of greatness never rose
10 Upon his simple brain;
  The wealth on which a nation grows,
  And builds its power to reign,

All darkly lay beneath his tread,
  Where many a stream did wind,
15 Deep slumbering in its yellow bed,
  The charm that rules mankind.

---

[1] *fabulous* I.e., fabled; of mythological reputation.

[2] *the Sunday law* Lobbying by Protestant religious leaders among the white American settlers in California led to the passage of California's first "Sunday law," outlawing noisy amusements on Sundays, in 1855. A more stringent version of the law, outlawing all business on Sundays, was passed in 1858 and was not repealed until 1883.

[3] *Digger* Highly derogatory term for the Indigenous peoples of California, stemming from the hunter-gatherer way of life—including digging up roots to eat—practiced by many of them. The term epitomizes the contempt that many American settlers in California felt for Indigenous Californians, a contempt which greatly facilitated the near-total extermination of California's Indigenous population during the decades following the Gold Rush.

Had he and his dark brethren known
Of gold the countless worth,
They now beyond that power had grown
20   Which sweeps them from the earth.

But happier he perchance, by far,
Still digging for his roots,
Than thousand paler wanderers are
Whose toil hath had no fruits. …

25   Far off among the mountains stern,
Shall thousands meet with blight,
And many a raven lock shall turn
To hairs of frosty white;

And many a lonely grave shall hide
30   The mouldering form of him
For whom sad eyes are never dried,
With age and sorrow dim.

Yet, though the wayside all be strewn
With sorrows and with graves,
35   The glory of the race is shown
By what it does and braves.

What though the desert's mouldering heaps
Affright the startled eye—
What though in wilds the venturer sleeps,
40   His bones uncovered lie,

'Tis not the living that have won
Alone the victory:
But each dead soldier, too, has done
His part as loftily.

45   'Tis they—the living and the dead—
Who have redeemed our land;
Have cities reared, the arts have spread,
And placed us where we stand.

As led Adventure bold before,
50   The Arts and Learning came;
And now, behold I upon this shore
They have a place and name.

Where roamed erewhile the rugged bear
Amid these oaks of green,
55   And wandering from his mountain lair
The cougar's steps were seen,

Lo! Peace hath built her quiet nest;
And "mild-eyed Science"[1] roves,
As was her wont° when Greece was blest,   *habit*
60   In Academic groves.[2]

Oh! tranquil be these shades for aye,°   *forever*
These groves forever green;
And youth and age still bless their day
That here their steps have been.

65   May Learning here still have her seat,
Her empire of the mind
The home of Genius, Wit's Retreat,
Whate'er is pure refined.

And thus the proudest boast shall be
70   Of young Ambition crowned—
"The woods of Oakland sheltered me,
Their leaves my brow have bound."[3]

---

[1]   *mild-eyed Science*   Ridge may be thinking of the English writer
and academic Robert Blakey's translation, published in 1845, of
"Lines on the Burning of the Alexandrian Library" by Saint Ammon,
a fourth-century Christian ascetic, in which these words appear.

[2]   *Academic groves*   The words "academic" and "academy" come
from *Akademia*, the name for a sacred grove of olive trees outside of
Athens that was the site of the philosophical school (also called the
Academy) founded by the Greek philosopher Plato (c. 427–347 BCE).

[3]   *Their leaves … bound*   In ancient Greece, oak trees were sacred
to the god Zeus, and the wearing of oak leaf crowns symbolized
wisdom.

Sarah Moore Grimké
<u>1792 – 1873</u>

Born into the height of privilege on a plantation in South Carolina, Sarah Moore Grimké defied convention to become, in the 1830s, one of the most influential abolitionists in the United States, as well as a progressive thinker on women's rights. Working closely with her sister Angelina, Grimké drew on the Bible, on contemporary political and sociological writings, and on her own experiences in the slaveholding South in building her arguments against racial prejudice and gender constraints in nineteenth-century America; her writings, which often utilized the popular epistolary form, would go on to influence later writers and activists, including Harriet Beecher Stowe and Elizabeth Cady Stanton.

Sarah Moore Grimké was born in Charleston in 1792, the sixth child of Mary and John Grimké. The family divided their time between fashionable Charleston and their large cotton plantation in the north of the state. As a child, Grimké expressed discomfort with her family's slaveholding practices, and she was once punished for teaching her enslaved handmaid to read (a violation of South Carolina law); it was not until much later in life, though, that she began unequivocally to oppose slavery as an institution. She took private lessons with her brother Thomas until 1805, when he left the state to enter Yale College; her parents discouraged her from pursuing further "unfeminine" education. Angelina Grimké was born not long thereafter; Grimké was, at her own request, named Angelina's godmother, initiating a close bond that would endure until the end of her life.

In her twenties, Grimké began seeking religious fulfilment outside the Episcopalian Church of her family, experiencing an emotionally exhausting cycle of mystical visions, conversions, and relapses that lasted many years. Drawn initially to the Presbyterian Church, she was introduced to the Society of Friends (the Quakers) in 1818, while on a visit to Philadelphia. Though initially put off by the Quakers' somber ethos and outsider status, Grimké was by 1821 sufficiently moved by the faith to return to Philadelphia and take up residence with a Quaker family; she was an official member of the Society of Friends by 1823. Private spiritual concerns continued to dominate Grimké's life over the following years, but she began too to contemplate larger social issues, and on her occasional returns to South Carolina she found her sister increasingly beginning to probe the religious and ethical questions surrounding plantation slavery. Grimké was joined by Angelina in Philadelphia in 1829; it was Angelina who would ultimately push her to embrace the abolitionist cause in the coming decade.

Though the Society of Friends had for over a century been officially opposed to slavery, and though its doctrines upheld the spiritual equality of all people, the Grimké sisters found themselves often frustrated by the relative indifference to slavery of most Quaker individuals, and by the frequency with which they were, as women, expected to keep especially silent on the topic. Sarah herself remained hesitant to speak on the matter or to attend abolitionist meetings until mid-1835. A diary entry for May 12 of that year records her change of heart: "Truly," she wrote, "I often feel ready to go to prison or to death in this cause of justice, mercy, and love; and I do fully believe if I am called to return to Carolina, it will not be long before I shall suffer persecution of some kind or other." In late 1836, she incurred the anger of the Philadelphia Quakers by accompanying Angelina to New York, where the sisters then became the first female agents for the American Anti-Slavery Society; the following three years would comprise the most productive period of Grimké's abolitionist activism.

Grimké's first abolitionist work, *An Epistle to the Clergy of the Southern States*, was published by the American Anti-Slavery Society that year. A theologically charged admonition to Southern religious authorities to relinquish their support of slavery, the text emphasizes biblical arguments—refuting the biblical defenses of slavery often put forward in the South—but also shows Grimké's familiarity with Thomas Jefferson's *Notes on the State of Virginia* (1787) and other secular works describing American slavery. Grimké and her sister began to hold "parlor meetings" on slavery in the North—attended, controversially, by both men and women—and spent much of 1837 on a speaking tour of New England, aiming particularly to draw women into the abolitionist movement.

During this period Grimké began working on a series of letters in which she further developed her theory of women's rights; these letters were eventually published in *The New England Spectator* and the abolitionist newspaper *The Liberator*. Her arguments addressed matters of class as well as race and gender, highlighting issues such as the pay gap between laboring men and women. The series was deeply influenced by Lydia Maria Child's recent *The History of the Condition of Women in Various Ages and Nations* (1835); Grimké had had little opportunity to read other works on women's rights, and she opened the collection by describing her topic as "nearly untrodden ground." The letters were later published as a single volume titled *Letters on the Equality of the Sexes* (1838).

In 1839, the sisters collaborated with abolitionist Theodore Weld (whom Angelina had married the previous year) to publish *American Slavery as It Is: Testimony of a Thousand Witnesses*, a monumental work to which Grimké contributed substantial research as well as numerous accounts of slavery on her family's plantation. The book was enormously influential, providing abolitionists with an invaluable trove of incontrovertible evidence (the raw material was derived from personal testimony, from thousands of newspaper reports, and—tellingly—from advertisements that had been placed in newspapers by the slaveholders themselves). In turn, the book helped to provide raw material for some of the most influential abolitionist works of fiction later in the century—chief among them Stowe's *Uncle Tom's Cabin*.

Grimké lived with the Welds for the rest of her life. The household eventually expanded to include not only the Welds's children but also two nephews, Archibald and Francis James Grimké, mixed-race sons of Henry Grimké and his enslaved mistress; both men would become prominent African American rights activists in the late nineteenth and early twentieth centuries. *American Slavery* was Grimké's last published work to be widely influential, but she continued to be involved in the fight for social justice, including in the burgeoning women's suffrage movement, until late in her life. Her private writings reveal a continuing engagement with early feminist works (including Elizabeth Barrett Browning's *Aurora Leigh* [1856] and John Stuart Mill's *The Subjection of Women* [1869]). Her translation of Lamartine's biography of Joan of Arc was published with a small print run in 1867. Her unpublished writings include a novel, now lost, about an interracial marriage.

Throughout much of her life, Grimké's accomplishments were frequently overshadowed by those of her more outspoken and oratorically talented sister. Both Grimkés were in 1885 the subject of a biography (written by Catherine Birney), but they were thereafter largely neglected in twentieth-century scholarship of the abolitionist movement—as were most female and African American abolitionists. Dwight Dumond's 1961 *Antislavery: The Crusade for Freedom in America* devotes a chapter to Angelina Grimké, but makes little mention of Sarah. It was not until the publication of Gerda Lerner's landmark *The Grimké Sisters from South Carolina: Pioneers for Women's Rights and Abolition* in 1967 that Sarah Grimké's achievements as a pioneering feminist as well as an abolitionist began to receive renewed attention from scholars.

———————————————

NOTE ON THE TEXT: The text of "Letter 8: On the Condition of Women in the United States" is based on that published in the first edition of Sarah Moore Grimké's *Letters on the Equality of the Sexes* (1838). Spelling and punctuation have been modernized in accordance with the practices of this anthology.

⌘⌘⌘

from *Letters on the Equality of the Sexes and the Condition of Woman*

LETTER 8
ON THE CONDITION OF WOMEN
IN THE UNITED STATES

Brookline, 1837

My dear Sister[1]—I have now taken a brief survey of the condition of woman in various parts of the world. I regret that my time has been so much occupied by other things, that I have been unable to bestow that attention upon the subject which it merits, and that my constant change of place has prevented me from having access to books, which might probably have assisted me in this part of my work. I hope that the principles I have asserted will claim the attention of some of my sex, who may be able to bring into view, more thoroughly than I have done, the situation and degradation of woman. I shall now proceed to make a few remarks on the condition of women in my own country.

During the early part of my life, my lot was cast among the butterflies of the *fashionable* world; and of this class of women, I am constrained to say, both from experience and observation, that their education is miserably deficient; that they are taught to regard marriage as the one thing needful, the only avenue to distinction; hence to attract the notice and win the attentions of men, by their external charms, is the chief business of fashionable girls. They seldom think that men will be allured by intellectual acquirements, because they find, that where any mental superiority exists, a woman is generally shunned and regarded as stepping out of her "appropriate sphere," which, in their view, is to dress, to dance, to set out to the best possible advantage her person,[2] to read the novels which inundate the press, and which do more to destroy her character

as a rational creature, than anything else. Fashionable women regard themselves, and are regarded by men, as pretty toys or as mere instruments of pleasure; and the vacuity of mind, the heartlessness, the frivolity which is the necessary result of this false and debasing estimate of women, can only be fully understood by those who have mingled in the folly and wickedness of fashionable life; and who have been called from such pursuits by the voice of the Lord Jesus, inviting their weary and heavy laden souls to come unto Him and learn of Him, that they may find something worthy of their immortal spirit, and their intellectual powers; that they may learn the high and holy purposes of their creation, and consecrate themselves unto the service of God; and not, as is now the case, to the pleasure of man.

There is another and much more numerous class in this country who are withdrawn by education or circumstances from the circle of fashionable amusements, but who are brought up with the dangerous and absurd idea that *marriage* is a kind of preferment;[3] and that to be able to keep their husband's house, and render his situation comfortable, is the end of her being. Much that she does and says and thinks is done in reference to this situation; and to be married is too often held up to the view of girls as the *sine qua non*[4] of human happiness and human existence. For this purpose, more than for any other, I verily believe the majority of girls are trained. This is demonstrated by the imperfect education which is bestowed upon them, and the little pains[5] taken to cultivate their minds, after they leave school, by the little time allowed them for reading, and by the idea being constantly inculcated, that although all household concerns should be attended to with scrupulous punctuality at particular seasons, the improvement of their intellectual capacities is only a secondary consideration, and may serve as an occupation to fill up the odds and ends of time. In most families, it is considered a matter of far more consequence to call a girl off from making a pie, or a pudding, than to interrupt her whilst engaged in her studies. This mode of training necessarily exalts, in their view, the animal above the intellectual and spiritual nature, and teaches women to regard themselves as a kind of machinery,

---

[1]   *My dear Sister*   The letters in this book, which were first published individually in *The New England Spectator*, were addressed to Mary S. Parker, who was then president of the Boston Female Anti-Slavery Society. Grimké's habit of addressing people as "Sister" or "Brother," and her occasional use of the pronouns "thee," "thou," and "thine," stemmed in part from Quaker customs.

[2]   *person*   I.e., body; physical appearance.

[3]   *preferment*   Promotion.

[4]   *sine qua non*   Latin: indispensable attribute.

[5]   *pains*   Effort.

necessary to keep the domestic engine in order, but of little value as the *intelligent* companions of men.

Let no one think, from these remarks, that I regard a knowledge of housewifery as beneath the acquisition of women. Far from it: I believe that a complete knowledge of household affairs is an indispensable requisite in a woman's education—that by the mistress of a family, whether married or single, doing her duty thoroughly and *understandingly*, the happiness of the family is increased to an incalculable degree, as well as a vast amount of time and money saved. All I complain of is that our education consists so almost exclusively in culinary and other manual operations. I do long to see the time, when it will no longer be necessary for women to expend so many precious hours in furnishing "a well spread table," but that their husbands will forego some of their accustomed indulgences in this way, and encourage their wives to devote some portion of their time to mental cultivation, even at the expense of having to dine sometimes on baked potatoes, or bread and butter.

I believe the sentiment expressed by the author of *Live and Let Live*[1] is true:

> Other things being equal, a woman of the highest mental endowments will always be the best housekeeper, for domestic economy,[2] is a science that brings into action the qualities of the mind, as well as the graces of the heart. A quick perception, judgment, discrimination, decision and order are high attributes of mind, and are all in daily exercise in the well ordering of a family. If a sensible woman, an intellectual woman, a woman of genius, is not a good housewife, it is not because she is either, or all of those, but because there is some deficiency in her character, or some omission of duty which should make her very humble, instead of her indulging in any secret self-complacency on account of a certain superiority, which only aggravates her fault.

The influence of women over the minds and character of *children* of both sexes is allowed[3] to be far greater than that of men. This being the case by the very ordering of nature, women should be prepared by education for the performance of their sacred duties as mothers and as sisters. A late American writer,[4] speaking on this subject, says in reference to an article in the *Westminster Review*:

> I agree entirely with the writer in the high estimate which he places on female education, and have long since been satisfied that the subject not only merits, but *imperiously demands* a thorough reconsideration. The whole scheme must, in my opinion, be reconstructed. The great elements of usefulness and duty are too little attended to. Women ought, in my view of the subject, to approach to the best education now given to men (I except mathematics and the classics), far more I believe than has ever yet been attempted. Give me a host of educated, pious mothers and sisters, and I will do more to revolutionize a country, in moral and religious taste, in manners and in social virtues and intellectual cultivation, than I can possibly do in double or treble the time, with a similar host of educated men. I cannot but think that the miserable condition of the great body of the people in all ancient communities, is to be ascribed in a very great degree to the degradation of women.

There is another way in which the general opinion, that women are inferior to men, is manifested, that bears with tremendous effect on the laboring class, and indeed on almost all who are obliged to earn a subsistence, whether it be by mental or physical exertion—I allude to the disproportionate value set on the time and labor of men and women. A man who is engaged in teaching, can always, I believe, command a higher price for tuition than a woman—even when he teaches the same branches, and is not in any respect superior to the woman. This I know is the case in boarding and other schools with which I have been acquainted, and it is so in every occupation in which the sexes engage indiscriminately. As for example, in tailoring, a man has twice or three times as much, for making a waistcoat

---

[1]   *the author of Live and Let Live*   American novelist Catharine Maria Sedgwick (1789–1867); this 1837 novel focuses on the experiences of domestic servants and other working-class women.

[2]   *domestic economy*   Household management.

[3]   *allowed*   Admitted; acknowledged.

[4]   [Grimké's note]   Thomas S. Grimke. [Grimké here refers to her elder brother, with whom she had studied as a child, and who had died in 1834. As a lawyer and noted orator, Thomas Grimke was known for supporting various reform movements, including that of women's education (though he was far less radical than either of his sisters on the topic of abolition).]

or pantaloons, as a woman, although the work done by each may be equally good. In those employments which are peculiar to women, their time is estimated at only half the value of that of men. A woman who goes out to wash[1] works as hard in proportion as a wood sawyer, or a coal heaver, but she is not generally able to make more than half as much by a day's work. The low remuneration which women receive for their work has claimed the attention of a few philanthropists, and I hope it will continue to do so until some remedy is applied for this enormous evil. I have known a widow, left with four or five children to provide for, unable to leave home because her helpless babes demand her attention, compelled to earn a scanty subsistence, by making coarse shirts at 12 ½ cents a piece, or by taking in washing, for which she was paid by some wealthy persons 12 ½ cents per dozen. All these things evince the low estimation in which woman is held. There is yet another and more disastrous consequence arising from this unscriptural notion—women being educated, from earliest childhood, to regard themselves as inferior creatures, have not that self-respect which conscious equality would engender, and hence when their virtue[2] is assailed, they yield to temptation with facility, under the idea that it rather exalts than debases them to be connected with a superior being.

There is another class of women in this country to whom I cannot refer without feelings of the deepest shame and sorrow. I allude to our female slaves. Our southern cities are whelmed beneath a tide of pollution; the virtue of female slaves is wholly at the mercy of irresponsible tyrants, and women are bought and sold in our slave markets, to gratify the brutal lust of those who bear the name of Christians. In our slave states, if amid all her degradation and ignorance, a woman desires to preserve her virtue unsullied, she is either bribed or whipped into compliance, or if she dares resist her seducer, her life by the laws of some of the slave states may be, and has actually been sacrificed to the fury of disappointed passion. Where such laws do not exist, the power which is necessarily vested in the master over his property leaves the defenceless slave entirely at his mercy, and the sufferings of some females on this account, both physical and mental, are intense. Mr. Gholson, in the House of Delegates of Virginia, in 1832, said, "He really had been under the impression that he owned his slaves. He had lately purchased four women and ten children, in whom he thought he had obtained a great bargain; for he supposed they were his own property, *as were his brood mares*." But even if any laws existed in the United States, as in Athens formerly, for the protection of female slaves, they would be null and void, because the evidence of a colored person is not admitted against a white, in any of our Courts of Justice in the slave states. "In Athens, if a female slave had cause to complain of any want[3] of respect to the laws of modesty, she could seek the protection of the temple, and demand a change of owners; and such appeals were never discountenanced, or neglected by the magistrate." In Christian America, the slave has no refuge from unbridled cruelty and lust.

S.A. Forrall,[4] speaking of the state of morals at the South, says, "Negresses, when young and likely,[5] are often employed by the planter, or his friends, to administer to their sensual desires. This frequently is a matter of speculation, for if the offspring, a mulatto, be a handsome female, 800 or 1000 dollars may be obtained for her in the New Orleans market. It is an occurrence of no uncommon nature to see a Christian father sell his own daughter, and the brother his own sister." The following is copied by the *N.Y. Evening Star* from the *Picayune*, a paper published in New Orleans. "A very beautiful girl, belonging to the estate of John French, a deceased gambler at New Orleans, was sold a few days since for the round sum of $7,000. An ugly-looking bachelor named Gouch, a member of the Council of one of the Principalities, was the purchaser. The girl is a brunette; remarkable for her beauty and intelligence, and there was considerable contention, who should be the purchaser. She was, however, persuaded to accept Gouch, he having made

---

[1]   *wash* I.e., launder clothing. In middle- or upper-class households, this task—which, carried out without the help of modern implements, was very physically demanding—was usually performed by servants or hired launderers. Laundering was one of few options available to women who needed to earn money, and was often considered particularly lowly work.

[2]   *virtue* I.e., chastity.

[3]   *want* Lack.

[4]   *S.A. Forrall* Author of the 1832 book *A Ramble of Six Thousand Miles Through the United States of America*, from which the following quotation is taken.

[5]   *likely* Attractive.

her princely promises." I will add but one more from the numerous testimonies respecting the degradation of female slaves, and the licentiousness of the South. It is from the *Circular* of the Kentucky Union, for the moral and religious improvement of the colored race. "To the female character among our black population, we cannot allude but with feelings of the bitterest shame. A similar condition of moral pollution and utter disregard of a pure and virtuous reputation, is to be found *only without the pale of Christendom*. That such a state of society should exist in a Christian nation, claiming to be the most enlightened upon earth, without calling forth any *particular attention* to its existence, though ever before our eyes and *in our families*, is a moral phenomenon at once unaccountable and disgraceful." Nor does the colored woman suffer alone: the moral purity of the white woman is deeply contaminated. In the daily habit of seeing the virtue of her enslaved sister sacrificed without hesitancy or remorse, she looks upon the crimes of seduction and illicit intercourse without horror, and although not personally involved in the guilt, she loses that value for innocence in her own, as well as the other sex, which is one of the strongest safeguards to virtue. She lives in habitual intercourse[1] with men, whom she knows to be polluted by licentiousness, and often is she compelled to witness in her own domestic circle, those disgusting and heart-sickening jealousies and strifes which disgraced and distracted the family of Abraham.[2] In addition to all this, the female slaves suffer every species of degradation and cruelty, which the most wanton barbarity can inflict; they are indecently divested of their clothing, sometimes tied up and severely whipped, sometimes prostrated on the earth, while their naked bodies are torn by the scorpion lash.

> The whip on WOMAN's shrinking flesh!
>   Our soil yet reddening with the stains
> Caught from her scourging warm and fresh.[3]

Can any American woman look at these scenes of shocking licentiousness and cruelty, and fold her hands in apathy, and say, "I have nothing to do with slavery"? *She cannot and be guiltless.*

I cannot close this letter without saying a few words on the benefits to be derived by men, as well as women, from the opinions I advocate relative to the equality of the sexes. Many women are now supported, in idleness and extravagance, by the industry of their husbands, fathers, or brothers, who are compelled to toil out their existence at the counting house, or in the printing office, or some other laborious occupation, while the wife and daughters and sisters take no part in the support of the family, and appear to think that their sole business is to spend the hard bought earnings of their male friends. I deeply regret such a state of things, because I believe that if women felt their responsibility, for the support of themselves, or their families, it would add strength and dignity to their characters, and teach them more true sympathy for their husbands, than is now generally manifested—a sympathy which would be exhibited by actions as well as words. Our brethren may reject my doctrine, because it runs counter to common opinions, and because it wounds their pride; but I believe they would be "partakers of the benefit" resulting from the Equality of the Sexes, and would find that woman, as their equal, was unspeakably more valuable than woman as their inferior, both as a moral and an intellectual being.

Thine in the bonds of womanhood,
SARAH M. GRIMKÉ
—1837

---

[1]   *intercourse* Communication; contact.

[2]   *jealousies and strifes ... Abraham* In the Book of Genesis, the patriarch Abraham is described as having one wife, Sarah, and two concubines, Hagar and Keturah. Abraham's fathering of Ishmael by Hagar when Sarah was unable to conceive causes considerable tension in their household; eventually, this leads to the exile of Ishmael and Hagar.

[3]   *The whip ... and fresh* From "Stanzas" by American Quaker antislavery poet John Greenleaf Whittier (1807–92).

RALPH WALDO EMERSON

1803 – 1882

In 1885, poet Oliver Wendell Holmes wrote that Ralph Waldo Emerson was "the poet whom some admired without understanding, a few understood, or thought they did, without admiring, and many both understood and admired—among these there being not a small number who went far beyond admiration, and lost themselves in devout worship." Even today, few nineteenth-century American figures are as frequently discussed, paraphrased, quoted, and even idolized as the New England orator, philosopher, and poet—though some critics have seen him, in the words of Edgar Allan Poe, as a "mystic for mysticism's sake." Partly because of the complex and sometimes self-contradictory qualities of Emerson's essays, his name is frequently invoked by writers, thinkers, and politicians in disparate realms, from environmentalism to economics, and for varied, even conflicting, ends. His writings themselves espouse not so much a certain set of values as a certain understanding of the relationship between the self and the external world, as well as between the self and the divine. It is in large part through Emerson's influence that the values of individualism, anti-traditionalism, and anti-institutionalism have come to dominate so much of American literary and political culture. And Emerson's Americanism has itself been influential; his work posed a prominent challenge to the idea that in order for Americans to develop a literary tradition, they needed to imitate the English one.

Emerson was born in 1803 to Bostoners William and Ruth Haskins Emerson. He followed in the footsteps of his minister father and grandfather when he himself joined the Unitarian ministry as a young man; it was largely from his mother Ruth's influence that he developed strong religious feeling. Emerson's aunt, Mary Moody Emerson—a significant writer and diarist in her own right—was also an important educational influence, and though they later disagreed on many religious principles, Emerson would continue to cite Mary Moody as his best early teacher. The Emersons lived in poverty for many years following William's early death, but Ruth managed to earn enough money to send the Emerson children to Harvard College; Emerson performed unexceptionally, but developed a voracious literary appetite outside class, and kept detailed journals of his readings; he would later call these journals the "Wide World."

Emerson entered Harvard's Divinity School in 1825, and soon met Ellen Louisa Tucker, with whom he appears to have had a profound and spiritual relationship. They married in 1829, and that same year he accepted a post as assistant pastor in Boston's Second Church. The next several years would be fraught with private difficulty, however, as Ellen died of tuberculosis in 1831, less than two years into their marriage. During the same period, Emerson became increasingly dissatisfied with Unitarian theology and conventional Christian rites in general, writing in 1832 that "The profession [of minister] is antiquated. In an altered age, we worship in the dead forms of our forefathers." Emerson formally broke with the Church, and, in December of 1832, he embarked on a tour of Europe that lasted until the following autumn. Traveling to popular cultural centers in Italy, Switzerland, France, and Britain, he met many of the leading literary and intellectual figures of the day, among them the Romantic poets Wordsworth and Coleridge—whose *Aids to Reflection* (1825) would prove highly influential in Emerson's future works— and the essayist and translator Thomas Carlyle, with whom he would maintain a lasting correspondence.

The year after his return to the United States in 1833, Emerson received his late wife's legacy, an annual sum of over one thousand dollars that granted him the financial freedom to pursue his re-invigorated intellectual interests. Inspired as much by the literature of the Romantics as by contemporary developments in natural science, Emerson was increasingly engrossed by ideas about the relationship between nature and the soul. Having come home to a New England just beginning to be taken over by the Lyceum movement (which aimed to disseminate knowledge among the general population by providing public lectures on the ethical, intellectual, and scientific questions of the day), he entered himself into the ranks of public educators. His lectures were the early anchors of Emerson's future success; well into his career as a writer, he was known as much for his passionate and invigorating delivery at the podium as for the ideas he delivered on paper.

During this period Emerson met Lydia (later Lidian) Jackson, whom he married in 1835; the couple then moved to Concord. The following year, Emerson published his first book, *Nature*—a work that laid the groundwork for the Transcendentalist thought with which he would be associated for the rest of his life. A loose company of intellectuals drawn to the philosophy of *Nature* began to gather, designating Emerson as their informal leader. The members of the Transcendental Club, though varying in their philosophical approaches, shared with Emerson essential beliefs in the primacy of the individual, in the ability to apprehend truth through the synthesis of the self with nature, and in the immanent divinity of nature and the human soul. *Nature* weaves together intellectual threads from an extraordinarily wide array of sources, ranging from the scientific mysticism of Emanuel Swedenborg to the novels and letters of Madame de Staël; from classical philosophy and Neoplatonism to Quakerism; from English and German Romanticism to Hindu mythology and scripture. *Nature* abounds with quotations, misquotations, and paraphrases from all these, woven into a uniquely Emersonian work.

While *Nature* began almost immediately to be influential, it did not make Emerson well-known among the general public. He first attracted wide public notice in 1837, after he had delivered a speech before the Phi Beta Kappa students graduating from Harvard College. The speech, now known as "The American Scholar," encouraged his audience not to succumb to unreflective bookishness and academic hero-worship, but to trust the genius that could be found within their own selves. His next major speech, the "Divinity School Address," was delivered at Harvard in 1838. The Harvard Divinity School was then considered a center of Unitarian theology, and Emerson's speech provoked controversy by challenging many tenets of Unitarianism and appearing to utterly undermine the authority of Christian traditions and texts. He condemned what he called "historical Christianity" for its obsession with "the personal, the positive, the ritual," and for dwelling overly on Jesus as a "*person*" and miracle-worker, rather than simply as a prophet of the divine. Many were shocked by the speech, and a public debate over what came to be known as the "miracles controversy" ensued.

Though scandalous, the event helped crystallize Emerson's status as an important and innovative American voice. The Transcendentalist movement continued to grow, and in 1840 the Club—whose members now included such New England intellectuals as Margaret Fuller, Elizabeth Peabody, Amos Bronson Alcott, and Henry David Thoreau—established a periodical called *The Dial* (1840–44), for which Emerson wrote the introduction to the first issue. In 1841, Emerson cemented his growing international renown with *Essays* (later retitled *Essays: First Series*), a volume of writings drawn largely from lectures he had previously delivered. The volume, which included the now-classic essay "Self-Reliance," was a popular as well as a critical success in both the United States and Europe.

Emerson again faced personal tragedy, however, when his son Waldo died of scarlet fever in 1842, at the age of five. Wrestling with sorrow, Emerson wrote the essay "Experience" (1844), in which he attempted to reconcile the optimistic self-assuredness of his previous writings with the apparent impotency of human effort against the "lords of life." Around this time Emerson began more seriously engaging with Eastern religion and philosophy, and especially with Hindu texts such as the *Bhagavad Gita* and the *Vishnu Purana*; their influence can be seen in his first volume of poetry, *Poems* (1846), as well as in later work.

In 1847 Emerson embarked again on a tour of Europe, this time as a famous speaker and writer, and in Scotland and England he delivered numerous lectures. These provided raw material for successful books such as *Representative Men* (1850), a collection of semi-biographical pieces on influential historical figures—all men—each of whom are posited as representatives of a particular human virtue or type (among them Plato as the "philosopher," Shakespeare as the "poet," and Swedenborg as the "mystic"). The collection was influenced by Carlyle's similarly structured *On Heroes, Hero-Worship, and The Heroic in History* (1841), which expounded what is sometimes known as the "great man theory" of history.

Emerson long defined himself as "a seeing eye and not a useful hand," and his suspicions of social institutions and of conformity held him back from associating himself with the various social and political movements of the day. Partly thanks to the influence of his wife Lidian, however, Emerson eventually came to support the abolitionist movement. He became more strongly committed to the abolitionist cause after the passing of the Fugitive Slave Law in 1850, and delivered multiple addresses against slavery throughout the 1850s. He welcomed the outbreak of the Civil War in 1861, believing it to be the crisis that would lead America to a new age. (Emerson's dedication to abolitionism, like that of many white activists of the era, should not be misconstrued as implying an unqualified egalitarianism; he continued throughout his life to hold many false ideas regarding racial hierarchy.)

Though he began to experience degenerative memory problems and his output slowed after the War, Emerson continued to lecture and write until not long before his death. He died of pneumonia-related complications in 1882, and was buried in Sleepy Hollow Cemetery, Concord. Emerson's many journals, edited by his son Edward Waldo, were published posthumously; these private writings have contributed greatly to scholarly understanding of Emerson's personal, professional, and philosophical development.

It is difficult to overstate Emerson's importance to American intellectual history—or his influence on American literature. The extraordinary degree to which he lent emotional as well as intellectual force to other leading nineteenth-century writers is suggested in a comment made by Walt Whitman, who sent Emerson a copy of his first volume of poetry, *Leaves of Grass* (1855). "I was simmering, simmering, simmering," Whitman later wrote; "Emerson brought me to a boil."

NOTE ON THE TEXTS: The selections presented here are based on the following editions and printings: *Nature* (1836); "Self-Reliance" in *Essays: First Series* (1841); "The Poet" in *Essays: Second Series* (1844); and "Brahma" on the version that appeared in the *Atlantic Monthly* in 1857.

Spelling and punctuation have been modernized in accordance with the practices of this anthology; Emerson's original capitalization has, however, for the most part been preserved.

⌘ ⌘ ⌘

from *Nature*

Nature is but an image or imitation of wisdom, the last thing of the soul; nature being a thing which doth only do, but not know.

PLOTINUS[1]

---

[1] *PLOTINUS* Roman-Egyptian philosopher (205–270 CE) whose theories of emanation postulated the existence of one supreme source that creates the possibility of all other existences; this philosophical system, which was largely derived from the earlier Greek philosopher Plato (c. 427–c. 347 BCE), was named Neoplatonism by medieval scholars. In his 1849 edition of *Nature*, Emerson replaced this epigraph with lines from his own poem, "Nature": "A subtle chain of countless rings / The next unto the farthest brings; / The eye reads omens where it goes, / And speaks all languages the rose; /

INTRODUCTION

Our age is retrospective. It builds the sepulchres of the fathers. It writes biographies, histories, and criticism. The foregoing generations beheld God and nature face to face; we, through their eyes. Why should not we also enjoy an original relation to the universe? Why should not we have a poetry and philosophy of insight and not of tradition, and a religion by revelation to us, and not the history of theirs? Embosomed for a season in nature, whose floods of life stream around and through us, and invite us by the powers

---

And, striving to be man, the worm / Mounts through all the spires of form."

they supply, to action proportioned to nature, why should we grope among the dry bones of the past, or put the living generation into masquerade out of its faded wardrobe? The sun shines today also. There is more wool and flax in the fields. There are new lands, new men, new thoughts. Let us demand our own works and laws and worship.

Undoubtedly we have no questions to ask which are unanswerable. We must trust the perfection of the creation so far, as to believe that whatever curiosity the order of things has awakened in our minds, the order of things can satisfy. Every man's condition is a solution in hieroglyphic to those inquiries he would put. He acts it as life, before he apprehends it as truth. In like manner, nature is already, in its forms and tendencies, describing its own design. Let us interrogate the great apparition, that shines so peacefully around us. Let us inquire, to what end[1] is nature?

All science has one aim, namely, to find a theory of nature. We have theories of races and of functions, but scarcely yet a remote approximation to an idea of creation. We are now so far from the road to truth, that religious teachers dispute and hate each other, and speculative men are esteemed unsound and frivolous. But to a sound judgment, the most abstract truth is the most practical. Whenever a true theory appears, it will be its own evidence. Its test is, that it will explain all phenomena. Now many are thought not only unexplained but inexplicable; as language, sleep, dreams, beasts, sex.

Philosophically considered, the universe is composed of Nature and the Soul. Strictly speaking, therefore, all that is separate from us, all which Philosophy distinguishes as the NOT ME, that is, both nature and art, all other men and my own body, must be ranked under this name, NATURE. In enumerating the values of nature and casting up their sum, I shall use the word in both senses—in its common and in its philosophical import. In inquiries so general as our present one, the inaccuracy is not material; no confusion of thought will occur. *Nature*, in the common sense, refers to essences unchanged by man; space, the air, the river, the leaf. *Art* is applied to the mixture of his will with the same things, as in a house, a canal, a statue, a picture. But his operations taken together are so insignificant,

a little chipping, baking, patching, and washing, that in an impression so grand as that of the world on the human mind, they do not vary the result.

CHAPTER I
NATURE

To go into solitude, a man needs to retire as much from his chamber as from society. I am not solitary whilst I read and write, though nobody is with me. But if a man would be alone, let him look at the stars. The rays that come from those heavenly worlds, will separate between him and vulgar things. One might think the atmosphere was made transparent with this design, to give man, in the heavenly bodies, the perpetual presence of the sublime. Seen in the streets of cities, how great they are! If the stars should appear one night in a thousand years, how would men believe and adore; and preserve for many generations the remembrance of the city of God which had been shown! But every night come out these preachers of beauty, and light the universe with their admonishing smile.

The stars awaken a certain reverence, because though always present, they are always inaccessible; but all natural objects make a kindred impression, when the mind is open to their influence. Nature never wears a mean[2] appearance. Neither does the wisest man extort all her secret, and lose his curiosity by finding out all her perfection. Nature never became a toy to a wise spirit. The flowers, the animals, the mountains, reflected all the wisdom of his best hour, as much as they had delighted the simplicity of his childhood.

When we speak of nature in this manner, we have a distinct but most poetical sense in the mind. We mean the integrity of impression made by manifold natural objects. It is this which distinguishes the stick of timber of the wood-cutter, from the tree of the poet. The charming landscape which I saw this morning is indubitably made up of some twenty or thirty farms. Miller owns this field, Locke that, and Manning[3] the woodland beyond. But none of them owns the landscape. There is a property in the horizon which no man has but he whose eye can integrate all the parts, that is,

---

1   *end*   Purpose.

2   *mean*   Lowly or insignificant.

3   *Miller ... Manning*   Common, generic surnames in Emerson's area.

the poet. This is the best part of these men's farms, yet to this their land-deeds give them no title.

To speak truly, few adult persons can see nature. Most persons do not see the sun. At least they have a very superficial seeing. The sun illuminates only the eye of the man, but shines into the eye and the heart of the child. The lover of nature is he whose inward and outward senses are still truly adjusted to each other; who has retained the spirit of infancy even into the era of manhood. His intercourse with heaven and earth becomes part of his daily food. In the presence of nature, a wild delight runs through the man, in spite of real sorrows. Nature says—he is my creature, and maugre[1] all his impertinent griefs, he shall be glad with me. Not the sun or the summer alone, but every hour and season yields its tribute of delight; for every hour and change corresponds to and authorizes a different state of the mind, from breathless noon to grimmest midnight. Nature is a setting that fits equally well a comic or a mourning piece. In good health, the air is a cordial of incredible virtue. Crossing a bare common,[2] in snow puddles, at twilight, under a clouded sky, without having in my thoughts any occurrence of special good fortune, I have enjoyed a perfect exhilaration. Almost I fear to think how glad I am. In the woods too, a man casts off his years, as the snake his slough, and at what period soever of life, is always a child. In the woods, is perpetual youth. Within these plantations of God, a decorum and sanctity reign, a perennial festival is dressed, and the guest sees not how he should tire of them in a thousand years. In the woods, we return to reason and faith. There I feel that nothing can befall me in life—no disgrace, no calamity (leaving me my eyes) which nature cannot repair. Standing on the bare ground—my head bathed by the blithe air, and uplifted into infinite space—all mean egotism vanishes. I become a transparent eyeball. I am nothing. I see all. The currents of the Universal Being circulate through me; I am part or particle of God. The name of the nearest friend sounds then foreign and accidental.[3] To be brothers, to be acquaintances, master or servant, is then a trifle and a disturbance. I am the lover of uncontained and immortal beauty.

In the wilderness, I find something more dear and connate[4] than in streets or villages. In the tranquil landscape, and especially in the distant line of the horizon, man beholds somewhat[5] as beautiful as his own nature.

The greatest delight which the fields and woods minister, is the suggestion of an occult[6] relation between man and the vegetable.[7] I am not alone and unacknowledged. They nod to me and I to them. The waving of the boughs in the storm, is new to me and old. It takes me by surprise, and yet is not unknown. Its effect is like that of a higher thought or a better emotion coming over me, when I deemed I was thinking justly or doing right.

Yet it is certain that the power to produce this delight, does not reside in nature, but in man, or in a harmony of both. It is necessary to use these pleasures with great temperance. For, nature is not always tricked in holiday attire, but the same scene which yesterday breathed perfume and glittered as for the frolic of the nymphs, is overspread with melancholy today. Nature always wears the colors of the spirit. To a man laboring under calamity, the heat of his own fire hath sadness in it. Then, there is a kind of contempt of the landscape felt by him who has just lost by death a dear friend. The sky is less grand as it shuts down over less worth in the population.

— 1836

[NOTE: The full text of *Nature* is included in the online component of this anthology.]

---

1   *maugre*   In spite of.

2   *common*   Tract of land belonging collectively to the public.

3   *accidental*   Inessential.

4   *connate*   Inborn; corresponding deeply with one's inner being.

5   *somewhat*   Something.

6   *occult*   Mysterious; secret.

7   *vegetable*   I.e., vegetation; plants.

IN CONTEXT: ILLUSTRATIONS OF EMERSON'S *NATURE*

Artist and poet Christopher Cranch (1813–92) ardently embraced Emerson's ideas and abandoned his intended career as a Unitarian minister in favor of Transcendentalist artistic and intellectual circles. The drawing reproduced here, commonly known as "the transparent eyeball," is his best-known work. As Cranch would later write, the drawing had its origin in a series of casually drawn "comic illustrations of some of Emerson's quaint sentences"; he then expanded the project into a bound manuscript titled *Illustrations of the New Philosophy*, a collection of caricatures based on statements quoted from Emerson's writings. These drawings remained in manuscript form until they were published in the mid-twentieth century.

"I expand and live in the warm day, like corn & melons." From Christopher Cranch, *Illustrations of the New Philosophy*, manuscript c. 1837–39 (MS Am 1506, Houghton Library, Harvard University).

"Few grown-up persons see the Sun." From Christopher Cranch, *Illustrations of the New Philosophy* (MS Am 1506, Houghton Library, Harvard University).

"Standing on the bare ground,—my head bathed by the blithe air, & uplifted into infinite space,—all mean egotism vanishes. I become a Transparent Eyeball." From Christopher Cranch, *Illustrations of the New Philosophy* (MS Am 1506, Houghton Library, Harvard University).

Self-Reliance

Ne te quaesiveris extra.[1]

Man is his own star, and the soul that can
Render an honest and a perfect man,
Command all light, all influence, all fate,
Nothing to him falls early or too late.
Our acts our angels are, or good or ill,
Our fatal shadows that walk by us still.
    Epilogue to Beaumont and Fletcher's *Honest Man's
    Fortune.*[2]

Cast the bantling° on the rocks,   *infant*
Suckle him with the she-wolf's teat:
Wintered with the hawk and fox,
Power and speed be hands and feet.[3]

I read the other day some verses written by an eminent painter[4] which were original and not conventional. Always the soul hears an admonition in such lines, let the subject be what it may. The sentiment they instill is of more value than any thought they may contain. To believe your own thought, to believe that what is true for you in your private heart, is true for all men—that is genius. Speak your latent conviction and it shall be the universal sense; for always the inmost becomes the outmost—and our first thought is rendered back to us by the trumpets of the Last Judgment. Familiar as the voice of the mind is to each, the highest merit we ascribe to Moses, Plato, and Milton,[5] is that they set at naught books and traditions, and spoke not what men but what they thought. A man should learn to detect and watch that gleam of light which flashes across his mind from within, more than the lustre of the firmament[6] of bards and sages. Yet he dismisses without notice his thought, because it is his. In every work of genius we recognize our own rejected thoughts: they come back to us with a certain alienated majesty. Great works of art have no more affecting lesson for us than this. They teach us to abide by our spontaneous impression with good humored inflexibility then most when the whole cry of voices is on the other side. Else, tomorrow a stranger will say with masterly good sense precisely what we have thought and felt all the time, and we shall be forced to take with shame our own opinion from another.

There is a time in every man's education when he arrives at the conviction that envy is ignorance; that imitation is suicide; that he must take himself for better, for worse, as his portion; that though the wide universe is full of good, no kernel of nourishing corn can come to him but through his toil bestowed on that plot of ground which is given to him to till. The power which resides in him is new in nature, and none but he knows what that is which he can do, nor does he know until he has tried. Not for nothing one face, one character, one fact makes much impression on him, and another none. It is not without pre-established harmony, this sculpture in the memory. The eye was placed where one ray should fall, that it might testify of that particular ray. We but half express ourselves, and are ashamed of that divine idea which each of us represents. It may be safely trusted as proportionate and of good issues, so it be faithfully imparted, but God will not have his work made manifest by cowards. It needs a divine man to exhibit anything divine. A man is relieved and gay when he has put his heart into his work and done his best; but what he has said or done otherwise shall give him no peace. It is a deliverance which does not deliver. In the attempt his genius deserts him; no muse befriends; no invention, no hope.

Trust thyself:[7] every heart vibrates to that iron string. Accept the place the divine Providence has found for you; the society of your contemporaries, the connection of events. Great men have always done so and confided themselves childlike to the genius of their age, betraying their perception that the Eternal was

---

[1] *Ne te quaesiveris extra*   Latin: Do not search outside yourself. See *Satire* 1.7 by Roman poet Persius (34–62 CE).

[2] *Epilogue to ... Man's Fortune*   A slight misattribution; *The Honest Man's Fortune* (written c. 1613) was most likely written by John Fletcher in collaboration with Nathan Field and Philip Massinger.

[3] *Cast the ... and feet*   Stanza written by Emerson.

[4] *eminent painter*   Likely Washington Allston (1779–1843), American painter and poet.

[5] *Moses*   Old Testament prophet; *Plato*   Greek philosopher (c. 427–c. 347 BCE); *Milton*   English poet John Milton (1608–74).

[6] *firmament*   Sky; the heavens.

[7] *Trust thyself*   Variation of the famous ancient Greek maxim "know thyself."

stirring at their heart, working through their hands, predominating in all their being. And we are now men, and must accept in the highest mind the same transcendent destiny; and not pinched in a corner, not cowards fleeing before a revolution, but redeemers and benefactors, pious aspirants to be noble clay, plastic[1] under the Almighty effort, let us advance and advance on Chaos and the Dark.

What pretty oracles nature yields us on this text in the face and behavior of children, babes and even brutes. That divided and rebel mind, that distrust of a sentiment because our arithmetic has computed the strength and means opposed to our purpose, these have not. Their mind being whole, their eye is as yet unconquered, and when we look in their faces, we are disconcerted. Infancy conforms to nobody: all conform to it, so that one babe commonly makes four or five out of the adults who prattle and play to it. So God has armed youth and puberty and manhood no less with its own piquancy and charm, and made it enviable and gracious and its claims not to be put by, if it will stand by itself. Do not think the youth has no force because he cannot speak to you and me. Hark![2] in the next room, who spoke so clear and emphatic? Good Heaven! it is he! it is that very lump of bashfulness and phlegm which for weeks has done nothing but eat when you were by, that now rolls out these words like bell-strokes. It seems he knows how to speak to his contemporaries. Bashful or bold, then, he will know how to make us seniors very unnecessary.

The nonchalance of boys who are sure of a dinner, and would disdain as much as a lord to do or say aught to conciliate one, is the healthy attitude of human nature. How is a boy the master of society; independent, irresponsible, looking out from his corner on such people and facts as pass by, he tries and sentences them on their merits, in the swift summary way of boys, as good, bad, interesting, silly, eloquent, troublesome. He cumbers himself never about consequences, about interests: he gives an independent, genuine verdict. You must court him: he does not court you. But the man is, as it were, clapped into jail by his consciousness. As soon as he has once acted or spoken

with éclat,[3] he is a committed person, watched by the sympathy or the hatred of hundreds whose affections must now enter into his account. There is no Lethe[4] for this. Ah, that he could pass again into his neutral, godlike independence! Who can thus lose all pledge, and having observed, observe again from the same unaffected, unbiased, unbribable, unaffrighted innocence, must always be formidable, must always engage the poet's and the man's regards. Of such an immortal youth the force would be felt. He would utter opinions on all passing affairs, which being seen to be not private but necessary, would sink like darts into the ear of men, and put them in fear.

These are the voices which we hear in solitude, but they grow faint and inaudible as we enter into the world. Society everywhere is in conspiracy against the manhood of every one of its members. Society is a joint-stock company[5] in which the members agree, for the better securing of his bread to each shareholder, to surrender the liberty and culture of the eater. The virtue in most request is conformity. Self-reliance is its aversion. It loves not realities and creators, but names and customs.

Whoso would be a man must be a nonconformist. He who would gather immortal palms[6] must not be hindered by the name of goodness, but must explore if it be goodness. Nothing is at last sacred but the integrity of our own mind. Absolve you to yourself, and you shall have the suffrage[7] of the world. I remember an answer which when quite young I was prompted to make to a valued adviser who was wont[8] to importune me with the dear old doctrines of the church. On my saying, What have I to do with the sacredness of traditions, if I live wholly from within? my friend suggested—"But these impulses may be from below, not from above." I replied, "They do not seem to me to be such; but if I am the devil's child, I will live then from

---

1   *plastic*   Flexible; able to be molded.

2   *Hark!*   Listen!

3   *éclat*   Brilliance.

4   *Lethe*   In Classical mythology, river in the underworld that causes forgetfulness, so that the dead may forget their earthly existence.

5   *joint-stock company*   Company in which capital is divided into a common, shared fund.

6   *palms*   I.e., honors.

7   *suffrage*   Support; prayers.

8   *was wont*   Had the tendency.

the devil." No law can be sacred to me but that of my nature. Good and bad are but names very readily transferable to that or this; the only right is what is after my constitution, the only wrong what is against it. A man is to carry himself in the presence of all opposition as if everything were titular[1] and ephemeral but he. I am ashamed to think how easily we capitulate to badges and names, to large societies and dead institutions. Every decent and well-spoken individual affects and sways me more than is right. I ought to go upright and vital, and speak the rude[2] truth in all ways. If malice and vanity wear the coat of philanthropy, shall that pass? If an angry bigot assumes this bountiful cause of Abolition, and comes to me with his last news from Barbados,[3] why should I not say to him, "Go love thy infant; love thy wood-chopper: be good-natured and modest: have that grace; and never varnish your hard, uncharitable ambition with this incredible tenderness for black folk a thousand miles off. Thy love afar is spite at home." Rough and graceless would be such greeting, but truth is handsomer than the affectation of love. Your goodness must have some edge to it—else it is none. The doctrine of hatred must be preached as the counteraction of the doctrine of love when that pules[4] and whines. I shun father and mother and wife and brother, when my genius calls me. I would write on the lintels of the door-post, *Whim.*[5] I hope it is somewhat better than whim at last, but we cannot spend the day in explanation. Expect me not to show cause why I seek or why I exclude company. Then, again, do not tell me, as a good man did today, of my obligation to put all poor men in good situations. Are they *my* poor?

I tell thee, thou foolish philanthropist, that I grudge the dollar, the dime, the cent I give to such men as do not belong to me and to whom I do not belong. There is a class of persons to whom by all spiritual affinity I am bought and sold; for them I will go to prison, if need be; but your miscellaneous popular charities; the education at college of fools; the building of meeting-houses to the vain end to which many now stand; alms to sots; and the thousandfold Relief Societies—though I confess with shame I sometimes succumb and give the dollar, it is a wicked dollar which by-and-by I shall have the manhood to withhold.

Virtues are in the popular estimate rather the exception than the rule. There is the man *and* his virtues. Men do what is called a good action, as some piece of courage or charity, much as they would pay a fine in expiation of daily non-appearance on parade.[6] Their works are done as an apology or extenuation of their living in the world—as invalids and the insane pay a high board. Their virtues are penances. I do not wish to expiate, but to live. My life is not an apology, but a life. It is for itself and not for a spectacle. I much prefer that it should be of a lower strain, so it be genuine and equal, than that it should be glittering and unsteady. I wish it to be sound and sweet, and not to need diet and bleeding.[7] My life should be unique; it should be an alms, a battle, a conquest, a medicine. I ask primary evidence that you are a man, and refuse this appeal from the man to his actions. I know that for myself it makes no difference whether I do or forbear those actions which are reckoned excellent. I cannot consent to pay for a privilege where I have intrinsic right. Few and mean[8] as my gifts may be, I actually am, and do not need for my own assurance or the assurance of my fellows any secondary testimony.

What I must do, is all that concerns me, not what the people think. This rule, equally arduous in actual and in intellectual life, may serve for the whole distinction between greatness and meanness. It is the harder, because you will always find those who think they know what is your duty better than you know it. It is

1   *titular* I.e., possessing a seemingly important title but having no real importance.

2   *rude* Unembellished.

3   *Barbados* Slavery had been abolished in most of the British Empire with the Slavery Abolition Act of 1833. The Act's passage was in large part motivated by a series of rebellions held by enslaved people in British territories, including one in Barbados in 1816. Before Emerson became a committed abolitionist in the years leading up to the Civil War, he expressed ambivalence about the matter, as can be seen here.

4   *pules* Cries or whimpers.

5   *I would ... Whim* See Exodus 12, in which God instructs the Israelites to mark their lintels (or doorframes) with blood to identify their homes so that he can spare them when he punishes the Egyptians with a plague.

6   *daily non-appearance on parade* Failure of military personnel to appear in uniform for daily drills or inspection.

7   *bleeding* Archaic medical treatment in which a person's blood is extracted.

8   *mean* Lowly.

easy in the world to live after the world's opinion; it is easy in solitude to live after our own; but the great man is he who in the midst of the crowd keeps with perfect sweetness the independence of solitude.

The objection to conforming to usages that have become dead to you is that it scatters your force. It loses your time and blurs the impression of your character. If you maintain a dead church, contribute to a dead Bible Society, vote with a great party either for the Government or against it, spread your table like base housekeepers—under all these screens, I have difficulty to detect the precise man you are. And, of course, so much force is withdrawn from your proper life. But do your thing, and I shall know you. Do your work, and you shall reinforce yourself. A man must consider what a blindman's-buff is this game of conformity. If I know your sect, I anticipate your argument. I hear a preacher announce for his text and topic the expediency of one of the institutions of his church. Do I not know beforehand that not possibly can he say a new and spontaneous word? Do I not know that with all this ostentation of examining the grounds of the institution, he will do no such thing? Do I not know that he is pledged to himself not to look but at one side; the permitted side, not as a man, but as a parish minister? He is a retained attorney, and these airs of the bench are the emptiest affectation. Well, most men have bound their eyes with one or another handkerchief, and attached themselves to some one of these communities of opinion. This conformity makes them not false in a few particulars, authors of a few lies, but false in all particulars. Their every truth is not quite true. Their two is not the real two, their four not the real four: so that every word they say chagrins us, and we know not where to begin to set them right. Meantime nature is not slow to equip us in the prison-uniform of the party to which we adhere. We come to wear one cut of face and figure, and acquire by degrees the gentlest asinine expression. There is a mortifying experience in particular which does not fail to wreak itself also in the general history; I mean, "the foolish face of praise,"[1] the forced smile which we put on in company where we do not feel at ease in answer to conversation which does not interest us. The muscles, not spontaneously moved, but moved by a low usurping willfulness, grow tight about the outline of the face and make the most disagreeable sensation, a sensation of rebuke and warning which no brave young man will suffer twice.

For non-conformity the world whips you with its displeasure. And therefore a man must know how to estimate a sour face. The bystanders look askance on him in the public street or in the friend's parlor. If this aversation[2] had its origin in contempt and resistance like his own, he might well go home with a sad countenance; but the sour faces of the multitude, like their sweet faces, have no deep cause, disguise no god, but are put on and off as the wind blows, and a newspaper directs. Yet is the discontent of the multitude more formidable than that of the senate and the college. It is easy enough for a firm man who knows the world to brook the rage of the cultivated classes. Their rage is decorous and prudent, for they are timid as being very vulnerable themselves. But when to their feminine rage the indignation of the people is added, when the ignorant and the poor are aroused, when the unintelligent brute force that lies at the bottom of society is made to growl and mow,[3] it needs the habit[4] of magnanimity and religion to treat it godlike as a trifle of no concernment.

The other terror that scares us from self-trust is our consistency; a reverence for our past act or word, because the eyes of others have no other data for computing our orbit than our past acts, and we are loath to disappoint them.

But why should you keep your head over your shoulder? Why drag about this monstrous corpse of your memory, lest you contradict somewhat you have stated in this or that public place? Suppose you should contradict yourself; what then? It seems to be a rule of wisdom never to rely on your memory alone, scarcely even in acts of pure memory, but to bring the past for judgment into the thousand-eyed present, and live ever in a new day. Trust your emotion. In your metaphysics you have denied personality to the Deity: yet when the devout motions of the soul come, yield to them heart and life, though they should clothe God with shape

---

[1] *the foolish face of praise*   See "Epistle to Dr. Arbuthnot" (1735) by English satirical poet Alexander Pope.

[2] *aversation* Rejection.

[3] *mow* Grimace.

[4] *habit* Clothing.

and color. Leave your theory as Joseph his coat in the hand of the harlot,[1] and flee.

A foolish consistency is the hobgoblin of little minds, adored by little statesmen and philosophers and divines. With consistency a great soul has simply nothing to do. He may as well concern himself with his shadow on the wall. Out upon your guarded lips! Sew them up with packthread, do. Else, if you would be a man, speak what you think today in words as hard as cannon balls, and tomorrow speak what tomorrow thinks in hard words again, though it contradict everything you said today. Ah, then, exclaim the aged ladies, you shall be sure to be misunderstood. Misunderstood! It is a right fool's word. Is it so bad then to be misunderstood? Pythagoras was misunderstood, and Socrates, and Jesus, and Luther, and Copernicus, and Galileo, and Newton,[2] and every pure and wise spirit that ever took flesh. To be great is to be misunderstood.

I suppose no man can violate his nature. All the sallies[3] of his will are rounded in by the law of his being as the inequalities[4] of Andes and Himmaleh[5] are insignificant in the curve of the sphere. Nor does it matter how you gauge and try him. A character is like an acrostic or Alexandrian stanza[6]—read it forward, backward, or across, it still spells the same thing. In this pleasing contrite wood-life which God allows me, let me record day by day my honest thought without prospect or retrospect, and, I cannot doubt, it will be found symmetrical, though I mean it not, and see it not. My book should smell of pines and resound with the hum of insects. The swallow over my window should interweave that thread or straw he carries in his bill into my web also. We pass for what we are. Character teaches above our wills. Men imagine that they communicate their virtue or vice only by overt actions and do not see that virtue or vice emit a breath every moment.

Fear never but you shall be consistent in whatever variety of actions, so they be each honest and natural in their hour. For of one will, the actions will be harmonious, however unlike they seem. These varieties are lost sight of at a little distance, at a little height of thought. One tendency unites them all. The voyage of the best ship is a zigzag line of a hundred tacks. This is only microscopic criticism. See the line from a sufficient distance, and it straightens itself to the average tendency. Your genuine action will explain itself and will explain your other genuine actions. Your conformity explains nothing. Act singly, and what you have already done singly, will justify you now. Greatness always appeals to the future. If I can be great enough now to do right and scorn eyes, I must have done so much right before, as to defend me now. Be it how it will, do right now. Always scorn appearances, and you always may. The force of character is cumulative. All the foregone days of virtue work their health into this. What makes the majesty of the heroes of the senate and the field, which so fills the imagination? The consciousness of a train of great days and victories behind. There they all stand and shed an united light on the advancing actor. He is attended as by a visible escort of angels to every man's eye. That is it which throws thunder into Chatham's[7] voice, and dignity into Washington's[8] port, and

---

1   *as Joseph … the harlot*   Joseph, who has been sold into slavery by his jealous brothers, flees from his master's wife when she tries to seduce him. See Genesis 39.12: "And she caught him by his garment, saying, Lie with me: and he left his garment in her hand, and fled, and got him out."

2   *Pythagoras*   Ancient Greek philosopher, mathematician, and mystic (c. 570–c. 495 BCE); *Socrates*   Ancient Greek philosopher and teacher (c. 470–399 BCE) who was famously executed by the Athenian authorities for his supposed crimes of impiety and of corrupting the minds of his students; *Luther*   Martin Luther (1483–1546), German theologian and foremost leader of the Protestant Reformation who in 1520 was excommunicated by the Pope for his controversial writings; *Copernicus*   Nicolaus Copernicus (1473–1543), Polish-Prussian astronomer who posited that the Sun, not the Earth, is at the center of the solar system; *Galileo*   Galileo Galilei (1564–1642), Italian astronomer and physicist who was considered a heretic for his championing of the Copernican model of the Solar System; *Newton*   Sir Isaac Newton (1642–1727), English physicist who formulated a number of revolutionary theories about the physical world, including the law of gravity.

3   *sallies*   Ventures forth (the term especially refers to a military force attacking from a position of retreat).

4   *inequalities*   I.e., peaks and valleys.

5   *Andes and Himmaleh*   Large mountain ranges in South America and Asia.

6   *Alexandrian stanza*   Here, a palindrome, a word or line that reads the same forwards or backwards; usually, an "Alexandrian" is a poetic line with twelve syllables.

7   *Chatham*   William Pitt, first Earl of Chatham (1708–78), British prime minister known for his oratorical skills.

8   *Washington*   George Washington (1732–99).

America into Adams's[1] eye. Honor is venerable to us because it is no ephemeris.[2] It is always ancient virtue. We worship it today, because it is not of today. We love it and pay it homage, because it is not a trap for our love and homage, but is self-dependent, self-derived, and therefore of an old immaculate pedigree, even if shown in a young person.

I hope in these days we have heard the last of conformity and consistency. Let the words be gazetted[3] and ridiculous henceforward. Instead of the gong for dinner, let us hear a whistle from the Spartan fife.[4] Let us bow and apologize never more. A great man is coming to eat at my house. I do not wish to please him: I wish that he should wish to please me. I will stand here for humanity, and though I would make it kind, I would make it true. Let us affront and reprimand the smooth mediocrity and squalid contentment of the times, and hurl in the face of custom, and trade, and office, the fact which is the upshot of all history, that there is a great responsible Thinker and Actor moving wherever moves a man; that a true man belongs to no other time or place, but is the centre of things. Where he is, there is nature. He measures you, and all men, and all events. You are constrained to accept his standard. Ordinarily everybody in society reminds us of somewhat else or of some other person. Character, reality, reminds you of nothing else. It takes place of the whole creation. The man must be so much that he must make all circumstances indifferent—put all means into the shade. This all great men are and do. Every true man is a cause, a country, and an age; requires infinite spaces and numbers and time fully to accomplish his thought—and posterity seem to follow his steps as a procession. A man Caesar is born, and for ages after, we have a Roman Empire. Christ is born, and millions of minds so grow and cleave to his genius, that he is confounded with virtue and the possible of man. An institution is the lengthened shadow of one man; as, the Reformation, of Luther; Quakerism, of Fox; Methodism, of Wesley; Abolition, of Clarkson.[5] Scipio,[6] Milton called "the height of Rome";[7] and all history resolves itself very easily into the biography of a few stout and earnest persons.

Let a man then know his worth, and keep things under his feet. Let him not peep or steal, or skulk up and down with the air of a charity-boy, a bastard, or an interloper, in the world which exists for him. But the man in the street finding no worth in himself which corresponds to the force which built a tower or sculptured a marble god, feels poor when he looks on these. To him a palace, a statue, a costly book have an alien and forbidding air, much like a gay equipage,[8] and seem to say like that, "Who are you, sir?" Yet they all are his, suitors for his notice, petitioners to his faculties that they will come out and take possession. The picture waits for my verdict: it is not to command me, but I am to settle its claims to praise. That popular fable of the sot who was picked up dead drunk in the street, carried to the duke's house, washed and dressed and laid in the duke's bed, and, on his waking, treated with all obsequious ceremony like the duke, and assured that he had been insane,[9] owes its popularity to the fact that it symbolizes so well the state of man, who is in the world a sort of sot, but now and then wakes up, exercises his reason, and finds himself a true prince.

Our reading is mendicant[10] and sycophantic. In history, our imagination makes fools of us, plays us false. Kingdom and lordship, power and estate are a gaudier vocabulary than private John and Edward in a small house and common day's work: but the things of life are the same to both: the sum total of both is the same. Why all this deference to Alfred, and Scanderbeg, and

---

[1]   *Adams*   Probably John Adams (1735–1826), second president of the United States and one of the nation's founders.

[2]   *ephemeris*   Ephemeral thing.

[3]   *gazetted*   Announced in a newspaper.

[4]   *Spartan fife*   Military flute of the Spartans, an ancient Greek people known for their emphasis on strength and military prowess.

[5]   *Fox*   George Fox (1624–91), founder of the Religious Society of Friends, more commonly known as the Quakers; *Wesley*   John Wesley (1703–91), founder of Methodism; *Clarkson*   Thomas Clarkson (1760–1846), prominent English abolitionist.

[6]   *Scipio*   Publius Cornelius Scipio Africanus (236–183 BCE), Roman general who conquered Spain and Carthage and defeated Hannibal in the Punic Wars.

[7]   *the height of Rome*   See *Paradise Lost* 9.510.

[8]   *equipage*   Carriage and horses, with attendants.

[9]   *That popular ... been insane*   See Shakespeare's *The Taming of the Shrew*, "Induction."

[10]   *mendicant*   Like a beggar.

Gustavus?[1] Suppose they were virtuous: did they wear out virtue? As great a stake depends on your private act today, as followed their public and renowned steps. When private men shall act with vast views, the lustre will be transferred from the actions of kings to those of gentlemen.

The world has indeed been instructed by its kings, who have so magnetized the eyes of nations. It has been taught by this colossal symbol the mutual reverence that is due from man to man. The joyful loyalty with which men have everywhere suffered the king, the noble, or the great proprietor to walk among them by a law of his own, make his own scale of men and things, and reverse theirs, pay for benefits not with money but with honor, and represent the Law in his person, was the hieroglyphic by which they obscurely signified their consciousness of their own right and comeliness, the right of every man.

The magnetism which all original action exerts is explained when we inquire the reason of self-trust. Who is the Trustee? What is the aboriginal[2] Self on which a universal reliance may be grounded? What is the nature and power of that science-baffling star, without parallax,[3] without calculable elements, which shoots a ray of beauty even into trivial and impure actions, if the least mark of independence appear? The inquiry leads us to that source, at once the essence of genius, the essence of virtue, and the essence of life, which we call Spontaneity or Instinct. We denote this primary wisdom as Intuition, whilst all later teachings are tuitions. In that deep force, the last fact behind which analysis cannot go, all things find their common origin. For the sense of being which in calm hours rises, we know not how, in the soul, is not diverse from things, from space, from light, from time, from man, but one with them, and proceedeth obviously from the same source whence their life and being also proceedeth. We first share the life by which things exist, and afterwards see them as appearances in nature, and forget that we have shared their cause. Here is the fountain of action and the fountain of thought. Here are the lungs of that inspiration which giveth man wisdom, of that inspiration of man which cannot be denied without impiety and atheism. We lie in the lap of immense intelligence, which makes us organs of its activity and receivers of its truth. When we discern justice, when we discern truth, we do nothing of ourselves, but allow a passage to its beams. If we ask whence this comes, if we seek to pry into the soul that causes—all metaphysics, all philosophy is at fault. Its presence or its absence is all we can affirm. Every man discerns between the voluntary acts of his mind, and his involuntary perceptions. And to his involuntary perceptions, he knows a perfect respect is due. He may err in the expression of them, but he knows that these things are so, like day and night, not to be disputed. All my willful actions and acquisitions are but roving—the most trivial reverie, the faintest native emotion, are domestic and divine. Thoughtless people contradict as readily the statement of perceptions as of opinions, or rather much more readily; for they do not distinguish between perception and notion. They fancy that I choose to see this or that thing. But perception is not whimsical, but fatal.[4] If I see a trait, my children will see it after me, and in course of time, all mankind—although it may chance that no one has seen it before me. For my perception of it is as much a fact as the sun.

The relations of the soul to the divine spirit are so pure that it is profane to seek to interpose helps. It must be that when God speaketh, he should communicate not one thing, but all things; should fill the world with his voice; should scatter forth light, nature, time, souls, from the centre of the present thought; and new date and new create the whole. Whenever a mind is simple, and receives a divine wisdom, old things pass away—means, teachers, texts, temples fall; it lives now and absorbs past and future into the present hour. All things are made sacred by relation to it— one as much as another. All things are dissolved to their centre by their cause, and in the universal miracle petty and particular miracles disappear. This is and must be. If, therefore, a man claims to know and speak of God, and carries you backward to the phraseology of some

---

1   *Alfred* King Alfred the Great of England (849–99); *Scanderbeg* Albanian military commander (1405–68) who rebelled against the Turkish occupation of Albania; *Gustavus* King Gustavus Adolphus of Sweden (1594–1632).

2   *aboriginal* Inherent.

3   *parallax* Change in an object's apparent position caused by an actual change in the position from which it is being observed, such as the apparent movement of the stars caused by the movement of the Earth.

---

4   *fatal* I.e., determined by fate.

old mouldered nation in another country, in another world, believe him not. Is the acorn better than the oak which is its fullness and completion? Is the parent better than the child into whom he has cast his ripened being? Whence then this worship of the past? The centuries are conspirators against the sanity and majesty of the soul. Time and space are but physiological colors which the eye maketh, but the soul is light; where it is, is day; where it was, is night; and history is an impertinence and an injury, if it be anything more than a cheerful apologue[1] or parable of my being and becoming.

Man is timid and apologetic. He is no longer upright. He dares not say "I think," "I am," but quotes some saint or sage. He is ashamed before the blade of grass or the blowing rose. These roses under my window make no reference to former roses or to better ones; they are for what they are; they exist with God today. There is no time to them. There is simply the rose; it is perfect in every moment of its existence. Before a leaf-bud has burst, its whole life acts; in the full-blown flower, there is no more; in the leafless root, there is no less. Its nature is satisfied, and it satisfies nature, in all moments alike. There is no time to it. But man postpones or remembers; he does not live in the present, but with reverted eye laments the past, or, heedless of the riches that surround him, stands on tiptoe to foresee the future. He cannot be happy and strong until he too lives with nature in the present, above time.

This should be plain enough. Yet see what strong intellects dare not yet hear God himself, unless he speak the phraseology of I know not what David, or Jeremiah, or Paul.[2] We shall not always set so great a price on a few texts, on a few lives. We are like children who repeat by rote the sentences of grandames and tutors, and, as they grow older, of the men of talents and character they chance to see, painfully recollecting the exact words they spoke; afterwards, when they come into the point of view which those had who uttered these sayings, they understand them, and are willing to let the words go; for, at any time, they can use words as good, when occasion comes. So was it

with us, so will it be, if we proceed. If we live truly, we shall see truly. It is as easy for the strong man to be strong, as it is for the weak to be weak. When we have new perception, we shall gladly disburden the memory of its hoarded treasures as old rubbish. When a man lives with God, his voice shall be as sweet as the murmur of the brook and the rustle of the corn.

And now at last the highest truth on this subject remains unsaid; probably, cannot be said; for all that we say is the far off remembering of the intuition. That thought, by what I can now nearest approach to say it, is this. When good is near you, when you have life in yourself, it is not by any known or appointed way; you shall not discern the footprints of any other; you shall not see the face of man; you shall not hear any name; the way, the thought, the good shall be wholly strange and new. It shall exclude all other being. You take the way from man not to man. All persons that ever existed are its fugitive ministers. There shall be no fear in it. Fear and hope are alike beneath it. It asks nothing. There is somewhat low even in hope. We are then in vision. There is nothing that can be called gratitude nor properly joy. The soul is raised over passion. It seeth identity and eternal causation. It is a perceiving that Truth and Right are. Hence it becomes a Tranquillity out of the knowing that all things go well. Vast spaces of nature; the Atlantic Ocean, the South Sea; vast intervals of time, years, centuries, are of no account. This which I think and feel, underlay that former state of life and circumstances, as it does underlie my present, and will always all circumstance, and what is called life, and what is called death.

Life only avails, not the having lived. Power ceases in the instant of repose; it resides in the moment of transition from a past to a new state; in the shooting of the gulf; in the darting to an aim. This one fact the world hates, that the soul *becomes;* for that forever degrades the past; turns all riches to poverty; all reputation to shame; confounds the saint with the rogue; shoves Jesus and Judas[3] equally aside. Why then do we prate of self-reliance? Inasmuch as the soul is present, there will be power not confident but agent. To talk of reliance is a poor external way of speaking. Speak rather of that which relies, because it works and is. Who has more

---

[1]   *apologue* Allegory.

[2]   *David, or Jeremiah, or Paul* Biblical King of Israel, biblical prophet, and one of Jesus' apostles, all of whom have been credited with the authorship of portions of the Bible.

[3]   *Judas* The apostle who is said to have betrayed Jesus to the authorities.

soul than I, masters me, though he should not raise his finger. Round him I must revolve by the gravitation of spirits; who has less, I rule with like facility. We fancy it rhetoric when we speak of eminent virtue. We do not yet see that virtue is Height, and that a man or a company of men plastic and permeable to principles, by the law of nature must overpower and ride all cities, nations, kings, rich men, poets, who are not.

This is the ultimate fact which we so quickly reach on this as on every topic, the resolution of all into the ever blessed One. Virtue is the governor, the creator, the reality. All things real are so by so much of virtue as they contain. Hardship, husbandry, hunting, whaling, war, eloquence, personal weight, are somewhat, and engage my respect as examples of the soul's presence and impure action. I see the same law working in nature for conservation and growth. The poise of a planet, the bended tree recovering itself from the strong wind, the vital resources of every vegetable and animal, are also demonstrations of the self-sufficing, and therefore self-relying soul. All history from its highest to its trivial passages is the various record of this power.

Thus all concentrates; let us not rove; let us sit at home with the cause. Let us stun and astonish the intruding rabble of men and books and institutions by a simple declaration of the divine fact. Bid them take the shoes from off their feet, for God is here within.[1] Let our simplicity judge them, and our docility to our own law demonstrate the poverty of nature and fortune beside our native riches.

But now we are a mob. Man does not stand in awe of man, nor is the soul admonished to stay at home, to put itself in communication with the internal ocean, but it goes abroad to beg a cup of water of the urns of men. We must go alone. Isolation must precede true society. I like the silent church before the service begins, better than any preaching. How far off, how cool, how chaste the persons look, begirt[2] each one with a precinct or sanctuary. So let us always sit. Why should we assume the faults of our friend, or wife, or father, or child, because they sit around our hearth, or are said to have the same blood? All men have my blood, and I have all men's. Not for that will I adopt their petulance or folly,

even to the extent of being ashamed of it. But your isolation must not be mechanical, but spiritual, that is, must be elevation. At times the whole world seems to be in conspiracy to importune you with emphatic trifles. Friend, client, child, sickness, fear, want, charity, all knock at once at thy closet door and say, "Come out unto us." Do not spill thy soul; do not all descend; keep thy state; stay at home in thine own heaven; come not for a moment into their facts, into their hubbub of conflicting appearances, but let in the light of thy law on their confusion. The power men possess to annoy me, I give them by a weak curiosity. No man can come near me but through my act. "What we love that we have, but by desire we bereave ourselves of the love."[3]

If we cannot at once rise to the sanctities of obedience and faith, let us at least resist our temptations, let us enter into the state of war, and wake Thor and Woden,[4] courage and constancy in our Saxon breasts. This is to be done in our smooth times by speaking the truth. Check[5] this lying hospitality and lying affection. Live no longer to the expectation of these deceived and deceiving people with whom we converse. Say to them, O father, O mother, O wife, O brother, O friend, I have lived with you after appearances hitherto. Henceforward I am the truth's. Be it known unto you that henceforward I obey no law less than the eternal law. I will have no covenants but proximities. I shall endeavor to nourish my parents, to support my family, to be the chaste husband of one wife—but these relations I must fill after a new and unprecedented way. I appeal from your customs. I must be myself. I cannot break myself any longer for you, or you. If you can love me for what I am, we shall be the happier. If you cannot, I will still seek to deserve that you should. I must be myself. I will not hide my tastes or aversions. I will so trust that what is deep is holy, that I will do strongly before the sun and moon whatever inly rejoices me, and the heart appoints. If you are noble, I will love you; if you are not, I will not hurt you and myself by hypocritical attentions. If you

---

[1]   *Bid them ... here within*   See Exodus 3.5: "put off thy shoes from off thy feet, for the place whereon thou standest is holy ground."

[2]   *begirt*   Surround.

[3]   *What we ... the love*   Emerson's own loose translation of the first line of "Love and Desire" by German poet Friedrich Schiller (1759–1805).

[4]   *Thor and Woden*   Norse gods associated with strength and warfare.

[5]   *Check*   Stop; restrain.

are true, but not in the same truth with me, cleave to your companions; I will seek my own. I do this not selfishly, but humbly and truly. It is alike your interest and mine and all men's, however long we have dwelt in lies, to live in truth. Does this sound harsh today? You will soon love what is dictated by your nature as well as mine, and if we follow the truth, it will bring us out safe at last.—But so you may give these friends pain. Yes, but I cannot sell my liberty and my power, to save their sensibility. Besides, all persons have their moments of reason when they look out into the region of absolute truth; then will they justify me and do the same thing.

The populace think that your rejection of popular standards is a rejection of all standard, and mere antinomianism;[1] and the bold sensualist will use the name of philosophy to gild his crimes. But the law of consciousness abides. There are two confessionals, in one or the other of which we must be shriven. You may fulfill your round of duties by clearing yourself in the *direct*, or, in the *reflex* way. Consider whether you have satisfied your relations to father, mother, cousin, neighbor, town, cat, and dog; whether any of these can upbraid you. But I may also neglect this reflex standard, and absolve me to myself. I have my own stern claims and perfect circle. It denies the name of duty to many offices that are called duties. But if I can discharge its debts, it enables me to dispense with the popular code. If anyone imagines that this law is lax, let him keep its commandment one day.

And truly it demands something godlike in him who has cast off the common motives of humanity, and has ventured to trust himself for a task-master. High be his heart, faithful his will, clear his sight, that he may in good earnest be doctrine, society, law to himself, that a simple purpose may be to him as strong as iron necessity is to others.

If any man consider the present aspects of what is called by distinction *society*, he will see the need of these ethics. The sinew and heart of man seem to be drawn out, and we are become timorous desponding whimperers. We are afraid of truth, afraid of fortune, afraid of death, and afraid of each other. Our age yields no great and perfect persons. We want men and women who shall renovate life and our social state, but we see that most natures are insolvent; cannot satisfy their own wants, have an ambition out of all proportion to their practical force, and so do lean and beg day and night continually. Our housekeeping is mendicant, our arts, our occupations, our marriages, our religion we have not chosen, but society has chosen for us. We are parlor soldiers. The rugged battle of fate, where strength is born, we shun.

If our young men miscarry[2] in their first enterprises, they lose all heart. If the young merchant fails, men say he is *ruined*. If the finest genius studies at one of our colleges, and is not installed in an office within one year afterwards in the cities or suburbs of Boston or New York, it seems to his friends and to himself that he is right in being disheartened and in complaining the rest of his life. A sturdy lad from New Hampshire or Vermont, who in turn tries all the professions, who *teams it*,[3] *farms it*, *peddles*, keeps a school, preaches, edits a newspaper, goes to Congress, buys a township, and so forth, in successive years, and always, like a cat, falls on his feet, is worth a hundred of these city dolls. He walks abreast with his days, and feels no shame in not "studying a profession," for he does not postpone his life, but lives already. He has not one chance, but a hundred chances. Let a stoic arise who shall reveal the resources of man, and tell men they are not leaning willows, but can and must detach themselves; that with the exercise of self-trust, new powers shall appear; that a man is the word made flesh,[4] born to shed healing to the nations,[5] that he should be ashamed of our compassion, and that the moment he acts from himself, tossing the laws, the books, idolatries, and customs out of the window, we pity him no more but thank and revere him—and that teacher shall restore the life of man to splendor, and make his name dear to all History.

It is easy to see that a greater self-reliance—a new respect for the divinity in man—must work a

---

1   *antinomianism* Doctrine held to by some Christians that salvation is derived from faith and divine grace alone, and that therefore the saved are not bound by moral laws such as those of the Ten Commandments.

2   *miscarry* Fail.

3   *teams it* Drives a team of horses or other animals.

4   *word made flesh* Phrase applied to Jesus in John 1.14.

5   *shed healing to the nations* See Revelation 2.22: "on either side of the river [of life], was there the tree of life ... and the leaves of the tree were for the healing of the nations."

revolution in all the offices and relations of men; in their religion; in their education; in their pursuits; their modes of living; their association; in their property; in their speculative views.

1. In what prayers do men allow themselves! That which they call a holy office, is not so much as brave and manly. Prayer looks abroad and asks for some foreign addition to come through some foreign virtue, and loses itself in endless mazes of natural and supernatural, and mediatorial and miraculous. Prayer that craves a particular commodity—anything less than all good—is vicious. Prayer is the contemplation of the facts of life from the highest point of view. It is the soliloquy of a beholding and jubilant soul. It is the spirit of God pronouncing his works good. But prayer as a means to effect a private end, is theft and meanness. It supposes dualism and not unity in nature and consciousness. As soon as the man is at one with God, he will not beg. He will then see prayer in all action. The prayer of the farmer kneeling in his field to weed it, the prayer of the rower kneeling with the stroke of his oar, are true prayers heard throughout nature, though for cheap ends. Caratach, in Fletcher's *Bonduca*,[1] when admonished to inquire the mind of the god Audate, replies,

> His hidden meaning lies in our endeavors,
> Our valors are our best gods.

Another sort of false prayers are our regrets. Discontent is the want of self-reliance: it is infirmity of will. Regret calamities, if you can thereby help the sufferer; if not, attend your own work, and already the evil begins to be repaired. Our sympathy is just as base. We come to them who weep foolishly, and sit down and cry for company, instead of imparting to them truth and health in rough electric shocks, putting them once more in communication with the soul. The secret of fortune is joy in our hands. Welcome evermore to gods and men is the self-helping man. For him all doors are flung wide. Him all tongues greet, all honors crown, all eyes follow with desire. Our love goes out to him and embraces him, because he did not need it. We solicitously and apologetically caress and celebrate him, because he held on his way and scorned our

disapprobation. The gods love him because men hated him. "To the persevering mortal," said Zoroaster,[2] "the blessed Immortals are swift."

As men's prayers are a disease of the will, so are their creeds a disease of the intellect. They say with those foolish Israelites, "Let not God speak to us, lest we die. Speak thou, speak any man with us, and we will obey."[3] Everywhere I am bereaved of meeting God in my brother, because he has shut his own temple doors, and recites fables merely of his brother's, or his brother's brother's God. Every new mind is a new classification. If it prove a mind of uncommon activity and power, a Locke, a Lavoisier, a Hutton, a Bentham, a Spurzheim,[4] it imposes its classification on other men, and lo! a new system. In proportion always to the depth of the thought, and so to the number of the objects it touches and brings within reach of the pupil, is his complacency. But chiefly is this apparent in creeds and churches, which are also classifications of some powerful mind acting on the elemental thought of Duty, and man's relation to the Highest. Such is Calvinism, Quakerism, Swedenborgianism.[5] The pupil takes the same delight in subordinating everything to the new terminology that a girl does who has just learned botany, in seeing a new earth and new seasons thereby. It will happen for a time that the pupil will feel a real debt to the teacher—will find his intellectual power has grown by the study of his writings. This will continue until he has exhausted his master's mind. But in all unbalanced minds, the classification is idolized, passes for the end, and not for a speedily exhaustible means, so that the walls of the system blend to their eye in the remote horizon with the walls of the universe; the luminaries of heaven seem to them hung on the

---

1   *Fletcher's Bonduca*   See *Bonduca* 3.1 (c. 1613) by John Fletcher.

2   *Zoroaster*   Ancient Persian prophet who founded the religion of Zoroastrianism.

3   *Let not … will obey*   See Exodus 20.19.

4   *Locke*   John Locke (1632–1704), English philosopher; *Lavoisier* Antoine Lavoisier (1743–97), French chemist; *Hutton* James Hutton (1726–97), Scottish geologist; *Bentham* Jeremy Bentham (1748–1832), English utilitarian philosopher; *Spurzheim* Johann Gaspar Spurzheim (1776–1832), proponent of the popular pseudoscience of phrenology. Emerson amended the 1847 edition of this text to refer to French mathematician Joseph Fourier instead of Spurzheim, as phrenology was losing its credibility in the United States.

5   *Calvinism, Quakerism, Swedenborgianism*   Schools of Christian thought.

arch their master built. They cannot imagine how you aliens have any right to see—how you can see; "It must be somehow that you stole the light from us." They do not yet perceive that light, unsystematic, indomitable, will break into any cabin, even into theirs. Let them chirp awhile and call it their own. If they are honest and do well, presently their neat new pinfold[1] will be too strait and low, will crack, will lean, will rot and vanish, and the immortal light, all young and joyful, million-orbed, million-colored, will beam over the universe as on the first morning.

2. It is for want of self-culture that the idol of Travelling, the idol of Italy, of England, of Egypt, remains for all educated Americans. They who made England, Italy, or Greece venerable in the imagination, did so not by rambling round creation as a moth round a lamp, but by sticking fast where they were, like an axis of the earth. In manly hours, we feel that duty is our place, and that the merrymen of circumstance should follow as they may. The soul is no traveller: the wise man stays at home with the soul, and when his necessities, his duties, on any occasion call him from his house, or into foreign lands, he is at home still, and is not gadding abroad from himself, and shall make men sensible by the expression of his countenance, that he goes the missionary of wisdom and virtue, and visits cities and men like a sovereign, and not like an interloper or a valet.

I have no churlish[2] objection to the circumnavigation of the globe, for the purposes of art, of study, and benevolence, so that the man is first domesticated, or does not go abroad with the hope of finding somewhat greater than he knows. He who travels to be amused, or to get somewhat which he does not carry, travels away from himself, and grows old even in youth among old things. In Thebes, in Palmyra,[3] his will and mind have become old and dilapidated as they. He carries ruins to ruins.

Travelling is a fool's paradise. We owe to our first journeys the discovery that place is nothing. At home I dream that at Naples, at Rome, I can be intoxicated with beauty, and lose my sadness. I pack my trunk, embrace my friends, embark on the sea, and at last wake up in Naples, and there beside me is the stern Fact, the sad self, unrelenting, identical, that I fled from. I seek the Vatican, and the palaces. I affect to be intoxicated with sights and suggestions, but I am not intoxicated. My giant goes with me wherever I go.

3. But the rage of travelling is itself only a symptom of a deeper unsoundness affecting the whole intellectual action. The intellect is vagabond, and the universal system of education fosters restlessness. Our minds travel when our bodies are forced to stay at home. We imitate; and what is imitation but the travelling of the mind? Our houses are built with foreign taste; our shelves are garnished with foreign ornaments; our opinions, our tastes, our whole minds lean, and follow the Past and the Distant, as the eyes of a maid follow her mistress. The soul created the arts wherever they have flourished. It was in his own mind that the artist sought his model. It was an application of his own thought to the thing to be done and the conditions to be observed. And why need we copy the Doric or the Gothic[4] model? Beauty, convenience, grandeur of thought, and quaint expression are as near to us as to any, and if the American artist will study with hope and love the precise thing to be done by him, considering the climate, the soil, the length of the day, the wants of the people, the habit and form of the government, he will create a house in which all these will find themselves fitted, and taste and sentiment will be satisfied also.

Insist on yourself; never imitate. Your own gift you can present every moment with the cumulative force of a whole life's cultivation; but of the adopted talent of another, you have only an extemporaneous, half possession. That which each can do best, none but his Maker can teach him. No man yet knows what it is, nor can, till that person has exhibited it. Where is the master who could have taught Shakespeare? Where is the master who could have instructed Franklin, or Washington, or Bacon,[5] or Newton? Every great man is an unique. The Scipionism of Scipio is precisely

---

1   *pinfold* Enclosure for livestock.

2   *churlish* Lowly or boorish.

3   *Thebes … Palmyra* Ancient, ruined cities in Egypt and what is now Syria.

4   *Doric or the Gothic* Traditional modes of architecture from ancient Greece and medieval Europe, respectively.

5   *Where is … or Washington* Neither Benjamin Franklin (1706–90) nor George Washington (1732–99) received extensive formal education; *Bacon* Francis Bacon (1561–1626), English philosopher.

that part he could not borrow. If anybody will tell me whom the great man imitates in the original crisis[1] when he performs a great act, I will tell him who else than himself can teach him. Shakespeare will never be made by the study of Shakespeare. Do that which is assigned thee, and thou canst not hope too much or dare too much. There is at this moment, there is for me an utterance bare and grand as that of the colossal chisel of Phidias,[2] or trowel of the Egyptians, or the pen of Moses, or Dante,[3] but different from all these. Not possibly will the soul all rich, all eloquent, with thousand-cloven tongue, deign to repeat itself; but if I can hear what these patriarchs say, surely I can reply to them in the same pitch of voice: for the ear and the tongue are two organs of one nature. Dwell up there in the simple and noble regions of thy life, obey thy heart, and thou shalt reproduce the Foreworld[4] again.

4. As our Religion, our Education, our Art look abroad, so does our spirit of society. All men plume themselves on the improvement of society, and no man improves.

Society never advances. It recedes as fast on one side as it gains on the other. Its progress is only apparent, like the workers of a treadmill.[5] It undergoes continual changes: it is barbarous, it is civilized, it is christianized, it is rich, it is scientific; but this change is not amelioration. For everything that is given, something is taken. Society acquires new arts and loses old instincts. What a contrast between the well-clad, reading, writing, thinking American, with a watch, a pencil, and a bill of exchange in his pocket, and the naked New Zealander, whose property is a club, a spear, a mat, and an undivided twentieth of a shed to sleep under. But compare the health of the two men, and you shall see that his aboriginal strength the white man has lost. If the traveller tell us truly, strike the savage with a broad axe, and in a day or two the flesh shall unite and heal

as if you struck the blow into soft pitch, and the same blow shall send the white to his grave.

The civilized man has built a coach, but has lost the use of his feet. He is supported on crutches, but loses so much support of muscle. He has got a fine Geneva watch, but he has lost the skill to tell the hour by the sun. A Greenwich nautical almanac[6] he has, and so being sure of the information when he wants it, the man in the street does not know a star in the sky. The solstice he does not observe; the equinox he knows as little; and the whole bright calendar of the year is without a dial in his mind. His notebooks impair his memory; his libraries overload his wit; the insurance office increases the number of accidents; and it may be a question whether machinery does not encumber; whether we have not lost by refinement some energy, by a christianity entrenched in establishments and forms, some vigor of wild virtue. For every stoic[7] was a stoic; but in Christendom where is the Christian?

There is no more deviation in the moral standard than in the standard of height or bulk. No greater men are now than ever were. A singular equality may be observed between the great men of the first and of the last ages; nor can all the science, art, religion and philosophy of the nineteenth century avail to educate greater men than Plutarch's[8] heroes, three or four and twenty centuries ago. Not in time is the race progressive. Phocion, Socrates, Anaxagoras, Diogenes,[9] are great men, but they leave no class. He who is really of their class will not be called by their name, but be wholly his own man, and in his turn the founder of a sect. The arts and inventions of each period are only its costume, and do not invigorate men. The harm of the improved machinery may compensate

---

1   *crisis*   Critically important stage; turning point.

2   *Phidias*   Ancient Greek sculptor and architect (c. 480–430 BCE) involved in many renowned projects, such as the construction of the Parthenon in Athens.

3   *Dante*   Italian poet Dante Alighieri (1265–1321).

4   *Foreworld*   I.e., the past.

5   *treadmill*   In the nineteenth century, treadmills were used to power mills and other machines; they were also operated as a punishment for prisoners sentenced to hard labor.

6   *Greenwich nautical almanac*   Published by the Royal Greenwich Observatory, almanac providing the data needed to determine one's longitude at sea.

7   *stoic*   Follower of stoicism, an ancient Greek philosophy that emphasized virtue and the importance of intellectual pursuits over emotional and bodily concerns.

8   *Plutarch*   Greek writer (c. 46–c. 120 CE) best known for *Lives of the Noble Greeks and Romans*, a collection of biographies focused on the moral character of historical figures.

9   *Phocion*   Athenian politician (402–318 BCE); *Anaxagoras* Ancient Greek philosopher (c. 510–c. 428 BCE); *Diogenes* Ancient Greek philosopher (c. 412–323 BCE).

its good. Hudson and Behring[1] accomplished so much in their fishing-boats, as to astonish Parry and Franklin,[2] whose equipment exhausted the resources of science and art. Galileo, with an opera-glass,[3] discovered a more splendid series of facts than anyone since. Columbus found the New World in an undecked boat. It is curious to see the periodical disuse and perishing of means and machinery which were introduced with loud laudation, a few years or centuries before. The great genius returns to essential man. We reckoned the improvements of the art of war among the triumphs of science, and yet Napoleon conquered Europe by the Bivouac,[4] which consisted of falling back on naked valor, and disencumbering it of all aids. The Emperor held it impossible to make a perfect army, says Las Casas,[5] "without abolishing our arms, magazines, commissaries, and carriages, until in imitation of the Roman custom, the soldier should receive his supply of corn, grind it in his hand-mill, and bake his bread himself."

Society is a wave. The wave moves onward, but the water of which it is composed does not. The same particle does not rise from the valley to the ridge. Its unity is only phenomenal. The persons who make up a nation today, next year die, and their experience with them.

And so the reliance on Property, including the reliance on governments which protect it, is the want of self-reliance. Men have looked away from themselves and at things so long that they have come to esteem what they call the soul's progress, namely, the religious, learned, and civil institutions, as guards of property, and they deprecate assaults on these, because they feel them to be assaults on property. They measure their esteem of each other, by what each has, and not by what each is. But a cultivated man becomes ashamed of his property, ashamed of what he has, out of new respect for his being. Especially he hates what he has, if he see that it is accidental—came to him by inheritance, or gift, or crime; then he feels that it is not having; it does not belong to him, has no root in him, and merely lies there, because no revolution or no robber takes it away. But that which a man is, does always by necessity acquire, and what the man acquires is permanent and living property, which does not wait the beck of rulers, or mobs, or revolutions, or fire, or storm, or bankruptcies, but perpetually renews itself wherever the man is put. "Thy lot or portion of life," said the Caliph Ali,[6] "is seeking after thee; therefore be at rest from seeking after it." Our dependence on these foreign goods leads us to our slavish respect for numbers. The political parties meet in numerous conventions; the greater the concourse, and with each new uproar of announcement, The delegation from Essex! The Democrats from New Hampshire! The Whigs of Maine! the young patriot feels himself stronger than before by a new thousand of eyes and arms. In like manner the reformers summon conventions, and vote and resolve in multitude. But not so, O friends! will the God deign to enter and inhabit you, but by a method precisely the reverse. It is only as a man puts off from himself all external support, and stands alone, that I see him to be strong and to prevail. He is weaker by every recruit to his banner. Is not a man better than a town? Ask nothing of men, and in the endless mutation, thou only firm column must presently appear the upholder of all that surrounds thee. He who knows that power is in the soul, that he is weak only because he has looked for good out of him and elsewhere, and so perceiving, throws himself unhesitatingly on his thought, instantly rights himself, stands in the erect position, commands his limbs, works miracles; just as a man who stands on his feet is stronger than a man who stands on his head.

So use all that is called Fortune. Most men gamble with her, and gain all, and lose all, as her wheel rolls. But do thou leave as unlawful these winnings, and deal with Cause and Effect, the chancellors of God. In the Will work and acquire, and thou hast chained the wheel of Chance, and shalt always drag her after

---

[1] *Hudson and Behring* Henry Hudson (c. 1565–1611), English Arctic explorer who sought the Northwest Passage, and Vitus Bering (1681–1741), Danish explorer who led two Russian expeditions exploring the ocean around China and Siberia.

[2] *Parry and Franklin* William Edward Parry (1790–1855) and John Franklin (1786–1847), English Arctic explorers who sought the Northwest Passage.

[3] *Galileo, with an opera-glass* Galileo made landmark discoveries in astronomy using small, basic telescopes.

[4] *Bivouac* Temporary, makeshift encampment.

[5] *Las Casas* Emmanuel, comte de Las Cases; the quotation is from his *Mémorial de Sainte-Hélène* (1823), a record of his conversations with Napoleon.

[6] *Caliph Ali* Ali ibn Abi Talib (c. 600–61 CE), early Muslim leader; the quoted line is attributed to him in Simon Ockley's *History of the Saracens* (1708–18).

thee. A political victory, a rise of rents, the recovery of your sick, or the return of your absent friend, or some other quite external event, raises your spirits, and you think good days are preparing for you. Do not believe it. It can never be so. Nothing can bring you peace but yourself. Nothing can bring you peace but the triumph of principles.

—1841

from *The Poet*

A moody child and wildly wise
Pursued the game with joyful eyes,
Which chose, like meteors, their way,
And rived° the dark with private ray: *split*
They overleapt the horizon's edge,
Searched with Apollo's[1] privilege;
Through man, and woman, and sea, and star,
Saw the dance of nature forward far;
Through worlds, and races, and terms, and times,
Saw musical order, and pairing rhymes.

Olympian bards[2] who sung
Divine ideas below,
Which always find us young,
And always keep us so.

Those who are esteemed umpires of taste, are often persons who have acquired some knowledge of admired pictures or sculptures, and have an inclination for whatever is elegant; but if you inquire whether they are beautiful souls, and whether their own acts are like fair pictures, you learn that they are selfish and sensual. Their cultivation is local, as if you should rub a log of dry wood in one spot to produce fire, all the rest remaining cold. Their knowledge of the fine arts is some study of rules and particulars, or some limited judgment of color or form, which is exercised for amusement or for show. It is a proof of the shallowness of the doctrine of beauty, as it lies in the minds of our amateurs, that men seem to have lost the perception of

the instant dependence of form upon soul. There is no doctrine of forms[3] in our philosophy. We were put into our bodies, as fire is put into a pan, to be carried about; but there is no accurate adjustment between the spirit and the organ, much less is the latter the germination of the former. So in regard to other forms, the intellectual men do not believe in any essential dependence of the material world on thought and volition. Theologians think it a pretty air-castle to talk of the spiritual meaning of a ship or a cloud, of a city or a contract, but they prefer to come again to the solid ground of historical evidence; and even the poets are contented with a civil and conformed manner of living, and to write poems from the fancy, at a safe distance from their own experience. But the highest minds of the world have never ceased to explore the double meaning, or, shall I say, the quadruple, or the centuple, or much more manifold meaning, of every sensuous fact: Orpheus, Empedocles, Heraclitus, Plato, Plutarch, Dante, Swedenborg,[4] and the masters of sculpture, picture, and poetry. For we are not pans and barrows,[5] nor even porters of the fire and torch-bearers, but children of the fire, made of it, and only the same divinity transmuted, and at two or three removes, when we know least about it. And this hidden truth, that the fountains whence all this river of Time, and its creatures, floweth, are intrinsically ideal and beautiful, draws us to the consideration of the nature and functions of the Poet, or

---

[1]   *Apollo*   In Greek mythology, Apollo was god of music, poetry, and the sun.

[2]   *Olympian bards*   Divine poets. In Greek mythology, Mount Olympus was the home of the gods.

[3]   *doctrine of forms*   Platonic philosophy posits an ideal realm of forms, with the perceivable, physical world a mere shadow of these forms.

[4]   *Orpheus*   In Greek mythology, Orpheus was a poet and prophet whose music could charm trees, stones, and wild animals into following his will; *Empedocles* Greek philosopher (c. 494–c. 434 BCE); *Heraclitus* Greek philosopher (c. 535–475 BCE); *Plato* Greek philosopher (c. 427–c. 347 BCE) whose system of philosophy—which argues for the essentially immaterial origins of reality—had a shaping influence on Western thought; *Plutarch* Greek essayist, biographer, and Platonic philosopher whose book *Parallel Lives of Noble Greeks and Romans* (c. second century CE) Emerson described as a "bible for heroes"; *Dante* Dante Alighieri was a Renaissance Italian poet whose *Divine Comedy* (c. 1308–20) is widely acknowledged as a major work of world literature; *Swedenborg* Swedish scientist and mystic Emanuel Swedenborg. His work, particularly the spiritual vision in his *Heaven and Hell* (1758), strongly influenced Emerson and the Transcendentalist movement more generally.

[5]   *barrows*   Tools for carrying loads, i.e., stretchers or wheelbarrows.

the man of Beauty, to the means and materials he uses, and to the general aspect of the art in the present time.

The breadth of the problem is great, for the poet is representative. He stands among partial men for the complete man, and apprises us not of his wealth, but of the commonwealth. The young man reveres men of genius, because, to speak truly, they are more himself than he is. They receive of the soul as he also receives, but they more. Nature enhances her beauty, to the eye of loving men, from their belief that the poet is beholding her shows at the same time. He is isolated among his contemporaries, by truth and by his art, but with this consolation in his pursuits, that they will draw all men sooner or later. For all men live by truth, and stand in need of expression. In love, in art, in avarice, in politics, in labor, in games, we study to utter our painful secret. The man is only half himself, the other half is his expression.

Notwithstanding this necessity to be published,[1] adequate expression is rare. I know not how it is that we need an interpreter; but the great majority of men seem to be minors, who have not yet come into possession of their own, or mutes, who cannot report the conversation they have had with nature. There is no man who does not anticipate a supersensual[2] utility in the sun, and stars, earth, and water. These stand and wait to render him a peculiar[3] service. But there is some obstruction, or some excess of phlegm[4] in our constitution, which does not suffer them to yield the due effect. Too feeble fall the impressions of nature on us to make us artists. Every touch should thrill. Every man should be so much an artist, that he could report in conversation what had befallen him. Yet, in our experience, the rays or appulses[5] have sufficient force to arrive at the

senses, but not enough to reach the quick,[6] and compel the reproduction of themselves in speech. The poet is the person in whom these powers are in balance, the man without impediment, who sees and handles that which others dream of, traverses the whole scale of experience, and is representative of man, in virtue of being the largest power to receive and to impart.

For the Universe has three children, born at one time, which reappear, under different names, in every system of thought, whether they be called cause, operation, and effect; or, more poetically, Jove, Pluto, Neptune;[7] or, theologically, the Father, the Spirit, and the Son; but which we will call here, the Knower, the Doer, and the Sayer. These stand respectively for the love of truth, for the love of good, and for the love of beauty. These three are equal. Each is that which he is essentially, so that he cannot be surmounted or analyzed, and each of these three has the power of the others latent in him, and his own patent.

The poet is the sayer, the namer, and represents beauty. He is a sovereign, and stands on the centre. For the world is not painted, or adorned, but is from the beginning beautiful; and God has not made some beautiful things, but Beauty is the creator of the universe. Therefore the poet is not any permissive potentate, but is emperor in his own right. Criticism is infested with a cant of materialism, which assumes that manual skill and activity is the first merit of all men, and disparages such as say and do not, overlooking the fact, that some men, namely, poets, are natural sayers, sent into the world to the end[8] of expression, and confounds them with those whose province is action, but who quit it to imitate the sayers. But Homer's[9] words are as costly and admirable to Homer, as Agamemnon's victories are to Agamemnon.[10] The poet does not wait for the hero or the sage, but, as they act and think primarily, so he writes primarily what will and must be spoken, reckoning the others, though primaries also, yet, in respect

---

[1] *to be published* To be heard, to be made public.

[2] *supersensual* I.e., beyond the material; spiritual.

[3] *peculiar* Particular, distinctive.

[4] *excess of phlegm* Phlegm was considered one of the "bodily humors," four fluids which, according to classical and medieval medical theory, must be balanced within the body in order for a person to be healthy. According to this theory, when one fluid predominates, the temperament associated with it is exacerbated; a person suffering an excess of phlegm was thought to become apathetic, lacking energy to act.

[5] *appulses* Propelled motions, such as those that govern the planets and stars.

[6] *quick* Vital part, the life-blood.

[7] *Jove, Pluto, Neptune* Roman gods of the sky, the underworld, and the sea, respectively.

[8] *end* Purpose.

[9] *Homer* Traditionally said to be the author of the ancient Greek epic poems the *Iliad* and the *Odyssey*.

[10] *Agamemnon* Commander of the Greek army that lays siege to the city of Troy in Homer's *Iliad*.

to him, secondaries and servants; as sitters or models in the studio of a painter, or as assistants who bring building materials to an architect.

For poetry was all written before time was, and whenever we are so finely organized that we can penetrate into that region where the air is music, we hear those primal warblings, and attempt to write them down, but we lose ever and anon[1] a word, or a verse, and substitute something of our own, and thus miswrite the poem. The men of more delicate ear write down these cadences more faithfully, and these transcripts, though imperfect, become the songs of the nations. For nature is as truly beautiful as it is good, or as it is reasonable, and must as much appear, as it must be done, or be known. Words and deeds are quite indifferent modes of the divine energy. Words are also actions, and actions are a kind of words.

The sign and credentials of the poet are, that he announces that which no man foretold. He is the true and only doctor;[2] he knows and tells; he is the only teller of news, for he was present and privy to the appearance which he describes. He is a beholder of ideas, and utterer of the necessary and causal. For we do not speak now of men of poetical talents, or of industry and skill in metre, but of the true poet. ...

For it is not metres, but a metre-making argument, that makes a poem—a thought so passionate and alive, that, like the spirit of a plant or an animal, it has architecture of its own, and adorns nature with a new thing. The thought and the form are equal in the order of time, but in the order of genesis the thought is prior to the form. The poet has a new thought: he has a whole new experience to unfold; he will tell us how it was with him, and all men will be the richer in his fortune. For, the experience of each new age requires a new confession, and the world seems always waiting for its poet. ... We know that the secret of the world is profound, but who or what shall be our interpreter, we know not. A mountain ramble, a new style of face, a new person, may put the key into our hands. Of course, the value of genius to us is in the veracity of its report. Talent may frolic and juggle; genius realizes and adds. Mankind, in good earnest, have arrived so far in

understanding themselves and their work, that the foremost watchman on the peak announces his news. It is the truest word ever spoken and the phrase will be the fittest, most musical, and the unerring voice of the world for that time.

All that we call sacred history attests that the birth of a poet is the principal event in chronology. Man, never so often deceived, still watches for the arrival of a brother who can hold him steady to a truth, until he has made it his own. With what joy I begin to read a poem, which I confide in as an inspiration! And now my chains are to be broken; I shall mount about these clouds and opaque airs in which I live—opaque, though they seem transparent—and from the heaven of truth I shall see and comprehend my relations. That will reconcile me to life, and renovate nature, to see trifles animated by a tendency,[3] and to know what I am doing. Life will no more be a noise; now I shall see men and women, and know the signs by which they may be discerned from fools and satans. This day shall be better than my birthday: then I became an animal: now I am invited into the science of the real. Such is the hope, but the fruition is postponed. Oftener it falls, that this winged man, who will carry me into the heaven, whirls me into mists, then leaps and frisks about with me from cloud to cloud, still affirming that he is bound heavenward; and I, being myself a novice, am slow in perceiving that he does not know the way into the heavens, and is merely bent that I should admire his skill to rise, like a fowl or a flying fish, a little way from the ground or the water; but the all-piercing, all-feeding, and ocular[4] air of heaven, that man shall never inhabit. I tumble down again soon into my old nooks, and lead the life of exaggerations as before, and have lost some faith in the possibility of any guide who can lead me thither where I would be.

But leaving these victims of vanity, let us, with new hope, observe how nature, by worthier impulses, has ensured the poet's fidelity to his office of announcement and affirming, namely, by the beauty of things, which becomes a new, and higher beauty, when expressed. Nature offers all her creatures to him as a picture-language. Being used as a type, a second wonderful value appears in the object, far better than its

---

[1]   *ever and anon*   I.e., every now and then.

[2]   *doctor*   Expert, teacher.

[3]   *tendency*   Conscious aim or purpose.

[4]   *ocular*   Visible.

old value, as the carpenter's stretched cord,[1] if you hold your ear close enough, is musical in the breeze. "Things more excellent than every image," says Jamblichus,[2] "are expressed through images." Things admit of being used as symbols, because nature is a symbol, in the whole, and in every part. …

The Universe is the externization of the soul. Wherever the life is, that bursts into appearance around it. Our science is sensual, and therefore superficial. The earth, and the heavenly bodies, physics, and chemistry, we sensually treat, as if they were self-existent; but these are the retinue of that Being we have. "The mighty heaven," said Proclus, "exhibits, in its transfigurations, clear images of the splendor of intellectual perceptions; being moved in conjunction with the unapparent periods of intellectual natures." Therefore, science always goes abreast with the just elevation of the man, keeping step with religion and metaphysics; or, the state of science is an index of our self-knowledge. Since everything in nature answers to a moral power, if any phenomenon remains brute and dark, it is because the corresponding faculty in the observer is not yet active.

No wonder, then, if these waters be so deep, that we hover over them with a religious regard. The beauty of the fable proves the importance of the sense; to the poet, and to all others; or, if you please, every man is so far a poet as to be susceptible of these enchantments of nature; for all men have the thoughts whereof the universe is the celebration. I find that the fascination resides in the symbol. Who loves nature? Who does not? Is it only poets, and men of leisure and cultivation, who live with her? No; but also hunters, farmers, grooms, and butchers, though they express their affection in their choice of life, and not in their choice of words. The writer wonders what the coachman or the hunter values in riding, in horses, and dogs. It is not superficial qualities. When you talk with him, he holds these at as slight a rate as you. His worship is sympathetic; he has no definitions, but he is commanded in nature, by the living power which he feels to be there present. No imitation, or playing of these things, would content him; he loves the earnest of the north

wind, of rain, of stone, and wood, and iron. A beauty not explicable, is dearer than a beauty which we can see to the end of. It is nature the symbol, nature certifying the supernatural, body overflowed by life, which he worships, with coarse, but sincere rites.

The inwardness, and mystery, of this attachment, drive men of every class to the use of emblems. The schools of poets, and philosophers, are not more intoxicated with their symbols, than the populace with theirs. In our political parties, compute the power of badges and emblems. See the great ball which they roll from Baltimore to Bunker hill![3] In the political processions, Lowell goes in a loom, and Lynn in a shoe, and Salem[4] in a ship. Witness the cider-barrel, the log-cabin, the hickory-stick, the palmetto, and all the cognizances[5] of party. See the power of national emblems. Some stars, lilies, leopards, a crescent, a lion, an eagle, or other figure, which came into credit God knows how, on an old rag of bunting, blowing in the wind, on a fort, at the ends of the earth, shall make the blood tingle under the rudest, or the most conventional exterior. The people fancy they hate poetry, and they are all poets and mystics!

… We are far from having exhausted the significance of the few symbols we use. We can come to use them yet with a terrible simplicity. It does not need that a poem should be long. Every word was once a poem. Every new relation is a new word. …

For, as it is dislocation and detachment from the life of God, that makes things ugly, the poet, who

---

1   *carpenter's … cord*   Cord that is stretched taut for use as a measuring tool.

2   *Jamblichus*   Iamblichus (c. 242–325) was a Syrian Neoplatonist philosopher.

3   *great ball … Bunker hill*   In the 1840 election, the Whigs, seeking to unseat President Martin Van Buren, used various songs, slogans, and campaign stunts, one of which was rolling balls made of twine and paper called "Harrison balls"—named after the Whig presidential candidate William Henry Harrison—down the streets of towns. This activity was inspired by campaign slogans such as "Keep the Ball Rolling." The balls were at times as big as twelve feet in diameter.

4   *Lowell … Salem*   Three cities in Massachusetts, each here accompanied by a symbol of their primary industry: textiles for Lowell; shoemaking for Lynn; and shipping for Salem.

5   *cider-barrel … log-cabin*   Symbols used by William Henry Harrison in his presidential campaign, as an effort to connect to the common people; *hickory-stick*   Symbol associated with President Andrew Jackson (1767–1845), also known as "Old Hickory," who defended himself against assassination in 1835 with a cane of hickory wood; *palmetto*   The palmetto tree is a symbol associated with the state of South Carolina; *cognizances*   Badges.

re-attaches things to nature and the Whole—re-attaching even artificial things, and violations of nature, to nature, by a deeper insight—disposes very easily of the most disagreeable facts. Readers of poetry see the factory-village, and the railway, and fancy that the poetry of the landscape is broken up by these, for these works of art are not yet consecrated in their reading; but the poet sees them fall within the great Order not less than the bee-hive, or the spider's geometrical web. Nature adopts them very fast into her vital circles, and the gliding train of cars she loves like her own. …

… We are symbols, and inhabit symbols; workmen, work, and tools, words and things, birth and death, all are emblems; but we sympathize with the symbols, and, being infatuated with the economical uses of things, we do not know that they are thoughts. The poet, by an ulterior intellectual perception, gives them power which makes their old use forgotten, and puts eyes, and a tongue, into every dumb[1] and inanimate object. … All the facts of the animal economy,[2] sex, nutriment, gestation, birth, growth, are symbols of the passage of the world into the soul of man, to suffer there a change, and reappear a new and higher fact. He uses forms according to the life, and not according to the form. This is true science. The poet alone knows astronomy, chemistry, vegetation, and animation,[3] for he does not stop at these facts, but employs them as signs. He knows why the plain, or meadow of space, was strown with these flowers we call suns, and moons, and stars; why the great deep is adorned with animals, with men, and gods; for, in every word he speaks he rides on them as the horses of thought.

By virtue of this science the poet is the Namer, or Language-maker, naming things sometimes after their appearance, sometimes after their essence, and giving to every one its own name and not another's, thereby rejoicing the intellect, which delights in detachment or boundary. The poets made all the words, and therefore language is the archives of history, and, if we must say it, a sort of tomb of the muses. For, though the origin of most of our words is forgotten, each word was at a stroke of genius, and obtained currency, because for the moment it symbolized the world to the first speaker

and to the hearer. The etymologist finds the deadest word to have been once a brilliant picture. Language is fossil poetry. As the limestone of the continent consists of infinite masses of the shells of animalcules,[4] so language is made up of images, or tropes, which now, in their secondary use, have long ceased to remind us of their poetic origin. But the poet names the thing because he sees it, or comes one step nearer to it than any other. This expression, or naming, is not art, but a second nature, grown out of the first, as a leaf out of a tree. What we call nature, is a certain self-regulated motion, or change; and nature does all things by her own hands, and does not leave another to baptise her, but baptises herself; and this through the metamorphosis again. …

… The poet knows that he speaks adequately, then, only when he speaks somewhat wildly, or, "with the flower of the mind"; not with the intellect, used as an organ, but with the intellect released from all service, and suffered to take its direction from its celestial life; or, as the ancients were wont to express themselves, not with intellect alone, but with the intellect inebriated by nectar. …

This is the reason why bards love wine, mead, narcotics, coffee, tea, opium, the fumes of sandalwood and tobacco, or whatever other species of animal exhilaration. All men avail themselves of such means as they can, to add this extraordinary power to their normal powers; and to this end they prize conversation, music, pictures, sculpture, dancing, theatres, travelling, war, mobs, fires, gaming, politics, or love, or science, or animal intoxication, which are several coarser or finer *quasi*-mechanical substitutes for the true nectar, which is the ravishment of the intellect by coming nearer to the fact. These are auxiliaries to the centrifugal tendency of a man, to his passage out into free space, and they help him to escape the custody of that body in which he is pent up, and of that jail-yard of individual relations in which he is enclosed. Hence a great number of such as were professionally expressors of Beauty, as painters, poets, musicians, and actors, have been more than others wont to lead a life of pleasure and indulgence; all but the few who received the true nectar; and, as it was a spurious mode of attaining freedom, as it was an emancipation not into the heavens,

---

[1] *dumb* Silent.

[2] *economy* In this context, the organization of the body.

[3] *animation* Art of bringing things to life.

[4] *animalcules* Small organisms.

but into the freedom of baser places, they were punished for that advantage they won, by a dissipation and deterioration. But never can any advantage be taken of nature by a trick. The spirit of the world, the great calm presence of the creator, comes not forth to the sorceries of opium or of wine. The sublime vision comes to the pure and simple soul in a clean and chaste body. ... It is with this as it is with toys. We fill the hands and nurseries of our children with all manner of dolls, drums, and horses, withdrawing their eyes from the plain face and sufficing objects of nature, the sun, and moon, the animals, the water, and stones, which should be their toys. So the poet's habit of living should be set on a key so low and plain, that the common influences should delight him. His cheerfulness should be the gift of the sunlight; the air should suffice for his inspiration, and he should be tipsy with water. ... If thou fill thy brain with Boston and New York, with fashion and covetousness, and wilt stimulate thy jaded senses with wine and French coffee, thou shalt find no radiance of wisdom in the lonely waste of the pinewoods.

If the imagination intoxicates the poet, it is not inactive in other men. The metamorphosis excites in the beholder an emotion of joy. The use of symbols has a certain power of emancipation and exhilaration for all men. We seem to be touched by a wand, which makes us dance and run about happily, like children. We are like persons who come out of a cave or cellar into the open air. This is the effect on us of tropes, fables, oracles, and all poetic forms. Poets are thus liberating gods. Men have really got a new sense, and found within their world, another world, or nest of worlds; for, the metamorphosis once seen, we divine that it does not stop. ...

The poets are thus liberating gods. The ancient British bards had for the title of their order, "Those who are free throughout the world." They are free, and they make free. An imaginative book renders us much more service at first, by stimulating us through its tropes, than afterward, when we arrive at the precise sense of the author. I think nothing is of any value in books, excepting the transcendental and extraordinary. ...

There is good reason why we should prize this liberation. The fate of the poor shepherd, who, blinded and lost in the snowstorm, perishes in a drift within a few feet of his cottage door, is an emblem of the state of man. On the brink of the waters of life and truth, we are miserably dying. The inaccessibleness of every thought but that we are in, is wonderful. What if you come near to it—you are as remote, when you are nearest, as when you are farthest. Every thought is also a prison; every heaven is also a prison. Therefore we love the poet, the inventor, who in any form, whether in an ode, or in an action, or in looks and behavior, has yielded us a new thought. He unlocks our chains, and admits us to a new scene.

This emancipation is dear to all men, and the power to impart it, as it must come from greater depth and scope of thought, is a measure of intellect. Therefore all books of the imagination endure, all which ascend to that truth, that the writer sees nature beneath him, and uses it as his exponent. Every verse or sentence, possessing this virtue, will take care of its own immortality. The religions of the world are the ejaculations[1] of a few imaginative men. ...

I look in vain for the poet whom I describe. We do not, with sufficient plainness, or sufficient profoundness, address ourselves to life, nor dare we chaunt our own times and social circumstance. If we filled the day with bravery, we should not shrink from celebrating it. Time and nature yield us many gifts, but not yet the timely man, the new religion, the reconciler, whom all things await. Dante's praise is, that he dared to write his autobiography in colossal cipher, or into universality. We have yet had no genius in America, with tyrannous eye, which knew the value of our incomparable materials, and saw, in the barbarism and materialism of the times, another carnival of the same gods whose picture he so much admires in Homer; then in the middle age; then in Calvinism.[2] Banks and tariffs, the newspaper and caucus, methodism and unitarianism,[3] are flat and dull to dull people, but rest on the same

---

[1] *ejaculations* Brief, often spontaneous prayers or expressions of emotion.

[2] *Calvinism* Branch of Protestant belief based on the teachings of French dissenter John Calvin (1509–64); many of the Puritans who settled in America followed Calvinistic doctrine.

[3] *methodism and unitarianism* Protestant denominations that began to take root in America in the latter half of the eighteenth century; both of these more liberal denominations rejected some of the harsher tenets of Calvinism, such as that of predestination (the idea that one is unalterably destined by God for heaven or hell).

foundations of wonder as the town of Troy, and the temple of Delphos,[1] and are as swiftly passing away. Our logrolling, our stumps[2] and their politics, our fisheries, our Negroes, and Indians, our boasts, and our repudiations, the wrath of rogues, and the pusillanimity of honest men, the northern trade, the southern planting, the western clearing, Oregon, and Texas, are yet unsung. Yet America is a poem in our eyes; its ample geography dazzles the imagination, and it will not wait long for metres.[3] If I have not found that excellent combination of gifts in my countrymen which I seek, neither could I aid myself to fix the idea of the poet by reading now and then in Chalmers's collection of five centuries of English poets.[4] These are wits, more than poets, though there have been poets among them. But when we adhere to the ideal of the poet, we have our difficulties even with Milton and Homer. Milton is too literary, and Homer too literal and historical.

But I am not wise enough for a national criticism, and must use the old largeness a little longer, to discharge my errand from the muse to the poet concerning his art.

Art is the path of the creator to his work. The paths, or methods, are ideal and eternal, though few men ever see them, not the artist himself for years, or for a lifetime, unless he come into the conditions. The painter, the sculptor, the composer, the epic rhapsodist, the orator, all partake one desire, namely, to express themselves symmetrically and abundantly, not dwarfishly and fragmentarily. They found or put themselves in certain conditions, as, the painter and sculptor before some impressive human figures; the orator, into the assembly of the people; and the others, in such scenes as each has found exciting to his intellect; and each presently feels the new desire. He hears a voice, he sees a beckoning. Then he is apprised, with wonder, what herds of daemons hem him in. He can no more rest; he says, with the old painter, "By God, it is in me, and must go forth of me." He pursues a beauty, half

seen, which flies before him. The poet pours out verses in every solitude. Most of the things he says are conventional, no doubt; but by and by he says something which is original and beautiful. That charms him. He would say nothing else but such things. In our way of talking, we say, "That is yours, this is mine"; but the poet knows well that it is not his; that it is as strange and beautiful to him as to you; he would fain hear the like eloquence at length. Once having tasted this immortal ichor,[5] he cannot have enough of it, and, as an admirable creative power exists in these intellections, it is of the last importance that these things get spoken. What a little of all we know is said! What drops of all the sea of our science are baled up! and by what accident it is that these are exposed, when so many secrets sleep in nature! Hence the necessity of speech and song; hence these throbs and heart-beatings in the orator, at the door of the assembly, to the end, namely, that thought may be ejaculated as Logos,[6] or Word.

Doubt not, O poet, but persist. Say, "It is in me, and shall out." Stand there, baulked and dumb, stuttering and stammering, hissed and hooted, stand and strive, until, at last, rage draw out of thee that dream-power which every night shows thee is thine own; a power transcending all limit and privacy, and by virtue of which a man is the conductor of the whole river of electricity. Nothing walks, or creeps, or grows, or exists, which must not in turn arise and walk before him as exponent of his meaning. Comes he to that power, his genius is no longer exhaustible. All the creatures, by pairs and by tribes, pour into his mind as into a Noah's ark, to come forth again to people a new world. This is like the stock of air for our respiration, or for the combustion of our fireplace, not a measure of gallons, but the entire atmosphere if wanted. And therefore the rich poets, as Homer, Chaucer, Shakespeare, and Raphael,[7] have obviously no limits to their works, except the limits of their lifetime, and resemble a mirror carried through the street, ready to render an image of every created thing.

---

[1]   *temple of Delphos*   The temple at Delphi was dedicated to Apollo, the Greek god of the sun, music, and poetry. It was also the location of the Pythia, a renowned oracle.

[2]   *stumps*   Stumps of big trees were used as platforms for oratory.

[3]   *metres*   I.e., lines of poetry.

[4]   *Chalmers's ... English poets*   Alexander Chalmers's collection *The Works of the English Poets, from Chaucer to Cowper* (1801).

[5]   *immortal ichor*   In Greek mythology, the fluid that runs through the veins of the gods.

[6]   *Logos*   Greek word meaning both "reason" and "word"; it also has specialized meanings in classical and Christian theology.

[7]   *Raphael*   Italian Renaissance painter (1483–1520).

O poet! a new nobility is conferred in groves and pastures, and not in castles, or by the sword-blade, any longer. The conditions are hard, but equal. Thou shalt leave the world, and know the muse only. Thou shalt not know any longer the times, customs, graces, politics, or opinions of men, but shalt take all from the muse. For the time of towns is tolled from the world by funereal chimes, but in nature the universal hours are counted by succeeding tribes of animals and plants, and by growth of joy on joy. God wills also that thou abdicate a manifold and duplex life, and that thou be content that others speak for thee. Others shall be thy gentlemen, and shall represent all courtesy and worldly life for thee; others shall do the great and resounding actions also. Thou shalt lie close hid with nature, and canst not be afforded to the Capitol or the Exchange. The world is full of renunciations and apprenticeships, and this is thine: thou must pass for a fool and a churl for a long season. This is the screen and sheath in which Pan[1] has protected his well-beloved flower, and thou shalt be known only to thine own, and they shall console thee with tenderest love. And thou shalt not be able to rehearse the names of thy friends in thy verse, for an old shame before the holy ideal. And this is the reward: that the ideal shall be real to thee, and the impressions of the actual world shall fall like summer rain, copious, but not troublesome, to thy invulnerable essence. Thou shalt have the whole land for thy park and manor, the sea for thy bath and navigation, without tax and without envy; the woods and the rivers thou shalt own; and thou shalt possess that wherein others are only tenants and boarders. Thou true landlord! sea-lord! air-lord! Wherever snow falls, or water flows, or birds fly, wherever day and night meet in twilight, wherever the blue heaven is hung by clouds, or sown with stars, wherever are forms with transparent boundaries, wherever are outlets into celestial space, wherever is danger, and awe, and love, there is Beauty, plenteous as rain, shed for thee, and though thou shouldest walk the world over, thou shalt not be able to find a condition inopportune or ignoble.
—1844

Brahma[2]

If the red slayer[3] think he slays,
Or if the slain think he is slain,
They know not well the subtle ways
I keep, and pass, and turn again.[4]

5 Far or forgot to me is near,
Shadow and sunlight are the same,
The vanished gods to me appear,
And one to me are shame and fame.

They reckon ill who leave me out;
10 When me they fly, I am the wings;
I am the doubter and the doubt,
And I the hymn the Brahmin[5] sings.

The strong gods[6] pine for my abode,
And pine in vain the sacred Seven;[7]
15 But thou, meek lover of the good!
Find me, and turn thy back on heaven.
—1857

---

1 *Pan* In Greek mythology, Pan was the god of the wilderness, often depicted with a pipe or flute. He was associated with the land and fertility.

---

2 *Brahma* Here Emerson may be conflating two concepts in Hinduism: Brahma, the Hindu creator god, and Brahman, the unifying principle that pervades all reality, simultaneously creative and unchanging. Emerson was familiar with discussions of Brahman in ancient Sanskrit texts such as the *Katha Upanishad* and the *Bhagavad Gita*.

3 *red slayer* Rudra, a terrifying god whose name may derive from the Sanskrit word for "red"; Rudra is sometimes identified with Shiva, a major deity associated with destruction.

4 *If the … turn again* See *Katha Upanishad* 1.2.19; the stanza bears a resemblance to lines from other Hindu texts as well.

5 *Brahmin* Member of the Brahmin caste, the highest caste in Hinduism, associated with priesthood.

6 *strong gods* Devas, divine beings in Hinduism.

7 *sacred Seven* Highly extolled sages or saints, sometimes known as the saptarishis, who appear in Hindu literature.

Mà-ka-tai-me-she-kià-kiàk / Black Hawk
1767? – 1838

The year 1833 saw the publication of a searing account of Native American removal: *Life of Ma-Ka-Tai-Me-She-Kia-Kiak or Black Hawk*, significantly subtitled "Dictated by Himself." The book told the story of Black Hawk, a Sauk leader who had recently come to celebrity—or, in the views of some, to notoriety—for his involvement in a movement of resistance to the enforced migration of his people. The narrative was indeed based upon a dictation by Black Hawk, who was, at the time of the dictation, nearing the end of his term of imprisonment for his role in what became known as the Black Hawk War; the recording of his story was a joint effort shared by Antoine LeClaire, a Pottawatomi and French-Canadian government interpreter, and John Barton Patterson, a Virginian newspaper editor. In the context of a literary scene gripped by "frontier" romances such as James Fenimore  Cooper's *The Last of the Mohicans* (1826)—which were narrated from the colonial point of view and tended to depict the suppression of Native American life and culture as tragic but inevitable—*Life of Black Hawk* stood out as monumental in its depiction of the active fight for the preservation of Sauk land, autonomy, and culture, and in the vital challenge Black Hawk presented to colonial assumptions regarding land rights, Native American culture, and the presumed national destiny.

Mà-ka-tai-me-she-kià-kiàk, whose name translates roughly to Black Sparrow Hawk or simply Black Hawk, was probably born around 1767, based on estimates of his age at the time he dictated his *Life*. His native village was Saukenuk, on Rock Island (now Arsenal Island), Illinois. The opening pages of Black Hawk's narrative recount the first stages of his people's relationship with white settlers as well as the ancestral origin of his own claim to Sauk Chiefdom. He says nothing of his childhood; his account of his own life begins around age fifteen, when he participated in his first battle against the Osages, a longstanding enemy of the Sauk. Though Black Hawk was neither a hereditary nor an elected civil chief, he was clearly a charismatic leader and a highly competent warrior, and is often referred to as a war chief in recognition of his leadership role. After siding with the British in the War of 1812—a war which was divisive among the Sauk—Black Hawk and his "British band" entered into a period of rising conflict with American settlers, which eventually led to the enforced migration of the Sauk out of their traditional territory, to which Black Hawk led a movement of resistance in the early 1830s.

The Black Hawk War (also known as the U.S.–Sauk War), may be understood in relation to President Andrew Jackson's genocidal "Indian removal" policies, which sought to banish numerous Native American tribes from their homelands to lands west of the Mississippi River. More narrowly, the origin of this particular 1832 conflict can be traced to the 1804 Treaty of St. Louis, which Black Hawk openly condemns in his *Life*. The treaty stipulated the ceding of millions of acres of Sauk land east of the Mississippi River to the United States, in exchange for a supply of provisions and a $1000 annuity. Black Hawk continually insisted on the invalidity of this treaty: deviating from the precedent afforded by earlier treaties, and from the consensus-based political practices of the Sauk, it had been signed by only four delegates from the Sauk nation and one member of the closely allied Meskwaki (referred to throughout the *Life* as the Fox), all of whom were reportedly intoxicated at the time of the signing and none of whom is believed to have understood the full extent and consequences of the treaty's claims. Though the tribe was for a time permitted to continue living and hunting upon the land, its members came into frequent conflict with white settlers and were eventually forced out when the land was officially sold to colonists. While many Sauk—including those following the leadership of Black Hawk's rival, Ke-o-kuck—complied with this demand, Black Hawk and his band continually resisted expulsion, making numerous attempts to return to their homeland. Black Hawk's band was finally defeated in August 1832 after a brutal struggle at Bad Axe, in which U.S. forces fired upon families who were trying to cross the Mississippi. Approximately 150 to 300 members of Black Hawk's band died in the massacre; the U.S. forces lost five men.

Three weeks after the events at Bad Axe, Black Hawk surrendered himself to U.S. forces. Along with several fellow leaders, he was held in captivity at the Jefferson Barracks in Missouri for eight months, a period he describes in his *Life* as tedious and degrading. Following this, Black Hawk's life took an extraordinary turn; though released from prison, he was compelled to go on a tour of the northeastern states under continued military custody. He was both shown to the American public and introduced to various political and military figures. The intention behind the enforced tour is unclear: it may have been a show of American military prowess and social superiority, and it may have been designed to further humiliate Black Hawk by publicly displaying him as a kind of trophy. To the inhabitants of New York, Philadelphia, Baltimore, and other northeastern cities, Black Hawk was evidently a spectacle to behold, and crowds gathered to meet and gawk at him. Nevertheless, it is evident from Black Hawk's own narrative that he enjoyed much of his time on tour, and that he used it as an opportunity to learn about U.S. culture and society. After several months—during which he crossed paths a number of times with President Jackson, and was once introduced to him—Black Hawk was finally released.

It is likely that some of the people Black Hawk met during this period encouraged him to have his story recorded. Though all documentation regarding the origins of his collaboration with LeClaire and Patterson has been lost, LeClaire claims in his introductory note to the *Life* that it was Black Hawk himself who first approached him with the intention of sharing his version of events. LeClaire was the official government interpreter for the Sauk and Meskwaki nations; Patterson was a Virginian newspaper editor, and was likely responsible for many editorial modifications, such as bracketed insertions, italicized words and phrases, and exclamation marks. Many reviewers at the time of *Life*'s publication thought the work had to be a hoax; many others, however, received it as the first published work to give expression to a truly "Indian" voice. (In so doing, they drew a contrast between the *Life* and earlier works written by literate Native Americans such as William Apess, whom such readers considered to be too fully assimilated to be capable of authentic cultural expression.)

Life of Black Hawk was an instant success, going through five editions in its first year. For the next few years of his life Black Hawk was something of a celebrity, and became a popular subject for portraits by artists such as George Catlin. The year 1838 saw the publication of another biography, *Life and Adventures of Black Hawk*, by Benjamin Drake, and he was the central figure of an 1839 long poem entitled *Ma-ka-tai-me-she-kia-kiak; or, Black Hawk, and Scenes in the West* by Elbert H. Smith. In 1882 J.B. Patterson, this time acting on his own rather than with LeClaire, released a new edition of the *Life* which further modified the text's language and introduced new narrative elements (now believed to be complete fabrications).

Another new edition appeared in 1916, with annotations and a new preface and introduction by historian Milo Milton Quaife. Quaife saw the story of Black Hawk as illuminating, "as with a flash of lightning, the viewpoint and state of mind of a typical representative of the vanquished race," but his appreciation of Black Hawk's autobiography was colored throughout by prejudice; he took it as a given that "the red man" was, "as measured by civilized standards ..., vastly the white man's inferior"; that whatever wisdom a Native American might possess was "the wisdom of the child of the forest"; and that the conquest of the American Indian was "an essential accompaniment to the progress of the human race." Similar views held sway among white historians and literary historians well into the second half of the twentieth century; as recently as 1995 the sixth edition of *The Oxford Companion to American Literature* continued to reprint James D. Hart's summation of Black Hawk's story from the 1943 first edition, portraying him as a leader who "refused to accept" the provisions of a legitimate treaty, and "instead, made war in frontier settlements." By then, however, a fuller and fairer interpretation of Black Hawk's life and writings had begun to emerge, most notably with the publication of Roger L. Nichols's *Black Hawk and the Warrior's Path* (1992, second edition 2017). New editions of the *Life* edited by Nichols (1999) and by J.

Gerald Kennedy (2008) have furthered our understanding of the degree to which Black Hawk's story, in Kennedy's words, "exposes the dark side of America's blind faith in its own sacred destiny."

Black Hawk died in 1838 while living in Iowa; his body was buried on a friend's farm. His remains were stolen the following year, and kept on display at the Burlington Geological and Historical Society in Iowa until 1855, when the building burned down. *Life* is a testament to Black Hawk's persistent defense of Sauk land and culture.

NOTE ON THE TEXT: The text presented below is based on that of the first edition of *Life of Ma-Ka-Tai-Me-She-Kia-Kiak or Black Hawk, Embracing the Tradition of His Nation* (1833). Bracketed words or phrases in this text represent editorial additions on the parts of Patterson and LeClaire. Spelling and punctuation have been modernized in accordance with the practices of this anthology. The full text of Black Hawk's *Life* is included in the website component of this anthology.

⌘ ⌘ ⌘

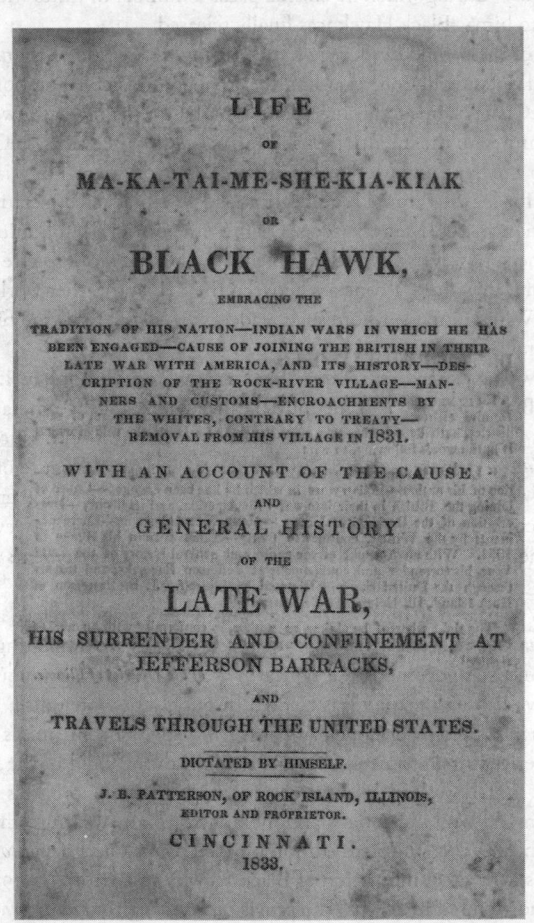

from *Life of Ma-Ka-Tai-Me-She-Kia-Kiak, or Black Hawk*

[By this point in Black Hawk's narrative, the War of 1812 has come to an end. The Sauk have been invited to Portage des Sioux to participate in the peace treaty signing, but their chief dies along the way, and his successor refuses to continue the journey, angering the U.S. leaders. The excerpt below picks up just after an interlude in which Black Hawk recounts a story shared to him by his Potawatomi friend Gomo, about a young Potawatomi man killed when his hunting party had been violently attacked by a group of white cattle herders.]

Here Gomo ended his story. I could relate many similar ones that have come within my own knowledge and observation; but I dislike to look back and bring on sorrow afresh. I will resume my narrative.

The great chief at St. Louis[1] having sent word for us to go down and confirm the treaty of peace, we did not hesitate, but started immediately, that we might smoke the *peace-pipe* with him. On our arrival, we met the great chiefs in council. They explained to us the words of our Great Father at Washington, accusing us of heinous crimes and diverse[2] misdemeanors, particularly in not coming down when first invited. We knew very well that *our Great Father had deceived us*, and thereby *forced* us to join the British, and could not believe that he had put this speech into the mouths of these chiefs to deliver to us. I was not a civil chief, and consequently made no reply: but our chiefs told the commissioners that "what they had said was a *lie*! That our Great Father had sent no such speech, he knowing the situation in which we had been placed had been *caused by him*!" The white chiefs appeared very angry at this reply, and said they "would break off the treaty with us, and *go to war*, as they would not be insulted."

Our chiefs had no intention of insulting them, and told them so—"that they merely wished to explain to them that *they had told a lie*, without making them angry; in the same manner that the whites do, when

they do not believe what is told them!" The council then proceeded, and the pipe of peace was smoked.

Here, for the first time, I touched the goose quill to the treaty—not knowing, however, that, by that act, I consented to give away my village. Had that been explained to me, I should have opposed it, and never would have signed their treaty, as my recent conduct will clearly prove.[3]

What do we know of the manner of the laws and customs of the white people? They might buy our bodies for dissection, and we would touch the goose quill to confirm it, without knowing what we are doing. This was the case with myself and people in touching the goose quill the first time.

We can only judge of what is proper and right by our standard of right and wrong, which differs widely from the whites, if I have been correctly informed. The whites *may do bad* all their lives, and then, if they are *sorry for it* when about to die, *all is well*! But with us it is different: we must continue throughout our lives to do what we conceive to be good. If we have corn and meat, and know of a family that have none, we divide with them. If we have more blankets than sufficient, and others have not enough, we must give to them that want. But I will presently explain our customs, and the manner we live.

We were friendly treated by the white chiefs, and started back to our village on Rock River. Here we found that troops had arrived to build a fort at Rock Island.[4] This, in our opinion, was a contradiction to what we had done—"to prepare for war in time of peace." We did not, however, object to their building their fort on the island, but were very sorry, as this was the best island on the Mississippi, and had long been the resort of our young people during the summer. It was our garden (like the white people have near to their big villages) which supplied us with strawberries, blackberries, gooseberries, plums, apples, and nuts of different kinds; and its waters supplied us with fine fish, being situated in the rapids of the river. In my early life, I spent many happy days on this island. A good spirit had care of it, who lived in a cave in the

---

1   *great chief at St. Louis* William Clark (1770–1838), Missouri governor who had famously explored western North America with Meriwether Lewis.

2   *diverse* Various.

3   *Here, for the … clearly prove* Unbeknownst to Black Hawk, this peace treaty also reaffirmed the terms of the 1804 treaty.

4   *build a fort at Rock Island* This was to become Fort Armstrong, construction of which began in 1816.

rocks immediately under the place where the fort now stands, and has often been seen by our people. He was white, with large wings like a *swan's*, but ten times larger. We were particular not to make much noise in that part of the island which he inhabited, for fear of disturbing him. But the noise of the fort has since driven him away, and no doubt a *bad spirit* has taken his place!

Our village was situate on the north side of Rock River, at the foot of its rapids, and on the point of land between Rock River and the Mississippi. In its front, a prairie extended to the bank of the Mississippi; and in our rear, a continued bluff, gently ascending from the prairie. On the side of this bluff we had our corn-fields, extending about two miles up, running parallel with the Mississippi; where we joined those of the Foxes, whose village was on the bank of the Mississippi, opposite the lower end of Rock Island, and three miles distant from ours. We had about eight hundred acres in cultivation, including what we had on the islands of Rock River. The land around our village, uncultivated, was covered with blue-grass, which made excellent pasture for our horses. Several fine springs broke out of the bluff, nearby, from which we were supplied with good water. The rapids of Rock River furnished us with an abundance of excellent fish, and the land, being good, never failed to produce good crops of corn, beans, pumpkins, and squashes. We always had plenty—our children never cried with hunger, nor our people were never in want. Here our village had stood for more than a hundred years, during all which time we were the undisputed possessors of the valley of the Mississippi, from the Ouisconsin to the Portage des Sioux, near the mouth of the Missouri, being about seven hundred miles in length.

At this time we had very little intercourse with the whites, except our traders. Our village was healthy, and there was no place in the country possessing such advantages, nor no hunting grounds better than those we had in possession. If another prophet had come to our village in those days, and told us what has since taken place, none of our people would have believed him. What! to be driven from our village and hunting grounds, and not even permitted to visit the graves of our forefathers, and relations, and friends!

This hardship is not known to the whites. With us it is a custom to visit the graves of our friends, and keep them in repair for many years. The mother will go alone to weep over the grave of her child! The brave, with pleasure, visits the grave of his father, after he has been successful in war, and repaints the post that shows where he lies! There is no place like that where the bones of our forefathers lie, to go to when in grief. Here the Great Spirit will take pity on us!

But, how different is our situation now, from what it was in those days! Then were we as happy as the buffalo on the plains—but now, we are as miserable as the hungry howling wolf in the prairie! But I am digressing from my story. Bitter reflection crowds upon my mind, and must find utterance.

When we returned to our village in the spring, from our wintering grounds, we would finish trading with our traders, who always followed us to our village. We purposely kept some of our fine furs for this trade; and, as there was great opposition among them, who should get these skins, we always got our goods cheap. After this trade was over, the traders would give us a few kegs of rum, which was generally promised in the fall, to encourage us to make a good hunt, and not go to war. They would then start with their furs and peltries for their homes. Our old men would take a frolic (at this time our young men never drank). When this was ended, the next thing to be done was to bury our dead (such as had died during the year). This is a great *medicine feast*. The relations of those who have died, give all the goods they have purchased, as presents to their friends—thereby reducing themselves to poverty, to show the Great Spirit that they are humble, so that he will take pity on them. We would next open the caches, and take out corn and other provisions, which had been put up in the fall—and then commence repairing our lodges. As soon as this is accomplished, we repair the fences around our fields, and clean them off, ready for planting corn. This work is done by our women. The men, during this time, are feasting on dried venison, bear's meat, wild fowl, and corn, prepared in different ways; and recounting to each other what took place during the winter.

Our women plant the corn, and as soon as they get done, we make a feast and dance the *crane* dance, in which they join us, dressed in their best, and decorated with feathers. At this feast our young braves select the young woman they wish to have for a wife. He then informs his mother, who calls on the mother of the girl, when the arrangement is made, and the time appointed for him to come. He goes to the lodge when all are asleep (or pretend to be), lights his matches, which have been provided for the purpose, and soon finds where his intended sleeps. He then awakens her, and holds the light to his face that she may know him—after which he places the light close to her. If she blows it out, the ceremony is ended, and he appears in the lodge the next morning, as one of the family. If she does not blow out the light, but leaves it to burn out, he retires from the lodge. The next day he places himself in full view of it, and plays his flute. The young women go out, one by one, to see who he is playing for. The tune changes, to let them know he is not playing for them. When his intended makes her appearance at the door, he continues his *courting* tune, until she returns to the lodge. He then gives over playing, and makes another trial at night, which generally turns out favorable. During the first year they ascertain whether they can agree with each other, and can be happy—if not, they part, and each looks out again. If we were to live together and disagree we should be as foolish as the whites. No indiscretion can banish a woman from her parental lodge—no difference how many children she may bring home, she is always welcome—the kettle is over the fire to feed them.

The crane dance often lasts two or three days. When this is over, we feast again, and have our *national dance*. The large square in the village is swept and prepared for the purpose. The chiefs and old warriors, take seats on mats which have been spread at the upper end of the square—the drummers and singers come next, and the braves and women form the sides, leaving a large space in the middle. The drums beat, and the singers commence. A warrior enters the square, keeping time with the music. He shows the manner he started on a war party—how he approached the enemy—he strikes, and describes the way he killed him. All join in applause. He then leaves the square, and another enters and takes his place. Such of our young men as have not been out in war parties, and killed an enemy, stand back ashamed—not being able to enter the square. I remember that I was ashamed to look where our young women stood, before I could take my stand in the square as a warrior.

What pleasure it is to an old warrior, to see his son come forward and relate his exploits—it makes him feel young, and induces him to enter the square, and "fight his battles o'er again."[1]

This national dance makes our warriors. When I was travelling last summer, on a steam boat, on a large river, going from New York to Albany, I was shown the place where the Americans dance their national dance [West Point[2]]; where the old warriors recount to their young men, what they have done, to stimulate them to go and do likewise. This surprised me, as I did not think the whites understood our way of making braves.

When our national dance is over—our corn-fields hoed, and every weed dug up, and our corn about knee-high, all our young men would start in a direction towards sundown, to hunt deer and buffalo—being prepared also to kill Sioux, if any are found on our hunting grounds—a part of our old men and women to the lead mines to make lead—and the remainder of our people start to fish, and get mat stuff.[3] Everyone leaves the village, and remains about forty days. They then return: the hunting party bringing in dried buffalo and deer meat, and sometimes *Sioux scalps*, when they are found trespassing on our hunting grounds. At other times they are met by a party of Sioux too strong for them, and are driven in. If the Sioux have killed the Sacs last, they expect to be retaliated upon, and will fly before them, and vice versa. Each party knows that the other has a right to retaliate, which induces those who have killed last, to give way before their enemy—as neither wish to strike, except to avenge the death of their relatives. All our wars are predicated by the relatives of those killed; or by aggressions upon our hunting grounds.

The party from the lead mines bring lead, and the others dried fish, and mats for our winter lodges. Presents are now made by each party; the first, giving to the others dried buffalo and deer, and they, in exchange, presenting them with lead, dried fish and

---

[1] *fight his battles o'er again* Loose quotation from John Dryden's *Alexander's Feast* (1697), evidently an insertion on the part of LeClaire or Patterson.

[2] *West Point* Large military academy in New York.

[3] *mat stuff* I.e., material for making mats for the lodges.

mats. This is a happy season of the year—having plenty of provisions, such as beans, squashes, and other produce, with our dried meat and fish, we continue to make feasts and visit each other, until our corn is ripe. Some lodge in the village makes a feast daily, to the Great Spirit. I cannot explain this so that the white people would comprehend me, as we have no regular standard among us. Everyone makes his feast as he thinks best, to please the Great Spirit, who has the care of all beings created. Others believe in two Spirits: one good and one bad, and make feasts for the Bad Spirit, *to keep him quiet*! If they can make peace with him, the Good Spirit will not hurt them! For my part, I am of opinion, that so far as we have *reason*, we have a right to use it, in determining what is right or wrong; and should pursue that path which we believe to be right— believing, that "whatever is, is right." If the Great and Good Spirit wished us to believe and do as the whites, he could easily change our opinions, so that we would see, and think, and act as they do. We are *nothing* compared to His power, and we feel and know it. We have men among us, like the whites, who pretend to know the right path, but will not consent to show it without *pay*! I have no faith in their paths—but believe that every man must make his own path!

When our corn is getting ripe, our young people watch with anxiety for the signal to pull roasting ears—as none dare touch them until the proper time. When the corn is fit to use, another great ceremony takes place, with feasting, and returning thanks to the Great Spirit for giving us corn.

I will here relate the manner in which corn first came. According to tradition, handed down to our people, a beautiful woman was seen to descend from the clouds, and alight upon the earth, by two of our ancestors, who had killed a deer, and were sitting by a fire, roasting a part of it to eat. They were astonished at seeing her, and concluded that she must be hungry, and had smelt the meat—and immediately went to her, taking with them a piece of the roasted venison. They presented it to her, and she eat—and told them to return to the spot where she was sitting, at the end of one year, and they would find a reward for their kindness and generosity. She then ascended to the clouds, and disappeared. The two men returned to their village, and explained to the nation what they had seen, done, and heard—but were laughed at by their people. When the period arrived, for them to visit this consecrated ground, where they were to find a reward for their attention to the beautiful woman of the clouds, they went with a large party, and found, where her right hand had rested on the ground, *corn* growing—and where the left hand had rested, *beans*, and immediately where she had been seated, *tobacco*.

The two first have, ever since, been cultivated by our people, as our principal provisions—and the last used for smoking. The white people have since found out the latter, and seem to relish it as much as we do—as they use it in different ways, viz. smoking, snuffing and eating![1]

We thank the Great Spirit for all the benefits he has conferred upon us. For myself, I never take a drink of water from a spring, without being mindful of his goodness.

We next have our great ball play—from three to five hundred on a side, play this game. We play for horses, guns, blankets, or any other kind of property we have. The successful party take the stakes, and all retire to our lodges in peace and friendship.

We next commence horse-racing, and continue our sport and feasting, until the corn is all secured. We then prepare to leave our village for our hunting grounds. The traders arrive, and give us credit for such articles as we want to clothe our families, and enable us to hunt. We first, however, hold a council with them, to ascertain the price they will give for our skins, and what they will charge us for goods. We inform them where we intend hunting—and tell them where to build their houses. At this place, we deposit part of our corn, and leave our old people. The traders have always been kind to them and relieved them when in want. They were always much respected by our people—and never since we have been a nation, has one of them been killed by any of our people.

We disperse, in small parties, to make our hunt, and as soon as it is over, we return to our traders establishment, with our skins, and remain feasting, playing cards, and other pastimes, until near the close of the winter. Our young men then start on the beaver hunt; others to hunt racoons and muskrats—and the remainder of our people go to the sugar camps to make

---

1   *eating* I.e., chewing.

sugar. All leave our encampment, and appoint a place to meet on the Mississippi, so that we may return to our village together, in the spring. We always spent our time pleasantly at the sugar camp. It being the season for wild fowl, we lived well, and always had plenty, when the hunters came in, that we might make a feast for them. After this is over, we return to our village, accompanied, sometimes, by our traders. In this way, the year rolled round happily. But these are times that were!

On returning in the spring, from our hunting ground, I had the pleasure of meeting our old friend, the trader of Peoria, at Rock Island. He came up in a boat from St. Louis, not as a trader, as in times past, but as our *agent*. We were all pleased to see him. He told us, that he narrowly escaped falling into the hands of Dixon. He remained with us a short time, gave us good advice, and then returned to St. Louis.

The Sioux having committed depredations on our people, we sent out war parties that summer who succeeded in killing *fourteen*. I paid several visits to Fort Armstrong during the summer, and was always well treated. We were not as happy then in our village as formerly. Our people got more liquor than customary. I used all my influence to prevent drunkenness, but without effect. As the settlements progressed towards us, we became worse off, and more unhappy. Many of our people, instead of going to their old hunting grounds, where game was plenty, would go near to the settlements to hunt—and, instead of saving their skins to pay the trader for goods furnished them in the fall, would sell them to the settlers for whisky! and return in the spring without the means of getting anything for them.

About this time my eldest son was taken sick and died. He had always been a dutiful child, and had just grown to manhood. Soon after, my youngest daughter, an interesting and affectionate child, died also. This was a hard stroke, because I loved my children. In my distress, I left the noise of the village, and built my lodge on a mound in my corn-field, and enclosed it with a fence, around which I planted corn and beans. Here I was with my family alone. I gave everything I had away, and reduced myself to poverty. The only covering I retained, was a piece of buffalo robe. I resolved on blacking my face and fasting, for two years, for the

loss of my two children—drinking only of water in the middle of the day, and eating sparingly of boiled corn at sunset. I fulfilled my promise, hoping that the Great Spirit would take pity on me.

My nation had now some difficulty with the Ioways, with whom we wished to be at peace. Our young men had repeatedly killed some of the Ioways; and these breaches had always been made up by giving presents to the relations of those killed. But the last council we had with them, we promised that, in case any more of their people were killed ours, instead of presents, we would give up the person, or persons, that had done the injury. We made this determination known to our people; but, notwithstanding, one of our young men killed an Ioway the following winter.

A party of our people were about starting for the Ioway village to give the young man up. I agreed to accompany them. When we were ready to start, I called at the lodge for the young man to go with us. He was sick, but willing to go. His brother, however, prevented him, and insisted on going to die in his place, as his brother was unable to travel. We started, and on the seventh day arrived in sight of the Ioway village, and when within a short distance of it, halted and dismounted. We all bid farewell to our young brave, who entered the village alone, singing his *death-song*, and sat down in the square in the middle of the village. One of the Ioway chiefs came out to us. We told him that we had fulfilled our promise—that we had brought the brother of the young man who had killed one of their people—that he had volunteered to come in his place, in consequence of his brother being unable to travel from sickness. We had no further conversation, but mounted our horses and rode off. As we started, I cast my eye towards the village, and observed the Ioways coming out of their lodges with spears and war clubs. We took our trail back, and travelled until dark—then encamped and made a fire. We had not been here long, before we heard the sound of horses coming towards us. We seized our arms; but instead of an enemy, it was our young brave with two horses. He told me that after we had left him, they menaced him with death for sometime—then gave him something to eat—smoked the pipe with him—and made him a present of the two horses and some goods, and started him after us. When we arrived at our village, our people were much pleased; and for the noble and generous conduct of the Ioways, on this occasion, not one of their people has been killed since by any of our nation.

That fall I visited Malden[1] with several of my band, and were well treated by our British father, who gave us a variety of presents. He also gave me a medal, and told me there never would be war between England and America again; but, for my fidelity to the British during the war that had terminated sometime before, requested me to come with my band every year and get presents, as Col. Dixon had promised me.

I returned, and hunted that winter on the Two Rivers. The whites were now settling the country fast. I was out one day hunting in a bottom,[2] and met three white men. They accused me of killing their hogs; I denied it; but they would not listen to me. One of them took my gun out of my hand and fired it off—then took out the flint, gave back my gun, and commenced beating me with sticks, and ordered me off. I was so much bruised that I could not sleep for several nights.

Some time after this occurrence, one of my camp cut a bee-tree,[3] and carried the honey to his lodge. A party of white men soon followed, and told him that the bee-tree was theirs, and that he had no right to cut it. He pointed to the honey, and told them to take it; they were not satisfied with this, but took all the packs of skins that he had collected during the winter, to pay his trader and clothe his family with in the spring, and carried them off!

How could we like such people, who treated us so unjustly? We determined to break up our camp, for fear that they would do worse—and when we joined our people in the spring, a great many of them complained of similar treatment.

This summer our agent[4] came to live at Rock Island. He treated us well, and gave us good advice. I visited him and the trader very often during the summer, and, for the first time, heard talk of our having to leave my village. The trader explained to me the terms of the treaty that had been made, and said we would be obliged to leave the Illinois side of the Mississippi, and advised us to select a good place for our village, and remove to it in the spring. He pointed out the difficulties we would have to encounter, if we remained at our village on Rock River. He had great influence with the principal Fox chief (his adopted brother), and persuaded him to leave his village, and go to the west side of the Mississippi River, and build another—which he did the spring following.

Nothing was now talked of but leaving our village. Ke-o-kuck had been persuaded to consent to go; and was using all his influence, backed by the war chief at fort Armstrong, and our agent and trader at Rock Island, to induce others to go with him. He sent the crier through the village to inform our people that it was the wish of our Great Father that we should remove to the west side of the Mississippi—and recommended the Ioway River[5] as a good place for the new village—and wished his party to make such arrangements, before they started on their winter's hunt, as to preclude the necessity of their returning to the village in the spring.

The party opposed to removing, called upon me for my opinion. I gave it freely—and after questioning Quàsh-quà-me about the sale of the lands, he assured me that he "never had consented to the sale of our village." I now promised this party to be their leader, and raised the standard of opposition to Ke-o-kuck, with a full determination not to leave my village. I had an interview with Ke-o-kuck, to see if this difficulty could not be settled with our Great Father—and told him to propose to give other land (any that our Great Father might choose, even our *lead mines*), to be peaceably permitted to keep the small point of land on which our village and fields were situate. I was of opinion that the white people had plenty of land, and would never take our village from us. Ke-o-kuck promised to make an exchange if possible; and applied to our agent, and the great chief at St. Louis (who has charge of all the agents), for permission to go to Washington to see our Great Father for that purpose. This satisfied us for some time. We started to our hunting grounds, in good hopes that something would be done for us. During the winter, I received information that three families of whites had arrived at our village, and destroyed some

---

[1] *Malden*   British-held fort located in present-day Ontario, visited annually by Black Hawk and his band.

[2] *bottom*   Valley or lowland.

[3] *bee-tree*   Tree in which honeybees have built their hive.

[4] *our agent*   This would have been English trader George Davenport (1783–1845), a close friend of Antoine LeClaire.

[5] *Ioway River*   I.e., the Iowa River.

of our lodges, and were making fences and dividing our corn-fields for their own use—*and were quarrelling among themselves about their lines, in the division!* I immediately started for Rock River, a distance of ten day's travel, and on my arrival, found the report to be true. I went to my lodge, and saw a family occupying it. I wished to talk with them, but they could not understand me. I then went to Rock Island, and (the agent being absent) told the interpreter what I wanted to say to those people, viz: "Not to settle on our lands—nor trouble our lodges or fences—that there was plenty of land in the country for them to settle upon—and they must leave our village, as we were coming back to it in the spring." The interpreter wrote me a paper, and I went back to the village, and showed it to the intruders, but could not understand their reply. I expected, however, that they would remove, as I requested them. I returned to Rock Island, passed the night there, and had a long conversation with the trader. He again advised me to give up, and make my village with Ke-o-kuck, on the Ioway River. I told him that I would not. The next morning I crossed the Mississippi, on very bad ice—but the Great Spirit made it strong, that I might pass over safe. I travelled three days farther to see the Winnebago sub-agent, and converse with him on the subject of our difficulties. He gave me no better news than the trader had done. I started then, by way of Rock River, to see the prophet,[1] believing that he was a man of great knowledge. When we met, I explained to him everything as it was. He at once agreed that I was right, and advised me never to give up our village, for the whites to plough up the bones of our people. He said, that if we remained at our village, the whites would not trouble us—and advised me to get Ke-o-kuck, and the party that had consented to go with him to the Ioway in the spring, to return, and remain at our village.

I returned to my hunting ground, after an absence of one moon, and related what I had done. In a short time we came up to our village, and found that the whites had not left it—but that others had come, and that the greater part of our corn-fields had been enclosed. When we landed, the whites appeared displeased because we had come back. We repaired the lodges that had been left standing, and built others. Ke-o-kuck came to the village; but his object was to persuade others to follow him to the Ioway. He had accomplished nothing towards making arrangements for us to remain, or to exchange other lands for our village. There was no more friendship existing between us. I looked upon him as a coward, and no brave, to abandon his village to be occupied by strangers. What *right* had these people to our village, and our fields which the Great Spirit had given us to live upon?

My reason teaches me that *land cannot be sold*. The Great Spirit gave it to his children to live upon, and cultivate, as far as is necessary for their subsistence; and so long as they occupy and cultivate it, they have the right to the soil—but if they voluntarily leave it, then any other people have a right to settle upon it. Nothing can be sold, but such things as can be carried away.

In consequence of the improvements of the intruders on our fields, we found considerable difficulty to get ground to plant a little corn. Some of the whites permitted us to plant small patches in the fields they had fenced, keeping all the best ground for themselves. Our women had great difficulty in climbing their fences (being unaccustomed to the kind), and were ill-treated if they left a rail down.

One of my old friends thought he was safe. His corn-field was on a small island of Rock River. He planted his corn; it came up well—but the white man saw it! He wanted the island, and took his team over, ploughed up the corn, and re-planted it for himself! The old man shed tears; not for himself, but the distress his family would be in if they raised no corn.

The white people brought whisky into our village, made our people drunk, and cheated them out of their homes, guns and traps! This fraudulent system was carried to such an extent that I apprehended serious difficulties might take place, unless a stop was put to it. Consequently, I visited all the whites and begged them not to sell whisky to my people. One of them continued the practice openly. I took a party of my young men, went to his house, and took out his barrel and broke in the head and turned out the whisky. I did this for fear some of the whites might be killed by my people when drunk.

---

[1]   *the prophet* This would have been the influential medicine man Wabokieshiek (c. 1794–c. 1841), also known as White Cloud and as the Winnebago Prophet.

Our people were treated badly by the whites on many occasions. At one time, a white man beat one of our women cruelly, for pulling a few suckers[1] of corn out of his field, to suck, when hungry! At another time, one of our young men was beat with clubs by two white men for opening a fence which crossed our road, to take his horse through. His shoulder blade was broken, and his body badly bruised, from which he soon after *died*!

Bad, and cruel, as our people were treated by the whites, not one of them was hurt or molested by any of my band. I hope this will prove that we are a peaceable people—having permitted ten men to take possession of our corn-fields; prevent us from planting corn; burn and destroy our lodges; ill-treat our women; and *beat to death* our men, without offering resistance to their barbarous cruelties. This is a lesson worthy for the white man to learn: to use forbearance when injured.

We acquainted our agent daily with our situation, and through him, the great chief at St. Louis—and hoped that something would be done for us. The whites were *complaining* at the same time that *we* were *intruding* upon *their rights*! They made themselves out the *injured* party, and *we* the *intruders*! and called loudly to the great war chief to protect *their* property!

How smooth must be the language of the whites, when they can make right look like wrong, and wrong like right.

During this summer, I happened at Rock Island, when a great chief arrived, whom I had known as the great chief of Illinois [governor Cole[2]], in company with another chief, who, I have been told, is a great writer [judge Jas. Hall[3]]. I called upon them, and begged to explain to them the grievances under which me and my people were laboring, hoping that they could do something for us. The great chief, however, did not seem disposed to council with me. He said he was no longer the chief of Illinois—that his children had selected another father in his stead, and that he now only ranked as they did. I was surprised at this talk, as

I had always heard that he was a good, brave, and great chief. But the white people never appear to be satisfied. When they get a good father, they hold councils (at the suggestion of some bad, ambitious man, who wants the place himself), and conclude, among themselves, that this man, or some other equally ambitious, would make a better father than they have, and nine times out of ten they don't get as good a one again.

I insisted on explaining to these two chiefs the true situation of my people. They gave their assent: I rose and made a speech, in which I explained to them the treaty made by Quàsh-quà-me, and three of our braves, according to the manner the trader and others had explained it to me. I then told them that Quàsh-quà-me and his party *denied*, positively, having ever sold my village; and that, as I had never known them to *lie*, I was determined to keep it in possession.

I told them that the white people had already entered our village, *burnt our lodges, destroyed our fences, ploughed up our corn, and beat our people*: that they had brought *whisky* into our country, *made our people drunk*, and taken from them their *horses, guns, and traps*; and that I had borne all this injury, without suffering any of my braves to raise a hand against the whites.

My object in holding this council was to get the opinion of these two chiefs, as to the best course for me to pursue. I had appealed in vain, time after time, to our agent, who regularly represented our situation to the great chief at St. Louis, whose duty it was to call upon our Great Father to have justice done to us; but instead of this, we are told *that the white people want our country, and we must leave it to them*!

I did not think it possible that our Great Father wished us to leave our village, where we had lived so long, and where the bones of so many of our people had been laid. The great chief said that, as he was no longer a chief, he could do nothing for us; and felt sorry that it was not in his power to aid us—nor did he know how to advise us. Neither of them could do anything for us; but both evidently appeared very sorry. It would give me great pleasure, at all times, to take these two chiefs by the hand.

That fall I paid a visit to the agent, before we started to our hunting grounds, to hear if he had any good news for me. He had news! He said that the land on

---

1   *suckers*   Young shoots growing from the base of the stalk.

2   *governor Cole*   Edward Coles (1786–1868), secretary to President James Madison and governor of Illinois from 1822 to 1826.

3   *judge Jas. Hall*   James Hall (1793–1868), who published a collection of biographical sketches of significant Native Americans between 1836 and 1844.

which our village stood was now ordered to be sold to individuals; and that, when sold, *our right* to remain, by treaty, would be at an end, and that if we returned next spring, we would be *forced* to remove!

We learned during the winter, that *part* of the lands where our village stood had been sold to individuals, and that the *trader* at Rock Island had bought the greater part that had been sold.[1] The reason was now plain to me, why *he* urged us to remove. His object, we thought, was to get our lands. We held several councils that winter to determine what we should do, and resolved, in one of them, to return to our village in the spring, as usual: and concluded, that if we were removed by force, that the *trader*, agent, and others, must be the cause; and that, if found guilty of having us driven from our village, they should be *killed!* The trader stood foremost on this list. He had purchased the land on which my lodge stood, and that of our *graveyard* also! Ne-a-pope proposed to kill him, and the agent, interpreter, the great chief at St. Louis, the war chief at fort Armstrong, Rock Island, and Ke-o-kuck—these being the principal persons to blame for endeavoring to remove us.

Our women received bad accounts from the women that had been raising corn at the new village—the difficulty of breaking the new prairie with hoes—and the small quantity of corn raised. We were nearly in the same situation in regard to the latter, It being the first time I ever knew our people to be in want of provision.

I prevailed upon some of Ke-o-kuck's band to return this spring to the Rock River village. Ke-o-kuck would not return with us. I hoped that we would get permission to go to Washington to settle our affairs with our Great Father. I visited the agent at Rock Island. He was displeased because we had returned to our village, and told me that we *must* remove to the west of the Mississippi. I told him plainly that we *would not!* I visited the interpreter at his house, who advised me to do as the agent had directed me. I then went to see the trader, and upbraided him for buying our lands. He said that if he had not purchased them, some person else would, and that if our Great Father would make an exchange with us, he would willingly give up the land he had purchased to the government. This I

thought was fair, and began to think that he had not acted as badly as I had suspected. We again repaired our lodges, and built others, as most of our village had been burnt and destroyed. Our women selected small patches to plant corn (where the whites had not taken them within their fences), and worked hard to raise something for our children to subsist upon.

I was told that, according to the treaty, we had no *right* to remain on the lands *sold*, and that the government would *force* us to leave them. There was but a small portion, however, that *had been sold*; the balance, remaining in the hands of the government, we claimed the right (if we had no other) to "live and hunt upon, as long as it remained the property of the government," by a stipulation in the same treaty that required us to evacuate it *after* it had been sold. This was the land that we wished to inhabit, and thought we had the best right to occupy.

I heard that there was a great chief on the Wabash, and sent a party to get his advice. They informed him that we had not sold our village. He assured them then, that if we had not sold the land on which our village stood, our Great Father would not take it from us.

I started early to Malden to see the chief of my British Father, and told him my story. He gave the same reply that the chief on the Wabash had given; and, in justice to him, I must say, that he never gave me any bad advice: but advised me to apply to our American Father, who, he said, would do us justice. I next called on the great chief at Detroit,[2] and made the same statement to him that I had to the chief of our British father. He gave me the same reply. He said, if we had not sold our lands, and would remain peaceably on them, that we would not be disturbed. This assured me that I was right, and determined me to hold out, as I had promised my people.

I returned from Malden late in the fall. My people were gone to their hunting ground, whither I followed. Here I learned that they had been badly treated all summer by the whites; and that a treaty had been held at Prairie du Chien. Ke-o-kuck and some of our people attended it, and found out that our Great Father had exchanged a small strip of the land that was ceded by Quàsh-quà-me and his party, with the Pottowatomies,

---

[1] *the trader ... been sold* Davenport purchased the land on Rock Island around 1829.

[2] *great chief at Detroit* Lewis Cass (1782–1866), territorial governor of Michigan.

for a portion of their land, near Chicago; and that the object of this treaty was to get it back again; and that the United States had agreed to give them *sixteen thousand dollars a year forever*, for this small strip of land— it being less than the twentieth part of that taken from our nation, for *one thousand dollars a year*! This bears evidence of something I cannot explain. This land, they say, belonged to the United States. What reason, then, could have induced them to exchange it with the Pottowatomies? If it was so valuable, why not keep it? Or, if they found that they had made a bad bargain with the Pottowatomies, why not take back their land at a fair proportion of what they gave our nation for it? If this small portion of the land that they took from us for *one thousand dollars* a year, be worth *sixteen thousand dollars a year forever*, to the Pottowatomies, then the whole tract of country taken from us ought to be worth, to our nation, *twenty times* as much as this small fraction.

Here I was again puzzled to find out how the white people reasoned; and began to doubt whether they had any standard of right and wrong!

—1833

Elias Boudinot / Gallegina
c. 1804 – 1839

Cherokee speaker, printer, and journalist Elias Boudinot was among the most influential Indigenous writers of his day. As editor of America's first Native American newspaper—and the first American paper to be published in an Indigenous language—Boudinot facilitated a lively written discourse on pertinent social issues within the Cherokee Nation, and contributed to a broader awareness of contemporary Cherokee society and its relationship to American settler culture.

Elias Boudinot was born Gallegina, or "Buck," Watie, in Oothcalga, Georgia in around 1804. His father Oo'Watie, or David Watie, had been among the founding figures of Oothcalga in the post-Revolutionary period, during which many Cherokee had begun to move away from their former village system onto small, independent homesteads. (The U.S. government enthusiastically supported such moves, seeing them as signs of the progressing "assimilation" of Indigenous peoples.) Gallegina was first educated in a Moravian missionary school, where Indigenous children were not only taught religious and academic subjects but were also encouraged to learn "civilized" arts such as farming, weaving, and sewing. Seen as a promising student, Gallegina was sent north in 1817 to continue his education at the American Board of Commissioners Foreign Mission School in Cornwall, Connecticut. It was on his way there that he met the respected lawyer and politician Elias Boudinot, whose name he adopted as a mark of respect.

The ABC Foreign Mission School aimed to educate and Christianize youth from foreign nations (including Hawaii and China), with the expectation that they would eventually return to their home communities and spread Christianity there themselves. As with the Moravian mission, the focus was at least as much on teaching students European-style agricultural practices as it was on academic learning. Boudinot excelled as a student, and was considered a strong candidate for entry into the Andover Theological Seminary in Massachusetts; in 1822, however, a severe illness caused him to return temporarily to his family home in Georgia.

While in Georgia, Boudinot kept up a written correspondence with Harriet Gold (whose family were involved in the running of the Foreign Mission School). The public announcement of their engagement in 1825 caused an uproar in Cornwall, where newspapers denounced the interracial relationship, and effigies of the couple were burned in the street. The Gold family at first refused to give their consent to the marriage, but when Harriet herself became severely ill they saw it as a sign from God and relented; Gold and Boudinot married in 1826. The Foreign Mission School never recovered from the scandal, with former white supporters now seeing the school as a breeding ground for interracial marriage. It closed permanently not long thereafter.

Now married, the Boudinots established a home in New Echota, Georgia, then the capital of the Cherokee Nation. Boudinot was subsequently appointed by the Cherokee Council to return to the northeast on a speaking tour to raise funds for a Cherokee national academy and printing press. Boudinot's lectures centered on subjects such as racial equality, and also emphasized the "progress" made in recent years by the Cherokee Nation in adopting many aspects of Euro-American political, agricultural, and social life. The lectures were heavily attended; he went on to publish a pamphlet, *An Address to the Whites* (1826)—based on a speech given in Philadelphia—with the aim of spreading awareness to an even wider audience.

The tour was a modest financial success; sufficient funds were raised for the Nation to launch a newspaper, the *Cherokee Phoenix*, in early 1828, with Boudinot as editor. The *Cherokee Phoenix* was remarkable for printing its content both in English and in Cherokee, using the recently invented Cherokee syllabary. The paper's subscription base came to include most households in the Cherokee Nation, as well as numerous non-Indigenous subscribers in America and Europe. Its content included poetry, religious writings, local reporting, and editorials written by Boudinot on subjects such as racism, Cherokee progress, and Indian removal.

For the first two years of his position as editor, Boudinot fervently opposed removal, describing Georgia's calls for Cherokee relocation as "tyrannical and unchristian," and writing that they threatened "to blast all [the Cherokee's] rising hopes and expectations." As Georgia's actions against the Cherokee Nation grew more aggressive, Boudinot gradually changed his position, seeing peaceful coexistence between the Cherokee and white settlers as impossible, and compliance with the state's demands, however unjust they might have been, as being in the Nation's best interests. By 1832, pressure from the anti-removal Cherokee Council led to Boudinot's resignation. Partly due to a sudden loss of federal government funding, the *Cherokee Phoenix* ceased publication indefinitely in 1834. (A version of the paper was revived as *The Cherokee Advocate* from 1844 to 1906, and it operates today under its original name.)

In December 1835, Boudinot held a conference in his home with U.S. treaty commissioners and a group of Cherokee known as the Treaty Party, which consisted of around two hundred members—less than two per cent of the Nation's population. The resultant Treaty of New Echota—which ceded all Cherokee land east of the Mississippi to Georgia—was protested by the Cherokee Council, who asserted that they represented the majority of the Cherokee population and petitioned the Supreme Court to declare the document invalid. Nevertheless, removal was enforced in 1838. Some four thousand Cherokee died either in internment camps or on the trail to Indian Territory, which would come to be known as the Trail of Tears. Boudinot would continue to defend his actions regarding removal for the rest of his life; in an 1837 letter he wrote, "I cannot hesitate. Whether it is right and justifiable on the part of the United States that the Cherokees should remove, is not now the question. That it is right for the Cherokees to save themselves from destruction, bears no question in my opinion."

Harriet Gold died of complications related to childbirth in 1836; Boudinot married a New England missionary, Delight Sargent, the following year, and moved with his family to Oklahoma before the U.S. enforcement of removal. He was attacked and killed in 1839 by a group of Cherokee men, in compliance with a Cherokee Nation law that punished with death anyone who sold Cherokee lands without the Council's approval. Boudinot's complex and changing positions on some of the most important social and political issues of his age have ensured that he remains a controversial but widely discussed writer to this day.

NOTE ON THE TEXT: The text of "To the Public" is based on that printed in the first issue of the *Cherokee Phoenix* on 21 February 1828. Spelling and punctuation have been modernized in accordance with the practices of this anthology; Boudinot's inconsistency in his use of American and British spellings, however, has been retained.

⌘ ⌘ ⌘

To the Public

New Echota
Thursday, February 21, 1828

We are happy in being able, at length, to issue the first number of our paper, although after a longer delay than we anticipated. This delay has been owing to unavoidable circumstances, which, we think, will be sufficient to acquit us, and though our readers and patrons may be wearied in the expectation of gratifying their eyes on this paper of no ordinary novelty, yet we hope their patience will not be so exhausted, but that they will give it a calm perusal, and pass upon it a candid[1] judgment. It is far from our expectation that it will meet with entire and universal approbation, particularly from those who consider learning and science necessary to the merits of newspapers. Such must not expect to be gratified here, for the merits (if merits they can be called) on which our paper is expected to exist, are not alike with those which keep alive the political and religious papers of the day. We lay no claim to extensive information; and we sincerely hope this public disclosure will save us from the severe criticisms to which our ignorance of many things will frequently expose us, in the future course of our editorial labors. Let the public but consider our motives, and the design[2] of this paper, which is, the benefit of the Cherokees, and we are sure, those who wish well to the Indian race, will keep out of view all the failings and deficiencies of the Editor, and give a prompt support to the first paper ever published in an Indian country, and under the direction of some of the remnants of those who by the most mysterious course of providence have dwindled into oblivion. To prevent us from the like destiny, is certainly a laudable undertaking, which the Christian, the Patriot, and the Philanthropist will not be ashamed to aid. Many are now engaged, by various means and with various success, in attempting to rescue, not only us, but all our kindred tribes, from the impending danger which has been so fatal to our forefathers; and we are happy to be in a situation to tender them our public acknowledgements for their unwearied efforts. Our present undertaking is intended to be nothing more than a feeble auxiliary to these efforts. Those, therefore, who are engaged for the good of the Indians of every tribe, and who pray that salvation, peace, and the comforts of civilized life may be extended to every Indian fireside on this continent, will consider us as co-workers together in their benevolent labors. To them we make our appeal for patronage, and pledge ourselves to encourage and assist them, in whatever appears to be for the benefit of the Aborigines.

In the commencement of our labours, it is due to our readers that we should acquaint them with the general principles which we have prescribed to ourselves as rules in conducting this paper. These principles we shall accordingly state briefly. It may, however, be proper to observe that the establishment which has been lately purchased, principally with the charities of our white brethren, is the property of the Nation,[3] and that the paper, which is now offered to the public, is patronized by, and under the direction of, the Cherokee Legislature, as will be seen in the Prospectus already before the public. As servants we are bound to that body, from which, however, we have not received any instructions, but are left at liberty to form such regulations for our conduct as will appear to us most conducive to the interests of the people, for whose benefit this paper has been established.

As the *Phoenix* is a national paper, we shall feel ourselves bound to devote it to national purposes. "The laws and public documents of the Nation," and matters relating to the welfare and condition of the Cherokees as a people, will be faithfully published in English and Cherokee.

As the liberty of the press is so essential to the improvement of the mind, we shall consider our paper a *free paper*, with, however, proper and usual restrictions. We shall reserve to ourselves the liberty of rejecting such communications as tend to evil, and such as are too intemperate and too personal. But the columns of this paper shall always be open to free and temperate discussions on matters of politics, religion, etc.

We shall avoid as much as possible controversy on disputed doctrinal points in religion. Though we have our particular belief on this important subject, and perhaps are as strenuous upon it, as some of our

---

1   *candid* Unbiased.

2   *design* Purpose.

3   *the Nation* I.e., the Cherokee Nation.

brethren of a different faith, yet we conscientiously think—and in this thought we are supported by men of judgment—that it would be injudicious, perhaps highly pernicious, to introduce to this people the various minor differences of Christians. Our object is not sectarian; and if we had a wish to support, in our paper, the denomination with which we have the honor and privilege of being connected, yet we know our incompetency for the task.

We will not unnecessarily intermeddle with the politics and affairs of our neighbors. As we have no particular interest in the concerns of the surrounding states, we shall only expose ourselves to contempt and ridicule by improper intrusion. And though at times we should do ourselves injustice to be silent on matters of great interest to the Cherokees, yet we will not return railing for railing, but consult mildness, for we have been taught to believe, that "A soft answer turneth away wrath; but grievous words stir up anger."[1] The unpleasant controversy existing with the state of Georgia,[2] of which many of our readers are aware, will frequently make our situation trying, by having hard sayings and threatenings thrown out against us, a specimen of which will be found in our next. We pray God that we may be delivered from such spirit.

In regard to the controversy with Georgia, and the present policy of the General Government, in removing and concentrating the Indians out of the limits of any state, which, by the way, appears to be gaining strength, we will invariably and faithfully state the feelings of the majority of our people. Our views, as a people, on this subject, have been most sadly misrepresented. These views we do not wish to conceal, but are willing that the public should know what we think of this policy, which, in our opinion, if carried into effect, will prove pernicious to us.

We have been asked which side of the Presidential question[3] we should take. Our answer is, we think best to take a neutral stand, and we know that such a course is most prudent, as we have no vote on the question,[4] and although we have our individual choice, yet it would be folly for us to spend words and time on a subject which has engrossed very much the attention of the public already.

In fine, we shall pay a sacred regard to truth, and avoid, as much as possible, that partiality to which we shall be exposed. In relating facts of a local nature, whether political, moral, or religious, we shall take care that exaggeration shall not be our crime. We shall also feel ourselves bound to correct all misstatements relating to the present condition of the Cherokees.

How far we shall be successful in advancing the improvement of our people is not now for us to decide. We hope, however, our efforts will not be altogether in vain. Now is the moment when mere speculation on the practicability of civilizing us is out of the question. Sufficient and repeated evidence has been given, that Indians can be reclaimed from a savage state, and that with proper advantages, they are as capable of improvement in mind as any other people; and let it be remembered, notwithstanding the assertions of those who talk to the contrary, that this improvement can be made, not only by the Cherokees, but by all the Indians, *in their present locations*. We are rendered bold in making this assertion, by considering the history of our people within the last fifteen years. There was a time within our remembrance, when darkness was sadly prevalent, and ignorance abounded amongst us—when strong and deep-rooted prejudices were directed against many things relating to civilized life and when it was thought a disgrace for a Cherokee to appear in the costume of a white man. We mention these things not by way of boasting, but to show to our readers that it is not a

---

[1]   *A soft ... anger*   See Proverbs 15.1.

[2]   *The unpleasant ... Georgia*   I.e., the efforts on the part of the state and federal governments to arrange for the removal of the Cherokee people from their land in Georgia to "Indian territory," to which the vast majority of Cherokee were opposed.

[3]   *the Presidential question*   The two main candidates of the 1828 presidential election were the incumbent President John Quincy Adams, leader of the National Republican Party, and Andrew Jackson, leader of the Democratic Party. Jackson, a staunch

proponent of Indian Removal, won the election in December 1828; he remained in office until 1837.

[4]   *we have ... the question*   The right to vote was withheld from the vast majority of Native Americans until the passage of the Indian Citizenship Act in 1924, which granted birthright citizenship to all Native Americans born after its passage. Prior to that time, citizenship could only be attained by Indigenous individuals if they were considered to be fully "assimilated" and to have abandoned any tribal affiliations. Even after 1924, voter suppression prevented many Native Americans from voting in state and federal elections; only with the passage of the Voting Rights Act in 1965 did Native Americans attain full voting rights.

visionary thing to attempt to civilize and Christianize all the Indians, but highly practicable.

It is necessary for our white patrons to know that this paper is not intended to be a source of profit, and that its continuance must depend, in a great measure, on the liberal support which they may be pleased to grant us. Though our object is not gain, yet we wish as much patronage, as will enable us to support the establishment without subjecting it to pecuniary difficulties. Those of our friends who have done so much already for us by instructing us in the arts of civilized life, and enabling us to enjoy the blessings of education, and the comforts of religion, and to whose exertions may be attributed the present means of improvement in this Nation, will not think it a hard matter that their aid should now be respectfully requested. In order that our paper may have an extensive circulation in this Nation and out of it, we have fixed upon the most liberal terms possible; such, in our opinion, as will render it as cheap as most of the Southern papers; and in order that our subscribers may be prompt in their remittances, we have made considerable difference between the first and the last payments. Those who have any experience in the management of periodicals will be sensible how important it is that the payments of subscribers should be prompt and regular, particularly where the existence of a paper depends upon its own income. We sincerely hope that we shall never have any occasion to complain of the delinquency of any of our patrons.

We would now commit our feeble efforts to the good will and indulgence of the public, praying that God will attend them with his blessings, and hoping for that happy period when all the Indian tribes of America shall arise, Phoenix-like, from their ashes, and when the terms, "Indian depredation," "war whoop," "scalping knife," and the like, shall become obsolete, and forever be "buried deep under ground."

—1828

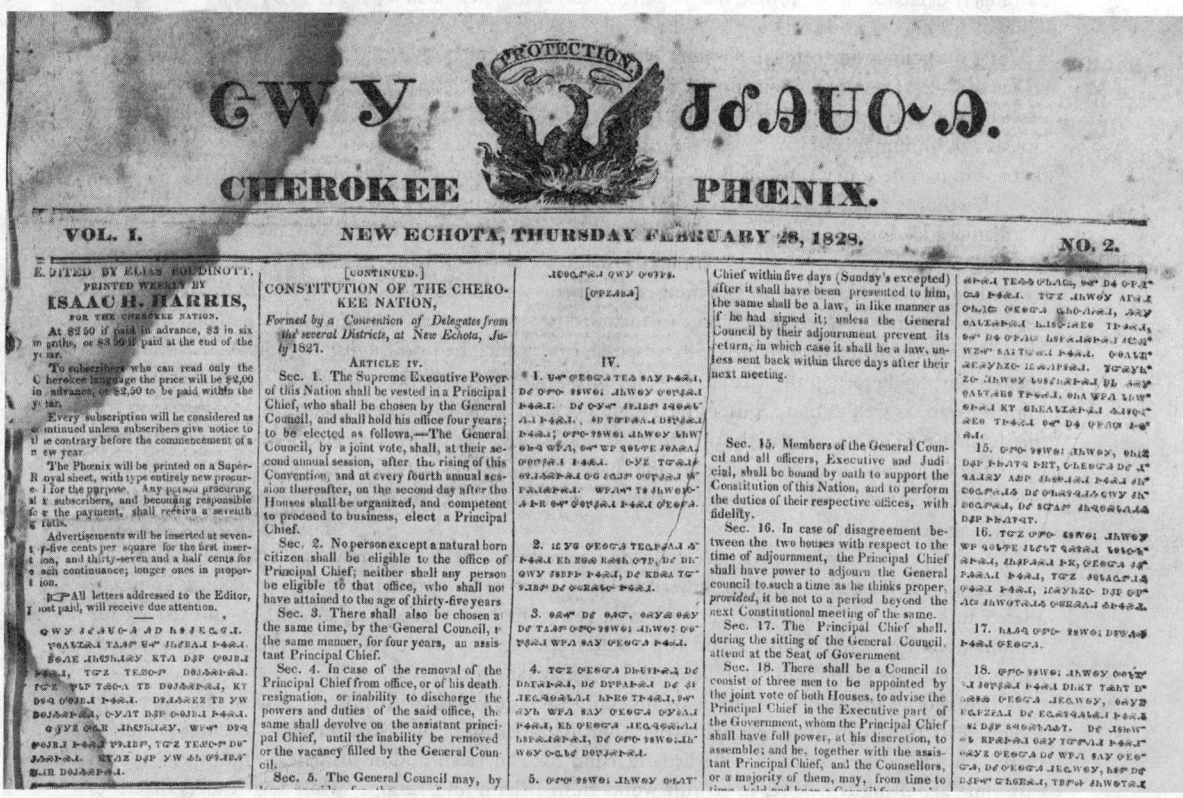

Front page of the second issue of the *Cherokee Phoenix*, with content in both English and Cherokee.

NATHANIEL HAWTHORNE
1804 – 1864

Descended from a long line of Massachusetts Puritan settlers, Nathaniel Hawthorne was born into a cultural and psychological inheritance that deeply affected a body of work that has long been accorded a central place in American literature. His fiction is renowned for its psychological depth, for its dark and richly symbolic character, and for its evocative historical portrayals. Novels such as *The Scarlet Letter* (1850) and *The House of the Seven Gables* (1851) and stories such as "Young Goodman Brown" (1835) and "My Kinsman, Major Molineux" (1832) depict imagined moments of the American past, interrogating and re-interpreting the American legacy of Puritan beliefs and values; our understanding of early colonial society continues to be substantially shaped by Hawthorne's depictions. So too does our sense of the human psyche, and what it is capable of; Hawthorne's work remains widely read not least of all for the deep understanding it offers to the human sense of sinfulness—and the human capacity for self-righteousness. But his fiction also continues to provoke debate, and to spin off questions in rich profusion. For all their historical and psychological depth, Hawthorne's writings embody a strangely detached stance toward the pressing ethical and societal concerns of his era; even on the topic of the Civil War, his work shows a strong disinclination to make themes clear or morals obvious. That

stance troubled some of his contemporaries—his enigmatic 1862 essay "Chiefly about War Matters" was described by one contemporary as "pure intellect, without emotion, without sympathy, without principles ... as unhuman and passionless as a disembodied intelligence." Yet in spite of such detachment—or perhaps in part because of it—readers continue to engage passionately with Hawthorne's work.

Hawthorne was born in July 1804 in Salem, Massachusetts; his ancestors included John Hathorne (Nathaniel added the "w" to his last name later in life), one of the fiercest and least repentant judges in the 1692 Salem witch trials. His sea-captain father died of yellow fever while in Suriname when Hawthorne was only four years old; Hawthorne's mother, Elizabeth, was forced to move with her three children into her parents' home—a large household that included her two unmarried sisters and her several brothers. Here Hawthorne had a large library at his disposal, from which he read English authors such as Edmund Spenser and Shakespeare, the satirists Joseph Addison and Richard Steele, and the Christian allegorist John Bunyan, as well as more contemporary authors such as the Scottish Romantic Sir Walter Scott. At the insistence of an uncle, Hawthorne attended Bowdoin College in Maine from 1821 to 1825; there he made the acquaintance of future literary luminary Henry Wadsworth Longfellow and future president Franklin Pierce (who became a lifelong friend). Hawthorne was an unexceptional student, however, graduating in the middle of his class.

By this point Hawthorne had determined to become a writer, and he returned to Salem after graduation to devote himself to his new ambition. He appears to have anticipated the struggle to come: in a letter to his mother he once wrote, "What do you think of my becoming an author, and relying for support upon my pen? ... How proud you would feel to see my works praised by the reviewers. ... But authors are always poor devils, and therefore Satan may take them."

Hawthorne lived comfortably with his mother's family, but with little income of his own. For several years he struggled agonizingly—once burning a manuscript in frustration—to enter a literary market in which there seemed to be little demand for American fiction. American publishers had an easy time acquiring the rights to reprint works from Britain and Europe, while few readers or critics took seriously the idea of American "literature" (popular New York writers Washington Irving and James

Fenimore Cooper were among the few recognized as having made distinctive contributions). In 1828 Hawthorne published—privately, anonymously, and at his own expense—the novel *Fanshawe*. Heavily autobiographical and influenced by eighteenth-century British Romanticism, Gothicism, and literary melodrama, the novel sold poorly and received very mixed reviews; Hawthorne destroyed all the copies he could get his hands on, and later refused to acknowledge his authorship.

Despite this evidently profound disappointment, Hawthorne did not abandon his literary pursuits. He had a minor triumph in 1830 with the publication of "The Hollow of the Three Hills" in a periodical, and continued throughout the decade to find outlets for his short works in newspapers, magazines, and gift books. He developed a talent for historical settings and symbolic imagery with stories such as "My Kinsman, Major Molineux" and "Young Goodman Brown." Such stories provided a notable contrast to the often sentimental and light-hearted contents of gift books such as *The Token*. Hawthorne seems to have endured some anxiety over his association with this "feminine" literature, which may help explain why he published anonymously throughout this period.

Recognizing that Hawthorne's fiction deserved another chance at stand-alone publication, in 1837 a Bowdoin friend, Horatio Bridge, secretly gave a publisher $250 to finance the publication of the first volume of Hawthorne's collection *Twice-Told Tales* (a second volume appeared in 1842). *Twice-Told Tales* was his first real critical success; those praising the book included Edgar Allan Poe.

In 1838 Hawthorne worked briefly as a "weigher and gauger" at the Boston Custom House; despite the humble job description the position was something of a political sinecure, with a substantial salary of $1,200 a year. In the same year he became engaged to Sophia Peabody, an accomplished artist whose better-known sister Elizabeth was a prominent Transcendentalist (and would become a leading progressive educator).

Hawthorne resigned from his Custom House position in 1841 to spend a period of several months working at Brook Farm, a utopian Transcendentalist community and joint-stock company that he had invested in. In July 1842 he and Sophia were finally married; they rented the Old Manse in Concord, Massachusetts, and moved in immediately. In Concord, they befriended leading Transcendentalists such as Ralph Waldo Emerson, Henry David Thoreau, and Margaret Fuller, though Hawthorne never became fully integrated into this group or its ideals—and at times expressed distaste for Fuller's feminism.

By 1844 the family had begun to grow (Una, the first of their three children, was born that year), but their financial resources had shrunk, and they were forced to give up the large house in Concord and return to Salem. Hawthorne's third collection, *Mosses from an Old Manse* (1846), did little to alleviate the growing family's financial burden. Through his connection with Pierce and other Democrats he obtained another Custom House appointment, this time in Salem to the more senior position of surveyor. The work was remunerative, but Hawthorne found it unfulfilling.

The year 1849 marked a low point for him. The 1848 electoral defeat of the Democrats led to the dismissal of many political appointees in 1849; Hawthorne received word on June 8 that he had lost his job. He protested vigorously but unsuccessfully (arguing that he had in fact acted above party politics while in the position), and the unauthorized publication of one of his letters led to a substantial controversy over the matter. Hawthorne felt he had been dragged down among "the common political brawlers" (as he termed them in a letter to Longfellow), and he became alienated from many of his old acquaintances in Salem. The controversy had not yet died down when, in late July, his mother died; Hawthorne described it as "the darkest hour I ever lived."

In the ensuing grief and financial distress, Hawthorne began work on his first full-length novel, *The Scarlet Letter: A Romance*. Published the following year, the "romance" was prefaced by "The Custom-House: Introductory to *The Scarlet Letter*," a satirical sketch based on his own experiences in Salem and bearing little connection (at least on the surface) to the body of the work. (Then, as now, critics have disagreed as to the degree to which strong connections between the two do in fact exist.) A historical novel, *The Scarlet Letter* was a full-length treatment of themes such as sinfulness, guilt, and Puritan social hypocrisy that had sounded throughout Hawthorne's shorter work. The story of Hester Prynne—a young woman accused of (and punished for) adultery—was likely inspired by stories of other Puritan women persecuted for their sexual relationships; laws punishing adultery with the enforced wearing of a letter

"A" had existed in Plymouth, for instance. The novel's "revolting subject," as it was deemed by a writer for the *North American Review*, was controversial, even though the narrative never explicitly condemned the social code under which Hester was punished; indeed, one reviewer commended the novel for the "great moral lesson" it provided against the sin of adultery. Nevertheless, the novel was a popular success, and most critics admired its power. The London magazine *The Athenaeum* declared Hawthorne "among the most original and peculiar writers of American fiction," and the *Boston Transcript* speculated that not only was he among the best American writers of the "last half century," but that he had "not been eclipsed by the higher class of European minds which have led the way in that department to which his genius belongs."

Having at last established a reputation, over the following decade Hawthorne continued to focus on longer works. *The Scarlet Letter* was followed by two more works of fiction that have come to be regarded as classics: *The House of the Seven Gables* (1851), a historical novel in the Gothic mode; and *The Blithedale Romance* (1852), a novel touching on a wide range of the most controversial issues of the day, among them the fight for prison reform and the nascent struggle for women's rights. *The Blithedale Romance* had clearly been partially inspired by his time living communally at Brook Farm, but Hawthorne intended it (as he wrote in a preface) to be read as "a little removed" from "the actual events of real lives" and to imply no conclusion, "favorable or otherwise, in respect to Socialism."

Also in 1852, Hawthorne published *The Life of Franklin Pierce*, a campaign biography of the presidential candidate and Hawthorne's great friend from Bowdoin College. Pierce ran as a Democrat (which in those days meant support for American expansionism—as a military commander Pierce had played a significant role in the Mexican–American War—and opposition to any measures that might threaten the institution of slavery). In supporting Pierce, Hawthorne was very clear in his opposition to the abolitionists, suggesting that it might be wise to regard slavery

> as one of those evils which divine Providence does not leave to be remedied by human contrivances, but which, in its own good time, by some means impossible to be anticipated, but of the simplest and easiest operation, when all its uses shall have been fulfilled, it causes to vanish like a dream.

Pierce won the election, taking office in 1853; later that year Hawthorne was appointed American Consul at Liverpool, England, the center of the cotton trade. It was a sinecure, but Hawthorne took his duties seriously. Once again, politics led to the loss of his position; Hawthorne resigned in 1857 after Pierce had been defeated in his bid for re-nomination as presidential candidate of the Democratic Party.

Hawthorne and his family spent a good deal of 1858 and 1859 in Europe, with extended stays in Rome and Florence; his next novel, *The Marble Faun* (1860), was set in a romanticized Italy and inspired by their travels.

As the Civil War took hold in America, Hawthorne became even more distanced from the political stance taken by many of his fellow New Englanders. Unlike friends such as Emerson—who had been openly wary of causes and movements earlier in his career but was eventually persuaded by the injustice of slavery to join the abolitionist cause—Hawthorne stayed clear of the fray. In 1862 he wrote his only piece on the Civil War, "Chiefly about War Matters," in which he dismissed Lincoln, criticized the war, and appeared completely uninterested in the conflict's causes. Scholars continue to wrestle with the meanings of this layered and iconoclastic piece.

The last work published during Hawthorne's lifetime was *Our Old Home* (1863), a series of English travel sketches dedicated—controversially—to Pierce. Toward the following year Hawthorne's health started to decline; he died in the spring of 1864, aged fifty-nine, during a trip with Pierce to the White Mountains of New Hampshire.

In 1847, Edgar Allan Poe had remarked that Hawthorne was "*the* example ... in this country, of the privately-admired and publicly-underappreciated man of genius." But by the time he died his reputation had grown considerably. An appreciative piece published in *The Atlantic Monthly* in 1870 gave expression to what had become the prevailing view of Hawthorne's unique talent:

[H]is genius, as all the world knows, was of masculine force and sweep. But, on the other hand, no man had more of the feminine element than he. He was feminine in his quick perceptions, his fine insight, his sensibility to beauty, his delicate reserve, his purity of feeling. No man comprehended woman more perfectly; none has painted woman with a more exquisite and ethereal pencil. ... *The Scarlet Letter, The Blithedale Romance, The House of the Seven Gables, The Marble Faun*, and many of his smaller stories, have one marked characteristic in common, which maybe defined a taste for studying and delineating the night-side of human nature. He had a passion for exploring the crypts and caverns of the soul. ... *The Scarlet Letter* is the highest expression of his genius in this respect—a work of prodigious power, but so painful in the impression that it leaves that many can never read it a second time.

By the end of the century, though, many saw the dark symbolism of Hawthorne's "romances" as out of step with the trend toward realism in fiction; Henry James, for one, faulted *The Scarlet Letter* for what seemed to him a lack "of reality" and for "superficial symbolism." It was not until the mid-twentieth century that Hawthorne's reputation was fully restored. The critic F.O. Matthiessen, in setting out an array of enormously influential historical/aesthetic concepts, devoted almost 200 of the 650 pages of his *American Renaissance* (1941) to Hawthorne— to the importance of allegory and symbolism in his works, and to the importance of Hawthorne himself in American literature.

In the late twentieth and early twenty-first centuries feminist, deconstructionist, and new histori-cist critics have opened many other windows onto Hawthorne and his work in the context of his era. Particularly notable has been the work of Nina Baym, whose arguments for reading "Hawthorne as a feminist writer" have sparked lively discussion among literary scholars (many of whom have perceived ambivalence rather than feminism in his presentation of female characters). There continues to be lively discussion as well over Hawthorne's treatment of slavery and other ethical/political issues—a discussion given new life in the late twentieth century by Eric Cheyfitz's suggestion that Hawthorne scholars have too often felt the need to "explain, that is, complicate" what to Cheyfitz was a plain fact—"Hawthorne's simply reprehensible stand on the slavery issue." Few in the twenty-first century have defended that stand—but many have continued to draw nuanced distinctions between the author and the aesthetic and affective aspects of his work.

NOTE ON THE TEXTS: Unless otherwise noted, the texts of the works presented here are based on their first published appearances. Spelling and punctuation have been modernized in accordance with the practices of this anthology.

⌘ ⌘ ⌘

Young Goodman Brown

Young Goodman[1] Brown came forth, at sunset, into the street of Salem village, but put his head back, after crossing the threshold, to exchange a parting kiss with his young wife. And Faith, as the wife was aptly named, thrust her own pretty head into the street, letting the wind play with the pink ribbons of her cap, while she called to Goodman Brown.

"Dearest heart," whispered she, softly and rather sadly, when her lips were close to his ear, "pr'y thee, put off your journey until sunrise, and sleep in your own bed tonight. A lone woman is troubled with such dreams and such thoughts, that she's afeard of herself, sometimes. Pray, tarry with me this night, dear husband, of all nights in the year!"

"My love and my Faith," replied young Goodman Brown, "of all nights in the year, this one night must I tarry away from thee. My journey, as thou callest it, forth and back again, must needs be done 'twixt now and sunrise. What, my sweet, pretty wife, dost thou doubt me already, and we but three months married?"

"Then God bless you!" said Faith, with the pink ribbons, "and may you find all well, when you come back."

"Amen!" cried Goodman Brown. "Say thy prayers, dear Faith, and go to bed at dusk, and no harm will come to thee."

So they parted; and the young man pursued his way, until, being about to turn the corner by the meeting-house, he looked back, and saw the head of Faith still peeping after him, with a melancholy air, in spite of her pink ribbons.

"Poor little Faith!" thought he, for his heart smote him. "What a wretch am I, to leave her on such an errand! She talks of dreams, too. Methought, as she spoke, there was trouble in her face, as if a dream had warned her what work is to be done tonight. But, no, no! 't would kill her to think it. Well, she's a blessed angel on earth; and after this one night, I'll cling to her skirts and follow her to Heaven."

With this excellent resolve for the future, Goodman Brown felt himself justified in making more haste on his present evil purpose. He had taken a dreary road, darkened by all the gloomiest trees of the forest, which barely stood aside to let the narrow path creep through, and closed immediately behind. It was all as lonely as could be; and there is this peculiarity in such a solitude, that the traveler knows not who may be concealed by the innumerable trunks and the thick boughs overhead; so that, with lonely footsteps, he may yet be passing through an unseen multitude.

"There may be a devilish Indian behind every tree," said Goodman Brown, to himself; and he glanced fearfully behind him, as he added, "What if the devil himself should be at my very elbow!"

His head being turned back, he passed a crook of the road, and looking forward again, beheld the figure of a man, in grave and decent attire, seated at the foot of an old tree. He arose, at Goodman Brown's approach, and walked onward, side by side with him.

"You are late, Goodman Brown," said he. "The clock of the Old South was striking as I came through Boston; and that is full fifteen minutes agone."[2]

"Faith kept me back a while," replied the young man, with a tremor in his voice caused by the sudden appearance of his companion, though not wholly unexpected.

It was now deep dusk in the forest, and deepest in that part of it where these two were journeying. As nearly as could be discerned, the second traveler was about fifty years old, apparently in the same rank of life as Goodman Brown, and bearing a considerable resemblance to him, though perhaps more in expression than features. Still, they might have been taken for father and son. And yet, though the elder person was as simply clad as the younger, and as simple in manner too, he had an indescribable air of one who knew the world, and would not have felt abashed at the governor's dinner-table, or in King William's[3] court, were it possible that his affairs should call him thither. But the only thing about him that could be fixed upon as remarkable was his staff, which bore the likeness of a great black snake, so curiously wrought, that it might almost be seen to twist and wriggle itself, like a living

---

[1]   *Goodman*   Respectful title for the male head of a household.

[2]   *The clock … minutes agone*   Reference to the Old South Church in Boston; to have walked the sixteen miles from Boston to Salem in fifteen minutes suggests unnatural power;   *agone*   Ago.

[3]   *King William*   William III (r. 1689–1702), monarch of England along with his wife, Mary II (r. 1689–94).

serpent. This, of course, must have been an ocular deception, assisted by the uncertain light.

"Come, Goodman Brown!" cried his fellow traveler, "this is a dull pace for the beginning of a journey. Take my staff, if you are so soon weary."

"Friend," said the other, exchanging his slow pace for a full stop, "having kept covenant by meeting thee here, it is my purpose now to return whence I came. I have scruples, touching the matter thou wot'st[1] of."

"Sayest thou so?" replied he of the serpent, smiling apart. "Let us walk on, nevertheless, reasoning as we go; and if I convince thee not, thou shalt turn back. We are but a little way in the forest, yet."

"Too far, too far!" exclaimed the Goodman, unconsciously resuming his walk. "My father never went into the woods on such an errand, nor his father before him. We have been a race of honest men and good Christians, since the days of the martyrs.[2] And shall I be the first of the name of Brown, that ever took this path, and kept—"

"Such company, thou wouldst say," observed the elder person, interpreting his pause. "Good, Goodman Brown! I have been as well acquainted with your family as with ever a one among the Puritans; and that's no trifle to say. I helped your grandfather, the constable, when he lashed the Quaker woman so smartly through the streets of Salem.[3] And it was I that brought your father a pitch-pine knot, kindled at my own hearth, to set fire to an Indian village, in King Philip's War.[4] They were my good friends, both; and many a pleasant walk have we had along this path, and returned merrily after midnight. I would fain be friends with you, for their sake."

"If it be as thou sayest," replied Goodman Brown, "I marvel they never spoke of these matters. Or, verily,

I marvel not, seeing that the least rumor of the sort would have driven them from New England. We are a people of prayer, and good works to boot, and abide[5] no such wickedness."

"Wickedness or not," said the traveler with the twisted staff, "I have a very general acquaintance here in New England. The deacons of many a church have drunk the communion wine with me; the selectmen of diverse[6] towns make me their chairman; and a majority of the Great and General Court[7] are firm supporters of my interest. The governor and I, too—but these are state secrets."

"Can this be so!" cried Goodman Brown, with a stare of amazement at his undisturbed companion. "Howbeit, I have nothing to do with the governor and council; they have their own ways, and are no rule for a simple husbandman,[8] like me. But, were I to go on with thee, how should I meet the eye of that good old man, our minister, at Salem village? Oh, his voice would make me tremble, both Sabbath day and lecture day!"[9]

Thus far, the elder traveler had listened with due gravity, but now burst into a fit of irrepressible mirth, shaking himself so violently, that his snake-like staff actually seemed to wriggle in sympathy.

"Ha! ha! ha!" shouted he, again and again; then composing himself, "Well, go on, Goodman Brown, go on; but, pr'y thee, don't kill me with laughing!"

"Well, then, to end the matter at once," said Goodman Brown, considerably nettled, "there is my wife, Faith. It would break her dear little heart; and I'd rather break my own!"

"Nay, if that be the case," answered the other, "e'en go thy ways, Goodman Brown. I would not, for twenty old women like the one hobbling before us, that Faith should come to any harm."

As he spoke, he pointed his staff at a female figure on the path, in whom Goodman Brown recognized a very pious and exemplary dame who had taught him

---

[1] *wot'st* Wotest; knows.

[2] *days of the martyrs* I.e., the period during which Protestants were persecuted in Europe, especially, in England, during the reign (1553–58) of the Catholic Mary I.

[3] *your grandfather ... of Salem* Hawthorne's ancestor William Hathorne was an oppressive Puritan leader in 1600s Salem, and was also known to have had a Quaker woman publicly lashed.

[4] *pitch-pine* Type of coniferous tree which produces pitch or turpentine; *King Philip's War* Conflict between English settlers and the Wanpanoag and other Native American tribes of the region; the Wanpanoag leader Metacom (1638–76) was called "King Philip" by some of the English.

[5] *to boot, and abide* As well, and tolerate.

[6] *diverse* Various.

[7] *Great and General Court* Legislative bodies.

[8] *husbandman* Holder of a small farm or simply a man of common status.

[9] *lecture day* Sermon day held during the week, rather than on a Sunday.

his catechism[1] in youth, and was still his moral and spiritual adviser, jointly with the minister and deacon Gookin.[2]

"A marvel, truly, that Goody Cloyse[3] should be so far in the wilderness, at nightfall!" said he. "But, with your leave, friend, I shall take a cut through the woods, until we have left this Christian woman behind. Being a stranger to you, she might ask whom I was consorting with, and whither I was going."

"Be it so," said his fellow traveler. "Betake you to the woods, and let me keep the path."

Accordingly, the young man turned aside, but took care to watch his companion, who advanced softly along the road, until he had come within a staff's length of the old dame. She, meanwhile, was making the best of her way, with singular speed for so aged a woman, and mumbling some indistinct words, a prayer, doubtless, as she went. The traveler put forth his staff, and touched her withered neck with what seemed the serpent's tail.

"The devil!" screamed the pious old lady.

"Then Goody Cloyse knows her old friend?" observed the traveler, confronting her, and leaning on his writhing stick.

"Ah, forsooth, and is it your worship, indeed?" cried the good dame. "Yea, truly is it, and in the very image of my old gossip, Goodman Brown, the grandfather of the silly fellow that now is. But, would your worship believe it? my broomstick hath strangely disappeared, stolen, as I suspect, by that unhanged witch, Goody Cory,[4] and that, too, when I was all anointed with the juice of smallage and cinque-foil and wolf's bane[5]—"

"Mingled with fine wheat and the fat of a new-born babe," said the shape of old Goodman Brown.

"Ah, your worship knows the receipt,"[6] cried the old lady, cackling aloud. "So, as I was saying, being all ready for the meeting, and no horse to ride on, I made up my mind to foot it; for they tell me, there is a nice young man to be taken into communion[7] tonight. But now your good worship will lend me your arm, and we shall be there in a twinkling."

"That can hardly be," answered her friend. "I may not spare you my arm, Goody Cloyse, but here is my staff, if you will."

So saying, he threw it down at her feet, where, perhaps, it assumed life, being one of the rods which its owner had formerly lent to the Egyptian Magi.[8] Of this fact, however, Goodman Brown could not take cognizance. He had cast up his eyes in astonishment, and looking down again, beheld neither Goody Cloyse nor the serpentine staff, but his fellow-traveler alone, who waited for him as calmly as if nothing had happened.

"That old woman taught me my catechism!" said the young man; and there was a world of meaning in this simple comment.

They continued to walk onward, while the elder traveler exhorted his companion to make good speed and persevere in the path, discoursing so aptly, that his arguments seemed rather to spring up in the bosom of his auditor, than to be suggested by himself. As they went, he plucked a branch of maple, to serve for a walking stick, and began to strip it of the twigs and little boughs, which were wet with evening dew. The moment his fingers touched them, they became strangely withered and dried up, as with a week's sunshine. Thus the pair proceeded, at a good free pace, until suddenly, in a gloomy hollow of the road, Goodman Brown sat himself down on the stump of a tree, and refused to go any farther.

"Friend," said he, stubbornly, "my mind is made up. Not another step will I budge on this errand. What if a wretched old woman do choose to go to the devil, when I thought she was going to Heaven! Is that any

---

[1] *catechism* Formal Christian instruction given to children, often given from church-ordained books.

[2] *deacon Gookin* Daniel Gookin (1612–87) was a Boston politician; *deacon* Church officer.

[3] *Goody Cloyse* A woman named Sarah Cloyse was among the people imprisoned for witchcraft during the Salem witch trials; *Goody* Short form of *goodwife*, female variant of the title Goodman.

[4] *Goody Cory* Martha Cory or Corey was hanged for witchcraft in Salem in 1692.

[5] *smallage … wolf's bane* Herbs associated with witchcraft.

[6] *receipt* Recipe.

[7] *communion* Ordinarily, Christian ceremony initiating a young person into the ceremonies of the church.

[8] *it assumed life … Egyptian Magi* See Exodus 7.11, where the Egyptian magi copy Aaron's feat by throwing their rods before the Pharaoh and turning them into serpents.

reason why I should quit my dear Faith, and go after her?"

"You will think better of this, by-and-by," said his acquaintance, composedly. "Sit here and rest yourself awhile; and when you feel like moving again, there is my staff to help you along."

Without more words, he threw his companion the maple stick, and was as speedily out of sight as if he had vanished into the deepening gloom. The young man sat a few moments by the roadside, applauding himself greatly, and thinking with how clear a conscience he should meet the minister, in his morning walk, nor shrink from the eye of good old deacon Gookin. And what calm sleep would be his, that very night, which was to have been spent so wickedly, but so purely and sweetly now, in the arms of Faith! Amidst these pleasant and praiseworthy meditations, Goodman Brown heard the tramp of horses along the road, and deemed it advisable to conceal himself within the verge of the forest, conscious of the guilty purpose that had brought him thither, though now so happily turned from it.

On came the hoof tramps and the voices of the riders, two grave old voices, conversing soberly as they drew near. These mingled sounds appeared to pass along the road, within a few yards of the young man's hiding place; but owing, doubtless, to the depth of the gloom at that particular spot, neither the travelers nor their steeds were visible. Though their figures brushed the small boughs by the wayside, it could not be seen that they intercepted, even for a moment, the faint gleam from the strip of bright sky, athwart which they must have passed. Goodman Brown alternately crouched and stood on tiptoe, pulling aside the branches, and thrusting forth his head as far as he durst,[1] without discerning so much as a shadow. It vexed him the more because he could have sworn, were such a thing possible, that he recognized the voices of the minister and deacon Gookin, jogging along quietly, as they were wont to do, when bound to some ordination or ecclesiastical council. While yet within hearing, one of the riders stopped to pluck a switch.

"Of the two, reverend Sir," said the voice like the deacon's, "I had rather miss an ordination dinner than tonight's meeting. They tell me that some of our community are to be here from Falmouth and beyond, and others from Connecticut and Rhode Island; besides several of the Indian powows[2] who, after their fashion, know almost as much deviltry as the best of us. Moreover, there is a goodly young woman to be taken into communion."

"Mighty well, deacon Gookin!" replied the solemn old tones of the minister. "Spur up, or we shall be late. Nothing can be done, you know, until I get on the ground."

The hoofs clattered again, and the voices, talking so strangely in the empty air, passed on through the forest, where no church had ever been gathered, nor solitary Christian prayed. Whither, then, could these holy men be journeying, so deep into the heathen wilderness? Young Goodman Brown caught hold of a tree, for support, being ready to sink down on the ground, faint and overburdened with the heavy sickness of his heart. He looked up to the sky, doubting whether there really was a Heaven above him. Yet, there was the blue arch, and the stars brightening in it.

"With Heaven above, and Faith below, I will yet stand firm against the devil!" cried Goodman Brown.

While he still gazed upward, into the deep arch of the firmament, and had lifted his hands to pray, a cloud, though no wind was stirring, hurried across the zenith, and hid the brightening stars. The blue sky was still visible, except directly overhead, where this black mass of cloud was sweeping swiftly northward. Aloft in the air, as if from the depths of the cloud, came a confused and doubtful sound of voices. Once, the listener fancied that he could distinguish the accents of townspeople of his own, men and women, both pious and ungodly, many of whom he had met at the communion table, and had seen others rioting at the tavern. The next moment, so indistinct were the sounds, he doubted whether he had heard aught but the murmur of the old forest, whispering without a wind. Then came a stronger swell of those familiar tones, heard daily in the sunshine at Salem village, but never, until now, from a cloud of night. There was one voice, of a young woman, uttering lamentations, yet with an uncertain sorrow, and entreating for some favor, which, perhaps, it would grieve her to obtain. And all the unseen multitude, both saints and sinners, seemed to encourage her onward.

---

[1] *durst* Dared.

[2] *powows* Medicine men; shamans.

"Faith!" shouted Goodman Brown, in a voice of agony and desperation; and the echoes of the forest mocked him, crying—"Faith! Faith!" as if bewildered wretches were seeking her, all through the wilderness.

The cry of grief, rage, and terror was yet piercing the night, when the unhappy husband held his breath for a response. There was a scream, drowned immediately in a louder murmur of voices, fading into far-off laughter, as the dark cloud swept away, leaving the clear and silent sky above Goodman Brown. But something fluttered lightly down through the air, and caught on the branch of a tree. The young man seized it, and beheld a pink ribbon.

"My Faith is gone!" cried he, after one stupefied moment. "There is no good on earth; and sin is but a name. Come, devil! for to thee is this world given."

And maddened with despair, so that he laughed loud and long, did Goodman Brown grasp his staff and set forth again, at such a rate, that he seemed to fly along the forest path, rather than to walk or run. The road grew wilder and drearier, and more faintly traced, and vanished at length, leaving him in the heart of the dark wilderness, still rushing onward, with the instinct that guides mortal man to evil. The whole forest was peopled with frightful sounds; the creaking of the trees, the howling of wild beasts, and the yell of Indians; while, sometimes, the wind tolled like a distant church bell, and sometimes gave a broad roar around the traveler, as if all Nature were laughing him to scorn. But he was himself the chief horror of the scene, and shrank not from its other horrors.

"Ha! ha! ha!" roared Goodman Brown, when the wind laughed at him. "Let us hear which will laugh loudest! Think not to frighten me with your deviltry! Come witch, come wizard, come Indian powow, come devil himself! and here comes Goodman Brown. You may as well fear him as he fear you!"

In truth, all through the haunted forest, there could be nothing more frightful than the figure of Goodman Brown. On he flew, among the black pines, brandishing his staff with frenzied gestures, now giving vent to an inspiration of horrid blasphemy, and now shouting forth such laughter, as set all the echoes of the forest laughing like demons around him. The fiend[1] in his own shape is less hideous than when he rages in the breast of man. Thus sped the demoniac on his course, until, quivering among the trees, he saw a red light before him, as when the felled trunks and branches of a clearing have been set on fire, and throw up their lurid blaze against the sky, at the hour of midnight. He paused, in a lull of the tempest that had driven him onward, and heard the swell of what seemed a hymn, rolling solemnly from a distance, with the weight of many voices. He knew the tune; it was a familiar one in the choir of the village meeting-house. The verse died heavily away, and was lengthened by a chorus, not of human voices, but of all the sounds of the benighted wilderness, pealing in awful harmony together. Goodman Brown cried out; and his cry was lost to his own ear, by its unison with the cry of the desert.[2]

In the interval of silence he stole forward, until the light glared full upon his eyes. At one extremity of an open space, hemmed in by the dark wall of the forest, arose a rock, bearing some rude, natural resemblance either to an altar or a pulpit, and surrounded by four blazing pines, their tops aflame, their stems untouched, like candles at an evening meeting. The mass of foliage that had overgrown the summit of the rock was all on fire, blazing high into the night, and fitfully illuminating the whole field. Each pendent twig and leafy festoon was in a blaze. As the red light arose and fell, a numerous congregation alternately shone forth, then disappeared in shadow, and again grew, as it were, out of the darkness, peopling the heart of the solitary woods at once.

"A grave and dark-clad company!" quoth Goodman Brown.

In truth, they were such. Among them, quivering to-and-fro between gloom and splendor, appeared faces that would be seen, next day, at the council board of the province, and others which, Sabbath after Sabbath, looked devoutly heavenward, and benignantly over the crowded pews, from the holiest pulpits in the land. Some affirm that the lady of the governor was there. At least, there were high dames well known to her, and wives of honored husbands, and widows, a great multitude, and ancient maidens, all of excellent repute, and fair young girls who trembled lest their mothers should espy them. Either the sudden gleams of light, flashing over the obscure field, bedazzled Goodman Brown, or

---

[1] *The fiend* I.e., the devil.

[2] *desert* Wilderness.

he recognized a score of the church members of Salem village, famous for their especial sanctity. Good old deacon Gookin had arrived, and waited at the skirts of that venerable saint, his revered pastor. But, irreverently consorting with these grave, reputable, and pious people, these elders of the church, these chaste dames and dewy virgins, there were men of dissolute lives and women of spotted fame, wretches given over to all mean and filthy vice, and suspected even of horrid crimes. It was strange to see that the good shrank not from the wicked, nor were the sinners abashed by the saints. Scattered, also, among their pale-faced enemies, were the Indian priests, or powows, who had often scared their native forest with more hideous incantations than any known to English witchcraft.

"But, where is Faith?" thought Goodman Brown; and, as hope came into his heart, he trembled.

Another verse of the hymn arose, a slow and solemn strain such as the pious love, but joined to words which expressed all that our nature can conceive of sin, and darkly hinted at far more. Unfathomable to mere mortals is the lore of fiends. Verse after verse was sung, and still the chorus of the desert swelled between, like the deepest tone of a mighty organ. And, with the final peal of that dreadful anthem, there came a sound, as if the roaring wind, the rushing streams, the howling beasts, and every other voice of the unconverted wilderness, were mingling and according with the voice of guilty man, in homage to the prince of all. The four blazing pines threw up a loftier flame, and obscurely discovered shapes and visages of horror on the smoke wreaths, above the impious assembly. At the same moment, the fire on the rock shot redly forth, and formed a glowing arch above its base, where now appeared a figure. With reverence be it spoken, the figure bore no slight similitude, both in garb and manner, to some grave divine of the New England churches.

"Bring forth the converts!" cried a voice, that echoed through the field and rolled into the forest.

At the word, Goodman Brown stepped forth from the shadow of the trees, and approached the congregation, with whom he felt a loathful brotherhood, by the sympathy of all that was wicked in his heart. He could have well nigh sworn that the shape of his own dead father beckoned him to advance, looking downward from a smoke wreath, while a woman, with dim features of despair, threw out her hand to warn him back.[1] Was it his mother? But he had no power to retreat one step, nor to resist, even in thought, when the minister and good old deacon Gookin, seized his arms, and led him to the blazing rock. Thither came also the slender form of a veiled female, led between Goody Cloyse, that pious teacher of the catechism, and Martha Carrier,[2] who had received the devil's promise to be queen of hell. A rampant hag was she! And there stood the proselytes, beneath the canopy of fire.

"Welcome, my children," said the dark figure, "to the communion of your race![3] Ye have found, thus young, your nature and your destiny. My children, look behind you!"

They turned; and flashing forth, as it were, in a sheet of flame, the fiend worshippers were seen; the smile of welcome gleamed darkly on every visage.

"There," resumed the sable[4] form, "are all whom ye have reverenced from youth. Ye deemed them holier than yourselves, and shrank from your own sin, contrasting it with their lives of righteousness, and prayerful aspirations heavenward. Yet, here are they all, in my worshipping assembly! This night it shall be granted you to know their secret deeds; how hoary bearded elders of the church have whispered wanton words to the young maids of their households; how many a woman, eager for widows' weeds,[5] has given her husband a drink at bedtime, and let him sleep his last sleep in her bosom; how beardless youths have made haste to inherit their fathers' wealth; and how fair damsels— blush not, sweet ones!—have dug little graves in the garden, and bidden me, the sole guest, to an infant's funeral. By the sympathy of your human hearts for sin,

---

1   *shape of … him back* Allusion to the belief in "spectral evidence" during the witch trials. Many of the accusers claimed to have seen or been attacked by the "specters" of the accused, proving them to be witches; spectral evidence became less accepted as people suspected that the devil could also take the shape of the innocent.

2   *Martha Carrier* Another of the accused in the Salem witch trials. She vehemently denied all accusations against herself; nevertheless, she was hanged in 1692. In his summary of her trial, Cotton Mather called Carrier a "rampant hag" and asserted that "the Devil had promised her, she should be Queen of Hell."

3   *race* Appearing as "grave" in the original printing, this was corrected in *Mosses from an Old Manse* (1846).

4   *sable* Dark.

5   *widow's weeds* Mourning clothes of a widow.

ye shall scent out all the places—whether in church, bedchamber, street, field, or forest—where crime has been committed, and shall exult to behold the whole earth one stain of guilt, one mighty blood spot. Far more than this! It shall be yours to penetrate, in every bosom, the deep mystery of sin, the fountain of all wicked arts, and which, inexhaustibly supplies more evil impulses than human power—than my power, at its utmost!—can make manifest in deeds. And now, my children, look upon each other."

They did so; and, by the blaze of the hell-kindled torches, the wretched man beheld his Faith, and the wife her husband, trembling before that unhallowed altar.

"Lo! there ye stand, my children," said the figure, in a deep and solemn tone, almost sad, with its despairing awfulness, as if his once angelic nature could yet mourn for our miserable race. "Depending upon one another's hearts, ye had still hoped, that virtue were not all a dream. Now are ye undeceived! Evil is the nature of mankind. Evil must be your only happiness. Welcome, again, my children, to the communion of your race!"

"Welcome!" repeated the fiend worshippers, in one cry of despair and triumph.

And there they stood, the only pair, as it seemed, who were yet hesitating on the verge of wickedness, in this dark world. A basin was hollowed, naturally, in the rock. Did it contain water, reddened by the lurid light? or was it blood? or, perchance, a liquid flame? Herein did the Shape of Evil dip his hand, and prepare to lay the mark of baptism upon their foreheads, that they might be partakers of the mystery of sin, more conscious of the secret guilt of others, both in deed and thought, than they could now be of their own. The husband cast one look at his pale wife, and Faith at him. What polluted wretches would the next glance show them to each other, shuddering alike at what they disclosed and what they saw!

"Faith! Faith!" cried the husband, "look up to Heaven, and resist the Wicked One!"

Whether Faith obeyed, he knew not. Hardly had he spoken, when he found himself amid calm night and solitude, listening to a roar of the wind, which died heavily away through the forest. He staggered against the rock and felt it chill and damp, while a hanging twig, that had been all on fire, besprinkled his cheek with the coldest dew.

The next morning, young Goodman Brown came slowly into the street of Salem village, staring around him like a bewildered man. The good old minister was taking a walk along the graveyard, to get an appetite for breakfast and meditate his sermon, and bestowed a blessing, as he passed, on Goodman Brown. He shrank from the venerable saint, as if to avoid an anathema.[1] Old deacon Gookin was at domestic worship, and the holy words of his prayer were heard through the open window. "What God doth the wizard pray to?" quoth Goodman Brown. Goody Cloyse, that excellent old Christian, stood in the early sunshine, at her own lattice, catechising a little girl who had brought her a pint of morning's milk. Goodman Brown snatched away the child, as from the grasp of the fiend himself. Turning the corner by the meeting-house, he spied the head of Faith, with the pink ribbons, gazing anxiously forth, and bursting into such joy at sight of him that she skipped along the street, and almost kissed her husband before the whole village.[2] But, Goodman Brown looked sternly and sadly into her face, and passed on without a greeting.

Had Goodman Brown fallen asleep in the forest, and only dreamed a wild dream of a witch-meeting?

Be it so, if you will. But, alas! it was a dream of evil omen for young Goodman Brown. A stern, a sad, a darkly meditative, a distrustful, if not a desperate man did he become, from the night of that fearful dream. On the Sabbath day, when the congregation were singing a holy psalm, he could not listen, because an anthem of sin rushed loudly upon his ear, and drowned all the blessed strain. When the minister spoke from the pulpit, with power and fervid eloquence, and, with his hand on the open Bible, of the sacred truths of our religion, and of saint-like lives and triumphant deaths, and of future bliss or misery unutterable, then did Goodman Brown turn pale, dreading, lest the roof should thunder down upon the gray blasphemer and his hearers. Often, waking suddenly at midnight, he

---

1   *anathema*   Curse denouncing a person, and excommunicating them from church and God.

2   *almost kissed ... village*   Publicly kissing one's spouse was generally frowned upon, and even punishable by law, in seventeenth-century Massachusetts.

shrank from the bosom of Faith, and at morning or eventide, when the family knelt down at prayer, he scowled, and muttered to himself, and gazed sternly at his wife, and turned away. And when he had lived long, and was borne to his grave, a hoary corpse, followed by Faith, an aged woman, and children and grandchildren, a goodly procession, besides neighbors, not a few, they carved no hopeful verse upon his tombstone; for his dying hour was gloom.

—1835

The Minister's Black Veil

A Parable[1]

The sexton stood in the porch of Milford[2] meeting house, pulling busily at the bell-rope. The old people of the village came stooping along the street. Children, with bright faces, tripped merrily beside their parents, or mimicked a graver gait, in the conscious dignity of their Sunday clothes. Spruce bachelors looked sidelong at the pretty maidens, and fancied that the sabbath sunshine made them prettier than on weekdays. When the throng had mostly streamed into the porch, the sexton began to toll the bell, keeping his eye on the Reverend Mr. Hooper's door. The first glimpse of the clergyman's figure was the signal for the bell to cease its summons.

"But what has good Parson Hooper got upon his face?" cried the sexton in astonishment.

All within hearing immediately turned about, and beheld the semblance of Mr. Hooper, pacing slowly his meditative way towards the meeting house. With one accord they started, expressing more wonder than if some strange minister were coming to dust the cushions of Mr. Hooper's pulpit.

"Are you sure it is our parson?" inquired Goodman[3] Gray of the sexton.

"Of a certainty it is good Mr. Hooper," replied the sexton. "He was to have exchanged pulpits with Parson Shute of Westbury; but Parson Shute sent to excuse himself yesterday, being to preach a funeral sermon."

The cause of so much amazement may appear sufficiently slight. Mr. Hooper, a gentlemanly person of about thirty, though still a bachelor, was dressed with due clerical neatness, as if a careful wife had starched his band,[4] and brushed the weekly dust from his Sunday's garb. There was but one thing remarkable in his appearance. Swathed about his forehead, and hanging down over his face, so low as to be shaken by his breath, Mr. Hooper had on a black veil. On a nearer view, it seemed to consist of two folds of crape,[5] which entirely concealed his features, except the mouth and chin, but probably did not intercept his sight, farther than to give a darkened aspect to all living and inanimate things. With this gloomy shade before him, good Mr. Hooper walked onward, at a slow and quiet pace, stooping somewhat and looking on the ground, as is customary with abstracted men, yet nodding kindly to those of his parishioners who still waited on the meeting house steps. But so wonder-struck were they, that his greeting hardly met with a return.

"I can't really feel as if good Mr. Hooper's face was behind that piece of crape," said the sexton.

"I don't like it," muttered an old woman, as she hobbled into the meeting house. "He has changed himself into something awful,[6] only by hiding his face."

"Our parson has gone mad!" cried Goodman Gray, following him across the threshold.

A rumor of some unaccountable phenomenon had preceded Mr. Hooper into the meeting house, and set all the congregation astir. Few could refrain from twisting their heads towards the door; many stood upright, and turned directly about; while several little boys clambered upon the seats, and came down again with a terrible racket. There was a general bustle, a rustling of the women's gowns and shuffling of the men's feet, greatly at variance with that hushed repose which

---

[1]   [Hawthorne's note]   Another clergyman in New-England, Mr. Joseph Moody, of York, Maine, who died about eighty years since, made himself remarkable by the same eccentricity that is here related of the Reverend Mr. Hooper. In his case, however, the symbol had a different import. In early life he had accidentally killed a beloved friend; and from that day till the hour of his own death, he hid his face from men.

[2]   *sexton*   Officer responsible for maintaining a church; *Milford*   Town in Massachusetts, near Boston.

[3]   *Goodman*   Respectful title for the male head of a household.

[4]   *band*   Collar (usually white) worn by a cleric.

[5]   *crape*   Thin, gauzy fabric frequently used for mourning attire.

[6]   *awful*   Inspiring of awe and reverential fear.

should attend the entrance of the minister. But Mr. Hooper appeared not to notice the perturbation of his people. He entered with an almost noiseless step, bent his head mildly to the pews on each side, and bowed as he passed his oldest parishioner, a white-haired great-grandsire, who occupied an armchair in the centre of the aisle. It was strange to observe how slowly this venerable man became conscious of something singular in the appearance of his pastor. He seemed not fully to partake of the prevailing wonder, till Mr. Hooper had ascended the stairs, and showed himself in the pulpit, face to face with his congregation, except for the black veil. That mysterious emblem was never once withdrawn. It shook with his measured breath as he gave out the psalm; it threw its obscurity between him and the holy page, as he read the Scriptures; and while he prayed, the veil lay heavily on his uplifted countenance. Did he seek to hide it from the dread Being whom he was addressing?

Such was the effect of this simple piece of crape, that more than one woman of delicate nerves was forced to leave the meeting house. Yet perhaps the pale-faced congregation was almost as fearful a sight to the minister, as his black veil to them.

Mr. Hooper had the reputation of a good preacher, but not an energetic one: he strove to win his people heavenward by mild, persuasive influences, rather than to drive them thither by the thunders of the Word. The sermon which he now delivered was marked by the same characteristics of style and manner as the general series of his pulpit oratory. But there was something, either in the sentiment of the discourse itself, or in the imagination of the auditors, which made it greatly the most powerful effort that they had ever heard from their pastor's lips. It was tinged, rather more darkly than usual, with the gentle gloom of Mr. Hooper's temperament. The subject had reference to secret sin, and those sad mysteries which we hide from our nearest and dearest, and would fain conceal from our own consciousness, even forgetting that the Omniscient can detect them. A subtle power was breathed into his words. Each member of the congregation, the most innocent girl, and the man of hardened breast, felt as if the preacher had crept upon them, behind his awful veil, and discovered their hoarded iniquity of deed or thought. Many spread their clasped hands on their bosoms. There was nothing terrible in what Mr. Hooper said, at least, no violence; and yet, with every tremor of his melancholy voice, the hearers quaked. An unsought pathos came hand in hand with awe. So sensible were the audience of some unwonted attribute in their minister, that they longed for a breath of wind to blow aside the veil, almost believing that a stranger's visage would be discovered, though the form, gesture, and voice were those of Mr. Hooper.

At the close of the services, the people hurried out with indecorous confusion, eager to communicate their pent-up amazement, and conscious of lighter spirits the moment they lost sight of the black veil. Some gathered in little circles, huddled closely together, with their mouths all whispering in the centre; some went homeward alone, wrapped in silent meditation; some talked loudly, and profaned the Sabbath day with ostentatious laughter. A few shook their sagacious heads, intimating that they could penetrate the mystery; while one or two affirmed that there was no mystery at all, but only that Mr. Hooper's eyes were so weakened by the midnight lamp, as to require a shade. After a brief interval, forth came good Mr. Hooper also, in the rear of his flock. Turning his veiled face from one group to another, he paid due reverence to the hoary heads, saluted the middle aged with kind dignity as their friend and spiritual guide, greeted the young with mingled authority and love, and laid his hands on the little children's heads to bless them. Such was always his custom on the Sabbath day. Strange and bewildered looks repaid him for his courtesy. None, as on former occasions, aspired to the honor of walking by their pastor's side. Old Squire Saunders, doubtless by an accidental lapse of memory, neglected to invite Mr. Hooper to his table, where the good clergyman had been wont to bless the food almost every Sunday since his settlement. He returned, therefore, to the parsonage, and, at the moment of closing the door, was observed to look back upon the people, all of whom had their eyes fixed upon the minister. A sad smile gleamed faintly from beneath the black veil, and flickered about his mouth, glimmering as he disappeared.

"How strange," said a lady, "that a simple black veil, such as any woman might wear on her bonnet, should become such a terrible thing on Mr. Hooper's face!"

"Something must surely be amiss with Mr. Hooper's intellects," observed her husband, the physician of the village. "But the strangest part of the affair is the effect of this vagary, even on a sober-minded man like myself. The black veil, though it covers only our pastor's face, throws its influence over his whole person, and makes him ghostlike from head to foot. Do you not feel it so?"

"Truly do I," replied the lady; "and I would not be alone with him for the world. I wonder he is not afraid to be alone with himself!"

"Men sometimes are so," said her husband.

The afternoon service was attended with similar circumstances. At its conclusion, the bell tolled for the funeral of a young lady. The relatives and friends were assembled in the house, and the more distant acquaintances stood about the door, speaking of the good qualities of the deceased, when their talk was interrupted by the appearance of Mr. Hooper, still covered with his black veil. It was now an appropriate emblem. The clergyman stepped into the room where the corpse was laid, and bent over the coffin, to take a last farewell of his deceased parishioner. As he stooped, the veil hung straight down from his forehead, so that, if her eyelids had not been closed forever, the dead maiden might have seen his face. Could Mr. Hooper be fearful of her glance, that he so hastily caught back the black veil? A person who watched the interview between the dead and living, scrupled not to affirm that, at the instant when the clergyman's features were disclosed, the corpse had slightly shuddered, rustling the shroud and muslin cap, though the countenance retained the composure of death. A superstitious old woman was the only witness of this prodigy. From the coffin, Mr. Hooper passed into the chamber of the mourners, and thence to the head of the staircase, to make the funeral prayer. It was a tender and heart-dissolving prayer, full of sorrow, yet so imbued with celestial hopes, that the music of a heavenly harp, swept by the fingers of the dead, seemed faintly to be heard among the saddest accents of the minister. The people trembled, though they but darkly understood him when he prayed that they, and himself, and all of mortal race, might be ready, as he trusted this young maiden had been, for the dreadful hour that should snatch the veil from their faces. The bearers went heavily forth, and the mourners followed, saddening all the street, with the dead before them, and Mr. Hooper in his black veil behind.

"Why do you look back?" said one in the procession to his partner.

"I had a fancy," replied she, "that the minister and the maiden's spirit were walking hand in hand."

"And so had I, at the same moment," said the other.

That night, the handsomest couple in Milford village were to be joined in wedlock. Though reckoned a melancholy man, Mr. Hooper had a placid cheerfulness for such occasions, which often excited a sympathetic smile where livelier merriment would have been thrown away. There was no quality of his disposition which made him more beloved than this. The company at the wedding awaited his arrival with impatience, trusting that the strange awe which had gathered over him throughout the day would now be dispelled. But such was not the result. When Mr. Hooper came, the first thing that their eyes rested on was the same horrible black veil, which had added deeper gloom to the funeral, and could portend nothing but evil to the wedding. Such was its immediate effect on the guests, that a cloud seemed to have rolled duskily from beneath the black crape, and dimmed the light of the candles. The bridal pair stood up before the minister. But the bride's cold fingers quivered in the tremulous hand of the bridegroom, and her death-like paleness caused a whisper that the maiden who had been buried a few hours before was come from her grave to be married. If ever another wedding were so dismal, it was that famous one where they tolled the wedding knell.[1] After performing the ceremony, Mr. Hooper raised a glass of wine to his lips, wishing happiness to the new-married couple in a strain of mild pleasantry that ought to have brightened the features of the guests, like a cheerful gleam from the hearth. At that instant, catching a glimpse of his figure in the looking-glass, the black veil involved his own spirit in the horror with which it overwhelmed all others. His frame shuddered—his lips grew white—he spilt the untasted wine upon the carpet—and rushed forth into the darkness. For the Earth, too, had on her Black Veil.

---

1   *that famous ... wedding knell* Allusion to Hawthorne's own story *The Wedding Knell*, first published along with this story in the gift-book *The Token* in 1836;   *knell* Sound of a funeral bell.

The next day, the whole village of Milford talked of little else than Parson Hooper's black veil. That, and the mystery concealed behind it, supplied a topic for discussion between acquaintances meeting in the street, and good women gossiping at their open windows. It was the first item of news that the tavern-keeper told to his guests. The children babbled of it on their way to school. One imitative little imp covered his face with an old black handkerchief, thereby so affrighting his playmates that the panic seized himself, and he well nigh lost his wits by his own waggery.[1]

It was remarkable that, of all the busybodies and impertinent people in the parish, not one ventured to put the plain question to Mr. Hooper, wherefore he did this thing. Hitherto, whenever there appeared the slightest call for such interference, he had never lacked advisers, nor shown himself averse to be guided by their judgment. If he erred at all, it was by so painful a degree of self-distrust, that even the mildest censure would lead him to consider an indifferent action as a crime. Yet, though so well acquainted with this amiable weakness, no individual among his parishioners chose to make the black veil a subject of friendly remonstrance. There was a feeling of dread, neither plainly confessed nor carefully concealed, which caused each to shift the responsibility upon another, till at length it was found expedient to send a deputation to the church, in order to deal with Mr. Hooper about the mystery, before it should grow into a scandal. Never did an embassy so ill discharge its duties. The minister received them with friendly courtesy, but became silent after they were seated, leaving to his visitors the whole burden of introducing their important business. The topic, it might be supposed, was obvious enough. There was the black veil swathed round Mr. Hooper's forehead, and concealing every feature above his placid mouth, on which, at times, they could perceive the glimmering of a melancholy smile. But that piece of crape, to their imagination, seemed to hang down before his heart, the symbol of a fearful secret between him and them. Were the veil but cast aside, they might speak freely of it, but not till then. Thus they sat a considerable time, speechless, confused, and shrinking uneasily from Mr. Hooper's eye, which they felt to be fixed upon them with an invisible glance. Finally, the deputies returned abashed to their constituents, pronouncing the matter too weighty to be handled, except by a council of the churches, if, indeed, it might not require a general synod.[2]

But there was one person in the village unappalled by the awe with which the black veil had impressed all besides herself. When the deputies returned without an explanation, or even venturing to demand one, she, with the calm energy of her character, determined to chase away the strange cloud that appeared to be settling round Mr. Hooper, every moment more darkly than before. As his plighted wife, it should be her privilege to know what the black veil concealed. At the minister's first visit, therefore, she entered upon the subject with a direct simplicity, which made the task easier both for him and her. After he had seated himself, she fixed her eyes steadfastly upon the veil, but could discern nothing of the dreadful gloom that had so overawed the multitude: it was but a double fold of crape, hanging down from his forehead to his mouth, and slightly stirring with his breath.

"No," she said aloud, and smiling, "there is nothing terrible in this piece of crape, except that it hides a face which I am always glad to look upon. Come, good sir, let the sun shine from behind the cloud. First lay aside your black veil: then tell me why you put it on."

Mr. Hooper's smile glimmered faintly.

"There is an hour to come," said he, "when all of us shall cast aside our veils. Take it not amiss, beloved friend, if I wear this piece of crape till then."

"Your words are a mystery, too," returned the young lady. "Take away the veil from them, at least."

"Elizabeth, I will," said he, "so far as my vow may suffer[3] me. Know, then, this veil is a type[4] and a symbol, and I am bound to wear it ever, both in light and darkness, in solitude and before the gaze of multitudes, and as with strangers, so with my familiar friends. No mortal eye will see it withdrawn. This dismal shade must separate me from the world: even you, Elizabeth, can never come behind it!"

"What grievous affliction hath befallen you," she earnestly inquired, "that you should thus darken your eyes forever?"

---

[1]   *waggery* Mischievousness.

[2]   *synod* Large assemblage of the clergy of a given church.

[3]   *suffer* Allow.

[4]   *type* Embodiment of a religious theme.

"If it be a sign of mourning," replied Mr. Hooper, "I, perhaps, like most other mortals, have sorrows dark enough to be typified by a black veil."

"But what if the world will not believe that it is the type of an innocent sorrow?" urged Elizabeth. "Beloved and respected as you are, there may be whispers that you hide your face under the consciousness of secret sin. For the sake of your holy office, do away this scandal!"

The color rose into her cheeks as she intimated the nature of the rumors that were already abroad in the village. But Mr. Hooper's mildness did not forsake him. He even smiled again—that same sad smile, which always appeared like a faint glimmering of light, proceeding from the obscurity beneath the veil.

"If I hide my face for sorrow, there is cause enough," he merely replied; "and if I cover it for secret sin, what mortal might not do the same?"

And with this gentle but unconquerable obstinacy did he resist all her entreaties. At length Elizabeth sat silent. For a few moments she appeared lost in thought, considering, probably, what new methods might be tried to withdraw her lover from so dark a fantasy, which, if it had no other meaning, was perhaps a symptom of mental disease. Though of a firmer character than his own, the tears rolled down her cheeks. But, in an instant, as it were, a new feeling took the place of sorrow: her eyes were fixed insensibly on the black veil, when, like a sudden twilight in the air, its terrors fell around her. She arose, and stood trembling before him.

"And do you feel it then at last?" said he mournfully.

She made no reply, but covered her eyes with her hand, and turned to leave the room. He rushed forward and caught her arm.

"Have patience with me, Elizabeth!" cried he passionately. "Do not desert me, though this veil must be between us here on earth. Be mine, and hereafter there shall be no veil over my face, no darkness between our souls! It is but a mortal veil—it is not for eternity! Oh! you know not how lonely I am, and how frightened to be alone behind my black veil. Do not leave me in this miserable obscurity forever!"

"Lift the veil but once, and look me in the face," said she.

"Never! It cannot be!" replied Mr. Hooper.

"Then farewell!" said Elizabeth.

She withdrew her arm from his grasp, and slowly departed, pausing at the door, to give one long, shuddering gaze, that seemed almost to penetrate the mystery of the black veil. But, even amid his grief, Mr. Hooper smiled to think that only a material emblem had separated him from happiness, though the horrors which it shadowed forth must be drawn darkly between the fondest of lovers.

From that time no attempts were made to remove Mr. Hooper's black veil, or, by a direct appeal, to discover the secret which it was supposed to hide. By persons who claimed a superiority to popular prejudice, it was reckoned merely an eccentric whim, such as often mingles with the sober actions of men otherwise rational, and tinges them all with its own semblance of insanity. But with the multitude, good Mr. Hooper was irreparably a bugbear.[1] He could not walk the street with any peace of mind, so conscious was he that the gentle and timid would turn aside to avoid him, and that others would make it a point of hardihood to throw themselves in his way. The impertinence of the latter class compelled him to give up his customary walk, at sunset, to the burial ground; for when he leaned pensively over the gate, there would always be faces behind the gravestones, peeping at his black veil. A fable went the rounds, that the stare of the dead people drove him thence. It grieved him, to the very depth of his kind heart, to observe how the children fled from his approach, breaking up their merriest sports, while his melancholy figure was yet afar off. Their instinctive dread caused him to feel, more strongly than aught else, that a preternatural horror was interwoven with the threads of the black crape. In truth, his own antipathy to the veil was known to be so great, that he never willingly passed before a mirror, nor stooped to drink at a still fountain, lest, in its peaceful bosom, he should be affrighted by himself. This was what gave plausibility to the whispers, that Mr. Hooper's conscience tortured him for some great crime too horrible to be entirely concealed, or otherwise than so obscurely intimated. Thus, from beneath the black veil, there rolled a cloud into the sunshine, an ambiguity of sin or sorrow, which enveloped the poor minister, so that love or sympathy could never reach him. It was said that ghost and fiend

---

[1] *bugbear* Creature that causes great fear or anxiety.

consorted with him there. With self-shudderings and outward terrors, he walked continually in its shadow, groping darkly within his own soul, or gazing through a medium that saddened the whole world. Even the lawless wind, it was believed, respected his dreadful secret, and never blew aside the veil. But still good Mr. Hooper sadly smiled at the pale visages of the worldly throng as he passed by.

Among all its bad influences, the black veil had the one desirable effect, of making its wearer a very efficient clergyman. By the aid of his mysterious emblem—for there was no other apparent cause—he became a man of awful power over souls that were in agony for sin. His converts always regarded him with a dread peculiar to themselves, affirming, though but figuratively, that, before he brought them to celestial light, they had been with him behind the black veil. Its gloom, indeed, enabled him to sympathize with all dark affections. Dying sinners cried aloud for Mr. Hooper, and would not yield their breath till he appeared; though ever, as he stooped to whisper consolation, they shuddered at the veiled face so near their own. Such were the terrors of the black veil, even when death had bared his visage! Strangers came long distances to attend service at his church, with the mere idle purpose of gazing at his figure, because it was forbidden them to behold his face. But many were made to quake ere they departed! Once, during Governor Belcher's administration, Mr. Hooper was appointed to preach the election sermon.[1] Covered with his black veil, he stood before the chief magistrate, the council, and the representatives, and wrought so deep an impression that the legislative measures of that year were characterized by all the gloom and piety of our earliest ancestral sway.

In this manner Mr. Hooper spent a long life, irreproachable in outward act, yet shrouded in dismal suspicions; kind and loving, though unloved, and dimly feared; a man apart from men, shunned in their health and joy, but ever summoned to their aid in mortal anguish. As years wore on, shedding their snows above his sable veil, he acquired a name throughout the New England churches, and they called him Father Hooper.

Nearly all his parishioners, who were of mature age when he was settled, had been borne away by many a funeral: he had one congregation in the church, and a more crowded one in the churchyard; and having wrought so late into the evening, and done his work so well, it was now good Father Hooper's turn to rest.

Several persons were visible by the shaded candle-light, in the death chamber of the old clergyman. Natural connections[2] he had none. But there was the decorously grave, though unmoved, physician, seeking only to mitigate the last pangs of the patient whom he could not save. There were the deacons, and other eminently pious members of his church. There, also, was the Reverend Mr. Clark, of Westbury, a young and zealous divine, who had ridden in haste to pray by the bedside of the expiring minister. There was the nurse, no hired handmaiden of death, but one whose calm affection had endured thus long in secrecy, in solitude, amid the chill of age, and would not perish, even at the dying hour. Who, but Elizabeth! And there lay the hoary head of good Father Hooper upon the death pillow, with the black veil still swathed about his brow and reaching down over his face, so that each more difficult gasp of his faint breath caused it to stir. All through life that piece of crape had hung between him and the world: it had separated him from cheerful brotherhood and woman's love, and kept him in that saddest of all prisons, his own heart; and still it lay upon his face, as if to deepen the gloom of his darksome chamber, and shade him from the sunshine of eternity.

For some time previous, his mind had been confused, wavering doubtfully between the past and the present, and hovering forward, as it were, at intervals, into the indistinctness of the world to come. There had been feverish turns, which tossed him from side to side, and wore away what little strength he had. But in his most convulsive struggles, and in the wildest vagaries of his intellect, when no other thought retained its sober influence, he still showed an awful solicitude lest the black veil should slip aside. Even if his bewildered soul could have forgotten, there was a faithful woman at his pillow, who, with averted eyes, would have covered that aged face, which she had last beheld in the comeliness of manhood. At length the death-stricken old man lay quietly in the torpor of mental and bodily

---

[1]   *Governor Belcher … election sermon*   Jonathan Belcher (1682–1757) was governor of Massachusetts and New Hampshire. Election sermons were preached at the beginning of a governor's administration, upon election.

[2]   *Natural connections*   I.e., blood relations; family.

exhaustion, with an imperceptible pulse, and breath that grew fainter and fainter, except when a long, deep, and irregular inspiration seemed to prelude the flight of his spirit.

The minister of Westbury approached the bedside.

"Venerable Father Hooper," said he, "the moment of your release is at hand. Are you ready for the lifting of the veil, that shuts in time from eternity?"

Father Hooper at first replied merely by a feeble motion of his head; then, apprehensive, perhaps, that his meaning might be doubtful, he exerted himself to speak.

"Yea," said he, in faint accents; "my soul hath a patient weariness until that veil be lifted."

"And is it fitting," resumed the Reverend Mr. Clark, "that a man so given to prayer, of such a blameless example, holy in deed and thought, so far as mortal judgment may pronounce; is it fitting that a father in the church should leave a shadow on his memory, that may seem to blacken a life so pure? I pray you, my venerable brother, let not this thing be! Suffer us to be gladdened by your triumphant aspect as you go to your reward. Before the veil of eternity be lifted, let me cast aside this black veil from your face!"

And thus speaking, the Reverend Mr. Clark bent forward to reveal the mystery of so many years. But, exerting a sudden energy, that made all the beholders stand aghast, Father Hooper snatched both his hands from beneath the bedclothes, and pressed them strongly on the black veil, resolute to struggle, if the minister of Westbury would contend with a dying man.

"Never!" cried the veiled clergyman. "On earth, never!"

"Dark old man!" exclaimed the affrighted minister, "with what horrible crime upon your soul are you now passing to the judgment?"

Father Hooper's breath heaved; it rattled in his throat; but, with a mighty effort, grasping forward with his hands, he caught hold of life, and held it back till he should speak. He even raised himself in bed; and there he sat, shivering with the arms of death around him, while the black veil hung down, awful, at that last moment, in the gathered terrors of a lifetime. And yet the faint, sad smile, so often there, now seemed to glimmer from its obscurity, and linger on Father Hooper's lips.

"Why do you tremble at me alone?" cried he, turning his veiled face round the circle of pale spectators. "Tremble also at each other! Have men avoided me, and women shown no pity, and children screamed and fled, only for my black veil? What, but the mystery which it obscurely typifies, has made this piece of crape so awful? When the friend shows his inmost heart to his friend; the lover to his best-beloved; when man does not vainly shrink from the eye of his Creator, loathsomely treasuring up the secret of his sin; then deem me a monster, for the symbol beneath which I have lived, and die! I look around me, and lo! on every visage a black veil!"

While his auditors shrank from one another, in mutual affright, Father Hooper fell back upon his pillow, a veiled corpse, with a faint smile lingering on the lips. Still veiled, they laid him in his coffin, and a veiled corpse they bore him to the grave. The grass of many years has sprung up and withered on that grave; the burial stone is moss-grown, and good Mr. Hooper's face is dust; but awful is still the thought that it moldered beneath the black veil!

—1836

The Birthmark

In the latter part of the last century, there lived a man of science—an eminent proficient in every branch of natural philosophy—who, not long before our story opens, had made experience of a spiritual affinity, more attractive than any chemical one. He had left his laboratory to the care of an assistant, cleared his fine countenance from the furnace smoke, washed the stain of acids from his fingers, and persuaded a beautiful woman to become his wife. In those days, when the comparatively recent discovery of electricity, and other kindred mysteries of nature, seemed to open paths into the region of miracle, it was not unusual for the love of science to rival the love of woman, in its depth and absorbing energy. The higher intellect, the imagination, the spirit, and even the heart, might all find their congenial aliment in pursuits which, as some of their ardent votaries[1] believed, would ascend

---

[1]   *aliment* Nourishment; *votaries* Devotees.

from one step of powerful intelligence to another, until the philosopher should lay his hand on the secret of creative force, and perhaps make new worlds for himself. We know not whether Aylmer possessed this degree of faith in man's ultimate control over nature. He had devoted himself, however, too unreservedly to scientific studies, ever to be weaned from them by any second passion. His love for his young wife might prove the stronger of the two; but it could only be by intertwining itself with his love of science, and uniting the strength of the latter to his own.

Such a union accordingly took place, and was attended with truly remarkable consequences, and a deeply impressive moral. One day, very soon after their marriage, Aylmer sat gazing at his wife, with a trouble in his countenance that grew stronger, until he spoke.

"Georgiana," said he, "has it never occurred to you that the mark upon your cheek might be removed?"

"No, indeed," said she, smiling; but perceiving the seriousness of his manner, she blushed deeply. "To tell you the truth, it has been so often called a charm, that I was simple enough to imagine it might be so."

"Ah, upon another face, perhaps it might," replied her husband. "But never on yours! No, dearest Georgiana, you came so nearly perfect from the hand of Nature, that this slightest possible defect—which we hesitate whether to term a defect or a beauty—shocks me, as being the visible mark of earthly imperfection."

"Shocks you, my husband!" cried Georgiana, deeply hurt; at first reddening with momentary anger, but then bursting into tears. "Then why did you take me from my mother's side? You cannot love what shocks you!"

To explain this conversation, it must be mentioned that, in the centre of Georgiana's left cheek, there was a singular mark, deeply interwoven, as it were, with the texture and substance of her face. In the usual state of her complexion—a healthy, though delicate, bloom—the mark wore a tint of deeper crimson, which imperfectly defined its shape amid the surrounding rosiness. When she blushed, it gradually became more indistinct, and finally vanished amid the triumphant rush of blood that bathed the whole cheek with its brilliant glow. But, if any shifting emotion caused her to turn pale, there was the mark again, a crimson stain upon the snow, in what Aylmer

sometimes deemed an almost fearful distinctness. Its shape bore not a little similarity to the human hand, though of the smallest pigmy size. Georgiana's lovers were wont to say that some fairy, at her birth hour, had laid her tiny hand upon the infant's cheek, and left this impress there, in token of the magic endowments that were to give her such sway over all hearts. Many a desperate swain would have risked life for the privilege of pressing his lips to the mysterious hand. It must not be concealed, however, that the impression wrought by this fairy sign-manual varied exceedingly, according to the difference of temperament in the beholders. Some fastidious persons—but they were exclusively of her own sex—affirmed that the Bloody Hand, as they chose to call it, quite destroyed the effect of Georgiana's beauty, and rendered her countenance even hideous. But it would be as reasonable to say, that one of those small blue stains, which sometimes occur in the purest statuary marble, would convert the Eve of Powers[1] to a monster. Masculine observers, if the birthmark did not heighten their admiration, contented themselves with wishing it away, that the world might possess one living specimen of ideal loveliness, without the semblance of a flaw. After his marriage—for he thought little or nothing of the matter before—Aylmer discovered that this was the case with himself.

Had she been less beautiful—if Envy's self could have found aught else to sneer at—he might have felt his affection heightened by the prettiness of this mimic hand, now vaguely portrayed, now lost, now stealing forth again, and glimmering to-and-fro with every pulse of emotion that throbbed within her heart. But, seeing her otherwise so perfect, he found this one defect grow more and more intolerable, with every moment of their united lives. It was the fatal flaw of humanity, which Nature, in one shape or another, stamps ineffaceably on all her productions, either to imply that they are temporary and finite, or that their perfection must be wrought by toil and pain. The Crimson Hand expressed the ineludible grip, in which mortality clutches the highest and purest of earthly mould, degrading them into kindred with the lowest, and even with the very brutes, like whom their visible

1   *Eve of Powers* Marble sculpture (variously known as *Eve Before the Fall* or *Eve Tempted*) by American sculptor Hiram Powers (1805–73).

frames return to dust. In this manner, selecting it as the symbol of his wife's liability to sin, sorrow, decay, and death, Aylmer's sombre imagination was not long in rendering the birthmark a frightful object, causing him more trouble and horror than ever Georgiana's beauty, whether of soul or sense, had given him delight.

At all the seasons which should have been their happiest, he invariably, and without intending it—nay, in spite of a purpose to the contrary—reverted to this one disastrous topic. Trifling as it at first appeared, it so connected itself with innumerable trains of thought, and modes of feeling, that it became the central point of all. With the morning twilight, Aylmer opened his eyes upon his wife's face, and recognized the symbol of imperfection; and when they sat together at the evening hearth, his eyes wandered stealthily to her cheek, and beheld, flickering with the blaze of the wood fire, the spectral Hand that wrote mortality where he would fain have worshipped. Georgiana soon learned to shudder at his gaze. It needed but a glance, with the peculiar expression that his face often wore, to change the roses of her cheek into a deathlike paleness, amid which the Crimson Hand was brought strongly out, like a *bas-relief*[1] of ruby on the whitest marble.

Late, one night, when the lights were growing dim, so as hardly to betray the stain on the poor wife's cheek, she herself, for the first time, voluntarily took up the subject.

"Do you remember, my dear Aylmer," said she, with a feeble attempt at a smile—"have you any recollection of a dream, last night, about this odious Hand?"

"None! none whatever!" replied Aylmer, starting; but then he added in a dry, cold tone, affected for the sake of concealing the real depth of his emotion—"I might well dream of it; for, before I fell asleep, it had taken a pretty firm hold of my fancy."

"And you did dream of it," continued Georgiana, hastily; for she dreaded lest a gush of tears should interrupt what she had to say—"A terrible dream! I wonder that you can forget it. Is it possible to forget this one expression? 'It is in her heart now—we must have it out!' Reflect, my husband; for by all means I would have you recall that dream."

The mind is in a sad state, when Sleep, the all-involving, cannot confine her spectres within the dim region of her sway, but suffers them to break forth, affrighting this actual life with secrets that perchance belong to a deeper one. Aylmer now remembered his dream. He had fancied himself, with his servant Aminidab, attempting an operation for the removal of the birthmark. But the deeper went the knife, the deeper sank the Hand, until at length its tiny grasp appeared to have caught hold of Georgiana's heart; whence, however, her husband was inexorably resolved to cut or wrench it away.

When the dream had shaped itself perfectly in his memory, Aylmer sat in his wife's presence with a guilty feeling. Truth often finds its way to the mind close-muffled in robes of sleep, and then speaks with uncompromising directness of matters in regard to which we practise an unconscious self-deception, during our waking moments. Until now, he had not been aware of the tyrannizing influence acquired by one idea over his mind, and of the lengths which he might find in his heart to go, for the sake of giving himself peace.

"Aylmer," resumed Georgiana, solemnly, "I know not what may be the cost to both of us, to rid me of this fatal birthmark. Perhaps its removal may cause cureless deformity. Or, it may be, the stain goes as deep as life itself. Again, do we know that there is a possibility, on any terms, of unclasping the firm grip of this little Hand, which was laid upon me before I came into the world?"

"Dearest Georgiana, I have spent much thought upon the subject," hastily interrupted Aylmer—"I am convinced of the perfect practicability of its removal."

"If there be the remotest possibility of it," continued Georgiana, "let the attempt be made, at whatever risk. Danger is nothing to me; for life—while this hateful mark makes me the object of your horror and disgust—life is a burden which I would fling down with joy. Either remove this dreadful Hand, or take my wretched life! You have deep science! All the world bears witness of it. You have achieved great wonders! Cannot you remove this little, little mark, which I cover with the tips of two small fingers? Is this beyond your power, for the sake of your own peace, and to save your poor wife from madness?"

---

[1] *bas-relief* Low relief sculpture, characterized by slightly raised features that project from a flat background.

"Noblest—dearest—tenderest wife!" cried Aylmer, rapturously. "Doubt not my power. I have already given this matter the deepest thought—thought which might almost have enlightened me to create a being less perfect than yourself. Georgiana, you have led me deeper than ever into the heart of science. I feel myself fully competent to render this dear cheek as faultless as its fellow; and then, most beloved, what will be my triumph, when I shall have corrected what Nature left imperfect, in her fairest work! Even Pygmalion, when his sculptured woman assumed life,[1] felt not greater ecstasy than mine will be."

"It is resolved, then," said Georgiana, faintly smiling. "And, Aylmer, spare me not, though you should find the birthmark take refuge in my heart at last."

Her husband tenderly kissed her cheek—her right cheek, not that which bore the impress of the Crimson Hand.

The next day, Aylmer apprized his wife of a plan that he had formed, whereby he might have opportunity for the intense thought and constant watchfulness, which the proposed operation would require; while Georgiana, likewise, would enjoy the perfect repose essential to its success. They were to seclude themselves in the extensive apartments occupied by Aylmer as a laboratory, and where, during his toilsome youth, he had made discoveries in the elemental powers of nature, that had roused the admiration of all the learned societies in Europe. Seated calmly in this laboratory, the pale philosopher had investigated the secrets of the highest cloud-region, and of the profoundest mines; he had satisfied himself of the causes that kindled and kept alive the fires of the volcano; and had explained the mystery of fountains, and how it is that they gush forth, some so bright and pure, and others with such rich medicinal[2] virtues, from the dark bosom of the earth. Here, too, at an earlier period, he had studied the wonders of the human frame, and attempted to fathom the very process by which Nature assimilates all her precious influences from earth and air, and from

the spiritual world, to create and foster Man, her masterpiece. The latter pursuit, however, Aylmer had long laid aside, in unwilling recognition of the truth, against which all seekers sooner or later stumble, that our great creative Mother, while she amuses us with apparently working in the broadest sunshine, is yet severely careful to keep her own secrets, and, in spite of her pretended openness, shows us nothing but results. She permits us, indeed, to mar, but seldom to mend, and, like a jealous patentee,[3] on no account to make. Now, however, Aylmer resumed these half-forgotten investigations; not, of course, with such hopes or wishes as first suggested them; but because they involved much physiological truth, and lay in the path of his proposed scheme for the treatment of Georgiana.

As he led her over the threshold of the laboratory, Georgiana was cold and tremulous. Aylmer looked cheerfully into her face, with intent to reassure her, but was so startled with the intense glow of the birthmark upon the whiteness of her cheek, that he could not restrain a strong convulsive shudder. His wife fainted.

"Aminidab! Aminidab!" shouted Aylmer, stamping violently on the floor.

Forthwith, there issued from an inner apartment a man of low stature, but bulky frame, with shaggy hair hanging about his visage, which was grimed with the vapors of the furnace. This personage had been Aylmer's underworker during his whole scientific career, and was admirably fitted for that office by his great mechanical readiness, and the skill with which, while incapable of comprehending a single principle, he executed all the practical details of his master's experiments. With his vast strength, his shaggy hair, his smoky aspect, and the indescribable earthiness that incrusted him, he seemed to represent man's physical nature; while Aylmer's slender figure, and pale, intellectual face, were no less apt a type of the spiritual element.

"Throw open the door of the boudoir, Aminidab," said Aylmer, "and burn a pastille."[4]

"Yes, master," answered Aminadab, looking intently at the lifeless form of Georgiana; and then he muttered

---

[1]   *Pygmalion ... assumed life*   In Greek myth—best known from Ovid's *Metamorphoses*—Pygmalion sculpted a woman of ivory so beautiful that he fell in love with her; upon hearing his lovelorn prayers, the goddess Aphrodite brought the sculpture to life.

[2]   *medicinal*   Appearing as "medical" in the first 1843 printing, this was corrected when the story was reprinted in *Mosses from an Old Manse* (1846).

[3]   *jealous*   Suspicious and overprotective; *patentee*   Someone who holds a patent on an invention.

[4]   *pastille*   Small tablet which releases a fragrance when burned, often for therapeutic purposes.

to himself—"If she were my wife, I'd never part with that birthmark."

When Georgiana recovered consciousness, she found herself breathing an atmosphere of penetrating fragrance, the gentle potency of which had recalled her from her deathlike faintness. The scene around her looked like enchantment. Aylmer had converted those smoky, dingy, sombre rooms, where he had spent his brightest years in recondite pursuits, into a series of beautiful apartments,[1] not unfit to be the secluded abode of a lovely woman. The walls were hung with gorgeous curtains, which imparted the combination of grandeur and grace, that no other species of adornment can achieve; and as they fell from the ceiling to the floor, their rich and ponderous folds, concealing all angles and straight lines, appeared to shut in the scene from infinite space. For aught Georgiana knew, it might be a pavilion among the clouds. And Aylmer, excluding the sunshine, which would have interfered with his chemical processes, had supplied its place with perfumed lamps, emitting flames of various hue, but all uniting in a soft, empurpled radiance. He now knelt by his wife's side, watching her earnestly, but without alarm; for he was confident in his science, and felt that he could draw a magic circle round her, within which no evil might intrude.

"Where am I? Ah, I remember!" said Georgiana, faintly; and she placed her hand over her cheek, to hide the terrible mark from her husband's eyes.

"Fear not, dearest!" exclaimed he, "Do not shrink from me! Believe me, Georgiana, I even rejoice in this single imperfection, since it will be such rapture to remove it."

"Oh, spare me!" sadly replied his wife—"Pray do not look at it again. I never can forget that convulsive shudder."

In order to soothe Georgiana, and, as it were, to release her mind from the burden of actual things, Aylmer now put in practice some of the light and playful secrets which science had taught him among its profounder lore. Airy figures, absolutely bodiless ideas, and forms of unsubstantial beauty, came and danced before her, imprinting their momentary footsteps on beams of light. Though she had some indistinct idea of the method of these optical phenomena, still the illusion was almost perfect enough to warrant the belief that her husband possessed sway over the spiritual world. Then again, when she felt a wish to look forth from her seclusion, immediately, as if her thoughts were answered, the procession of external existence flitted across a screen. The scenery and the figures of actual life were perfectly represented, but with that bewitching, yet indescribable difference, which always makes a picture, an image, or a shadow, so much more attractive than the original. When wearied of this, Aylmer bade her cast her eyes upon a vessel, containing a quantity of earth. She did so, with little interest at first, but was soon startled to perceive the germ of a plant, shooting upward from the soil. Then came the slender stalk—the leaves gradually unfolded themselves—and amid them was a perfect and lovely flower.

"It is magical!" cried Georgiana, "I dare not touch it."

"Nay, pluck it," answered Aylmer, "pluck it, and inhale its brief perfume while you may. The flower will wither in a few moments, and leave nothing save its brown seed-vessels—but thence may be perpetuated a race as ephemeral as itself."

But Georgiana had no sooner touched the flower than the whole plant suffered a blight, its leaves turning coal-black, as if by the agency of fire.

"There was too powerful a stimulus," said Aylmer thoughtfully.

To make up for this abortive[2] experiment, he proposed to take her portrait by a scientific process of his own invention. It was to be effected by rays of light striking upon a polished plate of metal. Georgiana assented—but, on looking at the result, was affrighted to find the features of the portrait blurred and indefinable; while the minute figure of a hand appeared where the cheek should have been. Aylmer snatched the metallic plate, and threw it into a jar of corrosive acid.

Soon, however, he forgot these mortifying failures. In the intervals of study and chemical experiment, he came to her, flushed and exhausted, but seemed invigorated by her presence, and spoke in glowing language of the resources of his art. He gave a history of the long dynasty of the Alchemists, who spent so many ages in quest of the universal solvent, by which the Golden Principle might be elicited from all things vile and

---

[1] *apartments* Rooms.

[2] *abortive* Unfulfilled.

base.[1] Aylmer appeared to believe that, by the plainest scientific logic, it was altogether within the limits of possibility to discover this long-sought medium; but, he added, a philosopher who should go deep enough to acquire the power, would attain too lofty a wisdom to stoop to the exercise of it. Not less singular were his opinions in regard to the Elixir Vitae.[2] He more than intimated that it was at his option to concoct a liquid that should prolong life for years—perhaps interminably—but that it would produce a discord in nature, which all the world, and chiefly the quaffer of the immortal nostrum,[3] would find cause to curse.

"Aylmer, are you in earnest?" asked Georgiana, looking at him with amazement and fear; "it is terrible to possess such power, or even to dream of possessing it!"

"Oh, do not tremble, my love!" said her husband, "I would not wrong either you or myself by working such inharmonious effects upon our lives. But I would have you consider how trifling, in comparison, is the skill requisite to remove this little Hand."

At the mention of the birthmark, Georgiana, as usual, shrank, as if a red-hot iron had touched her cheek.

Again Aylmer applied himself to his labors. She could hear his voice in the distant furnace-room, giving directions to Aminidab, whose harsh, uncouth, misshapen tones were audible in response, more like the grunt or growl of a brute than human speech. After hours of absence, Aylmer re-appeared, and proposed that she should now examine his cabinet of chemical products, and natural treasures of the earth. Among the former he showed her a small vial, in which, he remarked, was contained a gentle, yet most powerful fragrance, capable of impregnating all the breezes that blow across a kingdom. They were of inestimable value, the contents of that little vial; and, as he said so, he threw some of the perfume into the air, and filled the room with piercing and invigorating delight.

"And what is this?" asked Georgiana, pointing to a small crystal globe, containing a gold-colored liquid. "It is so beautiful to the eye, that I could imagine it the Elixir of Life."

"In one sense it is," replied Aylmer, "or rather the Elixir of Immortality. It is the most precious poison that ever was concocted in this world. By its aid, I could apportion the lifetime of any mortal at whom you might point your finger. The strength of the dose would determine whether he were to linger out years, or drop dead in the midst of a breath. No king, on his guarded throne, could keep his life, if I, in my private station, should deem that the welfare of millions justified me in depriving him of it."

"Why do you keep such a terrific[4] drug?" inquired Georgiana in horror.

"Do not mistrust me, dearest!" said her husband, smiling; "its virtuous potency is yet greater than its harmful one. But, see! here is a powerful cosmetic. With a few drops of this, in a vase of water, freckles may be washed away as easily as the hands are cleansed. A stronger infusion would take the blood out of the cheek, and leave the rosiest beauty a pale ghost."

"Is it with this lotion that you intend to bathe my cheek?" asked Georgiana anxiously.

"Oh, no!" hastily replied her husband—"this is merely superficial. Your case demands a remedy that shall go deeper."

In his interviews with Georgiana, Aylmer generally made minute inquiries as to her sensations, and whether the confinement of the rooms, and the temperature of the atmosphere, agreed with her. These questions had such a particular drift, that Georgiana began to conjecture that she was already subjected to certain physical influences, either breathed in with the fragrant air, or taken with her food. She fancied, likewise—but it might be altogether fancy—that there was a stirring up of her system—a strange, indefinite sensation creeping through her veins, and tingling, half painfully, half pleasurably, at her heart. Still, whenever she dared to look into the mirror, there she beheld herself, pale as a white rose, and with the crimson birthmark stamped upon her cheek. Not even Aylmer now hated it so much as she.

---

[1]   *Alchemists ... vile and base* Alchemy was a protoscientific school, widespread during the medieval and Early Modern periods, which sought to discover the nature of physical substances and how to transform them, particularly how to transform "baser" materials into gold.

[2]   *Elixir Vitae* Elixir of Life; another substance sought by the Alchemists, thought to delay death indefinitely.

[3]   *nostrum* Concoction.

[4]   *terrific* I.e., terrible; of awe-inspiring power.

To dispel the tedium of the hours which her husband found it necessary to devote to the processes of combination and analysis, Georgiana turned over the volumes of his scientific library. In many dark old tomes, she met with chapters full of romance and poetry. They were the works of the philosophers of the middle ages, such as Albertus Magnus, Cornelius Agrippa, Paracelsus, and the famous friar who created the prophetic Brazen Head.[1] All these antique naturalists stood in advance of their centuries, yet were imbued with some of their[2] credulity, and therefore were believed, and perhaps imagined themselves, to have acquired from the investigation of nature a power above nature, and from physics a sway over the spiritual world. Hardly less curious and imaginative were the early volumes of the Transactions of the Royal Society,[3] in which the members, knowing little of the limits of natural possibility, were continually recording wonders, or proposing methods whereby wonders might be wrought.

But, to Georgiana, the most engrossing volume was a large folio from her husband's own hand, in which he had recorded every experiment of his scientific career, with its original aim, the methods adopted for its development, and its final success or failure, with the circumstances to which either event was attributable. The book, in truth, was both the history and emblem of his ardent, ambitious, imaginative, yet practical and laborious life. He handled physical details, as if there were nothing beyond them; yet spiritualized them all, and redeemed himself from materialism by his strong and eager aspiration towards the infinite. In his grasp, the veriest clod of earth assumed a soul. Georgiana, as she read, reverenced Aylmer, and loved him more profoundly than ever, but with a less entire dependence on his judgment than heretofore. Much as he had accomplished, she could not but observe that his most splendid successes were almost invariably failures, if compared with the ideal at which he aimed. His brightest diamonds were the merest pebbles, and felt to be so by himself, in comparison with the inestimable gems which lay hidden beyond his reach. The volume, rich with achievements that had won renown for its author, was yet as melancholy a record as ever mortal hand had penned. It was the sad confession, and continual exemplification, of the short-comings of the composite man—the spirit burdened with clay and working in matter—and of the despair that assails the higher nature, at finding itself so miserably thwarted by the earthly part. Perhaps every man of genius, in whatever sphere, might recognise the image of his own experience in Aylmer's journal.

So deeply did these reflections affect Georgiana, that she laid her face upon the open volume, and burst into tears. In this situation she was found by her husband.

"It is dangerous to read in a sorcerer's books," said he, with a smile, though his countenance was uneasy and displeased. "Georgiana, there are pages in that volume which I can scarcely glance over and keep my senses. Take heed lest it prove as detrimental to you!"

"It has made me worship you more than ever," said she.

"Ah! wait for this one success," rejoined he, "then worship me if you will. I shall deem myself hardly unworthy of it. But, come! I have sought you for the luxury of your voice. Sing to me, dearest!"

So she poured out the liquid music of her voice to quench the thirst of his spirit. He then took his leave, with a boyish exuberance of gaiety, assuring her that her seclusion would endure but a little longer, and that the result was already certain. Scarcely had he departed, when Georgiana felt irresistibly impelled to follow him. She had forgotten to inform Aylmer of a symptom, which, for two or three hours past, had begun to excite her attention. It was a sensation in the fatal birthmark, not painful, but which induced a restlessness throughout her system. Hastening after her husband, she intruded, for the first time, into the laboratory.

The first thing that struck her eye was the furnace, that hot and feverish worker, with the intense glow of its fire, which, by the quantities of soot clustered above it, seemed to have been burning for ages. There was a

---

[1] *Albertus Magnus ... Brazen Head* European scientists and philosophers of the Middle Ages and Renaissance, whose works were associated with alchemy and the occult (although any alchemical texts associated with Magnus have likely been misattributed); the Brazen Head, a talking head which could answer questions, was reputedly created by the medieval scholar Roger Bacon.

[2] *their* This was corrected from "its" in *Mosses from an Old Manse.*

[3] *Royal Society* Scientific community founded in London in the mid-1600s.

distilling apparatus in full operation. Around the room were retorts, tubes, cylinders, crucibles,[1] and other apparatus of chemical research. An electrical machine stood ready for immediate use. The atmosphere felt oppressively close, and was tainted with gaseous odors, which had been tormented forth by the processes of science. The severe and homely simplicity of the apartment, with its naked walls and brick pavement, looked strange, accustomed as Georgiana had become to the fantastic elegance of her boudoir. But what chiefly, indeed almost solely, drew her attention, was the aspect of Aylmer himself.

He was pale as death, anxious, and absorbed, and hung over the furnace as if it depended upon his utmost watchfulness whether the liquid, which it was distilling, should be the draught of immortal happiness or misery. How different from the sanguine and joyous mien that he had assumed for Georgiana's encouragement!

"Carefully now, Aminidab! Carefully, thou human machine! Carefully, thou man of clay!" muttered Aylmer, more to himself than his assistant. "Now, if there be a thought too much or too little, it is all over!"

"Hoh! hoh!" mumbled Aminadab—"look, master, look!"

Aylmer raised his eyes hastily, and at first reddened, then grew paler than ever, on beholding Georgiana. He rushed towards her, and seized her arm with a grip that left the print of his fingers upon it.

"Why do you come hither? Have you no trust in your husband?" cried he impetuously. "Would you throw the blight of that fatal birthmark over my labors? It is not well done. Go, prying woman, go!"

"Nay, Aylmer," said Georgiana, with the firmness of which she possessed no stinted endowment, "it is not you that have a right to complain. You mistrust your wife! You have concealed the anxiety with which you watch the development of this experiment. Think not so unworthily of me, my husband! Tell me all the risk we run; and fear not that I shall shrink, for my share in it is far less than your own!"

"No, no, Georgiana!" said Aylmer impatiently, "it must not be."

"I submit," replied she, calmly. "And, Aylmer, I shall quaff whatever draught you bring me; but it will be on the same principle that would induce me to take a dose of poison, if offered by your hand."

"My noble wife," said Aylmer, deeply moved, "I knew not the height and depth of your nature, until now. Nothing shall be concealed. Know, then, that this Crimson Hand, superficial as it seems, has clutched its grasp into your being, with a strength of which I had no previous conception. I have already administered agents powerful enough to do aught except to change your entire physical system. Only one thing remains to be tried. If that fail us, we are ruined!"

"Why did you hesitate to tell me this?" asked she.

"Because, Georgiana," said Aylmer, in a low voice, "there is danger!"

"Danger? There is but one danger—that this horrible stigma shall be left upon my cheek!" cried Georgiana. "Remove it! remove it!—whatever be the cost—or we shall both go mad!"

"Heaven knows, your words are too true," said Aylmer, sadly. "And now, dearest, return to your boudoir. In a little while, all will be tested."

He conducted her back, and took leave of her with a solemn tenderness, which spoke far more than his words how much was now at stake. After his departure, Georgiana became rapt in musings. She considered the character of Aylmer, and did it completer justice than at any previous moment. Her heart exulted, while it trembled, at his honorable love, so pure and lofty that it would accept nothing less than perfection, nor miserably make itself contented with an earthlier nature than he had dreamed of. She felt how much more precious was such a sentiment, than that meaner kind which would have borne with the imperfection for her sake, and have been guilty of treason to holy love, by degrading its perfect idea to the level of the actual. And, with her whole spirit, she prayed that, for a single moment, she might satisfy his highest and deepest conception. Longer than one moment, she well knew, it could not be; for his spirit was ever on the march—ever ascending—and each instant required something that was beyond the scope of the instant before.

The sound of her husband's footsteps aroused her. He bore a crystal goblet, containing a liquor colorless as water, but bright enough to be the draught of

---

[1]   *retorts* Vessels used to distill liquids; *crucibles* Heat-resistant vessels for the fusing of molten metals.

immortality. Aylmer was pale; but it seemed rather the consequence of a highly wrought state of mind, and tension of spirit, than of fear or doubt.

"The concoction of the draught has been perfect," said he, in answer to Georgiana's look. "Unless all my science have deceived me, it cannot fail."

"Save on your account, my dearest Aylmer," observed his wife, "I might wish to put off this birth-mark of mortality by relinquishing mortality itself, in preference to any other mode. Life is but a sad possession to those who have attained precisely the degree of moral advancement at which I stand. Were I weaker and blinder, it might be happiness. Were I stronger, it might be endured hopefully. But, being what I find myself, methinks I am of all mortals the most fit to die."

"You are fit for heaven without tasting death!" replied her husband. "But why do we speak of dying? The draught cannot fail. Behold its effect upon this plant!"

On the window-seat there stood a geranium, dis-eased with yellow blotches, which had overspread all its leaves. Aylmer poured a small quantity of the liquid upon the soil in which it grew. In a little time, when the roots of the plant had taken up the moisture, the unsightly blotches began to be extinguished in a living verdure.

"There needed no proof," said Georgiana, quietly. "Give me the goblet. I joyfully stake all upon your word."

"Drink, then, thou lofty creature!" exclaimed Aylmer, with fervid admiration. "There is no taint of imperfection on thy spirit. Thy sensible frame, too, shall soon be all perfect!"

She quaffed the liquid, and returned the goblet to his hand.

"It is grateful," said she, with a placid smile. "Methinks it is like water from a heavenly fountain; for it contains I know not what of unobtrusive fragrance and deliciousness. It allays a feverish thirst, that had parched me for many days. Now, dearest, let me sleep. My earthly senses are closing over my spirit, like the leaves around the heart of a rose, at sunset."

She spoke the last words with a gentle reluctance, as if it required almost more energy than she could command to pronounce the faint and lingering syllables.

Scarcely had they loitered through her lips, ere she was lost in slumber. Aylmer sat by her side, watching her aspect with the emotions proper to a man, the whole value of whose existence was involved in the process now to be tested. Mingled with this mood, however, was the philosophic investigation, characteristic of the man of science. Not the minutest symptom escaped him. A heightened flush of the cheek—a slight irregu-larity of breath—a quiver of the eyelid—a hardly perceptible tremor through the frame—such were the details which, as the moments passed, he wrote down in his folio[1] volume. Intense thought had set its stamp upon every previous page of that volume; but the thoughts of years were all concentrated upon the last.

While thus employed, he failed not to gaze often at the fatal Hand, and not without a shudder. Yet once, by a strange and unaccountable impulse, he pressed it with his lips. His spirit recoiled, however, in the very act, and Georgiana, out of the midst of her deep sleep, moved uneasily and murmured, as if in remonstrance. Again, Aylmer resumed his watch. Nor was it with-out avail. The Crimson Hand, which at first had been strongly visible upon the marble paleness of Georgiana's cheek, now grew more faintly outlined. She remained not less pale than ever; but the birthmark, with every breath that came and went, lost somewhat of its former distinctness. Its presence had been awful;[2] its departure was more awful still. Watch the stain of the rainbow fading out of the sky, and you will know how that mys-terious symbol passed away.

"By Heaven, it is well nigh gone!" said Aylmer to himself, in almost irrepressible ecstasy. "I can scarcely trace it now. Success! Success! And now it is like the faintest rose-color. The slightest flush of blood across her cheek would overcome it. But she is so pale!"

He drew aside the window-curtain, and suffered the light of natural day to fall into the room, and rest upon her cheek. At the same time, he heard a gross, hoarse chuckle, which he had long known as his servant Aminidab's expression of delight.

"Ah, clod! Ah, earthly mass!" cried Aylmer, laughing in a sort of frenzy. "You have served me well! Matter and Spirit—Earth and Heaven—have both done their

---

[1] *folio* Ledger or notebook.

[2] *awful* Awe-inspiring.

part in this! Laugh, thing of the senses! You have earned the right to laugh."

These exclamations broke Georgiana's sleep. She slowly unclosed her eyes, and gazed into the mirror, which her husband had arranged for that purpose. A faint smile flitted over her lips, when she recognized how barely perceptible was now that Crimson Hand, which had once blazed forth with such disastrous brilliancy as to scare away all their happiness. But then her eyes sought Aylmer's face, with a trouble and anxiety that he could by no means account for.

"My poor Aylmer!" murmured she.

"Poor? Nay, richest! Happiest! Most favored!" exclaimed he. "My peerless bride, it is successful! You are perfect!"

"My poor Aylmer!" she repeated, with a more than human tenderness. "You have aimed loftily! you have done nobly! Do not repent that, with so high and pure a feeling, you have rejected the best that earth could offer. Aylmer—dearest Aylmer—I am dying!"

Alas, it was too true! The fatal Hand had grappled with the mystery of life, and was the bond by which an angelic spirit kept itself in union with a mortal frame. As the last crimson tint of the birthmark—that sole token of human imperfection—faded from her cheek, the parting breath of the now perfect woman passed into the atmosphere, and her soul, lingering a moment near her husband, took its heavenward flight. Then a hoarse, chuckling laugh was heard again! Thus ever does the gross Fatality of Earth exult in its invariable triumph over the immortal essence, which, in this dim sphere of half-development, demands the completeness of a higher state. Yet, had Alymer reached a profounder wisdom, he need not thus have flung away the happiness, which would have woven his mortal life of the self-same texture with the celestial. The momentary circumstance was too strong for him; he failed to look beyond the shadowy scope of Time, and living once for all in Eternity, to find the perfect Future in the present.
—1843

HENRY WADSWORTH LONGFELLOW

1807 – 1882

Throughout the second half of the nineteenth century there could be no doubt as to the identity of the best-known, most widely read and most highly esteemed American poet: Henry Wadsworth Longfellow. In a century when accentual syllabic meters dominated the world of English-language poetry, Longfellow was an accomplished versifier in virtually every accentual syllabic form. In an era when short lyric poetry had not yet crowded out longer narrative forms, Longfellow was an acknowledged master of narrative in verse. In a nation that largely looked to its poets to clothe in romance a history too often driven by acquisitiveness and cruelty, Longfellow shaped a sense of gentle and cooperative nationhood—and shaped it in words that adults and schoolchildren alike could readily commit to memory. When, as President, Lincoln asked his friend Noah Brooks to recite part of "The Building of the Ship," Lincoln's "eyes filled with tears and his cheeks were wet" as Brooks delivered the final section ("sail on, O ship of State / Sail on, O Union, strong and great"); Lincoln was so moved that he "did not speak for several minutes. He finally said, with simplicity, 'It is a wonderful gift, to be able to stir men like that.'"

Longfellow's background was one of privilege. He was born in Portland, Maine (at a time when Maine was still a district within the state of Massachusetts) on 27 February, 1807. His mother, the former Zilpah Wadsworth, was an accomplished pianist whose family could trace their ancestors to the families who had come to America on the *Mayflower* in 1620, and his father, Stephen Longfellow, was one of Maine's leading citizens—a Harvard graduate and a lawyer who would later serve as a judge and as a member of Congress. Longfellow's childhood was quiet and bookish, and his literary ambitions were evident early on; his first poem was published in the *Portland Gazette* when he was just thirteen. At fifteen he entered Maine's leading college, Bowdoin (where his father, a former overseer of the school, remained a trustee). Not long after his graduation in 1825, Longfellow successfully applied for the post of professor of Modern Languages at Bowdoin—though the appointment was conditional on his willingness to spend several years abroad familiarizing himself with the languages he would be expected to teach. Longfellow spent the next three years traveling and studying in Europe, and retuned to Bowdoin to take up his professorship in 1829, by then conversant with the languages and literatures of France, Italy, Spain, and Germany. In 1831 he married Mary Potter, a friend of his sister's who, like Longfellow, was of a distinguished legal family. And within a few years he had published a number of textbooks, as well as numerous articles on European literatures—and he had written a good deal of poetry, most of it in the form of translations.

From the beginning, Longfellow had grand aspirations that he felt could not be realized among the "dust and cobwebs of this country college"—as he described Bowdoin. He had cultivated a relationship with George Ticknor, Harvard's distinguished Professor of Modern Languages, and when Ticknor retired in 1834, Longfellow (at the age of 27) was offered the post. He followed his previous pattern of going abroad for an extended period to immerse himself in foreign languages and literatures, this time spending a year and a half in Europe.

When he returned from Europe to take up his Harvard post, Longfellow was a widower; Mary had died in 1835, following a miscarriage. Eight months after Mary's death, however, while still traveling in Europe, he had met Frances ("Fanny") Appleton, a well-educated and witty young woman from an established and very wealthy Massachusetts family. Appleton rejected Longfellow when, in 1837, he first proposed marriage to her—and she was further alienated when in 1839 he published *Hyperion*, a prose romance informed by the history of their relationship that enjoyed little success. Longfellow's 1839 volume of verse, *Voices of the Night*, however, was met with an enthusiastic reception; one of the poems included in it, "A Psalm of Life," became one of nineteenth-century America's most frequently recited poems. Popular too was his 1841 volume, *Ballads and Other Poems*; of the poems in that volume, "The Wreck of the Hesperus," "The Village Blacksmith," and "Excelsior" received particular praise, with "Excelsior" being reprinted in newspapers across America and becoming popular too in a version set to music.

Longfellow's passion for Appleton remained undimmed through these years, and eventually he won her over. The two were married in 1843, and Longfellow's father purchased for them the large, historic house in Cambridge, Massachusetts in which Longfellow had until then been renting rooms.

The previous year, with little fanfare, Longfellow had published a pamphlet of antislavery verse, *Poems on Slavery*, which was widely distributed by abolitionist societies. Though he steered clear thereafter of public engagement in the controversial political issues of the day, his abolitionist commitment was unwavering; during the 1850s he is now known to have purchased the freedom of a number of enslaved people.

For the next twelve years Longfellow combined his professorship with a prolific output, and became more popular with each passing year. His long narrative poems *Evangeline* (1847) and *The Song of Hiawatha* (1855) were particular successes (by 1857 the former had sold close to 36,000 copies and the latter over 50,000 copies) and they were critical successes as well, in Britain as well as in America. His poems were acclaimed above all for their sonorousness and for their affective qualities—for instilling in readers a love of nature and (though Longfellow always eschewed crude or overtly jingoistic appeals) an appreciation of America and its history. They were acclaimed too for the sincere goodwill that they were felt to convey—and for the moral effect that such goodwill was felt to exert upon readers. The view of Longfellow and his poetry that was expressed by the *Huntington Democrat* may seem extravagant to twenty-first-century sensibilities, but it was not untypical: "No person has ever read his writings without feeling bettered thereby, and without feeling filled with a love for the good, true, and pure."

By the late 1850s Longfellow was firmly established as one of America's leading literary figures—sufficiently so that he felt able to resign his professorship at Harvard in order to focus exclusively on his writing. His marriage was a happy one, and the couple had six children. On 9 July 1861, however, the family was devastated by a catastrophic accident. As the *New York Times* reported it,

> [Mrs. Fanny Longfellow was] seated at her library table, making seals for the entertainment of her two youngest children. A match or a piece of lighted paper caught her dress, and she was in a moment enveloped in flames. Professor Longfellow, who was in his study, ran to her assistance, and succeeded in extinguishing the flames, with considerable injury to himself, but too late for the rescue of her life.

Over the next several years Longfellow increasingly turned to translation, though he continued to publish original work as well throughout the 1860s and 1870s. When he died, aged 75, he was mourned throughout America, and his passing was soon commemorated in Poets' Corner, Westminster Abbey, in London; he was the first American to be so honored.

Poems such as "A Psalm of Life" and "Paul Revere's Ride" continued to be memorized by schoolchildren well into the twentieth century, and continued to be enormously popular among adults as well; when a National Poetry Poll to choose America's favorite poem was run in over 250 newspapers in 1929, two Longfellow poems placed in the top ten ("A Psalm of Life" at number 1, and *Evangeline* at number 6), and no fewer than ten Longfellow poems were among the top fifty. In the literary and scholarly community, however, Longfellow's sonorousness was more and more devalued, and the substance of his poetry was more and more often dismissed as shallow, simplistic, and sentimental. Even in the late nineteenth century educated opinion had often expressed reservations about Longfellow's supposed greatness as a poet. An obituary that appeared on 25 March 1882 in the Philadelphia *Times*, for example, delicately qualified its praise for his poetic accomplishment:

His verse, while it is not always artistically exact, has always a natural ease, a graceful movement, that conveys the impression of great elevation of thought, even where the thought does not really rise very far from earth.

By the mid-twentieth century, Longfellow's importance was widely viewed as being merely historical; it was considered to be to his credit that he had come "nearer than anyone else to being the voice of the [nineteenth-century] man in the street and on the farm" (as Henry Seidel Canby put it in 1947), but the poems themselves (with the exception of a few lyrics) came to be less and less thought of as an important part of the canon of American literature. In his influential *Oxford Companion to American Literature* (which went through six editions between 1944 and 1995), James D. Hart dismissed Longfellow as "lacking in passion and high imagination, and ... too decorous, benign, and sweet."

The twenty-first century has brought new questions as to Longfellow's place in American literature. In 1947 it was considered a sign of the breadth of a writer's appeal if he could be described as "the voice of the man in the street"; by the twenty-first century the maleness and the presumed whiteness of the "voice of the man in the street" paradigm was becoming increasingly evident—and Longfellow's vision as a highly privileged white male has come on those grounds to seem if anything even more limited than it did to mid-twentieth-century critics.

Several other twenty-first-century trends have worked in the other direction, though, and have helped to renew serious interest in Longfellow as a poet of real importance. One is simply the increased interest in literary history that has characterized literary studies since the early 1990s. A second has been a revival of interest in the force that appeals to the emotions can exert in the interplay between a text and an audience; whereas modernism and postmodernism tended to distrust or to disparage overt expressions of sentiment in literary works, sentiment has become a topic of considerable interest to many twenty-first-century critics. And a third has been a renewed interest in traditional poetic forms. That renewed interest has led to a renewed appreciation of the extraordinary range of Longfellow's formal accomplishment, even in unusual and highly challenging meters. Finally, increased engagement with transatlantic and transnational approaches to literature has fostered a greater appreciation of Longfellow's lifelong interest in reaching across cultural and linguistic barriers. Where Longfellow will settle into the canon of American literature as it continues to be re-shaped in the twenty-first century remains a question of considerable interest, with no clear answer.

Newspaper notice of "Longfellow Entertainment," from the *Carolina Watchman* (Salisbury, Carolina), 23 February 1888. Events of this sort were common throughout the United States in the years following Longfellow's death.

NOTE ON THE TEXTS: Where possible we have based our text on the first-published text. Longfellow's poetry presents few large textual issues, but with several of his best-known poems the texts of the originally published magazine versions differ in some respects from those of the versions published later in bound book collections. In a number of such cases, we have drawn attention in the footnotes to significant differences between the texts. Where no magazine version exists, we have used the first published version in book form as our base text, while also consulting other editions—notably the Cambridge *Complete Poetical Works* (1893), edited by H.E. Scudder, and the Library of America *Poems and Other Writings* (2000), edited by J.D. McClatchy. Spelling and punctuation have been modernized in accordance with the practices of this anthology.

⌘⌘⌘

A Psalm of Life[1]

What the Heart of the Young Man Said to the Psalmist[2]

Tell me not, in mournful numbers,[3]
　　Life is but an empty dream!
For the soul is dead that slumbers,
　　And things are not what they seem.

5　Life is real! Life is earnest![4]
　　And the grave is not its goal;
Dust thou art, to dust returnest,[5]
　　Was not spoken of the soul.

Not enjoyment, and not sorrow,
10　　Is our destined end or way;

But to act,[6] that each tomorrow
　　Find us farther than today.

Art is long, and Time is fleeting,
　　And our hearts, though stout° and brave,　　*resolute*
15　Still, like muffled drums, are beating
　　Funeral marches to the grave.

In the world's broad field of battle,
　　In the bivouac of Life,
Be not like dumb,° driven cattle!　　*silent*
20　　Be a hero in the strife!

Trust no Future, howe'er pleasant!
　　Let the dead Past bury its dead!
Act—act in the living Present!
　　Heart within, and God o'erhead!

25　Lives of great men all remind us
　　We can make our[7] lives sublime,
And, departing, leave behind us
　　Footprints on the sands of time;

Footprints,[8] that perhaps another,
30　　Sailing o'er life's solemn main,°　　*ocean*
A forlorn and shipwrecked brother,
　　Seeing, shall take heart again.

Let us, then, be up and doing,
　　With a heart for any fate;
35　Still achieving, still pursuing,
　　Learn to labor and to wait.
　　　　—1838, 1839

---

[1]　When first published (in the September 1838 issue of *The Knickerbocker: or, New-York Monthly Magazine*) the poem was prefaced by three lines adapted from seventeenth-century English poet Richard Crashaw's "Wishes to His (Supposed) Mistress": "[I wish her] life that shall send / A challenge to its end, And when it comes, say, 'Welcome, friend.'" (Longfellow either misremembered two words from the Crashaw stanza, or intentionally altered them; Crashaw's poem reads "dares send" in the first line, and "his end" in the second.) The magazine version numbered the stanzas with the Roman numerals I to IX. Longfellow removed the epigram and the stanza numbers when the poem was published in *Voices of the Night* (1839), and altered some of the punctuation; that version became one of the best-known poems of the nineteenth and early twentieth centuries. Longfellow, who had written the poem soon after the death of his first wife, later said that he had "kept it some time in manuscript, unwilling to show it to anyone, it being a voice from my inmost heart, at a time when I was rallying from depression."

[2]　*the Psalmist* David is traditionally said to have been the author of many of the psalms in the biblical Book of Psalms—including Psalm 103, which includes these lines: "… the Lord has compassion on those who fear him; / for he knows how we are formed, / he remembers that we are dust. / The life of mortals is like grass, they flourish like a flower of the field; / the wind blows over it and it is gone, and its place remembers it no more."

[3]　*numbers* In its metrical pattern, any accentual-syllabic poem is divisible into numbers—regularly patterned groups of stressed and unstressed syllables.

[4]　*Life is real … earnest* The 1838 *Knickerbocker* version has dashes rather than exclamation marks in this line.

[5]　*Dust … returnest* The phrase "earth to earth, ashes to ashes, dust to dust" occurs in the text of the funeral service in the *Book of Common Prayer*. The phrase has its roots in biblical verses such as Ecclesiastes 3.20: "All go unto one place; all are of the dust, and all turn to dust again." See also above regarding Psalm 103.

[6]　*act* In the 1838 *Knickerbocker* version this word is italicized.

[7]　*our* In the 1838 *Knickerbocker* version this word is italicized.

[8]　*Footprints* In both the 1838 *Knickerbocker* version and the 1839 *Voices of the Night* version, footsteps rather than *footprints*. Longfellow revised to *footprints* for his 1850 two-volume *Poems*, and "footprints on the sands of time" became one of the most often quoted lines of American poetry.

The Wreck of the Hesperus[1]

It was the schooner Hesperus,
That sailed the wintry sea;
And the skipper had taken his little daughter,
To bear him company.

5 Blue were her eyes as the fairy-flax,
Her cheeks like the dawn of day,
And her bosom white as the hawthorn buds,
That ope in the month of May.

The skipper he stood beside the helm,
10 His pipe was in his mouth,
And he watched how the veering flaw° did blow *gust*
The smoke now West, now South.

Then up and spake an old Sailòr,
Had sailed to the Spanish Main,[2]
15 "I pray thee, put into yonder port,
For I fear a hurricane.

"Last night, the moon had a golden ring,
And tonight no moon we see!"
The skipper, he blew a whiff from his pipe,
20 And a scornful laugh laughed he.[3]

Colder and louder blew the wind,
A gale from the Northeast.
The snow fell hissing in the brine,
And the billows frothed like yeast.

25 Down came the storm, and smote amain° *quickly*
The vessel in its strength;
She shuddered and paused, like a frighted steed,
Then leaped her cable's length.

"Come hither! come hither! my little daughter,
30 And do not tremble so;
For I can weather the roughest gale
That ever wind did blow."

He wrapped her warm in his seaman's coat
Against the stinging blast;
35 He cut a rope from a broken spar,
And bound her to the mast.

"O father! I hear the church-bells ring,
O say, what may it be?"
"'Tis a fog-bell on a rock-bound coast!"—
40 And he steered for the open sea.

"O father! I hear the sound of guns,
O say, what may it be?"
"Some ship in distress, that cannot live
In such an angry sea!"

45 "O father! I see a gleaming light,
O say, what may it be?"
But the father answered never a word,
A frozen corpse was he.

Lashed to the helm, all stiff and stark,
50 With his face turned to the skies,
The lantern gleamed through the gleaming snow
On his fixed and glassy eyes.

Then the maiden clasped her hands and prayed
That savèd she might be;
55 And she thought of Christ, who stilled the wave,
On the Lake of Galilee.[4]

[1] First published 11 January 1840 in *The New World* (a New York weekly newspaper), this ballad had by the end of that year been widely published in other American newspapers, as well as in Britain in the literary magazine *Bentley's Miscellany*. It became one of Longfellow's most popular poems, and remained so until the second half of the twentieth century, when the ballad form fell from fashion. The poem was twice made into a film (in 1927, and in 1948).
Though the story of Longfellow's ballad is fiction, it has some basis in fact. The poet made this entry in his journal on 17 December 1839: "News of shipwrecks horrible on the coast. Twenty bodies washed ashore near Gloucester, one lashed to a piece of the wreck. There is a reef called Norman's Woe where many of these took place; among others the schooner *Hesperus*. Also the *Sea-flower* on Black Rock. I must write a ballad upon this."

[2] *Spanish Main* Northern coast of South America.

[3] *laughed he* An additional stanza appears at this point in the *New World* version: "I would not put into yonder port, / Nor yet into yonder bay / Though it blew a gale, with fiery hail, / As on the Judgment Day!" This stanza does not appear in later versions—including in the text of the poem as it was published in other newspapers later in the same year.

[4] *Christ ... Galilee* See Matthew 8, Mark 4, and Luke 8; all three gospels recount this incident, in which Jesus is reported to have miraculously calmed the waves when a great storm has blown up on the Sea of Galilee.

And fast through the midnight dark and drear,
    Through the whistling sleet and snow,
Like a sheeted ghost, the vessel swept
60   Tow'rds the reef of Norman's Woe.[1]

And ever the fitful gusts between
    A sound came from the land;
It was the sound of the trampling surf
    On the rocks and the hard sea-sand.

65 The breakers were right beneath her bows,
    She drifted a dreary wreck,
And a whooping billow swept the crew
    Like icicles from her deck.

She struck where the white and fleecy waves
70   Looked soft as carded wool,[2]
But the cruel rocks, they gored her side
    Like the horns of an angry bull.

Her rattling shrouds, all sheathed in ice,
    With the masts went by the board;
75 Like a vessel of glass, she stove and sank,
    Ho! ho! the breakers roared!

At daybreak, on the bleak sea-beach,
    A fisherman stood aghast,
To see the form of a maiden fair,
80   Lashed close to a drifting mast.

The salt sea was frozen on her breast,
    The salt tears in her eyes;
And he saw her hair, like the brown sea-weed,
    On the billows fall and rise.

85 Such was the wreck of the Hesperus,
    In the midnight and the snow!
Christ save us all from a death like this,
    On the reef of Norman's Woe!
—1840

D. Huntington, Illustration for "The Wreck of the Hesperus," *Poems* (Carey and Hart edition), 1845.

---

[1] *Norman's Woe* Reef off the shore of Cape Ann, Gloucester, Massachusetts; the site of many shipwrecks.

[2] *carded wool* Unprocessed wool that has been cleaned and disentangled.

John Gilbert, Illustration for "The Wreck of the Hesperus," *Longfellow's Poetical Works* (Ticknor & Fields edition), 1856.

from *Poems on Slavery*

During the six months Longfellow spent in Europe in 1842 he met with his German translator, Ferdinand Freiligrath, a political radical who was a vehement opponent of slavery. He also corresponded with his close friend Charles Sumner (later to become a leading figure among the Radical Republicans in the American Senate); Sumner suggested that Longfellow write some antislavery poems—"some stirring words that shall move the whole land."

Longfellow liked to steer clear of controversy, but he clearly felt strongly about slavery; for years he made a practice of devoting a portion of his earnings to purchasing freedom for enslaved African Americans, and he predicted following the execution of John Brown in 1859 that a new revolution was coming—"a new Revolution quite as much needed" as that of 1776 had been.

Longfellow published the antislavery poems on their own as a slim volume in 1842. He prefaced the volume with a brief note regarding the death of William Ellery Channing, a leading abolitionist, a leading figure in the Unitarian Church, and one of America's most influential intellectuals. The first of Longfellow's eight poems is dedicated to Channing. The others in the group, as Longfellow noted in his preface, "were written at sea, in the latter part of October, 1842."

The Slave's Dream

Beside the ungathered rice[1] he lay,
　His sickle in his hand;
His breast was bare, his matted hair
　Was buried in the sand.
5　Again, in the mist and shadow of sleep,
　He saw his Native Land.

Wide through the landscape of his dreams
　The lordly Niger[2] flowed;
Beneath the palm-trees on the plain
10　Once more a king he strode;
And heard the tinkling caravans
　Descend the mountain-road.[3]

He saw once more his dark-eyed queen
　Among her children stand;
15　They clasped his neck, they kissed his cheeks,
　They held him by the hand!—
A tear burst from the sleeper's lids
　And fell into the sand.

---

[1]　*ungathered rice* Conditions for enslaved workers were notoriously brutal on American plantations in the South—for workers assigned to harvest rice as much as for those forced to pick cotton or cut sugar cane.

[2]　*Niger* The largest river in West Africa.

[3]　*the tinkling caravans ... road* Trade caravans from the ancient Ghana and Mali empires in the upper reaches of the Niger traveled south and west to the Atlantic coast; north to Marrakech and Morocco; and east to Egypt and Ethiopia. Such caravans operated into the twentieth century.

And then at furious speed he rode
20   Along the Niger's bank;
His bridle-reins were golden chains,
    And, with a martial clank,
At each leap he could feel his scabbard of steel
    Smiting his stallion's flank.

25 Before him, like a blood-red flag,
    The bright flamingoes flew;
From morn till night he followed their flight,
    O'er plains where the tamarind grew,
Till he saw the roofs of Caffre[1] huts,
30   And the ocean rose to view.

At night he heard the lion roar,
    And the hyena scream,
And the river-horse,[2] as he crushed the reeds
    Beside some hidden stream;
35 And it passed, like a glorious roll of drums,
    Through the triumph of his dream.

The forests, with their myriad tongues,
    Shouted of liberty;
And the Blast of the Desert cried aloud,
40   With a voice so wild and free,
That he started in his sleep and smiled
    At their tempestuous glee.

He did not feel the driver's whip,
    Nor the burning heat of day;
45 For Death had illumined the Land of Sleep,
    And his lifeless body lay
A worn-out fetter, that the soul
    Had broken and thrown away!
    —1842

The Slave Singing at Midnight

Loud he sang the psalm of David!
He, a Negro and enslaved,
Sang of Israel's victory,
Sang of Zion,° bright and free.[3]   *Israel*

5   In that hour, when night is calmest,
Sang he from the Hebrew Psalmist,
In a voice so sweet and clear
That I could not choose but hear,

Songs of triumph, and ascriptions,
10 Such as reached the swart° Egyptians,   *swarthy*
When upon the Red Sea coast
Perished Pharaoh and his host.°   *multitude*

And the voice of his devotion
Filled my soul with strange emotion;
15 For its tones by turns were glad,
Sweetly solemn, wildly sad.

Paul and Silas, in their prison,
Sang of Christ, the Lord arisen,
And an earthquake's arm of might
20 Broke their dungeon-gates at night.[4]

But, alas! what holy angel
Brings the Slave this glad evangel?[5]
And what earthquake's arm of might
Breaks his dungeon-gates at night?
    —1842

---

[1] *Caffre* Term (also spelled "Kaffir") widely used in the nine-teenth century to denote sub-Saharan African peoples. (In the twentieth century the term came to be used almost exclusively in pejorative ways, and it is now considered extremely offensive.)

[2] *river-horse* The roots of the word "hippopotamus" are the ancient Greek words for "horse" and "river."

[3] *the psalm ... and free* Several of the biblical psalms (tradition-ally attributed to David) reference the escape of the Israelites from slavery in Egypt, across the Red Sea to freedom; the story has it that God parts the waters of the sea, allowing the Israelites to cross unharmed. When the Egyptian Pharaoh and his forces try to follow, however, the waters close up again, and they perish.

[4] *Paul and Silas ... at night* As recounted in Acts 16.25–31, the apostles Paul and Silas, who had been imprisoned unjustly, prayed for deliverance; the prison was soon shaken by an earthquake, and they were able to escape.

[5] *glad evangel* Good news.

The Quadroon[1] Girl

The slaver in the broad lagoon
    Lay moored with idle sail;
He waited for the rising moon,
    And for the evening gale.

5 Under the shore his boat was tied,
    And all her listless crew
Watched the gray alligator slide
    Into the still bayou.

Odors of orange-flowers, and spice,
10   Reached them from time to time,
Like airs that breathe from Paradise
    Upon a world of crime.

The planter, under his roof of thatch,
    Smoked thoughtfully and slow;
15 The slaver's thumb was on the latch,
    He seemed in haste to go.

He said, "My ship at anchor rides
    In yonder broad lagoon;
I only wait the evening tides,
20   And the rising of the moon."

Before them, with her face upraised,
    In timid attitude,
Like one half curious, half amazed,
    A quadroon maiden stood.

25 Her eyes were large, and full of light,
    Her arms and neck were bare;
No garment she wore save° a kirtle[2] bright,   *except*
    And her own long, raven hair.

And on her lips there played a smile
30   As holy, meek, and faint,
As lights in some cathedral aisle
    The features of a saint.

"The soil is barren—the farm is old,"
    The thoughtful planter said;
35 Then looked upon the slaver's gold,
    And then upon the maid.

His heart within him was at strife
    With such accursed gains:
For he knew whose passions gave her life,
40   Whose blood ran in her veins.

But the voice of nature was too weak;
    He took the glittering gold!
Then pale as death grew the maiden's cheek,
    Her hands as icy cold.

45 The slaver led her from the door,
    He led her by the hand,
To be his slave and paramour
    In a strange and distant land!
 —1842

Whereas, one of the most efficient means of spreading anti-slavery truth, is by the circulation of publications which contain that truth; therefore

Resolved, That 'Longfellow's Poems on slavery' and Mr. O'Connell's 'Letter to the Cincinnati Repealers' which has been recently published in a cheap form, in our judgment, should be extensively circulated, and we recommend that they be placed in every family in our respective neighborhoods.

Resolution passed by the Worcester County Anti-Slavery Society at their annual meeting, held Friday 12 January 1844 (as reported in *The Liberator*, 26 January 1844).

---

1 *Quadroon* Term commonly used in the nineteenth century to classify a person of mixed racial background—specifically, someone with one black and three white grandparents.

2 *kirtle* Simple, one-piece garment.

The Jewish Cemetery at Newport[1]

How strange it seems! These Hebrews in their
   graves,
   Close by the street of this fair seaport town,
Silent beside the never-silent waves,
   At rest in all this moving up and down!

5 The trees are white with dust, that o'er their sleep
   Wave their broad curtains in the south-wind's
      breath,
While underneath these leafy tents they keep
   The long, mysterious Exodus of Death.

And these sepulchral stones, so old and brown,
10   That pave with level flags their burial-place,
Seem like the tablets of the Law, thrown down
   And broken by Moses at the mountain's base.[2]

The very names recorded here are strange,
   Of foreign accent, and of different climes;
15 Alvares and Rivera[3] interchange

With Abraham and Jacob of old times.

"Blessed be God! for he created Death!"
   The mourners said, "and Death is rest and peace";
Then added, in the certainty of faith,
20   "And giveth Life that nevermore shall cease."[4]

Closed are the portals of their Synagogue,
   No Psalms of David now the silence break,
No Rabbi reads the ancient Decalogue[5]
   In the grand dialect the Prophets spake.

25 Gone are the living, but the dead remain,
   And not neglected; for a hand unseen,[6]
Scattering its bounty, like a summer rain,
   Still keeps their graves and their remembrance
      green.

How came they here? What burst of Christian hate,
30   What persecution, merciless and blind,
Drove o'er the sea—that desert desolate—
   These Ishmaels and Hagars[7] of mankind?

They lived in narrow streets and lanes obscure,
   Ghetto and Judenstrass,[8] in mirk and mire;

---

[1] Longfellow visited this cemetery while in Newport, Rhode Island in 1852; the poem was first published in *Putnam's Magazine* in July of that year. The synagogue was founded in 1763 by Isaac Touro; by the end of the century, however (according to an 1869 *Harper's* report, the Jews' Newport "temple was deserted, though from time to time a few of their race congregated to celebrate a feast, a marriage, or funeral; for they reverently brought back their dead, and laid them to rest with the ashes of their forefathers." One of those ceremonies occurred earlier in 1854; Judah Touro (younger son of Isaac) died 28 January 1854; he had long been a resident of New Orleans, but he asked that his remains be buried in Newport. His death and burial were was widely reported, though it is not clear if Longfellow read of them.

[2] *the tablets … mountain's base* See Exodus 32.19. In the biblical story, Moses has ascended Mount Sinai to receive the stone tablets from God (with the commandments inscribed upon them); when he discovers that the Israelites have been worshipping a golden calf—an idol—he becomes infuriated and smashes the tablets.

[3] *Alvares and Rivera* The name "Alvares" (like the name "Touro") is of Portuguese origin, the name "Rivera" of Spanish origin. Both countries expelled their Jewish populations, beginning in the 1490s (as England had done two centuries earlier); Jews from Portugal or Spain had the option of converting to Christianity or leaving their homeland. Many emigrated as a result (to various Mediterranean destinations, as well as across the Atlantic), and emigration continued over the next two hundred years, as many Marranos (those who had converted to Christianity under duress, and who still faced

considerable discrimination) continued to become alienated from the other residents of their Spanish and Portuguese homelands.

[4] *Blessed be … shall cease* The Jewish funeral service involves prayers such as the Tziduk Hadin, which includes these lines: "He brings death and restores life, brings down to the grave and raises up from there. … Righteous are You, Lord, to bring death and to restore life, for in Your hands are entrusted all spirits."

[5] *Decalogue* The Ten Commandments.

[6] *a hand unseen* Abraham Touro, one of the sons of Isaac Touro, the founder of the Touro synagogue, made a bequest to the town of Newport when he died in 1822, in order that the cemetery, the synagogue, and the adjacent street be kept in good repair in perpetuity. In 1854 the *Providence Journal* reported (in an article reporting the death of his brother, Judah) that the "Touro Fund" had grown to "more than $15,000"—in those days a very large sum.

[7] *Ishmaels and Hagars* Outcasts. See Genesis 21 for the story of how Hagar and her son Ishmael are forced to leave their home.

[8] *Ghetto and Judenstrass* In parts of Europe where anti-Semitism had not led to the outright expulsion of Jews, Jews nevertheless faced substantial discrimination. Forms of employment were severely restricted, as was residency; in many cities Jews were restricted to a single, small neighborhood, where cramped conditions prevailed. Venice created the first such neighborhood in 1516, and called it a

35   Taught in the school of patience to endure
          The life of anguish and the death of fire.

      All their lives long, with the unleavened bread
          And bitter herbs of exile[1] and its fears,
      The wasting famine of the heart they fed,
40   And slaked its thirst with marah[2] of their tears.

      Anathema maranatha![3] was the cry
          That rang from town to town, from street to
              street;
      At every gate the accursed Mordecai[4]
          Was mocked and jeered, and spurned by Christian
              feet.

45   Pride and humiliation hand in hand
          Walked with them through the world where'er
              they went;
      Trampled and beaten were they as the sand,
          And yet unshaken as the continent.

      For in the background figures vague and vast
50   Of patriarchs and of prophets rose sublime,
      And all the great traditions of the Past
          They saw reflected in the coming time.

      And thus forever with reverted look
          The mystic volume of the world they read,
55   Spelling it backward, like a Hebrew book,[5]
          Till life became a Legend of the Dead.

But ah! what once has been shall be no more!
    The groaning earth in travail and in pain
Brings forth its races, but does not restore,
60   And the dead nations never rise again.
—1854

from *The Song of Hiawatha*

In the second half of the nineteenth century (and well into the twentieth) Longfellow's *The Song of Hiawatha* was celebrated as a foundational work of American literature. A note that Longfellow provided to accompany the work provides a good deal of the background to the poem:

> This Indian Edda—if I may so call it—is founded on a tradition prevalent among the North American Indians, of a personage of miraculous birth, who was sent among them to clear their rivers, forests, and fishing-grounds, and to teach them the arts of peace. He was known among different tribes by the several names of Michabou, Chiabo, Manabozo, Tarenyawagon, and Hiawatha. Mr. Schoolcraft gives an account of him in his *Algic Researches*, Vol. 1., p. 134; and in his *History, Condition, and Prospects of the Indian Tribes of the United States*, Part 3., p. 314, may be found the Iroquois form of the tradition, derived from the verbal narrations of an Onondaga chief.
>
> Into this old tradition I have woven other curious Indian legends, drawn chiefly from the various and valuable writings of Mr. Schoolcraft, to whom the literary world is greatly indebted for his indefatigable zeal in rescuing from oblivion so much of the legendary lore of the Indians.
>
> The scene of the poem is among the Ojibways on the southern shore of Lake Superior, in the region between the Pictured Rocks and the Grand Sable.

The "Edda" that Longfellow refers to is a collection of medieval Old Norse poems known as *The Poetic Edda*. In addition to being influenced by the heroic tone of such poems, Longfellow was influenced by the form; the unusual meter that he chose for *The*

---

new "ghetto"; soon the name was being used to denote Jewish areas in Florence, Rome, and many other cities; *Judenstrass* German: Jews street.

[1]   *unleavened bread … herbs of exile*   Bitter herbs and unleavened bread are among the foods traditionally eaten at Passover, commemorating the Exodus—the Jews' escape from slavery across the Red Sea into Egypt.

[2]   *marah*   Bitter water; see Exodus 15.22–25.

[3]   *Anathema maranatha!*   See 1 Corinthians 21–22; the apostle Paul calls for anyone who does not love Jesus Christ to be cursed ("Anathema Maranatha").

[4]   *Mordecai*   A central figure in the biblical book of Esther—but here, simply a common Jewish name.

[5]   *Spelling … Hebrew book*   Lines of Hebrew are read right to left.

Song of Hiawatha—trochaic tetrameter[1]—has some affinities with the rhythms of old Scandinavian verse. For the subject matter of his poem, Longfellow largely relied, as he says, on the writings of Henry Rowe Schoolcraft—who had himself relied extensively on the work of his wife, Jane Johnston Schoolcraft, the daughter of an Ojibwe mother and a Scotch-Irish father. (See Jane Johnston Schoolcraft's author entry elsewhere in this anthology.)

As is now universally accepted by historians, there was a historical figure named Hiawatha, who played a central role in bringing peace to his people.[2] Longfellow's poem, however, is as much about myth and legend as it is about history. As he had discovered in Schoolcraft's writings, the "personage of miraculous birth, … sent to teach the arts of peace" was a traditional mythic figure who went by different names in many different native traditions. Drawing on the mythology of the "Noble Savage" that had become established in white culture, as well as on Indigenous myths and traditions (in particular, those of the Ojibwe), Longfellow crafted a poem that millions of readers on both sides of the Atlantic found deeply affecting. The exuberant response of the reviewer of the *Aberdeen Journal* (who had obtained an advance copy in November 1855) gives some sense of the degree of enthusiasm that *The Song of Hiawatha* inspired in many quarters:

> As we read [the sections of the poem], at every line we become enchanted more and more with their wild and mystic, yet simple and homely beauty. Each of them, after the first two, relates a separate adventure of Hiawatha, the hero of the poem. This

Hiawatha is a kind of demigod—a semi-mythical personage. …

Situating his poem in a semi-mythical past made it possible for Longfellow to steer clear of the pressing controversies of his own time regarding the settler colonists and the Indigenous peoples of America. *The Song of Hiawatha* ends with the arrival of white people in North America, and Hiawatha experiences a vague vision of how the settler colonialists will sweep across the continent:

> In the woodlands rang their axes,
> Smoked their towns in all the valleys,
> Over all the lakes and rivers
> Rushes their great canoes of thunder.

A partial exception has been made with this poem to the anthology policy of modernizing spelling and punctuation; Longfellow often capitalizes words such as "Winter" or "Prairie" in the poem; though in many cases these entities are not clearly personified, it seems likely that he intended there to be a suggestion of personification; on that assumption we have retained such capitalizations in the text provided here.

One chapter of *The Song of Hiawatha* is included in these pages; a much more substantial set of excerpts is included as part of the website component of this anthology.

Introduction

Should you ask me, whence these stories?
Whence these legends and traditions,
With the odors of the forest
With the dew and damp of meadows,
5   With the curling smoke of wigwams,
With the rushing of great rivers,
With their frequent repetitions,
And their wild reverberations
As of thunder in the mountains?
10   I should answer, I should tell you,
"From the forests and the prairies,
From the great lakes of the Northland,
From the land of the Ojibways,
From the land of the Dacotahs,
15   From the mountains, moors, and fen-lands° *marshlands*

---

1   *trochaic tetrameter*   In verse written in trochaic tetrameter, a line typically consists of four groups of syllables, with each group typically consisting of a stressed syllable followed by an unstressed syllable.

2   *Hiawatha … his people*   Following a long period of conflict within the Iroquois Confederacy, the prophet Dekanawida and his disciple Hayonhwatha (variously spelled Deganawida and Hiawatha) arranged a series of meetings of the feuding Iroquois nations, and managed to negotiate a lasting peace accord—the Great Law of Peace. Modern historians have not reached a consensus of precisely when these momentous developments occurred; some are of the view that the peace accord was reached in the sixteenth century CE, others that it occurred some centuries earlier. But all agree that the legend of Deganawida and Hiawatha is based on a series of historical events—events that were crucial to the formation of what became the most powerful and influential Indigenous group in the northeast of the continent.

Where the heron, the Shuh-shuh-gah,
Feeds among the reeds and rushes.
I repeat them as I heard them
From the lips of Nawadaha,
20 The musician, the sweet singer."
     Should you ask where Nawadaha
Found these songs so wild and wayward,
Found these legends and traditions,
I should answer, I should tell you,
25 "In the bird's-nests of the forest,
In the lodges of the beaver,
In the hoof-prints of the bison,
In the eyry[1] of the eagle!
     "All the wild-fowl sang them to him,
30 In the moorlands and the fen-lands,
In the melancholy marshes;
Chetowaik, the plover, sang them,
Mahng, the loon, the wild-goose, Wawa,
The blue heron, the Shuh-shuh-gah,
35 And the grouse, the Mushkodasa!"
     If still further you should ask me,
Saying, "Who was Nawadaha?
Tell us of this Nawadaha,"
I should answer your inquiries
40 Straightway in such words as follow.
     "In the Vale of Tawasentha,[2]
In the green and silent valley,
By the pleasant water-courses,
Dwelt the singer Nawadaha.
45 Round about the Indian village
Spread the meadows and the corn-fields,
And beyond them stood the forest,
Stood the groves of singing pine-trees,
Green in Summer, white in Winter,
50 Ever sighing, ever singing.
     "And the pleasant water-courses,
You could trace them through the valley,
By the rushing in the Spring-time,
By the alders in the Summer,
55 By the white fog in the Autumn,
By the black line in the Winter;
And beside them dwelt the singer,
In the Vale of Tawasentha,

In the green and silent valley.
60   "There he sang of Hiawatha,
Sang the Song of Hiawatha,
Sang his wondrous birth and being,
How he prayed and how he fasted,
How he lived, and toiled, and suffered,
65 That the tribes of men might prosper,
That he might advance his people!"
     Ye who love the haunts of Nature,
Love the sunshine of the meadow,
Love the shadow of the forest,
70 Love the wind among the branches,
And the rain-shower and the snow-storm,
And the rushing of great rivers
Through their palisades of pine-trees,
And the thunder in the mountains,
75 Whose innumerable echoes
Flap like eagles in their eyries;
Listen to these wild traditions,
To this Song of Hiawatha!
     Ye who love a nation's legends,
80 Love the ballads of a people,
That like voices from afar off
Call to us to pause and listen,
Speak in tones so plain and childlike,
Scarcely can the ear distinguish
85 Whether they are sung or spoken;
Listen to this Indian Legend,
To this Song of Hiawatha!
     Ye whose hearts are fresh and simple,
Who have faith in God and Nature,
90 Who believe that in all ages
Every human heart is human,
That in even savage bosoms
There are longings, yearnings, strivings
For the good they comprehend not,
95 That the feeble hands and helpless,
Groping blindly in the darkness,
Touch God's right hand in that darkness
And are lifted up and strengthened;
Listen to this simple story,
100 To this Song of Hiawatha!
     Ye, who sometimes, in your rambles
Through the green lanes of the country,
Where the tangled barberry-bushes
Hang their tufts of crimson berries

---

1   *eyry*   Nest built in a high, inaccessible place.
2   *Vale of Tawasentha*   Traditional Iroquois burial ground at the
mouth of a creek in upstate New York.

105 Over stone walls gray with mosses,
Pause by some neglected graveyard,
For a while to muse, and ponder
On a half-effaced inscription,
Written with little skill of song-craft,
110 Homely phrases, but each letter
Full of hope and yet of heart-break,
Full of all the tender pathos
Of the Here and the Hereafter;
Stay and read this rude inscription,
115 Read this Song of Hiawatha!

14
PICTURE-WRITING[1]

In those days said Hiawatha,
"Lo! how all things fade and perish!
From the memory of the old men
Pass away the great traditions,
5 The achievements of the warriors,
The adventures of the hunters,
All the wisdom of the Medas,
All the craft of the Wabenos,
All the marvellous dreams and visions
10 Of the Jossakeeds, the Prophets![2]
     "Great men die and are forgotten,
Wise men speak; their words of wisdom
Perish in the ears that hear them,
Do not reach the generations
15 That, as yet unborn, are waiting
In the great, mysterious darkness
Of the speechless days that shall be!
     "On the grave-posts of our fathers
Are no signs, no figures painted;
20 Who are in those graves we know not,
Only know they are our fathers.
Of what kith[3] they are and kindred,

From what old, ancestral Totem,
Be it Eagle, Bear, or Beaver,[4]
25 They descended, this we know not,
Only know they are our fathers.
     "Face to face we speak together,
But we cannot speak when absent,
Cannot send our voices from us
30 To the friends that dwell afar off;
Cannot send a secret message,
But the bearer learns our secret,
May pervert it, may betray it,
May reveal it unto others."
35 Thus said Hiawatha, walking
In the solitary forest,
Pondering, musing in the forest,
On the welfare of his people.
     From his pouch he took his colors,
40 Took his paints of different colors,
On the smooth bark of a birch-tree
Painted many shapes and figures,
Wonderful and mystic figures,
And each figure had a meaning,
45 Each some word or thought suggested.
     Gitche Manito[5] the Mighty,
He, the Master of Life, was painted
As an egg, with points projecting
To the four winds of the heavens.
50 Everywhere is the Great Spirit,
Was the meaning of this symbol.
     Mitche Manito the Mighty,
He the dreadful Spirit of Evil,
As a serpent was depicted,
55 As Kenabeek, the great serpent.
Very crafty, very cunning,
Is the creeping Spirit of Evil,
Was the meaning of this symbol.
     Life and Death he drew as circles,
60 Life was white, but Death was darkened;
Sun and moon and stars he painted,
Man and beast, and fish and reptile,
Forests, mountains, lakes, and rivers.

---

[1] Longfellow draws heavily in this section of the poem on information provided by George Copway in his 1850 book, *The Traditional History and Characteristic Sketches of the Ojibway Nation.* (See "Indigenous Oral and Visual Literatures," elsewhere in this anthology, for excerpts from Copway's work.)

[2] *All the wisdom ... the Prophets* According to Henry Rowe Schoolcraft (whose writings Longfellow relied on), the Medas, Wabenos, and Jossakeeds were members of mystical secret societies respectively practicing medicine, magic, and prophecy.

[3] *kith* Friends, neighbors, acquaintances.

[4] *ancestral Totem ... Beaver* Totems are objects emblematic of a particular native group—most commonly, of clans within a particular tribe. Eagle, Bear, and Beaver clans may all be found within the Ojibwe (and the broader Anishinaabe group); the word *totem* itself derives from the Ojibwe language.

[5] *Gitche Manito* Algonquian term for "great spirit."

For the earth he drew a straight line,
65　For the sky a bow above it;
White the space between for daytime,
Filled with little stars for nighttime;
On the left a point for sunrise,
On the right a point for sunset,
70　On the top a point for noontide,
And for rain and cloudy weather
Waving lines descending from it.
　　Footprints pointing towards a wigwam
Were a sign of invitation,
75　Were a sign of guests assembling;
Bloody hands with palms uplifted
Were a symbol of destruction,
Were a hostile sign and symbol.
　　All these things did Hiawatha
80　Show unto his wondering people,
And interpreted their meaning,
And he said: "Behold, your grave-posts
Have no mark, no sign, nor symbol,
Go and paint them all with figures;
85　Each one with its household symbol,
With its own ancestral Totem;
So that those who follow after
May distinguish them and know them."
　　And they painted on the grave-posts
90　On the graves yet unforgotten,
Each his own ancestral Totem,
Each the symbol of his household;
Figures of the Bear and Reindeer,
Of the Turtle, Crane, and Beaver,
95　Each inverted as a token
That the owner was departed,
That the chief who bore the symbol
Lay beneath in dust and ashes.
　　And the Jossakeeds, the Prophets,
100　The Wabenos, the Magicians,
And the Medicine-men, the Medas,
Painted upon bark and deer-skin
Figures for the songs they chanted,
For each song a separate symbol,
105　Figures mystical and awful,
Figures strange and brightly colored;
And each figure had its meaning,
Each some magic song suggested.
　　The Great Spirit, the Creator,

110　Flashing light through all the heaven;
The Great Serpent, the Kenabeek,
With his bloody crest erected,
Creeping, looking into heaven;
In the sky the sun, that listens,
115　And the moon eclipsed and dying;
Owl and eagle, crane and hen-hawk,
And the cormorant, bird of magic;
Headless men, that walk the heavens,
Bodies lying pierced with arrows,
120　Bloody hands of death uplifted,
Flags on graves, and great war-captains
Grasping both the earth and heaven!
　　Such as these the shapes they painted
On the birch-bark and the deer-skin;
125　Songs of war and songs of hunting,
Songs of medicine and of magic,
All were written in these figures,
For each figure had its meaning,
Each its separate song recorded.
130　　Nor forgotten was the Love-Song,
The most subtle of all medicines,
The most potent spell of magic,
Dangerous more than war or hunting!
Thus the Love-Song was recorded,
135　Symbol and interpretation.
　　First a human figure standing,
Painted in the brightest scarlet;
'Tis the lover, the musician,
And the meaning is, "My painting
140　Makes me powerful over others."
　　Then the figure seated, singing,
Playing on a drum of magic,
And the interpretation, "Listen!
'Tis my voice you hear, my singing!"
145　　Then the same red figure seated
In the shelter of a wigwam,
And the meaning of the symbol,
"I will come and sit beside you
In the mystery of my passion!"
150　　Then two figures, man and woman,
Standing hand in hand together,
With their hands so clasped together
That they seemed in one united,
And the words thus represented
155　Are, "I see your heart within you,

And your cheeks are red with blushes!"
    Next the maiden on an island,
In the centre of an island;
And the song this shape suggested
160 Was, "Though you were at a distance,
Were upon some far-off island,
Such the spell I cast upon you,
Such the magic power of passion,
I could straightway draw you to me!"
165   Then the figure of the maiden
Sleeping, and the lover near her,
Whispering to her in her slumbers,
Saying, "Though you were far from me
In the land of Sleep and Silence,
170 Still the voice of love would reach you!"
    And the last of all the figures
Was a heart within a circle,
Drawn within a magic circle;
And the image had this meaning:
175 "Naked lies your heart before me,
To your naked heart I whisper!"
    Thus it was that Hiawatha,
In his wisdom, taught the people
All the mysteries of painting,
180 All the art of Picture-Writing,
On the smooth bark of the birch-tree,
On the white skin of the reindeer,
On the grave-posts of the village.
—1855

Nature

As a fond mother, when the day is o'er,
Leads by the hand her little child to bed,
Half willing, half reluctant to be led,
And leave his broken playthings on the floor,
5 Still gazing at them through the open door,
Nor wholly reassured and comforted
By promises of others in their stead,
Which, though more splendid, may not please
    him more;
So Nature deals with us, and takes away
10 Our playthings one by one, and by the hand
Leads us to rest so gently, that we go
Scarce knowing if we wish to go or stay,
Being too full of sleep to understand
How far the unknown transcends the what we
    know.
—1877

My Cathedral

Like two cathedral towers these stately pines
Uplift their fretted summits tipped with cones;
The arch beneath them is not built with stones,
Not Art but Nature traced these lovely lines,
5 And carved this graceful arabesque[1] of vines;
No organ but the wind here sighs and moans,
No sepulchre conceals a martyr's bones.
No marble bishop on his tomb reclines.
Enter! the pavement, carpeted with leaves,
10 Gives back a softened echo to thy tread!
Listen! the choir is singing; all the birds,
In leafy galleries beneath the eaves,
Are singing! listen, ere the sound be fled,
And learn there may be worship without words.
—1880

---

1   *arabesque*   Complex decorative design.

IN CONTEXT

Images of Longfellow

Albert Sands Southworth and Josiah Johnson Hawes, Henry Wadsworth Longfellow, 1850.

Henry Wadsworth Longfellow, 1858.

Photographer unknown, Longfellow Family, c. 1849. Pictured along with Longfellow are his wife, Frances "Fanny" Appleton Longfellow, and their sons Charles and Ernest.

Julia Margaret Cameron, Henry Wadsworth Longfellow, 1868. This famous photograph was taken when Longfellow visited Alfred, Lord Tennyson at his home on the Isle of Wight. Julia Margaret Cameron, who was already becoming recognized as an extraordinary photographer, was a neighbor of Tennyson's, and had photographed the famous British poet several times; it was at Tennyson's suggestion that Cameron photographed Longfellow.

Longfellow grew a beard after his face had been burned when he attempted to rescue his wife from the flames in 1861.

ABRAHAM LINCOLN

1809 – 1865

Revered by many for his leadership of the United States during the Civil War, Abraham Lincoln is scarcely less renowned for his oratorical accomplishments. The elegant balance of his sentences and the gentle but insistent repetitions embedded within them bring clarity to ideas and engender an emotional response among those reading or hearing them. Lincoln's reputation as a skilled rhetorician was well established before the election of 1860, but it was the speeches he delivered as president—especially the Gettysburg Address and the Second Inaugural Address (the latter delivered mere weeks before his assassination)—that cemented his reputation as one of history's most extraordinary orators. As President, Lincoln saw the nation through the most dramatic crisis it had yet experienced, and his memorable expressions of that crisis shaped the way subsequent generations came to understand the Civil War.

The story of Lincoln's youth is widely known. His parents were poor farmers in southwestern Kentucky who later moved to Indiana and then Illinois. Lincoln was bookishly inclined from an early age, much to the chagrin of his father, who often beat young Abraham for neglecting his farm duties in order to read books. In his early twenties, Lincoln left his family for town life in New Salem, Illinois, where he purchased a shop and became a popular local figure (with a reputation for telling exceptionally vulgar jokes). Following a brief period serving in the Black Hawk War, Lincoln ran for and was elected to the Illinois General Assembly (while he was at the same time studying to become a lawyer). By 1837 he had moved to the state capital of Springfield, where he established a successful law practice while serving in the state legislature. It was in Springfield that he met Mary Todd, whose parents were members of an illustrious slaveholding Kentucky family. Todd and Lincoln married in 1842.

Lincoln continued to engage in politics throughout the 1840s, and served for one term in the U.S. House of Representatives; but in 1849 he chose not to run for re-election, and it appeared that he had finished with political life. The passage of the controversial Kansas-Nebraska Act in 1854 drew Lincoln back into politics. As a vocal, if moderate, critic of slavery, Lincoln was infuriated by the new legislation and decided to seek election to the U.S. Senate.

From this point onward, Lincoln's national reputation grew rapidly. In 1856 he was significantly involved in the creation of the new Republican Party of Illinois, and in 1858, he was pitted against Democratic leader Stephen A. Douglas—one of the primary voices behind the Kansas-Nebraska Act—in the campaign to represent Illinois in the Senate. The now-famous seven debates in which Lincoln and Douglas engaged were particularly remarkable for their highly public nature; the telegraph, the railroad, and the greater prevalence of shorthand in journalism made possible the widespread dissemination of Lincoln's and Douglas's words even to those who could not attend the events. Slavery was the predominant topic. Lincoln, perhaps more so than any major American politician before him, insisted that the future of slavery was a moral question. Yet in the face of Douglas's accusations that he was an "abolitionist," Lincoln asserted repeatedly that he had no intention of interfering with the institution of slavery in areas where it was already established. Lincoln also repeatedly denied Douglas's allegations that he desired full political and social equality for African Americans.

The Illinois legislature awarded Douglas the Senate seat—though it was clear that, if the popular vote had determined the state's senator (as would not be the case until after the Seventeenth Amendment was enacted in 1913), Lincoln would have emerged victorious. Lincoln's impressive performance in the debates was followed by his Cooper Union address in New York City in early 1860—a long and intensely researched oration arguing (contrary to the claims of Democrats such as Douglas) that the Founders had included no clause in the Constitution that would prevent Congress from forbidding the extension of slavery. The speech's success made it clear that Lincoln was a contender for the presidency. He was nominated at the Republican Convention that spring; on November 6 he was elected as the sixteenth President (and first Republican President) of the United States.

By the time Lincoln took office in March of 1861, however, the country was in turmoil. South Carolina seceded from the Union in December 1860, and six other Southern states quickly followed; little more than a month after Lincoln's inauguration in 1861, the Civil War broke out.

As the incoming president of a broken nation, Lincoln's overriding goal was not to end slavery but to preserve the Union. His first inaugural address repeated sentiments he had expressed during the Douglas debates: "I have no purpose, directly or indirectly, to interfere with the institution of slavery in the States where it exists. I believe I have no lawful right to do so, and I have no inclination to do so." In a personal letter dated 22 August 1862, over a year after the war had begun, Lincoln wrote, "If I could save the Union without freeing any slave I would do it, and if I could save it by freeing all the slaves I would do it." As the war dragged on, however, the second of those alternatives came to the fore. On 1 January 1863 Lincoln issued the Emancipation Proclamation, an executive order declaring the freedom of all enslaved residents of the Confederacy (this did not include the enslaved in states that had not seceded: Kentucky, Missouri, Maryland, and Delaware), and inviting all emancipated men to join the Union Army. That August Lincoln met for the first time with the prominent black abolitionist Frederick Douglass to discuss the treatment of black Union soldiers. And in January 1865, the Thirteenth Amendment passed, ending slavery in all states.

The occasion for the most memorable of all Lincoln's speeches was the dedication in November 1863 before a crowd of some 15,000 people of a national cemetery at Gettysburg, Pennsylvania, which the previous summer had been the site of one of the most violent battles of the war. Lincoln followed a two-and-a-half-hour speech given by celebrated orator Edward Everett with a two-and-a-half-minute address that stunned the audience with its brevity. Everett wrote the president the next day, "I should be glad if I could flatter myself that I came as near to the central idea of the occasion, in two hours, as you did in two minutes." Lincoln's Gettysburg Address was being anthologized in texts on elocution within the next two years.

Lincoln delivered his Second Inaugural Address on 4 March 1865, as the war was nearing its end. Though the ground outside the Capitol building (with its newly completed dome) was muddy following weeks of rain, many thousands turned out to hear the President's speech. Among them was John Wilkes Booth, an actor and proslavery radical, who would assassinate Lincoln just a few weeks later. Of all Lincoln's speeches, the Second Inaugural most eloquently frames the moral crisis at the center of the Civil War; Frederick Douglass described the speech as a "sacred effort."

Less than two months after the inauguration, Lincoln was shot in the back of the head by Booth while attending a theater performance with his wife; he died the following morning. The assassination of Lincoln seemed to many a martyrdom. Walt Whitman penned four poems in memory of Lincoln, picturing him as a fallen ship's captain, a drooping star, a dear commander, and a gentle, just man. The abolitionist preacher Henry Ward Beecher, brother to Harriet Beecher Stowe, evoked the biblical narrative of Moses in his eulogy for the fallen President, claiming that Lincoln had been sent by God "to lead them [the enslaved] out of the land of bondage." The eloquent president did indeed die as slavery legally ended. However, the struggle for African American equality turned out to be very far from over.

NOTE ON THE TEXTS: The text of the speech popularly known as "A House Divided" is based on that printed in the *Chicago Tribune* for 19 June 1858; this is the version of the speech Lincoln sent to the editors of an 1860 edition of the Lincoln-Douglas debates. The version of the Gettysburg Address reproduced here (of which Lincoln wrote five drafts) is known as the Bliss copy, after Colonel Alexander Bliss. It is the only version to have been signed and dated by Lincoln, and it is also the version etched into the wall of the Lincoln Memorial. The text of the Second Inaugural Address is based on the handwritten manuscript, which is thought to have been the copy used by Lincoln when he delivered the speech; scans of this manuscript are available online through the Library of Congress. Spelling and punctuation have been lightly modernized.

⌘ ⌘ ⌘

from *Speech delivered at the Republican State Convention in Springfield, Illinois* [*"A House Divided"*]

The speech excerpted below, popularly known as the "House Divided" speech for the biblical metaphor used in its opening lines, is often considered to have initiated the famous Lincoln-Douglas debates. It was delivered immediately following Lincoln's nomination by the Illinois Republican Party for the position of state senator, against incumbent Democratic senator Stephen A. Douglas. Both Lincoln and Douglas referred back to the ideas of the "House Divided" speech several times over the course of their series of debates.

If we could first know where we are, and whither we are tending, we could better judge what to do, and how to do it. We are now far into the fifth year, since a policy was initiated with the avowed object, and confident promise, of putting an end to slavery agitation.[1] Under the operation of that policy, that agitation has not only not ceased, but has constantly augmented. In my opinion, it will not cease, until a crisis shall have been reached and passed. "A house divided against itself cannot stand."[2] I believe this government cannot endure permanently half slave and half free. I do not expect the Union to be dissolved—I do not expect the house to fall—but I do expect it will cease to be divided. It will become all one thing, or all the other. Either the opponents of slavery will arrest the further spread of it, and place it where the public mind shall rest in the belief that it is in the course of ultimate extinction; or its advocates will push it forward, till it shall become alike lawful in all the States, old as well as new—North as well as South.

Have we no tendency to the latter condition?

Let anyone who doubts, carefully contemplate that now almost complete legal combination—piece of machinery so to speak—compounded of the Nebraska doctrine, and the Dred Scott decision.[3] ...

... Put this and that together, and we have another nice little niche, which we may, ere long, see filled with another Supreme Court decision, declaring that the Constitution of the United States does not permit a *State* to exclude slavery from its limits. And this may especially be expected if the doctrine of "care not whether slavery be voted down or voted up"[4] shall gain

---

1   *a policy ... slavery agitation* Lincoln refers to the Kansas-Nebraska Act of May 1854, which had been drafted by Stephen Douglas; it repealed the Missouri Compromise and allowed new states to determine by popular vote whether or not they would allow slavery. To the surprise of Douglas, President Franklin Pierce, and other supporters of the Act, it had virtually the opposite effect to ending the national debate over slavery, and led to the period of violence between proslavery and antislavery agitators popularly known as "Bleeding Kansas."

2   *A house ... cannot stand* See Mark 3.25: "And if a house be divided against itself, that house cannot stand."

3   *Dred Scott decision* 1857 Supreme Court decision in which it was declared that persons of African descent, whether free or enslaved, could not be considered American citizens, and thereby had no legal standing in court. The decision came after the formerly enslaved Dred Scott attempted to secure the court's further confirmation of his freedom so that the children of his deceased former owner could not claim inherited ownership of Scott's daughters.

4   *care not ... voted up* Statement made in a speech by Stephen Douglas referring to his support of popular sovereignty on the question of slavery as Kansas sought to enter the Union.

upon the public mind sufficiently to give promise that such a decision can be maintained when made.

Such a decision is all that slavery now lacks of being alike lawful in all the States. Welcome or unwelcome, such decision is probably coming, and will soon be upon us, unless the power of the present political dynasty shall be met and overthrown. We shall lie down pleasantly dreaming that the people of Missouri are on the verge of making their State free, and we shall awake to the reality, instead, that the Supreme Court has made Illinois a slave state. To meet and overthrow the power of that dynasty, is the work now before all those who would prevent that consummation. That is what we have to do. ...

... Two years ago the Republicans of the nation mustered over thirteen hundred thousand strong. We did this under the single impulse of resistance to a common danger, with every external circumstance against us. Of strange, discordant, and even hostile elements, we gathered from the four winds, and formed and fought the battle through, under the constant hot fire of a disciplined, proud and pampered enemy. Did we brave all them to falter now? now, when that same enemy is wavering, dissevered and belligerent? The result is not doubtful. We shall not fail—if we stand firm, we *shall not fail*. Wise counsels may accelerate, or mistake delay it, but, sooner or later, the victory is sure to come. —1858

Dedication of the Soldiers' National Cemetery in Gettysburg, 19 November 1863, where Lincoln delivered the Gettysburg Address.

The "Bliss copy" of the Gettysburg Address. This is the last known version of the speech written in Lincoln's hand, and the only one that bears his signature.

Address Delivered at the Dedication of the Cemetery at Gettysburg

Four score and seven years ago our fathers brought forth on this continent, a new nation, conceived in Liberty, and dedicated to the proposition that all men are created equal.

Now we are engaged in a great civil war, testing whether that nation, or any nation so conceived and so dedicated, can long endure. We are met on a great battle-field of that war. We have come to dedicate a portion of that field, as a final resting place for those who here gave their lives, that that nation might live. It is altogether fitting and proper that we should do this.

But, in a larger sense, we cannot dedicate—we cannot consecrate—we cannot hallow—this ground. The brave men, living and dead, who struggled here, have consecrated it, far above our poor power to add or detract. The world will little note, nor long remember what we say here, but it can never forget what they did here. It is for us the living, rather, to be dedicated here to the unfinished work which they who fought here have thus far so nobly advanced. It is rather for us to be here dedicated to the great task remaining before us—that from these honored dead we take increased devotion to that cause for which they gave the last full measure of devotion—that we here highly resolve that these dead shall not have died in vain—that this nation, under God, shall have a new birth of freedom—and that government of the people, by the people, for the people, shall not perish from the earth.

—1863

Second Inaugural Address

Fellow-Countrymen:

At this second appearing to take the oath of the presidential office, there is less occasion for an extended address than there was at the first.[1] Then a statement, somewhat in detail, of a course to be pursued, seemed fitting and proper. Now, at the expiration of four years, during which public declarations have been constantly called forth on every point and phase of the great contest which still absorbs the attention, and engrosses the energies of the nation, little that is new could be presented. The progress of our arms,[2] upon which all else chiefly depends, is as well known to the public as to myself; and it is, I trust, reasonably satisfactory and encouraging to all. With high hope for the future, no prediction in regard to it is ventured.

On the occasion corresponding to this four years ago, all thoughts were anxiously directed to an impending civil war. All dreaded it—all sought to avert it. While the inaugural address was being delivered from this place, devoted altogether to *saving* the Union without war, insurgent agents[3] were in the city seeking to *destroy* it without war—seeking to dissolve the Union, and divide effects,[4] by negotiation. Both parties deprecated war;[5] but one of them would *make* war rather than let the nation survive; and the other would *accept* war rather than let it perish. And the war came.

One eighth of the whole population were colored slaves, not distributed generally over the Union, but localized in the Southern part of it. These slaves constituted a peculiar and powerful interest. All knew that this interest was, somehow, the cause of the war. To strengthen, perpetuate, and extend this interest was the object for which the insurgents would rend the Union, even by war; while the government claimed no right to do more than to restrict the territorial enlargement of it. Neither party expected for the war, the magnitude, or the duration, which it has already attained. Neither anticipated that the *cause* of the conflict might cease with, or even before, the conflict itself should cease. Each looked for an easier triumph, and a result less fundamental and astounding. Both read the same Bible, and pray to the same God; and each invokes His aid against the other. It may seem strange that any men should dare to ask a just God's assistance in wringing

---

[1] *less occasion ... the first* Lincoln's first inaugural address, delivered on 4 March 1861, was, at over three-and-a-half thousand words, far longer than the second one; it is included in full in the website component of this anthology.

[2] *of our arms* Of the Union forces in the Civil War.

[3] *insurgent agents* Representatives attempting to undermine the government.

[4] *effects* Possessions (of the United States as a whole).

[5] *Both parties deprecated war* Both Northerners and Southerners expressed their disapproval of the idea of going to war.

Photograph taken at the United States Capitol during the delivery of Lincoln's Second Inaugural Address, by the Scottish-American photographer Alexander Gardner; Lincoln can be seen at the center of the photograph with the manuscript of his speech in hand.

their bread from the sweat of other men's faces; but let us judge not that we be not judged.[1] The prayers of both could not be answered; that of neither has been answered fully. The Almighty has His own purposes. "Woe unto the world because of offences! for it must needs be that offences come; but woe to that man by whom the offence cometh!"[2] If we shall suppose that American slavery is one of those offenses which, in the providence of God, must needs come, but which, having continued through His appointed time, He now wills to remove, and that He gives to both North and South this terrible war, as the woe due to those by whom the offence came, shall we discern therein any departure from those divine attributes which the believers in a living God always ascribe to Him? Fondly do we hope—fervently do we pray—that this mighty scourge of war may speedily pass away. Yet, if God wills that it continue, until all the wealth piled by the bondsman's two hundred and fifty years of unrequited toil shall be sunk, and until every drop of blood drawn with the lash, shall be paid by another drawn with the sword, as was said three thousand years ago, so still it must be said "the judgments of the Lord, are true and righteous altogether."[3]

With malice toward none; with charity for all; with firmness in the right, as God gives us to see the right, let us strive on to finish the work we are in; to bind up the nation's wounds; to care for him who shall have borne the battle, and for his widow, and his orphan— to do all which may achieve and cherish a just and a lasting peace, among ourselves, and with all nations. —1865

---

[1] *let us ... not judged*   See Matthew 7.1.

[2] *Woe unto ... cometh*   See Matthew 18.7.

[3] *the judgments ... altogether*   See Psalm 9.19.

Edgar Allan Poe

1809 – 1849

Edgar Allan Poe is a legendary figure in popular culture, a writer famous for his alienation, his madness and substance abuse, and his mastery of eerie and gruesome tales. Poe broadened, through his critical writings as well as through the example of his own fiction, the expressive powers of the American short story. Yet, during his own lifetime, he barely scraped by on his earnings as a writer and rarely experienced more than modest popular success. What renown he did earn prior to his death rested largely on his work as a literary critic; in 1845 poet James Russell Lowell called him "the most discriminating, philosophical, and fearless critic upon imaginative works who has written in America." In the years following his death, however, his fiction and poetry found enthusiastic adherents (as well as detractors), and his influence on literature and popular culture ever since has been profound: he is widely considered an originator of the detective story, wrote several pioneering tales of science fiction, and penned some of the most evocative and disturbing tales of the supernatural and macabre to be found in nineteenth-century literature.

Edgar Poe was born in Boston in 1809 to itinerant stage actors Elizabeth Arnold and David Poe, but after his father left the family and his mother died, Poe was brought up by John and Frances Allan, a wealthy Virginian merchant couple. Poe spent most of his childhood in Richmond, Virginia, but the family also lived in London for a few years. He entered the University of Virginia in 1826, where he excelled academically, though numerous letters sent home reveal Poe's distress at John Allan's inadequate financial support, which at times left Poe seriously impoverished. He also fell into the institution's rampant drinking and gambling culture, incurring significant debts. After intense quarreling with Allan, who cut him off financially, Poe left the university after one year and departed Richmond for Boston.

It is unclear when exactly Poe began writing seriously, but by 1827 he had composed enough poems to make up a short volume. His first published collections, *Tamerlane and Other Poems* (1827, published anonymously) and its expanded edition, *Al Aaraaf, Tamerlane, and Minor Poems* (1829), were virtually ignored by critics and were acknowledged by Poe himself to be of generally indifferent quality. Already evident in this early work, however, is Poe's debt to German and British Romanticism—particularly to the work of Lord Byron and Thomas Moore— and to such poets' fascination with the art and culture of the Middle East. Poe achieved slightly more critical (but not popular) success with his third collection, *Poems by Edgar A. Poe* (1831). Many of these poems reflect their author's increasing preoccupation with the theme of death—especially that of a beloved or beautiful woman, which he would later describe as "the most poetical topic in the world." After the financial failure of *Poems*, Poe began to experiment with the short story, publishing his first tale in 1832.

Poe was one of the first Americans to live solely, and precariously, on the profits of his writing, and he considered himself a "magazinist," contributing fiction, poetry, and criticism to periodicals as well as taking on editorial roles. By mid-decade Poe was working as an editorial assistant at the *Southern Literary Messenger* back in Richmond, while also continuing to contribute poems and stories to various journals and annual gift books. Over the course of his career, Poe worked for several magazines and earned a good deal of both respect and notoriety for his literary reviews. Frustrated by an American reviewing practice that he saw as overly moralizing and didactic, Poe advocated a rigorously analytical practice. Indeed, he believed that his role as a critic meant exposing bad writing, and his ruthless reviews sparked notoriously combative relationships with many of his contemporaries. Among them were many intellectual figures from New England, a region which Poe saw as disproportionately represented in literary media and whose most prominent authors—among them Emerson, Longfellow, and Whittier—he often dismissed as unimaginative and overly regional in their literary vision. Poe sometimes used his critical platform to praise the works of other Southerners whom he saw as unjustly overlooked by the New England literary establishment, such as William Gilmore Simms—whose "Murder Will Out" Poe called the "best ghost-story ever written by an American"—Philip Pendleton Cooke, and John Pendleton Kennedy.

In 1836, Poe moved to Baltimore and married his first cousin, Virginia Clemm, who was then only thirteen years old—though on their marriage certificate her age was given as twenty-one (closer to the average age of a bride in the nineteenth century). Virginia was passionately devoted to Poe, who claimed to love her "as no man ever loved before." The ongoing threat of severe poverty, however, posed difficulties, as did Poe's continuing struggles with depression and alcohol abuse and Virginia's failing health due to tuberculosis, of which she died in 1847. In popular accounts of Poe's life, Virginia's early death is often framed as precipitating a decline into alcoholism and madness, and as inspiring the macabre content for which he is famous; in fact, he had already written his best-known Gothic pieces before she died, and while he grieved her loss deeply, he was in the midst of planning a second marriage at the time of his own death less than three years after hers.

Unable to find a publisher interested in a collection of his short stories, Poe turned to the more popular novel form, and managed to secure the publication of *The Narrative of Arthur Gordon Pym of Nantucket* in 1838. The short novel—whose protagonist was dubbed "the American Robinson Crusoe" by a London reviewer—owed much to the genre of the sea tale (popularized by New York writer James Fenimore Cooper) as well as to the travel literature then popular. Today, the novel is deemed by some to be among Poe's best works; it also, however, gives expression to the racist views that Poe held throughout his life. John Allan's business relied on enslaved people for its operation, and at eighteen Poe expressed to his father outrage at being subjected to the "authority of the blacks" in the household. Poe rarely stated opinions on slavery directly in his writing, but as a critic he disparaged abolitionist works for their "fanaticism" and "misrepresentation" of how the enslaved were treated. Relatively few scholars drew attention to Poe's racism until the 1980s, when it became a focus of academic discussion; interest in Poe's treatment of race intensified in 1993, when Toni Morrison argued that Poe had been instrumental in developing white American ideas of blackness. Following Morrison, many scholars have been less interested in determining the extent of Poe's personal racism than in considering what Poe's depictions of servile black characters, racialized monsters, and tyrannical white oppressors suggest about white American anxieties surrounding blackness and slavery.

In 1840 Poe published *Tales of the Grotesque and Arabesque*, a short-story collection that, like so much of his earlier work, sold poorly but was critically well received. Many of Poe's most famous stories were released either in this collection or in periodicals over the next few years, during which he wrote comic and satirical tales as well as the dark, Gothic, and horror-inducing fiction he would come to be most strongly associated with. Poe's dark humor—his delight in hoaxes, word play, and subversive mockery—is present, to varying degrees, in much of his work. His remarkably influential series of mystery stories, featuring the detective C. Auguste Dupin, initiated the trope of the crime-solving protagonist who uses painstaking rational inquiry to solve complex or dramatic crimes. Stories such as Poe's "The Fall of the House of Usher" (1839)—with its ruined manor house, gloomy landscape, and a psychologically tortured character—build on the late eighteenth-century Gothic tradition developed by writers such as Ann Radcliffe. Though such Gothic elements were mainly drawn from British and other European literature, Poe also had American predecessors and contemporaries, including Charles Brockden Brown, William Dunlap, and James Kirke. He was also influenced by the African American ghost stories he heard as a child from the enslaved woman, Judith or Juliet (the record is unclear), who helped raise him in the Allan household.

Poe's greatest success in his lifetime was "The Raven" (1845), a poem whose speaker is a psychologically tortured student grieving the loss of his beloved. The poem was reprinted widely in both the United States and Britain; among its many enthusiastic readers was poet Elizabeth Barrett Browning, who wrote that it had "produced a sensation, a 'fit of horror,' here in England." Following up on the poem's popularity, Poe wrote "The Philosophy of Composition," which professed to detail his writing process. By his account, "The Raven" appears to have been a culmination of all his artistic aims; Poe claimed to value "unity of impression" (a work should ideally be short enough to be read in one sitting), a near-mathematical degree of attention to aesthetic and compositional detail, and the evocation of pleasure and beauty rather than of realism or truth. Due to ineffective copyright laws, "The Raven" earned Poe little money, leaving him and his wife as deeply in poverty as ever.

In 1848, Poe published the prose poem *Eureka*, a work in which he put forward his intuitive understanding of "the material and spiritual universe"; audiences were largely bewildered by the book's mysticism, though Poe himself claimed it was his most important work. In October of the following year, Poe was found delirious in Baltimore. He died in a hospital a few days later; the cause of his death remains unclear. Poe's character was torn apart in a scathing *New York Tribune* obituary, in which literary critic Rufus Griswold described him as a "naturally unamiable" cynic who "walked the streets, in madness or melancholy, with lips moving in indistinct curses." Griswold wrote a further memoir about Poe that emphasized his alcoholism and dishonesty, though even he had to acknowledge Poe's force of character, reporting that his conversation was "supra-mortal in its eloquence." For decades, controversy surrounded Poe's character, and many interpreted his tales of horror and melancholy as direct reflections of his own psyche.

Poe's work, however, became increasingly renowned in Europe—and especially in France, where the poet Charles Baudelaire translated much of his work in the mid-nineteenth century. The French Symbolists were heavily influenced by Poe, as were writers in the Aesthetic movement, whose motto "Art for Art's Sake" had been anticipated by Poe in a posthumously published essay, "The Poetic Principle" (1850), in which he praises the nobility of a "poem written solely for the poem's sake." The Anglo-American literary scene was slower to warm up to Poe, but in these countries, too, his influence grew. American authors from H.P. Lovecraft and Shirley Jackson to Richard Wright were indebted to Poe's legacy, as was the film director Alfred Hitchcock. In England, Sir Arthur Conan Doyle acknowledged Poe as a key precursor for his Sherlock Holmes tales: "Where was the detective story until Poe breathed the breath of life into it?" Indeed, the genres of detective fiction, horror fiction, and science fiction all find in Poe a significant influence, as do related genres in film and television. While Poe's work continues to find detractors and skeptics, the balance over the last hundred years has swung decidedly in his favor, and his stories, poems, and essays continue to be read and reinterpreted by both literary critics and a wide general readership.

NOTE ON THE TEXTS: Poe often revised his stories and poems, particularly as he prepared for book publication works that had originally appeared in periodicals. Texts reprinted in this anthology are based upon his latest authorized versions, as these include his corrections and additions. The text of "Sonnet—To Science" is based upon that published in *The Raven and Other Poems* (1845). For the text of "Ligeia," the editors have consulted the version printed in the S.H. Whitman copy of the *Broadway Journal* (1845–46), which includes corrections penciled in by Poe. The text of "The Tell-Tale Heart" is based upon the version printed in Griswold's 1850–56 four-volume edition, *The Works of the Late Edgar Allan Poe*, and "The Fall of the House of Usher" and "The Black Cat" are based upon the versions appearing in the 1845 *Tales by Edgar Allan Poe*. The version of "The Raven" reprinted here is based upon the text that appeared in the *Richmond Semi-Weekly Examiner* on 25 September 1849, and our excerpts from "The Philosophy of Composition" are based on the version printed in *Graham's Magazine* in 1846. For "Annabel Lee," the editors have consulted the "Griswold" manuscript, the version Poe sent to his editor in May 1849. Unless otherwise noted, spelling and punctuation have been modernized in accordance with the practices of this anthology.

⌘⌘⌘

Sonnet—To Science

Science! true daughter of Old Time thou art!
　Who alterest all things with thy peering eyes.
Why preyest thou thus upon the poet's heart,
　　Vulture,[1] whose wings are dull realities?
5　How should he love thee? or how deem thee wise?
　　Who wouldst not leave him in his wandering
To seek for treasure in the jewelled skies,
　　Albeit he soared with an undaunted wing?[2]
Hast thou not dragged Diana[3] from her car?
10　　And driven the Hamadryad[4] from the wood
To seek a shelter in some happier star?
　　Hast thou not torn the Naiad[5] from her flood,
The Elfin[6] from the green grass, and from me
The summer dream beneath the tamarind tree?
　—1829

---

[1]　*Why preyest … Vulture*　Allusion to Prometheus, a Greek mythical figure who stole fire from the gods to give to humankind; for this, his punishment was to be chained to a rock while a vulture (in some versions, an eagle) devoured his liver each day.

[2]　*Albeit … wing*　Allusion to the Greek myth of Icarus, a young man who flew using wings made from wax. When he ascended too close to the sun, the wax melted, and Icarus fell to his death.

[3]　*Diana*　Roman goddess of chastity, childbirth, wilderness, and the hunt. As she is here, she is often equated with the moon goddess Selene, who rides a chariot across the sky.

[4]　*Hamadryad*　In Greek mythology, a nymph whose life is bound to a tree.

[5]　*Naiad*　Nymph associated with small bodies of water such as streams or springs.

[6]　*Elfin*　I.e., elf.

Ligeia[7]

And the will therein lieth, which dieth not. Who knoweth the mysteries of the will, with its vigor? For God is but a great will pervading all things by nature of its intentness. Man doth not yield himself to the angels, nor unto death utterly, save only through the weakness of his feeble will.

　　　　　　　　　　　—Joseph Glanvill[8]

I cannot, for my soul, remember how, when, or even precisely where, I first became acquainted with the lady Ligeia. Long years have since elapsed, and my memory is feeble through much suffering. Or, perhaps, I cannot *now* bring these points to mind, because, in truth, the character of my beloved, her rare learning, her singular yet placid cast of beauty, and the thrilling and enthralling eloquence of her low musical language, made their way into my heart by paces so steadily and stealthily progressive that they have been unnoticed and unknown. Yet I believe that I met her first and most frequently in some large, old, decaying city near the Rhine.[9] Of her family—I have surely heard her speak. That it is of a remotely ancient date cannot be doubted. Ligeia! Ligeia! Buried in studies of a nature more than all else adapted to deaden impressions of the outward world, it is by that sweet word alone— by Ligeia—that I bring before mine eyes in fancy the image of her who is no more. And now, while I write, a recollection flashes upon me that I have *never known* the paternal name of her who was my friend and my betrothed, and who became the partner of my studies, and finally the wife of my bosom. Was it a playful charge[10] on the part of my Ligeia? or was it a test of my strength of affection, that I should institute no

---

[7]　*Ligeia*　In Greek mythology, Ligeia is one of the Sirens, a group of creatures that combine the features of beautiful women and birds. They were said to live on island cliffs and to sing entrancing music that enticed sailors to crash their ships on the rocks.

[8]　*And the … Joseph Glanvill*　Poe apparently fabricated this epigraph; Joseph Glanvill (1636–80) was, however, a real person, an English philosopher with an interest in science and the supernatural.

[9]　*Rhine*　River in Europe that stretches from the Swiss Alps to cross Germany and the Netherlands, emptying into the North Sea.

[10]　*charge*　Command.

inquiries upon this point? or was it rather caprice of my own—a wildly romantic offering on the shrine of the most passionate devotion? I but indistinctly recall the fact itself—what wonder that I have utterly forgotten the circumstances which originated or attended it? And, indeed, if ever that spirit which is entitled *Romance*—if ever she, the wan, and the misty-winged *Ashtophet*[1] of idolatrous Egypt, presided, as they tell, over marriages ill-omened, then most surely she presided over mine.

There is one dear topic, however, on which my memory faileth me not. It is the *person*[2] of Ligeia. In stature she was tall, somewhat slender, and, in her latter days, even emaciated. I would in vain attempt to portray the majesty, the quiet ease, of her demeanor, or the incomprehensible lightness and elasticity of her footfall. She came and departed as a shadow. I was never made aware of her entrance into my closed study save by the dear music of her low sweet voice, as she placed her marble hand upon my shoulder. In beauty of face no maiden ever equalled her. It was the radiance of an opium dream—an airy and spirit-lifting vision more wildly divine than the phantasies which hovered about the slumbering souls of the daughters of Delos.[3] Yet her features were not of that regular mould which we have been falsely taught to worship in the classical labors of the heathen.[4] "There is no exquisite beauty," says Bacon, Lord Varulam, speaking truly of all the forms and *genera* of beauty, "without some *strangeness* in the proportions."[5] Yet, although I saw that the features of Ligeia were not of a classic regularity, although I perceived that her loveliness was indeed "exquisite," and felt that there was much of "strangeness" pervading it, yet I have tried in vain to detect the irregularity and to trace home my own perception of "the strange." I

examined the contour of the lofty and pale forehead—it was faultless—how cold indeed that word when applied to a majesty so divine! The skin rivaling the purest ivory, the commanding extent and repose, the gentle prominence of the regions above the temples,[6] and then the raven-black, the glossy, the luxuriant and naturally-curling tresses, setting forth the full force of the Homeric epithet, "hyacinthine!"[7] I looked at the delicate outlines of the nose—and nowhere but in the graceful medallions of the Hebrews had I beheld a similar perfection. There were the same luxurious smoothness of surface, the same scarcely perceptible tendency to the aquiline, the same harmoniously curved nostril speaking the free spirit. I regarded the sweet mouth. Here was indeed the triumph of all things heavenly—the magnificent turn of the short upper lip—the soft, voluptuous slumber of the under—the dimples which sported, and the color which spoke—the teeth glancing back, with a brilliancy almost startling, every ray of the holy light which fell upon them in her serene and placid, yet most exultingly radiant of all smiles. I scrutinized the formation of the chin—and here, too, I found the gentleness of breadth, the softness and the majesty, the fullness and the spirituality, of the Greek—the contour which the God Apollo revealed but in a dream, to Cleomenes, the son of the Athenian.[8] And then I peered into the large eyes of Ligeia.

For eyes we have no models in the remotely antique. It might have been, too, that in these eyes of my beloved lay the secret to which Lord Verulam alludes. They were, I must believe, far larger than the ordinary eyes of our own race.[9] They were even far fuller than the fullest of the gazelle eyes of the tribe of the valley of

---

[1] *Ashtophet* Also known as Astarte or Astoreth, goddess of fertility, sexuality, and war historically worshipped in various regions of the Middle East, including Egypt.

[2] *person* I.e., physical body, appearance.

[3] *Delos* Important religious center of ancient Greece.

[4] *her features ... the heathen* I.e., her beauty was not of the type glorified in classical Greek and Roman art, which emphasized an extremely proportional and idealized figure.

[5] *There is ... the proportions* This is a slight misquotation from "Of Beauty" (1612) by English philosopher Francis Bacon, Baron Verulam; the original line reads "excellent" rather than "exquisite."

[6] *I examined ... the temples* In the pseudoscience of phrenology, according to which the shape of one's skull indicates one's personality traits, a high forehead suggests a great intellect. The region immediately above the temple is associated with strong desire to live; the region just above that is linked to "alimentiveness" (i.e., appetite).

[7] *hyacinthine* Allusion to the *Odyssey*, in which the speaker compares Odysseus' curling hair to a hyacinth in bloom.

[8] *the God Apollo ... Athenian* Cleomenes is the reputed sculptor of the Venus de' Medici, a depiction of the Greek goddess of love; Apollo is the Greek god of art.

[9] *larger than ... race* Phrenology associates large eyes with enhanced linguistic ability.

Nourjahad.[1] Yet it was only at intervals—in moments of intense excitement—that this peculiarity became more than slightly noticeable in Ligeia. And at such moments was her beauty—in my heated fancy thus it appeared perhaps—the beauty of beings either above or apart from the earth—the beauty of the fabulous Houri[2] of the Turk. The hue of the orbs was the most brilliant of black, and, far over them, hung jetty[3] lashes of great length. The brows, slightly irregular in outline, had the same tint. The "strangeness," however, which I have found in the eyes, was of a nature distinct from the formation, or the color, or the brilliancy of the features, and must, after all, be referred to the *expression*. Ah, word of no meaning! behind whose vast latitude of mere sound we entrench our ignorance of so much of the spiritual. The expression of the eyes of Ligeia! How for long hours have I pondered upon it! How have I, through the whole of a mid-summer night, struggled to fathom it! What was it—that something more profound than the well of Democritus[4]—which lay far within the pupils of my beloved? What *was* it? I was possessed with a passion to discover. Those eyes! those large, those shining, those divine orbs! they became to me twin stars of Leda,[5] and I to them devoutest of astrologers.

There is no point, among the many incomprehensible anomalies of the science of mind, more thrillingly exciting than the fact—never, I believe noticed in the schools—that in our endeavors to recall to memory something long forgotten, we often find ourselves *upon the very verge* of remembrance, without being able, in the end, to remember. And thus how frequently, in my intense scrutiny of Ligeia's eyes, have I felt approaching the full knowledge of their expression—felt it

approaching—yet not quite be mine—and so at length entirely depart! And (strange, oh strangest mystery of all!) I found, in the commonest objects of the universe, a circle of analogies to that expression. I mean to say that, subsequently to the period when Ligeia's beauty passed into my spirit, there dwelling as in a shrine, I derived from many existences in the material world, a sentiment such as I felt always aroused within me by her large and luminous orbs. Yet not the more could I define that sentiment, or analyze, or even steadily view it. I recognized it, let me repeat, sometimes in the survey of a rapidly-growing vine—in the contemplation of a moth, a butterfly, a chrysalis, a stream of running water. I have felt it in the ocean; in the falling of a meteor. I have felt it in the glances of unusually aged people. And there are one or two stars in heaven (one especially, a star of the sixth magnitude, double and changeable, to be found near the large star in Lyra[6]) in a telescopic scrutiny of which I have been made aware of the feeling. I have been filled with it by certain sounds from stringed instruments, and not unfrequently by passages from books. Among innumerable other instances, I well remember something in a volume of Joseph Glanvill, which (perhaps merely from its quaintness—who shall say?) never failed to inspire me with the sentiment; "And the will therein lieth, which dieth not. Who knoweth the mysteries of the will, with its vigor? For God is but a great will pervading all things by nature of its intentness. Man doth not yield him to the angels, nor unto death utterly, save only through the weakness of his feeble will."

Length of years, and subsequent reflection, have enabled me to trace, indeed, some remote connexion between this passage in the old English moralist and a portion of the character of Ligeia. An *intensity* in thought, action, or speech was possibly, in her, a result, or at least an index, of that gigantic volition which, during our long intercourse, failed to give other and more immediate evidence of its existence. Of all the women whom I have ever known, she, the outwardly calm, the ever-placid Ligeia, was the most violently a prey to the tumultuous vultures of stern passion. And

---

1   *gazelle eyes ... Nourjahad*   Allusion to the orientalist novel *The History of Nourjahad* (1767) by Irish writer Frances Sheridan.

2   *Houri*   Beautiful maidens said to await devout Muslims in Paradise.

3   *jetty*   Rich, glossy black.

4   *well of Democritus*   The proverbial statement "truth lies at the bottom of a well" is often attributed to the ancient Greek philosopher Democritus (c. 460–c. 370 BCE), who is best known for espousing an early version of atomic theory.

5   *twin stars of Leda*   Castor and Pollux, twin sons of Leda, a Spartan queen. Pollux was born immortal, but Castor was not; Pollux shared his immortality with his brother, and they were transformed into stars in the constellation Gemini.

6   *Lyra*   Constellation within which can be found Vega (one of the brightest stars in the sky). It is not entirely clear what "star of the sixth magnitude" is meant, but Lyra does contain the famous star system Epsilon Lyrae, which appears to be one star but includes two pairs of stars that orbit each other.

of such passion I could form no estimate, save by the miraculous expansion of those eyes which at once so delighted and appalled me—by the almost magical melody, modulation, distinctness and placidity of her very low voice—and by the fierce energy (rendered doubly effective by contrast with her manner of utterance) of the wild words which she habitually uttered.

I have spoken of the learning of Ligeia: it was immense—such as I have never known in woman. In all the classical tongues was she deeply proficient, and as far as my own acquaintance extended in regard to the modern dialects of Europe, I have never known her at fault. Indeed upon any theme of the most admired, because simply the most abstruse of the boasted erudition of the academy, have I *ever* found Ligeia at fault? How singularly—how thrillingly, this one point in the nature of my wife has forced itself, at this late period only, upon my attention! I said her knowledge was such as I had never known in woman—but where breathes the man who has traversed, and successfully, *all* the wide areas of moral, physical, and mathematical science? I saw not then what I now clearly perceive, that the acquisitions of Ligeia were gigantic, were astounding; yet I was sufficiently aware of her infinite supremacy to resign myself, with a child-like confidence, to her guidance through the chaotic world of metaphysical investigation at which I was most busily occupied during the earlier years of our marriage. With how vast a triumph—with how vivid a delight—with how much of all that is ethereal in hope—did I *feel*, as she bent over me in studies but little sought—but less known—that delicious vista by slow degrees expanding before me, down whose long, gorgeous, and all untrodden path, I might at length pass onward to the goal of a wisdom too divinely precious not to be forbidden!

How poignant, then, must have been the grief with which, after some years, I beheld my well-grounded expectations take wings to themselves and flee away! Without Ligeia I was but as a child groping benighted. Her presence, her readings alone, rendered vividly luminous the many mysteries of the transcendentalism[1]

in which we were immersed. Wanting the radiant lustre of her eyes, letters, lambent and golden, grew duller than Saturnian[2] lead. And now those eyes shone less and less frequently upon the pages over which I pored. Ligeia grew ill. The wild eyes blazed with a too—too glorious effulgence; the pale fingers became of the transparent waxen hue of the grave, and the blue veins upon the lofty forehead swelled and sunk impetuously with the tides of the most gentle emotion. I saw that she must die—and I struggled desperately in spirit with the grim Azrael.[3] And the struggles of the passionate wife were, to my astonishment, even more energetic than my own. There had been much in her stern nature to impress me with the belief that, to her, death would have come without its terrors—but not so. Words are impotent to convey any just idea of the fierceness of resistance with which she wrestled with the Shadow. I groaned in anguish at the pitiable spectacle. I would have soothed—I would have reasoned; but, in the intensity of her wild desire for life—for life—*but for life*—solace and reason were alike the uttermost of folly. Yet not until the last instance, amid the most convulsive writhings of her fierce spirit, was shaken the external placidity of her demeanor. Her voice grew more gentle—grew more low—yet I would not wish to dwell upon the wild meaning of the quietly uttered words. My brain reeled as I hearkened entranced, to a melody more than mortal—to assumptions and aspirations which mortality had never before known.

That she loved me, I should not have doubted; and I might have been easily aware that, in a bosom such as hers, love would have reigned no ordinary passion. But in death only, was I fully impressed with the intensity of her affection. For long hours, detaining my hand, would she pour out before me the overflowing of a heart whose more than passionate devotion amounted to idolatry. How had I deserved to be so blessed by such confessions? How had I deserved to be so cursed with the removal of my beloved in the hour of her making them? But upon this subject I cannot bear to dilate. Let me say only, that in Ligeia's more than womanly abandonment to a love, alas! all unmerited,

---

1   *transcendentalism* Probably referring to the transcendental philosophy discussed by European philosophers such as Immanuel Kant (1724–1804), rather than to the American Transcendentalist movement developed by writers such as Emerson in the mid-to-late 1830s; Poe was noted throughout his career for his distaste for the New England Transcendentalists.

2   *Wanting* I.e., without; *lambent* Radiant; *Saturnian* Dull, gloomy; the descriptor also alludes to the practice of alchemy, in which lead was associated with the planet Saturn.

3   *Azrael* Angel of Death in Islam and Judaism.

all unworthily bestowed, I at length recognised the principle of her longing with so wildly earnest a desire for the life which was now fleeing so rapidly away. It is this wild longing—it is this eager intensity of desire for life—*but* for life—that I have no power to portray—no utterance capable of expressing.

At high noon of the night in which she departed, beckoning me, peremptorily, to her side, she bade me repeat certain verses composed by herself not many days before. I obeyed her. They were these:

> Lo! 'tis a gala night
> Within the lonesome latter years!
>   An angel throng, bewinged,
>   bedight°   *arrayed*
> In veils, and drowned in tears,
> 5 Sit in a theatre, to see
> A play of hopes and fears,
> While the orchestra breathes fitfully
> The music of the spheres.[1]
>
> Mimes, in the form of God on high,
> 10 Mutter and mumble low,
> And hither and thither fly—
> Mere puppets they, who come and go
> At bidding of vast formless things
> That shift the scenery to and fro,
> 15 Flapping from out their Condor wings
> Invisible Woe!
>
> That motley drama!—oh, be sure
> It shall not be forgot!
>   With its Phantom°   *illusion*
>   chased forevermore,
> 20 By a crowd that seize it not,
> Through a circle that ever returneth in
> To the self-same spot,
> And much of Madness and more of Sin,
> And Horror the soul of the plot.
>
> 25 But see, amid the mimic rout,
> A crawling shape intrude!
> A blood-red thing that writhes from out
> The scenic solitude!
> It writhes!—it writhes!—with mortal pangs
> 30 The mimes become its food,

And the seraphs sob at vermin fangs
In human gore imbued.
Out—out are the lights—out all!
And over each quivering form,
35 The curtain, a funeral pall,
Comes down with the rush of a storm,
And the angels, all pallid and wan,
Uprising, unveiling, affirm
That the play is the tragedy, "Man,"
40 And its hero the Conqueror Worm.

"O God!" half shrieked Ligeia, leaping to her feet and extending her arms aloft with a spasmodic movement, as I made an end of these lines—"O God! O Divine Father!—shall these things be undeviatingly so?—shall this Conqueror be not once conquered? Are we not part and parcel in Thee? Who—who knoweth the mysteries of the will with its vigor? Man doth not yield him to the angels, *nor unto death utterly*, save only through the weakness of his feeble will."

And now, as if exhausted with emotion, she suffered her white arms to fall, and returned solemnly to her bed of Death. And as she breathed her last sighs, there came mingled with them a low murmur from her lips. I bent to them my ear and distinguished, again, the concluding words of the passage in Glanvill. "*Man doth not yield him to the angels, nor unto death utterly, save only through the weakness of his feeble will.*"

She died;—and I, crushed into the very dust with sorrow, could no longer endure the lonely desolation of my dwelling in the dim and decaying city by the Rhine. I had no lack of what the world calls wealth. Ligeia had brought me far more, very far more than ordinarily falls to the lot of mortals. After a few months, therefore, of weary and aimless wandering, I purchased, and put in some repair, an abbey, which I shall not name, in one of the wildest and least frequented portions of fair England. The gloomy and dreary grandeur of the building, the almost savage aspect[2] of the domain, the many melancholy and time-honored memories connected with both, had much in unison with the feelings of utter abandonment which had driven me into that remote and unsocial region of the country. Yet, although the external abbey, with its verdant decay hanging about it, suffered but little alteration, I gave

---

[1] *of the spheres* Heavenly.

[2] *aspect* Appearance.

way, with a child-like perversity, and perchance with a faint hope of alleviating my sorrows, to a display of more than regal magnificence within. For such follies, even in childhood, I had imbibed a taste and now they came back to me as if in the dotage of grief. Alas, I now feel how much even of incipient madness might have been discovered in the gorgeous and fantastic draperies, in the solemn carvings of Egypt, in the wild cornices and furniture, in the Bedlam[1] patterns of the carpets of tufted gold! I had become a bounden slave in the trammels[2] of opium, and my labors and my orders had taken a coloring from my dreams. But these absurdities I must not pause to detail. Let me speak only of that one chamber, ever accursed, whither, in a moment of mental alienation, I led from the altar as my bride—as the successor of the unforgotten Ligeia—the fair-haired and blue-eyed Lady Rowena Trevanion, of Tremaine.

There is no individual portion of the architecture and decoration of that bridal chamber which is not now visibly before me. Where were the souls of the haughty family of the bride, when, through thirst of gold, they permitted to pass the threshold of an apartment *so* bedecked, a maiden and a daughter so beloved? I have said that I minutely remember the details of the chamber—yet I am sadly forgetful on topics of deep moment—and here there was no system, no keeping, in the fantastic display, to take hold upon the memory. The room lay in a high turret of the castellated[3] abbey, was pentagonal in shape, and of capacious size. Occupying the whole southern face of the pentagon was the sole window—an immense sheet of unbroken glass from Venice—a single pane, and tinted of a leaden hue, so that the rays of either the sun or moon, passing through it, fell with a ghastly lustre upon the objects within. Over the upper portion of this huge window extended the open trellis-work of an aged vine, which clambered up the massy[4] walls of the turret. The ceiling, of gloomy-looking oak, was excessively lofty, vaulted, and elaborately fretted with the wildest and most grotesque specimens of a semi-Gothic,

semi-Druidical[5] device. From out the most central recess of this melancholy vaulting, depended, by a single chain of gold with long links, a huge censer of the same metal, Saracenic[6] in pattern, and with many perforations so contrived that there writhed in and out of them, as if endued[7] with a serpent vitality, a continual succession of parti-colored fires.

Some few ottomans and golden candelabra, of Eastern figure, were in various stations about—and there was the couch, too—the bridal couch—of an Indian model, and low, and sculptured of solid ebony, with a pall-like canopy above. In each of the angles of the chamber stood on end a gigantic sarcophagus of black granite, from the tombs of the kings over against Luxor,[8] with their aged lids full of immemorial sculpture. But in the draping of the apartment lay, alas! the chief phantasy of all. The lofty walls—gigantic in height—even unproportionally so—were hung from summit to foot, in vast folds, with a heavy and massive-looking tapestry— tapestry of a material which was found alike as a carpet on the floor, as a covering for the ottomans and the ebony bed, as a canopy for the bed, and as the gorgeous volutes[9] of the curtains which partially shaded the window. This material was the richest cloth of gold. It was spotted all over, at irregular intervals, with arabesque[10] figures, about a foot in diameter, and wrought upon the cloth in patterns of the most jetty black. But these figures partook of the true character of the arabesque only when regarded from a single point of view. By a contrivance now common, and indeed traceable to a very remote period of antiquity, they were made changeable in aspect. To one entering the room, they bore the appearance of simple monstrosities; but upon a farther advance, this appearance gradually departed; and step by step, as

---

[1] *cornices*   Ornamental wall moldings, usually just beneath the ceiling; *Bedlam*   Chaotic, mad (Bedlam was a London hospital for the mentally ill).

[2] *trammels*   Nets; shackles.

[3] *castellated*   Having many turrets, like a castle fortress.

[4] *massy*   Massive, heavy.

[5] *fretted*   Carved with interweaving patterns; *semi-Druidical*   Likely meaning Celtic in design; the Druids were Celtic priests or magicians.

[6] *censer*   Incense burner; *Saracenic*   Intricately ornamented, with complex patterns associated with Islamic architecture.

[7] *endued*   Endowed.

[8] *Luxor*   Egyptian city near the ruins of ancient Thebes.

[9] *volutes*   Curved or twisted shapes.

[10] *arabesque*   Ornate, especially incorporating a complex interweaving pattern; the term is associated with Middle Eastern decorative arts.

the visitor moved his station in the chamber, he saw himself surrounded by an endless succession of the ghastly forms which belong to the superstition of the Norman,[1] or arise in the guilty slumbers of the monk. The phantasmagoric[2] effect was vastly heightened by the artificial introduction of a strong continual current of wind behind the draperies—giving a hideous and uneasy animation to the whole.

In halls such as these—in a bridal chamber such as this—I passed, with the Lady of Tremaine, the unhallowed hours of the first month of our marriage—passed them with but little disquietude. That my wife dreaded the fierce moodiness of my temper—that she shunned me and loved me but little—I could not help perceiving; but it gave me rather pleasure than otherwise. I loathed her with a hatred belonging more to demon than to man. My memory flew back (oh, with what intensity of regret!) to Ligeia, the beloved, the august, the beautiful, the entombed. I revelled in recollections of her purity, of her wisdom, of her lofty, her ethereal nature, of her passionate, her idolatrous love. Now, then, did my spirit fully and freely burn with more than all the fires of her own. In the excitement of my opium dreams (for I was habitually fettered in the shackles of the drug) I would call aloud upon her name, during the silence of the night, or among the sheltered recesses of the glens by day, as if, through the wild eagerness, the solemn passion, the consuming ardor of my longing for the departed, I could restore her to the pathway she had abandoned—ah, *could* it be forever?—upon earth.

About the commencement of the second month of the marriage, the lady Rowena was attacked with sudden illness, from which her recovery was slow. The fever which consumed her, rendered her nights uneasy; and in her perturbed state of half-slumber, she spoke of sounds, and of motions, in and about the chamber of the turret, which I concluded had no origin save in the distemper of her fancy, or perhaps in the phantasmagoric influences of the chamber itself. She became at length convalescent—finally well. Yet but a brief period elapsed, ere a second more violent disorder again threw her upon a bed of suffering; and from this attack her frame, at all times feeble, never altogether recovered. Her illnesses were, after this epoch, of alarming character, and of more alarming recurrence, defying alike the knowledge and the great exertions of her physicians. With the increase of the chronic disease which had thus, apparently, taken too sure hold upon her constitution to be eradicated by human means, I could not fail to observe a similar increase in the nervous irritability of her temperament, and in her excitability by trivial causes of fear. She spoke again, and now more frequently and pertinaciously, of the sounds—of the slight sounds—and of the unusual motions among the tapestries, to which she had formerly alluded.

One night, near the closing in of September, she pressed this distressing subject with more than usual emphasis upon my attention. She had just awakened from an unquiet slumber, and I had been watching, with feelings half of anxiety, half of a vague terror, the workings of her emaciated countenance. I sat by the side of her ebony bed, upon one of the ottomans of India. She partly arose, and spoke, in an earnest low whisper, of sounds which she *then* heard, but which I could not hear—of motions which she *then* saw, but which I could not perceive. The wind was rushing hurriedly behind the tapestries, and I wished to show her (what, let me confess it, I could not *all* believe) that those almost inarticulate breathings, and those very gentle variations of the figures upon the wall, were but the natural effects of that customary rushing of the wind. But a deadly pallor, overspreading her face, had proved to me that my exertions to reassure her would be fruitless. She appeared to be fainting, and no attendants were within call. I remembered where was deposited a decanter of light wine which had been ordered by her physicians, and hastened across the chamber to procure it. But, as I stepped beneath the light of the censer, two circumstances of a startling nature attracted my attention. I had felt that some palpable although invisible object had passed lightly by my person; and I saw that there lay upon the golden carpet, in the very middle of the rich lustre thrown from the censer, a shadow—a faint, indefinite shadow of angelic aspect—such as might be fancied for the

---

[1]   *the ghastly … Norman* The folklore of medieval Normandy incorporated a wide range of monsters.

[2]   *phantasmagoric* Reference to phantasmagoria, entertainments in which optical illusions—usually of supernatural phenomena—are created by means of projection.

shadow of a shade.[1] But I was wild with the excitement of an immoderate dose of opium, and heeded these things but little, nor spoke of them to Rowena. Having found the wine, I recrossed the chamber, and poured out a goblet-full, which I held to the lips of the fainting lady. She had now partially recovered, however, and took the vessel herself, while I sank upon an ottoman near me, with my eyes fastened upon her person. It was then that I became distinctly aware of a gentle foot-fall upon the carpet, and near the couch; and in a second thereafter, as Rowena was in the act of raising the wine to her lips, I saw, or may have dreamed that I saw, fall within the goblet, as if from some invisible spring in the atmosphere of the room, three or four large drops of a brilliant and ruby colored fluid. If this I saw—not so Rowena. She swallowed the wine unhesitatingly, and I forbore to speak to her of a circumstance which must, after all, I considered, have been but the suggestion of a vivid imagination, rendered morbidly active by the terror of the lady, by the opium, and by the hour.

Yet I cannot conceal it from my own perception that, immediately subsequent to the fall of the ruby-drops, a rapid change for the worse took place in the disorder of my wife; so that, on the third subsequent night, the hands of her menials prepared her for the tomb, and on the fourth, I sat alone, with her shrouded body, in that fantastic chamber which had received her as my bride. Wild visions, opium-engendered, flitted, shadow-like, before me. I gazed with unquiet eye upon the sarcophagi in the angles of the room, upon the varying figures of the drapery, and upon the writhing of the parti-colored fires in the censer overhead. My eyes then fell, as I called to mind the circumstances of a former night, to the spot beneath the glare of the censer where I had seen the faint traces of the shadow. It was there, however, no longer, and, breathing with greater freedom, I turned my glances to the pallid and rigid figure upon the bed. Then rushed upon me a thousand memories of Ligeia—and then came back upon my heart, with the turbulent violence of a flood, the whole of that unutterable woe with which I had regarded *her* thus enshrouded. The night waned; and still, with a bosom full of bitter thoughts of the one only and supremely beloved, I remained gazing upon the body of Rowena.

It might have been midnight, or perhaps earlier, or later, for I had taken no note of time, when a sob, low, gentle, but very distinct, startled me from my reverie. I *felt* that it came from the bed of ebony—the bed of death. I listened in an agony of superstitious terror—but there was no repetition of the sound; I strained my vision to detect any motion in the corpse—but there was not the slightest perceptible. Yet I could not have been deceived. I *had* heard the noise, however faint, and my whole soul was awakened within me. I resolutely and perseveringly kept my attention riveted upon the body. Many minutes elapsed before any circumstance occurred tending to throw light upon the mystery. At length it became evident that a slight, a very feeble, and barely noticeable tinge of color had flushed up within the cheeks, and along the sunken small veins of the eyelids. Through a species of unutterable horror and awe, for which the language of mortality has no sufficiently energetic expression, I felt my heart cease to beat, my limbs grow rigid where I sat. Yet a sense of duty finally operated to restore my self-possession. I could no longer doubt that we had been precipitate in our preparations—that Rowena still lived. It was necessary that some immediate exertion be made; yet the turret was altogether apart from the portion of the abbey tenanted by the servants—there were none within call—I had no means of summoning them to my aid without leaving the room for many minutes—and this I could not venture to do. I therefore struggled alone in my endeavors to call back the spirit still hovering. In a short period it was certain, however, that a relapse had taken place; the color disappeared from both eyelid and cheek, leaving a wanness even more than that of marble; the lips became doubly shrivelled and pinched up in the ghastly expression of death; a repulsive clamminess and coldness overspread rapidly the surface of the body; and all the usual rigorous stiffness immediately supervened. I fell back with a shudder upon the couch from which I had been so startlingly aroused, and again gave myself up to passionate waking visions of Ligeia.

An hour thus elapsed when (could it be possible?) I was a second time aware of some vague sound issuing from the region of the bed. I listened—in extremity of horror. The sound came again—it was a sigh. Rushing to the corpse, I saw—distinctly saw—a tremor upon

---

[1] *shade* Ghost.

the lips. In a minute afterward they relaxed, disclosing a bright line of the pearly teeth. Amazement now struggled in my bosom with the profound awe which had hitherto reigned there alone. I felt that my vision grew dim, that my reason wandered; and it was only by a violent effort that I at length succeeded in nerving myself to the task which duty thus once more had pointed out. There was now a partial glow upon the forehead, upon the cheek and throat; a perceptible warmth pervaded the whole frame; there was even a slight pulsation at the heart. The lady *lived*; and with redoubled ardor I betook myself to the task of restoration. I chafed and bathed the temples and the hands, and used every exertion which experience, and no little medical reading, could suggest. But in vain. Suddenly, the color fled, the pulsation ceased, the lips resumed the expression of the dead, and, in an instant afterwards, the whole body took upon itself the icy chilliness, the livid hue, the intense rigidity, the sunken outline, and each and all of the loathsome peculiarities of that which has been, for many days, a tenant of the tomb.

And again I sunk into visions of Ligeia—and again (what marvel that I shudder while I write?) *again* there reached my ears a low sob from the region of the ebony bed. But why shall I minutely detail the unspeakable horrors of that night? Why shall I pause to relate how, time after time, until near the period of the gray dawn, this hideous drama of revivification was repeated; and how each terrific relapse was only into a sterner and apparently more irredeemable death; how each agony wore the aspect of a struggle with some invisible foe; and how each struggle was succeeded by I know not what of wild change in the personal appearance of the corpse? Let me hurry to a conclusion.

The greater part of the fearful night had worn away, and she who had been dead, once again stirred—and now more vigorously than hitherto, although arousing from a dissolution more appalling in its utter hopelessness than any. I had long ceased to struggle or to move, and remained sitting rigidly upon the ottoman, a helpless prey to a whirl of violent emotions, of which extreme awe was perhaps the least terrible, the least consuming. The corpse, I repeat, stirred, and now more vigorously than before. The hues of life flushed up with unwonted energy into the countenance—the limbs relaxed—and, save that the eyelids were yet pressed heavily together, and that the bandages and draperies of the grave still imparted their charnel[1] character to the figure, I might have dreamed that Rowena had indeed shaken off, utterly, the fetters of Death. But if this idea was not, even then, altogether adopted, I could at least doubt no longer, when, arising from the bed, tottering, with feeble steps, with closed eyes, and with the manner of one bewildered in a dream, the thing that was enshrouded advanced bodily and palpably into the middle of the apartment.

I trembled not—I stirred not—for a crowd of unutterable fancies connected with the air, the stature, the demeanor of the figure, rushing hurriedly through my brain, had paralyzed—had chilled me into stone. I stirred not—but gazed upon the apparition. There was a mad disorder in my thoughts—a tumult unappeasable. Could it indeed be Rowena *at all*—the fair-haired, the blue-eyed Lady Rowena Trevanion of Tremaine? Why, *why* should I doubt it? The bandage lay heavily about the mouth—but then might it not be the mouth of the breathing Lady of Tremaine? And the cheeks—there were the roses as in her noon of life— yes, these might indeed be the fair cheeks of the living Lady of Tremaine. And the chin, with its dimples, as in health, might it not be hers?—but *had she then grown taller since her malady*? What inexpressible madness seized me with that thought? One bound, and I had reached her feet! Shrinking from my touch, she let fall from her head, unloosened, the ghastly cerements[2] which had confined it, and there streamed forth, into the rushing atmosphere of the chamber, huge masses of long and dishevelled hair; *it was blacker than the raven wings of the midnight*! And now slowly opened *the eyes* of the figure which stood before me. "Here then, at least," I shrieked aloud, "can I never—can I never be mistaken—these are the full, and the black, and the wild eyes—of my lost love—of the lady—of the Lady Ligeia!"

—1838 (REVISED 1845, 1848)

---

[1]   *charnel* Deathlike.

[2]   *cerements* Waxed cloths for wrapping the dead.

The Fall of the House of Usher

Son coeur est un luth suspendu;
Sitôt qu'on le touche il résonne.[1]
De Béranger.

During the whole of a dull, dark, and soundless day in the autumn of the year, when the clouds hung oppressively low in the heavens, I had been passing alone, on horseback, through a singularly dreary tract of country; and at length found myself, as the shades of the evening drew on, within view of the melancholy House of Usher. I know not how it was—but, with the first glimpse of the building, a sense of insufferable gloom pervaded my spirit. I say insufferable; for the feeling was unrelieved by any of that half-pleasurable, because poetic, sentiment, with which the mind usually receives even the sternest natural images of the desolate or terrible. I looked upon the scene before me—upon the mere house, and the simple landscape features of the domain—upon the bleak walls—upon the vacant eye-like windows—upon a few rank sedges—and upon a few white trunks of decayed trees—with an utter depression of soul which I can compare to no earthly sensation more properly than to the after-dream of the reveller upon opium—the bitter lapse into every-day life,—the hideous dropping off of the veil. There was an iciness, a sinking, a sickening of the heart—an unredeemed dreariness of thought which no goading of the imagination could torture into aught of the sublime. What was it—I paused to think—what was it that so unnerved me in the contemplation of the House of Usher? It was a mystery all insoluble; nor could I grapple with the shadowy fancies that crowded upon me as I pondered. I was forced to fall back upon the unsatisfactory conclusion, that while, beyond doubt, there *are* combinations of very simple natural objects which have the power of thus affecting us, still the analysis of this power lies among considerations beyond our depth. It was possible, I reflected, that a mere different arrangement of the particulars of the scene, of the details of the picture, would be sufficient to modify, or

perhaps to annihilate its capacity for sorrowful impression; and, acting upon this idea, I reined my horse to the precipitous brink of a black and lurid tarn[2] that lay in unruffled lustre by the dwelling, and gazed down—but with a shudder even more thrilling than before—upon the re-modelled and inverted images of the gray sedge, and the ghastly tree-stems, and the vacant and eye-like windows.

Nevertheless, in this mansion of gloom I now proposed to myself a sojourn of some weeks. Its proprietor, Roderick Usher, had been one of my boon companions in boyhood; but many years had elapsed since our last meeting. A letter, however, had lately reached me in a distant part of the country—a letter from him—which, in its wildly importunate nature, had admitted of no other than a personal reply. The MS.[3] gave evidence of nervous agitation. The writer spoke of acute bodily illness—of a mental disorder which oppressed him—and of an earnest desire to see me, as his best, and indeed his only personal friend, with a view of attempting, by the cheerfulness of my society, some alleviation of his malady. It was the manner in which all this, and much more, was said—it was the apparent *heart* that went with his request—which allowed me no room for hesitation; and I accordingly obeyed forthwith what I still considered a very singular summons.

Although, as boys, we had been even intimate associates, yet I really knew little of my friend. His reserve had been always excessive and habitual. I was aware, however, that his very ancient family had been noted, time out of mind, for a peculiar sensibility of temperament, displaying itself, through long ages, in many works of exalted art, and manifested, of late, in repeated deeds of munificent yet unobtrusive charity, as well as in a passionate devotion to the intricacies, perhaps even more than to the orthodox and easily recognizable beauties, of musical science. I had learned, too, the very remarkable fact, that the stem of the Usher race, all time-honored as it was, had put forth, at no period, any enduring branch; in other words, that the entire family lay in the direct line of descent, and had always, with very trifling and very temporary variation, so lain. It was this deficiency, I considered, while running over in thought the perfect keeping

---

[1]   *Son coeur … résonne*   French: His or her heart is a suspended lute; it resounds as soon as it is touched. The quotation is slightly altered from Pierre Jean de Béranger's song "Le Refus" (1830).

[2]   *tarn*   Small mountain lake.

[3]   *MS.*   Manuscript; also, handwriting.

of the character of the premises with the accredited character of the people, and while speculating upon the possible influence which the one, in the long lapse of centuries, might have exercised upon the other—it was this deficiency, perhaps, of collateral issue,[1] and the consequent undeviating transmission, from sire to son, of the patrimony with the name, which had, at length, so identified the two as to merge the original title of the estate in the quaint and equivocal appellation of the "House of Usher"—an appellation which seemed to include, in the minds of the peasantry who used it, both the family and the family mansion.

I have said that the sole effect of my somewhat childish experiment—of looking down within the tarn—had been to deepen the first singular impression. There can be no doubt that the consciousness of the rapid increase of my superstition—for why should I not so term it?—served mainly to accelerate the increase itself. Such, I have long known, is the paradoxical law of all sentiments having terror as a basis. And it might have been for this reason only, that, when I again uplifted my eyes to the house itself, from its image in the pool, there grew in my mind a strange fancy—a fancy so ridiculous, indeed, that I but mention it to show the vivid force of the sensations which oppressed me. I had so worked upon my imagination as really to believe that about the whole mansion and domain there hung an atmosphere peculiar to themselves and their immediate vicinity—an atmosphere which had no affinity with the air of heaven, but which had reeked up from the decayed trees, and the gray wall, and the silent tarn—a pestilent and mystic vapor, dull, sluggish, faintly discernible, and leaden-hued.

Shaking off from my spirit what *must* have been a dream, I scanned more narrowly the real aspect[2] of the building. Its principal feature seemed to be that of an excessive antiquity. The discoloration of ages had been great. Minute fungi overspread the whole exterior, hanging in a fine tangled web-work from the eaves. Yet all this was apart from any extraordinary dilapidation. No portion of the masonry had fallen; and there appeared to be a wild inconsistency between its still perfect adaptation of parts, and the crumbling condition of the individual stones. In this there was much that reminded me of the specious totality of old wood-work which has rotted for long years in some neglected vault, with no disturbance from the breath of the external air. Beyond this indication of extensive decay, however, the fabric[3] gave little token of instability. Perhaps the eye of a scrutinizing observer might have discovered a barely perceptible fissure, which, extending from the roof of the building in front, made its way down the wall in a zig-zag direction, until it became lost in the sullen waters of the tarn.

Noticing these things, I rode over a short causeway to the house. A servant in waiting took my horse, and I entered the Gothic archway of the hall. A valet,[4] of stealthy step, thence conducted me, in silence, through many dark and intricate passages in my progress to the *studio* of his master. Much that I encountered on the way contributed, I know not how, to heighten the vague sentiments of which I have already spoken. While the objects around me—while the carvings of the ceilings, the sombre tapestries of the walls, the ebon blackness of the floors, and the phantasmagoric[5] armorial trophies which rattled as I strode, were but matters to which, or to such as which, I had been accustomed from my infancy—while I hesitated not to acknowledge how familiar was all this—I still wondered to find how unfamiliar were the fancies which ordinary images were stirring up. On one of the staircases, I met the physician of the family. His countenance, I thought, wore a mingled expression of low cunning and perplexity. He accosted me with trepidation and passed on. The valet now threw open a door and ushered me into the presence of his master.

The room in which I found myself was very large and lofty. The windows were long, narrow, and pointed, and at so vast a distance from the black oaken floor as to be altogether inaccessible from within. Feeble gleams of encrimsoned light made their way through

---

1 *collateral issue* Blood relatives outside the direct line of descent, i.e., siblings, cousins, aunts, uncles, etc.

2 *aspect* Physical appearance.

3 *fabric* Frame of the building.

4 *valet* Gentleman's servant.

5 *phantasmagoric* Illusory, continuously transforming; here the word describes optical illusions created by the reflection of light off metal, in this case off armor or weaponry that is displayed on the walls of the house.

the trellissed panes,[1] and served to render sufficiently distinct the more prominent objects around; the eye, however, struggled in vain to reach the remoter angles of the chamber, or the recesses of the vaulted and fretted ceiling. Dark draperies hung upon the walls. The general furniture was profuse, comfortless, antique, and tattered. Many books and musical instruments lay scattered about, but failed to give any vitality to the scene. I felt that I breathed an atmosphere of sorrow. An air of stern, deep, and irredeemable gloom hung over and pervaded all.

Upon my entrance, Usher rose from a sofa upon which he had been lying at full length, and greeted me with a vivacious warmth which had much in it, I at first thought, of an overdone cordiality—of the constrained effort of the *ennuyé*[2] man of the world. A glance, however, at his countenance convinced me of his perfect sincerity. We sat down; and for some moments, while he spoke not, I gazed upon him with a feeling half of pity, half of awe. Surely, man had never before so terribly altered, in so brief a period, as had Roderick Usher! It was with difficulty that I could bring myself to admit the identity of the wan[3] being before me with the companion of my early boyhood. Yet the character of his face had been at all times remarkable. A cadaverousness of complexion; an eye large, liquid, and luminous beyond comparison; lips somewhat thin and very pallid, but of a surpassingly beautiful curve; a nose of a delicate Hebrew model, but with a breadth of nostril unusual in similar formations; a finely moulded chin, speaking, in its want of prominence, of a want of moral energy; hair of a more than web-like softness and tenuity; these features, with an inordinate expansion above the regions of the temple,[4] made up altogether a countenance not easily to be forgotten. And now in the mere exaggeration of the prevailing character of these features, and of the expression

they were wont to convey, lay so much of change that I doubted to whom I spoke. The now ghastly pallor of the skin, and the now miraculous lustre of the eye, above all things startled and even awed me. The silken hair, too, had been suffered to grow all unheeded, and as, in its wild gossamer texture, it floated rather than fell about the face, I could not, even with effort, connect its Arabesque[5] expression with any idea of simple humanity.

In the manner of my friend I was at once struck with an incoherence—an inconsistency; and I soon found this to arise from a series of feeble and futile struggles to overcome an habitual trepidancy—an excessive nervous agitation. For something of this nature I had indeed been prepared, no less by his letter, than by reminiscences of certain boyish traits, and by conclusions deduced from his peculiar physical conformation and temperament. His action was alternately vivacious and sullen. His voice varied rapidly from a tremulous indecision (when the animal spirits seemed utterly in abeyance) to that species of energetic concision—that abrupt, weighty, unhurried, and hollow-sounding enunciation—that leaden, self-balanced and perfectly modulated guttural utterance, which may be observed in the lost drunkard, or the irreclaimable eater of opium, during the periods of his most intense excitement.

It was thus that he spoke of the object of my visit, of his earnest desire to see me, and of the solace he expected me to afford him. He entered, at some length, into what he conceived to be the nature of his malady. It was, he said, a constitutional and a family evil, and one for which he despaired to find a remedy—a mere nervous affection, he immediately added, which would undoubtedly soon pass off. It displayed itself in a host of unnatural sensations. Some of these, as he detailed them, interested and bewildered me; although, perhaps, the terms, and the general manner of the narration had their weight. He suffered much from a morbid acuteness of the senses; the most insipid food was alone endurable; he could wear only garments of certain texture; the odors of all flowers were oppressive; his eyes were tortured by even a faint light; and there were but

---

[1] *trellissed panes* Gothic-style windows with tracery—decorative stonework that keeps the glass in place.

[2] *ennuyé* French: bored.

[3] *wan* Pale and sickly.

[4] *inordinate expansion ... temple* In the pseudoscience of phrenology, according to which the shape of one's skull indicates one's personality traits, a person whose skull is enlarged above the temple is particularly strong in the trait of "ideality" (i.e., imagination, especially the capacity to imagine and appreciate perfection).

[5] *Arabesque* Ornate, especially with a complex interweaving pattern; the term can also refer to things perceived to possess "Arabian" qualities.

peculiar sounds, and these from stringed instruments, which did not inspire him with horror.

To an anomalous species of terror I found him a bounden slave. "I shall perish," said he, "I *must* perish in this deplorable folly. Thus, thus, and not otherwise, shall I be lost. I dread the events of the future, not in themselves, but in their results. I shudder at the thought of any, even the most trivial, incident, which may operate upon this intolerable agitation of soul. I have, indeed, no abhorrence of danger, except in its absolute effect—in terror. In this unnerved—in this pitiable condition—I feel that the period will sooner or later arrive when I must abandon life and reason together, in some struggle with the grim phantasm, FEAR."

I learned, moreover, at intervals, and through broken and equivocal hints, another singular feature of his mental condition. He was enchained by certain superstitious impressions in regard to the dwelling which he tenanted, and whence, for many years, he had never ventured forth—in regard to an influence whose supposititious force was conveyed in terms too shadowy here to be re-stated—an influence which some peculiarities in the mere form and substance of his family mansion, had, by dint of long sufferance, he said, obtained over his spirit—an effect which the *physique* of the gray walls and turrets, and of the dim tarn into which they all looked down, had, at length, brought about upon the *morale* of his existence.

He admitted, however, although with hesitation, that much of the peculiar gloom which thus afflicted him could be traced to a more natural and far more palpable origin—to the severe and long-continued illness—indeed to the evidently approaching dissolution—of a tenderly beloved sister—his sole companion for long years—his last and only relative on earth. "Her decease," he said, with a bitterness which I can never forget, "would leave him (him the hopeless and the frail) the last of the ancient race of the Ushers." While he spoke, the lady Madeline (for so was she called) passed slowly through a remote portion of the apartment, and, without having noticed my presence, disappeared. I regarded her with an utter astonishment not unmingled with dread—and yet I found it impossible to account for such feelings. A sensation of stupor oppressed me, as my eyes followed her retreating steps.

When a door, at length, closed upon her, my glance sought instinctively and eagerly the countenance of the brother—but he had buried his face in his hands, and I could only perceive that a far more than ordinary wanness had overspread the emaciated fingers through which trickled many passionate tears.

The disease of the lady Madeline had long baffled the skill of her physicians. A settled apathy, a gradual wasting away of the person, and frequent although transient affections of a partially cataleptical character,[1] were the unusual diagnosis. Hitherto she had steadily borne up against the pressure of her malady, and had not betaken herself finally to bed; but, on the closing in of the evening of my arrival at the house, she succumbed (as her brother told me at night with inexpressible agitation) to the prostrating power of the destroyer; and I learned that the glimpse I had obtained of her person would thus probably be the last I should obtain—that the lady, at least while living, would be seen by me no more.

For several days ensuing, her name was unmentioned by either Usher or myself; and, during this period I was busied in earnest endeavors to alleviate the melancholy of my friend. We painted and read together; or I listened, as if in a dream, to the wild improvisations of his speaking guitar. And thus, as a closer and still closer intimacy admitted me more unreservedly into the recesses of his spirit, the more bitterly did I perceive the futility of all attempt at cheering a mind from which darkness, as if an inherent positive quality, poured forth upon all objects of the moral and physical universe, in one unceasing radiation of gloom.

I shall ever bear about me a memory of the many solemn hours I thus spent alone with the master of the House of Usher. Yet I should fail in any attempt to convey an idea of the exact character of the studies, or of the occupations, in which he involved me, or led me the way. An excited and highly distempered ideality threw a sulphureous[2] lustre over all. His long improvised dirges[3] will ring for ever in my ears. Among other things, I bear painfully in mind a certain singular

---

[1]   *affections ... cataleptical character*   Medical complaints that involve loss of consciousness, such as fainting spells, trances, and seizures.

[2]   *sulphureous*   I.e., smoky, unclear; also, more figuratively, hellish.

[3]   *dirges*   Somber, funereal songs.

perversion and amplification of the wild air of the last waltz of Von Weber.[1] From the paintings over which his elaborate fancy brooded, and which grew, touch by touch, into vaguenesses at which I shuddered the more thrillingly, because I shuddered knowing not why—from these paintings (vivid as their images now are before me) I would in vain endeavor to educe[2] more than a small portion which should lie within the compass of merely written words. By the utter simplicity, by the nakedness, of his designs, he arrested and overawed attention. If ever mortal painted an idea, that mortal was Roderick Usher. For me at least—in the circumstances then surrounding me—there arose out of the pure abstractions which the hypochondriac contrived to throw upon his canvass, an intensity of intolerable awe, no shadow of which felt I ever yet in the contemplation of the certainly glowing yet too concrete reveries of Fuseli.[3]

One of the phantasmagoric conceptions of my friend, partaking not so rigidly of the spirit of abstraction, may be shadowed forth, although feebly, in words. A small picture presented the interior of an immensely long and rectangular vault or tunnel, with low walls, smooth, white, and without interruption or device.[4] Certain accessory points of the design served well to convey the idea that this excavation lay at an exceeding depth below the surface of the earth. No outlet was observed in any portion of its vast extent, and no torch, or other artificial source of light was discernible; yet a flood of intense rays rolled throughout, and bathed the whole in a ghastly and inappropriate splendor.

I have just spoken of that morbid condition of the auditory nerve which rendered all music intolerable to the sufferer, with the exception of certain effects of stringed instruments. It was, perhaps, the narrow limits to which he thus confined himself upon the guitar, which gave birth, in great measure, to the fantastic character of his performances. But the fervid

facility of his *impromptus* could not be so accounted for. They must have been, and were, in the notes, as well as in the words of his wild fantasias (for he not unfrequently accompanied himself with rhymed verbal improvisations), the result of that intense mental collectedness and concentration to which I have previously alluded as observable only in particular moments of the highest artificial excitement. The words of one of these rhapsodies I have easily remembered. I was, perhaps, the more forcibly impressed with it, as he gave it, because, in the under or mystic current of its meaning, I fancied that I perceived, and for the first time, a full consciousness on the part of Usher, of the tottering of his lofty reason upon her throne. The verses, which were entitled "The Haunted Palace,"[5] ran very nearly, if not accurately, thus:

1.

In the greenest of our valleys,
    By good angels tenanted,
Once a fair and stately palace—
    Radiant palace—reared its head.
5 In the monarch Thought's dominion—
    It stood there!
Never seraph° spread a pinion°   *angel | wing*
    Over fabric half so fair.

2.

Banners yellow, glorious, golden,
10   On its roof did float and flow;
(This—all this—was in the olden
    Time long ago)
And every gentle air that dallied,
    In that sweet day,
15 Along the ramparts plumed and pallid,
    A winged odor went away.

3.

Wanderers in that happy valley
    Through two luminous windows saw
Spirits moving musically
20   To a lute's well-tunèd law,

---

[1] *Von Weber* Carl Maria von Weber (1786–1826) German Romantic composer, to whom "Von Weber's Last Waltz" was long attributed; the piece was in fact composed by Carl Gottlieb Reissiger (1798–1859).

[2] *educe* Draw out; come up with.

[3] *Fuseli* Swiss painter Henry Fuseli (1741–1825), known for depictions of dark, Gothic, and supernatural subjects.

[4] *device* Design; carving or other decoration.

[5] *The Haunted Palace* An endnote in the original *Burton's* publication of this story reads as follows: "The ballad of 'The Haunted Palace,' introduced in this tale, was published separately, some months ago, in the Baltimore 'Museum.'"

Round about a throne, where sitting
   (Porphyrogene![1])
In state his glory well befitting,
   The ruler of the realm was seen.

4.

25 And all with pearl and ruby glowing
   Was the fair palace door,
Through which came flowing, flowing, flowing,
   And sparkling evermore,
A troop of Echoes whose sole duty
30   Was but to sing,
In voices of surpassing beauty,
   The wit and wisdom of their king.

5.

But evil things, in robes of sorrow,
   Assailed the monarch's high estate;
35 (Ah, let us mourn, for never morrow
   Shall dawn upon him, desolate!)
And, round about his home, the glory
   That blushed and bloomed
Is but a dim-remembered story
40   Of the old time entombed.

6.

And travellers now within that valley,
   Through the red-litten windows, see
Vast forms that move fantastically
   To a discordant melody;
45 While, like a rapid ghastly river,
   Through the pale door,
A hideous throng rush out forever,
   And laugh—but smile no more.

I well remember that suggestions arising from this ballad, led us into a train of thought wherein there became manifest an opinion of Usher's which I mention not so much on account of its novelty (for other men[2] have thought thus) as on account of the per-

tinacity with which he maintained it. This opinion, in its general form, was that of the sentience of all vegetable things. But, in his disordered fancy, the idea had assumed a more daring character, and trespassed, under certain conditions, upon the kingdom of inorganization.[3] I lack words to express the full extent, or the earnest *abandon* of his persuasion. The belief, however, was connected (as I have previously hinted) with the gray stones of the home of his forefathers. The condition of the sentience had been here, he imagined, fulfilled in the method of collocation of these stones—in the order of their arrangement, as well as in that of the many *fungi* which overspread them, and of the decayed trees which stood around—above all, in the long undisturbed endurance of this arrangement, and in its reduplication in the still waters of the tarn. Its evidence—the evidence of the sentience—was to be seen, he said (and I here started as he spoke), in the gradual yet certain condensation of an atmosphere of their own about the waters and the walls. The result was discoverable, he added, in that silent, yet importunate and terrible influence which for centuries had moulded the destinies of his family, and which made *him* what I now saw him—what he was. Such opinions need no comment, and I will make none.

Our books—the books which, for years, had formed no small portion of the mental existence of the invalid—were, as might be supposed, in strict keeping with this character of phantasm. We pored together over such works as the Ververt et Chartreuse of Gresset; the Belphegor of Machiavelli; the Heaven and Hell of Swedenborg; the Subterranean Voyage of Nicholas Klimm de Holberg; the Chiromancy of Robert Flud, of Jean D'Indaginé, and of De la Chambre; the Journey into the Blue Distance of Tieck; and the City of the Sun of Campanella.[4] One favorite volume was a small

---

[1] *Porphyrogene* Born into purple (the color of royalty); of noble birth.

[2] [Poe's note] Watson, Dr. Percival, Spallanzani, and especially the Bishop of Landaff. See "Chemical Essays," vol. v. [Poe refers to Richard Watson, Bishop of Landaff (1737–1816), who wrote extensively on chemistry and other sciences as well as on theology; Thomas Percival (1740–1804), English writer on medical ethics; and

Lazzaro Spallanzani (1729–99), Italian biologist and Catholic priest. All three writers speculated on the possibility that plant matter may be sensitive or in some way perceptive.]

[3] *kingdom of inorganization* World of inanimate matter.

[4] *Our books ... Campanella* The narrator lists works (many of them rather obscure) whose themes include religion, science, mysticism, and the supernatural; the authors are French poet Jean-Baptiste-Louis Gresset (1709–77), Italian political philosopher Niccolò Machiavelli (1469–1527), Swedish scientist and mystic Emanuel Swedenborg (1688–1772), Danish-Norwegian playwright and philosopher Ludvig Holberg (1684–1754), English scientist and

octavo edition of the *Directorium Inquisitorium*, by the Dominican Eymeric de Gironne; and there were passages in Pomponius Mela, about the old African Satyrs and œgipans,[1] over which Usher would sit dreaming for hours. His chief delight, however, was found in the earnest and repeated perusal of an exceedingly rare and curious book in quarto Gothic—the manual of a forgotten church—the *Vigiliae Mortuorum secundum Chorum Ecclesiae Maguntinae*.[2]

I could not help thinking of the wild ritual of this work, and of its probable influence upon the hypochondriac, when, one evening, having informed me abruptly that the lady Madeline was no more, he stated his intention of preserving her corpse for a fortnight (previously[3] to its final interment) in one of the numerous vaults within the main walls of the building. The worldly reason, however, assigned for this singular proceeding, was one which I did not feel at liberty to dispute. The brother had been led to his resolution (so he told me) by consideration of the unusual character of the malady of the deceased, of certain obtrusive and eager inquiries on the part of her medical men, and of the remote and exposed situation of the burial ground of the family. I will not deny that when I called to mind the sinister countenance of the person whom I met upon the staircase, on the day of my arrival at the house, I had no desire to oppose what I regarded as

at best but a harmless, and by no means an unnatural, precaution.[4]

At the request of Usher, I personally aided him in the arrangements for the temporary entombment. The body having been encoffined, we two alone bore it to its rest. The vault in which we placed it (and which had been so long unopened that our torches, half smothered in its oppressive atmosphere, gave us little opportunity for investigation) was small, damp, and utterly without means of admission for light; lying, at great depth, immediately beneath that portion of the building in which was my own sleeping apartment. It had been used, apparently, in remote feudal times, for the worst purposes of a donjon-keep,[5] and, in later days, as a place of deposit for powder, or some other highly combustible substance, as a portion of its floor, and the whole interior of a long archway through which we reached it, were carefully sheathed with copper. The door, of massive iron, had been, also, similarly protected. Its immense weight caused an unusually sharp grating sound, as it moved upon its hinges.

Having deposited our mournful burden upon trestles[6] within this region of horror, we partially turned aside the yet unscrewed lid of the coffin, and looked upon the face of the tenant. A striking similitude between the brother and sister now first arrested my attention; and Usher, divining, perhaps, my thoughts, murmured out some few words from which I learned that the deceased and himself had been twins, and that sympathies of a scarcely intelligible nature had always existed between them. Our glances, however, rested not long upon the dead—for we could not regard her unawed. The disease which had thus entombed the lady in the maturity of youth, had left, as usual in all maladies of a strictly cataleptical character, the mockery of a faint blush upon the bosom and the face, and that suspiciously lingering smile upon the lip which is so terrible in death. We replaced and screwed down

---

occultist Robert Fludd (1574–1637), German astrologer Johannes Indagine (c. 1467–1537), French writer on palmistry Maria Cireau de la Chambre (1594–1669), German poet Ludwig Tieck (1773–1853), and Italian Utopian philosopher Tommaso Campanella (1568–1639); *Chiromancy* Palm-reading.

[1] *octavo* Small book size, created by folding sheets of paper so as to produce eight pages per sheet; *Directorium Inquisitorium* Written by Spanish theologian Nicholas Eymeric de Gerone (c. 1316–99), the *Directorium Inquisitorum* was a definitive text on Inquisitorial procedure and the means of extracting confessions from suspected heretics (especially through torture); *Pomponius Mela* Roman geographer (c. 43 CE) who wrote about bizarre foreign mythological creatures; *Satyrs and œgipans* Mythological creatures who are half human and half goat.

[2] *quarto* Book size created by folding sheets of paper so as to produce four pages per sheet; *Gothic* Ornate typeface also known as black letter; *Vigiliae … Maguntinae* Roman Catholic book of prayers for the dead, printed c. 1500.

[3] *previously* Prior.

[4] *The worldly reason … precaution* Grave-robbing was common in nineteenth-century America, as the rise of medicine produced an increasing need for bodies to be dissected for study; fresh graves were thus more susceptible. Usher may also have been concerned over the possibility of premature burial—in case Madeline were not actually dead, but in a deep coma—which was a rare but not unheard-of occurrence during this period.

[5] *donjon-keep* Dungeon.

[6] *trestles* Braces for supporting the coffin.

the lid, and, having secured the door of iron, made our way, with toil, into the scarcely less gloomy apartments of the upper portion of the house.

And now, some days of bitter grief having elapsed, an observable change came over the features of the mental disorder of my friend. His ordinary manner had vanished. His ordinary occupations were neglected or forgotten. He roamed from chamber to chamber with hurried, unequal, and objectless step. The pallor of his countenance had assumed, if possible, a more ghastly hue—but the luminousness of his eye had utterly gone out. The once occasional huskiness of his tone was heard no more; and a tremulous quaver, as if of extreme terror, habitually characterized his utterance. There were times, indeed, when I thought his unceasingly agitated mind was laboring with some oppressive secret, to divulge which he struggled for the necessary courage. At times, again, I was obliged to resolve all into the mere inexplicable vagaries of madness, for I beheld him gazing upon vacancy for long hours, in an attitude of the profoundest attention, as if listening to some imaginary sound. It was no wonder that his condition terrified—that it infected me. I felt creeping upon me, by slow yet certain degrees, the wild influences of his own fantastic yet impressive superstitions.

It was, especially, upon retiring to bed late in the night of the seventh or eighth day after the placing of the lady Madeline within the donjon, that I experienced the full power of such feelings. Sleep came not near my couch—while the hours waned and waned away. I struggled to reason off the nervousness which had dominion over me. I endeavored to believe that much, if not all of what I felt, was due to the bewildering influence of the gloomy furniture of the room—of the dark and tattered draperies, which, tortured into motion by the breath of a rising tempest, swayed fitfully to and fro upon the walls, and rustled uneasily about the decorations of the bed. But my efforts were fruitless. An irrepressible tremor gradually pervaded my frame; and, at length, there sat upon my very heart an incubus[1] of utterly causeless alarm. Shaking this off with a gasp and a struggle, I uplifted myself upon the pillows, and, peering earnestly within the intense darkness of the chamber, harkened—I know not why,

except that an instinctive spirit prompted me—to certain low and indefinite sounds which came, through the pauses of the storm, at long intervals, I knew not whence. Overpowered by an intense sentiment of horror, unaccountable yet unendurable, I threw on my clothes with haste (for I felt that I should sleep no more during the night) and endeavored to arouse myself from the pitiable condition into which I had fallen, by pacing rapidly to and fro through the apartment.

I had taken but few turns in this manner, when a light step on an adjoining staircase arrested my attention. I presently recognized it as that of Usher. In an instant afterwards he rapped, with a gentle touch, at my door, and entered, bearing a lamp. His countenance was, as usual, cadaverously wan—but, moreover, there was a species of mad hilarity in his eyes—an evidently restrained *hysteria* in his whole demeanor. His air appalled me—but anything was preferable to the solitude which I had so long endured, and I even welcomed his presence as a relief.

"And you have not seen it?" he said abruptly, after having stared about him for some moments in silence—"you have not then seen it? But, stay! you shall." Thus speaking, and having carefully shaded his lamp, he hurried to one of the casements,[2] and threw it freely open to the storm.

The impetuous fury of the entering gust nearly lifted us from our feet. It was, indeed, a tempestuous yet sternly beautiful night, and one wildly singular in its terror and its beauty. A whirlwind had apparently collected its force in our vicinity; for there were frequent and violent alterations in the direction of the wind; and the exceeding density of the clouds (which hung so low as to press upon the turrets of the house) did not prevent our perceiving the life-like velocity with which they flew careering from all points against each other, without passing away into the distance. I say that even their exceeding density did not prevent our perceiving this—yet we had no glimpse of the moon or stars, nor was there any flashing forth of the lightning. But the under surfaces of the huge masses of agitated vapor, as well as all terrestrial objects immediately around us, were glowing in the unnatural light of a faintly luminous and distinctly visible gaseous exhalation which hung about and enshrouded the mansion.

---

[1]   *incubus* Evil spirit said to sit upon people's chests in their sleep, causing nightmares.

[2]   *casements* Window panes that open outward.

"You must not—you shall not behold this!" said I, shuddering, to Usher, as I led him, with a gentle violence, from the window to a seat. "These appearances, which bewilder you, are merely electrical phenomena not uncommon—or it may be that they have their ghastly origin in the rank miasma of the tarn. Let us close this casement—the air is chilling and dangerous to your frame. Here is one of your favorite romances.[1] I will read, and you shall listen—and so we will pass away this terrible night together."

The antique volume which I had taken up was the "Mad Trist" of Sir Launcelot Canning[2]—but I had called it a favorite of Usher's more in sad jest than in earnest; for, in truth, there is little in its uncouth and unimaginative prolixity which could have had interest for the lofty and spiritual ideality of my friend. It was, however, the only book immediately at hand; and I indulged a vague hope that the excitement which now agitated the hypochondriac might find relief (for the history of mental disorder is full of similar anomalies) even in the extremeness of the folly which I should read. Could I have judged, indeed, by the wild, over-strained air of vivacity with which he harkened, or apparently harkened, to the words of the tale, I might well have congratulated myself upon the success of my design.

I had arrived at that well-known portion of the story where Ethelred, the hero of the Trist, having sought in vain for peaceable admission into the dwelling of the hermit, proceeds to make good an entrance by force. Here, it will be remembered, the words of the narrative run thus:

"And Ethelred, who was by nature of a doughty heart, and who was now mighty withal, on account of the powerfulness of the wine which he had drunken, waited no longer to hold parley with the hermit, who, in sooth,[3] was of an obstinate and maliceful turn, but, feeling the rain upon his shoulders, and fearing the rising of the tempest, uplifted his mace outright, and, with blows, made quickly room in the plankings of the door for his gauntleted hand; and now pulling therewith sturdily, he so cracked, and ripped, and tore all asunder, that the noise of the dry and hollow-sounding wood alarummed[4] and reverberated throughout the forest."

At the termination of this sentence I started, and for a moment, paused; for it appeared to me (although I at once concluded that my excited fancy had deceived me)—it appeared to me that, from some very remote portion of the mansion, there came, indistinctly, to my ears, what might have been, in its exact similarity of character, the echo (but a stifled and dull one certainly) of the very cracking and ripping sound which Sir Launcelot had so particularly described. It was, beyond doubt, the coincidence alone which had arrested my attention; for, amid the rattling of the sashes of the casements, and the ordinary commingled noises of the still increasing storm, the sound, in itself, had nothing, surely, which should have interested or disturbed me. I continued the story:

"But the good champion Ethelred, now entering within the door, was sore enraged and amazed to perceive no signal of the maliceful hermit; but, in the stead thereof, a dragon of a scaly and prodigious demeanor, and of a fiery tongue, which sate in guard before a palace of gold, with a floor of silver; and upon the wall there hung a shield of shining brass with this legend enwritten—

Who entereth herein, a conqueror hath bin,
Who slayeth the dragon, the shield he shall win.

And Ethelred uplifted his mace, and struck upon the head of the dragon, which fell before him, and gave up his pesty[5] breath, with a shriek so horrid and harsh, and withal so piercing, that Ethelred had fain to close his ears with his hands against the dreadful noise of it, the like whereof was never before heard."

Here again I paused abruptly, and now with a feeling of wild amazement—for there could be no doubt whatever that, in this instance, I did actually hear (although from what direction it proceeded I found it impossible to say) a low and apparently distant, but harsh, protracted, and most unusual screaming or grating sound—the exact counterpart of what my fancy

---

[1] *romances* I.e., heroic tales of adventure and chivalry.

[2] *"Mad Trist" … Launcelot Canning* Both the book and its author are fictional; *Trist* Meeting or encounter.

[3] *sooth* Truth.

[4] *alarummed* Rang out; sounded loudly.

[5] *pesty* Putrid.

had already conjured up as the sound of the dragon's unnatural shriek as described by the romancer.

Oppressed, as I certainly was, upon the occurrence of this second and most extraordinary coincidence, by a thousand conflicting sensations, in which wonder and extreme terror were predominant, I still retained sufficient presence of mind to avoid exciting, by any observation, the sensitive nervousness of my companion. I was by no means certain that he had noticed the sounds in question; although, assuredly, a strange alteration had, during the last few minutes, taken place in his demeanor. From a position fronting my own, he had gradually brought round his chair, so as to sit with his face to the door of the chamber; and thus I could but partially perceive his features, although I saw that his lips trembled as if he were murmuring inaudibly. His head had dropped upon his breast—yet I knew that he was not asleep, from the wide and rigid opening of the eye, as I caught a glance of it in profile. The motion of his body, too, was at variance with this idea—for he rocked from side to side with a gentle yet constant and uniform sway. Having rapidly taken notice of all this, I resumed the narrative of Sir Launcelot, which thus proceeded:

"And now, the champion, having escaped from the terrible fury of the dragon, bethinking himself of the brazen[1] shield, and of the breaking up of the enchantment which was upon it, removed the carcass from out of the way before him, and approached valorously over the silver pavement of the castle to where the shield was upon the wall; which in sooth tarried not for his full coming, but fell down at his feet upon the silver floor, with a mighty great and terrible ringing sound."

No sooner had these syllables passed my lips, than—as if a shield of brass had indeed, at the moment, fallen heavily upon a floor of silver—I became aware of a distinct, hollow, metallic, and clangorous, yet apparently muffled reverberation. Completely unnerved, I leaped to my feet; but the measured rocking movement of Usher was undisturbed. I rushed to the chair in which he sat. His eyes were bent fixedly before him, and throughout his whole countenance there reigned a stony rigidity. But, as I laid my hand upon his shoulder, there came a strong shudder over his whole person; a sickly smile quivered about his lips; and I saw that he

spoke in a low, hurried, and gibbering murmur, as if unconscious of my presence. Bending closely over his person, I at length drank in the hideous import of his words.

"Not hear it? yes, I hear it, and *have* heard it. Long—long—long—many minutes, many hours, many days, have I heard it—yet I dared not—oh, pity me, miserable wretch that I am!—I dared not—*I dared* not speak! *We have put her living in the tomb!* Said I not that my senses were acute? I *now* tell you that I heard her first feeble movements in the hollow coffin. I heard them—many, many days ago—yet I dared not—*I dared not speak!* And now—tonight—Ethelred—ha! ha!—the breaking of the hermit's door, and the death-cry of the dragon, and the clangor of the shield! say, rather, the rending of the coffin, and the grating of the iron hinges, and her struggles within the coppered archway of the vault! Oh whither shall I fly? Will she not be here anon? Is she not hurrying to upbraid me for my haste? Have I not heard her footstep on the stair? Do I not distinguish that heavy and horrible beating of her heart? Madman!"—here he sprang furiously to his feet, and shrieked out his syllables, as if in the effort he were giving up his soul—"*Madman! I tell you that she now stands without*[2] *the door!*"

As if in the superhuman energy of his utterance there had been found the potency of a spell—the huge antique panels to which the speaker pointed, threw slowly back, upon the instant, their ponderous and ebony jaws. It was the work of the rushing gust—but then without those doors there *did* stand the lofty and enshrouded figure of the lady Madeline of Usher. There was blood upon her white robes, and the evidence of some bitter struggle upon every portion of her emaciated frame. For a moment she remained trembling and reeling to and fro upon the threshold—then, with a low moaning cry, fell heavily inward upon the person of her brother, and in her violent and now final death-agonies, bore him to the floor a corpse, and a victim to the terrors he had anticipated.

From that chamber, and from that mansion, I fled aghast. The storm was still abroad in all its wrath as I found myself crossing the old causeway. Suddenly there shot along the path a wild light, and I turned to see whence a gleam so unusual could have issued; for

---

[1] *brazen* Brass.

[2] *without* Outside.

the vast house and its shadows were alone behind me. The radiance was that of the full, setting, and blood-red moon, which now shone vividly through that once barely-discernible fissure, of which I have before spoken as extending from the roof of the building, in a zig-zag direction, to the base. While I gazed, this fissure rapidly widened—there came a fierce breath of the whirlwind—the entire orb of the satellite burst at once upon my sight—my brain reeled as I saw the mighty walls rushing asunder—there was a long tumultuous shouting sound like the voice of a thousand waters—and the deep and dank tarn at my feet closed sullenly and silently over the fragments of the "*House of Usher.*"
—1839 (REVISED 1845)

The Tell-Tale Heart[1]

TRUE!—nervous—very, very dreadfully nervous I had been and am; but why *will* you say that I am mad? The disease had sharpened my senses—not destroyed—not dulled them. Above all was the sense of hearing acute. I heard all things in the heaven and in the earth. I heard many things in hell. How, then, am I mad? Hearken! and observe how healthily—how calmly I can tell you the whole story.

It is impossible to say how first the idea entered my brain; but once conceived, it haunted me day and night. Object there was none. Passion there was none. I loved the old man. He had never wronged me. He had never given me insult. For his gold I had no desire. I think it was his eye! yes, it was this! One of his eyes resembled that of a vulture—a pale blue eye, with a film over it. Whenever it fell upon me, my blood ran cold; and so by degrees—very gradually—I made up my mind to take the life of the old man, and thus rid myself of the eye forever.

Now this is the point. You fancy me mad. Madmen know nothing. But you should have seen *me*. You should have seen how wisely I proceeded—with what caution—with what foresight—with what dissimulation I went to work! I was never kinder to the old man than during the whole week before I killed him. And every night, about midnight, I turned the latch of his door and opened it—oh, so gently! And then, when I had made an opening sufficient for my head, I put in a dark lantern, all closed, closed, so that no light shone out, and then I thrust in my head. Oh, you would have laughed to see how cunningly I thrust it in! I moved it slowly—very, very slowly, so that I might not disturb the old man's sleep. It took me an hour to place my whole head within the opening so far that I could see him as he lay upon his bed. Ha!—would a madman have been so wise as this? And then, when my head was well in the room, I undid the lantern cautiously—oh, so cautiously—cautiously (for the hinges creaked)—I undid it just so much that a single thin ray fell upon the vulture eye. And this I did for seven long nights—every night just at midnight—but I found the eye always closed; and so it was impossible to do the work; for it was not the old man who vexed me, but his Evil Eye. And every morning, when the day broke, I went boldly into the chamber, and spoke courageously to him, calling him by name in a hearty tone, and inquiring how he had passed the night. So you see he would have been a very profound old man, indeed, to suspect that every night, just at twelve, I looked in upon him while he slept.

Upon the eighth night I was more than usually cautious in opening the door. A watch's minute hand moves more quickly than did mine. Never before that night, had I *felt* the extent of my own powers—of my sagacity. I could scarcely contain my feelings of triumph. To think that there I was, opening the door, little by little, and he not even to dream of my secret deeds or thoughts. I fairly chuckled at the idea; and perhaps he heard me; for he moved on the bed suddenly, as if startled. Now you may think that I drew back—but no. His room was as black as pitch with the thick darkness, (for the shutters were close fastened, through fear of robbers,) and so I knew that he could not see the opening of the door, and I kept pushing it on steadily, steadily.

I had my head in, and was about to open the lantern, when my thumb slipped upon the tin fastening, and the old man sprang up in the bed, crying out—"Who's there?"

I kept quite still and said nothing. For a whole hour I did not move a muscle, and in the mean time I did

[1] Diverging from this anthology's standard practice, spelling and punctuation have been left unmodernized throughout this story.

not hear him lie down. He was still sitting up in the bed, listening;—just as I have done, night after night, hearkening to the death watches[1] in the wall.

Presently I heard a slight groan, and I knew it was the groan of mortal terror. It was not a groan of pain or of grief—oh, no!—it was the low stifled sound that arises from the bottom of the soul when overcharged with awe. I knew the sound well. Many a night, just at midnight, when all the world slept, it has welled up from my own bosom, deepening, with its dreadful echo, the terrors that distracted me. I say I knew it well. I knew what the old man felt, and pitied him, although I chuckled at heart. I knew that he had been lying awake ever since the first slight noise, when he had turned in the bed. His fears had been ever since growing upon him. He had been trying to fancy them causeless, but could not. He had been saying to himself—"It is nothing but the wind in the chimney—it is only a mouse crossing the floor," or "it is merely a cricket which has made a single chirp." Yes, he had been trying to comfort himself with these suppositions: but he had found all in vain. *All in vain*; because Death, in approaching him, had stalked with his black shadow before him, and enveloped the victim. And it was the mournful influence of the unperceived shadow that caused him to feel—although he neither saw nor heard—to *feel* the presence of my head within the room.

When I had waited a long time, very patiently, without hearing him lie down, I resolved to open a little—a very, very little crevice in the lantern. So I opened it—you cannot imagine how stealthily, stealthily—until, at length, a single dim ray, like the thread of the spider, shot from out the crevice and fell upon the vulture eye.

It was open—wide, wide open—and I grew furious as I gazed upon it. I saw it with perfect distinctness—all a dull blue, with a hideous veil over it that chilled the very marrow in my bones; but I could see nothing else of the old man's face or person: for I had directed the ray as if by instinct, precisely upon the damned spot.

And now have I not told you that what you mistake for madness is but over acuteness of the senses?—now,

I say, there came to my ears a low, dull, quick sound, such as a watch makes when enveloped in cotton. I knew *that* sound well, too. It was the beating of the old man's heart. It increased my fury, as the beating of a drum stimulates the soldier into courage.

But even yet I refrained and kept still. I scarcely breathed. I held the lantern motionless. I tried how steadily I could maintain the ray upon the eye. Meantime the hellish tattoo of the heart increased. It grew quicker and quicker, and louder and louder every instant. The old man's terror *must* have been extreme! It grew louder, I say, louder every moment!—do you mark[2] me well? I have told you that I am nervous: so I am. And now at the dead hour of the night, amid the dreadful silence of that old house, so strange a noise as this excited me to uncontrollable terror. Yet, for some minutes longer I refrained and stood still. But the beating grew louder, louder! I thought the heart must burst. And now a new anxiety seized me—the sound would be heard by a neighbor! The old man's hour had come! With a loud yell, I threw open the lantern and leaped into the room. He shrieked once—once only. In an instant I dragged him to the floor, and pulled the heavy bed over him. I then smiled gaily, to find the deed so far done. But, for many minutes, the heart beat on with a muffled sound. This, however, did not vex me; it would not be heard through the wall. At length it ceased. The old man was dead. I removed the bed and examined the corpse. Yes, he was stone, stone dead. I placed my hand upon the heart and held it there many minutes. There was no pulsation. He was stone dead. His eye would trouble me no more.

If still you think me mad, you will think so no longer when I describe the wise precautions I took for the concealment of the body. The night waned, and I worked hastily, but in silence. First of all I dismembered the corpse. I cut off the head and the arms and the legs.

I then took up three planks from the flooring of the chamber, and deposited all between the scantlings.[3] I then replaced the boards so cleverly, so cunningly, that no human eye—not even *his*—could have detected any thing wrong. There was nothing to wash out—no

original spelling

---

[1]   *death watches*   Beetles that bore into wood, especially the wood of old buildings. They make a tapping sound that resembles the ticking of a watch, and their presence is thought by some to be an omen of death.

[2]   *mark*   Attend, listen to.

[3]   *scantlings*   Joists; supporting beams.

stain of any kind—no blood-spot whatever. I had been too wary for that. A tub had caught all—ha! ha!

When I had made an end of these labors, it was four o'clock—still dark as midnight. As the bell sounded the hour, there came a knocking at the street door. I went down to open it with a light heart,—for what had I *now* to fear? There entered three men, who introduced themselves, with perfect suavity, as officers of the police. A shriek had been heard by a neighbor during the night; suspicion of foul play had been aroused; information had been lodged at the police office, and they (the officers) had been deputed to search the premises.

I smiled,—for *what* had I to fear? I bade the gentlemen welcome. The shriek, I said, was my own in a dream. The old man, I mentioned, was absent in the country. I took my visiters all over the house. I bade them search—search *well*. I led them, at length, to *his* chamber. I showed them his treasures, secure, undisturbed. In the enthusiasm of my confidence, I brought chairs into the room, and desired them *here* to rest from their fatigues, while I myself, in the wild audacity of my perfect triumph, placed my own seat upon the very spot beneath which reposed the corpse of the victim.

The officers were satisfied. My *manner* had convinced them. I was singularly at ease. They sat, and while I answered cheerily, they chatted of familiar things. But, ere long, I felt myself getting pale and wished them gone. My head ached, and I fancied a ringing in my ears: but still they sat and still chatted. The ringing became more distinct:—it continued and became more distinct: I talked more freely to get rid of the feeling: but it continued and gained definitiveness—until, at length, I found that the noise was *not* within my ears.

No doubt I now grew *very* pale;—but I talked more fluently, and with a heightened voice. Yet the sound increased—and what could I do? It was *a low, dull, quick sound—much such a sound as a watch makes when enveloped in cotton.* I gasped for breath—and yet the officers heard it not. I talked more quickly—more vehemently; but the noise steadily increased. I arose and argued about trifles, in a high key and with violent gesticulations; but the noise steadily increased. Why *would* they not be gone? I paced the floor to and fro with heavy strides, as if excited to fury by the observations

of the men—but the noise steadily increased. Oh God! what *could* I do? I foamed—I raved—I swore! I swung the chair upon which I had been sitting, and grated it upon the boards, but the noise arose over all and continually increased. It grew louder—louder—*louder*! And still the men chatted pleasantly, and smiled. Was it possible they heard not? Almighty God!—no, no! They heard!—they suspected!—they *knew*!—they were making a mockery of my horror!—this I thought, and this I think. But anything was better than this agony! Anything was more tolerable than this derision! I could bear those hypocritical smiles no longer! I felt that I must scream or die!—and now—again!—hark! louder! louder! louder! *louder*!—

"Villains!" I shrieked, "dissemble[1] no more! I admit the deed!—tear up the planks!—here, here!—it is the beating of his hideous heart!"

—1843

The Black Cat

For the most wild, yet most homely narrative which I am about to pen, I neither expect nor solicit belief. Mad indeed would I be to expect it, in a case where my very senses reject their own evidence. Yet, mad am I not—and very surely do I not dream. But tomorrow I die, and today I would unburden my soul. My immediate purpose is to place before the world, plainly, succinctly, and without comment, a series of mere household events. In their consequences, these events have terrified—have tortured—have destroyed me. Yet I will not attempt to expound them. To me, they have presented little but Horror—to many they will seem less terrible than *barroques*.[2] Hereafter, perhaps, some intellect may be found which will reduce my phantasm[3] to the common-place—some intellect more calm, more logical, and far less excitable than my own, which will perceive, in the circumstances I detail

---

[1] *dissemble* Pretend.

[2] *barroques* Gothic ornamentation, such as gargoyles or grotesques.

[3] *phantasm* Delusion or frightening apparition.

with awe, nothing more than an ordinary succession of very natural causes and effects.

From my infancy I was noted for the docility and humanity of my disposition. My tenderness of heart was even so conspicuous as to make me the jest of my companions. I was especially fond of animals, and was indulged by my parents with a great variety of pets. With these I spent most of my time, and never was so happy as when feeding and caressing them. This peculiarity of character grew with my growth, and, in my manhood, I derived from it one of my principal sources of pleasure. To those who have cherished an affection for a faithful and sagacious dog, I need hardly be at the trouble of explaining the nature or the intensity of the gratification thus derivable. There is something in the unselfish and self-sacrificing love of a brute, which goes directly to the heart of him who has had frequent occasion to test the paltry friendship and gossamer fidelity of mere *Man*.

I married early, and was happy to find in my wife a disposition not uncongenial with my own. Observing my partiality for domestic pets, she lost no opportunity of procuring those of the most agreeable kind. We had birds, goldfish, a fine dog, rabbits, a small monkey, and *a cat*.

This latter was a remarkably large and beautiful animal, entirely black, and sagacious to an astonishing degree. In speaking of his intelligence, my wife, who at heart was not a little tinctured with superstition, made frequent allusion to the ancient popular notion, which regarded all black cats as witches in disguise. Not that she was ever *serious* upon this point—and I mention the matter at all for no better reason than that it happens, just now, to be remembered.

Pluto[1]—this was the cat's name—was my favorite pet and playmate. I alone fed him, and he attended me wherever I went about the house. It was even with difficulty that I could prevent him from following me through the streets.

Our friendship lasted, in this manner, for several years, during which my general temperament and character—through the instrumentality of the Fiend Intemperance[2]—had (I blush to confess it) experienced

a radical alteration for the worse. I grew, day by day, more moody, more irritable, more regardless of the feelings of others. I suffered myself to use intemperate language to my wife. At length, I even offered her personal violence. My pets, of course, were made to feel the change in my disposition. I not only neglected, but ill-used them. For Pluto, however, I still retained sufficient regard to restrain me from maltreating him, as I made no scruple of maltreating the rabbits, the monkey, or even the dog, when by accident, or through affection, they came in my way. But my disease grew upon me—for what disease is like Alcohol!—and at length even Pluto, who was now becoming old, and consequently somewhat peevish—even Pluto began to experience the effects of my ill temper.

One night, returning home, much intoxicated, from one of my haunts about town, I fancied that the cat avoided my presence. I seized him; when, in his fright at my violence, he inflicted a slight wound upon my hand with his teeth. The fury of a demon instantly possessed me. I knew myself no longer. My original soul seemed, at once, to take its flight from my body; and a more than fiendish malevolence, gin-nurtured, thrilled every fibre of my frame. I took from my waistcoat-pocket a pen-knife, opened it, grasped the poor beast by the throat, and deliberately cut one of its eyes from the socket! I blush, I burn, I shudder, while I pen the damnable atrocity.

When reason returned with the morning—when I had slept off the fumes of the night's debauch—I experienced a sentiment half of horror, half of remorse, for the crime of which I had been guilty; but it was, at best, a feeble and equivocal feeling, and the soul remained untouched. I again plunged into excess, and soon drowned in wine all memory of the deed.

In the meantime the cat slowly recovered. The socket of the lost eye presented, it is true, a frightful appearance, but he no longer appeared to suffer any pain. He went about the house as usual, but, as might be expected, fled in extreme terror at my approach. I had so much of my old heart left, as to be at first grieved by this evident dislike on the part of a creature which had once so loved me. But this feeling soon gave place to irritation. And then came, as if to my final and irrevocable overthrow, the spirit of PERVERSENESS. Of this spirit philosophy takes no account. Yet I am not more

---

[1]   *Pluto* God of the underworld in Roman mythology.

[2]   *Intemperance* I.e., excessive indulgence or lack of restraint, in this case, excessive consumption of alcohol.

sure that my soul lives, than I am that perverseness is one of the primitive impulses of the human heart—one of the indivisible primary faculties, or sentiments, which give direction to the character of Man. Who has not, a hundred times, found himself committing a vile or a silly action, for no other reason than because he knows he should *not*? Have we not a perpetual inclination, in the teeth of our best judgment, to violate that which is *Law*, merely because we understand it to be such? This spirit of perverseness, I say, came to my final overthrow. It was this unfathomable longing of the soul *to vex itself*—to offer violence to its own nature—to do wrong for the wrong's sake only—that urged me to continue and finally to consummate the injury I had inflicted upon the unoffending brute. One morning, in cool blood, I slipped a noose about its neck and hung it to the limb of a tree—hung it with the tears streaming from my eyes, and with the bitterest remorse at my heart—hung it *because* I knew that it had loved me, and *because* I felt it had given me no reason of offence—hung it *because* I knew that in so doing I was committing a sin—a deadly sin that would so jeopardize my immortal soul as to place it—if such a thing were possible—even beyond the reach of the infinite mercy of the Most Merciful and Most Terrible God.

On the night of the day on which this cruel deed was done, I was aroused from sleep by the cry of fire. The curtains of my bed were in flames. The whole house was blazing. It was with great difficulty that my wife, a servant, and myself, made our escape from the conflagration. The destruction was complete. My entire worldly wealth was swallowed up, and I resigned myself thenceforward to despair.

I am above the weakness of seeking to establish a sequence of cause and effect, between the disaster and the atrocity. But I am detailing a chain of facts—and wish not to leave even a possible link imperfect. On the day succeeding the fire, I visited the ruins. The walls, with one exception, had fallen in. This exception was found in a compartment wall, not very thick, which stood about the middle of the house, and against which had rested the head of my bed. The plastering had here, in great measure, resisted the action of the fire—a fact which I attributed to its having been recently spread. About this wall a dense crowd were collected, and many persons seemed to be examining a particular portion of it with very minute and eager attention. The words "strange!" "singular!" and other similar expressions, excited my curiosity. I approached and saw, as if graven in *bas relief*[1] upon the white surface, the figure of a gigantic *cat*. The impression was given with an accuracy truly marvellous. There was a rope about the animal's neck.

When I first beheld this apparition—for I could scarcely regard it as less—my wonder and my terror were extreme. But at length reflection came to my aid. The cat, I remembered, had been hung in a garden adjacent to the house. Upon the alarm of fire, this garden had been immediately filled by the crowd—by some one of whom the animal must have been cut from the tree and thrown, through an open window, into my chamber. This had probably been done with the view of arousing me from sleep. The falling of other walls had compressed the victim of my cruelty into the substance of the freshly-spread plaster; the lime of which, with the flames, and the *ammonia* from the carcass, had then accomplished the portraiture as I saw it.

Although I thus readily accounted to my reason, if not altogether to my conscience, for the startling fact just detailed, it did not the less fail to make a deep impression upon my fancy. For months I could not rid myself of the phantasm of the cat; and, during this period, there came back into my spirit a half-sentiment that seemed, but was not, remorse. I went so far as to regret the loss of the animal, and to look about me, among the vile haunts which I now habitually frequented, for another pet of the same species, and of somewhat similar appearance, with which to supply its place.

One night as I sat, half stupefied, in a den of more than infamy, my attention was suddenly drawn to some black object, reposing upon the head of one of the immense hogsheads[2] of Gin, or of Rum, which constituted the chief furniture of the apartment. I had been looking steadily at the top of this hogshead for some minutes, and what now caused me surprise was the fact that I had not sooner perceived the object thereupon. I approached it, and touched it with my

---

[1]   *bas relief* Relief sculpture characterized by slightly raised features that project from a flat background.

[2]   *hogsheads* Casks.

hand. It was a black cat—a very large one—fully as large as Pluto, and closely resembling him in every respect but one. Pluto had not a white hair upon any portion of his body; but this cat had a large, although indefinite splotch of white, covering nearly the whole region of the breast.

Upon my touching him, he immediately arose, purred loudly, rubbed against my hand, and appeared delighted with my notice. This, then, was the very creature of which I was in search. I at once offered to purchase it of the landlord; but this person made no claim to it—knew nothing of it—had never seen it before.

I continued my caresses, and, when I prepared to go home, the animal evinced a disposition to accompany me. I permitted it to do so; occasionally stooping and patting it as I proceeded. When it reached the house it domesticated itself at once, and became immediately a great favorite with my wife.

For my own part, I soon found a dislike to it arising within me. This was just the reverse of what I had anticipated; but—I know not how or why it was—its evident fondness for myself rather disgusted and annoyed. By slow degrees, these feelings of disgust and annoyance rose into the bitterness of hatred. I avoided the creature; a certain sense of shame, and the remembrance of my former deed of cruelty, preventing me from physically abusing it. I did not, for some weeks, strike, or otherwise violently ill use it; but gradually—very gradually—I came to look upon it with unutterable loathing, and to flee silently from its odious presence, as from the breath of a pestilence.

What added, no doubt, to my hatred of the beast, was the discovery, on the morning after I brought it home, that, like Pluto, it also had been deprived of one of its eyes. This circumstance, however, only endeared it to my wife, who, as I have already said, possessed, in a high degree, that humanity of feeling which had once been my distinguishing trait, and the source of many of my simplest and purest pleasures.

With my aversion to this cat, however, its partiality for myself seemed to increase. It followed my footsteps with a pertinacity which it would be difficult to make the reader comprehend. Whenever I sat, it would crouch beneath my chair, or spring upon my knees, covering me with its loathsome caresses. If I arose to walk it would get between my feet and thus nearly throw me down, or, fastening its long and sharp claws in my dress, clamber, in this manner, to my breast. At such times, although I longed to destroy it with a blow, I was yet withheld from so doing, partly by a memory of my former crime, but chiefly—let me confess it at once—by absolute *dread* of the beast.

This dread was not exactly a dread of physical evil—and yet I should be at a loss how otherwise to define it. I am almost ashamed to own—yes, even in this felon's cell, I am almost ashamed to own—that the terror and horror with which the animal inspired me, had been heightened by one of the merest chimaeras[1] it would be possible to conceive. My wife had called my attention, more than once, to the character of the mark of white hair, of which I have spoken, and which constituted the sole visible difference between the strange beast and the one I had destroyed. The reader will remember that this mark, although large, had been originally very indefinite; but, by slow degrees—degrees nearly imperceptible, and which for a long time my Reason struggled to reject as fanciful—it had, at length, assumed a rigorous distinctness of outline. It was now the representation of an object that I shudder to name—and for this, above all, I loathed, and dreaded, and would have rid myself of the monster *had I dared*—it was now, I say, the image of a hideous—of a ghastly thing—of the GALLOWS! Oh, mournful and terrible engine of Horror and of Crime—of Agony and of Death!

And now was I indeed wretched beyond the wretchedness of mere Humanity. And *a brute beast*—whose fellow I had contemptuously destroyed—*a brute beast* to work out for *me*—for me a man, fashioned in the image of the High God—so much of insufferable woe! Alas! neither by day nor by night knew I the blessing of Rest anymore! During the former the creature left me no moment alone; and, in the latter, I started, hourly, from dreams of unutterable fear, to find the hot breath of *the thing* upon my face, and its vast weight—an incarnate Night-Mare[2] that I had no power to shake off—incumbent eternally upon my *heart*!

Beneath the pressure of torments such as these, the feeble remnant of the good within me succumbed.

---

1   *chimaeras*   Illusory or monstrous things.

2   *Night-Mare*   In European folklore, nightmares are personified as demons who sit upon one's chest during the night, causing bad dreams.

Evil thoughts became my sole intimates—the darkest and most evil of thoughts. The moodiness of my usual temper increased to hatred of all things and of all mankind; while, from the sudden, frequent, and ungovernable outbursts of a fury to which I now blindly abandoned myself, my uncomplaining wife, alas! was the most usual and the most patient of sufferers.

One day she accompanied me, upon some household errand, into the cellar of the old building which our poverty compelled us to inhabit. The cat followed me down the steep stairs, and, nearly throwing me headlong, exasperated me to madness. Uplifting an axe, and forgetting, in my wrath, the childish dread which had hitherto stayed my hand, I aimed a blow at the animal which, of course, would have proved instantly fatal had it descended as I wished. But this blow was arrested by the hand of my wife. Goaded, by the interference, into a rage more than demoniacal, I withdrew my arm from her grasp and buried the axe in her brain. She fell dead upon the spot, without a groan.

This hideous murder accomplished, I set myself forthwith, and with entire deliberation, to the task of concealing the body. I knew that I could not remove it from the house, either by day or by night, without the risk of being observed by the neighbors. Many projects entered my mind. At one period I thought of cutting the corpse into minute fragments, and destroying them by fire. At another, I resolved to dig a grave for it in the floor of the cellar. Again, I deliberated about casting it in the well in the yard—about packing it in a box, as if merchandize, with the usual arrangements, and so getting a porter to take it from the house. Finally I hit upon what I considered a far better expedient than either of these. I determined to wall it up in the cellar—as the monks of the middle ages are recorded to have walled up their victims.

For a purpose such as this the cellar was well adapted. Its walls were loosely constructed, and had lately been plastered throughout with a rough plaster, which the dampness of the atmosphere had prevented from hardening. Moreover, in one of the walls was a projection, caused by a false chimney, or fireplace, that had been filled up, and made to resemble the rest of the cellar. I made no doubt that I could readily displace the bricks at this point, insert the corpse, and wall the whole up as before, so that no eye could detect anything suspicious.

And in this calculation I was not deceived. By means of a crow-bar I easily dislodged the bricks, and, having carefully deposited the body against the inner wall, I propped it in that position, while, with little trouble, I re-laid the whole structure as it originally stood. Having procured mortar, sand, and hair,[1] with every possible precaution, I prepared a plaster which could not be distinguished from the old, and with this I very carefully went over the new brick-work. When I had finished, I felt satisfied that all was right. The wall did not present the slightest appearance of having been disturbed. The rubbish on the floor was picked up with the minutest care. I looked around triumphantly, and said to myself—"Here at least, then, my labor has not been in vain."

My next step was to look for the beast which had been the cause of so much wretchedness; for I had, at length, firmly resolved to put it to death. Had I been able to meet with it, at the moment, there could have been no doubt of its fate; but it appeared that the crafty animal had been alarmed at the violence of my previous anger, and forebore to present itself in my present mood. It is impossible to describe, or to imagine, the deep, the blissful sense of relief which the absence of the detested creature occasioned in my bosom. It did not make its appearance during the night—and thus for one night at least, since its introduction into the house, I soundly and tranquilly slept; aye, *slept* even with the burden of murder upon my soul!

The second and the third day passed, and still my tormentor came not. Once again I breathed as a free man. The monster, in terror, had fled the premises forever! I should behold it no more! My happiness was supreme! The guilt of my dark deed disturbed me but little. Some few inquiries had been made, but these had been readily answered. Even a search had been instituted—but of course nothing was to be discovered. I looked upon my future felicity as secured.

Upon the fourth day of the assassination, a party of the police came, very unexpectedly, into the house, and proceeded again to make rigorous investigation of the premises. Secure, however, in the inscrutability of my place of concealment, I felt no embarrassment whatever. The officers bade me accompany them in their

---

[1] *hair* The addition of animal hair to mortar increases its durability.

search. They left no nook or corner unexplored. At length, for the third or fourth time, they descended into the cellar. I quivered not in a muscle. My heart beat calmly as that of one who slumbers in innocence. I walked the cellar from end to end. I folded my arms upon my bosom, and roamed easily to and fro. The police were thoroughly satisfied and prepared to depart. The glee at my heart was too strong to be restrained. I burned to say if but one word, by way of triumph, and to render doubly sure their assurance of my guiltlessness.

"Gentlemen," I said at last, as the party ascended the steps, "I delight to have allayed your suspicions. I wish you all health, and a little more courtesy. By the bye, gentlemen, this—this is a very well constructed house." [In the rabid desire to say something easily, I scarcely knew what I uttered at all.] "I may say an *excellently* well constructed house. These walls—are you going, gentlemen?—these walls are solidly put together"; and here, through the mere frenzy of bravado, I rapped heavily, with a cane which I held in my hand, upon that very portion of the brick-work behind which stood the corpse of the wife of my bosom.

But may God shield and deliver me from the fangs of the Arch-Fiend! No sooner had the reverberation of my blows sunk into silence, than I was answered by a voice from within the tomb! By a cry, at first muffled and broken, like the sobbing of a child, and then quickly swelling into one long, loud, and continuous scream, utterly anomalous and inhuman—a howl—a wailing shriek, half of horror and half of triumph, such as might have arisen only out of hell, conjointly from the throats of the damned in their agony and of the demons that exult in the damnation.

Of my own thoughts it is folly to speak. Swooning, I staggered to the opposite wall. For one instant the party upon the stairs remained motionless, through extremity of terror and of awe. In the next, a dozen stout arms were toiling at the wall. It fell bodily. The corpse, already greatly decayed and clotted with gore, stood erect before the eyes of the spectators. Upon its head, with red extended mouth and solitary eye of fire, sat the hideous beast whose craft had seduced me into murder, and whose informing voice had consigned me to the hangman. I had walled the monster up within the tomb!

—1843

Aubrey Vincent Beardsley, *The Black Cat,* for *Edgar Allan Poe's "Tales of Mystery and the Imagination,"* Chicago, 1895–96, 1894. Beardsley was commissioned by the Chicago publisher Stone and Kimball to create illustrations for an edition of Poe's *Tales of Mystery and Imagination*; this image of the black cat upon the dead wife's head is one of four illustrations that Beardsley created for the 1895–96 edition.

The Raven

Once upon a midnight dreary, while I pondered, weak and weary,
Over many a quaint and curious volume of forgotten lore—
While I nodded, nearly napping, suddenly there came a tapping,
As of someone gently rapping, rapping at my chamber door—
5   "'Tis some visitor," I muttered, "tapping at my chamber door—
       Only this and nothing more."

Ah, distinctly I remember it was in the bleak December;
And each separate dying ember wrought its ghost upon the floor.
Eagerly I wished the morrow; vainly I had tried to borrow
10   From my books surcease° of sorrow—sorrow for the lost Lenore—   *stoppage*
For the rare and radiant maiden whom the angels name Lenore—
       Nameless *here* for evermore.

And the silken, sad, uncertain rustling of each purple curtain
Thrilled me—filled me with fantastic terrors never felt before;
15   So that now, to still the beating of my heart, I stood repeating
       "'Tis some visitor entreating entrance at my chamber door—
Some late visitor entreating entrance at my chamber door;—
       This it is and nothing more."

Presently my soul grew stronger; hesitating then no longer,
20   "Sir," said I, "or Madam, truly your forgiveness I implore;
But the fact is I was napping, and so gently you came rapping,
And so faintly you came tapping, tapping at my chamber door,
That I scarce was sure I heard you"—here I opened wide the door;
       Darkness there and nothing more.

25   Deep into that darkness peering, long I stood there wondering, fearing,
Doubting, dreaming dreams no mortal ever dared to dream before;
But the silence was unbroken, and the darkness gave no token,
And the only word there spoken was the whispered word, "Lenore?"
This I whispered, and an echo murmured back the word, "Lenore!"
30   Merely this and nothing more.

Back into the chamber turning, all my soul within me burning,
Soon I heard again a tapping somewhat louder than before.
"Surely," said I, "surely that is something at my window lattice;
Let me see, then, what thereat is, and this mystery explore—
35   Let my heart be still a moment and this mystery explore—
       'Tis the wind, and nothing more!"

Open here I flung the shutter, when, with many a flirt° and flutter,   *dart, flick*
In there stepped a stately Raven of the saintly days of yore;
Not the least obeisance made he; not an instant stopped or stayed he;

40 But, with mien of lord or lady, perched above my chamber door—
Perched upon a bust of Pallas[1] just above my chamber door—
    Perched, and sat, and nothing more.

Then this ebony bird beguiling my sad fancy into smiling,
By the grave and stern decorum of the countenance it wore,
45 "Though thy crest be shorn and shaven, thou," I said, "art sure no craven,[2]
Ghastly grim and ancient Raven wandering from the Nightly shore—
Tell me what thy lordly name is on the Night's Plutonian[3] shore!"
    Quoth the Raven "Nevermore."

Much I marvelled this ungainly fowl to hear discourse so plainly,
50 Though its answer little meaning—little relevancy bore;
For we cannot help agreeing that no living human being
Ever yet was blessed with seeing bird above his chamber door—
Bird or beast upon the sculptured bust above his chamber door,
    With such name as "Nevermore."

55 But the Raven, sitting lonely on the placid bust, spoke only
That one word, as if his soul in that one word he did outpour.
Nothing farther then he uttered—not a feather then he fluttered—
Till I scarcely more than muttered "Other friends have flown before—
On the morrow *he* will leave me, as my Hopes have flown before."
60   Then the bird said "Nevermore."

Startled at the stillness broken by reply so aptly spoken,
"Doubtless," said I, "what it utters is its only stock and store
Caught from some unhappy master whom unmerciful Disaster
Followed fast and followed faster till his songs one burden[4] bore—
65 Till the dirges[5] of his Hope that melancholy burden bore
      Of 'Never—nevermore.'"

But the Raven still beguiling all my sad fancy into smiling,
Straight I wheeled a cushioned seat in front of bird, and bust and door;
Then upon the velvet sinking, I betook myself to linking
70 Fancy unto fancy, thinking what this ominous bird of yore—
What this grim, ungainly, ghastly, gaunt, and ominous bird of yore
    Meant in croaking "Nevermore."

This I sat engaged in guessing, but no syllable expressing
To the fowl whose fiery eyes now burned into my bosom's core;

---

[1] *bust* Sculpture of the head and shoulders; *Pallas* Epithet of Athena, Greek goddess of wisdom, warfare, and art.

[2] *Though thy crest … craven* Reference to the practice of punishing cowardly knights by shaving their heads.

[3] *Plutonian* Dark or gloomy, alluding to Pluto as the Roman god of the underworld.

[4] *burden* Refrain, chorus.

[5] *dirges* Funeral songs.

75 This and more I sat divining, with my head at ease reclining
On the cushion's velvet lining that the lamp-light gloated o'er,
But whose velvet-violet lining with the lamp-light gloating o'er,
     She shall press, ah, nevermore!

Then, methought, the air grew denser, perfumed from an unseen censer[1]
80 Swung by seraphim° whose footfalls tinkled on the tufted° floor.   *angels / carpeted*
"Wretch," I cried, "thy God hath lent thee—by these angels he hath sent thee
Respite—respite and nepenthe[2] from thy memories of Lenore;
Quaff,[3] oh quaff this kind nepenthe and forget this lost Lenore!"
     Quoth the Raven "Nevermore."

85 "Prophet!" said I, "thing of evil! prophet still, if bird or devil!
Whether Tempter sent, or whether tempest tossed thee here ashore,
Desolate yet all undaunted, on this desert land enchanted—
On this home by Horror haunted—tell me truly, I implore—
Is there—*is* there balm in Gilead?[4]—tell me—tell me, I implore!"
90   Quoth the Raven "Nevermore."

"Prophet!" said I, "thing of evil! prophet still, if bird or devil!
By that Heaven that bends above us—by that God we both adore—
Tell this soul with sorrow laden if, within the distant Aidenn,°   *Eden*
It shall clasp a sainted maiden whom the angels name Lenore—
95 Clasp a rare and radiant maiden whom the angels name Lenore."
     Quoth the Raven "Nevermore."

"Be that word our sign of parting, bird or fiend!" I shrieked, upstarting—
"Get thee back into the tempest and the Night's Plutonian shore!
Leave no black plume° as a token of that lie thy soul hath spoken!   *feather*
100 Leave my loneliness unbroken! quit the bust above my door!
Take thy beak from out my heart, and take thy form from off my door!"
     Quoth the Raven "Nevermore."

And the Raven, never flitting, still is sitting, *still* is sitting
On the pallid bust of Pallas just above my chamber door;
105 And his eyes have all the seeming of a demon's that is dreaming,
And the lamp-light o'er him streaming throws his shadow on the floor;
And my soul from out that shadow that lies floating on the floor
     Shall be lifted—nevermore!
—1845 (REVISED 1849)

---

1   *censer*   Incense burner.

2   *nepenthe*   Legendary drug supposed to banish sorrow by inducing forgetfulness.

3   *Quaff*   Drink quickly and deeply.

4   *balm in Gilead*   See Jeremiah 8.22: "Is there no balm in Gilead?" Balm is a medicinal ointment, and, proverbially, the balm of Gilead is a powerful cure; Christian interpretation identifies the balm with Christ.

IN CONTEXT

"The Raven" in Nineteenth-Century Visual Culture

Widely considered one of the most famous poems in history, "The Raven" began early on to be interpreted, celebrated, and parodied by artists in a variety of media, including engravings, drawings, and paintings. This fascination continued through the twentieth century and into the twenty-first, with new literary interpretations emerging as well as graphic novels, films, and television adaptations. "The Raven" was also translated widely, contributing to Poe's international reputation—especially in France, where the following illustrations of the poem originate. Poe's fame became so closely entwined with his poem that he was nicknamed "Mr. Raven," and depictions of him in popular culture often included a raven perched nearby.

Edouard Manet, "Once upon a Midnight Dreary." Illustration from Stéphane Mallarmé's translation of *Le Corbeau* [*The Raven*], 1875.

This edition had a considerable impact. Manet's fellow post-Impressionist Paul Gauguin, for example, included Poe's raven in his 1891 engraving of Manet—as well as in *Mana'o tupapa'u* (1892) and several other of his well-known paintings of the 1890s.

Edouard Manet, "Design for the poster and cover." Illustration to Stéphane Mallarmé's translation of *Le Corbeau* [*The Raven*], 1875.

Gustave Doré, "Illustration 14," *The Raven*, 1884. Doré's engravings of *The Raven* have proved enduringly popular; his illustrated version of the poem was widely distributed in America and in Europe.

"Edgar A. Poe," Great Americans cigarette card, 1888. Poe's fame led to his appearance as one of fifty "great Americans" illustrated in an 1888 series of cards included in packs of W. Duke, Sons & Co. cigarettes. The raven perched on the statue of Pallas is conspicuous in the background.

from *The Philosophy of Composition*

... Nothing is more clear than that every plot, worth the name, must be elaborated to its *dénouement* before anything be attempted with the pen. It is only with the *dénouement* constantly in view that we can give a plot its indispensable air of consequence, or causation, by making the incidents, and especially the tone at all points, tend to the development of the intention.

There is a radical error, I think, in the usual mode of constructing a story. Either history affords a thesis[1]—or one is suggested by an incident of the day—or, at best, the author sets himself to work in the combination of striking events to form merely the basis of his narrative—designing, generally, to fill in with description, dialogue, or authorial comment, whatever crevices of fact, or action, may, from page to page, render themselves apparent.

I prefer commencing with the consideration of an *effect*. Keeping originality *always* in view—for he is false to himself who ventures to dispense with so obvious and so easily attainable a source of interest—I say to myself, in the first place, "Of the innumerable effects, or impressions, of which the heart, the intellect, or (more generally) the soul is susceptible, what one shall I, on the present occasion, select?" Having chosen a novel, first, and secondly a vivid effect, I consider whether it can best be wrought by incident or tone—whether by ordinary incidents and peculiar tone, or the converse, or by peculiarity both of incident and tone—afterward looking about me (or rather within) for such combinations of event, or tone, as shall best aid me in the construction of the effect. ...

... If any literary work is too long to be read at one sitting, we must be content to dispense with the immensely important effect derivable from unity of impression—for, if two sittings be required, the affairs of the world interfere, and everything like totality is at once destroyed. But since, *ceteris paribus*,[2] no poet can afford to dispense with *anything* that may advance his design, it but remains to be seen whether there is, in extent, any advantage to counterbalance the loss of unity which attends it. Here I say no, at once. What we term a long poem is, in fact, merely a succession of brief ones—that is to say, of brief poetical effects. It is needless to demonstrate that a poem is such, only inasmuch as it intensely excites, by elevating, the soul; and all intense excitements are, through a psychal[3] necessity, brief. For this reason, at least one half of the "Paradise Lost"[4] is essentially prose—a succession of poetical excitements interspersed, *inevitably*, with corresponding depressions—the whole being deprived, through the extremeness of its length, of the vastly important artistic element, totality, or unity, of effect.

It appears evident, then, that there is a distinct limit, as regards length, to all works of literary art—the limit of a single sitting—and that, although in certain classes of prose composition, such as "Robinson Crusoe"[5] (demanding no unity), this limit may be advantageously overpassed, it can never properly be overpassed in a poem. Within this limit, the extent of a poem may be made to bear mathematical relation to its merit—in other words, to the excitement or elevation—again in other words, to the degree of the true poetical effect which it is capable of inducing; for it is clear that the brevity must be in direct ratio of the intensity of the intended effect: this, with one proviso—that a certain degree of duration is absolutely requisite for the production of any effect at all. ...

—1846

Annabel Lee

It was many and many a year ago,
    In a kingdom by the sea,
That a maiden there lived whom you may know
    By the name of Annabel Lee;
5 And this maiden she lived with no other thought
    Than to love and be loved by me.

I was a child and *she* was a child,
    In a kingdom by the sea;

---

1   *thesis*   Theme.

2   *ceteris paribus*   Latin: all things being equal.

3   *psychal*   Psychological.

4   *Paradise Lost*   1667 epic poem by John Milton, often ranked among the most important works of English literature.

5   *Robinson Crusoe*   Influential 1719 novel by Daniel Defoe.

But we loved with a love that was more than love—
10   I and my Annabel Lee—
With a love that the wingèd seraphs° in Heaven   *angels*
        Coveted her and me.

And this was the reason that, long ago,
        In this kingdom by the sea,
15 A wind blew out of a cloud, chilling
        My beautiful Annabel Lee;
So that her high-born kinsmen came
        And bore her away from me,
To shut her up in a sepulchre,
20   In this kingdom by the sea.

The angels, not half so happy in Heaven,
        Went envying her and me—
Yes!—that was the reason (as all men know,
        In this kingdom by the sea)
25 That the wind came out of the cloud by night,
        Chilling and killing my Annabel Lee.

But our love it was stronger by far than the love
        Of those who were older than we—
        Of many far wiser than we—
30 And neither the angels in Heaven above,
        Nor the demons down under the sea,
Can ever dissever my soul from the soul
        Of the beautiful Annabel Lee:

For the moon never beams, without bringing me
    dreams
35   Of the beautiful Annabel Lee;
And the stars never rise, but I feel the bright eyes
        Of the beautiful Annabel Lee:
And so, all the night-tide, I lie down by the side
Of my darling—my darling—my life and my bride,
40   In her sepulchre there by the sea—
        In her tomb by the sounding sea.

—1849

Margaret Fuller

1810 – 1850

At the peak of her career in the 1840s, writer, journalist, and literary critic Margaret Fuller was among the most influential nonfiction writers in America. She was an important friend of the Transcendentalist school that sprouted in Massachusetts in late 1830s, but her career also took her beyond the scope of that movement, and into the arena of social and political reform. Praised by her friend and fellow Transcendentalist Ralph Waldo Emerson as "the greatest woman, I believe, of ancient or modern times," Fuller was remarkable not least of all for achieving literary prominence and independent financial success at a time when many considered the quietude of the domestic sphere to be the only appropriate place for women. But the range of Fuller's writing, the scope of her ambition, and her profound enthusiasm for the life of the mind were also recognized as being extraordinary for any human being, male or female. The admiration expressed by Scottish writer Thomas Carlyle was widely shared: "Such a predetermination to eat this big universe as her oyster or her egg, and to be absolute empress of all height and glory in it that her heart could conceive, I have not before seen in any human soul."

Born in Cambridgeport, Massachusetts in May 1810, Sarah Margaret Fuller was the eldest child of Timothy and Margarett Crane Fuller. Timothy seems to have had few, if any, qualms about providing his daughter with an education most of his peers would have seen as "unfeminine" at best, and thus set about educating Margaret in the rigorous manner commonly imposed upon boys of the era. By four she was reading *Aesop's Fables*; by seven she was reading the classics of Greek and Latin philosophy and literature; and by her teens she rose daily before five in the morning to begin a twelve-hour study schedule. Similarly intensive instruction was not uncommon for boys of her era, who often entered college around the age of fifteen, and Fuller had a natural zeal to learn and to improve her mind that was well nurtured by these high expectations. But if her education provided her with the grounds for her future success, some would say it also underlaid a great deal of her future personal anguish. Throughout her childhood, Fuller suffered from hallucinations, nightmares, and episodes of somnambulism, and she continued to exhibit "nervous" tendencies and frequent headaches in adulthood.

Beginning in 1819, Fuller was enrolled in a series of private schools, beginning with the Cambridgeport Private Grammar School and including two "finishing schools" for young ladies. She returned to live with her family in 1826, where she continued to study from her father's library. When not reading, Fuller began in earnest to write; fascinated by German Romanticism, she completed her first translation of Goethe in 1833, and in 1834 published a first essay, "In Defense of Brutus," in the *Boston Daily Advertiser*.

Fuller's father died the following year; the sudden need to contribute financially to the family brought a temporary end to her scholarly ambitions, and she spent a little over a year working as a schoolteacher. Fuller was beloved by many of her students, but the work did not fully engage her; after resigning from her post, she found a more fulfilling outlet for her teaching abilities in the "Conversations" she began holding in Boston—a series of intellectual seminars for women, held between 1839 and 1844, and addressing various topics including literature, ethics, pedagogy, and the place of women in society. The Conversations brought Fuller her first dose of fame, and at their peak became so popular that she was impelled to allow men to join her audience. The same year she began holding the Conversations, Fuller published the first English translation of *Conversations with Goethe* by Johann Peter Eckermann, to a good deal of acclaim.

In 1840, the Transcendental Movement coalesced to form *The Dial* (1840–44), the periodical that had been long envisioned by Ralph Waldo Emerson and his companions. Fuller was chosen as the magazine's first editor, and she published one of her most significant works in its pages; "The Great Lawsuit. Man *versus* Men. Woman *versus* Women" appeared in the July 1843 issue. In this long essay Fuller not only demands equal treatment of the sexes, but also explores the very concept of gender, suggesting that there may be masculine women and feminine men. The piece caught the eye of *New-York Tribune* editor Horace Greeley, who contacted Fuller and encouraged her to expand the work into book form: the result was *Woman in the Nineteenth Century* (1845). Though not without its detractors, the work was praised by many, and has since come to be regarded as a classic of American writing on gender and women's rights.

Greeley hired Fuller on as a critic for the *Tribune* in 1844. Over the span of less than two years she wrote well over two hundred articles for the paper, which was among the most widely-read papers in the nation. She developed a deeper interest in dominant social issues of the age, among them the incarceration of women, the treatment of mental patients, prostitution, and abolition. Her position with the *Tribune* also took Fuller abroad for the first time in her life. In 1846 she sailed for Britain and France, and she traveled to Italy the following year. When revolutions began to sweep the Italian states in 1848, Fuller reported on these events for the *Tribune*, while also participating in running a military hospital in Rome. Here Fuller met and fell in love with revolutionary Giovanni Angelo Ossoli, with whom she had a son. The family set sail for America in 1850; their ship was wrecked just off the New York coast, killing all on board, and Fuller's body was never found.

Fuller's death was a blow to her intellectual community at home, as was the loss of her rumored final work, a history of the Italian Revolution. The work left behind, however, was more than enough to secure her place in the canon of nineteenth-century American writers. In the first volume of their *History of Woman Suffrage* (1881), Elizabeth Cady Stanton and her co-authors concluded that Fuller had done more to influence "the thought of American women than any woman previous to her time." To be sure, there was a period in the late nineteenth and early twentieth centuries when Fuller's star was in decline. Literary historian Barrett Wendell, for example, wrote in 1925 of the Transcendentalists that "few have proved immortal. Bronson Alcott and Theodore Parker seem fading with Margaret Fuller into mere memories." By the second half of the twentieth century, however, Fuller's importance was again becoming widely acknowledged. When the first edition of *The Norton Anthology of American Literature* was published in 1979, she was one of only three women writers from the 1820–65 period to be included. In the twenty-first century, the publication of the concluding volume of Charles Capper's acclaimed *Margaret Fuller: An American Romantic Life* helped to confirm her reputation as (in scholar Mary Kelley's words) "one of America's most expansive intellectuals."

NOTE ON THE TEXT: The text of "The Great Lawsuit: Man *versus* Men. Woman *versus* Women" presented below is based on that published in volume 4 of *The Dial* in July 1843. Spelling and punctuation have been modernized in accordance with the practices of this anthology.

⌘⌘⌘

from *The Great Lawsuit: Man* versus *Men.* *Woman* versus *Women.*[1]

... Lord Herbert's[2] was a marriage of convention, made for him at fifteen; he was not discontented with it, but looked only to the advantages it brought of perpetuating his family on the basis of a great fortune. He paid, in act, what he considered a dutiful attention to the bond; his thoughts travelled elsewhere, and, while forming a high ideal of the companionship of minds in marriage, he seems never to have doubted that its realization must be postponed to some other stage of being. Dante, almost immediately after the death of Beatrice, married a lady chosen for him by his friends.[3]

Centuries have passed since, but civilized Europe is still in a transition state about marriage, not only in practice, but in thought. A great majority of societies and individuals are still doubtful whether earthly marriage is to be a union of souls, or merely a contract of convenience and utility. Were woman established in the rights of an immortal being, this could not be. She would not in some countries be given away by her father, with scarcely more respect for her own feelings than is shown by the Indian chief, who sells his daughter for a horse, and beats her if she runs away from her new home. Nor, in societies where her choice is left free, would she be perverted, by the current of opinion that seizes her, into the belief that she must marry, if it be only to find a protector, and a home of her own.

Neither would man, if he thought that the connection was of permanent importance, enter upon it so lightly. He would not deem it a trifle, that he was to enter into the closest relations with another soul, which, if not eternal in themselves, must eternally affect his growth.

Neither, did he believe woman capable of friendship, would he, by rash haste, lose the chance of finding a friend in the person who might, probably, live half a century by his side. Did love to his mind partake of infinity, he would not miss his chance of its revelations, that he might the sooner rest from his weariness by a bright fireside, and have a sweet and graceful attendant, "devoted to him alone." Were he a step higher, he would not carelessly enter into a relation, where he might not be able to do the duty of a friend, as well as a protector from external ill, to the other party, and have a being in his power pining for sympathy, intelligence, and aid, that he could not give.

Where the thought of equality has become pervasive, it shows itself in four kinds.

The household partnership. In our country the woman looks for a "smart but kind" husband, the man for a "capable, sweet-tempered" wife.

The man furnishes the house, the woman regulates it. Their relation is one of mutual esteem, mutual dependence. Their talk is of business, their affection shows itself by practical kindness. They know that life goes more smoothly and cheerfully to each for the other's aid; they are grateful and content. The wife praises her husband as a "good provider," the husband in return compliments her as a "capital housekeeper." This relation is good as far as it goes.

Next comes a closer tie which takes the two forms, either of intellectual companionship, or mutual idolatry. The last, we suppose, is to no one a pleasing subject of contemplation. The parties weaken and narrow one another; they lock the gate against all the glories of the universe that they may live in a cell together. To themselves they seem the only wise, to all others steeped in infatuation, the gods smile as they look forward to the crisis of cure, to men the woman seems an unlovely siren,[4] to women the man an effeminate boy.

The other form, of intellectual companionship, has become more and more frequent. Men engaged in public life, literary men, and artists have often found in their wives companions and confidants in thought no less than in feeling. And, as in the course of things the intellectual development of woman has spread wider and risen higher, they have, not unfrequently, shared

---

[1] The full text of *The Great Lawsuit* is available in the website component of this anthology.

[2] *Lord Herbert* English poet Edward Herbert, 1st Baron of Cherbury (1583–1648).

[3] *Dante ... his friends* Italian poet Dante Alighieri (c. 1265–1321) immortalized his childhood sweetheart Beatrice Portinari (1265–90) in his epic Christian allegory *The Divine Comedy*, where she serves as the protagonist's guide through Paradise. Dante was betrothed to Gemma Donati around the age of eleven, and married her around 1285.

[4] *siren* Mythical creature, part woman and part bird, whose enchanted song is said to lure sailors to their destruction.

the same employment. As in the case of Roland and his wife,[1] who were friends in the household and the nation's councils, read together, regulated home affairs, or prepared public documents together indifferently.

It is very pleasant, in letters begun by Roland and finished by his wife, to see the harmony of mind and the difference of nature, one thought, but various ways of treating it.

This is one of the best instances of a marriage of friendship. It was only friendship, whose basis was esteem; probably neither party knew love, except by name.

Roland was a good man, worthy to esteem and be esteemed, his wife as deserving of admiration as able to do without it. Madame Roland is the fairest specimen we have yet of her class, as clear to discern her aim, as valiant to pursue it, as Spenser's Britomart,[2] austerely set apart from all that did not belong to her, whether as woman or as mind. She is an antetype[3] of a class to which the coming time will afford a field, the Spartan[4] matron, brought by the culture of a book-furnishing age to intellectual consciousness and expansion.

Self-sufficing strength and clear-sightedness were in her combined with a power of deep and calm affection. The page of her life is one of unsullied dignity.

Her appeal to posterity is one against the injustice of those who committed such crimes in the name of liberty. She makes it in behalf of herself and her husband. I would put beside it on the shelf a little volume, containing a similar appeal from the verdict of contemporaries to that of mankind, that of Godwin in behalf of his wife, the celebrated, the by most men detested Mary Wollstonecraft.[5] In his view it was an appeal from the injustice of those who did such wrong in the name of virtue.

Were this little book interesting for no other cause, it would be so for the generous affection evinced under the peculiar circumstances. This man had courage to love and honor this woman in the face of the world's verdict, and of all that was repulsive in her own past history. He believed he saw of what soul she was, and that the thoughts she had struggled to act out were noble. He loved her and he defended her for the meaning and tendency of her inner life. It was a good fact.

Mary Wollstonecraft, like Madame Dudevant[6] (commonly known as George) in our day, was a woman whose existence better proved the need of some new interpretation of woman's rights, than anything she wrote. Such women as these, rich in genius, of most tender sympathies, and capable of high virtue and a chastened harmony, ought not to find themselves by birth in a place so narrow, that in breaking bonds they become outlaws. Were there as much room in the world for such, as in Spenser's poem for Britomart, they would not run their heads so wildly against its laws. They find their way at last to purer air, but the world will not take off the brand it has set upon them. The champion of the rights of woman found in Godwin one who pleads her own cause like a brother. George Sand smokes, wears male attire, wishes to be addressed as *Mon frère*;[7] perhaps, if she found those who were as brothers indeed, she would not care whether she were brother or sister.

We rejoice to see that she, who expresses such a painful contempt for men in most of her works, as shows she must have known great wrong from them, in *La Roche Mauprat*,[8] depicting one raised, by the workings of love, from the depths of savage sensualism to a moral and intellectual life. It was love for a pure object,

---

[1] *Roland and his wife* Fuller refers to the French intellectuals and revolutionaries Marie-Jeanne (1754–93) and Jean-Marie (1734–93) de la Platiere.

[2] *Spenser's Britomart* Fuller alludes to Edmund Spenser's epic poem *The Faerie Queene* (1590–96), an allegory of the reign of Elizabeth I. Its wide cast of allegorical female characters includes the woman knight Britomart, an allegory of Chastity.

[3] *antetype* Predecessor.

[4] *Spartan* With the spirit of the ancient Greek culture known for valuing bravery and militarism.

[5] *Godwin ... Mary Wollstonecraft* Mary Wollstonecraft's 1792 *A Vindication of the Rights of Woman* was among the most influential works to argue for women's education and intellectual rights in the eighteenth century. Her husband, philosopher William Godwin,

---

published the biography *Memoirs of the Author of A Vindication of the Rights of Woman* in 1798 after her death, inciting controversy in Britain for his frank treatment of her unconventional life.

[6] *Madame Dudevant* Reference to the popular French novelist Amantine Lucile Aurore Dupin (married to Casimir Dudevant until their separation in 1835), famous for wearing men's clothes and for adopting the masculine pseudonym George Sand.

[7] *Mon frère* French: My brother.

[8] *La Roche Mauprat* 1837 novel by Sand.

for a steadfast woman, one of those who, the Italian said, could make the stair to heaven.

Women like Sand will speak now, and cannot be silenced; their characters and their eloquence alike foretell an era when such as they shall easier learn to lead true lives. But though such forebode, not such shall be the parents of it. Those who would reform the world must show that they do not speak in the heat of wild impulse; their lives must be unstained by passionate error; they must be severe lawgivers to themselves. As to their transgressions and opinions, it may be observed, that the resolve of Eloisa to be only the mistress of Abelard, was that of one who saw the contract of marriage a seal of degradation. Wherever abuses of this sort are seen, the timid will suffer, the bold protest. But society is in the right to outlaw them till she has revised her law, and she must be taught to do so, by one who speaks with authority, not in anger and haste.

If Godwin's choice of the calumniated authoress of the "Rights of Woman," for his honored wife, be a sign of a new era, no less so is an article of great learning and eloquence, published several years since in an English review, where the writer, in doing full justice to Eloisa, shows his bitter regret that she lives not now to love him, who might have known better how to prize her love than did the egotistical Abelard.

These marriages, these characters, with all their imperfections, express an onward tendency. They speak of aspiration of soul, of energy of mind, seeking clearness and freedom. Of a like promise are the tracts now publishing by Goodwyn Barmby (the European Pariah as he calls himself) and his wife Catharine.[1] Whatever we may think of their measures, we see them in wedlock, the two minds are wed by the only contract that can permanently avail, of a common faith, and a common purpose.

We might mention instances, nearer home, of minds, partners in work and in life, sharing together, on equal terms, public and private interests, and which have not on any side that aspect of offence which characterizes the attitude of the last named; persons who steer straight onward, and in our freer life have not been obliged to run their heads against any wall. But

the principles which guide them might, under petrified or oppressive institutions, have made them warlike, paradoxical, or, in some sense, Pariahs. The phenomenon is different, the law the same, in all these cases. Men and women have been obliged to build their house from the very foundation. If they found stone ready in the quarry, they took it peaceably, otherwise they alarmed the country by pulling down old towers to get materials.

These are all instances of marriage as intellectual companionship. The parties meet mind to mind, and a mutual trust is excited which can buckler[2] them against a million. They work together for a common purpose, and, in all these instances, with the same implement, the pen.

A pleasing expression in this kind is afforded by the union in the names of the Howitts. William and Mary Howitt[3] we heard named together for years, supposing them to be brother and sister; the equality of labors and reputation, even so, was auspicious, more so, now we find them man and wife. In his late work on Germany, Howitt mentions his wife with pride, as one among the constellation of distinguished English women, and in a graceful, simple manner.

In naming these instances we do not mean to imply that community of employment is an essential to union of this sort, more than to the union of friendship. Harmony exists in difference no less than in likeness, if only the same keynote govern both parts. Woman the poem, man the poet; woman the heart, man the head; such divisions are only important when they are never to be transcended. If nature is never bound down, nor the voice of inspiration stifled, that is enough. We are pleased that women should write and speak, if they feel the need of it, from having something to tell; but silence for a hundred years would be as well, if that silence be from divine command, and not from man's tradition.

While Goetz von Berlichingen[4] rides to battle, his wife is busy in the kitchen; but difference of occupation

---

1   *Goodwyn Barmby ... his wife Catharine*   English philosophers and supporters of socialism and women's rights (1820–81 and 1816–53, respectively).

2   *buckler*   Shield.

3   *William and Mary Howitt*   English authors and translators (1792–1879 and 1799–1888, respectively) who worked closely together throughout their careers.

4   *Goetz von Berlichingen*   Famed German knight and mercenary (1480–1562), depicted by Goethe in his 1773 play of the same name, from which Fuller quotes below.

does not prevent that community of life, that perfect esteem, with which he says,

Whom God loves, to him gives he such a wife!

Manzoni thus dedicates his *Adelchi*:[1]

To his beloved and venerated wife, Enrichetta Luigia Blondel, who, with conjugal affections and maternal wisdom, has preserved a virgin mind, the author dedicates this Adelchi, grieving that he could not, by a more splendid and more durable monument, honor the dear name and the memory of so many virtues.

The relation could not be fairer, nor more equal, if she too had written poems. Yet the position of the parties might have been the reverse as well; the woman might have sung the deeds, given voice to the life of the man, and beauty would have been the result, as we see in pictures of Arcadia[2] the nymph singing to the shepherds, or the shepherd with his pipe allures the nymphs, either makes a good picture. The sounding lyre requires not muscular strength, but energy of soul to animate the hand which can control it. Nature seems to delight in varying her arrangements, as if to show that she will be fettered by no rule, and we must admit the same varieties that she admits.

I have not spoken of the higher grade of marriage union, the religious, which may be expressed as pilgrimage towards a common shrine. This includes the others; home sympathies, and household wisdom, for these pilgrims must know how to assist one another to carry their burdens along the dusty way; intellectual communion, for how sad it would be on such a journey to have a companion to whom you could not communicate thoughts and aspirations, as they sprang to life, who would have no feeling for the more and more glorious prospects that open as we advance, who would never see the flowers that may be gathered by the most industrious traveler. It must include all these. Such a

fellow pilgrim Count Zinzendorf[3] seems to have found in his countess of whom he thus writes.

Twenty-five years' experience has shown me that just the help-mate whom I have is the only one that could suit my vocation. Who else could have so carried through my family affairs? Who lived so spotlessly before the world? Who so wisely aided me in my rejection of a dry morality? Who so clearly set aside the Pharisaism[4] which, as years passed, threatened to creep in among us? Who so deeply discerned as to the spirits of delusion which sought to bewilder us? Who would have governed my whole economy so wisely, richly, and hospitably when circumstances commanded? Who have taken indifferently the part of servant or mistress, without on the one side affecting an especial spirituality, on the other being sullied by any worldly pride? Who, in a community where all ranks are eager to be on a level, would, from wise and real causes, have known how to maintain inward and outward distinctions? Who, without a murmur, have seen her husband encounter such dangers by land and sea? Who undertaken with him and sustained such astonishing pilgrimages? Who amid such difficulties always held up her head, and supported me? Who found so many hundred thousands and acquitted them on her own credit? And, finally, who, of all human beings, would so well understand and interpret to others my inner and outer being as this one, of such nobleness in her way of thinking, such great intellectual capacity, and free from the theological perplexities that enveloped me?

An observer[5] adds this testimony.

We may in many marriages regard it as the best arrangement, if the man has so much advantage over

---

[1]   *Adelchi*   Tragic 1822 play written by Alessandro Manzoni.

[2]   *Arcadia*   Region of Greece, often depicted as a bucolic paradise in classical literature.

[3]   *Count Zinzendorf*   Nikolaus Ludwig, Count von Zinzendorf (1700–60), German Protestant religious leader, bishop of the Moravian Church. His first wife was hymnodist Erdmuthe Dorothea (1700–56).

[4]   *Pharisaism*   Hypocrisy; reference to the Pharisees, an ancient orthodox Jewish sect often referred to in the New Testament as overly invested in religious law.

[5]   [Fuller's note]   Spangenberg.   [August Gottlieb Spangenberg (1704–92), German theologian, who became bishop of the Moravian Church after the death of Count Zinzendorf.]

his wife that she can, without much thought of her own, be, by him, led and directed, as by a father. But it was not so with the Count and his consort. She was not made to be a copy; she was an original; and, while she loved and honored him, she thought for herself on all subjects with so much intelligence, that he could and did look on her as sister and friend also.

Such a woman is the sister and friend of all beings, as the worthy man is their brother and helper.

Another sign of the time is furnished by the triumphs of female authorship. These have been great and constantly increasing. They have taken possession of so many provinces for which men had pronounced them unfit, that though these still declare there are some inaccessible to them, it is difficult to say just *where* they must stop. ...

The late Dr. Channing,[1] whose enlarged and tender and religious nature shared every onward impulse of his time, though his thoughts followed his wishes with a deliberative caution, which belonged to his habits and temperament, was greatly interested in these expectations for women. His own treatment of them was absolutely and thoroughly religious. He regarded them as souls, each of which had a destiny of its own, incalculable to other minds, and whose leading it must follow, guided by the light of a private conscience. He had sentiment, delicacy, kindness, taste, but they were all pervaded and ruled by this one thought, that all beings had souls, and must vindicate their own inheritance. Thus all beings were treated by him with an equal, and sweet, though solemn courtesy. The young and unknown, the woman and the child, all felt themselves regarded with an infinite expectation, from which there was no reaction to vulgar prejudice. He demanded of all he met, to use his favorite phrase, "great truths."

His memory, every way dear and reverend, is by many especially cherished for this intercourse of unbroken respect.

At one time when the progress of Harriet Martineau[2] through this country, Angelina Grimke's[3] appearance in public, and the visit of Mrs. Jameson[4] had turned his thoughts to this subject, he expressed high hopes as to what the coming era would bring to woman. He had been much pleased with the dignified courage of Mrs. Jameson in taking up the defence of her sex in a way from which women usually shrink, because, if they express themselves on such subjects with sufficient force and clearness to do any good, they are exposed to assaults whose vulgarity makes them painful. In intercourse with such a woman, he had shared her indignation at the base injustice, in many respects, and in many regions done to the sex; and been led to think of it far more than ever before. He seemed to think that he might some time write upon the subject. That his aid is withdrawn from the cause is a subject of great regret, for on this question, as on others, he would have known how to sum up the evidence and take, in the noblest spirit, middle ground. He always furnished a platform on which opposing parties could stand, and look at one another under the influence of his mildness and enlightened candor.

Two younger thinkers, men both, have uttered noble prophecies, auspicious for woman. Kinmont,[5] all whose thoughts tended towards the establishment of the reign of love and peace, thought that the inevitable means of this would be an increased predominance given to the idea of woman. Had he lived longer to see the growth of the peace party, the reforms in life and medical practice which seek to substitute water for

---

[1] *The late Dr. Channing* William Ellery Channing (1780–1842), prominent Unitarian preacher.

[2] *Harriet Martineau* British sociologist who described her tour of the United States in 1834 in the influential (and controversial) text *Society in America* (1837).

[3] *Angelina Grimke* Prominent abolitionist and women's rights activist who earned fame as an orator during a time when political oratory was almost exclusively the field of men (1805–79).

[4] *Mrs. Jameson* Anglo-Irish art historian and traveler Anna Brownell Jameson, author of the travel memoir *Winter Studies and Summer Rambles in Canada* (1838).

[5] *Kinmont* Scottish educator Alexander Kinmont (1799–1838).

wine and drugs, pulse for animal food,[1] he would have been confirmed in his view of the way in which the desired changes are to be effected.

In this connection I must mention Shelley,[2] who, like all men of genius, shared the feminine development, and unlike many, knew it. His life was one of the first pulse-beats in the present reform-growth. He, too, abhorred blood and heat, and, by his system and his song, tended to reinstate a plant-like gentleness in the development of energy. In harmony with this his ideas of marriage were lofty, and of course no less so of woman, her nature, and destiny.

For woman, if by a sympathy as to outward condition she is led to aid the enfranchisement of the slave, must no less so, by inward tendency, to favor measures which promise to bring the world more thoroughly and deeply into harmony with her nature. When the lamb takes place of the lion as the emblem of nations, both women and men will be as children of one spirit, perpetual learners of the word and doers thereof, not hearers only.

A writer in a late number of the New York Pathfinder, in two articles headed "Femality," has uttered a still more pregnant word than any we have named. He views woman truly from the soul, and not from society, and the depth and leading of his thoughts is proportionably remarkable. He views the feminine nature as a harmonizer of the vehement elements, and this has often been hinted elsewhere; but what he expresses most forcibly is the lyrical, the inspiring and inspired apprehensiveness of her being.

Had I room to dwell upon this topic, I could not say anything so precise, so near the heart of the matter, as may be found in that article; but, as it is, I can only indicate, not declare, my view.

There are two aspects of woman's nature, expressed by the ancients as Muse and Minerva.[3] It is the former to which the writer in the Pathfinder looks. It is the latter which Wordsworth[4] has in mind, when he says,

> With a placid brow,
> Which woman ne'er should forfeit, keep thy vow.

The especial genius of woman I believe to be electrical in movement, intuitive in function, spiritual in tendency. She is great not so easily in classification, or re-creation, as in an instinctive seizure of causes, and a simple breathing out of what she receives that has the singleness of life, rather than the selecting or energizing of art.

More native to her is it to be the living model of the artist, than to set apart from herself any one form in objective reality; more native to inspire and receive the poem than to create it. In so far as soul is in her completely developed, all soul is the same; but as far as it is modified in her as woman, it flows, it breathes, it sings, rather than deposits soil, or finishes work, and that which is especially feminine flushes in blossom the face of earth, and pervades like air and water all this seeming solid globe, daily renewing and purifying its life. Such may be the especially feminine element, spoken of as Femality. But it is no more the order of nature that it should be incarnated pure in any form, than that the masculine energy should exist unmingled with it in any form.

Male and female represent the two sides of the great radical dualism. But, in fact, they are perpetually passing into one another. Fluid hardens to solid, solid rushes to fluid. There is no wholly masculine man, no purely feminine woman.

History jeers at the attempts of physiologists to bind great original laws by the forms which flow from them. They make a rule; they say from observation, what can and cannot be. In vain! Nature provides exceptions to every rule. She sends women to battle, and

---

1   *pulse for animal food*   It was beginning to be recognized in the 1840s that humans could obtain needed protein from plant food—in particular, from pulses such as beans and chickpeas—rather than from eating other animals. (A small group of vegetarians became vocal in New England in the 1840s; Transcendentalist thinker Amos Bronson Alcott, who was what would today be described as vegan, was the best known of the group.)

2   *Shelley*   English Romantic poet Percy Bysshe Shelley (1792–1822), husband of novelist Mary Shelley (1797–1851) and proponent of various reform movements such as vegetarianism and nonviolence.

3   *Muse*   One of the nine female personifications of art and inspiration described in Greek and Roman mythology; *Minerva*   Roman goddess of wisdom and strategic warfare.

4   *Wordsworth*   English Romantic poet William Wordsworth (1770–1850); Fuller quotes from his 1829 poem "Liberty" below.

sets Hercules spinning;[1] she enables women to bear immense burdens, cold, and frost; she enables the man, who feels maternal love, to nourish his infant like a mother. Of late she plays still gayer pranks. Not only she deprives organizations, but organs, of a necessary end. She enables people to read with the top of the head, and see with the pit of the stomach. Presently she will make a female Newton,[2] and a male Siren.

Man partakes of the feminine in the Apollo,[3] woman of the masculine as Minerva.

Let us be wise and not impede the soul. Let her work as she will. Let us have one creative energy, one incessant revelation. Let it take what form it will, and let us not bind it by the past to man or woman, black or white. Jove sprang from Rhea, Pallas from Jove.[4] So let it be.

If it has been the tendency of the past remarks to call woman rather to the Minerva side—if I, unlike the more generous writer, have spoken from society no less than the soul—let it be pardoned. It is love that has caused this, love for many incarcerated souls that might be freed could the idea of religious self-dependence be established in them, could the weakening habit of dependence on others be broken up.

Every relation, every gradation of nature, is incalculably precious, but only to the soul which is poised upon itself, and to whom no loss, no change, can bring dull discord, for it is in harmony with the central soul.

If any individual live too much in relations, so that he becomes a stranger to the resources of his own nature, he falls after a while into a distraction,[5] or imbecility, from which he can only be cured by a time of isolation, which gives the renovating fountains time to rise up. With a society it is the same. Many minds, deprived of the traditory or instinctive means of passing a cheerful existence, must find help in self-impulse or perish. It is therefore that while any elevation, in the view of union, is to be hailed with joy, we shall not decline celibacy as the great fact of the time. It is one from which no vow, no arrangement, can at present save a thinking mind. For now the rowers are pausing on their oars, they wait a change before they can pull together. All tends to illustrate the thought of a wise contemporary. Union is only possible to those who are units. To be fit for relations in time, souls, whether of man or woman, must be able to do without them in the spirit.

It is therefore that I would have woman lay aside all thought, such as she habitually cherishes, of being taught and led by men. I would have her, like the Indian girl, dedicate herself to the Sun, the Sun of Truth, and go nowhere if his beams did not make clear the path. I would have her free from compromise, from complaisance, from helplessness, because I would have her good enough and strong enough to love one and all beings, from the fulness, not the poverty of being.

Men, as at present instructed, will not help this work, because they also are under the slavery of habit. I have seen with delight their poetic impulses. A sister is the fairest ideal, and how nobly Wordsworth, and even Byron,[6] have written of a sister.

There is no sweeter sight than to see a father with his little daughter. Very vulgar men become refined to the eye when leading a little girl by the hand. At that moment the right relation between the sexes seems established, and you feel as if the man would aid in the noblest purpose, if you ask him in behalf of his little daughter. Once two fine figures stood before me, thus. The father of very intellectual aspect, his falcon eye softened by affection as he looked down on his fair child, she the image of himself, only more graceful and brilliant in expression. I was reminded of Southey's Kehama,[7] when lo, the dream was rudely broken. They were talking of education, and he said,

---

[1] *sets Hercules spinning* Several Greek and Roman myths describe a period during which the hero Hercules was made a servant to the Lydian queen Omphale, who forced him to perform traditionally feminine tasks such as spinning wool.

[2] *Newton* Reference to the English scientist and mathematician Isaac Newton (1642–1726).

[3] *Apollo* Greek god of the sun, music, and poetry.

[4] *Jove ... Jove* In Greek and Roman mythology, the Titaness Rhea is the mother of Zeus (known by the Romans as Jove); Athena, often referred to with the honorific Pallas, was born from the head of Zeus.

[5] *distraction* Distress or madness.

[6] *Wordsworth, and even Byron* Both Wordsworth and Lord Byron wrote poetry addressed to their beloved sisters (in Byron's case a half-sister) Dorothy Wordsworth (1771–1855) and Augusta Mary Leigh (1783–1851), respectively. (Byron is also known, however, for his numerous affairs and his occasionally abusive relationships with women.)

[7] *Southey's Kehama* Reference to Robert Southey's epic poem *The Curse of Kehama* (1810).

"I shall not have Maria brought too forward. If she knows too much, she will never find a husband; superior women hardly ever can."

"Surely," said his wife, with a blush, "you wish Maria to be as good and wise as she can, whether it will help her to marriage or not."

"No," he persisted, "I want her to have a sphere and a home, and someone to protect her when I am gone."

It was a trifling incident, but made a deep impression. I felt that the holiest relations fail to instruct the unprepared and perverted mind. If this man, indeed, would have looked at it on the other side, he was the last that would have been willing to have been taken himself for the home and protection he could give, but would have been much more likely to repeat the tale of Alcibiades with his phials.

But men do *not* look at both sides, and women must leave off asking them and being influenced by them, but retire within themselves, and explore the groundwork of being till they find their peculiar secret. Then when they come forth again, renovated and baptized, they will know how to turn all dross[1] to gold, and will be rich and free though they live in a hut, tranquil if in a crowd. Then their sweet singing shall not be from passionate impulse, but the lyrical overflow of a divine rapture, and a new music shall be elucidated from this many-chorded world.

Grant her then for a while the armor and the javelin. Let her put from her the press of other minds and meditate in virgin loneliness. The same idea shall reappear in due time as Muse, or Ceres, the all-kindly, patient Earth-Spirit.

I tire everyone with my Goethean illustrations. But it cannot be helped.

Goethe, the great mind which gave itself absolutely to the leadings of truth, and let rise through him the waves which are still advancing through the century, was its intellectual prophet. Those who know him see, daily, his thought fulfilled more and more, and they must speak of it, till his name weary and even nauseate, as all great names have in their time. And I cannot spare the reader, if such there be, his wonderful sight as to the prospects and wants of women.

As his Wilhelm grows in life and advances in wisdom, he becomes acquainted with women of more and more character, rising from Mariana to Macaria.[2]

Macaria, bound with the heavenly bodies in fixed revolutions, the centre of all relations, herself unrelated, expresses the Minerva side.

Mignon, the electrical, inspired lyrical nature.

All these women, though we see them in relations, we can think of as unrelated. They all are very individual, yet seem nowhere restrained. They satisfy for the present, yet arouse an infinite expectation.

The economist Theresa, the benevolent Natalia,[3] the fair Saint, have chosen a path, but their thoughts are not narrowed to it. The functions of life to them are not ends, but suggestions.

Thus to them all things are important, because none is necessary. Their different characters have fair play, and each is beautiful in its minute indications, for nothing is enforced or conventional, but everything, however slight, grows from the essential life of the being.

Mignon and Theresa wear male attire when they like, and it is graceful for them to do so, while Macaria is confined to her arm chair behind the green curtain, and the Fair Saint could not bear a speck of dust on her robe.

All things are in their places in this little world because all is natural and free, just as "there is room for everything out of doors." Yet all is rounded in by natural harmony which will always arise where Truth and Love are sought in the light of freedom.

Goethe's book bodes an era of freedom like its own, of "extraordinary generous seeking," and new revelations. New individualities shall be developed in the actual world, which shall advance upon it as gently as the figures come out upon his canvass.

A profound thinker has said "no married woman can represent the female world, for she belongs to her husband. The idea of woman must be represented by a virgin."[4]

---

[1]   *dross*   Waste matter produced during the smelting process.

[2]   *As his Wilhelm … Macaria*   Here and over the next few paragraphs, Fuller references numerous female characters from Goethe's *Wilhelm Meister's Apprenticeship*.

[3]   *Natalia*   Natalia of Nicomedia, wife of the martyr Saint Adrian (d. 306).

[4]   *no married … a virgin*   The source of this quotation is unknown.

But that is the very fault of marriage, and of the present relation between the sexes, that the woman does belong to the man, instead of forming a whole with him. Were it otherwise there would be no such limitation to the thought.

Woman, self-centred, would never be absorbed by any relation; it would be only an experience to her as to man. It is a vulgar error that love, *a* love to woman is her whole existence; she also is born for Truth and Love in their universal energy. Would she but assume her inheritance, Mary would not be the only Virgin Mother. Not Manzoni[1] alone would celebrate in his wife the virgin mind with the maternal wisdom and conjugal affections. The soul is ever young, ever virgin.

And will not she soon appear? The woman who shall vindicate their birthright for all women; who shall teach them what to claim, and how to use what they obtain? Shall not her name be for her era Victoria, for her country and her life Virginia? Yet predictions are rash; she herself must teach us to give her the fitting name.

—1843

---

[1]   *Manzoni*   Italian novelist Alessandro Manzoni (1785–1873).

DAVID WALKER

c. 1785/96 – 1830

First published in 1829, David Walker's *Appeal to the Coloured Citizens of the World* was among the most controversial publications of the antebellum period. Written in language as impassioned as it is deliberate, the pamphlet is an incisive condemnation of the institution of slavery and all who profited from it, calling for immediate emancipation and for the rise of a nationwide racial consciousness among both enslaved and free African Americans. Perceived by many at the time as dangerously radical, the *Appeal* was immediately vilified by Southern slaveholders as well as by moderate Northern abolitionists, its author deemed by detractors to be at best misguided and at worst a threat to the very foundations of American society. To threaten and overthrow those cruel and unjust foundations, however, was one of Walker's primary aims. The *Appeal*, which helped usher in abolitionism as one of the most important concerns of nineteenth-century America, has been influential in the struggle for racial justice ever since its publication, and echoes of it can be heard in the work of Maria W. Stewart, Frederick Douglass, W.E.B. Du Bois, Martin Luther King Jr., and Malcolm X, among others.

Though Walker's father had been enslaved, his mother was free and therefore Walker himself was born into freedom. Nevertheless, the legal and social restraints experienced by even free African Americans in the antebellum South were severe. At an unknown date he left his native North Carolina for Charleston, South Carolina, where he joined the African Methodist Episcopal Church—a leading force in the fight for racial justice throughout the nineteenth century—and likely encountered the formerly enslaved Denmark Vesey, whose radical, revolutionary approach to abolitionism would see echoes in Walker's later work. After traveling numerous Southern and Western states, Walker settled in Boston, where, though black people continued to experience severe discrimination and outright violence, there was nonetheless a flourishing black intellectual and political community. Here he purchased a used-clothing store and married Eliza Butler. Walker joined the influential Prince Hall Masonic Lodge, which advocated for black education rights among other causes; helped found the Massachusetts General Colored Association, before which he frequently lectured; wrote for and helped distribute *Freedom's Journal*, the first African American-owned newspaper in the country; and used his shop and home as a shelter, often for those escaping slavery via the Underground Railroad.

Published in 1829, *Walker's Appeal, in Four Articles, together with a Preamble, to the Coloured Citizens of the World*, was a consummation of years of antislavery thought, calling upon African Americans to recognize and resist the oppression under which they lived, and invoking ancient and biblical examples of slavery to demonstrate the historically exceptional injustice of the American institution. In part, Walker's text was a response to Thomas Jefferson's influential *Notes on the State of Virginia* (1787)—often considered a foundational expression of American political culture—in which Jefferson defends slavery on the basis of the "real distinctions which nature has made" between black and white people, and claims that African Americans should, if free, be "removed beyond the reach of mixture" with whites. Walker addresses the way this latter infamous claim had recently been taken up by the American Colonization Society, which advocated for the deportation of black people to Africa; from the 1820s to the 1840s the Society sent thousands of African Americans to colonize Liberia, where more than half died.

Though *Walker's Appeal* was not the first stand-alone publication of its sort—a number of abolitionist tracts had, for instance, been previously published by Boston's African Society—it was among the most ambitious. Anticipating the negative response his pamphlet would likely elicit among white authorities if distributed conventionally, Walker used a varied network of supporters to circulate the *Appeal* among people who would otherwise have been unable to access it, and to read it aloud to those who were illiterate; this network may have included sympathetic sailors and ship workers—a large proportion of whom were free blacks—as well as activists and ministers to whom Walker mailed crates of the pamphlet directly. The pamphlet soon reached thousands of people around the country, with copies found as far south as New Orleans. In 1830 the work was already in its third revised edition, with each revision featuring additional material, as well as a shift towards increasingly radical language.

By this point the pamphlet had attracted the notice of many outraged Southern slaveholders, who took quick action to suppress knowledge of the text among the people they enslaved. Southern newspapers reported on the pamphlet extensively, and proslavery Southerners called for Walker's capture and execution—with a large reward offered to those willing to do the deed. Georgia's Governor Gilmer accused Boston of harboring "highly inflammatory" literature and demanded that the pamphlet's circulation be brought to an end (the city's mayor declined to take such action). The legislature of North Carolina met secretly about the *Appeal* and passed harsh laws forbidding anyone from teaching enslaved people how to read or write, and from circulating what was considered seditious literature. On the whole, many Southern states saw a surge in racist legislation during the early 1830s, likely in part as a response to the increasingly vigorous antislavery resistance represented by texts like the *Appeal*. White abolitionists, too, were disturbed by the forceful language of the pamphlet: Benjamin Lundy, for instance, declared the *Appeal* "a labored attempt to rouse the worst passions of human nature, and inflame the minds of those to whom it is addressed," while William Lloyd Garrison commented that "We deprecate its circulation, though we cannot but wonder at the bravery and intelligence of its author." (Though Garrison's personal response to the *Appeal* was mixed, the text appears to have influenced his own growing support for immediate abolition—and his rejection of the aims of the American Colonization Society.)

Despite the attempts to suppress its influence, Walker's *Appeal* was an important catalyst for the explosion of abolitionist culture throughout the country in the post-1830 era. It had a profound influence on the abolitionist and feminist work of Walker's protégée Maria Stewart, who built upon Walker's rhetoric of racial uplift even while rejecting his controversial endorsement of violent means. The slave rebellion led by Nat Turner in 1831—a struggle for freedom in which rebels killed fifty-five whites, widely depicted as a massacre in the South—reflected Walker's revolutionary rhetoric, though we cannot be certain that Turner himself had encountered Walker's work. While the *Appeal* was somewhat forgotten over the following decade, it experienced a revival in 1848, when it was republished by black Northern abolitionist Henry Highland Garnet, who wrote in his brief "Sketch" of the author, "They said that he went too far, and was making trouble. So the Jews spoke of Moses." Walker's fiery rhetoric, and his openness to armed revolt as an appropriate response to slavery, have led some historians to see his work as influential in the development of the later Black Power and Black Nationalist movements.

Walker died unexpectedly not long after the release of the *Appeal*'s third edition. The cause of his death has long been disputed and never resolved—many in Boston's black community believed he had been murdered, though the official cause of death was recorded as tuberculosis. Walker's only child to live to adulthood, Edward Garrison Walker, was born after his father's death; in 1866 he became one of the first black men elected to the Massachusetts State Legislature.

NOTE ON THE TEXT: The text of the work presented here is based on the third edition of the *Appeal*, the last edition published during Walker's lifetime, with the full title *Walker's Appeal, in Four Articles, together with a Preamble, to the Coloured Citizens of the World, but in particular, and very expressly, to those of The United States of America* (1830). Spelling and punctuation have been modernized in accordance with the practices of this anthology. Inconsistencies in the use of American and British spelling conventions have not been corrected.

⌘ ⌘ ⌘

from *Walker's Appeal, in Four Articles*

APPEAL, ETC.

My dearly beloved Brethren and Fellow Citizens. Having travelled over a considerable portion of these United States, and having, in the course of my travels, taken the most accurate observations of things as they exist—the result of my observations has warranted the full and unshaken conviction, that we (coloured people of these United States) are the most degraded, wretched, and abject set of beings that ever lived since the world began; and I pray God that none like us ever may live again until time shall be no more. They tell us of the Israelites in Egypt, the Helots in Sparta,[1] and of the Roman Slaves, which last were made up from almost every nation under heaven, whose sufferings under those ancient and heathen nations, were, in comparison with ours, under this enlightened and Christian nation, no more than a cypher[2]—or, in other words, those heathen nations of antiquity, had but little more among them than the name and form of slavery; while wretchedness and endless miseries were reserved, apparently in a phial, to be poured out upon our fathers, ourselves and our children, by *Christian* Americans!

These positions I shall endeavour, by the help of the Lord, to demonstrate in the course of this *Appeal*, to the satisfaction of the most incredulous mind—and may God Almighty, who is the Father of our Lord Jesus Christ, open your hearts to understand and believe the truth.

The *causes*, my brethren, which produce our wretchedness and miseries, are so very numerous and aggravating, that I believe the pen only of a Josephus or a Plutarch,[3] can well enumerate and explain them. Upon subjects, then, of such incomprehensible magnitude, so impenetrable, and so notorious, I shall be obliged to omit a large class of, and content myself with giving you an exposition of a few of those, which do indeed rage to such an alarming pitch, that they cannot but be a perpetual source of terror and dismay to every reflecting mind.

I am fully aware, in making this appeal to my much afflicted and suffering brethren, that I shall not only be assailed by those whose greatest earthly desires are, to keep us in abject ignorance and wretchedness, and who are of the firm conviction that Heaven has designed us and our children to be slaves and *beasts of burden* to them and their children. I say, I do not only expect to be held up to the public as an ignorant, impudent and restless disturber of the public peace, by such avaricious creatures, as well as a mover of insubordination—and perhaps put in prison or to death, for giving a superficial exposition of our miseries, and exposing tyrants. But I am persuaded, that many of my brethren, particularly those who are ignorantly in league with slaveholders or tyrants, who acquire their daily bread by the blood and sweat of their more ignorant brethren—and not a few of those too, who are too ignorant to see an inch beyond their noses, will rise up and call me cursed—Yea, the jealous ones among us will perhaps use more abject subtlety, by affirming that this work is not worth perusing, that we are well situated, and there is no use in trying to better our condition, for we cannot. I will ask one question here. Can our condition be any worse? Can it be more mean[4] and abject? If there are any changes, will they not be for the better, though they may appear for the worst at first? Can they get us any lower? Where can they get us? They are afraid to treat us worse, for they know well, the day they do it they are gone. But against all accusations which may or can be preferred against me, I appeal to Heaven for my motive in writing—who knows that my object is, if possible, to awaken in the breasts of my afflicted, degraded and slumbering brethren, a spirit of

---

1 *Israelites in Egypt ... in Sparta* Historical examples of slavery. The Israelites' enslavement to the Egyptians, and their subsequent emancipation through the intervention of God, is the primary subject of the Book of Exodus. The Helots were a class of people in Spartan society; their exact status has been the subject of historical debate, with some uncertainty as to whether they were fully considered slaves by the Spartans or whether they occupied a status between slave and citizen.

2 *cypher* Literally, the digit zero; i.e., of no comparative importance.

3 *Josephus* Roman-Jewish scholar (37–100 CE) best known for his works on Jewish history; *Plutarch* Influential Greek essayist and biographer (46–120 CE).

4 *mean* Base, impoverished.

inquiry and investigation respecting our miseries and wretchedness in this *Republican Land of Liberty!!!!!!*

The sources from which our miseries are derived, and on which I shall comment, I shall not combine in one, but shall put them under distinct heads and expose them in their turn; in doing which, keeping truth on my side, and not departing from the strictest rules of morality, I shall endeavour to penetrate, search out, and lay them open for your inspection. If you cannot or will not profit by them, I shall have done *my* duty to you, my country and my God.

And as the inhuman system of *slavery* is the *source* from which most of our miseries proceed, I shall begin with that *curse to nations*, which has spread terror and devastation through so many nations of antiquity, and which is raging to such a pitch at the present day in Spain and in Portugal.[1] It had one tug in England, in France, and in the United States of America;[2] yet the inhabitants thereof, do not learn wisdom, and erase it entirely from their dwellings and from all with whom they have to do. The fact is, the labour of slaves comes so cheap to the avaricious usurpers, and is (as they think) of such great utility to the country where it exists, that those who are actuated by sordid avarice only, overlook the evils, which will as sure as the Lord lives, follow after the good. In fact, they are so happy to keep in ignorance and degradation, and to receive the homage and labour of the slaves, they forget that God rules in the armies of heaven and among the inhabitants of the earth, having his ears continually open to the cries, tears and groans of his oppressed people; and being a just and holy Being will at one day appear fully in behalf of the oppressed, and arrest the progress of the avaricious oppressors; for although the destruction of the oppressors God may not effect by the oppressed, yet the Lord our God will bring other destructions upon them—for not unfrequently will he cause them to rise up one against another, to be split and divided, and to oppress each other, and sometimes to open hostilities with sword in hand. Some may ask, what is the matter with this united and happy people? Some say it is the cause of political usurpers, tyrants, oppressors, &c. But has not the Lord an oppressed and suffering people among them? Does the Lord condescend to hear their cries and see their tears in consequence of oppression? Will he let the oppressors rest comfortably and happy always? Will he not cause the very children of the oppressors to rise up against them, and oftimes put them to death? "God works in many ways his wonders to perform."[3] ...

All persons who are acquainted with history, and particularly the Bible, who are not blinded by the God of this world, and are not actuated by avarice—who are able to lay aside prejudice long enough to view candidly and impartially, things as they were, are, and probably will be—who are willing to admit that God made man to serve Him *alone*, and that man should have no other Lord or Lords but Himself—that God Almighty is the *sole proprietor* or *master* of the WHOLE human family, and will not on any consideration admit of a colleague, being unwilling to divide his glory with another—and who can dispense with prejudice long enough to admit that we are *men*, notwithstanding our *impriminent noses* and *woolly heads*, and believe that we feel for our fathers, mothers, wives and children, as well as the whites do for theirs. I say, all who are permitted to see and believe these things, can easily recognize the judgments of God among the Spaniards. Though others may lay the cause of the fierceness with which they cut each other's throats, to some other circumstance, yet they who believe that God is a God of justice, will believe that SLAVERY *is the principal cause.*

---

1   *And as ... in Portugal* Walker is referring to the theory that slavery, as a morally corrupt institution, would inherently lead to dissolution and unrest within the societies that upheld it; as an example, he alludes to the bloody civil conflicts and economic crises that occurred in the formerly slave-trading countries of Spain and Portugal in the first few decades of the nineteenth century. (Both countries also lost possession of slaveholding colonies in the early decades of the nineteenth century; though in most cases these colonies were established as non-slaveholding nations, the formerly Portuguese colony Brazil did not abolish slavery until 1888.)

2   *It had one tug ... of America* The Atlantic slave trade was abolished by the United Kingdom in 1807, and in the United States the importation of enslaved people was banned that same year. Slavery was abolished, re-instated, and then re-abolished by France between 1794 and 1826. Though considered an important victory by abolitionists, the abolition of the Atlantic slave trade did not ban the actual possession and sale of enslaved people within the U.S. or within British and French colonies, nor did it stop the illegal importation of enslaved people into the country.

---

3   *God works ... to perform* Paraphrase of the opening lines of English poet William Cowper's abolitionist hymn "Light Shining Out of Darkness" (1773).

While the Spaniards are running about upon the field of battle cutting each other's throats, has not the Lord an afflicted and suffering people in the midst of them, whose cries and groans in consequence of oppression are continually pouring into the ears of the God of justice? Would they not cease to cut each other's throats, if they could? But how can they? The very support which they draw from government to aid them in perpetrating such enormities, does it not arise in a great degree from the wretched victims of oppression among them? And yet they are calling for *Peace! Peace!!* Will any peace be given unto them? Their destruction may indeed be procrastinated awhile, but can it continue long, while they are oppressing the Lord's people? Has He not the hearts of all men in His hand? Will he suffer one part of his creatures to go on oppressing another like brutes always, with impunity? And yet, those avaricious wretches are calling for *Peace!!!!* I declare, it does appear to me, as though some nations think God is asleep, or that he made the Africans for nothing else but to dig their mines and work their farms, or they cannot believe history, sacred or profane. I ask every man who has a heart, and is blessed with the privilege of believing—Is not God a God of justice to *all* his creatures? Do you say he is? Then if he gives peace and tranquility to tyrants, and permits them to keep our fathers, our mothers, ourselves and our children in eternal ignorance and wretchedness, to support them and their families, would he be to us a God of *justice*? I ask, O ye *Christians!!!* who hold us and our children in the most abject ignorance and degradation, that ever a people were afflicted with since the world began—I say, if God gives you peace and tranquility, and suffers you thus to go on afflicting us, and our children, who have never given you the least provocation—would he be to us *a God of justice?* If you will allow that we are MEN, who feel for each other, does not the blood of our fathers and of us their children, cry aloud to the Lord of Sabaoth[1] against you, for the cruelties and murders with which you have, and do continue to afflict us. But it is time for me to close my remarks on the suburbs, just to enter more fully into the interior of this system of cruelty and oppression.

ARTICLE I.
OUR WRETCHEDNESS IN CONSEQUENCE OF SLAVERY.

My beloved brethren: The Indians of North and of South America—the Greeks—the Irish, subjected under the king of Great Britain—the Jews, that ancient people of the Lord—the inhabitants of the islands of the sea—in fine,[2] all the inhabitants of the earth (except however, the sons of Africa) are called *men*, and of course are, and ought to be free. But we (coloured people) and our children are *brutes!!* and of course are, and *ought to be* SLAVES to the American people and their children forever!! to dig their mines and work their farms; and thus go on enriching them, from one generation to another with our *blood* and our *tears!!!!*

I promised in a preceding page to demonstrate to the satisfaction of the most incredulous, that we (coloured people of these United States of America) are the *most wretched, degraded* and *abject* set of beings that *ever lived* since the world began, and that the white Americans having reduced us to the wretched state of *slavery,* treat us in that condition *more cruel* (they being an enlightened and Christian people), than any heathen nation did any people whom it had reduced to our condition. These affirmations are so well confirmed in the minds of all unprejudiced men, who have taken the trouble to read histories, that they need no elucidation from me. But to put them beyond all doubt, I refer you in the first place to the children of Jacob,[3] or of Israel in Egypt, under Pharaoh and his people. Some of my brethren do not know who Pharaoh and the Egyptians were—I know it to be a fact, that some of them take the Egyptians to have been a gang of *devils,* not knowing any better, and that they (Egyptians) having got possession of the Lord's people, treated them *nearly* as cruel as *Christian Americans* do us, at the present day. For the information of such, I would only mention that the Egyptians, were Africans or coloured people, such as we are—some of them yellow and others dark—a mixture of Ethiopians and the natives of Egypt—about the same as you see the coloured people of the United States at the present day. I say, I call your attention then, to the children

---

[1] *Lord of Sabaoth* Lord of Hosts or God of armies; used to refer to God in his capacity as a military leader of the heavenly host.

[2] *in fine* To summarize.

[3] *the children of Jacob* I.e., the Israelites; Jacob is an Israelite patriarch also referred to by the name "Israel."

of Jacob, while I point out particularly to you his son Joseph,[1] among the rest, in Egypt.

"And Pharaoh, said unto Joseph, thou shalt be over my house, and according unto thy word shall all my people be ruled: only in the throne will I be greater than thou."[2]

"And Pharaoh said unto Joseph, see, I have set thee over all the land of Egypt."[3]

"And Pharaoh said unto Joseph, I am Pharaoh, and without thee shall no man lift up his hand or foot in all the land of Egypt."[4]

Now I appeal to heaven and to earth, and particularly to the American people themselves, who cease not to declare that our condition is not *hard*, and that we are comparatively satisfied to rest in wretchedness and misery, under them and their children. Not, indeed, to show me a coloured President, a Governor, a Legislator, a Senator, a Mayor, or an Attorney at the Bar. But to show me a man of colour, who holds the low office of a Constable, or one who sits in a Juror Box, even on a case of one of his wretched brethren, throughout this great Republic!! But let us pass Joseph the son of Israel a little farther in review, as he existed with that heathen nation.

"And Pharaoh called Joseph's name Zaphnath-paaneah; and he gave him to wife Asenath the daughter of Potipherah priest of On. And Joseph went out over all the land of Egypt."[5]

Compare the above, with the American institutions. Do they not institute laws to prohibit us from marrying among the whites?[6] I would wish, candidly, however, before the Lord, to be understood, that I would not give a *pinch of snuff* to be married to any white person I ever saw in all the days of my life. And I do say it, that the black man, or man of colour, who will leave his own colour (provided he can get one, who is good for any thing) and marry a white woman, to be a double slave to her, just because she is *white*, ought to be treated by her as he surely will be, viz:[7] as a NIGER ! ! ! ![8] It is not, indeed, what I care about inter-marriages with the whites, which induced me to pass this subject in review; for the Lord knows, that there is a day coming when they will be glad enough to get into the company of the blacks, notwithstanding, we are, in this generation, levelled by them, almost on a level with the brute creation: and some of us they treat even worse than they do the brutes that perish. I only made this extract to show how much lower we are held, and how much more cruel we are treated by the Americans, than were the children of Jacob, by the Egyptians.—We will notice the sufferings of Israel some further, under *heathen Pharaoh*, compared with ours under the *enlightened Christians of America*.

"And Pharaoh spake unto Joseph, saying, thy father and thy brethren are come unto thee:

"The land of Egypt is before thee: in the best of the land make thy father and brethren to dwell; in the land of Goshen let them dwell: and if thou knowest any men of activity among them, then make them rulers over my cattle."[9]

I ask those people who treat us so *well*, Oh! I ask them, where is the most barren spot of land which they have given unto us? Israel had the most fertile land in all Egypt. Need I mention the very notorious fact, that I have known a poor man of colour, who laboured night and day, to acquire a little money, and having acquired it, he vested it in a small piece of land, and got him a house erected thereon, and having paid for the whole, he moved his family into it, where he was suffered to remain but nine months, when he was cheated out of his property by a white man, and driven out of door! And is not this the case generally? Can a man of colour buy a piece of land and keep it peaceably? Will

original spelling—

original spelling—

---

[1] *Joseph*   One of Jacob's twelve sons, Joseph is sold into slavery to a man named Potiphar by his jealous brothers. The Book of Genesis narrates the story of Joseph's rise from slavery to the status of vizier, second only to the Pharaoh in power.

[2] [Walker's note]   See Genesis, chap. xli. v. 40.

[3] [Walker's note]   v. 41.

[4] [Walker's note]   v. 44.

[5] [Walker's note]   v. 45.

[6] *Do they not ... the whites?*   Numerous anti-miscegenation laws were in place in the United States in this period in both the South and the North (Massachusetts, for instance, first enacted legislation barring black people from intermarrying with whites in 1705, and did not repeal the law until 1843).

[7] *viz:*   Abbreviation for the Latin videlicet, meaning "namely" or "that is to say."

[8] *NIGER*   As the context here suggests, the "n word" had by this time firmly established itself in the vernacular as an emphatically pejorative alternative to the then-more-neutral term "negro." This spelling (with a single g) remained in occasional use until the mid-nineteenth century.

[9] [Walker's note]   Genesis, xlvii.—v. 5–6.

not some white man try to get it from him, even if it is in a *mud hole*? I need not comment any farther on a subject, which all, both black and white, will readily admit. But I must, really, observe that in this very city, when a man of colour dies, if he owned any real estate it most generally falls into the hands of some white person. The wife and children of the deceased may weep and lament if they please, but the estate will be kept snug enough by its white possessor.

But to prove farther that the condition of the Israelites was better under the Egyptians than ours is under the whites. I call upon the professing Christians, I call upon the philanthropist, I call upon the very tyrant himself, to show me a page of history, either sacred or profane, on which a verse can be found, which maintains, that the Egyptians heaped the *insupportable insult* upon the children of Israel, by telling them that they were not of the *human family*. Can the whites deny this charge? Have they not, after having reduced us to the deplorable condition of slaves under their feet, held us up as descending originally from the tribes of *Monkeys*, or *Orang-Outangs?* O! my God! I appeal to every man of feeling—is not this insupportable? Is it not heaping the most gross insult upon our miseries, because they have got us under their feet and we cannot help ourselves? Oh! pity us we pray thee, Lord Jesus, Master. Has Mr. Jefferson declared to the world, that we are inferior to the whites, both in the endowments of our bodies and of minds?[1] It is indeed surprising, that a man of such great learning, combined with such excellent natural parts, should speak so of a set of men in chains. I do not know what to compare it to, unless, like putting one wild deer in an iron cage, where it will be secured, and hold another by the side of the same, then let it go, and expect the one in the cage to run as fast as the one at liberty. So far, my brethren, were the Egyptians from heaping these insults upon their slaves, that Pharaoh's daughter took Moses, a son of Israel for her own, as will appear by the following.

"And Pharaoh's daughter said unto her, [Moses' mother] take this child away, and nurse it for me, and I will pay thee thy wages. And the woman took the child [Moses] and nursed it.

"And the child grew, and she brought him unto Pharaoh's daughter and he became her son. And she called his name Moses: and she said because I drew him out of the water."[2]

In all probability, Moses would have become Prince Regent to the throne, and no doubt, in process of time but he would have been seated on the throne of Egypt. But he had rather suffer shame, with the people of God, than to enjoy pleasures with that wicked people for a season. O! that the coloured people were long since of Moses' excellent disposition, instead of courting favour with, and telling news and lies to our *natural enemies*, against each other—aiding them to keep their hellish chains of slavery upon us. Would we not long before this time, have been respectable men, instead of such wretched victims of oppression as we are? Would they be able to drag our mothers, our fathers, our wives, our children and ourselves, around the world in chains and hand-cuffs as they do, to dig up gold and silver for them and theirs? This question, my brethren, I leave for you to digest; and may God Almighty force it home to your hearts. Remember that unless you are united, keeping your tongues within your teeth, you will be afraid to trust your secrets to each other, and thus perpetuate our miseries under the *Christians!!!!!* ❧ ADDITION.— Remember, also to lay humble at the feet of our Lord and Master Jesus Christ, with prayers and fastings. Let our enemies go on with their butcheries, and at once fill up their cup. Never make an attempt to gain our freedom or *natural right*, from under our cruel oppressors and murderers, until you see your way clear[3]—when

---

[1] *Mr. Jefferson ... of minds?* Here and throughout the text Walker refers to Thomas Jefferson's *Notes on the State of Virginia* (1787). A work of political commentary on subjects such as the separation of church and state, individual liberty, and freedom of speech, the book also expresses Jefferson's racialist scientific theories on what he considered to be the "natural" inequality of white and black people. Jefferson presents these theories to support his argument that Virginia should not yet emancipate its enslaved people.

[2] [Walker's note] See Exodus, chap. 11. v. 9, 10.

[3] [Walker's note] It is not to be understood here, that I mean for us to wait until God shall take us by the hair of our heads and drag us out of abject wretchedness and slavery, nor do I mean to convey the idea for us to wait until our enemies shall make preparations, and call us to seize those preparations, take it away from them, and put everything before us to death, in order to gain our freedom which God has given us. For you must remember that we are men as well as they. God has been pleased to give us two eyes, two hands, two feet, and some sense in our heads as well as they. They have no more right to hold us in slavery than we have to hold them, we have just as much right, in the sight of God, to hold them and their children in slavery and wretchedness, as they have to hold us, and no more.

that hour arrives and you move, be not afraid or dismayed; for be you assured that Jesus Christ the King of heaven and of earth who is the God of justice and of armies, will surely go before you. And those enemies who have for hundreds of years stolen our *rights*, and kept us ignorant of Him and His divine worship, he will remove. Millions of whom, are this day, so ignorant and avaricious, that they cannot conceive how God can have an attribute of justice, and show mercy to us because it pleased Him to make us black—which colour, Mr. Jefferson calls unfortunate!!!!!! As though we are not as thankful to our God, for having made us as it pleased himself, as they (the whites) are for having made them white. They think because they hold us in their infernal chains of slavery, that we wish to be white, or of their color—but they are dreadfully deceived—we wish to be just as it pleased our Creator to have made us, and no avaricious and unmerciful wretches, have any business to make slaves of, or hold us in slavery. How would they like for us to make slaves of, and hold them in cruel slavery, and murder them as they do us? But is Mr. Jefferson's assertion true? viz. "that it is unfortunate for us that our Creator has been pleased to make us *black*." We will not take his say so, for the fact. The world will have an opportunity to see whether it is unfortunate for us, that our Creator *has made us* darker than the *whites*.

Fear not the number and education of our *enemies*, against whom we shall have to contend for our lawful right; guaranteed to us by our Maker; for why should we be afraid, when God is, and will continue (if we continue humble) to be on our side?

The man who would not fight under our Lord and Master Jesus Christ, in the glorious and heavenly cause of freedom and of God—to be delivered from the most wretched, abject and servile slavery, that ever a people was afflicted with since the foundation of the world, to the present day—ought to be kept with all of his children or family, in slavery, or in chains, to be butchered by his *cruel enemies*. ☙

I saw a paragraph, a few years since, in a South Carolina paper, which, speaking of the barbarity of the Turks, it said: "The Turks are the most barbarous people in the world—they treat the Greeks more like *brutes* than human beings." And in the same paper was an advertisement, which said: "Eight well built

Virginia and Maryland *Negro fellows* and four *wenches* will positively be *sold* this day, *to the highest bidder!*" And what astonished me still more was, to see in this same *humane* paper!! the cuts of three men, with clubs and budgets[1] on their backs, and an advertisement offering a considerable sum of money for their apprehension and delivery. I declare, it is really so amusing to hear the Southerners and Westerners of this country talk about *barbarity*, that it is positively, enough to make a man *smile*.

The suffering of the Helots among the Spartans, were somewhat severe, it is true, but to say that theirs, were as severe as ours among the Americans, I do most strenuously deny—for instance, can any man show me an article on a page of ancient history which specifies, that, the Spartans chained, and hand-cuffed the Helots, and dragged them from their wives and children, children from their parents, mothers from their suckling babes, wives from their husbands, driving them from one end of the country to the other? Notice the Spartans were heathens, who lived long before our Divine Master made his appearance in the flesh. Can Christian Americans deny these barbarous cruelties? Have you not, Americans, having subjected us under you, added to these miseries, by insulting us in telling us to our face, because we are helpless, that we are not of the human family? I ask you, O! Americans, I ask you, in the name of the Lord, can you deny these charges? Some perhaps may deny, by saying, that they never thought or said that we were not men. But do not actions speak louder than words? Have they not made provisions for the Greeks, and Irish?[2] Nations who have never done the least thing for them, while *we*, who have enriched their country with our blood and tears—have dug up gold and silver for them and their children, from generation to generation, and are in more miseries than any other people under heaven, are not seen, but by comparatively, a handful of the American people? There are indeed, more ways to kill a dog, besides choking it to death with butter. Further—The Spartans or Lacedemonians, had some frivolous pretext, for enslaving the Helots, for they (Helots) while being free inhabitants of Sparta, stirred

---

[1]   *cuts* I.e., woodcuts; engravings;   *budgets* Leather bags.

[2]   *made provisions ... Irish* I.e., provided them with rights.

up an intestine[1] commotion, and were, by the Spartans subdued, and made prisoners of war. Consequently they and their children were condemned to perpetual slavery.[2]

I have been for years troubling the pages of historians, to find out what our fathers have done to the *white Christians of America*, to merit such condign[3] punishment as they have inflicted on them, and do continue to inflict on us their children. But I must aver, that my researches have hitherto been to no effect. I have therefore, come to the immovable conclusion, that they (Americans) have, and do continue to punish us for nothing else, but for enriching them and their country. For I cannot conceive of anything else. Nor will I believe otherwise, until the Lord shall convince me.

The world knows, that slavery as it existed among the Romans, (which was the primary cause of their destruction) was, comparatively speaking, no more than a *cypher*, when compared with ours under the Americans. Indeed I should not have noticed the Roman slaves, had not the very learned and penetrating Mr. Jefferson said, "when a master was murdered, all his slaves in the same house, or within hearing, were condemned to death."[4] Here let me ask Mr. Jefferson, (but he is gone to answer at the bar of God, for the deeds done in his body while living), I therefore ask the whole American people, had I not rather die, or be put to death, than to be a slave to any tyrant, who takes not only my own, but my wife and children's lives by the inches? Yea, would I meet death with avidity far! far!! in preference to such *servile submission* to the murderous hands of tyrants. Mr. Jefferson's very severe remarks on us have been so extensively argued upon by men whose attainments in literature, I shall never be able to reach, that I would not have meddled with it, were it not to solicit each of my brethren, who has the spirit of a man, to buy a copy of Mr. Jefferson's "Notes on Virginia," and put it in the hand of his son. For let no one of us suppose that the refutations which have been written

by our white friends are enough—they are *whites*, we are *blacks*. We, and the world wish to see the charges of Mr. Jefferson refuted by the blacks *themselves*, according to their chance; for we must remember that what the whites have written respecting this subject, is other men's labours, and did not emanate from the blacks. I know well, that there are some talents and learning among the coloured people of this country, which we have not a chance to develop, in consequence of oppression; but our oppression ought not to hinder us from acquiring all we can. For we will have a chance to develop them by and by. God will not suffer us, always to be oppressed. Our sufferings will come to an *end*, in spite of all the Americans this side of *eternity*. Then we will want all the learning and talents among ourselves, and perhaps more, to govern ourselves. "Every dog must have its day," the American's is coming to an end.

But let us review Mr. Jefferson's remarks respecting us some further. Comparing our miserable fathers, with the learned philosophers of Greece, he says: "Yet notwithstanding these and other discouraging circumstances among the Romans, their slaves were often their rarest artists. They excelled too, in science, insomuch as to be usually employed as tutors to their master's children; Epictetus, Terence and Phaedrus,[5] were slaves—but they were of the race of whites. It is not their *condition* then, but *nature*, which has produced the distinction."[6] See this, my brethren!! Do you believe that this assertion is swallowed by millions of the whites? Do you know that Mr. Jefferson was one of as great characters as ever lived among the whites? See his writings for the world, and public labours for the United States of America. Do you believe that the assertions of such a man, will pass away into oblivion unobserved by this people and the world? If you do you are much mistaken—See how the American people treat us—have we souls in our bodies? Are we men who have any spirits at all? I know that there are many *swell-bellied* fellows among us, whose greatest object is to fill their stomachs. Such

1   *intestine* Internal, as in a civil conflict.

2   [Walker's note]   See Dr. Goldsmith's *History of Greece*—page 9. See also, Plutarch's *Lives*. The Helots [were] subdued by Agis, king of Sparta.

3   *condign* Deserved; fitting.

4   [Walker's note] See his *Notes on Virginia*, page 210.

5   *Epictetus* Greek stoic philosopher (c. 55–135 CE) who was born enslaved in Phrygia but later became free; *Terence* Roman playwright (c. 195–159 BCE), enslaved by a Roman senator and later freed; *Phaedrus* Probably Gaius Julius Phaedrus, a first-century Roman writer of fables who was born enslaved and likely freed under the reign of Augustus.

6   [Walker's note] See his *Notes on Virginia*, page 211.

I do not mean—I am after those who know and feel, that we are MEN, as well as other people; to them, I say, that unless we try to refute Mr. Jefferson's arguments respecting us, we will only establish them.

But the slaves among the Romans. Everybody who has read history, knows, that as soon as a slave among the Romans obtained his freedom, he could rise to the greatest eminence in the State, and there was no law instituted to hinder a slave from buying his freedom. Have not the Americans instituted laws to hinder us from obtaining our freedom? Do any deny this charge? Read the laws of Virginia, North Carolina, &c. Further: have not the Americans instituted laws to prohibit a man of colour from obtaining and holding any office whatever, under the government of the United States of America? Now, Mr. Jefferson tells us, that our condition is not so hard, as the slaves' were under the Romans!!!!!!

It is time for me to bring this article to a close. But before I close it, I must observe to my brethren that at the close of the first Revolution in this country, with Great Britain, there were but thirteen States in the Union, now there are twenty-four, most of which are slave-holding States, and the whites are dragging us around in chains and in hand-cuffs, to their new States and Territories to work their mines and farms, to enrich them and their children—and millions of them believing firmly that we being a little darker than they, were made by our Creator to be an inheritance to them and their children forever—the same as a parcel of *brutes*.

Are we MEN!!—I ask you, O my brethren! are we MEN? Did our Creator make us to be slaves to dust and ashes like ourselves? Are they not dying worms as well as we? Have they not to make their appearance before the tribunal of Heaven, to answer for the deeds done in the body, as well as we? Have we any other Master but Jesus Christ alone? Is he not their Master as well as ours? What right then, have we to obey and call any other Master, but Himself? How we could be so *submissive* to a gang of men, whom we cannot tell whether they are *as good* as ourselves or not, I never could conceive. However, this is shut up with the Lord, and we cannot precisely tell—but I declare, we judge men by their works.

The whites have always been an unjust, jealous, unmerciful, avaricious and blood-thirsty set of beings, always seeking after power and authority. We view them all over the confederacy of Greece, where they were first known to be anything (in consequence of education) we see them there, cutting each other's throats—trying to subject each other to wretchedness and misery—to effect which, they used all kinds of deceitful, unfair, and unmerciful means. We view them next in Rome, where the spirit of tyranny and deceit raged still higher. We view them in Gaul, Spain, and in Britain. In fine, we view them all over Europe, together with what were scattered about in Asia and Africa, as heathens, and we see them acting more like devils than accountable men. But some may ask, did not the blacks of Africa, and the mulattoes of Asia,[1] go on in the same way as did the whites of Europe. I answer, no—they never were half so avaricious, deceitful and unmerciful as the whites, according to their knowledge.

But we will leave the whites or Europeans as heathens, and take a view of them as Christians, in which capacity we see them as cruel, if not more so than ever. In fact, take them as a body, they are ten times more cruel, avaricious and unmerciful than ever they were; for while they were heathens, they were bad enough it is true, but it is positively a fact that they were not quite so audacious as to go and take vessel loads of men, women and children, and in cold blood, and through devilishness, throw them into the sea, and murder them in all kind of ways. While they were heathens, they were too ignorant for such barbarity. But being Christians, enlightened and sensible, they are completely prepared for such hellish cruelties. Now suppose God were to give them more sense, what would they do? If it were possible, would they not *dethrone* Jehovah and seat themselves upon his throne? I therefore, in the name and fear of the Lord God of Heaven and of earth, divested of prejudice either on the side of my colour or that of the whites, advance my suspicion of them, whether they are *as good by nature* as we are or not. Their actions, since they were known as a people, have been the reverse, I do indeed suspect them, but

---

[1]   *mulattoes of Asia* Though the term "mulatto" (which is today considered archaic and offensive) generally referred to people of mixed black and white parentage, it would occasionally be used to refer more vaguely to persons of other ethnicities perceived to have a skin tone between black and white.

this, as I before observed, is shut up with the Lord, we cannot exactly tell, it will be proved in succeeding generations. The whites have had the essence of the gospel as it was preached by my master and his apostles—the Ethiopians have not, who are to have it in its meridian[1] splendor—the Lord will give it to them to their satisfaction. I hope and pray to my God, that they will make good use of it, that it may be well with them.[2]

from ARTICLE 4.
OUR WRETCHEDNESS IN CONSEQUENCE OF THE COLONIZING PLAN.[3]

My dearly beloved brethren: This is a scheme on which so many able writers, together with that very judicious coloured Baltimorean,[4] have commented, that I feel my delicacy about touching it. But as I am compelled to do the will of my Master, I declare, I will give you my sentiments upon it. Previous, however, to giving my sentiments, either for or against it, I shall give that of Mr. Henry Clay, together with that of Mr. Elias B. Caldwell,[5] Esq. of the District of Columbia, as extracted from the *National Intelligencer*, by Dr. Torrey, author of a series of "Essays on Morals, and the Diffusion of Useful Knowledge."

At a meeting which was convened in the District of Columbia, for the express purpose of agitating the subject of colonizing us in some part of the world, Mr. Clay was called to the chair, and having been seated a little while, he rose and spake, in substance, as follows: says he[6]—"That class of the mixt population of our country [coloured people] was peculiarly situated; they neither enjoyed the immunities of freemen, nor were they subjected to the incapacities of slaves, but partook, in some degree, of the qualities of both. From their condition, and the unconquerable prejudices resulting from their colour, they never could amalgamate with the free whites of this country. It was desirable, therefore, as it respected them, and the residue of the population of the country, to drain them off. Various schemes of colonization had been thought of, and a part of our continent, it was supposed by some, might furnish a suitable establishment for them. But, for his part, Mr. C. said, he had a decided preference for some part of the Coast of Africa. There ample provision might be made for the colony itself, and it might be rendered instrumental to the introduction into that extensive quarter of the globe, of the arts, civilization, and Christianity." [Here I ask Mr. Clay, what kind of Christianity? Did he mean such as they have among the Americans—distinction, whip, blood and oppression? I pray the Lord Jesus Christ to forbid it.] "There," said he, "was a peculiar, a moral fitness, in restoring them to the land of their fathers, and if instead of the evils and sufferings which we had been the innocent cause of inflicting upon the inhabitants of Africa, we can transmit to her the blessings of our arts, our civilization, and our religion. May we not hope that America will extinguish a great portion of that moral debt which she has contracted to that unfortunate continent? Can there be

---

[1]   *meridian* Highest; zenith.

[2]   [Walker's note] It is my solemn belief, that if ever the world becomes Christianized, (which must certainly take place before long) it will be through the means, under God of the *Blacks*, who are now held in wretchedness, and degradation, by the white *Christians* of the world, who before they learn to do justice to us before our Maker—and be reconciled to us, and reconcile us to them, and by that means have clear consciences before God and man. Send out Missionaries to convert the Heathens, many of whom after they cease to worship gods, which neither see nor hear, become ten times more the children of Hell, than ever they were, why what is the reason? Why the reason is obvious, they must learn to do justice at home, before they go into distant lands, to display their charity, Christianity, and benevolence; when they learn to do justice, God will accept their offering (no man may think that I am against Missionaries for I am not, my object is to see justice done at home, before we go convert the Heathens).

[3]   THE *COLONIZING PLAN* The American Colonization Society, founded by a group of white politicians in 1816, aimed to deport free African Americans to the newly established colony of Liberia. The society's leaders included both supporters of slavery and abolitionists; though its supporters claimed that colonization would benefit black people, many black activists, and later some white abolitionists, were strongly opposed to the endeavor, believing it to be a means of protecting the institution of slavery from the influence of free African Americans. The mortality rate in the colony of Liberia was extremely high.

[4]   *coloured Baltimorean* William Watkins (1801–58), antislavery and anti-colonization speaker who wrote numerous articles for the abolitionist newspapers *The Liberator* and *The Genius of Universal Emancipation* under the alias "The Colored Baltimorean."

[5]   *Mr. Henry Clay … Elias B. Caldwell* White politicians who were involved in the establishment of the American Colonization Society.

[6]   [Walker's note] See Dr. Torrey's *Portraiture of Domestic Slavery in the United States*, page 85, 86.

a nobler cause than that which, whilst it proposes, &c. ******* [you know what this means.][1] contemplates the spreading of the arts of civilized life, and the possible redemption from ignorance and barbarism of a benighted quarter of the globe?"

Before I proceed any further, I solicit your notice, brethren, to the foregoing part of Mr. Clay's speech, in which he says, (☞ look above) "and if, instead of the evils and sufferings, which we had been the innocent cause of inflicting," &c. What this very learned statesman could have been thinking about, when he said in his speech, "we had been the innocent cause of inflicting," &c., I have never been able to conceive. Are Mr. Clay and the rest of the Americans, innocent of the blood and groans of our fathers and us, their children? Every individual may plead innocence, if he pleases, but God will, before long, separate the innocent from the guilty, unless something is speedily done—which I suppose will hardly be, so that their destruction may be sure. Oh Americans! let me tell you, in the name of the Lord, it will be good for you, if you listen to the voice of the Holy Ghost, but if you do not, you are ruined!!! Some of you are good men; but the will of my God must be done. Those avaricious and ungodly tyrants among you, I am awfully afraid will drag down the vengeance of God upon you. When God Almighty commences his battle on the continent of America, for the oppression of his people, tyrants will wish they never were born.

But to return to Mr. Clay, whence I digressed. He says, "It was proper and necessary distinctly to state, that he understood it constituted no part of the object of this meeting, to touch or agitate in the slightest degree, a delicate question, connected with another portion of the coloured population of our country. It was not proposed to deliberate upon or consider at all, any question of emancipation, or that which was connected with the abolition of slavery. It was upon that condition alone, he was sure, that many gentlemen from the South and the West, whom he saw present,

had attended, or could be expected to co-operate. It was upon that condition only, that he himself had attended." That is to say, to fix a plan to get those of the coloured people, who are said to be free, away from among those of our brethren whom they unjustly hold in bondage, so that they may be enabled to keep them the more secure in ignorance and wretchedness, to support them and their children, and consequently they would have the more obedient slaves. For if the free are allowed to stay among the slaves, they will have intercourse together, and, of course, the free will learn[2] the slaves *bad habits*, by teaching them that they are MEN, as well as other people, and certainly *ought* and *must* be FREE. ...

The Americans of North and of South America, including the West India Islands—no trifling portion of whom were, for stealing, murdering, &c. compelled to flee from Europe, to save their necks or banishment,[3] have effected their escape to this continent, where God blessed them with all the comforts of life—He gave them a plenty of every thing calculated to do them good—not satisfied with this, however, they wanted slaves, and wanted us for their slaves, who belong to the Holy Ghost, and no other, who we shall have to serve us instead of tyrants. I say, the Americans want us, the property of the Holy Ghost, to serve them. But there is a day fast approaching, when (unless there is a universal repentance on the part of the whites, which will scarcely take place, they have got to be so hardened in consequence of our blood, and so wise in their own conceit). To be plain and candid with you, Americans! I say that the day is fast approaching, when there will be a greater time on the continent of America, than ever was witnessed upon this earth, since it came from the hand of its Creator. Some of you have done us so much injury, that you will never be able to repent. Your cup must be filled. You want us for your slaves, and shall have enough of us—God is just, *who will give you your fill of us*. ...

---

1   *&c. ... [you know what this means.]*   Clay's original 1816 speech here reads, "... whilst it proposes to rid our own country of a useless and pernicious, if not a dangerous portion of its population." In Walker's source for this passage, Jesse Torrey—a white supporter of colonization—euphemistically omits this portion of the sentence and replaces it with "&c." Walker himself added the asterisks and bracketed comment.

2   *intercourse* I.e., interactions, communication; *learn* Teach.

3   *The Americans ... banishment* Walker is referring to the practice of penal transportation, whereby people convicted of crimes in their home countries (especially Britain) were deported to one of that country's colonies. (This practice ceased in the United States after the American Revolution.)

I shall now pass in review of the speech of Mr. Elias B. Caldwell, Esq. of the District of Columbia, extracted from the same page on which Mr. Clay's will be found. Mr. Caldwell, giving his opinion respecting us, at that ever memorable meeting, he says: "The more you improve the condition of these people, the more you cultivate their minds, the more miserable you make them in their present state. You give them a higher relish for those privileges which they can never attain, and turn what we intend for a blessing into a curse." Let me ask this benevolent man, what he means by a blessing intended for us? Did he mean sinking us and our children into ignorance and wretchedness, to support him and his family? What he meant will appear evident and obvious to the most ignorant in the world. ☞ See Mr. Caldwell's intended blessings for us, O! my Lord! ! "No," said he, "if they must remain in their present situation, keep them in the *lowest state of degradation and ignorance.* The nearer you bring them to the condition of brutes, the better chance do you give them of possessing their *apathy*." Here I pause to get breath, having laboured to extract the above clause of this gentleman's speech, at that colonizing meeting. I presume that everybody knows the meaning of the word "*apathy*"—if any do not, let him get Sheridan's Dictionary, in which he will find it explained in full. I solicit the attention of the world, to the foregoing part of Mr. Caldwell's speech, that they may see what man will do with his fellow men, when he had them under his feet. To what length will not man go in iniquity when given up to a hard heart, and reprobate mind, in consequence of blood and oppression? The last clause of this speech, which was written in a very artful manner, and which will be taken for the speech of a friend, without close examination and deep penetration, I shall now present. He says, "surely, Americans ought to be the last people on earth, to advocate such slavish doctrines, to cry peace and contentment to those who are deprived of the privileges of civil liberty, they who have so largely partaken of its blessings, who know so well how to estimate its value, ought to be among the foremost to extend it to others." The real sense and meaning of the last part of Mr. Caldwell's speech is, get the free people of colour away to Africa, from among the slaves, where they may at once be blessed and happy, and those who we hold in slavery, will be contented to rest in ignorance and wretchedness, to dig up gold and silver for us and our children. Men have indeed got to be so cunning, these days, that it would take the eye of a Solomon[1] to penetrate and find them out. ...

God will show the whites what we are, yet. I say, from the beginning, I do not think that we were natural enemies to each other. But the whites having made us so wretched, by subjecting us to slavery, and having murdered so many millions of us, in order to make us work for them, and out of devilishness—and they taking our wives, whom we love as we do ourselves—our mothers, who bore the pains of death to give us birth—our fathers and dear little children, and ourselves, and strip and beat us one before the other—chain, hand-cuff, and drag us about like rattle-snakes—shoot us down like wild bears, before each other's faces, to make us submissive to, and work to support them and their families. They (the whites) know well, if we are *men*—and there is a secret monitor in their hearts which tells them we are—they know, I say, if we *are* men, and see them treating us in the manner they do, that there can be nothing in our hearts but death alone, for them, notwithstanding we may appear cheerful, when we see them murdering our dear mothers and wives, because we cannot help ourselves. ... Consequently they, themselves, (and not us) render themselves our natural enemies, by treating us so cruel. They keep us miserable now, and call us their property, but some of them will have enough of us by and by—their stomachs shall run over with us; they want us for their slaves, and shall have us to their fill. We are all in the world together!! I said above, because we cannot help ourselves, (viz. we cannot help the whites murdering our mothers and our wives) but this statement is incorrect—for we can help ourselves; for, if we lay aside abject servility, and be determined to act like men, and not brutes—the murderers among the whites would be afraid to show their cruel heads. But O, my God!—in sorrow I must say it, that my colour, all over the world, have a mean, servile spirit. They yield in a moment to the whites, let them be right or wrong—the reason they are able to keep their feet on our throats. Oh! my coloured brethren, all over the world, when shall we arise from this death-like apathy?—And be men!! You will notice, if

---

[1]   *Solomon*   Ancient King of Israel, known for his great wisdom.

ever we become men, I mean *respectable* men, such as other people are, we must exert ourselves to the full. For remember, that it is the greatest desire and object of the greater part of the whites, to keep us ignorant, and make us work to support them and their families.—Here now, in the Southern and Western sections of this country, there are at least three coloured persons for one white, why is it, that those few weak, good-for-nothing whites, are able to keep so many able men, one of whom, can put to flight a dozen whites, in wretchedness and misery? It shows at once, what the blacks are, we are ignorant, abject, servile and mean—and the whites know it—they know that we are too servile to assert our rights as men—or they would not fool with us as they do. Would they fool with any other people as they do with us? No, they know too well, that they would get themselves ruined. Why do they not bring the inhabitants of Asia to be body servants to them? They know they would get their bodies rent and torn from head to foot. Why do they not get the Aborigines of this country to be slaves to them and their children, to work their farms and dig their mines? They know well that the Aborigines of this country, or (Indians) would tear them from the earth. The Indians would not rest day or night, they would be up all times of night, cutting their cruel throats. But my colour, (some, not all,) are willing to stand still and be murdered by the cruel whites. In some of the West-India Islands, and over a large part of South America, there are six or eight coloured persons for one white.[1] Why

do they not take possession of those places? Who hinders them? It is not the avaricious whites—for they are too busily engaged in laying up money—derived from the blood and tears of the blacks. The fact is, they are too servile, they love to have Masters too well!! …

… Will any of us leave our homes and go to Africa? I hope not.[2] Let them commence their attack upon us as they did on our brethren in Ohio,[3] driving and beating us from our country, and my soul for theirs, they will have enough of it. Let no man of us budge one step, and let slave-holders come to beat us from our country. America is more our country, than it is the whites'—we have enriched it with our *blood and tears*. The greatest riches in all America have arisen from our blood and tears—and will they drive us from our property and homes, which we have earned with our *blood*? They must look sharp or this very thing will bring swift destruction upon them. The Americans have got so fat on our blood and groans, that they have almost forgotten the God of armies. But let them go on. …

---

[1]   [Walker's note]   For instance in the two States of Georgia, and South Carolina, there are, perhaps, not much short of six or seven hundred thousand persons of colour; and if I was a gambling character, I would not be afraid to stake down upon the board FIVE CENTS against TEN, that there are in the single State of Virginia, five or six hundred thousand coloured persons. Four hundred and fifty thousand of whom (let them be well equipt for war) I would put against every white person on the whole continent of America. (Why? why because I know that the Blacks, once they get involved in a war, had rather die than to live, they either kill or be killed.) The whites know this too, which makes them quake and tremble. To show the world further, how servile the coloured people are, I will only hold up to view, the one Island of Jamaica, as a specimen of our meanness.

In that Island, there are three hundred and fifty thousand souls—of whom fifteen thousand are whites, the remainder, three hundred and thirty-five thousand are coloured people! and this Island is ruled by the white people!!!!!!!! (15,000) ruling and tyrannizing over 335,000 persons!!!!!!!!—O! coloured men!! O! coloured

men!!! O! coloured men!!!! Look!! look!!! at this!!!! and, tell me if we are not abject and servile enough, how long, O! how long my colour shall we be dupes and dogs to the cruel whites?—I only passed Jamaica, and its inhabitants, in review as a specimen to show the world, the condition of the Blacks at this time, now coloured people of the whole world, I beg you to look at the (15000 white,) and (Three Hundred and Thirty-Five Thousand coloured people) in that Island, and tell me how can the white tyrants of the world but say that we are not men, but were made to be slaves and Dogs to them and their children forever!!!!!!!—why my friends only look at the thing!!!! (15000) whites keeping in wretchedness and degradation (335000) viz. 22 coloured persons for one white!!!!!!!! when at the same time, an equal number (15000) Blacks, would almost take the whole of South America, because where they go as soldiers to fight death follows in their train.

[2]   [Walker's note]   Those who are ignorant enough to go to Africa, the coloured people ought to be glad to have them go, for if they are ignorant enough to let the whites *fool* them off to Africa, they would be no small injury to us if they reside in this country.

[3]   *Let them … in Ohio*   Although Ohio had been established as a free state in 1803, shortly thereafter the state passed laws known as "Black Codes" or "Black Laws," severely restricting black immigration into the state as well as the movement and employment of free black people within the state. Free black people found in the state without free papers and other such documents (which could cost as much as $500 to obtain) would be subject to severe prosecution. The year 1829 in particular saw a rise in anti-black violence, and a number of riots resulted in the burning down of numerous black communities.

And now, brethren, having concluded these four Articles, I submit them, together with my Preamble, dedicated to the Lord, for your inspection, in language so very simple, that the most ignorant, who can read at all, may easily understand—of which you may make the best you possibly can.[1] Should tyrants take it into their heads to emancipate any of you, remember that your freedom is your natural right. You are men, as well as they, and instead of returning thanks to them for your freedom, return it to the Holy Ghost, who is our rightful owner. ...

—1829, 1830

[NOTE: The full text of *Walker's Appeal, in Four Articles* is included in the online component of this anthology.]

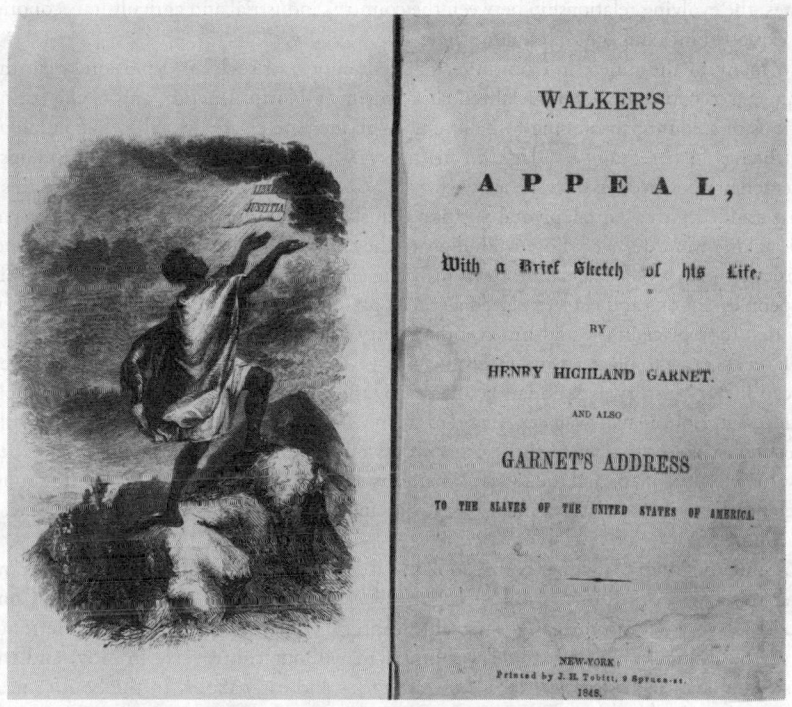

Walker's Appeal was reprinted by black abolitionist Henry Highland Garnet in 1848, in an edition that also featured Garnet's *Address to the Slaves of the United States of America.* That edition also included this engraving as a new "frontispiece" to Walker's pamphlet. The identity of the artist is not known.

---

[1] [Walker's note] Some of my brethren, who are sensible, do not take an interest in enlightening the minds of our more ignorant brethren respecting this Book, and in reading it to them, just as though they will not have either to stand or fall by what is written in this book. Do they believe that I would be so foolish as to put out a book of this kind without strict—ah! very strict commandments of the Lord? Surely the blacks and whites must think that I am ignorant enough. Do they think that I would have the audacious wickedness to take the name of my God in vain? Notice, I said in the concluding clause of Article 3 [omitted here]—I call God, I call Angels, I call men to witness, that the destruction of the Americans is at hand, and will be speedily consummated unless they repent. Now I wonder if the world think that I would take the name of God in this way in vain? What do they think I take God to be? Do they suppose that I would trifle with that God who will not have his Holy name taken in vain? He will show you and the world, in due time, whether this book is for his glory, or written by me through envy to the whites, as some have represented.

SLAVERY AND ABOLITION

CONTEXTS

In 1853, the abolitionist orator Wendell Phillips called the question of slavery—its morality, its status, its future—"the question of this generation." This characterization is hard to dispute. By the time of Phillips's 1853 speech, the debate about slavery had come to dominate the nation's politics and pervade its literature; the debate intersected with or subsumed all sorts of other urgent issues of the time—westward expansion, regional and sectional rivalries, the distribution of power between the federal government and the states, the evolving relationship between the country's industrial and agricultural economies—and in 1861 it exploded into outright internal warfare.

To many in the nineteenth century, such centrality, and such an explosion, were the inevitable consequence of two centuries of racialized enslavement in North America, and of the constitutive contradictions of a country professing to believe that "all men are created equal" while holding millions of human beings in hereditary bondage. In his same 1853 speech, however, Wendell Phillips provided a complementary perspective when he avowed that "*Slavery has been made* the question of this generation" (emphasis added). The central, pivotal position that slavery, and the drive to end it, had come to occupy in national life was due, according to Phillips, to the efforts of numerous people—white and black, free and enslaved—"to waken the nation to its real state, and chain it to the consideration of this one duty." These peoples' actions and choices played a crucial part in bringing on the great national reckoning with slavery that took place in the mid-nineteenth century.

Slavery's central place in nineteenth-century America, and specifically in nineteenth-century American literary history, is abundantly attested by the many works throughout this anthology volume that address it, from David Walker's *Appeal* to the poems and speeches of Frances Ellen Watkins Harper. This section aims to supplement those other works by providing a necessarily brief and selective survey of how, between the 1820s and the 1870s, Americans of all stripes thought about, wrote about, contested, and defended race-based slavery, and of what did and did not change for enslaved people, and for the whole country, as a result.

Despite the intense arguments that took place during the constitutional convention over how and whether the U.S. Constitution would recognize slavery—arguments that shaped the Constitution in key ways—slavery had, in the early nineteenth century, largely receded from the forefront of national politics. The international slave trade was outlawed without controversy in 1807, and the Northern states steadily abolished slavery itself in the late 1700s and early 1800s. In the South, meanwhile, the invention of the cotton gin in the 1790s, and the subsequent massive growth of the cotton industry, made slavery newly important, even vital, to the region's economy. This re-entrenchment of slavery in the South, however, did not substantively affect the national political scene until 1820, when the dispute surrounding Missouri's admission to the Union as a slave state, resulting in the Missouri Compromise, brought the conflicting interests and divergent trajectories of the so-called "slave" and "free" states into the open.

One major contributor to these divergent trajectories was the growth in the North, in the years after the Missouri Compromise, of "modern abolitionism" (as the activist William Goodell termed it): a movement, building on the transatlantic campaign against the international slave trade in the eighteenth and early nineteenth centuries, that sought to end slavery in the United States on moral grounds. Abolitionism drew from and incorporated various communities, including free Northern black people, such as Samuel Cornish and John Russwurm, the editors of the first African American-run newspaper, *Freedom's Journal*; white members of various antislavery Christian denominations, such as Quakers and Unitarians; and escapees from slavery such as Frederick Douglass and Harriet Jacobs. Abolitionist activism also took a huge variety of forms, some of which are represented in the bound book and website portions of this section, including sentimental appeals such as Annie Parker's poem "Story Telling"; rigorous legal and constitutional argumentation, as in Goodell's *The American Slave Code in Theory and Practice* and Douglass's *The Dred Scott Decision*; and impassioned, unflinching documentation of slavery's inhumanity, as in the enormously influential collection *American Slavery as It Is*. This diversity of abolitionist voices gave rise to occasional internal fissures: the movement split between supporters and opponents of armed resistance to slavery, as well as between those such as Goodell and Douglass who believed slavery could be ended under the Constitution as it existed and those, such as William Lloyd Garrison, who held that the Constitution, and indeed the whole country in its current form, were irreparably tainted by slavery.

Abolitionism existed alongside, and sometimes augmented or joined forces with, the efforts to escape, defy, or overthrow slavery undertaken by enslaved people in the South. Many thousands of enslaved people made difficult and dangerous journeys to freedom in the Northern states or in Canada, assisted by the extensive infrastructure of the "Underground Railroad" and the abolitionists who maintained it. The many different forms such journeys could take are illustrated in this section by the anonymous poem "Escape from Slavery of Henry Box Brown" and the selections from *Narratives of Fugitive Slaves in Canada*. A smaller but still significant number of enslaved people made even more difficult and dangerous journeys southward to freedom in Mexico, as the website excerpt from Frederick Law Olmsted's *A Journey Through Texas* attests. Still other enslaved people rose up against their enslavement or plotted to do so, including Denmark Vesey in South Carolina in 1822, Nat Turner in Virginia in 1831, Joseph Cinqué on the *Amistad* in 1839, and Madison Washington on the *Creole* in 1841. Similar, smaller-scale acts of defiance—no less powerful, and even more poignant, for the hopeless circumstances in which they were undertaken—are documented below in the excerpts from Bethany Veney's slave narrative and the newspaper article "Arrest of Fugitive Slaves" covering the famous case of Margaret Garner, who chose to kill her children rather than let them be taken back to slavery.

Faced with the condemnation of abolitionists and the active resistance, in various forms, of enslaved people themselves, enslavers and supporters of slavery increasingly sought to defend the institution and combat attempts to restrict, escape, or resist it. These efforts of enslavers and their allies also took a wide variety of forms, including the advertisements for fugitives placed in newspapers; the justifications of slavery penned by writers such as Zephaniah Kingsley, John P. Kennedy, and Caroline Lee Hentz; and political and legal mandates such as the 1850 Fugitive Slave Act and the 1857 *Dred Scott* decision. Slavery, and the racism which allowed it to endure, were further bolstered by—and left deep imprints on—institutions and cultural practices in the North. As the excerpt from Austin Reed's memoir *The Life and Adventures of a Haunted Convict* included in the website portion of this section demonstrates, often-racialized forms of involuntary servitude, including indenture and forced convict labor, continued in the North after slavery per se was abolished there (and the Thirteenth Amendment would later explicitly permit the continuation of penal servitude even as it abolished slavery per se nationwide). The massive popularity of blackface minstrelsy also helped the cause of slavery in the "free" states: the idealization of slavery and derogatory depiction of enslaved people in minstrel songs such as "Old Uncle Ned" (also included in this section's website portion) did much to make especially working-class white Northerners—many of whom felt threatened by the prospect of abolition, which they believed would increase competition for low-wage jobs—sympathetic towards slavery. While numerous white Northerners thus came to passively or actively support slavery, some white Southerners with daily, face-to-face acquaintance with the institution, such as the diarist Mary Chesnut, came to dislike it—albeit in Chesnut's case for reasons that centered on the opportunities for the sexual exploitation of enslaved women that slavery afforded to white men, and the attendant shame this brought on white women like herself.

The slavery debate came to a head in the 1850s in a series of escalating crises, including the bitter disputes over slavery's expansion into the western territories, the passage of and response to the Fugitive Slave Act, the argument surrounding Harriet Beecher Stowe's *Uncle Tom's Cabin*, the violence of "Bleeding Kansas," and the *Dred Scott* decision. In 1860, this chain of crises resulted in Southern secession. The ensuing Civil War brought about the downfall of slavery, though in a contingent, haphazard way: a contingency and haphazardness evident in the two versions, preliminary and final, of President Lincoln's Emancipation Proclamation, which reveal the political calculations that went into this epochal measure and the limitations of its scope and efficacy. Victory over secession in 1865 made emancipation a reality for enslaved African Americans throughout the South, but their legal status remained unclear until slavery was formally and universally abolished by the Thirteenth Amendment, which did not take effect until December 1865—and then it took two more constitutional amendments, in 1868 and 1870, to legally ensure the citizenship and voting rights of formerly enslaved people (or at least of formerly enslaved men).

The struggle between emancipated African Americans (and their allies) and erstwhile enslavers continued after the end of the Civil War. Formerly enslaved people sought to make the most of their newfound—but often only nominal—freedom, while former enslavers sought to restrict that freedom and reimpose a social and economic system as much like slavery as possible. This section tells this continuing story through documents such as Jourdon Anderson's witheringly deadpan response to his former enslaver's request for his continued labor; the advertisements placed by formerly enslaved people trying to reunite their broken, dispersed families; and examples of the many attempts made by white Southerners, by means of oratory, legal codes, and terrorist violence alike, to keep African Americans subordinated. By the 1870s—despite the ongoing efforts of such African American champions of civil rights as Robert B. Elliott and Frederick Douglass—these white Southern attempts to reimpose legalized racial subordination in another form had met with substantial success. Opponents of such racism would have to build on the activism of abolitionists into the Reconstruction era and beyond, as they pursued a vision of an America in which all citizens could be free, prosperous, and equal before the law.

⌘ ⌘ ⌘

Masthead and opening of the first issue (16 March 1827) of *Freedom's Journal*, a pioneering African American newspaper that greatly influenced the development of the abolitionist movement. For the full text of the introductory editorial, "To Our Patrons," the beginning of which appears here, see the first selection below.

Samuel Cornish and John B. Russwurm, "To Our Patrons," *Freedom's Journal* (16 March 1827)

Founded in 1827 by leaders of the free black community in New York City, *Freedom's Journal* was the first newspaper owned and operated by African Americans to be published in the United States. The paper's initial editors were Samuel Cornish (1795–1858) and John B. Russwurm (1799–1851). Cornish was the first African American to become a Presbyterian minister; after *Freedom's Journal* ceased publication in 1829, he founded a new paper, *The Rights of All*. Russwurm was the second African American to have earned a bachelor's degree from a U.S. university. In addition to regional, national, and international news, the paper—which circulated in eleven states and the District of Columbia, as well as in Haiti, Europe, and Canada—published editorials opposing slavery, lynching, and other manifestations of white American racism; biographical and historical information relevant to African Americans; and announcements of births, marriages, and deaths in the New York black community. The paper folded in 1829, but it wielded a lasting influence on the abolitionist movement, as well as on the political consciousness of its African American readers: for example, David Walker, the antislavery activist who published his landmark *Appeal to the Coloured Citizens of the World* in 1829, was one of *Freedom's Journal*'s subscription agents.

The rationale, agenda, and contents of *Freedom's Journal* are aptly summarized in Cornish and Russwurm's introductory editorial to its first issue, presented below.

In presenting our first number to our patrons, we feel all the diffidence of persons entering upon a new and untried line of business. But a moment's reflection upon the noble objects which we have in view by the publication of this journal; the expediency of its appearance at this time, when so many schemes are in action concerning our people—encourage us to come boldly before an enlightened public. For we believe that a paper devoted to the dissemination of useful knowledge among our brethren, and to their moral and religious improvement, must meet with the cordial approbation of every friend to humanity.

The peculiarities of this journal render it important that we should advertise to the world the motives by which we are actuated, and the objects which we contemplate.

We wish to plead our own cause. Too long have others spoken for us. Too long has the public been deceived by misrepresentations, in things which concern us dearly, though in the estimation of some mere trifles; for though there are many in society who exercise towards us benevolent feelings; still (with sorrow we confess it) there are others who make it their business to enlarge upon the least trifle which tends to the discredit of any person of colour; and pronounce anathemas and denounce our whole body for the misconduct of this guilty one. We are aware that there are many instances of vice among us, but we avow that it is because no one has taught its subjects to be virtuous; many instances of poverty, because no sufficient efforts accommodated to minds contracted by slavery and deprived of early education have been made, to teach them how to husband their hard earnings, and to secure to themselves comforts.

Education being an object of the highest importance to the welfare of society, we shall endeavour to present just and adequate views of it, and to urge upon our brethren the necessity and expediency of training their children, while young, to habits of industry, and thus forming them for becoming useful members of society. It is surely time that we should awake from this lethargy of years, and make a concentrated effort for the education of our youth. We form a spoke in the human wheel, and it is necessary that we should understand our pendence[1] on the different parts, and theirs on us, in order to perform our part with propriety.

Though not desirous of dictating, we shall feel it our incumbent duty to dwell occasionally upon the general principles and rules of economy. The world has grown too enlightened, to estimate any man's character by his personal appearance. Though all men acknowledge

---

1   *pendence* I.e., dependence.

the excellency of Franklin's maxims,[1] yet comparatively few practise upon them. We may deplore when it is too late, the neglect of these self-evident truths,[2] but it avails little to mourn. Ours will be the task of admonishing our brethren on these points.

The civil rights of a people being of the greatest value, it shall ever be our duty to vindicate our brethren, when oppressed; and to lay the case before the public. We shall also urge upon our brethren (who are qualified by the laws of the different states) the expediency of using their elective franchise;[3] and of making an independent use of the same. We wish them not to become the tools of party.

And as much time is frequently lost, and wrong principles instilled, by the perusal of works of trivial importance, we shall consider it a part of our duty to recommend to our young readers such authors as will not only enlarge their stock of useful knowledge, but such as will also serve to stimulate them to higher attainments in science.[4]

We trust also, that through the columns of the Freedom's Journal, many practical pieces, having for their bases the improvement of our brethren, will be presented to them, from the pens of many of our respected friends, who have kindly promised their assistance.

It is our earnest wish to make our journal a medium of intercourse[5] between our brethren in the different states of this great confederacy: that through its columns an expression of our sentiments, on many interesting subjects which concern us, may be offered to the public: that the plans which apparently are beneficial may be candidly discussed and properly weighed; if worthy, receive our cordial approbation; if not, our marked disapprobation.

Useful knowledge of every kind, and everything that relates to Africa, shall find a ready admission into our columns; and as that vast continent becomes daily more known, we trust that many things will come to light, proving that the natives of it are neither so ignorant nor stupid as they have generally been supposed to be.

And while these important subjects shall occupy the columns of the Freedom's Journal, we would not be unmindful of our brethren who are still in the iron fetters of bondage. They are our kindred by all the ties of nature; and though but little can be effected by us, still let our sympathies be poured forth, and our prayers in their behalf ascend to Him who is able to succour them.

From the press and the pulpit we have suffered much by being incorrectly represented. Men whom we equally love and admire have not hesitated to represent us disadvantageously, without becoming personally acquainted with the true state of things, nor discerning between virtue and vice among us. The virtuous part of our people feel themselves sorely aggrieved under the existing state of things—they are not appreciated.

Our vices and our degradation are ever arrayed against us, but our virtues are passed by unnoticed. And what is still more lamentable, our friends, to whom we concede all the principles of humanity and religion, from these very causes seem to have fallen into the current of popular feeling and are imperceptibly floating on the stream—actually living in the practice of prejudice, while they abjure it in theory, and feel it not in their hearts. Is it not very desirable that such should know more of our actual condition; and of our efforts and feelings, that in forming or advocating plans for our amelioration, they may do it more understandingly? In the spirit of candor and humility we intend by a simple representation of facts to lay our case before the public, with a view to arrest the progress of prejudice, and to shield ourselves against the consequent evils. We wish to conciliate all and to

---

[1] *Franklin's maxims*   I.e., the aphorisms and tips regarding how to manage one's economic affairs that the American colonial politician, intellectual, and writer Benjamin Franklin published in the yearly issues of his *Poor Richard's Almanack* (1732–58) and later collected in his essay "The Way to Wealth" (1758). Many of these maxims, such as "A penny saved is a penny earned" and "Early to bed, and early to rise, makes a man healthy, wealthy and wise," counsel industry and frugality and have become commonplaces in modern American vernacular.

[2] *self-evident truths*   See the second sentence of the Declaration of Independence: "We hold these truths to be self-evident, that all men are created equal, that they are endowed by their Creator with certain unalienable Rights, that among these are Life, Liberty and the pursuit of Happiness."

[3] *using … franchise*   I.e., voting.

[4] *science*   Intellectual study.

[5] *intercourse*   Communication.

irritate none, yet we must be firm and unwavering in our principles, and persevering in our efforts.

If ignorance, poverty and degradation have hitherto been our unhappy lot; has the eternal decree gone forth, that our race alone are to remain in this state, while knowledge and civilization are shedding their enlivening rays over the rest of the human family? The recent travels of Denham and Clapperton in the interior of Africa, and the interesting narrative which they have published;[1] the establishment of the republic of Haiti after years of sanguinary warfare;[2] its subsequent progress in all the arts of civilization; and the advancement of liberal ideas in South America, where despotism has given place to free governments,[3] and where many of our brethren now fill important civil and military stations, prove the contrary.

The interesting fact that there are five hundred thousand free persons of colour, one half of whom might peruse, and the whole be benefitted by the publication of the journal; that no publication, as yet, has been devoted exclusively to their improvement—that many selections from approved standard authors, which are within the reach of few, may occasionally be made—and more important still, that this large body of our citizens have no public channel—all serve to prove the real necessity, at present, for the appearance of the Freedom's Journal.

It shall ever be our desire so to conduct the editorial department of our paper as to give offence to none of our patrons; as nothing is farther from us than to make it the advocate of any partial[4] views, either in politics or religion. What few days we can number have been devoted to the improvement of our brethren; and it is our earnest wish that the remainder may be spent in the same delightful service.

In conclusion, whatever concerns us as a people will ever find a ready admission into the Freedom's Journal, interwoven with all the principal news of the day.

And while everything in our power shall be performed to support the character of our journal, we would respectfully invite our numerous friends to assist by their communications, and our coloured brethren to strengthen our hands by their subscriptions, as our labour is one of common cause, and worthy of their consideration and support. And we do most earnestly solicit the latter, that if at any time we should seem to be zealous, or too pointed in the inculcation of any important lesson, they will remember that they are equally interested in the cause in which we are engaged, and attribute our zeal to the peculiarities of our situation; and our earnest engagedness in their well-being.

THE EDITORS.

from Zephaniah Kingsley, *A Treatise on the Patriarchal, or Cooperative System of Society* (1828)

Zephaniah Kingsley (1765–1843), an English-born Quaker, merchant, and slave trader, settled in Florida, then a Spanish colony, in 1803, where he became a major plantation owner; after Spain ceded Florida to the United States in 1821, he helped mediate Florida's transition to U.S. administration. Kingsley published *A Treatise on the Patriarchal, or Co-operative System of Society as It Exists in Some Governments and Colonies in America, and in the United States, Under the Name of Slavery, with Its Necessity and Advantages*—to give the work its full title—in 1828. The treatise defended the institution of slavery, albeit in terms that were heavily influenced by Kingsley's experience in Spanish Florida, where enslaved people were often encouraged to purchase their freedom and free black people were tolerated and permitted

---

[1] *The recent travels ... published* Between 1822 and 1825, the British military officers Dixon Denham and Hugh Clapperton traveled from Tripoli, on the Mediterranean coast of what is now Libya, to present-day Nigeria and back. Their account of the journey, *Narrative of Travels and Discoveries in Northern and Central Africa in the Years 1822–23 and 1824*, was published in 1826.

[2] *the establishment ... warfare* The Haitian Revolution began in 1791 in what was then the French colony of Saint-Domingue (also known as St. Domingo), when the colony's enslaved black population rose in revolt. After over a decade of conflict, the Republic of Haiti won its independence in 1804, making the revolution the first successful large-scale rebellion by enslaved people in modern history. As such, the Haitian Revolution loomed large in the imagination of early nineteenth-century African Americans, including the founders and editors of *Freedom's Journal*.

[3] *the advancement ... free governments* By 1827, all of the Spanish colonies in mainland North, Central, and South America had achieved independence from Spain.

---

[4] *partial* Biased; unduly favoring one party over others.

some civil rights. Kingsley—who took four of his enslaved women as common-law wives or concubines, all of whom he eventually freed—was troubled by Florida's transition to the U.S.'s more rigid form of race-based slavery, in which the existence of free black people was viewed as a threat, and he left the state for Haiti in the 1830s. His treatise was reprinted in 1829, 1833, and 1834; despite some criticism of Kingsley's support for a class of free black people existing alongside enslaved people, the treatise continued to inform Southern defenses of slavery as a "positive good" down to the Civil War.

The treatise's preface, summarizing its main arguments, is presented below; the text is based on the treatise's 1829 second edition. A longer excerpt from the body of the work can be found in the website portion of this anthology.

PREFACE

It will be allowed[1] by everyone that agriculture is the great foundation of the wealth and prosperity of our Southern states. This important science has already attracted some share of attention from men of the first talents, by whose improvements in cultivation several valuable productions promise, from their superiority, to maintain a preference in foreign markets; and the recent introduction of new articles of tropical produce into the southern districts, where they bid fair to succeed, offers still greater incitements to agricultural enterprise, and opens a new and extensive range for future speculation.

While this great field of wealth and independence promises now to be well understood and duly appreciated, the primary cause and means by which alone it can be realized, has either escaped attention, or been designedly overlooked: I mean the perpetuation of that kind of labor which now produces it, and which seems best adapted, under all circumstances, to render it profitable to the Southern capitalist.

The idea of slavery, when associated with cruelty and injustice, is revolting to every philanthropic mind; but when that idea is associated with justice and benevolence, slavery, commonly so called, easily amalgamates with the ordinary conditions of life.

---

[1]   *allowed* Admitted.

To counteract the existing prejudice against slavery, by making it evident that the condition of slaves may be equally happy and more independent of the ordinary evils of life, than that of the common class of whites denominated free—that they are now equally virtuous, moral and less corrupted than the ordinary class of laboring whites—that their labor is far more

Robert Douglass, Jr., *The Booroom Slave,* 1834. This pen-and-ink wash drawing by Douglass (1809–87), a Philadelphia-based African American artist, appears on one of the first pages of the friendship album of Mary Anne Dickerson, another black Philadelphian. (Friendship albums were scrapbooks in which friends of the album's owner could leave notes, poems, sketches, or other keepsakes.) The image reworks a well-known abolitionist painting by the English artist Henry Thomson. The lines underneath, taken from a 1744 poem by the English writer William Shenstone, read "When the grim lion urged his cruel chase, / When the stern panther sought his midnight prey, / What fate reserved me for this Christian race? / A race more polished, more severe than they!"

productive—that they yield more support and benefit to the State; which, under a well regulated system of management, is better fitted to endure a state of war than it would be with an equal number of free white people of ordinary means and condition; and, finally, that the slave or patriarchal system of society (so often commiserated[1] as a subject of deep regret) which constitutes the bond of social compact of the southern seaboard of the United States, is better adapted for strength, durability and independence, than any other state of society hitherto adopted. To endeavor to prove all this, and to destroy the prejudice existing against slavery, under the circumstances with which it is now associated in the South, is the object of the present essay; dedicated to the people of Florida, and to political economists throughout the Southern states, by a votary of rational policy, and

most respectfully

their humble servant,

Z. KINGSLEY

from Theodore Dwight Weld, Angelina Grimké Weld, and Sarah Grimké, *American Slavery as It Is: Testimony of a Thousand Witnesses* (1839)

A compendious, impassioned compilation of firsthand testimony about slavery, *American Slavery as It Is* influenced the development of the American abolitionist movement more than quite possibly any other single work. The degree of the book's importance can be measured by the fact that its primary rival for the title of most influential abolitionist work, Harriet Beecher Stowe's *Uncle Tom's Cabin* (1852), relied heavily on it. The book was co-authored by Theodore Dwight Weld (1803–95), a prominent abolitionist during the movement's formative years in the 1830s and 40s, and the Grimké sisters, Angelina (1805–79) and Sarah (1792–1873), antislavery activists originally from South Carolina (Angelina Grimké was also Weld's wife). Weld and the Grimkés put together the book largely from numerous direct descriptions of, or examples of, slavery's brutality, most of

them written by observers in the slave states and especially by enslavers themselves; newspaper advertisements offering rewards for fugitive enslaved people were a particularly useful resource. (The book emphasized the accounts of enslavers over those of enslaved people, because, as its authors put it, "That [enslavers] should utter falsehoods, for the sake of proclaiming their own infamy, is not probable.") The book's impact thus derived not just from its array of factual evidence about what slavery was actually like, but specifically from the way in which it derived this evidence in large part from enslavers' own words.

I... t is assumed by slaveholders that "public opinion" at the South[2] so frowns on cruelty to the slaves, that *fear of disgrace* would restrain from the infliction of it, were there no other consideration.

Now, that this is sheer fiction is shown by the fact that the newspapers in the slaveholding states teem with advertisements for runaway slaves, in which the masters and mistresses describe their men and women as having been "branded with a hot iron," on their "cheeks," "jaws," "breasts," "arms," "legs," and "thighs"; also as "scarred," "very much scarred," "cut up," "marked," etc. "with the whip," also with "iron collars on," "chains," "bars of iron," "fetters," "bells," "horns,"[3] "shackles," etc. They also describe them as having been wounded by "buckshot," "rifle-balls," etc. fired at them by their "owners," and others when in pursuit; also, as having "notches" cut in their ears, the tops or bottoms of their ears "cut off," or "slit," or "one ear cut off," or "both ears cut off," etc. etc. The masters and mistresses who thus advertise their runaway slaves coolly sign their names to their advertisements, giving the street and number of their residences, if in cities, their post office address, etc. if in the country; thus making public proclamation as widely as possible that *they* "brand,"

---

[1] *commiserated* Lamented.

[2] *at the South* I.e., in the South.

[3] *bells, horns* Enslaved people—especially those who had previously attempted to escape—were sometimes forced to wear metal collars with bells attached, often known as a "bell and horns," to prevent further escape attempts. Moses Roper's *Narrative of the Adventures and Escape of Moses Roper, from American Slavery* (1838) described the use of "iron horns, with bells, attached to the back of the slave's neck," calling such implements (which could be several feet in height) an "instrument of torture."

"scar," "gash," "cut up," etc. the flesh of their slaves; load them with irons, cut off their ears, etc.; they speak of these things with the utmost *sang froid*,[1] not seeming to think it possible that any one will esteem them at all the less because of these outrages upon their slaves; further, these advertisements swarm in many of the largest and most widely circulated political and commercial papers that are published in the slave states. The editors of those papers constitute the main body of the literati of the slave states; they move in the highest circle of society, are among the "popular" men in the community, and *as a class*, are more influential than any other; yet these editors publish these advertisements with iron indifference. So far from proclaiming to such felons, homicides, and murderers, that they will not be their bloodhounds, to hunt down the innocent and mutilated victims who have escaped from their torture, they freely furnish them with every facility,[2] become their accomplices and share their spoils; and instead of outraging "public opinion" by doing it, they are the men after its own heart, its organs, its representatives, its *self*.

To show that the "public opinion" of the slave states towards the slaves is absolutely *diabolical*, we will insert a few, out of a multitude, of similar advertisements from a variety of southern papers now before us.

The North Carolina Standard, of July 18, 1838, contains the following:

"TWENTY DOLLARS REWARD. Ran away from the subscriber, a negro woman and two children; the woman is tall and black, and *a few days before she went off*, I burnt her with a hot iron on the left side of her face; I tried to make the letter M, *and she kept a cloth over her head and face and a fly bonnet on her head so as to cover the burn*; her children are both boys, the oldest is in his seventh year; he is a *mulatto*[3] and has blue eyes; the youngest is black and is in his fifth year. The woman's name is Betty, commonly called Bet.

MICAJAH RICKS.

Nash County, July 7, 1838."

---

1   *sang froid*   French: cold blood.

2   *facility*   Opportunity, accommodation.

3   *mulatto*   Term, now universally regarded as offensive, that was widely used in the nineteenth century to classify individuals of mixed racial background—typically, someone with one white parent and one parent of African descent.

Hear the wretch tell his story, with as much indifference as if he were describing the cutting of his initials in the bark of a tree.

"*I burnt her with a hot iron on the left side of her face,*" "*I tried to make the letter M,*" and this he says in a newspaper, and puts his name to it, and the editor of the paper, who is also its proprietor, publishes it for him and pockets his fee. …

J.P. Ashford advertises as follows in the "Natchez Courier," August 24, 1838.

"Ran away, a negro girl called Mary, has a small scar over her eye, a *good many teeth missing,* the letter A. *is branded on her cheek and forehead.*"

A.B. Metcalf thus advertises a woman in the same paper, June 15, 1838.

"Ran away, Mary, a black woman, has a *scar* on her back and right arm near the shoulder, *caused by a rifle ball.*"

John Henderson, in the "Grand Gulf Advertiser," August 29, 1838, advertises Betsey.

"Ran away, a black woman Betsey, has an *iron bar on her right leg.*"

Robert Nicoll, whose residence is in Mobile, in Dauphin street, between Emmanuel and Conception streets, thus advertises a woman in the "Mobile Commercial Advertiser."

"TEN DOLLARS REWARD will be given for my negro woman Liby. The said Liby is about 30 years old, and VERY MUCH SCARRED ABOUT THE NECK AND EARS, occasioned by whipping, had on a handkerchief tied round her ears, as she COMMONLY wears it to HIDE THE SCARS."

To show that slaveholding brutality now is the same that it was the eighth of a century ago, we publish the following advertisement from the "Charleston (S.C.) Courier," of 1825.

"TWENTY DOLLARS REWARD—Ran away from the subscriber, on the 14th instant,[4] a negro girl named Molly.

"The said girl was sold by Messrs. Wm. Payne & Sons, as the property of an estate of a Mr. Gearrall, and purchased by a Mr. Moses, and sold by him to a Thomas Prisley, of Edgefield District, of whom I

---

4   *instant*   Anglicization of the Latin instante mense, meaning "[of] this month."

bought her on the 17th of April, 1819. She is 16 or 17 years of age, slim made, LATELY BRANDED ON THE LEFT CHEEK, THUS, R, and a piece taken off of her ear on the same side; the same letter on the inside of both her legs.

ABNER ROSS, Fairfield District."

But instead of filling pages with similar advertisements, illustrating the horrible brutality of slaveholders towards their slaves, the reader is referred to the preceding pages of this work, to the scores of advertisements written by slaveholders, printed by slaveholders, published by slaveholders, in newspapers edited by slaveholders, and patronized by slaveholders; advertisements describing not only men and boys, but women, aged and middle-aged, matrons and girls of tender years, their necks chafed with iron collars with prongs, their limbs galled with iron rings, and chains, and bars of iron, iron hobbles and shackles, all parts of their persons scarred with the lash, and branded with hot irons, and torn with rifle bullets, pistol balls and buck shot, and gashed with knives, their eyes out, their ears cut off, their teeth drawn out, and their bones broken. He is referred also to the cool and shocking indifference with which these slaveholders, "gentlemen" and "ladies," Reverends, and Honorables, and Excellencies, write and print, and publish and pay, and take money for, and read and circulate, and sanction, such infernal barbarity. Let the reader ponder all this, and then lay it to heart, that this is that "public opinion" of the slaveholders which protects their slaves from all injury, and is an effectual guarantee of personal security. ...

But we are not yet quite ready to dismiss this protector, "Public Opinion." To illustrate the hardened brutality with which slaveholders regard their slaves, the shameless and apparently unconscious indecency with which they speak of their female slaves, examine their persons, and describe them, under their own signatures, in newspapers, hand-bills, etc. just as they would describe the marks of cattle and swine, on all parts of their bodies; we will make a few extracts from southern papers. Reader, as we proceed to these extracts, remember our motto—"True humanity consists *not* in a squeamish ear."

Mr. P. Abdie, of New Orleans, advertises in the New Orleans Bee, of January 29, 1838, for one of his female slaves, as follows;

"Ran away, the negro wench[1] named Betsey, aged about 22 years, handsome-faced, and good countenance; having the marks of the whip behind her neck, and several others on her rump. The above reward ($10) will be given to whoever will bring that wench to P. Abdie." ...

Mr. William Robinson, Georgetown, District of Columbia, advertised for his slave in the National Intelligencer, of Washington City, Oct. 2, 1837, as follows:

"Eloped from my residence a young negress, 22 years old, of a chesnut, or brown color. She has a very singular mark—this mark, to the best of my recollection, covers a part of her *breasts*, *body*, and *limbs*; and when her neck and arms are uncovered, is very perceptible; she has been frequently seen east and south of the Capitol Square, and is harbored by ill-disposed persons, of every complexion, for her services."

Mr. John C. Beasley, near Huntsville, Alabama, thus advertises a young girl of eighteen, in the Huntsville Democrat, of August 1st, 1837. "Ran away Maria, about 18 years old, *very far advanced with child.*" He then offers a reward to any one who will commit this young girl, in this condition, *to jail.* ...

The above are a few specimens of the gross[2] details, in describing the persons of females, of all ages, and the marks upon all parts of their bodies; proving incontestably, that slaveholders are in the habit not only of stripping their female slaves of their clothing, and inflicting punishment upon their "shrinking flesh,"[3] but of subjecting their naked persons to the most minute and revolting inspection, and then of publishing to the world the results of their examination, as well as the scars left by their own inflictions upon them, their length, size, and exact position on the body; and all this without impairing in the least, the standing in the community of the shameless wretches who thus proclaim their own abominations. That such things should not at all affect the standing of such persons in

---

1 *wench* In American usage, this word, a now-derogatory term for a female servant, was exclusively applied to black women.

2 *gross* Repulsively immoral or uncivilized.

3 *shrinking flesh* See the abolitionist poet John Greenleaf Whittier's "Stanzas," later retitled "Expostulation" (1834): "What, ho!—*our* countrymen in chains! / The whip on woman's shrinking flesh!"

society, is certainly no marvel: how could they affect it, when the same communities enact laws *requiring* their own legal officers to inspect minutely the persons and bodily marks of all slaves taken up as runaways, and to publish in the newspapers a particular description of all such marks and peculiarities of their persons, their size, appearance, position on the body, etc. Yea, verily, when the "public opinion" of the community, in the solemn form of law, commands jailors, sheriffs, captains of police, etc. to divest of their clothing aged matrons and young girls, minutely examine their naked persons, and publish the results of their examination—who can marvel, that the same "public opinion" should tolerate the slaveholders themselves, in doing the same things to their own property, which they have appointed legal officers to do as their proxies.[1] ...

Runaway Advertisements

For nearly two centuries, advertisements for fugitive enslaved people—posted either by enslavers offering rewards for their return or by authorities announcing their capture—were an extremely common feature of American newspapers. Such advertisements began to appear almost as soon as the first newspapers were founded in the American colonies, and they continued to be printed—as the final example below indicates—even after the official abolition of slavery, as the so-called "Black Codes" (bodies of law introduced immediately after the Civil War in many Southern states that imposed numerous restrictions on the freedom

of emancipated African Americans, including labor requirements) attempted to perpetuate legal African American servitude in a different form. The examples of runaway advertisements from the early and mid-nineteenth century included here provide insight into how enslavers thought about their "property"; they also offer small but valuable windows into the lives of enslaved people who may otherwise have left no trace in the historical record.

FROM THE *RALEIGH REGISTER AND NORTH CAROLINA WEEKLY ADVERTISER* (19 MAY 1820)

RUNAWAY NEGROES

On the 10th of this month I bought at a Sheriff's sale, a stout black negro woman by the name of Sooky, considerably advanced in years, and her female child, called Olive, about four years old. They were sold as the property of Samuel G. Briggs, of Raleigh. They formerly belonged to a Miss Hart, who lived in Mr. Briggs's family, and were, as I understand, brought from Northampton County. They were at my house in the night after the sale, and apparently contented, but in the morning were missing. Whether they have attempted to make their way to Northampton; or whether they are harbored in or about Raleigh; or what has become of them, I am at a loss to conjecture.

Any useful information on this subject will be thankfully received; and I will give a reward of ten dollars to any person who will deliver the negroes to me, together with a suitable reward for any services beyond my present expectation.

HENRY POTTER.
Raleigh, May 18, 1820.

---

[1] [Authors' note]   As a sample of these laws, we give the following extract from one of the laws of Maryland, where slaveholding "public opinion" exists in its mildest form.

"It shall be the duty of the sheriffs of the several counties of this state, upon any runaway servant or slave being committed to his custody, to cause the same to be advertised, etc. and to make particular and minute descriptions of the *person and bodily marks* of such runaway." –*Laws of Maryland of* 1802, Chap. 96, Sec. 1 and 2.

That the sheriffs, jailors, etc. do not neglect this part of their official "duty" is plain from the minute description which they give in the advertisements of marks upon all parts of the persons of females, as well as males; and also from the occasional declaration "no scars discoverable on any part," or "no marks discoverable *about* her"; which last is taken from an advertisement in the Milledgeville (Geo.) Journal, June 26, 1838, signed "T.S. Densler, Jailor."

FROM THE *MOBILE COMMERCIAL REGISTER*
(2 JUNE 1826)

NOTICE.

COMMITTED to the Jail of Mobile County, on the 23d of January last, a Negro Man, named GUY, five feet, eight inches high, with a scar on his right cheek, & also a small scar on the right side of his nose. Appears to be 35 years of age, says he came from Monticello, in Mississippi, to this place, and professes to be free. If he is not taken out in the time prescribed by law, he will be sold to pay jail fees.

    James P. Bates,
    Sheriff.

Runaway advertisement from the *Milledgeville Federal Union*, 8 June 1841.

FROM THE *MILLEDGEVILLE FEDERAL UNION*
(1 NOVEMBER 1853)

$400 Reward.

RAN AWAY or stolen from my negro mart in Columbus,[1] in December last, TWO NEGRO MEN, one named Simon, the other named John, both carpenters. Simon is a yellow[2] copper-colored man, about forty years old, middling height, stout built, he has a scar in one corner of his mouth cut with a knife; since his departure he has been seen lurking about Mr. Bowin's in Coweta County, where he has a wife. He was purchased of E.C. Bowin in the neighborhood of Griffin; he may be in that section, or he may be in Carroll County. John is a mulatto about 45 or 50 years of age, middling height, stout built, in a previous runaway scrape he tried to pass himself off as a Frenchman, he can talk French a little. A few days previous to his leaving he received a severe scar on his forehead in a fight with a negro. I presume the scar is still to be seen; he is considerably gray, perhaps half gray, the black hairs are very black. It is not likely that he will acknowledge himself a slave. When he was apprehended before, he claimed to be a free Frenchman, and threatened to prosecute the party that took him for unlawfully detaining him. They were on the point of releasing him, when he was recognized by a carpenter that he had worked for. The above reward will be given for the delivery of the two negroes if stolen with sufficient proof to convict the thief, or ONE HUNDRED DOLLARS for either of the negroes, if delivered to me by the fifteenth of November next, or FIFTY DOLLARS, if delivered any time after the 15th of November or placed in any jail so that I can get them.

    H.H. LOWE.

---

[1] *negro mart* I.e., establishment of a trader and seller of enslaved people; *Columbus* City in western Georgia. Milledgeville, where this newspaper was published, was at the time the Georgia state capital.

[2] *yellow* Term, now considered offensive except in African American usage, for a (usually mixed-race) African American with light brown skin.

TWENTY-FIVE DOLLARS REWARD—For the apprehension of the griffe[1] woman JOSEPHINE, about 34 years of age, of medium height, some teeth missing, and rather polite or modest. She formerly lived at Algiers,[2] and was until recently owned by Mr. J.C. Wilson at the Balize,[3] where she has a daughter about 16 years of age, of whom she appears to be very fond.

She left on Friday last, 18th inst.,[4] about 2 o'clock P.M., was dressed ordinarily, had no shoes on and appeared to be intoxicated.

The above reward will be paid by

MAJOR HARBIN, 169 Gravier street, or at No. 30 Poydras street.

Runaway—GEORGE WASHINGTON, a negro boy aged about 15 years who was indentured to the undersigned by the Assistant Superintendent of the Freedmen's Bureau[5] on the 25th day of September, 1865, has absconded from my service and employment, without any just cause or provocation. This is to forewarn all persons against harboring or employing the said indentured boy, as in such cases the law will be rigidly enforced against those so employing or harboring the said George. And for the apprehension and return of him to me in Greensboro[6] a reasonable reward will be paid.

JAMES F. PEARCE.

anonymous, "Escape from Slavery of Henry Box Brown" (c. 1849)

Henry Brown (c. 1815–97), an enslaved Virginian man, resolved to escape in August 1848, when his wife Nancy and their three children were all sold away to North Carolina. With the help of two citizens of Richmond, Virginia, one of whom was a free black man, Brown arranged to have himself shipped in a box from Richmond to the office of an abolitionist Quaker merchant in Philadelphia. His journey in the box, which measured three feet long, two and a half feet deep, and two feet wide, took place in March 1849 and lasted just over a full day before he arrived safely in Philadelphia. During Brown's subsequent tour on the abolitionist lecture circuit, he added "Box" to his name. The first of two published versions of Brown's life story, *Narrative of Henry Box Brown*, appeared in Boston in 1849, and Brown used his share of its proceeds to fund a live theatrical experience, *Henry Box Brown's Mirror of Slavery*, which featured a moving panorama—a very long canvas with a series of paintings that was progressively unrolled on stage—together with music and narration. He toured with the panorama throughout New England and—after the Fugitive Slave Act was passed in 1850—Great Britain, where he settled and where the second version of his narrative was published. In his later life, Brown made his living as a magician and entertainer; after returning to the U.S. in 1875, he moved to Canada in 1886 and died there in 1897.

One of the many renditions of Brown's famous escape that circulated, in various mediums, in the years after it took place was the song given below, the lyrics to which were printed (probably in the summer of 1849) in Boston as a broadside, here reproduced in facsimile. The song was composed to the tune of—and satirically rewrites the lyrics of—a minstrel song, "Old Uncle Ned," the words to which can be found in the website portion of this section.

---

[1] *griffe* Term for a person with three-quarters black and one-quarter white ancestry. Like all such nineteenth-century terms classifying people in terms of their racial background, it is today considered archaic and offensive.

[2] *Algiers* Neighborhood in New Orleans, Louisiana, the second-oldest neighborhood in the city.

[3] *the Balize* La Balize, Louisiana, a community at the mouth of the Mississippi River; it was abandoned in 1860 after being destroyed by a hurricane.

[4] *inst.* Abbreviation of Latin *instante mense*, meaning "[of] this month."

[5] *Freedmen's Bureau* U.S. government agency established after the Civil War to provide essential services to formerly enslaved people ("freedmen"), including food, medical care, education, locating and communicating with family members, and employment.

[6] *Greensboro* Town in North Carolina.

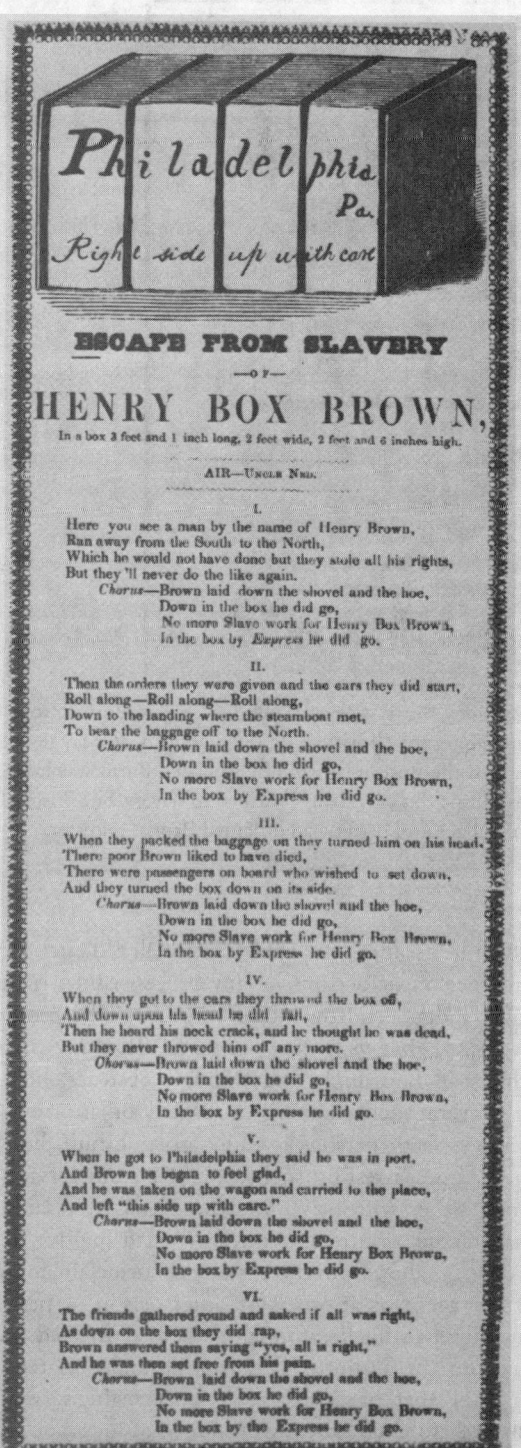

from the Fugitive Slave Act (1850)

The right of enslavers to apprehend enslaved people who had escaped into another state and to have them returned to slavery was codified in the so-called "Fugitive Slave Clause" of the U.S. Constitution, and was further enforced by a Fugitive Slave Act passed in 1793. By the 1840s, however, the steady stream of enslaved people escaping to the North, the extent of the assistance they were receiving from Northern abolitionists, and various measures taken by local and state courts and legislatures in the North, and by the U.S. Supreme Court, that made it more difficult for enslavers to reclaim fugitive "property" in other states all convinced many Southerners that a more rigorous update of the 1793 act was needed. The resultant 1850 Fugitive Slave Act formed a key part of the Compromise of 1850, a package of laws designed to settle the intensifying disputes between North and South over slavery and its westward expansion (or, as many Northern abolitionists saw it, to appease the South). The act penalized anyone—not just law enforcement officers but common citizens—who sought to aid fugitive enslaved people or did not cooperate in their capture; gave officials financial incentives to return fugitives to slavery; and denied alleged fugitives the right to a jury trial or even to testify on their own behalf—a provision that resulted in free black Northerners being kidnapped, accused of being fugitives, and enslaved. The Fugitive Slave Act convinced many African Americans that they could not live safely anywhere in the United States, while the act's attempt, in effect, to make every American citizen responsible for enforcing slavery intensified the antislavery commitment of abolitionists and pushed many white Northerners who had previously believed slavery was no concern of theirs to oppose the institution.

... **S**ec. 6. *And be it further enacted*, That when a person held to service or labor in any State or Territory of the United States, has heretofore or shall hereafter escape into another State or Territory of the United States, the person or persons to whom such service or labor may be due, or his, her, or their agent

KIDNAPPING
AGAIN!!
A MAN WAS STOLEN LAST NIGHT BY THE
Fugitive Slave Bill COMMISSIONER!
HE WILL HAVE HIS
MOCK TRIAL
ON SATURDAY, MAY 27, AT 9 O'CLOCK,
In the Kidnapper's 'Court,' before the Hon. Slave Bill Commissioner,
AT THE COURT HOUSE, IN COURT SQUARE.
SHALL BOSTON STEAL ANOTHER MAN?
Thursday, May 25, 1854.

This broadside, distributed in Boston in 1854, publicizes the case of Anthony Burns (1834–62), who escaped to Boston from slavery in Virginia. His capture under the 1850 Fugitive Slave Act sparked intense opposition; on the evening of 26 May 1854, the day after this broadside was printed, a group of abolitionists attacked the Boston courthouse in which Burns was held in an unsuccessful attempt to free him. With the aid of federal troops, Burns was eventually returned to slavery, but Boston sympathizers later purchased his freedom. He then attended Oberlin College and became an ordained Baptist minister.

or attorney, duly authorized, by power of attorney, in writing, … may pursue and reclaim such fugitive person, either by procuring a warrant from some one of the courts, judges, or commissioners aforesaid, … or by seizing and arresting such fugitive, where the same can be done without process, and by taking, or causing such person to be taken, forthwith before such court, judge, or commissioner, whose duty it shall be to hear and determine the case of such claimant in a summary manner[.][1] … In no trial or hearing under this act shall the testimony of such alleged fugitive be admitted in evidence; and the certificates in this and the first [fourth] section mentioned, shall be conclusive of the right of the person or persons in whose favor granted, to remove such fugitive to the State or Territory from

which he escaped, and shall prevent all molestation of such person or persons by any process issued by any court, judge, magistrate, or other person whomsoever.

Sec. 7. *And be it further enacted*, That any person who shall knowingly and willingly obstruct, hinder, or prevent such claimant, his agent or attorney, or any person or persons lawfully assisting him, her, or them, from arresting such a fugitive from service or labor, either with or without process as aforesaid, or shall rescue, or attempt to rescue, such fugitive from service or labor, from the custody of such claimant, his or her agent or attorney, or other person or persons lawfully assisting as aforesaid, when so arrested, pursuant to the authority herein given and declared; or shall aid, abet, or assist such person so owing service or labor as aforesaid, directly or indirectly, to escape from such claimant, his agent or attorney, or other person or

[1]   *in a summary manner*   Quickly, without jury trial or other usual judicial procedures.

persons legally authorized as aforesaid; or shall harbor or conceal such fugitive, so as to prevent the discovery and arrest of such person, after notice or knowledge of the fact that such person was a fugitive from service or labor as aforesaid, shall, for either of said offences, be subject to a fine not exceeding one thousand dollars, and imprisonment not exceeding six months, by indictment and conviction before the District Court of the United States for the district in which such offence may have been committed, or before the proper court of criminal jurisdiction, if committed within any one of the organized Territories of the United States; and shall moreover forfeit and pay, by way of civil damages to the party injured by such illegal conduct, the sum of one thousand dollars for each fugitive so lost as aforesaid, to be recovered by action of debt, in any of the District or Territorial Courts aforesaid, within whose jurisdiction the said offence may have been committed.

Sec. 8. *And be it further enacted*, That the marshals, their deputies, and the clerks of the said District and Territorial Courts, shall be paid, for their services, the like fees as may be allowed for similar services in other cases; ... and in all cases where the proceedings are before a commissioner, he shall be entitled to a fee of ten dollars in full for his services in each case, upon the delivery of the said certificate[1] to the claimant, his agent or attorney; or a fee of five dollars in cases where the proof shall not, in the opinion of such commissioner, warrant such certificate and delivery, inclusive of all services incident to such arrest and examination, to be paid, in either case, by the claimant, his or her agent or attorney. ...

from Bethany Veney, *The Narrative of Bethany Veney: A Slave Woman* (1889)

Bethany Veney (c. 1815–1916) was born into slavery on a plantation in the Shenandoah Valley, in Virginia. She endured a forced separation from her first husband, Jerry Fickland, when he was sold further south; many years later, she was to dedicate her *Narrative* to Fickland. Veney herself endured being sold to several plantation owners before she was purchased in the 1850s by a Northern entrepreneur and abolitionist who freed her and her son. This purchase, while it gave Veney and her child freedom, led to Veney's permanent separation from her second husband, Frank Veney. The selection below from Bethany Veney's memoir, which she dictated in the 1880s, describes her separation from Fickland; a longer excerpt, detailing the couple's courtship and marriage, is included in the website component of this anthology.

CHAPTER 5
MEETING—A LAST INTERVIEW—SEPARATION

The place where I was to meet Jerry[2] was, as I have said, across the run,[3] in a corn-field, near the blacksmith's shop, the time Friday night.

It had rained hard all day, and the stream was swollen, and pouring and rushing at a fearful rate. I waited till everybody was in bed and asleep, when I lighted my pine knot,[4] and started for the Pass. It was still raining, and the night was very dark. Only by my torch could I see a step before me; and, when I attempted to wade in, as I did in many different places, I found it was no use. I should surely be drowned if I persisted. So, disappointed and grieved, I gave up and went home. The next morning I was able to get over on horseback to milk the cows, but I neither heard nor saw anything of Jerry.

Saturday night came. I knew well that, if not caught by White,[5] Jerry would be round. At last, everyone was in bed, and all was still. I waited and listened. I listened and waited. Then I heard his step at the door. I hurriedly opened it, and he came in. His clothes were

---

[1]   *the said certificate*   I.e., the certificate mentioned in Section 6 authorizing the enslaver or their representative(s) to remove the captured fugitive or fugitives back to the state or territory in which they were enslaved.

[2]   *The place ... Jerry*   In the previous chapter of Veney's *Narrative*, included in the website portion of this section, she and Jerry discover that he is to be sold to help pay the debts of his enslaver's family. Jerry is permitted to visit his wife before being sent south; during the visit, they decide that he will try to escape and hide in the mountains, where Bethany will meet him to discuss their further course of action.

[3]   *run*   Creek, stream.

[4]   *pine knot*   Piece of pinewood carried as a torch.

[5]   *White*   Frank White, the slave trader to whom Jerry has been sold.

still damp and stiff from the rain of yesterday. He was frightened and uneasy. He had been hiding around in different places, constantly fearing detection. He had seen me from behind the old blacksmith's shop when I had tried the night before, with my pine knot, to ford the stream; and he was glad, he said, when he saw me go back, for he knew I should be carried down by the current and be drowned, if I had persisted. I went to my mistress's bedroom, and asked her if I might go to the cellar. She knew at once what I meant, and whispered softly, "Betty, has Jerry come?" then, without waiting for reply, added, "get him some milk and light bread and butter." I was not long in doing so; and the poor fellow ate like one famishing. Then he wanted to know all that had happened, and what White had said when he found he was gone. We talked a long time, and tried to devise some plans for our mutual safety and possible escape from slavery altogether; but, every way we looked, the path was beset with danger and exposure. We were both utterly disheartened. But sleep came at last and, for the time being, relieved us of our fears.

In the morning, which was Sunday, we had our breakfast together, and, as the hours passed, began to feel a little comforted. After dinner, we walked out to the field and strolled about for some time; and, when ready to go back to the house, we each took an armful of fodder along for the horses. As we laid it down and turned to go into the house, David McCoy[1] rode up on horseback. He saw Jerry at once, and called him to come to the fence. The excitement of the last days— the fasting and the fear—had completely cowed and broken whatever of manhood, or even of brute courage, a slave might by any possibility be presumed at any time to be possessed of, and the last remains of these qualities in poor Jerry were gone. He mutely obeyed; and when, with an oath, McCoy commanded him to mount the horse behind him, he mutely seated himself there. McCoy then called to me to go to the house and bring Jerry's clothes. "Never," I screamed back to him—"never, not to save your miserable life." But Jerry said: "O Betty, 'tis no use. We can't help it." I knew this was so. I stifled my anger and my grief, brought his little bundle, into which I tucked a testament and catechism

someone had given me, and shook hands "good-bye" with him. So we *parted forever*, in this world.

from "Arrest of Fugitive Slaves," *Cincinnati Gazette* (29 January 1856)

One especially well-publicized case of an enslaved person's attempt to escape or resist enslavement was that of Margaret Garner, an enslaved woman who escaped from northern Kentucky along with her husband Robert, her four children—the three younger of whom were most likely fathered by her enslaver, Archibald Gaines—and a group of relatives and other enslaved families. When the Garners were caught outside Cincinnati, Ohio, Margaret—in an attempt to prevent her children from being taken back to slavery—killed her two-year-old daughter Mary with a butcher's knife and wounded her other children before being subdued. In the hearing that followed, Margaret's defenders, who included the prominent women's-rights activist Lucy Stone, argued that she should stand trial in Ohio rather than being immediately returned to slavery in Kentucky, but she was eventually returned to her enslaver, who then sent her and her husband "down the river" to the Deep South; she died in Mississippi in 1858. Margaret Garner's case became instantly famous and has inspired numerous literary and artistic responses ever since, from Frances Harper's 1859 poem "The Slave Mother: A Tale of Ohio" to Toni Morrison's renowned 1987 novel *Beloved*.

This article reporting on the case, originally published in the *Cincinnati Gazette*, was reprinted in the 2 February 1856 issue of *The Anti-Slavery Bugle*, an abolitionist Ohio newspaper, on which the text presented below is based. In its accompanying editorial, the *Bugle* wrote, "Let the spirit of this despairing mother seize upon her oppressed race over the South and the whole Union cannot enslave them."

---

[1]   *David McCoy* Another slave trader, with whom Frank White has made an agreement to find Jerry and send him along to White.

Lewis Miller, *Slave Trader, Sold to Tennessee,* 1850. This watercolor sketch comes from *Sketchbook of Landscapes in the State of Virginia,* in which Miller (1796–1882), a Pennsylvanian, documented his visits to Virginia, where he had family. The sketch depicts a group of recently-sold enslaved people being marched— barefoot—to their new enslaver in Tennessee. Miller's accompanying caption notes that such sights were common in Virginia, "with the negro's in droves Sold." The lines Miller wrote above the scene put a seemingly positive spin on it: they contain an injunction to "weep no more" and call the location of the people's new enslavement "that happy shore."

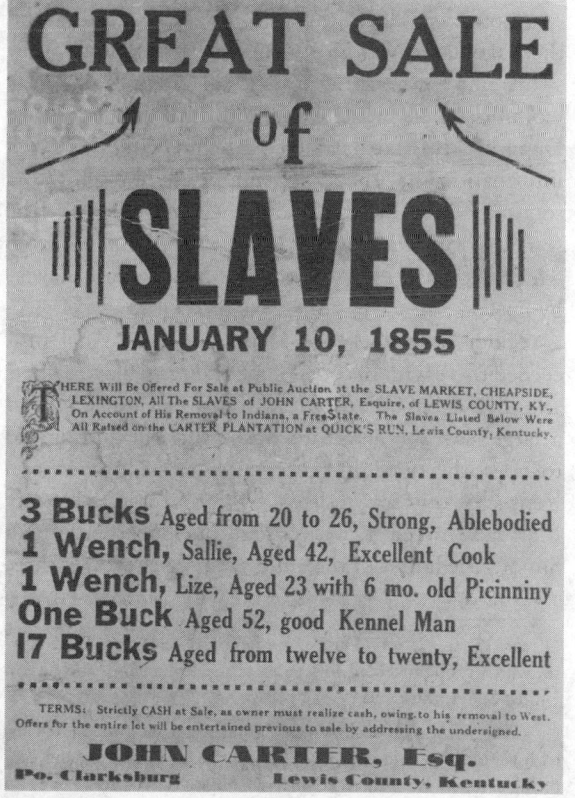

Poster advertising an auction of enslaved people in Kentucky, 1855. The poster exemplifies the demeaning racist terminology often used to categorize enslaved African Americans: "buck" and "wench" for men and women, respectively, and "picinniny" (also spelled various other ways) for children.

ARREST OF FUGITIVE SLAVES.

A SLAVE MOTHER MURDERS HER CHILD RATHER THAN SEE IT RETURNED TO SLAVERY.

Great excitement existed throughout the city the whole of yesterday, in consequence of the arrest of a party of slaves, and the murder of her child by a slave mother, while the officers were in the act of making the arrest. A party of seventeen slaves escaped from Boone and Kenton counties, in Kentucky (about sixteen miles from the Ohio), on Sunday night last, and taking with them two horses and a sled, drove that night to the Ohio River, opposite to Western Row, in this city. Leaving the horses and sled standing there, they crossed the river on foot on the ice.[1]

Five of them were the slaves of Archibald K. Gaines, three of John Marshall, both living in Boone County, a short distance beyond Florence, and six of Levi F. Daugherty, of Kenton County. We have not learned who claims the other three.

About 7 o'clock this morning the masters and their agents arrived in pursuit of their property. They swore out a warrant before J.L. Pendery, Esq., U.S. Commissioner, which was put into the hands of Deputy U.S. Marshal Geo. S. Bennet, who obtained information that they were in a house belonging to a son of Jo. Kite, the third house beyond Millcreek. The son was formerly owned in the neighborhood from which they had escaped and was bought from slavery by his father.

About 10 o'clock the Deputy U.S. Marshal proceeded there with his posse,[2] including the slave owners and their agent and Major Murphy, a Kentuckian, and a large slave holder. Kite was called out and agreed to open the door, but afterwards refused, when two Kentucky officers, assisted by some of the Deputy Marshals, forced it, whereupon the young negro man Simon, the father of the children, fired a revolver three times before he was overpowered. By one of these shots, Special Marshal John Patterson, who raised his arm to reach the pistol, had two of his fingers of his right hand shot off, the ball afterward striking his lip.

In the house were found four adults, viz:[3] old Simon and his wife, and young Simon and his wife and four children of the latter, the oldest near six years and the youngest a babe of about nine months. One of these, however, was lying on the floor dying, its head cut almost entirely off. There was also a gash about four inches long in the throat of the eldest, and a wound on the head of the other boy.

The officers state that when they questioned the boys about their wounds they said the folks threw them down and tried to kill them.

The young woman, Peggy, and her four children belonged to Marshall, and her husband and the old man Simon and the old woman Mary to Gaines. Old Simon and Mary are the parents of young Simon.

The other nine of the party, we were informed, were put upon the cars yesterday, by a director of the underground railway, and furnished with through tickets.[4]

Those arrested in Kite's house were taken to the U.S. Court Rooms about 12 o'clock, and guarded there until 3 o'clock, when Commissioner Pendery came and opened his Court.

Gaines appeared to claim his negroes. Marshall was represented by his son, but as he has no power of attorney from his father, the case was postponed until 9 o'clock this morning, in order to give him time to supply this omission.

The fugitives were then taken to the Hammond Street station house to be kept overnight. The Marshal attempted to get a hack to carry them there, but the crowd frightened all the hackmen[5] that were called so that they declined. They were afraid their carriages would be broken by the mob.

About an hour after they were taken there Mr. Gaines came along with the dead body of the murdered

---

[1]   *they crossed … ice*   During the famously severe winter of 1855–56, which brought record low temperatures to much of the eastern United States, the Ohio River froze over.

[2]   *posse*   Group of local men that a sheriff could call upon to assist with various law enforcement duties: in this case, pursuing and capturing escapees from slavery under the Fugitive Slave Act.

[3]   *viz.*   Abbreviation of the Latin videlicet, meaning "namely" or "that is to say."

[4]   *put upon … through tickets*   The author of this article is here elaborating on the metaphor of the "Underground Railroad": i.e., the escapees were secretly helped further north toward Canada by abolitionist sympathizers.

[5]   *hack*   Hired coach;   *hackmen*   People hired to drive carriages and transport goods.

child. He was taking it to Covington[1] for interment that it might rest in ground consecrated to slavery.[2] ...

It is said that it can be proven that these slaves have frequently been in Ohio in company with their masters, and the question will be raised ... whether such bringing them into a free State has not rendered them free.

from *The Narratives of Fugitive Slaves in Canada* (1856)

The only collection ever compiled of first-hand interviews of black people who had escaped slavery by taking the Underground Railroad to Canada, *The Narratives of Fugitive Slaves in Canada* was published in 1856 by the Massachusetts abolitionist Benjamin Drew (1812–1903). The book—the full title of which is *A North-Side View of Slavery. The Refugee: or the Narratives of Fugitive Slaves in Canada*—was partially a response to *A South-Side View of Slavery* (1855), a book by Drew's fellow white Massachusetts writer Nehemiah Adams that described the supposed moral and religious benefits that enslavement conferred on African Americans and criticized the abolition movement's ostensible radicalism. In order to rebut Adams's arguments, Drew traveled widely in Canada West (the present-day Canadian province of Ontario), interviewing some of the thousands of escapees from slavery who had settled there and recording their accounts of their lives in slavery, their journeys to freedom, and their experiences in Canada.

A larger sample of narratives from this book can be found in the website portion of this anthology.

WILLIAM JOHNSON

I look upon slavery as I do upon a deadly poison. The slaves are not contented nor happy in their lot. Neither on the farm where I was in Virginia, nor in the neighborhood were the slaves satisfied. The man I belonged to did not give us enough to eat. My feet were frostbitten on my way North, but I would rather have died on the way than to go back.

It would not do to stop at all about our work—if the people should try to get a little rest, there would be a cracking spell amongst them.[3] I have had to go through a great deal of affliction; I have been compelled to work when I was sick. I used to have rheumatism,[4] and could not always do so much work as those who were well—then I would sometimes be whipped. I have never seen a runaway that wanted to go back—I have never heard of one.

I knew a very smart young man—he was a fellow-servant of mine, who had recently professed religion[5]—who was tied up by a quick-tempered overseer, and whipped terribly. He died not long after, and the people there believed it was because of the whipping. Some of the slaves told the owner, but he did not discharge the overseer. He will have to meet it at the day of judgment.

I had grown up quite large, before I thought anything about liberty. The fear of being sold South[6] had more influence in inducing me to leave than any other thing. Master used to say, that if we didn't suit him, he would put us in his pocket quick—meaning he would sell us. He never gave me a great coat[7] in his life—he said he knew he ought to do it, but that he couldn't get ahead far enough. His son had a child by a colored woman, and he would have sold it—his own grandchild—if the other folks hadn't opposed it.

I have found good friends in Canada, but have been able to do no work on account of my frozen feet—I lost two toes from my right foot. My determination is to go to work as soon as I am able. I have been about

---

[1] *Covington* City in Kentucky, just across the Ohio River from Cincinnati.

[2] *ground ... slavery* I.e., in the soil of a slave state.

[3] *there would ... amongst them* I.e., they would be beaten severely.

[4] *rheumatism* Term for a class of disorders affecting the joints, such as arthritis.

[5] *professed religion* Publicly embraced Christianity.

[6] *The fear ... South* Conditions for enslaved people in the Deep South, where most large-scale cotton cultivation took place, were generally much worse than in the more northerly slave states; consequently, enslaved people in "Upper South" states such as Virginia greatly feared being sold to new enslavers in the Deep South.

[7] *great coat* Long, warm overcoat.

among the colored people in St. Catharines[1] considerably, and have found them industrious and frugal. No person has offered me any liquor since I have been here: I have seen no colored person use it. I have been trying to learn to read since I came here, and I know a great many fugitives who are trying to learn.

HARRIET TUBMAN[2]

I grew up like a neglected weed—ignorant of liberty, having no experience of it. Then I was not happy or contented: every time I saw a white man, I was afraid of being carried away. I had two sisters carried away in a chain-gang—one of them left two children. We were always uneasy. Now I've been free, I know what a dreadful condition slavery is. I have seen hundreds of escaped slaves, but I never saw one who was willing to go back and be a slave. I have no opportunity to see my friends in my native land. We would rather stay in our native land, if we could be as free there as we are here. I think slavery is the next thing to hell. If a person would send another into bondage, he would, it appears to me, be bad enough to send him into hell, if he could.

MRS. CHRISTOPHER HAMILTON

I left Mississippi about fourteen years ago. I was raised a house servant, and was well used,[3] but I saw and heard a great deal of the cruelty of slavery. I saw more than I wanted to—I never want to see so much again. The slaveholders say their slaves are better off than if they were free, and that they prefer slavery to freedom. I do not, and never saw one that wished to go back. It would be a hard trial to make me a slave again. I had

HARRIET TUBMAN.

Harriet Tubman as she appeared during the Civil War, in which she served as a scout and spy for the U.S. Army. Tubman guided federal troops on an 1863 raid on plantations along the Combahee River in South Carolina, an action in which more than 750 enslaved people were freed. This image was printed as a frontispiece to *Scenes in the Life of Harriet Tubman* (1869).

rather live in Canada, on one potato a day, than to live in the South with all the wealth they have got. I am now my own mistress, and need not work when I am sick. I can do my own thinkings, without having any one to think for me—to tell me when to come, what to do, and to sell me when they get ready. I wish I could have my relatives here. I might say a great deal more against slavery—nothing for it.

The people who raised me failed; they borrowed money and mortgaged me. I went to live with people whose ways did not suit me, and I thought it best to come to Canada, and live as I pleased.

BEN BLACKBURN

I was born in Maysville, Ky. I got here last Tuesday evening, and spent the Fourth of July in Canada. I felt as big and free as any man could feel, and I worked part of the day for my own benefit: I guess my master's

---

[1] *St. Catharines* Town in what is now the Canadian province of Ontario, not far from the U.S. border, that became a center of abolitionist activity and a place of refuge and settlement for enslaved people who took the Underground Railroad to Canada. By the mid-1850s, about 800 black people lived there, out of a total population of approximately 6,000.

[2] *HARRIET TUBMAN* African American abolitionist and activist (c. 1822–1913) who was one of the most famous "conductors" on the Underground Railroad. After herself escaping from slavery in Maryland in 1849, she guided first her family and then numerous other enslaved people to freedom, for which she became known as "Moses." Tubman lived in St. Catharines from 1851 to 1858.

[3] *well used* I.e., well treated.

time is out. Seventeen came away in the same gang that I did.

LYDIA ADAMS

[Mrs. A. lives in a very comfortable log-house on the road from Windsor to the Refugees' Home.[1]]

I am seventy or eighty years old. I was from Fairfax County, old Virginia. I was married and had three children when I left there for Wood County, where I lived twenty years: thence to Missouri, removing with my master's family. One by one they sent four of my children away from me, and sent them to the South: and four of my grandchildren all to the South but one. My oldest son, Daniel—then Sarah—all gone. "It's no use to cry about it," said one of the young women, "she's got to go." That's what she said when Esther went away. Esther's husband is here now, almost crazy about her: they took her and sold her away from him. They were all Methodist people—great Methodists—all belonged to the church. My master died—he left no testimony whether he was willing to go or not. ... I have been in Canada about one year, and like it as far as I have seen.

I've been wanting to be free ever since I was a little child. I said to them I didn't believe God ever meant me to be a slave, if my skin was black—at any rate not all my lifetime: why not have it as in old times, seven years' servants?[2] Master would say, "No, you were made to wait on white people: what was niggers[3] made for? Why, just to wait on us all."

I am afraid the slaveholders will go to a bad place—I am really afraid they will. I don't think any slaveholder can get to the kingdom.[4]

DAVID GRIER

I was born free in Maryland—was stolen and sold in Kentucky, when between eight and nine years old. In Kentucky I was set free by will,[5] and as they were trying to break the will up, some of my claimant's friends persuaded me to come off to Ohio. From Ohio, I came here on account of the oppressive laws demanding security for good behavior[6]—I was a stranger and could not give it. I had to leave my family in Kentucky.

I came in 1831. I have cleared land on lease for five or six years, then have to leave it, and go into the bush again. I worked so about thirteen years. I could do no better, and the white people, I believe, took advantage of it to get the land cleared. This has kept me poor. I guess I have cleared not short of seventy or eighty acres, and got no benefit. I have now six acres cleared.

from Roger Taney, the *Dred Scott* Decision (1857)

In 1846, Dred Scott, an enslaved Missouri man, sued for his freedom (assisted by white abolitionists), arguing that because he had been taken by his enslavers for extended periods to Illinois and Wisconsin Territory, where slavery was illegal, he had automatically become free. The St. Louis Circuit Court ruled in favor of Scott, but the Missouri Supreme Court reversed that ruling, whereupon Scott sued again in federal court; the case reached the U.S. Supreme Court, as *Dred Scott v. Sandford*, in 1856. In a 7–2 decision issued on 6 March 1857, the Court

---

1   *on the road ... Refugees' Home* In 1851, the Refugee Home Society, an international Canadian–American abolitionist organization, founded a settlement for fugitive enslaved people twenty miles from Windsor, a Canadian city directly across the U.S.–Canada border from Detroit, Michigan.

2   *why not ... servants* Reference to the practice of indentured servitude, widespread during the early colonial period, according to which the indentured person was obliged to perform unpaid labor for a fixed period of time—usually four to seven years—after which they would be free.

3   *niggers* By the nineteenth century, as the context here suggests, "the n-word" (today universally acknowledged to be an utterly unacceptable expression of racism) had achieved its current, emphatically pejorative meaning in white American vernacular.

4   *the kingdom* The kingdom of God—i.e., heaven.

5   *by will* I.e., according to the written will of his enslaver after his enslaver's death.

6   *the oppressive ... good behavior* Ohio's so-called "Black Laws," passed in 1807 in order to discourage African American migration to the state, required, among other things, that black residents find at least two people who would guarantee a surety of five hundred dollars—an amount of money designed to be prohibitively expensive—for their good behavior.

ruled that African Americans were not recognized as U.S. citizens under the Constitution and that federal courts therefore had no jurisdiction in the case and no right to end Scott's enslavement under Missouri law. In addition, the majority decision, written by Chief Justice Roger Taney, went on to declare any attempt by the federal government to impose restrictions on the expansion of slavery unconstitutional. The decision, which the Court had hoped would definitively settle the debate surrounding slavery, was predictably hailed in the slave states and bitterly decried in the free states, thereby further deepening the national polarization that would spark civil war a few years later.

... The question is simply this: Can a negro, whose ancestors were imported into this country, and sold as slaves, become a member of the political community formed and brought into existence by the Constitution of the United States, and as such become entitled to all the rights, and privileges, and immunities, guaranteed by that instrument to the citizen? One of which rights is the privilege of suing in a court of the United States in the cases specified in the Constitution. ...

In the opinion of the court, the legislation and histories of the times, and the language used in the Declaration of Independence, show that neither the class of persons who had been imported as slaves, nor their descendants, whether they had become free or not, were then acknowledged as a part of the people, nor intended to be included in the general words used in that memorable instrument.

It is difficult at this day to realize the state of public opinion in relation to that unfortunate race, which prevailed in the civilized and enlightened portions of the world at the time of the Declaration of Independence, and when the Constitution of the United States was framed and adopted. But the public history of every European nation displays it in a manner too plain to be mistaken.

They had for more than a century before been regarded as beings of an inferior order, and altogether unfit to associate with the white race, either in social or political relations; and so far inferior, that they had no rights which the white man was bound to respect; and that the negro might justly and lawfully be reduced to slavery for his benefit. He was bought and sold, and treated as an ordinary article of merchandise and traffic,[1] whenever a profit could be made by it. This opinion was at that time fixed and universal in the civilized portion of the white race. It was regarded as an axiom in morals as well as in politics, which no one thought of disputing, or supposed to be open to dispute; and men in every grade and position in society daily and habitually acted upon it in their private pursuits, as well as in matters of public concern, without doubting for a moment the correctness of this opinion. ...

No one, we presume, supposes that any change in public opinion or feeling, in relation to this unfortunate race, in the civilized nations of Europe or in this country, should induce the court to give to the words of the Constitution a more liberal construction in their favor than they were intended to bear when the instrument was framed and adopted. Such an argument would be altogether inadmissible in any tribunal called on to interpret it. If any of its provisions are deemed unjust, there is a mode prescribed in the instrument itself by which it may be amended; but while it remains unaltered, it must be construed now as it was understood at the time of its adoption. ...

Upon the whole, therefore, it is the judgment of this court, ... that the plaintiff in error is not a citizen of Missouri, in the sense in which that word is used in the Constitution; and that the Circuit Court of the United States, for that reason, had no jurisdiction in the case, and could give no judgment in it. Its judgment for the defendant must, consequently, be reversed, and a mandate issued, directing the suit to be dismissed for want[2] of jurisdiction.

---

[1] *traffic* Trade.

[2] *want* Lack.

from Mary Chesnut, Diary, 18 March 1861

The Civil War diary of Mary Boykin Chesnut (1823–86) is widely considered by modern historians to be a masterpiece of the diary genre. The wife of a wealthy Southern planter, Senator, and eventual aide to Jefferson Davis, president of the secessionist Southern government during the Civil War, Chesnut kept a journal from February 1861 through July 1865 in which she chronicled her wartime experiences. Though she belonged to the South's enslaving elite, Chesnut herself disliked slavery; many of her diary entries reveal passionate opposition to the institution, although more because of what she perceived as its ill effects on white enslavers, especially white women, than out of any strong sympathy with enslaved people themselves. (In fact, the diary makes it painfully clear that Chesnut shared many of her society's racist prejudices.) Chesnut revised her wartime diary in the 1880s, though she died before she could complete this project; it was this version that was first published in the early 1900s and earned Chesnut literary acclaim. An authoritative scholarly edition published in 1981 made available much of her original wartime writing; the excerpt presented below is based on one of these original diary entries.

March 18, 1861

… I wonder if it be a sin to think slavery a curse to any land. Sumner[1] said not one word of this hated institution which is not true. Men and women are punished when their masters and mistresses are brutes and not when they do wrong—and then we live surrounded by prostitutes.[2] An abandoned woman[3] is sent out of any decent house elsewhere. Who thinks any worse of a negro or mulatto[4] woman for being a thing we can't name? God forgive us, but ours is a *monstrous* system and wrong and iniquity. Perhaps the rest of the world is as bad—this *only* I see. Like the patriarchs of old[5] our men live all in one house with their wives and their concubines, and the mulattoes one sees in every family exactly resemble the white children—and every lady tells you who is the father of all the mulatto children in everybody's household, but those in her own she seems to think drop from the clouds, or pretends so to think. Good women we have, *but* they talk of all *nastiness* … —but they are, I believe, in conduct the purest women God ever made. Thank God for my countrywomen—alas for the men! No worse than men everywhere, but the lower their mistresses, the more degraded they must be. …

Mr. Harris said it was so patriarchal. So it is—flocks and herds and slaves—and wife Leah does not suffice. Rachel must be *added*, if not *married*.[6] And all the time they seem to think themselves patterns—models of husbands and fathers.

… And again I say, my countrywomen are as pure as angels, though surrounded by another race who are the social evil![7] …

---

[1] *Sumner* Charles Sumner (1811–74), U.S. Senator for Massachusetts noted for his fervent opposition to slavery.

[2] *prostitutes* Though the core meaning of prostitute is *person who engages in sexual activity in exchange for money*, enslaved women were of course not paid for the sexual acts they were coerced into taking part in with their enslavers. Then (as now) the word was often used loosely as a slur against any woman who had engaged in sexual activity considered to be inappropriate—whether coerced or not, whether for payment or not.

[3] *An abandoned woman* I.e., a woman who has been seduced or sexually exploited and then deserted.

[4] *mulatto* Term used in the nineteenth century, today considered archaic and offensive, to refer to an individual of mixed racial background—typically, someone with one white parent and one parent of African descent.

[5] *patriarchs of old* Reference to the male figures of the biblical book of Genesis, who are typically described as ruling over large tribal households that include one or more wives as well as concubines (unmarried women, often enslaved, who are kept as sexual partners).

[6] *wife Leah … married* Chesnut refers here to the story of Jacob (later renamed Israel), one of the biblical patriarchs and the traditional ancestor of the Israelites, who fell in love with Rachel, was tricked by her father into marrying her older sister Leah instead, but was eventually able to marry Rachel as well. See Genesis 29.

[7] *the social evil* In the nineteenth century, this phrase was often used to refer specifically to prostitution.

Wilson.

Branded Slave from New Orleans.

LEARNING IS WEALTH.

WILSON, CHARLEY, REBECCA & ROSA.

Slaves from New Orleans

Charles Paxson, *Wilson. Branded Slave from New Orleans* and *Learning Is Wealth. Wilson, Charley, Rebecca & Rosa. Slaves from New Orleans*, 1863–64. These photographs depict formerly enslaved people freed when the U.S. Army occupied New Orleans, Louisiana during the Civil War. The first photograph portrays Wilson Chinn, "about 60 years old," posing with instruments of restraint and torture commonly used on enslaved people, including a collar, a whipping paddle, and chains. Chinn appears again in the second photograph, together with three mixed-race children, Charles Taylor, Rebecca Huger, and Rosina Downs; this second photograph exemplifies the genre of "white slave propaganda," in which images or descriptions of enslaved people who appeared white were used to shock white audiences. The photographs, and others like them, were reproduced and copies of them sold to raise funds for the education of emancipated people, and more generally to build support for abolition.

from Abraham Lincoln, Emancipation Proclamation, 1 January 1863

Opposition to slavery, and especially to its expansion, formed one of the cornerstones of Abraham Lincoln's Republican Party. After the Civil War broke out, however, President Lincoln long resisted taking any broad or systematic steps to end slavery, due largely to political considerations: he was mindful of the fact that most Northerners saw the war—as he himself at first saw it—as a war to preserve the Union and would likely resist an attempt to redefine it as a war for abolition. He also feared that any federal measures against slavery would drive the four slave states that had remained in the Union (Missouri, Kentucky, Maryland, and Delaware) to secede and join the other secessionist slave states. These considerations also shaped the Emancipation Proclamation that Lincoln eventually did issue in September 1862, and which was formalized on 1 January 1863. The Proclamation's scope was further limited by Lincoln's sense that he lacked any constitutional authority to take unilateral measures against slavery beyond that which he possessed as Commander-in-Chief of the U.S. armed forces in time of war.

The text of the final Emancipation Proclamation, given below, bears comparison to the so-called "Preliminary" Emancipation Proclamation, the text of which appears in the website portion of this section.

By the President of the United States
of America:
A Proclamation.

Whereas, on the twenty-second day of September, in the year of our Lord one thousand eight hundred and sixty-two, a proclamation was issued by the President of the United States, containing, among other things, the following, to wit:

"That on the first day of January, in the year of our Lord one thousand eight hundred and sixty-three, all persons held as slaves within any State or designated part of a State, the people whereof shall then be in rebellion against the United States, shall be then, thenceforward,

and forever free; and the Executive Government of the United States, including the military and naval authority thereof, will recognize and maintain the freedom of such persons, and will do no act or acts to repress such persons, or any of them, in any efforts they may make for their actual freedom. ..."

Now, therefore, I, Abraham Lincoln, President of the United States, by virtue of the power in me vested as Commander-in-Chief, of the Army and Navy of the United States in time of actual armed rebellion against the authority and government of the United States, and as a fit and necessary war measure for suppressing said rebellion, do, on this first day of January, in the year of our Lord one thousand eight hundred and sixty-three, and in accordance with my purpose so to do publicly proclaimed for the full period of one hundred days, from the day first above mentioned, order and designate as the States and parts of States wherein the people thereof respectively are this day in rebellion against the United States, the following, to wit:

Arkansas, Texas, Louisiana (except the Parishes of St. Bernard, Plaquemines, Jefferson, St. John, St. Charles, St. James Ascension, Assumption, Terrebonne, Lafourche, St. Mary, St. Martin, and Orleans, including the City of New Orleans),[1] Mississippi, Alabama, Florida, Georgia, South Carolina, North Carolina, and Virginia (except the forty-eight counties designated as West Virginia, and also the counties of Berkley, Accomac, Northampton, Elizabeth City, York, Princess Ann, and Norfolk, including the cities of Norfolk and Portsmouth),[2] and which excepted parts are for the present left precisely as if this proclamation were not issued.

And by virtue of the power and for the purpose aforesaid, I do order and declare that all persons held

---

[1] *the Parishes ... New Orleans* Portions of the state of Louisiana that were, at the time the Emancipation Proclamation was issued, under Union military occupation.

[2] *except the forty-eight ... Portsmouth* In 1861, after Virginia seceded from the Union, what was then the northwestern portion of the state, which had a very small enslaved population and correspondingly low support for secession, broke away in turn from Virginia (aided by the fact that the Union Army had occupied the region). The area was admitted to the Union as the new state of West Virginia on 20 June 1863. The other parts of Virginia named in this parenthesis were all portions of the state that Union forces had also occupied.

as slaves within said designated States, and parts of States, are and henceforward shall be free; and that the Executive government of the United States, including the military and naval authorities thereof, will recognize and maintain the freedom of said persons.

And I hereby enjoin upon the people so declared to be free to abstain from all violence, unless in necessary self-defence; and I recommend to them that, in all cases when allowed, they labor faithfully for reasonable wages.

And I further declare and make known, that such persons of suitable condition will be received into the armed service of the United States to garrison forts, positions, stations, and other places, and to man vessels of all sorts in said service.

And upon this act, sincerely believed to be an act of justice, warranted by the Constitution, upon military necessity, I invoke the considerate judgment of mankind, and the gracious favor of Almighty God.

In witness whereof, I have hereunto set my hand and caused the seal of the United States to be affixed.

Done at the City of Washington, this first day of January, in the year of our Lord one thousand eight hundred and sixty-three, and of the Independence of the United States of America the eighty-seventh.

By the President: Abraham Lincoln
William H. Seward, Secretary of State.

Jourdon Anderson, "Letter from a Freedman to His Old Master" (1865)

Jourdon Anderson (1825–1907) was enslaved for nearly three decades on a plantation in Wilson County, Tennessee. In 1848, he married Amanda (Mandy) McGregor, with whom he eventually had eleven children. They and their family gained their freedom in 1864, when U.S. Army troops camped at the plantation of their enslaver, Patrick Henry Anderson. By the summer of 1865, Jourdon Anderson and his family were living in Dayton, Ohio, where Patrick contacted him with a request that he return to work on the plantation, which was in deep financial trouble. Anderson, who was illiterate, dictated his response to this request

to his employer, the Dayton banker and abolitionist Valentine Winters, who published it in the *Cincinnati Commercial*. The letter quickly became a sensation and was widely reprinted, including in the *New York Daily Tribune* and in Lydia Maria Child's anthology *The Freedmen's Book* (1865); it even appeared in French translation in Switzerland. Anderson spent the remaining forty years of his life in Dayton, working as a janitor, coachman, hostler, and church sexton; his former enslaver was forced to sell his estate in September 1865 and died two years later.

DAYTON, Ohio, August 7, 1865.

To my Old Master, Col. P.H. ANDERSON, *Big Spring, Tennessee.*

Sir: I got your letter and was glad to find that you had not forgotten Jordan, and that you wanted me to come back and live with you again, promising to do better for me than anybody else can. I have often felt uneasy about you. I thought the Yankees would have hung you long before this for harboring Rebs they found at your house. I suppose they never heard about your going to Col. Martin's to kill the Union soldier that was left by his company in their stable. Although you shot at me twice before I left you, I did not want to hear of your being hurt, and am glad you are still living. It would do me good to go back to the dear old home again and see Miss Mary and Miss Martha[1] and Allen, Esther, Green, and Lee. Give my love to them all, and tell them I hope we will meet in the better world, if not in this. I would have gone back to see you all when I was working in the Nashville Hospital, but one of the neighbors told me Henry[2] intended to shoot me if he ever got a chance.

I want to know particularly what the good chance is you propose to give me. I am doing tolerably well here; I get $25 a month, with victuals and clothing; have a comfortable home for Mandy (the folks here call her Mrs. Anderson), and the children, Milly Jane and Grundy, go to school and are learning well; the teacher says Grundy has a head for a preacher. They go

---

[1]   *Miss ... Martha*   Patrick Henry Anderson's wife and daughter.

[2]   *Henry*   Probably Patrick Henry Anderson's son, Patrick Henry Jr., who was generally known as Henry.

to Sunday School, and Mandy and me attend church regularly. We are kindly treated; sometimes we overhear others saying, "Them colored people were slaves" down in Tennessee. The children feel hurt when they hear such remarks, but I tell them it was no disgrace in Tennessee to belong to Col. Anderson. Many darkies would have been proud, as I used to was, to call you master. Now, if you will write and say what wages you will give me, I will be better able to decide whether it would be to my advantage to move back again.

As to my freedom, which you say I can have, there is nothing to be gained on that score, as I got my free papers in 1864 from the Provost-Marshal-General of the Department of Nashville. Mandy says she would be afraid to go back without some proof that you are sincerely disposed to treat us justly and kindly—and we have concluded to test your sincerity by asking you to send us our wages for the time we served you. This will make us forget and forgive old scores, and rely on your justice and friendship in the future. I served you faithfully for thirty-two years, and Mandy twenty years. At $25 a month for me, and $2 a week for Mandy, our earnings would amount to $11,680. Add to this the interest for the time our wages has been kept back and deduct what you paid for our clothing and three doctor's visits to me, and pulling a tooth for Mandy, and the balance will show what we are in justice entitled to. Please send the money by Adams Express, in care of V. Winters,[1] esq., Dayton, Ohio. If you fail to pay us for faithful labors in the past we can have little faith in your promises in the future. We trust the good Maker has opened your eyes to the wrongs which you and your fathers have done to me and my fathers, in making us toil for you for generations without recompense. Here I draw my wages every Saturday night, but in Tennessee there was never any pay-day for the Negroes any more than for the horses and cows. Surely there will be a day of reckoning for those who defraud the laborer of his hire.[2]

In answering this letter please state if there would be any safety for my Milly and Jane, who are now grown up and both good-looking girls. You know how it was with poor Matilda and Catherine. I would rather stay here and starve and die if it come to that than have my girls brought to shame by the violence and wickedness of their young masters. You will also please state if there has been any schools opened for the colored children in your neighborhood, the great desire of my life now is to give my children an education, and have them form virtuous habits.

From your old servant, Jourdon Anderson.

P.S. Say howdy to George Carter,[3] and thank him for taking the pistol from you when you were shooting at me.

from William Marvin, Speech to the Freedmen of Marianna, 17 September 1865

William Marvin (1808–1902), a native New Yorker, moved to Florida in the 1830s, where he served as a U.S. attorney and district court judge; he remained loyal to the Union when Florida seceded. In July 1865, President Andrew Johnson appointed him Provisional Governor of Florida. Marvin gave the speech excerpted below to an audience of more than a thousand formerly enslaved people in the northern Florida city of Marianna.

With this war you had nothing to do; you neither commenced it, nor did you end it, nor is the result attributable to you at all. It was a white man's war. It is true that a few colored men were enlisted in the army of the U.S., but they fought no battles; or if [they] engaged at all in such, they were trifling affairs.[4] Indeed, you had nothing to do with it; you remained at home, worked, behaved yourselves, and the blood of no man is on your hands. ...

At the beginning, the war was neither intended nor prosecuted ... to liberate you from slavery. Neither

---

[1] *V. Winters* Jourdon Anderson's employer, Valentine Winters; Anderson and his wife later named one of their sons after him, who grew up to become a friend and collaborator of the African American author Paul Laurence Dunbar.

[2] *Surely ... his hire* Anderson here echoes several Bible verses, including Leviticus 19.13 and James 5.4.

[3] *George Carter* A carpenter in Wilson County, Tennessee.

[4] *It is true ... trifling affairs* African American Union troops took part in a battle in Marianna itself on 27 September 1864, just a year before Marvin gave this speech.

the Northern white man nor the Southern white man expected nor intended such a result; neither, therefore, is entitled to your thanks or gratitude. ... To a higher power should you feel grateful for your freedom—the Providence and tender mercies of Almighty God. You are free—as free as the white man—and never again so long as the U.S. exist ... will you be reduced to slavery. ...

If you ask me the question, whether the white man of the North or the white man of the South is your friend, I will answer you by saying that I hope and believe both of them are; but if it comes to a question of certainty as to which of the two is your better friend, I shall answer plainly and tell you: the white man of the South. I was born in the North, raised and educated there, but I have spent the last thirty years of my life in the South, and I consider myself capable of judging between the two people, particularly in reference to yourselves. I know the Northern man, or Yankee, as you call him, from the crown of his head to the sole of his foot, and I tell you today as your friend, that the Southern white man, with whom you were raised and who is acquainted with your habits and customs, is the best friend you have. ...

I know, that though I am here as the governor of the state, and tell you that you are free, that you will not believe it. You are prepared to say that you remain on the same plantations and are controlled and directed by the same owners, for whom, as before, you have to work, and that you do not understand by such facts that you are free.[1] And on and after the first of January next,[2] I know, as well as if I witnessed it now, what you will do. You will leave your old homes—drift about the country—float from plantation to plantation; hundreds of you will come to town, and everywhere

you will be looking for freedom, and it will only be when your old masters and mistresses do not pursue you that you will be convinced that you are no longer slaves. And when you shall find as you will that you are free—find it with hungry stomachs and with nothing to eat, with the fact that none cares for you, and that you are driven more than ever to care for yourselves, you will then begin wisely to consider what is best to be done. ...

My advice is to remain on the plantations where you have been accustomed to work, with your former owners if they will make a contract with you. Make the best contract you can with them, and show to them that you are willing to work better, now that you are compensated for your work, than you ever have done before. Be faithful, be truthful, be honest, be interested in the affairs of the plantation; see that the mules are well fed, that the hogs get good attention and that the things entrusted to you be not neglected. ...

Your masters, influenced by interest aside from human feelings, which none question many of them having, have fed you, clothed you, and when sick have nursed you and when necessary have employed medical attendance. The raising of your children has received almost their exclusive care; they furnished the old women to watch over them during the absence of their mothers, who came two or three times to nurse them during the day. Now, as freed men and women, you are by your work to feed yourselves, clothe yourselves, employ medical attendance, [and] raise and educate your children. ...

Do not think that, because you are free, you have a right to be impudent, uncivil, or impolite to white people. You have no such right. Impoliteness is not justifiable in anyone. You should be as civil, as polite as you always have been. ... You do not wish to make white people hate you. It is to them that you are to look for almost everything: you want to be instructed by them; you want to learn from them; so you must be polite and civil to them, and don't put on airs and flaunt and look insolent at them, and don't, as I have heard has been done in places, jostle, or rub, or shove up against them when passing them on the road. Such a course is highly wrong and will get you into trouble. Some of the most polite men I have ever seen were colored men who have been raised in good families. They

---

[1]   *You are prepared ... free* Florida, like many other former secessionist slave states, imposed so-called "Black Codes" in the immediate aftermath of the Civil War. Among numerous other restrictions on the freedom of formerly enslaved people, these laws mandated annual labor contracts, which kept many African Americans working for their former enslavers on terms that were frequently little better than slavery. (An example of Mississippi's Black Code can be found in the website portion of this section.)

[2]   *on and after ... next* Marvin delivered this speech in part to refute rumors circulating among formerly enslaved people that, in January 1866, they were to receive distributions of land belonging to their former enslavers.

SCENES IN MEMPHIS, TENNESSEE, DURING THE RIOT—SHOOTING DOWN NEGROES ON THE MORNING OF MAY 2, 1866.—[SKETCHED BY A. R. W.]

Alfred Waud, *Scenes in Memphis, Tennessee, During the Riot—Shooting Down Negroes on the Morning of May 2, 1866*, 1866. This illustration by Waud—an English-born artist who had previously sketched many combat scenes during the Civil War—was published in the 26 May 1866 issue of *Harper's Weekly*. It depicts the massacre that had occurred earlier that month in Memphis, Tennessee: a coordinated assault in which, over the first three days of May, a white mob, including many police officers, killed over forty black citizens of the city and destroyed numerous black churches, schools, and private homes. The Memphis Massacre typified the white supremacist violence whereby, over the next decade, white Southerners would reimpose their hegemony over emancipated African Americans. A selection of firsthand accounts of the Memphis Massacre can be found in the website component of this section.

were naturally polite and knew well how to be so, and it is so with you. You can be as polite as anyone, and you ought not to be otherwise. It is a duty which is due to yourselves; it is gentlemanly and ladylike, and, now that you are free, you should try and be gentlemen and ladies. You have a greater inducement now than you ever had before, and if you wish to be esteemed as ladies and gentlemen, you must conduct yourselves accordingly. Call your old master, Master, and your old mistress, Mistress. It is right that you should; it is proper, it is polite. You do not mean, by calling them so, that you belong to them, but that you wish to be respectful and polite, and to give no cause for offence, but rather desire to please. I don't say that you must call them Master or Mistress, but

I say it is civil and polite in you to do it, and you ought, therefore, to do it. I have known many white servants; and there are thousands in the North where I was raised, and it is so in England, too; who call those who employ them Master and Mistress. It is a term of respect and deference, and they call them thus because this is so. There they, as I said before, are white servants, and they till the land, feed the stock and do other work that is done here, and they are respected and all of them find employment, as you may do if you will conduct yourselves properly. …

[Do not conclude that] the mantle of freedom makes you the equal of the white man. [For that to happen] you would have to be able to write a book, build a railroad, a steam engine, a steamboat and thousands of other things. ... [It would be foolish] to think they are not superior to you and will ever be. ...

Before the war each one of you was worth, in dollars and cents to your owners, eight hundred, or a thousand, or fifteen hundred dollars—worth more than fifty acres, or eighty acres of land and a mule thrown in. Well, the president[1] has, in giving you your freedom, taken so many dollars and cents from your old masters, and he thinks, as I do, they have lost enough, and you by it have had enough given to you. If he were to give you more it would prove a curse to you. God has directed the president how much to give you and he will give no more. ...

Will you promise me to do the best you can, be kindly disposed to all, to be good men and women? ("We will.") ... God help you do it.

Advertisements Taken Out by Formerly Enslaved People Seeking Family Members

In the years after the end of slavery, thousands of advertisements were placed in African American newspapers throughout the country by formerly enslaved people searching for family members from whom they had been separated, usually by sale into the domestic slave trade. The advertisements were typically published in special sections titled "Information Wanted," "Last Seen," or (as in the *Southwestern Christian Advocate*) "Lost Friends," and were also frequently read aloud in churches; they were a fixture of black periodicals for decades and continued to appear into the twentieth century. How many such advertisements resulted in reunions it is impossible to know, but that at least some proved successful is demonstrated by the final example included below.

FROM THE *COLORED TENNESSEAN* (24 MARCH 1866)

Information Wanted

Of my daughter, Martha James. When last heard from was in Montgomery, Ala., but is supposed to have gone to Mobile. She formerly belonged to Dr. Barnett, Princeton, Ky., and was sold to Mr. John James, Nashville, Tenn., about nine years ago, since which time she has not been seen by me. Information of her will be thankfully received by her mother by addressing Colored Tennessean, Box 1150, Nashville, Tenn.

HANNAH BARNETT ...

Of our five children, whom we have not seen for four years. Their names are as follows, viz.:[2] Josephine, aged 20 years; Celia, aged 14 years; Caroline, aged 13 years; Ellen, aged 10 years; and Augusta, aged 8 years. They were in Charlotte, N.C., or at Rock Hill[3] when we last heard from them.

Any information concerning these children will be thankfully received by their mother. Our address is, Augusta, Ga.

AUGUSTUS BRYANT
LUTITIA BRYANT

N.B.—These persons were formerly owned by John L. and Virginia Moon, of Augusta, Ga.

FROM THE *CHRISTIAN RECORDER*[4] (24 MARCH 1866)

Information Wanted

By Lucy Walker, of my husband, Anderson Walker. The last time I saw him was on September 2, 1864, at Athens, Georgia. His former owner was Ferdinand

---

[1] *the president* Andrew Johnson, U.S. President from 1865 to 1869. A Tennessee politician and enslaver, Johnson supported the Union when his state seceded. In a bid to obtain the support of the Southern Unionists Johnson represented, President Lincoln made Johnson his running mate in the 1864 presidential election; as vice-president, Johnson then assumed the presidency after Lincoln's assassination. During his presidency, Johnson opposed federal attempts to protect and promote the rights of formerly enslaved people and supported the reestablishment of white supremacist governments in the Southern states on the grounds of "states' rights."

[2] *viz.* Abbreviation of the Latin videlicet, meaning "namely" or "that is to say."

[3] *Rock Hill* City in northern South Carolina, about twenty-five miles south of Charlotte.

[4] *CHRISTIAN RECORDER* Official newspaper, published in Philadelphia, of the African Methodist Episcopal Church; founded in 1848, it is the oldest continuously-published African American periodical in the United States.

Phirwell. Lucy was owned by Marcella Bloomfield. Any information will be thankfully received by the undersigned. Address

Lucy Walker
Care of Rev. Cyrus Boey,
Elder of Bethel Church,
Oswego City, N.Y.

FROM THE *CHRISTIAN RECORDER* (28 JANUARY 1871)

Information wanted of my sister Rosanna. We parted in Richmond, Va., thirty-five years ago. Learned that she was carried to Alabama by a man named Templeman. She is now about 58 years old. My name then was Anthony Terrill. Also, information wanted of Harriet Chapman, mother of Sidney Oliver. When last heard from she was at Chapman's Mill, Monroe County, Ga., upward of 40 years ago. Any information address,

Anthony Fleming,
Plaquemine, La.

FROM THE *SOUTHWESTERN CHRISTIAN ADVOCATE*[1] (12 JULY 1877)

I am searching for my mother, whose name is Mary Hall. In 1859 she belonged to Bill Lawson, in Wharton County;[2] he sold her to a cousin of his, whose name I think was also Lawson, and that he lived near Powderhorn, Texas. My name was formerly Henry Hall, I had a sister named Caroline. Address, Henry Wharton, San Filipe, Texas.

FROM THE *SOUTHWESTERN CHRISTIAN ADVOCATE* (24 APRIL 1884)

Mr. Editor—I have got a letter from Turner Petty's people through the inquiry in the paper. God bless the paper. It is bringing the people together.
W.H. JACKSON.
Brenham, Texas.

This certificate, issued by the Wilson County, Tennessee office of the federal Freedmen's Bureau on 23 April 1866, formalizes the marriage of Joseph and Mary Province, formerly enslaved people who had, according to the certificate, "been living together as man and wife for about twenty-one years" and had a nineteen-year-old son. Because marriages between enslaved people were not recognized under slavery, emancipated African Americans frequently asked for and received such certificates from Freedmen's Bureau agents, legalizing marriages that had often existed informally for many years. The bureau also helped African Americans find spouses or other family members from whom they had been separated during slavery.

---

[1] *SOUTHWESTERN ... ADVOCATE* Newspaper published in New Orleans, Louisiana.

[2] *Wharton County* County in southeast Texas.

from Robert B. Elliott, Speech to the House of Representatives, 6 January 1874

Robert Brown Elliott (1842–84) was one of the first African American men to win a seat in Congress in the wake of the abolition of slavery and the passage of the Fourteenth Amendment. Elliott's early life is obscure, but he was likely born and educated in England before settling in South Carolina in 1867, where he practiced law (and helped form the first known African American law firm), served in state government, and led the South Carolina National Guard in its efforts to suppress the Ku Klux Klan. He was elected to the U.S. House of Representatives in 1870 and was reelected in 1872. In Congress, he opposed granting amnesty to former secessionists and worked to pass legislation to weaken the KKK. He made his greatest impact with the speech excerpted below, given in support of a proposed Civil Rights Bill to outlaw discrimination in public transportation, public accommodations, and schools. Elliott's forceful defense of the cause of civil rights, and his eloquence on behalf of his formerly enslaved compatriots, won praise across the country. The Civil Rights Bill passed Congress and was signed into law in 1875, though it went largely unenforced as white supremacist governments regained control of the South. The same reimposition of white hegemony in the South also put an end to Elliott's political career, and he died in poverty in New Orleans in 1884.

While I am sincerely grateful for this high mark of courtesy that has been accorded to me by this House, it is a matter of regret to me that it is necessary at this day that I should rise in the presence of an American Congress to advocate a bill which simply asserts equal rights and equal public privileges for all classes of American citizens. I regret, sir, that the dark hue of my skin may lend a color to the imputation that I am controlled by motives personal to myself in my advocacy of this great measure of national justice. Sir, the motive that impels me is restricted by no such narrow boundary, but is as broad as your Constitution. I advocate it, sir, because it is right. The bill, however, not only appeals to your justice, but it demands a response from your gratitude. …

… The negro, true to that patriotism and love of country that have ever characterized and marked his history on this continent, came to the aid of the government in its efforts to maintain the Constitution. To that government he now appeals; that Constitution he now invokes for protection against outrage and unjust prejudices founded upon caste.

But, sir, we are told by the distinguished gentleman from Georgia [Mr. Stephens[1]] that Congress has no power under the Constitution to pass such a law, and that the passage of such an act is in direct contravention of the rights of the states. I cannot assent to any such proposition. The constitution of a free government ought always to be construed in favor of human rights. Indeed, the Thirteenth, Fourteenth, and Fifteenth Amendments, in positive words, invest Congress with the power to protect the citizen in his civil and political rights. …

These amendments, one and all, are … declared to have as their all-pervading design and end the security to the recently enslaved race, not only their nominal freedom, but their complete protection from those who had formerly exercised unlimited dominion over them. It is in this broad light that all these amendments must be read: the purpose to secure the perfect equality before the law of all citizens of the United States. What you give to one class you must give to all; what you deny to one class you shall deny to all[.] …

… [I]n this discussion I cannot and I will not forget that the welfare and rights of my whole race in this country are involved. When, therefore, the honorable gentleman from Georgia lends his voice and influence to defeat this measure, I do not shrink from saying that it is not from him that the American House of Representatives should take lessons in matters touching human rights or the joint relations of the state and national governments. While the honorable gentleman contented himself with harmless speculations in his study, or in the columns of a newspaper, we might well smile at the impotence of his efforts to turn back

---

[1]   *Mr. Stephens*   Alexander H. Stephens (1812–83), politician from Georgia who served as vice-president of the secessionist Southern government throughout the Civil War. After the war, he was briefly imprisoned before being elected, in 1873, to the U.S. House of Representatives, in which he had also served before the war.

the advancing tide of opinion and progress; but, when he comes again upon this national arena, and throws himself with all his power and influence across the path which leads to the full enfranchisement of my race, I meet him only as an adversary; nor shall age or any other consideration restrain me from saying that he now offers this government, which he has done his utmost to destroy, a very poor return for its magnanimous treatment, to come here and seek to continue, by the assertion of doctrines obnoxious to the true principles of our Government, the burdens and oppressions which rest upon five millions of his countrymen who never failed to lift their earnest prayers for the success of this government when the gentleman was seeking to break up the Union of these states and to blot the American republic from the galaxy of nations. [Loud applause.]

Sir, it is scarcely twelve years since that gentleman shocked the civilized world by announcing the birth of a government which rested on human slavery as its cornerstone.[1] The progress of events has swept away that *pseudo*-government which rested on greed, pride, and tyranny; and the race whom he then ruthlessly spurned and trampled on are here to meet him in debate, and to demand that the rights which are enjoyed by their former oppressors—who vainly sought to overthrow a government which they could not prostitute to the base uses of slavery—shall be accorded to those who even in the darkness of slavery kept their allegiance true to freedom and the Union. ...

... Technically, this bill is to decide upon the civil status of the colored American citizen: a point disputed at the very formation of our present government, when by a short-sighted policy, a policy repugnant to true republican government, one negro counted as three-fifths of a man.[2] The logical result of this mistake of the framers of the Constitution strengthened the cancer of slavery, which finally spread its poisonous tentacles over the southern portion of the body-politic. To arrest its growth and save the nation we have passed through the harrowing operation of intestine[3] war, dreaded at all times, resorted to at the last extremity, like the surgeon's knife, but absolutely necessary to extirpate the disease which threatened with the life of the nation the overthrow of civil and political liberty on this continent. In that dire extremity the members of the race which I have the honor in part to represent— the race which pleads for justice at your hands today, forgetful of their inhuman and brutalizing servitude at the South, their degradation and ostracism at the North—flew willingly and gallantly to the support of the national government. Their sufferings, assistance, privations, and trials in the swamps and in the rice-fields, their valor on the land and on the sea, is a part of the ever-glorious record which makes up the history of a nation preserved, and might, should I urge the claim, incline you to respect and guarantee their rights and privileges as citizens of our common republic. But I remember that valor, devotion, and loyalty are not always rewarded according to their just deserts, and that after the battle some who have borne the brunt of the fray may, through neglect or contempt, be assigned to a subordinate place, while the enemies in war may be preferred to the sufferers.

The results of the war, as seen in reconstruction, have settled forever the political status of my race. The passage of this bill will determine the civil status, not only of the negro, but of any other class of citizens who may feel themselves discriminated against. It will form the capstone of that temple of liberty, begun on this continent under discouraging circumstances, carried on in spite of the sneers of monarchists and the

---

[1] *it is ... cornerstone* On 21 March 1861, Alexander Stephens gave a speech explaining and interpreting the new constitution of the Confederate States of America—as the government formed by the secessionist states called itself—in which he declared that the Confederacy's "foundations are laid, its cornerstone rests, upon the great truth, that the negro is not equal to the white man; that slavery—subordination to the superior race—is his natural and normal condition." The speech—which, after the war, Stephens attempted to revise and downplay—became known as "The Cornerstone Speech"; excerpts of it can be found in the Contexts section on the Civil War, included in the website component of this volume.

[2] *one ... man* Reference to the so-called "Three-Fifths Compromise" made during the drafting of the U.S. Constitution. According to the compromise, each enslaved person in states permitting slavery would count as three-fifths of a person when determining that state's representation in the House of Representatives (and, by extension, its number of electoral votes in the Electoral College). The compromise was enshrined in Article 1, Section 2, Clause 3 of the Constitution but was superseded and repudiated by the Fourteenth Amendment in 1868.

[3] *intestine* Internal, as in a civil conflict.

cavils of pretended friends of freedom, until at last it stands in all its beautiful symmetry and proportions, a building the grandest of which the world has ever seen, realizing the most sanguine expectations and the highest hopes of those who, in the name of equal, impartial, and universal liberty, laid the foundation stones.

The Holy Scriptures tell us of an humble handmaiden who long, faithfully, and patiently gleaned in the rich fields of her wealthy kinsman; and we are told further that at last, in spite of her humble antecedents, she found complete favor in his sight.[1] For over two centuries our race had "reaped down your fields." The cries and woes which we have uttered have "entered into the ears of the Lord of Sabaoth,"[2] and we are at last politically free. The last vestiture only is needed—civil rights. Having gained this, we may, with hearts overflowing with gratitude, and thankful that our prayer has been granted, repeat the prayer of Ruth: "entreat me not to leave thee, or to return from following after thee; for whither thou goest, I will go; and where thou lodgest, I will lodge; thy people shall be my people, and thy god my God; where thou diest, will I die, and there will I be buried; the Lord do so to me, and more also, if aught but death part thee and me."[3] [Great applause.]

---

[1]   *The Holy … his sight*   Elliott here briefly summarizes the biblical Book of Ruth;   *gleaned*   Gathered the grain left behind after the fields were harvested. This was a means of obtaining food for poor or marginalized people that was explicitly identified as a legal right of theirs in the biblical books of Leviticus and Deuteronomy and, later, in parts of medieval and early modern Europe.

[2]   *For over … Sabaoth*   See James 5.4: "Behold, the hire of the labourers who have reaped down your fields, which is of you kept back by fraud, crieth: and the cries of them which have reaped are entered into the ears of the Lord of Sabaoth." The expression "Lord of Sabaoth," meaning "Lord of Hosts" or "God of armies," is a biblical term used to refer to God in his capacity as a military leader of either the Israelite army or the heavenly host of angels.

[3]   *entreat … thee and me*   See Ruth 1.16–17. In this passage, Ruth, a Moabite—i.e., non-Israelite—woman who married an Israelite and has now been widowed, tells her mother-in-law Naomi that she still intends to follow and remain loyal to her, even now that her husband, Naomi's son, is dead;   *aught*   Anything.

SOJOURNER TRUTH

c. 1797 – 1883

Abolitionist and women's rights activist Sojourner Truth was among the most celebrated and compelling orators of nineteenth-century America. Born into slavery near the turn of the century, Truth spent the first seventeen years of her free life working as a domestic servant in New York City before undergoing the spiritual transformation that, in 1843, compelled her to begin a career as an itinerant evangelist. Truth soon became a national celebrity, renowned both for her moving religious exhortations and for her uniquely powerful campaigning for racial and gender equality. Throughout her career, Truth thought and spoke about the intersections of race, class, and gender in a way that few of her fellow activists fully appreciated. Truth never learned to read or write herself; her ideas have come down to us primarily through the accounts of her contemporaries—a fact that has for decades challenged scholars seeking an "authentic" account of this exceptionally charismatic figure.

Isabella (Truth's birth name) was born to parents Elizabeth and James Baumfree or Bomefree around 1797 in Ulster County, two years before the passage of New York State's Gradual Abolition Act, and three decades before that act would take effect for all enslaved people in the state. Speaking Low Dutch as her first language, Isabella learned English when she was sold to an English-speaker, John Neely, around the age of nine. She lived under five different enslavers over the course of her enslaved life, enduring forced separation from her family as well as numerous instances of severe abuse. Forbidden from marrying her first love, Robert, because he belonged to another owner, Isabella was instead arranged to be married to Thomas, with whom she had five children.

Isabella's final enslaver was John Dumont, under whom some scholars speculate she experienced sexual abuse, and with whom she lived for sixteen years until the autumn of 1826. When Dumont broke a promise he had made to emancipate her that summer, Isabella emancipated herself. Leaving in the early hours of the morning, she walked twelve miles to a Quaker settlement with her youngest daughter in tow, leaving her other children with their father, who did not join her. The Quakers provided shelter for Isabella, and provided for her purchase from Dumont when he later came to demand her return. She was taken into the household of Isaac Van Wagenen, for whom she worked voluntarily—though legally still enslaved—as a domestic helper over the course of the next year. While working for Van Wagenen, Isabella discovered that her five year-old son Peter had been illegally sold into slavery in Alabama by Dumont. When the Gradual Abolition Act came into effect and she was officially freed, Isabella sued to regain custody of her son, and, remarkably, succeeded.

In 1828 Isabella underwent a conversion experience, upon which she moved to New York City; she lived there for the next fifteen years, working as a domestic servant, preaching in various contexts including within the Methodist Church and at revivalist camp meetings, and briefly becoming involved in a controversial cult called the Kingdom of Matthias. She underwent a second religious experience in 1843; leaving behind what she now believed to be a sinful city, Isabella adopted the new name Sojourner Truth and began her travels to spread God's word.

Truth discovered a talent for oratory and religious ministry, and soon became something of a regional celebrity. As her fame increased, Truth took to posing for photographs, which she had printed in the popular form of *cartes de visite* that she then sold to collectors to fund her missionary travels. Though she did not initially demonstrate a vocal interest in either abolitionism or women's rights, the religious circles in which she moved often had a strongly antislavery bent. In the mid-1840s, Truth began living at the Northampton Association for Education and Industry, one of the era's many utopian, reform-minded communities. Here she met several prominent abolitionists—among them William Lloyd Garrison, David Ruggles, and, perhaps most significantly, the formerly enslaved orator Frederick Douglass. Douglass and Truth, though very different in their personalities, made profound impressions on one another here; it was at this point that Truth seems to have dedicated herself to the antislavery cause.

Around 1848, Garrison encouraged Truth to compose an autobiography focused on her time in slavery, in the vein of similar slave narratives by individuals such as Douglass. Having never learned to read or write, Truth dictated her life story to abolitionist Olive Gilbert, and had it published in 1850 as *The Narrative of Sojourner Truth, A Northern Slave*. It was printed cheaply, and sold in large numbers at abolitionist conferences. The *Narrative* contributed to Truth's growing abolitionist fame; she began speaking publicly on the subject that fall.

In May 1851, Truth spoke at a women's rights conference held at a church in Akron, Ohio, at which she appears to have been the only African American woman in attendance. In contemporary records of the speech, Truth affirmed the physical capabilities of women, using herself as an example; argued for their intellectual rights; and sharply repudiated the biblically derived objections to the equality of women that opponents of women's rights commonly offered. In the best-known contemporaneous report of the speech, Marius Robinson claimed that it was "impossible to transfer it to paper, or convey any adequate idea of the effect [Truth's speech] produced upon the audience." Another account of Truth's speech, however, eventually became more famous; it was produced in 1863, over a decade after the speech had been given, by Frances Dana Gage, who had presided over the Akron convention. In her version, Gage significantly expanded upon the content of Truth's speech, portraying her as speaking in a strong dialect reflective of stereotypical Southern "slave" accents. (Truth, as a native Dutch speaker from the North, would almost certainly not have spoken with such an accent.) Gage also added the famous refrain, "Ar'n't I a Woman?," which has since lent the speech its popular name. Gage's version appeared in revised editions of Truth's *Narrative* published in the 1870s and 1880s, as well as in the first volume of Elizabeth Cady Stanton's monumental *History of Woman Suffrage* (1881); it remained throughout much of the twentieth century the most widely known and reproduced.

Truth's speeches continued to garner her influence and notoriety. Her highly animated, song-filled lectures were the subject of much comment, as was her physical appearance; she stood nearly six feet tall, and is said to have bared both her arms and her breasts on stage to prove her strength and womanhood to skeptics. She was regularly discussed in abolitionist and feminist media; Harriet Beecher Stowe famously wrote of her in *The Atlantic Monthly* in 1863, describing her as "the Libyan Sibyl."

Though a pacifist at heart, Truth welcomed the Civil War as a national spiritual purge. She met (and posed for a photograph with) Abraham Lincoln during the period at which the Emancipation Proclamation was being drafted, and, after the end of the war, she provided aid and advice to newly emancipated men and women. Over the following years she agitated for healthcare, housing, and land reform for African Americans; for the desegregation of transportation; for temperance; for the abolition of capital punishment; and for universal suffrage.

Truth died in 1883, at the age of eighty-six, having by then established a vivid presence in the American public imagination. She had often aroused puzzlement in her admirers, including in Frederick Douglass, who described her as a "strange compound of wit and wisdom, of wild enthusiasm and flint-like common sense. She was a genuine specimen of the uncultured negro. She cared very little for elegance of speech or refinement of manners." Long after her death, monikers such as "the Negro Joan of Arc" remained associated with her name. Later scholarship has often pivoted on the question of authenticity, especially as it relates to her apparently intentional rejection of conventional literacy; on her highly dynamic lectures; and on her intersectional politics. Her life, career, and words continue to both challenge and fascinate.

NOTE ON THE TEXTS: The text of Truth's narrative is taken from the first edition of the *Narrative of Sojourner Truth, a Northern Slave, emancipated from bodily servitude by the state of New York, in 1828* (1850). Truth's famous 1851 speech is presented in two versions: the first is based on that printed in *The Anti-Slavery Bugle* on 21 June 1851, transcribed with commentary by Marius Robinson; the second is based on that published in the 1875 edition *Narrative of Sojourner Truth; A Bondswoman of Olden Time, emancipated by the New York Legislature in the early part of the present century; with a history of her Labors and Correspondence, drawn from her "Book of life,"* edited by Frances Titus with reminiscences by Frances Dana Gage. Spelling and punctuation have been lightly modernized in accordance with the practices of this anthology, but any writing that aims to reproduce (authentically or not) Truth's speech patterns remains unaltered.

⌘ ⌘ ⌘

from *The Narrative of Sojourner Truth, A Northern Slave*

HER RELIGIOUS INSTRUCTION

Isabella[1] and Peter (her youngest brother) remained, with their parents, the legal property of Charles Ardinburgh till his decease, which took place when Isabella was near nine years old.

After this event, she was often surprised to find her mother in tears; and when, in her simplicity, she inquired, "Mau-mau, what makes you cry?" she would answer, "Oh, my child, I am thinking of your brothers and sisters that have been sold away from me." And she would proceed to detail many circumstances respecting them. But Isabella long since concluded that it was the impending fate of her only remaining children, which her mother but too well understood, even then, that called up those memories from the past, and made them crucify her heart afresh.

In the evening, when her mother's work was done, she would sit down under the sparkling vault of heaven, and calling her children to her, would talk to them of the only Being that could effectually aid or protect them. Her teachings were delivered in Low Dutch, her only language, and, translated into English, ran nearly as follows:

"My children, there is a God, who hears and sees you."

"A *God*, mau-mau! Where does he live?" asked the children.

"He lives in the sky," she replied; "and when you are beaten, or cruelly treated, or fall into any trouble, you must ask help of him, and he will always hear and help you." She taught them to kneel and say the Lord's Prayer. She entreated them to refrain from lying and stealing, and to strive to obey their masters.

At times, a groan would escape her, and she would break out in the language of the Psalmist—"Oh Lord, how long?[2] Oh Lord, how long?" And in reply to Isabella's question—"What ails you, mau-mau?" her only answer was, "Oh, a good deal ails me—Enough ails me." Then again, she would point them to the stars, and say, in her peculiar language, "Those are the same stars, and that is the same moon, that look down upon your brothers and sisters, and which they see as they look up to them, though they are ever so far away from us, and each other."

Thus, in her humble way, did she endeavor to show them their Heavenly Father, as the only being who could protect them in their perilous condition; at the same time, she would strengthen and brighten the chain of family affection, which she trusted extended itself sufficiently to connect the widely scattered members of her precious flock. These instructions of the mother were treasured up and held sacred by Isabella, as our future narrative will show.

THE AUCTION

At length, the never-to-be-forgotten day of the terrible auction arrived, when the "slaves, horses, and other cattle" of Charles Ardinburgh, deceased, were to be

---

[1] *Isabella* Truth's birth name.

[2] *Oh Lord, how long?* See Psalm 13.1: "How long wilt thou forget me, O Lord? for ever? how long wilt thou hide thy face from me?"

put under the hammer, and again change masters. Not only Isabella and Peter, but their mother, were now destined to the auction block, and would have been struck off with the rest to the highest bidder, but for the following circumstance: A question arose among the heirs, "Who shall be burdened with Bomefree, when we have sent away his faithful Mau-mau Bett?"[1] He was becoming weak and infirm; his limbs were painfully rheumatic and distorted—more from exposure and hardship than from old age, though he was several years older than Mau-mau Bett; he was no longer considered of value, but must soon be a burden and care to some one. After some contention on the point at issue, none being willing to be burdened with him, it was finally agreed, as most expedient for the heirs, that the price of Mau-mau Bett should be sacrificed, and she receive her freedom, on condition that she take care of and support her faithful James—faithful, not only to her as a husband, but proverbially faithful as a slave to those who would not willingly sacrifice a dollar for *his* comfort, now that he had commenced his descent into the dark vale of decrepitude and suffering. This important decision was received as joyful news indeed to our ancient couple, who were the objects of it, and who were trying to prepare their hearts for a severe struggle, and one altogether new to them, as they had never before been separated; for, though ignorant, helpless, crushed in spirit, and weighed down with hardship and cruel bereavement, they were still human, and their human hearts beat within them with as true an affection as ever caused a human heart to beat. And their anticipated separation now, in the decline of life, after the last child had been torn from them, must have been truly appalling. Another privilege was granted them—that of remaining occupants of the same dark, humid cellar I have before described: otherwise, they were to support themselves as they best could. And as her mother was still able to do considerable work, and her father a little, they got on for some time very comfortably. The strangers who rented the house were humane people, and very kind to them; they were not rich, and owned no slaves. How long this state of things continued, we are unable to say, as Isabella had

not then sufficiently cultivated her organ[2] of time to calculate years, or even weeks or hours. But she thinks her mother must have lived several years after the death of Master Charles. She remembers going to visit her parents some three or four times before the death of her mother, and a good deal of time seemed to her to intervene between each visit.

At length her mother's health began to decline—a fever-sore made its ravages on one of her limbs, and the palsy[3] began to shake her frame; still, she and James tottered about, picking up a little here and there, which, added to the mites[4] contributed by their kind neighbors, sufficed to sustain life, and drive famine from the door. ...

THE CAUSE OF HER LEAVING THE CITY

The first years spent by Isabella in the city, she accumulated more than enough to satisfy all her wants, and she placed all the overplus in the Savings Bank. Afterwards, while living with Mr. Pierson,[5] he prevailed on her to take it all thence, and invest it in a common fund which he was about establishing, as a fund to be drawn from by all the faithful; the faithful, of course, were the handful that should subscribe to his peculiar creed. This fund, commenced by Mr. Pierson, afterwards became part and parcel of the kingdom of which Matthias assumed to be head;[6] and at the breaking up of the kingdom, her little property was merged in the general ruin—or went to enrich those who profited by the loss of others, if any such there were. Mr. Pierson and others had so assured her that the fund would supply all her wants, at all times, and in all emergencies, and to the end of life, that she became perfectly careless on the subject—asking for no interest when she drew her money from the bank, and

---

[1] *Bomefree* Truth's father, James Baum-free; *Mau-mau Bett* Truth's mother Elizabeth.

[2] *organ* Mental sense.

[3] *palsy* Paralysis or tremor.

[4] *mites* Small donations.

[5] *Mr. Pierson* Isabella's employer, businessperson Elias Pierson.

[6] *the kingdom ... head* Elias Pierson had been converted by itinerant preacher Robert Matthews, also known as Matthias, in the 1830s, following which he helped fund a new religious cult called the Kingdom of Matthias. Matthias became a notorious figure both for his unorthodox—and rampantly misogynistic—theology and for the controversy that surrounded his cult's dissolution.

taking no account of the sum she placed in the fund. She recovered a few articles of the furniture from the wreck of the kingdom, and received a small sum of money from Mr. B. Folger, as the price of Mrs. Folger's attempt to convict her of murder.[1] With this to start upon, she commenced anew her labors, in the hope of yet being able to accumulate a sufficiency to make a little home for herself, in her advancing age. With this stimulus before her, she toiled hard, working early and late, doing a great deal for a little money, and turning her hand to almost anything that promised good pay. Still, she did not prosper, and somehow, could not contrive to lay by a single dollar for a "rainy day."

When this had been the state of her affairs some time, she suddenly paused, and taking a retrospective view of what had passed, inquired within herself why it was that, for all her unwearied labors, she had nothing to show; why it was that others, with much less care and labor, could hoard up treasures for themselves and children? She became more and more convinced, as she reasoned, that everything she had undertaken in the city of New York had finally proved a failure; and where her hopes had been raised the highest, there she felt the failure had been the greatest, and the disappointment most severe.

After turning it in her mind for some time, she came to the conclusion that she had been taking part in a great drama, which was, in itself, but one great system of robbery and wrong. "Yes," she said, "the rich rob the poor, and the poor rob one another." True, she had not received labor from others, and stinted their pay, as she felt had been practised against her; but she had taken their work from them, which was their only means to get money, and was the same to them in the end. For instance—a gentleman where she lived would give her a dollar to hire a poor man to clear the new-fallen snow from the steps and sidewalks. She would arise early, and perform the labor herself, putting the money into her own pocket. A poor man would come along, saying she ought to have let him have the job; he was poor, and needed the pay for his family. She would harden her heart against him, and

answer—"I am poor too, and I need it for mine." But, in her retrospection, she thought of all the misery she might have been adding to, in her selfish grasping, and it troubled her conscience sorely; and this insensibility to the claims of human brotherhood, and the wants of the destitute and wretched poor, she now saw, as she never had done before, to be unfeeling, selfish and wicked. These reflections and convictions gave rise to a sudden revulsion of feeling in the heart of Isabella, and she began to look upon money and property with great indifference, if not contempt—being at that time unable, probably, to discern any difference between a miserly grasping at and hoarding of money and means, and a true use of the good things of this life for one's own comfort, and the relief of such as she might be enabled to befriend and assist. One thing she was sure of—that the precepts, "Do unto others as ye would that others should do unto you," "Love your neighbor as yourself,"[2] and so forth, were maxims that had been but little thought of by herself, or practised by those about her.

Her next decision was that she must leave the city; it was no place for her; yea, she felt called in spirit to leave it, and to travel east and lecture. She had never been further east than the city, neither had she any friends there of whom she had particular reason to expect anything; yet to her it was plain that her mission lay in the east, and that she would find friends there. She determined on leaving; but these determinations and convictions she kept close locked in her own breast, knowing that if her children and friends were aware of it, they would make such an ado about it as would render it very unpleasant, if not distressing to all parties. Having made what preparations for leaving she deemed necessary—which was, to put up a few articles of clothing in a pillow-case, all else being deemed an unnecessary incumbrance—about an hour before she left, she informed Mrs. Whiting, the woman of the house where she was stopping, that her name was no longer Isabella, but SOJOURNER, and that she was going east. And to her inquiry, "What are you going east for?" her answer was, "The Spirit calls me there, and I must go."

---

1   *Mr. B. Folger ... murder*   The Kingdom of Matthias fell apart after Pierson died under suspicious circumstances, upon which both Matthias and Isabella were accused of his murder. Isabella successfully sued their accusers, the Folgers, for libel.

2   *Do unto others ... as yourself*   See Luke 6.31 and Mark 12.31, respectively.

She left the city on the morning of the 1st of June, 1843, crossing over to Brooklyn, L.I.;[1] and taking the rising sun for her only compass and guide, she "remembered Lot's wife,"[2] and hoping to avoid her fate, she resolved not to look back till she felt sure the wicked city from which she was fleeing was left too far behind to be visible in the distance; and when she first ventured to look back, she could just discern the blue cloud of smoke that hung over it, and she thanked the Lord that she was thus far removed from what seemed to *her* a second Sodom.

She was now fairly started on her pilgrimage; her bundle in one hand, and a little basket of provisions in the other, and two York shillings[3] in her purse—her heart strong in the faith that her true work lay before her, and that the Lord was her director; and she doubted not he would provide for and protect her, and that it would be very censurable in her to burden herself with anything more than a moderate supply for her then present needs. Her mission was not merely to travel east, but to "lecture," as she designated it, "testifying of the hope that was in her"—exhorting the people to embrace Jesus, and refrain from sin, the nature and origin of which she explained to them in accordance with her own most curious and original views. Through her life, and all its chequered changes, she has ever clung fast to her first permanent impressions on religious subjects.

Wherever night overtook her, there she sought for lodgings—free, if she might—if not, she paid; at a tavern, if she chanced to be at one—if not, at a private dwelling; with the rich, if they would receive her—if not, with the poor.

But she soon discovered that the largest houses were nearly always full; if not quite full, company was soon expected; and that it was much easier to find an unoccupied corner in a small house than in a large one; and if a person possessed but a miserable roof over his head, you might be sure of a welcome to part of it.

But this, she had penetration enough to see, was quite as much the effect of a want of sympathy as of benevolence; and this was also very apparent in her religious conversations with people who were strangers to her. She said, "she never could find out that the rich had any religion. If *I* had been rich and accomplished, I could; for the rich could always find religion in the rich, and *I* could find it among the poor."

At first, she attended such meetings as she heard of, in the vicinity of her travels, and spoke to the people as she found them assembled. Afterwards, she advertised meetings of her own, and held forth to large audiences, having, as she said, "a good time."

When she became weary of travelling, and wished a place to stop a while and rest herself, she said some opening for her was always near at hand; and the first time she needed rest, a man accosted her as she was walking, inquiring if she was looking for work. She told him that was not the object of her travels, but that she would willingly work a few days, if anyone wanted. He requested her to go to his family, who were sadly in want of assistance, which he had been thus far unable to supply. She went to the house where she was directed, and was received by his family, one of whom was ill, as a "Godsend"; and when she felt constrained to resume her journey, they were very sorry, and would fain have detained her longer; but as she urged the necessity of leaving, they offered her what seemed in her eyes a great deal of money as a remuneration for her labor, and an expression of their gratitude for her opportune assistance; but she would only receive a very little of it; enough, as she says, to enable her to pay tribute to Cæsar,[4] if it was demanded of her; and two or three York shillings at a time were all she allowed herself to take; and then, with purse replenished, and strength renewed, she would once more set out to perform her mission.

---

1   *L.I.*   Long Island.

2   *remembered Lot's wife*   In Genesis 19, the virtuous man Lot and his unnamed wife are permitted by God to flee the city of Sodom, which God is about to destroy because its inhabitants have been sinful; Lot and his wife are instructed not to look back upon the burning city, but Lot's wife disobeys, and as a punishment is turned into a pillar of salt. The story is referenced in the New Testament; Luke 17.32 instructs Christians to "Remember Lot's wife."

3   *York shillings*   Colonial form of currency still then in circulation in New York; one shilling was the equivalent of approximately twelve cents.

4   *pay tribute to Cæsar*   Truth is likely referencing the biblical saying regarding taxation, "Render unto Caesar the things that are Caesar's, and unto God the things that are God's" (Matthew 22.21); the "things that are Caesar's" referred to taxes or other fees relating to secular matters. In other words, Truth will accept only as much money as she needs to pay for the demands of earthly life, which may have included road and bridge taxes as well as things such as food and shelter.

THE CONSEQUENCES OF REFUSING A TRAVELLER A NIGHT'S LODGING

As she drew near the centre of the Island,[1] she commenced, one evening at nightfall, to solicit the favor of a night's lodging. She had repeated her request a great many, it seemed to her some twenty times, and as many times she received a negative answer. She walked on, the stars and the tiny horns of the new moon shed but a dim light on her lonely way, when she was familiarly accosted by two Indians, who took her for an acquaintance. She told them they were mistaken in the person; she was a stranger there, and asked them the direction to a tavern. They informed her it was yet a long way—some two miles or so—and inquired if she were alone. Not wishing for their protection, or knowing what might be the character of their kindness, she answered, "No, not exactly," and passed on. At the end of a weary way, she came to the tavern—rather, to a large building, which was occupied as a courthouse, tavern, and jail—and on asking for a night's lodging, was informed she could stay, if she would consent to be locked in. This to her mind was an insuperable objection. To have a key turned on her was a thing not to be thought of, at least not to be endured, and she again took up her line of march, preferring to walk beneath the open sky, to being locked up by a stranger in such a place. She had not walked far, before she heard the voice of a woman under an open shed; she ventured to accost her, and inquired if she knew where she could get in for the night. The woman answered that she did not, unless she went home with them; and turning to her "good man," asked him if the stranger could not share their home for the night, to which he cheerfully assented. Sojourner thought it evident he had been taking a drop too much, but as he was civil and good-natured, and she did not feel inclined to spend the night alone in the open air, she felt driven to the necessity of accepting their hospitality, whatever it might prove to be. The woman soon informed her that there was a ball in the place, at which they would like to drop in a while, before they went to their home.

Balls being no part of Sojourner's mission, she was not desirous of attending; but her hostess could be satisfied with nothing short of a taste of it, and she was forced to go with her, or relinquish their company at once, in which move there might be more exposure than in accompanying her. She went, and soon found herself surrounded by an assemblage of people, collected from the very dregs of society, too ignorant and degraded to understand, much less entertain, a high or bright idea—in a dirty hovel, destitute of every comfort, and where the fumes of whiskey were abundant and powerful.

Sojourner's guide there was too much charmed with the combined entertainments of the place to be able to tear herself away, till she found her faculties for enjoyment failing her, from a too free use of liquor; and she betook herself to bed till she could recover them. Sojourner, seated in a corner, had time for many reflections, and refrained from lecturing them, in obedience to the recommendation, "Cast not your pearls,"[2] etc. When the night was far spent, the husband of the sleeping woman aroused the sleeper, and reminded her that she was not very polite to the woman she had invited to sleep at her house, and of the propriety of returning home. They once more emerged into the pure air, which to our friend Sojourner, after so long breathing the noisome air of the ballroom, was most refreshing and grateful. Just as day dawned, they reached the place they called their home. Sojourner now saw that she had lost nothing in the shape of rest by remaining so long at the ball, as their miserable cabin afforded but one bunk or pallet for sleeping; and had there been many such, she would have preferred sitting up all night to occupying one like it. They very politely offered her the bed, if she would use it; but civilly declining, she waited for morning with an eagerness of desire she never felt before on the subject, and was never more happy than when the eye of day shed its golden light once more over the earth. She was once more free, and while daylight should last, independent, and needed no invitation to pursue her journey. Let these facts teach us that every pedestrian in the world is not a vagabond, and that it is a dangerous thing to compel anyone to receive that hospitality from the vicious and abandoned which they should

---

[1] *the Island* I.e., Long Island.

[2] *Cast not your pearls* See Matthew 7.6: "Give not that which is holy unto the dogs, neither cast ye your pearls before swine, lest they trample them under their feet, and turn again and rend you."

have received from us—as thousands can testify, who have thus been caught in the snares of the wicked.

The fourth of July, Isabella arrived at Huntingdon; from thence she went to Cold Springs, where she found the people making preparations for a mass temperance meeting. With her usual alacrity, she entered into their labors, getting up dishes *à la New York*,[1] greatly to the satisfaction of those she assisted. After remaining at Cold Springs some three weeks, she returned to Huntingdon, where she took boat for Connecticut. Landing at Bridgeport, she again resumed her travels towards the northeast, lecturing some, and working some, to get wherewith to pay tribute to Cæsar, as she called it; and in this manner she presently came to the city of New Haven, where she found many meetings, which she attended—at some of which, she was allowed to express her views freely, and without reservation. She also called meetings expressly to give herself an opportunity to be heard; and found in the city many true friends of Jesus, as she judged, with whom she held communion of spirit, having no preference for one sect more than another, but being well satisfied with all who gave her evidence of having known or loved the Saviour.

After thus delivering her testimony in this pleasant city, feeling she had not as yet found an abiding place, she went from thence to Bristol, at the request of a zealous sister who desired her to go to the latter place and hold a religious conversation with some friends of hers there. She went as requested, found the people kindly and religiously disposed, and through them she became acquainted with several very interesting persons.

A spiritually-minded brother in Bristol, becoming interested in her new views and original opinions, requested as a favor that she would go to Hartford, to see and converse with friends of his there. Standing ready to perform any service in the Lord, she went to Hartford as desired, bearing in her hand the following note from this brother:

SISTER—I send you this living messenger, as I believe her to be one that God loves. Ethiopia is stretching forth her hands unto God.[2] You can see by this sister, that God does by his Spirit alone teach his own children things to come. Please receive her, and she will tell you some new things. Let her tell her story without interrupting her, and give close attention, and you will see she has got the lever of truth, that God helps her to pry where but few can. She cannot read or write, but the law is in her heart.

Send her to brother—brother—and where she can do the most good.

From your brother,   H.L.B.

SOME OF HER VIEWS AND REASONINGS

As soon as Isabella saw God as an all-powerful, all-pervading spirit, she became desirous of hearing all that had been written of him, and listened to the account of the creation of the world and its first inhabitants, as contained in the first chapters of Genesis, with peculiar interest. For some time she received it all literally, though it appeared strange to her that "God worked by the day, got tired, and stopped to rest," etc. But after a little time, she began to reason upon it, thus—"Why, if God works by the day, and one day's work tires him, and he is obliged to rest, either from weariness or on account of darkness, or if he waited for the 'cool of the day to walk in the garden,'[3] because he was inconvenienced by the heat of the sun, why then it seems that God cannot do as much as *I* can; for *I* can bear the sun at noon, and work several days and nights in succession without being much tired. Or, if he rested nights because of the darkness, it is very queer that he should make the night so dark that he could not see himself. If *I* had been God, I would have made the night light enough for my own convenience, surely." But the moment she placed this idea of God by the side

---

[1]   *getting up dishes à la New York* Preparing meals in New York style. The expression "à la New York" is tongue-in-cheek; nineteenth-century American cuisine was typically quite unrefined, but restaurants often tried to suggest a higher level of sophistication by dressing up the dishes they served with French or other European names (*potatoes Parisienne, macaroni à la Milanese*, etc.).

[2]   *Ethiopia … unto God* See Psalm 68.31: "Princes shall come out of Egypt; Ethiopia shall soon stretch out her hands unto God." In the nineteenth century, this biblical line was often referenced by abolitionists, with "Ethiopia" being used as a shorthand for the African continent and African-descended people as a whole.

[3]   *cool of … the garden* See Genesis 3.8: "And they [Adam and Eve] heard the voice of the Lord God walking in the garden in the cool of the day."

of the impression she had once so suddenly received of his inconceivable greatness and entire spirituality, that moment she exclaimed mentally, "No, God does not stop to rest, for he is a spirit, and cannot tire; he cannot want for light, for he hath all light in himself. And if 'God is all in all,' and 'worketh all in all,'[1] as I have heard them read, then it is impossible he should rest at all; for if he did, every other thing would stop and rest too; the waters would not flow, and the fishes could not swim; and all motion must cease. God could have no pauses in his work, and he needed no Sabbaths of rest. Man might need them, and he should take them when he needed them, whenever he required rest. As it regarded the worship of God, he was to be worshipped at all times and in all places; and one portion of time never seemed to her more holy than another."

These views, which were the results of the workings of her own mind, assisted solely by the light of her own experience and very limited knowledge, were, for a long time after their adoption, closely locked in her own breast, fearing lest their avowal might bring upon her the imputation of "infidelity"—the usual charge preferred by all religionists, against those who entertain religious views and feelings differing materially from their own. If, from their own sad experience, they are withheld from shouting the cry of "infidel," they fail not to see and to feel, ay, and to say, that the dissenters are not of the right spirit, and that their spiritual eyes have never been unsealed.

While travelling in Connecticut, she met a minister, with whom she held a long discussion on these points, as well as on various other topics, such as the origin of all things, especially the origin of evil, at the same time bearing her testimony strongly against a paid ministry. He belonged to that class, and, as a matter of course, as strongly advocated his own side of the question.

I had forgotten to mention, in its proper place, a very important fact, that when she was examining the scriptures, she wished to hear them without comment; but if she employed adult persons to read them to her, and she asked them to read a passage over again, they invariably commenced to explain, by giving her their version of it; and in this way, they tried her feelings exceedingly. In consequence of this, she ceased to ask

adult persons to read the Bible to her, and substituted children in their stead. Children, as soon as they could read distinctly, would re-read the same sentence to her, as often as she wished, and without comment—and in that way she was enabled to see what her own mind could make out of the record, and that, she said, was what she wanted, and not what others thought it to mean. She wished to compare the teachings of the Bible with the witness within her; and she came to the conclusion, that the spirit of truth spoke in those records, but that the recorders of those truths had intermingled with them ideas and suppositions of their own. This is one among the many proofs of her energy and independence of character.

When it became known to her children that Sojourner had left New York, they were filled with wonder and alarm. Where could she have gone, and why had she left? were questions no one could answer satisfactorily. Now, their imaginations painted her as a wandering maniac—and again they feared she had been left to commit suicide; and many were the tears they shed at the loss of her.

But when she reached Berlin, Conn., she wrote to them by amanuensis, informing them of her where-abouts, and waiting an answer to her letter; thus quieting their fears, and gladdening their hearts once more with assurances of her continued life and her love.
—1850

Speech at the Akron, Ohio Women's Rights Convention, 1851

On the 29th of May 1851, Sojourner Truth attended a women's rights convention held at the Old Stone Church in Akron, Ohio, where she ventured before the crowd, apparently spontaneously, and delivered what would become one of the most famous speeches of the burgeoning women's rights movement. Numerous reports of her speech were published in newspapers at the time; most notable among them was that written by Marius Robinson for the Salem *Anti-Slavery Bugle*. Nearly twelve years later, another account was published in the 23 April 1863 issue of the *New York Independent*, written by Frances Dana Gage, who had presided over the 1851 Akron event. This version differed substantially from the earlier

---

[1]   *God is ... in all*   See 1 Corinthians 12.6: "And there are diversities of operations, but it is the same God which worketh all in all."

transcription, portraying Truth as speaking with a dialect that modern scholars argue was almost certainly not representative of her actual mode of speaking. Nevertheless, Gage's version was reprinted in an 1875 edition of the *Narrative of Sojourner Truth; A Bondswoman of Olden Time*, and again in Volume 1 of Elizabeth Cady Stanton's *History of Woman Suffrage* (1881). It prevailed as the standard rendition of Truth's speech well into the twentieth century.

[*1851 version*]

WOMEN'S RIGHTS CONVENTION

SOJOURNER TRUTH

One of the most unique and interesting speeches of the Convention was made by Sojourner Truth, an emancipated slave. It is impossible to transfer it to paper, or convey any adequate idea of the effect it produced upon the audience. Those only can appreciate it who saw her powerful form, her whole-souled, earnest gesture, and listened to her strong and truthful tones. She came forward to the platform and addressing the President said with great simplicity:

May I say a few words? Receiving an affirmative answer, she proceeded: I want to say a few words about this matter. I am a woman's rights. I have as much muscle as any man, and can do as much work as any man. I have plowed and reaped and husked and chopped and mowed, and can any man do more than that? I have heard much about the sexes being equal; I can carry as much as any man, and can eat as much too, if I can get it. I am as strong as any man that is now. As for intellect, all I can say is, if woman have a pint and man a quart—why can't she have her little pint full? You need not be afraid to give us our rights for fear we will take too much—for we can't take more than our pint'll hold. The poor men seem to be all in confusion, and don't know what to do. Why children, if you have woman's rights give it to her and you will feel better. You will have your own rights, and they won't be so much trouble. I can't read, but I can hear. I have heard the Bible and have learned that Eve caused man to sin. Well if woman upset the world, do give her a chance to set it right side up again. The Lady has spoken about

Jesus, how he never spurned woman from him, and she was right. When Lazarus died, Mary and Martha came to him with faith and love and besought him to raise their brother. And Jesus wept—and Lazarus came forth.[1] And how came Jesus into the world? Through God who created him and woman who bore him. Man, where is your part? But the women are coming up blessed by God and a few of the men are coming up with them. But man is in a tight place, the poor slave is on him, woman is coming on him, and he is surely between a hawk and a buzzard.

—1851

[*1875 version*]

The cause [of women's rights] was unpopular then. The leaders of the movement trembled on seeing a tall, gaunt black woman, in a gray dress and white turban, surmounted by an uncouth sun-bonnet, march deliberately into the church, walk with the air of a queen up the aisle, and take her seat upon the pulpit steps. A buzz of disapprobation was heard all over the house, and such words as these fell upon listening ears:

"An abolition affair!" "Woman's rights and niggers!" "We told you so!" "Go it, old darkey!"

I chanced upon that occasion to wear my first laurels in public life as president of the meeting. At my request, order was restored and the business of the hour went on. The morning session was held; the evening exercises came and went. Old Sojourner, quiet and reticent as the "Libyan Statue,"[2] sat crouched against the wall on the corner of the pulpit stairs, her sun-bonnet shading her eyes, her elbows on her knees, and her chin resting upon her broad, hard palm. At intermission she was busy, selling "The Life of Sojourner Truth," a narrative of her own strange and adventurous life. Again and again timorous and trembling ones came to me and said with earnestness, "Don't let her speak, Mrs.

1 *When Lazarus ... came forth* In John 11, Jesus is asked by Mary and Martha of Bethany to come to the aid of their ailing brother Lazarus. Jesus arrives in Bethany four days after Lazarus' death, but because of the sisters' faith, Jesus raises Lazarus from the dead.

2 *Libyan Statue* Reference to an 1861 marble sculpture by William Wetmore Story; see the contextual materials in the website component of this anthology.

Gage, it will ruin us. Every newspaper in the land will have our cause mixed with abolition and niggers, and we shall be utterly denounced." My only answer was, "We shall see when the time comes."

The second day the work waxed warm. Methodist, Baptist, Episcopal, Presbyterian, and Universalist ministers came in to hear and discuss the resolutions presented. One claimed superior rights and privileges for man on the ground of superior intellect; another, because of the manhood of Christ. "If God had desired the equality of woman, he would have given some token of his will through the birth, life, and death of the Saviour." Another gave us a theological view of the sin of our first mother. There were few women in those days that dared to "speak in meeting," and the august teachers of the people were seeming to get the better of us, while the boys in the galleries and the sneerers among the pews were hugely enjoying the discomfiture, as they supposed, of the "strong minded." Some of the tender-skinned friends were on the point of losing dignity, and the atmosphere of the convention betokened a storm.

Slowly from her seat in the corner rose Sojourner Truth, who, till now, had scarcely lifted her head. "Don't let her speak!" gasped half a dozen in my ear. She moved slowly and solemnly to the front, laid her old bonnet at her feet, and turned her great, speaking eyes to me. There was a hissing sound of disapprobation above and below. I rose and announced "Sojourner Truth," and begged the audience to keep silence for a few moments. The tumult subsided at once, and every eye was fixed on this almost Amazon[1] form, which stood nearly six feet high, head erect, and eye piercing the upper air, like one in a dream. At her first word, there was a profound hush. She spoke in deep tones, which, though not loud, reached every ear in the house, and away through the throng at the doors and windows:

"Well, chilern, whar dar is so much racket dar must be something out o' kilter. I tink dat 'twixt de niggers of de Souf and de women at de Norf all a talkin' 'bout rights, de white men will be in a fix pretty soon. But what's all dis here talkin' 'bout? Dat man ober dar say dat women needs to be helped into carriages, and lifted ober ditches, and to have de best place every whar. Nobody eber help me into carriages, or ober mud puddles, or gives me any best place," and raising herself to her full height and her voice to a pitch like rolling thunder, she asked, "and ar'n't I a woman? Look at me! Look at my arm!" And she bared her right arm to the shoulder, showing her tremendous muscular power. "I have plowed, and planted, and gathered into barns, and no man could head me—and ar'n't I a woman? I could work as much and eat as much as a man (when I could get it), and bear de lash as well—and ar'n't I a woman? I have borne thirteen chilern and seen 'em mos' all sold off into slavery,[2] and when I cried out with a mother's grief, none but Jesus heard—and ar'n't I a woman? Den dey talks 'bout dis ting in de head— what dis dey call it?" "Intellect," whispered some one near. "Dat's it honey. What's dat got to do with women's rights or nigger's rights? If my cup won't hold but a pint and yourn holds a quart, would n't ye be mean[3] not to let me have my little half-measure full?" And she pointed her significant finger and sent a keen glance at the minister who had made the argument. The cheering was long and loud.

"Den dat little man in black dar, he say woman can't have as much rights as man, cause Christ want[4] a woman. Whar did your Christ come from?" Rolling thunder could not have stilled that crowd as did those deep, wonderful tones, as she stood there with outstretched arms and eye of fire. Raising her voice still louder, she repeated, "Whar did your Christ come from? From God and a woman. Man had nothing to do with him." Oh! what a rebuke she gave the little man.

Turning again to another objector, she took up the defense of mother Eve.[5] I cannot follow her through

---

[1] *Amazon* Legendary race of tall, strong women warriors in Greek mythology.

[2] *I have ... into slavery* In fact, as Truth relates in her *Narrative*, she had only five children, all of whom were born into slavery, and all of whom she lived with until she left Dumont's farm in 1826. (One son was sold—illegally—to a slaveholder in Alabama shortly before New York emancipated all its enslaved inhabitants, but Truth successfully sued for his return.)

[3] *mean* Selfish; small-minded.

[4] *want* Wasn't.

[5] *defense of mother Eve* I.e., an attack against Christian arguments by which Eve is considered to have introduced sin to the world through her actions in the Garden of Eden, and thereby to have rendered all women sinful.

it all. It was pointed, and witty, and solemn, eliciting at almost every sentence deafening applause; and she ended by asserting that "if de fust woman God ever made was strong enough to turn the world upside down, all 'lone, dese togedder," and she glanced her eye over us, "ought to be able to turn it back and get it right side up again, and now dey is asking to do it, de men better let em." Long continued cheering. "Bleeged[1] to ye for hearin' on me, and now ole Sojourner ha'n't got nothing more to say."

Amid roars of applause, she turned to her corner, leaving more than one of us with streaming eyes and

hearts beating with gratitude. She had taken us up in her strong arms and carried us safely over the slough of difficulty, turning the whole tide in our favor. I have never in my life seen anything like the magical influence that subdued the mobbish spirit of the day and turned the jibes and sneers of an excited crowd into notes of respect and admiration. Hundreds rushed up to shake hands, and congratulate the glorious old mother and bid her God speed on her mission of "testifying again concerning the wickedness of this 'ere people."

—1875

IN CONTEXT

Sojourner Truth's *cartes de visite*

In the 1860s, Sojourner Truth started regularly posing for photographs, which she printed in mass and sold at speeches and events to fund her activist travels. In 1864 she began having her photographs copyrighted under her own name—as opposed to that of the photographer—and adding the distinctive caption: "I sell the Shadow to Support the Substance." Many of her early portraits were printed in the form of *cartes de visite*, small (approximately the size of modern playing cards), inexpensive photo cards that in the 1860s became hugely popular as collectors' items, especially those that depicted politicians and celebrities. The *carte de visite* was among several innovations in early photography that led many at the time to praise photography as democratizing the tradition of portraiture, both by making it more accessible and affordable and by making portraits easier to reproduce and share. In the late 1870s the *cartes de visite* format was largely supplanted by that of the somewhat larger cabinet card, and Truth adapted her practice to suit. She continued posing for and selling her photographs until not long before her death.

---

[1] *Bleeged* Obliged.

Photographer unknown. The first known extant photograph of Truth, this 1861 portrait depicts Truth just prior to her appearance at an event in Indiana, whose state constitution included an article forbidding African Americans from traveling into the state. Some reports suggest that Truth's unusual outfit, consisting of numerous layers of heavy, padded, red-white-and-blue garments, was given her by her white colleagues as a sort of coat of soft armor against the disorderly and potentially hostile crowd. Truth was also escorted to the event by the state's Home Guard. She was arrested and released several times over the course of her Indiana speaking tour, but her abolitionist following also grew with every speech.

Photographer unknown, 1864. This photograph is among the few which clearly show Truth's right hand, which had lost part of its index finger in an accident during her time enslaved by John Dumont.

I SELL THE SHADOW TO SUPPORT THE SUBSTANCE.
SOJOURNER TRUTH.

I Sell the Shadow to Support the Substance.
SOJOURNER TRUTH.

Photographer unknown, 1864. Knitting exploded in popularity during the Civil War, with many women knitting garments, especially socks, to be sent to the soldiers. Several photographs depict Truth with her knitting.

Photographer unknown, 1866. The framed portrait sitting on her lap is a photograph of her grandson, James Caldwell, who had fought with the 54th Massachusetts Regiment during the Civil War.

Randall Studio, c. 1870. The backdrop in this photograph (which would have been supplied by the studio) is among the most ornate of those to be seen in Truth's portraits.

AFRICAN AMERICAN ORAL LITERATURE

In a famous passage in his 1845 *Narrative of the Life of Frederick Douglass, an American Slave*, Douglass pays tribute to the vital importance that the music and oral literature created by enslaved African Americans had for his life, politics, and writing. He relates how his fellow enslaved people on a Maryland plantation "would compose and sing as they went along": "Every tone was a testimony against slavery[.] … Those songs still follow me, to deepen my hatred of slavery, and quicken my sympathies for my brethren in bonds." Douglass's sense of the power of such oral creations has today become nearly universal: African American oral literature is now commonly valued as a rich and compelling artform. This genre of music and oral storytelling attests to how enslaved people resisted dehumanization, maintained their creativity, and fostered a culture of their own, and it has wielded incalculable influence on the subsequent course of not just African American literature but the whole of American literature, culture, and language.

African American oral literature comprises a huge array of different forms, including spirituals (or, as W.E.B. Du Bois termed them, "sorrow songs"), work songs, and a variety of more irreverent or light-hearted songs and poems, as well as animal fables, supernatural tales, tall tales, and anecdotal narratives both serious and comic.[1] This varied body of literature stems from an equally wide array of sources. In the twentieth century, many scholars of slavery (including both white writers such as historian Stanley Elkins and black writers such as sociologist E. Franklin Frazier) argued that the experience of the Middle Passage and subsequent enslavement completely severed enslaved Africans from their previous identities and cultural traditions. While enslavement certainly constituted a profound culture shock, however, it is clear—as many African Americans had always known, and as black writers such as Du Bois and historian Carter G. Woodson were already emphasizing in the late nineteenth and early twentieth centuries—that enslaved people did in fact preserve and perpetuate stories, myths, characters, and traditions of storytelling, performance, and recitation from various African cultures. These African elements in African American oral literature include trickster tales centering on mythological figures such as the spider Anansi (who survived as Ah Nancy in the Gullah communities of the South Carolina and Georgia coast), the West African deities Eshu and Legba, and the trickster hares found in South, Central, and East African folklore—one potential source for the stories of Brer Rabbit.

The development of African American oral literature was also shaped by African institutions and practices such as the call-and-response mode of group recitation. In their explanation of this practice, the white editors of *Slave Songs of the United States* (1867), the first published collection of such songs, describe how call-and-response could serve as a form of improvisatory composition as well as performance: "the leading singer starts the words of each verse, often improvising, and the others, who 'base' him, as it is called, strike in with the refrain, or even join in the solo, when the words are familiar." Oral literature, which by definition requires the simultaneous presence of a speaker or speakers and a hearer or hearers, is inherently communal in a way that written literature is not; the solitary reader, privately taking in the disembodied written words of someone far distant from them in space, time, or both, has no equivalent in an oral-literary world. Call-and-response, by involving the whole group in the work of oral creation, amplifies this inherently communal nature. As a participatory, communal form that blurs the line between leader or speaker and audience and emphasizes (in the words of African American linguist Geneva Smitherman) "group cohesiveness, cooperation, and the collective common good," call-and-response embodies the creation and affirmation of community among enslaved people that was a core aim of black oral literature.

---

[1]   Though it is not included in the following section, being instead represented in the Nineteenth-Century Oratory section, included in the website component of this volume, as well as in individual author entries, African American oratory also certainly merits consideration as another variety of African American oral literature.

Alongside such enduring African legacies, the stories and songs of enslaved people also attest to the encounter with different cultural traditions that took place in America. Similarities between African American oral narratives (such as "Why Brer Possum Has No Hair on His Tail," a modern version of which is presented in this volume's website component) and Native American stories (such as "Why the Possum's Tail Is Bare," which appears in this volume's section on Indigenous Oral and Visual Literatures) have been noted ever since the former were first collected in the late nineteenth century; debate continues as to the primary direction of cultural transmission between African American and Native American oral literatures, but that there was cross-fertilization between the two literatures seems clear. Additionally, the culture of enslaved African Americans was shaped in more overt and immediate ways by that of Euro-American enslavers. The genre of the spiritual exemplifies how enslaved people took one of the centerpieces of the Euro-American culture imposed on them, Christianity, and made it into a source of consolation, an expression of their deepest aspirations, and even a means of resistance.

African American oral literature often repurposes the materials it draws from various different cultural traditions to codify and express the experience of living through slavery, as well as the hope of escape. Spirituals, for instance, abundantly attest to enslaved people's yearning for freedom, in their ubiquitous expressions of longing for deliverance from hardship and suffering and their frequent references to the biblical story of the Israelites' escape from slavery in Egypt. In addition, particular songs such as "Swing Low, Sweet Chariot" and "Steal Away" have been interpreted as coded messages referring specifically to escape plans or attempts. (Whether enslaved people actually used such so-called "Underground Railroad songs" in these ways, though, has been disputed.) Similarly, a longstanding interpretation of trickster tales such as those of Brer Rabbit—in which smaller and weaker creatures such as rabbits consistently escape and even prevail over larger, more powerful predators by means of their wits—views them as describing the means whereby enslaved people could survive and resist their enslavers; as Abigail Christensen, one of the first collectors of these tales, succinctly put it, "The Rabbit represents the colored man." More recent interpreters, however, have called into question this view as well, pointing to the fact that the weaker animals in these stories sometimes behave just as unscrupulously, obtusely, and even cruelly as the predators, in ways that complicate any easy correspondence to enslavers and enslaved.

Whether or not it specifically addressed the circumstances of life under slavery, enslaved people's oral literature was crucial for surviving enslavement and for imagining—and enacting—an identity not defined or confined by it. In their oral creations, enslaved black people used what was available to them, from their own cultural pasts as well as from the other cultural traditions they had assimilated, to forge community, wield agency, and show that there was more to them than the fact of their enslavement. It is in this sense, even more than on the level of content, that, in Douglass's words, "every tone" of his fellow enslaved people's songs "was a testimony against slavery." In this way, black oral literature is intrinsically a literature of hope and resistance. The strategies, mentalities, and practices that fostered and were fostered by enslaved people's oral culture would go on to inform the attitudes of African Americans towards literacy and written literature, according to which—as the scholar Gholdy Muhammad has put it of the literary societies developed in the nineteenth century by black people in the North—literacy and literature were fundamentally about "liberation and power."

While the oral literature of enslaved people was first and foremost something they created among and for themselves, black oral culture—song in particular—was already appealing to certain white observers by the mid-eighteenth century. Samuel Davies, a Presbyterian minister who evangelized to enslaved people in Virginia from 1748 to 1759 (and whose missionary work likely inspired a spiritual, "Lord, I Want to Be a Christian"), described the religious singing of his African American parishioners as "a torrent of sacred harmony" that "carried my mind away to Heaven," while Thomas Jefferson noted more clinically some years later that enslaved people "are more generally gifted than the whites with accurate ears for tune and time." Others were more dismissive: in 1819, the Philadelphia minister John Fanning Watson condemned as "a growing evil" the songs "composed and first sung by the illiterate *blacks* of the society," which he called "miserable as poetry, and senseless as matter." In the decades after Watson wrote, blackface minstrelsy, with its racist white representations and parodies of black musical culture, became an enormously popular genre of mass entertainment: the first—but certainly not the last—white American appropriation of a black American expressive form. Despite—or because of—minstrelsy's popularity (and despite the fact that certain African Americans performed in minstrel shows and even formed their own troupes), practically no examples of actual African American song were collected or published until the 1860s; Frederick Douglass's printing, in *My Bondage and My Freedom* (1855), of the slave song beginning "We raise de wheat," presented in this section's website component, is one of the few exceptions.

The first intensive efforts to record black oral literature in print took place during, and because of, the Civil War, which brought large numbers of white Northern intellectuals—mainly abolitionists belonging to or accompanying the Union Army—into sustained contact with communities of enslaved or formerly-enslaved people for the first time. Some of these white observers admired the songs they heard from the black people they worked with and arranged for their publication. The words and music for two such songs, including "Poor Rosy, Poor Gal" (in this anthology's online component), were published in Philadelphia in 1862 by Lucy McKim, the twenty-year-old daughter of an antislavery Pennsylvania family. Five years later, McKim (who by then had married the son of the antislavery leader William Lloyd Garrison) collaborated with two other abolitionists, William Francis Allen and Charles Pickard Ware—both of whom, like her, had spent time during the war with the African American inhabitants of the Sea Islands off the South Carolina and Georgia coast—to publish *Slave Songs of the United States*. This pioneering collection assembled 136 African American songs from throughout the states practicing slavery, but primarily from the Sea Islands; most were spirituals, but the collection also included non-religious songs such as "Charleston Gals" and "Run, N—, Run!"

The musical, poetic dimension of African American oral literature was further popularized in the decade after the Civil War by the Fisk Jubilee Singers, an a cappella ensemble founded in 1871 to raise funds for Fisk University, a black educational institution in Nashville, Tennessee. The Singers' tours gave many white Americans their first real exposure to black music; according to one reviewer of the group, "Those who have only heard the burnt cork caricatures of negro minstrelsy have not the slightest conception of what it really is." (The Singers had, however, learned Euro-American musical and choral conventions from George White, the white Northern teacher who organized the group, and they were likely able to connect with white audiences in part because their manner of performing spirituals was adapted to these Euro-American conventions.) When the Singers began touring, many African Americans resisted disseminating spirituals beyond their own communities, though for divergent reasons. Some black people viewed spirituals as relics of an enslaved past that they did not wish to perpetuate, while others saw these songs as profoundly meaningful centerpieces of their own culture and hence resisted sharing them with white audiences, precisely because—as Ella Sheppard, one of the most prominent of the Jubilee Singers, put it—"they were sacred to our parents." The Singers themselves only reluctantly agreed to the idea of performing spirituals, when this was first broached by the white managers of the group, but once (in Sheppard's words) "we began to appreciate the wonderful beauty and power of our songs," they collected and arranged over one hundred for their repertoire, many of which were published in *The Story of the Jubilee Singers; With Their Songs* (1877). By then, the Jubilee Singers had become internationally popular, introducing spirituals to white audiences that included the likes of Mark Twain and Queen Victoria (while also experiencing constant racial discrimination in the process). How their popularization of spirituals was viewed by other African Americans is harder to gauge; black periodicals, notably, gave the Singers practically no coverage. The Singers did win the esteem of black leaders such as Douglass, however, and their efforts helped make the case within their own community, as well as beyond it, that this aspect of the black oral tradition had enduring value and could resonate with audiences very different from the groups that had birthed it.

Other collections of the song and poetry of enslaved people continued to appear into the twentieth century; a volume published in 1922 by the Fisk University chemistry professor Thomas W. Talley, *Negro Folk Rhymes: Wise and Otherwise*, deserves particular mention as the first such collection published by an African American scholar, as well as one of the first to emphasize other genres besides spirituals. In the meantime, another dimension of black oral literature had also been made extensively available to a mass readership: prose folktales. By far the most influential collector and transmitter of such tales was

Joel Chandler Harris, a white Southerner whose 1880 book *Uncle Remus: His Songs and His Sayings: The Folk-lore of the Old Plantation* threaded together stories Harris heard during the Civil War years from several enslaved people at a plantation in Georgia, presenting them in a frame story as narratives told to a young white boy by the fictional "Uncle Remus." The book, in which the exploits of Brer Rabbit featured prominently, was a bestseller, and Harris followed it up with eight other Uncle Remus collections (three of them posthumous). Undeniably significant in American literary history, Harris's work also remains deeply controversial: critics debate whether his collections should be primarily seen as works of preservation or appropriation, as well as how to weigh his commitment, as a politically-engaged journalist and editor, to racial reconciliation and equality in the Reconstruction-era South against his books' idealization of "the old plantation."

Harris, however, was neither the first nor the only collector of African American oral prose. Abigail Christensen, a folklorist who spent most of her life in South Carolina after moving there from Massachusetts with her abolitionist parents, published a version of the story of Brer Rabbit and the Tar-Baby that she heard on the Sea Islands (which appears in the website component of this volume) in 1874, six years before Harris's first book appeared, leading an admirer to dub her "The Original Uncle Remus." Christensen's full collection, *Afro-American Folk Lore: Told Round Cabin Fires on the Sea Islands of South Carolina*, was published in 1892. Other notable collectors of black folktales during this period included Robert Roosevelt—uncle of future president Theodore Roosevelt, who also preceded Harris in the publication of Brer Rabbit stories—and Alcée Fortier, whose research into Louisiana Creole culture included documenting stories about that tradition's equivalent of Brer Rabbit, "Compair Lapin."

The work of studying and publishing the oral culture of enslaved black people continued into the twentieth century, carried forward by both white and black collectors. One of the best-known stories today to have come out of slavery, "All God's Chillen Had Wings," was recorded by the Ohio-born white writer John Bennett, who followed in Abigail Christensen's footsteps by moving to South Carolina and developing an interest in the language and culture of the local Gullah people. Bennett first heard a version of a widespread story of people flying away from slavery in 1907; however, his research scandalized Charleston's white upper-class society (into which he had married), and he did not publish this and other stories he collected until the 1940s. African American documenters of the oral literature of slavery include some of the foremost names in twentieth-century African American literature, such as W.E.B. Du Bois—who ended his epochal *The Souls of Black Folk* (1903) with an influential study of the nature and importance of the "sorrow songs"—and Zora Neale Hurston, an academically-trained anthropologist who collected black Southern folktales, including stories of slavery like "Big Sixteen," which she published in the collection *Mules and Men* (1935).

Hurston's and Du Bois's work with black oral literature also highlights the degree to which, as a creative medium fundamentally tied to live speech or song, this literature eludes, and can even be distorted by, representation in print. Hurston's collections attest to this issue precisely because of the care she took to contextualize the stories she heard in the circumstances in which they were related; her attempts to bring readers as close to these circumstances as possible also have the effect of foregrounding the inevitable difference and distance between readers and hearers. Du Bois, for his part, identified something intangible in the "sorrow songs" that could be fully conveyed only in person, not on the page: "the true Negro folk-song ... lives in the hearts of those who have heard them truly sung and in the hearts of the Negro people." The fact that, as oral literature, African American spirituals or folktales cannot be encapsulated by—or bound by—any one printed version of them has been embraced by such recent transmitters of this literature as Julius Lester, who rewrote Harris's "Uncle Remus" stories in the 1980s and 90s to make them better able to speak to a contemporary American audience—not least by removing the condescending if not demeaning aspects of Harris's renderings.

As the oral literature of enslaved people has undergone repeated revitalization and reinvention, this literature has also powerfully shaped American literature and culture from the late nineteenth century on. Just as it inspired Douglass, so black oral literature has galvanized the work of numerous African American writers since his time, from Du Bois and Hurston, through Langston Hughes, Ralph Ellison, and Richard Wright, to Alice Walker and Toni Morrison. In addition, some of the foremost white American writers, including Mark Twain and William Faulkner, owe a deep stylistic and thematic debt to African American oral culture. Brer Rabbit stories have become a cornerstone of modern children's literature (while also continuing to interest and delight adult readers); the words and themes of the spirituals are integrally woven into the fabric of American life and resonate around the world; and the musical traditions that originated in slavery have become one of the most all-pervasive forces in American culture, engendering gospel, the blues, and jazz (and thence rock 'n' roll and its descendants in modern popular culture), as well as influencing countless novelists and poets, including writers as different as T.S. Eliot and Allen Ginsberg. If, in the early twentieth century, John Bennett, disappointed by the initial reception of the Gullah folktales he had collected, could only hope that "maybe somebody, some day, will appreciate these really uncommon things," today that hope has been abundantly realized. Not only do the songs and stories crafted by enslaved people, in Douglass's words, "still follow" all Americans; in important respects, they have led the country on its ongoing literary, cultural, and political journey.

––––––––––––––––

NOTE ON THE TEXTS: The works included in the following section were selected with an eye to conveying something of the breadth and diversity of African American oral literature: song and poetry as well as oral prose, non-religious as well as religious material, relatively obscure works as well as famous ones. Some of the works included in this section, such as the songs from *Slave Songs of the United States*, were initially printed in a rendition—often, but not always, a white editor's or collector's rendition—of an African American dialect, while other works, such as the songs from *The Story of the Jubilee Singers* and "All God's Chillen Had Wings," were initially printed in standard English. In all cases, the style and form of a work's initial publication has been retained.

⌘ ⌘ ⌘

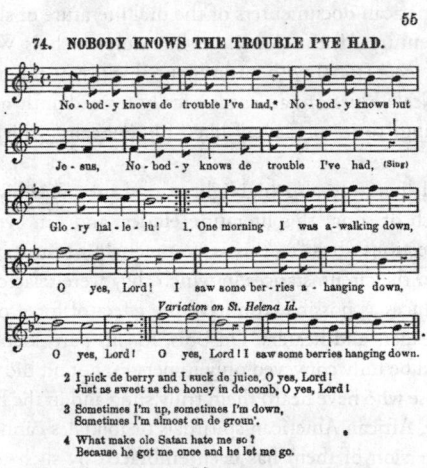

"Nobody Knows the Trouble I've Had," as printed in *Slave Songs of the United States* (1867). This song, under the alternate title "Nobody Knows the Trouble I've Seen," has since become one of the most famous and often-performed African American spirituals.

ROLL, JORDAN, ROLL[1]

as recorded by Lucy McKim Garrison, William Francis Allen, and Charles Pickard Ware, *Slave Songs of the United States* (1867)

My brudder[2] sittin' on de tree of life,
An' he yearde° when Jordan[3] roll.   *hear*

[Chorus]
Roll, Jordan, Roll,
Roll, Jordan Roll!
5   O march de angel march,
O march de angel march;
O my soul arise in Heaven, Lord,
For to yearde when Jordan roll.

Little chil'en, learn to fear de Lord,
10 And let your days be long.

O, let no false nor spiteful word
Be found upon your tongue.

MICHAEL ROW THE BOAT ASHORE

as recorded by Lucy McKim Garrison, William Francis Allen, and Charles Pickard Ware, *Slave Songs of the United States* (1867)

Michael[4] row the boat ashore, Hallelujah!
Michael boat a gospel boat, Hallelujah!

I wonder where my mudder deh,° Hallelujah!   *there*
See my mudder on de rock gwine° home,   *going*
   Hallelujah!
5   On de rock gwine home in Jesus' name, Hallelujah!
Michael boat a music boat, Hallelujah!
Gabriel blow de trumpet horn,[5] Hallelujah!
O you mind your boastin' talk, Hallelujah!
Boastin' talk will sink your soul, Hallelujah!
10 Brudder, lend a helpin' hand, Hallelujah!
Sister, help for trim dat boat, Hallelujah!
Jordan stream is wide and deep, Hallelujah!
Jesus stand on t' oder side, Hallelujah!
I wonder if my maussa deh, Hallelujah!
15 My fader gone to unknown land, Hallelujah!
O de Lord he plant his garden deh, Hallelujah!
He raise de fruit for you to eat, Hallelujah!
He dat eat shall neber die, Hallelujah!
When de riber overflow, Hallelujah!
20 O poor sinner, how you land? Hallelujah!
Riber run and darkness comin', Hallelujah!
Sinner row to save your soul, Hallelujah!

Words from Hilton Head[6]
Michael haul the boat ashore.
Then you'll hear the horn they blow.
Then you'll hear the trumpet sound.
Trumpet sound the world around.
Trumpet sound for rich and poor.
Trumpet sound the jubilee,[7]
Trumpet sound for you and me.

---

[1]   *ROLL, JORDAN, ROLL*   According to the editors of *Slave Songs of the United States*, "This spiritual probably extends from South Carolina to Florida, and is one of the best known and noblest of the songs."

[2]   *My brudder*   The editors of *Slave Songs of the United States* note, as variants of these words in other renditions of the song, "Parson Fuller, Deacon Henshaw, Brudder Mosey [Moses], Massa Linkum [Lincoln], etc."

[3]   *Jordan*   The Jordan River, which today forms the boundary between Israel and the West Bank, on one side, and Jordan, on the other, has great symbolic significance in the Jewish and Christian traditions. According to the Bible, the Israelites entered the Promised Land, after their escape from slavery in Egypt, by crossing the Jordan, and Jesus was later baptized in it at the beginning of his ministry. The Jordan was also frequently used to symbolize the transition from this world to the next.

[4]   *Michael*   According to Christian tradition, the archangel Michael conducts souls to the afterlife and protects the souls of the virtuous from Satan.

[5]   *Gabriel ... horn*   In Christian tradition, the second coming of Christ, and the consequent Last Judgment, will be heralded by a trumpet blown by the archangel Gabriel; this motif appears frequently in African American spirituals.

[6]   *Hilton Head*   Island off the coast of South Carolina, one of the Sea Islands that extend along the South Carolina, Georgia, and Florida coasts. The version of the song given previously was first recorded on St. Helena Island, another of the Sea Islands not far from Hilton Head.

[7]   *jubilee*   The biblical Book of Leviticus mandates a Jubilee year every fiftieth year, in which debts would be forgiven and slaves and prisoners set free: "Then shalt thou cause the trumpet of the jubilee to sound[.] ... And ye shall hallow the fiftieth year, and proclaim liberty throughout all the land unto all the inhabitants thereof: it shall be a jubilee unto you; and ye shall return every man unto his possession, and ye shall return every man unto his family" (Leviticus 25.9–10).

CHARLESTON GALS

as recorded by Lucy McKim Garrison, William Francis
Allen, and Charles Pickard Ware, *Slave Songs of the United
States* (1867)

As I walked down the new-cut road,
I met the tap[1] and then the toad;
The toad commenced to whistle and sing,
And the possum cut the pigeon-wing.[2]

5   Along come an old man riding by:
Old man, if you don't mind,[3] your horse will die;
If he dies I'll tan his skin,
And if he lives I'll ride him agin.
Hi ho, for Charleston gals!
10 Charleston gals are the gals for me.

As I went a-walking down the street,
Up steps Charleston gals to take a walk with me.
I kep' a-walking and they kep' a-talking,
I danced with a gal with a hole in her stocking.

SWING LOW, SWEET CHARIOT

as recorded in J.B.I. Marsh, ed., *The Story of the Jubilee
Singers; With Their Songs* (1877)

[Chorus]
Swing low, sweet chariot,
Coming for to carry me home,[4]
Swing low, sweet chariot,
Coming for to carry me home.

5   I looked over Jordan, and what did I see,
Coming for to carry me home?
A band of angels coming after me,
Coming for to carry me home.

If you get there before I do,
10 Coming for to carry me home,
Tell all my friends I'm coming too,
Coming for to carry me home.

The brightest day that ever I saw,
Coming for to carry me home,
15 When Jesus washed my sins away,
Coming for to carry me home.

I'm sometimes up and sometimes down,
Coming for to carry me home,
But still my soul feels heavenly bound,
20 Coming for to carry me home.

MANY THOUSAND GONE

as recorded in J.B.I. Marsh, ed., *The Story of the Jubilee
Singers; With Their Songs* (1877)

No more auction block for me,
No more, no more;
No more auction block for me,
Many thousand gone.

5   No more peck o' corn[5] for me,
No more, no more;
No more peck o' corn for me,
Many thousand gone.

No more driver's lash for me,
10 No more, no more;
No more driver's lash for me,
Many thousand gone.

No more pint o' salt[6] for me,

---

[1]   *tap*   Terrapin, a type of turtle (often abbreviated "t'apin," and
thence "tap").

[2]   *cut the pigeon-wing*   The "pigeon wing" was a dance move that
imitated a bird.

[3]   *if you don't mind*   I.e., if you're not careful.

[4]   *Swing … home*   In the Second Book of Kings, the great Israelite
prophet Elijah, at the end of his life, is taken up to heaven by "a
chariot of fire" in the view of his disciple and successor Elisha after
crossing the River Jordan. See 2 Kings 2.1–12.

[5]   *peck o' corn*   A peck is a unit of measure equivalent to two gallons. A "peck of corn" would have been the ration of corn given to
enslaved fieldworkers (corn being less valued than other foods).

[6]   *pint o' salt*   Compare Frederick Douglass's description, in his
autobiography *The Life and Times of Frederick Douglass* (1881), of the
rations at the plantation at which he was enslaved: "The men and the
women slaves on Col. Lloyd's farm received as their monthly allowance of food, eight pounds of pickled pork, or its equivalent in fish.
The pork was often tainted, and the fish were of the poorest quality.
With their pork or fish, they had given them one bushel of Indian
meal [corn] … of which quite fifteen per cent. was more fit for pigs
than for men. With this one pint of salt was given, and this was the

No more, no more;
15 No more pint o' salt for me,
Many thousand gone.

No more hundred lash for me,
No more, no more;
No more hundred lash for me,
20 Many thousand gone.

No more mistress's call for me,
No more, no more;
No more mistress's call for me,
Many thousand gone.

SLAVE MARRIAGE CEREMONY SUPPLEMENT
as recorded by Thomas W. Talley, *Negro Folk Rhymes: Wise and Otherwise, With a Study* (1922)

Dark an' stormy may come de wedder;
I jines dis he-male an' dis she-male togedder.
Let none, but Him dat makes de thunder,
Put dis he-male an' dis she-male asunder.
5 I darfore 'nounce you bofe de same.
Be good, go 'long, an' keep up yo' name.
De broomstick's jumped,[1] de worl's not wide.
She's now yo' own. Salute yo' bride!

ALL GOD'S CHILLEN HAD WINGS
as recorded by John Bennett, *Doctor to the Dead* (1943, 1946)

Once all Africans could fly like birds; but owing to their many transgressions, their wings were taken away. There remained, here and there, in the Sea Islands and out-of-the-way places in the low country,[2]

some who had been overlooked, and had retained the power of flight, though they looked like other men.

There was a cruel master on one of the sea islands who worked his people till they died. When they died he bought others to take their places. These also he killed with overwork in the burning summer sun, through the middle hours of the day, although this was against the law.

One day, when all the worn-out Negroes were dead of overwork, he bought, of a broker in the town, a company of native Africans just brought into the country, and put them at once to work in the cottonfield.

He drove them hard. They went to work at sunrise and did not stop until dark. They were driven with unsparing harshness all day long, men, women and children. There was no pause for rest during the unendurable heat of the midsummer noon, though trees were plenty and near. But through the hardest hours, when fair plantations gave their Negroes rest, this man's driver pushed the work along without a moment's stop for breath, until all grew weak with heat and thirst.

There was among them one young woman who had lately borne a child. It was her first; she had not fully recovered from bearing, and should not have been sent to the field until her strength had come back. She had her child with her, as the other women had, astraddle on her hip, or piggyback.

The baby cried. She spoke to quiet it. The driver could not understand her words. She took her breast with her hand and threw it over her shoulder that the child might suck and be content. Then she went back to chopping knot-grass; but being very weak, and sick with the great heat, she stumbled, slipped and fell.

The driver struck her with his lash until she rose and staggered on.

She spoke to an old man near her, the oldest man of them all, tall and strong, with a forked beard. He replied; but the driver could not understand what they said; their talk was strange to him.

She returned to work; but in a little while she fell again. Again the driver lashed her until she got to her feet. Again she spoke to the old man. But he said:

---

entire monthly allowance of a full-grown slave, working constantly in the open field from morning till night every day in the month except Sunday."

[1] *De broomstick's jumped* During the 1840s and 50s, it became a widespread practice at marriages between enslaved people for the newly-married couple to jump over a broomstick. Because slave marriages were not legally recognized, jumping over the broomstick served as a public ceremony symbolizing the couple's commitment. The practice still forms part of some African American marriage ceremonies today.

[2] *Sea Islands* Chain of islands off the coast of South Carolina, Georgia, and Florida; *low country* Coastal region of South Carolina and Georgia, including the Sea Islands as well as the

mainland coastal plain. The enslaved African Americans brought to work on the cotton, indigo, and rice plantations of the Low Country developed a distinctive creole language, known as Gullah, and a culture that preserved many aspects of various African traditions.

"Not yet, daughter; not yet." So she went on working, though she was very ill.

Soon she stumbled and fell again. But when the driver came running with his lash to drive her on with her work, she turned to the old man and asked: "Is it time yet, daddy?" He answered: "Yes, daughter; the time has come. Go; and peace be with you!" ... and stretched out his arms toward her ... so.

With that she leaped straight up into the air and was gone like a bird, flying over field and wood.

The driver and overseer ran after her as far as the edge of the field; but she was gone, high over their heads, over the fence, and over the top of the woods, gone, with her baby astraddle of her hip, sucking at her breast.

Then the driver hurried the rest to make up for her loss; and the sun was very hot indeed. So hot that soon a man fell down. The overseer himself lashed him to his feet. As he got up from where he had fallen the old man called to him in an unknown tongue. My grandfather told me the words he said; but it was a long time ago, and I have forgotten them. But when he had spoken, the man turned and laughed at the overseer, and leaped up into the air, and was gone, like a gull, flying over field and wood.

Soon another man fell. The driver lashed him. He turned to the old man. The old man cried out to him, and stretched out his arms as he had done for the other two; and he, like them, leaped up, and was gone through the air, flying like a bird over field and wood.

Then the overseer cried to the driver, and the master cried to them both: "Beat the old devil! He is the doer!"

The overseer and the driver ran at the old man with lashes ready; and the master ran too, with a picket pulled from the fence, to beat the life out of the old man who had made those Negroes fly.

But the old man laughed in their faces, and said something loudly to all the Negroes in the field, the new Negroes and the old Negroes.

And as he spoke to them they all remembered what they had forgotten, and recalled the power which once had been theirs. Then all the Negroes, old and new, stood up together; the old man raised his hands; and they all leaped up into the air with a great shout; and in a moment were gone, flying, like a flock of crows, over the field, over the fence, and over the top of the wood; and behind them flew the old man.

The men went clapping their hands; and the women went singing; and those who had children gave them their breasts; and the children laughed and sucked as their mothers flew, and were not afraid.

The master, the overseer, and the driver looked after them as they flew, beyond the wood, beyond the river, miles on miles, until they passed beyond the last rim of the world and disappeared in the sky like a handful of leaves. They were never seen again.

Where they went I do not know; I never was told. Nor what it was that the old man said ... that I have forgotten. But as he went over the last fence he made a sign in the master's face, and cried "Kuli-ba! Kuli-ba!" I don't know what that means.

But if I could only find the old wood sawyer,[1] he could tell you more; for he was there at the time, and saw the Africans fly away with their women and children. He is an old, old man, over ninety years of age, and remembers a great many things.

As told by Caesar Grant, of John's Island,[2] carter and laborer.

---

[1] *wood sawyer* Workman who saws wood.

[2] *John's Island* Coastal island near Charleston, South Carolina; the largest of the Sea Islands.

HARRIET BEECHER STOWE

1811 – 1896

Harriet Beecher Stowe's first novel, *Uncle Tom's Cabin* (1852), may well have excited more controversy than any other work of fiction in American history. In the 1850s it was welcomed by abolitionists for the impetus it gave to their movement—and met with furious indignation by white Southerners. Its characters and dramatic scenes were absorbed into the nation's consciousness, and the novel spawned—largely without Stowe's approval—a veritable industry of crude "Tom shows" whose characters hardened into racist cultural artefacts, at once wildly popular and routinely mocked. By the mid-twentieth century, *Uncle Tom's Cabin* was widely dismissed as irrelevant politically, a failure artistically, and—in what would have struck readers of the 1850s as an extraordinary irony—pervasively racist in its portrayal of black people. In our own century, its estimation as literature and as a political work engaged with the most serious political and moral questions of its era has continued to fluctuate wildly, although no one can deny its significance or popularity.

Harriet Beecher was born in Litchfield, Connecticut in 1811, the seventh child of Lyman Beecher, a Congregational minister, and Roxana Foote Beecher. Roxana died in 1816; her death (and subsequent idolization in the family's collective memory) had a lasting psychological impact upon Stowe. Lyman (who promptly remarried, and had four more children) was a strong shaping force in her life in large part through his passionate Calvinist religious convictions.

Stowe attended the Litchfield Female Academy and later her elder sister Catharine's Hartford Female Seminary, an influential and progressive institution that, in addition to teaching the "domestic arts," offered a level of academic instruction rarely available to young women in the early nineteenth century. Stowe proved an enthusiastic student with a particular talent for writing, especially on moral, philosophical, and religious themes. By 1827 her formal education was considered complete and she took on a teaching position at the Seminary, where she remained for five more years.

In 1832 the Beecher family moved to Cincinnati, Ohio, a rapidly growing city then considered the westernmost outpost of "civilized" America. The following year Harriet and Catharine together wrote and published a geography textbook, *Primary Geography for Children*, which sold well; they also helped form the Semi-Colon Club, an informal literary association where Stowe received encouragement to start writing sketches (some of which were published in the local *Western Monthly Magazine*). In 1836 she met and married Calvin Stowe, a teacher at the Lane Seminary where her father taught; they had their first children, twin daughters, later that year. The couple had a companionate, intellectually fulfilling relationship, though differences in their temperaments and Calvin's frequent trips away from home in the early years of their marriage led to recurring tensions.

In the mid-1830s, Cincinnati, just across the border from the slave state of Kentucky, saw an explosion in public debate over slavery, with radical abolitionists increasingly unwilling to tolerate the passive antislavery sentiments of respected community leaders such as Lyman Beecher. Several anti- and pro-slavery riots shook the city; in their aftermath, many of the Beecher children, including Stowe, began to distance themselves from their father's careful tolerance of slavery and to interest themselves in the movement for immediate abolition.

To supplement the income for her growing family, Stowe began in the late 1830s to write short fiction for commercial magazines, including the new and increasingly popular *Godey's Lady's Book*; she experimented with various genres including brief domestic sketches, tales of the frontier, and religious and morally instructive stories. Her stories were in sufficient demand that in 1843 a selection was published in Boston in book form as *The Mayflower*. Throughout much of the 1840s, however, Stowe wrote little fiction; tensions in her marriage were recurrent, and household duties were utterly exhausting (by the end of the 1840s she would have six children, five of them living; her seventh child was born in 1850).

At the end of the decade, two dramatic events combined to provide Stowe with the impetus to begin writing *Uncle Tom's Cabin*. The first was the death of her infant son, Charley, during a cholera epidemic in 1849; Stowe's grief and devastation would inform much of her depiction of the sufferings of enslaved women and mothers in the novel. The second was the passage of the Fugitive Slave Act in September 1850. Part of the Compromise of 1850—a package of federal legislation meant to diffuse the increasing political tensions between the North and the South—the Act protected the right of slaveowners to pursue individuals who had fled North and re-enslave them; more than that, it required Northerners to assist in the pursuit, and threatened substantial fines or jail time for those found to be assisting fugitives. The Act was widely hated in the North, and made the injustices of slavery impossible to ignore. Stowe, who was already a supporter of immediate abolition, was enraged by the Fugitive Slave Act—"I have felt almost choked sometimes with pent-up wrath that does no good," she wrote to her sister. But her rage was transformative. She turned toward what was arguably the most effective means for American women to have their say in moral and political affairs—the pen.

The first installment of *Uncle Tom's Cabin* was published in the Washington, D.C., abolitionist paper *The National Era* on 5 June 1851, the last on 1 April 1852. The novel follows the interrelated stories of several enslaved characters: George Harris, a mixed-race man who defies his cruel enslaver and escapes to Canada; his wife Eliza, who flees her otherwise "kind" enslaver when she discovers he intends to sell both her and her young son; and the titular Uncle Tom, a deeply pious middle-aged man who is sold onto a Louisiana plantation and defies slavery not through violence or escape but through Christian forbearance. The serialized novel was moderately successful, eliciting many passionate responses from readers who wrote Stowe to share their feelings. However, it was the novel's publication in book format on 20 March 1852 that turned *Uncle Tom's Cabin* into a phenomenon. "Reader, buy *Uncle Tom's Cabin*," commanded an 1852 review in the New Hampshire *Morning Star*; "By all means do not go out of this world without having read 'the Story of the Age.'" The two-volume book became a bestseller almost overnight, selling over ten thousand copies in its first few days and over 300,000 within the year in the United States alone. In Britain (which had abolished slavery in the 1830s), it sold over one million copies in its first year.

As influential literary figure Edwin Percy Whipple observed in an 1876 essay in *Harper's Monthly Magazine*, the publication of *Uncle Tom's Cabin* turned out to be "an important political event. It was one of the most powerful agencies in building up the Republican party, in electing Abraham Lincoln to the Presidency,[1] and in raising earnest volunteers for the great crusade against slavery." The novel was widely praised for its effective combination of political suasion, religious feeling, and sentiment. And, as one letter-writer put it, the story was "peculiarly calculated to enlist the moral and religious sympathies, and call to action the latent energies of the female heart." But while the novel's sentimental rhetoric in many ways sought to appeal to women particularly, male readers were clearly affected too: the story of prominent newspaper editor Horace Greeley, who was said to have sobbed his way through the book in a hotel room in Ohio, is far from unique. The narrative inspired writers such as William Wells Brown and Mary Hayden Green Pike to write abolitionist novels of their own, and it inspired poets as well—including Quaker abolitionist John Greenleaf Whittier and activist Frances Ellen Watkins Harper (whose 1854 "Eliza Harris" is directly based on the novel).

In the other direction, countless proslavery apologists characterized Stowe's novel as an "infamous book of lies," and some questioned the propriety of Stowe's delving into the subject at all—as a Northerner, and as a woman. As one reviewer for *The Southern Literary Messenger* put it, "It is a horrible

---

[1]   The most frequently recounted Stowe anecdote concerns Lincoln, who is said to have greeted her in 1862 with these words: "So you're the little woman who wrote the book that made this great war." But the anecdote, which originated decades after the fact in family lore, cannot be said to have any basis in fact. Stowe and Lincoln did meet in November of 1862, but there is no reliable record of their conversation.

thought that a woman should write or a lady should read such productions as those by which [Stowe's] celebrity has been acquired." Proslavery authors began writing "anti-Tom" novels—novels portraying a romanticized view of the South and of relations between the enslaver and the enslaved; Virginia author Mary Henderson Eastman's *Aunt Phillis's Cabin; or Southern Life as It Is* (1852) enjoyed considerable popularity in the North as well as in the South.

Though most abolitionists welcomed Stowe's success in awakening "the strongest compassion for the oppressed and the utmost abhorrence of the system which grinds them to the dust" (as William Lloyd Garrison put in *The Liberator*), Garrison and others were deeply uncomfortable with the degree to which Stowe portrayed passivity in the face of oppression to be appropriate for the enslaved; they found the portrayal of the titular Uncle Tom particularly troubling in this respect. The novel's conclusion—which appears to endorse the controversial, primarily white-led movement to transport free African Americans to the colony of Liberia—was also deeply troubling to many. (Stowe would renounce the colonizationist movement in later years, partly as a result of her correspondence with the black abolitionist and anti-colonizationist Frederick Douglass.)

In 1853, Stowe responded to charges that she was ill-qualified to tackle the subject of slavery with *A Key to Uncle Tom's Cabin*, in which she provided exhaustive documentation of the facts on which she had based her novel (and also revealed that the character of Uncle Tom had been heavily based on that of the formerly enslaved minister Josiah Henson). The Stowes subsequently embarked on a tour of England and continental Europe, where her novel's egalitarian themes resonated with many who had supported the various democratic revolutions of 1848.

Stowe's next book was a second novel, *Dred: A Tale of the Great Dismal Swamp* (1856), which offered a more radical view of the struggle against slavery; her detailed appendix of research sources made it clear that her title character was a composite of the early nineteenth-century slave revolt leaders Nat Turner and Denmark Vesey. *Dred* sold modestly well, but had far less impact on America than had *Uncle Tom's Cabin*. Stowe's fame nevertheless continued unabated; she wrote several more novels over the next decade, including *The Minister's Wooing* (1859), a work set in eighteenth-century New England that turned a critical eye on the legacy of Calvinism, and *A Pearl of Orr's Island: A Story of the Coast of Maine* (1862).

Stowe's career was sufficiently lucrative that Calvin decided to retire in early 1864. Stowe courted controversy again in 1869 with "The True Story of Lady Byron's Life," which discussed English poet Lord Byron's incestuous affair with his half sister; though rumors of the affair had been widespread for years, the article was nevertheless explosive, nearly ruining both the prestigious *Atlantic Monthly* magazine in which it had been published and Stowe's own reputation. For decades scholars and biographers puzzled over this turn in Stowe's literary career; in recent years some scholars have read "The True Story" and the subsequent *Lady Byron Vindicated* (1870) as proto-feminist explorations of nineteenth-century gender roles and of the subjugation of women in sexual relationships.

Stowe's final novel was the 1878 *Poganuc People*, a regional novel that evoked the New England of her childhood. Her physical and mental health deteriorated rapidly over the next few years, especially after Calvin's death in 1886; Stowe herself died in July 1896.

The legacy of *Uncle Tom's Cabin* in American culture far outlived Stowe herself. The first stage adaptation had been written shortly after the novel's publication by George Aiken, a white playwright who also starred in the production as the novel's mixed-race hero George Harris. The novel was adapted countless additional times over the following decades, with many productions substantially altering the plot and exaggerating the racial stereotypes that had underlain the original narrative. These stage plays came to be known as "Tom Shows," and though their popularity was waning by the 1930s, they were still occasionally encountered even in the North as late as the 1940s. Some Tom Shows were wildly melodramatic, while others added song-and-dance numbers and comic scenes, adopting racist tropes from the minstrel show genre.

The "Tom Shows" were disdained by the literary establishment, but the novel itself continued to have broad appeal through the late-nineteenth century and into the twentieth. It was admired by respected European novelists such as George Eliot, George Sand, and Leo Tolstoy, who in 1897 declared it as an example "of the highest art flowing from love of God and man." By the 1920s, however, the novel had begun to be dismissed by the literary establishment as a hackneyed work of sentimentalism, with little in the way of aesthetic or intellectual value, and by mid century it was being attacked as downright pernicious. In his famous 1955 essay "Everybody's Protest Novel," James Baldwin dismissed the novel's "self-righteous, virtuous sentimentality" and condemned its two-dimensional characters. Baldwin treated *Uncle Tom's Cabin* as the paradigmatical protest novel, and condemned all such novels for their sentimentality—"sentimentality is the mark of dishonesty, the inability to feel," he proclaimed—and for the way in which, as he saw it, they simplified and distorted complex psychological and cultural truths; in his view, Stowe's "self-righteous sentimentality" and "catalog of violence" left "unanswered and unnoticed the only question that actually matters: what it was, after all, that moved her [i.e., white] people to such deeds." In another famous essay published a year later, J.C. Furnas focused more narrowly on Stowe's portrayal of black people, crediting her work for contributing significantly to "the wrongheadedness, distortions and wishful thinkings about Negroes in general and American Negroes in particular that still plague us today."

The reception history of *Uncle Tom's Cabin* has continued to take new turns in the twenty-first century. The literature of sentiment and the literature of protest are being read more sympathetically than they were for much of the twentieth century. Since the 1970s, critics have come to take the works of many nineteenth-century female writers much more seriously—and to question the gendered biases that often underlaid twentieth-century dismissals of popular and sentimental fiction as unworthy of study. Increasingly, twenty-first-century critics are interested in examining *Uncle Tom's Cabin*'s strategies in the context of the 1850s and 1860s as well as its legacy for race relations in subsequent periods; some critics also use Stowe's novel as a springboard for discussions about the role of emotion in literature more generally. The novel continues to entrance, infuriate, and, most of all, intrigue readers and scholars into our own day.

NOTE ON THE TEXT: The excerpts presented below are based on the 1852 first edition of *Uncle Tom's Cabin; or, Life Among the Lowly*. Spelling and punctuation have been modernized in accordance with the practices of this anthology.

⌘⌘⌘

from *Uncle Tom's Cabin; or, Life Among the Lowly*

CHAPTER I
IN WHICH THE READER IS INTRODUCED TO A MAN OF HUMANITY

Late in the afternoon of a chilly day in February, two gentlemen were sitting alone over their wine, in a well-furnished dining parlor, in the town of P——, in Kentucky. There were no servants present, and the gentlemen, with chairs closely approaching, seemed to be discussing some subject with great earnestness.

For convenience sake, we have said, hitherto, two *gentlemen*. One of the parties, however, when critically examined, did not seem, strictly speaking, to come under the species. He was a short, thick-set man, with coarse, commonplace features, and that swaggering air of pretension which marks a low man who is trying to elbow his way upward in the world. He was much over-dressed, in a gaudy vest of many colors, a blue neckerchief, bedropped gayly with yellow spots, and arranged with a flaunting tie, quite in keeping with the general air of the man. His hands, large and coarse, were plentifully bedecked with rings; and he wore a heavy gold watch-chain, with a bundle of seals of portentous size, and a great variety of colors, attached to it—which, in the ardor of conversation, he was in the habit of flourishing and jingling with evident satisfaction. His conversation was in free and easy defiance of Murray's Grammar,[1] and was garnished at convenient

---

[1] *Murray's Grammar* American scholar Lindley Murray's widely used textbook *English Grammar* (1795), which dictated rules of grammar and usage.

intervals with various profane expressions, which not even the desire to be graphic in our account shall induce us to transcribe.

His companion, Mr. Shelby, had the appearance of a gentleman; and the arrangements of the house, and the general air of the housekeeping, indicated easy and even opulent circumstances. As we before stated, the two were in the midst of an earnest conversation.

"That is the way I should arrange the matter," said Mr. Shelby.

"I can't make trade that way—I positively can't, Mr. Shelby," said the other, holding up a glass of wine between his eye and the light.

"Why, the fact is, Haley, Tom is an uncommon fellow; he is certainly worth that sum anywhere—steady, honest, capable, manages my whole farm like a clock."

"You mean honest, as niggers[1] go," said Haley, helping himself to a glass of brandy.

"No; I mean, really, Tom is a good, steady, sensible, pious fellow. He got religion at a camp meeting,[2] four years ago; and I believe he really *did* get it. I've trusted him, since then, with everything I have—money, house, horses—and let him come and go round the country; and I always found him true and square in everything."

"Some folks don't believe there is pious niggers, Shelby," said Haley, with a candid flourish of his hand, "but *I do*. I had a fellow, now, in this yer last lot I took to Orleans—'t was as good as a meetin, now, really, to hear that critter pray; and he was quite gentle and quiet like. He fetched me a good sum, too, for I bought him cheap of a man that was 'bliged to sell out; so I realized six hundred on him. Yes, I consider religion a valeyable thing in a nigger, when it's the genuine article, and no mistake."

"Well, Tom's got the real article, if ever a fellow had," rejoined the other. "Why, last fall, I let him go to Cincinnati alone, to do business for me, and bring home five hundred dollars. 'Tom,' says I to him, 'I trust you, because I think you're a Christian—I know you wouldn't cheat.' Tom comes back, sure enough; I knew he would. Some low fellows, they say, said to him—'Tom, why don't you make tracks for Canada?'[3] 'Ah, master trusted me, and I couldn't,'—they told me about it. I am sorry to part with Tom, I must say. You ought to let him cover the whole balance of the debt; and you would, Haley, if you had any conscience."

"Well, I've got just as much conscience as any man in business can afford to keep—just a little, you know, to swear by, as 't were," said the trader, jocularly; "and, then, I'm ready to do anything in reason to 'blige friends; but this yer, you see, is a leetle too hard on a fellow—a leetle too hard." The trader sighed contemplatively, and poured out some more brandy.

"Well, then, Haley, how will you trade?" said Mr. Shelby, after an uneasy interval of silence.

"Well, haven't you a boy or gal that you could throw in with Tom?"

"Hum! none that I could well spare; to tell the truth, it's only hard necessity makes me willing to sell at all. I don't like parting with any of my hands, that's a fact."

Here the door opened, and a small quadroon[4] boy, between four and five years of age, entered the room. There was something in his appearance remarkably beautiful and engaging. His black hair, fine as floss silk, hung in glossy curls about his round, dimpled face, while a pair of large dark eyes, full of fire and softness, looked out from beneath the rich, long lashes, as he peered curiously into the apartment. A gay robe of scarlet and yellow plaid, carefully made and neatly fitted, set off to advantage the dark and rich style of his beauty; and a certain comic air of assurance, blended with bashfulness, showed that he had been not unused to being petted and noticed by his master.

---

1   *nigger* By the mid-nineteenth century, this word, when used by white speakers, had acquired the extremely derogatory connotations it carries today, though it was sometimes used by African Americans without any derogatory intention; "negro" was, by contrast, considered a polite term by both black and white Americans.

2   *camp meeting* Outdoor religious gathering; camp meetings were associated particularly with evangelical Christian denominations, and provided a form of worship that was more accessible to the enslaved communities of the South.

3   *why don't … for Canada?* Due to its location along the border between Kentucky and the free state of Ohio, Cincinnati was an important center of the Underground Railroad, a secret network that aided enslaved people escaping to freedom in Canada.

4   *quadroon* Term commonly used in the nineteenth century to classify a person of mixed racial ancestry, generally with one black and three white grandparents.

"Hulloa, Jim Crow!"[1] said Mr. Shelby, whistling, and snapping a bunch of raisins towards him, "pick that up, now!"

The child scampered, with all his little strength, after the prize, while his master laughed.

"Come here, Jim Crow," said he. The child came up, and the master patted the curly head, and chucked him under the chin.

"Now, Jim, show this gentleman how you can dance and sing." The boy commenced one of those wild, grotesque songs common among the negroes, in a rich, clear voice, accompanying his singing with many comic evolutions of the hands, feet, and whole body, all in perfect time to the music.

"Bravo!" said Haley, throwing him a quarter of an orange.

"Now, Jim, walk like old Uncle Cudjoe, when he has the rheumatism," said his master.

Instantly the flexible limbs of the child assumed the appearance of deformity and distortion, as, with his back humped up, and his master's stick in his hand, he hobbled about the room, his childish face drawn into a doleful pucker, and spitting from right to left, in imitation of an old man.

Both gentlemen laughed uproariously.

"Now, Jim," said his master, "show us how old Elder Robbins leads the psalm." The boy drew his chubby face down to a formidable length, and commenced toning a psalm tune through his nose, with imperturbable gravity.

"Hurrah! bravo! what a young 'un!" said Haley; "that chap's a case, I'll promise. Tell you what," said he, suddenly clapping his hand on Mr. Shelby's shoulder, "fling in that chap, and I'll settle the business—I will. Come, now, if that ain't doing the thing up about the rightest!"

At this moment, the door was pushed gently open, and a young quadroon woman, apparently about twenty-five, entered the room.

There needed only a glance from the child to her, to identify her as its mother. There was the same rich, full, dark eye, with its long lashes; the same ripples of silky black hair. The brown of her complexion gave way on the cheek to a perceptible flush, which deepened as she saw the gaze of the strange man fixed upon her in bold and undisguised admiration. Her dress was of the neatest possible fit, and set off to advantage her finely moulded shape; a delicately formed hand and a trim foot and ankle were items of appearance that did not escape the quick eye of the trader, well used to run up at a glance the points of a fine female article.

"Well, Eliza?" said her master, as she stopped and looked hesitatingly at him.

"I was looking for Harry, please, sir"; and the boy bounded toward her, showing his spoils, which he had gathered in the skirt of his robe.

"Well, take him away, then," said Mr. Shelby; and hastily she withdrew, carrying the child on her arm.

"By Jupiter," said the trader, turning to him in admiration, "there's an article, now! You might make your fortune on that ar gal in Orleans, any day. I've seen over a thousand, in my day, paid down for gals not a bit handsomer."

"I don't want to make my fortune on her," said Mr. Shelby, dryly; and, seeking to turn the conversation, he uncorked a bottle of fresh wine, and asked his companion's opinion of it.

"Capital, sir—first chop!" said the trader; then turning, and slapping his hand familiarly on Shelby's shoulder, he added—

"Come, how will you trade about the gal? What shall I say for her—what'll you take?"

"Mr. Haley, she is not to be sold," said Shelby. "My wife would not part with her for her weight in gold."

"Ay, ay! women always say such things, cause they ha'nt no sort of calculation. Just show 'em how many watches, feathers, and trinkets, one's weight in gold would buy, and that alters the case, *I* reckon."

"I tell you, Haley, this must not be spoken of; I say no, and I mean no," said Shelby, decidedly.

"Well, you'll let me have the boy, though," said the trader; "you must own I've come down pretty handsomely for him."

"What on earth can you want with the child?" said Shelby.

"Why, I've got a friend that's going into this yer branch of the business—wants to buy up handsome boys to raise for the market. Fancy articles entirely—sell

---

[1]   *Jim Crow* While the origins of this pejorative term for an enslaved African American are unclear, its widespread usage by whites in the mid-nineteenth century stems from the popular 1828 song and dance "Jump Jim Crow" by Thomas Dartmouth Rice, a white performer of blackface minstrelsy.

for waiters,[1] and so on, to rich 'uns, that can pay for handsome 'uns. It sets off one of yer great places—a real handsome boy to open door, wait, and tend. They fetch a good sum; and this little devil is such a comical, musical concern, he's just the article."

"I would rather not sell him," said Mr. Shelby, thoughtfully; "the fact is, sir, I'm a humane man, and I hate to take the boy from his mother, sir."

"O, you do? La! yes—something of that ar natur. I understand, perfectly. It is mighty onpleasant getting on with women, sometimes. I al'ays hates these yer screachin', screamin' times. They are *mighty* onpleasant; but, as I manages business, I generally avoids 'em, sir. Now, what if you get the girl off for a day, or a week, or so; then the thing's done quietly—all over before she comes home. Your wife might get her some earrings, or a new gown, or some such truck, to make up with her."

"I'm afraid not."

"Lor bless ye, yes! These critters an't like white folks, you know; they gets over things, only manage right. Now, they say," said Haley, assuming a candid and confidential air, "that this kind o' trade is hardening to the feelings; but I never found it so. Fact is, I never could do things up the way some fellers manage the business. I've seen 'em as would pull a woman's child out of her arms, and set him up to sell, and she screechin' like mad all the time; very bad policy—damages the article—makes 'em quite unfit for service sometimes. I knew a real handsome gal once, in Orleans, as was entirely ruined by this sort o' handling. The fellow that was trading for her didn't want her baby; and she was one of your real high sort, when her blood was up. I tell you, she squeezed up her child in her arms, and talked, and went on real awful. It kinder makes my blood run cold to think on't; and when they carried off the child, and locked her up, she jest went ravin' mad, and died in a week. Clear waste, sir, of a thousand dollars, just for want of management—there's where 't is. It's always best to do the humane thing, sir; that's been *my* experience." And the trader leaned back in his chair, and folded his arm, with an air of virtuous decision, apparently considering himself a second Wilberforce.[2]

The subject appeared to interest the gentleman deeply; for while Mr. Shelby was thoughtfully peeling an orange, Haley broke out afresh, with becoming diffidence, but as if actually driven by the force of truth to say a few words more.

"It don't look well, now, for a feller to be praisin' himself; but I say it jest because it's the truth. I believe I'm reckoned to bring in about the finest droves of niggers that is brought in—at least, I've been told so; if I have once, I reckon I have a hundred times—all in good case—fat and likely, and I lose as few as any man in the business. And I lays it all to my management, sir; and humanity, sir, I may say, is the great pillar of *my* management."

Mr. Shelby did not know what to say, and so he said, "Indeed!"

"Now, I've been laughed at for my notions, sir, and I've been talked to. They an't pop'lar, and they an't common; but I stuck to 'em, sir; I've stuck to 'em, and realized well on 'em; yes, sir, they have paid their passage, I may say," and the trader laughed at his joke.

There was something so piquant and original in these elucidations of humanity, that Mr. Shelby could not help laughing in company. Perhaps you laugh too, dear reader; but you know humanity comes out in a variety of strange forms now-a-days, and there is no end to the odd things that humane people will say and do.

Mr. Shelby's laugh encouraged the trader to proceed.

"It's strange, now, but I never could beat this into people's heads. Now, there was Tom Loker, my old partner, down in Natchez;[3] he was a clever fellow, Tom was, only the very devil with niggers—on principle 't was, you see, for a better hearted feller never broke bread; 't was his *system*, sir. I used to talk to Tom. 'Why, Tom,' I used to say, 'when your gals takes on and cry, what's the use o' crackin on 'em over the head, and knockin' on 'em round? It's ridiculous,' says I, 'and don't do no sort o' good. Why, I don't see no harm in their cryin',' says I; 'it's natur,' says I, 'and if natur can't blow off one way, it will another. Besides, Tom,' says

---

1   *waiters* Personal servants.

2   *Wilberforce* English politician and abolitionist William Wilberforce (1759–1833), a leading figure in the movement to end

British involvement in slavery and the slave trade; the Slavery Abolition Act of 1833 (which took effect in August, 1834) ended slavery in most of the British colonies.

3   *Natchez* City in Mississippi, an important center of plantation agriculture.

I, 'it jest spiles[1] your gals; they get sickly, and down in the mouth; and sometimes they gets ugly—particular yallow[2] gals do—and it's the devil and all gettin' on 'em broke in. Now,' says I, 'why can't you kinder coax 'em up, and speak 'em fair? Depend on it, Tom, a little humanity, thrown in along, goes a heap further than all your jawin' and crackin'; and it pays better,' says I, 'depend on't.' But Tom couldn't get the hang on 't; and he spiled so many for me, that I had to break off with him, though he was a good-hearted fellow, and as fair a business hand as is goin'."

"And do you find your ways of managing do the business better than Tom's?" said Mr. Shelby.

"Why, yes, sir, I may say so. You see, when I any ways can, I takes a leetle care about the onpleasant parts, like selling young uns and that—get the gals out of the way—out of sight, out of mind, you know—and when it's clean done, and can't be helped, they naturally gets used to it. 'Tan't, you know, as if it was white folks, that's brought up in the way of 'spectin' to keep their children and wives, and all that. Niggers, you know, that's fetched up properly, ha'n't no kind of 'spectations of no kind; so all these things comes easier."

"I'm afraid mine are not properly brought up, then," said Mr. Shelby.

"S'pose not; you Kentucky folks spile your niggers. You mean well by 'em, but 'tan't no real kindness, arter all. Now, a nigger, you see, what's got to be hacked and tumbled round the world, and sold to Tom, and Dick, and the Lord knows who, 'tan't no kindness to be givin' on him notions and expectations, and bringin' on him up too well, for the rough and tumble comes all the harder on him arter. Now, I venture to say, your niggers would be quite chop-fallen in a place where some of your plantation niggers would be singing and whooping like all possessed. Every man, you know, Mr. Shelby, naturally thinks well of his own ways; and I think I treat niggers just about as well as it's ever worthwhile to treat 'em."

"It's a happy thing to be satisfied," said Mr. Shelby, with a slight shrug, and some perceptible feelings of a disagreeable nature.

"Well," said Haley, after they had both silently picked their nuts for a season, "what do you say?"

"I'll think the matter over, and talk with my wife," said Mr. Shelby. "Meantime, Haley, if you want the matter carried on in the quiet way you speak of, you'd best not let your business in this neighborhood be known. It will get out among my boys, and it will not be a particularly quiet business getting away any of my fellows, if they know it, I'll promise you."

"O! certainly, by all means, mum! of course. But I'll tell you, I'm in a devil of a hurry, and shall want to know, as soon as possible, what I may depend on," said he, rising and putting on his overcoat.

"Well, call up this evening, between six and seven, and you shall have my answer," said Mr. Shelby, and the trader bowed himself out of the apartment.

"I'd like to have been able to kick the fellow down the steps," said he to himself, as he saw the door fairly closed, "with his impudent assurance; but he knows how much he has me at advantage. If anybody had ever said to me that I should sell Tom down south to one of those rascally traders, I should have said, 'Is thy servant a dog, that he should do this thing?'[3] And now it must come, for aught I see. And Eliza's child, too! I know that I shall have some fuss with wife about that; and, for that matter, about Tom, too. So much for being in debt—heigho! The fellow sees his advantage, and means to push it."

Perhaps the mildest form of the system of slavery is to be seen in the State of Kentucky. The general prevalence of agricultural pursuits of a quiet and gradual nature, not requiring those periodic seasons of hurry and pressure that are called for in the business of more southern districts, makes the task of the negro a more healthful and reasonable one; while the master, content with a more gradual style of acquisition, has not those temptations to hardheartedness which always overcome frail human nature when the prospect of sudden and rapid gain is weighed in the balance, with no heavier counterpoise than the interests of the helpless and unprotected.

Whoever visits some estates there, and witnesses the good-humored indulgence of some masters and mistresses, and the affectionate loyalty of some slaves, might be tempted to dream the oft-fabled poetic

---

[1] *spiles* Spoils.

[2] *yallow* Racial descriptor designating individuals of mixed racial ancestry with light brown skin.

[3] *Is ... thing?* See 2 Kings 8.13: "But what, is thy servant a dog, that he should do this great thing?"

legend of a patriarchal institution,[1] and all that; but over and above the scene there broods a portentous shadow—the shadow of *law*. So long as the law considers all these human beings, with beating hearts and living affections, only as so many *things* belonging to a master—so long as the failure, or misfortune, or imprudence, or death of the kindest owner, may cause them any day to exchange a life of kind protection and indulgence for one of hopeless misery and toil—so long it is impossible to make anything beautiful or desirable in the best regulated administration of slavery.

Mr. Shelby was a fair average kind of man, good-natured and kindly, and disposed to easy indulgence of those around him, and there had never been a lack of anything which might contribute to the physical comfort of the negroes on his estate. He had, however, speculated largely and quite loosely; had involved himself deeply, and his notes[2] to a large amount had come into the hands of Haley; and this small piece of information is the key to the preceding conversation.

Now, it had so happened that, in approaching the door, Eliza had caught enough of the conversation to know that a trader was making offers to her master for somebody.

She would gladly have stopped at the door to listen, as she came out; but her mistress just then calling, she was obliged to hasten away.

Still she thought she heard the trader make an offer for her boy—could she be mistaken? Her heart swelled and throbbed, and she involuntarily strained him so tight that the little fellow looked up into her face in astonishment.

"Eliza, girl, what ails you today?" said her mistress, when Eliza had upset the wash-pitcher, knocked down the work-stand, and finally was abstractedly offering her mistress a long night-gown in place of the silk dress she had ordered her to bring from the wardrobe.

Eliza started. "O, missis!" she said, raising her eyes; then, bursting into tears, she sat down in a chair, and began sobbing.

"Why, Eliza, child! what ails you?" said her mistress.

"O! missis, missis," said Eliza, "there's been a trader talking with master in the parlor! I heard him."

"Well, silly child, suppose there has."

"O, missis, *do* you suppose mas'r would sell my Harry?" And the poor creature threw herself into a chair, and sobbed convulsively.

"Sell him! No, you foolish girl! You know your master never deals with those southern traders, and never means to sell any of his servants, as long as they behave well. Why, you silly child, who do you think would want to buy your Harry? Do you think all the world are set on him as you are, you goosie? Come, cheer up, and hook my dress. There now, put my back hair up in that pretty braid you learnt the other day, and don't go listening at doors anymore."

"Well, but, missis, *you* never would give your consent—to—to—"

"Nonsense, child! to be sure, I shouldn't. What do you talk so for? I would as soon have one of my own children sold. But really, Eliza, you are getting altogether too proud of that little fellow. A man can't put his nose into the door, but you think he must be coming to buy him."

Reassured by her mistress' confident tone, Eliza proceeded nimbly and adroitly with her toilet,[3] laughing at her own fears, as she proceeded.

Mrs. Shelby was a woman of a high class, both intellectually and morally. To that natural magnanimity and generosity of mind which one often marks as characteristic of the women of Kentucky, she added high moral and religious sensibility and principle, carried out with great energy and ability into practical results. Her husband, who made no professions to any particular religious character, nevertheless reverenced and respected the consistency of hers, and stood, perhaps, a little in awe of her opinion. Certain it was that he gave her unlimited scope in all her benevolent efforts for the comfort, instruction, and improvement of her servants, though he never took any decided part in them himself. In fact, if not exactly a believer in the doctrine of the efficiency of the extra good works of saints,[4] he really seemed somehow or other to fancy that his

---

1   *patriarchal institution* I.e., an institution in which enslavers are perceived as benevolent, fatherly figures.

2   *notes* Documents outlining debt and repayment terms.

3   *toilet* Dressing and personal grooming.

4   *the doctrine ... of saints* Reference to the belief held by Catholics and some other Christians that the good works of the saints have direct benefits for the souls of the living (the importance of earthly "good works" was generally held in low esteem by nineteenth-century Calvinists in comparison with the inner quality of grace).

wife had piety and benevolence enough for two—to indulge a shadowy expectation of getting into heaven through her superabundance of qualities to which he made no particular pretension.

The heaviest load on his mind, after his conversation with the trader, lay in the foreseen necessity of breaking to his wife the arrangement contemplated—meeting the importunities and opposition which he knew he should have reason to encounter.

Mrs. Shelby, being entirely ignorant of her husband's embarrassments,[1] and knowing only the general kindliness of his temper, had been quite sincere in the entire incredulity with which she had met Eliza's suspicions. In fact, she dismissed the matter from her mind, without a second thought; and being occupied in preparations for an evening visit, it passed out of her thoughts entirely.

[The following chapters introduce the reader further to the novel's enslaved characters, including Uncle Tom and his wife Aunt Chloe, their children Pete and Mose, and Eliza's husband George Harris, who is enslaved on a neighboring plantation under a cruel master. Also introduced is young Master George, the Shelbys' son, a good-natured boy who enjoys spending his time at Uncle Tom's cabin. George Harris reveals to Eliza that he intends on escaping to Canada, with the hope of eventually purchasing Eliza and Harry their freedom. Meanwhile, Mr. Shelby reluctantly signs a contract selling Harry and Tom to the trader Haley.]

Chapter 5
Showing the Feelings of Living Property on Changing Owners

Mr. and Mrs. Shelby had retired to their apartment for the night. He was lounging in a large easy-chair, looking over some letters that had come in the afternoon mail, and she was standing before her mirror, brushing out the complicated braids and curls in which Eliza had arranged her hair; for, noticing her pale cheeks and haggard eyes, she had excused her attendance that night, and ordered her to bed. The employment, naturally enough, suggested her conversation with the girl

in the morning; and, turning to her husband, she said, carelessly,

"By the by, Arthur, who was that low-bred fellow that you lugged in to our dinner-table today?"

"Haley is his name," said Shelby, turning himself rather uneasily in his chair, and continuing with his eyes fixed on a letter.

"Haley! Who is he, and what may be his business here, pray?"

"Well, he's a man that I transacted some business with, last time I was at Natchez," said Mr. Shelby.

"And he presumed on it to make himself quite at home, and call and dine here, ay?"

"Why, I invited him; I had some accounts with him," said Shelby.

"Is he a negro-trader?" said Mrs. Shelby, noticing a certain embarrassment in her husband's manner.

"Why, my dear, what put that into your head?" said Shelby, looking up.

"Nothing—only Eliza came in here, after dinner, in a great worry, crying and taking on, and said you were talking with a trader, and that she heard him make an offer for her boy—the ridiculous little goose!"

"She did, hey?" said Mr. Shelby, returning to his paper, which he seemed for a few moments quite intent upon, not perceiving that he was holding it bottom upwards.

"It will have to come out," said he, mentally; "as well now as ever."

"I told Eliza," said Mrs. Shelby, as she continued brushing her hair, "that she was a little fool for her pains, and that you never had anything to do with that sort of persons. Of course, I knew you never meant to sell any of our people—least of all, to such a fellow."

"Well, Emily," said her husband, "so I have always felt and said; but the fact is that my business lies so that I cannot get on without. I shall have to sell some of my hands."

"To that creature? Impossible! Mr. Shelby, you cannot be serious."

"I'm sorry to say that I am," said Mr. Shelby. "I've agreed to sell Tom."

"What! our Tom? that good, faithful creature! been your faithful servant from a boy! O, Mr. Shelby! and you have promised him his freedom, too—you and I have spoken to him a hundred times of it. Well, I

---

[1]   *embarrassments*   Financial difficulties.

can believe anything now—I can believe *now* that you could sell little Harry, poor Eliza's only child!" said Mrs. Shelby, in a tone between grief and indignation.

"Well, since you must know all, it is so. I have agreed to sell Tom and Harry both; and I don't know why I am to be rated as if I were a monster for doing what everyone does every day."

"But why, of all others, choose these?" said Mrs. Shelby. "Why sell them, of all on the place, if you must sell at all?"

"Because they will bring the highest sum of any— that's why. I could choose another, if you say so. The fellow made me a high bid on Eliza, if that would suit you any better," said Mr. Shelby.

"The wretch!" said Mrs. Shelby, vehemently.

"Well, I didn't listen to it, a moment—out of regard to your feelings, I wouldn't—so give me some credit."

"My dear," said Mrs. Shelby, recollecting herself, "forgive me. I have been hasty. I was surprised, and entirely unprepared for this—but surely you will allow me to intercede for these poor creatures. Tom is a noble-hearted, faithful fellow, if he is black. I do believe, Mr. Shelby, that if he were put to it, he would lay down his life for you."

"I know it, I dare say; but what's the use of all this? I can't help myself."

"Why not make a pecuniary sacrifice? I'm willing to bear my part of the inconvenience. O, Mr. Shelby, I have tried—tried most faithfully, as a Christian woman should—to do my duty to these poor, simple, dependent creatures. I have cared for them, instructed them, watched over them, and known all their little cares and joys, for years; and how can I ever hold up my head again among them if, for the sake of a little paltry gain, we sell such a faithful, excellent, confiding creature as poor Tom, and tear from him in a moment all we have taught him to love and value? I have taught them the duties of the family, of parent and child, and husband and wife; and how can I bear to have this open acknowledgement that we care for no tie, no duty, no relation, however sacred, compared with money? I have talked with Eliza about her boy—her duty to him as a Christian mother, to watch over him, pray for him, and bring him up in a Christian way; and now what can I say, if you tear him away, and sell him, soul and body, to a profane, unprincipled man,

just to save a little money? I have told her that one soul is worth more than all the money in the world; and how will she believe me when she sees us turn round and sell her child? sell him, perhaps, to certain ruin of body and soul!"

"I'm sorry you feel so about it, Emily—indeed I am," said Mr. Shelby; "and I respect your feelings, too, though I don't pretend to share them to their full extent; but I tell you now, solemnly, it's of no use—I can't help myself. I didn't mean to tell you this, Emily; but, in plain words, there is no choice between selling these two and selling everything. Either they must go, or *all* must. Haley has come into possession of a mortgage, which, if I don't clear off with him directly, will take everything before it. I've raked, and scraped, and borrowed, and all but begged—and the price of these two was needed to make up the balance, and I had to give them up. Haley fancied the child; he agreed to settle the matter that way, and no other. I was in his power, and *had* to do it. If you feel so to have them sold, would it be any better to have *all* sold?"

Mrs. Shelby stood like one stricken. Finally, turning to her toilet, she rested her face in her hands, and gave a sort of groan.

"This is God's curse on slavery! a bitter, bitter, most accursed thing! a curse to the master and a curse to the slave! I was a fool to think I could make anything good out of such a deadly evil. It is a sin to hold a slave under laws like ours—I always felt it was—I always thought so when I was a girl—I thought so still more after I joined the church; but I thought I could gild it over—I thought, by kindness, and care, and instruction, I could make the condition of mine better than freedom—fool that I was!"

"Why, wife, you are getting to be an abolitionist, quite."

"Abolitionist! if they knew all I know about slavery, they *might* talk! We don't need them to tell us; you know I never thought that slavery was right—never felt willing to own slaves."

"Well, therein you differ from many wise and pious men," said Mr. Shelby. "You remember Mr. B.'s sermon, the other Sunday?"

"I don't want to hear such sermons; I never wish to hear Mr. B. in our church again. Ministers can't help the evil, perhaps—can't cure it, any more than we can—but defend it! it always went against my common sense. And I think you didn't think much of that sermon, either."

"Well," said Shelby, "I must say these ministers sometimes carry matters further than we poor sinners would exactly dare to do. We men of the world must wink pretty hard at various things, and get used to a deal that isn't the exact thing. But we don't quite fancy, when women and ministers come out broad and square, and go beyond us in matters of either modesty or morals, that's a fact. But now, my dear, I trust you see the necessity of the thing, and you see that I have done the very best that circumstances would allow."

"O yes, yes!" said Mrs. Shelby, hurriedly and abstractedly fingering her gold watch, "I haven't any jewelry of any amount," she added, thoughtfully; "but would not this watch do something? it was an expensive one, when it was bought. If I could only at least save Eliza's child, I would sacrifice anything I have."

"I'm sorry, very sorry, Emily," said Mr. Shelby, "I'm sorry this takes hold of you so; but it will do no good. The fact is, Emily, the thing's done; the bills of sale are already signed, and in Haley's hands; and you must be thankful it is no worse. That man has had it in his power to ruin us all—and now he is fairly off. If you knew the man as I do, you'd think that we had had a narrow escape."

"Is he so hard, then?"

"Why, not a cruel man, exactly, but a man of leather—a man alive to nothing but trade and profit—cool, and unhesitating, and unrelenting, as death and the grave. He'd sell his own mother at a good percentage—not wishing the old woman any harm, either."

"And this wretch owns that good, faithful Tom, and Eliza's child!"

"Well, my dear, the fact is that this goes rather hard with me; it's a thing I hate to think of. Haley wants to drive matters, and take possession tomorrow. I'm going to get out my horse bright and early, and be off. I can't see Tom, that's a fact; and you had better arrange a drive somewhere, and carry Eliza off. Let the thing be done when she is out of sight."

"No, no," said Mrs. Shelby; "I'll be in no sense accomplice or help in this cruel business. I'll go and see poor old Tom, God help him, in his distress! They shall see, at any rate, that their mistress can feel for and with

them. As to Eliza, I dare not think about it. The Lord forgive us! What have we done, that this cruel necessity should come on us?"

There was one listener to this conversation whom Mr. and Mrs. Shelby little suspected.

Communicating with their apartment was a large closet, opening by a door into the outer passage. When Mrs. Shelby had dismissed Eliza for the night, her feverish and excited mind had suggested the idea of this closet; and she had hidden herself there, and, with her ear pressed close against the crack of the door, had not lost a word of the conversation.

When the voices died into silence, she rose and crept stealthily away. Pale, shivering, with rigid features and compressed lips, she looked an entirely altered being from the soft and timid creature she had been hitherto. She moved cautiously along the entry, paused one moment at her mistress' door, and raised her hands in mute appeal to Heaven, and then turned and glided into her own room. It was a quiet, neat apartment, on the same floor with her mistress. There was the pleasant sunny window, where she had often sat singing at her sewing; there a little case of books, and various little fancy articles, ranged by them, the gifts of Christmas holidays; there was her simple wardrobe in the closet and in the drawers: here was, in short, her home; and, on the whole, a happy one it had been to her. But there, on the bed, lay her slumbering boy, his long curls falling negligently around his unconscious face, his rosy mouth half open, his little fat hands thrown out over the bedclothes, and a smile spread like a sunbeam over his whole face.

"Poor boy! poor fellow!" said Eliza; "they have sold you! but your mother will save you yet!"

No tear dropped over that pillow; in such straits as these, the heart has no tears to give—it drops only blood, bleeding itself away in silence. She took a piece of paper and a pencil, and wrote, hastily,

"O, Missis! dear Missis! don't think me ungrateful—don't think hard of me, any way—I heard all you and master said tonight. I am going to try to save my boy—you will not blame me! God bless and reward you for all your kindness!"

Hastily folding and directing this, she went to a drawer and made up a little package of clothing for her boy, which she tied with a handkerchief firmly round her waist; and, so fond is a mother's remembrance, that, even in the terrors of that hour, she did not forget to put in the little package one or two of his favorite toys, reserving a gayly painted parrot to amuse him, when she should be called on to awaken him. It was some trouble to arouse the little sleeper; but, after some effort, he sat up, and was playing with his bird, while his mother was putting on her bonnet and shawl.

"Where are you going, mother?" said he, as she drew near the bed, with his little coat and cap.

His mother drew near, and looked so earnestly into his eyes, that he at once divined that something unusual was the matter.

"Hush, Harry," she said; "mustn't speak loud, or they will hear us. A wicked man was coming to take little Harry away from his mother, and carry him 'way off in the dark; but mother won't let him—she's going to put on her little boy's cap and coat, and run off with him, so the ugly man can't catch him."

Saying these words, she had tied and buttoned on the child's simple outfit, and, taking him in her arms, she whispered to him to be very still; and, opening a door in her room which led into the outer verandah, she glided noiselessly out.

It was a sparkling, frosty, starlight night, and the mother wrapped the shawl close round her child, as, perfectly quiet with vague terror, he clung round her neck.

Old Bruno, a great Newfoundland who slept at the end of the porch, rose, with a low groan, as she came near. She gently spoke his name, and the animal, an old pet and playmate of hers, instantly, wagging his tail, prepared to follow her, though apparently revolving much, in his simple dog's head, what such an indiscreet midnight promenade might mean. Some dim ideas of imprudence or impropriety in the measure seemed to embarrass him considerably; for he often stopped, as Eliza glided forward, and looked wistfully, first at her and then at the house, and then, as if reassured by reflection, he pattered along after her again. A few minutes brought them to the window of Uncle Tom's cottage, and Eliza, stopping, tapped lightly on the window-pane.

The prayer-meeting at Uncle Tom's had, in the order of hymn-singing, been protracted to a very late hour; and, as Uncle Tom had indulged himself in a few

lengthy solos afterwards, the consequence was, that, although it was now between twelve and one o'clock, he and his worthy helpmeet were not yet asleep.

"Good Lord! what's that?" said Aunt Chloe, starting up and hastily drawing the curtain. "My sakes alive, if it an't Lizy! Get on your clothes, old man, quick! there's old Bruno, too, a pawin' round; what on airth! I'm gwine to open the door."

And, suiting the action to the word, the door flew open, and the light of the tallow candle, which Tom had hastily lighted, fell on the haggard face and dark, wild eyes of the fugitive.

"Lord bless you! I'm skeered to look at ye, Lizy! Are ye tuck[1] sick, or what's come over ye?"

"I'm running away—Uncle Tom and Aunt Chloe—carrying off my child—Master sold him!"

"Sold him?" echoed both, lifting up their hands in dismay.

"Yes, sold him!" said Eliza, firmly; "I crept into the closet by Mistress' door tonight, and I heard Master tell Missis that he had sold my Harry, and you, Uncle Tom, both, to a trader; and that he was going off this morning on his horse, and that the man was to take possession today."

Tom had stood, during this speech, with his hands raised, and his eyes dilated, like a man in a dream. Slowly and gradually, as its meaning came over him, he collapsed, rather than seated himself, on his old chair, and sunk his head down upon his knees.

"The good Lord have pity on us!" said Aunt Chloe. "O! it don't seem as if it was true! What has he done, that Mas'r should sell *him*?"

"He hasn't done anything—it isn't for that. Master don't want to sell; and Missis—she's always good. I heard her plead and beg for us; but he told her 'twas no use; that he was in this man's debt, and that this man had got the power over him; and that if he didn't pay him off clear, it would end in his having to sell the place and all the people, and move off. Yes, I heard him say there was no choice between selling these two and selling all, the man was driving him so hard. Master said he was sorry; but oh, Missis—you ought to have heard her talk! If she an't a Christian and an angel, there never was one. I'm a wicked girl to leave her so; but, then, I can't help it. She said, herself, one soul

---

[1] *tuck* Took; taken.

was worth more than the world; and this boy has a soul, and if I let him be carried off, who knows what'll become of it? It must be right: but, if it an't right, the Lord forgive me, for I can't help doing it!"

"Well, old man!" said Aunt Chloe, "why don't you go, too? Will you wait to be toted down river, where they kill niggers with hard work and starving? I'd a heap rather die than go there, any day! There's time for ye—be off with Lizy—you've got a pass to come and go any time.[1] Come, bustle up, and I'll get your things together."

Tom slowly raised his head, and looked sorrowfully but quietly around, and said,

"No, no—I an't going. Let Eliza go—it's her right! I wouldn't be the one to say no—'tan't in *natur* for her to stay; but you heard what she said! If I must be sold, or all the people on the place, and everything go to rack, why, let me be sold. I s'pose I can b'ar it as well as any on 'em," he added, while something like a sob and a sigh shook his broad, rough chest convulsively. "Mas'r always found me on the spot—he always will. I never have broke trust, nor used my pass no ways contrary to my word, and I never will. It's better for me alone to go, than to break up the place and sell all. Mas'r an't to blame, Chloe, and he'll take care of you and the poor—"

Here he turned to the rough trundle-bed full of little woolly heads, and broke fairly down. He leaned over the back of the chair, and covered his face with his large hands. Sobs, heavy, hoarse and loud, shook the chair, and great tears fell through his fingers on the floor: just such tears, sir, as you dropped into the coffin where lay your first-born son; such tears, woman, as you shed when you heard the cries of your dying babe. For, sir, he was a man—and you are but another man. And, woman, though dressed in silk and jewels, you are but a woman, and, in life's great straits and mighty griefs, ye feel but one sorrow!

"And now," said Eliza, as she stood in the door, "I saw my husband only this afternoon, and I little knew then what was to come. They have pushed him to the very last standing-place, and he told me, today, that he was going to run away. Do try, if you can, to get word

to him. Tell him how I went, and why I went; and tell him I'm going to try and find Canada. You must give my love to him, and tell him, if I never see him again,"—she turned away, and stood with her back to them for a moment, and then added, in a husky voice, "tell him to be as good as he can, and try and meet me in the kingdom of heaven."

"Call Bruno in there," she added. "Shut the door on him, poor beast! He mustn't go with me!"

A few last words and tears, a few simple adieus and blessings, and, clasping her wondering and affrighted child in her arms, she glided noiselessly away.

Chapter 7
The Mother's Struggle

It is impossible to conceive of a human creature more wholly desolate and forlorn than Eliza, when she turned her footsteps from Uncle Tom's cabin.

Her husband's suffering and dangers, and the danger of her child, all blended in her mind, with a confused and stunning sense of the risk she was running, in leaving the only home she had ever known, and cutting loose from the protection of a friend whom she loved and revered. Then there was the parting from every familiar object—the place where she had grown up, the trees under which she had played, the groves where she had walked many an evening in happier days, by the side of her young husband—everything, as it lay in the clear, frosty starlight, seemed to speak reproachfully to her, and ask her whither could she go from a home like that?

But stronger than all was maternal love, wrought into a paroxysm of frenzy by the near approach of a fearful danger. Her boy was old enough to have walked by her side, and, in an indifferent case, she would only have led him by the hand; but now the bare thought of putting him out of her arms made her shudder, and she strained him to her bosom with a convulsive grasp, as she went rapidly forward.

The frosty ground creaked beneath her feet, and she trembled at the sound; every quaking leaf and fluttering shadow sent the blood backward to her heart, and quickened her footsteps. She wondered within herself at the strength that seemed to be come upon her; for she felt the weight of her boy as if it had been a feather,

---

[1] *you've got … any time* In order to travel on their own, enslaved persons often required written documents from their enslavers, granting them permission to do so.

and every flutter of fear seemed to increase the supernatural power that bore her on, while from her pale lips burst forth, in frequent ejaculations,[1] the prayer to a Friend above—"Lord, help! Lord, save me!"

If it were *your* Harry, mother, or your Willie, that were going to be torn from you by a brutal trader, tomorrow morning—if you had seen the man, and heard that the papers were signed and delivered, and you had only from twelve o'clock till morning to make good your escape—how fast could *you* walk? How many miles could you make in those few brief hours, with the darling at your bosom—the little sleepy head on your shoulder—the small, soft arms trustingly holding on to your neck?

For the child slept. At first, the novelty and alarm kept him waking; but his mother so hurriedly repressed every breath or sound, and so assured him that if he were only still she would certainly save him, that he clung quietly round her neck, only asking, as he found himself sinking to sleep,

"Mother, I don't need to keep awake, do I?"

"No, my darling; sleep, if you want to."

"But, mother, if I do get asleep, you won't let him get me?"

"No! so may God help me!" said his mother, with a paler cheek, and a brighter light in her large dark eyes.

"You're *sure*, an't you, mother?"

"Yes, *sure*!" said the mother, in a voice that startled herself; for it seemed to her to come from a spirit within, that was no part of her; and the boy dropped his little weary head on her shoulder, and was soon asleep. How the touch of those warm arms, the gentle breathings that came in her neck, seemed to add fire and spirit to her movements! It seemed to her as if strength poured into her in electric streams, from every gentle touch and movement of the sleeping, confiding child. Sublime is the dominion of the mind over the body, that, for a time, can make flesh and nerve impregnable, and string the sinews like steel, so that the weak become so mighty.

The boundaries of the farm, the grove, the wood-lot, passed by her dizzily, as she walked on; and still she went, leaving one familiar object after another, slacking not, pausing not, till reddening daylight found her many a long mile from all traces of any familiar objects upon the open highway.

She had often been, with her mistress, to visit some connections, in the little village of T——, not far from the Ohio River, and knew the road well. To go thither, to escape across the Ohio River, were the first hurried outlines of her plan of escape; beyond that, she could only hope in God.

When horses and vehicles began to move along the highway, with that alert perception peculiar to a state of excitement, and which seems to be a sort of inspiration, she became aware that her headlong pace and distracted air might bring on her remark and suspicion. She therefore put the boy on the ground and, adjusting her dress and bonnet, she walked on at as rapid a pace as she thought consistent with the preservation of appearances. In her little bundle she had provided a store of cakes[2] and apples, which she used as expedients for quickening the speed of the child, rolling the apple some yards before them, when the boy would run with all his might after it; and this ruse, often repeated, carried them over many a half-mile.

After a while, they came to a thick patch of woodland, through which murmured a clear brook. As the child complained of hunger and thirst, she climbed over the fence with him; and, sitting down behind a large rock which concealed them from the road, she gave him a breakfast out of her little package. The boy wondered and grieved that she could not eat; and when, putting his arms round her neck, he tried to wedge some of his cake into her mouth, it seemed to her that the rising in her throat would choke her.

"No, no, Harry darling! mother can't eat till you are safe! We must go on—on—till we come to the river!" And she hurried again into the road, and again constrained herself to walk regularly and composedly forward.

She was many miles past any neighborhood where she was personally known. If she should chance to meet any who knew her, she reflected that the well-known kindness of the family would be of itself a blind to suspicion, as making it an unlikely supposition that she could be a fugitive. As she was also so white as not to be known as of colored lineage, without a critical

---

1   *ejaculations* Outbursts; exclamations.

2   *cakes* Likely including leavened breads, corn cakes, and fruit cakes rather than confections.

survey, and her child was white also, it was much easier for her to pass on unsuspected.

On this presumption, she stopped at noon at a neat farmhouse, to rest herself, and buy some dinner for her child and self; for, as the danger decreased with the distance, the supernatural tension of the nervous system lessened, and she found herself both weary and hungry.

The good woman, kindly and gossiping, seemed rather pleased than otherwise with having somebody come in to talk with; and accepted, without examination, Eliza's statement, that she "was going on a little piece, to spend a week with her friends,"—all which she hoped in her heart might prove strictly true.

An hour before sunset, she entered the village of T——, by the Ohio River, weary and foot-sore, but still strong in heart. Her first glance was at the river, which lay, like Jordan, between her and the Canaan[1] of liberty on the other side.

It was now early spring, and the river was swollen and turbulent; great cakes of floating ice were swinging heavily to and fro in the turbid waters. Owing to the peculiar form of the shore on the Kentucky side, the land bending far out into the water, the ice had been lodged and detained in great quantities, and the narrow channel which swept round the bend was full of ice, piled one cake over another, thus forming a temporary barrier to the descending ice, which lodged, and formed a great, undulating raft, filling up the whole river, and extending almost to the Kentucky shore.

Eliza stood, for a moment, contemplating this unfavorable aspect of things, which she saw at once must prevent the usual ferry-boat from running, and then turned into a small public house[2] on the bank, to make a few inquiries.

The hostess, who was busy in various fizzing and stewing operations over the fire, preparatory to the evening meal, stopped, with a fork in her hand, as Eliza's sweet and plaintive voice arrested her.

"What is it?" she said.

"Isn't there any ferry or boat, that takes people over to B——, now?" she said.

"No, indeed!" said the woman; "the boats has stopped running."

Eliza's look of dismay and disappointment struck the woman, and she said, inquiringly,

"Maybe you're wanting to get over? anybody sick? Ye seem mighty anxious?"

"I've got a child that's very dangerous,"[3] said Eliza. "I never heard of it till last night, and I've walked quite a piece today, in hopes to get to the ferry."

"Well, now, that's onlucky," said the woman, whose motherly sympathies were much aroused; "I'm re'lly consarned for ye. Solomon!" she called, from the window, towards a small back building. A man, in leather apron and very dirty hands, appeared at the door.

"I say, Sol," said the woman, "is that ar man going to tote them bar'ls over tonight?"

"He said he should try, if 't was any way prudent," said the man.

"There's a man a piece down here, that's going over with some truck[4] this evening, if he durs' to; he'll be in here to supper tonight, so you'd better set down and wait. That's a sweet little fellow," added the woman, offering him a cake.

But the child, wholly exhausted, cried with weariness.

"Poor fellow! he isn't used to walking, and I've hurried him on so," said Eliza.

"Well, take him into this room," said the woman, opening into a small bedroom, where stood a comfortable bed. Eliza laid the weary boy upon it, and held his hands in hers till he was fast asleep. For her there was no rest. As a fire in her bones, the thought of the pursuer urged her on; and she gazed with longing eyes on the sullen, surging waters that lay between her and liberty.

Here we must take our leave of her for the present, to follow the course of her pursuers.

———

Though Mrs. Shelby had promised that the dinner should be hurried on table, yet it was soon seen, as the

---

1   *like Jordan ... Canaan*   In the Old Testament, Canaan is a prosperous region west of the Jordan River that is promised by God to the Israelites after their liberation from slavery in Egypt. "Crossing Jordan" became a widespread metaphor for escaping from slavery.

2   *public house*   Business providing food, drink, and often accommodation.

3   *dangerous*   I.e., dangerously ill.

4   *truck*   Goods for transport.

thing has often been seen before, that it required more than one to make a bargain. So, although the order was fairly given out in Haley's hearing, and carried to Aunt Chloe by at least half a dozen juvenile messengers, that dignitary only gave certain very gruff snorts, and tosses of her head, and went on with every operation in an unusually leisurely and circumstantial manner.

For some singular reason, an impression seemed to reign among the servants generally that Missis would not be particularly disobliged by delay; and it was wonderful what a number of counter accidents occurred constantly, to retard the course of things. One luckless wight contrived to upset the gravy; and then gravy had to be got up *de novo*,[1] with due care and formality, Aunt Chloe watching and stirring with dogged precision, answering shortly, to all suggestions of haste, that she "warn't a going to have raw gravy on the table, to help nobody's catchings." One tumbled down with the water, and had to go to the spring for more; and another precipitated the butter into the path of events; and there was from time to time giggling news brought into the kitchen that "Mas'r Haley was mighty oneasy, and that he couldn't sit in his cheer no ways, but was a walkin' and stalkin' to the winders and through the porch."

"Sarves him right!" said Aunt Chloe, indignantly. "He'll get wus nor oneasy,[2] one of these days, if he don't mend his ways. *His* master'll be sending for him, and then see how he'll look!"

"He'll go to torment, and no mistake," said little Jake.

"He desarves it!" said Aunt Chloe, grimly; "he's broke a many, many, many hearts—I tell ye all!" she said, stopping, with a fork uplifted in her hands; "it's like what Mas'r George reads in Ravelations—souls a callin' under the altar! and a callin' on the Lord for vengeance on sich! and by and by the Lord he'll hear 'em—so he will!"[3]

Aunt Chloe, who was much revered in the kitchen, was listened to with open mouth; and, the dinner being now fairly sent in, the whole kitchen was at leisure to gossip with her, and to listen to her remarks.

"Sich'll be burnt up forever, and no mistake; won't ther?" said Andy.

"I'd be glad to see it, I'll be boun'," said little Jake.

"Chil'en!" said a voice, that made them all start. It was Uncle Tom, who had come in, and stood listening to the conversation at the door.

"Chil'en!" he said, "I'm afeard you don't know what ye're sayin'. Forever is a *dre'ful* word, chil'en; it's awful to think on't. You oughtenter wish that ar to any human crittur."

"We wouldn't to anybody but the soul-drivers,"[4] said Andy; "nobody can help wishing it to them, they's so awful wicked."

"Don't natur herself kinder cry out on em?" said Aunt Chloe. "Don't dey tear der suckin' baby right off his mother's breast, and sell him, and der little children as is crying and holding on by her clothes—don't dey pull 'em off and sells em? Don't dey tear wife and husband apart?" said Aunt Chloe, beginning to cry, "when it's jest takin' the very life on 'em? and all the while does they feel one bit—don't dey drink and smoke, and take it oncommon easy? Lor, if the devil don't get them, what's he good for?" And Aunt Chloe covered her face with her checked apron, and began to sob in good earnest.

"Pray for them that 'spitefully use you, the good book says,"[5] says Tom.

"Pray for 'em!" said Aunt Chloe; "Lor, it's too tough! I can't pray for 'em."

"It's natur, Chloe, and natur's strong," said Tom, "but the Lord's grace is stronger; besides, you oughter think what an awful state a poor crittur's soul's in that'll do them ar things—you oughter thank God that you an't *like* him, Chloe. I'm sure I'd rather be sold, ten thousand times over, than to have all that ar poor crittur's got to answer for."

---

1 *wight* Creature; person; *de novo* Latin: once again.

2 *wus nor oneasy* I.e., worse than uneasy.

3 *it's like … he will!"* See Revelation 6.9–10, in which Christ opens the seven seals of a book, instigating the beginning of the Apocalypse: "And when he had opened the fifth seal, I saw under the altar the souls of them that were slain for the word of God, and for the testimony which they held: / And they cried with a loud voice, saying, How long, O Lord, holy and true, dost thou not judge and avenge our blood on them that dwell on the earth?"

4 *soul-drivers* Phrase commonly used to refer either to slave traders or to plantation overseers.

5 *Pray for … book says* See Matthew 5.44: "But I say unto you, Love your enemies, bless them that curse you, do good to them that hate you, and pray for them which despitefully use you, and persecute you," and Luke 6.28: "Bless them that curse you, and pray for them which despitefully use you."

"So'd I, a heap," said Jake. "Lor, *shouldn't* we cotch it, Andy?"

Andy shrugged his shoulders, and gave an acquiescent whistle.

"I'm glad Mas'r didn't go off this morning, as he looked to," said Tom; "that ar hurt me more than sellin', it did. Mebbe it might have been natural for him, but 't would have come desp't hard on me, as has known him from a baby; but I've seen Mas'r, and I begin ter feel sort o' reconciled to the Lord's will now. Mas'r couldn't help hisself; he did right, but I'm feared things will be kinder goin' to rack,[1] when I'm gone. Mas'r can't be spected to be a pryin' round everywhar, as I've done, a keepin' up all the ends. The boys all means well, but they's powerful car'less. That ar troubles me."

The bell here rang, and Tom was summoned to the parlor.

"Tom," said his master, kindly, "I want you to notice that I give this gentleman bonds to forfeit a thousand dollars if you are not on the spot when he wants you; he's going today to look after his other business, and you can have the day to yourself. Go anywhere you like, boy."

"Thank you, Mas'r," said Tom.

"And mind yerself," said the trader, "and don't come it over your master with any o' yer nigger tricks; for I'll take every cent out of him, if you an't thar. If he'd hear to me, he wouldn't trust any on ye—slippery as eels!"

"Mas'r," said Tom—and he stood very straight—"I was jist eight years old when ole Missis put you into my arms, and you wasn't a year old. 'Thar,' says she, 'Tom, that's to be *your* young Mas'r; take good care on him,' says she. And now I jist ask you, Mas'r, have I ever broke word to you, or gone contrary to you, 'specially since I was a Christian?"

Mr. Shelby was fairly overcome, and the tears rose to his eyes.

"My good boy," said he, "the Lord knows you say but the truth; and if I was able to help it, all the world shouldn't buy you."

"And sure as I am a Christian woman," said Mrs. Shelby, "you shall be redeemed as soon as I can any way bring together means. Sir," she said to Haley, "take good account of who you sell him to, and let me know."

"Lor, yes, for that matter," said the trader, "I may bring him up in a year, not much the wuss for wear, and trade him back."

"I'll trade with you then, and make it for your advantage," said Mrs. Shelby.

"Of course," said the trader, "all's equal with me; li'ves trade 'em up as down, so I does a good business. All I want is a livin', you know, ma'am; that's all any on us wants, I s'pose."

Mr. and Mrs. Shelby both felt annoyed and degraded by the familiar[2] impudence of the trader, and yet both saw the absolute necessity of putting a constraint on their feelings. The more hopelessly sordid and insensible he appeared, the greater became Mrs. Shelby's dread of his succeeding in recapturing Eliza and her child, and of course the greater her motive for detaining him by every female artifice. She therefore graciously smiled, assented, chatted familiarly, and did all she could to make time pass imperceptibly.

At two o'clock Sam and Andy[3] brought the horses up to the posts, apparently greatly refreshed and invigorated by the scamper of the morning.

Sam was there new oiled from dinner, with an abundance of zealous and ready officiousness. As Haley approached, he was boasting, in flourishing style, to Andy, of the evident and eminent success of the operation, now that he had "farly come to it."

"Your master, I s'pose, don't keep no dogs," said Haley, thoughtfully, as he prepared to mount.

"Heaps on 'em," said Sam, triumphantly; "thar's Bruno—he's a roarer! and, besides that, 'bout every nigger of us keeps a pup of some natur or uther."

"Poh!" said Haley—and he said something else, too, with regard to the said dogs, at which Sam muttered,

"I don't see no use cussin' on 'em, no way."

"But your master don't keep no dogs (I pretty much know he don't) for trackin' out niggers."

Sam knew exactly what he meant, but he kept on a look of earnest and desperate simplicity.

"Our dogs all smells round considable sharp. I spect they's the kind, though they han't never had no practice. They's *far* dogs, though, at most anything, if you'd get 'em started. Here, Bruno," he called, whistling to

---

[1]   *rack* Wreck.

[2]   *familiar* Inappropriately informal.

[3]   *Sam and Andy* Two other men enslaved by the Shelbys, commanded by Mr. Shelby to aid Haley in finding Eliza.

the lumbering Newfoundland, who came pitching tumultuously toward them.

"You go hang!" said Haley, getting up. "Come, tumble up now."

Sam tumbled up accordingly, dexterously contriving to tickle Andy as he did so, which occasioned Andy to split out into a laugh, greatly to Haley's indignation, who made a cut at him with his riding-whip.

"I's 'stonished at yer, Andy," said Sam, with awful gravity. "This yer's a seris bisness, Andy. Yer mustn't be a makin' game. This yer an't no way to help Mas'r."

"I shall take the straight road to the river," said Haley, decidedly, after they had come to the boundaries of the estate. "I know the way of all of 'em—they makes tracks for the underground."[1]

"Sartin," said Sam, "dat's de idee. Mas'r Haley hits de thing right in de middle. Now, der's two roads to de river—de dirt road and der pike[2]—which Mas'r mean to take?"

Andy looked up innocently at Sam, surprised at hearing this new geographical fact, but instantly confirmed what he said, by a vehement reiteration.

"Cause," said Sam, "I'd rather be 'clined to 'magine that Lizy'd take de dirt road, bein' it's the least travelled."

Haley, notwithstanding that he was a very old bird, and naturally inclined to be suspicious of chaff,[3] was rather brought up by this view of the case.

"If yer warn't both on yer such cussed liars, now!" he said, contemplatively, as he pondered a moment.

The pensive, reflective tone in which this was spoken appeared to amuse Andy prodigiously, and he drew a little behind, and shook so as apparently to run a great risk of falling off his horse, while Sam's face was immovably composed into the most doleful gravity.

"Course," said Sam, "Mas'r can do as he'd ruther; go de straight road, if Mas'r thinks best—it's all one to us. Now, when I study 'pon it, I think de straight road de best, *decidedly*."

"She would naturally go a lonesome way," said Haley, thinking aloud, and not minding Sam's remark.

"Dar an't no sayin'," said Sam; "gals is pecular; they never does nothin' ye thinks they will; mose gen'lly the contrar. Gals is nat'lly made contrary; and so, if you thinks they've gone one road, it is sartin you'd better go t' other, and then you'll be sure to find 'em. Now, my private 'pinion is, Lizy took der dirt road; so I think we'd better take de straight one."

This profound generic view of the female sex did not seem to dispose Haley particularly to the straight road; and he announced decidedly that he should go the other, and asked Sam when they should come to it.

"A little piece ahead," said Sam, giving a wink to Andy with the eye which was on Andy's side of the head; and he added, gravely, "but I've studded on de matter, and I'm quite clar we ought not to go dat ar way. I nebber been over it no way. It's despit[4] lonesome, and we might lose our way—whar we'd come to, de Lord only knows."

"Nevertheless," said Haley, "I shall go that way."

"Now I think on't, I think I hearn 'em tell that dat ar road was all fenced up and down by der creek, and thar, an't it, Andy?"

Andy wasn't certain; he'd only "hearn tell" about that road, but never been over it. In short, he was strictly noncommittal.

Haley, accustomed to strike the balance of probabilities between lies of greater or lesser magnitude, thought that it lay in favor of the dirt road aforesaid. The mention of the thing he thought he perceived was involuntary on Sam's part at first, and his confused attempts to dissuade him he set down to a desperate lying on second thoughts, as being unwilling to implicate Eliza.

When, therefore, Sam indicated the road, Haley plunged briskly into it, followed by Sam and Andy.

Now, the road, in fact, was an old one, that had formerly been a thoroughfare to the river, but abandoned for many years after the laying of the new pike. It was open for about an hour's ride, and after that it was cut across by various farms and fences. Sam knew this fact perfectly well—indeed, the road had been so long closed up, that Andy had never heard of it. He therefore rode along with an air of dutiful submission,

---

[1] *underground* The Underground Railroad, a secret traveling network (and network of safe-houses) by means of which many enslaved persons escaped to the North.

[2] *pike* Paid road; highway.

[3] *old bird ... chaff* Allusion to the proverbial phrase "You cannot catch old birds with chaff," meaning that those who are old and wise are not easily deceived; *chaff* Empty grain husks.

[4] *despit* Desperate.

only groaning and vociferating occasionally that 't was "desp't rough, and bad for Jerry's[1] foot."

"Now, I jest give yer warning," said Haley, "I know yer; yer won't get me to turn off this yer road, with all yer fussin'—so you shet up!"

"Mas'r will go his own way!" said Sam, with rueful submission, at the same time winking most portentously to Andy, whose delight was now very near the explosive point.

Sam was in wonderful spirits—professed to keep a very brisk look-out—at one time exclaiming that he saw "a gal's bonnet" on the top of some distant eminence, or calling to Andy "if that thar wasn't 'Lizy' down in the hollow"; always making these exclamations in some rough or craggy part of the road, where the sudden quickening of speed was a special inconvenience to all parties concerned, and thus keeping Haley in a state of constant commotion.

After riding about an hour in this way, the whole party made a precipitate and tumultuous descent into a barnyard belonging to a large farming establishment. Not a soul was in sight, all the hands being employed in the fields; but, as the barn stood conspicuously and plainly square across the road, it was evident that their journey in that direction had reached a decided finale.

"Wan't dat ar what I told Mas'r?" said Sam, with an air of injured innocence. "How does strange gentleman spect to know more about a country dan de natives born and raised?"

"You rascal!" said Haley, "you knew all about this."

"Didn't I tell yer I *know'd*, and yer wouldn't believe me? I told Mas'r 't was all shet up, and fenced up, and I didn't spect we could get through—Andy heard me."

It was all too true to be disputed, and the unlucky man had to pocket his wrath with the best grace he was able, and all three faced to the right about, and took up their line of march for the highway.

In consequence of all the various delays, it was about three-quarters of an hour after Eliza had laid her child to sleep in the village tavern that the party came riding into the same place. Eliza was standing by the window, looking out in another direction, when Sam's quick eye caught a glimpse of her. Haley and Andy were two yards behind. At this crisis, Sam contrived to have his hat blown off, and uttered a loud and characteristic

ejaculation, which startled her at once; she drew suddenly back; the whole train swept by the window, round to the front door.

A thousand lives seemed to be concentrated in that one moment to Eliza. Her room opened by a side door to the river. She caught her child, and sprang down the steps towards it. The trader caught a full glimpse of her, just as she was disappearing down the bank; and throwing himself from his horse, and calling loudly on Sam and Andy, he was after her like a hound after a deer. In that dizzy moment her feet to her scarce seemed to touch the ground, and a moment brought her to the water's edge. Right on behind they came; and, nerved with strength such as God gives only to the desperate, with one wild cry and flying leap, she vaulted sheer over the turbid current by the shore, on to the raft of ice beyond. It was a desperate leap—impossible to anything but madness and despair; and Haley, Sam, and Andy instinctively cried out, and lifted up their hands, as she did it.

The huge green fragment of ice on which she alighted pitched and creaked as her weight came on it, but she stayed there not a moment. With wild cries and desperate energy she leaped to another and still another cake; stumbling—leaping—slipping—springing upwards again! Her shoes are gone—her stockings cut from her feet—while blood marked every step; but she saw nothing, felt nothing, till dimly, as in a dream, she saw the Ohio side, and a man helping her up the bank.

"Yer a brave gal, now, whoever ye ar!" said the man, with an oath.

Eliza recognized the voice and face of a man who owned a farm not far from her old home.

"O, Mr. Symmes! save me—do save me—do hide me!" said Eliza.

"Why, what's this?" said the man. "Why, if 'tan't Shelby's gal!"

"My child! this boy! he'd sold him! There is his Mas'r," said she, pointing to the Kentucky shore. "O, Mr. Symmes, you've got a little boy!"

"So I have," said the man, as he roughly, but kindly, drew her up the steep bank. "Besides, you're a right brave gal. I like grit, wherever I see it."

When they had gained the top of the bank, the man paused.

---

[1] *Jerry* Andy's horse.

"I'd be glad to do something for ye," said he; "but then there's nowhar I could take ye. The best I can do is to tell ye to go *thar*," said he, pointing to a large white house which stood by itself, off the main street of the village. "Go thar; they're kind folks. Thar's no kind o' danger but they'll help you—they're up to all that sort o' thing."

"The Lord bless you!" said Eliza, earnestly.

"No 'casion, no 'casion in the world," said the man. "What I've done's of no 'count."

"And, oh, surely, sir, you won't tell anyone!"

"Go to thunder, gal! What do you take a feller for? In course not," said the man. "Come, now, go along like a likely,[1] sensible gal, as you are. You've arnt your liberty, and you shall have it, for all me."

The woman folded her child to her bosom, and walked firmly and swiftly away. The man stood and looked after her.

"Shelby, now, mebbe won't think this yer the most neighborly thing in the world; but what's a feller to do? If he catches one of my gals in the same fix, he's welcome to pay back. Somehow I never could see no kind o' critter a strivin' and pantin', and trying to clar theirselves, with the dogs arter 'em, and go agin 'em. Besides, I don't see no kind of 'casion for me to be hunter and catcher for other folks, neither."

So spoke this poor, heathenish Kentuckian, who had not been instructed in his constitutional relations,[2] and consequently was betrayed into acting in a sort of Christianized manner, which, if he had been better situated and more enlightened, he would not have been left to do.

Haley had stood a perfectly amazed spectator of the scene, till Eliza had disappeared up the bank, when he turned a blank, inquiring look on Sam and Andy.

"That ar was a tolable fair stroke of business," said Sam.

"The gal's got seven devils in her, I believe!" said Haley. "How like a wildcat she jumped!"

"Wal, now," said Sam, scratching his head, "I hope Mas'r'll 'scuse us tryin' dat ar road. Don't think I feel spry enough for dat ar, no way!" and Sam gave a hoarse chuckle.

"*You* laugh!" said the trader, with a growl.

"Lord bless you, Mas'r, I couldn't help it, now," said Sam, giving way to the long pent-up delight of his soul. "She looked so curi's, a leapin' and springin'—ice a crackin'—and only to hear her—plump! ker chunk! ker splash! Spring! Lord! how she goes it!" and Sam and Andy laughed till the tears rolled down their cheeks.

"I'll make ye laugh t'other side yer mouths!" said the trader, laying about their heads with his riding-whip.

Both ducked, and ran shouting up the bank, and were on their horses before he was up.

"Good evening, Mas'r!" said Sam, with much gravity. "I berry much spect Missis be anxious 'bout Jerry. Mas'r Haley won't want us no longer. Missis wouldn't hear of our ridin' the critters over Lizy's bridge tonight"; and, with a facetious poke into Andy's ribs, he started off, followed by the latter, at full speed—their shouts of laughter coming faintly on the wind.

—1852

[NOTE: Chapters 1, 3–5, 7–12, 20, 26, 40, 41, and 45 are included in full in the website component of this anthology.]

---

1   *likely* Term suggesting strength or capability, but also frequently physical attractiveness.

2   *constitutional relations* The recently passed Fugitive Slave Act made it a federal crime to aid persons escaping from slavery, and placed increased pressures on ordinary citizens to aid in their capture.

IN CONTEXT

Visualizing *Uncle Tom's Cabin* in the Nineteenth Century

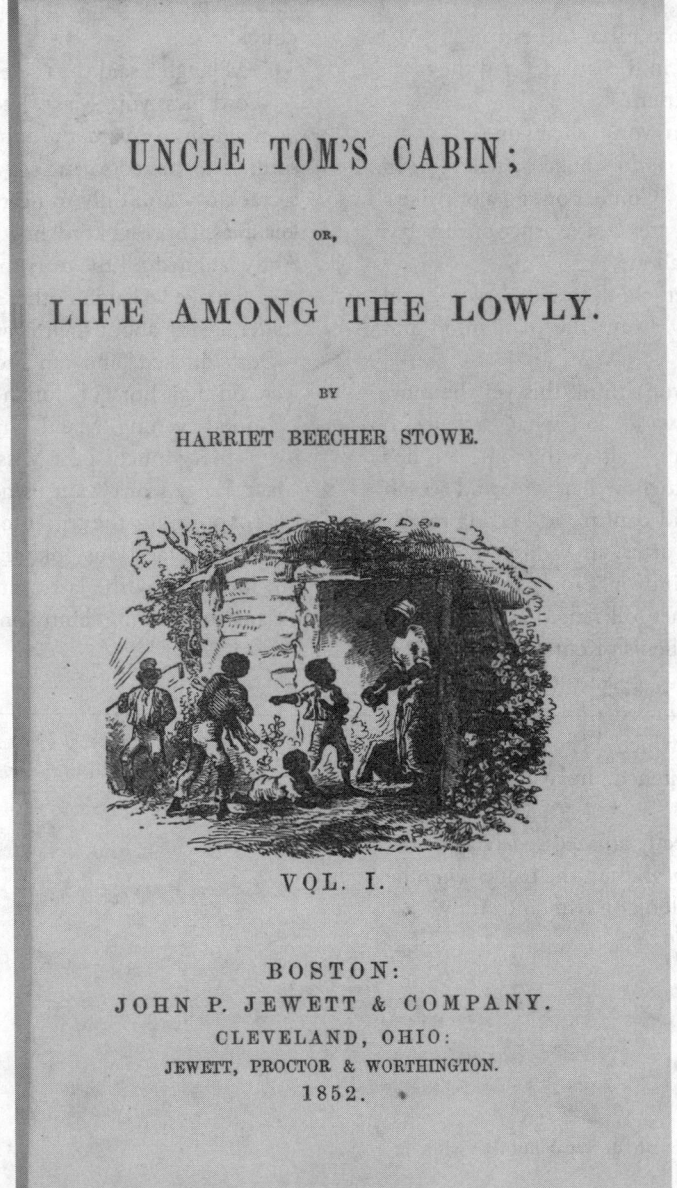

Frontispiece of the first edition of *Uncle Tom's Cabin*, which featured seven illustrations by Boston-based engraver Hammatt Billings (1818–74). Billings was already known for his work on the illustrated magazine *Gleason's Pictorial*, and in 1850 had redesigned the iconic masthead for the influential abolitionist newspaper *The Liberator*.

Hammatt Billings, *Little Eva Reading the Bible to Uncle Tom in the Arbor*, 1852. Billings's illustrations of the friendship between Eva and Uncle Tom were extremely influential and formed the basis for countless later visualizations of the novel. (See the anthology's online component for passages featuring the character of Eva—and of Topsy, who is depicted in the image below and on the following page.)

Louisa Corbaux, *Eva and Topsy*, 1852. Colored lithograph.

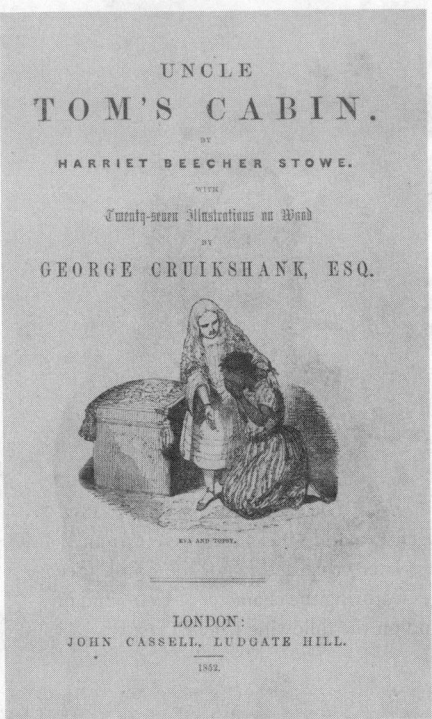

George Cruikshank, *Topsy with Miss Ophelia's Wardrobe*, 1852.

Frontispiece to the 1852 London edition, illustrated by George Cruikshank. Earlier in his career, Cruikshank (1792–1878) was best known as a caricaturist, his cartoons often targeting the royal family, contemporary fashions, and political ideologies on either side of the spectrum; interestingly, many of his cartoons targeted the abolitionist movement in particular, and were highly racist. He turned increasingly to book illustration in the 1830s, providing illustrations for several novels by Charles Dickens. The London edition featured twenty-seven engravings designed by Cruikshank.

George Cruikshank, *Eliza Crosses the Ohio on the Floating Ice*, 1852.

White actor Caroline Howard in blackface as the character of Topsy in the 1852 stage adaptation of *Uncle Tom's Cabin*, written by George Aiken. The play was produced by Caroline's father, George C. Howard, who himself starred as George Harris; other members of the Howard family also acted in the play.

For Christmas 1852, Jewett and Co. commissioned a second edition of *Uncle Tom's Cabin*, a lavishly illustrated "gift book" featuring over one hundred new images by Hammatt Billings. One of the last images in the edition is this one depicting a crowd of freed people reaching towards the African continent. The narrative of George and Eliza Harris in the novel concludes with them emigrating to Liberia, a colony that had been established by white politicians expressly for freed African Americans. The first edition of *Uncle Tom's Cabin* had sold for around $1.50; the Christmas edition sold for $15.

Advertisement for the 1881 stage play *Jay Rial's Ideal Uncle Tom's Cabin*. Eliza's dramatic escape over the Ohio was among the most popular scenes for stage adaptations of the novel, which often featured live bloodhounds—even though Eliza is not pursued by dogs in this scene in the original novel.

HARRIET JACOBS

c. 1813 – 1897

For a hundred and twenty years, Harriet Jacobs's groundbreaking narrative, *Incidents in the Life of a Slave Girl* (1861), went largely unnoticed. When it did receive commentary, it was assumed that the narrative was not autobiography but fiction, and that its true author was the white abolitionist writer Lydia Maria Child (who in fact edited the volume). It was not until scholar Jean Fagan Yellin published a groundbreaking article on the narrative in 1981 that Jacobs's authorship was authenticated. This meant that Jacobs's gripping and eloquent narrative, one of the earliest written by an enslaved woman in the United States, did not impact American literature and history until late in the twentieth century. Since then, Jacobs's achievement as a writer and activist has been widely recognized, and her profound influence on American literature has taken firm root. Jacobs's *Incidents* is brave and revolutionary in that it openly discusses the particular evils that slavery systemically inflicted on women—sexual abuse, rape, and the knowledge that any children born would be born enslaved. As critic Henry Louis Gates Jr. wrote, "Whereas the black male slave narrators' accounts of sexual brutality remain suggestive, if gruesome, Jacobs's … charts in vivid detail precisely how the shape of her life and the choices she makes are defined by her reduction to a sexual object, an object to be raped, bred or abused." Jacobs herself put it very simply: "Slavery is terrible for men; but it is far more terrible for women."

Jacobs was born in Edenton, North Carolina; most biographers date her birth in 1813, though her tombstone states she was born in 1815. Her mother, Delilah Horniblow, was enslaved by Margaret Horniblow, and her father, Elijah Knox, was enslaved by Andrew Knox. As a young child, Jacobs was unaware of her own enslaved condition; her father, a skilled carpenter, was allowed to keep a portion of his earnings, and the family lived in tolerable independence. Jacobs's maternal grandmother, Molly Horniblow, was a formative influence and support to the family, particularly to Jacobs. "I was so fondly shielded," she recalled, "that I never dreamed I was a piece of merchandise." Jacobs's mother died when she was six, breaking up the family circle; Margaret Horniblow, who had owned Delilah and thus owned her daughter, brought Jacobs to her home. Jacobs was treated kindly, and Horniblow taught her to read, write, and sew. When Jacobs was almost twelve years old, Horniblow died. Although Jacobs had believed that her mistress would set her free, she was instead bequeathed to Horniblow's five-year-old niece. Jacobs came under the control of the girl's father, Dr. James Norcom (who is given the pseudonym Dr. Flint in *Incidents*), a cruel man who soon began persecuting Jacobs with unwanted sexual attention.

Norcom's harassment of Jacobs was persistent, and her life in his house became more and more unbearable, both because of the sexual pressure and because of Mrs. Norcom's jealousy. Jacobs was increasingly isolated by what she perceived to be the shame of her situation: she usually went to her grandmother for advice, but she did not want to communicate the sexual nature of Norcom's persecution. In an effort to find security, Jacobs took a lover, Samuel Tredwell Sawyer, a local white attorney. With Sawyer, Jacobs would have two children, Joseph and Louisa. "I knew nothing would enrage [Norcom] so much as to know that I favored another," Jacobs wrote, "and it was something to triumph over my tyrant even in that small way." This relationship did not free her, however, from Norcom's threats, and, in the summer of 1835, Jacobs ran away and hid in a small crawlspace just below her grandmother's roof. She spent seven years in this tiny garret, watching her children grow up through a small hole she made to peer through. She managed to sew and read the Bible, but those years in hiding were plagued by isolation, by discomfort brought on by the weather—cold, heat, and rain all made her hideaway a miserable place—and by illness. In 1842, Jacobs escaped and went by boat to Pennsylvania, and from there to New York City.

While Jacobs was in hiding, Sawyer, who had been elected to Congress in 1837, had managed to purchase his and Jacobs's two children from Norcom, and he had sent the girl, Louisa, to Brooklyn to work as a servant (he did not keep his promise to free the children). Jacobs settled in New York to be close to her daughter—her son also eventually joined them—and took a job as nursemaid in the house of Mary Stace Willis, wife of the well-known poet and editor Nathaniel Parker Willis. Periodically, Norcom would try to find Jacobs, and she would have to temporarily leave New York. On one such occasion in 1845, while Jacobs was hiding in Boston, her employer, Mary Willis, died; when Nathaniel Willis subsequently decided to take a trip to England with his daughter, Jacobs accepted his offer to go with them and act as nursemaid. Jacobs experienced little racism in England, and she was impressed that the poor people in that country had access to education. In 1849, again fleeing Norcom, Jacobs went to Rochester, New York, where she worked with her brother, John Jacobs, in an antislavery reading room and bookstore. Rochester was a thriving center for abolitionist and feminist activism—Jacobs and her brother's reading room was located above the offices of Frederick Douglass's newspaper—and Jacobs began to find likeminded friends there, including Amy Post, who encouraged Jacobs to write and publish her experience.

In the meantime, Nathaniel Parker Willis remarried, and his second wife, Cornelia Grinell, employed Jacobs as a nursemaid for her new baby. In 1852, when Jacobs was again threatened with capture, Cornelia bought her for $300, ensuring her freedom. Though it deflated Jacobs to be traded like merchandise, having her freedom was a significant relief, and in 1853 she began her writing career in earnest. She wrote anonymous letters to the *New York Tribune*, including "Letter from a Fugitive Slave. Slaves Sold under Peculiar Circumstances" (21 June 1853), which touches on what would become a central theme in *Incidents*: the sexual abuse faced by enslaved women, and the struggle enslaved mothers endured to attempt to protect their children. Jacobs wrote *Incidents* while still working as a nursemaid in the Willis household; she kept her writing private, because she was not convinced that Nathaniel Willis supported abolition (though his wife certainly did). In the summer of 1857, Jacobs wrote to Amy Post that she had finished "a true and just account of my own life in Slavery," and that she hoped it "might do something for the Antislavery Cause."

Jacobs faced hurdles, however, in publishing *Incidents*, traveling to England in 1858 in an unsuccessful search for a publisher. The Boston company Phillips and Samson eventually agreed to take the book if Willis, Jacobs's employer, or Harriet Beecher Stowe would write an introduction. Jacobs didn't feel Willis would support the book, so she asked Stowe, but Stowe rejected the idea of collaborating with Jacobs. A different publisher, Thayer and Eldridge, then agreed to publish, stipulating this time an introduction by Lydia Maria Child, and, though very reluctant to do so, Jacobs asked Child if she would contribute to the project. Child agreed to not only write an introduction, but to edit the book. Though many people thought Child's involvement was extensive, Jean Fagan Yellin's research makes it clear that Child did not exceed the role she herself described in the introduction to the volume: "I have not added anything to the incidents, or changed the import of [Jacobs's] very pertinent remarks. With trifling exceptions, both the ideas and the language are her own. I pruned excrescences a little, but otherwise I had no reason for changing her lively and dramatic way of telling her own story."

When Thayer and Eldridge dissolved as a company, Jacobs secured the typeset pages of *Incidents* and determined to publish it herself; it was finally published in 1861, followed by a British edition in 1862. Jacobs used a pseudonym, Linda Brent, and she changed the names of all the characters in the book to protect their anonymity. *Incidents* was warmly received by audiences in the North and across the Atlantic, but it was not financially successful, and the Civil War soon drew much of the public's attention. After the war, Jacobs's work fell into obscurity, and only since the 1980s have readership and scholarship of it flourished; it has since become one of the most often-taught and frequently-read slave narratives.

Jacobs's writing style was influenced by the Bible, by other slave narratives—such as those by Olaudah Equiano and Frederick Douglass—and by the work of various contemporary women writers, including Lydia Maria Child, Fanny Fern, and Harriet Beecher Stowe. Like Stowe, Jacobs uses the rhetorical tools of the sentimental novel to add emotional power to her attack on slavery, and to frame some of her own experiences. In sentimental novels such as Samuel Richardson's *Pamela* (1740), for example, a servant girl is persecuted by the sexual attentions of her master, whom she continually rejects, thereby preserving her virtue. Jacobs's persistence in escaping Norcom is presented within this framework, as she bravely and successfully keeps her abuser at bay; on the other hand, the shame she feels at having an unmarried affair with Sawyer is felt as a failure to live up to the idealization of what it means to be a virtuous young woman. While Jacobs clearly judged herself against such ideals, she also forcefully questions their application to a person who is trapped in the misery of slavery: "… in looking back, calmly, on the events of my life, I feel that the slave woman ought not to be judged by the same standard as others."

Jacobs's story, focusing as it does on the bonds of women and seeking as it does an inter-racial and inter-regional political alliance, has become a crucial feminist text. *Incidents* has also taken a vital place in the history of African American literature, influencing writers such as Toni Morrison, Alice Walker, bell hooks, Ta-Nehisi Coates, and Claudia Rankine, among many others. As writers consider what it means to lead a dignified life in an America still convulsed with sexism and racism, Jacobs's narrative is a touchstone and inspiration. It has been translated into many languages and is read and taught around the world.

Jacobs dedicated her life not only to exposing the sexual violence of slavery—a secret she said was "concealed like those of the Inquisition"—but also to bettering the condition of black people across the United States. Following the publication of *Incidents*, Jacobs delivered numerous speeches in support of abolition, nursed wounded black troops during the Civil War, and assisted newly-emancipated African Americans. In 1864, she established a school for black children in Alexandria, Virginia, where her daughter Louisa was a teacher. Jacobs died in Washington, D.C. in 1897 and was buried in Cambridge, Massachusetts, in Mount Auburn Cemetery.

NOTE ON THE TEXT: The excerpts presented here are based on the first 1861 Boston edition of Jacobs's *Incidents in the Life of a Slave Girl, Written by Herself*, edited by Lydia Maria Child.

⌘ ⌘ ⌘

from *Incidents in the Life of a Slave Girl, Written by Herself*

Northerners know nothing at all about Slavery. They think it is perpetual bondage only. They have no conception of the depth of *degradation* involved in that word, SLAVERY; if they had, they would never cease their efforts until so horrible a system was overthrown.

A WOMAN OF NORTH CAROLINA

Rise up, ye women that are at ease! Hear my voice, ye careless daughters! Give ear unto my speech.

ISAIAH 32.9

PREFACE BY THE AUTHOR

Reader, be assured this narrative is no fiction. I am aware that some of my adventures may seem incredible; but they are, nevertheless, strictly true. I have not exaggerated the wrongs inflicted by Slavery; on the contrary, my descriptions fall far short of the facts. I have concealed the names of places, and given persons fictitious names. I had no motive for secrecy on my own account, but I deemed it kind and considerate towards others to pursue this course.

I wish I were more competent to the task I have undertaken. But I trust my readers will excuse deficiencies in consideration of circumstances. I was born and reared in Slavery; and I remained in a Slave State twenty-seven years. Since I have been at the North, it has been necessary for me to work diligently for my own support, and the education of my children. This has not left me much leisure to make up for the loss of early opportunities to improve myself; and it has compelled me to write these pages at irregular intervals, whenever I could snatch an hour from household duties.

When I first arrived in Philadelphia, Bishop Paine[1] advised me to publish a sketch of my life, but I told him I was altogether incompetent to such an undertaking. Though I have improved my mind somewhat since that time, I still remain of the same opinion; but I trust my motives will excuse what might otherwise seem presumptuous. I have not written my experiences in order to attract attention to myself; on the contrary, it would have been more pleasant to me to have been silent about my own history. Neither do I care to excite sympathy for my own sufferings. But I do earnestly desire to arouse the women of the North to a realizing sense of the condition of two millions of women at the South, still in bondage, suffering what I suffered, and most of them far worse. I want to add my testimony to that of abler pens to convince the people of the Free States what Slavery really is. Only by experience can anyone realize how deep, and dark, and foul is that pit of abominations. May the blessing of God rest on this imperfect effort in behalf of my persecuted people!

Linda Brent[2]

INTRODUCTION BY THE EDITOR

The author of the following autobiography is personally known to me, and her conversation and manners inspire me with confidence. During the last seventeen years, she has lived the greater part of the time with a distinguished family in New York, and has so deported[3] herself as to be highly esteemed by them. This fact is sufficient, without further credentials of her character.

I believe those who know her will not be disposed to doubt her veracity, though some incidents in her story are more romantic[4] than fiction.

At her request, I have revised her manuscript; but such changes as I have made have been mainly for purposes of condensation and orderly arrangement. I have not added anything to the incidents, or changed the import of her very pertinent remarks. With trifling exceptions, both the ideas and the language are her own. I pruned excrescences a little, but otherwise I had no reason for changing her lively and dramatic way of telling her own story. The names of both persons and places are known to me; but for good reasons I suppress them.

It will naturally excite surprise that a woman reared in Slavery should be able to write so well. But circumstances will explain this. In the first place, nature endowed her with quick perceptions. Secondly, the mistress, with whom she lived till she was twelve years old, was a kind, considerate friend, who taught her to read and spell. Thirdly, she was placed in favorable circumstances after she came to the North; having frequent intercourse with intelligent persons, who felt a friendly interest in her welfare, and were disposed to give her opportunities for self-improvement.

I am well aware that many will accuse me of indecorum for presenting these pages to the public; for the experiences of this intelligent and much-injured woman belong to a class which some call delicate subjects, and others indelicate. This peculiar phase of Slavery[5] has generally been kept veiled; but the public ought to be made acquainted with its monstrous features, and I willingly take the responsibility of presenting them with the veil withdrawn. I do this for the sake of my sisters in bondage, who are suffering wrongs so foul, that our ears are too delicate to listen to them. I do it with the hope of arousing conscientious and reflecting women at the North to a sense of their duty in the exertion of moral influence on the question of Slavery, on all possible occasions. I do it with the hope that every man who reads this narrative will swear solemnly before God that, so far as he has power to prevent it, no fugitive from Slavery shall ever

---

[1] *Bishop Paine* Daniel Alexander Payne was a writer, educator, and bishop in the African Methodist Episcopal Church. In the early 1840s, he worked on the Philadelphia Vigilance Committee, which provided clothing and shelter for enslaved people escaping to the North.

[2] *Linda Brent* Harriet Jacobs's pseudonym.

[3] *deported* Conducted.

[4] *romantic* Unlikely or implausible.

[5] *peculiar phase of Slavery* I.e., the particular abuses, such as sexual violence, that slavery systemically encouraged and enabled.

be sent back to suffer in that loathsome den of corruption and cruelty.

L. Maria Child

CHAPTER I. CHILDHOOD

I was born a slave; but I never knew it till six years of happy childhood had passed away. My father was a carpenter, and considered so intelligent and skillful in his trade, that, when buildings out of the common line were to be erected, he was sent for from long distances, to be head workman. On condition of paying his mistress two hundred dollars a year,[1] and supporting himself, he was allowed to work at his trade, and manage his own affairs. His strongest wish was to purchase his children; but, though he several times offered his hard earnings for that purpose, he never succeeded. In complexion my parents were a light shade of brownish yellow, and were termed mulattoes.[2] They lived together in a comfortable home; and, though we were all slaves, I was so fondly shielded that I never dreamed I was a piece of merchandise, trusted to them for safe keeping, and liable to be demanded of them at any moment. I had one brother, William, who was two years younger than myself—a bright, affectionate child. I had also a great treasure in my maternal grandmother, who was a remarkable woman in many respects. She was the daughter of a planter in South Carolina, who, at his death, left her mother and his three children free, with money to go to St. Augustine,[3] where they had relatives. It was during the Revolutionary War; and they were captured on their passage, carried back, and sold to different purchasers. Such was the story my grandmother used to tell me; but I do not remember all the particulars. She was a little girl when she was captured and sold to the keeper of a large hotel. I have often heard her tell how hard she fared during childhood. But as she grew older she evinced so much intelligence, and was so faithful, that her master and mistress could not help seeing it was

for their interest to take care of such a valuable piece of property. She became an indispensable personage in the household, officiating in all capacities, from cook and wet nurse to seamstress. She was much praised for her cooking; and her nice[4] crackers became so famous in the neighborhood that many people were desirous of obtaining them. In consequence of numerous requests of this kind, she asked permission of her mistress to bake crackers at night, after all the household work was done; and she obtained leave to do it, provided she would clothe herself and her children from the profits. Upon these terms, after working hard all day for her mistress, she began her midnight bakings, assisted by her two oldest children. The business proved profitable; and each year she laid by a little, which was saved for a fund to purchase her children. Her master died, and the property was divided among his heirs. The widow had her dower in the hotel, which she continued to keep open. My grandmother remained in her service as a slave; but her children were divided among her master's children. As she had five, Benjamin, the youngest one, was sold, in order that each heir might have an equal portion of dollars and cents. There was so little difference in our ages that he seemed more like my brother than my uncle. He was a bright, handsome lad, nearly white; for he inherited the complexion my grandmother had derived from Anglo-Saxon ancestors. Though only ten years old, seven hundred and twenty dollars were paid for him. His sale was a terrible blow to my grandmother; but she was naturally hopeful, and she went to work with renewed energy, trusting in time to be able to purchase some of her children. She had laid up three hundred dollars, which her mistress one day begged as a loan, promising to pay her soon. The reader probably knows that no promise or writing given to a slave is legally binding; for, according to Southern laws, a slave, being property, can hold no property. When my grandmother lent her hard earnings to her mistress, she trusted solely to her honor. The honor of a slaveholder to a slave!

To this good grandmother I was indebted for many comforts. My brother Willie and I often received portions of the crackers, cakes, and preserves, she made to sell; and after we ceased to be children we were indebted to her for many more important services.

---

[1]   *two hundred dollars a year*   Equivalent to about $6,000.

[2]   *mulattoes*   The term "mulatto," which is today considered archaic and offensive, was commonly used in the nineteenth century to classify individuals of mixed racial background—most frequently, those with one white and one black parent.

[3]   *St. Augustine*   City on the northeast coast of Florida.

[4]   *nice*   Tasty, delicate.

Such were the unusually fortunate circumstances of my early childhood. When I was six years old, my mother died; and then, for the first time, I learned, by the talk around me, that I was a slave. My mother's mistress was the daughter of my grandmother's mistress. She was the foster sister of my mother; they were both nourished at my grandmother's breast. In fact, my mother had been weaned at three months old, that the babe of the mistress might obtain sufficient food. They played together as children; and, when they became women, my mother was a most faithful servant to her whiter foster sister. On her death-bed her mistress promised that her children should never suffer for anything; and during her lifetime she kept her word. They all spoke kindly of my dead mother, who had been a slave merely in name, but in nature was noble and womanly. I grieved for her, and my young mind was troubled with the thought who would now take care of me and my little brother. I was told that my home was now to be with her mistress; and I found it a happy one. No toilsome or disagreeable duties were imposed upon me. My mistress was so kind to me that I was always glad to do her bidding, and proud to labor for her as much as my young years would permit. I would sit by her side for hours, sewing diligently, with a heart as free from care as that of any free-born white child. When she thought I was tired, she would send me out to run and jump; and away I bounded, to gather berries or flowers to decorate her room. Those were happy days—too happy to last. The slave child had no thought for the morrow; but there came that blight, which too surely waits on every human being born to be a chattel.

When I was nearly twelve years old, my kind mistress sickened and died. As I saw the cheek grow paler, and the eye more glassy, how earnestly I prayed in my heart that she might live! I loved her; for she had been almost like a mother to me. My prayers were not answered. She died, and they buried her in the little churchyard, where, day after day, my tears fell upon her grave.

I was sent to spend a week with my grandmother. I was now old enough to begin to think of the future; and again and again I asked myself what they would do with me. I felt sure I should never find another mistress so kind as the one who was gone. She had promised my dying mother that her children should never suffer for

anything; and when I remembered that, and recalled her many proofs of attachment to me, I could not help having some hopes that she had left me free. My friends were almost certain it would be so. They thought she would be sure to do it, on account of my mother's love and faithful service. But, alas! we all know that the memory of a faithful slave does not avail much to save her children from the auction block.

After a brief period of suspense, the will of my mistress was read, and we learned that she had bequeathed me to her sister's daughter, a child of five years old. So vanished our hopes. My mistress had taught me the precepts of God's Word: "Thou shalt love thy neighbor as thyself." "Whatsoever ye would that men should do unto you, do ye even so unto them."[1] But I was her slave, and I suppose she did not recognize me as her neighbor. I would give much to blot out from my memory that one great wrong. As a child, I loved my mistress; and, looking back on the happy days I spent with her, I try to think with less bitterness of this act of injustice. While I was with her, she taught me to read and spell; and for this privilege, which so rarely falls to the lot of a slave, I bless her memory.

She possessed but few slaves; and at her death those were all distributed among her relatives. Five of them were my grandmother's children, and had shared the same milk that nourished her mother's children. Notwithstanding my grandmother's long and faithful service to her owners, not one of her children escaped the auction block. These God-breathing machines are no more, in the sight of their masters, than the cotton they plant, or the horses they tend.

CHAPTER 2. THE NEW MASTER AND MISTRESS

Dr. Flint, a physician in the neighborhood, had married the sister of my mistress, and I was now the property of their little daughter. It was not without murmuring[2] that I prepared for my new home; and what added to my unhappiness, was the fact that my

---

[1]   *Thou shalt ... thyself*   The second of Christ's commandments, see Matthew 22.39; *Whatsoever ye would ... unto them*   This saying is known as the "golden rule." See Leviticus 19.18 and Matthew 7.12.

[2]   *not without murmuring*   See Philippians 2.14–15: "Do all things without murmurings and disputings; / That ye may be blameless and harmless, the sons of God, without rebuke, in the midst of a crooked and perverse nation, among whom ye shine as lights in the world."

brother William was purchased by the same family. My father, by his nature, as well as by the habit of transacting business as a skillful mechanic, had more of the feelings of a freeman than is common among slaves. My brother was a spirited boy; and being brought up under such influences, he early detested the name of master and mistress. One day, when his father and his mistress both happened to call him at the same time, he hesitated between the two; being perplexed to know which had the strongest claim upon his obedience. He finally concluded to go to his mistress. When my father reproved him for it, he said, "You both called me, and I didn't know which I ought to go to first."

"You are *my* child," replied our father, "and when I call you, you should come immediately, if you have to pass through fire and water."[1]

Poor Willie! He was now to learn his first lesson of obedience to a master. Grandmother tried to cheer us with hopeful words, and they found an echo in the credulous hearts of youth.

When we entered our new home we encountered cold looks, cold words, and cold treatment. We were glad when the night came. On my narrow bed I moaned and wept, I felt so desolate and alone.

I had been there nearly a year, when a dear little friend of mine was buried. I heard her mother sob, as the clods fell on the coffin of her only child, and I turned away from the grave, feeling thankful that I still had something left to love. I met my grandmother, who said, "Come with me, Linda"; and from her tone I knew that something sad had happened. She led me apart from the people, and then said, "My child, your father is dead." Dead! How could I believe it? He had died so suddenly I had not even heard that he was sick. I went home with my grandmother. My heart rebelled against God, who had taken from me mother, father, mistress, and friend. The good grandmother tried to comfort me. "Who knows the ways of God?" said she. "Perhaps they have been kindly taken from the evil days to come." Years afterwards I often thought of this. She promised to be a mother to her grandchildren, so far as she might be permitted to do so; and

strengthened by her love, I returned to my master's. I thought I should be allowed to go to my father's house the next morning; but I was ordered to go for flowers, that my mistress's house might be decorated for an evening party. I spent the day gathering flowers and weaving them into festoons, while the dead body of my father was lying within a mile of me. What cared my owners for that? he was merely a piece of property. Moreover, they thought he had spoiled his children, by teaching them to feel that they were human beings. This was blasphemous doctrine for a slave to teach; presumptuous in him, and dangerous to the masters.

The next day I followed his remains to a humble grave beside that of my dear mother. There were those who knew my father's worth, and respected his memory.

My home now seemed more dreary than ever. The laugh of the little slave-children sounded harsh and cruel. It was selfish to feel so about the joy of others. My brother moved about with a very grave face. I tried to comfort him, by saying, "Take courage, Willie; brighter days will come by and by."

"You don't know anything about it, Linda," he replied. "We shall have to stay here all our days; we shall never be free."

I argued that we were growing older and stronger, and that perhaps we might, before long, be allowed to hire our own time, and then we could earn money to buy our freedom. William declared this was much easier to say than to do; moreover, he did not intend to buy his freedom. We held daily controversies upon this subject.

Little attention was paid to the slaves' meals in Dr. Flint's house. If they could catch a bit of food while it was going, well and good. I gave myself no trouble on that score, for on my various errands I passed my grandmother's house, where there was always something to spare for me. I was frequently threatened with punishment if I stopped there; and my grandmother, to avoid detaining me, often stood at the gate with something for my breakfast or dinner. I was indebted to her for all my comforts, spiritual or temporal. It was her labor that supplied my scanty wardrobe. I have a vivid recollection of the linsey-woolsey[2] dress given me

---

1   *pass through fire and water*   See Isaiah 43.2: "When thou passest through the waters, I will be with thee; and through the rivers, they shall not overflow thee: when thou walkest through the fire, thou shalt not be burned; neither shall the flame kindle upon thee."

2   *linsey-woolsey*   Coarse fabric made of the cheapest wool and linen.

every winter by Mrs. Flint. How I hated it! It was one of the badges of slavery.

While my grandmother was thus helping to support me from her hard earnings, the three hundred dollars she had lent her mistress were never repaid. When her mistress died, her son-in-law, Dr. Flint, was appointed executor. When grandmother applied to him for payment, he said the estate was insolvent, and the law prohibited payment. It did not, however, prohibit him from retaining the silver candelabra, which had been purchased with that money. I presume they will be handed down in the family, from generation to generation.

My grandmother's mistress had always promised her that, at her death, she should be free; and it was said that in her will she made good the promise. But when the estate was settled, Dr. Flint told the faithful old servant that, under existing circumstances, it was necessary she should be sold.

On the appointed day, the customary advertisement was posted up, proclaiming that there would be "a public sale of negroes, horses, &c." Dr. Flint called to tell my grandmother that he was unwilling to wound her feelings by putting her up at auction, and that he would prefer to dispose of her at private sale. My grandmother saw through his hypocrisy; she understood very well that he was ashamed of the job. She was a very spirited woman, and if he was base enough to sell her, when her mistress intended she should be free, she was determined the public should know it. She had for a long time supplied many families with crackers and preserves; consequently, "Aunt Marthy," as she was called, was generally known, and everybody who knew her respected her intelligence and good character. Her long and faithful service in the family was also well known, and the intention of her mistress to leave her free. When the day of sale came, she took her place among the chattels, and at the first call she sprang upon the auction-block. Many voices called out, "Shame! Shame! Who is going to sell *you*, Aunt Marthy? Don't stand there! That is no place for *you*." Without saying a word, she quietly awaited her fate. No one bid for her. At last, a feeble voice said, "Fifty dollars." It came from a maiden lady, seventy years old, the sister of my grandmother's deceased mistress. She had lived forty years under the same roof with my grandmother; she knew how faithfully she had served her owners, and how cruelly she had been defrauded of her rights; and she resolved to protect her. The auctioneer waited for a higher bid; but her wishes were respected; no one bid above her. She could neither read nor write; and when the bill of sale was made out, she signed it with a cross. But what consequence was that, when she had a big heart overflowing with human kindness? She gave the old servant her freedom.

At that time, my grandmother was just fifty years old. Laborious years had passed since then; and now my brother and I were slaves to the man who had defrauded her of her money, and tried to defraud her of her freedom. One of my mother's sisters, called Aunt Nancy, was also a slave in his family. She was a kind, good aunt to me; and supplied the place of both housekeeper and waiting maid to her mistress. She was, in fact, at the beginning and end of everything.

Mrs. Flint, like many southern women, was totally deficient in energy. She had not strength to superintend her household affairs; but her nerves were so strong, that she could sit in her easy chair and see a woman whipped, till the blood trickled from every stroke of the lash. She was a member of the church; but partaking of the Lord's supper[1] did not seem to put her in a Christian frame of mind. If dinner was not served at the exact time on that particular Sunday, she would station herself in the kitchen, and wait till it was dished, and then spit in all the kettles and pans that had been used for cooking. She did this to prevent the cook and her children from eking out their meagre fare with the remains of the gravy and other scrapings. The slaves could get nothing to eat except what she chose to give them. Provisions were weighed out by the pound and ounce, three times a day. I can assure you she gave them no chance to eat wheat bread from her flour barrel. She knew how many biscuits a quart of flour would make, and exactly what size they ought to be.

Dr. Flint was an epicure.[2] The cook never sent a dinner to his table without fear and trembling; for if there happened to be a dish not to his liking, he would

---

[1]   *Lord's supper* I.e., sacrament of the Eucharist, in which the faithful drink wine and eat bread that is considered, symbolically, the blood and body of Christ.

[2]   *epicure* Person devoted to sensual pleasure.

either order her to be whipped, or compel her to eat every mouthful of it in his presence. The poor, hungry creature might not have objected to eating it; but she did object to having her master cram it down her throat till she choked.

They had a pet dog, that was a nuisance in the house. The cook was ordered to make some Indian mush[1] for him. He refused to eat, and when his head was held over it, the froth flowed from his mouth into the basin. He died a few minutes after. When Dr. Flint came in, he said the mush had not been well cooked, and that was the reason the animal would not eat it. He sent for the cook, and compelled her to eat it. He thought that the woman's stomach was stronger than the dog's; but her sufferings afterwards proved that he was mistaken. This poor woman endured many cruelties from her master and mistress; sometimes she was locked up, away from her nursing baby, for a whole day and night.

When I had been in the family a few weeks, one of the plantation slaves was brought to town, by order of his master. It was near night when he arrived, and Dr. Flint ordered him to be taken to the work house, and tied up to the joist, so that his feet would just escape the ground. In that situation he was to wait till the doctor had taken his tea. I shall never forget that night. Never before, in my life, had I heard hundreds of blows fall, in succession, on a human being. His piteous groans, and his "O, pray don't, massa," rang in my ear for months afterwards. There were many conjectures as to the cause of this terrible punishment. Some said master accused him of stealing corn; others said the slave had quarrelled with his wife, in presence of the overseer, and had accused his master of being the father of her child. They were both black, and the child was very fair.

I went into the work house next morning, and saw the cowhide[2] still wet with blood, and the boards all covered with gore. The poor man lived, and continued to quarrel with his wife. A few months afterwards Dr. Flint handed them both over to a slave-trader. The guilty man put their value into his pocket, and had the satisfaction of knowing that they were out of sight and hearing. When the mother was delivered into the trader's hands, she said, "You *promised* to treat me

well." To which he replied, "You have let your tongue run too far; damn you!" She had forgotten that it was a crime for a slave to tell who was the father of her child.

From others than the master persecution also comes in such cases. I once saw a young slave girl dying soon after the birth of a child nearly white. In her agony she cried out, "O Lord, come and take me!" Her mistress stood by, and mocked at her like an incarnate fiend. "You suffer, do you?" she exclaimed. "I am glad of it. You deserve it all, and more too."

The girl's mother said, "The baby is dead, thank God; and I hope my poor child will soon be in heaven, too."

"Heaven!" retorted the mistress. "There is no such place for the like of her and her bastard."

The poor mother turned away, sobbing. Her dying daughter called her, feebly, and as she bent over her, I heard her say, "Don't grieve so, mother; God knows all about it; and HE will have mercy upon me."

Her sufferings, afterwards, became so intense, that her mistress felt unable to stay; but when she left the room, the scornful smile was still on her lips. Seven children called her mother. The poor black woman had but the one child, whose eyes she saw closing in death, while she thanked God for taking her away from the greater bitterness of life.

CHAPTER 5. THE TRIALS OF GIRLHOOD

During the first years of my service in Dr. Flint's family, I was accustomed to share some indulgences with the children of my mistress. Though this seemed to me no more than right, I was grateful for it, and tried to merit the kindness by the faithful discharge of my duties. But I now entered on my fifteenth year—a sad epoch in the life of a slave girl. My master began to whisper foul words in my ear. Young as I was, I could not remain ignorant of their import. I tried to treat them with indifference or contempt. The master's age, my extreme youth, and the fear that his conduct would be reported to my grandmother, made him bear this treatment for many months. He was a crafty man, and resorted to many means to accomplish his purposes. Sometimes he had stormy, terrific[3] ways, that made his victims tremble; sometimes he assumed a gentleness that he thought must surely subdue. Of the two,

---

[1]   *Indian mush*   Porridge made of corn.

[2]   *cowhide*   Heavy whip made of cow's hide.

[3]   *terrific*   I.e., terrifying.

I preferred his stormy moods, although they left me trembling. He tried his utmost to corrupt the pure principles my grandmother had instilled. He peopled my young mind with unclean images, such as only a vile monster could think of. I turned from him with disgust and hatred. But he was my master. I was compelled to live under the same roof with him—where I saw a man forty years my senior daily violating the most sacred commandments of nature. He told me I was his property; that I must be subject to his will in all things. My soul revolted against the mean tyranny. But where could I turn for protection? No matter whether the slave girl be as black as ebony or as fair as her mistress. In either case, there is no shadow of law to protect her from insult, from violence, or even from death; all these are inflicted by fiends who bear the shape of men. The mistress, who ought to protect the helpless victim, has no other feelings towards her but those of jealousy and rage. The degradation, the wrongs, the vices, that grow out of slavery, are more than I can describe. They are greater than you would willingly believe. Surely, if you credited one half the truths that are told you concerning the helpless millions suffering in this cruel bondage, you at the north would not help to tighten the yoke.[1] You surely would refuse to do for the master, on your own soil, the mean and cruel work which trained bloodhounds and the lowest class of whites do for him at the south.

Everywhere the years bring to all enough of sin and sorrow; but in slavery the very dawn of life is darkened by these shadows. Even the little child, who is accustomed to wait on her mistress and her children, will learn, before she is twelve years old, why it is that her mistress hates such and such a one among the slaves. Perhaps the child's own mother is among those hated ones. She listens to violent outbreaks of jealous passion, and cannot help understanding what is the cause. She will become prematurely knowing in evil things. Soon she will learn to tremble when she hears her master's footfall. She will be compelled to realize that she is no longer a child. If God has bestowed beauty upon her, it will prove her greatest curse. That which commands admiration in the white woman only hastens the degradation of the female slave. I know that some are too much brutalized by slavery to feel the humiliation of their position; but many slaves feel it most acutely, and shrink from the memory of it. I cannot tell how much I suffered in the presence of these wrongs, nor how I am still pained by the retrospect. My master met me at every turn, reminding me that I belonged to him, and swearing by heaven and earth that he would compel me to submit to him. If I went out for a breath of fresh air, after a day of unwearied toil, his footsteps dogged me. If I knelt by my mother's grave, his dark shadow fell on me even there. The light heart which nature had given me became heavy with sad forebodings. The other slaves in my master's house noticed the change. Many of them pitied me; but none dared to ask the cause. They had no need to inquire. They knew too well the guilty practices under that roof; and they were aware that to speak of them was an offence that never went unpunished.

I longed for someone to confide in. I would have given the world to have laid my head on my grandmother's faithful bosom, and told her all my troubles. But Dr. Flint swore he would kill me, if I was not as silent as the grave. Then, although my grandmother was all in all to me, I feared her as well as loved her. I had been accustomed to look up to her with a respect bordering upon awe. I was very young, and felt shamefaced about telling her such impure things, especially as I knew her to be very strict on such subjects. Moreover, she was a woman of a high spirit. She was usually very quiet in her demeanor; but if her indignation was once roused, it was not very easily quelled. I had been told that she once chased a white gentleman with a loaded pistol, because he insulted one of her daughters. I dreaded the consequences of a violent outbreak; and both pride and fear kept me silent. But though I did not confide in my grandmother, and even evaded her vigilant watchfulness and inquiry, her presence in the neighborhood was some protection to me. Though she had been a slave, Dr. Flint was afraid of her. He dreaded her scorching rebukes. Moreover, she was known and patronized by many people; and he did not wish to have his villainy made public. It was

---

[1]   *north ... yoke* Reference to the hope that Northerners would actively resist the terms of the Fugitive Slave Act of 1850, under which it became illegal for anyone, whether in the North or the South, to give aid to people escaping slavery; citizens throughout the country were expected to actively participate in the apprehension and return of fugitives to the South. The Fugitive Slave Act was fiercely resisted by Northern abolitionists, but it was not repealed until 1864.

lucky for me that I did not live on a distant plantation, but in a town not so large that the inhabitants were ignorant of each other's affairs. Bad as are the laws and customs in a slaveholding community, the doctor, as a professional man, deemed it prudent to keep up some outward show of decency.

O, what days and nights of fear and sorrow that man caused me! Reader, it is not to awaken sympathy for myself that I am telling you truthfully what I suffered in slavery. I do it to kindle a flame of compassion in your hearts for my sisters who are still in bondage, suffering as I once suffered.

I once saw two beautiful children playing together. One was a fair white child; the other was her slave, and also her sister. When I saw them embracing each other, and heard their joyous laughter, I turned sadly away from the lovely sight. I foresaw the inevitable blight that would fall on the little slave's heart. I knew how soon her laughter would be changed to sighs. The fair child grew up to be a still fairer woman. From childhood to womanhood her pathway was blooming with flowers, and overarched by a sunny sky. Scarcely one day of her life had been clouded when the sun rose on her happy bridal morning.

How had those years dealt with her slave sister, the little playmate of her childhood? She, also, was very beautiful; but the flowers and sunshine of love were not for her. She drank the cup of sin, and shame, and misery, whereof her persecuted race are compelled to drink.

In view of these things, why are ye silent, ye free men and women of the north? Why do your tongues falter in maintenance of the right? Would that I had more ability! But my heart is so full, and my pen is so weak! There are noble men and women who plead for us, striving to help those who cannot help themselves. God bless them! God give them strength and courage to go on! God bless those, everywhere, who are laboring to advance the cause of humanity!

CHAPTER 6. THE JEALOUS MISTRESS

I would ten thousand times rather that my children should be the half-starved paupers of Ireland than to be the most pampered among the slaves of America. I would rather drudge out my life on a cotton plantation, till the grave opened to give me rest, than to live

with an unprincipled master and a jealous mistress. The felon's home in a penitentiary is preferable. He may repent, and turn from the error of his ways, and so find peace; but it is not so with a favorite slave. She is not allowed to have any pride of character. It is deemed a crime in her to wish to be virtuous.

Mrs. Flint possessed the key to her husband's character before I was born. She might have used this knowledge to counsel and to screen the young and the innocent among her slaves; but for them she had no sympathy. They were the objects of her constant suspicion and malevolence. She watched her husband with unceasing vigilance; but he was well practiced in means to evade it. What he could not find opportunity to say in words he manifested in signs. He invented more than were ever thought of in a deaf and dumb[1] asylum. I let them pass, as if I did not understand what he meant; and many were the curses and threats bestowed on me for my stupidity. One day he caught me teaching myself to write. He frowned, as if he was not well pleased, but I suppose he came to the conclusion that such an accomplishment might help to advance his favorite scheme. Before long, notes were often slipped into my hand. I would return them, saying, "I can't read them, sir." "Can't you?" he replied; "then I must read them to you." He always finished the reading by asking, "Do you understand?" Sometimes he would complain of the heat of the tea room, and order his supper to be placed on a small table in the piazza.[2] He would seat himself there with a well-satisfied smile, and tell me to stand by and brush away the flies. He would eat very slowly, pausing between the mouthfuls. These intervals were employed in describing the happiness I was so foolishly throwing away, and in threatening me with the penalty that finally awaited my stubborn disobedience. He boasted much of the forbearance he had exercised towards me, and reminded me that there was a limit to his patience. When I succeeded in avoiding opportunities for him to talk to me at home, I was ordered to come to his office, to do some errand. When there, I was obliged to stand and listen to such language as he saw fit to address to me. Sometimes I so openly expressed my contempt for him that he would become violently enraged, and I wondered why he did

---

1   *dumb*   Unable to speak.

2   *piazza*   Veranda.

not strike me. Circumstanced as he was, he probably thought it was better policy to be forbearing. But the state of things grew worse and worse daily. In desperation I told him that I must and would apply to my grandmother for protection. He threatened me with death, and worse than death, if I made any complaint to her. Strange to say, I did not despair. I was naturally of a buoyant disposition, and always I had hope of somehow getting out of his clutches. Like many a poor, simple slave before me, I trusted that some threads of joy would yet be woven into my dark destiny.

I had entered my sixteenth year, and every day it became more apparent that my presence was intolerable to Mrs. Flint. Angry words frequently passed between her and her husband. He had never punished me himself, and he would not allow anybody else to punish me. In that respect, she was never satisfied; but, in her angry moods, no terms were too vile for her to bestow upon me. Yet I, whom she detested so bitterly, had far more pity for her than he had, whose duty it was to make her life happy. I never wronged her, or wished to wrong her; and one word of kindness from her would have brought me to her feet.

After repeated quarrels between the doctor and his wife, he announced his intention to take his youngest daughter, then four years old, to sleep in his apartment. It was necessary that a servant should sleep in the same room, to be on hand if the child stirred. I was selected for that office, and informed for what purpose that arrangement had been made. By managing to keep within sight of people, as much as possible during the day time, I had hitherto succeeded in eluding my master, though a razor was often held to my throat to force me to change this line of policy. At night I slept by the side of my great aunt, where I felt safe. He was too prudent to come into her room. She was an old woman, and had been in the family many years. Moreover, as a married man, and a professional man, he deemed it necessary to save appearances in some degree. But he resolved to remove the obstacle in the way of his scheme; and he thought he had planned it so that he should evade suspicion. He was well aware how much I prized my refuge by the side of my old aunt, and he determined to dispossess me of it. The first night the doctor had the little child in his room alone. The next morning, I was ordered to take my station as nurse the following night.

A kind Providence interposed in my favor. During the day Mrs. Flint heard of this new arrangement, and a storm followed. I rejoiced to hear it rage.

After a while my mistress sent for me to come to her room. Her first question was, "Did you know you were to sleep in the doctor's room?"

"Yes, ma'am."

"Who told you?"

"My master."

"Will you answer truly all the questions I ask?"

"Yes, ma'am."

"Tell me, then, as you hope to be forgiven, are you innocent of what I have accused you?"

"I am."

She handed me a Bible, and said, "Lay your hand on your heart, kiss this holy book, and swear before God that you tell me the truth."

I took the oath she required, and I did it with a clear conscience.

"You have taken God's holy word to testify your innocence," said she. "If you have deceived me, beware! Now take this stool, sit down, look me directly in the face, and tell me all that has passed between your master and you."

I did as she ordered. As I went on with my account her color changed frequently, she wept, and sometimes groaned. She spoke in tones so sad, that I was touched by her grief. The tears came to my eyes; but I was soon convinced that her emotions arose from anger and wounded pride. She felt that her marriage vows were desecrated, her dignity insulted, but she had no compassion for the poor victim of her husband's perfidy. She pitied herself as a martyr; but she was incapable of feeling for the condition of shame and misery in which her unfortunate, helpless slave was placed.

Yet perhaps she had some touch of feeling for me; for when the conference was ended, she spoke kindly, and promised to protect me. I should have been much comforted by this assurance if I could have had confidence in it; but my experiences in slavery had filled me with distrust. She was not a very refined woman, and had not much control over her passions. I was an object of her jealousy, and, consequently, of her hatred; and I knew I could not expect kindness or confidence from her under the circumstances in which I was placed. I could not blame her. Slave-holders' wives feel as other women would under similar circumstances. The fire of her temper kindled from small sparks, and now the flame became so intense that the doctor was obliged to give up his intended arrangement.

I knew I had ignited the torch, and I expected to suffer for it afterwards; but I felt too thankful to my mistress for the timely aid she rendered me to care much about that. She now took me to sleep in a room adjoining her own. There I was an object of her especial care, though not of her especial comfort, for she spent many a sleepless night to watch over me. Sometimes I woke up, and found her bending over me. At other times she whispered in my ear, as though it was her husband who was speaking to me, and listened to hear what I would answer. If she startled me, on such occasions, she would glide stealthily away; and the next morning she would tell me I had been talking in my sleep, and ask who I was talking to. At last, I began to be fearful for my life. It had been often threatened; and you can imagine, better than I can describe, what an unpleasant sensation it must produce to wake up in the dead of night and find a jealous woman bending over you. Terrible as this experience was, I had fears that it would give place to one more terrible.

My mistress grew weary of her vigils; they did not prove satisfactory. She changed her tactics. She now tried the trick of accusing my master of crime, in my presence, and gave my name as the author of the accusation. To my utter astonishment, he replied, "I don't believe it; but if she did acknowledge it, you tortured her into exposing me." Tortured into exposing him! Truly, Satan had no difficulty in distinguishing the color of his soul! I understood his object in making this false representation. It was to show me that I gained nothing by seeking the protection of my mistress; that the power was still all in his own hands. I pitied Mrs. Flint. She was a second wife, many years the junior of her husband; and the hoary-headed[1] miscreant was enough to try the patience of a wiser and better woman. She was completely foiled, and knew not how to proceed. She would gladly have had me flogged for my supposed false oath; but, as I have already stated, the doctor never allowed anyone to whip me. The old sinner was politic. The application of the lash might have led to remarks that would have exposed him in the eyes of his children and grandchildren. How often did I rejoice that I lived in a town where all the inhabitants knew each other! If I had been on a remote plantation, or lost among the multitude of a crowded city, I should not be a living woman at this day.

The secrets of slavery are concealed like those of the Inquisition. My master was, to my knowledge, the father of eleven slaves. But did the mothers dare to tell who was the father of their children? Did the other slaves dare to allude to it, except in whispers among themselves? No, indeed! They knew too well the terrible consequences.

My grandmother could not avoid seeing things which excited her suspicions. She was uneasy about me, and tried various ways to buy me; but the never-changing answer was always repeated: "Linda does not belong to me. She is my daughter's property, and I have no legal right to sell her." The conscientious man! He was too scrupulous to sell me; but he had no scruples whatever about committing a much greater wrong against the helpless young girl placed under his guardianship, as his daughter's property. Sometimes my persecutor would ask me whether I would like to be sold. I told him I would rather be sold to anybody than to lead such a life as I did. On such occasions he would assume the air of a very injured individual, and reproach me for my ingratitude. "Did I not take you into the house, and make you the companion of my own children?" he would say. "Have I ever treated you like a negro? I have never allowed you to be punished, not even to please your mistress. And this is the recompense I get, you ungrateful girl!" I answered that he had reasons of his own for screening me from punishment, and that the course he pursued made my mistress hate me and persecute me. If I wept, he would say, "Poor child! Don't cry! don't cry! I will make peace for you with your mistress. Only let me arrange matters in my own way. Poor, foolish girl! you don't know what is for your own good. I would cherish you. I would make a lady of you. Now go, and think of all I have promised you."

I did think of it.

Reader, I draw no imaginary pictures of southern homes. I am telling you the plain truth. Yet when victims make their escape from this wild beast of Slavery, northerners consent to act the part of bloodhounds,

---

[1]   *hoary-headed* I.e., white-haired.

and hunt the poor fugitive back into his den, "full of dead men's bones, and all uncleanness."[1] Nay, more, they are not only willing, but proud, to give their daughters in marriage to slaveholders. The poor girls have romantic notions of a sunny clime, and of the flowering vines that all the year round shade a happy home. To what disappointments are they destined! The young wife soon learns that the husband in whose hands she has placed her happiness pays no regard to his marriage vows. Children of every shade of complexion play with her own fair babies, and too well she knows that they are born unto him of his own household. Jealousy and hatred enter the flowery home, and it is ravaged of its loveliness.

Southern women often marry a man knowing that he is the father of many little slaves. They do not trouble themselves about it. They regard such children as property, as marketable as the pigs on the plantation; and it is seldom that they do not make them aware of this by passing them into the slave-trader's hands as soon as possible, and thus getting them out of their sight. I am glad to say there are some honorable exceptions.

I have myself known two southern wives who exhorted their husbands to free those slaves towards whom they stood in a "parental relation"; and their request was granted. These husbands blushed before the superior nobleness of their wives' natures. Though they had only counselled them to do that which it was their duty to do, it commanded their respect, and rendered their conduct more exemplary. Concealment was at an end, and confidence took the place of distrust.

Though this bad institution deadens the moral sense, even in white women, to a fearful extent, it is not altogether extinct. I have heard southern ladies say of Mr. Such a one, "He not only thinks it no disgrace to be the father of those little niggers,[2] but he is not ashamed to call himself their master. I declare, such things ought not to be tolerated in any decent society!"

CHAPTER 7. THE LOVER

Why does the slave ever love? Why allow the tendrils of the heart to twine around objects which may at any moment be wrenched away by the hand of violence? When separations come by the hand of death, the pious soul can bow in resignation, and say, "Not my will, but thine be done, O Lord!" But when the ruthless hand of man strikes the blow, regardless of the misery he causes, it is hard to be submissive. I did not reason thus when I was a young girl. Youth will be youth. I loved, and I indulged the hope that the dark clouds around me would turn out a bright lining. I forgot that in the land of my birth the shadows are too dense for light to penetrate. A land

> Where laughter is not mirth; nor thought the mind;
> Nor words a language; nor e'en men mankind.
> Where cries reply to curses, shrieks to blows,
> And each is tortured in his separate hell.[3]

There was in the neighborhood a young colored carpenter; a free born man. We had been well acquainted in childhood, and frequently met together afterwards. We became mutually attached, and he proposed to marry me. I loved him with all the ardor of a young girl's first love. But when I reflected that I was a slave, and that the laws gave no sanction to the marriage of such, my heart sank within me. My lover wanted to buy me; but I knew that Dr. Flint was too willful and arbitrary a man to consent to that arrangement. From him, I was sure of experiencing all sorts of opposition, and I had nothing to hope from my mistress. She would have been delighted to have got rid of me, but not in that way. It would have relieved her mind of a burden if she could have seen me sold to some distant state, but if I was married near home I should be just as much in her husband's power as I had previously been—for the husband of a slave has no power to protect her. Moreover, my mistress, like many others, seemed to think that slaves had no right to any family ties of their own; that they were created merely to wait upon the family of the mistress. I once heard her abuse a young slave girl, who told her that a colored man

---

[1] *full ... uncleanness* See Matthew 23.27: "Woe unto you, scribes and Pharisees, hypocrites! for ye are like unto whited sepulchers, which indeed appear beautiful outward, but are within full of dead men's bones, and of all uncleanness."

[2] *niggers* By the mid-nineteenth century, this word, when used by white people of black people, had acquired the extremely derogatory connotations it carries today.

[3] *Where laughter ... separate hell* These lines are from Byron's "The Lament of Tasso," 4.84–87 (1817).

wanted to make her his wife. "I will have you peeled and pickled, my lady," said she, "if I ever hear you mention that subject again. Do you suppose that I will have you tending my children with the children of that nigger?"[1] The girl to whom she said this had a mulatto child, of course not acknowledged by its father. The poor black man who loved her would have been proud to acknowledge his helpless offspring.

Many and anxious were the thoughts I revolved in my mind. I was at a loss what to do. Above all things, I was desirous to spare my lover the insults that had cut so deeply into my own soul. I talked with my grandmother about it, and partly told her my fears. I did not dare to tell her the worst. She had long suspected all was not right, and if I confirmed her suspicions I knew a storm would rise that would prove the overthrow of all my hopes.

This love-dream had been my support through many trials; and I could not bear to run the risk of having it suddenly dissipated. There was a lady in the neighborhood, a particular friend of Dr. Flint's, who often visited the house. I had a great respect for her, and she had always manifested a friendly interest in me. Grandmother thought she would have great influence with the doctor. I went to this lady, and told her my story. I told her I was aware that my lover's being a free-born man would prove a great objection; but he wanted to buy me; and if Dr. Flint would consent to that arrangement, I felt sure he would be willing to pay any reasonable price. She knew that Mrs. Flint disliked me; therefore, I ventured to suggest that perhaps my mistress would approve of my being sold, as that would rid her of me. The lady listened, with kindly sympathy, and promised to do her utmost to promote my wishes. She had an interview with the doctor, and I believe she pleaded my cause earnestly; but it was all to no purpose.

How I dreaded my master now! Every minute I expected to be summoned to his presence; but the day passed, and I heard nothing from him. The next morning, a message was brought to me: "Master wants you in his study." I found the door ajar, and I stood a moment gazing at the hateful man who claimed a right to rule me, body and soul. I entered, and tried to appear calm. I did not want him to know how my heart was bleeding. He looked fixedly at me, with an expression which seemed to say, "I have half a mind to kill you on the spot." At last he broke the silence, and that was a relief to both of us.

"So you want to be married, do you?" said he, "and to a free nigger."

"Yes, sir."

"Well, I'll soon convince you whether I am your master, or the nigger fellow you honor so highly. If you *must* have a husband, you may take up with one of my slaves."

What a situation I should be in, as the wife of one of *his* slaves, even if my heart had been interested!

I replied, "Don't you suppose, sir, that a slave can have some preference about marrying? Do you suppose that all men are alike to her?"

"Do you love this nigger?" said he, abruptly.

"Yes, sir."

"How dare you tell me so!" he exclaimed, in great wrath. After a slight pause, he added, "I supposed you thought more of yourself; that you felt above the insults of such puppies."

I replied, "If he is a puppy I am a puppy, for we are both of the negro race. It is right and honorable for us to love each other. The man you call a puppy never insulted me, sir; and he would not love me if he did not believe me to be a virtuous woman."

He sprang upon me like a tiger, and gave me a stunning blow. It was the first time he had ever struck me; and fear did not enable me to control my anger. When I had recovered a little from the effects, I exclaimed, "You have struck me for answering you honestly. How I despise you!"

There was silence for some minutes. Perhaps he was deciding what should be my punishment; or, perhaps, he wanted to give me time to reflect on what I had said, and to whom I had said it. Finally, he asked, "Do you know what you have said?"

"Yes, sir; but your treatment drove me to it."

"Do you know that I have a right to do as I like with you—that I can kill you, if I please?"

"You have tried to kill me, and I wish you had; but you have no right to do as you like with me."

"Silence!" he exclaimed, in a thundering voice. "By heavens, girl, you forget yourself too far! Are you mad?

---

[1]   *nigger* By the mid-nineteenth century this word, when used by white people of black people, had acquired the extremely derogatory connotations it carries today.

If you are, I will soon bring you to your senses. Do you think any other master would bear what I have borne from you this morning? Many masters would have killed you on the spot. How would you like to be sent to jail for your insolence?"

"I know I have been disrespectful, sir," I replied; "but you drove me to it; I couldn't help it. As for the jail, there would be more peace for me there than there is here."

"You deserve to go there," said he, "and to be under such treatment, that you would forget the meaning of the word *peace*. It would do you good. It would take some of your high notions out of you. But I am not ready to send you there yet, notwithstanding your ingratitude for all my kindness and forbearance. You have been the plague of my life. I have wanted to make you happy, and I have been repaid with the basest ingratitude; but though you have proved yourself incapable of appreciating my kindness, I will be lenient towards you, Linda. I will give you one more chance to redeem your character. If you behave yourself and do as I require, I will forgive you and treat you as I always have done; but if you disobey me, I will punish you as I would the meanest slave on my plantation. Never let me hear that fellow's name mentioned again. If I ever know of your speaking to him, I will cowhide you both; and if I catch him lurking about my premises, I will shoot him as soon as I would a dog. Do you hear what I say? I'll teach you a lesson about marriage and free niggers! Now go, and let this be the last time I have occasion to speak to you on this subject."

Reader, did you ever hate? I hope not. I never did but once; and I trust I never shall again. Somebody has called it "the atmosphere of hell";[1] and I believe it is so.

For a fortnight[2] the doctor did not speak to me. He thought to mortify me; to make me feel that I had disgraced myself by receiving the honorable addresses of a respectable colored man, in preference to the base proposals of a white man. But though his lips disdained to address me, his eyes were very loquacious. No animal ever watched its prey more narrowly than he watched me. He knew that I could write, though he had failed to make me read his letters; and he was now troubled

lest I should exchange letters with another man. After a while he became weary of silence; and I was sorry for it. One morning, as he passed through the hall, to leave the house, he contrived to thrust a note into my hand. I thought I had better read it, and spare myself the vexation of having him read it to me. It expressed regret for the blow he had given me, and reminded me that I myself was wholly to blame for it. He hoped I had become convinced of the injury I was doing myself by incurring his displeasure. He wrote that he had made up his mind to go to Louisiana; that he should take several slaves with him, and intended I should be one of the number. My mistress would remain where she was; therefore I should have nothing to fear from that quarter. If I merited kindness from him, he assured me that it would be lavishly bestowed. He begged me to think over the matter, and answer the following day.

The next morning I was called to carry a pair of scissors to his room. I laid them on the table with the letter beside them. He thought it was my answer, and did not call me back. I went as usual to attend my young mistress to and from school. He met me in the street, and ordered me to stop at his office on my way back. When I entered, he showed me his letter, and asked me why I had not answered it. I replied, "I am your daughter's property, and it is in your power to send me, or take me, wherever you please." He said he was very glad to find me so willing to go, and that we should start early in the autumn. He had a large practice in the town, and I rather thought he had made up the story merely to frighten me. However that might be, I was determined that I would never go to Louisiana with him.

Summer passed away, and early in the autumn Dr. Flint's eldest son was sent to Louisiana to examine the country, with a view to emigrating. That news did not disturb me. I knew very well that I should not be sent with *him*. That I had not been taken to the plantation before this time, was owing to the fact that his son was there. He was jealous of his son; and jealousy of the overseer had kept him from punishing me by sending me into the fields to work. Is it strange that I was not proud of these protectors? As for the overseer, he was a man for whom I had less respect than I had for a bloodhound.

Young Mr. Flint did not bring back a favorable report of Louisiana, and I heard no more of that scheme. Soon

1 *Somebody … hell* English writer Martin Farquhar Tupper wrote that "hatred is the atmosphere of hell" in his book *Proverbial Philosophy* (1838).

2 *a fortnight* Two weeks.

after this, my lover met me at the corner of the street, and I stopped to speak to him. Looking up, I saw my master watching us from his window. I hurried home, trembling with fear. I was sent for, immediately, to go to his room. He met me with a blow. "When is mistress to be married?" said he, in a sneering tone. A shower of oaths and imprecations followed. How thankful I was that my lover was a free man! that my tyrant had no power to flog him for speaking to me in the street!

Again and again I revolved in my mind how all this would end. There was no hope that the doctor would consent to sell me on any terms. He had an iron will, and was determined to keep me, and to conquer me. My lover was an intelligent and religious man. Even if he could have obtained permission to marry me while I was a slave, the marriage would give him no power to protect me from my master. It would have made him miserable to witness the insults I should have been subjected to. And then, if we had children, I knew they must "follow the condition of the mother."[1] What a terrible blight that would be on the heart of a free, intelligent father! For *his* sake, I felt that I ought not to link his fate with my own unhappy destiny. He was going to Savannah to see about a little property left him by an uncle; and hard as it was to bring my feelings to it, I earnestly entreated him not to come back. I advised him to go to the Free States, where his tongue would not be tied, and where his intelligence would be of more avail to him. He left me, still hoping the day would come when I could be bought. With me the lamp of hope had gone out. The dream of my girlhood was over. I felt lonely and desolate.

Still I was not stripped of all. I still had my good grandmother, and my affectionate brother. When he put his arms round my neck, and looked into my eyes, as if to read there the troubles I dared not tell, I felt that I still had something to love. But even that pleasant emotion was chilled by the reflection that he might be torn from me at any moment, by some sudden freak of my master. If he had known how we loved each other,

I think he would have exulted in separating us. We often planned together how we could get to the north. But, as William remarked, such things are easier said than done. My movements were very closely watched, and we had no means of getting any money to defray our expenses. As for grandmother, she was strongly opposed to her children's undertaking any such project. She had not forgotten poor Benjamin's sufferings,[2] and she was afraid that if another child tried to escape, he would have a similar or a worse fate. To me, nothing seemed more dreadful than my present life. I said to myself, "William *must* be free. He shall go to the north, and I will follow him." Many a slave sister has formed the same plans.

CHAPTER 8. WHAT SLAVES ARE TAUGHT TO THINK OF THE NORTH

Slaveholders pride themselves upon being honorable men; but if you were to hear the enormous lies they tell their slaves, you would have small respect for their veracity. I have spoken plain English. Pardon me. I cannot use a milder term. When they visit the north, and return home, they tell their slaves of the runaways they have seen, and describe them to be in the most deplorable condition. A slaveholder once told me that he had seen a runaway friend of mine in New York, and that she besought him to take her back to her master, for she was literally dying of starvation; that many days she had only one cold potato to eat, and at other times could get nothing at all. He said he refused to take her, because he knew her master would not thank him for bringing such a miserable wretch to his house. He ended by saying to me, "This is the punishment she brought on herself for running away from a kind master."

---

1   *follow ... mother*   From 1662 onwards, slave law in Britain and America had followed the doctrine that children followed the status of their mother (i.e., any child born to an enslaved woman would be themselves enslaved). This law meant that enslavers who fathered children with enslaved women were not held in any way accountable and in fact profited from the practice, as they could then exploit or sell their own children.

---

2   *Benjamin's sufferings*   In Chapter Four, "The Slave Who Dared to Feel Like a Man," the narrator relates the story of Benjamin, a character based on Joseph Horniblow, Jacobs's uncle, who, being close in age, "seemed more like my brother than my uncle." Joseph Horniblow ran away from his enslaver to avoid being whipped, was caught, paraded through town in chains, and put in jail, where his enslavers deliberately kept him in vermin-infested conditions in order to break his spirit. He was sold to a new enslaver in New Orleans and eventually escaped to New York. Jacobs and her brother both named their sons after Joseph Horniblow.

This whole story was false. I afterwards stayed with that friend in New York, and found her in comfortable circumstances. She had never thought of such a thing as wishing to go back to slavery. Many of the slaves believe such stories, and think it is not worthwhile to exchange slavery for such a hard kind of freedom. It is difficult to persuade such that freedom could make them useful men, and enable them to protect their wives and children. If those heathen in our Christian land had as much teaching as some Hindoos, they would think otherwise. They would know that liberty is more valuable than life. They would begin to understand their own capabilities, and exert themselves to become men and women.

But while the Free States sustain a law[1] which hurls fugitives back into slavery, how can the slaves resolve to become men? There are some who strive to protect wives and daughters from the insults of their masters; but those who have such sentiments have had advantages above the general mass of slaves. They have been partially civilized and Christianized by favorable circumstances. Some are bold enough to *utter* such sentiments to their masters. O, that there were more of them!

Some poor creatures have been so brutalized by the lash that they will sneak out of the way to give their masters free access to their wives and daughters. Do you think this proves the black man to belong to an inferior order of beings? What would *you* be, if you had been born and brought up a slave, with generations of slaves for ancestors? I admit that the black man *is* inferior. But what is it that makes him so? It is the ignorance in which white men compel him to live; it is the torturing whip that lashes manhood out of him; it is the fierce bloodhounds of the South, and the scarcely less cruel human bloodhounds of the north, who enforce the Fugitive Slave Law. *They* do the work.

Southern gentlemen indulge in the most contemptuous expressions about the Yankees, while they,[2] on their part, consent to do the vilest work for them, such as the ferocious bloodhounds and the despised negro-hunters are employed to do at home. When southerners go to

the north, they are proud to do them honor;[3] but the northern man is not welcome south of Mason Dixon's line, unless he suppresses every thought and feeling at variance with their "peculiar institution."[4] Nor is it enough to be silent. The masters are not pleased, unless they obtain a greater degree of subservience than that; and they are generally accommodated. Do they respect the northerner for this? I trow[5] not. Even the slaves despise "a northern man with southern principles"; and that is the class they generally see. When northerners go to the south to reside, they prove very apt scholars. They soon imbibe the sentiments and disposition of their neighbors, and generally go beyond their teachers. Of the two, they are proverbially the hardest masters.

They seem to satisfy their consciences with the doctrine that God created the Africans to be slaves. What a libel upon the heavenly Father, who "made of one blood all nations of men"![6] And then who are Africans? Who can measure the amount of Anglo-Saxon blood coursing in the veins of American slaves?

I have spoken of the pains slaveholders take to give their slaves a bad opinion of the north; but, notwithstanding this, intelligent slaves are aware that they have many friends in the Free States. Even the most ignorant have some confused notions about it. They knew that I could read; and I was often asked if I had seen anything in the newspapers about white folks over in the big north, who were trying to get their freedom for them. Some believe that the abolitionists have already made them free, and that it is established by law, but that their masters prevent the law from going into effect. One woman begged me to get a newspaper and read it over. She said her husband told her that the black people had sent word to the queen of 'Merica that they were all slaves; that she didn't believe it, and went to Washington city to see the president about it.

---

1   *Free States sustain a law*   See note 1 on page 961 above.

2   *Yankees*   In common American usage, this term referred originally to New Englanders, and later to Northerners in general—the sense in which Jacobs is using it here;   *they*   I.e., the Yankees.

3   *they ... honor*   I.e., the Northerners are respectful of visiting Southerners.

4   *Mason Dixon's line*   Line separating parts of Pennsylvania and Delaware from parts of Maryland and Virginia; the phrase was used as shorthand for the boundary between the Northern free states and the Southern slave states;   *peculiar institution*   I.e., slavery.

5   *trow*   Believe.

6   *made ... men*   See Acts 17.26.

They quarrelled; she drew her sword upon him, and swore that he should help her to make them all free.

That poor, ignorant woman thought that America was governed by a Queen, to whom the President was subordinate. I wish the President was subordinate to Queen Justice.

Chapter 10. A Perilous Passage in the Slave Girl's Life

After my lover went away, Dr. Flint contrived a new plan. He seemed to have an idea that my fear of my mistress was his greatest obstacle. In the blandest tones, he told me that he was going to build a small house for me, in a secluded place, four miles away from the town. I shuddered; but I was constrained to listen, while he talked of his intention to give me a home of my own, and to make a lady of me. Hitherto, I had escaped my dreaded fate, by being in the midst of people. My grandmother had already had high words with my master about me. She had told him pretty plainly what she thought of his character, and there was considerable gossip in the neighborhood about our affairs, to which the open-mouthed jealousy of Mrs. Flint contributed not a little. When my master said he was going to build a house for me, and that he could do it with little trouble and expense, I was in hopes something would happen to frustrate his scheme; but I soon heard that the house was actually begun. I vowed before my Maker that I would never enter it. I had rather toil on the plantation from dawn till dark; I had rather live and die in jail, than drag on, from day to day, through such a living death. I was determined that the master, whom I so hated and loathed, who had blighted the prospects of my youth, and made my life a desert, should not, after my long struggle with him, succeed at last in trampling his victim under his feet. I would do anything, everything, for the sake of defeating him. What *could* I do? I thought and thought, till I became desperate, and made a plunge into the abyss.

And now, reader, I come to a period in my unhappy life, which I would gladly forget if I could. The remembrance fills me with sorrow and shame. It pains me to tell you of it; but I have promised to tell you the truth, and I will do it honestly, let it cost me what it may. I will not try to screen myself behind the plea of compulsion from a master; for it was not so. Neither can I plead ignorance or thoughtlessness. For years, my master had done his utmost to pollute my mind with foul images, and to destroy the pure principles inculcated by my grandmother, and the good mistress of my childhood. The influences of slavery had had the same effect on me that they had on other young girls; they had made me prematurely knowing, concerning the evil ways of the world. I know what I did, and I did it with deliberate calculation.

But, O, ye happy women, whose purity has been sheltered from childhood, who have been free to choose the objects of your affection, whose homes are protected by law, do not judge the poor desolate slave girl too severely! If slavery had been abolished, I, also, could have married the man of my choice; I could have had a home shielded by the laws; and I should have been spared the painful task of confessing what I am now about to relate; but all my prospects had been blighted by slavery. I wanted to keep myself pure; and, under the most adverse circumstances, I tried hard to preserve my self-respect; but I was struggling alone in the powerful grasp of the demon Slavery; and the monster proved too strong for me. I felt as if I was forsaken by God and man; as if all my efforts must be frustrated; and I became reckless in my despair.

I have told you that Dr. Flint's persecutions and his wife's jealousy had given rise to some gossip in the neighborhood. Among others, it chanced that a white unmarried gentleman had obtained some knowledge of the circumstances in which I was placed. He knew my grandmother, and often spoke to me in the street. He became interested for me, and asked questions about my master, which I answered in part. He expressed a great deal of sympathy, and a wish to aid me. He constantly sought opportunities to see me, and wrote to me frequently. I was a poor slave girl, only fifteen years old.

So much attention from a superior person was, of course, flattering; for human nature is the same in all. I also felt grateful for his sympathy, and encouraged by his kind words. It seemed to me a great thing to have such a friend. By degrees, a more tender feeling crept into my heart. He was an educated and eloquent gentleman; too eloquent, alas, for the poor slave girl who trusted in him. Of course I saw whither all this was tending. I knew the impassable gulf between us; but to be an object of interest to a man who is not married, and who is not her master, is agreeable to the pride and feelings of a slave, if her miserable situation has left her any pride or sentiment. It seems less degrading to give one's self, than to submit to compulsion. There is something akin to freedom in having a lover who has no control over you, except that which he gains by kindness and attachment. A master may treat you as rudely as he pleases, and you dare not speak; moreover, the wrong does not seem so great with an unmarried man, as with one who has a wife to be made unhappy. There may be sophistry in all this; but the condition of a slave confuses all principles of morality, and, in fact, renders the practice of them impossible.

When I found that my master had actually begun to build the lonely cottage, other feelings mixed with those I have described. Revenge, and calculations of interest, were added to flattered vanity and sincere gratitude for kindness. I knew nothing would enrage Dr. Flint so much as to know that I favored another; and it was something to triumph over my tyrant even in that small way. I thought he would revenge himself by selling me, and I was sure my friend, Mr. Sands, would buy me. He was a man of more generosity and feeling than my master, and I thought my freedom could be easily obtained from him. The crisis of my fate now came so near that I was desperate. I shuddered to think of being the mother of children that should be owned by my old tyrant. I knew that as soon as a new fancy took him, his victims were sold far off to get rid of them; especially if they had children. I had seen several women sold, with his babies at the breast. He never allowed his offspring by slaves to remain long in sight of himself and his wife. Of a man who was not my master I could ask to have my children well supported; and in this case, I felt confident I should obtain the boon. I also felt quite sure that they would be made free. With all these thoughts revolving in my mind, and seeing no other way of escaping the doom I so much dreaded, I made a headlong plunge. Pity me, and pardon me, O virtuous reader! You never knew what it is to be a slave; to be entirely unprotected by law or custom; to have the laws reduce you to the condition of a chattel, entirely subject to the will of another. You never exhausted your ingenuity in avoiding the snares,

and eluding the power of a hated tyrant; you never shuddered at the sound of his footsteps, and trembled within hearing of his voice. I know I did wrong. No one can feel it more sensibly than I do. The painful and humiliating memory will haunt me to my dying day. Still, in looking back, calmly, on the events of my life, I feel that the slave woman ought not to be judged by the same standard as others.

The months passed on. I had many unhappy hours. I secretly mourned over the sorrow I was bringing on my grandmother, who had so tried to shield me from harm. I knew that I was the greatest comfort of her old age, and that it was a source of pride to her that I had not degraded myself, like most of the slaves. I wanted to confess to her that I was no longer worthy of her love; but I could not utter the dreaded words.

As for Dr. Flint, I had a feeling of satisfaction and triumph in the thought of telling *him*. From time to time he told me of his intended arrangements, and I was silent. At last, he came and told me the cottage was completed, and ordered me to go to it. I told him I would never enter it. He said, "I have heard enough of such talk as that. You shall go, if you are carried by force; and you shall remain there." I replied, "I will never go there. In a few months I shall be a mother."

He stood and looked at me in dumb amazement, and left the house without a word. I thought I should be happy in my triumph over him. But now that the truth was out, and my relatives would hear of it, I felt wretched. Humble as were their circumstances, they had pride in my good character. Now, how could I look them in the face? My self-respect was gone! I had resolved that I would be virtuous, though I was a slave. I had said, "Let the storm beat! I will brave it till I die." And now, how humiliated I felt!

I went to my grandmother. My lips moved to make confession, but the words stuck in my throat. I sat down in the shade of a tree at her door and began to sew. I think she saw something unusual was the matter with me. The mother of slaves is very watchful. She knows there is no security for her children. After they have entered their teens she lives in daily expectation of trouble. This leads to many questions. If the girl is of a sensitive nature, timidity keeps her from answering truthfully, and this well-meant course has a tendency to drive her from maternal counsels. Presently, in came my mistress, like a mad woman, and accused me concerning her husband. My grandmother, whose suspicions had been previously awakened, believed what she said. She exclaimed, "O Linda! has it come to this? I had rather see you dead than to see you as you now are. You are a disgrace to your dead mother." She tore from my fingers my mother's wedding ring and her silver thimble. "Go away!" she exclaimed, "and never come to my house, again." Her reproaches fell so hot and heavy, that they left me no chance to answer. Bitter tears, such as the eyes never shed but once, were my only answer. I rose from my seat, but fell back again, sobbing. She did not speak to me; but the tears were running down her furrowed cheeks, and they scorched me like fire. She had always been so kind to me! So kind! How I longed to throw myself at her feet, and tell her all the truth! But she had ordered me to go, and never to come there again. After a few minutes, I mustered strength, and started to obey her. With what feelings did I now close that little gate, which I used to open with such an eager hand in my childhood! It closed upon me with a sound I never heard before.

Where could I go? I was afraid to return to my master's. I walked on recklessly, not caring where I went, or what would become of me. When I had gone four or five miles, fatigue compelled me to stop. I sat down on the stump of an old tree. The stars were shining through the boughs above me. How they mocked me, with their bright, calm light! The hours passed by, and as I sat there alone a chilliness and deadly sickness came over me. I sank on the ground. My mind was full of horrid thoughts. I prayed to die; but the prayer was not answered. At last, with great effort I roused myself, and walked some distance further, to the house of a woman who had been a friend of my mother. When I told her why I was there, she spoke soothingly to me; but I could not be comforted. I thought I could bear my shame if I could only be reconciled to my grandmother. I longed to open my heart to her. I thought if she could know the real state of the case, and all I had been bearing for years, she would perhaps judge me less harshly. My friend advised me to send for her. I did so; but days of agonizing suspense passed before she came. Had she utterly forsaken me? No. She came at last. I knelt before her, and told her the things that had poisoned my life; how long I had been persecuted; that

I saw no way of escape; and in an hour of extremity I had become desperate. She listened in silence. I told her I would bear anything and do anything, if in time I had hopes of obtaining her forgiveness. I begged of her to pity me, for my dead mother's sake. And she did pity me. She did not say, "I forgive you"; but she looked at me lovingly, with her eyes full of tears. She laid her old hand gently on my head, and murmured, "Poor child! Poor child!"

[In the chapter omitted here, the narrator Linda is living at her Aunt Martha's house (though she is still owned by Dr. Flint). Linda falls ill and her baby boy is born early; it takes Linda a year to recover from her illness and the birth. Dr. Flint continues to persecute her with his attention even though she is no longer under his roof.]

Chapter 12. Fear of Insurrection

Not far from this time Nat Turner's insurrection[1] broke out; and the news threw our town into great commotion. Strange that they should be alarmed when their slaves were so "contented and happy"! But so it was.

It was always the custom to have a muster[2] every year. On that occasion every white man shouldered his musket. The citizens[3] and the so-called country gentlemen wore military uniforms. The poor whites took their places in the ranks in every-day dress, some without shoes, some without hats. This grand occasion had already passed; and when the slaves were told there was to be another muster, they were surprised and rejoiced. Poor creatures! They thought it was going to be a holiday. I was informed of the true state of affairs, and imparted it to the few I could trust. Most gladly

---

[1] *Nat Turner's insurrection* In 1831, the enslaved preacher Nat Turner led an antislavery rebellion in Virginia; at least 51 white people were killed, and the rebellion was suppressed after four days of fighting, after which over a hundred black people were killed in retaliation. The revolt was widely depicted as a massacre in Southern media, and the events led to new restrictions on education for black people as well as to rules preventing enslaved people from meeting without a white person present.

[2] *muster* Gathering or roll-call for a militia unit, in order to count the number of persons available for potential military service.

[3] *citizens* Likely a reference to those who were entitled to vote—men in the community who paid taxes or owned property.

would I have proclaimed it to every slave; but I dared not. All could not be relied on. Mighty is the power of the torturing lash.

By sunrise, people were pouring in from every quarter within twenty miles of the town. I knew the houses were to be searched; and I expected it would be done by country bullies and the poor whites. I knew nothing annoyed them so much as to see colored people living in comfort and respectability; so I made arrangements for them with especial care. I arranged everything in my grandmother's house as neatly as possible. I put white quilts on the beds, and decorated some of the rooms with flowers. When all was arranged, I sat down at the window to watch. Far as my eye could reach, it rested on a motley crowd of soldiers. Drums and fifes were discoursing[1] martial music. The men were divided into companies of sixteen, each headed by a captain. Orders were given, and the wild scouts rushed in every direction, wherever a colored face was to be found.

It was a grand opportunity for the low whites, who had no negroes of their own to scourge. They exulted in such a chance to exercise a little brief authority, and show their subserviency to the slaveholders; not reflecting that the power which trampled on the colored people also kept themselves in poverty, ignorance, and moral degradation. Those who never witnessed such scenes can hardly believe what I know was inflicted at this time on innocent men, women, and children, against whom there was not the slightest ground for suspicion. Colored people and slaves who lived in remote parts of the town suffered in an especial manner. In some cases the searchers scattered powder and shot among their clothes, and then sent other parties to find them, and bring them forward as proof that they were plotting insurrection. Everywhere men, women, and children were whipped till the blood stood in puddles at their feet. Some received five hundred lashes; others were tied hands and feet, and tortured with a bucking paddle,[2] which blisters the skin terribly. The dwellings of the colored people, unless they happened to be

protected by some influential white person, who was nigh at hand, were robbed of clothing and everything else the marauders thought worth carrying away. All day long these unfeeling wretches went round, like a troop of demons, terrifying and tormenting the helpless. At night, they formed themselves into patrol bands, and went wherever they chose among the colored people, acting out their brutal will. Many women hid themselves in woods and swamps, to keep out of their way. If any of the husbands or fathers told of these outrages, they were tied up to the public whipping post, and cruelly scourged for telling lies about white men. The consternation was universal. No two people that had the slightest tinge of color in their faces dared to be seen talking together.

I entertained no positive fears about our household, because we were in the midst of white families who would protect us. We were ready to receive the soldiers whenever they came. It was not long before we heard the tramp of feet and the sound of voices. The door was rudely pushed open; and in they tumbled, like a pack of hungry wolves. They snatched at everything within their reach. Every box, trunk, closet, and corner underwent a thorough examination. A box in one of the drawers containing some silver change was eagerly pounced upon. When I stepped forward to take it from them, one of the soldiers turned and said angrily, "What d'ye foller us fur? D'ye s'pose white folks is come to steal?"

I replied, "You have come to search; but you have searched that box, and I will take it, if you please."

At that moment I saw a white gentleman who was friendly to us; and I called to him, and asked him to have the goodness to come in and stay till the search was over. He readily complied. His entrance into the house brought in the captain of the company, whose business it was to guard the outside of the house, and see that none of the inmates left it. This officer was Mr. Litch, the wealthy slaveholder whom I mentioned, in the account of neighboring planters, as being notorious for his cruelty. He felt above soiling his hands with the search. He merely gave orders; and, if a bit of writing was discovered, it was carried to him by his ignorant followers, who were unable to read.

My grandmother had a large trunk of bedding and table cloths. When that was opened, there was a great

---

[1] *fifes* Small flutes that are played along with drums in military music; *discoursing* Pouring forth.

[2] *bucking paddle* Wooden paddle—also called a "spanking paddle"—with holes in it, designed to create blisters when repeatedly used to whip someone.

shout of surprise; and one exclaimed, "Where'd the damned niggers git all dis sheet an' table clarf?"

My grandmother, emboldened by the presence of our white protector, said, "You may be sure we didn't pilfer 'em from *your* houses."

"Look here, mammy," said a grim-looking fellow without any coat, "you seem to feel mighty gran' 'cause you got all them 'ere fixens. White folks oughter have 'em all."

His remarks were interrupted by a chorus of voices shouting, "We's got 'em! We's got 'em! Dis 'ere yaller gal's[1] got letters!"

There was a general rush for the supposed letter, which, upon examination, proved to be some verses written to me by a friend. In packing away my things, I had overlooked them. When their captain informed them of their contents, they seemed much disappointed. He inquired of me who wrote them. I told him it was one of my friends. "Can you read them?" he asked. When I told him I could, he swore, and raved, and tore the paper into bits. "Bring me all your letters!" said he, in a commanding tone. I told him I had none. "Don't be afraid," he continued, in an insinuating way. "Bring them all to me. Nobody shall do you any harm." Seeing I did not move to obey him, his pleasant tone changed to oaths and threats. "Who writes to you? half free niggers?" inquired he. I replied, "O, no; most of my letters are from white people. Some request me to burn them after they are read, and some I destroy without reading."

An exclamation of surprise from some of the company put a stop to our conversation. Some silver spoons which ornamented an old-fashioned buffet had just been discovered. My grandmother was in the habit of preserving fruit for many ladies in the town, and of preparing suppers for parties; consequently she had many jars of preserves. The closet that contained these was next invaded, and the contents tasted. One of them, who was helping himself freely, tapped his neighbor on the shoulder, and said, "Wal done! Don't wonder de niggers want to kill all de white folks, when dey live on 'sarves" [meaning preserves]. I stretched out my hand to take the jar, saying, "You were not sent here to search for sweetmeats."

"And what *were* we sent for?" said the captain, bristling up to me. I evaded the question.

The search of the house was completed, and nothing found to condemn us. They next proceeded to the garden, and knocked about every bush and vine with no better success. The captain called his men together, and, after a short consultation, the order to march was given. As they passed out of the gate, the captain turned back, and pronounced a malediction on the house. He said it ought to be burned to the ground, and each of its inmates receive thirty-nine lashes. We came out of this affair very fortunately; not losing anything except some wearing apparel.

Towards evening the turbulence increased. The soldiers, stimulated by drink, committed still greater cruelties. Shrieks and shouts continually rent the air. Not daring to go to the door, I peeped under the window curtain. I saw a mob dragging along a number of colored people, each white man, with his musket upraised, threatening instant death if they did not stop their shrieks. Among the prisoners was a respectable old colored minister. They had found a few parcels of shot in his house, which his wife had for years used to balance her scales. For this they were going to shoot him on Court House Green. What a spectacle was that for a civilized country! A rabble, staggering under intoxication, assuming to be the administrators of justice!

The better class of the community exerted their influence to save the innocent, persecuted people; and in several instances they succeeded, by keeping them shut up in jail till the excitement abated. At last the white citizens found that their own property was not safe from the lawless rabble they had summoned to protect them. They rallied[2] the drunken swarm, drove them back into the country, and set a guard over the town.

The next day, the town patrols were commissioned to search colored people that lived out of the city; and the most shocking outrages were committed with perfect impunity. Every day for a fortnight, if I looked out, I saw horsemen with some poor panting negro tied to their saddles, and compelled by the lash to keep up with their speed, till they arrived at the jail yard. Those who had been whipped too unmercifully to

---

[1]   *yaller gal* I.e., mulatto girl.

[2]   *rallied* Brought back together.

walk were washed with brine, tossed into a cart, and carried to jail. One black man, who had not fortitude to endure scourging, promised to give information about the conspiracy. But it turned out that he knew nothing at all. He had not even heard the name of Nat Turner. The poor fellow had, however, made up a story, which augmented his own sufferings and those of the colored people.

The day patrol continued for some weeks, and at sundown a night guard was substituted. Nothing at all was proved against the colored people, bond or free. The wrath of the slaveholders was somewhat appeased by the capture of Nat Turner. The imprisoned were released. The slaves were sent to their masters, and the free were permitted to return to their ravaged homes. Visiting was strictly forbidden on the plantations. The slaves begged the privilege of again meeting at their little church in the woods, with their burying ground around it. It was built by the colored people, and they had no higher happiness than to meet there and sing hymns together, and pour out their hearts in spontaneous prayer. Their request was denied, and the church was demolished. They were permitted to attend the white churches, a certain portion of the galleries being appropriated to their use. There, when everybody else had partaken of the communion, and the benediction had been pronounced, the minister said, "Come down, now, my colored friends." They obeyed the summons, and partook of the bread and wine, in commemoration of the meek and lowly Jesus, who said, "God is your Father, and all ye are brethren."

[Linda relates how the slaveholders in her community try to use religion to instill obedience, and she explicates the hypocrisy of Christian slaveholders, particularly of Dr. Flint, who tries to convince Linda that sex with him—unlike sex with another enslaved person—wouldn't affect her virtue in God's eyes. Linda rejects this argument as not in keeping with her reading of the Bible.]

CHAPTER 14. ANOTHER LINK TO LIFE

I had not returned to my master's house since the birth of my child. The old man raved to have me thus removed from his immediate power; but his wife vowed, by all that was good and great, she would kill me if I came back; and he did not doubt her word. Sometimes he would stay away for a season. Then he would come and renew the old threadbare discourse about his forbearance and my ingratitude. He labored, most unnecessarily, to convince me that I had lowered myself. The venomous old reprobate had no need of descanting on that theme. I felt humiliated enough. My unconscious babe was the ever-present witness of my shame. I listened with silent contempt when he talked about my having forfeited *his* good opinion; but I shed bitter tears that I was no longer worthy of being respected by the good and pure. Alas! slavery still held me in its poisonous grasp. There was no chance for me to be respectable. There was no prospect of being able to lead a better life.

Sometimes, when my master found that I still refused to accept what he called his kind offers, he would threaten to sell my child. "Perhaps that will humble you," said he.

Humble *me*! Was I not already in the dust? But his threat lacerated my heart. I knew the law gave him power to fulfil it; for slaveholders have been cunning enough to enact that "the child shall follow the condition of the *mother*," not of the *father*; thus taking care that licentiousness shall not interfere with avarice. This reflection made me clasp my innocent babe all the more firmly to my heart. Horrid visions passed through my mind when I thought of his liability to fall into the slave trader's hands. I wept over him, and said, "O my child! perhaps they will leave you in some cold cabin to die, and then throw you into a hole, as if you were a dog."

When Dr. Flint learned that I was again to be a mother, he was exasperated beyond measure. He rushed from the house, and returned with a pair of shears. I had a fine head of hair; and he often railed about my pride of arranging it nicely. He cut every hair close to my head, storming and swearing all the time. I replied to some of his abuse, and he struck me. Some months before, he had pitched me down stairs in a fit of passion; and the injury I received was so serious that I was unable to turn myself in bed for many days. He then said, "Linda, I swear by God I will never raise my hand against you again"; but I knew that he would forget his promise.

After he discovered my situation, he was like a restless spirit from the pit. He came every day; and I was subjected to such insults as no pen can describe. I would not describe them if I could; they were too low, too revolting. I tried to keep them from my grandmother's knowledge as much as I could. I knew she had enough to sadden her life, without having my troubles to bear. When she saw the doctor treat me with violence, and heard him utter oaths terrible enough to palsy a man's tongue, she could not always hold her peace. It was natural and motherlike that she should try to defend me; but it only made matters worse.

When they told me my new-born babe was a girl, my heart was heavier than it had ever been before. Slavery is terrible for men; but it is far more terrible for women. Superadded to the burden common to all, *they* have wrongs, and sufferings, and mortifications peculiarly their own.

Dr. Flint had sworn that he would make me suffer, to my last day, for this new crime against *him*, as he called it; and as long as he had me in his power he kept his word. On the fourth day after the birth of my babe, he entered my room suddenly, and commanded me to rise and bring my baby to him. The nurse who took care of me had gone out of the room to prepare some nourishment, and I was alone. There was no alternative. I rose, took up my babe, and crossed the room to where he sat. "Now stand there," said he, "till I tell you to go back!" My child bore a strong resemblance to her father, and to the deceased Mrs. Sands, her grandmother. He noticed this; and while I stood before him, trembling with weakness, he heaped upon me and my little one every vile epithet he could think of. Even the grandmother in her grave did not escape his curses. In the midst of his vituperations[1] I fainted at his feet. This recalled him to his senses. He took the baby from my arms, laid it on the bed, dashed cold water on my face, took me up, and shook me violently, to restore my consciousness before anyone entered the room. Just then my grandmother came in, and he hurried out of the house. I suffered in consequence of this treatment; but I begged my friends to let me die, rather than send for the doctor. There was nothing I dreaded so much as his presence. My life was spared; and I was glad for the sake of my little ones. Had it not been for these ties to life, I should have been glad to be released by death, though I had lived only nineteen years.

Always it gave me a pang that my children had no lawful claim to a name. Their father offered his; but, if I had wished to accept the offer, I dared not while my master lived. Moreover, I knew it would not be accepted at their baptism. A Christian name they were at least entitled to; and we resolved to call my boy for our dear good Benjamin, who had gone far away from us.

My grandmother belonged to the church; and she was very desirous of having the children christened. I knew Dr. Flint would forbid it, and I did not venture to attempt it. But chance favored me. He was called to visit a patient out of town, and was obliged to be absent during Sunday. "Now is the time," said my grandmother; "we will take the children to church, and have them christened."

When I entered the church, recollections of my mother came over me, and I felt subdued in spirit. There she had presented me for baptism, without any reason to feel ashamed. She had been married, and had such legal rights as slavery allows to a slave. The vows had at least been sacred to *her*, and she had never violated them. I was glad she was not alive, to know under what different circumstances her grandchildren were presented for baptism. Why had my lot been so different from my mother's? *Her* master had died when she was a child; and she remained with her mistress till she married. She was never in the power of any master; and thus she escaped one class of the evils that generally fall upon slaves.

When my baby was about to be christened, the former mistress of my father stepped up to me, and proposed to give it her Christian name. To this I added the surname of my father, who had himself no legal right to it; for my grandfather on the paternal side was a white gentleman. What tangled skeins are the genealogies of slavery! I loved my father; but it mortified me to be obliged to bestow his name on my children.

---

[1]   *vituperations* Abusive rantings.

When we left the church, my father's old mistress invited me to go home with her. She clasped a gold chain round my baby's neck. I thanked her for this kindness; but I did not like the emblem. I wanted no chain to be fastened on my daughter, not even if its links were of gold. How earnestly I prayed that she might never feel the weight of slavery's chain, whose iron entereth into the soul!

[Dr. Flint continues to terrorize and abuse Linda, threatening to sell her children, and at one point throwing her small son Benjamin across the room, causing him to lose consciousness. The boy recovers, but Linda almost wanted him to die rather than be subject to the cruelties of slavery. Dr. Flint tells Linda she can either have sex with him or go to his son's plantation; Linda moves to the plantation with her daughter Ellen (Benjamin is too ill to go). Renewed threats to her children, and the cruelty of the younger Mr. Flint and his wife, determine Linda to escape.]

CHAPTER 17. THE FLIGHT

Mr. Flint was hard pushed for house servants, and rather than lose me he had restrained his malice. I did my work faithfully, though not, of course, with a willing mind. They were evidently afraid I should leave them. Mr. Flint wished that I should sleep in the great house instead of the servants' quarters. His wife agreed to the proposition, but said I mustn't bring my bed into the house, because it would scatter feathers on her carpet. I knew when I went there that they would never think of such a thing as furnishing a bed of any kind for me and my little one. I therefore carried my own bed, and now I was forbidden to use it. I did as I was ordered. But now that I was certain my children were to be put in their power, in order to give them a stronger hold on me, I resolved to leave them that night. I remembered the grief this step would bring upon my dear old grandmother; and nothing less than the freedom of my children would have induced me to disregard her advice. I went about my evening work with trembling steps. Mr. Flint twice called from his chamber door to inquire why the house was not locked up. I replied that I had not done my work. "You have

had time enough to do it," said he. "Take care how you answer me!"

I shut all the windows, locked all the doors, and went up to the third story, to wait till midnight. How long those hours seemed, and how fervently I prayed that God would not forsake me in this hour of utmost need! I was about to risk everything on the throw of a die; and if I failed, O what would become of me and my poor children? They would be made to suffer for my fault.

At half past twelve I stole softly down stairs. I stopped on the second floor, thinking I heard a noise. I felt my way down into the parlor, and looked out of the window. The night was so intensely dark that I could see nothing. I raised the window very softly and jumped out. Large drops of rain were falling, and the darkness bewildered me. I dropped on my knees, and breathed a short prayer to God for guidance and protection. I groped my way to the road, and rushed towards the town with almost lightning speed. I arrived at my grandmother's house, but dared not see her. She would say, "Linda, you are killing me"; and I knew that would unnerve me. I tapped softly at the window of a room, occupied by a woman, who had lived in the house several years. I knew she was a faithful friend, and could be trusted with my secret. I tapped several times before she heard me. At last she raised the window, and I whispered, "Sally, I have run away. Let me in, quick." She opened the door softly, and said in low tones, "For God's sake, don't. Your grandmother is trying to buy you and de chillern. Mr. Sands was here last week. He tole her he was going away on business, but he wanted her to go ahead about buying you and de chillern, and he would help her all he could. Don't run away, Linda. Your grandmother is all bowed down wid trouble now."

I replied, "Sally, they are going to carry my children to the plantation tomorrow; and they will never sell them to anybody so long as they have me in their power. Now, would you advise me to go back?"

"No, chile, no," answered she. "When dey finds you is gone, dey won't want de plague ob de chillern; but where is you going to hide? Dey knows ebery inch ob dis house."

I told her I had a hiding-place, and that was all it was best for her to know. I asked her to go into my room as soon as it was light, and take all my clothes out of my trunk, and pack them in hers; for I knew Mr. Flint and the constable would be there early to search my room. I feared the sight of my children would be too much for my full heart; but I could not go out into the uncertain future without one last look. I bent over the bed where lay my little Benny and baby Ellen. Poor little ones! fatherless and motherless! Memories of their father came over me. He wanted to be kind to them; but they were not all to him, as they were to my womanly heart. I knelt and prayed for the innocent little sleepers. I kissed them lightly, and turned away.

As I was about to open the street door, Sally laid her hand on my shoulder, and said, "Linda, is you gwine all alone? Let me call your uncle."

"No Sally," I replied, "I want no one to be brought into trouble on my account."

I went forth into the darkness and rain. I ran on till I came to the house of the friend who was to conceal me.

Early the next morning Mr. Flint was at my grandmother's inquiring for me. She told him she had not seen me, and supposed I was at the plantation. He watched her face narrowly, and said, "Don't you know anything about her running off?" She assured him that she did not. He went on to say, "Last night she ran off without the least provocation. We had treated her very kindly. My wife liked her. She will soon be found and brought back. Are her children with you?" When told that they were, he said, "I am very glad to hear that. If they are here, she cannot be far off. If I find out that any of my niggers have had anything to do with this damned business, I'll give 'em five hundred lashes." As he started to go to his father's, he turned round and added, persuasively, "Let her be brought back, and she shall have her children to live with her."

The tidings made the old doctor rave and storm at a furious rate. It was a busy day for them. My grandmother's house was searched from top to bottom. As my trunk was empty, they concluded I had taken my clothes with me. Before ten o'clock every vessel northward bound was thoroughly examined, and the law against harboring fugitives was read to all on board. At night a watch was set over the town. Knowing how distressed my grandmother would be, I wanted to send her a message; but it could not be done. Everyone who went in or out of her house was closely watched.

The doctor said he would take my children, unless she became responsible for them; which of course she willingly did. The next day was spent in searching. Before night, the following advertisement was posted at every corner, and in every public place for miles round:

"$300 REWARD! Ran away from the subscriber, an intelligent, bright, mulatto girl, named Linda, 21 years age. Five feet four inches high. Dark eyes, and black hair inclined to curl; but it can be made straight. Has a decayed spot on a front tooth. She can read and write, and in all probability will try to get to the Free States. All persons are forbidden, under penalty of the law, to harbor or employ said slave. $150 will be given to whoever takes her in the state, and $300 if taken out of the state and delivered to me, or lodged in jail.
DR. FLINT."

. . .

[Linda moves to new hiding places several times; Dr. Flint imagines she has gone North, and he goes to New York to find her. The father of Linda's children, Mr. Sands, uses an agent to buy the children and Linda's brother, William, from Dr. Flint. When Dr. Flint discovers who the buyer is, he is incensed and vows never to sell Linda. Linda needs to change hiding places again, and even spends a night hiding in the aptly named Snaky Swamp.]

Chapter 21. The Loophole of Retreat

A small shed had been added to my grandmother's house years ago. Some boards were laid across the joists at the top, and between these boards and the roof was a very small garret, never occupied by anything but rats and mice. It was a pent roof, covered with nothing but shingles, according to the southern custom for such buildings. The garret was only nine feet long, and seven wide. The highest part was three feet high, and sloped down abruptly to the loose board floor. There was no admission for either light or air. My uncle Phillip, who was a carpenter, had very skillfully made a concealed trap door, which communicated with the storeroom. He had been doing this while I was waiting in the swamp. The storeroom opened upon a piazza. To this hole I was conveyed as soon as I entered the house. The air was stifling; the darkness total. A bed had been spread on the floor. I could sleep quite comfortably on one side; but the slope was so sudden that I could not turn on the other without hitting the roof. The rats and mice ran over my bed; but I was weary, and I slept such sleep as the wretched may, when a tempest has passed over them. Morning came. I knew it only by the noises I heard; for in my small den day and night were all the same. I suffered for air even more than for light. But I was not comfortless. I heard the voices of my children. There was joy and there was sadness in the sound. It made my tears flow. How I longed to speak to them! I was eager to look on their faces; but there was no hole, no crack, through which I could peep. This continued darkness was oppressive. It seemed horrible to sit or lie in a cramped position day after day, without one gleam of light. Yet I would have chosen this, rather than my lot as a slave, though white people considered it an easy one; and it was so compared with the fate of others. I was never cruelly over-worked; I was never lacerated with the whip from head to foot; I was never so beaten and bruised that I could not turn from one side to the other; I never had my heel-strings cut to prevent my running away; I was never chained to a log and forced to drag it about, while I toiled in the fields from morning till night; I was never branded with hot iron, or torn by bloodhounds. On the contrary, I had always been kindly treated, and tenderly cared for, until I came into the hands of Dr. Flint. I had never wished for freedom till then. But though my life in slavery was comparatively devoid of hardships, God pity the woman who is compelled to lead such a life!

My food was passed up to me through the trap-door my uncle had contrived; and my grandmother, my uncle Phillip, and aunt Nancy would seize such opportunities as they could, to mount up there and chat with me at the opening. But of course this was not safe in the daytime. It must all be done in darkness. It was impossible for me to move in an erect position, but I crawled about my den for exercise. One day I hit my head against something, and found it was a gimlet.[1] My uncle had left it sticking there when he made the

trap-door. I was as rejoiced as Robinson Crusoe[2] could have been in finding such a treasure. It put a lucky thought into my head. I said to myself, "Now I will have some light. Now I will see my children." I did not dare to begin my work during the daytime, for fear of attracting attention. But I groped round; and having found the side next the street, where I could frequently see my children, I stuck the gimlet in and waited for evening. I bored three rows of holes, one above another; then I bored out the interstices between. I thus succeeded in making one hole about an inch long and an inch broad. I sat by it till late into the night, to enjoy the little whiff of air that floated in. In the morning I watched for my children. The first person I saw in the street was Dr. Flint. I had a shuddering, superstitious feeling that it was a bad omen. Several familiar faces passed by. At last I heard the merry laughing of children, and presently two sweet little faces were looking up at me, as though they knew I was there, and were conscious of the joy they imparted. How I longed to *tell* them I was there!

My condition was now a little improved. But for weeks I was tormented by hundreds of little red insects, fine as a needle's point, that pierced through my skin, and produced an intolerable burning. The good grandmother gave me herb teas and cooling medicines, and finally I got rid of them. The heat of my den was intense, for nothing but thin shingles protected me from the scorching summer's sun. But I had my consolations. Through my peeping-hole I could watch the children, and when they were near enough, I could hear their talk. Aunt Nancy brought me all the news she could hear at Dr. Flint's. From her I learned that the doctor had written to New York to a colored woman, who had been born and raised in our neighborhood, and had breathed his contaminating atmosphere. He offered her a reward if she could find out anything about me. I know not what was the nature of her reply; but he soon after started for New York in haste, saying to his family that he had business of importance to transact. I peeped at him as he passed on his way to the steamboat. It was a satisfaction to have miles of land and

---

1   *gimlet* Tool used for boring holes.

2   *Robinson Crusoe* Protagonist of Daniel Defoe's novel of the same name (1719). In the novel, Crusoe is shipwrecked on an uninhabited island and manages to build a dwelling and farm for himself with the few tools he successfully scavenges from the shipwreck.

water between us, even for a little while; and it was a still greater satisfaction to know that he believed me to be in the Free States. My little den seemed less dreary than it had done. He returned, as he did from his former journey to New York, without obtaining any satisfactory information. When he passed our house next morning, Benny was standing at the gate. He had heard them say that he had gone to find me, and he called out, "Dr. Flint, did you bring my mother home? I want to see her." The doctor stamped his foot at him in a rage, and exclaimed, "Get out of the way, you little damned rascal! If you don't, I'll cut off your head."

Benny ran terrified into the house, saying, "You can't put me in jail again. I don't belong to you now." It was well that the wind carried the words away from the doctor's ear. I told my grandmother of it, when we had our next conference at the trap-door; and begged of her not to allow the children to be impertinent to the irascible old man.

Autumn came, with a pleasant abatement of heat. My eyes had become accustomed to the dim light, and by holding my book or work in a certain position near the aperture I contrived to read and sew. That was a great relief to the tedious monotony of my life. But when winter came, the cold penetrated through the thin shingle roof, and I was dreadfully chilled. The winters there are not so long, or so severe, as in northern latitudes; but the houses are not built to shelter from cold, and my little den was peculiarly comfortless. The kind grandmother brought me bed-clothes and warm drinks. Often I was obliged to lie in bed all day to keep comfortable; but with all my precautions, my shoulders and feet were frostbitten. O, those long, gloomy days, with no object for my eye to rest upon, and no thoughts to occupy my mind, except the dreary past and the uncertain future! I was thankful when there came a day sufficiently mild for me to wrap myself up and sit at the loophole to watch the passersby. Southerners have the habit of stopping and talking in the streets, and I heard many conversations not intended to meet my ears. I heard slave-hunters planning how to catch some poor fugitive. Several times I heard allusions to Dr. Flint, myself, and the history of my children, who, perhaps, were playing near the gate. One would say, "I wouldn't move my little finger to catch her, as old Flint's property." Another would say,

"I'll catch *any* nigger for the reward. A man ought to have what belongs to him, if he *is* a damned brute." The opinion was often expressed that I was in the Free States. Very rarely did anyone suggest that I might be in the vicinity. Had the least suspicion rested on my grandmother's house, it would have been burned to the ground. But it was the last place they thought of. Yet there was no place, where slavery existed, that could have afforded me so good a place of concealment.

Dr. Flint and his family repeatedly tried to coax and bribe my children to tell something they had heard said about me. One day the doctor took them into a shop, and offered them some bright little silver pieces and gay handkerchiefs if they would tell where their mother was. Ellen shrank away from him, and would not speak; but Benny spoke up, and said, "Dr. Flint, I don't know where my mother is. I guess she's in New York; and when you go there again, I wish you'd ask her to come home, for I want to see her; but if you put her in jail, or tell her you'll cut her head off, I'll tell her to go right back."

[Linda continues to live in her roof-top garret, sewing for the children, suffering from the weather, falling ill and watching her children endure illness. Mr. Sands is elected to Congress; he promises to someday free the children but so far has not. Linda tricks Dr. Flint into thinking she is in Boston, which allows her to occasionally get out of her garret and stretch her legs.]

CHAPTER 29. PREPARATIONS FOR ESCAPE

I hardly expect that the reader will credit me, when I affirm that I lived in that little dismal hole, almost deprived of light and air, and with no space to move my limbs, for nearly seven years. But it is a fact; and to me a sad one, even now; for my body still suffers from the effects of that long imprisonment, to say nothing of my soul. Members of my family, now living in New York and Boston, can testify to the truth of what I say.

Countless were the nights that I sat late at the little loophole scarcely large enough to give me a glimpse of one twinkling star. There, I heard the patrols and slave-hunters conferring together about the capture of runaways, well knowing how rejoiced they would be to catch me.

Season after season, year after year, I peeped at my children's faces, and heard their sweet voices, with a heart yearning all the while to say, "Your mother is here." Sometimes it appeared to me as if ages had rolled away since I entered upon that gloomy, monotonous existence. At times, I was stupefied and listless; at other times I became very impatient to know when these dark years would end, and I should again be allowed to feel the sunshine, and breathe the pure air.

After Ellen left us, this feeling increased. Mr. Sands had agreed that Benny might go to the north whenever his uncle Phillip could go with him; and I was anxious to be there also, to watch over my children, and protect them so far as I was able. Moreover, I was likely to be drowned out of my den, if I remained much longer; for the slight roof was getting badly out of repair, and uncle Phillip was afraid to remove the shingles, lest someone should get a glimpse of me. When storms occurred in the night, they spread mats and bits of carpet, which in the morning appeared have been laid out to dry; but to cover the roof in the daytime might have attracted attention. Consequently, my clothes and bedding were often drenched; a process by which the pains and aches in my cramped and stiffened limbs were greatly increased. I revolved various plans of escape in my mind, which I sometimes imparted to my grandmother, when she came to whisper with me at the trap-door. The kind-hearted old woman had an intense sympathy for runaways. She had known too much of the cruelties inflicted on those who were captured. Her memory always flew back at once to the sufferings of her bright and handsome son, Benjamin, the youngest and dearest of her flock. So, whenever I alluded to the subject, she would groan out, "O, don't think of it, child. You'll break my heart." I had no good old aunt Nancy now to encourage me; but my brother William and my children were continually beckoning me to the north.

And now I must go back a few months in my story. I have stated that the first of January was the time for selling slaves, or leasing them out to new masters. If time were counted by heart-throbs, the poor slaves might reckon years of suffering during that festival so joyous to the free. On the New Year's day preceding my aunt's death, one of my friends, named Fanny, was to be sold at auction to pay her master's debts. My thoughts were with her during all the day, and at night I anxiously inquired what had been her fate. I was told that she had been sold to one master, and her four little girls to another master, far distant; that she had escaped from her purchaser, and was not to be found. Her mother was the old Aggie I have spoken of. She lived in a small tenement belonging to my grandmother, and built on the same lot with her own house. Her dwelling was searched and watched, and that brought the patrols so near me that I was obliged to keep very close in my den. The hunters were somehow eluded; and not long afterwards Benny accidentally caught sight of Fanny in her mother's hut. He told his grandmother, who charged him never to speak of it, explaining to him the frightful consequences; and he never betrayed the trust. Aggie little dreamed that my grandmother knew where her daughter was concealed, and that the stooping form of her old neighbor was bending under a similar burden of anxiety and fear; but these dangerous secrets deepened the sympathy between the two old persecuted mothers.

My friend Fanny and I remained many weeks hidden within call of each other; but she was unconscious of the fact. I longed to have her share my den, which seemed a more secure retreat than her own; but I had brought so much trouble on my grandmother, that it seemed wrong to ask her to incur greater risks. My restlessness increased. I had lived too long in bodily pain and anguish of spirit. Always I was in dread that by some accident, or some contrivance, slavery would succeed in snatching my children from me. This thought drove me nearly frantic, and I determined to steer for the North Star at all hazards. At this crisis, Providence opened an unexpected way for me to escape. My friend Peter came one evening, and asked to speak with me. "Your day has come, Linda," said he. "I have found a chance for you to go to the Free States. You have a fortnight to decide." The news seemed too good to be true; but Peter explained his arrangements, and told me all that was necessary was for me to say I would go. I was going to answer him with a joyful yes, when the thought of Benny came to my mind. I told him the temptation was exceedingly strong, but I was terribly afraid of Dr. Flint's alleged power over my child, and that I could not go and leave him behind. Peter remonstrated earnestly. He said such a good chance might never occur again; that Benny was free, and could be sent to me; and that for the sake of my children's welfare I ought not to hesitate a moment. I told him I would consult with uncle Phillip. My uncle rejoiced in the plan, and bade me to go by all means. He promised, if his life was spared, that he would either bring or send my son to me as soon as I reached a place of safety. I resolved to go, but thought nothing had better be said to my grandmother till very near the time of departure. But my uncle thought she would feel it more keenly if I left her so suddenly. "I will reason with her," said he, "and convince her how necessary it is, not only for your sake, but for hers also. You cannot be blind to the fact that she is sinking under her burdens." I was not blind to it. I knew that my concealment was an ever-present source of anxiety, and that the older she grew the more nervously fearful she was of discovery. My uncle talked with her, and finally succeeded in persuading her that it was absolutely necessary for me to seize the chance so unexpectedly offered.

The anticipation of being a free woman proved almost too much for my weak frame. The excitement stimulated me, and at the same time bewildered me. I made busy preparations for my journey, and for my son to follow me. I resolved to have an interview with him before I went, that I might give him cautions and advice, and tell him how anxiously I should be waiting for him at the north. Grandmother stole up to me as often as possible to whisper words of counsel. She insisted upon my writing to Dr. Flint, as soon as I arrived in the Free States, and asking him to sell me to her. She said she would sacrifice her house, and all she had in the world, for the sake of having me safe with my children in any part of the world. If she could only live to know *that* she could die in peace. I promised the dear old faithful friend that I would write to her as soon as I arrived, and put the letter in a safe way to reach her; but in my own mind I resolved that not another cent of her hard earnings should be spent to pay rapacious slaveholders for what they called their property. And even if I had not been unwilling to buy what I had already a right to possess, common humanity would have prevented me from accepting the generous offer, at the expense of turning my aged

relative out of house and home, when she was trembling on the brink of the grave.

I was to escape in a vessel; but I forbear to mention any further particulars. I was in readiness, but the vessel was unexpectedly detained several days. Meantime, news came to town of a most horrible murder committed on a fugitive slave, named James. Charity, the mother of this unfortunate young man, had been an old acquaintance of ours. I have told the shocking particulars of his death, in my description of some of the neighboring slaveholders. My grandmother, always nervously sensitive about runaways, was terribly frightened. She felt sure that a similar fate awaited me, if I did not desist from my enterprise. She sobbed, and groaned, and entreated me not to go. Her excessive fear was somewhat contagious, and my heart was not proof against her extreme agony. I was grievously disappointed, but I promised to relinquish my project.

When my friend Peter was apprised of this, he was disappointed and vexed. He said, that judging from our past experience, it would be a long time before I had such another chance to throw away. I told him it need not be thrown away; that I had a friend concealed nearby, who would be glad enough to take the place that had been provided for me. I told him about poor Fanny, and the kind-hearted, noble fellow, who never turned his back upon anybody in distress, white or black, expressed his readiness to help her. Aggie was much surprised when she found that we knew her secret. She was rejoiced to hear of such a chance for Fanny, and arrangements were made for her to go on board the vessel the next night. They both supposed that I had long been at the north, therefore my name was not mentioned in the transaction. Fanny was carried on board at the appointed time, and stowed away in a very small cabin. This accommodation had been purchased at a price that would pay for a voyage to England. But when one proposes to go to fine old England, they stop to calculate whether they can afford the cost of the pleasure; while in making a bargain to escape from slavery, the trembling victim is ready to say, "Take all I have, only don't betray me!"

The next morning I peeped through my loophole, and saw that it was dark and cloudy. At night I received news that the wind was ahead,[1] and the vessel had not sailed. I was exceedingly anxious about Fanny, and Peter too, who was running a tremendous risk at my instigation. Next day the wind and weather remained the same. Poor Fanny had been half dead with fright when they carried her on board, and I could readily imagine how she must be suffering now. Grandmother came often to my den, to say how thankful she was I did not go. On the third morning she rapped for me to come down to the storeroom. The poor old sufferer was breaking down under her weight of trouble. She was easily flurried now. I found her in a nervous, excited state, but I was not aware that she had forgotten to lock the door behind her, as usual. She was exceedingly worried about the detention of the vessel. She was afraid all would be discovered, and then Fanny, and Peter, and I, would all be tortured to death, and Phillip should be utterly ruined, and her house would be torn down. Poor Peter! If he should die such a horrible death as the poor slave James had lately done, and all for his kindness in trying to help me, how dreadful it would be for us all! Alas, the thought was familiar to me, and had sent many a sharp pang through my heart. I tried to suppress my own anxiety, and speak soothingly to her. She brought in some allusion to aunt Nancy, the dear daughter she had recently buried, and then she lost all control of herself. As she stood there, trembling and sobbing, a voice from the piazza called out, "Whar is you, aunt Marthy?" Grandmother was startled, and in her agitation opened the door, without thinking of me. In stepped Jenny, the mischievous housemaid, who had tried to enter my room, when I was concealed in the house of my white benefactress. "I's bin huntin ebery whar for you, aunt Marthy," said she. "My missis wants you to send her some crackers." I had slunk down behind a barrel, which entirely screened me, but I imagined that Jenny was looking directly at the spot, and my heart beat violently. My grandmother immediately thought what she had done, and went out quickly with Jenny to count the crackers, locking the door behind her. She returned to me, in a few minutes, the perfect picture of despair. "Poor child!" she exclaimed, "my carelessness has ruined you. The boat ain't gone yet. Get ready immediately, and go

with Fanny. I ain't got another word to say against it now; for there's no telling what may happen this day."

Uncle Phillip was sent for, and he agreed with his mother in thinking that Jenny would inform Dr. Flint in less than twenty-four hours. He advised getting me on board the boat, if possible; if not, I had better keep very still in my den, where they could not find me without tearing the house down. He said it would not do for him to move in the matter, because suspicion would be immediately excited; but he promised to communicate with Peter. I felt reluctant to apply to him again, having implicated him too much already; but there seemed to be no alternative. Vexed as Peter had been by my indecision, he was true to his generous nature, and said at once that he would do his best to help me, trusting I should show myself a stronger woman this time.

He immediately proceeded to the wharf, and found that the wind had shifted, and the vessel was slowly beating downstream. On some pretext of urgent necessity, he offered two boatmen a dollar apiece to catch up with her. He was of lighter complexion than the boatmen he hired, and when the captain saw them coming so rapidly, he thought officers were pursuing his vessel in search of the runaway slave he had on board. They hoisted sails, but the boat gained upon them, and the indefatigable Peter sprang on board.

The captain at once recognized him. Peter asked him to go below, to speak about a bad bill he had given him. When he told his errand, the captain replied, "Why, the woman's here already; and I've put her where you or the devil would have a tough job to find her."

"But it is another woman I want to bring," said Peter. "She is in great distress, too, and you shall be paid anything within reason, if you'll stop and take her."

"What's her name?" inquired the captain.

"Linda," he replied.

"That's the name of the woman already here," rejoined the captain. "By George! I believe you mean to betray me."

"O!" exclaimed Peter, "God knows I wouldn't harm a hair of your head. I am too grateful to you. But there really is another woman in great danger. Do have the humanity to stop and take her!"

After a while they came to an understanding. Fanny, not dreaming I was anywhere about in that region, had

---

[1]   *wind was ahead*   I.e., there was a head wind, making it difficult to sail.

assumed my name, though she called herself Johnson. "Linda is a common name," said Peter, "and the woman I want to bring is Linda Brent."

The captain agreed to wait at a certain place till evening, being handsomely paid for his detention.

Of course, the day was an anxious one for us all. But we concluded that if Jenny had seen me, she would be too wise to let her mistress know of it; and that she probably would not get a chance to see Dr. Flint's family till evening, for I knew very well what were the rules in that household. I afterwards believed that she did not see me; for nothing ever came of it, and she was one of those base characters that would have jumped to betray a suffering fellow being for the sake of thirty pieces of silver.[1]

I made all my arrangements to go on board as soon as it was dusk. The intervening time I resolved to spend with my son. I had not spoken to him for seven years, though I had been under the same roof, and seen him every day, when I was well enough to sit at the loophole. I did not dare to venture beyond the storeroom; so they brought him there, and locked us up together, in a place concealed from the piazza door. It was an agitating interview for both of us. After we had talked and wept together for a little while, he said, "Mother, I'm glad you're going away. I wish I could go with you. I knew you was here; and I have been so afraid they would come and catch you!"

I was greatly surprised, and asked him how he had found it out.

He replied, "I was standing under the eaves, one day, before Ellen went away, and I heard somebody cough up over the wood shed. I don't know what made me think it was you, but I did think so. I missed Ellen, the night before she went away; and grandmother brought her back into the room in the night; and I thought maybe she'd been to see *you*, before she went, for I heard grandmother whisper to her, 'Now go to sleep; and remember never to tell.'"

I asked him if he ever mentioned his suspicions to his sister. He said he never did; but after he heard the cough, if he saw her playing with other children on that side of the house, he always tried to coax her round to the other side, for fear they would hear me cough, too.

He said he had kept a close lookout for Dr. Flint, and if he saw him speak to a constable, or a patrol, he always told grandmother. I now recollected that I had seen him manifest uneasiness, when people were on that side of the house, and I had at the time been puzzled to conjecture a motive for his actions. Such prudence may seem extraordinary in a boy of twelve years, but slaves, being surrounded by mysteries, deceptions, and dangers, early learn to be suspicious and watchful, and prematurely cautious and cunning. He had never asked a question of grandmother, or uncle Phillip, and I had often heard him chime in with other children, when they spoke of my being at the north.

I told him I was now really going to the Free States, and if he was a good, honest boy, and a loving child to his dear old grandmother, the Lord would bless him, and bring him to me, and we and Ellen would live together. He began to tell me that grandmother had not eaten anything all day. While he was speaking, the door was unlocked, and she came in with a small bag of money, which she wanted me to take. I begged her to keep a part of it, at least, to pay for Benny's being sent to the north; but she insisted, while her tears were falling fast, that I should take the whole. "You may be sick among strangers," she said, "and they would send you to the poorhouse to die." Ah, that good grandmother!

For the last time I went up to my nook. Its desolate appearance no longer chilled me, for the light of hope had risen in my soul. Yet, even with the blessed prospect of freedom before me, I felt very sad at leaving forever that old homestead, where I had been sheltered so long by the dear old grandmother; where I had dreamed my first young dream of love; and where, after that had faded away, my children came to twine themselves so closely round my desolate heart. As the hour approached for me to leave, I again descended to the storeroom. My grandmother and Benny were there. She took me by the hand, and said, "Linda, let us pray." We knelt down together, with my child pressed to my heart, and my other arm round the faithful, loving old friend I was about to leave forever. On no other occasion has it ever been my lot to listen to so fervent a supplication for mercy and protection. It thrilled through my heart, and inspired me with trust in God.

Peter was waiting for me in the street. I was soon by his side, faint in body, but strong of purpose. I did

---

[1]   *thirty pieces of silver*   Before the Last Supper, Judas Iscariot betrays Jesus for thirty silver coins (see Matthew 26.15).

not look back upon the old place, though I felt that I should never see it again.

[Linda and Fanny make it safely to Philadelphia on the boat and soon after head to New York. Linda's children Ellen and Benny have in the meantime also both gone North, Ellen to live with a relation of Mr. Sands and Benny with Uncle Phillip. Linda finds on her arrival that Ellen was not going to school as planned but instead was working as a servant for a Mrs. Hobbs. Linda takes a job as nursemaid to a Mrs. Bruce, a very kind and considerate woman. Dr. Flint comes to New York to find Linda, and she goes to Boston for a month to avoid him. While on a trip with Mrs. Bruce and the baby, Linda experiences the full extent of racism in the North, as she is treated scornfully and rudely. On their return, Dr. Flint returns again, as he had learned where Linda was staying, and she and her children flee to Boston for several months. On the death of Mrs. Bruce, Linda is distraught, but Mr. Bruce keeps her employed as a nurse for the child, Mary. They go to England, where Linda is impressed that the poor in that country have rights and access to education; she does not experience racism in England. Upon her return, she goes to Boston to look after her daughter Ellen.]

CHAPTER 39. THE CONFESSION

For two years my daughter and I supported ourselves comfortably in Boston. At the end of that time, my brother William offered to send Ellen to a boarding school. It required a great effort for me to consent to part with her, for I had few near ties, and it was her presence that made my two little rooms seem homelike. But my judgment prevailed over my selfish feelings. I made preparations for her departure. During the two years we had lived together I had often resolved to tell her something about her father; but I had never been able to muster sufficient courage. I had a shrinking dread of diminishing my child's love. I knew she must have curiosity on the subject, but she had never asked a question. She was always very careful not to say anything to remind me of my troubles. Now that she was going from me, I thought if I should die before she returned, she might hear my story from someone who did not understand the palliating circumstances; and

that if she were entirely ignorant on the subject, her sensitive nature might receive a rude shock.

When we retired for the night, she said, "Mother, it is very hard to leave you alone. I am almost sorry I am going, though I do want to improve myself. But you will write to me often; won't you, mother?"

I did not throw my arms round her. I did not answer her. But in a calm, solemn way, for it cost me great effort, I said, "Listen to me, Ellen; I have something to tell you!" I recounted my early sufferings in slavery, and told her how nearly they had crushed me. I began to tell her how they had driven me into a great sin, when she clasped me in her arms, and exclaimed, "O, don't, mother! Please don't tell me any more."

I said, "But, my child, I want you to know about your father."

"I know all about it, mother," she replied; "I am nothing to my father, and he is nothing to me. All my love is for you. I was with him five months in Washington, and he never cared for me. He never spoke to me as he did to his little Fanny. I knew all the time he was my father, for Fanny's nurse told me so; but she said I must never tell anybody, and I never did. I used to wish he would take me in his arms and kiss me, as he did Fanny; or that he would sometimes smile at me, as he did at her. I thought if he was my own father, he ought to love me. I was a little girl then, and didn't know any better. But now I never think anything about my father. All my love is for you." She hugged me closer as she spoke, and I thanked God that the knowledge I had so much dreaded to impart had not diminished the affection of my child. I had not the slightest idea she knew that portion of my history. If I had, I should have spoken to her long before; for my pent-up feelings had often longed to pour themselves out to someone I could trust. But I loved the dear girl better for the delicacy she had manifested towards her unfortunate mother.

The next morning, she and her uncle started on their journey to the village in New York, where she was to be placed at school. It seemed as if all the sunshine had gone away. My little room was dreadfully lonely. I was thankful when a message came from a lady, accustomed to employ me, requesting me to come and sew in her family for several weeks. On my return, I found a letter from brother William. He thought of opening an anti-slavery reading room in Rochester, and combining with it the sale of some books and stationery; and he wanted me to unite with him. We tried it, but it was not successful. We found warm anti-slavery friends there, but the feeling was not general enough to support such an establishment. I passed nearly a year in the family of Isaac and Amy Post, practical believers in the Christian doctrine of human brotherhood. They measured a man's worth by his character, not by his complexion. The memory of those beloved and honored friends will remain with me to my latest hour.

CHAPTER 40. THE FUGITIVE SLAVE LAW

My brother, being disappointed in his project, concluded to go to California; and it was agreed that Benjamin should go with him. Ellen liked her school, and was a great favorite there. They did not know her history, and she did not tell it, because she had no desire to make capital out of their sympathy. But when it was accidentally discovered that her mother was a fugitive slave, every method was used to increase her advantages and diminish her expenses.

I was alone again. It was necessary for me to be earning money, and I preferred that it should be among those who knew me. On my return from Rochester, I called at the house of Mr. Bruce, to see Mary, the darling little babe that had thawed my heart, when it was freezing into a cheerless distrust of all my fellow-beings. She was growing a tall girl now, but I loved her always. Mr. Bruce had married again, and it was proposed that I should become nurse to a new infant. I had but one hesitation, and that was my feeling of insecurity in New York, now greatly increased by the passage of the Fugitive Slave Law. However, I resolved to try the experiment. I was again fortunate in my employer. The new Mrs. Bruce was an American, brought up under aristocratic influences and still living in the midst of them; but if she had any prejudice against color, I was never made aware of it; and as for the system of slavery, she had a most hearty dislike of it. No sophistry of Southerners could blind her to its enormity. She was a person of excellent principles and a noble heart. To me, from that hour to the present, she has been a true and sympathizing friend. Blessings be with her and hers!

About the time that I reentered the Bruce family, an event occurred of disastrous import to the colored people. The slave Hamlin,[1] the first fugitive that came under the new law, was given up by the bloodhounds of the north to the bloodhounds of the south. It was the beginning of a reign of terror to the colored population. The great city rushed on in its whirl of excitement, taking no note of the "short and simple annals of the poor."[2] But while fashionables were listening to the thrilling voice of Jenny Lind[3] in Metropolitan Hall, the thrilling voices of poor hunted colored people went up, in an agony of supplication, to the Lord, from Zion's church. Many families, who had lived in the city for twenty years, fled from it now. Many a poor washerwoman, who, by hard labor, had made herself a comfortable home, was obliged to sacrifice her furniture, bid a hurried farewell to friends, and seek her fortune among strangers in Canada. Many a wife discovered a secret she had never known before— that her husband was a fugitive, and must leave her to ensure his own safety. Worse still, many a husband discovered that his wife had fled from slavery years ago, and as "the child follows the condition of its mother," the children of his love were liable to be seized and carried into slavery. Everywhere, in those humble homes, there was consternation and anguish. But what cared the legislators of the "dominant race" for the blood they were crushing out of trampled hearts?

When my brother William spent his last evening with me, before he went to California, we talked nearly all the time of the distress brought on our oppressed people by the passage of this iniquitous law; and never had I seen him manifest such bitterness of spirit, such stern hostility to our oppressors. He was himself free from

---

[1] *Hamlin* James Hamlet was the first victim of the Fugitive Slave Act; he was arrested in Manhattan and sent to Baltimore in 1850. Hamlet insisted he was a free man, but a Mary Brown of Maryland succeeded in having the law seize hold of him, separating him from his wife and two children. Hamlet was then brought to the Baltimore slave market, where he was bought by his home community in Williamsburgh, Brooklyn for eight hundred dollars, after which he was able to return to his family and his job.

[2] *short ... poor* Quotation is from line 32 of Thomas Gray's "Elegy Written in a Country Churchyard" (1751). The line refers to main life events—births, deaths, marriages, and christenings—that are recorded in parish registers.

[3] *Jenny Lind* Renowned Swedish opera singer who, from 1850 to 1852, toured the United States. The excitement surrounding her concerts came to be referred to as "Lind Mania."

the operation of the law; for he did not run from any Slaveholding State, being brought into the Free States by his master. But I was subject to it; and so were hundreds of intelligent and industrious people all around us. I seldom ventured into the streets; and when it was necessary to do an errand for Mrs. Bruce, or any of the family, I went as much as possible through back streets and by-ways. What a disgrace to a city calling itself free, that inhabitants, guiltless of offence, and seeking to perform their duties conscientiously, should be condemned to live in such incessant fear, and have nowhere to turn for protection! This state of things, of course, gave rise to many impromptu vigilance committees. Every colored person, and every friend of their persecuted race, kept their eyes wide open. Every evening I examined the newspapers carefully, to see what Southerners had put up at the hotels. I did this for my own sake, thinking my young mistress and her husband might be among the list; I wished also to give information to others, if necessary; for if many were "running to and fro," I resolved that "knowledge should be increased."[1]

This brings up one of my Southern reminiscences, which I will here briefly relate. I was somewhat acquainted with a slave named Luke, who belonged to a wealthy man in our vicinity. His master died, leaving a son and daughter heirs to his large fortune. In the division of the slaves, Luke was included in the son's portion. This young man became a prey to the vices growing out of the "patriarchal institution," and when he went to the north, to complete his education, he carried his vices with him. He was brought home, deprived of the use of his limbs, by excessive dissipation. Luke was appointed to wait upon his bed-ridden master, whose despotic habits were greatly increased by exasperation at his own helplessness. He kept a cowhide beside him, and, for the most trivial occurrence, he would order his attendant to bare his back, and kneel beside the couch, while he whipped him till his strength was exhausted. Some days he was not allowed to wear anything but his shirt, in order to be in readiness to be flogged. A day seldom passed without his receiving more or less blows. If the slightest

resistance was offered, the town constable was sent for to execute the punishment, and Luke learned from experience how much more the constable's strong arm was to be dreaded than the comparatively feeble one of his master. The arm of his tyrant grew weak, and was finally palsied;[2] and then the constable's services were in constant requisition. The fact that he was entirely dependent on Luke's care, and was obliged to be tended like an infant, instead of inspiring any gratitude or compassion towards his poor slave, seemed only to increase his irritability and cruelty. As he lay there on his bed, a mere disgraced wreck of manhood, he took into his head the strangest freaks of despotism; and if Luke hesitated to submit to his orders, the constable was immediately sent for. Some of these freaks were of a nature too filthy to be repeated. When I fled from the house of bondage, I left poor Luke still chained to the bedside of this cruel and disgusting wretch.

One day, when I had been requested to do an errand for Mrs. Bruce, I was hurrying through back streets, as usual, when I saw a young man approaching, whose face was familiar to me. As he came nearer, I recognized Luke. I always rejoiced to see or hear of anyone who had escaped from the black pit; but, remembering this poor fellow's extreme hardships, I was peculiarly glad to see him on Northern soil, though I no longer called it *free* soil. I well remembered what a desolate feeling it was to be alone among strangers, and I went up to him and greeted him cordially. At first, he did not know me; but when I mentioned my name, he remembered all about me. I told him of the Fugitive Slave Law, and asked him if he did not know that New York was a city of kidnappers.

He replied, "De risk ain't so bad for me, as 'tis fur you. 'Cause I runned away from de speculator,[3] and you runned away from de massa. Dem speculators vont spen dar money to come here fur a runaway, if dey ain't sartin sure to put dar hans right on him. An I tell you I's tuk good car 'bout dat. I had too hard times down dar, to let 'em ketch dis nigger."

He then told me of the advice he had received, and the plans he had laid. I asked if he had money enough to take him to Canada. "'Pend upon it, I hab," he replied. "I tuk car fur dat. I'd bin workin all my

---

[1] *running ... increased* These quotations are both from Daniel 12.4, where the prophet Daniel is finishing a description of what was revealed to him about the end of the world: "But thou, O Daniel, shut up the words, and seal the book, even to the time of the end: many shall run to and fro, and knowledge shall be increased."

[2] *palsied* Affected by tremors and paralysis; rendered incapable.

[3] *speculator* Interregional slave trader.

days fur dem cussed whites, an got no pay but kicks and cuffs. So I tought dis nigger had a right to money nuff to bring him to de Free States. Massa Henry he lib till ebery body vish him dead; an ven he did die, I knowed de debbil would hab him, an vouldn't vant him to bring his money 'long too. So I tuk some of his bills, and put 'em in de pocket of his ole trousers. An ven he was buried, dis nigger ask fur dem ole trousers, an dey gub 'em to me." With a low, chuckling laugh, he added, "You see I didn't *steal* it; dey *gub* it to me. I tell you, I had mighty hard time to keep de speculator from findin it; but he didn't git it."

This is a fair specimen of how the moral sense is educated by slavery. When a man has his wages stolen from him, year after year, and the laws sanction and enforce the theft, how can he be expected to have more regard to honesty than has the man who robs him? I have become somewhat enlightened, but I confess that I agree with poor, ignorant, much-abused Luke, in thinking he had a *right* to that money, as a portion of his unpaid wages. He went to Canada forthwith, and I have not since heard from him.

All that winter I lived in a state of anxiety. When I took the children out to breathe the air, I closely observed the countenances of all I met. I dreaded the approach of summer, when snakes and slaveholders make their appearance. I was, in fact, a slave in New York, as subject to slave laws as I had been in a Slave State. Strange incongruity in a State called free!

Spring returned, and I received warning from the south that Dr. Flint knew of my return to my old place, and was making preparations to have me caught. I learned afterwards that my dress, and that of Mrs. Bruce's children, had been described to him by some of the Northern tools, which slaveholders employ for their base purposes, and then indulge in sneers at their cupidity and mean servility.

I immediately informed Mrs. Bruce of my danger, and she took prompt measures for my safety. My place as nurse could not be supplied immediately, and this generous, sympathizing lady proposed that I should carry her baby away. It was a comfort to me to have the child with me; for the heart is reluctant to be torn away from every object it loves. But how few mothers would have consented to have one of their own babes become a fugitive, for the sake of a poor, hunted nurse,

on whom the legislators of the country had let loose the bloodhounds! When I spoke of the sacrifice she was making, in depriving herself of her dear baby, she replied, "It is better for you to have baby with you, Linda; for if they get on your track, they will be obliged to bring the child to me; and then, if there is a possibility of saving you, you shall be saved."

This lady had a very wealthy relative, a benevolent gentleman in many respects, but aristocratic and pro-slavery. He remonstrated with her for harboring a fugitive slave; told her she was violating the laws of her country; and asked her if she was aware of the penalty. She replied, "I am very well aware of it. It is imprisonment and one thousand dollars fine. Shame on my country that it *is* so! I am ready to incur the penalty. I will go to the state's prison, rather than have any poor victim torn from *my* house, to be carried back to slavery."

The noble heart! The brave heart! The tears are in my eyes while I write of her. May the God of the helpless reward her for her sympathy with my persecuted people!

I was sent into New England, where I was sheltered by the wife of a senator, whom I shall always hold in grateful remembrance. This honorable gentleman would not have voted for the Fugitive Slave Law, as did the senator in "Uncle Tom's Cabin";[1] on the contrary, he was strongly opposed to it; but he was enough under its influence to be afraid of having me remain in his house many hours. So I was sent into the country, where I remained a month with the baby. When it was supposed that Dr. Flint's emissaries had lost track of me, and given up the pursuit for the present, I returned to New York.

CHAPTER 41. FREE AT LAST

Mrs. Bruce, and every member of her family, were exceedingly kind to me. I was thankful for the blessings of my lot, yet I could not always wear a cheerful countenance. I was doing harm to no one; on the contrary, I was doing all the good I could in my small way; yet I could never go out to breathe God's free air without

---

[1] *senator in "Uncle Tom's Cabin"* In Harriet Beecher Stowe's novel *Uncle Tom's Cabin*, a state law prohibiting people from helping enslaved fugitives is signed by Senator Bird.

trepidation at my heart. This seemed hard; and I could not think it was a right state of things in any civilized country.

From time to time I received news from my good old grandmother. She could not write; but she employed others to write for her. The following is an extract from one of her last letters:

"Dear Daughter: I cannot hope to see you again on earth; but I pray to God to unite us above, where pain will no more rack this feeble body of mine; where sorrow and parting from my children will be no more. God has promised these things if we are faithful unto the end. My age and feeble health deprive me of going to church now; but God is with me here at home. Thank your brother for his kindness. Give much love to him, and tell him to remember the Creator in the days of his youth, and strive to meet me in the Father's kingdom. Love to Ellen and Benjamin. Don't neglect him. Tell him for me, to be a good boy. Strive, my child, to train them for God's children. May he protect and provide for you, is the prayer of your loving old mother."

These letters both cheered and saddened me. I was always glad to have tidings from the kind, faithful old friend of my unhappy youth; but her messages of love made my heart yearn to see her before she died, and I mourned over the fact that it was impossible. Some months after I returned from my flight to New England, I received a letter from her, in which she wrote, "Dr. Flint is dead. He has left a distressed family. Poor old man! I hope he made his peace with God."

I remembered how he had defrauded my grandmother of the hard earnings she had loaned; how he had tried to cheat her out of the freedom her mistress had promised her, and how he had persecuted her children; and I thought to myself that she was a better Christian than I was, if she could entirely forgive him. I cannot say, with truth, that the news of my old master's death softened my feelings towards him. There are wrongs which even the grave does not bury. The man was odious to me while he lived, and his memory is odious now.

His departure from this world did not diminish my danger. He had threatened my grandmother that his heirs should hold me in slavery after he was gone; that I never should be free so long as a child of his survived.

As for Mrs. Flint, I had seen her in deeper afflictions than I supposed the loss of her husband would be, for she had buried several children; yet I never saw any signs of softening in her heart. The doctor had died in embarrassed circumstances, and had little to will to his heirs, except such property as he was unable to grasp. I was well aware what I had to expect from the family of Flints; and my fears were confirmed by a letter from the south, warning me to be on my guard, because Mrs. Flint openly declared that her daughter could not afford to lose so valuable a slave as I was.

I kept close watch of the newspapers for arrivals; but one Saturday night, being much occupied, I forgot to examine the Evening Express as usual. I went down into the parlor for it, early in the morning, and found the boy about to kindle a fire with it. I took it from him and examined the list of arrivals. Reader, if you have never been a slave, you cannot imagine the acute sensation of suffering at my heart, when I read the names of Mr. and Mrs. Dodge,[1] at a hotel in Courtland Street. It was a third-rate hotel, and that circumstance convinced me of the truth of what I had heard, that they were short of funds and had need of my value, as *they* valued me; and that was by dollars and cents. I hastened with the paper to Mrs. Bruce. Her heart and hand were always open to everyone in distress, and she always warmly sympathized with mine. It was impossible to tell how near the enemy was. He might have passed and repassed the house while we were sleeping. He might at that moment be waiting to pounce upon me if I ventured out of doors. I had never seen the husband of my young mistress, and therefore I could not distinguish him from any other stranger. A carriage was hastily ordered; and, closely veiled, I followed Mrs. Bruce, taking the baby again with me into exile. After various turnings and crossings and returnings, the carriage stopped at the house of one of Mrs. Bruce's friends, where I was kindly received. Mrs. Bruce returned immediately, to instruct the domestics what to say if anyone came to inquire for me.

It was lucky for me that the evening paper was not burned up before I had a chance to examine the list of arrivals. It was not long after Mrs. Bruce's return to her house, before several people came to inquire for me. One inquired for me, another asked for my daughter

---

[1] *Mr. and Mrs. Dodge* Dr. Flint's daughter and her husband.

Ellen, and another said he had a letter from my grandmother, which he was requested to deliver in person.

They were told, "She *has* lived here, but she has left."

"How long ago?"

"I don't know, sir."

"Do you know where she went?"

"I do not, sir." And the door was closed.

This Mr. Dodge, who claimed me as his property, was originally a Yankee peddler in the south; then he became a merchant, and finally a slaveholder. He managed to get introduced into what was called the first society, and married Miss Emily Flint. A quarrel arose between him and her brother, and the brother cowhided him. This led to a family feud, and he proposed to remove to Virginia. Dr. Flint left him no property, and his own means had become circumscribed, while a wife and children depended upon him for support. Under these circumstances, it was very natural that he should make an effort to put me into his pocket.

I had a colored friend, a man from my native place, in whom I had the most implicit confidence. I sent for him, and told him that Mr. and Mrs. Dodge had arrived in New York. I proposed that he should call upon them to make inquiries about his friends at the south, with whom Dr. Flint's family were well acquainted. He thought there was no impropriety in his doing so, and he consented. He went to the hotel, and knocked at the door of Mr. Dodge's room, which was opened by the gentleman himself, who gruffly inquired, "What brought you here? How came you to know I was in the city?"

"Your arrival was published in the evening papers, sir; and I called to ask Mrs. Dodge about my friends at home. I didn't suppose it would give any offence."

"Where's that negro girl, that belongs to my wife?"

"What girl, sir?"

"You know well enough. I mean Linda, that ran away from Dr. Flint's plantation, some years ago. I dare say you've seen her, and know where she is."

"Yes, sir, I've seen her, and know where she is. She is out of your reach, sir."

"Tell me where she is, or bring her to me, and I will give her a chance to buy her freedom."

"I don't think it would be of any use, sir. I have heard her say she would go to the ends of the earth, rather than pay any man or woman for her freedom, because

she thinks she has a right to it. Besides, she couldn't do it, if she would, for she has spent her earnings to educate her children."

This made Mr. Dodge very angry, and some high words passed between them. My friend was afraid to come where I was; but in the course of the day I received a note from him. I supposed they had not come from the south, in the winter, for a pleasure excursion; and now the nature of their business was very plain.

Mrs. Bruce came to me and entreated me to leave the city the next morning. She said her house was watched, and it was possible that some clue to me might be obtained. I refused to take her advice. She pleaded with an earnest tenderness, that ought to have moved me; but I was in a bitter, disheartened mood. I was weary of flying from pillar to post.[1] I had been chased during half my life, and it seemed as if the chase was never to end. There I sat, in that great city, guiltless of crime, yet not daring to worship God in any of the churches. I heard the bells ringing for afternoon service, and, with contemptuous sarcasm, I said, "Will the preachers take for their text, 'Proclaim liberty to the captive, and the opening of prison doors to them that are bound'?[2] or will they preach from the text, 'Do unto others as ye would they should do unto you'?"[3] Oppressed Poles and Hungarians could find a safe refuge in that city; John Mitchell was free to proclaim in the City Hall his desire for "a plantation well stocked with slaves";[4] but there I sat, an oppressed American, not daring to show my face. God forgive the black and bitter thoughts I indulged on that Sabbath day! The Scripture says,

---

[1] *flying ... post* Futile traveling from place to place.

[2] *Proclaim ... bound* See Isaiah 61.1: "The Spirit of the Lord God is upon me; because the Lord hath anointed me to preach good tidings unto the meek; he hath sent me to bind up the brokenhearted, to proclaim liberty to the captives, and the opening of the prison to them that are bound."

[3] *Do unto others ... unto you* See Matthew 7.12: "Therefore all things whatsoever ye would that men should do to you, do ye even so to them: for this is the law and the prophets."

[4] *John Mitchell ... stocked with slaves* John Mitchel was an Irish activist and journalist who escaped to America in 1853, where he became a proslavery Southern secessionist. In 1854 he claimed that he would like to have "a good plantation well-stocked with healthy negroes in Alabama."

"Oppression makes even a wise man mad";[1] and I was not wise.

I had been told that Mr. Dodge said his wife had never signed away her right to my children, and if he could not get me, he would take them. This it was, more than anything else, that roused such a tempest in my soul. Benjamin was with his uncle William in California, but my innocent young daughter had come to spend a vacation with me. I thought of what I had suffered in slavery at her age, and my heart was like a tiger's when a hunter tries to seize her young.

Dear Mrs. Bruce! I seem to see the expression of her face, as she turned away discouraged by my obstinate mood. Finding her expostulations unavailing, she sent Ellen to entreat me. When ten o'clock in the evening arrived and Ellen had not returned, this watchful and unwearied friend became anxious. She came to us in a carriage, bringing a well-filled trunk for my journey—trusting that by this time I would listen to reason. I yielded to her, as I ought to have done before.

The next day, baby and I set out in a heavy snow storm, bound for New England again. I received letters from the City of Iniquity,[2] addressed to me under an assumed name. In a few days one came from Mrs. Bruce, informing me that my new master was still searching for me, and that she intended to put an end to this persecution by buying my freedom. I felt grateful for the kindness that prompted this offer, but the idea was not so pleasant to me as might have been expected. The more my mind had become enlightened, the more difficult it was for me to consider myself an article of property; and to pay money to those who had so grievously oppressed me seemed like taking from my sufferings the glory of triumph. I wrote to Mrs. Bruce, thanking her, but saying that being sold from one owner to another seemed too much like slavery; that such a great obligation could not be easily cancelled; and that I preferred to go to my brother in California.

Without my knowledge, Mrs. Bruce employed a gentleman in New York to enter into negotiations with Mr. Dodge. He proposed to pay three hundred dollars down, if Mr. Dodge would sell me, and enter into obligations to relinquish all claim to me or my children forever after. He who called himself my master said he scorned so small an offer for such a valuable servant. The gentleman replied, "You can do as you choose, sir. If you reject this offer you will never get anything; for the woman has friends who will convey her and her children out of the country."

Mr. Dodge concluded that "half a loaf was better than no bread," and he agreed to the proffered terms. By the next mail I received this brief letter from Mrs. Bruce: "I am rejoiced to tell you that the money for your freedom has been paid to Mr. Dodge. Come home tomorrow. I long to see you and my sweet babe."

My brain reeled as I read these lines. A gentleman near me said, "It's true; I have seen the bill of sale." "The bill of sale!" Those words struck me like a blow. So I was *sold* at last! A human being *sold* in the free city of New York! The bill of sale is on record, and future generations will learn from it that women were articles of traffic in New York, late in the nineteenth century of the Christian religion. It may hereafter prove a useful document to antiquaries, who are seeking to measure the progress of civilization in the United States. I well know the value of that bit of paper; but much as I love freedom, I do not like to look upon it. I am deeply grateful to the generous friend who procured it, but I despise the miscreant who demanded payment for what never rightfully belonged to him or his.

I had objected to having my freedom bought, yet I must confess that when it was done I felt as if a heavy load had been lifted from my weary shoulders. When I rode home in the cars I was no longer afraid to unveil my face and look at people as they passed. I should have been glad to have met Daniel Dodge himself; to have had him seen me and known me, that he might have mourned over the untoward circumstances which compelled him to sell me for three hundred dollars.

When I reached home, the arms of my benefactress were thrown round me, and our tears mingled. As soon as she could speak, she said, "O Linda, I'm so glad it's all over! You wrote to me as if you thought you were going to be transferred from one owner to another. But I did not buy you for your services. I should have done just the same, if you had been going to sail for

---

[1] *Oppression ... mad* See Ecclesiastes 7.7: "Surely oppression maketh a wise man mad; and a gift destroyeth the heart."

[2] *City of Iniquity* See Habakkuk 2.12: "Woe to him that buildeth a town with blood, and stablisheth a city by iniquity!"

California tomorrow. I should, at least, have the satisfaction of knowing that you left me a free woman."

My heart was exceedingly full. I remembered how my poor father had tried to buy me, when I was a small child, and how he had been disappointed. I hoped his spirit was rejoicing over me now. I remembered how my good old grandmother had laid up her earnings to purchase me in later years, and how often her plans had been frustrated. How that faithful, loving old heart would leap for joy, if she could look on me and my children now that we were free! My relatives had been foiled in all their efforts, but God had raised me up a friend among strangers, who had bestowed on me the precious, long-desired boon. Friend! It is a common word, often lightly used. Like other good and beautiful things, it may be tarnished by careless handling; but when I speak of Mrs. Bruce as my friend, the word is sacred.

My grandmother lived to rejoice in my freedom; but not long after, a letter came with a black seal. She had gone "where the wicked cease from troubling, and the weary are at rest."[1]

Time passed on, and a paper came to me from the south, containing an obituary notice of my uncle Phillip. It was the only case I ever knew of such an honor conferred upon a colored person. It was written by one of his friends, and contained these words: "Now that death has laid him low, they call him a good man and a useful citizen; but what are eulogies to the black man, when the world has faded from his vision? It does not require man's praise to obtain rest in God's kingdom." So they called a colored man a *citizen*! Strange words to be uttered in that region!

Reader, my story ends with freedom; not in the usual way, with marriage. I and my children are now free! We are as free from the power of slaveholders as are the white people of the north; and though that, according to my ideas, is not saying a great deal, it is a vast improvement in *my* condition. The dream of my life is not yet realized. I do not sit with my children in a home of my own. I still long for a hearthstone of my own, however humble. I wish it for my children's sake far more than for my own. But God so orders circumstances as to keep me with my friend Mrs. Bruce. Love, duty, gratitude, also bind me to her side. It is a privilege to serve her who pities my oppressed people, and who has bestowed the inestimable boon of freedom on me and my children.

It has been painful to me, in many ways, to recall the dreary years I passed in bondage. I would gladly forget them if I could. Yet the retrospection is not altogether without solace; for with those gloomy recollections come tender memories of my good old grandmother, like light, fleecy clouds floating over a dark and troubled sea.

—1861

---

[1] *where the wicked ... at rest* See Job 3.17: "There the wicked cease from troubling; and there the weary be at rest."

IN CONTEXT

Fugitive Slave Advertisement for Harriet Jacobs

The following advertisement was placed by Dr. James Norcom in the *American Beacon* on 4 July 1835; in it, he offers a $100 dollar reward for the return of his "servant girl," Harriet Jacobs.

$100 REWARD

WILL be given for the apprehension and delivery of my Servant Girl HARRIET. She is a light mulatto, 21 years of age, about 5 feet 4 inches high, of a thick and corpulent habit, having on her head a thick covering of black hair that curls naturally, but which can be easily combed straight. She speaks easily and fluently, and has an agreeable carriage and address. Being a good seamstress, she has been accustomed to dress well, has a variety of very fine clothes, made in the prevailing fashion, and will probably appear, if abroad, tricked out in gay and fashionable finery. As this girl absconded from the plantation of my son without any known cause or provocation, it is probable she designs to transport herself to the North.

The above reward, with all reasonable charges, will be given for apprehending her, or securing her in any prison or jail within the U. States.

All persons are hereby forewarned against harboring or entertaining her, or being in any way instrumental in her escape, under the most rigorous penalties of the law.

JAMES NORCOM.

Edenton, N. C. June 30

Henry David Thoreau

1817 – 1862

The works of Henry David Thoreau comprise the most influential outgrowth of the nineteenth-century Transcendentalist movement; from Thoreau's own day through to the twenty-first century they have taken on a life of their own, inspiring passionate engagement among generation after generation of readers. Thoreau's "Resistance to Civil Government" (1849) is a foundational text in the literature of non-violent political resistance. And *Walden; or, Life in the Woods* (1854), which has been read as a poetic meditation on nature and the spiritual life, as a work of social criticism, and as a philosophical tract, remains *the* foundational text of American environmental writing.

Thoreau's public literary career was inextricably entwined with the events of his private life, in which he endeavored to live according to his various dictums of anti-materialistic simplicity and moral integrity. Thoreau was one who set himself apart—in "Civil Disobedience," apart from the political mainstream, and in *Walden*, apart from his human neighbors and from "civilized life," answering what he felt to be an invitation to make his life equal in "simplicity, and ... innocence, with Nature herself." But the setting-apart was performed very publicly; that is among the many paradoxes of Thoreau's writings, and of his life, that continue to provoke discussion and to engage readers. "Simplicity! Simplicity! Simplicity!" is his clarion call, yet it is impossible to escape complexity and paradox in his writing.

David Henry Thoreau (he started putting his middle name first shortly after college) was born in 1817 to Cynthia Dunbar—an enthusiastic member of an early antislavery society—and John Thoreau in Concord, Massachusetts. Thoreau spent four years at Harvard College, studying modern European and Indigenous American languages alongside the usual ancient Greek and Latin, after which he found work as a schoolteacher. But following a confrontation with a school board member (who insisted that Thoreau flog his students), he left the position. Sometime after this Thoreau met and befriended local preacher and intellectual Ralph Waldo Emerson. Emerson's *Nature* (1836) had recently energized the Transcendentalist movement with its rousing assertions about the relationship between the human self and the natural world; Emerson took on the younger man as a kind of intellectual protégé, initiating what would become a lifelong friendship. It was Emerson who first encouraged Thoreau to write a journal, a habit he would maintain for the rest of his life.

Massachusetts in the 1830s was simmering with the energy of the Lyceum Movement, which aimed to disseminate knowledge of science, art, literature, and philosophy to a wider and generalized audience. Thoreau was among those invited to lecture at the Concord Lyceum; he gave his first public talk there in 1838; his journal notes on the lecture (the full text of which has not survived) provide an early glimpse into Thoreau's ambitions as a thinker. Entitled "Society," the talk gave voice to his skepticism as to the efficacy of democracy in America, and his resistance to the Aristotelian idea that "man was made for society"; in Thoreau's view, "society was made for man."

In 1838 Thoreau accepted another teaching position—this time at the Concord Academy, where his brother, John Thoreau Jr., soon joined him as a teacher and co-director. Less than two years later, however, John's health had started to fail, and they closed the school. John's death on New Year's Day, 1842 was a devastating blow; Thoreau's first book, *A Week on the Concord and Merrimack Rivers* (1849), is in large part an elegy to John.

Throughout the 1840s, Thoreau contributed numerous poems, essays, and book reviews to *The Dial*, a Transcendentalist periodical launched in 1840 by Emerson, Margaret Fuller, and other local figures.

Some of Thoreau's contributions to the journal were prose meditations on the natural environment; many appeared in the *Dial*'s "Ethnical Scriptures" column, where Thoreau commented on various scriptural writings from Hinduism, Buddhism, Confucianism, and other Eastern traditions. Like Emerson, Thoreau was fascinated by the religions and philosophy of Asia and the Middle East, and ardently read translations of Indian texts such as the *Bhagavad Gita* and the Vedas.

By about 1845, Thoreau had in mind a book that would reflect on a boating journey he and his brother had taken together before John Thoreau Jr.'s death. It was partly in search of writerly solitude that Thoreau made his now-famous move to Walden Pond, a small, fairly secluded lake a couple of miles from the center of the village of Concord. There, on a tract of forested land owned by Emerson, he built a small cabin. This was not the first time he had considered some form of alternative lifestyle; earlier in the decade he had been urged to join two Utopian agricultural communities inspired by Transcendentalist principles—Brook Farm and Fruitlands. Both times he had said no. By the middle of the decade those communities had foundered; Thoreau embarked on a solitary initiative that would eventually have a far wider impact than either of those religiously-focused communal experiments.

Thoreau's solitary experiment began with little fanfare, though it sparked a good deal of interest among his Concord neighbors, who were puzzled by this eccentric Harvard graduate who had seemingly chosen to throw away his education and talents to live as a hermit in the woods. Thoreau ended up living at Walden Pond for two years (1845–47), spending his days reading, walking, observing Nature (unlike Emerson, Thoreau generally capitalized the noun), tending his bean fields, entertaining curious visitors, and beginning work on the only two books he would publish—first the elegiac *A Week on the Concord* and later *Walden*, an account of his present experiment.

A Week on the Concord (1849) was praised by friends for its powerful prose, but sold poorly. *Walden*, on the other hand, which was published five years later, sold well and for the most part received enthusiastic reviews, both in the United States and in England. English novelist George Eliot praised Thoreau's "deep poetic sensibility" and concluded that as readers "we feel throughout the book the presence of a refined as well as a hardy mind," while Emerson wrote (perhaps hyperbolically) that "all American kind are delighted with 'Walden' as far as they have dared say." Several reviewers predicted that *Walden* would hold a lasting place in American literature—and they have been proved right, though there was a period in the late nineteenth and early twentieth centuries when Thoreau's reputation dipped somewhat. Late nineteenth-century editions of *The American Cyclopedia* devote a page and a half to Emerson and over two pages to Hawthorne, but give Thoreau an entry less than a quarter page long. And Barrett Wendell's influential *A Literary History of America*, while praising *Walden* for the "artistic form" of its descriptions (the book "remains a vital bit of literature for anyone who loves to read about nature," Wendell concluded), lumps Thoreau together with Bronson Alcott in a chapter entitled "The Lesser Men of Concord." In the mid-twentieth century Thoreau and *Walden* came to be granted a more central place in the canon of American literature. Environmentalists such as Aldo Leopold were profoundly influenced by *Walden*, as were leading literary figures such as Annie Dillard (whose MA thesis was on the subject of Thoreau and *Walden*).

Much as Nature as a large concept was fundamental to Thoreau's thinking, so too did the details of the natural world come to fascinate him, and to occupy considerable space in his writing. Thoreau had become intrigued by Charles Darwin's *Journal of the Voyage of the Beagle* (1839) and other botanical and scientific writings, and that interest began to color both his daily pursuits and his writing; some of the best-loved and most widely cited passages from *Walden* involve detailed description of natural phenomena. At least one passage in the text—in which a battle between two species of ant is dramatically described—connects directly to similar descriptions of insect wars in Darwin's work.

In the years between leaving Walden Pond and writing *Walden*, Thoreau continued to expand on his reading as well as on the observations he had made of the natural world; in addition to numerous works of natural philosophy he absorbed the latest in American nature writing. (Among his influences were Susan Fenimore Cooper, author of *Rural Hours* [1850], and ornithologist John James Audubon.) Overall, *Walden* is noteworthy not least of all for paying far more attention to material, ecological details than had any of the nature writings of previous Transcendentalists. But the relationship within Thoreau's own mind between Nature as an idea and the natural world as a subject for detailed scientific interest was not without tension. His detailed observations brought him excitement but also, on occasion, concern; in an 1851 journal entry he wrote, "I fear that the character of my knowledge is from year to year becoming more distinct and scientific—that, in exchange for views as wide as heaven's cope, I am being narrowed down to the field of the microscope." Another, oft-quoted (and, like many of Thoreau's writings, oft-misquoted) line from an 1851 journal entry is his assertion that "the question is not what you look at, but what you see." It is often taken to be an unqualified endorsement of the value of sustained and observant engagement with the natural world—and his journal entry for that day does indeed include descriptions that exemplify such sustained and observant engagement. But the context of the famous quotation itself is one in which Thoreau is praising the poetic sensibility and dismissing the "mere science" of the astronomer who is blind to the true significance of the phenomena he is looking at.

Arguably, then, Thoreau's writing about Nature is in large part the product of ideas continually in tension within his own mind. Certainly *Walden* itself continues to command attention not least of all because of the tensions and paradoxes—even the contradictions—the text gives voice to. Even in the twenty-first century, *Walden* continues to excite not only interest, but heated debate; in 2015, for example, a passionate attack on Thoreau and *Walden* in *The New Yorker* by Pulitzer Prize-winning journalist Kathryn Schultz was met with equally passionate defenses (of both author and book) in other leading magazines by, among others, Columbia University law professor Jedediah Britton-Purdy. What seems to Schultz and some others as "an unnavigable thicket of contradiction" in *Walden* strikes others as an immensely readable and engaging expression of various ideas in tension with one another. What seems to some an unattractive degree of self-absorption in Thoreau's writing (Isaac Hecker, one of the few to review *Walden* negatively on its initial appearance, complained of what he read as Thoreau's "pride" and "pretension"), strikes others as lively individualism. *Walden* has become established as a central text in the canon of American literature in large part because of its continuing capacity to excite passionate debate.

While residing at Walden, Thoreau was embroiled in an unrelated controversy—arrested and briefly imprisoned in 1846 for refusing to pay his taxes. Although Thoreau was not the first local figure to be enmeshed in such a dispute—Concord teacher Amos Bronson Alcott, previously a leading member of Fruitlands, had been arrested on the same charge in 1843—curiosity and confusion regarding Thoreau's motives continued until well after his departure from the Walden cabin in 1847. The following year he returned to the Lyceum to speak about his decision to face imprisonment rather than pay the required fee. This lecture eventually grew into the essay "Resistance to Civil Government," an essay published in the sole issue of Transcendental educator Elizabeth Peabody's periodical *Aesthetic Papers* in 1849. "Civil Disobedience" (as the essay is popularly known) posed an important question: how is it possible for an individual to retain moral integrity within the confines of an unjust society? Thoreau framed his action as a form of political protest against both slavery and the Mexican–American War. (The two were not unconnected; many opponents of the war regarded it as a means of extending the domain of American slavery.)

"Civil Disobedience" was among Thoreau's earliest public expressions of support for the abolitionist movement that would soon be coming to its crisis—though Thoreau would in some ways remain aloof from the movement itself. "Civil Disobedience" did little to dispel public disapproval of Thoreau's tax resistance, with one reviewer comparing Thoreau unfavorably to the "red republicans" of revolutionary France. But in the generations since, "Civil Disobedience" has been cited as inspiration by the Russian novelist and pacifist Leo Tolstoy, by the revolutionary Indian leader Mohandas Gandhi, and by the Civil Rights leader Martin Luther King Jr.; Thoreau's notion that "non-cooperation with evil is as much a moral obligation as is cooperation with good" continues to provoke heated debate—and to inspire resistance to authority.

Thoreau's participation on the New England lecture circuit increased following the favorable reception of *Walden*. He also worked with his mother in helping those fleeing slavery to escape along the Underground Railroad. Thoreau found his abolitionist zeal stimulated by the Fugitive Slave Act of 1850. In 1854 he delivered an acclaimed lecture, "Slavery in Massachusetts," in response to the Act and to the trial and re-enslavement of Anthony Burns; the lecture made Thoreau an abolitionist figure of some renown, and in the process solidified the reputation of Concord as a center of antebellum abolitionism. Here too, however, some observers have detected tensions and paradoxes—one of the great exemplars of American individualists was sometimes perhaps an uneasy participant in community activism.

Thoreau's health began to fail in the early 1860s, and in 1862, not halfway into the Civil War, he succumbed to the tuberculosis that had troubled him since young adulthood. Numerous volumes of his lectures and writings were published posthumously—as were his collected journals in 1906, which contribute vastly to our understanding of his intellectual development and provide insight into some of his unrecorded lectures. After his death his old friend Emerson wrote of him that "few lives contain so many renunciations. ... [H]e never married; he lived alone; he never went to church; he never voted; ... he ate no flesh; he drank no wine; he never knew the use of tobacco; and, though a naturalist, he used neither trap nor gun."

Thoreau remains a vitally important reference point in discussions of the place of individual humans in human society as a whole, and of the place of humans (both individually and collectively) in the natural world. *Walden*—its status now secure as a foundational text of American nature writing and of twentieth- and twenty-first-century environmental movements—continues to strike a sympathetic chord among a wide range of readers. Thoreau at one and the same time posits Nature as a magnet attracting all that is best in humanity and presents a compelling vision of Nature as standing apart from human-ity—even in opposition to human society. "I love Nature partly because she is not man, but a retreat from him," wrote Thoreau. "None of his institutions control or pervade her."

NOTE ON THE TEXTS: The text of "Resistance to Civil Government" presented here is based on its first published appearance in 1849 in Elizabeth Peabody's periodical *Aesthetic Papers*. The text of *Walden; or, Life in the Woods* presented here is based on that reproduced in *The Writings of Henry David Thoreau* (1906). Spelling and punc-tuation have been modernized in accordance with the practices of this anthology.

⌘ ⌘ ⌘

Resistance to Civil Government

In 1846, during the time he was living at Walden Pond, Thoreau was making a trip into the nearby town of Concord when he was arrested by Sam Staples, the local constable, for having failed to pay the local poll tax for the past several years. Staples initially offered to lend Thoreau enough money to pay the tax, but Thoreau refused, arguing that it was a matter of principle. He spent the night in jail—until the debt was paid, to his irritation, by an anonymous friend—and continued to make an issue of the principles involved, most notably in a lecture he gave in Concord on 26 January 1848, which was published as "Resistance to Civil Government" in 1849. The essay was later republished as "Civil Disobedience," and under that name has taken its place among the best known of all American essays. But the historical background to the famous piece remains unfamiliar to many modern readers.

In nineteenth-century America, a poll tax was a fixed annual amount charged to any individual who was eligible to go to the polls—to vote in an election. At the time, poll taxes were levied in several of the states; poll tax revenue accounted for at least a quarter of the total revenue of the state of Massachusetts. Though poll taxes were levied by the individual states, rather than by the federal government, Thoreau treated the state as a fundamental piece of the larger State—of American government as a whole. As a citizen, one was required to pay the poll tax in order to vote, whether for local, state, or federal positions, and Thoreau thus saw the politics of the United States as a whole as vitally relevant to the paying of the poll tax in the town of Concord, Massachusetts.

Thoreau's arguments were focused on two interconnected areas in which he saw America as having acted immorally—the Mexican–American War of 1846–47, and the American institution of slavery. He was not alone in seeing the two as connected; a substantial minority of Americans (and a majority in much of the North) suspected President James K. Polk, a slaveholder, of having provoked the war with the intent not only of adding new territory to the United States, but also of eventually increasing the number of states in which slavery was permitted, and thereby giving the slave states a controlling interest in the politics of the republic. Whether or not that was Polk's express intent,

it was certainly the case that the vast territory acquired by the United States as a result of the war lay almost entirely south of latitude 36°30'—the line that had been established under the terms of the 1820 Missouri Compromise as the northernmost limit of territory in which slavery would be permitted.

Opposition to the war (and to slavery) was particularly strong in the state of Massachusetts, where the government had in 1847 passed a resolution condemning the American government's actions. To Thoreau, however, words or resolutions on paper were not enough; those opposed to the war and to slavery should demonstrate their opposition through concrete actions. Above all, those opposing slavery should never be willing—as Massachusetts senator Daniel Webster was notoriously willing—to compromise with supporters of slavery.

The controversy over slavery and the new territories was further complicated for some time by passionate differences of opinion among those supporting slavery as to whether or not the nation should be interested in incorporating large parts of what had been Mexico into the United States. A significant faction was of the view that the racial "purity" of the American nation would be jeopardized if large numbers of dark-skinned Mexicans were allowed to live within American borders. It was only on the assurance that the territories being annexed were not heavily populated, and that they could readily be "Americanized," that majority opinion in America had swung unreservedly behind Polk.

The 1848 presidential election represented a dispiriting moment for opponents of the war, and of slavery. The issue of slavery in the newly acquired territories was a divisive one in both parties. Polk, a Democrat, chose not to run for another term, but his administration had been popular among a majority of Americans for having added to American territory through its prosecution of the war with Mexico, and it was widely expected that another Democrat would be elected. (That expectation remained strong even after a break-away faction of antislavery Democrats under the leadership of Martin Van Buren contested the election under a new antislavery banner as the Free Soil Party.) Many members of the Whig Party—the Democrats' main rival—had been highly critical of the war. But they had no confidence that anyone in their own ranks could stand a chance against almost any Democrat in the election. When the Whigs found that Zachary Taylor, a general who had led the American forces in the war effort but who had no discernable allegiance to Whig principles, was available as a candidate, they set principle to one side and nominated him at their convention. Taylor did indeed defeat the Democrats' nominee, Lewis Cass. (The 1848 popular vote was forty-seven per cent for Taylor and forty-three per cent for Cass, with Van Buren's Free Soil Party taking ten per cent.)

It was against this political background that Thoreau penned his famous essay on democratic principles.

I heartily accept the motto, "That government is best which governs least";[1] and I should like to see it acted up to more rapidly and systematically. Carried out, it finally amounts to this, which also I believe, "That government is best which governs not at all"; and when men are prepared for it, that will be the kind of government which they will have. Government is at best but an expedient; but most governments are usually, and all governments are sometimes, inexpedient. The objections which have been brought against a standing army, and they are many and weighty, and deserve to prevail, may also at last be brought against a standing government. The standing army is only an arm of the standing government. The government itself, which is only the mode which the people have chosen to execute their will, is equally liable to be abused and perverted before the people can act through it. Witness the present Mexican war,[2] the work of comparatively a few individuals using the standing government as their tool; for, in the outset, the people would not have consented to this measure.

This American government—what is it but a tradition, though a recent one, endeavoring to transmit itself unimpaired to posterity, but each instant losing some of its integrity? It has not the vitality and force of a single living man; for a single man can bend it to his will. It is a sort of wooden gun to the people themselves; and, if ever they should use it in earnest as

a real one against each other, it will surely split. But it is not the less necessary for this; for the people must have some complicated machinery or other, and hear its din, to satisfy that idea of government which they have. Governments show thus how successfully men can be imposed on, even impose on themselves, for their own advantage. It is excellent, we must all allow; yet this government never of itself furthered any enterprise, but by the alacrity with which it got out of its way. *It* does not keep the country free. *It* does not settle the West. *It* does not educate. The character inherent in the American people has done all that has been accomplished; and it would have done somewhat more, if the government had not sometimes got in its way. For government is an expedient by which men would fain succeed in letting one another alone; and, as has been said, when it is most expedient, the governed are most let alone by it. Trade and commerce, if they were not made of India rubber, would never manage to bounce over the obstacles which legislators are continually putting in their way; and, if one were to judge these men wholly by the effects of their actions, and not partly by their intentions, they would deserve to be classed and punished with those mischievous persons who put obstructions on the railroads.

But, to speak practically and as a citizen, unlike those who call themselves no-government men, I ask for, not at once no government, but *at once* a better government. Let every man make known what kind of government would command his respect, and that will be one step toward obtaining it.

After all, the practical reason why, when the power is once in the hands of the people, a majority are permitted, and for a long period continue, to rule, is not because they are most likely to be in the right, nor because this seems fairest to the minority, but because they are physically the strongest. But a government in which the majority rule in all cases cannot be based on justice, even as far as men understand it. Can there not be a government in which majorities do not virtually decide right and wrong, but conscience? in which majorities decide only those questions to which the rule of expediency is applicable? Must the citizen ever for a moment, or in the least degree, resign his conscience to the legislator? Why has every man a conscience, then? I think that we should be men first, and subjects

---

[1] *That government … governs least* Paraphrase of the motto of the *United States Magazine and Democratic Review*, which has often been erroneously attributed to Thomas Jefferson.

[2] *Mexican war* Many Northerners and abolitionists opposed the Mexican–American War, which had broken out in 1846, fearing that it would expand and strengthen the domain of Southern slavery.

afterward. It is not desirable to cultivate a respect for the law, so much as for the right. The only obligation which I have a right to assume, is to do at any time what I think right. It is truly enough said, that a corporation has no conscience;[1] but a corporation of conscientious men is a corporation *with* a conscience. Law never made men a whit more just; and, by means of their respect for it, even the well-disposed are daily made the agents of injustice. A common and natural result of an undue respect for law is, that you may see a file of soldiers, colonel, captain, corporal, privates, powder-monkeys[2] and all, marching in admirable order over hill and dale to the wars, against their wills, aye, against their common sense and consciences, which makes it very steep marching indeed, and produces a palpitation of the heart. They have no doubt that it is a damnable business in which they are concerned; they are all peaceably inclined. Now, what are they? Men at all? or small moveable forts and magazines,[3] at the service of some unscrupulous man in power? Visit the Navy Yard, and behold a marine, such a man as an American government can make, or such as it can make a man with its black arts, a mere shadow and reminiscence of humanity, a man laid out alive and standing, and already, as one may say, buried under arms with funeral accompaniments, though it may be

Not a drum was heard, nor a funeral note,
As his corse to the ramparts we hurried;
Not a soldier discharged his farewell shot
O'er the grave where our hero we buried.[4]

The mass of men serve the State thus, not as men mainly, but as machines, with their bodies. They are the standing army, and the militia, jailers, constables, *posse comitatus*,[5] &c. In most cases there is no free exercise whatever of the judgment or of the moral sense; but they put themselves on a level with wood and earth and stones; and wooden men can perhaps be manufactured that will serve the purpose as well. Such command no more respect than men of straw, or a lump of dirt. They have the same sort of worth only as horses and dogs. Yet such as these even are commonly esteemed good citizens. Others, as most legislators, politicians, lawyers, ministers, and office-holders, serve the State chiefly with their heads; and, as they rarely make any moral distinctions, they are as likely to serve the devil, without intending it, as God. A very few, as heroes, patriots, martyrs, reformers in the great sense, and men, serve the State with their consciences also, and so necessarily resist it for the most part; and they are commonly treated by it as enemies. A wise man will only be useful as a man, and will not submit to be "clay," and "stop a hole to keep the wind away,"[6] but leave that office to his dust at least:

I am too high-born to be propertied,
To be a secondary at control,
Or useful serving-man and instrument
To any sovereign state throughout the world.[7]

He who gives himself entirely to his fellow-men appears to them useless and selfish; but he who gives himself partially to them is pronounced a benefactor and philanthropist.

How does it become a man to behave toward this American government today? I answer that he cannot without disgrace be associated with it. I cannot for an instant recognize that political organization as *my* government which is the *slave's* government also.

All men recognize the right of revolution; that is, the right to refuse allegiance to and to resist the government, when its tyranny or its inefficiency are great and unendurable. But almost all say that such is not the case now. But such was the case, they think, in the Revolution of '75.[8] If one were to tell me that this was a bad government because it taxed certain foreign

---

[1]   *a corporation ... no conscience*   Idea erroneously attributed to English jurist and politician Sir Edward Coke (1552–1634) by later English philosopher Jeremy Bentham (1748–1832).

[2]   *powder-monkeys*   Boys hired to carry gunpowder from storage rooms to the guns.

[3]   *magazines*   Military storehouses.

[4]   *Not a ... we buried*   See "Burial of Sir John Moore at Corunna" by Irish poet Charles Wolfe (1791–1823);   *corse*   Corpse.

[5]   *posse comitatus*   Latin: enabling group of companions; temporary police force recruited from the general population.

[6]   *clay ... wind away*   See Shakespeare's *Hamlet* 5.1.220–21.

[7]   *I am ... the world*   See Shakespeare's *King John* 5.2.79–82.

[8]   *Revolution of '75*   I.e., the American Revolutionary War; unjust taxation by the British government was one of the primary grievances among the revolution's leaders.

commodities brought to its ports, it is most probable that I should not make an ado about it, for I can do without them: all machines have their friction; and possibly this does enough good to counterbalance the evil. At any rate, it is a great evil to make a stir about it. But when the friction comes to have its machine, and oppression and robbery are organized, I say, let us not have such a machine any longer. In other words, when a sixth of the population of a nation which has undertaken to be the refuge of liberty are slaves, and a whole country is unjustly overrun and conquered by a foreign army, and subjected to military law, I think that it is not too soon for honest men to rebel and revolutionize. What makes this duty the more urgent is the fact, that the country so overrun is not our own, but ours is the invading army.

Paley,[1] a common authority with many on moral questions, in his chapter on the "Duty of Submission to Civil Government," resolves all civil obligation into expediency; and he proceeds to say, "that so long as the interest of the whole society requires it, that is, so long as the established government cannot be resisted or changed without public inconveniency, it is the will of God that the established government be obeyed, and no longer." "This principle being admitted, the justice of every particular case of resistance is reduced to a computation of the quantity of the danger and grievance on the one side, and of the probability and expense of redressing it on the other." Of this, he says, every man shall judge for himself. But Paley appears never to have contemplated those cases to which the rule of expediency does not apply, in which a people, as well as an individual, must do justice, cost what it may. If I have unjustly wrested a plank from a drowning man, I must restore it to him though I drown myself. This, according to Paley, would be inconvenient. But he that would save his life, in such a case, shall lose it.[2] This people must cease to hold slaves, and to make

war on Mexico, though it cost them their existence as a people.

In their practice, nations agree with Paley; but does anyone think that Massachusetts does exactly what is right at the present crisis?

> A drab of state, a cloth-o'-silver slut,
> To have her train borne up, and her soul trail in the dirt.[3]

Practically speaking, the opponents to a reform in Massachusetts are not a hundred thousand politicians at the South, but a hundred thousand merchants and farmers here, who are more interested in commerce and agriculture than they are in humanity, and are not prepared to do justice to the slave and to Mexico, *cost what it may*.[4] I quarrel not with far-off foes, but with those who, near at home, co-operate with, and do the bidding of those far away, and without whom the latter would be harmless. We are accustomed to say, that the mass of men are unprepared; but improvement is slow, because the few are not materially wiser or better than the many. It is not so important that many should be as good as you, as that there be some absolute goodness somewhere; for that will leaven the whole lump. There are thousands who are *in opinion* opposed to slavery and to the war, who yet in effect do nothing to put an end to them; who, esteeming themselves children of Washington and Franklin, sit down with their hands in their pockets, and say that they know not what to do, and do nothing; who even postpone the question of freedom to the question of free-trade, and quietly read

---

[1] *Paley* English theologian and philosopher William Paley (1743–1805); the quotation is from his *Principles of Moral and Political Philosophy* (1785).

[2] *But he ... lose it* See Matthew 10.39: "He that findeth his life shall lose it: and he that loseth his life for my sake shall find it." The drowning man analogy stems from a question posed by Roman philosopher Cicero (106–43 BCE) in his book on ethics and moral philosophy, *De Officiis*.

[3] *A drab ... the dirt* See *The Revenger's Tragedy* 4.4 by Thomas Middleton (1580–1627). The quotation suggests that a person whose soul is unclean cannot change their nature by dressing themselves in fine clothes. Massachusetts, Thoreau suggests, has dressed itself in fine clothes with its resolution against slavery, but its soul remains unclean. (The term "slut," in this context, refers to an unkempt or unclean person, and does not necessarily have derogatory sexual connotations.)

[4] *more interested ... what it may* The legislature of Massachusetts had passed a resolution in 1847 condemning the war and the annexation of Mexican territories as a war "waged ingloriously, by a powerful nation against a weak neighbor, unnecessarily and without just cause ... with the triple object of extending slavery ... [and] of obtaining control of the Free States, under the Constitution of the United States." But few in Massachusetts were calling for concrete action beyond this.

the prices-current along with the latest advices from Mexico, after dinner, and, it may be, fall asleep over them both. What is the price-current of an honest man and patriot today? They hesitate, and they regret, and sometimes they petition; but they do nothing in earnest and with effect. They will wait, well disposed, for others to remedy the evil, that they may no longer have it to regret. At most, they give only a cheap vote, and a feeble countenance and Godspeed, to the right, as it goes by them. There are nine hundred and ninety-nine patrons of virtue to one virtuous man; but it is easier to deal with the real possessor of a thing than with the temporary guardian of it.

All voting is a sort of gaming, like chequers or backgammon, with a slight moral tinge to it, a playing with right and wrong, with moral questions; and betting naturally accompanies it. The character of the voters is not staked. I cast my vote, perchance, as I think right; but I am not vitally concerned that that right should prevail. I am willing to leave it to the majority. Its obligation, therefore, never exceeds that of expediency. Even voting *for the right* is *doing* nothing for it. It is only expressing to men feebly your desire that it should prevail. A wise man will not leave the right to the mercy of chance, nor wish it to prevail through the power of the majority. There is but little virtue in the action of masses of men. When the majority shall at length vote for the abolition of slavery, it will be because they are indifferent to slavery, or because there is but little slavery left to be abolished by their vote. *They* will then be the only slaves. Only *his* vote can hasten the abolition of slavery who asserts his own freedom by his vote.

I hear of a convention to be held at Baltimore,[1] or elsewhere, for the selection of a candidate for the Presidency, made up chiefly of editors, and men who are politicians by profession; but I think, what is it to any independent, intelligent, and respectable man what decision they may come to, shall we not have the advantage of his wisdom and honesty, nevertheless? Can we not count upon some independent votes? Are there not many individuals in the country who do not attend conventions? But no: I find that the respectable man, so called, has immediately drifted from his

position, and despairs of his country, when his country has more reason to despair of him. He forthwith adopts one of the candidates thus selected as the only *available* one, thus proving that he is himself *available* for any purposes of the demagogue. His vote is of no more worth than that of any unprincipled foreigner or hireling native, who may have been bought. Oh for a man who is a *man*, and, as my neighbor says, has a bone in his back which you cannot pass your hand through! Our statistics are at fault: the population has been returned too large. How many *men* are there to a square thousand miles in this country? Hardly one. Does not America offer any inducement for men to settle here? The American has dwindled into an Odd Fellow[2]—one who may be known by the development of his organ of gregariousness, and a manifest lack of intellect and cheerful self-reliance; whose first and chief concern, on coming into the world, is to see that the alms-houses are in good repair; and, before yet he has lawfully donned the virile garb,[3] to collect a fund for the support of the widows and orphans that may be; who, in short, ventures to live only by the aid of the mutual insurance company, which has promised to bury him decently.

It is not a man's duty, as a matter of course, to devote himself to the eradication of any, even the most enormous wrong; he may still properly have other concerns to engage him; but it is his duty, at least, to wash his hands of it, and, if he gives it no thought longer, not to give it practically his support. If I devote myself to other pursuits and contemplations, I must first see, at least, that I do not pursue them sitting upon another man's shoulders. I must get off him first, that he may pursue his contemplations too. See what gross inconsistency is tolerated. I have heard some of my townsmen say, "I should like to have them order me out to help put down an insurrection of the slaves, or to march to Mexico—see if I would go"; and yet these very men have each, directly by their allegiance, and so indirectly, at least, by their money, furnished a substitute. The soldier is applauded who refuses to serve in an unjust war by those who do not refuse to sustain the

1   *convention to ... at Baltimore* The 1848 Democratic National Convention. See the headnote to this essay for further information.

2   *Odd Fellow* Ironic allusion to the Independent Order of Odd Fellows, a fraternal organization with benevolent social aims.

3   *virile garb* The "toga virilis," robe donned by boys in ancient Rome upon reaching the age of adulthood.

unjust government which makes the war; is applauded by those whose own act and authority he disregards and sets at nought; as if the State were penitent to that degree that it hired one to scourge it while it sinned, but not to that degree that it left off sinning for a moment. Thus, under the name of order and civil government, we are all made at last to pay homage to and I support our own meanness. After the first blush of sin, comes its indifference; and from immoral it becomes, as it were, *un*moral, and not quite unnecessary to that life which we have made.

The broadest and most prevalent error requires the most disinterested virtue to sustain it. The slight reproach to which the virtue of patriotism is commonly liable, the noble are most likely to incur. Those who, while they disapprove of the character and measures of a government, yield to it their allegiance and support, are undoubtedly its most conscientious supporters, and so frequently the most serious obstacles to reform. Some are petitioning the State to dissolve the Union, to disregard the requisitions of the President. Why do they not dissolve it themselves—the union between themselves and the State—and refuse to pay their quota into its treasury? Do not they stand in the same relation to the State, that the State does to the Union? And have not the same reasons prevented the State from resisting the Union, which have prevented them from resisting the State?

How can a man be satisfied to entertain an opinion merely, and enjoy *it*? Is there any enjoyment in it, if his opinion is that he is aggrieved? If you are cheated out of a single dollar by your neighbor, you do not rest satisfied with knowing that you are cheated, or with saying that you are cheated, or even with petitioning him to pay you your due; but you take effectual steps at once to obtain the full amount, and see that you are never cheated again. Action from principle—the perception and the performance of right—changes things and relations; it is essentially revolutionary, and does not consist wholly with anything which was. It not only divides states and churches, it divides families; aye, it divides the *individual*, separating the diabolical in him from the divine.

Unjust laws exist: shall we be content to obey them, or shall we endeavor to amend them, and obey them until we have succeeded, or shall we transgress them at once? Men generally, under such a government as this, think that they ought to wait until they have persuaded the majority to alter them. They think that, if they should resist, the remedy would be worse than the evil. But it is the fault of the government itself that the remedy *is* worse than the evil. *It* makes it worse. Why is it not more apt to anticipate and provide for reform? Why does it not cherish its wise minority? Why does it cry and resist before it is hurt? Why does it not encourage its citizens to be on the alert to point out its faults, and *do* better than it would have them? Why does it always crucify Christ, and excommunicate Copernicus and Luther,[1] and pronounce Washington and Franklin rebels?

One would think, that a deliberate and practical denial of its authority was the only offence never contemplated by government; else, why has it not assigned its definite, its suitable and proportionate penalty? If a man who has no property refuses but once to earn nine shillings for the State, he is put in prison for a period unlimited by any law that I know, and determined only by the discretion of those who placed him there; but if he should steal ninety times nine shillings from the State, he is soon permitted to go at large again.

If the injustice is part of the necessary friction of the machine of government, let it go, let it go: perchance it will wear smooth—certainly the machine will wear out. If the injustice has a spring, or a pulley, or a rope, or a crank, exclusively for itself, then perhaps you may consider whether the remedy will not be worse than the evil; but if it is of such a nature that it requires you to be the agent of injustice to another, then, I say, break the law. Let your life be a counter friction to stop the machine. What I have to do is to see, at any rate, that I do not lend myself to the wrong which I condemn.

As for adopting the ways which the State has provided for remedying the evil, I know not of such ways. They take too much time, and a man's life will be gone. I have other affairs to attend to. I came into this world, not chiefly to make this a good place to live in, but to live in it, be it good or bad. A man has not everything to do, but something; and because he cannot do

---

1   *Copernicus and Luther* Renaissance astronomer Nicolaus Copernicus (1473–1543) and German theologian Martin Luther (1483–1546), who were both excommunicated from the church for their revolutionary ideas.

everything, it is not necessary that he should do *some-thing* wrong. It is not my business to be petitioning the governor or the legislature any more than it is theirs to petition me; and, if they should not hear my petition, what should I do then? But in this case the State has provided no way: its very Constitution is the evil. This may seem to be harsh and stubborn and unconciliatory; but it is to treat with the utmost kindness and consideration the only spirit that can appreciate or deserves it. So is all change for the better, like birth and death which convulse the body.

I do not hesitate to say, that those who call themselves abolitionists should at once effectually withdraw their support, both in person and property, from the government of Massachusetts, and not wait till they constitute a majority of one, before they suffer the right to prevail through them. I think that it is enough if they have God on their side, without waiting for that other one. Moreover, any man more right than his neighbors, constitutes a majority of one already.

I meet this American government, or its representative the State government, directly, and face to face, once a year, no more, in the person of its tax-gatherer; this is the only mode in which a man situated as I am necessarily meets it; and it then says distinctly, Recognize me; and the simplest, the most effectual, and, in the present posture of affairs, the indispensablest mode of treating with it on this head, of expressing your little satisfaction with and love for it, is to deny it then. My civil neighbor, the tax-gatherer, is the very man I have to deal with—for it is, after all, with men and not with parchment that I quarrel—and he has voluntarily chosen to be an agent of the government. How shall he ever know well what he is and does as an officer of the government, or as a man, until he is obliged to consider whether he shall treat me, his neighbor, for whom he has respect, as a neighbor and well-disposed man, or as a maniac and disturber of the peace, and see if he can get over this obstruction to his neighborliness without a ruder and more impetuous thought or speech corresponding with his action? I know this well, that if one thousand, if one hundred, if ten men whom I could name—if ten *honest* men only—aye, if *one* HONEST man, in this State of Massachusetts, *ceasing to hold slaves*, were actually to withdraw from this co-partnership, and be locked up in the county

jail therefore, it would be the abolition of slavery in America. For it matters not how small the beginning may seem to be: what is once well done is done for ever. But we love better to talk about it: that we say is our mission. Reform keeps many scores of newspapers in its service, but not one man. If my esteemed neighbor, the State's ambassador,[1] who will devote his days to the settlement of the question of human rights in the Council Chamber, instead of being threatened with the prisons of Carolina, were to sit down the prisoner of Massachusetts, that State which is so anxious to foist the sin of slavery upon her sister—though at present she can discover only an act of inhospitality to be the ground of a quarrel with her—the Legislature would not wholly waive the subject the following winter.

Under a government which imprisons any unjustly, the true place for a just man is also a prison. The proper place today, the only place which Massachusetts has provided for her freer and less desponding spirits, is in her prisons, to be put out and locked out of the State by her own act, as they have already put themselves out by their principles. It is there that the fugitive slave, and the Mexican prisoner on parole, and the Indian come to plead the wrongs of his race, should find them; on that separate, but more free and honorable ground, where the State places those who are not *with* her but *against* her—the only house in a slave-state in which a free man can abide with honor. If any think that their influence would be lost there, and their voices no longer afflict the ear of the State, that they would not be as an enemy within its walls, they do not know by how much truth is stronger than error, nor how much more eloquently and effectively he can combat injustice who has experienced a little in his own person. Cast your whole vote, not a strip of paper merely, but your whole influence. A minority is powerless while it conforms to the majority; it is not even a minority then; but it is irresistible when it clogs by its whole weight. If the alternative is to keep all just men in prison, or give up war and slavery, the State will not hesitate which to choose. If a thousand

---

[1]   *my esteemed ... State's ambassador* Samuel Hoar (1778–1856), Concord politician who in 1844 was forcibly expelled from South Carolina when he went there to protest the seizure of free black seamen from Massachusetts, whose freedom was not acknowledged by South Carolina and who were thus at risk of being sold into slavery.

men were not to pay their tax-bills this year, that would not be a violent and bloody measure, as it would be to pay them, and enable the State to commit violence and shed innocent blood. This is, in fact, the definition of a peaceable revolution, if any such is possible. If the tax-gatherer, or any other public officer, asks me, as one has done, "But what shall I do?" my answer is, "If you really wish to do anything, resign your office." When the subject has refused allegiance, and the officer has resigned his office, then the revolution is accomplished. But even suppose blood should flow. Is there not a sort of bloodshed when the conscience is wounded? Through this wound a man's real manhood and immortality flow out, and he bleeds to an everlasting death. I see this blood flowing now.

I have contemplated the imprisonment of the offender, rather than the seizure of his goods—though both will serve the same purpose—because they who assert the purest right, and consequently are most dangerous to a corrupt State, commonly have not spent much time in accumulating property. To such the State renders comparatively small service, and a slight tax is wont to appear exorbitant, particularly if they are obliged to earn it by special labor with their hands. If there were one who lived wholly without the use of money, the State itself would hesitate to demand it of him. But the rich man—not to make any invidious comparison—is always sold to the institution which makes him rich. Absolutely speaking, the more money, the less virtue; for money comes between a man and his objects, and obtains them for him; and it was certainly no great virtue to obtain it. It puts to rest many questions which he would otherwise be taxed to answer; while the only new question which it puts is the hard but superfluous one, how to spend it. Thus his moral ground is taken from under his feet. The opportunities of living are diminished in proportion as what are called the "means" are increased. The best thing a man can do for his culture when he is rich is to endeavour to carry out those schemes which he entertained when he was poor. Christ answered the Herodians according to their condition. "Show me the tribute-money," said he—and one took a penny out of his pocket—If you use money which has the image of Cæsar on it, and which he has made current and valuable, that is, *if you are men of the State*, and gladly enjoy the advantages of

Cæsar's government, then pay him back some of his own when he demands it; "Render therefore to Cæsar that which is Cæsar's, and to God those things which are God's,"[1]—leaving them no wiser than before as to which was which; for they did not wish to know.

When I converse with the freest of my neighbors, I perceive that, whatever they may say about the magnitude and seriousness of the question, and their regard for the public tranquillity, the long and the short of the matter is, that they cannot spare the protection of the existing government, and they dread the consequences of disobedience to it to their property and families. For my own part, I should not like to think that I ever rely on the protection of the State. But, if I deny the authority of the State when it presents its tax-bill, it will soon take and waste all my property, and so harass me and my children without end. This is hard. This makes it impossible for a man to live honestly and at the same time comfortably in outward respects. It will not be worth the while to accumulate property; that would be sure to go again. You must hire or squat somewhere, and raise but a small crop, and eat that soon. You must live within yourself, and depend upon yourself, always tucked up and ready for a start, and not have many affairs. A man may grow rich in Turkey even, if he will be in all respects a good subject of the Turkish government. Confucius said, "If a State is governed by the principles of reason, poverty and misery are subjects of shame; if a State is not governed by the principles of reason, riches and honors are the subjects of shame."[2] No: until I want the protection of Massachusetts to be extended to me in some distant southern port, where my liberty is endangered, or until I am bent solely on building up an estate at home by peaceful enterprise, I can afford to refuse allegiance to Massachusetts, and her right to my property and life. It costs me less in every sense to incur the penalty of disobedience to the State, than it would to obey. I should feel as if I were worth less in that case.

---

[1] *Christ answered … are God's* See Matthew 22.16–21, in which the Herodians, in an attempt to slander him before the authorities, ask Jesus whether he thinks it lawful to pay taxes to Roman authorities.

[2] *If a … of shame* From the *Analects* 8.13 by Chinese philosopher Confucius (551–479 BCE).

Some years ago, the State met me in behalf of the church, and commanded me to pay a certain sum toward the support of a clergyman whose preaching my father attended, but never I myself. "Pay it," it said, "or be locked up in the jail." I declined to pay. But, unfortunately, another man saw fit to pay it. I did not see why the schoolmaster should be taxed to support the priest, and not the priest the schoolmaster; for I was not the State's schoolmaster, but I supported myself by voluntary subscription. I did not see why the lyceum should not present its tax-bill, and have the State to back its demand, as well as the church. However, at the request of the selectmen, I condescended to make some such statement as this in writing: "Know all men by these presents, that I, Henry Thoreau, do not wish to be regarded as a member of any incorporated society which I have not joined." This I gave to the town-clerk; and he has it. The State, having thus learned that I did not wish to be regarded as a member of that church, has never made a like demand on me since; though it said that it must adhere to its original presumption that time. If I had known how to name them, I should then have signed off in detail from all the societies which I never signed on to; but I did not know where to find a complete list.

I have paid no poll-tax for six years. I was put into a jail once on this account, for one night;[1] and, as I stood considering the walls of solid stone, two or three feet thick, the door of wood and iron, a foot thick, and the iron grating which strained the light, I could not help being struck with the foolishness of that institution which treated me as if I were mere flesh and blood and bones, to be locked up. I wondered that it should have concluded at length that this was the best use it could put me to, and had never thought to avail itself of my services in some way. I saw that, if there was a wall of stone between me and my townsmen, there was a still more difficult one to climb or break through, before they could get to be as free as I was. I did not for a moment feel confined, and the walls seemed a great waste of stone and mortar. I felt as if I alone of all my townsmen had paid my tax. They plainly did not know how to treat me, but behaved like persons who are underbred. In every threat and in every compliment there was a blunder; for they thought that my chief desire was to stand the other side of that stone wall. I could not but smile to see how industriously they locked the door on my meditations, which followed them out again without let or hindrance, and *they* were really all that was dangerous. As they could not reach me, they had resolved to punish my body; just as boys, if they cannot come at some person against whom they have a spite, will abuse his dog. I saw that the State was half-witted, that it was timid as a lone woman with her silver spoons, and that it did not know its friends from its foes, and I lost all my remaining respect for it, and pitied it.

Thus the State never intentionally confronts a man's sense, intellectual or moral, but only his body, his senses. It is not armed with superior wit or honesty, but with superior physical strength. I was not born to be forced. I will breathe after my own fashion. Let us see who is the strongest. What force has a multitude? They only can force me who obey a higher law than I. They force me to become like themselves. I do not hear of *men* being *forced* to live this way or that by masses of men. What sort of life were that to live? When I meet a government which says to me, "Your money or your life," why should I be in haste to give it my money? It may be in a great strait, and not know what to do: I cannot help that. It must help itself; do as I do. It is not worth the while to snivel about it. I am not responsible for the successful working of the machinery of society. I am not the son of the engineer. I perceive that, when an acorn and a chestnut fall side by side, the one does not remain inert to make way for the other, but both obey their own laws, and spring and grow and flourish as best they can, till one, perchance, overshadows and destroys the other. If a plant cannot live according to its nature, it dies; and so a man.

The night in prison was novel and interesting enough. The prisoners in their shirt-sleeves were enjoying a chat and the evening air in the door-way, when I entered. But the jailer said, "Come, boys, it is time to lock up"; and so they dispersed, and I heard the sound of their steps returning into the hollow apartments. My room-mate was introduced to me by the jailer, as "a first-rate fellow and a clever man." When the door was locked, he showed me where to hang

---

1   *I was ... one night*   In July 1846.

my hat, and how he managed matters there. The rooms were whitewashed once a month; and this one, at least, was the whitest, most simply furnished, and probably the neatest apartment in the town. He naturally wanted to know where I came from, and what brought me there; and, when I had told him, I asked him in my turn how he came there, presuming him to be an honest man, of course; and, as the world goes, I believe he was. "Why," said he, "they accuse me of burning a barn; but I never did it." As near as I could discover, he had probably gone to bed in a barn when drunk, and smoked his pipe there; and so a barn was burnt. He had the reputation of being a clever man, had been there some three months waiting for his trial to come on, and would have to wait as much longer; but he was quite domesticated and contented, since he got his board for nothing, and thought that he was well treated.

He occupied one window, and I the other; and I saw, that, if one stayed there long, his principal business would be to look out the window. I had soon read all the tracts that were left there, and examined where former prisoners had broken out, and where a grate had been sawed off, and heard the history of the various occupants of that room; for I found that even here there was a history and a gossip which never circulated beyond the walls of the jail. Probably this is the only house in the town where verses are composed, which are afterward printed in a circular form,[1] but not published. I was shown quite a long list of verses which were composed by some young men who had been detected in an attempt to escape, who avenged themselves by singing them.

I pumped my fellow-prisoner as dry as I could, for fear I should never see him again; but at length he showed me which was my bed, and left me to blow out the lamp.

It was like traveling into a far country, such as I had never expected to behold, to lie there for one night. It seemed to me that I never had heard the town-clock strike before, nor the evening sounds of the village; for we slept with the windows open, which were inside the grating. It was to see my native village in the light of the middle ages, and our Concord was turned into a Rhine stream, and visions of knights and castles passed before me. They were the voices of old burghers that I heard in the streets. I was an involuntary spectator and auditor of whatever was done and said in the kitchen of the adjacent village-inn—a wholly new and rare experience to me. It was a closer view of my native town. I was fairly inside of it. I never had seen its institutions before. This is one of its peculiar institutions; for it is a shire town.[2] I began to comprehend what its inhabitants were about.

In the morning, our breakfasts were put through the hole in the door, in small oblong-square tin pans, made to fit, and holding a pint of chocolate, with brown bread, and an iron spoon. When they called for the vessels again, I was green enough to return what bread I had left; but my comrade seized it, and said that I should lay that up for lunch or dinner. Soon after, he was let out to work at haying in a neighboring field, whither he went every day, and would not be back till noon; so he bade me good-day, saying that he doubted if he should see me again.

When I came out of prison—for someone interfered, and paid the tax[3]—I did not perceive that great changes had taken place on the common, such as he observed who went in a youth, and emerged a tottering and gray-headed man; and yet a change had to my eyes come over the scene—the town, and State, and country—greater than any that mere time could effect. I saw yet more distinctly the State in which I lived. I saw to what extent the people among whom I lived could be trusted as good neighbors and friends; that their friendship was for summer weather only; that they did not greatly purpose to do right; that they were a distinct race from

---

[1]   *circular form*   I.e., to be distributed among many people.

[2]   *shire town*   County seat, meaning it held the county jail.

[3]   *for someone ... the tax*   There has been a good deal of speculation as to the identity of this person, though no conclusions can be made; suggested persons have included Emerson, Samuel Hoar, and Thoreau's Aunt Maria.

me by their prejudices and superstitions, as the Chinamen and Malays are; that, in their sacrifices to humanity, they ran no risks, not even to their property; that, after all, they were not so noble but they treated the thief as he had treated them, and hoped, by a certain outward observance and a few prayers, and by walking in a particular straight though useless path from time to time, to save their souls. This may be to judge my neighbors harshly; for I believe that most of them are not aware that they have such an institution as the jail in their village.

It was formerly the custom in our village, when a poor debtor came out of jail, for his acquaintances to salute him, looking through their fingers, which were crossed to represent the grating of a jail window, "How do ye do?" My neighbors did not thus salute me, but first looked at me, and then at one another, as if I had returned from a long journey. I was put into jail as I was going to the shoemaker's to get a shoe which was mended. When I was let out the next morning, I proceeded to finish my errand, and, having put on my mended shoe, joined a huckleberry party, who were impatient to put themselves under my conduct; and in half an hour—for the horse was soon tackled—was in the midst of a huckleberry field, on one of our highest hills, two miles off; and then the State was nowhere to be seen.

This is the whole history of "My Prisons."[1]

I have never declined paying the highway tax, because I am as desirous of being a good neighbor as I am of being a bad subject; and, as for supporting schools, I am doing my part to educate my fellow-countrymen now. It is for no particular item in the tax-bill that I refuse to pay it. I simply wish to refuse allegiance to the State, to withdraw and stand aloof from it effectually. I do not care to trace the course of my dollar, if I could, till it buys a man, or a musket to shoot one with— the dollar is innocent—but I am concerned to trace the effects of my allegiance. In fact, I quietly declare war with the State, after my fashion, though I will still

make what use and get what advantage of her I can, as is usual in such cases.

If others pay the tax which is demanded of me, from a sympathy with the State, they do but what they have already done in their own case, or rather they abet injustice to a greater extent than the State requires. If they pay the tax from a mistaken interest in the individual taxed, to save his property or prevent his going to jail, it is because they have not considered wisely how far they let their private feelings interfere with the public good.

This, then, is my position at present. But one cannot be too much on his guard in such a case, lest his action be biased by obstinacy, or an undue regard for the opinions of men. Let him see that he does only what belongs to himself and to the hour.

I think sometimes, Why, this people mean well; they are only ignorant; they would do better if they knew how: why give your neighbors this pain to treat you as they are not inclined to? But I think, again, this is no reason why I should do as they do, or permit others to suffer much greater pain of a different kind. Again, I sometimes say to myself, When many millions of men, without heat, without ill-will, without personal feeling of any kind, demand of you a few shillings only, without the possibility, such is their constitution, of retracting or altering their present demand, and without the possibility, on your side, of appeal to any other millions, why expose yourself to this overwhelming brute force? You do not resist cold and hunger, the winds and the waves, thus obstinately; you quietly submit to a thousand similar necessities. You do not put your head into the fire. But just in proportion as I regard this as not wholly a brute force, but partly a human force, and consider that I have relations to those millions as to so many millions of men, and not of mere brute or inanimate things, I see that appeal is possible, first and instantaneously, from them to the Maker of them, and, secondly, from them to themselves. But, if I put my head deliberately into the fire, there is no appeal to fire or to the Maker of fire, and I have only myself to blame. If I could convince myself that I have any right to be satisfied with men as they are, and to treat them accordingly, and not according, in some respects, to my requisitions and expectations of what they and I

---

[1] *My Prisons* Allusion to the prison memoir of Silvio Pellico (1788–1854).

ought to be, then, like a good Mussulman[1] and fatalist, I should endeavor to be satisfied with things as they are, and say it is the will of God. And, above all, there is this difference between resisting this and a purely brute or natural force, that I can resist this with some effect; but I cannot expect, like Orpheus,[2] to change the nature of the rocks and trees and beasts.

I do not wish to quarrel with any man or nation. I do not wish to split hairs, to make fine distinctions, or set myself up as better than my neighbors. I seek rather, I may say, even an excuse for conforming to the laws of the land. I am but too ready to conform to them. Indeed I have reason to suspect myself on this head; and each year, as the tax-gatherer comes round, I find myself disposed to review the acts and position of the general and state governments, and the spirit of the people, to discover a pretext for conformity. I believe that the State will soon be able to take all my work of this sort out of my hands, and then I shall be no better a patriot than my fellow countrymen. Seen from a lower point of view, the Constitution, with all its faults, is very good; the law and the courts are very respectable; even this State and this American government are, in many respects, very admirable and rare things, to be thankful for, such as a great many have described them; but seen from a point of view a little higher, they are what I have described them; seen from a higher still, and the highest, who shall say what they are, or that they are worth looking at or thinking of at all?

However, the government does not concern me much, and I shall bestow the fewest possible thoughts on it. It is not many moments that I live under a government, even in this world. If a man is thought-free, fancy-free, imagination-free, that which *is not* never for a long time appearing *to be* to him, unwise rulers or reformers cannot fatally interrupt him.

I know that most men think differently from myself; but those whose lives are by profession devoted to the study of these or kindred subjects, content me as little as any. Statesmen and legislators, standing so completely within the institution, never distinctly and nakedly behold it. They speak of moving society, but have no resting-place without it. They may be men of a certain experience and discrimination, and have no doubt invented ingenious and even useful systems, for which we sincerely thank them; but all their wit and usefulness lie within certain not very wide limits. They are wont to forget that the world is not governed by policy and expediency. Webster[3] never goes behind government, and so cannot speak with authority about it. His words are wisdom to those legislators who contemplate no essential reform in the existing government; but for thinkers, and those who legislate for all time, he never once glances at the subject. I know of those whose serene and wise speculations on this theme would soon reveal the limits of his mind's range and hospitality. Yet, compared with the cheap professions of most reformers, and the still cheaper wisdom and eloquence of politicians in general, his are almost the only sensible and valuable words, and we thank Heaven for him. Comparatively, he is always strong, original, and, above all, practical. Still his quality is not wisdom, but prudence. The lawyer's truth is not Truth, but consistency, or a consistent expediency. Truth is always in harmony with herself, and is not concerned chiefly to reveal the justice that may consist with wrong-doing. He well deserves to be called, as he has been called, the Defender of the Constitution. There are really no blows to be given by him but defensive ones. He is not a leader, but a follower. His leaders are the men of '87.[4] "I have never made an effort," he says, "and never propose to make an effort; I have never countenanced an effort, and never mean to countenance an effort, to disturb the arrangement as originally made, by which the various States came into the Union." Still thinking of the sanction which the Constitution gives to slavery, he says, "Because it was a part of the original compact, let it stand." Notwithstanding his special acuteness and ability, he is unable to take a fact out

---

[1]   *Mussulman*   Antiquated term for a Muslim.

[2]   *Orpheus*   According to Ovid's *Metamorphoses*, Orpheus was able to charm trees, stones, and wild beasts into following him by the beautiful playing of his lyre.

[3]   *Webster*   Daniel Webster (1782–1852), Whig politician and at the time Senator from Massachusetts. Webster played a key role in persuading the Senate to accept the Compromise of 1850, under the terms of which California would be admitted to the Union as a free state, but Utah and New Mexico could choose if they wished to allow slavery. The Compromise also committed the government to strengthen the Fugitive Slave Act.

[4]   *men of '87*   Those who drafted the United States Constitution in 1787.

of its merely political relations, and behold it as it lies absolutely to be disposed of by the intellect—what, for instance, it behoves a man to do here in America today with regard to slavery—but ventures, or is driven, to make some such desperate answer as the following, while professing to speak absolutely, and as a private man—from which what new and singular code of social duties might be inferred? "The manner," says he, "in which the government of those States where slavery exists are to regulate it, is for their own consideration, under their responsibility to their constituents, to the general laws of propriety, humanity, and justice, and to God. Associations formed elsewhere, springing from a feeling of humanity, or any other cause, have nothing whatever to do with it. They have never received any encouragement from me, and they never will."[1]

They who know of no purer sources of truth, who have traced up its stream no higher, stand, and wisely stand, by the Bible and the Constitution, and drink at it there with reverence and humility; but they who behold where it comes trickling into this lake or that pool, gird up their loins once more, and continue their pilgrimage toward its fountain-head.

No man with a genius for legislation has appeared in America. They are rare in the history of the world. There are orators, politicians, and eloquent men, by the thousand; but the speaker has not yet opened his mouth to speak, who is capable of settling the much-vexed questions of the day. We love eloquence for its own sake, and not for any truth which it may utter, or any heroism it may inspire. Our legislators have not yet learned the comparative value of free-trade and of freedom, of union, and of rectitude, to a nation. They have no genius or talent for comparatively humble questions of taxation and finance, commerce and manufactures and agriculture. If we were left solely to the wordy wit of legislators in Congress for our guidance, uncorrected by the seasonable experience and the effectual complaints of the people, America would not long retain her rank among the nations. For eighteen hundred years, though perchance I have no right to say it, the New Testament has been written; yet where

is the legislator who has wisdom and practical talent enough to avail himself of the light which it sheds on the science of legislation?

The authority of government, even such as I am willing to submit to—for I will cheerfully obey those who know and can do better than I, and in many things even those who neither know nor can do so well—is still an impure one: to be strictly just, it must have the sanction and consent of the governed. It can have no pure right over my person and property but what I concede to it. The progress from an absolute to a limited monarchy, from a limited monarchy to a democracy, is a progress toward a true respect for the individual. Is a democracy, such as we know it, the last improvement possible in government? Is it not possible to take a step further towards recognizing and organizing the rights of man? There will never be a really free and enlightened State, until the State comes to recognize the individual as a higher and independent power, from which all its own power and authority are derived, and treats him accordingly. I please myself with imagining a State at last which can afford to be just to all men, and to treat the individual with respect as a neighbor; which even would not think it inconsistent with its own repose, if a few were to live aloof from it, not meddling with it, nor embraced by it, who fulfilled all the duties of neighbors and fellow-men. A State which bore this kind of fruit, and suffered it to drop off as fast as it ripened, would prepare the way for a still more perfect and glorious State, which also I have imagined, but not yet anywhere seen.

—1849

---

[1] [Thoreau's note]   These extracts have been inserted since the Lecture was read.   [Thoreau presumably refers to the two latter quotations, which are taken from speeches delivered by Webster before Congress in 1848.]

from *Walden; or, Life in the Woods*[1]

FROM CHAPTER 1
ECONOMY

When I wrote the following pages, or rather the bulk of them, I lived alone, in the woods, a mile from any neighbor, in a house which I had built myself, on the shore of Walden Pond, in Concord, Massachusetts, and earned my living by the labor of my hands only. I lived there two years and two months. At present I am a sojourner in civilized life again.

I should not obtrude my affairs so much on the notice of my readers if very particular inquiries had not been made by my townsmen concerning my mode of life, which some would call impertinent, though they do not appear to me at all impertinent, but, considering the circumstances, very natural and pertinent. Some have asked what I got to eat; if I did not feel lonesome; if I was not afraid; and the like. Others have been curious to learn what portion of my income I devoted to charitable purposes; and some, who have large families, how many poor children I maintained. I will therefore ask those of my readers who feel no particular interest in me to pardon me if I undertake to answer some of these questions in this book. In most books, the *I*, or first person, is omitted; in this it will be retained; that, in respect to egotism, is the main difference. We commonly do not remember that it is, after all, always the first person that is speaking. I should not talk so much about myself if there were anybody else whom I knew as well. Unfortunately, I am confined to this theme by the narrowness of my experience. Moreover, I, on my side, require of every writer, first or last, a simple and sincere account of his own life, and not merely what he has heard of other men's lives; some such account as he would send to his kindred from a distant land; for if he has lived sincerely, it must have been in a distant land to me. Perhaps these pages are more particularly addressed to poor students. As for the rest of my readers, they will accept such portions as apply to them. I trust that none will stretch the seams in putting on the coat, for it may do good service to him whom it fits.

I would fain say something, not so much concerning the Chinese and Sandwich Islanders[2] as you who read these pages, who are said to live in New England; something about your condition, especially your outward condition or circumstances in this world, in this town, what it is, whether it is necessary that it be as bad as it is, whether it cannot be improved as well as not. I have travelled a good deal in Concord; and everywhere, in shops, and offices, and fields, the inhabitants have appeared to me to be doing penance in a thousand remarkable ways. What I have heard of Bramins[3] sitting exposed to four fires and looking in the face of the sun; or hanging suspended, with their heads downward, over flames; or looking at the heavens over their shoulders "until it becomes impossible for them to resume their natural position, while from the twist of the neck nothing but liquids can pass into the stomach"; or dwelling, chained for life, at the foot of a tree; or measuring with their bodies, like caterpillars, the breadth of vast empires; or standing on one leg on the tops of pillars—even these forms of conscious penance are hardly more incredible and astonishing than the scenes which I daily witness. The twelve labors of Hercules[4] were trifling in comparison with those which my neighbors have undertaken; for they were only twelve, and had an end; but I could never see that these men slew or captured any monster or finished any labor. They have no friend Iolas to burn with a hot iron the root of the hydra's head,[5] but as soon as one head is crushed, two spring up.

I see young men, my townsmen, whose misfortune it is to have inherited farms, houses, barns, cattle, and farming tools; for these are more easily acquired than got rid of. Better if they had been born in the open pasture and suckled by a wolf, that they might have seen

---

[1]   Excerpts from *Walden* are included below; the full text is included as part of the website component of this anthology.

[2]   *Sandwich Islanders* Indigenous Hawaiians; the Hawaiian Islands were generally known to English speakers as the Sandwich Islands, after the British Earl of Sandwich, from 1778 until the mid-1800s.

[3]   *Bramins* Brahmins, members of the priest caste in Hindu culture. Thoreau's source for the following descriptions of Brahmin spiritual practices is James Mill's *The History of India* (1817).

[4]   *twelve labors of Hercules* The Greek mythological demigod Hercules was given twelve dangerous feats to perform.

[5]   *friend Iolas ... hydra's head* The hydra was a many-headed monster who could re-grow two heads from every one that was cut off; Hercules's friend Iolaus helped him defeat the monster.

with clearer eyes what field they were called to labor in. Who made them serfs of the soil? Why should they eat their sixty acres, when man is condemned to eat only his peck of dirt? Why should they begin digging their graves as soon as they are born? They have got to live a man's life, pushing all these things before them, and get on as well as they can. How many a poor immortal soul have I met well nigh crushed and smothered under its load, creeping down the road of life, pushing before it a barn seventy-five feet by forty, its Augean stables[1] never cleansed, and one hundred acres of land, tillage, mowing, pasture, and wood-lot! The portionless, who struggle with no such unnecessary inherited encumbrances, find it labor enough to subdue and cultivate a few cubic feet of flesh.

But men labor under a mistake. The better part of the man is soon plowed into the soil for compost. By a seeming fate, commonly called necessity, they are employed, as it says in an old book, laying up treasures which moth and rust will corrupt and thieves break through and steal. It is a fool's life, as they will find when they get to the end of it, if not before. …

Most men, even in this comparatively free country, through mere ignorance and mistake, are so occupied with the factitious cares and superfluously coarse labors of life that its finer fruits cannot be plucked by them. Their fingers, from excessive toil, are too clumsy and tremble too much for that. Actually, the laboring man has not leisure for a true integrity day by day; he cannot afford to sustain the manliest relations to men; his labor would be depreciated in the market. He has no time to be anything but a machine. How can he remember well his ignorance—which his growth requires—who has so often to use his knowledge? We should feed and clothe him gratuitously sometimes, and recruit him with our cordials, before we judge of him. The finest qualities of our nature, like the bloom on fruits, can be preserved only by the most delicate handling. Yet we do not treat ourselves nor one another thus tenderly.

Some of you, we all know, are poor, find it hard to live, are sometimes, as it were, gasping for breath. I have no doubt that some of you who read this book are unable to pay for all the dinners which you have actually eaten, or for the coats and shoes which are fast wearing or are already worn out, and have come to this page to spend borrowed or stolen time, robbing your creditors of an hour. It is very evident what mean[2] and sneaking lives many of you live, for my sight has been whetted by experience; always on the limits, trying to get into business and trying to get out of debt, … always promising to pay, promising to pay, tomorrow, and dying today, insolvent; seeking to curry favor, to get custom, by how many modes, only not state-prison offences; lying, flattering, voting, contracting yourselves into a nutshell of civility or dilating into an atmosphere of thin and vaporous generosity, that you may persuade your neighbor to let you make his shoes, or his hat, or his coat, or his carriage, or import his groceries for him; making yourselves sick, that you may lay up something against a sick day, something to be tucked away in an old chest, or in a stocking behind the plastering, or, more safely, in the brick bank; no matter where, no matter how much or how little.

I sometimes wonder that we can be so frivolous, I may almost say, as to attend to the gross but somewhat foreign form of servitude called Negro Slavery; there are so many keen and subtle masters that enslave both north and south. It is hard to have a southern overseer; it is worse to have a northern one; but worst of all when you are the slave-driver of yourself. Talk of a divinity in man! Look at the teamster on the highway, wending to market by day or night; does any divinity stir within him? His highest duty to fodder and water his horses! What is his destiny to him compared with the shipping interests? Does not he drive for Squire Make-a-stir? How godlike, how immortal, is he? See how he cowers and sneaks, how vaguely all the day he fears, not being immortal nor divine, but the slave and prisoner of his own opinion of himself, a fame won by his own deeds. Public opinion is a weak tyrant compared with our own private opinion. What a man thinks of himself, that it is which determines, or rather indicates, his fate. Self-emancipation even in the West Indian provinces of the fancy and imagination—what Wilberforce[3] is there to bring that about? Think, also, of the ladies of

---

[1]   *Augean stables* As one of his labors, Hercules had to clean the massive Augean stables.

[2]   *mean* Lowly.

[3]   *Wilberforce* William Wilberforce, English politician and abolitionist (1759–1833).

the land weaving toilet cushions[1] against the last day, not to betray too green an interest in their fates! As if you could kill time without injuring eternity.

The mass of men lead lives of quiet desperation. What is called resignation is confirmed desperation. From the desperate city you go into the desperate country, and have to console yourself with the bravery of minks and muskrats. A stereotyped but unconscious despair is concealed even under what are called the games and amusements of mankind. There is no play in them, for this comes after work. But it is a characteristic of wisdom not to do desperate things.

When we consider what, to use the words of the catechism, is the chief end of man,[2] and what are the true necessaries and means of life, it appears as if men had deliberately chosen the common mode of living because they preferred it to any other. Yet they honestly think there is no choice left. But alert and healthy natures remember that the sun rose clear. It is never too late to give up our prejudices. No way of thinking or doing, however ancient, can be trusted without proof. What everybody echoes or in silence passes by as true today may turn out to be falsehood tomorrow, mere smoke of opinion, which some had trusted for a cloud that would sprinkle fertilizing rain on their fields. What old people say you cannot do you try and find that you can. Old deeds for old people, and new deeds for new. Old people did not know enough once, perchance, to fetch fresh fuel to keep the fire a-going; new people put a little dry wood under a pot, and are whirled round the globe with the speed of birds, in a way to kill old people, as the phrase is. Age is no better, hardly so well, qualified for an instructor as youth, for it has not profited so much as it has lost. One may almost doubt if the wisest man has learned anything of absolute value by living. Practically, the old have no very important advice to give the young, their own experience has been so partial, and their lives have been such miserable failures, for private reasons, as they must believe; and it may be that they have some faith left which belies that experience, and they are only less young than they were. I have lived some thirty years on this planet, and I have yet to hear the first syllable of valuable or even earnest advice from my seniors. They have told me nothing, and probably cannot tell me anything to the purpose. Here is life, an experiment to a great extent untried by me; but it does not avail me that they have tried it. If I have any experience which I think valuable, I am sure to reflect that this my Mentors said nothing about.

One farmer says to me, "You cannot live on vegetable food solely, for it furnishes nothing to make bones with"; and so he religiously devotes a part of his day to supplying his system with the raw material of bones; walking all the while he talks behind his oxen, which, with vegetable-made bones, jerk him and his lumbering plough along in spite of every obstacle. Some things are really necessaries of life in some circles, the most helpless and diseased, which in others are luxuries merely, and in others still are entirely unknown.

The whole ground of human life seems to some to have been gone over by their predecessors, both the heights and the valleys, and all things to have been cared for. ... Undoubtedly the very tedium and ennui which presume to have exhausted the variety and the joys of life are as old as Adam. But man's capacities have never been measured; nor are we to judge of what he can do by any precedents, so little has been tried. Whatever have been thy failures hitherto, "be not afflicted, my child, for who shall assign to thee what thou hast left undone?"[3]

We might try our lives by a thousand simple tests; as, for instance, that the same sun which ripens my beans illumines at once a system of earths like ours. If I had remembered this it would have prevented some mistakes. This was not the light in which I hoed them. The stars are the apexes of what wonderful triangles! What distant and different beings in the various mansions of the universe are contemplating the same one at the same moment! Nature and human life are as various as our several constitutions. Who shall say what prospect

---

1   *toilet cushions* Decorative cushions kept at one's dressing table or on the accompanying chair. (The noun "toilet" could refer either to the dressing room or table or to the action of getting dressed, doing one's hair, etc.)

2   *the words ... of man* The catechism is a church-authorized primer on Christian doctrine usually presented in the form of questions and conventionally accepted answers. The first question in *The New England Primer* is "What is the chief end of man?" with the answer being, "Man's chief end is to glorify God, and to enjoy him forever."

3   *be not afflicted ... undone?* From Horace Haymen Wilson's 1840 translation of *The Vishnu Purana*, a sacred Hindu text.

life offers to another? Could a greater miracle take place than for us to look through each other's eyes for an instant? We should live in all the ages of the world in an hour; ay, in all the worlds of the ages. History, Poetry, Mythology! I know of no reading of another's experience so startling and informing as this would be.

The greater part of what my neighbors call good I believe in my soul to be bad, and if I repent of anything, it is very likely to be my good behavior. What demon possessed me that I behaved so well? You may say the wisest thing you can, old man—you who have lived seventy years, not without honor of a kind—I hear an irresistible voice which invites me away from all that. One generation abandons the enterprises of another like stranded vessels.

I think that we may safely trust a good deal more than we do. We may waive just so much care of ourselves as we honestly bestow elsewhere. Nature is as well adapted to our weakness as to our strength. The incessant anxiety and strain of some is a well nigh incurable form of disease. We are made to exaggerate the importance of what work we do; and yet how much is not done by us! or, what if we had been taken sick? How vigilant we are! determined not to live by faith if we can avoid it; all the day long on the alert, at night we unwillingly say our prayers and commit ourselves to uncertainties. So thoroughly and sincerely are we compelled to live, reverencing our life, and denying the possibility of change. This is the only way, we say; but there are as many ways as there can be drawn radii from one centre. All change is a miracle to contemplate; but it is a miracle which is taking place every instant. Confucius said, "To know that we know what we know, and that we do not know what we do not know, that is true knowledge."[1] When one man has reduced a fact of the imagination to be a fact to his understanding, I foresee that all men at length establish their lives on that basis.

Let us consider for a moment what most of the trouble and anxiety which I have referred to is about, and how much it is necessary that we be troubled, or, at least, careful. It would be some advantage to live a primitive and frontier life, though in the midst of an outward civilization, if only to learn what are the gross necessaries of life and what methods have been taken to obtain them; or even to look over the old day-books of the merchants, to see what it was that men most commonly bought at the stores, what they stored, that is, what are the grossest groceries. For the improvements of ages have had but little influence on the essential laws of man's existence; as our skeletons, probably, are not to be distinguished from those of our ancestors.

By the words, *necessary of life*, I mean whatever, of all that man obtains by his own exertions, has been from the first, or from long use has become, so important to human life that few, if any, whether from savageness, or poverty, or philosophy, ever attempt to do without it. To many creatures there is in this sense but one necessary of life, Food. To the bison of the prairie it is a few inches of palatable grass, with water to drink; unless he seeks the Shelter of the forest or the mountain's shadow. None of the brute creation requires more than Food and Shelter. The necessaries of life for man in this climate may, accurately enough, be distributed under the several heads of Food, Shelter, Clothing, and Fuel; for not till we have secured these are we prepared to entertain the true problems of life with freedom and a prospect of success. Man has invented, not only houses, but clothes and cooked food; and possibly from the accidental discovery of the warmth of fire, and the consequent use of it, at first a luxury, arose the present necessity to sit by it. We observe cats and dogs acquiring the same second nature. By proper Shelter and Clothing we legitimately retain our own internal heat; but with an excess of these, or of Fuel, that is, with an external heat greater than our own internal, may not cookery properly be said to begin? Darwin, the naturalist, says of the inhabitants of Tierra del Fuego, that while his own party, who were well clothed and sitting close to a fire, were far from too warm, these naked savages, who were farther off, were observed, to his great surprise, "to be streaming with perspiration at undergoing such a roasting."[2] So, we are told, the New Hollander[3] goes naked with impunity, while

[1] *Confucius said ... knowledge* Thoreau's translation from Guillaume Pauthier's *Confucius et Mencius*, itself a French translation of the Confucian book *The Doctrine of the Mean*.

[2] *Darwin ... roasting* See Charles Darwin's *Narrative of the Surveying Voyages of His Majesty's Ships Adventure and Beagle* (1839).

[3] *New Hollander* Aboriginal Australian; Australia was named New Holland after its discovery by Dutch travelers in the seventeenth century.

the European shivers in his clothes. Is it impossible to combine the hardiness of these savages with the intellectualness of the civilized man? According to Liebig,[1] man's body is a stove, and food the fuel which keeps up the internal combustion in the lungs. In cold weather we eat more, in warm less. The animal heat is the result of a slow combustion, and disease and death take place when this is too rapid; or for want of fuel, or from some defect in the draught, the fire goes out. Of course the vital heat is not to be confounded with fire; but so much for analogy. It appears, therefore, from the above list, that the expression, *animal life*, is nearly synonymous with the expression, *animal heat*; for while Food may be regarded as the Fuel which keeps up the fire within us—and Fuel serves only to prepare that Food or to increase the warmth of our bodies by addition from without—Shelter and Clothing also serve only to retain the *heat* thus generated and absorbed.

The grand necessity, then, for our bodies, is to keep warm, to keep the vital heat in us. What pains we accordingly take, not only with our Food, and Clothing, and Shelter, but with our beds, which are our night-clothes, robbing the nests and breasts of birds to prepare this shelter within a shelter, as the mole has its bed of grass and leaves at the end of its burrow! The poor man is wont to complain that this is a cold world; and to cold, no less physical than social, we refer directly a great part of our ails. The summer, in some climates, makes possible to man a sort of Elysian[2] life. Fuel, except to cook his Food, is then unnecessary; the sun is his fire, and many of the fruits are sufficiently cooked by its rays; while Food generally is more various, and more easily obtained, and Clothing and Shelter are wholly or half unnecessary. At the present day, and in this country, as I find by my own experience, a few implements, a knife, an axe, a spade, a wheelbarrow, etc., and for the studious, lamplight, stationery, and access to a few books, rank next to necessaries, and can all be obtained at a trifling cost. Yet some, not wise, go to the other side of the globe, to barbarous and unhealthy regions, and devote themselves to trade for ten or twenty years, in order that they may live—that is, keep comfortably warm—and die in New England at last.

The luxuriously rich are not simply kept comfortably warm, but unnaturally hot; as I implied before, they are cooked, of course à la mode.

Most of the luxuries, and many of the so-called comforts of life, are not only not indispensable, but positive hindrances to the elevation of mankind. With respect to luxuries and comforts, the wisest have ever lived a more simple and meagre life than the poor. The ancient philosophers, Chinese, Hindoo, Persian, and Greek, were a class than which none has been poorer in outward riches, none so rich in inward. We know not much about them. It is remarkable that we know so much of them as we do. The same is true of the more modern reformers and benefactors of their race. None can be an impartial or wise observer of human life but from the vantage ground of what *we* should call voluntary poverty. Of a life of luxury the fruit is luxury, whether in agriculture, or commerce, or literature, or art. There are nowadays professors of philosophy, but not philosophers. Yet it is admirable to profess because it was once admirable to live. To be a philosopher is not merely to have subtle thoughts, nor even to found a school, but so to love wisdom as to live according to its dictates, a life of simplicity, independence, magnanimity, and trust. It is to solve some of the problems of life, not only theoretically, but practically. The success of great scholars and thinkers is commonly a courtier-like success, not kingly, not manly. They make shift to live merely by conformity, practically as their fathers did, and are in no sense the progenitors of a nobler race of men. But why do men degenerate ever? What makes families run out? What is the nature of the luxury which enervates and destroys nations? Are we sure that there is none of it in our own lives? The philosopher is in advance of his age even in the outward form of his life. He is not fed, sheltered, clothed, warmed, like his contemporaries. How can a man be a philosopher and not maintain his vital heat by better methods than other men?

When a man is warmed by the several modes which I have described, what does he want next? Surely not more warmth of the same kind, as more and richer food, larger and more splendid houses, finer and more abundant clothing, more numerous incessant and hotter fires, and the like. When he has obtained those things which are necessary to life, there is another

---

[1]   *Liebig*   German chemist Baron Justus von Liebig (1803–73).

[2]   *Elysian*   Blissful. Referring to Elysium, where, according to classical mythology, the blessed reside after death.

alternative than to obtain the superfluities; and that is, to adventure on life now, his vacation from humbler toil having commenced. The soil, it appears, is suited to the seed, for it has sent its radicle[1] downward, and it may now send its shoot upward also with confidence. Why has man rooted himself thus firmly in the earth, but that he may rise in the same proportion into the heavens above?—for the nobler plants are valued for the fruit they bear at last in the air and light, far from the ground, and are not treated like the humbler esculents,[2] which, though they may be biennials, are cultivated only till they have perfected their root, and often cut down at top for this purpose, so that most would not know them in their flowering season.

I do not mean to prescribe rules to strong and valiant natures, who will mind their own affairs whether in heaven or hell, and perchance build more magnificently and spend more lavishly than the richest, without ever impoverishing themselves, not knowing how they live—if, indeed, there are any such, as has been dreamed; nor to those who find their encouragement and inspiration in precisely the present condition of things, and cherish it with the fondness and enthusiasm of lovers—and, to some extent, I reckon myself in this number; I do not speak to those who are well employed, in whatever circumstances—and they know whether they are well employed or not—but mainly to the mass of men who are discontented, and idly complaining of the hardness of their lot or of the times, when they might improve them. There are some who complain most energetically and inconsolably of any, because they are, as they say, doing their duty. I also have in my mind that seemingly wealthy, but most terribly impoverished class of all, who have accumulated dross,[3] but know not how to use it, or get rid of it, and thus have forged their own golden or silver fetters.

If I should attempt to tell how I have desired to spend my life in years past, it would probably surprise those of my readers who are somewhat acquainted with its actual history; it would certainly astonish those who know nothing about it. I will only hint at some of the enterprises which I have cherished.

In any weather, at any hour of the day or night, I have been anxious to improve the nick of time, and notch it on my stick too; to stand on the meeting of two eternities, the past and future, which is precisely the present moment; to toe that line. You will pardon some obscurities, for there are more secrets in my trade than in most men's, and yet not voluntarily kept, but inseparable from its very nature. I would gladly tell all that I know about it, and never paint "No Admittance" on my gate.

I long ago lost a hound, a bay horse, and a turtle-dove, and am still on their trail. Many are the travellers I have spoken concerning them, describing their tracks and what calls they answered to. I have met one or two who had heard the hound, and the tramp of the horse, and even seen the dove disappear behind a cloud, and they seemed as anxious to recover them as if they had lost them themselves.

To anticipate, not the sunrise and the dawn merely, but, if possible, Nature herself! How many mornings, summer and winter, before yet any neighbor was stirring about his business, have I been about mine! No doubt, many of my townsmen have met me returning from this enterprise, farmers starting for Boston in the twilight, or woodchoppers going to their work. It is true, I never assisted the sun materially in his rising, but, doubt not, it was of the last[4] importance only to be present at it.

So many autumn, ay, and winter days, spent outside the town, trying to hear what was in the wind, to hear and carry it express! I well-nigh sunk all my capital in it, and lost my own breath into the bargain, running in the face of it. If it had concerned either of the political parties, depend upon it, it would have appeared in the Gazette with the earliest intelligence. At other times watching from the observatory of some cliff or tree, to telegraph any new arrival; or waiting at evening on the hill-tops for the sky to fall, that I might catch something, though I never caught much, and that, manna-wise, would dissolve again in the sun.

For a long time I was reporter to a journal, of no very wide circulation, whose editor has never yet seen fit to print the bulk of my contributions, and, as is

---

[1]   *radicle* Root of a seedling.

[2]   *esculents* Edibles.

[3]   *dross* Substance left over from melting metals; more broadly, extraneous matter of little inherent value.

---

[4]   *last* Greatest.

too common with writers, I got only my labor for my pains. However, in this case my pains were their own reward.

For many years I was self-appointed inspector of snow storms and rain storms, and did my duty faithfully; surveyor, if not of highways, then of forest paths and all across-lot routes, keeping them open, and ravines bridged and passable at all seasons, where the public heel had testified to their utility.

I have looked after the wild stock of the town, which give a faithful herdsman a good deal of trouble by leaping fences; and I have had an eye to the unfrequented nooks and corners of the farm; though I did not always know whether Jonas or Solomon worked in a particular field to-day; that was none of my business. I have watered the red huckleberry, the sand cherry and the nettle tree, the red pine and the black ash, the white grape and the yellow violet, which might have withered else in dry seasons.

In short, I went on thus for a long time, I may say it without boasting, faithfully minding my business, till it became more and more evident that my townsmen would not after all admit me into the list of town officers, nor make my place a sinecure[1] with a moderate allowance. My accounts, which I can swear to have kept faithfully, I have, indeed, never got audited, still less accepted, still less paid and settled. However, I have not set my heart on that.

Not long since, a strolling Indian went to sell baskets at the house of a well-known lawyer in my neighborhood. "Do you wish to buy any baskets?" he asked. "No, we do not want any," was the reply. "What!" exclaimed the Indian as he went out the gate, "do you mean to starve us?" Having seen his industrious white neighbors so well off—that the lawyer had only to weave arguments, and by some magic, wealth and standing followed—he had said to himself; I will go into business; I will weave baskets; it is a thing which I can do. Thinking that when he had made the baskets he would have done his part, and then it would be the white man's to buy them. He had not discovered that it was necessary for him to make it worth the other's while to buy them, or at least make him think that it was so, or to make something else which it would be worth his while to buy. I too had woven a kind of basket of a delicate texture, but I had not made it worth any one's while to buy them. Yet not the less, in my case, did I think it worth my while to weave them, and instead of studying how to make it worth men's while to buy my baskets, I studied rather how to avoid the necessity of selling them. The life which men praise and regard as successful is but one kind. Why should we exaggerate any one kind at the expense of the others?

Finding that my fellow citizens were not likely to offer me any room in the court house, or any curacy[2] or living anywhere else, but I must shift for myself, I turned my face more exclusively than ever to the woods, where I was better known. I determined to go into business at once, and not wait to acquire the usual capital, using such slender means as I had already got. My purpose in going to Walden Pond was not to live cheaply nor to live dearly there, but to transact some private business with the fewest obstacles; to be hindered from accomplishing which for want of a little common sense, a little enterprise and business talent, appeared not so sad as foolish.

I have always endeavored to acquire strict business habits; they are indispensable to every man. …

I have thought that Walden Pond would be a good place for business, not solely on account of the railroad and the ice trade; it offers advantages which it may not be good policy to divulge; it is a good port and a good foundation. …

As this business was to be entered into without the usual capital, it may not be easy to conjecture where those means, that will still be indispensable to every such undertaking, were to be obtained. As for Clothing, to come at once to the practical part of the question, perhaps we are led oftener by the love of novelty, and a regard for the opinions of men, in procuring it, than by a true utility. Let him who has work to do recollect that the object of clothing is, first, to retain the vital heat, and secondly, in this state of society, to cover nakedness, and he may judge how much of any necessary or important work may be accomplished without adding to his wardrobe. Kings and queens who wear a suit but once, though made by some tailor or dressmaker to their majesties, cannot know the comfort of wearing a suit that fits. They are no better than wooden horses to hang the clean clothes on. Every day

---

[1] *sinecure* Position that requires little or no actual work.

[2] *curacy* Ecclesiastical position.

our garments become more assimilated to ourselves, receiving the impress of the wearer's character, until we hesitate to lay them aside, without such delay and medical appliances and some such solemnity even as our bodies. No man ever stood the lower in my estimation for having a patch in his clothes; yet I am sure that there is greater anxiety, commonly, to have fashionable, or at least clean and unpatched clothes, than to have a sound conscience. But even if the rent is not mended, perhaps the worst vice betrayed is improvidence. I sometimes try my acquaintances by such tests as this: Who could wear a patch, or two extra seams only, over the knee? Most behave as if they believed that their prospects for life would be ruined if they should do it. It would be easier for them to hobble to town with a broken leg than with a broken pantaloon. Often if an accident happens to a gentleman's legs, they can be mended; but if a similar accident happens to the legs of his pantaloons, there is no help for it; for he considers, not what is truly respectable, but what is respected. We know but few men, a great many coats and breeches. Dress a scarecrow in your last shift, you standing shiftless by, who would not soonest salute the scarecrow? Passing a cornfield the other day, close by a hat and coat on a stake, I recognized the owner of the farm. He was only a little more weather-beaten than when I saw him last. I have heard of a dog that barked at every stranger who approached his master's premises with clothes on, but was easily quieted by a naked thief. It is an interesting question how far men would retain their relative rank if they were divested of their clothes. Could you, in such a case, tell surely of any company of civilized men, which belonged to the most respected class? … Even in our democratic New England towns the accidental possession of wealth, and its manifestation in dress and equipage alone, obtain for the possessor almost universal respect. But they yield such respect, numerous as they are, are so far heathen, and need to have a missionary sent to them. Beside, clothes introduced sewing, a kind of work which you may call endless; a woman's dress, at least, is never done.[1]

A man who has at length found something to do will not need to get a new suit to do it in; for him the old will do, that has lain dusty in the garret[2] for an indeterminate period. Old shoes will serve a hero longer than they have served his valet—if a hero ever has a valet—bare feet are older than shoes, and he can make them do. Only they who go to soirées and legislative halls must have new coats, coats to change as often as the man changes in them. But if my jacket and trousers, my hat and shoes, are fit to worship God in, they will do; will they not? Who ever saw his old clothes—his old coat, actually worn out, resolved into its primitive elements, so that it was not a deed of charity to bestow it on some poor boy, by him perchance to be bestowed on some poorer still, or shall we say richer, who could do with less? I say, beware of all enterprises that require new clothes, and not rather a new wearer of clothes. If there is not a new man, how can the new clothes be made to fit? If you have any enterprise before you, try it in your old clothes. All men want, not something to *do with*, but something to *do*, or rather something to *be*. Perhaps we should never procure a new suit, however ragged or dirty the old, until we have so conducted, so enterprised or sailed in some way, that we feel like new men in the old, and that to retain it would be like keeping new wine in old bottles. Our moulting season, like that of the fowls, must be a crisis in our lives. The loon retires to solitary ponds to spend it. Thus also the snake casts its slough, and the caterpillar its wormy coat, by an internal industry and expansion; for clothes are but our outmost cuticle and mortal coil.[3] Otherwise we shall be found sailing under false colors, and be inevitably cashiered[4] at last by our own opinion, as well as that of mankind.

We don garment after garment, as if we grew like exogenous plants[5] by addition without. Our outside and often thin and fanciful clothes are our epidermis, or false skin, which partakes not of our life, and may be stripped off here and there without fatal injury; our thicker garments, constantly worn, are our cellular

---

1   *a woman's dress … never done* Reference to the proverbial expression, "A woman's work is never done."

2   *garret* Small, often unpleasant living space at the top of a building.

3   *mortal coil* I.e., the body. See Shakespeare's *Hamlet* 3.1.74–76: "For in that sleep of death what dreams may come, / When we have shuffled off this mortal coil, / Must give us pause."

4   *cashiered* Discredited; lowered in position.

5   *exogenous plants* Plants that grow additional outer layers with each growth cycle, such as trees.

integument, or cortex; but our shirts are our liber or true bark, which cannot be removed without girdling and so destroying the man. I believe that all races at some seasons wear something equivalent to the shirt. It is desirable that a man be clad so simply that he can lay his hands on himself in the dark, and that he live in all respects so compactly and preparedly, that, if an enemy take the town, he can, like the old philosopher, walk out the gate empty-handed without anxiety. While one thick garment is, for most purposes, as good as three thin ones, and cheap clothing can be obtained at prices really to suit customers; while a thick coat can be bought for five dollars, which will last as many years, thick pantaloons for two dollars, cowhide boots for a dollar and a half a pair, a summer hat for a quarter of a dollar, and a winter cap for sixty-two and a half cents, or a better be made at home at a nominal cost, where is he so poor that, clad in such a suit, *of his own earning*, there will not be found wise men to do him reverence?

When I ask for a garment of a particular form, my tailoress tells me gravely, "They do not make them so now," not emphasizing the "They" at all, as if she quoted an authority as impersonal as the Fates, and I find it difficult to get made what I want, simply because she cannot believe that I mean what I say, that I am so rash. When I hear this oracular sentence, I am for a moment absorbed in thought, emphasizing to myself each word separately that I may come at the meaning of it, that I may find out by what degree of consanguinity *They* are related to *me*, and what authority they may have in an affair which affects me so nearly …

On the whole, I think that it cannot be maintained that dressing has in this or any country risen to the dignity of an art. At present men make shift to wear what they can get. Like shipwrecked sailors, they put on what they can find on the beach, and at a little distance, whether of space or time, laugh at each other's masquerade. Every generation laughs at the old fashions, but follows religiously the new. We are amused at beholding the costume of Henry VIII, or Queen Elizabeth, as much as if it was that of the King and Queen of the Cannibal Islands. All costume off a man is pitiful or grotesque. It is only the serious eye peering from and the sincere life passed within it, which restrain laughter and consecrate the costume of any

people. Let Harlequin[1] be taken with a fit of the colic[2] and his trappings will have to serve that mood too. When the soldier is hit by a cannonball rags are as becoming as purple. …

I cannot believe that our factory system is the best mode by which men may get clothing. The condition of the operatives is becoming every day more like that of the English; and it cannot be wondered at, since, as far as I have heard or observed, the principal object is, not that mankind may be well and honestly clad, but, unquestionably, that corporations may be enriched. In the long run men hit only what they aim at. Therefore, though they should fail immediately, they had better aim at something high.

As for a Shelter, I will not deny that this is now a necessary of life, though there are instances of men having done without it for long periods in colder countries than this. Samuel Laing[3] says that "the Laplander[4] in his skin dress, and in a skin bag which he puts over his head and shoulders, will sleep night after night on the snow, in a degree of cold which would extinguish the life of one exposed to it in any woollen clothing." He had seen them asleep thus. Yet he adds, "They are not hardier than other people." But, probably, man did not live long on the earth without discovering the convenience which there is in a house, the domestic comforts, which phrase may have originally signified the satisfactions of the house more than of the family; though these must be extremely partial and occasional in those climates where the house is associated in our thoughts with winter or the rainy season chiefly, and two thirds of the year, except for a parasol, is unnecessary. In our climate, in the summer, it was formerly almost solely a covering at night. In the Indian gazettes[5] a wigwam was the symbol of a day's march, and a row of them cut or painted on the bark of a tree

---

1   *Harlequin*   Stock character in Italian stage comedies, known for his distinctive costume patterned in colorful diamond shapes.

2   *colic*   Illness of the stomach or bowels.

3   *Samuel Laing*   Scottish traveler and writer; Thoreau quotes from his 1837 *Journal of a Residence in Norway during the Years 1834, 1835, and 1836.*

4   *Laplander*   I.e., a Sami, or Indigenous person of northern Scandinavia; the term "Lapland" today refers more specifically to a region of northern Finland.

5   *gazettes*   Engravings.

signified that so many times they had camped. Man was not made so large limbed and robust but that he must seek to narrow his world, and wall in a space such as fitted him. He was at first bare and out of doors; but though this was pleasant enough in serene and warm weather, by daylight, the rainy season and the winter, to say nothing of the torrid sun, would perhaps have nipped his race in the bud if he had not made haste to clothe himself with the shelter of a house. Adam and Eve, according to the fable, wore the bower before other clothes. Man wanted a home, a place of warmth, or comfort, first of physical warmth, then the warmth of the affections.

We may imagine a time when, in the infancy of the human race, some enterprising mortal crept into a hollow in a rock for shelter. Every child begins the world again, to some extent, and loves to stay out-doors, even in wet and cold. It plays house, as well as horse, having an instinct for it. Who does not remember the interest with which when young he looked at shelving rocks, or any approach to a cave? It was the natural yearning of that portion of our most primitive ancestor which still survived in us. From the cave we have advanced to roofs of palm leaves, of bark and boughs, of linen woven and stretched, of grass and straw, of boards and shingles, of stones and tiles. At last, we know not what it is to live in the open air, and our lives are domestic in more senses than we think. From the hearth to the field is a great distance. It would be well perhaps if we were to spend more of our days and nights without any obstruction between us and the celestial bodies, if the poet did not speak so much from under a roof, or the saint dwell there so long. Birds do not sing in caves, nor do doves cherish their innocence in dovecots.

However, if one designs to construct a dwelling house, it behooves him to exercise a little Yankee shrewdness, lest after all he find himself in a work-house, a labyrinth without a clue, a museum, an almshouse, a prison, or a splendid mausoleum instead. Consider first how slight a shelter is absolutely nec-essary. I have seen Penobscot Indians, in this town, living in tents of thin cotton cloth, while the snow was nearly a foot deep around them, and I thought that they would be glad to have it deeper to keep out the wind. Formerly, when how to get my living honestly, with freedom left for my proper pursuits, was a ques-tion which vexed me even more than it does now, for unfortunately I am become somewhat callous,[1] I used to see a large box by the railroad, six feet long by three wide, in which the laborers locked up their tools at night, and it suggested to me that every man who was hard pushed might get such a one for a dollar, and, having bored a few auger holes in it, to admit the air at least, get into it when it rained and at night, and hook down the lid, and so have freedom in his love, and in his soul be free. This did not appear the worst, nor by any means a despicable alternative. You could sit up as late as you pleased, and, whenever you got up, go abroad without any landlord or house-lord dogging you for rent. Many a man is harassed to death to pay the rent of a larger and more luxurious box who would not have frozen to death in such a box as this. I am far from jesting. Economy is a subject which admits of being treated with levity, but it cannot so be disposed of. A comfortable house for a rude and hardy race, that lived mostly out of doors, was once made here almost entirely of such materials as Nature furnished ready to their hands. Gookin,[2] who was superintendent of the Indians subject to the Massachusetts Colony, writ-ing in 1674, says, "The best of their houses are cov-ered very neatly, tight and warm, with barks of trees, slipped from their bodies at those seasons when the sap is up, and made into great flakes, with pressure of weighty timber, when they are green. The meaner sort are covered with mats which they make of a kind of bulrush, and are also indifferently tight and warm, but not so good as the former. Some I have seen, sixty or a hundred feet long and thirty feet broad. I have often lodged in their wigwams, and found them as warm as the best English houses." He adds, that they were com-monly carpeted and lined within with well-wrought embroidered mats, and were furnished with various utensils. The Indians had advanced so far as to regulate the effect of the wind by a mat suspended over the hole in the roof and moved by a string. Such a lodge was in the first instance constructed in a day or two at most,

---

[1] *callous* Hardened (with no suggestion of having become unfeeling toward the sufferings of others).

[2] *Gookin* Irish-born Puritan settler Daniel Gookin (1612–87), who lived in Vermont and Massachusetts, and was known for his interest in and writings about Native American cultures.

and taken down and put up in a few hours; and every family owned one, or its apartment in one.

In the savage state[1] every family owns a shelter as good as the best, and sufficient for its coarser and simpler wants; but I think that I speak within bounds when I say that, though the birds of the air have their nests, and the foxes their holes,[2] and the savages their wigwams, in modern civilized society not more than one half the families own a shelter. In the large towns and cities, where civilization especially prevails, the number of those who own a shelter is a very small fraction of the whole. The rest pay an annual tax for this outside garment of all, become indispensable summer and winter, which would buy a village of Indian wigwams, but now helps to keep them poor as long as they live. I do not mean to insist here on the disadvantage of hiring[3] compared with owning, but it is evident that the savage owns his shelter because it costs so little, while the civilized man hires his commonly because he cannot afford to own it; nor can he, in the long run, any better afford to hire. But, answers one, by merely paying this tax the *poor* civilized man secures an abode which is a palace compared with the savage's. An annual rent of from twenty-five to a hundred dollars (these are the country rates) entitles him to the benefit of the improvements of centuries, spacious apartments, clean paint and paper, Rumford fireplace,[4] back plastering, Venetian blinds, copper pump, spring lock, a commodious cellar, and many other things. But how happens it that he who is said to enjoy these things is so commonly a poor civilized man, while the savage, who has them not, is rich as a savage? If it is asserted that civilization is a real advance in the condition of man—and I think that it is, though only the wise improve their advantages—it must be shown that it has produced better dwellings without making them more costly; and the cost of a thing is the amount of what I will call life which is required to be exchanged for it, immediately or in the long run. An average house in this neighborhood costs perhaps eight hundred dollars, and to lay up this sum will take from ten to fifteen years of the laborer's life, even if he is not encumbered with a family—estimating the pecuniary value of every man's labor at one dollar a day, for if some receive more, others receive less—so that he must have spent more than half his life commonly before *his* wigwam will be earned. If we suppose him to pay a rent instead, this is but a doubtful choice of evils. Would the savage have been wise to exchange his wigwam for a palace on these terms?

It may be guessed that I reduce almost the whole advantage of holding this superfluous property as a fund in store against the future, so far as the individual is concerned, mainly to the defraying of funeral expenses. But perhaps a man is not required to bury himself. Nevertheless this points to an important distinction between the civilized man and the savage; and, no doubt, they have designs on us for our benefit, in making the life of a civilized people an *institution*, in which the life of the individual is to a great extent absorbed, in order to preserve and perfect that of the race. But I wish to show at what a sacrifice this advantage is at present obtained, and to suggest that we may possibly so live as to secure all the advantage without suffering any of the disadvantage. What mean ye by saying that the poor ye have always with you, or that the fathers have eaten sour grapes, and the children's teeth are set on edge?

"As I live, saith the Lord God, ye shall not have occasion any more to use this proverb in Israel."

"Behold all souls are mine; as the soul of the father, so also the soul of the son is mine: the soul that sinneth, it shall die."[5]

When I consider my neighbors, the farmers of Concord, who are at least as well off as the other classes, I find that for the most part they have been toiling twenty, thirty, or forty years, that they may become the real owners of their farms, which commonly they have inherited with encumbrances, or else bought with hired money—and we may regard one third of that toil as the cost of their houses—but commonly they have not paid for them yet. It is true, the encumbrances

---

[1] *In the savage state* In a state of simplicity (with no suggestion of being prone to savagery); living according to nature, without any of the trappings of civilization.

[2] *the birds … their holes* See Matthew 8.20: "The foxes have holes, and the birds of the air have nests, but the Son of man hath not where to lay his head."

[3] *hiring* Renting.

[4] *Rumford fireplace* Fireplace designed to prevent smoke from being carried downward by drafts.

[5] *What mean ye … shall die* See Ezekiel 18.2–4.

sometimes outweigh the value of the farm, so that the farm itself becomes one great encumbrance, and still a man is found to inherit it, being well acquainted with it, as he says. On applying to the assessors, I am surprised to learn that they cannot at once name a dozen in the town who own their farms free and clear. If you would know the history of these homesteads, inquire at the bank where they are mortgaged. The man who has actually paid for his farm with labor on it is so rare that every neighbor can point to him. I doubt if there are three such men in Concord. What has been said of the merchants, that a very large majority, even ninety-seven in a hundred, are sure to fail, is equally true of the farmers. With regard to the merchants, however, one of them says pertinently that a great part of their failures are not genuine pecuniary failures, but merely failures to fulfil their engagements, because it is inconvenient; that is, it is the moral character that breaks down. But this puts an infinitely worse face on the matter, and suggests, beside, that probably not even the other three succeed in saving their souls, but are perchance bankrupt in a worse sense than they who fail honestly. Bankruptcy and repudiation are the springboards from which much of our civilization vaults and turns its somersets,[1] but the savage stands on the unelastic plank of famine. Yet the Middlesex Cattle Show goes off here with éclat[2] annually, as if all the joints of the agricultural machine were suent.[3]

The farmer is endeavoring to solve the problem of a livelihood by a formula more complicated than the problem itself. To get his shoestrings[4] he speculates in herds of cattle. With consummate skill he has set his trap with a hair spring to catch comfort and independence, and then, as he turned away, got his own leg into it. This is the reason he is poor; and for a similar reason we are all poor in respect to a thousand savage comforts, though surrounded by luxuries. As Chapman sings,

The false society of men—
            —for earthly greatness

All heavenly comforts rarefies to air.[5]

And when the farmer has got his house, he may not be the richer but the poorer for it, and it be the house that has got him. ... our houses are such unwieldy property that we are often imprisoned rather than housed in them; and the bad neighborhood to be avoided is our own scurvy selves. I know one or two families, at least, in this town, who, for nearly a generation, have been wishing to sell their houses in the outskirts and move into the village, but have not been able to accomplish it, and only death will set them free.

Granted that the *majority* are able at last either to own or hire the modern house with all its improvements. While civilization has been improving our houses, it has not equally improved the men who are to inhabit them. It has created palaces, but it was not so easy to create noblemen and kings. *And if the civilized man's pursuits are no worthier than the savage's, if he is employed the greater part of his life in obtaining gross necessaries and comforts merely, why should he have a better dwelling than the former?*

But how do the poor *minority* fare? Perhaps it will be found, that just in proportion as some have been placed in outward circumstances above the savage, others have been degraded below him. The luxury of one class is counterbalanced by the indigence of another. On the one side is the palace, on the other are the almshouse and "silent poor."[6] The myriads who built the pyramids to be the tombs of the Pharaohs were fed on garlic, and it may be were not decently buried themselves. The mason who finishes the cornice of the palace returns at night perchance to a hut not so good as a wigwam. It is a mistake to suppose that, in a country where the usual evidences of civilization exist, the condition of a very large body of the inhabitants may not be as degraded

---

1   *somersets* Somersaults.

2   *éclat* Dazzling effect.

3   *suent* Running smoothly.

4   *shoestrings* Generally made of leather in the 1800s.

5   *Chapman ... rarefies to air* I.e., Human society leads us, for the sake of pursuing greatness on earth, to treat heavenly comforts as insubstantial. Chapman (1559–1634) was an English poet and dramatist; the quotation is from his *The Tragedy of Caesar and Pompey* 5.2; in which the character Sacrifice argues in a long speech that humans pay too much attention to expensive ornament and, more generally, to building in the outward, physical world; he expresses his own intent to "build all inward" and commends those who turn "their back to all the world / And only look at heaven."

6   *silent poor* Those who neither complain of their poverty nor seek charity.

as that of savages. I refer to the degraded poor, not now to the degraded rich. To know this I should not need to look farther than to the shanties which everywhere border our railroads, that last improvement in civilization; where I see in my daily walks human beings living in sties, and all winter with an open door, for the sake of light, without any visible, often imaginable, wood pile, and the forms of both old and young are permanently contracted by the long habit of shrinking from cold and misery, and the development of all their limbs and faculties is checked. It certainly is fair to look at that class by whose labor the works which distinguish this generation are accomplished. Such too, to a greater or less extent, is the condition of the operatives of every denomination in England, which is the great workhouse of the world. Or I could refer you to Ireland,[1] which is marked as one of the white or enlightened spots on the map. Contrast the physical condition of the Irish with that of the North American Indian, or the South Sea Islander, or any other savage race before it was degraded by contact with the civilized man. Yet I have no doubt that that people's rulers are as wise as the average of civilized rulers. Their condition only proves what squalidness may consist with civilization. I hardly need refer now to the laborers in our Southern States who produce the staple exports of this country, and are themselves a staple production of the South.[2] But to confine myself to those who are said to be in *moderate* circumstances.

Most men appear never to have considered what a house is, and are actually though needlessly poor all their lives because they think that they must have such a one as their neighbors have. As if one were to wear any sort of coat which the tailor might cut out for him, or, gradually leaving off palmleaf hat or cap of woodchuck skin, complain of hard times because he could not afford to buy him a crown! It is possible to invent a house still more convenient and luxurious than we have, which yet all would admit that man could not afford to pay for. Shall we always study to obtain more of these things, and not sometimes to be content with less? Shall the respectable citizen thus gravely teach, by precept and example, the necessity of the young man's

providing a certain number of superfluous glow-shoes,[3] and umbrellas, and empty guest chambers for empty guests, before he dies? Why should not our furniture be as simple as the Arab's or the Indian's? …

It is the luxurious and dissipated who set the fashions which the herd so diligently follow. The traveller who stops at the best houses, so called, soon discovers this, for the publicans presume him to be a Sardanapalus,[4] and if he resigned himself to their tender mercies he would soon be completely emasculated. I think that in the railroad car we are inclined to spend more on luxury than on safety and convenience, and it threatens without attaining these to become no better than a modern drawing room, with its divans, and ottomans, and sun-shades, and a hundred other oriental things, which we are taking west with us, invented for the ladies of the harem and the effeminate natives of the Celestial Empire,[5] which Jonathan[6] should be ashamed to know the names of. I would rather sit on a pumpkin and have it all to myself than be crowded on a velvet cushion. I would rather ride on earth in an ox cart with a free circulation, than go to heaven in the fancy car of an excursion train and breathe a *malaria*[7] all the way.

The very simplicity and nakedness of man's life in the primitive ages imply this advantage at least, that they left him still but a sojourner in nature. When he was refreshed with food and sleep he contemplated his journey again. He dwelt, as it were, in a tent in this world, and was either threading the valleys, or crossing the plains, or climbing the mountain tops. But lo! men have become the tools of their tools. The man who independently plucked the fruits when he was hungry is become a farmer; and he who stood under a tree for shelter, a housekeeper. We now no longer camp as for a night, but have settled down on earth and forgotten heaven. We have adopted Christianity merely as an improved method of *agri*-culture.[8] We have built

1   *Ireland*   At the time of Thoreau's residence at Walden Pond, Ireland was going through the Great Famine, which resulted in the deaths of approximately one million people.

2   *the laborers … the South*   I.e., enslaved people.

3   *glow-shoes*   I.e., galoshes; rubber boots.

4   *a Sardanapalus*   I.e., as a king surrounded by his enemies, defeated; Sardanapalus was according to legend the last king of Assyria (c. seventh century BCE).

5   *Celestial Empire*   Term formerly used to refer to China.

6   *Jonathan*   Generic name for a stereotypical American man.

7   *a malaria*   I.e., tainted, diseased air.

8   *agri-culture*   Play on words emphasizing the Latin root agri, meaning the tilling of fields.

for this world a family mansion, and for the next a family tomb. The best works of art are the expression of man's struggle to free himself from this condition, but the effect of our art is merely to make this low state comfortable and that higher state to be forgotten. There is actually no place in this village for a work of *fine* art, if any had come down to us, to stand, for our lives, our houses and streets, furnish no proper pedestal for it. There is not a nail to hang a picture on, nor a shelf to receive the bust of a hero or a saint. When I consider how our houses are built and paid for, or not paid for, and their internal economy managed and sustained, I wonder that the floor does not give way under the visitor while he is admiring the gewgaws[1] upon the mantel-piece, and let him through into the cellar, to some solid and honest though earthy foundation. I cannot but perceive that this so called rich and refined life is a thing jumped at, and I do not get on in the enjoyment of the *fine* arts which adorn it, my attention being wholly occupied with the jump; for I remember that the greatest genuine leap, due to human muscles alone, on record, is that of certain wandering Arabs, who are said to have cleared twenty-five feet on level ground. Without factitious support, man is sure to come to earth again beyond that distance. The first question which I am tempted to put to the proprietor of such great impropriety is, Who bolsters you? Are you one of the ninety-seven who fail, or of the three who succeed? Answer me these questions, and then perhaps I may look at your baubles and find them ornamental. The cart before the horse is neither beautiful nor useful. Before we can adorn our houses with beautiful objects the walls must be stripped, and our lives must be stripped, and beautiful housekeeping and beautiful living be laid for a foundation: now, a taste for the beautiful is most cultivated out of doors, where there is no house and no housekeeper. ...

In this course which our ancestors took there was a show of prudence at least, as if their principle were to satisfy the more pressing wants first. But are the more pressing wants satisfied now? When I think of acquiring for myself one of our luxurious dwellings, I am deterred, for, so to speak, the country is not yet adapted to *human* culture, and we are still forced to cut our *spiritual* bread far thinner than our forefathers did

their wheaten. Not that all architectural ornament is to be neglected even in the rudest periods; but let our houses first be lined with beauty, where they come in contact with our lives, like the tenement of the shellfish, and not overlaid with it. But, alas! I have been inside one or two of them, and know what they are lined with.

Though we are not so degenerate but that we might possibly live in a cave or a wigwam or wear skins to-day, it certainly is better to accept the advantages, though so dearly bought, which the invention and industry of mankind offer. In such a neighborhood as this, boards and shingles, lime and bricks, are cheaper and more easily obtained than suitable caves, or whole logs, or bark in sufficient quantities, or even well-tempered clay or flat stones. I speak understandingly on this subject, for I have made myself acquainted with it both theoretically and practically. With a little more wit we might use these materials so as to become richer than the richest now are, and make our civilization a blessing. The civilized man is a more experienced and wiser savage. But to make haste to my own experiment.

Near the end of March, 1845, I borrowed an axe and went down to the woods by Walden Pond, nearest to where I intended to build my house, and began to cut down some tall, arrowy white pines, still in their youth, for timber. It is difficult to begin without borrowing, but perhaps it is the most generous course thus to permit your fellow-men to have an interest in your enterprise. The owner of the axe, as he released his hold on it, said that it was the apple of his eye; but I returned it sharper than I received it. It was a pleasant hillside where I worked, covered with pine woods, through which I looked out on the pond, and a small open field in the woods where pines and hickories were springing up. The ice in the pond was not yet dissolved, though there were some open spaces, and it was all dark-colored and saturated with water. There were some slight flurries of snow during the days that I worked there; but for the most part when I came out on to the railroad, on my way home, its yellow sand-heap stretched away gleaming in the hazy atmosphere, and the rails shone in the spring sun, and I heard the lark and pewee and other birds already come to commence another year with us. They were pleasant spring days, in which the

---

[1]   *gewgaws* Frivolous ornaments.

winter of man's discontent[1] was thawing as well as the earth, and the life that had lain torpid began to stretch itself. One day, when my axe had come off and I had cut a green hickory for a wedge, driving it with a stone, and had placed the whole to soak in a pond hole in order to swell the wood, I saw a striped snake run into the water, and he lay on the bottom, apparently without inconvenience, as long as I stayed there, or more than a quarter of an hour; perhaps because he had not yet fairly come out of the torpid state. It appeared to me that for a like reason men remain in their present low and primitive condition; but if they should feel the influence of the spring of springs arousing them, they would of necessity rise to a higher and more ethereal life. I had previously seen the snakes in frosty mornings in my path with portions of their bodies still numb and inflexible, waiting for the sun to thaw them. On the 1st of April it rained and melted the ice, and in the early part of the day, which was very foggy, I heard a stray goose groping about over the pond and cackling as if lost, or like the spirit of the fog.

So I went on for some days cutting and hewing timber, and also studs and rafters, all with my narrow axe, not having many communicable or scholar-like thoughts, singing to myself,

Men say they know many things;
But lo! they have taken wings—
The arts and sciences,
And a thousand appliances;

The wind that blows
Is all that anybody knows.[2]

I hewed the main timbers six inches square, most of the studs on two sides only, and the rafters and floor timbers on one side, leaving the rest of the bark on, so that they were just as straight and much stronger than sawed ones. Each stick was carefully mortised or tenoned[3] by its stump, for I had borrowed other tools by this time. My days in the woods were not very

---

[1]   *winter of man's discontent* See Shakespeare's *Richard III* 1.1.1: "Now is the winter of our discontent."

[2]   *Men say ... anybody knows* The poem is Thoreau's own.

[3]   *mortised or tenoned* Types of joint connecting two pieces of wood.

long ones; yet I usually carried my dinner of bread and butter, and read the newspaper in which it was wrapped, at noon, sitting amid the green pine boughs which I had cut off, and to my bread was imparted some of their fragrance, for my hands were covered with a thick coat of pitch. Before I had done I was more the friend than the foe of the pine tree, though I had cut down some of them, having become better acquainted with it. Sometimes a rambler in the wood was attracted by the sound of my axe, and we chatted pleasantly over the chips which I had made.

By the middle of April, for I made no haste in my work, but rather made the most of it, my house was framed and ready for the raising. I had already bought the shanty of James Collins, an Irishman who worked on the Fitchburg Railroad, for boards. James Collins' shanty was considered an uncommonly fine one. When I called to see it he was not at home. I walked about the outside, at first unobserved from within, the window was so deep and high. It was of small dimensions, with a peaked cottage roof, and not much else to be seen, the dirt being raised five feet all around as if it were a compost heap. The roof was the soundest part, though a good deal warped and made brittle by the sun. Door-sill there was none, but a perennial passage for the hens under the door board. Mrs. C. came to the door and asked me to view it from the inside. The hens were driven in by my approach. It was dark, and had a dirt floor for the most part, dank, clammy, and aguish, only here a board and there a board which would not bear removal. She lighted a lamp to show me the inside of the roof and the walls, and also that the board floor extended under the bed, warning me not to step into the cellar, a sort of dust hole two feet deep. In her own words, they were "good boards overhead, good boards all around, and a good window"—of two whole squares originally, only the cat had passed out that way lately. There was a stove, a bed, and a place to sit, an infant in the house where it was born, a silk parasol, gilt-framed looking-glass, and a patent new coffee mill nailed to an oak sapling, all told. The bargain was soon concluded, for James had in the meanwhile returned. I to pay four dollars and twenty-five cents tonight, he to vacate at five tomorrow morning, selling to nobody else meanwhile: I to take possession at six. It were well, he said, to be there early, and anticipate certain indistinct but wholly unjust claims on the score of ground rent and fuel. This he assured me was the only encumbrance. At six I passed him and his family on the road. One large bundle held their all,—bed, coffee-mill, looking-glass, hens—all but the cat, she took to the woods and became a wild cat, and, as I learned afterward, trod in a trap set for woodchucks, and so became a dead cat at last.

I took down this dwelling the same morning, drawing the nails, and removed it to the pond side by small cartloads, spreading the boards on the grass there to bleach and warp back again in the sun. One early thrush gave me a note or two as I drove along the woodland path. I was informed treacherously by a young Patrick[1] that neighbor Seeley, an Irishman, in the intervals of the carting, transferred the still tolerable, straight, and drivable nails, staples, and spikes to his pocket, and then stood when I came back to pass the time of day, and look freshly up, unconcerned, with spring thoughts, at the devastation; there being a dearth of work, as he said. He was there to represent spectatordom, and help make this seemingly insignificant event one with the removal of the gods of Troy.[2]

I dug my cellar in the side of a hill sloping to the south, where a woodchuck had formerly dug his burrow, down through sumach and blackberry roots, and the lowest stain of vegetation, six feet square by seven deep, to a fine sand where potatoes would not freeze in any winter. The sides were left shelving, and not stoned; but the sun having never shone on them, the sand still keeps its place. It was but two hours' work. I took particular pleasure in this breaking of ground, for in almost all latitudes men dig into the earth for an equable temperature. Under the most splendid house in the city is still to be found the cellar where they store their roots as of old, and long after the superstructure has disappeared posterity remark its dent in the earth. The house is still but a sort of porch at the entrance of a burrow.

At length, in the beginning of May, with the help of some of my acquaintances, rather to improve so good an occasion for neighborliness than from any necessity, I set up the frame of my house. No man was ever more honored in the character of his raisers[3] than I. They are destined, I trust, to assist at the raising of loftier structures one day. I began to occupy my house on the 4th of July, as soon as it was boarded and roofed, for the boards were carefully feather-edged and lapped, so that it was perfectly impervious to rain; but before boarding I laid the foundation of a chimney at one end, bringing two cartloads of stones up the hill from the pond in my arms. I built the chimney after my hoeing in the fall, before a fire became necessary for warmth, doing my cooking in the meanwhile out of doors on the ground, early in the morning: which mode I still think is in some respects more convenient and agreeable than the usual one. When it stormed before my bread was baked, I fixed a few boards over the fire, and sat under them to watch my loaf, and passed some pleasant hours in that way. In those days, when my hands were much employed, I read but little, but the least scraps of paper which lay on the ground, my holder, or tablecloth, afforded me as much entertainment, in fact answered the same purpose as the *Iliad*.[4]

It would be worth the while to build still more deliberately than I did, considering, for instance, what foundation a door, a window, a cellar, a garret, have in the nature of man, and perchance never raising any superstructure until we found a better reason for it than our temporal necessities even. There is some of the same fitness in a man's building his own house that there is in a bird's building its own nest. Who knows but if men constructed their dwellings with their own hands, and provided food for themselves and families simply and honestly enough, the poetic faculty would be universally developed, as birds universally sing when they are so engaged? But alas! we do like cowbirds and cuckoos, which lay their eggs in nests which other birds have built, and cheer no traveller with their chattering and unmusical notes. Shall we forever resign the pleasure of construction to the carpenter? What does architecture amount to in the experience of the mass of men?

---

1. *Patrick*   Generic name for a stereotypical Irishman.

2. *the removal ... of Troy*   Allusion to Virgil's *Aeneid*, in which Aeneas and his family escape Troy before its destruction, carrying with them their household gods.

3. *his raisers*   At least a half dozen others assisted Thoreau in raising his cabin—among them Ralph Waldo Emerson, Bronson Alcott, and William Ellery Channing.

4. *the Iliad*   Epic Greek poem about the Trojan War, generally attributed to the 8th century BCE poet Homer.

I never in all my walks came across a man engaged in so simple and natural an occupation as building his house. We belong to the community. It is not the tailor alone who is the ninth part of a man; it is as much the preacher, and the merchant, and the farmer. Where is this division of labor to end? and what object does it finally serve? No doubt another *may* also think for me; but it is not therefore desirable that he should do so to the exclusion of my thinking for myself.

True, there are architects so called in this country, and I have heard of one at least possessed with the idea of making architectural ornaments have a core of truth, a necessity, and hence a beauty, as if it were a revelation to him.[1] All very well perhaps from his point of view, but only a little better than the common dilettantism. A sentimental reformer in architecture, he began at the cornice, not at the foundation. It was only how to put a core of truth within the ornaments, that every sugar plum in fact might have an almond or caraway seed in it—though I hold that almonds are most wholesome without the sugar—and not how the inhabitant, the indweller, might build truly within and without, and let the ornaments take care of themselves. What reasonable man ever supposed that ornaments were something outward and in the skin merely—that the tortoise got his spotted shell, or the shell-fish its mother-o'-pearl tints, by such a contract as the inhabitants of Broadway their Trinity Church?[2] But a man has no more to do with the style of architecture of his house than a tortoise with that of its shell: nor need the soldier be so idle as to try to paint the precise *color* of his virtue on his standard. The enemy will find it out. He may turn pale when the trial comes. This man seemed to me to lean over the cornice, and timidly whisper his half truth to the rude occupants who really knew it better than he. What of architectural beauty I now see, I know has gradually grown from within outward, out of the necessities and character of the indweller, who is the only builder—out of some unconscious

truthfulness, and nobleness, without ever a thought for the appearance and whatever additional beauty of this kind is destined to be produced will be preceded by a like unconscious beauty of life. The most interesting dwellings in this country, as the painter knows, are the most unpretending, humble log huts and cottages of the poor commonly; it is the life of the inhabitants whose shells they are, and not any peculiarity in their surfaces merely, which makes them *picturesque*; and equally interesting will be the citizen's suburban box, when his life shall be as simple and as agreeable to the imagination, and there is as little straining after effect in the style of his dwelling. A great proportion of architectural ornaments are literally hollow, and a September gale would strip them off, like borrowed plumes, without injury to the substantials. They can do without *architecture* who have no olives nor wines in the cellar. ...

Before winter I built a chimney, and shingled the sides of my house, which were already impervious to rain, with imperfect and sappy shingles made of the first slice of the log, whose edges I was obliged to straighten with a plane.

I have thus a tight shingled and plastered house, ten feet wide by fifteen long, and eight-feet posts, with a garret and a closet, a large window on each side, two trap doors, one door at the end, and a brick fireplace opposite. The exact cost of my house, paying the usual price for such materials as I used, but not counting the work, all of which was done by myself, was as follows; and I give the details because very few are able to tell exactly what their houses cost, and fewer still, if any, the separate cost of the various materials which compose them:

Boards	$ 8.03 ½, mostly shanty boards.
Refuse shingles for roof and sides	4.00
Laths	1.25
Two second-hand windows with glass	2.43
One thousand old brick	4.00
Two casks of lime	2.40 That was high.
Hair	0.31 More than I needed.
Mantle-tree iron	0.15

---

[1]   *one at least ... revelation to him*   Horatio Greenough (1805–52), a sculptor and a friend of both Emerson and Thoreau, published several influential essays on architectural subjects; opposing unnecessary ornament, he defined beauty in architecture as "the promise of function."

[2]   *Trinity Church*   Heavily ornamented neo-Gothic style church, located at 79 Broadway in New York City. Completed in 1846, it remained the tallest building in the city until 1890.

Nails	3.90
Hinges and screws . . .	0.14
Latch	0.10
Chalk	0.01
Transportation	1.40 I carried a good
	part on my back.
In all	$28.12 ½

These are all the materials, excepting the timber, stones, and sand, which I claimed by squatter's right. I have also a small wood-shed adjoining, made chiefly of the stuff which was left after building the house.

I intend to build me a house which will surpass any on the main street in Concord in grandeur and luxury, as soon as it pleases me as much and will cost me no more than my present one.

I thus found that the student who wishes for a shelter can obtain one for a lifetime at an expense not greater than the rent which he now pays annually. If I seem to boast more than is becoming, my excuse is that I brag for humanity rather than for myself; and my shortcomings and inconsistencies do not affect the truth of my statement. Notwithstanding much cant and hypocrisy—chaff which I find it difficult to separate from my wheat, but for which I am as sorry as any man—I will breathe freely and stretch myself in this respect, it is such a relief to both the moral and physical system; and I am resolved that I will not through humility become the devil's attorney. I will endeavor to speak a good word for the truth. At Cambridge College[1] the mere rent of a student's room, which is only a little larger than my own, is thirty dollars each year, though the corporation had the advantage of building thirty-two side by side and under one roof, and the occupant suffers the inconvenience of many and noisy neighbors, and perhaps a residence in the fourth story. I cannot but think that if we had more true wisdom in these respects, not only less education would be needed, because, forsooth, more would already have been acquired, but the pecuniary expense of getting an education would in a great measure vanish. Those conveniences which the student requires at Cambridge or elsewhere cost him or somebody else ten times as great a sacrifice of life as they would with proper management on both sides.

Those things for which the most money is demanded are never the things which the student most wants. Tuition, for instance, is an important item in the term bill, while for the far more valuable education which he gets by associating with the most cultivated of his contemporaries no charge is made. The mode of founding a college is, commonly, to get up a subscription of dollars and cents, and then following blindly the principles of a division of labor to its extreme, a principle which should never be followed but with circumspection—to call in a contractor who makes this a subject of speculation, and he employs Irishmen or other operatives actually to lay the foundations, while the students that are to be are said to be fitting themselves for it; and for these oversights successive generations have to pay. I think that it would be *better than this*, for the students, or those who desire to be benefited by it, even to lay the foundation themselves. The student who secures his coveted leisure and retirement by systematically shirking any labor necessary to man obtains but an ignoble and unprofitable leisure, defrauding himself of the experience which alone can make leisure fruitful. "But," says one, "you do not mean that the students should go to work with their hands instead of their heads?" I do not mean that exactly, but I mean something which he might think a good deal like that; I mean that they should not *play* life, or *study* it merely, while the community supports them at this expensive game, but earnestly *live* it from beginning to end. How could youths better learn to live than by at once trying the experiment of living? Methinks this would exercise their minds as much as mathematics. If I wished a boy to know something about the arts and sciences, for instance, I would not pursue the common course, which is merely to send him into the neighborhood of some professor, where anything is professed and practised but the art of life—to survey the world through a telescope or a microscope, and never with his natural eye; to study chemistry, and not learn how his bread is made, or mechanics, and not learn how it is earned; to discover new satellites to Neptune, and not detect the motes in his eyes,[2] or to what vagabond he is a satellite himself; or to be devoured by the monsters that swarm

---

1   *Cambridge College* Harvard (located in Cambridge, Massachusetts).

2   *detect … his eyes* See Luke 6.41: "And why beholdest thou the mote that is in thy brother's eye, but perceivest not the beam that is in thine own eye?"

all around him, while contemplating the monsters in a drop of vinegar. Which would have advanced the most at the end of a month—the boy who had made his own jackknife from the ore which he had dug and smelted, reading as much as would be necessary for this—or the boy who had attended the lectures on metallurgy at the Institute in the meanwhile, and had received a Rodgers' penknife[1] from his father? Which would be most likely to cut his fingers? To my astonishment I was informed on leaving college that I had studied navigation! Why, if I had taken one turn down the harbor I should have known more about it. Even the *poor* student studies and is taught only *political* economy, while that economy of living which is synonymous with philosophy is not even sincerely professed in our colleges. The consequence is, that while he is reading Adam Smith, Ricardo, and Say,[2] he runs his father in debt irretrievably.

As with our colleges, so with a hundred "modern improvements"; there is an illusion about them; there is not always a positive advance. The devil goes on exacting compound interest to the last for his early share and numerous succeeding investments in them. Our inventions are wont to be pretty toys, which distract our attention from serious things. They are but improved means to an unimproved end, an end which it was already but too easy to arrive at; as railroads lead to Boston or New York. We are in great haste to construct a magnetic telegraph from Maine to Texas; but Maine and Texas, it may be, have nothing important to communicate. Either is in such a predicament as the man who was earnest to be introduced to a distinguished deaf woman, but when he was presented, and one end of her ear trumpet was put into his hand, had nothing to say. As if the main object were to talk fast and not to talk sensibly. We are eager to tunnel under the Atlantic and bring the old world some weeks nearer to the new; but perchance the first news that will leak through into the broad, flapping American ear will be that the Princess Adelaide[3] has the whooping cough. ...

One says to me, "I wonder that you do not lay up money; you love to travel; you might take the cars and go to Fitchburg today and see the country." But I am wiser than that. I have learned that the swiftest traveller is he that goes afoot. I say to my friend, Suppose we try who will get there first. The distance is thirty miles; the fare ninety cents. That is almost a day's wages. I remember when wages were sixty cents a day for laborers on this very road. Well, I start now on foot, and get there before night; I have travelled at that rate by the week together. You will in the meanwhile have earned your fare, and arrive there some time tomorrow, or possibly this evening, if you are lucky enough to get a job in season. Instead of going to Fitchburg, you will be working here the greater part of the day. And so, if the railroad reached round the world, I think that I should keep ahead of you; and as for seeing the country and getting experience of that kind, I should have to cut your acquaintance altogether.

Such is the universal law, which no man can ever outwit, and with regard to the railroad even we may say it is as broad as it is long. To make a railroad round the world available to all mankind is equivalent to grading the whole surface of the planet. Men have an indistinct notion that if they keep up this activity of joint stocks and spades long enough all will at length ride somewhere, in next to no time, and for nothing; but though a crowd rushes to the depot, and the conductor shouts "All aboard!" when the smoke is blown away and the vapor condensed, it will be perceived that a few are riding, but the rest are run over—and it will be called, and will be, "A melancholy accident." No doubt they can ride at last who shall have earned their fare, that is, if they survive so long, but they will probably have lost their elasticity and desire to travel by that time. This spending of the best part of one's life earning money in order to enjoy a questionable liberty during the least valuable part of it, reminds me of the Englishman who went to India to make a fortune first, in order that he might return to England and live the life of a poet. He should have gone up garret[4] at once. "What!" exclaim

---

[1] *Rodgers' penknife* High quality penknife manufactured in England.

[2] *Adam Smith* Scottish economist (1723–90); *Ricardo* English economist David Ricardo (1772–1823); *Say* French economist Jean-Baptiste Say (1767–1832).

[3] *Princess Adelaide* Adelaide of Saxe-Meiningen, queen consort of the United Kingdom and Hanover until the death of her husband, King William IV, in 1837.

[4] *gone up garret* I.e., become a poet. (The death of English poet Thomas Chatterton [1752–70] established in the public mind a long-lasting image of the poet as a dedicated soul who chooses to live in poverty in a tiny attic room.)

a million Irishmen[1] starting up from all the shanties in the land, "is not this railroad which we have built a good thing?" Yes, I answer, *comparatively* good, that is, you might have done worse; but I wish, as you are brothers of mine, that you could have spent your time better than digging in this dirt.

Before I finished my house, wishing to earn ten or twelve dollars by some honest and agreeable method, in order to meet my unusual expenses, I planted about two acres and a half of light and sandy soil near it chiefly with beans, but also a small part with potatoes, corn, peas, and turnips. The whole lot contains eleven acres, mostly growing up to pines and hickories, and was sold the preceding season for eight dollars and eight cents an acre. One farmer said that it was "good for nothing but to raise cheeping squirrels on." I put no manure whatever on this land, not being the owner, but merely a squatter, and not expecting to cultivate so much again, and I did not quite hoe it all once. I got out several cords of stumps in ploughing, which supplied me with fuel for a long time, and left small circles of virgin mould, easily distinguishable through the summer by the greater luxuriance of the beans there. The dead and for the most part unmerchantable wood behind my house, and the driftwood from the pond, have supplied the remainder of my fuel. I was obliged to hire a team and a man for the ploughing, though I held the plough myself. My farm outgoes for the first season were, for implements, seed, work, etc., $14.72½. The seed corn was given me. This never costs anything to speak of, unless you plant more than enough. I got twelve bushels of beans, and eighteen bushels of potatoes, beside some peas and sweet corn. The yellow corn and turnips were too late to come to anything. My whole income from the farm was

	$23.44
Deducting the outgoes . . .	14.72½
There are left	$8.71½,

beside produce consumed and on hand at the time this estimate was made of the value of $4.50—the amount on hand much more than balancing a little

grass which I did not raise. All things considered, that is, considering the importance of a man's soul and of today, notwithstanding the short time occupied by my experiment, nay, partly even because of its transient character, I believe that that was doing better than any farmer in Concord did that year.

The next year I did better still, for I spaded up all the land which I required, about a third of an acre, and I learned from the experience of both years, not being in the least awed by many celebrated works on husbandry, Arthur Young[2] among the rest, that if one would live simply and eat only the crop which he raised, and raise no more than he ate, and not exchange it for an insufficient quantity of more luxurious and expensive things, he would need to cultivate only a few rods[3] of ground, and that it would be cheaper to spade up that than to use oxen to plough it, and to select a fresh spot from time to time than to manure the old, and he could do all his necessary farm work as it were with his left hand at odd hours in the summer; and thus he would not be tied to an ox, or horse, or cow, or pig, as at present. I desire to speak impartially on this point, and as one not interested in the success or failure of the present economical and social arrangements. I was more independent than any farmer in Concord, for I was not anchored to a house or farm, but could follow the bent of my genius, which is a very crooked one, every moment. Beside being better off than they already, if my house had been burned or my crops had failed, I should have been nearly as well off as before.

I am wont to think that men are not so much the keepers of herds as herds are the keepers of men, the former are so much the freer. Men and oxen exchange work; but if we consider necessary work only, the oxen will be seen to have greatly the advantage, their farm is so much the larger. Man does some of his part of the exchange work in his six weeks of haying, and it is no boy's play. Certainly no nation that lived simply in all respects, that is, no nation of philosophers, would commit so great a blunder as to use the labor of animals. True, there never was and is not likely soon to be a nation of philosophers, nor am I certain it is desirable that there should be. However, *I* should never have broken a horse or bull and taken him to board for any

---

[1]   *a million Irishmen* A substantial portion of laborers on the railroads of the nineteenth century were immigrants from Ireland.

[2]   *Arthur Young* English writer on agriculture (1741–1820).

[3]   *rods* Units of measurement equivalent to about 5.5 yards.

work he might do for me, for fear I should become a horse-man or a herds-man merely; and if society seems to be the gainer by so doing, are we certain that what is one man's gain is not another's loss, and that the stable-boy has equal cause with his master to be satisfied? Granted that some public works would not have been constructed without this aid, and let man share the glory of such with the ox and horse; does it follow that he could not have accomplished works yet more worthy of himself in that case? When men begin to do, not merely unnecessary or artistic, but luxurious and idle work, with their assistance, it is inevitable that a few do all the exchange work with the oxen, or, in other words, become the slaves of the strongest. Man thus not only works for the animal within him, but, for a symbol of this, he works for the animal without him. Though we have many substantial houses of brick or stone, the prosperity of the farmer is still measured by the degree to which the barn overshadows the house. This town is said to have the largest houses for oxen, cows, and horses hereabouts, and it is not behindhand in its public buildings; but there are very few halls for free worship or free speech in this county. It should not be by their architecture, but why not even by their power of abstract thought, that nations should seek to commemorate themselves? How much more admirable the Bhagvat-Geeta[1] than all the ruins of the East! Towers and temples are the luxury of princes. ... The religion and civilization which are barbaric and heathenish build splendid temples; but what you might call Christianity does not. Most of the stone a nation hammers goes toward its tomb only. It buries itself alive. As for the Pyramids, there is nothing to wonder at in them so much as the fact that so many men could be found degraded enough to spend their lives constructing a tomb for some ambitious booby, whom it would have been wiser and manlier to have drowned in the Nile, and then given his body to the dogs. I might possibly invent some excuse for them and him, but I have no time for it. As for the religion and love of art of the builders, it is much the same all the world over, whether the building be an Egyptian temple or the United States Bank. It costs more than it comes to. The mainspring is vanity, assisted by the love of garlic and bread and butter. ... But to proceed with my statistics.

By surveying, carpentry, and day-labor of various other kinds in the village in the meanwhile, for I have as many trades as fingers, I had earned $13.34. The expense of food for eight months, namely, from July 4th to March 1st, the time when these estimates were made, though I lived there more than two years—not counting potatoes, a little green corn, and some peas, which I had raised, nor considering the value of what was on hand at the last date—was

Rice	$ 1.73½	
Molasses	1.73	Cheapest form of the saccharine.
Rye meal . . .	1.04¾	
Indian meal . .	0.99¾}	Cheaper than rye.
Pork	0.22	
Flour	0.88 {	Costs more than Indian meal, both money and trouble.
Sugar	0.80	
Lard	0.65	
Apples	0.25	
Dried apple . .	0.22	
Sweet potatoes .	0.10	
One pumpkin .	0.06	
One watermelon .	0.02	
Salt	0.03	

All experiments which failed.

Yes, I did eat $8.74, all told; but I should not thus unblushingly publish my guilt, if I did not know that most of my readers were equally guilty with myself, and that their deeds would look no better in print. The next year I sometimes caught a mess of fish for my dinner, and once I went so far as to slaughter a woodchuck which ravaged my bean-field—effect his transmigration, as a Tartar would say[2]—and devour him, partly for experiment's sake; but though it afforded me a momentary enjoyment, notwithstanding a musky flavor, I saw that the longest use would not make that

---

[1] *Bhagvat-Geeta* The *Bhagavad Gita*, important work of Hindu scripture.

[2] *effect ... would say* "Transmigration" refers to the transmigration of the soul into a new body after death, a principle important to the belief systems of many cultures; the Tatars are a Turkic ethnic group of eastern Europe and northwestern Asia.

a good practice, however it might seem to have your woodchucks ready dressed by the village butcher.

Clothing and some incidental expenses within the same dates, though little can be inferred from this item, amounted to

$8.40 ¾

Oil and some household utensils   2.00

So that all the pecuniary outgoes, excepting for washing and mending,[1] which for the most part were done out of the house, and their bills have not yet been received—and these are all and more than all the ways by which money necessarily goes out in this part of the world—were

House	$28.12 ½
Farm one year	14.72 ½
Food eight months	8.74
Clothing, etc., eight months .	8.40 ¾
Oil, etc., eight months . . .	2.00
In all, ...	$61.99 ¾

I address myself now to those of my readers who have a living to get. And to meet this I have for farm produce sold

$23.44

Earned by day-labor . . .   13.34

In all $36.78,

which subtracted from the sum of the outgoes leaves a balance of $25.21¾ on the one side—this being very nearly the means with which I started, and the measure of expenses to be incurred—and on the other, beside the leisure and independence and health thus secured, a comfortable house for me as long as I choose to occupy it.

These statistics, however accidental and therefore uninstructive they may appear, as they have a certain completeness, have a certain value also. Nothing was given me of which I have not rendered some account. It appears from the above estimate, that my food alone cost me in money about twenty-seven cents a week.[2] It was, for nearly two years after this, rye and Indian meal without yeast, potatoes, rice, a very little salt pork, molasses, and salt, and my drink water. It was fit that I should live on rice, mainly, who loved so well the philosophy of India. To meet the objections of some inveterate cavillers,[3] I may as well state, that if I dined out occasionally, as I always had done, and I trust shall have opportunities to do again, it was frequently to the detriment of my domestic arrangements. But the dining out, being, as I have stated, a constant element, does not in the least affect a comparative statement like this.

I learned from my two years' experience that it would cost incredibly little trouble to obtain one's necessary food, even in this latitude; that a man may use as simple a diet as the animals, and yet retain health and strength. I have made a satisfactory dinner, satisfactory on several accounts, simply off a dish of purslane[4] (*Portulaca oleracea*) which I gathered in my cornfield, boiled and salted. I give the Latin on account of the savoriness of the trivial name. And pray what more can a reasonable man desire, in peaceful times, in ordinary noons, than a sufficient number of ears of green sweet-corn boiled, with the addition of salt? Even the little variety which I used was a yielding to the demands of appetite, and not of health. Yet men have come to such a pass that they frequently starve, not for want of necessaries, but for want of luxuries; and I know a good woman who thinks that her son lost his life because he took to drinking water only.

The reader will perceive that I am treating the subject rather from an economic than a dietetic point of view, and he will not venture to put my abstemiousness to the test unless he has a well-stocked larder.

Bread I at first made of pure Indian meal and salt, genuine hoe-cakes, which I baked before my fire out of doors on a shingle or the end of a stick of timber sawed off in building my house; but it was wont to get[5] smoked and to have a piny flavor. I tried flour also; but

---

[1] *excepting for washing and mending* These tasks were done by Thoreau's mother and sisters.

[2] *twenty-seven cents a week* Though exact comparisons are impossible, the equivalent buying power today would probably require something close to $10.

[3] *cavillers* People raising frivolous objections.

[4] *purslane* Leafy green vegetable.

[5] *was wont to get* Had a tendency to become.

have at last found a mixture of rye and Indian meal most convenient and agreeable. In cold weather it was no little amusement to bake several small loaves of this in succession, tending and turning them as carefully as an Egyptian his hatching eggs.[1] They were a real cereal fruit which I ripened, and they had to my senses a fragrance like that of other noble fruits, which I kept in as long as possible by wrapping them in cloths. I made a study of the ancient and indispensable art of bread-making, consulting such authorities as offered, going back to the primitive days and first invention of the unleavened kind, when from the wildness of nuts and meats men first reached the mildness and refinement of this diet, and travelling gradually down in my studies through that accidental souring of the dough which, it is supposed, taught the leavening process, and through the various fermentations thereafter, till I came to "good, sweet, wholesome bread," the staff of life. Leaven, which some deem the soul of bread, the *spiritus* which fills its cellular tissue, which is religiously preserved like the vestal fire[2]—some precious bottle-full, I suppose, first brought over in the Mayflower, did the business for America, and its influence is still rising, swelling, spreading, in cerealian[3] billows over the land—this seed I regularly and faithfully procured from the village, till at length one morning I forgot the rules, and scalded my yeast; by which accident I discovered that even this was not indispensable—for my discoveries were not by the synthetic but analytic process—and I have gladly omitted it since, though most housewives earnestly assured me that safe and wholesome bread without yeast might not be, and elderly people prophesied a speedy decay of the vital forces. Yet I find it not to be an essential ingredient, and after going without it for a year am still in the land of the living; and I am glad to escape the trivialness of carrying a bottle-full in my pocket, which would sometimes pop and discharge its contents[4] to my

discomfiture. It is simpler and more respectable to omit it. Man is an animal who more than any other can adapt himself to all climates and circumstances. …

Every New Englander might easily raise all his own breadstuffs in this land of rye and Indian corn, and not depend on distant and fluctuating markets for them. Yet so far are we from simplicity and independence that, in Concord, fresh and sweet meal is rarely sold in the shops, and hominy and corn in a still coarser form are hardly used by any. For the most part the farmer gives to his cattle and hogs the grain of his own producing, and buys flour, which is at least no more wholesome, at a greater cost, at the store. I saw that I could easily raise my bushel or two of rye and Indian corn, for the former will grow on the poorest land, and the latter does not require the best, and grind them in a hand-mill, and so do without rice and pork; and if I must have some concentrated sweet, I found by experiment that I could make a very good molasses either of pumpkins or beets, and I knew that I needed only to set out a few maples to obtain it more easily still, and while these were growing I could use various substitutes beside those which I have named. "For," as the Forefathers sang,

> we can make liquor to sweeten our lips
> Of pumpkins and parsnips and walnut-tree chips.[5]

Finally, as for salt, that grossest[6] of groceries, to obtain this might be a fit occasion for a visit to the seashore, or, if I did without it altogether, I should probably drink the less water. I do not learn that the Indians ever troubled themselves to go after it.

Thus I could avoid all trade and barter, so far as my food was concerned, and having a shelter already, it would only remain to get clothing and fuel. The pantaloons which I now wear were woven in a farmer's family—thank Heaven there is so much virtue still in man; for I think the fall from the farmer to the operative as great and memorable as that from the man to the farmer—and in a new country, fuel is an encumbrance.

---

[1] *an Egyptian his hatching eggs*   Reference to the artificial incubation of eggs said to have been practiced by Ancient Egyptians.

[2] *vestal fire*   Fire kept perpetually burning in the Temple of Vesta, goddess of the hearth, in ancient Rome.

[3] *cerealian*   Word coined by Thoreau, referencing both cereals (or grains), and the Roman goddess of agriculture.

[4] *bottle-full … its contents*   Baker's yeast during this period came in a liquid form, usually obtained from local brewers as a by-product of the beer brewing process.

[5] *we can … chips*   Lines from a folk song known as the "Forefathers' Song."

[6] *grossest*   Most basic or common grocery item; possibly also with the meaning "most commonly purchased in bulk" (or "by the gross").

As for a habitat, if I were not permitted still to squat, I might purchase one acre at the same price for which the land I cultivated was sold—namely, eight dollars and eight cents. But as it was, I considered that I enhanced the value of the land by squatting on it.

There is a certain class of unbelievers who sometimes ask me such questions as, if I think that I can live on vegetable food alone; and to strike at the root of the matter at once—for the root is faith—I am accustomed to answer such, that I can live on board nails. If they cannot understand that, they cannot understand much that I have to say. For my part, I am glad to hear of experiments of this kind being tried; as that a young man tried for a fortnight to live on hard, raw corn on the ear, using his teeth for all mortar. The squirrel tribe tried the same and succeeded. The human race is interested in these experiments, though a few old women who are incapacitated for them, or who own their thirds in mills, may be alarmed.

My furniture—part of which I made myself, and the rest cost me nothing of which I have not rendered an account—consisted of a bed, a table, a desk, three chairs, a looking-glass three inches in diameter, a pair of tongs and andirons, a kettle, a skillet, and a frying-pan, a dipper, a wash-bowl, two knives and forks, three plates, one cup, one spoon, a jug for oil, a jug for molasses, and a japanned[1] lamp. None is so poor that he need sit on a pumpkin. That is shiftlessness. There is a plenty of such chairs as I like best in the village garrets to be had for taking them away. Furniture! Thank God, I can sit and I can stand without the aid of a furniture warehouse. What man but a philosopher would not be ashamed to see his furniture packed in a cart and going up country exposed to the light of heaven and the eyes of men, a beggarly account of empty boxes?[2] That is Spaulding's furniture.[3] I could never tell from inspecting such a load whether it belonged to a so called rich man or a poor one; the owner always

seemed poverty-stricken. Indeed, the more you have of such things the poorer you are. Each load looks as if it contained the contents of a dozen shanties; and if one shanty is poor, this is a dozen times as poor. ... I cannot but feel compassion when I hear some trig,[4] compact-looking man, seemingly free, all girded and ready, speak of his "furniture," as whether it is insured or not. "But what shall I do with my furniture?" My gay[5] butterfly is entangled in a spider's web then. Even those who seem for a long while not to have any, if you inquire more narrowly you will find have some stored in somebody's barn. I look upon England today as an old gentleman who is travelling with a great deal of baggage, trumpery which has accumulated from long housekeeping, which he has not the courage to burn; great trunk, little trunk, bandbox[6] and bundle. Throw away the first three at least. It would surpass the powers of a well man nowadays to take up his bed and walk, and I should certainly advise a sick one to lay down his bed and run. When I have met an immigrant tottering under a bundle which contained his all—looking like an enormous wen[7] which had grown out of the nape of his neck—I have pitied him, not because that was his all, but because he had all that to carry. If I have got to drag my trap, I will take care that it be a light one and do not nip me in a vital part. But perchance it would be wisest never to put one's paw into it.

I would observe, by the way, that it costs me nothing for curtains, for I have no gazers to shut out but the sun and moon, and I am willing that they should look in. The moon will not sour milk nor taint meat of mine, nor will the sun injure my furniture or fade my carpet, and if he is sometimes too warm a friend, I find it still better economy to retreat behind some curtain which nature has provided, than to add a single item to the details of housekeeping. A lady once offered me a mat, but as I had no room to spare within the house, nor time to spare within or without to shake it, I declined it, preferring to wipe my feet on the sod before my door. It is best to avoid the beginnings of evil. ...

The customs of some savage nations might, perchance, be profitably imitated by us, for they at least

---

1   *japanned* Decorated and finished in lacquer (in Japanese style).

2   *beggarly account of empty boxes* See Shakespeare's *Romeo and Juliet* 5.1.48.

3   *Spaulding's furniture* Commercially-fabricated furniture (perhaps referencing Elbridge G. Spaulding, later to be credited with the invention of the greenback. Spaulding's Exchange in Buffalo, founded in 1845, was an emporium housing numerous retail outlets and offering a wide variety of commercial goods for sale).

4   *trig* Secure, steady.

5   *gay* Brightly colored.

6   *bandbox* Small box for storing hats and millinery accessories.

7   *wen* Protuberance.

go through the semblance of casting their slough annually; they have the idea of the thing, whether they have the reality or not. Would it not be well if we were to celebrate such a "busk," or "feast of first fruits," as Bartram[1] describes to have been the custom of the Mucclasse Indians? "When a town celebrates the busk," says he, "having previously provided themselves with new clothes, new pots, pans, and other household utensils and furniture, they collect all their worn out clothes and other despicable things, sweep and cleanse their houses, squares, and the whole town of their filth, which with all the remaining grain and other old provisions they cast together into one common heap, and consume it with fire. After having taken medicine, and fasted for three days, all the fire in the town is extinguished. During this fast they abstain from the gratification of every appetite and passion whatever. A general amnesty is proclaimed; all malefactors may return to their town."

"On the fourth morning, the high priest, by rubbing dry wood together, produces new fire in the public square, from whence every habitation in the town is supplied with the new and pure flame."

They then feast on the new corn and fruits, and dance and sing for three days, "and the four following days they receive visits and rejoice with their friends from neighboring towns who have in like manner purified and prepared themselves."

The Mexicans also practised a similar purification at the end of every fifty-two years, in the belief that it was time for the world to come to an end.

I have scarcely heard of a truer sacrament—that is, as the dictionary defines it, "outward and visible sign of an inward and spiritual grace"—than this, and I have no doubt that they were originally inspired directly from Heaven to do thus, though they have no biblical record of the revelation.

For more than five years I maintained myself thus solely by the labor of my hands, and I found, that by working about six weeks in a year, I could meet all the expenses of living. The whole of my winters, as well as most of my summers, I had free and clear for study. I have thoroughly tried school-keeping, and found that

my expenses were in proportion, or rather out of proportion, to my income, for I was obliged to dress and train, not to say think and believe, accordingly, and I lost my time into the bargain. As I did not teach for the good of my fellow-men, but simply for a livelihood, this was a failure. I have tried trade; but I found that it would take ten years to get under way in that, and that then I should probably be on my way to the devil. I was actually afraid that I might by that time be doing what is called a good business. When formerly I was looking about to see what I could do for a living, some sad experience in conforming to the wishes of friends being fresh in my mind to tax my ingenuity, I thought often and seriously of picking huckleberries; that surely I could do, and its small profits might suffice—for my greatest skill has been to want but little—so little capital it required, so little distraction from my wonted moods, I foolishly thought. While my acquaintances went unhesitatingly into trade or the professions, I contemplated this occupation as most like theirs; ranging the hills all summer to pick the berries which came in my way, and thereafter carelessly dispose of them; so, to keep the flocks of Admetus.[2] I also dreamed that I might gather the wild herbs, or carry evergreens to such villagers as loved to be reminded of the woods, even to the city, by hay-cart loads. But I have since learned that trade curses everything it handles; and though you trade in messages from heaven, the whole curse of trade attaches to the business.

As I preferred some things to others, and especially valued my freedom, as I could fare hard and yet succeed well, I did not wish to spend my time in earning rich carpets or other fine furniture, or delicate cookery, or a house in the Grecian or the Gothic style just yet. … For myself I found that the occupation of a day-laborer was the most independent of any, especially as it required only thirty or forty days in a year to support one. The laborer's day ends with the going down of the sun, and he is then free to devote himself to his chosen pursuit, independent of his labor; but his employer, who speculates[3] from month to month, has no respite from one end of the year to the other.

---

[1] *Bartram* William Bartram, American botanist and ethnographer, author of *Travels through North and South Carolina* (1791).

[2] *keep the flocks of Admetus* King of Pherae in Greek mythology, whose flocks the god Apollo was forced to tend.

[3] *speculates* Takes business and investment risks.

In short, I am convinced, both by faith and experience, that to maintain one's self on this earth is not a hardship but a pastime, if we will live simply and wisely; as the pursuits of the simpler nations are still the sports of the more artificial. It is not necessary that a man should earn his living by the sweat of his brow, unless he sweats easier than I do.

One young man of my acquaintance, who has inherited some acres, told me that he thought he should live as I did, *if he had the means*. I would not have anyone adopt *my* mode of living on any account; for, beside that before he has fairly learned it I may have found out another for myself, I desire that there may be as many different persons in the world as possible; but I would have each one be very careful to find out and pursue *his own* way, and not his father's or his mother's or his neighbor's instead. The youth may build or plant or sail, only let him not be hindered from doing that which he tells me he would like to do. It is by a mathematical point only that we are wise, as the sailor or the fugitive slave keeps the polestar[1] in his eye; but that is sufficient guidance for all our life. We may not arrive at our port within a calculable period, but we would preserve the true course.

Undoubtedly, in this case, what is true for one is truer still for a thousand, as a large house is not proportionally more expensive than a small one, since one roof may cover, one cellar underlie, and one wall separate several apartments. But for my part, I preferred the solitary dwelling. Moreover, it will commonly be cheaper to build the whole yourself than to convince another of the advantage of the common wall; and when you have done this, the common partition, to be much cheaper, must be a thin one, and that other may prove a bad neighbor, and also not keep his side in repair. The only coöperation which is commonly possible is exceedingly partial and superficial; and what little true coöperation there is, is as if it were not, being a harmony inaudible to men. If a man has faith, he will coöperate with equal faith everywhere; if he has not faith, he will continue to live like the rest of the world, whatever company he is joined to. To coöperate, in the highest as well as the lowest sense, means *to get our living together*. I heard it proposed lately that two young men should travel together over the world,

the one without money, earning his means as he went, before the mast and behind the plow, the other carrying a bill of exchange in his pocket. It was easy to see that they could not long be companions or coöperate, since one would not *operate* at all. They would part at the first interesting crisis in their adventures. Above all, as I have implied, the man who goes alone can start today; but he who travels with another must wait till that other is ready, and it may be a long time before they get off.

But all this is very selfish, I have heard some of my townsmen say. I confess that I have hitherto indulged very little in philanthropic enterprises. I have made some sacrifices to a sense of duty, and among others have sacrificed this pleasure also. There are those who have used all their arts to persuade me to undertake the support of some poor family in the town; and if I had nothing to do—for the devil finds employment for the idle—I might try my hand at some such pastime as that. However, when I have thought to indulge myself in this respect, and lay their Heaven under an obligation by maintaining certain poor persons in all respects as comfortably as I maintain myself, and have even ventured so far as to make them the offer, they have one and all unhesitatingly preferred to remain poor. While my townsmen and women are devoted in so many ways to the good of their fellows, I trust that one at least may be spared to other and less humane pursuits. You must have a genius for charity as well as for anything else. As for Doing-good, that is one of the professions which are full. Moreover, I have tried it fairly, and, strange as it may seem, am satisfied that it does not agree with my constitution. Probably I should not consciously and deliberately forsake my particular calling to do the good which society demands of me, to save the universe from annihilation; and I believe that a like but infinitely greater steadfastness elsewhere is all that now preserves it. But I would not stand between any man and his genius; and to him who does this work, which I decline, with his whole heart and soul and life, I would say, Persevere, even if the world call it doing evil, as it is most likely they will. …

There is no odor so bad as that which arises from goodness tainted. It is human, it is divine, carrion. If I knew for a certainty that a man was coming to my house with the conscious design of doing me good, I

---

1   *polestar* I.e., the North Star.

should run for my life, as from that dry and parching wind of the African deserts called the simoom, which fills the mouth and nose and ears and eyes with dust till you are suffocated, for fear that I should get some of his good done to me—some of its virus mingled with my blood. No—in this case I would rather suffer evil the natural way. A man is not a good *man* to me because he will feed me if I should be starving, or warm me if I should be freezing, or pull me out of a ditch if I should ever fall into one. I can find you a Newfoundland dog that will do as much. Philanthropy is not love for one's fellow-man in the broadest sense. Howard[1] was no doubt an exceedingly kind and worthy man in his way, and has his reward; but, comparatively speaking, what are a hundred Howards to *us*, if their philanthropy do not help *us* in our best estate, when we are most worthy to be helped? I never heard of a philanthropic meeting in which it was sincerely proposed to do any good to me, or the like of me. …

Be sure that you give the poor the aid they most need, though it be your example which leaves them far behind. If you give money, spend yourself with it, and do not merely abandon it to them. We make curious mistakes sometimes. Often the poor man is not so cold and hungry as he is dirty and ragged and gross. It is partly his taste, and not merely his misfortune. If you give him money, he will perhaps buy more rags with it. I was wont to pity the clumsy Irish laborers who cut ice on the pond, in such mean and ragged clothes, while I shivered in my more tidy and somewhat more fashionable garments, till, one bitter cold day, one who had slipped into the water came to my house to warm him, and I saw him strip off three pairs of pants and two pairs of stockings ere he got down to the skin, though they were dirty and ragged enough, it is true, and that he could afford to refuse the *extra*[2] garments which I offered him, he had so many *intra*[3] ones. This ducking[4] was the very thing he needed. Then I began to pity myself, and I saw that it would be a greater charity to bestow on me a flannel shirt than a whole slop-shop on him. There are a thousand hacking at the branches of evil to one who is striking at the root, and

---

[1] *Howard* John Howard, English prison reformer (1726–90).

[2] *extra* Latin: outer.

[3] *intra* Latin: inner.

[4] *ducking* Submersion in water.

it may be that he who bestows the largest amount of time and money on the needy is doing the most by his mode of life to produce that misery which he strives in vain to relieve. It is the pious slave-breeder devoting the proceeds of every tenth slave to buy a Sunday's liberty for the rest. Some show their kindness to the poor by employing them in their kitchens. Would they not be kinder if they employed themselves there? You boast of spending a tenth part of your income in charity; maybe you should spend the nine tenths so, and done with it. Society recovers only a tenth part of the property then. Is this owing to the generosity of him in whose possession it is found, or to the remissness of the officers of justice?

Philanthropy is almost the only virtue which is sufficiently appreciated by mankind. Nay, it is greatly overrated[.] …

I would not subtract anything from the praise that is due to philanthropy, but merely demand justice for all who by their lives and works are a blessing to mankind. I do not value chiefly a man's uprightness and benevolence, which are, as it were, his stem and leaves. Those plants of whose greenness withered we make herb tea for the sick, serve but a humble use, and are most employed by quacks. I want the flower and fruit of a man; that some fragrance be wafted over from him to me, and some ripeness flavor our intercourse. His goodness must not be a partial and transitory act, but a constant superfluity, which costs him nothing and of which he is unconscious. This is a charity that hides a multitude of sins. The philanthropist too often surrounds mankind with the remembrance of his own cast-off griefs as an atmosphere, and calls it sympathy. We should impart our courage, and not our despair, our health and ease, and not our disease, and take care that this does not spread by contagion. …

I believe that what so saddens the reformer is not his sympathy with his fellows in distress, but, though he be the holiest son of God, is his private ail. Let this be righted, let the spring come to him, the morning rise over his couch, and he will forsake his generous companions without apology. My excuse for not lecturing against the use of tobacco is, that I never chewed it; that is a penalty which reformed tobacco-chewers have to pay; though there are things enough I have chewed, which I could lecture against. If you should ever be betrayed into any of these philanthropies, do not let your left hand know what your right hand does,[1] for it is not worth knowing. Rescue the drowning and tie your shoe-strings. Take your time, and set about some free labor.

Our manners have been corrupted by communication with the saints.[2] Our hymn-books resound with a melodious cursing of God and enduring him forever. One would say that even the prophets and redeemers had rather consoled the fears than confirmed the hopes of man. There is nowhere recorded a simple and irrepressible satisfaction with the gift of life, any memorable praise of God. All health and success does me good, however far off and withdrawn it may appear; all disease and failure helps to make me sad and does me evil, however much sympathy it may have with me or I with it. If, then, we would indeed restore mankind by truly Indian, botanic, magnetic,[3] or natural means, let us first be as simple and well as Nature ourselves, dispel the clouds which hang over our own brows, and take up a little life into our pores. Do not stay to be an overseer of the poor, but endeavor to become one of the worthies of the world. ...

CHAPTER 2
WHERE I LIVED, AND WHAT I LIVED FOR

At a certain season of our life we are accustomed to consider every spot as the possible site of a house. I have thus surveyed the country on every side within a dozen miles of where I live. In imagination I have bought all the farms in succession, for all were to be bought, and I knew their price. I walked over each farmer's premises, tasted his wild apples, discoursed on husbandry[4] with him, took his farm at his price, at any price, mortgaging it to him in my mind; even put a higher price on it, took everything but a deed of it—took his word for his deed, for I dearly love to talk—cultivated it, and him too to some extent, I trust, and withdrew when I had enjoyed it long enough, leaving him to carry it on. This experience entitled me to be regarded as a sort of real-estate broker by my friends. Wherever I sat, there I might live, and the landscape radiated from me accordingly. What is a house but a *sedes*, a seat? Better if a country seat. I discovered many a site for a house not likely to be soon improved, which some might have thought too far from the village, but to my eyes the village was too far from it. Well, there I might live, I said; and there I did live, for an hour, a summer and a winter life; saw how I could let the years run off, buffet the winter through, and see the spring come in. The future inhabitants of this region, wherever they may place their houses, may be sure that they have been anticipated. An afternoon sufficed to lay out the land into orchard, wood-lot, and pasture, and to decide what fine oaks or pines should be left to stand before the door, and whence each blasted tree could be seen to the best advantage; and then I let it lie, fallow, perchance, for a man is rich in proportion to the number of things which he can afford to let alone.

My imagination carried me so far that I even had the refusal of several farms—the refusal was all I wanted—but I never got my fingers burned by actual possession. The nearest that I came to actual possession was when I bought the Hollowell place, and had begun to sort my seeds, and collected materials with which to make a wheelbarrow to carry it on or off with; but before the owner gave me a deed of it, his wife—every man has such a wife—changed her mind and wished to keep it, and he offered me ten dollars to release him. Now, to speak the truth, I had but ten cents in the world, and it surpassed my arithmetic to tell, if I was that man who had ten cents, or who had a farm, or ten dollars, or all together. However, I let him keep the ten dollars and the farm too, for I had carried it far enough; or rather, to be generous, I sold him the farm for just what I gave for it, and, as he was not a rich man, made him a present of ten dollars, and still had my ten cents, and seeds, and materials for a wheelbarrow left. I found thus that I had been a rich man without any damage to my poverty. But I retained the landscape, and I have since annually carried off what it yielded without a wheelbarrow. With respect to landscapes,

---

[1] *left hand ... right hand does* See Matthew 6.3–4: "But when thou doest alms, let not thy left hand know what thy right hand doeth: That thine alms may be in secret: and thy Father which seeth in secret himself shall reward thee openly."

[2] *Our manners ... the saints* See 1 Corinthians 15.33: "Be not deceived: evil communications corrupt good manners."

[3] *magnetic* I.e., related to animal magnetism, an invisible bodily force believed to exist in the bodies of all living things and to be able to facilitate what was later known as hypnotism.

[4] *husbandry* Agriculture.

I am monarch of all I *survey*,
My right there is none to dispute.[1]

I have frequently seen a poet withdraw, having enjoyed the most valuable part of a farm, while the crusty farmer supposed that he had got a few wild apples only. Why, the owner does not know it for many years when a poet has put his farm in rhyme, the most admirable kind of invisible fence, has fairly impounded it, milked it, skimmed it, and got all the cream, and left the farmer only the skimmed milk.

The real attractions of the Hollowell farm, to me, were: its complete retirement, being about two miles from the village, half a mile from the nearest neighbor, and separated from the highway by a broad field; its bounding on the river, which the owner said protected it by its fogs from frosts in the spring, though that was nothing to me; the gray color and ruinous state of the house and barn, and the dilapidated fences, which put such an interval between me and the last occupant; the hollow and lichen-covered apple trees, gnawed by rabbits, showing what kind of neighbors I should have; but above all, the recollection I had of it from my earliest voyages up the river, when the house was concealed behind a dense grove of red maples, through which I heard the house dog bark. I was in haste to buy it, before the proprietor finished getting out some rocks, cutting down the hollow apple trees, and grubbing up some young birches which had sprung up in the pasture, or, in short, had made any more of his improvements. To enjoy these advantages I was ready to carry it on; like Atlas,[2] to take the world on my shoulders—I never heard what compensation he received for that— and do all those things which had no other motive or excuse but that I might pay for it and be unmolested in my possession of it; for I knew all the while that it would yield the most abundant crop of the kind I wanted, if I could only afford to let it alone. But it turned out as I have said.

All that I could say, then, with respect to farming on a large scale—I have always cultivated a garden—was,

that I had had my seeds ready. Many think that seeds improve with age. I have no doubt that time discriminates between the good and the bad; and when at last I shall plant, I shall be less likely to be disappointed. But I would say to my fellows, once for all, As long as possible live free and uncommitted. It makes but little difference whether you are committed to a farm or the county jail.

Old Cato,[3] whose "De Re Rusticâ" is my "Cultivator,"[4] says—and the only translation I have seen makes sheer nonsense of the passage—"When you think of getting a farm turn it thus in your mind, not to buy greedily; nor spare your pains to look at it, and do not think it enough to go round it once. The oftener you go there the more it will please you, if it is good." I think I shall not buy greedily, but go round and round it as long as I live, and be buried in it first, that it may please me the more at last.

The present was my next experiment of this kind, which I purpose to describe more at length, for convenience putting the experience of two years into one. As I have said, I do not propose to write an ode to dejection, but to brag as lustily as chanticleer[5] in the morning, standing on his roost, if only to wake my neighbors up.

When first I took up my abode in the woods, that is, began to spend my nights as well as days there, which, by accident, was on Independence Day, or the Fourth of July, 1845, my house was not finished for winter, but was merely a defense against the rain, without plastering or chimney, the walls being of rough, weather-stained boards, with wide chinks, which made it cool at night. The upright white hewn studs and freshly planed door and window casings gave it a clean and airy look, especially in the morning, when its timbers were saturated with dew, so that I fancied that by noon some sweet gum would exude from them. To my imagination it retained throughout the day more or less of this auroral[6] character, reminding me of a

---

1   *I am ... to dispute*   See "Verses Supposed to Be Written by Alexander Selkirk" by William Cowper (1731–1800); Thoreau italicizes "survey" to emphasize his pun on the word.

2   *Atlas*   Greek god who was said to hold up the pillars of the universe.

3   *Old Cato*   Cato the Elder (234–149 BCE), Roman senator who wrote *De Agricultura* (On Agriculture).

4   *Cultivator*   Monthly journal on farming practices in circulation during the 1800s.

5   *chanticleer*   Literary name for a cockerel; rooster.

6   *auroral*   Dawn-like.

certain house on a mountain which I had visited a year before. This was an airy and unplastered cabin, fit to entertain a traveling god, and where a goddess might trail her garments. The winds which passed over my dwelling were such as sweep over the ridges of mountains, bearing the broken strains, or celestial parts only, of terrestrial music. The morning wind forever blows, the poem of creation is uninterrupted; but few are the ears that hear it. Olympus[1] is but the outside of the earth everywhere.

The only house I had been the owner of before, if I except a boat, was a tent, which I used occasionally when making excursions in the summer, and this is still rolled up in my garret; but the boat, after passing from hand to hand, has gone down the stream of time. With this more substantial shelter about me, I had made some progress toward settling in the world. This frame, so slightly clad, was a sort of crystallization around me, and reacted on the builder. It was suggestive somewhat as a picture in outlines. I did not need to go outdoors to take the air, for the atmosphere within had lost none of its freshness. It was not so much within doors as behind a door where I sat, even in the rainiest weather. The Harivansa[2] says, "An abode without birds is like a meat without seasoning." Such was not my abode, for I found myself suddenly neighbor to the birds; not by having imprisoned one, but having caged myself near them. I was not only nearer to some of those which commonly frequent the garden and the orchard, but to those wilder and more thrilling songsters of the forest which never, or rarely, serenade a villager—the wood thrush, the veery, the scarlet tanager, the field sparrow, the whip-poor-will, and many others.

I was seated by the shore of a small pond, about a mile and a half south of the village of Concord and somewhat higher than it, in the midst of an extensive wood between that town and Lincoln, and about two miles south of that our only field known to fame, Concord Battle Ground;[3] but I was so low in the woods that the opposite shore, half a mile off, like the rest, covered with wood, was my most distant horizon. For the first

week, whenever I looked out on the pond it impressed me like a tarn[4] high up on the side of a mountain, its bottom far above the surface of other lakes, and, as the sun arose, I saw it throwing off its nightly clothing of mist, and here and there, by degrees, its soft ripples or its smooth reflecting surface was revealed, while the mists, like ghosts, were stealthily withdrawing in every direction into the woods, as at the breaking up of some nocturnal conventicle.[5] The very dew seemed to hang upon the trees later into the day than usual, as on the sides of mountains.

This small lake was of most value as a neighbor in the intervals of a gentle rain-storm in August, when, both air and water being perfectly still, but the sky overcast, mid-afternoon had all the serenity of evening, and the wood thrush sang around, and was heard from shore to shore. A lake like this is never smoother than at such a time; and the clear portion of the air above it being shallow and darkened by clouds, the water, full of light and reflections, becomes a lower heaven itself so much the more important. From a hill-top nearby, where the wood had been recently cut off, there was a pleasing vista southward across the pond, through a wide indentation in the hills which form the shore there, where their opposite sides sloping toward each other suggested a stream flowing out in that direction through a wooded valley, but stream there was none. That way I looked between and over the near green hills to some distant and higher ones in the horizon, tinged with blue. Indeed, by standing on tiptoe I could catch a glimpse of some of the peaks of the still bluer and more distant mountain ranges in the northwest, those true-blue coins from heaven's own mint, and also of some portion of the village. But in other directions, even from this point, I could not see over or beyond the woods which surrounded me. It is well to have some water in your neighborhood, to give buoyancy to and float the earth. One value even of the smallest well is, that when you look into it you see that earth is not continent but insular. This is as important as that it keeps butter cool.[6] When I looked across the pond from this peak toward the Sudbury meadows, which in time of flood I distinguished elevated perhaps

---

[1] *Olympus* Mount Olympus, home of the gods in Greek mythology.

[2] *Harivansa* Sacred Hindu text.

[3] *Concord Battle Ground* Site of one of the first battles of the American Revolutionary War; it took place on 19 April 1775.

[4] *tarn* Small mountain lake.

[5] *conventicle* Religious gathering.

[6] *keeps butter cool* Referring to the practice of storing butter in wells, prior to the invention of refrigeration.

by a mirage in their seething valley, like a coin in a basin, all the earth beyond the pond appeared like a thin crust insulated and floated even by this small sheet of intervening water, and I was reminded that this on which I dwelt was but *dry land*.

Though the view from my door was still more contracted, I did not feel crowded or confined in the least. There was pasture enough for my imagination. The low shrub oak plateau to which the opposite shore arose stretched away toward the prairies of the West and the steppes of Tartary,[1] affording ample room for all the roving families of men. "There are none happy in the world but beings who enjoy freely a vast horizon," said Damodara,[2] when his herds required new and larger pastures.

Both place and time were changed, and I dwelt nearer to those parts of the universe and to those eras in history which had most attracted me. Where I lived was as far off as many a region viewed nightly by astronomers. We are wont to imagine rare and delectable places in some remote and more celestial corner of the system, behind the constellation of Cassiopeia's Chair,[3] far from noise and disturbance. I discovered that my house actually had its site in such a withdrawn, but forever new and unprofaned, part of the universe. If it were worth the while to settle in those parts near to the Pleiades or the Hyades, to Aldebaran or Altair,[4] then I was really there, or at an equal remoteness from the life which I had left behind, dwindled and twinkling with as fine a ray to my nearest neighbor, and to be seen only in moonless nights by him. Such was that part of creation where I had squatted—

There was a shepherd that did live,
And held his thoughts as high
As were the mounts whereon his flocks
Did hourly feed him by.[5]

What should we think of the shepherd's life if his flocks always wandered to higher pastures than his thoughts?

Every morning was a cheerful invitation to make my life of equal simplicity, and I may say innocence, with Nature herself. I have been as sincere a worshipper of Aurora[6] as the Greeks. I got up early and bathed in the pond; that was a religious exercise, and one of the best things which I did. They say that characters were engraven on the bathing tub of King Tching-thang[7] to this effect: "Renew thyself completely each day; do it again, and again, and forever again." I can understand that. Morning brings back the heroic ages. I was as much affected by the faint hum of a mosquito making its invisible and unimaginable tour through my apartment at earliest dawn, when I was sitting with door and windows open, as I could be by any trumpet that ever sang of fame. It was Homer's[8] requiem; itself an Iliad and Odyssey in the air, singing its own wrath and wanderings. There was something cosmical about it; a standing advertisement, till forbidden, of the everlasting vigor and fertility of the world. The morning, which is the most memorable season of the day, is the awakening hour. Then there is least somnolence in us; and for an hour, at least, some part of us awakes which slumbers all the rest of the day and night. Little is to be expected of that day, if it can be called a day, to which we are not awakened by our Genius, but by the mechanical nudgings of some servitor, are not awakened by our own newly acquired force and aspirations from within, accompanied by the undulations of celestial music, instead of factory bells, and a fragrance filling the air—to a higher life than we fell asleep from; and thus the darkness bear its fruit, and prove itself to be good, no less than the light. That man who does not believe that each day contains an earlier, more sacred, and auroral hour than he has yet profaned, has despaired of life, and is pursuing a descending and darkening way. After a partial cessation of his sensuous life, the soul of man, or its organs rather, are reinvigorated each day, and his Genius tries again what noble life it can make. All

---

1   *steppes of Tartary*   Plains of central and northern Asia, including parts of what are now Siberia and Mongolia.

2   *Damodara*   Name for the Hindu god Krishna; Thoreau derives the quotation from a French edition of the *Harivansa*.

3   *Cassiopeia's Chair*   Set of stars in the constellation Cassiopeia, which form the shape of the queen's chair.

4   *Pleiades ... Altair*   Other constellations.

5   *There was ... him by*   Early seventeenth-century verse by an anonymous author, which Thoreau would probably have discovered in Thomas Evans's *Old Ballads* (1810).

---

6   *Aurora*   Classical goddess of the dawn.

7   *King Tching-thang*   Emperor Tang, founder of the Shang dynasty in China. The quotation that follows is from the Confucian text *The Great Learning*.

8   *Homer*   Author of the *Iliad* and *Odyssey*, epic works of Classical Greek poetry.

memorable events, I should say, transpire in morning time and in a morning atmosphere. The Vedas[1] say, "All intelligences awake with the morning." Poetry and art, and the fairest and most memorable of the actions of men, date from such an hour. All poets and heroes, like Memnon,[2] are the children of Aurora, and emit their music at sunrise. To him whose elastic and vigorous thought keeps pace with the sun, the day is a perpetual morning. It matters not what the clocks say or the attitudes and labors of men. Morning is when I am awake and there is a dawn in me. Moral reform is the effort to throw off sleep. Why is it that men give so poor an account of their day if they have not been slumbering? They are not such poor calculators. If they had not been overcome with drowsiness, they would have performed something. The millions are awake enough for physical labor; but only one in a million is awake enough for effective intellectual exertion, only one in a hundred millions to a poetic or divine life. To be awake is to be alive. I have never yet met a man who was quite awake. How could I have looked him in the face?

We must learn to reawaken and keep ourselves awake, not by mechanical aids, but by an infinite expectation of the dawn, which does not forsake us in our soundest sleep. I know of no more encouraging fact than the unquestionable ability of man to elevate his life by a conscious endeavor. It is something to be able to paint a particular picture, or to carve a statue, and so to make a few objects beautiful; but it is far more glorious to carve and paint the very atmosphere and medium through which we look, which morally we can do. To affect the quality of the day, that is the highest of arts. Every man is tasked to make his life, even in its details, worthy of the contemplation of his most elevated and critical hour. If we refused, or rather used up, such paltry information as we get, the oracles would distinctly inform us how this might be done.

I went to the woods because I wished to live deliberately, to front only the essential facts of life, and see if I could not learn what it had to teach, and not, when I came to die, discover that I had not lived. I did not wish to live what was not life, living is so dear; nor did I wish to practice resignation, unless it was quite necessary. I wanted to live deep and suck out all the marrow of life, to live so sturdily and Spartan-like[3] as to put to rout all that was not life, to cut a broad swath and shave close, to drive life into a corner, and reduce it to its lowest terms, and, if it proved to be mean,[4] why then to get the whole and genuine meanness of it, and publish its meanness to the world; or if it were sublime, to know it by experience, and be able to give a true account of it in my next excursion. For most men, it appears to me, are in a strange uncertainty about it, whether it is of the devil or of God, and have *somewhat hastily* concluded that it is the chief end of man here to "glorify God and enjoy him forever."[5]

Still we live meanly, like ants; though the fable tells us that we were long ago changed into men; like pygmies we fight with cranes;[6] it is error upon error, and clout upon clout, and our best virtue has for its occasion a superfluous and evitable wretchedness. Our life is frittered away by detail. An honest man has hardly need to count more than his ten fingers, or in extreme cases he may add his ten toes, and lump the rest. Simplicity, simplicity, simplicity! I say, let your affairs be as two or three, and not a hundred or a thousand; instead of a million count half a dozen, and keep your accounts on your thumbnail. In the midst of this chopping sea of civilized life, such are the clouds and storms and quicksands and thousand-and-one items to be allowed for, that a man has to live, if he would not founder and go to the bottom and not make his port at all, by dead reckoning, and he must be a great calculator indeed who succeeds. Simplify, simplify. Instead of three meals a day, if it be necessary eat but one; instead

---

[1]   *Vedas* Collection of four texts which comprise some of the most significant scriptures of Hinduism; the actual source of the following quotation is unknown.

[2]   *Memnon* In Greek mythology, son of Eos (also known as Aurora) and king of the Ethiopians; he was killed by Achilles in the Trojan War.

[3]   *Spartan-like* Akin to the citizens of the ancient Greek state of Sparta, who were known for their bravery and disciplined simplicity of living.

[4]   *mean* Base, lowly, undignified.

[5]   *the chief ... him forever* From the Shorter Catechism in *The New England Primer*: Question: "What is the chief end of man?" Answer: "Man's chief end is to glorify God and enjoy him forever." See also Psalm 86.12: "and I will glorify thy name for evermore."

[6]   *like pygmies ... with cranes* See Homer's *Iliad*, book 3, in which the warring Trojans are likened to the pygmies, a mythological race of small humans who were said to be at constant war with cranes.

of a hundred dishes, five; and reduce other things in proportion. Our life is like a German Confederacy,[1] made up of petty states, with its boundary forever fluctuating, so that even a German cannot tell you how it is bounded at any moment. The nation itself, with all its so-called internal improvements, which, by the way are all external and superficial, is just such an unwieldy and overgrown establishment, cluttered with furniture and tripped up by its own traps, ruined by luxury and heedless expense, by want of calculation and a worthy aim, as the million households in the land; and the only cure for it, as for them, is in a rigid economy, a stern and more than Spartan simplicity of life and elevation of purpose. It lives too fast. Men think that it is essential that the *Nation* have commerce, and export ice, and talk through a telegraph, and ride thirty miles an hour, without a doubt, whether *they* do or not; but whether we should live like baboons or like men, is a little uncertain. If we do not get out sleepers,[2] and forge rails, and devote days and nights to the work, but go to tinkering upon our *lives* to improve *them*, who will build railroads? And if railroads are not built, how shall we get to heaven in season?[3] But if we stay at home and mind our business, who will want railroads? We do not ride on the railroad; it rides upon us. Did you ever think what those sleepers are that underlie the railroad? Each one is a man, an Irishman, or a Yankee man. The rails are laid on them, and they are covered with sand, and the cars run smoothly over them. They are sound sleepers, I assure you. And every few years a new lot is laid down and run over; so that, if some have the pleasure of riding on a rail, others have the misfortune to be ridden upon. And when they run over a man that is walking in his sleep, a supernumerary sleeper in the wrong position, and wake him up, they suddenly stop the cars, and make a hue and cry about it, as if this were an exception. I am glad to know that it takes a gang of men for every five miles to keep the sleepers down and level in their beds as it is, for this is a sign that they may sometime get up again.

Why should we live with such hurry and waste of life? We are determined to be starved before we are hungry. Men say that a stitch in time saves nine, and so they take a thousand stitches today to save nine tomorrow. As for *work*, we haven't any of any consequence. We have the Saint Vitus' dance,[4] and cannot possibly keep our heads still. If I should only give a few pulls at the parish bell-rope, as for a fire, that is, without setting the bell, there is hardly a man on his farm in the outskirts of Concord, notwithstanding that press of engagements which was his excuse so many times this morning, nor a boy, nor a woman, I might almost say, but would forsake all and follow that sound, not mainly to save property from the flames, but, if we will confess the truth, much more to see it burn, since burn it must, and we, be it known, did not set it on fire—or to see it put out, and have a hand in it, if that is done as handsomely; yes, even if it were the parish church itself. Hardly a man takes a half-hour's nap after dinner, but when he wakes he holds up his head and asks, "What's the news?" as if the rest of mankind had stood his sentinels. Some give directions to be waked every half-hour, doubtless for no other purpose; and then, to pay for it, they tell what they have dreamed. After a night's sleep the news is as indispensable as the breakfast. "Pray tell me anything new that has happened to a man anywhere on this globe,"—and he reads it over his coffee and rolls, that a man has had his eyes gouged out this morning on the Wachito River; never dreaming the while that he lives in the dark unfathomed mammoth cave of this world, and has but the rudiment of an eye himself.

For my part, I could easily do without the post-office. I think that there are very few important communications made through it. To speak critically, I never received more than one or two letters in my life—I wrote this some years ago—that were worth the postage. The penny-post[5] is, commonly, an institution through which you seriously offer a man that penny for his thoughts which is so often safely offered in jest. And I am sure that I never read any memorable news

---

[1] *German Confederacy*   Germany was not unified until 1871; prior to that, it comprised numerous states, which were often at war with one another.

[2] *sleepers*   Wooden planks upon which train rails are built; also a pun.

[3] *in season*   In time.

---

[4] *Saint Vitus' dance*   Chorea, a disorder of the nerves causing jerking motions in the face, hands, and feet; named after the patron saint of the disease, Saint Vitus.

[5] *penny-post*   Postal service by which letters could be sent for the cost of one penny.

in a newspaper. If we read of one man robbed, or murdered, or killed by accident, or one house burned, or one vessel wrecked, or one steamboat blown up, or one cow run over on the Western Railroad, or one mad dog killed, or one lot of grasshoppers in the winter—we never need read of another. One is enough. If you are acquainted with the principle, what do you care for a myriad instances and applications? To a philosopher all *news*, as it is called, is gossip, and they who edit and read it are old women over their tea. Yet not a few are greedy after this gossip. There was such a rush, as I hear, the other day at one of the offices to learn the foreign news by the last arrival, that several large squares of plate glass belonging to the establishment were broken by the pressure—news which I seriously think a ready wit might write a twelvemonth, or twelve years, beforehand with sufficient accuracy. As for Spain, for instance, if you know how to throw in Don Carlos and the Infanta, and Don Pedro and Seville and Granada,[1] from time to time in the right proportions—they may have changed the names a little since I saw the papers—and serve up a bull-fight when other entertainments fail, it will be true to the letter, and give us as good an idea of the exact state or ruin of things in Spain as the most succinct and lucid reports under this head in the newspapers: and as for England, almost the last significant scrap of news from that quarter was the revolution of 1649;[2] and if you have learned the history of her crops for an average year, you never need attend to that thing again, unless your speculations are of a merely pecuniary character. If one may judge who rarely looks into the newspapers, nothing new does ever happen in foreign parts, a French revolution[3] not excepted.

What news! how much more important to know what that is which was never old! "Kieou-he-yu (great dignitary of the state of Wei) sent a man to Khoung-tseu[4] to know his news. Khoung-tseu caused the messenger to be seated near him, and questioned him in these terms: What is your master doing? The messenger answered with respect: My master desires to diminish the number of his faults, but he cannot come to the end of them. The messenger being gone, the philosopher remarked: What a worthy messenger! What a worthy messenger!" The preacher, instead of vexing the ears of drowsy farmers on their day of rest at the end of the week—for Sunday is the fit conclusion of an ill-spent week, and not the fresh and brave beginning of a new one—with this one other draggle-tail of a sermon, should shout with thundering voice, "Pause! Avast! Why so seeming fast, but deadly slow?"

Shams and delusions are esteemed for soundest truths, while reality is fabulous.[5] If men would steadily observe realities only, and not allow themselves to be deluded, life, to compare it with such things as we know, would be like a fairy tale and the Arabian Nights' Entertainments.[6] If we respected only what is inevitable and has a right to be, music and poetry would resound along the streets. When we are unhurried and wise, we perceive that only great and worthy things have any permanent and absolute existence, that petty fears and petty pleasures are but the shadow of the reality. This is always exhilarating and sublime. By closing the eyes and slumbering, and consenting to be deceived by shows, men establish and confirm their daily life of routine and habit everywhere, which still is built on purely illusory foundations. Children, who play life, discern its true law and relations more clearly than men, who fail to live it worthily, but who think that they are wiser by experience, that is, by failure. I have read in a Hindoo book, that "there was a king's son, who, being expelled in infancy from his native city, was brought up by a forester, and, growing up to maturity in that state, imagined himself to belong

---

[1] *Don Carlos ... and Granada* Examples of typical figures of Spanish history; Carlos of Spain (1788–1855) was a pretender to the Spanish throne, eventually ousted by the Infanta Isabella (1830–1904), the daughter of Carlos's brother and the previous king, Ferdinand VII (1784–1833). "Don Pedro" refers to the Castilian king known as Peter the Cruel (1334–69).

[2] *revolution of 1649* Year in which Charles I of England was executed by the Parliamentarians in the English Civil War, signaling the beginning of the Puritan Commonwealth of England, lasting until 1660.

[3] *a French revolution* At the time *Walden* was being written, the most recent revolution in France had been that of 1848, which led to the establishment of the Second French Empire under Napoleon III (1808–73).

[4] *Khoung-tseu* Antiquated English spelling of the Mandarin name of Confucius; the story is from Book Fourteen of the *Analects*, a collection of sayings traditionally attributed to Confucius.

[5] *fabulous* Mythical, fictional.

[6] *Arabian Nights' Entertainments* Also known as *One Thousand and One Nights*, a collection of Arabic, Indian, and Persian folk tales.

to the barbarous race with which he lived. One of his father's ministers having discovered him, revealed to him what he was, and the misconception of his character was removed, and he knew himself to be a prince. So soul," continues the Hindoo philosopher, "from the circumstances in which it is placed, mistakes its own character, until the truth is revealed to it by some holy teacher, and then it knows itself to be *Brahme*."[1] I perceive that we inhabitants of New England live this mean life that we do because our vision does not penetrate the surface of things. We think that that *is* which *appears* to be. If a man should walk through this town and see only the reality, where, think you, would the "Mill-dam"[2] go to? If he should give us an account of the realities he beheld there, we should not recognize the place in his description. Look at a meeting-house, or a court-house, or a jail, or a shop, or a dwelling-house, and say what that thing really is before a true gaze, and they would all go to pieces in your account of them. Men esteem truth remote, in the outskirts of the system, behind the farthest star, before Adam and after the last man. In eternity there is indeed something true and sublime. But all these times and places and occasions are now and here. God himself culminates in the present moment, and will never be more divine in the lapse of all the ages. And we are enabled to apprehend at all what is sublime and noble only by the perpetual instilling and drenching of the reality that surrounds us. The universe constantly and obediently answers to our conceptions; whether we travel fast or slow, the track is laid for us. Let us spend our lives in conceiving then. The poet or the artist never yet had so fair and noble a design but some of his posterity at least could accomplish it.

Let us spend one day as deliberately as Nature, and not be thrown off the track by every nutshell and mosquito's wing that falls on the rails. Let us rise early and fast, or break fast, gently and without perturbation; let company come and let company go, let the bells ring and the children cry, determined to make a day of it. Why should we knock under and go with the stream?

Let us not be upset and overwhelmed in that terrible rapid and whirlpool called a dinner, situated in the meridian shallows. Weather this danger and you are safe, for the rest of the way is downhill. With unrelaxed nerves, with morning vigor, sail by it, looking another way, tied to the mast like Ulysses.[3] If the engine whistles, let it whistle till it is hoarse for its pains. If the bell rings, why should we run? We will consider what kind of music they are like. Let us settle ourselves, and work and wedge our feet downward through the mud and slush of opinion, and prejudice, and tradition, and delusion, and appearance, that alluvion[4] which covers the globe, through Paris and London, through New York and Boston and Concord, through Church and State, through poetry and philosophy and religion, till we come to a hard bottom and rocks in place, which we can call *reality*, and say, This is, and no mistake; and then begin, having a *point d'appui*,[5] below freshet and frost and fire, a place where you might found a wall or a state, or set a lamp-post safely, or perhaps a gauge, not a Nilometer,[6] but a Realometer, that future ages might know how deep a freshet of shams and appearances had gathered from time to time. If you stand right fronting and face to face to a fact, you will see the sun glimmer on both its surfaces, as if it were a scimitar, and feel its sweet edge dividing you through the heart and marrow, and so you will happily conclude your mortal career. Be it life or death, we crave only reality. If we are really dying, let us hear the rattle in our throats and feel cold in the extremities; if we are alive, let us go about our business.

Time is but the stream I go a-fishing in. I drink at it; but while I drink I see the sandy bottom and detect how shallow it is. Its thin current slides away, but eternity remains. I would drink deeper; fish in the sky, whose bottom is pebbly with stars. I cannot count one. I know not the first letter of the alphabet. I have always

---

1   *there was … be Brahme* Thoreau's source for the story is unclear; *Brahme* likely refers to Brahman, which in Hinduism is the unifying principle that pervades all reality, simultaneously creative and unchanging.

2   *Mill-dam* Center in which business was conducted in Concord.

3   *tied to … like Ulysses* In Homer's *Odyssey*, Odysseus (also known by the Roman name Ulysses) ties himself to the mast of his ship so that he can hear the seductive song of the Sirens without succumbing to their call—as they were known in mythology to lead sailors to their deaths.

4   *alluvion* Flood.

5   *point d'appui* French: point of support.

6   *Nilometer* Structure used in ancient Egypt to measure the rising and falling levels of the Nile.

been regretting that I was not as wise as the day I was born. The intellect is a cleaver; it discerns and rifts its way into the secret of things. I do not wish to be any more busy with my hands than is necessary. My head is hands and feet. I feel all my best faculties concentrated in it. My instinct tells me that my head is an organ for burrowing, as some creatures use their snout and fore paws, and with it I would mine and burrow my way through these hills. I think that the richest vein is somewhere hereabouts; so by the divining-rod and thin rising vapors I judge; and here I will begin to mine.

from Chapter 5
SOLITUDE

This is a delicious evening, when the whole body is one sense, and imbibes delight through every pore. I go and come with a strange liberty in Nature, a part of herself. As I walk along the stony shore of the pond in my shirt-sleeves, though it is cool as well as cloudy and windy, and I see nothing special to attract me, all the elements are unusually congenial to me. The bull-frogs trump to usher in the night, and the note of the whip-poor-will is borne on the rippling wind from over the water. Sympathy with the fluttering alder and poplar leaves almost takes away my breath; yet, like the lake, my serenity is rippled but not ruffled. These small waves raised by the evening wind are as remote from storm as the smooth reflecting surface. Though it is now dark, the wind still blows and roars in the wood, the waves still dash, and some creatures lull the rest with their notes. The repose is never complete. The wildest animals do not repose, but seek their prey now; the fox, and skunk, and rabbit, now roam the fields and woods without fear. They are Nature's watchmen—links which connect the days of animated life.

When I return to my house I find that visitors have been there and left their cards, either a bunch of flowers, or a wreath of evergreen, or a name in pencil on a yellow walnut leaf or a chip. They who come rarely to the woods take some little piece of the forest into their hands to play with by the way, which they leave, either intentionally or accidentally. One has peeled a willow wand, woven it into a ring, and dropped it on my table. I could always tell if visitors had called in my absence, either by the bended twigs or grass, or the print of their

shoes, and generally of what sex or age or quality they were by some slight trace left, as a flower dropped, or a bunch of grass plucked and thrown away, even as far off as the railroad, half a mile distant, or by the lingering odor of a cigar or pipe. Nay, I was frequently notified of the passage of a traveller along the highway sixty rods[1] off by the scent of his pipe.

There is commonly sufficient space about us. Our horizon is never quite at our elbows. The thick wood is not just at our door, nor the pond, but somewhat is always clearing, familiar and worn by us, appropriated and fenced in some way, and reclaimed from Nature. For what reason have I this vast range and circuit, some square miles of unfrequented forest, for my privacy, abandoned to me by men? My nearest neighbor is a mile distant, and no house is visible from any place but the hilltops within half a mile of my own. I have my horizon bounded by woods all to myself; a distant view of the railroad where it touches the pond on the one hand, and of the fence which skirts the woodland road on the other. But for the most part it is as solitary where I live as on the prairies. It is as much Asia or Africa as New England. I have, as it were, my own sun and moon and stars, and a little world all to myself. At night there was never a traveller passed my house, or knocked at my door, more than if I were the first or last man; unless it were in the spring, when at long intervals some came from the village to fish for pouts—they plainly fished much more in the Walden Pond of their own natures, and baited their hooks with darkness—but they soon retreated, usually with light baskets, and left "the world to darkness and to me,"[2] and the black kernel of the night was never profaned by any human neighborhood. I believe that men are generally still a little afraid of the dark, though the witches are all hung, and Christianity and candles have been introduced.

Yet I experienced sometimes that the most sweet and tender, the most innocent and encouraging society may be found in any natural object, even for the poor misanthrope and most melancholy man. There can be no very black melancholy to him who lives in the

---

[1]   *rods* Units of measurement, derived from the surveyor's tool; a rod is equivalent to approximately 5.5 yards.

[2]   *the world … to me* See Thomas Gray's "Elegy Written in a Country Churchyard" (1751).

midst of nature and has his senses still. There was never yet such a storm but it was Aeolian[1] music to a healthy and innocent ear. Nothing can rightly compel a simple and brave man to a vulgar sadness. While I enjoy the friendship of the seasons I trust that nothing can make life a burden to me. The gentle rain which waters my beans and keeps me in the house today is not drear and melancholy, but good for me too. Though it prevents my hoeing them, it is of far more worth than my hoeing. If it should continue so long as to cause the seeds to rot in the ground and destroy the potatoes in the low lands, it would still be good for the grass on the uplands, and, being good for the grass, it would be good for me. Sometimes, when I compare myself with other men, it seems as if I were more favored by the gods than they, beyond any deserts that I am conscious of; as if I had a warrant and surety at their hands which my fellows have not, and were especially guided and guarded. I do not flatter myself, but if it be possible they flatter me. I have never felt lonesome, or in the least oppressed, by a sense of solitude, but once, and that was a few weeks after I came to the woods, when, for an hour, I doubted if the near neighborhood of man was not essential to a serene and healthy life. To be alone was something unpleasant. But I was at the same time conscious of a slight insanity in my mood, and seemed to foresee my recovery. In the midst of a gentle rain while these thoughts prevailed, I was suddenly sensible of such sweet and beneficent society in Nature, in the very pattering of the drops, and in every sound and sight around my house, an infinite and unaccountable friendliness all at once like an atmosphere sustaining me, as made the fancied advantages of human neighborhood insignificant, and I have never thought of them since. Every little pine needle expanded and swelled with sympathy and befriended me. I was so distinctly made aware of the presence of something kindred to me, even in scenes which we are accustomed to call wild and dreary, and also that the nearest of blood to me and humanest was not a person nor a villager, that I thought no place could ever be strange to me again.

Mourning untimely consumes the sad;
Few are their days in the land of the living,
Beautiful daughter of Toscar.[2]

Some of my pleasantest hours were during the long rain-storms in the spring or fall, which confined me to the house for the afternoon as well as the forenoon, soothed by their ceaseless roar and pelting, when an early twilight ushered in a long evening in which many thoughts had time to take root and unfold themselves. In those driving northeast rains which tried the village houses so, when the maids stood ready with mop and pail in front entries to keep the deluge out, I sat behind my door in my little house, which was all entry, and thoroughly enjoyed its protection. In one heavy thunder-shower the lightning struck a large pitch pine across the pond, making a very conspicuous and perfectly regular spiral groove from top to bottom, an inch or more deep, and four or five inches wide, as you would groove a walking-stick. I passed it again the other day, and was struck with awe on looking up and beholding that mark, now more distinct than ever, where a terrific and resistless bolt came down out of the harmless sky eight years ago. Men frequently say to me, "I should think you would feel lonesome down there, and want to be nearer to folks, rainy and snowy days and nights especially." I am tempted to reply to such—This whole earth which we inhabit is but a point in space. How far apart, think you, dwell the two most distant inhabitants of yonder star, the breadth of whose disk cannot be appreciated by our instruments? Why should I feel lonely? is not our planet in the Milky Way? This which you put seems to me not to be the most important question. What sort of space is that which separates a man from his fellows and makes him solitary? I have found that no exertion of the legs can bring two minds much nearer to one another. What do we want most to dwell near to? Not to many men surely—the depot, the post-office, the bar-room, the meeting-house, the school-house, the grocery, Beacon Hill,[3] or the Five Points,[4] where men

---

[1] *Aeolian* Of Aeolus, the Greek god of the winds; the Aeolian harp, an instrument designed to be "played" by the blowing of the wind, had been popularized during the Romantic era, and was favored by Thoreau.

[2] *Mourning ... of Toscar* See the poem "Croma" in *The Genuine Remains of Ossian* (1841) by Patrick MacGregor.

[3] *Beacon Hill* Neighborhood in Boston.

[4] *Five Points* Manhattan district known at the time both for its dense population and for its prevalence of crime.

most congregate—but to the perennial source of our life, whence in all our experience we have found that to issue, as the willow stands near the water and sends out its roots in that direction. This will vary with different natures, but this is the place where a wise man will dig his cellar. I one evening overtook one of my townsmen, who has accumulated what is called "a handsome property"—though I never got a *fair* view of it—on the Walden road, driving a pair of cattle to market, who inquired of me how I could bring my mind to give up so many of the comforts of life. I answered that I was very sure I liked it passably well; I was not joking. And so I went home to my bed, and left him to pick his way through the darkness and the mud to Brighton[1]—or Bright-town—which place he would reach sometime in the morning.

Any prospect of awakening or coming to life to a dead man makes indifferent all times and places. The place where that may occur is always the same, and indescribably pleasant to all our senses. For the most part we allow only outlying and transient circumstances to make our occasions. They are, in fact, the cause of our distraction. Nearest to all things is that power which fashions their being. *Next* to us the grandest laws are continually being executed. *Next* to us is not the workman whom we have hired, with whom we love so well to talk, but the workman whose work we are.

"How vast and profound is the influence of the subtle powers of Heaven and of Earth!"

"We seek to perceive them, and we do not see them; we seek to hear them, and we do not hear them; identified with the substance of things, they cannot be separated from them."

"They cause that in all the universe men purify and sanctify their hearts, and clothe themselves in their holiday garments to offer sacrifices and oblations to their ancestors. It is an ocean of subtile intelligences. They are everywhere, above us, on our left, on our right; they environ us on all sides."[2]

We are the subjects of an experiment which is not a little interesting to me. Can we not do without the society of our gossips a little while under these circumstances—have our own thoughts to cheer us? Confucius says truly, "Virtue does not remain as an abandoned orphan; it must of necessity have neighbors."[3]

With thinking we may be beside ourselves in a sane sense. By a conscious effort of the mind we can stand aloof from actions and their consequences; and all things, good and bad, go by us like a torrent. We are not wholly involved in Nature. I may be either the driftwood in the stream, or Indra[4] in the sky looking down on it. I *may* be affected by a theatrical exhibition; on the other hand, I *may not* be affected by an actual event which appears to concern me much more. I only know myself as a human entity—the scene, so to speak, of thoughts and affections—and am sensible of a certain doubleness by which I can stand as remote from myself as from another. However intense my experience, I am conscious of the presence and criticism of a part of me, which, as it were, is not a part of me, but spectator, sharing no experience, but taking note of it; and that is no more I than it is you. When the play—it may be the tragedy—of life is over, the spectator goes his way. It was a kind of fiction, a work of the imagination only, so far as he was concerned. This doubleness may easily make us poor neighbors and friends sometimes.

I find it wholesome to be alone the greater part of the time. To be in company, even with the best, is soon wearisome and dissipating. I love to be alone. I never found the companion that was so companionable as solitude. We are for the most part more lonely when we go abroad among men than when we stay in our chambers. A man thinking or working is always alone, let him be where he will. Solitude is not measured by the miles of space that intervene between a man and his fellows. The really diligent student in one of the crowded hives of Cambridge College is as solitary as a dervish[5] in the desert. The farmer can work alone in the field or the woods all day, hoeing or chopping, and not feel lonesome, because he is employed; but when he comes home at night he cannot sit down in a room

---

[1]   *Brighton*   Town, now part of Boston, known in the nineteenth century for housing farm markets and slaughterhouses.

[2]   *How vast ... all sides*   Thoreau's translation from Guillaume Pauthier's *Confucius et Mencius*, itself a French translation of the Confucian book *The Doctrine of the Mean*.

[3]   *Virtue ... neighbors*   Thoreau's translation of Confucius's *Analects*, again from Pauthier's French translation.

[4]   *Indra*   Hindu deity associated with the heavens, thunder, and rain.

[5]   *dervish*   Sufi Muslim ascetic.

alone, at the mercy of his thoughts, but must be where he can "see the folks," and recreate, and, as he thinks, remunerate himself for his day's solitude; and hence he wonders how the student can sit alone in the house all night and most of the day without ennui and "the blues"; but he does not realize that the student, though in the house, is still at work in *his* field, and chopping in *his* woods, as the farmer in his, and in turn seeks the same recreation and society that the latter does, though it may be a more condensed form of it.

Society is commonly too cheap. We meet at very short intervals, not having had time to acquire any new value for each other. We meet at meals three times a day, and give each other a new taste of that old musty cheese that we are. We have had to agree on a certain set of rules, called etiquette and politeness, to make this frequent meeting tolerable and that we need not come to open war. We meet at the post-office, and at the sociable, and about the fireside every night; we live thick and are in each other's way, and stumble over one another, and I think that we thus lose some respect for one another. Certainly less frequency would suffice for all important and hearty communications. Consider the girls in a factory—never alone, hardly in their dreams. It would be better if there were but one inhabitant to a square mile, as where I live. The value of a man is not in his skin, that we should touch him.

I have heard of a man lost in the woods and dying of famine and exhaustion at the foot of a tree, whose loneliness was relieved by the grotesque visions with which, owing to bodily weakness, his diseased imagination surrounded him, and which he believed to be real. So also, owing to bodily and mental health and strength, we may be continually cheered by a like but more normal and natural society, and come to know that we are never alone.

I have a great deal of company in my house; especially in the morning, when nobody calls. Let me suggest a few comparisons, that some one may convey an idea of my situation. I am no more lonely than the loon in the pond that laughs so loud, or than Walden Pond itself. What company has that lonely lake, I pray? And yet it has not the blue devils,[1] but the blue angels in it, in the azure tint of its waters. The sun is alone, except in thick weather, when there sometimes appear

to be two, but one is a mock sun.[2] God is alone—but the devil, he is far from being alone; he sees a great deal of company; he is legion. I am no more lonely than a single mullein or dandelion in a pasture, or a bean leaf, or sorrel, or a horse-fly, or a humblebee.[3] I am no more lonely than the Mill Brook, or a weathercock, or the north star, or the south wind, or an April shower, or a January thaw, or the first spider in a new house. …

Chapter 17
Spring

The opening of large tracts by the ice-cutters[4] commonly causes a pond to break up earlier; for the water, agitated by the wind, even in cold weather, wears away the surrounding ice. But such was not the effect on Walden that year, for she had soon got a thick new garment to take the place of the old. This pond never breaks up so soon as the others in this neighborhood, on account both of its greater depth and its having no stream passing through it to melt or wear away the ice. I never knew it to open in the course of a winter, not excepting that of '52–3, which gave the ponds so severe a trial. It commonly opens about the first of April, a week or ten days later than Flint's Pond and Fair-Haven, beginning to melt on the north side and in the shallower parts where it began to freeze. It indicates better than any water hereabouts the absolute progress of the season, being least affected by transient changes of temperature. A severe cold of a few days' duration in March may very much retard the opening of the former ponds, while the temperature of Walden increases almost uninterruptedly. A thermometer thrust into the middle of Walden on the 6th of March, 1847, stood at 32°, or freezing point; near the shore at 33°; in the middle of Flint's Pond, the same day, at 32½°; at a dozen rods from the shore, in shallow water, under ice a foot thick, at 36°. This difference of three and a half degrees between the temperature of the deep water and the shallow in the latter pond, and the fact that a great proportion of it is comparatively shallow, show why it should break up so much sooner than Walden. The ice

---

[1] *blue devils* Demons that cause melancholy.

[2] *mock sun* Sundog; bright spot appearing next to the sun.

[3] *humblebee* Bumblebee.

[4] *ice-cutters* Referring to the harvesting of ice from Walden Pond.

in the shallowest part was at this time several inches thinner than in the middle. In midwinter the middle had been the warmest and the ice thinnest there. So, also, everyone who has waded about the shores of the pond in summer must have perceived how much warmer the water is close to the shore, where only three or four inches deep, than a little distance out, and on the surface where it is deep, than near the bottom. In spring the sun not only exerts an influence through the increased temperature of the air and earth, but its heat passes through ice a foot or more thick, and is reflected from the bottom in shallow water, and so also warms the water and melts the underside of the ice, at the same time that it is melting it more directly above, making it uneven, and causing the air bubbles which it contains to extend themselves upward and downward until it is completely honeycombed, and at last disappears suddenly in a single spring rain. Ice has its grain as well as wood, and when a cake begins to rot or "comb," that is, assume the appearance of honeycomb, whatever may be its position, the air cells are at right angles with what was the water surface. Where there is a rock or a log rising near to the surface the ice over it is much thinner, and is frequently quite dissolved by this reflected heat; and I have been told that in the experiment at Cambridge to freeze water in a shallow wooden pond, though the cold air circulated underneath, and so had access to both sides, the reflection of the sun from the bottom more than counterbalanced this advantage. When a warm rain in the middle of the winter melts off the snow-ice from Walden, and leaves a hard dark or transparent ice on the middle, there will be a strip of rotten though thicker white ice, a rod or more wide, about the shores, created by this reflected heat. Also, as I have said, the bubbles themselves within the ice operate as burning-glasses to melt the ice beneath.

The phenomena of the year take place every day in a pond on a small scale. Every morning, generally speaking, the shallow water is being warmed more rapidly than the deep, though it may not be made so warm after all, and every evening it is being cooled more rapidly until the morning. The day is an epitome of the year. The night is the winter, the morning and evening are the spring and fall, and the noon is the summer. The cracking and booming of the ice indicate a change of temperature. One pleasant morning after a cold night, February 24th, 1850, having gone to Flint's Pond to spend the day, I noticed with surprise, that when I struck the ice with the head of my axe, it resounded like a gong for many rods around, or as if I had struck on a tight drum-head. The pond began to boom about an hour after sunrise, when it felt the influence of the sun's rays slanted upon it from over the hills; it stretched itself and yawned like a waking man with a gradually increasing tumult, which was kept up three or four hours. It took a short siesta at noon, and boomed once more toward night, as the sun was withdrawing his influence. In the right stage of the weather a pond fires its evening gun with great regularity. But in the middle of the day, being full of cracks, and the air also being less elastic, it had completely lost its resonance, and probably fishes and muskrats could not then have been stunned by a blow on it. The fishermen say that the "thundering of the pond" scares the fishes and prevents their biting. The pond does not thunder every evening, and I cannot tell surely when to expect its thundering; but though I may perceive no difference in the weather, it does. Who would have suspected so large and cold and thick-skinned a thing to be so sensitive? Yet it has its law to which it thunders obedience when it should as surely as the buds expand in the spring. The earth is all alive and covered with papillae. The largest pond is as sensitive to atmospheric changes as the globule of mercury in its tube.

One attraction in coming to the woods to live was that I should have leisure and opportunity to see the Spring come in. The ice in the pond at length begins to be honeycombed, and I can set my heel in it as I walk. Fogs and rains and warmer suns are gradually melting the snow; the days have grown sensibly longer; and I see how I shall get through the winter without adding to my wood-pile, for large fires are no longer necessary. I am on the alert for the first signs of spring, to hear the chance note of some arriving bird, or the striped squirrel's chirp, for his stores must be now nearly exhausted, or see the woodchuck venture out of his winter quarters. On the 13th of March, after I had heard the bluebird, song sparrow, and red-wing, the ice was still nearly a foot thick. As the weather grew warmer it was not sensibly worn away by the water, nor broken up and floated off as in rivers, but, though it was completely melted for half a rod in width about the shore, the middle was merely honeycombed and saturated with water, so that you could put your foot through it when six inches thick; but by the next day evening, perhaps, after a warm rain followed by fog, it would have wholly disappeared, all gone off with the fog, spirited away. One year I went across the middle only five days before it disappeared entirely. In 1845 Walden was first completely open on the 1st of April; in '46, the 25th of March; in '47, the 8th of April; in '51, the 28th of March; in '52, the 18th of April; in '53, the 23d of March; in '54, about the 7th of April.

Every incident connected with the breaking up of the rivers and ponds and the settling of the weather is particularly interesting to us who live in a climate of so great extremes. When the warmer days come, they who dwell near the river hear the ice crack at night with a startling whoop as loud as artillery, as if its icy fetters were rent from end to end, and within a few days see it rapidly going out. So the alligator comes out of the mud with quakings of the earth. One old man, who has been a close observer of Nature, and seems as thoroughly wise in regard to all her operations as if she had been put upon the stocks when he was a boy, and he had helped to lay her keel—who has come to his growth, and can hardly acquire more of natural lore if he should live to the age of Methuselah[1]—told me—and I was surprised to hear him express wonder at any of Nature's operations, for I thought that there were no secrets between them—that one spring day he took his gun and boat, and thought that he would have a little sport with the ducks. There was ice still on the meadows, but it was all gone out of the river, and he dropped down without obstruction from Sudbury, where he lived, to Fair-Haven Pond, which he found, unexpectedly, covered for the most part with a firm field of ice. It was a warm day, and he was surprised to see so great a body of ice remaining. Not seeing any ducks, he hid his boat on the north or back side of an island in the pond, and then concealed himself in the bushes on the south side, to await them. The ice was melted for three or four rods from the shore, and there was a smooth and warm sheet of water, with a muddy bottom, such as the ducks love, within, and he thought it likely that some would be along pretty soon. After he had lain still there about an hour he heard a low and seemingly very distant sound, but singularly grand and impressive, unlike anything he had ever heard, gradually swelling and increasing as if it would have a universal and memorable ending, a sullen rush and roar, which seemed to him all at once like the sound of a vast body of fowl coming in to settle there, and, seizing his gun, he started up in haste and excited; but he found, to his surprise, that the whole body of the ice had started while he lay there, and drifted in to the shore, and the sound he had heard was made by its edge grating on the shore—at first gently nibbled and crumbled off, but at length heaving up and scattering its wrecks along the island to a considerable height before it came to a standstill.

At length the sun's rays have attained the right angle, and warm winds blow up mist and rain and melt the snowbanks, and the sun dispersing the mist smiles on a checkered landscape of russet and white smoking with incense, through which the traveler picks his way from islet to islet, cheered by the music of a thousand tinkling rills and rivulets whose veins are filled with the blood of winter which they are bearing off.

Few phenomena gave me more delight than to observe the forms which thawing sand and clay assume in flowing down the sides of a deep cut on the railroad through which I passed on my way to the village, a phenomenon not very common on so large a scale, though the number of freshly exposed banks of the right material must have been greatly multiplied since railroads were invented. The material was sand of every degree of fineness and of various rich colors, commonly mixed with a little clay. When the frost comes out in the spring, and even in a thawing day in the winter, the sand begins to flow down the slopes like lava, sometimes bursting out through the snow and overflowing it where no sand was to be seen before. Innumerable little streams overlap and interlace one with another, exhibiting a sort of hybrid product, which obeys half way the law of currents, and half way that of vegetation. As it flows it takes the forms of sappy leaves or vines, making heaps of pulpy sprays a foot or more in depth, and resembling, as you look down on them, the

---

[1] *Methuselah* According to Genesis 5.27, Methuselah lived to be 969 years old.

laciniated, lobed, and imbricated thalluses[1] of some lichens; or you are reminded of coral, of leopards' paws or birds' feet, of brains or lungs or bowels, and excrements of all kinds. It is a truly *grotesque* vegetation, whose forms and color we see imitated in bronze, a sort of architectural foliage more ancient and typical than acanthus, chiccory, ivy, vine, or any vegetable leaves; destined perhaps, under some circumstances, to become a puzzle to future geologists. The whole cut impressed me as if it were a cave with its stalactites laid open to the light. The various shades of the sand are singularly rich and agreeable, embracing the different iron colors, brown, gray, yellowish, and reddish. When the flowing mass reaches the drain at the foot of the bank it spreads out flatter into *strands*, the separate streams losing their semi-cylindrical form and gradually becoming more flat and broad, running together as they are more moist, till they form an almost flat *sand*, still variously and beautifully shaded, but in which you can trace the original forms of vegetation; till at length, in the water itself, they are converted into *banks*, like those formed off the mouths of rivers, and the forms of vegetation are lost in the ripple marks on the bottom.

The whole bank, which is from twenty to forty feet high, is sometimes overlaid with a mass of this kind of foliage, or sandy rupture, for a quarter of a mile on one or both sides, the produce of one spring day. What makes this sand foliage remarkable is its springing into existence thus suddenly. When I see on the one side the inert bank—for the sun acts on one side first—and on the other this luxuriant foliage, the creation of an hour, I am affected as if in a peculiar sense I stood in the laboratory of the Artist who made the world and me—had come to where he was still at work, sporting on this bank, and with excess of energy strewing his fresh designs about. I feel as if I were nearer to the vitals of the globe, for this sandy overflow is something such a foliaceous mass as the vitals of the animal body. You find thus in the very sands an anticipation of the vegetable leaf. No wonder that the earth expresses itself outwardly in leaves, it so labors with the idea inwardly. The atoms have already learned this

law, and are pregnant by it. The overhanging leaf sees here its prototype. *Internally*, whether in the globe or animal body, it is a moist thick *lobe*, a word especially applicable to the liver and lungs and the *leaves* of fat (λειβω, *labor, lapsus*, to flow or slip downward, a lapsing; λοβός, *globus*, lobe, globe; also lap, flap, and many other words); *externally* a dry thin *leaf*, even as the *f* and *v* are a pressed and dried *b*. The radicals of *lobe* are *lb*, the soft mass of the *b* (single lobed, or B, double lobed), with the liquid *l* behind it pressing it forward. In globe, *glb*, the guttural *g* adds to the meaning the capacity of the throat. The feathers and wings of birds are still drier and thinner leaves. Thus, also, you pass from the lumpish grub in the earth to the airy and fluttering butterfly. The very globe continually transcends and translates itself, and becomes winged in its orbit. Even ice begins with delicate crystal leaves, as if it had flowed into moulds which the fronds of water plants have impressed on the watery mirror. The whole tree itself is but one leaf, and rivers are still vaster leaves whose pulp is intervening earth, and towns and cities are the ova of insects in their axils.

When the sun withdraws the sand ceases to flow, but in the morning the streams will start once more and branch and branch again into a myriad of others. You here see perchance how blood-vessels are formed. If you look closely you observe that first there pushes forward from the thawing mass a stream of softened sand with a drop-like point, like the ball of the finger, feeling its way slowly and blindly downward, until at last with more heat and moisture, as the sun gets higher, the most fluid portion, in its effort to obey the law to which the most inert also yields, separates from the latter and forms for itself a meandering channel or artery within that, in which is seen a little silvery stream glancing like lightning from one stage of pulpy leaves or branches to another, and ever and anon swallowed up in the sand. It is wonderful how rapidly yet perfectly the sand organizes itself as it flows, using the best material its mass affords to form the sharp edges of its channel. Such are the sources of rivers. In the silicious matter which the water deposits is perhaps the bony system, and in the still finer soil and organic matter the fleshy fiber or cellular tissue. What is man but a mass of thawing clay? The ball of the human finger is but a drop congealed. The fingers and toes flow to

---

[1] *laciniated* Divided into irregular lobes; *imbricated* Overlapping; *thalluses* Plant structures (such as those of mosses and lichens) which have no differentiation between leaf and stem and lack true roots.

their extent from the thawing mass of the body. Who knows what the human body would expand and flow out to under a more genial heaven? Is not the hand a spreading *palm* leaf with its lobes and veins? The ear may be regarded, fancifully, as a lichen, *umbilicaria*, on the side of the head, with its lobe or drop. The lip— *labium*, from *labor* (?)—laps or lapses from the sides of the cavernous mouth. The nose is a manifest congealed drop or stalactite. The chin is a still larger drop, the confluent dripping of the face. The cheeks are a slide from the brows into the valley of the face, opposed and diffused by the cheek bones. Each rounded lobe of the vegetable leaf, too, is a thick and now loitering drop, larger or smaller; the lobes are the fingers of the leaf; and as many lobes as it has, in so many directions it tends to flow, and more heat or other genial influences would have caused it to flow yet farther.

Thus it seemed that this one hillside illustrated the principle of all the operations of Nature. The Maker of this earth but patented a leaf. What Champollion[1] will decipher this hieroglyphic for us, that we may turn over a new leaf at last? This phenomenon is more exhilarating to me than the luxuriance and fertility of vineyards. True, it is somewhat excrementitious in its character, and there is no end to the heaps of liver, lights,[2] and bowels, as if the globe were turned wrong side outward; but this suggests at least that Nature has some bowels, and there again is mother of humanity. This is the frost coming out of the ground; this is Spring. It precedes the green and flowery spring, as mythology precedes regular poetry. I know of nothing more purgative of winter fumes and indigestions. It convinces me that Earth is still in her swaddling-clothes, and stretches forth baby fingers on every side. Fresh curls spring from the baldest brow. There is nothing inorganic. These foliaceous heaps lie along the bank like the slag[3] of a furnace, showing that Nature is "in full blast" within. The earth is not a mere fragment of dead history, stratum upon stratum like the leaves of a book,

to be studied by geologists and antiquaries chiefly, but living poetry like the leaves of a tree, which precede flowers and fruit—not a fossil earth, but a living earth; compared with whose great central life all animal and vegetable life is merely parasitic. Its throes will heave our exuviæ from their graves. You may melt your metals and cast them into the most beautiful molds you can; they will never excite me like the forms which this molten earth flows out into. And not only it, but the institutions upon it are plastic like clay in the hands of the potter.

Ere long, not only on these banks, but on every hill and plain and in every hollow, the frost comes out of the ground like a dormant quadruped from its burrow, and seeks the sea with music, or migrates to other climes in clouds. Thaw with his gentle persuasion is more powerful than Thor[4] with his hammer. The one melts, the other but breaks in pieces.

When the ground was partially bare of snow, and a few warm days had dried its surface somewhat, it was pleasant to compare the first tender signs of the infant year just peeping forth with the stately beauty of the withered vegetation which had withstood the winter— life-everlasting, goldenrods, pinweeds, and graceful wild grasses, more obvious and interesting frequently than in summer even, as if their beauty was not ripe till then; even cotton-grass, cat-tails, mulleins, johnswort, hard-hack, meadow-sweet, and other strong-stemmed plants, those unexhausted granaries which entertain the earliest birds—decent weeds, at least, which widowed Nature wears.[5] I am particularly attracted by the arching and sheaf-like top of the wool-grass; it brings back the summer to our winter memories, and is among the forms which art loves to copy, and which, in the vegetable kingdom, have the same relation to types already in the mind of man that astronomy has. It is an antique style, older than Greek or Egyptian. Many of the phenomena of Winter are suggestive of an inexpressible tenderness and fragile delicacy. We are accustomed to hear this king described as a rude and

---

[1] *Champollion* Jean-François Champollion (1790–1832), French scholar responsible for deciphering the hieroglyphics carved onto the Rosetta Stone, thereby providing the means for understanding ancient Egyptian writing.

[2] *lights* Lungs.

[3] *slag* Refuse created as a by-product during the process of smelting metal.

[4] *Thor* Norse god of thunder, often depicted with his fearsome hammer, Mjolnir.

[5] *decent weeds … Nature wears* Punning on a secondary use of the word "weeds," meaning the clothing worn by a widow.

boisterous tyrant; but with the gentleness of a lover he adorns the tresses of Summer.

At the approach of spring the red squirrels got under my house, two at a time, directly under my feet as I sat reading or writing, and kept up the queerest chuckling and chirruping and vocal pirouetting and gurgling sounds that ever were heard; and when I stamped they only chirruped the louder, as if past all fear and respect in their mad pranks, defying humanity to stop them. No, you don't—chickaree—chickaree. They were wholly deaf to my arguments, or failed to perceive their force, and fell into a strain of invective that was irresistible.

The first sparrow of spring! The year beginning with younger hope than ever! The faint silvery warblings heard over the partially bare and moist fields from the bluebird, the song sparrow, and the red-wing, as if the last flakes of winter tinkled as they fell! What at such a time are histories, chronologies, traditions, and all written revelations? The brooks sing carols and glees to the spring. The marsh hawk, sailing low over the meadow, is already seeking the first slimy life that awakes. The sinking sound of melting snow is heard in all dells, and the ice dissolves apace in the ponds. The grass flames up on the hillsides like a spring fire, "*et primitus oritur herba imbribus primoribus evocata,*"[1] as if the earth sent forth an inward heat to greet the returning sun; not yellow but green is the color of its flame; the symbol of perpetual youth, the grass-blade, like a long green ribbon, streams from the sod into the summer, checked indeed by the frost, but anon pushing on again, lifting its spear of last year's hay with the fresh life below. It grows as steadily as the rill oozes out of the ground. It is almost identical with that, for in the growing days of June, when the rills are dry, the grass-blades are their channels, and from year to year the herds drink at this perennial green stream, and the mower draws from it betimes their winter supply. So our human life but dies down to its root, and still puts forth its green blade to eternity.

Walden is melting apace. There is a canal two rods wide along the northerly and westerly sides, and wider still at the east end. A great field of ice has cracked off

from the main body. I hear a song sparrow singing from the bushes on the shore—*olit, olit, olit—chip, chip, chip, che char—che wiss, wiss, wiss.* He too is helping to crack it. How handsome the great sweeping curves in the edge of the ice, answering somewhat to those of the shore, but more regular! It is unusually hard, owing to the recent severe but transient cold, and all watered or waved like a palace floor. But the wind slides eastward over its opaque surface in vain, till it reaches the living surface beyond. It is glorious to behold this ribbon of water sparkling in the sun, the bare face of the pond full of glee and youth, as if it spoke the joy of the fishes within it, and of the sands on its shore—a silvery sheen as from the scales of a leuciscus,[2] as it were all one active fish. Such is the contrast between winter and spring. Walden was dead and is alive again. But this spring it broke up more steadily, as I have said.

The change from storm and winter to serene and mild weather, from dark and sluggish hours to bright and elastic ones, is a memorable crisis which all things proclaim. It is seemingly instantaneous at last. Suddenly an influx of light filled my house, though the evening was at hand, and the clouds of winter still overhung it, and the eaves were dripping with sleety rain. I looked out the window, and lo! where yesterday was cold gray ice there lay the transparent pond already calm and full of hope as in a summer evening, reflecting a summer evening sky in its bosom, though none was visible overhead, as if it had intelligence with some remote horizon. I heard a robin in the distance, the first I had heard for many a thousand years, methought, whose note I shall not forget for many a thousand more—the same sweet and powerful song as of yore. O the evening robin, at the end of a New England summer day! If I could ever find the twig he sits upon! I mean *he*; I mean *the twig*. This at least is not the *Turdus migratorius*.[3] The pitch pines and shrub oaks about my house, which had so long drooped, suddenly resumed their several characters, looked brighter, greener, and more erect and alive, as if effectually cleansed and restored by the rain. I knew that it would not rain anymore. You may tell by looking at any twig of the forest, ay, at your very wood-pile, whether its winter is past or not. As it grew darker, I was startled by the honking

---

1   *et primitus … primoribus evocata* From *Rerum Rusticarum* by Marcus Terentius Varro (116–27 BCE), Roman scholar: "and the grass which is called forth by the early rains is just growing."

2   *leuciscus* Genus of freshwater fish.

3   *Turdus migratorius* The American robin.

of geese flying low over the woods, like weary travelers getting in late from Southern lakes, and indulging at last in unrestrained complaint and mutual consolation. Standing at my door, I could hear the rush of their wings; when, driving toward my house, they suddenly spied my light, and with hushed clamor wheeled and settled in the pond. So I came in, and shut the door, and passed my first spring night in the woods.

In the morning I watched the geese from the door through the mist, sailing in the middle of the pond, fifty rods off, so large and tumultuous that Walden appeared like an artificial pond for their amusement. But when I stood on the shore they at once rose up with a great flapping of wings at the signal of their commander, and when they had got into rank circled about over my head, twenty-nine of them, and then steered straight to Canada, with a regular *honk* from the leader at intervals, trusting to break their fast in muddier pools. A "plump" of ducks rose at the same time and took the route to the north in the wake of their noisier cousins.

For a week I heard the circling, groping clangor of some solitary goose in the foggy mornings, seeking its companion, and still peopling the woods with the sound of a larger life than they could sustain. In April the pigeons were seen again flying express in small flocks, and in due time I heard the martins twittering over my clearing, though it had not seemed that the township contained so many that it could afford me any, and I fancied that they were peculiarly of the ancient race that dwelt in hollow trees ere white men came. In almost all climes the tortoise and the frog are among the precursors and heralds of this season, and birds fly with song and glancing plumage, and plants spring and bloom, and winds blow, to correct this slight oscillation of the poles and preserve the equilibrium of nature.

As every season seems best to us in its turn, so the coming in of spring is like the creation of Cosmos out of Chaos and the realization of the Golden Age.[1]

Eurus ad Auroram, Nabathaeaque regna recessit,
Persidaque, et radiis juga subdita matutinis.

The East-Wind withdrew to Aurora and the
    Nabathæan kingdom,
And the Persian, and the ridges placed under the
    morning rays.

* * * * * * * * * * * * *

Man was born. Whether that Artificer of things,
The origin of a better world, made him from the
    divine seed;
Or the earth, being recent and lately sundered from
    the high
Ether, retained some seeds of cognate heaven.

A single gentle rain makes the grass many shades greener. So our prospects brighten on the influx of better thoughts. We should be blessed if we lived in the present always, and took advantage of every accident that befell us, like the grass which confesses the influence of the slightest dew that falls on it; and did not spend our time in atoning for the neglect of past opportunities, which we call doing our duty. We loiter in winter while it is already spring. In a pleasant spring morning all men's sins are forgiven. Such a day is a truce to vice. While such a sun holds out to burn, the vilest sinner may return. Through our own recovered innocence we discern the innocence of our neighbors. You may have known your neighbor yesterday for a thief, a drunkard, or a sensualist, and merely pitied or despised him, and despaired of the world; but the sun shines bright and warm this first spring morning, recreating the world, and you meet him at some serene work, and see how his exhausted and debauched veins expand with still joy and bless the new day, feel the spring influence with the innocence of infancy, and all his faults are forgotten. There is not only an atmosphere of good will about him, but even a savor of holiness groping for expression, blindly and ineffectually perhaps, like a new-born instinct, and for a short hour the south hill-side echoes to no vulgar jest. You see some innocent fair shoots preparing to burst from his gnarled rind and try another year's life, tender and fresh as the youngest plant. Even he has entered into

---

[1] *the creation ... Golden Age* In Classical mythology, Cosmos, or the universe, was created out of the primordial state of Chaos, ushering in the peaceful and prosperous Golden Age of human history. The myth was recounted by many Classical authors; the quotations here are from the *Metamorphoses*, by the Roman writer Ovid (43 BCE–C. 17 CE), translated by Thoreau. The two quotations are of

---

1.61–62 and 1.78–81. (Oddly, Thoreau provides the Latin for only the first of these.)

the joy of his Lord. Why the jailer does not leave open his prison doors—why the judge does not dismiss his case—why the preacher does not dismiss his congregation! It is because they do not obey the hint which God gives them, nor accept the pardon which he freely offers to all.

"A return to goodness produced each day in the tranquil and beneficent breath of the morning, causes that in respect to the love of virtue and the hatred of vice, one approaches a little the primitive nature of man, as the sprouts of the forest which has been felled. In like manner the evil which one does in the interval of a day prevents the germs of virtues which began to spring up again from developing themselves and destroys them.

"After the germs of virtue have thus been prevented many times from developing themselves, then the beneficent breath of evening does not suffice to preserve them. As soon as the breath of evening does not suffice longer to preserve them, then the nature of man does not differ much from that of the brute. Men seeing the nature of this man like that of the brute, think that he has never possessed the innate faculty of reason. Are those the true and natural sentiments of man?"[1]

The Golden Age was first created, which without any
    avenger
Spontaneously without law cherished fidelity and
    rectitude.
Punishment and fear were not; nor were threatening
    words read
On suspended brass; nor did the suppliant crowd fear
The words of their judge; but were safe without an
    avenger.
Not yet the pine felled on its mountains had descended
To the liquid waves that it might see a foreign world,
And mortals knew no shores but their own.

*   *   *   *   *   *   *   *   *   *   *   *

There was eternal spring, and placid zephyrs with
    warm
Blasts soothed the flowers born without seed.[2]

On the 29th of April, as I was fishing from the bank of the river near the Nine-Acre-Corner bridge, standing on the quaking grass and willow roots, where the muskrats lurk, I heard a singular rattling sound, somewhat like that of the sticks which boys play with their fingers, when, looking up, I observed a very slight and graceful hawk, like a nighthawk, alternately soaring like a ripple and tumbling a rod or two over and over, showing the underside of its wings, which gleamed like a satin ribbon in the sun, or like the pearly inside of a shell. This sight reminded me of falconry and what nobleness and poetry are associated with that sport. The Merlin it seemed to me it might be called: but I care not for its name. It was the most ethereal flight I had ever witnessed. It did not simply flutter like a butterfly, nor soar like the larger hawks, but it sported with proud reliance in the fields of air; mounting again and again with its strange chuckle, it repeated its free and beautiful fall, turning over and over like a kite, and then recovering from its lofty tumbling, as if it had never set its foot on *terra firma*.[3] It appeared to have no companion in the universe, sporting there alone, and to need none but the morning and the ether with which it played. It was not lonely, but made all the earth lonely beneath it. Where was the parent which hatched it, its kindred, and its father in the heavens? The tenant of the air, it seemed related to the earth but by an egg hatched sometime in the crevice of a crag; or was its native nest made in the angle of a cloud, woven of the rainbow's trimmings and the sunset sky, and lined with some soft midsummer haze caught up from earth? Its eyrie now some cliffy cloud.

Beside this I got a rare mess of golden and silver and bright cupreous[4] fishes, which looked like a string of jewels. Ah! I have penetrated to those meadows on the morning of many a first spring day, jumping from hummock to hummock, from willow root to willow root, when the wild river valley and the woods were bathed in so pure and bright a light as would have waked the dead, if they had been slumbering in their graves, as some suppose. There needs no stronger proof of immortality. All things must live in such a light. O

---

[1]   *A return ... of man*   Quotation from the *Works* by Chinese philosopher Mencius or Meng-tzu (372–289 BCE).

[2]   *The Golden ... without seed*   See Ovid's *Metamorphoses* 1.89–96, 1.107–08.

[3]   *terra firma*   Latin: solid land.

[4]   *cupreous*   Copper-colored.

Death, where was thy sting? O Grave, where was thy victory, then?[1]

Our village life would stagnate if it were not for the unexplored forests and meadows which surround it. We need the tonic of wildness—to wade sometimes in marshes where the bittern and the meadow-hen lurk, and hear the booming of the snipe; to smell the whispering sedge where only some wilder and more solitary fowl builds her nest, and the mink crawls with its belly close to the ground. At the same time that we are earnest to explore and learn all things, we require that all things be mysterious and unexplorable, that land and sea be infinitely wild, unsurveyed and unfathomed by us because unfathomable. We can never have enough of nature. We must be refreshed by the sight of inexhaustible vigor, vast and titanic features, the sea-coast with its wrecks, the wilderness with its living and its decaying trees, the thundercloud, and the rain which lasts three weeks and produces freshets.[2] We need to witness our own limits transgressed, and some life pasturing freely where we never wander. We are cheered when we observe the vulture feeding on the carrion which disgusts and disheartens us, and deriving health and strength from the repast. There was a dead horse in the hollow by the path to my house, which compelled me sometimes to go out of my way, especially in the night when the air was heavy, but the assurance it gave me of the strong appetite and inviolable health of Nature was my compensation for this. I love to see that Nature is so rife with life that myriads can be afforded to be sacrificed and suffered to prey on one another; that tender organizations can be so serenely squashed out of existence like pulp—tadpoles which herons gobble up, and tortoises and toads run over in the road; and that sometimes it has rained flesh and blood! With the liability to accident, we must see how little account is to be made of it. The impression made on a wise man is that of universal innocence. Poison is not poisonous after all, nor are any wounds fatal. Compassion is a very untenable ground. It must be expeditious. Its pleadings will not bear to be stereotyped.

Early in May, the oaks, hickories, maples, and other trees, just putting out amidst the pine woods around the pond, imparted a brightness like sunshine to the landscape, especially in cloudy days, as if the sun were breaking through mists and shining faintly on the hill-sides here and there. On the third or fourth of May I saw a loon in the pond, and during the first week of the month I heard the whippoorwill, the brown-thrasher, the veery, the wood-pewee, the chewink, and other birds. I had heard the wood-thrush long before. The phoebe had already come once more and looked in at my door and window, to see if my house was cavern-like enough for her, sustaining herself on humming wings with clinched talons, as if she held by the air, while she surveyed the premises. The sulphur-like pollen of the pitch-pine soon covered the pond and the stones and rotten wood along the shore, so that you could have collected a barrelful. This is the "sulphur showers" we hear of. Even in Calidas' drama of Sacontala,[3] we read of "rills dyed yellow with the golden dust of the lotus." And so the seasons went rolling on into summer, as one rambles into higher and higher grass.

Thus was my first year's life in the woods completed; and the second year was similar to it. I finally left Walden September 6th, 1847.

CHAPTER 18
CONCLUSION

To the sick the doctors wisely recommend a change of air and scenery. Thank Heaven, here is not all the world. The buck-eye[4] does not grow in New England, and the mockingbird is rarely heard here. The wild goose is more of a cosmopolite[5] than we; he breaks his fast in Canada, takes a luncheon in the Ohio, and plumes himself for the night in a southern bayou. Even the bison, to some extent, keeps pace with the seasons, cropping the pastures of the Colorado only till a greener and sweeter grass awaits him by the Yellowstone. Yet we think that if rail fences are pulled down, and stone walls piled up on our farms, bounds are henceforth set to our lives and our fates decided. If you are chosen town clerk, forsooth, you cannot go to

---

[1] *O Death ... victory, then?* See 1 Corinthians 15.55: "O death, where is thy sting? O grave, where is thy victory?"

[2] *freshets* Freshwater streams.

[3] *Calidas' drama of Sacontala* Referring to a Sanskrit play *Shakuntala* by Kalidasa.

[4] *buck-eye* Chestnut tree.

[5] *cosmopolite* Citizen of the world; person at home in a wide variety of different environments.

Tierra del Fuego[1] this summer: but you may go to the land of infernal fire nevertheless. The universe is wider than our views of it.

Yet we should oftener look over the tafferel[2] of our craft, like curious passengers, and not make the voyage like stupid sailors picking oakum.[3] The other side of the globe is but the home of our correspondent. Our voyaging is only great-circle sailing, and the doctors prescribe for diseases of the skin merely. One hastens to southern Africa to chase the giraffe; but surely that is not the game he would be after. How long, pray, would a man hunt giraffes if he could? Snipes and woodcocks also may afford rare sport; but I trust it would be nobler game to shoot one's self.

> Direct your eye right inward, and you'll find
> A thousand regions in your mind
> Yet undiscovered. Travel them, and be
> Expert in home-cosmography.[4]

What does Africa, what does the West stand for? Is not our own interior white on the chart? black though it may prove, like the coast, when discovered. Is it the source of the Nile, or the Niger, or the Mississippi, or a Northwest Passage around this continent, that we would find? Are these the problems which most concern mankind? Is Franklin the only man who is lost, that his wife should be so earnest to find him?[5] Does Mr. Grinnell[6] know where he himself is? Be rather the Mungo Park, the Lewis and Clark and Frobisher,[7] of your own streams and oceans; explore your own higher latitudes, with shiploads of preserved meats to support you, if they be necessary; and pile the empty cans sky-high for a sign. Were preserved meats invented to preserve meat merely? Nay, be a Columbus to whole new continents and worlds within you, opening new channels, not of trade, but of thought. Every man is the lord of a realm beside which the earthly empire of the Czar is but a petty state, a hummock left by the ice. Yet some can be patriotic who have no *self*-respect, and sacrifice the greater to the less. They love the soil which makes their graves, but have no sympathy with the spirit which may still animate their clay.[8] Patriotism is a maggot in their heads. What was the meaning of that South-Sea Exploring Expedition,[9] with all its parade and expense, but an indirect recognition of the fact that there are continents and seas in the moral world to which every man is an isthmus or an inlet, yet unexplored by him, but that it is easier to sail many thousand miles through cold and storm and cannibals, in a government ship, with five hundred men and boys to assist one, than it is to explore the private sea, the Atlantic and Pacific Ocean of one's being alone.

> *Erret, et extremos alter scrutetur Iberos.*
> *Plus habet hic vitae, plus habet ille viae.*[10]

> Let them wander and scrutinize the outlandish
>   Australians.
> I have more of God, they more of the road.

It is not worth the while to go round the world to count the cats in Zanzibar.[11] Yet do this even till you can do better, and you may perhaps find some "Symmes'

---

[1]   *Tierra del Fuego*   Archipelago off the southwest coast of South America; Thoreau puns on the Spanish translation of the name, "Land of Fire."

[2]   *tafferel*   Upper part of a ship's stern.

[3]   *picking oakum*   Picking apart the ship's ropes in order to use their fibers to make caulking for the ship—painstaking and tedious work often assigned to prisoners, or to sailors when there was nothing better to do.

[4]   *Direct your ... home-cosmography*   From "To My Honoured Friend Sir Ed. P. Knight" by English poet William Habington (1605–54).

[5]   *Is Franklin ... find him?*   Referring to the lost Arctic expedition of English explorer Sir John Franklin (1786–1847); his wife Jane Franklin launched one of many searches to find him and his crewmembers.

[6]   *Mr. Grinnell*   Henry Grinnell (1799–1874), New York merchant who spent much of his retirement after 1850 participating in efforts to find Franklin's remains.

[7]   *Mungo Park ... and Frobisher*   Mungo Park (1771–1806); Meriwether Lewis (1774–1809) and William Clark (1770–1838); and Martin Frobisher (c. 1535–94), all famous explorers.

[8]   *clay*   I.e., bodies.

[9]   *South-Sea Exploring Expedition*   Led by Charles Wilkes (1798–1877), American expedition of the Pacific Ocean and Antarctica undertaken from 1838 to 1842.

[10]   *Erret, et ... ille viae*   From "The Old Man of Verona" by Latin poet Claudian (c. 370–c. 404); the following is Thoreau's rather loose translation of the lines.

[11]   *cats in Zanzibar*   Allusion to *The Races of Man* (1851) by American anthropologist Charles Pickering; the book describes his travels in Africa, and his study of the domestic cats of Zanzibar.

Hole"[1] by which to get at the inside at last. England and France, Spain and Portugal, Gold Coast and Slave Coast, all front on this private sea; but no bark[2] from them has ventured out of sight of land, though it is without doubt the direct way to India. If you would learn to speak all tongues and conform to the customs of all nations, if you would travel farther than all travelers, be naturalized in all climes, and cause the Sphinx[3] to dash her head against a stone, even obey the precept of the old philosopher, and Explore thyself.[4] Herein are demanded the eye and the nerve. Only the defeated and deserters go to the wars, cowards that run away and enlist. Start now on that farthest western way, which does not pause at the Mississippi or the Pacific, nor conduct toward a worn-out China or Japan, but leads on direct, a tangent to this sphere, summer and winter, day and night, sun down, moon down, and at last earth down too.

It is said that Mirabeau[5] took to highway robbery "to ascertain what degree of resolution was necessary in order to place one's self in formal opposition to the most sacred laws of society." He declared that "a soldier who fights in the ranks does not require half so much courage as a foot-pad," —"that honor and religion have never stood in the way of a well-considered and a firm resolve." This was manly, as the world goes; and yet it was idle, if not desperate. A saner man would have found himself often enough "in formal opposition" to what are deemed "the most sacred laws of society," through obedience to yet more sacred laws, and so have tested his resolution without going out of his way. It is not for a man to put himself in such an attitude to society, but to maintain himself in whatever attitude he find himself through obedience to the laws of his being, which will never be one of opposition to a just government, if he should chance to meet with such.

I left the woods for as good a reason as I went there. Perhaps it seemed to me that I had several more lives to live, and could not spare any more time for that one. It is remarkable how easily and insensibly we fall into a particular route, and make a beaten track for ourselves. I had not lived there a week before my feet wore a path from my door to the pond-side; and though it is five or six years since I trod it, it is still quite distinct. It is true, I fear that others may have fallen into it, and so helped to keep it open. The surface of the earth is soft and impressible by the feet of men; and so with the paths which the mind travels. How worn and dusty, then, must be the highways of the world, how deep the ruts of tradition and conformity! I did not wish to take a cabin passage, but rather to go before the mast and on the deck of the world, for there I could best see the moonlight amid the mountains. I do not wish to go below now.

I learned this, at least, by my experiment; that if one advances confidently in the direction of his dreams, and endeavors to live the life which he has imagined, he will meet with a success unexpected in common hours. He will put some things behind, will pass an invisible boundary; new, universal, and more liberal laws will begin to establish themselves around and within him; or the old laws be expanded, and interpreted in his favor in a more liberal sense, and he will live with the license of a higher order of beings. In proportion as he simplifies his life, the laws of the universe will appear less complex, and solitude will not be solitude, nor poverty poverty, nor weakness weakness. If you have built castles in the air, your work need not be lost; that is where they should be. Now put the foundations under them.

It is a ridiculous demand which England and America make, that you shall speak so that they can understand you. Neither men nor toadstools grow so. As if that were important, and there were not enough to understand you without them. As if Nature could support but one order of understandings, could not sustain birds as well as quadrupeds, flying as well as creeping things, and *hush* and *who*, which Bright[6] can understand, were the best English. As if there were

---

[1] *Symmes' Hole* Referring to the theory expanded upon by John Symmes (1780–1829), which posits that the Earth is hollow and that its "habitable" interior can be accessed through holes at the North and South Poles.

[2] *bark* Ship.

[3] *Sphinx* In Greek mythology, the winged guardian of Thebes, who killed those who could not answer her riddles; when Oedipus did solve her riddle, she dashed her head against a stone.

[4] *the precept ... Explore thyself* Allusion to the ancient Greek aphorism "know thyself," made famous in particular by its use in works by Plato (c. 427–c. 347 BCE).

[5] *Mirabeau* French Revolutionary leader Honoré Gabriel Riqueti, comte de Mirabeau (1749–91).

[6] *Bright* Common name for an ox.

safety in stupidity alone. I fear chiefly lest my expression may not be *extra-vagant*[1] enough, may not wander far enough beyond the narrow limits of my daily experience, so as to be adequate to the truth of which I have been convinced. *Extra vagance!* it depends on how you are yarded. The migrating buffalo, which seeks new pastures in another latitude, is not extravagant like the cow which kicks over the pail, leaps the cowyard fence, and runs after her calf, in milking time. I desire to speak somewhere *without* bounds; like a man in a waking moment, to men in their waking moments; for I am convinced that I cannot exaggerate enough even to lay the foundation of a true expression. Who that has heard a strain of music feared then lest he should speak extravagantly anymore forever? In view of the future or possible, we should live quite laxly and undefined in front, our outlines dim and misty on that side; as our shadows reveal an insensible perspiration toward the sun. The volatile truth of our words should continually betray the inadequacy of the residual statement. Their truth is instantly *translated*; its literal monument alone remains. The words which express our faith and piety are not definite; yet they are significant and fragrant like frankincense to superior natures.

Why level downward to our dullest perception always, and praise that as common sense? The commonest sense is the sense of men asleep, which they express by snoring. Sometimes we are inclined to class those who are once-and-a-half-witted with the half-witted, because we appreciate only a third part of their wit. Some would find fault with the morning red, if they ever got up early enough. "They pretend," as I hear, "that the verses of Kabir have four different senses; illusion, spirit, intellect, and the exoteric doctrine of the Vedas";[2] but in this part of the world it is considered a ground for complaint if a man's writings admit of more than one interpretation. While England endeavors to cure the potato-rot,[3] will not any

endeavor to cure the brain-rot, which prevails so much more widely and fatally?

I do not suppose that I have attained to obscurity, but I should be proud if no more fatal fault were found with my pages on this score than was found with the Walden ice. Southern customers objected to its blue color, which is the evidence of its purity, as if it were muddy, and preferred the Cambridge ice, which is white, but tastes of weeds. The purity men love is like the mists which envelop the earth, and not like the azure ether beyond.

Some are dinning in our ears that we Americans, and moderns generally, are intellectual dwarfs compared with the ancients, or even the Elizabethan men. But what is that to the purpose? A living dog is better than a dead lion.[4] Shall a man go and hang himself because he belongs to the race of pygmies, and not be the biggest pygmy that he can? Let everyone mind his own business, and endeavor to be what he was made.

Why should we be in such desperate haste to succeed and in such desperate enterprises? If a man does not keep pace with his companions, perhaps it is because he hears a different drummer. Let him step to the music which he hears, however measured or far away. It is not important that he should mature as soon as an apple tree or an oak. Shall he turn his spring into summer? If the condition of things which we were made for is not yet, what were any reality which we can substitute? We will not be shipwrecked on a vain reality. Shall we with pains erect a heaven of blue glass over ourselves, though when it is done we shall be sure to gaze still at the true ethereal heaven far above, as if the former were not?

There was an artist in the city of Kouroo[5] who was disposed to strive after perfection. One day it came into his mind to make a staff. Having considered that in an imperfect work time is an ingredient, but into a perfect work time does not enter, he said to himself, It shall be perfect in all respects, though I should do nothing else in my life. He proceeded instantly to

---

1   *extra-vagant*   Play on the Latin origins of the word: *extra* meaning "outside," *vagant* meaning "to wander."

2   *They pretend … the Vedas*   From *Histoire de la littérature hindoui et hindoustani* (1839) by French scholar Garcin de Tassy; *Kabir*   Indian poet and mystic of the fifteenth century, influenced by both Hinduism and Islam.

3   *potato-rot*   Potato blight, which affected much of Europe in the 1840s but especially Ireland, then under the rule of England, where

it caused a devastating famine; close to one million people are estimated to have died between 1845 and 1848.

4   *A living … dead lion*   See Ecclesiastes 9.4.

5   *There was … of Kouroo*   The source of the following fable is unclear; though influences from Hindu texts are evident, Thoreau likely made up the substance of the tale himself.

the forest for wood, being resolved that it should not be made of unsuitable material; and as he searched for and rejected stick after stick, his friends gradually deserted him, for they grew old in their works and died, but he grew not older by a moment. His singleness of purpose and resolution, and his elevated piety, endowed him, without his knowledge, with perennial youth. As he made no compromise with Time, Time kept out of his way, and only sighed at a distance because he could not overcome him. Before he had found a stock in all respects suitable the city of Kouroo was a hoary ruin, and he sat on one of its mounds to peel the stick. Before he had given it the proper shape the dynasty of the Candahars was at an end, and with the point of the stick he wrote the name of the last of that race in the sand, and then resumed his work. By the time he had smoothed and polished the staff Kalpa was no longer the pole-star; and ere he had put on the ferule and the head adorned with precious stones, Brahma[1] had awoke and slumbered many times. But why do I stay to mention these things? When the finishing stroke was put to his work, it suddenly expanded before the eyes of the astonished artist into the fairest of all the creations of Brahma. He had made a new system in making a staff, a world with full and fair proportions; in which, though the old cities and dynasties had passed away, fairer and more glorious ones had taken their places. And now he saw by the heap of shavings still fresh at his feet, that, for him and his work, the former lapse of time had been an illusion, and that no more time had elapsed than is required for a single scintillation from the brain of Brahma to fall on and inflame the tinder of a mortal brain. The material was pure, and his art was pure; how could the result be other than wonderful?

No face which we can give to a matter will stead us so well at last as the truth. This alone wears well. For the most part, we are not where we are, but in a false position. Through an infinity of our natures, we suppose a case, and put ourselves into it, and hence are in two cases at the same time, and it is doubly difficult to get out. In sane moments we regard only the facts, the case that is. Say what you have to say, not what you ought. Any truth is better than make-believe. Tom

Hyde, the tinker, standing on the gallows, was asked if he had anything to say. "Tell the tailors," said he, "to remember to make a knot in their thread before they take the first stitch." His companion's prayer is forgotten.[2]

However mean your life is, meet it and live it; do not shun it and call it hard names. It is not so bad as you are. It looks poorest when you are richest. The fault-finder will find faults even in paradise. Love your life, poor as it is. You may perhaps have some pleasant, thrilling, glorious hours, even in a poor-house. The setting sun is reflected from the windows of the alms-house as brightly as from the rich man's abode; the snow melts before its door as early in the spring. I do not see but a quiet mind may live as contentedly there, and have as cheering thoughts, as in a palace. The town's poor seem to me often to live the most independent lives of any. Maybe they are simply great enough to receive without misgiving. Most think that they are above being supported by the town; but it oftener happens that they are not above supporting themselves by dishonest means, which should be more disreputable. Cultivate poverty like a garden herb, like sage. Do not trouble yourself much to get new things, whether clothes or friends. Turn the old; return to them. Things do not change; we change. Sell your clothes and keep your thoughts. God will see that you do not want society. If I were confined to a corner of a garret all my days, like a spider, the world would be just as large to me while I had my thoughts about me. The philosopher said: "From an army of three divisions one can take away its general, and put it in disorder; from the man the most abject and vulgar one cannot take away his thought."[3] Do not seek so anxiously to be developed, to subject yourself to many influences to be played on; it is all dissipation. Humility like darkness reveals the heavenly lights. The shadows of poverty and meanness gather around us, "and lo! creation widens to our view."[4] We are often reminded that if there were bestowed on us

---

1 *Brahma* Hindu creator god.

2 *Tom Hyde ... is forgotten* Thoreau's source for this story and figure is unclear.

3 *The philosopher ... his thought* From the *Analects* of Confucius 9.26.

4 *and lo! ... our view* Slight misquotation from "Night and Day" or "To Night" by Spanish-born poet and theologian Joseph Blanco White (1775–1841).

the wealth of Croesus,[1] our aims must still be the same, and our means essentially the same. Moreover, if you are restricted in your range by poverty, if you cannot buy books and newspapers, for instance, you are but confined to the most significant and vital experiences; you are compelled to deal with the material which yields the most sugar and the most starch. It is life near the bone where it is sweetest. You are defended from being a trifler. No man loses ever on a lower level by magnanimity on a higher. Superfluous wealth can buy superfluities only. Money is not required to buy one necessary of the soul.

I live in the angle of a leaden wall, into whose composition was poured a little alloy of bell metal. Often, in the repose of my mid-day, there reaches my ears a confused *tintinnabulum* from without. It is the noise of my contemporaries. My neighbors tell me of their adventures with famous gentlemen and ladies, what notabilities they met at the dinner-table; but I am no more interested in such things than in the contents of the Daily Times. The interest and the conversation are about costume and manners chiefly; but a goose is a goose still, dress it as you will. They tell me of California and Texas, of England and the Indies, of the Hon. Mr. —— of Georgia or of Massachusetts, all transient and fleeting phenomena, till I am ready to leap from their courtyard like the Mameluke bey.[2] I delight to come to my bearings—not walk in procession with pomp and parade, in a conspicuous place, but to walk even with the Builder of the universe, if I may—not to live in this restless, nervous, bustling, trivial Nineteenth Century, but stand or sit thoughtfully while it goes by. What are men celebrating? They are all on a committee of arrangements, and hourly expect a speech from somebody. God is only the president of the day, and Webster[3] is his orator. I love to weigh, to settle, to gravitate toward that which most strongly and rightfully attracts me—not hang by the beam of the scale and try to weigh less, not suppose a case, but take the case that is; to travel the only path I can, and that on which no power can resist me. It affords me no satisfaction to commence to spring an arch before I have got a solid foundation. Let us not play at kittly-benders.[4] There is a solid bottom everywhere. We read that the traveler asked the boy if the swamp before him had a hard bottom. The boy replied that it had. But presently the traveler's horse sank in up to the girths, and he observed to the boy, "I thought you said that this bog had a hard bottom." "So it has," answered the latter, "but you have not got half way to it yet." So it is with the bogs and quicksands of society; but he is an old boy that knows it. Only what is thought, said, or done at a certain rare coincidence is good. I would not be one of those who will foolishly drive a nail into mere lath and plastering; such a deed would keep me awake nights. Give me a hammer, and let me feel for the furring.[5] Do not depend on the putty. Drive a nail home and clinch it so faithfully that you can wake up in the night and think of your work with satisfaction—a work at which you would not be ashamed to invoke the Muse. So will help you God, and so only. Every nail driven should be as another rivet in the machine of the universe, you carrying on the work.

Rather than love, than money, than fame, give me truth. I sat at a table where were rich food and wine in abundance, and obsequious attendance, but sincerity and truth were not; and I went away hungry from the inhospitable board. The hospitality was as cold as the ices. I thought that there was no need of ice to freeze them. They talked to me of the age of the wine and the fame of the vintage; but I thought of an older, a newer, and purer wine, of a more glorious vintage, which they had not got, and could not buy. The style, the house and grounds and "entertainment" pass for nothing with me. I called on the king, but he made me wait in his hall, and conducted like a man incapacitated for hospitality. There was a man in my neighborhood who lived in a hollow tree. His manners were truly regal. I should have done better had I called on him.

---

1   *Croesus* Famously affluent king of Lydia (r. c. 585–c. 546 BCE), whose name came to be applied to anyone of great wealth.

2   *Mameluke bey* Reference to the massacre of the Mamluks, an Egyptian military caste, in 1811; according to legend, all died but for one "bey" or officer, who leapt from the citadel with his horse.

3   *Webster* Massachusetts senator Daniel Webster (1782–1852), renowned for his oratorical skill and admired by many but often criticized by Thoreau, who disliked Webster for his willingness to compromise with supporters of slavery (notably in the Compromise of 1850).

4   *kittlybenders* Game of trying to run atop thin ice without breaking through.

5   *furring* Thin boards nailed to a surface in order to raise it to be lathed.

How long shall we sit in our porticoes practicing idle and musty virtues, which any work would make impertinent? As if one were to begin the day with long-suffering, and hire a man to hoe his potatoes; and in the afternoon go forth to practice Christian meekness and charity with goodness aforethought! Consider the China pride[1] and stagnant self-complacency of mankind. This generation inclines a little to congratulate itself on being the last of an illustrious line; and in Boston and London and Paris and Rome, thinking of its long descent, it speaks of its progress in art and science and literature with satisfaction. There are the Records of the Philosophical Societies, and the public Eulogies of *Great Men*! It is the good Adam contemplating his own virtue. "Yes, we have done great deeds, and sung divine songs, which shall never die,"—that is, as long as *we* can remember them. The learned societies and great men of Assyria,[2] where are they? What youthful philosophers and experimentalists we are! There is not one of my readers who has yet lived a whole human life. These may be but the spring months in the life of the race. If we have had the seven-years' itch,[3] we have not seen the seventeen-year locust yet in Concord. We are acquainted with a mere pellicle[4] of the globe on which we live. Most have not delved six feet beneath the surface, nor leaped as many above it. We know not where we are. Beside, we are sound asleep nearly half our time. Yet we esteem ourselves wise, and have an established order on the surface. Truly, we are deep thinkers, we are ambitious spirits! As I stand over the insect crawling amid the pine needles on the forest floor, and endeavoring to conceal itself from my sight, and ask myself why it will cherish those humble thoughts, and hide its head from me who might, perhaps, be its benefactor, and impart to its race some cheering information, I am reminded of the greater Benefactor and Intelligence that stands over me the human insect.

There is an incessant influx of novelty into the world, and yet we tolerate incredible dullness. I need only suggest what kind of sermons are still listened to in the most enlightened countries. There are such words as joy and sorrow, but they are only the burden of a psalm, sung with a nasal twang, while we believe in the ordinary and mean. We think that we can change our clothes only. It is said that the British Empire is very large and respectable, and that the United States are a first-rate power. We do not believe that a tide rises and falls behind every man which can float the British Empire like a chip, if he should ever harbor it in his mind. Who knows what sort of seventeen-year locust will next come out of the ground? The government of the world I live in was not framed, like that of Britain, in after-dinner conversations over the wine.

The life in us is like the water in the river. It may rise this year higher than man has ever known it, and flood the parched uplands; even this may be the eventful year, which will drown out all our muskrats. It was not always dry land where we dwell. I see far inland the banks which the stream anciently washed, before science began to record its freshets. Everyone has heard the story which has gone the rounds of New England, of a strong and beautiful bug which came out of the dry leaf of an old table of apple-tree wood, which had stood in a farmer's kitchen for sixty years, first in Connecticut, and afterward in Massachusetts, from an egg deposited in the living tree many years earlier still, as appeared by counting the annual layers beyond it; which was heard gnawing out for several weeks, hatched perchance by the heat of an urn. Who does not feel his faith in a resurrection and immortality strengthened by hearing of this? Who knows what beautiful and winged life, whose egg has been buried for ages under many concentric layers of woodenness in the dead dry life of society, deposited at first in the alburnum[5] of the green and living tree, which has been gradually converted into the semblance of its well-seasoned tomb—heard perchance gnawing out now for years by the astonished family of man, as they sat round the festive board—may unexpectedly come forth from amidst society's most trivial and handselled[6] furniture, to enjoy its perfect summer life at last!

---

[1] *China pride* Tensions arose between China and Britain in the 1830s, when the Chinese government refused to relax its longstanding isolationist foreign policy; thereafter, a widespread stereotype of the Chinese as proud and arrogant took root in the West.

[2] *Assyria* Empire of ancient Mesopotamia.

[3] *seven-years' itch* Scabies.

[4] *pellicle* Surface; skin.

[5] *alburnum* Sapwood.

[6] *handselled* Unwanted.

I do not say that John or Jonathan[1] will realize all this; but such is the character of that morrow which mere lapse of time can never make to dawn. The light which puts out our eyes is darkness to us. Only that day dawns to which we are awake. There is more day to dawn. The sun is but a morning star.

—1854

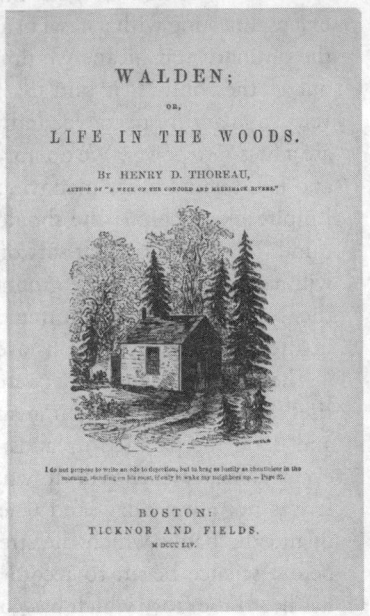

Title page of the first edition of *Walden; or, Life in the Woods.*

In Context

The Photographs of Herbert Wendell Gleason

At the age of 44, Congregationalist minister Herbert Wendell Gleason (1855–1937) gave up his position in order to pursue a new calling—studying, photographing, and writing about the natural world. In subsequent decades he became well known as a photographer as he traveled throughout North America, but he was known above all as a photographer of the New England landscapes that Thoreau had made famous half a century earlier. When Houghton Mifflin reproduced his photographs in their 1906 *Works of Henry David Thoreau,* the publisher described Gleason's contribution in glowing terms:

> Mr. Gleason has made a careful study of all Thoreau's writings … and has explored with equal thoroughness the woods and fields of Concord, visiting the localities mentioned in the Journal and getting photographs, not only of the places themselves, but also of many of the fleeting phenomena of the natural year in the very spots where Thoreau observed them.

In 1917 Gleason published *Through the Year with Thoreau,* in which he included many more of his photographs of Thoreau-related landscapes. A small selection is included here.

---

[1] *John or Jonathan* John Bull or Brother Jonathan, common personifications of England and America, respectively.

Thoreau's Cove, Walden Pond, 11 June 1901.

Fitchburg Railroad Train with Walden Pond in Winter, 24 March 1920.

Skunk Cabbage, from *Through the Year with Thoreau* (1917).

Eastern Shore, Walden Pond, 6 November 1899.

Ferns in the area Thoreau named Clintonia Swamp, just north of Walden Pond.

Cairn marking the site of Thoreau's cabin at Walden Pond. In 1881, Walt Whitman described this scene in his *Specimen Days*: "On the spot in the woods where Thoreau had his solitary house is now quite a cairn of stones, to mark the place; I too carried one and deposited on the heap." Elsewhere, Whitman declared that Thoreau, who had been a friend of his, "is not easily grasped—is elusive: yet he is one of the native forces—stands for a fact, a movement, an upheaval: Thoreau belongs to America, to the transcendental, to the protestors. ... Thoreau was not so precious, tender, a personality as Emerson: but he was a force—he looms up bigger and bigger[.]"

Frederick Douglass

1818 – 1895

Author of the most powerfully written and most widely read slave narrative of the antebellum era, Frederick Douglass became the foremost voice in the abolitionist movement, and, following the Civil War, one of the foremost critics of the horrors of the new "Jim Crow" system of oppression. He spoke up too against the oppression of women and against all forms of prejudice and inequality, and he spoke up consistently in favor of speaking up—in favor of resistance. "Power concedes nothing without a demand," he famously wrote. "It never did and it never will." He occupies a unique place in American literature, American history, and American political thought.

Douglass was born Frederick Augustus Washington Bailey in Talbot County, Maryland. A degree of mystery surrounds the circumstances of Douglass's birth; like many enslaved people, he was denied full knowledge of his parentage or date of birth. He inherited the enslavement of his mother, Harriet Bailey, but his father was almost certainly a white man, quite likely his enslaver, Aaron Anthony (though other possibilities have been suggested). Douglass came to accept a tentative birth year of 1817; however, we now know that he was born in February 1818.

In 1826 Douglass was acquired by the slaveholder Thomas Auld, and was sent to live in Baltimore with Auld's brother and sister-in-law. In 1833 Douglass was removed from his situation in Baltimore and forced to work on Thomas Auld's plantation. Emboldened by his growing consciousness of slavery's injustice, Douglass grew increasingly rebellious, and was sent to work for a man named Edward Covey, locally famous as a so-called slave-breaker. Douglass attempted escape twice. In 1836 he was part of a failed plot organized by several enslaved companions, and was briefly jailed for his participation. Two years later, Douglass's second attempt was successful. Douglass left unexplained in the first and second versions of his autobiography any of the details of this escape, on the grounds—as he explains in Chapter 11—that telling the story would probably cause "difficulties" for those who helped him and "would most undoubtedly induce greater vigilance on the part of slaveholders"; it is only the third and final version—the 1881 *Life and Times of Frederick Douglass*—that includes the story of his escape.

Douglass presents the escape very largely as a solo endeavor; as we now know, he was in fact aided by several people—very much including the free black woman Anna Murray, to whom he had become engaged shortly before the escape. It was largely from Anna that Douglass obtained the funds that enabled him to travel from slavery in Baltimore to freedom in New York on 3 September 1838. Anna made the same trip a week later, and on 15 September the two were married in the home of David Ruggles, a black grocer and printer who led an organization devoted to assisting fugitive slaves. It was Ruggles who suggested that Frederick Bailey change his name—as was often done by those wishing to minimize the chances of being captured and returned to bondage. For a few days Douglass called himself Frederick Johnson, and it was under that name that he and Anna were married.

Ruggles also suggested that the couple move to New Bedford, Massachusetts, a community more friendly than was New York to fugitives who had been enslaved, and one where he felt Douglass would be able to find employment. There the Douglasses stayed initially at the home of an abolitionist named Nathan Johnson—evidently one of many Johnsons in New Bedford. Feeling that another name was necessary to distinguish himself from the other Johnsons, Frederick asked Nathan Johnson to suggest a new name; according to the narrative, it was Johnson who suggested the name under which Douglass would become famous.

In the North Douglass found a land of remarkable prosperity but also of profound contradiction; though an ordinary white laborer might enjoy a more luxurious existence and higher education level than an upper-class southern slaveholder, a free black citizen could expect continual discrimination from employers, church congregations, and other groups. Eventually Douglass—whose religious conversion experiences are given more emphasis in his two later memoirs—found employment as a licensed preacher in the African Methodist Episcopal Zion Church. Douglass also became a regular reader of the *Liberator*, an antislavery newspaper founded by leading white abolitionist William Lloyd Garrison. Douglass began attending antislavery meetings, where he soon began to share his own story and to make a local name for himself. In August 1841 he delivered his first formal speech before an antislavery audience in Nantucket. His moving story and evident oratorical talents caught Garrison's attention; Douglass became a valued contributor to the *Liberator*, and was appointed to a paid position with the Massachusetts Anti-Slavery Society not long thereafter.

Over the following years Douglass traveled widely and delivered speech after speech to audiences throughout the Northern states; he came to occupy a central place in the abolitionist movement. When Emerson was invited to deliver a major speech on slavery in August 1844, for example, Frederick Douglass was among the three others rounding out the program. People everywhere found something extraordinary about him. Nathaniel P. Rogers, editor of the *Herald of Freedom* abolitionist newspaper, described in 1843 the effect of Douglass's words when the speaker was in full flight as "sterner, darker, deeper" than oratory or eloquence. "It was the volcanic outbreak of human nature, long pent up in slavery and at last bursting its imprisonment. It was the storm of insurrection."

Douglass's celebrated status also often made him a target; he endured egg- and brick-throwing and, in Pennsylvania in 1843, a mob attack resulted in a permanent injury to his right hand. Even those who ostensibly supported Douglass's goals were often unable or unwilling to reconcile the distinguished and eloquent speaker they saw with the enslaved life he described, and insisted that his story must have been falsified. (Douglass averred in the second version of his autobiography that "prejudice against color is stronger in the north than [in the] south; it hangs around my neck like a heavy weight.")

Emboldened rather than intimidated by the challenges to his story, Douglass began work on an autobiography in which he would provide factual details to corroborate his claims. Written in the space of just a few months beginning in December 1844, *Narrative of the Life of Frederick Douglass, an American Slave. Written by Himself,* was published in the spring of 1845 by the Anti-Slavery Office in Boston. The book was welcomed with enthusiasm in the abolitionist press; most notably, the *New York Tribune* on 10 June 1845 printed on its front page a long and highly favorable review (written by Margaret Fuller), along with a substantial excerpt from the book. By contrast, the *New York Herald* accorded it only a few words—"a neatly printed volume, which abolitionists may find interesting"—and most mainstream newspapers in northern states ignored it altogether. (In most southern states the dissemination of such works was strictly prohibited; a *Richmond Enquirer* article from April 1849 details a case in which a preacher named Jarvis C. Bacon was prosecuted for having circulated copies of Douglass's *Narrative* and another antislavery publication.)

By the 1840s the "slave narrative" was a well-established literary genre; in America alone at least ten such volumes were published between 1830 and 1845. Douglass's *Narrative* closely follows the conventions of the genre in several respects. The inclusion of a prefatory address by a white activist attesting to the book's authorship; the repeated assertions, near the beginning of the text, of un-hyperbolic truthfulness; the visceral descriptions of whippings, auction blocks, and other gruesome realities of enslaved life—all these are typical of the genre. Yet from the beginning Douglass's work was recognized as extraordinary in the quality of its writing and the depth of feeling it conveys; Fuller was not alone in finding the *Narrative* to be "glowing with … life and fertile in invention," "more simple, true, coherent, and warm with genuine feeling" than any other work of its kind. Writing in the 1860s, black abolitionist William Wells Brown reminisced that "the narrative of [Douglass's] life … gave a new impetus to the black man's literature. All other stories of fugitive slaves faded away before the beautifully written, highly descriptive, and thrilling memoir of Frederick Douglass." Within less than four months the *Narrative* had sold almost 5,000 copies, and by 1850 some 30,000 copies had been printed.

The book's broad readership and Douglass's increasing fame, however, did nothing to alter his legal status. With the threat of discovery and capture by fugitive-slave hunters in mind, Douglass embarked in late 1845 on a lecture tour of Great Britain—a tour that broadened Douglass's readership and led to several European editions of his *Narrative*. While he was abroad a group of English friends purchased his manumission for a sum of £150; Douglass returned to the United States a legally free man in 1847, and moved with his family to Rochester, New York.

That same year Douglass established a new antislavery weekly newspaper, *The North Star* (a collaboration with the free-born black abolitionist Martin Delany). The ideals emblazoned on its masthead—"Right is of no Sex—Truth is of no Color—God is the Father of us all, and we are all Brethren"—may seem unexceptionable today, but in 1847 they were revolutionary on several fronts. Douglass struggled to build a readership (in 1851 he merged *The North Star* with another weekly to form *Frederick Douglass' Paper*, and in 1858 he began to publish monthly rather than weekly), but he managed in one form or another to keep publishing a newspaper until 1863, and each issue is believed to have had several thousand readers.

William Lloyd Garrison did not entirely welcome the competition with his *Liberator*. By 1851, Douglass and Garrison had reached a formal parting of the ways, with issues of principle having come to separate the two. Garrison was an uncompromising believer in "immediatism"—the doctrine that slavery should be abolished immediately rather than gradually—but he remained reluctant to countenance the use of force to overcome the evils of slavery; Douglass, by contrast, was more and more strongly convinced that the use of force in certain circumstances was entirely justified. Douglass's revised and expanded 1855 autobiography, *My Bondage and My Freedom*, puts forward even more powerfully than the *Narrative* the case for forceful resistance to slavery. (A passage from the 1855 autobiography is provided for comparison in the online component of this anthology.)

Douglass had also begun to feel a desire to distance himself from the sometimes patronizing guidance of white abolitionists such as Garrison; his declared goal in founding *The North Star* had been to provide "a printing-press and paper, permanently established, under the complete control and direction of the immediate victims of slavery and oppression." Increasingly, questions about the appropriate means of resisting oppression became matters not only of the moral imperatives involved, but also matters of character formation; like Emerson, Douglass took the idea of self-reliance very much to heart. As early as 1848, in an essay entitled "What Are the Colored People Doing for Themselves?," Douglass had written against "that lazy, mean, and cowardly spirit that robs us of all self-reliance, and teaches us to depend upon others for the accomplishment of that which we should achieve with our own hands." For Douglass, the principle of self-reliance had a special resonance for African Americans.

In many of Douglass's writings, self-reliance (and self-fashioning) appears to be heavily gendered; "manhood" is given a central place. But Douglass was also involved in the fight for women's rights. In 1848 he spoke at both the Rochester and the Seneca Falls Women's Rights Conventions. One of Douglass's most celebrated speeches, commonly titled "What to the Slave Is the Fourth of July?," was given at an Independence Day event hosted by the Rochester Ladies' Anti-Slavery Society. During this period, then, Douglass saw activism on behalf of African Americans and activism for women's rights as connected causes. "When the true history of the antislavery cause shall be written," he wrote, "woman will occupy a large space in its pages, for the cause of the slave has been peculiarly a woman's cause." In the wake of the Civil War, however, there was for some years a significant rift between Douglass and leading campaigners for women's rights such as Elizabeth Cady Stanton and Susan B. Anthony, as debate intensified over the 1868 Fourteenth Amendment (affirming citizenship for all people born in the United States, regardless of color, but affirming the right to vote only for *male* citizens) and the 1870 Fifteenth Amendment (affirming that the right to vote was not to "be denied ... on account of race"). Anthony and Stanton were among those who opposed the Fifteenth Amendment; they saw no reason why the vote should be granted to black men before it had been granted to white women. Douglass, on the other hand, was outspoken in his belief that the former was a more urgent imperative than the latter. (Throughout the controversy, the voices of black women activists such as Frances Harper and Mary Ann Shadd Cary were too seldom heard.)

In addition to his autobiographical writings, Douglass published hundreds of speeches and essays—and one novella, *The Heroic Slave* (1852). After the war he became a prominent member of the Republican Party (which remained for many decades after Lincoln's death a party sympathetic to and supportive of African Americans). He received several government appointments, including United States Marshall for the District of Columbia and Minister (ambassador) to Haiti. In 1884, two years after Anna Murray-Douglass's death, he married Helen Pitts, a college-educated activist who had been working with Douglass in the office of the Recorder of Deeds. That she was white and he black led to accusations of betrayal and to her estrangement from several members of her family, but the two weathered the storm, and their marriage was a happy one.

Douglass lived for thirty years after the end of the Civil War, received many honors, and continued to speak out powerfully on a wide variety of topics. But in the years following the Compromise of 1887 and the rebirth of legalized oppression in the southern states, the tide was running against Douglass. His eloquence could do little to stop the spread of revisionist versions of the Civil War that downplayed the centrality of slavery to the struggle and framed the Confederacy as a noble "lost cause." As the years went by the genre of 'slave narrative' received less and less attention. Douglass's final great act of self-fashioning—his 1881 *Life and Times of Frederick Douglass*—sold poorly. By 1900 such writing had been nearly forgotten by mainstream white America. That year saw the publication of *A Literary History of America* by Harvard Professor of English Barrett Wendell; Wendell's eighteen-page chapter on the literature of the antislavery movement makes no mention whatsoever of Douglass—or of any other African American author. Douglass remained more consistently renowned among black readers in the late-nineteenth and early-twentieth centuries. He was honored in a long elegy by popular African American poet Paul Laurence Dunbar upon his death in 1895, and in 1899 was the subject of a biography written by black novelist Charles Chesnutt for the popular series Beacon Biographies of Eminent Americans; in 1906 Booker T. Washington wrote, "No negro can read and study the life of Frederick Douglass without deriving from it courage to look up and forward."

Nevertheless, in the first half of the twentieth century Douglass's *Narrative* went out of print. Not until 1960 did Harvard University Press bring out a new edition of the work—and even then with some timidity, the editor suggesting in his introduction that "perhaps Douglass seemed to protest too much in making slavery out as a 'soul-killing' institution." Only in the twenty-first century has Douglass come once again to be acknowledged without apology or equivocation as a uniquely towering presence, of enduring importance to America.

NOTE ON THE TEXTS: The texts of the works presented here are based on their first published editions. Spelling and punctuation have been modernized in accordance with the practices of this anthology.

⌘ ⌘ ⌘

Narrative of the Life of Frederick Douglass, an American Slave. Written by Himself

PREFACE[1]

In the month of August, 1841, I attended an anti-slavery convention in Nantucket, at which it was my happiness to become acquainted with Frederick Douglass, the writer of the following Narrative. He was a stranger to nearly every member of that body; but, having recently made his escape from the southern prison-house of bondage, and feeling his curiosity excited to ascertain the principles and measures of the abolitionists—of whom he had heard a somewhat vague description while he was a slave—he was induced to give his attendance, on the occasion alluded to, though at that time a resident in New Bedford.[2]

Fortunate, most fortunate occurrence!—fortunate for the millions of his manacled brethren, yet panting for deliverance from their awful thraldom!—fortunate for the cause of negro emancipation, and of universal liberty!—fortunate for the land of his birth, which he has already done so much to save and bless!—fortunate for a large circle of friends and acquaintances, whose sympathy and affection he has strongly secured by the many sufferings he has endured, by his virtuous traits of character, by his ever-abiding remembrance of those who are in bonds, as being bound with them!—fortunate for the multitudes, in various parts of our republic, whose minds he has enlightened on the subject of slavery, and who have been melted to tears by his pathos, or roused to virtuous indignation by his stirring eloquence against the enslavers of men!—fortunate for himself, as it at once brought him into the field of public usefulness, "gave the world assurance of a MAN,"[3] quickened the slumbering energies of his soul, and consecrated him to the great work of breaking the rod of the oppressor, and letting the oppressed go free!

I shall never forget his first speech at the convention—the extraordinary emotion it excited in my own mind—the powerful impression it created upon a crowded auditory, completely taken by surprise—the applause which followed from the beginning to the end of his felicitous remarks. I think I never hated slavery so intensely as at that moment; certainly, my perception of the enormous outrage which is inflicted by it, on the godlike nature of its victims, was rendered far more clear than ever. There stood one, in physical proportion and stature commanding and exact—in intellect richly endowed—in natural eloquence a prodigy—in soul manifestly "created but a little lower than the angels"[4]—yet a slave, ay, a fugitive slave—trembling for his safety, hardly daring to believe that on the American soil, a single white person could be found who would befriend him at all hazards, for the love of God and humanity! Capable of high attainments as an intellectual and moral being—needing nothing but a comparatively small amount of cultivation to make him an ornament to society and a blessing to his race—by the law of the land, by the voice of the people, by the terms of the slave code, he was only a piece of property, a beast of burden, a chattel[5] personal, nevertheless!

A beloved friend[6] from New Bedford prevailed on Mr. DOUGLASS to address the convention: He came forward to the platform with a hesitancy and embarrassment, necessarily the attendants of a sensitive mind in such a novel position. After apologizing for his ignorance, and reminding the audience that slavery was a poor school for the human intellect and heart, he proceeded to narrate some of the facts in his own history as a slave, and in the course of his speech gave utterance to many noble thoughts and thrilling reflections. As soon as he had taken his seat, filled with hope and admiration, I rose, and declared that PATRICK HENRY,[7]

---

1   *PREFACE*   Written by prominent white abolitionist William Lloyd Garrison (1805–79). It was common practice for the slave narratives of black authors to be prefaced by white authors, whose testimonials were thought to authenticate the text. This practice was not followed with Douglass's two subsequent autobiographies.

2   *New Bedford*   Douglass settled in New Bedford, Massachusetts with his wife after his self-emancipation in 1838.

3   *gave the world ... a MAN*   See Shakespeare's *Hamlet* 3.4.72.

4   *created but ... the angels*   See Psalm 8.5: "For thou hast made him [humankind] a little lower than the angels"; and Hebrews 2.7: "But we see Jesus, who was made a little lower than the angels."

5   *chattel*   Property.

6   *A beloved friend*   William C. Coffin, prominent white abolitionist in and around New Bedford and a supporter of Douglass.

7   *PATRICK HENRY*   American revolutionary orator and Founding Father (1736–99), famous for the speech in which he proclaimed: "Forbid it, Almighty God! I know not what course others may take; but as for me, give me liberty or give me death!"

of revolutionary fame, never made a speech more eloquent in the cause of liberty, than the one we had just listened to from the lips of that hunted fugitive. So I believed at that time—such is my belief now. I reminded the audience of the peril which surrounded this self-emancipated young man at the North—even in Massachusetts, on the soil of the Pilgrim Fathers, among the descendants of revolutionary sires;[1] and I appealed to them, whether they would ever allow him to be carried back into slavery—law or no law, constitution or no constitution. The response was unanimous and in thunder-tones—"NO!" "Will you succor and protect him as a brother-man—a resident of the old Bay State?"[2] "YES!" shouted the whole mass, with an energy so startling, that the ruthless tyrants south of Mason and Dixon's line[3] might almost have heard the mighty burst of feeling, and recognized it as the pledge of an invincible determination, on the part of those who gave it, never to betray him that wanders, but to hide the outcast, and firmly to abide the consequences.

It was at once deeply impressed upon my mind, that, if Mr. DOUGLASS could be persuaded to consecrate his time and talents to the promotion of the anti-slavery enterprise, a powerful impetus would be given to it, and a stunning blow at the same time inflicted on northern prejudice against a colored complexion. I therefore endeavored to instil hope and courage into his mind, in order that he might dare to engage in a vocation so anomalous and responsible for a person in his situation; and I was seconded in this effort by warm-hearted friends, especially by the late General Agent of the Massachusetts Anti-Slavery Society, Mr. JOHN A. COLLINS,[4] whose judgment in this instance entirely coincided with my own. At first, he could give no encouragement; with unfeigned diffidence, he expressed his conviction that he was not adequate to the performance of so great a task; the path marked out was wholly an untrodden one; he was sincerely apprehensive that he should do more harm than good. After much deliberation, however, he consented to make a trial; and ever since that period, he has acted as a lecturing agent, under the auspices either of the American or the Massachusetts Anti-Slavery Society.[5] In labors he has been most abundant; and his success in combating prejudice, in gaining proselytes, in agitating the public mind, has far surpassed the most sanguine expectations that were raised at the commencement of his brilliant career. He has borne himself with gentleness and meekness, yet with true manliness of character. As a public speaker, he excels in pathos, wit, comparison, imitation, strength of reasoning, and fluency of language. There is in him that union of head and heart, which is indispensable to an enlightenment of the heads and a winning of the hearts of others. May his strength continue to be equal to his day! May he continue to "grow in grace, and in the knowledge of God,"[6] that he may be increasingly serviceable in the cause of bleeding humanity, whether at home or abroad!

It is certainly a very remarkable fact, that one of the most efficient advocates of the slave population, now before the public, is a fugitive slave, in the person of FREDERICK DOUGLASS; and that the free colored population of the United States are as ably represented by one of their own number, in the person of CHARLES LENOX REMOND,[7] whose eloquent appeals have extorted the highest applause of multitudes on both sides of the Atlantic. Let the calumniators[8] of the colored race despise themselves for their baseness and illiberality of spirit, and henceforth cease to talk of the natural inferiority of those who require nothing but time and opportunity to attain to the highest point of human excellence.

---

[1] *Pilgrim Fathers ... revolutionary sires* "Pilgrim Fathers" refers to the English colonists who arrived in Plymouth, Massachusetts in 1620; *revolutionary sires* Ancestors who participated in the American Revolution.

[2] *old Bay State* Massachusetts.

[3] *Mason and Dixon's line* Drawn in the 1760s by English surveyors Charles Mason and Jeremiah Dixon, the Mason-Dixon line separated parts of Pennsylvania and Delaware from parts of Maryland and Virginia; it came to signify the border between the American North and South, and thereby the literal and symbolic border between the free states and the slave states.

[4] *JOHN A. COLLINS* White antislavery activist (1810–79).

---

[5] *American or ... Society* The Massachusetts Anti-Slavery Society was an auxiliary of the American Anti-Slavery Society; both were associated with William Lloyd Garrison.

[6] *grow in grace ... of God* See 2 Peter 3.18: "But grow in grace, and in the knowledge of our Lord and Saviour Jesus Christ."

[7] *CHARLES LENOX REMOND* Free-born African American abolitionist from Salem, Massachusetts (1810–73), a close friend of Douglass after whom Douglass named his youngest son.

[8] *calumniators* Slanderers.

It may, perhaps, be fairly questioned, whether any other portion of the population of the earth could have endured the privations, sufferings and horrors of slavery, without having become more degraded in the scale of humanity than the slaves of African descent. Nothing has been left undone to cripple their intellects, darken their minds, debase their moral nature, obliterate all traces of their relationship to mankind; and yet how wonderfully they have sustained the mighty load of a most frightful bondage, under which they have been groaning for centuries! To illustrate the effect of slavery on the white man—to show that he has no powers of endurance, in such a condition, superior to those of his black brother—DANIEL O'CONNELL,[1] the distinguished advocate of universal emancipation, and the mightiest champion of prostrate but not conquered Ireland, relates the following anecdote in a speech delivered by him in the Conciliation Hall, Dublin, before the Loyal National Repeal Association,[2] March 31, 1845. "No matter," said Mr. O'CONNELL, "under what specious term it may disguise itself, slavery is still hideous. It has a natural, an inevitable tendency to brutalize every noble faculty of man. An American sailor, who was cast away on the shore of Africa, where he was kept in slavery for three years, was, at the expiration of that period, found to be imbruted and stultified—he had lost all reasoning power; and having forgotten his native language, could only utter some savage gibberish between Arabic and English, which nobody could understand, and which even he himself found difficulty in pronouncing. So much for the humanizing influence of THE DOMESTIC INSTITUTION!" Admitting this to have been an extraordinary case of mental deterioration, it proves at least that the white slave can sink as low in the scale of humanity as the black one.

Mr. DOUGLASS has very properly chosen to write his own Narrative, in his own style, and according to the best of his ability, rather than to employ someone else. It is, therefore, entirely his own production; and, considering how long and dark was the career he had to run as a slave—how few have been his opportunities to improve his mind since he broke his iron fetters—it is, in my judgment, highly creditable to his head and heart. He who can peruse it without a tearful eye, a heaving breast, an afflicted spirit—without being filled with an unutterable abhorrence of slavery and all its abettors, and animated with a determination to seek the immediate overthrow of that execrable system—without trembling for the fate of this country in the hands of a righteous God, who is ever on the side of the oppressed, and whose arm is not shortened that it cannot save—must have a flinty heart, and be qualified to act the part of a trafficker "in slaves and the souls of men."[3] I am confident that it is essentially true in all its statements; that nothing has been set down in malice, nothing exaggerated, nothing drawn from the imagination; that it comes short of the reality, rather than overstates a single fact in regard to SLAVERY AS IT Is.[4] The experience of FREDERICK DOUGLASS, as a slave, was not a peculiar one; his lot was not especially a hard one; his case may be regarded as a very fair specimen of the treatment of slaves in Maryland, in which State it is conceded that they are better fed and less cruelly treated than in Georgia, Alabama, or Louisiana. Many have suffered incomparably more, while very few on the plantations have suffered less, than himself. Yet how deplorable was his situation! what terrible chastisements were inflicted upon his person! what still more shocking outrages were perpetrated upon his mind! with all his noble powers and sublime aspirations, how like a brute was he treated, even by those professing to have the same mind in them that was in Christ Jesus! to what dreadful liabilities was he continually subjected! how destitute of friendly counsel and aid, even in his greatest extremities! how heavy was the midnight of woe which shrouded in blackness the last ray of hope, and filled the future with terror and gloom! what longings after freedom took possession of his breast, and how his misery augmented, in proportion as he grew reflective and intelligent—thus demonstrating that a happy slave is an extinct man! how he thought, reasoned, felt, under the lash of the

---

[1]   DANIEL O'CONNELL   Irish politician (1775–1847) who fought to obtain equal rights for Catholics (a goal that was partially achieved with the so-called "Catholic Emancipation" of 1829) and to obtain for Ireland a degree of independence from English rule.

[2]   Repeal Association   Founded by O'Connell to call for repeal of the 1800 Acts of Union (which had abolished the Irish Parliament in order to bring Ireland under the direct control of Britain).

[3]   in slaves … souls of men   See Revelation 18.13.

[4]   SLAVERY AS IT IS   Allusion to white abolitionist Theodore Dwight Weld's influential 1839 antislavery book American Slavery as It Is: A Testimony of a Thousand Witnesses.

driver, with the chains upon his limbs! what perils he encountered in his endeavors to escape from his horrible doom! and how signal have been his deliverance and preservation in the midst of a nation of pitiless enemies!

This Narrative contains many affecting incidents, many passages of great eloquence and power; but I think the most thrilling one of them all is the description DOUGLASS gives of his feelings, as he stood soliloquizing respecting his fate, and the chances of his one day being a freeman, on the banks of the Chesapeake Bay—viewing the receding vessels as they flew with their white wings before the breeze, and apostrophizing[1] them as animated by the living spirit of freedom. Who can read that passage, and be insensible to its pathos and sublimity? Compressed into it is a whole Alexandrian library[2] of thought, feeling, and sentiment—all that can, all that need be urged, in the form of expostulation, entreaty, rebuke, against that crime of crimes—making man the property of his fellow-man! O, how accursed is that system, which entombs the godlike mind of man, defaces the divine image, reduces those who by creation were crowned with glory and honor to a level with four-footed beasts, and exalts the dealer in human flesh above all that is called God! Why should its existence be prolonged one hour? Is it not evil, only evil, and that continually? What does its presence imply but the absence of all fear of God, all regard for man, on the part of the people of the United States? Heaven speed its eternal overthrow!

So profoundly ignorant of the nature of slavery are many persons, that they are stubbornly incredulous whenever they read or listen to any recital of the cruelties which are daily inflicted on its victims. They do not deny that the slaves are held as property; but that terrible fact seems to convey to their minds no idea of injustice, exposure to outrage, or savage barbarity. Tell them of cruel scourgings, of mutilations and brandings, of scenes of pollution and blood, of the banishment of all light and knowledge, and they affect to be greatly indignant at such enormous exaggerations, such wholesale misstatements, such abominable

libels on the character of the southern planters! As if all these direful outrages were not the natural results of slavery! As if it were less cruel to reduce a human being to the condition of a thing, than to give him a severe flagellation, or to deprive him of necessary food and clothing! As if whips, chains, thumb-screws, paddles, blood-hounds, overseers, drivers, patrols, were not all indispensable to keep the slaves down, and to give protection to their ruthless oppressors! As if, when the marriage institution is abolished, concubinage, adultery, and incest, must not necessarily abound; when all the rights of humanity are annihilated, any barrier remains to protect the victim from the fury of the spoiler; when absolute power is assumed over life and liberty, it will not be wielded with destructive sway! Skeptics of this character abound in society. In some few instances, their incredulity arises from a want of reflection; but, generally, it indicates a hatred of the light, a desire to shield slavery from the assaults of its foes, a contempt of the colored race, whether bond or free. Such will try to discredit the shocking tales of slaveholding cruelty which are recorded in this truthful Narrative; but they will labor in vain. Mr. DOUGLASS has frankly disclosed the place of his birth, the names of those who claimed ownership in his body and soul, and the names also of those who committed the crimes which he has alleged against them. His statements, therefore, may easily be disproved, if they are untrue.

In the course of his Narrative, he relates two instances of murderous cruelty—in one of which a planter deliberately shot a slave belonging to a neighboring plantation, who had unintentionally gotten within his lordly domain in quest of fish; and in the other, an overseer blew out the brains of a slave who had fled to a stream of water to escape a bloody scourging. Mr. DOUGLASS states that in neither of these instances was anything done by way of legal arrest or judicial investigation. *The Baltimore American*, of March 17, 1845, relates a similar case of atrocity, perpetrated with similar impunity—as follows: "Shooting a slave.—We learn, upon the authority of a letter from Charles County, Maryland, received by a gentleman of this city, that a young man, named Matthews, a nephew of General Matthews, and whose father, it is believed, holds an office at Washington, killed one of the slaves upon his

---

[1]   *apostrophizing* Addressing inanimate objects directly in a poetic fashion.

[2]   *Alexandrian library* Renowned ancient library located in Alexandria, Egypt.

father's farm by shooting him. The letter states that young Matthews had been left in charge of the farm; that he gave an order to the servant, which was disobeyed, when he proceeded to the house, obtained a gun, and, returning, shot the servant. He immediately, the letter continues, fled to his father's residence, where he still remains unmolested." Let it never be forgotten, that no slaveholder or overseer can be convicted of any outrage perpetrated on the person of a slave, however diabolical it may be, on the testimony of colored witnesses, whether bond or free. By the slave code, they are adjudged to be as incompetent to testify against a white man, as though they were indeed a part of the brute creation. Hence, there is no legal protection in fact, whatever there may be in form, for the slave population; and any amount of cruelty may be inflicted on them with impunity. Is it possible for the human mind to conceive of a more horrible state of society?

The effect of a religious profession on the conduct of southern masters is vividly described in the following Narrative, and shown to be anything but salutary. In the nature of the case, it must be in the highest degree pernicious. The testimony of Mr. DOUGLASS, on this point, is sustained by a cloud of witnesses, whose veracity is unimpeachable. "A slaveholder's profession of Christianity is a palpable imposture. He is a felon of the highest grade. He is a man-stealer. It is of no importance what you put in the other scale."

Reader! are you with the man-stealers in sympathy and purpose, or on the side of their down-trodden victims? If with the former, then are you the foe of God and man. If with the latter, what are you prepared to do and dare in their behalf? Be faithful, be vigilant, be untiring in your efforts to break every yoke, and let the oppressed go free. Come what may—cost what it may—inscribe on the banner which you unfurl to the breeze, as your religious and political motto—"NO COMPROMISE WITH SLAVERY! NO UNION WITH SLAVEHOLDERS!"

WM. LLOYD GARRISON.
BOSTON, May 1, 1845.

LETTER FROM WENDELL PHILLIPS,[1] ESQ

BOSTON, April 22, 1845

My Dear Friend

You remember the old fable of "The Man and the Lion,"[2] where the lion complained that he should not be so misrepresented "when the lions wrote history."

I am glad the time has come when the "lions write history." We have been left long enough to gather the character of slavery from the involuntary evidence of the masters. One might, indeed, rest sufficiently satisfied with what, it is evident, must be, in general, the results of such a relation, without seeking farther to find whether they have followed in every instance. Indeed, those who stare at the half-peck of corn a week, and love to count the lashes on the slave's back, are seldom the "stuff" out of which reformers and abolitionists are to be made. I remember that, in 1838, many were waiting for the results of the West India experiment,[3] before they could come into our ranks. Those "results" have come long ago; but, alas! few of that number have come with them, as converts. A man must be disposed to judge of emancipation by other tests than whether it has increased the produce of sugar—and to hate slavery for other reasons than because it starves men and whips women—before he is ready to lay the first stone of his anti-slavery life.

I was glad to learn, in your story, how early the most neglected of God's children waken to a sense of their rights, and of the injustice done them. Experience is a keen teacher; and long before you had mastered your A

1   WENDELL PHILLIPS Massachusetts-based abolitionist and social activist (1811–84).

2   The Man and the Lion Allusion to one of Aesop's Fables, in which a man gestures towards a sculpture of a male figure conquering a lion as evidence of human superiority; the lion counters that if lions could sculpt, they would be the ones depicted as victorious. Tradition has long held that the Greek storyteller Aesop was himself enslaved.

3   West India experiment Referring to the British West Indies Emancipation Act that formally abolished slavery in the British West Indies. It was enacted in 1833, and began to take effect a year later, but its provisions were for a phased abolition; until at least 1838 many previously enslaved people were still bound to their former enslavers as apprentices.

B C, or knew where the "white sails" of the Chesapeake were bound, you began, I see, to gauge the wretchedness of the slave, not by his hunger and want, not by his lashes and toil, but by the cruel and blighting death which gathers over his soul.

In connection with this, there is one circumstance which makes your recollections peculiarly valuable, and renders your early insight the more remarkable. You come from that part of the country where we are told slavery appears with its fairest features. Let us hear, then, what it is at its best estate—gaze on its bright side, if it has one; and then imagination may task her powers to add dark lines to the picture, as she travels southward to that (for the colored man) Valley of the Shadow of Death,[1] where the Mississippi sweeps along.

Again, we have known you long, and can put the most entire confidence in your truth, candor, and sincerity. Everyone who has heard you speak has felt, and, I am confident, every one who reads your book will feel, persuaded that you give them a fair specimen of the whole truth. No one-sided portrait—no wholesale complaints—but strict justice done, whenever individual kindliness has neutralized, for a moment, the deadly system with which it was strangely allied. You have been with us, too, some years, and can fairly compare the twilight of rights, which your race enjoy at the North, with that "noon of night" under which they labor south of Mason and Dixon's line. Tell us whether, after all, the half-free colored man of Massachusetts is worse off than the pampered slave of the rice swamps!

In reading your life, no one can say that we have unfairly picked out some rare specimens of cruelty. We know that the bitter drops, which even you have drained from the cup, are no incidental aggravations, no individual ills, but such as must mingle always and necessarily in the lot of every slave. They are the essential ingredients, not the occasional results, of the system.

After all, I shall read your book with trembling for you. Some years ago, when you were beginning to tell me your real name and birthplace, you may remember I stopped you, and preferred to remain ignorant of all. With the exception of a vague description, so I continued, till the other day, when you read me your memoirs. I hardly knew, at the time, whether to thank you or not for the sight of them, when I reflected that it was still dangerous, in Massachusetts, for honest men to tell their names! They say the fathers, in 1776, signed the Declaration of Independence with the halter about their necks. You, too, publish your declaration of freedom with danger compassing you around. In all the broad lands which the Constitution of the United States overshadows, there is no single spot—however narrow or desolate—where a fugitive slave can plant himself and say, "I am safe." The whole armory of Northern Law has no shield for you. I am free to say that, in your place, I should throw the MS.[2] into the fire.

You, perhaps, may tell your story in safety, endeared as you are to so many warm hearts by rare gifts, and a still rarer devotion of them to the service of others. But it will be owing only to your labors, and the fearless efforts of those who, trampling the laws and Constitution of the country under their feet, are determined that they will "hide the outcast,"[3] and that their hearths shall be, spite of the law, an asylum for the oppressed, if, some time or other, the humblest may stand in our streets, and bear witness in safety against the cruelties of which he has been the victim.

Yet it is sad to think, that these very throbbing hearts which welcome your story, and form your best safeguard in telling it, are all beating contrary to the "statute in such case made and provided." Go on, my dear friend, till you, and those who, like you, have been saved, so as by fire, from the dark prison-house, shall stereotype these free, illegal pulses into statutes; and New England, cutting loose from a blood-stained Union, shall glory in being the house of refuge for the oppressed—till we no longer merely "hide the outcast," or make a merit of standing idly by while he is hunted in our midst; but, consecrating anew the soil of the Pilgrims as an asylum for the oppressed, proclaim our welcome to the slave so loudly, that the tones shall reach every hut in the Carolinas, and make the broken-hearted bondman leap up at the thought of old Massachusetts.

God speed the day!

Till then, and ever,
Yours truly,
WENDELL PHILLIPS

---

[1] *Valley of the Shadow of Death*   See Psalms 23.4.

[2] *MS*   Manuscript.

[3] *hide the outcast*   See Isaiah 16.3.

CHAPTER 1

I was born in Tuckahoe, near Hillsborough, and about twelve miles from Easton, in Talbot county, Maryland. I have no accurate knowledge of my age, never having seen any authentic record containing it. By far the larger part of the slaves know as little of their ages as horses know of theirs, and it is the wish of most masters within my knowledge to keep their slaves thus ignorant. I do not remember to have ever met a slave who could tell of his birthday. They seldom come nearer to it than planting-time, harvest-time, cherry-time, spring-time, or fall-time. A want of information concerning my own was a source of unhappiness to me even during childhood. The white children could tell their ages. I could not tell why I ought to be deprived of the same privilege. I was not allowed to make any inquiries of my master concerning it. He deemed all such inquiries on the part of a slave improper and impertinent, and evidence of a restless spirit. The nearest estimate I can give makes me now between twenty-seven and twenty-eight years of age. I come to this, from hearing my master say, some time during 1835, I was about seventeen years old.[1]

My mother was named Harriet Bailey. She was the daughter of Isaac and Betsey Bailey, both colored, and quite dark. My mother was of a darker complexion than either my grandmother or grandfather.

My father was a white man. He was admitted to be such by all I ever heard speak of my parentage. The opinion was also whispered that my master was my father; but of the correctness of this opinion, I know nothing; the means of knowing was withheld from me. My mother and I were separated when I was but an infant—before I knew her as my mother. It is a common custom, in the part of Maryland from which I ran away, to part children from their mothers at a very early age. Frequently, before the child has reached its twelfth month, its mother is taken from it, and hired out on some farm a considerable distance off, and the child is placed under the care of an old woman, too old for field labor. For what this separation is done, I do not know, unless it be to hinder the development of the child's affection toward its mother, and to blunt and destroy the natural affection of the mother for the child. This is the inevitable result.

I never saw my mother, to know her as such, more than four or five times in my life; and each of these times was very short in duration, and at night. She was hired by a Mr. Stewart,[2] who lived about twelve miles from my home. She made her journeys to see me in the night, travelling the whole distance on foot, after the performance of her day's work. She was a field hand, and a whipping is the penalty of not being in the field at sunrise, unless a slave has special permission from his or her master to the contrary—a permission which they seldom get, and one that gives to him that gives it the proud name of being a kind master. I do not recollect of ever seeing my mother by the light of day. She was with me in the night. She would lie down with me, and get me to sleep, but long before I waked she was gone. Very little communication ever took place between us. Death soon ended what little we could have while she lived, and with it her hardships and suffering. She died when I was about seven years old, on one of my master's farms, near Lee's Mill. I was not allowed to be present during her illness, at her death, or burial. She was gone long before I knew any thing about it. Never having enjoyed, to any considerable extent, her soothing presence, her tender and watchful care, I received the tidings of her death with much the same emotions I should have probably felt at the death of a stranger.

Called thus suddenly away, she left me without the slightest intimation of who my father was. The whisper that my master was my father, may or may not be true; and, true or false, it is of but little consequence to my purpose whilst the fact remains, in all its glaring odiousness, that slaveholders have ordained, and by law established, that the children of slave women shall in all cases follow the condition of their mothers; and this is done too obviously to administer to their own lusts, and make a gratification of their wicked desires profitable as well as pleasurable; for by this cunning arrangement, the slaveholder, in cases not a few, sustains to his slaves the double relation of master and father.

---

1   *I have no accurate knowledge ... years old*   Records made available after Douglass's death reveal that he was born in February 1818 (though the exact date remains unknown).

2   *hired by a Mr. Stewart*   I.e., her owner hired her out to a Mr. Stewart; the transaction would not have involved Douglass's mother being paid.

I know of such cases; and it is worthy of remark that such slaves invariably suffer greater hardships, and have more to contend with, than others. They are, in the first place, a constant offence to their mistress. She is ever disposed to find fault with them; they can seldom do anything to please her; she is never better pleased than when she sees them under the lash, especially when she suspects her husband of showing to his mulatto children favors which he witholds from his black slaves. The master is frequently compelled to sell this class of his slaves, out of deference to the feelings of his white wife; and, cruel as the deed may strike anyone to be, for a man to sell his own children to human flesh-mongers, it is often the dictate of humanity for him to do so; for, unless he does this, he must not only whip them himself, but must stand by and see one white son tie up his brother, of but few shades darker complexion than himself, and ply the gory lash to his naked back; and if he lisp one word of disapproval, it is set down to his parental partiality, and only makes a bad matter worse, both for himself and the slave whom he would protect and defend.

Every year brings with it multitudes of this class of slaves. It was doubtless in consequence of a knowledge of this fact, that one great statesman of the south predicted the downfall of slavery by the inevitable laws of population. Whether this prophecy is ever fulfilled or not, it is nevertheless plain that a very different-looking class of people are springing up at the south, and are now held in slavery, from those originally brought to this country from Africa; and if their increase do no other good, it will do away the force of the argument, that God cursed Ham, and therefore American slavery is right.[1] If the lineal descendants of Ham are alone to be scripturally enslaved, it is certain that slavery at the south must soon become unscriptural; for thousands are ushered into the world, annually, who, like myself, owe their existence to white fathers, and those fathers most frequently their own masters.

I have had two masters. My first master's name was Anthony. I do not remember his first name. He was generally called Captain Anthony—a title which, I presume, he acquired by sailing a craft on the Chesapeake Bay. He was not considered a rich slaveholder. He owned two or three farms, and about thirty slaves. His farms and slaves were under the care of an overseer. The overseer's name was Plummer. Mr. Plummer was a miserable drunkard, a profane swearer, and a savage monster. He always went armed with a cowskin[2] and a heavy cudgel. I have known him to cut and slash the women's heads so horribly, that even master would be enraged at his cruelty, and would threaten to whip him if he did not mind himself. Master, however, was not a humane slaveholder. It required extraordinary barbarity on the part of an overseer to affect him. He was a cruel man, hardened by a long life of slaveholding. He would at times seem to take great pleasure in whipping a slave. I have often been awakened at the dawn of day by the most heart-rending shrieks of an own aunt of mine, whom he used to tie up to a joist, and whip upon her naked back till she was literally covered with blood. No words, no tears, no prayers, from his gory victim, seemed to move his iron heart from its bloody purpose. The louder she screamed, the harder he whipped; and where the blood ran fastest, there he whipped longest. He would whip her to make her scream, and whip her to make her hush; and not until overcome by fatigue, would he cease to swing the blood-clotted cowskin. I remember the first time I ever witnessed this horrible exhibition. I was quite a child, but I well remember it. I never shall forget it whilst I remember anything. It was the first of a long series of such outrages, of which I was doomed to be a witness and a participant. It struck me with awful force. It was the blood-stained gate, the entrance to the hell of slavery, through which I was about to pass. It was a most terrible spectacle. I wish I could commit to paper the feelings with which I beheld it.

This occurrence took place very soon after I went to live with my old master, and under the following circumstances. Aunt Hester went out one night—where or for what I do not know—and happened to be absent when my master desired her presence. He had ordered her not to go out evenings, and warned her that she must never let him catch her in company with a young man, who was paying attention to her, belonging to Colonel Lloyd. The young man's name was Ned

---

1   *God cursed Ham ... is right*   Some proslavery apologists claimed that a biblical justification for slavery could be found in Genesis 9.25, in which God curses Canaan, the son of Ham, declaring that "a servant of servants shall he be unto his brethren."

2   *cowskin*   Whip made from cowhide.

Roberts, generally called Lloyd's Ned. Why master was so careful of her, may be safely left to conjecture. She was a woman of noble form, and of graceful proportions, having very few equals, and fewer superiors, in personal appearance, among the colored or white women of our neighborhood.

Aunt Hester had not only disobeyed his orders in going out, but had been found in company with Lloyd's Ned; which circumstance, I found, from what he said while whipping her, was the chief offence. Had he been a man of pure morals himself, he might have been thought interested in protecting the innocence of my aunt; but those who knew him will not suspect him of any such virtue. Before he commenced whipping Aunt Hester, he took her into the kitchen, and stripped her from neck to waist, leaving her neck, shoulders, and back, entirely naked. He then told her to cross her hands, calling her at the same time a d——d b——h. After crossing her hands, he tied them with a strong rope, and led her to a stool under a large hook in the joist, put in for the purpose. He made her get upon the stool, and tied her hands to the hook. She now stood fair for his infernal purpose. Her arms were stretched up at their full length, so that she stood upon the ends of her toes. He then said to her, "Now, you d——d b——h, I'll learn[1] you how to disobey my orders!" and after rolling up his sleeves, he commenced to lay on the heavy cowskin, and soon the warm, red blood (amid heart-rending shrieks from her, and horrid oaths from him) came dripping to the floor. I was so terrified and horror-stricken at the sight, that I hid myself in a closet, and dared not venture out till long after the bloody transaction was over. I expected it would be my turn next. It was all new to me. I had never seen anything like it before. I had always lived with my grandmother on the outskirts of the plantation, where she was put to raise the children of the younger women. I had therefore been, until now, out of the way of the bloody scenes that often occurred on the plantation.

CHAPTER 2

My master's family consisted of two sons, Andrew and Richard; one daughter, Lucretia, and her husband,

Captain Thomas Auld. They lived in one house, upon the home plantation of Colonel Edward Lloyd. My master was Colonel Lloyd's clerk and superintendent. He was what might be called the overseer of the overseers. I spent two years of childhood on this plantation in my old master's family. It was here that I witnessed the bloody transaction recorded in the first chapter; and as I received my first impressions of slavery on this plantation, I will give some description of it, and of slavery as it there existed. The plantation is about twelve miles north of Easton, in Talbot county, and is situated on the border of Miles River. The principal products raised upon it were tobacco, corn, and wheat. These were raised in great abundance; so that, with the products of this and the other farms belonging to him, he was able to keep in almost constant employment a large sloop,[2] in carrying them to market at Baltimore. This sloop was named Sally Lloyd, in honor of one of the colonel's daughters. My master's son-in-law, Captain Auld, was master of the vessel; she was otherwise manned by the colonel's own slaves. Their names were Peter, Isaac, Rich, and Jake. These were esteemed very highly by the other slaves, and looked upon as the privileged ones of the plantation; for it was no small affair, in the eyes of the slaves, to be allowed to see Baltimore.

Colonel Lloyd kept from three to four hundred slaves on his home plantation, and owned a large number more on the neighboring farms belonging to him. The names of the farms nearest to the home plantation were Wye Town and New Design. "Wye Town" was under the overseership of a man named Noah Willis. New Design was under the overseership of a Mr. Townsend. The overseers of these, and all the rest of the farms, numbering over twenty, received advice and direction from the managers of the home plantation. This was the great business place. It was the seat of government for the whole twenty farms. All disputes among the overseers were settled here. If a slave was convicted of any high misdemeanor, became unmanageable, or evinced a determination to run away, he was brought immediately here, severely whipped, put on board the sloop, carried to Baltimore, and sold to Austin Woolfolk, or some other slave-trader, as a warning to the slaves remaining.

---

1   *learn* Teach.

2   *sloop* Small, single-masted sailing vessel.

Here, too, the slaves of all the other farms received their monthly allowance of food, and their yearly clothing. The men and women slaves received, as their monthly allowance of food, eight pounds of pork, or its equivalent in fish, and one bushel of corn meal. Their yearly clothing consisted of two coarse linen shirts, one pair of linen trousers, like the shirts, one jacket, one pair of trousers for winter, made of coarse negro cloth,[1] one pair of stockings, and one pair of shoes; the whole of which could not have cost more than seven dollars. The allowance of the slave children was given to their mothers, or the old women having the care of them. The children unable to work in the field had neither shoes, stockings, jackets, nor trousers, given to them; their clothing consisted of two coarse linen shirts per year. When these failed them, they went naked until the next allowance-day. Children from seven to ten years old, of both sexes, almost naked, might be seen at all seasons of the year.

There were no beds given the slaves, unless one coarse blanket be considered such, and none but the men and women had these. This, however, is not considered a very great privation. They find less difficulty from the want of beds, than from the want of time to sleep; for when their day's work in the field is done, the most of them having their washing, mending, and cooking to do, and having few or none of the ordinary facilities for doing either of these, very many of their sleeping hours are consumed in preparing for the field the coming day; and when this is done, old and young, male and female, married and single, drop down side by side, on one common bed—the cold, damp floor—each covering himself or herself with their miserable blankets; and here they sleep till they are summoned to the field by the driver's horn. At the sound of this, all must rise, and be off to the field. There must be no halting; everyone must be at his or her post; and woe betides them who hear not this morning summons to the field; for if they are not awakened by the sense of hearing, they are by the sense of feeling: no age nor sex finds any favor. Mr. Severe, the overseer, used to stand by the door of the quarter, armed with a large hickory stick[2] and heavy cowskin, ready to whip anyone who

was so unfortunate as not to hear, or, from any other cause, was prevented from being ready to start for the field at the sound of the horn.

Mr. Severe was rightly named: he was a cruel man. I have seen him whip a woman, causing the blood to run half an hour at the time; and this, too, in the midst of her crying children, pleading for their mother's release. He seemed to take pleasure in manifesting his fiendish barbarity. Added to his cruelty, he was a profane swearer. It was enough to chill the blood and stiffen the hair of an ordinary man to hear him talk. Scarce a sentence escaped him but that was commenced or concluded by some horrid oath. The field was the place to witness his cruelty and profanity. His presence made it both the field of blood and of blasphemy. From the rising till the going down of the sun, he was cursing, raving, cutting, and slashing among the slaves of the field, in the most frightful manner. His career was short. He died very soon after I went to Colonel Lloyd's; and he died as he lived, uttering, with his dying groans, bitter curses and horrid oaths. His death was regarded by the slaves as the result of a merciful providence.

Mr. Severe's place was filled by a Mr. Hopkins. He was a very different man. He was less cruel, less profane, and made less noise, than Mr. Severe. His course was characterized by no extraordinary demonstrations of cruelty. He whipped, but seemed to take no pleasure in it. He was called by the slaves a good overseer.

The home plantation of Colonel Lloyd wore the appearance of a country village. All the mechanical operations for all the farms were performed here. The shoemaking and mending, the blacksmithing, cartwrighting, coopering,[3] weaving, and grain-grinding, were all performed by the slaves on the home plantation. The whole place wore a business-like aspect very unlike the neighboring farms. The number of houses, too, conspired to give it advantage over the neighboring farms. It was called by the slaves the Great House Farm. Few privileges were esteemed higher, by the slaves of the out-farms, than that of being selected to do errands at the Great House Farm. It was associated in their minds with greatness. A representative could not be prouder of his election to a seat in the American Congress, than a slave on one of the out-farms would

---

[1] *negro cloth* General term referring to the poor-quality fabric used to make clothing for enslaved people.

[2] *hickory stick* Made from the tough wood of the hickory tree.

[3] *cartwrighting* Carpentry; *coopering* Making of wooden casks, barrels, and other vessels for storing goods.

be of his election to do errands at the Great House Farm. They regarded it as evidence of great confidence reposed in them by their overseers; and it was on this account, as well as a constant desire to be out of the field from under the driver's lash, that they esteemed it a high privilege, one worth careful living for. He was called the smartest and most trusty fellow, who had this honor conferred upon him the most frequently. The competitors for this office sought as diligently to please their overseers, as the office-seekers in the political parties seek to please and deceive the people. The same traits of character might be seen in Colonel Lloyd's slaves, as are seen in the slaves of the political parties.

The slaves selected to go to the Great House Farm, for the monthly allowance for themselves and their fellow-slaves, were peculiarly enthusiastic. While on their way, they would make the dense old woods, for miles around, reverberate with their wild songs, revealing at once the highest joy and the deepest sadness. They would compose and sing as they went along, consulting neither time nor tune. The thought that came up, came out—if not in the word, in the sound; and as frequently in the one as in the other. They would sometimes sing the most pathetic sentiment in the most rapturous tone, and the most rapturous sentiment in the most pathetic tone. Into all of their songs they would manage to weave something of the Great House Farm. Especially would they do this, when leaving home. They would then sing most exultingly the following words:

"I am going away to the Great House Farm!
O, yea! O, yea! O!"

This they would sing, as a chorus, to words which to many would seem unmeaning jargon, but which, nevertheless, were full of meaning to themselves. I have sometimes thought that the mere hearing of those songs would do more to impress some minds with the horrible character of slavery, than the reading of whole volumes of philosophy on the subject could do.

I did not, when a slave, understand the deep meaning of those rude and apparently incoherent songs. I was myself within the circle; so that I neither saw nor heard as those without might see and hear. They told

a tale of woe which was then altogether beyond my feeble comprehension; they were tones loud, long, and deep; they breathed the prayer and complaint of souls boiling over with the bitterest anguish. Every tone was a testimony against slavery, and a prayer to God for deliverance from chains. The hearing of those wild notes always depressed my spirit, and filled me with ineffable sadness. I have frequently found myself in tears while hearing them. The mere recurrence to those songs, even now, afflicts me; and while I am writing these lines, an expression of feeling has already found its way down my cheek. To those songs I trace my first glimmering conception of the dehumanizing character of slavery. I can never get rid of that conception. Those songs still follow me, to deepen my hatred of slavery, and quicken my sympathies for my brethren in bonds. If any one wishes to be impressed with the soul-killing effects of slavery, let him go to Colonel Lloyd's plantation, and, on allowance-day, place himself in the deep pine woods, and there let him, in silence, analyze the sounds that shall pass through the chambers of his soul—and if he is not thus impressed, it will only be because "there is no flesh in his obdurate heart."[1]

I have often been utterly astonished, since I came to the north, to find persons who could speak of the singing, among slaves, as evidence of their contentment and happiness. It is impossible to conceive of a greater mistake. Slaves sing most when they are most unhappy. The songs of the slave represent the sorrows of his heart; and he is relieved by them, only as an aching heart is relieved by its tears. At least, such is my experience. I have often sung to drown my sorrow, but seldom to express my happiness. Crying for joy,

---

[1] *there is ... obdurate heart*   Douglass is quoting from an approximately 50-line passage dealing with slavery (sometimes printed as if it were a separate poem, and given the title "Slavery") that appears in Book 2 of English poet William Cowper's long poem *The Task* (1785). It reads in part as follows:

My soul is sick, with every day's report
Of wrong and outrage with which earth is filled;
There is no flesh in man's obdurate heart...;
He finds his fellow guilty of a skin
Not colored like his own[.] ...

In America as well as in Britain, editions of Cowper's poetic works remained very widely read well into the second half of the nineteenth century, often outselling poets such as Milton and Wordsworth; it is likely that many of Douglass's readers would have been familiar with this quotation.

and singing for joy, were alike uncommon to me while in the jaws of slavery. The singing of a man cast away upon a desolate island might be as appropriately considered as evidence of contentment and happiness, as the singing of a slave; the songs of the one and of the other are prompted by the same emotion.

CHAPTER 3

Colonel Lloyd kept a large and finely cultivated garden, which afforded almost constant employment for four men, besides the chief gardener, (Mr. M'Durmond). This garden was probably the greatest attraction of the place. During the summer months, people came from far and near—from Baltimore, Easton, and Annapolis—to see it. It abounded in fruits of almost every description, from the hardy apple of the north to the delicate orange of the south. This garden was not the least source of trouble on the plantation. Its excellent fruit was quite a temptation to the hungry swarms of boys, as well as the older slaves, belonging to the colonel, few of whom had the virtue or the vice to resist it. Scarcely a day passed, during the summer, but that some slave had to take the lash for stealing fruit. The colonel had to resort to all kinds of stratagems to keep his slaves out of the garden. The last and most successful one was that of tarring his fence all around; after which, if a slave was caught with any tar upon his person, it was deemed sufficient proof that he had either been into the garden, or had tried to get in. In either case, he was severely whipped by the chief gardener. This plan worked well; the slaves became as fearful of tar as of the lash. They seemed to realize the impossibility of touching tar without being defiled.

The colonel also kept a splendid riding equipage. His stable and carriage-house presented the appearance of some of our large city livery[1] establishments. His horses were of the finest form and noblest blood. His carriage-house contained three splendid coaches, three or four gigs, besides dearborns and barouches[2] of the most fashionable style.

This establishment was under the care of two slaves—old Barney and young Barney—father and son. To attend to this establishment was their sole work. But it was by no means an easy employment; for in nothing was Colonel Lloyd more particular than in the management of his horses. The slightest inattention to these was unpardonable, and was visited upon those, under whose care they were placed, with the severest punishment; no excuse could shield them, if the colonel only suspected any want of attention to his horses—a supposition which he frequently indulged, and one which, of course, made the office of old and young Barney a very trying one. They never knew when they were safe from punishment. They were frequently whipped when least deserving, and escaped whipping when most deserving it. Everything depended upon the looks of the horses, and the state of Colonel Lloyd's own mind when his horses were brought to him for use. If a horse did not move fast enough, or hold his head high enough, it was owing to some fault of his keepers. It was painful to stand near the stable-door, and hear the various complaints against the keepers when a horse was taken out for use. "This horse has not had proper attention. He has not been sufficiently rubbed and curried, or he has not been properly fed; his food was too wet or too dry; he got it too soon or too late; he was too hot or too cold; he had too much hay, and not enough of grain; or he had too much grain, and not enough of hay; instead of old Barney's attending to the horse, he had very improperly left it to his son." To all these complaints, no matter how unjust, the slave must answer never a word. Colonel Lloyd could not brook any contradiction from a slave. When he spoke, a slave must stand, listen, and tremble; and such was literally the case. I have seen Colonel Lloyd make old Barney, a man between fifty and sixty years of age, uncover his bald head, kneel down upon the cold, damp ground, and receive upon his naked and toil-worn shoulders more than thirty lashes at the time. Colonel Lloyd had three sons—Edward, Murray, and Daniel—and three sons-in-law, Mr. Winder, Mr. Nicholson, and Mr. Lowndes. All of these lived at the Great House Farm, and enjoyed the luxury of whipping the servants when they pleased, from old Barney down to William Wilkes, the coach-driver. I have seen Winder make one of the house-servants stand off from

---

[1] *livery* Stable.

[2] *gigs* Light two-wheeled, one-horse carriages; *dearborns* Light four-wheeled carriages; *barouches* Heavier, four-wheeled carriages, considered quite luxurious.

him a suitable distance to be touched with the end of his whip, and at every stroke raise great ridges upon his back.

To describe the wealth of Colonel Lloyd would be almost equal to describing the riches of Job.[1] He kept from ten to fifteen house-servants. He was said to own a thousand slaves, and I think this estimate quite within the truth. Colonel Lloyd owned so many that he did not know them when he saw them; nor did all the slaves of the out-farms know him. It is reported of him, that, while riding along the road one day, he met a colored man, and addressed him in the usual manner of speaking to colored people on the public highways of the south: "Well, boy, whom do you belong to?" "To Colonel Lloyd," replied the slave. "Well, does the colonel treat you well?" "No, sir," was the ready reply. "What, does he work you too hard?" "Yes, sir." "Well, don't he give you enough to eat?" "Yes, sir, he gives me enough, such as it is."

The colonel, after ascertaining where the slave belonged, rode on; the man also went on about his business, not dreaming that he had been conversing with his master. He thought, said, and heard nothing more of the matter, until two or three weeks afterwards. The poor man was then informed by his overseer that, for having found fault with his master, he was now to be sold to a Georgia trader. He was immediately chained and handcuffed; and thus, without a moment's warning, he was snatched away, and forever sundered, from his family and friends, by a hand more unrelenting than death. This is the penalty of telling the truth, of telling the simple truth, in answer to a series of plain questions.

It is partly in consequence of such facts, that slaves, when inquired of as to their condition and the character of their masters, almost universally say they are contented, and that their masters are kind. The slaveholders have been known to send in spies among their slaves, to ascertain their views and feelings in regard to their condition. The frequency of this has had the effect to establish among the slaves the maxim, that a still tongue makes a wise head. They suppress the truth rather than take the consequences of telling it, and in

so doing prove themselves a part of the human family. If they have anything to say of their masters, it is generally in their masters' favor, especially when speaking to an untried man. I have been frequently asked, when a slave, if I had a kind master, and do not remember ever to have given a negative answer; nor did I, in pursuing this course, consider myself as uttering what was absolutely false; for I always measured the kindness of my master by the standard of kindness set up among slaveholders around us. Moreover, slaves are like other people, and imbibe prejudices quite common to others. They think their own better than that of others. Many, under the influence of this prejudice, think their own masters are better than the masters of other slaves; and this, too, in some cases, when the very reverse is true. Indeed, it is not uncommon for slaves even to fall out and quarrel among themselves about the relative goodness of their masters, each contending for the superior goodness of his own over that of the others. At the very same time, they mutually execrate their masters when viewed separately. It was so on our plantation. When Colonel Lloyd's slaves met the slaves of Jacob Jepson, they seldom parted without a quarrel about their masters; Colonel Lloyd's slaves contending that he was the richest, and Mr. Jepson's slaves that he was the smartest, and most of a man. Colonel Lloyd's slaves would boast his ability to buy and sell Jacob Jepson. Mr. Jepson's slaves would boast his ability to whip Colonel Lloyd. These quarrels would almost always end in a fight between the parties, and those that whipped were supposed to have gained the point at issue. They seemed to think that the greatness of their masters was transferable to themselves. It was considered as being bad enough to be a slave; but to be a poor man's slave was deemed a disgrace indeed!

CHAPTER 4

Mr. Hopkins remained but a short time in the office of overseer. Why his career was so short, I do not know, but suppose he lacked the necessary severity to suit Colonel Lloyd. Mr. Hopkins was succeeded by Mr. Austin Gore, a man possessing, in an eminent degree, all those traits of character indispensable to what is called a first-rate overseer. Mr. Gore had served Colonel Lloyd, in the capacity of overseer, upon one of

---

[1]   *riches of Job*   The biblical figure Job is best known for the brutal test of faith he is put under by God, but prior to these events he is described as wealthy and prosperous.

the out-farms, and had shown himself worthy of the high station of overseer upon the home or Great House Farm.

Mr. Gore was proud, ambitious, and persevering. He was artful, cruel, and obdurate. He was just the man for such a place, and it was just the place for such a man. It afforded scope for the full exercise of all his powers, and he seemed to be perfectly at home in it. He was one of those who could torture the slightest look, word, or gesture, on the part of the slave, into impudence, and would treat it accordingly. There must be no answering back to him; no explanation was allowed a slave, showing himself to have been wrong-fully accused. Mr. Gore acted fully up to the maxim laid down by slaveholders, "It is better that a dozen slaves should suffer under the lash, than that the over-seer should be convicted, in the presence of the slaves, of having been at fault." No matter how innocent a slave might be—it availed him nothing, when accused by Mr. Gore of any misdemeanor. To be accused was to be convicted, and to be convicted was to be punished; the one always following the other with immutable certainty. To escape punishment was to escape accu-sation; and few slaves had the fortune to do either, under the overseership of Mr. Gore. He was just proud enough to demand the most debasing homage of the slave, and quite servile enough to crouch, himself, at the feet of the master. He was ambitious enough to be contented with nothing short of the highest rank of overseers, and persevering enough to reach the height of his ambition. He was cruel enough to inflict the severest punishment, artful enough to descend to the lowest trickery, and obdurate enough to be insensible to the voice of a reproving conscience. He was, of all the overseers, the most dreaded by the slaves. His pres-ence was painful; his eye flashed confusion; and seldom was his sharp, shrill voice heard, without producing horror and trembling in their ranks.

Mr. Gore was a grave man, and, though a young man, he indulged in no jokes, said no funny words, seldom smiled. His words were in perfect keeping with his looks, and his looks were in perfect keeping with his words. Overseers will sometimes indulge in a witty word, even with the slaves; not so with Mr. Gore. He spoke but to command, and commanded but to be obeyed; he dealt sparingly with his words,

and bountifully with his whip, never using the former where the latter would answer as well. When he whipped, he seemed to do so from a sense of duty, and feared no consequences. He did nothing reluctantly, no matter how disagreeable; always at his post, never inconsistent. He never promised but to fulfil. He was, in a word, a man of the most inflexible firmness and stone like coolness.

His savage barbarity was equalled only by the consummate coolness with which he committed the grossest and most savage deeds upon the slaves under his charge. Mr. Gore once undertook to whip one of Colonel Lloyd's slaves, by the name of Demby. He had given Demby but few stripes,[1] when, to get rid of the scourging, he ran and plunged himself into a creek, and stood there at the depth of his shoulders, refusing to come out. Mr. Gore told him that he would give him three calls, and that, if he did not come out at the third call, he would shoot him. The first call was given. Demby made no response, but stood his ground. The second and third calls were given with the same result. Mr. Gore then, without consultation or deliberation with anyone, not even giving Demby an additional call, raised his musket to his face, taking deadly aim at his standing victim, and in an instant poor Demby was no more. His mangled body sank out of sight, and blood and brains marked the water where he had stood.

A thrill of horror flashed through every soul upon the plantation, excepting Mr. Gore. He alone seemed cool and collected. He was asked by Colonel Lloyd and my old master, why he resorted to this extraordinary expedient. His reply was (as well as I can remember) that Demby had become unmanageable. He was set-ting a dangerous example to the other slaves—one which, if suffered to pass without some such dem-onstration on his part, would finally lead to the total subversion of all rule and order upon the plantation. He argued that if one slave refused to be corrected, and escaped with his life, the other slaves would soon copy the example; the result of which would be, the free-dom of the slaves, and the enslavement of the whites. Mr. Gore's defence was satisfactory. He was continued in his station as overseer upon the home plantation. His fame as an overseer went abroad. His horrid crime was not even submitted to judicial investigation. It was

---

[1] *stripes* I.e., lash-marks.

committed in the presence of slaves, and they of course could neither institute a suit, nor testify against him; and thus the guilty perpetrator of one of the bloodiest and most foul murders goes unwhipped of justice, and uncensured by the community in which he lives. Mr. Gore lived in St. Michael's, Talbot county, Maryland, when I left there; and if he is still alive, he very probably lives there now; and if so, he is now, as he was then, as highly esteemed and as much respected as though his guilty soul had not been stained with his brother's blood.

I speak advisedly when I say this—that killing a slave, or any colored person, in Talbot county, Maryland, is not treated as a crime, either by the courts or the community. Mr. Thomas Lanman, of St. Michael's, killed two slaves, one of whom he killed with a hatchet, by knocking his brains out. He used to boast of the commission of the awful and bloody deed. I have heard him do so laughingly, saying, among other things, that he was the only benefactor of his country in the company, and that when others would do as much as he had done, we should be relieved of "the d——d niggers."

The wife of Mr. Giles Hicks, living but a short distance from where I used to live, murdered my wife's cousin, a young girl between fifteen and sixteen years of age, mangling her person in the most horrible manner, breaking her nose and breastbone with a stick, so that the poor girl expired in a few hours afterward. She was immediately buried, but had not been in her untimely grave but a few hours before she was taken up and examined by the coroner, who decided that she had come to her death by severe beating. The offence for which this girl was thus murdered was this: She had been set that night to mind Mrs. Hicks's baby, and during the night she fell asleep, and the baby cried. She, having lost her rest for several nights previous, did not hear the crying. They were both in the room with Mrs. Hicks. Mrs. Hicks, finding the girl slow to move, jumped from her bed, seized an oak stick of wood by the fireplace, and with it broke the girl's nose and breastbone, and thus ended her life. I will not say that this most horrid murder produced no sensation in the community. It did produce sensation, but not enough to bring the murderess to punishment. There was a warrant issued for her arrest, but it was never served.

Thus she escaped not only punishment, but even the pain of being arraigned before a court for her horrid crime.

Whilst I am detailing bloody deeds which took place during my stay on Colonel Lloyd's plantation, I will briefly narrate another, which occurred about the same time as the murder of Demby by Mr. Gore.

Colonel Lloyd's slaves were in the habit of spending a part of their nights and Sundays in fishing for oysters, and in this way made up the deficiency of their scanty allowance. An old man belonging to Colonel Lloyd, while thus engaged, happened to get beyond the limits of Colonel Lloyd's, and on the premises of Mr. Beal Bondly. At this trespass, Mr. Bondly took offence, and with his musket came down to the shore, and blew its deadly contents into the poor old man.

Mr. Bondly came over to see Colonel Lloyd the next day, whether to pay him for his property, or to justify himself in what he had done, I know not. At any rate, this whole fiendish transaction was soon hushed up. There was very little said about it at all, and nothing done. It was a common saying, even among little white boys, that it was worth a half-cent to kill a "nigger," and a half-cent to bury one.

CHAPTER 5

As to my own treatment while I lived on Colonel Lloyd's plantation, it was very similar to that of the other slave children. I was not old enough to work in the field, and there being little else than field work to do, I had a great deal of leisure time. The most I had to do was to drive up the cows at evening, keep the fowls out of the garden, keep the front yard clean, and run of errands for my old master's daughter, Mrs. Lucretia Auld. The most of my leisure time I spent in helping Master Daniel Lloyd in finding his birds, after he had shot them. My connection with Master Daniel was of some advantage to me. He became quite attached to me, and was a sort of protector of me. He would not allow the older boys to impose upon me, and would divide his cakes with me.

I was seldom whipped by my old master, and suffered little from anything else than hunger and cold. I suffered much from hunger, but much more from cold. In hottest summer and coldest winter, I was kept almost naked—no shoes, no stockings, no jacket, no trousers, nothing on but a coarse tow linen[1] shirt, reaching only to my knees. I had no bed. I must have perished with cold, but that, the coldest nights, I used to steal a bag which was used for carrying corn to the mill. I would crawl into this bag, and there sleep on the cold, damp, clay floor, with my head in and feet out. My feet have been so cracked with the frost, that the pen with which I am writing might be laid in the gashes.

We were not regularly allowanced. Our food was coarse corn meal boiled. This was called mush. It was put into a large wooden tray or trough, and set down upon the ground. The children were then called, like so many pigs, and like so many pigs they would come and devour the mush; some with oyster-shells, others with pieces of shingle, some with naked hands, and none with spoons. He that ate fastest got most; he that was strongest secured the best place; and few left the trough satisfied.

I was probably between seven and eight years old when I left Colonel Lloyd's plantation. I left it with joy. I shall never forget the ecstasy with which I received the intelligence that my old master (Anthony) had determined to let me go to Baltimore, to live with Mr. Hugh Auld, brother to my old master's son-in-law, Captain Thomas Auld. I received this information about three days before my departure. They were three of the happiest days I ever enjoyed. I spent the most part of all these three days in the creek, washing off the plantation scurf, and preparing myself for my departure.

The pride of appearance which this would indicate was not my own. I spent the time in washing, not so much because I wished to, but because Mrs. Lucretia had told me I must get all the dead skin off my feet and knees before I could go to Baltimore; for the people in Baltimore were very cleanly, and would laugh at me if I looked dirty. Besides, she was going to give me a pair of trousers, which I should not put on unless I got all the dirt off me. The thought of owning a pair of trousers was great indeed! It was almost a sufficient motive, not only to make me take off what would be called by pig-drovers the mange, but the skin itself. I went at it in good earnest, working for the first time with the hope of reward.

The ties that ordinarily bind children to their homes were all suspended in my case. I found no severe trial in my departure. My home was charmless; it was not home to me; on parting from it, I could not feel that I was leaving anything which I could have enjoyed by staying. My mother was dead, my grandmother lived far off, so that I seldom saw her. I had two sisters and one brother, that lived in the same house with me; but the early separation of us from our mother had well nigh blotted the fact of our relationship from our memories. I looked for home elsewhere, and was confident of finding none which I should relish less than the one which I was leaving. If, however, I found in my new home hardship, hunger, whipping, and nakedness, I had the consolation that I should not have escaped any one of them by staying. Having already had more than a taste of them in the house of my old master, and having endured them there, I very naturally inferred my ability to endure them elsewhere, and especially at Baltimore; for I had something of the feeling about Baltimore that is expressed in the proverb, that "being hanged in England is preferable to dying a natural death in Ireland." I had the strongest desire to see Baltimore. Cousin Tom, though not fluent in speech, had inspired me with that desire by his eloquent description of the place. I could never point out anything at the Great House, no matter how beautiful or powerful, but that he had seen something at Baltimore far exceeding, both in beauty and strength, the object which I pointed out to him. Even the Great House itself, with all its pictures, was far inferior to many buildings in Baltimore. So strong was my desire, that I thought a gratification of it would fully compensate for whatever loss of comforts I should sustain by the exchange. I left without a regret, and with the highest hopes of future happiness.

We sailed out of Miles River for Baltimore on a Saturday morning. I remember only the day of the week, for at that time I had no knowledge of the days of the month, nor the months of the year. On setting sail, I walked aft, and gave to Colonel Lloyd's plantation what I hoped would be the last look. I then placed myself in the bows of the sloop, and there spent the remainder of the day in looking ahead, interesting myself in what was in the distance rather than in things near by or behind.

---

[1]   *tow linen* Material made from shorter, unworked strands of flax fibers, resulting in a coarser cloth than regular linen.

In the afternoon of that day, we reached Annapolis, the capital of the State. We stopped but a few moments, so that I had no time to go on shore. It was the first large town that I had ever seen, and though it would look small compared with some of our New England factory villages, I thought it a wonderful place for its size—more imposing even than the Great House Farm!

We arrived at Baltimore early on Sunday morning, landing at Smith's Wharf, not far from Bowley's Wharf. We had on board the sloop a large flock of sheep; and after aiding in driving them to the slaughterhouse of Mr. Curtis on Louden Slater's Hill, I was conducted by Rich, one of the hands belonging on board of the sloop, to my new home in Alliciana Street, near Mr. Gardner's shipyard, on Fells Point.

Mr. and Mrs. Auld were both at home, and met me at the door with their little son Thomas, to take care of whom I had been given. And here I saw what I had never seen before; it was a white face beaming with the most kindly emotions; it was the face of my new mistress, Sophia Auld. I wish I could describe the rapture that flashed through my soul as I beheld it. It was a new and strange sight to me, brightening up my pathway with the light of happiness. Little Thomas was told, there was his Freddy—and I was told to take care of little Thomas; and thus I entered upon the duties of my new home with the most cheering prospect ahead.

I look upon my departure from Colonel Lloyd's plantation as one of the most interesting events of my life. It is possible, and even quite probable, that but for the mere circumstance of being removed from that plantation to Baltimore, I should have today, instead of being here seated by my own table, in the enjoyment of freedom and the happiness of home, writing this Narrative, been confined in the galling chains of slavery. Going to live at Baltimore laid the foundation, and opened the gateway, to all my subsequent prosperity. I have ever regarded it as the first plain manifestation of that kind providence which has ever since attended me, and marked my life with so many favors. I regarded the selection of myself as being somewhat remarkable. There were a number of slave children that might have been sent from the plantation to Baltimore. There were those younger, those older, and those of the same age. I was chosen from among them all, and was the first, last, and only choice.

I may be deemed superstitious, and even egotistical, in regarding this event as a special interposition of divine Providence in my favor. But I should be false to the earliest sentiments of my soul, if I suppressed the opinion. I prefer to be true to myself, even at the hazard of incurring the ridicule of others, rather than to be false, and incur my own abhorrence. From my earliest recollection, I date the entertainment of a deep conviction that slavery would not always be able to hold me within its foul embrace; and in the darkest hours of my career in slavery, this living word of faith and spirit of hope departed not from me, but remained like ministering angels to cheer me through the gloom. This good spirit was from God, and to him I offer thanksgiving and praise.

CHAPTER 6

My new mistress proved to be all she appeared when I first met her at the door—a woman of the kindest heart and finest feelings. She had never had a slave under her control previously to myself, and prior to her marriage she had been dependent upon her own industry for a living. She was by trade a weaver; and by constant application to her business, she had been in a good degree preserved from the blighting and dehumanizing effects of slavery. I was utterly astonished at her goodness. I scarcely knew how to behave towards her. She was entirely unlike any other white woman I had ever seen. I could not approach her as I was accustomed to approach other white ladies. My early instruction was all out of place. The crouching servility, usually so acceptable a quality in a slave, did not answer when manifested toward her. Her favor was not gained by it; she seemed to be disturbed by it. She did not deem it impudent or unmannerly for a slave to look her in the face. The meanest slave was put fully at ease in her presence, and none left without feeling better for having seen her. Her face was made of heavenly smiles, and her voice of tranquil music.

But, alas! this kind heart had but a short time to remain such. The fatal poison of irresponsible power was already in her hands, and soon commenced its infernal work. That cheerful eye, under the influence of slavery, soon became red with rage; that voice, made all of sweet accord, changed to one of harsh and horrid discord; and that angelic face gave place to that of a demon.

Very soon after I went to live with Mr. and Mrs. Auld, she very kindly commenced to teach me the A, B, C. After I had learned this, she assisted me in learning to spell words of three or four letters. Just at this point of my progress, Mr. Auld found out what was going on, and at once forbade Mrs. Auld to instruct me further, telling her, among other things, that it was unlawful, as well as unsafe, to teach a slave to read. To use his own words, further, he said, "If you give a nigger an inch, he will take an ell.[1] A nigger should know nothing but to obey his master—to do as he is told to do. Learning would spoil the best nigger in the world. Now," said he, "if you teach that nigger (speaking of myself) how to read, there would be no keeping him. It would forever unfit him to be a slave. He would at once become unmanageable, and of no value to his master. As to himself, it could do him no good, but a great deal of harm. It would make him discontented and unhappy." These words sank deep into my heart, stirred up sentiments within that lay slumbering, and called into existence an entirely new train of thought. It was a new and special revelation, explaining dark and mysterious things, with which my youthful understanding had struggled, but struggled in vain. I now understood what had been to me a most perplexing difficulty—to wit, the white man's power to enslave the black man. It was a grand achievement, and I prized it highly. From that moment, I understood the pathway from slavery to freedom. It was just what I wanted, and I got it at a time when I the least expected it. Whilst I was saddened by the thought of losing the aid of my kind mistress, I was gladdened by the invaluable instruction which, by the merest accident, I had gained from my master. Though conscious of the difficulty of learning without a teacher, I set out with high hope, and a fixed purpose, at whatever cost of trouble, to learn how to read. The very decided manner with which he spoke, and strove to impress his wife with the evil consequences of giving me instruction, served to convince me that he was deeply sensible of the truths he was uttering. It gave me the best assurance that I might rely with the utmost confidence on the results which, he said, would flow from teaching me to read.

What he most dreaded, that I most desired. What he most loved, that I most hated. That which to him was a great evil, to be carefully shunned, was to me a great good, to be diligently sought; and the argument which he so warmly urged, against my learning to read, only served to inspire me with a desire and determination to learn. In learning to read, I owe almost as much to the bitter opposition of my master, as to the kindly aid of my mistress. I acknowledge the benefit of both.

I had resided but a short time in Baltimore before I observed a marked difference, in the treatment of slaves, from that which I had witnessed in the country. A city slave is almost a freeman, compared with a slave on the plantation. He is much better fed and clothed, and enjoys privileges altogether unknown to the slave on the plantation. There is a vestige of decency, a sense of shame, that does much to curb and check those outbreaks of atrocious cruelty so commonly enacted upon the plantation. He is a desperate slaveholder, who will shock the humanity of his non-slaveholding neighbors with the cries of his lacerated slave. Few are willing to incur the odium attaching to the reputation of being a cruel master; and above all things, they would not be known as not giving a slave enough to eat. Every city slaveholder is anxious to have it known of him, that he feeds his slaves well; and it is due to them to say, that most of them do give their slaves enough to eat. There are, however, some painful exceptions to this rule. Directly opposite to us, on Philpot Street, lived Mr. Thomas Hamilton. He owned two slaves. Their names were Henrietta and Mary. Henrietta was about twenty-two years of age, Mary was about fourteen; and of all the mangled and emaciated creatures I ever looked upon, these two were the most so. His heart must be harder than stone, that could look upon these unmoved. The head, neck, and shoulders of Mary were literally cut to pieces. I have frequently felt her head, and found it nearly covered with festering sores, caused by the lash of her cruel mistress. I do not know that her master ever whipped her, but I have been an eye-witness to the cruelty of Mrs. Hamilton. I used to be in Mr. Hamilton's house nearly every day. Mrs. Hamilton used to sit in a large chair in the middle of the room, with a heavy cowskin always by her side, and scarce an hour passed during the day but was marked by the blood of one of these slaves. The girls seldom

---

[1]   *an ell*   Approximately 45 inches.

passed her without her saying, "Move faster, you black gip!" at the same time giving them a blow with the cowskin over the head or shoulders, often drawing the blood. She would then say, "Take that, you black gip!" continuing, "If you don't move faster, I'll move you!" Added to the cruel lashings to which these slaves were subjected, they were kept nearly half-starved. They seldom knew what it was to eat a full meal. I have seen Mary contending with the pigs for the offal thrown into the street. So much was Mary kicked and cut to pieces, that she was oftener called "pecked" than by her name.

CHAPTER 7

I lived in Master Hugh's family about seven years. During this time, I succeeded in learning to read and write. In accomplishing this, I was compelled to resort to various stratagems. I had no regular teacher. My mistress, who had kindly commenced to instruct me, had, in compliance with the advice and direction of her husband, not only ceased to instruct, but had set her face against my being instructed by anyone else. It is due, however, to my mistress to say of her, that she did not adopt this course of treatment immediately. She at first lacked the depravity indispensable to shutting me up in mental darkness. It was at least necessary for her to have some training in the exercise of irresponsible power, to make her equal to the task of treating me as though I were a brute.

My mistress was, as I have said, a kind and tender-hearted woman; and in the simplicity of her soul she commenced, when I first went to live with her, to treat me as she supposed one human being ought to treat another. In entering upon the duties of a slaveholder, she did not seem to perceive that I sustained to her the relation of a mere chattel, and that for her to treat me as a human being was not only wrong, but dangerously so. Slavery proved as injurious to her as it did to me. When I went there, she was a pious, warm, and tender-hearted woman. There was no sorrow or suffering for which she had not a tear. She had bread for the hungry, clothes for the naked, and comfort for every mourner that came within her reach. Slavery soon proved its ability to divest her of these heavenly qualities. Under its influence, the tender heart became stone, and the lamblike disposition gave way to one of tiger-like fierceness. The first step in her downward course was in her ceasing to instruct me. She now commenced to practise her husband's precepts. She finally became even more violent in her opposition than her husband himself. She was not satisfied with simply doing as well as he had commanded; she seemed anxious to do better. Nothing seemed to make her more angry than to see me with a newspaper. She seemed to think that here lay the danger. I have had her rush at me with a face made all up of fury, and snatch from me a newspaper, in a manner that fully revealed her apprehension. She was an apt woman; and a little experience soon demonstrated, to her satisfaction, that education and slavery were incompatible with each other.

From this time I was most narrowly[1] watched. If I was in a separate room any considerable length of time, I was sure to be suspected of having a book, and was at once called to give an account of myself. All this, however, was too late. The first step had been taken. Mistress, in teaching me the alphabet, had given me the inch, and no precaution could prevent me from taking the ell.

The plan which I adopted, and the one by which I was most successful, was that of making friends of all the little white boys whom I met in the street. As many of these as I could, I converted into teachers. With their kindly aid, obtained at different times and in different places, I finally succeeded in learning to read. When I was sent of errands, I always took my book with me, and by going one part of my errand quickly, I found time to get a lesson before my return. I used also to carry bread with me, enough of which was always in the house, and to which I was always welcome; for I was much better off in this regard than many of the poor white children in our neighborhood. This bread I used to bestow upon the hungry little urchins, who, in return, would give me that more valuable bread of knowledge. I am strongly tempted to give the names of two or three of those little boys, as a testimonial of the gratitude and affection I bear them; but prudence forbids;—not that it would injure me, but it might embarrass them; for it is almost an unpardonable offence to teach slaves to read in this Christian country. It is enough to say of the dear little fellows, that they

---

1   *narrowly* Closely.

lived on Philpot Street, very near Durgin and Bailey's ship-yard. I used to talk this matter of slavery over with them. I would sometimes say to them, I wished I could be as free as they would be when they got to be men. "You will be free as soon as you are twenty-one, but I am a slave for life! Have not I as good a right to be free as you have?" These words used to trouble them; they would express for me the liveliest sympathy, and console me with the hope that something would occur by which I might be free.

I was now about twelve years old, and the thought of being a slave for life began to bear heavily upon my heart. Just about this time, I got hold of a book entitled "The Columbian Orator."[1] Every opportunity I got, I used to read this book. Among much of other interesting matter, I found in it a dialogue between a master and his slave. The slave was represented as having run away from his master three times. The dialogue represented the conversation which took place between them, when the slave was retaken the third time. In this dialogue, the whole argument in behalf of slavery was brought forward by the master, all of which was disposed of by the slave. The slave was made to say some very smart as well as impressive things in reply to his master—things which had the desired though unexpected effect; for the conversation resulted in the voluntary emancipation of the slave on the part of the master.

In the same book, I met with one of Sheridan's[2] mighty speeches on and in behalf of Catholic emancipation. These were choice documents to me. I read them over and over again with unabated interest. They gave tongue to interesting thoughts of my own soul, which had frequently flashed through my mind, and died away for want of utterance. The moral which I

gained from the dialogue was the power of truth over the conscience of even a slaveholder. What I got from Sheridan was a bold denunciation of slavery, and a powerful vindication of human rights. The reading of these documents enabled me to utter my thoughts, and to meet the arguments brought forward to sustain slavery; but while they relieved me of one difficulty, they brought on another even more painful than the one of which I was relieved. The more I read, the more I was led to abhor and detest my enslavers. I could regard them in no other light than a band of successful robbers, who had left their homes, and gone to Africa, and stolen us from our homes, and in a strange land reduced us to slavery. I loathed them as being the meanest as well as the most wicked of men. As I read and contemplated the subject, behold! that very discontentment which Master Hugh had predicted would follow my learning to read had already come, to torment and sting my soul to unutterable anguish. As I writhed under it, I would at times feel that learning to read had been a curse rather than a blessing. It had given me a view of my wretched condition, without the remedy. It opened my eyes to the horrible pit, but to no ladder upon which to get out. In moments of agony, I envied my fellow-slaves for their stupidity. I have often wished myself a beast. I preferred the condition of the meanest reptile to my own. Anything, no matter what, to get rid of thinking! It was this everlasting thinking of my condition that tormented me. There was no getting rid of it. It was pressed upon me by every object within sight or hearing, animate or inanimate. The silver trump of freedom had roused my soul to eternal wakefulness. Freedom now appeared, to disappear no more forever. It was heard in every sound, and seen in every thing. It was ever present to torment me with a sense of my wretched condition. I saw nothing without seeing it, I heard nothing without hearing it, and felt nothing without feeling it. It looked from every star, it smiled in every calm, breathed in every wind, and moved in every storm.

I often found myself regretting my own existence, and wishing myself dead; and but for the hope of being free, I have no doubt but that I should have killed myself, or done something for which I should have been killed. While in this state of mind, I was eager to hear anyone speak of slavery. I was a ready listener.

---

1 *The Columbian Orator* Anthology of speeches and essays collected by New England educator Caleb Bingham (1757–1817), popular as a schoolbook.

2 *Sheridan* Douglass is misremembering here. Richard Brinsley Sheridan (1751–1816) was an Irish poet, playwright, and politician; a short Parliamentary speech by Sheridan is included in the contents of the *Orator*, but it bears little resemblance to what Douglass describes here. The text to which he likely meant to refer is the speech for Catholic Emancipation given by United Irishman Arthur O'Connor in 1795, which directly follows the "Dialogue between a Master and Slave." (This speech is often further misidentified as having been given by Daniel O'Connell.)

Every little while, I could hear something about the abolitionists. It was some time before I found what the word meant. It was always used in such connections as to make it an interesting word to me. If a slave ran away and succeeded in getting clear, or if a slave killed his master, set fire to a barn, or did anything very wrong in the mind of a slaveholder, it was spoken of as the fruit of abolition. Hearing the word in this connection very often, I set about learning what it meant. The dictionary afforded me little or no help. I found it was "the act of abolishing"; but then I did not know what was to be abolished. Here I was perplexed. I did not dare to ask anyone about its meaning, for I was satisfied that it was something they wanted me to know very little about. After a patient waiting, I got one of our city papers, containing an account of the number of petitions from the north, praying for the abolition of slavery in the District of Columbia, and of the slave trade between the States. From this time I understood the words abolition and abolitionist, and always drew near when that word was spoken, expecting to hear something of importance to myself and fellow-slaves. The light broke in upon me by degrees. I went one day down on the wharf of Mr. Waters; and seeing two Irishmen unloading a scow of stone, I went, unasked, and helped them. When we had finished, one of them came to me and asked me if I were a slave. I told him I was. He asked, "Are ye a slave for life?" I told him that I was. The good Irishman seemed to be deeply affected by the statement. He said to the other that it was a pity so fine a little fellow as myself should be a slave for life. He said it was a shame to hold me. They both advised me to run away to the north; that I should find friends there, and that I should be free. I pretended not to be interested in what they said, and treated them as if I did not understand them; for I feared they might be treacherous. White men have been known to encourage slaves to escape, and then, to get the reward, catch them and return them to their masters. I was afraid that these seemingly good men might use me so; but I nevertheless remembered their advice, and from that time I resolved to run away. I looked forward to a time at which it would be safe for me to escape. I was too young to think of doing so immediately; besides, I wished to learn how to write, as I might have occasion to write my own pass. I consoled myself with the hope

that I should one day find a good chance. Meanwhile, I would learn to write.

The idea as to how I might learn to write was suggested to me by being in Durgin and Bailey's shipyard, and frequently seeing the ship carpenters, after hewing, and getting a piece of timber ready for use, write on the timber the name of that part of the ship for which it was intended. When a piece of timber was intended for the larboard[1] side, it would be marked thus—"L." When a piece was for the starboard side, it would be marked thus—"S." A piece for the larboard side forward, would be marked thus—"L. F." When a piece was for starboard side forward, it would be marked thus—"S. F." For larboard aft, it would be marked thus—"L. A." For starboard aft, it would be marked thus—"S. A." I soon learned the names of these letters, and for what they were intended when placed upon a piece of timber in the ship-yard. I immediately commenced copying them, and in a short time was able to make the four letters named. After that, when I met with any boy who I knew could write, I would tell him I could write as well as he. The next word would be, "I don't believe you. Let me see you try it." I would then make the letters which I had been so fortunate as to learn, and ask him to beat that. In this way I got a good many lessons in writing, which it is quite possible I should never have gotten in any other way. During this time, my copy-book was the board fence, brick wall, and pavement; my pen and ink was a lump of chalk. With these, I learned mainly how to write. I then commenced and continued copying the italics in Webster's Spelling Book,[2] until I could make them all without looking on the book. By this time, my little Master Thomas had gone to school, and learned how to write, and had written over a number of copybooks. These had been brought home, and shown to some of our near neighbors, and then laid aside. My mistress used to go to class meeting at the Wilk Street meetinghouse every Monday afternoon, and leave me to take care of the house. When left thus, I used to spend the time in writing in the spaces left in Master

---

1 *larboard* Left (or "port") side of a ship; the right side is referred to as the "starboard."

2 *Webster's Spelling Book* Refers to *The American Spelling Book* by American educator Noah Webster (1758–1843); first published in 1783, the book was a steady bestseller into the second half of the nineteenth century.

Thomas's copy-book, copying what he had written. I continued to do this until I could write a hand very similar to that of Master Thomas. Thus, after a long, tedious effort for years, I finally succeeded in learning how to write.

CHAPTER 8

In a very short time after I went to live at Baltimore, my old master's youngest son Richard died; and in about three years and six months after his death, my old master, Captain Anthony, died, leaving only his son, Andrew, and daughter, Lucretia, to share his estate. He died while on a visit to see his daughter at Hillsborough. Cut off thus unexpectedly, he left no will as to the disposal of his property. It was therefore necessary to have a valuation of the property, that it might be equally divided between Mrs. Lucretia and Master Andrew. I was immediately sent for, to be valued with the other property. Here again my feelings rose up in detestation of slavery. I had now a new conception of my degraded condition. Prior to this, I had become, if not insensible to my lot, at least partly so. I left Baltimore with a young heart overborne with sadness, and a soul full of apprehension. I took passage with Captain Rowe, in the schooner Wild Cat, and, after a sail of about twenty-four hours, I found myself near the place of my birth. I had now been absent from it almost, if not quite, five years. I, however, remembered the place very well. I was only about five years old when I left it, to go and live with my old master on Colonel Lloyd's plantation; so that I was now between ten and eleven years old.

We were all ranked together at the valuation. Men and women, old and young, married and single, were ranked with horses, sheep, and swine. There were horses and men, cattle and women, pigs and children, all holding the same rank in the scale of being, and were all subjected to the same narrow examination. Silvery-headed age and sprightly youth, maids and matrons, had to undergo the same indelicate inspection. At this moment, I saw more clearly than ever the brutalizing effects of slavery upon both slave and slaveholder.

After the valuation, then came the division. I have no language to express the high excitement and deep anxiety which were felt among us poor slaves during this time. Our fate for life was now to be decided. We had no more voice in that decision than the brutes among whom we were ranked. A single word from the white men was enough—against all our wishes, prayers, and entreaties—to sunder forever the dearest friends, dearest kindred, and strongest ties known to human beings. In addition to the pain of separation, there was the horrid dread of falling into the hands of Master Andrew. He was known to us all as being a most cruel wretch—a common drunkard, who had, by his reckless mismanagement and profligate dissipation, already wasted a large portion of his father's property. We all felt that we might as well be sold at once to the Georgia traders, as to pass into his hands; for we knew that that would be our inevitable condition—a condition held by us all in the utmost horror and dread.

I suffered more anxiety than most of my fellow-slaves. I had known what it was to be kindly treated; they had known nothing of the kind. They had seen little or nothing of the world. They were in very deed men and women of sorrow, and acquainted with grief. Their backs had been made familiar with the bloody lash, so that they had become callous; mine was yet tender; for while at Baltimore I got few whippings, and few slaves could boast of a kinder master and mistress than myself; and the thought of passing out of their hands into those of Master Andrew—a man who, but a few days before, to give me a sample of his bloody disposition, took my little brother by the throat, threw him on the ground, and with the heel of his boot stamped upon his head till the blood gushed from his nose and ears—was well calculated to make me anxious as to my fate. After he had committed this savage outrage upon my brother, he turned to me, and said that was the way he meant to serve me one of these days—meaning, I suppose, when I came into his possession.

Thanks to a kind Providence, I fell to the portion of Mrs. Lucretia, and was sent immediately back to Baltimore, to live again in the family of Master Hugh. Their joy at my return equalled their sorrow at my departure. It was a glad day to me. I had escaped a worse than lion's jaws. I was absent from Baltimore, for the purpose of valuation and division, just about one month, and it seemed to have been six.

Very soon after my return to Baltimore, my mistress, Lucretia, died, leaving her husband and one child,

Amanda; and in a very short time after her death, Master Andrew died. Now all the property of my old master, slaves included, was in the hands of strangers—strangers who had had nothing to do with accumulating it. Not a slave was left free. All remained slaves, from the youngest to the oldest. If any one thing in my experience, more than another, served to deepen my conviction of the infernal character of slavery, and to fill me with unutterable loathing of slaveholders, it was their base ingratitude to my poor old grandmother. She had served my old master faithfully from youth to old age. She had been the source of all his wealth; she had peopled his plantation with slaves; she had become a great grandmother in his service. She had rocked him in infancy, attended him in childhood, served him through life, and at his death wiped from his icy brow the cold death-sweat, and closed his eyes forever. She was nevertheless left a slave—a slave for life—a slave in the hands of strangers; and in their hands she saw her children, her grandchildren, and her great-grandchildren, divided, like so many sheep, without being gratified with the small privilege of a single word, as to their or her own destiny. And, to cap the climax of their base ingratitude and fiendish barbarity, my grandmother, who was now very old, having outlived my old master and all his children, having seen the beginning and end of all of them, and her present owners finding she was of but little value, her frame already racked with the pains of old age, and complete helplessness fast stealing over her once active limbs, they took her to the woods, built her a little hut, put up a little mud-chimney, and then made her welcome to the privilege of supporting herself there in perfect loneliness; thus virtually turning her out to die! If my poor old grandmother now lives, she lives to suffer in utter loneliness; she lives to remember and mourn over the loss of children, the loss of grandchildren, and the loss of great-grandchildren. They are, in the language of the slave's poet, Whittier,[1]

Gone, gone, sold and gone
To the rice swamp dank and lone,
Where the slave-whip ceaseless swings,

Where the noisome insect stings,
Where the fever-demon strews
Poison with the falling dews,
Where the sickly sunbeams glare
Through the hot and misty air:—
  Gone, gone, sold and gone
  To the rice swamp dank and lone,
  From Virginia hills and waters—
  Woe is me, my stolen daughters!

The hearth is desolate. The children, the unconscious children, who once sang and danced in her presence, are gone. She gropes her way, in the darkness of age, for a drink of water. Instead of the voices of her children, she hears by day the moans of the dove, and by night the screams of the hideous owl. All is gloom. The grave is at the door. And now, when weighed down by the pains and aches of old age, when the head inclines to the feet, when the beginning and ending of human existence meet, and helpless infancy and painful old age combine together—at this time, this most needful time, the time for the exercise of that tenderness and affection which children only can exercise towards a declining parent—my poor old grandmother, the devoted mother of twelve children, is left all alone, in yonder little hut, before a few dim embers. She stands—she sits—she staggers—she falls—she groans—she dies—and there are none of her children or grandchildren present, to wipe from her wrinkled brow the cold sweat of death, or to place beneath the sod her fallen remains. Will not a righteous God visit for these things?[2]

In about two years after the death of Mrs. Lucretia, Master Thomas married his second wife. Her name was Rowena Hamilton. She was the eldest daughter of Mr. William Hamilton. Master now lived in St. Michael's. Not long after his marriage, a misunderstanding took place between himself and Master Hugh; and as a means of punishing his brother, he took me from him to live with himself at St. Michael's. Here I underwent another most painful separation. It, however, was not so severe as the one I dreaded at the division of property; for, during this interval, a great change had taken

---

[1] *the slave's poet, Whittier* John Greenleaf Whittier (1807–92), white Quaker poet and abolitionist who was associated with William Lloyd Garrison. The quotation is from "The Farewell of a Virginia Slave Mother to Her Daughters Sold into Southern Bondage."

[2] *Will not … these things?* See Jeremiah 5.29: "Shall I not visit for these things? saith the Lord: shall not my soul be avenged on such a nation as this?"

place in Master Hugh and his once kind and affectionate wife. The influence of brandy upon him, and of slavery upon her, had effected a disastrous change in the characters of both; so that, as far as they were concerned, I thought I had little to lose by the change. But it was not to them that I was attached. It was to those little Baltimore boys that I felt the strongest attachment. I had received many good lessons from them, and was still receiving them, and the thought of leaving them was painful indeed. I was leaving, too, without the hope of ever being allowed to return. Master Thomas had said he would never let me return again. The barrier betwixt himself and brother he considered impassable.

I then had to regret that I did not at least make the attempt to carry out my resolution to run away; for the chances of success are tenfold greater from the city than from the country.

I sailed from Baltimore for St. Michael's in the sloop Amanda, Captain Edward Dodson. On my passage, I paid particular attention to the direction which the steamboats took to go to Philadelphia. I found, instead of going down, on reaching North Point they went up the bay, in a north-easterly direction. I deemed this knowledge of the utmost importance. My determination to run away was again revived. I resolved to wait only so long as the offering of a favorable opportunity. When that came, I was determined to be off.

CHAPTER 9

I have now reached a period of my life when I can give dates. I left Baltimore, and went to live with Master Thomas Auld, at St. Michael's, in March, 1832. It was now more than seven years since I lived with him in the family of my old master, on Colonel Lloyd's plantation. We of course were now almost entire strangers to each other. He was to me a new master, and I to him a new slave. I was ignorant of his temper and disposition; he was equally so of mine. A very short time, however, brought us into full acquaintance with each other. I was made acquainted with his wife not less than with himself. They were well matched, being equally mean[1] and cruel. I was now, for the first time

during a space of more than seven years, made to feel the painful gnawings of hunger—a something which I had not experienced before since I left Colonel Lloyd's plantation. It went hard enough with me then, when I could look back to no period at which I had enjoyed a sufficiency. It was tenfold harder after living in Master Hugh's family, where I had always had enough to eat, and of that which was good. I have said Master Thomas was a mean man. He was so. Not to give a slave enough to eat, is regarded as the most aggravated development of meanness even among slaveholders. The rule is, no matter how coarse the food, only let there be enough of it. This is the theory; and in the part of Maryland from which I came, it is the general practice—though there are many exceptions. Master Thomas gave us enough of neither coarse nor fine food. There were four slaves of us in the kitchen—my sister Eliza, my aunt Priscilla, Henny, and myself; and we were allowed less than a half of a bushel of corn-meal per week, and very little else, either in the shape of meat or vegetables. It was not enough for us to subsist upon. We were therefore reduced to the wretched necessity of living at the expense of our neighbors. This we did by begging and stealing, whichever came handy in the time of need, the one being considered as legitimate as the other. A great many times have we poor creatures been nearly perishing with hunger, when food in abundance lay mouldering in the safe and smoke-house,[2] and our pious mistress was aware of the fact; and yet that mistress and her husband would kneel every morning, and pray that God would bless them in basket and store!

Bad as all slaveholders are, we seldom meet one destitute of every element of character commanding respect. My master was one of this rare sort. I do not know of one single noble act ever performed by him. The leading trait in his character was meanness; and if there were any other element in his nature, it was made subject to this. He was mean; and, like most other mean men, he lacked the ability to conceal his meanness. Captain Auld was not born a slaveholder. He had been a poor man, master only of a Bay craft. He came into possession of all his slaves by marriage; and of all men, adopted slaveholders are the worst. He was cruel, but cowardly. He commanded without firmness. In the enforcement of his rules, he was at times rigid,

---

[1]   *mean* Lowly and undignified; also, miserly.

[2]   *safe and smoke-house* Storage-places for meat.

and at times lax. At times, he spoke to his slaves with the firmness of Napoleon and the fury of a demon; at other times, he might well be mistaken for an inquirer who had lost his way. He did nothing of himself. He might have passed for a lion, but for his ears. In all things noble which he attempted, his own meanness shone most conspicuous. His airs, words, and actions, were the airs, words, and actions of born slaveholders, and, being assumed, were awkward enough. He was not even a good imitator. He possessed all the disposition to deceive, but wanted the power. Having no resources within himself, he was compelled to be the copyist of many, and being such, he was forever the victim of inconsistency; and of consequence he was an object of contempt, and was held as such even by his slaves. The luxury of having slaves of his own to wait upon him was something new and unprepared for. He was a slaveholder without the ability to hold slaves. He found himself incapable of managing his slaves either by force, fear, or fraud. We seldom called him "master"; we generally called him "Captain Auld," and were hardly disposed to title him at all. I doubt not that our conduct had much to do with making him appear awkward, and of consequence fretful. Our want of reverence for him must have perplexed him greatly. He wished to have us call him master, but lacked the firmness necessary to command us to do so. His wife used to insist upon our calling him so, but to no purpose. In August, 1832, my master attended a Methodist camp-meeting[1] held in the Bay-side, Talbot county, and there experienced religion. I indulged a faint hope that his conversion would lead him to emancipate his slaves, and that, if he did not do this, it would, at any rate, make him more kind and humane. I was disappointed in both these respects. It neither made him to be humane to his slaves, nor to emancipate them. If it had any effect on his character, it made him more cruel and hateful in all his ways; for I believe him to have been a much worse man after his conversion than before. Prior to his conversion, he relied upon his own depravity to shield and sustain him in his savage barbarity; but after his conversion, he found religious sanction and support for his slaveholding cruelty. He made the greatest pretensions to piety. His house was the house of prayer. He prayed morning, noon, and night. He

very soon distinguished himself among his brethren, and was soon made a class-leader and exhorter. His activity in revivals was great, and he proved himself an instrument in the hands of the church in converting many souls. His house was the preachers' home. They used to take great pleasure in coming there to put up; for while he starved us, he stuffed them. We have had three or four preachers there at a time. The names of those who used to come most frequently while I lived there, were Mr. Storks, Mr. Ewery, Mr. Humphry, and Mr. Hickey. I have also seen Mr. George Cookman[2] at our house. We slaves loved Mr. Cookman. We believed him to be a good man. We thought him instrumental in getting Mr. Samuel Harrison, a very rich slaveholder, to emancipate his slaves; and by some means got the impression that he was laboring to effect the emancipation of all the slaves. When he was at our house, we were sure to be called in to prayers. When the others were there, we were sometimes called in and sometimes not. Mr. Cookman took more notice of us than either of the other ministers. He could not come among us without betraying his sympathy for us, and, stupid as we were, we had the sagacity to see it.

While I lived with my master in St. Michael's, there was a white young man, a Mr. Wilson, who proposed to keep a Sabbath school for the instruction of such slaves as might be disposed to learn to read the New Testament. We met but three times, when Mr. West and Mr. Fairbanks, both class-leaders, with many others, came upon us with sticks and other missiles, drove us off, and forbade us to meet again. Thus ended our little Sabbath school in the pious town of St. Michael's.

I have said my master found religious sanction for his cruelty. As an example, I will state one of many facts going to prove the charge. I have seen him tie up a lame young woman, and whip her with a heavy cowskin upon her naked shoulders, causing the warm red blood to drip; and, in justification of the bloody deed, he would quote this passage of Scripture—"He that knoweth his master's will, and doeth it not, shall be beaten with many stripes."[3]

---

1   *camp-meeting*   Outdoor meeting.

2   *Mr. George Cookman*   Methodist minister (1800–41) who served as Chaplain to the Senate and promoted emancipation.

3   *He that knoweth … many stripes*   See Luke 12.47.

Master would keep this lacerated young woman tied up in this horrid situation four or five hours at a time. I have known him to tie her up early in the morning, and whip her before breakfast; leave her, go to his store, return at dinner, and whip her again, cutting her in the places already made raw with his cruel lash. The secret of master's cruelty toward "Henny" is found in the fact of her being almost helpless. When quite a child, she fell into the fire, and burned herself horribly. Her hands were so burnt that she never got the use of them. She could do very little but bear heavy burdens. She was to master a bill of expense; and as he was a mean man, she was a constant offence to him. He seemed desirous of getting the poor girl out of existence. He gave her away once to his sister; but, being a poor gift, she was not disposed to keep her. Finally, my benevolent master, to use his own words, "set her adrift to take care of herself." Here was a recently-converted man, holding on upon the mother, and at the same time turning out her helpless child, to starve and die! Master Thomas was one of the many pious slaveholders who hold slaves for the very charitable purpose of taking care of them.

My master and myself had quite a number of differences. He found me unsuitable to his purpose. My city life, he said, had had a very pernicious effect upon me. It had almost ruined me for every good purpose, and fitted me for every thing which was bad. One of my greatest faults was that of letting his horse run away, and go down to his father-in-law's farm, which was about five miles from St. Michael's. I would then have to go after it. My reason for this kind of carelessness, or carefulness, was, that I could always get something to eat when I went there. Master William Hamilton, my master's father-in-law, always gave his slaves enough to eat. I never left there hungry, no matter how great the need of my speedy return. Master Thomas at length said he would stand it no longer. I had lived with him nine months, during which time he had given me a number of severe whippings, all to no good purpose. He resolved to put me out, as he said, to be broken; and, for this purpose, he let me for one year to a man named Edward Covey. Mr. Covey was a poor man, a farm-renter. He rented the place upon which he lived, as also the hands with which he tilled it. Mr. Covey had acquired a very high reputation for breaking young slaves, and this reputation was of immense value

to him. It enabled him to get his farm tilled with much less expense to himself than he could have had it done without such a reputation. Some slaveholders thought it not much loss to allow Mr. Covey to have their slaves one year, for the sake of the training to which they were subjected, without any other compensation. He could hire young help with great ease, in consequence of this reputation. Added to the natural good qualities of Mr. Covey, he was a professor of religion—a pious soul—a member and a class-leader in the Methodist church. All of this added weight to his reputation as a "nigger-breaker." I was aware of all the facts, having been made acquainted with them by a young man who had lived there. I nevertheless made the change gladly; for I was sure of getting enough to eat, which is not the smallest consideration to a hungry man.

CHAPTER 10

I had left Master Thomas's house, and went to live with Mr. Covey, on the 1st of January, 1833. I was now, for the first time in my life, a field hand. In my new employment, I found myself even more awkward than a country boy appeared to be in a large city. I had been at my new home but one week before Mr. Covey gave me a very severe whipping, cutting my back, causing the blood to run, and raising ridges on my flesh as large as my little finger. The details of this affair are as follows: Mr. Covey sent me, very early in the morning of one of our coldest days in the month of January, to the woods, to get a load of wood. He gave me a team of unbroken oxen. He told me which was the in-hand ox, and which the off-hand one.[1] He then tied the end of a large rope around the horns of the in-hand ox, and gave me the other end of it, and told me, if the oxen started to run, that I must hold on upon the rope. I had never driven oxen before, and of course I was very awkward. I, however, succeeded in getting to the edge of the woods with little difficulty; but I had got a very few rods into the woods, when the oxen took fright, and started full tilt, carrying the cart against trees, and over stumps, in the most frightful manner. I expected every moment that my brains would be dashed out against the trees. After running thus for a considerable

---

[1] *in-hand ox … off-hand one* Oxen on the right- and left-hand sides of a pair, respectively.

distance, they finally upset the cart, dashing it with great force against a tree, and threw themselves into a dense thicket. How I escaped death, I do not know. There I was, entirely alone, in a thick wood, in a place new to me. My cart was upset and shattered, my oxen were entangled among the young trees, and there was none to help me. After a long spell of effort, I succeeded in getting my cart righted, my oxen disentangled, and again yoked to the cart. I now proceeded with my team to the place where I had, the day before, been chopping wood, and loaded my cart pretty heavily, thinking in this way to tame my oxen. I then proceeded on my way home. I had now consumed one half of the day. I got out of the woods safely, and now felt out of danger. I stopped my oxen to open the woods gate; and just as I did so, before I could get hold of my ox-rope, the oxen again started, rushed through the gate, catching it between the wheel and the body of the cart, tearing it to pieces, and coming within a few inches of crushing me against the gate-post. Thus twice, in one short day, I escaped death by the merest chance. On my return, I told Mr. Covey what had happened, and how it happened. He ordered me to return to the woods again immediately. I did so, and he followed on after me. Just as I got into the woods, he came up and told me to stop my cart, and that he would teach me how to trifle away my time, and break gates. He then went to a large gum-tree, and with his axe cut three large switches, and, after trimming them up neatly with his pocketknife, he ordered me to take off my clothes. I made him no answer, but stood with my clothes on. He repeated his order. I still made him no answer, nor did I move to strip myself. Upon this he rushed at me with the fierceness of a tiger, tore off my clothes, and lashed me till he had worn out his switches, cutting me so savagely as to leave the marks visible for a long time after. This whipping was the first of a number just like it, and for similar offences.

I lived with Mr. Covey one year. During the first six months, of that year, scarce a week passed without his whipping me. I was seldom free from a sore back. My awkwardness was almost always his excuse for whipping me. We were worked fully up to the point of endurance. Long before day we were up, our horses fed, and by the first approach of day we were off to the field with our hoes and ploughing teams. Mr. Covey gave us enough to eat, but scarce time to eat it. We were often less than five minutes taking our meals. We were often in the field from the first approach of day till its last lingering ray had left us; and at saving-fodder time, midnight often caught us in the field binding blades.[1]

Covey would be out with us. The way he used to stand it, was this. He would spend the most of his afternoons in bed. He would then come out fresh in the evening, ready to urge us on with his words, example, and frequently with the whip. Mr. Covey was one of the few slaveholders who could and did work with his hands. He was a hard-working man. He knew by himself just what a man or a boy could do. There was no deceiving him. His work went on in his absence almost as well as in his presence; and he had the faculty of making us feel that he was ever present with us. This he did by surprising us. He seldom approached the spot where we were at work openly, if he could do it secretly. He always aimed at taking us by surprise. Such was his cunning, that we used to call him, among ourselves, "the snake." When we were at work in the cornfield, he would sometimes crawl on his hands and knees to avoid detection, and all at once he would rise nearly in our midst, and scream out, "Ha, ha! Come, come! Dash on, dash on!" This being his mode of attack, it was never safe to stop a single minute. His comings were like a thief in the night. He appeared to us as being ever at hand. He was under every tree, behind every stump, in every bush, and at every window, on the plantation. He would sometimes mount his horse, as if bound to St. Michael's, a distance of seven miles, and in half an hour afterwards you would see him coiled up in the corner of the wood-fence, watching every motion of the slaves. He would, for this purpose, leave his horse tied up in the woods. Again, he would sometimes walk up to us, and give us orders as though he was upon the point of starting on a long journey, turn his back upon us, and make as though he was going to the house to get ready; and, before he would get half way thither, he would turn short and crawl into a fence-corner, or behind some tree, and there watch us till the going down of the sun.

---

[1]   *saving-fodder time* Harvest time; *binding blades* Binding wheat sheaves.

Mr. Covey's *forte*[1] consisted in his power to deceive. His life was devoted to planning and perpetrating the grossest deceptions. Everything he possessed in the shape of learning or religion, he made conform to his disposition to deceive. He seemed to think himself equal to deceiving the Almighty. He would make a short prayer in the morning, and a long prayer at night; and, strange as it may seem, few men would at times appear more devotional than he. The exercises of his family devotions were always commenced with singing; and, as he was a very poor singer himself, the duty of raising the hymn generally came upon me. He would read his hymn, and nod at me to commence. I would at times do so; at others, I would not. My non-compliance would almost always produce much confusion. To show himself independent of me, he would start and stagger through with his hymn in the most discordant manner. In this state of mind, he prayed with more than ordinary spirit. Poor man! such was his disposition, and success at deceiving, I do verily believe that he sometimes deceived himself into the solemn belief, that he was a sincere worshipper of the most high God; and this, too, at a time when he may be said to have been guilty of compelling his woman slave to commit the sin of adultery. The facts in the case are these: Mr. Covey was a poor man; he was just commencing in life; he was only able to buy one slave; and, shocking as is the fact, he bought her, as he said, for a breeder. This woman was named Caroline. Mr. Covey bought her from Mr. Thomas Lowe, about six miles from St. Michael's. She was a large, able-bodied woman, about twenty years old. She had already given birth to one child, which proved her to be just what he wanted. After buying her, he hired a married man of Mr. Samuel Harrison, to live with him one year; and him he used to fasten up with her every night! The result was, that, at the end of the year, the miserable woman gave birth to twins. At this result Mr. Covey seemed to be highly pleased, both with the man and the wretched woman. Such was his joy, and that of his wife, that nothing they could do for Caroline during her confinement was too good, or too hard, to be done. The children were regarded as being quite an addition to his wealth.

If at any one time of my life more than another, I was made to drink the bitterest dregs of slavery, that time was during the first six months of my stay with Mr. Covey. We were worked in all weathers. It was never too hot or too cold; it could never rain, blow, hail, or snow, too hard for us to work in the field. Work, work, work, was scarcely more the order of the day than of the night. The longest days were too short for him, and the shortest nights too long for him. I was somewhat unmanageable when I first went there, but a few months of this discipline tamed me. Mr. Covey succeeded in breaking me. I was broken in body, soul, and spirit. My natural elasticity was crushed, my intellect languished, the disposition to read departed, the cheerful spark that lingered about my eye died; the dark night of slavery closed in upon me; and behold a man transformed into a brute!

Sunday was my only leisure time. I spent this in a sort of beast-like stupor, between sleep and wake, under some large tree. At times I would rise up, a flash of energetic freedom would dart through my soul, accompanied with a faint beam of hope, that flickered for a moment, and then vanished. I sank down again, mourning over my wretched condition. I was sometimes prompted to take my life, and that of Covey, but was prevented by a combination of hope and fear. My sufferings on this plantation seem now like a dream rather than a stern reality.

Our house stood within a few rods of the Chesapeake Bay, whose broad bosom was ever white with sails from every quarter of the habitable globe. Those beautiful vessels, robed in purest white, so delightful to the eye of freemen, were to me so many shrouded ghosts, to terrify and torment me with thoughts of my wretched condition. I have often, in the deep stillness of a summer's Sabbath, stood all alone upon the lofty banks of that noble bay, and traced, with saddened heart and tearful eye, the countless number of sails moving off to the mighty ocean. The sight of these always affected me powerfully. My thoughts would compel utterance; and there, with no audience but the Almighty, I would pour out my soul's complaint, in my rude way, with an apostrophe[2] to the moving multitude of ships:

---

1 *forte* Italian: strength; particular ability.

2 *apostrophe* Exclamatory speech made either to one or more people who are unable to respond (whether because they are not present or because they are not alive) or to one or more inanimate objects.

"You are loosed from your moorings, and are free; I am fast in my chains, and am a slave! You move merrily before the gentle gale, and I sadly before the bloody whip! You are freedom's swift-winged angels, that fly round the world; I am confined in bands of iron! O that I were free! O, that I were on one of your gallant decks, and under your protecting wing! Alas! betwixt me and you, the turbid waters roll. Go on, go on. O that I could also go! Could I but swim! If I could fly! O, why was I born a man, of whom to make a brute! The glad ship is gone; she hides in the dim distance. I am left in the hottest hell of unending slavery. O God, save me! God, deliver me! Let me be free! Is there any God? Why am I a slave? I will run away. I will not stand it. Get caught, or get clear, I'll try it. I had as well die with ague as the fever.[1] I have only one life to lose. I had as well be killed running as die standing. Only think of it; one hundred miles straight north, and I am free! Try it? Yes! God helping me, I will. It cannot be that I shall live and die a slave. I will take to the water. This very bay shall yet bear me into freedom. The steamboats steered in a north-east course from North Point. I will do the same; and when I get to the head of the bay, I will turn my canoe adrift, and walk straight through Delaware into Pennsylvania. When I get there, I shall not be required to have a pass; I can travel without being disturbed. Let but the first opportunity offer, and, come what will, I am off. Meanwhile, I will try to bear up under the yoke. I am not the only slave in the world. Why should I fret? I can bear as much as any of them. Besides, I am but a boy, and all boys are bound to someone. It may be that my misery in slavery will only increase my happiness when I get free. There is a better day coming."

Thus I used to think, and thus I used to speak to myself; goaded almost to madness at one moment, and at the next reconciling myself to my wretched lot.

I have already intimated that my condition was much worse, during the first six months of my stay at Mr. Covey's, than in the last six. The circumstances leading to the change in Mr. Covey's course toward me form an epoch in my humble history. You have seen how a man was made a slave; you shall see how a slave was made a man. On one of the hottest days of the month of August, 1833, Bill Smith, William Hughes, a slave named Eli, and myself, were engaged in fanning wheat.[2] Hughes was clearing the fanned wheat from before the fan. Eli was turning, Smith was feeding, and I was carrying wheat to the fan. The work was simple, requiring strength rather than intellect; yet, to one entirely unused to such work, it came very hard. About three o'clock of that day, I broke down; my strength failed me; I was seized with a violent aching of the head, attended with extreme dizziness; I trembled in every limb. Finding what was coming, I nerved myself up, feeling it would never do to stop work. I stood as long as I could stagger to the hopper with grain. When I could stand no longer, I fell, and felt as if held down by an immense weight. The fan of course stopped; every one had his own work to do; and no one could do the work of the other, and have his own go on at the same time.

Mr. Covey was at the house, about one hundred yards from the treading-yard where we were fanning. On hearing the fan stop, he left immediately, and came to the spot where we were. He hastily inquired what the matter was. Bill answered that I was sick, and there was no one to bring wheat to the fan. I had by this time crawled away under the side of the post and rail-fence by which the yard was enclosed, hoping to find relief by getting out of the sun. He then asked where I was. He was told by one of the hands. He came to the spot, and, after looking at me awhile, asked me what was the matter. I told him as well as I could, for I scarce had strength to speak. He then gave me a savage kick in the side, and told me to get up. I tried to do so, but fell back in the attempt. He gave me another kick, and again told me to rise. I again tried, and succeeded in gaining my feet; but, stooping to get the tub with which I was feeding the fan, I again staggered and fell. While down in this situation, Mr. Covey took up the hickory slat with which Hughes had been striking off the half-bushel measure, and with it gave me a heavy blow upon the head, making a large wound, and the blood ran freely; and with this again told me to get up. I made no effort to comply, having now made up my mind to let him do his worst. In a short time after

---

[1] *ague ... fever* The point here is that there is little difference between the two; "ague" was a term given to a range of infectious maladies for which a high fever was a key symptom.

[2] *fanning wheat* Separating chaff from the wheat by means of a large fanning mill.

receiving this blow, my head grew better. Mr. Covey had now left me to my fate. At this moment I resolved, for the first time, to go to my master, enter a complaint, and ask his protection. In order to [do] this, I must that afternoon walk seven miles; and this, under the circumstances, was truly a severe undertaking. I was exceedingly feeble; made so as much by the kicks and blows which I received, as by the severe fit of sickness to which I had been subjected. I, however, watched my chance, while Covey was looking in an opposite direction, and started for St. Michael's. I succeeded in getting a considerable distance on my way to the woods, when Covey discovered me, and called after me to come back, threatening what he would do if I did not come. I disregarded both his calls and his threats, and made my way to the woods as fast as my feeble state would allow; and thinking I might be overhauled by him if I kept the road, I walked through the woods, keeping far enough from the road to avoid detection, and near enough to prevent losing my way. I had not gone far before my little strength again failed me. I could go no farther. I fell down, and lay for a considerable time. The blood was yet oozing from the wound on my head. For a time I thought I should bleed to death; and think now that I should have done so, but that the blood so matted my hair as to stop the wound. After lying there about three quarters of an hour, I nerved myself up again, and started on my way, through bogs and briers, barefooted and bareheaded, tearing my feet sometimes at nearly every step; and after a journey of about seven miles, occupying some five hours to perform it, I arrived at master's store. I then presented an appearance enough to affect any but a heart of iron. From the crown of my head to my feet, I was covered with blood. My hair was all clotted with dust and blood; my shirt was stiff with blood. I suppose I looked like a man who had escaped a den of wild beasts, and barely escaped them. In this state I appeared before my master, humbly entreating him to interpose his authority for my protection. I told him all the circumstances as well as I could, and it seemed, as I spoke, at times to affect him. He would then walk the floor, and seek to justify Covey by saying he expected I deserved it. He asked me what I wanted. I told him, to let me get a new home; that as sure as I lived with Mr. Covey again, I should live with but to die with him;

that Covey would surely kill me; he was in a fair way for it. Master Thomas ridiculed the idea that there was any danger of Mr. Covey's killing me, and said that he knew Mr. Covey; that he was a good man, and that he could not think of taking me from him; that, should he do so, he would lose the whole year's wages; that I belonged to Mr. Covey for one year, and that I must go back to him, come what might; and that I must not trouble him with any more stories, or that he would himself get hold of me. After threatening me thus, he gave me a very large dose of salts,[1] telling me that I might remain in St. Michael's that night (it being quite late), but that I must be off back to Mr. Covey's early in the morning; and that if I did not, he would get hold of me, which meant that he would whip me. I remained all night, and, according to his orders, I started off to Covey's in the morning (Saturday morning), wearied in body and broken in spirit. I got no supper that night, or breakfast that morning. I reached Covey's about nine o'clock; and just as I was getting over the fence that divided Mrs. Kemp's fields from ours, out ran Covey with his cowskin, to give me another whipping. Before he could reach me, I succeeded in getting to the cornfield; and as the corn was very high, it afforded me the means of hiding. He seemed very angry, and searched for me a long time. My behavior was altogether unaccountable. He finally gave up the chase, thinking, I suppose, that I must come home for something to eat; he would give himself no further trouble in looking for me. I spent that day mostly in the woods, having the alternative before me—to go home and be whipped to death, or stay in the woods and be starved to death. That night, I fell in with Sandy Jenkins, a slave with whom I was somewhat acquainted. Sandy had a free wife[2] who lived about four miles from Mr. Covey's; and it being Saturday, he was on his way to see her. I told him my circumstances, and he very kindly invited me to go home with him. I went home with him, and talked this whole matter over, and got his advice as to what course

---

1   *large dose of salts*   I.e., smelling salts, comprising a mixture of carbonate of ammonia and other scented components, used to restore people from spells of fainting or dizziness.

2   *a free wife*   Because slavery often resulted in spouses being sold to different slaveholders, it sometimes occurred that one would be granted their freedom while the other remained enslaved.

it was best for me to pursue. I found Sandy an old adviser. He told me, with great solemnity, I must go back to Covey; but that before I went, I must go with him into another part of the woods, where there was a certain root, which, if I would take some of it with me, carrying it always on my right side, would render it impossible for Mr. Covey, or any other white man, to whip me. He said he had carried it for years; and since he had done so, he had never received a blow, and never expected to while he carried it. I at first rejected the idea, that the simple carrying of a root in my pocket would have any such effect as he had said, and was not disposed to take it; but Sandy impressed the necessity with much earnestness, telling me it could do no harm, if it did no good. To please him, I at length took the root, and, according to his direction, carried it upon my right side. This was Sunday morning. I immediately started for home; and upon entering the yard gate, out came Mr. Covey on his way to meeting. He spoke to me very kindly, bade me drive the pigs from a lot near by, and passed on towards the church. Now, this singular conduct of Mr. Covey really made me begin to think that there was something in the root which Sandy had given me; and had it been on any other day than Sunday, I could have attributed the conduct to no other cause than the influence of that root; and as it was, I was half inclined to think the root to be something more than I at first had taken it to be. All went well till Monday morning. On this morning, the virtue of the root was fully tested. Long before daylight, I was called to go and rub, curry,[1] and feed, the horses. I obeyed, and was glad to obey. But whilst thus engaged, whilst in the act of throwing down some blades from the loft, Mr. Covey entered the stable with a long rope; and just as I was half out of the loft, he caught hold of my legs, and was about tying me. As soon as I found what he was up to, I gave a sudden spring, and as I did so, he holding to my legs, I was brought sprawling on the stable floor. Mr. Covey seemed now to think he had me, and could do what he pleased; but at this moment—from whence came the spirit I don't know—I resolved to fight; and, suiting my action to the resolution, I seized Covey hard by the throat; and as I did so, I rose. He held on to me, and I to him. My resistance was so entirely unexpected that

Covey seemed taken all aback. He trembled like a leaf. This gave me assurance, and I held him uneasy, causing the blood to run where I touched him with the ends of my fingers. Mr. Covey soon called out to Hughes for help. Hughes came, and, while Covey held me, attempted to tie my right hand. While he was in the act of doing so, I watched my chance, and gave him a heavy kick close under the ribs. This kick fairly sickened Hughes, so that he left me in the hands of Mr. Covey. This kick had the effect of not only weakening Hughes, but Covey also. When he saw Hughes bending over with pain, his courage quailed. He asked me if I meant to persist in my resistance. I told him I did, come what might; that he had used me like a brute for six months, and that I was determined to be used so no longer. With that, he strove to drag me to a stick that was lying just out of the stable door. He meant to knock me down. But just as he was leaning over to get the stick, I seized him with both hands by his collar, and brought him by a sudden snatch to the ground. By this time, Bill came. Covey called upon him for assistance. Bill wanted to know what he could do. Covey said, "Take hold of him, take hold of him!" Bill said his master hired him out to work, and not to help to whip me; so he left Covey and myself to fight our own battle out. We were at it for nearly two hours. Covey at length let me go, puffing and blowing at a great rate, saying that if I had not resisted, he would not have whipped me half so much. The truth was, that he had not whipped me at all. I considered him as getting entirely the worst end of the bargain; for he had drawn no blood from me, but I had from him. The whole six months afterwards, that I spent with Mr. Covey, he never laid the weight of his finger upon me in anger. He would occasionally say, he didn't want to get hold of me again. "No," thought I, "you need not; for you will come off worse than you did before."

This battle with Mr. Covey was the turning-point in my career as a slave. It rekindled the few expiring embers of freedom, and revived within me a sense of my own manhood. It recalled the departed self-confidence, and inspired me again with a determination to be free. The gratification afforded by the triumph was a full compensation for whatever else might follow, even death itself. He only can understand the deep satisfaction which I experienced, who has himself repelled by

---

[1]   *curry*   Brush.

force the bloody arm of slavery. I felt as I never felt before. It was a glorious resurrection, from the tomb of slavery, to the heaven of freedom. My long-crushed spirit rose, cowardice departed, bold defiance took its place; and I now resolved that, however long I might remain a slave in form, the day had passed forever when I could be a slave in fact. I did not hesitate to let it be known of me, that the white man who expected to succeed in whipping, must also succeed in killing me.

From this time I was never again what might be called fairly whipped, though I remained a slave four years afterwards. I had several fights, but was never whipped.

It was for a long time a matter of surprise to me why Mr. Covey did not immediately have me taken by the constable to the whipping-post, and there regularly whipped for the crime of raising my hand against a white man in defence of myself. And the only explanation I can now think of does not entirely satisfy me; but such as it is, I will give it. Mr. Covey enjoyed the most unbounded reputation for being a first-rate overseer and negro-breaker. It was of considerable importance to him. That reputation was at stake; and had he sent me—a boy about sixteen years old—to the public whipping-post, his reputation would have been lost; so, to save his reputation, he suffered me to go unpunished.

My term of actual service to Mr. Edward Covey ended on Christmas day, 1833. The days between Christmas and New Year's Day are allowed as holidays; and, accordingly, we were not required to perform any labor, more than to feed and take care of the stock. This time we regarded as our own, by the grace of our masters; and we therefore used or abused it nearly as we pleased. Those of us who had families at a distance, were generally allowed to spend the whole six days in their society. This time, however, was spent in various ways. The staid, sober, thinking and industrious ones of our number would employ themselves in making corn-brooms, mats, horse-collars, and baskets; and another class of us would spend the time in hunting opossums, hares, and coons. But by far the larger part engaged in such sports and merriments as playing ball, wrestling, running foot-races, fiddling, dancing, and drinking whisky; and this latter mode of spending the time was by far the most agreeable to the feelings of our masters. A slave who would work during the holidays was considered by our masters as scarcely deserving them. He was regarded as one who rejected the favor of his master. It was deemed a disgrace not to get drunk at Christmas; and he was regarded as lazy indeed, who had not provided himself with the necessary means, during the year, to get whisky enough to last him through Christmas.

From what I know of the effect of these holidays upon the slave, I believe them to be among the most effective means in the hands of the slaveholder in keeping down the spirit of insurrection. Were the slaveholders at once to abandon this practice, I have not the slightest doubt it would lead to an immediate insurrection among the slaves. These holidays serve as conductors, or safety-valves, to carry off the rebellious spirit of enslaved humanity. But for these, the slave would be forced up to the wildest desperation; and woe betide the slaveholder, the day he ventures to remove or hinder the operation of those conductors! I warn him that, in such an event, a spirit will go forth in their midst, more to be dreaded than the most appalling earthquake.

The holidays are part and parcel of the gross fraud, wrong, and inhumanity of slavery. They are professedly a custom established by the benevolence of the slaveholders; but I undertake to say, it is the result of selfishness, and one of the grossest frauds committed upon the down-trodden slave. They do not give the slaves this time because they would not like to have their work during its continuance, but because they know it would be unsafe to deprive them of it. This will be seen by the fact, that the slaveholders like to have their slaves spend those days just in such a manner as to make them as glad of their ending as of their beginning. Their object seems to be, to disgust their slaves with freedom, by plunging them into the lowest depths of dissipation. For instance, the slaveholders not only like to see the slave drink of his own accord, but will adopt various plans to make him drunk. One plan is, to make bets on their slaves, as to who can drink the most whisky without getting drunk; and in this way they succeed in getting whole multitudes to drink to excess. Thus, when the slave asks for virtuous freedom, the cunning slaveholder, knowing his ignorance, cheats him with a dose of vicious dissipation, artfully labelled with the name of liberty. The most of us used to drink it down, and the result was just what might be supposed; many of us were led to think that there was little to choose between liberty and slavery. We felt, and very properly too, that we had almost as well be slaves to man as to rum. So, when the holidays ended, we staggered up from the filth of our wallowing, took a long breath, and marched to the field—feeling, upon the whole, rather glad to go, from what our master had deceived us into a belief was freedom, back to the arms of slavery.

I have said that this mode of treatment is a part of the whole system of fraud and inhumanity of slavery. It is so. The mode here adopted to disgust the slave with freedom, by allowing him to see only the abuse of it, is carried out in other things. For instance, a slave loves molasses; he steals some. His master, in many cases, goes off to town, and buys a large quantity; he returns, takes his whip, and commands the slave to eat the molasses, until the poor fellow is made sick at the very mention of it. The same mode is sometimes adopted to make the slaves refrain from asking for more food than their regular allowance. A slave runs through his allowance, and applies for more. His master is enraged at him; but, not willing to send him off without food, gives him more than is necessary, and compels him to eat it within a given time. Then, if he complains that he cannot eat it, he is said to be satisfied neither full nor fasting, and is whipped for being hard to please! I have an abundance of such illustrations of the same principle, drawn from my own observation, but think the cases I have cited sufficient. The practice is a very common one.

On the first of January, 1834, I left Mr. Covey, and went to live with Mr. William Freeland, who lived about three miles from St. Michael's. I soon found Mr. Freeland a very different man from Mr. Covey. Though not rich, he was what would be called an educated southern gentleman. Mr. Covey, as I have shown, was a well-trained negro-breaker and slave-driver. The former (slaveholder though he was) seemed to possess some regard for honor, some reverence for justice, and some respect for humanity. The latter seemed totally insensible to all such sentiments. Mr. Freeland had many of the faults peculiar to slaveholders, such as being very

passionate and fretful; but I must do him the justice to say, that he was exceedingly free from those degrading vices to which Mr. Covey was constantly addicted. The one was open and frank, and we always knew where to find him. The other was a most artful deceiver, and could be understood only by such as were skilful enough to detect his cunningly-devised frauds. Another advantage I gained in my new master was, he made no pretensions to, or profession of, religion; and this, in my opinion, was truly a great advantage. I assert most unhesitatingly, that the religion of the south is a mere covering for the most horrid crimes—a justifier of the most appalling barbarity—a sanctifier of the most hateful frauds—and a dark shelter under, which the darkest, foulest, grossest, and most infernal deeds of slaveholders find the strongest protection. Were I to be again reduced to the chains of slavery, next to that enslavement, I should regard being the slave of a religious master the greatest calamity that could befall me. For of all slaveholders with whom I have ever met, religious slaveholders are the worst. I have ever found them the meanest and basest, the most cruel and cowardly, of all others. It was my unhappy lot not only to belong to a religious slaveholder, but to live in a community of such religionists. Very near Mr. Freeland lived the Rev. Daniel Weeden, and in the same neighborhood lived the Rev. Rigby Hopkins. These were members and ministers in the Reformed Methodist Church. Mr. Weeden owned, among others, a woman slave, whose name I have forgotten. This woman's back, for weeks, was kept literally raw, made so by the lash of this merciless, religious wretch. He used to hire hands. His maxim was, Behave well or behave ill, it is the duty of a master occasionally to whip a slave, to remind him of his master's authority. Such was his theory, and such his practice.

Mr. Hopkins was even worse than Mr. Weeden. His chief boast was his ability to manage slaves. The peculiar feature of his government was that of whipping slaves in advance of deserving it. He always managed to have one or more of his slaves to whip every Monday morning. He did this to alarm their fears, and strike terror into those who escaped. His plan was to whip for the smallest offences, to prevent the commission of large ones. Mr. Hopkins could always find some excuse for whipping a slave. It would astonish one, unaccustomed to a slaveholding life, to see with what wonderful ease a slaveholder can find things, of which to make occasion to whip a slave. A mere look, word, or motion—a mistake, accident, or want of power—are all matters for which a slave may be whipped at any time. Does a slave look dissatisfied? It is said, he has the devil in him, and it must be whipped out. Does he speak loudly when spoken to by his master? Then he is getting high-minded, and should be taken down a button-hole lower. Does he forget to pull off his hat at the approach of a white person? Then he is wanting in reverence, and should be whipped for it. Does he ever venture to vindicate his conduct, when censured for it? Then he is guilty of impudence—one of the greatest crimes of which a slave can be guilty. Does he ever venture to suggest a different mode of doing things from that pointed out by his master? He is indeed presumptuous, and getting above himself; and nothing less than a flogging will do for him. Does he, while ploughing, break a plough—or, while hoeing, break a hoe? It is owing to his carelessness, and for it a slave must always be whipped. Mr. Hopkins could always find something of this sort to justify the use of the lash, and he seldom failed to embrace such opportunities. There was not a man in the whole county, with whom the slaves who had the getting their own home, would not prefer to live, rather than with this Rev. Mr. Hopkins. And yet there was not a man anywhere round, who made higher professions of religion, or was more active in revivals—more attentive to the class, love-feast, prayer and preaching meetings, or more devotional in his family— that prayed earlier, later, louder, and longer— than this same reverend slave-driver, Rigby Hopkins.

But to return to Mr. Freeland, and to my experience while in his employment. He, like Mr. Covey, gave us enough to eat; but, unlike Mr. Covey, he also gave us sufficient time to take our meals. He worked us hard, but always between sunrise and sunset. He required a good deal of work to be done, but gave us good tools with which to work. His farm was large, but he employed hands enough to work it, and with ease, compared with many of his neighbors. My treatment, while in his employment, was heavenly, compared with what I experienced at the hands of Mr. Edward Covey.

Mr. Freeland was himself the owner of but two slaves. Their names were Henry Harris and John Harris. The rest of his hands he hired. These consisted of myself,

Sandy Jenkins,[1] and Handy Caldwell. Henry and John were quite intelligent, and in a very little while after I went there, I succeeded in creating in them a strong desire to learn how to read. This desire soon sprang up in the others also. They very soon mustered up some old spelling-books, and nothing would do but that I must keep a Sabbath school. I agreed to do so, and accordingly devoted my Sundays to teaching these my loved fellow-slaves how to read. Neither of them knew his letters when I went there. Some of the slaves of the neighboring farms found what was going on, and also availed themselves of this little opportunity to learn to read. It was understood, among all who came, that there must be as little display about it as possible. It was necessary to keep our religious masters at St. Michael's unacquainted with the fact, that, instead of spending the Sabbath in wrestling, boxing, and drinking whisky, we were trying to learn how to read the will of God; for they had much rather see us engaged in those degrading sports, than to see us behaving like intellectual, moral, and accountable beings. My blood boils as I think of the bloody manner in which Messrs. Wright Fairbanks and Garrison West, both class-leaders, in connection with many others, rushed in upon us with sticks and stones, and broke up our virtuous little Sabbath school, at St. Michael's—all calling themselves Christians! humble followers of the Lord Jesus Christ! But I am again digressing.

I held my Sabbath school at the house of a free colored man, whose name I deem it imprudent to mention; for should it be known, it might embarrass him greatly, though the crime of holding the school was committed ten years ago. I had at one time over forty scholars, and those of the right sort, ardently desiring to learn. They were of all ages, though mostly men and women. I look back to those Sundays with an amount of pleasure not to be expressed. They were great days to my soul. The work of instructing my dear fellow-slaves was the sweetest engagement with which I was ever blessed. We loved each other, and to leave them at the

---

[1] [Douglass's note]   This is the same man who gave me the roots to prevent my being whipped by Mr. Covey. He was "a clever soul." We used frequently to talk about the fight with Covey, and as often as we did so, he would claim my success as the result of the roots which he gave me. This superstition is very common among the more ignorant slaves. A slave seldom dies but that his death is attributed to trickery.

close of the Sabbath was a severe cross indeed. When I think that these precious souls are today shut up in the prison-house of slavery, my feelings overcome me, and I am almost ready to ask, "Does a righteous God govern the universe? and for what does he hold the thunders in his right hand, if not to smite the oppressor, and deliver the spoiled out of the hand of the spoiler?"[1] These dear souls came not to Sabbath school because it was popular to do so, nor did I teach them because it was reputable to be thus engaged. Every moment they spent in that school, they were liable to be taken up, and given thirty-nine lashes. They came because they wished to learn. Their minds had been starved by their cruel masters. They had been shut up in mental darkness. I taught them, because it was the delight of my soul to be doing something that looked like bettering the condition of my race. I kept up my school nearly the whole year I lived with Mr. Freeland; and, beside my Sabbath school, I devoted three evenings in the week, during the winter, to teaching the slaves at home. And I have the happiness to know, that several of those who came to Sabbath school learned how to read; and that one, at least, is now free through my agency.

The year passed off smoothly. It seemed only about half as long as the year which preceded it. I went through it without receiving a single blow. I will give Mr. Freeland the credit of being the best master I ever had, till I became my own master. For the ease with which I passed the year, I was, however, somewhat indebted to the society of my fellow-slaves. They were noble souls; they not only possessed loving hearts, but brave ones. We were linked and interlinked with each other. I loved them with a love stronger than anything I have experienced since. It is sometimes said that we slaves do not love and confide in each other. In answer to this assertion, I can say, I never loved any or confided in any people more than my fellow-slaves, and especially those with whom I lived at Mr. Freeland's. I believe we would have died for each other. We never undertook to do anything, of any importance, without a mutual consultation. We never moved separately. We were one; and as much so by our tempers and

dispositions, as by the mutual hardships to which we were necessarily subjected by our condition as slaves.

At the close of the year 1834, Mr. Freeland again hired me of my master, for the year 1835. But, by this time, I began to want to live upon free land as well as with Freeland; and I was no longer content, therefore, to live with him or any other slaveholder. I began, with the commencement of the year, to prepare myself for a final struggle, which should decide my fate one way or the other. My tendency was upward. I was fast approaching manhood, and year after year had passed, and I was still a slave. These thoughts roused me—I must do something. I therefore resolved that 1835 should not pass without witnessing an attempt, on my part, to secure my liberty. But I was not willing to cherish this determination alone. My fellow-slaves were dear to me. I was anxious to have them participate with me in this, my life-giving determination. I therefore, though with great prudence, commenced early to ascertain their views and feelings in regard to their condition, and to imbue their minds with thoughts of freedom. I bent myself to devising ways and means for our escape, and meanwhile strove, on all fitting occasions, to impress them with the gross fraud and inhumanity of slavery. I went first to Henry, next to John, then to the others. I found, in them all, warm hearts and noble spirits. They were ready to hear, and ready to act when a feasible plan should be proposed. This was what I wanted. I talked to them of our want of manhood, if we submitted to our enslavement without at least one noble effort to be free. We met often, and consulted frequently, and told our hopes and fears, recounted the difficulties, real and imagined, which we should be called on to meet. At times we were almost disposed to give up, and try to content ourselves with our wretched lot; at others, we were firm and unbending in our determination to go. Whenever we suggested any plan, there was shrinking—the odds were fearful. Our path was beset with the greatest obstacles; and if we succeeded in gaining the end of it, our right to be free was yet questionable—we were yet liable to be returned to bondage. We could see no spot, this side of the ocean, where we could be free. We knew nothing about Canada. Our knowledge of the north did not extend farther than New York; and to go there, and be forever harassed with the frightful liability of

---

[1]   *Does a righteous ... the spoiler*   These lines contain allusions to several biblical passages, including Exodus 15 and Isaiah 33.1.

being returned to slavery—with the certainty of being treated tenfold worse than before—the thought was truly a horrible one, and one which it was not easy to overcome. The case sometimes stood thus: At every gate through which we were to pass, we saw a watchman—at every ferry a guard—on every bridge a sentinel—and in every wood a patrol. We were hemmed in upon every side. Here were the difficulties, real or imagined—the good to be sought, and the evil to be shunned. On the one hand, there stood slavery, a stern reality, glaring frightfully upon us—its robes already crimsoned with the blood of millions, and even now feasting itself greedily upon our own flesh. On the other hand, away back in the dim distance, under the flickering light of the north star, behind some craggy hill or snow-covered mountain, stood a doubtful freedom—half frozen—beckoning us to come and share its hospitality. This in itself was sometimes enough to stagger us; but when we permitted ourselves to survey the road, we were frequently appalled. Upon either side we saw grim death, assuming the most horrid shapes. Now it was starvation, causing us to eat our own flesh; now we were contending with the waves, and were drowned; now we were overtaken, and torn to pieces by the fangs of the terrible bloodhound. We were stung by scorpions, chased by wild beasts, bitten by snakes, and finally, after having nearly reached the desired spot—after swimming rivers, encountering wild beasts, sleeping in the woods, suffering hunger and nakedness—we were overtaken by our pursuers, and, in our resistance, we were shot dead upon the spot! I say, this picture sometimes appalled us, and made us

> rather bear those ills we had,
> Than fly to others, that we knew not of.[1]

In coming to a fixed determination to run away, we did more than Patrick Henry, when he resolved upon liberty or death. With us it was a doubtful liberty at most, and almost certain death if we failed. For my part, I should prefer death to hopeless bondage.

Sandy, one of our number, gave up the notion, but still encouraged us. Our company then consisted of Henry Harris, John Harris, Henry Bailey, Charles Roberts, and myself. Henry Bailey was my uncle, and belonged to my master. Charles married my aunt: he belonged to my master's father-in-law, Mr. William Hamilton.

The plan we finally concluded upon was, to get a large canoe belonging to Mr. Hamilton, and upon the Saturday night previous to Easter holidays, paddle directly up the Chesapeake Bay. On our arrival at the head of the bay, a distance of seventy or eighty miles from where we lived, it was our purpose to turn our canoe adrift, and follow the guidance of the north star till we got beyond the limits of Maryland. Our reason for taking the water route was, that we were less liable to be suspected as runaways; we hoped to be regarded as fishermen; whereas, if we should take the land route, we should be subjected to interruptions of almost every kind. Anyone having a white face, and being so disposed, could stop us, and subject us to examination.

The week before our intended start, I wrote several protections, one for each of us. As well as I can remember, they were in the following words, to wit:

> This is to certify that I, the undersigned, have given the bearer, my servant, full liberty to go to Baltimore, and spend the Easter holidays. Written with mine own hand, &c., 1835.
> WILLIAM HAMILTON,
> Near St. Michael's, in Talbot county, Maryland

We were not going to Baltimore; but, in going up the bay, we went toward Baltimore, and these protections were only intended to protect us while on the bay.

As the time drew near for our departure, our anxiety became more and more intense. It was truly a matter of life and death with us. The strength of our determination was about to be fully tested. At this time, I was very active in explaining every difficulty, removing every doubt, dispelling every fear, and inspiring all with the firmness indispensable to success in our undertaking; assuring them that half was gained the instant we made the move; we had talked long enough; we were now ready to move; if not now, we never should be; and if we did not intend to move now, we had as well fold our arms, sit down, and acknowledge ourselves fit only to be slaves. This, none of us were

---

1   *rather bear ... knew not of*   See Shakespeare's *Hamlet* 3.1.89–90.

prepared to acknowledge. Every man stood firm; and at our last meeting, we pledged ourselves afresh, in the most solemn manner, that, at the time appointed, we would certainly start in pursuit of freedom. This was in the middle of the week, at the end of which we were to be off. We went, as usual, to our several fields of labor, but with bosoms highly agitated with thoughts of our truly hazardous undertaking. We tried to conceal our feelings as much as possible; and I think we succeeded very well.

After a painful waiting, the Saturday morning, whose night was to witness our departure, came. I hailed it with joy, bring what of sadness it might. Friday night was a sleepless one for me. I probably felt more anxious than the rest, because I was, by common consent, at the head of the whole affair. The responsibility of success or failure lay heavily upon me. The glory of the one, and the confusion of the other, were alike mine. The first two hours of that morning were such as I never experienced before, and hope never to again. Early in the morning, we went, as usual, to the field. We were spreading manure; and all at once, while thus engaged, I was overwhelmed with an indescribable feeling, in the fulness of which I turned to Sandy, who was near by, and said, "We are betrayed!" "Well," said he, "that thought has this moment struck me." We said no more. I was never more certain of anything.

The horn was blown as usual, and we went up from the field to the house for breakfast. I went for the form, more than for want of anything to eat that morning. Just as I got to the house, in looking out at the lane gate, I saw four white men, with two colored men. The white men were on horseback, and the colored ones were walking behind, as if tied. I watched them a few moments till they got up to our lane gate. Here they halted, and tied the colored men to the gate-post. I was not yet certain as to what the matter was. In a few moments, in rode Mr. Hamilton, with a speed betokening great excitement. He came to the door, and inquired if Master William was in. He was told he was at the barn. Mr. Hamilton, without dismounting, rode up to the barn with extraordinary speed. In a few moments, he and Mr. Freeland returned to the house. By this time, the three constables rode up, and in great haste dismounted, tied their horses, and met Master William and Mr. Hamilton returning from the barn; and after talking awhile, they all walked up to the kitchen door. There was no one in the kitchen but myself and John. Henry and Sandy were up at the barn. Mr. Freeland put his head in at the door, and called me by name, saying, there were some gentlemen at the door who wished to see me. I stepped to the door, and inquired what they wanted. They at once seized me, and, without giving me any satisfaction, tied me—lashing my hands closely together. I insisted upon knowing what the matter was. They at length said, that they had learned I had been in a "scrape," and that I was to be examined before my master; and if their information proved false, I should not be hurt.

In a few moments, they succeeded in tying John. They then turned to Henry, who had by this time returned, and commanded him to cross his hands. "I won't!" said Henry, in a firm tone, indicating his readiness to meet the consequences of his refusal. "Won't you?" said Tom Graham, the constable. "No, I won't!" said Henry, in a still stronger tone. With this, two of the constables pulled out their shining pistols, and swore, by their Creator, that they would make him cross his hands or kill him. Each cocked his pistol, and, with fingers on the trigger, walked up to Henry, saying, at the same time, if he did not cross his hands, they would blow his damned heart out. "Shoot me, shoot me!" said Henry; "you can't kill me but once. Shoot, shoot—and be damned! I won't be tied!" This he said in a tone of loud defiance; and at the same time, with a motion as quick as lightning, he with one single stroke dashed the pistols from the hand of each constable. As he did this, all hands fell upon him, and, after beating him some time, they finally overpowered him, and got him tied.

During the scuffle, I managed, I know not how, to get my pass out, and, without being discovered, put it into the fire. We were all now tied; and just as we were to leave for Easton jail, Betsy Freeland, mother of William Freeland, came to the door with her hands full of biscuits, and divided them between Henry and John. She then delivered herself of a speech, to the following effect: addressing herself to me, she said, "You devil! You yellow devil! it was you that put it into the heads of Henry and John to run away. But for you, you long-legged mulatto devil! Henry nor John would never have thought of such a thing." I made no reply, and was immediately hurried off towards St. Michael's. Just a moment previous to the scuffle with Henry, Mr. Hamilton suggested the propriety of making a search for the protections which he had understood Frederick had written for himself and the rest. But, just at the moment he was about carrying his proposal into effect, his aid was needed in helping to tie Henry; and the excitement attending the scuffle caused them either to forget, or to deem it unsafe, under the circumstances, to search. So we were not yet convicted of the intention to run away.

When we got about half way to St. Michael's, while the constables having us in charge were looking ahead, Henry inquired of me what he should do with his pass. I told him to eat it with his biscuit, and own nothing; and we passed the word around, "Own nothing"; and "Own nothing!" said we all. Our confidence in each other was unshaken. We were resolved to succeed or fail together, after the calamity had befallen us as much as before. We were now prepared for anything. We were to be dragged that morning fifteen miles behind horses, and then to be placed in the Easton jail. When we reached St. Michael's, we underwent a sort of examination. We all denied that we ever intended to run away. We did this more to bring out the evidence against us, than from any hope of getting clear of being sold; for, as I have said, we were ready for that. The fact was, we cared but little where we went, so we went together. Our greatest concern was about separation. We dreaded that more than anything this side of death. We found the evidence against us to be the testimony of one person; our master would not tell who it was; but we came to a unanimous decision among ourselves as to who their informant was. We were sent off to the jail at Easton. When we got there, we were delivered up to the sheriff, Mr. Joseph Graham, and by him placed in jail. Henry, John, and myself, were placed in one room together—Charles, and Henry Bailey, in another. Their object in separating us was to hinder concert.

We had been in jail scarcely twenty minutes, when a swarm of slave traders, and agents for slave traders, flocked into jail to look at us, and to ascertain if we were for sale. Such a set of beings I never saw before! I felt myself surrounded by so many fiends from perdition.[1] A band of pirates never looked more like their father, the devil. They laughed and grinned over us, saying, "Ah, my boys! we have got you, haven't we?" And after taunting us in various ways, they one by one went into an examination of us, with intent to ascertain our value. They would impudently ask us if we would not like to have them for our masters. We would make them no answer, and leave them to find out as best they could. Then they would curse and swear at us, telling us that they could take the devil out of us in a very little while, if we were only in their hands.

While in jail, we found ourselves in much more comfortable quarters than we expected when we went there. We did not get much to eat, nor that which was very good; but we had a good clean room, from the windows of which we could see what was going on in the street, which was very much better than though we had been placed in one of the dark, damp cells. Upon the whole, we got along very well, so far as the jail and its keeper were concerned. Immediately after the holidays were over, contrary to all our expectations, Mr. Hamilton and Mr. Freeland came up to Easton, and took Charles, the two Henrys, and John, out of jail, and carried them home, leaving me alone. I regarded this separation as a final one. It caused me more pain than anything else in the whole transaction. I was ready for anything rather than separation. I supposed that they had consulted together, and had decided that, as I was the whole cause of the intention of the others to run away, it was hard to make the innocent suffer with the guilty; and that they had, therefore, concluded to take the others home, and sell me, as a warning to the others that remained. It is due to the noble Henry to say, he seemed almost as reluctant at leaving the prison as at leaving home to come to the prison. But we knew we should, in all probability, be separated, if we were sold; and since he was in their hands, he concluded to go peaceably home.

I was now left to my fate. I was all alone, and within the walls of a stone prison. But a few days before, and I was full of hope. I expected to have been safe in a land of freedom; but now I was covered with gloom, sunk down to the utmost despair. I thought the possibility of freedom was gone. I was kept in this way about one week, at the end of which, Captain Auld, my master, to my surprise and utter astonishment, came up, and took me out, with the intention of sending me, with

---

[1] *perdition* Hell.

a gentleman of his acquaintance, into Alabama. But, from some cause or other, he did not send me to Alabama, but concluded to send me back to Baltimore, to live again with his brother Hugh, and to learn a trade.

Thus, after an absence of three years and one month, I was once more permitted to return to my old home at Baltimore. My master sent me away, because there existed against me a very great prejudice in the community, and he feared I might be killed.

In a few weeks after I went to Baltimore, Master Hugh hired me to Mr. William Gardner, an extensive ship-builder, on Fell's Point. I was put there to learn how to caulk.[1] It, however, proved a very unfavorable place for the accomplishment of this object. Mr. Gardner was engaged that spring in building two large man-of-war brigs, professedly for the Mexican government. The vessels were to be launched in the July of that year, and in failure thereof, Mr. Gardner was to lose a considerable sum; so that when I entered, all was hurry. There was no time to learn anything. Every man had to do that which he knew how to do. In entering the shipyard, my orders from Mr. Gardner were, to do whatever the carpenters commanded me to do. This was placing me at the beck and call of about seventy-five men. I was to regard all these as masters. Their word was to be my law. My situation was a most trying one. At times I needed a dozen pair of hands. I was called a dozen ways in the space of a single minute. Three or four voices would strike my ear at the same moment. It was—"Fred., come help me to cant[2] this timber here."—"Fred., come carry this timber yonder."—"Fred., bring that roller here."—"Fred., go get a fresh can of water."—"Fred., come help saw off the end of this timber."—"Fred., go quick, and get the crowbar."—"Fred., hold on the end of this fall."[3]—"Fred., go to the blacksmith's shop, and get a new punch."—"Hurra, Fred! run and bring me a cold chisel."—"I say, Fred., bear a hand, and get up a fire as quick as lightning under that steam-box."—"Halloo, nigger! come, turn this grindstone."—"Come, come!

move, move! and bowse[4] this timber forward."—"I say, darky, blast your eyes, why don't you heat up some pitch?"—"Halloo! halloo! halloo!" (Three voices at the same time.) "Come here!—Go there!—Hold on where you are! Damn you, if you move, I'll knock your brains out!"

This was my school for eight months; and I might have remained there longer, but for a most horrid fight I had with four of the white apprentices, in which my left eye was nearly knocked out, and I was horribly mangled in other respects. The facts in the case were these: Until a very little while after I went there, white and black ship-carpenters worked side by side, and no one seemed to see any impropriety in it. All hands seemed to be very well satisfied. Many of the black carpenters were freemen. Things seemed to be going on very well. All at once, the white carpenters knocked off, and said they would not work with free colored workmen. Their reason for this, as alleged, was, that if free colored carpenters were encouraged, they would soon take the trade into their own hands, and poor white men would be thrown out of employment. They therefore felt called upon at once to put a stop to it. And, taking advantage of Mr. Gardner's necessities, they broke off, swearing they would work no longer, unless he would discharge his black carpenters. Now, though this did not extend to me in form, it did reach me in fact. My fellow-apprentices very soon began to feel it degrading to them to work with me. They began to put on airs, and talk about the "niggers" taking the country, saying we all ought to be killed; and, being encouraged by the journeymen, they commenced making my condition as hard as they could, by hectoring me around, and sometimes striking me. I, of course, kept the vow I made after the fight with Mr. Covey, and struck back again, regardless of consequences; and while I kept them from combining, I succeeded very well; for I could whip the whole of them, taking them separately. They, however, at length combined, and came upon me, armed with sticks, stones, and heavy handspikes. One came in front with a half brick. There was one at each side of me, and one behind me. While I was attending to those in front, and on either side, the one behind ran up with the handspike, and struck me a heavy blow upon the head. It stunned me. I fell, and

---

[1] *caulk* Seal the wooden seams of a boat against leakage with oakum and melted tar.

[2] *cant* Smoothen a sharp angle.

[3] *fall* Free end of a rope used for hauling.

[4] *bowse* Haul.

with this they all ran upon me, and fell to beating me with their fists. I let them lay on for a while, gathering strength. In an instant, I gave a sudden surge, and rose to my hands and knees. Just as I did that, one of their number gave me, with his heavy boot, a powerful kick in the left eye. My eyeball seemed to have burst. When they saw my eye closed, and badly swollen, they left me. With this I seized the handspike, and for a time pursued them. But here the carpenters interfered, and I thought I might as well give it up. It was impossible to stand my hand against so many. All this took place in sight of not less than fifty white ship-carpenters, and not one interposed a friendly word; but some cried, "Kill the damned nigger! Kill him! kill him! He struck a white person." I found my only chance for life was in flight. I succeeded in getting away without an additional blow, and barely so; for to strike a white man is death by Lynch law[1]—and that was the law in Mr. Gardner's shipyard; nor is there much of any other out of Mr. Gardner's shipyard.

I went directly home, and told the story of my wrongs to Master Hugh; and I am happy to say of him, irreligious as he was, his conduct was heavenly, compared with that of his brother Thomas under similar circumstances. He listened attentively to my narration of the circumstances leading to the savage outrage, and gave many proofs of his strong indignation at it. The heart of my once overkind mistress was again melted into pity. My puffed-out eye and blood-covered face moved her to tears. She took a chair by me, washed the blood from my face, and, with a mother's tenderness, bound up my head, covering the wounded eye with a lean piece of fresh beef. It was almost compensation for my suffering to witness, once more, a manifestation of kindness from this, my once affectionate old mistress. Master Hugh was very much enraged. He gave expression to his feelings by pouring out curses upon the heads of those who did the deed. As soon as I got a little the better of my bruises, he took me with him

to Esquire Watson's, on Bond Street, to see what could be done about the matter. Mr. Watson inquired who saw the assault committed. Master Hugh told him it was done in Mr. Gardner's ship-yard at midday, where there were a large company of men at work. "As to that," he said, "the deed was done, and there was no question as to who did it." His answer was, he could do nothing in the case, unless some white man would come forward and testify. He could issue no warrant on my word. If I had been killed in the presence of a thousand colored people, their testimony combined would have been insufficient to have arrested one of the murderers. Master Hugh, for once, was compelled to say this state of things was too bad. Of course, it was impossible to get any white man to volunteer his testimony in my behalf, and against the white young men. Even those who may have sympathized with me were not prepared to do this. It required a degree of courage unknown to them to do so; for just at that time, the slightest manifestation of humanity toward a colored person was denounced as abolitionism, and that name subjected its bearer to frightful liabilities. The watchwords of the bloody-minded in that region, and in those days, were, "Damn the abolitionists!" and "Damn the niggers!" There was nothing done, and probably nothing would have been done if I had been killed. Such was, and such remains, the state of things in the Christian city of Baltimore.

Master Hugh, finding he could get no redress, refused to let me go back again to Mr. Gardner. He kept me himself, and his wife dressed my wound till I was again restored to health. He then took me into the ship-yard of which he was foreman, in the employment of Mr. Walter Price. There I was immediately set to calking, and very soon learned the art of using my mallet and irons. In the course of one year from the time I left Mr. Gardner's, I was able to command the highest wages given to the most experienced caulkers. I was now of some importance to my master. I was bringing him from six to seven dollars per week. I sometimes brought him nine dollars per week: my wages were a dollar and a half a day. After learning how to caulk, I sought my own employment, made my own contracts, and collected the money which I earned. My pathway became much more smooth than before; my condition was now much more comfortable. When I

---

[1] *is death by Lynch law* Will lead inevitably to being lynched (i.e., killed by a vigilante mob falsely claiming to be administering justice). Though some lynchings targeted Jews and other minorities, the vast majority were racially motivated murders of black persons by white mobs; the practice became increasingly widespread following the end of Reconstruction in 1877, and remained common throughout the early decades of the twentieth century, during the Jim Crow era of segregation.

could get no calking to do, I did nothing. During these leisure times, those old notions about freedom would steal over me again. When in Mr. Gardner's employment, I was kept in such a perpetual whirl of excitement, I could think of nothing, scarcely, but my life; and in thinking of my life, I almost forgot my liberty. I have observed this in my experience of slavery—that whenever my condition was improved, instead of its increasing my contentment, it only increased my desire to be free, and set me to thinking of plans to gain my freedom. I have found that, to make a contented slave, it is necessary to make a thoughtless one. It is necessary to darken his moral and mental vision, and, as far as possible, to annihilate the power of reason. He must be able to detect no inconsistencies in slavery; he must be made to feel that slavery is right; and he can be brought to that only when he ceases to be a man.

I was now getting, as I have said, one dollar and fifty cents per day. I contracted for it; I earned it; it was paid to me; it was rightfully my own; yet, upon each returning Saturday night, I was compelled to deliver every cent of that money to Master Hugh. And why? Not because he earned it—not because he had any hand in earning it—not because I owed it to him—nor because he possessed the slightest shadow of a right to it; but solely because he had the power to compel me to give it up. The right of the grim-visaged pirate upon the high seas is exactly the same.

CHAPTER II

I now come to that part of my life during which I planned, and finally succeeded in making, my escape from slavery. But before narrating any of the peculiar circumstances, I deem it proper to make known my intention not to state all the facts connected with the transaction. My reasons for pursuing this course may be understood from the following: First, were I to give a minute statement of all the facts, it is not only possible, but quite probably, that others would thereby be involved in the most embarrassing difficulties. Secondly, such a statement would most undoubtedly induce greater vigilance on the part of slaveholders than has existed heretofore among them; which would, of course, be the means of guarding a door whereby some dear brother bondsman might escape his galling

chains. I deeply regret the necessity that impels me to suppress anything of importance connected with my experience in slavery. It would afford me great pleasure indeed, as well as materially add to the interest of my narrative, were I at liberty to gratify a curiosity, which I know exists in the minds of many, by an accurate statement of all the facts pertaining to my most fortunate escape. But I must deprive myself of this pleasure, and the curious of the gratification which such a statement would afford. I would allow myself to suffer under the greatest imputations which evil-minded men might suggest, rather than exculpate myself, and thereby run the hazard of closing the slightest avenue by which a brother slave might clear himself of the chains and fetters of slavery.

I have never approved of the very public manner in which some of our western friends have conducted what they call the underground railroad,[1] but which I think, by their open declarations, has been made most emphatically the upper-ground railroad. I honor those good men and women for their noble daring, and applaud them for willingly subjecting themselves to bloody persecution, by openly avowing their participation in the escape of slaves. I, however, can see very little good resulting from such a course, either to themselves or the slaves escaping; while, upon the other hand, I see and feel assured that those open declarations are a positive evil to the slaves remaining, who are seeking to escape. They do nothing towards enlightening the slave, whilst they do much towards enlightening the master. They stimulate him to greater watchfulness, and enhance his power to capture his slave. We owe something to the slave south of the line as well as to those north of it; and in aiding the latter on their way to freedom, we should be careful to do nothing which would be likely to hinder the former from escaping from slavery. I would keep the merciless slaveholder profoundly ignorant of the means of flight adopted by the slave. I would leave him to imagine himself surrounded by myriads of invisible tormentors, ever ready to snatch from his infernal grasp his trembling prey. Let him be left to feel his way in the dark; let darkness commensurate with his crime hover

---

1   *underground railroad*   Secret network of people and safe-houses by means of which many enslaved persons escaped to the North.

over him; and let him feel that at every step he takes, in pursuit of the flying bondman, he is running the frightful risk of having his hot brains dashed out by an invisible agency. Let us render the tyrant no aid; let us not hold the light by which he can trace the footprints of our flying brother. But enough of this. I will now proceed to the statement of those facts, connected with my escape, for which I am alone responsible, and for which no one can be made to suffer but myself.

In the early part of the year 1838, I became quite restless. I could see no reason why I should, at the end of each week, pour the reward of my toil into the purse of my master. When I carried to him my weekly wages, he would, after counting the money, look me in the face with a robber-like fierceness, and ask, "Is this all?" He was satisfied with nothing less than the last cent. He would, however, when I made him six dollars, sometimes give me six cents, to encourage me. It had the opposite effect. I regarded it as a sort of admission of my right to the whole. The fact that he gave me any part of my wages was proof, to my mind, that he believed me entitled to the whole of them. I always felt worse for having received anything; for I feared that the giving me a few cents would ease his conscience, and make him feel himself to be a pretty honorable sort of robber. My discontent grew upon me. I was ever on the look-out for means of escape; and, finding no direct means, I determined to try to hire my time, with a view of getting money with which to make my escape. In the spring of 1838, when Master Thomas came to Baltimore to purchase his spring goods, I got an opportunity, and applied to him to allow me to hire my time. He unhesitatingly refused my request, and told me this was another stratagem by which to escape. He told me I could go nowhere but that he could get me; and that, in the event of my running away, he should spare no pains in his efforts to catch me. He exhorted me to content myself, and be obedient. He told me, if I would be happy, I must lay out no plans for the future. He said, if I behaved myself properly, he would take care of me. Indeed, he advised me to complete thoughtlessness of the future, and taught me to depend solely upon him for happiness. He seemed to see fully the pressing necessity of setting aside my intellectual nature, in order to contentment in slavery. But in spite of him, and even in spite of myself, I continued to think, and to think about the injustice of my enslavement, and the means of escape.

About two months after this, I applied to Master Hugh for the privilege of hiring my time. He was not acquainted with the fact that I had applied to Master Thomas, and had been refused. He too, at first, seemed disposed to refuse; but, after some reflection, he granted me the privilege, and proposed the following terms: I was to be allowed all my time, make all contracts with those for whom I worked, and find my own employment; and, in return for this liberty, I was to pay him three dollars at the end of each week; find myself in calking tools, and in board and clothing. My board was two dollars and a half per week. This, with the wear and tear of clothing and calking tools, made my regular expenses about six dollars per week. This amount I was compelled to make up, or relinquish the privilege of hiring my time. Rain or shine, work or no work, at the end of each week the money must be forthcoming, or I must give up my privilege. This arrangement, it will be perceived, was decidedly in my master's favor. It relieved him of all need of looking after me. His money was sure. He received all the benefits of slaveholding without its evils; while I endured all the evils of a slave, and suffered all the care and anxiety of a freeman. I found it a hard bargain. But, hard as it was, I thought it better than the old mode of getting along. It was a step towards freedom to be allowed to bear the responsibilities of a freeman, and I was determined to hold on upon it. I bent myself to the work of making money. I was ready to work at night as well as day, and by the most untiring perseverance and industry, I made enough to meet my expenses, and lay up a little money every week. I went on thus from May till August. Master Hugh then refused to allow me to hire my time longer. The ground for his refusal was a failure on my part, one Saturday night, to pay him for my week's time. This failure was occasioned by my attending a camp meeting about ten miles from Baltimore. During the week, I had entered into an engagement with a number of young friends to start from Baltimore to the camp ground early Saturday evening; and being detained by my employer, I was unable to get down to Master Hugh's without disappointing the company. I knew that Master Hugh was in no special need of the money that night. I therefore decided to go to camp meeting, and upon my return pay him the three dollars. I stayed at the camp meeting one day longer than I intended when I left. But as soon as I returned, I called upon him to pay him what he considered his due. I found him very angry; he could scarce restrain his wrath. He said he had a great mind to give me a severe whipping. He wished to know how I dared to go out of the city without asking his permission. I told him I hired my time and while I paid him the price which he asked for it, I did not know that I was bound to ask him when and where I should go. This reply troubled him; and, after reflecting a few moments, he turned to me, and said I should hire my time no longer; that the next thing he should know of, I would be running away. Upon the same plea, he told me to bring my tools and clothing home forthwith. I did so; but instead of seeking work, as I had been accustomed to do previously to hiring my time, I spent the whole week without the performance of a single stroke of work. I did this in retaliation. Saturday night, he called upon me as usual for my week's wages. I told him I had no wages; I had done no work that week. Here we were upon the point of coming to blows. He raved, and swore his determination to get hold of me. I did not allow myself a single word; but was resolved, if he laid the weight of his hand upon me, it should be blow for blow. He did not strike me, but told me that he would find me in constant employment in future. I thought the matter over during the next day, Sunday, and finally resolved upon the third day of September, as the day upon which I would make a second attempt to secure my freedom. I now had three weeks during which to prepare for my journey. Early on Monday morning, before Master Hugh had time to make any engagement for me, I went out and got employment of Mr. Butler, at his ship-yard near the drawbridge, upon what is called the City Block, thus making it unnecessary for him to seek employment for me. At the end of the week, I brought him between eight and nine dollars. He seemed very well pleased, and asked why I did not do the same the week before. He little knew what my plans were. My object in working steadily was to remove any suspicion he might entertain of my intent to run away; and in this I succeeded admirably. I suppose he thought I was never better satisfied with my condition than at the very time during which I was planning my escape. The second week passed, and again I carried him my full wages; and so well pleased was he, that he gave me twenty-five cents (quite a large sum for a slaveholder to give a slave), and bade me to make a good use of it. I told him I would.

Things went on without very smoothly indeed, but within there was trouble.[1] It is impossible for me to describe my feelings as the time of my contemplated start drew near. I had a number of warmhearted friends in Baltimore—friends that I loved almost as I did my life—and the thought of being separated from them forever was painful beyond expression. It is my opinion that thousands would escape from slavery, who now remain, but for the strong cords of affection that bind them to their friends. The thought of leaving my friends was decidedly the most painful thought with which I had to contend. The love of them was my tender point, and shook my decision more than all things else. Besides the pain of separation, the dread and apprehension of a failure exceeded what I had experienced at my first attempt. The appalling defeat I then sustained returned to torment me. I felt assured that, if I failed in this attempt, my case would be a hopeless one—it would seal my fate as a slave forever. I could not hope to get off with anything less than the severest punishment, and being placed beyond the means of escape. It required no very vivid imagination to depict the most frightful scenes through which I should have to pass, in case I failed. The wretchedness of slavery, and the blessedness of freedom, were perpetually before me. It was life and death with me. But I remained firm, and, according to my resolution, on the third day of September, 1838, I left my chains, and succeeded in reaching New York without the slightest interruption of any kind. How I did so—what means I adopted, what direction I travelled, and by what mode of conveyance—I must leave unexplained, for the reasons before mentioned.

I have been frequently asked how I felt when I found myself in a free State. I have never been able to answer the question with any satisfaction to myself. It was a moment of the highest excitement I ever experienced. I suppose I felt as one may imagine the unarmed mariner to feel when he is rescued by a friendly man-of-war[2]

---

1   *within there was trouble*   I felt troubled within myself.

2   *man-of-war*   Large warship.

from the pursuit of a pirate. In writing to a dear friend, immediately after my arrival at New York, I said I felt like one who had escaped a den of hungry lions. This state of mind, however, very soon subsided; and I was again seized with a feeling of great insecurity and loneliness. I was yet liable to be taken back, and subjected to all the tortures of slavery.[1] This in itself was enough to damp the ardor of my enthusiasm. But the loneliness overcame me. There I was in the midst of thousands, and yet a perfect stranger; without home and without friends, in the midst of thousands of my own brethren—children of a common Father, and yet I dared not to unfold to any one of them my sad condition. I was afraid to speak to anyone for fear of speaking to the wrong one, and thereby falling into the hands of money-loving kidnappers, whose business it was to lie in wait for the panting fugitive, as the ferocious beasts of the forest lie in wait for their prey. The motto which I adopted when I started from slavery was this—"Trust no man!" I saw in every white man an enemy, and in almost every colored man cause for distrust. It was a most painful situation; and, to understand it, one must needs experience it, or imagine himself in similar circumstances. Let him be a fugitive slave in a strange land—a land given up to be the hunting-ground for slaveholders—whose inhabitants are legalized kidnappers—where he is every moment subjected to the terrible liability of being seized upon by his fellowmen, as the hideous crocodile seizes upon his prey!—I say, let him place himself in my situation—without home or friends—without money or credit—wanting[2] shelter, and no one to give it—wanting bread, and no money to buy it—and at the same time let him feel that he is pursued by merciless men-hunters, and in total darkness as to what to do, where to go, or where to stay—perfectly helpless both as to the means of defence and means of escape—in the midst of plenty, yet suffering the terrible gnawings of hunger—in the midst of houses, yet having no home—among fellow-men, yet feeling as if in the midst of wild beasts, whose greediness

to swallow up the trembling and half-famished fugitive is only equalled by that with which the monsters of the deep swallow up the helpless fish upon which they subsist—I say, let him be placed in this most trying situation—the situation in which I was placed—then, and not till then, will he fully appreciate the hardships of, and know how to sympathize with, the toil-worn and whip-scarred fugitive slave.

Thank Heaven, I remained but a short time in this distressed situation. I was relieved from it by the humane hand of Mr. David Ruggles,[3] whose vigilance, kindness, and perseverance, I shall never forget. I am glad of an opportunity to express, as far as words can, the love and gratitude I bear him. Mr. Ruggles is now afflicted with blindness, and is himself in need of the same kind offices which he was once so forward in the performance of toward others. I had been in New York but a few days, when Mr. Ruggles sought me out, and very kindly took me to his boarding-house at the corner of Church and Lespenard Streets. Mr. Ruggles was then very deeply engaged in the memorable Darg case,[4] as well as attending to a number of other fugitive slaves, devising ways and means for their successful escape; and, though watched and hemmed in on almost every side, he seemed to be more than a match for his enemies.

Very soon after I went to Mr. Ruggles, he wished to know of me where I wanted to go; as he deemed it unsafe for me to remain in New York. I told him I was a caulker, and should like to go where I could get work. I thought of going to Canada; but he decided against it, and in favor of my going to New Bedford, thinking I should be able to get work there at my trade. At this time, Anna,[5] my intended wife, came on; for I wrote to her immediately after my arrival at New York (notwithstanding my homeless, houseless, and helpless condition), informing her of my successful flight, and wishing her to come on forthwith. In a few days after her arrival, Mr. Ruggles called in the Rev. J.W.C.

---

[1] *I was yet liable ... tortures of slavery* When an enslaved person escaped, under the provisions of the Fugitive Slave Act of 1793 a slaveholder was guaranteed the right to seek out, capture, and return that person to enslavement. (Later, the Fugitive Slave Act of 1850 made these provisions even harsher.)

[2] *wanting* Lacking.

[3] *Mr. David Ruggles* Free-born black abolitionist from Connecticut (1810–49), who aided fugitives via the Underground Railroad.

[4] *Darg case* In 1838, Ruggles had been involved in assisting the enslaved man Thomas Hughes in escaping from the enslaver John P. Darg, for which involvement Ruggles was briefly imprisoned.

[5] [Douglass's note] She was free.

Pennington,[1] who, in the presence of Mr. Ruggles, Mrs. Michaels, and two or three others, performed the marriage ceremony, and gave us a certificate, of which the following is an exact copy:

This may certify, that I joined together in holy matrimony Frederick Johnson[2] and Anna Murray, as man and wife, in the presence of Mr. David Ruggles and Mrs. Michaels.

JAMES W.C. PENNINGTON
New York, Sept. 15, 1838

Upon receiving this certificate, and a five-dollar bill from Mr. Ruggles, I shouldered one part of our baggage, and Anna took up the other, and we set out forthwith to take passage on board of the steamboat John W. Richmond for Newport, on our way to New Bedford. Mr. Ruggles gave me a letter to a Mr. Shaw in Newport, and told me, in case my money did not serve me to New Bedford, to stop in Newport and obtain further assistance; but upon our arrival at Newport, we were so anxious to get to a place of safety, that, notwithstanding we lacked the necessary money to pay our fare, we decided to take seats in the stage,[3] and promise to pay when we got to New Bedford. We were encouraged to do this by two excellent gentlemen, residents of New Bedford, whose names I afterward ascertained to be Joseph Ricketson and William C. Taber. They seemed at once to understand our circumstances, and gave us such assurance of their friendliness as put us fully at ease in their presence. It was good indeed to meet with such friends, at such a time. Upon reaching New Bedford, we were directed to the house of Mr. Nathan Johnson, by whom we were kindly received, and hospitably provided for. Both Mr. and Mrs. Johnson took a deep and lively interest in our welfare. They proved themselves quite worthy of the name of abolitionists. When the stage-driver found us unable to pay our fare, he held on upon our baggage as security for the debt. I had but to mention the fact to Mr. Johnson, and he forthwith advanced the money.

We now began to feel a degree of safety, and to prepare ourselves for the duties and responsibilities of a life of freedom. On the morning after our arrival at New Bedford, while at the breakfast-table, the question arose as to what name I should be called by. The name given me by my mother was, "Frederick Augustus Washington Bailey." I, however, had dispensed with the two middle names long before I left Maryland so that I was generally known by the name of "Frederick Bailey." I started from Baltimore bearing the name of "Stanley." When I got to New York, I again changed my name to "Frederick Johnson," and thought that would be the last change. But when I got to New Bedford, I found it necessary again to change my name. The reason of this necessity was, that there were so many Johnsons in New Bedford, it was already quite difficult to distinguish between them. I gave Mr. Johnson the privilege of choosing me a name, but told him he must not take from me the name of "Frederick." I must hold on to that, to preserve a sense of my identity. Mr. Johnson had just been reading the "Lady of the Lake,"[4] and at once suggested that my name be "Douglass." From that time until now I have been called "Frederick Douglass"; and as I am more widely known by that name than by either of the others, I shall continue to use it as my own.

I was quite disappointed at the general appearance of things in New Bedford. The impression which I had received respecting the character and condition of the people of the north, I found to be singularly erroneous. I had very strangely supposed, while in slavery, that few of the comforts, and scarcely any of the luxuries, of life were enjoyed at the north, compared with what were enjoyed by the slaveholders of the south. I probably came to this conclusion from the fact that northern people owned no slaves. I supposed that they were about upon a level with the non-slaveholding population of the south. I knew they were exceedingly poor, and I had been accustomed to regard their poverty as the necessary consequence of their being non-slaveholders. I had somehow imbibed the opinion that, in the absence of slaves, there could be no wealth, and

---

[1]   *J.W.C. Pennington*   Formerly enslaved abolitionist and minister (1807–70).

[2]   [Douglass's note]   I had changed my name from Frederick *Bailey* to that of *Johnson*.

[3]   *stage*   Stagecoach.

[4]   *Lady of the Lake*   Narrative poem by Scottish author Sir Walter Scott (1771–1832). Two of the main characters are James Douglas, an exiled former mentor of King James V of Scotland, and Douglas's daughter Ellen Douglas.

very little refinement. And upon coming to the north, I expected to meet with a rough, hard-handed, and uncultivated population, living in the most Spartan-like[1] simplicity, knowing nothing of the ease, luxury, pomp, and grandeur of southern slaveholders. Such being my conjectures, anyone acquainted with the appearance of New Bedford may very readily infer how palpably I must have seen my mistake.

In the afternoon of the day when I reached New Bedford, I visited the wharves, to take a view of the shipping. Here I found myself surrounded with the strongest proofs of wealth. Lying at the wharves, and riding in the steam, I saw many ships of the finest model, in the best order, and of the largest size. Upon the right and left, I was walled in by granite warehouses of the widest dimensions, stowed to their utmost capacity with the necessaries and comforts of life. Added to this, almost everybody seemed to be at work, but noiselessly so, compared with what I had been accustomed to in Baltimore. There were no loud songs heard from those engaged in loading and unloading ships. I heard no deep oaths or horrid curses on the laborer. I saw no whipping of men; but all seemed to go smoothly on. Every man appeared to understand his work, and went at it with a sober, yet cheerful earnestness, which betokened the deep interest which he felt in what he was doing, as well as a sense of his own dignity as a man. To me this looked exceedingly strange. From the wharves I strolled around and over the town, gazing with wonder and admiration at the splendid churches, beautiful dwellings, and finely-cultivated gardens; evincing an amount of wealth, comfort, taste, and refinement, such as I had never seen in any part of slaveholding Maryland.

Everything looked clean, new, and beautiful. I saw few or no dilapidated houses, with poverty-stricken inmates; no half-naked children and barefooted women, such as I had been accustomed to see in Hillsborough, Easton, St. Michael's, and Baltimore. The people looked more able, stronger, healthier, and happier, than those of Maryland. I was for once made glad by a view of extreme wealth, without being saddened by seeing extreme poverty. But the most astonishing as well as the most interesting thing to me was the condition of the colored people, a great many of whom, like myself, had escaped thither as a refuge from the hunters of men. I found many, who had not been seven years out of their chains, living in finer houses, and evidently enjoying more of the comforts of life, than the average slaveholders in Maryland. I will venture to assert, that my friend Mr. Nathan Johnson (of whom I can say with a grateful heart, "I was hungry, and he gave me meat; I was thirsty, and he gave me drink; I was a stranger, and he took me in"[2]) lived in a neater house; dined at a better table; took, paid for, and read, more newspapers; better understood the moral, religious, and political character of the nation—than nine tenths of the slaveholders in Talbot county, Maryland. Yet Mr. Johnson was a working man. His hands were hardened by toil, and not his alone, but those also of Mrs. Johnson. I found the colored people much more spirited than I had supposed they would be. I found among them a determination to protect each other from the blood-thirsty kidnapper, at all hazards. Soon after my arrival, I was told of a circumstance which illustrated their spirit. A colored man and a fugitive slave were on unfriendly terms. The former was heard to threaten the latter with informing his master of his whereabouts. Straightway a meeting was called among the colored people, under the stereotyped[3] notice, "Business of importance!" The betrayer was invited to attend. The people came at the appointed hour, and organized the meeting by appointing a very religious old gentleman as president, who, I believe, made a prayer, after which he addressed the meeting as follows: "Friends, we have got him here, and I would recommend that you young men just take him outside the door, and kill him!" With this, a number of them bolted at him; but they were intercepted by some more timid than themselves, and the betrayer escaped their vengeance, and has not been seen in New Bedford since. I believe there have been no more such threats, and should there be hereafter, I doubt not that death would be the consequence.

---

[1]   *Spartan-like* Resembling the Spartans, who were known for their militaristic self-discipline and material plainness of living.

[2]   *I was hungry ... took me in* See Matthew 25.35.

[3]   *stereotyped* Printed. (Stereotyping was a then-new method of printing identical copies using metal plates.)

I found employment, the third day after my arrival, in stowing a sloop with a load of oil.[1] It was new, dirty, and hard work for me; but I went at it with a glad heart and a willing hand. I was now my own master. It was a happy moment, the rapture of which can be understood only by those who have been slaves. It was the first work, the reward of which was to be entirely my own. There was no Master Hugh standing ready, the moment I earned the money, to rob me of it. I worked that day with a pleasure I had never before experienced. I was at work for myself and newly-married wife. It was to me the starting-point of a new existence. When I got through with that job, I went in pursuit of a job of caulking; but such was the strength of prejudice against color, among the white caulkers, that they refused to work with me, and of course I could get no employment.[2] Finding my trade of no immediate benefit, I threw off my caulking habiliments, and prepared myself to do any kind of work I could get to do. Mr. Johnson kindly let me have his wood-horse and saw, and I very soon found myself a plenty of work. There was no work too hard—none too dirty. I was ready to saw wood, shovel coal, carry wood, sweep the chimney, or roll oil casks—all of which I did for nearly three years in New Bedford, before I became known to the anti-slavery world.

In about four months after I went to New Bedford, there came a young man to me, and inquired if I did not wish to take the "Liberator."[3] I told him I did; but, just having made my escape from slavery, I remarked that I was unable to pay for it then. I, however, finally became a subscriber to it. The paper came, and I read it from week to week with such feelings as it would be quite idle for me to attempt to describe. The paper became my meat and my drink. My soul was set all on fire. Its sympathy for my brethren in bonds—its scathing denunciations of slaveholders—its faithful exposures of slavery—and its powerful attacks upon the upholders of the institution—sent a thrill of joy through my soul, such as I had never felt before!

I had not long been a reader of the "Liberator" before I got a pretty correct idea of the principles, measures, and spirit of the anti-slavery reform. I took right hold of the cause. I could do but little; but what I could, I did with a joyful heart, and never felt happier than when in an anti-slavery meeting. I seldom had much to say at the meetings, because what I wanted to say was said so much better by others. But, while attending an anti-slavery convention at Nantucket, on the 11th of August, 1841, I felt strongly moved to speak, and was at the same time much urged to do so by Mr. William C. Coffin, a gentleman who had heard me speak in the colored people's meeting at New Bedford.[4] It was a severe cross, and I took it up reluctantly. The truth was, I felt myself a slave, and the idea of speaking to white people weighed me down. I spoke but a few moments, when I felt a degree of freedom, and said what I desired with considerable ease. From that time until now, I have been engaged in pleading the cause of my brethren—with what success, and with what devotion, I leave those acquainted with my labors to decide.

APPENDIX

I find, since reading over the foregoing Narrative, that I have, in several instances, spoken in such a tone and manner, respecting religion, as may possibly lead those unacquainted with my religious views to suppose me an opponent of all religion. To remove the liability of such misapprehension, I deem it proper to append the following brief explanation. What I have said respecting and against religion, I mean strictly to apply to the slaveholding religion of this land, and with no possible reference to Christianity proper; for, between the Christianity of this land, and the Christianity of Christ, I recognize the widest possible difference—so wide, that to receive the one as good, pure, and holy, is of necessity to reject the other as bad, corrupt, and wicked. To be the friend of the one, is of necessity to be the enemy of the other. I love the pure, peaceable, and impartial Christianity of Christ: I therefore hate

---

1   *stowing a sloop with a load of oil*   Loading casks of [whale] oil onto a cargo sailing ship.

2   [Douglass's note]   I am told that colored persons can now get employment at caulking in New Bedford—a result of anti-slavery effort.

3   *take* Subscribe to; *the "Liberator"* Radical abolitionist newspaper established in 1831 and published by William Lloyd Garrison.

4   *colored people's ... New Bedford* I.e., at the meeting of the African Methodist Episcopal Zion Church, where Douglass had begun preaching in 1839.

the corrupt, slaveholding, women-whipping, cradle-plundering, partial and hypocritical Christianity of this land. Indeed, I can see no reason, but the most deceitful one, for calling the religion of this land Christianity. I look upon it as the climax of all misnomers, the boldest of all frauds, and the grossest of all libels. Never was there a clearer case of "stealing the livery of the court of heaven to serve the devil in."[1] I am filled with unutterable loathing when I contemplate the religious pomp and show, together with the horrible inconsistencies, which everywhere surround me. We have men-stealers for ministers, women-whippers for missionaries, and cradle-plunderers for church members. The man who wields the blood-clotted cowskin during the week fills the pulpit on Sunday, and claims to be a minister of the meek and lowly Jesus. The man who robs me of my earnings at the end of each week meets me as a class-leader on Sunday morning, to show me the way of life, and the path of salvation. He who sells my sister, for purposes of prostitution, stands forth as the pious advocate of purity. He who proclaims it a religious duty to read the Bible denies me the right of learning to read the name of the God who made me. He who is the religious advocate of marriage robs whole millions of its sacred influence, and leaves them to the ravages of wholesale pollution. The warm defender of the sacredness of the family relation is the same that scatters whole families—sundering husbands and wives, parents and children, sisters and brothers—leaving the hut vacant, and the hearth desolate. We see the thief preaching against theft, and the adulterer against adultery. We have men sold to build churches, women sold to support the gospel, and babes sold to purchase Bibles for the Poor Heathen! All For The Glory Of God And The Good Of Souls! The slave auctioneer's bell and the church-going bell chime in with each other, and the bitter cries of the heart-broken slave are drowned in the religious shouts of his pious master. Revivals of religion and revivals in the slave-trade go hand in hand together. The slave prison and the church stand near each other. The clanking of fetters and the rattling of chains in the prison, and the pious psalm and solemn prayer in the church, may be heard at the same time. The dealers in the bodies and souls of men erect their stand in the presence of the pulpit, and they mutually help each other. The dealer gives his blood-stained gold to support the pulpit, and the pulpit, in return, covers his infernal business with the garb of Christianity. Here we have religion and robbery the allies of each other—devils dressed in angels' robes, and hell presenting the semblance of paradise.

> Just God! and these are they,
>   Who minister at thine altar, God of right!
> Men who their hands, with prayer and blessing, lay
>   On Israel's ark of light.[2]
>
> What! preach, and kidnap men?
>   Give thanks, and rob thy own afflicted poor?
> Talk of thy glorious liberty, and then
>   Bolt hard the captive's door?
>
> What! servants of thy own
>   Merciful Son, who came to seek and save
> The homeless and the outcast, fettering down
>   The tasked and plundered slave!
>
> Pilate and Herod[3] friends!
>   Chief priests and rulers, as of old, combine!
> Just God and holy! is that church which lends
>   Strength to the spoiler thine?[4]

The Christianity of America is a Christianity, of whose votaries it may be as truly said, as it was of the ancient scribes and Pharisees,[5] "They bind heavy burdens, and grievous to be borne, and lay them on men's shoulders, but they themselves will not move them

---

[1] *stealing the livery ... devil in*   From Book 8 of Scottish poet Robert Pollok's popular poem *The Course of Time* (1827).

[2] *Israel's ark of light*   I.e., the Ark of the Covenant, containing the two stone tablets upon which the Ten Commandments were written, and thus symbolizing religious law as a whole.

[3] *Pilate and Herod*   Pontius Pilate, the Roman ruler who approved Jesus' crucifixion; and the Galilean ruler Herod Antipas, who was involved in the executions both of John the Baptist and Jesus.

[4] *Just God ... spoiler thine?*   The above comprises the first four stanzas of John Greenleaf Whittier's poem "Clerical Oppressors" (1835).

[5] *ancient scribes and Pharisees*   The scribes were professional scholars of religious law, while the Pharisees were a sect whose members insisted on strict adherence to oral and written religious laws; the lines that follow are taken from Matthew 23.4–28, wherein Jesus denounces the scribes and Pharisees for hypocrisy.

with one of their fingers. All their works they do for to be seen of men. They love the uppermost rooms at feasts, and the chief seats in the synagogues, ... and to be called of men, Rabbi, Rabbi. But woe unto you, scribes and Pharisees, hypocrites! for ye shut up the kingdom of heaven against men; for ye neither go in yourselves, neither suffer ye them that are entering to go in. Ye devour widows' houses, and for a pretence make long prayers; therefore ye shall receive the greater damnation. Ye compass sea and land to make one proselyte, and when he is made, ye make him twofold more the child of hell than yourselves. Woe unto you, scribes and Pharisees, hypocrites! for ye pay tithe of mint, and anise, and cumin, and have omitted the weightier matters of the law, judgment, mercy, and faith; these ought ye to have done, and not to leave the other undone. Ye blind guides! which strain at a gnat, and swallow a camel. Woe unto you, scribes and Pharisees, hypocrites! for ye make clean the outside of the cup and of the platter; but within, they are full of extortion and excess. Woe unto you, scribes and Pharisees, hypocrites! for ye are like unto whited sepulchres, which indeed appear beautiful outward, but are within full of dead men's bones, and of all uncleanness. Even so ye also outwardly appear righteous unto men, but within ye are full of hypocrisy and iniquity."

Dark and terrible as is this picture, I hold it to be strictly true of the overwhelming mass of professed Christians in America. They strain at a gnat, and swallow a camel. Could anything be more true of our churches? They would be shocked at the proposition of fellowshipping a sheep-stealer; and at the same time they hug to their communion a man-stealer, and brand me with being an infidel, if I find fault with them for it. They attend with Pharisaical strictness to the outward forms of religion, and at the same time neglect the weightier matters of the law, judgment, mercy, and faith. They are always ready to sacrifice, but seldom to show mercy. They are they who are represented as professing to love God whom they have not seen, whilst they hate their brother whom they have seen. They love the heathen on the other side of the globe. They can pray for him, pay money to have the Bible put into his hand, and missionaries to instruct him; while they despise and totally neglect the heathen at their own doors.

Such is, very briefly, my view of the religion of this land; and to avoid any misunderstanding, growing out of the use of general terms, I mean by the religion of this land, that which is revealed in the words, deeds, and actions, of those bodies, north and south, calling themselves Christian churches, and yet in union with slaveholders. It is against religion, as presented by these bodies, that I have felt it my duty to testify.

I conclude these remarks by copying the following portrait of the religion of the south (which is, by communion and fellowship, the religion of the north), which I soberly affirm is "true to the life," and without caricature or the slightest exaggeration. It is said to have been drawn, several years before the present anti-slavery agitation began, by a northern Methodist preacher, who, while residing at the south, had an opportunity to see slaveholding morals, manners, and piety, with his own eyes. "Shall I not visit for these things? saith the Lord. Shall not my soul be avenged on such a nation as this?"[1]

A PARODY

Come, saints and sinners, hear me tell
How pious priests whip Jack and Nell,
And women buy and children sell,
And preach all sinners down to hell,
      And sing of heavenly union.

They'll bleat and baa, dona like goats,
Gorge down black sheep, and strain at motes,
Array their backs in fine black coats,
Then seize their negroes by their throats,
      And choke, for heavenly union.

They'll church you if you sip a dram,
And damn you if you steal a lamb;
Yet rob old Tony, Doll, and Sam,
Of human rights, and bread and ham;
      Kidnapper's heavenly union.

---

1   *Shall I not … as this?*   See Jeremiah 5.9. The identity of the preacher to whom Douglass refers is unknown; the following poem, which parodies the popular Southern hymn "Heavenly Union," seems to have been written by Douglass himself.

They'll talk loudly of Christ's reward,
And bind his image with a cord,
And scold, and swing the lash abhorred,
And sell their brother in the Lord
    To handcuffed heavenly union.

They'll read and sing a sacred song,
And make a prayer both loud and long,
And teach the right and do the wrong,
Hailing the brother, sister throng,
    With words of heavenly union.

We wonder how such saints can sing,
Or praise the Lord upon the wing,
Who roar, and scold, and whip, and sting,
And to their slaves and mammon cling,
    In guilty conscience union.

They'll raise tobacco, corn, and rye,
And drive, and thieve, and cheat, and lie,
And lay up treasures in the sky,
By making switch and cowskin fly,
    In hope of heavenly union.

They'll crack old Tony on the skull,
And preach and roar like Bashan bull,[1]
Or braying ass, of mischief full,
Then seize old Jacob by the wool,
    And pull for heavenly union.

A roaring, ranting, sleek man-thief,
Who lived on mutton, veal, and beef,
Yet never would afford relief
To needy, sable sons of grief,
    Was big with heavenly union.

"Love not the world," the preacher said,
And winked his eye, and shook his head;
He seized on Tom, and Dick, and Ned,
Cut short their meat, and clothes, and bread,
    Yet still loved heavenly union.

Another preacher whining spoke
Of One whose heart for sinners broke:
He tied old Nanny to an oak,

And drew the blood at every stroke,
    And prayed for heavenly union.

Two others oped their iron jaws,
And waved their children-stealing paws;
There sat the children in gewgaws;[2]
By stinting negroes' backs and maws,
    They kept up heavenly union.

All good from Jack another takes,
And entertains their flirts and rakes[3]
Who dress as sleek as glossy snakes,
And cram their mouths with sweetened cakes;
    And this goes down for union.

Sincerely and earnestly hoping that this little book may do something toward throwing light on the American slave system, and hastening the glad day of deliverance to the millions of my brethren in bonds—faithfully relying upon the power of truth, love, and justice, for my success in my humble efforts—and solemnly pledging my self anew to the sacred cause—I subscribe myself,

        FREDERICK DOUGLASS
        LYNN, Mass., April 28, 1845

—1845

from *To My Old Master*

Douglass published this as an open letter in the 8 September 1848 issue of the *North Star*; the letter was reprinted in William Lloyd Garrison's abolitionist newspaper *The Liberator* two weeks later, and Douglass also included it, with minor revisions, in the appendices to his second autobiography, *My Bondage and My Freedom* (1855).

THOMAS AULD—SIR:

… I have often thought I should like to explain to you the grounds upon which I have justified myself in running away from you. I am almost ashamed to do so

---

1   *Bashan bull* Strong bull mentioned in Psalm 22.12–13.

2   *gewgaws* Ornamental or showy clothing.

3   *rakes* Licentious or immoral men.

now, for by this time you may have discovered them yourself. I will, however, glance at them. When yet but a child about six years old, I imbibed the determination to run away. The very first mental effort that I now remember on my part, was an attempt to solve the mystery, Why am I a slave? and with this question my youthful mind was troubled for many days, pressing upon me more heavily at times than others. When I saw the slave-driver whip a slave-woman, cut the blood out of her neck, and heard her piteous cries, I went away into the corner of the fence, wept and pondered over this mystery. I had, through some medium, I know not what, got some idea of God, the Creator of all mankind, the black and the white, and that he had made the blacks to serve the whites as slaves. How he could do this and be *good*, I could not tell. I was not satisfied with this theory, which made God responsible for slavery, for it pained me greatly, and I have wept over it long and often. At one time, your first wife, Mrs. Lucretia, heard me singing and saw me shedding tears, and asked of me the matter, but I was afraid to tell her. I was puzzled with this question, till one night, while sitting in the kitchen, I heard some of the old slaves talking of their parents having been stolen from Africa by white men, and were sold here as slaves. The whole mystery was solved at once. Very soon after this, my aunt Jinny and uncle Noah ran away, and the great noise made about it by your father-in-law, made me for the first time acquainted with the fact, that there were free States as well as slave States. From that time, I resolved that I would someday run away. The morality of the act, I dispose of as follows: I am myself; you are yourself; we are two distinct persons, equal persons. What you are I am. You are a man, so am I. God created both, and made us separate beings. I am not by nature bound to you, or you to me. Nature does not make your existence depend upon me, or mine to depend upon yours. I cannot walk upon your legs, or you upon mine. I cannot breathe for you, or you for me; I must breathe for myself, and you for yourself. We are distinct persons, and are each equally provided with faculties necessary to our individual existence. In leaving you, I took nothing but what belonged to me, and in no way lessened your means of obtaining an *honest* living. Your faculties remained yours, and mine became useful to their rightful owner. I therefore see

no wrong in any part of the transaction. It is true, I went off secretly, but that was more your fault than mine. Had I let you into the secret, you would have defeated the enterprise entirely; but for this, I should have been really glad to have made you acquainted with my intention to leave.

You may perhaps want to know how I like my present condition. I am free to say, I greatly prefer it to that which I occupied in Maryland. I am, however, by no means prejudiced against that State as such. Its geography, climate, fertility, and products, are such as to make it a very desirable abode for any man; and but for the existence of slavery there, it is not impossible that I might again take up my abode in that State. It is not that I love Maryland less, but freedom more.[1] You will be surprised to learn that people at the North labor under the strange delusion that if the slaves were emancipated at the South, they would all flock to the North. So far from this being the case, in that event, you would see many old and familiar faces back again at the South. The fact is, there are few here who would not return to the South in the event of emancipation. We want to live in the land of our birth, and to lay our bones by the side of our fathers'; and nothing short of an intense love of personal freedom keeps us from the South. For the sake of this, most of us would live on a crust of bread and a cup of cold water.

Since I left you, I have had a rich experience. I have occupied stations which I never dreamed of when a slave. Three out of the ten years since I left you, I spent as a common laborer on the wharves of New Bedford, Massachusetts. It was there I earned my first free dollar. It was mine. I could spend it as I pleased. I could buy hams or herring with it, without asking any odds of anybody. That was a precious dollar to me. You remember when I used to make seven or eight, and even nine dollars a week in Baltimore, you would take every cent of it from me every Saturday night, saying that I belonged to you, and my earnings also. I never liked this conduct on your part—to say the best, I thought it a little mean.[2] I would not have served you so. But let

---

1   *not that … freedom more*   See Shakespeare's *Julius Caesar* 3.2.21–24: "If then that friend demand why Brutus rose against Caesar, this is my answer: not that I loved Caesar less, but that I loved Rome more."

2   *mean*   Ungenerous; ignoble.

that pass. I was a little awkward about counting money in New Bedford. I like to have betrayed myself several times. I caught myself saying phip,[1] for four pence; and one time a man actually charged me with being a runaway, whereupon I was silly enough to become one by running away from him, for I was greatly afraid he might adopt measures to get me again into slavery, a condition I then dreaded more than death.

I soon, however, learned to count money as well as to make it, and got on swimmingly. I married soon after leaving you:[2] in fact, I was engaged to be married before I left you; and instead of finding my companion a burden, she was truly a helpmeet. She went to live— at service, and I to work on the wharf, and though we toiled hard the first winter, we never lived more happily. After remaining in New Bedford for three years, I met with Wm. Lloyd Garrison,[3] a person of whom you have *possibly* heard, as he is pretty generally known among slaveholders. He put it into my head that I might make myself serviceable to the cause of the slave by devoting a portion of my time to telling my own sorrows, and those of other slaves which had come under my observation. This was the commencement of a higher state of existence than any to which I had ever aspired. I was thrown into society the most pure, enlightened and benevolent that the country affords. Among these, I have never forgotten you, but have invariably made you the topic of conversation—thus giving you all the notoriety I could do. I need not tell you that the opinion formed of you in these circles, is far from being favorable. They have little respect for your honesty, and less for your religion.

But I was going on to relate to you something of my interesting experience. I had not long enjoyed the excellent society to which I have referred, before the light of its excellence exerted a beneficial influence on my mind and heart. Much of my early dislike of white persons was removed, and their manners, habits and customs, so entirely unlike what I have been used to in the kitchen-quarters on the plantations of the South, fairly charmed me, and gave me a strong disrelish for the coarse and degrading customs of my former condition. I therefore made an effort so to improve my mind and deportment, as to be somewhat fitted to the station to which I seemed almost Providentially called. The transition from degradation to respectability was indeed great, and to get from one to the other without carrying some marks of one's former condition, is truly a difficult matter. I would not have you think that I am now entirely clear of all plantation peculiarities, but my friends here, while they entertain the strongest dislike to them, regard me with that charity to which my past life somewhat entitles me, so that my condition in this respect is exceedingly pleasant. So far as my domestic affairs are concerned, I can boast of as comfortable a dwelling as your own. I have an industrious and neat companion, and four dear children—the oldest a girl of nine years, and three fine boys, the oldest eight, the next six, and the youngest four years old. The three oldest are now going regularly to school—two can read and write, and the other can spell with tolerable correctness words of two syllables. Dear fellows! they are all in comfortable beds, and are sound asleep, perfectly secure under my own roof. There are no slaveholders here to rend my heart by snatching them from my arms, or blast a proud mother's dearest hopes by tearing them from her bosom. These dear children are ours—not to work up into rice, sugar, and tobacco, but to watch over, regard, and protect, and to rear them up in the nurture and admonition of the gospel—to train them up in the paths of wisdom and virtue, and, as far as we can, to make them useful to the world and to themselves. Oh! sir, a slaveholder never appears to me so completely an agent of hell, as when I think of and look upon my dear children. It is then that my feelings rise above my control. I meant to have said more with respect to my own prosperity and happiness, but thoughts and feelings which this recital has quickened, unfits me to proceed further in that direction. The grim horrors of slavery rise in all their ghastly terror before me, the wails of millions pierce my heart, and chill my blood. I remember the chain, the gag, the bloody whip, the deathlike gloom overshadowing the broke spirit of the fettered bondman, the appalling liability of his being

---

[1] *phip* Maryland slang for a four-pence coin.

[2] *I married ... leaving you* Douglass's first wife, Anna Murray-Douglass (1813–82) was born free in Maryland, and provided Douglass with crucial aid in his self-emancipation.

[3] *Wm. Lloyd Garrison* Among the most prominent white abolitionists of the era, William Lloyd Garrison (1805–79) founded the abolitionist newspaper *The Liberator* as well as the American Anti-Slavery Society.

torn away from wife and children and sold like a beast in the market. Say not this is a picture of fancy.[1] You well know that I wear stripes[2] on my back inflicted by your direction; and that you, while we were brothers in the same church, caused this right hand, with which I am now penning this letter, to be closely tied to my left, and my person dragged at the pistol's mouth, fifteen miles, from the Bay side to Easton, to be sold like a beast in the market, for the alleged crime of intending to escape from your possession. All this and more you remember, and know to be perfectly true, not only of yourself, but of nearly all of the slaveholders around you.

At this moment, you are probably the guilty holder of at least three of my own dear sisters, and my only brother in bondage. These you regard as your property. They are recorded on your ledger, or perhaps have been sold to human flesh mongers, with a view to filling your own ever-hungry purse. Sir, I desire to know how and where these dear sisters are. Have you sold them? or are they still in your possession? What has become of them? are they living or dead? And my dear old grandmother, whom you turned out like an old horse, to die in the woods—is she still alive? Write and let me know all about them. If my grandmother be still alive, she is of no service to you, for by this time she must be nearly eighty years old—too old to be cared for by one to whom she has ceased to be of service; send her to me at Rochester,[3] or bring her to Philadelphia,[4] and it shall be the crowning happiness of my life to take care of her in her old age. Oh! she was to me a mother, and a father, so far as hard toil for my comfort could make her such. Send me my grandmother! that I may watch over and take care of her in her old age. And my sisters, let me know all about them. I would write to them, and learn all I want to know of them, without disturbing you in

any way, but that, through your unrighteous conduct, they have been entirely deprived of the power to read and write. You have kept them in utter ignorance, and have therefore robbed them of the sweet enjoyments of writing or receiving letters from absent friends and relatives. Your wickedness and cruelty committed in this respect on your fellow-creatures, are greater than all the stripes you have laid upon my back, or theirs. It is an outrage upon the soul—a war upon the immortal spirit, and one for which you must give account at the bar of our common Father and Creator.

The responsibility which you have assumed in this regard is truly awful—and how you could stagger under it these many years is marvellous. Your mind must have become darkened, your heart hardened, your conscience seared and petrified, or you would have long since thrown off the accursed load and sought relief at the hands of a sin forgiving God. How, let me ask, would you look upon me, were I some dark night in company with a band of hardened villains, to enter the precincts of your own elegant dwelling and seize the person of your own lovely daughter Amanda, and carry her off from your family, friends, and all the loved ones of her youth—make her my slave—compel her to work, and I take her wages—place her name on my ledger as property—disregard her personal rights—fetter the powers of her immortal soul by denying her the right and privilege of learning to read and write—feed her coarsely—clothe her scantily, and whip her on the naked back occasionally; more and still more horrible, leave her unprotected—a degraded victim to the brutal lust of fiendish overseers who would pollute, blight, and blast her fair soul—rob her of all dignity—destroy her virtue, and annihilate all in her person the graces that adorn the character of virtuous womanhood? I ask how would you regard me, if such were my conduct? Oh! the vocabulary of the damned would not afford a word sufficiently infernal, to express your idea of my God-provoking wickedness. Yet sir, your treatment of my beloved sisters is in all essential points, precisely like the case I have now supposed. Damning as would be such a deed on my part, it would be no more so than that which you have committed against me and my sisters.

I will now bring this letter to a close; you shall hear from me again unless you let me hear from you. I

---

1   *fancy*   Imagination; a fiction.

2   *stripes*   I.e., scars from having been whipped.

3   *Rochester*   The home of Douglass and his family, in New York.

4   *Philadelphia*   One of Douglass's first stops on his way to freedom, Philadelphia was largely populated by Quakers, who generally opposed slavery. (Though Pennsylvania was the first state to pass an act abolishing slavery in 1780, its gradual nature meant that there were still people living enslaved in the state well into the early nineteenth century.)

intend to make use of you as a weapon with which to assail the system of slavery—as a means of concentrating public attention on the system, and deepening the horror of trafficking in the souls and bodies of men. I shall make use of you as a means of exposing the character of the American church and clergy—and as a means of bringing this guilty nation with yourself to repentance. In doing this I entertain no malice towards you personally. There is no roof under which you would be more safe than mine, and there is nothing in my house which you might need for your comfort, which I would not readily grant. Indeed, I should esteem it a privilege, to set you an example as to how mankind ought to treat each other.

I am your fellow man but not your slave,
FREDERICK DOUGLASS
P.S. I send a copy of the paper containing this letter, to save postage.—F.D.
—1848

What to the Slave Is the Fourth of July?

In 1852, Douglass was invited by the Rochester Ladies' Anti-Slavery Society to deliver an oration before the citizenry of Rochester, as part of the local Independence Day celebrations. He did not give the resulting speech a title; it is often referred to as "What to the Slave Is the Fourth of July?" and often, in excerpted form, given the title "The Hypocrisy of American Slavery." The full speech was issued in pamphlet form later in 1852, titled simply "Oration, Delivered in Corinthian Hall, Rochester." In 1855 Douglass published an extract from the speech in the appendices to *My Bondage and My Freedom*. That extract omits some of the speech's more inflammatory passages.

M r. President, Friends and Fellow Citizens: He who could address this audience without a quailing sensation has stronger nerves than I have. I do not remember ever to have appeared as a speaker before any assembly more shrinkingly, nor with greater distrust of my ability, than I do this day. A feeling has crept over me, quite unfavorable to the exercise of my limited powers of speech. The task before me is one

which requires much previous thought and study for its proper performance. I know that apologies of this sort are generally considered flat and unmeaning. I trust, however, that mine will not be so considered. Should I seem at ease, my appearance would much misrepresent me. The little experience I have had in addressing public meetings, in country schoolhouses, avails me nothing on the present occasion.

The papers and placards say that I am to deliver a 4th of July oration. This certainly sounds large and out of the common way for me. It is true that I have often had the privilege to speak in this beautiful Hall, and to address many who now honor me with their presence. But neither their familiar faces, nor the perfect gage I think I have of Corinthian Hall, seems to free me from embarrassment.

The fact is, ladies and gentlemen, the distance between this platform and the slave plantation, from which I escaped, is considerable—and the difficulties to be overcome in getting from the latter to the former, are by no means slight. That I am here today is, to me, a matter of astonishment as well as of gratitude. You will not, therefore, be surprised, if in what I have to say I evince no elaborate preparation, nor grace my speech with any high sounding exordium.[1] With little experience and with less learning, I have been able to throw my thoughts hastily and imperfectly together; and trusting to your patient and generous indulgence, I will proceed to lay them before you.

This, for the purpose of this celebration, is the 4th of July.[2] It is the birthday of your National Independence, and of your political freedom. This, to you, is what the Passover[3] was to the emancipated people of God. It carries your minds back to the day, and to the act of your great deliverance, and to the signs, and to the wonders, associated with that act, and that day. This celebration also marks the beginning of another year of your national life, and reminds you that the

---

1   *exordium* Introduction.

2   *This … 4th of July* Though the address was part of the Independence Day festivities, it was delivered on the 5th of July rather than the 4th.

3   *Passover* Event described in the Book of Exodus in which God frees the Israelites from slavery in Egypt by punishing the Egyptians with ten plagues, the last of which is the death of all the first-born children. God passes over the homes of the Israelites when he brings this final plague.

Republic of America is now 76 years old. I am glad, fellow-citizens, that your nation is so young. Seventy-six years, though a good old age for a man, is but a mere speck in the life of a nation. Three score years and ten is the allotted time for individual men; but nations number their years by thousands. According to this fact, you are, even now, only in the beginning of your national career, still lingering in the period of childhood. I repeat, I am glad this is so. There is hope in the thought, and hope is much needed, under the dark clouds which lower above the horizon. The eye of the reformer is met with angry flashes, portending disastrous times; but his heart may well beat lighter at the thought that America is young, and that she is still in the impressible stage of her existence. May he not hope that high lessons of wisdom, of justice and of truth, will yet give direction to her destiny? Were the nation older, the patriot's heart might be sadder, and the reformer's brow heavier. Its future might be shrouded in gloom, and the hope of its prophets go out in sorrow. There is consolation in the thought that America is young. Great streams are not easily turned from channels, worn deep in the course of ages. They may sometimes rise in quiet and stately majesty, and inundate the land, refreshing and fertilizing the earth with their mysterious properties. They may also rise in wrath and fury, and bear away, on their angry waves, the accumulated wealth of years of toil and hardship. They, however, gradually flow back to the same old channel, and flow on as serenely as ever. But, while the river may not be turned aside, it may dry up, and leave nothing behind but the withered branch, and the unsightly rock, to howl in the abyss-sweeping wind, the sad tale of departed glory. As with rivers so with nations.

Fellow citizens, I shall not presume to dwell at length on the associations that cluster about this day. The simple story of it is that, 76 years ago, the people of this country were British subjects. The style and title of your "sovereign people" (in which you now glory) was not then born. You were under the British Crown. Your fathers esteemed the English Government as the home government, and England as the fatherland. This home government, you know, although a considerable distance from your home, did, in the exercise of its parental prerogatives, impose upon its colonial children such restraints, burdens and limitations as, in its mature judgment, it deemed wise, right and proper.

But your fathers, who had not adopted the fashionable idea of this day of the infallibility of government, and the absolute character of its acts, presumed to differ from the home government in respect to the wisdom and the justice of some of those burdens and restraints. They went so far in their excitement as to pronounce the measures of government unjust, unreasonable, and oppressive, and altogether such as ought not to be quietly submitted to. I scarcely need say, fellow citizens, that my opinion of those measures fully accords with that of your fathers. Such a declaration of agreement on my part would not be worth much to anybody. It would, certainly, prove nothing, as to what part I might have taken, had I lived during the great controversy of 1776. To say *now* that America was right, and England wrong, is exceedingly easy. Everybody can say it; the dastard, not less than the noble brave, can flippantly descant on[1] the tyranny of England towards the American Colonies. It is fashionable to do so; but there was a time when to pronounce against England, and in favor of the cause of the colonies, tried men's souls. They who did so were accounted in their day plotters of mischief, agitators and rebels, dangerous men. To side with the right against the wrong, with the weak against the strong, and with the oppressed against the oppressor! *here* lies the merit, and the one which, of all others, seems unfashionable in our day. The cause of liberty may be stabbed by the men who glory in the deeds of your fathers. But, to proceed.

Feeling themselves harshly and unjustly treated by the home government, your fathers, like men of honesty, and men of spirit, earnestly sought redress. They petitioned and remonstrated; they did so in a decorous, respectful, and loyal manner. Their conduct was wholly unexceptionable. This, however, did not answer the purpose. They saw themselves treated with sovereign indifference, coldness and scorn. Yet they persevered. They were not the men to look back.

As the sheet anchor takes a firmer hold, when the ship is tossed by the storm, so did the cause of your fathers grow stronger, as it breasted the chilling blasts

---

[1]   *descant on* Discuss.

of kingly displeasure. The greatest and best of British statesmen admitted its justice, and the loftiest eloquence of the British Senate came to its support. But, with that blindness which seems to be the unvarying characteristic of tyrants, since Pharaoh and his hosts were drowned in the Red Sea,[1] the British Government persisted in the exactions complained of.

The madness of this course, we believe, is admitted now, even by England; but we fear the lesson is wholly lost on our present rulers.

Oppression makes a wise man mad. Your fathers were wise men, and if they did not go mad, they became restive under this treatment. They felt themselves the victims of grievous wrongs, wholly incurable in their colonial capacity. With brave men there is always a remedy for oppression. Just here, the idea of a total separation of the colonies from the crown was born! It was a startling idea, much more so, than we, at this distance of time, regard it. The timid and the prudent (as has been intimated) of that day, were, of course, shocked and alarmed by it.

Such people lived then, had lived before, and will, probably, ever have a place on this planet; and their course, in respect to any great change (no matter how great the good to be attained, or the wrong to be redressed by it), may be calculated with as much precision as can be the course of the stars. They hate all changes, but silver, gold and copper change! Of this sort of change they are always strongly in favor.

These people were called Tories[2] in the days of your fathers; and the appellation probably conveyed the same idea that is meant by a more modern, though a somewhat less euphonious term,[3] which we often find in our papers, applied to some of our old politicians.

Their opposition to the then dangerous thought was earnest and powerful; but, amid all their terror and affrighted vociferations against it, the alarming and revolutionary idea moved on, and the country with it.

On the 2d of July, 1776, the old Continental Congress, to the dismay of the lovers of ease, and the worshipers of property, clothed that dreadful idea with all the authority of national sanction.[4] They did so in the form of a resolution; and as we seldom hit upon resolutions, drawn up in our day, whose transparency is at all equal to this, it may refresh your minds and help my story if I read it.

Resolved, That these united colonies are, and of right, ought to be free and Independent States; that they are absolved from all allegiance to the British Crown; and that all political connection between them and the State of Great Britain is, and ought to be, dissolved.

Citizens, your fathers made good that resolution. They succeeded; and today you reap the fruits of their success. The freedom gained is yours; and you, therefore, may properly celebrate this anniversary. The 4th of July is the first great fact in your nation's history—the very ringbolt in the chain of your yet undeveloped destiny.

Pride and patriotism, not less than gratitude, prompt you to celebrate and to hold it in perpetual remembrance. I have said that the Declaration of Independence is the RINGBOLT to the chain of your nation's destiny; so, indeed, I regard it. The principles contained in that instrument are saving principles. Stand by those principles, be true to them on all occasions, in all places, against all foes, and at whatever cost.

From the round top of your ship of state, dark and threatening clouds may be seen. Heavy billows, like mountains in the distance, disclose to the leeward[5] huge forms of flinty rocks! That *bolt* drawn, that *chain* broken, and all is lost. *Cling to this day—cling to it,*

---

[1] *since Pharaoh … Red Sea* Douglass refers to the crossing of the Red Sea in the Book of Exodus, when God parts the sea to allow the Israelites to pass through and then drowns the pursuing Egyptian army.

[2] *Tories* Term used in Britain and elsewhere to refer to Conservative politicians and their supporters; it came during the American Revolutionary War to refer to Loyalists to the British cause.

[3] *somewhat … term* Douglass is likely alluding to the term "hunker," which was often applied to conservative politicians in the United States in the mid-nineteenth century; *euphonious* Pleasant-sounding.

[4] *On the 2d … sanction* The Declaration of Independence was passed by the Second Continental Congress on the 2nd of July, and ratified on the 4th.

[5] *leeward* Side facing away from the wind.

and to its principles, with the grasp of a storm-tossed mariner to a spar[1] at midnight.

The coming into being of a nation, in any circumstances, is an interesting event. But, besides general considerations, there were peculiar circumstances which make the advent of this republic an event of special attractiveness.

The whole scene, as I look back to it, was simple, dignified and sublime.

The population of the country, at the time, stood at the insignificant number of three millions. The country was poor in the munitions of war. The population was weak and scattered, and the country a wilderness unsubdued. There were then no means of concert[2] and combination such as exist now. Neither steam nor lightning[3] had then been reduced to order and discipline. From the Potomac to the Delaware was a journey of many days. Under these, and innumerable other disadvantages, your fathers declared for liberty and independence and triumphed.

Fellow Citizens, I am not wanting[4] in respect for the fathers of this republic. The signers of the Declaration of Independence were brave men. They were great men too—great enough to give fame to a great age. It does not often happen to a nation to raise, at one time, such a number of truly great men. The point from which I am compelled to view them is not, certainly, the most favorable; and yet I cannot contemplate their great deeds with less than admiration. They were statesmen, patriots and heroes, and for the good they did, and the principles they contended for, I will unite with you to honor their memory.

They loved their country better than their own private interests; and, though this is not the highest form of human excellence, all will concede that it is a rare virtue, and that when it is exhibited, it ought to command respect. He who will, intelligently, lay down his life for his country, is a man whom it is not in human nature to despise. Your fathers staked their lives, their fortunes, and their sacred honor, on the cause of their country. In their admiration of liberty, they lost sight of all other interests.

They were peace men; but they preferred revolution to peaceful submission to bondage. They were quiet men; but they did not shrink from agitating against oppression. They showed forbearance; but that they knew its limits. They believed in order; but not in the order of tyranny. With them, nothing was "*settled*" that was not right. With them, justice, liberty and humanity were "*final*"; not slavery and oppression. You may well cherish the memory of such men. They were great in their day and generation. Their solid manhood stands out the more as we contrast it with these degenerate times.

How circumspect, exact and proportionate were all their movements! How unlike the politicians of an hour! Their statesmanship looked beyond the passing moment, and stretched away in strength into the distant future. They seized upon eternal principles, and set a glorious example in their defense. Mark them!

Fully appreciating the hardship to be encountered, firmly believing in the right of their cause, honorably inviting the scrutiny of an onlooking world, reverently appealing to heaven to attest their sincerity, soundly comprehending the solemn responsibility they were about to assume, wisely measuring the terrible odds against them, your fathers, the fathers of this republic, did, most deliberately, under the inspiration of a glorious patriotism, and with a sublime faith in the great principles of justice and freedom, lay deep the cornerstone of the national superstructure, which has risen and still rises in grandeur around you.

Of this fundamental work, this day is the anniversary. Our eyes are met with demonstrations of joyous enthusiasm. Banners and pennants[5] wave exultingly on the breeze. The din of business, too, is hushed. Even mammon[6] seems to have quitted his grasp on this day. The ear-piercing fife and the stirring drum unite their accents with the ascending peal of a thousand church bells. Prayers are made, hymns are sung, and sermons are preached in honor of this day; while the quick martial tramp of a great and multitudinous nation, echoed back by all the hills, valleys and mountains of a vast continent, bespeak the occasion one of thrilling and universal interest—a nation's jubilee.

---

1   *spar*   Mast or other pole used to support a ship's sails.

2   *concert*   Coming together.

3   *steam nor lightning*   I.e., neither steam power nor electricity.

4   *wanting*   Lacking.

5   *pennants*   Narrow, triangular flags.

6   *mammon*   Wealth and profit (regarded as a false god).

Friends and citizens, I need not enter further into the causes which led to this anniversary. Many of you understand them better than I do. You could instruct me in regard to them. That is a branch of knowledge in which you feel, perhaps, a much deeper interest than your speaker. The causes which led to the separation of the colonies from the British crown have never lacked for a tongue. They have all been taught in your common schools, narrated at your firesides, unfolded from your pulpits, and thundered from your legislative halls, and are as familiar to you as household words. They form the staple of your national poetry and eloquence.

I remember, also, that, as a people, Americans are remarkably familiar with all facts which make in their own favor. This is esteemed by some as a national trait—perhaps a national weakness. It is a fact that whatever makes for the wealth or for the reputation of Americans—and can be had *cheap*!—will be found by Americans. I shall not be charged with slandering Americans, if I say I think the American side of any question may be safely left in American hands.

I leave, therefore, the great deeds of your fathers to other gentlemen whose claim to have been regularly descended will be less likely to be disputed than mine!

THE PRESENT

My business, if I have any here today, is with the present. The accepted time with God and his cause is the ever-living now.

> Trust no future, however pleasant,
>   Let the dead past bury its dead;
> Act, act in the living present,
>   Heart within, and God overhead.[1]

We have to do with the past only as we can make it useful to the present and to the future. To all inspiring motives, to noble deeds which can be gained from the past, we are welcome. But now is the time, the important time. Your fathers have lived, died, and have done their work, and have done much of it well. You live and must die, and you must do your work. You have no right to enjoy a child's share in the labor of your fathers, unless your children are to be blessed by your labors. You have no right to wear out and waste the hard-earned fame of your fathers to cover your indolence. Sydney Smith[2] tells us that men seldom eulogize the wisdom and virtues of their fathers, but to excuse some folly or wickedness of their own. This truth is not a doubtful one. There are illustrations of it near and remote, ancient and modern. It was fashionable, hundreds of years ago, for the children of Jacob to boast, we have "Abraham to our father," when they had long lost Abraham's faith and spirit.[3] That people contented themselves under the shadow of Abraham's great name, while they repudiated the deeds which made his name great. Need I remind you that a similar thing is being done all over this country today? Need I tell you that the Jews are not the only people who built the tombs of the prophets, and garnished the sepulchres of the righteous? Washington could not die till he had broken the chains of his slaves. Yet his monument is built up by the price of human blood,[4] and the traders in the bodies and souls of men, shout—"We have Washington to '*our father.*'" Alas! that it should be so; yet so it is.

> The evil that men do, lives after them,
> The good is oft' interred with their bones.[5]

Fellow citizens, pardon me, allow me to ask, why am I called upon to speak here today?[6] What have I, or those I represent, to do with your national independence? Are the great principles of political freedom and of natural justice, embodied in that Declaration of Independence, extended to us? and am I, therefore,

---

[1]   *Trust no … God overhead*   See Henry Wadsworth Longfellow's "A Psalm of Life" (1838).

[2]   *Sydney Smith* English humorist and Anglican minister (1771–1845).

[3]   *children of Jacob … spirit*   See Matthew 3.9; Jacob, a biblical patriarch and grandson of Abraham, appears in the Book of Genesis.

[4]   *Washington … human blood*   At the time of his death in 1799, George Washington owned 124 enslaved people, all of whom were freed under the terms of his will. The monument to which Douglass refers is the Washington Monument, construction of which had begun in 1848 (though it was not completed until 1884); given that slavery in Washington, D.C. did not end until 1862, it is highly likely that enslaved people played a large role in the early stages of construction.

[5]   *The evil … their bones*   See Shakespeare's *Julius Caesar* 3.2.84–85.

[6]   *Fellow citizens … today?*   Douglass begins his 1855 "Extract" here.

called upon to bring our humble offering to the national altar, and to confess the benefits and express devout gratitude for the blessings resulting from your independence to us?

Would to God, both for your sakes and ours, that an affirmative answer could be truthfully returned to these questions! Then would my task be light, and my burden easy and delightful. For *who* is there so cold that a nation's sympathy could not warm him? Who so obdurate and dead to the claims of gratitude, that would not thankfully acknowledge such priceless benefits? Who so stolid and selfish, that would not give his voice to swell the hallelujahs of a nation's jubilee, when the chains of servitude had been torn from his limbs? I am not that man. In a case like that, the dumb[1] might eloquently speak, and the "lame man leap as an hart."[2]

But such is not the state of the case. I say it with a sad sense of the disparity between us. I am not included within the pale of this glorious anniversary! Your high independence only reveals the immeasurable distance between us. The blessings in which you, this day, rejoice, are not enjoyed in common. The rich inheritance of justice, liberty, prosperity and independence, bequeathed by your fathers, is shared by you, not by me. The sunlight that brought life and healing to you, has brought stripes[3] and death to me. This Fourth July is *yours*, not *mine*. *You* may rejoice, *I* must mourn. To drag a man in fetters into the grand illuminated temple of liberty, and call upon him to join you in joyous anthems, were inhuman mockery and sacrilegious irony. Do you mean, citizens, to mock me, by asking me to speak today? If so, there is a parallel to your conduct.[4] And let me warn you that it is dangerous to copy the example of a nation whose crimes, towering up to heaven, were thrown down by the breath of the Almighty, burying that nation in irrecoverable ruin![5] I can today take up the plaintive lament of a peeled[6] and woe-smitten people!

> By the rivers of Babylon, there we sat down. Yea! we wept when we remembered Zion. We hanged our harps upon the willows in the midst thereof. For there, they that carried us away captive, required of us a song; and they who wasted us required of us mirth, saying, Sing us one of the songs of Zion. How can we sing the Lord's song in a strange land? If I forget thee, O Jerusalem, let my right hand forget her cunning. If I do not remember thee, let my tongue cleave to the roof of my mouth.

Fellow citizens; above your national, tumultuous joy, I hear the mournful wail of millions! whose chains, heavy and grievous yesterday, are today rendered more intolerable by the jubilee shouts that reach them. If I do forget, if I do not faithfully remember those bleeding children of sorrow this day, "may my right hand forget her cunning, and may my tongue cleave to the roof of my mouth"! To forget them, to pass lightly over their wrongs, and to chime in with the popular theme, would be treason most scandalous and shocking, and would make me a reproach before God and the world. My subject, then fellow citizens, is American Slavery. I shall see this day, and its popular characteristics, from the slave's point of view. Standing, there, identified with the American bondman, making his wrongs mine, I do not hesitate to declare, with all my soul, that the character and conduct of this nation never looked blacker to me than on this 4th of July! Whether we turn to the declarations of the past, or to the professions of the present, the conduct of the nation seems equally hideous and revolting. America is false to the past, false to the present, and solemnly binds herself to be false to the future. Standing with God and the crushed and bleeding slave on this occasion, I will, in the name of humanity which is outraged, in the name of liberty which is fettered, in the name of the constitution and

---

[1] *dumb* Mute.

[2] *lame man … hart* See Isaiah 35.6: "Then shall the lame man leap as an hart, and the tongue of the dumb sing: for in the wilderness shall waters break out, and streams in the desert"; *hart* Stag.

[3] *stripes* I.e., wounds caused by being whipped.

[4] *there is … your conduct* Douglass alludes to the treatment of the Israelites during their period as captives of the Babylonian King Nebuchadnezzar. Psalm 137 (quoted from below) describes how the Israelites refuse their captor's demand that they "sing the Lord's song in a strange land."

[5] *a nation … irrecoverable ruin* The destruction of the kingdom of Babylon is prophesied in the Old Testament, and described in the Book of Revelations, where the kingdom's sinful history is symbolized by the figure of the "Whore of Babylon."

[6] *peeled* Wretched.

the Bible, which are disregarded and trampled upon, dare to call in question and to denounce, with all the emphasis I can command, everything that serves to perpetuate slavery—the great sin and shame of America! "I will not equivocate; I will not excuse";[1] I will use the severest language I can command; and yet not one word shall escape me that any man, whose judgment is not blinded by prejudice, or who is not at heart a slaveholder, shall not confess to be right and just.

But I fancy I hear some one of my audience say, it is just in this circumstance that you and your brother abolitionists fail to make a favorable impression on the public mind. Would you argue more, and denounce less,[2] would you persuade more, and rebuke less, your cause would be much more likely to succeed. But, I submit, where all is plain, there is nothing to be argued. What point in the anti-slavery creed would you have me argue? On what branch of the subject do the people of this country need light? Must I undertake to prove that the slave is a man? That point is conceded already. Nobody doubts it. The slaveholders themselves acknowledge it in the enactment of laws for their government. They acknowledge it when they punish disobedience on the part of the slave. There are seventy-two crimes in the State of Virginia, which, if committed by a black man (no matter how ignorant he be), subject him to the punishment of death; while only two of the same crimes will subject a white man to the like punishment. What is this but the acknowledgement that the slave is a moral, intellectual and responsible being? The manhood of the slave is conceded. It is admitted in the fact that Southern statute books are covered with enactments forbidding, under severe fines and penalties, the teaching of the slave to read or to write. When you can point to any such laws, in reference to the beasts of the field, then I may consent to argue the manhood of the slave. When the dogs in your streets, when the fowls of the air, when the cattle on your hills, when the fish of the sea, and the reptiles that crawl, shall be unable to distinguish the slave from a brute, *then* will I argue with you that the slave is a man!

For the present, it is enough to affirm the equal manhood of the negro race. Is it not astonishing that, while we are ploughing, planting and reaping, using all kinds of mechanical tools, erecting houses, constructing bridges, building ships, working in metals of brass, iron, copper, silver and gold; that, while we are reading, writing and cyphering,[3] acting as clerks, merchants and secretaries, having among us lawyers, doctors, ministers, poets, authors, editors, orators and teachers; that, while we are engaged in all manner of enterprises common to other men, digging gold in California, capturing the whale in the Pacific, feeding sheep and cattle on the hill-side, living, moving, acting, thinking, planning, living in families as husbands, wives and children, and, above all, confessing and worshipping the Christian's God, and looking hopefully for life and immortality beyond the grave, we are called upon to prove that we are men!

Would you have me argue that man is entitled to liberty? that he is the rightful owner of his own body? You have already declared it. Must I argue the wrongfulness of slavery? Is that a question for republicans?[4] Is it to be settled by the rules of logic and argumentation, as a matter beset with great difficulty, involving a doubtful application of the principle of justice, hard to be understood? How should I look today, in the presence of Americans, dividing and subdividing a discourse, to show that men have a natural right to freedom? speaking of it relatively, and positively, negatively, and affirmatively? To do so would be to make myself ridiculous, and to offer an insult to your understanding. There is not a man beneath the canopy of heaven, that does not know that slavery is wrong *for him*.

What, am I to argue that it is wrong to make men brutes, to rob them of their liberty, to work them without wages, to keep them ignorant of their relations to their fellow men, to beat them with sticks, to flay their flesh with the lash, to load their limbs with irons, to hunt them with dogs, to sell them at auction, to sunder their families, to knock out their teeth, to burn their flesh, to starve them into obedience and submission to their masters? Must I argue that a system thus marked

---

[1] *I will ... not excuse* Douglass here quotes from William Lloyd Garrison's opening article in the first issue of *The Liberator* (1831), an influential antislavery newspaper.

[2] *argue ... less* I.e., present more arguments in favor of your goals, and make fewer denunciations of the present state.

[3] *cyphering* Doing calculations.

[4] *republicans* I.e., citizens of a republic.

with blood, and stained with pollution, is *wrong*? No I will not. I have better employment for my time and strength than such arguments would imply.

What, then, remains to be argued? Is it that slavery is not divine; that God did not establish it; that our doctors of divinity are mistaken? There is blasphemy in the thought. That which is inhuman, cannot be divine! *Who* can reason on such a proposition? They that can, may; I cannot. The time for such argument is past.

At a time like this, scorching irony, not convincing argument, is needed. O! had I the ability, and could I reach the nation's ear, I would, today, pour out a fiery stream of biting ridicule, blasting reproach, withering sarcasm, and stern rebuke. For it is not light that is needed, but fire; it is not the gentle shower, but thunder. We need the storm, the whirlwind, and the earthquake. The feeling of the nation must be quickened; the conscience of the nation must be roused; the propriety of the nation must be startled; the hypocrisy of the nation must be exposed; and its crimes against God and man must be proclaimed and denounced.

What, to the American slave, is your 4th of July? I answer: a day that reveals to him, more than all other days in the year, the gross injustice and cruelty to which he is the constant victim. To him, your celebration is a sham; your boasted liberty, an unholy license; your national greatness, swelling vanity; your sounds of rejoicing are empty and heartless; your denunciations of tyrants, brass fronted impudence; your shouts of liberty and equality, hollow mockery; your prayers and hymns, your sermons and thanksgivings, with all your religious parade, and solemnity, are, to him, mere bombast, fraud, deception, impiety, and hypocrisy—a thin veil to cover up crimes which would disgrace a nation of savages. There is not a nation on the earth guilty of practices more shocking and bloody than are the people of these United States, at this very hour.

Go where you may, search where you will, roam through all the monarchies and despotisms of the old world, travel through South America, search out every abuse, and when you have found the last, lay your facts by the side of the everyday practices of this nation, and you will say with me, that, for revolting barbarity and shameless hypocrisy, America reigns without a rival.[1]

The Internal Slave Trade

Take the American slave-trade, which, we are told by the papers, is especially prosperous just now. Ex-Senator Benton[2] tells us that the price of men was never higher than now. He mentions the fact to show that slavery is in no danger. This trade is one of the peculiarities of American institutions. It is carried on in all the large towns and cities in one-half of this confederacy; and millions are pocketed every year by dealers in this horrid traffic. In several states, this trade is a chief source of wealth. It is called (in contradistinction to the foreign slave-trade) "*the internal slave-trade.*" It is, probably, called so, too, in order to divert from it the horror with which the foreign slave-trade is contemplated. That trade has long since been denounced by this government, as piracy.[3] It has been denounced with burning words, from the high places of the nation, as an execrable traffic. To arrest it, to put an end to it, this nation keeps a squadron, at immense cost, on the coast of Africa. Everywhere, in this country, it is safe to speak of this foreign slave-trade as a most inhuman traffic, opposed alike to the laws of God and of man. The duty to extirpate and destroy it, is admitted even by our Doctors of Divinity. In order to put an end to it, some of these last have consented that their colored brethren (nominally free) should leave this country, and establish themselves on the western coast of Africa![4] It is, however, a notable fact that, while so much execration is poured out by Americans upon those engaged in the foreign slave-trade, the men engaged in the slave-trade between the states pass without condemnation, and their business is deemed honorable.

Behold the practical operation of this internal slave-trade, the American slave-trade, sustained by American politics and American religion. Here you will see men

---

1   *without a rival*   The "Extract" in Douglass's *My Bondage and My Freedom* ends here.

2   *Ex-Senator Benton*   Thomas Hart Benton (1782–1858), Democratic senator who, though he owned enslaved people for much of his life, came to oppose the institution.

3   *That trade ... as piracy*   The Atlantic slave trade was abolished by the United States in 1808.

4   *In order ... of Africa*   Douglass alludes to the colonization movement, led chiefly by the American Colonization Society, whose members (many of whom were clergymen, and all of whom were white) advocated for the relocation of free African Americans to the African continent. This movement was widely condemned by many—though not all—abolitionists in the nineteenth century.

and women, reared like swine for the market. You know what is a swine-drover? I will show you a man-drover.[1] They inhabit all our Southern States. They perambulate the country, and crowd the highways of the nation, with droves of human stock. You will see one of these human flesh jobbers,[2] armed with pistol, whip and bowie-knife,[3] driving a company of a hundred men, women, and children, from the Potomac to the slave market at New Orleans. These wretched people are to be sold singly, or in lots, to suit purchasers. They are food for the cotton-field, and the deadly sugar-mill. Mark the sad procession, as it moves wearily along, and the inhuman wretch who drives them. Hear his savage yells and his blood-chilling oaths, as he hurries on his affrighted captives! There, see the old man, with locks thinned and gray. Cast one glance, if you please, upon that young mother, whose shoulders are bare to the scorching sun, her briny tears falling on the brow of the babe in her arms. See, too, that girl of thirteen, weeping, *yes*! weeping, as she thinks of the mother from whom she has been torn! The drove moves tardily. Heat and sorrow have nearly consumed their strength; suddenly you hear a quick snap, like the discharge of a rifle; the fetters clank, and the chain rattles simultaneously; your ears are saluted with a scream, that seems to have torn its way to the centre of your soul! The crack you heard, was the sound of the slave-whip; the scream you heard, was from the woman you saw with the babe. Her speed had faltered under the weight of her child and her chains! that gash on her shoulder tells her to move on. Follow the drove to New Orleans. Attend the auction; see men examined like horses; see the forms of women rudely and brutally exposed to the shocking gaze of American slave-buyers. See this drove sold and separated forever; and never forget the deep, sad sobs that arose from that scattered multitude. Tell me citizens, where, under the sun, you can witness a spectacle more fiendish and shocking. Yet this is but a glance at the American slave-trade, as it exists, at this moment, in the ruling part of the United States.

I was born amid such sights and scenes. To me the American slave-trade is a terrible reality. When a child, my soul was often pierced with a sense of its horrors. I lived on Philpot Street, Fell's Point, Baltimore, and have watched from the wharves, the slave ships in the Basin, anchored from the shore, with their cargoes of human flesh, waiting for favorable winds to waft them down the Chesapeake. There was, at that time, a grand slave mart kept at the head of Pratt Street, by Austin Woldfolk. His agents were sent into every town and county in Maryland, announcing their arrival, through the papers, and on flaming "*hand-bills*," headed cash for negroes. These men were generally well dressed men, and very captivating in their manners. Ever ready to drink, to treat, and to gamble. The fate of many a slave has depended upon the turn of a single card; and many a child has been snatched from the arms of its mother, by bargains arranged in a state of brutal drunkenness.

The flesh-mongers gather up their victims by dozens, and drive them, chained, to the general depot at Baltimore. When a sufficient number have been collected here, a ship is chartered, for the purpose of conveying the forlorn crew to Mobile, or to New Orleans. From the slave prison to the ship, they are usually driven in the darkness of night; for since the antislavery agitation, a certain caution is observed.

In the deep still darkness of midnight, I have been often aroused by the dead heavy footsteps, and the piteous cries of the chained gangs that passed our door. The anguish of my boyish heart was intense; and I was often consoled, when speaking to my mistress in the morning, to hear her say that the custom was very wicked; that she hated to hear the rattle of the chains, and the heart-rending cries. I was glad to find one who sympathized with me in my horror.

Fellow citizens, this murderous traffic is, today, in active operation in this boasted republic. In the solitude of my spirit, I see clouds of dust raised on the highways of the South; I see the bleeding footsteps; I hear the doleful wail of fettered humanity, on the way to the slave-markets, where the victims are to be sold like *horses*, *sheep*, and *swine*, knocked off to the highest bidder. There I see the tenderest ties ruthlessly broken, to gratify the lust, caprice and rapacity of the buyers and sellers of men. My soul sickens at the sight.

---

[1] *drover* Herder; one who is in charge of moving a herd (or "drove") of animals from place to place.

[2] *jobbers* Dealers.

[3] *bowie-knife* Short fighting-knife often associated with the American South.

Is this the land your Fathers loved,
    The freedom which they toiled to win?
Is this the earth whereon they moved?
    Are these the graves they slumber in?[1]

But a still more inhuman, disgraceful, and scandalous state of things remains to be presented.

By an act of the American Congress, not yet two years old, slavery has been nationalized in its most horrible and revolting form. By that act, Mason & Dixon's line has been obliterated; New York has become as Virginia; and the power to hold, hunt, and sell men, women, and children as slaves remains no longer a mere state institution, but is now an institution of the whole United States.[2] The power is co-extensive with the star-spangled banner, and American Christianity. Where these go, may also go the merciless slave-hunter. Where these are, man is not sacred. He is a bird for the sportsman's gun. By that most foul and fiendish of all human decrees, the liberty and person of every man are put in peril. Your broad republican domain is hunting ground for *men*. *Not* for thieves and robbers, enemies of society, merely, but for men guilty of no crime. Your lawmakers have commanded all good citizens to engage in this hellish sport. Your President, your Secretary of State, your *lords*, *nobles*, and ecclesiastics, enforce, as a duty you owe to your free and glorious country, and to your God, that you do this accursed thing. Not fewer than forty Americans have, within the past two years, been hunted down, and, without a moment's warning, hurried away in chains, and consigned to slavery and excruciating torture. Some of these have had wives and children, dependent on them for bread; but of this,

no account was made. The right of the hunter to his prey stands superior to the right of marriage, and to *all* rights in this republic, the rights of God included! For black men there are neither law, justice, humanity, nor religion. The Fugitive Slave *Law* makes mercy to them, a crime; and bribes the judge who tries them. An American Judge gets ten dollars for every victim he consigns to slavery, and five, when he fails to do so. The oath of any two villains is sufficient, under this hell-black enactment, to send the most pious and exemplary black man into the remorseless jaws of slavery! His own testimony is nothing. He can bring no witnesses for himself. The minister of American justice is bound, by the law, to hear but *one* side; and *that* side, is the side of the oppressor. Let this damning fact be perpetually told. Let it be thundered around the world, that, in tyrant-killing, king-hating, people-loving, democratic, Christian America, the seats of justice are filled with judges, who hold their offices under an open and palpable *bribe*, and are bound, in deciding in the case of a man's liberty, *to hear only his accusers!*

In glaring violation of justice, in shameless disregard of the forms of administering law, in cunning arrangement to entrap the defenseless, and in diabolical intent, this Fugitive Slave Law stands alone in the annals of tyrannical legislation. I doubt if there be another nation on the globe, having the brass and the baseness to put such a law on the statute-book. If any man in this assembly thinks differently from me in this matter, and feels able to disprove my statements, I will gladly confront him at any suitable time and place he may select.

RELIGIOUS LIBERTY

I take this law to be one of the grossest infringements of Christian Liberty, and, if the churches and ministers of our country were not stupidly blind, or most wickedly indifferent, they, too, would so regard it.

At the very moment that they are thanking God for the enjoyment of civil and religious liberty, and for the right to worship God according to the dictates of their own consciences, they are utterly silent in respect to a law which robs religion of its chief significance, and makes it utterly worthless to a world lying in wickedness. Did this law concern the "*mint, anise* and

---

[1]   *Is this ... slumber in?*   See "Stanzas for the Times" by antislavery poet John Greenleaf Whittier.

[2]   *By an act ... United States*   Douglass refers to the Fugitive Slave Act of 1850 (a part of the Compromise of 1850), under the terms of which it became illegal for anyone, whether in the North or the South, to give aid to people escaping slavery; citizens throughout the country were expected to actively participate in the apprehension and return of such fugitives. Given that the testimony of captured African Americans was not accepted in court, the Act inevitably resulted in the capture and enslavement of many free African Americans, as well as of many who had been previously enslaved; *Mason & Dixon's line*   Line separating parts of Pennsylvania and Delaware from parts of Maryland and Virginia; the phrase was used as shorthand for the boundary between the Northern free states and the Southern slave states.

cumin"[1]—abridge the right to sing psalms, to partake of the sacrament, or to engage in any of the ceremonies of religion, it would be smitten by the thunder of a thousand pulpits. A general shout would go up from the church, demanding *repeal, repeal, instant repeal*! And it would go hard with that politician who presumed to solicit the votes of the people without inscribing this motto on his banner. Further, if this demand were not complied with, another Scotland would be added to the history of religious liberty, and the stern old covenanters[2] would be thrown into the shade. A John Knox would be seen at every church door, and heard from every pulpit, and Fillmore would have no more quarter than was shown by Knox to the beautiful but treacherous queen Mary of Scotland.[3] The fact that the church of our country (with fractional exceptions) does not esteem "the Fugitive Slave Law" as a declaration of war against religious liberty, implies that that church regards religion simply as a form of worship, an empty ceremony, and *not* a vital principle, requiring active benevolence, justice, love and good will towards man. It esteems sacrifice above mercy; psalm-singing above right doing; solemn meetings above practical righteousness. A worship that can be conducted by persons who refuse to give shelter to the houseless, to give bread to the hungry, clothing to the naked, and who enjoin obedience to a law forbidding these acts of mercy, is a curse, not a blessing to mankind. The Bible addresses all such persons as "scribes, pharisees, hypocrites, who pay tithe of *mint, anise,* and *cumin,* and have omitted the weightier matters of the law, judgment, mercy and faith."

THE CHURCH RESPONSIBLE

But the church of this country is not only indifferent to the wrongs of the slave, it actually takes sides with the oppressors. It has made itself the bulwark of American slavery, and the shield of American slave-hunters. Many of its most eloquent Divines, who stand as the very lights of the church, have shamelessly given the sanction of religion, and the Bible, to the whole slave system. They have taught that man may, properly, be a slave; that the relation of master and slave is ordained of God; that to send back an escaped bondman to his master is clearly the duty of all the followers of the Lord Jesus Christ; and this horrible blasphemy is palmed off upon the world for Christianity.

For my part, I would say, welcome infidelity! welcome atheism! welcome anything! in preference to the gospel, *as preached by those Divines*! They convert the very name of religion into an engine of tyranny, and barbarous cruelty, and serve to confirm more infidels, in this age, than all the infidel writings of Thomas Paine, Voltaire, and Bolingbroke,[4] put together, have done! These ministers make religion a cold and flinty-hearted thing, having neither principles of right action, nor bowels of compassion. They strip the love of God of its beauty, and leave the throng of religion a huge, horrible, repulsive form. It is a religion for oppressors, tyrants, man-stealers, and *thugs*. It is not that "*pure and undefiled religion*"[5] which is from above, and which is "*first pure, then peaceable, easy to be entreated,* full of mercy and good fruits, *without partiality, and without hypocrisy.*" But a religion which favors the rich against the poor; which exalts the proud above the humble; which divides mankind into two classes, tyrants and slaves; which says to the man in chains, *stay there*; and to the oppressor, *oppress*

---

1   *mint, anise and cumin*   See Matthew 23.23: "Woe unto you, scribes and Pharisees, hypocrites! for ye pay tithe of mint and anise and cumin, and have omitted the weightier matters of the law, judgment, mercy, and faith: these ought ye to have done, and not to leave the other undone."

2   *covenanters*   Name given to the Scottish Presbyterians who signed the National Covenant in 1638, seeking to uphold the Presbyterian Church in Scotland in the face of persecution by King Charles I.

3   *A John Knox ... Scotland*   John Knox (1514–72), religious dissenter and founder of the Scottish Presbyterian Church, was an ardent opponent of the Catholic Mary Queen of Scots, who was executed for treason in 1587. Millard Fillmore, who was President of the United States at the time of Douglass's speech, was instrumental in the passage of the Fugitive Slave Act.

4   *Thomas Paine*   English-born political theorist whose *Common Sense* (1776) was profoundly influential during the time of the American Revolution, and whose *The Age of Reason* (1794–1807) was highly critical of organized religion;   *Voltaire*   French Enlightenment philosopher (1694–1778) who advocated freedom of speech and the separation of church and state, and was often accused of atheism;   *Bolingbroke*   Henry St. John, 1st Viscount Bolingbroke (1678–1751), English political philosopher whose antireligious views were influential on Voltaire as well as on numerous key figures of the American Revolution.

5   *pure and undefiled religion*   See James 1.27.

on; it is a religion which may be professed and enjoyed by all the robbers and enslavers of mankind; it makes God a respecter of persons,[1] denies his fatherhood of the race, and tramples in the dust the great truth of the brotherhood of man. All this we affirm to be true of the popular church, and the popular worship of our land and nation—a religion, a church, and a worship which, on the authority of inspired wisdom, we pronounce to be an abomination in the sight of God. In the language of Isaiah, the American church might be well addressed, "Bring no more vain oblations; incense is an abomination unto me: the new moons and Sabbaths, the calling of assemblies, I cannot away with; it is iniquity, even the solemn meeting. Your new moons, and your appointed feasts my soul hateth. They are a trouble to me; I am weary to bear them; and when ye spread forth your hands I will hide mine eyes from you. Yea! when ye make many prayers, I will not hear. YOUR HANDS ARE FULL OF BLOOD; cease to do evil, learn to do well; seek judgment; relieve the oppressed; judge for the fatherless; plead for the widow."[2]

The American church is guilty, when viewed in connection with what it is doing to uphold slavery; but it is superlatively guilty when viewed in connection with its ability to abolish slavery.

The sin of which it is guilty is one of omission as well as of commission. Albert Barnes[3] but uttered what the common sense of every man at all observant of the actual state of the case will receive as truth, when he declared that "There is no power out of the church that could sustain slavery an hour, if it were not sustained in it."

Let the religious press, the pulpit, the Sunday school, the conference meeting, the great ecclesiastical, missionary, Bible and tract associations of the land array their immense powers against slavery, and slave-holding; and the whole system of crime and blood would be scattered to the winds; and that

they do not do this involves them in the most awful responsibility of which the mind can conceive.

In prosecuting the anti-slavery enterprise, we have been asked to spare the church, to spare the ministry; but *how*, we ask, could such a thing be done? We are met on the threshold of our efforts for the redemption of the slave, by the church and ministry of the country, in battle arrayed against us; and we are compelled to fight or flee. From *what* quarter, I beg to know, has proceeded a fire so deadly upon our ranks, during the last two years, as from the Northern pulpit? As the champions of oppressors, the chosen men of American theology have appeared—men, honored for their so-called piety, and their real learning. The Lords of Buffalo, the Springs of New York, the Lathrops of Auburn, the Coxes and Spencers of Brooklyn, the Gannets and Sharps of Boston, the Deweys of Washington,[4] and other great religious lights of the land, have, in utter denial of the authority of *Him*, by whom they professed to be called to the ministry, deliberately taught us, against the example of the Hebrews, and against the remonstrance of the Apostles, they teach *that we ought to obey man's law before the law of God.*[5]

My spirit wearies of such blasphemy; and how such men can be supported, as the "standing types and representatives of Jesus Christ," is a mystery which I leave others to penetrate. In speaking of the American church, however, let it be distinctly understood that I mean the *great mass* of the religious organizations of our land. There are exceptions, and I thank God that there are. Noble men may be found, scattered all over these Northern States, of whom Henry Ward Beecher of Brooklyn, Samuel J. May[6] of Syracuse, and my esteemed friend[7] on the platform, are shining

---

1   *respecter of persons*   In Acts 10.34, Peter claims that "God is no respecter of persons"; i.e., that he does not favor people of higher status.

2   *In the language ... the widow*   See Isaiah 1.13–17.

3   *Albert Barnes*   American antislavery theologian (1798–1870) who wrote numerous books on the subject of slavery and religion.

4   *The Lords ... of Washington*   Douglass alludes to a number of religious leaders who were either explicitly proslavery or who were morally opposed to slavery but favored not interfering with the institution.

5   *that we ... of God*   See Acts 5.29: "Then Peter and the other apostles answered and said, We ought to obey God rather than men."

6   *Henry Ward Beecher*   American Congregationalist minister (1813–87) and antislavery activist; *Samuel J. May* American Unitarian minister (1797–1871) and abolitionist.

7   [Douglass's note] Rev. R.R. Raymond. [Baptist minister and abolitionist who contributed to Julia Griffiths's 1853 abolitionist collection *Autographs for Freedom*.]

examples; and let me say further, that, upon these men lies the duty to inspire our ranks with high religious faith and zeal, and to cheer us on in the great mission of the slave's redemption from his chains.

RELIGION IN ENGLAND AND RELIGION IN AMERICA

One is struck with the difference between the attitude of the American church towards the anti-slavery movement, and that occupied by the churches in England towards a similar movement in that country. There, the church, true to its mission of ameliorating, elevating, and improving the condition of mankind, came forward promptly, bound up the wounds of the West Indian slave, and restored him to his liberty. There, the question of emancipation was a high religious question. It was demanded, in the name of humanity, and according to the law of the living God. The Sharps, the Clarksons, the Wilberforces, the Buxtons, and Burchells and the Knibbs,[1] were alike famous for their piety, and for their philanthropy. The anti slavery movement *there* was not an anti-church movement, for the reason that the church took its full share in prosecuting that movement: and the anti-slavery movement in this country will cease to be an anti-church movement, when the church of this country shall assume a favorable, instead of a hostile position towards that movement.

Americans! your republican politics, not less than your republican religion, are flagrantly inconsistent. You boast of your love of liberty, your superior civilization, and your pure Christianity, while the whole political power of the nation, as embodied in the two great political parties, is solemnly pledged to support and perpetuate the enslavement of three millions of your countrymen. You hurl your anathemas at the crowned headed tyrants of Russia and Austria, and pride yourselves on your Democratic institutions, while you yourselves consent to be the mere *tools* and *bodyguards* of the tyrants of Virginia and Carolina. You invite to your shores fugitives of oppression from abroad, honor them with banquets, greet them with ovations, cheer them, toast them, salute them, protect them, and pour out your money to them like water; but the fugitives from your own land, you advertise, hunt, arrest, shoot and kill. You glory in your refinement, and your universal education; yet you maintain a system as barbarous and dreadful, as ever stained the character of a nation—a system begun in avarice, supported in pride, and perpetuated in cruelty. You shed tears over fallen Hungary,[2] and make the sad story of her wrongs the theme of your poets, statesmen and orators, till your gallant sons are ready to fly to arms to vindicate her cause against her oppressors; but, in regard to the ten thousand wrongs of the American slave, you would enforce the strictest silence, and would hail him as an enemy of the nation who dares to make those wrongs the subject of public discourse! You are all on fire at the mention of liberty for France or for Ireland; but are as cold as an iceberg at the thought of liberty for the enslaved of America. You discourse eloquently on the dignity of labor; yet you sustain a system which, in its very essence, casts a stigma upon labor. You can bare your bosom to the storm of British artillery, to throw off a three-penny tax on tea;[3] and yet wring the last hard-earned farthing from the grasp of the black laborers of your country. You profess to believe "that, of one blood, God made all nations of men to dwell on the face of all the earth,"[4] and hath commanded all men, everywhere to love one another; yet you notoriously hate (and glory in your hatred) all men whose skins are not colored like your own. You declare, before the world, and are understood by the world to declare, that you "*hold these truths to be self evident, that all men are created equal; and are endowed by their Creator with certain inalienable rights; and that, among these are, life, liberty, and the pursuit of happiness*";[5] and yet, you hold securely, in a bondage which, according to your own

---

[1] *The Sharps ... the Knibbs* Douglass alludes to numerous English abolitionists active in the eighteenth and early nineteenth centuries, among them the influential politician William Wilberforce (1759–1833).

[2] *fallen Hungary* The Hungarian Revolution, which many Americans supported, took place in 1848; it was violently suppressed by the Austrian Empire.

[3] *throw off ... on tea* Douglass alludes to the Boston Tea Party of 1773, in which colonists protested the British Tea Act on the grounds that they would not tolerate taxation without representation.

[4] *that ... the earth* See Acts 17.26.

[5] *hold these truths ... of happiness* From the Declaration of Independence.

Thomas Jefferson, "*is worse than ages of that which your fathers rose in rebellion to oppose*,"[1] a *seventh part* of the inhabitants of your country.

Fellow-citizens! I will not enlarge further on your national inconsistencies. The existence of slavery in this country brands your republicanism as a sham, your humanity as a base pretence, and your Christianity as a lie. It destroys your moral power abroad; it corrupts your politicians at home. It saps the foundation of religion; it makes your name a hissing, and a by word to a mocking earth. It is the antagonistic force in your government, the only thing that seriously disturbs and endangers your *Union*. It fetters your progress; it is the enemy of improvement, the deadly foe of education; it fosters pride; it breeds insolence; it promotes vice; it shelters crime; it is a curse to the earth that supports it; and yet, you cling to it, as if it were the sheet anchor of all your hopes. Oh! be warned! be warned! a horrible reptile is coiled up in your nation's bosom; the venomous creature is nursing at the tender breast of your youthful republic; *for the love of God, tear away*, and fling from you the hideous monster, and *let the weight of twenty millions crush and destroy it forever*!

THE CONSTITUTION

But it is answered in reply to all this, that precisely what I have now denounced is, in fact, guaranteed and sanctioned by the Constitution of the United States; that the right to hold, and to hunt slaves is a part of that Constitution framed by the illustrious Fathers of this Republic.

Then, I dare to affirm, notwithstanding all I have said before, your fathers stooped, basely stooped.

> To palter with us in a double sense:
> And keep the word of promise to the ear,
> But break it to the heart.[2]

And instead of being the honest men I have before declared them to be, they were the veriest imposters that ever practiced on mankind. *This* is the inevitable conclusion, and from it there is no escape; but I differ from those who charge this baseness on the framers of the Constitution of the United States.[3] *It is a slander upon their memory*, at least, so I believe. There is not time now to argue the constitutional question at length; nor have I the ability to discuss it as it ought to be discussed. The subject has been handled with masterly power by Lysander Spooner, Esq., by William Goodell, by Samuel E. Sewall, Esq., and last, though not least, by Gerritt Smith, Esq.[4] These gentlemen have, as I think, fully and clearly vindicated the Constitution from any design to support slavery for an hour.

Fellow citizens! there is no matter in respect to which the people of the North have allowed themselves to be so ruinously imposed upon, as that of the pro-slavery character of the Constitution. In *that* instrument I hold there is neither warrant, license, nor sanction of the hateful thing; but, interpreted as it *ought* to be interpreted, the Constitution is a Glorious Liberty Document. Read its preamble, consider its purposes. Is slavery among them? Is it at the gateway? or is it in the temple? It is neither. While I do not intend to argue this question on the present occasion, let me ask, if it be not somewhat singular that, if the Constitution were intended to be, by its framers and adopters, a slave-holding instrument, why neither *slavery*, *slaveholding*, nor *slave* can anywhere be found in it. What would be thought of an instrument, drawn up, *legally* drawn up, for the purpose of entitling the city of Rochester to a track of land, in which no mention of land was made? Now, there are certain rules of interpretation, for the proper understanding of all legal instruments. These rules are well established. They are plain, common-sense rules, such as you and I, and all of us, can understand and apply, without having passed years in the study of law. I scout the idea

---

[1]   *Thomas Jefferson ... to oppose* Douglass paraphrases text included in a letter sent by Thomas Jefferson to Jean-Nicolas Démeunier in 1786, in which he decried the hypocrisy of American slavery. (Jefferson was himself a slaveholder.)

[2]   *To palter ... heart* Paraphrase from Shakespeare's *Macbeth* 5.8.24–26.

[3]   *but I differ ... United States* This disagreement was among the factors that led to Douglass's falling-out with his former colleague William Lloyd Garrison, who strongly believed the Constitution to be an inherently proslavery document.

[4]   *Lysander ... Esq.* Douglass names several abolitionists who argued that slavery was unconstitutional.

that the question of the constitutionality, or unconstitutionality of slavery, is not a question for the people. I hold that every American citizen has a right to form an opinion of the constitution, and to propagate that opinion, and to use all honorable means to make his opinion the prevailing one. Without this right, the liberty of an American citizen would be as insecure as that of a Frenchman. Ex-Vice-President Dallas[1] tells us that the constitution is an object to which no American mind can be too attentive, and no American heart too devoted. He further says, the constitution, in its words, is plain and intelligible, and is meant for the home-bred, unsophisticated understandings of our fellow-citizens. Senator Berrien[2] tell us that the Constitution is the fundamental law, that which controls all others. The charter of our liberties, which every citizen has a personal interest in understanding thoroughly. The testimony of Senator Breese, Lewis Cass,[3] and many others that might be named, who are everywhere esteemed as sound lawyers, so regard the constitution. I take it, therefore, that it is not presumption in a private citizen to form an opinion of that instrument.

Now, take the constitution according to its plain reading, and I defy the presentation of a single proslavery clause in it. On the other hand it will be found to contain principles and purposes, entirely hostile to the existence of slavery.

I have detained my audience entirely too long already. At some future period I will gladly avail myself of an opportunity to give this subject a full and fair discussion.

Allow me to say, in conclusion, notwithstanding the dark picture I have this day presented of the state of the nation, I do not despair of this country. There are forces in operation, which must inevitably work the downfall of slavery. "*The arm of the Lord is not*

shortened,"[4] and the doom of slavery is certain. I, therefore, leave off where I began, with *hope*. While drawing encouragement from the "Declaration of Independence," the great principles it contains, and the genius of American Institutions, my spirit is also cheered by the obvious tendencies of the age. Nations do not now stand in the same relation to each other that they did ages ago. No nation can now shut itself up, from the surrounding world, and trot round in the same old path of its fathers without interference. The time *was* when such could be done. Long established customs of hurtful character could formerly fence themselves in, and do their evil work with social impunity. Knowledge was then confined and enjoyed by the privileged few, and the multitude walked on in mental darkness. But a change has now come over the affairs of mankind. Walled cities and empires have become unfashionable. The arm of commerce has borne away the gates of the strong city. Intelligence is penetrating the darkest corners of the globe. It makes its pathway over and under the sea, as well as on the earth. Wind, steam, and lightning are its chartered agents. Oceans no longer divide, but link nations together. From Boston to London is now a holiday excursion. Space is comparatively annihilated. Thoughts expressed on one side of the Atlantic, are distinctly heard on the other.

The far off and almost fabulous[5] Pacific rolls in grandeur at our feet. The Celestial Empire, the mystery of ages, is being solved. The fiat of the Almighty, "*Let there be Light*,"[6] has not yet spent its force. No abuse, no outrage whether in taste, sport or avarice, can now hide itself from the all-pervading light. The iron shoe, and crippled foot of China must be seen, in contrast with nature. *Afric must rise and put on her yet unwoven garment. "Ethiopia shall stretch out her hand unto God."*[7] In the fervent aspirations of William Lloyd Garrison, I say, and let every heart join in saying it:

---

[1] *Ex-Vice-President Dallas* George Dallas (1792–1864), Vice President to James K. Polk.

[2] *Senator Berrien* John Berrien (1781–1856), Georgia Senator who argued that slavery was fundamental to the Constitution.

[3] *Senator Breese* Sidney Breese (1800–78), Illinois Senator who favored the rule of popular sovereignty on the question of slavery; *Lewis Cass* Michigan Senator who campaigned for the Presidency in 1848 and was opposed to limiting the spread of slavery.

---

[4] *The arm ... not shortened* See Isaiah 59.1.

[5] *fabulous* I.e., fabled; of mythological reputation.

[6] *Let there be Light* See Genesis 1.3.

[7] *Ethiopia ... unto God* See Psalms 68.31; in the nineteenth century, Ethiopia was often thought of as symbolizing all Africa and all people of African descent.

God speed the year of jubilee
 The wide world o'er!
When from their galling chains set free,
Th' oppressed shall vilely bend the knee,
And wear the yoke of tyranny
 Like brutes no more.
That year will come, and freedom's reign,
To man his plundered rights again
 Restore.

God speed the day when human blood
 Shall cease to flow!
In every clime be understood,
The claims of human brotherhood,
And each return for evil, good,
 Not blow for blow;
That day will come all feuds to end,
And change into a faithful friend
 Each foe.

God speed the hour, the glorious hour,
 When none on earth
Shall exercise a lordly power,
Nor in a tyrant's presence cower;
But all to manhood's stature tower,
 By equal birth!
THAT HOUR WILL COME, to each, to all,
And from his prison-house, the thrall
 Go forth.

Until that year, day, hour, arrive,
With head, and heart, and hand I'll strive,
To break the rod, and rend the gyve,[1]
The spoiler of his prey deprive—
 So witness Heaven!
And never from my chosen post,
Whate'er the peril or the cost,
 Be driven.[2]

—1852

In Context

Photographs of Frederick Douglass

Frederick Douglass was a great proponent of the new art of photography. He saw it as a fundamentally democratic medium as well as a crucial tool in the fight to end slavery and racial discrimination. Douglass used photography as a means to assert greater control over his public image as a black man, sitting for at least 160 distinct portraits over the course of his life (as identified by John Stauffer, Zoe Trodd, and Celeste-Marie Bernier in their 2015 *Picturing Frederick Douglass*). By contrast, there are only 126 photographs of Abraham Lincoln known to exist, and only 127 of Walt Whitman.

---

[1] *gyve* Shackle.

[2] *God speed ... Be driven* See William Lloyd Garrison's "The Triumph of Freedom" (1852).

Daguerreotype taken c. 1841, artist unknown. This is the first known photograph of Douglass.

Daguerreotype taken in July or August 1843, two years before the publication of Douglass's *Narrative*, artist unknown.

Daguerreotype taken in May 1848 by Edward White Gallery.

Daguerreotype taken c. 1853, two years before the publication of Douglass's second autobiography, *My Bondage and My Freedom*. Artist unknown.

Engraving of a photograph taken by John Howe Kent on 3 November 1882, used as the frontispiece to Douglass's revised third autobiography, *The Life and Times of Frederick Douglass* (1893).

Photograph taken on 31 October 1894 by Phineas C. Headley, Jr. and James E. Reed, a few months before Douglass's death. Douglass very rarely smiled in his photographs.

Portrait of Douglass seated with his second wife, Helen Pitts (right). Helen's sister, Eva Pitts, stands in the center. Taken c. 1884, shortly after their marriage, artist unknown.

Engraving used as the frontispiece to the first edition of Douglass's 1845 *Narrative*, artist unknown.

Cover of an 1847 anti-abolitionist pamphlet reprinting one of Douglass's speeches. The pamphlet described Douglass as a "presumptive negro" and as a "runaway slave from Baltimore," despite the fact that he had been manumitted some months before.

WALT WHITMAN
1819 – 1892

Walt Whitman forged a radical and fundamentally American poetics that would come to inspire generations of writers and social reformers. His work communicates a democratic vision that is at once spiritual, sexual, and political, one that embraces the dignity of the human body and the dignity of working-class labor. His poetic "I" claimed to speak for and to channel the full swath of society—plants and animals as well as all people, including, especially, the marginalized. During Whitman's life, public reception of his work was frequently mixed; while many readers applauded him for his innovative style and bold choice of subject matter, those same innovations of form and theme caused many more conservative readers to take affront, and Whitman frequently faced the threat of obscenity charges throughout his career. Today, he is broadly considered one of the most influential writers in American literary history, as well as one of the most beloved. While readers and critics across the world continue to connect passionately with Whitman's democratic vision and linguistic virtuosity, since the late-twentieth century they have also brought nuanced criticism to bear on his poetry, journalism, and correspondence, particularly on the subjects of race and American expansionism.

Walter Whitman was born into a Long Island family with Quaker ties in May 1819, the second of Walter and Louisa Van Velsor Whitman's eight surviving children. The family moved to Brooklyn in 1823, as Walter Sr., a carpenter and farmer by trade, undertook to engage in the city's booming real estate market. As a young man, Whitman had a somewhat strained relationship with his father, an enthusiastic Democrat and free thinker whom he respected but also found to be stern and occasionally tyrannical. Whitman's relationship to his mother was much warmer; they would remain close well into Whitman's adulthood.

Whitman received only minimal formal schooling in Brooklyn before beginning a series of apprenticeships at the age of eleven, first as a lawyer's assistant and later as a printer for the Long Island *Patriot*, a Democrat newspaper. His experience at the *Patriot* helped cultivate his commitment to the Northern Democratic Party and to its urban, working-class (and mostly white) constituency. His early newspaper work also trained him in the art of typesetting—which he would later put to use in self-publishing *Leaves of Grass*—and granted him a platform for his first articles and short stories. Whitman developed a strong attachment to the city and remained in Brooklyn even after the rest of his family returned to rural Long Island in 1833. In his free time, he attended the theater and public lectures, visited museums and galleries, and read widely from circulating libraries, developing a taste in particular for popular novelists such as James Fenimore Cooper and the Scottish Sir Walter Scott. Still, it was journalism, which he came to see as the lifeblood of a healthy democracy, that would be the formative influence on his early career.

Strained financial circumstances, stemming in part from the national recession of 1837, induced Whitman to switch careers at the age of seventeen, when he moved back to Long Island to work as a schoolteacher. This initiated a period of profound depression: Whitman didn't enjoy being cut off from the intellectual energy of Brooklyn, and he felt lonely, describing himself to a friend as "forsaken of all God's creation." While teaching, Whitman maintained his connection to the literary world by writing poems and short stories, some of which he published in a variety of periodicals (and some of which he seems to have taught in his classes). Little in this early work indicates the stylistic and thematic innovation that would be a hallmark of his later work; much of it is sentimental, moralistic, and stylistically conventional. His first novel, *Franklin Evans, or the Inebriate*, was published in 1842; a temperance novel, the work was later dismissed by Whitman as having been written during a fit of drunkenness. Whatever its origin, the novel proved quite successful; in fact, it sold more copies than any individual edition of *Leaves of Grass* ever would during Whitman's lifetime.

By 1841, Whitman was able to quit teaching and again leave Long Island, first for New York City and later for his beloved Brooklyn. He attended lectures by the likes of Ralph Waldo Emerson, and it was also during this period that Whitman became enamored of the opera, which he would later describe as a foundational influence on his poetry. Throughout much of the duration of the Mexican–American War (1846–48), Whitman was chief editor of the Brooklyn *Eagle*, a daily aligned with the presiding Democratic Party. In that role, Whitman wrote numerous editorials in support of the controversial conflict, through which the United States aimed to expand its territorial claims into the southwest. Though Whitman shared the fears of many northerners that a U.S. victory in the war would result in the further expansion of slavery into the newly acquired territories, his enthusiasm for western expansion and the ideals of Manifest Destiny dominated; as he put it in an 1846 editorial: "Mexico must be thoroughly chastised!"

By 1848 Whitman had become a supporter of the new Free Soil Party, established by northern Democrats disenchanted with their party's refusal to challenge slavery. Whitman's increasingly vocal condemnations of the institution led the *Eagle* to dismiss him from his editorial role in early 1848. Mere weeks later, a chance encounter with a Louisiana journalist resulted in an offer of work at the *Crescent*, a newly established New Orleans paper. Whitman ventured south in February. Though his time at the *Crescent* ultimately lasted only a few months, the experience was, by all accounts, personally transformative. Basking in the racially, culturally, linguistically, and religiously diverse community of New Orleans, Whitman also witnessed at close range the unforgettable horrors of the domestic slave trade—for which New Orleans functioned as a key port. Many biographers have also speculated that Whitman's New Orleans experience included a passionate love affair with a man, suggested most strongly by the unpublished manuscript version of the poem eventually titled "Once I Pass'd Through a Populous City."

Scholars have long puzzled over the origins of *Leaves of Grass*, for whose stylistic innovations there appears to have been little precedent in Whitman's writing prior to 1855; for some, the New Orleans experience is a plausible answer to part of the mystery. Some scholars have also suggested that the tense social climate growing out of the Compromise of 1850 and the Fugitive Slave Law—widely seen by even proslavery northerners as an unacceptable concession to the southern slave states—led to Whitman's political and creative ideals becoming more radical in the early 1850s; his new poetry would feature a more active imaginative engagement with the theme of racial equality. Later in life Whitman remembered his literary development as follows: "At the age of thirty-one to thirty-three, a desire that had been flitting through my previous life, or hovering on the flanks, mostly indefinite hitherto, had steadily advanced to the front, defined itself, and finally dominated everything else."

The first edition of *Leaves of Grass* was published, at Whitman's expense, in late June 1855. It featured a lengthy prose preface, clearly influenced by Emerson's 1844 essay "The Poet," establishing his cultural project and his conviction that "the United States themselves are essentially the greatest poem." The volume included twelve as-yet untitled poems, whose unrhymed, unmetered, and expansively long lines were unlike almost anything that had been seen in English literature to that date. Whitman's name appeared neither on the book's elegantly leather-bound and embossed cover nor on its title page, but only in the body of the opening poem eventually titled "Song of Myself," in which the speaker declares himself to be "Walt Whitman, an American, one of the roughs, a kosmos."

Reviews were relatively slow to appear—though they were not, as has often been assumed, predominantly negative. The first, by prominent critic Charles A. Dana, was moderately positive. An anonymous reviewer for *Life Illustrated* enthusiastically described *Leaves of Grass* as "like no other book that ever was written," describing its poems as "lines of rhythmical prose, or a series of *utterances* (we know not what else to call them), unconnected, curious, and original." Still, dissatisfied with the book's initial reception, Whitman soon took matters into his own hands and began submitting anonymous reviews himself: "Not a borrower from other lands, but a prodigal user of his own land is Walt Whitman," declares one he wrote for the *American Phrenological Journal* in October. Another memorably opens, "An American bard at last!" Whitman also sent a copy of the collection to Emerson, who gratified the poet with an enthusiastic and congratulatory letter, calling *Leaves of Grass* "the most extraordinary piece of wit and wisdom that America has yet contributed." The first truly negative review came in November from the notoriously harsh critic Rufus Griswold, who described the book as "a mass of stupid filth," and as the literary culmination of a transcendental philosophy that was "fast rotting the healthy core of all the social virtues." The book's transgressions were thematic at least as much as formal: Whitman's eagerness to express the poetic beauties of the human body, bodily functions, and sex provoked substantial controversy. On this front, the popular journalist and novelist Fanny Fern defended Whitman, declaring that "I extract no poison from these *Leaves*—to me they have brought only healing."

Whitman had begun writing additional material almost as soon as the first edition was released, and a second edition came out in autumn 1856. The new edition dispensed with the preface but added twenty new poems, expanding the previous ninety-five pages to well over three hundred. The poems were now given titles, and the back of the book contained a selection of reviews of the first edition—including Emerson's letter of congratulations (which was reprinted without Emerson's permission). The second edition still sold poorly, and Whitman's financial situation became strained, instigating a temporary return to journalism. During this period he also wrote the pamphlet *The Eighteenth Presidency!*, not published until 1928, which reveals his increasing anger at contemporary politics and at the continuation of slavery, calling on members of the white working class to "abolish slavery, or it will abolish you." He also penned a series of newspaper articles in September 1858 entitled "Manly Health and Training," a health manual and political manifesto arguing for the vitality of the body as the bedrock of a healthy democracy.

A third edition of *Leaves of Grass* appeared in 1860, this time initiated by an offer of publication from Thayer & Eldridge, Boston publishers with close ties to the abolitionist movement. With this edition Whitman aimed more than ever to make the work marketable, arranging his poems into thematic clusters and including several illustrations throughout the volume. The thematic clusters included "Enfans d'Adam" (later renamed "Children of Adam"), a sequence of poems centered on heterosexual love and procreation, which prompted new accusations of obscenity from more conservative readers, who were outraged at this frank discussion of women's desire that was not clearly contained within marriage. The new "Calamus" sequence, meanwhile, was a celebration of what Whitman called "manly love"—of what modern readers usually interpret as a romance. Some biographers have speculated that the "Calamus" poems originated from a love affair Whitman had with a man in the late 1850s, but the sequence provoked less controversy in a society that, while it condemned overt sexuality between men, was nonetheless accustomed to passionate expressions of male friendship. The poems today remain widely cherished for their moving depictions of emotional passion and physical affection between men. For all the controversy it did provoke, the third edition of *Leaves of Grass* was by far Whitman's most successful, selling upwards of four thousand copies.

The onset of the Civil War in 1861 prompted a swift change in the trajectory of Whitman's career and personal life. His first attempt at war poetry was "Beat! Beat! Drums!," a propagandistic piece intended to encourage new recruits to the Union Army; the poem was published in several prominent papers in September 1861. But Whitman's involvement in the war effort became substantially more direct after his brother George was wounded while fighting for the Union in December 1862. Whitman traveled to Virginia to find his brother, later describing his search among the wounded as "the greatest suffering I ever experienced in my life." George's wounds turned out to be minor, but the horror of the hospital environment was transformative for Whitman. He soon moved to Washington, D.C., taking on a part-time job as a clerk in the Union paymaster's office that allowed him to spend the rest of his time volunteering at nearby military hospitals. Whitman offered practical service as a nurse but also endeavored to offer friendship and emotional support to the wounded, reading to them, helping them write letters home, and developing in many cases passionate attachments. His experiences deeply informed a new work of poetry, *Drum-Taps*, first published as an independent volume in 1865 and incorporated into later editions of *Leaves of Grass*. Whitman later published prose accounts of his time in the military hospitals, which he collected under the title *Memoranda During the War* (1875) and later incorporated into the autobiographical *Specimen Days & Collect* (1882), a narrative composed of personal sketches, essays, and notes touching on the poet's life from childhood to the year 1880.

Drum-Taps was already at press when the news broke of Lincoln's assassination in April 1865. Whitman, who had by then developed (if at first grudgingly) a profound admiration for the Republican president, wrote several elegies for him, including "When Lilacs Last in the Dooryard Bloom'd." These were added to *Sequel to Drum-Taps*, published shortly after the first volume. Whitman remained in Washington after the end of the war, where he maintained government employment until the 1870s, while continuing to expand and revise *Leaves of Grass*, which was reissued in further editions in 1867 and 1871.

In 1867 Whitman began composing the essays that would eventually form the pamphlet *Democratic Vistas* (1871). The work expressed his frustration at the inequality and cultural vapidity he saw at the heart of Reconstruction-era America, as well as his enduring hopes that literature would ultimately lift the nation out of moral and political stagnation. On some of the central questions of the Reconstruction, however—namely, African American citizenship and suffrage—Whitman adopted a highly conservative stance, describing universal suffrage as a "danger" and expressing doubts about the ability of African Americans to participate fully in American society; he appears also to have had little to say about the dramatic upsurge of racial violence that began in the late 1860s. While Whitman was a committed abolitionist, and while he embraced and promoted the idea that America should be open to immigrants of all backgrounds, he did express in his journalism and correspondence racist views about African Americans and about America's Indigenous peoples, who he imagined would gradually disappear as their lands were colonized, giving way to a United States shaped by, and belonging to, the white working class. Twenty-first-century scholars working with the critical lenses of race, gender, sexuality, ability, and the environment, have contributed to a reassessment of Whitman that acknowledges his limitations, revealing a poet who broke through many—but not all—of the prejudices of his own time. Before his death Whitman reflected upon, and regretted, some of his earlier views: "After all I may have been tainted a bit, just a little bit," he wrote, with the pernicious racism that suffused his culture, "yet I have been anti-slavery always—was then and am now: and to all and any other slaveries, too, black or white, mental or physical." Whitman suffered a stroke in 1873, prompting him to travel to New Jersey, where many of his family members now resided. Whitman's mother died only days after his arrival, an event that devastated him. Physically weakened, he moved in with his brother George and his wife in a working-class neighborhood in Camden, where he would reside for the following decade.

Personal tragedies notwithstanding, as an artist and public figure Whitman's prospects had by now improved substantially. Over the course of the 1870s and 80s he became a regular correspondent of various intellectuals both at home and abroad, having developed an enthusiastic following in Britain in particular. In the early 1870s his correspondents included English critic John Addington Symonds, an early scholar of homosexuality and one of the first writers to prominently suggest that the "Calamus" poems were expressive of what he termed "Greek love"—a suggestion that Whitman ardently denied. Despite his increased prominence, Whitman was wounded by the omission of his work from a number of prominent literary anthologies around this time, most notably from Emerson's collection *Parnassus* (1874). Such omissions prompted his anonymous submission in 1876 of "Walt Whitman's Actual American Position" to the *West Jersey Press*, which claimed that his work had been systematically vilified and ignored by the American literary establishment.

The poems in the 1881–82 edition of *Leaves of Grass* appeared in their final versions and arrangement. Whitman suffered another stroke in 1888, after which his physical condition deteriorated significantly. In his final year he worked on what is commonly termed the "Deathbed Edition" of *Leaves of Grass* (1891), identical to the 1881 edition but for the inclusion of two more poem clusters, which he termed "annexes," at the end of the volume; he also worked on compiling his *Complete Prose Works*, published in 1892. Whitman died of complications resulting from pneumonia in March 1892, at the age of seventy-two.

During his lifetime and after his death, Whitman became an icon of democratic poetics and politics, the quintessential "outsider," a queer, working-class writer who made his own books and worked on the margins of elite literary culture. In the words of poet June Jordan, he is "the one white father who shares the systematic disadvantages of his heterogenous offspring." He became a central figure in emerging Anglo-American gay culture, with British writers such as Edward Carpenter and John Addington Symonds viewing him as a prophet heralding a new, modern sexuality that would be divested of shame and would include the liberation of homoerotic desire. In the twentieth century he was revered as a radical, inclusive, antiracist poet who celebrated the working class. He had a profound influence, for example, on many Harlem Renaissance, modernist, Beat, and queer writers, such as Langston Hughes, Alain Locke, Jean Toomer, T.S. Eliot, H.D., Wallace Stevens, Hart Crane, Adrienne Rich, and Allen Ginsberg, who wrote that "Whitman's exposure of a new self of man or woman empowered every particular soul who heard his long breathed inspiration." Whitman's influence has also stretched to poets around the world, particularly in Latin and South America and in Europe, including Federico García Lorca and Pablo Neruda. While our understanding of Whitman as a person and writer grows ever more nuanced and complex, his poems continue to act as a catalyst for a new generation of artists, which was just what Whitman himself called for: "I am a man who, sauntering along without fully stopping, turns a casual look upon you and then averts his face, / Leaving it to you to prove and define it, / Expecting the main things from you."

NOTE ON THE TEXTS: The texts of the poems presented below are based on the 1881 version of *Leaves of Grass*, with two exceptions: the poem later titled "Song of Myself," which we have included in its untitled 1855 version, and the sequence "Live Oak, with Moss," which was not published in Whitman's lifetime and which is here based on the notebook manuscript of 1859. By 1881, "Song of Myself" had undergone numerous revisions, including being divided by Whitman into fifty-two numbered sections; for ease of reference, and to accommodate those readers more familiar with the 1881 text, we include section numbers in the left-hand margins of the 1855 text roughly where they appear in the 1881 version.

   Given the evidence of intentional idiosyncrasies of spelling and punctuation on Whitman's part, we have in his case departed from this anthology's conventional practice of modernizing spelling and punctuation. We have departed as well from our usual two-column format for Whitman's poetry; printing Whitman's often very long lines in two-column format would lead to a distracting number of line breaks.

   We are deeply indebted to the Whitman Archive (whitmanarchive.org) for making facsimiles of *Leaves of Grass* in the various editions published during Whitman's lifetime freely available online.

⌘ ⌘ ⌘

from *1855 Leaves of Grass* [*Preface*]

America does not repel the past or what it has produced under its forms or amid other politics or the idea of castes[1] or the old religions . . . . accepts the lesson with calmness . . . is not so impatient as has been supposed that the slough[2] still sticks to opinions and manners and literature while the life which served its requirements has passed into the new life of the new forms . . . perceives that the corpse is slowly borne from the eating and sleeping rooms of the house . . . perceives that it waits a little while in the door . . . that it was fittest for its days . . . that its action has descended to the stalwart and wellshaped heir who approaches . . . and that he shall be fittest for his days.

   The Americans of all nations at any time upon the earth have probably the fullest poetical nature. The United States themselves are essentially the greatest poem. In the history of the earth hitherto the largest and most stirring appear tame and orderly to their ampler largeness and stir. Here at last is something in the doings of man that corresponds with the broadcast doings of the day and night. Here is not merely a nation but a teeming nation of nations. Here is action untied from strings necessarily blind to particulars and details magnificently moving in vast masses. Here is the hospitality which forever indicates heroes . . . . Here

---

1   *castes*   Hereditary social hierarchies.

2   *slough*   Mud, or the dead tissue that forms over a wound.

are the roughs and beards and space and ruggedness and nonchalance that the soul loves. Here the performance disdaining the trivial unapproached in the tremendous audacity of its crowds and groupings and the push of its perspective spreads with crampless and flowing breadth and showers its prolific and splendid extravagance. One sees it must indeed own the riches of the summer and winter, and need never be bankrupt while corn grows from the ground or the orchards drop apples or the bays contain fish or men beget children upon women.

Other states indicate themselves in their deputies . . . . but the genius of the United States is not best or most in its executives or legislatures, nor in its ambassadors or authors or colleges or churches or parlors, nor even in its newspapers or inventors . . . but always most in the common people. Their manners speech dress friendships—the freshness and candor of their physiognomy[1]—the picturesque looseness of their carriage . . . their deathless attachment to freedom—their aversion to anything indecorous or soft or mean[2]—the practical acknowledgment of the citizens of one state by the citizens of all other states—the fierceness of their roused resentment—their curiosity and welcome of novelty—their self-esteem and wonderful sympathy—their susceptibility to a slight[3]—the air they have of persons who never knew how it felt to stand in the presence of superiors—the fluency of their speech—their delight in music, the sure symptom of manly tenderness and native elegance of soul . . . their good temper and openhandedness—the terrible[4] significance of their elections—the President's taking off his hat to them not they to him—these too are unrhymed poetry. It awaits the gigantic and generous treatment worthy of it.

The largeness of nature or the nation were monstrous without a corresponding largeness and generosity of the spirit of the citizen. Not nature nor swarming states nor streets and steamships nor prosperous business nor farms nor capital nor learning may suffice for the ideal of man . . . nor suffice the poet. No reminiscences may suffice either. A live nation can always cut a deep mark and can have the best authority the cheapest . . . namely from its own soul. This is the sum of the profitable uses of individuals or states and of present action and grandeur and of the subjects of poets.—As if it were necessary to trot back generation after generation to the eastern records! As if the beauty and sacredness of the demonstrable must fall behind that of the mythical! As if men do not make their mark out of any times! As if the opening of the western continent by discovery and what has transpired since in North and South America were less than the small theatre of the antique or the aimless sleepwalking of the middle ages! The pride of the United States leaves the wealth and finesse of the cities and all returns of commerce and agriculture and all the magnitude of geography or shows of exterior victory to enjoy the breed of full sized men or one full sized man unconquerable and simple.

The American poets are to enclose old and new for America is the race of races. Of them a bard[5] is to be commensurate with a people. To him the other continents arrive as contributions . . . he gives them reception for their sake and his own sake. His spirit responds to his country's spirit . . . . he incarnates its geography and natural life and rivers and lakes. Mississippi with annual freshets[6] and changing chutes, Missouri and Columbia and Ohio and Saint Lawrence with the falls and beautiful masculine Hudson, do not embouchure[7] where they spend themselves more than they embouchure into him. The blue breadth over the inland sea of Virginia and Maryland and the sea off Massachusetts and Maine and over Manhattan bay and over Champlain and Erie and over Ontario and Huron and Michigan and Superior, and over the Texan and Mexican and Floridian and Cuban seas and over the seas off California and Oregon, is not tallied by the blue breadth of the waters below more than the breadth of above and below is tallied by him. When the long Atlantic coast stretches longer and the Pacific coast stretches longer he easily stretches with them

---

[1] *physiognomy* Facial appearance (especially as considered to reveal one's personality).

[2] *mean* Small-minded.

[3] *slight* Insult.

[4] *terrible* I.e., awe-inspiring.

[5] *bard* Wandering poet or minstrel who records the important events of the day in verse.

[6] *freshets* Flooded areas or streams caused by heavy rainfall.

[7] *embouchure* As a noun, "embouchure" can refer to the mouth of a river or to the part of a wind instrument that touches the mouth of the player; Whitman here may be using it as a verb to mean "flow out."

north or south. He spans between them also from east to west and reflects what is between them. On him rise solid growths that offset the growths of pine and cedar and hemlock and liveoak and locust and chestnut and cypress and hickory and limetree and cottonwood and tuliptree and cactus and wildvine and tamarind and persimmon . . . . and tangles as tangled as any canebrake[1] or swamp . . . . and forests coated with transparent ice and icicles hanging from the boughs and crackling in the wind . . . . and sides and peaks of mountains . . . . and pasturage sweet and free as savannah or upland or prairie . . . . with flights and songs and screams that answer those of the wildpigeon and highhold[2] and orchard-oriole and coot and surf-duck and redshouldered-hawk and fish-hawk and white-ibis and indian-hen and cat-owl and water-pheasant and qua-bird and pied-sheldrake[3] and blackbird and mockingbird and buzzard and condor and night-heron and eagle. To him the hereditary countenance descends both mother's and father's. To him enter the essences of the real things and past and present events—of the enormous diversity of temperature and agriculture and mines—the tribes of red aborigines—the weatherbeaten vessels entering new ports or making landings on rocky coasts—the first settlements north or south—the rapid stature and muscle—the haughty defiance of '76,[4] and the war and peace and formation of the constitution . . . . the union always surrounded by blatherers and always calm and impregnable—the perpetual coming of immigrants—the wharf hem'd cities and superior marine—the unsurveyed interior—the loghouses and clearings and wild animals and hunters and trappers . . . . the free commerce—the fisheries and whaling and gold-digging—the endless gestation of new states—the convening of Congress every December,[5] the members duly coming up from all climates and the uttermost parts . . . . the noble character of the young mechanics and of all free American workmen and workwomen . . . . the general ardor and friendliness and enterprise—the perfect equality of the female with the male . . . . the large amativeness[6]—the fluid movement of the population—the factories and mercantile life and laborsaving machinery—the Yankee swap[7]—the New-York firemen and the target excursion[8]—the southern plantation life—the character of the northeast and of the northwest and southwest—slavery and the tremulous spreading of hands to protect it, and the stern opposition to it which shall never cease till it ceases or the speaking of tongues and the moving of lips cease. For such the expression of the American poet is to be transcendant and new. It is to be indirect and not direct or descriptive or epic. Its quality goes through these to much more. Let the age and wars of other nations be chanted and their eras and characters be illustrated and that finish the verse. Not so the great psalm of the republic. Here the theme is creative and has vista. Here comes one among the wellbeloved stonecutters and plans with decision and science and sees the solid and beautiful forms of the future where there are now no solid forms.

Of all nations the United States with veins full of poetical stuff most needs poets and will doubtless have the greatest and use them the greatest. Their Presidents shall not be their common referee so much as their poets shall. Of all mankind the great poet is the equable man. Not in him but off from him things are grotesque or eccentric or fail of their sanity. Nothing out of its place is good and nothing in its place is bad. He bestows on every object or quality its fit proportions neither more nor less. He is the arbiter of the diverse

---

1   *liveoak* Evergreen oaks, primarily found in the southeastern United States; they often are draped with Spanish moss; *limetree* More commonly known as basswood or linden trees; *wildvine* Species of grapevine, also known as the fox grape; *tamarind* Grown commercially in southern Florida; *persimmon* American persimmon; *canebrake* Thicket of sugarcane.

2   *highhold* The northern flicker, a species of woodpecker.

3   *surf-duck* Surf scoter; *indian-hen* Pileated woodpecker; *cat-owl* Long-eared owl; *qua-bird* Black-crowned night heron; *pied-sheldrake* Likely a reference to the common shelduck.

4   *haughty defiance of '76* I.e., the signing of the Declaration of Independence in 1776.

5   *convening … December* Before 1933, Congress would convene on the first Monday in December.

6   *amativeness* Love, especially sexual love; the term is derived from the pseudoscience of phrenology, and in that context refers to an individual's alleged propensity for sexual passion.

7   *the Yankee swap* Trade of two dissimilar things, typically in which the item given away turns out to be worth considerably less than the one received.

8   *target excursion* Day-long excursion by the members of a local militia or gun-club for the purposes of target practice (often also an occasion for general merry-making).

and he is the key. He is the equalizer of his age and land . . . . he supplies what wants supplying and checks what wants checking. If peace is the routine out of him speaks the spirit of peace, large, rich, thrifty, building vast and populous cities, encouraging agriculture and the arts and commerce—lighting the study of man, the soul, immortality—federal, state or municipal government, marriage, health, freetrade, intertravel by land and sea . . . . nothing too close, nothing too far off . . . the stars not too far off. In war he is the most deadly force of the war. Who recruits him recruits horse and foot . . . he fetches parks of artillery[1] the best that engineer ever knew. If the time becomes slothful and heavy he knows how to arouse it . . . he can make every word he speaks draw blood. Whatever stagnates in the flat of custom or obedience or legislation he never stagnates. Obedience does not master him, he masters it. High up out of reach he stands turning a concentrated light . . . he turns the pivot with his finger[2] . . . he baffles the swiftest runners as he stands and easily overtakes and envelops them. The time straying toward infidelity and confections and persiflage[3] he withholds by his steady faith . . . he spreads out his dishes . . . he offers the sweet firmfibred meat that grows men and women. His brain is the ultimate brain. He is no arguer . . . he is judgment. He judges not as the judge judges but as the sun falling around a helpless thing. As he sees the farthest he has the most faith. His thoughts are the hymns of the praise of things. In the talk on the soul and eternity and God off of his equal plane he is silent. He sees eternity less like a play with a prologue and denouement . . . . he sees eternity in men and women . . . he does not see men and women as dreams or dots. Faith is the antiseptic of the soul . . . it pervades the common people and preserves them . . . they never give up believing and expecting and trusting. There is that indescribable freshness and unconsciousness about an illiterate person that humbles and mocks the power of the noblest expressive genius. The poet sees for a certainty how one not a great artist may be just as sacred and perfect as the greatest artist. . . . . . The power to

destroy or remould is freely used by him but never the power of attack. What is past is past. If he does not expose superior models and prove himself by every step he takes he is not what is wanted. The presence of the greatest poet conquers . . . not parleying or struggling or any prepared attempts. Now he has passed that way see after him! there is not left any vestige of despair or misanthropy or cunning or exclusiveness or the ignominy of a nativity or color or delusion of hell or the necessity of hell . . . . . and no man thenceforward shall be degraded for ignorance or weakness or sin.

The greatest poet hardly knows pettiness or triviality. If he breathes into any thing that was before thought small it dilates with the grandeur and life of the universe. He is a seer . . . . he is individual . . . he is complete in himself . . . . the others are as good as he, only he sees it and they do not. He is not one of the chorus[4] . . . . he does not stop for any regulation . . . he is the president of regulation. What the eyesight does to the rest he does to the rest. Who knows the curious mystery of the eyesight? The other senses corroborate themselves, but this is removed from any proof but its own and foreruns the identities of the spiritual world. A single glance of it mocks all the investigations of man and all the instruments and books of the earth and all reasoning. What is marvellous? what is unlikely? what is impossible or baseless or vague? after you have once just opened the space of a peachpit and given audience to far and near and to the sunset and had all things enter with electric swiftness softly and duly without confusion or jostling or jam.

The land and sea, the animals fishes and birds, the sky of heaven and the orbs, the forests mountains and rivers, are not small themes . . . but folks expect of the poet to indicate more than the beauty and dignity which always attach to dumb[5] real objects . . . . they expect him to indicate the path between reality and their souls. Men and women perceive the beauty well enough . . probably as well as he. The passionate tenacity of hunters, woodmen, early risers, cultivators of gardens and orchards and fields, the love of healthy women for the manly form, seafaring persons, drivers of horses, the passion for light and the open

---

[1] *parks of artillery* Artillery units.

[2] *High up ... his finger* American poets are here likened to lighthouse keepers, who guide beams of light to illumine sections of dark sea and sky.

[3] *persiflage* Banter or light mockery.

---

[4] *chorus* In classical Greek theater, a group of performers who comment collectively on the action of the play.

[5] *dumb* Incapable of speech; silent.

air, all is an old varied sign of the unfailing perception of beauty and of a residence of the poetic in outdoor people. They can never be assisted by poets to perceive . . . . some may but they never can. The poetic quality is not marshalled in rhyme or uniformity or abstract addresses to things nor in melancholy complaints or good precepts, but is the life of these and much else and is in the soul. The profit of rhyme is that it drops seeds of a sweeter and more luxuriant rhyme, and of uniformity that it conveys itself into its own roots in the ground out of sight. The rhyme and uniformity of perfect poems show the free growth of metrical laws and bud from them as unerringly and loosely as lilacs or roses on a bush, and take shapes as compact as the shapes of chestnuts and oranges and melons and pears, and shed the perfume impalpable to form. The fluency and ornaments of the finest poems or music or orations or recitations are not independent but dependent. All beauty comes from beautiful blood and a beautiful brain. If the greatnesses are in conjunction in a man or woman it is enough . . . . the fact will prevail through the universe . . . . but the gaggery and gilt[1] of a million years will not prevail. Who troubles himself about his ornaments or fluency is lost. This is what you shall do: Love the earth and sun and the animals, despise riches, give alms to every one that asks, stand up for the stupid and crazy, devote your income and labor to others, hate tyrants, argue not concerning God, have patience and indulgence toward the people, take off your hat to nothing known or unknown or to any man or number of men, go freely with powerful uneducated persons and with the young and with the mothers of families, read these leaves in the open air every season of every year of your life, reexamine all you have been told at school or church or in any book, dismiss whatever insults your own soul, and your very flesh shall be a great poem and have the richest fluency not only in its words but in the silent lines of its lips and face and between the lashes of your eyes and in every motion and joint of your body . . . . The poet shall not spend his time in unneeded work. He shall know that the ground is always ready ploughed and manured . . . . others may not know it but he shall. He shall go directly to the creation. His trust shall master the trust of everything he touches . . . . and shall master all attachment.

The known universe has one complete lover and that is the greatest poet. He consumes an eternal passion and is indifferent which chance happens and which possible contingency of fortune or misfortune and persuades daily and hourly his delicious pay. What balks or breaks others is fuel for his burning progress to contact and amorous joy. Other proportions of the reception of pleasure dwindle to nothing to his proportions. All expected from heaven or from the highest he is rapport with in the sight of the daybreak or a scene of the winter woods or the presence of children playing or with his arm round the neck of a man or woman. His love above all love has leisure and expanse . . . . he leaves room ahead of himself. He is no irresolute or suspicious lover . . . he is sure . . . he scorns intervals. His experience and the showers and thrills are not for nothing. Nothing can jar him . . . . suffering and darkness cannot—death and fear cannot. To him complaint and jealousy and envy are corpses buried and rotten in the earth . . . . he saw them buried. The sea is not surer of the shore or the shore of the sea than he is of the fruition of his love and of all perfection and beauty.

The fruition of beauty is no chance of hit or miss . . . it is inevitable as life . . . . it is exact and plumb as gravitation. From the eyesight proceeds another eyesight and from the hearing proceeds another hearing and from the voice proceeds another voice eternally curious of the harmony of things with man. To these respond perfections not only in the committees that were supposed to stand for the rest but in the rest themselves just the same. These understand the law of perfection in masses and floods . . . that its finish is to each for itself and onward from itself . . . that it is profuse and impartial . . . that there is not a minute of the light or dark nor an acre of the earth or sea without it—nor any direction of the sky nor any trade or employment nor any turn of events. This is the reason that about the proper expression of beauty there is precision and balance . . . one part does not need to be thrust above another. The best singer is not the one who has the most lithe and powerful organ[2] . . . the pleasure of

---

[1] *gaggery* Deceit; *gilt* Thin layer of gold.

[2] *organ* I.e., organ of singing; voice.

poems is not in them that take the handsomest measure and similes and sound.

Without effort and without exposing in the least how it is done the greatest poet brings the spirit of any or all events and passions and scenes and persons some more and some less to bear on your individual character as you hear or read. To do this well is to compete with the laws that pursue and follow time. What is the purpose must surely be there and the clue of it must be there . . . . and the faintest indication is the indication of the best and then becomes the clearest indication. Past and present and future are not disjoined but joined. The greatest poet forms the consistence of what is to be from what has been and is. He drags the dead out of their coffins and stands them again on their feet . . . . he says to the past, Rise and walk before me that I may realize you. He learns the lesson . . . . he places himself where the future becomes present. The greatest poet does not only dazzle his rays over character and scenes and passions . . . he finally ascends and finishes all . . . he exhibits the pinnacles that no man can tell what they are for or what is beyond . . . . he glows a moment on the extremest verge. He is most wonderful in his last half-hidden smile or frown . . . by that flash of the moment of parting the one that sees it shall be encouraged or terrified afterward for many years. The greatest poet does not moralize or make applications of morals . . . . he knows the soul. The soul has that measureless pride which consists in never acknowledging any lessons but its own. But it has sympathy as measureless as its pride and the one balances the other and neither can stretch too far while it stretches in company with the other. The inmost secrets of art sleep with the twain. The greatest poet has lain close betwixt both and they are vital in his style and thoughts.

The art of art, the glory of expression and the sunshine of the light of letters is simplicity. Nothing is better than simplicity . . . . nothing can make up for excess or for the lack of definiteness. To carry on the heave of impulse and pierce intellectual depths and give all subjects their articulations are powers neither common nor very uncommon. But to speak in literature with the perfect rectitude and insousiance[1] of the movements of animals and the unimpeachableness of the sentiment of trees in the woods and grass by

the roadside is the flawless triumph of art. If you have looked on him who has achieved it you have looked on one of the masters of the artists of all nations and times. You shall not contemplate the flight of the graygull over the bay or the mettlesome[2] action of the blood horse or the tall leaning of sunflowers on their stalk or the appearance of the sun journeying through heaven or the appearance of the moon afterward with any more satisfaction than you shall contemplate him. The greatest poet has less a marked style and is more the channel of thoughts and things without increase or diminution, and is the free channel of himself. He swears to his art, I will not be meddlesome, I will not have in my writing any elegance or effect or originality to hang in the way between me and the rest like curtains. I will have nothing hang in the way, not the richest curtains. What I tell I tell for precisely what it is. Let who may exalt or startle or fascinate or sooth I will have purposes as health or heat or snow has and be as regardless of observation. What I experience or portray shall go from my composition without a shred of my composition. You shall stand by my side and look in the mirror with me.

The old red blood and stainless gentility of great poets will be proved by their unconstraint. A heroic person walks at his ease through and out of that custom or precedent or authority that suits him not. Of the traits of the brotherhood of writers savans[3] musicians inventors and artists nothing is finer than silent defiance advancing from new free forms. In the need of poems philosophy politics mechanism science behaviour, the craft of art, an appropriate native grand-opera, shipcraft, or any craft, he is greatest forever and forever who contributes the greatest original practical example. The cleanest expression is that which finds no sphere worthy of itself and makes one.

The messages of great poets to each man and woman are, Come to us on equal terms, Only then can you understand us, We are no better than you, What we enclose you enclose, What we enjoy you may enjoy. Did you suppose there could be only one Supreme? We affirm there can be unnumbered Supremes, and that one does not countervail another any more than one eyesight countervails another . . and that men

---

[1]   *insousiance* Indifference.

[2]   *mettlesome* Spirited or playful.

[3]   *savans* Learned people (savants).

can be good or grand only of the consciousness of their supremacy within them. What do you think is the grandeur of storms and dismemberments and the deadliest battles and wrecks and the wildest fury of the elements and the power of the sea and the motion of nature and of the throes of human desires and dignity and hate and love? It is that something in the soul which says, Rage on, Whirl on, I tread master here and everywhere, Master of the spasms of the sky and of the shatter of the sea, Master of nature and passion and death, And of all terror and all pain.

The American bards shall be marked for generosity and affection and for encouraging competitors . . They shall be kosmos . . without monopoly or secrecy . . glad to pass any thing to any one . . hungry for equals night and day. They shall not be careful of riches and privilege . . . . they shall be riches and privilege . . . . they shall perceive who the most affluent man is. The most affluent man is he that confronts all the shows he sees by equivalents out of the stronger wealth of himself. The American bard shall delineate no class of persons nor one or two out of the strata of interests nor love most nor truth most nor the soul most nor the body most . . . . and not be for the eastern states more than the western or the northern states more than the southern.

Exact science and its practical movements are no checks on the greatest poet but always his encouragement and support. The outset and remembrance are there . . there the arms that lifted him first and brace him best . . . . there he returns after all his goings and comings. The sailor and traveler . . the anatomist chemist astronomer geologist phrenologist[1] spiritualist mathematician historian and lexicographer[2] are not poets, but they are the lawgivers of poets and their construction underlies the structure of every perfect poem. No matter what rises or is uttered they sent the seed of the conception of it . . . of them and by them stand the visible proofs of souls . . . . . always of their fatherstuff must be begotten the sinewy races of bards. If there shall be love and content between the father and the son and if the greatness of the son is the exuding of the greatness of the father there shall be love between the poet and the man of demonstrable science. In the beauty of poems are the tuft and final applause of science.

Great is the faith of the flush of knowledge and of the investigation of the depths of qualities and things. Cleaving and circling here swells the soul of the poet yet it [is] president of itself always. The depths are fathomless and therefore calm. The innocence and nakedness are resumed . . . they are neither modest nor immodest. The whole theory of the special and supernatural and all that was twined with it or educed out of it departs as a dream. What has ever happened . . . . what happens and whatever may or shall happen, the vital laws enclose all . . . . they are sufficient for any case and for all cases . . . none to be hurried or retarded . . . . any miracle of affairs or persons inadmissible in the vast clear scheme where every motion and every spear of grass and the frames and spirits of men and women and all that concerns them are unspeakably perfect miracles all referring to all and each distinct and in its place. It is also not consistent with the reality of the soul to admit that there is anything in the known universe more divine than men and women.

Men and women and the earth and all upon it are simply to be taken as they are, and the investigation of their past and present and future shall be unintermitted and shall be done with perfect candor. Upon this basis philosophy speculates ever looking toward the poet, ever regarding the eternal tendencies of all toward happiness never inconsistent with what is clear to the senses and to the soul. For the eternal tendencies of all toward happiness make the only point of sane philosophy. Whatever comprehends less than that . . . whatever is less than the laws of light and of astronomical motion . . . or less than the laws that follow the thief the liar the glutton and the drunkard through this life and doubtless afterward . . . . . . or less than vast stretches of time or the slow formation of density or the patient upheaving of strata—is of no account. Whatever would put God in a poem or system of philosophy as contending against some being or influence is also of no account. Sanity and ensemble characterise the great master . . . spoilt in one principle all is spoilt. The great master has nothing to do with miracles. He

---

[1]   *phrenologist* One who practices the pseudoscience phrenology, according to which the shape of an individual's head is indicative of certain personality traits; phrenology was very influential in the nineteenth century and was a subject of fascination to Whitman.

[2]   *lexicographer* Compiler of dictionaries.

sees health for himself in being one of the mass . . . . he sees the hiatus in singular eminence. To the perfect shape comes common ground. To be under the general law is great for that is to correspond with it. The master knows that he is unspeakably great and that all are unspeakably great . . . . that nothing for instance is greater than to conceive children and bring them up well . . . that to be is just as great as to perceive or tell.

In the make of the great masters the idea of political liberty is indispensible. Liberty takes the adherence of heroes wherever men and women exist . . . . but never takes any adherence or welcome from the rest more than from poets. They are the voice and exposition of liberty. They out of ages are worthy the grand idea . . . . to them it is confided and they must sustain it. Nothing has precedence of it and nothing can warp or degrade it. The attitude of great poets is to cheer up slaves and horrify despots. The turn of their necks, the sound of their feet, the motions of their wrists, are full of hazard to the one and hope to the other. Come nigh them awhile and though they neither speak or advise you shall learn the faithful American lesson. Liberty is poorly served by men whose good intent is quelled from one failure or two failures or any number of failures, or from the casual indifference or ingratitude of the people, or from the sharp show of the tushes[1] of power, or the bringing to bear soldiers and cannon or any penal statutes. Liberty relies upon itself, invites no one, promises nothing, sits in calmness and light, is positive and composed, and knows no discouragement. The battle rages with many a loud alarm and frequent advance and retreat . . . . the enemy triumphs . . . . the prison, the handcuffs, the iron necklace and anklet, the scaffold, garrote[2] and leadballs do their work . . . . the cause is asleep . . . . the strong throats are choked with their own blood . . . . the young men drop their eyelashes toward the ground when they pass each other . . . . and is liberty gone out of that place? No never. When liberty goes it is not the first to go nor the second or third to go . . it waits for all the rest to go . . it is the last. . . When the memories of the old martyrs are faded utterly away . . . . when the large names of patriots are laughed at in the public halls from the lips of the orators . . . . when the boys are no more christened after the same but christened after tyrants and traitors instead . . . . when the laws of the free are grudgingly permitted and laws for informers and bloodmoney are sweet to the taste of the people . . . . when I and you walk abroad upon the earth stung with compassion at the sight of numberless brothers answering our equal friendship and calling no man master—and when we are elated with noble joy at the sight of slaves . . . . when the soul retires in the cool communion of the night and surveys its experience and has much extasy over the word and deed that put back a helpless innocent person into the gripe of the gripers or into any cruel inferiority . . . . when those in all parts of these states who could easier realize the true American character but do not yet—when the swarms of cringers, suckers, doughfaces,[3] lice of politics, planners of sly involutions for their own preferment to city offices or state legislatures or the judiciary or congress or the presidency, obtain a response of love and natural deference from the people whether they get the offices or no . . . . when it is better to be a bound booby and rogue in office at a high salary than the poorest free mechanic or farmer with his hat unmoved from his head and firm eyes and a candid and generous heart . . . . and when servility by town or state or the federal government or any oppression on a large scale or small scale can be tried on without its own punishment following duly after in exact proportion against the smallest chance of escape . . . . or rather when all life and all the souls of men and women are discharged from any part of the earth—then only shall the instinct of liberty be discharged from that part of the earth.

As the attributes of the poets of the kosmos concentre[4] in the real body and soul and in the pleasure of things they possess the superiority of genuineness over all fiction and romance. As they emit themselves facts are showered over with light . . . . the daylight is lit with more volatile light . . . . also the deep between the setting and rising sun goes deeper many fold. Each precise object or condition or combination or process

[1] *tushes* Dismissive exclamations that express contempt or disapproval.

[2] *garrote* Implement for execution via strangulation.

[3] *doughfaces* Politicians who are overly willing to be led by the ideas or interests of others; at this period, the term often referred in particular to Northerners who were seen as being overly sympathetic with the South in political matters.

[4] *concentre* Concentrate.

exhibits a beauty . . . . the multiplication table its—old age its—the carpenter's trade its—the grand-opera its . . . . the hugehulled cleanshaped New-York clipper at sea under steam or full sail gleams with unmatched beauty . . . . the American circles and large harmonies of government gleam with theirs . . . . and the commonest definite intentions and actions with theirs. The poets of the kosmos advance through all interpositions and coverings and turmoils and stratagems to first principles. They are of use . . . . they dissolve poverty from its need and riches from its conceit. You large proprietor they say shall not realize or perceive more than any one else. The owner of the library is not he who holds a legal title to it having bought and paid for it. Anyone and every one is owner of the library who can read the same through all the varieties of tongues and subjects and styles, and in whom they enter with ease and take residence and force toward paternity and maternity, and make supple and powerful and rich and large. . . . . These American states strong and healthy and accomplished shall receive no pleasure from violations of natural models and must not permit them. In paintings or mouldings or carvings in mineral or wood, or in the illustrations of books or newspapers, or in any comic or tragic prints, or in the patterns of woven stuffs or any thing to beautify rooms or furniture or costumes, or to put upon cornices or monuments or on the prows or sterns of ships, or to put anywhere before the human eye indoors or out, that which distorts honest shapes or which creates unearthly beings or places or contingencies is a nuisance and revolt. Of the human form especially it is so great it must never be made ridiculous. Of ornaments to a work nothing outre[1] can be allowed . . but those ornaments can be allowed that conform to the perfect facts of the open air and that flow out of the nature of the work and come irrepressibly from it and are necessary to the completion of the work. Most works are most beautiful without ornament. . . Exaggerations will be revenged in human physiology. Clean and vigorous children are jetted and conceived only in those communities where the models of natural forms are public every day. . . . . Great genius and the people of these states must never be demeaned to romances.

As soon as histories are properly told there is no more need of romances.

The great poets are also to be known by the absence in them of tricks and by the justification of perfect personal candor. Then folks echo a new cheap joy and a divine voice leaping from their brains: How beautiful is candor! All faults may be forgiven of him who has perfect candor. Henceforth let no man of us lie, for we have seen that openness wins the inner and outer world and that there is no single exception, and that never since our earth gathered itself in a mass have deceit or subterfuge or prevarication attracted its smallest particle or the faintest tinge of a shade—and that through the enveloping wealth and rank of a state or the whole republic of states a sneak or sly person shall be discovered and despised . . . . and that the soul has never been once fooled and never can be fooled . . . . and thrift without the loving nod of the soul is only a fœtid[2] puff . . . . and there never grew up in any of the continents of the globe nor upon any planet or satellite or star, nor upon the asteroids, nor in any part of ethereal space, nor in the midst of density, nor under the fluid wet of the sea, nor in that condition which precedes the birth of babes, nor at any time during the changes of life, nor in that condition that follows what we term death, nor in any stretch of abeyance or action afterward of vitality, nor in any process of formation or reformation anywhere, a being whose instinct hated the truth.

Extreme caution or prudence, the soundest organic health, large hope and comparison and fondness for women and children, large alimentiveness and destructiveness and causality,[3] with a perfect sense of the oneness of nature and the propriety of the same spirit applied to human affairs . . these are called up of the float[4] of the brain of the world to be parts of the greatest poet from his birth out of his mother's womb and from her birth out of her mother's. Caution seldom goes far enough. It has been thought that the prudent citizen was the citizen who applied himself to solid

---

[1]   *outre*   French: unusual, unorthodox, or extravagant.

[2]   *fœtid*   Rank, stinking.

[3]   *large alimentiveness . . . destructiveness . . . causality*   Phrenological terms that suggest pronounced development of certain personality traits: appetite for food, energy and self-preservation, and logical thinking (respectively).

[4]   *float*   For Whitman, the word "float" often suggests the life-giving cosmos before bodies take form and become matter.

gains and did well for himself and his family and completed a lawful life without debt or crime. The greatest poet sees and admits these economies as he sees the economies of food and sleep, but has higher notions of prudence than to think he gives much when he gives a few slight attentions at the latch of the gate. The premises of the prudence of life are not the hospitality of it or the ripeness and harvest of it. Beyond the independence of a little sum laid aside for burial-money, and of a few clapboards around and shingles overhead on a lot of American soil owned, and the easy dollars that supply the year's plain clothing and meals, the melancholy prudence of the abandonment of such a great being as a man is to the toss and pallor of years of moneymaking with all their scorching days and icy nights and all their stifling deceits and underhanded dodgings, or infinitessimals[1] of parlors, or shameless stuffing while others starve . . and all the loss of the bloom and odor of the earth and of the flowers and atmosphere and of the sea and of the true taste of the women and men you pass or have to do with in youth or middle age, and the issuing sickness and desperate revolt at the close of a life without elevation or naivete, and the ghastly chatter of a death without serenity or majesty, is the great fraud upon modern civilization and forethought, blotching the surface and system which civilization undeniably drafts, and moistening with tears the immense features it spreads and spreads with such velocity before the reached kisses of the soul . . . Still the right explanation remains to be made about prudence. The prudence of the mere wealth and respectability of the most esteemed life appears too faint for the eye to observe at all when little and large alike drop quietly aside at the thought of the prudence suitable for immortality. What is wisdom that fills the thinness of a year or seventy or eighty years to wisdom spaced out by ages and coming back at a certain time with strong reinforcements and rich presents and the clear faces of wedding-guests as far as you can look in every direction running gaily toward you? Only the soul is of itself . . . . all else has reference to what ensues. All that a person does or thinks is of consequence. Not a move can a man or woman make that affects him or her in a day or a month or any part of the direct lifetime or the hour of death but the same affects him or her onward

afterward through the indirect lifetime. The indirect is always as great and real as the direct. The spirit receives from the body just as much as it gives to the body. Not one name of word or deed . . not of venereal sores[2] or discolorations . . not the privacy of the onanist[3] . . not of the putrid veins of gluttons or rumdrinkers . . . not peculation[4] or cunning or betrayal or murder . . no serpentine poison of those that seduce women . . not the foolish yielding of women . . not prostitution . . not of any depravity of young men . . not of the attainment of gain by discreditable means . . not any nastiness of appetite . . not any harshness of officers to men or judges to prisoners or fathers to sons or sons to fathers or of husbands to wives or bosses to their boys . . not of greedy looks or malignant wishes . . . nor any of the wiles practised by people upon themselves . . . ever is or ever can be stamped on the programme but it is duly realized and returned, and that returned in further performances . . . and they returned again. Nor can the push of charity or personal force ever be any thing else than the profoundest reason, whether it bring arguments to hand or no. No specification is necessary . . to add or subtract or divide is in vain. Little or big, learned or unlearned, white or black, legal or illegal, sick or well, from the first inspiration down the windpipe to the last expiration out of it, all that a male or female does that is vigorous and benevolent and clean is so much sure profit to him or her in the unshakable order of the universe and through the whole scope of it forever. If the savage or felon is wise it is well . . . . if the greatest poet or savan is wise it is simply the same . . if the President or chief justice is wise it is the same . . . if the young mechanic or farmer is wise it is no more or less . . if the prostitute is wise it is no more nor less. The interest will come round . . all will come round. All the best actions of war and peace . . . all help given to relatives and strangers and the poor and old and sorrowful and young children and widows and the sick, and to all shunned persons . . all furtherance of fugitives and of the escape of slaves . . all the self-denial that stood steady and aloof on wrecks and saw others take the seats of the boats . . .

---

[2] *venereal sores* I.e., sores arising from a sexually transmitted infection, here most likely referring to syphilis.

[3] *onanist* Masturbator.

[4] *peculation* Embezzlement.

---

[1] *infinitessimals* Minutiae, trivialities.

all offering of substance or life for the good old cause, or for a friend's sake or opinion's sake . . . all pains of enthusiasts scoffed at by their neighbors . . all the vast sweet love and precious suffering of mothers . . . all honest men baffled in strifes recorded or unrecorded . . . . all the grandeur and good of the few ancient nations whose fragments of annals we inherit . . and all the good of the hundreds of far mightier and more ancient nations unknown to us by name or date or location . . . . all that was ever manfully begun, whether it succeeded or no . . . . all that has at any time been well suggested out of the divine heart of man or by the divinity of his mouth or by the shaping of his great hands . . and all that is well thought or done this day on any part of the surface of the globe . . or on any of the wandering stars[1] or fixed stars by those there as we are here . . or that is henceforth to be well thought or done by you whoever you are, or by any one—these singly and wholly inured at their time and inure now and will inure always to the identities from which they sprung or shall spring . . . Did you guess any of them lived only its moment? The world does not so exist . . no parts palpable or impalpable so exist . . . no result exists now without being from its long antecedent result, and that from its antecedent, and so backward without the farthest mentionable spot coming a bit nearer the beginning than any other spot. . . . . Whatever satisfies the soul is truth. The prudence of the greatest poet answers at last the craving and glut of the soul, is not contemptuous of less ways of prudence if they conform to its ways, puts off nothing, permits no let-up for its own case or any case, has no particular sabbath or judgment-day, divides not the living from the dead or the righteous from the unrighteous, is satisfied with the present, matches every thought or act by its correlative, knows no possible forgiveness or deputed atonement . . knows that the young man who composedly periled his life and lost it has done exceeding well for himself, while the man who has not periled his life and retains it to old age in riches and ease has perhaps achieved nothing for himself worth mentioning . . and that only that person has no great prudence to learn who has learnt to prefer real longlived things, and favors body and soul the same, and perceives the indirect assuredly

following the direct, and what evil or good he does leaping onward and waiting to meet him again—and who in his spirit in any emergency whatever neither hurries or avoids death.

The direct trial of him who would be the greatest poet is today. If he does not flood himself with the immediate age as with vast oceanic tides . . . . . and if he does not attract his own land body and soul to himself and hang on its neck with incomparable love and plunge his semitic muscle[2] into its merits and demerits . . . and if he be not himself the age transfigured . . . . and if to him is not opened the eternity which gives similitude to all periods and locations and processes and animate and inanimate forms, and which is the bond of time, and rises up from its inconceivable vagueness and infiniteness in the swimming shape of today, and is held by the ductile anchors of life, and makes the present spot the passage from what was to what shall be, and commits itself to the representation of this wave of an hour and this one of the sixty beautiful children of the wave—let him merge in the general run and wait his developement . . . . Still the final test of poems or any character or work remains. The prescient poet projects himself centuries ahead and judges performer or performance after the changes of time. Does it live through them? Does it still hold on untired? Will the same style and the direction of genius to similar points be satisfactory now? Has no new discovery in science or arrival at superior planes of thought and judgment and behaviour fixed him or his so that either can be looked down upon? Have the marches of tens and hundreds and thousands of years made willing detours to the right hand and the left hand for his sake? Is he beloved long and long after he is buried? Does the young man think often of him? and the young woman think often of him? and do the middleaged and the old think of him?

A great poem is for ages and ages in common and for all degrees and complexions and all departments and sects and for a woman as much as a man and a man as much as a woman. A great poem is no finish to a man or woman but rather a beginning. Has any one fancied he could sit at last under some due authority and rest

---

[1]   *wandering stars* I.e., the planets, which, unlike the immobile "fixed stars," change their positions in the night sky.

[2]   *semitic muscle* I.e., penis; in a later version of "A Woman Waits for Me," which also uses this phrase, Whitman corrects "semitic" to "seminal."

satisfied with explanations and realize and be content and full? To no such terminus does the greatest poet bring . . . he brings neither cessation or sheltered fatness and ease. The touch of him tells in action. Whom he takes he takes with firm sure grasp into live regions previously unattained . . . . thenceforward is no rest . . . . they see the space and ineffable sheen that turn the old spots and lights into dead vacuums. The companion of him beholds the birth and progress of stars and learns one of the meanings. Now there shall be a man cohered out of tumult and chaos . . . . the elder encourages the younger and shows him how . . . they two shall launch off fearlessly together till the new world fits an orbit for itself and looks unabashed on the lesser orbits of the stars and sweeps through the ceaseless rings and shall never be quiet again.

There will soon be no more priests. Their work is done. They may wait awhile . . perhaps a generation or two . . dropping off by degrees. A superior breed shall take their place . . . . the gangs of kosmos and prophets en masse shall take their place. A new order shall arise and they shall be the priests of man, and every man shall be his own priest. The churches built under their umbrage shall be the churches of men and women. Through the divinity of themselves shall the kosmos and the new breed of poets be interpreters of men and women and of all events and things. They shall find their inspiration in real objects today, symptoms of the past and future . . . . They shall not deign to defend immortality or God or the perfection of things or liberty or the exquisite beauty and reality of the soul. They shall arise in America and be responded to from the remainder of the earth.

The English language befriends the grand American expression . . . . it is brawny enough and limber and full enough. On the tough stock of a race who through all change of circumstance was never without the idea of political liberty, which is the animus[1] of all liberty, it has attracted the terms of daintier and gayer and subtler and more elegant tongues. It is the powerful language of resistance . . . it is the dialect of common sense. It is the speech of the proud and melancholy races and of all who aspire. It is the chosen tongue to express growth faith self-esteem freedom justice equality friendliness amplitude prudence decision and courage. It is the medium that shall well nigh express the inexpressible.

No great literature nor any like style of behaviour or oratory or social intercourse or household arrangements or public institutions or the treatment by bosses of employed people, nor executive detail or detail of the army or navy, nor spirit of legislation or courts or police or tuition or architecture or songs or amusements or the costumes of young men, can long elude the jealous and passionate instinct of American standards. Whether or no the sign appears from the mouths of the people, it throbs a live interrogation in every freeman's and freewoman's heart after that which passes by or this built to remain. Is it uniform with my country? Are its disposals without ignominious distinctions? Is it for the evergrowing communes of brothers and lovers, large, well-united, proud beyond the old models, generous beyond all models? Is it something grown fresh out of the fields or drawn from the sea for use to me today here? I know that what answers for me an American must answer for any individual or nation that serves for a part of my materials. Does this answer? or is it without reference to universal needs? or sprung of the needs of the less developed society of special ranks? or old needs of pleasure overlaid by modern science and forms? Does this acknowledge liberty with audible and absolute acknowledgement, and set slavery at nought for life and death? Will it help breed one goodshaped and wellhung man, and a woman to be his perfect and independent mate? Does it improve manners? Is it for the nursing of the young of the republic? Does it solve readily with the sweet milk of the nipples of the breasts of the mother of many children? Has it too the old ever-fresh forbearance and impartiality? Does it look with the same love on the last born and on those hardening toward stature, and on the errant, and on those who disdain all strength of assault outside of their own?

The poems distilled from other poems will probably pass away. The coward will surely pass away. The expectation of the vital and great can only be satisfied by the demeanor of the vital and great. The swarms of the polished deprecating and reflectors and the polite float off and leave no remembrance. America prepares with composure and goodwill for the visitors that have sent

---

1 *animus* Motivating impulse.

word. It is not intellect that is to be their warrant[1] and welcome. The talented, the artist, the ingenious, the editor, the statesman, the erudite . . they are not unappreciated . . they fall in their place and do their work. The soul of the nation also does its work. No disguise can pass on it . . no disguise can conceal from it. It rejects none, it permits all. Only toward as good as itself and toward the like of itself will it advance halfway. An individual is as superb as a nation when he has the qualities which make a superb nation. The soul of the largest and wealthiest and proudest nation may well go half-way to meet that of its poets. The signs are effectual. There is no fear of mistake. If the one is true the other is true. The proof of a poet is that his country absorbs him as affectionately as he has absorbed it.
—1855

from *1855 Leaves of Grass* [*Song of Myself*]

[1]   I celebrate myself,
      And what I assume you shall assume,
      For every atom belonging to me as good belongs to you.

      I loafe and invite my soul,
5   I lean and loafe at my ease . . . . observing a spear of summer grass.

[2]   Houses and rooms are full of perfumes . . . . the shelves are crowded with perfumes,
      I breathe the fragrance myself, and know it and like it,
      The distillation would intoxicate me also, but I shall not let it.

      The atmosphere is not a perfume . . . . it has no taste of the distillation . . . . it is odorless,
10   It is for my mouth forever . . . . I am in love with it,
      I will go to the bank by the wood and become undisguised and naked,
      I am mad for it to be in contact with me.

      The smoke of my own breath,
      Echos, ripples, and buzzed whispers . . . . loveroot,[2] silkthread, crotch and vine,
15   My respiration and inspiration . . . . the beating of my heart . . . . the passing of blood and air
          through my lungs,
      The sniff of green leaves and dry leaves, and of the shore and darkcolored sea-rocks, and of
          hay in the barn,
      The sound of the belched words of my voice . . . . words loosed to the eddies of the wind,
      A few light kisses . . . . a few embraces . . . . a reaching around of arms,
      The play of shine and shade on the trees as the supple boughs wag,
20   The delight alone or in the rush of the streets, or along the fields and hillsides,
      The feeling of health . . . . the full-noon trill . . . . the song of me rising from bed and meet-
          ing the sun.

---

1   *warrant* Guarantee.
2   *loveroot* White wildflower of the American Southwest.

Have you reckoned a thousand acres much? Have you reckoned the earth much?
Have you practiced so long to learn to read?
Have you felt so proud to get at the meaning of poems?

25 Stop this day and night with me and you shall possess the origin of all poems,
You shall possess the good of the earth and sun . . . . there are millions of suns left,
You shall no longer take things at second or third hand . . . . nor look through the eyes of the
      dead . . . . nor feed on the spectres in books,
You shall not look through my eyes either, nor take things from me,
You shall listen to all sides and filter them from yourself.

[3] I have heard what the talkers were talking . . . . the talk of the beginning and the end,
But I do not talk of the beginning or the end.

There was never any more inception than there is now,
Nor any more youth or age than there is now;
And will never be any more perfection than there is now,
35 Nor any more heaven or hell than there is now.

Urge and urge and urge,
Always the procreant urge of the world.

Out of the dimness opposite equals advance . . . . Always substance and increase,
Always a knit of identity . . . . always distinction . . . . always a breed of life.

40 To elaborate is no avail . . . . Learned and unlearned feel that it is so.

Sure as the most certain sure . . . . plumb in the uprights, well entretied,[1] braced in the beams,
Stout as a horse, affectionate, haughty, electrical,
I and this mystery here we stand.

Clear and sweet is my soul . . . . and clear and sweet is all that is not my soul.

45 Lack one lacks both . . . . and the unseen is proved by the seen,
Till that becomes unseen and receives proof in its turn.

Showing the best and dividing it from the worst, age vexes age,
Knowing the perfect fitness and equanimity of things, while they discuss I am silent, and go
      bathe and admire myself.

Welcome is every organ and attribute of me, and of any man hearty and clean,
50 Not an inch nor a particle of an inch is vile, and none shall be less familiar than the rest.

I am satisfied . . . . I see, dance, laugh, sing;
As God comes a loving bedfellow and sleeps at my side all night and close on the peep of the
      day,

_____

1 *entretied* Plastered.

And leaves for me baskets covered with white towels bulging the house with their plenty,
Shall I postpone my acceptation and realization and scream at my eyes,
55   That they turn from gazing after and down the road,
And forthwith cipher[1] and show me to a cent,
Exactly the contents of one, and exactly the contents of two, and which is ahead?

[4]   Trippers and askers surround me,
People I meet . . . . . the effect upon me of my early life . . . . of the ward and city I live in . . . .
   of the nation,
60   The latest news . . . . discoveries, inventions, societies . . . . authors old and new,
My dinner, dress, associates, looks, business, compliments, dues,
The real or fancied indifference of some man or woman I love,
The sickness of one of my folks—or of myself . . . . or ill-doing . . . . or loss or lack of money
   . . . . or depressions or exaltations,
They come to me days and nights and go from me again,
65   But they are not the Me myself.

Apart from the pulling and hauling stands what I am,
Stands amused, complacent, compassionating, idle, unitary,
Looks down, is erect, bends an arm on an impalpable certain rest,
Looks with its sidecurved head curious what will come next,
70   Both in and out of the game, and watching and wondering at it.

Backward I see in my own days where I sweated through fog with linguists and contenders,
I have no mockings or arguments . . . . I witness and wait.

[5]   I believe in you my soul . . . . the other I am must not abase itself to you,
And you must not be abased to the other.

75   Loafe with me on the grass . . . . loose the stop from your throat,
Not words, not music or rhyme I want . . . . not custom or lecture, not even the best,
Only the lull I like, the hum of your valved voice.

I mind how we lay in June, such a transparent summer morning;
You settled your head athwart my hips and gently turned over upon me,
80   And parted the shirt from my bosom-bone, and plunged your tongue to my barestript heart,
And reached till you felt my beard, and reached till you held my feet.

Swiftly arose and spread around me the peace and joy and knowledge that pass all the art and
   argument of the earth;[2]
And I know that the hand of God is the elderhand[3] of my own,
And I know that the spirit of God is the eldest brother of my own,

---

[1]   *cipher* Calculate.

[2]   *peace … earth* See Philippians 4.7: "And the peace of God, which passeth all understanding, shall keep your hearts and minds through Jesus Christ."

[3]   *elderhand* Guiding hand, pattern; in card-playing, the "elder hand" is a term used for the first player.

85 And that all the men ever born are also my brothers .... and the women my sisters and
    lovers,
And that a kelson¹ of the creation is love;
And limitless are leaves stiff or drooping in the fields,
And brown ants in the little wells beneath them,
And mossy scabs of the wormfence,² and heaped stones, and elder and mullen³ and pokeweed.

[6] A child said, What is the grass? fetching it to me with full hands;
How could I answer the child? .... I do not know what it is any more than he.

I guess it must be the flag of my disposition, out of hopeful green stuff woven.

Or I guess it is the handkerchief of the Lord,
A scented gift and remembrancer designedly dropped,
95 Bearing the owner's name someway in the corners,⁴ that we may see and remark, and say
    Whose?

Or I guess the grass is itself a child .... the produced babe of the vegetation.

Or I guess it is a uniform hieroglyphic,
And it means, Sprouting alike in broad zones and narrow zones,
Growing among black folks as among white,
100 Kanuck, Tuckahoe, Congressman, Cuff,⁵ I give them the same, I receive them the same.

And now it seems to me the beautiful uncut hair of graves.

Tenderly will I use you curling grass,
It may be you transpire from the breasts of young men,
It may be if I had known them I would have loved them;
105 It may be you are from old people and from women, and from offspring taken soon out of
    their mothers' laps,
And here you are the mothers' laps.

This grass is very dark to be from the white heads of old mothers,
Darker than the colorless beards of old men,
Dark to come from under the faint red roofs of mouths.

110 O I perceive after all so many uttering tongues!
And I perceive they do not come from the roofs of mouths for nothing.

---

¹ *kelson* Foundational piece of a ship's structure: the timber that connects the keel and the floor-timbers together.

² *wormfence* Also known as a "snake-fence," a rough fence made with rails put together in a zigzag pattern.

³ *mullen* I.e., mullein plants, which grow along roadsides and in empty fields (as do elderberries and pokeweed).

⁴ *designedly ... corners* I.e., a handkerchief dropped on purpose as a gift or love-token, with the owner's initials embroidered on one of the corners.

⁵ *Kanuck* American slang term for a French Canadian; *Tuckahoe* Person living in Lower Virginia; *Cuff* Slang term, often derogatory, for an African American.

I wish I could translate the hints about the dead young men and women,
And the hints about old men and mothers, and the offspring taken soon out of their laps.

What do you think has become of the young and old men?
115   And what do you think has become of the women and children?

They are alive and well somewhere;
The smallest sprout shows there is really no death,
And if ever there was it led forward life, and does not wait at the end to arrest it,
And ceased the moment life appeared.

120   All goes onward and outward . . . . and nothing collapses,
And to die is different from what any one supposed, and luckier.

[7]   Has any one supposed it lucky to be born?
I hasten to inform him or her it is just as lucky to die, and I know it.

I pass death with the dying, and birth with the new-washed babe . . . . and am not contained
        between my hat and boots,
125   And peruse manifold objects, no two alike, and every one good,
The earth good, and the stars good, and their adjuncts all good.

I am not an earth nor an adjunct of an earth,
I am the mate and companion of people, all just as immortal and fathomless as myself;
They do not know how immortal, but I know.

130   Every kind for itself and its own . . . . for me mine male and female,
For me all that have been boys and that love women,
For me the man that is proud and feels how it stings to be slighted,
For me the sweetheart and the old maid . . . . for me mothers and the mothers of mothers,
For me lips that have smiled, eyes that have shed tears,
135   For me children and the begetters of children.

Who need be afraid of the merge?
Undrape . . . . you are not guilty to me, nor stale nor discarded,
I see through the broadcloth and gingham[1] whether or no,
And am around, tenacious, acquisitive, tireless . . . . and can never be shaken away.

[8]   The little one sleeps in its cradle,
I lift the gauze and look a long time, and silently brush away flies with my hand.

The youngster and the redfaced girl turn aside up the bushy hill,
I peeringly view them from the top.

---

1   *broadcloth* Fine wool fabric, often used for men's jackets and trousers; *gingham* Checked cotton fabric, commonly used for dresses, aprons, and shirts.

The suicide sprawls on the bloody floor of the bedroom,
145 It is so . . . . I witnessed the corpse . . . . there the pistol had fallen.

The blab of the pave . . . . the tires of carts and sluff of bootsoles and talk of the promenaders,
The heavy omnibus,[1] the driver with his interrogating thumb, the clank of the shod horses on
    the granite floor,
The carnival of sleighs, the clinking and shouted jokes and pelts of snowballs;
The hurrahs for popular favorites . . . . the fury of roused mobs,
150 The flap of the curtained litter[2]—the sick man inside, borne to the hospital,
The meeting of enemies, the sudden oath,[3] the blows and fall,
The excited crowd—the policeman with his star quickly working his passage to the centre of
    the crowd;
The impassive stones that receive and return so many echoes,
The souls moving along . . . . are they invisible while the least atom of the stones is visible?
155 What groans of overfed or half-starved who fall on the flags sunstruck or in fits,
What exclamations of women taken suddenly, who hurry home and give birth to babes,
What living and buried speech is always vibrating here . . . . what howls restrained by
    decorum,
Arrests of criminals, slights, adulterous offers made, acceptances, rejections with convex lips,
I mind them or the resonance of them . . . . I come again and again.

[9] The big doors of the country-barn stand open and ready,
The dried grass of the harvest-time loads the slow-drawn wagon,
The clear light plays on the brown gray and green intertinged,
The armfuls are packed to the sagging mow:[4]
I am there . . . . I help . . . . I came stretched atop of the load,
165 I felt its soft jolts . . . . one leg reclined on the other,
I jump from the crossbeams, and seize the clover and timothy,[5]
And roll head over heels, and tangle my hair full of wisps.

[10] Alone far in the wilds and mountains I hunt,
Wandering amazed at my own lightness and glee,
170 In the late afternoon choosing a safe spot to pass the night,
Kindling a fire and broiling the freshkilled game,
Soundly falling asleep on the gathered leaves, my dog and gun by my side.

The Yankee clipper is under her three skysails . . . . she cuts the sparkle and scud,[6]
My eyes settle the land . . . . I bend at her prow or shout joyously from the deck.

---

1 *omnibus* Bus.

2 *litter* Frame supporting a couch or bed; used to carry a sick person from one place to another.

3 *oath* Utterance of an expletive; swearing.

4 *mow* Place where hay is stacked in the barn.

5 *timothy* Timothy grass, a popular cultivar for hay.

6 *clipper* Fast sailing ship, with a sharp bow; *skysails* Light sails located above the royal sails; *scud* Ocean
spray.

175   The boatmen and clamdiggers arose early and stopped for me,
       I tucked my trowser-ends in my boots and went and had a good time,
       You should have been with us that day round the chowder-kettle.

       I saw the marriage of the trapper in the open air in the far-west . . . . the bride was a red girl,
       Her father and his friends sat near by crosslegged and dumbly[1] smoking . . . . they had moc-
           casins to their feet and large thick blankets hanging from their shoulders;
180   On a bank lounged the trapper . . . . he was dressed mostly in skins . . . . his luxuriant beard
           and curls protected his neck,
       One hand rested on his rifle . . . . the other hand held firmly the wrist of the red girl,
       She had long eyelashes . . . . her head was bare . . . . her coarse straight locks descended upon
           her voluptuous limbs and reached to her feet.[2]

       The runaway slave came to my house and stopped outside,
       I heard his motions crackling the twigs of the woodpile,
185   Through the swung half-door of the kitchen I saw him limpsey[3] and weak,
       And went where he sat on a log, and led him in and assured him,
       And brought water and filled a tub for his sweated body and bruised feet,
       And gave him a room that entered from my own, and gave him some coarse clean clothes,
       And remember perfectly well his revolving eyes and his awkwardness,
190   And remember putting plasters on the galls[4] of his neck and ankles;
       He staid with me a week before he was recuperated and passed north,
       I had him sit next me at table . . . . my firelock[5] leaned in the corner.

[11]   Twenty-eight young men bathe by the shore,
       Twenty-eight young men, and all so friendly,
195   Twenty-eight years of womanly life, and all so lonesome.

       She owns the fine house by the rise of the bank,
       She hides handsome and richly drest aft[6] the blinds of the window.

       Which of the young men does she like the best?
       Ah the homeliest of them is beautiful to her.

200   Where are you off to, lady? for I see you,
       You splash in the water there, yet stay stock still in your room.

       Dancing and laughing along the beach came the twenty-ninth bather,
       The rest did not see her, but she saw them and loved them.

---

1   *dumbly*   Silently.

2   *I saw … her feet*   This passage describes the scene depicted in *The Trapper's Bride*, a painting by Alfred Jacob Miller
     (1810–74).

3   *limpsey*   Limp.

4   *plasters*   Bandages, dressings;   *galls*   Wounds caused by chafing.

5   *firelock*   Gun.

6   *aft*   Behind.

The beards of the young men glistened with wet, it ran from their long hair,
205   Little streams passed all over their bodies.

An unseen hand also passed over their bodies,
It descended tremblingly from their temples and ribs.

The young men float on their backs, their white bellies swell to the sun . . . . they do not ask who seizes fast to them,
They do not know who puffs and declines with pendant and bending arch,
210   They do not think whom they souse[1] with spray.

[12]   The butcher-boy puts off his killing-clothes, or sharpens his knife at the stall in the market,
I loiter enjoying his repartee and his shuffle and breakdown.[2]

Blacksmiths with grimed and hairy chests environ[3] the anvil,
Each has his main-sledge[4] . . . . they are all out . . . . there is a great heat in the fire.

215   From the cinder-strewed threshold I follow their movements,
The lithe sheer of their waists plays even with their massive arms,
Overhand the hammers roll—overhand so slow—overhand so sure,
They do not hasten, each man hits in his place.

[13]   The negro holds firmly the reins of his four horses . . . . the block swags underneath on its tied-over chain,
220   The negro that drives the huge dray of the stoneyard . . . . steady and tall he stands poised on one leg on the stringpiece,[5]
His blue shirt exposes his ample neck and breast and loosens over his hipband,
His glance is calm and commanding . . . . he tosses the slouch of his hat away from his forehead,
The sun falls on his crispy hair and moustache . . . . falls on the black of his polish'd and perfect limbs.

I behold the picturesque giant and love him . . . . and I do not stop there,
225   I go with the team also.

---

[1]   *souse* Soak.

[2]   *repartee* Clever and witty questions and replies; *shuffle* Slow, sliding dance; *breakdown* Riotous, exuberant dance. Both dances had origins in the folkdance traditions of African Americans, and had been adapted by white performers for use in popular entertainments—including blackface minstrel shows.

[3]   *environ* Surround.

[4]   *main-sledge* Large hammer used by blacksmiths.

[5]   *dray* Low cart used for carrying or dragging heavy loads; *stoneyard* Place where stone is cut; *stringpiece* Connecting piece of timber used in the framework of the cart.

In me the caresser of life wherever moving . . . . backward as well as forward slueing,[1]
To niches aside and junior bending.

Oxen that rattle the yoke or halt in the shade, what is that you express in your eyes?
It seems to me more than all the print I have read in my life.

230   My tread scares the wood-drake[2] and wood-duck on my distant and daylong ramble,
They rise together, they slowly circle around.
. . . . I believe in those winged purposes,
And acknowledge the red yellow and white playing within me,
And consider the green and violet and the tufted crown[3] intentional;
235   And do not call the tortoise unworthy because she is not something else,
And the mockingbird in the swamp never studied the gamut,[4] yet trills pretty well to me,
And the look of the bay mare shames silliness out of me.

[14]   The wild gander leads his flock through the cool night,
Ya-honk! he says, and sounds it down to me like an invitation;
240   The pert[5] may suppose it meaningless, but I listen closer,
I find its purpose and place up there toward the November sky.

The sharphoofed moose of the north, the cat on the housesill, the chickadee, the prairie-dog,
The litter of the grunting sow as they tug at her teats,
The brood of the turkeyhen, and she with her halfspread wings,
245   I see in them and myself the same old law.

The press of my foot to the earth springs a hundred affections,
They scorn the best I can do to relate them.

I am enamoured of growing outdoors,
Of men that live among cattle or taste of the ocean or woods,
250   Of the builders and steerers of ships, of the wielders of axes and mauls,[6] of the drivers of
horses,
I can eat and sleep with them week in and week out.

What is commonest and cheapest and nearest and easiest is Me,
Me going in for my chances, spending for vast returns,
Adorning myself to bestow myself on the first that will take me,
255   Not asking the sky to come down to my goodwill,
Scattering it freely forever.

---

[1]   *slueing*   Turning or twisting.

[2]   *wood-drake*   Male of the wood duck.

[3]   *red ... tufted crown*   The male wood duck has all these colors in his plumage, and he has tufted white feathers
flaring from his crown down his neck.

[4]   *gamut*   Complete series of notes in a formal musical scale.

[5]   *pert*   Saucy or impertinent person.

[6]   *mauls*   Sledgehammers.

[15]   The pure contralto sings in the organloft,

The carpenter dresses his plank . . . . the tongue of his foreplane[1] whistles its wild ascending lisp,

The married and unmarried children ride home to their thanksgiving dinner,

260   The pilot seizes the king-pin,[2] he heaves down with a strong arm,

The mate stands braced in the whaleboat, lance and harpoon are ready,

The duck-shooter walks by silent and cautious stretches,

The deacons are ordained with crossed hands at the altar,

The spinning-girl[3] retreats and advances to the hum of the big wheel,

265   The farmer stops by the bars of a Sunday and looks at the oats and rye,

The lunatic is carried at last to the asylum a confirmed case,

He will never sleep any more as he did in the cot in his mother's bedroom;

The jour printer with gray head and gaunt jaws works at his case,[4]

He turns his quid of tobacco,[5] his eyes get blurred with the manuscript;

270   The malformed limbs are tied to the anatomist's table,

What is removed drops horribly in a pail;

The quadroon[6] girl is sold at the stand . . . . the drunkard nods by the barroom stove,

The machinist rolls up his sleeves . . . . the policeman travels his beat . . . . the gate-keeper
        marks who pass,

The young fellow drives the express-wagon . . . . I love him though I do not know him;

275   The half-breed[7] straps on his light boots to compete in the race,

The western turkey-shooting draws old and young . . . . some lean on their rifles, some sit on
        logs,

Out from the crowd steps the marksman and takes his position and levels his piece;[8]

The groups of newly-come immigrants cover the wharf or levee,

The woollypates[9] hoe in the sugarfield, the overseer views them from his saddle;

280   The bugle calls in the ballroom, the gentlemen run for their partners, the dancers bow to
        each other;

The youth lies awake in the cedar-roofed garret and harks[10] to the musical rain,

The Wolverine sets traps on the creek that helps fill the Huron,[11]

The reformer ascends the platform, he spouts with his mouth and nose,

---

[1] *foreplane* Carpenter's tool used to smooth the wood after it has been cut.

[2] *pilot* Person who steers a ship; the navigator; *king-pin* Central bolt used to pivot an axle; in this context, the steering wheel of the ship's helm.

[3] *spinning-girl* I.e., girl at work making yarn or thread on a spinning wheel.

[4] *jour printer* Journeyman printer, one who has finished an apprenticeship but still works as the employee of someone else; *case* Tray divided into sections to hold printing type.

[5] *turns* Chews; *quid of tobacco* Lump of chewing tobacco.

[6] *quadroon* Term (now considered offensive) for a person who has three white grandparents and one black grandparent.

[7] *half-breed* Offensive term for a person of mixed ethnic origin (in the U.S., this term was usually applied to a person with one black or white parent and one Indigenous parent).

[8] *piece* Gun.

[9] *woollypates* I.e., wooly-haired, offensive term applied to African Americans.

[10] *harks* Listens.

[11] *Wolverine* Person from Michigan; *the Huron* Any one of three Huron rivers in Michigan or Lake Huron.

The company returns from its excursion, the darkey brings up the rear and bears the well-
    riddled[1] target,
285   The squaw[2] wrapt in her yellow-hemmed cloth is offering moccasins and beadbags for sale,
The connoisseur peers along the exhibition-gallery with halfshut eyes bent sideways,
The deckhands make fast the steamboat, the plank is thrown for the shoregoing passengers,
The young sister holds out the skein,[3] the elder sister winds it off in a ball and stops now and
    then for the knots,
The one-year wife is recovering and happy, a week ago she bore her first child,
290   The cleanhaired Yankee girl works with her sewing-machine or in the factory or mill,
The nine months' gone is in the parturition chamber,[4] her faintness and pains are advancing;
The pavingman leans on his twohanded rammer[5]—the reporter's lead[6] flies swiftly over the
    notebook—the signpainter is lettering with red and gold,
The canal-boy trots on the towpath[7]—the bookkeeper counts at his desk—the shoemaker
    waxes his thread,
The conductor beats time for the band and all the performers follow him,
295   The child is baptised—the convert is making the first professions,[8]
The regatta is spread on the bay . . . . how the white sails sparkle!
The drover watches his drove,[9] he sings out to them that would stray,
The pedlar sweats with his pack on his back—the purchaser higgles about the odd cent,
The camera and plate are prepared, the lady must sit for her daguerreotype,
300   The bride unrumples her white dress, the minutehand of the clock moves slowly,
The opium eater reclines with rigid head and just-opened lips,
The prostitute draggles her shawl, her bonnet bobs on her tipsy and pimpled neck,
The crowd laugh at her blackguard oaths,[10] the men jeer and wink to each other,
(Miserable! I do not laugh at your oaths nor jeer you,)
305   The President holds a cabinet council, he is surrounded by the great secretaries,
On the piazza walk five friendly matrons with twined arms;
The crew of the fish-smack[11] pack repeated layers of halibut in the hold,
The Missourian crosses the plains toting his wares and his cattle,
The fare-collector goes through the train—he gives notice by the jingling of loose change,
310   The floormen are laying the floor—the tinners are tinning the roof—the masons are calling
    for mortar,

---

1   *well-riddled*   Shot through (containing many bullet holes).

2   *squaw*   Offensive term for an Indigenous woman; while by this point it carried negative connotations, it was still
used frequently by English speakers, even by those who did not intend it derogatorily.

3   *skein*   Large coil of thread or yarn.

4   *parturition chamber*   Birthing room.

5   *rammer*   Instrument used to set paving stones.

6   *lead*   Pencil.

7   *towpath*   Path that runs alongside a canal.

8   *professions*   Statements of faith.

9   *drover*   Cattle dealer;   *drove*   Herd of cattle.

10   *blackguard oaths*   Coarse swearing.

11   *fish-smack*   Single-masted sailing ship used for fishing.

In single file each shouldering his hod[1] pass onward the laborers;

Seasons pursuing each other the indescribable crowd is gathered . . . . it is the Fourth of July
     . . . . what salutes of cannon and small arms!

Seasons pursuing each other the plougher ploughs and the mower mows and the wintergrain
     falls in the ground;

Off on the lakes the pikefisher watches and waits by the hole in the frozen surface,

315   The stumps stand thick round the clearing, the squatter[2] strikes deep with his axe,

The flatboatmen make fast toward dusk near the cottonwood or pekantrees,[3]

The coon-seekers go now through the regions of the Red river, or through those drained by
     the Tennessee, or through those of the Arkansas,

The torches shine in the dark that hangs on the Chattahoochee or Altamahaw;[4]

Patriarchs sit at supper with sons and grandsons and great grandsons around them,

320   In walls of abode,[5] in canvass tents, rest hunters and trappers after their day's sport.

The city sleeps and the country sleeps,

The living sleep for their time . . . . the dead sleep for their time,

The old husband sleeps by his wife and the young husband sleeps by his wife;

And these one and all tend inward to me, and I tend outward to them,

325   And such as it is to be of these more or less I am.

[16]   I am of old and young, of the foolish as much as the wise,

Regardless of others, ever regardful of others,

Maternal as well as paternal, a child as well as a man,

Stuffed with the stuff that is coarse, and stuffed with the stuff that is fine,

330   One of the great nation, the nation of many nations—the smallest the same and the largest
     the same,

A southerner soon as a northerner, a planter nonchalant and hospitable,

A Yankee bound my own way . . . . ready for trade . . . . my joints the limberest joints on
     earth and the sternest joints on earth,

A Kentuckian walking the vale of the Elkhorn in my deerskin leggings,

A boatman over the lakes or bays or along coasts . . . . a Hoosier, a Badger, a Buckeye,[6]

335   A Louisianian or Georgian, a poke-easy[7] from sandhills and pines,

At home on Canadian snowshoes or up in the bush, or with fishermen off Newfoundland,

At home in the fleet of iceboats, sailing with the rest and tacking,

At home on the hills of Vermont or in the woods of Maine or the Texan ranch,

Comrade of Californians . . . . comrade of free northwesterners, loving their big proportions,

340   Comrade of raftsmen and coalmen—comrade of all who shake hands and welcome to drink
     and meat;

---

1   *hod* Open container used to carry mortar or bricks.

2   *squatter* Settler with no formal title to the land, or a settler on land that the government has not yet surveyed.

3   *pekantrees* I.e., pecan trees, which grow in the southern United States, particularly near the Mississippi River.

4   *Chattahoochee* River that stretches from northern Georgia to the Florida panhandle; *Altamahaw* River that stretches from central to southeastern Georgia.

5   *abode* Whitman changed this to "adobe" in the 1856 edition of *Leaves of Grass*.

6   *Hoosier ... Badger ... Buckeye* Residents of Indiana, Wisconsin, and Ohio, respectively.

7   *poke-easy* Easy-going person that takes it slow (regional term used chiefly in the Southern U.S.).

A learner with the simplest, a teacher of the thoughtfulest,
A novice beginning experient¹ of myriads of seasons,
Of every hue and trade and rank, of every caste and religion,
Not merely of the New World but of Africa Europe or Asia . . . . a wandering savage,
345 A farmer, mechanic, or artist . . . . a gentleman, sailor, lover or quaker,²
A prisoner, fancy-man,³ rowdy, lawyer, physician or priest.

I resist anything better than my own diversity,
And breathe the air and leave plenty after me,
And am not stuck up, and am in my place.

350 The moth and the fisheggs are in their place,
The suns I see and the suns I cannot see are in their place,
The palpable is in its place and the impalpable is in its place.

[17] These are the thoughts of all men in all ages and lands, they are not original with me,
If they are not yours as much as mine they are nothing or next to nothing,
355 If they do not enclose everything they are next to nothing,
If they are not the riddle and the untying of the riddle they are nothing,
If they are not just as close as they are distant they are nothing.

This is the grass that grows wherever the land is and the water is,
This is the common air that bathes the globe.

[18] This is the breath of laws and songs and behaviour,
This is the tasteless water of souls . . . . this is the true sustenance,
It is for the illiterate . . . . it is for the judges of the supreme court . . . . it is for the federal
  capitol and the state capitols,
It is for the admirable communes of literary men and composers and singers and lecturers
  and engineers and savans,⁴
It is for the endless races of working people and farmers and seamen.

365 This is the trill of a thousand clear cornets and scream of the octave flute⁵ and strike of
  triangles.

I play not a march for victors only . . . . I play great marches for conquered and slain persons.

Have you heard that it was good to gain the day?
I also say it is good to fall . . . . battles are lost in the same spirit in which they are won.

---

1 *experient* Having knowledge of, experience in.

2 *quaker* One that trembles from love or from religious zeal; Whitman could also mean a Quaker, a member of the religious sect the Society of Friends.

3 *fancy-man* A sweetheart; alternatively, a man who lives on the earnings of a prostitute.

4 *savans* Learned people (savants).

5 *octave flute* Also known as a piccolo, a small flute that plays an octave higher than the typical flute.

I sound triumphal drums for the dead . . . . I fling through my embouchures[1] the loudest
    and gayest music to them,
370 Vivas[2] to those who have failed, and to those whose war-vessels sank in the sea, and those
    themselves who sank in the sea,
And to all generals that lost engagements, and all overcome heroes, and the numberless
    unknown heroes equal to the greatest heroes known.

[19] This is the meal pleasantly set . . . . this is the meat and drink for natural hunger,
It is for the wicked just the same as the righteous . . . . I make appointments with all,
I will not have a single person slighted or left away,
375 The keptwoman and sponger[3] and thief are hereby invited . . . . the heavy-lipped slave is
    invited . . . . the venerealee[4] is invited,
There shall be no difference between them and the rest.

This is the press of a bashful hand . . . . this is the float and odor of hair,
This is the touch of my lips to yours . . . . this is the murmur of yearning,
This is the far-off depth and height reflecting my own face,
380 This is the thoughtful merge of myself and the outlet again.

Do you guess I have some intricate purpose?
Well I have . . . . for the April rain has, and the mica on the side of a rock has.

Do you take it I would astonish?
Does the daylight astonish? or the early redstart[5] twittering through the woods?
385 Do I astonish more than they?

This hour I tell things in confidence,
I might not tell everybody but I will tell you.

[20] Who goes there! hankering, gross, mystical, nude?
How is it I extract strength from the beef I eat?

390 What is a man anyhow? What am I? and what are you?
All I mark as my own you shall offset it with your own,
Else it were time lost listening to me.

I do not snivel that snivel the world over,
That months are vacuums and the ground but wallow and filth,
395 That life is a suck and a sell, and nothing remains at the end but threadbare crape[6] and tears.

---

[1] *embouchures*   In music, the part of the instrument that touches the mouth of the player.

[2] *Vivas*   Cheers of applause.

[3] *keptwoman*   Woman who is "kept" (i.e., supported financially) in exchange for sexual services; a mistress; *sponger*   Someone living at another person's expense.

[4] *venerealee*   Person who has a venereal disease (sexually transmitted infection).

[5] *redstart*   Migratory eastern North American wood warbler.

[6] *suck*   Deception; *sell*   Hoax, disappointment; *crape*   Thin fabric often dyed black and used for mourning garments.

Whimpering and truckling fold with powders¹ for invalids . . . . conformity goes to the
    fourth-removed,
I cock my hat as I please indoors or out.

Shall I pray? Shall I venerate and be ceremonious?
I have pried through the strata and analyzed to a hair,
400 And counselled with doctors and calculated close and found no sweeter fat than sticks to my
    own bones.

In all people I see myself, none more and not one a barleycorn² less,
And the good or bad I say of myself I say of them.

And I know I am solid and sound,
To me the converging objects of the universe perpetually flow,
405 All are written to me, and I must get what the writing means.

And I know I am deathless,
I know this orbit of mine cannot be swept by a carpenter's compass,
I know I shall not pass like a child's carlacue cut with a burnt stick at night.³

I know I am august,⁴
410 I do not trouble my spirit to vindicate itself or be understood,
I see that the elementary laws never apologize,
I reckon I behave no prouder than the level I plant my house by after all.

I exist as I am, that is enough,
If no other in the world be aware I sit content,
415 And if each and all be aware I sit content.

One world is aware, and by far the largest to me, and that is myself,
And whether I come to my own today or in ten thousand or ten million years,
I can cheerfully take it now, or with equal cheerfulness I can wait.

My foothold is tenoned and mortised⁵ in granite,
420 I laugh at what you call dissolution,
And I know the amplitude of time.

---

¹ *truckling* Servile, submissive behavior; *powders* Medicinal powders. Doses were wrapped in a folded piece of paper.

² *barleycorn* A grain of barley, but also a unit of measurement equivalent to one third of an inch.

³ *carlacue . . . night* Usually spelled "curlicue," which is a curl or twist. In American slang, "to cut a carlicue" was to pull off a boyish caper or trick—in this case, the child perhaps is writing something with a charred stick, which would wash away with the first rain.

⁴ *august* Respected, eminent, reverenced.

⁵ *tenoned and mortised* Securely fixed together. In carpentry, a tenon—a projection at the end of a wooden piece—is fixed into a mortise—a hole or cavity in another piece of wood. Together they form a strong joint.

[21]   I am the poet of the body,
        And I am the poet of the soul.

        The pleasures of heaven are with me, and the pains of hell are with me,
425   The first I graft and increase upon myself . . . . the latter I translate into a new tongue.

        I am the poet of the woman the same as the man,
        And I say it is as great to be a woman as to be a man,
        And I say there is nothing greater than the mother of men.

        I chant a new chant of dilation[1] or pride,
430   We have had ducking[2] and deprecating about enough,
        I show that size is only development.

        Have you outstript the rest? Are you the President?
        It is a trifle . . . . they will more than arrive there every one, and still pass on.

        I am he that walks with the tender and growing night;
435   I call to the earth and sea half-held by the night.

        Press close barebosomed night! Press close magnetic nourishing night!
        Night of south winds! Night of the large few stars!
        Still nodding night! Mad naked summer night!

        Smile O voluptuous coolbreathed earth!
440   Earth of the slumbering and liquid trees!
        Earth of departed sunset! Earth of the mountains misty-topt!
        Earth of the vitreous[3] pour of the full moon just tinged with blue!
        Earth of shine and dark mottling the tide of the river!
        Earth of the limpid gray of clouds brighter and clearer for my sake!
445   Far-swooping elbowed earth! Rich apple-blossomed earth!
        Smile, for your lover comes!

        Prodigal![4] you have given me love! . . . . therefore I to you give love!
        O unspeakable passionate love!

        Thruster holding me tight and that I hold tight!
450   We hurt each other as the bridegroom and the bride hurt each other.

[22]   You sea! I resign myself to you also . . . . I guess what you mean,
        I behold from the beach your crooked inviting fingers,

---

1   *dilation* Expansion.
2   *ducking* Evading, side-stepping.
3   *vitreous* Glass-like.
4   *Prodigal* Christ's Parable of the Prodigal Son is told in Luke 15.11–32. The story focuses on redemption: a way-ward son who has wasted his inheritance is welcomed home by his father without reproach.

I believe you refuse to go back without feeling of me;
We must have a turn together . . . . I undress . . . . hurry me out of sight of the land,
455   Cushion me soft . . . . rock me in billowy drowse,
Dash me with amorous wet . . . . I can repay you.

Sea of stretched ground-swells!
Sea breathing broad and convulsive breaths!
Sea of the brine of life! Sea of unshovelled and always-ready graves!
460   Howler and scooper of storms! Capricious and dainty sea!
I am integral with you . . . . I too am of one phase and of all phases.

Partaker of influx and efflux . . . . extoler of hate and conciliation,
Extoler of amies[1] and those that sleep in each others' arms.

I am he attesting sympathy;
465   Shall I make my list of things in the house and skip the house that supports them?

I am the poet of commonsense and of the demonstrable and of immortality;
And am not the poet of goodness only . . . . I do not decline to be the poet of wickedness also.
Washes and razors for foofoos[2] . . . . for me freckles and a bristling beard.

What blurt is it about virtue and about vice?
470   Evil propels me, and reform of evil propels me . . . . I stand indifferent,
My gait is no faultfinder's or rejecter's gait,
I moisten the roots of all that has grown.

Did you fear some scrofula out of the unflagging[3] pregnancy?
Did you guess the celestial laws are yet to be worked over and rectified?

475   I step up to say that what we do is right and what we affirm is right . . . . and some is only
      the ore[4] of right,
Witnesses of us . . . . one side a balance and the antipodal side a balance,
Soft doctrine as steady help as stable doctrine,
Thoughts and deeds of the present our rouse and early start.

This minute that comes to me over the past decillions,
480   There is no better than it and now.

What behaved well in the past or behaves well today is not such a wonder,
The wonder is always and always how there can be a mean man or an infidel.

---

1   *amies*   Friends, lovers.

2   *foofoos*   Offensive slang term for men who fussed over their appearance.

3   *scrofula*   Swelling of the lymph glands: a type of tuberculosis; *unflagging*   Untiring, energetic.

4   *ore*   Material mined from the earth containing valuable metal that has not yet been refined.

[23]   Endless unfolding of words of ages!
       And mine a word of the modern . . . . a word en masse.

485   A word of the faith that never balks,
       One time as good as another time . . . . here or henceforward it is all the same to me.

       A word of reality . . . . materialism first and last imbueing.

       Hurrah for positive science! Long live exact demonstration!
       Fetch stonecrop[1] and mix it with cedar and branches of lilac;
490   This is the lexicographer or chemist . . . . this made a grammar of the old cartouches,[2]
       These mariners put the ship through dangerous unknown seas,
       This is the geologist, and this works with the scalpel, and this is a mathematician.

       Gentlemen I receive you, and attach and clasp hands with you,
       The facts are useful and real . . . . they are not my dwelling . . . . I enter by them to an area of
          the dwelling.

495   I am less the reminder of property or qualities, and more the reminder of life,
       And go on the square[3] for my own sake and for others' sakes,
       And make short account of neuters and geldings,[4] and favor men and women fully equipped,
       And beat the gong of revolt, and stop with fugitives and them that plot and conspire.

[24]   Walt Whitman, an American, one of the roughs, a kosmos,
500   Disorderly fleshy and sensual . . . . eating drinking and breeding,
       No sentimentalist . . . . no stander above men and women or apart from them . . . . no more
          modest than immodest.

       Unscrew the locks from the doors!
       Unscrew the doors themselves from their jambs!

       Whoever degrades another degrades me . . . . and whatever is done or said returns at last to me,
505   And whatever I do or say I also return.

       Through me the afflatus[5] surging and surging . . . . through me the current and index.

       I speak the password primeval . . . . I give the sign of democracy;
       By God! I will accept nothing which all cannot have their counterpart of on the same terms.

---

[1]   *stonecrop*   Sedum plant with small flowers that grows on rocks and old stone walls.

[2]   *cartouches*   Circled areas in Egyptian hieroglyphs containing images that denote a royal name; inscribed tablets
made to look like a scroll of paper are also referred to as cartouches.

[3]   *go on the square*   Act and speak honestly and openly.

[4]   *neuters and geldings*   Castrated or spayed animals; by extension, people perceived to be unsexed or sexually
repressed.

[5]   *afflatus*   Divine inspiration, the passing on of spiritual wisdom.

Through me many long dumb voices,
510   Voices of the interminable generations of slaves,
Voices of prostitutes and of deformed persons,
Voices of the diseased and despairing, and of thieves and dwarfs,
Voices of cycles of preparation and accretion,
And of the threads that connect the stars—and of wombs, and of the fatherstuff,
515   And of the rights of them the others are down upon,
Of the trivial and flat and foolish and despised,
Of fog in the air and beetles rolling balls of dung.

Through me forbidden voices,
Voices of sexes and lusts . . . . voices veiled, and I remove the veil,
520   Voices indecent by me clarified and transfigured.

I do not press my finger across my mouth,
I keep as delicate around the bowels as around the head and heart,
Copulation is no more rank to me than death is.

I believe in the flesh and the appetites,
525   Seeing hearing and feeling are miracles, and each part and tag of me is a miracle.

Divine am I inside and out, and I make holy whatever I touch or am touched from;
The scent of these arm-pits is aroma finer than prayer,
This head is more than churches or bibles or creeds.

If I worship any particular thing it shall be some of the spread of my body;
530   Translucent mould of me it shall be you,
Shaded ledges and rests, firm masculine coulter,[1] it shall be you,
Whatever goes to the tilth[2] of me it shall be you,
You my rich blood, your milky stream pale strippings of my life;
Breast that presses against other breasts it shall be you,
535   My brain it shall be your occult convolutions,
Root of washed sweet-flag, timorous pond-snipe,[3] nest of guarded duplicate eggs, it shall be
    you,
Mixed tussled hay of head and beard and brawn it shall be you,
Trickling sap of maple, fibre of manly wheat, it shall be you;
Sun so generous it shall be you,
540   Vapors lighting and shading my face it shall be you,
You sweaty brooks and dews it shall be you,
Winds whose soft-tickling genitals rub against me it shall be you,

---

[1] *coulter* Blade on a plough that cuts the soil.

[2] *tilth* Cultivation, ploughing.

[3] *sweet-flag* Flowering wetland plant, also called the calamus, which produces a striking, phallic spadix when in flower, and which has long been symbolically associated (in Greek mythology and elsewhere) with love between men; *pond-snipe* Shorebird, likely the Wilson's snipe or the common snipe, both of which catch worms and insects along the muddy shores of ponds and in wet fields.

Broad muscular fields, branches of liveoak,[1] loving lounger in my winding paths, it shall be you,
Hands I have taken, face I have kissed, mortal I have ever touched, it shall be you.

545   I dote on myself . . . . there is that lot of me, and all so luscious,
Each moment and whatever happens thrills me with joy.

I cannot tell how my ankles bend . . . . nor whence the cause of my faintest wish,
Nor the cause of the friendship I emit . . . . nor the cause of the friendship I take again.

To walk up my stoop is unaccountable . . . . I pause to consider if it really be,
550   That I eat and drink is spectacle enough for the great authors and schools,
A morning-glory at my window satisfies me more than the metaphysics of books.

To behold the daybreak!
The little light fades the immense and diaphanous shadows,
The air tastes good to my palate.

555   Hefts of the moving world at innocent gambols, silently rising, freshly exuding,
Scooting obliquely high and low.

Something I cannot see puts upward libidinous prongs,
Seas of bright juice suffuse heaven.

The earth by the sky staid with . . . . the daily close of their junction,
560   The heaved challenge from the east that moment over my head,
The mocking taunt, See then whether you shall be master!

[25]   Dazzling and tremendous how quick the sunrise would kill me,
If I could not now and always send sunrise out of me.

We also ascend dazzling and tremendous as the sun,
565   We found our own my soul in the calm and cool of the daybreak.

My voice goes after what my eyes cannot reach,
With the twirl of my tongue I encompass worlds and volumes of worlds.

Speech is the twin of my vision . . . . it is unequal to measure itself.

It provokes me forever,
570   It says sarcastically, Walt, you understand enough . . . . why don't you let it out then?

Come now I will not be tantalized . . . . you conceive too much of articulation.

Do you not know how the buds beneath are folded?
Waiting in gloom protected by frost,

---

1   *liveoak* Evergreen oaks, primarily found in the southeastern United States.

The dirt receding before my prophetical screams,
575   I underlying causes to balance them at last,
My knowledge my live parts . . . . it keeping tally with the meaning of things,
Happiness . . . . which whoever hears me let him or her set out in search of this day.

My final merit I refuse you . . . . I refuse putting from me the best I am.

Encompass worlds but never try to encompass me,
580   I crowd your noisiest talk by looking toward you.

Writing and talk do not prove me,
I carry the plenum[1] of proof and every thing else in my face,
With the hush of my lips I confound the topmost skeptic.

[26]   I think I will do nothing for a long time but listen,
585   And accrue what I hear into myself . . . . and let sounds contribute toward me.

I hear the bravuras of birds . . . . the bustle of growing wheat . . . . gossip of flames . . . . clack
of sticks cooking my meals.

I hear the sound of the human voice . . . . a sound I love,
I hear all sounds as they are tuned to their uses . . . . sounds of the city and sounds out of the
city . . . . sounds of the day and night;
Talkative young ones to those that like them . . . . the recitative[2] of fish-pedlars and fruit-
pedlars . . . . the loud laugh of workpeople at their meals,
590   The angry base of disjointed friendship . . . . the faint tones of the sick,
The judge with hands tight to the desk, his shaky lips pronouncing a death-sentence,
The heave'e'yo of stevedores[3] unlading ships by the wharves . . . . the refrain of the
anchor-lifters;
The ring of alarm-bells . . . . the cry of fire . . . . the whirr of swift-streaking engines and hose-
carts with premonitory tinkles and colored lights,
The steam-whistle . . . . the solid roll of the train of approaching cars;
595   The slow-march played at night at the head of the association,
They go to guard some corpse . . . . the flag-tops are draped with black muslin.

I hear the violincello or man's heart's complaint,
And hear the keyed cornet or else the echo of sunset.

I hear the chorus . . . . it is a grand-opera . . . . this indeed is music!

---

1   *plenum*   Entirety of space filled with matter.

2   *recitative*   Type of musical utterance that lies between speaking and singing, often used in religious services and
in oratorios and operas.

3   *stevedores*   Laborers who load and unload merchant ships.

600 A tenor large and fresh as the creation fills me,
The orbic[1] flex of his mouth is pouring and filling me full.

I hear the trained soprano . . . . she convulses me like the climax of my love-grip;
The orchestra whirls me wider than Uranus flies,
It wrenches unnamable ardors from my breast,
605 It throbs me to gulps of the farthest down horror,
It sails me . . . . I dab with bare feet . . . . they are licked by the indolent waves,
I am exposed . . . . cut by bitter and poisoned hail,
Steeped amid honeyed morphine . . . . my windpipe squeezed in the fakes of death,[2]
Let up again to feel the puzzle of puzzles,
610 And that we call Being.

[27] To be in any form, what is that?
If nothing lay more developed the quahaug[3] and its callous shell were enough.

Mine is no callous shell,
I have instant conductors all over me whether I pass or stop,
615 They seize every object and lead it harmlessly through me.

I merely stir, press, feel with my fingers, and am happy,
To touch my person to some one else's is about as much as I can stand.

[28] Is this then a touch? . . . . quivering me to a new identity,
Flames and ether[4] making a rush for my veins,
620 Treacherous tip of me reaching and crowding to help them,
My flesh and blood playing out lightning, to strike what is hardly different from myself,
On all sides prurient provokers stiffening my limbs,
Straining the udder of my heart for its withheld drip,
Behaving licentious toward me, taking no denial,
625 Depriving me of my best as for a purpose,
Unbuttoning my clothes and holding me by the bare waist,
Deluding my confusion with the calm of the sunlight and pasture fields,
Immodestly sliding the fellow-senses away,
They bribed to swap off with touch, and go and graze at the edges of me,
630 No consideration, no regard for my draining strength or my anger,
Fetching the rest of the herd around to enjoy them awhile,
Then all uniting to stand on a headland and worry[5] me.

---

[1] *orbic* Round, spherical.

[2] *fakes of death* "Fakes" is a nautical term for coils of rope, so this phrase likely suggests the "coils" (or snares) of death.

[3] *quahaug* Narraganset: Atlantic clam.

[4] *ether* Flammable liquid made by combining sulfuric acid and ethanol.

[5] *worry* Take by the throat and injure or kill by biting and shaking (said of dogs or wolves when they catch a sheep). Also used to refer to greedy, excessively fond kisses and hugs and, more generally, to physical harassment and distress.

The sentries desert every other part of me,
They have left me helpless to a red marauder,
635   They all come to the headland to witness and assist against me.

I am given up by traitors;
I talk wildly . . . . I have lost my wits . . . . I and nobody else am the greatest traitor,
I went myself first to the headland . . . . my own hands carried me there.

You villain touch! what are you doing? . . . . my breath is tight in its throat;
640   Unclench your floodgates! you are too much for me.

[29]   Blind loving wrestling touch! Sheathed hooded sharptoothed touch!
Did it make you ache so leaving me?

Parting tracked by arriving . . . . perpetual payment of the perpetual loan,
Rich showering rain, and recompense richer afterward.

645   Sprouts take and accumulate . . . . stand by the curb prolific and vital,
Landscapes projected masculine full-sized and golden.

[30]   All truths wait in all things,
They neither hasten their own delivery nor resist it,
They do not need the obstetric forceps of the surgeon,
650   The insignificant is as big to me as any,
What is less or more than a touch?

Logic and sermons never convince,
The damp of the night drives deeper into my soul.

Only what proves itself to every man and woman is so,
655   Only what nobody denies is so.

A minute and a drop of me settle my brain;
I believe the soggy clods shall become lovers and lamps,
And a compend[1] of compends is the meat of a man or woman,
And a summit and flower there is the feeling they have for each other,
660   And they are to branch boundlessly out of that lesson until it becomes omnific,[2]
And until every one shall delight us, and we them.

[31]   I believe a leaf of grass is no less than the journeywork[3] of the stars,
And the pismire[4] is equally perfect, and a grain of sand, and the egg of the wren,

---

1   *compend*   Compendium, a condensed embodiment.
2   *omnific*   All-making; having the power to create everything.
3   *journeywork*   Work done for pay.
4   *pismire*   Ant.

And the tree-toad is a chef-d'oeuvre[1] for the highest,
665   And the running blackberry would adorn the parlors of heaven,
And the narrowest hinge in my hand puts to scorn all machinery,
And the cow crunching with depressed[2] head surpasses any statue,
And a mouse is miracle enough to stagger sextillions of infidels,
And I could come every afternoon of my life to look at the farmer's girl boiling her iron tea-
        kettle and baking shortcake.

670   I find I incorporate gneiss and coal and long-threaded moss and fruits and grains and escu-
        lent[3] roots,
And am stucco'd with quadrupeds and birds all over,
And have distanced what is behind me for good reasons,
And call any thing close again when I desire it.

In vain the speeding or shyness,
675   In vain the plutonic rocks[4] send their old heat against my approach,
In vain the mastadon[5] retreats beneath its own powdered bones,
In vain objects stand leagues off and assume manifold shapes,
In vain the ocean settling in hollows and the great monsters lying low,
In vain the buzzard houses herself with the sky,
680   In vain the snake slides through the creepers and logs,
In vain the elk takes to the inner passes of the woods,
In vain the razorbilled auk[6] sails far north to Labrador,
I follow quickly . . . . I ascend to the nest in the fissure of the cliff.

[32]   I think I could turn and live awhile with the animals . . . . they are so placid and
        self contained,
685   I stand and look at them sometimes half the day long.

They do not sweat and whine about their condition,
They do not lie awake in the dark and weep for their sins,
They do not make me sick discussing their duty to God,
Not one is dissatisfied . . . . not one is demented with the mania of owning things,
690   Not one kneels to another nor to his kind that lived thousands of years ago,
Not one is respectable or industrious over the whole earth.

So they show their relations to me and I accept them;
They bring me tokens of myself . . . . they evince them plainly in their possession.

---

1   *chef-d'oeuvre*   French: masterpiece.

2   *depressed*   Lowered.

3   *gneiss*   Granite-like rock composed of quartz, feldspar, and mica;   *esculent*   Edible.

4   *plutonic rocks*   Rocks created by heat at great depths in the earth (as opposed to volcanic rocks, which are created at the earth's surface). "Plutonic" can also mean "infernal" or "hellish" (because of the association with the Roman god of the underworld, Pluto).

5   *mastadon*   Extinct elephant-like mammal.

6   *razorbilled auk*   North Atlantic seabird.

I do not know where they got those tokens,
695   I must have passed that way untold times ago and negligently dropt them,
Myself moving forward then and now and forever,
Gathering and showing more always and with velocity,
Infinite and omnigenous¹ and the like of these among them;
Not too exclusive toward the reachers of my remembrancers,
700   Picking out here one that shall be my amie,
Choosing to go with him on brotherly terms.

A gigantic beauty of a stallion, fresh and responsive to my caresses,
Head high in the forehead and wide between the ears,
Limbs glossy and supple, tail dusting the ground,
705   Eyes well apart and full of sparkling wickedness . . . . ears finely cut and flexibly moving.

His nostrils dilate . . . . my heels embrace him . . . . his well built limbs tremble with pleasure
      . . . . we speed around and return.

I but use you a moment and then I resign you stallion . . . . and do not need your paces, and
      outgallop them,
And myself as I stand or sit pass faster than you.

[33]   Swift wind! Space! My Soul! Now I know it is true what I guessed at;
710   What I guessed when I loafed on the grass,
What I guessed while I lay alone in my bed . . . . and again as I walked the beach under the
      paling stars of the morning.

My ties and ballasts² leave me . . . . I travel . . . . I sail . . . . my elbows rest in the sea-gaps,
I skirt the sierras . . . . my palms cover continents,
I am afoot with my vision.

715   By the city's quadrangular houses . . . . in log-huts, or camping with lumbermen,
Along the ruts of the turnpike³ . . . . along the dry gulch and rivulet bed,
Hoeing my onion-patch, and rows of carrots and parsnips . . . . crossing savannas . . . trailing
      in forests,
Prospecting . . . . gold-digging . . . . girdling the trees of a new purchase,
Scorched ankle-deep by the hot sand . . . . hauling my boat down the shallow river;
720   Where the panther walks to and fro on a limb overhead . . . . where the buck turns furiously
      at the hunter,
Where the rattlesnake suns his flabby length on a rock . . . . where the otter is feeding on fish,
Where the alligator in his tough pimples sleeps by the bayou,
Where the black bear is searching for roots or honey . . . . where the beaver pats the mud
      with his paddle-tail;
Over the growing sugar . . . . over the cottonplant . . . . over the rice in its low moist field;

---

¹   *omnigenous* Infinitely diverse.
²   *ballasts* Weights placed in the holds of a ship to keep it steadier on the sea.
³   *turnpike* Toll road, usually a main road or highway.

725 Over the sharp-peaked farmhouse with its scalloped scum[1] and slender shoots from the
    gutters;
Over the western persimmon[2] . . . . over the longleaved corn and the delicate blue-flowered
    flax;
Over the white and brown buckwheat, a hummer and a buzzer there with the rest,
Over the dusky green of the rye as it ripples and shades in the breeze;
Scaling mountains . . . . pulling myself cautiously up . . . . holding on by low scragged[3] limbs,
730 Walking the path worn in the grass and beat through the leaves of the brush;
Where the quail is whistling betwixt the woods and the wheatlot,
Where the bat flies in the July eve . . . . where the great goldbug[4] drops through the dark;
Where the flails[5] keep time on the barn floor,
Where the brook puts out of the roots of the old tree and flows to the meadow,
735 Where cattle stand and shake away flies with the tremulous shuddering of their hides,
Where the cheese-cloth hangs in the kitchen, and andirons[6] straddle the hearth-slab, and
    cobwebs fall in festoons from the rafters;
Where triphammers[7] crash . . . . where the press is whirling its cylinders;
Wherever the human heart beats with terrible throes out of its ribs;
Where the pear-shaped balloon is floating aloft . . . . floating in it myself and looking com-
    posedly down;
740 Where the life-car is drawn on the slipnoose[8] . . . . where the heat hatches pale-green eggs in
    the dented sand,
Where the she-whale swims with her calves and never forsakes them,
Where the steamship trails hindways its long pennant of smoke,
Where the ground-shark's[9] fin cuts like a black chip out of the water,
Where the half-burned brig[10] is riding on unknown currents,
745 Where shells grow to her slimy deck, and the dead are corrupting below;
Where the striped and starred flag is borne at the head of the regiments;
Approaching Manhattan, up by the long-stretching island,
Under Niagara, the cataract falling like a veil over my countenance;
Upon a door-step . . . . upon the horse-block[11] of hard wood outside,
750 Upon the race-course, or enjoying pic-nics or jigs or a good game of base-ball,

---

1 *scum* Froth or sediment on the rainwater that has gathered in the house's gutters.

2 *persimmon* American persimmon, a tree that grows as far west as Texas and Oklahoma.

3 *scragged* Thin, rough, scraggly.

4 *great goldbug* Unclear, but likely the golden tortoise beetle.

5 *flails* Instruments used to thresh grain.

6 *andirons* Pair of iron bars used to support wood in a fireplace.

7 *triphammers* Huge hammers that work by triggering a tripping device, usually a wheel that raises the hammer and then allows it to fall.

8 *life-car* Type of watertight life-boat attached to a rope and used to pull people through heavy seas to safety; *slipnoose* Noose that tightens and loosens with a slip-knot.

9 *ground-shark* Also known as the Greenland shark.

10 *brig* Ship with two square-rigged masts.

11 *horse-block* Cement or wooden structure with steps, used to help climb up onto a horse.

At he-festivals with blackguard jibes and ironical license and bull-dances[1] and drinking and
    laughter,

At the cider-mill, tasting the sweet of the brown sqush[2] . . . . sucking the juice through a
    straw,

At apple-pealings,[3] wanting kisses for all the red fruit I find,

At musters and beach-parties and friendly bees and huskings and house-raisings;[4]

755 Where the mockingbird sounds his delicious gurgles, and cackles and screams and weeps,

Where the hay-rick stands in the barnyard, and the dry-stalks are scattered, and the brood
    cow[5] waits in the hovel,

Where the bull advances to do his masculine work, and the stud to the mare, and the cock is
    treading the hen,

Where the heifers browse, and the geese nip their food with short jerks;

Where the sundown shadows lengthen over the limitless and lonesome prairie,

760 Where the herds of buffalo make a crawling spread of the square miles far and near;

Where the hummingbird shimmers . . . . where the neck of the longlived swan is curving and
    winding;

Where the laughing-gull scoots by the slappy shore and laughs her near-human laugh;

Where beehives range on a gray bench in the garden half-hid by the high weeds;

Where the band-necked partridges roost in a ring on the ground with their heads out;

765 Where burial coaches enter the arched gates of a cemetery;

Where winter wolves bark amid wastes of snow and icicled trees;

Where the yellow-crowned heron comes to the edge of the marsh at night and feeds upon
    small crabs;

Where the splash of swimmers and divers cools the warm noon;

Where the katydid works her chromatic reed[6] on the walnut-tree over the well;

770 Through patches of citrons[7] and cucumbers with silver-wired leaves,

Through the salt-lick[8] or orange glade . . . . or under conical furs;

Through the gymnasium . . . . through the curtained saloon . . . . through the office or public
    hall;

Pleased with the native and pleased with the foreign . . . . pleased with the new and old,

Pleased with women, the homely as well as the handsome,

---

[1] *he-festivals* A coinage of Whitman's; *jibes* Taunts, jeers; *bull-dances* Dances with only men present (typically these were dances held by sailors aboard ship). Also called stag-dances.

[2] *sqush* Colloquial term for a pulpy, squeezed-out mush.

[3] *apple-pealings* Social gatherings at apple-harvest time to bring in the apples and prepare them for cider-making and other uses. Also called an apple-bee.

[4] *musters* Social gatherings of firefighters in which skill competitions were held; *bees* Neighborhood gatherings that bring people together to complete labor-heavy tasks, such as gathering in harvests or building houses and barns. There was often a festival atmosphere to lighten the work; *huskings* Gatherings held to husk the corn harvest; *house-raisings* Gatherings held to build homes.

[5] *brood cow* Cow ready to conceive calves.

[6] *katydid works her chromatic reed* Reference to the sound of the katydid, or bush cricket, a type of grasshopper common to the central and eastern parts of the U.S.

[7] *citrons* Lemons.

[8] *salt-lick* Place where animals come to lick salt (either a place built by humans for this purpose or a place with naturally-occurring salt).

775   Pleased with the quakeress as she puts off her bonnet and talks melodiously,[1]
Pleased with the primitive tunes of the choir of the whitewashed church,
Pleased with the earnest words of the sweating Methodist preacher, or any preacher . . . .
    looking seriously at the camp-meeting;[2]
Looking in at the shop-windows in Broadway the whole forenoon . . . . pressing the flesh of
    my nose to the thick plate-glass,[3]
Wandering the same afternoon with my face turned up to the clouds;
780   My right and left arms round the sides of two friends and I in the middle;
Coming home with the bearded and dark-cheeked bush-boy . . . . riding behind him at the
    drape[4] of the day;
Far from the settlements studying the print of animals' feet, or the moccasin print;
By the cot in the hospital reaching lemonade to a feverish patient,
By the coffined corpse when all is still, examining with a candle;
785   Voyaging to every port to dicker[5] and adventure;
Hurrying with the modern crowd, as eager and fickle as any,
Hot toward one I hate, ready in my madness to knife him;
Solitary at midnight in my back yard, my thoughts gone from me a long while,
Walking the old hills of Judea[6] with the beautiful gentle god by my side;
790   Speeding through space . . . . speeding through heaven and the stars,
Speeding amid the seven satellites and the broad ring and the diameter of eighty thousand miles,[7]
Speeding with tailed meteors . . . . throwing fire-balls like the rest,
Carrying the crescent child that carries its own full mother in its belly;
Storming enjoying planning loving cautioning,
795   Backing and filling, appearing and disappearing,
I tread day and night such roads.

I visit the orchards of God and look at the spheric product,
And look at quintillions ripened, and look at quintillions green.

I fly the flight of the fluid and swallowing soul,
800   My course runs below the soundings of plummets.

I help myself to material and immaterial,
No guard can shut me off, no law can prevent me.

---

1   *the quakeress … talks melodiously*   The Quakers, or Society of Friends, were known for the gender equality of their religious services and for encouraging women to speak in church and become ministers. Quakers also employed an old-fashioned, and many would say musical and charming, style of speech.

2   *camp-meeting*   Religious meeting that takes place outside, usually over the course of several days. Attendees would set up camp at the location for the duration of the meeting.

3   *plate-glass*   High-quality glass used in shop windows to allow passers-by a clear view.

4   *bush-boy*   Usually a term that was applied to an Indigenous boy from Australia or South Africa who lives in the wilderness (here transferred to the American scene);   *drape*   I.e., close.

5   *dicker*   Bargain, set up deals.

6   *Judea*   Biblical location of Bethlehem, the birthplace of Jesus Christ.

7   *seven … miles*   I.e., the planet Saturn, of whose numerous moons seven were known by the mid-1800s, and which has a diameter of 72,367 miles.

I anchor my ship for a little while only,
My messengers continually cruise away or bring their returns to me.

805 I go hunting polar furs and the seal . . . . leaping chasms with a pike-pointed staff . . . . clinging to topples[1] of brittle and blue.

I ascend to the foretruck . . . . I take my place late at night in the crow's nest[2] . . . . we sail
through the arctic sea . . . . it is plenty light enough,
Through the clear atmosphere I stretch around on the wonderful beauty,
The enormous masses of ice pass me and I pass them . . . . the scenery is plain in all
directions,
The white-topped mountains point up in the distance . . . . I fling out my fancies toward
them;
810 We are about approaching some great battlefield in which we are soon to be engaged,
We pass the colossal outposts of the encampments . . . . we pass with still feet and caution;
Or we are entering by the suburbs some vast and ruined city . . . . the blocks and fallen
architecture more than all the living cities of the globe.

I am a free companion . . . . I bivouac[3] by invading watchfires.

I turn the bridegroom out of bed and stay with the bride myself,
815 And tighten her all night to my thighs and lips.

My voice is the wife's voice, the screech by the rail of the stairs,
They fetch my man's body up dripping and drowned.

I understand the large hearts of heroes,
The courage of present times and all times;
820 How the skipper[4] saw the crowded and rudderless wreck of the steamship, and death chasing
it up and down the storm,
How he knuckled tight and gave not back one inch, and was faithful of days and faithful of
nights,
And chalked in large letters on a board, Be of good cheer, We will not desert you;
How he saved the drifting company at last,
How the lank loose-gowned women looked when boated from the side of their prepared
graves,
825 How the silent old-faced infants, and the lifted sick, and the sharp-lipped unshaved men;
All this I swallow and it tastes good . . . . I like it well, and it becomes mine,
I am the man . . . . I suffered . . . . I was there.[5]

---

1   *topples*   High crests or ledges (here presumably referring to ice formations).

2   *foretruck*   The top of the foremast (in the front of the vessel);   *crow's nest*   Sheltered lookout at the top of a ship's
masthead.

3   *bivouac*   Sleep in the open air.

4   *skipper*   Captain of a small ship.

5   *I understand ... was there*   This stanza describes a naval disaster that took place in late December 1853; the steamship
San Francisco departed New York for San Francisco on 22 December 1853 and was devastated by a storm that began on

The disdain and calmness of martyrs,

The mother condemned for a witch and burnt with dry wood, and her children gazing on;

830 The hounded slave that flags[1] in the race and leans by the fence, blowing and covered with
    sweat,

The twinges that sting like needles his legs and neck,

The murderous buckshot and the bullets,

All these I feel or am.

I am the hounded slave . . . . I wince at the bite of the dogs,

835 Hell and despair are upon me . . . . crack and again crack the marksmen,

I clutch the rails of the fence . . . . my gore dribs thinned with the ooze[2] of my skin,

I fall on the weeds and stones,

The riders spur their unwilling horses and haul close,

They taunt my dizzy ears . . . . they beat me violently over the head with their whip-stocks.[3]

840 Agonies are one of my changes of garments;

I do not ask the wounded person how he feels . . . . I myself become the wounded person,

My hurt turns livid upon me as I lean on a cane and observe.

I am the mashed fireman with breastbone broken . . . . tumbling walls buried me in their
    debris,

Heat and smoke I inspired . . . . I heard the yelling shouts of my comrades,

845 I heard the distant click of their picks and shovels;

They have cleared the beams away . . . . they tenderly lift me forth.

I lie in the night air in my red shirt . . . . the pervading hush is for my sake,

Painless after all I lie, exhausted but not so unhappy,

White and beautiful are the faces around me . . . . the heads are bared of their fire-caps,

850 The kneeling crowd fades with the light of the torches.

Distant and dead resuscitate,

They show as the dial or move as the hands of me . . . . and I am the clock myself.

I am an old artillerist, and tell of some fort's bombardment . . . . and am there again.

Again the reveille of drummers . . . . again the attacking cannon and mortars and howitzers,[4]

855 Again the attacked send their cannon responsive.

---

the night of the 24th. Approximately two hundred passengers were swept overboard in the initial storm; others died by suicide or from disease in the following days as they awaited rescue. The survivors were rescued by the *Kilby* on the 28th, though, due to the violent weather, they were not able to disembark in New York until mid-January.

[1]   *flags*   Loses speed.

[2]   *gore*   Blood;   *ooze*   Sweat.

[3]   *whip-stocks*   Handles of whips, or the sticks to which whips are attached.

[4]   *reveille*   Music played to wake people up in the morning;   *mortars*   Artillery guns that fire missiles at high angles;   *howitzers*   Light-weight artillery guns.

I take part . . . . I see and hear the whole,
The cries and curses and roar . . . . the plaudits for well aimed shots,
The ambulanza[1] slowly passing and trailing its red drip,
Workmen searching after damages and to make indispensible repairs,
860   The fall of grenades through the rent[2] roof . . . . the fan-shaped explosion,
The whizz of limbs heads stone wood and iron high in the air.

Again gurgles the mouth of my dying general . . . . he furiously waves with his hand,
He gasps through the clot . . . . Mind not me . . . . mind . . . . the entrenchments.

[34]   I tell not the fall of Alamo[3] . . . . not one escaped to tell the fall of Alamo,
865   The hundred and fifty are dumb yet at Alamo.

Hear now the tale of a jetblack sunrise,
Hear of the murder in cold blood of four hundred and twelve young men.[4]

Retreating they had formed in a hollow square with their baggage for breastworks,[5]
Nine hundred lives out of the surrounding enemy's nine times their number was the price
    they took in advance,
870   Their colonel was wounded and their ammunition gone,
They treated[6] for an honorable capitulation, received writing and seal, gave up their arms,
    and marched back prisoners of war.

They were the glory of the race of rangers,[7]
Matchless with a horse, a rifle, a song, a supper or a courtship,
Large, turbulent, brave, handsome, generous, proud and affectionate,
875   Bearded, sunburnt, dressed in the free costume of hunters,
Not a single one over thirty years of age.

The second Sunday morning they were brought out in squads and massacred . . . . it was
    beautiful early summer,
The work commenced about five o'clock and was over by eight.

None obeyed the command to kneel,
880   Some made a mad and helpless rush . . . . some stood stark and straight,

---

1   *ambulanza* Italian: ambulance.

2   *rent* Torn.

3   *Alamo* The Battle of the Alamo (1836) took place in San Antonio, Texas, during the Texas Revolution. Close to two hundred Texans were killed by the Mexican Army.

4   *murder … young men* From here to line 889, Whitman is describing the events of the Goliad Massacre, which took place during the Texas Revolution on 27 March 1836. Between 423 and 445 Texian prisoners were killed by the Mexican Army in the town of Goliad. The prisoners were killed by firing squad and by being beaten and stabbed to death.

5   *breastworks* Temporary chest-high military barriers.

6   *treated* Negotiated.

7   *rangers* Organized group of armed individuals dedicated to protecting a certain area of land.

A few fell at once, shot in the temple or heart . . . . the living and dead lay together,
The maimed and mangled dug in the dirt . . . . the new-comers saw them there;
Some half-killed attempted to crawl away,
These were dispatched[1] with bayonets or battered with the blunts of muskets;
885 A youth not seventeen years old seized his assassin till two more came to release him,
The three were all torn, and covered with the boy's blood.

At eleven o'clock began the burning of the bodies;
And that is the tale of the murder of the four hundred and twelve young men,
And that was a jetblack sunrise.

[35] Did you read in the seabooks of the oldfashioned frigate-fight?[2]
Did you learn who won by the light of the moon and stars?

Our foe was no skulk in his ship, I tell you,
His was the English pluck, and there is no tougher or truer, and never was, and never will be;
Along the lowered eve he came, horribly raking[3] us.

895 We closed with him . . . . the yards[4] entangled . . . . the cannon touched,
My captain[5] lashed fast with his own hands.

We had received some eighteen-pound shots under the water,
On our lower-gun-deck two large pieces had burst at the first fire, killing all around and
    blowing up overhead.

Ten o'clock at night, and the full moon shining and the leaks on the gain, and five feet of
    water reported,
900 The master-at-arms[6] loosing the prisoners confined in the after-hold to give them a chance
    for themselves.

The transit to and from the magazine[7] was now stopped by the sentinels,
They saw so many strange faces they did not know whom to trust.

---

[1] *dispatched* Killed.

[2] *oldfashioned frigate-fight* The naval war scene that follows describes the events of the Battle of Flamborough Head, which took place on 23 September 1779 during the American Revolutionary War. The battle occurred in the North Sea, between the Franco-American alliance and the British navy, which was protecting a convoy of merchant ships. The battle ended in a victory for the Franco-American side, though the merchant convoy escaped without harm.

[3] *raking* Sweeping the ship from bow to stern with gunfire.

[4] *yards* Wooden supports for sails on the masts.

[5] *captain* Reference to Navy captain John Paul Jones (1747–92), who is often referred to as the "father of the American Navy." His bravery and persistence in the Battle of Flamborough Head became legendary.

[6] *master-at-arms* Officer in charge of discipline aboard ship.

[7] *magazine* Area of a warship where ammunition, arms, and explosives were kept.

Our frigate was afire .... the other asked if we demanded quarters? if our colors were struck[1] and the fighting done?

I laughed content when I heard the voice of my little captain,

905   We have not struck, he composedly cried, We have just begun our part of the fighting.

Only three guns were in use,
One was directed by the captain himself against the enemy's mainmast,
Two well-served with grape and canister[2] silenced his musketry and cleared his decks.

The tops alone seconded the fire of this little battery, especially the maintop,[3]

910   They all held out bravely during the whole of the action.

Not a moment's cease,
The leaks gained fast on the pumps .... the fire eat toward the powder-magazine,[4]
One of the pumps was shot away .... it was generally thought we were sinking.

Serene stood the little captain,

915   He was not hurried .... his voice was neither high nor low,
His eyes gave more light to us than our battle-lanterns.

Toward twelve at night, there in the beams of the moon they surrendered to us.

[36]   Stretched and still lay the midnight,
Two great hulls motionless on the breast of the darkness,

920   Our vessel riddled and slowly sinking .... preparations to pass to the one we had conquered,
The captain on the quarter deck coldly giving his orders through a countenance white as a sheet,
Near by the corpse of the child that served in the cabin,
The dead face of an old salt with long white hair and carefully curled whiskers,
The flames spite of all that could be done flickering aloft and below,

925   The husky voices of the two or three officers yet fit for duty,
Formless stacks of bodies and bodies by themselves .... dabs of flesh upon the masts and spars,
The cut of cordage and dangle of rigging .... the slight shock of the soothe of waves,
Black and impassive guns, and litter of powder-parcels, and the strong scent,
Delicate sniffs of the seabreeze .... smells of sedgy grass and fields by the shore ... death-messages given in charge to survivors,

930   The hiss of the surgeon's knife and the gnawing teeth of his saw,
The wheeze, the cluck, the swash of falling blood .... the short wild scream, the long dull tapering groan,
These so .... these irretrievable.

---

1   *colors were struck*   To lower the ship's flag—a symbol of surrender.

2   *grape and canister*   I.e., grapeshot and canister-shot, two types of iron balls that were shot from cannons.

3   *tops ... maintop*   Sailors stationed at the tops of the masts.

4   *eat*   Ate;   *powder-magazine*   Place where the gunpowder was stored.

[37] O Christ! My fit is mastering me!
      What the rebel said gaily adjusting his throat to the rope-noose,

935   What the savage at the stump, his eye-sockets empty, his mouth spirting whoops and
          defiance,
      What stills the traveler come to the vault at Mount Vernon,[1]
      What sobers the Brooklyn boy as he looks down the shores of the Wallabout and remembers
          the prison ships,[2]
      What burnt the gums of the redcoat at Saratoga when he surrendered his brigades,[3]
      These become mine and me every one, and they are but little,

940   I become as much more as I like.

      I become any presence or truth of humanity here,
      And see myself in prison shaped like another man,
      And feel the dull unintermitted pain.

      For me the keepers of convicts shoulder their carbines[4] and keep watch,

945   It is I let out in the morning and barred at night.

      Not a mutineer walks handcuffed to the jail, but I am handcuffed to him and walk by his
          side,
      I am less the jolly one there, and more the silent one with sweat on my twitching lips.

      Not a youngster is taken for larceny, but I go up too and am tried and sentenced.

      Not a cholera patient lies at the last gasp, but I also lie at the last gasp,

950   My face is ash-colored, my sinews gnarl . . . . away from me people retreat.

      Askers embody themselves in me, and I am embodied in them,
      I project my hat and sit shamefaced and beg.

[38] I rise extatic through all, and sweep with the true gravitation,
      The whirling and whirling is elemental within me.

955   Somehow I have been stunned. Stand back!
      Give me a little time beyond my cuffed head and slumbers and dreams and gaping,
      I discover myself on a verge of the usual mistake.

---

1   *vault at Mount Vernon*   Where George Washington (1732–99) is buried.

2   *Brooklyn boy . . . prison ships*   Whitman himself grew up near Wallabout Bay and the Brooklyn Naval Yard. During
the Revolutionary War British prison ships were moored at Wallabout, where the terrible conditions resulted in over
10,000 American prisoner-of-war deaths.

3   *redcoat at Saratoga*   British General John Burgoyne led the British army during the Battles of Saratoga (19
September and 7 October 1777);   *surrendered his brigades*   The British surrendered to the Americans on 17 October
1777.

4   *carbines*   Medium-sized firearms.

That I could forget the mockers and insults!
That I could forget the trickling tears and the blows of the bludgeons and hammers!
960   That I could look with a separate look on my own crucifixion and bloody crowning![1]

I remember . . . . I resume the overstaid fraction,
The grave of rock multiplies what has been confided to it . . . . or to any graves,
The corpses rise . . . . the gashes heal . . . . the fastenings roll away.[2]

I troop forth replenished with supreme power, one of an average unending procession,
965   We walk the roads of Ohio and Massachusetts and Virginia and Wisconsin and New
        York and New Orleans and Texas and Montreal and San Francisco and Charleston and
        Savannah and Mexico,
Inland and by the seacoast and boundary lines . . . . and we pass the boundary lines.

Our swift ordinances[3] are on their way over the whole earth,
The blossoms we wear in our hats are the growth of two thousand years.

Eleves[4] I salute you,
970   I see the approach of your numberless gangs . . . . I see you understand yourselves and me,
And know that they who have eyes are divine, and the blind and lame are equally divine,
And that my steps drag behind yours yet go before them,
And are aware how I am with you no more than I am with everybody.

[39]   The friendly and flowing savage . . . . Who is he?
975   Is he waiting for civilization or past it and mastering it?

Is he some southwesterner raised outdoors? Is he Canadian?
Is he from the Mississippi country? or from Iowa, Oregon or California? or from the moun-
        tains? or prairie life or bush-life? or from the sea?

Wherever he goes men and women accept and desire him,
They desire he should like them and touch them and speak to them and stay with them.

980   Behaviour lawless as snow-flakes . . . . words simple as grass . . . . uncombed head and laugh-
        ter and naivete;
Slowstepping feet and the common features, and the common modes and emanations,
They descend in new forms from the tips of his fingers,
They are wafted with the odor of his body or breath . . . . they fly out of the glance of his
        eyes.

---

1   *bloody crowning*   Christ was given a crown of thorns to wear during his crucifixion.

2   *fastenings roll away*   See Luke 24.1–12, which describes the resurrection of Christ, particularly the moment when
the body of Christ is discovered to be missing from the grave: "And they found the stone rolled away from the sepulchre" (24.2).

3   *ordinances*   Decrees, commands.

4   *Eleves*   French: Students.

[40] Flaunt of the sunshine I need not your bask . . . . lie over,[1]
985   You light surfaces only . . . . I force the surfaces and the depths also.

Earth! you seem to look for something at my hands,
Say old topknot![2] what do you want?

Man or woman! I might tell how I like you, but cannot,
And might tell what it is in me and what it is in you, but cannot,
990   And might tell the pinings I have . . . . the pulse of my nights and days.

Behold I do not give lectures or a little charity,
What I give I give out of myself.

You there, impotent, loose in the knees, open your scarfed chops[3] till I blow grit within you,
Spread your palms and lift the flaps of your pockets,
995   I am not to be denied . . . . I compel . . . . I have stores plenty and to spare,
And any thing I have I bestow.

I do not ask who you are . . . . that is not important to me,
You can do nothing and be nothing but what I will infold you.

To a drudge of the cottonfields or emptier of privies I lean . . . . on his right cheek I put the
    family kiss,
1000   And in my soul I swear I never will deny him.

On women fit for conception I start bigger and nimbler babes,
This day I am jetting the stuff of far more arrogant republics.

To any one dying . . . . thither I speed and twist the knob of the door,
Turn the bedclothes toward the foot of the bed,
1005   Let the physician and the priest go home.

I seize the descending man . . . . I raise him with resistless will.

O despairer, here is my neck,
By God! you shall not go down! Hang your whole weight upon me.

I dilate you with tremendous breath . . . . I buoy you up;
1010   Every room of the house do I fill with am armed[4] force . . . . lovers of me, bafflers of graves:
Sleep! I and they keep guard all night;
Not doubt, not decease shall dare to lay finger upon you,

---

[1]   *lie over* Wait, defer until later.

[2]   *topknot* Slang term to refer to an Indigenous person—or, simply, to mean "head."

[3]   *scarfed chops* Jaws and mouth wrapped in a scarf.

[4]   *am armed* Whitman changed this in the 1856 edition to "an armed."

I have embraced you, and henceforth possess you to myself,
And when you rise in the morning you will find what I tell you is so.

[41]   I am he bringing help for the sick as they pant on their backs,
And for strong upright men I bring yet more needed help.

I heard what was said of the universe,
Heard it and heard of several thousand years;
It is middling well as far as it goes .... but is that all?

1020   Magnifying and applying come I,
Outbidding at the start the old cautious hucksters,[1]
The most they offer for mankind and eternity less than a spirt of my own seminalwet,
Taking myself the exact dimensions of Jehovah[2] and laying them away,
Lithographing Kronos and Zeus his son, and Hercules[3] his grandson,
1025   Buying drafts of Osiris and Isis and Belus and Brahma and Adonai,[4]
In my portfolio placing Manito[5] loose, and Allah on a leaf, and the crucifix engraved,
With Odin, and the hideous-faced Mexitli,[6] and all idols and images,
Honestly taking them all for what they are worth, and not a cent more,
Admitting they were alive and did the work of their day,
1030   Admitting they bore mites as for unfledged birds who have now to rise and fly and sing for
            themselves,
Accepting the rough deific sketches to fill out better in myself .... bestowing them freely on
            each man and woman I see,
Discovering as much or more in a framer framing a house,
Putting higher claims for him there with his rolled-up sleeves, driving the mallet and chisel;
Not objecting to special revelations .... considering a curl of smoke or a hair on the back of
            my hand as curious as any revelation;
1035   Those ahold of fire-engines and hook-and-ladder ropes more to me than the gods of the
            antique wars,
Minding their voices peal through the crash of destruction,
Their brawny limbs passing safe over charred laths[7] .... their white foreheads whole and
            unhurt out of the flames;

---

[1] *hucksters* Pedlars, people selling goods at stalls or booths.

[2] *Jehovah* Latinized Hebrew word for God.

[3] *Kronos* In Greek mythology, the ruler of the Titans and father of Zeus; *Zeus* Greek god of the sky and
thunderbolt who rules the gods as king; *Hercules* Greek hero and son of Zeus.

[4] *drafts* Plans, sketches; *Osiris* Egyptian fertility god of the dead and the underworld; *Isis* Egyptian goddess
of the sky and natural world, sister and wife of Osiris; *Belus* Babylonian god of war; *Brahma* Hindu god of
creation; *Adonai* Another Hebrew name for God.

[5] *Manito* Algonquian name for the lifeforce—the great spirit—that infuses all things.

[6] *Odin* In Norse mythology, the supreme god, associated with wisdom, death, poetry, war, and healing; *Mexitli* Legendary Aztec leader and priest.

[7] *laths* Strips of wood that hold up the plaster on walls and ceilings.

By the mechanic's wife with her babe at her nipple interceding for every person born;[1]

Three scythes at harvest whizzing in a row from three lusty angels with shirts bagged out at their waists;

1040 The snag-toothed hostler[2] with red hair redeeming sins past and to come,

Selling all he possesses and traveling on foot to fee[3] lawyers for his brother and sit by him while he is tried for forgery:

What was strewn in the amplest strewing the square rod[4] about me, and not filling the square rod then;

The bull and the bug never worshipped half enough,

Dung and dirt more admirable than was dreamed,

1045 The supernatural of no account . . . . myself waiting my time to be one of the supremes,

The day getting ready for me when I shall do as much good as the best, and be as prodigious,

Guessing when I am it will not tickle me much to receive puffs[5] out of pulpit or print;

By my life-lumps![6] becoming already a creator!

Putting myself here and now to the ambushed womb of the shadows!

[42]   . . . . A call in the midst of the crowd,

My own voice, orotund[7] sweeping and final.

Come my children,

Come my boys and girls, and my women and household and intimates,

Now the performer launches his nerve . . . . he has passed his prelude on the reeds within.

1055 Easily written loose fingered chords! I feel the thrum[8] of their climax and close.

My head evolves on my neck,

Music rolls, but not from the organ . . . . folks are around me, but they are no household of mine.

Ever the hard and unsunk ground,

Ever the eaters and drinkers . . . . ever the upward and downward sun . . . . ever the air and the ceaseless tides,

1060 Ever myself and my neighbors, refreshing and wicked and real,

Ever the old inexplicable query . . . . ever that thorned thumb— that breath of itches and thirsts,

Ever the vexer's hoot! hoot! till we find where the sly one hides and bring him forth;

---

1   *interceding . . . born*   In Catholic tradition the Virgin Mary acts as an intercessor—one that mediates between God and humankind to answer the prayers of the faithful.

2   *hostler*   Person who stables horses at an inn.

3   *fee*   Pay.

4   *square rod*   Unit of land measuring 30¼ square yards.

5   *puffs*   Extravagant words of praise in reviews or comments.

6   *life-lumps*   Perhaps a reference to the pseudoscience phrenology, which seeks to trace a person's character and fate by interpreting the shapes of various parts of the head.

7   *orotund*   Resonant, powerful.

8   *thrum*   Tones made by thrumming—playing—a stringed instrument.

Ever love . . . . ever the sobbing liquid of life,
Ever the bandage under the chin . . . . ever the tressels[1] of death.

1065   Here and there with dimes on the eyes walking,[2]
To feed the greed of the belly the brains liberally spooning,
Tickets buying or taking or selling, but in to the feast never once going;
Many sweating and ploughing and thrashing, and then the chaff[3] for payment receiving,
A few idly owning, and they the wheat continually claiming.

1070   This is the city . . . . and I am one of the citizens;
Whatever interests the rest interests me . . . . politics, churches, newspapers, schools,
Benevolent societies, improvements, banks, tariffs, steamships, factories, markets,
Stocks and stores and real estate and personal estate.

They who piddle[4] and patter here in collars and tailed coats . . . . I am aware who they are . . . .
    and that they are not worms or fleas,
1075   I acknowledge the duplicates of myself under all the scrape-lipped and pipe-legged[5]
    concealments.

The weakest and shallowest is deathless with me,
What I do and say the same waits for them,
Every thought that flounders in me the same flounders in them.

I know perfectly well my own egotism,
1080   And know my omniverous words, and cannot say any less,
And would fetch you whoever you are flush with myself.

My words are words of a questioning, and to indicate reality;
This printed and bound book . . . . but the printer and the printing-office boy?
The marriage estate and settlement . . . . but the body and mind of the bridegroom? also
    those of the bride?
1085   The panorama of the sea . . . . but the sea itself?

The well-taken photographs . . . . but your wife or friend close and solid in your arms?
The fleet of ships of the line[6] and all the modern improvements . . . . but the craft and pluck
    of the admiral?
The dishes and fare and furniture . . . . but the host and hostess, and the look out of their
    eyes?
The sky up there . . . . yet here or next door or across the way?

---

[1] *tressels* Trestles—wooden supports—were used to hold up coffins during funerals and wakes.

[2] *dimes … walking* Reference to ancient burial practices, particularly in Greece and Rome, in which coins are placed on the eyes or mouths of the dead so they can pay for their passage to the underworld.

[3] *thrashing* Process of separating grains from the husks and straw; *chaff* Husks.

[4] *piddle* Waste time.

[5] *scrape-lipped* Shaved; *pipe-legged* Likely a reference to those who wear suit pants.

[6] *ships of the line* Steam and wind-powered naval warships designed to hold a line in battle.

1090   The saints and sages in history . . . . but you yourself?

Sermons and creeds and theology . . . . but the human brain, and what is called reason, and what is called love, and what is called life?

[43]   I do not despise you priests;

My faith is the greatest of faiths and the least of faiths,

Enclosing all worship ancient and modern, and all between ancient and modern,

1095   Believing I shall come again upon the earth after five thousand years,

Waiting responses from oracles . . . . honoring the gods . . . . saluting the sun,

Making a fetish of the first rock or stump . . . . powowing with sticks in the circle of obis,[1]

Helping the lama or brahmin[2] as he trims the lamps of the idols,

Dancing yet through the streets in a phallic procession . . . . rapt and austere in the woods, a gymnosophist,[3]

1100   Drinking mead from the skull-cup . . . . to shasta and vedas admirant[4] . . . . minding the koran,

Walking the teokallis, spotted with gore from the stone and knife—beating the serpent-skin drum;[5]

Accepting the gospels, accepting him that was crucified, knowing assuredly that he is divine,

To the mass kneeling—to the puritan's prayer rising—sitting patiently in a pew,

Ranting and frothing in my insane crisis—waiting dead-like till my spirit arouses me;

1105   Looking forth on pavement and land, and outside of pavement and land,

Belonging to the winders of the circuit of circuits.[6]

One of that centripetal and centrifugal gang,

I turn and talk like a man leaving charges before a journey.

Down-hearted doubters, dull and excluded,

1110   Frivolous sullen moping angry affected disheartened atheistical,

I know every one of you, and know the unspoken interrogatories,

By experience I know them.

---

1   *powowing* Participating in a powwow, a ceremony held in many Indigenous communities that involves feasting, dancing, and music; *obis* Igbo word that can mean both "house" and "chief."

2   *lama* In Tibetan Buddhism, the title of a teacher; *brahmin* Hindu priest and teacher.

3   *gymnosophist* Hindu mystic who is dedicated to prayer and lives ascetically.

4   *skull-cup* Vessel made out of a skull (used perhaps by religious devotees as a "memento mori," a reminder of death); *shasta* Usually spelled "shastra," a name for any of the Hindu sacred texts; *vedas* The four sacred texts of the Hindus; *admirant* Admiring.

5   *teokallis* A teocalli is a four-sided pyramid built for religious purposes by ancient Mexicans and Central Americans, including the Aztecs; *spotted with gore* Likely a reference to the practice of human sacrifice, which would occur on top of the teocalli; *serpent-skin drum* Aztec drums, called "huehuetls," were covered with a skin and would be played by priests during religious rituals. Snakes were sacred to the Aztecs, as they were associated symbolically with their god Quetzalcoatl, so a drum made from snake-skin would be appropriate for ceremonies.

6   *winders ... circuits* Preachers in the nineteenth century would follow a travel circuit so they could speak at churches or outdoors at predetermined locations in a wide area; such preachers were known as "circuit winders."

How the flukes[1] splash!
How they contort rapid as lightning, with spasms and spouts of blood!

1115 Be at peace bloody flukes of doubters and sullen mopers,
I take my place among you as much as among any;
The past is the push of you and me and all precisely the same,
And the day and night are for you and me and all,
And what is yet untried and afterward is for you and me and all.

1120 I do not know what is untried and afterward,
But I know it is sure and alive and sufficient.

Each who passes is considered, and each who stops is considered, and not a single one can it
    fail.

It cannot fail the young man who died and was buried,
Nor the young woman who died and was put by his side,
1125 Nor the little child that peeped in at the door and then drew back and was never seen again,
Nor the old man who has lived without purpose, and feels it with bitterness worse than gall,
Nor him in the poorhouse tubercled by rum and the bad disorder,[2]
Nor the numberless slaughtered and wrecked . . . . nor the brutish koboo,[3] called the ordure
    of humanity,
Nor the sacs merely floating with open mouths for food to slip in,
1130 Nor any thing in the earth, or down in the oldest graves of the earth,
Nor any thing in the myriads of spheres, nor one of the myriads of myriads that inhabit them,
Nor the present, nor the least wisp that is known.

[44] It is time to explain myself . . . . let us stand up.

What is known I strip away . . . . I launch all men and women forward with me into the
    unknown.

1135 The clock indicates the moment . . . . but what does eternity indicate?

Eternity lies in bottomless reservoirs . . . . its buckets are rising forever and ever,
They pour and they pour and they exhale away.

We have thus far exhausted trillions of winters and summers;
There are trillions ahead, and trillions ahead of them.

1140 Births have brought us richness and variety,
And other births will bring us richness and variety.

---

1   *flukes*   Whale's tail (which extends horizontally on both sides).

2   *tubercled*   I.e., afflicted with tuberculosis;   *bad disorder*   Slang or euphemism for a venereal disease (sexually
transmitted infection).

3   *koboo*   Offensive Malay name for the Orang Batin Sembilan or Anak Dalam people of southeast Sumatra.

I do not call one greater and one smaller,
That which fills its period and place is equal to any.

Were mankind murderous or jealous upon you my brother or my sister?

1145 I am sorry for you . . . . they are not murderous or jealous upon me;
All has been gentle with me . . . . . . I keep no account with lamentation;
What have I to do with lamentation?

I am an acme of things accomplished, and I an encloser of things to be.

My feet strike an apex of the apices[1] of the stairs,
1150 On every step bunches of ages, and larger bunches between the steps,
All below duly traveled—and still I mount and mount.

Rise after rise bow the phantoms behind me,
Afar down I see the huge first Nothing, the vapor from the nostrils of death,
I know I was even there . . . . I waited unseen and always,
1155 And slept while God carried me through the lethargic mist,
And took my time . . . . and took no hurt from the fœtid[2] carbon.

Long I was hugged close . . . . long and long.

Immense have been the preparations for me,
Faithful and friendly the arms that have helped me.

1160 Cycles ferried my cradle, rowing and rowing like cheerful boatmen;
For room to me stars kept aside in their own rings,
They sent influences to look after what was to hold me.

Before I was born out of my mother generations guided me,
My embryo has never been torpid . . . . nothing could overlay it;
1165 For it the nebula cohered to an orb . . . . the long slow strata piled to rest it on . . . . vast
    vegetables gave it sustenance,
Monstrous sauroids[3] transported it in their mouths and deposited it with care.

All forces have been steadily employed to complete and delight me,
Now I stand on this spot with my soul.

[45] Span of youth! Ever-pushed elasticity! Manhood balanced and florid and full!

1170 My lovers suffocate me!
Crowding my lips, and thick in the pores of my skin,

---

1   *apices*   Plural for "apex."

2   *fœtid*   Rank, stinking.

3   *sauroids*   Lizard-like creatures.

Jostling me through streets and public halls . . . . coming naked to me at night,
Crying by day Ahoy from the rocks of the river . . . . swinging and chirping over my head,
Calling my name from flowerbeds or vines or tangled underbrush,
1175   Or while I swim in the bath . . . . or drink from the pump at the corner . . . . or the curtain is
       down at the opera . . . . or I glimpse at a woman's face in the railroad car;
Lighting on every moment of my life,
Bussing my body with soft and balsamic[1] busses,
Noiselessly passing handfuls out of their hearts and giving them to be mine.

Old age superbly rising! Ineffable grace of dying days!

1180   Every condition promulges not only itself . . . . it promulges what grows after and out of
       itself,
And the dark hush promulges as much as any.

I open my scuttle[2] at night and see the far-sprinkled systems,
And all I see, multiplied as high as I can cipher, edge but the rim of the farther systems.

Wider and wider they spread, expanding and always expanding,
1185   Outward and outward and forever outward.

My sun has his sun, and round him obediently wheels,
He joins with his partners a group of superior circuit,
And greater sets follow, making specks of the greatest inside them.

There is no stoppage, and never can be stoppage;
1190   If I and you and the worlds and all beneath or upon their surfaces, and all the palpable life,
       were this moment reduced back to a pallid float,[3] it would not avail in the long run,
We should surely bring up again where we now stand,
And as surely go as much farther, and then farther and farther.

A few quadrillions of eras, a few octillions of cubic leagues, do not hazard the span, or make
       it impatient,
They are but parts . . . . any thing is but a part.

1195   See ever so far . . . . there is limitless space outside of that,
Count ever so much . . . . there is limitless time around that.

Our rendezvous is fitly appointed . . . . God will be there and wait till we come.

---

1   *Bussing* Kissing; *balsamic* Fragrant, delicious, healing, restorative.

2   *scuttle* Opening in a ship's side or deck with a moveable lid.

3   *float* For Whitman, the word "float" often suggests the life-giving cosmos before bodies take form and become
matter.

[46]   I know I have the best of time and space—and that I was never measured, and never will be
            measured.

        I tramp a perpetual journey,
1200   My signs are a rain-proof coat and good shoes and a staff cut from the woods;
        No friend of mine takes his ease in my chair,
        I have no chair, nor church nor philosophy;
        I lead no man to a dinner-table or library or exchange,
        But each man and each woman of you I lead upon a knoll,
1205   My left hand hooks you round the waist,
        My right hand points to landscapes of continents, and a plain public road.

        Not I, not any one else can travel that road for you,
        You must travel it for yourself.

        It is not far . . . . it is within reach,
1210   Perhaps you have been on it since you were born, and did not know,
        Perhaps it is every where on water and on land.

        Shoulder your duds,[1] and I will mine, and let us hasten forth;
        Wonderful cities and free nations we shall fetch as we go.

        If you tire, give me both burdens, and rest the chuff[2] of your hand on my hip,
1215   And in due time you shall repay the same service to me;
        For after we start we never lie by again.

        This day before dawn I ascended a hill and looked at the crowded heaven,
        And I said to my spirit, When we become the enfolders of those orbs and the pleasure and
            knowledge of every thing in them, shall we be filled and satisfied then?
        And my spirit said No, we level that lift to pass and continue beyond.

1220   You are also asking me questions, and I hear you;
        I answer that I cannot answer . . . . you must find out for yourself.

        Sit awhile wayfarer,
        Here are biscuits to eat and here is milk to drink,
        But as soon as you sleep and renew yourself in sweet clothes I will certainly kiss you with my
            goodbye kiss and open the gate for your egress hence.

1225   Long enough have you dreamed contemptible dreams,
        Now I wash the gum from your eyes,
        You must habit[3] yourself to the dazzle of the light and of every moment of your life

_____

[1]   *duds*   Clothes; here the word implies clothes and personal things packed in a bag or satchel.

[2]   *chuff*   This term usually means a swollen cheek; here it seems to refer to the raised curve of the palm below the
        thumb.

[3]   *habit*   Habituate, accustom.

Long have you timidly waded, holding a plank by the shore,
Now I will you to be a bold swimmer,
1230   To jump off in the midst of the sea, and rise again and nod to me and shout, and laughingly
    dash with your hair.

[47]   I am the teacher of athletes,
He that by me spreads a wider breast than my own proves the width of my own,
He most honors my style who learns under it to destroy the teacher.

The boy I love, the same becomes a man not through derived power but in his own right,
1235   Wicked, rather than virtuous out of conformity or fear,
Fond of his sweetheart, relishing well his steak,
Unrequited love or a slight cutting him worse than a wound cuts,
First rate to ride, to fight, to hit the bull's eye, to sail a skiff, to sing a song or play on the
    banjo,
Preferring scars and faces pitted with smallpox over all latherers and those that keep out of
    the sun.

1240   I teach straying from me, yet who can stray from me?
I follow you whoever you are from the present hour;
My words itch at your ears till you understand them.

I do not say these things for a dollar, or to fill up the time while I wait for a boat;
It is you talking just as much as myself . . . . I act as the tongue of you,
1245   It was tied in your mouth . . . . in mine it begins to be loosened.

I swear I will never mention love or death inside a house,
And I swear I never will translate myself at all, only to him or her who privately stays with
    me in the open air.

If you would understand me go to the heights or water-shore,
The nearest gnat is an explanation and a drop or the motion of waves a key,
1250   The maul the oar and the handsaw second my words.

No shuttered room or school can commune with me,
But roughs and little children better than they.

The young mechanic is closest to me . . . . he knows me pretty well,
The woodman that takes his axe and jug with him shall take me with him all day,
1255   The farmboy ploughing in the field feels good at the sound of my voice,
In vessels that sail my words must sail . . . . I go with fishermen and seamen, and love them,
My face rubs to the hunter's face when he lies down alone in his blanket,
The driver thinking of me does not mind the jolt of his wagon,
The young mother and old mother shall comprehend me,
1260   The girl and the wife rest the needle a moment and forget where they are,
They and all would resume what I have told them.

[48]   I have said that the soul is not more than the body,
   And I have said that the body is not more than the soul,
   And nothing, not God, is greater to one than one's-self is,
1265   And whoever walks a furlong[1] without sympathy walks to his own funeral, dressed in his shroud,
   And I or you pocketless of a dime may purchase the pick of the earth,
   And to glance with an eye or show a bean in its pod confounds the learning of all times,
   And there is no trade or employment but the young man following it may become a hero,
   And there is no object so soft but it makes a hub for the wheeled universe,
1270   And any man or woman shall stand cool and supercilious before a million universes.

   And I call to mankind, Be not curious about God,
   For I who am curious about each am not curious about God,
   No array of terms can say how much I am at peace about God and about death.

   I hear and behold God in every object, yet I understand God not in the least,
1275   Nor do I understand who there can be more wonderful than myself.

   Why should I wish to see God better than this day?
   I see something of God each hour of the twenty-four, and each moment then,
   In the faces of men and women I see God, and in my own face in the glass;
   I find letters from God dropped in the street, and every one is signed by God's name,
1280   And I leave them where they are, for I know that others will punctually come forever and ever.

[49]   And as to you death, and you bitter hug of mortality . . . . it is idle to try to alarm me.

   To his work without flinching the accoucheur[2] comes,
   I see the elderhand pressing receiving supporting,
   I recline by the sills of the exquisite flexible doors . . . . and mark the outlet, and mark the relief and escape.

1285   And as to you corpse I think you are good manure, but that does not offend me,
   I smell the white roses sweetscented and growing,
   I reach to the leafy lips . . . . I reach to the polished breasts of melons.

   And as to you life, I reckon you are the leavings of many deaths,
   No doubt I have died myself ten thousand times before.

1290   I hear you whispering there O stars of heaven,
   O suns . . . . O grass of graves . . . . O perpetual transfers and promotions . . . . if you do not say anything how can I say anything?

---

[1]   *furlong* Unit of measurement that varies historically but is now stated to be 220 yards.

[2]   *accoucheur* Midwife.

Of the turbid pool that lies in the autumn forest,
Of the moon that descends the steeps of the soughing[1] twilight,
Toss, sparkles of day and dusk . . . . toss on the black stems that decay in the muck,
1295   Toss to the moaning gibberish of the dry limbs.

I ascend from the moon . . . . I ascend from the night,
And perceive of the ghastly glitter the sunbeams reflected,
And debouch[2] to the steady and central from the offspring great or small.

[50]   There is that in me . . . . I do not know what it is . . . . but I know it is in me.

1300   Wrenched and sweaty . . . . calm and cool then my body becomes;
I sleep . . . . I sleep long.

I do not know it . . . . it is without name . . . . it is a word unsaid,
It is not in any dictionary or utterance or symbol.

Something it swings on more than the earth I swing on,
1305   To it the creation is the friend whose embracing awakes me.

Perhaps I might tell more . . . . Outlines! I plead for my brothers and sisters.

Do you see O my brothers and sisters?
It is not chaos or death . . . . it is form and union and plan . . . . it is eternal life . . . . it is
    happiness.

[51]   The past and present wilt . . . . I have filled them and emptied them,
1310   And proceed to fill my next fold of the future.

Listener up there! Here you . . . . what have you to confide to me?
Look in my face while I snuff the sidle[3] of evening,
Talk honestly, for no one else hears you, and I stay only a minute longer.

Do I contradict myself?
1315   Very well then . . . . I contradict myself;
I am large . . . . I contain multitudes.

I concentrate toward them that are nigh . . . . I wait on the door-slab.

Who has done his day's work and will soonest be through with his supper?
Who wishes to walk with me?

1320   Will you speak before I am gone? Will you prove already too late?

---

1   *soughing*   Rustling, sighing.
2   *debouch*   Emerge from a narrow to a wider space.
3   *sidle*   Shy approach.

[52]   The spotted hawk swoops by and accuses me . . . . he complains of my gab and my loitering.

I too am not a bit tamed . . . . I too am untranslatable,
I sound my barbaric yawp over the roofs of the world.

The last scud[1] of day holds back for me,
1325   It flings my likeness after the rest and true as any on the shadowed wilds,
It coaxes me to the vapor and the dusk.

I depart as air . . . . I shake my white locks at the runaway sun,
I effuse my flesh in eddies and drift it in lacy jags.[2]

I bequeath myself to the dirt to grow from the grass I love,
1330   If you want me again look for me under your bootsoles.

You will hardly know who I am or what I mean,
But I shall be good health to you nevertheless,
And filter and fibre your blood.

Failing to fetch me at first keep encouraged,
1335   Missing me one place search another,
I stop some where waiting for you.[3]
—1855

---

[1]   *scud*   Hurry; quick movement of light clouds before the wind.

[2]   *jags*   Fragments, shreds.

[3]   The 1855 ["Song of Myself"] has generally been printed without a period at the end, as the period is missing in some extant copies of the 1855 *Leaves of Grass*. However, Ed Folsom's "Census of the 1855 *Leaves of Grass*" (2006) shows that many other copies *did* in fact include a period, proving that the missing punctuation in other copies was a simple printing error, and that in all likelihood Whitman intended to have a period close the poem.

IN CONTEXT

1855 *Leaves of Grass* [*Song of Myself*][1]

Alfred Jacob Miller, *The Trapper's Bride*, 1845. Whitman describes a striking scene in lines 178–82 of the 1855 *Leaves of Grass* [*Song of Myself*] that closely resembles the details of this painting by Baltimore artist Alfred Jacob Miller. Miller had taken an expedition in 1837 into what is now western Wyoming, where he recorded his observations of the culture surrounding the Western fur trade. In 1856 he made notes for a sketch of the scene that is depicted in this earlier painting: "The scene represents a trapper taking a wife, or purchasing one. The prices varying in accordance with circumstance. He (the trapper) is seated with his friend, to the left of the sketch, his hand extended to his promised wife, supported by her father and accompanied by a chief, who holds the calumet, an article indispensable in all grand ceremonies. ... A free trapper (white or half-breed), being ton[2] or upper circle, is a most desirable match, but it is conceded that he is a ruined man after such an investment, the lady running into unheard of extravagancies. She wants a dress, horse, gorgeous saddle, trappings, and the deuce[3] knows what besides. For this the poor devil trapper sells himself, body and soul, to the Fur Company for a number of years. He traps beaver, hunts the buffalo and bear, elk and etc. The fur and robes of which the company credit to his account."

Common-law marriages between Indigenous women and trappers were not unusual in the seventeenth to early nineteenth centuries—they were known as marriage "à la façon du pays" ("in the style of the country")—and they forged important trade and diplomatic alliances. Indigenous women helped the American and European fur traders survive and acted as intermediaries between the fur companies and the Indigenous populations; the Métis people are considered the descendants of these inter-cultural alliances.

---

[1]   Materials relating to the battle of the Alamo and the Goliad Massacre—both of which Whitman describes in the 1855 *Leaves of Grass*—can be found in this anthology's "Expansion, Native American Expulsion, and 'Manifest Destiny'" contexts section.

[2]   *ton* High society.

[3]   *deuce* Devil.

THE WRECK OF THE STEAM SHIP "SAN FRANCISCO".

The Wreck of the Steam Ship "San Francisco," c. 1854. The caption reads: "The ships ANTARCTIC of New York, Captain Stouffer, and THREE BELLS of Glasgow, Captain Creighton, rescuing the passengers and crew from the wreck of the steamship SAN FRANCISCO, disabled and sinking on her voyage from New York to San Francisco, 24 December 1853. The bark KILBY of Bunten, Captain Low, had previously fallen in with the wreck and taken off some passengers but, during a gale in the night, was separated from SAN FRANCISCO and could not find her again." The storm that disabled the *San Francisco* made the rescue extraordinarily risky, but of the 800 passengers (most of whom were U.S. Army members and their families) around 500 were saved. Whitman describes in lines 818–27 the moment when Captain Creighton arrived to save the passengers from the *San Francisco* and told them "Be of good cheer, We will not desert you." The dramatic rescue—and the heroism of the captains who participated in it—was the compelling subject of countless newspaper articles; personal accounts by survivors of the incident were also widely published. The captains Stouffer, Creighton, and Low were given Congressional Life Saving Medals in 1866.

John Paul Jones During the Battle, from James C. Bradford's *The Reincarnation of John Paul Jones: The Navy Discovers Its Professional Roots* (c. 1896). On 23 September 1779, Commodore John Paul Jones led the Continental Navy (American and French forces) into battle against the British at Flamborough Head, off the coast of northeastern England. During the battle, and after his ship had been severely damaged, Jones was asked if he was ready to strike the colors (i.e., surrender, by lowering the new American flag). Jones famously replied that "I have not yet begun to fight." In the end, the Continental Navy prevailed in the battle.

In the nineteenth century, Jones was remembered as a dashing, fearless American naval hero, and he was frequently portrayed as such in works of fiction—among them James Fenimore Cooper's *The Pilot* (1824) and Herman Melville's *Israel Potter* (1854–55). Whitman describes scenes from the Battle of Flamborough Head in lines 890–917 of the 1855 *Leaves of Grass* [*Song of Myself*].

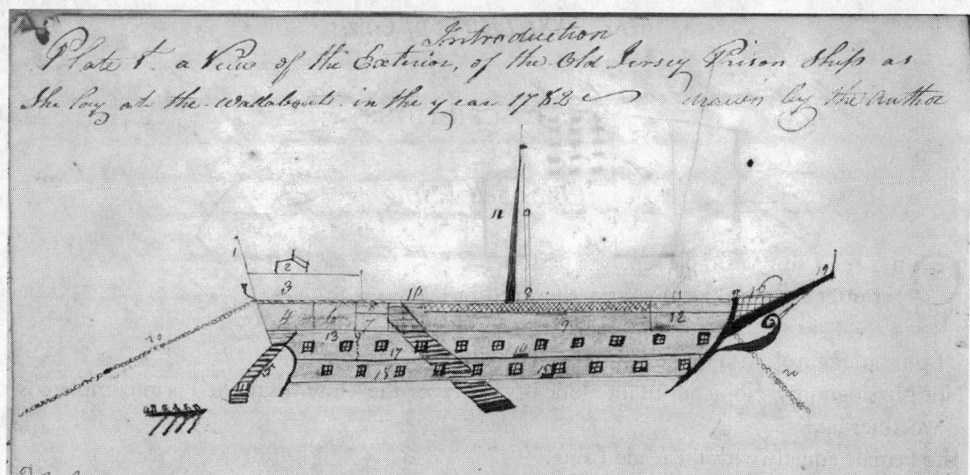

Thomas Dring, *The Jersey Prison Ship as Moored at the Wallabout Near Long Island, in the Year 1782* from *Recollections of Life on the Prison Ship* Jersey, 1829. During the Revolutionary War, British ships anchored in Wallabout Bay, Brooklyn, served as prisons for American prisoners of war. The conditions onboard these ships were unspeakably awful, and it is estimated that between 8,000 and 11,000 American prisoners died while confined, mainly of disease and starvation—more casualties than were incurred on land during the war. Bodies of the dead were either thrown overboard or buried in shallow graves along the sandy shore; human bones were found in the bay for many decades afterwards. Most notorious of all the ships was the HMS *Jersey*, nicknamed "The Hell Afloat," pictured above. Whitman grew up near Wallabout Bay and describes, in line 937 of [*Song of Myself*], what it felt like to live in proximity to such a gruesome history: "What sobers the Brooklyn boy as he looks down the shores of the Wallabout and remembers the prison ships."

The following account of imprisonment aboard the *Jersey* in the autumn of 1780 is by Captain Silas Talbot, as recorded in Danske Dandridge's book *American Prisoners of the Revolution* (1910): "All her port holes were closed. … There were about 1,100 prisoners on board. There were no berths or seats, to lie down on, not a bench to sit on. Many were almost without clothes. The dysentery, fever, phrenzy and despair prevailed among them, and filled the place with filth, disgust and horror. The scantiness of the allowance, the bad quality of the provisions, the brutality of the guards, and the sick, pining for comforts they could not obtain, altogether furnished continually one of the greatest scenes of human distress and misery ever beheld. It was now the middle of October, the weather was cool and clear, with frosty nights, so that the number of deaths per day was reduced to an average of ten, and this number was considered by the survivors a small one, when compared with the terrible mortality that had prevailed for three months before. The human bones and skulls, yet bleaching on the shore of Long Island, and daily exposed, by the falling down of the high bank on which the prisoners were buried, is a shocking sight, and manifestly demonstrates that the *Jersey* prison ship had been as destructive as a field of battle."

from *1881 Leaves of Grass*

from INSCRIPTIONS

One's Self I Sing

One's self I sing, a simple separate person,
Yet utter the word Democratic, the word En-Masse.

Of physiology from top to toe I sing,
Not physiognomy[1] alone nor brain alone is worthy for the Muse, I say the Form complete is
   worthier far,
5 The Female equally with the Male I sing.

Of Life immense in passion, pulse, and power,
Cheerful, for freest action form'd under the laws divine,
The Modern Man I sing.
—1867, 1881

from CHILDREN OF ADAM

I Sing the Body Electric

1

I sing the body electric,
The armies of those I love engirth[2] me and I engirth them,
They will not let me off till I go with them, respond to them,
And discorrupt them, and charge them full with the charge of the soul.

5 Was it doubted that those who corrupt their own bodies conceal themselves?
And if those who defile the living are as bad as they who defile the dead?
And if the body does not do fully as much as the soul?
And if the body were not the soul, what is the soul?

2

The love of the body of man or woman balks account,[3] the body itself balks account,
10 That of the male is perfect, and that of the female is perfect.

The expression of the face balks account,
But the expression of a well-made man appears not only in his face,

---

1 *physiognomy* Facial appearance (especially as considered to reveal one's personality).

2 *engirth* Surround.

3 *balks account* Resists description; cannot be explained.

It is in his limbs and joints also, it is curiously in the joints of his hips and wrists,
It is in his walk, the carriage of his neck, the flex of his waist and knees, dress does not hide him,

15 The strong sweet quality he has strikes through the cotton and broadcloth,[1]
To see him pass conveys as much as the best poem, perhaps more,
You linger to see his back, and the back of his neck and shoulder-side.

The sprawl and fulness of babes, the bosoms and heads of women, the folds of their dress, their style as we pass in the street, the contour of their shape downwards,
The swimmer naked in the swimming-bath, seen as he swims through the transparent green-shine, or lies with his face up and rolls silently to and fro in the heave of the water,

20 The bending forward and backward of rowers in row-boats, the horseman in his saddle,
Girls, mothers, house-keepers, in all their performances,
The group of laborers seated at noon-time with their open dinner-kettles, and their wives waiting,
The female soothing a child, the farmer's daughter in the garden or cow-yard,
The young fellow hoeing corn, the sleigh-driver driving his six horses through the crowd,

25 The wrestle of wrestlers, two apprentice-boys, quite grown, lusty, good-natured, native-born, out on the vacant lot at sun-down after work,
The coats and caps thrown down, the embrace of love and resistance,
The upper-hold and under-hold, the hair rumpled over and blinding the eyes;
The march of firemen in their own costumes, the play of masculine muscle through clean-setting trowsers and waist-straps,
The slow return from the fire, the pause when the bell strikes suddenly again, and the listening on the alert,

30 The natural, perfect, varied attitudes, the bent head, the curv'd neck and the counting;
Such-like I love—I loosen myself, pass freely, am at the mother's breast with the little child,
Swim with the swimmers, wrestle with wrestlers, march in line with the firemen, and pause, listen, count.

3

I knew a man, a common farmer, the father of five sons,
And in them the fathers of sons, and in them the fathers of sons.

35 This man was of wonderful vigor, calmness, beauty of person,
The shape of his head, the pale yellow and white of his hair and beard, the immeasurable meaning of his black eyes, the richness and breadth of his manners,
These I used to go and visit him to see, he was wise also,
He was six feet tall, he was over eighty years old, his sons were massive, clean, bearded, tan-faced, handsome,
They and his daughters loved him, all who saw him loved him,

40 They did not love him by allowance, they loved him with personal love,
He drank water only, the blood show'd like scarlet through the clear-brown skin of his face,

---

1   *broadcloth*   Fine wool fabric, often used to make men's pants and jackets.

He was a frequent gunner and fisher, he sail'd his boat himself, he had a fine one presented to
    him by a ship-joiner, he had fowling-pieces[1] presented to him by men that loved him,
When he went with his five sons and many grand-sons to hunt or fish, you would pick him
    out as the most beautiful and vigorous of the gang,
You would wish long and long to be with him, you would wish to sit by him in the boat that
    you and he might touch each other.

4

45   I have perceiv'd that to be with those I like is enough,
To stop in company with the rest at evening is enough,
To be surrounded by beautiful, curious, breathing, laughing flesh is enough,
To pass among them or touch any one, or rest my arm ever so lightly round his or her neck
    for a moment, what is this then?
I do not ask any more delight, I swim in it as in a sea.

50   There is something in staying close to men and women and looking on them, and in the
    contact and odor of them, that pleases the soul well,
All things please the soul, but these please the soul well.

5

This is the female form,
A divine nimbus[2] exhales from it from head to foot,
It attracts with fierce undeniable attraction,
55   I am drawn by its breath as if I were no more than a helpless vapor, all falls aside but myself
    and it,
Books, art, religion, time, the visible and solid earth, and what was expected of heaven or
    fear'd of hell, are now consumed,
Mad filaments, ungovernable shoots play out of it, the response likewise ungovernable,
Hair, bosom, hips, bend of legs, negligent falling hands all diffused, mine too diffused,
Ebb stung by the flow and flow stung by the ebb, love-flesh swelling and deliciously aching,
60   Limitless limpid jets of love hot and enormous, quivering jelly of love, white-blow and deliri-
    ous juice,
Bridegroom night of love working surely and softly into the prostrate dawn,
Undulating into the willing and yielding day,
Lost in the cleave of the clasping and sweet-flesh'd day.

This the nucleus—after the child is born of woman, man is born of woman,
65   This the bath of birth, this the merge of small and large, and the outlet again.

Be not ashamed women, your privilege encloses the rest, and is the exit of the rest,
You are the gates of the body, and you are the gates of the soul.

---

[1]   *fowling-pieces* Shotguns for hunting fowl.
[2]   *nimbus* Halo.

The female contains all qualities and tempers them,
She is in her place and moves with perfect balance,
70 She is all things duly veil'd, she is both passive and active,
She is to conceive daughters as well as sons, and sons as well as daughters.

As I see my soul reflected in Nature,
As I see through a mist, One with inexpressible completeness, sanity, beauty,
See the bent head and arms folded over the breast, the Female I see.

6

75 The male is not less the soul nor more, he too is in his place,
He too is all qualities, he is action and power,
The flush of the known universe is in him,
Scorn becomes him well, and appetite and defiance become him well,
The wildest largest passions, bliss that is utmost, sorrow that is utmost become him well,
    pride is for him,
80 The full-spread pride of man is calming and excellent to the soul,
Knowledge becomes him, he likes it always, he brings every thing to the test of himself,
Whatever the survey, whatever the sea and the sail he strikes soundings at last only here,
(Where else does he strike soundings except here?)

The man's body is sacred and the woman's body is sacred,
85 No matter who it is, it is sacred—is it the meanest[1] one in the laborers' gang?
Is it one of the dull-faced immigrants just landed on the wharf?
Each belongs here or anywhere just as much as the well-off, just as much as you,
Each has his or her place in the procession.

(All is a procession,
90 The universe is a procession with measured and perfect motion.)

Do you know so much yourself that you call the meanest ignorant?
Do you suppose you have a right to a good sight, and he or she has no right to a sight?
Do you think matter has cohered together from its diffuse float,[2] and the soil is on the
    surface, and water runs and vegetation sprouts,
For you only, and not for him and her?

7

95 A man's body at auction,
(For before the war I often go to the slave-mart and watch the sale,)
I help the auctioneer, the sloven[3] does not half know his business.

---

[1] *meanest* Lowliest (especially in terms of social or financial status).

[2] *float* For Whitman, the word "float" often suggests the life-giving cosmos before bodies take form and become matter.

[3] *sloven* Untidy person.

Gentlemen look on this wonder,
Whatever the bids of the bidders they cannot be high enough for it,
100   For it the globe lay preparing quintillions of years without one animal or plant,
For it the revolving cycles truly and steadily roll'd.

In this head the all-baffling brain,
In it and below it the makings of heroes.

Examine these limbs, red, black, or white, they are cunning in tendon and nerve,
105   They shall be stript that you may see them.

Exquisite senses, life-lit eyes, pluck,[1] volition,
Flakes of breast-muscle, pliant backbone and neck, flesh not flabby, good-sized arms and legs,
And wonders within there yet.

Within there runs blood,
110   The same old blood! the same red-running blood!
There swells and jets a heart, there all passions, desires, reachings, aspirations,
(Do you think they are not there because they are not express'd in parlors and lecture-rooms?)

This is not only one man, this the father of those who shall be fathers in their turns,
In him the start of populous states and rich republics,
115   Of him countless immortal lives with countless embodiments and enjoyments.

How do you know who shall come from the offspring of his offspring through the centuries?
(Who might you find you have come from yourself, if you could trace back through the
    centuries?)

8

A woman's body at auction,
She too is not only herself, she is the teeming mother of mothers,
120   She is the bearer of them that shall grow and be mates to the mothers.

Have you ever loved the body of a woman?
Have you ever loved the body of a man?
Do you not see that these are exactly the same to all in all nations and times all over the
    earth?

If any thing is sacred the human body is sacred,
125   And the glory and sweet of a man is the token of manhood untainted,
And in man or woman a clean, strong, firm-fibred body, is more beautiful than the most
    beautiful face.

---

[1]   *pluck*   In the sense of courage or spiritedness.

Have you seen the fool that corrupted his own live body? or the fool that corrupted her own live body?

For they do not conceal themselves, and cannot conceal themselves.

9

O my body! I dare not desert the likes of you in other men and women, nor the likes of the parts of you,

130 I believe the likes of you are to stand or fall with the likes of the soul, (and that they are the soul,)

I believe the likes of you shall stand or fall with my poems, and that they are my poems,

Man's, woman's, child's, youth's, wife's, husband's, mother's, father's, young man's, young woman's poems,

Head, neck, hair, ears, drop and tympan of the ears,[1]

Eyes, eye-fringes, iris of the eye, eyebrows, and the waking or sleeping of the lids,

135 Mouth, tongue, lips, teeth, roof of the mouth, jaws, and the jaw-hinges,

Nose, nostrils of the nose, and the partition,

Cheeks, temples, forehead, chin, throat, back of the neck, neck-slue,[2]

Strong shoulders, manly beard, scapula, hind-shoulders, and the ample side-round of the chest,

Upper-arm, armpit, elbow-socket, lower-arm, arm-sinews, arm-bones,

140 Wrist and wrist-joints, hand, palm, knuckles, thumb, forefinger, finger-joints, finger-nails,

Broad breast-front, curling hair of the breast, breast-bone, breast-side,

Ribs, belly, backbone, joints of the backbone,

Hips, hip-sockets, hip-strength, inward and outward round, man-balls, man-root,

Strong set of thighs, well carrying the trunk above,

145 Leg-fibres, knee, knee-pan, upper-leg, under-leg,

Ankles, instep, foot-ball, toes, toe-joints, the heel;

All attitudes, all the shapeliness, all the belongings of my or your body or of any one's body, male or female,

The lung-sponges, the stomach-sac, the bowels sweet and clean,

The brain in its folds inside the skull-frame,

150 Sympathies, heart-valves, palate-valves, sexuality, maternity,

Womanhood, and all that is a woman, and the man that comes from woman,

The womb, the teats, nipples, breast-milk, tears, laughter, weeping, love-looks, love-perturbations and risings,

The voice, articulation, language, whispering, shouting aloud,

Food, drink, pulse, digestion, sweat, sleep, walking, swimming,

155 Poise on the hips, leaping, reclining, embracing, arm-curving and tightening,

The continual changes of the flex of the mouth, and around the eyes,

The skin, the sunburnt shade, freckles, hair,

The curious sympathy one feels when feeling with the hand the naked meat of the body,

The circling rivers the breath, and breathing it in and out,

160 The beauty of the waist, and thence of the hips, and thence downward toward the knees,

---

[1] *tympan of the ears* Eardrum.

[2] *neck-slue* I.e., the turn of the neck.

The thin red jellies within you or within me, the bones and the marrow in the bones,
The exquisite realization of health;
O I say these are not the parts and poems of the body only, but of the soul,
O I say now these are the soul!
—1855, 1881

Crossing Brooklyn Ferry[1]

1

Flood-tide[2] below me! I see you face to face!
Clouds of the west—sun there half an hour high—I see you also face to face.

Crowds of men and women attired in the usual costumes, how curious you are to me!
On the ferry-boats the hundreds and hundreds that cross, returning home, are more curious
  to me than you suppose,
5 And you that shall cross from shore to shore years hence are more to me, and more in my
  meditations, than you might suppose.

2

The impalpable sustenance of me from all things at all hours of the day,
The simple, compact, well-join'd scheme, myself disintegrated, every one disintegrated yet
  part of the scheme,
The similitudes of the past and those of the future,
The glories strung like beads on my smallest sights and hearings, on the walk in the street and
  the passage over the river,
10 The current rushing so swiftly and swimming with me far away,
The others that are to follow me, the ties between me and them,
The certainty of others, the life, love, sight, hearing of others.

Others will enter the gates of the ferry and cross from shore to shore,
Others will watch the run of the flood-tide,
15 Others will see the shipping of Manhattan north and west, and the heights of Brooklyn to
  the south and east,
Others will see the islands large and small;
Fifty years hence, others will see them as they cross, the sun half an hour high,
A hundred years hence, or ever so many hundred years hence, others will see them,
Will enjoy the sunset, the pouring-in of the flood-tide, the falling-back to the sea of the
  ebb-tide.

---

1   This poem was added to *Leaves of Grass* in the second edition (1856), where it was entitled "Sun-Down Poem." It
was renamed "Crossing Brooklyn Ferry" in 1860. In the 1881 edition of *Leaves of Grass*, the poem appears independently rather than within a cluster of other poems.

2   *Flood-tide*   Incoming tide.

3

20 It avails not, time nor place—distance avails not,
I am with you, you men and women of a generation, or ever so many generations hence,
Just as you feel when you look on the river and sky, so I felt,
Just as any of you is one of a living crowd, I was one of a crowd,
Just as you are refresh'd by the gladness of the river and the bright flow, I was refresh'd,
25 Just as you stand and lean on the rail, yet hurry with the swift current, I stood yet was
    hurried,
Just as you look on the numberless masts of ships and the thick-stemm'd pipes of steamboats,
    I look'd.

I too many and many a time cross'd the river of old,
Watched the Twelfth-month[1] sea-gulls, saw them high in the air floating with motionless
    wings, oscillating their bodies,
Saw how the glistening yellow lit up parts of their bodies and left the rest in strong shadow,
30 Saw the slow-wheeling circles and the gradual edging toward the south,
Saw the reflection of the summer sky in the water,
Had my eyes dazzled by the shimmering track of beams,
Look'd at the fine centrifugal spokes of light round the shape of my head in the sunlit water,
Look'd on the haze on the hills southward and south-westward,
35 Look'd on the vapor as it flew in fleeces tinged with violet,
Look'd toward the lower bay to notice the vessels arriving,
Saw their approach, saw aboard those that were near me,
Saw the white sails of schooners and sloops, saw the ships at anchor,
The sailors at work in the rigging or out astride the spars,[2]
40 The round masts, the swinging motion of the hulls, the slender serpentine pennants,[3]
The large and small steamers in motion, the pilots in their pilot-houses,[4]
The white wake left by the passage, the quick tremulous whirl of the wheels,
The flags of all nations, the falling of them at sunset,
The scallop-edged waves in the twilight, the ladled cups, the frolicsome crests and glistening,
45 The stretch afar growing dimmer and dimmer, the gray walls of the granite storehouses by
    the docks,
On the river the shadowy group, the big steam-tug closely flank'd on each side by the barges,
    the hay-boat, the belated lighter,[5]
On the neighboring shore the fires from the foundry[6] chimneys burning high and glaringly
    into the night,
Casting their flicker of black contrasted with wild red and yellow light over the tops of
    houses, and down into the clefts of streets.

---

[1] *Twelfth-month* I.e., December (Quakers followed what they call the "plain calendar," naming the months of the
year in this numerical manner).

[2] *spars* Yards, booms, and gaffs—wooden beams—supporting the sails of a ship.

[3] *pennants* Flags.

[4] *pilots* Those who steer the ship, navigators; *pilot-house* Place where the ship's steering-wheel is located.

[5] *lighter* Flat-bottomed barge used to load and unload larger ships at harbor.

[6] *foundry* Factory where metal and glass are melted and cast into molds.

4

These and all else were to me the same as they are to you,
50 I loved well those cities, loved well the stately and rapid river,
The men and women I saw were all near to me,
Others the same—others who look back on me because I look'd forward to them,
(The time will come, though I stop here to-day and to-night.)

5

What is it then between us?
55 What is the count of the scores or hundreds of years between us?

Whatever it is, it avails not—distance avails not, and place avails not,
I too lived, Brooklyn of ample hills was mine,
I too walk'd the streets of Manhattan island, and bathed in the waters around it,
I too felt the curious abrupt questionings stir within me,
60 In the day among crowds of people sometimes they came upon me,
In my walks home late at night or as I lay in my bed they came upon me,
I too had been struck from the float[1] forever held in solution,
I too had receiv'd identity by my body,
That I was I knew was of my body, and what I should be I knew I should be of my body.

6

65 It is not upon you alone the dark patches fall,
The dark threw its patches down upon me also,
The best I had done seem'd to me blank and suspicious,
My great thoughts as I supposed them, were they not in reality meagre?
Nor is it you alone who know what it is to be evil,
70 I am he who knew what it was to be evil,
I too knitted the old knot of contrariety,
Blabb'd, blush'd, resented, lied, stole, grudg'd,
Had guile, anger, lust, hot wishes I dared not speak,
Was wayward, vain, greedy, shallow, sly, cowardly, malignant,
75 The wolf, the snake, the hog, not wanting in me,
The cheating look, the frivolous word, the adulterous wish, not wanting,
Refusals, hates, postponements, meanness, laziness, none of these wanting,
Was one with the rest, the days and haps[2] of the rest,
Was call'd by my nighest[3] name by clear loud voices of young men as they saw me approach-
    ing or passing,
80 Felt their arms on my neck as I stood, or the negligent leaning of their flesh against me as I
    sat,
Saw many I loved in the street or ferry-boat or public assembly, yet never told them a word,

---

1 *float* For Whitman, the word "float" often suggests the life-giving cosmos before bodies take form and become matter.

2 *haps* Chances, luck.

3 *nighest* Closest, most intimate.

Lived the same life with the rest, the same old laughing, gnawing, sleeping,
Play'd the part that still looks back on the actor or actress,
The same old role, the role that is what we make it, as great as we like,
85 Or as small as we like, or both great and small.

7

Closer yet I approach you,
What thought you have of me now, I had as much of you—I laid in my stores in advance,
I consider'd long and seriously of you before you were born.

Who was to know what should come home to me?
90 Who knows but I am enjoying this?
Who knows, for all the distance, but I am as good as looking at you now, for all you cannot
see me?

8

Ah, what can ever be more stately and admirable to me than mast-hemm'd Manhattan?
River and sunset and scallop-edg'd waves of flood-tide?
The sea-gulls oscillating their bodies, the hay-boat in the twilight, and the belated lighter?

95 What gods can exceed these that clasp me by the hand, and with voices I love call me
promptly and loudly by my nighest name as I approach?
What is more subtle than this which ties me to the woman or man that looks in my face?
Which fuses me into you now, and pours my meaning into you?

We understand then do we not?
What I promis'd without mentioning it, have you not accepted?
100 What the study could not teach—what the preaching could not accomplish is accomplish'd,
is it not?

9

Flow on, river! flow with the flood-tide, and ebb with the ebb-tide!
Frolic on, crested and scallop-edg'd waves!
Gorgeous clouds of the sunset! drench with your splendor me, or the men and women
generations after me!
Cross from shore to shore, countless crowds of passengers!
105 Stand up, tall masts of Mannahatta![1] stand up, beautiful hills of Brooklyn!
Throb, baffled and curious brain! throw out questions and answers!
Suspend here and everywhere, eternal float of solution!
Gaze, loving and thirsting eyes, in the house or street or public assembly!
Sound out, voices of young men! loudly and musically call me by my nighest name!
110 Live, old life! play the part that looks back on the actor or actress!
Play the old role, the role that is great or small according as one makes it!

---

1 *Mannahatta* Leni Lenape name for Manhattan, which means "land of many hills."

Consider, you who peruse me, whether I may not in unknown ways be looking upon you;

Be firm, rail over the river, to support those who lean idly, yet haste with the hasting current;

Fly on, sea-birds! fly sideways, or wheel in large circles high in the air;

115 Receive the summer sky, you water, and faithfully hold it till all downcast eyes have time to take it from you!

Diverge, fine spokes of light, from the shape of my head, or any one's head, in the sunlit water!

Come on, ships from the lower bay! pass up or down, white-sail'd schooners, sloops, lighters!

Flaunt away, flags of all nations! be duly lower'd at sunset!

Burn high your fires, foundry chimneys! cast black shadows at nightfall! cast red and yellow light over the tops of the houses!

120 Appearances, now or henceforth, indicate what you are,

You necessary film,[1] continue to envelop the soul,

About my body for me, and your body for you, be hung our divinest aromas,

Thrive, cities—bring your freight, bring your shows, ample and sufficient rivers,

Expand, being than which none else is perhaps more spiritual,

125 Keep your places, objects than which none else is more lasting.

You have waited, you always wait, you dumb,[2] beautiful ministers,

We receive you with free sense at last, and are insatiate henceforward,

Not you any more shall be able to foil us, or withhold yourselves from us,

We use you, and do not cast you aside—we plant you permanently within us,

130 We fathom you not—we love you—there is perfection in you also,

You furnish your parts toward eternity,

Great or small, you furnish your parts toward the soul.

—1856, 1881

from SEA-DRIFT

Out of the Cradle Endlessly Rocking

Out of the cradle endlessly rocking,
  Out of the mocking-bird's throat, the musical shuttle,[3]

Out of the Ninth-month[4] midnight,

Over the sterile sands[5] and the fields beyond, where the child leaving his bed wander'd alone, bareheaded, barefoot,

---

1   *film*   Thin membrane, covering.

2   *dumb*   Silent.

3   *shuttle*   Tool used in weaving that moves the thread across the cloth and interweaves it, from one edge to the other. The sound of a shuttle moving across the loom is rhythmic, as well as ascending and descending.

4   *Ninth-month*   I.e., September (Quakers followed what they call the "plain calendar," naming the months of the year in this numerical manner).

5   *sterile sands*   Beach with no vegetation.

5   Down from the shower'd halo,
Up from the mystic play of shadows twining and twisting as if they were alive,
Out from the patches of briers and blackberries,
From the memories of the bird that chanted to me,
From your memories sad brother, from the fitful risings and fallings I heard,
10 From under that yellow half-moon late-risen and swollen as if with tears,
From those beginning notes of yearning and love there in the mist,
From the thousand responses of my heart never to cease,
From the myriad thence-arous'd words,
From the word stronger and more delicious than any,
15 From such as now they start the scene revisiting,
As a flock, twittering, rising, or overhead passing,
Borne hither, ere all eludes me, hurriedly,
A man, yet by these tears a little boy again,
Throwing myself on the sand, confronting the waves,
20 I, chanter of pains and joys, uniter of here and hereafter,
Taking all hints to use them, but swiftly leaping beyond them,
A reminiscence sing.

Once Paumanok,[1]
When the lilac-scent was in the air and Fifth-month grass was growing,
25 Up this seashore in some briers,
Two feather'd guests from Alabama, two together,
And their nest, and four light-green eggs spotted with brown,
And every day the he-bird to and fro near at hand,
And every day the she-bird crouch'd on her nest, silent, with bright eyes,
30 And every day I, a curious boy, never too close, never disturbing them,
Cautiously peering, absorbing, translating.

Shine! shine! shine!
Pour down your warmth, great sun!
While we bask, we two together.

35 *Two together!*
Winds blow south, or winds blow north,
Day come white, or night come black,
Home, or rivers and mountains from home,
Singing all time, minding no time,
40 *While we two keep together.*

Till of a sudden,
May-be kill'd, unknown to her mate,
One forenoon the she-bird crouch'd not on the nest,
Nor return'd that afternoon, nor the next,
45 Nor ever appear'd again.

---

1 *Paumanok* Indigenous name for Long Island.

And thenceforward all summer in the sound of the sea,
And at night under the full of the moon in calmer weather,
Over the hoarse surging of the sea,
Or flitting from brier to brier by day,
50 I saw, I heard at intervals the remaining one, the he-bird,
The solitary guest from Alabama.

Blow! blow! blow!
Blow up sea-winds along Paumanok's shore;
I wait and I wait till you blow my mate to me.

55 Yes, when the stars glisten'd,
All night long on the prong of a moss-scallop'd stake,
Down almost amid the slapping waves,
Sat the lone singer wonderful causing tears.

He call'd on his mate,
60 He pour'd forth the meanings which I of all men know.

Yes my brother I know,
The rest might not, but I have treasur'd every note,
For more than once dimly down to the beach gliding,
Silent, avoiding the moonbeams, blending myself with the shadows,
65 Recalling now the obscure shapes, the echoes, the sounds and sights after their sorts,
The white arms out in the breakers tirelessly tossing,
I, with bare feet, a child, the wind wafting my hair,
Listen'd long and long.

Listen'd to keep, to sing, now translating the notes,
70 Following you my brother.

Soothe! soothe! soothe!
Close on its wave soothes the wave behind,
And again another behind embracing and lapping, every one close,
But my love soothes not me, not me.

75 *Low hangs the moon, it rose late,*
It is lagging—O I think it is heavy with love, with love.

O madly the sea pushes upon the land,
With love, with love.

O night! do I not see my love fluttering out among the breakers?
80 *What is that little black thing I see there in the white?*

Loud! loud! loud!
Loud I call to you, my love!

High and clear I shoot my voice over the waves,
Surely you must know who is here, is here,
85 You must know who I am, my love.

Low-hanging moon!
What is that dusky spot in your brown yellow?
O it is the shape, the shape of my mate!
O moon do not keep her from me any longer.

90 Land! land! O land!
Whichever way I turn, O I think you could give me my mate back again if you only would,
For I am almost sure I see her dimly whichever way I look.
O rising stars!
Perhaps the one I want so much will rise, will rise with some of you.

95 O throat! O trembling throat!
Sound clearer through the atmosphere!
Pierce the woods, the earth,
Somewhere listening to catch you must be the one I want.

Shake out carols!
100 Solitary here, the night's carols!
Carols of lonesome love! Death's carols!
Carols under that lagging, yellow, waning moon!
O under that moon where she droops almost down into the sea!
O reckless despairing carols.

105 But soft! sink low!
Soft! let me just murmur,
And do you wait a moment you husky-nois'd sea,
For somewhere I believe I heard my mate responding to me,
So faint, I must be still, be still to listen,
110 But not altogether still, for then she might not come immediately to me.

Hither my love!
Here I am! here!
With this just-sustain'd note I announce myself to you,
This gentle call is for you my love, for you.

115 Do not be decoy'd elsewhere,
That is the whistle of the wind, it is not my voice,
That is the fluttering, the fluttering of the spray,
Those are the shadows of leaves.
O darkness! O in vain!
120 O I am very sick and sorrowful.

O brown halo in the sky near the moon, drooping upon the sea!
O troubled reflection in the sea!
O throat! O throbbing heart!
And I singing uselessly, uselessly all the night.

125   *O past! O happy life! O songs of joy!*
In the air, in the woods, over fields,
Loved! loved! loved! loved! loved!
But my mate no more, no more with me!
We two together no more.

130   The aria sinking,
All else continuing, the stars shining,
The winds blowing, the notes of the bird continuous echoing,
With angry moans the fierce old mother incessantly moaning,
On the sands of Paumanok's shore gray and rustling,
135   The yellow half-moon enlarged, sagging down, drooping, the face of the sea almost touching,
The boy ecstatic, with his bare feet the waves, with his hair the atmosphere dallying,
The love in the heart long pent, now loose, now at last tumultuously bursting,
The aria's meaning, the ears, the soul, swiftly depositing,
The strange tears down the cheeks coursing,
140   The colloquy there, the trio, each uttering,
The undertone, the savage old mother incessantly crying,
To the boy's soul's questions sullenly timing, some drown'd secret hissing,
To the outsetting bard.

Demon or bird! (said the boy's soul,)
145   Is it indeed toward your mate you sing? or is it really to me?
For I, that was a child, my tongue's use sleeping, now I have heard you,
Now in a moment I know what I am for, I awake,
And already a thousand singers, a thousand songs, clearer, louder and more sorrowful than
        yours,
A thousand warbling echoes have started to life within me, never to die.

150   O you singer solitary, singing by yourself, projecting me,
O solitary me listening, never more shall I cease perpetuating you,
Never more shall I escape, never more the reverberations,
Never more the cries of unsatisfied love be absent from me,
Never again leave me to be the peaceful child I was before what there in the night,
155   By the sea under the yellow and sagging moon,
The messenger there arous'd, the fire, the sweet hell within,
The unknown want, the destiny of me.

O give me the clew![1] (it lurks in the night here somewhere,)
O if I am to have so much, let me have more!

---

1   *clew* Clue.

160 A word then, (for I will conquer it,)
The word final, superior to all,
Subtle, sent up—what is it?—I listen;
Are you whispering it, and have been all the time, you sea-waves?
Is that it from your liquid rims and wet sands?

165 Whereto answering, the sea,
Delaying not, hurrying not,
Whisper'd me through the night, and very plainly before daybreak,
Lisp'd to me the low and delicious word death,
And again death, death, death, death,
170 Hissing melodious, neither like the bird nor like my arous'd child's heart,
But edging near as privately for me rustling at my feet,
Creeping thence steadily up to my ears and laving[1] me softly all over,
Death, death, death, death, death.

Which I do not forget,
175 But fuse the song of my dusky demon and brother,
That he sang to me in the moonlight on Paumanok's gray beach,
With the thousand responsive songs at random,
My own songs awaked from that hour,
And with them the key, the word up from the waves,
180 The word of the sweetest song and all songs,
That strong and delicious word which, creeping to my feet,
(Or like some old crone rocking the cradle, swathed in sweet garments, bending aside,)
The sea whisper'd me.
—1859, 1881

from By the Roadside

When I Heard the Learn'd Astronomer

When I heard the learn'd astronomer,
　　When the proofs, the figures, were ranged in columns before me,
When I was shown the charts and diagrams, to add, divide, and measure them,
When I sitting heard the astronomer where he lectured with much applause in the
　　lecture-room,
5 How soon unaccountable I became tired and sick,
Till rising and gliding out I wander'd off by myself,
In the mystical moist night-air, and from time to time,
Look'd up in perfect silence at the stars.
—1865, 1881

1　*laving*　Washing, bathing.

from DRUM-TAPS[1]

The Wound-Dresser[2]

1

An old man bending I come among new faces,
    Years looking backward resuming in answer to children,
Come tell us old man, as from young men and maidens that love me,
(Arous'd and angry, I'd thought to beat the alarum, and urge relentless war,
5 But soon my fingers fail'd me, my face droop'd and I resign'd myself,
To sit by the wounded and soothe them, or silently watch the dead);
Years hence of these scenes, of these furious passions, these chances,
Of unsurpass'd heroes (was one side so brave? the other was equally brave);
Now be witness again, paint the mightiest armies of earth,
10 Of those armies so rapid so wondrous what saw you to tell us?
What stays with you latest and deepest? of curious panics,
Of hard-fought engagements or sieges tremendous what deepest remains?

2

O maidens and young men I love and that love me,
What you ask of my days those the strangest and sudden your talking recalls,
15 Soldier alert I arrive after a long march cover'd with sweat and dust,
In the nick of time I come, plunge in the fight, loudly shout in the rush of successful charge,
Enter the captur'd works[3]—yet lo, like a swift-running river they fade,
Pass and are gone they fade—I dwell not on soldiers' perils or soldiers' joys,
(Both I remember well—many the hardships, few the joys, yet I was content).

20 But in silence, in dreams' projections,
While the world of gain and appearance and mirth goes on,
So soon what is over forgotten, and waves wash the imprints off the sand,
With hinged knees returning I enter the doors (while for you up there,
Whoever you are, follow without noise and be of strong heart).

25 Bearing the bandages, water and sponge,
Straight and swift to my wounded I go,
Where they lie on the ground after the battle brought in,
Where their priceless blood reddens the grass the ground,
Or to the rows of the hospital tent, or under the roof'd hospital,
30 To the long rows of cots up and down each side I return,

---

[1] Inspired by Whitman's experience as a volunteer nurse during the Civil War, *Drum-Taps* was first published as an independent volume in October 1865. Already at press at the time of Lincoln's assassination, it was followed later that same month by *Sequel to Drum-Taps*, which included several elegies for the late President. The poems from both volumes were incorporated into subsequent editions of *Leaves of Grass*.

[2] In the 1865, 1867, and 1871 editions, this poem was entitled "The Dresser."

[3] *works* Fortifications.

To each and all one after another I draw near, not one do I miss,
An attendant follows holding a tray, he carries a refuse pail,
Soon to be fill'd with clotted rags and blood, emptied, and fill'd again.

I onward go, I stop,
35 With hinged knees and steady hand to dress wounds,
I am firm with each, the pangs are sharp yet unavoidable,
One turns to me his appealing eyes—poor boy! I never knew you,
Yet I think I could not refuse this moment to die for you, if that would save you.

3

On, on I go (open doors of time! open hospital doors!),
40 The crush'd head I dress (poor crazed hand tear not the bandage away),
The neck of the cavalry-man with the bullet through and through I examine,
Hard the breathing rattles, quite glazed already the eye, yet life struggles hard
(Come sweet death! be persuaded O beautiful death!
In mercy come quickly).

45 From the stump of the arm, the amputated hand,
I undo the clotted lint, remove the slough,[1] wash off the matter and blood,
Back on his pillow the soldier bends with curv'd neck and side-falling head,
His eyes are closed, his face is pale, he dares not look on the bloody stump,
And has not yet look'd on it.

50 I dress a wound in the side, deep, deep,
But a day or two more, for see the frame all wasted and sinking,
And the yellow-blue countenance see.

I dress the perforated shoulder, the foot with the bullet-wound,
Cleanse the one with a gnawing and putrid gangrene, so sickening, so offensive,
55 While the attendant stands behind aside me holding the tray and pail.

I am faithful, I do not give out,
The fractur'd thigh, the knee, the wound in the abdomen,
These and more I dress with impassive hand (yet deep in my breast a fire, a burning flame).

4

Thus in silence in dreams' projections,
60 Returning, resuming, I thread my way through the hospitals,
The hurt and wounded I pacify with soothing hand,
I sit by the restless all the dark night, some are so young,
Some suffer so much, I recall the experience sweet and sad,
(Many a soldier's loving arms about this neck have cross'd and rested,
65 Many a soldier's kiss dwells on these bearded lips.)
   —1865, 1881

---

1 *slough* Layer of dead tissue forming over a wound.

from MEMORIES OF PRESIDENT LINCOLN[1]

When Lilacs Last in the Dooryard Bloom'd

1

When lilacs last in the dooryard bloom'd,
   And the great star[2] early droop'd in the western sky in the night,
I mourn'd, and yet shall mourn with ever-returning spring.

Ever-returning spring, trinity sure to me you bring,
5   Lilac blooming perennial and drooping star in the west,
And thought of him I love.

2

O powerful western fallen star!
O shades of night—O moody, tearful night!
O great star disappear'd—O the black murk that hides the star!
10   O cruel hands that hold me powerless—O helpless soul of me!
O harsh surrounding cloud that will not free my soul.

3

In the dooryard fronting an old farm-house near the white-wash'd palings,
Stands the lilac-bush tall-growing with heart-shaped leaves of rich green,
With many a pointed blossom rising delicate, with the perfume strong I love,
15   With every leaf a miracle—and from this bush in the dooryard,
With delicate-color'd blossoms and heart-shaped leaves of rich green,
A sprig with its flower I break.

4

In the swamp in secluded recesses,
A shy and hidden bird is warbling a song.

20   Solitary the thrush,
The hermit[3] withdrawn to himself, avoiding the settlements,
Sings by himself a song.

---

[1]   This title was first applied to a group of four poems in the 1881 edition of *Leaves of Grass*; the poems had appeared in the 1871 *Passage to India* under the title *President Lincoln's Burial Hymn*. "When Lilacs Last in the Dooryard Bloom'd" and "O Captain! My Captain!" had first been published in *Sequel to Drum-Taps* in October 1865.
        President Lincoln died on 15 April 1865 after being shot by Confederate loyalist and spy, John Wilkes Booth; after lying in state in Washington until 21 April, Lincoln's body was brought on a tour aboard the *Lincoln Special*, a funeral train, stopping in major cities along the way, before being buried in Springfield, Illinois. Mourners gathered along the tracks and at the official stops; the shock and sorrow following Lincoln's death were profound.

[2]   *great star*   I.e., Venus, which at certain times of the year can be seen low in the sky just after sunset.

[3]   *hermit*   The hermit thrush, a reclusive bird with a beautiful, melancholy song, heard only in the early morning or late evening during the spring and early summer.

Song of the bleeding throat,
Death's outlet song of life, (for well dear brother I know,
25 If thou wast not granted to sing thou would'st surely die.)

5

Over the breast of the spring, the land, amid cities,
Amid lanes and through old woods, where lately the violets peep'd from the ground, spotting
     the gray debris,
Amid the grass in the fields each side of the lanes, passing the endless grass,
Passing the yellow-spear'd wheat, every grain from its shroud in the dark-brown fields
     uprisen,
30 Passing the apple-tree blows[1] of white and pink in the orchards,
Carrying a corpse to where it shall rest in the grave,
Night and day journeys a coffin.

6

Coffin that passes through lanes and streets,
Through day and night with the great cloud darkening the land,
35 With the pomp of the inloop'd flags with the cities draped in black,
With the show of the States themselves as of crape-veil'd[2] women standing,
With processions long and winding and the flambeaus[3] of the night,
With the countless torches lit, with the silent sea of faces and the unbared heads,
With the waiting depot, the arriving coffin, and the sombre faces,
40 With dirges through the night, with the thousand voices rising strong and solemn,
With all the mournful voices of the dirges pour'd around the coffin,
The dim-lit churches and the shuddering organs—where amid these you journey,
With the tolling tolling bells' perpetual clang,
Here, coffin that slowly passes,
45 I give you my sprig of lilac.

7

(Nor for you, for one alone,
Blossoms and branches green to coffins all I bring,
For fresh as the morning, thus would I chant a song for you O sane and sacred death.

All over bouquets of roses,
50 O death, I cover you over with roses and early lilies,
But mostly and now the lilac that blooms the first,
Copious I break, I break the sprigs from the bushes,
With loaded arms I come, pouring for you,
For you and the coffins all of you O death.)

---

1 *blows* Blossomings.

2 *crape-veil'd* I.e., wearing veils of crape, a fabric traditionally used for mourning garments.

3 *flambeaus* Torches, but also referring here to the bonfires that the mourners lit as they waited for the funeral train
to come.

8

55   O western orb sailing the heaven,
Now I know what you must have meant as a month since I walk'd,
As I walk'd in silence the transparent shadowy night,
As I saw you had something to tell as you bent to me night after night,
As you droop'd from the sky low down as if to my side, (while the other stars all look'd on,)
60   As we wander'd together the solemn night, (for something I know not what kept me from
    sleep,)
As the night advanced, and I saw on the rim of the west how full you were of woe,
As I stood on the rising ground in the breeze in the cool transparent night,
As I watch'd where you pass'd and was lost in the netherward black of the night,
As my soul in its trouble dissatisfied sank, as where you sad orb,
65   Concluded, dropt in the night, and was gone.

9

Sing on there in the swamp,
O singer bashful and tender, I hear your notes, I hear your call,
I hear, I come presently, I understand you,
But a moment I linger, for the lustrous star has detain'd me,
70   The star my departing comrade holds and detains me.

10

O how shall I warble myself for the dead one there I loved?
And how shall I deck my song for the large sweet soul that has gone?
And what shall my perfume be for the grave of him I love?

Sea-winds blown from east and west,
75   Blown from the Eastern sea and blown from the Western sea, till there on the prairies
    meeting,
These and with these and the breath of my chant,
I'll perfume the grave of him I love.

11

O what shall I hang on the chamber walls?
And what shall the pictures be that I hang on the walls,
80   To adorn the burial-house of him I love?

Pictures of growing spring and farms and homes,
With the Fourth-month[1] eve at sundown, and the gray smoke lucid and bright,
With floods of the yellow gold of the gorgeous, indolent, sinking sun, burning, expanding
    the air,
With the fresh sweet herbage under foot, and the pale green leaves of the trees prolific,
85   In the distance the flowing glaze, the breast of the river, with a wind-dapple here and there,

---

1   *Fourth-month* I.e., April (Quakers followed what they call the "plain calendar," naming the months of the year
in this numerical manner).

With ranging hills on the banks, with many a line against the sky, and shadows,
And the city at hand with dwellings so dense, and stacks of chimneys,
And all the scenes of life and the workshops, and the workmen homeward returning.

12

Lo, body and soul—this land,
90 My own Manhattan with spires, and the sparkling and hurrying tides, and the ships,
The varied and ample land, the South and the North in the light, Ohio's shores and flashing Missouri,
And ever the far-spreading prairies cover'd with grass and corn.

Lo, the most excellent sun so calm and haughty,
The violet and purple morn with just-felt breezes,
95 The gentle soft-born measureless light,
The miracle spreading bathing all, the fulfill'd noon,
The coming eve delicious, the welcome night and the stars,
Over my cities shining all, enveloping man and land.

13

Sing on, sing on you gray-brown bird,
100 Sing from the swamps, the recesses, pour your chant from the bushes,
Limitless out of the dusk, out of the cedars and pines.

Sing on dearest brother, warble your reedy song,
Loud human song, with voice of uttermost woe.

O liquid and free and tender!
105 O wild and loose to my soul—O wondrous singer!
You only I hear—yet the star holds me, (but will soon depart,)
Yet the lilac with mastering odor holds me.

14

Now while I sat in the day and look'd forth,
In the close of the day with its light and the fields of spring, and the farmers preparing their crops,
110 In the large unconscious scenery of my land with its lakes and forests,
In the heavenly aerial beauty, (after the perturb'd winds and the storms,)
Under the arching heavens of the afternoon swift passing, and the voices of children and women,
The many-moving sea-tides, and I saw the ships how they sail'd,
And the summer approaching with richness, and the fields all busy with labor,
115 And the infinite separate houses, how they all went on, each with its meals and minutia of daily usages,
And the streets how their throbbings throbb'd, and the cities pent—lo, then and there,
Falling upon them all and among them all, enveloping me with the rest,

Appear'd the cloud, appear'd the long black trail,
And I knew death, its thought, and the sacred knowledge of death.

120   Then with the knowledge of death as walking one side of me,
And the thought of death close-walking the other side of me,
And I in the middle as with companions, and as holding the hands of companions,
I fled forth to the hiding receiving night that talks not,
Down to the shores of the water, the path by the swamp in the dimness,
125   To the solemn shadowy cedars and ghostly pines so still.

And the singer so shy to the rest receiv'd me,
The gray-brown bird I know receiv'd us comrades three,
And he sang the carol of death, and a verse for him I love.

From deep secluded recesses,
130   From the fragrant cedars and the ghostly pines so still,
Came the carol of the bird.

And the charm of the carol rapt me,
As I held as if by their hands my comrades in the night,
And the voice of my spirit tallied the song of the bird.

135   *Come lovely and soothing death,*
Undulate round the world, serenely arriving, arriving,
In the day, in the night, to all, to each,
Sooner or later delicate death.

Prais'd be the fathomless universe,
140   *For life and joy, and for objects and knowledge curious,*
And for love, sweet love—but praise! praise! praise!
For the sure-enwinding arms of cool-enfolding death.

Dark mother always gliding near with soft feet,
Have none chanted for thee a chant of fullest welcome?
145   *Then I chant it for thee, I glorify thee above all,*
I bring thee a song that when thou must indeed come, come unfalteringly.

Approach strong deliveress,
When it is so, when thou hast taken them I joyously sing the dead,
Lost in the loving floating ocean of thee,
150   *Laved*[1] *in the flood of thy bliss O death.*

From me to thee glad serenades,
Dances for thee I propose saluting thee, adornments and feastings for thee,
And the sights of the open landscape and the high-spread sky are fitting,
And life and the fields, and the huge and thoughtful night.

---

1   *Laved* Bathed, washed.

155   *The night in silence under many a star,*
The ocean shore and the husky whispering wave whose voice I know,
And the soul turning to thee O vast and well-veil'd death,
And the body gratefully nestling close to thee.

   Over the tree-tops I float thee a song,
160   *Over the rising and sinking waves, over the myriad fields and the prairies wide,*
Over the dense-pack'd cities all and the teeming wharves and ways,
I float this carol with joy, with joy to thee O death.

15

To the tally of my soul,
Loud and strong kept up the gray-brown bird,
165   With pure deliberate notes spreading filling the night.

Loud in the pines and cedars dim,
Clear in the freshness moist and the swamp-perfume,
And I with my comrades there in the night.

While my sight that was bound in my eyes unclosed,
170   As to long panoramas of visions.

And I saw askant the armies,
I saw as in noiseless dreams hundreds of battle-flags,
Borne through the smoke of the battles and pierc'd with missiles I saw them,
And carried hither and yon through the smoke, and torn and bloody,
175   And at last but a few shreds left on the staffs, (and all in silence,)
And the staffs all splinter'd and broken.

I saw battle-corpses, myriads of them,
And the white skeletons of young men, I saw them,
I saw the debris and debris of all the slain soldiers of the war,
180   But I saw they were not as was thought,
They themselves were fully at rest, they suffer'd not,
The living remain'd and suffer'd, the mother suffer'd,
And the wife and the child and the musing comrade suffer'd,
And the armies that remain'd suffer'd.

16

185   Passing the visions, passing the night,
Passing, unloosing the hold of my comrades' hands,
Passing the song of the hermit bird and the tallying song of my soul,
Victorious song, death's outlet song, yet varying ever-altering song,
As low and wailing, yet clear the notes, rising and falling, flooding the night,
190   Sadly sinking and fainting, as warning and warning, and yet again bursting with joy,

Covering the earth and filling the spread of the heaven,
As that powerful psalm in the night I heard from recesses,
Passing, I leave thee lilac with heart-shaped leaves,
I leave thee there in the door-yard, blooming, returning with spring.

195   I cease from my song for thee,
From my gaze on thee in the west, fronting the west, communing with thee,
O comrade lustrous with silver face in the night.

Yet each to keep and all, retrievements out of the night,
The song, the wondrous chant of the gray-brown bird,
200   And the tallying chant, the echo arous'd in my soul,
With the lustrous and drooping star with the countenance full of woe,
With the holders holding my hand nearing the call of the bird,
Comrades mine and I in the midst, and their memory ever to keep, for the dead I loved so well,
For the sweetest, wisest soul of all my days and lands—and this for his dear sake,
205   Lilac and star and bird twined with the chant of my soul,
There in the fragrant pines and the cedars dusk and dim.
      —1865, 1881

Live Oak,[1] with Moss

In 1859, Whitman copied a series of twelve poems into a small notebook under the title "Live Oak, with Moss" (later crossed out and changed to "Calamus-Leaves"). The sequence is apparently an autobiographical reflection on a love affair with a man—a possibility supported by the notes Whitman wrote on the back of a draft of the title poem:

> A Cluster of poems, sonnets expressing the thoughts, pictures, aspirations &c.
> Fit to be perused during the days of the approach of Death.
> that I have prepared myself for that purpose—
> Remember now——
> Remember then——

The "Live Oak" poems appear in *Leaves of Grass* as part of the *Calamus* cluster; there are some changes and revisions in the published versions, but by far the most significant change is that the poems are split up and reordered to an extent that obscures the narrative implied in the original sequence. It is unclear whether Whitman's motivations were purely artistic, or whether, as many critics speculate, he felt the need to partially censor such an explicit portrayal of same-sex love. The poems were not reprinted in their "Live Oak" order until 1953, and were not commonly available in that form until the late twentieth century. The text provided below is based on the notebook manuscript; versions that appeared in *Leaves of Grass* in the *Calamus* cluster are included in the anthology's website component.

---

[1]   *Live Oak*   Evergreen oak primarily found in the southeastern United States. The tree is often overgrown with dense, beard-like hanging mosses.

1

Not the heat flames up and consumes,
      Not the sea-waves hurry in and out,
Not the air, delicious and dry, the air of the ripe summer, bears lightly along white down-
      balls of myriads of seeds, wafted, sailing gracefully, to drop where they may,
Not these—O none of these, more than the flames of me, consuming, burning for his love
      whom I love—O none, more than I, hurrying in and out;
5 Does the tide hurry, seeking something, and never give up?—O I, the same, to seek my life-
      long lover;
O nor down-balls, nor perfumes, nor the high rain-emitting clouds, are borne through the
      open air, more than my copious soul is borne through the open air, wafted in all directions,
      for friendship, for love.—

2

I saw in Louisiana a live-oak growing,
All alone stood it, and the moss hung down from the branches,
Without any companion it grew there, glistening out with joyous leaves of dark green,
10 And its look, rude,[1] unbending, lusty, made me think of myself;
But I wondered how it could utter joyous leaves, standing alone there without its friend, its
      lover—For I knew I could not;
And I plucked a twig with a certain number of leaves upon it, and twined around it a little
      moss, and brought it away—And I have placed it in sight in my room,
It is not needed to remind me as of my friends, (for I believe lately I think of little else than
      of them,)
Yet it remains to me a curious token—it makes me think of manly love,
15 For all that, and though the live oak glistens there in Louisiana, solitary in a wide flat space,
      uttering joyous leaves all its life, without a friend, a lover, near—I know very well I could not.

3

When I heard at the close of the day how I had been praised in the Capitol, still it was not a
      happy night for me that followed;
Nor when I caroused—Nor when my favorite plans were accomplished—was I really happy;
But that day I rose at dawn from the bed of perfect health, electric, inhaling sweet breath,
When I saw the full moon in the west grow pale and disappear in the morning light,
20 When I wandered alone over the beach, and undressing, bathed, laughing with the waters,
      and saw the sun rise,
And when I thought how my friend, my lover, was coming, then O I was happy;
Each breath tasted sweeter—and all that day my food nourished me more—And the beauti-
      ful day passed well,
And the next came with equal joy—And with the next, at evening, came my friend,
And that night, while all was still, I heard the waters roll slowly continually up the shores
25 I heard the hissing rustle of the liquid and sands, as directed to me, whispering, to congratu-
      late me,—For the friend I love lay sleeping by my side,
In the stillness his face was inclined towards me, while the moon's clear beams shone, And his
      arm lay lightly over my breast—And that night I was happy.

---

[1] *rude* Rough or uncultivated.

II II II

When I heard at the close of
    the Day how I had been
    praised in the Capitol, still
    it was not a happy night
    for me that followed;
Nor
And else, when I caroused—Or
—*Nor* when my *favorite* plans were accom-
    plished—*it was* I *really happy*
    it was well enough—
Still, I was not happy;
the that that when
But that Day when I rose
    at dawn from the bed of
    perfect health, electric, in-
    haling sweet breath,
When I saw the full moon
    in the west grow pale and
    disappear in the morning light,
When I wandered alone over the
    beach and undressing, bathed,
    laughing with the waters, and
    saw the sun rise,

4

4

This moment as I sit alone, yearning and pensive, it seems to me there are other men, in
    other lands, yearning and pensive.
It seems to me I can look over and behold them, in Germany, France, Spain—Or far away in
    China, India, or Russia—talking other dialects,
And it seems to me if I could know those men I should love them as I love men in my own
    lands;
30   It seems to me they are as wise, beautiful, benevolent, as any in my own lands;
O I think we should be brethren—I think I should be happy with them.

5

Long I thought that knowledge alone would suffice me—O if I could but obtain knowledge!

Then the Land of the Prairies engrossed me—the south savannas engrossed me—For them I would live—I would be their orator;

Then I met the examples of old and new heroes—I heard of warriors, sailors, and all daunt-less persons—And it seemed to me I too had it in me to be as dauntless as any, and would be so;

35 And then to finish all, it came to me to strike up the songs of the New World—And then I believed my life must be spent in singing;

But now take notice, Land of the prairies, Land of the south savannas, Ohio's land,

Take notice, you Kanuck[1] woods—and you, Lake Huron—and all that with you roll toward Niagara—and you Niagara also,

And you, Californian mountains—that you all find some one else that he be your singer of songs,

For I can be your singer of songs no longer—I have ceased to enjoy them.

40 I have found him who loves me, as I him in perfect love,

With the rest I dispense—I sever from all that I thought would suffice me, for it does not—it is now empty and tasteless to me,

I heed knowledge, and the grandeur of The States, and the examples of heroes, no more,

I am indifferent to my own songs—I am to go with him I love, and he is to go with me,

It is to be enough for each of us that we are together—We never separate again.—

6

45 What think you I have taken my pen to record?

Not the battle-ship, perfect-model'd, majestic, that I saw to day arrive in the offing,[2] under full sail,

Nor the splendors of the past day   nor the splendors of the night that envelopes me—Nor the glory and growth of the great city spread around me,

But the two men I saw to-day on the pier, parting the parting of dear friends.

The one to remain hung on the other's neck and passionately kissed him—while the one to depart tightly prest the one to remain in his arms.

7

50 You bards of ages hence! when you refer to me, mind not so much my poems,

Nor speak to me that I prophesied of The States and led them the way of their glories,

But come, I will inform who I was underneath that impassive exterior—I will tell you what to say of me,

Publish my name and hang up my picture as that of the tenderest lover,

The friend, the lover's portrait, of whom his friend, his lover was fondest,

55 Who was not proud of his songs, but of the measureless ocean of love within him—and freely poured it forth,

Who often walked lonesome walks thinking of his dearest friends, his lovers,

Who pensive, away from one he loved, often lay sleepless and dissatisfied at night,

---

1   *Kanuck*   American slang meaning "French Canadian."

2   *offing*   Area of the sea that is some distance from the shoreline but can be seen from land.

Who, dreading lest the one he loved might after all be indifferent to him, felt the sick feeling—O sick! sick!

Whose happiest days were those, far away through fields, in woods, on hills, he and another, wandering hand in hand, they twain,[1] apart from other men.

60 Who ever, as he sauntered the streets, curved with his arm the manly shoulder of his friend—while the curving arm of his friend rested upon him also.

8

Hours continuing long, sore and heavy-hearted,

Hours of the dusk, when I withdraw to a lonesome and unfrequented spot, seating myself, leaning my face in my hands,

Hours sleepless, deep in the night, when I go forth, speeding swiftly the country roads, or through the city streets, or pacing miles and miles, stifling plaintive cries,

Hours discouraged, distracted—For he, the one I cannot content myself without—soon I saw him content himself without me,

65 Hours when I am forgotten—(O weeks and months are passing, but I believe I am never to forget!)

Sullen and suffering hours—(I am ashamed—but it is useless—I am what I am;)

Hours of my torment—I wonder if other men ever have the like out of the like feelings?

Is there even one other like me—distracted—his friend, his lover, lost to him?

Is he too as I am now? Does he still rise in the morning, dejected, thinking who is lost to him? And at night, awaking, think who is lost?

70 Does he too harbor his friendship silent and endless? Harbor his anguish and passion?

Does some stray reminder, or the casual mention of a name, bring the fit back upon him, taciturn and deprest?

Does he see himself reflected in me? In these hours does he see the face of his hours reflected?

9

I dreamed in a dream of a city where all the men were like brothers,

O I saw them tenderly love each other—I often saw them, in numbers, walking hand in hand;

75 I dreamed that was the city of robust friends—Nothing was greater there than manly love—it led the rest,

It was seen every hour in the actions of the men of that city, and in all their looks and words.—

10

O you whom I often and silently come where you are, that I may be with you,

As I walk by your side, or sit near, or remain in the same room with you,

Little you know the subtle electric fire that for your sake is playing within me.—

---

1   *twain*   Two; paired.

11

80 Earth! Though you look so impassive, ample and spheric there—I now suspect that is not all,
I now suspect there is something terrible in you, ready to break forth,
For an athlete loves me, and I him—But toward him there is something fierce and terrible in me,
I dare not tell it in words—not even in these songs.

12

To the young man, many things to absorb, to engraft, to develop, I teach, that he be my eleve,[1]
85 But if through him speed not the blood of friendship, hot and red—If he be not silently
selected by lovers, and do not silently select lovers—of what use were it for him to seek to become eleve of mine?
—WRITTEN 1858–59 (PUBLISHED 1953)

---

[1] *eleve* Student.

HERMAN MELVILLE

1819 – 1891

Herman Melville is widely acknowledged to be one of America's most significant literary figures, a formidable writer of the sea, and a strong voice for the quintessentially American ideals of democracy, freedom, and equality; he was also fierce in condemning the forces that impeded the fulfillment of those ideals. Though Melville died in relative obscurity, his novels and short fiction have become enduringly popular and highly acclaimed for their narrative power, philosophical depth, thematic richness, and stylistic innovation. One biographer wrote of *Moby-Dick* (1851) that it is "the most daring and prolonged aesthetic adventure that had ever been conducted in the hemisphere in the English language." A persistent and eloquent defender of those who suffer within hierarchical, patriarchal, and racist power structures, Melville wrote about the lives of sailors, enslaved people, office clerks, and factory workers, defying dominant ideologies of masculinity, capitalism, "whiteness," and colonialism.

Herman Melvill was born in 1819 to Allan Melvill and Maria Gansevoort Melvill (the "e" was added later). He was descended on both sides from prominent families: his paternal grandfather played a part in the Boston Tea Party, and his maternal grandfather, General Peter Gansevoort, was a Revolutionary War hero. The Melvill children were raised in Maria's Dutch Reformed Calvinist faith, with its emphasis on original sin, damnation, and predestination; while Melville came to reject this interpretation of Christianity, it had a profound effect on his imagination. Melville began his education in New York City, but when Allan Melvill's importing business failed, the family moved to Albany, where Herman was enrolled at Albany Academy. He was educated there only for a year, before he was withdrawn for financial reasons. When Herman was twelve, his father died after descending into madness, leaving the family in debt, and in 1832 the twelve-year-old Herman began work as a clerk in the New York State Bank. It was at this time that Maria added the "e" to the family name, perhaps in an effort to distance themselves from Allan Melvill's bankruptcy.

Over the next five years, Melville worked at his brother Gansevoort's fur store and attended the Albany Academy again. In 1837, he took up a teaching post near Pittsfield, and in 1838 enrolled at the Lansingburgh Academy to study engineering, but in the following year he changed course dramatically by signing up as a cabin boy on the merchant ship *St. Lawrence*, which sailed from New York to Liverpool and back. On his return, Melville took up teaching, first in Greenbush and then in Brunswick, New York. In 1840 he decided to go to sea again, this time aboard a whaling ship, the *Acushnet*, which sailed from New Bedford to the South Seas on 3 January 1841. After sailing for over a year, Melville jumped ship on 9 July 1842 with his friend Richard Tobias Greene at the Marquesas Islands, where he lived with the islanders of the Taipi Valley for four weeks before joining an Australian whaling crew aboard the *Lucy Ann*. He shortly afterwards went to shore in Tahiti, where he was imprisoned as a mutineer; after escaping in October 1842, he signed on with a Nantucket whaling ship, the *Charles and Henry*. Upon completing the cruise in 1843, Melville spent time in the Hawaiian Islands, where he worked various jobs, including as a pin setter in a bowling alley. Later that year, Melville enlisted in the United States Navy and sailed on a frigate, the *United States*, until 1844, when he landed in Boston and was discharged.

In 1846, Melville published *Typee,* an account of his time among the Marquesas islanders; the book was first printed in London and then in New York. This travel narrative, and its sequel, *Omoo*, which recounts Melville's adventures in Tahiti, were very popular in America and Britain, establishing the young Melville as a literary celebrity known for sultry, action-packed adventure stories. While successes,

Typee and *Omoo* were also controversial: in both books, Melville attacked the Christian missionaries who sought to "civilize" the Indigenous peoples of the islands. While Melville's depiction of the islanders partook of the racial stereotypes of his day, he asserted very clearly that the barbarism of white people far exceeded any that could be found among the islanders: "the fiend-like skill we display in the invention of all manner of death-dealing engines, the vindictiveness with which we carry on our wars, and the misery and desolation that follow in their train, are enough of themselves to distinguish the white civilized man as the most ferocious animal on the face of the earth." Such statements proved provocative enough that the publishers of *Typee* chose to soften the book's comments on missionaries in the second printing.

Typee was dedicated to Lemuel Shaw, Chief Justice of the Massachusetts Supreme Court and father of Elizabeth Shaw, whom Melville married in 1847; the couple would in time have four children. Melville and Elizabeth settled first in New York City, and most of Melville's family moved in with them: his mother Maria, his four sisters, and his brother and sister-in-law. Melville's early fame brought him into the literary circle of the Duyckinck brothers in New York, from whose libraries Melville borrowed many books. He entered on a course of intense reading, which in turn exerted a profound influence over his future writing; in addition to the Old Testament prophets, he read Shakespeare with increasing wonderment, as well as Defoe, Milton, Rabelais, Swift, Mary Shelley, Byron, Montaigne, and Sir Thomas Browne.

In 1849, Melville turned from writing semi-autobiographical travel narratives to more inventive forms of fiction, as he felt an "invincible distaste" for facts and "a longing to plume my pinions for flight." Looking to engage a more sophisticated audience in addition to the "superficial skimmer of pages" whom he believed had enjoyed his earlier works, Melville's first fully fictional novel, *Mardi* (1849), shifted away from the realist mode to engage in a philosophical allegory that emphasizes the supreme importance of freedom and equality. The book sold poorly and was rejected by critics, and Melville responded by writing two more books in quick succession: *Redburn* in 1849 and *White-Jacket* in 1850. In a letter to his father-in-law, Melville wrote of these books that "they are two jobs, which I have done for money—being forced to it, as other men are to sawing wood." These two novels, which were in many ways a return to his earlier style, found a wide readership. After members of Congress read Melville's scathing denunciation of flogging in *White-Jacket*, as well as his depiction of the authoritarian, unequal conditions of naval life, they banned flogging on all American ships. *Redburn,* which delves into themes of sexuality, nationalism, and the place of refugees in antebellum society, has been receiving increased critical attention, with one scholar deeming it "one of the great nineteenth-century works about race and emigration."

In September 1850, Melville and his growing family moved out of New York City to Arrowhead, a farm in Pittsville, Massachusetts, which Melville bought with money borrowed from his father-in-law. While in the area earlier in the summer, Melville had met Nathaniel Hawthorne, and the two quickly became friends. In late August 1850, Melville published "Hawthorne and His Mosses" in the *Literary World* magazine, in which he praises Hawthorne's genius, as well as his originality, darkness, and Americanness: "the smell of your beeches and hemlocks is upon him; your own prairies are in his soul ... you will hear the far roar of his Niagara." Viewed as an early expression of the Young America movement, the essay argues for the excellence and potential of American writers, with Hawthorne as an exemplary figure "who breathe[s] that unshackled, democratic spirit of Christianity in all things."

Melville's friendship with Hawthorne, and Hawthorne's literary influence on Melville, came at a time of great creativity—he was in the process of writing *Moby-Dick*. His passionate letters to Hawthorne, as well as the frequent expression of homoerotic desire in his work, have led many to suppose the friendship between the two writers was a romantic one. If so, evidence for it is one-sided: while Melville was clearly passionately attached to Hawthorne, and while Hawthorne very much admired Melville and his work, only one letter from Hawthorne to Melville exists, and it is a request for Melville to pick up some mail. Though there is no clear biographical proof that Melville had sexual relationships with men, his work certainly celebrates homoerotic desire, linking it with, among other things, creativity and resistance to conventional power structures based on heterosexual norms. For this reason, Melville is frequently hailed as a trailblazer, one of the most significant early writers in the queer American literary tradition.

At Arrowhead during the winter of 1850–51, Melville worked on *Moby-Dick* from early in the morning through to the afternoon. His sister Augusta would every day copy out the work from the day before, and she wrote in a letter that she found the book "very fine." After finishing the manuscript, Melville wrote to Hawthorne that "I have written a wicked book, and feel spotless as a lamb." Unfortunately, though British reviews contained favorable impressions of the novel, American critics at the time were unappreciative and overwhelmed, complaining that the book was too long, too mystical, and over-wrought. A reviewer for *The New York Evangelist* wrote in 1851 that "oddity is the governing character [of *Moby-Dick*]" and that Melville "has reached the very limbo of eccentricity." In the wake of the public dismissal of both *Mardi* and *Moby-Dick*, Melville grew increasingly embittered with his readers and reviewers, but continued writing fiction, publishing the novel *Pierre; or, the Ambiguities* in 1852. Critics were even more bewildered by this novel, calling it "morbid and unhealthy…[like] a horrid fit of the night-mare." *Pierre* did not increase Melville's income or reputation, and neither did his final novel, *The Confidence-Man* (1857). Now considered a masterly, metafictional tour-de-force, *The Confidence-Man* confused Melville's contemporary readership, confirming critics in their opinion that Melville had not developed his potential. He himself knew he had; in a letter to Hawthorne he wrote: "Though I wrote the Gospels in this century, I should die in the gutter."

Between 1853 and 1855, Melville turned to a form of fiction that was, at that time, often more lucrative than novels by contributing short stories to *Putnam's Monthly*. Melville was a keen reader of periodicals, and he created works for *Putnam's* that reflected the influence of contemporary writers of short fiction, including Hawthorne, Edgar Allan Poe, and Charles Dickens. Melville continued, in these stories, to explore themes from his novels—the dehumanizing effects of capitalist, patriarchal social structures, the inhumanity of white supremacist attitudes, the mystery of the sea, and the draw of travel. He collected six of his stories and published them as *The Piazza Tales* (1856), including the now well-known tales *Benito Cereno*, "Bartleby, the Scrivener," and "The Encantadas." Reviews for the volume were quite positive, but sales were not, and this disappointment, when paired with the discouraging reception of *Mardi*, *Moby-Dick*, and *Pierre*, contributed to Melville's decision to stop writing fiction for the foreseeable future.

The ensuing decade in Melville's life was a dark one, and one that coincided with the national crisis of the Civil War. In 1856–57, he took a trip to Europe and the Middle East in an attempt to regain his spirits, but things did not improve, and he struggled to support his family on his return. In 1866 he took a job at the New York Custom House, a position he worked for nineteen years, earning four dollars a day. Melville's mental state deteriorated to a point where his wife Elizabeth nearly left him in 1867; that same year Melville's eldest son, Malcolm, died by suicide at the age of eighteen.

Melville did not stop writing, however; instead of fiction, he turned to poetry. *Battle-Pieces*, a collection of poems reflecting on the Civil War, was published in 1866; in an appendix, Melville urged the North to treat the South with mercy. His next work, *Clarel* (1876), was a seven-thousand-line poem inspired by his spiritual crisis and by his trip to the Middle East. *Clarel* was Melville's last publication during his lifetime. Two more books of poetry, *John Marr and Other Sailors* (1888) and *Timoleon* (1891), were printed in runs of twenty-five copies each and circulated privately. Melville's poetry has, until recently, been largely absent from accounts of American literary history, which long held Walt Whitman and Emily Dickinson to be the only great post-bellum nineteenth-century poets. The formal innovations of Melville's poems are being increasingly recognized, including their shift away from Romantic subjectivity, and scholars are integrating Melville's three decades of poetic output into a more nuanced history of nineteenth-century American poetry. In addition to another book of poems, *Weeds and Wildings Chiefly*, an unfinished novella, *Billy Budd*, was found in manuscript after Melville's death in 1891; it was not published until 1924. At once hailed as a masterpiece by Thomas Mann, among others, the story of the execution of the beautiful young sailor has taken its place alongside *Moby-Dick* as one of Melville's most critically acclaimed and often adapted works.

When Melville died, the *North American Review* printed a notice, which said that he "wrote out of his heart … [but] his books are now but little read. When he died the other day … men who could give you the names of fifty living poets and perhaps a hundred living American novelists owned that they had never heard of Herman Melville." The *New York Times* encapsulated Melville's obscurity when it printed a brief article in honor of his life entitled "The Late Hiram Melville." It was not until the height of the Modernist movement in the 1920s that the so-called "Melville Revival" brought Melville's work, particularly *Moby-Dick*, into prominence. Raymond Weaver's *Herman Melville: Mariner and Mystic* (1921) launched the revival, and writers such as Virginia Woolf, D.H. Lawrence, and Lewis Mumford wrote essays highlighting Melville's formal and linguistic innovations. His influence on these writers, and on many writers that followed in the twentieth and twenty-first centuries, has been profound; poets such as W.H. Auden and Hart Crane have commemorated Melville in verse, and Ralph Ellison's groundbreaking novel *Invisible Man* (1952) creatively interprets aspects of *The Confidence-Man* and bears an epigraph drawn from *Benito Cereno*. Melville's reputation among readers and critics has only increased in the century that followed the Revival, but for a long time his fame was based almost solely on *Moby-Dick*, and to a lesser extent *Billy Budd*; it was not until the 1960s that critics and readers began engaging with the short fiction, and not until even more recently that his poetry has found an appreciative audience.

Twenty-first-century scholars have continued to explore the aesthetic, generic, and formal dimensions of Melville's work, and his fiction and poetry are essential to discourses in American literary studies on sexuality, transatlanticism, ecocriticism, and race, as well as to conversations around settler colonialism, imperialism, and the excesses of capitalism—his story "Bartleby, the Scrivener," for example, was an inspirational text for the Occupy Wall Street movement. As American literary studies move away from a nationalist approach and towards a more hemispheric one, Melville has taken on a more global identity—one anticipated, in the 1950s, by the Trinidadian anticolonial activist C.L.R. James's enthusiastic admiration for him. Melville's "ruthless democracy," as he himself called it, made him a voice for the displaced and oppressed; his unwavering commitment to depict the "meanest mariners, and renegades, and castaways" and "weave around them tragic graces" continues to forge connections with new generations of readers, who come to his allusive, complex texts again and again for their sheer linguistic power, but also for their unique ability to bring the reader to the outer edges of perception, where change becomes possible.

———————————

NOTE ON THE TEXTS: The texts of Melville's works presented here are based on their earliest printings. The text of *Moby Dick* has been prepared while consulting the first American edition of *Moby Dick*, the first British edition (*The Whale*), and the authoritative Northwestern-Newberry edition (1998). This anthology's usual practices of modernization have not been followed in the case of *Moby-Dick*; spelling and punctuation from the original printings have been retained. The shorter stories "Bartleby, the Scrivener" and *Benito Cereno* are based on Brian Yothers's Broadview edition of *The Piazza Tales*, which is in turn based on the 1856 first edition of *The Piazza Tales* published by Dix & Edwards. Where the first edition and the initial magazine publication of the stories in *Putnam's Monthly* are in substantial conflict, Yothers followed the versions in *The Piazza Tales* (1856). The texts from *Battle-Pieces* are based on the first edition printed in New York by Harper & Brothers in 1866.

⌘ ⌘ ⌘

from *Moby-Dick, or The Whale*

CHAPTER 42. THE WHITENESS OF THE WHALE.

What the white whale was to Ahab,[1] has been hinted; what, at times, he was to me, as yet remains unsaid. Aside from those more obvious considerations touching Moby Dick, which could not but occasionally awaken in any man's soul some alarm, there was another thought, or rather vague, nameless horror concerning him, which at times by its intensity completely overpowered all the rest; and yet so mystical and well nigh ineffable was it, that I almost despair of putting it in a comprehensible form. It was the whiteness of the whale that above all things appalled me. But how can I hope to explain myself here; and yet, in some dim, random way, explain myself I must, else all these chapters might be naught.

Though in many natural objects, whiteness refiningly enhances beauty, as if imparting some special virtue of its own, as in marbles, japonicas,[2] and pearls; and though various nations have in some way recognised a certain royal preeminence in this hue; even the barbaric, grand old kings of Pegu[3] placing the title "Lord of the White Elephants" above all their other magniloquent ascriptions of dominion; and the modern kings of Siam[4] unfurling the same snow-white quadruped in the royal standard; and the Hanoverian flag[5] bearing the one figure of a snow-white charger; and the great Austrian Empire, Cæsarian heir to overlording Rome,[6] having for the imperial colour the same impe-

rial hue; and though this pre-eminence in it applies to the human race itself, giving the white man ideal mastership over every dusky tribe; and though, besides all this, whiteness has been even made significant of gladness, for among the Romans a white stone marked a joyful day; and though in other mortal sympathies and symbolizings, this same hue is made the emblem of many touching, noble things—the innocence of brides, the benignity of age; though among the Red Men of America the giving of the white belt of wampum[7] was the deepest pledge of honor; though in many climes, whiteness typifies the majesty of Justice in the ermine of the Judge, and contributes to the daily state of kings and queens drawn by milk-white steeds; though even in the higher mysteries of the most august religions it has been made the symbol of the divine spotlessness and power; by the Persian fire worshippers,[8] the white forked flame being held the holiest on the altar; and in the Greek mythologies, Great Jove himself being made incarnate in a snow-white bull; and though to the noble Iroquois, the midwinter sacrifice of the sacred White Dog was by far the holiest festival of their theology, that spotless, faithful creature being held the purest envoy they could send to the Great Spirit with the annual tidings of their own fidelity; and though directly from the Latin word for white, all Christian priests derive the name of one part of their sacred vesture, the alb or tunic, worn beneath the cassock; and though among the holy pomps of the Romish faith, white is specially employed in the celebration of the Passion of our Lord; though in the Vision of St. John, white robes are given to the redeemed, and the four-and-twenty elders stand clothed in white before the great white throne, and the Holy One that sitteth there white like wool;[9] yet for all these accumulated asso-

---

1   *Ahab*   Captain of the *Pequod*, the whaling ship on which the speaker, Ishmael, is embarked as a member of the crew. A grim mystery surrounds Captain Ahab, who lost his leg to a legendary white sperm whale known as Moby Dick and is now obsessed with hunting down and killing the whale. Ahab is described in the Bible as a wicked king who did "evil in the sight of the Lord above all that were before him" (1 Kings 16.30).

2   *japonicas*   Flowering camellia plants from Japan.

3   *Pegu*   Region that is located in what is now south-central Myanmar.

4   *Siam*   Thailand.

5   *Hanoverian flag*   Flag of the Electorate (later Kingdom) of Hanover, a German state from 1692–1807 and again from 1814–37.

6   *Austrian Empire ... overlording Rome*   The Austrian Empire (1804–1918) evolved from the Holy Roman Empire, the emperor of

which claimed his legitimacy from the ancient Roman emperors or "Caesars."

7   *wampum*   Shell beads used by various Indigenous peoples for purposes including gifts, record-keeping, and trade.

8   *Persian fire worshippers*   Zoroastrians. Members of this faith pray in the presence of fire due to its association with wisdom and spiritual insight. A "fire worshipper" named Fedallah plays a significant role in *Moby-Dick* as Ahab's sinister "shadow" and voice of the fate that supposedly awaits him.

9   *Vision of St. John ... wool*   See the Book of Revelation (traditionally believed to have been written by St. John), especially 7.9–14, 4.4, and 1.14.

ciations, with whatever is sweet, and honorable, and sublime, there yet lurks an elusive something in the innermost idea of this hue, which strikes more of panic to the soul than that redness which affrights in blood.

This elusive quality it is, which causes the thought of whiteness, when divorced from more kindly associations, and coupled with any object terrible in itself, to heighten that terror to the furthest bounds. Witness the white bear of the poles, and the white shark of the tropics; what but their smooth, flaky whiteness makes them the transcendent horrors they are? That ghastly whiteness it is which imparts such an abhorrent mildness, even more loathsome than terrific, to the dumb gloating of their aspect. So that not the fierce-fanged tiger in his heraldic coat can so stagger courage as the white-shrouded bear or shark.[1]

Bethink thee of the albatross, whence come those clouds of spiritual wonderment and pale dread, in which that white phantom sails in all imaginations? Not Coleridge first threw that spell;[2] but God's great, unflattering laureate, Nature.[3]

Most famous in our Western annals and Indian traditions is that of the White Steed of the Prairies; a magnificent milk-white charger, large-eyed, small-headed, bluff-chested, and with the dignity of a thousand monarchs in his lofty, overscorning carriage. He was the elected Xerxes[4] of vast herds of wild horses, whose pastures in those days were only fenced by the Rocky Mountains and the Alleghanies. At their flaming head he westward trooped it like that chosen star which every evening leads on the hosts of light. The flashing cascade of his mane, the curving comet of his tail, invested him with housings[5] more resplendent than gold and silver-beaters could have furnished him. A most imperial and archangelical apparition of that

embrace some holy ark. Wondrous flutterings and throbbings shook it. Though bodily unharmed, it uttered cries, as some king's ghost in supernatural distress. Through its inexpressible, strange eyes, methought I peeped to secrets which took hold of God. As Abraham before the angels, I bowed myself [see Genesis 18.2]; the white thing was so white, its wings so wide, and in those for ever exiled waters, I had lost the miserable warping memories of traditions and of towns. Long I gazed at that prodigy of plumage. I cannot tell, can only hint, the things that darted through me then. But at last I awoke; and turning, asked a sailor what bird was this. A goney, he replied. Goney! I never had heard that name before; is it conceivable that this glorious thing is utterly unknown to men ashore! never! But some time after, I learned that goney was some seaman's name for albatross. So that by no possibility could Coleridge's wild Rhyme have had aught to do with those mystical impressions which were mine, when I saw that bird upon our deck. For neither had I then read the Rhyme, nor knew the bird to be an albatross. Yet, in saying this, I do but indirectly burnish a little brighter the noble merit of the poem and the poet.

I assert, then, that in the wondrous bodily whiteness of the bird chiefly lurks the secret of the spell; a truth the more evinced in this, that by a solecism of terms there are birds called grey albatrosses; and these I have frequently seen, but never with such emotions as when I beheld the Antarctic fowl.

But how had the mystic thing been caught? Whisper it not, and I will tell; with a treacherous hook and line, as the fowl floated on the sea. At last the Captain made a postman of it; tying a lettered, leathern tally [stick with carved messages] round its neck, with the ship's time and place; and then letting it escape. But I doubt not, that leathern tally, meant for man, was taken off in Heaven, when the white fowl flew to join the wing-folding, the invoking, and adoring cherubim!

---

[1] [Melville's note] With reference to the Polar bear, it may possibly be urged by him who would fain go still deeper into this matter, that it is not the whiteness, separately regarded, which heightens the intolerable hideousness of that brute; for, analysed, that heightened hideousness, it might be said, only rises from the circumstance, that the irresponsible ferociousness of the creature stands invested in the fleece of celestial innocence and love; and hence, by bringing together two such opposite emotions in our minds, the Polar bear frightens us with so unnatural a contrast. But even assuming all this to be true; yet, were it not for the whiteness, you would not have that intensified terror.

   As for the white shark, the white gliding ghostliness of repose in that creature, when beheld in his ordinary moods, strangely tallies with the same quality in the Polar quadruped. This peculiarity is most vividly hit by the French in the name they bestow upon that fish. The Romish mass for the dead begins with "Requiem eternam" (eternal rest), whence Requiem denominating the mass itself, and any other funeral music. Now, in allusion to the white, silent stillness of death in this shark, and the mild deadliness of his habits, the French call him *Requin*.

[2] *Coleridge … spell* Melville is referring to Samuel Taylor Coleridge's famous poem featuring an albatross, *The Rime of the Ancient Mariner* (1798).

[3] [Melville's note] I remember the first albatross I ever saw. It was during a prolonged gale, in waters hard upon the Antarctic seas. From my forenoon watch below, I ascended to the overclouded deck; and there, dashed upon the main hatches, I saw a regal, feathery thing of unspotted whiteness, and with a hooked, Roman bill sublime. At intervals, it arched forth its vast archangel wings, as if to

[4] *Xerxes* King of Persia (c. 518–465 BCE) who gained inherited, not elected, power.

[5] *housings* Trappings or ornaments that extend from the horse's saddle over its back and sides.

unfallen, western world,[1] which to the eyes of the old trappers and hunters revived the glories of those primeval times when Adam walked majestic as a god, bluff-browed and fearless as this mighty steed. Whether marching amid his aides and marshals in the van[2] of countless cohorts that endlessly streamed it over the plains, like an Ohio; or whether with his circumambient subjects browsing all around at the horizon, the White Steed gallopingly reviewed them with warm nostrils reddening through his cool milkiness; in whatever aspect he presented himself, always to the bravest Indians he was the object of trembling reverence and awe. Nor can it be questioned from what stands on legendary record of this noble horse, that it was his spiritual whiteness chiefly, which so clothed him with divineness; and that this divineness had that in it which, though commanding worship, at the same time enforced a certain nameless terror.

But there are other instances where this whiteness loses all that accessory and strange glory which invests it in the White Steed and Albatross.

What is it that in the Albino man so peculiarly repels and often shocks the eye, as that sometimes he is loathed by his own kith[3] and kin! It is that whiteness which invests him, a thing expressed by the name he bears.[4] The Albino is as well made as other men—has no substantive deformity—and yet this mere aspect of all-pervading whiteness makes him more strangely hideous than the ugliest abortion.[5] Why should this be so?

Nor, in quite other aspects, does Nature in her least palpable but not the less malicious agencies, fail to enlist among her forces this crowning attribute of the terrible. From its snowy aspect, the gauntleted ghost of the Southern Seas has been denominated the White Squall. Nor, in some historic instances, has the art of human malice omitted so potent an auxiliary. How wildly it heightens the effect of that passage in Froissart, when, masked in the snowy symbol of their faction, the desperate White Hoods of Ghent murder their bailiff in the market-place![6]

Nor, in some things, does the common, hereditary experience of all mankind fail to bear witness to the supernaturalism of this hue. It cannot well be doubted, that the one visible quality in the aspect of the dead which most appals the gazer, is the marble pallor lingering there; as if indeed that pallor were as much like the badge of consternation in the other world, as of mortal trepidation here. And from that pallor of the dead, we borrow the expressive hue of the shroud in which we wrap them. Nor even in our superstitions do we fail to throw the same snowy mantle round our phantoms; all ghosts rising in a milk-white fog—Yea, while these terrors seize us, let us add, that even the king of terrors, when personified by the evangelist, rides on his pallid horse.[7]

Therefore, in his other moods, symbolize whatever grand or gracious thing he will by whiteness, no man can deny that in its profoundest idealized significance it calls up a peculiar apparition to the soul.

But though without dissent this point be fixed, how is mortal man to account for it? To analyse it, would seem impossible. Can we, then, by the citation of some of those instances wherein this thing of whiteness—though for the time either wholly or in great part stripped of all direct associations calculated to impart to it aught fearful, but nevertheless, is found to exert over us the same sorcery, however modified;—can we thus hope to light upon some chance clue to conduct us to the hidden cause we seek?

Let us try. But in a matter like this, subtlety appeals to subtlety, and without imagination no man can follow another into these halls. And though, doubtless, some at least of the imaginative impressions about to be presented may have been shared by most men,

---

1   *unfallen, western world*   North America before European colonial encroachment.

2   *van*   Forefront.

3   *kith*   Friends and acquaintances.

4   *Albino ... name he bears*   "Albino" is a borrowing from Portuguese, referring to a person lacking the pigment melanin; the term is based on the Latin "albus," meaning "white."

5   *abortion*   In this context, a person imperfectly made, a monstrosity.

6   *Froissart ... market-place*   This description is from the *Chronicles* (written c. 1379–c. 1405) of the medieval French historian Jean Froissart. The White Hoods were a militia in medieval Ghent and Bruges; in the incident referred to here, a city bailiff was sent to arrest the leaders of the White Hoods, but the White Hoods kill the bailiff before he can do so.

7   *king of terrors ... pallid horse*   See Revelation 6.8, attributed to St. John the Evangelist: "And I looked, and behold a pale horse: and his name that sat on him was Death, and Hell followed with him."

yet few perhaps were entirely conscious of them at the time, and therefore may not be able to recall them now.

Why to the man of untutored ideality,[1] who happens to be but loosely acquainted with the peculiar character of the day, does the bare mention of Whitsuntide[2] marshal in the fancy such long, dreary, speechless processions of slow-pacing pilgrims, down-cast and hooded with new-fallen snow? Or, to the unread, unsophisticated Protestant of the Middle American States, why does the passing mention of a White Friar or a White Nun,[3] evoke such an eyeless statue in the soul?

Or what is there apart from the traditions of dungeoned warriors and kings (which will not wholly account for it) that makes the White Tower of London tell so much more strongly on the imagination of an untravelled American, than those other storied structures, its neighbors—the Byward Tower, or even the Bloody?[4] And those sublimer towers, the White Mountains of New Hampshire, whence, in peculiar moods, comes that gigantic ghostliness over the soul at the bare mention of that name, while the thought of Virginia's Blue Ridge is full of a soft, dewy, distant dreaminess? Or why, irrespective of all latitudes and longitudes, does the name of the White Sea exert such a spectralness over the fancy, while that of the Yellow Sea[5] lulls us with mortal thoughts of long lacquered mild afternoons on the waves, followed by the gaudiest and yet sleepiest of sunsets? Or, to choose a wholly unsubstantial instance, purely addressed to the fancy, why, in reading the old fairy tales of Central Europe, does "the tall pale man" of the Hartz forests, whose changeless pallor unrustlingly glides through the green of the groves—why is this phantom more terrible than all the whooping imps of the Blocksburg?[6]

Nor is it, altogether, the remembrance of her cathedral-toppling earthquakes; nor the stampedoes of her frantic seas; nor the tearlessness of arid skies that never rain;[7] nor the sight of her wide field of leaning spires, wrenched cope-stones, and crosses all adroop (like canted yards[8] of anchored fleets); and her suburban avenues of house-walls lying over upon each other, as a tossed pack of cards;[9]—it is not these things alone which make tearless Lima, the strangest, saddest city thou can'st see. For Lima has taken the white veil;[10] and there is a higher horror in this whiteness of her woe. Old as Pizarro,[11] this whiteness keeps her ruins for ever new; admits not the cheerful greenness of complete decay; spreads over her broken ramparts the rigid pallor of an apoplexy[12] that fixes its own distortions.

I know that, to the common apprehension, this phenomenon of whiteness is not confessed to be the prime agent in exaggerating the terror of objects otherwise terrible; nor to the unimaginative mind is there aught of terror in those appearances whose awfulness to another mind almost solely consists in this one phenomenon, especially when exhibited under any form at all approaching to muteness or universality. What I

---

[1] *ideality* Imaginativeness.

[2] *Whitsuntide* Church season of Pentecost, beginning on Whitsunday (a contraction of "White Sunday"), that celebrated the descent of the Holy Spirit upon the Apostles. Confirmation and baptismal ceremonies are frequently held on Pentecost, for which white robes are traditionally worn.

[3] *White Friar ... White Nun* Ghostly nuns and friars are common motifs in Gothic fiction.

[4] *White Tower ... Byward Tower ... Bloody* Individual towers in the fortress known as the Tower of London. The White Tower, built between 1078 and 1097, is the keep of the castle and housed soldiers and acted as a prison. It was whitewashed inside and out in 1240 on the orders of Henry III. The Bloody Tower was built between 1238 and 1272 and was thought to be the site of the murder of the two "Princes in the Tower"—Edward V and his brother the Duke of York—as well as the site of the death of Henry VI. Byward Tower, also built between 1238 and 1272, was the gatehouse to the Outer Ward of the fortress.

[5] *White Sea* Inlet of the Barents Sea off the northwest Russian coast; *Yellow Sea* Inlet off the Pacific Ocean between China and the Korean peninsula.

[6] *tall pale man ... Hartz forests* Der Grossman, or the "Tall Man" or "Slenderman" is a medieval folktale figure who lives in the Black Forest, luring children to the woods; *imps of the Blocksburg* Blocksberg is the highest mountain in the Harz range in Germany; the mountain has long been thought to be peopled with devils and witches.

[7] *never rain* Lima, Peru, receives less than two inches of rain per year.

[8] *canted yards* Supports for the sails that are tilted while a vessel is at anchor.

[9] *wrenched ... cards* An earthquake in 1746 caused extensive damage to Lima, which was still evident when Melville visited in 1844.

[10] *Lima ... white veil* Some of the most prominent architecture in Lima at this time was made with white stone (the Presidential Palace, the Cathedral of Lima, the Archbishop's Palace, and Aliaga House, for example). When initiates become nuns, they "take the white veil" as a symbolic representation of their marriage with Christ.

[11] *Pizarro* Francisco Pizarro (c. 1470–1541) founded Lima in 1535.

[12] *apoplexy* Sudden loss of consciousness, a stroke.

mean by these two statements may perhaps be respectively elucidated by the following examples.

First: The mariner, when drawing nigh the coasts of foreign lands, if by night he hear the roar of breakers, starts to vigilance, and feels just enough of trepidation to sharpen all his faculties; but under precisely similar circumstances, let him be called from his hammock to view his ship sailing through a midnight sea of milky whiteness—as if from encircling headlands shoals of combed white bears were swimming round him, then he feels a silent, superstitious dread; the shrouded phantom of the whitened waters is horrible to him as a real ghost; in vain the lead assures him he is still off soundings;[1] heart and helm they both go down; he never rests till blue water is under him again. Yet where is the mariner who will tell thee, "Sir, it was not so much the fear of striking hidden rocks, as the fear of that hideous whiteness that so stirred me"?

Second: To the native Indian of Peru, the continual sight of the snow-howdahed[2] Andes conveys naught of dread, except, perhaps, in the mere fancying of the eternal frosted desolateness reigning at such vast altitudes, and the natural conceit of what a fearfulness it would be to lose oneself in such inhuman solitudes. Much the same is it with the backwoodsman of the West, who with comparative indifference views an unbounded prairie sheeted with driven snow, no shadow of tree or twig to break the fixed trance of whiteness. Not so the sailor, beholding the scenery of the Antarctic seas; where at times, by some infernal trick of legerdemain[3] in the powers of frost and air, he, shivering and half shipwrecked, instead of rainbows speaking hope and solace to his misery, views what seems a boundless church-yard grinning upon him with its lean ice monuments and splintered crosses.

But thou sayest, methinks that white-lead[4] chapter about whiteness is but a white flag hung out from a craven soul; thou surrenderest to a hypo,[5] Ishmael.

Tell me, why this strong young colt, foaled in some peaceful valley of Vermont, far removed from all beasts of prey—why is it that upon the sunniest day, if you but shake a fresh buffalo robe behind him, so that he cannot even see it, but only smells its wild animal muskiness—why will he start, snort, and with bursting eyes paw the ground in phrensies[6] of affright? There is no remembrance in him of any gorings of wild creatures in his green northern home, so that the strange muskiness he smells cannot recall to him anything associated with the experience of former perils; for what knows he, this New England colt, of the black bisons of distant Oregon?

No: but here thou beholdest even in a dumb brute, the instinct of the knowledge of the demonism in the world. Though thousands of miles from Oregon, still when he smells that savage musk, the rending, goring bison herds are as present as to the deserted wild foal of the prairies, which this instant they may be trampling into dust.

Thus, then, the muffled rollings of a milky sea; the bleak rustlings of the festooned frosts of mountains; the desolate shiftings of the windrowed[7] snows of prairies; all these, to Ishmael, are as the shaking of that buffalo robe to the frightened colt!

Though neither knows where lie the nameless things of which the mystic sign gives forth such hints; yet with me, as with the colt, somewhere those things must exist. Though in many of its aspects this visible world seems formed in love, the invisible spheres were formed in fright.

But not yet have we solved the incantation of this whiteness, and learned why it appeals with such power to the soul; and more strange and far more portentous—why, as we have seen, it is at once the most meaning symbol of spiritual things, nay, the very veil of the Christian's Deity; and yet should be as it is, the intensifying agent in things the most appalling to mankind.

Is it that by its indefiniteness it shadows forth the heartless voids and immensities of the universe, and thus stabs us from behind with the thought of annihilation, when beholding the white depths of the milky way? Or is it, that as in essence whiteness is not so much

---

1   *off soundings*   In water deep enough that the soundings—the lines and weights used to test the depth of surrounding water—do not hit bottom.

2   *snow-howdahed*   Snow-topped (a howdah is the structure placed on top of an elephant's back to seat riders).

3   *legerdemain*   Sleight of hand.

4   *white-lead*   Carbonate of lead used to make white pigments.

5   *hypo*   Episode of anxiety or hypochondria.

6   *phrensies*   I.e., frenzies.

7   *windrowed*   Blown into rows by the wind.

a color as the visible absence of color; and at the same time the concrete of all colors; is it for these reasons that there is such a dumb blankness, full of meaning, in a wide landscape of snows—a colorless, all-color of atheism from which we shrink? And when we consider that other theory of the natural philosophers,[1] that all other earthly hues—every stately or lovely emblazoning—the sweet tinges of sunset skies and woods; yea, and the gilded velvets of butterflies, and the butterfly cheeks of young girls; all these are but subtile deceits, not actually inherent in substances, but only laid on from without; so that all deified Nature absolutely paints like the harlot, whose allurements cover nothing but the charnel-house within;[2] and when we proceed further, and consider that the mystical cosmetic which produces every one of her hues, the great principle of light, for ever remains white or colorless in itself, and if operating without medium upon matter, would touch all objects, even tulips and roses, with its own blank tinge—pondering all this, the palsied universe lies before us a leper; and like wilful travellers in Lapland, who refuse to wear colored and coloring glasses[3] upon their eyes, so the wretched infidel gazes himself blind at the monumental white shroud that wraps all the prospect around him. And of all these things the Albino whale was the symbol. Wonder ye then at the fiery hunt?

—1851

[NOTE: Further selections from *Moby-Dick* are included in the online component of this anthology.]

Bartleby, the Scrivener

I am a rather elderly man. The nature of my avocations, for the last thirty years, has brought me into more than ordinary contact with what would seem an interesting and somewhat singular set of men, of whom, as yet, nothing, that I know of, has ever been written—I mean, the law-copyists, or scriveners.[4] I have known very many of them, professionally and privately, and, if I pleased, could relate diverse histories, at which good-natured gentlemen might smile, and sentimental souls might weep. But I waive the biographies of all other scriveners, for a few passages in the life of Bartleby, who was a scrivener, the strangest I ever saw, or heard of. While, of other law-copyists, I might write the complete life, of Bartleby nothing of that sort can be done. I believe that no materials exist, for a full and satisfactory biography of this man. It is an irreparable loss to literature. Bartleby was one of those beings of whom nothing is ascertainable, except from the original sources, and, in his case, those are very small. What my own astonished eyes saw of Bartleby, *that* is all I know of him, except, indeed, one vague report, which will appear in the sequel.[5]

Ere introducing the scrivener, as he first appeared to me, it is fit I make some mention of myself, my *employés*,[6] my business, my chambers, and general surroundings; because some such description is indispensable to an adequate understanding of the chief character about to be presented. Imprimis:[7] I am a man who, from his youth upwards, has been filled with a profound conviction that the easiest way of life is the best. Hence, though I belong to a profession proverbially energetic and nervous, even to turbulence, at times, yet nothing of that sort have I ever suffered to invade my peace. I am one of those unambitious lawyers who never addresses a jury, or in any way draws

---

1   *natural philosophers* Those studying the physical and natural world, precursors to today's scientists. Some, such as John Locke (1628–1704), believed that "secondary" qualities in physical objects (like color) are painted on by the mind and are not inherent in the object itself.

2   *allurements … within* See Matthew 23.27: "Woe unto you, scribes and Pharisees, hypocrites! for ye are like unto whited sepulchres, which indeed appear beautiful outward, but are within full of dead men's bones, and of all uncleanness."

3   *colored and coloring glasses* I.e., sunglasses.

---

4   *avocations* Employments, vocations; *scriveners* People employed to copy or write documents.

5   *sequel* Refers not to a follow-up story, but to the "vague report" that is relayed to the reader at the end of this story.

6   *employés* French: employees.

7   *Imprimis* Latin: In the first place; often used by lawyers to introduce the first in a list of items (in a will, for instance).

down public applause; but, in the cool tranquility of a snug retreat, do a snug business among rich men's bonds, and mortgages, and title-deeds. All who know me, consider me an eminently *safe* man. The late John Jacob Astor,[1] a personage little given to poetic enthusiasm, had no hesitation in pronouncing my first grand point to be prudence; my next, method. I do not speak it in vanity, but simply record the fact, that I was not unemployed in my profession by the late John Jacob Astor; a name which, I admit, I love to repeat; for it hath a rounded and orbicular sound to it, and rings like unto bullion.[2] I will freely add, that I was not insensible to the late John Jacob Astor's good opinion.

Some time prior to the period at which this little history begins, my avocations had been largely increased. The good old office, now extinct in the State of New York, of a Master in Chancery,[3] had been conferred upon me. It was not a very arduous office, but very pleasantly remunerative. I seldom lose my temper; much more seldom indulge in dangerous indignation at wrongs and outrages; but, I must be permitted to be rash here, and declare, that I consider the sudden and violent abrogation of the office of Master in Chancery, by the new Constitution, as a ———[4] premature act; inasmuch as I had counted upon a life-lease of the profits, whereas I only received those of a few short years. But this is by the way.

My chambers were up stairs, at No. —— Wall street. At one end, they looked upon the white wall of the interior of a spacious skylight shaft, penetrating the building from top to bottom.

This view might have been considered rather tame than otherwise, deficient in what landscape painters call "life." But, if so, the view from the other end of my chambers offered, at least, a contrast, if nothing more. In that direction, my windows commanded an unobstructed view of a lofty brick wall, black by age and everlasting shade; which wall required no spy-glass[5] to bring out its lurking beauties, but, for the benefit of all near-sighted spectators, was pushed up to within ten feet of my window panes. Owing to the great height of the surrounding buildings, and my chambers being on the second floor, the interval between this wall and mine not a little resembled a huge square cistern.[6]

At the period just preceding the advent of Bartleby, I had two persons as copyists in my employment, and a promising lad as an office-boy. First, Turkey; second, Nippers; third, Ginger Nut. These may seem names, the like of which are not usually found in the Directory. In truth, they were nicknames, mutually conferred upon each other by my three clerks, and were deemed expressive of their respective persons or characters. Turkey was a short, pursy[7] Englishman, of about my own age—that is, somewhere not far from sixty. In the morning, one might say, his face was of a fine florid hue, but after twelve o'clock, meridian[8]—his dinner hour—it blazed like a grate full of Christmas coals; and continued blazing—but, as it were, with a gradual wane—till six o'clock, P.M., or thereabouts; after which, I saw no more of the proprietor of the face, which, gaining its meridian with the sun, seemed to set with it, to rise, culminate, and decline the following day, with the like regularity and undiminished glory. There are many singular coincidences I have known in the course of my life, not the least among which was the fact, that, exactly when Turkey displayed his fullest beams from his red and radiant countenance, just then, too, at that critical moment, began the daily period when I considered his business capacities as seriously disturbed for the remainder of the twenty-four hours. Not that he was absolutely idle, or averse to business, then; far from it. The difficulty was, he was apt to be altogether too energetic. There was a strange, inflamed, flurried, flighty recklessness of activity about him. He would be incautious in dipping his pen into his ink-stand. All his blots upon my documents were dropped there after twelve o'clock, meridian. Indeed, not only

---

[1] *John Jacob Astor* Wealthy American businessperson (1763–1848) who made his fortune in the fur trade.

[2] *orbicular* Spherical; *bullion* Raw gold or silver.

[3] *Master in Chancery* Senior supervisory role at the Court of Chancery. The New York Chancery Court, which existed from 1701 to 1847, dealt with equity matters and functioned as a court of appeals for the state Supreme Court.

[4] *abrogation ... new Constitution* The Court of Chancery was abolished in 1847 when the New York state judicial system was overhauled in accordance with the State Constitutional Convention of 1846; —— The dashes are marking an expletive.

[5] *spy-glass* Telescope.

[6] *cistern* Water tank (often these were set high up on a building to supply it with water).

[7] *pursy* Fat.

[8] *meridian* Noon.

would he be reckless, and sadly given to making blots in the afternoon, but, some days, he went further, and was rather noisy. At such times, too, his face flamed with augmented blazonry, as if cannel coal had been heaped on anthracite.[1] He made an unpleasant racket with his chair; spilled his sand-box;[2] in mending his pens, impatiently split them all to pieces, and threw them on the floor in a sudden passion; stood up, and leaned over his table, boxing his papers about in a most indecorous manner, very sad to behold in an elderly man like him. Nevertheless, as he was in many ways a most valuable person to me, and all the time before twelve o'clock, meridian, was the quickest, steadiest creature, too, accomplishing a great deal of work in a style not easily to be matched—for these reasons, I was willing to overlook his eccentricities, though, indeed, occasionally, I remonstrated with him. I did this very gently, however, because, though the civilest, nay, the blandest and most reverential of men in the morning, yet, in the afternoon, he was disposed, upon provocation, to be slightly rash with his tongue—in fact, insolent. Now, valuing his morning services as I did, and resolved not to lose them—yet, at the same time, made uncomfortable by his inflamed ways after twelve o'clock—and being a man of peace, unwilling by my admonitions to call forth unseemly retorts from him, I took upon me, one Saturday noon (he was always worse on Saturdays)[3] to hint to him, very kindly, that, perhaps, now that he was growing old, it might be well to abridge his labors; in short, he need not come to my chambers after twelve o'clock, but, dinner over, had best go home to his lodgings, and rest himself till tea-time.[4] But no; he insisted upon his afternoon devotions. His countenance became intolerably fervid, as he oratorically assured me—gesticulating with a long ruler at the other end of the room—that if his services

in the morning were useful, how indispensable, then, in the afternoon?

"With submission, sir," said Turkey, on this occasion, "I consider myself your right-hand man. In the morning I but marshal and deploy my columns; but in the afternoon I put myself at their head, and gallantly charge the foe, thus"—and he made a violent thrust with the ruler.

"But the blots, Turkey," intimated I.

"True; but, with submission, sir, behold these hairs! I am getting old. Surely, sir, a blot or two of a warm afternoon is not to be severely urged against gray hairs. Old age—even if it blot the page—is honorable. With submission, sir, we *both* are getting old."

This appeal to my fellow-feeling was hardly to be resisted. At all events, I saw that go he would not. So, I made up my mind to let him stay, resolving, nevertheless, to see to it that, during the afternoon, he had to do with my less important papers.

Nippers, the second on my list, was a whiskered, sallow, and, upon the whole, rather piratical-looking young man, of about five and twenty. I always deemed him the victim of two evil powers—ambition and indigestion. The ambition was evinced by a certain impatience of the duties of a mere copyist, an unwarrantable usurpation of strictly professional affairs, such as the original drawing up of legal documents. The indigestion seemed betokened in an occasional nervous testiness and grinning irritability, causing the teeth to audibly grind together over mistakes committed in copying; unnecessary maledictions, hissed, rather than spoken, in the heat of business; and especially by a continual discontent with the height of the table where he worked. Though of a very ingenious mechanical turn, Nippers could never get this table to suit him. He put chips under it, blocks of various sorts, bits of pasteboard, and at last went so far as to attempt an exquisite adjustment, by final pieces of folded blotting-paper. But no invention would answer.[5] If, for the sake of easing his back, he brought the table lid at a sharp angle well up towards his chin, and wrote there like a man using the steep roof of a Dutch house for his desk, then he declared that it stopped the circulation in his arms. If now he lowered the table to his waistbands, and stooped over it in writing, then there was

---

[1] *blazonry* The art of depicting armorial symbols, but in this case used figuratively to mean "coloring"; *cannel coal* Hard coal with a bright flame; *anthracite* Hard, high-quality coal that burns with little flame or smoke.

[2] *sand-box* Box filled with sand used to blot ink.

[3] *on Saturdays* It was customary to work a six-day work week in the nineteenth century (the five-day work week was only instituted in the U.S. in the mid-twentieth century).

[4] *tea-time* Four or five o'clock in the afternoon.

[5] *answer* Suffice.

a sore aching in his back. In short, the truth of the matter was, Nippers knew not what he wanted. Or, if he wanted anything, it was to be rid of a scrivener's table altogether. Among the manifestations of his diseased ambition was a fondness he had for receiving visits from certain ambiguous-looking fellows in seedy coats, whom he called his clients. Indeed, I was aware that not only was he, at times, considerable of a ward-politician, but he occasionally did a little business at the Justices' courts, and was not unknown on the steps of the Tombs.[1] I have good reason to believe, however, that one individual who called upon him at my chambers, and who, with a grand air, he insisted was his client, was no other than a dun,[2] and the alleged title-deed, a bill. But, with all his failings, and the annoyances he caused me, Nippers, like his compatriot Turkey, was a very useful man to me; wrote a neat, swift hand; and, when he chose, was not deficient in a gentlemanly sort of deportment. Added to this, he always dressed in a gentlemanly sort of way; and so, incidentally, reflected credit upon my chambers. Whereas, with respect to Turkey, I had much ado to keep him from being a reproach to me. His clothes were apt to look oily, and smell of eating-houses. He wore his pantaloons very loose and baggy in summer. His coats were execrable; his hat not to be handled. But while the hat was a thing of indifference to me, inasmuch as his natural civility and deference, as a dependent[3] Englishman, always led him to doff it the moment he entered the room, yet his coat was another matter. Concerning his coats, I reasoned with him; but with no effect. The truth was, I suppose, that a man with so small an income could not afford to sport such

a lustrous face and a lustrous coat at one and the same time. As Nippers once observed, Turkey's money went chiefly for red ink.[4] One winter day, I presented Turkey with a highly respectable-looking coat of my own—a padded gray coat, of a most comfortable warmth, and which buttoned straight up from the knee to the neck. I thought Turkey would appreciate the favor, and abate his rashness and obstreperousness of afternoons. But no; I verily believe that buttoning himself up in so downy and blanket-like a coat had a pernicious effect upon him—upon the same principle that too much oats are bad for horses. In fact, precisely as a rash, restive horse is said to feel his oats, so Turkey felt his coat. It made him insolent. He was a man whom prosperity harmed.

Though, concerning the self-indulgent habits of Turkey, I had my own private surmises, yet, touching Nippers, I was well persuaded that, whatever might be his faults in other respects, he was, at least, a temperate[5] young man. But, indeed, nature herself seemed to have been his vintner, and, at his birth, charged him so thoroughly with an irritable, brandy-like disposition, that all subsequent potations[6] were needless. When I consider how, amid the stillness of my chambers, Nippers would sometimes impatiently rise from his seat, and stooping over his table, spread his arms wide apart, seize the whole desk, and move it, and jerk it, with a grim, grinding motion on the floor, as if the table were a perverse voluntary agent, intent on thwarting and vexing him, I plainly perceive that, for Nippers, brandy-and-water were altogether superfluous.

It was fortunate for me that, owing to its peculiar cause—indigestion—the irritability and consequent nervousness of Nippers were mainly observable in the morning, while in the afternoon he was comparatively mild. So that, Turkey's paroxysms only coming on about twelve o'clock, I never had to do with their eccentricities at one time. Their fits relieved each other, like guards. When Nippers's was on, Turkey's was off; and *vice versa*. This was a good natural arrangement, under the circumstances.

---

[1]   *considerable of a ward-politician*   Of importance to a local politician; this phrase can also be interpreted to mean that Nippers has ambitions of becoming a local politician; *Justices' courts*   I.e., the courts of the State judges;   *the Tombs*   Informal name for the city prison, known formally as the New York City Halls of Justice and House of Detention. Built in the Egyptian Revival style, the prison was situated on what had been the Collect Pond. The area had been drained and filled in, but not very successfully, and soon after the Tombs was built it began to sink into the ground, creating damp and unhealthy conditions for the inmates. After visiting the prison in 1842, Charles Dickens wrote that "such indecent and disgusting dungeons as these cells, would bring disgrace upon the most despotic empire in the world."

[2]   *dun*   Debt collector.

[3]   *dependent*   Subordinate.

[4]   *red ink*   Wine.

[5]   *temperate*   Moderate, avoiding alcohol.

[6]   *vintner*   Seller of wine;   *potations*   Alcoholic drinks.

Ginger Nut, the third on my list, was a lad, some twelve years old. His father was a car-man,[1] ambitious of seeing his son on the bench instead of a cart, before he died. So he sent him to my office, as student at law, errand-boy, cleaner and sweeper, at the rate of one dollar a week. He had a little desk to himself, but he did not use it much. Upon inspection, the drawer exhibited a great array of the shells of various sorts of nuts. Indeed, to this quick-witted youth, the whole noble science of the law was contained in a nut-shell. Not the least among the employments of Ginger Nut, as well as one which he discharged with the most alacrity, was his duty as cake and apple purveyor for Turkey and Nippers. Copying law-papers being proverbially a dry, husky[2] sort of business, my two scriveners were fain to moisten their mouths very often with Spitzenbergs,[3] to be had at the numerous stalls nigh the Custom House and Post Office. Also, they sent Ginger Nut very frequently for that peculiar cake—small, flat, round, and very spicy—after which he had been named by them. Of a cold morning, when business was but dull, Turkey would gobble up scores of these cakes, as if they were mere wafers—indeed, they sell them at the rate of six or eight for a penny—the scrape of his pen blending with the crunching of the crisp particles in his mouth. Of all the fiery afternoon blunders and flurried rashnesses of Turkey, was his once moistening a ginger-cake between his lips, and clapping it on to a mortgage, for a seal. I came within an ace[4] of dismissing him then. But he mollified me by making an oriental bow, and saying—

"With submission, sir, it was generous of me to find you in stationery on my own account."

Now my original business—that of a conveyancer and title hunter,[5] and drawer-up of recondite documents of all sorts—was considerably increased by receiving the master's office. There was now great work for scriveners. Not only must I push the clerks already with me, but I must have additional help.

In answer to my advertisement, a motionless young man one morning stood upon my office threshold, the door being open, for it was summer. I can see that figure now—pallidly neat, pitiably respectable, incurably forlorn! It was Bartleby.

After a few words touching his qualifications, I engaged him, glad to have among my corps of copyists a man of so singularly sedate an aspect, which I thought might operate beneficially upon the flighty temper of Turkey, and the fiery one of Nippers.

I should have stated before that ground glass folding-doors divided my premises into two parts, one of which was occupied by my scriveners, the other by myself. According to my humor, I threw open these doors, or closed them. I resolved to assign Bartleby a corner by the folding-doors, but on my side of them, so as to have this quiet man within easy call, in case any trifling thing was to be done. I placed his desk close up to a small side-window in that part of the room, a window which originally had afforded a lateral view of certain grimy backyards and bricks, but which, owing to subsequent erections, commanded at present no view at all, though it gave some light. Within three feet of the panes was a wall, and the light came down from far above, between two lofty buildings, as from a very small opening in a dome. Still further to a satisfactory arrangement, I procured a high green folding screen, which might entirely isolate Bartleby from my sight, though not remove him from my voice. And thus, in a manner, privacy and society were conjoined.

At first, Bartleby did an extraordinary quantity of writing. As if long famishing for something to copy, he seemed to gorge himself on my documents. There was no pause for digestion. He ran a day and night line,[6] copying by sun-light and by candle-light. I should have been quite delighted with his application, had he been cheerfully industrious. But he wrote on silently, palely, mechanically.

It is, of course, an indispensable part of a scrivener's business to verify the accuracy of his copy, word by word. Where there are two or more scriveners in an office, they assist each other in this examination, one reading from the copy, the other holding the original. It is a very dull, wearisome, and lethargic affair. I can

---

[1] *car-man* A person who drives a cart.

[2] *husky* Tough and dry like husks.

[3] *Spitzenbergs* Variety of apple.

[4] *came within an ace* Was on the point of.

[5] *conveyancer* Lawyer who prepares documents for the exchange of property; *title hunter* Lawyer who investigates the legal ownership of land and property.

[6] *ran … line* I.e., he copied both day and night.

readily imagine that, to some sanguine[1] temperaments, it would be altogether intolerable. For example, I cannot credit that the mettlesome poet, Byron,[2] would have contentedly sat down with Bartleby to examine a law document of, say five hundred pages, closely written in a crimpy[3] hand.

Now and then, in the haste of business, it had been my habit to assist in comparing some brief document myself, calling Turkey or Nippers for this purpose. One object I had, in placing Bartleby so handy to me behind the screen, was, to avail myself of his services on such trivial occasions. It was on the third day, I think, of his being with me, and before any necessity had arisen for having his own writing examined, that, being much hurried to complete a small affair I had in hand, I abruptly called to Bartleby. In my haste and natural expectancy of instant compliance, I sat with my head bent over the original on my desk, and my right hand sideways, and somewhat nervously extended with the copy, so that, immediately upon emerging from his retreat, Bartleby might snatch it and proceed to business without the least delay.

In this very attitude did I sit when I called to him, rapidly stating what it was I wanted him to do—namely, to examine a small paper with me. Imagine my surprise, nay, my consternation, when, without moving from his privacy, Bartleby, in a singularly mild, firm voice, replied, "I would prefer not to."

I sat awhile in perfect silence, rallying my stunned faculties. Immediately it occurred to me that my ears had deceived me, or Bartleby had entirely misunderstood my meaning. I repeated my request in the clearest tone I could assume; but in quite as clear a one came the previous reply, "I would prefer not to."

"Prefer not to," echoed I, rising in high excitement, and crossing the room with a stride. "What do you mean? Are you moon-struck?[4] I want you to help me compare this sheet here—take it," and I thrust it towards him.

"I would prefer not to," said he.

I looked at him steadfastly. His face was leanly composed; his gray eye dimly calm. Not a wrinkle of agitation rippled him. Had there been the least uneasiness, anger, impatience or impertinence in his manner; in other words, had there been anything ordinarily human about him, doubtless I should have violently dismissed him from the premises. But as it was, I should have as soon thought of turning my pale plaster-of-paris bust of Cicero[5] out of doors. I stood gazing at him awhile, as he went on with his own writing, and then reseated myself at my desk. This is very strange, thought I. What had one best do? But my business hurried me. I concluded to forget the matter for the present, reserving it for my future leisure. So calling Nippers from the other room, the paper was speedily examined.

A few days after this, Bartleby concluded four lengthy documents, being quadruplicates of a week's testimony taken before me in my High Court of Chancery. It became necessary to examine them. It was an important suit, and great accuracy was imperative. Having all things arranged, I called Turkey, Nippers and Ginger Nut, from the next room, meaning to place the four copies in the hands of my four clerks, while I should read from the original. Accordingly, Turkey, Nippers, and Ginger Nut had taken their seats in a row, each with his document in his hand, when I called to Bartleby to join this interesting group.

"Bartleby! quick, I am waiting."

I heard a slow scrape of his chair legs on the uncarpeted floor, and soon he appeared standing at the entrance of his hermitage.

"What is wanted?" said he, mildly.

"The copies, the copies," said I, hurriedly. "We are going to examine them. There"—and I held towards him the fourth quadruplicate.

"I would prefer not to," he said, and gently disappeared behind the screen.

For a few moments I was turned into a pillar of salt,[6] standing at the head of my seated column of clerks.

---

1 *sanguine* Brave and amorous.

2 *Byron* George Gordon, Lord Byron (1788–1824), a Romantic poet famous for his passionate and energetic personality as well as for his verse.

3 *crimpy* Wobbly.

4 *moon-struck* Insane (the moon was long thought to unsettle the mental faculties).

5 *Cicero* Marcus Tullius Cicero (106–43 BCE) was a Roman lawyer and consul admired for his intellect, oratorical skills, and integrity.

6 *pillar of salt* In chapter 15 of the book of Genesis, God rains fire and brimstone on Sodom and Gomorrah, but angels warn Lot and

Recovering myself, I advanced towards the screen, and demanded the reason for such extraordinary conduct.

"*Why* do you refuse?"

"I would prefer not to."

With any other man I should have flown outright into a dreadful passion, scorned all further words, and thrust him ignominiously from my presence. But there was something about Bartleby that not only strangely disarmed me, but, in a wonderful[1] manner, touched and disconcerted me. I began to reason with him.

"These are your own copies we are about to examine. It is labor saving to you, because one examination will answer for your four papers. It is common usage. Every copyist is bound to help examine his copy. Is it not so? Will you not speak? Answer!"

"I prefer not to," he replied in a flutelike tone. It seemed to me that, while I had been addressing him, he carefully revolved every statement that I made; fully comprehended the meaning; could not gainsay the irresistible conclusion; but, at the same time, some paramount consideration prevailed with him to reply as he did.

"You are decided, then, not to comply with my request—a request made according to common usage and common sense?"

He briefly gave me to understand, that on that point my judgment was sound. Yes: his decision was irreversible.

It is not seldom the case that, when a man is browbeaten in some unprecedented and violently unreasonable way, he begins to stagger in his own plainest faith. He begins, as it were, vaguely to surmise that, wonderful as it may be, all the justice and all the reason is on the other side. Accordingly, if any disinterested persons are present, he turns to them for some reinforcement for his own faltering mind.

"Turkey," said I, "what do you think of this? Am I not right?"

"With submission, sir," said Turkey, in his blandest tone, "I think that you are."

"Nippers," said I, "what do *you* think of it?"

"I think I should kick him out of the office."

(The reader, of nice[2] perceptions, will here perceive that, it being morning, Turkey's answer is couched in polite and tranquil terms, but Nippers replies in ill-tempered ones. Or, to repeat a previous sentence, Nippers's ugly mood was on duty, and Turkey's off.)

"Ginger Nut," said I, willing to enlist the smallest suffrage in my behalf, "what do *you* think of it?"

"I think, sir, he's a little *luny*,"[3] replied Ginger Nut, with a grin.

"You hear what they say," said I, turning towards the screen, "come forth and do your duty."

But he vouchsafed no reply. I pondered a moment in sore perplexity. But once more business hurried me. I determined again to postpone the consideration of this dilemma to my future leisure. With a little trouble we made out to examine the papers without Bartleby, though at every page or two Turkey deferentially dropped his opinion, that this proceeding was quite out of the common; while Nippers, twitching in his chair with a dyspeptic[4] nervousness, ground out, between his set teeth, occasional hissing maledictions against the stubborn oaf behind the screen. And for his (Nippers's) part, this was the first and the last time he would do another man's business without pay.

Meanwhile Bartleby sat in his hermitage, oblivious to everything but his own peculiar business there.

Some days passed, the scrivener being employed upon another lengthy work. His late remarkable conduct led me to regard his ways narrowly. I observed that he never went to dinner; indeed, that he never went anywhere. As yet I had never, of my personal knowledge, known him to be outside of my office. He was a perpetual sentry in the corner. At about eleven o'clock though, in the morning, I noticed that Ginger Nut would advance toward the opening in Bartleby's screen, as if silently beckoned thither by a gesture invisible to me where I sat. The boy would then leave the office, jingling a few pence, and reappear with a handful of ginger-nuts, which he delivered in the hermitage, receiving two of the cakes for his trouble.

He lives, then, on ginger-nuts, thought I; never eats a dinner, properly speaking; he must be a vegetarian,

---

his wife and daughters to flee to the mountains without looking back before the destruction comes. Lot's wife does look back and is turned into a pillar of salt.

1   *wonderful*   Astonishing, unusual.

2   *nice*   Accurate, discerning, discriminating.

3   *luny*   I.e., loony, the shortened form of lunatic, which is another way of saying "moon-struck" ("luna" means "moon" in Latin).

4   *dyspeptic*   Uneasy, uncomfortable (resulting from indigestion).

then; but no; he never eats even vegetables, he eats nothing but ginger-nuts. My mind then ran on in reveries concerning the probable effects upon the human constitution of living entirely on ginger-nuts. Ginger-nuts are so called, because they contain ginger as one of their peculiar constituents, and the final flavoring one. Now, what was ginger? A hot, spicy thing. Was Bartleby hot and spicy? Not at all. Ginger, then, had no effect upon Bartleby. Probably, he preferred it should have none.

Nothing so aggravates an earnest person as a passive resistance. If the individual so resisted be of a not inhumane temper, and the resisting one perfectly harmless in his passivity, then, in the better moods of the former, he will endeavor charitably to construe to his imagination what proves impossible to be solved by his judgment. Even so, for the most part, I regarded Bartleby and his ways. Poor fellow! thought I, he means no mischief; it is plain he intends no insolence; his aspect sufficiently evinces that his eccentricities are involuntary. He is useful to me. I can get along with him. If I turn him away, the chances are he will fall in with some less-indulgent employer, and then he will be rudely treated, and perhaps driven forth miserably to starve. Yes. Here I can cheaply purchase a delicious self-approval. To befriend Bartleby; to humor him in his strange willfulness, will cost me little or nothing, while I lay up in my soul what will eventually prove a sweet morsel for my conscience. But this mood was not invariable, with me. The passiveness of Bartleby sometimes irritated me. I felt strangely goaded on to encounter him in new opposition—to elicit some angry spark from him answerable to my own. But, indeed, I might as well have essayed to strike fire with my knuckles against a bit of Windsor soap.[1] But one afternoon the evil impulse in me mastered me, and the following little scene ensued:

"Bartleby," said I, "when those papers are all copied, I will compare them with you."

"I would prefer not to."

"How? Surely you do not mean to persist in that mulish vagary?"

No answer.

I threw open the folding-doors near by, and, turning upon Turkey and Nippers, exclaimed:

"Bartleby a second time says, he won't examine his papers. What do you think of it, Turkey?"

It was afternoon, be it remembered. Turkey sat glowing like a brass boiler; his bald head steaming; his hands reeling among his blotted papers.

"Think of it?" roared Turkey; "I think I'll just step behind his screen, and black his eyes for him!"

So saying, Turkey rose to his feet and threw his arms into a pugilistic[2] position. He was hurrying away to make good his promise, when I detained him, alarmed at the effect of incautiously rousing Turkey's combativeness after dinner.

"Sit down, Turkey," said I, "and hear what Nippers has to say. What do you think of it, Nippers? Would I not be justified in immediately dismissing Bartleby?"

"Excuse me, that is for you to decide, sir. I think his conduct quite unusual, and, indeed, unjust, as regards Turkey and myself. But it may only be a passing whim."

"Ah," exclaimed I, "you have strangely changed your mind, then—you speak very gently of him now."

"All beer," cried Turkey; "gentleness is effects of beer—Nippers and I dined together to-day. You see how gentle *I* am, sir. Shall I go and black his eyes?"

"You refer to Bartleby, I suppose. No, not to-day, Turkey," I replied; "pray, put up[3] your fists."

I closed the doors, and again advanced towards Bartleby. I felt additional incentives tempting me to my fate. I burned to be rebelled against again. I remembered that Bartleby never left the office.

"Bartleby," said I, "Ginger Nut is away; just step around to the Post Office, won't you? (it was but a three minutes' walk), and see if there is anything for me."

"I would prefer not to."

"You *will* not?"

"I *prefer* not."

I staggered to my desk, and sat there in a deep study. My blind inveteracy[4] returned. Was there any other thing in which I could procure myself to be ignominiously repulsed by this lean, penniless wight?[5]—my hired clerk? What added thing is there, perfectly reasonable, that he will be sure to refuse to do?

---

[1]   *Windsor soap*   Brown, scented soap.

[2]   *pugilistic*   Ready-to-fight.

[3]   *put up*   Put away.

[4]   *inveteracy*   Hostility.

[5]   *wight*   Person, but can also be used to refer to a ghost.

"Bartleby!"

No answer.

"Bartleby," in a louder tone.

No answer.

"Bartleby," I roared.

Like a very ghost, agreeably to the laws of magical invocation, at the third summons, he appeared at the entrance of his hermitage.

"Go to the next room, and tell Nippers to come to me."

"I prefer not to," he respectfully and slowly said, and mildly disappeared.

"Very good, Bartleby," said I, in a quiet sort of serenely-severe self-possessed tone, intimating the unalterable purpose of some terrible retribution very close at hand. At the moment I half intended something of the kind. But upon the whole, as it was drawing towards my dinner-hour, I thought it best to put on my hat and walk home for the day, suffering much from perplexity and distress of mind.

Shall I acknowledge it? The conclusion of this whole business was, that it soon became a fixed fact of my chambers, that a pale young scrivener, by the name of Bartleby, had a desk there; that he copied for me at the usual rate of four cents a folio (one hundred words); but he was permanently exempt from examining the work done by him, that duty being transferred to Turkey and Nippers, out of compliment, doubtless, to their superior acuteness; moreover, said Bartleby was never, on any account, to be dispatched on the most trivial errand of any sort; and that even if entreated to take upon him such a matter, it was generally understood that he would "prefer not to"—in other words, that he would refuse point-blank.

As days passed on, I became considerably reconciled to Bartleby. His steadiness, his freedom from all dissipation, his incessant industry (except when he chose to throw himself into a standing revery behind his screen), his great stillness, his unalterableness of demeanor under all circumstances, made him a valuable acquisition. One prime thing was this—*he was always there*—first in the morning, continually through the day, and the last at night. I had a singular confidence in his honesty. I felt my most precious papers perfectly safe in his hands. Sometimes, to be sure, I could not, for the very soul of me, avoid falling

into sudden spasmodic passions with him. For it was exceeding difficult to bear in mind all the time those strange peculiarities, privileges, and unheard of exemptions, forming the tacit stipulations on Bartleby's part under which he remained in my office. Now and then, in the eagerness of dispatching pressing business, I would inadvertently summon Bartleby, in a short, rapid tone, to put his finger, say, on the incipient tie of a bit of red tape[1] with which I was about compressing some papers. Of course, from behind the screen the usual answer, "I prefer not to," was sure to come; and then, how could a human creature, with the common infirmities of our nature, refrain from bitterly exclaiming upon such perverseness—such unreasonableness. However, every added repulse of this sort which I received only tended to lessen the probability of my repeating the inadvertence.

Here it must be said, that according to the custom of most legal gentlemen occupying chambers in densely-populated law buildings, there were several keys to my door. One was kept by a woman residing in the attic, which person weekly scrubbed and daily swept and dusted my apartments. Another was kept by Turkey for convenience sake. The third I sometimes carried in my own pocket. The fourth I knew not who had.

Now, one Sunday morning I happened to go to Trinity Church,[2] to hear a celebrated preacher, and finding myself rather early on the ground I thought I would walk round to my chambers for a while. Luckily I had my key with me; but upon applying it to the lock, I found it resisted by something inserted from the inside. Quite surprised, I called out; when to my consternation a key was turned from within; and thrusting his lean visage at me, and holding the door ajar, the apparition of Bartleby appeared, in his shirt sleeves, and otherwise in a strangely tattered dishabille,[3] saying quietly that he was sorry, but he was deeply engaged just then, and—preferred not admitting me at present. In a brief word or two, he moreover added, that perhaps I had better walk round the block two or three

---

[1]   *put his finger ... red tape*   The speaker is tying up legal documents in the typical red or pink tape that was customarily used for such purposes.

[2]   *Trinity Church*   Episcopal church near Wall Street that catered to wealthy and money-minded New Yorkers.

[3]   *dishabille*   Disheveled style of dress.

times, and by that time he would probably have concluded his affairs.

Now, the utterly unsurmised[1] appearance of Bartleby, tenanting my law-chambers of a Sunday morning, with his cadaverously gentlemanly *nonchalance*, yet withal firm and self-possessed, had such a strange effect upon me, that incontinently[2] I slunk away from my own door, and did as desired. But not without sundry twinges of impotent rebellion against the mild effrontery of this unaccountable scrivener. Indeed, it was his wonderful mildness chiefly, which not only disarmed me, but unmanned me as it were. For I consider that one, for the time, is a sort of unmanned when he tranquilly permits his hired clerk to dictate to him, and order him away from his own premises. Furthermore, I was full of uneasiness as to what Bartleby could possibly be doing in my office in his shirt sleeves, and in an otherwise dismantled condition of a Sunday morning. Was anything amiss going on? Nay, that was out of the question. It was not to be thought of for a moment that Bartleby was an immoral person. But what could he be doing there?—copying? Nay again, whatever might be his eccentricities, Bartleby was an eminently decorous person. He would be the last man to sit down to his desk in any state approaching to nudity. Besides, it was Sunday; and there was something about Bartleby that forbade the supposition that he would by any secular occupation violate the proprieties of the day.[3]

Nevertheless, my mind was not pacified; and full of a restless curiosity, at last I returned to the door. Without hindrance I inserted my key, opened it, and entered. Bartleby was not to be seen. I looked round anxiously, peeped behind his screen; but it was very plain that he was gone. Upon more closely examining the place, I surmised that for an indefinite period Bartleby must have ate, dressed, and slept in my office, and that, too without plate, mirror, or bed. The cushioned seat of a ricketty old sofa in one corner bore the faint impress of a lean, reclining form. Rolled away under his desk, I found a blanket; under the empty grate, a blacking box[4] and brush; on a chair, a tin basin, with soap and a ragged towel; in a newspaper a few crumbs of ginger-nuts and a morsel of cheese. Yes, thought I, it is evident enough that Bartleby has been making his home here, keeping bachelor's hall all by himself. Immediately then the thought came sweeping across me, what miserable friendlessness and loneliness are here revealed! His poverty is great; but his solitude, how horrible! Think of it. Of a Sunday, Wall-street is deserted as Petra;[5] and every night of every day it is an emptiness. This building, too, which of week-days hums with industry and life, at nightfall echoes with sheer vacancy, and all through Sunday is forlorn. And here Bartleby makes his home; sole spectator, of a solitude which he has seen all populous—a sort of innocent and transformed Marius brooding among the ruins of Carthage![6]

For the first time in my life a feeling of overpowering stinging melancholy seized me. Before, I had never experienced aught but a not unpleasing sadness. The bond of a common humanity now drew me irresistibly to gloom. A fraternal melancholy! For both I and Bartleby were sons of Adam.[7] I remembered the bright silks and sparkling faces I had seen that day, in gala trim, swan-like sailing down the Mississippi of Broadway; and I contrasted them with the pallid copyist, and thought to myself, Ah, happiness courts the light, so we deem the world is gay; but misery hides aloof, so we deem that misery there is none. These sad fancyings—chimeras, doubtless, of a sick and silly brain—led on to other and more special thoughts, concerning the eccentricities of Bartleby. Presentiments of strange discoveries hovered round me. The scrivener's pale form appeared to me laid out, among uncaring strangers, in its shivering winding sheet.[8]

---

[1] *unsurmised* Unimagined, unexpected.

[2] *incontinently* Lacking in resolution.

[3] *proprieties of the day* Nineteenth-century American Protestants, following the Puritan tradition, treated Sunday (the Sabbath) as a day of rest, when no secular work could take place.

[4] *blacking box* Box containing shoe polish.

[5] *Petra* Deserted city in what is now Jordan.

[6] *Marius … Carthage* When Roman general Gaius Marius was exiled in 88 CE, he went to Carthage (which had been destroyed by Rome in the Punic Wars, between 264–146 BCE). There is a well-known Neoclassical painting of Marius "brooding" in Carthage by Dutch-American painter John Vanderlyn, entitled "Marius Amid the Ruins of Carthage" (1808).

[7] *sons of Adam* I.e., human beings, sharing the fate of Adam, who, in the book of Genesis, eats from the tree of knowledge and is punished with loss of paradise, a life of toil, and mortality.

[8] *winding sheet* Burial shroud.

Suddenly I was attracted by Bartleby's closed desk, the key in open sight left in the lock.

I mean no mischief, seek the gratification of no heartless curiosity, thought I; besides, the desk is mine, and its contents, too, so I will make bold to look within. Everything was methodically arranged, the papers smoothly placed. The pigeon holes were deep, and removing the files of documents, I groped into their recesses. Presently I felt something there, and dragged it out. It was an old bandanna handkerchief, heavy and knotted. I opened it, and saw it was a savings' bank.

I now recalled all the quiet mysteries which I had noted in the man. I remembered that he never spoke but to answer; that, though at intervals he had considerable time to himself, yet I had never seen him reading—no, not even a newspaper; that for long periods he would stand looking out, at his pale window behind the screen, upon the dead brick wall; I was quite sure he never visited any refectory[1] or eating house; while his pale face clearly indicated that he never drank beer like Turkey, or tea and coffee even, like other men; that he never went anywhere in particular that I could learn; never went out for a walk, unless, indeed, that was the case at present; that he had declined telling who he was, or whence he came, or whether he had any relatives in the world; that though so thin and pale, he never complained of ill health. And more than all, I remembered a certain unconscious air of pallid—how shall I call it?—of pallid haughtiness, say, or rather an austere reserve about him, which had positively awed me into my tame compliance with his eccentricities, when I had feared to ask him to do the slightest incidental thing for me, even though I might know, from his long-continued motionlessness, that behind his screen he must be standing in one of those dead-wall reveries of his.

Revolving all these things, and coupling them with the recently discovered fact, that he made my office his constant abiding place and home, and not forgetful of his morbid moodiness; revolving all these things, a prudential feeling began to steal over me. My first emotions had been those of pure melancholy and sincerest pity; but just in proportion as the forlornness of Bartleby grew and grew to my imagination, did that same melancholy merge into fear, that pity into repulsion. So true it is, and so terrible, too, that up to a certain point the thought or sight of misery enlists our best affections; but, in certain special cases, beyond that point it does not. They err who would assert that invariably this is owing to the inherent selfishness of the human heart. It rather proceeds from a certain hopelessness of remedying excessive and organic ill. To a sensitive being, pity is not seldom pain. And when at last it is perceived that such pity cannot lead to effectual succor, common sense bids the soul be rid of it. What I saw that morning persuaded me that the scrivener was the victim of innate and incurable disorder. I might give alms[2] to his body; but his body did not pain him; it was his soul that suffered, and his soul I could not reach.

I did not accomplish the purpose of going to Trinity Church that morning. Somehow, the things I had seen disqualified me for the time from church-going. I walked homeward, thinking what I would do with Bartleby. Finally, I resolved upon this—I would put certain calm questions to him the next morning, touching his history, etc., and if he declined to answer them openly and unreservedly (and I supposed he would prefer not), then to give him a twenty dollar bill over and above whatever I might owe him, and tell him his services were no longer required; but that if in any other way I could assist him, I would be happy to do so, especially if he desired to return to his native place, wherever that might be, I would willingly help to defray the expenses. Moreover, if, after reaching home, he found himself at any time in want of aid, a letter from him would be sure of a reply.

The next morning came.

"Bartleby," said I, gently calling to him behind his screen.

No reply.

"Bartleby," said I, in a still gentler tone, "come here; I am not going to ask you to do anything you would prefer not to do—I simply wish to speak to you."

Upon this he noiselessly slid into view.

"Will you tell me, Bartleby, where you were born?"

"I would prefer not to."

"Will you tell me *anything* about yourself?"

"I would prefer not to."

---

[1]   *refectory*   Communal dining hall.

[2]   *give alms*   Offer charity.

"But what reasonable objection can you have to speak to me? I feel friendly towards you."

He did not look at me while I spoke, but kept his glance fixed upon my bust of Cicero, which, as I then sat, was directly behind me, some six inches above my head.

"What is your answer, Bartleby," said I, after waiting a considerable time for a reply, during which his countenance remained immovable, only there was the faintest conceivable tremor of the white attenuated mouth.

"At present I prefer to give no answer," he said, and retired into his hermitage.

It was rather weak in me I confess, but his manner, on this occasion, nettled me. Not only did there seem to lurk in it a certain calm disdain, but his perverseness seemed ungrateful, considering the undeniable good usage and indulgence he had received from me.

Again I sat ruminating what I should do. Mortified as I was at his behavior, and resolved as I had been to dismiss him when I entered my office, nevertheless I strangely felt something superstitious knocking at my heart, and forbidding me to carry out my purpose, and denouncing me for a villain if I dared to breathe one bitter word against this forlornest of mankind. At last, familiarly drawing my chair behind his screen, I sat down and said: "Bartleby, never mind, then, about revealing your history; but let me entreat you, as a friend, to comply as far as may be with the usages of this office. Say now, you will help to examine papers to-morrow or next day: in short, say now, that in a day or two you will begin to be a little reasonable:—say so, Bartleby."

"At present I would prefer not to be a little reasonable," was his mildly cadaverous reply.

Just then the folding-doors opened, and Nippers approached. He seemed suffering from an unusually bad night's rest, induced by severer indigestion than common. He overheard those final words of Bartleby.

"*Prefer not*, eh?" gritted Nippers—"I'd *prefer* him, if I were you, sir," addressing me—"I'd *prefer* him; I'd give him preferences, the stubborn mule! What is it, sir, pray, that he *prefers* not to do now?"

Bartleby moved not a limb.

"Mr. Nippers," said I, "I'd prefer that you would withdraw for the present."

Somehow, of late, I had got into the way of involuntarily using this word "prefer" upon all sorts of not exactly suitable occasions. And I trembled to think that my contact with the scrivener had already and seriously affected me in a mental way. And what further and deeper aberration might it not yet produce? This apprehension had not been without efficacy in determining me to summary[1] measures.

As Nippers, looking very sour and sulky, was departing, Turkey blandly and deferentially approached.

"With submission, sir," said he, "yesterday I was thinking about Bartleby here, and I think that if he would but prefer to take a quart of good ale every day, it would do much towards mending him, and enabling him to assist in examining his papers."

"So you have got the word, too," said I, slightly excited.

"With submission, what word, sir," asked Turkey, respectfully crowding himself into the contracted space behind the screen, and by so doing, making me jostle the scrivener. "What word, sir?"

"I would prefer to be left alone here," said Bartleby, as if offended at being mobbed in his privacy.

"*That's* the word, Turkey," said I—"*that's* it."

"Oh, *prefer*? oh yes—queer word. I never use it myself. But, sir, as I was saying, if he would but prefer—"

"Turkey," interrupted I, "you will please withdraw."

"Oh certainly, sir, if you prefer that I should."

As he opened the folding-door to retire, Nippers at his desk caught a glimpse of me, and asked whether I would prefer to have a certain paper copied on blue paper or white. He did not in the least roguishly accent the word prefer. It was plain that it involuntarily rolled from his tongue. I thought to myself, surely I must get rid of a demented man, who already has in some degree turned the tongues, if not the heads of myself and clerks. But I thought it prudent not to break the dismission[2] at once.

The next day I noticed that Bartleby did nothing but stand at his window in his dead-wall revery. Upon asking him why he did not write, he said that he had decided upon doing no more writing.

---

1   *summary*   Quick and determined.

2   *dismission*   Dismissal.

"Why, how now? what next?" exclaimed I, "do no more writing?"

"No more."

"And what is the reason?"

"Do you not see the reason for yourself," he indifferently replied.

I looked steadfastly at him, and perceived that his eyes looked dull and glazed. Instantly it occurred to me, that his unexampled diligence in copying by his dim window for the first few weeks of his stay with me might have temporarily impaired his vision.

I was touched. I said something in condolence with him. I hinted that of course he did wisely in abstaining from writing for a while; and urged him to embrace that opportunity of taking wholesome exercise in the open air. This, however, he did not do. A few days after this, my other clerks being absent, and being in a great hurry to dispatch certain letters by the mail, I thought that, having nothing else earthly to do, Bartleby would surely be less inflexible than usual, and carry these letters to the post-office. But he blankly declined. So, much to my inconvenience, I went myself.

Still added days went by. Whether Bartleby's eyes improved or not, I could not say. To all appearance, I thought they did. But when I asked him if they did, he vouchsafed no answer. At all events, he would do no copying. At last, in reply to my urgings, he informed me that he had permanently given up copying.

"What!" exclaimed I; "suppose your eyes should get entirely well—better than ever before—would you not copy then?"

"I have given up copying," he answered, and slid aside.

He remained as ever, a fixture in my chamber. Nay—if that were possible—he became still more of a fixture than before. What was to be done? He would do nothing in the office; why should he stay there? In plain fact, he had now become a millstone[1] to me, not only useless as a necklace, but afflictive to bear. Yet I was sorry for him. I speak less than truth when I say that, on his own account, he occasioned me uneasiness. If he would but have named a single relative or friend, I would instantly have written, and urged

their taking the poor fellow away to some convenient retreat. But he seemed alone, absolutely alone in the universe. A bit of wreck in the mid Atlantic. At length, necessities connected with my business tyrannized over all other considerations. Decently as I could, I told Bartleby that in six days time he must unconditionally leave the office. I warned him to take measures, in the interval, for procuring some other abode. I offered to assist him in this endeavor, if he himself would but take the first step towards a removal. "And when you finally quit me, Bartleby," added I, "I shall see that you go not away entirely unprovided. Six days from this hour, remember."

At the expiration of that period, I peeped behind the screen, and lo! Bartleby was there.

I buttoned up my coat, balanced myself; advanced slowly towards him, touched his shoulder, and said, "The time has come; you must quit this place; I am sorry for you; here is money; but you must go."

"I would prefer not," he replied, with his back still towards me.

"You *must*."

He remained silent.

Now I had an unbounded confidence in this man's common honesty. He had frequently restored to me sixpences and shillings carelessly dropped upon the floor, for I am apt to be very reckless in such shirt-button affairs.[2] The proceeding, then, which followed will not be deemed extraordinary.

"Bartleby," said I, "I owe you twelve dollars on account; here are thirty-two; the odd twenty are yours—Will you take it?" and I handed the bills towards him.

But he made no motion.

"I will leave them here, then," putting them under a weight on the table. Then taking my hat and cane and going to the door, I tranquilly turned and added—"After you have removed your things from these offices, Bartleby, you will of course lock the door—since every-one is now gone for the day but you—and if you please, slip your key underneath the mat, so that I may have it in the morning. I shall not see you again; so good-by to you. If, hereafter, in your new place of abode, I can be of any service to you, do not fail to advise me by letter. Good-by, Bartleby, and fare you well."

---

[1] *millstone* Heavy stone used to grind corn; a "millstone around one's neck" is a common saying, meaning that one is burdened by a heavy problem.

[2] *reckless … affairs* I.e., careless about such small things.

But he answered not a word; like the last column of some ruined temple, he remained standing mute and solitary in the middle of the otherwise deserted room.

As I walked home in a pensive mood, my vanity got the better of my pity. I could not but highly plume[1] myself on my masterly management in getting rid of Bartleby. Masterly I call it, and such it must appear to any dispassionate thinker. The beauty of my procedure seemed to consist in its perfect quietness. There was no vulgar bullying, no bravado of any sort, no choleric[2] hectoring, and striding to and fro across the apartment, jerking out vehement commands for Bartleby to bundle himself off with his beggarly traps.[3] Nothing of the kind. Without loudly bidding Bartleby depart—as an inferior genius might have done—I *assumed* the ground that depart he must; and upon that assumption built all I had to say. The more I thought over my procedure, the more I was charmed with it. Nevertheless, next morning, upon awakening, I had my doubts— I had somehow slept off the fumes of vanity. One of the coolest and wisest hours a man has, is just after he awakes in the morning. My procedure seemed as sagacious as ever—but only in theory. How it would prove in practice—there was the rub.[4] It was truly a beautiful thought to have assumed Bartleby's departure; but, after all, that assumption was simply my own, and none of Bartleby's. The great point was, not whether I had assumed that he would quit me, but whether he would prefer so to do. He was more a man of preferences than assumptions.

After breakfast, I walked down town, arguing the probabilities *pro* and *con*. One moment I thought it would prove a miserable failure, and Bartleby would be found all alive at my office as usual; the next moment it seemed certain that I should find his chair empty. And so I kept veering about. At the corner of Broadway and Canal street, I saw quite an excited group of people standing in earnest conversation.

"I'll take odds he doesn't," said a voice as I passed.

"Doesn't go?—done!" said I, "put up your money."

I was instinctively putting my hand in my pocket to produce my own, when I remembered that this was an election day. The words I had overheard bore no reference to Bartleby, but to the success or non-success of some candidate for the mayoralty. In my intent frame of mind, I had, as it were, imagined that all Broadway shared in my excitement, and were debating the same question with me. I passed on, very thankful that the uproar of the street screened my momentary absent-mindedness.

As I had intended, I was earlier than usual at my office door. I stood listening for a moment. All was still. He must be gone. I tried the knob. The door was locked. Yes, my procedure had worked to a charm; he indeed must be vanished. Yet a certain melancholy mixed with this: I was almost sorry for my brilliant success. I was fumbling under the door mat for the key, which Bartleby was to have left there for me, when accidentally my knee knocked against a panel, producing a summoning sound, and in response a voice came to me from within—"Not yet; I am occupied."

It was Bartleby.

I was thunderstruck. For an instant I stood like the man who, pipe in mouth, was killed one cloudless afternoon long ago in Virginia, by summer lightning; at his own warm open window he was killed, and remained leaning out there upon the dreamy afternoon till someone touched him, when he fell.

"Not gone!" I murmured at last. But again obeying that wondrous ascendancy which the inscrutable scrivener had over me, and from which ascendancy, for all my chafing, I could not completely escape, I slowly went down stairs and out into the street, and while walking round the block, considered what I should next do in this unheard-of perplexity. Turn the man out by an actual thrusting I could not; to drive him away by calling him hard names would not do; calling in the police was an unpleasant idea; and yet, permit him to enjoy his cadaverous triumph over me—this, too, I could not think of. What was to be done? or, if nothing could be done, was there anything further that I could *assume* in the matter? Yes, as before I had prospectively assumed that Bartleby would depart, so now I might retrospectively assume that departed he

---

1   *plume* Congratulate.

2   *choleric* Angry.

3   *traps* Belongings.

4   *there was the rub* See Shakespeare's *Hamlet* (1609) Act 3, Scene 1, where Hamlet considers what might follow after death: "To die, To sleep; / To sleep, perchance to dream—ay, there's the rub, / For in that sleep of death what dreams may come / When we have shuffled off this mortal coil, / Must give us pause" (65–69).

was. In the legitimate carrying out of this assumption, I might enter my office in a great hurry, and pretending not to see Bartleby at all, walk straight against him as if he were air. Such a proceeding would in a singular degree have the appearance of a home-thrust.[1] It was hardly possible that Bartleby could withstand such an application of the doctrine of assumptions. But upon second thoughts the success of the plan seemed rather dubious. I resolved to argue the matter over with him again.

"Bartleby," said I, entering the office, with a quietly severe expression, "I am seriously displeased. I am pained, Bartleby. I had thought better of you. I had imagined you of such a gentlemanly organization, that in any delicate dilemma a slight hint would suffice—in short, an assumption. But it appears I am deceived. Why," I added, unaffectedly starting, "you have not even touched that money yet," pointing to it, just where I had left it the evening previous.

He answered nothing.

"Will you, or will you not, quit me?" I now demanded in a sudden passion, advancing close to him.

"I would prefer *not* to quit you," he replied gently emphasizing the *not*.

"What earthly right have you to stay here? Do you pay any rent? Do you pay my taxes? Or is this property yours?"

He answered nothing.

"Are you ready to go on and write now? Are your eyes recovered? Could you copy a small paper for me this morning? or help examine a few lines? or step round to the post-office? In a word, will you do anything at all, to give a coloring to your refusal to depart the premises?"

He silently retired into his hermitage.

I was now in such a state of nervous resentment that I thought it but prudent to check myself at present from further demonstrations. Bartleby and I were alone. I remembered the tragedy of the unfortunate Adams and the still more unfortunate Colt in the solitary office of the latter; and how poor Colt, being dreadfully incensed by Adams, and imprudently permitting himself to get wildly excited, was at unawares hurried into his fatal act—an act which certainly no man could possibly deplore more than the actor himself.[2] Often it had occurred to me in my ponderings upon the subject, that had that altercation taken place in the public street, or at a private residence, it would not have terminated as it did. It was the circumstance of being alone in a solitary office, upstairs, of a building entirely unhallowed by humanizing domestic associations—an uncarpeted office, doubtless, of a dusty, haggard sort of appearance—this it must have been, which greatly helped to enhance the irritable desperation of the hapless Colt.

But when this old Adam[3] of resentment rose in me and tempted me concerning Bartleby, I grappled him and threw him. How? Why, simply by recalling the divine injunction: "A new commandment give I unto you, that ye love one another."[4] Yes, this it was that saved me. Aside from higher considerations, charity often operates as a vastly wise and prudent principle—a great safeguard to its possessor. Men have committed murder for jealousy's sake, and anger's sake, and hatred's sake, and selfishness' sake, and spiritual pride's sake; but no man, that ever I heard of, ever committed a diabolical murder for sweet charity's sake. Mere self-interest, then, if no better motive can be enlisted, should, especially with high-tempered men, prompt all beings to charity and philanthropy. At any rate, upon the occasion in question, I strove to drown my exasperated feelings towards the scrivener by benevolently construing his conduct.—Poor fellow, poor fellow! thought I, he don't mean anything; and besides, he has seen hard times, and ought to be indulged.

I endeavored, also, immediately to occupy myself, and at the same time to comfort my despondency. I tried to fancy, that in the course of the morning, at such time as might prove agreeable to him, Bartleby, of his own free accord, would emerge from his hermitage and take up some decided line of march in the

---

[1]   *home-thrust*   I.e., move that strikes home (hits its target).

[2]   *tragedy … himself*   The story that the lawyer alludes to here is one of the more infamous murder cases in New York City. John Caldwell Colt (1810–42), brother of the firearms inventor Samuel Colt (1814–62), murdered a printer named Samuel Adams with a hatchet, covered up the crime, and died by suicide on the day he was scheduled to be executed.

[3]   *Adam*   I.e., sin, human weakness. Adam, as the original sinner, stands here for the sinful tendencies of all humanity.

[4]   *A new … another*   See John 13.34; these words are spoken by Christ to his disciples after the Last Supper.

direction of the door. But no. Half-past twelve o'clock came; Turkey began to glow in the face, overturn his inkstand, and become generally obstreperous; Nippers abated down into quietude and courtesy; Ginger Nut munched his noon apple; and Bartleby remained standing at his window in one of his profoundest dead-wall reveries. Will it be credited? Ought I to acknowledge it? That afternoon I left the office without saying one further word to him.

Some days now passed, during which, at leisure intervals I looked a little into "Edwards on the Will," and "Priestley on Necessity."[1] Under the circumstances, those books induced a salutary feeling. Gradually I slid into the persuasion that these troubles of mine, touching the scrivener, had been all predestinated[2] from eternity, and Bartleby was billeted[3] upon me for some mysterious purpose of an allwise Providence, which it was not for a mere mortal like me to fathom. Yes, Bartleby, stay there behind your screen, thought I; I shall persecute you no more; you are harmless and noiseless as any of these old chairs; in short, I never feel so private as when I know you are here. At last I see it, I feel it; I penetrate to the predestinated purpose of my life. I am content. Others may have loftier parts to enact; but my mission in this world, Bartleby, is to furnish you with office-room for such period as you may see fit to remain.

I believe that this wise and blessed frame of mind would have continued with me, had it not been for the unsolicited and uncharitable remarks obtruded upon me by my professional friends who visited the rooms. But thus it often is, that the constant friction of illiberal minds wears out at last the best resolves of the more generous. Though to be sure, when I reflected upon it, it was not strange that people entering my office should be struck by the peculiar aspect of the unaccountable Bartleby, and so be tempted to throw out some sinister observations concerning him. Sometimes an attorney, having business with me, and calling at my office, and finding no one but the scrivener there, would undertake to obtain some sort of precise information from him touching my whereabouts; but without heeding his idle talk, Bartleby would remain standing immovable in the middle of the room. So after contemplating him in that position for a time, the attorney would depart, no wiser than he came.

Also, when a reference[4] was going on, and the room full of lawyers and witnesses, and business driving fast, some deeply-occupied legal gentleman present, seeing Bartleby wholly unemployed, would request him to run round to his (the legal gentleman's) office and fetch some papers for him. Thereupon, Bartleby would tranquilly decline, and yet remain idle as before. Then the lawyer would give a great stare, and turn to me. And what could I say? At last I was made aware that all through the circle of my professional acquaintance, a whisper of wonder was running round, having reference to the strange creature I kept at my office. This worried me very much. And as the idea came upon me of his possibly turning out a long-lived man, and keep occupying my chambers, and denying my authority; and perplexing my visitors; and scandalizing my professional reputation; and casting a general gloom over the premises; keeping soul and body together to the last upon his savings (for doubtless he spent but half a dime a day), and in the end perhaps outlive me, and claim possession of my office by right of his perpetual occupancy: as all these dark anticipations crowded upon me more and more, and my friends continually intruded their relentless remarks upon the apparition in my room; a great change was wrought in me. I resolved to gather all my faculties together, and forever rid me of this intolerable incubus.[5]

Ere revolving any complicated project, however, adapted to this end, I first simply suggested to Bartleby the propriety of his permanent departure. In a calm and serious tone, I commanded the idea to his careful and mature consideration. But, having taken three days to meditate upon it, he apprised me, that his original

---

[1] *Edwards on the Will* Calvinist theologian Jonathan Edwards's *Freedom of the Will* (1754) argues that human will is depraved, and that humanity is consequently reliant on God's grace for salvation; *Priestley on Necessity* Joseph Priestley was an eminent English materialist philosopher. In his *Doctrine of Philosophical Necessity* (1777) he denies the reality of both the soul and free will.

[2] *predestinated* Edwards was a vigorous proponent of the doctrine of predestination: that God predestined people to salvation or damnation without reference to their own works.

[3] *billeted* Lodged.

[4] *reference* Meeting to resolve a legal matter or dispute.

[5] *incubus* Demon who has sexual intercourse with sleeping victims, usually women; it can also mean "nightmare," and is often used to describe an oppressive or parasitic person.

determination remained the same; in short, that he still preferred to abide with me.

What shall I do? I now said to myself, buttoning up my coat to the last button. What shall I do? what ought I to do? what does conscience say I *should* do with this man, or, rather, ghost. Rid myself of him, I must; go, he shall. But how? You will not thrust him, the poor, pale, passive mortal—you will not thrust such a helpless creature out of your door? you will not dishonor yourself by such cruelty? No, I will not, I cannot do that. Rather would I let him live and die here, and then mason up his remains in the wall.[1] What, then, will you do? For all your coaxing, he will not budge. Bribes he leaves under your own paper-weight on your table; in short, it is quite plain that he prefers to cling to you.

Then something severe, something unusual must be done. What! surely you will not have him collared by a constable, and commit his innocent pallor to the common jail? And upon what ground could you procure such a thing to be done?—a vagrant, is he? What! he a vagrant, a wanderer, who refuses to budge? It is because he will *not* be a vagrant, then, that you seek to count him *as* a vagrant. That is too absurd. No visible means of support: there I have him. Wrong again: for indubitably he *does* support himself, and that is the only unanswerable proof that any man can show of his possessing the means so to do. No more, then. Since he will not quit me, I must quit him. I will change my offices; I will move elsewhere, and give him fair notice, that if I find him on my new premises I will then proceed against him as a common trespasser.

Acting accordingly, next day I thus addressed him: "I find these chambers too far from the City Hall; the air is unwholesome. In a word, I propose to remove my offices next week, and shall no longer require your services. I tell you this now, in order that you may seek another place."

He made no reply, and nothing more was said.

On the appointed day I engaged carts and men, proceeded to my chambers, and, having but little furniture, everything was removed in a few hours. Throughout, the scrivener remained standing behind the screen, which I directed to be removed the last thing. It was

withdrawn; and, being folded up like a huge folio, left him the motionless occupant of a naked room. I stood in the entry watching him a moment, while something from within me upbraided me.

I re-entered, with my hand in my pocket—and—and my heart in my mouth.

"Good-by, Bartleby; I am going—good-by, and God some way bless you; and take that," slipping something in his hand. But it dropped upon the floor, and then—strange to say—I tore myself from him whom I had so longed to be rid of.

Established in my new quarters, for a day or two I kept the door locked, and started at every footfall in the passages. When I returned to my rooms, after any little absence, I would pause at the threshold for an instant, and attentively listen, ere applying my key. But these fears were needless. Bartleby never came nigh me.

I thought all was going well, when a perturbed-looking stranger visited me, inquiring whether I was the person who had recently occupied rooms at No. —— Wall street.

Full of forebodings, I replied that I was.

"Then, sir," said the stranger, who proved a lawyer, "you are responsible for the man you left there. He refuses to do any copying; he refuses to do anything; he says he prefers not to; and he refuses to quit the premises."

"I am very sorry, sir," said I, with assumed tranquility, but an inward tremor, "but, really, the man you allude to is nothing to me—he is no relation or apprentice of mine, that you should hold me responsible for him."

"In mercy's name, who is he?"

"I certainly cannot inform you. I know nothing about him. Formerly I employed him as a copyist; but he has done nothing for me now for some time past."

"I shall settle him, then—good morning, sir."

Several days passed, and I heard nothing more; and, though I often felt a charitable prompting to call at the place and see poor Bartleby, yet a certain squeamishness, of I know not what, withheld me.

All is over with him, by this time, thought I, at last, when, through another week, no further intelligence reached me. But, coming to my room the day after, I found several persons waiting at my door in a high state of nervous excitement.

1 *mason up ... wall* In Edgar Allan Poe's story "The Cask of Amontillado" (1846), the murderer buries his victim alive by immurement (bricking him up behind a wall).

"That's the man—here he comes," cried the foremost one, whom I recognized as the lawyer who had previously called upon me alone.

"You must take him away, sir, at once," cried a portly person among them, advancing upon me, and whom I knew to be the landlord of No. —— Wall street. "These gentlemen, my tenants, cannot stand it any longer; Mr. B——," pointing to the lawyer, "has turned him out of his room, and he now persists in haunting the building generally, sitting upon the banisters of the stairs by day, and sleeping in the entry by night. Everybody is concerned; clients are leaving the offices; some fears are entertained of a mob; something you must do, and that without delay."

Aghast at this torrent, I fell back before it, and would fain have locked myself in my new quarters. In vain I persisted that Bartleby was nothing to me—no more than to anyone else. In vain—I was the last person known to have anything to do with him, and they held me to the terrible account. Fearful, then, of being exposed in the papers (as one person present obscurely threatened), I considered the matter, and, at length, said, that if the lawyer would give me a confidential interview with the scrivener, in his (the lawyer's) own room, I would, that afternoon, strive my best to rid them of the nuisance they complained of.

Going up stairs to my old haunt, there was Bartleby silently sitting upon the banister at the landing.

"What are you doing here, Bartleby?" said I.

"Sitting upon the banister," he mildly replied.

I motioned him into the lawyer's room, who then left us.

"Bartleby" said I, "are you aware that you are the cause of great tribulation to me, by persisting in occupying the entry after being dismissed from the office?"

No answer.

"Now one of two things must take place. Either you must do something, or something must be done to you. Now what sort of business would you like to engage in? Would you like to re-engage in copying for some one?"

"No; I would prefer not to make any change."

"Would you like a clerkship in a dry-goods store?"

"There is too much confinement about that. No, I would not like a clerkship; but I am not particular."

"Too much confinement," I cried, "why you keep yourself confined all the time!"

"I would prefer not to take a clerkship," he rejoined, as if to settle that little item at once.

"How would a bar-tender's business suit you? There is no trying of the eye-sight in that."

"I would not like it at all; though, as I said before, I am not particular."

His unwonted wordiness inspirited me. I returned to the charge.

"Well, then, would you like to travel through the country collecting bills for the merchants? That would improve your health."

"No, I would prefer to be doing something else."

"How, then, would going as a companion to Europe, to entertain some young gentleman with your conversation—how would that suit you?"

"Not at all. It does not strike me that there is anything definite about that. I like to be stationary. But I am not particular."

"Stationary you shall be, then," I cried, now losing all patience, and, for the first time in all my exasperating connection with him, fairly flying into a passion. "If you do not go away from these premises before night, I shall feel bound—indeed, I *am* bound—to—to—to quit the premises myself!" I rather absurdly concluded, knowing not with what possible threat to try to frighten his immobility into compliance. Despairing of all further efforts, I was precipitately leaving him, when a final thought occurred to me—one which had not been wholly unindulged before.

"Bartleby," said I, in the kindest tone I could assume under such exciting circumstances, "will you go home with me now—not to my office, but my dwelling—and remain there till we can conclude upon some convenient arrangement for you at our leisure? Come, let us start now, right away."

"No: at present I would prefer not to make any change at all."

I answered nothing; but, effectually dodging every one by the suddenness and rapidity of my flight, rushed from the building, ran up Wall street towards Broadway, and, jumping into the first omnibus, was soon removed from pursuit. As soon as tranquility returned, I distinctly perceived that I had now done all that I possibly could, both in respect to the demands of the landlord and his tenants, and with regard to my own desire and sense of duty, to benefit Bartleby, and shield him from rude persecution, I now strove to be entirely care-free and quiescent; and my conscience justified me in the attempt; though, indeed, it was not so successful as I could have wished. So fearful was I of being again hunted out by the incensed landlord and his exasperated tenants, that, surrendering my business to Nippers, for a few days, I drove about the upper part of the town and through the suburbs, in my rockaway;[1] crossed over to Jersey City and Hoboken, and paid fugitive visits to Manhattanville and Astoria.[2] In fact, I almost lived in my rockaway for the time.

When again I entered my office, lo, a note from the landlord lay upon the desk. I opened it with trembling hands. It informed me that the writer had sent to the police, and had Bartleby removed to the Tombs as a vagrant. Moreover, since I knew more about him than anyone else, he wished me to appear at that place, and make a suitable statement of the facts. These tidings had a conflicting effect upon me. At first I was indignant; but, at last, almost approved. The landlord's energetic, summary disposition, had led him to adopt a procedure which I do not think I would have decided upon myself; and yet, as a last resort, under such peculiar circumstances, it seemed the only plan.

As I afterwards learned, the poor scrivener, when told that he must be conducted to the Tombs, offered not the slightest obstacle, but, in his pale, unmoving way, silently acquiesced.

Some of the compassionate and curious bystanders joined the party; and headed by one of the constables arm in arm with Bartleby, the silent procession filed its way through all the noise, and heat, and joy of the roaring thoroughfares at noon.

The same day I received the note, I went to the Tombs, or, to speak more properly, the Halls of Justice. Seeking the right officer, I stated the purpose of my call, and was informed that the individual I described was, indeed, within. I then assured the functionary that Bartleby was a perfectly honest man, and greatly to be compassionated, however unaccountably eccentric. I narrated all I knew and closed by suggesting the idea of letting him remain in as indulgent confinement as possible, till something less harsh might be done—though, indeed, I hardly knew what. At all events, if nothing else could be decided upon, the alms-house[3] must receive him. I then begged to have an interview.

Being under no disgraceful charge, and quite serene and harmless in all his ways, they had permitted him freely to wander about the prison, and, especially, in the inclosed grass-platted yards thereof. And so I found him there, standing all alone in the quietest of the yards, his face towards a high wall, while all around, from the narrow slits of the jail windows, I thought I saw peering out upon him the eyes of murderers and thieves.

"Bartleby!"

"I know you," he said, without looking round— "and I want nothing to say to you."

"It was not I that brought you here, Bartleby," said I, keenly pained at his implied suspicion. "And to you, this should not be so vile a place. Nothing reproachful attaches to you by being here. And see, it is not so sad a place as one might think. Look, there is the sky, and here is the grass."

"I know where I am," he replied, but would say nothing more, and so I left him.

As I entered the corridor again, a broad meat-like man, in an apron, accosted me, and, jerking his thumb over his shoulder, said—"Is that your friend?"

"Yes."

"Does he want to starve? If he does, let him live on the prison fare, that's all."

"Who are you?" asked I, not knowing what to make of such an unofficially speaking person in such a place.

"I am the grub-man. Such gentlemen as have friends here, hire me to provide them with something good to eat."

"Is this so?" said I, turning to the turnkey.

He said it was.

"Well, then," said I, slipping some silver into the grub-man's hands (for so they called him), "I want you to give particular attention to my friend there; let him

---

[1] *rockaway* Carriage.

[2] *Jersey City … Hoboken* Cities in New Jersey, both located on the Hudson River; *Manhattanville* Neighborhood in Manhattan, also called West Harlem; *Astoria* Neighborhood in the borough of Queens, New York.

[3] *alms-house* Charitable house or building that offered shelter to the poor.

have the best dinner you can get. And you must be as polite to him as possible."

"Introduce me, will you?" said the grub-man, looking at me with an expression which seem to say he was all impatience for an opportunity to give a specimen of his breeding.

Thinking it would prove of benefit to the scrivener, I acquiesced; and, asking the grub-man his name, went up with him to Bartleby.

"Bartleby, this is a friend; you will find him very useful to you."

"Your sarvant, sir, your sarvant," said the grub-man, making a low salutation behind his apron. "Hope you find it pleasant here, sir; nice grounds—cool apartments—hope you'll stay with us some time—try to make it agreeable. What will you have for dinner to-day?"

"I prefer not to dine to-day," said Bartleby, turning away. "It would disagree with me; I am unused to dinners." So saying, he slowly moved to the other side of the inclosure, and took up a position fronting the dead-wall.

"How's this?" said the grub-man, addressing me with a stare of astonishment. "He's odd, ain't he?"

"I think he is a little deranged," said I, sadly.

"Deranged? deranged is it? Well, now, upon my word, I thought that friend of yourn was a gentleman forger; they are always pale, and genteel-like, them forgers. I can't help pity 'em—can't help it, sir. Did you know Monroe Edwards?"[1] he added, touchingly, and paused. Then, laying his hand piteously on my shoulder, sighed, "he died of consumption at Sing-Sing.[2] So you weren't acquainted with Monroe?"

"No, I was never socially acquainted with any forgers. But I cannot stop longer. Look to my friend yonder. You will not lose by it. I will see you again."

Some few days after this, I again obtained admission to the Tombs, and went through the corridors in quest of Bartleby; but without finding him.

"I saw him coming from his cell not long ago," said a turnkey, "may be he's gone to loiter in the yards."

So I went in that direction.

"Are you looking for the silent man?" said another turnkey, passing me. "Yonder he lies—sleeping in the yard there. 'Tis not twenty minutes since I saw him lie down."

The yard was entirely quiet. It was not accessible to the common prisoners. The surrounding walls, of amazing thickness, kept off all sounds behind them. The Egyptian character of the masonry weighed upon me with its gloom. But a soft imprisoned turf grew under foot. The heart of the eternal pyramids, it seemed, wherein, by some strange magic, through the clefts, grass-seed, dropped by birds, had sprung.

Strangely huddled at the base of the wall, his knees drawn up, and lying on his side, his head touching the cold stones, I saw the wasted Bartleby. But nothing stirred. I paused; then went close up to him; stooped over, and saw that his dim eyes were open; otherwise he seemed profoundly sleeping. Something prompted me to touch him. I felt his hand, when a tingling shiver ran up my arm and down my spine to my feet.

The round face of the grub-man peered upon me now. "His dinner is ready. Won't he dine to-day, either? Or does he live without dining?"

"Lives without dining," said I, and closed the eyes.

"Eh!—He's asleep, ain't he?"

"With kings and counselors,"[3] murmured I.

* * * * * *

There would seem little need for proceeding further in this history. Imagination will readily supply the meagre recital of poor Bartleby's interment. But, ere parting with the reader, let me say, that if this little narrative has sufficiently interested him, to awaken curiosity as to who Bartleby was, and what manner of life he led prior to the present narrator's making his acquaintance, I can only reply, that in such curiosity I fully share, but am wholly unable to gratify it. Yet here I hardly know whether I should divulge one little item of rumor, which came to my ear a few months after the scrivener's decease. Upon what basis it rested,

[1] *Monroe Edwards* Infamous slave trader and forger (1808–47) whose trial gained considerable prominence in the years preceding Melville's writing of "Bartleby."

[2] *Sing-Sing* Prison in New York state.

[3] *With kings and counselors* See the book of Job, Chapter 3, where Job curses the day he was born: "'Why died I not from the womb? ... For now should I have lain still and been quiet ... / With kings and counsellors of the earth, who built desolate places for themselves'" (3.11–14). The full chapter appears as an In Context section in this volume's website component.

I could never ascertain; and hence, how true it is I cannot now tell. But, inasmuch as this vague report has not been without a certain suggestive interest to me, however sad, it may prove the same with some others; and so I will briefly mention it. The report was this: that Bartleby had been a subordinate clerk in the Dead Letter Office[1] at Washington, from which he had been suddenly removed by a change in the administration. When I think over this rumor, hardly can I express the emotions which seize me. Dead letters! does it not sound like dead men? Conceive a man by nature and misfortune prone to a pallid hopelessness, can any business seem more fitted to heighten it than that of continually handling these dead letters, and assorting them for the flames? For by the cart-load they are annually burned. Sometimes from out the folded paper the pale clerk takes a ring—the finger it was meant for, perhaps, moulders in the grave; a banknote sent in swiftest charity—he whom it would relieve, nor eats nor hungers anymore; pardon for those who died despairing; hope for those who died unhoping; good tidings for those who died stifled by unrelieved calamities. On errands of life, these letters speed to death.

Ah, Bartleby! Ah, humanity!

—1853

Benito Cereno

An important context for *Benito Cereno* is the history of the Haitian Revolution, which was underway in 1799, the year the story is set. Beginning in 1791 and ending in 1804, the Haitian Revolution led to the foundation of a black state free from slavery.

In August 1791, the enslaved people of what was then the French colony of Saint-Domingue rose in revolt against their white enslavers—whom they outnumbered by at least a ten to one ratio—killing the whites and burning their plantations. In the following years the rebel army defeated not only French forces, but also those sent by Britain to seize control of the lucrative colony. By 1801, the formerly enslaved population controlled the entire island (Saint-Domingue as well as the neighboring Spanish colony of Santo Domingo), and Toussaint Louverture, the commander of the rebel army, created a new constitution that abolished slavery across the territory. In 1802, French forces renewed efforts to retake the colony and reinstitute slavery. Toussaint was captured and imprisoned in France, but the fighting continued, with the French perpetrating mass executions of captured soldiers. Toussaint died in prison in 1803; in November of that year, the rebel army, now under the leadership of Jean-Jacques Dessalines, drove the French off the island. Dessalines declared independence for Haiti on 1 January 1804. He then ordered the massacre of the remaining white population.

In America, news of the Haitian Revolution elicited mixed responses. Many abolitionists were supportive and saw the conflict as further proof that societies built on slavery were inherently unstable, whereas Southern enslavers and their supporters reacted in terror that similar events would occur on their plantations. Haiti became a source of hope to enslaved people across the world, and to black resistance in America particularly. As Frederick Douglass said in 1893, "Until [Haiti] spoke no Christian nation had abolished Negro slavery. Until she spoke no Christian nation had given to the world an organized effort to abolish slavery. Until she spoke the slave ship, followed by hungry sharks, greedy to devour the dead and dying slaves flung overboard to feed them, ploughed in peace the South Atlantic, painting the sea with the Negro's blood." Melville sets his story mid-way through the Haitian Revolution, before Louverture created a constitution but after the enslaved population had taken the upper hand in the conflict.

In the year 1799, Captain Amasa Delano,[2] of Duxbury, in Massachusetts, commanding a large sealer[3] and general trader, lay at anchor with a valuable cargo, in the harbor of St. Maria—a small, desert, uninhabited island toward the southern extremity of the long coast of Chili.[4] There he had touched[5] for water.

On the second day, not long after dawn, while lying in his berth, his mate came below, informing him that a strange sail was coming into the bay. Ships were then

---

[1] *Dead Letter Office* Place where undeliverable mail is stored and eventually destroyed.

[2] *Amasa Delano* This character is based on a real American sea captain, best known for his book *Narrative of Voyages and Travels in the Northern and Southern Hemispheres, Comprising Three Voyages Round the World* (1817).

[3] *sealer* Seal-hunting vessel.

[4] *Chili* Modern-day Chile.

[5] *touched* Landed.

not so plenty in those waters as now. He rose, dressed, and went on deck.

The morning was one peculiar to that coast. Everything was mute and calm; everything gray. The sea, though undulated into long roods[1] of swells, seemed fixed, and was sleeked at the surface like waved lead that has cooled and set in the smelter's mould. The sky seemed a gray surtout.[2] Flights of troubled gray fowl, kith and kin[3] with flights of troubled gray vapors among which they were mixed, skimmed low and fitfully over the waters, as swallows over meadows before storms.

Shadows present, foreshadowing deeper shadows to come.

To Captain Delano's surprise, the stranger, viewed through the glass, showed no colors; though to do so upon entering a haven, however uninhabited in its shores, where but a single other ship might be lying, was the custom among peaceful seamen of all nations. Considering the lawlessness and loneliness of the spot, and the sort of stories, at that day, associated with those seas, Captain Delano's surprise might have deepened into some uneasiness had he not been a person of a singularly undistrustful good-nature, not liable, except on extraordinary and repeated incentives, and hardly then, to indulge in personal alarms, any way involving the imputation of malign evil in man. Whether, in view of what humanity is capable, such a trait implies, along with a benevolent heart, more than ordinary quickness and accuracy of intellectual perception, may be left to the wise to determine.

But whatever misgivings might have obtruded on first seeing the stranger, would almost, in any seaman's mind, have been dissipated by observing that, the ship, in navigating into the harbor, was drawing too near the land; a sunken reef making out off her bow. This seemed to prove her a stranger, indeed, not only to the sealer, but the island; consequently, she could be no wonted freebooter[4] on that ocean. With no small interest, Captain Delano continued to watch her—a proceeding not much facilitated by the vapors partly mantling[5] the hull, through which the far matin light[6] from her cabin streamed equivocally enough; much like the sun—by this time hemisphered on the rim of the horizon, and, apparently, in company with the strange ship entering the harbor—which, wimpled by the same low, creeping clouds, showed not unlike a Lima intriguante's one sinister eye peering across the Plaza from the Indian loop-hole of her dusk *saya-y-manta*.[7]

It might have been but a deception of the vapors, but, the longer the stranger was watched the more singular appeared her manoeuvres. Ere long it seemed hard to decide whether she meant to come in or no— what she wanted, or what she was about. The wind, which had breezed up a little during the night, was now extremely light and baffling,[8] which the more increased the apparent uncertainty of her movements. Surmising, at last, that it might be a ship in distress, Captain Delano ordered his whale-boat to be dropped, and, much to the wary opposition of his mate, prepared to board her, and, at the least, pilot[9] her in. On the night previous, a fishing-party of the seamen had gone a long distance to some detached rocks out of sight from the sealer, and, an hour or two before daybreak, had returned, having met with no small success. Presuming that the stranger might have been long off soundings,[10] the good captain put several baskets of the fish, for presents, into his boat, and so pulled away. From her continuing too near the sunken reef, deeming her in danger, calling to his men, he made all haste to apprise those on board of their situation. But, some time ere the boat came up, the wind, light though it was, having shifted, had headed the vessel off, as well as partly broken the vapors from about her.

---

[1]   *roods* Units of land measurement, each equivalent to a quarter of an acre. A rood can also be a Christian cross.

[2]   *surtout* Overcoat.

[3]   *kith and kin* Friends and family.

[4]   *wonted freebooter* Practiced pirate.

[5]   *mantling* Cloaking; covering.

[6]   *matin light* Morning light, but with the suggestion of morning prayer-time (matins).

[7]   *wimpled* Veiled; *Lima* Capital of Peru; *intriguante* Woman who engages in an intrigue—here, perhaps, an extramarital affair; *saya-y-manta* Dress with a hood that partially covers the face, which women wore in colonial Peru and could conceal their identities.

[8]   *baffling* Variable, shifting.

[9]   *pilot* Steer, guide.

[10]   *off soundings* In waters so deep that the soundings—the line and lead used by a ship to ascertain water depth—could not reach the bottom. When in water so deep there are few fish to be caught; shallower seas contain more sea life.

Upon gaining a less remote view, the ship, when made signally visible on the verge of the leaden-hued swells, with the shreds of fog here and there raggedly furring her, appeared like a white-washed monastery after a thunder-storm, seen perched upon some dun cliff among the Pyrenees. But it was no purely fanciful resemblance which now, for a moment, almost led Captain Delano to think that nothing less than a ship-load of monks was before him. Peering over the bulwarks were what really seemed, in the hazy distance, throngs of dark cowls; while, fitfully revealed through the open port-holes, other dark moving figures were dimly descried, as of Black Friars[1] pacing the cloisters.

Upon a still nigher approach, this appearance was modified, and the true character of the vessel was plain—a Spanish merchantman of the first class, carrying negro slaves, amongst other valuable freight, from one colonial port to another. A very large, and, in its time, a very fine vessel, such as in those days were at intervals encountered along that main;[2] sometimes superseded Acapulco treasure-ships,[3] or retired frigates of the Spanish king's navy, which, like superannuated Italian palaces, still, under a decline of masters, preserved signs of former state.

As the whale-boat drew more and more nigh, the cause of the peculiar pipe-clayed aspect[4] of the stranger was seen in the slovenly neglect pervading her. The spars,[5] ropes, and great part of the bulwarks,[6] looked woolly, from long unacquaintance with the scraper, tar, and the brush. Her keel[7] seemed laid, her ribs put together, and she launched, from Ezekiel's Valley of Dry Bones.[8]

In the present business in which she was engaged, the ship's general model and rig appeared to have undergone no material change from their original warlike and Froissart pattern.[9] However, no guns were seen.

The tops[10] were large, and were railed about with what had once been octagonal net-work, all now in sad disrepair. These tops hung overhead like three ruinous aviaries, in one of which was seen, perched, on a ratlin, a white noddy,[11] a strange fowl, so called from its lethargic, somnambulistic character, being frequently caught by hand at sea. Battered and mouldy, the castellated forecastle[12] seemed some ancient turret, long ago taken by assault, and then left to decay. Toward the stern, two high-raised quarter galleries—the balustrades here and there covered with dry, tindery sea-moss—opening out from the unoccupied state-cabin, whose dead-lights,[13] for all the mild weather, were hermetically closed and calked—these tenantless balconies hung over the sea as if it were the grand Venetian canal. But the principal relic of faded grandeur was the ample oval of the shield-like stern-piece,[14] intricately carved with

---

[1] *Black Friars* Members of the Order of Preachers, or Dominicans, who wear black cloaks.

[2] *main* Sea.

[3] *Acapulco treasure-ships* Also known as Manila Galleons, ships that for over two centuries (1565–1815) moved between Acapulco and the Philippines (both were part of what was known as New Spain). This trade route brought the treasures of the Far East to the Americas.

[4] *pipe-clayed aspect* Look of having been whitened (pipes were made of white clay).

[5] *spars* Wooden masts, and the wooden parts of sails (booms and yards).

[6] *bulwarks* Sides of the ship above the level of the deck.

[7] *keel* Bottom centerline structure of a ship; the rest of the hull is built around the keel.

[8] *Ezekiel's ... Bones* Ezekiel 37.1–14 recounts the prophet's vision of a valley of dry human bones, which God tells Ezekiel are the exiled bones of the people of Israel, waiting to be resurrected in their homeland.

[9] *Froissart pattern* Jean Froissart (1337–1405) was a French historian of the Hundred Years' War (1337–1453) who celebrated chivalry and the feudal aristocracy. Illustrated editions of Froissart's *Chronicles* (c. 1391)—one of which was published in New York in 1854, shortly before the publication of *Benito Cereno*—contain stylized illustrations of medieval warships, which typically contain one mast and sail and a high turreted forecastle and after castle. By the time Melville's story takes place, this style of shipbuilding had been obsolete for a century and a half.

[10] *tops* Topsails.

[11] *ratlin* Small rope used in forming a ship's ladder; *white noddy* Small seabird, also known as a tern.

[12] *castellated forecastle* Forecastle (the raised deck at the front of a ship) that is built like a castle wall for defensive purposes (the ships in the Froissart illustrations have this appearance).

[13] *dead-lights* Shutters placed over port-holes and cabin-windows to keep water out in a storm.

[14] *stern-piece* Flat piece of wood at the stern, to which the side planks are attached.

the arms of Castile and Leon,[1] medallioned about by groups of mythological or symbolical devices; uppermost and central of which was a dark satyr[2] in a mask, holding his foot on the prostrate neck of a writhing figure, likewise masked.

Whether the ship had a figure-head, or only a plain beak,[3] was not quite certain, owing to canvas wrapped about that part, either to protect it while undergoing a re-furbishing, or else decently to hide its decay. Rudely painted or chalked, as in a sailor freak,[4] along the forward side of a sort of pedestal below the canvas, was the sentence, "*Seguid vuestro jefe*" (follow your leader); while upon the tarnished headboards,[5] near by, appeared, in stately capitals, once gilt, the ship's name, "SAN DOMINICK,"[6] each letter streakingly corroded with tricklings of copper-spike rust; while, like mourning weeds, dark festoons of sea-grass slimily swept to and fro over the name, with every hearse-like roll of the hull.

As, at last, the boat was hooked from the bow along toward the gangway[7] amidship, its keel, while yet some inches separated from the hull, harshly grated as on a sunken coral reef. It proved a huge bunch of conglobated[8] barnacles adhering below the water to the side like a wen[9]—a token of baffling airs and long calms passed somewhere in those seas.

Climbing the side, the visitor was at once surrounded by a clamorous throng of whites and blacks, but the latter outnumbering the former more than could have been expected, negro transportation-ship as the stranger in port was. But, in one language, and as with one voice, all poured out a common tale of suffering; in which the negresses, of whom there were not a few, exceeded the others in their dolorous vehemence. The scurvy,[10] together with the fever, had swept off a great part of their number, more especially the Spaniards. Off Cape Horn they had narrowly escaped shipwreck;[11] then, for days together, they had lain tranced[12] without wind; their provisions were low; their water next to none; their lips that moment were baked.

While Captain Delano was thus made the mark[13] of all eager tongues, his one eager glance took in all faces, with every other object about him. Always upon first boarding a large and populous ship at sea, especially a foreign one, with a nondescript crew such as Lascars or Manilla men,[14] the impression varies in a peculiar way from that produced by first entering a strange house with strange inmates in a strange land. Both house and ship—the one by its walls and blinds, the other by its high bulwarks like ramparts—hoard from view their interiors till the last moment: but in the case of the ship there is this addition; that the living spectacle it contains, upon its sudden and complete disclosure, has, in contrast with the blank ocean which zones it, something of the effect of enchantment. The ship seems unreal; these strange costumes, gestures, and faces, but a shadowy tableau just emerged from the deep, which directly must receive back what it gave.

Perhaps it was some such influence, as above is attempted to be described, which, in Captain Delano's mind, heightened whatever, upon a staid scrutiny, might have seemed unusual; especially the conspicuous figures of four elderly grizzled negroes, their heads like black, doddered[15] willow tops, who, in venerable

---

[1] *arms of Castile and Leon* The symbols (arms) of the Spanish region of Castile and León are two lions and two castles.

[2] *satyr* Woodland deity; often represented as part human, part animal, and in a state of sexual arousal.

[3] *figure-head* Ornamental sculpture, usually a woman's figure, that is placed at the head of a ship; *plain beak* Undecorated projection at the head of the ship (beak-shaped).

[4] *freak* Eccentric behavior.

[5] *headboards* Planking between the headrails—the timbers that extend on each side from the head of the ship.

[6] *SAN DOMINICK* Name suggestive of the Roman Catholic Order of Preachers, or Dominicans, who took their name from St. Dominic, and also of the Haitian Revolution: "Saint-Domingue" is the name of the French colony in which the revolution took place. Melville invented this name for the ship.

[7] *gangway* Passage between stowed cargo in the hold.

[8] *conglobated* Gathered together in a round mass.

[9] *wen* Tumor.

[10] *scurvy* A disease caused by vitamin C deficiency, once common among sailors.

[11] *Off Cape … shipwreck* Rounding Cape Horn (the southernmost tip of South America) was one of the more dangerous tasks that mariners could confront, as the seas are particularly rough, and storms are common.

[12] *tranced* I.e., entranced, becalmed.

[13] *mark* Target.

[14] *Lascars* Sailors from Asia, especially the Indian subcontinent; *Manilla men* Filipinos.

[15] *doddered* Made unsteady, trembling.

contrast to the tumult below them, were couched, sphynx-like, one on the starboard cat-head, another on the larboard, and the remaining pair face to face on the opposite bulwarks above the main-chains.[1] They each had bits of unstranded old junk in their hands, and, with a sort of stoical self-content, were picking the junk into oakum,[2] a small heap of which lay by their sides. They accompanied the task with a continuous, low, monotonous, chant; droning and drilling away like so many gray-headed bag-pipers playing a funeral march.

The quarter-deck rose into an ample elevated poop,[3] upon the forward verge of which, lifted, like the oakum-pickers, some eight feet above the general throng, sat along in a row, separated by regular spaces, the cross-legged figures of six other blacks; each with a rusty hatchet in his hand, which, with a bit of brick and a rag, he was engaged like a scullion in scouring;[4] while between each two was a small stack of hatchets, their rusted edges turned forward awaiting a like operation. Though occasionally the four oakum-pickers would briefly address some person or persons in the crowd below, yet the six hatchet-polishers neither spoke to others, nor breathed a whisper among themselves, but sat intent upon their task, except at intervals, when, with the peculiar love in negroes of uniting industry with pastime, two and two they sideways clashed their hatchets together, like cymbals, with a barbarous din. All six, unlike the generality, had the raw aspect of unsophisticated Africans.

But that first comprehensive glance which took in those ten figures, with scores less conspicuous, rested but an instant upon them, as, impatient of the hubbub of voices, the visitor turned in quest of whomsoever it might be that commanded the ship.

But as if not unwilling to let nature make known her own case among his suffering charge, or else in despair of restraining it for the time, the Spanish captain, a gentlemanly, reserved-looking, and rather young man to a stranger's eye, dressed with singular richness, but bearing plain traces of recent sleepless cares and disquietudes, stood passively by, leaning against the main-mast, at one moment casting a dreary, spiritless look upon his excited people, at the next an unhappy glance toward his visitor. By his side stood a black of small stature, in whose rude face, as occasionally, like a shepherd's dog, he mutely turned it up into the Spaniard's, sorrow and affection were equally blended.

Struggling through the throng, the American advanced to the Spaniard, assuring him of his sympathies, and offering to render whatever assistance might be in his power. To which the Spaniard returned for the present but grave and ceremonious acknowledgments, his national formality dusked by the saturnine[5] mood of ill-health.

But losing no time in mere compliments, Captain Delano, returning to the gangway, had his basket of fish brought up; and as the wind still continued light, so that some hours at least must elapse ere the ship could be brought to the anchorage, he bade his men return to the sealer, and fetch back as much water as the whale-boat could carry, with whatever soft bread the steward might have, all the remaining pumpkins on board, with a box of sugar, and a dozen of his private bottles of cider.

Not many minutes after the boat's pushing off, to the vexation of all, the wind entirely died away, and the tide turning, began drifting back the ship helplessly seaward. But trusting this would not long last, Captain Delano sought, with good hopes, to cheer up the strangers, feeling no small satisfaction that, with persons in their condition, he could—thanks to his frequent voyages along the Spanish main—converse with some freedom in their native tongue.

While left alone with them, he was not long in observing some things tending to heighten his first impressions; but surprise was lost in pity, both for the Spaniards and blacks, alike evidently reduced from scarcity of water and provisions; while long-continued suffering seemed to have brought out the

---

[1] *cat-head* Beam that sticks out from the ship's bows and is used to raise and lower the anchor without hitting the bows; *main-chains* Tackle that is either near or attached to the mainmast.

[2] *junk* Old ropes; *oakum* Fibers from hemp ropes that have been unwound and separated, often used as a caulking material on ships. Picking ropes to make oakum was a painful job.

[3] *quarter-deck* Upper deck behind the mainmast; *poop* Stern of the ship.

[4] *bit of brick ... scouring* These men were using bricks of pumice stone to polish (scour) the rust from the hatchets. A "scullion" was the lowest rank of servant, who was given the worst jobs in the household.

[5] *saturnine* Gloomy.

less good-natured qualities of the negroes, besides, at the same time, impairing the Spaniard's authority over them. But, under the circumstances, precisely this condition of things was to have been anticipated. In armies, navies, cities, or families, in nature herself, nothing more relaxes good order than misery. Still, Captain Delano was not without the idea, that had Benito Cereno been a man of greater energy, misrule would hardly have come to the present pass. But the debility,[1] constitutional or induced by hardships, bodily and mental, of the Spanish captain, was too obvious to be overlooked. A prey to settled dejection, as if long mocked with hope he would not now indulge it, even when it had ceased to be a mock, the prospect of that day, or evening at furthest, lying at anchor, with plenty of water for his people, and a brother captain to counsel and befriend, seemed in no perceptible degree to encourage him. His mind appeared unstrung, if not still more seriously affected. Shut up in these oaken walls, chained to one dull round of command, whose unconditionality cloyed him, like some hypochondriac abbot he moved slowly about, at times suddenly pausing, starting, or staring, biting his lip, biting his fingernail, flushing, paling, twitching his beard, with other symptoms of an absent or moody mind. This distempered spirit was lodged, as before hinted, in as distempered a frame. He was rather tall, but seemed never to have been robust, and now with nervous suffering was almost worn to a skeleton. A tendency to some pulmonary complaint appeared to have been lately confirmed. His voice was like that of one with lungs half gone—hoarsely suppressed, a husky whisper. No wonder that, as in this state he tottered about, his private servant apprehensively followed him. Sometimes the negro gave his master his arm, or took his handkerchief out of his pocket for him; performing these and similar offices with that affectionate zeal which transmutes into something filial or fraternal acts in themselves but menial; and which has gained for the negro the repute of making the most pleasing bodyservant in the world; one, too, whom a master need be on no stiffly superior terms with, but may treat with familiar trust; less a servant than a devoted companion.

Marking the noisy indocility[2] of the blacks in general, as well as what seemed the sullen inefficiency of the whites it was not without humane satisfaction that Captain Delano witnessed the steady good conduct of Babo.

But the good conduct of Babo, hardly more than the ill-behavior of others, seemed to withdraw the half-lunatic Don Benito from his cloudy languor. Not that such precisely was the impression made by the Spaniard on the mind of his visitor. The Spaniard's individual unrest was, for the present, but noted as a conspicuous feature in the ship's general affliction. Still, Captain Delano was not a little concerned at what he could not help taking for the time to be Don Benito's unfriendly indifference towards himself. The Spaniard's manner, too, conveyed a sort of sour and gloomy disdain, which he seemed at no pains to disguise. But this the American in charity ascribed to the harassing effects of sickness, since, in former instances, he had noted that there are peculiar natures on whom prolonged physical suffering seems to cancel every social instinct of kindness; as if, forced to black bread themselves, they deemed it but equity that each person coming nigh them should, indirectly, by some slight or affront, be made to partake of their fare.

But ere long Captain Delano bethought him that, indulgent as he was at the first, in judging the Spaniard, he might not, after all, have exercised charity enough. At bottom it was Don Benito's reserve which displeased him; but the same reserve was shown towards all but his faithful personal attendant. Even the formal reports which, according to sea-usage, were, at stated times, made to him by some petty underling, either a white, mulatto or black, he hardly had patience enough to listen to, without betraying contemptuous aversion. His manner upon such occasions was, in its degree, not unlike that which might be supposed to have been his imperial countryman's, Charles V., just previous to the anchoritish retirement[3] of that monarch from the throne. This splenetic[4] disrelish of his place

---

[1]   *debility*   Weakness.

[2]   *indocility*   Unruliness, lack of submissiveness.

[3]   *anchoritish retirement*   In 1556, Charles V (1500–58) abdicated his throne as Holy Roman Emperor and joined a monastery. An anchorite is a person who withdraws from society to lead a life of religious seclusion.

[4]   *splenetic*   Melancholic, grumpy.

was evinced in almost every function pertaining to it. Proud as he was moody, he condescended to no personal mandate. Whatever special orders were necessary, their delivery was delegated to his body-servant, who in turn transferred them to their ultimate destination, through runners, alert Spanish boys or slave boys, like pages or pilot-fish[1] within easy call continually hovering round Don Benito. So that to have beheld this undemonstrative invalid gliding about, apathetic and mute, no landsman could have dreamed that in him was lodged a dictatorship beyond which, while at sea, there was no earthly appeal.

Thus, the Spaniard, regarded in his reserve, seemed the involuntary victim of mental disorder. But, in fact, his reserve might, in some degree, have proceeded from design. If so, then here was evinced the unhealthy climax of that icy though conscientious policy, more or less adopted by all commanders of large ships, which, except in signal emergencies, obliterates alike the manifestation of sway with every trace of sociality; transforming the man into a block, or rather into a loaded cannon, which, until there is call for thunder, has nothing to say.

Viewing him in this light, it seemed but a natural token of the perverse habit induced by a long course of such hard self-restraint, that, notwithstanding the present condition of his ship, the Spaniard should still persist in a demeanor, which, however harmless, or, it may be, appropriate, in a well-appointed vessel, such as the San Dominick might have been at the outset of the voyage, was anything but judicious now. But the Spaniard, perhaps, thought that it was with captains as with gods: reserve, under all events, must still be their cue. But probably this appearance of slumbering dominion might have been but an attempted disguise to conscious imbecility—not deep policy, but shallow device. But be all this as it might, whether Don Benito's manner was designed or not, the more Captain Delano noted its pervading reserve, the less he felt uneasiness at any particular manifestation of that reserve towards himself.

Neither were his thoughts taken up by the captain alone. Wonted to the quiet orderliness of the sealer's comfortable family of a crew, the noisy confusion of the San Dominick's suffering host repeatedly challenged his eye. Some prominent breaches, not only of discipline but of decency, were observed. These Captain Delano could not but ascribe, in the main, to the absence of those subordinate deck-officers to whom, along with higher duties, is intrusted what may be styled the police department of a populous ship. True, the old oakum-pickers appeared at times to act the part of monitorial constables to their countrymen, the blacks; but though occasionally succeeding in allaying trifling outbreaks now and then between man and man, they could do little or nothing toward establishing general quiet. The San Dominick was in the condition of a transatlantic emigrant ship, among whose multitude of living freight are some individuals, doubtless, as little troublesome as crates and bales; but the friendly remonstrances of such with their ruder companions are of not so much avail as the unfriendly arm of the mate. What the San Dominick wanted was, what the emigrant ship has, stern superior officers. But on these decks not so much as a fourth-mate was to be seen.

The visitor's curiosity was roused to learn the particulars of those mishaps which had brought about such absenteeism, with its consequences; because, though deriving some inkling of the voyage from the wails which at the first moment had greeted him, yet of the details no clear understanding had been had. The best account would, doubtless, be given by the captain. Yet at first the visitor was loth to ask it, unwilling to provoke some distant rebuff. But plucking up courage, he at last accosted Don Benito, renewing the expression of his benevolent interest, adding, that did he (Captain Delano) but know the particulars of the ship's misfortunes, he would, perhaps, be better able in the end to relieve them. Would Don Benito favor him with the whole story.

Don Benito faltered; then, like some somnambulist suddenly interfered with, vacantly stared at his visitor, and ended by looking down on the deck. He maintained this posture so long, that Captain Delano, almost equally disconcerted, and involuntarily almost as rude, turned suddenly from him, walking forward to accost one of the Spanish seamen for the desired information. But he had hardly gone five paces, when,

---

[1] *pages* Attendants on a person of high-rank; *pilot-fish* Fish that swim alongside, and eat parasites from, sharks. They also eat leftover bits from a shark's kill.

with a sort of eagerness, Don Benito invited him back, regretting his momentary absence of mind, and professing readiness to gratify him.

While most part of the story was being given, the two captains stood on the after part of the main-deck, a privileged spot, no one being near but the servant.

"It is now a hundred and ninety days," began the Spaniard, in his husky whisper, "that this ship, well officered and well manned, with several cabin passengers—some fifty Spaniards in all—sailed from Buenos Ayres bound to Lima, with a general cargo, hardware, Paraguay tea[1] and the like—and," pointing forward, "that parcel of negroes, now not more than a hundred and fifty, as you see, but then numbering over three hundred souls. Off Cape Horn we had heavy gales. In one moment, by night, three of my best officers, with fifteen sailors, were lost, with the main-yard; the spar snapping under them in the slings, as they sought, with heavers,[2] to beat down the icy sail. To lighten the hull, the heavier sacks of mata were thrown into the sea, with most of the water-pipes[3] lashed on deck at the time. And this last necessity it was, combined with the prolonged detentions[4] afterwards experienced, which eventually brought about our chief causes of suffering. When—"

Here there was a sudden fainting attack of his cough, brought on, no doubt, by his mental distress. His servant sustained him, and drawing a cordial from his pocket placed it to his lips. He a little revived. But unwilling to leave him unsupported while yet imperfectly restored, the black with one arm still encircled his master, at the same time keeping his eye fixed on his face, as if to watch for the first sign of complete restoration, or relapse, as the event might prove.

The Spaniard proceeded, but brokenly and obscurely, as one in a dream.

—"Oh, my God! rather than pass through what I have, with joy I would have hailed the most terrible gales; but—"

His cough returned and with increased violence; this subsiding; with reddened lips and closed eyes he fell heavily against his supporter.

"His mind wanders. He was thinking of the plague that followed the gales," plaintively sighed the servant; "my poor, poor master!" wringing one hand, and with the other wiping the mouth. "But be patient, Señor," again turning to Captain Delano, "these fits do not last long; master will soon be himself."

Don Benito reviving, went on; but as this portion of the story was very brokenly delivered, the substance only will here be set down.

It appeared that after the ship had been many days tossed in storms off the Cape, the scurvy broke out, carrying off numbers of the whites and blacks. When at last they had worked round into the Pacific, their spars and sails were so damaged, and so inadequately handled by the surviving mariners, most of whom were become invalids, that, unable to lay her northerly course by the wind, which was powerful, the unmanageable ship, for successive days and nights, was blown northwestward, where the breeze suddenly deserted her, in unknown waters, to sultry calms. The absence of the water-pipes now proved as fatal to life as before their presence had menaced it. Induced, or at least aggravated, by the more than scanty allowance of water, a malignant fever followed the scurvy; with the excessive heat of the lengthened calm, making such short work of it as to sweep away, as by billows, whole families of the Africans, and a yet larger number, proportionably, of the Spaniards, including, by a luckless fatality, every remaining officer on board. Consequently, in the smart west winds eventually following the calm, the already rent sails, having to be simply dropped, not furled, at need, had been gradually reduced to the beggars' rags they were now. To procure substitutes for his lost sailors, as well as supplies of water and sails, the captain, at the earliest opportunity, had made for Baldivia, the southernmost civilized port of Chili and South America; but upon nearing the coast the thick weather had prevented him from so much as sighting that harbor. Since which period, almost without a crew, and almost without

---

[1] *Paraguay tea* I.e., yerba mate, a major export from Paraguay in the nineteenth century.

[2] *slings* Middle part of a yard; *heavers* Wooden bars used to tighten ropes.

[3] *mata* I.e., the yerba mate; *water-pipes* Barrels of drinking water.

[4] *detentions* Periods of being delayed (in this case, becalmed).

canvas and almost without water, and, at intervals giving its added dead to the sea, the San Dominick had been battle-dored[1] about by contrary winds, inveigled by currents, or grown weedy in calms. Like a man lost in woods, more than once she had doubled upon her own track.

"But throughout these calamities," huskily continued Don Benito, painfully turning in the half embrace of his servant, "I have to thank those negroes you see, who, though to your inexperienced eyes appearing unruly, have, indeed, conducted themselves with less of restlessness than even their owner could have thought possible under such circumstances."

Here he again fell faintly back. Again his mind wandered; but he rallied, and less obscurely proceeded.

"Yes, their owner was quite right in assuring me that no fetters[2] would be needed with his blacks; so that while, as is wont in this transportation, those negroes have always remained upon deck—not thrust below, as in the Guinea-men[3]—they have, also, from the beginning, been freely permitted to range within given bounds at their pleasure."

Once more the faintness returned—his mind roved—but, recovering, he resumed:

"But it is Babo here to whom, under God, I owe not only my own preservation, but likewise to him, chiefly, the merit is due, of pacifying his more ignorant brethren, when at intervals tempted to murmurings."

"Ah, master," sighed the black, bowing his face, "don't speak of me; Babo is nothing; what Babo has done was but duty."

"Faithful fellow!" cried Captain Delano. "Don Benito, I envy you such a friend; slave I cannot call him."

As master and man stood before him, the black upholding the white, Captain Delano could not but bethink him of the beauty of that relationship which could present such a spectacle of fidelity on the one hand and confidence on the other. The scene was heightened by the contrast in dress, denoting their relative positions. The Spaniard wore a loose Chili jacket of dark velvet; white small-clothes[4] and stockings, with silver buckles at the knee and instep; a high-crowned sombrero, of fine grass; a slender sword, silver mounted, hung from a knot in his sash—the last being an almost invariable adjunct, more for utility than ornament, of a South American gentleman's dress to this hour. Excepting when his occasional nervous contortions brought about disarray, there was a certain precision in his attire curiously at variance with the unsightly disorder around; especially in the belittered Ghetto,[5] forward of the main-mast, wholly occupied by the blacks.

The servant wore nothing but wide trowsers, apparently, from their coarseness and patches, made out of some old topsail; they were clean, and confined at the waist by a bit of unstranded rope, which, with his composed, deprecatory air at times, made him look something like a begging friar of St. Francis.[6]

However unsuitable for the time and place, at least in the blunt-thinking American's eyes, and however strangely surviving in the midst of all his afflictions, the toilette[7] of Don Benito might not, in fashion at least, have gone beyond the style of the day among South Americans of his class. Though on the present voyage sailing from Buenos Ayres, he had avowed himself a native and resident of Chili, whose inhabitants had not so generally adopted the plain coat and once plebeian pantaloons; but, with a becoming modification, adhered to their provincial costume, picturesque as any in the world. Still, relatively to the pale history of the voyage, and his own pale face, there seemed something so incongruous in the Spaniard's apparel, as almost to suggest the image of an invalid courtier tottering about London streets in the time of the plague.

The portion of the narrative which, perhaps, most excited interest, as well as some surprise, considering

---

[1] *battle-dored* Shunted back and forth like a shuttlecock between battledores (the rackets used in badminton).

[2] *fetters* Shackles, restraints.

[3] *Guinea-men* Slave ships used in the transatlantic slave trade.

[4] *small-clothes* Knee-breeches.

[5] *Ghetto* Area of the ship likened to a segregated ghetto in a city (in the nineteenth century a "ghetto" referred most often to the Jewish quarter of a European city).

[6] *unstranded* Unbroken; *friar of St. Francis* Franciscans are mendicant friars; their iconic habit is a brown woolen robe belted with a white rope, which is knotted three times to remind the wearer of the three central vows of Franciscan life: poverty, chastity, and obedience. The Franciscans and Dominicans were frequent rivals during the Middle Ages.

[7] *toilette* Style of dress.

the latitudes in question, was the long calms spoken of, and more particularly the ship's so long drifting about. Without communicating the opinion, of course, the American could not but impute at least part of the detentions both to clumsy seamanship and faulty navigation. Eying Don Benito's small, yellow hands, he easily inferred that the young captain had not got into command at the hawse-hole, but the cabin-window;[1] and if so, why wonder at incompetence, in youth, sickness, and gentility united?

But drowning criticism in compassion, after a fresh repetition of his sympathies, Captain Delano, having heard out his story, not only engaged, as in the first place, to see Don Benito and his people supplied in their immediate bodily needs, but, also, now farther promised to assist him in procuring a large permanent supply of water, as well as some sails and rigging; and, though it would involve no small embarrassment to himself, yet he would spare three of his best seamen for temporary deck officers; so that without delay the ship might proceed to Conception,[2] there fully to refit for Lima, her destined port.

Such generosity was not without its effect, even upon the invalid. His face lighted up; eager and hectic, he met the honest glance of his visitor. With gratitude he seemed overcome.

"This excitement is bad for master," whispered the servant, taking his arm, and with soothing words gently drawing him aside.

When Don Benito returned, the American was pained to observe that his hopefulness, like the sudden kindling in his cheek, was but febrile[3] and transient.

Ere long, with a joyless mien, looking up towards the poop, the host invited his guest to accompany him there, for the benefit of what little breath of wind might be stirring.

As during the telling of the story, Captain Delano had once or twice started at the occasional cymballing of the hatchet-polishers, wondering why such an interruption should be allowed, especially in that part of the ship, and in the ears of an invalid; and moreover, as the hatchets had anything but an attractive look, and the handlers of them still less so, it was, therefore, to tell the truth, not without some lurking reluctance, or even shrinking, it may be, that Captain Delano, with apparent complaisance, acquiesced in his host's invitation. The more so, since, with an untimely caprice of punctilio,[4] rendered distressing by his cadaverous aspect, Don Benito, with Castilian bows, solemnly insisted upon his guest's preceding him up the ladder leading to the elevation; where, one on each side of the last step, sat for armorial supporters and sentries two of the ominous file.[5] Gingerly enough stepped good Captain Delano between them, and in the instant of leaving them behind, like one running the gauntlet, he felt an apprehensive twitch in the calves of his legs.

But when, facing about, he saw the whole file, like so many organ-grinders, still stupidly intent on their work, unmindful of everything beside, he could not but smile at his late fidgety panic.

Presently, while standing with his host, looking forward upon the decks below, he was struck by one of those instances of insubordination previously alluded to. Three black boys, with two Spanish boys, were sitting together on the hatches, scraping a rude wooden platter, in which some scanty mess had recently been cooked. Suddenly, one of the black boys, enraged at a word dropped by one of his white companions, seized a knife, and, though called to forbear by one of the oakum-pickers, struck the lad over the head, inflicting a gash from which blood flowed.

In amazement, Captain Delano inquired what this meant. To which the pale Don Benito dully muttered, that it was merely the sport of the lad.

"Pretty serious sport, truly," rejoined Captain Delano. "Had such a thing happened on board the Bachelor's Delight, instant punishment would have followed."

At these words the Spaniard turned upon the American one of his sudden, staring, half-lunatic looks;

---

[1] *got into … cabin-window* I.e., he is a landsman who gained his captaincy through connections rather than through experience at sea. When one "climbs through the hawse-hole" one rises through the ranks from the bottom up (the hawse-hole is one of two small holes that the ship's cable runs through); climbing through the "cabin window," on the other hand, means gaining command of a ship by jumping straight into the captain's cabin (by virtue of one's wealth and connections).

[2] *Conception* Port in south-central Chile.

[3] *febrile* Feverish.

[4] *punctilio* Politeness, adherence to formal etiquette.

[5] *file* Line of workers polishing the hatchets.

then, relapsing into his torpor, answered, "Doubtless, doubtless, Señor."

Is it, thought Captain Delano, that this hapless man is one of those paper captains I've known, who by policy wink at what by power they cannot put down? I know no sadder sight than a commander who has little of command but the name.

"I should think, Don Benito," he now said, glancing towards the oakum-picker who had sought to interfere with the boys, "that you would find it advantageous to keep all your blacks employed, especially the younger ones, no matter at what useless task, and no matter what happens to the ship. Why, even with my little band, I find such a course indispensable. I once kept a crew on my quarter-deck thrumming mats[1] for my cabin, when, for three days, I had given up my ship—mats, men, and all—for a speedy loss, owing to the violence of a gale, in which we could do nothing but helplessly drive before it."

"Doubtless, doubtless," muttered Don Benito.

"But," continued Captain Delano, again glancing upon the oakum-pickers and then at the hatchet-polishers, near by, "I see you keep some, at least, of your host employed."

"Yes," was again the vacant response.

"Those old men there, shaking their pows[2] from their pulpits," continued Captain Delano, pointing to the oakum-pickers, "seem to act the part of old dominies[3] to the rest, little heeded as their admonitions are at times. Is this voluntary on their part, Don Benito, or have you appointed them shepherds to your flock of black sheep?"

"What posts they fill, I appointed them," rejoined the Spaniard, in an acrid tone, as if resenting some supposed satiric reflection.

"And these others, these Ashantee[4] conjurors here," continued Captain Delano, rather uneasily eying the brandished steel of the hatchet-polishers, where, in spots, it had been brought to a shine, "this seems a curious business they are at, Don Benito?"

"In the gales we met," answered the Spaniard, "what of our general cargo was not thrown overboard was much damaged by the brine. Since coming into calm weather, I have had several cases of knives and hatchets daily brought up for overhauling and cleaning."

"A prudent idea, Don Benito. You are part owner of ship and cargo, I presume; but none of the slaves, perhaps?"

"I am owner of all you see," impatiently returned Don Benito, "except the main company of blacks, who belonged to my late friend, Alexandro Aranda."

As he mentioned this name, his air was heart-broken; his knees shook; his servant supported him.

Thinking he divined the cause of such unusual emotion, to confirm his surmise, Captain Delano, after a pause, said: "And may I ask, Don Benito, whether—since awhile ago you spoke of some cabin passengers—the friend, whose loss so afflicts you, at the outset of the voyage accompanied his blacks?"

"Yes."

"But died of the fever?"

"Died of the fever. Oh, could I but—"

Again quivering, the Spaniard paused.

"Pardon me," said Captain Delano, lowly, "but I think that, by a sympathetic experience, I conjecture, Don Benito, what it is that gives the keener edge to your grief. It was once my hard fortune to lose, at sea, a dear friend, my own brother, then supercargo.[5] Assured of the welfare of his spirit, its departure I could have borne like a man; but that honest eye, that honest hand—both of which had so often met mine—and that warm heart; all, all—like scraps to the dogs—to throw all to the sharks! It was then I vowed never to have for fellow-voyager a man I loved, unless, unbeknown to him, I had provided every requisite, in case of a fatality, for embalming his mortal part for interment on shore. Were your friend's remains now on board this ship, Don Benito, not thus strangely would the mention of his name affect you."

"On board this ship?" echoed the Spaniard. Then, with horrified gestures, as directed against some

---

[1] *thrumming mats* Sewing rope over mats or sails to create a rough thick surface that could be used to stop leaks.

[2] *pows* Scottish word meaning "heads."

[3] *dominies* Preachers within the Dutch Reformed Church, in which denomination Melville was brought up; alternatively, schoolmasters.

[4] *Ashantee* The Ashanti or Asante people are among the Akan peoples of West Africa. They resisted British colonization and had a reputation for martial prowess in the nineteenth century.

[5] *supercargo* A representative of the ship's owner who sails aboard the ship to guard the cargo.

spectre, he unconsciously fell into the ready arms of his attendant, who, with a silent appeal toward Captain Delano, seemed beseeching him not again to broach a theme so unspeakably distressing to his master.

This poor fellow now, thought the pained American, is the victim of that sad superstition which associates goblins with the deserted body of man, as ghosts with an abandoned house. How unlike are we made! What to me, in like case, would have been a solemn satisfaction, the bare suggestion, even, terrifies the Spaniard into this trance. Poor Alexandro Aranda! what would you say could you here see your friend—who, on former voyages, when you, for months, were left behind, has, I dare say, often longed, and longed, for one peep at you—now transported with terror at the least thought of having you anyway nigh him.

At this moment, with a dreary grave-yard toll, betokening a flaw, the ship's forecastle bell, smote by one of the grizzled oakum-pickers, proclaimed ten o'clock, through the leaden calm; when Captain Delano's attention was caught by the moving figure of a gigantic black, emerging from the general crowd below, and slowly advancing towards the elevated poop. An iron collar was about his neck, from which depended a chain, thrice wound round his body; the terminating links padlocked together at a broad band of iron, his girdle.

"How like a mute Atufal moves," murmured the servant.

The black mounted the steps of the poop, and, like a brave prisoner, brought up to receive sentence, stood in unquailing muteness before Don Benito, now recovered from his attack.

At the first glimpse of his approach, Don Benito had started, a resentful shadow swept over his face; and, as with the sudden memory of bootless[1] rage, his white lips glued together.

This is some mulish mutineer, thought Captain Delano, surveying, not without a mixture of admiration, the colossal form of the negro.

"See, he waits your question, master," said the servant.

Thus reminded, Don Benito, nervously averting his glance, as if shunning, by anticipation, some rebellious response, in a disconcerted voice, thus spoke:—

"Atufal, will you ask my pardon, now?"

The black was silent.

"Again, master," murmured the servant, with bitter upbraiding eying his countryman, "Again, master; he will bend to master yet."

"Answer," said Don Benito, still averting his glance, "say but the one word, *pardon*, and your chains shall be off."

Upon this, the black, slowly raising both arms, let them lifelessly fall, his links clanking, his head bowed; as much as to say, "no, I am content."

"Go," said Don Benito, with inkept[2] and unknown emotion.

Deliberately as he had come, the black obeyed.

"Excuse me, Don Benito," said Captain Delano, "but this scene surprises me; what means it, pray?"

"It means that that negro alone, of all the band, has given me peculiar cause of offense. I have put him in chains; I—"

Here he paused; his hand to his head, as if there were a swimming there, or a sudden bewilderment of memory had come over him; but meeting his servant's kindly glance seemed reassured, and proceeded:—

"I could not scourge[3] such a form. But I told him he must ask my pardon. As yet he has not. At my command, every two hours he stands before me."

"And how long has this been?"

"Some sixty days."

"And obedient in all else? And respectful?"

"Yes."

"Upon my conscience, then," exclaimed Captain Delano, impulsively, "he has a royal spirit in him, this fellow."

"He may have some right to it," bitterly returned Don Benito, "he says he was king in his own land."

"Yes," said the servant, entering a word, "those slits in Atufal's ears once held wedges of gold; but poor Babo here, in his own land, was only a poor slave; a black man's slave was Babo, who now is the white's."

Somewhat annoyed by these conversational familiarities, Captain Delano turned curiously upon the attendant, then glanced inquiringly at his master; but, as if long wonted to these little informalities, neither master nor man seemed to understand him.

---

[1]   *bootless* Unavailing.

[2]   *inkept* Suppressed.

[3]   *scourge* Whip, torture.

"What, pray, was Atufal's offense, Don Benito?" asked Captain Delano; "if it was not something very serious, take a fool's advice, and, in view of his general docility, as well as in some natural respect for his spirit, remit him his penalty."

"No, no, master never will do that," here murmured the servant to himself, "proud Atufal must first ask master's pardon. The slave there carries the padlock, but master here carries the key."

His attention thus directed, Captain Delano now noticed for the first,[1] that, suspended by a slender silken cord, from Don Benito's neck, hung a key. At once, from the servant's muttered syllables, divining the key's purpose, he smiled, and said:—"So, Don Benito—padlock and key—significant symbols, truly."

Biting his lip, Don Benito faltered.

Though the remark of Captain Delano, a man of such native simplicity as to be incapable of satire or irony, had been dropped in playful allusion to the Spaniard's singularly evidenced lordship over the black; yet the hypochondriac seemed some way to have taken it as a malicious reflection upon his confessed inability thus far to break down, at least, on a verbal summons, the entrenched will of the slave. Deploring this supposed misconception, yet despairing of correcting it, Captain Delano shifted the subject; but finding his companion more than ever withdrawn, as if still sourly digesting the lees[2] of the presumed affront above-mentioned, by-and-by Captain Delano likewise became less talkative, oppressed, against his own will, by what seemed the secret vindictiveness of the morbidly sensitive Spaniard. But the good sailor, himself of a quite contrary disposition, refrained, on his part, alike from the appearance as from the feeling of resentment, and if silent, was only so from contagion.

Presently the Spaniard, assisted by his servant somewhat discourteously crossed over[3] from his guest; a procedure which, sensibly enough, might have been allowed to pass for idle caprice of ill-humor, had not master and man, lingering round the corner of the elevated skylight, began whispering together in low voices. This was unpleasing. And more; the moody air of the Spaniard, which at times had not been without a sort of valetudinarian[4] stateliness, now seemed anything but dignified; while the menial familiarity of the servant lost its original charm of simple-hearted attachment.

In his embarrassment, the visitor turned his face to the other side of the ship. By so doing, his glance accidentally fell on a young Spanish sailor, a coil of rope in his hand, just stepped from the deck to the first round of the mizzen-rigging.[5] Perhaps the man would not have been particularly noticed, were it not that, during his ascent to one of the yards, he, with a sort of covert intentness, kept his eye fixed on Captain Delano, from whom, presently, it passed, as if by a natural sequence, to the two whisperers.

His own attention thus redirected to that quarter, Captain Delano gave a slight start. From something in Don Benito's manner just then, it seemed as if the visitor had, at least partly, been the subject of the withdrawn consultation going on—a conjecture as little agreeable to the guest as it was little flattering to the host.

The singular alternations of courtesy and ill-breeding in the Spanish captain were unaccountable, except on one of two suppositions—innocent lunacy, or wicked imposture.

But the first idea, though it might naturally have occurred to an indifferent observer, and, in some respect, had not hitherto been wholly a stranger to Captain Delano's mind, yet, now that, in an incipient way, he began to regard the stranger's conduct something in the light of an intentional affront, of course the idea of lunacy was virtually vacated.

But if not a lunatic, what then? Under the circumstances, would a gentleman, nay, any honest boor, act the part now acted by his host? The man was an impostor. Some low-born adventurer, masquerading as an oceanic grandee; yet so ignorant of the first requisites of mere gentlemanhood as to be betrayed into the present remarkable indecorum.

That strange ceremoniousness, too, at other times evinced, seemed not uncharacteristic of one playing a

1   *the first*   The *Putnam's* edition of "Benito Cereno" reads "for the first time," but the later *Piazza Tales* edition omits the word "time."

2   *lees*   Dregs.

3   *discourteously crossed over*   Rudely walked away across the poop deck without excusing themselves from the conversation.

4   *valetudinarian*   Invalid.

5   *mizzen-rigging*   Rigging on the smaller mast in the aft (rear) portion of the ship.

part above his real level. Benito Cereno—Don Benito Cereno—a sounding name. One, too, at that period, not unknown, in the surname, to super-cargoes and sea captains trading along the Spanish Main, as belonging to one of the most enterprising and extensive mercantile families in all those provinces; several members of it having titles; a sort of Castilian Rothschild,[1] with a noble brother, or cousin, in every great trading town of South America. The alleged Don Benito was in early manhood, about twenty-nine or thirty. To assume a sort of roving cadetship in the maritime affairs of such a house, what more likely scheme for a young knave of talent and spirit? But the Spaniard was a pale invalid. Never mind. For even to the degree of simulating mortal disease, the craft of some tricksters had been known to attain. To think that, under the aspect of infantile weakness, the most savage energies might be couched—those velvets of the Spaniard but the silky paw to his fangs.

From no train of thought did these fancies come; not from within, but from without; suddenly, too, and in one throng, like hoar frost; yet as soon to vanish as the mild sun of Captain Delano's good-nature regained its meridian.

Glancing over once more towards his host—whose side-face, revealed above the skylight, was now turned towards him—he was struck by the profile, whose clearness of cut was refined by the thinness, incident to ill-health, as well as ennobled about the chin by the beard. Away with suspicion. He was a true off-shoot of a true hidalgo[2] Cereno.

Relieved by these and other better thoughts, the visitor, lightly humming a tune, now began indifferently pacing the poop, so as not to betray to Don Benito that he had at all mistrusted incivility, much less duplicity; for such mistrust would yet be proved illusory, and by the event; though, for the present, the circumstance which had provoked that distrust remained unexplained. But when that little mystery should have been cleared up, Captain Delano thought he might extremely regret it, did he allow Don Benito to become aware that he had indulged in ungenerous surmises. In

short, to the Spaniard's black-letter text, it was best, for awhile, to leave open margin.[3]

Presently, his pale face twitching and overcast, the Spaniard, still supported by his attendant, moved over towards his guest, when, with even more than his usual embarrassment, and a strange sort of intriguing intonation in his husky whisper, the following conversation began:—

"Señor, may I ask how long you have lain at this isle?"

"Oh, but a day or two, Don Benito."

"And from what port are you last?"

"Canton."

"And there, Señor, you exchanged your sealskins for teas and silks, I think you said?"

"Yes. Silks, mostly."

"And the balance you took in specie,[4] perhaps?"

Captain Delano, fidgeting a little, answered—

"Yes; some silver; not a very great deal, though."

"Ah—well. May I ask how many men have you, Señor?"

Captain Delano slightly started, but answered—

"About five-and-twenty, all told."

"And at present, Señor, all on board, I suppose?"

"All on board, Don Benito," replied the Captain, now with satisfaction.

"And will be to-night, Señor?"

At this last question, following so many pertinacious[5] ones, for the soul of him Captain Delano could not but look very earnestly at the questioner, who, instead of meeting the glance, with every token of craven discomposure dropped his eyes to the deck; presenting an unworthy contrast to his servant, who, just then, was kneeling at his feet, adjusting a loose shoe-buckle; his disengaged face meantime, with humble curiosity, turned openly up into his master's downcast one.

The Spaniard, still with a guilty shuffle, repeated his question:

"And—and will be to-night, Señor?"

---

1   *Rothschild*   Major European banking family in the nineteenth century.

2   *hidalgo*   Member of the Spanish nobility.

3   *black-letter text … open margin*   A black-letter text is a heavy Gothic typeface. To leave open margin is to leave space for more text to be added to a page—i.e., Captain Delano is leaving space for Cereno to redeem his rude behavior.

4   *specie*   Coins (currency).

5   *pertinacious*   Annoyingly persistent.

"Yes, for aught I know," returned Captain Delano—"but nay," rallying himself into fearless truth, "some of them talked of going off on another fishing party about midnight."

"Your ships generally go—go more or less armed, I believe, Señor?"

"Oh, a six-pounder[1] or two, in case of emergency," was the intrepidly indifferent reply, "with a small stock of muskets, sealing-spears, and cutlasses, you know."

As he thus responded, Captain Delano again glanced at Don Benito, but the latter's eyes were averted; while abruptly and awkwardly shifting the subject, he made some peevish allusion to the calm, and then, without apology, once more, with his attendant, withdrew to the opposite bulwarks, where the whispering was resumed.

At this moment, and ere Captain Delano could cast a cool thought upon what had just passed, the young Spanish sailor, before mentioned, was seen descending from the rigging. In act of stooping over to spring inboard to the deck, his voluminous, unconfined frock, or shirt, of coarse woolen, much spotted with tar, opened out far down the chest, revealing a soiled under garment of what seemed the finest linen, edged, about the neck, with a narrow blue ribbon, sadly faded and worn. At this moment the young sailor's eye was again fixed on the whisperers, and Captain Delano thought he observed a lurking significance in it, as if silent signs, of some Freemason sort, had that instant been interchanged.

This once more impelled his own glance in the direction of Don Benito, and, as before, he could not but infer that himself formed the subject of the conference. He paused. The sound of the hatchet-polishing fell on his ears. He cast another swift side-look at the two. They had the air of conspirators. In connection with the late questionings, and the incident of the young sailor, these things now begat such return of involuntary suspicion, that the singular guilelessness of the American could not endure it. Plucking up a gay and humorous expression, he crossed over to the two rapidly, saying:—"Ha, Don Benito, your black here seems high in your trust; a sort of privy-counselor, in fact."

Upon this, the servant looked up with a good-natured grin, but the master started as from a venomous bite. It was a moment or two before the Spaniard sufficiently recovered himself to reply; which he did, at last, with cold constraint:—"Yes, Señor, I have trust in Babo."

Here Babo, changing his previous grin of mere animal humor into an intelligent smile, not ungratefully eyed his master.

Finding that the Spaniard now stood silent and reserved, as if involuntarily, or purposely giving hint that his guest's proximity was inconvenient just then, Captain Delano, unwilling to appear uncivil even to incivility itself, made some trivial remark and moved off; again and again turning over in his mind the mysterious demeanor of Don Benito Cereno.

He had descended from the poop, and, wrapped in thought, was passing near a dark hatchway, leading down into the steerage, when, perceiving motion there, he looked to see what moved. The same instant there was a sparkle in the shadowy hatchway, and he saw one of the Spanish sailors, prowling there hurriedly placing his hand in the bosom of his frock, as if hiding something. Before the man could have been certain who it was that was passing, he slunk below out of sight. But enough was seen of him to make it sure that he was the same young sailor before noticed in the rigging.

What was that which so sparkled? thought Captain Delano. It was no lamp—no match—no live coal. Could it have been a jewel? But how come sailors with jewels?—or with silk-trimmed under-shirts either? Has he been robbing the trunks of the dead cabin-passengers? But if so, he would hardly wear one of the stolen articles on board ship here. Ah, ah—if, now, that was, indeed, a secret sign I saw passing between this suspicious fellow and his captain awhile since; if I could only be certain that, in my uneasiness, my senses did not deceive me, then—

Here, passing from one suspicious thing to another, his mind revolved the strange questions put to him concerning his ship.

By a curious coincidence, as each point was recalled, the black wizards of Ashantee would strike up with their hatchets, as in ominous comment on the white stranger's thoughts. Pressed by such enigmas and portents, it would have been almost against nature, had not, even into the least distrustful heart, some ugly misgivings obtruded.

---

[1] *six-pounder* Cannon that shoots balls weighing six pounds.

Observing the ship, now helplessly fallen into a current, with enchanted sails, drifting with increased rapidity seaward; and noting that, from a lately intercepted projection of the land, the sealer was hidden, the stout mariner began to quake at thoughts which he barely durst confess to himself. Above all, he began to feel a ghostly dread of Don Benito. And yet, when he roused himself, dilated his chest, felt himself strong on his legs, and coolly considered it—what did all these phantoms amount to?

Had the Spaniard any sinister scheme, it must have reference not so much to him (Captain Delano) as to his ship (the Bachelor's Delight). Hence the present drifting away of the one ship from the other, instead of favoring any such possible scheme, was, for the time, at least, opposed to it. Clearly any suspicion, combining such contradictions, must need be delusive. Beside, was it not absurd to think of a vessel in distress—a vessel by sickness almost dismanned of her crew—a vessel whose inmates were parched for water—was it not a thousand times absurd that such a craft should, at present, be of a piratical character; or her commander, either for himself or those under him, cherish any desire but for speedy relief and refreshment? But then, might not general distress, and thirst in particular, be affected? And might not that same undiminished Spanish crew, alleged to have perished off to a remnant, be at that very moment lurking in the hold? On heart-broken pretense of entreating a cup of cold water, fiends in human form had got into lonely dwellings, nor retired until a dark deed had been done. And among the Malay pirates,[1] it was no unusual thing to lure ships after them into their treacherous harbors, or entice boarders from a declared enemy at sea, by the spectacle of thinly manned or vacant decks, beneath which prowled a hundred spears with yellow arms ready to upthrust them through the mats. Not that Captain Delano had entirely credited such things. He had heard of them—and now, as stories, they recurred. The present destination of the ship was the anchorage. There she would be near his own vessel. Upon gaining that vicinity, might not the San Dominick, like a slumbering volcano, suddenly let loose energies now hid?

He recalled the Spaniard's manner while telling his story. There was a gloomy hesitancy and subterfuge about it. It was just the manner of one making up his tale for evil purposes, as he goes. But if that story was not true, what was the truth? That the ship had unlawfully come into the Spaniard's possession? But in many of its details, especially in reference to the more calamitous parts, such as the fatalities among the seamen, the consequent prolonged beating about, the past sufferings from obstinate calms, and still continued suffering from thirst; in all these points, as well as others, Don Benito's story had corroborated not only the wailing ejaculations of the indiscriminate multitude, white and black, but likewise—what seemed impossible to be counterfeit—by the very expression and play of every human feature, which Captain Delano saw. If Don Benito's story was, throughout, an invention, then every soul on board, down to the youngest negress, was his carefully drilled recruit in the plot: an incredible inference. And yet, if there was ground for mistrusting his veracity, that inference was a legitimate one.

But those questions of the Spaniard. There, indeed, one might pause. Did they not seem put with much the same object with which the burglar or assassin, by day-time, reconnoitres the walls of a house? But, with ill purposes, to solicit such information openly of the chief person endangered, and so, in effect, setting him on his guard; how unlikely a procedure was that? Absurd, then, to suppose that those questions had been prompted by evil designs. Thus, the same conduct, which, in this instance, had raised the alarm, served to dispel it. In short, scarce any suspicion or uneasiness, however apparently reasonable at the time, which was not now, with equal apparent reason, dismissed.

At last he began to laugh at his former forebodings; and laugh at the strange ship for, in its aspect, someway siding with them, as it were; and laugh, too, at the odd-looking blacks, particularly those old scissors-grinders, the Ashantees; and those bed-ridden old knitting women, the oakum-pickers; and almost at the dark Spaniard himself, the central hobgoblin of all.

For the rest, whatever in a serious way seemed enigmatical, was now good-naturedly explained away by the thought that, for the most part, the poor invalid scarcely knew what he was about; either sulking in black vapors, or putting idle questions without sense

---

[1] *Malay pirates* Piracy in the Straight of Malacca (between the Malay Peninsula and the island of Sumatra) was particularly prevalent in the eighteenth and nineteenth centuries.

or object. Evidently for the present, the man was not fit to be intrusted with the ship. On some benevolent plea withdrawing the command from him, Captain Delano would yet have to send her to Conception, in charge of his second mate, a worthy person and good navigator—a plan not more convenient for the San Dominick than for Don Benito; for, relieved from all anxiety, keeping wholly to his cabin, the sick man, under the good nursing of his servant, would, probably, by the end of the passage, be in a measure restored to health, and with that he should also be restored to authority.

Such were the American's thoughts. They were tranquilizing. There was a difference between the idea of Don Benito's darkly pre-ordaining Captain Delano's fate, and Captain Delano's lightly arranging Don Benito's. Nevertheless, it was not without something of relief that the good seaman presently perceived his whale-boat in the distance. Its absence had been prolonged by unexpected detention at the sealer's side, as well as its returning trip lengthened by the continual recession of the goal.

The advancing speck was observed by the blacks. Their shouts attracted the attention of Don Benito, who, with a return of courtesy, approaching Captain Delano, expressed satisfaction at the coming of some supplies, slight and temporary as they must necessarily prove.

Captain Delano responded; but while doing so, his attention was drawn to something passing on the deck below: among the crowd climbing the landward bulwarks, anxiously watching the coming boat, two blacks, to all appearances accidentally incommoded by one of the sailors, violently pushed him aside, which the sailor someway resenting, they dashed him to the deck, despite the earnest cries of the oakum-pickers.

"Don Benito," said Captain Delano quickly, "do you see what is going on there? Look!"

But, seized by his cough, the Spaniard staggered, with both hands to his face, on the point of falling. Captain Delano would have supported him, but the servant was more alert, who, with one hand sustaining his master, with the other applied the cordial. Don Benito restored, the black withdrew his support, slipping aside a little, but dutifully remaining within call of a whisper. Such discretion was here evinced as quite

wiped away, in the visitor's eyes, any blemish of impropriety which might have attached to the attendant, from the indecorous conferences before mentioned; showing, too, that if the servant were to blame, it might be more the master's fault than his own, since, when left to himself, he could conduct thus well.

His glance called away from the spectacle of disorder to the more pleasing one before him, Captain Delano could not avoid again congratulating his host upon possessing such a servant, who, though perhaps a little too forward now and then, must upon the whole be invaluable to one in the invalid's situation.

"Tell me, Don Benito," he added, with a smile—"I should like to have your man here, myself—what will you take for him? Would fifty doubloons be any object?"

"Master wouldn't part with Babo for a thousand doubloons," murmured the black, overhearing the offer, and taking it in earnest, and, with the strange vanity of a faithful slave, appreciated by his master, scorning to hear so paltry a valuation put upon him by a stranger. But Don Benito, apparently hardly yet completely restored, and again interrupted by his cough, made but some broken reply.

Soon his physical distress became so great, affecting his mind, too, apparently, that, as if to screen the sad spectacle, the servant gently conducted his master below.

Left to himself, the American, to while away the time till his boat should arrive, would have pleasantly accosted some one of the few Spanish seamen he saw; but recalling something that Don Benito had said touching their ill conduct, he refrained; as a shipmaster indisposed to countenance cowardice or unfaithfulness in seamen.

While, with these thoughts, standing with eye directed forward towards that handful of sailors, suddenly he thought that one or two of them returned the glance and with a sort of meaning. He rubbed his eyes, and looked again; but again seemed to see the same thing. Under a new form, but more obscure than any previous one, the old suspicions recurred, but, in the absence of Don Benito, with less of panic than before. Despite the bad account given of the sailors, Captain Delano resolved forthwith to accost one of them. Descending the poop, he made his way through the blacks, his movement drawing a queer cry from the oakum-pickers, prompted by whom, the negroes, twitching each other aside, divided before him; but, as if curious to see what was the object of this deliberate visit to their Ghetto, closing in behind, in tolerable order, followed the white stranger up. His progress thus proclaimed as by mounted kings-at-arms, and escorted as by a Caffre[1] guard of honor, Captain Delano, assuming a good-humored, off-handed air, continued to advance; now and then saying a blithe word to the negroes, and his eye curiously surveying the white faces, here and there sparsely mixed in with the blacks, like stray white pawns venturously involved in the ranks of the chess-men opposed.

While thinking which of them to select for his purpose, he chanced to observe a sailor seated on the deck engaged in tarring the strap of a large block, a circle of blacks squatted round him inquisitively eying the process.

The mean employment of the man was in contrast with something superior in his figure. His hand, black with continually thrusting it into the tar-pot held for him by a negro, seemed not naturally allied to his face, a face which would have been a very fine one but for its haggardness. Whether this haggardness had aught to do with criminality, could not be determined; since, as intense heat and cold, though unlike, produce like sensations, so innocence and guilt, when, through casual association with mental pain, stamping any visible impress, use one seal—a hacked one.

Not again that this reflection occurred to Captain Delano at the time, charitable man as he was. Rather another idea. Because observing so singular a haggardness combined with a dark eye, averted as in trouble and shame, and then again recalling Don Benito's confessed ill opinion of his crew, insensibly he was operated upon by certain general notions which, while disconnecting pain and abashment from virtue, invariably link them with vice.

If, indeed, there be any wickedness on board this ship, thought Captain Delano, be sure that man there has fouled his hand in it, even as now he fouls it in the pitch. I don't like to accost him. I will speak to this other, this old Jack here on the windlass.[2]

He advanced to an old Barcelona tar,[3] in ragged red breeches and dirty night-cap, cheeks trenched and bronzed, whiskers dense as thorn hedges. Seated between two sleepy-looking Africans, this mariner, like his younger shipmate, was employed upon some rigging—splicing a cable—the sleepy-looking blacks performing the inferior function of holding the outer parts of the ropes for him.

Upon Captain Delano's approach, the man at once hung his head below its previous level; the one necessary for business. It appeared as if he desired to be thought absorbed, with more than common fidelity, in his task. Being addressed, he glanced up, but with what seemed a furtive, diffident air, which sat strangely enough on his weather-beaten visage, much as if a grizzly bear, instead of growling and biting, should simper and cast sheep's eyes. He was asked several questions concerning the voyage—questions purposely referring to several particulars in Don Benito's narrative, not previously corroborated by those impulsive cries greeting the visitor on first coming on board. The questions were briefly answered, confirming all that remained to be confirmed of the story. The negroes about the windlass joined in with the old sailor; but, as they became talkative, he by degrees became mute, and at length quite glum, seemed morosely unwilling to answer more questions, and yet, all the while, this ursine[4] air was somehow mixed with his sheepish one.

Despairing of getting into unembarrassed talk with such a centaur,[5] Captain Delano, after glancing round for a more promising countenance, but seeing none, spoke pleasantly to the blacks to make way for him; and so, amid various grins and grimaces, returned to the poop, feeling a little strange at first, he could hardly tell why, but upon the whole with regained confidence in Benito Cereno.

---

1   *Caffre*   Variant on caffer or kaffir, a racial slur usually applied to a black person from southern Africa. Since the mid-twentieth century, this term has been considered highly offensive (and in South Africa its use is legally actionable).

2   *windlass*   An instrument—a roller on supports—used on a ship to wind rope or chain (for example to haul an anchor up and down).

3   *tar*   Sailor.

4   *ursine*   Bear-like.

5   *centaur*   Hybrid creature; in Greek mythology, centaurs were half-human, half-horse.

How plainly, thought he, did that old whiskerando yonder betray a consciousness of ill desert.[1] No doubt, when he saw me coming, he dreaded lest I, apprised by his Captain of the crew's general misbehavior, came with sharp words for him, and so down with his head. And yet—and yet, now that I think of it, that very old fellow, if I err not, was one of those who seemed so earnestly eying me here awhile since. Ah, these currents spin one's head round almost as much as they do the ship. Ha, there now's a pleasant sort of sunny sight; quite sociable, too.

His attention had been drawn to a slumbering negress, partly disclosed through the lacework of some rigging, lying, with youthful limbs carelessly disposed, under the lee of the bulwarks, like a doe in the shade of a woodland rock. Sprawling at her lapped breasts, was her wide-awake fawn, stark naked, its black little body half lifted from the deck, crosswise with its dam's; its hands, like two paws, clambering upon her; its mouth and nose ineffectually rooting to get at the mark; and meantime giving a vexatious half-grunt, blending with the composed snore of the negress.

The uncommon vigor of the child at length roused the mother. She started up, at a distance facing Captain Delano. But as if not at all concerned at the attitude in which she had been caught, delightedly she caught the child up, with maternal transports, covering it with kisses.

There's naked nature, now; pure tenderness and love, thought Captain Delano, well pleased.

This incident prompted him to remark the other negresses more particularly than before. He was gratified with their manners: like most uncivilized women, they seemed at once tender of heart and tough of constitution; equally ready to die for their infants or fight for them. Unsophisticated as leopardesses; loving as doves. Ah! thought Captain Delano, these, perhaps, are some of the very women whom Ledyard[2] saw in Africa, and gave such a noble account of.

These natural sights somehow insensibly deepened his confidence and ease. At last he looked to see how his boat was getting on; but it was still pretty remote. He turned to see if Don Benito had returned; but he had not.

To change the scene, as well as to please himself with a leisurely observation of the coming boat, stepping over into the mizzen-chains,[3] he clambered his way into the starboard quarter-gallery—one of those abandoned Venetian-looking water-balconies[4] previously mentioned—retreats cut off from the deck. As his foot pressed the half-damp, half-dry sea-mosses matting the place, and a chance phantom cats-paw[5]—an islet of breeze, unheralded, unfollowed—as this ghostly cats-paw came fanning his cheek; as his glance fell upon the row of small, round dead-lights—all closed like coppered eyes of the coffined—and the state-cabin door, once connecting with the gallery, even as the dead-lights had once looked out upon it, but now calked fast like a sarcophagus[6] lid; and to a purple-black tarred-over, panel, threshold, and post; and he bethought him of the time, when that state-cabin and this state-balcony had heard the voices of the Spanish king's officers, and the forms of the Lima viceroy's daughters had perhaps leaned where he stood—as these and other images flitted through his mind, as the cats-paw through the calm, gradually he felt rising a dreamy inquietude, like that of one who alone on the prairie feels unrest from the repose of the noon.

He leaned against the carved balustrade, again looking off toward his boat; but found his eye falling upon the ribbon grass, trailing along the ship's water-line, straight as a border of green box;[7] and parterres of sea-weed, broad ovals and crescents, floating nigh and far, with what seemed long formal alleys between, crossing the terraces of swells, and sweeping round as if leading to the grottoes below. And overhanging all was the balustrade by his arm, which, partly stained with pitch and partly embossed with moss, seemed the charred

---

1   *desert*   Merit.

2   *Ledyard*   American explorer John Ledyard (1751–89). In the *Putnam*'s publication of *Benito Cereno*, Melville mentions the Scottish explorer Mungo Park (1771–1806) here instead, who led more extensive explorations into West Africa.

3   *mizzen-chains*   Set of chains used to work the mizzen-sail (attached to the mizzen-mast, which is located to the rear of the main mast).

4   *water-balconies*   Balconies in Venice overlook canals, as these do the sea. Balconies in Venice were also often used as settings in popular nineteenth-century Gothic tales.

5   *cats-paw*   Wind that slightly and momentarily ruffles the sea.

6   *sarcophagus*   Ancient stone coffin.

7   *box*   I.e., box-hedges.

ruin of some summer-house in a grand garden long running to waste.

Trying to break one charm, he was but becharmed anew. Though upon the wide sea, he seemed in some far inland country; prisoner in some deserted château, left to stare at empty grounds, and peer out at vague roads, where never wagon or wayfarer passed.

But these enchantments were a little disenchanted as his eye fell on the corroded main-chains. Of an ancient style, massy and rusty in link, shackle and bolt, they seemed even more fit for the ship's present business than the one for which she had been built.

Presently he thought something moved nigh the chains. He rubbed his eyes, and looked hard. Groves of rigging were about the chains; and there, peering from behind a great stay, like an Indian from behind a hemlock, a Spanish sailor, a marlingspike[1] in his hand, was seen, who made what seemed an imperfect gesture towards the balcony, but immediately as if alarmed by some advancing step along the deck within, vanished into the recesses of the hempen forest, like a poacher.

What meant this? Something the man had sought to communicate, unbeknown to any one, even to his captain. Did the secret involve aught unfavorable to his captain? Were those previous misgivings of Captain Delano's about to be verified? Or, in his haunted mood at the moment, had some random, unintentional motion of the man, while busy with the stay, as if repairing it, been mistaken for a significant beckoning?

Not unbewildered, again he gazed off for his boat. But it was temporarily hidden by a rocky spur of the isle. As with some eagerness he bent forward, watching for the first shooting view of its beak, the balustrade gave way before him like charcoal. Had he not clutched an outreaching rope he would have fallen into the sea. The crash, though feeble, and the fall, though hollow, of the rotten fragments, must have been overheard. He glanced up. With sober curiosity peering down upon him was one of the old oakum-pickers, slipped from his perch to an outside boom; while below the old negro, and, invisible to him, reconnoitering from a port-hole like a fox from the mouth of its den, crouched the Spanish sailor again. From something suddenly suggested by the man's air, the mad idea now darted into Captain Delano's mind, that Don Benito's plea of indisposition, in withdrawing below, was but a pretense: that he was engaged there maturing his plot, of which the sailor, by some means gaining an inkling, had a mind to warn the stranger against; incited, it may be, by gratitude for a kind word on first boarding the ship. Was it from foreseeing some possible interference like this, that Don Benito had, beforehand, given such a bad character of his sailors, while praising the negroes; though, indeed, the former seemed as docile as the latter the contrary? The whites, too, by nature, were the shrewder race. A man with some evil design, would he not be likely to speak well of that stupidity which was blind to his depravity, and malign that intelligence from which it might not be hidden? Not unlikely, perhaps. But if the whites had dark secrets concerning Don Benito, could then Don Benito be any way in complicity with the blacks? But they were too stupid. Besides, who ever heard of a white so far a renegade as to apostatize from his very species almost, by leaguing in against it with negroes? These difficulties recalled former ones. Lost in their mazes, Captain Delano, who had now regained the deck, was uneasily advancing along it, when he observed a new face; an aged sailor seated cross-legged near the main hatchway. His skin was shrunk up with wrinkles like a pelican's empty pouch; his hair frosted; his countenance grave and composed. His hands were full of ropes, which he was working into a large knot. Some blacks were about him obligingly dipping the strands for him, here and there, as the exigencies of the operation demanded.

Captain Delano crossed over to him, and stood in silence surveying the knot; his mind, by a not uncongenial transition, passing from its own entanglements to those of the hemp. For intricacy, such a knot he had never seen in an American ship, nor indeed any other. The old man looked like an Egyptian priest, making Gordian knots for the temple of Ammon.[2] The knot seemed a combination of double-bowline-knot, treble-crown-knot, back-handed-well-knot, knot-in-and-out-knot, and jamming-knot.

At last, puzzled to comprehend the meaning of such a knot, Captain Delano addressed the knotter:—

"What are you knotting there, my man?"

---

[1]   *marlingspike*   Tool used in when splicing rope (to separate the strands).

[2]   *Gordian knots*   Knots too complex to be untangled, but they can be cut;   *Ammon*   Amun-Ra, chief Egyptian deity.

"The knot," was the brief reply, without looking up.

"So it seems; but what is it for?"

"For some one else to undo," muttered back the old man, plying his fingers harder than ever, the knot being now nearly completed.

While Captain Delano stood watching him, suddenly the old man threw the knot towards him, saying in broken English—the first heard in the ship—something to this effect: "Undo it, cut it, quick." It was said lowly, but with such condensation of rapidity, that the long, slow words in Spanish, which had preceded and followed, almost operated as covers to the brief English between.

For a moment, knot in hand, and knot in head, Captain Delano stood mute; while, without further heeding him, the old man was now intent upon other ropes. Presently there was a slight stir behind Captain Delano. Turning, he saw the chained negro, Atufal, standing quietly there. The next moment the old sailor rose, muttering, and, followed by his subordinate negroes, removed to the forward part of the ship, where in the crowd he disappeared.

An elderly negro, in a clout[1] like an infant's, and with a pepper and salt head, and a kind of attorney air, now approached Captain Delano. In tolerable Spanish, and with a good-natured, knowing wink, he informed him that the old knotter was simple-witted, but harmless; often playing his odd tricks. The negro concluded by begging the knot, for of course the stranger would not care to be troubled with it. Unconsciously, it was handed to him. With a sort of congé,[2] the negro received it, and, turning his back, ferreted into it like a detective custom-house officer after smuggled laces. Soon, with some African word, equivalent to pshaw, he tossed the knot overboard.

All this is very queer now, thought Captain Delano, with a qualmish sort of emotion; but, as one feeling incipient sea-sickness, he strove, by ignoring the symptoms, to get rid of the malady. Once more he looked off for his boat. To his delight, it was now again in view, leaving the rocky spur astern.

The sensation here experienced, after at first relieving his uneasiness, with unforeseen efficacy soon began to remove it. The less distant sight of that well-known boat—showing it, not as before, half blended with the haze, but with outline defined, so that its individuality, like a man's, was manifest; that boat, Rover by name, which, though now in strange seas, had often pressed the beach of Captain Delano's home, and, brought to its threshold for repairs, had familiarly lain there, as a Newfoundland dog; the sight of that household boat evoked a thousand trustful associations, which, contrasted with previous suspicions, filled him not only with lightsome confidence, but somehow with half humorous self-reproaches at his former lack of it.

"What, I, Amasa Delano—Jack of the Beach, as they called me when a lad—I, Amasa; the same that, duck-satchel in hand, used to paddle along the water-side to the school-house made from the old hulk[3]—I, little Jack of the Beach, that used to go berrying with cousin Nat and the rest; I to be murdered here at the ends of the earth, on board a haunted pirate-ship by a horrible Spaniard? Too nonsensical to think of! Who would murder Amasa Delano? His conscience is clean. There is some one above. Fie, fie, Jack of the Beach! you are a child indeed; a child of the second childhood, old boy; you are beginning to dote and drule,[4] I'm afraid."

Light of heart and foot, he stepped aft, and there was met by Don Benito's servant, who, with a pleasing expression, responsive to his own present feelings, informed him that his master had recovered from the effects of his coughing fit, and had just ordered him to go present his compliments to his good guest, Don Amasa, and say that he (Don Benito) would soon have the happiness to rejoin him.

There now, do you mark that? again thought Captain Delano, walking the poop. What a donkey I was. This kind gentleman who here sends me his kind compliments, he, but ten minutes ago, dark-lantern in hand, was dodging round some old grind-stone in the hold, sharpening a hatchet for me, I thought. Well, well; these long calms have a morbid effect on the mind, I've often heard, though I never believed it before. Ha! Glancing towards the boat; there's Rover; good dog; a white bone in her mouth. A pretty big bone though,

---

1   *clout*   Scrap of clothing.

2   *congé*   Ceremonious departure.

3   *duck-satchel*   Bag made of linen canvas ("duck canvas"), a thick, heavy cotton. Sailors often had a bag made of this material to move personal items from ship to shore;   *hulk*   Dismantled ship that is still afloat but put to other uses (in this case as a school-house).

4   *drule*   I.e., drool.

seems to me.—What? Yes, she has fallen afoul of the bubbling tide-rip there. It sets her the other way, too, for the time. Patience.

It was now about noon, though, from the grayness of everything, it seemed to be getting towards dusk.

The calm was confirmed. In the far distance, away from the influence of land, the leaden ocean seemed laid out and leaded up, its course finished, soul gone, defunct. But the current from landward, where the ship was, increased; silently sweeping her further and further towards the tranced waters beyond.

Still, from his knowledge of those latitudes, cherishing hopes of a breeze, and a fair and fresh one, at any moment, Captain Delano, despite present prospects, buoyantly counted upon bringing the San Dominick safely to anchor ere night. The distance swept over was nothing; since, with a good wind, ten minutes' sailing would retrace more than sixty minutes, drifting. Meantime, one moment turning to mark "Rover" fighting the tide-rip, and the next to see Don Benito approaching, he continued walking the poop.

Gradually he felt a vexation arising from the delay of his boat; this soon merged into uneasiness; and at last—his eye falling continually, as from a stage-box into the pit, upon the strange crowd before and below him, and, by-and-by, recognizing there the face—now composed to indifference—of the Spanish sailor who had seemed to beckon from the main-chains—something of his old trepidations returned.

Ah, thought he—gravely enough—this is like the ague:[1] because it went off, it follows not that it won't come back.

Though ashamed of the relapse, he could not altogether subdue it; and so, exerting his good-nature to the utmost, insensibly he came to a compromise.

Yes, this is a strange craft; a strange history, too, and strange folks on board. But—nothing more.

By way of keeping his mind out of mischief till the boat should arrive, he tried to occupy it with turning over and over, in a purely speculative sort of way, some lesser peculiarities of the captain and crew. Among others, four curious points recurred:

First, the affair of the Spanish lad assailed with a knife by the slave boy; an act winked at by Don Benito. Second, the tyranny in Don Benito's treatment of Atufal, the black; as if a child should lead a bull of the Nile[2] by the ring in his nose. Third, the trampling of the sailor by the two negroes; a piece of insolence passed over without so much as a reprimand. Fourth, the cringing submission to their master, of all the ship's underlings, mostly blacks; as if by the least inadvertence they feared to draw down his despotic displeasure.

Coupling these points, they seemed somewhat contradictory. But what then, thought Captain Delano, glancing towards his now nearing boat—what then? Why, Don Benito is a very capricious commander. But he is not the first of the sort I have seen; though it's true he rather exceeds any other. But as a nation—continued he in his reveries—these Spaniards are all an odd set; the very word Spaniard has a curious, conspirator, Guy-Fawkish[3] twang to it. And yet, I dare say, Spaniards in the main are as good folks as any in Duxbury, Massachusetts. Ah good! At last "Rover" has come.

As, with its welcome freight, the boat touched the side, the oakum-pickers, with venerable gestures, sought to restrain the blacks, who, at the sight of three gurried[4] water-casks in its bottom, and a pile of wilted pumpkins in its bow, hung over the bulwarks in disorderly raptures.

Don Benito, with his servant, now appeared; his coming, perhaps, hastened by hearing the noise. Of him Captain Delano sought permission to serve out the water, so that all might share alike, and none injure themselves by unfair excess. But sensible, and, on Don Benito's account, kind as this offer was, it was received with what seemed impatience; as if aware that he lacked energy as a commander, Don Benito, with the true jealousy of weakness, resented as an affront any interference. So, at least, Captain Delano inferred.

In another moment the casks were being hoisted in, when some of the eager negroes accidentally jostled Captain Delano, where he stood by the gangway; so that, unmindful of Don Benito, yielding to the

---

[1]   *ague* Fever.

[2]   *bull of the Nile* In Ancient Egypt, sacred bulls were worshipped as manifestations of the god Apis.

[3]   *Guy-Fawkish* Guy Fawkes (1570–1606) was a leader of the Gunpowder Plot of 1605, which aimed to blow up Parliament and restore Catholicism in England. Fawkes also fought in the Spanish army during the Eighty Years' War against the Protestant Dutch.

[4]   *gurried* Slimed with fish waste.

impulse of the moment, with good-natured authority he bade the blacks stand back; to enforce his words making use of a half-mirthful, half-menacing gesture. Instantly the blacks paused, just where they were, each negro and negress suspended in his or her posture, exactly as the word had found them—for a few seconds continuing so—while, as between the responsive posts of a telegraph, an unknown syllable ran from man to man among the perched oakum-pickers. While the visitor's attention was fixed by this scene, suddenly the hatchet-polishers half rose, and a rapid cry came from Don Benito.

Thinking that at the signal of the Spaniard he was about to be massacred, Captain Delano would have sprung for his boat, but paused, as the oakum-pickers, dropping down into the crowd with earnest exclamations, forced every white and every negro back, at the same moment, with gestures friendly and familiar, almost jocose, bidding him, in substance, not be a fool. Simultaneously the hatchet-polishers resumed their seats, quietly as so many tailors, and at once, as if nothing had happened, the work of hoisting in the casks was resumed, whites and blacks singing at the tackle.

Captain Delano glanced towards Don Benito. As he saw his meagre form in the act of recovering itself from reclining in the servant's arms, into which the agitated invalid had fallen, he could not but marvel at the panic by which himself had been surprised, on the darting supposition that such a commander, who, upon a legitimate occasion, so trivial, too, as it now appeared, could lose all self-command, was, with energetic iniquity, going to bring about his murder.

The casks being on deck, Captain Delano was handed a number of jars and cups by one of the steward's aids, who, in the name of his captain, entreated him to do as he had proposed—dole out the water. He complied, with republican impartiality as to this republican element, which always seeks one level, serving the oldest white no better than the youngest black; excepting, indeed, poor Don Benito, whose condition, if not rank, demanded an extra allowance. To him, in the first place, Captain Delano presented a fair pitcher of the fluid; but, thirsting as he was for it, the Spaniard quaffed not a drop until after several grave bows and salutes. A reciprocation of courtesies which the sight-loving Africans hailed with clapping of hands.

Two of the less wilted pumpkins being reserved for the cabin table, the residue were minced up on the spot for the general regalement. But the soft bread, sugar, and bottled cider, Captain Delano would have given the whites alone, and in chief Don Benito; but the latter objected; which disinterestedness not a little pleased the American; and so mouthfuls all around were given alike to whites and blacks; excepting one bottle of cider, which Babo insisted upon setting aside for his master.

Here it may be observed that as, on the first visit of the boat, the American had not permitted his men to board the ship, neither did he now; being unwilling to add to the confusion of the decks.

Not uninfluenced by the peculiar good-humor at present prevailing, and for the time oblivious of any but benevolent thoughts, Captain Delano, who, from recent indications, counted upon a breeze within an hour or two at furthest, dispatched the boat back to the sealer, with orders for all the hands that could be spared immediately to set about rafting casks to the watering-place and filling them. Likewise he bade word be carried to his chief officer, that if, against present expectation, the ship was not brought to anchor by sunset, he need be under no concern; for as there was to be a full moon that night, he (Captain Delano) would remain on board ready to play the pilot, come the wind soon or late.

As the two Captains stood together, observing the departing boat—the servant, as it happened, having just spied a spot on his master's velvet sleeve, and silently engaged rubbing it out—the American expressed his regrets that the San Dominick had no boats; none, at least, but the unseaworthy old hulk of the long-boat, which, warped as a camel's skeleton in the desert, and almost as bleached, lay pot-wise inverted amidships, one side a little tipped, furnishing a subterraneous sort of den for family groups of the blacks, mostly women and small children; who, squatting on old mats below, or perched above in the dark dome, on the elevated seats, were descried, some distance within, like a social circle of bats, sheltering in some friendly cave; at intervals, ebon[1] flights of naked boys and girls, three or four years old, darting in and out of the den's mouth.

---

1   *ebon*   Black (like ebony).

"Had you three or four boats now, Don Benito," said Captain Delano, "I think that, by tugging at the oars, your negroes here might help along matters some. Did you sail from port without boats, Don Benito?"

"They were stove in the gales, Señor."

"That was bad. Many men, too, you lost then. Boats and men. Those must have been hard gales, Don Benito."

"Past all speech," cringed the Spaniard.

"Tell me, Don Benito," continued his companion with increased interest, "tell me, were these gales immediately off the pitch of Cape Horn?"

"Cape Horn?—who spoke of Cape Horn?"

"Yourself did, when giving me an account of your voyage," answered Captain Delano, with almost equal astonishment at this eating of his own words, even as he ever seemed eating his own heart, on the part of the Spaniard. "You yourself, Don Benito, spoke of Cape Horn," he emphatically repeated.

The Spaniard turned, in a sort of stooping posture, pausing an instant, as one about to make a plunging exchange of elements, as from air to water.

At this moment a messenger-boy, a white, hurried by, in the regular performance of his function carrying the last expired half hour forward to the forecastle, from the cabin time-piece, to have it struck at the ship's large bell.

"Master," said the servant, discontinuing his work on the coat sleeve, and addressing the rapt Spaniard with a sort of timid apprehensiveness, as one charged with a duty, the discharge of which, it was foreseen, would prove irksome to the very person who had imposed it, and for whose benefit it was intended, "master told me never mind where he was, or how engaged, always to remind him to a minute, when shaving-time comes. Miguel has gone to strike the half-hour afternoon. It is *now*, master. Will master go into the cuddy?"[1]

"Ah—yes," answered the Spaniard, starting, as from dreams into realities; then turning upon Captain Delano, he said that ere long he would resume the conversation.

"Then if master means to talk more to Don Amasa," said the servant, "why not let Don Amasa sit by master in the cuddy, and master can talk, and Don Amasa can listen, while Babo here lathers and strops."[2]

"Yes," said Captain Delano, not unpleased with this sociable plan, "yes, Don Benito, unless you had rather not, I will go with you."

"Be it so, Señor."

As the three passed aft, the American could not but think it another strange instance of his host's capriciousness, this being shaved with such uncommon punctuality in the middle of the day. But he deemed it more than likely that the servant's anxious fidelity had something to do with the matter; inasmuch as the timely interruption served to rally his master from the mood which had evidently been coming upon him.

The place called the cuddy was a light deck-cabin formed by the poop, a sort of attic to the large cabin below. Part of it had formerly been the quarters of the officers; but since their death all the partitioning had been thrown down, and the whole interior converted into one spacious and airy marine hall; for absence of fine furniture and picturesque disarray of odd appurtenances, somewhat answering to the wide, cluttered hall of some eccentric bachelor-squire in the country, who hangs his shooting-jacket and tobacco-pouch on deer antlers, and keeps his fishing-rod, tongs, and walking-stick in the same corner.

The similitude was heightened, if not originally suggested, by glimpses of the surrounding sea; since, in one aspect, the country and the ocean seem cousins-german.[3]

The floor of the cuddy was matted. Overhead, four or five old muskets were stuck into horizontal holes along the beams. On one side was a claw-footed old table lashed to the deck; a thumbed missal[4] on it, and over it a small, meagre crucifix attached to the bulkhead. Under the table lay a dented cutlass or two, with a hacked harpoon, among some melancholy old rigging, like a heap of poor friars' girdles.[5] There were also two

---

[1] *cuddy* Cabin near the stern, often used to serve the officers' meals. It can also refer to the captain's cabin.

[2] *strops* Sharpens the razor for shaving.

[3] *cousins-german* First cousins.

[4] *missal* Catholic book of devotional prayers, often richly decorated.

[5] *girdles* Belts. Franciscan mendicant friars tied their habits with rope.

long, sharp-ribbed settees of Malacca cane,[1] black with age, and uncomfortable to look at as inquisitors' racks, with a large, misshapen arm-chair, which, furnished with a rude barber's crotch[2] at the back, working with a screw, seemed some grotesque engine of torment. A flag locker was in one corner, open, exposing various colored bunting,[3] some rolled up, others half unrolled, still others tumbled. Opposite was a cumbrous wash-stand, of black mahogany, all of one block, with a pedestal, like a font, and over it a railed shelf, containing combs, brushes, and other implements of the toilet.[4] A torn hammock of stained grass swung near; the sheets tossed, and the pillow wrinkled up like a brow, as if who ever slept here slept but illy, with alternate visitations of sad thoughts and bad dreams.

The further extremity of the cuddy, overhanging the ship's stern, was pierced with three openings, windows or port-holes, according as men or cannon might peer, socially or unsocially, out of them. At present neither men nor cannon were seen, though huge ring-bolts and other rusty iron fixtures of the wood work hinted of twenty-four-pounders.[5]

Glancing towards the hammock as he entered, Captain Delano said, "You sleep here, Don Benito?"

"Yes, Señor, since we got into mild weather."

"This seems a sort of dormitory, sitting-room, sail-loft, chapel, armory, and private closet all together, Don Benito," added Captain Delano, looking round.

"Yes, Señor; events have not been favorable to much order in my arrangements."

Here the servant, napkin on arm, made a motion as if waiting his master's good pleasure. Don Benito signified his readiness, when, seating him in the Malacca arm-chair, and for the guest's convenience drawing opposite one of the settees, the servant commenced operations by throwing back his master's collar and loosening his cravat.

There is something in the negro which, in a peculiar way, fits him for avocations about one's person. Most negroes are natural valets and hair-dressers; taking to the comb and brush congenially as to the castinets,[6] and flourishing them apparently with almost equal satisfaction. There is, too, a smooth tact about them in this employment, with a marvelous, noiseless, gliding briskness, not ungraceful in its way, singularly pleasing to behold, and still more so to be the manipulated subject of. And above all is the great gift of good-humor. Not the mere grin or laugh is here meant. Those were unsuitable. But a certain easy cheerfulness, harmonious in every glance and gesture; as though God had set the whole negro to some pleasant tune.

When to this is added the docility arising from the unaspiring contentment of a limited mind and that susceptibility of blind attachment sometimes inhering in indisputable inferiors, one readily perceives why those hypochondriacs, Johnson and Byron[7]—it may be, something like the hypochondriac Benito Cereno—took to their hearts, almost to the exclusion of the entire white race, their serving men, the negroes, Barber and Fletcher.[8] But if there be that in the negro which exempts him from the inflicted sourness of the morbid or cynical mind, how, in his most prepossessing aspects, must he appear to a benevolent one? When at ease with respect to exterior things, Captain Delano's nature was not only benign, but familiarly and humorously so. At home, he had often taken rare satisfaction in sitting in his door, watching some free man of color at his work or play. If on a voyage he chanced to have a black sailor, invariably he was on chatty and half-gamesome terms with him. In fact, like most men of a good, blithe heart, Captain Delano took to negroes, not philanthropically, but genially, just as other men to Newfoundland dogs.

1   *settees of Malacca cane*   Sofas made with interwoven pieces of Malacca cane, a type of rattan palm from Sumatra.

2   *barber's crotch*   Forked peg on which the barber could hang implements.

3   *flag locker*   Locker on a ship used for storing various flags; *bunting* Flags.

4   *toilet*   Process of grooming and dressing.

5   *twenty-four-pounders*   I.e., cannons that fire twenty-four-pound balls of shot.

6   *castinets*   Pair of instruments made of concave shells that are attached to the thumbs and hit by the middle fingers to produce a rattling sound; they are traditionally used in Spanish dances.

7   *Johnson*   Samuel Johnson (1709–84), British intellectual of the eighteenth century; *Byron* George Gordon, Lord Byron (1788–1824), Romantic poet.

8   *Barber*   Jamaican-born Francis Barber (c. 1742/43–1801) was Samuel Johnson's servant and literary assistant for over 30 years; *Fletcher* William Fletcher (c. 1775–1839) was Byron's valet for nearly two decades; contrary to what Melville suggests here, he was a white Englishman.

Hitherto, the circumstances in which he found the San Dominick had repressed the tendency. But in the cuddy, relieved from his former uneasiness, and, for various reasons, more sociably inclined than at any previous period of the day, and seeing the colored servant, napkin on arm, so debonair about his master, in a business so familiar as that of shaving, too, all his old weakness for negroes returned.

Among other things, he was amused with an odd instance of the African love of bright colors and fine shows, in the black's informally taking from the flag-locker a great piece of bunting of all hues, and lavishly tucking it under his master's chin for an apron.

The mode of shaving among the Spaniards is a little different from what it is with other nations. They have a basin, specifically called a barber's basin, which on one side is scooped out, so as accurately to receive the chin, against which it is closely held in lathering; which is done, not with a brush, but with soap dipped in the water of the basin and rubbed on the face.

In the present instance salt-water was used for lack of better; and the parts lathered were only the upper lip, and low down under the throat, all the rest being cultivated beard.

The preliminaries being somewhat novel to Captain Delano, he sat curiously eying them, so that no conversation took place, nor, for the present, did Don Benito appear disposed to renew any.

Setting down his basin, the negro searched among the razors, as for the sharpest, and having found it, gave it an additional edge by expertly strapping[1] it on the firm, smooth, oily skin of his open palm; he then made a gesture as if to begin, but midway stood suspended for an instant, one hand elevating the razor, the other professionally dabbling among the bubbling suds on the Spaniard's lank neck. Not unaffected by the close sight of the gleaming steel, Don Benito nervously shuddered; his usual ghastliness[2] was heightened by the lather, which lather, again, was intensified in its hue by the contrasting sootiness of the negro's body. Altogether the scene was somewhat peculiar, at least to Captain Delano, nor, as he saw the two thus postured, could he resist the vagary, that in the black he saw a headsman,[3] and in the white a man at the block. But this was one of those antic conceits,[4] appearing and vanishing in a breath, from which, perhaps, the best regulated mind is not always free.

Meantime the agitation of the Spaniard had a little loosened the bunting from around him, so that one broad fold swept curtain-like over the chair-arm to the floor, revealing, amid a profusion of armorial bars and ground-colors—black, blue, and yellow—a closed castle in a blood red field diagonal with a lion rampant in a white.[5]

"The castle and the lion," exclaimed Captain Delano—"why, Don Benito, this is the flag of Spain you use here. It's well it's only I, and not the King, that sees this," he added, with a smile, "but"—turning towards the black—"it's all one, I suppose, so the colors be gay"; which playful remark did not fail somewhat to tickle the negro.

"Now, master," he said, readjusting the flag, and pressing the head gently further back into the crotch of the chair; "now, master," and the steel glanced nigh the throat.

Again Don Benito faintly shuddered.

"You must not shake so, master. See, Don Amasa, master always shakes when I shave him. And yet master knows I never yet have drawn blood, though it's true, if master will shake so, I may some of these times. Now master," he continued. "And now, Don Amasa, please go on with your talk about the gale, and all that; master can hear, and, between times, master can answer."

"Ah yes, these gales," said Captain Delano; "but the more I think of your voyage, Don Benito, the more I wonder, not at the gales, terrible as they must have been, but at the disastrous interval following them. For here, by your account, have you been these two months and more getting from Cape Horn to St. Maria, a distance which I myself, with a good wind, have sailed in a few days. True, you had calms, and long ones, but to be becalmed for two months, that is, at least, unusual.

---

1   *strapping* I.e., "stropping," sharpening a razor on a piece of leather (in this case on Babo's hand).

2   *ghastliness* Paleness.

3   *vagary* Momentary play of the imagination; *headsman* Executioner (one that kills by beheading).

4   *conceits* Imaginings, fancies.

5   *armorial bars* In heraldry, lines drawn horizontally across a shield (or in this case flag); *ground-colors* Background colors; *closed castle … white* Describes the heraldic symbols on the flag of Castile and León.

Why, Don Benito, had almost any other gentleman told me such a story, I should have been half disposed to a little incredulity."

Here an involuntary expression came over the Spaniard, similar to that just before on the deck, and whether it was the start he gave, or a sudden gawky roll of the hull in the calm, or a momentary unsteadiness of the servant's hand, however it was, just then the razor drew blood, spots of which stained the creamy lather under the throat: immediately the black barber drew back his steel, and, remaining in his professional attitude, back to Captain Delano, and face to Don Benito, held up the trickling razor, saying, with a sort of half humorous sorrow, "See, master—you shook so—here's Babo's first blood."

No sword drawn before James the First of England,[1] no assassination in that timid King's presence, could have produced a more terrified aspect than was now presented by Don Benito.

Poor fellow, thought Captain Delano, so nervous he can't even bear the sight of barber's blood; and this unstrung, sick man, is it credible that I should have imagined he meant to spill all my blood, who can't endure the sight of one little drop of his own? Surely, Amasa Delano, you have been beside yourself this day. Tell it not when you get home, sappy Amasa. Well, well, he looks like a murderer, doesn't he? More like as if himself were to be done for. Well, well, this day's experience shall be a good lesson.

Meantime, while these things were running through the honest seaman's mind, the servant had taken the napkin from his arm, and to Don Benito had said—"But answer Don Amasa, please, master, while I wipe this ugly stuff off the razor, and strop it again."

As he said the words, his face was turned half round, so as to be alike visible to the Spaniard and the American, and seemed, by its expression, to hint, that he was desirous, by getting his master to go on with the conversation, considerately to withdraw his attention from the recent annoying accident. As if glad to snatch the offered relief, Don Benito resumed, rehearsing to Captain Delano, that not only were the calms of unusual duration, but the ship had fallen in with obstinate currents; and other things he added, some of which were but repetitions of former statements, to explain how it came to pass that the passage from Cape Horn to St. Maria had been so exceedingly long; now and then, mingling with his words, incidental praises, less qualified than before, to the blacks, for their general good conduct. These particulars were not given consecutively, the servant, at convenient times, using his razor, and so, between the intervals of shaving, the story and panegyric went on with more than usual huskiness.

To Captain Delano's imagination, now again not wholly at rest, there was something so hollow in the Spaniard's manner, with apparently some reciprocal hollowness in the servant's dusky comment of silence, that the idea flashed across him, that possibly master and man, for some unknown purpose, were acting out, both in word and deed, nay, to the very tremor of Don Benito's limbs, some juggling[2] play before him. Neither did the suspicion of collusion lack apparent support, from the fact of those whispered conferences before mentioned. But then, what could be the object of enacting this play of the barber before him? At last, regarding the notion as a whimsy, insensibly suggested, perhaps, by the theatrical aspect of Don Benito in his harlequin ensign,[3] Captain Delano speedily banished it.

The shaving over, the servant bestirred himself with a small bottle of scented waters, pouring a few drops on the head, and then diligently rubbing; the vehemence of the exercise causing the muscles of his face to twitch rather strangely.

His next operation was with comb, scissors, and brush; going round and round, smoothing a curl here, clipping an unruly whisker-hair there, giving a graceful sweep to the temple-lock, with other impromptu touches evincing the hand of a master; while, like any resigned gentleman in barber's hands, Don Benito bore all, much less uneasily, at least than he had done the razoring; indeed, he sat so pale and rigid now, that the

---

[1] *James the First of England* James I of England (r. 1603–25) was also James VI of Scotland (r. 1567–1625). Known for his vivid belief in the supernatural, he survived several conspiracies and assassination attempts, including Guy Fawkes's Gunpowder Plot (see note above).

[2] *juggling* Deceptive.

[3] *harlequin ensign* Multicolored costume (like the fabric worn by clowns) covered in heraldic symbols (i.e., the flag).

negro seemed a Nubian[1] sculptor finishing off a white statue-head.

All being over at last, the standard[2] of Spain removed, tumbled up, and tossed back into the flag-locker, the negro's warm breath blowing away any stray hair, which might have lodged down his master's neck; collar and cravat readjusted; a speck of lint whisked off the velvet lapel; all this being done; backing off a little space, and pausing with an expression of subdued self-complacency, the servant for a moment surveyed his master, as, in toilet at least, the creature of his own tasteful hands.

Captain Delano playfully complimented him upon his achievement; at the same time congratulating Don Benito.

But neither sweet waters, nor shampooing, nor fidelity, nor sociality, delighted the Spaniard. Seeing him relapsing into forbidding gloom, and still remaining seated, Captain Delano, thinking that his presence was undesired just then, withdrew, on pretense of seeing whether, as he had prophesied, any signs of a breeze were visible.

Walking forward to the main-mast, he stood awhile thinking over the scene, and not without some undefined misgivings, when he heard a noise near the cuddy, and turning, saw the negro, his hand to his cheek. Advancing, Captain Delano perceived that the cheek was bleeding. He was about to ask the cause, when the negro's wailing soliloquy enlightened him.

"Ah, when will master get better from his sickness; only the sour heart that sour sickness breeds made him serve Babo so; cutting Babo with the razor, because, only by accident, Babo had given master one little scratch; and for the first time in so many a day, too. Ah, ah, ah," holding his hand to his face.

Is it possible, thought Captain Delano; was it to wreak in private his Spanish spite against this poor friend of his, that Don Benito, by his sullen manner, impelled me to withdraw? Ah this slavery breeds ugly passions in man.—Poor fellow!

He was about to speak in sympathy to the negro, but with a timid reluctance he now re-entered the cuddy.

Presently master and man came forth; Don Benito leaning on his servant as if nothing had happened.

But a sort of love-quarrel, after all, thought Captain Delano.

He accosted Don Benito, and they slowly walked together. They had gone but a few paces, when the steward—a tall, rajah-looking mulatto, orientally set off with a pagoda turban formed by three or four Madras handkerchiefs wound about his head, tier on tier—approaching with a salaam,[3] announced lunch in the cabin.

On their way thither, the two captains were preceded by the mulatto, who, turning round as he advanced, with continual smiles and bows, ushered them on, a display of elegance which quite completed the insignificance of the small bare-headed Babo, who, as if not unconscious of inferiority, eyed askance the graceful steward. But in part, Captain Delano imputed his jealous watchfulness to that peculiar feeling which the full-blooded African entertains for the adulterated one. As for the steward, his manner, if not bespeaking much dignity of self-respect, yet evidenced his extreme desire to please; which is doubly meritorious, as at once Christian and Chesterfieldian.[4]

Captain Delano observed with interest that while the complexion of the mulatto was hybrid, his physiognomy was European—classically so.

"Don Benito," whispered he, "I am glad to see this usher-of-the-golden-rod[5] of yours; the sight refutes an

---

[1] *Nubian* Person from Nubia, a region in north-east Africa along the Nile river.

[2] *standard* Flag.

---

[3] *rajah-looking* Resembling Indian nobility; *mulatto* One of the terms commonly used in the nineteenth century to classify individuals of mixed racial background; "mulatto" generally meant a person with one white parent and one parent of African descent; *pagoda* Temple; *Madras handkerchiefs* Traditional, colorful head-wraps made of madras (Indian) cotton; *salaam* Bow.

[4] *Chesterfieldian* Allusion to Philip Stanhope, Earl of Chesterfield (1694–1773), whose posthumously published *Letters to His Son* (1774) contained extensive advice for gentlemen on topics including what he called "the art of pleasing" as well as ways to seduce women. Chesterfield emphasized the idea that gentlemen often need to make moral compromises in order to thrive in society.

[5] *usher-of-the-golden-rod* The Usher of the Black Rod keeps order in the House of Lords in the U.K. Parliament; other ushers (stewards) have different colored rods associated with their duties, though there is no usher of the golden rod. Francesco's light pigmentation causes Delano to use "golden" rather than "black" to describe him.

ugly remark once made to me by a Barbadoes planter;[1] that when a mulatto has a regular European face, look out for him; he is a devil. But see, your steward here has features more regular than King George's of England; and yet there he nods, and bows, and smiles; a king, indeed—the king of kind hearts and polite fellows. What a pleasant voice he has, too?"

"He has, Señor."

"But tell me, has he not, so far as you have known him, always proved a good, worthy fellow?" said Captain Delano, pausing, while with a final genuflexion[2] the steward disappeared into the cabin; "come, for the reason just mentioned, I am curious to know."

"Francesco is a good man," a sort of sluggishly responded Don Benito,[3] like a phlegmatic[4] appreciator, who would neither find fault nor flatter.

"Ah, I thought so. For it were strange, indeed, and not very creditable to us white-skins, if a little of our blood mixed with the African's, should, far from improving the latter's quality, have the sad effect of pouring vitriolic acid[5] into black broth; improving the hue, perhaps, but not the wholesomeness."

"Doubtless, doubtless, Señor, but"—glancing at Babo—"not to speak of negroes, your planter's remark I have heard applied to the Spanish and Indian intermixtures in our provinces. But I know nothing about the matter," he listlessly added.

And here they entered the cabin.

The lunch was a frugal one. Some of Captain Delano's fresh fish and pumpkins, biscuit and salt beef, the reserved bottle of cider, and the San Dominick's last bottle of Canary.[6]

As they entered, Francesco, with two or three colored aids, was hovering over the table giving the last adjustments. Upon perceiving their master they withdrew, Francesco making a smiling congé, and the Spaniard, without condescending to notice it, fastidiously remarking to his companion that he relished not superfluous attendance.

Without companions, host and guest sat down, like a childless married couple, at opposite ends of the table, Don Benito waving Captain Delano to his place, and, weak as he was, insisting upon that gentleman being seated before himself.

The negro placed a rug under Don Benito's feet, and a cushion behind his back, and then stood behind, not his master's chair, but Captain Delano's. At first, this a little surprised the latter. But it was soon evident that, in taking his position, the black was still true to his master; since by facing him he could the more readily anticipate his slightest want.

"This is an uncommonly intelligent fellow of yours, Don Benito," whispered Captain Delano across the table.

"You say true, Señor."

During the repast, the guest again reverted to parts of Don Benito's story, begging further particulars here and there. He inquired how it was that the scurvy and fever should have committed such wholesale havoc upon the whites, while destroying less than half of the blacks. As if this question reproduced the whole scene of plague before the Spaniard's eyes, miserably reminding him of his solitude in a cabin where before he had had so many friends and officers round him, his hand shook, his face became hueless, broken words escaped; but directly the sane memory of the past seemed replaced by insane terrors of the present. With starting eyes he stared before him at vacancy. For nothing was to be seen but the hand of his servant pushing the Canary over towards him. At length a few sips served partially to restore him. He made random reference to the different constitution of races, enabling one to offer more resistance to certain maladies than another. The thought was new to his companion.

Presently Captain Delano, intending to say something to his host concerning the pecuniary part of the business he had undertaken for him, especially—since he was strictly accountable to his owners—with reference to the new suit of sails, and other things of that sort; and naturally preferring to conduct such affairs in

---

[1] *Barbadoes planter* I.e., plantation owner and enslaver on the island of Barbados, a British colony in the Caribbean. By the time *Benito Cereno* was published, slavery on Barbados (and throughout the British Empire) had been abolished, but it was still legal at the time the story takes place.

[2] *genuflexion* Bow.

[3] *sluggishly ... Benito* It is impossible to make grammatical sense of this construction; it seems likely that "Don Benito responded sluggishly" may have been what was intended.

[4] *phlegmatic* Unexpressive, indifferent.

[5] *vitriolic acid* I.e., sulphuric acid (to call a person "vitriolic" suggests rebelliousness and ill-temper).

[6] *Canary* White wine from the Canary Islands.

private, was desirous that the servant should withdraw; imagining that Don Benito for a few minutes could dispense with his attendance. He, however, waited awhile; thinking that, as the conversation proceeded, Don Benito, without being prompted, would perceive the propriety of the step.

But it was otherwise. At last catching his host's eye, Captain Delano, with a slight backward gesture of his thumb, whispered, "Don Benito, pardon me, but there is an interference with the full expression of what I have to say to you."

Upon this the Spaniard changed countenance; which was imputed to his resenting the hint, as in some way a reflection upon his servant. After a moment's pause, he assured his guest that the black's remaining with them could be of no disservice; because since losing his officers he had made Babo (whose original office, it now appeared, had been captain of the slaves) not only his constant attendant and companion, but in all things his confidant.

After this, nothing more could be said; though, indeed, Captain Delano could hardly avoid some little tinge of irritation upon being left ungratified in so inconsiderable a wish, by one, too, for whom he intended such solid services. But it is only his querulousness, thought he; and so filling his glass he proceeded to business.

The price of the sails and other matters was fixed upon. But while this was being done, the American observed that, though his original offer of assistance had been hailed with hectic animation, yet now when it was reduced to a business transaction, indifference and apathy were betrayed. Don Benito, in fact, appeared to submit to hearing the details more out of regard to common propriety, than from any impression that weighty benefit to himself and his voyage was involved.

Soon, his manner became still more reserved. The effort was vain to seek to draw him into social talk. Gnawed by his splenetic mood, he sat twitching his beard, while to little purpose the hand of his servant, mute as that on the wall, slowly pushed over the Canary.

Lunch being over, they sat down on the cushioned transom;[1] the servant placing a pillow behind his master. The long continuance of the calm had now affected the atmosphere. Don Benito sighed heavily, as if for breath.

"Why not adjourn to the cuddy," said Captain Delano; "there is more air there." But the host sat silent and motionless.

Meantime his servant knelt before him, with a large fan of feathers. And Francesco coming in on tiptoes, handed the negro a little cup of aromatic waters, with which at intervals he chafed his master's brow; smoothing the hair along the temples as a nurse does a child's. He spoke no word. He only rested his eye on his master's, as if, amid all Don Benito's distress, a little to refresh his spirit by the silent sight of fidelity.

Presently the ship's bell sounded two o'clock; and through the cabin windows a slight rippling of the sea was discerned; and from the desired direction.

"There," exclaimed Captain Delano, "I told you so, Don Benito, look!"

He had risen to his feet, speaking in a very animated tone, with a view the more to rouse his companion. But though the crimson curtain of the stern-window near him that moment fluttered against his pale cheek, Don Benito seemed to have even less welcome for the breeze than the calm.

Poor fellow, thought Captain Delano, bitter experience has taught him that one ripple does not make a wind, any more than one swallow a summer.[2] But he is mistaken for once. I will get his ship in for him, and prove it.

Briefly alluding to his weak condition, he urged his host to remain quietly where he was, since he (Captain Delano) would with pleasure take upon himself the responsibility of making the best use of the wind.

Upon gaining the deck, Captain Delano started at the unexpected figure of Atufal, monumentally fixed at the threshold, like one of those sculptured porters of black marble guarding the porches of Egyptian tombs.

But this time the start was, perhaps, purely physical. Atufal's presence, singularly attesting docility even in sullenness, was contrasted with that of the hatchet-polishers, who in patience evinced their industry;

---

1   *transom*   Seat built into the side of a ship's cabin.

2   *one swallow a summer*   From the proverb "One swallow does not a summer make"—i.e., the arrival of one migrating swallow does not mean summer has arrived.

while both spectacles showed, that lax as Don Benito's general authority might be, still, whenever he chose to exert it, no man so savage or colossal but must, more or less, bow.

Snatching a trumpet which hung from the bulwarks, with a free step Captain Delano advanced to the forward edge of the poop, issuing his orders in his best Spanish. The few sailors and many negroes, all equally pleased, obediently set about heading the ship towards the harbor.

While giving some directions about setting a lower stu'n'-sail,[1] suddenly Captain Delano heard a voice faithfully repeating his orders. Turning, he saw Babo, now for the time acting, under the pilot, his original part of captain of the slaves. This assistance proved valuable. Tattered sails and warped yards were soon brought into some trim. And no brace or halyard was pulled but to the blithe songs of the inspirited negroes.

Good fellows, thought Captain Delano, a little training would make fine sailors of them. Why see, the very women pull and sing too. These must be some of those Ashantee negresses that make such capital soldiers, I've heard. But who's at the helm. I must have a good hand there.

He went to see.

The San Dominick steered with a cumbrous tiller, with large horizontal pullies attached. At each pully-end stood a subordinate black, and between them, at the tiller-head, the responsible post, a Spanish seaman, whose countenance evinced his due share in the general hopefulness and confidence at the coming of the breeze.

He proved the same man who had behaved with so shame-faced an air on the windlass.

"Ah,—it is you, my man," exclaimed Captain Delano—"well, no more sheep's-eyes now;—look straight forward and keep the ship so. Good hand, I trust? And want to get into the harbor, don't you?"

The man assented with an inward chuckle, grasping the tiller-head firmly. Upon this, unperceived by the American, the two blacks eyed the sailor intently.

Finding all right at the helm, the pilot went forward to the forecastle, to see how matters stood there.

The ship now had way[2] enough to breast the current. With the approach of evening, the breeze would be sure to freshen.[3]

Having done all that was needed for the present, Captain Delano, giving his last orders to the sailors, turned aft to report affairs to Don Benito in the cabin; perhaps additionally incited to rejoin him by the hope of snatching a moment's private chat while the servant was engaged upon deck.

From opposite sides, there were, beneath the poop, two approaches to the cabin; one further forward than the other, and consequently communicating with a longer passage. Marking the servant still above, Captain Delano, taking the nighest entrance—the one last named, and at whose porch Atufal still stood—hurried on his way, till, arrived at the cabin threshold, he paused an instant, a little to recover from his eagerness. Then, with the words of his intended business upon his lips, he entered. As he advanced toward the seated Spaniard, he heard another footstep, keeping time with his. From the opposite door, a salver[4] in hand, the servant was likewise advancing.

"Confound the faithful fellow," thought Captain Delano; "what a vexatious coincidence."

Possibly, the vexation might have been something different, were it not for the brisk confidence inspired by the breeze. But even as it was, he felt a slight twinge, from a sudden indefinite association in his mind of Babo with Atufal.

"Don Benito," said he, "I give you joy; the breeze will hold, and will increase. By the way, your tall man and time-piece, Atufal, stands without.[5] By your order, of course?"

Don Benito recoiled, as if at some bland satirical touch,[6] delivered with such adroit garnish of apparent good breeding as to present no handle for retort.

He is like one flayed alive, thought Captain Delano; where may one touch him without causing a shrink?

The servant moved before his master, adjusting a cushion; recalled to civility, the Spaniard stiffly replied:

---

1   *stu'n'-sail*   An additional sail set to increase the ship's speed.

2   *way*   Momentum.

3   *freshen*   Strengthen.

4   *salver*   Tray.

5   *without*   Outside.

6   *touch*   Rebuke.

"you are right. The slave appears where you saw him, according to my command; which is, that if at the given hour I am below, he must take his stand and abide my coming."

"Ah now, pardon me, but that is treating the poor fellow like an ex-king indeed. Ah, Don Benito," smiling, "for all the license you permit in some things, I fear lest, at bottom, you are a bitter hard master."

Again Don Benito shrank; and this time, as the good sailor thought, from a genuine twinge of his conscience.

Again conversation became constrained. In vain Captain Delano called attention to the now perceptible motion of the keel gently cleaving the sea; with lack-lustre eye, Don Benito returned words few and reserved.

By-and-by, the wind having steadily risen, and still blowing right into the harbor bore the San Dominick swiftly on. Sounding a point of land, the sealer at distance came into open view.

Meantime Captain Delano had again repaired to the deck, remaining there some time. Having at last altered the ship's course, so as to give the reef a wide berth, he returned for a few moments below.

I will cheer up my poor friend, this time, thought he.

"Better and better, Don Benito," he cried as he blithely re-entered: "there will soon be an end to your cares, at least for awhile. For when, after a long, sad voyage, you know, the anchor drops into the haven, all its vast weight seems lifted from the captain's heart. We are getting on famously, Don Benito. My ship is in sight. Look through this side-light here; there she is; all a-taunt-o![1] The Bachelor's Delight, my good friend. Ah, how this wind braces one up. Come, you must take a cup of coffee with me this evening. My old steward will give you as fine a cup as ever any sultan tasted. What say you, Don Benito, will you?"

At first, the Spaniard glanced feverishly up, casting a longing look towards the sealer, while with mute concern his servant gazed into his face. Suddenly the old ague of coldness returned, and dropping back to his cushions he was silent.

"You do not answer. Come, all day you have been my host; would you have hospitality all on one side?"

"I cannot go," was the response.

"What? it will not fatigue you. The ships will lie together as near as they can, without swinging foul. It will be little more than stepping from deck to deck; which is but as from room to room. Come, come, you must not refuse me."

"I cannot go," decisively and repulsively repeated Don Benito.

Renouncing all but the last appearance of courtesy, with a sort of cadaverous sullenness, and biting his thin nails to the quick, he glanced, almost glared, at his guest, as if impatient that a stranger's presence should interfere with the full indulgence of his morbid hour. Meantime the sound of the parted waters came more and more gurglingly and merrily in at the windows; as reproaching him for his dark spleen; as telling him that, sulk as he might, and go mad with it, nature cared not a jot; since, whose fault was it, pray?

But the foul mood was now at its depth, as the fair wind at its height.

There was something in the man so far beyond any mere unsociality or sourness previously evinced, that even the forbearing good-nature of his guest could no longer endure it. Wholly at a loss to account for such demeanor, and deeming sickness with eccentricity, however extreme, no adequate excuse, well satisfied, too, that nothing in his own conduct could justify it, Captain Delano's pride began to be roused. Himself became reserved. But all seemed one to the Spaniard. Quitting him, therefore, Captain Delano once more went to the deck.

The ship was now within less than two miles of the sealer. The whale-boat was seen darting over the interval.

To be brief, the two vessels, thanks to the pilot's skill, ere long neighborly style lay anchored together.

Before returning to his own vessel, Captain Delano had intended communicating to Don Benito the smaller details of the proposed services to be rendered. But, as it was, unwilling anew to subject himself to rebuffs, he resolved, now that he had seen the San Dominick safely moored, immediately to quit her, without further allusion to hospitality or business. Indefinitely postponing his ulterior plans, he would regulate his future actions according to future circumstances. His boat was ready to receive him; but his host

---

[1]   *a-taunt-o*   With all sails rigged.

still tarried below. Well, thought Captain Delano, if he has little breeding, the more need to show mine. He descended to the cabin to bid a ceremonious, and, it may be, tacitly rebukeful adieu. But to his great satisfaction, Don Benito, as if he began to feel the weight of that treatment with which his slighted guest had, not indecorously, retaliated upon him, now supported by his servant, rose to his feet, and grasping Captain Delano's hand, stood tremulous; too much agitated to speak. But the good augury hence drawn was suddenly dashed, by his resuming all his previous reserve, with augmented gloom, as, with half-averted eyes, he silently reseated himself on his cushions. With a corresponding return of his own chilled feelings, Captain Delano bowed and withdrew.

He was hardly midway in the narrow corridor, dim as a tunnel, leading from the cabin to the stairs, when a sound, as of the tolling for execution in some jail-yard, fell on his ears. It was the echo of the ship's flawed bell, striking the hour, drearily reverberated in this subterranean vault. Instantly, by a fatality not to be withstood, his mind, responsive to the portent, swarmed with superstitious suspicions. He paused. In images far swifter than these sentences, the minutest details of all his former distrusts swept through him.

Hitherto, credulous good-nature had been too ready to furnish excuses for reasonable fears. Why was the Spaniard, so superfluously punctilious at times, now heedless of common propriety in not accompanying to the side his departing guest? Did indisposition forbid? Indisposition had not forbidden more irksome exertion that day. His last equivocal demeanor recurred. He had risen to his feet, grasped his guest's hand, motioned toward his hat; then, in an instant, all was eclipsed in sinister muteness and gloom. Did this imply one brief, repentant relenting at the final moment, from some iniquitous plot, followed by remorseless return to it? His last glance seemed to express a calamitous, yet acquiescent farewell to Captain Delano forever. Why decline the invitation to visit the sealer that evening? Or was the Spaniard less hardened than the Jew, who refrained not from supping at the board of him whom the same night he meant to betray?[1] What imported all those day-long enigmas and contradictions, except

they were intended to mystify, preliminary to some stealthy blow? Atufal, the pretended rebel, but punctual shadow, that moment lurked by the threshold without. He seemed a sentry, and more. Who, by his own confession, had stationed him there? Was the negro now lying in wait?

The Spaniard behind—his creature before: to rush from darkness to light was the involuntary choice.

The next moment, with clenched jaw and hand, he passed Atufal, and stood unharmed in the light. As he saw his trim ship lying peacefully at anchor, and almost within ordinary call; as he saw his household boat, with familiar faces in it, patiently rising and falling, on the short waves by the San Dominick's side; and then, glancing about the decks where he stood, saw the oakum-pickers still gravely plying their fingers; and heard the low, buzzing whistle and industrious hum of the hatchet-polishers, still bestirring themselves over their endless occupation; and more than all, as he saw the benign aspect of nature, taking her innocent repose in the evening; the screened sun in the quiet camp of the west shining out like the mild light from Abraham's tent;[2] as charmed eye and ear took in all these, with the chained figure of the black, clenched jaw and hand relaxed. Once again he smiled at the phantoms which had mocked him, and felt something like a tinge of remorse, that, by harboring them even for a moment, he should, by implication, have betrayed an atheist doubt of the ever-watchful Providence above.

There was a few minutes' delay, while, in obedience to his orders, the boat was being hooked along to the gangway. During this interval, a sort of saddened satisfaction stole over Captain Delano, at thinking of the kindly offices he had that day discharged for a stranger. Ah, thought he, after good actions one's conscience is never ungrateful, however much so the benefited party may be.

Presently, his foot, in the first act of descent into the boat, pressed the first round of the side-ladder, his face presented inward upon the deck. In the same moment, he heard his name courteously sounded; and,

---

[1]   *Jew ... betray*   See John 13.2, where Judas Iscariot, after sharing the Last Supper with Jesus, betrays him. While Jesus and all his disciples were Jews, Judas' Jewishness is often emphasized in anti-Semitic rhetoric.

[2]   *mild light ... Abraham's tent*   In Genesis 18, God visits Abraham and Sarah in their tent on the plains of Mamre and tells Sarah she will bear a child in her old age.

to his pleased surprise, saw Don Benito advancing—an unwonted energy in his air, as if, at the last moment, intent upon making amends for his recent discourtesy. With instinctive good feeling, Captain Delano, withdrawing his foot, turned and reciprocally advanced. As he did so, the Spaniard's nervous eagerness increased, but his vital energy failed; so that, the better to support him, the servant, placing his master's hand on his naked shoulder, and gently holding it there, formed himself into a sort of crutch.

When the two captains met, the Spaniard again fervently took the hand of the American, at the same time casting an earnest glance into his eyes, but, as before, too much overcome to speak.

I have done him wrong, self-reproachfully thought Captain Delano; his apparent coldness has deceived me: in no instance has he meant to offend.

Meantime, as if fearful that the continuance of the scene might too much unstring his master, the servant seemed anxious to terminate it. And so, still presenting himself as a crutch, and walking between the two captains, he advanced with them towards the gangway; while still, as if full of kindly contrition, Don Benito would not let go the hand of Captain Delano, but retained it in his, across the black's body.

Soon they were standing by the side, looking over into the boat, whose crew turned up their curious eyes. Waiting a moment for the Spaniard to relinquish his hold, the now embarrassed Captain Delano lifted his foot, to overstep the threshold of the open gangway; but still Don Benito would not let go his hand. And yet, with an agitated tone, he said, "I can go no further; here I must bid you adieu. Adieu, my dear, dear Don Amasa. Go—go!" suddenly tearing his hand loose, "go, and God guard you better than me, my best friend."

Not unaffected, Captain Delano would now have lingered; but catching the meekly admonitory eye of the servant, with a hasty farewell he descended into his boat, followed by the continual adieus of Don Benito, standing rooted in the gangway.

Seating himself in the stern, Captain Delano, making a last salute, ordered the boat shoved off. The crew had their oars on end. The bowsmen pushed the boat a sufficient distance for the oars to be lengthwise dropped. The instant that was done, Don Benito sprang over the bulwarks, falling at the feet of Captain Delano; at the same time calling towards his ship, but in tones so frenzied, that none in the boat could understand him. But, as if not equally obtuse, three sailors, from three different and distant parts of the ship, splashed into the sea, swimming after their captain, as if intent upon his rescue.

The dismayed officer of the boat eagerly asked what this meant. To which, Captain Delano, turning a disdainful smile upon the unaccountable Spaniard, answered that, for his part, he neither knew nor cared; but it seemed as if Don Benito had taken it into his head to produce the impression among his people that the boat wanted to kidnap him. "Or else—give way for your lives," he wildly added, starting at a clattering hubbub in the ship, above which rang the tocsin[1] of the hatchet-polishers; and seizing Don Benito by the throat he added, "this plotting pirate means murder!" Here, in apparent verification of the words, the servant, a dagger in his hand, was seen on the rail overhead, poised, in the act of leaping, as if with desperate fidelity to befriend his master to the last; while, seemingly to aid the black, the three white sailors were trying to clamber into the hampered bow. Meantime, the whole host of negroes, as if inflamed at the sight of their jeopardized captain, impended in one sooty avalanche over the bulwarks.

All this, with what preceded, and what followed, occurred with such involutions of rapidity, that past, present, and future seemed one.

Seeing the negro coming, Captain Delano had flung the Spaniard aside, almost in the very act of clutching him, and, by the unconscious recoil, shifting his place, with arms thrown up, so promptly grappled the servant in his descent, that with dagger presented at Captain Delano's heart, the black seemed of purpose to have leaped there as to his mark. But the weapon was wrenched away, and the assailant dashed down into the bottom of the boat, which now, with disentangled oars, began to speed through the sea.

At this juncture, the left hand of Captain Delano, on one side, again clutched the half-reclined Don Benito, heedless that he was in a speechless faint, while his right foot, on the other side, ground the prostrate negro; and his right arm pressed for added speed on the after oar, his eye bent forward, encouraging his men to their utmost.

---

[1] *tocsin* Signal, alarm.

But here, the officer of the boat, who had at last succeeded in beating off the towing sailors, and was now, with face turned aft, assisting the bowsman at his oar, suddenly called to Captain Delano, to see what the black was about; while a Portuguese oarsman shouted to him to give heed to what the Spaniard was saying.

Glancing down at his feet, Captain Delano saw the freed hand of the servant aiming with a second dagger—a small one, before concealed in his wool—with this he was snakishly writhing up from the boat's bottom, at the heart of his master, his countenance lividly vindictive, expressing the centred purpose of his soul; while the Spaniard, half-choked, was vainly shrinking away, with husky words, incoherent to all but the Portuguese.

That moment, across the long-benighted mind of Captain Delano, a flash of revelation swept, illuminating, in unanticipated clearness, his host's whole mysterious demeanor, with every enigmatic event of the day, as well as the entire past voyage of the San Dominick. He smote Babo's hand down, but his own heart smote him harder. With infinite pity he withdrew his hold from Don Benito. Not Captain Delano, but Don Benito, the black, in leaping into the boat, had intended to stab.

Both the black's hands were held, as, glancing up towards the San Dominick, Captain Delano, now with scales dropped from his eyes, saw the negroes, not in misrule, not in tumult, not as if frantically concerned for Don Benito, but with mask torn away, flourishing hatchets and knives, in ferocious piratical revolt. Like delirious black dervishes, the six Ashantees danced on the poop. Prevented by their foes from springing into the water, the Spanish boys were hurrying up to the topmost spars, while such of the few Spanish sailors, not already in the sea, less alert, were descried, helplessly mixed in, on deck, with the blacks.

Meantime Captain Delano hailed his own vessel, ordering the ports up, and the guns run out. But by this time the cable of the San Dominick had been cut; and the fag-end,[1] in lashing out, whipped away the canvas shroud about the beak, suddenly revealing, as the bleached hull swung round towards the open ocean, death for the figure-head, in a human skeleton;

chalky comment on the chalked words below, "*Follow your leader.*"

At the sight, Don Benito, covering his face, wailed out: "'Tis he, Aranda! my murdered, unburied friend!"

Upon reaching the sealer, calling for ropes, Captain Delano bound the negro, who made no resistance, and had him hoisted to the deck. He would then have assisted the now almost helpless Don Benito up the side; but Don Benito, wan as he was, refused to move, or be moved, until the negro should have been first put below out of view. When, presently assured that it was done, he no more shrank from the ascent.

The boat was immediately dispatched back to pick up the three swimming sailors. Meantime, the guns were in readiness, though, owing to the San Dominick having glided somewhat astern of the sealer, only the aftermost one could be brought to bear. With this, they fired six times; thinking to cripple the fugitive ship by bringing down her spars. But only a few inconsiderable ropes were shot away. Soon the ship was beyond the gun's range, steering broad out of the bay; the blacks thickly clustering round the bowsprit, one moment with taunting cries towards the whites, the next with upthrown gestures hailing the now dusky moors of ocean—cawing crows escaped from the hand of the fowler.[2]

The first impulse was to slip the cables and give chase. But, upon second thoughts, to pursue with whale-boat and yawl[3] seemed more promising.

Upon inquiring of Don Benito what firearms they had on board the San Dominick, Captain Delano was answered that they had none that could be used; because, in the earlier stages of the mutiny, a cabin-passenger, since dead, had secretly put out of order the locks of what few muskets there were. But with all his remaining strength, Don Benito entreated the American not to give chase, either with ship or boat; for the negroes had already proved themselves such desperadoes, that, in case of a present assault, nothing but a total massacre of the whites could be looked for. But, regarding this warning as coming from one whose spirit had been crushed by misery the American did not give up his design.

---

1   *fag-end*   End of a loose rope.

2   *fowler*   Bird-catcher.

3   *yawl*   Small ship's boat with four to six oars.

The boats were got ready and armed. Captain Delano ordered his men into them. He was going himself when Don Benito grasped his arm.

"What! have you saved my life, Señor, and are you now going to throw away your own?"

The officers also, for reasons connected with their interests and those of the voyage, and a duty owing to the owners, strongly objected against their commander's going. Weighing their remonstrances a moment, Captain Delano felt bound to remain; appointing his chief mate—an athletic and resolute man, who had been a privateer's-man[1]—to head the party. The more to encourage the sailors, they were told, that the Spanish captain considered his ship good as lost; that she and her cargo, including some gold and silver, were worth more than a thousand doubloons. Take her, and no small part should be theirs. The sailors replied with a shout.

The fugitives had now almost gained an offing.[2] It was nearly night; but the moon was rising. After hard, prolonged pulling, the boats came up on the ship's quarters, at a suitable distance laying upon their oars to discharge their muskets. Having no bullets to return, the negroes sent their yells. But, upon the second volley, Indian-like, they hurtled their hatchets. One took off a sailor's fingers. Another struck the whaleboat's bow, cutting off the rope there, and remaining stuck in the gunwale like a woodman's axe. Snatching it, quivering from its lodgment, the mate hurled it back. The returned gauntlet now stuck in the ship's broken quarter-gallery, and so remained.

The negroes giving too hot a reception, the whites kept a more respectful distance. Hovering now just out of reach of the hurtling hatchets, they, with a view to the close encounter which must soon come, sought to decoy the blacks into entirely disarming themselves of their most murderous weapons in a hand-to-hand fight, by foolishly flinging them, as missiles, short of the mark, into the sea. But, ere long, perceiving the stratagem, the negroes desisted, though not before many of them had to replace their lost hatchets with handspikes; an exchange which, as counted upon, proved, in the end, favorable to the assailants.

Meantime, with a strong wind, the ship still clove the water; the boats alternately falling behind, and pulling up, to discharge fresh volleys.

The fire was mostly directed towards the stern, since there, chiefly, the negroes, at present, were clustering. But to kill or maim the negroes was not the object. To take them, with the ship, was the object. To do it, the ship must be boarded; which could not be done by boats while she was sailing so fast.

A thought now struck the mate. Observing the Spanish boys still aloft, high as they could get, he called to them to descend to the yards, and cut adrift the sails. It was done. About this time, owing to causes hereafter to be shown, two Spaniards, in the dress of sailors, and conspicuously showing themselves, were killed; not by volleys, but by deliberate marksman's shots; while, as it afterwards appeared, by one of the general discharges, Atufal, the black, and the Spaniard at the helm likewise were killed. What now, with the loss of the sails, and loss of leaders, the ship became unmanageable to the negroes.

With creaking masts, she came heavily round to the wind; the prow slowly swinging into view of the boats, its skeleton gleaming in the horizontal moonlight, and casting a gigantic ribbed shadow upon the water. One extended arm of the ghost seemed beckoning the whites to avenge it.

"Follow your leader!" cried the mate; and, one on each bow, the boats boarded. Sealing-spears and cutlasses crossed hatchets and hand spikes. Huddled upon the long-boat amidships, the negresses raised a wailing chant, whose chorus was the clash of the steel.

For a time, the attack wavered; the negroes wedging themselves to beat it back; the half-repelled sailors, as yet unable to gain a footing, fighting as troopers in the saddle, one leg sideways flung over the bulwarks, and one without, plying their cutlasses like carters' whips.

But in vain. They were almost overborne, when, rallying themselves into a squad as one man, with a huzza, they sprang inboard, where, entangled, they involuntarily separated again. For a few breaths' space, there was a vague, muffled, inner sound, as of submerged sword-fish rushing hither and thither through shoals of black-fish. Soon, in a reunited band, and joined by

---

[1]   *privateer's-man* Person who worked on a privateer, a ship privately owned but commissioned by a government to capture enemy merchant ships. Sailors on privateers were thus familiar with armed conflict on the sea.

[2]   *offing* Safe distance.

the Spanish seamen, the whites came to the surface, irresistibly driving the negroes toward the stern. But a barricade of casks and sacks, from side to side, had been thrown up by the main-mast. Here the negroes faced about, and though scorning peace or truce, yet fain would have had respite. But, without pause, over-leaping the barrier, the unflagging sailors again closed. Exhausted, the blacks now fought in despair. Their red tongues lolled, wolf-like, from their black mouths. But the pale sailors' teeth were set; not a word was spoken; and, in five minutes more, the ship was won.

Nearly a score of the negroes were killed. Exclusive of those by the balls,[1] many were mangled; their wounds—mostly inflicted by the long-edged sealing-spears, resembling those shaven ones of the English at Preston Pans,[2] made by the poled scythes of the Highlanders. On the other side, none were killed, though several were wounded; some severely, includ-ing the mate. The surviving negroes were temporarily secured, and the ship, towed back into the harbor at midnight, once more lay anchored.

Omitting the incidents and arrangements ensuing, suffice it that, after two days spent in refitting, the ships sailed in company for Conception, in Chili, and thence for Lima, in Peru; where, before the vice-regal courts, the whole affair, from the beginning, under-went investigation.

Though, midway on the passage, the ill-fated Spaniard, relaxed from constraint, showed some signs of regaining health with free-will; yet, agreeably to his own foreboding, shortly before arriving at Lima, he relapsed, finally becoming so reduced as to be carried ashore in arms. Hearing of his story and plight, one of the many religious institutions of the City of Kings opened an hospitable refuge to him, where both physi-cian and priest were his nurses, and a member of the order volunteered to be his one special guardian and consoler, by night and by day.

The following extracts, translated from one of the official Spanish documents, will, it is hoped, shed light on the preceding narrative, as well as, in the first place, reveal the true port of departure and true history of the San Dominick's voyage, down to the time of her touching at the island of St. Maria.

But, ere the extracts come, it may be well to preface them with a remark.

The document selected, from among many others, for partial translation, contains the deposition of Benito Cereno; the first taken in the case. Some disclo-sures therein were, at the time, held dubious for both learned and natural reasons. The tribunal inclined to the opinion that the deponent, not undisturbed in his mind by recent events, raved of some things which could never have happened. But subsequent deposi-tions of the surviving sailors, bearing out the revelations of their captain in several of the strangest particulars, gave credence to the rest. So that the tribunal, in its final decision, rested its capital sentences upon state-ments which, had they lacked confirmation, it would have deemed it but duty to reject.

———————

I, Don Jose De Abos and Padilla, His Majesty's Notary for the Royal Revenue, and Register of this Province, and Notary Public of the Holy Crusade of this Bishopric, etc.

Do certify and declare, as much as is requisite in law, that, in the criminal cause commenced the twenty-fourth of the month of September, in the year sev-enteen hundred and ninety-nine, against the negroes of the ship San Dominick, the following declaration before me was made:

Declaration of the first witness, Don Benito Cereno.

The same day, and month, and year, His Honor, Doctor Juan Martinez de Rozas, Councilor of the Royal Audience of this Kingdom, and learned in the law of this Intendency,[3] ordered the captain of the ship San Dominick, Don Benito Cereno, to appear; which he did, in his litter, attended by the monk Infelez; of whom he received the oath, which he took by God, our Lord, and a sign of the Cross; under which he promised to tell the truth of whatever he should know and should be asked;—and being interrogated agree-ably to the tenor of the act commencing the process, he said, that on the twentieth of May last, he set sail

———————

[1] *balls* Bullets.

[2] *Preston Pans* Rebel victory in the Jacobite rising of 1745, when Catholic Scottish Highlanders loyal to the Stuart dynasty attempted—and ultimately failed—to restore Charles Stuart to the throne of Great Britain.

[3] *Intendency* Administration (those in charge of the province).

with his ship from the port of Valparaiso, bound to that of Callao;[1] loaded with the produce of the country beside thirty cases of hardware and one hundred and sixty blacks, of both sexes, mostly belonging to Don Alexandro Aranda, gentleman, of the city of Mendoza;[2] that the crew of the ship consisted of thirty-six men, beside the persons who went as passengers; that the negroes were in part as follows:

[*Here, in the original, follows a list of some fifty names, descriptions, and ages, compiled from certain recovered documents of Aranda's, and also from recollections of the deponent, from which portions only are extracted.*]

—One, from about eighteen to nineteen years, named José, and this was the man that waited upon his master, Don Alexandro, and who speaks well the Spanish, having served him four or five years; * * * a mulatto, named Francesco, the cabin steward, of a good person and voice, having sung in the Valparaiso churches, native of the province of Buenos Ayres, aged about thirty-five years. * * * A smart negro, named Dago, who had been for many years a grave-digger among the Spaniards, aged forty-six years. * * * Four old negroes, born in Africa, from sixty to seventy, but sound, calkers[3] by trade, whose names are as follows:—the first was named Muri, and he was killed (as was also his son named Diamelo); the second, Nacta; the third, Yola, likewise killed; the fourth, Ghofan; and six full-grown negroes, aged from thirty to forty-five, all raw,[4] and born among the Ashantees—Matiluqui, Yan, Lecbe, Mapenda, Yambaio, Akim; four of whom were killed; * * * a powerful negro named Atufal, who being supposed to have been a chief in Africa, his owner set great store by him. * * * And a small negro of Senegal, but some years among the Spaniards, aged about thirty, which negro's name was Babo; * * * that he does not remember the names of the others, but that still expecting the residue of Don Alexandro's papers will be found,

will then take due account of them all, and remit to the court; * * * and thirty-nine women and children of all ages.

[*The catalogue over, the deposition goes on.*]

* * * That all the negroes slept upon deck, as is customary in this navigation, and none wore fetters, because the owner, his friend Aranda, told him that they were all tractable; * * * that on the seventh day after leaving port, at three o'clock in the morning, all the Spaniards being asleep except the two officers on the watch, who were the boatswain, Juan Robles, and the carpenter, Juan Bautista Gayete, and the helmsman and his boy, the negroes revolted suddenly, wounded dangerously the boatswain and the carpenter, and successively killed eighteen men of those who were sleeping upon deck, some with hand spikes and hatchets, and others by throwing them alive overboard, after tying them; that of the Spaniards upon deck, they left about seven, as he thinks, alive and tied, to manoeuvre the ship, and three or four more, who hid themselves, remained also alive. Although in the act of revolt the negroes made themselves masters of the hatchway, six or seven wounded went through it to the cockpit, without any hindrance on their part; that during the act of revolt, the mate and another person, whose name he does not recollect, attempted to come up through the hatchway, but being quickly wounded, were obliged to return to the cabin; that the deponent resolved at break of day to come up the companion-way, where the negro Babo was, being the ringleader, and Atufal, who assisted him, and having spoken to them, exhorted them to cease committing such atrocities, asking them, at the same time, what they wanted and intended to do, offering, himself, to obey their commands; that notwithstanding this, they threw, in his presence, three men, alive and tied, overboard; that they told the deponent to come up, and that they would not kill him; which having done, the negro Babo asked him whether there were in those seas any negro countries where they might be carried, and he answered them, No; that the negro Babo afterwards told him to carry them to Senegal, or to the neighboring

---

[1]   *Valparaiso*   Port in Chile;   *Callao*   Port in Peru.

[2]   *Mendoza*   City in Argentina.

[3]   *calkers*   Caulkers—those who waterproof the seams of ships by stuffing them with oakum (shredded hemp) and sealing them with pitch.

[4]   *raw*   I.e., from Africa.

islands of St. Nicholas;[1] and he answered, that this was impossible, on account of the great distance, the necessity involved of rounding Cape Horn, the bad condition of the vessel, the want of provisions, sails, and water; but that the negro Babo replied to him he must carry them in any way; that they would do and conform themselves to everything the deponent should require as to eating and drinking; that after a long conference, being absolutely compelled to please them, for they threatened to kill all the whites if they were not, at all events, carried to Senegal, he told them that what was most wanting for the voyage was water; that they would go near the coast to take it, and thence they would proceed on their course; that the negro Babo agreed to it; and the deponent steered towards the intermediate ports, hoping to meet some Spanish, or foreign vessel that would save them; that within ten or eleven days they saw the land, and continued their course by it in the vicinity of Nasca;[2] that the deponent observed that the negroes were now restless and mutinous, because he did not effect the taking in of water, the negro Babo having required, with threats, that it should be done, without fail, the following day; he told him he saw plainly that the coast was steep, and the rivers designated in the maps were not to be found, with other reasons suitable to the circumstances; that the best way would be to go to the island of Santa Maria, where they might water easily, it being a solitary island, as the foreigners did; that the deponent did not go to Pisco,[3] that was near, nor make any other port of the coast, because the negro Babo had intimated to him several times, that he would kill all the whites the very moment he should perceive any city, town, or settlement of any kind on the shores to which they should be carried: that having determined to go to the island of Santa Maria, as the deponent had planned,

for the purpose of trying whether, on the passage or near the island itself, they could find any vessel that should favor them, or whether he could escape from it in a boat to the neighboring coast of Arruco,[4] to adopt the necessary means he immediately changed his course, steering for the island; that the negroes Babo and Atufal held daily conferences, in which they discussed what was necessary for their design of returning to Senegal, whether they were to kill all the Spaniards, and particularly the deponent; that eight days after parting from the coast of Nasca, the deponent being on the watch a little after day-break, and soon after the negroes had their meeting, the negro Babo came to the place where the deponent was, and told him that he had determined to kill his master, Don Alexandro Aranda, both because he and his companions could not otherwise be sure of their liberty, and that to keep the seamen in subjection, he wanted to prepare a warning of what road they should be made to take did they or any of them oppose him; and that, by means of the death of Don Alexandro, that warning would best be given; but, that what this last meant, the deponent did not at the time comprehend, nor could not, further than that the death of Don Alexandro was intended; and moreover the negro Babo proposed to the deponent to call the mate Raneds, who was sleeping in the cabin, before the thing was done, for fear, as the deponent understood it, that the mate, who was a good navigator, should be killed with Don Alexandro and the rest; that the deponent, who was the friend, from youth, of Don Alexandro, prayed and conjured, but all was useless; for the negro Babo answered him that the thing could not be prevented, and that all the Spaniards risked their death if they should attempt to frustrate his will in this matter, or any other; that, in this conflict, the deponent called the mate, Raneds, who was forced to go apart, and immediately the negro Babo commanded the Ashantee Martinqui and the Ashantee Lecbe to go and commit the murder; that those two went down with hatchets to the berth of Don Alexandro; that, yet half alive and mangled, they dragged him on deck; that they were going to throw him overboard in that state, but the negro Babo stopped them, bidding the murder be completed on the deck before him, which was done, when, by his

---

[1]   *islands of St. Nicholas*   Probably the Cabo Verde (Cape Verde) Islands, an archipelago located approximately 400 miles off the coast of Senegal in West Africa, one of which is named São Nicolau (St. Nicholas). The town of Tarrafal on São Nicolau was an anchorage for whaling ships in the nineteenth century, which may be the basis for Melville's familiarity with it. Senegal and the Cabo Verde Islands were both major sites of embarkation in the transatlantic slave trade; the Cabo Verde Islands also served as a penal colony for their Portuguese colonizers and were the site of several anticolonial revolts.

[2]   *Nasca*   Province in southern Peru.

[3]   *Pisco*   Port city in southern Peru.

[4]   *Arruco*   I.e., Araucanía, a region in Chile.

orders, the body was carried below, forward; that nothing more was seen of it by the deponent for three days; * * * that Don Alonzo Sidonia, an old man, long resident at Valparaiso, and lately appointed to a civil office in Peru, whither he had taken passage, was at the time sleeping in the berth opposite Don Alexandro's; that awakening at his cries, surprised by them, and at the sight of the negroes with their bloody hatchets in their hands, he threw himself into the sea through a window which was near him, and was drowned, without it being in the power of the deponent to assist or take him up; * * * that a short time after killing Aranda, they brought upon deck his german-cousin, of middle-age, Don Francisco Masa, of Mendoza, and the young Don Joaquin, Marques de Aramboalaza, then lately from Spain, with his Spanish servant Ponce, and the three young clerks of Aranda, José Mozairi, Lorenzo Bargas, and Hermenegildo Gandix, all of Cadiz; that Don Joaquin and Hermenegildo Gandix, the negro Babo, for purposes hereafter to appear, preserved alive; but Don Francisco Masa, José Mozairi, and Lorenzo Bargas, with Ponce the servant, beside the boatswain, Juan Robles, the boatswain's mates, Manuel Viscaya and Roderigo Hurta, and four of the sailors, the negro Babo ordered to be thrown alive into the sea, although they made no resistance, nor begged for anything else but mercy; that the boatswain, Juan Robles, who knew how to swim, kept the longest above water, making acts of contrition, and, in the last words he uttered, charged this deponent to cause mass to be said for his soul to our Lady of Succor:[1] * * * that, during the three days which followed, the deponent, uncertain what fate had befallen the remains of Don Alexandro, frequently asked the negro Babo where they were, and, if still on board, whether they were to be preserved for interment ashore, entreating him so to order it; that the negro Babo answered nothing till the fourth day, when at sunrise, the deponent coming on deck, the negro Babo showed him a skeleton, which had been substituted for the ship's proper figure-head—the image of Christopher Colon,[2] the discoverer of the New World; that the negro Babo asked him whose skeleton that was, and whether, from its whiteness, he should not think it a white's; that, upon discovering his face, the negro Babo, coming close, said words to this effect: "Keep faith with the blacks from here to Senegal, or you shall in spirit, as now in body, follow your leader," pointing to the prow; * * * that the same morning the negro Babo took by succession each Spaniard forward, and asked him whose skeleton that was, and whether, from its whiteness, he should not think it a white's; that each Spaniard covered his face; that then to each the negro Babo repeated the words in the first place said to the deponent; * * * that they (the Spaniards), being then assembled aft, the negro Babo harangued them, saying that he had now done all; that the deponent (as navigator for the negroes) might pursue his course, warning him and all of them that they should, soul and body, go the way of Don Alexandro, if he saw them (the Spaniards) speak, or plot anything against them (the negroes)—a threat which was repeated every day; that, before the events last mentioned, they had tied the cook to throw him overboard, for it is not known what thing they heard him speak, but finally the negro Babo spared his life, at the request of the deponent; that a few days after, the deponent, endeavoring not to omit any means to preserve the lives of the remaining whites, spoke to the negroes peace and tranquillity, and agreed to draw up a paper, signed by the deponent and the sailors who could write, as also by the negro Babo, for himself and all the blacks, in which the deponent obliged himself to carry them to Senegal, and they not to kill any more, and he formally to make over to them the ship, with the cargo, with which they were for that time satisfied and quieted. * * But the next day, the more surely to guard against the sailors' escape, the negro Babo commanded all the boats to be destroyed but the long-boat, which was unseaworthy, and another, a cutter[3] in good condition, which knowing it would yet be wanted for towing the water casks, he had it lowered down into the hold.

* * * * * *

[*Various particulars of the prolonged and perplexed navigation ensuing here follow, with incidents of a calamitous calm, from which portion one passage is extracted, to wit:*]

---

1   *our Lady of Succor*   An epithet of the Virgin Mary.

2   *Christopher Colon*   Christopher Columbus.

3   *cutter*   Boat kept on a warship and typically used for carrying stores and passengers from ship to shore.

—That on the fifth day of the calm, all on board suffering much from the heat, and want of water, and five having died in fits, and mad, the negroes became irritable, and for a chance gesture, which they deemed suspicious—though it was harmless—made by the mate, Raneds, to the deponent in the act of handing a quadrant,[1] they killed him; but that for this they afterwards were sorry, the mate being the only remaining navigator on board, except the deponent.

*   *   *   *   *   *

—That omitting other events, which daily happened, and which can only serve uselessly to recall past misfortunes and conflicts, after seventy-three days' navigation, reckoned from the time they sailed from Nasca, during which they navigated under a scanty allowance of water, and were afflicted with the calms before mentioned, they at last arrived at the island of Santa Maria, on the seventeenth of the month of August, at about six o'clock in the afternoon, at which hour they cast anchor very near the American ship, Bachelor's Delight, which lay in the same bay, commanded by the generous Captain Amasa Delano; but at six o'clock in the morning, they had already descried the port, and the negroes became uneasy, as soon as at distance they saw the ship, not having expected to see one there; that the negro Babo pacified them, assuring them that no fear need be had; that straightway he ordered the figure on the bow to be covered with canvas, as for repairs, and had the decks a little set in order; that for a time the negro Babo and the negro Atufal conferred; that the negro Atufal was for sailing away, but the negro Babo would not, and, by himself, cast about what to do; that at last he came to the deponent, proposing to him to say and do all that the deponent declares to have said and done to the American captain; *   *   *   *   *   *   *   *   * that the negro Babo warned him that if he varied in the least, or uttered any word, or gave any look that should give the least intimation of the past events or present state, he would instantly kill him, with all his companions, showing a dagger, which he carried hid, saying something which, as he understood it, meant that that dagger would be alert as his eye;

that the negro Babo then announced the plan to all his companions, which pleased them; that he then, the better to disguise the truth, devised many expedients, in some of them uniting deceit and defense; that of this sort was the device of the six Ashantees before named, who were his bravoes; that them he stationed on the break of the poop, as if to clean certain hatchets (in cases, which were part of the cargo), but in reality to use them, and distribute them at need, and at a given word he told them; that, among other devices, was the device of presenting Atufal, his right hand man, as chained, though in a moment the chains could be dropped; that in every particular he informed the deponent what part he was expected to enact in every device, and what story he was to tell on every occasion, always threatening him with instant death if he varied in the least: that, conscious that many of the negroes would be turbulent, the negro Babo appointed the four aged negroes, who were calkers, to keep what domestic order they could on the decks; that again and again he harangued the Spaniards and his companions, informing them of his intent, and of his devices, and of the invented story that this deponent was to tell; charging them lest any of them varied from that story; that these arrangements were made and matured during the interval of two or three hours, between their first sighting the ship and the arrival on board of Captain Amasa Delano; that this happened about half-past seven o'clock in the morning, Captain Amasa Delano coming in his boat, and all gladly receiving him; that the deponent, as well as he could force himself, acting then the part of principal owner, and a free captain of the ship, told Captain Amasa Delano, when called upon, that he came from Buenos Ayres, bound to Lima, with three hundred negroes; that off Cape Horn, and in a subsequent fever, many negroes had died; that also, by similar casualties, all the sea officers and the greatest part of the crew had died.

*   *   *   *   *   *

[*And so the deposition goes on, circumstantially recounting the fictitious story dictated to the deponent by Babo, and through the deponent imposed upon Captain Delano; and also recounting the friendly offers of Captain Delano, with other things, but all of which is here omitted. After the fictitious story, etc. the deposition proceeds:*]

---

1   *quadrant*   Instrument for making measurements of angles up to 90 degrees; used for navigation.

* * * * * *

—that the generous Captain Amasa Delano remained on board all the day, till he left the ship anchored at six o'clock in the evening, deponent speaking to him always of his pretended misfortunes, under the fore-mentioned principles, without having had it in his power to tell a single word, or give him the least hint, that he might know the truth and state of things; because the negro Babo, performing the office of an officious servant with all the appearance of submission of the humble slave, did not leave the deponent one moment; that this was in order to observe the deponent's actions and words, for the negro Babo understands well the Spanish; and besides, there were thereabout some others who were constantly on the watch, and likewise understood the Spanish; * * * that upon one occasion, while deponent was standing on the deck conversing with Amasa Delano, by a secret sign the negro Babo drew him (the deponent) aside, the act appearing as if originating with the deponent; that then, he being drawn aside, the negro Babo proposed to him to gain from Amasa Delano full particulars about his ship, and crew, and arms; that the deponent asked "For what?" that the negro Babo answered he might conceive; that, grieved at the prospect of what might overtake the generous Captain Amasa Delano, the deponent at first refused to ask the desired questions, and used every argument to induce the negro Babo to give up this new design; that the negro Babo showed the point of his dagger; that, after the information had been obtained the negro Babo again drew him aside, telling him that that very night he (the deponent) would be captain of two ships, instead of one, for that, great part of the American's ship's crew being to be absent fishing, the six Ashantees, without any one else, would easily take it; that at this time he said other things to the same purpose; that no entreaties availed; that, before Amasa Delano's coming on board, no hint had been given touching the capture of the American ship: that to prevent this project the deponent was powerless; * * *—that in some things his memory is confused, he cannot distinctly recall every event; * * * —that as soon as they had cast anchor at six of the clock in the evening, as has before been stated, the American Captain took leave, to return to his vessel; that upon a sudden impulse, which the deponent

believes to have come from God and his angels, he, after the farewell had been said, followed the generous Captain Amasa Delano as far as the gunwale, where he stayed, under pretense of taking leave, until Amasa Delano should have been seated in his boat; that on shoving off, the deponent sprang from the gunwale into the boat, and fell into it, he knows not how, God guarding him; that—

* * * * * *

[*Here, in the original, follows the account of what further happened at the escape, and how the San Dominick was retaken, and of the passage to the coast; including in the recital many expressions of "eternal gratitude" to the "generous Captain Amasa Delano." The deposition then proceeds with recapitulatory remarks, and a partial renumeration of the negroes, making record of their individual part in the past events, with a view to furnishing, according to command of the court, the data whereon to found the criminal sentences to be pronounced. From this portion is the following;*]

—That he believes that all the negroes, though not in the first place knowing to the design of revolt, when it was accomplished, approved it. * * * That the negro, José, eighteen years old, and in the personal service of Don Alexandro, was the one who communicated the information to the negro Babo, about the state of things in the cabin, before the revolt; that this is known, because, in the preceding midnight, he used to come from his berth, which was under his master's, in the cabin, to the deck where the ringleader and his associates were, and had secret conversations with the negro Babo, in which he was several times seen by the mate; that, one night, the mate drove him away twice; * * that this same negro José was the one who, without being commanded to do so by the negro Babo, as Lecbe and Martinqui were, stabbed his master, Don Alexandro, after he had been dragged half-lifeless to the deck; * * that the mulatto steward, Francesco, was of the first band of revolters, that he was, in all things, the creature and tool of the negro Babo; that, to make his court, he, just before a repast in the cabin, proposed, to the negro Babo, poisoning a dish for the generous Captain Amasa Delano; this is known and believed, because the negroes have said it; but that the negro Babo, having another design, forbade Francesco; * * that the Ashantee Lecbe was one of the worst of them; for that, on the day the ship was retaken, he assisted in the defense of her, with a hatchet in each hand, with one of which he wounded, in the breast, the chief mate of Amasa Delano, in the first act of boarding; this all knew; that, in sight of the deponent, Lecbe struck, with a hatchet, Don Francisco Masa, when, by the negro Babo's orders, he was carrying him to throw him overboard, alive, beside participating in the murder, before mentioned, of Don Alexandro Aranda, and others of the cabin-passengers; that, owing to the fury with which the Ashantees fought in the engagement with the boats, but this Lecbe and Yan survived; that Yan was bad as Lecbe; that Yan was the man who, by Babo's command, willingly prepared the skeleton of Don Alexandro, in a way the negroes afterwards told the deponent, but which he, so long as reason is left him, can never divulge; that Yan and Lecbe were the two who, in a calm by night, riveted the skeleton to the bow; this also the negroes told him; that the negro Babo was he who traced the inscription below it; that the negro Babo was the plotter from first to last; he ordered every murder, and was the helm and keel of the revolt; that Atufal was his lieutenant in all; but Atufal, with his own hand, committed no murder; nor did the negro Babo; * * that Atufal was shot, being killed in the fight with the boats, ere boarding; * * that the negresses, of age, were knowing to the revolt, and testified themselves satisfied at the death of their master, Don Alexandro; that, had the negroes not restrained them, they would have tortured to death, instead of simply killing, the Spaniards slain by command of the negro Babo; that the negresses used their utmost influence to have the deponent made away with; that, in the various acts of murder, they sang songs and danced—not gaily, but solemnly; and before the engagement with the boats, as well as during the action, they sang melancholy songs to the negroes, and that this melancholy tone was more inflaming than a different one would have been, and was so intended; that all this is believed, because the negroes have said it.—that of the thirty-six men of the crew, exclusive of the passengers (all of whom are now dead), which the deponent had knowledge of, six only remained alive, with four cabin-boys and ship-boys, not included with

the crew; * *—that the negroes broke an arm of one of the cabin-boys and gave him strokes with hatchets.

[*Then follow various random disclosures referring to various periods of time. The following are extracted;*]

—That during the presence of Captain Amasa Delano on board, some attempts were made by the sailors, and one by Hermenegildo Gandix, to convey hints to him of the true state of affairs; but that these attempts were ineffectual, owing to fear of incurring death, and, furthermore, owing to the devices which offered contradictions to the true state of affairs, as well as owing to the generosity and piety of Amasa Delano incapable of sounding such wickedness; * * * that Luys Galgo, a sailor about sixty years of age, and formerly of the king's navy, was one of those who sought to convey tokens to Captain Amasa Delano; but his intent, though undiscovered, being suspected, he was, on a pretense, made to retire out of sight, and at last into the hold, and there was made away with. This the negroes have since said; * * * that one of the ship-boys feeling, from Captain Amasa Delano's presence, some hopes of release, and not having enough prudence, dropped some chance-word respecting his expectations, which being overheard and understood by a slave-boy with whom he was eating at the time, the latter struck him on the head with a knife, inflicting a bad wound, but of which the boy is now healing; that likewise, not long before the ship was brought to anchor, one of the seamen, steering at the time, endangered himself by letting the blacks remark some expression in his countenance, arising from a cause similar to the above; but this sailor, by his heedful after conduct, escaped; * * * that these statements are made to show the court that from the beginning to the end of the revolt, it was impossible for the deponent and his men to act otherwise than they did; * * *—that the third clerk, Hermenegildo Gandix, who before had been forced to live among the seamen, wearing a seaman's habit, and in all respects appearing to be one for the time; he, Gandix, was killed by a musket ball fired through mistake from the boats before boarding; having in his fright run up the mizzen-rigging, calling to the boats— "don't board," lest upon their boarding the negroes should kill him; that this inducing the Americans to believe he some way favored the cause of the negroes, they fired two balls at him, so that he fell wounded from the rigging, and was drowned in the sea; * * *—that the young Don Joaquin, Marques de Aramboalaza, like Hermenegildo Gandix, the third clerk, was degraded to the office and appearance of a common seaman; that upon one occasion when Don Joaquin shrank, the negro Babo commanded the Ashantee Lecbe to take tar and heat it, and pour it upon Don Joaquin's hands; * * *—that Don Joaquin was killed owing to another mistake of the Americans, but one impossible to be avoided, as upon the approach of the boats, Don Joaquin, with a hatchet tied edge out and upright to his hand, was made by the negroes to appear on the bulwarks; whereupon, seen with arms in his hands and in a questionable attitude, he was shot for a renegade seaman; * * *—that on the person of Don Joaquin was found secreted a jewel, which, by papers that were discovered, proved to have been meant for the shrine of our Lady of Mercy in Lima; a votive offering, beforehand prepared and guarded, to attest his gratitude, when he should have landed in Peru, his last destination, for the safe conclusion of his entire voyage from Spain; * * *—that the jewel, with the other effects of the late Don Joaquin, is in the custody of the brethren of the Hospital de Sacerdotes,[1] awaiting the disposition of the honorable court; * * *—that, owing to the condition of the deponent, as well as the haste in which the boats departed for the attack, the Americans were not forewarned that there were, among the apparent crew, a passenger and one of the clerks disguised by the negro Babo; * * *—that, beside the negroes killed in the action, some were killed after the capture and re-anchoring at night, when shackled to the ring-bolts on deck; that these deaths were committed by the sailors, ere they could be prevented. That so soon as informed of it, Captain Amasa Delano used all his authority, and, in particular with his own hand, struck down Martinez Gola, who, having found a razor in the pocket of an old jacket of his, which one of the shackled negroes had on, was aiming it at the negro's throat; that the noble Captain Amasa Delano also wrenched from the hand of Bartholomew Barlo a dagger, secreted at the time of the massacre of the whites, with which

he was in the act of stabbing a shackled negro, who, the same day, with another negro, had thrown him down and jumped upon him; * * *—that, for all the events, befalling through so long a time, during which the ship was in the hands of the negro Babo, he cannot here give account; but that, what he has said is the most substantial of what occurs to him at present, and is the truth under the oath which he has taken; which declaration he affirmed and ratified, after hearing it read to him.

He said that he is twenty-nine years of age, and broken in body and mind; that when finally dismissed by the court, he shall not return home to Chili, but betake himself to the monastery on Mount Agonia without; and signed with his honor, and crossed himself, and, for the time, departed as he came, in his litter, with the monk Infelez, to the Hospital de Sacerdotes.

BENITO CERENO.

DOCTOR ROZAS.

If the Deposition have served as the key to fit into the lock of the complications which precede it, then, as a vault whose door has been flung back, the San Dominick's hull lies open to-day.

Hitherto the nature of this narrative, besides rendering the intricacies in the beginning unavoidable, has more or less required that many things, instead of being set down in the order of occurrence, should be retrospectively, or irregularly given; this last is the case with the following passages, which will conclude the account:

During the long, mild voyage to Lima, there was, as before hinted, a period during which the sufferer a little recovered his health, or, at least in some degree, his tranquillity. Ere the decided relapse which came, the two captains had many cordial conversations—their fraternal unreserve in singular contrast with former withdrawments.

Again and again it was repeated, how hard it had been to enact the part forced on the Spaniard by Babo.

"Ah, my dear friend," Don Benito once said, "at those very times when you thought me so morose and ungrateful, nay, when, as you now admit, you half thought me plotting your murder, at those very times my heart was frozen; I could not look at you, thinking of what, both on board this ship and your own,

---

[1]   *Hospital de Sacerdotes*   A place where priests would take care of the sick or needy ("sacerdotes" means "priests" in Spanish).

hung, from other hands, over my kind benefactor. And as God lives, Don Amasa, I know not whether desire for my own safety alone could have nerved me to that leap into your boat, had it not been for the thought that, did you, unenlightened, return to your ship, you, my best friend, with all who might be with you, stolen upon, that night, in your hammocks, would never in this world have wakened again. Do but think how you walked this deck, how you sat in this cabin, every inch of ground mined into honey-combs under you. Had I dropped the least hint, made the least advance towards an understanding between us, death, explosive death—yours as mine—would have ended the scene."

"True, true," cried Captain Delano, starting, "you have saved my life, Don Benito, more than I yours; saved it, too, against my knowledge and will."

"Nay, my friend," rejoined the Spaniard, courteous even to the point of religion, "God charmed your life, but you saved mine. To think of some things you did—those smilings and chattings, rash pointings and gesturings. For less than these, they slew my mate, Raneds; but you had the Prince of Heaven's safe-conduct through all ambuscades."[1]

"Yes, all is owing to Providence, I know: but the temper of my mind that morning was more than commonly pleasant, while the sight of so much suffering, more apparent than real, added to my good-nature, compassion, and charity, happily interweaving the three. Had it been otherwise, doubtless, as you hint, some of my interferences might have ended unhappily enough. Besides, those feelings I spoke of enabled me to get the better of momentary distrust, at times when acuteness might have cost me my life, without saving another's. Only at the end did my suspicions get the better of me, and you know how wide of the mark they then proved."

"Wide, indeed," said Don Benito, sadly; "you were with me all day; stood with me, sat with me, talked with me, looked at me, ate with me, drank with me; and yet, your last act was to clutch for a monster, not only an innocent man, but the most pitiable of all men. To such degree may malign machinations and deceptions impose. So far may even the best man err, in judging the conduct of one with the recesses of whose condition he is not acquainted. But you were

forced to it; and you were in time undeceived. Would that, in both respects, it was so ever, and with all men."

"You generalize, Don Benito; and mournfully enough. But the past is passed; why moralize upon it? Forget it. See, yon bright sun has forgotten it all, and the blue sea, and the blue sky; these have turned over new leaves."

"Because they have no memory," he dejectedly replied; "because they are not human."

"But these mild trades[2] that now fan your cheek, do they not come with a human-like healing to you? Warm friends, steadfast friends are the trades."

"With their steadfastness they but waft me to my tomb, Señor," was the foreboding response.

"You are saved," cried Captain Delano, more and more astonished and pained; "you are saved: what has cast such a shadow upon you?"

"The negro."

There was silence, while the moody man sat, slowly and unconsciously gathering his mantle about him, as if it were a pall.[3]

There was no more conversation that day.

But if the Spaniard's melancholy sometimes ended in muteness upon topics like the above, there were others upon which he never spoke at all; on which, indeed, all his old reserves were piled. Pass over the worst, and, only to elucidate let an item or two of these be cited. The dress, so precise and costly, worn by him on the day whose events have been narrated, had not willingly been put on. And that silver-mounted sword, apparent symbol of despotic command, was not, indeed, a sword, but the ghost of one. The scabbard, artificially stiffened, was empty.

As for the black—whose brain, not body, had schemed and led the revolt, with the plot—his slight frame, inadequate to that which it held, had at once yielded to the superior muscular strength of his captor, in the boat. Seeing all was over, he uttered no sound, and could not be forced to. His aspect seemed to say, since I cannot do deeds, I will not speak words. Put in irons in the hold, with the rest, he was carried to Lima. During the passage, Don Benito did not visit him. Nor then, nor at any time after, would he look at him. Before the tribunal he refused. When pressed by

---

[1]   *ambuscades* Ambushes.

[2]   *trades* Trade winds.

[3]   *pall* A cloth spread over a coffin, or a shroud over a dead body.

the judges he fainted. On the testimony of the sailors alone rested the legal identity of Babo.

Some months after, dragged to the gibbet[1] at the tail of a mule, the black met his voiceless end. The body was burned to ashes; but for many days, the head, that hive of subtlety, fixed on a pole in the Plaza, met, unabashed, the gaze of the whites; and across the Plaza looked towards St. Bartholomew's church, in whose vaults slept then, as now, the recovered bones of Aranda: and across the Rimac bridge looked towards the monastery, on Mount Agonia without; where, three months after being dismissed by the court, Benito Cereno, borne on the bier, did, indeed, follow his leader.

—1856

from *Battle-Pieces and Aspects of the War*[2]

THE PORTENT
(1859)

*H*anging from the beam,
 Slowly swaying (such the law),
Gaunt the shadow on your green,

---

[1]   *gibbet*   Gallows; place of execution.

[2]   Melville added the following dedication: "The Battle-Pieces in this volume are dedicated to the memory of the three hundred thousand who in the war for the maintenance of the union fell devotedly under the flag of their fathers." An authorial note also follows the title page:

With few exceptions, the Pieces in this volume originated in an impulse imparted by the fall of Richmond [Sunday April 2, 1865; Richmond, Virginia, was the Confederate capital]. They were composed without reference to collective arrangement, but, being brought together in review, naturally fall into the order assumed.

The events and incidents of the conflict—making up a whole, in varied amplitude, corresponding with the geographical area covered by the war—from these but a few themes have been taken, such as for any cause chanced to imprint themselves upon the mind.

The aspects which the strife as a memory assumes are as manifold as are the moods of involuntary meditation—moods variable, and at times widely at variance. Yielding instinctively, one after another, to feelings not inspired from any one source exclusively, and unmindful, without purposing to be, of consistency, I seem, in most of these verses, to have but placed a harp in a window [an "aeolian" harp, that sounds out music passively when wind blows across it], and noted the contrasted airs which wayward winds have played upon the strings.

Shenandoah![3]
5 *The cut is on the crown*
(Lo, John Brown),[4]
And the stabs shall heal no more.

Hidden in the cap
Is the anguish none can draw;
10 *So your future veils its face,*
Shenandoah!
But the streaming beard is shown
(Weird° John Brown),   uncanny, fateful
The meteor[5] *of the war.*

—1866

A Utilitarian View of the Monitor's Fight[6]

*P*lain be the phrase, yet apt the verse,
 More ponderous than nimble;
For since grimed War here laid aside
His Orient pomp,[7] 'twould ill befit
5   Overmuch to ply

---

[3]   *Shenandoah*   River that runs through Virginia and joins the Potomac at Harpers Ferry.

[4]   *John Brown*   Abolitionist who initiated a planned campaign against slavery in the Southern states by raiding the U.S. arsenal at Harpers Ferry in Virginia (now West Virginia) on 16–18 October 1859. Brown was tried and hanged for treason on 2 December 1859; his last words were written down on a scrap of paper: "I John Brown am now quite certain that the crimes of this guilty land will never be purged away; but with Blood. I had as I now think vainly flattered myself that without very much bloodshed; it might be done." The raid on Harpers Ferry is widely seen by historians as a prelude to the Civil War that erupted in 1861.

[5]   *meteor*   Meteors and other atmospheric phenomena were often interpreted as presaging conflict and death; see also Henry David Thoreau's essay "The Last Days of John Brown" (1860): "John Brown's career for the last six weeks of his life was meteor-like, flashing through the darkness in which we live."

[6]   *Utilitarian*   Materialistic, practical; *Monitor's Fight*   Battle of Hampton Roads, a naval battle fought on 8–9 March 1862 where the Elizabeth, Nansemond, and James Rivers meet before flowing out into Chesapeake Bay in Virginia. The battle was the first in which armored, steam-powered warships fought each other (the *USS Monitor* vs. the *CSS Virginia*); neither ship was able to defeat the other, and the battle ended indecisively. The battle had a significant impact on navies around the world, triggering an arms race in which every navy sought to develop ironclad warships.

[7]   *Orient pomp*   Luxurious and splendid show.

The rhyme's barbaric cymbal.

Hail to victory without the gaud°   *showiness*
    Of glory; zeal that needs no fans
Of banners; plain mechanic power
10 Plied cogently in War now placed—
        Where War belongs—
        Among the trades and artisans.

Yet this was battle, and intense—
        Beyond the strife of flects heroic;
15 Deadlier, closer, calm 'mid storm;
No passion; all went on by crank,
        Pivot, and screw,
        And calculations of caloric.°   *heat*

Needless to dwell; the story's known.
20   The ringing of those plates on plates
Still ringeth round the world—
The clangor of the blacksmiths' fray.
        The anvil-din
        Resounds this message from the Fates:

25 War yet shall be, and to the end;
        But war-paint shows the streaks of weather;
War yet shall be, but warriors
Are now but operatives; War's made
        Less grand than Peace,
30   And a singe runs through lace and feather.
—1866

Popular Literature and Print Culture, 1820–Reconstruction: A Visual Sampler

The following images offer only a glimpse of popular print culture in the mid-nineteenth century. For a more thorough sampling of popular literature and print culture, see the "Popular Literature and Print Culture" omnibus sections in this anthology's online component.

⌘ ⌘ ⌘

anonymous, Davy Crockett Tales

In 1835, a year before Davy Crockett's death during the Texas Revolution, a Nashville company called Snag and Sawyer published *Davy Crockett's Almanac*, a short book that combined astronomical information (times of sunrise and sunset, dates of full and new moons, etc.) with essays regarding wildlife, and stories about Crockett and other figures. The *Almanac* became a regular annual publication, at first through Snag and Sawyer and then in the 1840s through the publishing firm of Turner and Fisher, with offices in Philadelphia and New York and nationwide distribution. The early editions may have exaggerated the facts to some extent in their telling of tales about Crockett, but they remained largely factual—as they did in their essays on such topics as "Methods of Catching Wild Horses on the Prairies of Texas." Under the Turner and Fisher imprint, however, the tall tales became more and more detached from reality, with Crockett portrayed in light-hearted fashion as an almost mythical figure—the nineteenth-century equivalent of a Marvel superhero in the twenty-first century. The tall tales featuring Crockett include "Crockett's Wonderful Escape Up Niagara Falls" (1844), "Crockett among the Cannibals" (1854), and "Crockett and the (Black) Emperor of Haiti" (1856). Later issues also include tall tales featuring other heroic figures—Kit Carson notable among them.

The tales reproduced on the following pages are from *Crockett's Almanac, 1846: Scenes in River Life, Feats on the Lakes, Manners in the Backwoods, Adventures in Texas, Etc. Etc.*

Crockett himself seems to have been a figure very different from that portrayed in many of the tall tales. Though renowned for his exploits as a "frontiersman," he also made a strong impression as a politician, serving in the U.S. House of Representatives from 1827 to 1831 and again from 1833 to 1835. Something of his character comes through in the report published in the 28 June 1830 issue of the Raleigh, North Carolina *Raleigh Register*, describing Crockett delivering a speech against Andrew Jackson's Indian Removal Act of 1830.

> There have been so many queer stories told of this gentleman, and so many quaint sayings attributed to him, that most persons … have taken up the idea that he is one of those rough bears. … Whoever reads these remarks will be soon convinced that he possesses qualities both of the head and heart which would do credit to any man, whatever may be the want of polish in his manners, or the homeliness of his language.

The speech itself is a powerful indictment of the provisions of an act designed to ensure that "the Indians were to have no privileges allowed them while the white men were to have all—now, if this was not oppression with a vengeance, he did not know what was."

For more on the Texas Revolution and the attack on the Alamo, in which Crockett likely died, see the "Contexts: Expansion, Native American Expulsion, and 'Manifest Destiny'" section elsewhere in this volume.

Chester Harding, *David Crockett*, 1834 (detail).

"I LEAVE THIS RULÆ FOR OTHERS, WHEN I'M DEAD,
BE ALWAYS SURE YOU'RE RIGHT, THEN GO-AHEAD."

CROCKETT'S
18 | ALMANAC. | 46

Scenes in River Life, Feats on the Lakes, Manners in the Back
Woods, Adventures in Texas, &c. &c.

Crockett's wonderful escape up the Niagara Falls, on his Pet Alligator.

PUBLISHED BY TURNER & FISHER:
No. 15 NORTH SIXTH STREET, PHILADELPHIA;
AND, N. CHATHAM STREET, NEW YORK.
Toy Books, Song Books, Almanacs, Colored Prints, Juvenile Works, Valentines, &c.

Cover, *Crockett's 1846 Almanac.*

CROCKETT DRINKING UP THE GULF
BETWEEN THE UNITED STATES AND TEXAS.

You see, I told you in my last year's speech, that I go in for Texas and Annexation, clar up to the very gravel stone, in spite o' all the Mixy Mexican Spanish brown an red niggars; an the Malgamation party in Uncle Sam's lands, who go in for Annexation with the blackies. I've heard all the four mile speeches, an ten mile petitions on the subject, an' I have come to the clar conclusion that the only thing that raley prevents the annexation, is the leetle deep bellied pond called a Gulf between Uncle Sam an Texas; it stands like the Gulf between the rich man and Lazarus in the big book. It struck me like a thunderbolt, that if we war only to take that are deep Allegator water out o' the way, it would put an end to all no-go-ciation legislation, an all that sort o' national nonsense, for then little Texas an the States would annex themselves jist as nat'ral as two pumpkin vines, or as a gal o' seventeen annexes herself to a walken sprout o' lightnin, without the advice an consent o' the old folks. So in order to remove this one little liquid obstacle out o' the way o' sich a great national wedding, I've jist straddled across the neck o' this pond, an like Captain Colossus straddlen the Roads, an commence drinkin it up instanter. You see, when I open my flesh tunnel, it must come like a walken water spout, swaller arter swaller, till the bottom walks up as bair as a pumpkin, an then, if any human crittur, Yankee, Texian or Mexican, dure's to oppose instanter annexation, saw me up if I don't swallow them too, an' arter that I'll jist mount my alligator, travel into the middle o' Mexico, lick all the tarnal Royalists out o' thar tarnal mustaches, strip Santa Anna of his powership, show him all naked in his villany, an' wooden-legged ambition; teach the natives, red niggers, creoles, and the true bred Yankee Independence an Republicanism; an, then run for President myself, an if a better man beat me, why it will be all the better for human natur, an' I'll jist treat him to as much hog snappen jelly and whiskey as he can eat for a bull term, and hold myself ready to lick all traitors an dishonest politicians into true Republican decency, an if the critturs can't get along arter that, why I'll drink every spoonful of water between her an the United States, and annex her myself, in spite o' old Spain, an all the monkies called monarchs in creation.

In addition to "Crockett Drinking Up the Gulf" and "Crockett Catching a Mexican Tigress" (see next page), the 1846 issue of the *Almanac* included a variety of other tall tales featuring Davy Crockett, among them "Crockett Riding His Pet Bear Up a Tree," "Crockett Dancing Fire out of a Rock, and Burning the Indians," "Crockett and Ben Hardin Skating a Party of Indians into an Air Hole," and "Crockett Splitting the Great Mississippi Snag Alligator."

CROCKETT CATCHING A MEXICAN TIGRESS.

While I was in Texas, I met my old friend General Jimmy Raymond, the wild beast collector for all creation; he wanted about fifty men to go into Mexico, to catch an all tearin she tiger, an her young cubs for his great Zoological Institute. Well, soon as he spoke o' fifty men, I broke out instinctively into a horse laugh fit that lasted nearly an hour, It fairly shook the clothes off my back. "Fifty men," says I? "Yes," says he "Why," says I, "jist you foller me, to the haunt of the crittur, you want, an if I don't kidnap the hull tiger family, then call me a sucken fawn." "Agreed," says he, an off we started; we soon got near the tarnal night swamp spot; I walked into it about a hundred yards, feelin my way, till I saw a couple o' small lights which turned out to be a he tiger's eyes keepin watch for his wife an family; he was just springin at me when I caught hold of the two paws of the crittur, twisted 'em, an tied 'em around his neck so tarnal tight, that he died an choked instanter. I then walked up to the nest, grabbed Mrs. Tiger by the throat, pared off her nails, an held her till I choked half of her temper out, put her four young ones in my great skin cap, an marched out to the General, draggen their mommy arter me by the throat as docile as a kitten.

anonymous, *Crockett Catching a Mexican Tigress*, 1846.

Popular Novels in Print Culture

See the website component of this anthology for selections from many of the popular novels whose title pages are reproduced below.

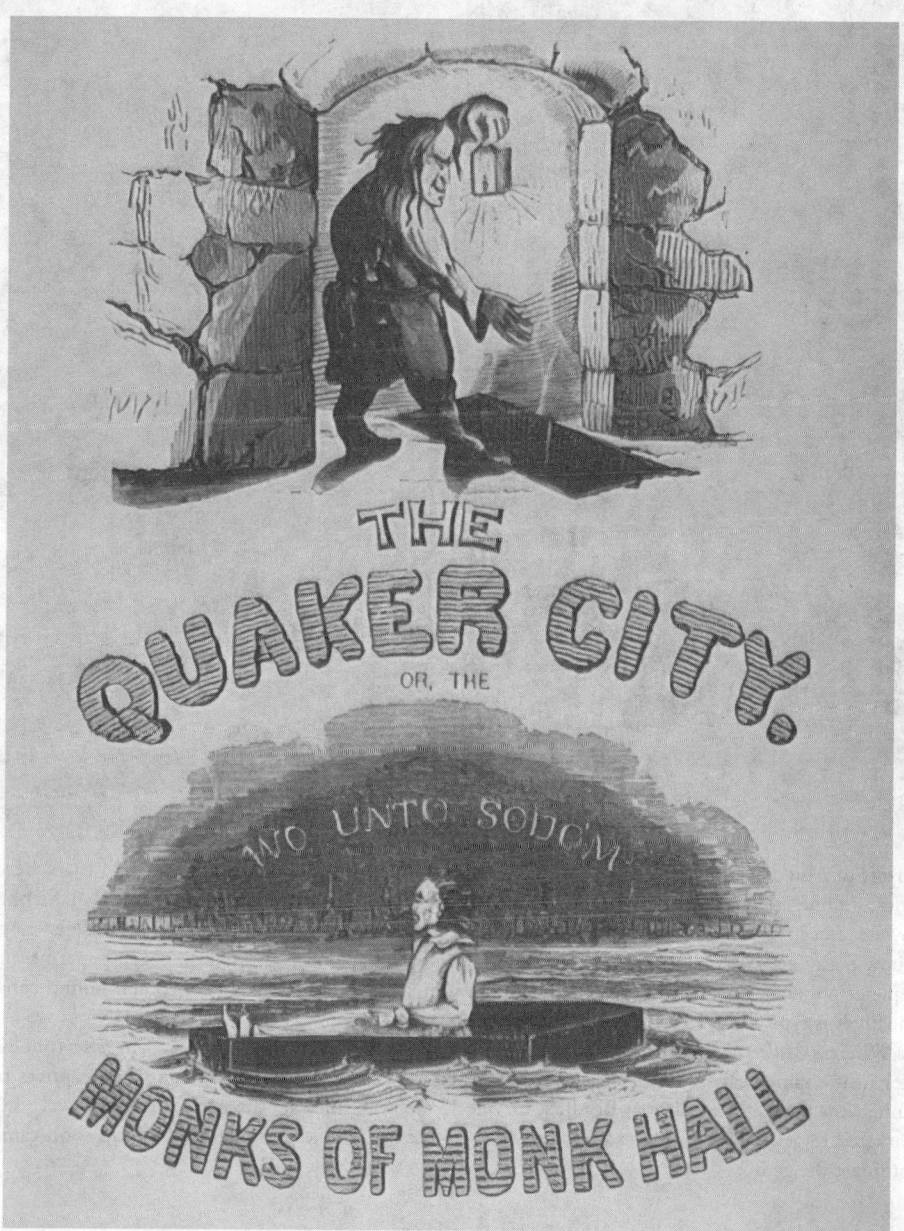

F.O.C. Darley, 1876 title page for George Lippard's *The Quaker City; or The Monks of Monk-Hall: A Romance of Philadelphia Life, Mystery, and Crime* (first published in 1845). A lurid account of crime and debauchery in Philadelphia, the novel is often considered the first American incarnation of the "city-mystery" genre, which purports to reveal the worlds of crime and moral debauchery that underlie the respectable exteriors of well-known cities.

Covers of Ann S. Stephens's *Malaeska: The Indian Wife of the White Hunter* (1860), the first in Beadle's series of dime novels; and of Edward S. Ellis, *Seth Jones; or, The Captives of the Frontier* (1860). Stephens's novel had been serialized over twenty years earlier (in the *Ladies' Companion*); reissued in this new format, it now became a great success in book form—and inexpensive novels printed on cheap paper became a staple of popular American literature. (By comparison, a one-volume novel printed and bound conventionally was typically priced in 1860 at 75 cents or more.)

Whereas *Malaeska* is focused on the experience of an Indigenous woman, Ellis's *Seth Jones* (published later in the same year by Beadle's) is a male-focused tale of a white hunter saving white captives from Mohawk warriors. The editor at Beadle's, Orville J. Victor, termed it "the perfect Dime Novel"; it was marketed to achieve even greater popularity than *Malaeska*, and stories of male heroism soon came to dominate the genre.

Horatio Alger's novel *Ragged Dick* (1867) was so popular that it formed the template not only for Alger's own subsequent novels but also for an entire sub-genre of fiction featuring a young white man who, faced with the hardships of poverty, retains his virtue and rises to respectability. Following the novel's initial success, the A.K. Loring book publishing company made *Ragged Dick* the first volume in the "Ragged Dick Series," using the above illustration in each. The four boys pictured include two boot-blacks (center and bottom right), a luggage boy (left), and a newspaper hawker (upper right). The "Ragged Dick Series" was followed by several other series of novels, including the "Luck and Pluck Series" (1871–75) and the "Ways to Success Series" (1887–90).

Frances Ellen Watkins Harper
1825 – 1911

One of the most important and most popular African American poets and novelists of the nineteenth century, Frances Ellen Watkins Harper was also among the century's most influential political activists; both through her writing and through her activism she was deeply involved in the antebellum and the post-Civil War struggles for black rights and for women's rights. As a speaker, Harper identified the interconnectedness of the injustices of nineteenth-century American society, declaring: "We are all bound up together in one great bundle of humanity, and society cannot trample on the weakest and feeblest of its members without receiving the curse in its own soul. ... Society cannot afford to neglect the enlightenment of any class of its members."

Harper was born Frances Ellen Watkins to free parents in Baltimore, Maryland, then a slaveholding state. Her parents both died when she was about three years old, leaving her to be raised by an uncle, the abolitionist educator, minister, and doctor William Watkins. Harper received a remarkably thorough education at the institution run by her uncle, the William Watkins Academy for Negro Youth, where she studied until the age of thirteen. She subsequently found employment as a seamstress and domestic servant in the home of a wealthy family, where she was encouraged to read from their extensive book collection in her spare time, and, as the years went on, to write her own poetry. By the age of about twenty Harper had written enough poems to fill a volume; *Forest Leaves* was published in the mid-to-late 1840s. (For many years this volume was deemed lost, but in May 2013 one extant, undated copy was discovered in the library of the Maryland Historical Society.) Many of the poems in this early collection would later be reworked and republished in periodicals and in Harper's later collections.

Harper left Maryland in 1850, shortly after the passage of the Fugitive Slave Act. Her first stop was Ohio, where she taught sewing at the Columbus Union Seminary; she then moved to Pennsylvania, where she continued to work as a teacher but also became more engaged in the antislavery movement (and, more broadly, in the struggle against racial prejudice). Following the passage of a law in Maryland in 1853 forbidding free African Americans from re-entering the state—making her effectively an exile—Harper decided to abandon her teaching post and become fully involved in the abolitionist cause. She began a lifelong friendship with William Still (later a renowned historian of the Underground Railroad) and was invited to live with him and his wife, where she continued to write poetry to support herself, submitting pieces to abolitionist newspapers such as *The Liberator* and *Frederick Douglass' Paper*. In 1854, Harper traveled to Massachusetts and delivered her first antislavery speech in New Bedford; she then traveled to Maine, where she found employment as an official paid lecturer for the Maine Anti-Slavery Society.

That same year, Harper released the collection *Poems on Miscellaneous Subjects*. The 48-page pamphlet was immensely successful; it was sold at Harper's lectures and went through about twenty editions over the next twenty years, selling 10,000 individual copies by 1857. The collection touched on themes such as Christian faith, alcoholism, and poverty as well as on slavery, and concluded with a number of short essays; in the final piece, "The Colored People in America," Harper comments on the oppression experienced by both free and enslaved African Americans across the country.

Harper ardently supported the abolitionist raid led by John Brown in 1859; she sent letters of support to his imprisoned followers, and sent her poem "Bury Me in a Free Land" (earlier published in the *Anti-Slavery Bugle*) to a man awaiting execution for his participation in the raid. That year Harper also published the story "The Two Offers" in the *Anglo-American Magazine*. Touching on themes such as class, marriage, and domestic abuse, the story featured a protagonist who, much like Harper, was unmarried and was trying to make a living as a writer. Harper herself did marry Fenton Harper, a widower, shortly after the story's publication, temporarily slowing the pace of her public antislavery career to adapt to her new role as a homemaker and as stepmother to his three children. The Harpers had one child together, Mary, before Fenton died in 1864. He left behind significant debts, and (although Frances had herself purchased the farm on which they'd lived) all her property as well as his was seized by authorities to pay off these debts. She was left almost destitute—a demeaning experience that helped to fuel Harper's passion for the cause of women's rights. "They left me one thing—and that was a looking glass!" she memorably proclaimed in a ground-breaking speech delivered in New York at the Eleventh National Women's Rights Convention in 1866 that has come to be known by the title "We Are All Bound Up Together." Though the speech was well received at the convention, it received little or no mention in nineteenth-century accounts of the suffrage movement; not until the twenty-first century has its importance as a statement of principles now associated with the concept of intersectionality become fully acknowledged.

During the early years of Reconstruction Harper traveled extensively in the South, where she lectured and helped establish educational institutions for freed men and women. She became highly renowned for her lectures, which were often very long and delivered extemporaneously, and in which she commented frequently on her hopes for the future of African Americans: "If we have had no past, it is well for us to look hopefully to the future—for the shadows bear the promise of a brighter coming day." In 1869 she returned to Pennsylvania—where she would live with her daughter Mary for the rest of her life—and began work on a new poetry collection, *Sketches of Southern Life* (1872). The collection included a cycle of poems featuring the character Aunt Chloe, a formerly enslaved woman whose reminiscences of slavery and of Reconstruction in the South presented a challenge to stereotypical literary portrayals of enslaved people, and would influence poetic portrayals of slavery and of African American vernacular speech for decades to come.

Between 1869 and 1882 Harper published three novels in serial form—*Minnie's Sacrifice* (1869), *Sowing and Reaping* (1876–77), and *Trial and Triumph* (1888–89)—while continuing to fight to better the lives of African Americans and of women. Harper's work was affected by the schism that occurred in the women's movement in the years leading up to the Fifteenth Amendment. Many white feminists, including Stanton and Anthony, decried the decision implicit in the Fifteenth Amendment to put the interests of African Americans—and of African American men in particular—ahead of those of women; their rhetoric in many cases became increasingly shaded with racism. For her own part, Harper supported the Fifteenth Amendment, predicting that black women would not receive justice under the law as women until they began to receive justice under the law as black.

Harper's fourth and final work of fiction, *Iola Leroy; or, Shadows Uplifted* (1892), explored themes such as mixed-race identity, racial "passing," and the sexual violence experienced by enslaved women. For many years *Iola Leroy* was thought to have been the first full-length novel published by a black woman in the United States. (*Our Nig*, which had been published anonymously in 1859 and long assumed to have been written by a white author, is now recognized as having been written by black author Harriet Wilson; Harper's first three novels, meanwhile, had escaped the attention of scholars until their rediscovery by literary historian Frances Smith Foster in the mid-1990s.) *Iola Leroy* received largely favorable reviews; it was praised not least of all for pleading "the cause of a race whose needs were never more pressing ... and whose destiny is now more closely interwoven with those of the nation than ever." Its significance, however, was downplayed in the twentieth century by various male African American authorities and white women scholars. Like her other work, it has received renewed attention in the twenty-first century.

Harper remained politically engaged until her death in 1911. Her reputation suffered considerably for many decades following her death. The sentimentalism of much of her poetry had fallen out of fashion, as had poetry that dealt explicitly with social, political, and moral concerns. The general neglect of black authors and activists by white scholars played a part as well; it is perhaps telling that in the multi-volume *History of Woman Suffrage* (1881–1922), authored in part by Stanton and Anthony, Harper is not mentioned once.

NOTE ON THE TEXTS: Most of the texts included here are the versions that first appeared in collected editions of Harper's poetry. To that generalization there is a notable exception; the text of "Bury Me in a Free Land" is taken from the 20 November 1858 issue of *The Anti-Slavery Bugle*. The text of "We Are All Bound Up Together" is taken from the transcription included in *Proceedings of the Eleventh Woman's Rights Convention, May 1866*. Spelling and punctuation have been modernized in accordance with the practices of this anthology.

⌘ ⌘ ⌘

The Slave Mother

Heard you that shriek? It rose
   So wildly on the air,
It seemed as if a burdened heart
   Was breaking in despair.

5 Saw you those hands so sadly clasped—
   The bowed and feeble head—
The shuddering of that fragile form—
   That look of grief and dread?

Saw you the sad, imploring eye?
10   Its every glance was pain,
As if a storm of agony
   Were sweeping through the brain.

She is a mother pale with fear,
   Her boy clings to her side,
15 And in her kirtle° vainly tries   *dress*
   His trembling form to hide.

He is not hers, although she bore
   For him a mother's pains;
He is not hers, although her blood
20   Is coursing through his veins!

He is not hers, for cruel hands
   May rudely tear apart
The only wreath of household love
   That binds her breaking heart.

25 His love has been a joyous light
   That o'er her pathway smiled,
A fountain gushing ever new,
   Amid life's desert wild.

His lightest word has been a tone
30   Of music round her heart,
Their lives a streamlet blent in° one—   *blended into*
   Oh, Father! must they part?

They tear him from her circling arms,
   Her last and fond embrace:
35 Oh! never more may her sad eyes
   Gaze on his mournful face.

No marvel, then, these bitter shrieks
   Disturb the listening air;
She is a mother, and her heart
40   Is breaking in despair.
   —1854

Bible Defense of Slavery

Take sackcloth[1] of the darkest dye,
  And shroud the pulpits round!
Servants of him that cannot lie,
  Sit mourning on the ground.

5 Let holy horror blanch each cheek,
  Pale every brow with fears;
And rocks and stones, if ye could speak,
  Ye well might melt to tears!

Let sorrow breathe in every tone,
10 In every strain ye raise;
Insult not God's majestic throne
  With th' mockery of praise.

A "reverend" man, whose light should be
  The guide of age and youth,
15 Brings to the shrine of Slavery
  The sacrifice of truth!

For the direst wrong by man imposed,
  Since Sodom's[2] fearful cry,
The word of life has been unclosed,
20 To give your God the lie.

Oh! when ye pray for heathen lands,
  And plead for their dark shores,
Remember Slavery's cruel hands
  Make heathens at your doors!
  —1854

Eliza Harris[3]

Like a fawn from the arrow, startled and wild,
  A woman swept by us, bearing a child;
In her eye was the night of a settled despair,
And her brow was o'ershaded with anguish and care.

5 She was nearing the river—in reaching the brink,
She heeded no danger, she paused not to think;
For she is a mother—her child is a slave—
And she'll give him his freedom, or find him a grave!

It was a vision to haunt us, that innocent face—
10 So pale in its aspect, so fair in its grace;
As the tramp of the horse and the bay of the hound,
With the fetters that gall,° were   *chafe*
  trailing the ground!

She was nerved by despair, and strengthened by woe,
As she leaped o'er the chasms that yawned from below;
15 Death howled in the tempest, and raved in the blast,
But she heard not the sound till the danger was past.

Oh! how shall I speak of my proud country's shame?
Of the stains on her glory, how give them their name?
How say that her banner in mockery waves—
20 Her "star spangled banner"—o'er millions of slaves?

How say that the lawless may torture and chase
A woman whose crime is the hue of her face?
How the depths of the forest may echo around
With the shrieks of despair, and the bay of the hound?

25 With her step on the ice, and her arm on her child,
The danger was fearful, the pathway was wild;
But, aided by Heaven, she gained a free shore,
Where the friends of humanity opened their door.

So fragile and lovely, so fearfully pale,
30 Like a lily that bends to the breath of the gale,

---

1 *sackcloth* Coarse fabric traditionally used for mourning or penitential garments.

2 *Sodom* City destroyed by God in the Book of Genesis as punishment for the sinfulness of its inhabitants.

3 The poem takes inspiration from the character of the same name in Harriet Beecher Stowe's 1852 *Uncle Tom's Cabin*; Eliza Harris, a young enslaved woman, decides to flee her enslavers when she finds out they intend on selling her young son Harry. Stowe's version of events is in turn said to have been inspired by that of a real woman who had escaped slavery.

Save the heave of her breast, and the sway of her hair,
You'd have thought her a statue of fear and despair.

In agony close to her bosom she pressed
The life of her heart, the child of her breast—
35 Oh! love from its tenderness gathering might,
Had strengthened her soul for the dangers of flight.

But she's free! yes, free from the land where the slave
From the hand of oppression must rest in the grave;
Where bondage and torture, where scourges and chains
40 Have placed on our banner indelible stains.

The bloodhounds have missed the scent of her way;
The hunter is rifled and foiled of his prey;
Fierce jargon and cursing, with clanking of chains,
Make sounds of strange discord on Liberty's plains.

45 With the rapture of love and fulness of bliss,
She placed on his brow a mother's fond kiss:
Oh! poverty, danger and death she can brave,
For the child of her love is no longer a slave!
—1854

Ethiopia[1]

Yes! Ethiopia yet shall stretch
     Her bleeding hands abroad;
Her cry of agony shall reach
     The burning throne of God.[2]

5 The tyrant's yoke from off her neck,
     His fetters from her soul,
The mighty hand of God shall break,
     And spurn the base control.

Redeemed from dust and freed from chains,
10   Her sons shall lift their eyes;
From cloud-capped hills and verdant plains
     Shall shouts of triumph rise.

Upon her dark, despairing brow,
     Shall play a smile of peace;
15 For God shall bend unto her woe,
     And bid her sorrows cease.

'Neath sheltering vines and stately palms
     Shall laughing children play,
And aged sires with joyous psalms
20   Shall gladden every day.

Secure by night, and blessed by day,
     Shall pass her happy hours;
Nor human tigers hunt for prey
     Within her peaceful bowers.

25 Then, Ethiopia! stretch, oh! stretch
     Thy bleeding hands abroad;
Thy cry of agony shall reach
     And find redress from God.
—1854

Advice to the Girls

Nay, do not blush! I only heard
     You had a mind to marry;
I thought I'd speak a friendly word,
     So just one moment tarry.

5 Wed not a man whose merit lies
     In things of outward show,
In raven hair or flashing eyes,
     That please your fancy so.

But marry one who's good and kind,
10   And free from all pretence;
Who, if without a gifted mind,
     At least has common sense.
—1854

---

[1]   The present text is the version that appeared in Harper's 1854 collection, *Poems on Miscellaneous Subjects*; a slightly different version had appeared in Harper's earlier collection, *Forest Leaves*. Throughout much of European history, the term "Ethiopia" often functioned as a metonym for the African continent or to represent people of African descent.

[2]   *Ethiopia ... of God* See Psalm 68.31: "Ethiopia shall soon stretch out her hands unto God."

A Mother's Heroism

When the noble mother of Lovejoy heard of her son's death, she said, "It is well! I had rather he should die so than desert his principles."[1]

The murmurs of a distant strife
    Fell on a mother's ear;
Her son had yielded up his life,
    Mid scenes of wrath and fear.

5 They told her how he'd spent his breath
    In pleading for the dumb,°   *mute*
And how the glorious martyr wreath
    Her child had nobly won.

They told her of his courage high,
10   Mid brutal force and might;
How he had nerved himself to die
    In battling for the right.

It seemed as if a tearful storm
    Swept wildly round her soul;
15 A moment, and her fragile form
    Bent 'neath its fierce control.

From lip and brow the color fled—
    But light flashed to her eye:
"'Tis well! 'tis well!" the mother said,
20   "That thus my child should die.

"'Tis well that, to his latest breath,
    He plead for liberty;
Truth nerved him for the hour of death,
    And taught him how to die.

25 "It taught him how to cast aside
    Earth's honors and renown;
To trample on her fame and pride,
    And win a martyr's crown."
    —1854

---

[1] *When the noble ... principles* The reference is to the case of abolitionist newspaper editor Elijah Parish Lovejoy, whose murder by a proslavery mob in 1837 sent shockwaves throughout the United States and spurred many abolitionists to further commit to the cause; his mother was Elizabeth Pattee Lovejoy.

The Fugitive's Wife

It was my sad and weary lot
    To toil in slavery;
But one thing cheered my lowly cot—
    My husband was with me.

5 One evening, as our children played
    Around our cabin door,
I noticed on his brow a shade
    I'd never seen before;

And in his eyes a gloomy night
10   Of anguish and despair—
I gazed upon their troubled light,
    To read the meaning there.

He strained me to his heaving heart—
    My own beat wild with fear;
15 I knew not, but I sadly felt
    There must be evil near.

He vainly strove to cast aside
    The tears that fell like rain:
Too frail, indeed, is manly pride,
20   To strive with grief and pain.

Again he clasped me to his breast,
    And said that we must part;
I tried to speak—but, oh! it seemed
    An arrow reached my heart.

25 "Bear not," I cried, "unto your grave,
    The yoke you've borne from birth;
No longer live a helpless slave,
    The meanest[2] thing on earth!"
    —1854

Bury Me in a Free Land

You may make my grave wherever you will,
  In a lowly vale or a lofty hill;
You may make it among earth's humblest graves,
    But not in a land where men are slaves.

---

[2] *meanest* Lowliest.

5 I could not sleep if around my grave
        I heard the steps of a trembling slave;
   His shadow above my silent tomb
        Would make it a place of fearful gloom.

   I could not rest if I heard the tread
10   Of a coffle-gang to the shambles[1] led,
   And the mother's shriek of wild despair
        Rise like a curse on the trembling air.

   I could not rest if I heard the lash
        Drinking her blood at each fearful gash,
15 And I saw her babes torn from her breast
        Like trembling doves from their parent nest.

   I'd shudder and start, if I heard the bay
        Of the bloodhounds seizing their human prey;
   If I heard the captive plead in vain
20   As they tightened afresh his galling chain.

   If I saw young girls, from their mothers' arms
        Bartered and sold for their youthful charms
   My eye would flash with a mournful flame,
        My death-paled cheek grow red with shame.

25 I would sleep, dear friends, where bloated might
        Can rob no man of his dearest right;
   My rest shall be calm in any grave.
        Where none calls his brother a slave.

   I ask no monument proud and high
30   To arrest the gaze of passers by;
   All that my spirit yearning craves,
        Is—bury me not in the land of slaves.[2]
   —1858

---

1 *coffle-gang* Group of people, especially enslaved people or prisoners, chained together; *shambles* Literally, a slaughterhouse, but
in this instance symbolizing a place of violence or suffering, likely a
slave-market.

2 *I ask … of slaves* The words of this final stanza are reproduced
as an epitaph on Harper's gravestone.

Vashti[3]

She leaned her head upon her hand
    And heard the king's decree—
"My lords are feasting in my halls,
    Bid Vashti come to me.

5 "I've shown the treasures of my house,
        My costly jewels rare,
   But with the glory of her eyes
        No rubies can compare.

   "Adorned and crowned I'd have her come,
10   With all her queenly grace,
   And, 'mid my lords and mighty men,
        Unveil her lovely face.

   "Each gem that sparkles in my crown,
        Or glitters on my throne,
15 Grows poor and pale when she appears,
        My beautiful, my own!"

   All waiting stood the chamberlains
        To hear the Queen's reply,
   They saw her cheek grow deathly pale,
20   But light flashed to her eye:

   "Go, tell the King," she proudly said,
        "That I am Persia's Queen,
   And by his crowds of merry men
        I never will be seen.

25 "I'll take their crown from off my head
        And tread it 'neath my feet
   Before their rude and careless gaze
        My shrinking eyes shall meet.

   "A queen unveiled before the crowd!
30   Upon each lip my name!
   Why, Persia's women all would blush
        And weep for Vashti's shame!

   "Go back!" she cried, and waived her hand,
        And grief was in her eye:

---

3 *Vashti* Persian queen whose story is recounted in the Book of
Esther.

35 "Go, tell the King," she sadly said,
    "That I would rather die."

They brought her message to the King,
    Dark flashed his angry eye;
'Twas as the lightning ere the storm
40   Hath swept in fury by.

Then bitterly outspoke the King,
    Through purple lips of wrath—
"What shall be done to her who dares
    To cross your monarch's path?"

45 Then spake his wily counsellors—
    "O King of this fair land!
From distant Ind to Ethiop,[1]
    All bow to thy command.

"But if, before thy servants' eyes,
50   This thing they plainly see,
That Vashti doth not heed thy will
    Nor yield herself to thee,

"The women, restive 'neath our rule,
    Would learn to scorn our name,
55 And from her deed to us would come
    Reproach and burning shame.

"Then, gracious King, sign with thy hand
    This stern but just decree
That Vashti lay aside her crown,
60   Thy Queen no more to be."

She heard again the King's command,
    And left her high estate,
Strong in her earnest womanhood,
    She calmly met her fate,

65 And left the palace of the King,
    Proud of her spotless name—
A woman who could bend to grief,
    But would not bow to shame.
        —1871

---

[1] *Ind* Term used in the nineteenth century to denote India, or for the East generally; *Ethiop* Term widely used in the nineteenth century to denote the African continent.

Learning to Read[2]

Very soon the Yankee teachers
    Came down and set up school;
But, oh! how the Rebs[3] did hate it—
    It was agin' their rule.

5 Our masters always tried to hide
    Book learning from our eyes;
Knowledge didn't agree with slavery—
    'Twould make us all too wise.

But some of us would try to steal
10   A little from the book,
And put the words together,
    And learn by hook or crook.

I remember Uncle Caldwell,
    Who took pot-liquor fat[4]
15 And greased the pages of his book,
    And hid it in his hat.

And had his master ever seen
    The leaves upon his head,
He'd have thought them greasy papers,
20   But nothing to be read.

And there was Mr. Turner's Ben,
    Who heard the children spell,
And picked the words right up by heart,
    And learned to read 'em well.

25 Well, the Northern folks kept sending
    The Yankee teachers down;
And they stood right up and helped us,
    Though Rebs did sneer and frown.

---

[2] *Learning to Read* This is the fourth of six poems in the "Aunt Chloe" cycle in *Sketches of Southern Life*, narrated from the perspective of a formerly enslaved woman on a plantation in the post-Civil War South; the full "Aunt Chloe" poem cycle is included in the website component of this anthology.

[3] *Rebs* Rebels; i.e., Confederates; supporters of the rebellion against the Union.

[4] *pot-liquor fat* Grease skimmed from cooking broth.

And, I longed to read my Bible,
30   For precious words it said;
But when I begun to learn it,
    Folks just shook their heads,

And said there is no use trying,
    Oh! Chloe, you're too late;
35 But as I was rising sixty,
    I had no time to wait.

So I got a pair of glasses,
    And straight to work I went,
And never stopped till I could read
40   The hymns and Testament.

Then I got a little cabin
    A place to call my own—
And I felt as independent
    As the queen upon her throne.
    —1872

In Context

Learning to Read and Write before Emancipation

from Elijah P. Marrs, *Life and History of the Rev. Elijah P. Marrs, First Pastor of Beargrass Baptist Church, and Author* (1885)

> Elijah P. Marrs (1840–1910) was born into slavery in Kentucky, and served in the Union Army during the final months of the Civil War. Following the war he worked as a Baptist minister and a teacher, and also organized and led various groups for the defense of African Americans against the Ku Klux Klan.

Very early in life I took up the idea that I wanted to learn to read and write. I was convinced that there would be something for me to do in the future that I could not accomplish by remaining in ignorance. I had heard so much about freedom, and of the colored people running off and going to Canada, that my mind was busy with this subject even in my young days. I sought the aid of the white boys, who did all they could in teaching me. They did not know that it was dangerous for a slave to read and write. I availed myself of every opportunity, daily I carried my book in my pocket, and every chance that offered would be learning my A, B, C's. Soon I learned to read. After this the white people would send me daily to the post office, at Simpsonville, K[entuck]y, a distance of two miles, when I would read the address of the letters; I also would read the newspapers the best I could. There was an old colored man on the place by the name of Ham Graves, who opened a night school, beginning at 10 o'clock at night. I attended his school one year and learned how to write my name and read writing. On every gatepost around the stable, as on the plow handles, you could see where I had been trying to write. Of course, I did not know the danger of it, and that fools' names, like fools' faces, are always seen in public places.

from Susie King Taylor, *Reminiscences of My Life in Camp with the 33d United States Colored Troops, late 1st S.C. Volunteers* (1902)

> Susie King Taylor (1848–1912) worked as a nurse, laundress, and teacher for the black freedmen of the 1st South Carolina Volunteers (which was later renamed the 33rd United States Colored Infantry Regiment). She continued to work as an educator after the end of the Civil War, dividing most of the rest of her life between Boston, where she found employment, and the South, where much of her family remained.

from CHAPTER 2
MY CHILDHOOD

I was born under the slave law in Georgia, in 1848, and was brought up by my grandmother in Savannah. There were three of us with her, my younger sister and brother. My brother and I being the two eldest, we were sent to a friend of my grandmother, Mrs. Woodhouse, a widow, to learn to read and write. She was a free woman and lived on Bay Lane, between Habersham and Price streets, about half a mile from my house. We went every day about nine o'clock, with our books wrapped in paper to prevent the police or white persons from seeing them. We went in, one at a time, through the gate, into the yard to the L kitchen, which was the schoolroom. She had twenty-five or thirty children whom she taught, assisted by her daughter, Mary Jane. The neighbors would see us going in sometimes, but they supposed we were there learning trades, as it was the custom to give children a trade of some kind. After school we left the same way we entered, one by one, when we would go to a square, about a block from the school, and wait for each other. We would gather laurel leaves and pop them on our hands, on our way home. I remained at her school for two years or more, when I was sent to a Mrs. Mary Beasley, where I continued until May 1860, when she told my grandmother she had taught me all she knew, and grandmother had better get someone else who could teach me more, so I stopped my studies for a while.

I had a white playmate about this time, named Katie O'Connor, who lived on the next corner of the street from my house, and who attended a convent. One day she told me, if I would promise not to tell her father, she would give me some lessons. On my promise not to do so, and getting her mother's consent, she gave me lessons about four months, every evening. At the end of this time she was put into the convent permanently, and I have never seen her since.

A month after this, James Blouis, our landlord's son, was attending the High School, and was very fond of grandmother, so she asked him to give me a few lessons, which he did until the middle of 1861, when the Savannah Volunteer Guards, to which he and his brother belonged, were ordered to the front under General Barton. In the first battle of Manassas,[1] his brother Eugene was killed, and James deserted over to the Union side, and at the close of the war went to Washington, D.C., where he has since resided.

We Are All Bound Up Together

I feel I am something of a novice upon this platform.[2] Born of a race whose inheritance has been outrage and wrong, most of my life had been spent in battling against those wrongs. But I did not feel as keenly as others, that I had these rights, in common with other women, which are now demanded. About two years ago, I stood within the shadows of my home. A great sorrow had fallen upon my life. My husband had died suddenly, leaving me a widow, with four children, one my own, and the others stepchildren. I tried to keep my children together. But my husband died in debt; and before he had been in his grave three months, the administrator had swept the very milk crocks and wash tubs from my hands. I was a farmer's wife and made butter for the Columbus market; but what could I do, when they had swept all away? They left me one thing—and that was a looking-glass! Had I died instead of my husband, how different would have been the result! By this time he would have had another wife, it is likely; and no administrator would have gone into his house, broken up his home, and sold his bed, and taken away his means of support.

I took my children in my arms, and went out to seek my living. While I was gone, a neighbor to whom I had once lent five dollars, went before a magistrate and swore that he believed I was a non-resident, and laid an attachment on my very bed. And I went back to

---

1   *first battle of Manassas*   First major battle of the Civil War, fought on 21 July 1861.
2   *this platform*   I.e., the cause of women's rights; Harper had dedicated most of her activism prior to this point to the causes of abolition and anti-racism.

Ohio with my orphan children in my arms, without a single feather bed in this wide world, that was not in the custody of the law. I say, then, that justice is not fulfilled so long as woman is unequal before the law.

We are all bound up together in one great bundle of humanity, and society cannot trample on the weakest and feeblest of its members without receiving the curse in its own soul. You tried that in the case of the negro. You pressed him down for two centuries; and in so doing you crippled the moral strength and paralyzed the spiritual energies of the white men of the country. When the hands of the black were fettered, white men were deprived of the liberty of speech and the freedom of the press. Society cannot afford to neglect the enlightenment of any class of its members. At the South, the legislation of the country was in behalf of the rich slaveholders, while the poor white man was neglected. What is the consequence today? From that very class of neglected poor white men comes the man who stands today with his hand upon the helm of the nation.[1] He fails to catch the watchword of the hour, and throws himself, the incarnation of meanness,[2] across the pathway of the nation. My objection to Andrew Johnson is not that he has been a poor white man; my objection is that he keeps "poor whits"[3] all the way through. (Applause.) That is the trouble with him.

This grand and glorious revolution which has commenced, will fail to reach its climax of success until throughout the length and breadth of the American Republic the nation shall be so color-blind as to know no man by the color of his skin or the curl of his hair. It will then have no privileged class, trampling upon and outraging the unprivileged classes, but will be then one great privileged nation, whose privilege will be to produce the loftiest manhood and womanhood that humanity can attain.

I do not believe that giving the woman the ballot is immediately going to cure all the ills of life. I do not believe that white women are dew-drops just exhaled from the skies. I think that like men they may be divided into three classes, the good, the bad, and the indifferent. The good would vote according to their convictions and principles; the bad, as dictated by prejudice or malice; and the indifferent will vote on the strongest side of the question, with the winning party.

You white women speak here of rights. I speak of wrongs. I, as a colored woman, have had in this country an education which has made me feel as if I were in the situation of Ishmael,[4] my hand against every man, and every man's hand against me. Let me go tomorrow morning and take my seat in one of your street cars—I do not know that they will do it in New York, but they will in Philadelphia—and the conductor will put up his hand and stop the car rather than let me ride.

A Lady—They will not do that here.

Mrs. Harper—They do in Philadelphia. Going from Washington to Baltimore this Spring, they put me in the smoking car. (Loud Voices—"Shame.") Aye, in the capital of the nation, where the black man consecrated himself to the nation's defence, faithful when the white man was faithless, they put me in the smoking car! They did it once; but the next time they tried it, they failed; for I would not go in. I felt the fight in me; but I don't want to have to fight all the time. Today I am puzzled where to make my home. I would like to make it in Philadelphia, near my own friends and relations. But if I want to ride in the streets of Philadelphia, they send me to ride on the platform with the driver. (Cries of "Shame.") Have women nothing to do with this? Not long since, a colored woman took her seat in an Eleventh Street car in Philadelphia, and the conductor stopped the car, and told the rest of the passengers to get out, and left the car with her in it alone, when they took it back to the station. One day I took my seat in a

---

[1] *From that very ... the nation* Harper refers to Andrew Johnson (1808–75), who had been vice president at the time of Lincoln's assassination in 1865 and thereafter assumed the Presidency. Johnson had been born into poverty in North Carolina, and had received no formal education. As President, Johnson was notoriously resistant to improving the civil and legal conditions of African Americans in the aftermath of the Civil War (for instance, he refused to interfere with the "Black Codes" passed by various state legislatures, which restricted black freedom to such an extent that they effectively re-established slavery).

[2] *meanness* Inferiority of character; stinginess.

[3] *keeps "poor whits"* Has unvaryingly displayed a lack of intelligence.

[4] *Ishmael* In the Book of Genesis, Ishmael is the son of Abraham by his wife's handmaid, Hagar. Abraham's wife, Sarai, casts out the expectant Hagar, who wanders the parched desert until God says to her, "Behold, thou art with child and shalt bear a son, and shalt call his name Ishmael; because the Lord hath heard thy affliction. And he will be a wild man; his hand will be against every man, and every man's hand against him" (Genesis 16.11–12).

car, and the conductor came to me and told me to take another seat. I just screamed "murder." The man said if I was black I ought to behave myself. I knew that if he was white he was not behaving himself. Are there not wrongs to be righted?

In advocating the cause of the colored man, since the Dred Scott decision,[1] I have sometimes said I thought the nation had touched bottom. But let me tell you there is a depth of infamy lower than that. It is when the nation, standing upon the threshold of a great peril, reached out its hands to a feebler race, and asked that race to help it, and when the peril was over, said, You are good enough for soldiers, but not good enough for citizens.[2] When Judge Taney[3] said that the men of my race had no rights which the white man was bound to respect, he had not seen the bones of the black man bleaching outside of Richmond. He had not seen the thinned ranks and the thickened graves of the Louisiana Second, a regiment which went into battle nine hundred strong, and came out with three hundred. He had not stood at Olustee and seen defeat and disaster crushing down the pride of our banner, until words was brought to Col. Hallowell, "The day is lost; go in and save it"; and black men stood in the gap, beat back the enemy, and saved your army.[4] (Applause.)

We have a woman in our country who has received the name of "Moses," not by lying about it, but by acting it out (applause)—a woman who has gone down into the Egypt of slavery and brought out hundreds of our people into liberty.[5] The last time I saw that woman, her hands were swollen. That woman who had led one of Montgomery's most successful expeditions,[6] who was brave enough and secretive enough to act as a scout for the American army, had her hands all swollen from a conflict with a brutal conductor, who undertook to eject her from her place. That woman, whose courage and bravery won a recognition from our army and from every black man in the land, is excluded from every thoroughfare of travel. Talk of giving women the ballot-box? Go on. It is a normal school,[7] and the white women of this country need it. While there exists this brutal element in society which tramples upon the feeble and treads down the weak, I tell you that if there is any class of people who need to be lifted out of their airy nothings and selfishness, it is the white women of America. (Applause.)

1866

---

[1] *Dred Scott decision* 1857 Supreme Court decision in which it was determined that persons of African descent, whether free or enslaved, could not be considered American citizens, and thereby had no legal standing in court. The decision came after the formerly enslaved Dred Scott attempted to secure the court's further confirmation of his freedom so that the children of his deceased former owner could not claim inherited ownership of Scott's daughters.

[2] *It is when … for citizens* Harper alludes to the participation of black soldiers in the Union Army during the Civil War, and especially following the Emancipation Proclamation (1863), which called for newly emancipated black men to join the Army.

[3] *Judge Taney* Author of the majority decision in the *Dred Scott* case.

[4] *Olustee … saved your army* Though the 1864 Battle of Olustee in Florida resulted in a Confederate victory, regiments comprised of African American soldiers, including the famous 54th Massachusetts Infantry, performed feats of bravery that prevented the total destruction of Union forces. The 54th Massachusetts was at the time under the command of Colonel Edward Needles Hallowell (1836–71).

[5] *We have … into liberty* Harper refers to Harriet Tubman, who escaped slavery in 1849 and subsequently became a dedicated Underground Railroad agent, helping to free hundreds of people; she also worked as a spy for the Union Army during the Civil War. Tubman was affectionately called "Moses" by her supporters, referring to the story in the Book of Exodus in which Moses leads the Israelites out of Egyptian slavery.

[6] *one of … successful expeditions* In 1863 Tubman, alongside Colonel James Montgomery, helped lead the Combahee Ferry raid, which resulted in the emancipation of over 700 people.

[7] *normal school* Institution for training schoolteachers. The implication is that suffrage for white women will only further empower them in what is already a socially accepted role, that of teachers and moral guides.

EMILY DICKINSON

1830 – 1886

Emily Dickinson wrote in a letter to a friend that "Biography first convinces us of the fleeing of the Biographied—." And indeed, as several generations of critics and biographers have approached this enigmatic poet's work and life, the poet herself remains elusive, though legends about her abound. Widely considered one of America's greatest writers, Dickinson has attracted a dedicated and passionate readership, as well as worldwide critical acclaim. Working entirely in compact poetic forms, she left us close to 1,800 poems, among which are some of the most incisive and psychologically powerful lyrics in English on the subjects of death, love, nature, and religion.

Emily Elizabeth Dickinson was born in Amherst, in the Connecticut Valley of Massachusetts, on 10 December 1830, and for most of her life she continued to live with her family in an Amherst mansion called the Homestead. She was the second of three children to Edward and Emily Norcross Dickinson. Edward Dickinson was a locally prominent lawyer and politician, who entered the United States House of Representatives in 1853. He was also a pious man who regularly read to his children from the Bible; Dickinson later said of him that "his heart was pure and terrible, and I think no other like it exists." Dickinson's mother, Emily Norcross Dickinson, came from a family that valued education for women, and she herself studied the sciences intently while at school. She suffered ill health throughout her life, and seems to have been emotionally distant; Dickinson said to Thomas Wentworth Higginson in 1870 that she "never had a mother. I suppose a mother is one to whom you hurry when you are troubled."

In 1840, Dickinson and her sister Lavinia were both enrolled at Amherst Academy, a converted boys' school with progressive educational ideals; here they studied subjects such as botany, chemistry, languages, and art, and attended lectures by visiting academics. By all accounts Dickinson was an engaged scholar, respected for her sense of humor and the strength of her intellect; she was also passionate about music and enjoyed dancing. In 1847, she began her secondary education at Mount Holyoke Female Seminary, where there was more emphasis on religious faith. Dickinson, who had not been baptized and who even at a young age maintained her distance from the established Puritanism of her community, publicly upheld her nonconformity. A fellow student, Clara Turner, remembered a day when the director of the school "asked all those who wanted to be Christians to rise." Dickinson remained in her seat and said to Clara: "They thought it queer I didn't rise—I thought a lie would be queerer." For reasons that remain somewhat unclear but that likely had to do with ill health, Dickinson left Mount Holyoke after a year, returning home in 1848.

In her time at school, Dickinson had developed several significant and intense friendships with both men and women. While at Amherst Academy, she became close to Leonard Humphrey, the principal of the school, who nurtured her love of reading. He was the first of a series of older male friends that Dickinson would refer to variously as "Tutor" or "Preceptor." The second was an attorney, Benjamin Franklin Newton, who worked with her father, and who introduced her to the works of William Wordsworth, Henry Wadsworth Longfellow, Ralph Waldo Emerson, and Lydia Maria Child. In the late 1840s, Dickinson met Susan Gilbert (later Susan Gilbert Dickinson), who was to become a life-long friend and eventually sister-in-law; the two formed a close bond and carried on a passionate correspondence; their letters have been interpreted by some later scholars as evidence of a romantic relationship. Dickinson wrote at least ninety-four poems to Susan, who—intelligent, sensitive, and open-minded—became very dear to the poet.

Dickinson's early life was also repeatedly marked by tragic loss. Her cousin and friend, Sophia Holland, died of typhus fever in 1844, and Dickinson's grief and ensuing depression were so deep that she was sent to Boston to recover. In May 1848, another friend, Jacob Holt, died, and two years later, Leonard Humphrey died of a brain aneurysm at the age of twenty-five. Three years later, Benjamin Newton died of tuberculosis when he was thirty-two. These were deep emotional blows to Dickinson, whose sensibility was marked by this series of young deaths; her poetry returns again and again to the themes of death, loss, and separation: "Parting is all we know of heaven / And all we need of hell."

When Dickinson returned home from school, she felt acutely the contrast between the relative freedom of school life and the constrictions of a home life in which a young woman was expected to devote her time to domestic duties. As she wrote to her friend Abiah Root in 1850, "God keep me from what they call households." Dickinson nonetheless took on many of these duties—and continued to do so throughout her life. She was a dedicated and gifted gardener; she baked the family desserts and bread; and she took care of her often-ailing mother. Dickinson also took steps, however, to secure some hours to herself, and she began in 1849 to write poetry. She refused to accept many of the social demands typically placed on the women of a prominent family like hers, withdrawing from the custom of "visiting" and receiving visitors; she saw only her family and closest friends.

Her need to preserve freedom may also have had a good deal to do with her decision not to marry. She wrote to Susan in 1852 about the merits of a single life: "How dull our lives must seem to the bride, and the plighted maiden, whose days are fed with gold, and who gathers pearls every evening; but to the *wife*, Susie, sometimes the *wife forgotten*, our lives perhaps seem dearer than all others in the world." Dickinson's choice to remain single did not mean that she lived without passionate attachments, however. She had intense relationships with both men and women throughout her life, mainly carried on through written correspondence (with the Reverend Charles Wadsworth, Benjamin Newton, and Susan Dickinson, among others). It is not clear to what degree these relationships were sexual, but it is abundantly clear that they could be passionate—and that, as the poet Adrienne Rich put it, Dickinson "was attracted by and interested in" men and women "whose minds had something to offer her."

In 1850 the Great Revival swept through Amherst, and Dickinson's father, sister, and many of her friends joined the local Congregationalist Church and declared themselves "for Christ." Dickinson did not join the church, as she had trouble accepting some of the tenets of the Congregationalist faith—particularly those surrounding predestination and hell. As she began to write more and more poetry, Dickinson often voiced religious concerns, but her spirituality was individual; she refused to adhere to a prescribed form of Christianity. In a letter to Jane Humphrey in 1850, she wrote: "Christ is calling everyone here, all my companions have answered … and I am standing alone in rebellion, and growing very careless. … I can't tell you *what* they have found, but *they* think it is something precious. I wonder if it *is*?"

At the Homestead, Dickinson continued to read widely in British and American literature, particularly the novelists and poets of her own century. She was also fond of the early modern poets—especially of William Shakespeare, of whose works she wrote to a friend, "Why is any other book needed?" Dickinson's own verse carries echoes of all these sources—as well as of the King James Bible, to whose rhetorical structures and poetic language she had been thoroughly introduced as a child.

However much she drew on literary traditions, Dickinson's own use of language, and the poetic forms she shaped, are unique. Most of her poetry is loosely organized according to stanzaic and metrical forms commonly used in Christian hymns—forms with relatively short rhymed lines, typically grouped in four-line stanzas. But Dickinson experiments with and transforms these traditional structures, using enjambment, imperfect and suspended rhymes, iconoclastic punctuation, and unusual word order to disrupt expectations and present compressed thoughts and feelings in extraordinarily suggestive ways.

Over the course of the 1850s the group of friends with whom Dickinson corresponded grew into something of a literary network. During her lifetime this was the primary audience for her poems, a quarter of which she sent to her friends in letters—letters which often also included reflections in prose that could be almost as cryptically expressive and fascinating as the poems themselves. "A letter," she wrote, "always feels to me like immortality because it is the mind alone without corporeal friend."

In the 1850s, Dickinson began to write to several correspondents from the literary world; these included two editors of the abolitionist newspaper *Springfield Republican*, Samuel Bowles and Josiah Holland. Bowles published seven of her lyrics in his paper, smoothing out a good deal of what he saw as Dickinson's idiosyncratic punctuation, rhymes, line breaks, and rhythms—a practice her other early editors also followed. Dickinson does not appear to have made any attempt to prevent such publication, and there is evidence in her letters with Susan that the two young women were looking forward to seeing "Safe in their Alabaster Chambers" in print. In other letters and poems, however, such as "A Narrow fellow in the Grass" (1863) and "Publication – is the Auction" (1865), the speaker expresses highly ambivalent views toward the ideas of publicity and fame.

Dickinson's most prolific period of writing began in the late 1850s and continued to the mid-1860s, by which time she had written over a thousand poems. In 1858, she began making fair copies, organizing the poems into groups later called "fascicles," which she sewed together by hand. In the spring of 1862, Dickinson read an article in *The Atlantic Monthly* by the literary critic Thomas Wentworth Higginson. Wanting an educated opinion on her work, she sent him four poems, asking if her poetry "breathed." This letter prompted the beginning of a correspondence with Higginson that would last until Dickinson's death. Though he offered her some criticism and some poetic advice, Higginson greatly admired the poetry and was sensitive to the power of her personality; he became a great support to her (she later told him that he had saved her life by responding to her query). Though she wrote to him in the language of a student to her teacher, she maintained a confident independence about her work; rarely if ever did she take his advice. For his part, Higginson may have suggested regularizing a good deal of her grammar and punctuation, but he described her poetry as "woven out of the heart's own atoms," and later acknowledged that "when a thought takes one's breath away, a lesson in grammar seems an impertinence."

In the early 1860s, Dickinson's reclusiveness increased, as did her creativity and poetic output. Her poems became even more experimental and dynamic, and she began increasingly to add variants to her manuscripts—alternative word choices that she wrote down in footnotes or in marginalia, allowing for at times radically different readings to coexist within a given poem. Scholars have noted that her most productive period coincided with the Civil War. She wrote in a letter that "Sorrow seems more general than it did, and not the estate of a few persons, since the war began; and if the anguish of others helped one with one's own, now would be many medicines. …"

The loss of Dickinson's father in 1874 caused prolonged grief, as her letters attest. "I dream about father every night," she wrote, "always a different dream, and forget what I am doing daytimes, wondering where he is. Without any body, I keep thinking. What kind can that be?" Her mother had a stroke the following year and broke her hip, and Dickinson became the primary caregiver until her mother's death in 1882. After a period of increasing ill health, Dickinson herself died on 15 May 1886, of kidney disease; she was buried beside her parents in Amherst.

The story of how the bulk of Dickinson's poems first saw publication after her death is complicated by a family disagreement. It began with the arrival in Amherst of David Todd, an astronomy professor, and his talented wife, Mabel Loomis Todd, in 1881. Dickinson's brother Austin and his wife, Susan Dickinson, both befriended Mabel. Dickinson also took an interest in her, albeit from afar: she would listen to Mabel sing and speak to her through a door, but the two never met. (Mabel, however, took a deep interest in Dickinson, and felt assured of her poetic genius.) The web of friendship frayed, however, when Austin and Mabel fell in love; the two began an affair that lasted for the remainder of Austin's life. After Dickinson's death, her sister Lavinia found a large cache of poems in Emily's chest of drawers; Lavinia eventually gave these to Mabel Todd to prepare for publication. Susan Dickinson, meanwhile, had a separate collection of poems and letters that Emily had given her over the course of their lifetime of friendship. The ensuing feud between Susan and Mabel over Dickinson's legacy continued down through their daughters' generation.

Mabel Todd, together with Higginson, edited the first two editions of Dickinson's verse, *Poems* (1890) and *Poems* (1891); these editions did not include any of the material from Susan Dickinson's collection. Todd and Higginson added titles to the poems, grouped them thematically—Dickinson did not title or number her work—and standardized much of her grammar and punctuation, with the intent of making the poetry more accessible. Their interventions received considerable censure in the late twentieth and early twenty-first centuries; the uncomplicated view that Helen McNeil expressed in the introduction to her 1986 edition—that Dickinson's "works were mangled by editors"—was widely shared. More recent scholarship has been less censorious and more alive to historical context—alive both to the extent that Dickinson's approach to poetry was ahead of her time, and to the sort of reception that her work would likely have received in the late nineteenth century had it been published with her manuscript capitalization, punctuation, and grammar intact. Even in Todd and Higginson's "cleaned up" versions, Dickinson's style met with a hostile reception from not a few critics; the reviewer for the popular *Scribner's Monthly*, for example, complained of her "neglect of form" and her "perverseness and eccentricity," while the famous British critic Andrew Lang was more caustic, writing in the *Daily News* that Dickinson "reminds us of no sane nor educated writer." Other critics were far more positive, however. The reviewer for the *New York Commercial Advertiser* termed Dickinson "the poet in quintessence," and in *Harper's*, William Dean Howells (perhaps the leading American arbiter of literary taste during the period) praised her "short, quick impulses of intense feeling or poignant thought," and concluded that her "strange poetry" constituted "a distinctive addition to the literature of the world." The poems were popular with the public as well—particularly among female readers; eleven editions were issued by the end of 1892.

After Susan Dickinson's death, her daughter, Martha Dickinson Bianchi, decided to publish the Dickinson poems and letters that had been in her mother's possession, under the title *The Single Hound* (1914). This volume sparked another surge of interest in Dickinson's poetry, one that launched her as a proto-modernist. In a review of *The Single Hound*, Harriet Monroe called Dickinson "an unconscious and uncatalogued Imagiste." This marked a moment in the history of Dickinson criticism when scholars began situating the poet within larger intellectual contexts—in relation not only to New England Transcendentalism and Puritanism, but also to international movements such as Imagism, the early twentieth-century literary movement that valued concision, clarity, and formal experimentation. Modernist critics also placed Dickinson within the tradition of seventeenth-century Metaphysical poets such as Henry Vaughan and John Donne. By the early 1920s, Dickinson was firmly established as a significant American poet. In Conrad Aiken's introduction to *Selected Poems of Emily Dickinson* (1924), he describes her poetry as "perhaps the finest, by a woman, in the English language." Interestingly, however, Dickinson remained marginalized in many conventional narratives of the development of American literature; neither the 1924 *Short History of American Literature* nor the 1925 *Literary History of America* include any mention of her at all.

In 1955, the scholar Thomas H. Johnson collected all the Dickinson poems and letters that were, at that time, known to exist; his edition presented the poems for the first time in an approximation of their original state, and in an attempt at chronological order. Johnson's edition sparked renewed interest in her poetry—and that interest has never let up in the intervening decades. Scholars in the 1960s focused largely on thematic and linguistic concerns, those in the 1970s largely on feminist and psychoanalytic readings. Scholars continued as well to research her life and build her biography, as well as to consider her within wider nineteenth-century contexts. In 1998 came another major editorial achievement, Ralph Franklin's edition of the poems, which offered a more reliable order and chronology than had that of Johnson (Franklin was able to trace, from watermarks and pinholes, the original order of poems in Dickinson's fascicles). In 2013, the online open-access Emily Dickinson Archive was launched, allowing all interested readers and scholars to engage with images of the manuscripts. And in 2016, Cristanne Miller published a ground-breaking new edition, *Emily Dickinson's Poems: As She Preserved Them*, presenting all the poems in Dickinson's canon as they were copied down—those that were sewn into her forty fascicles, and those that she had kept in draft form.

In the twenty-first century, critical approaches to Dickinson have emphasized the materiality of her manuscripts and probed into the history of her various editors, with a focus on gender politics. Critics have also been considering Dickinson's poetry from the perspectives of ecocriticism, animal studies, queer theory, disability studies, race studies, and digital humanities. Dickinson's influence on American and world literatures has been profound. Readers, poets, and critics alike return to Dickinson for her ability to push the boundaries of language and poetic form, and for her articulation of a vision of human experience that is unique in its suggestive power, its compressed emotion, and its ability to prompt questions. As Dickinson biographer Richard B. Sewall has put it, "We still are not quite sure of her. We ask and ask."

NOTE ON THE TEXTS: As do the editors of almost all anthologies, we make an exception in the case of Emily Dickinson to several of our usual practices. It is by this time a commonplace to acknowledge that Dickinson's style is so idiosyncratic as to make it entirely appropriate to suspend an anthology's conventions regarding modernizing or regularizing punctuation, and capitalization—as we have done in these pages. We have also suspended the anthology's conventions regarding the dating of works; our normal practice is to foreground the date of first publication of each work; in Dickinson's case it is for obvious reasons the date of composition that appears after each poem.

The texts printed in these pages are based on the handwritten manuscripts themselves, in the facsimile form in which the Emily Dickinson Archive, in cooperation with the Houghton Library at Harvard University (and other institutions holding the manuscripts), now makes the vast majority of Dickinson's manuscript versions available to the general public. (Like all editors—and all readers of Dickinson—we are greatly in their debt for the opportunity to experience her manuscripts directly.)

In preparing the texts of the poems included in this anthology we have also consulted the three major editions that are based directly on the manuscripts: Thomas H. Johnson's *The Complete Poems of Emily Dickinson* (1955); R.W. Franklin's *The Poems of Emily Dickinson* (1998); and Cristanne Miller's *Emily Dickinson's Poems: As She Preserved Them* (2016). In many cases where the transcriptions of these editors differ from one another, we provide information in the notes as to those differences, often indicating our reasoning in siding with one editor over another or—in a very few cases—in offering a reading different from those of any of the three.

We also in these pages provide examples of the manuscripts themselves in facsimile form. As those examples show very clearly, *any* transcription of Dickinson's poems into a printed form entails judgment calls as to what constitutes a dash and what a period; as to whether or not a letter is capitalized; as to where line breaks occur, and so on. Following Johnson, Franklin, and Miller, we standardize all marks perceived to be dashes (Johnson standardizes using an em dash; we, like Franklin and Miller, employ a spaced en dash). But as all editors acknowledge—and as anyone reading the manuscripts for themselves can plainly see—those marks in a substantial number of poems[1] vary very widely indeed. Some are high in the line, some in the middle, some well below the line; some are very long and emphatically rendered, others are so short as to make it difficult to be sure if they are intended as dashes or as periods. A great many marks—especially at the ends of lines—have a downwards left to right slant to them, and are distinctly below the line. Miller conjectures that, "like many of her contemporaries, [Dickinson] probably quite often wrote elongated periods—in a kind of rolling stop. She may also have written commas both high within her row of script and slanting right rather than left." Miller nevertheless decides not to "thoroughly revise earlier interpretations of these marks." Such decisions are entirely defensible; they have the merit of simplicity, and do not risk confusing readers who have, over the decades since the publication of Johnson's edition, become familiar with the convention of representing a wide variety of Dickinson's marks in the same way. (For that very reason we have maintained the "one-size dash" convention in the transcriptions found in these pages.) But such decisions implicitly concede that print transcriptions of Dickinson's handwritten manuscripts inevitably entail a good deal of interpretation. The reality is that it is simply not known, for example, whether Dickinson intended a mark that resembles a right-slanting comma to be read as some form of dash, as a comma, or as a mark with some other, special meaning. In recognition of these realities, we have also, in the case of a small number of the poems presented in these pages, presented alternative transcriptions alongside the conventional ones. (As part of the anthology's website component we present several more such alternative transcriptions.)

In the case of several poems, we have also provided examples of early editing practice; this anthology's two-column format allows us conveniently to place different versions side by side, providing a convenient portfolio for the purposes of comparison.

In these pages we order the poems chronologically, taking the lead of Johnson and Franklin (and drawing as well on the scholarship of Miller). As one other part of the website component of this anthology, however, we present one complete fascicle—Fascicle 13—for the benefit of those who wish to study a group of Dickinson's poems "as she preserved them," to use Miller's phrase. Miller's edition has many merits, not the least of which is the degree to which it encourages scholars, students, and readers generally, to think of Dickinson afresh; we hope that the various ways in which Dickinson is presented in these pages will, in much more modest fashion, serve a similar end.

⌘ ⌘ ⌘

---

[1]   Much as the transcription issues are of considerable interest and real significance, it is important too to make clear that they are not ubiquitous. A poem such as "These are the days when Birds come back" is in this respect not typical. Indeed, a great many of Dickinson's poems present few transcription issues, or none at all; all editors are in agreement as to what is capitalized, what is a dash and what is a comma, etc.

[*It's all I have to bring today –*][1]

It's all I have to bring today –
This, and my heart beside –
This, and my heart, and all the fields –
And all the meadows wide –
5 Be sure you count – sh'd I forget
Some one the sum could tell[2] –
This, and my heart, and all the Bees
Which in the Clover dwell.
—1858

[*I never lost as much but twice –*][3]

I never lost as much but[4] twice –
And that was in the sod.
Twice have I stood a beggar
Before the door of God!

5 Angels – twice descending
Reimbursed my store –
Burglar! Banker – Father!
I am poor once more!
—1858

[*I robbed the woods –*][5]

I robbed the Woods –
The trusting Woods –
The unsuspecting Trees
Brought out their
5 Burs[6] and mosses
My fantasy to please.
I scanned their trinkets curious –
I grasped – I bore away –
What will the solemn Hemlock[7] –
10 What will the Oak tree say?
—1859

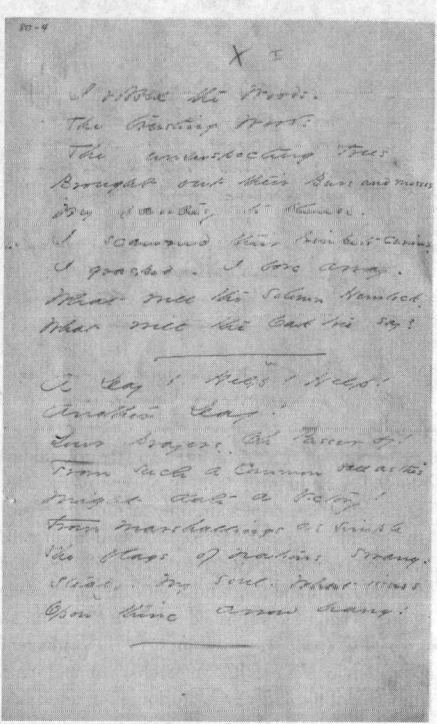

---

[1] This poem appears in Johnson as Poem 26; in Franklin as Poem 17; and in Miller as the second poem in Sheet 3 of Fascicle 1, page 38. The present text is in complete accord with the transcriptions of Franklin and Miller; the marks after "fields" and after "count," however, could plausibly be transcribed as right-slanting commas.

[2] *the sum could tell* I.e., it would be reflected in the total number.

[3] This poem appears in Johnson as Poem 49; in Franklin as Poem 39; and in Miller as the second poem in Sheet 3 of Fascicle 3, page 57. There are no transcription issues.

It is worth noting that Sheets 3 and 4 of this fascicle are made up of poems composed in 1858, whereas the fascicle's first two sheets are made up of poems dating from 1859.

[4] *but* Except.

[5] This poem appears in Johnson as Poem 41; in Franklin as Poem 57; and in Miller as the fourth poem in Sheet 3 of Fascicle 2, page 47. The present text is in agreement with Johnson in reading the mark at the end of the sixth line as a period, but in agreement with Franklin and Miller in reading the mark at the end of line 2 as a dash. The marks at the ends of lines 7, 8, and 9 could all plausibly be transcribed as right-slanting commas. A facsimile of the manuscript appears above.

[6] *Burs* Acorns from the bur oak tree.

[7] *Hemlock* The reference is to the North American hemlock pine, not to the poisonous plant of the same name.

[*These are the days when Birds come back*]¹

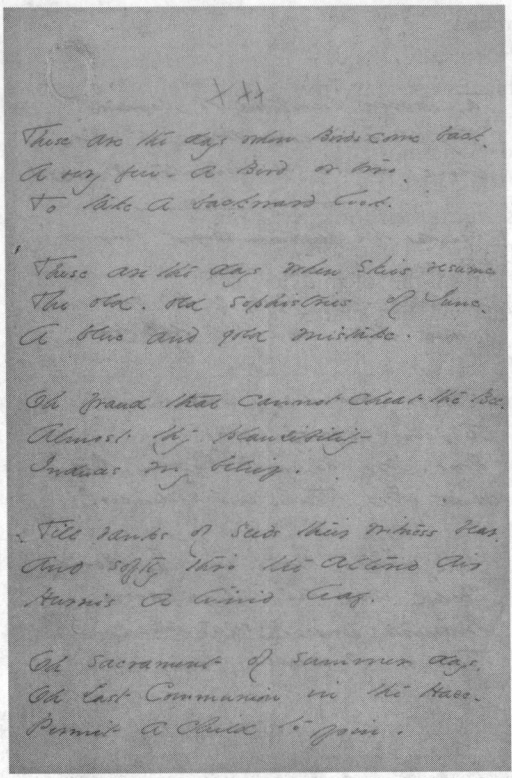

[*These are the days when Birds come back*]

These are the days when Birds come back,
A very few – a Bird or two,
To take a backward look.

These are the days when skies resume
5   The old . old sophistries² of June,
A blue and gold mistake.

Oh fraud that cannot cheat the Bee.
Almost thy plausibility
Induces my belief,

10   Till ranks of seeds their witness bear –
And softly thro' the altered air
Hurries a timid leaf.

Oh sacrament of summer days,
Oh Last Communion³ in the Haze,
15   Permit a child to join,

Thy sacred emblems to partake,
Thy consecrated bread to take
And thine immortal wine!
—1859

---

1   This poem appears in Johnson as Poem 130; in Franklin as Poem 122; and in Miller as the first poem in Sheet 3 of Fascicle 6, pages 81–82. The fascicle manuscript is the only manuscript version extant.

This poem is a good example of how difficult it is to transcribe Dickinson's manuscript writings into print with complete confidence. Karen Dandurand (the scholar who, in the 1980s, discovered that three poems had been published in *Drum Beat* in the 1860s) has fairly suggested of this poem that "most of the marks rendered by Johnson as dashes look as much, or more, like commas angled downward to the right, or like indeterminate dots." But subsequent editors have in this case followed Johnson; Franklin and Miller diverge from Johnson only in how they reproduce the mark at the end of one line ("Permit a child to join"), which Johnson prints as a period, Franklin prints as a dash, and Miller prints as a comma.

A facsimile of the first page of the 1859 manuscript version appears to the left. In the next column we offer a transcription that endeavors to present the marks more-or-less as they appear in the manuscript. In the third column a conventional transcription is provided, with the right-slanting marks interpreted as dashes. The fourth column prints the text as it was published (from a now-lost manuscript) in *Drum Beat*, 11 March 1864.

A version of the poem was included in Todd and Higginson's *Poems* (1890) under the title "Indian Summer."

---

2   *sophistries*   Deceptive reasonings.

3   *Last Communion*   Christian sacrament administered to the dying; the recipient eats bread and drinks wine in remembrance of Christ's sacrifice. The ritual is thought to bind the departing soul with Christ and thus with the promise of eternal life.

[*These are the days when Birds come back* —]

These are the days when Birds come back —
A very few — a Bird or two —
To take a backward look.

These are the days when skies resume
5   The old — old sophistries of June —
A blue and gold mistake.

Oh fraud that cannot cheat the Bee,
Almost thy plausibility
Induces my belief,

10   Till ranks of seeds their witness bear —
And softly thro' the altered air
Hurries a timid leaf.

Oh sacrament of summer days,
Oh Last Communion in the Haze —
15   Permit a child to join —

Thy sacred emblems to partake —
Thy consecrated bread to take
And thine immortal wine!
—1859

[*October*]

These are the days when birds come back,
A very few, a bird or two,
To take a backward look.

These are the days when skies resume
5   The old, old sophistries of June,—
A blue and gold mistake.

Oh, fraud that cannot cheat the bee!
Almost thy plausibility
Induces my belief,

10   Till ranks of seeds their witness bear,
And softly, through the altered air,
Hurries a timid leaf.

Oh, sacrament of summer days,
Oh last communion in the haze,
15   Permit a child to join!

Thy sacred emblems to partake,
Thy consecrated bread to take,
And thine immortal wine!
—1864

[*Success is counted sweetest*][1]

Success is counted sweetest
By those who ne'er succeed.
To comprehend a nectar
Requires sorest need.

5   Not one of all the purple Host
Who took the Flag[2] today
Can tell the definition
So clear of Victory

As he defeated – dying –
10   On whose forbidden ear
The distant strains of triumph
Burst agonized and clear!
—1859

SUCCESS.

SUCCESS is counted sweetest
By those who ne'er succeed.
To comprehend a Nectar
Requires the sorest need.
Not one of all the Purple Host
Who took the flag to-day,
Can tell the definition,
So plain, of Victory,
As he defeated, dying,
On whose forbidden ear
The distant strains of triumph
Break, agonizing clear.

---

[1]   This poem appears in Johnson as Poem 67; in Franklin as Poem 112; and in Miller as the third poem in Sheet 1 of Fascicle 5, page 69. The present transcription is in complete agreement with those of all three of these editors. The fascicle version probably dates from the summer of 1859; variant manuscript versions (in which the poem is not divided into stanzas) were sent to Susan Dickinson in 1859 and to Thomas Wentworth Higginson in July of 1862. The poem was first published in the *Brooklyn Daily Union*, 27 April 1862; that version (the source of which is presumed to have been a now-lost manuscript copy) was reprinted in 1878 in the anthology *A Masque of Poets*. Higginson and Todd made slight revisions for *Poems* (1890); this is the poem that opens that volume.

[2]   *took the Flag* Won the battle.

[*Safe in their Alabaster Chambers –*][1]

Safe in their Alabaster[2] Chambers –
Untouched by Morning
And untouched by Noon –
Sleep the meek members of the Resurrection[3] –
5   Rafter of satin,
And Roof of stone.

Light laughs the breeze
In her Castle above them –
Babbles the Bee in a stolid Ear,
10 Pipe the Sweet Birds in ignorant cadence –
Ah, what sagacity perished here!
—1859 VERSION

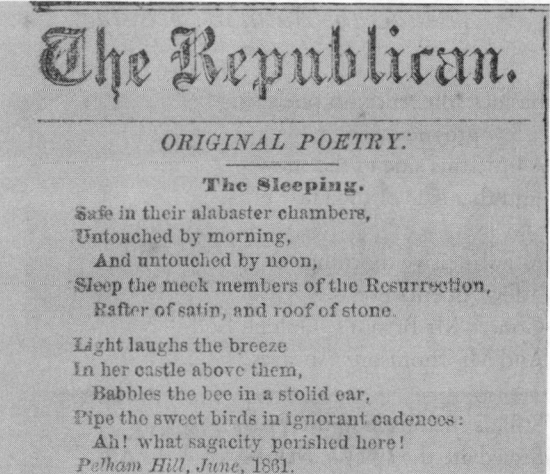

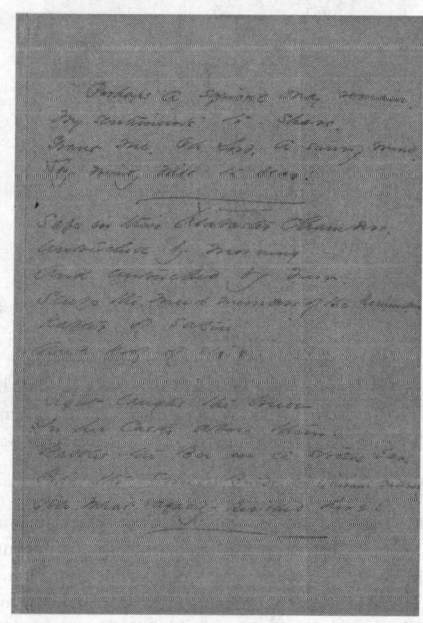

[*Safe in their Alabaster Chambers,*][4]

Safe in their Alabaster Chambers,
Untouched by Morning –
And untouched by Noon –
Lie the meek members of the Resurrection –
5   Rafter of Satin and Roof of Stone –

Grand go the Years – in the Crescent – above them –
Worlds scoop their Arcs –
And Firmaments – row –
Diadems – drop – and Doges[5] – surrender –
10 Soundless as dots – on a Disc of snow –
—1861 VERSION

---

[1] This poem appears in Johnson as Poem 216; in Franklin as Poem 124; and in Miller as the third poem in Sheet 3 of Fascicle 6, page 83 [the 1859 version] and also as the third poem in Sheet 4 of Fascicle 10, page 122 [the 1861 version]. The present transcription is in agreement with those of Franklin and Miller—though it is worth noting that the marks at the ends of lines 1, 3, and 4 may plausibly be read as right-slanting commas rather than dashes.

A variant of this 1859 version was published (with the title "The Sleeping") in the *Springfield Republican*, 1 March 1862.

[2] *Alabaster* Smooth, translucent white stone, frequently used for carving and statuary.

[3] *members of the Resurrection* I.e., the dead; those awaiting Judgment Day and the resurrection of the body.

[4] This 1861 version of the poem appears in Johnson as a variant of Poem 216; in Franklin as a variant of Poem 124; and in Miller as the third poem in Sheet 4 of Fascicle 10, page 122. The present transcription of the 1861 fascicle manuscript is in agreement with those of Franklin and Miller, except in two particulars: with Franklin, we read "Chambers" in line 1 as upper case; and, with Miller, we read "Noon" in line 3 as upper case. (Both can plausibly be read either way.)

An additional 1861 trial version of the second stanza is available under the heading *Dickinson's Personal Correspondence*, page 11, in the online component of this anthology.

[5] *Doges* Magistrates holding high civil office in the Venetian Republic from the seventh to the eighteenth centuries; the republic of Genoa also had a similar office.

[*Besides the Autumn poets sing*][1]

Besides[2] the Autumn poets sing
A few prosaic days
A little this side of the snow
And that side of the Haze.

5   A few incisive mornings –
A few Ascetic[3] eves –
Gone – Mr Bryant's "Golden Rod" –
And Mr Thomson's "sheaves."[4]

Still, is the bustle in the Brook –
10 Sealed are the spicy valves[5] –
Mesmeric fingers softly touch
The eyes of many Elves –

Perhaps a squirrel may remain –
My sentiments to share –
15 Grant me, Oh Lord, a sunny mind –
Thy windy will to bear!
—1859

[*All overgrown by cunning moss,*][6]

All overgrown by cunning[7] moss,
All interspersed with – weed,
The little cage of "Currer Bell"
In quiet "Haworth"[8] laid.

5   This Bird – observing others
When frosts too sharp became
Retire to other latitudes –
Quietly did the same –

But differed in returning –
10 Since Yorkshire hills are green –
Yet not in all the nests I meet –
Can Nightingale[9] be seen –

Or –

Gathered from many wanderings –
15 Gethsemane[10] can tell

---

[1]   This poem appears in Johnson as Poem 131; in Franklin as Poem 123; and in Miller as the second poem in Sheet 3 of Fascicle 6, page 82. The present transcription has been made according to conventional principles and, except for reading the mark after "Haze" as a period, is in accord with those of Johnson, Franklin, and Miller (all of whom print the poem with a dash after "Gone" in line 7, and with dashes at the ends of lines 5, 6, 7, 9, 10, 13, 14, and 15). These marks could all plausibly be read differently, however—the mark after "Gone" as a period; and the other marks as right-slanting commas. An alternative transcription appears in the website component of this anthology.

The poem appears in Todd and Higginson's *Poems* (1891) as Poem 49; they assign to it the title "November."

[2]   *Besides*   In addition to, beyond.

[3]   *Ascetic*   Austere, self-denying; Christian Ascetics withdrew from society and practiced abstinence and fasting, adhering to rigorous schedules of work and prayer.

[4]   *Mr Bryant's "Golden Rod"*   See "The Death of the Flowers," line 15, by American poet William Cullen Bryant (1794–1878); *Mr Thomson's "sheaves"*   See "Autumn," a section of the longer work *The Seasons*, by Scottish poet James Thomson (1700–48), lines 168 and 180.

[5]   *spicy valves*   I.e., flowers or seed pods that open or split like valves or doors; may refer more specifically to the "valves" of the flower's nectaries (which release scent as well as nectar).

[6]   This poem appears in Johnson as Poem 148; in Franklin as Poem 146; and in Miller as the second poem in Sheet 1, Fascicle 7, pages 86–87. The poem exists in only one manuscript version; at the end of the third stanza Dickinson writes "Or –" on a separate line, and then provides two more stanzas as alternatives. The poem is thus frequently printed including only the first three stanzas—although some editions have printed it as a three-stanza poem with Dickinson's alternative stanzas substituted for stanzas 2 and 3.

The transcription provided here is in agreement with those of Franklin and Miller except in one particular; the present editors read the mark between "with" and "weed" in line 2 as a dash, whereas Franklin and Miller have presumably read the mark between the two words as the cross from the "t" in "with." Dickinson certainly often places the crosses for her "t"s well beyond where the letter itself appears, but rarely so far forward as here—and rarely so low.

[7]   *cunning*   Skillful and crafty, as well as quaint, attractive.

[8]   *Currer Bell*   Pseudonym of English novelist and poet Charlotte Brontë (1816–55);   *Haworth*   Name of the parsonage where the Brontë family lived in Yorkshire, England (the graveyard attached to the church was directly adjacent to the parsonage house).

[9]   *Nightingale*   Migratory thrush whose beautiful, haunting song and habit of night-time singing have led to a symbolic association with poets and singers.

[10]   *Gethsemane*   Garden in Jerusalem where Christ prayed and endured agony of mind before his arrest and crucifixion.

Thro' what transporting anguish
She reached the Asphodel![1]

Soft fall the sounds of Eden
Upon her puzzled ear –
20 Oh what an afternoon for Heaven,
When "Bronte" entered there!
—1860

[I'm "wife" – I've finished that –][2]

I'm "wife" – I've finished that –
That other state –
I'm Czar[3] – I'm "Woman" now –
It's safer so –

5 How odd the Girl's life looks
Behind this soft Eclipse –
I think that Earth feels so
To folks in Heaven – now –

This being comfort – then
10 That other kind – was pain –
But why compare?
I'm "Wife"! Stop there!
—1861

[Title divine – is mine!][4]

Title divine – is mine!
The Wife – without the Sign!
Acute Degree – conferred on me –
Empress of Calvary![5]
5 Royal – all but the Crown!
Betrothed – without the swoon
God sends us Women –
When you – hold – Garnet to Garnet –
Gold – to Gold –
10 Born – Bridalled[6] – Shrouded –
In a Day –
Tri Victory
"My Husband" – women say –
Stroking the Melody –
15 Is this – the way?
—c. 1861

---

1 *Asphodel* In Greek mythology, this white flower covers the Elysian Fields, where heroes and virtuous souls rested after death.

2 This poem appears in Johnson as Poem 199; in Franklin as Poem 225; and in Miller as the fourth poem in Sheet 6, Fascicle 9, pages 112–13. There are few transcription issues—though the "dash" following "kind" in line 10 arguably might be better represented by a dot than a line of any length.

Todd and Higginson included the poem under the title "Apocalypse" in their edition of *Poems* (1890); aside from differences in punctuation, the version there includes two word changes in the second stanza; "feels" to "seems" and "folks" to "those."

3 *Czar* Title of the emperor of Russia.

4 This poem appears in Johnson as Poem 1072; in Franklin as Poem 194; and in Miller under "Poems Not Retained" on page 701. The poem exists in two manuscript versions (one to Samuel Bowles, the other to Susan Dickinson), both sent by Dickinson as letters, and both including this message following the poem itself: "Here's what I had to 'tell you'–you will tell no other; – Honor – is its own pawn." (Dickinson uses the "Honor is its own pawn" appeal in her 16 April 1862 letter to Thomas Wentworth Higginson.)

One line appears only in the version sent to Susan Dickinson; the Bowles version does not include the line "Tri Victory." In the Bowles version (but not in the Susan Dickinson) the word "this" in the final line is underlined. The present transcription is from the Susan Dickinson letter; Miller transcribes from the Bowles letter, while both Johnson (in *Final Harvest*) and Franklin (in *The Poems of Emily Dickinson: Reading Edition*) offer a composite version, including the "Tri Victory" line from the Susan Dickinson version and the underlining of "this" from the Bowles version.

An alternative transcription (in which this mark ˏ is used for "dashes" that have the form of right-slanting commas) appears in the website component of this anthology.

5 *Calvary* Place where Christ was crucified.

6 *Bridalled* I.e., married (with a pun on "bridled").

[*Faith is a fine invention*][1]

Faith is a fine invention
For Gentlemen who *see*.
But *Microscopes* are prudent
In an Emergency!
—1861

[*"Faith" is a fine invention*]

"Faith" is a fine invention
For Gentlemen who <u>see</u>!
But Microscopes are prudent
In an Emergency!
—1861

[*Some keep the Sabbath going to Church –*][2]

Some keep the Sabbath going to Church –
I keep it, staying at Home –
With a Bobolink[3] for a Chorister –
And an Orchard, for a Dome –

5 Some keep the Sabbath in Surplice[4] –
I just wear my Wings –
And instead of tolling the Bell, for Church,
Our little Sexton[5] – sings.

God preaches, a noted Clergyman –
10 And the sermon is never long,
So instead of getting to Heaven, at last –
I'm going, all along.
—1861

---

[1] The earliest extant version of this poem is that which appears in a letter to Samuel Bowles (dating probably from late 1860 or early 1861):

> Dear Mr Bowles
> Thank you.
>> "Faith" is a fine invention
>> When Gentlemen can see –
>> But Microscopes are prudent
>> In an Emergency.
> You spoke of the "East." I have thought about it this winter.
> Don't you think you and I should be shrewder, to take the <u>Mountain Road</u>?
>> That <u>Bareheaded life</u> – under the grass – worries one like a wasp.
>> The Rose is for Mary.
>>> Emily.

Dickinson included a revised version of the poem in Fascicle 10 (printed first above), and included a slightly different version in Fascicle 12 the next year (also printed above). The standard editions take different approaches to the poem: Johnson prints a transcription of the 1860 Bowles letter version as Poem 185; Franklin prints a transcription of the Fascicle 12 version as Poem 202; and Miller prints both fascicle versions (Fascicle 10, Sheet 1, page 119; Fascicle 12, Sheet 1, page 137), while noting in a footnote the existence of the Bowles letter version. Miller reads the punctuation at the end of the second line of the Fascicle 10 version as a dash; in other respects the present transcriptions are in accord with hers.

[2] This poem appears in Johnson as Poem 324; in Franklin as Poem 236; and in Miller as the final poem of Fascicle 9, Sheet 7, page 115. In their one-volume editions, both Johnson and Franklin print the version that Dickinson sent to Thomas Wentworth Higginson in July of 1861; that version is also used as the base text here. Miller prints the fascicle version (believed to date from the spring of 1861).

The poem was published (from a now-lost manuscript copy) in *Round Table*, 12 March 1864, under the title "My Sabbath," and was published by Todd and Higginson in *Poems* (1890) under the title "A Service of Song." As was standard practice when Dickinson's poems were published in her lifetime, capitalization, and punctuation were regularized; this resulted in the removal of most of the dashes—but also in the addition of one dash (both the *Round Table* version and the *Poems* [1890] version add a comma after "preaches" in line 9).

An alternative transcription (in which this mark ˌ is used for marks that have the form of right-slanting commas) appears in the website component of this anthology; the "dashes" at the ends of lines 2, 3, and 6 take this form, and the mark after "Heaven" is represented as a dot in the middle of the line rather than a comma, or, as it is sometimes transcribed, a dash.

[3] *Bobolink* North American songbird with a cheerful, tinkling song; its black and white plumage gives the bird a clerical look.

[4] *Surplice* Type of vestment worn by ministers, choristers, and other church officials.

[5] *Sexton* Caretaker of a church who traditionally rang the church bells.

[*The Lamp burns sure – within –*][1]

The Lamp burns sure – within –
Tho' Serfs[2] – supply the Oil –
It matters not the busy Wick –
At her phosphoric[3] toil!

5 The Slave – forgets – to fill –
The Lamp – burns golden – on –
Unconscious that the oil is out –
As that the Slave – is gone.
—1861

[*I came to buy a smile – today –*][4]

I came to buy a smile – today –
But just a single smile –
The smallest one upon your cheek
Will suit me just as well –

5 The one that no one else would miss
It shone so very small –
I'm pleading at the counter – sir –
Could you afford to sell?

I've Diamonds – on my fingers –
10 You know what Diamonds are!
I've Rubies – like the Evening Blood –
And Topaz – like the star!
'Twould be a bargain for a Jew![5]
Say – may I have it – Sir?
—1861

[*I'm Nobody! Who are you?*][6]

I'm Nobody! Who are you?
Are you – Nobody – too?
Then there's a pair of us!
Don't tell! they'd banish us – you know!

5 How dreary – to be – Somebody!
How public – like a Frog –
To tell your name – the livelong June –
To an admiring Bog!
—1861

---

1 This poem appears in Johnson as Poem 233; in Franklin as Poem 247; and in Miller as the fourth poem in Sheet 1 of Fascicle 10, page 117. The present text is in complete accord with the transcriptions of Johnson, Franklin, and Miller; the mark at the end of line 3, however, could plausibly be transcribed as a right-slanting comma.

2 *Serf* Person in servitude; slave.

3 *phosphoric* Phosphorescent, glowing in the dark.

4 This poem appears in Johnson as Poem 223; in Franklin as Poem 258; and in Miller as the only poem in Sheet 2 of Fascicle 11, page 127. The present text is in agreement with Franklin and Miller regarding the punctuation of the poem, and with Miller in emending "opon" to "upon" in line 3.

5 *'Twould ... Jew* I.e., you would get a good deal (Dickinson is referring to the racist stereotype that Jewish people get the better of others in financial dealings).

6 This poem appears in Johnson as Poem 288; in Franklin as Poem 260; and in Miller as part of Fascicle 11, Sheet 4, page 128. The poem was printed by Todd and Higginson in *Poems* (1891), with "Don't tell" printed at the end of the third line rather than the beginning of the fourth. There is only one manuscript version extant; transcriptions of the fourth line vary. The present editors follow Johnson in emending "Dont" to "Don't," while printing "they'd" in lower case; Franklin transcribes the line as-is ("Dont ... they'd"), while Miller emends "Dont" to "Don't" and capitalizes "They'd."

Dickinson provides two variant word choices in the manuscript: "advertise" for "banish" in line 4, and "one's" for "your" in line 7.

A facsimile of the manuscript appears above.

× 2

Wild nights – Wild nights!
Were I with thee
Wild nights should be
Our luxury!

Futile – the winds –
To a heart in port –
Done with the compass –
Done with the chart!

Rowing in Eden –
Ah, the sea!
Might I but moor –
Tonight –
In thee!

[*Wild nights – Wild nights!*][1]

Wild nights – Wild nights!
Were I with thee
Wild nights should[2] be
Our luxury!

5   Futile – the winds –
To a Heart in port –
Done with the Compass –
Done with the Chart!

Rowing in Eden –
10 Ah – the Sea!
Might I but moor – tonight –
In thee!
   —1861

[*Wild nights – Wild nights!*]

Wild nights – Wild nights!
Were I with thee
Wild nights should be
Our luxury!

5   Futile – the winds –
To a Heart in port –
Done with the Compass –
Done with the Chart!

Rowing in Eden –
10 Ah! the Sea!
Might I but moor –
Tonight –
In thee!
   —1861

[*Wild nights – Wild nights!*]

Wild nights! Wild nights!
Were I with thee,
Wild nights should be
Our luxury!

5   Futile the winds
To a heart in port,
Done with the compass,
Done with the chart.

Rowing in Eden!
10 Ah! the sea!
Might I but moor
To-night in thee!
   —1891

---

1   This poem appears in Johnson as Poem 249; in Franklin as Poem 269; and in Miller as part of Fascicle 11, Sheet 8, page 133. Here we present first a facsimile of the only manuscript version (see the facing page). Next is a conventional transcription of the poem, according to the principles followed by both Franklin and Miller—with the mark after "Ah" interpreted as a dash, and with "tonight" interpreted as the final word of the eleventh line, written in lower case. The next column presents an alternative transcription, with the mark after "Ah" interpreted as an exclamation mark missing its dot, and "Tonight" read as a capitalized word, forming a line on its own. Given that Dickinson capitalized with great frequency, and that she did not generally indent so as to make it clear if a word at the beginning of a line was intended to be carried over from the previous line or to begin a new line, other readings seem possible as well. Johnson reads the mark after "Ah" as a comma and capitalizes "Tonight," while keeping it as part of the eleventh line.

Todd and Higginson include the poem in their edition of *Poems*, second series (1891), with "To-night" capitalized and printed at the beginning of the twelfth line rather than at the end of the eleventh; their version is reproduced here last.

2   *should* Would.

[*I taste a liquor never brewed –*][1]

I taste a liquor never brewed –
From tankards scooped in Pearl –
Not all the Frankfort Berries[2]
Yield such an alcohol!

5 Inebriate of air – am I –
And Debauchee of Dew –
Reeling, thro' endless summer days,
From inns of molten Blue –

When "Landlords" turn the drunken Bee
10 Out of the foxglove's door –
When Butterflies – renounce their "drams"[3] –
I shall but drink the more!

Till Seraphs[4] swing their snowy Hats –
And Saints – to windows run –
15 To see the little Tippler
From Manzanilla[5] come!
    —1861

The May-Wine.

I taste a liquor never brewed,
  From tankards scooped in pearl;
Not Frankfort berries yield the sense
  Such a delirious whirl.

Inebriate of air am I,
  And debauchee of dew;—
Reeling through endless summer days,
  From inns of molten blue.

When landlords turn the drunken bee
  Out of the Fox-glove's door,
When butterflies renounce their drams,
  I shall but drink the more;

Till seraphs swing their snowy hats,
  And saints to windows run,
To see the little tippler
  Come staggering toward the sun.

---

[1] This poem appears in Johnson as Poem 214; in Franklin as Poem 207; and in Miller as the first poem in Sheet 1 of Fascicle 12, page 135 [the 1859 version] and also as the third poem in Sheet 4 of Fascicle 10, pages 122–23 [the 1861 version]. The fascicle manuscripts are the only manuscript versions extant. Dickinson provides two variant readings: "Vats upon the Rhine" for "Frankfort Berries" and "Leaning against the – Sun –" as an alternative last line (Franklin adopts the variant last line in his *Poems of Emily Dickinson*). The present transcription is in agreement with those of Franklin and Miller, except in one particular; we read the small mark at the end of line 7 (which resembles a right-slanting comma) as a comma rather than a dash.

    A variant of this poem (from a now-lost manuscript copy, with a different last line) was published in the *Springfield Republican*, 4 May 1861, under the title "The May-Wine."

[2] *Frankfort Berries* Grapes grown in Germany's Rhine Valley.

[3] *drams* Small cups of liquor or wine.

[4] *Seraphs* Angels.

[5] *Tippler* Habitual drinker, but not a full-fledged alcoholic; *Manzanilla* Spanish sherry.

[*There's a certain Slant of light,*][1]

There's a certain Slant of light,
Winter Afternoons –
That oppresses, like the Heft
Of Cathedral Tunes –

5   Heavenly Hurt, it gives us –
We can find no scar,
But internal difference –
Where the Meanings, are –

None may teach it – Any –
10 'Tis the Seal Despair –
An imperial affliction
Sent us of the Air –

When it comes, the Landscape listens –
Shadows – hold their breath –
15 When it goes, 'tis like the Distance
On the look of Death
—1862

[*"Hope" is the thing with feathers –*][2]

"Hope" is the thing with feathers –
That perches in the soul –
And sings the tune without the words –
And never stops – at all –

5   And sweetest – in the Gale – is heard –
And sore must be the storm –
That could abash the little Bird
That kept so many warm –

I've heard it in the chilliest land
10 And on the strangest Sea –
Yet, never, in Extremity,
It asked a crumb – of Me.
—1862

---

[1]   This poem appears in Johnson as Poem 258; in Franklin as Poem 320; and in Miller as the fourth poem in Sheet 3, Fascicle 13, page 153. Above is a conventional transcription of the poem following the principles established by Johnson, Franklin, and Miller; both Franklin and Miller read the poem as having thirteen dashes. (Johnson reads the mark after "difference" as a comma; in other respects his transcription is identical to those of Franklin and Miller.)

Todd and Higginson edited the poem for their edition of *Poems* (1890), with "weight" replacing "heft" in line 3, and with only one dash.

---

[2]   This poem appears in Johnson as Poem 254; in Franklin as Poem 314; and in Miller within Fascicle 13, Sheet 2, page 150. All three of those editors punctuate the poem identically, as have the editors of this anthology—which is an entirely defensible reading, though alternative readings are certainly possible in lines 6, 11, and 12, and perhaps line 4 as well.

[*I found the words to every thought*][1]

I found the words to every thought
I ever had – but One –
And that – defies me –
As a Hand did try to chalk[2] the Sun

5 To Races – nurtured in the Dark –
How would your own – begin?
Can Blaze be shown in Cochineal[3] –
Or Noon – in Mazarin?[4]
—1862

[*I like a look of Agony,*][5]

I like a look of Agony,
Because I know it's true –
Men do not sham Convulsion,
Nor simulate, a Throe –

5 The eyes glaze once – and that is Death –
Impossible to feign
The Beads upon the Forehead
By homely Anguish strung.
—1862

[*I felt a Funeral, in my Brain,*][6]

I felt a Funeral, in my Brain,
And Mourners to and fro
Kept treading – treading – till it seemed
That Sense[7] was breaking through –

5 And when they all were seated,
A Service, like a Drum –
Kept beating – beating – till I thought
My Mind was going numb –

And then I heard them lift a Box
10 And creak across my Soul
With those same Boots of Lead, again,
Then Space – began to toll,

As all the Heavens were a Bell,
And Being, but an Ear,
15 And I, and Silence, some strange Race
Wrecked, solitary, here –

And then a Plank in Reason, broke,
And I dropped down, and down –
And hit a World, at every plunge,
20 And Finished knowing – then –
—1862

---

1 This poem appears in Johnson as Poem 581; in Franklin as Poem 436; and in Miller as the last poem in Sheet 5 of Fascicle 15, page 175. Dickinson provides two variant word choices in the fascicle manuscript: "phrase" for "words" in line 1; and "done" for "shown" in line 7.

2 *chalk* Sketch, but also "make pale" or whiten.

3 *Cochineal* Lustrous scarlet color, made from a dye composed of the desiccated bodies of an insect, the *coccus cacti*, commonly found in Mexico.

4 *Mazarin* Deep shade of blue.

5 This poem appears in Johnson as Poem 339; in Franklin as Poem 241; and in Miller as the second poem in Sheet 2 of Fascicle 16, page 179. All three transcribe the poem in the same way—as is done here.

6 This poem appears in Johnson as Poem 280; in Franklin as Poem 340; and in Miller as the third poem in Sheet 2 of Fascicle 16, page 179. The present transcription of the fascicle manuscript is in complete agreement with those of Johnson, Franklin, and Miller. There are few transcription issues with the punctuation of the poem; the mark at the end of line 6 could plausibly be read as a right-slanting comma, and the mark at the end of line 8 as a period. Dickinson provides two variant word choices in the manuscript: "Crash" for "plunge" in line 19, and "Got through" for "Finished" in line 20. The poem was first published by Todd and Higginson in *Poems: Third Series* (1896), with the final stanza omitted and numerous smaller changes.

7 *Sense* Meaning, but also sensory perception, consciousness.

[*It was not Death, for I stood up,*][1]

It was not Death, for I stood up,
And all the Dead, lie down –
It was not Night, for all the Bells
Put Out their Tongues, for Noon.

5   It was not Frost, for on my Flesh
I felt Siroccos[2] – crawl –
Nor Fire – for just my Marble feet
Could keep a Chancel,[3] cool –

And yet, it tasted, like them all,
10 The Figures I have seen
Set orderly, for Burial,
Reminded me, of mine –

As if my life were shaven,
And fitted to a frame,
15 And could not breathe without a key,
And 'twas like Midnight, some –

When everything that ticked – has stopped –
And Space stares, all around,
Or Grisly frosts – first Autumn morns,
20 Repeal the Beating Ground –

But, most, like Chaos – Stopless – cool –
Without a Chance, or Spar[4] –
Or even a Report of Land –
To justify – Despair.
    —1862

---

[1]   This poem appears in Johnson as Poem 510; in Franklin as Poem 355; and in Miller as the first poem in Sheet 4 of Fascicle 17, pages 187–88. There is only one manuscript version extant; two alternative readings are written in the margins: "Knees" for "Flesh" in line 5, and "two" for "my" in line 7. Other than in line 18, the transcription here is in accord with the three standard editions. Miller and Johnson both transcribe the punctuation in line 18 as two dashes, while Franklin reads the line as having a dash at the end and no punctuation after "stares." In the manuscript the marks that appear after "stares" and after "around" are similar—both shaped like right-slanting commas.

[2]   *Siroccos*   Hot, dry winds from North Africa that sweep across the Mediterranean to Southern Europe.

[3]   *Chancel*   Section of a church where the services are performed.

[4]   *Spar*   Piece of timber, often used for supportive wooden structures on a ship, such as masts, booms, or gaffs.

[*A Bird came down the Walk –*][5]

A Bird came down the Walk –
He did not know I saw.
He bit an Angleworm[6] in halves
And ate the fellow, raw,

5   And then he drank a Dew
From a convenient Grass –
And then hopped sidewise to the Wall
To let a Beetle pass –

He glanced with rapid eyes
10 That hurried all around –
They looked like frightened Beads, I thought –
He stirred his Velvet Head

Like one in danger, Cautious,
I offered him a Crumb
15 And he unrolled his feathers
And rowed him softer home –

Than Oars divide the Ocean,
Too silver[7] for a seam –
Or Butterflies, off Banks of Noon
20 Leap, plashless as they swim.
    —1862

---

[5]   This poem appears in Johnson as Poem 328; in Franklin as Poem 359; and in Miller as the third and last poem in Sheet 5 of Fascicle 17, pages 189–90. There are two manuscript versions extant, both evidently from 1862; the punctuation of the two differs in several respects, beginning with the comma that appears after "Bird" in the first line of the version that both Franklin and Miller take as their primary copy text. The present text is (like that in Johnson's edition) transcribed from the variant manuscript; the transcriptions are identical except for the punctuation at the end of the second line, which Johnson reads as a dash. It is one of several points of uncertainty; several of the other dashes could well be read as right-slanting commas.

   Another now-lost manuscript version was sent to Higginson, who printed the full poem in his October 1891 *Atlantic Monthly* article on Dickinson (see the website component of this anthology); Todd and Higginson edited the poem for *Poems* (1890), giving it the title "In the Garden."

[6]   *Angleworm*   Earthworm (like those used by "anglers," or fishers).

[7]   *silver*   Glistening and in motion, like quicksilver (mercury), as well as silver in color. Dickinson describes the ocean in similar terms elsewhere, for example as an "everywhere of silver."

[*After great pain, a formal feeling comes –*][1]

After great pain, a formal feeling comes –
The Nerves sit ceremonious, like Tombs –
The stiff Heart questions 'was it He, that bore,'
And 'Yesterday, or Centuries before'?
5 The Feet, mechanical, go round –
A Wooden way
Of Ground, or Air, or Ought –
Regardless grown,
A Quartz contentment, like a stone –

10 This is the Hour of Lead –
Remembered, if outlived,
As Freezing persons, recollect the Snow –
First – Chill – then Stupor – then the letting go –
—1862

But positive, as Sound –
5 It beckons, and it baffles –
Philosophy, don't know –
And through a Riddle, at the last –
Sagacity, must go –
To guess it, puzzles scholars –
10 To gain it, Men have borne
Contempt of Generations
And Crucifixion, shown –
Faith slips – and laughs, and rallies –
Blushes, if any see –
15 Plucks at a twig of Evidence –
And asks a Vane,[4] the way –
Much Gesture, from the Pulpit –
Strong Hallelujahs roll –
Narcotics cannot still the – Tooth
20 That nibbles at the soul –
—1862

[*This World is not conclusion.*][2]

This World is not conclusion.
A Species[3] stands beyond –
Invisible, as Music –

[*I like to see it lap the Miles –*][5]

I like to see it lap the Miles –
And lick the Valleys up –
And stop to feed itself at Tanks[6] –
And then – prodigious step

5 Around a Pile of Mountains –
And supercilious peer
In Shanties – by the sides of Roads –
And then a Quarry pare

To fit its sides
10 And crawl between

---

1 This poem appears in Johnson as Poem 341; in Franklin as Poem 372; and in Miller as the third poem in Sheet 4 of Fascicle 18, page 198. The manuscript transcriptions by Franklin and Miller diverge in several respects from that by Johnson—most notably in that Johnson does not transcribe the quotation marks, and ignores the manuscript marks regarding the ordering of the lines in the second stanza. The present text agrees with those of Franklin and of Miller in every particular; it may be worth noting, however, that the mark at the end of line 7 could perhaps more plausibly be read as a right-slanting comma than as a dash, and that the mark after "First" in the last line appears to be a dot rather than a dash.

2 This poem appears in Johnson as Poem 501; in Franklin as Poem 373; and in Miller as the fourth poem in Sheet 4 of Fascicle 18, pages 198–99. There are several alternatives indicated in the manuscript: "sequel" for "Species" in line 2; "prove" for "guess" in line 9; "Sure" for "Strong" in line 18; and "Mouse" for "Tooth" in line 19. The transcriptions by Johnson, Franklin, and Miller are in agreement except in one particular; Franklin does not emend "dont" to "don't" in line 6. The present text agrees with those of Franklin and of Miller; it is worth noting, however, that several of the marks at the ends of lines could plausibly be read as right-slanting commas, and at least two others as periods.

3 *Species* Metaphysical ideal or vision.

---

4 *Vane* Weather-vane.

5 This poem appears in Johnson as Poem 585; in Franklin as Poem 383; and in Miller as the second poem in Sheet 2 of Fascicle 19, page 204. Franklin leaves "it's" uncorrected both in line 9 and in line 17; Dickinson provides several alternative readings in the fascicle manuscript: "hear it" for "see it" in line 1; "Ribs" for "sides" in line 9; "then" for "And" in line 14; and "punctual" for "prompter" in line 15. Todd and Higginson edited the poem for *Poems* (1890), giving it the title "The Railway Train."

6 *Tanks* Water stations (also called "water stops") for steam engines, where they could replenish their supply of water.

Complaining all the while
In horrid – hooting stanza –
Then chase itself down Hill –

And neigh like Boanerges[1] –
15 Then – prompter than a Star
Stop – docile and omnipotent
At its own stable door –
—1862

[*The Soul selects her own Society –*][2]

The Soul selects her own Society –
Then – shuts the Door –
To her divine Majority –
Present no more –

5 Unmoved – she notes the Chariots – pausing –
At her low Gate –
Unmoved – an Emperor be kneeling
Upon her Mat –

I've known her – from an ample nation –
10 Choose One –
Then – close the Valves of her attention –
Like Stone –
—1862

[*One need not be a Chamber – to be Haunted –*][3]

One need not be a Chamber – to be Haunted –
One need not be a House –
The Brain has Corridors – surpassing
Material Place –

5 Far safer, of a Midnight Meeting
External Ghost
Than its interior Confronting –
That Cooler Host.

Far safer, through an Abbey gallop,[4]
10 The Stones a'chase –
Than Unarmed, one's a'self encounter –
In lonesome Place –

Ourself behind ourself, concealed –
Should startle most –
15 Assassin hid in our Apartment
Be Horror's least.

The Body – borrows a Revolver –
He bolts the Door –
O'erlooking a superior spectre –
20 Or More –
—1862, 1864

---

1 *Boanerges* Loud, denunciatory preacher.

2 This poem appears in Johnson as Poem 303; in Franklin as Poem 409; and in Miller as the last poem in Sheet 4 of Fascicle 20, page 218. The present transcription of the fascicle manuscript is in complete agreement with those of the three standard editions; it is worth noting, however, that several of the marks at the ends of lines (notably, at the ends of lines 1, 3, 5, and 11) could plausibly be read as a right-slanting commas—as could the marks after "Chariots" in line 5 and "her" in line 9. Todd and Higginson include the poem under the title "Exclusion" in *Poems* (1890); they adopt the variant word choices Dickinson provides for lines 3 and 4: "On" for "To" in line 3, and "Obtrude" for "Present" in line 4. Dickinson also provides manuscript variant readings for line 8 ("On her Rush mat") and line 11 ("lids" for "Valves").

3 This poem appears in Johnson as Poem 670; in Franklin as Poem 407; and in Miller as the first poem in Sheet 4 of Fascicle 20, page 217. The present editors follow Johnson and Franklin in transcribing from the 1864 variant that Dickinson sent to Susan Dickinson; it differs in several small particulars from the 1862 fascicle text, and in one large one: the fascicle text ends with "More near" rather than "Or More." The fascicle manuscript also includes numerous variants. Like Johnson (but unlike Franklin), we emend "it's" to "its" in line 7. Todd and Higginson include the poem in *Poems* (1891) under the title "Ghosts," evidently using the fascicle manuscript as their base text, but adopting Dickinson's variant word choice for line 8 ("Whiter" for "cooler").

4 *through an Abbey gallop* Abbeys—usually haunted—are common settings in Gothic literature.

[*They shut me up in Prose –*][1]

They shut me up in Prose –
As when a little Girl
They put me in the Closet –
Because they liked me "still" –

5 Still! Could themself have peeped –
And seen my Brain – go round –
They might as wise have lodged a Bird
For Treason – in the Pound –

Himself[2] has but to will
10 And easy as a Star
Look down upon Captivity –
And laugh – No more have I –
—1862

[*This was a Poet –*][3]

This was a Poet –
It is That
Distills amazing sense
From ordinary Meanings –
5 And Attar[4] so immense

From the familiar species
That perished by the Door –
We wonder it was not Ourselves
Arrested[5] it – before –

10 Of Pictures, the Discloser –
The Poet – it is He –
Entitles Us – by Contrast –
To ceaseless Poverty –

Of Portion – so unconscious –
15 The Robbing – could not harm –
Himself – to Him – a Fortune –
Exterior – to Time –
—1862

[*I died for Beauty – but was scarce*][6]

I died for Beauty – but was scarce
Adjusted in the Tomb
When One who died for Truth, was lain
In an adjoining Room

5 He questioned softly "Why I failed"?
"For Beauty", I replied –
"And I – for Truth – Themself are One –
We Brethren, are", He said –

---

1   This poem appears in Johnson as Poem 613; in Franklin as Poem 445; and in Miller as the last poem in Sheet 2 of Fascicle 21, page 223. The present transcription of the fascicle manuscript is in complete agreement with those of Johnson and Miller; Franklin prints "opon" (for "upon") in line 11, rather than silently correcting, as is done by other editors. It is worth noting that several of the marks at the ends of lines (notably, at the ends of lines 1, 3, 5, 6, and 11) could plausibly be read as right-slanting commas. The manuscript provides a variant of line 11: "Abolish his Captivity" for "Look down upon Captivity."

2   *Himself* I.e., the bird.

3   This poem appears in Johnson as Poem 448; in Franklin as Poem 446; and in Miller as the first poem in Sheet 3 of Fascicle 21, page 224. The present transcription of the fascicle manuscript is in complete agreement with those of Franklin and Miller; Johnson reads what appear in the manuscript to be the poem's first two lines as one, thus regularizing the poem into stanzas of four lines each. It is worth noting that several of the marks at the ends of lines (notably, at the ends of lines 1, 4, 10, and 12) could plausibly be read as right-slanting commas.

4   *Attar* Essential oil made from roses.

5   *Arrested* Caught, laid hold of.

6   This poem appears in Johnson as Poem 449; in Franklin as Poem 448; and in Miller as the third poem in Sheet 3 of Fascicle 21, page 225. The present transcription of the fascicle manuscript is in complete agreement with that of Johnson, who emends "bretheren" to "brethren." (Franklin and Miller print the word with the additional "e.") The word was spelled (and presumably pronounced) with three syllables in late medieval times ("bretheryn"), though by Shakespeare's time it had become standardized as a two-syllable word. It is certainly possible that Dickinson intended the archaic spelling and pronunciation, but it seems at least as likely that this was an inadvertent misspelling; Dickinson was, as Miller says, "an erratic speller." It is also worth noting that, with the two-syllable "brethren," the line scans as iambic trimeter—as do the last lines of the other two stanzas.

There are few transcription issues with the punctuation of the poem, though the marks at the ends of lines 10 and 11 could plausibly be read as right-slanting commas.

And so, as Kinsmen, met a Night –
10 We talked between the Rooms –
Until the Moss had reached our lips –
And covered up – our names –
—1862

[*The Malay – took the Pearl –*][1]

The Malay[2] – took the Pearl –
Not – I – the Earl –
I – feared the Sea – too much
Unsanctified – to touch –

5 Praying that I might be
Worthy – the Destiny –
The Swarthy fellow swam –
And bore my Jewel – Home –

Home to the Hut! What lot
10 Had I – the Jewel – got –
Borne on a Dusky Breast –
I had not deemed a Vest
Of Amber – fit –

The Negro[3] never knew
15 I – wooed it – too –
To gain, or be undone –
Alike to Him – One –
—1862

[*Because I could not stop for Death –*][4]

Because I could not stop for Death –
He kindly stopped for me –
The Carriage held but just Ourselves –
And Immortality.

5 We slowly drove – He knew no haste
And I had put away
My labor and my leisure too,
For His Civility –

We passed the School, where Children strove[5]
10 At Recess – in the Ring –
We passed the Fields of Gazing Grain –
We passed the Setting Sun –

Or rather – He passed Us –
The Dews drew quivering and Chill –
15 For only Gossamer,[6] my Gown –
My Tippet – only Tulle[7] –

We paused before a House that seemed
A Swelling of the Ground –
The Roof was scarcely visible –
20 The Cornice[8] – in the Ground –

Since then – 'tis Centuries – and yet
Feels shorter than the Day
I first surmised the Horses' Heads
Were toward Eternity –
—1862

---

1   This poem appears in Johnson as Poem 452; in Franklin as Poem 451; and in Miller as the third poem in Sheet 4 of Fascicle 21, page 226. The present text is in agreement with Johnson, Franklin, and Miller regarding the punctuation of the poem—though the mark at the end of line 7 could plausibly be read as a right-slanting comma.

2   *Malay*   Person from the Malay Peninsula. Prior to the industrialization of the pearl industry, many pearls were harvested by divers in Southeast Asia.

3   *Negro*   In the nineteenth century, this term could be used to refer to any person perceived as having dark skin.

4   This poem appears in Johnson as Poem 712; in Franklin as Poem 479; and in Miller as the opening poem in Fascicle 23, Sheet 1, page 239. The transcriptions in the Johnson, Franklin, and Miller editions are in complete accord, interpreting the marks at the ends of lines 3, 12, 13, and 24 as dashes, and the mark after "Centuries" in line 21 as a dash as well; the transcription here takes the same approach. In the "Alternative Readings" section that appears as part of the website component of this anthology we present an alternative transcription, in which the same marks are read as reverse or right-slanting commas (‚).

The Todd and Higginson edition of *Poems* (1890) includes a version of this poem, under the title "The Chariot," in which there are several substantive changes—including the omission of the fourth stanza.

5   *strove*   Fought or quarreled.

6   *Gossamer*   Extremely fine material.

7   *Tippet*   Small shawl or capelet;   *Tulle*   Fine, netted fabric.

8   *Cornice*   Decorative molding that runs along the base of a building's roof.

[*I dwell in Possibility* –][1]

I dwell in Possibility –
A fairer House than Prose –
More numerous of Windows –
Superior – for Doors –

5 Of Chambers as the Cedars –
Impregnable of Eye –
And for an Everlasting Roof
The Gambrels[2] of the Sky –

Of Visitors – the fairest –
10 For Occupation – This –
The spreading wide my narrow Hands
To gather Paradise –
—1862

[*He fumbles at your Soul*][3]

He fumbles at your Soul
As Players at the Keys[4]
Before they drop full Music on –
He stuns you by degrees –
5 Prepares your brittle nature
For the ethereal Blow
By fainter Hammers – further heard –
Then nearer – Then so slow
Your Breath has time to straighten –
10 Your Brain – to bubble Cool –
Deals – One – imperial – Thunderbolt –
That scalps your naked Soul –

When Winds take Forests in their Paws –
The Universe – is still –
—1862

[*It feels a shame to be Alive* –][5]

It feels a shame to be Alive –
When Men so brave – are dead –
One envies the Distinguished Dust –
Permitted – such a Head –

---

1 This poem appears in Johnson as Poem 657; in Franklin as Poem 466; and in Miller as the first poem in Sheet 4 of Fascicle 22, page 233. The present transcription of the fascicle manuscript is in complete agreement with those of all three of these editors—all of whom silently emend "visiters" in line 9. There are few transcription issues with the punctuation of the poem, though the mark at the end of line 5 could plausibly be read as a right-slanting comma. Dickinson provides one alternative reading in the manuscript—"Gables" for "Gambrels" in line 8.

2 *Gambrels* Roofs with two slopes on each side. (This variety of roof was common in the northeastern states.)

3 This poem appears in Johnson as Poem 315; in Franklin as Poem 477; and in Miller as the third poem in Sheet 6 of Fascicle 22, pages 237–38. Miller transcribes from the fascicle manuscript, in which "substance" appears instead of "nature" in line 5; "chance" instead of "time" in line 9; "peels" instead of "scalps" in line 12; and "Firmaments – are" instead of "Universe – is" in line 14. The variant readings are included in the fascicle manuscript, and were adopted in the manuscript version sent to Susan Dickinson (also believed to date from late 1862), which is the basis for the present text. The first 12 lines in the fascicle version are organized into three four-line stanzas. Franklin's Poem 477 adopts all the variant readings of the Susan Dickinson version, but adopts the stanza structure of the fascicle version. Both Franklin and Miller retain the misspelling of "ethereal" as "etherial," which appears in both versions. There are few transcription issues with the punctuation of this poem.

4 *Keys* I.e., piano keys.

5 This poem appears in Johnson as Poem 444; in Franklin as Poem 524; and in Miller as the second poem in Sheet 6 of Fascicle 24, pages 257–58. The present text is in agreement with the transcriptions of both Franklin and Miller. It is perhaps worth noting that nineteenth-century reading habits in a poetic context such as line 15 of this poem would almost certainly have taken "dissolved" as having three syllables (dis-sol-ved).

5　The Stone – that tells defending Whom
　　This Spartan put away[1]
　　What little of Him we – possessed
　　In Pawn for Liberty

　　The price is great – Sublimely paid –
10　Do we deserve – a Thing –
　　That lives – like Dollars – must be piled
　　Before we may obtain?

　　Are we that wait – sufficient worth –
　　That such Enormous Pearl
15　As life – dissolved be[2] – for Us –
　　In Battle's – horrid Bowl?

　　It may be – a Renown to live –
　　I think the Men who die –
　　Those unsustained – Saviors –
20　Present Divinity –
　　—1863

[This is my letter to the World][3]

This is my letter to the World
That never wrote to Me –
The simple News that Nature told –
With tender Majesty

5　Her Message is committed
　　To Hands I cannot see –
　　For love of Her – Sweet – countrymen –
　　Judge tenderly – of Me
　　—1863

[I heard a Fly buzz – when I died –][4]

I heard a Fly buzz – when I died –
The Stillness in the Room
Was like the Stillness in the Air –
Between the Heaves of Storm –

5　The Eyes around – had wrung them dry –
　　And Breaths were gathering firm
　　For that last Onset – when the King
　　Be witnessed – in the Room –

　　I willed my Keepsakes – Signed away
10　What portion of me be
　　Assignable – and then it was
　　There interposed a Fly –

　　With Blue – uncertain stumbling Buzz –
　　Between the light – and me –
15　And then the Windows failed – and then
　　I could not see to see –
　　—1863

---

[1]　*The Stone … put away*　Allusion to the famous epitaph at the site of the Battle of Thermopylae (480 BCE), where all 300 of the Spartan soldiers who were sent to defend Greece against the Persian army died; one translation of the epitaph reads, "Go tell the Spartans, thou who passest by, / That here, obedient to their laws, we lie."

[2]　*Enormous Pearl … dissolved be*　Reference to the commonly held belief that pearls dissolve in strongly acidic solutions. See also Matthew 13.45–46: "Again, the kingdom of heaven is like unto a merchant man, seeking goodly pearls: Who, when he had found one pearl of great price, went and sold all that he had, and bought it."

[3]　This poem appears in Johnson as Poem 441; in Franklin as Poem 519; and in Miller as the second poem in Sheet 4 of Fascicle 24, page 254. The present transcription of the fascicle manuscript is in complete agreement with those of all three of these editors. There are few transcription issues with the punctuation of the poem, though the marks at the ends of lines 2 and 6 could plausibly be read as periods rather than dashes.

[4]　This poem appears in Johnson as Poem 465; in Franklin as Poem 591; and in Miller as the third poem in Sheet 1 of Fascicle 26, page 270. The present transcription of the fascicle manuscript is in complete agreement with those of Franklin and Miller. There are few transcription issues with the punctuation of the poem, though the marks at the ends of lines 3 and 12 could plausibly be read as right-slanting commas. The second dash in line 13—if dash it is—takes the form of an underline mark beneath the "s" of "stumbling"; Johnson does not read there as being any punctuation mark here.

[*The Brain – is wider than the Sky –*][1]

The Brain – is wider than the Sky –
For – put them side by side –
The one the other will contain
With ease – and You – beside –
5   The Brain is deeper than the sea –
For – hold them – Blue to Blue –
The one the other will absorb –
As Sponges – Buckets – do –

The Brain is just the weight of God –
10   For – Heft them – Pound for Pound –
And they will differ – if they do –
As Syllable from Sound –
—1863

[*Much Madness is divinest Sense –*][2]

Much Madness is divinest Sense –
To a discerning Eye –
Much Sense – the starkest Madness –
'Tis the Majority
5   In this, as all, prevail –
Assent – and you are sane –
Demur – you're straightway dangerous –
And handled with a Chain –
—1863

[*I started Early – Took my Dog –*][3]

I started Early – Took my Dog –
And visited the Sea –
The Mermaids in the Basement
Came out to look at me –

5   And Frigates – in the Upper Floor
Extended Hempen[4] Hands –
Presuming Me to be a Mouse –
Aground – upon the Sands –

But no Man moved Me – till the Tide
10   Went past my simple Shoe –

And past my Apron – and my Belt
And past my Boddice – too –

And made as He would eat me up –
As wholly as a Dew
15   Upon a Dandelion's Sleeve –
And then – I started – too –

And He – He followed – close behind –
I felt His Silver Heel
Upon my Ankle – Then my Shoes
20   Would overflow with Pearl –

Until We met the Solid Town –
No One He seemed to know –
And bowing – with a Mighty look –
At me – The Sea withdrew –
—1863

---

1   This poem appears in Johnson as Poem 632; in Franklin as Poem 598; and in Miller as the third poem in Sheet 3 of Fascicle 26, page 273. The present transcription of the fascicle manuscript is in complete agreement with those of Johnson, Franklin, and Miller. There are few transcription issues with the punctuation of the poem; the mark at the end of line 11 could plausibly be read as a right-slanting comma, and the mark at the end of line 12 as a period. Dickinson provides one variant word choice in the manuscript: "include" for "contain" in line 3.

2   This poem appears in Johnson as Poem 435; in Franklin as Poem 620; and in Miller as the fourth poem in Sheet 3 of Fascicle 29, page 304. Johnson and Franklin read "All" rather than "all" in line 5; a comparison of Dickinson's rendering in line 6 of a capital "A" followed by lower case letters (in "Assent") lends support to Miller's reading of the "a" in "all" as lower case.

3   This poem appears in Johnson as Poem 520; in Franklin as Poem 656; and in Miller as the first poem in Sheet 2 of Fascicle 30, pages 311–12. The present text follows Johnson in emending all three of the obvious misspellings in the manuscript: "opon" in line 8, and again in line 19; and "Ancle" in line 19. Franklin leaves all three uncorrected, while Miller emends "opon" but not "Ancle." The present text is in agreement with Johnson, Franklin, and Miller regarding the punctuation of the poem. The mark in the middle of line 11 could plausibly be read as a right-slanting comma, and the mark at the end of line 4 could plausibly be read as a period.

4   *Hempen*   Hemp fiber was and is commonly used to make ropes; in the nineteenth century it was also (somewhat less commonly) used to make ships' sails.

[*What Soft – Cherubic Creatures –*][1]

What Soft – Cherubic Creatures –
These Gentlewomen are –
One would as soon assault a Plush –
Or violate a Star –

5 Such Dimity[2] Convictions –
A Horror so refined
Of freckled Human Nature –
Of Deity – Ashamed –

It's such a common – Glory –
10 A Fisherman's – Degree –
Redemption – Brittle Lady –
Be so – ashamed of Thee.
—1863

[*My Life had stood – a Loaded Gun –*][3]

My Life had stood – a Loaded Gun –
In Corners – till a Day
The Owner passed – identified –
And carried Me away –

5 And now We roam in Sovreign Woods –
And now We hunt the Doe –
And every time I speak for Him –
The Mountains straight reply –

And do I smile, such cordial light
10 Upon the Valley glow –
It is as a Vesuvian[4] face
Had let its pleasure through –

And when at Night – Our good Day done –
I guard My Master's Head –
15 'Tis better than the Eider-Duck's[5]
Deep Pillow – to have shared –

To foe of His – I'm deadly foe –
None stir the second time –
On whom I lay a Yellow Eye –
20 Or an emphatic Thumb –

Though I than He – may longer live
He longer must – than I –
For I have but the power to kill,
Without – the power to die –
—1863

---

[1] This poem appears in Johnson as Poem 401; in Franklin as Poem 675; and in Miller as the third poem in Sheet 1 of "Unbound Sheets," page 418. Johnson and Miller read "Ashamed" as lower case both in line 8 and in line 12; Franklin reads the word as capitalized in line 8 but lowercase in line 12. Johnson, Franklin, and Miller all read a dash rather than a period at the end of the poem.

[2] *Dimity* Lightweight cotton.

[3] This poem appears in Johnson as Poem 754; in Franklin as Poem 764; and in Miller as the first poem in Sheet 4 of Fascicle 34, pages 354–55. The present transcription of the fascicle manuscript is with two exceptions in agreement with those of Johnson, Franklin, and Miller: Franklin spells "it's" in line 12 just as the word appears in Dickinson's manuscript, whereas other editors correct the error; Franklin and Miller both omit the mark that appears between "Eider" and "Duck" in line 15, whereas (like Johnson) the present editors transcribe it as a hyphen. There are a few other possible transcription issues with the punctuation of the poem; the marks at the end of lines 14 and 19 could plausibly be read as right-slanting commas, while the mark at the end of line 22 could very plausibly be read as a period. Dickinson provides four alternative readings in the manuscript: "the" for "in" in line 5; "Low" for "Deep" in line 16; "harm" for "stir" in line 18; and "art" for "power" in line 23.

[4] *Vesuvian* The southern Italian volcano Mount Vesuvius erupted in 79 CE, killing well over one thousand people, primarily in the city of Pompeii.

[5] *Eider-Duck* Genus of sea ducks, whose feathers are commonly used to stuff quilts and pillows.

[I could bring You Jewels – had I a mind to –][1]

I could bring You Jewels – had I a mind to –
But You have enough – of those –
I could bring You Odors from St Domingo[2] –
Colors – from Vera Cruz[3] –

5   Berries[4] of the Bahamas – have I –
But this little Blaze
Flickering to itself – in the Meadow –
Suits Me – more than those –

Never a Fellow matched this Topaz –
10 And his Emerald Swing –
Dower[5] itself – for Bobadilo[6] –
Better – Could I bring?
—1863

---

1   This poem appears in Johnson as Poem 697; in Franklin as Poem 726; and in Miller as the second poem in Sheet 4 of Fascicle 35, page 364. The present text is in complete accord with the transcriptions of Franklin and Miller; it may be worth noting, however, that the mark at the end of line 5 could plausibly be read as a period.

2   *Odors* I.e., fragrant ointments or perfumes; *St Domingo* While "Santo Domingo" is the name of the capital city of the Dominican Republic, it is more likely that Dickinson means to refer to the newly independent Haiti, which had been known as Saint-Domingue under the French colonial regime. The Haitian Revolution of the late eighteenth century had been led by a coalition of free and enslaved black Haitians, resulting in the abolition of slavery and the expulsion of most white colonials from the country. To many white Americans in the nineteenth century, "Domingo" remained shorthand both for Haiti itself and for the violence of revolution (though the success of the Haitian Revolution also remained an inspiration to many black abolitionists).

3   *Colors* I.e., pigments or dyes; *Vera Cruz* State in Mexico, located on the coast of the Gulf of Mexico.

4   *Berries* Here likely referring to melons, which botanically speaking are a type of berry.

5   *Dower* Dowry; money brought by a bride into her marriage.

6   *Bobadilo* Francisco de Bobadilla, Spanish-born governor of the colony of Saint-Domingue (1499–1502).

[Publication – is the Auction][7]

Publication – is the Auction
Of the Mind of Man –
Poverty – be justifying
For so foul a thing

5   Possibly – but We – would rather
From Our Garret go
White – Unto the White Creator –
Than invest – Our Snow –

Thought belong to Him who gave it –
10 Then – to Him Who bear
It's Corporeal illustration – Sell
The Royal Air –

In the Parcel – Be the Merchant
Of the Heavenly Grace –
15 But reduce no Human Spirit
To Disgrace of Price –
—1863

[I never saw a Moor –][8]

I never saw a Moor –
I never saw the Sea –
Yet know I how the Heather looks
And what a Billow[9] be.

5   I never spoke with God
Nor visited in Heaven –
Yet certain am I of the spot
As if the Checks[10] were given –
—1864

---

7   This poem appears in Johnson as Poem 709; in Franklin as Poem 788; and in Miller as the second poem in Sheet 5 of Fascicle 37, pages 386–87. The present text is in complete accord with the transcriptions of Johnson, Franklin, and Miller; it may be noted, however, that the mark at the end of line 7 could plausibly be read as a right-slanting comma.

8   This poem appears in Johnson as Poem 1052; in Franklin as Poem 800; and in Miller under "Loose Poems," page 532. The present text is in agreement with the transcriptions of Johnson, Franklin, and Miller.

9   *Billow* Wave.

10 *Checks* Train tickets.

[Color – Caste – Denomination –][1]

Color – Caste – Denomination –
These – are Time's Affair –
Death's diviner Classifying
Does not know they are –

5   As in sleep – All Hue forgotten –
Tenets – put behind –
Death's large – Democratic fingers
Rub away the Brand.[2]

If Circassian[3] – He is careless –
10 If He put away
Chrysalis of Blonde – or Umber –
Equal Butterfly –

They emerge from His Obscuring –
What Death – knows so well –
15 Our minuter intuitions –
Deem unplausible
—1864

[She rose to His Requirement – dropt][4]

She rose to His Requirement – dropt
The Playthings of Her Life
To take the honorable Work
Of Woman, and of Wife –

5   If ought[5] She missed in Her new Day,
Of Amplitude, or Awe –
Or first Prospective – Or the Gold
In using, wear away,

It lay unmentioned – as the Sea
10 Develope Pearl, and Weed,
But Only to Himself – be known
The Fathoms they abide –
—1864

[The Poets light but Lamps –][6]

The Poets light but Lamps –
Themselves – go out –
The Wicks they stimulate
If vital Light

5   Inhere as do the Suns –
Each Age a Lens
Disseminating their
Circumference –
—1865

[1] This poem appears in Johnson as Poem 970; in Franklin as Poem 836; and in Miller as the first poem in Sheet 6 of Fascicle 40, page 412. The present text is in agreement with the transcriptions of Johnson, Franklin, and Miller except in one particular; we read the mark at the end of line 8 as a period rather than a dash. (It may also be worth noting that the mark at the end of the first line could plausibly be read as a right-slanting comma.) Dickinson provides one variant word choice in the manuscript: "incredible" for "unplausible" in the final line.

[2] *Brand* Physical identifying mark, possibly with reference to a brand burned into the skin of an enslaved person.

[3] *Circassian* Of Circassia, a region in the North Caucasus in what is now southwestern Russia.

[4] This poem appears in Johnson as Poem 732; in Franklin as Poem 857; and in Miller as part of Fascicle 38, Sheet 4, pages 393–94. The present transcription of the manuscript is in agreement with those of Franklin and Miller—though it may be noted that the marks at the end of line 6 and after "unmentioned" in line 9 could plausibly be read as right-slanting commas.

The poem was published under the title "The Wife" in Todd and Higginson's *Poems* (1890); in that version "Develops" is substituted for "Develope" in line 10 and "is" for "be" in line 11.

[5] *ought* Aught.

[6] This poem appears in Johnson as Poem 883; in Franklin as Poem 930; and in Miller under "Unbound Sheets," as the first poem on Sheet 15, page 436. The present transcription of the manuscript is in agreement with those of Franklin and Miller; Johnson reads the mark at the end of line 3 as a dash, but it seems more plausible to read it as the crossing of the final "t" in "stimulate."

[*The Heart has narrow Banks*]¹

The Heart has narrow Banks
It measures like the Sea
In mighty – unremitting Bass
And Blue monotony

5   Till Hurricane bisect
And as itself discerns
Its insufficient Area
The Heart convulsive learns

That Calm is but a Wall
10   Of Unattempted Gauze
An instant's Push demolishes
A Questioning – dissolves.
—c. 1865

[*Could I but ride indefinite*]²

Could I but ride indefinite
As doth the Meadow Bee
And visit only where I liked
And no one visit me

5   And flirt all Day with Buttercups
And marry whom I may
And dwell a little everywhere
Or better, run away

With no Police to follow
10   Or chase Him if He do
Till He should jump Peninsulas
To get away from me –

I said "But just to be a Bee"
Upon a Raft of Air
15   And row in Nowhere all Day long
And anchor "off the Bar"

What Liberty! So Captives deem
Who tight in Dungeons are.
—c. 1865

Detail (buttercup) from Dickinson's *Herbarium*, Seq. 26. A facsimile page from the *Herbarium* is reproduced in this volume's color insert.

[*As the Starved Maelstrom laps the Navies*]³

As the Starved Maelstrom⁴ laps the Navies
As the Vulture teazed
Forces the Broods⁵ in lonely Valleys
As the Tiger eased

5   By but a Crumb of Blood, fasts Scarlet
Till he meet a Man
Dainty adorned with Veins and Tissues
And partakes – his Tongue

---

1   This poem appears in Johnson as Poem 928; in Franklin as Poem 960; and in Miller as the second poem of Sheet 21 in "Unbound Sheets," page 445. The present text, like those of Miller and Johnson, emends "It's" to "Its" in line 7. We agree with both Miller and Franklin in reading "monotony" in line 4 as lower case and "Unattempted" in line 10 as upper case (whereas Johnson reads the words as "Monotony" and "unattempted"). Dickinson provides one variant word choice in the manuscript—"paces" for "measures" in line 2.

2   This poem appears in Johnson as Poem 661; in Franklin as Poem 1056; and in Miller as the first poem in Sheet 43 under "Unbound Sheets," page 474. The present text is in agreement with the transcriptions of Franklin and Miller except in one particular; like Miller, we emend "Opon" to "Upon" in line 14.

3   This poem appears in Johnson as Poem 872; in Franklin as Poem 1064; and in Miller as the second poem in Sheet 45, under "Unbound Sheets," page 477. The present text is in agreement with the transcriptions of Johnson, Franklin, and Miller except in two particulars; we side with Franklin and Miller in retaining Dickinson's archaic variant spelling of "teazed," and with Johnson in reading the mark at the end of the poem as a period rather than a dash (though either reading is certainly defensible).

4   *Maelstrom*   Whirlpool.

5   *Forces*   I.e., overpowers; *Broods*   Young birds.

Cooled by the Morsel for a moment
10 Grows a fiercer thing
Till he esteem his Dates and Cocoa
A Nutrition mean

I, of a finer Famine
Deem my Supper dry
15 For but a Berry of Domingo[1]
And a Torrid[2] Eye.
—1865

[*A narrow Fellow in the Grass*]

This poem was first published on 14 February 1866, in the *Springfield Republican*, a newspaper edited by Dickinson's friend Samuel Bowles. Dickinson did not submit the poem for publication, however; it has been plausibly conjectured that Susan Dickinson passed along to Bowles a now-lost manuscript copy which Dickinson had given her. A facsimile of the 1865 manuscript page appears on the facing page, followed by a transcription. Next appears the 1866 published version, and finally a transcription of the 1872 manuscript version.

This is the only known instance in which Dickinson complained of any of the specifics relating to the publication of one of her poems; in a 17 March 1866 letter to Higginson she commented as follows on the publication of the poem in the *Springfield Republican* (it is presumed that she enclosed a clipping of the newspaper's printed version with her letter):

Lest you meet my Snake and suppose I deceive it was robbed of me—defeated too of the third line by the punctuation. The third and fourth were one—I had told you I did not print—I feared you might think me ostensible.[3] If I still entreat you to teach me, are you much displeased?

As is often the case with Dickinson's letters, it is difficult to be entirely clear of her meaning here. She does not want Higginson to think that she has deceived him—presumably in her protestations that she has not sought to have her work printed; she assures him that this poem was stolen from her. She asserts too that her intentions were "defeated" by the punctuation of the third line in the newspaper version, which retains the dash in the middle of the line but adds a question mark at the end of the line—whereas in the 1865 manuscript Dickinson has no punctuation. (Interestingly, Dickinson herself includes a question mark in her 1872 manuscript version—but in the middle of the line, not at its end.) On that point her complaint seems clear—but what does she mean by "The third and fourth were one"? Could she mean that the third and fourth [lines of the poem] were [intended to be set out as] one [line]? That would mean a line like this—

You may have met Him – did you not His notice sudden is –

which seems highly implausible. The alternative is that she means that the third and fourth [lines of the poem] were [wrongly made into] one [by the newspaper editors], when Dickinson herself had intended them to be separate lines—in other words, that Dickinson had intended the first stanza to have five lines. That appears to be how she writes the stanza in the 1872 version she sent to Susan Dickinson, in which she capitalizes the first letter of Did. With Dickinson it is frequently difficult to be sure of her intentions regarding line breaks, given that she so often capitalized words in the middle of lines, but in the 1872 version it seems clear that there would have been ample room on the page for Dickinson to write the word "Did," after "him?" if she had intended "You may have met him? Did you not" to form just one line. But here again, it is impossible to be entirely sure of Dickinson's intentions.

1   *Berry*   In this context, a melon; *Domingo*   Possibly a reference to Santo Domingo, the capital city of the Dominican Republic, but more likely to Saint-Domingue, the colonial name of Haiti prior to the 1791 Haitian Revolution, which had been led by free and enslaved black Haitians. Throughout the nineteenth century, "Domingo" remained common shorthand (especially to white Americans) both for Haiti itself and for the violence of revolution.

2   *Torrid*   Hot; also possibly a reference to the torrid zone, another name for the Tropics.

3   *ostensible*   Seeking visibility; ostentatious.

88-13

A narrow fellow in
the Grass
Occasionally rides -
You may have met Him -
Did you not -
His notice sudden is -

The Grass divides as
with a Comb -
A spotted shaft is
seen -
And then it closes
at your feet -
And opens further on -

He likes a Boggy
Acre
A Floor too cool
for Corn
Yet when a Boy, and
Barefoot -

[*A narrow Fellow in the Grass*][1]

A narrow Fellow in the Grass
Occasionally rides –
You may have met Him – did you not
His notice sudden is –

5 The Grass divides as with a Comb –
A spotted shaft is seen –
And then it closes at your feet
And opens further on –

He likes a Boggy Acre
10 A Floor too cool for Corn
Yet when a Boy, and Barefoot –
I more than once at Noon

Have passed, I thought, a Whip lash
Unbraiding in the Sun
15 When stooping to secure it
It wrinkled, and was gone –

Several of Nature's People
I know, and they know me –
I feel for them a transport[2]
20 Of cordiality –

But never met this Fellow
Attended, or alone
Without a tighter breathing
And Zero at the Bone –
   —1865

THE SNAKE.

A narrow fellow in the grass
Occasionally rides;
You may have met him—did you not?
His notice instant is,
The grass divides as with a comb,
A spotted shaft is seen,
And then it closes at your feet,
And opens further on.

He likes a boggy acre,
A floor too cool for corn,
Yet when a boy and barefoot,
I more than once at noon
Have passed, I thought, a whip-lash,
Unbraiding in the sun,
When stooping to secure it,
It wrinkled and was gone.

Several of nature's people
I know, and they know me;
I feel for them a transport
Of cordiality.
Yet never met this fellow,
Attended or alone,
Without a tighter breathing,
And zero at the bone.

[*A narrow Fellow in the Grass*]

A narrow Fellow in the Grass
Occasionally rides –
You may have met him?
Did you not
5 His notice instant is –

The Grass divides as with a Comb –
A spotted Shaft is seen,
And then it closes at your Feet
And opens further on –

10 He likes a Boggy Acre –
A Floor too cool for Corn –
But when a Boy and Barefoot
I more than once at Noon

Have passed I thought a Whip Lash
15 Unbraiding in the Sun
When stooping to secure it

---

1 This poem appears in Johnson as Poem 986; in Franklin as Poem 1096; and in Miller as part of Unbound Sheet 54, pages 489–90. There are two manuscript versions extant; the first dates from 1865, while the second is included in an 1872 letter to Susan Dickinson. Johnson and Miller transcribe from the 1865 version; the two differ only slightly (the first two lines of the third stanza are punctuated differently, with Miller reading a dash at the end of the first line and Johnson reading a dash at the end of the second line). The image in the righthand column shows the version printed under the title "The Snake" in the *Springfield Republican* on 14 February 1866.

2 *transport* Rush of emotion.

It wrinkled
And was gone –

Several of Nature's People
20 I know and they know me
I feel for them a transport
Of Cordiality

But never met this Fellow
Attended or alone
25 Without a tighter Breathing
And Zero at the Bone.
        —1872

[*The Bustle in a House*]¹

The Bustle in a House
The Morning after Death
Is solemnest of industries
Enacted upon Earth –

5 The Sweeping up the Heart
And putting Love away
We shall not want to use again
Until Eternity –
        —1865

[*A Spider sewed at Night*]²

A Spider sewed at Night
Without a Light
Upon an Arc of White –

If Ruff it was of Dame
5 Or Shroud of Gnome
Himself himself inform –

Of Immortality
His strategy
Was physiognomy³ –
        —1868

[*Tell all the Truth but tell it slant –*]⁴

Tell all the Truth but tell it slant –
Success in Circuit lies
Too bright for our infirm Delight
The Truth's superb surprise
5 As Lightning to the Children eased
With explanation kind
The Truth must dazzle gradually
Or every man be blind –
        —1872

---

2   This poem appears in Johnson as Poem 1138; in Franklin as Poem 1163; and in Miller under "Poems Not Retained," pages 705–06. The present text is in agreement with the transcriptions of Franklin and Miller except in one particular; like Miller, we emend "Opon" to "Upon" in line 3. The dashes in the manuscript sent to Susan Dickinson very much resemble commas.

3   *physiognomy* Study of a person's facial features to determine his or her character.

4   This poem appears in Johnson as Poem 1129; in Franklin as Poem 1263; and in Miller under "Loose Poems," pages 563–64. The present transcription of the manuscript is in complete agreement with those of Johnson, Franklin, and Miller. Dickinson provides two variant word choices in the manuscript: "bold" for "bright" in line 3, and "moderately" for "gradually" in line 7.

---

1   This poem appears in Johnson as Poem 1078; in Franklin as Poem 1108; and in Miller as the third poem in Sheet 57, under "Unbound Sheets," page 494. The present text is in agreement with the transcriptions of Johnson, Franklin, and Miller except in one particular; we side with Franklin and Miller in reading the mark at the end of the poem as a dash rather than (as Johnson reads it) a period.

372

Tell all the truth
but tell it slant -
Success in Circuit
Lies
Too bright for our
(cold

infirm delight
the truths superb
surprise
As Lightning to
the Children eased
With explanation kind
the Truth must
dazzle gradually
                moderately
Or every man be
blind -

The manuscript of "Tell all the Truth but tell it slant" (Amherst College, Amherst - Amherst Manuscript # 372 - Tell all the truth but tell it slant - asc:12240 - p. 1). Dickinson's handwriting varied considerably both from one manuscript to another and over time.

[*To pile like Thunder to its close*][1]

To pile like Thunder to its close
Then crumble grand away
While Everything created hid
This – would be Poetry –

5 Or Love – the two coeval[2] come –
We both and neither prove –
Experience either and consume –
For None see God and live –
—C. 1875

[*Apparently with no surprise*][3]

Apparently with no surprise
To any happy Flower
The Frost beheads it at its play –
In accidental power –
5 The blonde Assassin passes on –
The Sun proceeds unmoved
To measure off another Day
For an Approving God –
—C. 1884

[*My life closed twice before its close;*][4]

My life closed twice before its close;
It yet remains to see
If Immortality unveil
A third event to me,

5 So huge, so hopeless to conceive
As these that twice befell.
Parting is all we know of heaven,
And all we need of hell.
—DATE OF COMPOSITION UNKNOWN (FIRST PUBLISHED
1896)

[*To make a prairie it takes a clover and one bee,*][5]

To make a prairie it takes a clover and one bee,
One clover, and a bee,
And revery.
The revery alone will do,
5 If bees are few.
—DATE OF COMPOSITION UNKNOWN (FIRST PUBLISHED
1896)

---

[1] This poem appears in Johnson as Poem 1247; in Franklin as Poem 1353; and in Miller under "Poems Not Retained," page 713. The present text is in agreement with the transcriptions of Franklin and Miller except in one particular; like Miller, we emend "it's" to "its" in line 1.

[2] *coeval* Of contemporaneous duration or existence.

[3] This poem appears in Johnson as Poem 1624; in Franklin as Poem 1668; and in Miller under "Loose Poems," page 654. The present text is in agreement with the transcriptions of Johnson, Franklin, and Miller except in two particulars; like Johnson and Miller, we emend "it's" to "its" in line 3, and like Franklin and Miller we read the mark at the end of the poem as a dash rather than a period. Todd and Higginson edited the poem for *Poems* (1890), giving it the title "Death and Life."

[4] This poem appears in Johnson as Poem 1732; in Franklin as Poem 1773; and in Miller under "Poems Transcribed by Others," page 686. No Dickinson manuscript appears to have survived; a transcription by Mabel Todd has survived, and the poem appears in *Poems: Third Series* (1896). Franklin retains the spelling "it's" in line 1.

[5] This poem appears in Johnson as Poem 1755; in Franklin as Poem 1779; and in Miller under "Poems Transcribed by Others," page 688. No Dickinson manuscript appears to have survived; a transcription by Mabel Todd has survived, and the poem appears in *Poems: Third Series* (1896).

Rebecca Harding Davis
1831 – 1910

Rebecca Harding Davis became an overnight literary celebrity with the publication of her first major short story, "Life in the Iron-Mills." Immediately hailed as a work of outstanding strength and insight, the story has since been identified as an early and important contribution to literary realism, a movement that would not properly take hold in American fiction until two decades later, with the works of writers such as Mark Twain. Davis herself continued to develop her brand of realism over a long, prolific, and popularly successful career in which she strove, as she wrote, "to dig into this commonplace, this vulgar American life, and see what is in it." In addition to these realist works of pathos and social observation, she worked in a remarkable range of genres both highbrow and lowbrow, including serialized gothic and mystery fiction, children's stories, memoir, and essays. Raised in what is now West Virginia with ties to the South and to the North, Davis considered herself a "Westerner" and took an iconoclastic approach to the political issues of her day; her stance on matters from marriage to the Civil War did not align fully with either Southern or Northern intellectual traditions.

Born in Washington, Pennsylvania, in 1831, Rebecca Blaine Harding was the eldest of five children born to Rachel Leet Wilson and English-born Richard W. Harding. Washington was her mother's hometown, but the family's permanent residence at the time was in Alabama, after which they settled in 1836 in Wheeling, Virginia. The family was comfortably middle class; Richard, a great reader, stocked an ample library with British classics, which comprised Harding's first exposure to literature. She read widely, enjoying novels by the likes of Maria Edgeworth, John Bunyan, and Sir Walter Scott. Despite her father's bias against American literature, however, Harding was deeply influenced by the short fiction of American author Nathaniel Hawthorne, whom she credited with inspiring her initial interest in fiction that centered on "commonplace folk and things."

The Harding children all received an extensive home education, provided by their mother and various tutors; in 1844, Harding returned to her mother's hometown to attend the Washington Female Seminary, a prestigious girls' educational institution whose curriculum blended conventionally "feminine" topics such as music and drawing with the study of literature, philosophy, theology, mathematics, and various sciences. Students were exposed to lectures by prominent literary figures, and Washington society provided opportunities for Harding to attend abolitionist lectures by activists such as Horace Greeley and Francis LeMoyne.

Harding graduated from the seminary as valedictorian in 1848; despite this academic achievement, as a woman her prospects were limited. For the next fourteen years she lived at her family home, where, despite the extensive household duties expected of her, she began to build a writing career. Over the course of those years she published numerous—mostly anonymous—reviews, essays, stories, and poems in the local *Wheeling Intelligencer*, of which she also served as editor for a brief period in 1859. Her breakthrough came in the winter of 1861, when she had a story accepted by the *Atlantic Monthly*, a periodical which had been founded only a few years previously but had already become one of the most eminent literary publications in the country. Harding was paid fifty dollars for "Life in the Iron-Mills," which was printed anonymously in the April volume of the magazine that year (the same month in which the Civil War broke out). Written following a series of highly publicized workers' strikes across the country, the story is socially provocative: the protagonist is an industrial laborer who, despite his innate artistic abilities, lacks the means of escaping the hardships and injustice of the nineteenth-century class system.

"Life in the Iron-Mills" was an immediate success, its grim realism a distinguishing feature amidst the sentimental and romantic fiction that dominated the American literary scene.

Davis soon visited Boston and Concord, where she met Hawthorne and Ralph Waldo Emerson, and where she formed a long-lived friendship with Louisa May Alcott. Davis found, however, that her objections to Transcendentalism and to New England elitism were reaffirmed by her experience in Massachusetts. She would later write of "Emerson, Hawthorne, and the other members of the 'Atlantic' coterie" that "while they thought they were guiding the real world, they stood quite outside of it, and never would see it as it was."

Among the many letters of admiration Davis received for her first story was one from a man named L. Clarke Davis, a lawyer and newspaper editor from Philadelphia. The two met in Wheeling in 1862, and they became engaged that summer, marrying the following year and moving to Philadelphia, where their home would become a meeting place for local intellectuals. In 1864 Davis gave birth to the first of their three children, Richard Harding Davis.

Davis's writing provided the family's main income, and she continued to publish prolifically throughout the next decades. But although the realism of Davis's writing was largely well-received, she nevertheless faced a degree of editorial censorship when editors or publishers considered her sobering tone and political subject matter to be too much for readers' tastes. This pattern began with her second submission to the *Atlantic Monthly*: editor James T. Fields initially rejected the piece, a long story titled "The Deaf and the Dumb." His recommendations—which Davis followed—included changing the title and inserting a happier ending; the story was then serialized as "A Story of To-day" in 1862 (and later published as a single novel, *Margaret Howth*).

While she continued to publish with the *Atlantic Monthly* and to accept Fields's interventions in her work, Davis also began a long-term relationship with *Peterson's Magazine*, an inexpensive publication intended for middle-class women readers. It was far less prestigious than the *Atlantic Monthly*, but *Peterson's* paid significantly better and offered one of the largest audiences of any periodical of the era. Over the following decades, she would publish fourteen serialized novels and more than eighty short stories in the magazine, many of them works drawing on the gothic, mystery, and other popular genres.

Davis's work consistently tackled difficult social and political questions: "The Wife's Story" (1864), for instance, is an impassioned account of the anguish experienced by a new wife torn between domestic responsibilities and a desire to pursue an artistic career; and *Waiting for the Verdict* (1868), Davis's most ambitious novel, addresses the question of persisting systemic racism in postwar America. (Race was a topic of vital importance to Davis, though her fiction often presented a mixed bag of socially progressive ideals and pervasive racial stereotyping.) The same questions of class, race, and gender that inform her fiction also emerged repeatedly throughout her distinguished career as an editorial correspondent, during which she also reported on topics such as prostitution and asylum reform. For many years her primary journalistic relationship was with the *New York Tribune*, until she resigned from the paper when it tried to suppress her essay series criticizing some of its advertisers; later she wrote most frequently for the *New York Independent*, in addition to contributing to other publications such as Harriet Beecher Stowe's periodical *Hearth and Home*. Davis became at least as celebrated for her journalism as for her stories and novels; all in all, it is estimated that she published more than five hundred pieces of fiction and nonfiction.

At the age of seventy-three, Davis completed the memoir *Bits of Gossip* (1904), whose self-effacing title belies the greater ambition expressed in its opening line: "It has always seemed to me that each human being, before going out into the silence, should leave behind him, not the story of his own life, but of the time in which he lived." Davis died six years later. She was largely forgotten in the years following her death, perhaps in part overshadowed by the success of her son Richard, who had become a literary celebrity in his own right. In the early 1970s, however, a volume of Davis's stories was discovered in a junk shop by the feminist writer and activist Tillie Olsen, who was immediately taken by the power of "Life in the Iron-Mills." The story was re-published in 1972 by the Feminist Press, as the first of their series of rediscovered classics by women authors. Since then, the story has been considered a staple of the American literary canon, though many scholars of the late twentieth century felt that the quality of the rest of her work had been compromised by editorial intervention and a desire to appeal to a broad audience. Some twenty-first-century critics argue, however, that the quality of her oeuvre has been significantly underestimated, citing its political complexity, its deft deployment of genre conventions, and its pioneering achievement in American realism. As one critic wrote in 1868, "[t]he festering spots of society, from which so many writers shrink, she probes with the unerring blade."

NOTE ON THE TEXT: Except where otherwise noted, the text presented below is based on that printed in the *Atlantic Monthly* in 1861, with references to both the original manuscript version and the version later included in *Atlantic Tales* (1865) where relevant. Spelling and punctuation have been modernized in accordance with the practices of this anthology.

⌘ ⌘ ⌘

Life in the Iron-Mills

"Is this the end?
O Life, as futile, then, as frail!
What hope of answer or redress?"[1]

A cloudy day: do you know what that is in a town[2] of iron-works? The sky sank down before dawn, muddy, flat, immovable. The air is thick, clammy with the breath of crowded human beings. It stifles me. I open the window, and, looking out, can scarcely see through the rain the grocer's shop opposite, where a crowd of drunken Irishmen are puffing Lynchburg[3] tobacco in their pipes. I can detect the scent through all the foul smells ranging loose in the air.

The idiosyncrasy of this town is smoke. It rolls sullenly in slow folds from the great chimneys of the iron-foundries, and settles down in black, slimy pools on the muddy streets. Smoke on the wharves, smoke on the dingy boats, on the yellow river—clinging in a coating of greasy soot to the house-front, the two faded poplars, the faces of the passers-by. The long train of mules, dragging masses of pig-iron[4] through the narrow street, have a foul vapor hanging to their reeking sides. Here, inside, is a little broken figure of an angel pointing upward from the mantel-shelf; but even its wings are covered with smoke, clotted and black. Smoke everywhere! A dirty canary chirps desolately in a cage beside me. Its dream of green fields and sunshine is a very old dream—almost worn out, I think.

From the back-window I can see a narrow brick-yard sloping down to the river-side, strewed with rain-butts[5] and tubs. The river, dull and tawny-colored, (*la belle rivière!*[6]) drags itself sluggishly along, tired of the heavy weight of boats and coal-barges. What wonder? When I was a child, I used to fancy a look of weary, dumb[7] appeal upon the face of the negro-like river slavishly bearing its burden day after day. Something of the same idle notion comes to me today, when from the street-window I look on the slow stream of human life creeping past, night and morning, to the great mills. Masses of men, with dull, besotted[8] faces bent to the ground, sharpened here and there by pain or cunning; skin and muscle and flesh begrimed with smoke and ashes; stooping all night over boiling cauldrons of metal, laired by day in dens of drunkenness and infamy; breathing from infancy to death an air saturated with fog and grease and soot, vileness for soul and body. What do you make of a case like that,

---

1   *Is this … or redress?*   Lines adapted from Alfred, Lord Tennyson's *In Memoriam A.H.H.* (1850).

2   *town*   Though the town is never named in the text, it appears to be Davis's hometown of Wheeling, Virginia (now West Virginia).

3   *drunken Irishmen*   Nineteenth-century discourse was rife with negative stereotypes of the Irish, including an association between Irish people and drunkenness;   *Lynchburg*   Virginian city known for the production of inferior-quality dark-leaf tobacco.

4   *pig-iron*   Small blocks of crude iron.

5   *rain-butts*   Vessels designed to catch rainwater for various uses.

6   *la belle rivière*   French: the beautiful river, a name used by French explorers to refer to the Ohio River, which runs through Wheeling.

7   *dumb*   Silent.

8   *besotted*   Dull, stupefied.

amateur psychologist? You call it an altogether serious thing to be alive: to these men it is a drunken jest, a joke—horrible to angels perhaps, to them commonplace enough. My fancy about the river was an idle one: it is no type of such a life. What if it be stagnant and slimy here? It knows that beyond there waits for it odorous[1] sunlight—quaint old gardens, dusky with soft, green foliage of apple-trees, and flushing crimson with roses—air, and fields, and mountains. The future of the Welsh puddler[2] passing just now is not so pleasant. To be stowed away, after his grimy work is done, in a hole in the muddy graveyard, and after that—*not* air, nor green fields, nor curious roses.

Can you see how foggy the day is? As I stand here, idly tapping the window-pane, and looking out through the rain at the dirty back-yard and the coal-boats below, fragments of an old story float up before me—a story of this old house into which I happened to come today. You may think it a tiresome story enough, as foggy as the day, sharpened by no sudden flashes of pain or pleasure. I know: only the outline of a dull life, that long since, with thousands of dull lives like its own, was vainly lived and lost: thousands of them—massed, vile, slimy lives, like those of the torpid lizards in yonder stagnant water-butt. Lost? There is a curious point for you to settle, my friend, who study psychology in a lazy, *dilettante* way. Stop a moment. I am going to be honest. This is what I want you to do. I want you to hide your disgust, take no heed to your clean clothes, and come right down with me—here, into the thickest of the fog and mud and foul effluvia. I want you to hear this story. There is a secret down here, in this nightmare fog, that has lain dumb for centuries: I want to make it a real thing to you. You, Egoist, or Pantheist, or Arminian,[3] busy in making straight paths for your feet on the hills, do not see it clearly—this terrible question which men here have gone mad and died trying to answer. I dare

not put this secret into words. I told you it was dumb. These men, going by with drunken faces and brains full of unawakened power, do not ask it of Society or of God. Their lives ask it; their deaths ask it. There is no reply. I will tell you plainly that I have a great hope; and I bring it to you to be tested. It is this: that this terrible dumb question is its own reply; that it is not the sentence of death we think it, but, from the very extremity of its darkness, the most solemn prophecy which the world has known of the Hope to come. I dare make my meaning no clearer, but will only tell my story. It will, perhaps, seem to you as foul and dark as this thick vapor about us, and as pregnant with death; but if your eyes are free as mine are to look deeper, no perfume-tinted dawn will be so fair with promise of the day that shall surely come.

My story is very simple—only what I remember of the life of one of these men—a furnace-tender in one of Kirby & John's rolling-mills—Hugh Wolfe. You know the mills? They took the great order for Lower Virginia railroads there last winter; run usually with about a thousand men. I cannot tell why I choose the half-forgotten story of this Wolfe more than that of myriads of these furnace-hands. Perhaps because there is a secret underlying sympathy between that story and this day with its impure fog and thwarted sunshine—or perhaps simply for the reason that this house is the one where the Wolfes lived. There were the father and son—both hands,[4] as I said, in one of Kirby & John's mills for making railroad-iron—and Deborah, their cousin, a picker[5] in some of the cotton-mills. The house was rented then to half a dozen families. The Wolfes had two of the cellar-rooms. The old man, like many of the puddlers and feeders[6] of the mills, was Welsh—had spent half of his life in the Cornish tin-mines. You may pick the Welsh emigrants, Cornish miners, out of the throng passing the windows, any day. They are a trifle more filthy; their muscles are not so brawny; they stoop more. When they are drunk, they neither yell, nor shout, nor stagger, but skulk along like beaten hounds. A pure, unmixed blood,

---

[1] *odorous* Fragrant; sweet-smelling.

[2] *puddler* Worker who converts pig iron into steel or wrought iron by means of a labor-intensive process of melting and stirring.

[3] *Egoist* One who believes the pursuit of self-interest will lead to universal improvement; *Pantheist* One who believes that God is inherently present in all nature; *Arminian* Follower of the religious doctrines of Jacobus Arminius (1560–1607), which oppose the doctrines of Calvinism and assert that salvation can be attained through the performance of good works.

[4] *hands* I.e., workers.

[5] *picker* Worker who operated the machine, also called a picker, that separated cotton fibers in preparation for spinning.

[6] *feeders* Workers who feed molten metal into the iron-casting form.

I fancy: shows itself in the slight angular bodies and sharply-cut facial lines. It is nearly thirty years since the Wolfes lived here. Their lives were like those of their class: incessant labor, sleeping in kennel-like rooms, eating rank pork and molasses, drinking—God and the distillers only know what; with an occasional night in jail, to atone for some drunken excess. Is that all of their lives?—of the portion given to them and these their duplicates swarming the streets today?—nothing beneath?—all? So many a political reformer will tell you—and many a private reformer, too, who has gone among them with a heart tender with Christ's charity, and come out outraged, hardened.

One rainy night, about eleven o'clock, a crowd of half-clothed women stopped outside of the cellar-door. They were going home from the cotton-mill.

"Good-night, Deb," said one, a mulatto,[1] steadying herself against the gas-post. She needed the post to steady her. So did more than one of them.

"Dah's a ball to Miss Potts' tonight. Ye'd best come."

"Inteet, Deb, if hur'll[2] come, hur'll hef fun," said a shrill Welsh voice in the crowd.

Two or three dirty hands were thrust out to catch the gown of the woman, who was groping for the latch of the door.

"No."

"No? Where's Kit Small then?"

"Begorra![3] on the spools.[4] Alleys behint,[5] though we helped her, we dud. An wid ye! Let Deb alone! It's ondacent[6] frettin' a quite body. Be the powers, an' we'll have a night of it! there'll be lashin's o' drink—the Vargent[7] be blessed and praised for 't!"

They went on, the mulatto inclining for a moment to show fight, and drag the woman Wolfe off with them; but, being pacified, she staggered away.

Deborah groped her way into the cellar, and, after considerable stumbling, kindled a match, and lighted a tallow dip,[8] that sent a yellow glimmer over the room. It was low, damp—the earthen floor covered with a green, slimy moss—a fetid air smothering the breath. Old Wolfe lay asleep on a heap of straw, wrapped in a torn horse-blanket. He was a pale, meek little man, with a white face and red rabbit-eyes. The woman Deborah was like him; only her face was even more ghastly, her lips bluer, her eyes more watery. She wore a faded cotton gown and a slouching bonnet. When she walked, one could see that she was deformed, almost a hunchback. She trod softly, so as not to waken him, and went through into the room beyond. There she found by the half-extinguished fire an iron saucepan filled with cold boiled potatoes, which she put upon a broken chair with a pint-cup of ale. Placing the old candlestick beside this dainty repast, she untied her bonnet, which hung limp and wet over her face, and prepared to eat her supper. It was the first food that had touched her lips since morning. There was enough of it, however: there is not always. She was hungry— one could see that easily enough—and not drunk, as most of her companions would have been found at this hour. She did not drink, this woman—her face told that, too—nothing stronger than ale. Perhaps the weak, flaccid wretch had some stimulant in her pale life to keep her up—some love or hope, it might be, or urgent need. When that stimulant was gone, she would take to whiskey. Man cannot live by work alone. While she was skinning the potatoes, and munching them, a noise behind her made her stop.

"Janey!" she called, lifting the candle and peering into the darkness. "Janey, are you there?"

A heap of ragged coats was heaved up, and the face of a young girl emerged, staring sleepily at the woman.

"Deborah," she said, at last, "I'm here the night."

"Yes, child. Hur's welcome," she said, quietly eating on.

The girl's face was haggard and sickly; her eyes were heavy with sleep and hunger: real Milesian[9] eyes they were, dark, delicate blue, glooming out from black shadows with a pitiful fright.

"I was alone," she said, timidly.

"Where's the father?" asked Deborah, holding out a potato, which the girl greedily seized.

---

1 *mulatto* Antiquated term for a person of mixed race.

2 *hur'll* Throughout the story, "hur" is frequently used as a dialectical pronoun meaning him, her, she, he, or you.

3 *Begorra* Irish-English expression meaning "by God."

4 *spools* In a cotton mill, spindles on which cotton is stretched, spun, and wound.

5 *Alleys behint* Always behind.

6 *ondacent* Indecent.

7 *Vargent* Virgin; i.e., the Virgin Mary.

8 *tallow dip* Cheap candle.

9 *Milesian* Irish.

"He's beyant[1]—wid Haley—in the stone house." (Did you ever hear the word *jail* from an Irish mouth?) "I came here. Hugh told me never to stay me-lone."

"Hugh?"

"Yes."

A vexed frown crossed her face. The girl saw it, and added quickly—

"I have not seen Hugh the day, Deb. The old man says his watch[2] lasts till the mornin'."

The woman sprang up, and hastily began to arrange some bread and flitch[3] in a tin pail, and to pour her own measure of ale into a bottle. Tying on her bonnet, she blew out the candle.

"Lay ye down, Janey dear," she said, gently, covering her with the old rags. "Hur can eat the potatoes, if hur's hungry."

"Where are ye goin', Deb? The rain's sharp."

"To the mill, with Hugh's supper."

"Let him bide till th' morn. Sit ye down."

"No, no," sharply pushing her off. "The boy'll starve."

She hurried from the cellar, while the child wearily coiled herself up for sleep. The rain was falling heavily, as the woman, pail in hand, emerged from the mouth of the alley, and turned down the narrow street, that stretched out, long and black, miles before her. Here and there a flicker of gas lighted an uncertain space of muddy footwalk and gutter; the long rows of houses, except an occasional lager-bier shop, were closed; now and then she met a band of mill hands skulking to or from their work.

Not many even of the inhabitants of a manufacturing town know the vast machinery of system by which the bodies of workmen are governed, that goes on unceasingly from year to year. The hands of each mill are divided into watches that relieve each other as regularly as the sentinels of an army. By night and day the work goes on, the unsleeping engines groan and shriek, the fiery pools of metal boil and surge. Only for a day in the week, in half-courtesy to public censure, the fires are partially veiled; but as soon as the clock strikes midnight, the great furnaces break forth with renewed fury, the clamor begins with fresh, breathless vigor, the engines sob and shriek like "gods in pain."

As Deborah hurried down through the heavy rain, the noise of these thousand engines sounded through the sleep and shadow of the city like far-off thunder. The mill to which she was going lay on the river, a mile below the city-limits. It was far, and she was weak, aching from standing twelve hours at the spools. Yet it was her almost nightly walk to take this man his supper, though at every square she sat down to rest, and she knew she should receive small word of thanks.

Perhaps, if she possessed an artist's eye, the picturesque oddity of the scene might have made her step stagger less, and the path seem shorter; but to her the mills were only "summat deilish[4] to look at by night."

The road leading to the mills had been quarried from the solid rock, which rose abrupt and bare on one side of the cinder-covered road, while the river, sluggish and black, crept past on the other. The mills for rolling iron are simply immense tent-like roofs, covering acres of ground, open on every side. Beneath these roofs Deborah looked in on a city of fires, that burned hot and fiercely in the night. Fire in every horrible form: pits of flame waving in the wind; liquid metal-flames writhing in tortuous streams through the sand; wide cauldrons filled with boiling fire, over which bent ghastly wretches stirring the strange brewing; and through all, crowds of half-clad men, looking like revengeful ghosts in the red light, hurried, throwing masses of glittering fire. It was like a street in Hell. Even Deborah muttered, as she crept through, "'T looks like t' Devil's place!" It did—in more ways than one.

She found the man she was looking for, at last, heaping coal on a furnace. He had not time to eat his supper; so she went behind the furnace, and waited. Only a few men were with him, and they noticed her only by a "Hyur comes t' hunchback, Wolfe."

Deborah was stupid with sleep; her back pained her sharply; and her teeth chattered with cold, with the rain that soaked her clothes and dripped from her at every step. She stood, however, patiently holding the pail, and waiting.

"Hout, woman! ye look like a drowned cat. Come near to the fire," said one of the men, approaching to scrape away the ashes.

She shook her head. Wolfe had forgotten her. He turned, hearing the man, and came closer.

---

[1] *beyant* Beyond.

[2] *watch* Shift.

[3] *flitch* Bacon.

[4] *deilish* Devilish.

"I did no' think; gi' me my supper, woman."

She watched him eat with a painful eagerness. With a woman's quick instinct, she saw that he was not hungry—was eating to please her. Her pale, watery eyes began to gather a strange light.

"Is't good, Hugh? T' ale was a bit sour, I feared."

"No, good enough." He hesitated a moment. "Ye're tired, poor lass! Bide here till I go. Lay down there on that heap of ash, and go to sleep."

He threw her an old coat for a pillow, and turned to his work. The heap was the refuse of the burnt iron, and was not a hard bed; the half-smothered warmth, too, penetrated her limbs, dulling their pain and cold shiver.

Miserable enough she looked, lying there on the ashes like a limp, dirty rag—yet not an unfitting figure to crown the scene of hopeless discomfort and veiled crime: more fitting, if one looked deeper into the heart of things—at her thwarted woman's form, her colorless life, her waking stupor that smothered pain and hunger—even more fit to be a type[1] of her class. Deeper yet if one could look, was there nothing worth reading in this wet, faded thing, half-covered with ashes? no story of a soul filled with groping passionate love, heroic unselfishness, fierce jealousy? of years of weary trying to please the one human being whom she loved, to gain one look of real heart-kindness from him? If anything like this were hidden beneath the pale, bleared eyes, and dull, washed-out-looking face, no one had ever taken the trouble to read its faint signs: not the half-clothed furnace-tender, Wolfe, certainly. Yet he was kind to her: it was his nature to be kind, even to the very rats that swarmed in the cellar: kind to her in just the same way. She knew that. And it might be that very knowledge had given to her face its apathy and vacancy more than her low, torpid life. One sees that dead, vacant look steal sometimes over the rarest, finest of women's faces—in the very midst, it may be, of their warmest summer's day; and then one can guess at the secret of intolerable solitude that lies hid beneath the delicate laces and brilliant smile. There was no warmth, no brilliancy, no summer for this woman; so the stupor and vacancy had time to gnaw into her face perpetually. She was young, too, though no one guessed it; so the gnawing was the fiercer.

She lay quiet in the dark corner, listening, through the monotonous din and uncertain glare of the works,

to the dull plash of the rain in the far distance—shrinking back whenever the man Wolfe happened to look towards her. She knew, in spite of all his kindness, that there was that in her face and form which made him loathe the sight of her. She felt by instinct, although she could not comprehend it, the finer nature of the man, which made him among his fellow-workmen something unique, set apart. She knew, that, down under all the vileness and coarseness of his life, there was a groping passion for whatever was beautiful and pure—that his soul sickened with disgust at her deformity, even when his words were kindest. Through this dull consciousness, which never left her, came, like a sting, the recollection of the dark blue eyes and lithe figure of the little Irish girl she had left in the cellar. The recollection struck through even her stupid intellect with a vivid glow of beauty and of grace. Little Janey, timid, helpless, clinging to Hugh as her only friend: that was the sharp thought, the bitter thought, that drove into the glazed eyes a fierce light of pain. You laugh at it? Are pain and jealousy less savage realities down here in this place I am taking you to than in your own house or your own heart—your heart, which they clutch at sometimes? The note is the same, I fancy, be the octave high or low.

If you could go into this mill where Deborah lay, and drag out from the hearts of these men the terrible tragedy of their lives, taking it as a symptom of the disease of their class, no ghost Horror would terrify you more. A reality of soul-starvation, of living death, that meets you every day under the besotted faces on the street—I can paint nothing of this, only give you the outside outlines of a night, a crisis in the life of one man: whatever muddy depth of soul-history lies beneath you can read according to the eyes God has given you.

Wolfe, while Deborah watched him as a spaniel its master, bent over the furnace with his iron pole, unconscious of her scrutiny, only stopping to receive orders. Physically, Nature had promised the man but little. He had already lost the strength and instinct vigor of a man, his muscles were thin, his nerves weak, his face (a meek, woman's face) haggard, yellow with consumption.[2] In the mill he was known as one of the girl-men: "Molly Wolfe"

---

[1]   *type* Symbol; representative model.

[2]   *consumption* Extreme wasting of the body, typically due to tuberculosis. In reality, it is unlikely a person of Wolfe's physical weakness would have been capable of performing the demanding work of puddling.

was his *sobriquet*.[1] He was never seen in the cockpit, did not own a terrier,[2] drank but seldom; when he did, desperately. He fought sometimes, but was always thrashed, pommeled to a jelly. The man was game enough, when his blood was up: but he was no favorite in the mill; he had the taint of school-learning on him—not to a dangerous extent, only a quarter or so in the free-school in fact, but enough to ruin him as a good hand in a fight.

For other reasons, too, he was not popular. Not one of themselves, they felt that, though outwardly as filthy and ash-covered; silent, with foreign thoughts and longings breaking out through his quietness in innumerable curious ways: this one, for instance. In the neighboring furnace-buildings lay great heaps of the refuse from the ore after the pig-metal is run. *Korl* we call it here: a light, porous substance, of a delicate, waxen, flesh-colored tinge. Out of the blocks of this korl, Wolfe, in his off hours from the furnace, had a habit of chipping and moulding figures—hideous, fantastic enough, but sometimes strangely beautiful: even the mill-men saw that, while they jeered at him. It was a curious fancy in the man, almost a passion. The few hours for rest he spent hewing and hacking with his blunt knife, never speaking, until his watch came again—working at one figure for months, and, when it was finished, breaking it to pieces perhaps, in a fit of disappointment. A morbid, gloomy man, untaught, unled, left to feed his soul in grossness and crime, and hard, grinding labor.

I want you to come down and look at this Wolfe, standing there among the lowest of his kind, and see him just as he is, that you may judge him justly when you hear the story of this night. I want you to look back, as he does every day, at his birth in vice, his starved infancy; to remember the heavy years he has groped through as boy and man—the slow, heavy years of constant, hot work. So long ago he began, that he thinks sometimes he has worked there for ages. There is no hope that it will ever end. Think that God put into this man's soul a fierce thirst for beauty—to know it, to create it; to *be*—something, he knows not what—other than he is. There are moments when a

passing cloud, the sun glinting on the purple thistles, a kindly smile, a child's face, will rouse him to a passion of pain—when his nature starts up with a mad cry of rage against God, man, whoever it is that has forced this vile, slimy life upon him. With all this groping, this mad desire, a great blind intellect stumbling through wrong, a loving poet's heart, the man was by habit only a coarse, vulgar laborer, familiar with sights and words you would blush to name. Be just: when I tell you about this night, see him as he is. Be just—not like man's law, which seizes on one isolated fact, but like God's judging angel, whose clear, sad eye saw all the countless cankering days of this man's life, all the countless nights, when, sick with starving, his soul fainted in him, before it judged him for this night, the saddest of all.

I called this night the crisis of his life. If it was, it stole on him unawares. These great turning-days of life cast no shadow before, slip by unconsciously. Only a trifle, a little turn of the rudder, and the ship goes to heaven or hell.

Wolfe, while Deborah watched him, dug into the furnace of melting iron with his pole, dully thinking only how many rails the lump would yield. It was late—nearly Sunday morning; another hour, and the heavy work would be done—only the furnaces to replenish and cover for the next day. The workmen were growing more noisy, shouting, as they had to do, to be heard over the deep clamor of the mills. Suddenly they grew less boisterous—at the far end, entirely silent. Something unusual had happened. After a moment, the silence came nearer; the men stopped their jeers and drunken choruses. Deborah, stupidly lifting up her head, saw the cause of the quiet. A group of five or six men were slowly approaching, stopping to examine each furnace as they came. Visitors often came to see the mills after night: except by growing less noisy, the men took no notice of them. The furnace where Wolfe worked was near the bounds of the works; they halted there hot and tired: a walk over one of these great foundries is no trifling task. The woman, drawing out of sight, turned over to sleep. Wolfe, seeing them stop, suddenly roused from his indifferent stupor, and watched them keenly. He knew some of them: the overseer, Clarke; a son of Kirby, one of the mill-owners; and a Doctor May, one of the town-physicians. The other two were strangers.

---

[1]   *sobriquet*   Nickname.

[2]   *cockpit*   Arena in which roosters are made to fight one another to the death, for entertainment;   *terrier*   Some terrier breeds were commonly kept for the purpose of dogfighting.

Wolfe came closer. He seized eagerly every chance that brought him into contact with this mysterious class that shone down on him perpetually with the glamour of another order of being. What made the difference between them? That was the mystery of his life. He had a vague notion that perhaps tonight he could find it out. One of the strangers sat down on a pile of bricks, and beckoned young Kirby to his side.

"This *is* hot, with a vengeance. A match, please?"—lighting his cigar. "But the walk is worth the trouble. If it were not that you must have heard it so often, Kirby, I would tell you that your works look like Dante's Inferno."[1]

Kirby laughed.

"Yes. Yonder is Farinata[2] himself in the burning tomb,"—pointing to some figure in the shimmering shadows.

"Judging from some of the faces of your men," said the other, "they bid fair to try the reality of Dante's vision, someday."

Young Kirby looked curiously around, as if seeing the faces of his hands[3] for the first time.

"They're bad enough, that's true. A desperate set, I fancy. Eh, Clarke?"

The overseer did not hear him. He was talking of net profits just then—giving, in fact, a schedule of the annual business of the firm to a sharp peering little Yankee, who jotted down notes on a paper laid on the crown of his hat: a reporter for one of the city-papers, getting up a series of reviews of the leading manufactories. The other gentlemen had accompanied them merely for amusement. They were silent until the notes were finished, drying their feet at the furnaces, and sheltering their faces from the intolerable heat. At last the overseer concluded with—

"I believe that is a pretty fair estimate, Captain."

"Here, some of your men!" said Kirby, "bring up those boards. We may as well sit down, gentlemen, until the rain is over. It cannot last much longer at this rate."

"Pig-metal,"—mumbled the reporter, "um!—coal facilities—um!—hands employed, twelve hundred—bitumen—um!—all right, I believe, Mr. Clarke; sinking-fund[4]—what did you say was your sinking-fund?"

"Twelve hundred hands?" said the stranger, the young man who had first spoken. "Do you control their votes, Kirby?"

"Control? No." The young man smiled complacently. "But my father brought seven hundred votes to the polls for his candidate last November. No forcework, you understand—only a speech or two, a hint to form themselves into a society, and a bit of red and blue bunting to make them a flag. The Invincible Roughs—I believe that is their name. I forget the motto: 'Our country's hope,' I think."

There was a laugh. The young man talking to Kirby sat with an amused light in his cool gray eye, surveying critically the half-clothed figures of the puddlers, and the slow swing of their brawny muscles. He was a stranger in the city, spending a couple of months in the borders of a Slave State,[5] to study the institutions of the South—a brother-in-law of Kirby's—Mitchell. He was an amateur gymnast, hence his anatomical eye; a patron, in a *blasé* way, of the prize-ring; a man who sucked the essence out of a science or philosophy in an indifferent, gentlemanly way; who took Kant, Novalis, Humboldt,[6] for what they were worth in his own scales; accepting all, despising nothing, in heaven, earth, or hell, but one-idead men; with a temper yielding and brilliant as summer water, until his Self was touched, when it was ice, though brilliant still. Such men are not rare in the States.

As he knocked the ashes from his cigar, Wolfe caught with a quick pleasure the contour of the white hand, the blood-glow of a red ring he wore. His voice, too, and that of Kirby's, touched him like music—low, even, with chording cadences. About this man Mitchell hung the impalpable atmosphere belonging

---

[1] *Dante's Inferno* Hell, as described by the Italian poet Dante Alighieri (1265–1321) in *Inferno*, the first part of his epic three-part poem *The Divine Comedy*.

[2] *Farinata* Farinata degli Uberti, an aristocrat who in the *Inferno* is described as one among many heretics whose eternal torment is to be entombed in sepulchres surrounded by fire (see Cantos 9–10).

[3] *hands* I.e., workers.

[4] *sinking-fund* Money set aside for the purpose of paying down the principle of a company debt.

[5] *borders of a Slave State* The story was written prior to the establishment of West Virginia as a free state separate from the slave state of Virginia.

[6] *Kant* Immanuel Kant (1724–1804), German philosopher; *Novalis* Pen name of German poet and mystic philosopher Friedrich von Hardenberg (1772–1801); *Humboldt* German explorer and naturalist Alexander von Humboldt (1769–1859).

to the thorough-bred gentleman. Wolfe, scraping away the ashes beside him, was conscious of it, did obeisance to it with his artist sense, unconscious that he did so.

The rain did not cease. Clarke and the reporter left the mills; the others, comfortably seated near the furnace, lingered, smoking and talking in a desultory way. Greek would not have been more unintelligible to the furnace-tenders, whose presence they soon forgot entirely. Kirby drew out a newspaper from his pocket and read aloud some article, which they discussed eagerly. At every sentence, Wolfe listened more and more like a dumb, hopeless animal, with a duller, more stolid look creeping over his face, glancing now and then at Mitchell, marking acutely every smallest sign of refinement, then back to himself, seeing as in a mirror his filthy body, his more stained soul.

Never! He had no words for such a thought, but he knew now, in all the sharpness of the bitter certainty, that between them there was a great gulf never to be passed.[1] Never!

The bell of the mills rang for midnight. Sunday morning had dawned. Whatever hidden message lay in the tolling bells floated past these men unknown. Yet it was there. Veiled in the solemn music ushering the risen Savior was a key-note to solve the darkest secrets of a world gone wrong—even this social riddle which the brain of the grimy puddler grappled with madly tonight.

The men began to withdraw the metal from the cauldrons. The mills were deserted on Sundays, except by the hands who fed the fires, and those who had no lodgings and slept usually on the ash-heaps. The three strangers sat still during the next hour, watching the men cover the furnaces, laughing now and then at some jest of Kirby's.

"Do you know," said Mitchell, "I like this view of the works better than when the glare was fiercest? These heavy shadows and the amphitheatre of smoth-ered fires are ghostly, unreal. One could fancy these

red smouldering lights to be the half-shut eyes of wild beasts, and the spectral figures their victims in the den."

Kirby laughed. "You are fanciful. Come, let us get out of the den. The spectral figures, as you call them, are a little too real for me to fancy a close proximity in the darkness—unarmed, too."

The others rose, buttoning their overcoats, and light-ing cigars.

"Raining, still," said Doctor May, "and hard. Where did we leave the coach, Mitchell?"

"At the other side of the works. Kirby, what's that?"

Mitchell started back, half-frightened, as, suddenly turning a corner, the white figure of a woman faced him in the darkness—a woman, white, of giant pro-portions, crouching on the ground, her arms flung out in some wild gesture of warning.

"Stop! Make that fire burn there!" cried Kirby, stop-ping short.

The flame burst out, flashing the gaunt figure into bold relief.

Mitchell drew a long breath.

"I thought it was alive," he said, going up curiously. The others followed.

"Not marble, eh?" asked Kirby, touching it.

One of the lower overseers stopped.

"Korl, Sir."

"Who did it?"

"Can't say. Some of[2] the hands; chipped it out in off-hours."

"Chipped to some purpose, I should say. What a flesh-tint the stuff has! Do you see, Mitchell?"

"I see."

He had stepped aside where the light fell boldest on the figure, looking at it in silence. There was not one line of beauty or grace in it: a nude woman's form, muscular, grown coarse with labor, the powerful limbs instinct[3] with some one poignant longing. One idea: there it was in the tense, rigid muscles, the clutching hands, the wild, eager face, like that of a starving wolf's. Kirby and Doctor May walked around it, critical, curi-ous. Mitchell stood aloof, silent. The figure touched him strangely.

"Not badly done," said Doctor May. "Where did the fellow learn that sweep of the muscles in the arm and

---

1   *a great gulf ... be passed*   See Luke 16.25–26, where Abraham addresses a rich man who suffers in hell while Lazarus, who was a beggar in life, resides in heaven with Abraham: "Son, remember that thou in thy lifetime receivedst thy good things, and likewise Lazarus evil things: but now he is comforted, and thou art tormented. And beside all this, between us and you there is a great gulf fixed: so that they which would pass from hence to you cannot; neither can they pass to us, that would come from thence."

2   *Some of*   I.e., one of.

3   *instinct*   Charged, animated.

hand? Look at them! They are groping—do you see? clutching: the peculiar action of a man dying of thirst."

"They have ample facilities for studying anatomy," sneered Kirby, glancing at the half-naked figures.

"Look," continued the Doctor, "at this bony wrist, and the strained sinews of the instep! A working-woman—the very type of her class."

"God forbid!" muttered Mitchell.

"Why?" demanded May. "What does the fellow intend by the figure? I cannot catch the meaning."

"Ask him," said the other, dryly.

"There he stands," pointing to Wolfe, who stood with a group of men, leaning on his ash-rake.

The Doctor beckoned him with the affable smile which kind-hearted men put on, when talking to these people.

"Mr. Mitchell has picked you out as the man who did this—I'm sure I don't know why. But what did you mean by it?"

"She be hungry."

Wolfe's eyes answered Mitchell, not the Doctor.

"Oh-h! But what a mistake you have made, my fine fellow! You have given no sign of starvation to the body. It is strong—terribly strong. It has the mad, half-despairing gesture of drowning."

Wolfe stammered, glanced appealingly at Mitchell, who saw the soul of the thing, he knew. But the cool, probing eyes were turned on himself now—mocking, cruel, relentless.

"Not hungry for meat," the furnace-tender said at last.

"What then? Whiskey?" jeered Kirby, with a coarse laugh.

Wolfe was silent a moment, thinking.

"I dunno," he said, with a bewildered look. "It mebbe.[1] Summat to make her live, I think—like you. Whiskey ull do it, in a way."

The young man laughed again. Mitchell flashed a look of disgust somewhere—not at Wolfe.

"May," he broke out impatiently, "are you blind? Look at that woman's face! It asks questions of God, and says, 'I have a right to know.' Good God, how hungry it is!"

They looked a moment; then May turned to the mill-owner:

"Have you many such hands as this? What are you going to do with them? Keep them at puddling iron?"

Kirby shrugged his shoulders. Mitchell's look had irritated him.

"*Ce n'est pas mon affaire.*[2] I have no fancy for nursing infant geniuses. I suppose there are some stray gleams of mind and soul among these wretches. The Lord will take care of his own; or else they can work out their own salvation.[3] I have heard you call our American system a ladder which any man can scale. Do you doubt it? Or perhaps you want to banish all social ladders, and put us all on a flat table-land—eh, May?"

The Doctor looked vexed, puzzled. Some terrible problem lay hid in this woman's face, and troubled these men. Kirby waited for an answer, and, receiving none, went on, warming with his subject.

"I tell you, there's something wrong that no talk of '*Liberté*' or '*Egalité*'[4] will do away. If I had the making of men, these men who do the lowest part of the world's work should be machines—nothing more—hands. It would be kindness. God help them! What are taste, reason, to creatures who must live such lives as that?" He pointed to Deborah, sleeping on the ash-heap. "So many nerves to sting them to pain. What if God had put your brain, with all its agony of touch, into your fingers, and bid you work and strike with that?"

"You think you could govern the world better?" laughed the Doctor.

"I do not think at all."

"That is true philosophy. Drift with the stream, because you cannot dive deep enough to find bottom, eh?"

"Exactly," rejoined Kirby. "I do not think. I wash my hands of all social problems—slavery, caste, white or black. My duty to my operatives has a narrow limit—the pay-hour on Saturday night. Outside of that, if they cut korl, or cut each other's throats (the more popular amusement of the two), I am not responsible."

The Doctor sighed—a good honest sigh, from the depths of his stomach.

---

2 *Ce n'est ... mon affaire* French: This is none of my business.

3 *work out their own salvation* See Philippians 2.12, where Paul urges the people of Philippi to "not as in my presence only, but now much more in my absence, work out your own salvation with fear and trembling."

4 '*Liberté*' *or* '*Egalité*' Allusion to the national motto of France, originating in the French Revolution: "Liberty, Equality, Fraternity."

---

1 *mebbe* May be.

"God help us! Who is responsible?"

"Not I, I tell you," said Kirby, testily. "What has the man who pays them money to do with their souls' concerns, more than the grocer or butcher who takes it?"

"And yet," said Mitchell's cynical voice, "look at her! How hungry she is!"

Kirby tapped his boot with his cane. No one spoke. Only the dumb face of the rough image looking into their faces with the awful question, "What shall we do to be saved?" Only Wolfe's face, with its heavy weight of brain, its weak, uncertain mouth, its desperate eyes, out of which looked the soul of his class—only Wolfe's face turned towards Kirby's. Mitchell laughed—a cool, musical laugh.

"Money has spoken!" he said, seating himself lightly on a stone with the air of an amused spectator at a play. "Are you answered?"—turning to Wolfe his clear, magnetic face.

Bright and deep and cold as Arctic air, the soul of the man lay tranquil beneath. He looked at the furnace-tender as he had looked at a rare mosaic in the morning; only the man was the more amusing study of the two.

"Are you answered? Why, May, look at him! '*De profundis clamavi*.'[1] Or, to quote in English, 'Hungry and thirsty, his soul faints in him.'[2] And so Money sends back its answer into the depths through you, Kirby! Very clear the answer, too! I think I remember reading the same words somewhere: washing your hands in Eau de Cologne, and saying, 'I am innocent of the blood of this man.[3] See ye to it!'"

Kirby flushed angrily.

"You quote Scripture freely."

"Do I not quote correctly? I think I remember another line, which may amend my meaning: 'Inasmuch as ye did it unto one of the least of these, ye did it unto me.'[4]

Deist?[5] Bless you, man, I was raised on the milk of the Word. Now, Doctor, the pocket of the world having uttered its voice, what has the heart to say? You are a philanthropist, in a small way—*n'est ce pas*?[6] Here, boy, this gentleman can show you how to cut korl better—or your destiny. Go on, May!"

"I think a mocking devil possesses you tonight," rejoined the Doctor, seriously.

He went to Wolfe and put his hand kindly on his arm. Something of a vague idea possessed the Doctor's brain that much good was to be done here by a friendly word or two: a latent genius to be warmed into life by a waited-for sunbeam. Here it was: he had brought it. So he went on complacently:

"Do you know, boy, you have it in you to be a great sculptor, a great man?—do you understand?" (talking down to the capacity of his hearer: it is a way people have with children, and men like Wolfe), "to live a better, stronger life than I, or Mr. Kirby here? A man may make himself anything he chooses. God has given you stronger powers than many men—me, for instance."

May stopped, heated, glowing with his own magnanimity. And it was magnanimous. The puddler had drunk in every word, looking through the Doctor's flurry, and generous heat, and self-approval, into his will, with those slow, absorbing eyes of his.

"Make yourself what you will. It is your right."

"I know," quietly. "Will you help me?"

Mitchell laughed again. The Doctor turned now, in a passion—

"You know, Mitchell, I have not the means. You know, if I had, it is in my heart to take this boy and educate him for—"

"The glory of God, and the glory of John May."

May did not speak for a moment; then, controlled, he said,

"Why should one be raised, when myriads are left? I have not the money, boy," to Wolfe, shortly.

"Money?" He said it over slowly, as one repeats the guessed answer to a riddle, doubtfully. "That is it? Money?"

---

[1]   *De profundis clamavi*   First words of the Latin version of Psalm 130; in English, the Psalm begins, "Out of the depths have I cried unto thee, O Lord."

[2]   *Hungry and ... in him*   See Psalm 107.5.

[3]   *I am innocent ... this man*   See Matthew 27.24, where Pontius Pilate, the Roman governor who has consented to the crucifixion of Jesus, washes his hands before the mob and refuses to take personal responsibility for Jesus' death.

[4]   *Inasmuch as ... unto me*   See Matthew 25.40, where Jesus thanks the blessed for assisting him when he was in poverty and need, explaining that "Inasmuch as ye have done it unto one of the least of these my brethren, ye have done it unto me."

[5]   *Deist*   One who believes in a God who was the first cause and creator of the universe, but who has had little or no influence on the world and its inhabitants since. Deism became prominent in the United States in the eighteenth century, especially among scientists, philosophers, and those who were skeptical of organized religion.

[6]   *n'est ce pas*   French: isn't that so.

"Yes, money, that is it," said Mitchell, rising, and drawing his furred coat about him. "You've found the cure for all the world's diseases. Come, May, find your good-humor, and come home. This damp wind chills my very bones. Come and preach your Saint-Simonian[1] doctrines tomorrow to Kirby's hands. Let them have a clear idea of the rights of the soul, and I'll venture next week they'll strike for higher wages. That will be the end of it."

"Will you send the coach-driver to this side of the mills?" asked Kirby, turning to Wolfe.

He spoke kindly: it was his habit to do so. Deborah, seeing the puddler go, crept after him. The three men waited outside. Doctor May walked up and down, chafed. Suddenly he stopped.

"Go back, Mitchell! You say the pocket and the heart of the world speak without meaning to these people. What has its head to say? Taste, culture, refinement? Go!"

Mitchell was leaning against a brick wall. He turned his head indolently, and looked into the mills. There hung about the place a thick, unclean odor. The slightest motion of his hand marked that he perceived it, and his insufferable disgust. That was all. May said nothing, only quickened his angry tramp.

"Besides," added Mitchell, giving a corollary to his answer, "it would be of no use. I am not one of them."

"You do not mean"—said May, facing him.

"Yes, I mean just that. Reform is born of need, not pity. No vital movement of the people's has worked down, for good or evil; fermented, instead, carried up the heaving, cloggy mass. Think back through history, and you will know it. What will this lowest deep—thieves, Magdalens,[2] negroes—do with the light filtered through ponderous Church creeds, Baconian theories, Goethe schemes?[3] Some day, out of their bitter need will be thrown up their own light-bringer—their Jean Paul, their Cromwell,[4] their Messiah."

"Bah!" was the Doctor's inward criticism. However, in practice, he adopted the theory; for, when, night and morning, afterwards, he prayed that power might be given these degraded souls to rise, he glowed at heart, recognizing an accomplished duty.

Wolfe and the woman had stood in the shadow of the works as the coach drove off. The Doctor had held out his hand in a frank, generous way, telling him to "take care of himself, and to remember it was his right to rise." Mitchell had simply touched his hat, as to an equal, with a quiet look of thorough recognition. Kirby had thrown Deborah some money, which she found, and clutched eagerly enough. They were gone now, all of them. The man sat down on the cinder-road, looking up into the murky sky.

"'T be late, Hugh. Wunnot hur come?"

He shook his head doggedly, and the woman crouched out of his sight against the wall. Do you remember rare moments when a sudden light flashed over yourself, your world, God? when you stood on a mountain-peak, seeing your life as it might have been, as it is? one quick instant, when custom lost its force and everyday usage? when your friend, wife, brother, stood in a new light? your soul was bared, and the grave—a foretaste of the nakedness of the Judgment-Day? So it came before him, his life, that night. The slow tides of pain he had borne gathered themselves up and surged against his soul. His squalid daily life, the brutal coarseness eating into his brain, as the ashes into his skin: before, these things had been a dull aching

---

1 *Saint-Simonian* Saint-Simonism was a Christian proto-socialist movement in France based on the doctrines of the philosopher Henri, comte de Saint-Simon (1760–1825). Saint-Simon argued that the application of reason and scientific industry in conjunction with social cooperation could bring an end to poverty, war, and other excesses of capitalism; he also advocated a reformation of Christianity that would be centered on brotherly love.

2 *Magdalens* Prostitutes or former prostitutes (the term references Mary Magdalene, a follower of Jesus in the New Testament, apocryphally considered by some Christians to have been a repentant prostitute).

3 *Baconian theories* Sir Francis Bacon (1561–1624) was an English philosopher, jurist, and powerful political figure best known for his contributions to the development of the scientific method; *Goethe schemes* Johann Wolfgang von Goethe (1749–1832) was a German poet and philosopher who exerted a great influence on Romanticism.

4 *Jean Paul* Influential German novelist (1763–1825) associated with the Romantic movement; *Cromwell* Oliver Cromwell (1599–1658), English Puritan who was a leader in the uprising that overthrew King Charles I; he eventually established himself as Lord Protector of the nation, ruling for five years. He is a controversial figure, considered a violent dictator by some and a revolutionary hero by others.

into his consciousness; tonight, they were reality. He gripped the filthy red shirt that clung, stiff with soot, about him, and tore it savagely from his arm. The flesh beneath was muddy with grease and ashes—and the heart beneath that! And the soul? God knows.

Then flashed before his vivid poetic sense the man who had left him—the pure face, the delicate, sinewy limbs, in harmony with all he knew of beauty or truth. In his cloudy fancy he had pictured a Something like this. He had found it in this Mitchell, even when he idly scoffed at his pain: a Man all-knowing, all-seeing, crowned by Nature, reigning—the keen glance of his eye falling like a sceptre on other men. And yet his instinct taught him that he too—He! He looked at himself with sudden loathing, sick, wrung his hands with a cry, and then was silent. With all the phantoms of his heated, ignorant fancy, Wolfe had not been vague in his ambitions. They were practical, slowly built up before him out of his knowledge of what he could do. Through years he had day by day made this hope a real thing to himself—a clear, projected figure of himself, as he might become.

Able to speak, to know what was best, to raise these men and women working at his side up with him: sometimes he forgot this defined hope in the frantic anguish to escape—only to escape—out of the wet, the pain, the ashes, somewhere, anywhere—only for one moment of free air on a hill-side, to lie down and let his sick soul throb itself out in the sunshine. But tonight he panted for life. The savage strength of his nature was roused; his cry was fierce to God for justice.

"Look at me!" he said to Deborah, with a low, bitter laugh, striking his puny chest savagely. "What am I worth, Deb? Is it my fault that I am no better? My fault? My fault?"

He stopped, stung with a sudden remorse, seeing her hunchback shape writhing with sobs. For Deborah was crying thankless tears, according to the fashion of women.

"God forgi' me, woman! Things go harder wi' you nor me. It's a worse share."

He got up and helped her to rise; and they went doggedly down the muddy street, side by side.

"It's all wrong," he muttered, slowly—"all wrong! I dunnot understan'. But it'll end some day."

"Come home, Hugh!" she said, coaxingly; for he had stopped, looking around bewildered.

"Home—and back to the mill!" He went on saying this over to himself, as if he would mutter down every pain in this dull despair.

She followed him through the fog, her blue lips chattering with cold. They reached the cellar at last. Old Wolfe had been drinking since she went out, and had crept nearer the door. The girl Janey slept heavily in the corner. He went up to her, touching softly the worn white arm with his fingers. Some bitterer thought stung him, as he stood there. He wiped the drops from his forehead, and went into the room beyond, livid, trembling. A hope, trifling, perhaps, but very dear, had died just then out of the poor puddler's life, as he looked at the sleeping, innocent girl—some plan for the future, in which she had borne a part. He gave it up that moment, then and forever. Only a trifle, perhaps, to us: his face grew a shade paler—that was all. But, somehow, the man's soul, as God and the angels looked down on it, never was the same afterwards.

Deborah followed him into the inner room. She carried a candle, which she placed on the floor, closing the door after her. She had seen the look on his face, as he turned away: her own grew deadly. Yet, as she came up to him, her eyes glowed. He was seated on an old chest, quiet, holding his face in his hands.

"Hugh!" she said, softly.

He did not speak.

"Hugh, did hur hear what the man said—him with the clear voice? Did hur hear? Money, money—that it wud do all?"

He pushed her away—gently, but he was worn out; her rasping tone fretted him.

"Hugh!"

The candle flared a pale yellow light over the cobwebbed brick walls, and the woman standing there. He looked at her. She was young, in deadly earnest; her faded eyes, and wet, ragged figure caught from their frantic eagerness a power akin to beauty.

"Hugh, it is true! Money ull do it! Oh, Hugh, boy, listen till me! He said it true! It is money!"

"I know. Go back! I do not want you here."

"Hugh, it is t'last time. I'll never worrit[1] hur again."

---

[1]   *worrit* Worry; bother.

There were tears in her voice now, but she choked them back.

"Hear till me only tonight! If one of t' witch people wud come, them we heard of t' home, and gif hur all hur wants, what then? Say, Hugh!"

"What do you mean?"

"I mean money."

Her whisper shrilled through his brain.

"If one of t' witch dwarfs wud come from t' lane moors tonight, and gif hur money, to go out—*out*, I say—out, lad, where t' sun shines, and t' heath grows, and t' ladies walk in silken gownds, and God stays all t' time—where t' man lives that talked to us tonight—Hugh knows—Hugh could walk there like a king!"

He thought the woman mad, tried to check her, but she went on, fierce in her eager haste.

"If *I* were t' witch dwarf, if I had t' money, wud hur thank me? Wud hur take me out o' this place wid hur and Janey? I wud not come into the gran' house hur wud build, to vex hur wid t' hunch—only at night, when t' shadows were dark, stand far off to see hur."

Mad? Yes! Are many of us mad in this way?

"Poor Deb! poor Deb!" he said, soothingly.

"It is here," she said, suddenly jerking into his hand a small roll. "I took it! I did it! Me, me! not hur! I shall be hanged, I shall be burnt in hell, if anybody knows I took it! Out of his pocket, as he leaned against t' bricks. Hur knows?"

She thrust it into his hand, and then, her errand done, began to gather chips together to make a fire, choking down hysteric sobs.

"Has it come to this?"

That was all he said. The Welsh Wolfe blood was honest. The roll was a small green pocket-book containing one or two gold pieces, and a check for an incredible amount, as it seemed to the poor puddler. He laid it down, hiding his face again in his hands.

"Hugh, don't be angry wud me! It's only poor Deb—hur knows?"

He took the long skinny fingers kindly in his.

"Angry? God help me, no! Let me sleep. I am tired."

He threw himself heavily down on the wooden bench, stunned with pain and weariness. She brought some old rags to cover him.

It was late on Sunday evening before he awoke. I tell God's truth, when I say he had then no thought of keeping this money. Deborah had hid it in his pocket. He found it there. She watched him eagerly, as he took it out.

"I must gif it to him," he said, reading her face.

"Hur knows," she said with a bitter sigh of disappointment. "But it is hur right to keep it."

His right! The word struck him. Doctor May had used the same. He washed himself, and went out to find this man Mitchell. His right! Why did this chance word cling to him so obstinately? Do you hear the fierce devils whisper in his ear, as he went slowly down the darkening street?

The evening came on, slow and calm. He seated himself at the end of an alley leading into one of the larger streets. His brain was clear tonight, keen, intent, mastering. It would not start back, cowardly, from any hellish temptation, but meet it face to face. Therefore the great temptation of his life came to him veiled by no sophistry,[1] but bold, defiant, owning its own vile name, trusting to one bold blow for victory.

He did not deceive himself. Theft! That was it. At first the word sickened him; then he grappled with it. Sitting there on a broken cart-wheel, the fading day, the noisy groups, the church-bells' tolling passed before him like a panorama,[2] while the sharp struggle went on within. This money! He took it out, and looked at it. If he gave it back, what then? He was going to be cool about it.

People going by to church saw only a sickly mill-boy watching them quietly at the alley's mouth. They did not know that he was mad, or they would not have gone by so quietly: mad with hunger; stretching out his hands to the world, that had given so much to them, for leave to live the life God meant him to live. His soul within him was smothering to death; he wanted so much, thought so much, and *knew*—nothing. There was nothing of which he was certain, except the mill and things there. Of God and heaven he had heard so little, that they were to him what fairy-land is to a child: something real, but not here; very far off. His brain, greedy, dwarfed, full of thwarted energy and

---

1 *sophistry* Clever but fallacious reasoning.

2 *panorama* Long painting broken up into contiguous scenes, which would be unrolled or otherwise unveiled before audiences, sometimes with musical accompaniment; panoramas were popular entertainments during the nineteenth century.

unused powers, questioned these men and women going by, coldly, bitterly, that night. Was it not his right to live as they—a pure life, a good, true-hearted life, full of beauty and kind words? He only wanted to know how to use the strength within him. His heart warmed, as he thought of it. He suffered himself to think of it longer. If he took the money?

Then he saw himself as he might be, strong, helpful, kindly. The night crept on, as this one image slowly evolved itself from the crowd of other thoughts and stood triumphant. He looked at it. As he might be! What wonder, if it blinded him to delirium—the madness that underlies all revolution, all progress, and all fall?

You laugh at the shallow temptation? You see the error underlying its argument so clearly—that to him a true life was one of full development rather than self-restraint? that he was deaf to the higher tone in a cry of voluntary suffering for truth's sake than in the fullest flow of spontaneous harmony? I do not plead his cause. I only want to show you the mote in my brother's eye: then you can see clearly to take it out.[1]

The money—there it lay on his knee, a little blotted slip of paper, nothing in itself; used to raise him out of the pit; something straight from God's hand. A thief! Well, what was it to be a thief? He met the question at last, face to face, wiping the clammy drops of sweat from his forehead. God made this money—the fresh air, too—for his children's use. He never made the difference between poor and rich. The Something who looked down on him that moment through the cool gray sky had a kindly face, he knew—loved his children alike. Oh, he knew that!

There were times when the soft floods of color in the crimson and purple flames, or the clear depth of amber in the water below the bridge, had somehow given him a glimpse of another world than this—of an infinite depth of beauty and of quiet somewhere—somewhere—a depth of quiet and rest and love. Looking up now, it became strangely real. The sun had sunk quite below the hills, but his last rays struck upward, touching the zenith. The fog had risen, and the town and river were steeped in its thick, gray damp;

but overhead, the sun-touched smoke-clouds opened like a cleft ocean—shifting, rolling seas of crimson mist, waves of billowy silver veined with blood-scarlet, inner depths unfathomable of glancing light. Wolfe's artist-eye grew drunk with color. The gates of that other world! Fading, flashing before him now! What, in that world of Beauty, Content, and Right, were the petty laws, the mine and thine, of mill-owners and mill-hands?

A consciousness of power stirred within him. He stood up. A man, he thought, stretching out his hands—free to work, to live, to love! Free! His right! He folded the scrap of paper in his hand. As his nervous fingers took it in, limp and blotted, so his soul took in the mean temptation, lapped it in fancied rights, in dreams of improved existences, drifting and endless as the cloud-seas of color. Clutching it, as if the tightness of his hold would strengthen his sense of possession, he went aimlessly down the street. It was his watch at the mill. He need not go, need never go again, thank God!—shaking off the thought with unspeakable loathing.

Shall I go over the history of the hours of that night? how the man wandered from one to another of his old haunts, with a half-consciousness of bidding them farewell—lanes and alleys and backyards where the mill-hands lodged—noting, with a new eagerness, the filth and drunkenness, the pig-pens, the ash-heaps covered with potato-skins, the bloated, pimpled women at the doors—with a new disgust, a new sense of sudden triumph, and, under all, a new, vague dread, unknown before, smothered down, kept under, but still there? It left him but once during the night, when, for the second time in his life, he entered a church. It was a sombre Gothic pile, where the stained light lost itself in far-retreating arches; built to meet the requirements and sympathies of a far other class than Wolfe's. Yet it touched, moved him uncontrollably. The distances, the shadows, the still, marble figures, the mass of silent kneeling worshippers, the mysterious music, thrilled, lifted his soul with a wonderful pain. Wolfe forgot himself, forgot the new life he was going to live, the mean terror gnawing underneath. The voice of the speaker strengthened the charm; it was clear, feeling full, strong. An old man, who had lived much, suffered much; whose brain was keenly alive, dominant; whose

---

[1] *the mote ... take it out*   See Matthew 7.3–5: "And why beholdest thou the mote that is in thy brother's eye, but considerest not the beam [i.e., of timber] that is in thine own eye? ... Thou hypocrite, first cast out the beam out of thine own eye; and then shalt thou see clearly to cast out the mote out of thy brother's eye."

heart was summer-warm with charity. He taught it tonight. He held up Humanity in its grand total; showed the great world-cancer to his people. Who could show it better? He was a Christian reformer; he had studied the age thoroughly; his outlook at man had been free, world-wide, over all time. His faith stood sublime upon the Rock of Ages;[1] his fiery zeal guided vast schemes by which the gospel was to be preached to all nations. How did he preach it tonight? In burning, light-laden words he painted the incarnate Life, Love, the universal Man: words that became reality in the lives of these people, that lived again in beautiful words and actions, trifling, but heroic. Sin, as he defined it, was a real foe to them; their trials, temptations, were his. His words passed far over the furnace-tender's grasp, toned to suit another class of culture; they sounded in his ears a very pleasant song in an unknown tongue. He meant to cure this world-cancer with a steady eye that had never glared with hunger, and a hand that neither poverty nor strychnine-whiskey[2] had taught to shake. In this morbid, distorted heart of the Welsh puddler he had failed.

Years ago,[3] a mechanic[4] tried reform in the alleys of a city as swarming and vile as this mill town, who did

not fail. Could Wolfe have seen him as He was, that night, what then? A social Pariah, a man of the lowest caste, thrown up from among them, dying with their pain, starving with their hunger, tempted as they are to drink, to steal, to curse God and die. Theirs by blood, by birth. The son, they said, of Joseph the carpenter, his mother and sisters there among them. Terribly alone, one who loved and was not loved, and suffered from that pain; who dared to be pure and honest in that devil's den; who dared to die for us though he was a physical coward and feared death. If He had stood in the church that night, would not the wretch in the torn shirt there in the pew have "known the man"?[5] His brother first. And then, unveiled his God.

Wolfe rose at last, and turned from the church down the street. He looked up; the night had come on foggy, damp; the golden mists had vanished, and the sky lay dull and ash-colored. He wandered again aimlessly down the street, idly wondering what had become of the cloud-sea of crimson and scarlet. The trial-day of this man's life was over, and he had lost the victory. What followed was mere drifting circumstance—a quicker walking over the path—that was all. Do you want to hear the end of it? You wish me to make a tragic story out of it? Why, in the police-reports of the morning paper you can find a dozen such tragedies: hints of shipwrecks unlike any that ever befell on the high seas; hints that here a power was lost to heaven— that there a soul went down where no tide can ebb or flow. Commonplace enough the hints are—jocose sometimes, done up in rhyme.

Doctor May, a month after the night I have told you of, was reading to his wife at breakfast from this fourth column of the morning-paper: an unusual thing, these police-reports not being, in general, choice reading for ladies; but it was only one item he read.

"Oh, my dear! You remember that man I told you of, that we saw at Kirby's mill?—that was arrested for robbing Mitchell? Here he is; just listen: 'Circuit Court. Judge Day. Hugh Wolfe, operative in Kirby &

---

1   *Rock of Ages*   Common metaphor for Christ.

2   *strychnine-whiskey*   Slang term for cheap whiskey, to which poisons such as strychnine were sometimes added to allow producers to dilute the alcohol but achieve similar intoxicating effects.

3   *Years ago*   The following paragraph was censored from the original 1861 publication of the story; a revised form of it was restored when the text was reprinted in the 1865 anthology *Atlantic Tales*. Janice Milner Lasseter has persuasively argued that the manuscript version of the paragraph better reflects Davis's artistic vision; that version is reproduced above. In 1865, the paragraph was revised as follows:

Eighteen centuries ago, the Master of this man tried reform in the streets of a city as crowded and vile as this, and did not fail. His disciple, showing Him to-night to cultured hearers, showing the clearness of the God-power acting through Him, shrank back from one coarse fact; that in birth and habit the man Christ was thrown up from the lowest of the people: his flesh, their flesh; their blood, his blood; tempted like them, to brutalize day by day; to lie, to steal: the actual slime and want of their hourly life, and the wine-press he trod alone.

Yet, is there no meaning in this perpetually covered truth? If the son of the carpenter had stood in the church that night, as he stood with the fishermen and harlots by the sea of Galilee, before His Father and their Father, despised and rejected of men, without a place to lay His head, wounded for their iniquities, bruised for their transgressions, would not that hungry

mill-boy at least, in the back seat, have "known the man"? That Jesus did not stand there.

4   *mechanic*   Tradesperson; manual worker. Jesus is often described as a carpenter (also the trade of his mother's husband, Joseph).

5   *known the man*   See Matthew 26.72, where Peter denies that he was Jesus' disciple, saying "I do not know the man."

John's Loudon Mills. Charge, grand larceny. Sentence, nineteen years hard labor in penitentiary.' Scoundrel! Serves him right! After all our kindness that night! Picking Mitchell's pocket at the very time!"

His wife said something about the ingratitude of that kind of people, and then they began to talk of something else.

Nineteen years! How easy that was to read! What a simple word for Judge Day to utter! Nineteen years! Half a lifetime!

Hugh Wolfe sat on the window-ledge of his cell, looking out. His ankles were ironed. Not usual in such cases; but he had made two desperate efforts to escape. "Well," as Haley, the jailer, said, "small blame to him! Nineteen years' imprisonment was not a pleasant thing to look forward to." Haley was very good-natured about it, though Wolfe had fought him savagely.

"When he was first caught," the jailer said afterwards, in telling the story, "before the trial, the fellow was cut down at once—laid there on that pallet like a dead man, with his hands over his eyes. Never saw a man so cut down in my life. Time of the trial, too, came the queerest dodge[1] of any customer I ever had. Would choose no lawyer. Judge gave him one, of course. Gibson it was. He tried to prove the fellow crazy; but it wouldn't go. Thing was plain as daylight: money found on him. 'Twas a hard sentence, all the law allows; but it was for 'xample's sake. These millhands are gettin' onbearable. When the sentence was read, he just looked up, and said the money was his by rights, and that all the world had gone wrong. That night, after the trial, a gentleman came to see him here, name of Mitchell—him as he stole from. Talked to him for an hour. Thought he came for curiosity, like. After he was gone, thought Wolfe was remarkable quiet, and went into his cell. Found him very low; bed all bloody. Doctor said he had been bleeding at the lungs. He was as weak as a cat; yet, if ye'll b'lieve me, he tried to get a-past me and get out. I just carried him like a baby, and threw him on the pallet. Three days after, he tried it again: that time reached the wall. Lord help you! he fought like a tiger—giv' some terrible blow. Fightin' for life, you see; for he can't live long, shut up in the stone crib down yonder. Got a death-cough now. 'T took two of us to bring him down that day; so I just

put the irons on his feet. There he sits, in there. Goin' tomorrow, with a batch more of 'em. That woman, hunchback, tried with him—you remember?—she's only got three years. 'Complice. But *she's* a woman, you know. He's been quiet ever since I put on irons: giv' up, I suppose. Looks white, sick-lookin'. It acts different on 'em, bein' sentenced. Most of 'em gets reckless, devilish-like. Some prays awful, and sings them vile songs of the mills, all in a breath. That woman, now, she's desper't'. Been beggin' to see Hugh, as she calls him, for three days. I'm a-goin' to let her in. She don't go with him. Here she is in this next cell. I'm a-goin' now to let her in."

He let her in. Wolfe did not see her. She crept into a corner of the cell, and stood watching him. He was scratching the iron bars of the window with a piece of tin which he had picked up, with an idle, uncertain, vacant stare, just as a child or idiot would do.

"Tryin' to get out, old boy?" laughed Haley. "Them irons will need a crowbar beside your tin, before you can open 'em."

Wolfe laughed, too, in a senseless way.

"I think I'll get out," he said.

"I believe his brain's touched," said Haley, when he came out.

The puddler scraped away with the tin for half an hour. Still Deborah did not speak. At last she ventured nearer, and touched his arm.

"Blood?" she said, looking at some spots on his coat with a shudder.

He looked up at her. "Why, Deb!" he said, smiling—such a bright, boyish smile, that it went to poor Deborah's heart directly, and she sobbed and cried out loud.

"Oh, Hugh, lad! Hugh! dunnot look at me, when it wur my fault! To think I brought hur to it! And I loved hur so! Oh, lad, I dud!"

The confession, even in this wretch, came with the woman's blush through the sharp cry.

He did not seem to hear her, scraping away diligently at the bars with the bit of tin.

Was he going mad? She peered closely into his face. Something she saw there made her draw suddenly back, something which Haley had not seen, that lay beneath the pinched, vacant look it had caught since the trial, or the curious gray shadow that rested on it. That gray

---

[1]   *dodge*   Scheme; trick.

shadow—yes, she knew what that meant. She had often seen it creeping over women's faces for months, who died at last of slow hunger or consumption. That meant death, distant, lingering: but this——Whatever it was the woman saw, or thought she saw, used as she was to crime and misery, seemed to make her sick with a new horror. Forgetting her fear of him, she caught his shoulders, and looked keenly, steadily, into his eyes.

"Hugh!" she cried, in a desperate whisper, "oh, boy, not that! for God's sake, not *that*!"

The vacant laugh went off his face, and he answered her in a muttered word or two that drove her away. Yet the words were kindly enough. Sitting there on his pallet, she cried silently a hopeless sort of tears, but did not speak again. The man looked up furtively at her now and then. Whatever his own trouble was, her distress vexed him with a momentary sting.

It was market-day. The narrow window of the jail looked down directly on the carts and wagons drawn up in a long line, where they had unloaded. He could see, too, and hear distinctly the clink of money as it changed hands, the busy crowd of whites and blacks shoving, pushing one another, and the chaffering[1] and swearing at the stalls. Somehow, the sound, more than anything else had done, wakened him up—made the whole real to him. He was done with the world and the business of it. He let the tin fall, and looked out, pressing his face close to the rusty bars. How they crowded and pushed! And he—he should never walk that pavement again! There came Neff Sanders, one of the feeders at the mill, with a basket on his arm. Sure enough, Neff was married the other week. He whistled, hoping he would look up; but he did not. He wondered if Neff remembered he was there—if any of the boys thought of him up there, and thought that he never was to go down that old cinder-road again. Never again! He had not quite understood it before; but now he did. Not for days or years, but never!—that was it.

How clear the light fell on that stall in front of the market! and how like a picture it was, the dark-green heaps of corn, and the crimson beets, and golden melons! There was another with game: how the light flickered on that pheasant's breast, with the purplish blood dripping over the brown feathers! He could see the red shining of the drops, it was so near. In one

---

[1]   *chaffering* Bartering, haggling.

minute he could be down there. It was just a step. So easy, as it seemed, so natural to go! Yet it could never be—not in all the thousands of years to come—that he should put his foot on that street again! He thought of himself with a sorrowful pity, as of some one else. There was a dog down in the market, walking after his master with such a stately, grave look!—only a dog, yet he could go backwards and forwards just as he pleased: he had good luck! Why, the very vilest cur, yelping there in the gutter, had not lived his life, had been free to act out whatever thought God had put into his brain; while he—No, he would not think of that! He tried to put the thought away, and to listen to a dispute between a countryman and a woman about some meat; but it would come back. He, what had he done to bear this?

Then came the sudden picture of what might have been, and now. He knew what it was to be in the penitentiary, how it went with men there. He knew how in these long years he should slowly die, but not until soul and body had become corrupt and rotten—how, when he came out, if he lived to come, even the lowest of the mill-hands would jeer him—how his hands would be weak, and his brain senseless and stupid. He believed he was almost that now. He put his hand to his head, with a puzzled, weary look. It ached, his head, with thinking. He tried to quiet himself. It was only right, perhaps; he had done wrong. But was there right or wrong for such as he? What was right? And who had ever taught him? He thrust the whole matter away. A dark, cold quiet crept through his brain. It was all wrong; but let it be! It was nothing to him more than the others. Let it be!

The door grated, as Haley opened it.

"Come, my woman! Must lock up for t' night. Come, stir yerself!"

She went up and took Hugh's hand.

"Good-night, Deb," he said, carelessly.

She had not hoped he would say more; but the tired pain on her mouth just then was bitterer than death. She took his passive hand and kissed it.

"Hur'll never see Deb again!" she ventured, her lips growing colder and more bloodless.

What did she say that for? Did he not know it? Yet he would not be impatient with poor old Deb. She had trouble of her own, as well as he.

"No, never again," he said, trying to be cheerful.

She stood just a moment, looking at him. Do you laugh at her, standing there, with her hunchback, her rags, her bleared, withered face, and the great despised love tugging at her heart?

"Come, you!" called Haley, impatiently.

She did not move.

"Hugh!" she whispered.

It was to be her last word. What was it?

"Hugh, boy, not THAT!"

He did not answer. She wrung her hands, trying to be silent, looking in his face in an agony of entreaty. He smiled again, kindly.

"It is best, Deb. I cannot bear to be hurted any more."

"Hur knows," she said, humbly.

"Tell my father good-bye; and—and kiss little Janey."

She nodded, saying nothing, looked in his face again, and went out of the door. As she went, she staggered.

"Drinkin' today?" broke out Haley, pushing her before him. "Where the Devil did you get it? Here, in with ye!" and he shoved her into her cell, next to Wolfe's, and shut the door.

Along the wall of her cell there was a crack low down by the floor, through which she could see the light from Wolfe's. She had discovered it days before. She hurried in now, and, kneeling down by it, listened, hoping to hear some sound. Nothing but the rasping of the tin on the bars. He was at his old amusement again. Something in the noise jarred on her ear, for she shivered as she heard it. Hugh rasped away at the bars. A dull old bit of tin, not fit to cut korl with.

He looked out of the window again. People were leaving the market now. A tall mulatto girl, following her mistress, her basket on her head, crossed the street just below, and looked up. She was laughing; but, when she caught sight of the haggard face peering out through the bars, suddenly grew grave, and hurried by. A free, firm step, a clear-cut olive face, with a scarlet turban tied on one side, dark, shining eyes, and on the head the basket poised, filled with fruit and flowers, under which the scarlet turban and bright eyes looked out half-shadowed. The picture caught his eye. It was good to see a face like that. He would try tomorrow, and cut one like it. *Tomorrow*! He threw down the tin, trembling, and covered his face with his hands. When he looked up again, the daylight was gone.

Deborah, crouching nearby on the other side of the wall, heard no noise. He sat on the side of the low pallet, thinking. Whatever was the mystery which the woman had seen on his face, it came out now slowly, in the dark there, and became fixed—a something never seen on his face before. The evening was darkening fast. The market had been over for an hour; the rumbling of the carts over the pavement grew more infrequent: he listened to each, as it passed, because he thought it was to be for the last time. For the same reason, it was, I suppose, that he strained his eyes to catch a glimpse of each passer-by, wondering who they were, what kind of homes they were going to, if they had children—listening eagerly to every chance word in the street, as if— (God be merciful to the man! what strange fancy was this?)—as if he never should hear human voices again.

It was quite dark at last. The street was a lonely one. The last passenger, he thought, was gone. No—there was a quick step: Joe Hill, lighting the lamps. Joe was a good old chap; never passed a fellow without some joke or other. He remembered once seeing the place where he lived with his wife. "Granny Hill" the boys called her. Bedridden she was; but so kind as Joe was to her! kept the room so clean!—and the old woman, when he was there, was laughing at "some of t' lad's foolishness." The step was far down the street; but he could see him place the ladder, run up, and light the gas. A longing seized him to be spoken to once more.

"Joe!" he called, out of the grating. "Good-bye, Joe!"

The old man stopped a moment, listening uncertainly; then hurried on. The prisoner thrust his hand out of the window, and called again, louder; but Joe was too far down the street. It was a little thing; but it hurt him, this disappointment.

"Good-bye, Joe!" he called, sorrowfully enough.

"Be quiet!" said one of the jailers, passing the door, striking on it with his club.

Oh, that was the last, was it?

There was an inexpressible bitterness on his face, as he lay down on the bed, taking the bit of tin, which he had rasped to a tolerable degree of sharpness, in his hand—to play with, it may be. He bared his arms, looking intently at their corded veins and sinews. Deborah, listening in the next cell, heard a slight clicking sound, often repeated. She shut her lips tightly, that she might not scream; the cold drops of sweat broke over her, in her dumb agony.

"Hur knows best," she muttered at last, fiercely clutching the boards where she lay.

If she could have seen Wolfe, there was nothing about him to frighten her. He lay quite still, his arms outstretched, looking at the pearly stream of moonlight coming into the window. I think in that one hour that came then he lived back over all the years that had gone before. I think that all the low, vile life, all his wrongs, all his starved hopes, came then, and stung him with a farewell poison that made him sick unto death. He made neither moan nor cry, only turned his worn face now and then to the pure light, that seemed so far off, as one that said, "How long, O Lord? how long?"

The hour was over at last. The moon, passing over her nightly path, slowly came nearer, and threw the light across his bed on his feet. He watched it steadily, as it crept up, inch by inch, slowly. It seemed to him to carry with it a great silence. He had been so hot and tired there always in the mills! The years had been so fierce and cruel! There was coming now quiet and coolness and sleep. His tense limbs relaxed, and settled in a calm languor. The blood ran fainter and slow from his heart. He did not think now with a savage anger of what might be and was not; he was conscious only of deep stillness creeping over him. At first he saw a sea of faces: the mill-men—women he had known, drunken and bloated—Janeys timid and pitiful—poor old Debs: then they floated together like a mist, and faded away, leaving only the clear, pearly moonlight.

Whether, as the pure light crept up the stretched-out figure, it brought with it calm and peace, who shall say? His dumb soul was alone with God in judgment. A Voice may have spoken for it from far-off Calvary, "Father, forgive them, for they know not what they do!"[1] Who dare say? Fainter and fainter the heart rose and fell, slower and slower the moon floated from behind a cloud, until, when at last its full tide of white splendor swept over the cell, it seemed to wrap and fold into a deeper stillness the dead figure that never should move again. Silence deeper than the Night!

Nothing that moved, save the black, nauseous stream of blood dripping slowly from the pallet to the floor!

There was outcry and crowd enough in the cell the next day. The coroner and his jury, the local editors, Kirby himself; and boys with their hands thrust knowingly into their pockets and heads on one side, jammed into the corners. Coming and going all day. Only one woman. She came late, and outstayed them all. A Quaker,[2] or Friend, as they call themselves. I think this woman was known by that name in heaven. A homely body, coarsely dressed in gray and white. Deborah (for Haley had let her in) took notice of her. She watched them all—sitting on the end of the pallet, holding his head in her arms—with the ferocity of a watch-dog, if any of them touched the body. There was no meekness, no sorrow, in her face; the stuff out of which murderers are made, instead. All the time Haley and the woman were laying straight the limbs and cleaning the cell, Deborah sat still, keenly watching the Quaker's face. Of all the crowd there that day, this woman alone had not spoken to her—only once or twice had put some cordial to her lips. After they all were gone, the woman, in the same still, gentle way, brought a vase of wood-leaves and berries, and placed it by the pallet, then opened the narrow window. The fresh air blew in, and swept the woody fragrance over the dead face. Deborah looked up with a quick wonder.

"Did hur know my boy wud like it? Did hur know Hugh?"

"I know Hugh now."

The white fingers passed in a slow, pitiful way over the dead, worn face. There was a heavy shadow in the quiet eyes.

"Did hur know where they'll bury Hugh?" said Deborah in a shrill tone, catching her arm.

This had been the question hanging on her lips all day.

"In t' town-yard? Under t' mud and ash? T' lad'll smother, woman! He war born on t' lane[3] moor, where

---

[1]   *Calvary* Site of Jesus' crucifixion; *Father, forgive ... they do* Jesus' words at the crucifixion, referring to his persecutors; see Luke 23.34.

[2]   *Quaker* Member of the Religious Society of Friends, a Christian movement that has historically been associated with philanthropy and the pursuit of social justice causes such as abolitionism and prison reform. Quakers were also historically known for wearing simple, modest clothing, and for their use of what had originally been considered "plain speech," retaining the usage of words such as "thee" and "thou" after they had come to be considered antiquated.

[3]   *lane* Lone; lonely.

t' air is frick[1] and strong. Take hur out, for God's sake, take hur out where t' air blows!"

The Quaker hesitated, but only for a moment. She put her strong arm around Deborah and led her to the window.

"Thee sees the hills, friend, over the river? Thee sees how the light lies warm there, and the winds of God blow all the day? I live there, where the blue smoke is, by the trees. Look at me." She turned Deborah's face to her own, clear and earnest. "Thee will believe me? I will take Hugh and bury him there tomorrow."

Deborah did not doubt her. As the evening wore on, she leaned against the iron bars, looking at the hills that rose far off through the thick sodden clouds, like a bright, unattainable calm. As she looked, a shadow of their solemn repose fell on her face: its fierce discontent faded into a pitiful, humble quiet. Slow, solemn tears gathered in her eyes: the poor weak eyes turned so hopelessly to the place where Hugh was to rest, the grave heights looking higher and brighter and more solemn than ever before. The Quaker watched her keenly. She came to her at last, and touched her arm.

"When thee comes back," she said, in a low, sorrowful tone, like one who speaks from a strong heart deeply moved with remorse or pity, "thee shall begin thy life again—there on the hills. I came too late; but not for thee—by God's help, it may be."

Not too late. Three years after, the Quaker began her work. I end my story here. At evening-time it was light. There is no need to tire you with the long years of sunshine, and fresh air, and slow, patient Christ-love, needed to make healthy and hopeful this impure body and soul. There is a homely pine house, on one of these hills, whose windows overlook broad, wooded slopes and clover-crimsoned meadows—niched into the very place where the light is warmest, the air freest. It is the Friends' meeting-house.[2] Once a week they sit there, in their grave, earnest way, waiting for the Spirit of Love to speak, opening their simple hearts to receive His words. There is a woman, old, deformed, who takes a humble place among them: waiting like them: in

her gray dress, her worn face, pure and meek, turned now and then to the sky. A woman much loved by these silent, restful people; more silent than they, more humble, more loving. Waiting: with her eyes turned to hills higher and purer than these on which she lives—dim and far off now, but to be reached some day. There may be in her heart some latent hope to meet there the love denied her here—that she shall find him whom she lost, and that then she will not be all-unworthy. Who blames her? Something is lost in the passage of every soul from one eternity to the other—something pure and beautiful, which might have been and was not: a hope, a talent, a love, over which the soul mourns, like Esau deprived of his birthright.[3] What blame to the meek Quaker, if she took her lost hope to make the hills of heaven more fair?

Nothing remains to tell that the poor Welsh puddler once lived, but this figure of the mill-woman cut in korl. I have it here in a corner of my library. I keep it hid behind a curtain—it is such a rough, ungainly thing. Yet there are about it touches, grand sweeps of outline, that show a master's hand. Sometimes—tonight, for instance, the curtain is accidentally drawn back, and I see a bare arm stretched out imploringly in the darkness, and an eager, wolfish face watching mine: a wan, woeful face, through which the spirit of the dead korl-cutter looks out, with its thwarted life, its mighty hunger, its unfinished work. Its pale, vague lips seem to tremble with a terrible question. "Is this the End?" they say, "nothing beyond? no more?" Why, you tell me you have seen that look in the eyes of dumb brutes[4]—horses dying under the lash. I know.

The deep of the night is passing while I write. The gas-light wakens from the shadows here and there the objects which lie scattered through the room: only faintly, though; for they belong to the open sunlight. As I glance at them, they each recall some task or pleasure of the coming day. A half-moulded child's head; Aphrodite;[5] a bough of forest-leaves; music; work; homely fragments, in which lie the secrets of all eternal truth and beauty. Prophetic all! Only this dumb,

---

1   *frick*   Fresh.

2   *Friends' meeting-house*   Instead of holding conventional church services, some Quakers practice a form of unprogrammed worship in which they gather in meeting places and remain in contemplative silence, speaking to the group if compelled by divine inspiration.

3   *like Esau … his birthright*   See Genesis 25.33–34, where the starving Esau, a firstborn son, sells his inheritance to his younger brother Jacob in exchange for a bowl of food.

4   *dumb brutes*   Speechless animals.

5   *Aphrodite*   Greek goddess of love.

woeful face seems to belong to and end with the night. I turn to look at it. Has the power of its desperate need commanded the darkness away? While the room is yet steeped in heavy shadow, a cool, gray light suddenly touches its head like a blessing hand, and its groping arm points through the broken cloud to the far East, where, in the flickering, nebulous crimson, God has set the promise of the Dawn.

—1861

This 1870s photo of the First Point Bridge gives some sense of the degree to which smoke from the mills affected air quality in Pittsburgh, a city approximately eighty miles up the Ohio River from Wheeling, Virginia (where Davis's story is likely set) and likewise known in the mid-nineteenth century for its booming iron industry. (See the website component of this anthology for more material on the mills of Pittsburgh in the nineteenth century.)

GLOSSARY OF TERMS

Abolitionism: a social and political movement in the pre-Civil War era that sought to bring an end to the institution of slavery.

Accent: the natural emphasis (or stress) that speakers place on a syllable.

Accentual-Syllabic Verse: the most common metrical system in traditional English verse, in which a line is measured by the number of syllables and by the pattern of accented (stressed) and unaccented (unstressed) syllables.

Allegory: a narrative with both a literal meaning and secondary, often symbolic meaning or meanings, in which nearly every element, including such things as setting, characters, objects, and plot lines, may contribute to that symbolic meaning. See, for example, Nathaniel Hawthorne's "Young Goodman Brown."

Alliteration: the grouping of words with the same initial consonant (e.g., Longfellow's "In the world's broad field of battle / In the bivouac of Life"). The repetition of sound acts as a connector and adds auditory (and sometimes also thematic) emphasis.

Allusion: a reference, often indirect or unidentified, to a person, thing, or event. A reference in one literary work to another literary work, whether to its content or its form, also constitutes an allusion.

Almanac: an annual publication compiling information on many subjects, such as weather predictions for the year, cures for ailments, lists of roads, lists of government officials, poetry, and essays on current topics of interest.

Ambiguity: an "opening" of language created by the writer to allow for multiple meanings or differing interpretations. In literature, ambiguity may be deliberately employed by the writer to enrich meaning; this differs from any unintentional, unwanted ambiguity in non-literary prose.

Analogy: a broad term that refers to our processes of noting similarities among things or events. Specific forms of analogy in poetry include *simile* and *metaphor* (see below).

Antebellum: before, or existing before, a war; in American usage, particularly the period before the American Civil War but after the War of 1812. See also *postbellum*.

Antinomian Controversy / Free Grace Controversy: a conflict that took place from 1636 to 1638 involving religious and political leaders in the Massachusetts Bay Colony. The dispute originated with a difference in interpretation of the relationship between "works" (an individual's good acts) and "grace" (bestowed by God) as markers of spiritual salvation. Puritans generally agreed that salvation came through God's grace alone—people could not bring about their own salvation through good works—but most thought that a person who had been saved would necessarily think and act in accordance with the rules set out in the Bible. Proponents of "free grace" (called *antinomians* by their opponents) took the more extreme position that individuals who had been saved would simply know it, and that one's actions should not be treated as evidence of salvation—including one's adherence to civil or biblical law. Political and religious leaders responded to this challenge to their authority by banishing some of the movement's leaders—including, most famously, Anne Hutchinson—from the colony.

Aphorism: a pithy observation or saying that contains a general truth. For example: "Three may keep a secret, if two of them are dead" (Benjamin Franklin).

Apostrophe: a figure of speech (a trope; see *figures of speech* below) in which a writer directly addresses an object—or a dead or absent person—as if the imagined audience were actually listening. For example, James Monroe Whitfield's "America, it is to thee / Thou boasted land of liberty, / It is to thee I raise my song."

Archetype: in literature and mythology, a recurring idea, symbol, motif, character, or place. To some scholars and psychologists, an archetype represents universal human thought-patterns or experiences.

Arminianism: the theological doctrine that grew in opposition to the idea of predestination in Calvinism, holding instead that salvation was available to those who had faith in God and practiced good works; the movement influenced Methodism and, later, Unitarianism.

Autobiography: an account of a person's life, or portions of it, as written by that person and presumed to be factual.

Ballad: a folk song, or a poem originally recited to an audience, which tells a dramatic story based on legend or history. See, for example, Longfellow's "Paul Revere's Ride."

Ballad Stanza: a quatrain with alternating four-stress and three-stress lines, rhyming abcb. A variant is "common measure," in which the alternating lines are strictly iambic, and rhyme abab. Emily Dickinson used the technique to great effect; see, for example, "There is no Frigate like a Book."

Baptist: a member of a Protestant denomination that tends to adhere to Calvinist doctrine and advocates baptism for adult believers only—by total immersion, and after a confession of faith—in contrast to the practice of infant baptism among other denominations. See *Calvinism, Separatists.*

Bathos: an anticlimactic effect brought about by a writer's descent from an elevated subject or tone to the ordinary or trivial.

Bildungsroman: from the German words *bildung* (education) and *roman* (novel), a narrative (often a novel) of personal development typically about a young or innocent person who grows through a series of social, sexual, and political experiences.

Blank Verse: unrhymed lines written in iambic pentameter. See George Moses Horton's "Division of an Estate."

Bombast: inappropriately inflated or grandiose language.

Broadside: individual sheet of paper printed on only one side. Broadsides of a variety of different sorts (e.g., ballads, political tracts, short satires) were sold on the streets; they were also used to distribute information or as advertisements.

Brownists: a group of Separatists from the Church of England who adhered to the principles of church government espoused by Robert Browne (1550–1633), the founder of Congregationalism. See *Congregationalism.*

Burlesque: satire of a particularly exaggerated sort, particularly that which mocks its subject by emphasizing its vulgar or ridiculous aspects.

Calvinism: a branch of Protestantism based on the teachings of John Calvin (1509–64), stressing the absolute power of God and humanity's total depravity; central to Calvinist doctrine is the idea that human beings are innately and irreversibly sinful, and that only those who are predestined at birth to be saved—the elect—will be granted salvation. Many of the Separatists and Puritans who first settled in America followed Calvinist doctrine. See also *Protestantism.*

Canon: in literature, those works that are commonly accepted as possessing authority or importance. In practice, "canonical" texts or authors are those that are discussed most frequently by scholars and taught most frequently in university courses.

Canto: a sub-section of a long (usually epic) poem. See Melville's *Clarel* and Ezra Pound's *The Cantos.*

Captivity Narrative: a genre of literature that relates the experiences of a person who has been kidnapped; in American literature, the "Indian captivity narrative" was especially popular from the seventeenth through the nineteenth centuries. Conventions of this genre include a focus on the perspective of white captives, usually women; an emphasis on the subject's piety during the captivity; a tendency toward dehumanizing representations of Indigenous people; and detailed but prejudiced descriptions of Indigenous ways of life. *A Narrative of the Captivity and Restoration of Mrs. Mary Rowlandson* (1682) serves as an excellent example.

Catharsis: the arousal through the performance of a dramatic tragedy of "emotions of pity and fear" to a point where "purgation" or "purification" occurs and the feelings are released or transformed. The concept was developed by Aristotle in his *Poetics* from an ancient Greek medical concept, and adapted by him into an aesthetic principle.

Chiasmus: a figure of speech (a scheme) that reverses word order in successive parallel clauses; if the word order is A-B-C in the first clause, it becomes C-B-A in the second. See, for example, Frederick Douglass's phrase: "You have seen how a man was made a slave; you shall see how a slave was made a man."

Church of England/Anglican Church: Christian church established in the 1530s when the English King Henry VIII broke from the Roman Catholic Church and papal authority. In the sixteenth and seventeenth centuries, there was substantial conflict over whether or not the Anglican Church was sufficiently Protestant in its ideology and aesthetics; Puritans, Separatists, and related groups argued that the Church retained too much of what they saw as Catholic corruption. Some of the reforms advocated by the Puritans were taken up by the Anglican Church, but different factions within the Church continue to express a wide range of opinions on rituals and organization, from elaborate ceremony and a strict hierarchy to relatively informal religious services and more egalitarian governance. After the American Revolution, Anglican churches in America separated from the Church of England and, eventually, formed the Episcopal Church.

Civil Disobedience: title commonly applied to an 1849 essay by Henry David Thoreau ("Resistance to Civil Government"); more generally, a political view that recommends passive resistance to authority whenever laws or social obligations contradict individual beliefs.

Classical: originating in or relating to ancient Greek or Roman culture. As commonly conceived, classical implies a strong sense of formal order. The term neoclassical is often used with reference to literature (particularly of the eighteenth century) that was strongly influenced by ancient Greek and Roman models.

Closet Drama: a play (typically in verse) written for private performance. The term came into use in the first half of the nineteenth century.

Colonialism/Colonization: the system or policy by which a nation acquires control of another nation or nations by means of settlement, economic exploitation, and the subjugation of the region's original inhabitants. The term "colonization" may also refer to the idea, popular among white Americans in the early and mid-nineteenth century, of transporting freed enslaved people to Africa.

Colony: a settled area that is connected with a parent, often distant, country; the community of people in that area, and their descendants.

Color Line: a reference to the division between blacks and whites after the abolition of slavery, so named after an 1881 article by Frederick Douglass.

Colored Narrative: alternative term for *free indirect discourse*.

Comedy: as a literary term, used originally to denote that class of ancient Greek drama in which the action ends happily. More broadly the term has been used to describe a wide variety of literary forms of a more or less light-hearted or humorous character.

Conceit: an unusually elaborate metaphor or simile that presents a striking parallel between two apparently dissimilar things (see, for example, Edward Taylor's poem "Huswifery," in which God is cast as a cloth-maker and the speaker His spinning wheel). Ingenious or fanciful images and comparisons were especially popular with the metaphysical poets of seventeenth-century England, giving rise to the term "metaphysical conceit."

Confederacy: a group of people or nations joined together in political or social union for a particular purpose or mutual support; as, for example, the Iroquois Confederacy. The term is also used to denote the Confederate States of America, the self-proclaimed national government formed by the southern states that supported slavery and seceded from the United States.

Congregationalism: a Protestant religious movement in the Calvinist tradition in which each congregation runs its own affairs, independently from others. See also *Protestantism, Calvinism*.

Connotation: the implied, often unspoken meaning(s) of a given word, as distinct from its denotation, or literal meaning. Connotations may have highly emotional undertones and are usually culturally specific.

Contact: a reference to the physical and cultural meeting between European explorers and Indigenous peoples of North America, the repercussions of which included extensive loss of land and epidemic disease and death for the Indigenous population.

Convention: aesthetic approach, technique, or practice accepted as characteristic and appropriate for a particular form. It is a convention of certain sorts of plays, for example, that the characters speak in blank verse, of other sorts of plays that characters speak in rhymed couplets, and of still other sorts of dramatic performances that characters frequently break into song to express their feelings.

Coverture: a common-law doctrine stipulating that a married woman had no legal identity separate from that of her husband, and so was "covered" or controlled by him in the eyes of the law, with no property or economic rights of her own.

Creation Story: a story that narrates the origins of the world and its first inhabitants; creation stories may present a culture's fundamental worldview, including its moral and spiritual values; some may also chronicle significant geographical or historical events. The telling of creation stories is an act of great importance in many Indigenous cultures.

Creole: originally, a person of European descent who was born in the West Indies or Latin America; also, an enslaved person of African descent born in the colonies. These diverse groups of people settled in a variety of regions and established distinct social and political identities, and the term today can be defined variously; in Louisiana, the term refers to people who are descended from (mainly French) colonial settlers of the Louisiana region before the Louisiana Purchase in 1803. "Creole" may also refer to the hybrid language that develops as a result of the mixing of two or more such groups who speak a different parent language.

Declaration of Independence: the pronouncement adopted on 4 July 1776 that sets out to explain why the Thirteen Colonies felt it necessary to leave the British Empire and declare themselves independent states.

Deism: a school of religious and philosophical thought that grew to prominence during the Enlightenment, proposing that God exists only as the creator of the universe, and has had little or no influence on the world since creation; more generally, deists deny the literal truth of the Bible and other teachings of formal religion.

Democratic Party: a political party established in 1828; led by Andrew Jackson, the party supported a somewhat limited federal government, states' rights, and the removal of the central banking system. The party's nineteeth-century platform differed substantially from that of the Democratic Party in the twenty-first century. See also *Democratic-Republican Party*, *Whig Party*.

Democratic-Republican Party: one of the first two political parties of the United States; established in 1792 and led by Thomas Jefferson and James Madison, the party advocated a limited, decentralized federal government, agrarian and anti-aristocratic policies, and stronger ties to France in foreign affairs. Originally known as just the Republican Party, or the Jeffersonian Republicans, the party embraced the "Democratic-Republican Party" label in 1798, a name that had been intended by Federalist opponents to link them to the radicalism of the French Revolution. The party grew enormously during and after Jefferson's presidency—so much so that in 1824 it ran four candidates for the presidency; however, political division ensued, and the party eventually split in two, giving rise over the next decade to the Democratic Party and the Whig Party.

Denotation: See *connotation* above.

Dialogue: words spoken by characters to one another. (When a character is addressing themselves or the audience directly, the words spoken are referred to as a *monologue*.)

Diaspora: a group of people with a similar heritage or homeland who disperse across the globe to different locations, especially involuntarily; or, the dispersion itself.

Diction: word choice; the diction of a literary work (or of a literary character), whether colloquial, conversational, formal, or of some other type, contributes significantly to the tone of the text as well as to characterization.

Didacticism: aesthetic approach emphasizing moral instruction. See, for example, Harriet Beecher Stowe's novel, *Uncle Tom's Cabin*, or Frances Harper's temperance poems.

Disenfranchisement: the state of being deprived of civil privileges, especially the right to vote.

Doppelgänger: a look-alike (from the German *doppel*-double + -*gänger* walker); in folklore and literature, often an apparition of a living person, the sight of which spells doom or bad luck.

Dramatic Irony: This form of irony occurs when the audience's reception of a speech by a character on the stage is affected by the possession by the audience of information not available to the character.

Dred Scott v. Sandford: an 1857 Supreme Court decision in which the Court held that people of African descent were not United States citizens and so were not entitled to the rights and privileges laid out in the U.S. Constitution. The decision also held that the Missouri Compromise was unconstitutional, nullifying Congress's power to prevent the spread of slavery into new states. The decision came after the formerly enslaved Dred Scott attempted to secure the court's further confirmation of his freedom so that the children of his deceased former enslaver could not claim inherited ownership of Scott's daughters.

Elegy: a poem or other similar form of expression which formally mourns the death of a particular person (e.g., Whitman's "When Lilacs Last in the Dooryard Bloom'd") or in which the poet or speaker meditates on other serious subjects (e.g., Chief Seattle's 1854 speech concerning Indigenous worldviews and the environment).

Ellipsis: the omission of a word or words necessary for the complete grammatical construction of a sentence, but not necessary for our understanding of the sentence.

End-Stopped: a line of poetry is said to be end-stopped when the end of the line coincides with a natural pause in the syntax, such as the conclusion of a sentence; an end-stopped line is usually but not always marked by punctuation. For example, the first two lines of Longfellow's "The Arrow and the Song": "I shot an arrow into the air, / It fell to earth, I knew not where." Compare *enjambement*.

Enjambement: the "running-on" of the sense from one line of poetry to the next, with no pause created by punctuation or syntax. Longfellow's poem "The Arrow and the Song" provides an example, which follows on the heels of an end-stopped line: "For, so swiftly it flew, the sight / Could not follow it in its flight." Compare *end-stopped*.

Enlightenment: an intellectual movement of the seventeenth and eighteenth centuries broadly characterized by radically new scientific, political, and philosophical ideas that ushered in a wholesale reappraisal of society. Also referred to as the "Age of Reason," the period placed great stock in empirical observation and in the belief that human rationality, rather than faith and religious doctrine, would improve society. Enlightenment thinkers frequently called for the reform of existing political, religious, and social institutions, extending to—in the case of more radical figures—the separation of church and state, constitutional government, freedom of expression, and other kindred individual liberties. Enlightenment ideals directly inspired the American and other national revolutions.

Epic: a lengthy narrative poem, often divided into sections, that generally celebrates heroic deeds or events, and the style of which tends to be lofty and grand. Examples include Anne Bradstreet's *The Four Monarchies* and Michael Wigglesworth's *The Day of Doom*.

Epigraph: a quotation placed at the beginning of a discourse to indicate or foreshadow the theme.

Epiphany: a moment at which matters of significance are suddenly illuminated for a literary character (or for the reader), typically triggered by something small and seemingly of little import.

Episodic Plot: plot comprising a variety of episodes that are only loosely connected by threads of story material (as opposed to plots that present one or more continually unfolding narratives where successive episodes build one on another).

Eulogy: text expressing praise, especially for a distinguished person recently deceased. While not necessarily typical of the form, William Apess's *Eulogy on King Philip* provides an example.

Euphemism: mode of expression through which aspects of reality considered to be vulgar, crudely physical, or unpleasant are referred to indirectly rather than named explicitly. A variety of euphemisms exist for the processes of urination and defecation; *passed away* is often used as a euphemism for *died*.

Exposition: the setting out of material in an ordered form, either in speech or in writing. In a play those parts of the action that do not occur on stage but are rather recounted by the characters are frequently described as being presented in exposition. Similarly, when the background narrative is filled in near the beginning of a novel, such material is often described as having been presented in exposition.

Federalist Party: one of the first two political parties of the United States; led by Alexander Hamilton, George Washington, and John Adams, and favored by conservatives and business owners, the party dominated the national government from 1791 to 1801. Federalists advocated a strong centralized federal government, a national bank, and stronger ties to Britain in foreign affairs. The party faded after 1801 and dissolved soon thereafter. See also *Democratic-Republican Party*.

Fifteenth Amendment: an 1870 amendment to the U.S. Constitution guaranteeing that the right to vote could not be denied to anyone based on "race, color, or previous condition of servitude." Even after the amendment passed, threats, violence, and poll taxes continued to prevent some populations from voting in many places, and women were excluded from the amendment.

Figures of Speech: deliberate, highly concentrated uses of language intended to achieve particular purposes or effects on an audience. There are two kinds of figures: schemes and tropes. Schemes involve changes in word-sound and word-order, such as *alliteration* and *chiasmus*. Tropes play on our understandings of words to extend, alter, or transform meaning, as in *metaphor* and *personification*.

Fireside Poets: a group of nineteenth-century American poets who became widely popular especially in the latter half of the century, including Henry Wadsworth Longfellow, John Greenleaf Whittier, James Russell Lowell, William Cullen Bryant, and Oliver Wendell Holmes Sr. Their fame stemmed from their tendency to write in conventional meter on domestic themes and familiar moral and political issues.

First Great Awakening: the period of increased religious fervor that swept through the American colonies beginning in the 1730s. Having originated in Europe, the movement was introduced to New England through the preaching of figures like George Whitefield and Jonathan Edwards; it influenced many denominations, and led to, among other things, the emergence of evangelical Christianity. Proponents reinvigorated concepts of Calvinism as a reaction against the confidence placed in science and reason during the Age of Enlightenment and as an antidote to the prevailing materialism in the colonies. See also *Second Great Awakening*.

First-Person Narrative: narrative recounted using *I* and *me*. See also *narrative perspective*.

Folklore: the traditions and cultural artifacts shared by a given group of people; these include such things as tales and proverbs, handmade items and building styles, rituals and celebratory practices, and so on.

Folktale: a story that is passed down through generations orally and that, while often featuring fictional elements or characters, can communicate key aspects of a culture's knowledge, history, or beliefs; a genre of folklore.

Foot: a unit of a line of verse which contains a particular combination of stressed and unstressed syllables. Dividing a line into metrical feet (*iambs*, *trochees*, etc.), then counting the number of feet per line, is part of *scansion*. See also *meter*.

Founders/Founding Fathers: the leading figures in the founding of the United States who worked to unite the Thirteen Colonies, draft the Declaration of Independence and Constitution, lead the war for independence in various capacities, and build the ideological and functional framework of the country's democratic government.

Fourteenth Amendment: an 1868 amendment to the U.S. Constitution that granted citizenship to formerly enslaved people and guaranteed them "equal protection of the laws," thereby nullifying the Supreme Court's 1857 *Dred Scott* decision that had prevented people of African descent from becoming citizens. The amendment also gave the federal government authority to punish states for restricting citizens' right to vote; introduced hurdles that made it difficult for former Confederate leaders to hold office; invalidated federal and state debts owed to the now defunct Confederate states; and prohibited compensation to be paid to former enslavers.

Free Indirect Discourse: in prose fiction, third-person narration in which a seemingly objective and omniscient narrative voice assumes the point of view of one or more characters, and in which the thoughts and expressions are not typically set apart with indicators such as "he said" or "she thought"; the term may also be applied to situations in which it may not be entirely clear if the thoughts expressed emanate from the character, the narrator, or some combination of the two. When we hear through the third-person narrative voice of Melville's *Benito Cereno*, for example, the unsettling description of enslaved black sailors, we are likely to take it as being the view of the character Captain Delano. The narrator ascribes to the sailors the traits of "docility," "good-humour," and "cheerfulness"—"as though God had set the whole negro to some pleasant tune"—but it is difficult to imagine that the extreme incongruity between their enslavement and the narrator's description of their disposition is an objective statement of perceived truth on the part of the novel's third-person narrative voice.

Free Verse: poetry that does not follow any regular meter, line length, or rhyming scheme. In many respects, though, free verse follows the complex natural "rules" and rhythmic patterns (or cadences) of speech. Walt Whitman's long poetic lines provide a fine example.

Frontier: an extreme limit of settled land; as a concept in American history and culture, the frontier was an imagined border in the west beyond which lay wilderness. To many colonists, the idea of the frontier represented the opportunity for leading a new and better life; however, this idea frequently distorted the reality of the conditions in the frontier territory and either minimized or dismissed outright the Indigenous people who already inhabited it.

Fugitive Slave Acts: two federal laws, enacted in 1793 and 1850, that provided for the capture and return of escapees from slavery and imposed penalties on anyone who harbored or helped them; both acts were meant to quell the unrest emerging in southern states as a result of increasing antislavery sentiment in the north.

Genre: a particular literary form. The concept of genre may be used with different levels of generality. At the most general, poetry, drama, and prose fiction are distinguished as separate genres. At a lower level of generality various subgenres are frequently distinguished, such as (within drama) comedy and tragedy, or, at a still lower level of generality, minstrelsy, puppetry, burlesque, and so on.

Gilded Age: a period between the end of the Civil War and the start of the twentieth century in which tremendous industrial and technological growth led to extreme economic disparity between wealthy industrialists and financiers, on one hand, and the working class and immigrants, on the other; the term was coined by Mark Twain in reference to the façade of respectability that masked the era's greed and corruption.

Gold Coast: a region in West Africa named by imperial nations after its chief export, gold; modern-day Ghana. It was one of many coastal regions from Senegambia (modern-day Senegal) to Angola that were exploited during the era of the transatlantic slave trade.

Goodman/Goodwife: polite terms of address used in colonial America, generally in reference to those of lower or middling social status—laborers or farmers (and their wives)—as opposed to merchants and others of the wealthier classes.

Gospel: historically, the first four books of the New Testament, which narrate the life and relate the teachings of Jesus Christ, or the biblical message of Christ in general; also, a genre of music in which songs echo and elevate Christian worship, often featuring evangelical lyrics. See also *spiritual*.

Gothic: in literature, a term used to describe work with a sinister or grotesque tone that seeks to evoke a sense of terror on the part of the reader or audience. The term was used originally to describe styles prevalent in architecture and the visual arts in late Medieval Europe; Gothic literature originated in eighteenth-century England as a distinct genre in which works often featured medieval settings or themes, supernatural elements, and fantastic, macabre plots. Examples in American literature include much of Edgar

Allan Poe's work, Charles Brockden Brown's *Edgar Huntly*, and "The Legend of Sleepy Hollow" by Washington Irving.

Gullah/Geechee: a distinct group of African Americans who live in parts of Georgia, North Carolina, South Carolina, and Florida; the culture developed as various ethnic groups of enslaved people from Africa were forced to work on large and relatively isolated plantations in the region; also, the creole language that they speak.

Haitian Revolution: a large-scale revolution in Haiti that began in 1791 and was led by black and mixed-race Haitians, many of whom were enslaved; it ultimately resulted in the expulsion of French colonial forces and the establishment of Haiti as an independent nation in 1804. The revolution's success, along with Haiti's proximity to the fledgling United States, had a profound impact on American racial, social, and political history.

Homestead Act: a law enacted by Congress during the Civil War in 1862 that granted public lands to any private citizen or citizens-to-be who had not taken up arms against the Federal government; the law dealt a severe blow to Indigenous peoples.

Hoodoo: a set of spiritual practices and folk magic based in part on traditions and beliefs of enslaved Africans, including African spiritualism and Christianity. Hoodoo practice is also known as conjure or rootwork. See also *Obeah, Voodoo.*

Hudson River School: a group of New York-based landscape artists in the nineteenth century who were influenced by the ideas of Romanticism.

Humors: The four humors were believed until the sixteenth and seventeenth centuries to be elements in the makeup of all humans; a person's temperament was thought to be determined by the way in which the humors were combined. When the *choleric* humor was dominant, the person would tend toward anger; when the *sanguine* humor was dominant, toward pleasant affability; when the *phlegmatic* humor was dominant, toward a cool and calm attitude and/or a lack of feeling or enthusiasm; and when the *melancholic* humor was dominant, toward withdrawal and melancholy.

Hymn: a song whose theme is usually religious, in praise of divinity. Literary hymns may praise more secular subjects. African American spirituals provide abundant examples; see, for instance, "Swing Low, Sweet Chariot."

Hyperbole: a *figure of speech* (a trope) that deliberately exaggerates or inflates meaning to achieve particular effects, such as the theatrical tale of Pocahontas by John Smith, who describes her as laying her own head upon his to prevent him from being clubbed to death (see Smith's *General History of Virginia*), or, to more humorous effect, when Joel Chandler Harris's Uncle Remus describes sleep as an old man "ridin' on my eyeleds."

Iamb: the most common metrical foot in English verse, containing one unstressed syllable followed by a stressed syllable (e.g., between, achieve).

Idyll: traditionally, a short pastoral poem that idealizes country life, conveying impressions of innocence and happiness. See, for example, Longfellow's "The Village Blacksmith."

Image: the recreation in words of objects perceived by the senses, sometimes thought of as "pictures," although other senses besides sight are involved. Besides this literal application, the term also refers more generally to the descriptive effects of figurative language, especially in *metaphor* and *simile*.

Incantation: a chant or recitation of words that are believed to have magical power. A poem can achieve an "incantatory" effect through a compelling rhyme scheme and other repetitive patterns. For example, see Edgar Allan Poe's "The Raven."

Indentured Servant/Apprentice: a person who was bound to work without pay for a fixed period of time; indentures were usually at least somewhat voluntary, but the contracts were often liable to be sold to different employers with little to no consultation with the servant or apprentice in question.

Indian Expulsion: the forced removal of Indigenous people from their homes to facilitate settlement by predominantly white settlers, codified in the 1830 Indian Removal Act; also called Indian Removal.

Indian Territory: areas in modern-day Oklahoma, Missouri, and Kansas designated by the Federal government for Indigenous nations who had been forcibly removed from their homes; the territory shifted continuously throughout the eighteenth and nineteenth centuries, decreasing over time.

Indigenous people: the inhabitants of a region who are the descendants of the people who lived there prior to another ethnic group settling or colonizing that region.

Individualism: an ideology that emphasizes self-reliance, independence, and the value of one's own instincts and intelligence, especially with respect to aesthetic, social, or ethical judgments; in religion, an ideology that affirms the individual as the sole source of an authentic relationship with God, and the sole arbiter of one's social and intellectual responsibilities.

Irony: a subtle form of humor in which a statement is understood to convey a quite different (and often entirely opposite) meaning. A writer achieves this by carefully making sure that the statement occurs in a context which undermines or twists the statement's "literal" meaning. *Hyperbole* and *litotes* are often used for ironic effect. *Sarcasm* is a particularly strong or crude form of irony (usually spoken), in which the meaning is conveyed largely by the tone of voice adopted; something said sarcastically is meant clearly to imply its opposite.

See, for example, Washington Irving's *History of New York*, in which the narrator employs irony to relate one of the more disastrous effects that European colonization had on Indigenous people:

> ... no sooner did the benevolent inhabitants of Europe behold their sad condition than they immediately went to work to ameliorate and improve it. They ... made known to them a thousand remedies, by which the most inveterate diseases are alleviated and healed, and that they might comprehend the benefits and enjoy the comforts of these medicines, they previously introduced among them the diseases, which they were calculated to cure. By these and a variety of other methods was the condition of these poor savages, wonderfully improved. ...

Jacksonian Democracy: a nineteenth-century political movement associated with the presidency of Andrew Jackson; the movement saw expanded suffrage (for white men), a hands-off approach to the economy, and aggressive expansionism. While the movement had an egalitarian drive, many changes came at the expense of black and Indigenous people.

Jeffersonian Democracy: a late eighteenth-century and early nineteenth-century political movement named after Thomas Jefferson whose advocates staunchly supported the common people and ideas of republicanism, the tenets of which underpinned the values of the Democratic-Republican Party. See also *Democratic-Republican Party*, *Republicanism*.

Jeremiad: a literary work, often a sermon or speech, that expresses mourning, sorrow, or moral and spiritual disapproval; the form laments or decries perceived social or moral evils and prophesies doom unless the supposedly more wholesome spirit of an earlier time can be reawakened.

Jesuit: a member of the Society of Jesus, an order of the Roman Catholic Church; founded in the mid-sixteenth century during the rise of Protestantism, the order professed total obedience to the pope and sought to advance the Catholic faith, often by education or missionary activity.

Jim Crow: comic character commonly depicted by blackface performers in minstrel shows in the mid-nineteenth century; due to the popularity of such shows, "Jim Crow" was often used as a racist epithet for African Americans, and in the late nineteenth century the term came to refer to the legal and social systems that enforced racial segregation in southern states.

Know-Nothing Movement: an anti-immigrant and anti-Catholic movement that formed in the mid-nineteenth century in opposition to widespread German and Irish immigration.

Ku Klux Klan: a white supremacist group that emerged in the South in the wake of the Civil War and whose early members used organized violence, terror, and murder as a way to intimidate and abuse formerly enslaved people; the initial Klan's activities declined by the early 1880s, but there have been various resurgences throughout the twentieth and twenty-first centuries.

Künstlerroman: from the German for *künstler* (artist) and *roman* (novel), a narrative (often in novel form) about the personal and aesthetic growth of an artist. See, for example, Louisa May Alcott's *Little Women*.

Ledger Art/Ledger Drawing: narrative drawings developed by the Indigenous nations of the Great Plains as a means of historical representation; made with pencil, ink, crayon, and/or watercolor, and drawn on the pages of old ledgers (i.e., account books) that had earlier been used by white settlers. The practice flourished from the 1860s to the 1920s, continuing a long history of recording oral histories pictorially.

Litotes: a *figure of speech* (a trope) in which a writer deliberately uses understatement to paradoxically highlight significance, or, conversely, to convey an ironic attitude; this is often accomplished by affirming something through the negation of the opposite thing. For example, when the narrator of Melville's "Bartleby, the Scrivener" states that he was "not unemployed" by John Jacob Astor and "not insensible" to Astor's good opinion, the oddly constructed understatements cause the reader to pause, even stumble, and to call the narrator's reliability or purpose into question.

Local Color: a style of writing from the latter half of the nineteenth century that captures the character of a specific locale and the people who live there; practitioners sought to reproduce regional dialects and to give color to distinctive features of landscape, custom, and folklore. See also *Regionalism*.

Loyalist: a colonist who remained loyal to Britain in the American War of Independence. See also *Tory*.

Lyric: a poem, usually short, expressing an individual speaker's feelings or private thoughts. Originally a song performed with accompaniment on a lyre, the lyric poem is often noted for musicality of rhyme and rhythm. The lyric genre includes a variety of forms, including the *sonnet*, the *elegy*, the *ode*, and the *hymn*.

Manifest Destiny: a term, originating in the 1840s, used to communicate the belief that the United States was destined to expand westward across the North American continent; the doctrine of expansionism was couched in the terms of moral duty and God-given destiny, and its implementation had dire consequences for Indigenous and Hispanic people.

Mason-Dixon Line: Eighteenth-century survey line separating Pennsylvania and Delaware from Maryland and Virginia. In the *antebellum* United States, it and the Ohio River formed much of the dividing line between free and slave states and hence between North and South.

Mass: within Christianity, a church service that includes the sacrament of the Eucharist (Holy Communion), in which bread and wine are consumed; these are believed by those of many Christian denominations, especially Roman Catholics, to have been transubstantiated into the body and blood of Christ. Protestants do not generally use the term "Mass" and are more likely to believe that the bread and wine merely symbolize the body and blood.

Mayflower Compact: a document signed in 1620 aboard the *Mayflower* before it landed at Plymouth that committed the settlers to majority-rule government.

Melodrama: originally a term used to describe nineteenth-century plays featuring sensational story lines and a crude separation of characters into moral categories, with the pure and virtuous pitted against evil villains. Early melodramas employed background music throughout the action of the play as a means of heightening the emotional response of the audience. By extension, certain sorts of prose fictions or poems are often described as having melodramatic elements.

Mesoamerica: cultural region of Mexico and most of Central America where the Maya, Aztec, and other Indigenous peoples flourished before the Spanish Conquest. While the peoples of the region shared some cultural traits, geographical and linguistic differences were many.

Mestizo: a term used in Spanish America for a person of mixed Indigenous and European ancestry; from the Spanish word, meaning "mixed."

Metaphor: a *figure of speech* (in this case, a trope) in which a comparison is made or identity is asserted between two unrelated things or actions without the use of "like" or "as." The primary subject is known as the *tenor*; to illuminate its nature, the writer links it to wholly different images, ideas, or actions referred to as the *vehicle*. Unlike a *simile*, which is a direct comparison of two things, a metaphor "fuses" the separate qualities of two things, creating a new idea. For example, Dickinson's "'Hope' is the thing with feathers" is a metaphorical statement. The tenor, or primary subject, is "hope"; the vehicle of the metaphor is the image of an initially unnamed "thing with feathers," a bird. The line fuses the idea of hope with the qualities of a delicate bird perched in the soul and forever singing.

Meter: the pattern of stresses, syllables, and pauses that constitutes the regular rhythm of a line of verse. The meter of a poem is determined by identifying the stressed and unstressed syllables in a line of verse, and grouping them into recurring units known as feet. See also *accent*, *accentual-syllabic verse*, *foot*, and *scansion*.

Methodist: a member of a Protestant denomination formed in the eighteenth century as part of the religious movement led by John and Charles Wesley. Originally a sect within the Church of England, Methodism entailed enthusiastic evangelism, a strong emphasis on free will, and a strict, methodical regimen of Christian worship and living.

Metonymy: a *figure of speech* (a trope), meaning "change of name," in which a writer refers to an object or idea by substituting the name of another object or idea closely associated with it: for example, the substitution of "crown" for monarchy, "the press" for journalism, or "the pen" for writing. *Synecdoche* (see below) is a kind of metonymy.

Middle Passage: in the slave trade, the transatlantic journey from the coasts of Africa to the Americas and the West Indies; for the enslaved people in the slave ships, the one- to two-month voyage was horrific, brutal, and often deadly.

Minstrel Show/Minstrelsy: a form of Vaudeville theater popularized in the mid-nineteenth century that featured entertainers performing in blackface.

Miscegenation: the mixing of different racial or ethnic groups, or sexual relationships or reproduction between individuals of those groups, especially between white and non-white people; the term was coined in 1863.

Missouri Compromise: a deal made by Congress in 1820 to resolve the political imbalance that would have resulted if Missouri was admitted as a slave state; Maine was admitted as a free state, and slavery was prohibited thereafter anywhere north of Missouri's southern border.

Monologue: words spoken by a character to him or herself or to an audience directly.

Mood: This can describe the writer's attitude, implied or expressed, toward the subject (see *tone* below); or it may refer to the atmosphere that a writer creates in a passage of description or narration.

Mormonism: the teachings and doctrines of the Latter-Day Saint movement; started by Joseph Smith in the 1820s, Mormon theology embraces as sacred scripture both the Bible and the Book of Mormon; Smith claimed to have translated the latter from an ancient record shown to him by an angel.

Motif: an idea, image, action, or plot element that recurs throughout a literary work, creating new levels of meaning and strengthening structural coherence. The term is taken from music, where it describes recurring melodies or themes. See also *theme*.

Mulatto: term for a person with one white and one black parent; more loosely, a person with the appearance of being mixed-race. The designation is today considered offensive.

Myth: a traditional story that provides an explanation for a society or culture's early history or spiritual beliefs, or features of the natural world, usually involving a supernatural element of some kind.

Narrative Perspective: in fiction, the point of view from which the story is narrated. A first-person narrative is recounted using *I* and *me*, whereas a third-person narrative is recounted using *he, she, they*, and so on. When a narrative is written in the third person and the narrative voice evidently "knows" all that is being done and thought, the story is typically described as being recounted by an "omniscient narrator."

Neoclassical: adapted from or substantially influenced by the cultures of ancient Greece and Rome. The term *neoclassical* is often used to describe the ideals of eighteenth-century writers, thinkers, and artists who looked to ancient Greek and Roman civilization for models.

Non-Alphabetic Literature: a transmission or recording of knowledge, or a literary expression, that is inscribed without employing an alphabet; Indigenous literacies of this sort include objects such as baskets, wampum, pottery, tattoos, textiles, pictographs, and rock art.

Nonconformist: general term used to describe one who does not subscribe to the Church of England.

Obeah: a practice of spiritual healing and witchcraft, or folk medicine, originating among enslaved West Africans and developed in the Caribbean; the practice is more individual than it is collective. See also *Hoodoo, Voodoo*.

Ode: in English poetry, a long lyric poem of some gravity that is typically elevated in tone and complex in structure. Originally a classical poetic form, the ode was used by the Greeks and Romans to convey serious themes; later imitations of the form stemmed from the examples set by the Greek poet Pindar and the Roman poet Horace.

Onomatopoeia: a *figure of speech* (a scheme) in which a word "imitates" a sound, or in which the sound of a word seems to reflect its meaning.

Oral Literature: a form of literature communicated by spoken word and passed down from generation to generation; often taking the form of stories, oral literature may serve as a repository of history, mythology, spiritual belief, etc.

Oratory: the formal art of public speaking, especially with eloquence and with an eye toward persuasion.

Over-Soul: all-encompassing spiritual "unity" that animates the universe and resides in each human soul, and through which all of humanity is connected. The term was coined in 1841 by Ralph Waldo Emerson, but the concept is also a central principle in a number of Eastern religions.

Oxymoron: a *figure of speech* (a trope) in which two words whose meanings seem contradictory are placed together: for example, Fitzgerald's description in *The Great Gatsby* of Wolfsheim eating with "ferocious delicacy."

Parliament: in Britain, the combined legislative body, comprising both the House of Commons (the "lower house," made up of elected officials) and the House of Lords (the "upper house," comprised of members of the aristocracy). Unlike the American system, the British parliamentary system does not separate the executive and legislative functions of government.

Parody: a close, usually mocking imitation of a particular literary work, or of the well-known style of a particular author, in order to expose or magnify weaknesses. Parody is a form of satire—that is, humor that may ridicule and scorn its object. The poem "Counter-Jumps" parodies Whitman's sprawling "Song of Myself":   "I am the shop, and the counter, and the till, / But particularly the last. / And I explore and rummage the till, and am at home in it."

Pastiche: a discourse which borrows or imitates other writers' characters, forms, style, or ideas. Unlike a parody, a pastiche is usually intended as a compliment to the original writer.

Pastoral: in general, pertaining to country life; in prose, drama, and poetry, a stylized type of writing that idealizes the lives and innocence of country people, particularly shepherds and shepherdesses. See *idyll*.

Pathetic Fallacy: a form of personification in which inanimate objects are given human emotions: for example, rain clouds "weeping." The word "fallacy" in this connection is intended to suggest the distortion of reality or the false emotion that may result from an exaggerated use of personification.

Pathos: the emotional quality of a discourse; or the ability of a discourse to appeal to our emotions. It is usually applied to the mood conveyed by images of pain, suffering, or loss that arouse feelings of pity or sorrow in the reader.

Persona: the assumed identity or "speaking voice" that a writer projects in a discourse. The term "persona" literally means "mask." Even when a writer speaks in the first person, we should be aware that the attitudes or opinions we hear may not necessarily be those of the writer in real life. Much of Herman Melville's shorter fiction and essays, especially "Bartleby, the Scrivener" and *Benito Cereno*, makes extensive use of personas.

Personification: a *figure of speech* (a trope) in which a writer refers to inanimate objects, ideas, or animals as if they were human, or creates a human figure to represent an abstract entity such as Philosophy or Peace. For example, see Allen Ginsberg's "America": "America, when will you be angelic? / When will you take off your clothes?"

Picaresque: a genre of fiction that deals with the adventures of an unscrupulous but charismatic individual.

Pilgrims: Puritans who broke with the Church of England and settled the Plymouth Colony in 1620; their break from the church led to them being labeled Separatists. See also *Separatists*.

Pioneer: a person who is (or is deemed to be) among the first to explore or settle a new or unknown region or territory; the term is often used without considering prior Indigenous habitation.

Plantation: a large-scale agricultural enterprise that produces cash crops; in the American south, plantations varied greatly in size, but all relied on the forced labor of enslaved people. The term was also used in the seventeenth and eighteenth centuries to refer to the American colonies themselves.

Plot: the organization of story materials within a literary work. The order in which story material is presented (especially causes and consequences); the inclusion of elements that allow or encourage the reader or audience to form expectations as to what is likely to happen; the decision to present some story material through exposition rather than in more extended form as part of the main action of the narrative—all these are matters of plotting.

Postbellum: after, or existing after, a war; in American usage, especially the American Civil War. See also *antebellum*.

Predestination: the Calvinist belief that God has predetermined who is saved and who is damned. The belief thereby advances a doctrine of grace (rather than a doctrine of works): the actions, or works, of a person while alive have no influence on their fate. Rather, their salvation comes as a predetermined gift from God. See also *Calvinism*.

Presbyterian: term applied to a group of Protestants who advocated replacing the traditional hierarchy of the church (in which bishops and archbishops governed lower-level members of the clergy) with a system in which all presbyters, or ministers, would be equal; the Presbyterians were strongly influenced by Calvinism.

Prosody: the study and analysis of meter, rhythm, rhyme, stanzaic pattern, and other devices of versification.

Protagonist: the central character in a literary work.

Protestant Reformation/Reformation: a religious movement of the sixteenth century that set out to reform the Roman Catholic Church, and which resulted in the establishment of various Protestant churches throughout Europe and Britain and, eventually, its colonies; the movement effected a profound religious, political, intellectual, and cultural upheaval. See also *Protestantism*.

Protestantism: a branch of Christianity that formed as a result of the Protestant Reformation in the early sixteenth century. Protestant denominations reject the authority of the pope and of the Catholic Church, and they tend to place a greater emphasis than the Catholic Church on the Bible as the primary or sole source of religious doctrine.

Pun: a play on words, in which a word with two or more distinct meanings, or two words with similar sounds, may create humorous ambiguities.

Puritan: term applied to sixteenth- and seventeenth-century Protestants who felt that the Anglican Church was too similar to the Catholic Church and required further reform. Puritans played a leading role in the settlement of many New England colonies, including the Massachusetts Bay Colony in 1630. See also *Separatists*.

Quakerism/Religious Society of Friends: a Protestant sect committed to pacifism and the spiritual equality of all worshippers, and whose members stressed a direct relationship with God through Jesus Christ; many Quakers were also abolitionists and advocates of various social reforms.

Radical Republican: a mid-nineteenth century group within the Republican Party that, prior to the Civil War, was vehemently opposed to slavery and any form of compromise with the south; the group later advocated equal civil and political rights for former enslaved people during Reconstruction. See also *Republican Party*.

Realism: a literary movement that gained in prominence with the rise of social reform movements of the late nineteenth century. Proponents rejected the grandeur, sentimentalism, and idealism of Romanticism in favor of logic, fact, and objectivity; works feature a candid and detailed treatment of ordinary people living everyday lives. Rebecca Harding Davis's "Life in the Iron-Mills" (1861) provides a prime early example.

Reconstruction: the period from 1865 to 1877 during which the states that had seceded from the United States during the Civil War were readmitted to the federal system of government and reorganized; also, the process by which this reorganization was effected. The reorganization of the former secessionist states prominently featured efforts to secure the rights and promote the welfare of formerly enslaved people, including the ratification of the Fourteenth and Fifteenth Amendments. These efforts, however, were largely negated by the violent reimposition of white supremacy throughout the South and by the federal government's abandonment of Reconstruction in 1877.

Regionalism: a category of literature that emerged after the Civil War and that centers on the distinctiveness of regional, or local, culture and geography, rather than on broader national themes and issues. Bret Harte's coverage of the California Gold Rush in "The Luck of Roaring Camp" (1868) is an example. See also *local color*.

Renaissance, American: a term coined by literary critic F.O. Matthiessen to refer to the period in American literature between 1830 and 1865 during which, in Matthiessen's opinion, five main writers—Ralph Waldo Emerson, Nathaniel Hawthorne, Herman Melville, Henry David Thoreau, and Walt Whitman—helped to forge a literary style that was unique to the national spirit of the United States. Subsequent critics have taken Matthiessen to task for his exclusion of women and of African American and Indigenous writers, and have much broadened the list of those responsible for defining a national literature of the period. Some have also questioned whether such a uniform literature even exists. See also *Transcendentalism*, *Romanticism*.

Republican Party: a political party established in 1854 by a group of Whigs, Democrats, and other politicians who left their respective parties to form a party opposed to slavery's expansion. The Republicans nominated Abraham Lincoln as their presidential candidate in 1860; after the Civil War, the party sought for a time to protect and promote the rights of newly emancipated African Americans during Reconstruction, but the party gradually became more oriented toward economic and industrial growth. Not to be confused with the earlier political party of the same name that formed in opposition to the Federalist Party in the early 1790s. See also *Democratic-Republican Party*.

Republicanism: a political philosophy of the eighteenth century that rejected aristocracies and monarchies, and instead stressed liberty, the virtue of common citizens, and the uninfringeable rights of individuals. See also *Jeffersonian democracy*.

Reservation: an area of land set aside for a special purpose; in the context of America's Indigenous peoples, reservations were created by treaty, legislation, or executive order, and very often involved the forcible removal of Indigenous populations from their homelands.

Rhetoric: in classical Greece and Rome, the art of persuasion and public speaking. From the Middle Ages onwards, the study of rhetoric gave greater attention to style, particularly figures of speech. Today in poetics, the term rhetoric may encompass not only figures of speech, but also the persuasive effects of forms, sounds, and word choices.

Rhyme: the repetition of identical or similar sounds, usually in pairs and generally at the ends of metrical lines.

> End-Rhyme: a rhyming word or syllable at the end of a line.
>
> Eye-Rhyme: rhyming that pairs words whose spellings are alike but whose pronunciations are different: for example, move/love.
>
> Feminine Rhyme: a two-syllable (also known as "double") rhyme. The first syllable is stressed and the second unstressed: for example, hasty/tasty. See also *triple rhyme*.
>
> Interlocking Rhyme: the repetition of rhymes from one stanza to the next, creating links that add to the poem's continuity and coherence.

Internal Rhyme: the placement of rhyming words within lines so that at least two words in a line rhyme with each other.

Masculine Rhyme: a correspondence of sound between the final stressed syllables at the end of two or more lines, as in grieve/leave, arr-ive/sur-vive.

Slant Rhyme: an imperfect or partial rhyme (also known as "near" or "half" rhyme) in which the final consonants of stressed syllables match but the vowel sounds do not. E.g., spoiled/spilled, taint/stint.

Triple Rhyme: a three-syllable rhyme in which the first syllable of each rhyme-word is stressed and the other two unstressed (e.g., greenery/scenery).

True Rhyme: a rhyme in which everything but the initial consonant matches perfectly in sound and spelling.

Rhythm: in speech, the arrangement of stressed and unstressed syllables creates units of sound. In song or verse, these units usually form a regular rhythmic pattern, a kind of beat, described in prosody as *meter*.

Romanticism: a major social and cultural movement that originated in Europe as a reaction against the rationalism of the Enlightenment and that shaped much of Western artistic thought in the late eighteenth and nineteenth centuries; the movement emphasized the essential roles played by subjectivity and emotion in knowing and experiencing the world. Romantic works in literature tend to elevate the individual, to disparage the conventional, and to stress the value of contact with the natural world. Examples include William Cullen Bryant's poem "Thanatopsis" (1817). See also *Transcendentalism*.

Sarcasm: See *irony*.

Satire: literary work designed to make fun of or seriously criticize its subject. According to many literary theories of the Renaissance and neoclassical periods, the ridicule through satire of a certain sort of behavior may function for the reader or audience as a corrective of such behavior.

Scansion: the formal analysis of patterns of rhythm and rhyme in poetry. Each line of verse will have a certain number of fairly regular "beats" consisting of alternating stressed and unstressed syllables. To "scan" a poem is to count the beats in each line, to mark stressed and unstressed syllables and indicate their combination into "feet," to note pauses, and to identify rhyme schemes with letters of the alphabet.

Scheme: See *figures of speech*.

Secession: the action of withdrawing from membership of a political state, religious organization, or other similar alliance; in the United States, the insurrectionist withdrawal of eleven Southern states from the federal government that brought about the Civil War.

Second Great Awakening: a widespread Protestant religious revival during the early nineteenth century; the heart of the new evangelical movement stressed God's benevolence and humans' ability to endeavor to save themselves (where earlier Calvinist tradition emphasized the deep depravity of humanity, the inability to alter our fate, and salvation through God). See *First Great Awakening*.

Sermon: a discourse based upon scripture for the purpose of giving religious instruction or encouragement.

Seneca Falls Convention: 1848 New York convention often viewed as having launched the women's suffrage movement in America.

Separatists: a Protestant group in the Calvinist tradition whose members believed that the Church of England was too corrupt to be reformed and that it was necessary to separate from it, the Pilgrims aboard the *Mayflower* were Separatists. See also *Calvinism, Pilgrims*.

Simile: a *figure of speech* (a trope) which makes an explicit comparison between a particular object and another object or idea that is similar in some (often unexpected) way. A simile always uses "like" or "as" to signal the connection. Compare with *metaphor*.

Slave Narrative: an autobiographical account of the experiences of an enslaved person; numerous slave narratives were published in the United States from the late eighteenth to the mid-nineteenth century, and they contributed greatly to the rise of the abolitionist movement and the spread of opposition to slavery.

Sonnet: a highly structured lyric poem, which normally has fourteen lines of iambic pentameter. See the glossary of poetic terms in this anthology's online component.

Sons of Liberty: a loosely connected group of underground, grassroots organizations in Colonial America that formed in response to the Stamp Act with the goal of undermining British rule through acts of radical civil disobedience.

Spiritual: a genre of religious song that grew out of the collective experience of enslaved people and was adopted by black Christians of the southern United States especially; blending African, American, and African American musical elements, spirituals often express ideals of hope, justice, and salvation in the face of the oppressive experience of enslavement. See also *gospel*, *work song*.

Spiritualism: a nineteenth-century religious movement, especially popular among the upper and middle classes, whose adherents believed it was possible for the living to communicate with the spirits of the dead. It was closely linked to widely discussed scientific and pseudoscientific ideas.

Stanza: any lines of verse that are grouped together in a poem and separated from other similarly structured groups by a space.

Stress: See *accent*.

Sublime: a concept of the qualities of grandeur, power, and awe that may be inherent in or produced by undomesticated nature or great art. The sublime is generally thought of as higher and loftier than something that is merely beautiful; the concept plays a central role in many Romantic works.

Subplot: a line of story that is subordinate to the main storyline of a narrative. (Note that properly speaking a subplot is a category of story material, not of plot.)

Subtext: implied or suggested meaning of a passage of text, or of an entire work.

Suffrage: the right to vote.

Sun Dance: a large annual ceremony practiced primarily by Plains Indigenous cultures to honor the earth and sun, prove bravery, and pray for prowess in, for example, hunting or fighting; over several days, individuals endure exhaustion and self-torture as a path to spiritual renewal and enhanced prestige, or to establish stronger personal or tribal relationships.

Syllable: vocal sound or group of sounds forming a unit of speech; a syllable may be formed with a single effort of articulation. Some syllables consist of a single phoneme (e.g., the word *I*, or the first syllable in the word *u*-ni-ty) but others may be made up of several phonemes (as with one-syllable words such as *lengths*, *splurged*, and *through*). By contrast, the much shorter words *ago*, *any*, and *open* each have two syllables.

Symbol: a word, image, or idea that represents something more, or other, than for what it at first appears to stand. Like metaphor, the symbol extends meaning; but while the components of a metaphor are bound in a specific relationship, a symbol may have a range of connotations. For example, the image of a rose may call forth associations of love, passion, transience, fragility, youth, and beauty, among others. Often,

such meaning is implied rather than explicitly stated; indeed, much of the power of symbolic language lies in the reader's ability to make meaningful sense of it.

Synecdoche: a kind of *metonymy* in which a writer substitutes the name of a part of something to signify the whole: for example, "sail" for ship or "hand" for a member of the ship's crew.

Tall Tale: a form of folktale in which unbelievably exaggerated details are related as though they are historically factual. Tall tales may describe one's own supposed adventures or the adventures of a larger-than-life folk hero; examples of the latter include narratives about figures such as Davy Crockett and Johnny Appleseed, as well as African American oral stories such as "Big Sixteen."

Theme: the governing idea of a discourse, conveyed through the development of the subject, and through the recurrence of certain words, sounds, or metrical patterns. See also *motif*.

Third-Person Narrative: See *narrative perspective*.

Thirteenth Amendment: an 1865 amendment to the U.S. Constitution that abolished slavery throughout the nation; it was the first of three Reconstruction amendments following the Civil War that attempted to secure equal status and rights for African Americans.

Three-Fifths Clause: a provision in the U.S. Constitution that allowed for three-fifths of the enslaved population to be counted when determining each state's representation in the House of Representatives, thereby bolstering southern states' political power.

Tone: the writer's attitude toward a given subject or audience, as expressed through an authorial persona or "voice." Tone can be projected through particular choices of wording, imagery, figures of speech, and rhythmic devices. Compare *mood*.

Tory: a person who supported the British Crown; more generally, a political conservative who supports traditional political and social institutions. See also *Loyalist*.

Tragedy: in the traditional definition originating in discussions of ancient Greek drama, a serious narrative recounting the downfall of the protagonist. More loosely, the term has been applied to a wide variety of literary forms in which the tone is predominantly a dark one and the narrative does not end happily.

Trail of Tears: the expression used generally to invoke the suffering that Indigenous nations experienced when forcibly removed from their ancestral lands and driven, despite the threats of disease, exposure, starvation, and death, to "Indian Territory" west of the Mississippi; more specifically, the route traversed by the Cherokee nation during its expulsion in 1838 and 1839. See also *Indian Expulsion, Indian Territory*.

Transcendentalism: a philosophical and literary movement, centered mainly in New England, that flourished in the 1830s and 1840s; linked with the Romantic movement, its adherents held to a mystical, idealistic belief in the unity of all creation and the innate goodness of nature and of people, as well as a trust in one's own insight and intellect as a pathway to the deepest truths. Its members included Margaret Fuller, Ralph Waldo Emerson, and Henry David Thoreau. See also *Romanticism*.

Trickster: a figure in the mythology or oral literature of many cultures, including Indigenous peoples and African Americans, that turns its intelligence toward playing tricks or breaking rules and challenging conventions; in different cultures the figure takes different forms—often an animal such as Coyote or Raven (in various Indigenous cultures) or Brer Rabbit (in African American folklore).

Trope: any figure of speech that plays on our understandings of words to extend, alter, or transform "literal" meaning. Common tropes include *metaphor, simile, personification, hyperbole, metonymy, oxymoron, synecdoche,* and *irony*. See also *figures of speech*.

Uncle Sam: a personification of the United States and its people, typically represented as a white man with a severe gaze, white hair and chin whiskers, dressed in red, white, and blue; a symbol of American patriotism.

Uncle Tom: the enslaved title character of Harriet Beecher Stowe's 1852 novel; theatrical adaptations of the novel frequently transformed Uncle Tom into a subservient apologist for slavery, and the term "Uncle Tom" subsequently became a derogatory epithet for someone who accepts or willingly participates in their own subordination.

Underground Railroad: the secret network of support and safehouses by means of which many enslaved people escaped to the North, to Canada, or (in some cases) to Mexico.

Union: the United States; specifically, the group of northern states that were opposed to slavery and that remained loyal to the Federal government during the Civil War.

Unitarianism: a Christian movement beginning in the late eighteenth century that emphasized free will and universal salvation: the idea that all human beings can and will be saved, regardless of whether or not they belong to or accept the beliefs of a particular church. The movement was particularly influential upon Transcendentalists in the early nineteenth century (though it was also criticized by several of them, including by Emerson, himself a former Unitarian minister).

Verse: a general term for works of poetry, usually referring to poems that incorporate some kind of metrical structure. The term may also describe a line of poetry, though more frequently it is applied to a stanza.

Visual Literature: a form of literature in which images make up the primary means of communication, for example, sign language, rock art, winter counts, ledger art, etc.

Voodoo, or Vodou: a religion developed in the sixteenth century in Hispaniola (now Haiti) by enslaved Africans that blends elements from African religions with aspects of Roman Catholicism. See also *Hoodoo, Obeah*.

Wampum: beads made from shells, often threaded together in strings or belts, used by Indigenous peoples for ornamental, ceremonial, and record-keeping purposes.

Whig: during the American Revolution, a supporter of American independence; more generally, a supporter of the British or American Whig Party or its principles.

Whig Party: a political party that emerged in 1834 in opposition to the political platform of Andrew Jackson and his strong executive power; the party splintered in the 1850s over the issue of slavery, the northern faction joining with antislavery Democrats to form the Republican Party. See also *Democratic Party, Democratic-Republican Party*.

Winter Count: a pictographic record or calendar that records the major events in the history of an Indigenous community, especially Indigenous nations of the Plains.

Work Song: a song sung by physical laborers, especially enslaved people, as they worked, and usually linked rhythmically to the work being done. See also *spiritual*.

Yankee: a New Englander or, more generally, a person from a Northern state; outside of the United States, the term is often used to refer to any American.

Zeugma: a *figure of speech* (trope) in which one word links or "yokes" two others in the same sentence, often to comic or ironic effect. For example, a verb may govern two objects, as when Twain describes the fight between Tom Sawyer and the "new boy": "They … covered themselves with dust and glory."

MAPS

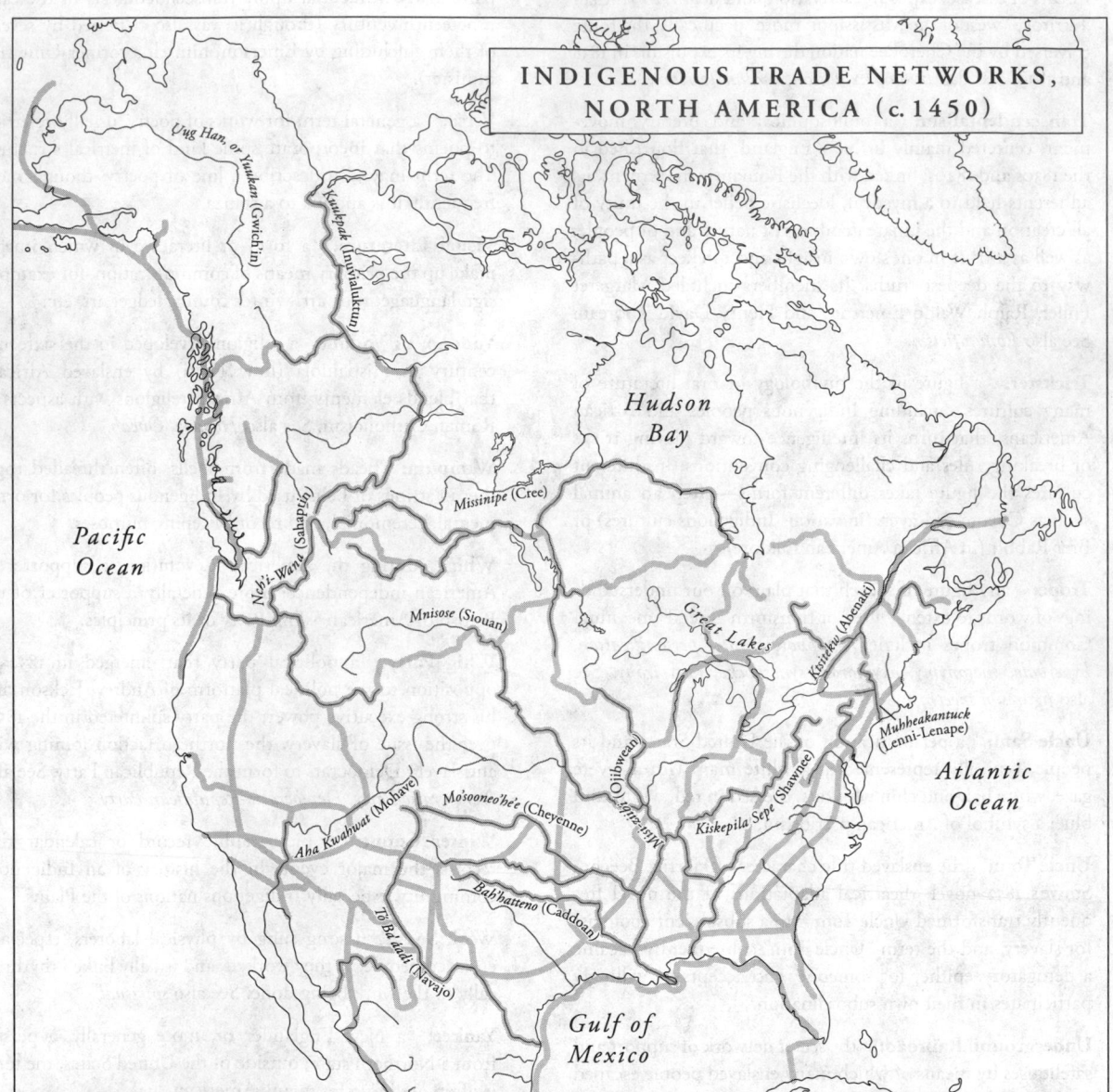

INDIGENOUS TRADE NETWORKS, NORTH AMERICA (c. 1450)

Uug Han, or Yuukan (Gwich'in)

Kuukpak (Inuvialuktun)

Hudson Bay

Missinipe (Cree)

Pacific Ocean

Nch'i-Wana (Sahaptin)

Mnisose (Siouan)

Great Lakes

Ksitekw (Abenaki)

Muhheakantuck (Lenni-Lenape)

Atlantic Ocean

Misi-ziibi (Ojibwean)

Aha Kwahwat (Mohave)

Mo'sooneo'he'e (Cheyenne)

Kiskepila Sepe (Shawnee)

Bah'hatteno (Caddoan)

Tó Ba áadi (Navajo)

Gulf of Mexico

This map suggests major Indigenous trade routes prior to European contact. Before contact, trade networks between and within Indigenous nations covered all manner of distances; many, of course, were smaller, localized networks, but major routes crisscrossed the continent. Traded items included products such as canoes, pottery, woven fabrics, and fishing nets; furs, shells, and feathers; turquoise, obsidian, and copper; and dried fish, maize, and tobacco—among many other goods. Trade centers also served as points for the exchange of oral literature and other forms of cultural expression.

Note that rivers, of significant importance to the trade networks depicted, are identified by Indigenous names; it should be recognized that these names are likely one of many applied to each river (or portion thereof) by different peoples over the centuries.

North American Indigenous Nations at Contact

The map on the following pages does not depict a specific historical moment, but rather shows the approximate locations of individual Indigenous nations at the time that each made contact with Europeans—a process that began in 1492 but extended over centuries. It is important to recognize that the names, locations, and cultures of many Indigenous groups changed significantly in the centuries before and after contact, and that individual peoples' relationships to their territories varied: some formed cities or other permanent settlements, others regularly migrated over vast distances, and some did both. We have attempted to include as many as possible of the nations that are named in works included in this anthology; regrettably, space constraints have necessitated the omission of hundreds of others. Despite its many limitations, we have included this map as a gesture toward representing the immense diversity of North America's Indigenous peoples, and as a rough geographical reference for readers encountering Indigenous peoples unfamiliar to them.

Indigenous nations appearing on the map are listed below, organized alphabetically within very general geographical regions. Where possible, the nations are identified by the names they use for themselves (autonyms), but variations in name, spelling, and orthography are many and may lead to irregularities. We have also included commonly used names imposed by Europeans or other Indigenous nations (exonyms); in a few cases, these exonyms are all we have available. Some modern nations formed after contact and are thus not represented on the map.

Many Indigenous scholars and knowledge-keepers have created maps intended to better represent Indigenous understandings of place and counter misrepresentations in traditional Euro-American maps. We encourage you to visit such resources as the Decolonial Atlas, Lisa Brooks's digital awikhigan, and Claudio Saunt's *Invasion of America*, all available online.

NORTH AMERICAN INDIGENOUS NATIONS AT CONTACT

Please refer to the table on the previous page in order to identify the Indigenous nations that correspond to numbers.

Pacific Ocean

Hudson Bay

Atlantic Ocean

Gulf of Mexico

Columbia R.

Missouri R.

St. Lawrence R.

Ohio R.

Mississippi R.

Colorado R.

Rio Grande

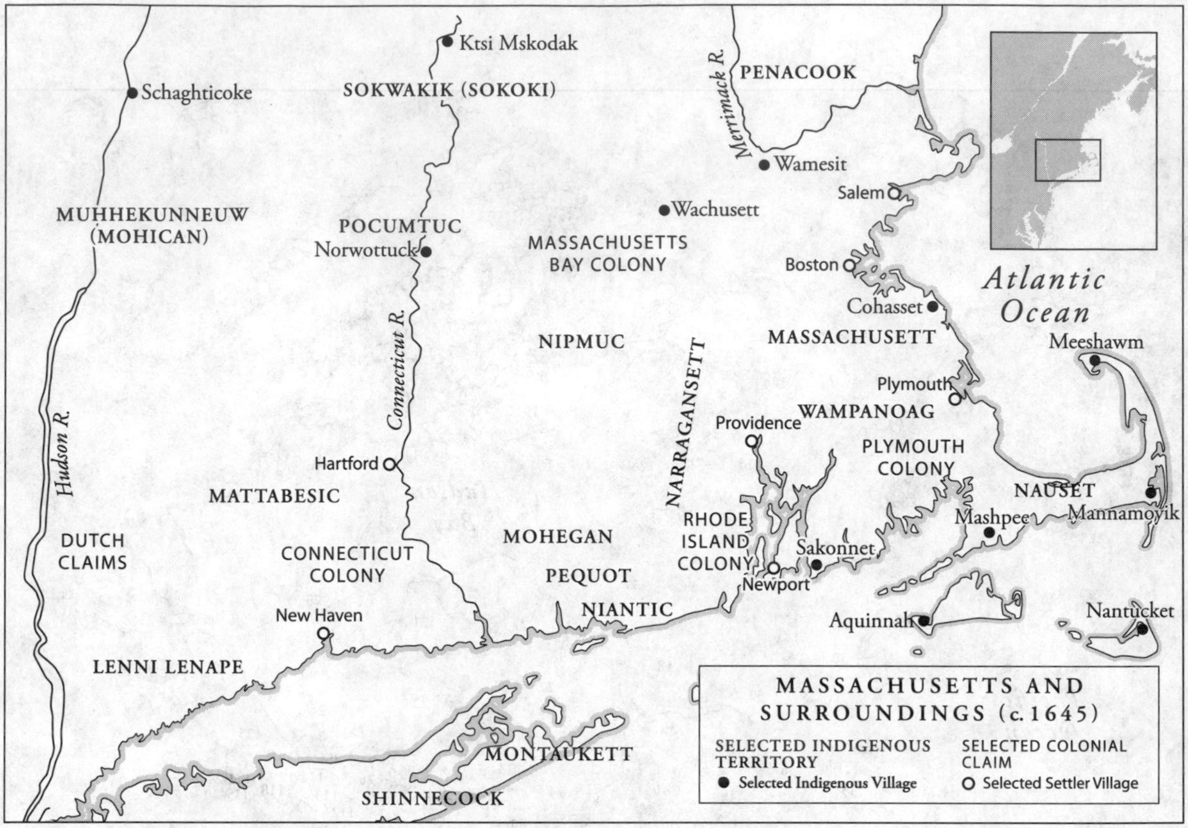

Schaghticoke

Ktsi Mskodak

SOKWAKIK (SOKOKI)

PENACOOK

MUHHEKUNNEUW
(MOHICAN)

Merrimack R.

Wamesit

POCUMTUC
Norwottuck

Wachusett

Salem

MASSACHUSETTS
BAY COLONY

Hudson R.

Connecticut R.

NIPMUC

Boston

Cohasset

MASSACHUSETT

Atlantic
Ocean

Meeshawm

Plymouth

NARRAGANSETT

WAMPANOAG

Providence

Hartford

MATTABESIC

PLYMOUTH
COLONY

NAUSET

DUTCH
CLAIMS

CONNECTICUT
COLONY

MOHEGAN

PEQUOT

RHODE
ISLAND
COLONY

Mashpee

Mannamoyik

Sakonnet

Newport

New Haven

LENNI LENAPE

NIANTIC

Aquinnah

Nantucket

MONTAUKETT

SHINNECOCK

MASSACHUSETTS AND
SURROUNDINGS (c. 1645)

SELECTED INDIGENOUS
TERRITORY
● Selected Indigenous Village

SELECTED COLONIAL
CLAIM
○ Selected Settler Village

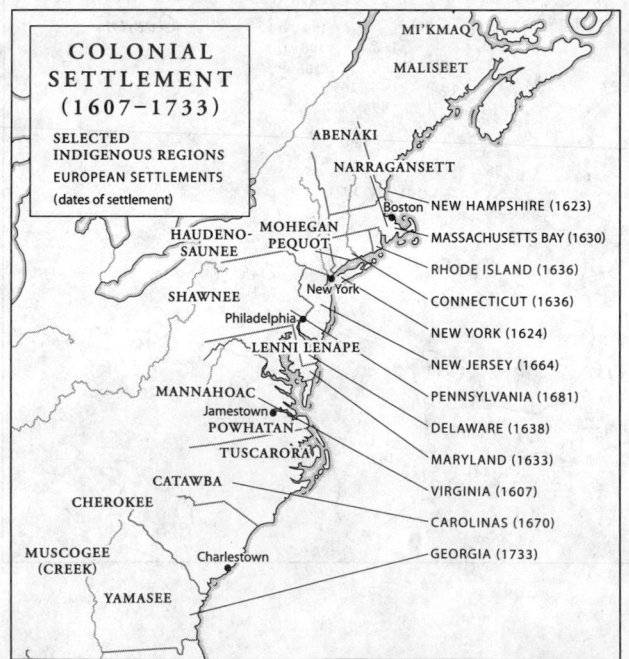

COLONIAL
SETTLEMENT
(1607–1733)

SELECTED
INDIGENOUS REGIONS
EUROPEAN SETTLEMENTS
(dates of settlement)

MI'KMAQ

MALISEET

ABENAKI

NARRAGANSETT

HAUDENO-
SAUNEE

MOHEGAN
PEQUOT

Boston   NEW HAMPSHIRE (1623)

MASSACHUSETTS BAY (1630)

RHODE ISLAND (1636)

SHAWNEE

New York

CONNECTICUT (1636)

NEW YORK (1624)

Philadelphia

LENNI LENAPE

NEW JERSEY (1664)

PENNSYLVANIA (1681)

MANNAHOAC

Jamestown

POWHATAN

DELAWARE (1638)

MARYLAND (1633)

TUSCARORA

VIRGINIA (1607)

CATAWBA

CHEROKEE

CAROLINAS (1670)

MUSCOGEE
(CREEK)

Charlestown

GEORGIA (1733)

YAMASEE

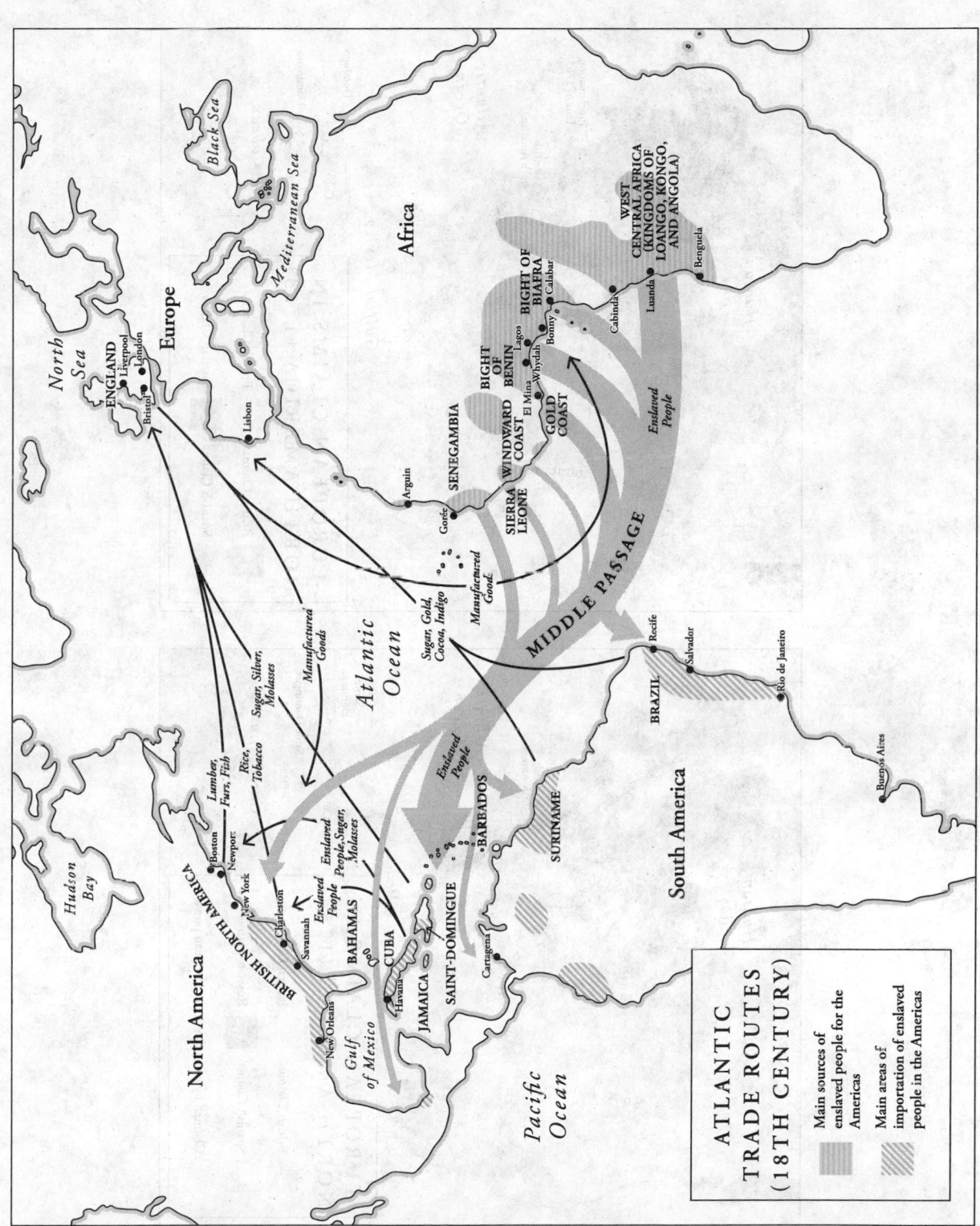

Black Sea

Mediterranean Sea

Africa

North Sea

ENGLAND
Liverpool
London
Europe
Bristol

Lisbon

WEST
CENTRAL AFRICA
(KINGDOMS OF
LOANGO, KONGO,
AND ANGOLA)

Benguela

Luanda
Cabinda

BIGHT OF
BIAFRA
Calabar
Bonny
Lagos
BIGHT
OF
BENIN
Whydah
El Mina
GOLD
COAST

Enslaved People

SENEGAMBIA
WINDWARD
COAST
SIERRA
LEONE

Arguin

Gorée

*Manufactured
Goods*

*Sugar, Gold,
Cocoa, Indigo*

MIDDLE PASSAGE

*Atlantic
Ocean*

*Manufactured
Goods*

*Sugar, Silver,
Molasses*

*Rice,
Tobacco*

*Lumber,
Furs, Fish*

Boston
Newport
New York

Charleston
Savannah

*Enslaved
People*

*Enslaved
People, Sugar,
Molasses*

BAHAMAS

CUBA
Havana

New Orleans
*Gulf
of Mexico*

JAMAICA

SAINT-DOMINGUE

Cartagena

BRITISH NORTH AMERICA

North America

*Hudson
Bay*

*Enslaved
People*

BARBADOS

SURINAME

BRAZIL

Recife
Salvador
Rio de Janeiro

Buenos Aires

South America

*Pacific
Ocean*

ATLANTIC
TRADE ROUTES
(18TH CENTURY)

Main sources of
enslaved people for the
Americas

Main areas of
importation of enslaved
people in the Americas

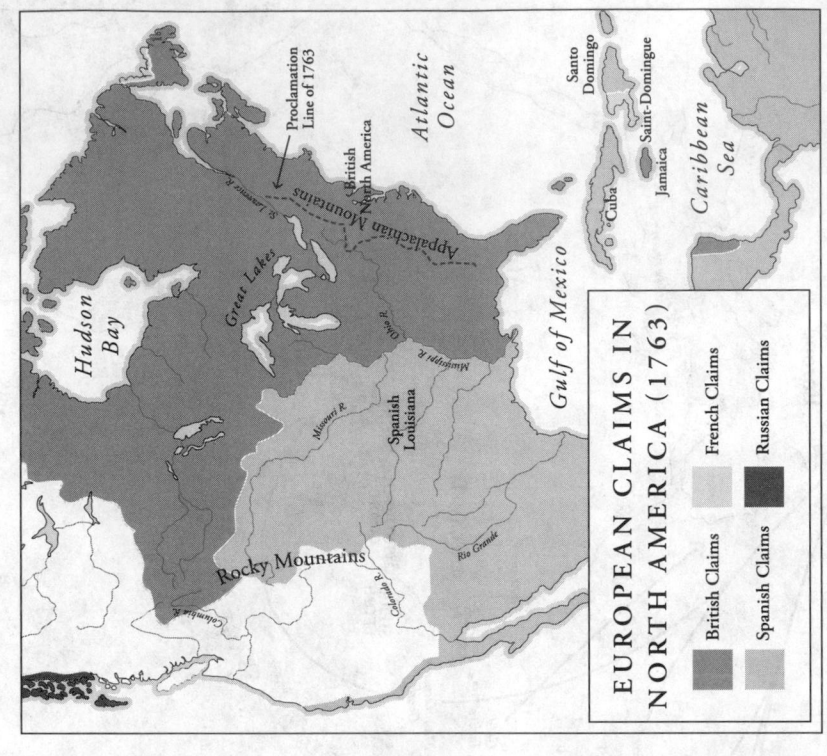

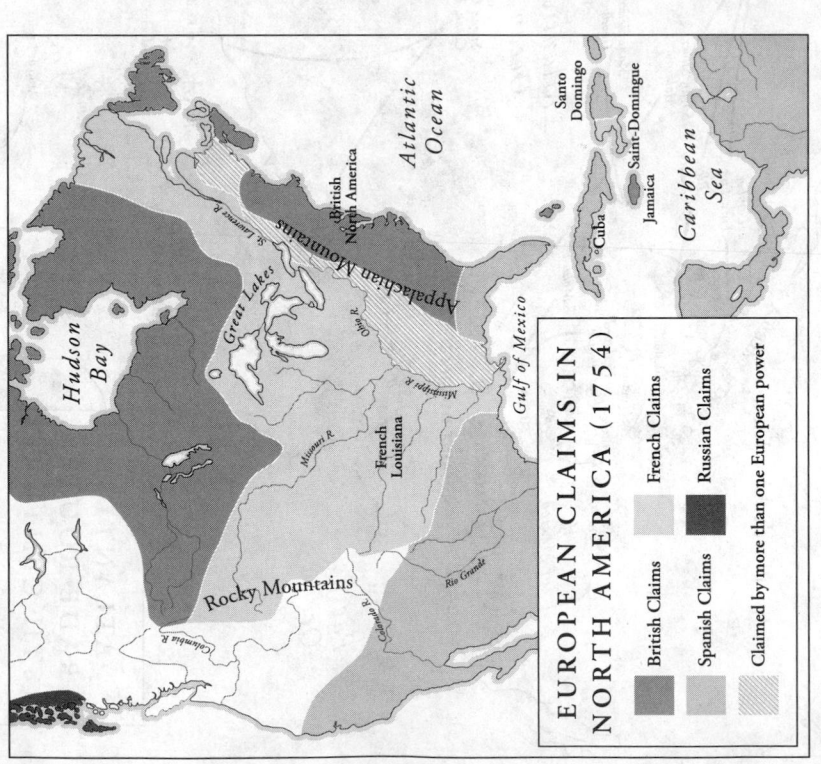

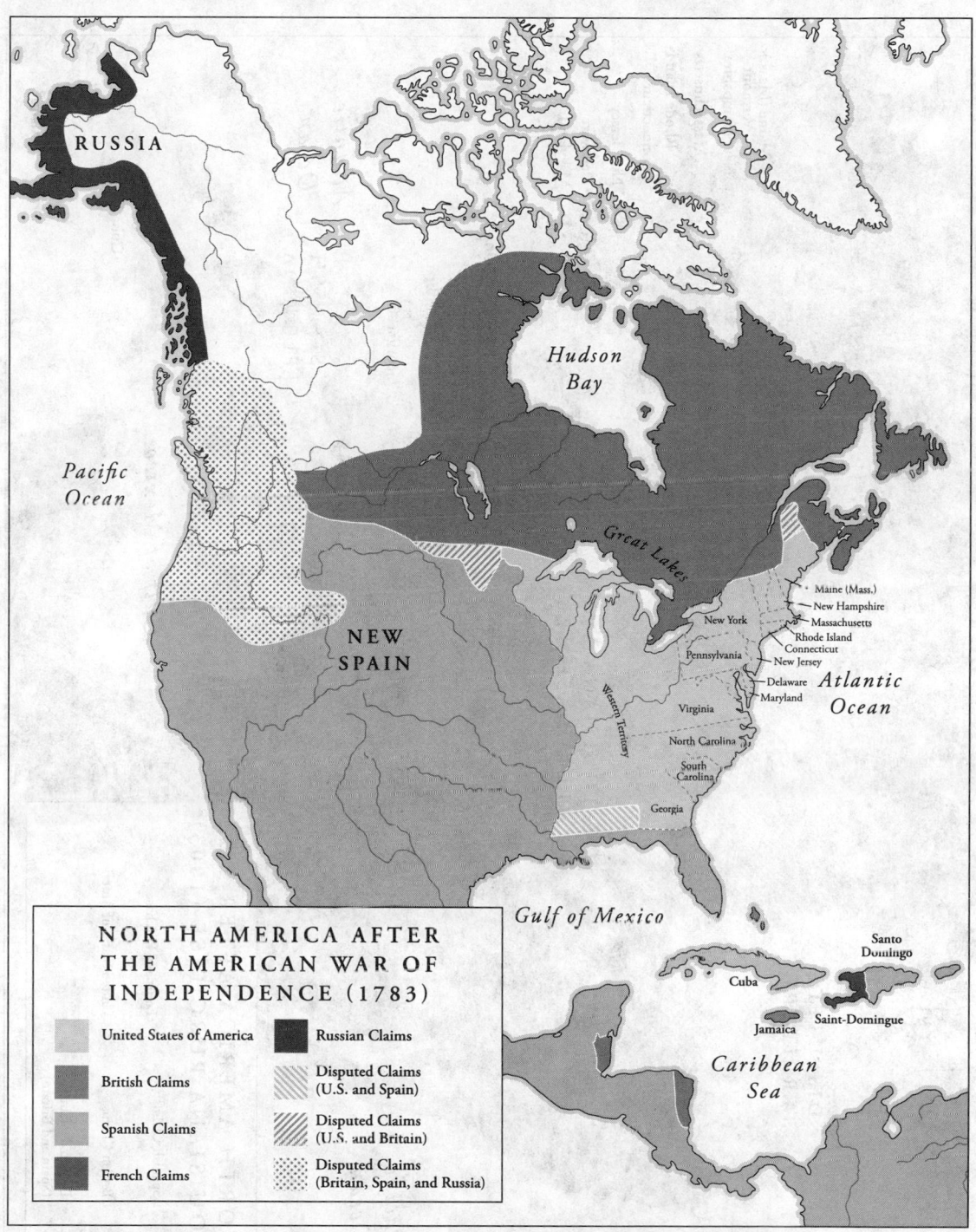

NORTH AMERICA AFTER THE AMERICAN WAR OF INDEPENDENCE (1783)

- United States of America
- British Claims
- Spanish Claims
- French Claims
- Russian Claims
- Disputed Claims (U.S. and Spain)
- Disputed Claims (U.S. and Britain)
- Disputed Claims (Britain, Spain, and Russia)

The Treaty of Paris in 1783 concluded the American War of Independence and established a boundary for the newly independent colonies that stretched west to the Mississippi River. States' claims to this new Western Territory were varied, overlapping, and dynamic, and are not depicted here.

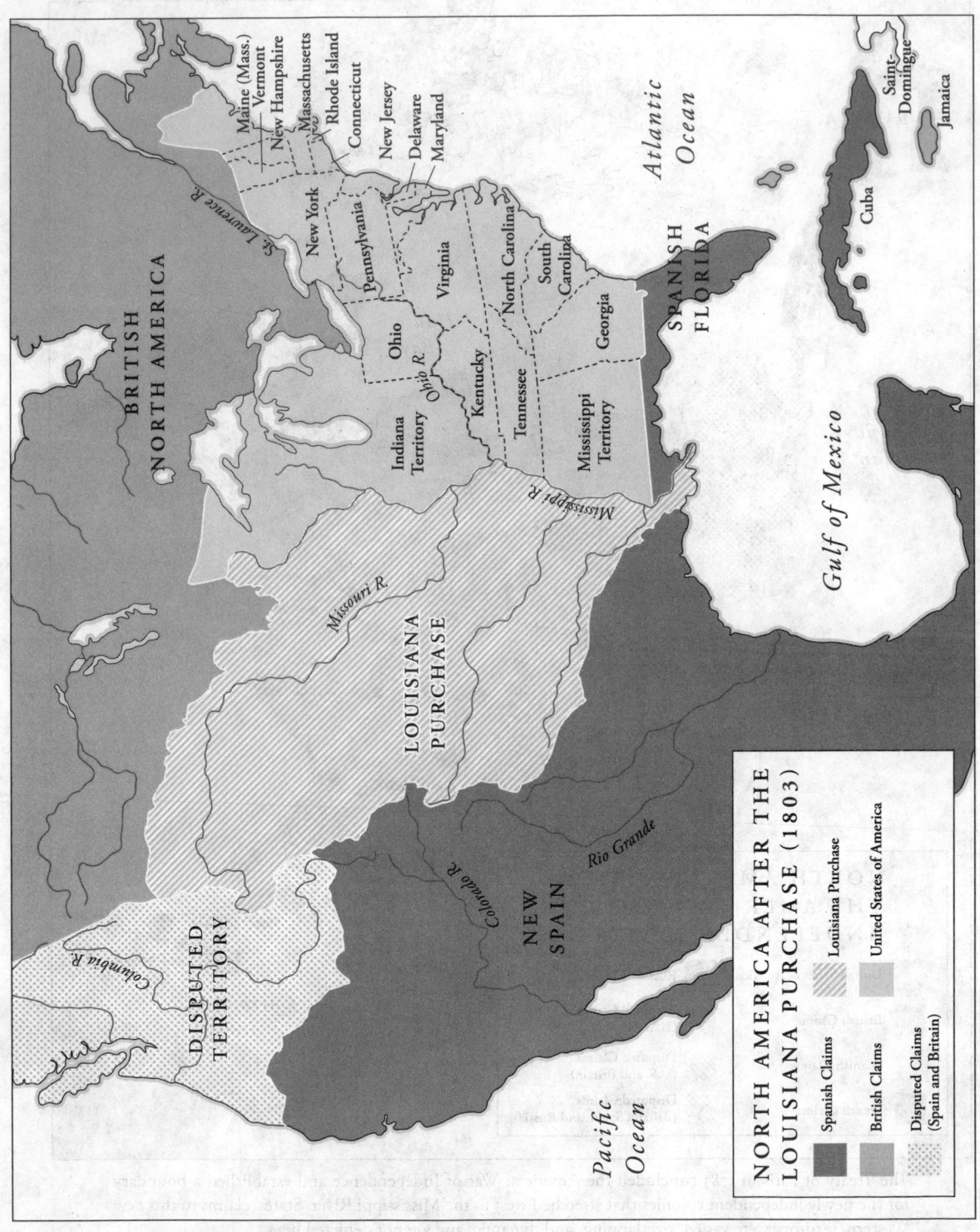

NORTH AMERICA AFTER THE LOUISIANA PURCHASE (1803)

Louisiana Purchase

United States of America

Spanish Claims

British Claims

Disputed Claims (Spain and Britain)

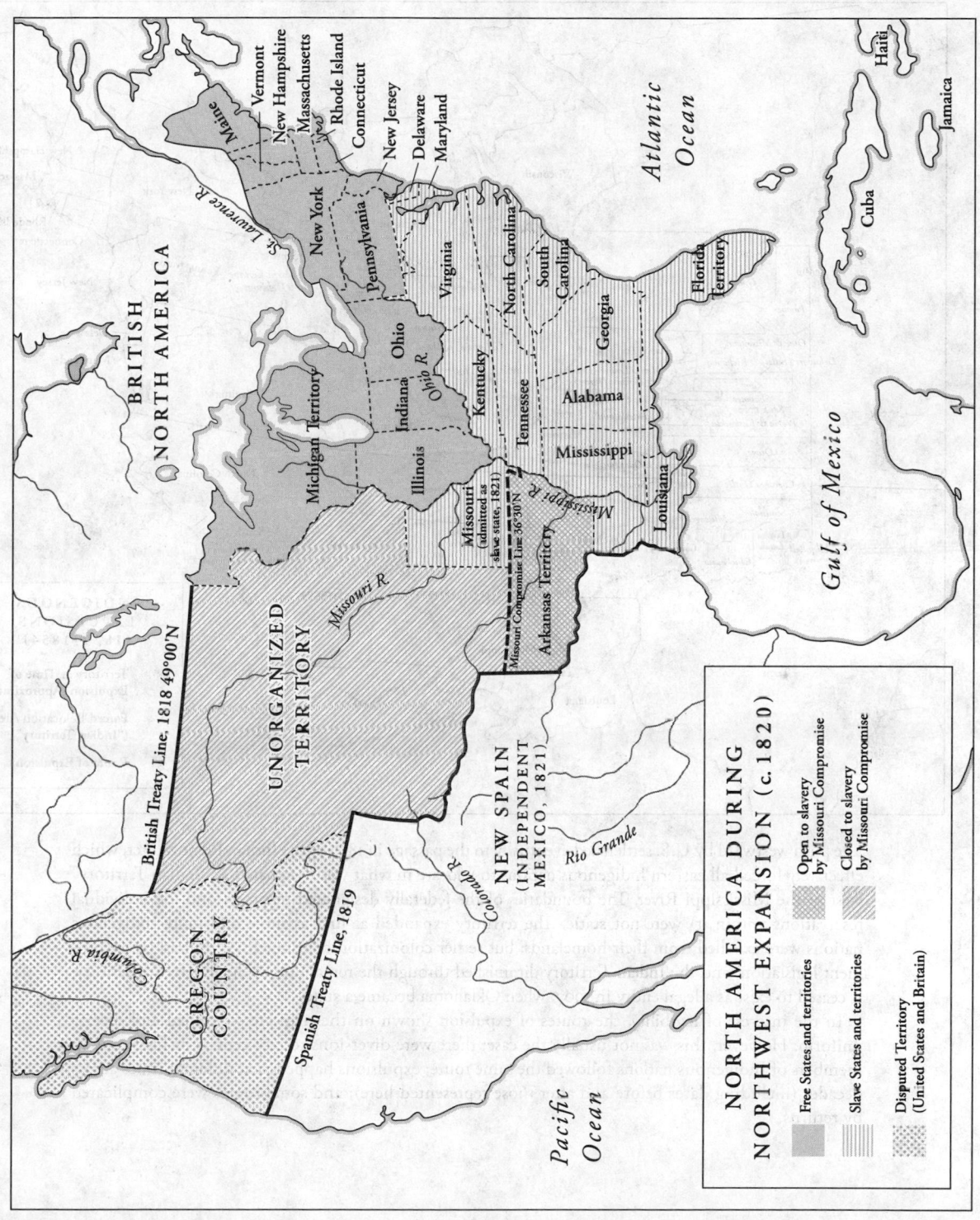

NORTH AMERICA DURING
NORTHWEST EXPANSION (c. 1820)

Free States and territories

Open to slavery
by Missouri Compromise

Slave States and territories

Closed to slavery
by Missouri Compromise

Disputed Territory
(United States and Britain)

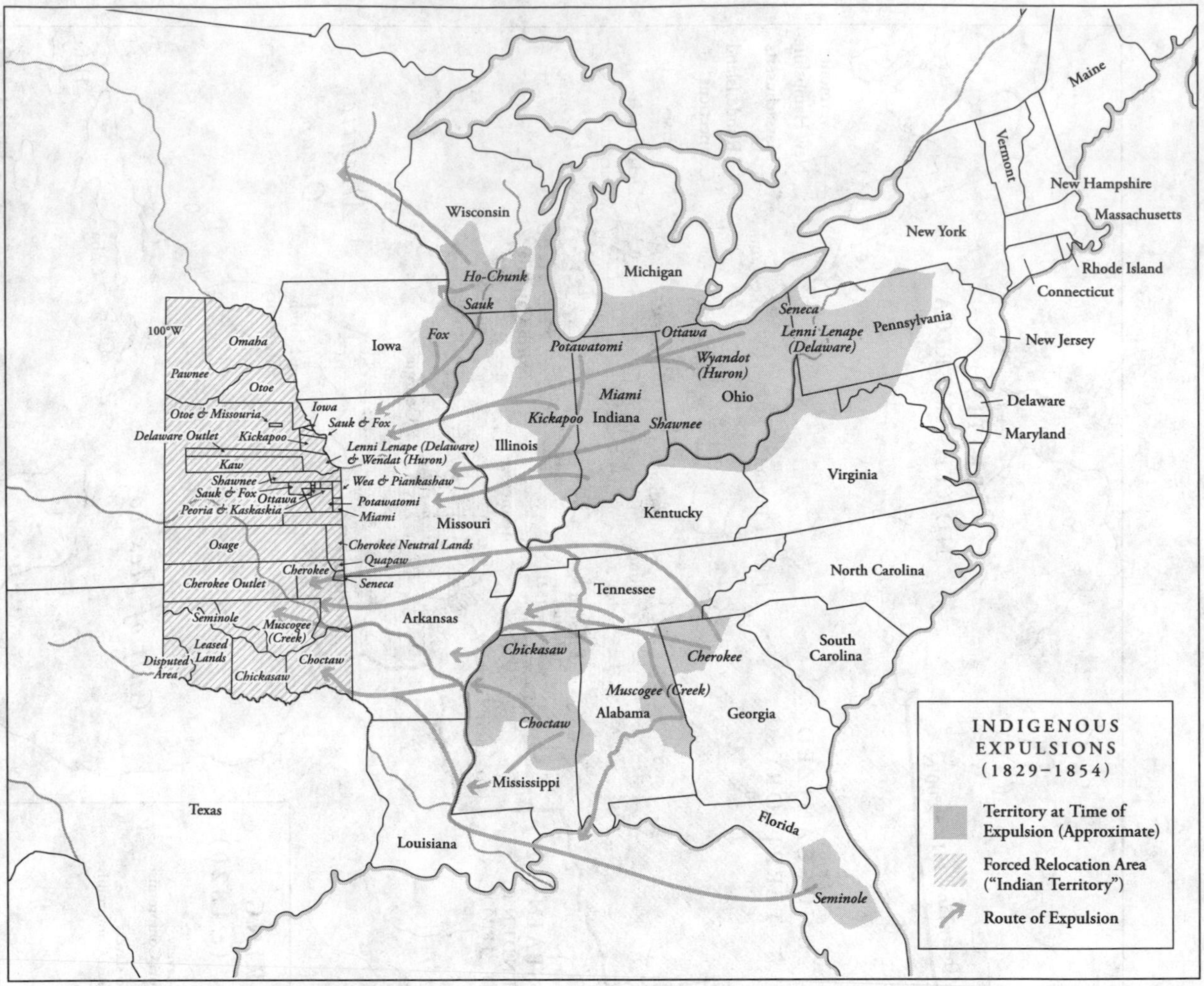
INDIGENOUS EXPULSIONS (1829–1854)
Territory at Time of Expulsion (Approximate)
Forced Relocation Area ("Indian Territory")
Route of Expulsion
100°W
Omaha
Pawnee
Otoe
Otoe & Missouria
Delaware Outlet
Kickapoo
Iowa
Sauk & Fox
Lenni Lenape (Delaware) & Wendat (Huron)
Kaw
Shawnee
Sauk & Fox
Ottawa
Peoria & Kaskaskia
Wea & Piankashaw
Potawatomi
Miami
Osage
Cherokee Neutral Lands
Quapaw
Cherokee
Cherokee Outlet
Seneca
Seminole
Muscogee (Creek)
Leased Lands
Disputed Area
Chickasaw
Choctaw
Wisconsin
Ho-Chunk
Sauk
Fox
Iowa
Michigan
Potawatomi
Ottawa
Miami
Kickapoo
Indiana
Illinois
Shawnee
Wyandot (Huron)
Ohio
Seneca
Lenni Lenape (Delaware)
Pennsylvania
New York
Maine
Vermont
New Hampshire
Massachusetts
Rhode Island
Connecticut
New Jersey
Delaware
Maryland
Virginia
Kentucky
Missouri
Tennessee
North Carolina
Arkansas
South Carolina
Chickasaw
Cherokee
Muscogee (Creek)
Alabama
Georgia
Choctaw
Mississippi
Texas
Louisiana
Florida
Seminole

The push westward by U.S. settlers led eventually to the passage in 1830 of the Indian Removal Act, which effectively forced all eastern Indigenous nations to relocate in what was designated as "Indian Territory" west of the Mississippi River. The boundaries of the federally designated territory (and the individual reservations within it) were not static. The territory expanded at first as more and more Indigenous nations were expelled from their homelands; but settler colonization continued, legitimized by government legislation, and the Indian Territory diminished through the remainder of the nineteenth century. It ceased to exist as a legal entity in 1907, when Oklahoma became a state.

In the interest of legibility, the routes of expulsion shown on the map are simplified and mostly uniform. However, this was not usually the case; there were diversions to city centers or forts; not all members of Indigenous nations followed the same route; expulsions happened at different times across decades (including dates before and after those represented here); and some routes were complicated by returns.

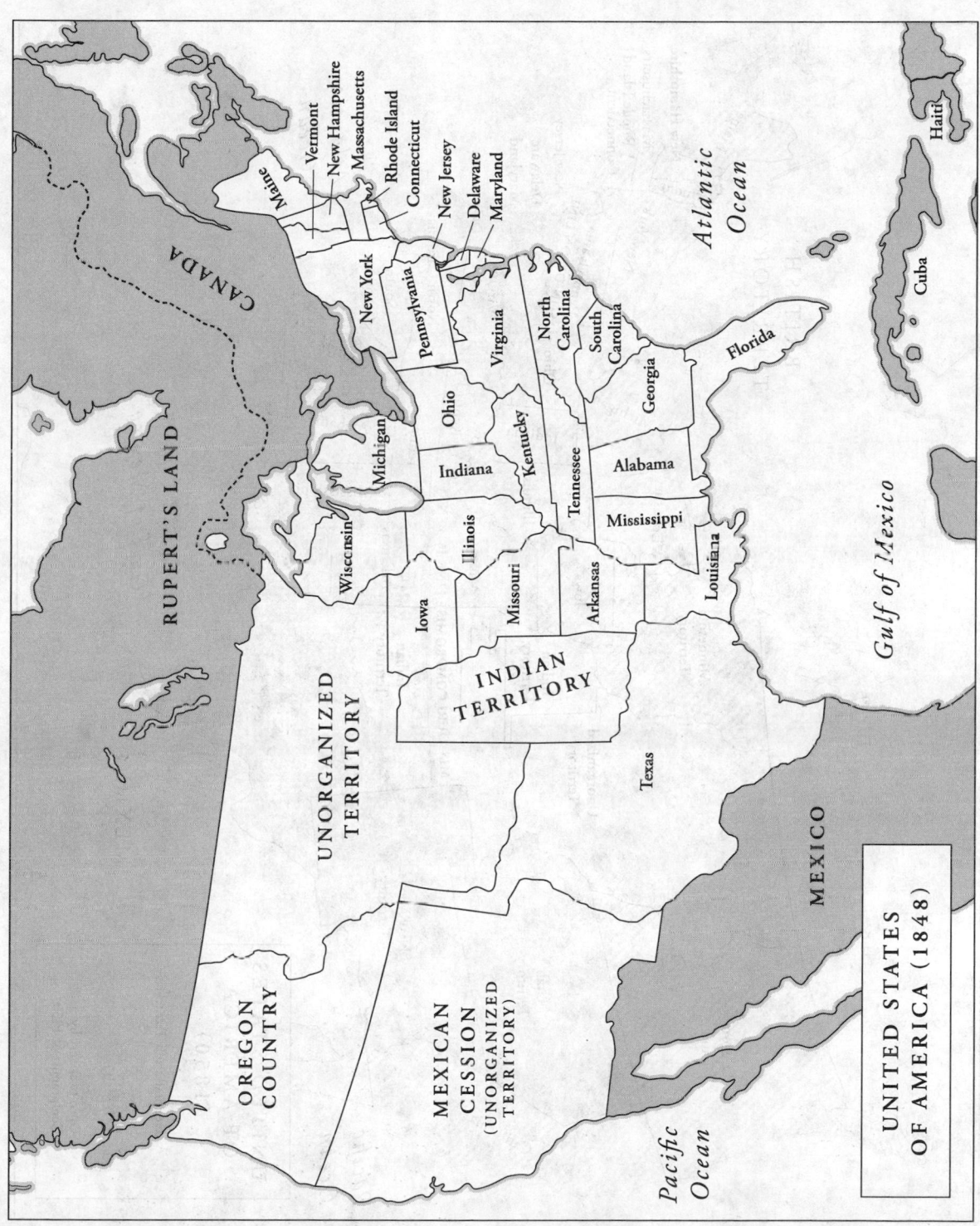

Maine
Vermont
New Hampshire
Massachusetts
Rhode Island
Connecticut
New Jersey
Delaware
Maryland

CANADA

RUPERT'S LAND

New York
Pennsylvania
Virginia
North Carolina
South Carolina
Georgia

Atlantic Ocean

Haiti

Cuba

Florida

Michigan
Ohio
Kentucky
Tennessee
Alabama

Indiana
Illinois
Wisconsin

Iowa
Missouri
Arkansas
Mississippi
Louisiana

Gulf of Mexico

UNORGANIZED TERRITORY

INDIAN TERRITORY

Texas

MEXICO

OREGON COUNTRY

MEXICAN CESSION
(UNORGANIZED TERRITORY)

Pacific Ocean

UNITED STATES
OF AMERICA (1848)

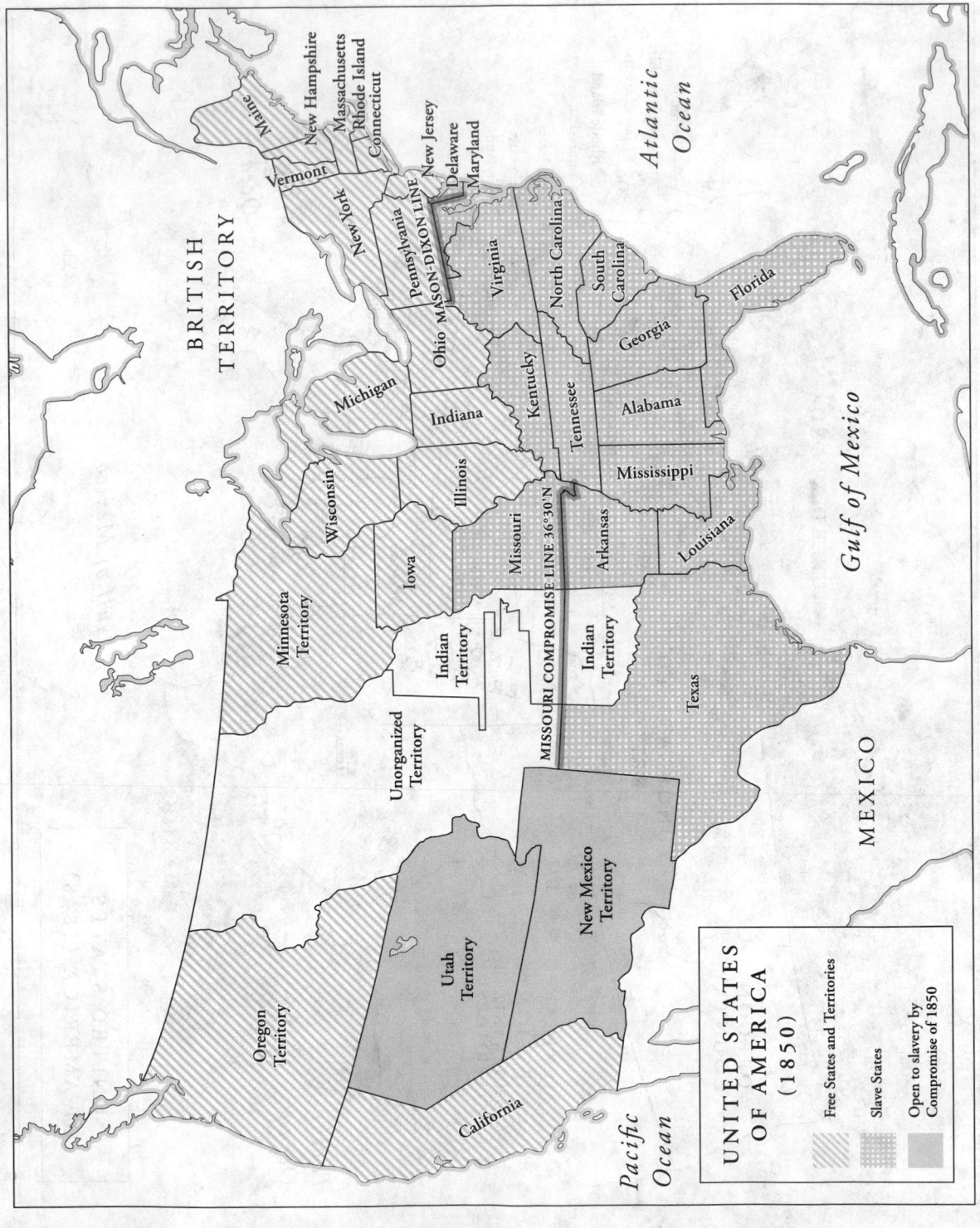

BRITISH TERRITORY

Maine

New Hampshire

Massachusetts

Rhode Island

Connecticut

Vermont

New York

New Jersey

Delaware

Maryland

MASON-DIXON LINE

Pennsylvania

Ohio

Virginia

North Carolina

South Carolina

Florida

Michigan

Indiana

Kentucky

Tennessee

Georgia

Alabama

Wisconsin

Illinois

Mississippi

Iowa

Missouri

Arkansas

Louisiana

MISSOURI COMPROMISE LINE 36°30'N

Minnesota Territory

Indian Territory

Indian Territory

Texas

Unorganized Territory

Oregon Territory

Utah Territory

New Mexico Territory

California

Atlantic Ocean

Gulf of Mexico

MEXICO

Pacific Ocean

UNITED STATES
OF AMERICA
(1850)

Free States and Territories

Slave States

Open to slavery by
Compromise of 1850

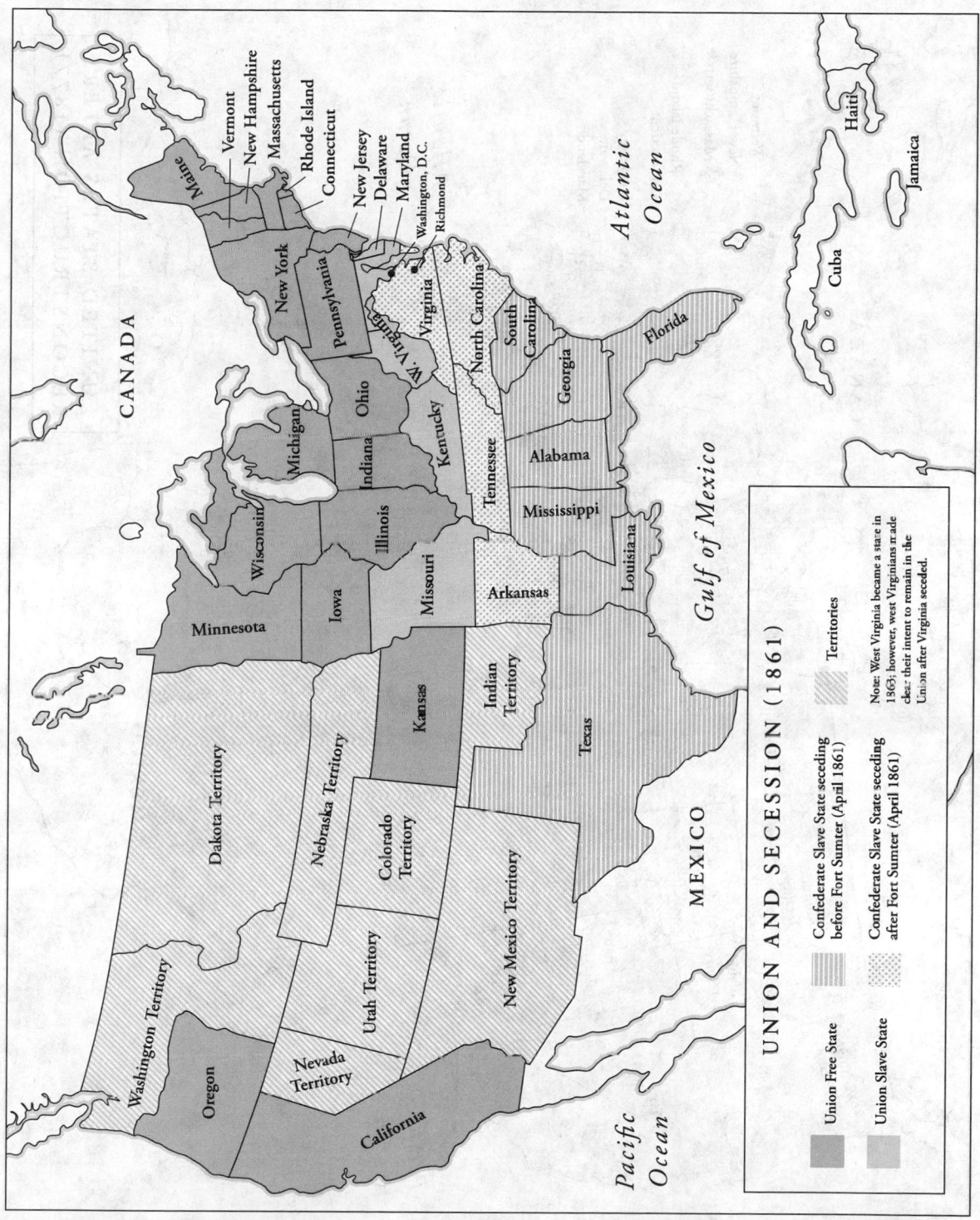

Vermont
New Hampshire
Massachusetts
Rhode Island
Connecticut
New Jersey
Delaware
Maryland
Washington, D.C.
Richmond

Maine

New York

Pennsylvania

W. Virginia

Virginia

North Carolina

South Carolina

Georgia

Florida

Ohio

Michigan

Indiana

Kentucky

Tennessee

Alabama

Illinois

Mississippi

Wisconsin

Missouri

Louisiana

Iowa

Arkansas

Minnesota

Indian Territory

Kansas

Texas

Dakota Territory

Nebraska Territory

Colorado Territory

New Mexico Territory

Washington Territory

Utah Territory

Nevada Territory

Oregon

California

Atlantic Ocean

Haiti

Jamaica

Cuba

Gulf of Mexico

MEXICO

Pacific Ocean

UNION AND SECESSION (1861)

Union Free State

Union Slave State

Confederate Slave State seceding before Fort Sumter (April 1861)

Confederate Slave State seceding after Fort Sumter (April 1861)

Territories

Note: West Virginia became a state in 1863; however, west Virginians made clear their intent to remain in the Union after Virginia seceded.

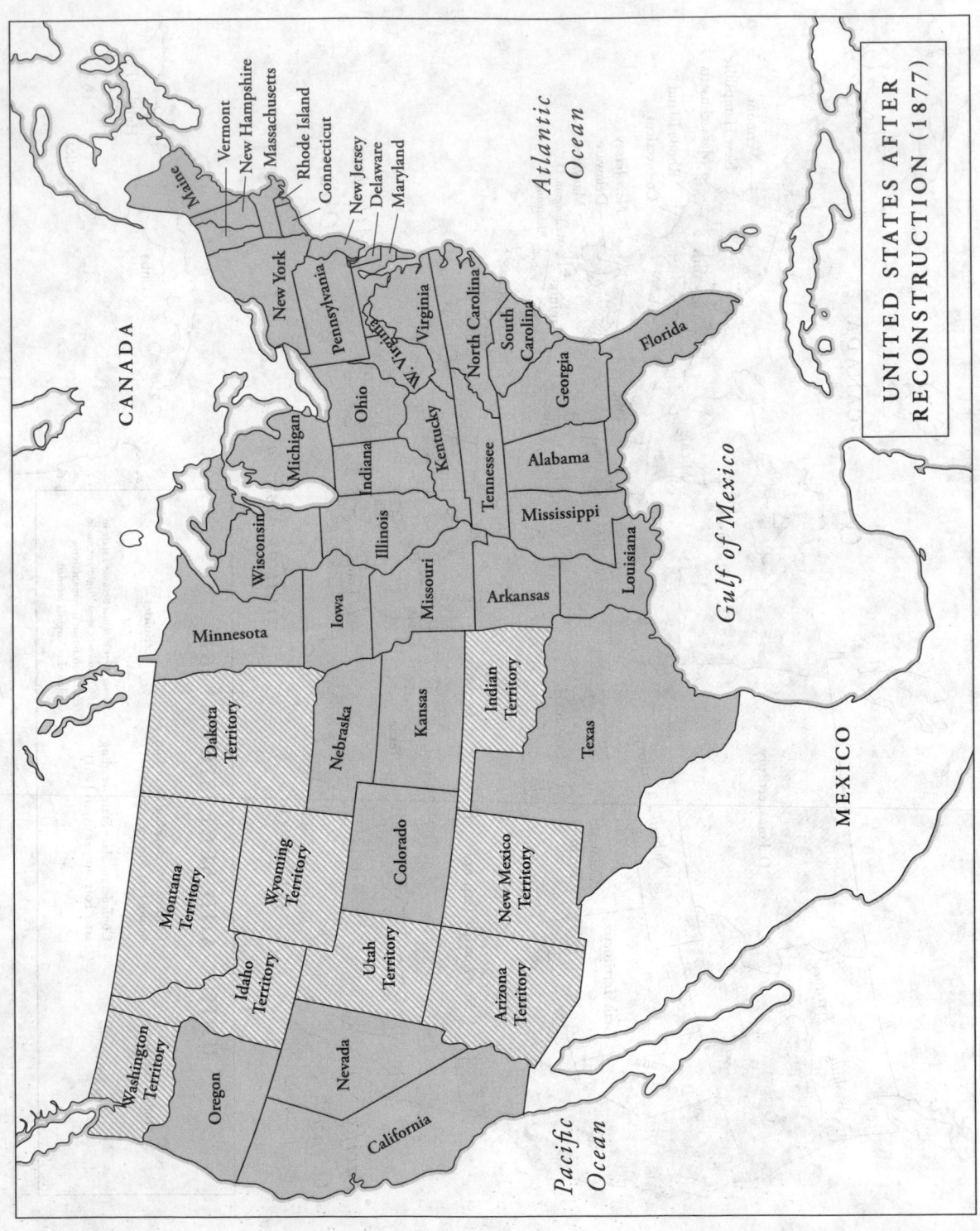

UNITED STATES AFTER
RECONSTRUCTION (1877)

Atlantic Ocean

CANADA

Maine
Vermont
New Hampshire
Massachusetts
Rhode Island
Connecticut
New Jersey
Delaware
Maryland

New York
Pennsylvania
W. Virginia
Virginia
North Carolina
South Carolina
Florida
Georgia

Ohio
Michigan
Indiana
Kentucky
Tennessee
Alabama
Mississippi

Wisconsin
Illinois
Missouri
Arkansas
Louisiana

Minnesota
Iowa
Kansas
Indian Territory
Texas

Gulf of Mexico

Dakota Territory
Nebraska
Colorado
New Mexico Territory

Montana Territory
Wyoming Territory
Utah Territory
Arizona Territory

MEXICO

Idaho Territory
Washington Territory
Oregon
Nevada
California

Pacific Ocean

PERMISSIONS ACKNOWLEDGMENTS

Dickinson, Emily. Images from Amherst Manuscript (Fascicle Set # 88, # 372) courtesy of Amherst College Archives and Special Collections. Images from *Herbarium*, c. 1839–46, call no. MS Am 1118.11 (Seq # 26, 32), Houghton Library, Harvard University. Manuscript poems, call no. MS Am 1118.3 (11a, 11b, 38b), Houghton Library, Harvard College Library. Copyright © President and Fellows of Harvard College. Used with permission.

Document no. 22. Dukes County Registry of Deed (DD 1:349) from *Native Writings in Massachusett*, ed. Ives Goddard and Kathleen J. Bradon. Vol. 1. Philadelphia: American Philosophical Society, 1988. (p. 94) Reproduced by permission of the American Philosophical Society.

Duncanson, Robert S. *Uncle Tom and Little Eva*, 1853, oil on canvas. Copyright © Detroit Institute of Arts / Gift of Mrs. Jefferson Butler and Miss Grace R. Conover / Bridgeman Images. Image no. DTR3081774. Reproduced with permission.

Franklin, Benjamin. "The Autobiography," from *Franklin: Writings*, ed. J.A. Leo Lemay, Library of America # 37, 1987. Reprinted with the permission of Dr. Kate Clarke Lemay.

Gleason, Herbert Wendell. *Eastern shore, Walden Pond*, 1899 Nov. 6; *The Fitchburg railroad and Walden Pond in winter*, 1920 Mar. 24; *H.W. Gleason at Thoreau's cairn, Walden Pond*, Concord, MA. 1908 May 19; *Northwest cove of Walden, ice breaking up (train in distance)*, 1920 Mar. 31; *South shore, Walden Pond*, 1903 May 30. Robbins-Mills Collection of Herbert Wendell Gleason Photographic Negatives. Courtesy of Special Collections, Concord Free Public Library.

Hasteen Klah. Excerpted from *Navajo Creation Myth: The Story of the Emergence*, recorded by Mary C. Wheelwright. Navajo Religion Series, Vol. 1. Copyright © 1942 Museum of Navajo Ceremonial Art, Santa Fe, NM. (pp. 78–79, 81–85) Reproduced by permission of the Wheelwright Museum of the American Indian.

Hochbruck, Wolfgang and Beatrix Dudensing-Reichel. Excerpt from "'Honoratissimi Benefactores': Native American Students and Two Seventeenth-Century Texts in the University Tradition," *Early Native American Writing: New Critical Essays*, ed. Helen Jaskoski. Copyright © Cambridge University Press, 1996. (pp. 5–6) Reproduced with the permission of Cambridge University Press through PLSclear.

Howling Wolf. *At the Sand Creek Massacre*, 1874–75, pen, ink, and watercolor on ledger paper. Allen Memorial Art Museum, Oberlin College. Copyright © Allen Memorial Art Museum / Gift of Mrs. Jacob D. Cox / Bridgeman Images. Image no. ALM741730. Reproduced with permission.

Manuscript of a Mi'kmaq prayer book, c. 1790, Image M18836. Copyright © McCord Museum. Reproduced by permission of the McCord Museum, Montreal, QC.

Color Insert

Anonymous. *John Freake* and *Mrs Elizabeth Freake and Baby Mary*, c. 1671–74, oil on canvas. Copyright © Worcester Art Museum / Bridgeman Images. Image numbers: WAM183405; WAM183406. Reproduced with permission.

Anonymous. Detail from *Plan of Civilization*, c. 1800, oil on canvas. Purchased by the Greenville County Museum of Art with funds from the Museum Association's 1990 and 1991 Collectors Groups and the 1989, 1990, and 1991 Museum Antiques Shows, sponsored by Elliott, Davis & Company, CPAs. Corporate Benefactors: Ernst and Young; Fluor Daniel; Mr. and Mrs. Alester G. Furman III; Mr. and Mrs. M. Dexter Hagy; Thomas P. Hartness; Mr. and Mrs. E. Erwin Maddrey II; Mary M. Pearce; Mr. and Mrs. John D. Pellett, Jr.; Mr. W. Thomas Smith; Mr. and Mrs. Edward H. Stall; Eleanor and Irvine Welling. Image courtesy of the Greenville County Museum of Art.

Barralet, John James. *The Apotheosis of Washington*, c. 1802. Image ID: BAWDNC. Contributor: John James Barralet / Alamy Stock Photo. Used with permission.

Dighton, Robert. *Keep within Compass*, August 16, 1785, object no. 1958-629,1; *Keep within Compass*, November 9, 1784, object no. 1958-629,2. The Colonial Williamsburg Foundation. Museum Purchase. Used with permission.

Fernández, Alejo. *The Virgin of the Navigators*, c. 1531–36. Image ID: BTGWT0. Contributor: Peter Horree / Alamy Stock Photo. Used with permission.

Krimmel, John Lewis. *Fourth of July Celebration in Center Square*, 1819. Image ID: 2E2MDAR. Contributor: ClassicStock / Alamy Stock Photo. Used with permission.

Punderson, Prudence. *The First, Second, and Last Scene of Mortality*, c. 1776–83. Item no. 1962.28.4. Image courtesy of the Connecticut Historical Society, Hartford, CT.

White, John. *The Manner of Their Fishing*, c.1585–93, The British Museum. Asset number: 22109001. Copyright © The Trustees of the British Museum. Used with permission.

Cover image: Detail from *Forget me not*, ca. 1843, Sarah Mapps Douglass, Martina Dickerson Album, Dickerson Family Collection; Print Department, Library Company of Philadelphia. Accession number: 13859.Q.83. Image courtesy of The Library Company of Philadelphia. www.librarycompany.org

Index of Authors and Titles

from the Publisher

A name never says it all, but the word "Broadview" expresses a good deal of the philosophy behind our company. We are open to a broad range of academic approaches and political viewpoints. We pay attention to the broad impact book publishing and book printing have in the wider world; for some years now we have used 100% recycled paper for most titles. Our publishing program is internationally broad in range. And we are committed to the principle that the successful operation of a publishing company need not depend on the exploitation of authors or readers.

Founded in 1985, Broadview remains a fully independent company owned by its shareholders—not an imprint or subsidiary of a larger multinational.

For the latest information on new titles, please visit www.broadviewpress.com

broadview press
www.broadviewpress.com

From the Publisher

A name never says it all, but the word "Broadview" expresses a good deal of the philosophy behind our company. We are open to a broad range of academic approaches and political viewpoints. We pay attention to the broad impact book publishing and book printing has in the wider world; for some years now we have used 100% recycled paper for most titles. Our publishing program is internationally oriented and broad-ranging. Our individual titles often appeal to a broad readership too; many are of interest as much to general readers as to academics and students.

Founded in 1985, Broadview remains a fully independent company owned by its shareholders—not an imprint or subsidiary of a larger multinational.

To order our books or obtain up-to-date information, please visit www.broadviewpress.com.

broadview press

www.broadviewpress.com